HARRAP
Paperback

DICTIONARY • DICTIONNAIRE
English–French • Français–Anglais

Editor/Rédactrice
Kate Nicholson

with/avec
Anna Stevenson

Publishing Manager/Direction éditoriale
Patrick White

Prepress Manager/Direction prépresse
Sharon McTeir

Prepress/Prépresse
Clair Simpson

HARRAP

This edition published in Great Britain 2005
by Chambers Harrap Publishers Ltd
7 Hopetoun Crescent, Edinburgh EH7 4AY

Previous edition published in 2001

ISBN 0 245 60744 7

Designed and typeset by Chambers Harrap Publishers Ltd
Printed and bound in Great Britain by Clays Ltd, St Ives plc

Contents/Table des matières

Preface

This pocket-sized dictionary from Harrap is aimed at students from beginners to intermediate level. For this brand new edition, the whole text has been thoroughly reread, revised and updated.

This informative little book packs as many words into its pages as possible, covering all the basic vocabulary students will need for everyday communication. It also features terms from a wide range of technical areas (computing, biology, education, finance etc), and, like all Harrap dictionaries, offers excellent coverage of colloquial and idiomatic language. In addition, many new words have been added from rapidly developing fields such as the Internet and mobile communication, including **broadband**, **chatroom**, **text** and **top-up card** (**connexion à haut débit**, **site de bavardage**, **texto** and **carte de recharge** in French). The most up-to-date words found in the press are also included, such as **cloning**, **reality TV** and **SARS** (**clonage**, **télé-réalité** and **SRAS** in French).

Another feature of the dictionary is the boxes on "false friends" which appear throughout the text, highlighting words that speakers of the other language often find confusing.

The dictionary has a clear, systematic layout which makes it a reliable and user-friendly tool for both finding translations of French items and translating from English into French. In order to be able to include as much information as possible, only the base forms are entered as headwords; derivatives (eg **commonly** from **common**) are given at the end of the entry in alphabetical order.

Structure of Entries

baccalauréat [bakalɔrea] *nm* = secondary school examination qualifying for entry to university, *Br* ≃ A-levels, *Am* ≃ high school diploma

- The equals sign = introduces an explanation when there is no translation possible.
- The sign ≃ introduces a word that has a roughly equivalent status but is not identical.

forcer [fɔrse] **1** *vt (obliger)* to force; *(porte)* to force open; *(voix)* to strain; **f. qn à faire qch** to force sb to do sth; **f. la main à qn** to force sb's hand; *Fam* **f. la dose** to overdo it **2** *vi (appuyer, tirer)* to force it; *(se surmener)* to overdo it **3** **se forcer** *vpr* to force oneself (**à faire** to do)

- The different grammatical categories are cleary indicated, introduced by a bold Arabic numeral.
- Usage labels are clearly shown.

échoir* [eʃwar] *vi* **é. à qn** to fall to sb

- The asterisk indicates that the verb is irregular. See the verb tables in the middle of the book for information on how to conjugate it.

agenda [aʒɛ̃da] *nm Br* diary, *Am* datebook; **a. électronique** electronic organizer

> Il faut noter que le nom anglais **agenda** est un faux ami. Il signifie **ordre du jour**.

- British and American translations clearly indicated.
- Usage notes warn users when a word is a false friend.

> **grand, -e** [grã, grãd] **1** *adj* big, large; *(en hauteur)* tall; *(chaleur, découverte, âge, mérite, ami)* great; *(bruit)* loud; *(différence)* big, great; *(adulte, mûr, plus âgé)* grown-up, big; *(âme)* noble; *(illustre)* great; **g. frère** *(plus âgé)* big brother; **le g. air** the open air; **il est g. temps que je parte** it's high time that I left; **il n'y avait pas g. monde** there were not many people **2** *adv* **g. ouvert** *(yeux, fenêtre)* wide open; **ouvrir g.** to open wide; **en g.** on a grand *or* large scale **3** *nmf (à l'école)* senior; *(adulte)* grown-up ▪**grandement** *adv (beaucoup)* greatly; *(généreusement)* grandly; **avoir g. de quoi vivre** to have plenty to live on ▪**grand-mère** *(pl* **grands-mères)** *nf* grandmother ▪**grand-père** *(pl* **grands-pères)** *nm* grandfather ▪**grand-route** *(pl* **grand-routes)** *nf* main road ▪**grands-parents** *nmpl* grandparents

- Derivatives are placed at the end of each entry in alphabetical order, introduced by ▪.

- The plural of compound French nouns is given systematically.

> **différence** [diferãs] *nf* difference (de in); **à la d. de qn/qch** unlike sb/sth; **faire la d. entre** to make a distinction between

- The most common prepositions used are given after the translation.

Préface

S'inscrivant dans la longue tradition Harrap, ce dictionnaire de poche s'adresse à l'utilisateur débutant ou de niveau intermédiaire et au voyageur qui souhaite avoir à portée de la main un ouvrage lui permettant de traduire les termes les plus fréquents de la langue. Reprenant les éditions précédentes, le texte a été entièrement revu, corrigé et mis à jour. Ouvrage fiable et de consultation aisée, il permet sans difficulté de sélectionner la traduction recherchée grâce à une présentation claire et systématique.

La langue familière y est bien représentée ainsi que les termes de base de divers domaines techniques (informatique, biologie, enseignement, finance, etc.) et le vocabulaire apparu le plus récemment y fait son entrée. De plus, de nombreux termes nouveaux issus de domaines en pleine expansion tels qu'Internet et la téléphonie mobile ont été ajoutés, tels que **connexion à haut débit**, **site de bavardage**, **carte de recharge** et **texto** (**broadband**, **chatroom**, **top-up card** et **text** en anglais). Les termes nouveaux les plus fréquemment utilisés dans la presse sont également présents : c'est le cas notamment de **clonage**, **SRAS** et **télé-réalité** (**cloning**, **SARS** et **reality TV** en anglais).

En outre, des notes sur les faux amis ont été inclues dans le texte pour mettre l'utilisateur en garde lorsqu'un terme anglais ressemble au français mais a une signification tout autre.

Par souci de concision, seuls les termes de base apparaissent en entrées : leurs dérivés (p.ex. **chanceux** de **chance**) sont donnés en fin d'article et présentés par ordre alphabétique. La prononciation et l'accent tonique du vocabulaire anglais ne sont repris pour les dérivés que s'ils diffèrent de la forme de base.

Structure des entrées

> **baccalauréat** [bakalɔrea] *nm* **=** secondary school examination qualifying for entry to university, *Br* ≃ A-levels, *Am* ≃ high school diploma

- Le signe = introduit une explication quand il n'y a pas de traduction possible.
- Le signe ≃ introduit les équivalents culturels.

> **forcer** [fɔrse] **1** *vt (obliger)* to force; *(porte)* to force open; *(voix)* to strain; **f. qn à faire qch** to force sb to do sth; **f. la main à qn** to force sb's hand; *Fam* **f. la dose** to overdo it **2** *vi (appuyer, tirer)* to force it; *(se surmener)* to overdo it **3 se forcer** *vpr* to force oneself (**à faire** to do)

- Les différentes catégories grammaticales ressortent clairement : elles sont introduites par un chiffre arabe et sont toujours présentées dans le même ordre.
- Des indicateurs d'usage sont donnés.

> **échoir*** [eʃwar] *vi* **é. à qn** to fall to sb

- * indique que le verbe est irrégulier. Se reporter aux pages centrales.

> **athlète** [atlɛt] *nmf* athlete ▪**athlétique** *adj* athletic ▪**athlétisme** *nm* athletics *(sing)*

- Indique le nombre lorsqu'une traduction est ambiguë.

grand, -e [grã, grãd] **1** *adj* big, large; *(en hauteur)* tall; *(chaleur, découverte, âge, mérite, ami)* great; *(bruit)* loud; *(différence)* big, great; *(adulte, mûr, plus âgé)* grown-up, big; *(âme)* noble; *(illustre)* great; **g. frère** *(plus âgé)* big brother; **le g. air** the open air; **il est g. temps que je parte** it's high time that I left; **il n'y avait pas g. monde** there were not many people **2** *adv* **g. ouvert** *(yeux, fenêtre)* wide open; **ouvrir g.** to open wide; **en g.** on a grand *or* large scale **3** *nmf (à l'école)* senior; *(adulte)* grown-up ▪**grandement** *adv (beaucoup)* greatly; *(généreusement)* grandly; **avoir g. de quoi vivre** to have plenty to live on ▪**grand-mère** *(pl* grands-mères) *nf* grandmother ▪**grand-père** *(pl* grands-pères) *nm* grandfather ▪**grand-route** *(pl* grand-routes) *nf* main road ▪**grands-parents** *nmpl* grandparents

- Les dérivés sont clairement placés en fin d'article et rangés par ordre alphabétique.
- Le pluriel des noms composés est donné à chaque fois.

agenda [aʒɛ̃da] *nm Br* diary, *Am* datebook; **a. électronique** electronic organizer

Il faut noter que le nom anglais **agenda** est un faux ami. Il signifie **ordre du jour**.

- La différence entre les termes anglais et américains est clairement indiquée.
- Une note d'usage avertit le lecteur qu'il a affaire à un faux ami.

différence [diferɑ̃s] *nf* difference (de in); **à la d. de qn/qch** unlike sb/sth; **faire la d. entre** to make a distinction between

- Les prépositions les plus courantes apparaissent à la suite de la traduction.

Abbreviations		Abréviations
gloss	=	glose
[introduces an explanation]		[introduit une explication]
cultural equivalent	≃	équivalent culturel
[introduces a translation which has a roughly equivalent status in the target language]		[introduit une traduction dont les connotations dans la langue cible sont comparables]
abbreviation	*abbr, abrév*	abréviation
adjective	*adj*	adjectif
adverb	*adv*	adverbe
agriculture	*Agr*	agriculture
American English	*Am*	anglais américain
anatomy	*Anat*	anatomie
architecture	*Archit*	architecture
slang	*Arg*	argot
article	*art*	article
cars	*Aut*	automobile
auxiliary	*aux*	auxiliaire
aviation	*Av*	aviation
Belgian French	*Belg*	belgicisme
biology	*Biol*	biologie
botany	*Bot*	botanique
British English	*Br*	anglais britannique
Canadian French	*Can*	canadianisme
chemistry	*Chem, Chim*	chimie
cinema	*Cin*	cinéma
commerce	*Com*	commerce
computing	*Comptr*	informatique
conjunction	*conj*	conjonction
cooking	*Culin*	cuisine
economics	*Econ, Écon*	économie
electricity, electronics	*El, Él*	électricité, électronique
exclamation	*exclam*	exclamation
feminine	*f*	féminin
familiar	*Fam*	familier
figurative	*Fig*	figuré
finance	*Fin*	finance
geography	*Geog, Géog*	géographie
geology	*Geol, Géol*	géologie
gymnastics	*Gym*	gymnastique
history	*Hist*	histoire
humorous	*Hum*	humoristique
industry	*Ind*	industrie
invariable	*inv*	invariable
journalism	*Journ*	journalisme
law	*Jur*	droit
law	*Law*	droit
linguistics	*Ling*	linguistique
masculine	*m*	masculin
mathematics	*Math*	mathématique
medicine	*Med, Méd*	médecine
meteorology	*Met, Météo*	météorologie
military	*Mil*	militaire
music	*Mus*	musique
noun	*n*	nom
shipping	*Naut*	nautisme
feminine noun	*nf*	nom féminin
feminine plural noun	*nfpl*	nom féminin pluriel

masculine noun	*nm*	nom masculin
masculine and feminine noun	*nmf*	nom masculin et féminin
masculine plural noun	*nmpl*	nom masculin pluriel
plural noun	*npl*	nom pluriel
computing	*Ordinat*	ordinateurs, informatique
pejorative	*Pej, Péj*	péjoratif
philosophy	*Phil*	philosophie
photography	*Phot*	photographie
physics	*Phys*	physique
plural	*pl*	pluriel
politics	*Pol*	politique
past participle	*pp*	participe passé
prefix	*pref, préf*	préfixe
preposition	*prep, prép*	préposition
pronoun	*pron*	pronom
past tense	*pt*	prétérit
something	*qch*	quelque chose
somebody	*qn*	quelqu'un
registered trademark	®	marque déposée
rail	*Rail*	chemins de fer
religion	*Rel*	religion
somebody	*sb*	quelqu'un
school	*Sch, Scol*	domaine scolaire
Scottish English	*Scot*	anglais d'Écosse
singular	*sing*	singulier
slang	*Sl*	argot
something	*sth*	quelque chose
suffix	*suff*	suffixe
technical term	*Tech*	terme technique
telecommunications	*Tel, Tél*	télécommunications
textiles	*Tex*	textile
very familiar	*très Fam*	très familier
television	*TV*	télévision
typography, printing	*Typ*	typographie, imprimerie
university	*Univ*	domaine universitaire
verb	*v*	verbe
very familiar	*very Fam*	très familier
intransitive verb	*vi*	verbe intransitif
reflexive verb	*vpr*	verbe pronominal
transitive verb	*vt*	verbe transitif
inseparable transitive verb	*vt insep*	verbe transitif à particule inséparable [par ex.: **he looks after the children** il s'occupe des enfants]
separable transitive verb	*vt sep*	verbe transitif à particule séparable [par ex.: **she sent the present back** *or* **she sent back the present** elle a rendu le cadeau]
vulgar	*Vulg*	vulgaire

Prononciation de l'anglais

Pour indiquer la prononciation anglaise, nous avons utilisé dans ce dictionnaire les symboles de l'API (Alphabet phonétique international). Pour chaque son anglais, vous trouverez dans le tableau ci-dessous des exemples de mots anglais, suivis de mots français présentant un son similaire. Une explication est donnée lorsqu'il n'y a pas d'équivalent en français.

Caractère API	Exemple en anglais	Exemple en français
Consonnes		
[b]	babble	bébé
[d]	dig	dent
[dʒ]	giant, jig	jean
[f]	fit, physics	face
[g]	grey, big	gag
[h]	happy	h aspiré : à quelques rares exceptions près, il est toujours prononcé en anglais
[j]	yellow	yaourt
[k]	clay, kick	car
[l]	lip, pill	lilas
[m]	mummy	maman
[n]	nip, pin	né
[ŋ]	sing	parking
[p]	pip	papa
[r]	rig, write	Pas d'équivalent français : se prononce en plaçant le bout de la langue au milieu du palais
[(r)]		Seulement prononcé en cas de liaison avec la voyelle qui suit comme dans : far away; the car is blue
[s]	sick, science	silence
[ʃ]	ship, nation	chèvre
[t]	tip, butt	tartine
[tʃ]	chip, batch	atchoum
[Θ]	thick	Son proche du /s/ français, il se prononce en plaçant le bout de la langue entre les dents du haut et celles du bas
[ð]	this, with	Son proche du /z/ français, il se prononce en plaçant le bout de la langue entre les dents du haut et celles du bas
[v]	vague, give	vie
[w]	wit, why	whisky

Caractère API	Exemple en anglais	Exemple en français
[z]	zip, physics	rose
[ʒ]	pleasure	je
[χ]	loch	Existe seulement dans certains mots écossais. Pas d'équivalent français : se prononce du fond de la gorge, comme Bach en allemand ou la 'jota' espagnole.
Voyelles		
[æ]	rag	natte
[ɑː]	large, half	pâte
[e]	set	/e/ moins ouvert que le [ɛ] français
[ɜː]	curtain, were	heure
[ə]	utter	cheval
[ɪ]	big, women	/i/ bref, à mi-chemin entre les sons [ɛ] et [i] français (plus proche de 'net' que de 'vite')
[iː]	leak, wee	/i/ plus long que le [i] français
[ɒ]	lock	bonne – mais plus ouvert et prononcé au fond du palais
[ɔː]	wall, cork	baume – mais plus ouvert et prononcé au fond du palais
[ʊ]	put, look	Son à mi-chemin entre un /ou/ bref et un /o/ ouvert
[uː]	moon	Son /ou/ prolongé
[ʌ]	cup	À mi-chemin entre un /a/ et un /e/ ouverts
Diphtongues : Elles sont rares en français et sont la combinaison de deux sons.		
[aɪ]	why, high, lie	aïe
[aʊ]	how	miaou, aoûtat – mais se prononce comme un seul son
[eə]	bear, share, where	flair
[eɪ]	day, make, main	merveille
[əʊ]	show, go	Combinaison d'un /o/ fermé et d'un /ou/
[ɪə]	here, gear	Combinaison d'un /i/ long suivi d'un /e/ ouvert bref
[ɔɪ]	boy, soil	langue d'oïl
[ʊə]	sure	Combinaison d'un son /ou/ suivi d'un /e/ ouvert bref

French Pronunciation

French pronunciation is shown in this dictionary using the symbols of the IPA (International Phonetic Alphabet). In the table below, examples of French words using these sounds are given, followed by English words which have a similar sound. Where there is no near-equivalent in English, an explanation is given.

IPA symbol	French example	English example
Consonants		
[b]	bébé	but
[d]	donner	door
[f]	forêt	fire
[g]	gare	get
[ʒ]	jour	pleasure
[k]	carte	kitten
[l]	lire	lonely
[m]	maman	mat
[n]	ni	now
[ŋ]	parking	singing
[ɲ]	campagne	canyon
[p]	patte	pat
[r]	rare	Like an English /r/ but pronounced at the back of the throat
[s]	soir	sit
[ʃ]	chose	sham
[t]	table	tap
[v]	valeur	value
[z]	zéro	zero
Vowels		
[a]	chat	cat
[ɑ]	âge	gasp
[e]	été	bay
[ɛ]	père	bed
[ə]	le	amend
[ø]	deux	Does not exist in English : [e] pronounced with the lips rounded
[œ]	seul	curtain
[i]	vite	bee – not quite as long as the English [i:]
[ɔ]	donner	cot – slightly more open than the English /o/
[o]	chaud	daughter – but higher than its English equivalent

IPA symbol	French example	English example
[u]	tout	**you** – but shorter than its English equivalent
[y]	voiture	Does not exist in English: [i] with lips rounded
[ã]	enfant	Nasal sound pronounced lower and further back in the mouth than [ɔ̃]

Vowels

[ɛ̃]	vin	Nasal sound: /a/ sound pronounced letting air pass through the nose
[ɔ̃]	bonjour	Nasal sound: closed /o/ sound pronounced letting air pass through the nose
[œ̃]	un	Nasal sound: like [ɛ̃] but with lips more rounded

Semi-vowels

[w]	voir	week
[j]	yoyo, paille	yard
[ɥ]	nuit	Does not exist in English: the vowel [y] elided with the following vowel

English-French
Anglais-Français

A, a[1] [eɪ] n (a) A, a m inv; **5A** (in address, street number) 5 bis; **to go from A to B** aller du point A au point B (b) Mus **A** la m (c) Sch (grade) **to get an A in French** = obtenir une très bonne note en français (d) (street atlas) **an A to Z of London** un plan de Londres

a[2] [ə, stressed eɪ]

a devient **an** [ən, stressed æn] devant voyelle ou h muet.

indefinite article (a) (in general) un, une; **a man** un homme; **an apple** une pomme; **an hour** une heure

(b) (definite article in French) **60 pence a kilo** 60 pence le kilo; **50 km an hour** 50 km à l'heure; **I have a broken arm** j'ai le bras cassé

(c) (article omitted in French) **he's a doctor/a father** il est médecin/père; **Caen, a town in Normandy** Caen, ville de Normandie; **what a man!** quel homme!; **a hundred** cent; **a thousand** mille

(d) (a certain) **a Mr Smith** un certain M. Smith

(e) (time) **twice a month** deux fois par mois

(f) (some) **to make a noise/a fuss** faire du bruit/des histoires

aback [ə'bæk] adv **taken a. (by)** déconcerté (par)

abandon [ə'bændən] **1** n (freedom of manner) abandon m **2** vt abandonner; **to a. ship** abandonner le navire ▪ **abandonment** n abandon m

abashed [ə'bæʃt] adj honteux, -euse (at de)

abate [ə'beɪt] vi (of storm, pain) se calmer; (of noise) diminuer; (of flood) baisser

abbey ['æbɪ] (pl -eys) n abbaye f

abbot ['æbət] n abbé m

abbreviate [ə'briːvɪeɪt] vt abréger ▪ **abbreviation** n abréviation f

abdicate ['æbdɪkeɪt] vti abdiquer ▪ **abdication** n abdication f

abdomen ['æbdəmən] n abdomen m ▪ **abdominal** [əb'dɒmɪnəl] adj abdominal ▪ **abdominals** npl abdominaux mpl

abduct [æb'dʌkt] vt (kidnap) enlever ▪ **abduction** n enlèvement m, rapt m

aberration [æbə'reɪʃən] n (folly, lapse) aberration f

abet [ə'bet] (pt & pp -tt-) vt Law **to aid and a. sb** être le complice de qn

abeyance [ə'beɪəns] n **in a.** (matter) en suspens; (law) en désuétude

abhor [əb'hɔː(r)] (pt & pp -rr-) vt avoir horreur de, exécrer ▪ **abhorrent** [-'hɒrənt] adj exécrable

abide [ə'baɪd] **1** vi **to a. by** (promise) tenir; (decision) se plier à **2** vt supporter; **I can't a. him** je ne peux pas le supporter

ability [ə'bɪlɪtɪ] (pl -ies) n capacité f (**to do** de faire); **he's a man of great a.** c'est quelqu'un de très compétent; **to the best of my a.** de mon mieux

abject ['æbdʒekt] adj (contemptible) abject; (poverty-stricken) misérable; **a. poverty** la misère noire

ablaze [ə'bleɪz] adj en feu; **to set sth a.** (person) mettre le feu à qch; (candle, spark) embraser qch; **a. with** (light) resplendissant de; **his eyes were a. with anger** il avait les yeux brillants de colère

able ['eɪbəl] adj capable; **to be a. to do sth** être capable de faire qch, pouvoir faire qch; **to be a. to swim/drive** savoir nager/conduire ▪ **able-'bodied** adj robuste ▪ **ably** adv habilement

abnormal [æb'nɔːməl] adj anormal ▪ **abnormality** [-'mælɪtɪ] (pl -ies) n anomalie f; (physical) difformité f ▪ **abnormally** adv (more than usually) exceptionnellement

aboard [ə'bɔːd] **1** adv (on ship, plane) à bord; **all a.** (on train) en voiture; **to go a.** monter à bord **2** prep **a. the ship/plane** à bord du navire/de l'avion; **a. the train** dans le train

abode [ə'bəʊd] n Literary demeure f; Law domicile m; **of no fixed a.** sans domicile fixe

abolish [ə'bɒlɪʃ] vt abolir ▪ **abolition** [æbə'lɪʃən] n abolition f

abominable [ə'bɒmɪnəbəl] adj abominable ▪ **abomination** [-'neɪʃən] n abomination f

Aborigine [æbə'rɪdʒɪnɪ] n Aborigène mf (d'Australie)

abort [ə'bɔːt] **1** vt (space flight, computer program) abandonner; Med **the foetus was aborted** la grossesse a été interrompue **2** vi Med faire une fausse couche ▪ **abortion** n avortement m; **to have an a.** se faire avorter ▪ **abortive** adj (plan, attempt) manqué, avorté

abound [ə'baʊnd] vi abonder (**in** or **with** en)

about [ə'baʊt] **1** adv (a) (approximately) à peu près, environ; **at a. two o'clock** vers deux heures; **a. time!** ce n'est pas trop tôt!

(b) (here and there) çà et là, ici et là; Fig **there's a lot of flu a. at the moment** il y a beaucoup de cas de grippe en ce moment; **there's a rumour**

a. (that…) il y a une rumeur qui circule (selon laquelle…); **to look a.** regarder autour de soi; **to follow someone a.** suivre quelqu'un partout; **there are lots a.** il y en a beaucoup; **(out and) a.** *(after illness)* sur pied; **(up and) a.** *(out of bed)* levé, debout

2 *prep* (**a**) *(around)* **a. the garden** autour du jardin; **a. the streets** par *or* dans les rues (**b**) *(near to)* **a. here** par ici (**c**) *(concerning)* au sujet de; **to talk a. sth** parler de qch; **a book a. sth** un livre sur qch; **what's it (all) a.?** de quoi s'agit-il?; **while you're a. it** pendant que vous y êtes (**d**) (*+ infinitive*) **a. to do** sur le point de faire; **I was a. to say…** j'étais sur le point de dire… ▪**about-'face, about-'turn** *n* Mil demi-tour *m*; *Fig* volte-face *f inv*

above [əˈbʌv] **1** *adv* au-dessus de; *(in book, document)* ci-dessus; **from a.** d'en haut; **the floor a.** l'étage *m* du dessus

2 *prep* (**a**) au-dessus de; **a. the bridge** *(on river)* en amont du pont; **he's a. me** *(in rank)* c'est mon supérieur; **she's not a. lying** elle n'est pas incapable de mentir; **he's not a. asking** il n'est pas trop fier pour demander; **a. all** surtout (**b**) *(with numbers)* plus de; **the temperature didn't rise above 2°C** la température n'a pas dépassé 2°C ▪**above-'board 1** *adj* honnête **2** *adv* sans tricherie ▪**above-mentioned** *adj* susmentionné

abrasion [əˈbreɪʒən] **1** *n* frottement *m*; *(wound)* écorchure *f* ▪**abrasive** [-sɪv] **1** *adj (substance)* abrasif, -ive; *Fig (person, manner)* caustique **2** *n* abrasif *m*

abreast [əˈbrest] *adv* côte à côte, de front; **four a.** par rangs de quatre; **to keep a. of** *or* **with** *(events)* se tenir au courant de

abridge [əˈbrɪdʒ] *vt (book)* abréger

abroad [əˈbrɔːd] *adv* (**a**) *(in or to a foreign country)* à l'étranger; **from a.** de l'étranger (**b**) *(over a wide area)* de tous côtés; **there's a rumour a. that…** il y a un bruit qui court comme quoi…

abrogate [ˈæbrəgeɪt] *vt* abroger

abrupt [əˈbrʌpt] *adj (sudden)* brusque, soudain; *(rude)* brusque, abrupt; *(slope, style)* abrupt ▪**abruptly** *adv (suddenly)* brusquement; *(rudely)* avec brusquerie

abscess [ˈæbses] *n* abcès *m*

abscond [əbˈskɒnd] *vi Formal* s'enfuir

absence [ˈæbsəns] *n* absence *f*; **in the a. of** *(person)* en l'absence de; *(thing)* faute de

absent 1 [ˈæbsənt] *adj* absent (**from** de) **2** [æbˈsent] *vt* **to a. oneself (from)** s'absenter (de) ▪**absent-'minded** *adj* distrait ▪**absent-'mindedness** *n* distraction *f*

absentee [æbsənˈtiː] *n* absent, -ente *mf* ▪**absenteeism** *n* absentéisme *m*

absolute [ˈæbsəluːt] *adj* absolu; *(proof)*

indiscutable; **he's an a. coward** c'est un vrai lâche; **he's an a. fool!** il est complètement idiot!; **it's an a. disgrace!** c'est une honte! ▪**absolutely** *adv* absolument; **a. forbidden** formellement interdit; **you're a. right** tu as tout à fait raison

absolve [əbˈzɒlv] *vt (sinner, accused)* absoudre; **to a. from** *(vow)* libérer de ▪**absolution** [æbsəˈluːʃən] *n* absolution *f*

absorb [əbˈzɔːb] *vt (liquid)* absorber; *(shock)* amortir; **to be absorbed in sth** être plongé dans qch ▪**absorbing** *adj (work)* absorbant; *(book, film)* passionnant ▪**absorption** *n* absorption *f*

absorbent [əbˈzɔːbənt] *adj* absorbant

abstain [əbˈsteɪn] *vi* Pol s'abstenir; **to a. from sth/from doing sth** s'abstenir de qch/de faire qch ▪**abstention** *n* Pol abstention *f*

abstemious [əbˈstiːmɪəs] *adj* sobre, frugal

abstinence [ˈæbstɪnəns] *n* abstinence *f*

abstract [ˈæbstrækt] **1** *adj* abstrait **2** *n* (**a**) *(notion)* **the a. l'abstrait** *m* (**b**) *(summary)* résumé *m* **3** [əbˈstrækt] *vt Formal* extraire (**de** from)

abstruse [əbˈstruːs] *adj* obscur

absurd [əbˈsɜːd] *adj* absurde, ridicule ▪**absurdity** *(pl* -ies*)* *n* absurdité *f* ▪**absurdly** *adv* absurdement

abundant [əˈbʌndənt] *adj* abondant ▪**abundance** *n* abondance *f* ▪**abundantly** *adv* **a. clear** parfaitement clair

abuse 1 [əˈbjuːs] *n (of power)* abus *m* (**of** de); *(of child)* mauvais traitements *mpl*; *(insults)* injures *fpl* **2** [əˈbjuːz] *vt (misuse)* abuser de; *(ill-treat)* maltraiter; *(insult)* injurier ▪**abusive** [əˈbjuːsɪv] *adj (person, language)* grossier, -ière

> Note that the French verb *abuser* is a false friend. It is never used to mean **to insult**.

abysmal [əˈbɪzməl] *adj Fam (bad)* exécrable

abyss [əˈbɪs] *n* abîme *m*

academic [ækəˈdemɪk] **1** *adj* (**a**) *(year, diploma)* *(of school)* scolaire; *(of university)* universitaire (**b**) *(scholarly)* intellectuel, -uelle (**c**) *(theoretical)* **the issue is of purely a. interest** cette question n'a d'intérêt que d'un point de vue théorique; **this is a. now** cela n'a plus d'importance (**d**) *(style)* académique **2** *n (teacher)* universitaire *mf*

academy [əˈkædəmɪ] *(pl* -ies*)* *n (society)* académie *f*; *(military)* école *f*; **a. of music** conservatoire *m*

accede [əkˈsiːd] *vi Formal* **to a. to** *(request, throne, position)* accéder à

accelerate [əkˈseləreɪt] **1** *vt* accélérer **2** *vi (of pace)* s'accélérer; *(of vehicle, driver)* accélérer ▪**accele'ration** *n* accélération *f* ▪**accelerator** *n* accélérateur *m*

accent [ˈæksənt] *n* accent *m* ▪**accentuate** [-ˈsentʃʊeɪt] *vt* accentuer

accept [ək'sept] *vt* accepter ▪ **acceptable** *adj (worth accepting, tolerable)* acceptable; **to be a. to sb** convenir à qn ▪ **acceptance** *n* acceptation *f*, *(approval, favour)* accueil *m* favorable ▪ **accepted** *adj (opinion)* reçu; *(fact)* reconnu

access ['ækses] **1** *n* accès *m* (**to sth** à qch; **to sb** auprès de qn); **a. road** route *f* d'accès; *Comptr* **a. code** code *m* d'accès; *Comptr* **a. provider** fournisseur *m* d'accès **2** *vt Comptr* accéder à ▪ **ac'cessible** *adj* accessible

accessories [ək'sesərɪz] *npl (objects)* accessoires *mpl*

accessory [ək'sesərɪ] *(pl* **-ies)** *n Law (accomplice)* complice *mf* (**to** de)

accident ['æksɪdənt] *n* accident *m*; **by a.** accidentellement; *(by chance)* par hasard ▪ **accident-prone** *adj* prédisposé aux accidents ▪ **accidental** [-'dentəl] *adj* accidentel, -elle ▪ **accidentally** [-'dentəlɪ] *adv* accidentellement; *(by chance)* par hasard

acclaim [ə'kleɪm] **1** *n* **(critical) a.** éloges *mpl*; **the film enjoys critical a.** ce film est salué par la critique **2** *vt (cheer)* acclamer; *(praise)* faire l'éloge de

acclimatize [ə'klaɪmətaɪz] *(Am* **acclimate** ['æklɪmeɪt]) **1** *vt* acclimater **2** *vi* s'acclimater ▪ **acclimatization** *(Am* **acclimation)** acclimatisation *f*

accolade ['ækəleɪd] *n Fig (praise)* louange *f*

accommodate [ə'kɒmədeɪt] *vt* **(a)** *(of house)* loger **(b)** *(reconcile)* concilier **(c)** *(supply)* fournir **(sb with sth** qch à qn) **(d)** *(oblige)* rendre service à ▪ **accommodating** *adj* accommodant, obligeant

> Note that the French verb **accommoder** is a false friend and is rarely a translation for the English verb **to accommodate**. Its most common translations are to **adapt** and to **prepare**.

accommodation [əkɒmə'deɪʃən] *n* **(a)** *(Am* **accommodations)** *(lodging)* logement *m*; *(rented room(s))* chambre(s) *f(pl)* **(b)** *Formal (compromise)* compromis *m*

accompany [ə'kʌmpənɪ] *(pt & pp* **-ied)** *vt* accompagner ▪ **accompaniment** *n* accompagnement *m* ▪ **accompanist** *n (musician)* accompagnateur, -trice *mf*

accomplice [ə'kʌmplɪs] *n* complice *mf*

accomplish [ə'kʌmplɪʃ] *vt (task, duty)* accomplir; *(aim)* atteindre ▪ **accomplished** *adj* accompli ▪ **accomplishment** *n (of task, duty)* accomplissement *m*; *(thing achieved)* réalisation *f*; **writing a novel is a great a.** écrire un roman, c'est vraiment quelque chose; **accomplishments** *(skills)* talents *mpl*

accord [ə'kɔːd] **1** *n* accord *m*; **of my own a.** de mon plein gré **2** *vt (grant)* accorder ▪ **accordance** *n* **in a. with** conformément à

according [ə'kɔːdɪŋ] **according to** *prep* selon, d'après ▪ **accordingly** *adv* en conséquence

accordion [ə'kɔːdɪən] *n* accordéon *m*

accost [ə'kɒst] *vt* accoster, aborder

account [ə'kaʊnt] **1** *n* **(a)** *(with bank or firm)* compte *m*; **accounts department** comptabilité *f* **(b)** *(report)* compte rendu *m*; *(explanation)* explication *f*; **to give a good a. of oneself** s'en tirer à son avantage **(c)** *(expressions)* **by all accounts** au dire de tous; **on a. of** à cause de; **on no a.** en aucun cas; **to take sth into a.** tenir compte de qch **2** *vi* **to a. for** *(explain)* expliquer; *(give reckoning of)* rendre compte de; *(represent)* représenter ▪ **accountable** *adj* responsable (**for** de; **to** devant)

accountant [ə'kaʊntənt] *n* comptable *mf* ▪ **accountancy** *n* comptabilité *f*

accrue [ə'kruː] *vi Fin (of interest)* s'accumuler; **to a. to sb** *(of advantage)* revenir à qn

accumulate [ə'kjuːmjʊleɪt] **1** *vt* accumuler **2** *vi* s'accumuler ▪ **accumulation** [-'leɪʃən] *n* accumulation *f*

accurate ['ækjʊrət] *adj* exact, précis ▪ **accuracy** *n* exactitude *f*, précision *f* ▪ **accurately** *adv* avec précision

accuse [ə'kjuːz] *vt* **to a. sb** (**of sth/doing sth**) accuser qn (de qch/faire qch) ▪ **accusation** [ækjʊ'zeɪʃən] *n* accusation *f*; **to make an a. against sb** lancer une accusation contre qn ▪ **accused** *n Law* **the a.** l'accusé, -ée *mf* ▪ **accusing** *adj* accusateur, -trice

accustom [ə'kʌstəm] *vt* habituer, accoutumer ▪ **accustomed** *adj* **to be a. to sth/to doing sth** être habitué à qch/à faire qch; **to get a. to sth/to doing sth** s'habituer à qch/à faire qch

ace [eɪs] *n* **(a)** *(card, person)* as *m* **(b)** *(at tennis)* ace *m*

acetate ['æsɪteɪt] *n* acétate *m*

acetic [ə'siːtɪk] *adj (acid)* acétique

ache [eɪk] **1** *n* douleur *f* **2** *vi* faire mal; **my head aches** j'ai mal à la tête; **I'm aching all over** j'ai mal partout; **it makes my heart a.** cela me fend le cœur; *Fam* **to be aching to do sth** brûler de faire qch ▪ **aching** *adj* douloureux, -euse

achieve [ə'tʃiːv] *vt (result)* obtenir; *(aim)* atteindre; *(ambition)* réaliser; *(victory)* remporter; **to a. success** réussir; **he'll never a. anything** il n'arrivera jamais à rien ▪ **achievement** *n (success)* réussite *f*; *(of ambition)* réalisation *f*; **writing a novel is quite an a.** écrire un roman, c'est vraiment quelque chose

> Note that the French words **achever** and **achèvement** are false friends and are never translations for the English words **to achieve** and **achievement**. Their most common meanings are respectively **to complete** and **completion**.

acid ['æsɪd] *adj & n* acide (*m*); **a. rain** pluies *fpl* acides ▪ **acidity** [ə'sɪdɪtɪ] *n* acidité *f*

acknowledge [ək'nɒlɪdʒ] *vt* reconnaître (**as** pour); (*greeting*) répondre à; **to a. (receipt of)** accuser réception de; **to a. defeat** s'avouer vaincu ▪ **acknowledg(e)ment** *n* (*of letter*) accusé *m* de réception; (*receipt*) reçu *m*; (*confession*) aveu *m* (**of** de); **in a. of** en reconnaissance de

acme ['ækmɪ] *n* sommet *m*, comble *m*

acne ['æknɪ] *n* acné *f*

acorn ['eɪkɔːn] *n* gland *m*

acoustic [ə'kuːstɪk] *adj* acoustique ▪ **acoustics** *npl* acoustique *f*

acquaint [ə'kweɪnt] *vt* **to a. sb with sth** informer qn de qch; **to be acquainted with** (*person*) connaître; (*fact*) savoir; **we are acquainted** on se connaît ▪ **acquaintance** *n* (*person, knowledge*) connaissance *f*

acquiesce [ækwɪ'es] *vi* (a) (*agree*) acquiescer (**in/to** à) (b) (*collude*) **to a. in sth** ne pas s'opposer à qch ▪ **acquiescence** *n* acquiescement *m*

acquire [ə'kwaɪə(r)] *vt* acquérir; (*taste*) prendre (**for** à); (*friends*) se faire; **acquired taste** goût *m* qui s'acquiert ▪ **acquisition** [ækwɪ'zɪʃən] *n* acquisition *f* ▪ **acquisitive** [ə'kwɪzɪtɪv] *adj* avide, cupide

acquit [ə'kwɪt] (*pt & pp* **-tt-**) *vt* (a) *Law* **to a. sb (of a crime)** acquitter qn (b) **to a. oneself badly/well** mal/bien s'en tirer ▪ **acquittal** *n* acquittement *m*

acre ['eɪkə(r)] *n* acre *f* (≃ *0,4 hectare*); *Fam* **acres of space** plein de place

acrid ['ækrɪd] *adj* (*smell, taste*) âcre

acrimonious [ækrɪ'məʊnɪəs] *adj* acerbe

acrobat ['ækrəbæt] *n* acrobate *mf* ▪ **acro'batic** *adj* acrobatique; **a. movement** or **feat** acrobatie *f* ▪ **acro'batics** *npl* acrobaties *fpl*

acronym ['ækrənɪm] *n* sigle *m*

across [ə'krɒs] **1** *prep* (*from side to side of*) d'un côté à l'autre de; (*on the other side of*) de l'autre côté de; (*crossways*) en travers de; **a bridge a. the river** un pont sur la rivière; **to walk** or **go a.** (*street, lawn*) traverser; **to run/swim a.** traverser en courant/à la nage **2** *adv* **to be a kilometre a.** (*wide*) avoir un kilomètre de large; **to get sth a. to sb** faire comprendre qch à qn

acrylic [ə'krɪlɪk] **1** *adj* (*paint, fibre*) acrylique; (*garment*) en acrylique **2** *n* acrylique *m*

act [ækt] **1** *n* (a) (*deed*) acte *m*; **a. (of parliament)** loi *f*; **caught in the a.** pris sur le fait; **a. of walking** action *f* de marcher; **an a. of folly** une folie (b) *Theatre* (*part of play*) acte *m*; (*in circus, cabaret*) numéro *m*; *Fig* **to get one's a. together** se secouer; *Fam* **to put on an a.** jouer la comédie; *Fam* **in on the a.** dans le coup **2** *vt* (*part in play or film*) jouer; **to a. the fool** faire

l'idiot **3** *vi* (a) (*take action, behave*) agir; **it's time to a.** il est temps d'agir; **to a. as secretary/etc** faire office de secrétaire/etc; **to a. as a warning** servir d'avertissement; **to a. (up)on** (*affect*) agir sur; (*advice*) suivre; **to a. on behalf of sb** représenter qn; *Fam* **to a. up** (*of person, machine*) faire des siennes (b) (*in play, film*) jouer; (*pretend*) jouer la comédie ▪ **acting 1** *adj* (*temporary*) intérimaire **2** *n* (*of play*) représentation *f*; (*actor's art*) jeu *m*; (*career*) théâtre *m*

action ['ækʃən] *n* action *f*; (*military*) combats *mpl*; (*legal*) procès *m*, action *f*; **to take a.** prendre des mesures; **to put into a.** (*plan*) exécuter; **out of a.** (*machine*) hors service; (*person*) hors de combat; **killed in a.** mort au champ d'honneur

activate ['æktɪveɪt] *vt* *Chem* activer; (*mechanism*) déclencher

active ['æktɪv] **1** *adj* actif, -ive; (*interest, dislike*) vif (*f* vive); (*volcano*) en activité **2** *n* *Grammar* actif *m* ▪ **ac'tivity** (*pl* **-ies**) *n* activité *f*; (*in street*) animation *f*

activist ['æktɪvɪst] *n* activiste *mf*

actor ['æktə(r)] *n* acteur *m*

actress ['æktrɪs] *n* actrice *f*

actual ['æktʃʊəl] *adj* réel (*f* réelle); (*example*) concret, -ète; **the a. book** le livre même; **in a. fact** en réalité ▪ **actually** *adv* (*truly*) réellement; (*in fact*) en réalité, en fait

> Note that the French words **actuel** and **actuellement** are false friends and are never translations for the English words **actual** and **actually**. They mean respectively **present** and **at present**.

actuary ['æktʃʊərɪ] (*pl* **-ies**) *n* actuaire *mf*

acumen [*Br* 'ækjʊmən, *Am* ə'kjuːmən] *n* perspicacité *f*; **to have business a.** avoir le sens des affaires

acupuncture ['ækjʊpʌŋktʃə(r)] *n* acuponcture *f* ▪ **acupuncturist** *n* acuponcteur, -trice *mf*

acute [ə'kjuːt] *adj* (*pain, angle*) aigu (*f* aiguë); (*anxiety, emotion*) vif (*f* vive); (*mind, observer*) perspicace; (*shortage*) grave ▪ **acutely** *adv* (*suffer, feel*) profondément; (*painful*) extrêmement; **he's a. aware that…** il a parfaitement conscience du fait que…

AD [eɪ'diː] (*abbr* **anno Domini**) *adv* apr. J.-C.

ad [æd] *n* *Fam* (*on radio, TV*) pub *f*; (*private, in newspaper*) annonce *f*; *Br* **small a.**, *Am* **want a.** petite annonce

Adam ['ædəm] *n* **A.'s apple** pomme *f* d'Adam

adamant ['ædəmənt] *adj* catégorique; **to be a. that…** maintenir que…

adapt [ə'dæpt] **1** *vt* adapter (**to** à); **to a. oneself to sth** s'adapter à qch **2** *vi* s'adapter ▪ **adaptable** *adj* (*person*) souple; (*instrument*) adaptable ▪ **adap'tation** *n* adaptation *f*

■**adapter, adaptor** n (for use abroad) adaptateur m; (for several plugs) prise f multiple

add [æd] 1 vt ajouter (**to** à; **that** que); **to a. (up or together)** (numbers) additionner; **to a. in** inclure 2 vi **to a. to** (increase) augmenter; **to a. up to** (total) s'élever à; (mean) signifier; (represent) constituer; Fam **it all adds up** tout s'explique

adder ['ædə(r)] n vipère f

addict ['ædɪkt] n drug **a.** toxicomane mf, drogué, -ée mf; **jazz/TV a.** fana(tique) mf du jazz/de la télé ■**addicted** [ə'dɪktɪd] adj **to be a. to drugs** être toxicomane; **to be a. to drink** être alcoolique; **to be a. to cigarettes** ne pas pouvoir se passer de tabac; **to be a. to sport** se passionner pour le sport; **to be a. to work** être un bourreau de travail; **to be a. to doing sth** (have the habit of) avoir la manie de faire qch ■**addiction** [ə'dɪkʃən] n (to drugs) dépendance f (to à); (to chocolate) passion f (to pour); **drug a.** toxicomanie f ■**addictive** adj (drug, TV) qui crée une dépendance

addition [ə'dɪʃən] n addition f; (increase) augmentation f; **in a.** de plus; **in a. to** en plus de ■**additional** adj supplémentaire

additive ['ædɪtɪv] n additif m

address [Br ə'dres, Am 'ædres] 1 n (on letter, parcel) adresse f; (speech) allocution f 2 [ə'dres] vt (person, audience) s'adresser à; (words, speech) adresser (**to** à); (letter) mettre l'adresse sur; **I addressed it to you** c'est à vous que je l'ai adressé ■**addressee** [ædre'siː] n destinataire mf

adenoids ['ædɪnɔɪdz] npl végétations fpl

adept [ə'dept] adj expert (**in** or **at** à)

adequate ['ædɪkwət] adj (enough) suffisant; (acceptable) convenable; (performance) acceptable ■**adequacy** n (of person) compétence f; **to doubt the a. of sth** douter que qch soit suffisant ■**adequately** adv (sufficiently) suffisamment; (acceptably) convenablement

adhere [əd'hɪə(r)] vi **to a. to** adhérer à; (decision, rule) s'en tenir à ■**adherence** n (support) adhésion f ■**adhesion** [-'hiːʒən] n (grip) adhérence f ■**adhesive** [-'hiːsɪv] adj & n adhésif (m)

ad infinitum [ædɪnfɪ'naɪtəm] adv à l'infini

adjacent [ə'dʒeɪsənt] adj (house, angle) adjacent (**to** à)

adjective ['ædʒɪktɪv] n adjectif m

adjoin [ə'dʒɔɪn] vt être attenant à ■**adjoining** adj attenant

adjourn [ə'dʒɜːn] 1 vt (postpone) ajourner; (session) suspendre 2 vi suspendre la séance; **to a. to another room** passer dans une autre pièce ■**adjournment** n ajournement m; (of session) suspension f (de séance)

adjudicate [ə'dʒuːdɪkeɪt] vti juger ■**adjudication** [-'keɪʃən] n jugement m ■**adjudicator** n juge m, arbitre m

adjust [ə'dʒʌst] vt (machine) régler; (machine part) ajuster, régler; (salaries, prices) (r)ajuster; (clothes) rajuster; **to a. (oneself) to sth** s'adapter à qch ■**adjustable** adj (seat) réglable ■**adjustment** n Tech réglage m; (of person) adaptation f; (of salaries, prices) réajustement m

ad-lib [æd'lɪb] 1 (pt & pp **-bb-**) vi improviser 2 adj (joke) improvisé 3 adv en improvisant

administer [əd'mɪnɪstə(r)] vt (manage, dispense) administrer (**to** à) ■**administration** [-'streɪʃən] n (administering, (government) gouvernement m ■**administrative** adj administratif, -ive ■**administrator** n administrateur, -trice mf

admirable ['ædmərəbəl] adj admirable ■**admiration** [-'reɪʃən] n admiration f

admiral ['ædmərəl] n amiral m

admire [əd'maɪə(r)] vt admirer (**for sth** pour qch; **for doing** de faire) ■**admirer** n admirateur, -trice mf ■**admiring** adj admiratif, -ive

admit [əd'mɪt] (pt & pp **-tt-**) 1 vt (let in) laisser entrer; (to hospital, college) admettre; (acknowledge) reconnaître, admettre (**that** que) 2 vi **to a. to sth** avouer qch; (mistake) reconnaître qch ■**admissible** adj admissible ■**admission** n (entry to theatre) entrée f (**to** à ou de); (to club, school) admission f; (acknowledgement) aveu m; **a. (charge)** (prix m d')entrée f ■**admittance** n entrée f; **'no a.'** 'entrée interdite' ■**admittedly** [-ɪdlɪ] adv de l'aveu général; **a., it was dark** je dois convenir qu'il faisait sombre

admonish [əd'mɒnɪʃ] vt (rebuke) réprimander; (warn) avertir

ado [ə'duː] n **without further a.** sans plus de façons

adolescent [ædə'lesənt] n adolescent, -ente mf ■**adolescence** n adolescence f

adopt [ə'dɒpt] vt (child, method, attitude) adopter; Pol (candidate) choisir ■**adopted** adj (child) adopté; (son, daughter) adoptif, -ive; (country) d'adoption ■**adoption** n adoption f ■**adoptive** adj (parent) adoptif, -ive

adore [ə'dɔː(r)] vt adorer (**doing** faire); **he adores being flattered** il adore qu'on le flatte ■**adorable** adj adorable ■**adoration** [ædə-'reɪʃən] n adoration f

adorn [ə'dɔːn] vt (room, book) orner (**with** de); (person, dress) parer (**with** de) ■**adornment** n ornements mpl; (finery) parure f

adrenalin(e) [ə'drenəlɪn] n adrénaline f

Adriatic [eɪdrɪ'ætɪk] n **the A.** l'Adriatique f

adrift [ə'drɪft] adj & adv (boat) à la dérive; **to come a.** (of rope, collar) se détacher; Fig **to turn sb a.** abandonner qn à son sort

adroit [ə'drɔɪt] adj habile

ADSL [eɪdiːes'el] (abbr **Asynchronous Digital Subscriber Line**) n Comptr ADSL f

adulation [ædjʊ'leɪʃən] *n* adulation *f*
adult ['ædʌlt, ə'dʌlt] **1** *n* adulte *mf* **2** *adj (animal)* adulte; **a. class/film** classe *f*/film *m* pour adultes ■ **adulthood** *n* âge *m* adulte
adulterate [ə'dʌltəreɪt] *vt (food)* empoisonner
adultery [ə'dʌltəri] *n* adultère *m*; **to commit a.** commettre l'adultère ■ **adulterous** *adj* adultère
advance [əd'vɑːns] **1** *n (movement, money)* avance *f*; *(of science)* progrès *mpl*; **advances** *(of love, friendship)* avances *fpl*; **in a.** *(book, inform, apply)* à l'avance; *(pay)* d'avance; *(arrive)* en avance; **in a. of sb** avant qn
2 *adj (payment)* anticipé; **a. booking** réservation *f*; **a. guard** avant-garde *f*
3 *vt* **(a)** *(put forward)* faire avancer; *(chess piece)* avancer **(b)** *(science, one's work)* faire progresser; *(opinion)* avancer
4 *vi (go forward, progress)* avancer; **to a. towards sb** s'avancer *ou* avancer vers qn ■ **advanced** *adj* avancé; *(studies, level)* supérieur; *(course)* de niveau supérieur; **a. in years** âgé; **she's very a. for her age** elle est très en avance pour son âge ■ **advancement** *n (progress, promotion)* avancement *m*
advantage [əd'vɑːntɪdʒ] *n* avantage *m* (**over** sur); **to take a. of** *(situation)* profiter de; *(person)* exploiter; *(woman)* séduire; **to show sth (off) to a.** mettre qch en valeur; *Sport* **a. Federer** *(in tennis)* avantage Federer ■ **advantageous** [ædvən'teɪdʒəs] *adj* avantageux, -euse (**to** pour)
advent ['ædvent] *n* arrivée *f*, avènement *m*; *Rel* **A.** l'Avent *m*
adventure [əd'ventʃə(r)] **1** *n* aventure *f* **2** *adj (film)* d'aventures ■ **adventurer** *n* aventurier, -ière *mf* ■ **adventurous** *adj* aventureux, -euse
adverb ['ædvɜːb] *n* adverbe *m*
adversary ['ædvəsəri] *(pl* **-ies)** *n* adversaire *mf*
adverse ['ædvɜːs] *adj* défavorable; *(effect)* négatif, -ive ■ **adversity** [əd'vɜːsɪti] *n* adversité *f*
advert ['ædvɜːt] *n Br* pub *f*; *(private, in newspaper)* annonce *f*
advertise ['ædvətaɪz] **1** *vt (commercially)* faire de la publicité pour; *(privately)* passer une annonce pour vendre; **he didn't want to a. his presence** il ne voulait pas se faire remarquer **2** *vi* faire de la publicité; *(privately)* passer une annonce (**for** pour trouver) ■ **advertiser** *n* annonceur, -euse *mf* ■ **advertising** *n* publicité *f*; **a. agency** agence *f* de publicité; **a. campaign** campagne *f* de publicité

> Note that the French verb **avertir** is a false friend and is never a translation for the English verb **to advertise**. Its most common meaning is **to warn**.

advertisement [*Br* əd'vɜːtɪsmənt, *Am* ædvər'taɪzmənt] *n* publicité *f*; *(private or in newspaper)* annonce *f*; *(poster)* affiche *f*; *TV* **the advertisements** la publicité

> Note that the French noun **avertissement** is a false friend and is never a translation for the English noun **advertisement**. It means **warning**.

advice [əd'vaɪs] *n* conseil(s) *m(pl)*; *Com (notification)* avis *m*; **a piece of a.** un conseil; **to ask sb's a.** demander conseil à qn; **to take sb's a.** suivre les conseils de qn
advise [əd'vaɪz] *vt* **(a)** *(counsel)* conseiller; *(recommend)* recommander; **to a. sb to do sth** conseiller à qn de faire qch; **to a. sb against doing sth** déconseiller à qn de faire qch; **he would be well advised to leave** il ferait bien de partir **(b)** *(inform)* **to a. sb that...** aviser qn que... ■ **advisable** *adj (action)* à conseiller; **it's a. to wait/***etc* il est plus prudent d'attendre/*etc* ■ **advisedly** [-ɪdlɪ] *adv* après réflexion ■ **adviser, advisor** *n* conseiller, -ère *mf*; **careers a.** conseiller, -ère *mf* d'orientation ■ **advisory** *adj* consultatif, -ive; **in an a. capacity** à titre consultatif
advocate 1 ['ædvəkət] *n (of cause)* défenseur *m*; *(lawyer)* avocat, -ate *mf* **2** ['ædvəkeɪt] *vt* préconiser
aegis ['iːdʒɪs] *n* **under the a. of** sous l'égide de
aeon ['iːɒn] *n* éternité *f*
aerial ['eərɪəl] **1** *n Br* antenne *f* **2** *adj (photo)* aérien, -ienne
aerobatics [eərə'bætɪks] *npl* acrobaties *fpl* aériennes
aerobics [eə'rəʊbɪks] *npl* aérobic *m*
aerodynamic [eərəʊdaɪ'næmɪk] *adj* aérodynamique
aeronautics [eərə'nɔːtɪks] *n* aéronautique *f*
aeroplane ['eərəpleɪn] *n Br* avion *m*
aerosol ['eərəsɒl] *n* aérosol *m*
aerospace ['eərəspeɪs] *adj (industry)* aérospatial
aesthetic [iːs'θetɪk] (*Am* **esthetic** [es'θetɪk]) *adj* esthétique
afar [ə'fɑː(r)] *adv Literary* **from a.** de loin
affable ['æfəbəl] *adj* affable
affair ['əfeə(r)] *n (matter, concern)* affaire *f*; **(love) a.** liaison *f*; **state of affairs** situation *f*

> Note that the French word **affaire** is a false friend. It is never used to mean **love affair**.

affect [ə'fekt] *vt (concern)* concerner; *(move, pretend to have)* affecter; *(harm)* nuire à; *(influence)* influer sur; **to be deeply affected by sth** être très affecté par qch; **to be affected by a disease/famine** être atteint par une maladie/touché par la famine ■ **affectation**

[æfek'teɪʃən] n affectation f ▪ **affected** adj (manner) affecté

affection [ə'fekʃən] n affection f (**for** pour) ▪ **affectionate** adj affectueux, -ueuse ▪ **affectionately** adv affectueusement

affiliate [ə'fɪlɪeɪt] vt affilier; **affiliated company** filiale f ▪ **affili'ation** n affiliation f; **what are his political affiliations?** quels sont ses liens avec les différents partis politiques?

affinity [ə'fɪnɪtɪ] (pl -ies) n affinité f

affirm [ə'fɜːm] vt affirmer ▪ **affirmation** [æfə'meɪʃən] n affirmation f ▪ **affirmative 1** adj affirmatif, -ive **2** n affirmative f; **to answer in the a.** répondre par l'affirmative

affix [ə'fɪks] vt (stamp, signature) apposer

afflict [ə'flɪkt] vt affliger (**with** de) ▪ **affliction** n (misery) affliction f; (disability) infirmité f

affluent ['æfluənt] adj riche; **a. society** société f d'abondance ▪ **affluence** n richesse f

afford [ə'fɔːd] vt (**a**) (pay for) **to be able to a. sth** avoir les moyens d'acheter qch, pouvoir se payer qch; **he can't a. the time (to read it)** il n'a pas le temps (de le lire); **I can a. to wait** je peux me permettre d'attendre (**b**) Formal (provide) fournir, donner; **to a. sb sth** fournir qch à qn ▪ **affordable** adj (price) abordable

affray [ə'freɪ] n Law rixe f

affront [ə'frʌnt] **1** n affront m **2** vt faire un affront à

Afghanistan [æf'gænɪstɑːn] n l'Afghanistan m

afield [ə'fiːld] adv **further a.** plus loin

afloat [ə'fləʊt] adv (ship, swimmer, business) à flot; (awash) submergé; **to stay a.** (of ship) rester à flot; (of business) se maintenir à flot

afoot [ə'fʊt] adv **there's something a.** il se trame quelque chose; **there's a plan a. to…** on prépare un projet pour…

aforementioned [ə'fɔːmenʃənd] adj susmentionné

afraid [ə'freɪd] adj **to be a.** avoir peur (**of sb/ sth** de qn/qch); **to be a. to do** or **of doing** avoir peur de faire; **to make sb a.** faire peur à qn; **I'm a. (that) he'll fall** j'ai peur qu'il (ne) tombe; **he's a. (that) she may be ill** il a peur qu'elle (ne) soit malade; **I'm a. he's out** (I regret to say) je regrette, il est sorti

afresh [ə'freʃ] adv de nouveau; **to start a.** recommencer

Africa ['æfrɪkə] n l'Afrique f ▪ **African 1** adj africain **2** n Africain, -aine mf

after ['ɑːftə(r)] **1** adv après; **soon/long a.** peu/ longtemps après; **the month a.** le mois d'après; **the day a.** le lendemain

2 prep après; **a. three days** au bout de trois jours; **the day a. the battle** le lendemain de la bataille; **a. eating** après avoir mangé; **day a. day** jour après jour; **a. you!** je vous en prie!; **a. all** après tout; **it's a. five** il est cinq heures

passées; Am **ten a. four** quatre heures dix; **to be a. sb/sth** (seek) chercher qn/qch

3 conj après que; **a. he saw you** après qu'il t'a vu ▪ **aftercare** n Med soins mpl postopératoires ▪ **aftereffects** npl suites fpl, séquelles fpl ▪ **afterlife** n vie f après la mort ▪ **aftermath** n suites fpl ▪ **aftersales 'service** n service m après-vente ▪ **after-shave (lotion)** n lotion f après-rasage, after-shave m inv ▪ **aftertaste** n arrière-goût m ▪ **afterthought** n réflexion f après coup; **to add/say sth as an a.** ajouter/ dire qch après coup ▪ **afterward(s)** adv après, plus tard

afternoon [ɑːftə'nuːn] n après-midi m ou f inv; **in the a.** l'après-midi; **at three in the a.** à trois heures de l'après-midi; **every Monday a.** tous les lundis après-midi; **good a.!** (hello) bonjour!; (goodbye) au revoir! ▪ **afternoons** adv Am l'après-midi

afters ['ɑːftəz] npl Br Fam dessert m

again [ə'gen, ə'geɪn] adv de nouveau, encore une fois; (furthermore) en outre; **to do a.** refaire; **to go down/up a.** redescendre/ remonter; **she won't do it a.** elle ne le fera plus; **never a.** plus jamais; **half as much a.** moitié plus; **a. and a.** bien des fois, maintes fois; **what's his name a.?** comment s'appelle-t-il déjà?

against [ə'genst, ə'geɪnst] prep contre; **to lean a. sth** s'appuyer contre qch; **to go** or **be a. sth** s'opposer à qch; **a. the law** illégal; **a law a. drinking** une loi qui interdit de boire; **his age is a. him** son âge lui est défavorable; **a. a background of** sur (un) fond de; **a. the light** à contre-jour; Br **a. the rules,** Am **a. the rule** interdit, contraire aux règlements; **the pound rose a. the dollar** la livre est en hausse par rapport au dollar

age [eɪdʒ] **1** n âge m; (old) a. vieillesse f; **what a. are you?, what's your a.?** quel âge as-tu?; **five years of a.** âgé de cinq ans; **to be of a.** être majeur; **to come of a.** atteindre sa majorité; **under a.** trop jeune, mineur; Fam **to wait (for) ages** attendre une éternité; **a. gap** différence f d'âge; **a. group** tranche f d'âge; **a. limit** limite f d'âge **2** vti (pres p **ag(e)ing**) vieillir ▪ **aged** adj (**a**) [eɪdʒd] **a. ten** âgé de dix ans (**b**) ['eɪdʒɪd] vieux (f vieille), âgé; **the a.** les personnes fpl âgées ▪ **ageless** adj toujours jeune ▪ **age-old** adj séculaire

agenda [ə'dʒendə] n ordre m du jour

Note that the French noun **agenda** is a false friend and is never a translation for the English noun **agenda**. It means **diary**.

agent ['eɪdʒənt] n agent m; (car dealer) concessionnaire mf ▪ **agency** n (**a**) (office) agence f (**b**) **through the a. of sb** par l'intermédiaire de qn

aggravate ['ægrəveɪt] vt (make worse) aggraver; Fam (person) exaspérer ■**aggra'vation** n aggravation f; Fam (bother) embêtements mpl

aggregate ['ægrɪgət] 1 adj global 2 n (total) ensemble m; **on a.** au total

aggression [ə'greʃən] n (act) agression f; (aggressiveness) agressivité f ■**aggressive** adj agressif, -ive ■**aggressiveness** n agressivité f ■**aggressor** n agresseur m

aggrieved [ə'griːvd] adj (offended) blessé, froissé; (tone) peiné

aggro ['ægrəʊ] n Br Fam (bother) embêtements mpl; (violence) bagarre f

aghast [ə'gɑːst] adj horrifié (at par)

agile [Br 'ædʒaɪl, Am 'ædʒəl] adj agile ■**agility** [ə'dʒɪlɪtɪ] n agilité f

agitate ['ædʒɪteɪt] 1 vt (worry) agiter; **to be agitated** être agité 2 vi **to a. for sth** faire campagne pour qch ■**agitation** [-'teɪʃən] n (anxiety, unrest) agitation f ■**agitator** n (political) agitateur, -trice mf

aglow [ə'gləʊ] adj (sky) embrasé; **to be a.** rayonner (**with** de)

agnostic [æg'nɒstɪk] adj & n agnostique (mf)

ago [ə'gəʊ] adv **a year a.** il y a un an; **how long a.?** il y a combien de temps (de cela)?; **long a.** il y a longtemps; **as long a. as 1800** déjà en 1800; **a short time a.** il y a peu de temps

agog [ə'gɒg] adj (excited) en émoi; (eager) impatient

agonize ['ægənaɪz] vi se faire beaucoup de souci ■**agonized** adj (look) angoissé; (cry) de douleur ■**agonizing** adj (pain) atroce; (situation) angoissant

> Note that the French verb **agoniser** is a false friend and is never a translation for the English verb **to agonize**. It means **to be dying**.

agony ['ægənɪ] (pl -ies) n (pain) douleur f atroce; (anguish) angoisse f; **to be in a.** être au supplice; **a. aunt** = responsable de la rubrique courrier du cœur; **a. column** (in newspaper) courrier m du cœur

> Note that the French noun **agonie** is a false friend and is never a translation for the English noun **agony**. It means **death throes**.

agree [ə'griː] 1 vi (come to an agreement) se mettre d'accord; (be in agreement) être d'accord (**with** avec); (of facts, dates) concorder; (of verb) s'accorder; **to a. (up)on** (decide) convenir de; **to a. to sth/to doing** consentir à qch/à faire; **it doesn't a. with me** (food, climate) ça ne me réussit pas 2 vt (plan) se mettre d'accord sur; (date, price) convenir de; (figures, sums) faire concorder; (approve) approuver; **to a. to do** accepter de faire; **to a. that...** admettre que... ■**agreed**

adj (time, place) convenu; **we are a.** nous sommes d'accord; **a.!** entendu! ■**agreement** n (contract, assent) & Grammar accord m (**with** avec); **to be in a. with sb** être d'accord avec qn; **to be in a. with a decision** approuver une décision; **to come to an a.** se mettre d'accord; **by mutual a.** d'un commun accord

> Note that the French noun **agrément** is a false friend and is never a translation for the English noun **agreement**. Its most common meaning is **pleasure** or **charm**.

agreeable [ə'griːəbəl] adj (pleasant) agréable; **to be a.** (agree) être d'accord; **to be a. to sth** consentir à qch

agriculture ['ægrɪkʌltʃə(r)] n agriculture f ■**agri'cultural** adj agricole

aground [ə'graʊnd] adv **to run a.** (of ship) (s')échouer

ah [ɑː] exclam ah!

ahead [ə'hed] adv (in space) en avant; (leading) en tête; (in the future) à l'avenir; **a. of** (space) devant; (time) avant; **one hour/etc a.** une heure/etc d'avance (**of** sur); **to be a. of schedule** être en avance; **to go on a.** partir devant; **to go a.** (advance) avancer; (continue) continuer; (start) commencer; **go a.!** allez-y!; **to go a. with** (task) mettre à exécution; **to get a.** (in race) prendre de l'avance; (succeed) réussir; **to think a.** prévoir

aid [eɪd] 1 n (help) aide f; (device) accessoire m; **with the a. of sb** avec l'aide de qn; **with the a. of sth** à l'aide de qch; **in a. of** (charity) au profit de; Fam **what's (all) this in a. of?** ça sert à quoi, tout ça? 2 vt aider (**sb to do** qn à faire)

aide [eɪd] n collaborateur, -trice mf

AIDS [eɪdz] (abbr Acquired Immune Deficiency Syndrome) n SIDA m; **A. victim/virus** malade mf/virus m du SIDA

ail [eɪl] vt **what ails you?** de quoi souffrez-vous? ■**ailing** adj (ill) souffrant; (company) en difficulté ■**ailment** n (petit) ennui m de santé

aim [eɪm] 1 n but m; **to take a. (at)** viser; **with the a. of** dans le but de 2 vt (gun) braquer (**at** sur); (lamp) diriger (**at** vers); (stone) lancer (**at** ou vers); (blow, remark) décocher (**at** à); **aimed at children** (product) destiné aux enfants 3 vi viser; **to a. at sb** viser qn; **to a. to do** or **at doing** avoir l'intention de faire ■**'aimless** adj (existence) sans but ■**'aimlessly** adv sans but

air [eə(r)] 1 n (a) (atmosphère) air m; **in the open a.** en plein air; **by a.** (travel) en ou par avion; (send letter or goods) par avion; **to be** or **go on the a.** (of person) passer à l'antenne; (of programme) être diffusé; **to throw (up) in(to) the a.** jeter en l'air; (up) in the a. (plan) incertain; Fig **there's something in the a.** il se prépare quelque chose (**b**) (appearance, tune) air *m*; **to put on airs** se donner des airs; **with an a. of sadness** d'un air triste

2 *adj (base)* aérien, -ienne; **a. bed** matelas *m* pneumatique; **a. fare** prix *m* du billet d'avion; **a. force** armée *f* de l'air

3 *vt (room)* aérer; *(views)* exposer; *Br* **airing cupboard** = placard où se trouve le chauffe-eau ▪**airbag** *n* Air Bag® *m* ▪**airborne** *adj (troops)* aéroporté; **to become a.** *(of aircraft)* décoller ▪**air-conditioned** *adj* climatisé ▪**air-conditioning** *n* climatisation *f* ▪**aircraft** *n inv* avion *m*; **a. carrier** porte-avions *m inv* ▪**airfield** *n* terrain *m* d'aviation ▪**air freshener** *n* désodorisant *m (pour la maison)* ▪**airgun** *n Br* carabine *f* à air comprimé ▪**air letter** *n* aérogramme *m* ▪**airlift 1** *n* pont *m* aérien **2** *vt* transporter par avion ▪**airline** *n* compagnie *f* aérienne; **a. ticket** billet *m* d'avion ▪**airlock** *n (in submarine, spacecraft)* sas *m*; *(in pipe)* poche *f* d'air ▪**airmail** *n* poste *f* aérienne; **by a.** par avion ▪**airman** *(pl -men)* *n* aviateur *m* ▪**airplane** *n Am* avion *m* ▪**airpocket** *n* trou *m* d'air ▪**airport** *n* aéroport *m* ▪**air-raid shelter** *n* abri *m* antiaérien ▪**airship** *n* dirigeable *m* ▪**airsick** *adj* **to be a.** avoir le mal de l'air ▪**airsickness** *n* mal *m* de l'air ▪**airstrip** *n* terrain *m* d'atterrissage ▪**airtight** *adj* hermétique ▪**air traffic controller** *n* contrôleur *m* aérien, aiguilleur *m* du ciel ▪**airway** *n (route)* couloir *m* aérien ▪**airworthy** *adj* en état de voler

airy ['eərɪ] *(-ier, -iest) adj (room)* clair et spacieux, -ieuse; *Fig (promise)* vain; *(manner)* désinvolte ▪**airy-'fairy** *adj Br Fam* farfelu ▪**airily** *adv (not seriously)* d'un ton léger

aisle [aɪl] *n (in supermarket, cinema)* allée *f*; *(in plane)* couloir *m*; *(in church) (on side)* nef *f* latérale; *(central)* allée centrale

ajar [ə'dʒɑː(r)] *adj & adv (door)* entrouvert

akin [ə'kɪn] *adj* **a. to** apparenté à

alabaster ['æləbɑːstə(r)] *n* albâtre *m*

alacrity [ə'lækrɪtɪ] *n* empressement *m*

à la mode [ælæ'məʊd] *adj Am (dessert)* avec de la crème glacée

alarm [ə'lɑːm] **1** *n (warning, fear, device)* alarme *f*; *(mechanism)* sonnerie *f* (d'alarme); **false a.** fausse alerte *f*; **a. clock** réveil *m* **2** *vt (frighten)* alarmer; *(worry)* inquiéter; **to get alarmed** s'alarmer; **they were alarmed at the news** la nouvelle les a beaucoup inquiétés ▪**alarmist** *n* alarmiste *mf*

alas [ə'læs] *exclam* hélas!

Albania [æl'beɪnɪə] *n* l'Albanie *f* ▪**Albanian 1** *adj* albanais **2** *n* Albanais, -aise *mf*

albatross ['ælbətrɒs] *n* albatros *m*

albeit [ɔːl'biːɪt] *conj Literary* quoique (+ *subjunctive*)

albino [*Br* æl'biːnəʊ, *Am* æl'baɪnəʊ] *(pl -os) n* albinos *mf*

album ['ælbəm] *n (book, record)* album *m*

alchemy ['ælkəmɪ] *n* alchimie *f* ▪**alchemist** *n* alchimiste *m*

alcohol ['ælkəhɒl] *n* alcool *m* ▪**alco'holic 1** *adj (person)* alcoolique; **a. drink** boisson *f* alcoolisée **2** *n (person)* alcoolique *mf* ▪**alcoholism** *n* alcoolisme *m*

alcopop ['ælkəʊpɒp] *n* prémix *m*

alcove ['ælkəʊv] *n* alcôve *f*

ale [eɪl] *n* bière *f*

alert [ə'lɜːt] **1** *adj (watchful)* vigilant; *(lively) (mind, baby)* éveillé **2** *n* alerte *f*; **on the a.** sur le qui-vive **3** *vt* alerter ▪**alertness** *n* vigilance *f*; *(of mind, baby)* vivacité *f*

A level ['eɪlevəl] *n Br (exam)* ≃ épreuve *f* de baccalauréat

alfalfa [æl'fælfə] *n Am* luzerne *f*

algebra ['ældʒɪbrə] *n* algèbre *f*

Algeria [æl'dʒɪərɪə] *n* l'Algérie *f* ▪**Algerian 1** *adj* algérien, -ienne **2** *n* Algérien, -ienne *mf*

alias ['eɪlɪəs] **1** *adv* alias **2** *(pl* **aliases)** *n* nom *m* d'emprunt

alibi ['ælɪbaɪ] *n* alibi *m*

alien ['eɪlɪən] **1** *adj* étranger, -ère **(to** à**)** **2** *n Formal (foreigner)* étranger, -ère *mf*; *(from outer space)* extraterrestre *mf* ▪**alienate** *vt (supporters, readers)* s'aliéner; **to a. sb** *(make unfriendly)* s'aliéner qn; **to feel alienated** se sentir exclu

alight¹ [ə'laɪt] *adj (fire)* allumé; *(building)* en feu; *(face)* éclairé; **to set sth a.** mettre le feu à qch

alight² [ə'laɪt] *(pt & pp* **alighted** *or* **alit)** *vi* **(a)** *Formal (from bus, train)* descendre **(from** de**)** **(b)** *(of bird)* se poser **(on** sur**)**

align [ə'laɪn] *vt* aligner; **to a. oneself with sb** s'aligner sur qn ▪**alignment** *n* alignement *m*; **in a. (with)** aligné (sur)

alike [ə'laɪk] **1** *adj (people, things)* semblables, pareils, -eilles; **to look** *or* **be a.** se ressembler **2** *adv* de la même manière; **summer and winter a.** été comme hiver

alimony [*Br* 'ælɪmənɪ, *Am* 'ælɪməʊnɪ] *n Law* pension *f* alimentaire

alit [ə'lɪt] *pt & pp of* **alight²**

alive [ə'laɪv] *adj* vivant, en vie; **a. to** conscient de; **a. with worms/***etc (crawling)* grouillant de vers/*etc*; **to stay a.** survivre; **to keep sb a.** maintenir qn en vie; **to keep a memory/custom a.** entretenir un souvenir/une tradition; **anyone** *or* **will tell you** n'importe qui vous le dira; **a. and well** bien portant; *Fam* **a. and kicking** plein de vie

all [ɔːl] **1** *adj* tout, toute, *pl* tous, toutes; **a. day** toute la journée; **a. men** tous les hommes; **a. the girls** toutes les filles; **a. four of them** tous les quatre; **with a. speed** à toute vitesse; **for a. his wealth** malgré toute sa fortune

2 *pron (everyone)* tous *mpl* toutes *fpl*; *(every-*

thing; **my sisters are a. here** toutes mes
sœurs sont ici; **he ate it a., he ate a. of it** il a
tout mangé; **take a. of it** prends (le) tout; **a. of
us** nous tous; **a. together** tous ensemble; **a.
(that) he has** tout ce qu'il a; **a. in a.** à tout
prendre; **in a., told** en tout; **a. but
impossible/etc (almost)** presque impossible/
etc; **anything at a.** quoi que ce soit; **if he
comes at a.** s'il vient effectivement; **if there's
any wind at a.** s'il y a le moindre vent; **nothing
at a.** rien du tout; **not at a.** pas du tout; *(after
'thank you')* il n'y a pas de quoi
3 *adv* tout; **a. alone** tout seul; **a. bad**
entièrement mauvais; **a. over** *(everywhere)*
partout; *(finished)* fini; **a. too soon** bien trop
tôt; *Sport* **six a.** six partout; *Fam* **a. there**
éveillé, intelligent; *Fam* **not a. there** un peu
fêlé; *Br Fam* **a. in** épuisé
4 *n Literary* **my a.** tout ce que j'ai **• all-'clear** *n*
Mil fin f d'alerte; *Fig* feu *m* vert **• all-important**
adj essentiel, -ielle *m* **• all-in** *adj Br* **a. price**
prix *m* global **• all-night** *adj (party)* qui dure
toute la nuit; *(shop)* ouvert toute la nuit **• all-
out** *adj (effort)* acharné; *(war, strike)* tous
azimuts **• all-powerful** *adj* tout-puissant (*f*
toute-puissante) **• all-purpose** *adj (tool)*
universel, -elle **• all-round** *adj (knowledge)*
approfondi; *(athlete)* complet, -ète **• all-
'rounder** *n* personne *f* qui est forte en tout
• all-star *adj* **an a. cast** une distribution
prestigieuse **• all-time** *adj (record)* jamais
battu; **to reach an a. low/high** arriver à son
point le plus bas/le plus haut

allay [ə'leɪ] *vt (fears)* calmer, apaiser; *(doubts)*
dissiper

allegation [ælɪ'geɪʃən] *n* accusation f

allege [ə'ledʒ] *vt* prétendre (**that** que)
• alleged *adj (so-called) (crime, fact)* prétendu;
(author, culprit) présumé; **he is a. to be...** on
prétend qu'il est... **• allegedly** [-ɪdlɪ] *adv* à
ce qu'on dit

allegiance [ə'liːdʒəns] *n (to party, cause)* fidélité
f (**to** à)

allegory ['ælɪgərɪ] *(pl* **-ies)** *n* allégorie *f*
• allegorical [-'gɒrɪkəl] *adj* allégorique

allergy ['ælədʒɪ] *(pl* **-ies)** *n* allergie *f* (**to** à)
• allergic [ə'lɜːdʒɪk] *adj* allergique (**to** à)

alleviate [ə'liːvɪeɪt] *vt (pain, suffering)*
soulager; *(burden, task)* alléger; *(problem)*
remédier à

alley ['ælɪ] *(pl* **-eys)** *n* ruelle *f*; *(in park)* allée *f*;
Fam **that's right up my a.** c'est mon rayon
• alleyway *n* ruelle *f*

alliance [ə'laɪəns] *n* alliance *f*

allied ['ælaɪd] *adj (country)* allié; *(matters)* lié

alligator ['ælɪgeɪtə(r)] *n* alligator *m*

allocate ['æləkeɪt] *vt (assign)* affecter (**to** à);
(distribute) répartir **• allocation** [-'keɪʃən] *n*
affectation *f*

allot [ə'lɒt] *(pt & pp* **-tt-)** *vt (assign)* attribuer (**to**
à); *(distribute)* répartir; **in the allotted time**
dans le temps imparti **• allotment** *n* (**a**)
(action) attribution f; *(share)* part f (**b**) *Br (land)*
jardin *m* ouvrier

allow [ə'laʊ] **1** *vt* permettre (**sb sth** qch à qn);
(give, grant) accorder (**sb sth** qch à qn);
(request) accéder à; **to a. a discount** accorder
une réduction; **to a. sb to do** permettre à qn
de faire; **to a. an hour/a metre/etc (estimated
period or quantity)** prévoir une heure/un
mètre/*etc;* **a. me!** permettez(-moi)!; **it's not
allowed** c'est interdit; **you're not allowed to
go** on vous interdit d'y aller **2** *vi* **to a. for sth**
tenir compte de qch **• allowable** *adj*
(acceptable) admissible; *(expense)* déductible

allowance [ə'laʊəns] *n* allocation f; *(for travel,
housing, food)* indemnité f; *(for duty-free goods)*
tolérance f; *(tax-free amount)* abattement *m;* **to
make allowances for** *(person)* être indulgent
envers; *(thing)* tenir compte de

alloy ['ælɔɪ] *n* alliage *m*

all right [ɔːl'raɪt] **1** *adj (satisfactory)* bien *inv;*
(unharmed) sain et sauf; *(undamaged)* intact;
(without worries) tranquille; **it's a.** ça va; **are
you a.?** ça va?; **I'm a.** *(healthy)* je vais bien;
(financially) je m'en sors; **he's a.** *(trustworthy)*
c'est quelqu'un de bien; **to be a. at maths** se
débrouiller en maths; **the TV is a. now** *(fixed)*
la télé marche maintenant **2** *adv (well)* bien;
a.! *(agreement)* d'accord!; **I received your
letter a.** *(emphatic)* j'ai bien reçu votre lettre; **is
it a. if I smoke?** ça ne vous dérange pas si je
fume?

allude [ə'luːd] *vi* **to a. to** faire allusion à
• allusion *n* allusion *f*

alluring [ə'ljʊərɪŋ] *adj* séduisant

ally 1 ['ælaɪ] *(pl* **-ies)** *n* allié, -iée *mf* **2** [ə'laɪ] *(pt
& pp* **-ied)** *vt* **to a. oneself with** s'allier à *ou* avec

almanac ['ɔːlmənæk] *n* almanach *m*

almighty [ɔːl'maɪtɪ] **1** *adj* (**a**) *(powerful)* tout-
puissant (*f* toute-puissante) (**b**) *Fam
(enormous)* terrible, formidable **2** *n* **the A.** le
Tout-Puissant

almond ['ɑːmənd] *n* amande *f*

almost ['ɔːlməʊst] *adv* presque; **he a. fell** il a
failli tomber

alms [ɑːmz] *npl* aumône *f*

aloft [ə'lɒft] *adv Literary* en haut

alone [ə'ləʊn] *adj & adv* seul; **an expert a.
can...** seul un expert peut...; **I did it (all) a.** je
l'ai fait (tout) seul; **to leave** *ou* **let a.** *(person)*
laisser tranquille; *(thing)* ne pas toucher à; **to
go it a.** faire cavalier seul; **they can't dance,
let a. sing** ils ne savent pas danser, et encore
moins chanter

along [ə'lɒŋ] **1** *prep (all)* **a.** (tout) le long de; **to
walk a. the shore** marcher le long du rivage; **to
go** *or* **walk a. the street** marcher dans la rue; **a.**

here par ici; *Fig* **somewhere a. the way** à un moment donné **2** *adv* **to move a.** avancer; **to hobble/plod a.** avancer en boitant/péniblement; **I'll be** *or* **come a. shortly** je viendrai tout à l'heure; **come a.!** venez donc!; **to bring sth a.** apporter qch; **to bring sb a.** amener qn; **all a.** *(all the time)* dès le début; *(all the way)* d'un bout à l'autre; **a. with** ainsi que

alongside [əlɒŋ'saɪd] *prep & adv* à côté de (de); **a. the kerb** le long du trottoir

aloof [ə'luːf] **1** *adj* distant **2** *adv* à distance; **to keep a. (from sth)** rester à l'écart (de qch)

aloud [ə'laud] *adv* à haute voix

alphabet ['ælfəbet] *n* alphabet *m* ▪ **alpha'betical** *adj* alphabétique

Alps [ælps] *npl* **the A.** les Alpes *fpl* ▪ **Alpine** ['ælpaɪn] *adj (club, range)* alpin; *(scenery)* alpestre

already [ɔːl'redɪ] *adv* déjà

alright [ɔːl'raɪt] *adv Fam* = **all right**

Alsatian [æl'seɪʃən] *n (dog)* berger *m* allemand

also ['ɔːlsəu] *adv* aussi, également; *(more-over)* de plus ▪ **also-ran** *n (person)* perdant,-ante *f*

altar ['ɔːltə(r)] *n* autel *m*

alter ['ɔːltə(r)] **1** *vt* changer; *(clothing)* retoucher **2** *vi* changer ▪ **alteration** [-'reɪʃən] *n* changement *m* (**in** de); *(of clothing)* retouche *f*; **alterations** *(to building)* travaux *mpl*

altercation [ɔːltə'keɪʃən] *n* altercation *f*

alternate **1** [ɔːl'tɜːnət] *adj* alterné; **on a. days** tous les deux jours **2** *vt* faire alterner **3** *vi* alterner (**with** avec); *El* **alternating current** courant *m* alternatif ▪ **al'ternately** *adv* alternativement ▪ **alter'nation** *n* alternance *f*

alternative [ɔːl'tɜːnətɪv] **1** *adj (other)* de remplacement; **an a. way** une autre façon; **a. answers** d'autres réponses (possibles); **a. energy** énergies *fpl* de substitution; **a. medicine** médecine *f* douce **2** *n (choice)* alternative *f*; **she had no a. but to obey** elle n'a pas pu faire autrement que d'obéir ▪ **alternatively** *adv* **(or) a.** *(or else)* ou alors, ou bien

although [ɔːl'ðəu] *adv* bien que (+ *subjunctive*)

altitude ['æltɪtjuːd] *n* altitude *f*

altogether [ɔːltə'geðə(r)] *adv (completely)* tout à fait; *(on the whole)* somme toute; **how much a.?** combien en tout?

aluminium [*Br* ælju'mɪnɪəm] (*Am* **aluminum** [ə'luːmɪnəm]) *n* aluminium *m*

alumnus [ə'lʌmnəs] (*pl* **-ni** [-naɪ]) *n* ancien(ienne) élève *mf*

always ['ɔːlweɪz] *adv* toujours; **he's a. criticizing** il est toujours à critiquer; **as a.** comme toujours

am [æm, *unstressed* əm] *see* **be**

a.m. [eɪ'em] *adv* du matin

amalgam [ə'mælgəm] *n (mix)* amalgame *m*

amalgamate [ə'mælgəmeɪt] *vti* fusionner

amass [ə'mæs] *vt (riches)* amasser

amateur ['æmətə(r)] **1** *n* amateur *m* **2** *adj (interest, sports, performance)* d'amateur; **a. painter/actress** peintre *m*/actrice *f* amateur ▪ **amateurish** *adj Pej (work)* d'amateur

amaze [ə'meɪz] *vt* stupéfier ▪ **amazed** *adj* stupéfait (**at sth** de qch); *(filled with wonder)* émerveillé; **a. at seeing** stupéfait de voir; **I was a. by his courage** son courage m'a stupéfié ▪ **amazing** *adj (surprising)* stupéfiant; *(incredible)* extraordinaire ▪ **amazingly** *adv* extraordinairement; *(miraculously)* par miracle

amazement [ə'meɪzmənt] *n* stupéfaction *f*; *(sense of wonder)* émerveillement *m*; **to my a.** à ma grande stupéfaction

ambassador [æm'bæsədə(r)] *n (man)* ambassadeur *m*; *(woman)* ambassadrice *f*

amber ['æmbə(r)] *n* ambre *m*; **a. (light)** *(of traffic signal)* (feu *m*) orange *m*; **the lights are at a.** le feu est à l'orange

ambidextrous [æmbɪ'dekstrəs] *adj* ambidextre

ambiguous [æm'bɪgjuəs] *adj* ambigu (*f* ambiguë) ▪ **ambiguously** *adv* de façon ambiguë ▪ **ambiguity** [-'gjuːɪtɪ] *n* ambiguïté *f*

ambition [æm'bɪʃən] *n* ambition *f* ▪ **ambitious** *adj* ambitieux, -ieuse

ambivalent [æm'bɪvələnt] *adj* ambivalent

amble ['æmbəl] *vi* marcher d'un pas tranquille

ambulance ['æmbjuləns] *n* ambulance *f*; **a. driver** ambulancier, -ière *mf*

ambush ['æmbuʃ] **1** *n* embuscade *f* **2** *vt* tendre une embuscade à; **to be ambushed** tomber dans une embuscade

amen [*Br* ɑː'men, *Am* eɪ'men] *exclam* amen

amenable [ə'miːnəbəl] *adj* docile; **a. to** *(responsive to)* sensible à; **a. to reason** raisonnable

amend [ə'mend] *vt (text)* modifier; *Pol (law)* amender; *(conduct)* corriger ▪ **amendment** *n Pol (to law, rule)* amendement *m*

amends [ə'mendz] *npl* **to make a.** se racheter; **to make a. for sth** réparer qch

amenities [*Br* ə'miːnɪtɪz, *Am* ə'menɪtɪz] *npl* *(pleasant things)* agréments *mpl*; *(of sports club)* équipement *m*; *(of town)* aménagements *mpl*; *(shops)* commerces *mpl*

America [ə'merɪkə] *n* l'Amérique *f*; **North/South A.** l'Amérique du Nord/du Sud ▪ **American 1** *adj* américain **2** *n* Américain, -aine *mf* ▪ **Americanism** *n* américanisme *m*

amethyst ['æməθɪst] *n* améthyste *f*

amiable ['eɪmɪəbəl] *adj* aimable

amicable ['æmɪkəbəl] *adj* amical ▪ **amicably** *adv (part)* amicalement; *Law (settle a dispute)* à l'amiable

amid(st) [ə'mɪd(st)] *prep* au milieu de, parmi

amiss [ə'mɪs] *adv & adj* **to take sth a.** mal prendre qch; **something is a.** *(wrong)* quelque chose ne va pas; **that wouldn't go a.** ça ne ferait pas de mal

ammonia [ə'məʊnɪə] *n (gas)* ammoniac *m*; *(liquid)* ammoniaque *f*

ammunition [æmjʊ'nɪʃən] *n* munitions *fpl*

amnesia [æm'niːzɪə] *n* amnésie *f*

amnesty ['æmnəstɪ] *(pl -ies)* *n* amnistie *f*

amniocentesis [æmnɪəʊsen'tiːsɪs] *n* amniocentèse *f*

amok [ə'mɒk] *adv* **to run a.** *(of crowd)* se déchaîner; *(of person, animal)* devenir fou furieux *(f* folle furieuse)

among(st) [ə'mʌŋ(st)] *prep (amidst)* parmi; *(between)* entre; **a. the crowd/books/others/** *etc* parmi la foule/les livres/les autres/*etc*; **a. themselves/friends** entre eux/amis; **a. other things** entre autres (choses)

amoral [eɪ'mɒrəl] *adj* amoral

amorous ['æmərəs] *adj (look, words)* polisson, -onne; *(person)* d'humeur polissonne; *(adventure)* amoureux, -euse

amount [ə'maʊnt] **1** *n* quantité *f*; *(sum of money)* somme *f*; *(total figure of invoice, debt)* montant *m*; *(scope, size)* importance *f* **2** *vi* **to a. to** *(bill)* s'élever à; *Fig* **it amounts to blackmail** ce n'est rien d'autre qu'du chantage; **it amounts to the same thing** ça revient au même

amp [æmp] *n (unit of electricity)* ampère *m*; *Br* **3-a. plug** prise *f* avec fusible de 3 ampères

amphibian [æm'fɪbɪən] *n & adj* amphibie (*m*) ▪**amphibious** *adj* amphibie

amphitheatre ['æmfɪθɪətə(r)] *n (Greek, Roman)* amphithéâtre *m*

ample ['æmpəl] *adj* **(a)** *(plentiful)* abondant; **to have a. time to do sth** avoir largement le temps de faire qch; **that's (quite) a.** c'est largement suffisant **(b)** *(large) (woman, bosom)* fort **(c)** *(roomy) (garment)* large ▪**amply** *adv* largement, amplement

amplify ['æmplɪfaɪ] *(pt & pp -ied)* *vt (essay, remarks)* développer; *(sound)* amplifier ▪**amplifier** *n* amplificateur *m*

amputate ['æmpjʊteɪt] *vt* amputer; **to a. sb's hand/***etc* amputer qn de la main/*etc* ▪**amputation** [-'teɪʃən] *n* amputation *f*

amuck [ə'mʌk] *adv* = **amok**

amuse [ə'mjuːz] *vt* amuser; **to keep sb amused** distraire qn ▪**amusement** *n* amusement *m*, divertissement *m*; *(pastime)* distraction *f*; **amusements** *(at fairground)* attractions *fpl*; *(gambling machines)* machines *fpl* à sous; **a. arcade** salle *f* de jeux; **a. park** parc *m* d'attractions ▪**amusing** *adj* amusant

an [æn, *unstressed* ən] *see* **a**

anachronism [ə'nækrənɪzəm] *n* anachronisme *m*

anaemia *(Am* **anemia)** [ə'niːmɪə] *n* anémie *f* ▪**anaemic** *(Am* **anemic)** *adj* anémique; **to become a.** faire de l'anémie

anaesthesia *(Am* **anesthesia)** [ænɪs'θiːzɪə] *n* anesthésie *f* ▪**anaesthetic** *(Am* **anesthetic)** [ænɪs'θetɪk] *n (process)* anesthésie *f*; *(substance)* anesthésique *m*; **under a.** sous anesthésie; **general/local a.** anesthésie générale/locale ▪**anaesthetize** *(Am* **anesthetize)** [ə'niːsθɪtaɪz] *vt* anesthésier

anagram ['ænəgræm] *n* anagramme *f*

anal ['eɪnəl] *adj* anal

analogy [ə'nælədʒɪ] *(pl -ies)* *n* analogie *f* (**with** avec) ▪**analogous** *adj* analogue (**to** à)

analyse ['ænəlaɪz] *vt* analyser ▪**analysis** [ə'næləsɪs] *(pl -yses* [-əsiːz]) *n* analyse *f*; *Fig* **in the final a.** en fin de compte ▪**analyst** [-lɪst] *n* analyste *mf* ▪**analytical** [-'lɪtɪkəl] *adj* analytique

anarchy ['ænəkɪ] *n* anarchie *f* ▪**anarchic** [æ'nɑːkɪk] *adj* anarchique ▪**anarchist** *n* anarchiste *mf*

anathema [ə'næθəmə] *n Rel* anathème *m*; **it is (an) a. to me** j'ai une sainte horreur de cela

anatomy [ə'nætəmɪ] *n* anatomie *f* ▪**anatomical** [ænə'tɒmɪkəl] *adj* anatomique

ancestor ['ænsestə(r)] *n* ancêtre *m* ▪**ancestral** [-'sestrəl] *adj* ancestral; **a. home** demeure *f* ancestrale ▪**ancestry** *n (lineage)* ascendance *f*; *(ancestors)* ancêtres *mpl*

anchor ['æŋkə(r)] **1** *n* ancre *f*; **to drop a.** jeter l'ancre; **to weigh a.** lever l'ancre **2** *vt (ship)* mettre à l'ancre **3** *vi* jeter l'ancre, mouiller ▪**anchored** *adj* ancré, à l'ancre

anchovy [*Br* 'æntʃəvɪ, *Am* æn'tʃəʊvɪ] *(pl -ies)* *n* anchois *m*

ancient ['eɪnʃənt] *adj* ancien, -ienne; *(premedieval)* antique; *Hum (person)* d'un grand âge; *Fig* **that's a. history!** c'est de l'histoire ancienne!

ancillary [æn'sɪlərɪ] *adj* auxiliaire

and [ænd, *unstressed* ən(d)] *conj* et; **a knife a. fork** un couteau et une fourchette; **my mother a. father** mon père et ma mère; **two hundred a. two** deux cent deux; **four a. three quarters** quatre trois quarts; **nice a. warm** bien chaud; **better a. better** de mieux en mieux; **she can read a. write** elle sait lire et écrire; **go a. see** va voir; **I knocked a. knocked** j'ai frappé pendant un bon moment

anecdote ['ænɪkdəʊt] *n* anecdote *f*

anemia [ə'niːmɪə] *n Am* = **anaemia**

anemic [ə'niːmɪk] *adj Am* = **anaemic**

anemone [ə'nemənɪ] *n* anémone *f*

anesthesia [ænɪs'θiːzɪə] *n Am* = **anaethesia**

anesthetic [ænɪs'θetɪk] *n Am* = **anaesthetic**

anesthetize [ə'niːsθɪtaɪz] *vt Am* = **anaesthetize**

anew [ə'njuː] *adv Literary* de nouveau; **to start a.** recommencer

angel ['eɪndʒəl] *n* ange *m* ▪**angelic** [æn'dʒelɪk] *adj* angélique

anger ['æŋgə(r)] **1** *n* colère *f*; **in a., out of a.** sous le coup de la colère **2** *vt* mettre en colère

angina [æn'dʒaɪnə] *n* angine *f* de poitrine

angle¹ ['æŋgəl] *n* angle *m*; **at an a.** en biais; *Fig* **seen from this a.** vu sous cet angle

angle² ['æŋgəl] *vi* (*to fish*) pêcher à la ligne; *Fig* **to a. for** (*compliments*) quêter ■**angler** *n* pêcheur, -euse *mf* à la ligne ■**angling** *n* pêche *f* à la ligne

Anglican ['æŋglɪkən] *adj & n* anglican, -ane (*mf*)

anglicism ['æŋglɪsɪzəm] *n* anglicisme *m*

Anglo- ['æŋgləʊ] *pref* anglo- ■**Anglo-'Saxon** *adj & n* anglo-saxon, -onne (*mf*)

angora [æŋ'gɔːrə] *n* (*wool*) angora *m*; **a. sweater**/*etc* pull *m*/*etc* en angora

angry ['æŋgrɪ] (**-ier, -iest**) *adj* (*person*) en colère, fâché; (*look*) furieux, -ieuse; **an a. letter** une lettre indignée; **a. words** des paroles indignées; **to get a.** se fâcher (**with** contre) ■**angrily** *adv* (*leave*) en colère; (*speak*) avec colère

angst [æŋst] *n* angoisse *f*

anguish ['æŋgwɪʃ] *n* angoisse *f* ■**anguished** *adj* (*look, voice*) angoissé; (*cry*) d'angoisse

angular ['æŋgjʊlə(r)] *adj* (*face*) anguleux, -euse

animal ['ænɪməl] **1** *adj* (*kingdom, fat*) animal **2** *n* animal *m*

animate 1 ['ænɪmeɪt] *vt* animer **2** ['ænɪmət] *adj* (*alive*) animé ■**animated** [-meɪtɪd] *adj* (*lively*) & *Cin* animé; **to become a.** s'animer ■**animation** [-'meɪʃən] *n* (*liveliness*) & *Cin* animation *f*

animosity [ænɪ'mɒsɪtɪ] *n* animosité *f*

aniseed ['ænɪsiːd] *n* (*as flavouring*) anis *m*; **a. drink** boisson *f* à l'anis

ankle ['æŋkəl] *n* cheville *f*; **a. boot** bottine *f*; **a. sock** socquette *f*

annals ['ænəlz] *npl* annales *fpl*

annex¹ [ə'neks] *vt* annexer

annex², *Br* **annexe** ['æneks] *n* (*building*) annexe *f*

annihilate [ə'naɪəleɪt] *vt* anéantir ■**annihi'lation** *n* anéantissement *m*

anniversary [ænɪ'vɜːsərɪ] (*pl* **-ies**) *n* (*of event*) anniversaire *m*

annotate ['ænəteɪt] *vt* annoter ■**annotation** [-'teɪʃən] *n* annotation *f*

announce [ə'naʊns] *vt* annoncer; (*birth, marriage*) faire part de ■**announcement** *n* (*statement*) annonce *f*; (*notice of birth, marriage, death*) avis *m*; (*private letter*) faire-part *m inv* ■**announcer** *n* (*on TV*) speaker *m*, speakerine *f*

annoy [ə'nɔɪ] *vt* (*inconvenience*) ennuyer; (*irritate*) agacer ■**annoyance** *n* contrariété *f*, ennui *m* ■**annoyed** *adj* fâché; **to get a.** se fâcher (**with** contre) ■**annoying** *adj* ennuyeux, -euse

Note that the French verb **ennuyer** can be a false friend. Its most common meaning is **to bore**.

annual ['ænjʊəl] **1** *adj* annuel, -uelle **2** *n* (*yearbook*) annuaire *m*; (*children's*) album *m*; (*plant*) plante *f* annuelle ■**annually** *adv* (*every year*) tous les ans; (*per year*) par an

annuity [ə'njʊətɪ] (*pl* **-ies**) *n* (*of retired person*) pension *f* viagère

annul [ə'nʌl] (*pt & pp* **-ll-**) *vt* (*contract, marriage*) annuler ■**annulment** *n* annulation *f*

anoint [ə'nɔɪnt] *vt* oindre (**with** de) ■**anointed** *adj* oint

anomalous [ə'nɒmələs] *adj* anormal ■**anomaly** (*pl* **-ies**) *n* anomalie *f*

anon [ə'nɒn] *adv Literary or Hum* tout à l'heure

anonymous [ə'nɒnɪməs] *adj* anonyme; **to remain a.** garder l'anonymat ■**anonymity** [ænə'nɪmɪtɪ] *n* anonymat *m*

anorak ['ænəræk] *n* anorak *m*

anorexia [ænə'reksɪə] *n* anorexie *f* ■**anorexic** *adj & n* anorexique (*mf*)

another [ə'nʌðə(r)] *adj & pron* un(e) autre; **a. man** (*different*) un autre homme; **a. month** (*additional*) encore un mois; **a. ten** encore dix; **one a.** l'un(e) l'autre, *pl* les un(e)s les autres; **they love one a.** ils s'aiment

answer ['ɑːnsə(r)] **1** *n* réponse *f*; (*to problem, riddle*) & *Math* solution *f* (**to** de); (*reason*) explication *f*; **in a. to your letter** en réponse à votre lettre
2 *vt* (*person, question, letter*) répondre à; (*prayer, wish*) exaucer; **he answered 'yes'** il a répondu 'oui'; **to a. the door** ouvrir la porte; **to a. the phone** répondre au téléphone; **to a. sb back** (*be rude to*) répondre à qn
3 *vi* répondre; **to a. back** (*rudely*) répondre, répliquer; **to a. for sb/sth** (*be responsible for*) répondre de qn/qch; **to a. (to) a description** (*of suspect*) correspondre à un signalement ■**answering machine** *n* répondeur *m*

answerable ['ɑːnsərəbəl] *adj* responsable (**for** sth de qch; **to sb** devant qn)

ant [ænt] *n* fourmi *f* ■**anthill** *n* fourmilière *f*

antagonism [æn'tægənɪzəm] *n* (*hostility*) hostilité *f* ■**antagonist** *n* adversaire *mf* ■**antago'nistic** *adj* (*hostile*) hostile (**to** à) ■**antagonize** *vt* provoquer (l'hostilité de)

Antarctic [æn'tɑːktɪk] **1** *adj* antarctique **2** *n* **the A.** l'Antarctique *m*

antecedent [æntɪ'siːdənt] *n* antécédent *m*

antechamber ['æntɪtʃeɪmbə(r)] *n* antichambre *f*

antedate ['æntɪdeɪt] *vt* (*letter*) antidater

antelope ['æntɪləʊp] *n* antilope *f*

antenatal [æntɪ'neɪtəl] *Br* **1** *adj* prénatal; **a. classes** préparation *f* à l'accouchement **2** *n* examen *m* prénatal

antenna¹ [æn'tenə] (pl **-ae** [-iː]) n (of insect) antenne f

antenna² [æn'tenə] (pl **-as**) n Am (for TV, radio) antenne f

anteroom ['æntırʊm] n antichambre f

anthem ['ænθəm] n national a. hymne m national

anthology [æn'θɒlədʒı] (pl **-ies**) n anthologie f

anthropology [ænθrə'pɒlədʒı] n anthropologie f

anti- [Br 'æntı, Am 'æntaı] pref anti-; Fam to be anti sth être contre qch ▪**anti-aircraft** adj antiaérien, -ienne ▪**antibiotic** [-baı'ɒtık] adj & n antibiotique (m) ▪**antibody** n anticorps m ▪**anticlimax** n déception f ▪**anticlockwise** adv Br dans le sens inverse des aiguilles d'une montre ▪**anticyclone** n anticyclone m ▪**antidote** n antidote m ▪**antifreeze** n (for vehicle) antigel m ▪**antihistamine** n (drug) antihistaminique m ▪**antiperspirant** n antisudoral m ▪**anti-Semitic** adj antisémite ▪**anti-Semitism** n antisémitisme m ▪**antiseptic** adj & n antiseptique (m) ▪**antisocial** adj (misfit) asocial; (measure, principles) antisocial; (unsociable) peu sociable

anticipate [æn'tısıpeıt] vt (foresee) anticiper; (expect) s'attendre à, prévoir; (forestall) devancer ▪**antici'pation** n (expectation) attente f, (foresight) prévision f, **in a. of** en prévision de; (in a. (thank, pay) d'avance

antics ['æntıks] npl singeries fpl; **he's up to his a. again** il a encore fait des siennes

antipathy [æn'tıpəθı] n antipathie f

antipodes [æn'tıpədiːz] npl antipodes mpl

antiquarian [æntı'kweərıən] adj a. bookseller libraire mf spécialisé(e) dans le livre ancien

antiquated ['æntıkweıtıd] adj (expression, custom) vieillot, -otte; (person) vieux jeu inv; (object, machine) antédiluvien, -ienne

antique [æn'tiːk] 1 adj (furniture) ancien, -ienne; (of Greek or Roman antiquity) antique; a. dealer antiquaire mf; a. shop magasin m d'antiquités 2 n antiquité f, objet m d'époque ▪**antiquity** [-'tıkwıtı] n (period) antiquité f

antithesis [æn'tıθəsıs] (pl **-eses** [-ısiːz]) n antithèse f

antlers ['æntləz] npl (of deer) bois mpl

antonym ['æntənım] n antonyme m

Antwerp ['æntwɜːp] n Anvers m ou f

anus ['eınəs] n anus m

anvil ['ænvıl] n enclume f

anxiety [æŋ'zaıətı] (pl **-ies**) n (worry) inquiétude f (about au sujet de); (fear) anxiété f, (eagerness) désir m (to do de faire; for sth de qch)

anxious ['æŋkʃəs] adj (worried) inquiet, -iète (about/for pour); (troubled) anxieux, -ieuse; (causing worry) angoissant; (eager) impatient (to do de faire); **I'm a. (that) he should leave** je tiens absolument à ce qu'il parte ▪**anxiously** adv (worriedly) avec inquiétude; (with impatience) impatiemment

any ['enı] 1 adj (a) (in questions) du, de la, des; **have you a. milk/tickets?** avez-vous du lait/des billets?; **is there a. man (at all) who…?** y a-t-il un homme qui…?
(b) (in negatives) de; (not the slightest) aucun; **he hasn't got a. milk/tickets** il n'a pas de lait/de billets; **there isn't a. doubt/problem** il n'y a aucun doute/problème
(c) (no matter which) n'importe quel; **ask a. doctor** demande à n'importe quel médecin
(d) (every) tout; **at a. moment** à tout moment; **in a. case, at a. rate** de toute façon
2 pron (a) (no matter which one) n'importe lequel; (somebody) quelqu'un; **if a. of you…** si l'un d'entre vous…, si quelqu'un parmi vous…
(b) (quantity) en; **have you got a.?** en as-tu?; **I don't see a.** je n'en vois pas
3 adv **not a. further/happier** pas plus loin/plus heureux, -euse; **I don't see him a. more** je ne le vois plus; **a. more tea?** encore un peu de thé?; **I'm not a. better** je ne vais pas mieux

anybody ['enıbɒdı] pron (a) (somebody) quelqu'un; **do you see a.?** tu vois quelqu'un?; **more than a.** plus que tout autre (b) (in negatives) personne; **he doesn't know a.** il ne connaît personne (c) (no matter who) n'importe qui; **a. would think that…** on croirait que…

anyhow ['enıhaʊ] adv (at any rate) de toute façon; Fam (badly) n'importe comment

anyone ['enıwʌn] pron = **anybody**

anyplace ['enıpleıs] adv Am = **anywhere**

anything ['enıθıŋ] pron (a) (something) quelque chose; **can you see a.?** tu vois quelque chose? (b) (in negatives) rien; **he doesn't do a.** il ne fait rien; **without a.** sans rien (c) (everything) tout; **a. you like** tout ce que tu veux; Fam **like a.** (work) comme un fou (d) (no matter what) **a. (at all)** n'importe quoi

anyway ['enıweı] adv (at any rate) de toute façon

anywhere ['enıweə(r)] adv (a) (no matter where) n'importe où (b) (everywhere) partout; **a. you go** où que vous alliez, partout où vous allez; **a. you like** (là) où tu veux (c) (somewhere) quelque part; **is he going a.?** va-t-il quelque part? (d) (in negatives) nulle part; **he doesn't go a.** il ne va nulle part; **without a. to put it** sans un endroit où le/la mettre

apace [ə'peıs] adv rapidement

apart [ə'pɑːt] adv (a) (separated) **we kept them a.** nous les tenions séparés; **with legs (wide) a.** les jambes écartées; **two years a.** à deux ans d'intervalle; **they are a metre a.** ils se trouvent à un mètre l'un de l'autre; **to come a.** (of two objects) se séparer; **to tell two things/**

people a. distinguer deux choses/personnes (l'une de l'autre); **worlds a.** *(very different)* diamétralement opposé (**b**) *(to pieces)* **to tear a. to take a.** démonter (**c**) *(to one side)* à part; **joking a.** sans blague; **a. from** *(except for)* à part

apartheid [ə'pɑːteɪt] *n* apartheid *m*

apartment [ə'pɑːtmənt] *n* appartement *m*; **a. building** immeuble *m* (d'habitation)

apathy ['æpəθɪ] *n* apathie *f* ■ **apa'thetic** *adj* apathique

ape [eɪp] **1** *n* grand singe *m* **2** *vt (imitate)* singer

aperitif [əperɪ'tiːf] *n* apéritif *m*

aperture ['æpətʃʊə(r)] *n* ouverture *f*

APEX ['eɪpeks] *adj Br Rail* **A. ticket** = billet d'avion ou de train à tarif réduit, soumis à certaines restrictions

apex ['eɪpeks] *n (of triangle) & Fig* sommet *m*

aphorism ['æfərɪzəm] *n* aphorisme *m*

aphrodisiac [æfrə'dɪzɪæk] *adj & n* aphrodisiaque *(m)*

apiece [ə'piːs] *adv* chacun; **£1 a.** 1 livre pièce *ou* chacun

apocalypse [ə'pɒkəlɪps] *n* apocalypse *f* ■ **apoca'lyptic** *adj* apocalyptique

apocryphal [ə'pɒkrɪfəl] *adj* apocryphe

apologetic [əpɒlə'dʒetɪk] *adj (letter)* plein d'excuses; **a. smile** sourire *m* d'excuse; **to be a.** *(about)* s'excuser (de) ■ **apologetically** *adv* en s'excusant

apology [ə'pɒlədʒɪ] *n (pl -ies)* excuses *fpl; Fam Pej* **an a. for a dinner** un dîner minable ■ **apologize** *vi* s'excuser (**for** de); **he apologized for being late** il s'est excusé de son retard; **to a. to sb** faire ses excuses à qn (**for** pour)

> Note that the French noun **apologie** is a false friend and is never a translation for the English verb **apology**. It means *defence*.

apoplexy ['æpəpleksɪ] *n* apoplexie *f* ■ **apo'plectic** *adj & n* apoplectique *(mf)*

apostle [ə'pɒsəl] *n* apôtre *m*

apostrophe [ə'pɒstrəfɪ] *n* apostrophe *f*

appal [ə'pɔːl] *(Am* **appall)** *(pt & pp* **-ll-)** *vt* consterner; **to be appalled (at)** être horrifié (par) ■ **appalling** *adj* épouvantable

apparatus [æpə'reɪtəs] *n (equipment, organization)* appareil *m; Br (in gym)* agrès *mpl*

apparent [ə'pærənt] *adj (seeming)* apparent; *(obvious)* **it's a. that...** il est clair que... ■ **apparently** *adv* apparemment; **she's going to Venice** il paraît qu'elle va à Venise

apparition [æpə'rɪʃən] *n (phantom)* apparition *f*

appeal [ə'piːl] **1** *n (charm)* attrait *m; (interest)* intérêt *m; (call)* appel *m; (pleading)* supplication *f; (to a court)* appel *m* **2** *vt* **to a. to sb** *(attract)* plaire à qn; *(interest)* intéresser qn;

(ask for help) faire appel à qn; **to a. to sb's generosity** faire appel à la générosité de qn; **to a. to sb for sth** demander qch à qn; **to a. to sb to do sth** supplier qn de faire qch **3** *vi (in court)* faire appel; **to a. against a decision** faire appel d'une décision ■ **appealing** *adj (attractive) (offer, idea)* séduisant; *(begging) (look)* suppliant

> Note that the French verb **appeler** is a false friend and is never a translation for the English verb **to appeal**. Its most common meaning is *to call*.

appear [ə'pɪə(r)] *vi (become visible)* apparaître; *(seem, be published)* paraître; *(on stage, in film)* jouer; *(in court)* comparaître; **it appears that...** *(it seems)* il semble que... (+ *subjunctive or indicative); (it is rumoured)* il paraîtrait que... (+ *indicative)* ■ **appearance** *n (act)* apparition *f, (look)* apparence *f; (of book)* parution *f;* **to put in an a.** faire acte de présence; **to keep up appearances** sauver les apparences

appease [ə'piːz] *vt (soothe)* apaiser; *(curiosity)* satisfaire

append [ə'pend] *vt* joindre, ajouter (**to** à) ■ **appendage** *n Anat* appendice *m*

appendix [ə'pendɪks] *(pl* **-ixes** [-ɪksɪz] *or* **-ices** [-ɪsiːz]) *n (in book, body)* appendice *m;* **to have one's a. out** se faire opérer de l'appendicite ■ **appendicitis** [-dɪ'saɪtɪs] *n* appendicite *f*

appetite ['æpɪtaɪt] *n* appétit *m;* **to take away sb's a.** couper l'appétit à qn ■ **appetizer** *n (drink)* apéritif *m; (food)* amuse-gueule *m inv* ■ **appetizing** *adj* appétissant

applaud [ə'plɔːd] **1** *vt (clap)* applaudir; *(approve of)* approuver, applaudir à **2** *vi* applaudir ■ **applause** *n* applaudissements *mpl*

apple ['æpəl] *n* pomme *f; Br* **stewed apples, Am a. sauce** compote *f* de pommes; **cooking a.** pomme *f* à cuire; **eating a.** pomme de dessert; **a. core** trognon *m* de pomme; **a. pie** tarte *f* aux pommes; **a. tree** pommier *m*

appliance [ə'plaɪəns] *n* appareil *m*

applicable [ə'plɪkəbəl] *adj (rule)* applicable (**to** à); *(relevant)* pertinent

applicant ['æplɪkənt] *n* candidat, -ate *mf* (**for** à)

application [æplɪ'keɪʃən] *n* (**a**) *(request)* demande *f* (**for** de); *(for job)* candidature *f* (**for** de); *(for membership)* demande d'inscription; **a. (form)** *(for job)* formulaire *m* de candidature; *(for club)* formulaire d'inscription (**b**) *(diligence)* application *f*

apply [ə'plaɪ] *(pt & pp* **-ied)** **1** *vt (put on, carry out)* appliquer; *(brake of vehicle)* appuyer sur; **to a. oneself** s'appliquer **2** *vi (be relevant)* s'appliquer (**to** à); **to a. for** *(job)* poser sa candidature à; **to a. to sb** *(ask)* s'adresser à qn (**for** pour) ■ **applied** *adj (maths, linguistics)* appliqué

appoint [ə'pɔɪnt] *vt (person)* nommer (**to a post** à un poste; **to do** pour faire); *(director, minister)* nommer; *(secretary, clerk)* engager; *(time, place)* fixer; **at the appointed time** à l'heure dite; **well-appointed** *(kitchen)* bien équipé ▪ **appointment** *n* nomination *f*; *(meeting)* rendez-vous *m inv*; *(post)* situation *f*; **to make an a. with** prendre rendez-vous avec

> Note that the French noun **appointements** is a false friend and is never a translation for the English noun **appointment**. It means **salary**.

apportion [ə'pɔ:ʃən] *vt* répartir; **to a. blame** dégager les responsabilités de chacun

appraise [ə'preɪz] *vt* évaluer ▪ **appraisal** *n* évaluation *f*

appreciable [ə'pri:ʃəbəl] *adj* appréciable, sensible

appreciate [ə'pri:ʃɪeɪt] **1** *vt (enjoy, value, assess)* apprécier; *(understand)* comprendre; *(be grateful for)* être reconnaissant de **2** *vi (of goods)* prendre de la valeur ▪ **appreciation** [-'eɪʃən] *n* (**a**) *(gratitude)* reconnaissance *f*; *(judgement)* appréciation *f* (**b**) *(rise in value)* augmentation *f* (de la valeur) ▪ **appreciative** [-ʃɪətɪv] *adj (grateful)* reconnaissant (**of** de); *(favourable)* élogieux, -ieuse; **to be a. of** *(enjoy)* apprécier

apprehend [æprɪ'hend] *vt (seize, arrest)* appréhender

apprehension [æprɪ'henʃən] *n (fear)* appréhension *f* ▪ **apprehensive** *adj* inquiet, -iète (**about** de, au sujet de); **to be a. of** appréhender

apprentice [ə'prentɪs] **1** *n* apprenti, -ie *mf* **2** *vt* **to a. sb to sb** placer qn en apprentissage chez qn ▪ **apprenticeship** *n* apprentissage *m*

approach [ə'prəʊtʃ] **1** *n (method)* façon *f* de s'y prendre; *(path, route)* voie *f* d'accès; *(of winter, vehicle)* approche *f*; **at the a. of** à l'approche de; **a. to a question** manière *f* d'aborder une question; **to make approaches to** faire des démarches auprès de; *(sexually)* faire des avances à **2** *vt (draw near to)* s'approcher de; *(go up to, tackle)* aborder; **to a. sb about sth** parler à qn de qch; **he's approaching forty** il va sur ses quarante ans **3** *vi (of person, vehicle)* s'approcher; *(of date)* approcher ▪ **approachable** *adj (person)* d'un abord facile; *(place)* accessible (**by road** par la route)

appropriate 1 [ə'prəʊprɪət] *adj (place, clothes, means)* approprié (**to** à); *(remark, time)* opportun; **a. to** *or* **for** qui convient à **2** [ə'prəʊprɪeɪt] *vt (steal)* s'approprier; *(set aside)* affecter (**for** à) ▪ **appropriately** *adv* convenablement

approval [ə'pru:vəl] *n* approbation *f*; **on a.** *(goods)* à l'essai

approve [ə'pru:v] *vt* approuver; **to a. of** *(conduct, decision, idea)* approuver; **I don't a. of him** il ne me plaît pas; **I a. of his going** je trouve bon qu'il y aille; **I a. of his accepting** *or* **having accepted** je l'approuve d'avoir accepté ▪ **approving** *adj (look)* approbateur, -trice

approximate 1 [ə'prɒksɪmət] *adj* approximatif, -ive **2** [ə'prɒksɪmeɪt] *vi* **to a. to sth** se rapprocher de qch ▪ **approximately** *adv* approximativement ▪ **approximation** *n* approximation *f*

apricot ['eɪprɪkɒt] *n* abricot *m*

April ['eɪprəl] *n* avril *m*; **A. fool!** poisson d'avril!

apron ['eɪprən] *n (garment)* tablier *m*

apt [æpt] *adj (remark, reply, means)* qui convient; *(word, name)* bien choisi; **she/it is a. to fall**/*etc (likely) (in general)* elle/ça a tendance à tomber/*etc*; *(on a particular occasion)* elle/ça pourrait bien tomber/*etc*; **a. at sth** *(manual work)* habile à qch; *(intellectual)* doué pour qch ▪ **aptly** *adv (described)* justement; *(chosen)* bien; **a. named** qui porte bien son nom

aptitude ['æptɪtju:d] *n* aptitude *f* (**for** pour); *(of student)* don *m* (**for** pour)

aqualung ['ækwəlʌŋ] *n* scaphandre *m* autonome

aquarium [ə'kweərɪəm] *n* aquarium *m*

Aquarius [ə'kweərɪəs] *n (sign)* le Verseau; **to be (an) A.** être Verseau

aquarobics [ækwə'rəʊbɪks] *n* aquagym *f*

aquatic [ə'kwætɪk] *adj (plant)* aquatique; *(sport)* nautique

aqueduct ['ækwɪdʌkt] *n* aqueduc *m*

aquiline ['ækwɪlaɪn] *adj (nose, profile)* aquilin

Arab ['ærəb] **1** *adj* arabe **2** *n* Arabe *mf* ▪ **Arabian** [ə'reɪbɪən] *adj* arabe ▪ **Arabic** *adj & n (language)* arabe *(m)*; **A. numerals** chiffres *mpl* arabes

arable ['ærəbəl] *adj (land)* arable

arbiter ['ɑ:bɪtə(r)] *n* arbitre *m*

arbitrary ['ɑ:bɪtrərɪ] *adj (decision, arrest)* arbitraire

arbitrate ['ɑ:bɪtreɪt] *vti* arbitrer ▪ **arbitration** [-'treɪʃən] *n* arbitrage *m*; **to go to a.** avoir recours à l'arbitrage ▪ **arbitrator** *n (in dispute)* médiateur, -trice *mf*

arc [ɑ:k] *n (of circle)* arc *m*

arcade [ɑ:'keɪd] *n (for shops) (small)* passage *m* couvert; *(large)* galerie *f* marchande

arch [ɑ:tʃ] **1** *n (of bridge)* arche *f*; *(of building)* voûte *f*, arc *m*; *(of foot)* cambrure *f* **2** *vt* **to a. one's back** *(inwards)* se cambrer; *(outwards)* se voûter ▪ **archway** *n* voûte *f*

arch- [ɑ:tʃ] *pref (hypocrite)* achevé, fini; **a.-enemy** ennemi *m* juré; **a.-rival** grand rival *m*

archaeology *(Am* **archeology)** [ɑ:kɪ'ɒlədʒɪ] *n* archéologie *f* ▪ **archaeologist** *(Am* **archeologist)** *n* archéologue *mf*

archaic [ɑ:'keɪɪk] *adj* archaïque

archangel ['ɑːkeɪndʒəl] n archange m
archbishop [ɑːtʃ'bɪʃəp] n archevêque m
archeologist [ɑːkɪ'ɒlədʒɪst] n Am = archaeologist
archeology [ɑːkɪ'ɒlədʒɪ] n Am = archaeology
archer ['ɑːtʃə(r)] n archer m ▪ **archery** n tir m à l'arc
archetype ['ɑːkɪtaɪp] n archétype m
archipelago [ɑːkɪ'pelǝgǝʊ] (pl -oes or -os) n archipel m
architect ['ɑːkɪtekt] n architecte mf ▪ **architecture** n architecture f
archives ['ɑːkaɪvz] npl archives fpl ▪ **archivist** ['ɑːkɪvɪst] n archiviste mf
arctic ['ɑːktɪk] 1 adj arctique; (weather) polaire, glacial 2 n the A. l'Arctique m
ardent ['ɑːdənt] adj (supporter) ardent, chaud ▪ **ardently** adv ardemment ▪ **ardour** (Am **ardor**) n ardeur f
arduous ['ɑːdjʊǝs] adj pénible, ardu ▪ **arduously** adv péniblement, ardument
are [ɑː(r)] see be
area ['eǝrɪǝ] n (of country) région f; (of town) quartier m; Mil zone f; (surface) superficie f; Fig (of knowledge) domaine m; dining a. coin-repas m; kitchen a. coin-cuisine m; play a. (in house) coin-jeux m; (outdoors) aire f de jeux; Tel a. code indicatif m
arena [ǝ'riːnǝ] n (for sports) & Fig arène f
aren't [ɑːnt] = are not
Argentina [ɑːdʒǝn'tiːnǝ] n l'Argentine f ▪ **Argentinian** [-'tɪnɪǝn] 1 adj argentin 2 n Argentin, -ine mf
arguable ['ɑːgjʊǝbǝl] adj discutable ▪ **arguably** adv it is a. the... on peut dire que c'est le/la...
argue ['ɑːgjuː] 1 vt (matter) discuter (de); (position) défendre; to a. that... soutenir que... 2 vi (quarrel) se disputer (with avec; about au sujet de); (reason) raisonner (with avec; about sur); to a. in favour of plaider en faveur de; don't a.! ne discute pas!
argument ['ɑːgjʊmǝnt] n (quarrel) dispute f; (debate) discussion f; (point) argument m; to have an a. with sb (quarrel) se disputer avec qn ▪ **argumentative** [-'mentǝtɪv] adj (person) querelleur, -euse
aria ['ɑːrɪǝ] n Mus aria f
arid ['ærɪd] adj aride
Aries ['eǝriːz] n (sign) le Bélier; to be (an) A. être Bélier
arise [ǝ'raɪz] (pt arose, pp arisen [ǝ'rɪzǝn]) vi (of problem, opportunity) se présenter; (of cry, objection) s'élever; (result) provenir (from de); Literary (get up) se lever
aristocracy [ærɪ'stɒkrǝsɪ] n aristocratie f ▪ **aristocrat** [Br 'ærɪstǝkræt, Am ǝ'rɪstǝkræt] n aristocrate mf ▪ **aristocratic** [Br ærɪstǝ'krætɪk, Am ǝrɪstǝ'krætɪk] adj aristocratique

arithmetic [ǝ'rɪθmǝtɪk] n arithmétique f
ark [ɑːk] n Noah's a. l'arche f de Noé
arm¹ [ɑːm] n bras m; a. in a. bras dessus bras dessous; with open arms à bras ouverts ▪ **armband** n brassard m ▪ **armchair** n fauteuil m ▪ **armful** n brassée f ▪ **armhole** n emmanchure f ▪ **armpit** n aisselle f ▪ **armrest** n accoudoir m
arm² [ɑːm] vt (with weapon) armer (**with** de) ▪ **armaments** npl armements mpl
armadillo [ɑːmǝ'dɪlǝʊ] (pl -os) n tatou m
armistice ['ɑːmɪstɪs] n armistice m
armour ['ɑːmǝ(r)] (Am **armor** ['ɑːmǝr]) n (of knight) armure f; (of tank) blindage m ▪ **armoured** (Am **armored**), **armour-'plated** (Am **armor-plated**) adj (car) blindé ▪ **armoury** (Am **armory**) n arsenal m
arms [ɑːmz] npl (weapons) armes fpl; the a. race la course aux armements
army ['ɑːmɪ] 1 (pl -ies) n armée f; to join the a. s'engager; the regular a. l'armée active 2 adj (uniform) militaire
A road ['eɪrǝʊd] n Br ≃ route f nationale
aroma [ǝ'rǝʊmǝ] n arôme m ▪ **aroma'therapy** n aromathérapie f ▪ **aromatic** [ærǝ'mætɪk] adj aromatique
arose [ǝ'rǝʊz] pp of arise
around [ǝ'raʊnd] 1 prep autour de; (approximately) environ; to travel a. the world faire le tour du monde 2 adv autour; all a. tout autour; a. here par ici; to follow sb a. suivre qn partout; to rush a. courir dans tous les sens; is Jack a.? est-ce que Jack est dans le coin?; he's still a. il est encore là; there's a lot of flu a. beaucoup de gens ont la grippe en ce moment
arouse [ǝ'raʊz] vt (suspicion, anger, curiosity) éveiller; (sexually) exciter; to a. sb from sleep tirer qn du sommeil
arrange [ǝ'reɪndʒ] vt arranger; (time, meeting) fixer; it was arranged that... il était convenu que...; to a. to do sth s'arranger pour faire qch ▪ **arrangement** n (layout, agreement, for music) arrangement m; arrangements (preparations) préparatifs mpl; (plans) projets mpl; to make arrangements to do sth prendre des dispositions pour faire qch
arrears [ǝ'rɪǝz] npl (payment) arriéré m; to be in a. avoir du retard dans ses paiements; to be three months in a. avoir trois mois de retard dans ses paiements; to be paid monthly in a. être payé à la fin du mois
arrest [ǝ'rest] 1 vt (criminal, progress) arrêter 2 n (of criminal) arrestation f; under a. en état d'arrestation ▪ **arresting** adj Fig (striking) frappant
arrive [ǝ'raɪv] vi arriver; to a. at (conclusion, decision) arriver à, parvenir à ▪ **arrival** n arrivée f; on my a. à mon arrivée; new a.

nouveau venu *m*, nouvelle venue *f*; *(baby)* nouveau-né, -ée *mf*

arrogant ['ærəgənt] *adj* arrogant ■**arrogance** *n* arrogance *f* ■**arrogantly** *adv* avec arrogance

arrow ['ærəʊ] *n* flèche *f*

arse [ɑːs] *n Br very Fam* cul *m*

arsenal ['ɑːsənəl] *n* arsenal *m*

arsenic ['ɑːsnɪk] *n* arsenic *m*

arson ['ɑːsən] *n* incendie *m* criminel ■**arsonist** *n* incendiaire *mf*

art [ɑːt] *n* art *m*; **faculty of arts, arts faculty** faculté *f* des lettres; **arts degree** ≃ licence *f* ès lettres; **a. exhibition** exposition *f* d'œuvres d'art; **a. gallery** *(museum)* musée *m*; *(shop)* galerie *f* d'art; **a. school** école *f* des beaux-arts

artefact ['ɑːtɪfækt] *n* objet *m*

artery ['ɑːtərɪ] *(pl* **-ies)** *n (in body, main route)* artère *f* ■**arterial** [ɑː'tɪərɪəl] *adj (blood)* artériel, -ielle; *Br* **a. road** route *f* principale

artful ['ɑːtfəl] *adj* astucieux, -ieuse ■**artfully** *adv* astucieusement

arthritis [ɑː'θraɪtɪs] *n* arthrite *f*

artichoke ['ɑːtɪtʃəʊk] *n (globe)* **a.** artichaut *m*; **Jerusalem a.** topinambour *m*

article ['ɑːtɪkəl] *n (object, clause, in newspaper)* & *Grammar* article *m*; **a. of clothing** vêtement *m*; **articles of value** objets *mpl* de valeur; *Br* **articles** *(of lawyer)* contrat *m* de stage

articulate 1 [ɑː'tɪkjʊlət] *adj (person)* qui s'exprime clairement; *(speech)* clair 2 [ɑː'tɪkjʊleɪt] *vti (speak)* articuler ■**articulated lorry** *n Br* semi-remorque *m* ■**articulation** [-'leɪʃən] *n* articulation *f*

artifact ['ɑːtɪfækt] *n* objet *m*

artifice ['ɑːtɪfɪs] *n* artifice *m*

artificial [ɑːtɪ'fɪʃəl] *adj* artificiel, -ielle ■**artificiality** [-fɪʃɪ'ælɪtɪ] *n* caractère *m* artificiel

artillery [ɑː'tɪlərɪ] *n* artillerie *f*

artisan [ɑːtɪ'zæn] *n* artisan *m*

artist ['ɑːtɪst] *n* artiste *mf* ■**artiste** [ɑː'tiːst] *n (singer, dancer)* artiste *mf* ■**ar'tistic** *adj (pattern, treasure)* artistique; *(person)* artiste ■**artistry** *n* art *m*

artless ['ɑːtləs] *adj* naturel, -elle

arty ['ɑːtɪ] *adj Pej* du genre artiste

as [æz, *unstressed* əz] 1 *adv* (a) *(with manner)* comme; **as promised/planned** comme promis/prévu; **A as in Anne** A comme Anne; **as you like** comme tu veux; **such as** comme, tel que; **as much** *or* **as hard as I can** (au)tant que je peux; **as it is** *(this being the case)* les choses étant ainsi; **to leave sth as it is** laisser qch comme ça *ou* tel quel; **it's late as it is** il est déjà tard; **as if, as though** comme si; **you look as if** *or* **as though you're tired** tu as l'air fatigué (b) *(comparison)* **as tall as you** aussi grand que vous; **as white as a sheet** blanc (*f* blanche) comme un linge; **as much** *or* **as hard as you** autant que vous; **as much money as** autant d'argent que; **as many people as** autant de gens que; **twice as big as** deux fois plus grand que; **the same as** le même que

2 *conj* (a) *(time)* **as always** comme toujours; **as I was leaving, as I left** comme je partais; **as one grows older** à mesure que l'on vieillit; **as he slept** pendant qu'il dormait; **one day as...** un jour que...; **as from, as of** *(time)* à partir de (b) *(reason)* puisque, comme; **as it's late...** puisqu'il est tard..., comme il est tard... (c) *(though)* **(as) clever as he is...** si intelligent qu'il soit... (d) *(concerning)* **as for that, as to that** quant à cela (e) *(+ infinitive)* **so as to...** de manière à...; **so stupid as to...** assez bête pour...

3 *prep* (a) comme; **she works as a cashier** elle est caissière, elle travaille comme caissière; **dressed up as a clown** déguisé en clown (b) *(capacity)* **as a teacher** en tant que professeur; **to act as a father** agir en père

asap [eɪeseɪ'piː] *(abbr* **as soon as possible)** dès que possible

asbestos [æs'bestəs] *n* amiante *f*

ascend [ə'send] 1 *vt (throne)* accéder à; *(stairs, mountain)* gravir 2 *vi* monter ■**ascent** *n* ascension *f (of* de); *(slope)* côte *f*

ascertain [æsə'teɪn] *vt (discover)* établir; *(truth)* découvrir; *(check)* s'assurer de; **to a. that...** s'assurer que...

ascetic [ə'setɪk] 1 *adj* ascétique 2 *n* ascète *mf*

ascribe [ə'skraɪb] *vt* attribuer (**to** à)

ash [æʃ] *n* (a) *(of cigarette, fire)* cendre *f*; **A. Wednesday** mercredi *m* des Cendres (b) *(tree)* frêne *m* ■**ashtray** *n* cendrier *m*

ashamed [ə'ʃeɪmd] *adj* **to be/feel a.** avoir honte (**of sb/sth** de qn/qch); **to be a. of oneself** avoir honte; **to make sb a.** faire honte à qn

ashen ['æʃən] *adj (pale grey)* cendré; *(face)* blême

ashore [ə'ʃɔː(r)] *adv* à terre; **to go a.** débarquer; **to put sb a.** débarquer qn

Asia ['eɪʃə, 'eɪʒə] *n* l'Asie *f* ■**Asian** 1 *adj* asiatique; *Br (from India)* indien, -ienne 2 *n* Asiatique *mf*; *Br (Indian)* Indien, -ienne *mf*

aside [ə'saɪd] 1 *adv* de côté; **to draw a.** *(curtain)* écarter; **to take** *or* **draw sb a.** prendre qn à part; **to step a.** s'écarter; *Am* **a. from** en dehors de 2 *n (in play, film)* aparté *m*

asinine ['æsɪnaɪn] *adj* stupide

ask [ɑːsk] 1 *vt (request, inquire about)* demander; *(invite)* inviter (**to sth** à qch); **to a. sb sth** demander qch à qn; **to a. sb about sb/sth** interroger qn sur qn/qch; **to a. (sb) a question** poser une question (à qn); **to a. sb the time/way** demander l'heure/son chemin à qn; **to a. sb for sth** demander qch à qn; **to a. sb to do** (request) demander à qn de faire; (invite) inviter qn à faire; **to a. to leave**/etc demander à partir/etc **2** vi (inquire) se renseigner (**about** sur); (request) demander; **to a. for sb/sth** demander qn/qch; **to a. for sth back** redemander qch; **to a. after** or **about sb** demander des nouvelles de qn; **the asking price** le prix demandé

askance [əˈskɑːns] adv **to look a. at sb** regarder qn de travers

askew [əˈskjuː] adv de travers

asleep [əˈsliːp] adj endormi; (arm, leg) engourdi; **to be a.** dormir; **to fall a.** s'endormir

asparagus [əˈspærəgəs] n (plant) asperge f; (food) asperges fpl

aspect [ˈæspekt] n aspect m; (of house) orientation f

aspersions [əˈspɜːʃənz] npl **to cast a. on** dénigrer

asphalt [ˈæsfɔːlt] n asphalte m

asphyxia [əsˈfɪksɪə] n asphyxie f ▪ **asphyxiate** vt asphyxier ▪ **asphyxi'ation** n asphyxie f

aspire [əˈspaɪə(r)] vi **to a. to** aspirer à ▪ **aspiration** [æspəˈreɪʃən] n aspiration f

aspirin [ˈæsprɪn] n aspirine f

ass [æs] n (**a**) (animal) âne m; Fam (person) imbécile mf, âne (**b**) Am very Fam cul m

assail [əˈseɪl] vt assaillir (**with** de) ▪ **assailant** n agresseur m

assassin [əˈsæsɪn] n assassin m ▪ **assassinate** vt assassiner ▪ **assassi'nation** n assassinat m

assault [əˈsɔːlt] **1** n (military) assaut m; (crime) agression f **2** vt (attack) agresser; **to be sexually assaulted** être victime d'une agression sexuelle

assemble [əˈsembəl] **1** vt (objects, ideas) assembler; (people) rassembler; (machine) monter **2** vi se rassembler ▪ **assembly** n (meeting) assemblée f; (of machine) montage m, assemblage m; (in school) rassemblement m (avant les cours); **a. line** (in factory) chaîne f de montage

assent [əˈsent] **1** n assentiment m **2** vi consentir (**to** à)

assert [əˈsɜːt] vt affirmer (**that** que); (rights) faire valoir; **to a. oneself** s'affirmer ▪ **assertion** n (statement) affirmation f; (of rights) revendication f ▪ **assertive** adj (forceful) (tone, person) affirmatif, -ive; (authoritarian) autoritaire

assess [əˈses] vt (value, damage) évaluer; (situation) analyser; (decide amount of) fixer le montant de; (person) juger ▪ **assessment** n évaluation f; (of situation) jugement m ▪ **assessor** n (valuer) expert m

asset [ˈæset] n (advantage) atout m; **assets** (of business) avoir m

assiduous [əˈsɪdjʊəs] adj assidu ▪ **assiduously** adv avec assiduité

assign [əˈsaɪn] vt (give) attribuer; (day, time) fixer; (appoint) nommer; (send, move) affecter (**to** à) ▪ **assignment** n (task) mission f; (for student) devoir m

assimilate [əˈsɪmɪleɪt] **1** vt (absorb) assimiler **2** vi (of immigrants) s'assimiler ▪ **assimilation** [-ˈleɪʃən] n assimilation f

assist [əˈsɪst] vti aider (**in doing** or **to do** à faire) ▪ **assistance** n aide f; **to be of a. to sb** aider qn ▪ **assistant 1** n assistant, -ante mf; Br (in shop) vendeur, -euse mf **2** adj adjoint

assizes [əˈsaɪzɪz] npl Br (court meetings) assises fpl

associate [əˈsəʊʃɪeɪt] **1** vt associer (**with sth** à ou avec qch; **with sb** à qn) **2** vi **to a. with sb** (mix socially) fréquenter qn; **to a. (oneself) with sb** (in business venture) s'associer à ou avec qn **3** [əˈsəʊʃɪət] n & adj associé, -iée (mf) ▪ **association** [-ˈeɪʃən] n association f; **associations** (memories) souvenirs mpl

assorted [əˈsɔːtɪd] adj (different) variés; (foods) assortis; **a well-a. couple**/etc un couple/etc bien assorti ▪ **assortment** n (of cheeses) assortiment m; **an a. of people** des gens de toutes sortes

assuage [əˈsweɪdʒ] vt Literary apaiser

assume [əˈsjuːm] vt (**a**) (suppose) supposer (**that** que); **let us a. that...** supposons que... (+ subjunctive) (**b**) (take on) (power, control) prendre; (responsibility, role) assumer; (attitude, name) adopter ▪ **assumed** adj (feigned) faux (f fausse); **a. name** nom m d'emprunt ▪ **assumption** [əˈsʌmpʃən] n (supposition) supposition f; **on the a. that...** en supposant que... (+ subjunctive)

> Note that the French verb **assumer** is a false friend and is never a translation for the English verb **to assume**. It never means **to suppose** or **to adopt**.

assurance [əˈʃʊərəns] n (**a**) (confidence, promise) assurance f (**b**) Br (insurance) assurance f

assure [əˈʃʊə(r)] vt assurer (**sb that** à qn que; **sb of sth** qn de qch) ▪ **assuredly** [-ɪdlɪ] adv assurément

asterisk [ˈæstərɪsk] n astérisque m

astern [əˈstɜːn] adv (in ship) à l'arrière

asthma [Br ˈæsmə, Am ˈæzmə] n asthme m ▪ **asthmatic** [-ˈmætɪk] adj & n asthmatique (mf)

astonish [əˈstɒnɪʃ] vt étonner; **to be astonished (at sth)** s'étonner (de qch) ▪ **astonishing** adj étonnant ▪ **astonishingly** adv étonnamment ▪ **astonishment** n étonnement m

astound [əˈstaʊnd] vt stupéfier ▪ **astounding** adj stupéfiant

astray [əˈstreɪ] adv **to go a.** s'égarer; **to lead a.** détourner du droit chemin

astride [ə'straɪd] **1** adv à califourchon **2** prep à cheval sur

astringent [ə'strɪndʒənt] adj astringent; Fig (harsh) sévère

astrology [ə'strɒlədʒɪ] n astrologie f **astrologer** n astrologue mf

astronaut ['æstrənɔːt] n astronaute mf

astronomy [ə'strɒnəmɪ] n astronomie f **astronomer** n astronome mf **astronomical** [æstrə'nɒmɪkəl] adj astronomique

astute [ə'stjuːt] adj (crafty) rusé; (clever) astucieux, -ieuse

asunder [ə'sʌndə(r)] adv Literary **to tear a.** (to pieces) mettre en pièces; **to break a.** (in two) casser en deux

asylum [ə'saɪləm] n asile m; Pej lunatic **a.** asile d'aliénés **asylum-seeker** n demandeur, -euse mf d'asile

at [æt, unstressed ət] prep (a) à; **at the end** à la fin; **at school** à l'école; **at work** au travail; **at six (o'clock)** à six heures; **at Easter** à Pâques; **to drive at 10 mph** ≃ rouler à 15 km; **to buy/sell at 3 euros a kilo** acheter/vendre (à) 3 euros le kilo

(b) chez; **at the doctor's** chez le médecin; **at home** chez soi, à la maison

(c) en; **at sea** en mer; **at war** en guerre; **good at maths** fort en maths

(d) contre; **angry at** fâché contre

(e) sur; **to shoot at** tirer sur; **at my request** sur ma demande

(f) de; **to laugh at sb/sth** rire de qn/qch; **surprised at sth** surpris de qch

(g) (au)près de; **at the window** près de la fenêtre

(h) par; **to come in at the door** entrer par la porte; **six at a time** six par six

(i) (phrases) **at night** la nuit; **to look at** regarder; **to be (hard) at it** travailler dur; **while you're at it** tant que tu y es; Br **he's always (on) at me** Fam il est toujours après moi

(j) Comptr (in e-mail addresses) **at (sign)** arrobas m; **'gwilson at transex, dot, co, dot, uk'** 'gwilson, arrobas, transex, point, co, point, uk'

atchoo [ə'tʃuː] exclam Am = **atishoo**

ate [eɪt] pt of **eat**

atheism ['eɪθɪɪzəm] n athéisme m **atheist** n athée mf

Athens ['æθənz] n Athènes m ou f

athlete ['æθliːt] n athlète mf; **a.'s foot** (disease) mycose f **athletic** [-'letɪk] adj athlétique; **a. meeting** Br réunion f d'athlétisme; Am réunion f sportive **athletics** [-'letɪks] npl Br athlétisme m; Am sport m

atishoo [ə'tɪʃuː] (Am **atchoo**) exclam atchoum!

Atlantic [ət'læntɪk] **1** adj (coast, ocean) atlantique **2** n **the A.** l'Atlantique m

atlas ['ætləs] n atlas m

atmosphere ['ætməsfɪə(r)] n atmosphère f **atmospheric** [-'ferɪk] adj atmosphérique

atom ['ætəm] n atome m; **a. bomb** bombe f atomique **atomic** [ə'tɒmɪk] adj atomique **atomizer** n atomiseur m

atone [ə'təʊn] vi **to a. for** (sin, crime) expier **atonement** n expiation f (**for** de)

atrocious [ə'trəʊʃəs] adj atroce **atrocity** [ə'trɒsɪtɪ] n (cruel action) atrocité f

atrophy ['ætrəfɪ] (pt & pp **-ied**) vi (of muscle) s'atrophier

attach [ə'tætʃ] vt attacher (**to** à); (document) joindre (**to** à); **attached to sb** (fond of) attaché à qn **attachment** n (**a**) (affection) attachement m (**to sb** à qn) (**b**) (tool) accessoire m (**c**) (to e-mail) fichier m joint

attaché [ə'tæʃeɪ] n (**a**) (in embassy) attaché, -ée mf (**b**) **a. case** attaché-case m

attack [ə'tæk] **1** n (**a**) (military) attaque f (**on** contre); (on sb's life) attentat m; (of illness) crise f; (of fever) accès m; **an a. of migraine** une migraine; **to launch an a. on** attaquer; **to be** or **come under a.** être attaqué **2** vt attaquer; (problem, plan) s'attaquer à **3** vi attaquer **attacker** n agresseur m

attain [ə'teɪn] vt (aim) atteindre; (ambition) réaliser; (rank) parvenir à **attainable** adj (aim) accessible; (ambition, result) réalisable **attainment** n (of ambition) réalisation f (**of** de); **attainments** (skills) talents mpl

attempt [ə'tempt] **1** n tentative f; **to make an a. to do** tenter de faire; **they made no a. to help her** ils n'ont rien fait pour l'aider; **to make an a. on** (record) faire une tentative pour battre; **to make an a. on sb's life** attenter à la vie de qn; **at the first a.** du premier coup **2** vt tenter; (task) entreprendre; **to a. to do** tenter de faire; **attempted murder** tentative f d'assassinat

attend [ə'tend] **1** vt (meeting) assister à; (course) suivre; (school, church) aller à; (patient) soigner; (wait on, serve) servir; (escort) accompagner; **well-attended course** cours m très suivi; **the meeting was well attended** il y a eu du monde à la réunion **2** vi assister; **to a.** (take care of) s'occuper de; Literary (pay attention to) prêter attention à **attendance** n présence f (**at** à); (people) assistance f; (school) **a.** scolarité f; **in a.** de service **attendant** n employé, -ée mf; (in service station) pompiste mf; Br (in museum) gardien, -ienne mf; **attendants** (of prince, king) suite f

attention [ə'tenʃən] n attention f; **to pay a.** faire ou prêter attention (**to** à); **for the a. of** à l'attention de; **to stand at a./to a.** (of soldier) être/se mettre au garde-à-vous; **a.!** garde-à-vous!; **a. to detail** minutie f

attentive [ə'tentɪv] adj (heedful) attentif, -ive (**to** à); (thoughtful) attentionné (**to** pour) **attentively** adv attentivement

attenuate [əˈtenjʊeɪt] *vt* atténuer

attest [əˈtest] **1** *vt (certify, confirm)* confirmer **2** *vi* **to a. to** témoigner de

attic [ˈætɪk] *n* grenier *m*

attire [əˈtaɪə(r)] *n Literary* vêtements *mpl*

attitude [ˈætɪtjuːd] *n* attitude *f*

attorney [əˈtɜːnɪ] *(pl -eys) n Am (lawyer)* avocat *m*

attract [əˈtrækt] *vt* attirer ■ **attraction** *n (charm, appeal)* attrait *m*; *(place, person)* attraction *f*; *(between people)* attirance *f*; *Phys* attraction terrestre; **attractions** *(at funfair)* attractions *fpl* ■ **attractive** *adj (house, room, person, car)* beau *(f* belle*)*; *(price, offer)* intéressant; *(landscape)* attrayant; **do you find her a.?** elle te plaît?

attribute 1 [ˈætrɪbjuːt] *n (quality)* attribut *m* **2** [əˈtrɪbjuːt] *vt (ascribe)* attribuer **(to** à*)* ■ **attributable** *adj* attribuable **(to** à*)*

attrition [əˈtrɪʃən] *n* **war of a.** guerre *f* d'usure

attuned [əˈtjuːnd] *adj* **a. to** *(of ideas, trends)* en accord avec; *(used to)* habitué à

atypical [eɪˈtɪpɪkəl] *adj* atypique

aubergine [ˈəʊbəʒiːn] *n Br* aubergine *f*

auburn [ˈɔːbən] *adj (hair)* auburn *inv*

auction [ˈɔːkʃən] **1** *n* vente *f* aux enchères **2** *vt* **to a. (off)** vendre aux enchères ■ **auctioneer** *n* commissaire-priseur *m*

audacious [ɔːˈdeɪʃəs] *adj* audacieux, -ieuse ■ **audacity** [ɔːˈdæsɪtɪ] *n* audace *f*

audible [ˈɔːdɪbəl] *adj (sound, words)* audible ■ **audibly** *adv* distinctement

audience [ˈɔːdɪəns] *n* **(a)** *(of speaker, musician, actor)* public *m*; *(of radio broadcast)* auditeurs *mpl*; **TV a.** téléspectateurs *mpl* **(b)** *(interview)* audience *f* **(with sb** avec qn*)*

audio [ˈɔːdɪəʊ] *adj (cassette, system)* audio *inv*; **a. tape** cassette *f* audio ■ **audiotypist** *n* audiotypiste *mf* ■ **audio'visual** *adj* audio-visuel, -uelle

audit [ˈɔːdɪt] **1** *n* audit *m* **2** *vt (accounts)* vérifier ■ **auditor** *n* commissaire *m* aux comptes

audition [ɔːˈdɪʃən] **1** *n* audition *f* **2** *vti* auditionner

auditorium [ɔːdɪˈtɔːrɪəm] *n* salle *f* de spectacle/de concert

augment [ɔːgˈment] *vt* augmenter **(with** *or* **by** de*)*

augur [ˈɔːgə(r)] **1** *vi* **to a. well** être de bon augure **2** *vt* présager

August [ˈɔːgəst] *n* août *m*

august [ɔːˈgʌst] *adj* auguste

aunt [ɑːnt] *n* tante *f* ■ **'auntie, 'aunty** *(pl* **aunties)** *n Fam* tata *f*

au pair [əʊˈpeə(r)] **1** *n* **a. (girl)** jeune fille *f* au pair **2** *adv* au pair

aura [ˈɔːrə] *n (of place)* atmosphère *f*; *(of person)* aura *f*

auspices [ˈɔːspɪsɪz] *npl* **under the a. of** sous les auspices de

auspicious [ɔːˈspɪʃəs] *adj* prometteur, -trice

austere [ɔːˈstɪə(r)] *adj* austère ■ **austerity** [ɔːˈsterɪtɪ] *n* austérité *f*

Australia [ɒˈstreɪlɪə] *n* l'Australie *f* ■ **Australian 1** *adj* australien, -ienne **2** *n* Australien, -ienne *mf*

Austria [ˈɒstrɪə] *n* l'Autriche *f* ■ **Austrian 1** *adj* autrichien, -ienne **2** *n* Autrichien, -ienne *mf*

authentic [ɔːˈθentɪk] *adj* authentique ■ **authenticate** *vt* authentifier ■ **authenticity** [ˈtɪsɪtɪ] *n* authenticité *f*

author [ˈɔːθə(r)] *n* auteur *m*

authoritarian [ɔːθɒrɪˈteərɪən] *adj & n* autoritaire *(mf)*

authoritative [ɔːˈθɒrɪtətɪv] *adj (report, book)* qui fait autorité; *(tone, person)* autoritaire

authority [ɔːˈθɒrɪtɪ] *(pl -ies) n* autorité *f*; *(permission)* autorisation *f* **(to do** de faire*)*; **to be in a.** *(in charge)* être responsable; **to be an a. on** faire autorité en ce qui concerne

authorize [ˈɔːθəraɪz] *vt* autoriser **(to do** à faire*)* ■ **authori'zation** *n* autorisation *f* **(to do** de faire*)*

autistic [ɔːˈtɪstɪk] *adj* autiste

auto [ˈɔːtəʊ] *(pl -os) n Am* auto *f*

autobiography [ɔːtəʊbaɪˈɒgrəfɪ] *(pl -ies) n* autobiographie *f* ■ **autobiographical** [-baɪə-ˈgræfɪkəl] *adj* autobiographique

autocrat [ˈɔːtəkræt] *n* autocrate *m* ■ **auto'cratic** *adj* autocratique

autograph [ˈɔːtəgrɑːf] **1** *n* autographe *m*; **a. book** album *m* d'autographes **2** *vt* dédicacer **(for sb** à qn*)*

automate [ˈɔːtəmeɪt] *vt* automatiser ■ **auto'mation** *n* automatisation *f*

automatic [ɔːtəˈmætɪk] *adj* automatique ■ **automatically** *adv* automatiquement

automaton [ɔːˈtɒmətən] *n* automate *m*

automobile [ˈɔːtəməbiːl] *n Am* automobile *f*

autonomous [ɔːˈtɒnəməs] *adj* autonome ■ **autonomy** *n* autonomie *f*

autopsy [ˈɔːtɒpsɪ] *(pl -ies) n* autopsie *f*

autumn [ˈɔːtəm] *n* automne *m*; **in a.** en automne ■ **autumnal** [ɔːˈtʌmnəl] *adj (weather, day)* d'automne

auxiliary [ɔːgˈzɪljərɪ] *(pl -ies) adj & n* auxiliaire *(mf)*; **a. (verb)** *(verbe m)* auxiliaire *m*

avail [əˈveɪl] **1** *n* **to no a.** en vain; **of no a.** inutile **2** *vt* **to a. oneself of** profiter de

available [əˈveɪləbəl] *adj* disponible; **a. to all** *(education, goal)* accessible à tous; **tickets are still a.** il reste des tickets; **this model is a. in black or green** ce modèle existe en noir et en vert ■ **availability** [-ˈbɪlɪtɪ] *n (of object)* disponibilité *f*; *(of education)* accessibilité *f*

avalanche [ˈævəlɑːnʃ] *n* avalanche *f*

avarice [ˈævərɪs] *n* avarice *f* ■ **avaricious** [-ˈrɪʃəs] *adj* avare

Ave *(abbr* **avenue)** *n* av.

avenge [ə'vendʒ] *vt* venger; **to a. oneself (on)** se venger (de)

avenue ['ævənjuː] *n* avenue *f*; *Fig (way to a result)* voie *f*

average ['ævərɪdʒ] **1** *n* moyenne *f*; **on a.** en moyenne; **above/below a.** au-dessus/au-dessous de la moyenne **2** *adj* moyen, -enne **3** *vt (do)* faire en moyenne; *(reach)* atteindre la moyenne de; *(figures)* faire la moyenne de

averse [ə'vɜːs] *adj* **to be a. to doing** répugner à faire ■ **aversion** [ə'vɜːʃən] *n (dislike)* aversion *f*; **to have an a. to sth/to doing** avoir de la répugnance pour qch/à faire

avert [ə'vɜːt] *vt (prevent)* éviter; **to a. one's eyes** *(turn away)* détourner les yeux (**from** de)

aviary ['eɪvɪərɪ] *(pl* **-ies)** *n* volière *f*

aviation [eɪvɪ'eɪʃən] *n* aviation *f* ■ **aviator** *n* aviateur, -trice *mf*

avid ['ævɪd] *adj* avide (**for** de) ■ **avidly** *adv* avidement

avocado [ævə'kɑːdəʊ] *(pl* **-os)** *n* **a. (pear)** avocat *m*

avoid [ə'vɔɪd] *vt* éviter; **to a. doing** éviter de faire; **I can't a. doing it** je ne peux pas ne pas le faire ■ **avoidable** *adj* évitable ■ **avoidance** *n* **his a. of danger/***etc* son désir d'éviter le danger/*etc*; **tax a.** évasion *f* fiscale

avowed [ə'vaʊd] *adj (enemy)* déclaré

await [ə'weɪt] *vt* attendre

awake [ə'weɪk] **1** *adj* réveillé, éveillé; **(wide-)a.** *(not feeling sleepy)* éveillé; **he's (still) a.** il ne dort pas (encore); **to keep sb a.** empêcher qn de dormir, tenir qn éveillé; **to lie a.** être incapable de dormir; **a. to** *(conscious of)* conscient de **2** *(pt* **awoke***, pp* **awoken)** *vi* se réveiller **3** *vt (person)* réveiller; *Literary (old memories)* éveiller, réveiller ■ **awaken 1** *vti =* **awake 2** *vt* **to a. sb to sth** faire prendre conscience de qch à qn ■ **awakening** *n* réveil *m*; **a rude a.** *(shock)* un réveil brutal

award [ə'wɔːd] **1** *n (prize)* prix *m*, récompense *f*; *(scholarship)* bourse *f* **2** *vt (money)* attribuer; *(prize)* décerner; **to a. damages** *(of judge)* accorder des dommages-intérêts

aware [ə'weə(r)] *adj* **to be a. of** *(conscious)* être conscient de; *(informed)* être au courant de; *(realize)* se rendre compte de; **to become a. of/that** se rendre compte de/que; **to be a. that...** se rendre compte que... ■ **awareness** *n* conscience *f*

awash [ə'wɒʃ] *adj* inondé (**with** de)

away [ə'weɪ] *adv* (**a**) *(distant)* loin; **5 km a.** à 5

km (de distance) (**b**) *(in time)* **ten days a.** dans dix jours (**c**) *(absent, gone)* absent; **a. with you!** va-t'en!; **to drive a.** partir (en voiture); **to fade/ melt a.** disparaître/fondre complètement (**d**) *(to one side)* **to look** *or* **turn a.** détourner les yeux (**e**) *(continuously)* **to work/talk a.** travailler/parler sans arrêt (**f**) *Br* **to play a.** *(of team)* jouer à l'extérieur

awe [ɔː] *n* crainte *f* (mêlée de respect); **to be in a. of sb** éprouver pour qn une crainte mêlée de respect ■ **awe-inspiring** *adj (impressive)* imposant ■ **awesome** *adj (impressive)* impressionnant; *(frightening)* effrayant; *Am Fam (excellent)* super *inv*

awful ['ɔːfəl] *adj* affreux, -euse; *(terrifying)* effroyable; *(ill)* malade; *Fam* **an a. lot of** un nombre incroyable de; **I feel a. (about it)** j'ai vraiment honte ■ **awfully** *adv (suffer)* affreusement; *(very) (good, pretty)* extrêmement; *(bad, late)* affreusement; **thanks a.** merci infiniment

awhile [ə'waɪl] *adv* quelque temps; *(stay, wait)* un peu

awkward ['ɔːkwəd] *adj* (**a**) *(clumsy) (person, gesture)* maladroit (**b**) *(difficult)* difficile; *(cumbersome)* gênant; *(tool)* peu commode; *(time)* mal choisi; *(silence)* gêné; **the a. age** l'âge ingrat; *Fam* **to be an a. customer** ne pas être commode ■ **awkwardly** *adv (walk)* maladroitement; *(speak)* d'un ton gêné; *(placed, situated)* à un endroit peu pratique ■ **awkwardness** *n* maladresse *f*; *(difficulty)* difficulté *f*; *(discomfort)* gêne *f*

awl [ɔːl] *n* poinçon *m*

awning ['ɔːnɪŋ] *n (of tent)* auvent *m*; *(over shop, window)* store *m*; *(canvas or glass canopy)* marquise *f*

awoke [ə'wəʊk] *pt of* **awake**

awoken [ə'wəʊkən] *pp of* **awake**

awry [ə'raɪ] *adv* **to go a.** *(of plan)* mal tourner

axe [æks] *(Am* **ax**) **1** *n* hache *f*; *Fig (reduction)* coupe *f* sombre; **to get the a.** *(of project)* être abandonné; *(of worker)* être mis à la porte; *Fig* **to have an a. to grind** agir dans un but intéressé **2** *vt (costs)* réduire; *(job)* supprimer; *(project)* abandonner

axiom ['æksɪəm] *n* axiome *m*

axis ['æksɪs] *(pl* **axes** ['æksiːz]) *n* axe *m*

axle ['æksəl] *n* essieu *m*

ay(e) [aɪ] **1** *adv* oui **2** *n* **the ayes** *(votes)* les voix *fpl* pour

azalea [ə'zeɪlɪə] *n (plant)* azalée *f*

B, b [biː] *n* B, b *m inv*; **2B** *(number)* 2 ter

BA [biːˈeɪ] *abbr* = **Bachelor of Arts**

babble [ˈbæbəl] **1** *vi (mumble)* bredouiller; *(of baby, stream)* gazouiller **2** *vt* **to b. (out)** *(words)* bredouiller **3** *n inv (of voices)* rumeur *f*; *(of baby, stream)* gazouillis *m*

babe [beɪb] *n* **(a)** *Literary* bébé *m* **(b)** *Fam (girl)* belle nana *f*

baboon [bəˈbuːn] *n* babouin *m*

baby [ˈbeɪbɪ] **1** *(pl -ies)* *n* bébé *m*; **b. boy** petit garçon *m*; **b. girl** petite fille *f*; **b. tiger**/*etc* bébé-tigre/*etc m*; **b. clothes/toys**/*etc* vêtements *mpl*/jouets *mpl*/*etc* de bébé; *Am* **b. carriage** landau *m*; **b. sling** kangourou *m*, porte-bébé *m*; **b. face** visage *m* poupin **2** *(pt & pp -ied)* *vt Fam* dorloter ▪**baby-minder** *n Br* nourrice *f* ▪**baby-sit** *(pt & pp -sat, pres p -sitting)* *vi* faire du baby-sitting; **to b. for sb** garder les enfants de qn ▪**baby-sitter** *n* baby-sitter *mf* ▪**baby-walker** *n* trotteur *m*

babyish [ˈbeɪbɪɪʃ] *adj* de bébé; *(puerile)* bébé *inv*, puéril

bachelor [ˈbætʃələ(r)] *n* **(a)** *(not married)* célibataire *m*; *Br* **b. flat** garçonnière *f* **(b)** *Univ* **B. of Arts/of Science** *(person)* ≃ licencié, -iée *mf* ès lettres/ès sciences; *(qualification)* ≃ licence *f* de lettres/sciences

back¹ [bæk] *n (of person, animal)* dos *m*; *(of chair)* dossier *m*; *(of hand)* revers *m*; *(of house, vehicle, train, head)* arrière *m*; *(of room)* fond *m*; *(of page)* verso *m*; *(of fabric)* envers *m*; *Football* arrière *m*; **at the b. of the book** à la fin du livre; **in** *or* **at the b. of the car** à l'arrière de la voiture; **at the b. of one's mind** derrière la tête; **b. to front** devant derrière, à l'envers; *Fam* **to get off sb's b.** ficher la paix à qn; *Am* **in b. of** derrière ▪**backache** *n* mal *m* de dos ▪**back'bencher** *n Br Pol* député *m* de base ▪**backbiting** *n Fam* médisance *f* ▪**backbone** *n* colonne *f* vertébrale; *(of fish)* grande arête *f*; *Fig (main support)* pivot *m* ▪**backbreaking** *adj* éreintant ▪**backchat** *n Br Fam* impertinence *f* ▪**backcloth** *n* toile *f* de fond ▪**back'date** *vt* antidater ▪**back'handed** *adj (compliment)* équivoque ▪**backhander** *n (stroke)* revers *m*; *Br Fam (bribe)* pot-de-vin *m* ▪**backpack** *n* sac *m* à dos ▪**backrest** *n* dossier *m* ▪**back'side** *n Fam (buttocks)* derrière *m* ▪**back'stage** *adv* dans les coulisses ▪**backstroke** *n (in swim-*

ming) dos *m* crawlé ▪**backtrack** *vi* rebrousser chemin ▪**backup** *n* appui *m*; *Am (tailback)* embouteillage *m*; *Comptr* sauvegarde *f* ▪**backwater** *n (place)* trou *m* perdu ▪**back-woods** *npl* forêt(s) *f(pl)* vierge(s); *Fig* **to live in the b.** habiter dans le bled ▪**back'yard** *n Br* arrière-cour *f*; *Am* jardin *m* (à l'arrière d'une maison)

back² [bæk] *adj (wheel, seat)* arrière *inv*; **b. door** porte *f* de derrière; **b. end** *(of bus)* arrière *m*; **b. issue** *(of magazine)* vieux numéro *m*; **b. pay** rappel *m* de salaire; **b. payments** arriéré *m*; **b. room** pièce *f* du fond; **b. street** rue *f* écartée; **b. taxes** arriéré *m* d'impôts; **b. tooth** molaire *f*

back³ [bæk] *adv (behind)* en arrière; **far b., a long way b.** loin derrière; **a long way b. in the past** à une époque reculée; **a month b.** il y a un mois; **to stand b.** *(of house)* être en retrait *(from the road* par rapport à la route)*; **to go b. and forth** aller et venir; **to come b.** revenir; **he's b.** il est de retour, il est rentré *ou* revenu; **the trip there and b.** le voyage aller et retour

back⁴ [bæk] **1** *vt (with money)* financer; *(horse)* parier sur; *(vehicle)* faire reculer; **to be backed with** *(of curtain, picture)* doublé de; **to b. sb (up)** *(support)* appuyer qn; *Comptr* **to b. up** sauvegarder **2** *vi (move backwards)* reculer; **to b. down** faire marche arrière; **to b. out** *(withdraw)* se retirer; *(of vehicle)* sortir en marche arrière; **to b. on to** *(of house)* donner par derrière sur; **to b. up** *(of vehicle)* faire marche arrière

backer [ˈbækə(r)] *n (supporter)* partisan *m*; *(on horses)* parieur, -ieuse *mf*; *(financial)* commanditaire *m*

backfire [bækˈfaɪə(r)] *vi* **(a)** *(of vehicle)* pétarader **(b)** *Fig* **to b. on sb** *(of plot)* se retourner contre qn

backgammon [ˈbækgæmən] *n* backgammon *m*

background [ˈbækgraʊnd] *n* fond *m*, arrière-plan *m*; *(educational)* formation *f*; *(professional)* expérience *f*; *(environment)* milieu *m*; *(circumstances)* contexte *m*; **to keep sb in the b.** tenir qn à l'écart; **b. music/noise** musique *f*/bruit *m* de fond

backing [ˈbækɪŋ] *n (aid)* soutien *m*; *(material)* support *m*

backlash [ˈbæklæʃ] *n* choc *m* en retour, retour *m* de flamme

backlog ['bæklɒg] *n* **b. of work** travail *m* en retard

backward ['bækwəd] **1** *adj* (*person, country*) arriéré; (*glance*) en arrière **2** *adv* = **backwards** ▪ **backwardness** *n* (*of person, country*) retard *m* ▪ **backwards** *adv* en arrière; (*to walk*) à reculons; (*to fall*) à la renverse; **to go** *or* **move b.** reculer; **to go b. and forwards** aller et venir

bacon ['beɪkən] *n* lard *m*; (*in rashers*) bacon *m*; **b. and eggs** œufs *mpl* au bacon

bacteria [bæk'tɪərɪə] *npl* bactéries *fpl*

bad [bæd] (*worse, worst*) *adj* mauvais; (*wicked*) méchant; (*sad*) triste; (*accident, wound*) grave; (*tooth*) carié; (*arm, leg*) malade; (*pain*) violent; **b. language** gros mots *mpl*; **b. cheque** chèque *m* sans provision; **it's b. to think that…** ce n'est pas bien de penser que…; **to feel b.** (*ill*) se sentir mal; **to feel b. about sth** s'en vouloir de qch; **to be b. at maths** être mauvais en maths; **things are b.** ça va mal; **that's not b.!** ce n'est pas mal!; **to go b.** (*of fruit, meat*) se gâter; (*of milk*) tourner; **in a b. way** (*sick*) mal en point; (*in trouble*) dans le pétrin; **too b.!** tant pis! ▪ **bad-'mannered** *adj* mal élevé ▪ **bad-'tempered** *adj* grincheux, -euse

bade [bæd] *pt of* **bid**

badge [bædʒ] *n* (*of plastic, bearing slogan or joke*) badge *m*; (*of metal, bearing logo*) pin's *m*; (*of postman, policeman*) plaque *f*; (*on school uniform*) insigne *m*

badger ['bædʒə(r)] **1** *n* (*animal*) blaireau *m* **2** *vt* importuner

badly ['bædlɪ] *adv* mal; (*hurt*) grièvement; **b. affected** très touché; **b. shaken** bouleversé; **to be b. mistaken** se tromper lourdement; **b. off** dans la gêne; **to be b. off for** manquer de; **to want sth b.** avoir grande envie de qch

badminton ['bædmɪntən] *n* badminton *m*

baffle ['bæfəl] *vt* (*person*) déconcerter

bag¹ [bæg] *n* sac *m*; **bags** (*luggage*) bagages *mpl*; (*under eyes*) poches *fpl*; *Fam* **bags of** (*lots of*) beaucoup de; *Fam Pej* **an old b.** une vieille taupe; *Fam* **in the b.** dans la poche; *Fam* **b. lady** clocharde *f* ▪ **bagful** *n* (plein) sac *m*

bag² [bæg] (*pt & pp* **-gg-**) *vt Fam* (*claim*) accaparer

baggage ['bægɪdʒ] *n* bagages *mpl*; (*of soldier*) équipement *m*; *Am* **b. car** fourgon *m*; **b. handler** (*in airport*) bagagiste *mf*; *Am* **b. room** consigne *f*

baggy ['bægɪ] (*-ier, -iest*) *adj* (*clothing*) (*out of shape*) déformé; (*deliberately loose*) large

bagpipes ['bægpaɪps] *npl* cornemuse *f*

Bahamas [bə'hɑːməz] *npl* **the B.** les Bahamas *fpl*

bail [beɪl] **1** *n Law* caution *f*; **on b.** sous caution; **to grant sb b.** libérer qn sous caution **2** *vt* **to b. sb out** *Law* se porter garant de qn; *Fig* tirer qn d'affaire; **to b. a company out** renflouer une entreprise **3** *vi* **to b. out** (*from aircraft*) s'éjecter

bailiff ['beɪlɪf] *n* (*law officer*) huissier *m*; *Br* (*of landowner*) régisseur *m*

bait [beɪt] **1** *n* appât *m* **2** *vt* (**a**) (*fishing hook*) amorcer (**b**) (*annoy*) tourmenter

baize [beɪz] *n* **green b.** (*on card table*) tapis *m* vert

bake [beɪk] **1** *vt* (faire) cuire au four **2** *vi* (*of cook*) faire de la pâtisserie/du pain; (*of cake*) cuire (au four); *Fam* **we're** *or* **it's baking (hot)** on crève de chaleur ▪ **baked** *adj* (*potatoes, apples*) au four; **b. beans** haricots *mpl* blancs à la tomate ▪ **baking** *n* cuisson *f*; **to do some b.** faire de la pâtisserie/du pain; **b. powder** levure *f* chimique; **b. tin** moule *m* à pâtisserie

baker ['beɪkə(r)] *n* boulanger, -ère *mf* ▪ **bakery** *n* boulangerie *f*

balaclava [bælə'klɑːvə] *n Br* **b. (helmet)** passe-montagne *m*

balance ['bæləns] **1** *n* (*equilibrium*) équilibre *m*; (*of account*) solde *m*; (*remainder*) reste *m*; (*in accounting*) bilan *m*; (*for weighing*) balance *f*; **to lose one's b.** perdre l'équilibre; **to strike a b.** trouver le juste milieu; **sense of b.** sens *m* de la mesure; **to be in the b.** être incertain; **on b.** à tout prendre; **b. of payments** balance *f* des paiements; **b. sheet** bilan *m* **2** *vt* maintenir en équilibre (**on** sur); (*budget, account*) équilibrer; (*compare*) mettre en balance; **to b. (out)** (*compensate for*) compenser **3** *vi* (*of person*) se tenir en équilibre; (*of accounts*) être en équilibre, s'équilibrer; **to b. (out)** (*even out*) s'équilibrer

> Note that the French word **balance** is a false friend. Its most common meaning is **scales**.

balcony ['bælkənɪ] (*pl* **-ies**) *n* balcon *m*

bald [bɔːld] (**-er, -est**) *adj* chauve; (*statement*) brutal; (*tyre*) lisse; **b. patch** *or* **spot** tonsure *f* ▪ **bald-'headed** *adj* chauve ▪ **balding** *adj* **to be b.** perdre ses cheveux ▪ **baldness** *n* calvitie *f*

bale [beɪl] **1** *n* (*of cotton*) balle *f* **2** *vi* **to b. out** (*from aircraft*) s'éjecter

baleful ['beɪlfəl] *adj Literary* sinistre

balk [bɔːk] *vi* reculer (**at** devant)

Balkans ['bɔːlkənz] *npl* **the B.** les Balkans *fpl*

ball¹ [bɔːl] *n* balle *f*; (*inflated, for football, rugby*) ballon *m*; *Billiards* bille *f*; (*of string, wool*) pelote *f*; (*sphere*) boule *f*; (*of meat, fish*) boulette *f*; *Fam* **to be on the b.** (*alert*) avoir de la présence d'esprit; (*knowledgeable*) connaître son affaire; **b. bearing** roulement *m* à billes; *Am* **b. game** match *m* de base-ball; *Fig* **it's a whole new b. game** c'est une tout autre affaire

ball² [bɔːl] *n* (*dance*) bal *m* (*pl* **bals**)

ballad ['bæləd] *n* (*poem*) ballade *f*; (*song*) romance *f*

ballast ['bæləst] **1** *n* lest *m* **2** *vt* lester

ballcock ['bɔːlkɒk] n Br robinet m à flotteur

ballerina [bælə'riːnə] n ballerine f

ballet [Br 'bæleɪ, Am bæ'leɪ] n ballet m

ballistic [bə'lɪstɪk] adj **b. missile** engin m balistique

balloon [bə'luːn] n (toy, airship) ballon m; (in cartoon) bulle f; **(weather) b.** ballon-sonde m

ballot ['bælət] 1 n (voting) scrutin m; **b. paper** bulletin m de vote; **b. box** urne f 2 vt (members) consulter (par un scrutin)

ballpoint (pen) ['bɔːlpɔɪnt(pen)] n stylo m à bille

ballroom ['bɔːlruːm] n salle f de danse; **b. dancing** danses fpl de salon

balm [bɑːm] n (oil, comfort) baume m ▪ **balmy** (-ier, -iest) adj (a) (mild) doux (f douce); Literary (fragrant) embaumé (b) Br Fam = **barmy**

baloney [bə'ləʊnɪ] n Am Culin (sausage) saucisse f bolognaise; Fam (nonsense) âneries fpl

Baltic ['bɔːltɪk] n the **B.** la Baltique

balustrade ['bæləstreɪd] n balustrade f

bamboo [bæm'buː] n bambou m; **b. shoots** pousses fpl de bambou

bamboozle [bæm'buːzəl] vt Fam (cheat) embobiner

ban [bæn] 1 n interdiction f; **to impose a b. on sth** interdire qch 2 (pt & pp -nn-) vt interdire; **to b. sb from doing sth** interdire à qn de faire qch; **to b. sb from** (club) exclure qn de

banal [bə'næl] adj banal (mpl -als)

banana [bə'nɑːnə] n banane f; **b. skin** peau f de banane

band [bænd] 1 n (a) (strip) bande f; (of hat) ruban m; **rubber** or **elastic b.** élastique m (b) (group of people) bande f; (of musicians) (petit) orchestre m; (pop group) groupe m 2 vi **to b. together** se (re)grouper

bandage ['bændɪdʒ] 1 n (strip) bande f; (dressing) bandage m 2 vt **to b. (up)** (arm, leg) bander; (wound) mettre un bandage sur; **to b. sb's arm** bander le bras à qn

Band-aid® ['bændeɪd] n Am pansement m adhésif

B and B [biːənd'biː] (abbr bed and breakfast) n Br see **bed**

bandit ['bændɪt] n bandit m

bandstand ['bændstænd] n kiosque m à musique

bandwagon ['bændwægən] n Fig **to jump on the b.** suivre le mouvement

bandwidth ['bændwɪdθ] n Radio & Comptr largeur f de bande

bandy¹ ['bændɪ] (-ier, -iest) adj **to have b. legs** avoir les jambes arquées

bandy² ['bændɪ] (pt & pp -ied) vt **to b. about** (story, rumour) faire circuler

bane [beɪn] n Literary fléau m; Fam **he's the b. of my life** il m'empoisonne l'existence

bang¹ [bæŋ] 1 n (blow, noise) coup m (violent); (of gun) détonation f; (of door) claquement m 2 vt (hit) cogner, frapper; (door) (faire) claquer; **to b. one's head** se cogner la tête; **to b. down** (lid) rabattre (violemment) 3 vi cogner, frapper; (of door) claquer; (of gun) détoner; (of firework) éclater; **to b. into sb/sth** heurter qn/qch 4 exclam vlan!, pan!; **to go b.** éclater

bang² [bæŋ] adv Br Fam (exactly) exactement; **b. in the middle** en plein milieu; **b. on six** à six heures tapantes

banger ['bæŋə(r)] n Br (a) Fam (sausage) saucisse f; **bangers and mash** purée f avec des saucisses (b) (firecracker) pétard m (c) Fam **old b.** (car) vieille guimbarde f

Bangladesh [bæŋglə'deʃ] n le Bangladesh ▪ **Bangladeshi** 1 adj bangladeshi 2 n Bangladeshi, -e mf

bangle ['bæŋgəl] n bracelet m

bangs [bæŋz] npl Am (of hair) frange f

banish ['bænɪʃ] vt bannir

banister ['bænɪstə(r)] n **banister(s)** rampe f (d'escalier)

banjo ['bændʒəʊ] (pl -os or -oes) n banjo m

bank¹ [bæŋk] 1 n (of river) bord m, rive f; (raised) berge f; (of earth) talus m; (of sand) banc m; **the Left B.** (in Paris) la Rive gauche 2 vt **to b. (up)** (earth) amonceler; (fire) couvrir 3 vi (of aircraft) virer

bank² [bæŋk] 1 n (for money) banque f; **b. account** compte m en banque; **b. card** carte f d'identité bancaire; **b. clerk** employé, -ée mf de banque; Br **b. holiday** jour m férié; Br **b. note** billet m de banque; **b. rate** taux m d'escompte 2 vt (money) mettre à la banque 3 vi avoir un compte en banque (**with** à) ▪ **banker** n banquier, -ière mf; Br **b.'s card** carte f d'identité bancaire ▪ **banking** 1 adj (transaction) bancaire 2 n (activity, profession) la banque

bank³ [bæŋk] vi **to b. on sb/sth** (rely on) compter sur qn/qch

bankrupt ['bæŋkrʌpt] 1 adj **to go b.** faire faillite; Fig **morally b.** qui a perdu toute crédibilité 2 vt mettre en faillite ▪ **bankruptcy** n faillite f

banner ['bænə(r)] n banderole f; (military flag) & Fig bannière f

banns [bænz] npl bans mpl; **to publish the b.** publier les bans

banoffee pie, banoffi pie [bə'nɒfɪ'paɪ] n Culin = gâteau m à la banane et au caramel

banquet ['bæŋkwɪt] n banquet m

banter ['bæntə(r)] 1 n plaisanteries fpl 2 vi plaisanter

baptism ['bæptɪzəm] n baptême m ▪ **Baptist** n & adj baptiste (mf)

baptize [bæp'taɪz] vt baptiser

bar [bɑː(r)] 1 n (a) (of metal) barre f; (of gold)

lingot m; (of chocolate) tablette f; (on window) barreau m; **b. of soap** savonnette f; **behind bars** (criminal) sous les verrous; **to be a b. to sth** faire obstacle à qch; Law **the B.** le barreau; **b. code** (on product) code-barres m (**b**) (pub) bar m; (counter) bar, comptoir m (**c**) (group of musical notes) mesure f **2** (pt & pp **-rr-**) vt (**a**) **to b. sb's way** barrer le passage à qn; **barred window** fenêtre f munie de barreaux (**b**) (prohibit) interdire (**sb from doing** à qn de faire); (exclude) exclure (**from** à) **3** prep (except) sauf; **b. none** sans exception ▪**barmaid** n serveuse f de bar ▪**barman** (pl **-men**) n barman m ▪**bartender** n Am barman m

Barbados [bɑːˈbeɪdɒs] n la Barbade

barbarian [bɑːˈbeərɪən] n barbare mf ▪**barbaric** [-ˈbærɪk] adj barbare ▪**barbarity** [-ˈbærɪtɪ] n barbarie f

barbecue [ˈbɑːbɪkjuː] **1** n barbecue m **2** vt cuire au barbecue

barbed wire [bɑːbdˈwaɪə(r)] n fil m de fer barbelé; (fence) barbelés mpl

barber [ˈbɑːbə(r)] n coiffeur m pour hommes

Barbie® [ˈbɑːbɪ] n **B. doll** poupée f Barbie®

barbiturate [bɑːˈbɪtjʊrət] n barbiturique m

bare [beə(r)] **1** (**-er, -est**) adj nu; (tree, hill) dénudé; (room, cupboard) vide; (mere) simple; **the b. necessities** le strict nécessaire; **with his b. hands** à mains nues **2** vt (arm, wire) dénuder; **to b. one's head** se découvrir ▪**bareback** adv **to ride b.** monter à cru ▪**barefaced** adj (lie) éhonté ▪**barefoot 1** adv nu-pieds **2** adj aux pieds nus ▪**bare'headed** adj & adv nu-tête inv

barely [ˈbeəlɪ] adv (scarcely) à peine; **b. enough** tout juste assez

bargain [ˈbɑːgɪn] **1** n (deal) marché m, affaire f; **a b.** (cheap buy) une occasion, une bonne affaire; **a real b.** une véritable occasion ou affaire; **it's a b.!** (agreed) c'est entendu!; **to make a b.** faire un marché (**with sb** avec qn); **into the b.** (in addition) par-dessus le marché; **b. price** prix m exceptionnel; **b. counter** rayon m des soldes **2** vi (negotiate) négocier; (haggle) marchander; **to b. for** or **on sth** (expect) s'attendre à qch; **he got more than he bargained for** il ne s'attendait pas à ça ▪**bargaining** n négociations fpl; (haggling) marchandage m

barge [bɑːdʒ] **1** n péniche f **2** vi **to b. in** (enter room) faire irruption; (interrupt) interrompre; **to b. into** (hit) se cogner contre

baritone [ˈbærɪtəʊn] n (voice, singer) baryton m

bark¹ [bɑːk] n (of tree) écorce f

bark² [bɑːk] **1** n aboiement m **2** vi aboyer; Fam Fig **you're barking up the wrong tree** tu fais fausse route ▪**barking 1** n aboiements mpl **2** adj Br Fam **b. (mad)** complètement cinglé

barley [ˈbɑːlɪ] n orge f; **b. sugar** sucre m d'orge

barmy [ˈbɑːmɪ] (**-ier, -iest**) adj Br Fam (crazy) dingue

barn [bɑːn] n (for crops) grange f; (for horses) écurie f; (for cattle) étable f

barometer [bəˈrɒmɪtə(r)] n baromètre m

baron [ˈbærən] n baron m; Fig (industrialist) magnat m; **press/oil b.** magnat de la presse/du pétrole ▪**baroness** n baronne f

baroque [Br bəˈrɒk, Am bəˈrəʊk] adj & n Archit & Mus baroque (m)

barracks [ˈbærəks] npl caserne f

> Note that the French word **baraque** is a false friend. Its most common translation is **shack**.

barrage [Br ˈbærɑːʒ, Am bəˈrɑːʒ] n (across river) barrage m; Fig **a b. of questions** un feu roulant de questions

barrel [ˈbærəl] n (**a**) (cask) tonneau m; (of oil) baril m (**b**) (of gun) canon m (**c**) **b. organ** orgue m de Barbarie

barren [ˈbærən] adj (land, woman, ideas) stérile; (style) aride

barrette [bəˈret] n Am (hair slide) barrette f

barricade [ˈbærɪkeɪd] **1** n barricade f **2** vt barricader; **to b. oneself (in)** se barricader (dans)

barrier [ˈbærɪə(r)] n also Fig barrière f; Br **(ticket) b.** (of station) portillon m; **sound b.** mur m du son

barring [ˈbɑːrɪŋ] prep sauf

barrister [ˈbærɪstə(r)] n Br ≃ avocat m

barrow [ˈbærəʊ] n (wheelbarrow) brouette f; (cart) charrette f ou voiture f à bras

barter [ˈbɑːtə(r)] **1** n troc m **2** vt troquer (**for** contre)

base [beɪs] **1** n (**a**) (bottom, main ingredient) base f; (of tree, lamp) pied m; **b. rate** (of bank) taux m de base (**b**) (military) base f **2** adj (**a**) (dishonourable) bas (f basse) (**b**) **b. metal** métal m vil **3** vt baser, fonder (**on** sur); **based in London** (person, company) basé à Londres ▪**baseless** adj sans fondement ▪**baseness** n bassesse f

baseball [ˈbeɪsbɔːl] n base-ball m

basement [ˈbeɪsmənt] n sous-sol m

bash [bæʃ] Fam **1** n (bang) coup m; Br **to have a b.** (try) essayer un coup **2** vt (hit) cogner; **to b. (about)** (ill-treat) malmener; **to b. sb up** tabasser qn; **to b. in** or **down** (door, fence) défoncer ▪**bashing** n Fam (thrashing) raclée f; **to get a b.** prendre une raclée

bashful [ˈbæʃfəl] adj timide

basic [ˈbeɪsɪk] **1** adj essentiel, -ielle, de base; (elementary) élémentaire; (pay, food) de base; (room, house, meal) tout simple **2** n Fam **the basics** l'essentiel m ▪**basically** [-klɪ] adv (on the whole) en gros; (in fact) en fait; (fundamentally) au fond

basil [Br ˈbæzəl, Am ˈbeɪzəl] n (herb) basilic m
basilica [bəˈzɪlɪkə] n basilique f
basin [ˈbeɪsən]n (**a**) (made of plastic) bassine f; (for soup, food) (grand) bol m; (portable washbasin) cuvette f; (sink) lavabo m (**b**) (of river) bassin m
basis [ˈbeɪsɪs] (pl **bases** [ˈbeɪsiːz]) n (for discussion) base f; (for opinion, accusation) fondement m; (of agreement) bases fpl; **on the b. of** d'après; **on that b.** dans ces conditions; **on a weekly b.** chaque semaine
bask [bɑːsk] vi (in the sun) se chauffer
basket [ˈbɑːskɪt] n panier m; (for bread, laundry, litter) corbeille f ▪ **basketball** n basket(-ball) m
Basque [bæsk] **1** adj basque **2** n (**a**) (person) Basque mf (**b**) (language) basque m
bass¹ [beɪs] **1** n Mus basse f **2** adj (note, voice, instrument) bas (f basse)
bass² [bæs] n (sea fish) bar m; (freshwater fish) perche f
bassoon [bəˈsuːn] n basson m
bastard [ˈbɑːstəd] **1** adj (child) bâtard **2** n (**a**) (child) bâtard, -arde mf (**b**) Vulg (unpleasant person) salaud m, salope f
baste [beɪst] vt (**a**) (fabric) bâtir (**b**) (meat) arroser de son jus
bastion [ˈbæstɪən] n also Fig bastion m
bat¹ [bæt] n (animal) chauve-souris f
bat² [bæt] **1** n Cricket & Baseball batte f; (in table-tennis) raquette f; **off my own b.** de ma propre initiative **2** (pt & pp **-tt-**) vt (**a**) (ball) frapper (**b**) **she didn't b. an eyelid** elle n'a pas sourcillé
batch [bætʃ] n (of people) groupe m; (of letters) paquet m; (of books) lot m; (of loaves) fournée f; (of papers) liasse f
bated [ˈbeɪtɪd] adj **with b. breath** en retenant son souffle
bath [bɑːθ] **1** (pl **baths** [bɑːðz]) n bain m; (tub) baignoire f; **to have** or **take a b.** prendre un bain; **b. towel** drap m de bain; Br swimming **baths** piscine f **2** vt Br baigner **3** vi Br prendre un bain ▪ **bathrobe** n Br peignoir m de bain; Am robe f de chambre ▪ **bathroom** n salle f de bain(s); Am (toilet) toilettes fpl ▪ **bathtub** n baignoire f
bathe [beɪð] **1** vt baigner; (wound) laver **2** vi se baigner; Am prendre un bain **3** n Old-fashioned bain m (de mer), baignade f; **to go for a b.** se baigner ▪ **bathing** n baignades fpl; **b. suit**, Br **b. costume** maillot m de bain
baton [Br ˈbætən, Am bəˈtɒn] n (of conductor) baguette f; (of policeman) matraque f; (of soldier, drum majorette) bâton m; (in relay race) témoin m
battalion [bəˈtæljən] n bataillon m
batter [ˈbætə(r)] **1** n pâte f à frire **2** vt (strike) cogner sur; (person) frapper; (town) pilonner; **to b. down** (door) défoncer ▪ **battered** adj (car, hat) cabossé; (house) délabré; (face)

meurtri; **b. child** enfant m martyr; **b. wife** femme f battue ▪ **battering** n **to take a b.** souffrir beaucoup
battery [ˈbætərɪ] (pl **-ies**) n (in vehicle, of guns, for hens) batterie f; (in radio, appliance) pile f; **b. hen** poule f de batterie
battle [ˈbætəl] **1** n bataille f; (struggle) lutte f; Fam **that's half the b.** la partie est à moitié gagnée **2** vi se battre, lutter ▪ **battlefield** n champ m de bataille ▪ **battleship** n cuirassé m
battlements [ˈbætəlmənts] npl (indentations) créneaux mpl; (wall) remparts mpl
batty [ˈbætɪ] (**-ier, -iest**) adj Br Fam toqué
baulk [bɔːk] vi reculer (**at** devant)
bawdy [ˈbɔːdɪ] (**-ier, -iest**) adj paillard
bawl [bɔːl] vti **to b. (out)** brailler; Am Fam **to b. sb out** engueuler qn
bay¹ [beɪ] **1** n (**a**) (part of coastline) baie f (**b**) (in room) renfoncement m; **b. window** bow-window m, oriel m (**c**) Br (for loading) aire f de chargement (**d**) **at b.** (animal, criminal) aux abois; **to keep** or **hold at b.** (enemy, wild dog) tenir en respect; (disease) juguler **2** vi aboyer **3** adj (horse) bai
bay² [beɪ] n (tree) laurier m; **b. leaf** feuille f de laurier
bayonet [ˈbeɪənɪt] n baïonnette f
bazaar [bəˈzɑː(r)] n (market, shop) bazar m; (charity sale) vente f de charité
bazooka [bəˈzuːkə] n bazooka m
BB gun [biːˈbiːgʌn] n Am carabine f à air comprimé
BBQ [biːbiːˈkjuː] (abbr **barbecue**) n Fam barbecue m
BC [biːˈsiː] (abbr **before Christ**) adv av. J.-C.
BCG [biːsiːˈdʒiː] (abbr **bacille Calmette-Guérin**) n Med BCG m
be [biː] (present tense **am, are, is**; past tense **was, were**; pp **been**; pres p **being**)

À l'oral et dans un style familier à l'écrit, le verbe be peut être contracté: **I am** devient **I'm**, **he/she/it is** deviennent **he's/she's/it's** et **you/ we/they are** deviennent **you're/we're/ they're**. Les formes négatives **is not/are not/ was not** et **were not** se contractent respectivement en **isn't/aren't/wasn't** et **weren't**.

1 vi (**a**) (gen) être; **it is green/small**/etc c'est vert/petit/etc; **he's a doctor** il est médecin; **he's an Englishman** c'est un Anglais; **it's him** c'est lui; **it's them** ce sont eux; **it's three (o'clock)** il est trois heures; **it's the sixth of May**, Am **it's May sixth** nous sommes le six mai (**b**) (with age, height) avoir; **to be twenty** (age) avoir vingt ans; **to be 2 m high** avoir 2 m de haut; **to be 6 f tall** ≃ mesurer 1,80 m (**c**) (with health) aller; **how are you?** comment vas-tu?; **I'm well/not well** je vais bien/mal

(**d**) *(with place, situation)* se trouver, être; **she's in York** elle se trouve *ou* elle est à York

(**e**) *(exist)* être; **the best painter there is** le meilleur peintre qui soit; **leave me be** laissez-moi (tranquille); **that may be** cela se peut

(**f**) *(go, come)* **I've been to see her** je suis allé la voir; **he's (already) been** il est (déjà) venu

(**g**) *(with weather, calculations)* faire; **it's fine** il fait beau; **it's foggy** il y a du brouillard; **2 and 2 are 4** 2 et 2 font 4

(**h**) *(cost)* coûter, faire; **it's 20 pence** ça coûte 20 pence; **how much is it?** ça fait combien?, c'est combien?

2 *v aux* (**a**) **I am/was doing** je fais/faisais; **I'll be staying** je vais rester; **I'm listening to the radio** je suis en train d'écouter la radio; **what has she been doing?** qu'est-ce qu'elle a fait?; **she's been there some time** elle est là depuis un moment; **he was killed** il a été tué; **I've been waiting (for) two hours** j'attends depuis deux heures; **it is said** on dit; **she's to be pitied** elle est à plaindre

(**b**) *(in questions and answers)* **isn't it?/aren't you?**/*etc* n'est-ce pas?, non?; **she's ill, is she?** *(surprise)* alors, comme ça, elle est malade?; **I am!/he is!**/*etc* oui!

(**c**) *(+ infinitive)* **he is to come at once** *(must)* il doit venir tout de suite; **he's shortly to go** *(intends to)* il va bientôt partir

(**d**) **there is/are** il y a; *(pointing)* voilà; **here is/ are** voici; **there she is** la voilà; **here they are** les voici

beach [biːtʃ] *n* plage *f*

beacon ['biːkən] *n (for ship, aircraft)* balise *f*; *(lighthouse)* phare *m*

bead [biːd] *n (small sphere)* perle *f*; *(of rosary)* grain *m*; *(of sweat)* goutte *f*, gouttelette *f*; **(string of) beads** collier *m*

beak [biːk] *n* bec *m*

beaker ['biːkə(r)] *n* gobelet *m*

beam [biːm] **1** *n* (**a**) *(of wood)* poutre *f* (**b**) *(of light, sunlight)* rayon *m*; *(of headlight, flashlight)* faisceau *m* (lumineux) **2** *vi (of light)* rayonner; *(of sun, moon)* briller; *(smile broadly)* sourire largement; **to b. with pride/joy** rayonner de fierté/joie **3** *vt (signals, programme)* transmettre (**to** à) ▪ **beaming** *adj (face, person, smile)* rayonnant

bean [biːn] *n* haricot *m*; *(of coffee)* grain *m*; *Fam* **to be full of beans** être plein d'énergie; **b. curd** pâte *f* de soja ▪ **beanshoots, beansprouts** *npl* germes *mpl* de soja

beanie hat ['biːnɪhæt] *n* bonnet *m*

bear[1] [beə(r)] *n (animal)* ours *m*; **b. cub** ourson *m*

bear[2] [beə(r)] **1** *(pt* **bore,** *pp* **borne)** *vt (carry, show)* porter; *(endure)* supporter; *(resemblance)* offrir; *(comparison)* soutenir; *(responsibility)* assumer; *(child)* donner naissance à; **I can't b.**

him/it je ne peux pas le supporter/supporter ça; **to b. sth in mind** *(remember)* se souvenir de qch; *(take into account)* tenir compte de qch; **to b. out** corroborer **2** *vi* **to b. left/right** *(turn)* tourner à gauche/droite; **to b. north**/*etc (go)* aller en direction du nord/*etc*; **to b. (up)on** *(relate to)* se rapporter à; *Fig* **to b. heavily on sb** *(of burden)* peser sur qn; **to b. with sb** être patient avec qn; **if you could b. with me** si vous voulez bien patienter; **to bring one's energies to b. on a task** consacrer toute son énergie à un travail; **to bring pressure to b. on sb** faire pression sur qn (**to do** pour faire); **to b. up** tenir le coup; **b. up!** courage!

bearable ['beərəbəl] *adj* supportable

beard [bɪəd] *n* barbe *f*; **to have a b.** porter la barbe ▪ **bearded** *adj* barbu

bearer ['beərə(r)] *n* porteur, -euse *mf*

bearing ['beərɪŋ] *n (relevance)* rapport *m* (**on** avec); *(posture, conduct)* port *m*; *(of ship, aircraft)* position *f*; **to get one's bearings** s'orienter

beast [biːst] *n* bête *f*; *Fam (person)* brute *f*

beastly ['biːstlɪ] *adj Br Fam (unpleasant)* horrible

beat [biːt] **1** *n (of heart, drum)* battement *m*; *(of policeman)* ronde *f*; *(in music)* rythme *m*

2 *(pt* **beat,** *pp* **beaten** [biːtən]) *vt* battre; **to b. a drum** battre du tambour; *Fam* **that beats me** ça me dépasse; *Fam* **b. it!** fiche le camp!; **to b. sb to it** devancer qn; **to b. back** *or* **off** repousser; **to b. down** *(price)* faire baisser; **to b. down** *or* **in** *(door)* défoncer; **to b. out** *(rhythm)* marquer; *(tune)* jouer; **to b. sb up** tabasser qn

3 *vi* battre; *(at door)* frapper (**at** à); *Fam* **to b. about** *or* **around the bush** tourner autour du pot; **to b. down** *(of rain)* tomber à verse; *(of sun)* taper ▪ **beating** *n (blows, defeat)* raclée *f*; *(of heart, drums)* battement *m*; **to take a b.** souffrir beaucoup

beater ['biːtə(r)] *n (for eggs)* fouet *m*

beautician [bjuːˈtɪʃən] *n* esthéticienne *f*

beautiful ['bjuːtɪfəl] *adj (très) beau (f belle); (superb)* merveilleux, -euse ▪ **beautifully** *adv (after verb)* à merveille; *(before adjective)* merveilleusement

beauty ['bjuːtɪ] *(pl* **-ies)** *n (quality, woman)* beauté *f*; **it's a b.!** *(car, house)* c'est une merveille!; **the b. of it is (that)...** le plus beau, c'est que...; **b. parlour** *or* **salon** institut *m* de beauté; **b. spot** *(on skin)* grain *m* de beauté; *Br (in countryside)* endroit *m* pittoresque; **b. therapist** esthéticienne *f*

beaver ['biːvə(r)] **1** *n* castor *m* **2** *vi* **to b. away** travailler dur (**at sth** à qch)

became [bɪˈkeɪm] *pt of* **become**

because [bɪˈkɒz] *conj* parce que; **b. of** à cause de

beck [bek] *n* **at sb's b. and call** aux ordres de qn

beckon ['bekən] *vti* to b. (to) sb faire signe à qn (to do de faire)

become [bɪ'kʌm] 1 (*pt* became, *pp* become) *vi* devenir; to b. a painter devenir peintre; to b. thin maigrir; to b. worried commencer à s'inquiéter; what has b. of her? qu'est-elle devenue? 2 *vt Formal* that hat becomes her ce chapeau lui va bien ▪ **becoming** *adj* (*clothes*) seyant; (*modesty*) bienséant

bed [bed] 1 *n* lit *m*; (*flowerbed*) parterre *m*; (*of vegetables*) carré *m*; (*of sea*) fond *m*; (*of river*) lit *m*; (*of rock*) couche *f*; to go to b. (aller) se coucher; to put sb to b. coucher qn; in b. couché; to get out of b. se lever; to make the b. faire le lit; b. and breakfast (*in hotel*) chambre *f* avec petit déjeuner; to stay in a b. and breakfast ≃ prendre une chambre d'hôte; *Br* ▪ b. settee (canapé *m*) convertible *m* 2 *vi* to b. down se coucher ▪ **bedbug** *n* punaise *f* ▪ **bedclothes** *npl*, ▪ **bedding** *n* couvertures *fpl* et draps *mpl* ▪ **bedpan** *n* bassin *m* (hygiénique) ▪ **bedridden** *adj* alité ▪ **bedroom** *n* chambre *f* à coucher ▪ **bedside** *n* chevet *m*; b. lamp/book/table lampe *f*/livre *m*/table *f* de chevet ▪ **bed'sit, bedsitter** *n Br* chambre *f* meublée ▪ **bedspread** *n* dessus-de-lit *m inv* ▪ **bedtime** *n* heure *f* du coucher; b.! c'est l'heure d'aller se coucher!; b. story histoire *f* (*pour endormir les enfants*)

bedevil [bɪ'devəl] (*Br* -ll-, *Am* -l-) *vt* (*plague*) tourmenter; (*confuse*) embrouiller; **bedevilled by** (*problems*) perturbé par

bedlam ['bedləm] *n Fam* (*noise*) chahut *m*

bedraggled [bɪ'drægəld] *adj* (*clothes, person*) débraillé et tout trempé

bee [bi:] *n* abeille *f* ▪ **beehive** *n* ruche *f*

beech [bi:tʃ] *n* (*tree, wood*) hêtre *m*

beef [bi:f] 1 *n* bœuf *m* 2 *vi Fam* (*complain*) rouspéter (about contre) ▪ **beefburger** *n* hamburger *m* ▪ **beefy** (-ier, -iest) *adj Fam* costaud

beekeeper ['bi:ki:pə(r)] *n* apiculteur, -trice *mf* ▪ **beekeeping** *n* apiculture *f*

beeline ['bi:laɪn] *n Fam* to make a b. for aller droit vers

been [bi:n] *pp* of **be**

beep [bi:p] 1 *n* (*of machine*) bip *m*, signal *m* sonore; (*of car horn*) coup *m* de klaxon 2 *vi* (*of machine*) faire bip, émettre un signal sonore; (*of car driver*) klaxonner 3 *vt* to b. the horn klaxonner ▪ **beeper** *n* récepteur *m* d'appels

beer [bɪə(r)] *n* bière *f*; b. garden = jardin où les clients d'un pub peuvent consommer; b. glass chope *f*

beet [bi:t] *n* betterave *f* ▪ **beetroot** *n* betterave *f*

beetle ['bi:təl] 1 *n* scarabée *m*; (*any beetle-like insect*) bestiole *f* 2 *vi Br* to b. off *Fam* (*run off*) se sauver

before [bɪ'fɔː(r)] 1 *adv* avant; (*already*) déjà; (*in front*) devant; the month b. le mois d'avant *ou* précédent; the day b. la veille; I've seen it b. je l'ai déjà vu; I've never done it b. je ne l'ai (encore) jamais fait 2 *prep* (*time*) avant; (*place*) devant; the year b. last il y a deux ans; b. my very eyes sous mes yeux 3 *conj* avant que (+ ne) (+ *subjunctive*), avant de (+ *infinitive*); b. he goes avant qu'il (ne) parte; b. going avant de partir ▪ **beforehand** *adv* à l'avance; check b. vérifiez au préalable

befriend [bɪ'frend] *vt* to b. sb se prendre d'amitié pour qn

befuddled [bɪ'fʌdəld] *adj* (*drunk*) ivre

beg [beg] 1 (*pt & pp* -gg-) *vt* to b. (for) (*favour, help*) demander; (*bread, money*) mendier; to b. sb to do sth supplier qn de faire qch; I b. to differ permettez-moi de ne pas être d'accord; to b. the question esquiver la question 2 *vi* (*in street*) mendier; (*ask earnestly*) supplier; to go begging (*of food, articles*) ne pas trouver d'amateurs

began [bɪ'gæn] *pt* of **begin**

beggar ['begə(r)] *n* mendiant, -iante *mf*; *Br Fam* (*person*) type *m*; lucky b. veinard, -arde *mf*

begin [bɪ'gɪn] 1 (*pt* began, *pp* begun, *pres p* beginning) *vt* commencer; (*fashion, campaign*) lancer; (*bottle, sandwich*) entamer; (*conversation*) engager; to b. doing *ou* to do sth commencer *ou* se mettre à faire qch; he began laughing il s'est mis à rire 2 *vi* commencer (with par; by doing par faire); to b. on sth commencer qch; beginning from à partir de; to b. with (*first of all*) d'abord

beginner [bɪ'gɪnə(r)] *n* débutant, -ante *mf*

beginning [bɪ'gɪnɪŋ] *n* commencement *m*, début *m*; in *or* at the b. au début, au commencement

begrudge [bɪ'grʌdʒ] *vt* (*envy*) envier (sb sth qch à qn); (*reproach*) reprocher (sb sth qch à qn); (*give unwillingly*) donner à contrecœur; to b. doing sth faire qch à contrecœur

begun [bɪ'gʌn] *pp* of **begin**

behalf [bɪ'hɑ:f] *n* on b. of sb, on sb's b. (*representing*) au nom de qn, de la part de qn; (*in the interests of*) en faveur de qn

behave [bɪ'heɪv] *vi* se conduire; (*of machine*) fonctionner; to b. (oneself) se tenir bien; (*of child*) être sage

behaviour [bɪ'heɪvjə(r)] (*Am* **behavior**) *n* conduite *f*, comportement *m*; to be on one's best b. se tenir particulièrement bien

behead [bɪ'hed] *vt* décapiter

behind [bɪ'haɪnd] 1 *prep* derrière; (*in terms of progress*) en retard sur; what's b. all this? qu'est-ce que ça cache? 2 *adv* derrière; (*late*) en retard; to be b. with the rent être en retard pour payer le loyer; to be b. with one's work avoir du travail en retard 3 *n Fam* (*buttocks*) derrière m ▪ **behindhand** adv en retard (**with** or **in** dans)

beige [beɪʒ] adj & n beige (m)

Beijing [beɪˈdʒɪŋ] n Beijing m ou f

being [ˈbiːɪŋ] n (person, soul) être m; **to come into b.** naître

belated [bɪˈleɪtɪd] adj tardif, -ive

belch [beltʃ] 1 n renvoi m 2 vi (of person) roter 3 vt **to b. (out)** (smoke) vomir

beleaguered [bɪˈliːɡəd] adj (besieged) assiégé

belfry [ˈbelfrɪ] (pl **belfries**) n beffroi m, clocher m

Belgium [ˈbeldʒəm] n la Belgique ▪ **Belgian** [-dʒən] 1 adj belge 2 n Belge mf

belie [bɪˈlaɪ] vt (feelings, background) ne pas refléter

belief [bɪˈliːf] n (believing, thing believed) croyance f (**in sb** en qn; **in sth** à ou en qch); (trust) confiance f, foi f (**in** en); (religious faith) foi; **to the best of my b.** pour autant que je sache

believe [bɪˈliːv] 1 vt croire; **I don't b. it** c'est pas possible; **I b. I'm right** je crois avoir raison, je crois que j'ai raison 2 vi croire (**in sth** à qch; **in God/sb** en Dieu/qn); **I b. so/not** je crois que oui/que non; **to b. in doing sth** croire qu'il faut faire qch; **he doesn't b. in smoking** il désapprouve que l'on fume ▪ **believable** adj crédible ▪ **believer** n (religious) croyant, -ante mf; **to be a b. in sth** croire à qch

belittle [bɪˈlɪtəl] vt dénigrer

bell [bel] n (large) (of church) cloche f; (small) clochette f; (in phone, mechanism, alarm) sonnerie f; (on door, bicycle) sonnette f; (on tambourine, dog) grelot m; **b. tower** clocher m ▪ **bellboy, bellhop** n Am groom m

belle [bel] n (woman) beauté f; **the b. of the ball** la reine du bal

belligerent [bɪˈlɪdʒərənt] adj & n belligérant, -ante (mf)

bellow [ˈbeləʊ] vi beugler, mugir

bellows [ˈbeləʊz] npl (**pair of**) **b.** soufflet m

belly [ˈbelɪ] (pl **-ies**) n ventre m; Fam **b. button** nombril m; **b. dancing** danse f du ventre ▪ **bellyache** Fam 1 n mal au ventre 2 vi (complain) rouspéter (**about sb** après qn; **about sth** au sujet de qch) ▪ **bellyful** n Fam **to have had a b.** en avoir plein le dos

belong [bɪˈlɒŋ] vi appartenir (**to** à); **to b. to a club** être membre d'un club; **that book belongs to me** ce livre m'appartient ou est à moi; **the cup belongs here** cette tasse se range ici; **he doesn't b.** il n'est pas à sa place ▪ **belongings** npl affaires fpl

beloved [bɪˈlʌvɪd] adj & n Literary bien-aimé, -ée (mf)

below [bɪˈləʊ] 1 prep (lower than) au-dessous de; (under) sous; (with numbers) moins de; Fig (unworthy of) indigne de 2 adv en dessous; (in

text) ci-dessous; **on the floor b.** à l'étage du dessous; **it's 10 degrees b.** il fait moins 10

belt [belt] 1 n ceinture f; (in machine) courroie f; (area) zone f, région f 2 vi **to b. up** (fasten seat belt) attacher sa ceinture; Br Fam **b. along** (rush) filer à toute allure; Br Fam **b. up!** (shut up) boucle-la! 3 vt Fam (hit) (ball) cogner dans; (person) flanquer un gnon à

bemoan [bɪˈməʊn] vt déplorer

bemused [bɪˈmjuːzd] adj perplexe

bench [bentʃ] n (seat) banc m; (work table) établi m; Law **the B.** (magistrates) la magistrature (assise); (court) le tribunal; Sport **to be on the b.** être remplaçant(e)

bend [bend] 1 n courbe f; (in river, pipe) coude m; (in road) virage m; (of arm, knee) pli m; Br **double b.** (on road) virage m en S, double virage m; Fam **round the b.** (mad) cinglé 2 (pt & pp **bent**) vt courber; (leg, arm) plier; **to b. one's head** baisser la tête; **to b. the rules** faire une entorse au règlement 3 vi (of branch) plier; (of road) tourner; (of river) faire un coude; **to b. (down)** (stoop) se courber; **to b. (over** or **forward)** se pencher; Fig **to b. over backwards to do sth** se mettre en quatre pour faire qch; **to b. to sb's will/etc** se soumettre à la volonté de qn/etc ▪ **bendy** (**-ier, -iest**) Br Fam (road) plein de virages; (flexible) souple

beneath [bɪˈniːθ] 1 prep sous; (unworthy of) indigne de 2 adv (au-)dessous

benediction [benɪˈdɪkʃən] n bénédiction f

benefactor [ˈbenɪfæktə(r)] n bienfaiteur m ▪ **benefactress** n bienfaitrice f

beneficial [benɪˈfɪʃəl] adj bénéfique

beneficiary [benɪˈfɪʃərɪ] (pl **-ies**) n bénéficiaire mf

benefit [ˈbenɪfɪt] 1 n (advantage) avantage m; (money) allocation f; **benefits** (of science, education) bienfaits mpl; **to sb's b.** dans l'intérêt de qn; **for your (own) b.** pour vous, pour votre bien; **to be of b.** faire du bien (**to sb** à qn); **to give sb the b. of the doubt** accorder à qn le bénéfice du doute; **b. concert** concert m de bienfaisance 2 vt faire du bien (**to** à); (be useful to) profiter à 3 vi **you'll b. from the rest** le repos vous fera du bien; **to b. from doing sth** gagner à faire qch

Benelux [ˈbenɪlʌks] n Benelux m

benevolent [bɪˈnevələnt] adj bienveillant ▪ **benevolence** n bienveillance f

benign [bɪˈnaɪn] adj (kind) bienveillant; (climate) doux (f douce); **b. tumour** tumeur f bénigne

bent [bent] 1 adj (nail, mind) tordu; Fam (dishonest) pourri; **b. on doing sth** résolu à faire qch 2 n (talent) aptitude f (**for** pour); (inclination, liking) penchant m, goût m (**for** pour); **to have a musical b.** avoir des dispositions pour la musique 3 pt & pp of **bend**

bequeath [bɪˈkwiːð] *vt Formal* léguer (**to** à) ▪ **bequest** [bɪˈkwest] *n Formal* legs *m*

bereaved [bɪˈriːvd] 1 *adj* endeuillé 2 *npl* **the b.** la famille du défunt/de la défunte ▪ **bereavement** *n* deuil *m*

bereft [bɪˈreft] *adj* **b. of** dénué de

beret [*Br* ˈbereɪ, *Am* bəˈreɪ] *n* béret *m*

berk [bɜːk] *n Br Fam* andouille *f*

Berlin [bɜːˈlɪn] *n* Berlin *m ou f*; **the B. Wall** le mur de Berlin

Bermuda [bəˈmjuːdə] *n* les Bermudes *fpl*

berry [ˈberɪ] (*pl* **-ies**) *n* baie *f*

berserk [bəˈzɜːk] *adj* **to go b.** devenir fou furieux (*f* folle furieuse)

berth [bɜːθ] 1 *n* (**a**) (*in ship, train*) couchette *f* (**b**) (*anchorage*) poste *m* à quai; *Fig* **to give sb a wide b.** éviter qn comme la peste 2 *vi* (*of ship*) aborder à quai

beseech [bɪˈsiːtʃ] (*pt & pp* **besought** *or* **beseeched**) *vt Literary* implorer (**to do** de faire)

beset [bɪˈset] (*pt & pp* **beset**, *pres p* **besetting**) *vt* assaillir; **b. with obstacles** semé d'obstacles; **b. with difficulties** en proie à toutes sortes de difficultés

beside [bɪˈsaɪd] *prep* à côté de; **that's b. the point** ça n'a rien à voir; **b. oneself** (*angry*) hors de soi; **to be b. oneself with joy/anger** être fou (*f* folle) de joie/de colère

besides [bɪˈsaɪdz] 1 *prep* (*in addition to*) en plus de; (*except*) excepté; **there are ten of us b. Paul** nous sommes dix sans compter Paul; **what else can you do b. singing?** que savez-vous faire à part chanter? 2 *adv* (*in addition*) en plus; (*moreover*) d'ailleurs; **there are more b.** il y en a d'autres encore

besiege [bɪˈsiːdʒ] *vt* (*of soldiers, crowd*) assiéger; *Fig* assaillir (**with** de)

besotted [bɪˈsɒtɪd] *adj* (*drunk*) abruti; **b. with** (*infatuated*) entiché de

bespatter [bɪˈspætə(r)] *vt* éclabousser (**with** de)

bespectacled [bɪˈspektəkəld] *adj* à lunettes

bespoke [bɪˈspəʊk] *adj* (*tailor*) à façon

best [best] 1 *adj* meilleur; **the b. page in the book** la meilleure page du livre; **my b. dress** ma plus belle robe; **the b. part of** (*most*) la plus grande partie de; **the b. thing is to accept** le mieux c'est d'accepter; **'b. before…'** (*on product*) 'à consommer avant…'; **b. man** (*at wedding*) témoin *m*

2 *n* **the b.** (**one**) le meilleur, la meilleure; **it's for the b.** c'est pour le mieux; **at b.** au mieux; **to do one's b.** faire de son mieux; **to look one's b.**, **to be at one's b.** être à son avantage; **to the b. of my knowledge** autant que je sache; **to make the b. of sth** (*accept*) s'accommoder de qch; **to get the b. out of sth** tirer le meilleur parti de qch; **to get the b. of it** avoir le dessus; **in one's Sunday b.** endimanché; **all the b.!** (*when leaving*) prends bien soin de toi!; (*good luck*) bonne chance!; (*in letter*) amicalement

3 *adv* (**the**) **b.** (*play, sing*) le mieux; **to like sb/ sth** (**the**) **b.** aimer qn/qch le plus; **the b. loved** le plus aimé; **I think it b. to wait** je juge prudent d'attendre ▪ **best-'seller** *n* (*book*) best-seller *m*

bestow [bɪˈstəʊ] *vt* accorder (**on** à)

bet [bet] 1 *n* pari *m* 2 (*pt & pp* **bet** *or* **betted**, *pres p* **betting**) *vt* parier (**on** sur; **that** que); *Fam* **you b.!** tu parles!

betray [bɪˈtreɪ] *vt* (*person, secret*) trahir; **to b. to sb** (*give away to*) livrer à qn ▪ **betrayal** *n* (*disloyalty*) trahison *f*; (*disclosure*) (*of secret*) révélation *f*

better [ˈbetə(r)] 1 *adj* meilleur (**than** que); **I need a b. car** j'ai besoin d'une meilleure voiture; **that's b.** c'est mieux; **she's (much) b.** (*in health*) elle va (beaucoup) mieux; **to get b.** (*recover*) se remettre; (*improve*) s'améliorer; **it's b. to go** il vaut mieux partir; **the b. part of** (*most*) la plus grande partie de

2 *adv* mieux (**than** que); **b. dressed/known/ etc** mieux habillé/connu/*etc*; **to look b.** (*of ill person*) avoir meilleure mine; **b. and b.** de mieux en mieux; **so much the b.**, **all the b.** tant mieux (**for** pour); **for b. and for worse** pour le meilleur et pour le pire; **I had b. go** il vaut mieux que je parte; **to be b. off** (*financially*) être plus à l'aise

3 *n* **to get the b. of sb** l'emporter sur qn; **to change for the b.** (*of person*) changer en bien; (*of situation*) s'améliorer; **one's betters** ses supérieurs *mpl*

4 *vt* (*improve*) améliorer; (*do better than*) dépasser; **to b. oneself** améliorer sa condition; **to b. sb's results**/*etc* (*do better than*) dépasser les résultats/*etc* de qn ▪ **betterment** *n* amélioration *f*

betting [ˈbetɪŋ] *n* paris *mpl*; *Br* **b. shop** *or* **office** ≃ PMU *m*

between [bɪˈtwiːn] 1 *prep* entre; **we did it b. us** nous l'avons fait à nous deux/trois/*etc*; **this is strictly b. you and me** que cela reste entre nous; **in b.** entre 2 *adv* **in b.** (*space*) au milieu; (*time*) dans l'intervalle

bevel [ˈbevəl] *n* (*edge*) biseau *m* ▪ **bevelled** (*Am* **beveled**) *adj* **b. edge** biseau *m*

beverage [ˈbevərɪdʒ] *n* boisson *f*

bevvy [ˈbevɪ] (*pl* **-ies**) *n Br Fam* **to have a b.** (*alcoholic drink*) boire un coup

bevy [ˈbevɪ] (*pl* **-ies**) *n* **a b. of** (*girls, reporters*) une nuée de

beware [bɪˈweə(r)] *vi* se méfier (**of** de); **b.!** attention!; **b. of falling** prenez garde de ne pas tomber; **'b. of the trains!'** 'attention aux trains!'; **'b. of the dog!'** 'attention, chien méchant!'; **'danger b.!'** 'attention! danger!'

bewilder [bɪˈwɪldə(r)] *vt* dérouter, laisser

perplexe ▪ **bewildering** adj déroutant ▪ **bewilderment** n perplexité f

bewitch [bɪˈwɪtʃ] vt ensorceler ▪ **bewitching** adj enchanteur, -eresse

beyond [bɪˈjɒnd] **1** prep (**a**) (further than) au-delà de; **b. a year** (longer than) plus d'un an; **b. reach/doubt** hors de portée/de doute; **b. belief** incroyable; **b. my/our/etc means** au-dessus de mes/nos/etc moyens; **due to circumstances b. our control** en raison de circonstances indépendantes de notre volonté; **it's b. me** ça me dépasse (**b**) (except) sauf **2** adv (further) au-delà

bias [ˈbaɪəs] **1** n (**a**) (inclination) penchant m (towards pour); (prejudice) préjugé m, parti pris m (**towards/against** en faveur de/contre) (**b**) **cut on the b.** (fabric) coupé dans le biais **2** (pt & pp -ss- or -s-) vt influencer (**towards/against** en faveur de/contre) ▪ **bias(s)ed** adj partial; **to be b. against** avoir des préjugés contre

bib [bɪb] n (for baby) bavoir m

bible [ˈbaɪbəl] n bible f; **the B.** la Bible ▪ **biblical** [ˈbɪblɪkəl] adj biblique

bibliography [bɪblɪˈɒɡrəfɪ] (pl -ies) n bibliographie f

bicarbonate [baɪˈkɑːbənət] n **b. of soda** bicarbonate m de soude

bicentenary [baɪsenˈtiːnərɪ] (Am **bicentennial** [baɪsenˈtenɪəl]) n bicentenaire m

biceps [ˈbaɪseps] n inv (muscle) biceps m

bicker [ˈbɪkə(r)] vi se chamailler ▪ **bickering** n chamailleries fpl

bicycle [ˈbaɪsɪkəl] n bicyclette f; **by b.** à bicyclette

bid¹ [bɪd] **1** n (**a**) (offer) offre f; (at auction) enchère f (**for** pour) (**b**) (attempt) tentative f; **a b. for attention/love** une tentative pour attirer l'attention/se faire aimer; **to make a b. for power** (legally) viser le pouvoir; (illegally) tenter une tentative de coup d'État **2** (pt & pp **bid**, pres p **bidding**) vt (sum of money) offrir; (at auction) faire une enchère de **3** vi faire une offre (**for** pour); (at auction) faire une enchère (**for** sur) ▪ **bidder** n (at auction) enchérisseur, -euse mf; **to the highest b.** au plus offrant ▪ **bidding** n (at auction) enchères fpl

bid² [bɪd] (pt **bade** [bæd], pp **bidden** [ˈbɪdən] or **bid**, pres p **bidding**) vt Literary (command) commander (**sb to do** à qn de faire); (say, wish) dire, souhaiter; **to b. sb good day** souhaiter le bonjour à qn ▪ **bidding** n **at sb's b.** sur les ordres de qn

bide [baɪd] vt **to b. one's time** attendre le bon moment

bier [bɪə(r)] n (for coffin) brancards mpl

bifocals [baɪˈfəʊkəlz] npl verres mpl à double foyer

big [bɪɡ] **1** (**bigger**, **biggest**) adj (tall, large) grand; (fat) gros (f grosse); (drop, increase) fort; **to get big(ger)** (taller) grandir; (fatter) grossir; **my b. brother** mon grand frère; Fam **b. mouth** grande gueule f; **b. toe** gros orteil m; Fam **the b. time** le succès **2** adv Fam **to do things b.** faire les choses en grand; **to think b.** voir grand; **to look b.** faire l'important; **to talk b.** fanfaronner ▪ **bighead** n Fam crâneur, -euse mf ▪ **big'headed** adj Fam crâneur, -euse ▪ **big-'hearted** adj généreux, -euse ▪ **bigshot**, **bigwig** n Fam gros bonnet m ▪ **big-time** adj Fam (criminal) de première

bigamy [ˈbɪɡəmɪ] n bigamie f ▪ **bigamist** n bigame mf ▪ **bigamous** adj bigame

bigot [ˈbɪɡət] n sectaire mf; (religious) bigot, -ote mf ▪ **bigoted** adj sectaire; (religious) bigot ▪ **bigotry** n sectarisme m; (religious) bigoterie f

> Note that the French word **bigot** is a false friend. It is only used to describe an excessively religious person and has no overtones of sectarianism.

bike [baɪk] n Fam vélo m; (motorbike) moto f

bikini [bɪˈkiːnɪ] n Bikini® m; **b. briefs** mini-slip m; **b. top/bottoms** haut m/bas m de maillot

bilberry [ˈbɪlbərɪ] (pl -ies) n myrtille f

bile [baɪl] n bile f

bilingual [baɪˈlɪŋɡwəl] adj bilingue

bill¹ [bɪl] **1** n (**a**) (invoice) facture f; (in restaurant) addition f; (in hotel) note f (**b**) Am (banknote) billet m (**c**) (bank draft) effet m; **b. of sale** acte m de vente (**d**) (notice) affiche f (**e**) Pol projet m de loi; **B. of Rights** = les dix premiers amendements de la Constitution américaine (**f**) (list) **b. of fare** menu m **2** vt (**a**) **to b. sb** envoyer la facture à qn (**b**) (publicize) annoncer ▪ **billboard** n Am panneau m d'affichage ▪ **billfold** n Am portefeuille m

bill² [bɪl] n (of bird) bec m

billet [ˈbɪlɪt] Mil **1** n cantonnement m **2** vt cantonner

billiards [ˈbɪljədz] n billard m

billion [ˈbɪljən] n milliard m ▪ **billio'naire** n milliardaire mf

billow [ˈbɪləʊ] **1** n (of smoke) volute f **2** vi (of smoke) tourbillonner; (of sea) se soulever; (of sail) se gonfler; **billowing smoke** des volutes fpl de fumée

billy-goat [ˈbɪlɪɡəʊt] n bouc m

bimbo [ˈbɪmbəʊ] (pl -os) n Fam minette f

bimonthly [baɪˈmʌnθlɪ] adj (every two weeks) bimensuel, -uelle; (every two months) bimestriel, -ielle

bin [bɪn] **1** n boîte f; (for litter) poubelle f **2** (pt & pp -nn-) vt Fam mettre à la poubelle

binary [ˈbaɪnərɪ] adj binaire

bind [baɪnd] **1** (pt & pp **bound**) vt (fasten) attacher; (book) relier; (fabric, hem) border; (unite) lier; **to b. sb hand and foot** ligoter qn;

to b. sb to do sth obliger qn à faire qch; **to be bound by sth** être lié par qch **2** *n Fam (bore)* plaie *f* ▪ **binding 1** *n (of book)* reliure *f* **2** *adj (contract)* qui lie; **to be b. on sb** *(legally)* lier qn

binder ['baɪndə(r)] *n (for papers)* classeur *m*

binge [bɪndʒ] *n Fam* **to go on a b.** *(drinking)* faire la bringue; *(eating)* se gaver ≃

bingo ['bɪŋɡəʊ] *n* ≃ loto *m*

binoculars [bɪ'nɒkjʊləz] *npl* jumelles *fpl*

biochemistry [baɪəʊ'kemɪstrɪ] *n* biochimie *f* ▪ **biochemical** *adj* biochimique

biodegradable [baɪəʊdɪ'ɡreɪdəbəl] *adj* biodégradable

biography [baɪ'ɒɡrəfɪ] *(pl -ies) n* biographie *f* ▪ **biographer** *n* biographe *mf* ▪ **bio'graphical** [baɪə'ɡræfɪkəl] *adj* biographique

biology [baɪ'ɒlədʒɪ] *n* biologie *f* ▪ **biological** [baɪə'lɒdʒɪkəl] *adj* biologique; **b. warfare** guerre *f* bactériologique ▪ **biologist** *n* biologiste *mf*

biped ['baɪped] *n* bipède *m*

birch [bɜːtʃ] **1** *n* **(silver) b.** bouleau *m*; **to give sb the b.** fouetter qn **2** *vt* fouetter

bird [bɜːd] *n* **(a)** *(animal)* oiseau *m*; *(fowl)* volaille *f*; **b. of prey** oiseau de proie; **b. table** mangeoire *f* pour oiseaux; **b.'s-eye view** perspective *f* à vol d'oiseau; *Fig* vue f d'ensemble **(b)** *Br Fam (girl)* nana *f* ▪ **birdseed** *n* graines *fpl* pour oiseaux

Biro® ['baɪrəʊ] *(pl -os) n Br* stylo *m* à bille

birth [bɜːθ] *n* naissance *f*; **to give b. to** donner naissance à; **from b.** *(blind, deaf)* de naissance; **b. certificate** acte *m* de naissance; **b. control** limitation *f* des naissances; **b. rate** (taux *m* de) natalité *f* ▪ **birthday** *n* anniversaire *m*; **happy b.!** joyeux anniversaire!; **b. party** fête *f* d'anniversaire; *Fig* **in one's b. suit** *(man)* en costume d'Adam; *(woman)* en costume d'Ève ▪ **birthmark** *n* tache *f* de naissance ▪ **birthplace** *n* lieu *m* de naissance; *(house)* maison *f* natale

biscuit ['bɪskɪt] *n Br* biscuit *m*, petit gâteau *m*; *Am* petit pain *m* au lait

bishop ['bɪʃəp] *n* évêque *m*; *(in chess)* fou *m*

bison ['baɪsən] *n inv* bison *m*

bit¹ [bɪt] *n* **(a)** *(of string, time)* bout *m*; **a b.** *(a little)* un peu; **a tiny b.** un tout petit peu; **quite a b.** *(very)* très; *(a lot)* beaucoup; **not a b.** pas du tout; **a b. of luck** une chance; **b. by b.** petit à petit; **in bits (and pieces)** en morceaux; **to come to bits** se démonter; **to do one's b.** participer; *Fam* **she's a b. of all right** elle est pas mal **(b)** *(coin)* pièce *f* **(c)** *(of horse)* mors *m* **(d)** *(of drill)* mèche *f* **(e)** *Comptr* bit *m*

bit² [bɪt] *pt of* **bite**

bitch [bɪtʃ] **1** *n* chienne *f*; *very Fam Pej (woman)* garce *f* **2** *vi Fam (complain)* râler *(about* après*)* ▪ **bitchy** *(-ier, -iest) adj Fam (remark, behaviour)* vache

bite [baɪt] **1** *n* **(a)** *(wound)* morsure *f*; *(from insect)* piqûre *f*; *Fishing* touche *f* **(b)** *(mouthful)* bouchée *f*; **to have a b. to eat** manger un morceau **(c)** *Fig (of style, text)* mordant *m* **2** *(pt bit, pp bitten* ['bɪtən]*) vt* mordre; *(of insect)* piquer; **to b. one's nails** se ronger les ongles; **to b. sth off** arracher qch d'un coup de dents; **to b. off a piece of apple** mordre dans une pomme **3** *vi (of person, dog)* mordre; *(of insect)* piquer; **to b. into sth** mordre dans qch ▪ **biting** *adj (cold, irony)* mordant; *(wind)* cinglant

bitter ['bɪtə(r)] **1** *n Br (beer)* = bière anglaise brune **2** *adj (person, taste, irony)* amer, -ère; *(cold, wind)* glacial; *(criticism)* acerbe; *(shock, fate)* cruel *(f* cruelle*); (conflict)* violent; **to feel b. (about sth)** être plein d'amertume (à cause de qch); **to the b. end** jusqu'au bout ▪ **bitterly** *adv* **to cry/regret b.** pleurer/regretter amèrement; **b. disappointed** cruellement déçu; **it's b. cold** il fait un froid de canard ▪ **bitterness** *n* amertume *f*; *(of the cold)* âpreté *f*; *(of conflict)* violence *f* ▪ **bitter'sweet** *adj* doux-amer *(f* douce-amère*); Am* **b. chocolate** chocolat *m* à croquer

bivouac ['bɪvʊæk] *Mil* **1** *n* bivouac *m* **2** *(pt & pp -ck-) vi* bivouaquer

bizarre [bɪ'zɑː(r)] *adj* bizarre

blab [blæb] *(pt & pp -bb-) vi* **(a)** *(chatter)* jaser **(b)** *(betray secret)* vendre la mèche

black [blæk] **1** *(-er, -est) adj* noir; **b. eye** œil *m* au beurre noir; **to give sb a b. eye** pocher l'œil à qn; **b. and blue** *(bruised)* couvert de bleus; *Av* **b. box** boîte *f* noire; *Br* **b. ice** verglas *m*; *Br* **b. pudding** boudin *m* noir; *Fig* **b. sheep** brebis *f* galeuse

2 *n (colour)* noir *m*; *(person)* Noir, -e *mf*; **it says here in b. and white** c'est écrit noir sur blanc

3 *vt* noircir; *(refuse to deal with)* boycotter

4 *vi* **to b. out** *(faint)* s'évanouir ▪ **blackberry** *(pl -ies) n* mûre *f* ▪ **blackbird** *n* merle *m* (noir) ▪ **blackboard** *n* tableau *m* (noir); **on the b.** au tableau ▪ **black'currant** *n* cassis *m* ▪ **blacken** *vti* noircir ▪ **blacklist 1** *n* liste *f* noire **2** *vt* mettre sur la liste noire ▪ **blackmail** *n* chantage *m* **2** *vt* faire chanter; **to b. sb into doing** faire chanter qn pour qu'il/elle fasse ▪ **blackmailer** *n* maître chanteur *m* ▪ **blackness** *n* noirceur *f*; *(of night)* ténèbres *fpl* ▪ **blackout** *n* panne *f* d'électricité; *(during war)* black-out *m inv*; *(fainting fit)* évanouissement *m*; *(news)* **b.** black-out ▪ **blacksmith** *n* forgeron *m*; *(working with horses)* maréchal-ferrant *m*

bladder ['blædə(r)] *n* vessie *f*

blade [bleɪd] *n* lame *f*; *(of windscreen wiper)* caoutchouc *m*; **b. of grass** brin *m* d'herbe

blame [bleɪm] **1** *n* responsabilité *f*; *(criticism)* blâme *m*; **to lay the b. (for sth) on sb** faire porter à qn la responsabilité (de qch); **to take**

the b. for sth endosser la responsabilité de qch 2 *vt* rendre responsable, faire porter la responsabilité à (**for** de); **to b. sb for doing sth** reprocher à qn d'avoir fait qch; **you're to b.** c'est de ta faute; **I b.** you for doing that je considère que c'est toi qui es responsable de cela ▪ **blameless** *adj* irréprochable

blanch [blɑːntʃ] 1 *vt* (*vegetables*) blanchir 2 *vi* (*turn pale*) blêmir

blancmange [bləˈmɒnʒ] *n Br* blanc-manger *m*

bland [blænd] (**-er, -est**) *adj* (*person*) terne; (*food*) insipide; (*remark, joke*) quelconque

blank [blæŋk] 1 *adj* (*paper, page*) blanc (*f* blanche), vierge; (*cheque*) en blanc; (*look, mind*) vide; (*puzzled*) ébahi; (*refusal*) absolu; *Comptr* (*disk, screen*) vide; (*unformatted*) vierge; **to leave b.** (*on form*) laisser en blanc; **b. tape** cassette *f* vierge 2 *n* (*space*) blanc *m*; (*cartridge*) cartouche *f* à blanc; **to fire blanks** tirer à blanc; **my mind's a b.** j'ai un trou ▪ **blankly** *adv* **to look b. at** (*without expression*) regarder, le visage inexpressif; (*without understanding*) regarder sans comprendre

blanket [ˈblæŋkɪt] 1 *n* (*on bed*) couverture *f*; (*of snow, leaves*) couche *f* 2 *vt Fig* (*cover*) recouvrir 3 *adj* (*term, remark*) général

blare [bleə(r)] 1 *n* (*noise*) beuglements *mpl*; (*of trumpet*) sonnerie *f* 2 *vi* **to b. (out)** (*of radio*) beugler; (*of music, car horn*) retentir

blarney [ˈblɑːnɪ] *n Fam* boniments *mpl*

blasé [ˈblɑːzeɪ] *adj* blasé

blaspheme [blæsˈfiːm] *vti* blasphémer ▪ **blasphemous** [ˈblæsfəməs] *adj* (*text*) blasphématoire; (*person*) blasphémateur, -trice ▪ **blasphemy** [ˈblæsfəmɪ] *n* blasphème *m*

blast [blɑːst] 1 *n* explosion *f*; (*air from explosion*) souffle *m*; (*of wind*) rafale *f*; (*of trumpet*) sonnerie *f*; (**at**) **full b.** (*loud*) à fond; (*fast*) à toute vitesse; **b. furnace** haut-fourneau *m* 2 *vt* (*hole, tunnel*) creuser (en dynamitant); *Fam* (*criticize*) démolir 3 *exclam Br Fam* zut! ▪ **blasted** *adj Br Fam* fichu ▪ **blast-off** *n* (*of spacecraft*) mise *f* à feu

blatant [ˈbleɪtənt] *adj* (*obvious*) flagrant; (*shameless*) éhonté ▪ **blatantly** *adv* de façon flagrante; **b. obvious** tout à fait évident

blaze [bleɪz] 1 *n* (*fire*) feu *m*; (*large*) incendie *m*; *Fig* (*splendour*) éclat *m*; **a b. of colour** une explosion de couleurs; **b. of light** torrent *m* de lumière 2 *vi* (*of fire, sun*) flamboyer; (*of light, eyes*) être éclatant 3 *vt Fig* **to b. a trail** ouvrir la voie ▪ **blazing** *adj* (*burning*) en feu; (*sun*) brûlant; *Fig* (*argument*) violent

blazer [ˈbleɪzə(r)] *n* blazer *m*

bleach [bliːtʃ] 1 *n* (*household*) (eau *f* de) Javel *f*; (*for hair*) décolorant *m* 2 *vt* (*clothes*) passer à l'eau de Javel; (*hair*) décolorer

bleachers [ˈbliːtʃərz] *npl Am* (*at stadium*) gradins *mpl*

bleak [bliːk] (**-er, -est**) *adj* (*appearance, countryside, weather*) morne; (*outlook*) lugubre; (*prospect*) peu encourageant

bleary [ˈblɪərɪ] *adj* (*eyes*) rouge

bleat [bliːt] *vi* bêler

bleed [bliːd] (*pt & pp* bled [bled]) 1 *vi* saigner; **to b. to death** saigner à mort; **her nose is bleeding** elle saigne du nez 2 *vt* (*radiator*) purger ▪ **bleeding** 1 *adj* (**a**) (*wound*) qui saigne (**b**) *Br very Fam* **a b. idiot** une espèce de con 2 *n* saignement; **has the b. stopped?** est-ce que ça saigne encore?

bleep [bliːp] 1 *n* bip *m* 2 *vt* appeler au bip 3 *vi* faire bip ▪ **bleeper** *n* (*pager*) bip *m*

blemish [ˈblemɪʃ] 1 *n* (*fault*) défaut *m*; (*mark*) marque *f*; *Fig* **it left a b. on his reputation** ça a entaché sa réputation 2 *vt Fig* (*reputation*) entacher

> Note that the French verb **blêmir** is a false friend and is never a translation for the English verb **to blemish**. It means **to go pale**.

blend [blend] 1 *n* mélange *m* 2 *vt* mélanger (**with** à *ou* avec) 3 *vi* se mélanger; (*of styles, colours*) se marier (**with** avec); **everything blends (in)** (*decor of room*) tout est assorti ▪ **blender** *n* mixer *m*

bless [bles] *vt* bénir; **to be blessed with sth** être doté de qch; **to be blessed with good health** avoir le bonheur d'être en bonne santé; **God b. you!** que Dieu te bénisse!; **b. you!** (*when sneezing*) à vos souhaits! ▪ **blessed** [blesɪd] *adj* (**a**) (*holy*) béni (**b**) *Fam* (*blasted*) fichu; **the whole b. day** toute la sainte journée; **I can't see a b. thing** je n'y vois absolument rien ▪ **blessing** *n Rel* bénédiction *f*; (*benefit*) bienfait *m*; **it was a b. in disguise** finalement, ça a été une bonne chose

blew [bluː] *pt of* **blow²**

blight [blaɪt] *n* (*on plants*) rouille *f*; *Fig* (*scourge*) fléau *m*; **urban b.** (*area*) quartier *m* délabré; (*condition*) délabrement *m* urbain

blimey [ˈblaɪmɪ] *exclam Br Fam* zut!

blind¹ [blaɪnd] 1 *adj* aveugle; **b. person** aveugle *mf*; **b. in one eye** borgne; **as b. as a bat** myope comme une taupe; *Fig* **b. with fury** aveuglé par la colère; *Fig* **to be b. to sth** ne pas voir qch; *Fig* **to turn a b. eye to sth** fermer les yeux sur qch; **b. alley** impasse *f*; **b. date** = rencontre arrangée avec quelqu'un qu'on ne connaît pas 2 *npl* **the b.** les aveugles *mpl* 3 *adv* **b. drunk** ivre mort 4 *vt* (*dazzle, make blind*) aveugler ▪ **blindly** *adv Fig* aveuglément ▪ **blindness** *n* cécité *f*

blind² [blaɪnd] *n Br* (*on window*) store *m*

blinders [ˈblaɪndərz] *npl Am* œillères *fpl*

blindfold [ˈblaɪndfəʊld] 1 *n* bandeau *m* 2 *vt* bander les yeux à 3 *adv* les yeux bandés

blink [blɪŋk] 1 *n* clignement *m*; *Br Fam* **on the b.**

(machine) détraqué **2** *vt* **to b. one's eyes** cligner des yeux **3** *vi (of person)* cligner des yeux; *(of eyes)* cligner; *(of light)* clignoter ■ **blinking** *adj Br Fam (for emphasis)* sacré; **you b. idiot!** espèce d'idiot!

blinkers ['blɪŋkəz] *npl Br (of horse)* œillères *fpl*; *Fam (indicators of vehicle)* clignotants *mpl*

bliss [blɪs] *n* félicité *f* ■ **blissful** *adj (wonderful)* merveilleux, -euse; *(very happy) (person)* aux anges ■ **blissfully** *adv (happy)* merveilleusement; **to be b. unaware that…** ne pas se douter le moins du monde que…

blister ['blɪstə(r)] **1** *n (on skin)* ampoule *f* **2** *vi* se couvrir d'ampoules

blithe [blaɪð] *adj Literary* joyeux, -euse

blitz [blɪts] **1** *n (air attack)* raid *m* éclair; *(bombing)* bombardement *m* aérien; *Fam (onslaught)* offensive *f* **2** *vt* bombarder

blizzard ['blɪzəd] *n* tempête *f* de neige

bloated ['bləʊtɪd] *adj (swollen)* gonflé

blob [blɒb] *n (of water)* grosse goutte *f*; *(of ink, colour)* tache *f*

bloc [blɒk] *n (political group)* bloc *m*

block [blɒk] **1** *n (of stone)* bloc *m*; *(of buildings)* pâté *m* de maisons; *(in pipe)* obstruction *f*; **b. of flats** immeuble *m*; *Am* **a b. away** une rue plus loin; **school b.** groupe *m* scolaire; **b. booking** réservation *f* de groupe; **b. capitals** *or* **letters** majuscules *fpl* **2** *vt (obstruct)* bloquer; *(pipe)* boucher; *(view)* cacher; **to b. off** *(road)* barrer; *(light)* intercepter; **to b. up** *(pipe, hole)* boucher ■ **blockage** *n* obstruction *f*

blockade [blɒ'keɪd] **1** *n* blocus *m* **2** *vt* bloquer

blockbuster ['blɒkbʌstə(r)] *n (film)* film *m* à grand spectacle

blog [blɒg] *(abbr* **weblog***)* *n Comptr* blog *m*

bloke [bləʊk] *n Br Fam* type *m*

blond [blɒnd] *adj & n* blond *(m)* ■ **blonde** *adj & n* blonde *(f)*

blood [blʌd] *n* sang *m*; **b. bank** banque *f* du sang; **b. bath** bain *m* de sang; **b. donor** donneur, -euse *mf* de sang; **b. group** groupe *m* sanguin; **b. poisoning** empoisonnement *m* du sang; **b. pressure** tension *f* artérielle; **high b. pressure** hypertension *f*; **to have high b. pressure** avoir de la tension; *Am* **b. sausage** boudin *m* **b. test** prise *f* de sang; ■ **bloodcurdling** *adj* à vous tourner le sang ■ **bloodhound** *n (dog, detective)* limier *m* ■ **bloodletting** *n Med* saignée *f* ■ **bloodshed** *n* effusion *f* de sang ■ **bloodshot** *adj (eye)* injecté de sang ■ **bloodstained** *adj* taché de sang ■ **bloodstream** *n* sang *m* ■ **bloodsucker** *n (insect, person)* sangsue *f* ■ **bloodthirsty** *adj* sanguinaire

bloody ['blʌdɪ] **1** *(*-ier, -iest*) adj (a)* ensanglanté *(b) Br very Fam* foutu; **a b. liar** un sale menteur; **b. weather!** sale temps!; **you b. fool!** conard! **2** *adv Br Fam (very)* vachement;

it's b. hot! il fait une putain de chaleur! ■ **bloody-'minded** *adj* pas commode

bloom [blu:m] **1** *n* fleur *f*; **in b.** *(tree)* en fleur(s); *(flower)* éclos **2** *vi (of tree, flower)* fleurir; *(of person)* s'épanouir ■ **blooming** *adj* **(a)** *(in bloom)* en fleur(s); *(person)* resplendissant; *(thriving)* florissant **(b)** *Br Fam (for emphasis)* sacré; **you b. idiot!** espèce d'idiot!

bloomer ['blu:mə(r)] *n* **(a)** *Br Fam (mistake)* gaffe *f* **(b)** *(bread)* ≃ bâtard *m* court

blossom ['blɒsəm] **1** *n* fleurs *fpl* **2** *vi* fleurir; **to b. (out)** *(of person)* s'épanouir

blot [blɒt] **1** *n* tache *f* **2** *(pt & pp* **-tt-***) vt (stain)* tacher; *(dry)* sécher; **to b. sth out** *(obliterate)* effacer qch ■ **blotting paper** *n* (papier *m*) buvard *m*

blotch [blɒtʃ] *n* tache *f* ■ **blotchy** *(*-ier, -iest*) adj* couvert de taches; *(face, skin)* marbré

blouse [blaʊz] *n* chemisier *m*

> Note that the French word **blouse** is a false friend. Its most common meaning is **overall**.

blow[1] [bləʊ] *n (hit, setback)* coup *m*; **to come to blows** en venir aux mains

blow[2] [bləʊ] **1** *(pt* **blew***, pp* **blown***) vt (of wind)* pousser; *(of person) (smoke, glass)* souffler; *(bubbles)* faire; *(trumpet)* souffler dans; *(kiss)* envoyer *(to* à); *Br Fam (money)* claquer *(on sth* pour s'acheter); **to b. a fuse** faire sauter un plomb; **to b. one's nose** se moucher; **to b. a whistle** donner un coup de sifflet **2** *vi (of wind, person)* souffler; *(of fuse)* sauter; *(of papers) (in wind)* s'éparpiller ■ **blowout** *n* **(a)** *(tyre)* éclatement *m* **(b)** *Br Fam (meal)* gueuleton *m* ■ **blow-up** *n (of photo)* agrandissement *m*

▸ **blow away 1** *vt sep (of wind)* emporter **2** *vi (of hat)* s'envoler

▸ **blow down 1** *vt sep (chimney, fence)* faire tomber **2** *vi (fall)* tomber

▸ **blow off** *vt sep (hat)* emporter; *(arm)* arracher

▸ **blow out 1** *vt sep (candle)* souffler; *(cheeks)* gonfler **2** *vi (of light)* s'éteindre

▸ **blow over 1** *vti* = **blow down 2** *vi (of quarrel)* se tasser

▸ **blow up 1** *vt sep (building)* faire sauter; *(pump up)* gonfler; *(photo)* agrandir **2** *vi (explode)* exploser

blow-dry ['bləʊdraɪ] **1** *n* Brushing® *m* **2** *vt* **to b. sb's hair** faire un Brushing® à qn

blowlamp ['bləʊlæmp] *n* chalumeau *m*

blown [bləʊn] *pp of* **blow**

blowtorch ['bləʊtɔːtʃ] *n* chalumeau *m*

blubber ['blʌbə(r)] *n* graisse *f* (de baleine)

bludgeon ['blʌdʒən] **1** *n* gourdin *m* **2** *vt* matraquer

blue [blu:] **1** *(*-er, -est*) adj* bleu; *Fam* **to feel b.** avoir le cafard; *Fam* **b. movie** film *m* porno **2** *n* bleu *m*; *Fam* **the blues** *(depression)* le cafard; *(music)* le blues; **out of the b.** *(unexpectedly)* sans crier gare **• bluebell** n jacinthe f des bois **• blueberry** (pl -ies) n airelle f **• bluebottle** n mouche f de la viande **• blueprint** n Fig plan m

bluff [blʌf] **1** adj (person) direct **2** n bluff m **3** vti bluffer

blunder ['blʌndə(r)] **1** n (mistake) gaffe f **2** vi faire une gaffe; **to b. along** (move awkwardly) avancer maladroitement **• blundering 1** adj (clumsy) maladroit **2** n maladresse f

blunt [blʌnt] **1** (-er, -est) adj (edge) émoussé; (pencil) mal taillé; (question, statement) direct; (person) brusque **2** vt (blade) émousser; (pencil) épointer **• bluntly** adv (say) franchement **• bluntness** n (of manner, statement) rudesse f; (of person) franchise f

blur [blɜː(r)] **1** n tache f floue **2** (pt & pp -rr-) vt (outline) brouiller **• blurred** adj (image, outline) flou

blurb [blɜːb] n (on book cover) notice f publicitaire

blurt [blɜːt] vt **to b. (out)** (secret) laisser échapper; (excuse) bredouiller

blush [blʌʃ] **1** n rougeur f; **with a b.** en rougissant; **to spare sb's blushes** éviter un embarras à qn **2** vi rougir (**with** de)

bluster ['blʌstə(r)] vi (of person) tempêter; (of wind) faire rage **• blustery** adj (weather) de grand vent; (wind) violent

BO [biːˈəʊ] (abbr body odour) n Fam **to have BO** sentir mauvais

boar [bɔː(r)] n **(wild) b.** sanglier m

board¹ [bɔːd] **1** n (piece of wood) planche f; (for notices) panneau m; (for games) tableau m; (cardboard) carton m; **on b. (a ship/plane)** à bord (d'un navire/avion); **to go on b.** monter à bord; Fig **to take sth on b.** tenir compte de qch; **to go by the b.** (of plan) être abandonné **2** vt (ship, plane) monter à bord de; (bus, train) monter dans; **to b. up** (door) condamner **3** vi flight Z001 is now boarding vol Z001, embarquement immédiat **• boarding** n (of passengers) embarquement m; **b. card/pass** carte f d'embarquement **• boardwalk** n Am (on beach) promenade f

board² [bɔːd] n (committee) conseil m; **b. (of directors)** conseil m d'administration; **b. (of examiners)** jury m (d'examen); **across the b.** (pay increase) global; (apply) globalement; **b. room** salle f du conseil

board³ [bɔːd] **1** n (food) pension f; **b. and lodging**, Br full b. pension f complète; Br half b. demi-pension f **2** vi (lodge) être en pension (**with** chez); **boarding house** pension f de famille; **boarding school** pensionnat m **• boarder** n pensionnaire mf

boast [bəʊst] **1** n vantardise f **2** vt se glorifier de; **to b. that one can do sth** se vanter de pouvoir faire qch **3** vi se vanter (**about** or **of** de) **• boasting** n vantardise f

boastful ['bəʊstfəl] adj vantard

boat [bəʊt] n bateau m; (small) canot m; (liner) paquebot m; **by b.** en bateau; Fig **in the same b.** logé à la même enseigne; **b. race** course f d'aviron **• boating** n canotage m; **to go b.** faire du canotage; **b. trip** excursion f en bateau

boatswain ['bəʊsən] n Naut maître m d'équipage

bob [bɒb] (pt & pp -bb-) vi **to b. (up and down)** (on water) danser sur l'eau

bobbin ['bɒbɪn] n bobine f

bobby ['bɒbɪ] (pl -ies) n (a) Br Fam (policeman) agent m (b) **b. pin** pince f à cheveux

bode [bəʊd] vi **to b. well/ill (for)** être de bon/mauvais augure (pour)

bodice ['bɒdɪs] n corsage m

bodily ['bɒdɪlɪ] **1** adj (need) physique **2** adv (lift, seize) à bras-le-corps; (carry) dans ses bras

body ['bɒdɪ] (pl -ies) n corps m; (of car) carrosserie f; (quantity) masse f; (institution) organisme m; **dead b.** cadavre m; **the main b. of the audience** le gros de l'assistance; **b. building** culturisme m; **b. piercing** piercing m; **b. warmer** gilet m matelassé **• bodyguard** n garde m du corps **• bodywork** n carrosserie f

boffin ['bɒfɪn] n Br Fam Hum scientifique mf

bog [bɒg] **1** n (swamp) marécage m **2** vt **to get bogged down in** (mud, work) s'enliser (dans); (details) se perdre (dans) **• boggy** (-ier, -iest) adj marécageux, -euse

bogey ['bəʊgɪ] (pl -eys) n (a) (source of fear) spectre m (b) Br Fam (in nose) crotte f de nez **• bogeyman** n croque-mitaine m

boggle ['bɒgəl] vi Fam **the mind boggles** ça laisse rêveur

bogus ['bəʊgəs] adj faux (f fausse)

boil¹ [bɔɪl] n (pimple) furoncle m

boil² [bɔɪl] **1** n **to come to the b.** bouillir; **to bring sth to the b.** amener qch à ébullition **2** vt **to b. (up)** faire bouillir; **to b. the kettle** mettre de l'eau à chauffer **3** vi bouillir; **to b. away** (until dry) s'évaporer; (on and on) bouillir sans arrêt; Fig **to b. down to** (of situation, question) revenir à; **to b. over** (of milk) déborder; Fig (of situation) empirer **• boiled** adj bouilli; **b. egg** œuf m à la coque **• boiling 1** n ébullition f; **to be at b. point** (of liquid) bouillir **2** adj **b. (hot)** bouillant; **it's b. (hot)** (weather) il fait une chaleur infernale

boiler ['bɔɪlə(r)] n chaudière f; Br **b. suit** bleus mpl de chauffe

boisterous ['bɔɪstərəs] adj (noisy) bruyant; (child) turbulent; (meeting) houleux, -euse

bold [bəʊld] (-er, -est) adj hardi; Typ **in b. (type)** en (caractères) gras **• boldness** n hardiesse f

Bolivia [bəˈlɪvɪə] n Bolivie f **• Bolivian 1** adj bolivien, -ienne **2** n Bolivien, -ienne mf

bollard ['bɒləd, 'bɒlɑːd] n Br (for traffic) borne f

bolster ['bəʊlstə(r)] **1** n (pillow) traversin m **2** vt (confidence, pride) renforcer, consolider

bolt [bəʊlt] **1** n (**a**) (on door) verrou m; (for nut) boulon m (**b**) (dash) **to make a b. for the door** se précipiter vers la porte (**c**) **b. of lightning** éclair m **2** adv **b. upright** tout droit **3** vt (**a**) (door) verrouiller (**b**) (food) engloutir **4** vi (dash) se précipiter; (run away) détaler; (of horse) s'emballer

bomb [bɒm] **1** n bombe f; **b. scare** alerte f à la bombe; Fam **it costs a b.** ça coûte les yeux de la tête **2** vt (from the air) bombarder; (of terrorist) faire sauter une bombe dans ou à ▪**bomber** n (aircraft) bombardier m; (terrorist) poseur m de bombe ▪**bombing** n bombardement m; (terrorist) attentat m à la bombe ▪**bombshell** n **to come as a b.** faire l'effet d'une bombe ▪**bombsite** n zone f bombardée; Fig **to look like a b.** ressembler à un champ de bataille

bombard [bɒm'bɑːd] vt (with bombs, questions) bombarder (**with** de) ▪**bombardment** n bombardement m

bona fide [bəʊnə'faɪd] adj véritable

bonanza [bə'nænzə] n aubaine f

bond [bɒnd] **1** n (link) lien m; (agreement) engagement m; Fin obligation f **2** vt (of glue) coller (**to** à) **3** vi (form attachment) créer des liens affectifs (**with** avec)

bondage ['bɒndɪdʒ] n esclavage m

bone [bəʊn] **1** n os m; (of fish) arête f; **b. of contention** pomme f de discorde; **b. china** porcelaine f tendre **2** vt (meat) désosser; (fish) ôter les arêtes de **3** vi Am Fam **to b. up on** (subject) bûcher ▪**bone-dry** adj complètement sec (f sèche) ▪**bone-'idle** adj Br paresseux, -euse ▪**bony** (**-ier, -iest**) adj (thin) maigre; (fish) plein d'arêtes

bonfire ['bɒnfaɪə(r)] n (for celebration) feu m de joie; (for dead leaves) feu m (de jardin)

bonkers ['bɒŋkəz] adj Br Fam dingue

bonnet ['bɒnɪt] n (hat) bonnet m; Br (of vehicle) capot m

bonus ['bəʊnəs] (pl **-uses** [-əsɪz]) n prime f; **no claims b.** (of car driver) bonus m; **b. number** (in lottery) numéro m complémentaire

boo [buː] **1** exclam (to frighten) hou! **2** n boos huées fpl **3** (pt & pp booed) vti huer

boob [buːb] Fam **1** n (**a**) Br (mistake) gaffe f (**b**) **boobs** (breasts) nénés mpl **2** vi Br gaffer

booby-trap ['buːbɪtræp] **1** n engin m piégé **2** (pt & pp **-pp-**) vt piéger

book¹ [bʊk] n livre m; (record) registre m; (of tickets) carnet m; (for exercises and notes) cahier m; **books** (accounts) comptes mpl; **b. club** club m du livre ▪**bookbinding** n reliure f ▪**bookcase** n bibliothèque f ▪**bookend** n serre-livres m inv ▪**bookie** n Br Fam bookmaker m ▪**bookkeeping** n comptabilité f ▪**booklet** n brochure f ▪**book-lover** n bibliophile mf ▪**bookmaker** n bookmaker m ▪**bookmark 1** n marque-page m; Comptr signet m **2** vt Comptr (Web page) créer un signet sur ▪**bookseller** n libraire mf ▪**bookshelf** n étagère f ▪**bookshop** (Am **bookstore**) n librairie f ▪**bookstall** n kiosque m à journaux ▪**bookworm** n passionné, -ée mf de lecture

book² [bʊk] **1** vt **to b. (up)** (seat) réserver; Br **to b. sb** (for traffic offence) dresser une contravention à qn; **fully booked (up)** (hotel, concert) complet, -ète; (person) pris **2** vi **to b. (up)** réserver des places; **to b. in** (to hotel) signer le registre; **to b. into a hotel** prendre une chambre dans un hôtel ▪**bookable** adj (seat) qu'on peut réserver ▪**booking** n réservation f; **b. clerk** guichetier, -ière mf; **b. office** bureau m de location

bookish ['bʊkɪʃ] adj (word, theory) livresque; (person) studieux, -ieuse

boom [buːm] **1** n (noise) grondement m (**b**) (economic) boom m **2** vi (**a**) (of thunder, gun) gronder (**b**) (of business, trade) être florissant

boomerang ['buːməræŋ] n boomerang m

boor [bʊə(r)] n rustre m ▪**boorish** adj rustre

boost [buːst] **1** n **to give sb a b.** remonter le moral à qn **2** vt (increase) augmenter; (product) faire de la réclame pour; (economy) stimuler; **to b. sb's morale** remonter le moral à qn; **to b. sb (up)** (push upwards) soulever qn ▪**booster** n **b.** (injection) rappel m

boot¹ [buːt] **1** n (**a**) (shoe) botte f; (ankle) **b.** bottillon m; (knee) **b.** bottine f; Fam **to get the b.** être mis à la porte; **b. polish** cirage m (**b**) Br (of vehicle) coffre m (**c**) **to b.** (in addition) en plus **2** vt Fam (kick) donner un coup ou des coups de pied à; **to b. sb out** mettre qn à la porte ▪**bootee** n (of baby) chausson m ▪**bootlace** n lacet m

boot² [buːt] Comptr **1** vt amorcer **2** vi s'amorcer

booth [buːθ, buːð] n (for phone, in language lab) cabine f; (at fair) stand m; (for voting) isoloir m

booty ['buːtɪ] n (loot) butin m

booze [buːz] Fam **1** n alcool m **2** vi picoler ▪**boozer** n Fam (person) poivrot, -ote mf; Br (pub) pub m ▪**booze-up** n Br Fam beuverie f

border ['bɔːdə(r)] **1** n (of country) & Fig frontière f; (edge) bord m; (of garden) bordure f **2** adj (town) frontière inv; (incident) de frontière **3** vt (street) border; **to b. (on)** (country) avoir une frontière commune avec; **to b. (up)on** (resemble, verge on) être voisin de ▪**borderline** n limite f; **b. case** cas m limite

bore¹ [bɔː(r)] **1** vt (weary) ennuyer; **to be bored** s'ennuyer; **I'm bored with that job** ce travail m'ennuie **2** n (person) raseur, -euse mf; **it's a b.** c'est ennuyeux ou rasoir ▪**boring** adj ennuyeux, -euse

bore² [bɔː(r)] **1** n (of gun) calibre m **2** vt (hole) percer; (rock, well) forer, creuser **3** vi forer

bore³ [bɔː(r)] pt of **bear²**

boredom ['bɔːdəm] n ennui m

born [bɔːn] adj né; **to be b.** naître; **he was b. in Paris/in 1980** il est né à Paris/en 1980

borne [bɔːn] pp of **bear²**

borough ['bʌrə] n circonscription f électorale urbaine

borrow ['bɒrəʊ] vt emprunter (**from** à) **• borrowing** n emprunt m

Bosnia ['bɒznɪə] n la Bosnie

bosom ['bʊzəm] n (chest, breasts) poitrine f; (breast) sein m; Fig (heart, soul) sein; **b. friend** ami, -ie mf intime

boss [bɒs] 1 n patron, -onne mf 2 vt **to b. sb around** or **about** donner des ordres à qn **• bossy** (-ier, -iest) adj autoritaire

boss-eyed ['bɒsaɪd] adj **to be b.** loucher

bosun ['bəʊsən] n Naut maître m d'équipage

botany ['bɒtənɪ] n botanique f **• botanical** [bə'tænɪkəl] adj botanique **• botanist** n botaniste mf

botch [bɒtʃ] vt Fam **to b. (up)** (spoil) bâcler; (repair badly) rafistoler

both [bəʊθ] 1 adj les deux; **b. brothers** les deux frères 2 pron tous/toutes (les) deux; **b. of the boys** les deux garçons; **b. of us** tous les deux; **b. of them died** ils sont morts tous les deux 3 adv (at the same time) à la fois; **b. in England and in France** en Angleterre comme en France; **b. you and I know that…** vous et moi, nous savons que…

bother ['bɒðə(r)] 1 n (trouble) ennui m; (effort) peine f; (inconvenience) dérangement m; Br **(oh) b.!** zut alors! 2 vt (annoy, worry) ennuyer; (disturb) déranger; (pester) importuner; (hurt, itch) (of foot, eye) gêner; **to b. doing** or **to do sth** se donner la peine de faire qch; **I can't be bothered!** ça m'embête! 3 vi **to b. about** (worry about) se préoccuper de; (deal with) s'occuper de; **don't b.!** ne prends pas cette peine!

bottle ['bɒtəl] 1 n bouteille f; (small) flacon m; (wide-mouthed) bocal m; (for baby) biberon m; **b. bank** conteneur m pour verre usagé; **b. opener** ouvre-bouteilles m inv 2 vt (milk, wine) mettre en bouteilles; **to b. up** (feeling) refouler **• bottle-feed** (pt & pp **-fed**) vt nourrir au biberon **• bottleneck** n (in road) goulot m d'étranglement; (traffic hold-up) bouchon m

bottom ['bɒtəm] 1 n (of sea, box) fond m; (of page, hill) bas m; (of table) bout m; Fam (buttocks) derrière m; **to be (at the) b. of the class** être le dernier/la dernière de la classe 2 adj (shelf) inférieur, du bas; **b. floor** rez-de-chaussée m; **b. gear** première vitesse f; **b. part** or **half** partie f inférieure f; Fig **the b. line is that…** le fait est que… **• bottomless** adj (funds) inépuisable; **b. pit** gouffre m

bough [baʊ] n Literary rameau m

bought [bɔːt] pt & pp of **buy**

boulder ['bəʊldə(r)] n rocher m

boulevard ['buːləvɑːd] n boulevard m

bounce [baʊns] 1 n rebond m 2 vt (ball) faire rebondir 3 vi (of ball) rebondir (**off** contre); (of person) faire des bonds; Fam (of cheque) être sans provision

bouncer ['baʊnsə(r)] n Fam (doorman) videur m

bound¹ [baʊnd] adj (a) **b. to do** (obliged) obligé de faire; (certain) sûr de faire; **it's b. to snow** il va sûrement neiger; **to be b. for** (of person, ship) être en route pour; (of train, plane) être à destination de (b) **b. up with** (connected) lié à

bound² [baʊnd] 1 n (leap) bond m 2 vi bondir

bound³ [baʊnd] pt & pp of **bind**

boundary ['baʊndərɪ] (pl -ies) n limite f

bounded ['baʊndɪd] adj **b. by** limité par

boundless ['baʊndləs] adj sans bornes

bounds [baʊndz] npl limites fpl; **out of b.** (place) interdit

bounty ['baʊntɪ] (pl -ies) n (reward) prime f

bouquet [bəʊ'keɪ] n (of flowers, wine) bouquet m

bourbon ['bɜːbən] n (whisky) bourbon m

bout [baʊt] n (of fever, coughing, violence) accès m; (of asthma, malaria) crise f; (session) séance f; (period) période f; Boxing combat m; **a b. of flu** une grippe

boutique [buː'tiːk] n boutique f (de mode)

bow¹ [bəʊ] n (weapon) arc m; (of violin) archet m; (knot) nœud m; **b. tie** nœud m papillon **• bow-legged** ['bəʊ'legɪd] adj aux jambes arquées

bow² [baʊ] 1 n (with knees bent) révérence f; (nod) salut m; **to take a b.** (of actor) saluer 2 vt **to b. one's head** incliner la tête 3 vi s'incliner (**to** devant); (nod) incliner la tête (**to** devant); **to b. down** (submit) s'incliner (**to** devant)

bow³ [baʊ] n (of ship) proue f

bowels ['baʊəlz] npl intestins mpl; Literary **in the b. of the earth** dans les entrailles de la terre

bowl¹ [bəʊl] n (small dish) bol m; (for salad) saladier m; (for soup) assiette f creuse; (of toilet) cuvette f

bowl² [bəʊl] 1 n bowls (game) boules fpl 2 vi (in cricket) lancer la balle **• bowling** n (tenpin) b. bowling m; **b. alley** bowling m; **b. ball** boule f de bowling; **b. green** terrain m de boules

▸ **bowl along** vi (of car, bicycle) rouler à toute vitesse

▸ **bowl over** vt sep (knock down) renverser; Fig (astound) **to be bowled over by sth** être stupéfié par qch

bowler ['bəʊlə(r)] n Br **b. (hat)** chapeau m melon

box [bɒks] 1 n boîte f; (larger) caisse f; (of cardboard) carton m; (in theatre) loge f; (for horse, in stable) box m; Br Fam (television) télé f;

b. number *(at post office)* numéro *m* de boîte postale; *(at newspaper)* référence *f* de petite annonce; **b. office** bureau *m* de location; *Br* **b. room** *(lumber room)* débarras *m*; *(bedroom)* petite chambre *f* **2** *vt* (**a**) **to b. (up)** mettre en boîte/caisse; **to b. in** *(enclose)* enfermer (**b**) **b. sb's ears** gifler qn **3** *vi* boxer; **to b. against sb** boxer contre qn ▪ **boxing** *n* (**a**) boxe *f*; **b. gloves/match** gants *mpl*/combat *m* de boxe; **b. ring** ring *m* (**b**) *Br* **B. Day** le lendemain de Noël

boxcar ['bɒkskɑːr] *n Am Rail* wagon *m* couvert

boxer ['bɒksə(r)] *n (fighter)* boxeur *m*; *(dog)* boxer *m*

boy [bɔɪ] *n* garçon *m*; **English b.** jeune Anglais *m*; *Br* **old b.** *(former pupil)* ancien élève *m*; *Fam* **the boys** *(pals)* les copains *mpl*; **my dear b.** mon cher ami; **oh b.!** mon Dieu! ▪ **boyband** *n* boys band *m* ▪ **boyfriend** *n* petit ami *m* ▪ **boyhood** *n* enfance *f* ▪ **boyish** *adj* de garçon; *Pej* puéril

boycott ['bɔɪkɒt] **1** *n* boycottage *m* **2** *vt* boycotter

bra [brɑː] *n* soutien-gorge *m*

brace [breɪs] **1** *n (dental)* appareil *m* dentaire; *(on leg, arm)* appareil *m* orthopédique; *(for fastening)* attache *f*; *Br* **braces** *(for trousers)* bretelles *fpl* **2** *vt* **to b. oneself for sth** *(news, shock)* se préparer à qch ▪ **bracing** *adj (air)* vivifiant

bracelet ['breɪslɪt] *n* bracelet *m*

bracken ['brækən] *n* fougère *f*

bracket ['brækɪt] *n (for shelves)* équerre *f*; *(round sign)* parenthèse *f*; *(square sign)* crochet *m*; *(group)* groupe *m*; *(for tax)* tranche *f*; **in brackets** entre parenthèses/crochets **2** *vt* mettre entre parenthèses/crochets; **to b. together** mettre dans le même groupe

brag [bræg] *(pt & pp* -gg-*) vi* se vanter (**about** or **of sth** de qch; **about doing** de faire)

braid [breɪd] **1** *n (of hair)* tresse *f*; *(trimming)* galon *m* **2** *vt (hair)* tresser; *(trim)* galonner

Braille [breɪl] *n* braille *m*; **in B.** en braille

brain [breɪn] *n* cerveau *m*; *(of animal, bird)* cervelle *f*; *Fam* **to have brains** *(sense)* être intelligent; *Fam* **to have money on the b.** être obsédé par l'argent; *Hum* **use your brain(s)!** réfléchis un peu!; **b. damage** lésions *fpl* cérébrales; **b. dead** dans un coma dépassé; **b. drain** fuite *f* des cerveaux; **b. surgeon** neurochirurgien, -ienne *mf* **2** *vt Fam (hit)* assommer ▪ **brainchild** ['breɪntʃaɪld] *n* trouvaille *f* ▪ **brainstorm** *n Br (mental confusion)* aberration *f*; *Am (brilliant idea)* idée *f* géniale ▪ **brainstorming** *n* brainstorming *m* ▪ **brainwash** *vt* faire un lavage de cerveau à ▪ **brainwashing** *n* lavage *m* de cerveau ▪ **brainwave** *n* idée *f* géniale ▪ **brainy** (-ier, -iest) *adj Fam* intelligent

braise [breɪz] *vt Culin* braiser

brake [breɪk] **1** *n* frein *m*; **b. fluid** liquide *m* de freins; **b. light** *(on vehicle)* stop *m* **2** *vi* freiner ▪ **braking** *n* freinage *m*

bramble ['bræmbəl] *n* ronce *f*

bran [bræn] *n* son *m*

branch [brɑːntʃ] **1** *n* branche *f*; *(of road)* embranchement *m*; *(of river)* bras *m*; *(of store)* succursale *f*; *(of bank)* agence *f*; **b. office** succursale **2** *vi* **to b. off** *(of road)* bifurquer; **to b. out** *(of firm, person)* étendre ses activités; *(of family, tree)* se ramifier

brand [brænd] **1** *n (on product, on cattle)* marque *f*; *(type)* type *m*, style *m*; **b. name** marque **2** *vt (mark)* marquer; *Fig* **to be branded as a liar/coward** avoir une réputation de menteur/lâche

brandish ['brændɪʃ] *vt* brandir

brand-new [brænd'njuː] *adj* tout neuf (*f* toute neuve)

brandy ['brændɪ] *(pl* -ies*) n* cognac *m*; *(made with fruit)* eau-de-vie *f*

brash [bræʃ] *adj* exubérant

brass [brɑːs] *n* cuivre *m*; *(instruments in orchestra)* cuivres *mpl*; *Fam* **the top b.** *(officers, executives)* les huiles *fpl*; **b. band** fanfare *f*

brassiere [*Br* 'bræzɪə(r), *Am* brə'zɪə(r)] *n* soutien-gorge *m*

brat [bræt] *n Pej (child)* morveux, -euse *mf*; *(badly behaved)* sale gosse *mf*

bravado [brə'vɑːdəʊ] *n* bravade *f*

brave [breɪv] **1** (-er, -est) *adj* courageux, -euse **2** *n (native American)* brave *m* **3** *vt (danger)* braver ▪ **bravely** *adv* courageusement ▪ **bravery** *n* courage *m*

> Note that the French word **brave** is a false friend. Its most common meaning is **kind**.

bravo [brɑː'vəʊ] *exclam* bravo!

brawl [brɔːl] **1** *n (fight)* bagarre *f* **2** *vi* se bagarrer ▪ **brawling 1** *adj* bagarreur, -euse **2** *n* bagarres *fpl*

brawn [brɔːn] *n Fam* muscles *mpl* ▪ **brawny** (-ier, -iest) *adj* musclé

bray [breɪ] *vi (of donkey)* braire

brazen ['breɪzən] **1** *adj (shameless)* effronté; *(lie)* éhonté **2** *vt* **to b. it out** s'en tirer au culot

Brazil [brə'zɪl] *n* le Brésil ▪ **Brazilian 1** *adj* brésilien, -ienne **2** *n* (**a**) *(person)* Brésilien, -ienne *mf* (**b**) *(wax)* épilation *f* maillot brésilien

breach [briːtʃ] **1** *n* (**a**) *(of rule)* violation *f* (**of** de); **b. of contract** rupture *f* de contrat; **b. of trust** abus *m* de confiance (**b**) *(in wall)* brèche *f* **2** *vt* (**a**) *(law, code)* enfreindre à; *(contract)* rompre (**b**) *(wall)* ouvrir une brèche dans

bread [bred] *n* pain *m*; *Fam (money)* blé *m*; **loaf of b.** pain; **brown b.** pain bis; **(slice** or **piece) of b. and butter** pain beurré; **it's my b. and butter** *(job)* c'est mon gagne-pain; **b. knife** couteau *m* à pain ▪ **breadbin** (*Am* **breadbox**) *n* boîte *f* à pain ▪ **breadboard** *n* planche *f* à pain ▪ **breadcrumb** *n* miette *f* de pain; **breadcrumbs** (*in cooking*) chapelure *f* ▪ **breaded** *adj* pané ▪ **breadline** *n* on the b. indigent ▪ **breadwinner** *n* to be the b. faire bouillir la marmite

breadth [bretθ] *n* largeur *f*

break [breɪk] **1** *n* cassure *f*; (*in bone*) fracture *f*; (*with person, group*) rupture *f*; (*in journey*) interruption *f*; (*rest*) repos *m*; (*in activity*) pause *f*; (*at school*) récréation *f*; (*holidays*) vacances *fpl*; *Fam* **to have a lucky b.** avoir de la veine; *Fam* **this could be your big b.** ça peut être la chance de ta vie; *Fam* **give him a b.!** laisse-le tranquille!

2 (*pt* **broke**, *pp* **broken**) *vt* casser; (*into pieces, with force*) briser; (*silence, spell, vow*) rompre; (*strike, will, ice*) briser; (*agreement, promise*) manquer à; (*treaty, law*) violer; (*record*) battre; (*journey*) interrompre; (*news*) annoncer (**to** à); (*habit*) se débarrasser de; **to b. one's arm** se casser le bras; **to b. sb's heart** briser le cœur à qn; *Fam* **b. a leg!** bonne chance!; **to b. the sound barrier** franchir le mur du son; **to b. a fall** amortir une chute; **to b. new ground** innover; **to b. open** (*safe*) percer

3 *vi* se casser; (*into pieces, of heart, of voice*) se briser; (*of boy's voice*) muer; (*of spell*) se rompre; (*of weather*) changer; (*of news*) éclater; (*of day*) se lever; (*of wave*) déferler; (*stop work*) faire la pause; **to b. in two** se casser en deux; **to b. free** se libérer; **to b. loose** se détacher ▪ **breakable** *adj* fragile ▪ **breakage** *n* **were there any breakages?** est-ce qu'il y a eu de la casse? ▪ **breakaway** *adj* (*group*) dissident ▪ **breakdown** *n* (*of machine*) panne *f*; (*of argument, figures*) analyse *f*; (*of talks*) échec *m*; (*of person*) dépression *f*; *Br* **b. lorry** *or* **van** dépanneuse *f* ▪ **breaker** *n* (*wave*) déferlante *f* ▪ **break-in** *n* cambriolage *m* ▪ **breaking-point** *n* **at b.** (*person, patience*) à bout; (*marriage*) au bord de la rupture ▪ **breakthrough** *n* (*discovery*) découverte *f* fondamentale ▪ **breakup** *n* fin *f*; (*in marriage, friendship*) rupture *f*

▸ **break away 1** *vi* se détacher **2** *vt sep* détacher

▸ **break down 1** *vt sep* (*door*) enfoncer; (*resistance*) briser; (*argument, figures*) analyser **2** *vi* (*of machine*) tomber en panne; (*of talks, negotiations*) échouer; (*of person*) (*collapse*) s'effondrer; (*have nervous breakdown*) craquer; (*start crying*) éclater en sanglots

▸ **break in 1** *vi* (*of burglar*) entrer par effraction; (*interrupt*) interrompre **2** *vt sep* (*door*) enfoncer; (*horse*) dresser

▸ **break into** *vt insep* (*house*) entrer par effraction; (*safe*) forcer; **to b. into song/a run** se mettre à chanter/courir; **to b. into**

laughter/tears éclater de rire/en sanglots

▸ **break off 1** *vt sep* (*detach*) (*twig, handle*) détacher; (*relations*) rompre **2** *vi* (*become detached*) se casser; (*stop*) s'arrêter; **to b. off with sb** rompre avec qn

▸ **break out** *vi* (*of war, fire*) éclater; (*escape*) s'échapper (**of** de); **to b. out in a rash** se couvrir de boutons

▸ **break through 1** *vi* (*of sun, army*) percer **2** *vt insep* (*defences*) percer; (*barrier*) forcer; (*wall*) faire une brèche dans

▸ **break up 1** *vt sep* (*reduce to pieces*) mettre en morceaux; (*marriage*) briser; (*fight*) mettre fin à **2** *vi* (*end*) prendre fin; (*of group*) se disperser; (*of marriage*) se briser; (*from school*) partir en vacances; **to b. up with sb** rompre avec qn

breakfast ['brekfəst] *n* petit déjeuner *m*; **to have b.** prendre le petit déjeuner; **b. TV** émissions *fpl* (télévisées) du matin

breakwater ['breɪkwɔːtə(r)] *n* brise-lames *m inv*

breast [brest] *n* (*of woman*) sein *m*; (*chest*) poitrine *f*; (*of chicken*) blanc *m* ▪ **breastfeed** (*pt & pp* **-fed**) *vt* allaiter ▪ **breaststroke** *n* (*in swimming*) brasse *f*

breath [breθ] *n* souffle *m*; **bad b.** mauvaise haleine *f*; **out of b.** à bout de souffle; **to take a deep b.** respirer profondément; **to hold one's b.** retenir son souffle; **to get a b. of fresh air** prendre l'air; **under one's b.** tout bas; **one's last b.** son dernier soupir ▪ **breathalyser®** *n* Alcotest® *m* ▪ **breathless** *adj* hors d'haleine ▪ **breathtaking** *adj* à couper le souffle

breathe [briːð] **1** *vi* (*of person, animal*) respirer; **to b. in** inhaler; **to b. out** expirer **2** *vt* respirer; **to b. air into sth** souffler dans qch; **to b. a sigh of relief** pousser un soupir de soulagement; **she didn't b. a word** (*about it*) elle n'en a pas soufflé mot ▪ **breathing** *n* respiration *f*; *Fig* **b. space** moment *m* de repos

breather ['briːðə(r)] *n Fam* pause *f*; **to take a b.** faire une pause

bred [bred] **1** *pt & pp of* **breed 2** *adj* **well-b.** bien élevé

breed [briːd] **1** *n* race *f* **2** (*pt & pp* **bred**) *vt* (*animals*) élever; *Fig* (*hatred, violence*) engendrer **3** *vi* (*of animals*) se reproduire ▪ **breeder** *n* éleveur, -euse *mf* ▪ **breeding** *n* (*of animals*) élevage *m*; (*procreation*) reproduction *f*; *Fig* (*manners*) éducation *f*

breeze [briːz] *n* brise *f* ▪ **breezy** (**-ier, -iest**) *adj* (**a**) (*weather, day*) frais (*f* fraîche), venteux, -euse (**b**) (*cheerful*) jovial; (*relaxed*) décontracté

breeze-block *n Br* parpaing *m*

brevity ['brevɪtɪ] *n* brièveté *f*

brew [bruː] **1** *n* (*drink*) breuvage *m*; (*of tea*) infusion *f* **2** *vt* (*beer*) brasser; *Fig* (*trouble, plot*) préparer; **to b. some tea** (*make*) préparer du thé **3** *vi* (*of beer*) fermenter; (*of tea*) infuser; *Fig* (*of storm*) se préparer; **something is brewing** il

se trame quelque chose ▪ **brewer** n brasseur m
▪ **brewery** (pl -ies) n brasserie f

bribe [braɪb] 1 n pot-de-vin m 2 vt acheter,
soudoyer; **to b. sb into doing sth** soudoyer qn
pour qu'il fasse qch ▪ **bribery** n corruption f

brick [brɪk] 1 n brique f; (child's) cube m; **b. wall**
mur en briques; Br Fam **to drop a b.** faire une
gaffe 2 vt **to b. up** (gap, door) murer
▪ **bricklayer** n maçon m ▪ **brickwork** n (bricks)
briques fpl; (construction) ouvrage m en briques

bridal ['braɪdəl] adj (ceremony, bed) nuptial; **b.
gown** robe f de mariée; **b. suite** (in hotel) suite
f nuptiale

bride [braɪd] n mariée f; **the b. and groom** les
mariés mpl ▪ **bridegroom** n marié m
▪ **bridesmaid** n demoiselle f d'honneur

bridge¹ [brɪdʒ] 1 n pont m; (on ship) passerelle
f; (of nose) arête f; (on teeth) bridge m 2 vt **to b. a
gap** combler une lacune

bridge² [brɪdʒ] n (game) bridge m

bridle ['braɪdəl] 1 n (for horse) bride f; **b. path**
allée f cavalière 2 vt (horse) brider

brief¹ [briːf] (-er, -est) adj bref (f brève); **in b.** en
résumé ▪ **briefly** adv (quickly) en vitesse; (say)
brièvement; (hesitate) un court instant

brief² [briːf] 1 n (instructions) instructions fpl;
(legal) dossier m; Fig (task) tâche f 2 vt donner
des instructions à; (inform) mettre au courant
(**on** de) ▪ **briefing** n (information) instructions
fpl; (meeting) briefing m

briefcase ['briːfkeɪs] n serviette f

briefs [briːfs] npl (underwear) slip m

brigade [brɪ'geɪd] n brigade f ▪ **brigadier**
[brɪgə'dɪə(r)] n général m de brigade

bright [braɪt] 1 (-er, -est) adj (star, eyes,
situation) brillant; (light, colour) vif (f vive);
(weather, room) clair; (clever) intelligent;
(happy) joyeux, -euse; (future) prometteur,
-euse; (idea) génial; **b. interval** (sunny period)
éclaircie f 2 adv **b. and early** (to get up) de bon
matin ▪ **brightly** adv (shine) avec éclat
▪ **brightness** n éclat m; (of person) intelligence f

brighten ['braɪtən] 1 vt **to b. (up)** (room) égayer
2 vi **to b. (up)** (of weather) s'éclaircir; (of face)
s'éclairer; (of person) s'égayer

brilliant ['brɪljənt] adj (light) éclatant; (person,
idea, career) brillant; Br Fam (fantastic) super inv
▪ **brilliance** n éclat m; (of person) intelligence f

brim [brɪm] 1 n (of hat, cup) bord m 2 (pt & pp
-mm-) vi **to b. over** déborder (**with** de)

brine [braɪn] n saumure f

bring [brɪŋ] (pt & pp **brought**) vt (person, animal,
car) amener; (object) apporter; (cause)
provoquer; **it has brought me great
happiness** cela m'a procuré un grand
bonheur; **to b. tears to sb's eyes** faire venir
les larmes aux yeux de qn; **to b. sth to sb's
attention** attirer l'attention de qn sur qch; **to b.
sth to an end** mettre fin à qch; **to b. sth to mind**

rappeler qch; **to b. sth on oneself** s'attirer qch; **I
can't b. myself to do it** je ne peux pas me
résoudre à le faire

▸ **bring about** vt sep provoquer

▸ **bring along** vt sep (object) apporter; (person)
amener

▸ **bring back** vt sep (person) ramener; (object)
rapporter; (memories) rappeler

▸ **bring down** vt sep (object) descendre;
(overthrow) faire tomber; (reduce) réduire;
(shoot down) (plane) abattre

▸ **bring forward** vt sep (in time or space)
avancer; (witness) produire

▸ **bring in** vt sep (object) rentrer; (person) faire
entrer/venir; (introduce) introduire; (income)
rapporter

▸ **bring off** vt sep (task) mener à bien

▸ **bring out** vt sep (object) sortir; (person) faire
sortir; (meaning) faire ressortir; (book) publier;
(product) lancer (revive)

▸ **bring round** vt sep ranimer; (convert)
convaincre; **she brought him round to her
point of view** elle a su le convaincre

▸ **bring to** vt sep **to b. sb to** ranimer qn

▸ **bring together** vt sep (friends, members)
réunir; (reconcile) réconcilier; (put in touch)
mettre en contact

▸ **bring up** vt sep (object) monter; (child) élever;
(question) soulever; (subject) mentionner;
(food) rendre

brink [brɪŋk] n bord m; **on the b. of sth** au bord
de qch

brisk [brɪsk] (-er, -est) adj (lively) vif (f vive); **at
a b. pace** vite; **trading is b.** le marché est actif;
business is b. les affaires marchent bien
▪ **briskly** adv vivement; (walk) d'un bon pas

bristle ['brɪsəl] 1 n poil m 2 vi se hérisser;
bristling with difficulties hérissé de difficultés

Britain ['brɪtən] n la Grande-Bretagne
▪ **British** 1 adj britannique; **the B. Isles** les îles
fpl Britanniques; **B. Summer Time** heure f d'été
(en Grande-Bretagne) 2 npl **the B.** les
Britanniques mpl ▪ **Briton** n Britannique mf

Brittany ['brɪtənɪ] n la Bretagne

brittle ['brɪtəl] adj cassant

broach [brəʊtʃ] vt (topic) aborder

broad¹ [brɔːd] (-er, -est) adj (wide) large;
(accent) prononcé; **in b. daylight** en plein jour;
the b. outline of (plan) les grandes lignes de; **b.
bean** fève f; Am Sport **b. jump** saut m en
longueur ▪ **broadband** Tel & Comptr 1 n
connexion f à haut débit ou à large bande 2
adj à haut débit, à large bande ▪ **'broad-
'minded** adj (person) à l'esprit large; **b.-
minded views** (**on**) des idées fpl larges (**sur**)
▪ **'broad-'shouldered** adj large d'épaules

broad² [brɔːd] n Am Fam (woman) gonzesse f

broadcast ['brɔːdkɑːst] 1 n émission f 2 (pt & pp
broadcast) vt diffuser 3 vi (of station) émettre;

(of person) parler à la radio/à la télévision ■**broadcaster** n journaliste mf de radio/ télévision ■**broadcasting** n Radio radiodiffusion f; TV télévision f

broaden ['brɔːdən] 1 vt élargir 2 vi s'élargir

broadly ['brɔːdlɪ] adv b. (speaking) en gros

broccoli ['brɒkəlɪ] n inv (plant) brocoli m; (food) brocolis mpl

brochure ['brəʊʃə(r)] n brochure f

brogue [brəʊg] n (Irish) accent m irlandais

broil [brɔɪl] vti griller ■**broiler** n Am poulet m (à rôtir); (apparatus) gril m

broke [brəʊk] 1 pt of **break** 2 adj Fam (penniless) fauché ■**broken** 1 pp of **break** 2 adj (man, voice, line) brisé; (ground) accidenté; (spirit) abattu; in **b. English** en mauvais anglais; **b. home** famille f désunie ■**broken-'down** adj (machine) détraqué

broker ['brəʊkə(r)] n (for shares, currency) agent m de change; (for goods, insurance) courtier, -ière mf

brolly ['brɒlɪ] (pl -ies) n Br Fam (umbrella) pépin m

bronchitis [brɒŋ'kaɪtɪs] n bronchite f

bronze [brɒnz] n bronze m; b. **statue** statue f en bronze

brooch [brəʊtʃ] n (ornament) broche f

brood [bruːd] 1 n couvée f 2 vi (of bird) couver; Fig **to b. over sth** (of person) ruminer qch ■**broody** (-ier, -iest) adj (person) (sulky) maussade; (dreamy) rêveur, -euse; Br Fam (woman) en mal d'enfant

brook [brʊk] 1 n ruisseau m 2 vt Formal (tolerate) tolérer

broom [bruːm] n (a) (for sweeping) balai m (b) (plant) genêt m ■**broomstick** n manche m à balai

Bros (abbr Brothers) npl Com Richard B. Richard Frères mpl

broth [brɒθ] n (thin) bouillon m; (thick) potage m

brothel ['brɒθəl] n maison f close

brother ['brʌðə(r)] n frère m ■**brother-in-law** (pl **brothers-in-law**) n beau-frère m ■**brotherhood** n fraternité f ■**brotherly** adj fraternel, -elle

brought [brɔːt] pt & pp of **bring**

brow [braʊ] n (a) (forehead) front m (b) (of hill) sommet m

browbeat ['braʊbiːt] (pt -beat, pp -beaten) vt intimider; **to b. sb into doing sth** faire faire qch à qn à force d'intimidation

brown [braʊn] 1 (-er, -est) adj marron inv; (hair) châtain; (tanned) bronzé 2 n marron m 3 vt (of sun) brunir; (food) faire dorer; Br Fam **to be browned off** en avoir marre 4 vi (of food) dorer

Brownie ['braʊnɪ] n (girl scout) ≃ jeannette f

brownie ['braʊnɪ] n (cake) brownie m

browse [braʊz] 1 vt Comptr **to b. the Web** naviguer sur le Web 2 vi (a) (in bookshop)

feuilleter des livres; (in shop, supermarket) regarder; **to b. through** (book) feuilleter (b) (of animal) brouter

bruise [bruːz] 1 n bleu m; (on fruit) meurtrissure f 2 vt **to b. one's knee/hand** se faire un bleu au genou/à la main; **to b. a fruit** taler un fruit ■**bruised** adj (covered in bruises) couvert de bleus ■**bruising** n (bruises) bleus mpl

brunch [brʌntʃ] n Fam brunch m

brunette [bruː'net] n brunette f

brunt [brʌnt] n **to bear the b. of** (attack, anger) subir le plus gros de; (expense) assumer la plus grosse part de

brush [brʌʃ] 1 n (tool) brosse f; (for shaving) blaireau m; (for sweeping) balayette f; **to give sth a b.** donner un coup de brosse à qch 2 vt (teeth, hair) brosser; (clothes) donner un coup de brosse à; **to b. sb/sth aside** écarter qn/ qch; **to b. sth away/off** enlever qch; **to b. up (on) one's French** se remettre au français 3 vi **to b. against sb/sth** effleurer qn/qch ■**brush-off** n Fam **to give sb the b.** envoyer promener qn ■**brush-up** n **to have a wash and b.** faire un brin de toilette

brushwood ['brʌʃwʊd] n broussailles fpl

brusque [bruːsk] adj brusque

Brussels ['brʌsəlz] n Bruxelles m ou f; **B. sprouts** choux mpl de Bruxelles

brutal ['bruːtəl] adj brutal; (attack) sauvage ■**bru'tality** [-'tælɪtɪ] n brutalité f; (of attack) sauvagerie f

brute [bruːt] 1 n (animal) bête f; (person) brute f 2 adj **by b. force** par la force

BSc [biːes'siː] (Am **BS** [biː'es]) abbr = **Bachelor of Science**

BSE [biːes'iː] (abbr **bovine spongiform encephalopathy**) n EBS f, maladie f de la vache folle

bubble ['bʌbəl] 1 n (of air, soap) bulle f; **b. bath** bain m moussant; **b. gum** chewing-gum m 2 vi (of liquid) bouillonner; **to b. over (with)** déborder (de) ■**bubbly** 1 adj (liquid) plein de bulles; (person, personality) débordant de vitalité 2 n Fam Hum (champagne) champ m

buck [bʌk] 1 n (a) Am Fam dollar m (b) (of rabbit) mâle m (c) Fam **to pass the b. (to sb)** refiler le bébé (à qn) 2 vt Fam **to b. sb up** remonter le moral à qn 3 vi Fam **to b. up** (become livelier) reprendre du poil de la bête; (hurry) se grouiller

bucket ['bʌkɪt] n seau m

buckle ['bʌkəl] 1 n boucle f 2 vt (a) (fasten) boucler (b) (deform) déformer 3 vi (deform) se déformer; **to b. down to a task** s'atteler à une tâche

buckshot ['bʌkʃɒt] n inv chevrotine f

buckteeth [bʌk'tiːθ] npl dents fpl de lapin

bud [bʌd] 1 n (on tree) bourgeon m; (on flower) bouton m 2 (pt & pp -dd-) vi bourgeonner; (of *flower)* pousser des boutons ■**budding** *adj (talent)* naissant; *(doctor)* en herbe

Buddhist ['bʊdɪst] *adj & n* bouddhiste *(mf)*

buddy ['bʌdɪ] *n Fam -ies)* in *Am Fam* pote *m*

budge [bʌdʒ] **1** *vi* bouger **2** *vt* faire bouger

budgerigar ['bʌdʒərɪgɑː(r)] *n Br* perruche *f*

budget ['bʌdʒɪt] **1** *n* budget *m* **2** *vi* dresser un budget; **to b. for sth** inscrire qch au budget

budgie ['bʌdʒɪ] *n Br Fam* perruche *f*

buff [bʌf] **1** *adj* **b.(-coloured)** chamois *inv* **2** *n Fam* (**a**) **jazz/film b.** fanatique *mf* de jazz/de cinéma (**b**) **in the b.** à poil **3** *vt (polish)* lustrer; **to b. one's nails** se polir les ongles

buffalo ['bʌfələʊ] *(pl -oes or -o)* *n* buffle *m*; **(American)** bison *m*

buffer ['bʌfə(r)] *n* (**a**) *(on train)* tampon *m*; *(at end of track)* butoir *m*; *Fig (safeguard)* protection *f* (**against** contre); **b. state** État *m* tampon (**b**) *(for polishing)* polissoir *m*

buffet¹ ['bʊfeɪ] *n (meal, café)* buffet *m*; **cold b.** viandes *fpl* froides; *Br* **b. car** *(on train)* wagon-restaurant *m*

buffet² ['bʌfɪt] *vt (of waves)* secouer; *(of wind, rain)* cingler

buffoon [bə'fuːn] *n* bouffon *m*

bug¹ [bʌg] *n* (**a**) *(insect)* bestiole *f*; *(bedbug)* punaise *f*; *Fam (germ)* microbe *m*; **the travel/skiing b.** le virus des voyages/du ski (**b**) *(in machine)* défaut *m*; *Comptr* bogue *m* (**c**) *(listening device)* micro *m* **2** *(pt & pp -gg-)* *vt (room)* installer des micros dans

bug² [bʌg] *(pt & pp -gg-)* *vt Fam (nag)* embêter

bugbear ['bʌgbeə(r)] *n Fam* cauchemar *m*

buggy ['bʌgɪ] *(pl -ies)* *n Br* **(baby) b.** *(pushchair)* poussette *f*; *Am (pram)* landau *m*

bugle ['bjuːgəl] *n (instrument)* clairon *m*

build [bɪld] **1** *n (of person)* carrure *f* **2** *(pt & pp built* [bɪlt]*)* *vt* construire; **to b. sth up** *(increase)* augmenter qch; *(business)* monter qch; **to b. up speed/one's strength** prendre de la vitesse/des forces **3** *vi* **to b. up** *(of tension, pressure)* augmenter; *(of dust, snow, interest)* s'accumuler; *(of traffic)* devenir dense ■**builder** *n (skilled)* maçon *m*; *(unskilled)* ouvrier *m*; *(contractor)* entrepreneur *m* ■**building** *n* bâtiment *m*; *(flats, offices)* immeuble *m*; *(action)* construction *f*; **b. site** chantier *m*; *Br* **b. society** ≃ société *f* de crédit immobilier ■**build-up** *n (increase)* augmentation *f*; *(of dust)* accumulation *f*; *(of troops)* concentration *f*; *(for author, book)* publicité *f*; **the b. to Christmas** la période précédant Noël

built-in [bɪlt'ɪn] *adj (cupboard)* encastré; *(part of machine)* incorporé; *Fig (innate)* inné

built-up ['bɪltʌp] *adj* urbanisé; **b. area** agglomération *f*

bulb [bʌlb] *n (of plant)* bulbe *m*; *(of lamp)* ampoule *f*

bulbous ['bʌlbəs] *adj (shape, nose)* gros et rond *(f* grosse et ronde); *(table leg)* renflé

Bulgaria [bʌl'geərɪə] *n* la Bulgarie ■**Bulgarian 1** *adj* bulgare **2** *n* Bulgare *mf*

bulge [bʌldʒ] **1** *n* renflement *m*; *Fam (increase)* augmentation *f* **2** *vi* **to b. (out)** bomber; *(of eyes)* sortir de la tête ■**bulging** *adj* bombé; *(eyes)* protubérant; **to be b.** *(of bag, pocket)* être bourré (**with** de)

bulimia [bʊ'lɪmɪə] *n* boulimie *f*

bulk [bʌlk] *n inv (of building, parcel)* volume *m*; *(of person)* grosseur *f*; **the b. of sth** la majeure partie de qch; **in b.** *(buy, sell)* en gros ■**bulky** *(-ier, -iest)* *adj* volumineux, -euse

bull [bʊl] *n* (**a**) *(animal)* taureau *m* (**b**) *very Fam (nonsense)* conneries *fpl* ■**bullfight** *n* corrida *f* ■**bullfighter** *n* torero *m* ■**bullring** *n* arène *f*

bulldog ['bʊldɒg] *n* bouledogue *m*; **b. clip** pince *f* (à dessin)

bulldoze ['bʊldəʊz] *vt (site)* passer au bulldozer; *(building)* démolir au bulldozer ■**bulldozer** *n* bulldozer *m*

bullet ['bʊlɪt] *n* balle *f* ■**bulletproof** *adj (car)* blindé; **it's b. glass** la vitre est blindée; **b. vest** gilet *m* pare-balles *inv*

bulletin ['bʊlətɪn] *n* bulletin *m*; *& Comptr* **b. board** panneau *m* d'affichage

bullion ['bʊljən] *n* **gold b.** lingots *mpl* d'or

bullock ['bʊlək] *n* bœuf *m*

bull's-eye ['bʊlzaɪ] *n (of target)* centre *m*; **to hit the b.** mettre dans le mille

bully ['bʊlɪ] **1** *(pl -ies)* *n* terreur *f* **2** *(pt & pp -ied)* *vt (ill-treat)* maltraiter; **to b. sb into doing sth** forcer qn à faire qch ■**bullying** *n* brimades *fpl*

bulwark ['bʊlwək] *n* rempart *m*

bum [bʌm] *Fam* **1** *n* (**a**) *Br (buttocks)* derrière *m*; **b. bag** banane *f* (**b**) *Am (tramp)* clochard, -arde *mf*; *(good-for-nothing)* bon *m* à rien, bonne *f* à rien **2** *(pt & pp -mm-)* *vi* **to b. (around)** *(be idle)* glander; *(travel)* vadrouiller **3** *vt Am* **to b. sth off sb** *(cigarette)* taxer qch à qn ■**bummer** *n* **what a b.!** quelle poisse!

bumblebee ['bʌmbəlbiː] *n* bourdon *m*

bumf [bʌmf] *n Br Fam* paperasse *f*

bump [bʌmp] **1** *n (impact)* choc *m*; *(jerk)* secousse *f*; *(on road, body)* bosse *f* **2** *vt (of car)* heurter; **to b. one's head/knee** se cogner la tête/le genou; **to b. into** *(of person)* se cogner contre; *(of car)* rentrer dans; *(meet)* tomber sur; *Fam* **to b. sb off** liquider qn; **to b. up** *(price)* augmenter **3** *vi* **to b. along** *(in car)* cahoter ■**bumper 1** *n (of car)* pare-chocs *m inv* **2** *adj (crop, year)* exceptionnel, -elle; **b. cars** autos *fpl* tamponneuses

bumpkin ['bʌmpkɪn] *n* **(country) b.** péquenaud, -aude *mf*

bumptious ['bʌmpʃəs] *adj* prétentieux, -ieuse

bumpy ['bʌmpɪ] *(-ier, -iest)* *adj (road, ride)*

cahoteux, -euse; **we had a b. flight** on a traversé des trous d'air pendant le vol

bun [bʌn] n (**a**) (cake) petit pain m au lait (**b**) (of hair) chignon m

bunch [bʌntʃ] n (of flowers) bouquet m; (of keys) trousseau m; (of bananas) régime m; (of grapes) grappe f; (of people) bande f; Fam **a b. of books/ideas** un tas de livres/d'idées; **to wear one's hair in bunches** porter des couettes

bundle ['bʌndəl] **1** n paquet m; (of papers) liasse f; (of firewood) fagot m **2** vt (put) fourrer (**into** dans); (push) pousser (**into** dans); **to b. sb off** expédier qn **3** vi **to b. (oneself) up** (bien) se couvrir

bung [bʌŋ] **1** n (stopper) bonde f **2** vt (**a**) Br Fam (toss) balancer (**b**) **to b. up** boucher

bungalow ['bʌŋɡələʊ] n pavillon m de plain-pied

bungee jumping ['bʌndʒiːdʒʌmpɪŋ] n saut m à l'élastique

bungle ['bʌŋɡəl] **1** vt gâcher **2** vi se tromper ▪ **bungler** n to be a b. faire du mauvais travail ▪ **bungling 1** adj (clumsy) maladroit **2** n gâchis m

bunion ['bʌnjən] n oignon m (au pied)

bunk [bʌŋk] n (in ship, train) couchette f; **b. beds** lits mpl superposés

bunker ['bʌŋkə(r)] n Mil & Golf bunker m; (for coal) coffre m à charbon

bunny ['bʌnɪ] (pl -ies) n Fam **b. (rabbit)** petit lapin m

bunting ['bʌntɪŋ] n (flags) guirlande f de drapeaux

buoy [bɔɪ] **1** n bouée f **2** vt Fig **to b. up** (support) soutenir

buoyant ['bɔɪənt] adj (in water) qui flotte; Fig (economy, prices) stable; Fig (person, mood) plein d'allant

burden ['bɜːdən] **1** n fardeau m; **the tax b.** la pression fiscale; Law **b. of proof** charge f de la preuve **2** vt charger (**with** de); Fig accabler (**with** de)

bureau ['bjʊərəʊ] (pl -**eaux** [-əʊz]) n (office) bureau m; Br (desk) secrétaire m; Am (chest of drawers) commode f

bureaucracy [bjʊə'rɒkrəsɪ] n bureaucratie f ▪ **bureaucrat** ['bjʊərəkræt] n bureaucrate mf

burger ['bɜːɡə(r)] n hamburger m

burglar ['bɜːɡlə(r)] n cambrioleur, -euse mf; **b. alarm** alarme f antivol ▪ **burglarize** vt Am cambrioler ▪ **burglary** (pl -ies) n cambriolage m ▪ **burgle** vt Br cambrioler

burial ['berɪəl] **1** n enterrement m **2** adj (service) funèbre; **b. ground** cimetière m

burly ['bɜːlɪ] (-ier, -iest) adj costaud

Burma ['bɜːmə] n Formerly la Birmanie ▪ **Burmese** [-'miːz] **1** adj birman **2** n Birman, -ane mf

burn [bɜːn] **1** n brûlure f **2** (pt & pp **burned** or **burnt**) vt brûler; **burnt alive** brûlé vif (f brûlée

vive); **to b. sth down** incendier qch; **to b. off** (paint) décaper au chalumeau; **to b. up** (energy) dépenser **3** vi brûler; **to b. down** (of house) être détruit par les flammes; **to b. out** (of fire) s'éteindre; (of fuse) sauter ▪ **burning 1** adj en feu; (fire) allumé; Fig (topic) brûlant; (fever) dévorant **2** n **smell of b.** odeur f de brûlé

burner ['bɜːnə(r)] n (on stove) brûleur m; Fig **to put sth on the back b.** remettre qch à plus tard

burp [bɜːp] Fam **1** n rot m **2** vi roter

burrow ['bʌrəʊ] **1** n (hole) terrier m **2** vti creuser

bursar ['bɜːsə(r)] n (in school) intendant, -ante mf

bursary ['bɜːsərɪ] (pl -ies) n (scholarship) bourse f

burst [bɜːst] **1** n (of shell) éclatement m, explosion f; (of laughter) éclat m; (of applause) salve f; (of thunder) coup m; (surge) élan m **2** (pt & pp **burst**) vt (bubble, balloon, boil) crever; (tyre) faire éclater; **to b. a blood vessel** se rompre une veine; **to b. open** (door) ouvrir brusquement; **the river b. its banks** le fleuve est sorti de son lit **3** vi (of bubble, balloon, boil, tyre, cloud) crever; (with force) (of shell, boiler, tyre) éclater; **to b. into a room** faire irruption dans une pièce; **to b. into flames** prendre feu; **to b. into tears** fondre en larmes; **to b. out laughing** éclater de rire; **to b. open** (of door) s'ouvrir brusquement ▪ **bursting** adj (full) (pockets) plein à craquer (**with** de); **b. with joy** débordant de joie; **to be b. to do** mourir d'envie de faire

bury ['berɪ] (pt & pp -**ied**) vt (body) enterrer; (hide) enfouir; (plunge) plonger (**in** dans); **to b. one's face into one's hands** enfouir son visage dans ses mains; **buried in one's work** plongé dans son travail

bus [bʌs] **1** (pl **buses** or **busses**) n autobus m, bus m; (long-distance) autocar m, car m; **by b.** en bus/en car; **b. driver/ticket** chauffeur m/ticket m de bus/car; **b. lane** couloir m de bus; **b. shelter** Abribus® m; **b. station** gare f routière; **b. stop** arrêt m de bus **2** (pt & pp **bused** or **bussed**) vt (children) transporter en bus

bush [bʊʃ] n buisson m; **the b.** (land) la brousse; **a b. of hair** une tignasse ▪ **bushy** (-ier, -iest) adj (hair, tail) touffu

bushed [bʊʃt] adj Fam (tired) crevé

busily ['bɪzɪlɪ] adv **to be b. doing sth** être très occupé à faire qch

business ['bɪznɪs] **1** n affaires fpl, commerce m; (shop) commerce m; (company, task, concern, matter) affaire f; **the textile/construction b.** l'industrie f du textile/de la construction; **the travel b.** le tourisme; **big b.** les grosses entreprises fpl; **to travel on b.** partir en voyage d'affaires; **to go out of b.** (stop trading) fermer; **to go about one's b.** vaquer à ses occupations; **it's quite a b.** c'est toute une affaire; **it's your b. to...** c'est à vous de...; **you have no b. to...** vous n'avez pas le droit de...;

that's none of your b.!, mind your own b.! ça ne vous regarde pas!; *Fam* **to mean b.** ne pas plaisanter **2** *adj* commercial; *(meeting, trip, lunch)* d'affaires; **b. card** carte *f* de visite; **b. hours** *(office)* heures *fpl* de bureau; *(shop)* heures d'ouverture; **b. school** école *f* de commerce; **b. studies** études *fpl* de commerce ▪ **businesslike** *adj* professionnel, -elle ▪ **businessman** *(pl* **-men)** *n* homme *m* d'affaires ▪ **businesswoman** *(pl* **-women)** *n* femme *f* d'affaires

busker ['bʌskə(r)] *n Br* musicien, -ienne *mf* des rues

bust [bʌst] **1** *n (statue)* buste *m*; *(of woman)* poitrine *f* **2** *adj Fam (broken)* fichu; **to go b.** *(bankrupt)* faire faillite **3** *(pt & pp* **bust** *or* **busted)** *vt Fam (break)* bousiller; *(arrest)* coffrer ▪ **bust-up** *n Fam (quarrel)* engueulade *f*; *(break-up)* rupture *f*

bustle ['bʌsəl] **1** *n* animation *f* **2** *vi* **to b. (about)** s'affairer

busy ['bɪzɪ] **1** **(-ier, -iest)** *adj* occupé; *(active)* actif, -ive; *(day)* chargé; *(street)* animé; *Am (phone, line)* occupé; **to be b. doing** *(in the process of)* être occupé à faire; **to keep sb b.** occuper qn; **to keep oneself b.** s'occuper; **the shops were very b.** il y avait plein de monde dans les magasins; *Am* **b. signal** sonnerie *f* 'occupé' **2** *vt* **to b. oneself** s'occuper *(with* **sth** à qch; **doing** à faire) ▪ **busybody** *(pl* **-ies)** *n Fam* fouineur, -euse *mf*

but [bʌt, *unstressed* bət] **1** *conj* mais **2** *prep (except)* sauf; **b. for that** sans cela; **b. for him** sans lui; **no one b. you** personne d'autre que toi; **the last b. one** l'avant-dernier, -ière *mf* **3** *adv Formal (only)* ne…que, seulement; **he's b. a child** ce n'est qu'un enfant; **one can b. try** on peut toujours essayer

butane ['bju:teɪn] *n* **b. (gas)** butane *m*

butcher ['bʊtʃə(r)] **1** *n* boucher *m*; **b.'s (shop)** boucherie *f* **2** *vt (people)* massacrer; *(animal)* abattre ▪ **butchery** *n* massacre *m* **(of** de)

butler ['bʌtlə(r)] *n* maître *m* d'hôtel

butt [bʌt] **1** *n (of cigarette)* mégot *m*; *(of gun)* crosse *f*; *Fig (of joke)* cible *f*; *Am Fam (buttocks)* derrière *m* **2** *vt (with head)* donner un coup de tête à **3** *vi* **to b. in** intervenir

butter ['bʌtə(r)] **1** *n* beurre *m*; *Br* **b. bean** = gros haricot blanc; **b. dish** beurrier *m* **2** *vt* beurrer; *Fam* **to b. sb up** passer de la pommade à qn ▪ **butterfingers** *n Fam* empoté, -ée *mf* ▪ **buttermilk** *n* babeurre *m* ▪ **butterscotch** *n* caramel *m* dur au beurre

buttercup ['bʌtəkʌp] *n* bouton-d'or *m*

butterfly ['bʌtəflaɪ] *(pl* **-ies)** *n* papillon *m*; *Fam* **to have butterflies** avoir l'estomac noué; **b. stroke** *(in swimming)* brasse *f* papillon

buttock ['bʌtək] *n* fesse *f*

button ['bʌtən] **1** *n* bouton *m*; *(of phone)* touche

f; *Am (badge)* badge *m* **2** *vt* **to b. (up)** boutonner **3** *vi* **to b. (up)** *(of garment)* se boutonner ▪ **buttonhole 1** *n* boutonnière *f* **2** *vt Fam (person)* coincer

buttress ['bʌtrɪs] **1** *n Archit* contrefort *m*; *Fig* soutien *m* **2** *vt Fig (support)* renforcer

buxom ['bʌksəm] *adj (full-bosomed)* à la poitrine généreuse

buy [baɪ] **1** *n* **a good b.** une bonne affaire **2** *(pt & pp* **bought)** *vt* **(a)** *(purchase)* acheter **(from sb** à qn; **for sb** à *ou* pour qn); **to b. back** racheter; **to b. over** *(bribe)* corrompre; **to b. up** acheter en bloc **(b)** *Am Fam (believe)* avaler; **I'll b. that!** je veux bien le croire! ▪ **buyer** *n* acheteur, -euse *mf*

buzz [bʌz] **1** *n* **(a)** *(noise)* bourdonnement *m* **(b)** *Fam (phone call)* **to give sb a b.** passer un coup de fil à qn **2** *vt* **to b. sb** *(using buzzer)* appeler qn **3** *vi* bourdonner; *Fam* **to b. off** se tirer ▪ **buzzer** *n (internal phone)* Interphone® *m*; *(of bell, clock)* sonnerie *f*

by [baɪ] **1** *prep* **(a)** *(agent)* par; de; **hit/chosen by** frappé/choisi par; **surrounded/followed by** entouré/suivi de; **a book/painting by…** un livre/tableau de…

(b) *(manner, means)* par; en; à; de; **by sea** par mer; **by mistake** par erreur; **by car/train** en voiture/train; **by bicycle** à bicyclette; **by moonlight** au clair de lune; **by doing** en faisant; **one by one** un à un; **day by day** jour en jour; **by sight/day** de vue/jour; **(all) by oneself** tout seul

(c) *(next to)* à côté de; *(near)* près de; **by the lake/sea** au bord du lac/de la mer; **to go** *or* **pass by** the bank/school passer devant la banque/l'école

(d) *(before in time)* avant; **by Monday** avant lundi, d'ici lundi; **by now** à cette heure-ci; **by yesterday** *(dès)* hier

(e) *(amount, measurement)* à; **by the kilo** au kilo; **taller by a metre** plus grand d'un mètre; **paid by the hour** payé à l'heure

(f) *(according to)* à, d'après; **by my watch** à ma montre; **it's fine** *or* **OK** *or* **all right by me** je n'y vois pas d'objection

2 *adv* **close by** tout près; **to go** *or* **pass by** passer; **by and large** en gros ▪ **by-election** *n* élection *f* partielle ▪ **by-law** *n* arrêté *m* *(municipal)* ▪ **by-product** *n* sous-produit *m* ▪ **by-road** *n* chemin *m* de traverse

bye(-bye) ['baɪ('baɪ)] *exclam Fam* salut!, au revoir!; **b. for now!** à bientôt!

bygone ['baɪgɒn] **1** *adj* **in b. days** jadis **2** *npl* **let bygones be bygones** oublions le passé

bypass ['baɪpɑːs] **1** *n* rocade *f*; **(heart) b. operation** pontage *m* **2** *vt (town)* contourner; *Fig (ignore)* court-circuiter

bystander ['baɪstændə(r)] *n* passant, -ante *mf*

byte [baɪt] *n Comptr* octet *m*

byword ['baɪwɜːd] *n* **a b. for** un synonyme de

C, c¹ [si:] *n* C, c *m inv*

c² *abbr* = **cent**

cab [kæb] *n* taxi *m*; *(of train, lorry)* cabine *f*; *Hist (horse-drawn)* fiacre *m*

cabaret ['kæbəreɪ] cabaret *m*

cabbage ['kæbɪdʒ] *n* chou *m* (*pl* choux)

cabbie, cabby ['kæbɪ] (*pl* -ies) *n Fam* chauffeur *m* de taxi

cabin ['kæbɪn] *n* (on ship, plane) cabine *f*; *(hut)* cabane *f*; *Av* **c. crew** équipage *m*

cabinet¹ ['kæbɪnɪt] *n* (cupboard) armoire *f*; (for display) vitrine *f*; **(filing) c.** classeur *m (meuble)*
■ **cabinet-maker** *n* ébéniste *m*

cabinet² ['kæbɪnɪt] *n* (government ministers) gouvernement *m*; **c. meeting** ≃ Conseil *m* des ministres; **c. minister** ministre *m*

cable ['keɪbəl] **1** *n* câble *m*; **c. car** *(with overhead cable)* téléphérique *m*; *(on tracks)* funiculaire *m*; **c. television** la télévision par câble; *Fam* **to have c.** avoir le câble **2** *vt (message)* câbler (**to** à)

cache [kæʃ] *n (place)* cachette *f*; **an arms c.** une cache d'armes

cachet ['kæfeɪ] *n (mark, character)* cachet *m*

cackle ['kækəl] **1** *n (of hen)* caquet *m*; *(laughter)* gloussement *m*; **2** *vi (of hen)* caqueter; *Fam (laugh)* glousser

cactus ['kæktəs] (*pl* **-ti** [-taɪ] *or* **-tuses** [-təsɪz]) *n* cactus *m*

cadaverous [kəˈdævərəs] *adj* cadavérique

caddie ['kædɪ] *n Golf* caddie *m*

caddy ['kædɪ] (*pl* -ies) *n* **(tea) c.** boîte *f* à thé

cadence ['keɪdəns] *n (rhythm)* & *Mus* cadence *f*

cadet [kəˈdet] *n* élève *m* officier

cadge [kædʒ] *vt Fam (meal)* se faire payer (**off sb** par qn); **to c. money from** *or* **off sb** taper qn

Caesarean [sɪˈzeərɪən] (*Am* **Cesarean**) *n* **C. (section)** césarienne *f*

caesar salad ['siːzəˈsæləd] (*Am* **cesar salad**) *n* = salade de romaine, de croûtons et d'une vinaigrette additionnée d'œuf

café ['kæfeɪ] *n* café *m*

cafeteria [kæfɪˈtɪərɪə] *n* cafétéria *f*

cafetière [kæfəˈtjeə(r)] *n (for making coffee)* cafetière *f* (à piston)

caffeine ['kæfiːn] *n* caféine *f*

cage [keɪdʒ] **1** *n* cage *f* **2** *vt* **to c. (up)** mettre en cage

cagey ['keɪdʒɪ] *adj (evasive)* évasif, -ive (**about** sur); *(cautious)* prudent

cahoots [kəˈhuːts] *n Fam* **in c.** de mèche (**with sb** avec qn)

Cairo ['kaɪərəʊ] *n* Le Caire

cajole [kəˈdʒəʊl] *vt* enjôler

cake¹ [keɪk] *n* gâteau *m*; *(small)* pâtisserie *f*; **c. shop** pâtisserie; **c. of soap** savonnette *f*; **it's a piece of c.** c'est du gâteau

cake² [keɪk] *vt* **caked with blood/mud** couvert de sang/boue

calamity [kəˈlæmɪtɪ] (*pl* -ies) *n* calamité *f*

calcium ['kælsɪəm] *n* calcium *m*

calculate ['kælkjʊleɪt] *vti* calculer; **to c. that...** *(estimate)* calculer que... ■ **calculated** *adj (deliberate)* délibéré; ■ **calculating** *adj (shrewd)* calculateur, -trice ■ **calculation** [-ˈleɪʃən] *n* calcul *m*

calculator ['kælkjʊleɪtə(r)] *n* calculatrice *f*

calculus ['kælkjʊləs] *n Math* & *Med* calcul *m*

calendar ['kælɪndə(r)] *n* calendrier *m*; *(directory)* annuaire *m*; *Am (for engagements)* agenda *m*; **c. month** mois *m* civil; **c. year** année *f* civile

calf [kɑːf] (*pl* **calves**) *n* (**a**) *(animal)* veau *m* (**b**) *(part of leg)* mollet *m*

calibre ['kælɪbə(r)] (*Am* **caliber**) *n* calibre *m* ■ **calibrate** *vt* calibrer

calico ['kælɪkəʊ] *n (fabric)* calicot *m*; *Am (printed)* indienne *f*

call [kɔːl] **1** *n (on phone)* appel *m*; *(shout)* cri *m*; *(vocation)* vocation *f*; *(visit)* visite *f*; **(telephone) c.** appel téléphonique; **to make a c.** téléphoner (**to** à); **to give sb a c.** téléphoner à qn; **to return sb's c.** rappeler qn; **on c.** *(doctor)* de garde; **there's no c. to do that** il n'y a aucune raison de faire cela; **there's no c. for that article** cet article n'est pas très demandé; *Br* **c. box** cabine *f* téléphonique; **c. centre** centre *m* d'appels; **c. girl** call-girl *f*

2 *vt (phone)* appeler; *(shout to)* crier; *(truce)* demander; **he's called David** il s'appelle David; **to c. a meeting** décider d'organiser une réunion; **to c. sb a liar** traiter qn de menteur; **she calls herself an expert** elle se dit expert; **to c. sth into question** mettre qch en question; *Fam* **let's c. it a day** ça suffit pour aujourd'hui

3 *vi* appeler; *(cry out)* crier; *(visit)* passer; **the train will c. at York** le train s'arrêtera à York

■ **call-up** n (of recruits) appel m (sous les drapeaux)

▶ **call back 1** vt sep rappeler **2** vi rappeler

▶ **call by** vi (visit) passer

▶ **call for** vt insep (require) demander; (summon) appeler; (collect) passer prendre

▶ **call in 1** vt sep (into room) faire entrer; (police) appeler; (product) rappeler **2** vi to c. in (on sb) (visit) passer (chez qn)

▶ **call off** vt sep (cancel) annuler; (strike) mettre fin à; (dog) rappeler

▶ **call on** vt insep (visit) passer voir; (invoke) invoquer; **to c. (up)on sb to do** inviter qn à faire; (urge) sommer qn de faire

▶ **call out 1** vt sep (shout) crier; (doctor) appeler; (workers) donner une consigne de grève à **2** vi (shout) crier; **to c. out to sb** interpeller qn; **to c. out for sth** demander qch à haute voix

▶ **call round** vi (visit) passer

▶ **call up** vt sep (phone) appeler; Mil (recruits) appeler (sous les drapeaux); (memories) évoquer

caller ['kɔːlə(r)] n visiteur, -euse mf; (on phone) correspondant, -ante mf; Tel **c. ID** identification f d'appel

calligraphy [kə'lɪgrəfɪ] n calligraphie f

calling ['kɔːlɪŋ] n vocation f; Am **c. card** carte f de visite

callous ['kæləs] adj (a) (cruel) insensible (b) (skin) calleux, -euse

callus ['kæləs] n cal m

calm [kɑːm] **1** (-er, -est) adj calme, tranquille; **keep c.!** restez calme! **2** n calme m **3** vt **to c. (down)** calmer **4** vi **to c. down** se calmer ■ **calmly** adv calmement ■ **calmness** n calme m

Calor Gas® ['kæləgæs] n Br Butagaz® m

calorie ['kælərɪ] n calorie f

calumny ['kæləmnɪ] n (pl -ies) n calomnie f

calve [kɑːv] vi (of cow) vêler

calves [kɑːvz] pl of **calf**

camcorder ['kæmkɔːdə(r)] n Caméscope® m

came [keɪm] pt of **come**

camel ['kæməl] n chameau m

cameo ['kæmɪəʊ] (pl -os) n (gem) camée m; **c. role** (in film) brève apparition f (d'un acteur connu)

camera ['kæmrə] n appareil photo m; **(TV or film) c.** caméra f ■ **cameraman** (pl -men) n cameraman m

camomile ['kæməmaɪl] n camomille f

camouflage ['kæməflɑːʒ] **1** n camouflage m **2** vt also Fig camoufler

camp¹ [kæmp] **1** n camp m, campement m; **c. bed** lit m de camp **2** vi **to c. (out)** camper ■ **camper** n (person) campeur, -euse mf; (vehicle) camping-car m ■ **campfire** n feu m de camp ■ **camping** n camping; **c. site** (terrain m de) camping m ■ **campsite** n camping m

camp² [kæmp] adj (effeminate) efféminé

campaign [kæm'peɪn] **1** n (political, military) campagne f; **press/publicity c.** campagne de presse/publicité **2** vi faire campagne (**for** pour; **against** contre) ■ **campaigner** n militant, -ante mf (**for** pour)

campus ['kæmpəs] n (of university) campus m

can¹ [kæn, unstressed kən] (pt **could**)

Le verbe **can** n'a ni infinitif, ni gérondif, ni participe. Pour exprimer l'infinitif ou le participe, on aura recours à la forme correspondante de **be able to** (he wanted to be able to speak English; she has always been able to swim). La forme négative est **can't**, qui s'écrit **cannot** dans la langue soutenue.

v aux (be able to) pouvoir; (know how to) savoir; **he couldn't help me** il ne pouvait pas m'aider; **she c. swim** elle sait nager; **if I could swim** si je savais nager; **he could do it tomorrow** il pourrait le faire demain; **he could have done it** il aurait pu le faire; **you could be wrong** (possibility) tu as peut-être tort; **he can't be dead** (probability) il ne peut pas être mort; **that can't be right!** ce n'est pas possible!; **c. I come in?** (permission) puis-je entrer?; **yes, you c.!** oui!; **I c. see** je vois; **as happy as c. be** aussi heureux, -euse que possible

can² [kæn] **1** n (for water) bidon m; (for food) boîte f; (for beer) can(n)ette f **2** (pt & pp -nn-) vt mettre en boîte ■ **canned** adj en boîte, en conserve; **c. beer** bière f en can(n)ette; **c. food** conserves fpl ■ **can-opener** n ouvre-boîtes m inv

Canada ['kænədə] n le Canada ■ **Canadian** [kə'neɪdɪən] **1** adj canadien, -ienne **2** n Canadien, -ienne mf

canal [kə'næl] n canal m

canary [kə'neərɪ] (pl -ies) n canari m

cancan ['kænkæn] n french cancan m

cancel ['kænsəl] **1** (Br -ll-, Am -l-) vt (flight, appointment) annuler; (goods, taxi) décommander; (train) supprimer; (word, paragraph) biffer; (cheque) faire opposition à; **to c. a ticket** (punch) (with date) composter un billet; (with hole) poinçonner un billet; **to c. each other out** s'annuler **2** vi se décommander ■ **cancellation** [-'leɪʃən] n annulation f; (of train) suppression f

Cancer ['kænsə(r)] n (sign) le Cancer; **to be (a) C.** être Cancer

cancer ['kænsə(r)] n cancer m; **stomach/skin c.** cancer de l'estomac/la peau; **c. patient** cancéreux, -euse mf; **c. specialist** cancérologue mf

candelabra [kændɪ'lɑːbrə] n candélabre m

candid ['kændɪd] adj franc (f franche) ■ **candour** (Am **candor**) n franchise f

Note that the French words **candide** and **candeur** are false friends and are never translations for the English words **candid** and **candour**. They mean **ingenuous** and **ingenuousness**.

candidate ['kændɪdeɪt] n candidat, -ate mf (**for** à); **to stand as a c.** être candidat ■**candidacy** [-dəsɪ], **candidature** [-dətʃə(r)] n candidature f

candle ['kændəl] n (wax) bougie f; (tallow) chandelle f; (in church) cierge m; **c. grease** suif m ■**candlelight** n **by c.** à la (lueur d'une) bougie; **to have dinner by c.** dîner aux chandelles ■**candlestick** n bougeoir m; (taller) chandelier m

candy ['kændɪ] (pl -ies) n Am bonbon m; (sweets) bonbons mpl; (sugar) **c.** sucre m candi; Am **c. store** confiserie f ■**candied** adj (fruit) confit ■**candyfloss** n Br barbe f à papa

cane [keɪn] **1** n (stick) canne f; (for basket) rotin m; (for punishment) baguette f **2** vt (punish) frapper avec une baguette

canine ['keɪnaɪn] **1** adj (tooth, race) canin **2** n (tooth) canine f

canister ['kænɪstə(r)] n boîte f (en métal)

cannabis ['kænəbɪs] n (drug) cannabis m; (plant) chanvre m indien

cannibal ['kænɪbəl] n cannibale mf

cannon ['kænən] (pl -s or **cannon**) n canon m ■**cannonball** n boulet m de canon

cannot ['kænɒt] = **can not**

canny ['kænɪ] (-ier, -iest) adj rusé

canoe [kə'nuː] **1** n canoë m; (dugout) pirogue f **2** vi faire du canoë-kayak ■**canoeing** n **to go c.** faire du canoë-kayak ■**canoeist** n canoëiste mf

canon ['kænən] n (law) & Fig canon m; (priest) chanoine m ■**canonize** vt Rel canoniser

canopy ['kænəpɪ] (pl -ies) n (of baby carriage) capote f; (awning) auvent m; (over bed) baldaquin m; (over altar) dais m; (made of glass) marquise f; Fig (of tree branches) canopée f

can't [kɑːnt] = **can not**

cantaloup(e) ['kæntəluːp] n (melon) cantaloup m

cantankerous [kæn'tæŋkərəs] adj acariâtre

cantata [kæn'tɑːtə] n Mus cantate f

canteen [kæn'tiːn] n (in school, factory) cantine f; (flask) gourde f; Br **c. of cutlery** ménagère f

canter ['kæntə(r)] **1** n petit galop m **2** vi aller au petit galop

canvas ['kænvəs] n (a) (cloth) (grosse) toile f; (for embroidery) canevas m; **under c.** (in a tent) sous la tente (b) Art toile f

canvass ['kænvəs] vt (area) faire du démarchage dans; (opinions) sonder; **to c. sb** (seek votes) solliciter le suffrage de qn; (seek orders) solliciter des commandes de qn ■**canvasser** n Pol agent m électoral; Com démarcheur, -euse mf ■**canvassing** n (for orders) démarchage m; (for votes) démarchage électoral

canyon ['kænjən] n cañon m, canyon m

CAP [siːeɪ'piː] (abbr common agricultural policy) n PAC f

cap¹ [kæp] n (a) (hat) casquette f; (for shower, of sailor) bonnet m; (of soldier) képi m (b) (of tube, valve) bouchon m; (of bottle) capsule f; (of pen) capuchon m (c) (of child's gun) amorce f (d) (Dutch) **c.** (contraceptive) diaphragme m

cap² [kæp] (pt & pp **-pp-**) vt (a) (outdo) surpasser; **to c. it all...** pour couronner le tout... (b) Br (spending) limiter (c) (cover) capped with recouvert de; **capped with snow** coiffé de neige

capable ['keɪpəbəl] adj (person) capable (**of sth** de qch; **of doing** de faire) ■**capa'bility** n capacité f ■**capably** adv avec compétence

capacity [kə'pæsɪtɪ] (pl -ies) n (of container) capacité f; (ability) aptitude f, capacité f (**for sth** pour qch; **for doing** à faire); (output) rendement m; **in my c. as a doctor** en ma qualité de médecin; **in an advisory c.** à titre consultatif; **filled to c.** (concert hall) comble

cape [keɪp] n (a) (cloak) cape f; (of cyclist) pèlerine f (b) (of coast) cap m; **C. Town** Le Cap

caper¹ ['keɪpə(r)] n Culin câpre f

caper² ['keɪpə(r)] **1** n (prank) cabriole f **2** vi (jump about) faire des cabrioles

capital ['kæpɪtəl] **1** adj (letter, importance) capital; **c. punishment** peine f capitale **2** n (a) **c. (city)** capitale f; **c. (letter)** majuscule f (b) (money) capital m ■**capitalism** n capitalisme m ■**capitalist** adj & n capitaliste (mf) ■**capitalize** vi **to c. on** tirer parti de

capitulate [kə'pɪtjʊleɪt] vi capituler (**to** devant) ■**capitu'lation** n capitulation f

cappuccino [kæpʊ'tʃiːnəʊ] n cappuccino m

caprice [kə'priːs] n caprice m ■**capricious** [kə'prɪʃəs] adj capricieux, -ieuse

Capricorn ['kæprɪkɔːn] n (sign) le Capricorne; **to be (a) C.** être Capricorne

capsicum ['kæpsɪkəm] n poivron m

capsize [kæp'saɪz] **1** vt faire chavirer **2** vi chavirer

capsule [Br 'kæpsjuːl, Am 'kæpsəl] n (of medicine) gélule f; (space) **c.** capsule f spatiale

captain ['kæptɪn] **1** n capitaine m **2** vt (ship) commander; (team) être le capitaine de

caption ['kæpʃən] n (of illustration) légende f; (of film, article) sous-titre m

captivate ['kæptɪveɪt] vt captiver ■**captivating** adj captivant

captive ['kæptɪv] n captif, -ive mf; **to be taken c.** être fait prisonnier ■**cap'tivity** n captivité f; **in c.** en captivité

capture ['kæptʃə(r)] **1** n capture f; (of town)

prise f **2** vt (person, animal, ship) capturer; (escaped prisoner or animal) reprendre; (town) prendre; (attention) capter; Fig (mood) rendre
car [kɑː(r)] n voiture f, automobile f; (train carriage) wagon m, voiture; **c. insurance/ industry** assurance f/industrie f automobile; **the c. door** la portière de la voiture; **c. bomb** voiture f piégée; Br **c. boot sale** = vente à la brocante où les marchandises sont exposées à l'arrière de voitures; **c. chase** poursuite f en voiture; **c. crash** accident m de voiture; **c. ferry** ferry m; Br **c. hire** location f de voitures; Br **c. park** parking m; **c. phone** téléphone m de voiture; **c. radio** autoradio m; **c. rental** location f de voitures; **c. wash** (machine) = station de lavage automatique pour voitures; (sign) lavage m automatique ▪**carpool** n = groupe de personnes effectuant régulièrement un trajet dans la même voiture ▪**carpooling** n covoiturage m ▪**carport** n abri m pour voiture ▪**carsick** adj to be c. être malade en voiture

Note that the French word **car** is a false friend and is never a translation for the English word **car**. It means **coach**.

carafe [kəˈræf] n carafe f
caramel [ˈkærəməl] n caramel m
carat [ˈkærət] (Am **karat**) n carat m; **18-c. gold** or m (à) 18 carats
caravan [ˈkærəvæn] n caravane f; (horse-drawn) roulotte f; **c. site** camping m pour caravanes
caraway [ˈkærəweɪ] n (plant) carvi m; **c. seeds** graines fpl de carvi
carbohydrates [kɑːbəʊˈhaɪdreɪts] npl hydrates mpl de carbone
carbon [ˈkɑːbən] n carbone m; **c. dioxide** dioxyde m de carbone, gaz m carbonique; **c. fibre** fibre f de carbone; **c. paper** (papier m) carbone
carburettor [kɑːbjʊˈretə(r)] (Am **carburetor** [ˈkɑːrbəreɪtər]) n carburateur m
carcass [ˈkɑːkəs] n carcasse f
card [kɑːd] n carte f; (cardboard) carton m; (index) fiche f; **c. game** jeu m de cartes; **c. index** fichier m; Rel cardinal m de jeu; **to play cards** jouer aux cartes; **it is** Br **on** or Am **in the cards that...** il est bien possible que... ▪**cardphone** n téléphone m à carte
cardboard [ˈkɑːdbɔːd] n carton m; **c. box** boîte f en carton, carton
cardiac [ˈkɑːdɪæk] adj cardiaque; **c. arrest** arrêt m du cœur
cardigan [ˈkɑːdɪɡən] n cardigan m
cardinal [ˈkɑːdɪnəl] **1** adj (number, point) cardinal **2** n Rel cardinal m
care [keə(r)] **1** n (attention) soin m; (protection) soins mpl; (worry) souci m; **to take c. to do** veiller à faire; **to take c. not to do** faire attention à ne pas faire; **to take c. of sb/sth**

s'occuper de qn/qch; **to take c. of oneself** (manage) savoir se débrouiller tout seul; (keep healthy) faire bien attention à soi; **that will take c. of itself** ça s'arrangera; **take c.!** (goodbye) au revoir!; **'c. of'** (on envelope) 'chez'
2 vt **I don't c. what he says** peu m'importe ce qu'il en dit; **would you c. to try?** voulez-vous essayer?
3 vi **I don't c.** ça m'est égal; **I couldn't c. less** ça m'est complètement égal; **who cares?** qu'est-ce que ça peut faire?; **to c. about** (feel concern about) se soucier de; **I don't c. for it (much)** je n'aime pas tellement ça; **to c. for a drink/a change** avoir envie d'un verre/d'un changement; **to c. about** or **for sb** (be fond of) avoir de la sympathie pour qn; **to c. for sb** (look after) soigner qn
career [kəˈrɪə(r)] **1** n carrière f; **to make a c. in sth** faire carrière dans qch **2** adj (diplomat) de carrière; **the job has c. prospects** cet emploi offre des perspectives de carrière; **it's a good c. move** c'est bon pour ma/ta/etc carrière **3** vi **to c. along** aller à vive allure
carefree [ˈkeəfriː] adj insouciant
careful [ˈkeəfəl] adj (exact, thorough) soigneux, -euse (about de); (work) minutieux, -ieuse; (cautious) prudent; **c. (about** or **with money)** regardant (à la dépense); **to be c. of** or **with sth** faire attention à qch; **to be c. to do** veiller à faire; **to be c. not to do** faire attention à ne pas faire; **be c.!** (fais) attention!; **be c. she doesn't see you!** (fais) attention qu'elle ne te voie pas! ▪**carefully** adv (thoroughly) avec soin; (cautiously) prudemment
careless [ˈkeələs] adj négligent; (absentminded) étourdi; (work) peu soigné; **c. about one's work** peu soigneux dans son travail; **c. about one's appearance** négligé; **c. mistake** faute f d'étourderie ▪**carelessness** n négligence f
carer [ˈkeərə(r)] n (relative) = personne s'occupant d'un parent malade ou âgé
caress [kəˈres] **1** n caresse f **2** vt (stroke) caresser; (kiss) embrasser
caretaker [ˈkeəteɪkə(r)] n gardien, -ienne mf, concierge mf
cargo [ˈkɑːɡəʊ] (pl -oes or -os) n cargaison f; **c. ship** cargo m

Note that the French word **cargo** is a false friend and is never a translation for the English word **cargo**. It means **cargo ship**.

Caribbean [Br kærɪˈbiːən, Am kəˈrɪbɪən] **1** adj caraïbe **2** n **the C. (islands)** les Antilles fpl
caricature [ˈkærɪkətʊə(r)] **1** n caricature f **2** vt caricaturer
caring [ˈkeərɪŋ] **1** adj (loving) aimant; (understanding) très humain **2** n affection f
carnage [ˈkɑːnɪdʒ] n carnage m
carnal [ˈkɑːnəl] adj charnel, -elle

carnation [kɑːˈneɪʃən] n œillet m

carnival [ˈkɑːnɪvəl] n carnaval m (pl -als)

carnivore [ˈkɑːnɪvɔː(r)] n carnivore m ▪ **carnivorous** [-ˈnɪvərəs] adj carnivore

carol [ˈkærəl] n chant m de Noël

carouse [kəˈraʊz] vi faire la fête

carp [kɑːp] 1 n inv (fish) carpe f 2 vi se plaindre (at de)

carpenter [ˈkɑːpɪntə(r)] n (for house building) charpentier m; (for light woodwork) menuisier m ▪ **carpentry** n charpenterie f; (for light woodwork) menuiserie f

carpet [ˈkɑːpɪt] 1 n (rug) & Fig tapis m; (fitted) moquette f; **c. sweeper** balai m mécanique 2 vt recouvrir d'un tapis/d'une moquette; Fig (of snow) recouvrir ▪ **carpeting** n (rugs) tapis mpl; **(wall-to-wall) c.** moquette f

> Note that the French word **carpette** is a false friend and is never a translation for the English word **carpet**. It means **small rug**.

carriage [ˈkærɪdʒ] n Br (of train) voiture f; (horse-drawn) voiture, équipage m; Br (transport of goods) transport m; (cost) frais mpl; (of typewriter) chariot m; Br **c. paid** port payé

carriageway [ˈkærɪdʒweɪ] n Br chaussée f

carrier [ˈkærɪə(r)] n (of illness) porteur, -euse mf; (company, airline) transporteur m; Br **c. (bag)** sac m en plastique; **c. pigeon** pigeon m voyageur

carrot [ˈkærət] n carotte f

carry [ˈkærɪ] (pt & pp **-ied**) 1 vt porter; (goods, passengers) transporter; (gun, money) avoir sur soi; (by wind) emporter; (sound) conduire; (disease) être porteur de; (sell) stocker; Pol (motion) faire passer, voter; Math (in calculation) retenir; **to c. water to** (of pipe) amener de l'eau à; **to c. responsibility** (of job) comporter des responsabilités; Fam **to c. the can** porter le chapeau; **to c. sth too far** pousser qch trop loin; **to c. oneself** se comporter 2 vi (of sound) porter ▪ **carryall** [ˈkærɪɔːl] n Am (bag) fourre-tout m inv ▪ **carrycot** [ˈkærɪkɒt] n Br porte-bébé m inv

▸ **carry away** vt sep emporter; Fig (of idea) transporter; **to be** or **get carried away** (excited) s'emballer

▸ **carry back** vt sep (thing) rapporter; (person) ramener; (in thought) reporter

▸ **carry forward** vt sep (in bookkeeping) reporter

▸ **carry off** vt sep (take away) emporter; (kidnap) enlever; (prize) remporter; **she carried it off** elle s'en est bien sortie

▸ **carry on 1** vt sep (continue) continuer (**doing** à faire); (negotiations) mener; (conversation) poursuivre 2 vi (continue) continuer; Pej (behave badly) se conduire mal; (complain) se plaindre; **to c. on with sth** continuer qch

▸ **carry out** vt sep (plan, promise) mettre à exécution; (order) exécuter; (repair, reform) effectuer; (duty) accomplir; Am (meal) emporter

▸ **carry through** vt sep (plan) mener à bien

cart [kɑːt] 1 n (horse-drawn) charrette f; (handcart) voiture f à bras; Am (in supermarket) Caddie® m 2 vt (goods, people) transporter; Fam **to c. (around)** trimbaler; **to c. away** emporter ▪ **carthorse** n cheval m de trait

cartel [kɑːˈtel] n Econ cartel m

cartilage [ˈkɑːtɪlɪdʒ] n cartilage m

carton [ˈkɑːtən] n (box) carton m; (of milk, fruit juice) brique f; (of cigarettes) cartouche f; (of cream) pot m

cartoon [kɑːˈtuːn] n (in newspaper) dessin m humoristique; (film) dessin animé; **c. (strip)** bande f dessinée

cartridge [ˈkɑːtrɪdʒ] n cartouche f; **c. belt** cartouchière f

cartwheel [ˈkɑːtwiːl] n **to do a c.** faire la roue

carve [kɑːv] vt (cut) tailler (**out of** dans); (name) graver; (sculpt) sculpter; **to c. (up)** (meat) découper; **to c. up** (country) morceler; **to c. out a career for oneself** faire carrière ▪ **carving 1** adj **c. knife** couteau m à découper 2 n (wood) **c.** sculpture f sur bois

cascade [kæsˈkeɪd] 1 n cascade f 2 vi tomber en cascade

case¹ [keɪs] n (instance, situation) & Med cas m; Law affaire f; Fig (arguments) arguments mpl; **in any c.** en tout cas; **in c. it rains** au cas où il pleuvrait; **in c. of** en cas de; **(just) in c.** au cas où

case² [keɪs] n (bag) valise f; (crate) caisse f; (for pen, glasses, camera, violin, cigarettes) étui m; (for jewels) écrin m

cash [kæʃ] 1 n (coins, banknotes) liquide m; Fam (money) sous mpl; **to pay (in) c.** payer en liquide; **to pay c. (down)** (not on credit) payer comptant; **to have c. flow problems** avoir des problèmes d'argent; **c. box** caisse f; Br **c. desk** caisse; **c. dispenser** or **machine** distributeur m de billets; **c. price** prix m (au) comptant; **c. register** caisse f enregistreuse 2 vt **to c. a cheque** or Am **check** (of person) encaisser un chèque; (of bank) payer un chèque; Fam **to c. in on** (situation) profiter de ▪ **cashback** n Br = espèces retirées de la caisse d'un magasin lors d'un paiement par carte

cashew [ˈkæʃuː] n **c. (nut)** noix f de cajou

cashier [kæˈʃɪə(r)] n caissier, -ière mf

cashmere [ˈkæʃmɪə(r)] n cachemire m

casing [ˈkeɪsɪŋ] n Tech boîtier m; (of sausage) boyau m

casino [kəˈsiːnəʊ] (pl -os) n casino m

cask [kɑːsk] n fût m, tonneau m ▪ **casket** n (box) coffret m; (coffin) cercueil m

casserole [ˈkæsərəʊl] n (covered dish) cocotte f; (stew) ragoût m

Note that the French word **casserole** is a false friend and is never a translation for the English word **casserole**. It means **saucepan**.

cassette [kə'set] *n (audio, video)* cassette *f*; *(for camera)* cartouche *f*; **c. player** lecteur *m* de cassettes; **c. recorder** magnétophone *m* à cassettes

cassock ['kæsək] *n* soutane *f*

cast [kɑːst] **1** *n (actors)* acteurs *mpl*; *(list of actors)* distribution *f*; *(mould)* moulage *m*; *(of dice)* coup *m*; *(for broken bone)* plâtre *m*; *Med* **in a c.** dans le plâtre; **to have a c. in one's eye** avoir une coquetterie dans l'œil **2** *(pt & pp* **cast)** *vt (throw)* jeter; *(light, shadow)* projeter; *(blame)* rejeter; *(glance)* jeter **(at** à *ou* sur); *(metal)* couler; *(theatrical role)* distribuer; *(actor)* donner un rôle à; **to c. doubt on sth** jeter le doute sur qch; **to c. a spell on sb** jeter un sort à qn; **to c. one's mind back** se reporter en arrière; **to c. a vote** voter; **to c. aside** rejeter; **c. iron** fonte *f* **3** *vi* **to c. off** *(of ship)* appareiller ▪ **cast-'iron** *adj (pan)* en fonte; *Fig (will)* de fer; *Fig (alibi, excuse)* en béton

castaway ['kɑːstəweɪ] *n* naufragé, -ée *mf*

caste [kɑːst] *n* caste *f*

caster ['kɑːstə(r)] *n (wheel)* roulette *f*; *Br* **c. sugar** sucre *m* en poudre

castle ['kɑːsəl] *n* château *m*; *(in chess)* tour *f*

castoffs ['kɑːstɒfs] *npl* vieux vêtements *mpl*

castor ['kɑːstə(r)] *n (wheel)* roulette *f*; **c. oil** huile *f* de ricin; *Br* **c. sugar** sucre *m* en poudre

castrate [kæ'streɪt] *vt* châtrer ▪ **castration** *n* castration *f*

casual ['kæʒjʊəl] *adj (offhand) (remark, glance)* en passant; *(relaxed, informal)* décontracté; *(conversation)* à bâtons rompus; *(clothes)* sport *inv*; *(careless)* désinvolte; *(meeting)* fortuit; *(employment, worker)* temporaire ▪ **casually** *adv (remark, glance)* en passant; *(informally)* avec décontraction; *(dress)* sport; *(carelessly)* avec désinvolture; *(meet)* par hasard

casualty ['kæʒjʊəltɪ] *(pl* **-ies)** *n* victime *f*; *Br* **c. (department)** *(in hospital)* (service *m* des) urgences *fpl*

cat [kæt] *n* chat *m*; *(female)* chatte *f*; **c. burglar** monte-en-l'air *m inv*; *Br* **c.'s eyes®** Cataphotes® *mpl*; **c. food** pâtée *f*

catalogue ['kætəlɒɡ] *(Am* **catalog)** **1** *n* catalogue *m* **2** *vt* cataloguer

catalyst ['kætəlɪst] *n Chem & Fig* catalyseur *m*

catapult ['kætəpʌlt] **1** *n (toy)* lance-pierres *m inv*; *(on aircraft carrier)* catapulte *f* **2** *vt* catapulter

cataract ['kætərækt] *n Med* cataracte *f*

catarrh [kə'tɑː(r)] *n Br* gros rhume *m*

catastrophe [kə'tæstrəfɪ] *n* catastrophe *f* ▪ **catastrophic** [kætə'strɒfɪk] *adj* catastrophique

catcall ['kætkɔːl] *n* sifflet *m*

catch [kætʃ] **1** *n (captured animal)* capture *f*, prise *f*; *(in fishing)* prise; *(of a whole day)* pêche *f*; *(difficulty)* piège *m*; *(on door)* loquet *m*; **there's a c.** il y a un piège **2** *(pt & pp* **caught)** *vt (ball, thief, illness)* attraper; *(fish, train, bus)* prendre; *(grab)* prendre, saisir; *(surprise)* surprendre; *(understand)* saisir; *(garment)* accrocher **(on** à); **to c. one's fingers in the door** se prendre les doigts dans la porte; **to c. sb's eye** *or* **attention** attirer l'attention de qn; **to c. sight of sb/sth** apercevoir qn/qch; **to c. fire** prendre feu; **to c. the sun** *(of garden, room)* être ensoleillé; *(of person)* prendre des couleurs; *Fam* **to c. sb (in)** trouver qn *(chez soi)*; **to c. one's breath** *(rest a while)* reprendre haleine; *(stop breathing)* retenir son souffle; **to c. sb doing** surprendre qn à faire; **to c. sb out** prendre qn en défaut; **to c. sb up** rattraper qn **3** *vi (of fire)* prendre; **her skirt (got) caught in the door** sa jupe s'est prise dans la porte; **to c. on** *(become popular)* prendre; *Fam (understand)* piger; **to c. up with sb** rattraper qn ▪ **catching** *adj (illness)* contagieux, -ieuse ▪ **catchphrase** *n (of politician)* slogan *m*; *(of comedian)* formule *f* favorite

catchy ['kætʃɪ] *(-ier, -iest)* *adj Fam (tune, slogan)* facile à retenir

catechism ['kætɪkɪzəm] *n* catéchisme *m*

category ['kætɪɡərɪ] *(pl* **-ies)** *n* catégorie *f* ▪ **categorical** [-'ɡɒrɪkəl] *adj* catégorique ▪ **categorize** *vt* classer *(par catégories)*

cater ['keɪtə(r)] *vi (provide food)* s'occuper des repas *(for* pour); **to c. to,** *Br* **to c. for** *(need, taste)* satisfaire; *(of book, newspaper)* s'adresser à ▪ **caterer** *n* traiteur *m* ▪ **catering** *n* restauration *f*; **to do the c.** s'occuper des repas

caterpillar ['kætəpɪlə(r)] *n* chenille *f*; **c. track** chenille

catgut ['kætɡʌt] *n (cord)* boyau *m*

cathedral [kə'θiːdrəl] *n* cathédrale *f*

Catholic ['kæθlɪk] *adj & n* catholique *(mf)* ▪ **Catholicism** [kə'çθɒlɪsɪzəm] *n* catholicisme *m*

cattle ['kætəl] *npl* bétail *m*

catty ['kætɪ] *(-ier, -iest)* *adj Fam (spiteful)* vache

catwalk ['kætwɔːk] *n Br (in fashion show)* podium *m*

caught [kɔːt] *pt & pp of* **catch**

cauldron ['kɔːldrən] *n* chaudron *m*

cauliflower ['kɒlɪflaʊə(r)] *n* chou-fleur *m*; *Br* **c. cheese** chou-fleur au gratin

cause [kɔːz] **1** *n (origin, ideal, aim) & Law* cause *f*; *(reason)* raison *f*, motif *m* **(of** de); **c. for complaint/dispute** sujet *m* de plainte/dispute; **to have c. for complaint** avoir des raisons de se plaindre; **to have no c. to worry** n'avoir aucune raison de s'inquiéter **2** *vt* causer, occasionner; **to c. trouble for sb** créer *ou* causer des ennuis à qn; **to c. sb/sth to fall** faire tomber qn/qch

causeway ['kɔːzweɪ] n chaussée f (sur un marécage)

caustic ['kɔːstɪk] adj (substance, remark) caustique; **c. soda** soude f caustique

cauterize ['kɔːtəraɪz] vt (wound) cautériser

caution ['kɔːʃən] 1 n (care) prudence f; (warning) avertissement m 2 vt (warn) avertir; Sport donner un avertissement à; **to c. sb against sth** mettre qn en garde contre qch; **to c. sb against doing sth** déconseiller à qn de faire qch

> Note that the French noun **caution** is a false friend and is never a translation for the English noun **caution**. Its most common meanings are **deposit** or **guarantee**. Note also that the French verb **cautionner** is a false friend. It never means **to warn**.

cautionary ['kɔːʃənərɪ] adj **c. tale** conte m moral

cautious ['kɔːʃəs] adj prudent ▪ **cautiously** adv prudemment

cavalier [kævə'lɪə(r)] 1 adj cavalier, -ière 2 n Hist (horseman, knight) cavalier m

cavalry ['kævəlrɪ] n cavalerie f

cave [keɪv] 1 n grotte f 2 vi **to c. in** (of ceiling) s'effondrer; (of floor) s'affaisser ▪ **caveman** (pl -men) n homme m des cavernes

> Note that the French word **cave** is a false friend and is never a translation for the English word **cave**. It means **cellar**.

cavern ['kævən] n caverne f

caviar(e) ['kævɪɑː(r)] n caviar m

cavity ['kævɪtɪ] n cavité f

cavort [kə'vɔːt] vi Fam faire des cabrioles; **to c. naked** se balader tout nu

CCTV [siːsiːtiːˈviː] (abbr **closed-circuit television**) n télévision f en circuit fermé

CD [siːˈdiː] (abbr **compact disc**) n CD m; **CD burner** or **writer** graveur m de CD; **CD player** lecteur m de CD

CD-ROM [siːdiːˈrɒm] (abbr **compact disc read-only memory**) n Comptr CD-ROM m inv

cease [siːs] 1 vt cesser (**doing** de faire); **to c. fire** cesser le feu 2 vi cesser (**from doing** de faire) ▪ **cease-fire** n cessez-le-feu m inv ▪ **ceaseless** adj incessant ▪ **ceaselessly** adv sans cesse

cedar ['siːdə(r)] n (tree, wood) cèdre m

cedilla [sɪˈdɪlə] n Grammar cédille f

ceiling ['siːlɪŋ] n (of room) & Fig (limit) plafond m; Fam **to hit the c.** piquer une crise

celebrate ['selɪbreɪt] 1 vt (event) célébrer, fêter; (mass) célébrer 2 vi faire la fête; **we should c.!** il faut fêter ça! ▪ **celebration** [-'breɪʃən] n (event) fête f; **the celebrations** les festivités fpl

celebrity [səˈlebrɪtɪ] (pl -ies) n célébrité f ▪ **celeb** n Br Fam célébrité f

celery ['selərɪ] n céleri m; **stick of c.** branche f de céleri

celibate ['selɪbət] adj **to be c.** ne pas avoir de rapports sexuels; (by choice) être chaste ▪ **celibacy** n absence f de rapports sexuels; (by choice) chasteté f

> Note that the French word **célibataire** is a false friend and is never a translation for the English word **celibate**. It means **unmarried**.

cell [sel] n cellule f; El élément m; Am **c. (phone)** portable m

cellar ['selə(r)] n cave f

> Note that the French word **cellier** is a false friend. It means **storeroom**.

cello ['tʃeləʊ] (pl -os) n violoncelle m ▪ **cellist** n violoncelliste mf

cellophane® ['seləfeɪn] n Br Cellophane® f

cellular ['seljʊlə(r)] adj cellulaire; **c. blanket** couverture f en cellular; Am **c. phone** téléphone m portable

celluloid® ['seljʊlɔɪd] n Celluloïd® m

cellulose ['seljʊləʊs] n cellulose f

Celsius ['selsɪəs] adj Celsius inv

Celt [kelt] n Celte mf ▪ **Celtic** adj celtique, celte

cement [sɪˈment] 1 n ciment m; **c. mixer** bétonnière f 2 vt cimenter

cemetery ['semətrɪ] (pl -ies) n cimetière m

cenotaph ['senətɑːf] n cénotaphe m

censor ['sensə(r)] 1 n censeur m 2 vt censurer ▪ **censorship** n censure f

censure ['senʃə(r)] 1 n critique f; **c. motion, vote of c.** motion f de censure 2 vt (criticize) blâmer

> Note that the French verb **censurer** is a false friend and is never a translation for the English verb **to censure**. It means **to censor**.

census ['sensəs] n recensement m

cent [sent] n (coin) cent m; Fam **not a c.** pas un sou

centenary [Br sen'tiːnərɪ, Am sen'tenərɪ] (pl -ies) n centenaire m

center ['sentə(r)] n Am = **centre**

centigrade ['sentɪgreɪd] adj centigrade

centimetre ['sentɪmiːtə(r)] n centimètre m

centipede ['sentɪpiːd] n mille-pattes m inv

central ['sentrəl] adj central; **C. London** le centre de Londres; **c. heating** chauffage m central; Br **c. reservation** (on motorway) terreplein m central ▪ **centralize** vt centraliser

centre ['sentə(r)] (Am **center**) 1 n centre m; Football **c. forward** avant-centre m 2 vt (attention, interest) concentrer (**on** sur)

centrifugal [sen'trɪfjʊgəl] adj centrifuge

century ['sentʃərɪ] (pl -ies) n siècle m; **in the twenty-first c.** au vingt et unième siècle

ceramic [sə'ræmɪk] *adj (tile)* en céramique **• ceramics 1** *npl (objects)* céramiques *fpl* **2** *n (art)* céramique *f*

cereal ['sɪərɪəl] *n* céréale *f*; **(breakfast) c.** céréales *fpl (pour petit déjeuner)*

cerebral [*Br* 'serɪbrəl, *Am* sə'riːbrəl] *adj* cérébral

ceremony ['serɪmənɪ] *(pl -ies) n (event)* cérémonie *f*; **to stand on c.** faire des façons **• ceremonial** [-'məʊnɪəl] **1** *adj* **c. dress** tenue *f* de cérémonie **2** *n* cérémonial *m* **• ceremonious** [-'məʊnɪəs] *adj* cérémonieux, -ieuse

certain ['sɜːtən] *adj* **(a)** *(sure)* certain *(that* que*)*; **she's c. to come, she'll come for c.** c'est certain qu'elle viendra; **I'm not c. what to do** je ne sais pas très bien quoi faire; **be c. you go!** il faut absolument que tu y ailles!; **to be c. of sth** être certain *ou* sûr de qch; **to make c. of sth** *(find out)* s'assurer de qch; *(be sure to get)* s'assurer qch; **for c.** *(say, know)* avec certitude **(b)** *(particular, some)* certain; **a c. person** une certaine personne; **c. people** certaines personnes **• certainly** *adv (undoubtedly)* certainement; *(yes)* bien sûr; *(without fail)* sans faute **• certainty** *(pl -ies) n* certitude *f*

certificate [sə'tɪfɪkɪt] *n* certificat *m*; *(from university)* diplôme *m*

certify ['sɜːtɪfaɪ] *(pt & pp -ied)* **1** *vt (document, signature)* certifier; **to c. sb (insane)** déclarer que l'état de santé de qn nécessite son internement psychiatrique; *Am* **certified letter** ≃ lettre *f* recommandée; *Am* **certified public accountant** expert-comptable *m* **2** *vi* **to c. to sth** attester qch

cervix ['sɜːvɪks] *(pl -vices* ['-vɪsiːz]) *n Anat* col *m* de l'utérus

cesspool ['sespuːl] *n* fosse *f* d'aisances; *Fig* cloaque *m*

CFC [siːef'siː] *(abbr* **chlorofluorocarbon**) *n* CFC *m*

chador [tʃa:dɔː(r)] *n (veil)* tchador *m*

chafe [tʃeɪf] *vt (skin)* irriter; *(of shoes)* blesser

chaff [tʃæf] *vt (tease)* taquiner

chaffinch ['tʃæfɪntʃ] *n (bird)* pinson *m*

chain [tʃeɪn] **1** *n (of rings, mountains)* chaîne *f*; *(of ideas)* enchaînement *m*; *(of events)* suite *f*; *(of lavatory)* chasse *f* d'eau; **c. reaction** réaction *f* en chaîne; **c. saw** tronçonneuse *f*; **c. store** magasin *m* à succursales multiples **2** *vt* **to c. (down)** enchaîner; **to c. (up)** *(dog)* mettre à l'attache **• chain-smoker** *n* **to be a c.** fumer cigarette sur cigarette

chair [tʃeə(r)] **1** *n* chaise *f*; *(armchair)* fauteuil *m*; *Univ (of professor)* chaire *f*; **the c.** *(office of chairperson)* la présidence; **c. lift** télésiège *m* **2** *vt (meeting)* présider **• chairman** *(pl -men) n* président, -ente *mf* **• chairmanship** *n* présidence *f*

chalet ['ʃæleɪ] *n* chalet *m*

chalk [tʃɔːk] **1** *n* craie *f*; **they are like c. and**

cheese c'est le jour et la nuit; *Fam* **not by a long c.** loin de là **2** *vt* marquer à la craie; *Fig* **to c. up** *(success)* remporter **• chalky (-ier, -iest)** *adj* crayeux, -euse

challenge ['tʃælɪndʒ] **1** *n* défi *m*; *(task)* challenge *m*, gageure *f*; **a c. for sth** *(bid)* une tentative d'obtenir qch **2** *vt* défier **(sb to do** qn de faire); *(question, dispute)* contester **• challenger** *n Sport* challenger *m* **• challenging** *adj (book, job)* stimulant

chamber ['tʃeɪmbə(r)] *n (room, assembly, of gun)* chambre *f*; *Br Law* **chambers** *(of judge)* cabinet *m*; **C. of Commerce** Chambre *f* de commerce; **c. music/orchestra** musique *f*/orchestre *m* de chambre; **c. pot** pot *m* de chambre **• chambermaid** *n* femme *f* de chambre

chameleon [kə'miːlɪən] *n* caméléon *m*

chamois ['ʃæmɪ] *n* **c. (leather)** peau *f* de chamois

champagne [ʃæm'peɪn] *n* champagne *m*

champion ['tʃæmpɪən] **1** *n* champion, -ionne *mf*; **c. skier, skiing c.** champion, -ionne de ski **2** *vt (support)* se faire le champion de **• championship** *n* championnat *m*

chance [tʃɑːns] **1** *n (luck)* hasard *m*; *(possibility)* chance *f*; *(opportunity)* occasion *f*; *(risk)* risque *m*; **by c.** par hasard; **by any c.** *(possibly)* par hasard; **to have the c. to do sth** *or* **of doing sth** avoir l'occasion de faire qch; **to give sb a c.** donner une chance à qn; **to take a c.** tenter le coup; **on the off c. (that) you could help me** au cas où tu pourrais m'aider **2** *adj (remark)* fait au hasard; **c. meeting** rencontre *f* fortuite; **c. occurrence** événement *m* fortuit **3** *vt* **to c. doing sth** prendre le risque de faire qch; **to c. to do sth** faire qch par hasard; **to c. it** risquer le coup

Note that the French noun **chance** is a false friend. Its most common meaning is **luck**.

chancellor ['tʃɑːnsələ(r)] *n Pol* chancelier *m* **• chancellery** *n* chancellerie *f*

chandelier [ʃændə'lɪə(r)] *n* lustre *m*

Note that the French word **chandelier** is a false friend. It means **candlestick**.

change [tʃeɪndʒ] **1** *n* changement *m*; *(money)* monnaie *f*; **for a c.** pour changer; **it makes a c. from...** ça change de...; **to have a c. of heart** changer d'avis; **a c. of clothes** des vêtements de rechange

2 *vt (modify)* changer; *(exchange)* échanger **(for** pour *ou* contre); *(money)* changer **(into** en); *(transform)* changer, transformer **(into** en); **to c. trains/one's skirt** changer de train/ de jupe; **to c. gear** *(in vehicle)* changer de vitesse; **to c. colour** changer de couleur; **to c. the subject** changer de sujet; **to get changed** *(put on other clothes)* se changer

3 *vi (alter)* changer; *(change clothes)* se changer; **to c. into sth** *(be transformed)* se changer *ou* se transformer en qch; **she changed into a dress** elle a mis une robe; **to c. over** passer *(from* de; *to* à) ▪ **changing** *n Br* **the c. of the guard** la relève de la garde; **c. room** vestiaire *m; (in shop)* cabine *f* d'essayage

changeable ['tʃeɪndʒəbəl] *adj (weather, mood)* changeant

changeover ['tʃeɪndʒəʊvə(r)] *n* passage *m* *(from* à; *to* à)

channel ['tʃænəl] **1** *n (on television)* chaîne *f; (for boats)* chenal *m; (groove)* rainure *f; (of communication, distribution)* canal *m; Geog* **the C.** la Manche; **the C. Islands** les îles Anglo-Normandes; **the C. Tunnel** le tunnel sous la Manche **2** *(Br* **-ll-,** *Am* **-l-)** *vt (energies, crowd, money)* canaliser *(into* vers)

chant [tʃɑːnt] **1** *n (of demonstrators)* slogan *m; (religious)* psalmodie *f* **2** *vt (slogan)* scander **3** *vi (of demonstrators)* scander des slogans; *(of monks)* psalmodier

> Note that the French words **chant** and **chanter** are false friends and are never translations for the English **chant** and **to chant**. They mean **song** and **to sing**.

chaos ['keɪɒs] *n* chaos *m* ▪ **chaotic** [-'ɒtɪk] *adj (situation, scene)* chaotique; *(room)* sens dessus dessous

chap¹ [tʃæp] *n Br Fam (fellow)* type *m;* **old c.!** mon vieux!

chap² [tʃæp] *(pt & pp* **-pp-)** *vt* gercer; **chapped hands/lips** des mains/lèvres gercées **2** *vi* se gercer

chapel ['tʃæpəl] *n* chapelle *f; (nonconformist church)* temple *m*

chaperon(e) ['ʃæpərəʊn] **1** *n* chaperon *m* **2** *vt* chaperonner

chaplain ['tʃæplɪn] *n* aumônier *m*

chapter ['tʃæptə(r)] *n* chapitre *m*

character ['kærɪktə(r)] *n* (**a**) *(of person, place)* caractère *m; (in book, film)* personnage *m; (person)* individu *m; (unusual person)* personnage; **he's a bit of a c.** c'est un personnage; **c. reference** *(for job)* références *fpl* (**b**) *(letter)* caractère *m;* **in bold characters** en caractères gras

characteristic ['kærɪktərɪstɪk] *adj & n* caractéristique *(f)* ▪ **characteristically** *adv* typiquement

characterize [kærɪktə'raɪz] *vt* caractériser

charade *(Br* ʃə'rɑːd, *Am* ʃə'reɪd] *n (travesty)* mascarade *f;* **charades** *(game)* charades *fpl* mimées

> Note that the French word **charade** is a false friend. It is a type of word game.

charcoal ['tʃɑːkəʊl] *n* charbon *m* de bois; *Art* fusain *m;* **c. grey** anthracite *inv*

charge¹ [tʃɑːdʒ] **1** *n (in battle)* charge *f; Law* chef *m* d'accusation; *(responsibility)* responsabilité *f,* charge; *(care)* garde *f;* **to take c. of sth** prendre qch en charge; **to be in c. of** être responsable de; **who's in c. here?** qui est le chef ici?; **the person in c.** le/la responsable; **the battery is on c.** la batterie est en charge **2** *vt (battery, soldiers)* charger; *Law (accuse)* inculper (**with** de) **3** *vi (rush)* se précipiter; *(soldiers)* charger; **to c. in/out** entrer/sortir en trombe ▪ **charged** *adj Fig* **a highly c. atmosphere** une atmosphère très tendue ▪ **charger** *n (for battery)* chargeur *m*

charge² [tʃɑːdʒ] **1** *n (cost)* prix *m;* **charges** *(expenses)* frais *mpl;* **there's a c. (for it)** c'est payant; **to make a c. for sth** faire payer qch; **free of c.** gratuit; **extra c.** supplément *m;* **c. card** carte *f* de paiement *(de magasin)* **2** *vt (amount)* demander (**for** pour); **to c. sb** faire payer qn; **to c. sth (up) to sb** mettre qch sur le compte de qn; **how much do you c.?** combien demandez-vous? ▪ **chargeable** *adj* **c. to sb** aux frais de qn

chariot ['tʃærɪət] *n* char *m*

charisma [kə'rɪzmə] *n* charisme *m*

charity ['tʃærɪtɪ] *(pl* **-ies)** *n (kindness, alms)* charité *f; (society)* œuvre *f* de charité; **to give to c.** faire des dons à des œuvres de charité ▪ **charitable** *adj (person, action)* charitable; *(organization)* caritatif, -ive

charlatan ['ʃɑːlətən] *n* charlatan *m*

charm [tʃɑːm] **1** *n (attractiveness, spell)* charme *m; (trinket)* breloque *f* **2** *vt* charmer ▪ **charming** *adj* charmant ▪ **charmingly** *adv* d'une façon charmante

charred [tʃɑːd] *adj (burnt until black)* carbonisé; *(scorched)* brûlé légèrement

chart [tʃɑːt] **1** *n (map)* carte *f; (table)* tableau *m; (graph)* graphique *m;* **charts** hit-parade *m* **2** *vt (route)* porter sur une carte; *(make a graph of)* faire le graphique de; *(of graph)* montrer; *Fig (observe)* suivre

charter ['tʃɑːtə(r)] **1** *n* (**a**) *(aircraft)* charter *m;* **the c. of** *(hiring)* l'affrètement *m* de; **c. flight** vol *m* charter (**b**) *(document)* charte *f* **2** *vt (aircraft)* affréter ▪ **chartered ac'countant** *n Br* expert-comptable *m*

chase [tʃeɪs] **1** *n* poursuite *f;* **to give c. to sb** se lancer à la poursuite de qn **2** *vt* poursuivre; **to c. sb away** *or* **off** chasser qn; *Fam* **to c. sth up** rechercher qch **3** *vi* **to c. after sb/sth** courir après qn/qch

> Note that the French verb **chasser** is a false friend. It means **to hunt**.

chasm ['kæzəm] *n also Fig* abîme *m,* gouffre *m*

chassis ['ʃæsɪ] *n (of vehicle)* châssis *m*

chaste [tʃeɪst] *adj* chaste ■**chastity** ['tʃæstɪtɪ] *n* chasteté *f*

chastening ['tʃeɪsənɪŋ] *adj (experience)* instructif, -ive

chastise [tʃæ'staɪz] *vt* punir

chat [tʃæt] **1** *n* petite conversation *f*; *Comptr* bavardage *m*; **to have a c.** causer (**with** avec) **2** *(pt & pp* **-tt-)** *vi (of person) Comptr* bavarder **3** *vt Br Fam* **to c. sb up** draguer qn ■**chatroom** *n Comptr* site *m* de bavardage

chatter ['tʃætə(r)] **1** *n* bavardage *m*; *(of birds)* jacassement *m* **2** *vi (of person)* bavarder; *(of birds, monkeys)* jacasser; **his teeth were chattering** il claquait des dents ■**chatterbox** *n* pie *f*

chatty ['tʃætɪ] *(-ier, -iest) adj (person)* bavard; *(letter)* plein de détails

chauffeur ['ʃəʊfə(r)] *n* chauffeur *m*

chauvinist ['ʃəʊvɪnɪst] *adj & n* chauvin, -ine *(mf)*; *Pej* **(male) c.** macho *m*

cheap [tʃiːp] **1** *(-er, -est) adj* bon marché *inv*, pas cher *(f* pas chère); *(rate, fare)* réduit; *(worthless)* sans valeur; *(vulgar)* de mauvais goût; *(superficial) (emotion, remark)* facile; *(mean, petty)* mesquin; **cheaper** meilleur marché *inv*, moins cher *(f* moins chère); **to feel c.** se sentir minable **2** *adv Fam (buy)* (à) bon marché, au rabais; **it was going c.** c'était bon marché **3** *n* **on the c.** à peu de frais ■**cheaply** *adv* (à) bon marché

cheapen ['tʃiːpən] *vt (degrade)* gâcher

cheat [tʃiːt] **1** *n (at games)* tricheur, -euse *mf*; *(crook)* escroc *m* **2** *vt (deceive)* tromper; *(defraud)* frauder; **to c. sb out of sth** escroquer qch à qn; **to c. on sb** tromper qn **3** *vi (at games)* tricher; *(defraud)* frauder ■**cheating** *n (at games)* tricherie *f*; *(deceit)* tromperie *f*; **it's a c.!** c'est de la triche!

check¹ [tʃek] **1** *adj (pattern)* à carreaux **2** *n* **c. (pattern)** carreaux *mpl* ■**checked** *adj (patterned)* à carreaux

check² [tʃek] **1** *n* vérification *f* (**on** de); *(inspection)* contrôle *m*; *(in chess)* échec *m*; *Am (tick)* ≃ croix *f*; *Am (receipt)* reçu *m*; *Am (restaurant bill)* addition *f*; *Am (cheque)* chèque *m*; **to keep a c. on sth** contrôler qch; **to put a c. on sth** mettre un frein à qch; **to keep sb in c.** tenir qn en échec; *Pol* **checks and balances** équilibre *m* des pouvoirs **2** *vt (examine)* vérifier; *(inspect)* contrôler; *(mark off)* cocher; *(inflation)* enrayer; *(emotion, impulse, enemy advance)* contenir; *Am (baggage)* mettre à la consigne **3** *vi* vérifier; **to c. on sth** vérifier qch; **to c. on sb** surveiller qn; **c. with her** pose-lui la question ■**checkbook** *n Am* carnet *m* de chèques ■**check-in** *n (at airport)* enregistrement *m* (des bagages) ■**checking account** *n Am* compte *m* courant ■**checklist** *n*

liste *f* de contrôle; *Av* check-list *f* ■**checkmate** *n (in chess)* échec *m* et mat ■**checkout** *n (in supermarket)* caisse *f* ■**checkpoint** *n* poste *m* de contrôle ■**checkroom** *n Am* vestiaire *m*; *Am (left-luggage office)* consigne *f* ■**checkup** *n (medical)* bilan *m* de santé; **to have a c.** faire un bilan de santé

▸ **check in 1** *vt sep (luggage)* enregistrer **2** *vi (arrive)* arriver; *(sign in)* signer le registre; *(at airport)* se présenter à l'enregistrement

▸ **check off** *vt sep (from list)* cocher

▸ **check out 1** *vt sep (confirm)* confirmer **2** *vi (at hotel)* régler sa note

▸ **check up** *vi* vérifier

checkered ['tʃekəd] *adj Am* = **chequered**

checkers ['tʃekərz] *npl Am* jeu *m* de dames ■**checkerboard** *n Am* damier *m*

cheddar ['tʃedə(r)] *n* cheddar *m (fromage)*

cheek [tʃiːk] *n* joue *f*; *Br Fam (impudence)* culot *m* ■**cheekbone** *n* pommette *f* ■**cheeky** *(-ier, -iest) adj Br (person, reply)* insolent

cheep [tʃiːp] *vi (of bird)* piailler

cheer [tʃɪə(r)] **1** *n* **cheers** *(shouts)* acclamations *fpl*; *Fam* **cheers!** *(when drinking)* à votre santé!; *Br (thanks)* merci! **2** *vt (applaud)* acclamer; **to c. sb on** encourager qn; **to c. sb (up)** *(comfort)* remonter le moral à qn; *(amuse)* faire sourire qn **3** *vi* applaudir; **to c. up** reprendre courage; *(be amused)* se dérider; **c. up!** (du) courage! ■**cheering 1** *adj (encouraging)* réjouissant **2** *n (shouts)* acclamations *fpl*

cheerful ['tʃɪəfəl] *adj* gai ■**cheerfully** *adv* gaiement ■**cheerless** *adj* morne

cheerio [tʃɪərɪ'əʊ] *exclam Br* salut!, au revoir!

cheese [tʃiːz] *n* fromage *m*; *Fam* **(say) c.!** *(for photograph)* souriez!; **c. board** plateau *m* de fromages; **c. sandwich** sandwich *m* au fromage ■**cheeseburger** *n* cheeseburger *m* ■**cheesecake** *n* tarte *f* au fromage blanc

cheesed [tʃiːzd] *adj Fam* **to be c. (off)** en avoir marre (**with** de)

cheesy ['tʃiːzɪ] *(-ier, -iest) adj Fam* ringard

cheetah ['tʃiːtə] *n* guépard *m*

chef [ʃef] *n* chef *m (cuisinier)*

chemical 1 *adj* chimique **2** *n* produit *m* chimique

chemist ['kemɪst] *n Br (pharmacist)* pharmacien, -ienne *mf*; *(scientist)* chimiste *mf*; *Br* **c.'s shop** pharmacie *f* ■**chemistry** *n* chimie *f*

chemotherapy [kiːməʊ'θerəpɪ] *n Med* chimiothérapie *f*; **to have c.** faire de la chimiothérapie

cheque [tʃek] *n Br* chèque *m*; **c. card** carte *f* d'identité bancaire *(sans laquelle un chéquier n'est pas valable)* ■**chequebook** *n Br* carnet *m* de chèques

chequered ['tʃekəd] *(Am* **checkered**) *adj Br (pattern)* à carreaux; *Fig (career)* en dents de scie; *Sport* **c. flag** drapeau *m* à damier

cherish ['tʃerɪʃ] vt (hope) nourrir, caresser; (person, memory) chérir

cherry ['tʃerɪ] 1 (pl -ies) n cerise f; (tree) cerisier m; **c. brandy** cherry m 2 adj **c.(-red)** cerise inv

chess [tʃes] n échecs mpl ▪ **chessboard** n échiquier m

chest [tʃest] n (a) (part of body) poitrine f; Fig to **get it off one's c.** dire ce qu'on a sur le cœur (b) (box) coffre m; **c. of drawers** commode f

chestnut ['tʃesnʌt] 1 n (nut) châtaigne f; (cooked) châtaigne, marron m; **c. (tree)** châtaignier m 2 adj (hair) châtain

chew [tʃu:] 1 vt to **c. (up)** mâcher; to **c. one's nails** se ronger les ongles; Fam to **c. over** (plan, problem) réfléchir à 2 vi mastiquer ▪ **chewing gum** n chewing-gum m

chewy ['tʃu:ɪ] adj (meat) caoutchouteux, -euse; (sweet) mou (f molle)

chick [tʃɪk] n (a) (chicken) poussin m; (bird) oisillon m (b) Fam (girl) nana f; **c. flick** = film qui plaît particulièrement aux femmes

chicken ['tʃɪkɪn] 1 n poulet m; Fam it's **c. feed!** c'est trois fois rien! 2 adj Fam (cowardly) froussard 3 vi Fam to **c. out** se dégonfler ▪ **chickenpox** n varicelle f

chickpea ['tʃɪkpi:] n pois m chiche

chicory ['tʃɪkərɪ] n inv (for salad) endive f; (for coffee) chicorée f

chief [tʃi:f] 1 n chef m; Fam (boss) patron m; Mil **c. of staff** chef d'état-major 2 adj (most important) principal; Com **c. executive** directeur m général ▪ **chiefly** adv principalement, surtout ▪ **chieftain** ['tʃi:ftən] n (of clan) chef m

chilblain ['tʃɪlbleɪn] n engelure f

child [tʃaɪld] (pl **children**) n enfant mf; it's **c.'s play** c'est un jeu d'enfant; **c. abuse** mauvais traitements mpl à enfant, maltraitance f; Br **c. benefit** ≃ allocations fpl familiales; **c. care** (for working parents) crèches fpl et garderies fpl; Br **c. minder** assistante f maternelle ▪ **childbearing** n (motherhood) maternité f; **of c. age** en âge d'avoir des enfants ▪ **childbirth** n accouchement m ▪ **childhood** n enfance f ▪ **childish** adj puéril ▪ **childishness** n puérilité f ▪ **childlike** adj enfantin ▪ **childproof** adj (lock, bottle) que les enfants ne peuvent pas ouvrir

children ['tʃɪldrən] pl of **child**

Chile ['tʃɪlɪ] n le Chili

chill [tʃɪl] 1 n froid m; (in feelings) froideur f; (illness) refroidissement m; to **catch a c.** prendre froid 2 vt (wine, melon) mettre au frais; (meat) réfrigérer; to **c. sb** faire frissonner qn; to **be chilled to the bone** être transi; **chilled wine** vin m frappé; **chilled dessert** dessert m frais ▪ **chilled** adj (a) (food, wine) refroidi; **best served c.** servir très frais (b)

Fam (relaxed) relax ▪ **chilling** adj (frightening) qui fait froid dans le dos ▪ **chilly** adj (-ier, -iest) froid; it's **c.** il fait (un peu) froid
▸ **chill out** vi Fam se détendre; **c. out!** relax!

chilli ['tʃɪlɪ] (pl -is or -ies) n (plant) piment m (rouge); (dish) **c. (con carne)** chili m (con carne); **c. powder** ≃ poivre m de Cayenne

chime [tʃaɪm] 1 n (of bells) carillon m; (of clock) sonnerie f 2 vi (of bell) carillonner; (of clock) sonner; Fam to **c. in** (interrupt) interrompre

chimney ['tʃɪmnɪ] (pl -eys) n cheminée f ▪ **chimneypot** n Br tuyau m de cheminée ▪ **chimneysweep** n ramoneur m

> Note that the French noun **cheminée** can be a false friend. It also means **fireplace** and **mantelpiece**.

chimpanzee [tʃɪmpæn'zi:] n chimpanzé m

chin [tʃɪn] n menton m; Fig to **keep one's c. up** tenir le coup

China ['tʃaɪnə] n la Chine ▪ **Chinese** [tʃaɪ'ni:z] 1 adj chinois; Br **C. leaves**, Am **C. cabbage** chou m chinois 2 n inv (person) Chinois, -oise mf; (language) chinois m; Fam (meal) repas m chinois; Fam (restaurant) restaurant m chinois

china ['tʃaɪnə] 1 n inv porcelaine f 2 adj en porcelaine

chink [tʃɪŋk] 1 n (a) (slit) fente f (b) (sound) tintement m 2 vt faire tinter 3 vi (of glasses) tinter

chip [tʃɪp] 1 n (splinter) éclat m; (break) ébréchure f; (counter) jeton m; Comptr puce f; **chips** Br (French fries) frites fpl; Am (crisps) chips fpl; Br **c. shop** = boutique où l'on vend du poisson pané et des frites; Fig to **have a c. on one's shoulder** en vouloir à tout le monde 2 (pt & pp -pp-) vt (cup, blade) ébrécher; (table) abîmer; (paint) écailler; (cut at) (stone, wood) tailler 3 vi Fam to **c. in** (contribute) contribuer; (interrupt) mettre son grain de sel ▪ **chipboard** n aggloméré m ▪ **chippings** npl **road** or **loose c.** gravillons mpl

> Note that the French word **chips** is a false friend for British English speakers. It means **crisps**.

chiropodist [kɪ'rɒpədɪst] n Br pédicure mf ▪ **chiropody** n Br soins mpl du pied

chirp [tʃɜ:p] 1 n pépiement m 2 vi (of bird) pépier

chirpy ['tʃɜ:pɪ] (-ier, -iest) adj d'humeur joyeuse

chisel ['tʃɪzəl] 1 n ciseau m 2 (Br -ll-, Am -l-) vt ciseler

chitchat ['tʃɪtʃæt] n Fam bavardage m

chivalry ['ʃɪvəlrɪ] n (courtesy) courtoisie f; (towards women) galanterie f; Hist (of knights) chevalerie f ▪ **chivalrous** adj (man) galant

chives [tʃaɪvz] npl ciboulette f

chlorine ['klɔːriːn] *n Chem* chlore *m*

chloroform ['klɔrəfɔːm] *n Chem* chloroforme *m*

choc-ice ['tʃɒkaɪs] *n Br* = glace individuelle enrobée de chocolat

chock [tʃɒk] **1** *n (wedge)* cale *f* **2** *vt* caler

chock-a-block [tʃɒkə'blɒk], **chock-full** [tʃɒk'fʊl] *adj Br Fam* archiplein

chocolate ['tʃɒklɪt] **1** *n* chocolat *m*; **drinking c.** chocolat en poudre; **hot c.** chocolat chaud; **milk/plain c.** chocolat au lait/à croquer **2** *adj (made of chocolate)* en chocolat; *(chocolate-flavoured)* au chocolat; *(colour)* chocolat *inv*; **c. egg** œuf *m* en chocolat ▪ **chocolate-coated** *adj* enrobé de chocolat

choice [tʃɔɪs] **1** *n* choix *m*; **to make a c.** choisir; **I had no c.** je n'ai pas eu le choix **2** *adj (goods)* de choix

choir ['kwaɪə(r)] *n* chœur *m* ▪ **choirboy** *n* jeune choriste *m*

choke [tʃəʊk] **1** *n (of car)* starter *m* **2** *vt (strangle)* étrangler; *(clog)* boucher **3** *vi* s'étrangler; **to c. with anger/laughter** s'étrangler de colère/de rire; **she choked on a fishbone** elle a failli s'étouffer avec une arête ▪ **choker** *n (necklace)* collier *m* (de chien)

cholera ['kɒlərə] *n* choléra *m*

cholesterol [kə'lestərɒl] *n* cholestérol *m*

choose [tʃuːz] **1** *(pt chose, pp chosen) vt* choisir; **to c. to do sth** choisir de faire qch **2** *vi* choisir; **as I/you/etc c.** comme il me/vous/etc plaît

choos(e)y ['tʃuːzɪ] *(choosier, choosiest) adj Fam* difficile (**about** sur)

chop [tʃɒp] **1** *n (of lamb, pork)* côtelette *f*; *Br Fam* **to get the c.** être flanqué à la porte **2** *(pt & pp -pp-) vt (wood)* couper (à la hache); *(food)* couper en morceaux; *(finely)* hacher; **to c. down** *(tree)* abattre; **to c. off** *(branch, finger)* couper; **to c. up** couper en morceaux **3** *vi* **to c. and change** changer sans cesse ▪ **chopper** *n (cleaver)* couperet *m*; *(axe)* hachette *f*; *Fam (helicopter)* hélico *m*

choppy ['tʃɒpɪ] *(-ier, -iest) adj (sea, river)* agité

chopsticks ['tʃɒpstɪks] *npl* baguettes *fpl (pour manger)*

choral ['kɔːrəl] *adj* choral; **c. society** chorale *f*

chord [kɔːd] *n Mus* accord *m*

chore [tʃɔː(r)] *n* corvée *f*; **(household) chores** travaux *mpl* du ménage; **to do the chores** faire le ménage

choreograph ['kɒrɪəgrɑːf] *vt* chorégraphier; *Fig* organiser ▪ **choreographer** [-'ɒgrəfə(r)] *n* chorégraphe *mf* ▪ **choreography** [-'ɒgrəfɪ] *n* chorégraphie *f*

chortle ['tʃɔːtəl] **1** *n* gloussement *m* (de joie) **2** *vi (laugh)* glousser (de joie)

chorus ['kɔːrəs] *n (of song)* refrain *m*; *(singers)* chœur *m*; *(dancers)* troupe *f*

chose [tʃəʊz] *pt of* **choose**

chosen ['tʃəʊzən] *pp of* **choose**

chowder ['tʃaʊdə(r)] *n Am Culin* = soupe de poissons épaisse

Christ [kraɪst] *n* le Christ ▪ **Christian** ['krɪstʃən] *adj & n* chrétien, -ienne *(mf)*; **C. name** prénom *m* ▪ **Christianity** [krɪstɪ'ænɪtɪ] *n* christianisme *m*

christen ['krɪsən] *vt (person, ship)* baptiser ▪ **christening** *n* baptême *m*

Christmas ['krɪsməs] **1** *n* Noël *m*; **at C. (time)** à Noël; **Merry** *or* **Happy C.!** Joyeux Noël! **2** *adj (tree, card, day, party)* de Noël; **C. Eve** la veille de Noël

chrome [krəʊm], **chromium** ['krəʊmɪəm] *n* chrome *m*

chronic ['krɒnɪk] *adj (disease, state)* chronique; *Fam (bad)* atroce

chronicle ['krɒnɪkəl] **1** *n* chronique *f* **2** *vt* faire la chronique de

chronology [krə'nɒlədʒɪ] *(pl -ies) n* chronologie *f* ▪ **chronological** [krɒnə'lɒdʒɪkəl] *adj* chronologique; **in c. order** par ordre chronologique

chronometer [krə'nɒmɪtə(r)] *n* chronomètre *m*

chrysanthemum [krɪ'sænθəməm] *n* chrysanthème *m*

chubby ['tʃʌbɪ] *(-ier, -iest) adj (person, hands)* potelé; *(cheeks)* rebondi

chuck [tʃʌk] *vt Fam (throw)* lancer; *(boyfriend, girlfriend)* plaquer; **to get chucked** se faire plaquer; **to c. away** *(old clothes)* balancer; *(money)* gaspiller; *(opportunity)* ficher en l'air; *Br* **to c. (in** *or* **up)** *(give up)* laisser tomber; **to c. out** *(throw away)* balancer; *(from house, school, club)* vider

chuckle ['tʃʌkəl] **1** *n* petit rire *m* **2** *vi* rire tout bas

chuffed [tʃʌft] *adj Br Fam* super content (**about** de)

chug [tʃʌg] *(pt & pp -gg-) vi* **to c. along** *(of vehicle)* avancer lentement; *(of train)* haleter

chum [tʃʌm] *n Fam* copain *m*, copine *f* ▪ **chummy** *(-ier, -iest) adj Fam* **to be c. with sb** être copain *(f* copine) avec qn

chunk [tʃʌŋk] *n (gros)* morceau *m*; *(of time)* partie *f* ▪ **chunky** *(-ier, -iest) adj Fam (person)* trapu; *(coat, sweater, material)* gros *(f* grosse)

church [tʃɜːtʃ] *n* église *f*; *(French Protestant)* temple *m*; **to go to c.** aller à l'église/au temple; **in c.** à l'église; **c. hall** salle *f* paroissiale ▪ **churchgoer** *n* pratiquant, -ante *f* ▪ **churchyard** *n* cimetière *m*

churlish ['tʃɜːlɪʃ] *adj (rude)* grossier, -ière; *(bad-tempered)* hargneux, -euse

churn [tʃɜːn] **1** *n (for making butter)* baratte *f*; *(milk can)* bidon *m* **2** *vt Pej* **to c. out** *(books)* pondre (en série); *(goods)* produire en série

chute [ʃuːt] *n Br (in pool, playground)* toboggan *m*; *(for rubbish)* vide-ordures *m inv*

chutney ['tʃʌtnɪ] n chutney m, = condiment épicé à base de fruits

CID [si:aɪ'di:] (abbr **Criminal Investigation Department**) n Br ≃ PJ f

cider ['saɪdə(r)] n cidre m

cigar [sɪ'gɑ:(r)] n cigare m

cigarette [sɪgə'ret] n cigarette f; **c. end** mégot m; **c. lighter** briquet m

cinch [sɪntʃ] n Fam **it's a c.** (easy) c'est un jeu d'enfant; (sure) c'est sûr et certain

cinder ['sɪndə(r)] n cendre f; **burnt to a c.** carbonisé; Br **c. track** (for running) cendrée f

Cinderella [sɪndə'relə] n Cendrillon f

cine camera ['sɪnɪkæmrə] n Br caméra f

cinema ['sɪnəmə] n (art) cinéma m; Br (place) cinéma; Br **to go to the c.** aller au cinéma ▪ **cinemagoer** n Br cinéphile mf

cinnamon ['sɪnəmən] n cannelle f

circle ['sɜːkəl] **1** n (shape, group, range) cercle m; (around eyes) cerne m; Theatre balcon m; **to sit in a c.** s'asseoir en cercle; Fig **to go round in circles** tourner en rond; **in political circles** dans les milieux mpl politiques **2** vt (move round) tourner autour de; (surround) entourer (**with** de) **3** vi (of aircraft, bird) décrire des cercles

circuit ['sɜːkɪt] n (electrical path, journey, for motor racing) circuit m; (of entertainers, judge) tournée f; El **c. breaker** disjoncteur m ▪ **circuitous** [sɜː'kju:ɪtəs] adj (route, means) indirect

circular ['sɜːkjʊlə(r)] **1** adj circulaire **2** n (letter) circulaire f; (advertisement) prospectus m

circulate ['sɜːkjʊleɪt] **1** vt faire circuler **2** vi circuler ▪ **circulation** [-'leɪʃən] n (of air, blood, money) circulation f; (of newspaper) tirage m; Fam **to be in c.** (person) être dans le circuit

circumcise ['sɜːkəmsaɪz] vt circoncire ▪ **circumcised** adj circoncis ▪ **circumcision** [-'sɪʒən] n circoncision f

circumference [sɜː'kʌmfərəns] n circonférence f

circumflex ['sɜːkəmfleks] n & adj **c. (accent)** accent m circonflexe

circumspect ['sɜːkəmspekt] adj circonspect

circumstance ['sɜːkəmstæns] n circonstance f; **circumstances** (financial) situation f financière; **in** or **under the circumstances** étant donné les circonstances; **in** or **under no circumstances** en aucun cas ▪ **circumstantial** [-'stænʃəl] adj Law **c. evidence** preuves fpl indirectes; **on c. evidence** sur la base de preuves indirectes

circumvent [sɜːkəm'vent] vt (rule, law, difficulty) contourner

circus ['sɜːkəs] n cirque m

cirrhosis [sɪ'rəʊsɪs] n Med cirrhose f

CIS (abbr **Commonwealth of Independent States**) n CEI f

cistern ['sɪstən] n citerne f; (for lavatory) réservoir m de chasse d'eau

citadel ['sɪtədəl] n citadelle f

cite [saɪt] vt (quote, commend) citer ▪ **ci'tation** n citation f

citizen ['sɪtɪzən] n citoyen, -enne mf; (of city) habitant, -ante mf ▪ **citizenship** n citoyenneté f; Br Sch instruction f civique

citrus ['sɪtrəs] adj **c. fruit(s)** agrumes mpl

city ['sɪtɪ] (pl -ies) n (grande) ville f, cité f; Br **the C.** la City (quartier des affaires de Londres); **c. centre** centre-ville m; **c. dweller** citadin, -ine mf; Am **c. hall** hôtel m de ville

civic ['sɪvɪk] adj (duty) civique; **c. centre** salle f municipale ▪ **civics** n Am Sch instruction f civique

civil ['sɪvəl] adj (**a**) (rights, war, marriage) civil; **c. servant** fonctionnaire mf; **c. service** fonction f publique (**b**) (polite) civil ▪ **civility** [sɪ'vɪlɪtɪ] n politesse f

civilian [sɪ'vɪljən] adj & n civil, -ile (mf)

civilize ['sɪvɪlaɪz] vt civiliser ▪ **civilization** [-'zeɪʃən] n civilisation f

civvies ['sɪvɪz] npl Fam **in c.** en civil

clad [klæd] adj Literary vêtu (**in** de)

claim [kleɪm] **1** n (demand) (for damages, compensation) demande f d'indemnisation; (as a right) revendication f; (statement) affirmation f; (right) droit m (**to** à); (insurance) **c.** demande d'indemnité; **to lay c. to sth** revendiquer qch **2** vt (as a right) réclamer, revendiquer; (payment, benefit, reduction) demander à bénéficier de; **to c. damages (from sb)** réclamer des dommages et intérêts (à qn); **to c. that...** (assert) prétendre que... ▪ **claimant** n Br (for social benefits, insurance) demandeur, -euse mf

clairvoyant [kleə'vɔɪənt] n voyant, -ante mf

clam [klæm] **1** n palourde f **2** (pt & pp -mm-) vi Fam **to c. up** (stop talking) se fermer comme une huître

clamber ['klæmbə(r)] vi **to c. up** grimper

clammy ['klæmɪ] (-ier, -iest) adj (hands) moite (et froid)

clamour ['klæmə(r)] (Am **clamor**) **1** n clameur f **2** vi **to c. for sth** demander qch à grands cris

clamp [klæmp] **1** n (clip-like) pince f; (in carpentry) serre-joint m; (wheel) **c.** (for vehicle) sabot m (de Denver) **2** vt serrer; (vehicle) mettre un sabot à **3** vi Fam **to c. down on** sévir contre ▪ **clampdown** n Fam coup m d'arrêt (**on** à)

clan [klæn] n also Fig clan m

clandestine [klæn'destɪn] adj clandestin

clang [klæŋ] n son m métallique

clanger ['klæŋə(r)] n Br Fam gaffe f; **to drop a c.** faire une gaffe

clap [klæp] **1** n battement m de mains; (on back) tape f; (of thunder) coup m **2** (pt & pp -pp-) vti (applaud) applaudir; **to c. (one's hands)** applaudir; (once) frapper dans ses mains

▪ **'clapped-'out** *adj Br Fam (person)* crevé; *(car, machine)* pourri ▪ **clapping** *n* applaudissements *mpl*

claptrap ['klæptræp] *n Fam* bêtises *fpl*; **to talk c.** dire des bêtises

claret ['klærət] *n (wine)* bordeaux *m* rouge

clarify ['klærɪfaɪ] *(pt & pp -ied) vt* clarifier ▪ **clarification** [-fɪ'keɪʃən] *n* clarification *f*

clarinet [klærɪ'net] *n* clarinette *f*

clarity ['klærətɪ] *n (of expression, argument)* clarté *f*; *(of sound)* pureté *f*; *(of water)* transparence *f*

clash [klæʃ] **1** *n (noise)* fracas *m*; *(of interests)* conflit *m*; *(of events)* coïncidence *f* **2** *vi (of objects)* s'entrechoquer; *(of interests, armies)* s'affronter; *(of colours)* jurer (**with** avec); *(coincide)* tomber en même temps (**with** que)

clasp [klɑːsp] **1** *n (fastener)* fermoir *m*; *(of belt)* boucle *f* **2** *vt (hold)* serrer; **to c. one's hands** joindre les mains

class [klɑːs] **1** *n* classe *f*; *(lesson)* cours *m*; *Br (university grade)* mention *f*; *Am* **the c. of 2003** la promotion de 2003; **to have c.** avoir de la classe **2** *vt* classer (**as** comme) ▪ **classmate** *n* camarade *mf* de classe ▪ **classroom** *n* (salle *f* de) classe *f*

classic ['klæsɪk] **1** *adj* classique **2** *n (writer, work)* classique *m* ▪ **classical** *adj* classique

classify ['klæsɪfaɪ] *(pt & pp -ied) vt* classer ▪ **classification** [-fɪ'keɪʃən] *n* classification *f* ▪ **classified** *adj (information, document)* confidentiel, -ielle; **c. advertisement** petite annonce *f*

classy ['klɑːsɪ] *(-ier, -iest) adj Fam* chic *inv*

clatter ['klætə(r)] *n* fracas *m*

clause [klɔːz] *n (in sentence)* proposition *f*; *(in legal document)* clause *f*

claustrophobia [klɔːstrə'fəʊbɪə] *n* claustrophobie *f* ▪ **claustrophobic** *adj (person)* claustrophobe; *(room, atmosphere)* oppressant

claw [klɔː] **1** *n (of lobster)* pince *f*; *(of cat, sparrow)* griffe *f*; *(of eagle)* serre *f* **2** *vt (scratch)* griffer; **to c. back** *(money)* récupérer

clay [kleɪ] *n* argile *f*

clean [kliːn] **1** *(-er, -est) adj* propre; *(clear-cut)* net *(f* nette); *(joke)* pour toutes les oreilles; *(game, fight)* dans les règles; **c. living** vie *f* saine; **a c. record** *(of suspect)* un casier judiciaire vierge; **to have a c. driving licence** avoir tous ses points sur son permis de conduire; **to make a c. breast of it, to come c.** tout avouer

2 *adv (utterly)* complètement; **to break c.** (se) casser net; **to cut c.** couper net

3 *n* **to give sth a c.** nettoyer qch

4 *vt* nettoyer; *(wash)* laver; **to c. one's teeth** se brosser *ou* se laver les dents; **to c. out** *(room)* nettoyer à fond; *(empty)* vider; **to c. up** *(room)* nettoyer; *Fig (reform)* épurer

5 *vi* **to c. (up)** faire le nettoyage ▪ **clean-cut** *adj* net *(f* nette) ▪ **cleaner** *n (in home)* femme *f* de ménage; **(dry) c.** teinturier, -ière *mf* ▪ **cleaning** *n* nettoyage *m*; *(housework)* ménage *m*; **c. lady** femme *f* de ménage ▪ **'clean-'living** *adj* honnête ▪ **cleanly** *adv (break, cut)* net ▪ **cleanness** *n* propreté *f* ▪ **'clean-'shaven** *adj (with no beard or moustache)* glabre; *(closely shaven)* rasé de près ▪ **clean-up** *n Fig* purge *f*

cleanliness ['klenlɪnɪs] *n* propreté *f*

cleanse [klenz] *vt* nettoyer; *Fig (soul, person)* purifier (**of** de); **cleansing cream** crème *f* démaquillante ▪ **cleanser** *n (for skin)* démaquillant *m*

clear [klɪə(r)] **1** *(-er, -est) adj (sky, water, sound, thought)* clair; *(glass)* transparent; *(outline, photo, skin, majority)* net *(f* nette); *(road)* libre; *(winner)* incontesté; *(obvious)* évident, clair; *(certain)* certain; **on a c. day** par temps clair; **all c.!** la voie est libre!; **to make oneself (completely or abundantly) c.** se faire (bien) comprendre; **it is c. that...** il est évident *ou* clair que...; **I wasn't c. what she meant** je n'étais pas sûr de la comprendre; **to have a c. conscience** avoir la conscience tranquille; **two c. weeks** *(complete)* deux semaines entières; **c. profit** bénéfice *m* net

2 *adv* **c. of** *(away from)* à l'écart de; **to keep** *or* **steer c. of** se tenir à l'écart de; **to get c. of** *(away from)* s'éloigner de

3 *vt (table)* débarrasser; *(road, area)* dégager; *(land)* défricher; *(fence)* franchir (sans toucher); *(obstacle)* éviter; *(accused person)* disculper; *(cheque)* compenser; *(debts, goods)* liquider; *(through customs)* dédouaner; *(for security)* autoriser; **to c. one's throat** s'éclaircir la gorge

4 *vi (of weather)* s'éclaircir; *(of fog)* se dissiper ▪ **clearing** *n (in woods)* clairière *f* ▪ **clearly** *adv (explain, write)* clairement; *(see, understand)* bien; *(obviously)* évidemment ▪ **clearness** *n (of sound)* clarté *f*, netteté *f*; *(of mind)* lucidité *f*

▸ **clear away 1** *vt sep (remove)* enlever **2** *vi (of fog)* se dissiper

▸ **clear off** *vi Fam (leave)* filer

▸ **clear out** *vt sep (empty)* vider; *(clean)* nettoyer; *(remove)* enlever

▸ **clear up 1** *vt sep (mystery)* éclaircir; *(room)* ranger **2** *vi (of weather)* s'éclaircir; *(of fog)* se dissiper; *(tidy)* ranger

clearance ['klɪərəns] *n (sale)* liquidation *f*; *(space)* dégagement *m*; *(permission)* autorisation *f*

clear-cut [klɪə'kʌt] *adj* net *(f* nette)

clear-headed [klɪə'hedɪd] *adj* lucide

cleavage ['kliːvɪdʒ] *n (split)* clivage *m*; *(of woman)* décolleté *m*

clef [klef] *n Mus* clef *f*

cleft [kleft] **1** *n* fissure *f* **2** *adj Anat* **c. palate** palais *m* fendu

clement ['klemənt] *adj (person, weather)* clément ▪ **clemency** *n* clémence *f*

clementine ['kleməntaɪn] *n* clémentine *f*

clench [klentʃ] *vt* **to c. one's fist/teeth** serrer le poing/les dents

clergy ['klɜːdʒɪ] *n* clergé *m* ▪ **clergyman** (*pl* -men) *n* ecclésiastique *m*

cleric ['klerɪk] *n Rel* ecclésiastique *m* ▪ **clerical** *adj (work)* de bureau; *(error)* d'écriture; *Rel* clérical

clerk [*Br* klɑːk, *Am* klɜːk] *n* employé, -ée *mf* de bureau; *Am (in store)* vendeur, -euse *mf*; *Law* **c. of the court** greffier *m*

clever ['klevə(r)] (-er, -est) *adj* intelligent; *(smart, shrewd)* astucieux, -ieuse; *(skilful)* habile (**at sth** à qch; **at doing** à faire); *(ingenious) (machine, plan)* ingénieux, -ieuse; *(gifted)* doué; **c. at English** fort en anglais; **c. with one's hands** adroit de ses mains ▪ **cleverly** *adv* intelligemment; *(ingeniously)* astucieusement; *(skilfully)* habilement ▪ **cleverness** *n* intelligence *f*; *(ingenuity)* astuce *f*; *(skill)* adresse *f*

cliché ['kliːʃeɪ] *n* cliché *m*

click [klɪk] **1** *n* bruit *m* sec; *Comptr (of mouse)* clic *m*; *Comptr* **d. click** double-clic *m* **2** *vt* **to c. one's heels** claquer des talons; **to c. one's tongue** faire claquer sa langue **3** *vi* faire un bruit sec; *Comptr (with mouse)* cliquer; *Fam (of lovers)* se plaire du premier coup; *Fam* **it suddenly clicked** ça a fait tilt; *Comptr* **to c. on sth** cliquer sur qch; *Comptr* **to double c. on sth** faire un double-clic sur qch

client ['klaɪənt] *n* client, -iente *mf* ▪ **clientele** [kliːən'tel] *n* clientèle *f*

cliff [klɪf] *n* falaise *f*

climate ['klaɪmɪt] *n (weather) & Fig (conditions)* climat *m*; **c. of opinion** opinion *f* générale ▪ **climatic** [-'mætɪk] *adj (changes)* climatique

climax ['klaɪmæks] **1** *n* point *m* culminant; *(sexual)* orgasme *m* **2** *vi* atteindre son point culminant; *(sexually)* atteindre l'orgasme

climb [klaɪm] **1** *n* montée *f* **2** *vt* **to c. (up)** *(steps, hill)* gravir; *(mountain)* faire l'ascension de; *(tree, ladder)* grimper à; **to c. (over)** *(wall)* escalader; **to c. down (from)** *(wall, tree)* descendre de; *(hill)* descendre **3** *vi (of plant)* grimper; **to c. (up)** *(steps, tree, hill)* monter; **to c. down** descendre; *Fig (back down)* revenir sur sa décision ▪ **climber** *n* grimpeur, -euse *mf*; *(mountaineer)* alpiniste *mf*; *(on rocks)* varappeur, -euse *mf*; *(plant)* plante *f* grimpante ▪ **climbing** *n* montée *f*; *(mountain)* **c.** alpinisme *m*; *(rock-)c.* varappe *f*; **c. frame** cage *f* à poule

climb-down ['klaɪmdaʊn] *n* reculade *f*

clinch [klɪntʃ] *vt (deal)* conclure

cling [klɪŋ] (*pt & pp* clung) *vi* s'accrocher (**to** à);

(stick) adhérer (**to** à) ▪ **clinging** *adj (clothes)* collant

clingfilm ['klɪŋfɪlm] *n Br* film *m* alimentaire

clinic ['klɪnɪk] *n Br (private)* clinique *f*; *(part of hospital)* service *m* ▪ **clinical** *adj Med* clinique; *Fig (attitude)* froid

clink [klɪŋk] **1** *n* tintement *m* **2** *vt* faire tinter **3** *vi* tinter

clip [klɪp] **1** *n* (a) *(fastener)* attache *f*; *(for paper)* trombone *m*; *(of brooch, of cyclist, for hair)* pince *f*; (b) *(of film)* extrait *m* (c) *Br Fam (blow)* taloche *f* (d) *Comptr* **c. art** clipart *m* **2** (*pt & pp* -pp-) *vt (paper)* attacher *(avec un trombone)*; *(cut)* couper; *(hedge)* tailler; *(ticket)* poinçonner; *(sheep)* tondre; **to c. sth out of** *(newspaper)* découper qch dans; **to c. (on)** *(attach)* attacher (**to** à) **3** *vi* **to c. together** s'emboîter ▪ **clippers** *npl (for hair)* tondeuse *f*; *(for fingernails)* coupe-ongles *m inv* ▪ **clipping** *n Am (from newspaper)* coupure *f*

clique [kliːk] *n Pej* clique *f* ▪ **cliquey** *adj Pej* très fermé

cloak [kləʊk] *n* cape *f* ▪ **cloakroom** *n* vestiaire *m*; *Br (lavatory)* toilettes *fpl*

clobber[1] ['klɒbə(r)] *n Br Fam (clothes)* fringues *fpl*; *(belongings)* barda *m*

clobber[2] ['klɒbə(r)] *vt Fam (hit)* tabasser

clock [klɒk] **1** *n (large)* horloge *f*; *(small)* pendule *f*; *Br Fam (mileometer)* compteur *m*; **a race against the c.** une course contre la montre; **round the c.** vingt-quatre heures sur vingt-quatre; **to put the clocks forward/back** *(in spring, autumn)* avancer/retarder les pendules; *Fig* **to turn the c. back** revenir en arrière; **c. radio** radioréveil *m*; **c. tower** clocher *m* **2** *vt (measure speed of)* chronométrer **3** *vi* **to c. in** *or* **out** *(of worker)* pointer ▪ **clockwise** *adv* dans le sens des aiguilles d'une montre

clockwork ['klɒkwɜːk] **1** *adj (toy)* mécanique **2** *n* **to go like c.** marcher comme sur des roulettes

clod [klɒd] *n* (a) *(of earth)* motte *f* (b) *Fam (oaf)* balourd, -ourde *mf*

clog [klɒg] **1** *n (shoe)* sabot *m* **2** (*pt & pp* -gg-) *vt* **to c. (up)** *(obstruct)* boucher

cloister ['klɔɪstə(r)] **1** *n* cloître *m* **2** *vt* cloîtrer

clone [kləʊn] **1** *n* clone *m* **2** *vt* cloner ▪ **cloning** *n* clonage *m*

close[1] [kləʊs] **1** (-er, -est) *adj (in distance, time, relationship)* proche; *(collaboration, resemblance, connection)* étroit; *(friend)* intime; *(contest)* serré; *(study)* rigoureux, -euse; *Ling (vowel)* fermé; *Br* **the weather is c., it's c.** il fait lourd; *Br* **it's c. in this room** cette pièce est mal aérée; **c. to** *(near)* près de, proche de; **c. to tears** au bord des larmes; **I'm very c. to her** *(friendly)* je suis très proche d'elle; **that was a c. shave** *or* **call** il s'en est fallu de peu

2 *adv* **c. (by)**, **c. at hand** tout près; **c. behind** juste derrière; *Fam* **c. on** *(almost)* pas loin de; **we stood/sat c. together** nous étions debout/assis serrés les uns contre les autres; **to follow c. behind** suivre de près; **to hold sb c.** tenir qn contre soi ▪**'close-'cropped** *adj (hair)* coupé ras ▪**'close-'fitting** *adj (clothes)* ajusté ▪**'close-'knit** *adj (group, family)* très uni ▪**closely** *adv (follow, guard)* de près; *(listen, examine)* attentivement; **c. linked** étroitement lié (**to** à); **c. contested** très disputé ▪**closeness** *n* proximité *f*; *(of collaboration)* étroitesse *f*; *(of friendship)* intimité *f*; *Br (of weather)* lourdeur *f* ▪**close-up** *n* gros plan *m*

close² [kləʊz] **1** *n (end)* fin *f*; **to bring to a c.** mettre fin à; **to draw to a c.** tirer à sa fin

2 *vt (door, shop, account, book, eye)* fermer; *(discussion)* clore; *(opening)* boucher; *(road)* barrer; *(gap)* réduire; *(deal)* conclure; **to c. the meeting** lever la séance; **to c. ranks** serrer les rangs

3 *vi (of door)* se fermer; *(of shop)* fermer; *(of wound)* se refermer; *(of meeting, festival)* se terminer ▪**closed** *adj (door, shop)* fermé; **c.-circuit television** télévision *f* en circuit fermé; **behind c. doors** à huis clos ▪**close-down** *n* fermeture *f* (définitive); *TV* fin *f* des émissions ▪**closing** **1** *n* fermeture *f*; *(of session)* clôture *f* 2 *adj (words, remarks)* dernier, -ière; **c. date** *(for application)* date *f* limite; **c. speech** discours *m* de clôture; **c. time** heure *f* de fermeture ▪**closure** ['kləʊʒə(r)] *n* fermeture *f* (définitive)

▸ **close down 1** *vt sep (business, factory)* fermer (définitivement) **2** *vi (of TV station)* terminer les émissions; *(of business, factory)* fermer (définitivement)

▸ **close in 1** *vt sep (enclose)* enfermer **2** *vi (approach)* approcher; **to c. in on sb** se rapprocher de qn

▸ **close up 1** *vt sep* fermer **2** *vi (of shopkeeper)* fermer; *(of wound)* se refermer; *(of line of people)* se resserrer

closet ['klɒzɪt] *n Am (cupboard)* placard *m*; *(wardrobe)* penderie *f*; *Fig* **to come out of the c.** révéler son homosexualité

clot [klɒt] **1** *n (of blood)* caillot *m*; *Br Fam (person)* andouille *f* **2** *(pt & pp* **-tt-)** *vt (blood)* coaguler **3** *vi (of blood)* (se) coaguler

cloth [klɒθ] *n* tissu *m*; *(of linen)* toile *f*; *(for dusting)* chiffon *m*; *(for dishes)* torchon *m*; *(tablecloth)* nappe *f*

clothe [kləʊð] *vt* vêtir (**in** de) ▪**clothing** *n (clothes)* vêtements *mpl*; **an article of c.** un vêtement

clothes [kləʊðz] *npl* vêtements *mpl*; **to put one's c. on** s'habiller; **to take one's c. off** se déshabiller; **c. brush** brosse *f* à habits; **c. line**

corde *f* à linge; *Br* **c. peg,** *Am* **c. pin** pince *f* à linge; **c. shop** magasin *m* de vêtements

cloud [klaʊd] **1** *n* nuage *m*; *Fig (of arrows, insects)* nuée *f* **2** *vt (window, mirror)* embuer; *(mind)* obscurcir; *(judgement)* affecter **3** *vi* **to c. (over)** *(of sky)* se couvrir ▪**cloudburst** *n* averse *f* ▪**cloudy** (**-ier, -iest**) *adj (weather, sky)* nuageux, -euse; *(liquid)* trouble; **it's c., it's a c. day** le temps est couvert

clout [klaʊt] *Fam* **1** *n (blow)* taloche *f*; *(influence)* influence *f*; **to have (plenty of) c.** avoir le bras long **2** *vt (hit)* flanquer une taloche à

clove [kləʊv] *n (spice)* clou *m* de girofle; **c. of garlic** gousse *f* d'ail

clover ['kləʊvə(r)] *n* trèfle *m*

clown [klaʊn] **1** *n* clown *m* **2** *vi* **to c. around** or **about** faire le clown

cloying ['klɔɪɪŋ] *adj (smell, sentiments)* écœurant

club [klʌb] **1** *n* **(a)** *(society)* club *m* **(b)** *(nightclub)* boîte *f* de nuit **(c)** *(weapon)* massue *f*; *(in golf)* club *m* **(d)** *Cards* **clubs** trèfle *m* **2** *(pt & pp* **-bb-)** *vt* frapper avec une massue **3** *vi* **(a)** *Br* **to c. together** se cotiser (**to buy sth** pour acheter qch) **(b)** **to go clubbing** aller en boîte ▪**clubhouse** *n* pavillon *m* ▪**club soda** *n Am* eau *f* gazeuse

cluck [klʌk] *vi (of hen)* glousser

clue [klu:] *n* indice *m*; *(of crossword)* définition *f*; *Fam* **I don't have a c.** je n'en ai pas la moindre idée ▪**clueless** *adj Br Fam* nul *(f* nulle)

clump [klʌmp] *n (of flowers, trees)* massif *m*

clumsy ['klʌmzɪ] (**-ier, -iest**) *adj* maladroit; *(tool)* peu commode ▪**clumsily** *adv* maladroitement ▪**clumsiness** *n* maladresse *f*

clung [klʌŋ] *pt & pp of* **cling**

cluster ['klʌstə(r)] **1** *n* groupe *m*; *(of stars)* amas *m* **2** *vi* se grouper

clutch [klʌtʃ] **1** *n* **(a)** *(in car)* embrayage *m*; *(pedal)* pédale *f* d'embrayage; **to let in/out the c.** embrayer/débrayer **(b)** **to fall into/escape from sb's clutches** tomber dans les griffes/ s'échapper des griffes de qn **2** *vt* tenir fermement **3** *vi* **to c. at** essayer de saisir

clutter ['klʌtə(r)] **1** *n (objects)* désordre *m* **2** *vt* **to c. (up)** *(room, table)* encombrer (**with** de)

cm *(abbr* **centimetre(s)** *n(pl)* cm *m(pl)*

Co *(abbr* **company)** *n* Cie *f*

co- [kəʊ] *pref* co-

c/o *(abbr* **care of)** *(on envelope)* chez

coach [kəʊtʃ] **1** *n* **(a)** *Br (train carriage)* voiture *f*, wagon *m*; *Br (bus)* car *m*; *(horse-drawn)* carrosse *m* **(b)** *(for sports)* entraîneur, -euse *mf* **2** *vt (sportsman, team)* entraîner; **to c. sb for an exam** préparer qn pour un examen *(en lui donnant des leçons particulières)*

coal [kəʊl] **1** *n* charbon *m* **2** *adj (merchant, fire)* de charbon; *(cellar, bucket)* à charbon; **c. industry** industrie *f* houillère ▪**coalfield** *n* bassin *m* houiller ▪**coalmine** *n* mine *f* de charbon ▪**coalminer** *n* mineur *m*

coalition [kəʊə'lɪʃən] *n* coalition *f*

coarse [kɔːs] (**-er, -est**) *adj* (*person, manners*) grossier, -ière, vulgaire; (*accent*) vulgaire; (*surface, fabric*) grossier; **to have c. hair** avoir les cheveux épais; **c. salt** gros sel *m* ▪**coarsely** *adv* grossièrement

coast [kəʊst] **1** *n* côte *f*; *Fig* **the c. is clear** la voie est libre **2** *vi* **to c. (down** or **along)** (*of vehicle, bicycle*) descendre en roue libre ▪**coastal** *adj* côtier, -ière ▪**coastguard** *n* (*person*) garde-côte *m* ▪**coastline** *n* littoral *m*

coaster ['kəʊstə(r)] *n* (*for glass*) dessous-de-verre *m inv*

coat [kəʊt] **1** *n* manteau *m*; (*overcoat*) pardessus *m*; (*jacket*) veste *f*; (*of animal*) pelage *m*; (*of paint*) couche *f*; **c. hanger** cintre *m*; **c. of arms** armoiries *fpl* **2** *vt* couvrir (**with** de); (*with chocolate, sugar*) enrober (**with** de) ▪**coating** *n* couche *f*

coax [kəʊks] *vt* enjôler; **to c. sb to do** or **into doing sth** amener qn à faire qch par des cajoleries; **she needed coaxing** elle s'est fait tirer l'oreille ▪**coaxing** *n* cajoleries *fpl*

cob [kɒb] *n* (*of corn*) épi *m*

cobble ['kɒbəl] **1** *n* pavé *m* **2** *vt* *Fam* **to c. together** (*text, compromise*) bricoler ▪**cobbled** *adj* (*street*) pavé ▪**cobble-stone** *n* pavé *m*

cobbler ['kɒblə(r)] *n* cordonnier *m*

cobra ['kəʊbrə] *n* (*snake*) cobra *m*

cobweb ['kɒbweb] *n* toile *f* d'araignée

Coca-Cola® [kəʊkə'kəʊlə] *n* Coca-Cola® *m*

cocaine [kəʊ'keɪn] *n* cocaïne *f*

cock [kɒk] **1** *n* (*rooster*) coq *m*; (*male bird*) mâle *m* **2** *vt* (*gun*) armer; **to c. one's ears** (*listen carefully*) dresser l'oreille ▪**cock-a-doodle-'doo** *n* & *exclam* cocorico (*m*) ▪**cock-and-'bull story** *n* histoire *f* à dormir debout

cockatoo [kɒkə'tuː] *n* cacatoès *m*

cocker ['kɒkə(r)] *n* **c. (spaniel)** cocker *m*

cockerel ['kɒkərəl] *n* jeune coq *m*

cock-eyed [kɒk'aɪd] *adj* *Fam* (*plan, idea*) farfelu

cockle ['kɒkəl] *n* (*shellfish*) coque *f*

cockney ['kɒknɪ] *adj* & *n* cockney (*mf*) (*natif des quartiers est de Londres*)

cockpit ['kɒkpɪt] *n* (*of aircraft*) poste *m* de pilotage

cockroach ['kɒkrəʊtʃ] *n* cafard *m*

cocksure [kɒk'ʃʊə(r)] *adj* *Fam* présomptueux, -ueuse

cocktail ['kɒkteɪl] *n* cocktail *m*; **fruit c.** macédoine *f* de fruits; **prawn c.** crevettes *fpl* à la mayonnaise; **c. party** cocktail *m*

cocky ['kɒkɪ] (**-ier, -iest**) *adj* *Fam* culotté

cocoa ['kəʊkəʊ] *n* cacao *m*

coconut ['kəʊkənʌt] *n* noix *f* de coco

cocoon [kə'kuːn] *n* cocon *m*

COD [siːəʊ'diː] (*abbr* **cash on delivery**) *n Br Com* paiement *m* à la livraison

cod [kɒd] *n* morue *f*; (*as food*) cabillaud *m* ▪**cod-liver 'oil** *n* huile *f* de foie de morue

coddle ['kɒdəl] *vt* dorloter

code [kəʊd] **1** *n* code *m*; **in c.** (*letter, message*) codé; **c. number** numéro *m* de code; **c. word** code **2** *vt* coder ▪**coding** *n* codage *m*

codeine ['kəʊdiːn] *n* codéine *f*

codify ['kəʊdɪfaɪ] (*pt & pp* **-ied**) *vt* codifier

co-educational [kəʊedjʊ'keɪʃənəl] *adj* (*school, teaching*) mixte

coefficient [kəʊɪ'fɪʃənt] *n* *Math* coefficient *m*

coerce [kəʊ'ɜːs] *vt* contraindre (**sb into doing** qn à faire) ▪**coercion** *n* contrainte *f*

coexist [kəʊɪg'zɪst] *vi* coexister ▪**coexistence** *n* coexistence *f*

coffee ['kɒfɪ] **1** *n* café *m*; **c. with milk**, *Br* **white c.** café au lait; **black c.** café noir; *Br* **c. bar** or **shop** café; **c. break** pause-café *f*; **c. cup** tasse *f* à café; **c. pot** cafetière *f*; **c. table** table *f* basse **2** *adj* **c.(-coloured)** café au lait *inv*

coffin ['kɒfɪn] *n* cercueil *m*

cog [kɒg] *n* dent *f*

cogitate ['kɒdʒɪteɪt] *vi* *Fml* méditer

cognac ['kɒnjæk] *n* cognac *m*

cohabit [kəʊ'hæbɪt] *vi* vivre en concubinage (**with** avec)

coherent [kəʊ'hɪərənt] *adj* (*logical*) cohérent; (*way of speaking*) compréhensible, intelligible ▪**cohesion** [-'hiːʒən] *n* cohésion *f*

coil [kɔɪl] **1** *n* (*of wire, rope*) rouleau *m*; (*single loop*) (*of hair*) boucle *f*; (*of snake*) anneau *m*; (*electrical*) bobine *f*; (*contraceptive*) stérilet *m* **2** *vt* (*rope, hair, hose*) enrouler (**around** autour de) **3** *vi* (*of snake*) s'enrouler (**around** autour de)

coin [kɔɪn] **1** *n* pièce *f* (de monnaie); *Am* **c. bank** tirelire *f* **2** *vt* (*money*) frapper; *Fig* (*word*) inventer; **to c. a phrase...** pour ainsi dire... ▪**coinage** *n* (*coins*) monnaie *f*; *Fig* invention *f*; **a recent c.** (*word*) un mot de formation récente ▪**coin-'operated** *adj* (*machine*) à pièces

coincide [kəʊɪn'saɪd] *vi* coïncider (**with** avec) ▪**coincidence** [-'ɪnsɪdəns] *n* coïncidence *f* ▪**coincidental** [-sɪ'dentəl] *adj* (*resemblance*) fortuit; **it's c.** c'est une coïncidence

coke [kəʊk] *n* (*fuel*) coke *m*; (*Coca-Cola®*) Coca® *m inv*

colander ['kʌləndə(r)] *n* (*for vegetables*) passoire *f*

cold [kəʊld] **1** (**-er, -est**) *adj* froid; **to be** or **feel c.** (*of person*) avoir froid; **to feel the c.** être frileux, -euse; **my hands are c.** j'ai froid aux mains; **it's c.** (*of weather*) il fait froid; **to get c.** (*of weather*) se refroidir; (*of food*) refroidir; **I'm getting c.** je commence à avoir froid; *Fam* **to get c. feet** se dégonfler; **in c. blood** de sang-froid; **c. cream** cold-cream *m*; *Br* **c. meats,** *Am*

c. cuts viandes *fpl* froides; c. sore bouton *m* de fièvre; c. war guerre *f* froide

2 *n* (**a**) *(temperature)* froid *m*; to be out in the c. être dehors dans le froid; *Fig* to be left out in the c. rester sur la touche (**b**) *(illness)* rhume *m*; a bad *or* nasty c. un gros rhume; to have a c. être enrhumé; to catch a c. attraper un rhume; to get a c. s'enrhumer ▪ **coldly** *adv* avec froideur ▪ **coldness** *n* froideur *f*

cold-blooded ['kəʊldblʌdɪd] *adj (person)* insensible; *(murder)* commis de sang-froid

cold-shoulder [kəʊld'ʃəʊldə(r)] *vt* snober

coleslaw ['kəʊlslɔː] *n* = salade de chou cru à la mayonnaise

colic ['kɒlɪk] *n* coliques *fpl*

collaborate [kə'læbəreɪt] *vi* collaborer (**on** à) ▪ **collaboration** [-'reɪʃən] *n* collaboration *f* ▪ **collaborator** *n* collaborateur, -trice *mf*

collage ['kɒlɑːʒ] *n (picture)* collage *m*

collapse [kə'læps] **1** *n* effondrement *m*; *(of government)* chute *f* **2** *vi (of person, building)* s'effondrer; *(faint)* se trouver mal; *(of government)* tomber ▪ **collapsible** *adj (chair)* pliant

collar ['kɒlə(r)] *n (on garment)* col *m*; *(of dog)* collier *m*; to seize sb by the c. saisir qn au collet ▪ **collarbone** *n* clavicule *f*

collate [kə'leɪt] *vt (documents) (gather)* rassembler; *(compare)* collationner

collateral [kəʊ'lætərəl] **1** *n Law & Fin (guarantee)* nantissement *m* **2** *adj* parallèle; *Law* collatéral; c. damage dégâts *mpl* ou dommages *mpl* collatéraux

colleague ['kɒliːg] *n* collègue *mf*

collect [kə'lekt] **1** *vt (pick up)* ramasser; *(gather)* rassembler; *(information)* recueillir; *(taxes)* percevoir; *(rent)* encaisser; *(stamps)* collectionner; to c. money *(in street, church)* quêter; to c. sb *(pick up)* passer prendre qn **2** *vi (of dust)* s'accumuler; *(of people)* se rassembler; *(in street, church)* quêter (**for** pour) **3** *adv Am* to call *or* phone sb c. téléphoner à qn en PCV

collection [kə'lekʃən] *n (of objects, stamps)* collection *f*; *(of poems)* recueil *m*; *(of money for church)* quête *f*; *(of mail, taxes)* levée *f*; *Br (of twigs, rubbish)* ramassage *m*

collective [kə'lektɪv] *adj* collectif, -ive ▪ **collectively** *adv* collectivement

collector [kə'lektə(r)] *n (of stamps)* collectionneur, -euse *mf*

college ['kɒlɪdʒ] *n Br (of further education)* établissement *m* d'enseignement supérieur; *Br (part of university)* = association d'enseignants et d'étudiants d'une même université qui dispose d'une semi-autonomie administrative; *Am (university)* université *f*; *Pol & Rel* collège *m*; to be at c. être étudiant; c. of music conservatoire *m* de musique

collide [kə'laɪd] *vi* entrer en collision (**with** avec) ▪ **collision** [-'lɪʒən] *n* collision *f*

colliery ['kɒlɪərɪ] *(pl* **-ies**) *n Br* houillère *f*

colloquial [kə'ləʊkwɪəl] *adj* familier, -ière ▪ **colloquialism** *n* expression *f* familière

collywobbles ['kɒlɪwɒbəlz] *npl Br Fam* to have the c. *(feel nervous)* avoir la frousse

cologne [kə'ləʊn] *n* eau *f* de Cologne

colon ['kəʊlən] *n* (**a**) *(punctuation mark)* deux-points *m* (**b**) *Anat* côlon *m*

colonel ['kɜːnəl] *n* colonel *m*

colonial [kə'ləʊnɪəl] *adj* colonial

colonize ['kɒlənaɪz] *vt* coloniser ▪ **colonization** [-'zeɪʃən] *n* colonisation *f*

colony ['kɒlənɪ] *(pl* **-ies**) *n* colonie *f*

colossal [kə'lɒsəl] *adj* colosse

colour ['kʌlə(r)] *(Am* **color**) **1** *n* couleur *f* **2** *adj (photo, television)* en couleurs; *(television set)* couleur *inv*; *(problem)* racial; c. supplement *(of newspaper)* supplément *m* en couleurs; to be off c. *(of person)* ne pas être dans son assiette **3** *vt* colorer; to c. (in) *(drawing)* colorier ▪ **coloured** *(Am* **colored**) *adj (person, pencil)* de couleur; *(glass, water)* coloré ▪ **colouring** *(Am* **coloring**) *n (in food)* colorant *m*; *(complexion)* teint *m*; *(with crayons)* coloriage *m*; *(shade, effect)* coloris *m*; *(blend of colours)* couleurs *fpl*; c. book album *m* de coloriages

colour-blind ['kʌləblaɪnd] *(Am* **color-blind**) *adj* daltonien, -ienne ▪ **colour-blindness** *(Am* **color-blindness**) *n* daltonisme *m*

colourfast ['kʌləfɑːst] *(Am* **colorfast**) *adj* grand teint *inv*

colourful ['kʌləfəl] *(Am* **colorful**) *adj (crowd, story)* coloré; *(person)* pittoresque

colt [kəʊlt] *n (horse)* poulain *m*

column ['kɒləm] *n* colonne *f*; *(newspaper feature)* rubrique *f*

coma ['kəʊmə] *n* coma *m*; in a c. dans le coma

comb [kəʊm] **1** *n* peigne *m* **2** *vt (hair)* peigner; *Fig (search)* ratisser, passer au peigne fin; to c. one's hair se peigner

combat ['kɒmbæt] **1** *n* combat *m*; *Br* c. trousers, *Am* c. pants battle-dress *m inv* **2** *vti* combattre (**for** pour)

combine¹ ['kɒmbaɪn] *n* (**a**) *(commercial)* association *f*; *(cartel)* cartel *m* (**b**) c. harvester *(machine)* moissonneuse-batteuse *f*

combine² [kəm'baɪn] **1** *vt (activities, qualities, features, elements, sounds)* combiner; *(efforts)* joindre, unir; to c. business with pleasure joindre l'utile à l'agréable; our combined efforts have produced a result en joignant nos efforts, nous avons obtenu un résultat; combined wealth/*etc* (put together) richesses/ *etc fpl* réunies **2** *vi (of teams, groups)* s'unir; *(of elements)* se combiner; *(of gases)* s'associer ▪ **combination** [kɒmbɪ'neɪʃən] *n* combinaison f; *(of qualities)* réunion f; **in c. with** en association avec; **c. lock** serrure f à combinaison

combustion [kəm'bʌstʃən] n combustion f

come [kʌm] *(pt came, pp come)* vi venir *(from* de; *to* à); **I've just c. from Glasgow/Scotland** j'arrive de Glasgow/d'Écosse; **to c. home** rentrer *(à la maison)*; **to c. first** *(in race, exam)* se classer premier; **c. and see me** viens me voir; **coming!** j'arrive!; **it came as a surprise to me** cela m'a surpris; **to c. near** *or* **close to** doing sth failllir faire qch; **to c. true** se réaliser; **c. next summer** l'été prochain; **in the years to c.** dans les années à venir; **nothing came of it** ça n'a abouti à rien; **c. what may** quoi qu'il arrive; **c. to think of it...** maintenant que j'y pense...; *Fam* **how c. ...?** comment se fait-il que...? ▪ **comeback** n **to make a c.** *(of fashion)* revenir; *(of actor, athlete)* faire un come-back ▪ **comedown** n *Fam* régression f

▸ **come about** vi *(happen)* arriver

▸ **come across** 1 vi **to c. across well/badly** bien/mal passer 2 vt insep *(find)* tomber sur

▸ **come along** vi venir *(with* avec*); (progress) (of work)* avancer; *(of student)* progresser; **c. along!** allons, pressons!

▸ **come at** vt insep *(attack)* attaquer

▸ **come away** vi *(leave, come off)* partir *(from* de*);* **to c. away from sb/sth** *(step or move back from)* s'écarter de qn/qch

▸ **come back** vi revenir; *(return home)* rentrer

▸ **come by** vt insep *(obtain)* obtenir; *(find)* trouver

▸ **come down** 1 vi descendre; *(of rain, temperature, price)* tomber; *(of building)* être démoli 2 vt insep *(stairs, hill)* descendre

▸ **come down with** vt insep *(illness)* attraper

▸ **come for** vt insep venir chercher

▸ **come forward** vi *(make oneself known, volunteer)* se présenter; **to c. forward with** *(suggestion)* offrir

▸ **come in** vi *(enter)* entrer; *(of tide)* monter; *(of train, athlete)* arriver; *(of money)* rentrer; **to c. in first** terminer premier; **to c. in useful** être bien utile

▸ **come in for** vt insep **to c. in for criticism** faire l'objet de critiques

▸ **come into** vt insep *(room)* entrer dans; *(money)* hériter de

▸ **come off** 1 vi *(of button)* se détacher; *(succeed)* réussir; *(happen)* avoir lieu 2 vt insep *(fall from)* tomber de; *(get down from)* descendre de

▸ **come on** vi *(make progress) (of work)* avancer; *(of student)* progresser; **c. on!** allez!

▸ **come out** vi sortir; *(of sun, book)* paraître; *(of stain)* s'enlever, partir; *(of secret)* être révélé; *(of photo)* réussir; **to c. out (on strike)** se mettre en grève

▸ **come over** 1 vi *(visit)* passer *(to* chez*);* **to c. over to** *(approach)* s'approcher de 2 vt insep **I don't know what came over me** je ne sais pas ce qui m'a pris

▸ **come round** vi *(visit)* passer *(to* chez*); (of date)* revenir; *(regain consciousness)* revenir à soi

▸ **come through** 1 vi *(survive)* s'en tirer 2 vt insep *(crisis)* sortir indemne de

▸ **come to** 1 vi *(regain consciousness)* revenir à soi 2 vt insep *(amount to)* revenir à; **to c. to a conclusion** arriver à une conclusion; **to c. to a decision** se décider; **to c. to an end** toucher à sa fin

▸ **come under** vt insep *(heading)* être classé sous; **to c. under sb's influence** subir l'influence de qn

▸ **come up** 1 vi *(rise)* monter; *(of question, job)* se présenter 2 vt insep *(stairs)* monter

▸ **come up against** vt insep *(problem)* se heurter à

▸ **come upon** vt insep *(book, reference)* tomber sur

▸ **come up to** vt insep *(reach)* arriver jusqu'à; *(approach)* s'approcher de; **the film didn't c. up to my expectations** le film n'était pas à la hauteur de mes espérances

▸ **come up with** vt insep *(idea, money)* trouver

comedy ['kɒmɪdɪ] *(pl* **-ies)** n comédie f ▪ **comedian** [kə'miːdɪən] n comique mf

> Note that the French word **comédien** is a false friend. It means **actor**.

comet ['kɒmɪt] n comète f

come-uppance [kʌm'ʌpəns] n *Fam* **he got his c.** il n'a eu que ce qu'il méritait

comfort ['kʌmfət] **1** n *(ease)* confort m; *(consolation)* réconfort m, consolation f; **to be a c. to sb** être d'un grand réconfort à qn; **too close for c.** trop près à mon/son/*etc* goût; *Am* **c. station** toilettes fpl publiques **2** vt *(console)* *(cheer)* réconforter ▪ **comfortable** adj *(chair, house)* confortable; *(rich)* aisé; **he's c.** *(in chair)* il est à son aise; *(of patient)* il ne souffre pas; **make yourself c.** mets-toi à ton aise ▪ **comfortably** adv *(sit)* confortablement; *(win)* facilement; **to live c.** avoir une vie aisée; **c. off** *(rich)* à l'aise financièrement ▪ **comforting** adj *(reassuring)* réconfortant

comforter ['kʌmfətər] n *Am (quilt)* édredon m; *(for baby)* sucette f

comfy ['kʌmfɪ] *(-ier, -iest)* adj *Fam (chair)* confortable; **I'm c.** je suis bien

comic ['kɒmɪk] **1** adj comique **2** n *(actor)* comique mf; *Br (magazine)* bande f dessinée, BD f; **c. book** bande f dessinée; **c. strip** *(in newspaper)* bande f dessinée ▪ **comical** adj comique

coming ['kʌmɪŋ] **1** adj *(future) (years, election,*

difficulties) à venir; **the c. month** le mois prochain; **the c. days** les prochains jours **2** *n* **comings and goings** allées *fpl* et venues

comma ['kɒmə] *n* virgule *f*

command [kə'mɑːnd] **1** *n* (*order*) ordre *m*; (*authority*) commandement *m*; (*mastery*) maîtrise *f* (**of** de); *Comptr* commande *f*; **at one's c.** (*disposal*) à sa disposition; **to be in c. (of)** (*ship, army*) commander; (*situation*) être maître (de); **under the c. of** sous le commandement de

2 *vt* (*order*) commander (**sb to do** à qn de faire); (*control*) (*ship, army*) commander; (*dominate*) (*of building*) dominer; (*be able to use*) disposer de; (*respect*) forcer

3 *vi* (*of captain*) commander ▪ **commanding** *adj* (*authoritative*) imposant; (*position*) dominant; **c. officer** commandant *m*

commandant ['kɒməndænt] *n Mil* commandant *m*

commandeer [kɒmən'dɪə(r)] *vt* réquisitionner

commander [kə'mɑːndə(r)] *n Mil* commandant *m*; **c.-in-chief** commandant *m* en chef

commandment [kə'mɑːndmənt] *n Rel* commandement *m*

commando [kə'mɑːndəʊ] (*pl* **-os** *or* **-oes**) *n* (*soldiers, unit*) commando *m*

commemorate [kə'meməreɪt] *vt* commémorer ▪ **commemoration** [-'reɪʃən] *n* commémoration *f* ▪ **commemorative** [-rətɪv] *adj* commémoratif, -ive

commence [kə'mens] *vti Formal* commencer (**doing** à faire) ▪ **commencement** *n* commencement *m*; *Am* (*ceremony*) remise *f* des diplômes

commend [kə'mend] *vt* (*praise*) louer; (*recommend*) recommander ▪ **commendable** *adj* louable

comment ['kɒment] **1** *n* commentaire *m* (**on** sur); **no c.!** sans commentaire! **2** *vi* faire des commentaires (**on** sur); **I won't c.** je n'ai rien à dire; **to c. on** (*text, event, news item*) commenter; **to c. that...** remarquer que... ▪ **commentary** [-əntərɪ] (*pl* **-ies**) *n* commentaire *m*; **live c.** (*on TV or radio*) reportage *m* en direct ▪ **commentate** [-ənteɪt] *vi* faire le commentaire; **to c. on sth** commenter qch ▪ **commentator** [-ənteɪtə(r)] *n* commentateur, -trice *mf* (**on** de)

commerce ['kɒmɜːs] *n* commerce *m* ▪ **commercial** [kə'mɜːʃəl] **1** *adj* commercial; **c. break** page *f* de publicité; **c. district** quartier *m* commerçant; *Br* **c. traveller** voyageur *m* de commerce **2** *n* (*advertisement*) publicité *f*; **the commercials** la publicité

commercialize [kə'mɜːʃəlaɪz] *vt Pej* (*event*) transformer en une affaire de gros sous ▪ **commercialized** *adj* (*district*) devenu trop commercial

commiserate [kə'mɪzəreɪt] *vi* **to c. with sb** être désolé pour qn ▪ **commiseration** [-'reɪʃən] *n* commisération *f*

commission [kə'mɪʃən] **1** *n* (*fee, group*) commission *f*; (*order for work*) commande *f*; **out of c.** (*machine*) hors service; *Mil* **to get one's c.** être nommé officier **2** *vt* (*artist*) passer une commande à; (*book*) commander; **to c. sb to do sth** charger qn de faire qch; *Mil* **to be commissioned** être nommé officier; **commissioned officer** officier *m* ▪ **commissioner** *n Pol* commissaire *m*; *Br* (**police**) **c.** commissaire de police

commissionaire [kəmɪʃə'neə(r)] *n Br* (*in hotel*) chasseur *m*

commit [kə'mɪt] (*pt & pp* **-tt-**) *vt* (*crime*) commettre; (*bind*) engager; (*devote*) consacrer; **to c. suicide** se suicider; **to c. sth to memory** apprendre qch par cœur; **to c. sb to prison** incarcérer qn; **to c. oneself** (*make a promise*) s'engager (**to** à) ▪ **commitment** *n* (*duty, responsibility*) obligation *f*; (*promise*) engagement *m*; (*devotion*) dévouement *m* (**to** à)

committee [kə'mɪtɪ] *n* comité *m*; (*parliamentary*) commission *f*

commodity [kə'mɒdɪtɪ] (*pl* **-ies**) *n Econ* marchandise *f*, produit *m*

common ['kɒmən] **1** (**-er, -est**) *adj* (*shared, vulgar*) commun; (*frequent*) courant, commun; **the c. man** l'homme *m* de la rue; **in c.** (*shared*) en commun (**with** avec); **to have nothing in c.** n'avoir rien de commun (**with** avec); **in c. with** (*like*) comme; **c. law** droit *m* coutumier; **c.-law wife** concubine *f*; **C. Market** Marché *m* commun; **c. room** (*for students*) salle *f* commune; (*for teachers*) salle *f* des professeurs; **c. sense** sens *m* commun, bon sens; **c. or garden** ordinaire

2 *n* (*land*) terrain *m* communal; **the Commons** les Communes *fpl*

▪ **commoner** *n* roturier, -ière *mf* ▪ **commonly** *adv* communément ▪ **commonness** *n* (*frequency*) fréquence *f*; (*vulgarity*) vulgarité *f*

commonplace ['kɒmənpleɪs] **1** *adj* courant **2** *n* banalité *f*

Commonwealth ['kɒmənwelθ] *n Br* **the C.** le Commonwealth

commotion [kə'məʊʃən] *n* (*disruption*) agitation *f*

communal [kə'mjuːnəl] *adj* (*shared*) (*bathroom, kitchen*) commun; (*of the community*) communautaire ▪ **communally** *adv* (*own*) en commun; (*live*) en communauté

commune 1 ['kɒmjuːn] *n* (*district*) commune *f*; (*group*) communauté *f* **2** [kə'mjuːn] *vi* **to c. with nature/God** être en communion avec la nature/Dieu ▪ **co'mmunion** *n* communion *f* (**with** avec); (**Holy**) **C.** communion; **to take C.** communier

communicate [kə'mju:nıkeıt] **1** vt communiquer; *(illness)* transmettre (**to** à) **2** vi *(of person, rooms)* communiquer (**with** avec) ▪ **communication** [-'keıʃən] n communication f; Br **c. cord** *(on train)* signal m d'alarme

communicative [kə'mju:nıkətıv] adj communicatif, -ive

communism ['kɒmjʊnızəm] n communisme m ▪ **communist** adj & n communiste *(mf)*

community [kə'mju:nıtı] **1** *(pl* **-ies)** n communauté f; **the student c.** les étudiants mpl **2** adj *(rights, life, spirit)* communautaire; **c. centre** centre m socioculturel; **c. worker** animateur, -trice mf socioculturel(le)

commute [kə'mju:t] **1** n *(journey)* trajet m **2** vt Law commuer (**to** en) **3** vi **to c. (to work)** faire la navette entre son domicile et son travail ▪ **commuter** n banlieusard, -arde mf; **c. town** cité-dortoir m; **c. train** train m de banlieue

compact¹ [kəm'pækt] adj *(car, crowd, substance)* compact; *(style)* condensé; **c. disc** ['kɒmpækt] disque m compact

compact² ['kɒmpækt] n *(for face powder)* poudrier m

companion [kəm'pænjən] n *(person)* compagnon m, compagne f; *(handbook)* manuel m ▪ **companionship** n camaraderie f

company ['kʌmpənı] *(pl* **-ies)** n *(companionship)* compagnie f; *(guests)* invités mpl, -ées fpl; *(people present)* assemblée f; *(business)* société f, compagnie f; **(theatre) c.** compagnie f (théâtrale); **to keep sb c.** tenir compagnie à qn; **in sb's c.** en compagnie de qn; **he's good c.** c'est un bon compagnon; **c. car** voiture f de société

comparable ['kɒmpərəbəl] adj comparable (**with** or **to** à)

comparative [kəm'pærətıv] **1** adj *(method)* comparatif, -ive; *(law, literature)* comparé; *(relative)(costs, comfort)* relatif, -ive **2** n Grammar comparatif m ▪ **comparatively** adv relativement

compare [kəm'peə(r)] **1** vt comparer (**with** or **to** à); **compared to** or **with** en comparaison de **2** vi être comparable (**with** à) ▪ **comparison** [-'pærısən] n comparaison f (**between** entre; **with** avec); **in c. with** en comparaison avec; **by** or **in c.** en comparaison; **there is no c.** il n'y a pas de comparaison

compartment [kəm'pɑ:tmənt] n compartiment m ▪ **compartmentalize** [kɒmpɑ:t'mentəlaiz] vt compartimenter

compass ['kʌmpəs] n **(a)** *(for finding direction)* boussole f; *(on ship)* compas m **(b) (pair of) compasses** compas m

compassion [kəm'pæʃən] n compassion f ▪ **compassionate** adj compatissant; **on c. grounds** pour raisons personnelles

compatible [kəm'pætıbəl] adj compatible ▪ **compati'bility** n compatibilité f

compatriot [kəm'pætrıət, kəm'peıtrıət] n compatriote mf

compel [kəm'pel] *(pt & pp* **-ll-)** vt forcer, obliger; *(respect, obedience)* forcer (**from sb** chez qn); **to c. sb to do sth** forcer qn à faire qch ▪ **compelling** adj *(film)* captivant; *(argument)* convaincant; *(urge)* irrésistible

compendium [kəm'pendıəm] n abrégé m

compensate ['kɒmpənseıt] **1** vt **to c. sb** *(with payment, reward)* dédommager qn (**for** de) **2** vi compenser; **to c. for sth** *(make up for)* compenser qch ▪ **compensation** [-'seıʃən] n *(financial)* dédommagement m; *(consolation)* compensation f; **in c. for** en dédommagement/compensation de

compère ['kɒmpeə(r)] **1** n animateur, -trice mf **2** vt animer

compete [kəm'pi:t] vi *(take part in race)* concourir (**in** à); **to c. (with sb)** rivaliser (avec qn); *(in business)* faire concurrence (à qn); **to c. for sth** se disputer qch; **to c. in a race/rally** participer à une course/un rallye

competent ['kɒmpıtənt] adj *(capable)* compétent (**to do** pour faire); *(sufficient)* *(knowledge)* suffisant ▪ **competence** n compétence f ▪ **competently** adv avec compétence

competition [kɒmpə'tıʃən] n **(a)** *(rivalry)* rivalité f; *(between companies)* concurrence f; **to be in c. with sb** être en concurrence avec qn **(b)** *(contest)* concours m; *(in sport)* compétition f

competitive [kəm'petıtıv] adj *(price, market)* compétitif, -ive; *(selection)* par concours; *(person)* qui a l'esprit de compétition; **c. examination** concours m ▪ **competitor** n concurrent, -ente mf

compile [kəm'paıl] vt *(list, catalogue)* dresser; *(documents)* compiler

complacent [kəm'pleısənt] adj content de soi ▪ **complacence, complacency** n autosatisfaction f; **there is no room for c.** ce n'est pas le moment de faire de l'autosatisfaction

complain [kəm'pleın] vi se plaindre (**to sb** à qn; **of** or **about sb/sth** de qn/qch; **that** que); **to c. of** or **about being tired** se plaindre d'être fatigué ▪ **complaint** n plainte f; *(in shop)* réclamation f; *(illness)* maladie f

complement 1 ['kɒmplımənt] n complément m **2** ['kɒmplıment] vt compléter ▪ **complementary** [-'mentərı] adj complémentaire; **c. medicine** médecines fpl douces

complete [kəm'pli:t] **1** adj *(whole)* complet, -ète; *(utter)* total; *(finished)* achevé; **he's a c. fool** il est complètement idiot **2** vt *(finish)* achever; *(form)* compléter ▪ **completely** adv complètement ▪ **completion** n achèvement m; *(of contract, sale)* exécution f

complex ['kɒmpleks] **1** *adj* complexe **2** *n* (*feeling, buildings*) complexe *m* ▪**complexity** [kəm'pleksɪtɪ] (*pl* **-ies**) *n* complexité *f*

complexion [kəm'plekʃən] *n* (*of face*) teint *m*; *Fig* caractère *m* (**of** de)

compliance [kəm'plaɪəns] *n* (*agreement*) conformité *f* (**with** avec)

complicate ['kɒmplɪkeɪt] *vt* compliquer (**with** de) ▪**complicated** *adj* compliqué ▪**complication** [-'keɪʃən] *n* complication *f*

compliment 1 ['kɒmplɪmənt] *n* compliment *m*; **compliments** (*of author*) hommages *mpl*; **to pay sb a c.** faire un compliment à qn; **compliments of the season** meilleurs vœux pour Noël et le nouvel an **2** ['kɒmplɪment] *vt* complimenter, faire des compliments à; **to c. sb on sth** (*bravery*) féliciter qn de qch; (*dress, haircut*) faire des compliments à qn sur qch ▪**complimentary** [-'mentərɪ] *adj* (**a**) (*praising*) élogieux, -ieuse (**b**) (*free*) gratuit; **c. ticket** billet *m* de faveur

comply [kəm'plaɪ] (*pt & pp* **-ied**) *vi* (*obey*) obéir; **to c. with** (*order*) obéir à; (*rule*) se conformer à; (*request*) accéder à

component [kəm'pəʊnənt] **1** *n* (*of structure, self-assembly furniture, problem*) élément *m*; (*of machine*) pièce *f*; (*chemical, electronic*) composant *m* **2** *adj* **c. part** pièce *f* détachée

compose [kəm'pəʊz] *vt* composer; **to c. oneself** se calmer ▪**composed** *adj* calme ▪**composer** *n* (*of music*) compositeur, -trice *mf* ▪**composition** [kɒmpə'zɪʃən] *n* (*in music, art, chemistry*) composition *f*; (*school essay*) rédaction *f*

compost ['kɒmpɒst] *n* compost *m*

composure [kəm'pəʊʒə(r)] *n* sang-froid *m*

compound 1 ['kɒmpaʊnd] **1** *n* (*word*) & *Chem* (*substance*) composé *m*; (*area*) enclos *m* **2** *adj* (*word, substance*) & *Fin* (*interest*) composé; (*sentence, number*) complexe **3** [kəm'paʊnd] *vt* (*problem*) aggraver

comprehend [kɒmprɪ'hend] *vt* comprendre ▪**comprehensible** *adj* compréhensible ▪**comprehension** *n* compréhension *f*

comprehensive [kɒmprɪ'hensɪv] **1** *adj* complet, -ète; (*study*) exhaustif, -ive; (*knowledge*) étendu; (*view, measure*) d'ensemble; (*insurance*) tous risques *inv* **2** *adj & n Br* **c. (school)** ≃ établissement *m* d'enseignement secondaire (*n'opérant pas de sélection à l'entrée*)

> Note that the French word **compréhensif** is a false friend and is never a translation for the English word **comprehensive**. It means **understanding**.

compress 1 ['kɒmpres] *n Med* compresse *f* **2** [kəm'pres] *vt* (*gas, air*) comprimer; *Fig* (*ideas, facts*) condenser ▪**compression** [-'preʃən] *n* compression *f*

comprise [kəm'praɪz] *vt* (*consist of*) comprendre; (*make up*) constituer; **to be comprised of** comprendre

compromise 1 ['kɒmprəmaɪz] **1** *n* compromis *m*; **c. solution** solution *f* de compromis **2** *vt* (*person, security*) compromettre; (*principles*) transiger sur; **to c. oneself** se compromettre **3** *vi* transiger (**on** sur) ▪**compromising** *adj* compromettant

compulsion [kəm'pʌlʃən] *n* (*urge*) besoin *m*; (*obligation*) contrainte *f* ▪**compulsive** *adj* (*behaviour*) compulsif, -ive; (*smoker, gambler, liar*) invétéré; **c. eater** boulimique *mf*

compulsory [kəm'pʌlsərɪ] *adj* obligatoire; **c. redundancy** licenciement *m* sec

compunction [kəm'pʌŋkʃən] *n* scrupule *m* (**about doing** à faire)

compute [kəm'pjuːt] *vt* calculer ▪**computing** *n* informatique *f*

computer [kəm'pjuːtə(r)] **1** *n* ordinateur *m* **2** *adj* (*program, system, network*) informatique; (*course, firm*) d'informatique; **to be c. literate** avoir des connaissances en informatique; **c. game** jeu *m* électronique; **c. language** langage *m* de programmation; **c. operator** opérateur, -trice *mf* sur ordinateur; **c. science** informatique *f*; **c. scientist** informaticien, -ienne *mf* ▪**computerization** [-raɪ'zeɪʃən] *n* informatisation *f* ▪**computerized** *adj* informatisé

comrade ['kɒmreɪd] *n* camarade *mf*

con [kɒn] *Fam* **1** *n* arnaque *f*; **c. man** arnaqueur *m* **2** (*pt & pp* **-nn-**) *vt* arnaquer; **to be conned** se faire arnaquer

concave [kɒn'keɪv] *adj* concave

conceal [kən'siːl] *vt* (*hide*) (*object*) dissimuler (**from** à qn); (*plan, news*) cacher (**from sb** à qn) ▪**concealment** *n* dissimulation *f*

concede [kən'siːd] **1** *vt* concéder (**to** à; **that** que); **to c. defeat** s'avouer vaincu **2** *vi* s'incliner

conceit [kən'siːt] *n* vanité *f* ▪**conceited** *adj* vaniteux, -euse

conceive [kən'siːv] **1** *vt* (*idea, child*) concevoir **2** *vi* (*of woman*) concevoir; **to c. of sth** concevoir qch ▪**conceivable** *adj* concevable; **it's c. that...** il est concevable que... (+ *subjunctive*) ▪**conceivably** *adv* **yes, c.** oui, c'est concevable

concentrate ['kɒnsəntreɪt] **1** *vt* concentrer (**on** sur) **2** *vi* se concentrer (**on** sur); **to c. on doing sth** s'appliquer à faire qch ▪**concentration** [-'treɪʃən] *n* concentration *f*; **to have a short c. span** ne pas avoir une grande capacité de concentration; **c. camp** camp *m* de concentration

concentric [kən'sentrɪk] *adj Math* concentrique

concept ['kɒnsept] *n* concept *m* ▪**conception** [kən'sepʃən] *n* (*of child, idea*) conception *f*

concern [kən'sɜːn] **1** *n (matter)* affaire *f; (worry)* inquiétude *f;* **his c. for** son souci de; **it's no c. of mine** cela ne me regarde pas; **(business)** c. entreprise *f* **2** *vt* concerner; **to c. oneself with sth, to be concerned with sth** *(be busy)* s'occuper de qch; **to be concerned about** *(be worried)* s'inquiéter de; **as far as I'm concerned...** en ce qui me concerne... ▪ **concerned** *adj (anxious)* inquiet, -iète (**about/at** au sujet de); **the department c.** *(relevant)* le service compétent ▪ **concerning** *prep* en ce qui concerne

concert ['kɒnsət] *n* concert *m;* **in c.** *(together)* de concert (**with** avec); **c. hall** salle *f* de concert; **c. pianist** concertiste *mf* ▪ **concert-goer** *n* habitué, -uée *mf* des concerts

concerted [kən'sɜːtɪd] *adj (effort)* concerté

concertina [kɒnsə'tiːnə] *n* concertina *m;* **c. crash** *(of vehicles)* carambolage *m*

concerto [kən'tʃɜːtəʊ] *(pl* **-os)** *n* concerto *m*

concession [kən'seʃən] *n* concession *f* (**to** à) ▪ **concessionary** *adj (rate, price)* réduit

conciliate [kən'sɪlɪeɪt] *vt* **to c. sb** *(win over)* se concilier qn; *(soothe)* apaiser qn ▪ **conciliation** [-'eɪʃən] *n* conciliation *f; (soothing)* apaisement *m* ▪ **conciliatory** [-lɪətərɪ, *Am* -tɔːrɪ] *adj (tone, person)* conciliant

concise [kən'saɪs] *adj* concis ▪ **concisely** *adv* avec concision ▪ **conciseness, concision** [-'sɪʒən] *n* concision *f*

conclude [kən'kluːd] **1** *vt (end, settle)* conclure; *(festival)* clore; **to c. that...** *(infer)* conclure que... **2** *vi (of event)* se terminer (**with** par); *(of speaker)* conclure ▪ **concluding** *adj (remarks, speech)* final *(mpl* **-als)** ▪ **conclusion** *n* conclusion *f;* **in c.** pour conclure; **to come to the c. that...** arriver à la conclusion que...

conclusive [kən'kluːsɪv] *adj* concluant ▪ **conclusively** *adv* de manière concluante

concoct [kən'kɒkt] *vt (dish, scheme)* concocter ▪ **concoction** *n (dish, drink)* mixture *f*

concord ['kɒŋkɔːd] *n* concorde *f*

concourse ['kɒŋkɔːs] *n (in airport, train station)* hall *m*

concrete ['kɒŋkriːt] **1** *n* béton *m;* **c. wall** mur *m* en béton; **c. mixer** bétonnière *f* **2** *adj (ideas, example)* concret, -ète

concur [kən'kɜː(r)] *(pt & pp* **-rr-)** *vi* **(a)** *(agree)* être d'accord (**with** avec) **(b)** *(happen together)* coïncider; **to c. to** *(contribute)* concourir à

concurrent [kən'kʌrənt] *adj* simultané ▪ **concurrently** *adv* simultanément

concussion [kən'kʌʃən] *n (injury)* commotion *f* cérébrale

condemn [kən'dem] *vt* condamner (**to** à); *(building)* déclarer inhabitable; **condemned man** condamné *m* à mort ▪ **condemnation** [kɒndem'neɪʃən] *n* condamnation *f*

condense [kən'dens] **1** *vt* condenser **2** *vi* se condenser ▪ **condensation** [kɒndən'seɪʃən] *n* condensation *f* (**of** de); *(mist)* buée *f*

condescend [kɒndɪ'send] *vi* condescendre (**to do** à faire) ▪ **condescension** *n* condescendance *f*

condiment ['kɒndɪmənt] *n* condiment *m*

condition ['kəndɪʃən] **1** *n (stipulation, circumstance, rank)* condition *f; (state)* état *m,* condition *f; (disease)* maladie *f;* **on the c. that...** à la condition que... (+ *subjunctive);* **on c. that I come with you** à condition que je t'accompagne; **in good c.** en bon état; **in/out of c.** en bonne/mauvaise forme **2** *vt (influence)* conditionner; *(hair)* mettre de l'après-shampooing sur; **to c. sb** *(train)* conditionner qn (**to do** à faire); **to be conditioned by sth** dépendre de qch ▪ **conditional 1** *adj* conditionnel, -elle; **to be c. upon** dépendre de **2** *n Grammar* conditionnel *m*

conditioner [kən'dɪʃənə(r)] *n (hair)* c. après-shampooing *m*

condo ['kɒndəʊ] *(pl* **-os)** *n Am* = **condominium**

condolences [kən'dəʊlənsɪz] *npl* condoléances *fpl*

condom ['kɒndəm, -dɒm] *n* préservatif *m*

condominium [kɒndə'mɪnɪəm] *n Am (building)* immeuble *m* en copropriété; *(apartment)* appartement *m* en copropriété

condone [kən'dəʊn] *vt (overlook)* fermer les yeux sur; *(forgive)* excuser

conducive [kən'djuːsɪv] *adj* **to be c. to** être favorable à; **not to be c. to** ne pas inciter à

conduct 1 ['kɒndʌkt] *n (behaviour, directing)* conduite *f* **2** [kən'dʌkt] *vt (campaign, inquiry, experiment)* mener; *(orchestra)* diriger; *(electricity, heat)* conduire; **to c. one's business** diriger ses affaires; **to c. oneself** se conduire; **conducted tour** *(of building, region)* visite *f* guidée

conductor [kən'dʌktə(r)] *n (of orchestra)* chef *m* d'orchestre; *Br (on bus)* receveur *m; Am (on train)* chef *m* de train; *(metal, cable)* conducteur *m*

> Note that the French word **conducteur** often is a false friend and is rarely a translation for the English word **conductor**.

cone [kəʊn] *n* cône *m; (for ice cream)* cornet *m;* **(paper) c.** cornet (de papier); **pine** *or* **fir c.** pomme *f* de pin; *Br* **traffic c.** cône de chantier

confectioner [kən'fekʃənə(r)] *n (of sweets)* confiseur, -euse *mf; (of cakes)* pâtissier, -ière *mf* ▪ **confectionery** *n (sweets)* confiserie *f; (cakes)* pâtisserie *f*

> Note that the French word **confectionneur** is a false friend and is not a translation for the English word **confectioner**. It means **clothes manufacturer**.

confederate [kən'fedərət] **1** *adj Pol* confédéré **2** *n (accomplice)* complice *mf* ▪ **confederacy, confederation** [-'reɪʃən] *n* confédération *f*

confer [kən'fɜː(r)] (*pt & pp* **-rr-**) **1** *vt (grant)* octroyer (**on** à) **2** *vi (talk together)* se consulter (**on** *or* **about** sur); **to c. with sb** consulter qn

conference ['kɒnfərəns] *n* conférence *f*; *(scientific, academic)* congrès *m*; **press** *or* **news c.** conférence de presse; **in c. (with)** en conférence (avec); *Tel* **c. call** téléconférence *f*

confess [kən'fes] **1** *vt* avouer, confesser (**that** que; **to** à qn); *Rel* confesser **2** *vi* avouer; *Rel* se confesser; **to c. to sth** *(crime)* avouer *ou* confesser qch; *(feeling)* avouer qch ▪ **confession** *n* aveu *m*, confession *f*; *Rel* confession; **to go to c.** aller à confesse ▪ **confessional** *n Rel* confessionnal *m*

confetti [kən'fetɪ] *n* confettis *mpl*

confidant [kɒnfɪ'dænt] *n* confident, -ente *mf*

confide [kən'faɪd] **1** *vt* confier (**to** à; **that** que) **2** *vi* **to c. in sb** se confier à qn

confidence ['kɒnfɪdəns] *n (trust)* confiance *f* (**in** en); *(secret)* confidence *f*; **(self-)c.** confiance *f* en soi; **in c.** *(adverb)* en confidence; *(adjective)* confidentiel, -ielle; **in strict c.** *(adverb)* tout à fait confidentiellement; *(adjective)* tout à fait confidentiel; **c. trick** escroquerie *f*; **c. trickster** escroc *m* ▪ **confident** *adj (smile, exterior)* confiant; **(self-)c.** sûr de soi ▪ **confidently** *adv* avec confiance

confidential [kɒnfɪ'denʃəl] *adj* confidentiel, -ielle ▪ **confidentially** *adv* en confidence

configuration [kənfɪgjʊ'reɪʃən] *n* configuration *f*

confine [kən'faɪn] *vt* (a) *(limit)* limiter (**to** à); **to c. oneself to doing sth** se limiter à faire qch (b) *(keep prisoner)* enfermer (**to/in** dans) ▪ **confined** *adj (atmosphere)* confiné; *(space)* réduit; **c. to bed** alité; **c. to the house/one's room** obligé de rester chez soi/de garder la chambre ▪ **confinement** *n (of prisoner)* emprisonnement *m*; *Old-fashioned Med (of pregnant woman)* couches *fpl*

confines ['kɒnfaɪnz] *npl* confins *mpl*; *Fig* limites *fpl*

confirm [kən'fɜːm] *vt* confirmer (**that** que); *Rel* **to be confirmed** recevoir la confirmation ▪ **confirmation** [kɒnfə'meɪʃən] *n & Rel* confirmation *f*; **it's subject to c.** c'est à confirmer ▪ **confirmed** *adj (bachelor)* endurci; *(smoker, habit)* invétéré

confiscate ['kɒnfɪskeɪt] *vt* confisquer (**from** à) ▪ **confiscation** [-'keɪʃən] *n* confiscation *f*

conflagration [kɒnflə'greɪʃən] *n* incendie *m*

conflict 1 ['kɒnflɪkt] *n* conflit *m* **2** [kən'flɪkt] *vi (of statement)* être en contradiction (**with** avec); *(of dates, events, programmes)* tomber en même temps (**with** que) ▪ **conflicting** *adj (views,*

theories, evidence) contradictoire; *(dates)* incompatible

confluence ['kɒnfluəns] *n (of rivers)* confluent *m*

conform [kən'fɔːm] *vi (of person)* se conformer (**to** *or* **with** à); *(of ideas, actions)* être en conformité (**to** with); *(of product)* être conforme (**to** *or* **with** à) ▪ **conformist** *adj & n* conformiste *(mf)* ▪ **conformity** *n* conformité *f*

confound [kən'faʊnd] *vt (surprise, puzzle)* laisser perplexe

confront [kən'frʌnt] *vt (danger)* affronter; *(problem)* faire face à; **to c. sb** *(be face to face with)* se trouver en face de qn; *(oppose)* s'opposer à qn; **to c. sb with sth** mettre qn en face de qch ▪ **confrontation** [kɒnfrən-'teɪʃən] *n* confrontation *f*

confuse [kən'fjuːz] *vt (make unsure)* embrouiller; **to c. sb/sth with** *(mistake for)* confondre qn/qch avec; **to c. matters** *or* **the issue** embrouiller la question ▪ **confused** *adj (situation, noises, idea)* confus; **to be c.** *(of person)* s'y perdre; **I'm (all** *or* **quite) c. (about it)** je m'y perds; **to get c.** s'embrouiller ▪ **confusing** *adj* déroutant ▪ **confusion** *n (bewilderment)* perplexité *f*; *(disorder, lack of clarity)* confusion *f*; **in (a state of) c.** en désordre

congeal [kən'dʒiːl] *vi (of blood)* (se) coaguler ▪ **congealed** *adj* **c. blood** sang *m* coagulé

congenial [kən'dʒiːnɪəl] *adj* sympathique

congenital [kən'dʒenɪtəl] *adj* congénital

congested [kən'dʒestɪd] *adj (street, town, lungs)* congestionné; *(nose)* bouché ▪ **congestion** *n (traffic)* encombrements *mpl*; *(overcrowding)* surpeuplement *m*

Congo ['kɒŋɡəʊ] *n* **(the) C.** le Congo

congratulate [kən'ɡrætʃʊleɪt] *vt* féliciter (**sb on sth** qn de qch; **sb on doing sth** qn d'avoir fait qch) ▪ **congratulations** [-'leɪʃənz] *npl* félicitations *fpl* (**on** pour) ▪ **congratulatory** *adj (telegram)* de félicitations

congregate ['kɒŋɡrɪgeɪt] *vi* se rassembler ▪ **congregation** [-'geɪʃən] *n (worshippers)* fidèles *mpl*

congress ['kɒŋɡres] *n* congrès *m*; *Am Pol* **C.** le Congrès *(assemblée législative américaine)* ▪ **Congressional** [kɒŋ'ɡreʃənəl] *adj Am Pol* du Congrès ▪ **Congressman** (*pl* **-men**) *n Am Pol* membre *m* du Congrès

conical ['kɒnɪkəl] *adj* conique

conifer ['kɒnɪfə(r)] *n* conifère *m*

conjecture [kən'dʒektʃə(r)] **1** *n* conjecture *f* **2** *vt* supposer **3** *vi* faire des conjectures

conjugal ['kɒndʒʊɡəl] *adj* conjugal

conjugate ['kɒndʒʊɡeɪt] *Grammar* **1** *vt (verb)* conjuguer **2** *vi* se conjuguer ▪ **conju'gation** *n* conjugaison *f*

conjunction [kən'dʒʌŋkʃən] *n Grammar* conjonction *f*; **in c. with** conjointement avec

conjunctivitis [kəndʒʌŋktɪ'vaɪtɪs] *n* conjonctivite *f*; **to have c.** avoir de la conjonctivite

conjure ['kʌndʒə(r)] *vt* **to c. (up)** *(by magic)* faire apparaître, *Fig* **to c. up** *(memories, images)* évoquer; **conjuring trick** tour *m* de prestidigitation ▪ **conjurer** *n* prestidigitateur, -trice *mf*

conk [kɒŋk] *Fam* **1** *n Br (nose)* pif *m*; *(blow)* gnon *m* **2** *vi* **c. out** *(break down)* tomber en panne; **the car conked out on me** la voiture m'a claqué entre les doigts

conker ['kɒŋkə(r)] *n Br Fam (chestnut)* marron *m* (d'Inde)

connect [kə'nekt] **1** *vt* relier (**with** *or* **to** à); *(telephone, washing machine)* brancher; **to c. sb with sb** *(on phone)* mettre qn en communication avec qn; **to c. sb/sth with sb/ sth** établir un lien entre qn/qch et qn/qch **2** *vi (be connected)* être relié; *(of rooms)* communiquer; *(of roads)* se rejoindre; **to c. with** *(of train, bus)* assurer la correspondance avec ▪ **connected** *adj (facts, events)* lié; **to be c. with** *(have to do with, relate to)* avoir un lien avec; *(have dealings with)* être lié à; *(by marriage)* être parent avec; **the two issues are not c.** les deux questions n'ont aucun rapport; **to be well c.** avoir des relations

connection [kə'nekʃən] *n (link)* rapport *m*, lien *m* (**with** avec); *(train, bus)* correspondance *f*; *(phone call)* communication *f*; *(between electrical wires)* contact *m*; *(between pipes)* raccord *m*; **connections** *(contacts)* relations *fpl*; **to have no c. with** n'avoir aucun rapport avec; **in c. with** à propos de; **in this** *or* **that c.** à ce propos; **there's a loose c.** *(in electrical appliance)* il y a un faux contact

connive [kə'naɪv] *vi* **to c. with sb** être de connivence avec qn; **to c. at sth** *(let happen)* laisser faire qch

connoisseur [kɒnə'sɜː(r)] *n* connaisseur *m*

connotation [kɒnə'teɪʃən] *n* connotation *f*

conquer ['kɒŋkə(r)] *vt (country, freedom)* conquérir; *(enemy, habit, difficulty)* vaincre ▪ **conquering** *adj* victorieux, -ieuse ▪ **conqueror** *n* vainqueur *m* ▪ **conquest** ['kɒŋkwest] *n* conquête *f*

cons [kɒnz] *npl* **the pros and c.** le pour et le contre

conscience ['kɒnʃəns] *n* conscience *f*; **to have sth on one's c.** avoir qch sur la conscience

conscientious [kɒnʃɪ'enʃəs] *adj* consciencieux, -ieuse; **c. objector** objecteur *m* de conscience ▪ **conscientiousness** *n* sérieux *m*

conscious ['kɒnʃəs] *adj (awake)* conscient; **to make a c. effort to do sth** faire un effort particulier pour faire qch; **to make a c. decision to do sth** chercher délibérément à faire qch; **c. of sth** *(aware)* conscient de qch; **c. that...** conscient que... ▪ **consciously** *adv*

(knowingly) consciemment ▪ **consciousness** *n* conscience *f* (**of** de); **to lose/regain c.** perdre/reprendre connaissance

conscript 1 ['kɒnskrɪpt] *n (soldier)* conscrit *m* **2** [kən'skrɪpt] *vt* enrôler ▪ **conscription** [kən'skrɪpʃən] *n* conscription *f*

consecrate ['kɒnsɪkreɪt] *vt Rel (church, place, bishop)* & *Fig* consacrer ▪ **consecration** [-'kreɪʃən] *n* consécration *f*

consecutive [kən'sekjʊtɪv] *adj* consécutif, -ive ▪ **consecutively** *adv* consécutivement

consensus [kən'sensəs] *n* consensus *m*

consent [kən'sent] **1** *n* consentement *m*; **by common c.** de l'aveu de tous; **by mutual c.** d'un commun accord **2** *vi* consentir (**to** à)

consequence ['kɒnsɪkwəns] *n (result)* conséquence *f*; *(importance)* importance *f*; **of no c.** sans importance ▪ **consequently** *adv* par conséquent

conservative [kən'sɜːvətɪv] **1** *adj (estimate)* modeste; *(view, attitude)* traditionnel, -elle; *(person)* traditionaliste; *Br Pol* conservateur, -trice; *Br Pol* **the C. Party** le Parti conservateur **2** *n Br Pol* conservateur, -trice *mf* ▪ **conservatism** *n (in behaviour)* & *Br Pol* conservatisme *m*

conservatory [kən'sɜːvətrɪ] *(pl* **-ies***) n Br (room)* véranda *f*

conserve [kən'sɜːv] *vt (energy, water, electricity)* faire des économies de; *(monument, language, tradition)* préserver; **to c. one's strength** ménager ses forces ▪ **conservation** [kɒnsə'veɪʃən] *n (of energy)* économies *fpl*; *(of nature)* protection *f* de l'environnement; **c. area** zone *f* naturelle protégée ▪ **conservationist** [kɒnsə'veɪʃənɪst] *n* défenseur *m* de l'environnement

consider [kən'sɪdə(r)] *vt (think over)* considérer; *(take into account)* tenir compte de; *(offer)* étudier; **I'll c. it** je vais y réfléchir; **to c. doing sth** envisager de faire qch; **to c. that...** considérer que...; **I c. her as a friend** je la considère comme une amie; **he's being considered for the job** sa candidature est à l'étude pour ce poste; **all things considered** tout bien considéré

considerable [kən'sɪdərəbəl] *adj (large)* considérable; *(much)* beaucoup de; **after c. difficulty** après bien des difficultés ▪ **considerably** *adv* considérablement

considerate [kən'sɪdərət] *adj* attentionné (**to** à l'égard de)

consideration [kənsɪdə'reɪʃən] *n (thought, thoughtfulness, reason)* considération *f*; **under c.** à l'étude; **out of c. for sb** par égard pour qn; **to take sth into c.** prendre qch en considération

considering [kən'sɪdərɪŋ] **1** *prep* étant donné **2** *conj* **c. (that)** étant donné que **3** *adv Fam* the result was good, c. c'est un bon résultat après tout

consign [kən'saɪn] *vt* (*send*) expédier; (*give, entrust*) confier (**to** à) ▪**consignment** *n* (*goods*) envoi *m*; (*sending*) expédition *f*

consist [kən'sɪst] *vi* consister (**of** en; **in** en; **in doing** à faire)

consistent [kən'sɪstənt] *adj* (*unchanging*) (*loyalty, quality, results*) constant; (*coherent*) (*ideas, argument*) cohérent, logique; **to be c. with** (*of statement*) concorder avec ▪**consistency** *n* (*of substance, liquid*) consistance *f*; (*of ideas, arguments*) cohérence *f* ▪**consistently** *adv* (*always*) constamment; (*regularly*) régulièrement; (*logically*) avec logique

> Note that the French word **consistant** is a false friend and is never a translation for the English word **consistent**. It means **substantial**.

console¹ [kən'səʊl] *vt* consoler (**for** de) ▪**consolation** [kɒnsə'leɪʃən] *n* consolation *f*; **c. prize** lot *m* de consolation

console² ['kɒnsəʊl] *n* (*control desk*) console *f*

consolidate [kən'sɒlɪdeɪt] **1** *vt* consolider **2** *vi* se consolider ▪**consoli'dation** *n* consolidation *f*

consonant ['kɒnsənənt] *n* consonne *f*

consort **1** ['kɒnsɔːt] *n* époux *m*, épouse *f* **2** [kən'sɔːt] *vi* **to c. with** (*criminals, addicts*) fréquenter

consortium [kən'sɔːtɪəm] (*pl* -**iums** *or* -**ia**) *n* Com consortium *m*

conspicuous [kən'spɪkjʊəs] *adj* (*noticeable*) bien visible; (*striking*) manifeste; (*showy*) voyant; **to look c.** ne pas passer inaperçu; **to be c. by one's absence** briller par son absence; **to make oneself c.** se faire remarquer; **in a c. position** bien en évidence ▪**conspicuously** *adv* visiblement

conspire [kən'spaɪə(r)] *vi* conspirer (**against** contre); **to c. to do sth** comploter de faire qch; **circumstances conspired against me** les circonstances se sont liguées contre moi ▪**conspiracy** [-'spɪrəsɪ] (*pl* -**ies**) *n* conspiration *f*

constable ['kʌnstəbəl] *n* Br (*police*) **c.** agent *m* de police; Br **chief c.** commissaire *m* de police divisionnaire

constant ['kɒnstənt] **1** *adj* (*frequent*) incessant; (*unchanging*) constant; (*faithful*) fidèle **2** *n* Math constante *f* ▪**constancy** *n* constance *f* ▪**constantly** *adv* constamment, sans cesse

constellation [kɒnstə'leɪʃən] *n* constellation *f*

consternation [kɒnstə'neɪʃən] *n* consternation *f*

constipate ['kɒnstɪpeɪt] *vt* constiper ▪**constipated** *adj* constipé ▪**consti'pation** *n* constipation *f*

constituent [kən'stɪtjʊənt] **1** *adj* (*element, part*) constitutif, -ive **2** *n* (**a**) (*part*) élément *m* constitutif (**b**) Pol (*voter*) électeur, -trice *mf* ▪**constituency** (*pl* -**ies**) *n* circonscription *f* électorale; (*voters*) électeurs *mpl*

constitute ['kɒnstɪtjuːt] *vt* constituer ▪**consti'tution** *n* constitution *f* ▪**constitutional** [-'tjuːʃənəl] *adj* Pol constitutionnel, -elle

constrain [kən'streɪn] *vt* (**a**) (*force*) contraindre (**sb to do**) qn à faire) (**b**) (*of clothing*) gêner ▪**constraint** *n* contrainte *f*

constrict [kən'strɪkt] *vt* (*tighten, narrow*) resserrer; (*movement*) gêner ▪**constriction** *n* (*of blood vessel*) constriction *f*; (*of person*) gêne *f*

construct [kən'strʌkt] *vt* construire ▪**construction** *n* (*building, structure*) & *Grammar* construction *f*; **under c.** en construction; **c. site** chantier *m* ▪**constructive** *adj* constructif, -ive

construe [kən'struː] *vt* interpréter

consul ['kɒnsəl] *n* consul *m* ▪**consular** [-sjʊlə(r)] *adj* consulaire ▪**consulate** [-sjʊlət] *n* consulat *m*

consult [kən'sʌlt] **1** *vt* consulter **2** *vi* **to c. with sb** discuter avec qn; Br **consulting room** (*of doctor*) cabinet *m* de consultation ▪**consultation** [kɒnsəl'teɪʃən] *n* consultation *f*; **in c. with** en consultation avec

consultancy [kən'sʌltənsɪ] (*pl* -**ies**) *n* **c.** (*firm*) cabinet-conseil *m*; **to do c. work** être consultant ▪**consultant** *n* Br (*doctor*) spécialiste *mf*; (*adviser*) consultant *m* **2** *adj* (*engineer*) consultant ▪**consultative** *adj* (*committee, role*) consultatif, -ive

consume [kən'sjuːm] *vt* (*food, supplies*) consommer; (*of fire*) consumer; (*of grief, hate*) dévorer; **to be consumed by** *or* **with jealousy** brûler de jalousie; **consuming ambition/ passion** ambition *f*/passion *f* dévorante ▪**consumer** *n* consommateur, -trice *mf*; **gas/ electricity c.** abonné, -ée *mf* au gaz/à l'électricité; **c. goods/society** biens *mpl*/ société *f* de consommation; **c. protection** défense *f* du consommateur ▪**consumerism** *n* consumérisme *m* ▪**consumption** [-'sʌmpʃən] *n* consommation *f*

consummate 1 [kən'sʌmɪt] *adj* (*linguist, cook*) de premier ordre; (*snob, hypocrite*) parfait **2** ['kɒnsəmeɪt] *vt* (*marriage, relationship*) consommer

contact ['kɒntækt] **1** *n* (*act of touching*) contact *m*; (*person*) relation *f*; **in c. with** en contact avec; **c. lenses** lentilles *fpl* de contact **2** *vt* contacter

contagious [kən'teɪdʒəs] *adj* (*disease*) contagieux, -ieuse; (*laughter*) communicatif, -ive

contain [kən'teɪn] *vt* (*enclose, hold back*) contenir; **to c. oneself** se contenir ▪**container** *n* (*box, jar*) récipient *m*; (*for transporting goods*) conteneur *m*

contaminate [kənˈtæmɪneɪt] *vt* contaminer ▪ **contamination** [-ˈneɪʃən] *n* contamination *f*

contemplate [ˈkɒntəmpleɪt] *vt (look at)* contempler; *(consider)* envisager (**doing** de faire) ▪ **contemplation** [-ˈpleɪʃən] *n* contemplation *f*; **deep in c.** en pleine contemplation

contemporary [kənˈtempərərɪ] 1 *adj* contemporain (**with** de); *(pattern, colour, style)* moderne 2 *(pl -ies) n (person)* contemporain, -aine *mf*

contempt [kənˈtempt] *n* mépris *m*; **to hold sb/ sth in c.** mépriser qn/qch ▪ **contemptible** *adj* méprisable ▪ **contemptuous** *adj* méprisant (**of** de); **to be c. of sth** mépriser qch

contend [kənˈtend] 1 *vi* **to c. with** *(problem)* faire face à; **to c. with sb** *(struggle)* se battre avec qn 2 *vt* **to c. that...** *(claim)* soutenir que... ▪ **contender** *n (in sport)* concurrent, -ente *mf*; *(in election, for job)* candidat, -ate *mf*

content¹ [kənˈtent] *adj (happy)* satisfait (**with** de) ▪ **contented** *adj* satisfait ▪ **contentment** *n* contentement *m*

content² [ˈkɒntent] *n (of book, text, film) (subject matter)* contenu *m*; **contents** contenu *m*; **contents page** *(of book)* table *f* des matières; **alcoholic/iron c.** teneur *f* en alcool/fer

contention [kənˈtenʃən] *n* (a) *(claim, belief)* affirmation *f* (b) *(disagreement)* désaccord *m*

contentious [kənˈtenʃəs] *adj (issue, views)* controversé

contest 1 [ˈkɒntest] *n (competition)* concours *m*; *(fight)* lutte *f*; *Boxing* combat *m* 2 [kənˈtest] *vt (dispute)* contester; **to c. a seat** se porter candidat; **a fiercely contested election** une élection très disputée ▪ **contestant** [kənˈtestənt] *n* concurrent, -ente *mf*; *(in fight)* adversaire *mf*

context [ˈkɒntekst] *n* contexte *m*; **in/out of c.** en/hors contexte ▪ **contextualize** *vt* contextualiser

continent [ˈkɒntɪnənt] *n* continent *m*; **the C.** l'Europe *f* continentale; **on the C.** en Europe ▪ **continental** [-ˈnentəl] 1 *adj (of Europe)* européen, -enne; *(of other continents)* continental; **c. breakfast** petit déjeuner *m* à la française 2 *n* Européen, -enne *mf* (continental(e))

contingent [kənˈtɪndʒənt] 1 *adj* contingent; **to be c. on sth** dépendre de qch 2 *n (group)* contingent *m* ▪ **contingency** *(pl -ies) n* éventualité *f*; **c. plan** plan *m* d'urgence

continual [kənˈtɪnjʊəl] *adj* continuel, -uelle ▪ **continually** *adv* continuellement

continue [kənˈtɪnjuː] 1 *vt* continuer (**to do** *ou* **doing** à *ou* de faire); **to c. (with)** *(work, speech)* poursuivre; *(resume)* reprendre 2 *vi* continuer; *(resume)* reprendre; **to c. in one's job** garder son emploi ▪ **continuation** [-ˈʊˈeɪʃən] *n*

continuation *f*; *(resumption)* reprise *f*; *(new episode)* suite *f* ▪ **continued** *adj (interest, attention)* soutenu; *(presence)* continuel, -uelle; **to be c.** *(of story)* à suivre

continuity [kɒntɪˈnjuːɪtɪ] *n* continuité *f*

continuous [kənˈtɪnjʊəs] *adj* continu; *Sch & Univ* **c. assessment** contrôle *m* continu des connaissances ▪ **continuously** *adv* sans interruption

contort [kənˈtɔːt] 1 *vt (twist)* tordre; **to c. oneself** se contorsionner 2 *vi* se tordre (**with** de) ▪ **contortion** *n* contorsion *f* ▪ **contortionist** *n (acrobat)* contorsionniste *mf*

contour [ˈkɒntʊə(r)] *n* contour *m*; **c. (line)** *(on map)* courbe *f* de niveau

contraband [ˈkɒntrəbænd] *n* contrebande *f*

contraception [kɒntrəˈsepʃən] *n* contraception *f* ▪ **contraceptive** *n* contraceptif *m*

contract¹ [ˈkɒntrækt] 1 *n* contrat *m*; **to be under c.** être sous contrat; **c. killer** tueur *m* à gages; **c. work** travail *m* en sous-traitance 2 *vt* **to c. to do sth** s'engager (par un contrat) à faire qch; **to c. work out** sous-traiter du travail 3 *vi* **to c. out** *(of policy, pension plan)* arrêter de souscrire ▪ **contractor** [kənˈtræktə(r)] *n* entrepreneur *m*

contract² [kənˈtrækt] 1 *vt (illness, debt)* contracter 2 *vi (shrink)* se contracter ▪ **contraction** *n* contraction *f*

contradict [kɒntrəˈdɪkt] *vt (person, statement)* contredire; *(deny)* démentir; **to c. oneself** se contredire ▪ **contradiction** *n* contradiction *f* ▪ **contradictory** *adj* contradictoire

contralto [kənˈtræltəʊ] *(pl -os) n* contralto *mf*

contraption [kənˈtræpʃən] *n Fam* machin *m*

contrary [ˈkɒntrərɪ] 1 *adj* (a) *(opposite)* contraire (**to** à) (b) [kənˈtreərɪ] *(awkward)* contrariant 2 *adv* **c. to** contrairement à 3 *n* contraire *m*; **on the c.** au contraire; **unless you/I/etc hear to the c.** sauf avis contraire

contrast [kənˈtrɑːst] 1 [ˈkɒntrɑːst] *n* contraste *m*; **in c. to** par opposition à 2 *vt* mettre en contraste 3 *vi* contraster (**with** avec) ▪ **contrasting** *adj (opinions)* opposé

contravene [kɒntrəˈviːn] *vt (law)* enfreindre ▪ **contravention** [-ˈvenʃən] *n* **in c. of a treaty** en violation d'un traité

contribute [kənˈtrɪbjuːt] 1 *vt (time, clothes)* donner (**to** à); *(article)* écrire (**to** pour); **to c. money to** verser de l'argent à 2 *vi* **to c. to** contribuer à; *(publication)* collaborer à; *(discussion)* prendre part à; *(charity)* donner à ▪ **contribution** [kɒntrɪˈbjuːʃən] *n* contribution *f* ▪ **contributor** *n (to newspaper)* collaborateur, -trice *mf*; *(of money)* donateur, -trice *mf* ▪ **contributory** *adj (cause, factor)* concourant; **to be a c. factor in sth** concourir à qch

contrite [kənˈtraɪt] *adj* contrit

contrivance [kənˈtraɪvəns] *n (device)* dispositif *m*; *(scheme)* système *m*

contrive [kən'traɪv] *vt* to c. to do sth trouver moyen de faire qch

contrived [kən'traɪvd] *adj* qui manque de naturel

control [kən'trəʊl] **1** *n* contrôle *m*; *(authority)* autorité *f* (**over** sur); **the controls** *(of plane)* les commandes *fpl*; *(of TV set, radio)* les boutons *mpl*; **(self-)c.** la maîtrise (de soi); **the situation or everything is under c.** je/il/*etc* contrôle la situation; **to lose c.** of *(situation, vehicle)* perdre le contrôle de; **out of c.** *(situation, crowd)* difficilement maîtrisable; *Comptr* **c. key** touche *f* de contrôle; **c. panel** tableau *m* de bord; **c. tower** *(at airport)* tour *f* de contrôle **2** *(pt & pp* **-ll-)** *vt (business, organization)* diriger; *(prices, quality)* contrôler; *(emotion, reaction)* maîtriser; *(disease)* enrayer; **to c. oneself** se contrôler

controversy ['kɒntrəvɜːsɪ] *(pl* **-ies)** *n* controverse *f* ▪**controversial** [-'vɜːʃəl] *adj* controversé

conundrum [kə'nʌndrəm] *n (riddle)* devinette *f*; *(mystery)* énigme *f*

conurbation [kɒnɜː'beɪʃən] *n* conurbation *f*

convalesce [kɒnvə'les] *vi (rest)* être en convalescence ▪**convalescence** *n* convalescence *f*

convene [kən'viːn] **1** *vt (meeting)* convoquer **2** *vi (meet)* se réunir

convenience [kən'viːnɪəns] *n* commodité *f*; **come at your (own) c.** venez quand vous voudrez; **all modern conveniences** tout le confort moderne; *Br* **(public) conveniences** toilettes *fpl*; **c. food(s)** plats *mpl* tout préparés; **c. store** magasin *m* de proximité

convenient [kən'viːnɪənt] *adj* commode, pratique; **to be c. (for)** *(suit)* convenir (à) ▪**conveniently** *adv (arrive, say)* à propos; **c. situated** bien situé

convent ['kɒnvənt] *n* couvent *m*; **c. school** école *f* des sœurs

convention [kən'venʃən] *n (custom)* usage *m*; *(agreement)* convention *f*; *(conference)* convention, congrès *m* ▪**conventional** *adj* conventionnel, -elle

converge [kən'vɜːdʒ] *vi* converger (**on** sur) ▪**convergence** *n* convergence *f* ▪**converging** *adj* convergent

conversation [kɒnvə'seɪʃən] *n* conversation *f* (**with** avec) ▪**conversational** *adj (tone)* de la conversation; *(person)* loquace ▪**conversationalist** *n* **to be a good c.** avoir de la conversation

converse 1 ['kɒnvɜːs] *adj & n* inverse *(m)* **2** [kən'vɜːs] *vi* s'entretenir (**with** avec) ▪**con'versely** [kən'vɜːslɪ] *adv* inversement

convert 1 ['kɒnvɜːt] *n* converti, -ie *mf* **2** *vt (change)* convertir (**into** *or* **to** en); *(building)* aménager (**into** *or* **to** en); *Rel* **to c.**

sb convertir qn (**to** à) **3** *vi (change religion)* se convertir (**to** à) ▪**conversion** *n* conversion *f*; *(of building)* aménagement *m*; *(in rugby)* transformation *f*

convertible [kən'vɜːtəbəl] **1** *adj (money, sofa)* convertible **2** *n (car)* décapotable *f*

convex [kɒn'veks] *adj* convexe

convey [kən'veɪ] *vt (transport)* transporter; *(communicate)* transmettre ▪**conveyor belt** *n* tapis *m* roulant

convict 1 ['kɒnvɪkt] *n* détenu *m* **2** [kən'vɪkt] *vt* déclarer coupable (**of** de) ▪**con'viction** [kən'vɪkʃən] *n (for crime)* condamnation *f*; *(belief)* conviction *f* (**that** que)

convince [kən'vɪns] *vt* convaincre (**of sth** de qch; **sb to do sth** qn de faire qch); **I was convinced that I was right** j'étais convaincu d'avoir raison ▪**convincing** *adj (argument, person)* convaincant ▪**convincingly** *adv (argue)* de façon convaincante

convivial [kən'vɪvɪəl] *adj (event)* joyeux, -euse; *(person)* chaleureux, -euse

convoluted [kɒnvə'luːtɪd] *adj (argument, style)* compliqué

convoy ['kɒnvɔɪ] *n* convoi *m*

convulse [kən'vʌls] *vt (shake)* ébranler; *(face)* convulser; **to be convulsed with pain** se tordre de douleur ▪**convulsion** *n Med* convulsion *f* ▪**convulsive** *adj* convulsif, -ive

coo [kuː] *(pt & pp* **cooed)** *vi (of dove)* roucouler

cook [kʊk] **1** *n (person)* cuisinier, -ière *mf* **2** *vt (meal)* préparer; *(food)* (faire) cuire; *Fam* **to c. the books** truquer les comptes; *Fam* **to c. up** inventer **3** *vi (of food)* cuire; *(of person)* faire la cuisine; *Fam* **what's cooking?** qu'est-ce qui se passe? ▪**cookbook** *n* livre *m* de cuisine ▪**cooker** *n Br (stove)* cuisinière *f* ▪**cookery** *n* cuisine *f*; *Br* **c. book** livre *m* de cuisine ▪**cooking** *n (activity, food)* cuisine *f*; *(process)* cuisson *f*; **to do the c.** faire la cuisine; **c. apple** pomme *f* à cuire; **c. utensils** ustensiles *mpl* de cuisine

cookie ['kʊkɪ] *n Am* biscuit *m*

cool [kuːl] **1** **(-er, -est)** *adj (weather, place, wind)* frais (*f* fraîche); *(tea, soup)* tiède; *(calm)* calme; *(unfriendly)* froid; *Fam (good)* cool *inv*; *Fam (trendy)* branché; **a (nice) c. drink** une boisson (bien) fraîche; **a c. £50** la coquette somme de 50 livres; **the weather is c., it's c.** il fait frais; **to keep sth c.** tenir qch au frais; **to keep a c. head** garder la tête froide **2** *n (of evening)* fraîcheur *f*; **to keep/lose one's c.** garder/perdre son sang-froid **3** *vt* **to c. (down)** refroidir, rafraîchir **4** *vi* **to c. (down** *or* **off)** *(of hot liquid)* refroidir; *(of enthusiasm)* se refroidir; *(of angry person)* se calmer; **to c. off** *(by drinking, swimming)* se rafraîchir ▪**cooler** *n (for food)* glacière *f* ▪**cool-'headed** *adj* calme ▪**coolly** *adv (calmly)* calmement; *(welcome)* froidement;

(boldly) effrontément ▪ **coolness** n fraîcheur f; *(unfriendliness)* froideur f

coop [ku:p] **1** n *(for chickens)* poulailler m **2** vt **to c. up** *(person, animal)* enfermer; **I've been cooped up** je suis resté enfermé

co-op ['kəʊɒp] n coopérative f

cooperate [kəʊ'ɒpəreɪt] vi coopérer (**in** à; **with** avec) ▪ **coope'ration** n coopération f

cooperative [kəʊ'ɒpərətɪv] **1** adj coopératif, -ive **2** n coopérative f

coopt [kəʊ'ɒpt] vt coopter (**onto** à)

coordinate [kəʊ'ɔ:dɪneɪt] vt coordonner ▪ **coordination** [-'neɪʃən] n coordination f ▪ **coordinator** n *(of project)* coordinateur, -trice mf

coordinates [kəʊ'ɔ:dɪnəts] npl Math coordonnées fpl; *(clothes)* coordonnés mpl

co-owner [kəʊ'əʊnə(r)] n copropriétaire mf

cop [kɒp] Fam **1** n *(policeman)* flic m **2** vi **to c. out** se défiler

cope [kəʊp] vi **to c. with** *(problem, demand)* faire face à; **to be able to c.** savoir se débrouiller; **I (just) can't c.** je n'y arrive plus

copier ['kɒpɪə(r)] n *(photocopier)* photocopieuse f

copilot ['kəʊpaɪlət] n copilote m

copious ['kəʊpɪəs] adj *(meal)* copieux, -ieuse; *(sunshine, amount)* abondant

copper ['kɒpə(r)] n **(a)** *(metal)* cuivre m; Br Fam **coppers** *(coins)* petite monnaie f **(b)** Br Fam *(policeman)* flic m

coppice ['kɒpɪs], **copse** [kɒps] n taillis m

copulate ['kɒpjʊleɪt] vi copuler

copy ['kɒpɪ] **1** (pl -ies) n *(of letter, document)* copie f; *(of book, magazine)* exemplaire m; *(of photo)* épreuve f; Comptr **c. and paste** copier-coller m **2** (pt & pp -ied) vt copier; **to c. out** or **down** *(text, letter)* copier; Comptr **to c. and paste sth** faire un copier-coller sur qch; Comptr **to c. sth to disk** copier qch sur disquette **3** vi copier ▪ **copyright** n copyright m

coral ['kɒrəl] n corail m

cord [kɔ:d] n **(a)** *(of curtain, bell, pyjamas)* cordon m; *(electrical)* cordon électrique m **(b)** *(corduroy)* velours m côtelé; **cords** *(trousers)* pantalon m en velours côtelé

cordial ['kɔ:dɪəl] **1** adj *(friendly)* cordial **2** n Br *(fruit)* **c.** sirop m

cordless ['kɔ:dləs] adj **c. phone** téléphone m sans fil

cordon ['kɔ:dən] **1** n cordon m **2** vt **to c. off** *(road)* barrer; *(area)* boucler

corduroy ['kɔ:dərɔɪ] n velours m côtelé

core [kɔ:(r)] **1** n *(of apple)* trognon m; *(of problem)* cœur m; *(group of people)* & Geol noyau m; **rotten to the c.** corrompu jusqu'à la moelle; Sch **c. curriculum** tronc m commun; **c. vocabulary** vocabulaire m de base **2** vt *(apple)* évider

cork [kɔ:k] **1** n *(material)* liège m; *(stopper)* bouchon m **2** vt *(bottle)* boucher ▪ **corkscrew** n tire-bouchon m

corn[1] [kɔ:n] n Br *(wheat)* blé m; Am *(maize)* maïs m; *(seed)* grain m; **c. on the cob** maïs m en épi, Can blé m en Inde

corn[2] [kɔ:n] n *(on foot)* cor m

corned beef [kɔ:nd'bi:f] n corned-beef m

corner ['kɔ:nə(r)] **1** n *(of street, room, page, screen)* coin m; *(bend in road)* virage m; Football corner m; Fig **in a (tight) c.** en situation difficile; **it's just round the c.** c'est juste au coin; Fig **Christmas is just round the c.** on est tout près de Noël; **c. shop** épicerie f du coin **2** vt *(person, animal)* acculer; **to c. the market** monopoliser le marché **3** vi *(of car, driver)* prendre un virage ▪ **cornerstone** n pierre f angulaire

cornet ['kɔ:nɪt] n Br *(of ice cream)* cornet m; *(instrument)* cornet m à pistons

cornflakes ['kɔ:nfleɪks] npl corn flakes mpl

cornflour ['kɔ:nflaʊə(r)] n Br farine f de maïs, Maïzena® f

cornflower ['kɔ:nflaʊə(r)] n bleuet m

cornstarch ['kɔ:nstɑ:tʃ] n Am = **cornflour**

Cornwall ['kɔ:nwəl] n Cornouailles f

corny ['kɔ:nɪ] (-ier, -iest) adj Fam *(joke)* nul (f nulle); *(film)* tarte

coronary ['kɒrənərɪ] (pl -ies) n infarctus m

coronation [kɒrə'neɪʃən] n couronnement m

coroner ['kɒrənə(r)] n Law coroner m

corporal ['kɔ:pərəl] **1** n *(in army)* caporal-chef m **2** adj corporel, -elle; **c. punishment** châtiment m corporel

corporate ['kɔ:pərət] adj *(budget)* de l'entreprise; *(decision)* collectif, -ive; **c. image** image f de marque de l'entreprise

corporation [kɔ:pə'reɪʃən] n *(business)* société f; Br *(of town)* conseil m municipal

corps [kɔ:(r), pl kɔ:z] n inv Mil & Pol corps m; **the press c.** les journalistes mpl

corpse [kɔ:ps] n cadavre m

corral [kə'ræl] n Am corral m (pl -s)

correct [kə'rekt] **1** adj *(accurate)* exact; *(proper)* correct; **he's c.** il a raison; **the c. time** l'heure exacte **2** vt corriger ▪ **correctly** adv correctement ▪ **correction** n correction f; **c. fluid** liquide m correcteur

correlate ['kɒrəleɪt] **1** vt mettre en corrélation (**with** avec) **2** vi être en corrélation (**with** à) ▪ **correlation** [-'leɪʃən] n corrélation f

correspond [kɒrɪ'spɒnd] vi correspondre ▪ **corresponding** adj *(matching)* correspondant; *(similar)* semblable

correspondence [kɒrɪ'spɒndəns] n correspondance f; **c. course** cours m par correspondance ▪ **correspondent** n correspondant, -ante mf

corridor ['kɒrɪdɔ:(r)] n couloir m, corridor m

corroborate [kə'rɒbəreɪt] vt corroborer

corrode [kə'rəʊd] **1** vt (metal) corroder **2** vi (of metal) se corroder ∎**corroded** adj (rusty) rouillé ∎**corrosion** n corrosion f

corrugated ['kɒrəgeɪtɪd] adj ondulé

corrupt [kə'rʌpt] **1** adj corrompu **2** vt corrompre ∎**corruption** n corruption f

Corsica ['kɔːsɪkə] n la Corse ∎**Corsican 1** adj corse **2** n Corse mf

cos [kɒs] n Br **c. (lettuce)** romaine f

cosh [kɒʃ] Br **1** n matraque f **2** vt matraquer

cosiness ['kəʊzɪnəs] n confort m

cosmetic [kɒz'metɪk] **1** adj Fig (change) superficiel, -ielle; **c. surgery** chirurgie f esthétique **2** n produit m de beauté

cosmopolitan [kɒzmə'pɒlɪtən] adj cosmopolite f

cost [kɒst] **1** n coût m; Econ **the c. of living** le coût de la vie; **at great c.** à grands frais; **to my c.** à mes dépens; **at any c., at all costs** à tout prix; Br **at c. price** au prix coûtant **2** (pt & pp **cost**) vti coûter; **how much does it c.?** ça coûte combien?; Fam **to c. the earth** or **an arm and a leg** coûter les yeux de la tête ∎**cost-effective** adj rentable ∎**costly** (-**ier**, -**iest**) adj (expensive) (car, trip) coûteux, -euse; (valuable) (jewel, antique) de (grande) valeur; **it was a c. mistake** c'est une erreur qui a coûté cher

co-star ['kəʊstɑː(r)] n (in film, play) partenaire mf

Costa Rica [kɒstə'riːkə] n le Costa Rica

costume ['kɒstjuːm] n costume m; (woman's suit) tailleur m; Br **(swimming) c.** maillot m de bain

cosy ['kəʊzɪ] **1** (-**ier**, -**iest**) adj Br (house) douillet, -ette; (atmosphere) intime; **make yourself (nice and) c.** mets-toi à l'aise; **we're c. on est bien ici 2** n **(tea) c.** couvre-théière m

cot [kɒt] n Br (for child) lit m d'enfant; Am (camp bed) lit de camp; Br **c. death** mort f subite du nourrisson

cottage ['kɒtɪdʒ] n petite maison f de campagne; **(thatched) c.** chaumière f; **c. cheese** fromage m blanc (maigre); **c. industry** industrie f artisanale; (at home) industrie familiale; Br **c. pie** ≃ hachis m Parmentier

cotton ['kɒtən] **1** n coton m; (yarn) fil m de coton; Br **c. wool,** Am **absorbent c.** coton m hydrophile, ouate f; **c. shirt** chemise f en coton; Am **c. candy** barbe f à papa **2** vi Fam **to c. on (to sth)** (realize) piger (qch)

couch [kaʊtʃ] **1** n (sofa) canapé m; (for doctor's patient) lit m **2** vt (express) formuler

couchette [kuː'ʃet] n Br (on train) couchette f

cough [kɒf] **1** n toux f; **c. syrup** or **medicine,** Br **c. mixture** sirop m pour la toux **2** vi tousser; Fam **to c. up** casquer **3** vt **to c. up** (blood) cracher; Fam (money) allonger

could [kʊd, unstressed kəd] pt of **can¹**

couldn't ['kʊdənt] = **could not**

council ['kaʊnsəl] n (assembly) conseil m; (local government) municipalité f; **(town/city) c.** conseil m municipal; **C. of Europe** Conseil de l'Europe; Br **c. flat/house** ≃ HLM f; Br **c. tax** = impôt regroupant taxe d'habitation et impôts locaux ∎**councillor** n conseiller, -ère mf; **(town) c.** conseiller m municipal

counsel ['kaʊnsəl] **1** n inv (advice) conseil m; Br (lawyer) avocat, -ate mf **2** (Br -**ll**-, Am -**l**-) vt conseiller **(sb to do** à qn de faire) ∎**counselling** (Am **counseling**) n assistance f psychosociale ∎**counsellor** (Am **counselor**) n conseiller, -ère mf

count¹ [kaʊnt] **1** n (calculation) compte m; Law (charge) chef m d'accusation; **to keep c. of sth** tenir le compte de qch **2** vt (find number of, include) compter; (consider) considérer; **not counting Paul** sans compter Paul; **to c. in** (include) inclure; **c. me in!** j'en suis!; **to c. out** (exclude) exclure; (money) compter; **c. me out!** ne compte pas sur moi! **3** vi compter; **to c. against sb** jouer contre qn; **to c. on sb/sth** (rely on) compter sur qn/qch; **to c. on doing sth** compter faire qch ∎**countdown** n compte m à rebours

count² [kaʊnt] n (title) comte m

counter ['kaʊntə(r)] **1** n **(a)** (in shop, bar) comptoir m; (in bank) guichet m; **the food c.** (in store) le rayon alimentation; Fig **under the c.** (buy, sell) au marché noir; **over the c.** (medicine) en vente libre **(b)** (in games) jeton m **(c)** (counting device) compteur m **2** adv **c. to** contrairement à; **to run c. to** aller à l'encontre de **3** vt (threat) répondre à; (effects) neutraliser; (blow) parer; **c. that...** riposter que... **4** vi riposter **(with** par)

counter- ['kaʊntə(r)] pref contre-

counteract [kaʊntə'rækt] vt (influence) contrecarrer; (effects) neutraliser

counterattack ['kaʊntərətæk] **1** n contre-attaque f **2** vti contre-attaquer

counterbalance ['kaʊntəbæləns] **1** n contre-poids m **2** vt contrebalancer

counterclockwise [kaʊntə'klɒkwaɪz] adj & adv Am dans le sens inverse des aiguilles d'une montre

counterfeit ['kaʊntəfɪt] **1** adj faux (f fausse) **2** n faux m **3** vt contrefaire

counterfoil ['kaʊntəfɔɪl] n souche f

counterpart ['kaʊntəpɑːt] n (thing) équivalent m; (person) homologue mf

counterproductive [kaʊntəprə'dʌktɪv] adj (action) contre-productif, -ive

countersign ['kaʊntəsaɪn] vt contresigner

countess ['kaʊntɪs] n comtesse f

countless ['kaʊntlɪs] adj innombrable; **on c. occasions** à maintes occasions

country ['kʌntrɪ] (pl -**ies**) **1** n pays m; (region) région f, pays; *(opposed to town)* campagne f; **in the c.** à la campagne **2** *adj (house, road)* de campagne; **c. and western music** country f, **c. dancing** danse f folklorique ∎**countryman** *(pl -men)* n **(fellow)** n compatriote r ∎**countryside** n campagne f; **in the c.** à la campagne

county ['kaʊntɪ] *(pl -ies)* n comté m; **c. council** ≃ conseil m général; *Br* **c. town**, *Am* **c. seat** chef-lieu m de comté

coup [kuː] *pl* k uːz] n *Pol* coup m d'État

couple ['kʌpəl] **1** n *(of people)* couple m; **a c. of** deux ou trois; *(a few)* quelques **2** vt *(connect)* accoupler

coupon ['kuːpɒn] n *(for discount)* bon m; *(form)* coupon m

courage ['kʌrɪdʒ] n courage m ∎**courageous** [kə'reɪdʒəs] *adj* courageux, -euse

courgette [kɔː'ʒet] n *Br* courgette f

courier ['kʊrɪə(r)] n *(for tourists)* guide mf; *(messenger)* messager m

course [kɔːs] **1** n (a) *(of river, time, events)* cours m; *(of ship)* route f; *(means)* moyen m; **c. of action** ligne f de conduite; **to be on c.** *Naut* suivre le cap; *Fig* être en bonne voie; **your best c. is to…** le mieux c'est de…; **as a matter of c.** normalement; **in the c. of** au cours de; **in the c. of time** avec le temps; **in due c.** en temps utile (b) *(lessons)* cours m; **c. of lectures** série f de conférences (c) *Med* **c. of treatment** traitement m (d) *(of meal)* plat m; **first c.** entrée f; **main c.** plat principal (e) *(for race)* parcours m; *(for horseracing)* champ m de courses; *(for golf)* terrain m **2** *adv* **of c.!** bien sûr!; **of c. not!** bien sûr que non!

court¹ [kɔːt] n *(of king)* cour f; *(for trials)* cour, tribunal m; *(for tennis)* court m; **c. of law** tribunal m; **to go to c.** aller en justice; **to take sb to c.** poursuivre qn en justice; *Br* **c. shoe** escarpin m ∎**courthouse** n *Am* palais m de justice ∎**courtroom** n *Law* salle f d'audience ∎**courtyard** n cour f

court² [kɔːt] **1** vt *(woman)* faire la cour à; *(danger)* aller au-devant de; *(death)* braver; *(friendship, favour)* rechercher **2** vi **to be courting** *(of couple)* se fréquenter ∎**courtship** n *(of person)* cour f; *(of animal)* parade f nuptiale

courteous ['kɜːtɪəs] *adj* poli, courtois ∎**courtesy** [-təsɪ] *(pl -ies)* n politesse f, courtoisie f; **c. car** = voiture mise à la disposition d'un client par un hôtel, un garage etc

courtier ['kɔːtɪə(r)] n *Hist* courtisan m

court-martial [kɔːt'mɑːʃəl] **1** n conseil m de guerre **2** vt *(Br* **-ll-**, *Am* **-l-)* **to be court-martialled** passer en cour martiale

cousin ['kʌzən] n cousin, -ine mf

cove [kəʊv] n crique f

Coventry ['kɒvəntrɪ] n *Br* **to send sb to C.** *(punish)* mettre qn en quarantaine

cover ['kʌvə(r)] **1** n *(lid)* couvercle m; *(of book)* couverture f; *(for furniture, typewriter)* housse f; *(bedspread)* dessus-de-lit m *inv*; **the covers** *(blankets)* les couvertures fpl; **to take c.** se mettre à l'abri; **under c.** *(sheltered)* à l'abri; **under separate c.** *(letter)* sous pli séparé; **under c. of darkness** à la faveur de la nuit; **c. charge** *(in restaurant)* couvert m; *Am* **c. letter** lettre f jointe; *Br* **c. note** *(insurance)* certificat m provisoire d'assurance

2 vt couvrir *(with* or **in** de); *(include)* englober; *(treat)* traiter; *(distance)* parcourir; *(event)* *(in newspaper, on TV)* couvrir; *(aim gun at)* tenir en joue; *(insure)* assurer *(against* contre); **to c. one's eyes** se couvrir les yeux; **to c. one's costs** couvrir ses frais; **to c. over** *(floor, saucepan)* recouvrir; **to c. up** recouvrir; *(truth, tracks)* dissimuler; *(scandal)* étouffer

3 vi **to c. (oneself) up** *(wrap up)* se couvrir; **to c. up for sb** cacher la vérité pour protéger qn ∎**cover-up** n **there was a c.** on a étouffé l'affaire

coverage ['kʌvərɪdʒ] n *(on TV, in newspaper)* couverture f médiatique

coveralls ['kʌvərɔːlz] npl *Am* bleu m de travail

covering ['kʌvərɪŋ] n *(wrapping)* enveloppe f; *(layer)* couche f; *Br* **c. letter** lettre f jointe

covert ['kəʊvɜːt, 'kʌvət] *adj* secret, -ète; *(look)* furtif, -ive

covet ['kʌvɪt] vt convoiter

cow¹ [kaʊ] n vache f; *Fam Pej (nasty woman)* peau f de vache; **c. elephant** éléphant f ∎**cowboy** n cow-boy m ∎**cowshed** n étable f

cow² [kaʊ] vt **to be cowed** *(frightened)* être intimidé *(by* par)

coward ['kaʊəd] n lâche mf ∎**cowardice** n lâcheté f ∎**cowardly** *adj* lâche

cower ['kaʊə(r)] vi *(crouch)* se tapir; *(with fear)* trembler; *(move back)* reculer *(par peur)*

cowslip ['kaʊslɪp] n *(plant)* coucou m

cox [kɒks] **1** n barreur, -euse mf **2** vt *(boat)* barrer

coy [kɔɪ] *(-er, -est)* *adj (shy)* timide; *Pej (affectedly shy)* *(faussement)* timide

coyote [kaɪ'əʊtɪ] n coyote m

cozy ['kəʊzɪ] *adj Am* = **cosy**

CPA [siːpiː'eɪ] *(abbr* **certified public accountant)** n *Am* expert-comptable m

crab [kræb] n (a) *(crustacean)* crabe m (b) **c. apple** pomme f sauvage

crabby ['kræbɪ] *(-ier, -iest)* *adj (person)* grincheux, -euse

crack¹ [kræk] **1** n *(split)* fente f; *(in glass, china, bone)* fêlure f; *(in skin)* crevasse f; *(noise)* craquement m; *(of whip)* claquement m; *(blow)* coup m; *Fam (joke)* plaisanterie f *(at* aux dépens de); *Fam* **to have a c. at doing sth**

essayer de faire qch; **at the c. of dawn** au point du jour **2** vt (glass, ice) fêler; (nut) casser; (ground, skin) crevasser; (whip) faire claquer; (problem) résoudre; (code) déchiffrer; (safe) percer; Fam (joke) raconter **3** vi se fêler; (of skin) se crevasser; (of branch, wood) craquer; Fam **to get cracking** (get to work) s'y mettre; (hurry) se grouiller

▸ **crack down** vi to c. down on sth prendre des mesures énergiques en matière de qch

▸ **crack up** Fam **1** vt sep **to c. sb up** faire éclater qn de rire; **it's not as hard as it's cracked up to be** ce n'est pas aussi dur qu'on le dit **2** vi **to c. up** (mentally) craquer; (laugh hysterically) éclater de rire

crack² [kræk] adj (first-rate) (driver, skier) d'élite; **c. shot** fin tireur m

crack³ [kræk] n (drug) crack m

crackdown [ˈkrækdaʊn] n mesures fpl énergiques (**on** en matière de)

cracked [krækt] adj Fam (crazy) cinglé

cracker [ˈkrækə(r)] n (**a**) (biscuit) biscuit m salé (**b**) (firework) pétard m; **Christmas c.** diablotin m (**c**) Br Fam **she's a c.** (attractive) elle est canon ▪ **crackers** adj Br Fam (mad) cinglé ▪ **crackpot** n Br Fam cinglé, -ée mf

crackle [ˈkrækəl] **1** n (of twigs) craquement m; (of fire) crépitement m; (of frying) grésillement m; (of radio) crachotement m **2** vi (of fire) crépiter; (of frying) grésiller; (of radio) crachoter

cradle [ˈkreɪdəl] **1** n berceau m **2** vt bercer

craft¹ [krɑːft] **1** n (skill) art m; (job) métier m **2** vt façonner ▪ **craftsman** (pl -men) n artisan m ▪ **craftsmanship** (skill) art m; **a fine piece of c.** une belle pièce

craft² [krɑːft] n (cunning) ruse f

craft³ [krɑːft] n inv (boat) bateau m

crafty [ˈkrɑːftɪ] (-ier, -iest) adj astucieux, -ieuse; Pej rusé

crag [kræg] n rocher m à pic ▪ **craggy** adj (rock) à pic; (face) anguleux, -euse

cram [kræm] (pt & pp -mm-) **1** vt **to c. sth into** (force) fourrer qch dans; **to c. with** (fill) bourrer de **2** vi **to c. into** (of people) s'entasser dans; **to c. (for an exam)** bûcher

cramp [kræmp] n (pain) crampe f (**in** à)

cramped [kræmpt] adj (surroundings) exigu (f exiguë); **in c. conditions** à l'étroit; **to be c. for space** être à l'étroit

cranberry [ˈkrænbərɪ] (pl -ies) n canneberge f

crane [kreɪn] **1** n (machine, bird) grue f **2** vt **to c. one's neck** tendre le cou

crank¹ [kræŋk] **1** n (handle) manivelle f **2** vt **to c. (up)** (vehicle) faire démarrer à la manivelle

crank² [kræŋk] n Fam (person) excentrique mf; (fanatic) fanatique mf ▪ **cranky** (-ier, -iest) adj Fam excentrique; Am (bad-tempered) grincheux, -euse

cranny [ˈkrænɪ] (pl -ies) n see nook

crap [kræp] **1** n Vulg (excrement) merde f; very Fam (nonsense) conneries fpl **2** adj very Fam (bad) nul (f nulle)

craps [kræps] n Am **to shoot c.** jouer aux dés

crash [kræʃ] **1** n (accident) accident m; (collapse of firm) faillite f; (noise) fracas m; (of thunder) coup m; **c. course/diet** cours m/régime m intensif; **c. barrier** (on road) glissière f de sécurité; **c. helmet** casque m; **c. landing** atterrissage m en catastrophe

2 exclam (of fallen object) patatras!

3 vt (car) avoir un accident avec; **to c. one's car into sth** rentrer dans qch (avec sa voiture)

4 vi (of car, plane) s'écraser; **to c. into** rentrer dans; **the cars crashed (into each other)** les voitures se sont percutées ▪ **crash-'land** vi atterrir en catastrophe

crass [kræs] adj grossier, -ière; **c. stupidity** immense bêtise f; **c. ignorance** ignorance f crasse

crate [kreɪt] n (large) caisse f; (small) cageot m; (for bottles) casier m

crater [ˈkreɪtə(r)] n cratère m; (**bomb**) **c.** entonnoir m

cravat [krəˈvæt] n foulard m

crave [kreɪv] vi **to c. for** avoir un besoin terrible de ▪ **craving** n envie f (**for** de)

craven [ˈkreɪvən] adj Literary (cowardly) lâche

crawl [krɔːl] **1** n (swimming stroke) crawl m; **to do the crawl** nager le crawl; **to move at a c.** (in vehicle) avancer au pas **2** vi (of snake, animal) ramper; (of child) marcher à quatre pattes; (of vehicle) avancer au pas; **to be crawling with** grouiller de

crayfish [ˈkreɪfɪʃ] n inv (freshwater) écrevisse f

crayon [ˈkreɪən] n (wax) crayon m gras

craze [kreɪz] n engouement m (**for** pour) ▪ **crazed** adj affolé

crazy [ˈkreɪzɪ] (-ier, -iest) adj fou (f folle); **to go c.** devenir fou; **to drive sb c.** rendre qn fou; **to be c. about sb/sth** être fou de qn/qch; **to run/work like c.** courir/travailler comme un fou; **c. paving** dallage m irrégulier ▪ **craziness** n folie f

cream [kriːm] **1** n (of milk, lotion) crème f; Fig **the c.** (the best) la crème de la crème; **c.(-coloured)** crème inv; **c. of tomato soup** crème de tomates; **c. cake** gâteau m à la crème; **c. cheese** fromage m à tartiner; **c. tea** = thé servi avec des scones, de la crème fouettée et de la confiture **2** vt (milk) écrémer; Fig **they c. off the best students** ils sélectionnent les meilleurs étudiants ▪ **creamy** (-ier, -iest) adj crémeux, -euse

crease [kriːs] **1** n pli m **2** vt froisser **3** vi se froisser ▪ **crease-resistant** adj infroissable

create [kriːˈeɪt] *vt* créer; **to c. a good impression** faire bonne impression ▪**creation** *n* création *f* ▪**creator** *n* créateur, -trice *f*

creative [kriːˈeɪtɪv] *adj (person, activity)* créatif, -ive ▪**creativeness, crea'tivity** *n* créativité *f*

creature [ˈkriːtʃə(r)] *n (animal)* bête *f*; *(person)* créature *f*; **one's c. comforts** ses aises *fpl*

crèche [kreʃ] *n Br (nursery)* crèche *f*; *Am (nativity scene)* crèche

credence [ˈkriːdəns] *n* **to give** or **lend c. to** ajouter foi à

credentials [krɪˈdenʃəlz] *npl (proof of ability)* références *fpl*; *(identity)* pièce *f* d'identité; *(of diplomat)* lettres *fpl* de créance

credible [ˈkredɪbəl] *adj* crédible; **it is hardly c. that…** on a peine à croire que… ▪**credi'bility** *n* crédibilité *f*

credit [ˈkredɪt] **1** *n (financial)* crédit *m*; *(merit)* mérite *m*; *(from university)* unité *f* de valeur; **credits** *(of film)* générique *m*; **to buy sth on c.** acheter qch à crédit; **to be in c.** *(of account)* être créditeur; *(of person)* avoir un solde positif; **to give c. to sb** *Fin* faire crédit à qn; *Fig* reconnaître le mérite de qn; **to give c. to sth** ajouter foi à qch; **she's a c. to the school** elle fait honneur à l'école; **to her c., she refused** c'est tout à son honneur d'avoir refusé; **c. balance** solde *m* créditeur; **c. card** carte *f* de crédit; **c. facilities** facilités *fpl* de paiement **2** *vt (of bank)* créditer (**sb with sth** qn de qch); *(believe)* croire; **to c. sb/sth with sth** *(qualities)* attribuer qch à qn/qch ▪**creditable** *adj* honorable ▪**creditor** *n* créancier, -ière *mf* ▪**creditworthy** *adj* solvable

credulous [ˈkredjʊləs] *adj* crédule

creed [kriːd] *n* credo *m*

creek [kriːk] *n (bay)* crique *f*; *Am (stream)* ruisseau *m*; *Br Fam* **to be up the c. (without a paddle)** être dans le pétrin

creep [kriːp] **1** *n Fam (unpleasant man)* type *m* répugnant; *(obsequious person)* lèche-bottes *mf inv*; *Fam* **it gives me the creeps** ça me fait froid dans le dos **2** *(pt & pp* **crept)** *vi* ramper; *(silently)* se glisser *(furtivement);* *(slowly)* avancer lentement; **it makes my flesh c.** ça me donne la chair de poule ▪**creepy** (-ier, -iest) *adj Fam* sinistre ▪**creepy-'crawly** *(pl* -ies) *(Am* creepy-crawler) *n Fam* bestiole *f*

cremate [krɪˈmeɪt] *vt* incinérer ▪**cremation** *n* crémation *f*

crematorium [kreməˈtɔːrɪəm] *(pl* -ia [-ɪə]) *(Am* **crematory** [ˈkriːmətəːrɪ]) *n* crématorium *m*

crêpe [kreɪp] *n (fabric)* crêpe *m*; **c. (rubber) soles** semelles *fpl* de crêpe; **c. bandage** bande *f* Velpeau®; **c. paper** papier *m* crépon

crept [krept] *pt & pp of* **creep**

crescent [ˈkresənt] *n (shape)* croissant *m*; *Br Fig (street)* rue *f* en demi-lune

cress [kres] *n* cresson *m*

crest [krest] *n (of wave, mountain, bird)* crête *f*; *(of hill)* sommet *m*; *(on seal, letters)* armoiries *fpl*

Crete [kriːt] *n* la Crète

cretin [ˈkretɪn] *n Fam* crétin, -ine *mf*

crevasse [krɪˈvæs] *n (in ice)* crevasse *f*

crevice [ˈkrevɪs] *n (crack)* fente *f*

crew [kruː] *n (of ship, plane)* équipage *m*; *Fam (gang)* équipe *f*; **c. cut** coupe *f* en brosse ▪**crew-neck(ed) sweater** *n* pull *m* ras du cou

crib [krɪb] **1** *n (a) Am (cot)* lit *m* d'enfant; *(cradle)* berceau *m*; *(nativity scene)* crèche *f* (**b**) *Br Fam* **c. (sheet)** antisèche *f* **2** *(pt & pp* **-bb-)** *vti Fam* pomper

crick [krɪk] *n* **c. in the neck** torticolis *m*; **c. in the back** tour *m* de reins

cricket¹ [ˈkrɪkɪt] *n (game)* cricket *m*; *Fig* **that's not c.!** ce n'est pas du jeu!

cricket² [ˈkrɪkɪt] *n (insect)* grillon *m*

crikey [ˈkraɪkɪ] *exclam Br Fam* zut alors!

crime [kraɪm] *n* crime *m*; *Law* délit *m*; *(criminal practice)* criminalité *f*; **c. wave** vague *f* de criminalité

criminal [ˈkrɪmɪnəl] *n* criminel, -elle *mf* **2** *adj* criminel, -elle; **c. offence** *(minor)* délit *m*; *(serious)* crime *m*; **c. record** casier *m* judiciaire

crimson [ˈkrɪmzən] *adj & n* cramoisi *(m)*

cringe [krɪndʒ] *vi (show fear)* avoir un mouvement de recul; *(be embarrassed)* avoir envie de rentrer sous terre

crinkle [ˈkrɪŋkəl] **1** *n (in paper, fabric)* pli *m* **2** *vt (paper, fabric)* froisser

cripple [ˈkrɪpəl] **1** *n (lame)* estropié, -iée *mf*; *(disabled)* infirme *mf* **2** *vt (disable)* rendre infirme; *Fig (nation, system)* paralyser ▪**crippled** *adj* infirme; *(ship)* désemparé

crisis [ˈkraɪsɪs] *(pl* **crises** [ˈkraɪsiːz]) *n* crise *f*

crisp [krɪsp] **1** *(-er, -est) adj (biscuit)* croustillant; *(apple, vegetables)* croquant; *(snow)* qui crisse sous les pas; *(air, style)* vif *(f* vive) **2** *n Br* **chips** *f*; *(potato)* **crisps** chips *fpl*; **packet of crisps** sachet *m* de chips ▪**crispbread** *n* pain *m* suédois

criss-cross [ˈkrɪskrɒs] **1** *adj (lines)* entre-croisé; *(muddled)* enchevêtré **2** *vi* s'entre-croiser **3** *vt* sillonner (en tous sens)

criterion [kraɪˈtɪərɪən] *(pl* -ia [-ɪə]) *n* critère *m*

critic [ˈkrɪtɪk] *n (reviewer)* critique *mf*; *(opponent)* détracteur, -trice *mf* ▪**critical** *adj* critique ▪**critically** *adv (examine)* en critique; *(harshly)* sévèrement; **to be c. ill** être dans un état critique ▪**criticism** [-sɪzəm] *n* critique *f* ▪**criticize** [-saɪz] *vti* critiquer ▪**critique** [krɪˈtiːk] *n (essay)* critique *f*

croak [krəʊk] *n* **1** croassement *m* **2** *vi (of frog)* croasser; *(of person)* parler d'une voix rauque

Croatia [krəʊˈeɪʃə] *n* la Croatie ▪**Croatian, Croat** [ˈkrəʊæt] **1** *adj* croate **2** *n (person)* Croate *mf*; *(language)* croate *m*

crochet ['krəʊʃeɪ] **1** n (travail m au) crochet m; **c. hook** crochet **2** vt faire au crochet **3** vi faire du crochet

crock [krɒk] n Fam **a c., an old c.** (person) un croulant; (car) un tacot

crockery ['krɒkərɪ] n vaisselle f

crocodile ['krɒkədaɪl] n crocodile m

crocus ['krəʊkəs] (pl -**uses** [-əsɪz]) n crocus m

croft [krɒft] n Br petite ferme f

crony ['krəʊnɪ] (pl -**ies**) n Fam Pej copain m, copine f

crook [krʊk] n (**a**) (thief) escroc m (**b**) (shepherd's stick) houlette f

crooked ['krʊkɪd] adj (hat, picture) de travers; (nose) tordu; (smile) en coin; (deal, person) malhonnête

croon [kruːn] vti chantonner

crop [krɒp] **1** n (harvest) récolte f; (produce) culture f; Fig (of questions) série f; (of people) groupe m; **c. of hair** chevelure f; **c. circle** = motif circulaire tracé dans un champ, attribué par certains à l'intervention d'extraterrestres **2** (pt & pp -**pp**-) vt (hair) couper ras **3** vi **to c. up** (of issue) survenir; (of opportunity) se présenter; (of name) être mentionné ▪ **cropper** n Br Fam **to come a c.** se ramasser une pelle

croquet ['krəʊkeɪ] n (game) croquet m

croquette [krəʊ'ket] n Culin croquette f

cross¹ [krɒs] **1** n croix f; **a c. between** (animal) un croisement entre; Fig **it's a c. between a car and a van** c'est un compromis entre une voiture et une camionnette; **c. street** rue f transversale

2 vt (street, room) traverser; (barrier, threshold) franchir; (legs, animals) croiser; (oppose) contrecarrer; (cheque) barrer; **to c. off** or **out** (word, name) rayer; **to c. over** (road) traverser; **it never crossed my mind that...** il ne m'est pas venu à l'esprit que...

3 vi (of paths) se croiser; **to c. over** traverser ▪ **crossbow** n arbalète f ▪ '**cross**-'**country** adj (walk) à travers champs; **c. race** cross m; **c. runner** coureur, -euse mf de fond ▪ '**cross-exami'nation** n Law contre-interrogatoire m ▪ '**cross-ex'amine** vt Law soumettre à un contre-interrogatoire ▪ '**cross-'eyed** adj qui louche ▪ '**crossfire** n feux mpl croisés ▪ **cross-legged** [-'leg(ɪ)d] adj & adv **to sit c.** être assis en tailleur ▪ '**cross-'purposes** npl **to be at c.** ne pas parler de la même chose ▪ '**cross-'reference** n renvoi m ▪ **crossroads** n carrefour m ▪ '**cross-'section** n coupe f transversale; (sample) échantillon m représentatif ▪ '**cross-'training** n = entraînement dans plusieurs disciplines ▪ **crosswalk** n Am passage m clouté ▪ **crosswind** n vent m de travers ▪ **crossword** (**puzzle**) n mots mpl croisés

cross² [krɒs] adj (angry) fâché (**with** contre); **to get c.** se fâcher (**with** contre)

crossing ['krɒsɪŋ] n (of sea, river) traversée f; Br (**pedestrian**) **c.** passage m clouté

crotch [krɒtʃ] n (of garment, person) entrejambe m

crotchet ['krɒtʃɪt] n Mus noire f

crotchety ['krɒtʃɪtɪ] adj Fam grognon, -onne

crouch [kraʊtʃ] vi **to c. (down)** (of person) s'accroupir; (of animal) se tapir

crow [krəʊ] **1** n corbeau m; **as the c. flies** à vol d'oiseau; **c.'s nest** (on ship) nid-de-pie m **2** vi (of cock) chanter; Fig (boast) se vanter (**about** de)

crowbar ['krəʊbɑː(r)] n levier m

crowd [kraʊd] **1** n foule f; Fam (group of people) bande f; Fam (of things) masse f; **there was quite a c.** il y avait beaucoup de monde; Fig **to follow the c.** suivre le mouvement **2** vt (fill) entasser; (street) envahir; **to c. people/objects into** entasser des gens/des objets dans; Fam **don't c. me!** ne me bouscule pas! **3** vi **to c. into** (of people) s'entasser dans; **to c. round sb/sth** se presser autour de qn/qch; **to c. together** se serrer ▪ **crowded** adj plein (**with** de); (train, room) bondé; (city) surpeuplé; **it's very c.** il y a beaucoup de monde

crown [kraʊn] **1** n (of king) couronne f; (of head, hill) sommet m; **the C.** (monarchy) la Couronne; Br Law **c. court** ≃ cour f d'assises; Br **c. jewels** joyaux mpl de la Couronne; **c. prince** prince m héritier **2** vt couronner ▪ **crowning** adj (glory) suprême; **c. achievement** (of career) couronnement m

crucial ['kruːʃəl] adj crucial

crucify ['kruːsɪfaɪ] (pt & pp -**ied**) vt crucifier ▪ **crucifix** [-fɪks] n crucifix m ▪ **crucifixion** [-'fɪkʃən] n crucifixion f

crude [kruːd] (-**er**, -**est**) adj (manners, person, language) grossier, -ière; (painting, work) rudimentaire; (fact) brut; **c. oil** pétrole m brut ▪ **crudely** adv (say, order) crûment; (build, paint) grossièrement ▪ **crudeness** n (of manners) grossièreté f; (of painting) état m rudimentaire

cruel [krʊəl] (**crueller**, **cruellest**) adj cruel (f cruelle) ▪ **cruelty** n cruauté f; **an act of c.** une cruauté

cruise [kruːz] **1** n croisière f; **to go on a c.** partir en croisière; Mil **c. missile** missile m de croisière; **c. ship** navire m de croisière **2** vi (of ship) croiser; (of vehicle) rouler; (of plane) voler; (of taxi) marauder; (of tourists) faire une croisière; **cruising speed** (of ship, plane) vitesse f de croisière

crumb [krʌm] n miette f; Fig (of comfort) brin m

crumble ['krʌmbəl] **1** n crumble m (dessert aux fruits recouvert de pâte sablée) **2** vt (bread) émietter **3** vi (of bread) s'émietter; (collapse) (of resistance) s'effondrer; **to c. (away)** (in small *pieces)* s'effriter; *(become ruined) (of building)* tomber en ruine ▪ **crumbly** *adj (pastry)* friable

crummy ['krʌmɪ] *(-ier, -iest) adj Fam* minable

crumpet ['krʌmpɪt] *n Br* = petite crêpe épaisse servie chaude et beurrée

crumple ['krʌmpəl] 1 *vt* froisser 2 *vi* se froisser

crunch [krʌntʃ] 1 *n Fam* **when it comes to the c.** au moment crucial 2 *vt (food)* croquer 3 *vi (of snow)* crisser ▪ **crunchy** *(-ier, -iest) adj (apple, vegetables)* croquant; *(bread)* croustillant

crusade [kru:'seɪd] 1 *n Hist & Fig* croisade *f* 2 *vi* faire une croisade ▪ **crusader** *n Hist* croisé *m*; *Fig* militant, -ante *mf*

crush [krʌʃ] 1 *n (crowd)* foule *f*; *(confusion)* bousculade *f*; *Fam* **to have a c. on sb** en pincer pour qn 2 *vt* écraser; *(hope)* détruire; *(clothes)* froisser; *(cram)* entasser (**into** dans) ▪ **crushing** *adj (defeat)* écrasant

crust [krʌst] *n* croûte *f* ▪ **crusty** *(-ier, -iest) n (bread)* croustillant

crutch [krʌtʃ] *n* (**a**) *(of invalid)* béquille *f* (**b**) *(crotch)* entrejambe *m*

crux [krʌks] *n* **the c. of the matter/problem** le nœud de l'affaire/du problème

cry [kraɪ] 1 *(pl cries) n (shout)* cri *m*; *Fam* **to have a good c.** pleurer un bon coup 2 *(pt & pp cried) vt* **to c. (out)** *(shout)* crier; **to c. one's eyes out** pleurer toutes les larmes de son corps 3 *vi (weep)* pleurer; **to c. (out)** pousser un cri; **to c. for help** appeler au secours; **to c. out for sth** *(of person)* demander qch à grands cris; **to be crying out for sth** *(of thing)* avoir grand besoin de qch; **to c. off** *(from invitation)* se décommander; **to c. over sb/sth** pleurer qn/qch ▪ **crying** 1 *adj* **a c. need of sth** un besoin urgent de qch; **a c. shame** un scandale 2 *n (shouts)* cris *mpl*; *(weeping)* pleurs *mpl*

crypt [krɪpt] *n* crypte *f*

cryptic ['krɪptɪk] *adj* énigmatique; **c. crossword** = mots croisés dont les définitions sont des énigmes

crystal ['krɪstəl] *n* cristal *m*; **c. ball** boule *f* de cristal; **c. vase** vase *m* en cristal ▪ **'crystal-'clear** *adj (water, sound)* cristallin; *(explanation)* clair comme de l'eau de roche

crystallize ['krɪstəlaɪz] 1 *vt* cristalliser 2 *vi (se)* cristalliser

cub [kʌb] *n* (**a**) *(of animal)* petit *m* (**b**) *(scout)* louveteau *m*

Cuba ['kju:bə] *n* Cuba *f* ▪ **Cuban** 1 *adj* cubain 2 *n* Cubain, -aine *mf*

cubbyhole ['kʌbɪhəʊl] *n* cagibi *m*

cube [kju:b] *n* cube *m*; *(of meat, vegetables)* dé *m*; *(of sugar)* morceau *m* ▪ **cubic** *adj (shape)* cubique; **c. capacity** volume *m*; *(of engine)* cylindrée *f*; **c. metre** mètre *m* cube

cubicle ['kju:bɪkəl] *n (for changing clothes)* cabine *f*; *(in hospital, dormitory)* box *m*

cuckoo [*Br* 'kʊku:, *Am* 'ku:ku:] *(pl* **-oos)** 1 *n*

(bird) coucou *m*; **c. clock** coucou *m* 2 *adj Fam (mad)* cinglé

cucumber ['kju:kʌmbə(r)] *n* concombre *m*

cuddle ['kʌdəl] 1 *n* câlin *m*; **to give sb a c.** faire un câlin à qn 2 *vt (hug)* serrer dans ses bras; *(caress)* câliner 3 *vi (of lovers)* se faire des câlins; **to (kiss and) c.** s'embrasser; **to c. up to sb** *(huddle)* se blottir contre qn ▪ **cuddly** *(-ier, -iest) adj (person)* mignon, -onne à croquer; **c. toy** peluche *f*

cudgel ['kʌdʒəl] *n* gourdin *m*

cue¹ [kju:] *n (in theatre)* réplique *f*; *(signal)* signal *m*; *Fig* **(right) on c.** au bon moment

cue² [kju:] *n* **(billiard) c.** queue *f* de billard

cuff [kʌf] 1 *n (of shirt)* poignet *m*; *Am (of trousers)* revers *m*; **off the c.** *(remark)* impromptu; **c. link** bouton *m* de manchette 2 *vt (strike)* gifler

cul-de-sac ['kʌldəsæk] *n Br* impasse *f*

culinary ['kʌlɪnərɪ] *adj* culinaire

cull [kʌl] *vt* choisir (**from** dans); *(animals)* abattre sélectivement

culminate ['kʌlmɪneɪt] *vi* **to c. in** aboutir à ▪ **culmination** [-'neɪʃən] *n* point *m* culminant

culprit ['kʌlprɪt] *n* coupable *mf*

cult [kʌlt] *n* culte *m*; **c. film** film *m* culte

cultivate ['kʌltɪveɪt] *vt (land, mind)* cultiver ▪ **cultivated** *adj* cultivé ▪ **cultivation** [-'veɪʃən] *n* culture *f*

culture ['kʌltʃə(r)] *n* culture *f* ▪ **cultural** *adj* culturel, -elle ▪ **cultured** *adj (person, mind)* cultivé

cumbersome ['kʌmbəsəm] *adj* encombrant

cumulative ['kju:mjʊlətɪv] *adj* cumulatif, -ive; **c. effect** *(long-term)* effet *m* à long terme

cunning ['kʌnɪŋ] 1 *adj (ingenious)* astucieux, -ieuse; *(devious)* rusé 2 *n* astuce *f*; *Pej* ruse *f* ▪ **cunningly** *adv* avec astuce; *Pej* avec ruse

cup [kʌp] *n* tasse *f*; *(goblet, prize)* coupe *f*; *Fam* **it's not my c. of tea** ce n'est pas mon truc; *Football* **c. final** finale *f* de la coupe ▪ **cupful** *n* tasse *f*

cupboard ['kʌbəd] *n Br* armoire *f*; *(built into wall)* placard *m*

cup-tie ['kʌptaɪ] *n Football* match *m* éliminatoire

curate ['kjʊərɪt] *n* vicaire *m*

curator [kjʊə'reɪtə(r)] *n (of museum)* conservateur *m*

curb [kɜ:b] 1 *n* (**a**) *(limit)* **to put a c. on** mettre un frein à (**b**) *Am (kerb)* bord *m* du trottoir 2 *vt (feelings)* refréner; *(ambitions)* modérer; *(expenses)* réduire

curd [kɜ:d] *n* **curd(s)** lait *m* caillé; **c. cheese** fromage *m* blanc battu

curdle ['kɜ:dəl] 1 *vt* cailler 2 *vi* se cailler

cure ['kjʊə(r)] 1 *n* remède *m* (**for** contre) 2 *vt* (**a**) *(person, illness)* guérir; *Fig (poverty)* éliminer; **to c. sb of** guérir qn de (**b**) *(meat, fish) (smoke)* fumer; *(salt)* saler; *(dry)* sécher ▪ **curable** *adj* guérissable

curfew ['kɜːfjuː] n couvre-feu m

curious ['kjʊərɪəs] adj (odd) curieux, -ieuse; (inquisitive) curieux, -ieuse (**about** de); **to be c. to know/see** être curieux de savoir/voir ▪ **curiously** adv (oddly) curieusement; (inquisitively) avec curiosité

curiosity [kjʊərɪ'ɒsɪtɪ] (pl -ies) n curiosité f (**about** de)

curl [kɜːl] **1** n (in hair) boucle f; Fig (of smoke) spirale f **2** vti (hair) boucler; (with small, tight curls) friser **3** vi **to c. up** (shrivel) se racornir; **to c. (oneself) up** (into a ball) se pelotonner ▪ **curler** n bigoudi m ▪ **curly** (**-ier**, **-iest**) adj (hair) bouclé; (with small, tight curls) frisé

currant ['kʌrənt] n (dried grape) raisin m de Corinthe; (fruit) groseille f

currency ['kʌrənsɪ] (pl -ies) n (**a**) (money) monnaie f; (**foreign**) **c.** devises fpl (étrangères) (**b**) **to gain c.** (of ideas) se répandre

current ['kʌrənt] **1** adj (fashion, trend) actuel, -uelle; (opinion, use, phrase) courant; (year, month) en cours; **c. account** (in bank) compte m courant; **c. affairs** questions fpl d'actualité; **c. events** actualité f; **the c. issue** (of magazine) le dernier numéro **2** n (of river, air, electricity) courant m ▪ **currently** adv actuellement

curriculum [kə'rɪkjʊləm] (pl -la [-lə]) n programme m scolaire; Br **c. vitae** curriculum vitae m inv

curry ['kʌrɪ] **1** (pl -ies) n (dish) curry m, cari m; **chicken c.** poulet m au curry **2** (pt & pp -ied) vt **to c. favour with sb** s'insinuer dans les bonnes grâces de qn

curse [kɜːs] **1** n malédiction f; (swearword) juron m; (scourge) fléau m **2** vt maudire; **cursed with sth** affligé de qch **3** vi (swear) jurer

cursor ['kɜːsə(r)] n Comptr curseur m

cursory ['kɜːsərɪ] adj superficiel, -ielle

curt [kɜːt] adj brusque ▪ **curtly** adv d'un ton brusque

curtail [kɜː'teɪl] vt (visit) écourter; (expenses) réduire ▪ **curtailment** n raccourcissement m; (of expenses) réduction f

curtain ['kɜːtən] n rideau m; **to draw the curtains** (close) tirer les rideaux; **c. call** (in theatre) rappel m

curts(e)y ['kɜːtsɪ] **1** (pl -ies or -eys) n révérence f **2** (pt & pp -ied) vi faire une révérence (**to** à)

curve [kɜːv] **1** n courbe f; (in road) virage m **2** vt courber **3** vi se courber; (of road) faire une courbe ▪ **curved** adj (line) courbe ▪ **curvy** adj (line) courbe; (woman) qui a des formes

cushion ['kʊʃən] **1** n coussin m **2** vt (shock) amortir ▪ **cushioned** adj (seat) rembourré

cushy ['kʊʃɪ] (-**ier**, -**iest**) adj Fam (job, life) pépère

custard ['kʌstəd] n crème f anglaise; (when set) crème renversée; **c. pie** tarte f à la crème

custody ['kʌstədɪ] n (of child, important papers) garde f; **in the c. of sb** sous la garde de qn; **to take sb into c.** placer qn en garde à vue ▪ **custodial** [kʌ'stəʊdɪəl] adj Law **c. sentence** peine f de prison ▪ **custodian** [kʌ'stəʊdɪən] n gardien, -ienne mf

custom ['kʌstəm] n coutume f; (of individual) habitude f; (customers) clientèle f ▪ '**custom-'built**, **customized** adj (car) (fait) sur commande ▪ '**custom-'made** adj (shirt) (fait) sur mesure ▪ **customize** vt personnaliser

customary ['kʌstəmərɪ] adj habituel, -uelle; **it is c. to...** il est d'usage de...

customer ['kʌstəmə(r)] n client, -iente mf; Pej (individual) individu m

customs ['kʌstəmz] npl (**the**) **c.** la douane; **c. duties** droits mpl de douane; **c. officer** douanier m; **c. union** union f douanière

cut [kʌt] **1** n (mark) coupure f; (stroke) coup m; (of clothes, hair) coupe f; (in salary, prices) réduction f; (of meat) morceau m; Comptr **c. and paste** couper-coller m

2 (pt & pp **cut**, pres p **cutting**) vt couper; (meat, chicken) découper; (glass, diamond, tree) tailler; (hay) faucher; (salary, prices, profits) réduire; **to c. sb's hair** couper les cheveux à qn; **to have one's hair c.** se faire couper les cheveux; **to c. a tooth** (of child) faire une dent; **to c. a corner** (in vehicle) prendre un virage à la corde; **to c. sth open** ouvrir qch avec un couteau/des ciseaux/etc; **to c. sth short** (visit) écourter qch; **to c. a long story short...** enfin, bref...; Comptr **to c. and paste sth** couper-coller qch

3 vi (of knife, scissors) couper; **this cloth cuts easily** ce tissu se coupe facilement ▪ **cutback** n réduction f ▪ **cutout** n (picture) découpage m; (electrical) coupe-circuit m inv

► **cut away** vt sep (remove) enlever

► **cut back** vt sep & vi réduire

► **cut down** **1** vt sep (**a**) (tree) abattre (**b**) (reduce) réduire **2** vi réduire

► **cut in** vi (interrupt) interrompre; (in vehicle) faire une queue de poisson (**on sb** à qn)

► **cut off** vt sep (piece, limb, hair) couper; (isolate) isoler

► **cut out** **1** vt sep (article) découper; (garment) tailler; (remove) enlever; (eliminate) supprimer; **to c. out drinking** (stop) s'arrêter de boire; Fam **c. it out!** ça suffit!; **c. out to be a doctor** fait pour être médecin **2** vi (of car engine) caler

► **cut up** vt sep couper en morceaux; (meat, chicken) découper; **to be very c. up about sth** (upset) être complètement chamboulé par qch

cute [kjuːt] (-**er**, -**est**) adj Fam mignon, -onne

cuticle ['kjuːtɪkəl] n cuticule f

cutlery ['kʌtlərɪ] n couverts mpl

cutlet ['kʌtlɪt] n côtelette f

cut-price [kʌt'praɪs] adj à prix réduit

cutthroat ['kʌtθrəʊt] **1** n assassin m **2** adj (competition) impitoyable

cutting ['kʌtɪŋ] **1** *n* coupe *f*; *(of glass, diamond)* taille *f*; *(from newspaper)* coupure *f*; *(plant)* bouture *f*; *(for train)* voie *f* en déblai **2** *adj (wind, remark)* cinglant; **c. edge** tranchant *m*

CV [siː'viː] *(abbr curriculum vitae) n Br* CV *m*

cyanide ['saɪənaɪd] *n* cyanure *m*

cybercafé ['saɪbəkæfeɪ] *n* cybercafé *m*

cybernetics [saɪbə'netɪks] *n Comptr* cyber-nétique *f*

cybersex ['saɪbəseks] *n Comptr* cybersexe *m*

cyberspace ['saɪbəspeɪs] *n Comptr* cyber-espace *m*

cycle¹ ['saɪkəl] **1** *n (bicycle)* bicyclette *f*; **c. lane** voie *f* réservée aux vélos; **c. path** piste *f* cyclable; **c. race** course *f* cycliste **2** *vi* aller à bicyclette **(to** à); *(as activity)* faire de la bicyclette ▪**cycling** *n* cyclisme *m* ▪**cyclist** *n* cycliste *mf*

cycle² ['saɪkəl] *n (series, period)* cycle *m* ▪**cyclical** ['sɪklɪkəl] *adj* cyclique

cyclone ['saɪkləʊn] *n* cyclone *m*

cylinder ['sɪlɪndə(r)] *n* cylindre *m* ▪**cylindrical** [sɪ'lɪndrɪkəl] *adj* cylindrique

cymbal ['sɪmbəl] *n* cymbale *f*

cynic ['sɪnɪk] *n* cynique *mf* ▪**cynical** *adj* cynique ▪**cynicism** [-sɪzm] *n* cynisme *m*

cypress ['saɪprəs] *n* cyprès *m*

Cyprus ['saɪprəs] *n* Chypre *f* ▪**Cypriot** ['sɪprɪət] **1** *adj* cypriote **2** *n* Cypriote *mf*

cyst [sɪst] *n Med* kyste *m*

cystitis [sɪ'staɪtəs] *n Med* cystite *f*

czar [zɑː(r)] *n* tsar *m*

Czech [tʃek] **1** *adj* tchèque; **the C. Republic** la République tchèque **2** *n (person)* Tchèque *mf*; *(language)* tchèque *m* ▪**Czechoslovakia** [tʃekəslə'vækɪə] *n Formerly* Tchécoslovaquie *f*

D, d [di:] *n* D, d *m inv* ■ **D.-day** *n* le jour J

dab [dæb] **1** *n* a **d. of** un petit peu de **2** (*pt & pp* **-bb-**) *vt* (*wound, brow*) tamponner; **to d. sth on sth** appliquer qch (à petits coups) sur qch

dabble ['dæbəl] *vi* **to d. in politics/journalism** faire vaguement de la politique/du journalisme

dad [dæd] *n Fam* papa *m* ■ **daddy** (*pl* **-ies**) *n Fam* papa *m*; *Br* **d. longlegs** (*cranefly*) tipule *f*; *Am* (*spider*) faucheur *m*

daffodil ['dæfədɪl] *n* jonquille *f*

daft [dɑːft] (**-er, -est**) *adj Fam* bête

dagger ['dægə(r)] *n* dague *f*; **at daggers drawn** à couteaux tirés (**with** avec)

dahlia ['deɪlɪə] *n* dahlia *m*

daily ['deɪlɪ] **1** *adj* quotidien, -ienne; (*wage*) journalier, -ière; *Br* **d. help** (*cleaning woman*) femme *f* de ménage; **d. paper** quotidien *m* **2** *adv* chaque jour, quotidiennement; **twice d.** deux fois par jour **3** (*pl* **-ies**) *n* quotidien *m*

dainty ['deɪntɪ] (**-ier, -iest**) *adj* délicat

dairy ['deərɪ] **1** (*pl* **-ies**) *n* (*factory*) laiterie *f*; (*shop*) crémerie *f* **2** *adj* laitier, -ière; **d. farm/ cow** ferme *f*/vache *f* laitière; **d. product** produit *m* laitier; **d. produce** produits *mpl* laitiers

daisy ['deɪzɪ] (*pl* **-ies**) *n* pâquerette *f*; (*bigger*) marguerite *f*; *Fam* **to push up the daisies** manger les pissenlits par la racine

dale [deɪl] *n Literary* vallée *f*

dally ['dælɪ] (*pt & pp* **-ied**) *vi* lambiner

dam [dæm] **1** *n* (*wall*) barrage *m* **2** (*pt & pp* **-mm-**) *vt* (*river*) construire un barrage sur

damage ['dæmɪdʒ] **1** *n* dégâts *mpl*; (*harm*) préjudice *m*; **damages** (*in court*) dommages-intérêts *mpl* **2** *vt* (*object*) endommager, abîmer; (*health*) nuire à; (*eyesight*) abîmer; (*plans, reputation*) compromettre ■ **damaging** *adj* (*harmful*) préjudiciable (**to** à)

damn [dæm] **1** *n Fam* **he doesn't care** *or* **give a d.** il s'en fiche pas mal **2** *adj Fam* (*awful*) fichu; **that d. car** cette fichue bagnole **3** *adv Fam* (*very*) vachement; *Br* **d. all** que dalle **4** *vt* (*condemn, doom*) condamner; (*of God*) damner; (*curse*) maudire; *Fam* **d. him!** qu'il aille se faire voir! **5** *exclam Fam* **d. (it)!** mince! ■ **damned 1** *adj* (a) (*soul*) damné (b) *Fam* (*awful*) fichu **2** *adv Fam* vachement ■ **damning** *adj* (*evidence*) accablant

damnation [dæm'neɪʃən] **1** *n* damnation *f* **2** *exclam Fam* bon sang!

damp [dæmp] **1** (**-er, -est**) *adj* humide; (*skin*) moite **2** *n* humidité *f* ■ **damp(en)** *vt* humecter; **to d. (down)** (*enthusiasm, zeal*) refroidir; (*ambition*) freiner; **to d. sb's spirits** décourager qn ■ **dampness** *n* humidité *f*

damper ['dæmpə(r)] *n* **to put a d. on** jeter un froid sur

damson ['dæmzən] *n* prune *f* de Damas

dance [dɑːns] **1** *n* danse *f*; (*social event*) bal *m* (*pl* bals); **d. floor** piste *f* de danse; **d. hall** dancing *m* **2** *vt* (*waltz, tango*) danser **3** *vi* danser; **to d. for joy** sauter de joie ■ **dancer** *n* danseur, -euse *mf* ■ **dancing** *n* danse *f*; **d. partner** cavalier, -ière *mf*

dandelion ['dændɪlaɪən] *n* pissenlit *m*

dandruff ['dændrʌf] *n* pellicules *fpl*

dandy ['dændɪ] *adj Am Fam* super *inv*

Dane [deɪn] *n* Danois, -oise *mf*

danger ['deɪndʒə(r)] *n* danger *m* (**to** pour); **in d.** en danger; **out of d.** hors de danger; **in d. of** (*threatened by*) menacé de; **to be in d. of doing sth** risquer de faire qch; **on the d. list** (*hospital patient*) dans un état critique; **'d. of fire'** 'risque d'incendie'; **d. zone** zone *f* dangereuse ■ **dangerous** *adj* dangereux, -euse (**to** pour) ■ **dangerously** *adv* dangereusement; **d. ill** gravement malade

dangle ['dæŋgəl] **1** *vt* balancer; *Fig* **to d. sth in front of sb** faire miroiter qch à qn **2** *vi* (*hang*) pendre; (*swing*) se balancer

Danish ['deɪnɪʃ] **1** *adj* danois **2** *n* (*language*) danois *m*

dank [dæŋk] (**-er, -est**) *adj* humide et froid

dapper ['dæpə(r)] *adj* soigné

dappled ['dæpəld] *adj* tacheté; (*horse*) pommelé

dare [deə(r)] **1** *n* défi *m*; **to do sth for a d.** faire qch par défi **2** *vt* **to d. to do sth** oser faire qch; **he doesn't d. (to) go** il n'ose pas y aller; **if you d. (to)** si tu l'oses; **I d. say he tried** il a essayé, c'est bien possible; **to d. sb to do sth** défier qn de faire qch

daredevil ['deədevəl] *n* casse-cou *mf inv*

daring ['deərɪŋ] **1** *adj* audacieux, -ieuse **2** *n* audace *f*

dark [dɑːk] **1** (**-er, -est**) *adj* (*room, night*) & *Fig* sombre; (*colour, skin, hair, eyes*) foncé; **it's d. at**

six il fait nuit à six heures; **d. glasses** lunettes *fpl* noires **2** *n* obscurité *f*; **after d.** une fois la nuit tombée; *Fig* **to keep sb in the d.** laisser qn dans l'ignorance (**about de**) ∎ **dark-'haired** *adj* aux cheveux bruns ∎ **dark-'skinned** *adj (person)* à peau brune

darken ['dɑːkən] **1** *vt* assombrir; *(colour)* foncer **2** *vi* s'assombrir; *(of colour)* foncer

darkness ['dɑːknəs] *n* obscurité *f*

darkroom ['dɑːkruːm] *n (for photography)* chambre *f* noire

darling ['dɑːlɪŋ] **1** *adj* chéri; *Fam (delightful)* adorable **2** *n (favourite)* chouchou, -oute *mf*; **(my) d.** (mon) chéri/(ma) chérie; **be a d.!** sois un ange!

darn [dɑːn] **1** *vt (mend)* repriser **2** *exclam* **d. it!** bon sang! ∎ **darning 1** *n* reprise *f* **2** *adj (needle, wool)* à repriser

dart [dɑːt] **1** *n (in game)* fléchette *f*; **darts** *(game)* fléchettes *fpl*; **to make a d.** se précipiter (**for** vers) **2** *vi (dash)* se précipiter (**for** vers) ∎ **dartboard** *n* cible *f (du jeu de fléchettes)*

dash [dæʃ] **1** *n* (a) *(run, rush)* ruée *f*; **to make a d. for sth** se ruer vers qch (b) **a d. of sth** un petit peu de qch; **a d. of milk** une goutte de lait (c) *(handwritten stroke)* trait *m*; *(punctuation sign)* tiret *m* **2** *vt (throw)* jeter; *Fig (destroy) (hopes)* briser; *Br Fam* **d. (it)!** zut!; **to d. off** *(letter)* écrire en vitesse **3** *vi* se précipiter; *(of waves)* se briser (**against** contre); **to d. in/out** entrer/sortir en vitesse; **to d. off** or **away** filer

dashboard ['dæʃbɔːd] *n (of vehicle)* tableau *m* de bord

dashing ['dæʃɪŋ] *adj (person)* fringant

data ['deɪtə] *npl* informations *fpl*; *Comptr* données *fpl*; **d. bank/base** banque *f*/base *f* de données; **d. capture** saisie *f* de données; **d. processing** informatique *f*

date¹ [deɪt] **1** *n (day)* date *f*; *Fam (meeting)* rendez-vous *m inv*; *Fam (person)* ami, -ie *mf*; **d. of birth** date de naissance; **up to d.** *(in fashion)* à la mode; *(information)* à jour; *(well-informed)* au courant (**on** de); **out of d.** *(old-fashioned)* démodé; *(expired)* périmé; **to d.** à ce jour; **d. rape** = viol commis par une connaissance; **d. stamp** *(object)* tampon *m* dateur; *(mark)* cachet *m* **2** *vt (letter)* dater; *(girl, boy)* sortir avec **3** *vi (go out of fashion)* dater; **to d. back to, to d. from** dater de; *(couple)* **they're dating** ils sortent ensemble; **dating agency** agence *f* matrimoniale

date² [deɪt] *n (fruit)* datte *f*

datebook ['deɪtbʊk] *n Am* agenda *m*

dated ['deɪtɪd] *adj* démodé

daub [dɔːb] *vt* barbouiller (**with** de)

daughter ['dɔːtə(r)] *n* fille *f* ∎ **daughter-in-law** *(pl* **daughters-in-law)** *n* belle-fille *f*

daunt [dɔːnt] *vt* intimider

dawdle ['dɔːdəl] *vi* traînasser

dawn [dɔːn] **1** *n* aube *f*; **at d.** à l'aube **2** *vi (of day)* se lever; *(of new era, idea)* naître; **it dawned upon him that...** il s'est rendu compte que...

day [deɪ] *n (period of daylight, 24 hours)* jour *m*; *(referring to duration)* journée *f*; **all d. (long)** toute la journée; **what d. is it?** quel jour sommes-nous?; **the following** or **next d.** le lendemain; **the d. before** la veille; **the d. before yesterday** or **before last** avant-hier; **the d. after tomorrow** après-demain; **to the d.** jour pour jour; **in my days** de mon temps; **in those days** en ce temps-là; **these days** de nos jours; *Br* **d. boarder** demi-pensionnaire *mf*; *Br* **d. nursery** crèche *f*; *Br* **d. return** *(on train)* aller et retour *m (valable une journée)*; *Br* **d. tripper** excursionniste *mf* ∎ **daybreak** ['deɪbreɪk] *n* point *m* du jour ∎ **daydream 1** *n* rêverie *f* **2** *vi* rêvasser ∎ **daylight** *n (lumière f* du) jour *m*; *(dawn)* point *m* du jour; **it's d.** il fait jour ∎ **daytime** *n* journée *f*, jour *m* ∎ **'day-to-'day** *adj* quotidien, -ienne; **on a d. basis** au jour le jour

daze [deɪz] **1** *n* **in a d.** étourdi; *(because of drugs)* hébété; *(astonished)* ahuri **2** *vt (by blow)* étourdir; *(of drug)* hébéter

dazzle ['dæzəl] *vt* éblouir

deacon ['diːkən] *n* diacre *m*

dead [ded] **1** *adj* mort; *(numb) (limb)* engourdi; *(party)* mortel, -elle; **the phone's d.** il n'y a pas de tonalité; **in (the) d. centre** au beau milieu; **d. end** *(street)* & *Fig* impasse *f*; **d.-end job** un travail sans avenir; *Fam* **to be a d. loss** *(of person)* être bon *(f* bonne) à rien; *Fam* **it's a d. loss** ça ne vaut rien; **the D. Sea** la mer Morte; **d. silence** silence *m* de mort; **a d. stop** un arrêt complet

2 *npl* **the d.** les morts *mpl*; **in the d. of night/ winter** au cœur de la nuit/l'hiver

3 *adv (completely)* totalement; *(very)* très; *Br Fam* **d. beat** éreinté; *Fam* **d. drunk** ivre mort; **'d. slow'** *(on sign)* 'roulez au pas'; **to stop d.** s'arrêter net ∎ **deadbeat** *n Am Fam (sponger)* parasite *m* ∎ **deadline** *n* date *f* limite; *(hour)* heure *f* limite ∎ **deadlock** *n Fig* impasse *f* ∎ **deadpan** *adj (face)* figé

deaden ['dedən] *vt (shock)* amortir; *(pain)* calmer; *(feeling)* émousser

deadly ['dedlɪ] **1** (**-ier, -iest**) *adj (poison, blow, enemy)* mortel, -elle; *(paleness, silence)* de mort; *Fam (boring)* mortel; **d. weapon** arme *f* meurtrière **2** *adv (pale, boring)* mortellement

deaf [def] **1** *adj* sourd; **d. and dumb** sourd-muet *(f* sourde-muette); **d. in one ear** sourd d'une oreille; **to go d.** devenir sourd; **to be d. to sb's requests** rester sourd aux prières de qn **2** *npl* **the d.** les sourds *mpl* ∎ **deafen** *vt* assourdir ∎ **deafness** *n* surdité *f*

deal¹ [diːl] *n* **a good** or **great d. (of)** *(a lot)* beaucoup (de)

deal² [di:l] *n* 1 *(in business)* marché *m*, affaire *f*; *Cards* donne *f*; **to make** *or* **do a d. (with sb)** conclure un marché (avec qn); **to give sb a fair d.** traiter qn équitablement; **to get a fair d. from sb** être traité équitablement par qn; **it's a d.!** d'accord!; *Ironic* **big d.!** la belle affaire!; **it's no big d.** ce n'est pas bien grave 2 *(pt & pp dealt)* *vt* **to d. sb a blow** porter un coup à qn; **to d. (out)** *(cards, money)* distribuer 3 *vi* *(trade)* traiter **(with sb** avec qn**)**; **to d. in** faire le commerce de; **to d. with** *(take care of)* s'occuper de; *(concern) (of book)* traiter de, parler de ■ **dealer** *n* marchand, -ande *mf* **(in** de**)**; *(agent)* dépositaire *mf*; *(for cars)* concessionnaire *mf*; *(in drugs)* revendeur, -euse *mf*; *Cards* donneur, -euse *mf* ■ **dealings** *npl* relations *fpl* **(with** avec**)**; *(in business)* transactions *fpl*

deal³ [di:l] *n (wood)* sapin *m*

dealt [delt] *pt & pp of* **deal**

dean [di:n] *n Br (in church, university)* doyen *m*; *Am (in secondary school)* conseiller, -ère *mf* principal(e) d'éducation

dear [dɪə(r)] 1 (**-er, -est**) *adj (loved, precious, expensive)* cher **(***f* chère**)**; *(price)* élevé; **D. Sir** *(in letter)* Monsieur; **D. Sirs** Messieurs; **D. Uncle** (mon) cher oncle; **oh d.!** oh là là! 2 *n* **(my) d.** *(darling)* (mon) chéri/(ma) chérie; *(friend)* mon cher/ma chère; **be a d.!** sois un ange! 3 *adv (cost, pay)* cher ■ **dearly** *adv (love)* tendrement; *(very much)* beaucoup; **to pay d. for sth** payer qch cher

dearth [dɜ:θ] *n* pénurie *f*

death [deθ] *n* mort *f*; **to put sb to d.** mettre qn à mort; **to be burnt to d.** mourir carbonisé; **to be bored to d.** s'ennuyer à mourir; **to be scared to d.** être mort de peur; **to be sick to d.** en avoir vraiment marre **(of** de**)**; **there were many deaths** il y a eu de nombreux morts; **d. certificate** acte *m* de décès; *Br* **d. duty** *or* **duties,** *Am* **d. taxes** droits *mpl* de succession; **d. march** marche *f* funèbre; **d. mask** masque *m* mortuaire; **d. penalty** peine *f* de mort; **d. rate** (taux *m* de) mortalité *f*; **d. sentence** condamnation *f* à mort; **d. wish** désir *m* de mort ■ **deathbed** *n* lit *m* de mort ■ **death-blow** *n* coup *m* mortel ■ **deathly** *adj (silence, pallor)* de mort

debar [dɪ'bɑ:(r)] *(pt & pp* **-rr-)** *vt* exclure **(from sth** de qch**)**; **to d. sb from doing sth** interdire à qn de faire qch

debase [dɪ'beɪs] *vt (person)* avilir; *(reputation)* ternir; *(coinage)* altérer

debate [dɪ'beɪt] 1 *n* débat *m* 2 *vti* discuter; **he debated whether to do it** il se demandait s'il devait le faire ■ **debatable** *adj* discutable; **it's d. whether she will succeed** il est difficile de dire si elle réussira

debilitate [dɪ'bɪlɪteɪt] *vt* débiliter ■ **debilitating** *adj* débilitant

debit ['debɪt] 1 *n* débit *m*; **in d.** *(account)* débiteur; **d. balance** solde *m* débiteur 2 *vt* débiter **(sb with sth** qn de qch**)**

debonair [debə'neə(r)] *adj* élégant et raffiné

debris ['debri:] *n (of building)* décombres *mpl*; *(of plane, car)* débris *mpl*

debt [det] *n* dette *f*; **to be in d.** avoir des dettes; **to be 50 dollars in d.** devoir 50 dollars; **to run** *or* **get into d.** faire des dettes ■ **debtor** *n* débiteur, -trice *mf*

debug [di:'bʌg] *(pt & pp* **-gg-)** *vt Comptr* déboguer

debunk [di:'bʌŋk] *vt Fam (idea, theory)* discréditer

debut ['debju:] *n (on stage)* début *m*; **to make one's d.** faire ses débuts

decade ['dekeɪd] *n* décennie *f*

> Note that the French word **décade** is a false friend. It usually refers to a period of ten days.

decadent ['dekədənt] *adj* décadent ■ **decadence** *n* décadence *f*

decaffeinated [di:'kæfɪneɪtɪd] *adj* décaféiné

decant [dɪ'kænt] *vt (wine)* décanter ■ **decanter** *n* carafe *f*

decapitate [dɪ'kæpɪteɪt] *vt* décapiter

decathlon [dɪ'kæθlɒn] *n Sport* décathlon *m*

decay [dɪ'keɪ] 1 *n (rot)* pourriture *f*; *(of building)* délabrement *m*; *(of tooth)* carie *f*; *(of nation)* déclin *m*; **to fall into d.** *(of building)* tomber en ruine 2 *vi (go bad)* se gâter; *(rot)* pourrir; *(of tooth)* se carier; *(of building)* tomber en ruine; *Fig (decline) (of nation)* décliner ■ **decaying** *adj (meat, fruit)* pourrissant; *(nation)* sur le déclin

deceased [dɪ'si:st] 1 *adj* décédé 2 *n* **the d.** le défunt/la défunte

deceit [dɪ'si:t] *n* tromperie *f* ■ **deceitful** *(person)* fourbe; *(behaviour)* malhonnête ■ **deceitfully** *adv* avec duplicité

deceive [dɪ'si:v] *vti* tromper; **to d. oneself** se faire des illusions

> Note that the French verb **décevoir** is a false friend and is never a translation for the English verb **to deceive**. It means **to disappoint**.

December [dɪ'sembə(r)] *n* décembre *m*

decent ['di:sənt] *adj (respectable)* convenable; *(good)* bon **(***f* bonne**)**; *(kind)* gentil, -ille; **that was d. (of you)** c'était chic de ta part ■ **decency** *n* décence *f*; *(kindness)* gentillesse *f* ■ **decently** *adv (respectably)* convenablement

deception [dɪ'sepʃən] *n* tromperie *f* ■ **deceptive** *adj* trompeur, -euse ■ **deceptively** *adv* **it looks d. straightforward** ça a l'air simple mais il ne faut pas s'y fier

Note that the French word **déception** is a false friend and is never a translation for the English word **deception**. It means **disappointment**.

decibel ['desɪbel] n décibel m

decide [dɪ'saɪd] 1 vt (outcome, future) décider de; (question, matter) régler; **to d. to do sth** décider de faire qch; **to d. that…** décider que…; **to d. sb to do sth** décider qn à faire qch 2 vi (make decisions) décider; (make up one's mind) se décider (**on doing** à faire); **to d. on sth** décider de qch; (choose) choisir qch; **the deciding factor** le facteur décisif ▪ **decided** adj (firm) décidé; (clear) net (f nette) ▪ **decidedly** [-ɪdlɪ] adv (firmly) résolument; (clearly) nettement

Note that the French word **décidément** is a false friend and is never a translation for the English word **decidedly**.

decimal ['desɪməl] 1 adj décimal; **d. point** virgule f 2 n décimale f ▪ **decimalization** [-aɪ'zeɪʃən] n décimalisation f

decimate ['desɪmeɪt] vt décimer

decipher [dɪ'saɪfə(r)] vt déchiffrer

decision [dɪ'sɪʒən] n décision f

decisive [dɪ'saɪsɪv] adj (action, event, tone) décisif, -ive; (person) résolu

deck [dek] 1 n (a) (of ship) pont m; **top d.** (of bus) impériale f (b) **d. of cards** jeu m de cartes (c) (of record player) platine f 2 vt **to d. (out)** (adorn) orner ▪ **deckchair** n chaise f longue

declare [dɪ'kleə(r)] vt déclarer (**that** que); (verdict, result) proclamer ▪ **declaration** [deklə'reɪʃən] n déclaration f; (of verdict) proclamation f

decline [dɪ'klaɪn] 1 n déclin m; (fall) baisse f 2 vt (offer) décliner; **to d. to do sth** refuser de faire qch 3 vi (become less) (of popularity, birthrate) être en baisse; (deteriorate) (of health, strength) décliner; (refuse) refuser; **to d. in importance** perdre de l'importance; **one's declining years** ses dernières années

decode [di:'kəʊd] vt (message) décoder ▪ **decoder** n Comptr & TV décodeur m

decompose [di:kəm'pəʊz] 1 vt (chemical compound) décomposer 2 vi (rot) se décomposer ▪ **decomposition** [-kɒmpə'zɪʃən] n décomposition f

decompression [di:kəm'preʃən] n décompression f; **d. chamber** sas m de décompression

decontaminate [di:kən'tæmɪneɪt] vt décontaminer

decor ['deɪkɔː(r)] n décor m

decorate ['dekəreɪt] vt (cake, house, soldier) décorer (**with** de); (hat, skirt) orner (**with** de); (paint) peindre; (wallpaper) tapisser

▪ **decorating** n **interior d.** décoration f d'intérieurs ▪ **decoration** [-'reɪʃən] n décoration f ▪ **decorative** [-rətɪv] adj décoratif, -ive ▪ **decorator** n Br (house painter) peintre m décorateur; (interior) d. décorateur, -trice mf

decorum [dɪ'kɔːrəm] n convenances fpl

decoy ['di:kɔɪ] n (artificial bird) appeau m; Fig leurre m; (police) d. policier m en civil

decrease 1 ['di:kri:s] n diminution f (**in** de) 2 [dɪ'kri:s] vti diminuer ▪ **decreasing** adj décroissant ▪ **decreasingly** adv de moins en moins

decree [dɪ'kri:] 1 n (by king) décret m; (by court) jugement m; (municipal) arrêté m 2 (pt & pp -eed) vt décréter (**that** que)

decrepit [dɪ'krepɪt] adj (building) en ruine; (person) décrépit

decry [dɪ'kraɪ] (pt & pp -ied) vt décrier

dedicate ['dedɪkeɪt] vt (devote) consacrer (**to** à); (book) dédier (**to** à); **to d. oneself to sth** se consacrer à qch ▪ **dedicated** adj (teacher) consciencieux, -ieuse ▪ **dedi'cation** n (in book) dédicace f; (devotion) dévouement m

deduce [dɪ'dju:s] vt (conclude) déduire (**from** de; **that** que)

deduct [dɪ'dʌkt] vt déduire (**from** de) ▪ **deductible** adj (from invoice) à déduire (**from** de); (from income) (expenses) déductible ▪ **deduction** n (subtraction, conclusion) déduction f

deed [di:d] n action f, acte m; (feat) exploit m; (legal document) acte m notarié

deem [di:m] vt Formal juger

deep [di:p] 1 (-er, -est) adj profond; (snow) épais (f épaisse); (voice) grave; (musical note) bas (f basse); (person) (difficult to understand) insondable; **to be 6 m d.** avoir 6 m de profondeur; **d. in thought** plongé dans ses pensées; **the d. end** (in swimming pool) le grand bain; **d. red** rouge foncé 2 adv profondément; **she went in d.** (into water) elle alla (jusqu')où elle n'avait pas pied; **d. into the night** tard dans la nuit 3 n Literary **the d.** l'océan m ▪ **deeply** adv profondément ▪ **'deep-'rooted**, **'deep-'seated** adj profondément enraciné ▪ **deep-sea 'diving** n plongée f sous-marine (en haute mer)

deepen ['di:pən] 1 vt (increase) augmenter; (canal, knowledge) approfondir 2 vi (of river, silence) devenir plus profond; (of mystery) s'épaissir; (of voice) devenir plus grave ▪ **deepening** adj (gap) grandissant; **the d. recession/crisis** l'aggravation f de la récession/crise

deep-freeze [di:p'fri:z] 1 n congélateur m 2 vt surgeler ▪ **deep-frozen** adj surgelé

deep-fry [di:p'fraɪ] vt faire cuire dans la friture ▪ **deep-'fryer** n friteuse f

deer [dɪə(r)] n inv cerf m

deface [dɪ'feɪs] *vt (damage)* dégrader; *(daub)* barbouiller

defamation [defə'meɪʃən] *n* diffamation *f* ▪**defamatory** [dɪ'fæmətərɪ] *adj* diffamatoire

default [dɪ'fɔ:lt] **1** *n* **by d.** par défaut; **to win by d.** gagner par forfait **2** *vi Law (fail to appear in court)* ne pas comparaître; **to d. on one's payments** être en rupture de paiement

defeat [dɪ'fi:t] **1** *n* défaite *f* **2** *vt (opponent, army)* vaincre; *(plan, effort)* faire échouer; **that defeats the purpose** or **object** ça va à l'encontre du but recherché ▪**defeatism** *n* défaitisme *m* ▪**defeatist** *adj & n* défaitiste *(mf)*

defect[1] ['di:fekt] *n* défaut *m*

defect[2] [dɪ'fekt] *vi (of party member, soldier)* déserter; **to d. to the enemy** passer à l'ennemi ▪**defection** *n* défection *f* ▪**defector** *n* transfuge *mf*

defective [dɪ'fektɪv] *adj (machine)* défectueux, -ueuse

defence [dɪ'fens] (*Am* **defense**) *n* défense *f*; (**against** contre); **to speak in d. of sb** prendre la défense de qn; **in his d.** à sa décharge ▪**defenceless** (*Am* **defenseless**) *adj* sans défense

defend [dɪ'fend] *vti* défendre ▪**defendant** *n (accused)* prévenu, -ue *mf* ▪**defender** *n* défenseur *m*; *(of sports title)* tenant, -ante *mf*

defense [dɪ'fens] *n Am* = **defence**

defensible [dɪ'fensəbəl] *adj* défendable

defensive [dɪ'fensɪv] **1** *adj* défensif, -ive; **to be d.** être sur la défensive **2** *n* **on the d.** sur la défensive

defer [dɪ'fɜ:(r)] *(pt & pp -rr-)* **1** *vt (postpone)* différer **2** *vi* **to d. to** s'en remettre à ▪**deferment** *n (postponement)* report *m*

defiant [dɪ'faɪənt] *adj (tone)* de défi; *(person)* provocant ▪**defiance** *n (resistance)* défi *m* (**of** à); **in d. of** *(contempt)* au mépris de ▪**defiantly** *adv* d'un air de défi

deficient [dɪ'fɪʃənt] *adj (not adequate)* insuffisant; *(faulty)* défectueux, -ueuse; **to be d. in** manquer de ▪**deficiency** *(pl -ies)* *n (shortage)* manque *m*; *(in vitamins, minerals)* carence *f* (**in** de); *(flaw)* défaut *m*

deficit ['defɪsɪt] *n* déficit *m*

defile [dɪ'faɪl] *vt (make dirty)* souiller

define [dɪ'faɪn] *vt* définir

definite ['defɪnɪt] *adj (exact) (date, plan, answer)* précis; *(clear) (improvement, advantage)* net (*f* nette); *(firm) (offer, order)* ferme; *(certain)* certain; **it's d. that...** il est certain que... *(+ indicative)*; **I was quite d.** j'ai été tout à fait formel; *Grammar* **d. article** article *m* défini ▪**definitely** *adv* certainement; *(improved, superior)* nettement; *(say)* catégoriquement

definition [defɪ'nɪʃən] *n* définition *f*

definitive [dɪ'fɪnɪtɪv] *adj* définitif, -ive

deflate [dɪ'fleɪt] *vt (tyre)* dégonfler ▪**deflation** *n* dégonflement *m*; *Econ* déflation *f*

deflect [dɪ'flekt] **1** *vt (bullet)* faire dévier; **to d. sb from a plan/aim** détourner qn d'un projet/ objectif **2** *vi (of bullet)* dévier

deform [dɪ'fɔ:m] *vt* déformer ▪**deformed** *adj (body)* difforme ▪**deformity** *n* difformité *f*

defraud [dɪ'frɔ:d] *vt (customs, State)* frauder; **to d. sb of sth** escroquer qch à qn

defrost [di:'frɒst] *vt (fridge)* dégivrer; *(food)* décongeler

deft [deft] *adj* adroit (**with** de) ▪**deftly** *adv* adroitement ▪**deftness** *n* adresse *f*

defunct [dɪ'fʌŋkt] *adj* défunt

defuse [di:'fju:z] *vt (bomb, conflict)* désamorcer

defy [dɪ'faɪ] *(pt & pp -ied)* *vt (person, death, logic)* défier; *(efforts)* résister à; **to d. sb to do sth** défier qn de faire qch; **it defies description** cela défie toute description

degenerate 1 [dɪ'dʒenərət] *adj & n* dégénéré, -ée *(mf)* **2** [dɪ'dʒenəreɪt] *vi* dégénérer (**into** en) ▪**degeneration** [-'reɪʃən] *n* dégénérescence *f*

degrade [dɪ'greɪd] *vt* dégrader ▪**degrading** *adj* dégradant

degree [dɪ'gri:] *n* (**a**) *(angle, temperature, extent)* degré *m*; **it's 20 degrees** il fait 20 degrés; **by degrees** peu à peu; **not in the slightest d.** pas du tout; **to some d., to a certain d.** jusqu'à un certain point; **to such a d.** à tel point (**that** que) (**b**) *(from university)* diplôme *m*; *(Bachelor's)* ≃ licence *f*; *(Master's)* ≃ maîtrise *f*; *(PhD)* ≃ doctorat *m*

dehumanize [di:'hju:mənaɪz] *vt* déshumaniser

dehydrated [di:haɪ'dreɪtɪd] *adj* déshydraté; **to get d.** se déshydrater

de-ice [di:'aɪs] *vt (car window)* dégivrer ▪**de-icer** *n* dégivreur *m*

deign [deɪn] *vt* daigner (**to do** faire)

deity ['di:ɪtɪ] *(pl -ies)* *n* dieu *m*

dejected [dɪ'dʒektɪd] *adj* abattu ▪**dejection** *n* abattement *m*

delay [dɪ'leɪ] **1** *n* (*lateness*) retard *m*; *(waiting period)* délai *m*; **without d.** sans tarder **2** *vt* retarder; *(payment)* différer; **to d. doing sth** tarder à faire qch; **to be delayed** avoir du retard **3** *vi (be slow)* tarder (**in doing** à faire); *(linger)* s'attarder; **don't d.!** faites vite! ▪**delayed-'action** *adj (bomb, fuse)* à retardement ▪**delaying** *adj* **d. tactics** or **actions** moyens *mpl* dilatoires

> Note that the French word **délai** is a false friend and is never a translation for the English word **delay**.

delectable [dɪ'lektəbəl] *adj* délectable

delegate 1 ['delɪgət] *n* délégué, -ée *mf* **2** ['delɪgeɪt] *vt* déléguer (**to** à) ▪**dele'gation** *n* délégation *f*

delete [dɪ'liːt] *vt* supprimer ▪**deletion** [-ʃən] *n* suppression *f*

deliberate¹ [dɪ'lɪbərət] *adj (intentional)* délibéré; *(cautious)* réfléchi; *(slow)* mesuré ▪**deliberately** *adv (intentionally)* délibérément; *(walk)* avec mesure

deliberate² [dɪ'lɪbəreɪt] **1** *vt (discuss)* délibérer sur **2** *vi* délibérer (**on** sur) ▪**deliberation** *n (discussion)* délibération *f*

delicate ['delɪkət] *adj* délicat ▪**delicacy** *(pl -ies) n (quality)* délicatesse *f; (food)* mets *m* délicat ▪**delicately** *adv* délicatement

delicatessen [delɪkə'tesən] *n (shop)* épicerie *f* fine

delicious [dɪ'lɪʃəs] *adj* délicieux, -ieuse

delight [dɪ'laɪt] **1** *n (pleasure)* plaisir *m*, joie *f; (food)* délice *m;* **delights** *(pleasures, things)* délices *fpl;* **to my (great) d.** à ma grande joie; **to be the d. of** faire les délices de; **to take d. in sth/in doing sth** se délecter de qch/à faire qch **2** *vt* ravir **3** *vi* **to d. in doing sth** prendre plaisir à faire qch ▪**delighted** *adj* ravi (**with** sth de qch; **to do** de faire; **that** que)

delightful [dɪ'laɪtfəl] *adj* charmant; *(meal, perfume, sensation)* délicieux, -ieuse ▪**delightfully** *adv (with charm)* avec beaucoup de charme; *(wonderfully)* merveilleusement

delineate [dɪ'lɪnɪeɪt] *vt (outline)* esquisser; *(plan, proposal)* définir

delinquent [dɪ'lɪŋkwənt] *adj & n* délinquant, -ante *(mf)* ▪**delinquency** *n* délinquance *f*

delirious [dɪ'lɪrɪəs] *adj* délirant; **to be d.** délirer ▪**delirium** [-rɪəm] *n (illness)* délire *m*

deliver [dɪ'lɪvə(r)] *vt* (a) *(goods)* livrer; *(letters)* distribuer; *(hand over)* remettre (**to** à) (b) *(rescue)* délivrer *(from* de) (c) *(give birth to)* mettre au monde; **to d. a woman's baby** accoucher une femme (d) *(speech)* prononcer; *(warning, ultimatum)* lancer; *(blow)* porter

deliverance [dɪ'lɪvərəns] *n* délivrance *f (from* de)

delivery [dɪ'lɪvərɪ] *(pl -ies) n* (a) *(of goods)* livraison *f; (of letters)* distribution *f; (handing over)* remise *f;* **d. man** *(pl -men)* livreur *m* (b) *(birth)* accouchement *m* (c) *(speaking)* débit *m*

delta ['deltə] *n (of river)* delta *m*

delude [dɪ'luːd] *vt* tromper; **to d. oneself** se faire des illusions ▪**delusion** *n* illusion *f; (in mental illness)* aberration *f* mentale

deluge ['deljuːdʒ] **1** *n (rain) & Fig (of water, questions)* déluge *m* **2** *vt* inonder (**with** de)

de luxe [dɪ'lʌks] *adj* de luxe

delve [delv] *vi* **to d. into** *(question)* creuser; *(past, books)* fouiller dans

demagogue ['deməgɒg] *n* démagogue *mf*

demand [dɪ'mɑːnd] **1** *n* exigence *f; (claim)* revendication *f; (for goods)* demande *f* (**for** pour); **to be in (great) d.** être très demandé; **to make demands on sb** exiger beaucoup de qn **2** *vt* exiger *(sth from sb* qch de qn); *(rights, more pay)* revendiquer; **to d. that...** exiger que...; **to d. to know** insister pour savoir ▪**demanding** *adj* exigeant

demarcation [diːmɑː'keɪʃən] *n* démarcation *f;* **d. line** ligne *f* de démarcation

demean [dɪ'miːn] *vt* **to d. oneself** s'abaisser ▪**demeaning** *adj* dégradant

demeanour [dɪ'miːnə(r)] *(Am* **demeanor**) *n (behaviour)* comportement *m*

demented [dɪ'mentɪd] *adj* dément

demerara [demə'reərə] *n Br* **d. sugar** cassonade *f*

demise [dɪ'maɪz] *n* disparition *f*

demister [diː'mɪstə(r)] *n Br (for vehicle)* dispositif *m* de désembuage

demo ['deməʊ] *(pl* **-os**) *n* (a) *Fam (demonstration)* manif *f* (b) *(of musician)* disque *m*/cassette *f*/vidéo *f* de démonstration; **d. tape** cassette *f* démo; *Comptr* **d. version** version *f* de démonstration

demobilize [diː'məʊbɪlaɪz] *vt* démobiliser

democracy [dɪ'mɒkrəsɪ] *(pl -ies) n* démocratie *f* ▪**democrat** ['deməkræt] *n* démocrate *mf* ▪**democratic** [demə'krætɪk] *adj (institution)* démocratique; *(person)* démocrate ▪**democratically** [demə'krætɪkəlɪ] *adv* démocratiquement

demography [dɪ'mɒgrəfɪ] *n* démographie *f*

demolish [dɪ'mɒlɪʃ] *vt* démolir ▪**demolition** [demə'lɪʃən] *n* démolition *f*

demon ['diːmən] *n* démon *m*

demonstrate ['demənstreɪt] **1** *vt* démontrer; *(machine)* faire une démonstration de; **to d. how to do sth** montrer comment faire qch **2** *vi (protest)* manifester ▪**demonstration** [-'streɪʃən] *n* démonstration *f; (protest)* manifestation *f;* **to hold** or **stage a d.** manifester ▪**demonstrator** *n (protester)* manifestant, -ante *mf; (of machine)* démonstrateur, -trice *mf*

demonstrative [dɪ'mɒnstrətɪv] **1** *adj (person, attitude)* démonstratif, -ive **2** *adj & n Grammar* démonstratif *(m)*

demoralize [dɪ'mɒrəlaɪz] *vt* démoraliser

demote [dɪ'məʊt] *vt* rétrograder

demure [dɪ'mjʊə(r)] *adj* réservé

den [den] *n (of lion, person)* antre *m*

denationalize [diː'næʃənəlaɪz] *vt* dénationaliser

denial [dɪ'naɪəl] *n (of rumour, allegation)* démenti *m; (psychological)* dénégation *f;* **to issue a d.** publier un démenti

denigrate ['denɪgreɪt] *vt* dénigrer

denim ['denɪm] *n* denim *m;* **denims** *(jeans)* jean *m*

Denmark ['denmɑːk] *n* le Danemark

denomination [dɪnɒmɪ'neɪʃən] n (religion) confession f; (of coin, banknote) valeur f

denominator [dɪ'nɒmɪneɪtə(r)] n Math & Fig dénominateur m; **lowest common d.** plus petit dénominateur m commun

denote [dɪ'nəʊt] vt dénoter

denounce [dɪ'naʊns] vt (person, injustice) dénoncer (to à); **to d. sb as a spy** accuser qn d'être un espion

dense [dens] (-er, -est) adj dense; Fam (stupid) lourd ■ **densely** adv **d. populated** très peuplé ■ **density** n densité f

dent [dent] 1 n (in car, metal) bosse f; **full of dents** (car) cabossé; **to make a d. in sth** cabosser qch; **to make a d. in one's savings** (of purchase) faire un trou dans ses économies 2 vt cabosser

dental ['dentəl] adj dentaire; **d. appointment** rendez-vous m inv chez le dentiste; **d. surgeon** chirurgien-dentiste m

dentist ['dentɪst] n dentiste mf; **to go to the d.('s)** aller chez le dentiste ■ **dentistry** n dentisterie f; **school of d.** école f dentaire

dentures ['dentʃəz] npl dentier m

Note that the French word **denture** is a false friend and is never a translation for the English word **dentures**. It means **a set of teeth**.

denunciation [dɪnʌnsɪ'eɪʃən] n dénonciation f; (public) accusation f publique

deny [dɪ'naɪ] (pt & pp -ied) vt nier (doing avoir fait; that que); (rumour) démentir; (authority) rejeter; (disown) renier; **to d. sb sth** refuser qch à qn

deodorant [diː'əʊdərənt] n déodorant m

depart [dɪ'pɑːt] 1 vi partir; (deviate) s'écarter (from de) 2 vt Literary **to d. this world** quitter ce monde ■ **departed** 1 adj (dead) défunt 2 n **the d.** le défunt/la défunte

department [dɪ'pɑːtmənt] n département m; (in office) service m; (in shop) rayon m; (of government) ministère m; Fig **that's your d.** c'est ton rayon; **d. store** grand magasin m ■ **departmental** [diːpɑːt'mentəl] adj **d. manager** (in office) chef m de service; (in shop) chef m de rayon

departure [dɪ'pɑːtʃə(r)] n départ m; Fig **a d. from the rule** une entorse au règlement; **to be a new d. for** constituer une nouvelle voie pour; **d. lounge** (in airport) salle f d'embarquement

depend [dɪ'pend] vi dépendre (**on** or **upon** de); **to d. (up)on** (rely on) compter sur (**for sth** pour qch); **you can d. on it!** tu peux compter là-dessus! ■ **dependable** adj (person, information) sûr; (machine) fiable ■ **dependant** n personne f à charge ■ **dependence** n dépendance f (**on** de) ■ **dependency** (pl -ies) n (country) dépendance f ■ **dependent** adj dépendant (**on** or **upon** de); (relative, child) à

charge; **to be d. (up)on** dépendre de; **to be d. on sb** (financially) être à la charge de qn

depict [dɪ'pɪkt] vt (describe) décrire; (in pictures) représenter ■ **depiction** n (description) peinture f; (in picture form) représentation f

deplete [dɪ'pliːt] vt (use up) épuiser; (reduce) réduire ■ **depletion** n épuisement m; (reduction) réduction f

deplore [dɪ'plɔː(r)] vt déplorer ■ **deplorable** adj déplorable ■ **deplorably** adv déplorablement

deploy [dɪ'plɔɪ] vt (troops) déployer

depopulate [diː'pɒpjʊleɪt] vt dépeupler ■ **depopulation** [-'leɪʃən] n dépeuplement m

deport [dɪ'pɔːt] vt (foreigner, criminal) expulser; Hist (to concentration camp) déporter ■ **deportation** [diːpɔː'teɪʃən] n expulsion f; Hist déportation f

deportment [dɪ'pɔːtmənt] n maintien m

depose [dɪ'pəʊz] vt (ruler) déposer

deposit [dɪ'pɒzɪt] 1 n (a) (in bank) dépôt m; (part payment) acompte m; (returnable) caution f; **d. account** compte m de dépôt (b) (sediment) dépôt m; (of gold, oil) gisement m 2 vt (object, money) déposer

depot [Br 'depəʊ, Am 'diːpəʊ] n (for goods) dépôt m; Am (railroad station) gare f; (bus) **d.** Br dépôt de bus; Am gare f routière

deprave [dɪ'preɪv] vt dépraver ■ **depraved** adj dépravé ■ **depravity** [dɪ'prævɪtɪ] n dépravation f

depreciate [dɪ'priːʃɪeɪt] 1 vt (reduce in value) déprécier 2 vi (fall in value) se déprécier ■ **depreciation** [-'eɪʃən] n dépréciation f

depress [dɪ'pres] vt (discourage) déprimer; (push down) appuyer sur ■ **depressed** adj (person, market) déprimé; (industry) in decline en déclin; (in crisis) en crise; **to get d.** se décourager ■ **depression** n dépression f

deprive [dɪ'praɪv] vt priver (**of** de) ■ **deprivation** [depra've'ɪʃən] n (hardship) privations fpl; (loss) perte f ■ **deprived** adj (child) défavorisé

depth [depθ] n profondeur f; (of snow) épaisseur f; (of interest) intensité f; **in the depths of** (forest, despair) au plus profond de; (winter) au cœur de; Fig **to get out of one's d.** (be unable to cope) ne pas être à la hauteur; **in d.** en profondeur

deputation [depjʊ'teɪʃən] n députation f

deputize ['depjʊtaɪz] 1 vt députer (**sb to do** qn pour faire) 2 vi assurer l'intérim (**for sb** de qn)

deputy ['depjʊtɪ] (pl -ies) n (replacement) remplaçant, -ante mf; (assistant) adjoint, -ointe mf; Am **d. (sheriff)** shérif m adjoint; **d. chairman** vice-président, -ente mf

derailed [dɪ'reɪld] adj **to be d.** (of train) dérailler ■ **derailment** n déraillement m

deranged [dɪ'reɪndʒd] adj **he's (mentally) d., his mind is d.** il a le cerveau dérangé

derby [Br 'dɑ:bɪ, Am 'dɜ:rbɪ] (pl **-ies**) n (**a**) Am (hat) chapeau m melon (**b**) Sport derby m

derelict ['derɪlɪkt] adj (building) abandonné

deride [dɪ'raɪd] vt tourner en dérision ▪ **derision** [-'rɪʒən] n dérision f ▪ **derisive** adj (laughter) moqueur, -euse; (amount) dérisoire ▪ **derisory** adj (amount) dérisoire

> Note that the French word **dérider** is a false friend and is never a translation for the English word to **deride**.

derive [dɪ'raɪv] 1 vt provenir (**from** de); **to d. pleasure from sth** prendre plaisir à qch; **to be derived from** provenir de 2 vi **to d. from** provenir de ▪ **derivative** [dɪ'rɪvətɪv] 1 adj banal 2 n Ling & Chem dérivé (m)

dermatitis [dɜ:mə'taɪtəs] n Med dermatite f

dermatologist [dɜ:mə'tɒlədʒɪst] n dermatologiste mf, dermatologue mf ▪ **dermatology** n dermatologie f

derogatory [dɪ'rɒɡətərɪ] adj (word) péjoratif, -ive; (remark) désobligeant (**to** pour)

derrick ['derɪk] n (of oil well) derrick m

descend [dɪ'send] 1 vt (stairs, hill) descendre; **to be descended from** descendre de 2 vi descendre (**from** de); (of darkness, rain) tomber; **to d. upon** (of tourists) envahir; (attack) faire une descente sur; **in descending order** en ordre décroissant

descendant [dɪ'sendənt] n descendant, -ante mf

descent [dɪ'sent] n (**a**) (of aircraft) descente f (**b**) (ancestry) origine f; **to be of Norman d.** être d'origine normande

describe [dɪ'skraɪb] vt décrire ▪ **description** [dɪ'skrɪpʃən] n description f; (on passport) signalement m; **of every d.** de toutes sortes ▪ **descriptive** [dɪ'skrɪptɪv] adj descriptif, -ive

desecrate ['desɪkreɪt] vt profaner ▪ **dese'cration** n profanation f

desegregate [di:'seɡrɪɡeɪt] vt (school) supprimer la ségrégation raciale dans ▪ **desegre'gation** n déségrégation f

desert[1] ['dezət] n désert m; **d. climate** climat m désertique; **d. animal/plant** animal m/plante f du désert; **d. island** île f déserte

desert[2] [dɪ'zɜ:t] 1 vt (person) abandonner; (place, cause) déserter 2 vi (of soldier) déserter ▪ **deserted** adj désert ▪ **deserter** n déserteur m

desertion [dɪ'zɜ:ʃən] n (by soldier) désertion f; (by spouse) abandon m du domicile conjugal

deserts [dɪ'zɜ:ts] npl **to get one's just d.** avoir ce qu'on mérite

deserve [dɪ'zɜ:v] vt mériter (**to do** de faire) ▪ **deservedly** [-ɪdlɪ] adv à juste titre ▪ **deserving** adj (person) méritant; (action, cause) méritoire; **to be d. of** (praise, love) être digne de

desiccated ['desɪkeɪtɪd] adj desséché

design [dɪ'zaɪn] 1 n (**a**) (pattern) motif m; (sketch) plan m; (of dress, car, furniture) modèle m; (planning) conception f; **industrial d.** dessin m industriel; **to study d.** étudier le design (**b**) (aim) dessein m; **by d.** intentionnellement; **to have designs on** avoir des vues sur 2 vt (car, building) concevoir; (dress) créer; **designed to do sth/for sth** conçu pour faire qch/pour qch; **well designed** bien conçu ▪ **designer** n (artistic) dessinateur, -trice mf; (industrial) concepteur-dessinateur m; (of clothes) styliste mf; (well-known) couturier m; **d. clothes** vêtements mpl de marque

designate ['dezɪɡneɪt] vt désigner ▪ **designation** [-'neɪʃən] n désignation f

desire [dɪ'zaɪə(r)] 1 n désir m; **I've got no d. to do that** je n'ai aucune envie de faire cela 2 vt désirer (**to do** faire) ▪ **desirable** adj désirable; **d. property** (in advertising) (très) belle propriété

desk [desk] n (in school) table f; (in office) bureau m; Br (in shop) caisse f; (**reception**) d. (in hotel) réception f; **the news d.** le service des informations; Am **d. clerk** (in hotel) réceptionniste mf; **d. job** travail m de bureau

desktop ['desktɒp] n **d. computer** ordinateur m de bureau; **d. publishing** publication f assistée par ordinateur

desolate ['desələt] adj (deserted) désolé; (in ruins) dévasté; (dreary, bleak) morne, triste; (person) abattu ▪ **desolation** [-'leɪʃən] n (ruin) dévastation f; (emptiness) solitude f; (of person) affliction f

despair [dɪ'speə(r)] 1 n désespoir m; **to drive sb to d.** désespérer qn; **to be in d.** être au désespoir 2 vi désespérer (**of sb** de qn; **of doing** de faire) ▪ **despairing** adj désespéré

despatch [dɪ'spætʃ] n & vt = dispatch

desperate ['despərət] adj désespéré; **to be d. for** (money, love) avoir désespérément besoin de; (cigarette, baby) mourir d'envie d'avoir ▪ **desperately** adv (ill) gravement; (in love) éperdument

desperation [despə'reɪʃən] n désespoir m; **in d.** en désespoir de cause

despicable [dɪ'spɪkəbəl] adj méprisable

despise [dɪ'spaɪz] vt mépriser

despite [dɪ'spaɪt] prep malgré

despondent [dɪ'spɒndənt] adj abattu ▪ **despondency** n abattement m

dessert [dɪ'zɜ:t] n dessert m ▪ **dessertspoon** n Br cuillère f à dessert

destabilize [di:'steɪbəlaɪz] vt déstabiliser

destination [destɪ'neɪʃən] n destination f

destine ['destɪn] vt destiner (**for** à; **to do** à faire); **it was destined to happen** ça devait arriver

destiny ['destɪnɪ] (pl **-ies**) n destin m, destinée f

destitute ['destɪtjuːt] adj (poor) indigent; **d. of** (lacking in) dénué de ▪ **desti'tution** n dénuement m

destroy [dɪ'strɔɪ] vt détruire; (horse, monkey) abattre; (cat, dog) faire piquer ▪ **destroyer** n (ship) contre-torpilleur m; (person) destructeur, -trice mf

destruction [dɪ'strʌkʃən] n destruction f ▪ **destructive** adj (person, war) destructeur, -trice; (power) destructif, -ive

detach [dɪ'tætʃ] vt détacher (**from** de) ▪ **detached** adj (indifferent) (person, manner) détaché; (without bias) (view) désintéressé; Br **d. house** maison f individuelle

detachable [dɪ'tætʃəbəl] adj amovible

detachment [dɪ'tætʃmənt] n (attitude, group of soldiers) détachement m; **the d. of** (action) la séparation de

detail ['diːteɪl] **1** n (a) (item of information) détail m; **in d.** en détail; **to go into d.** entrer dans les détails (b) Mil détachement m **2** vt (a) (describe) détailler (b) Mil **to d. sb to do sth** donner l'ordre à qn de faire qch ▪ **detailed** adj (account) détaillé

detain [dɪ'teɪn] vt (delay) retenir; (prisoner) placer en détention; (in hospital) garder ▪ **detainee** [diːteɪ'niː] n Pol & Law détenu, -ue mf ▪ **detention** [dɪ'tenʃən] n (at school) retenue f; (in prison) détention f

detect [dɪ'tekt] vt détecter ▪ **detection** n découverte f; (identification) identification f; (of mine) détection f

detective [dɪ'tektɪv] n (police officer) ≃ inspecteur m de police; (private) détective m privé; **d. film/novel** film m/roman m policier

detector [dɪ'tektə(r)] n détecteur m

deter [dɪ'tɜː(r)] (pt & pp **-rr-**) vt **to d. sb** (**from doing** or faire; **from sth** de qch)

detergent [dɪ'tɜːdʒənt] n détergent m

deteriorate [dɪ'tɪərɪəreɪt] vi se détériorer ▪ **deterioration** [-'reɪʃən] n détérioration f

determine [dɪ'tɜːmɪn] vt (cause, date) déterminer; (price) fixer; **to d. to do sth** décider de faire qch; **to d. sb to do sth** décider qn à faire qch; **to d. that...** décider que... ▪ **determined** adj (look, person, quantity) déterminé; **to be d. to do** or **on doing sth** être décidé à faire qch; **I'm d. she'll succeed** je suis bien décidé à ce qu'elle réussisse

deterrent [dɪ'terənt] n (military) force f de dissuasion; Fig **to be a d., to act as a d.** être dissuasif, -ive

detest [dɪ'test] vt détester (**doing** faire) ▪ **detestable** adj détestable

detonate ['detəneɪt] **1** vt faire exploser **2** vi exploser ▪ **detonation** [-'neɪʃən] n détonation f ▪ **detonator** n détonateur m

detour ['diːtʊə(r)] n détour m; **to make a d.** faire un détour

detract [dɪ'trækt] vi **to d. from** (make less) diminuer ▪ **detractor** n détracteur, -trice mf

detriment ['detrɪmənt] n **to the d. of** au détriment de ▪ **detrimental** [-'mentəl] adj préjudiciable (**to** à)

devalue [diː'væljuː] vt (money) dévaluer; (person, achievement) dévaloriser ▪ **devalu-'ation** n (of money) dévaluation f

devastate ['devəsteɪt] vt (crop, village) dévaster; (person) anéantir ▪ **devastating** adj (storm) dévastateur, -trice; (news, results) accablant; (shock) terrible; (charm) irrésistible

develop [dɪ'veləp] **1** vt (theory, argument) développer; (area, land) mettre en valeur; (habit, illness) contracter; (talent) manifester; (photo) développer; **to d. a liking for sth** prendre goût à qch **2** vi (grow) se développer; (of event, argument, crisis) se produire; (of talent, illness) se manifester; **to d. into** devenir ▪ **developing 1** adj **d. country** pays m en voie de développement **2** n (of photos) développement m

developer [dɪ'veləpə(r)] n (property) **d.** promoteur m

development [dɪ'veləpmənt] n (growth, progress) développement m; (of land) mise f en valeur; (housing) **d.** lotissement m; (large) grand ensemble m; **a (new) d.** (in situation) un fait nouveau

deviate ['diːvɪeɪt] vi dévier (**from** de); **to d. from the norm** s'écarter de la norme ▪ **deviant** [-ɪənt] adj (behaviour) anormal ▪ **deviation** [-'eɪʃən] n déviation f

device [dɪ'vaɪs] n (instrument, gadget) dispositif m; (scheme) procédé m; **explosive/nuclear d.** engin m explosif/nucléaire; **safety d.** dispositif de sécurité; **left to one's own devices** livré à soi-même

devil ['devəl] n diable m; Fam **a** or **the d. of a problem** un problème épouvantable; Fam **a** or **the d. of a noise** un bruit infernal; Fam **I had a** or **the d. of a job doing it** j'ai eu un mal fou à le faire; Fam **what/where/why the d....?** que/où/pourquoi diable...?; Fam **to run like the d.** courir comme un fou (f une folle) ▪ **devilish** adj diabolique

devious ['diːvɪəs] adj (mind, behaviour) tortueux, -ueuse; **he's d.** il a l'esprit tortueux

devise [dɪ'vaɪz] vt imaginer; (plot) ourdir

devitalize [diː'vaɪtəlaɪz] vt rendre exsangue

devoid [dɪ'vɔɪd] adj **d. of** dénué ou dépourvu de; (guilt) exempt de

devolution [diːvə'luːʃən] n Pol décentralisation f; **the d. of** (power) la délégation de

devolve [dɪ'vɒlv] vi **to d. upon** incomber à

devote [dɪ'vəʊt] vt consacrer (**to** à) ▪ **devoted** adj dévoué; (admirer) fervent

devotee [dɪvəʊˈtiː] *n (of music, sport)* passionné, -ée *mf* (**of** de)

devotion [dɪˈvəʊʃən] *n (to friend, family, cause)* dévouement *m* (**to sb** à qn); *(religious)* dévotion *f*; **devotions** *(prayers)* prières *fpl*

devour [dɪˈvaʊə(r)] *vt (eat, engulf, read)* dévorer

devout [dɪˈvaʊt] *adj* dévot; *(supporter, prayer)* fervent

dew [djuː] *n* rosée *f*

dext(e)rous [ˈdekstərəs] *adj* adroit ▪**dexterity** [-ˈsterɪtɪ] *n* dextérité *f*

diabetes [daɪəˈbiːtiːz] *n* diabète *m* ▪**diabetic** [-ˈbetɪk] **1** *adj* diabétique; **d. jam** confiture *f* pour diabétiques **2** *n* diabétique *mf*

diabolical [daɪəˈbɒlɪkəl] *adj* diabolique; *Fam (very bad)* épouvantable

diagnose [daɪəgˈnəʊz] *vt* diagnostiquer ▪**diagnosis** [-ˈnəʊsɪs] *(pl* **-oses** [-əʊsiːz]) *n* diagnostic *m*

diagonal [daɪˈægənəl] **1** *adj* diagonal **2** *n* diagonale *f* ▪**diagonally** *adv* en diagonale

diagram [ˈdaɪəgræm] *n* schéma *m*; *(geometrical)* figure *f*

dial [ˈdaɪəl] **1** *n* cadran *m* **2** *(Br* **-ll-,** *Am* **-l-)** *vt (phone number)* composer; *(person)* appeler ▪**dialling code** *n Br* indicatif *m* ▪**dialling tone** *n Br* tonalité *f* ▪**dial tone** *n Am* tonalité *f*

dialect [ˈdaɪəlekt] *n* dialecte *m*

dialogue [ˈdaɪəlɒg] *(Am* **dialog)** *n* dialogue *m*; *Comptr* **d. box** boîte *f* de dialogue

dialysis [daɪˈælɪsɪs] *n Med* dialyse *f*; **to be in d.** être sous dialyse

diameter [daɪˈæmɪtə(r)] *n* diamètre *m* ▪**diametrically** [daɪəˈmetrɪklɪ] *adv* **d. opposed** *(opinion)* diamétralement opposé

diamond [ˈdaɪəmənd] *n* **(a)** *(stone)* diamant *m*; *(shape)* losange *m*; *Am* **(baseball)** terrain *m* de baseball; **d. necklace** rivière *f* de diamants **(b)** *Cards* **diamond(s)** carreau *m*

diaper [ˈdaɪpər] *n Am* couche *f*

diaphragm [ˈdaɪəfræm] *n* diaphragme *m*

diarrhoea *(Am* **diarrhea)** [daɪəˈriːə] *n* diarrhée *f*; **to have d.** avoir la diarrhée

diary [ˈdaɪərɪ] *(pl* **-ies)** *n Br (calendar)* agenda *m*; *(private)* journal *m* (intime)

dice [daɪs] **1** *n inv* dé *m* **2** *vt (food)* couper en dés

dicey [ˈdaɪsɪ] *(-ier, -iest)* adj Fam* risqué

dichotomy [daɪˈkɒtəmɪ] *(pl* **-ies)** *n* dichotomie *f*

Dictaphone® [ˈdɪktəfəʊn] *n* Dictaphone® *m*

dictate [dɪkˈteɪt] **1** *vt (letter, conditions)* dicter (**to** à) **2** *vi* dicter; **to d. to sb** *(order around)* donner des ordres à qn ▪**dictation** *n* dictée *f*

dictates [ˈdɪkteɪts] *npl* préceptes *mpl*; **the d. of conscience** la voix de la conscience

dictator [dɪkˈteɪtə(r)] *n* dictateur *m* ▪**dicta'torial** [-təˈtɔːrɪəl] *adj* dictatorial ▪**dictatorship** *n* dictature *f*

dictionary [ˈdɪkʃənərɪ] *(pl* **-ies)** *n* dictionnaire *m*; **English d.** dictionnaire *m* d'anglais

did [dɪd] *pt of* **do**

diddle [ˈdɪdəl] *vt Br Fam (cheat)* rouler; **to d. sb out of sth** carotter qch à qn; **to get diddled out of sth** se faire refaire de qch

die¹ [daɪ] *(pt & pp* **died,** *pres p* **dying)** *vi* mourir (**of** *or* **from** de); *Fig* **to be dying to do sth** mourir d'envie de faire qch; **to be dying for sth** avoir une envie folle de qch; **to d. away** *(of noise)* mourir; **to d. down** *(of fire)* mourir; *(of storm)* se calmer; **to d. off** mourir (les uns après les autres); **to d. out** *(of custom)* mourir; *(of family)* s'éteindre

die² [daɪ] *n* **(a)** *(pl* **dice** [daɪs]) *(in games)* dé *m*; **the d. is cast** les dés sont jetés **(b)** *(mould)* matrice *f*

die-hard [ˈdaɪhɑːd] *n* réactionnaire *mf*

diesel [ˈdiːzəl] *adj & n* **d. (engine)** *(motor m)* diesel *m*; **d. (oil)** gazole *m*

diet [ˈdaɪət] **1** *n (usual food)* alimentation *f*; *(restricted food)* régime *m*; **to go on a d.** faire un régime; **d. foods** aliments *mpl* allégés **2** *vi* être au régime ▪**dietary** *adj* alimentaire; **d. fibre** fibres *fpl* alimentaires ▪**dietician** [-ˈtɪʃən] *n* diététicien, -ienne *mf*

differ [ˈdɪfə(r)] *vi* différer (**from** de); *(disagree)* ne pas être d'accord (**from** avec)

difference [ˈdɪfərəns] *n* différence *f* (**in** de); **d. of opinion** différend *m*; **it makes no d.** ça n'a pas d'importance; **it makes no d. to me** ça m'est égal; **that will make a big d.** ça va changer pas mal de choses

different [ˈdɪfərənt] *adj* différent (**from** de); *(another)* autre; *(various)* divers ▪**differently** *adv* différemment (**from** de)

differentiate [dɪfəˈrenʃɪeɪt] **1** *vt* différencier (**from** de) **2** *vi* faire la différence (**between** entre)

difficult [ˈdɪfɪkəlt] *adj* difficile (**to do** à faire); **it's d. for us to…** il nous est difficile de…; **the d. thing is to…** le plus difficile est de…

difficulty [ˈdɪfɪkəltɪ] *(pl* **-ies)** *n* difficulté *f*; **to have d. doing sth** avoir du mal à faire qch; **to be in d.** avoir des difficultés; **to have d.** *or* **difficulties with sb/sth** *(problems)* avoir des ennuis avec qn/qch

diffident [ˈdɪfɪdənt] *adj (person)* qui manque d'assurance; *(smile, tone)* mal assuré ▪**diffidence** *n* manque *m* d'assurance

diffuse 1 [dɪˈfjuːs] *adj (spread out, wordy)* diffus **2** [dɪˈfjuːz] *vt (spread)* diffuser ▪**diffusion** *n* diffusion *f*

dig [dɪg] **1** *n (in archaeology)* fouilles *fpl*; *(with spade)* coup *m* de bêche; *(with elbow)* coup de coude; *(with fist)* coup de poing; *Fam (remark)* pique *f* **2** *(pt & pp* **dug,** *pres p* **digging)** *vt (ground, garden)* bêcher; *(hole, grave)* creuser; **to d. sth into sth** *(push)* planter qch dans qch; **to d. out** *(animal, object)* déterrer; *(accident victim)* dégager; *Fam (find)* dénicher; **to d. up**

(from ground) déterrer; *(weed)* arracher; *(road)* excaver **3** *vi (dig a hole)* creuser; *(of pig)* fouiller; **to d. (oneself) in** *(of soldier)* se retrancher; **Fam to d. in** *(eat)* attaquer; **to d. into** *(past)* fouiller dans

digest 1 ['daɪdʒest] *n (summary)* condensé *m* **2** [daɪ'dʒest] *vti* digérer ▪**digestible** [-'dʒestəbəl] *adj* digeste ▪**di'gestion** *n* digestion *f* ▪**digestive** [-'dʒestɪv] *adj* digestif, -ive

digger ['dɪgə(r)] *n (machine)* pelleteuse *f*

digit ['dɪdʒɪt] *n (number)* chiffre *m* ▪**digital** *adj (TV, camera, computer)* numérique; *(tape, recording)* audionumérique; *(watch, clock)* à affichage numérique

dignified ['dɪgnɪfaɪd] *adj* digne ▪**dignitary** *(pl -ies)* *n* dignitaire *m* ▪**dignity** *n* dignité *f*

digress [daɪ'gres] *vi* faire une digression; **to d. from** s'écarter de ▪**digression** *n* digression *f*

digs [dɪgz] *npl Br Fam* chambre *f* meublée

dike [daɪk] *n Am* = **dyke**

dilapidated [dɪ'læpɪdeɪtɪd] *adj (house)* délabré

dilate [daɪ'leɪt] **1** *vt* dilater **2** *vi* se dilater ▪**dilation** *n* dilatation *f*

dilemma [daɪ'lemə] *n* dilemme *m*

diligent ['dɪlɪdʒənt] *adj* appliqué; **to be d. in doing sth** faire qch avec zèle ▪**diligence** *n* zèle *m*

dilly-dally ['dɪlɪ'dælɪ] *(pt & pp -ied)* *vi Fam (dawdle)* lambiner; *(hesitate)* tergiverser

dilute [daɪ'luːt] **1** *vt* diluer **2** *adj* dilué

dim [dɪm] **1** (**dimmer, dimmest**) *adj (light)* faible; *(colour)* terne; *(room)* sombre; *(memory, outline)* vague; *(person)* stupide **2** *(pt & pp -mm-)* *vt (light)* baisser; *(glory)* ternir; *(memory)* estomper; *Am* **to d. one's headlights** se mettre en code ▪**dimly** *adv (shine)* faiblement; *(vaguely)* vaguement; **d. lit** mal éclairé ▪**dimness** *n* faiblesse *f*; *(of memory)* flou *m*; *(of room)* pénombre *f*

dime [daɪm] *n Am* (pièce *f* de) dix cents *mpl*; **it's not worth a d.** ça ne vaut pas un clou; **a d. store** ≃ un Prisunic®, ≃ un Monoprix®

dimension [daɪ'menʃən] *n* dimension *f*

diminish [dɪ'mɪnɪʃ] *vti* diminuer ▪**diminishing** *adj* décroissant

diminutive [dɪ'mɪnjʊtɪv] **1** *adj (tiny)* minuscule **2** *adj & n Grammar* diminutif *(m)*

dimmer ['dɪmə(r)] *n* **d. (switch)** variateur *m*

dimmers ['dɪməz] *npl Am Aut* codes *mpl*

dimple ['dɪmpəl] *n* fossette *f* ▪**dimpled** *adj (chin, cheek)* à fossettes

dimwit ['dɪmwɪt] *n Fam* andouille *f* ▪**'dim'witted** *adj Fam* tarte

din [dɪn] **1** *n (noise)* vacarme *m* **2** *(pt & pp -nn-)* *vt* **to d. into sb that…** rabâcher à qn que…

dine [daɪn] *vi* dîner (**on** or **off** de); **to d. out** dîner dehors ▪**diner** *n (person)* dîneur, -euse *mf*; *Am (restaurant)* petit restaurant *m* ▪**dining**

car *n (on train)* wagon-restaurant *m* ▪**dining room** *n* salle *f* à manger

dinghy ['dɪŋgɪ] *(pl -ies)* *n* petit canot *m*; *(rubber)* **d.** canot pneumatique

dingy ['dɪndʒɪ] *(-ier, -iest)* *adj (room)* minable; *(colour)* terne

dinner ['dɪnə(r)] *n (evening meal)* dîner *m*; *(lunch)* déjeuner *m*; *(for dog, cat)* pâtée *f*; **to have d.** dîner; **to have sb to d.** avoir qn à dîner; **it's d. time** c'est l'heure de dîner; *(lunch)* c'est l'heure de déjeuner; **d. dance** dîner-dansant *m*; **d. jacket** smoking *m*; **d. party** dîner *m*; **d. plate** grande assiette *f*; **d. service, d. set** service *m* de table

dinosaur ['daɪnəsɔː(r)] *n* dinosaure *m*

dint [dɪnt] *n Formal* **by d. of sth/of doing** à force de qch/de faire

diocese ['daɪəsɪs] *n Rel* diocèse *m*

dip [dɪp] **1** *n (in road)* petit creux *m*; **to go for a d.** *(swim)* faire trempette **2** *(pt & pp -pp-)* *vt* plonger; *Br* **to d. one's headlights** se mettre en code **3** *vi (of road)* plonger; *(of sun)* descendre; **to d. into** *(pocket, savings)* puiser dans; *(book)* feuilleter

diphtheria [dɪf'θɪərɪə] *n Med* diphtérie *f*

diphthong ['dɪfθɒŋ] *n Ling* diphtongue *f*

diploma [dɪ'pləʊmə] *n* diplôme *m*

diplomacy [dɪ'pləʊməsɪ] *n* diplomatie *f*

diplomat ['dɪpləmæt] *n* diplomate *mf* ▪**diplo'matic** *adj* diplomatique; **to be d.** *(tactful)* être diplomate

dipper ['dɪpə(r)] *n Br* **the big d.** *(at fairground)* les montagnes *fpl* russes

dipstick ['dɪpstɪk] *n* jauge *f* de niveau d'huile

dire ['daɪə(r)] *adj (situation)* affreux, -euse; *(consequences)* tragique; *(poverty, need)* extrême; **to be in d. straits** être dans une mauvaise passe

direct¹ [daɪ'rekt] **1** *adj (result, flight, person)* direct; *(danger)* immédiat; *Br* **d. debit** prélèvement *m* automatique **2** *adv* directement ▪**directness** *n (of person, reply)* franchise *f*

direct² [daɪ'rekt] *vt (gaze, light, company, attention)* diriger (**at** sur); *(traffic)* régler; *(letter, remark)* adresser (**to** à); *(efforts)* consacrer (**towards** à); *(film)* réaliser; *(play)* mettre en scène; **to d. sb to** *(place)* indiquer à qn le chemin de; **to d. sb to do sth** charger qn de faire qch

direction [daɪ'rekʃən] *n* direction *f*, sens *m*; *(management)* direction; *(of film)* réalisation *f*; *(of play)* mise *f* en scène; **directions** *(orders)* indications *fpl*; **directions** *(for use)* mode *m* d'emploi; **in the opposite d.** en sens inverse

directive [dɪ'rektɪv] *n* directive *f*

directly [daɪ'rektlɪ] **1** *adv (without detour)* directement; *(exactly)* juste; *(at once)* tout de suite; *(speak)* franchement; **d. in front/behind**

juste devant/derrière **2** *conj Br Fam (as soon as)* aussitôt que *(+ indicative)*

director [daɪˈrektə(r)] *n* directeur, -trice *mf*; *(board member)* administrateur, -trice *mf*; *(of film)* réalisateur, -trice *mf*; *(of play)* metteur *m* en scène ▪ **directorship** *n* poste *m* de directeur; *(as board member)* poste d'administrateur

directory [daɪˈrektərɪ] *(pl* **-ies)** *n (phone book)* annuaire *m*; *(of streets)* guide *m*; *(of addresses)* & *Comptr* répertoire *m*; **telephone d.** annuaire *m* du téléphone; **Br d. enquiries** renseignements *mpl* téléphoniques

dirt [dɜːt] *n* saleté *f*; *(mud)* boue *f*; *(earth)* terre *f*; *Fig (talk)* obscénité(s) *f(pl)*; *Fam* **d. cheap** très bon marché; **d. road** chemin *m* de terre; *Sport* **d. track** cendrée *f*

dirty [ˈdɜːtɪ] **1** *(-ier, -iest) adj* sale; *(job)* salissant; *(word)* grossier, -ière; **to get d.** se salir; **to get sth d.** salir qch; **a d. joke** une histoire cochonne; **a d. trick** un sale tour; **a d. old man** un vieux cochon **2** *adv (fight)* déloyalement **3** *vt* salir; *(machine)* encrasser

disability [dɪsəˈbɪlɪtɪ] *(pl* **-ies)** *n (injury)* infirmité *f*; *(condition)* invalidité *f*; *Fig* désavantage *m*

disable [dɪsˈeɪbəl] *vt* rendre infirme ▪ **disabled 1** *adj* handicapé **2** *npl* **the d.** les handicapés *mpl*

disadvantage [dɪsədˈvɑːntɪdʒ] **1** *n* désavantage *m* **2** *vt* désavantager

disaffected [dɪsəˈfektɪd] *adj* mécontent ▪ **disaffection** *n* désaffection *f*

disagree [dɪsəˈgriː] *vi* ne pas être d'accord **(with** avec); *(of figures, reports)* ne pas concorder; **to d. with sb** *(of food, climate, medicine)* ne pas réussir à qn ▪ **disagreement** *n* désaccord *m*; *(quarrel)* différend *m*

disagreeable [dɪsəˈgriːəbəl] *adj* désagréable

disallow [dɪsəˈlaʊ] *vt Formal* rejeter

disappear [dɪsəˈpɪə(r)] *vi* disparaître ▪ **disappearance** *n* disparition *f*

disappoint [dɪsəˈpɔɪnt] *vt* décevoir; **I'm disappointed with it** ça m'a déçu ▪ **disappointing** *adj* décevant ▪ **disappointment** *n* déception *f*

disapproval [dɪsəˈpruːvəl] *n* désapprobation *f*

disapprove [dɪsəˈpruːv] *vi* **to d. of sb/sth** désapprouver qn/qch; **I d.** je suis contre ▪ **disapproving** *adj (look, tone)* désapprobateur, -trice

disarm [dɪsˈɑːm] *vti* désarmer ▪ **disarmament** *n* désarmement *m*

disarray [dɪsəˈreɪ] *n (distress)* désarroi *m*; *(disorder)* désordre *m*; **in d.** *(army, political party)* en plein désarroi; *(clothes, hair)* en désordre

disaster [dɪˈzɑːstə(r)] *n* désastre *m*, catastrophe *f*; **d. area** région *f* sinistrée ▪ **disastrous** *adj* désastreux, -euse

disband [dɪsˈbænd] **1** *vt* dissoudre **2** *vi* se dissoudre

disbelief [dɪsbəˈliːf] *n* incrédulité *f*

disc [dɪsk] *(Am* **disk)** *n* disque *m*; **d. jockey** disc-jockey *m*

discard [dɪsˈkɑːd] *vt (get rid of)* se débarrasser de; *(plan)* abandonner

discern [dɪˈsɜːn] *vt* discerner ▪ **discerning** *adj (person)* averti

discernible [dɪˈsɜːnəbəl] *adj* perceptible

discernment [dɪˈsɜːnmənt] *n* discernement *m*

discharge 1 [ˈdɪstʃɑːdʒ] *n (of gun, electricity)* décharge *f*; *(of pus, liquid)* écoulement *m*; *(dismissal)* renvoi *m*; *(freeing)* libération *f*; *(of unfit soldier)* réforme *f* **2** [dɪsˈtʃɑːdʒ] *vt (patient)* laisser sortir; *(employee)* renvoyer; *(soldier, prisoner)* libérer; *(unfit soldier)* réformer; *(gun)* décharger; *(liquid)* déverser

disciple [dɪˈsaɪpəl] *n* disciple *m*

disciplinary [dɪsɪˈplɪnərɪ] *adj (measure)* disciplinaire

discipline [ˈdɪsɪplɪn] **1** *n (behaviour, subject)* discipline *f* **2** *vt (control)* discipliner; *(punish)* punir

disclaim [dɪsˈkleɪm] *vt (renounce)* renoncer à; *(deny)* démentir

disclose [dɪsˈkləʊz] *vt* révéler ▪ **disclosure** [-ʒə(r)] *n* révélation *f*

disco [ˈdɪskəʊ] *(pl* **-os)** *n* discothèque *f* ▪ **discotheque** *n* discothèque *f*

discolour [dɪsˈkʌlə(r)] *(Am* **discolor) 1** *vt* décolorer; *(teeth)* jaunir **2** *vi* se décolorer; *(of teeth)* jaunir

discomfort [dɪsˈkʌmfət] *n (physical)* petite douleur *f*; *(mental)* malaise *m*

disconcerting [dɪskənˈsɜːtɪŋ] *adj* déconcertant

disconnect [dɪskəˈnekt] *vt (unfasten)* détacher; *(unplug)* débrancher; *(gas, telephone, electricity)* couper

discontent [dɪskənˈtent] *n* mécontentement *m* ▪ **discontented** *adj* mécontent (**with** de)

discontinue [dɪskənˈtɪnjuː] *vt* interrompre

discord [ˈdɪskɔːd] *n (disagreement)* discorde *f*; *Mus* dissonance *f*

discount 1 [ˈdɪskaʊnt] *n (on article)* réduction *f*; *(on account paid early)* escompte *m*; **at a d.** *(buy, sell)* au rabais; **d. store** solderie *f* **2** [dɪsˈkaʊnt] *vt (story)* ne pas tenir compte de

discourage [dɪsˈkʌrɪdʒ] *vt* décourager (**sb from doing** qn de faire); **to get discouraged** se décourager ▪ **discouragement** *n* découragement *m*

discourse [ˈdɪskɔːs] *n* discours *m*

discourteous [dɪsˈkɜːtɪəs] *adj* discourtois (**towards** envers)

discover [dɪsˈkʌvə(r)] *vt* découvrir (**that** que) ▪ **discovery** *(pl* **-ies)** *n* découverte *f*

discredit [dɪsˈkredɪt] **1** *n* discrédit *m* **2** *vt (cast* *slur on)* discréditer; *(refuse to believe)* ne pas croire ▪ **discreditable** *adj* indigne

discreet [dɪˈskriːt] *adj* discret, -ète

discrepancy [dɪˈskrepənsɪ] *(pl -ies)* n décalage *m* (**between** entre)

discretion [dɪˈskreʃən] n *(tact)* discrétion *f*; **I'll use my own d.** je jugerai par moi-même

discriminate [dɪˈskrɪmɪneɪt] *vi* **to d. against** faire de la discrimination envers; **to be discriminated against** être victime de discrimination; **to d. between** distinguer entre ▪ **discriminating** *adj* perspicace ▪ **discrimination** [-ˈneɪʃən] n *(bias)* discrimination *f*; *(judgement)* discernement *m*; *(distinction)* distinction *f* ▪ **discriminatory** [-nətərɪ] *adj* discriminatoire

discus [ˈdɪskəs] n *Sport* disque *m*

discuss [dɪˈskʌs] *vt* discuter de ▪ **discussion** n discussion *f*; **under d.** en discussion

disdain [dɪsˈdeɪn] **1** n dédain *m* **2** *vt* dédaigner (**to do** de faire) ▪ **disdainful** *adj* dédaigneux, -euse; **to be d. of** dédaigner

disease [dɪˈziːz] n maladie *f* ▪ **diseased** *adj* malade

disembark [dɪsɪmˈbɑːk] *vti* débarquer ▪ **disembarkation** [-embɑːˈkeɪʃən] n débarquement *m*

disembodied [dɪsɪmˈbɒdɪd] *adj* désincarné

disembowel [dɪsɪmˈbaʊəl] *(Br* **-ll-**, *Am* **-l-**) *vt* éviscérer

disenchanted [dɪsɪnˈtʃɑːntɪd] *adj* désenchanté

disengage [dɪsɪnˈgeɪdʒ] *vt (object)* dégager (**from** de); *(troops)* désengager; *Br* **to d. the clutch** débrayer

disentangle [dɪsɪnˈtæŋgəl] *vt (string)* démêler; **to d. oneself from** se dégager de

disfavour [dɪsˈfeɪvə(r)] *(Am* **disfavor**) n défaveur *f*

disfigure [dɪsˈfɪgə(r)] *vt* défigurer ▪ **disfigured** *adj* défiguré ▪ **disfigurement** n défigurement *m*

disgorge [dɪsˈgɔːdʒ] *vt Fig (water, passengers)* dégorger; *(food)* vomir

disgrace [dɪsˈgreɪs] **1** n *(shame)* honte *f* (**to** à); *(disfavour)* disgrâce *f* **2** *vt* déshonorer ▪ **disgraced** *adj* disgracié

disgraceful [dɪsˈgreɪsfəl] *adj* honteux, -euse ▪ **disgracefully** *adv* honteusement

Note that the French word **disgracieux** is a false friend and is never a translation for the English word **disgraceful**. It means **ungainly**.

disgruntled [dɪsˈgrʌntəld] *adj* mécontent

disguise [dɪsˈgaɪz] **1** n déguisement *m*; **in d.** déguisé **2** *vt* déguiser (**as** en)

disgust [dɪsˈgʌst] **1** n dégoût *m* (**for** or **at** or **with** de); **in d.** dégoûté **2** *vt* dégoûter

▪ **disgusted** *adj* dégoûté (**at** or **by** or **with** de); **to be d. with sb** *(annoyed)* être fâché contre qn; **I was d. to hear that...** j'ai été indigné d'apprendre que... ▪ **disgusting** *adj* dégoûtant

dish [dɪʃ] **1** n *(container, food)* plat *m*; **the dishes** la vaisselle; **to do the dishes** faire la vaisselle **2** *vt Fam* **to d. out** *(money, advice)* distribuer; **to d. out** or **up** *(food)* servir ▪ **dishtowel** n torchon *m* (à vaisselle) ▪ **dishwasher** n lave-vaisselle *m inv*

disharmony [dɪsˈhɑːmənɪ] n désaccord *m*; *(in music)* dissonance *f*

dishcloth [ˈdɪʃklɒθ] n *(for washing)* lavette *f*; *(for drying)* torchon *m*

dishevelled [dɪˈʃevəld] *(Am* **disheveled**) *adj (person, hair)* ébouriffé

dishonest [dɪsˈɒnɪst] *adj* malhonnête ▪ **dishonesty** n malhonnêteté *f*

dishonour [dɪsˈɒnə(r)] *(Am* **dishonor**) **1** n déshonneur *m* **2** *vt* déshonorer; *(cheque)* refuser d'honorer ▪ **dishonourable** *(Am* **dishonorable**) *adj* déshonorant ▪ **dishonourably** *(Am* **dishonorably**) *adv* avec déshonneur

disillusion [dɪsɪˈluːʒən] **1** n désillusion *f* **2** *vt* décevoir; **to be disillusioned (with)** être déçu (de) ▪ **disillusionment** n désillusion *f*

disinclined [dɪsɪnˈklaɪnd] *adj* peu disposé (**to do** à faire) ▪ **disinclination** [-klɪˈneɪʃən] n répugnance *f* (**to do** à faire)

disinfect [dɪsɪnˈfekt] *vt* désinfecter ▪ **disinfectant** *adj & n* désinfectant *(m)* ▪ **disinfection** n désinfection *f*

disinherit [dɪsɪnˈherɪt] *vt* déshériter

disintegrate [dɪsˈɪntɪgreɪt] **1** *vt* désintégrer **2** *vi* se désintégrer ▪ **disintegration** [-ˈgreɪʃən] n désintégration *f*

disinterested [dɪsˈɪntrɪstɪd] *adj (impartial)* désintéressé; *Fam (uninterested)* indifférent (**in** à)

disjointed [dɪsˈdʒɔɪntɪd] *adj (words, style)* décousu

disk [dɪsk] n **(a)** *Am* = **disc** **(b)** *Comptr* disque *m*; *(floppy)* disquette *f*; **on d.** sur disque; **hard d.** disque *m* dur; **d. drive** unité *f* de disques ▪ **diskette** [dɪsˈket] n *Comptr* disquette *f*

dislike [dɪsˈlaɪk] **1** n aversion *f* (**for** or **of** pour); **to take a d. to sb/sth** prendre qn/qch en grippe; **our likes and dislikes** nos goûts *mpl* **2** *vt* ne pas aimer (**doing** faire); **he doesn't d. it** ça ne lui déplaît pas

dislocate [ˈdɪsləkeɪt] *vt (limb)* démettre; *Fig (disrupt)* désorganiser; **to d. one's shoulder** se démettre l'épaule ▪ **dislo'cation** n dislocation *f*

dislodge [dɪsˈlɒdʒ] *vt* faire bouger, déplacer; *(enemy)* déloger

disloyal [dɪsˈlɔɪəl] *adj* déloyal ▪ **disloyally** *adv (act)* déloyalement ▪ **disloyalty** n déloyauté *f*

dismal ['dɪzməl] *adj* lugubre ▪**dismally** *adv* *(fail, behave)* lamentablement

dismantle [dɪs'mæntəl] *vt (machine)* démonter; *(organization)* démanteler

dismay [dɪs'meɪ] **1** *n* consternation *f* **2** *vt* consterner

dismiss [dɪs'mɪs] *vt (from job)* renvoyer (**from** de); *(official)* destituer; *(thought, suggestion)* écarter; **to d. an appeal** *(in court)* rejeter un appel; **to d. a case** *(of judge)* classer une affaire; **d.!** *(to soldiers)* rompez!; *(to class)* vous pouvez partir ▪**dismissal** *n* renvoi *m*; *(of official)* destitution *f*

dismount [dɪs'maʊnt] **1** *vi (of person)* descendre *(from de)* **2** *vt (of horse)* désarçonner

disobedience [dɪsə'biːdɪəns] *n* désobéissance *f* ▪**disobedient** *adj* désobéissant

disobey [dɪsə'beɪ] **1** *vt* désobéir à **2** *vi* désobéir

disorder [dɪs'ɔːdə(r)] *n (confusion)* désordre *m*; *(illness, riots)* troubles *mpl* ▪**disorderly** *adj (behaviour, person, room)* désordonné; *(meeting, crowd)* houleux, -euse

disorganize [dɪs'ɔːɡənaɪz] *vt* désorganiser; **to be disorganized** être désorganisé

disorientate [dɪs'ɔːrɪənteɪt] *(Am* **disorient** [dɪs'ɔːrɪənt]) *vt* désorienter

disown [dɪs'əʊn] *vt* renier

disparage [dɪs'pærɪdʒ] *vt* dénigrer ▪**disparaging** *adj (remark)* désobligeant

disparate ['dɪspərət] *adj* disparate ▪**disparity** [-'pærɪtɪ] *(pl* -ies) *n* disparité *f* (**between** entre)

dispassionate [dɪs'pæʃənət] *adj (unemotional)* calme; *(not biased)* impartial

dispatch [dɪ'spætʃ] **1** *n (sending)* expédition *f* (**of** de); *(message)* dépêche *f* **2** *vt (send, finish off)* expédier; *(troops, messenger)* envoyer

dispel [dɪ'spel] *(pt & pp* **-ll-**) *vt* dissiper

dispensary [dɪ'spensərɪ] *(pl* -ies) *n (in hospital)* pharmacie *f*; *(in chemist's shop)* officine *f*

dispense [dɪ'spens] **1** *vt (give out)* distribuer; *(justice)* administrer; *(medicine)* préparer; *Br* **dispensing chemist** pharmacien, -ienne *mf*; *(shop)* pharmacie *f* **2** *vi* **to d. with** *(do without)* se passer de; **that dispenses with the need for...** cela rend superflu... ▪**dispensation** [-'seɪʃən] *n* distribution *f*; **special d.** *(exemption)* dérogation *f* ▪**dispenser** *n (device)* distributeur *m*

disperse [dɪ'spɜːs] **1** *vt* disperser **2** *vi* se disperser ▪**dispersal, dispersion** *n* dispersion *f*

dispirited [dɪ'spɪrɪtɪd] *adj* découragé

displace [dɪs'pleɪs] *vt (shift)* déplacer; *(replace)* supplanter; **displaced person** personne *f* déplacée

display [dɪ'spleɪ] **1** *n (in shop)* étalage *m*; *(of paintings, handicrafts)* exposition *f*; *(of force)* déploiement *m*; *(of anger)* manifestation *f*; **d. (unit)** *(of computer)* moniteur *m*; **on d.** exposé

2 *vt (goods)* exposer; *(sign, notice)* afficher; *(emotion)* manifester; *(talent, concern, ignorance)* faire preuve de

displease [dɪs'pliːz] *vt* mécontenter ▪**displeased** *adj* mécontent (**with** de)

displeasure [dɪs'pleʒə(r)] *n* mécontentement *m*

disposable [dɪ'spəʊzəbəl] *adj Br (plate, nappy)* jetable; *(income)* disponible

disposal [dɪ'spəʊzəl] *n (sale)* vente *f*; *(of waste)* évacuation *f*; **at the d. of** à la disposition de

dispose[1] [dɪ'spəʊz] *vi* **to d. of** *(get rid of)* se débarrasser de; *(throw away)* jeter; *(matter, problem)* régler; *Fam (kill)* liquider

> Note that the French verb **disposer de** is a false friend. It only means **to have at one's disposal**.

dispose[2] [dɪ'spəʊz] *vt* **to d. sb to do** *(make willing)* disposer qn à faire; **to be disposed to do** être disposé à faire; **well-disposed towards** bien disposé envers

disposition [dɪspə'zɪʃən] *n (placing)* disposition *f*; *(character)* tempérament *m*; *(readiness)* inclination *f*

dispossess [dɪspə'zes] *vt* déposséder (**of** de)

disproportion [dɪsprə'pɔːʃən] *n* disproportion *f* ▪**disproportionate** *adj* disproportionné

disprove [dɪs'pruːv] *(pp* **disproved**, *Law* **disproven** [-'prəʊvən]) *vt* réfuter

dispute [dɪ'spjuːt] **1** *n (quarrel)* dispute *f*; *(debate)* controverse *f*; *(legal)* litige *m*; **beyond d.** incontestable; **in d.** *(matter)* débattu; *(facts, territory)* contesté; *(competence)* en question; **(industrial) d.** conflit *m* social **2** *vt (claim, will)* contester

disqualify [dɪs'kwɒlɪfaɪ] *(pt & pp* **-ied**) *vt (make unfit)* rendre inapte (**from** à); *Sport* disqualifier; **to d. sb from driving** retirer son permis à qn ▪**disqualification** [-fɪ'keɪʃən] *n Sport* disqualification *f*; **his d. from driving** le retrait de son permis de conduire

disquiet [dɪs'kwaɪət] **1** *n* inquiétude *f* **2** *vt* inquiéter ▪**disquieting** *adj* inquiétant

disregard [dɪsrɪ'ɡɑːd] **1** *n* mépris *m* (**for** de) **2** *vt* ne tenir aucun compte de

disrepair [dɪsrɪ'peə(r)] *n* **in (a state of) d.** délabré

disreputable [dɪs'repjʊtəbəl] *adj* peu recommandable; *(behaviour)* honteux, -euse

disrepute [dɪsrɪ'pjuːt] *n* discrédit *m*; **to bring sb/sth into d.** discréditer qn/qch

disrespect [dɪsrɪ'spekt] *n* irrespect *m* ▪**disrespectful** *adj* irrespectueux, -ueuse (**to** envers)

disrupt [dɪs'rʌpt] *vt (traffic, class)* perturber; *(communications)* interrompre; *(plan)* déranger ▪**disruption** *n* perturbation *f*; *(of communications)* interruption *f*; *(of plan)* dérangement *m*

disruptive [dɪsˈrʌptɪv] *adj* perturbateur, -trice
dissatisfied [dɪˈsætɪsfaɪd] *adj* mécontent
(**with** de) ■**dissatisfaction** [-ˈfækʃən] *n*
mécontentement *m* (**with** devant)
dissect [daɪˈsekt] *vt* disséquer ■**dissection** *n*
dissection *f*
disseminate [dɪˈsemɪneɪt] *vt* disséminer
dissension [dɪˈsenʃən] *n* dissension *f*
dissent [dɪˈsent] **1** *n* désaccord *m* **2** *vi* être en
désaccord (**from** avec) ■**dissenting** *adj*
(voice) dissident
dissertation [dɪsəˈteɪʃən] *n* mémoire *m*
disservice [dɪˈsɜːvɪs] *n* **to do sb a d.** rendre un
mauvais service à qn
dissident [ˈdɪsɪdənt] *adj & n* dissident, -ente
(mf) ■**dissidence** dissidence *f*
dissimilar [dɪˈsɪmɪlə(r)] *adj* différent (**to** de)
dissipate [ˈdɪsɪpeɪt] *vt (clouds, fog, fears)*
dissiper; *(energy, fortune)* gaspiller
dissociate [dɪˈsəʊʃɪeɪt] *vt* dissocier (**from** de)
dissolute [ˈdɪsəluːt] *adj* dissolu
dissolve [dɪˈzɒlv] **1** *vt* dissoudre **2** *vi* se
dissoudre ■**dissolution** [dɪsəˈluːʃən] *n* dissolution *f*
dissuade [dɪˈsweɪd] *vt* dissuader (**from doing**
de faire); **to d. sb from sth** détourner qn de qch
■**dissuasion** [-ʒən] *n* dissuasion *f*
distance [ˈdɪstəns] *n* distance *f*; **in the d.** au
loin; **from a d.** de loin; **at a d.** assez loin; **it's
within walking d.** on peut y aller à pied; **to
keep one's d.** garder ses distances
distant [ˈdɪstənt] *adj* lointain; *(relative)* éloigné;
(reserved) distant; **5 km d. from** à (une distance
de) 5 km de ■**distantly** *adv* **we're d. related**
nous sommes parents éloignés
distaste [dɪsˈteɪst] *n* aversion *f* (**for** pour)
■**distasteful** *adj* déplaisant
distemper[1] [dɪˈstempə(r)] *n (paint)* détrempe *f*
distemper[2] [dɪˈstempə(r)] *n (disease)* maladie *f*
de Carré
distil [dɪˈstɪl] *(pt & pp* **-ll-**) *vt* distiller; **distilled
water** *(for battery, iron)* eau *f* déminéralisée
■**distillation** [-ˈleɪʃən] *n* distillation *f*
■**distillery** *(pl* **-ies**) *n* distillerie *f*
distinct [dɪˈstɪŋkt] *adj* (a) *(clear)* clair; *f*
(preference, improvement, difference) net *(f*
nette) (b) *(different)* distinct (**from** de)
■**distinctly** *adv (see, hear)* distinctement;
(remember) très bien; *(better, easier)* nettement;
(stupid, ill-mannered) vraiment; **d. possible**
tout à fait possible
distinction [dɪˈstɪŋkʃən] *n* distinction *f*; *(in
exam)* mention *f* bien; **singer/writer of d.**
chanteur, -euse *mf*/écrivain *m* réputé(e)
distinctive [dɪˈstɪŋktɪv] *adj* distinctif, -ive
distinguish [dɪˈstɪŋgwɪʃ] *vti* distinguer (**from**
de; **between** entre); **to d. oneself** se
distinguer (**as** en tant que) ■**distinguished**
adj distingué

distort [dɪˈstɔːt] *vt* déformer ■**distorted** *adj*
déformé; *(false) (idea)* faux *(f* fausse)
■**distortion** *n (of features, sound)* distorsion *f*;
(of truth) déformation *f*
distract [dɪˈstrækt] *vt* distraire (**from** de)
■**distracted** *adj* préoccupé ■**distracting** *adj*
(noise) gênant

> Note that the French word **distrait** is a false
> friend. It means **absent-minded**.

distraction [dɪˈstrækʃən] *n (lack of attention,
amusement)* distraction *f*; **to drive sb to d.**
rendre qn fou/folle
distraught [dɪˈstrɔːt] *adj* éperdu
distress [dɪˈstres] **1** *n (mental)* détresse *f*;
(physical) douleur *f*; **in d.** *(ship, soul)* en
détresse; **in (great) d.** *(poverty)* dans la
détresse **2** *vt* bouleverser ■**distressing** *adj*
bouleversant
distribute [dɪˈstrɪbjuːt] *vt (give out)* & *Com
(supply)* distribuer; *(spread evenly)* répartir
■**distribution** [-ˈbjuːʃən] *n* distribution *f*; *(even
spread)* répartition *f* ■**distributor** *n (in car, of
films)* distributeur *m*; *(of cars)* concessionnaire
mf
district [ˈdɪstrɪkt] *n* région *f*; *(of town)* quartier
m; *(administrative)* district *m*; *Am* **d. attorney** ≃
procureur *m* de la République; *Br* **d. nurse**
infirmière *f* visiteuse
distrust [dɪsˈtrʌst] **1** *n* méfiance *f* (**of** à l'égard
de) **2** *vt* se méfier de ■**distrustful** *adj* méfiant;
to be d. of se méfier de
disturb [dɪˈstɜːb] *vt (sleep, water)* troubler;
(papers, belongings) déranger; **to d. sb** *(bother)*
déranger qn; *(worry, alarm)* troubler qn
■**disturbed** *adj (person) (worried, mentally
unbalanced)* perturbé; *(sleep)* agité
■**disturbing** *adj (worrying)* inquiétant;
(annoying, irksome) gênant
disturbance [dɪˈstɜːbəns] *n (noise)* tapage *m*;
disturbances *(riots)* troubles *mpl*
disunity [dɪsˈjuːnɪtɪ] *n* désunion *f*
disuse [dɪsˈjuːs] *n* **to fall into d.** tomber en
désuétude ■**disused** [-ˈjuːzd] *adj (building)*
désaffecté
ditch [dɪtʃ] **1** *n* fossé *m* **2** *vt* *Fam (get rid of)* se
débarrasser de; *(plan)* laisser tomber
dither [ˈdɪðə(r)] *vi Fam* tergiverser; **to d.
(around)** *(waste time)* tourner en rond
ditto [ˈdɪtəʊ] *adv* idem
diva [ˈdiːvə] *n (singer, star)* diva *f*
divan [dɪˈvæn] *n* divan *m*
dive [daɪv] **1** *n* (a) *(of swimmer, goalkeeper)*
plongeon *m*; *(of submarine)* plongée *f*; *(of
aircraft)* piqué *m* (b) *Fam Pej (bar)* boui-boui *m*
2 *(pt* **dived**, *Am* **dove**) *vi* plonger; *(of plane)*
piquer; **to d. for pearls** pêcher des perles; **to
d. for the exit/into the pub** se précipiter vers
la sortie/dans le pub ■**diver** *n* plongeur, -euse

mf; *(deep-sea)* scaphandrier *m* ▪**diving** *n* *(underwater)* plongée *f* sous-marine; **d. suit** scaphandre *m*; **d. board** plongeoir *m*

diverge [daɪ'vɜːdʒ] *vi* diverger (**from** de) ▪**divergence** *n* divergence *f* ▪**divergent** *adj* divergent

diverse [daɪ'vɜːs] *adj* divers ▪**diversify** (*pt & pp* -**ied**) **1** *vt* diversifier **2** *vi* (*of firm*) se diversifier ▪**diversity** *n* diversité *f*

diversion [daɪ'vɜːʃən] *n Br (on road)* déviation *f*; *(amusement)* distraction *f*; **to create a d.** faire diversion

divert [daɪ'vɜːt] *vt (attention, suspicions, river, plane)* détourner; *Br (traffic)* dévier; *(amuse)* divertir; **to d. sb from** détourner qn de

divest [daɪ'vest] *vt Formal* **to d. of** *(power, rights)* priver de

divide [dɪ'vaɪd] **1** *vt Math* diviser (**into** en; **by** par); *(food, money, time)* partager (**between** *or* **among** entre); **to d. sth (off) (from sth)** séparer qch (de qch); **to d. sth up** *(share out)* partager qch **2** *vi (of group, road)* se diviser (**into** en); **dividing line** ligne *f* de démarcation ▪**divided** *adj* divisé

dividend ['dɪvɪdend] *n* dividende *m*

divine [dɪ'vaɪn] *adj* divin ▪**divinity** [-'vɪnɪtɪ] (*pl* -**ies**) *n (quality, god)* divinité *f*; *(study)* théologie *f*

division [dɪ'vɪʒən] *n* division *f*; *(distribution)* partage *m*; *(dividing object)* séparation *f*; *Sport* **first d.** première division ▪**divisible** [-'vɪzɪbəl] *adj* divisible ▪**divisive** [-'vaɪsɪv] *adj* qui cause des dissensions

divorce [dɪ'vɔːs] **1** *n* divorce *m* **2** *vt (husband, wife)* divorcer de; *Fig (idea)* séparer (**from** de) **3** *vi* divorcer ▪**divorced** *adj* divorcé (**from** de); **to get a d.** divorcer ▪**divorcee** [*Br* dɪvɔː'siː, *Am* dɪvɔːr'seɪ] *n* divorcé, -ée *mf*

divulge [dɪ'vʌldʒ] *vt* divulguer

DIY [diːaɪ'waɪ] *(abbr* **do-it-yourself**) *n Br* bricolage *m*

dizzy ['dɪzɪ] (-**ier**, -**iest**) *adj* **to be** *or* **feel d.** avoir le vertige; **to make sb (feel) d.** donner le vertige à qn

DJ ['diːdʒeɪ] *abbr* = **disc jockey**

do [duː]

> Les formes négatives sont **don't/doesn't** et **didn't**, qui deviennent **do not/does not** et **did not** à l'écrit, dans un style plus soutenu.

1 *(3rd person sing present tense* **does**; *pt* **did**; *pp* **done**; *pres p* **doing**) *v aux* **do you do you know?** savez-vous?, est-ce que vous savez?; **I do not** *or* **don't see** je ne vois pas; **he DID say so** *(emphasis)* il l'a bien dit; **do stay** reste donc; **you know him, don't you?** tu le connais, n'est-ce pas?; **better than I do** mieux que je ne le fais; **neither do I** moi non plus; **so do I** moi aussi; **oh, does he?** *(surprise)* ah oui?; **don't!** non!

2 *vt* faire; **to do nothing but sleep** ne faire que

dormir; **what does she do?** *(in general)*, **what is she doing?** *(now)* qu'est-ce qu'elle fait?, que fait-elle?; **what have you done (with...)?** qu'as-tu fait (de...)?; **well done** *(congratulations)* bravo!; *(steak)* bien cuit; **it's over and done (with)** c'est fini; **that'll do me** *(suit)* ça m'ira; *Br Fam* **I've been done** *(cheated)* je me suis fait avoir; *Fam* **I'll do you!** je t'aurai!; **to do sb out of sth** escroquer qch à qn; **he's hard done by** on le traite durement; *Fam* **I'm done (in)** *(tired)* je suis claqué; *Fam* **he's done for** il est fichu; **to do in** *(kill)* zigouiller; **to do out** *(clean)* nettoyer; **to do over** *(redecorate)* refaire; **to do up** *(coat, buttons)* boutonner; *(zip)* fermer; *(house)* refaire; *(goods)* emballer; **do yourself up (well)!** *(wrap up)* couvre-toi (bien)!

3 *vi* **to do well/badly** bien/mal se débrouiller; **do as you're told** fais ce qu'on te dit; **that will do** *(be OK)* ça ira; *(be enough)* ça suffit; **have you done?** vous avez fini?; **business is doing well** les affaires marchent bien; **how are you doing?** *(comment)* ça va?; **how do you do** *(introduction)* enchanté; *(greeting)* bonjour; **he did well** *or* **right to leave** il a bien fait de partir; **do as I do** fais comme moi; **to make do** se débrouiller; **to do away with sb/sth** supprimer qn/qch; **I could do with a coffee** *(need, want)* je prendrais bien un café; **to do without sb/sth** se passer de qn/qch; **it has to do with...** *(relates to)* cela a à voir avec...; *(concerns)* cela concerne...; *Fam* **anything doing?** est-ce qu'il se passe quelque chose?

4 *n* (**a**) *(pl* **dos**) *Br Fam (party)* fête *f* (**b**) **the do's and don'ts** les choses à faire et à ne pas faire

docile ['dəʊsaɪl] *adj* docile

dock¹ [dɒk] **1** *n* (**a**) *(for ship)* dock *m* (**b**) *(in court)* banc *m* des accusés **2** *vi (of ship) (at quayside)* accoster; *(in port)* relâcher; *(of spacecraft)* s'arrimer ▪**docker** *n* docker *m* ▪**dockyard** *n* chantier *m* naval

dock² [dɒk] *vt* (**a**) *(wages)* rogner; **to d. sth from** *(wages)* retenir qch sur (**b**) *(animal's tail)* couper

doctor ['dɒktə(r)] **1** *n (medical)* médecin *m*, docteur *m*; *(having doctor's degree)* docteur **2** *vt (text, food)* altérer; *(cat)* châtrer ▪**doctorate** *n* doctorat *m* (**in** ès/en)

doctrine ['dɒktrɪn] *n* doctrine *f*

document 1 ['dɒkjʊmənt] *n* document *m* **2** ['dɒkjʊment] *vt (inform)* documenter; *(report in detail)* (*of film, author*) rendre compte de; *(support)* étayer; **well-documented** *(person)* bien renseigné; *(book)* bien documenté ▪**documentary** [-'mentərɪ] **1** *adj* documentaire **2** *(pl* -**ies**) *n (film)* documentaire *m*

doddering ['dɒdərɪŋ] *adj (senile)* gâteux, -euse; *(shaky)* branlant

doddle ['dɒdəl] *n Br Fam* **it's a d.** c'est simple comme bonjour

dodge [dɒdʒ] **1** *n (to one side)* mouvement *m* de côté; *Fig (trick)* truc *m* **2** *vt (question)* esquiver; *(person)* éviter; *(pursuer)* échapper à; *(tax)* éviter de payer **3** *vi (to one side)* faire un saut de côté; **to d. out of sight** s'esquiver, se mettre à l'abri des regards; **to d. through** *(crowd)* se faufiler dans

Dodgems® ['dɒdʒəmz] *npl* autos *fpl* tamponneuses

dodgy ['dɒdʒɪ] **(-ier, -iest)** *adj Fam (suspect)* louche; *(not working properly)* en mauvais état; *(risky)* risqué

doe [dəʊ] *n (deer)* biche *f*

does [dʌz] *see* **do** ▪**doesn't** ['dʌzənt] = **does not**

dog¹ [dɒg] *n* chien *m*; *(female)* chienne *f*; **d. biscuit** biscuit *m* pour chien; **d. collar** collier *m* de chien; *Fam (of clergyman)* col *m* de pasteur; **d. days** canicule *f*; **d. food** nourriture *f* pour chien ▪**dog-eared** *adj (page)* corné ▪**dog-'tired** *adj Fam* claqué

dog² [dɒg] *(pt & pp* **-gg-)** *vt (follow)* suivre de près

dogged ['dɒgɪd] *adj* obstiné ▪**doggedly** *adv* obstinément

doggy ['dɒgɪ] *(pl* **-ies)** *n Fam* toutou *m*; **d. bag** *(in restaurant)* = petit sac fourni par certains restaurants pour que les clients puissent emporter les restes

doghouse ['dɒghaʊs] *n Am (kennel)* niche *f; Fam* **to be in the d.** ne pas être en odeur de sainteté

dogsbody ['dɒgzbɒdɪ] *(pl* **-ies)** *n Br Fam Pej* factotum *m*

doily ['dɔɪlɪ] *(pl* **-ies)** *n* napperon *m*

doing ['duːɪŋ] *n* **that's your d.** c'est toi qui as fait ça; *Fam* **doings** *(activities)* activités *fpl*

do-it-yourself [duːɪtjə'self] *n Br* bricolage *m*; **d. store/book** magasin *m*/livre *m* de bricolage

doldrums ['dɒldrəmz] *npl* **to be in the d.** *(of person)* avoir le cafard; *(of business)* être en plein marasme

dole [dəʊl] **1** *n Br* **d. (money)** allocation *f* de chômage; **to go on the d.** s'inscrire au chômage **2** *vt* **to d. out** distribuer au compte-gouttes

doleful ['dəʊlfəl] *adj* triste

doll [dɒl] **1** *n* poupée *f*; *Br* **doll's house** maison *f* de poupée **2** *vt Fam* **to d. oneself up** se bichonner ▪**dollhouse** *n Am* maison *f* de poupée

dollar ['dɒlə(r)] *n* dollar *m*

dollop ['dɒləp] *n (of cream, purée)* grosse cuillerée *f*

dolly ['dɒlɪ] *(pl* **-ies)** *n Fam (doll)* poupée *f*

dolphin ['dɒlfɪn] *n* dauphin *m*

domain [dəʊ'meɪn] *n (land, sphere) & Comptr* domaine *m*; *Comptr* **d. name** nom *m* de domaine

dome [dəʊm] *n* dôme *m*

domestic [də'mestɪk] *adj (appliance, use, tasks)*

ménager, -ère; *(animal)* domestique; *(policy, flight, affairs)* intérieur; *(economy, currency)* national; *Br Sch* **d. science** cours *mpl* de couture et de cuisine ▪**domesticated** *adj* **to be d.** *(of person)* se débrouiller plutôt bien avec les travaux ménagers; *(of animal)* être domestiqué

domicile ['dɒmɪsaɪl] *n Law* domicile *m*

dominant ['dɒmɪnənt] *adj* dominant; *(person)* dominateur, -trice ▪**dominance** *n* prédominance *f*

dominate ['dɒmɪneɪt] *vti* dominer ▪**domination** [-'neɪʃən] *n* domination *f*

domineering [dɒmɪ'nɪərɪŋ] *adj (person, character)* dominateur, -trice

domino ['dɒmɪnəʊ] *(pl* **-oes)** *n* domino *m*; **dominoes** *(game)* dominos *mpl*

don [dɒn] **1** *n Br Univ* professeur *m* **2** *(pt & pp* **-nn-)** *vt Literary (clothing)* revêtir

donate [dəʊ'neɪt] **1** *vt* faire don de; *(blood)* donner **2** *vi* donner ▪**donation** *n* don *m*

done [dʌn] *pp of* **do**

donkey ['dɒŋkɪ] *(pl* **-eys)** *n* âne *m; Br Fam* **I haven't seen him for d.'s years** je ne l'ai pas vu depuis belle lurette; **d. work** travail *m* pénible

donor ['dəʊnə(r)] *n* donneur, -euse *mf*

don't [dəʊnt] = **do not**

donut ['dəʊnʌt] *n Am* beignet *m*

doodle ['duːdəl] *vi* griffonner

doom [duːm] **1** *n (fate)* destin *m*; **to be all d. and gloom** voir tout en noir **2** *vt* condamner (**to** à); **to be doomed** *(unlucky)* être marqué par le destin; *(about to die)* être perdu; **to be doomed (to failure)** *(of project)* être voué à l'échec

door [dɔː(r)] *n* porte *f*; *(of vehicle, train)* portière *f*; **out of doors** dehors; **d.-to-d. salesman** démarcheur *m* ▪**doorbell** *n* sonnette *f* ▪**door handle** *n* poignée *f* de porte ▪**doorknob** *n* bouton *m* de porte ▪**doorknocker** *n* marteau *m* ▪**doorman** *(pl* **-men)** *n (of hotel)* portier *m*; *(in block of flats)* concierge *m* ▪**doormat** *n* paillasson *m* ▪**doorstep** *n* seuil *m* ▪**doorstop(per)** *n* butoir *m* ▪**doorway** *n* **in the d.** dans l'embrasure de la porte

dope [dəʊp] *Fam* **1** *n* **(a)** *(drugs)* drogue *f*; *(for horse, athlete)* dopant *m* **(b)** *(idiot)* andouille *f* **2** *vt* doper

dopey ['dəʊpɪ] **(-ier, -iest)** *adj Fam (stupid)* abruti; *(sleepy)* endormi

dorm [dɔːm] *n Fam* = **dormitory**

dormant ['dɔːmənt] *adj (volcano)* en sommeil

dormer ['dɔːmə(r)] *n* **d. (window)** lucarne *f*

dormitory [*Br* 'dɔːmɪtrɪ, *Am* 'dɔːrmɪtɔːrɪ] *(pl* **-ies)** *n* dortoir *m; Am (university residence)* résidence *f* universitaire

dormouse ['dɔːmaʊs] *(pl* **-mice** [-maɪs]) *n* loir *m*

dose [dəʊs] **1** *n* dose *f*; *(of illness)* attaque *f*; **a d.**

of flu une grippe **2** *vt* **to d. oneself (up)** se bourrer de médicaments ▪ **dosage** ['dəʊsɪdʒ] *n (amount)* dose *f*

doss [dɒs] *vi Br Fam* **to d. down** crécher ▪ **dosshouse** *n Br Fam* asile *m* de nuit

dossier ['dɒsɪeɪ] *n (papers)* dossier *m*

dot [dɒt] **1** *n & Comptr* point *m; Fam* **on the d.** à l'heure pile; *Comptr* **d. com** start-up *f inv* **2** *(pt & pp* **-tt-**) *vt (letter)* mettre un point sur; **dotted with** parsemé de; **dotted line** pointillé *m* ▪ **dot-matrix printer** *n Comptr* imprimante *f* matricielle

dote [dəʊt] *vt* **to d. on** adorer

dotty ['dɒtɪ] (**-ier, -iest**) *adj Br Fam* cinglé

double ['dʌbəl] **1** *adj* double; **a d. bed** un grand lit; **a d. room** une chambre pour deux personnes; **d. 's'** deux 's'; **d. six** deux fois six; **d. three four two** *(phone number)* trente-trois quarante-deux **2** *adv (twice)* deux fois; *(fold)* en deux; **he earns d. what I earn** il gagne le double de moi; **to see d.** voir double **3** *n* double *m; (person)* double, sosie *m; (stand-in film)* doublure *f;* **on** *or* **at the d.** au pas de course **4** *vt* doubler; **to d. sth back** *or* **over** *(fold)* replier qch; **to be doubled over in pain** être plié (en deux) de douleur **5** *vi* doubler; **to d. back** *(of person)* revenir en arrière; **to d. up with pain/laughter** être plié (en deux) de douleur/rire ▪ **double-barrelled** [dʌbəl'bærəld] *adj (gun)* à deux canons; *(name)* à rallonges ▪ **double-bass** [dʌbəl'beɪs] *n Br (instrument)* contrebasse *f* ▪ **'double-'breasted** *adj (jacket)* croisé ▪ **'double-'check** *vti* revérifier ▪ **'double-'cross** *vt* doubler ▪ **'double-'dealing** *n* double jeu *m* ▪ **'double-'decker (bus)** *n* autobus *m* à impériale ▪ **double-'door(s)** *n* porte *f* à deux battants ▪ **double-'Dutch** *n Fam* baragouin *m* ▪ **double-'glazing** *(window)* double vitrage *m* ▪ **double-'jointed** *adj* désarticulé ▪ **double-'parking** *n* stationnement *m* en double file ▪ **double-'quick** *adv* en vitesse

doubly ['dʌblɪ] *adv* doublement

doubt [daʊt] **1** *n* doute *m;* **to be in d. about sth** avoir des doutes sur qch; **I have no d. about it** je n'en doute pas; **no d.** *(probably)* sans doute; **in d.** *(result, career)* dans la balance; **when in d.** dans le doute **2** *vt* douter de; **to d. whether** *or* **that** *or* **if...** douter que... *(+ subjunctive)*

doubtful ['daʊtfəl] *adj (person, future, success)* incertain; *(dubious) (quality)* douteux, -euse; **to be d.** *(about sth)* avoir des doutes *(sur qch);* **it's d. whether** *or* **that** *or* **if...** il n'est pas certain que... *(+ subjunctive)* ▪ **doubtless** *adv* sans doute

dough [dəʊ] *n* pâte *f; Fam (money)* blé *m*

doughnut ['dəʊnʌt] *n Br* beignet *m*

dour ['dʊə(r)] *adj* austère

douse [daʊs] *vt* arroser; *Fam (light)* éteindre

dove[1] [dʌv] *n* colombe *f* ▪ **dovecote** ['dʌvkɒt] *n* colombier *m*

dove[2] [dəʊv] *Am pt of* **dive**

Dover ['dəʊvə(r)] *n* Douvres *m ou f*

dovetail ['dʌvteɪl] **1** *n (wood joint)* queue-d'aronde *f* **2** *vi Fig (fit)* concorder (**with** avec)

dowdy ['daʊdɪ] (**-ier, -iest**) *adj* peu élégant

down[1] [daʊn] **1** *adv* en bas; *(to the ground)* à terre; **d. (in writing)** inscrit; **(lie) d.!** *(to dog)* couché!; **to come** *or* **go d.** descendre; **to come d. from** *(place)* arriver de; **to fall d.** tomber (par terre); **d. there** *or* **here** en bas; **d. with traitors!** à bas les traîtres!; **d. with (the) flu** grippé; *Fam* **to feel d.** *(depressed)* avoir le cafard; **d. to** *(in series, numbers, dates)* jusqu'à; **d. payment** acompte *m;* **d. under** aux antipodes, en Australie; *Br* **d. at heel,** *Am* **d. at the heels** miteux, -euse **2** *prep (at bottom of)* en bas de; *(from top to bottom of)* du haut en bas de; *(along)* le long de; **to go d.** *(hill, street, stairs)* descendre; **to live d. the street** habiter plus loin dans la rue **3** *vt (shoot down)* abattre; *(knock down)* terrasser; **to d. a drink** vider un verre ▪ **down-and-out** ['daʊnən'aʊt] **1** *adj* sur le pavé **2** *n* clochard, -arde *mf* ▪ **downbeat** *adj Fam (gloomy)* pessimiste ▪ **downcast** *adj* découragé ▪ **downfall** *n* chute *f* ▪ **downgrade** *vt (job)* déclasser; *(person)* rétrograder ▪ **down-'hearted** *adj* découragé ▪ **down-'hill** *adv* en pente; **to go d.** descendre; *(of sick person, business)* aller de plus en plus mal ▪ **download** **1** [daʊn'ləʊd] *vt* télécharger **2** ['daʊnləʊd] *n* téléchargement *m* ▪ **down-'market** *adj Br (car, furniture)* bas de gamme *inv; (neighbourhood, accent)* populaire; *(person, crowd)* ordinaire ▪ **downpour** *n* averse *f* ▪ **downright** **1** *adj (rogue)* véritable; *(refusal)* catégorique; *Br* **a d. nerve** *or* **cheek** un sacré culot **2** *adv (rude, disagreeable)* franchement ▪ **down'scale** *adj Am =* **down-market** ▪ **downstairs** **1** ['daʊnsteəz] *adj (room, neighbours) (below)* d'en bas; *(on the ground floor)* du rez-de-chaussée **2** [daʊn'steəz] *adv* en bas/au rez-de-chaussée; **to come** *or* **go d.** descendre l'escalier ▪ **down'stream** *adv* en aval ▪ **down-to-'earth** *adj* terre-à-terre *inv* ▪ **down-'town** *adv* en ville; **d. Chicago** le centre de Chicago ▪ **down-'trodden** *adj* opprimé ▪ **downward** *adj* vers le bas; *(path)* qui descend; *(trend)* à la baisse ▪ **downward(s)** *adv* vers le bas

down[2] [daʊn] *n (on bird, person)* duvet *m* ▪ **downy** (**-ier, -iest**) *adj (skin)* duveté

Downing Street ['daʊnɪŋstriːt] *nm Br Pol =* résidence officielle du Premier Ministre britannique (n° 10)

Down's [daʊnz] *adj* **D. syndrome** trisomie *f* 21; **a D. baby** un bébé trisomique *ou* mongolien

downs [daʊnz] *npl Br (hills)* collines *fpl*

dowry ['daʊərɪ] *(pl* **-ies)** *n* dot *f*

doze [dəʊz] **1** *n* petit somme *m* **2** *vi* sommeiller; **to d. off** s'assoupir ▪ **dozy (-ier, -iest)** *adj* somnolent; *Br Fam (silly)* gourde

dozen ['dʌzən] *n* douzaine *f*; **a d. books/eggs** une douzaine de livres/d'œufs; *Fig* **dozens of** des dizaines de

Dr *(abbr* **Doctor)** Docteur

drab [dræb] *adj* terne; *(weather)* gris

draft¹ [drɑːft] **1** *n* **(a)** *(outline)* ébauche *f*; *(of letter)* brouillon *m*; *(commercial document)* traite *f* **(b)** *Am (military)* conscription *f*; *(men)* contingent *m*; **d. dodger** insoumis *m* **2** *vt* **(a) to d. (out)** *(sketch out)* faire le brouillon de; *(write out)* rédiger **(b)** *(conscript)* appeler sous les drapeaux

draft² [drɑːft] *n Am* **= draught**

draftsman ['drɑːftsmən] *(pl* **-men)** *n Am* **= draughtsman**

drafty ['drɑːftɪ] *(-ier, -iest) adj Am* **= draughty**

drag [dræg] **1** *n Fam (boring task)* corvée *f*; *(boring person)* raseur, -euse *mf*; *(on cigarette)* taffe *f (on* **de)**; **what a d.!** quelle barbe!; **to be in d.** être travesti; *Am* **the main d.** la rue principale **2** *(pt & pp* **-gg-)** *vt* traîner; *(river)* draguer; *Fig* **to d. sth from sb** *(confession, promise)* arracher qch à qn; **to d. sb/sth along** (en)traîner qn/qch; **to d. sb away from** arracher qn à; **to d. sb into** entraîner qn dans **3** *vi* traîner; **to d. on** *or* **out** *(of film, day)* traîner en longueur

dragon ['drægən] *n* dragon *m*

dragonfly ['drægənflaɪ] *(pl* **-ies)** *n* libellule *f*

drain [dreɪn] **1** *n (sewer)* égout *m*; *(in street)* bouche *f* d'égout; **that's one year's work down the d.** voilà une année de travail perdue; **that's my holiday down the d.** mes vacances tombent à l'eau; **to be a d. on** *(resources, patience)* épuiser **2** *vt (glass, tank)* vider; *(vegetables)* égoutter; *(land)* drainer; *(resources)* épuiser; **to d. (off)** *(liquid)* faire écouler; **to d. sb/sth of** *(deprive of)* priver qn/qch de; **to feel drained** être épuisé **3** *vi* **to d. (off)** *(of liquid)* s'écouler; **to d. away** *(of strength)* s'épuiser; *Br* **draining board** paillasse *f* ▪ **drainage** *n* drainage *m* ▪ **drainboard** *n Am* paillasse *f* ▪ **drainer** *n (board)* paillasse *f*; *(rack, basket)* égouttoir *m*

drainpipe ['dreɪnpaɪp] *n* tuyau *m* d'évacuation

drake [dreɪk] *n* canard *m* (mâle)

dram [dræm] *n Fam (of whisky)* goutte *f*

drama ['drɑːmə] *n (event)* drame *m*; *(dramatic art)* théâtre *m*; **d. critic** critique *m* dramatique; *Fam* **don't be such a d. queen!** arrête ton cinéma!

dramatic [drə'mætɪk] *adj* dramatique; *(very great, striking)* spectaculaire ▪ **dramatics** *n* théâtre *m*

dramatist ['dræmətɪst] *n* dramaturge *m*

dramatize ['dræmətaɪz] *vt (exaggerate)* dramatiser; *(novel)* adapter pour la scène/l'écran

drank [dræŋk] *pt of* **drink**

drape [dreɪp] *vt (person, shoulders)* draper *(with* **de);** *(wall)* tapisser *(de tentures)* ▪ **drapes** *npl Am (curtains)* rideaux *mpl*

drastic ['dræstɪk] *adj (change, measure)* radical; *(remedy)* puissant; **d. reductions** *(in shop)* soldes *mpl* ▪ **drastically** *adv* radicalement; **d. reduced prices** prix *mpl* cassés

draught [drɑːft] *(Am* **draft)** *n* **(a)** *(wind)* courant *m* d'air; *(for fire)* tirage *m*; **d. excluder** bourrelet *m* **(b)** *Br* **draughts** *(game)* dames *fpl* ▪ **draught 'beer** *n* bière *f* (à la) pression ▪ **draughtboard** *n Br* damier *m*

draughtsman ['drɑːftsmən] *(Am* **draftsman)** *(pl* **-men)** *n* dessinateur, -trice *mf (industriel(le))*

draughty ['drɑːftɪ] *(Am* **drafty) (-ier, -iest)** *adj (room)* plein de courants d'air

draw¹ [drɔː] **1** *n Sport* match *m* nul; *(of lottery)* tirage *m* au sort; *(attraction)* attraction *f* **2** *(pt* **drew,** *pp* **drawn)** *vt* **(a)** *(pull)* tirer; *(pass, move)* passer *(over* **sur; into** dans); **to d. in** *(claws)* rentrer; **to d. out** *(meeting)* faire traîner en longueur; **to d. up** *(chair)* approcher *(contract, list, plan)* dresser, rédiger **(b)** *(extract)* retirer; *(pistol, sword)* dégainer; *(water, wine)* tirer; *Fig (strength, comfort)* retirer, puiser *(from* **de);** *(applause)* provoquer **(c)** *(attract)* attirer; **to d. a smile** faire sourire *(from* **sb** qn) **(d)** *Sport* **to d. a match** faire match nul **3** *vi Sport* faire match nul; **to d. near (to)** s'approcher *(de);* *(of time)* approcher *(de);* **to d. to a close** tirer à sa fin; **to d. aside** *(step aside)* s'écarter; **to d. away** *(go away)* s'éloigner; **to d. back** *(go backwards)* reculer; **to d. in** *(of days)* diminuer; *(of train)* arriver en gare; **to d. into the station** *(of train)* entrer en gare; **to d. on** *(of time)* s'avancer; **to d. up** *(of vehicle)* s'arrêter

draw² [drɔː] **1** *(pt* **drew,** *pp* **drawn)** *vt (picture)* dessiner; *(circle)* tracer; *Fig (parallel, distinction)* faire *(between* **entre) 2** *vi (as artist)* dessiner

drawback ['drɔːbæk] *n* inconvénient *m*

drawbridge ['drɔːbrɪdʒ] *n* pont-levis *m*

drawer [drɔː(r)] *n (in furniture)* tiroir *m*

drawing ['drɔːɪŋ] *n* dessin *m*; **d. board** planche *f* à dessin; *Br* **d. pin** punaise *f*; **d. room** salon *m*

drawl [drɔːl] **1** *n* voix *f* traînante **2** *vi* parler d'une voix traînante

drawn [drɔːn] **1** *pp of* **draw¹,²** **2** *adj (face)* tiré, crispé; **d. match** *or* **game** match *m* nul

dread [dred] **1** *n* terreur *f* **2** *vt* (*exam*) appréhender; **to d. doing sth** appréhender de faire qch

dreadful ['dredfəl] *adj* épouvantable; (*child*) insupportable; **I feel d.** (*ill*) je ne me sens vraiment pas bien; **I feel d. about it** j'ai vraiment honte ▪ **dreadfully** *adv* terriblement; **to be** *or* **feel d. sorry** regretter infiniment

dreadlocks ['dredlɒks] *npl* dreadlocks *fpl*

dream [driːm] **1** *n* rêve *m*; *Fam* (*wonderful thing or person*) merveille *f*; **to have a d.** faire un rêve (**about** de); **to have dreams of** rêver de; **a d. house** une maison de rêve; **a d. world** un monde imaginaire **2** (*pt & pp* **dreamed** *or* **dreamt** [dremt]) *vt* rêver (**that** que); **I never dreamt that…** (*imagined*) je n'aurais jamais songé que…; **to d. sth up** imaginer qch **3** *vi* rêver (**of** *or* **about sb/sth** de qn/qch; **of** *or* **about doing** de faire); **I wouldn't d. of it!** je n'y songerais même pas! ▪ **dreamer** *n* rêveur, -euse *mf* ▪ **dreamy** (**-ier, -iest**) *adj* rêveur, -euse

dreary ['drɪərɪ] (**-ier, -iest**) *adj* morne

dredge [dredʒ] **1** *n* drague *f* **2** *vt* (*river*) draguer

dregs [dregz] *npl* (*of wine*) lie *f*; *Fig* **the d. of society** les bas-fonds *mpl* de la société

drench [drentʃ] *vt* tremper; **to get drenched** se faire tremper (jusqu'aux os)

dress [dres] **1** *n* (*garment*) robe *f*; (*style of dressing*) tenue *f*; *Br* **d. circle** (*in theatre*) premier balcon *m*; **d. designer** styliste *mf*; (*well-known*) couturier *m*; **d. rehearsal** (*in theatre*) répétition *f*) générale *f*; **d. shirt** chemise *f* de soirée **2** *vt* (*person*) habiller; (*wound*) panser; (*salad*) assaisonner; (*chicken*) préparer; **to get dressed** s'habiller; **dressed for tennis** en tenue de tennis **3** *vi* s'habiller; **to d. up** (*smartly*) bien s'habiller; (*in disguise*) se déguiser (**as** en)

dresser ['dresə(r)] *n* (**a**) *Br* (*furniture*) vaisselier *m*; *Am* (*dressing table*) coiffeuse *f* (**b**) **she's a good d.** elle s'habille toujours bien

dressing ['dresɪŋ] *n* (*for wound*) pansement *m*; (*seasoning*) assaisonnement *m*; *Fam* **to give sb a d.-down** passer un savon à qn; *Br* **d. gown** robe *f* de chambre; (*of boxer*) peignoir *m*; **d. room** (*in theatre*) loge *f*; (*in store*) cabine *f* d'essayage; **d. table** coiffeuse *f*

dressmaker ['dresmeɪkə(r)] *n* couturière *f* ▪ **dressmaking** *n* couture *f*

dressy ['dresɪ] (**-ier, -iest**) *adj* (*smart*) chic *inv*; (*too*) **d.** trop habillé

drew [druː] *pt of* **draw**[1,2]

dribble ['drɪbəl] *vi* (**a**) (*of baby*) baver; (*of liquid*) tomber goutte à goutte (**b**) *Football* dribbler

dribs [drɪbz] *npl* **in d. and drabs** par petites quantités; (*arrive*) par petits groupes

dried [draɪd] *adj* (*fruit*) sec (*f* sèche); (*milk, eggs*) en poudre; (*flowers*) séché

drier ['draɪə(r)] *n* = **dryer**

drift [drɪft] **1** *n* (*movement*) mouvement *m*; (*direction*) sens *m*; (*of events*) cours *m*; (*of snow*) congère *f*; (*meaning*) sens général **2** *vi* (*through air*) être emporté par le vent; (*on water*) être emporté par le courant; (*of ship*) dériver; *Fig* (*of person, nation*) aller à la dérive; (*of snow*) s'amonceler; **to d. about** (**aimlessly**) (*walk around*) se promener sans but; **to d. apart** (*of husband and wife*) devenir des étrangers l'un pour l'autre ▪ **driftwood** *n* bois *m* flotté

drill [drɪl] **1** *n* (**a**) (*tool*) perceuse *f*; (*bit*) mèche *f*; (*pneumatic*) marteau *m* piqueur; (*dentist's*) roulette *f*; (*for rock*) foreuse *f* (**b**) (*exercise*) exercice *m*; (*correct procedure*) marche *f* à suivre **2** *vt* (**a**) (*wood*) percer; (*tooth*) fraiser; (*oil well*) forer (**b**) (*of troops*) faire faire l'exercice à **3** *vi* (**a**) **to d. for oil** faire de la recherche pétrolière (**b**) faire l'exercice

drily ['draɪlɪ] *adv* (*remark*) sèchement, d'un ton sec

drink [drɪŋk] **1** *n* boisson *f*; **to give sb a d.** donner (quelque chose) à boire à qn; **to have a d.** boire quelque chose; (*alcoholic*) prendre un verre **2** (*pt* **drank**, *pp* **drunk**) *vt* boire; **he drank himself to death** c'est l'alcool qui l'a tué; **to d. sth up** finir (de boire) qch **3** *vi* boire (**out of** dans); *Fam* **to d. like a fish** boire comme un trou; **to d. up** finir son verre; **to d. to sb** boire à la santé de qn; **drinking chocolate** chocolat *m* en poudre; **drinking fountain** fontaine *f* publique; **drinking trough** abreuvoir *m*; **drinking water** eau *f* potable

drinkable ['drɪŋkəbəl] *adj* (*fit for drinking*) potable; (*not unpleasant*) buvable

drip [drɪp] **1** *n* (*drop*) goutte *f*; (*sound*) bruit *m* de l'eau qui goutte; (*in hospital*) goutte-à-goutte *m inv*; *Fam* (*weak person*) mou *m*, molle *f*; **to be on a d.** être sous perfusion **2** (*pt & pp* **-pp-**) *vt* (*paint*) laisser tomber goutte à goutte; **you're dripping water everywhere!** tu mets de l'eau partout! **3** *vi* (*of water, rain*) goutter; (*of washing, vegetables*) s'égoutter; (*of tap*) fuir ▪ **'drip-'dry** *adj* (*shirt*) qui ne nécessite pas de repassage

dripping ['drɪpɪŋ] **1** *adj & adv* **d.** (**wet**) trempé **2** *n* (*fat*) graisse *f* de rôti

drive [draɪv] **1** *n* (*in car*) promenade *f* en voiture; (*road to private house*) allée *f*; (*energy*) énergie *f*; (*campaign*) campagne *f*; *Comptr* lecteur *m*; **an hour's d.** une heure de voiture; **left-hand d.** (*vehicle*) conduite *f* à gauche; **front-wheel d.** (*vehicle*) traction *f* avant; **sex d.** pulsion *f* sexuelle **2** (*pt* **drove**, *pp* **driven**) *vt* (*vehicle, train, passenger*) conduire (**to** à); (*machine*) actionner; (*chase away*) chasser; **to d. sb to do sth** pousser qn à faire qch; **to d. sb to despair** réduire qn au désespoir; **to d. sb mad** *or* **crazy**

rendre qn fou/folle; **to d. the rain/smoke against** *(of wind)* rabattre la pluie/fumée contre; **to d. sb hard** surmener qn; **he drives a Ford** il a une Ford

3 *vi (drive a car)* conduire; *(go by car)* rouler; **to d. on the left** rouler à gauche; **to d. to Paris** aller en voiture à Paris; **to d. to work** aller au travail en voiture; *Fig* **what are you driving at?** où veux-tu en venir?

▸ **drive along** *vi (in car)* rouler

▸ **drive away** **1** *vt sep (chase away)* chasser **2** *vi (in car)* partir en voiture

▸ **drive back** **1** *vt sep (passenger)* ramener (en voiture); *(enemy)* repousser **2** *vi (in car)* revenir (en voiture)

▸ **drive in** *vt sep (nail, knife)* enfoncer

▸ **drive off** *vi (in car)* partir (en voiture)

▸ **drive on** *vi (in car)* continuer sa route

▸ **drive out** *vt sep (chase away)* chasser

▸ **drive over** *vt insep (crush)* écraser

▸ **drive up** *vi (in car)* arriver (en voiture)

drive-in ['draɪvɪn] *adj Am* accessible en voiture; **d. (movie theater)** drive-in *m inv*; **d. (restaurant)** = restaurant où l'on est servi dans sa voiture

drivel ['drɪvəl] *n* idioties *fpl*

driven ['drɪvən] *pp of* **drive**

driver ['draɪvə(r)] *n (of car)* conducteur, -trice *mf*; *(of taxi, truck)* chauffeur *m*; **(train or engine) d.** mécanicien *m*; **she's a good d.** elle conduit bien; *Am* **d.'s license** permis *m* de conduire

driveway ['draɪvweɪ] *n (road to house)* allée *f*

driving ['draɪvɪŋ] **1** *n (in car)* conduite *f*; **d. conditions** état *m* des routes; **d. lesson** leçon *f* de conduite; *Br* **d. licence** permis *m* de conduire; **d. school** auto-école *f*; **d. test** examen *m* du permis de conduire **2** *adj (forceful)* **d. force** moteur *m*; **d. rain** pluie *f* battante

drizzle ['drɪzəl] **1** *n* bruine *f* **2** *vi* bruiner

droll [drəʊl] *adj* drôle, comique

dromedary ['drɒmədərɪ] *(pl -ies) n* dromadaire *m*

drone [drəʊn] **1** *n* (**a**) *(bee)* faux-bourdon *m* (**b**) *(hum)* bourdonnement *m*; *(purr)* ronronnement *m*; *Fig (of person)* débit *m* monotone **2** *vi (of engine)* ronronner; *(of bee)* bourdonner; *Fig* **to d. (on)** *(of person)* parler d'une voix monotone

drool [dru:l] *vi (slaver)* baver; *Fig (talk nonsense)* radoter; *Fig* **to d. over sb/sth** baver d'admiration devant qn/qch

droop [dru:p] *vi (of flower)* se faner; *(of head)* pencher; *(of eyelids, shoulders)* tomber

drop [drɒp] **1** *n* (**a**) *(of liquid)* goutte *f*; **eye/nose drops** gouttes *fpl* pour les yeux/le nez (**b**) *(fall)* baisse *f*, chute *f* (**in** de); *(distance of fall)* hauteur *f* de chute; *(slope)* descente *f*; *(of supplies from aircraft)* parachutage *m*

2 *(pt & pp -pp-) vt* laisser tomber; *(price, voice)* baisser; *(bomb)* larguer; *(passenger, goods from vehicle)* déposer; *(from boat)* débarquer; *(leave out)* faire sauter, omettre; *(remark)* laisser échapper; *(get rid of)* supprimer; *(habit)* abandonner; *(team member)* écarter; **to d. sb off** *(from vehicle)* déposer qn; **to d. sb a line/postcard to sb** écrire un petit mot/une carte postale à qn; **to d. a hint** faire une allusion; **to d. a hint that…** laisser entendre que…; **to d. one's h's** ne pas prononcer les h; **to d. a word in sb's ear** glisser un mot à l'oreille de qn

3 *vi (fall)* tomber; *(of person)* se laisser tomber; *(of price)* baisser; *Fam* **he's ready to d.** il tombe de fatigue; *Fam* **let it d.!** laisse tomber!; **to d. away** *(diminish)* diminuer; **to d. back** *or* **behind** rester en arrière; **to d. by** *or* **in** *(visit sb)* passer; **to d. off** *(fall asleep)* s'endormir; *(fall off)* tomber; *(of interest, sales)* diminuer; **to d. out** *(fall out)* tomber; *(withdraw)* se retirer; *(socially)* se mettre en marge de la société; *(of student)* laisser tomber ses études; **to d. over** *or* **round** *(visit sb)* passer

dropout ['drɒpaʊt] *n* marginal, -ale *mf*; *(student)* étudiant, -iante *mf* qui abandonne ses études

dropper ['drɒpə(r)] *n (for medicine)* compte-gouttes *m inv*

droppings ['drɒpɪŋz] *npl (of animal)* crottes *fpl*; *(of bird)* fiente *f*

dross [drɒs] *n Fam* rebut *m*

drought [draʊt] *n* sécheresse *f*

drove [drəʊv] *pt of* **drive**

droves [drəʊvz] *npl (of people)* foules *fpl*; **in d. en foule**

drown [draʊn] **1** *vt* noyer; **to d. oneself, to be drowned** se noyer **2** *vi* se noyer ▪ **drowning 1** *adj (person)* qui se noie **2** *n (death)* noyade *f*

drowse [draʊz] *vi* somnoler

drowsy ['draʊzɪ] *(-ier, -iest) adj* somnolent; **to be** *or* **feel d.** avoir sommeil; **to make sb (feel) d.** assoupir qn ▪ **drowsiness** *n* somnolence *f*

drudge [drʌdʒ] **1** *n (man)* homme *m* de peine; *(woman)* bonne *f* à tout faire **2** *vi* trimer ▪ **drudgery** *n* corvée *f*

drug [drʌg] **1** *n (against illness)* médicament *m*; *(narcotic)* drogue *f*; *Fig (activity, hobby)* drogue; **drugs** *(narcotics in general)* la drogue; **hard/soft drugs** drogues dures/douces; **to be on drugs, to take drugs** se droguer; **d. addict** drogué, -ée *mf*; **d. addiction** toxicomanie *f*; **d. dealer** *(large-scale)* trafiquant de drogue; *(small-scale)* petit trafiquant de drogue, dealer *m*; **d. squad** *(police)* brigade *f* des stupéfiants *ou Fam* des stups; **d. taking** usage *m* de la drogue **2** *(pt & pp -gg-) vt* droguer; *(drink)* mettre un médicament dans

druggist ['drʌgɪst] *n Am* pharmacien, -ienne *mf*

drugstore ['drʌgstɔːr] *n Am* drugstore *m*

drum [drʌm] **1** *n Mus* tambour *m*; *(for oil)* bidon *m*; *Mus* **the big** *or* **bass d.** la grosse caisse; **the drums** *(of rock group)* la batterie **2** *(pt & pp* **-mm-)** *vt* **to d. one's fingers** tambouriner avec ses doigts; **to d. sth into sb** enfoncer qch dans la tête de qn; **to d. up** *(support, interest)* rechercher; **to d. up business** *or* **custom** attirer les clients **3** *vi (with fingers)* tambouriner ▪**drummer** *n* tambour *m*; *(in pop or jazz group)* batteur *m* ▪**drumstick** *n (for drum)* baguette *f* de tambour; *(of chicken)* pilon *m*

drunk [drʌŋk] **1** *pp of* **drink 2** *adj* ivre; **to get d.** s'enivrer; *Fig* **d. with power/success** grisé par le pouvoir/le succès **3** *n* ivrogne *mf* ▪**drunkard** *n* ivrogne *mf* ▪**drunken** *adj (person) (regularly)* ivrogne; *(driver)* ivre; *(quarrel, brawl)* d'ivrogne; **d. driving** conduite *f* en état d'ivresse ▪**drunkenness** *n (state)* ivresse *f*; *(habit)* ivrognerie *f*

dry [draɪ] **1** *(drier, driest) adj* sec *(f* sèche*)*; *(well, river)* à sec; *(day)* sans pluie; *(toast)* sans beurre; *(wit)* caustique; *(subject, book)* aride; **on d. land** sur la terre ferme; **to keep sth d.** tenir qch au sec; **to wipe sth d.** essuyer qch; **to run d.** se tarir; **to feel** *or* **be d.** *(thirsty)* avoir soif; **to d. dock** cale *f* sèche; *Am* **d. goods store** épicerie *f*; **d. ice** neige *f* carbonique **2** *vt* sécher; *(by wiping)* essuyer; *(clothes)* faire sécher; **to d. the dishes** essuyer la vaisselle; **to d. sth off** *or* **up** sécher qch **3** *vi* sécher; **to d. off** sécher; **to d. up** sécher; *(dry the dishes)* essuyer la vaisselle; *(of stream)* se tarir ▪**dryer** *n (for hair, clothes)* séchoir *m*; *(helmet-style for hair)* casque *m* ▪**dryness** *n* sécheresse *f*; *(of wit)* causticité *f*; *(of book)* aridité *f*

dry-clean [draɪ'kliːn] *vt* nettoyer à sec ▪**dry-cleaner** *n* teinturier, -ière *mf*; **the d.'s** *(shop)* le pressing, la teinturerie

DTP [diːtiː'piː] *(abbr* **desktop publishing***) n Comptr* PAO *f*

dual ['djuːəl] *adj* double; *Br* **d. carriageway** route *f* à deux voies ▪**duality** [-'ælɪtɪ] *n* dualité *f*

dub [dʌb] *(pt & pp* **-bb-***) vt* **(a)** *(film)* doubler **(into** en*)* **(b)** *(nickname)* surnommer ▪**dubbing** *n (of film)* doublage *m*

dubious ['djuːbɪəs] *adj (offer, person)* douteux, -euse; **I'm d. about going** *or* **about whether to go** je me demande si je dois y aller

duchess ['dʌtʃɪs] *n* duchesse *f*

duck [dʌk] **1** *n* canard *m* **2** *vt (head)* baisser subitement; **to d. sb** plonger qn dans l'eau; *Fig* **to d. the issue** se dérober **3** *vi* se baisser ▪**duckling** *n* caneton *m*

duct [dʌkt] *n (tube in body, pipe)* conduit *m*

dud [dʌd] *Fam* **1** *adj (coin)* faux *(f* fausse*)*; *(cheque)* en bois; *(watch)* qui ne marche pas; *(bomb)* qui n'a pas éclaté **2** *n (person)* type *m* nul

dude [duːd] *n Am Fam* type *m* (-hôtel); **d. ranch** ranch *m*

due¹ [djuː] **1** *adj (money, sum)* dû *(f* due*)* (**to** à); *(rent, bill)* à payer; *(fitting, proper)* qui convient; **to fall d.** échoir; **she's d. for a pay rise** elle mérite une augmentation de salaire; **he's d. (to arrive)** il doit arriver d'un moment à l'autre; **I'm d. there** il faut que j'y sois; **when is the baby d.?** pour quand la naissance est-elle prévue?; **with all d. respect…** avec tout le respect que je vous dois…; **in d. course** *(when appropriate)* en temps voulu; *(eventually)* le moment venu; **d. to** par suite de, en raison de; *Fin* **d. date** échéance *f* **2** *n* dû *m*; **dues** *(of club)* cotisation *f*, *(official charges)* droits *mpl*; **to give him his d….** pour lui rendre justice…

due² [djuː] *adv* **d. north/south** plein nord/sud

duel ['djuːəl] **1** *n* duel *m* **2** *(Br* **ll-***, Am* **-l-***) vi* se battre en duel

duet [djuː'et] *n* duo *m*

duffel, duffle ['dʌfəl] *adj* **d. bag** sac *m* de marin; **d. coat** duffel-coat *m*

dug [dʌg] *pt & pp of* **dig** ▪**dugout** *n* **(a)** *(canoe)* pirogue *f* **(b)** *Mil* tranchée-abri *f*; *Sport* banc *m* de touche

duke [djuːk] *n* duc *m*

dull [dʌl] **1** **(1, -er)** *adj (boring)* ennuyeux, -euse; *(colour, character)* terne; *(weather)* maussade; *(sound, ache)* sourd; *(mind)* lent; *(edge, blade)* émoussé; *(hearing, sight)* faible **2** *vt (sound)* amortir; *(pain)* endormir; *(senses)* émousser; *(mind)* engourdir; *(colour)* ternir ▪**dullness** *n (of life, town)* monotonie *f*; *(of colour)* manque *m* d'éclat; *(of mind)* lourdeur *f*

duly ['djuːlɪ] *adv (properly)* dûment; *(as expected)* comme prévu

dumb [dʌm] **(-er, -est)** *adj* muet *(f* muette*)*; *Fam (stupid)* bête; **d. animals** les bêtes *fpl*

dumbbell ['dʌmbel] *n* haltère *m*

dumbfound [dʌm'faʊnd] *vt* sidérer

dumbwaiter [dʌm'weɪtə(r)] *n (lift for food)* monte-plats *m inv*

dummy ['dʌmɪ] **1** *(pl* **-ies***) n Br (of baby)* tétine *f*; *(for displaying clothes)* mannequin *m*; *(of ventriloquist)* pantin *m*; *Fam (fool)* idiot, -iote *mf* **2** *adj* factice

dump [dʌmp] **1** *n (for refuse)* décharge *f*, *(for ammunition)* dépôt *m*; *Fam Pej (town)* trou *m*; *Fam Pej (house)* baraque *f*; *Fam* **to be (down) in the dumps** avoir le cafard; **d. truck** tombereau *m* **2** *vt (rubbish)* déposer; *(waste)* déverser; *(bricks)* décharger; *Comptr (memory)* vider; **to d. (down)** déposer; *Fam* **to d. sb** plaquer qn ▪**dumper** *n Br* **d. (truck)** tombereau *m*

dumpling ['dʌmplɪŋ] *n (in stew)* boulette *f* de pâte; *Scot* = sorte de plum-pudding

Dumpster® ['dʌmpstə(r)] *n Am* benne *f* à ordures

dumpy ['dʌmpɪ] (**-ier, -iest**) adj Fam (person) boulot, -otte

dunce [dʌns] n cancre m

dune [djuːn] n (**sand**) **d.** dune f

dung [dʌŋ] n (of horse) crottin m; (of cattle) bouse f; (manure) fumier m

dungarees [dʌŋgəˈriːz] npl Br (of child, workman) salopette f; Am (jeans) jean m

dungeon ['dʌndʒən] n cachot m

dunk [dʌŋk] vt tremper

dupe [djuːp] **1** n dupe f **2** vt duper

duplex ['duːpleks] n Am (apartment) duplex m

duplicate 1 ['djuːplɪkət] n double m; **in d.** en deux exemplaires; **a d. copy** un duplicata; **a d. key** un double **2** ['djuːplɪkeɪt] vt (key, map) faire un double de; (on machine) photocopier ▪**duplication** [-'keɪʃən] n (on machine) reproduction f; (of effort) répétition f

durable ['djʊərəbəl] adj (material, shoes) résistant; (friendship, love) durable ▪**dura-'bility** n résistance f; (of friendship) durabilité f

duration [djʊə'reɪʃən] n durée f

duress [djʊ'res] n **under d.** sous la contrainte

during ['djʊərɪŋ] prep pendant, durant

dusk [dʌsk] n (twilight) crépuscule m

dusky ['dʌskɪ] (**-ier, -iest**) adj (complexion) basané

dust [dʌst] **1** n poussière f; **Am d. cloth** chiffon m; **d. cover** or **sheet** (for furniture) housse f; **d. cover** or **jacket** (for book) jaquette f **2** vt (**a**) (furniture) dépoussiérer (**b**) (sprinkle) saupoudrer (**with** de) **3** vi faire la poussière ▪**dustbin** n Br poubelle f ▪**dustcart** n Br benne f à ordures ▪**dustman** (pl **-men**) n Br éboueur m ▪**dustpan** n pelle f (à poussière)

duster ['dʌstə(r)] n Br chiffon m

dusty ['dʌstɪ] (**-ier, -iest**) adj poussiéreux, -euse

Dutch [dʌtʃ] **1** adj hollandais; Fam **to go D.** partager les frais (**with** avec) **2** n (**a**) **the D.** (people) les Hollandais mpl (**b**) (language) hollandais m ▪**Dutchman** (pl **-men**) n

Hollandais m ▪**Dutchwoman** (pl **-women**) n Hollandaise f

dutiful ['djuːtɪfəl] adj (son, child) obéissant

duty ['djuːtɪ] (pl **-ies**) n devoir m; (tax) droit m; **duties** (responsibilities) fonctions fpl; **to be on/off d.** être/ne pas être de service ▪**duty-'free** adj (goods, shop) hors taxe inv

duvet ['duːveɪ] n Br couette f

DVD [diːviːˈdiː] (abbr **Digital Video Disk, Digital Versatile Disk**) n DVD m inv; **D. player** lecteur m (de) DVD

DVD-ROM [diːviːdiːˈrɒm] (abbr **Digital Versatile Disk read-only memory**) n DVD-ROM m inv

dwarf [dwɔːf] **1** n nain m, naine f **2** vt (of building, trees) écraser; (of person) éclipser

dwell [dwel] (pt & pp **dwelt** [dwelt]) vi demeurer; **to d. (up)on** (think about) penser sans cesse à; (speak about) parler sans cesse de; (insist on) appuyer sur

dwindle ['dwɪndəl] vi diminuer (peu à peu) ▪**dwindling** adj (interest, resources) décroissant; (supplies) qui s'épuisent

dye [daɪ] **1** n teinture f **2** vt teindre; **to d. sth green** teindre qch en vert ▪**dyeing** n teinture f; (industry) teinturerie f ▪**dyer** n teinturier, -ière mf

dying ['daɪɪŋ] **1** pres p of **die¹ 2** adj (person, animal) mourant; (custom) qui se perd; (wish, words) dernier, -ière; **to my d. day** jusqu'à ma mort **3** n (death) mort f

dyke [daɪk] n (wall) digue f; (ditch) fossé m

dynamic [daɪ'næmɪk] adj dynamique ▪**dynamism** ['daɪnəmɪzəm] n dynamisme m

dynamite ['daɪnəmaɪt] **1** n dynamite f **2** vt dynamiter

dynamo ['daɪnəməʊ] (pl **-os**) n dynamo f

dynasty [Br 'dɪnəstɪ, Am 'daɪnəstɪ] (pl **-ies**) n dynastie f

dysentery ['dɪsəntrɪ] n (illness) dysenterie f

dyslexia [dɪs'leksɪə] n dyslexie f ▪**dyslexic** [-'leksɪk] adj & n dyslexique (mf)

E, e [iː] n (**a**) *(letter)* E, e m inv (**b**) *Mus* mi m (**c**) *Fam (ecstasy)* ecsta f, X f

each [iːtʃ] **1** adj chaque; **e. one** chacun, -une; **e. one of us** chacun d'entre nous **2** pron chacun, -une; **e. other** l'un(e) l'autre, pl les un(e)s les autres; **to see/greet e. other** se voir/se saluer; **separated from e. other** séparés l'un de l'autre; **e. of us** chacun, -une d'entre nous

eager ['iːgə(r)] adj impatient (**to do** de faire); *(enthusiastic)* plein d'enthousiasme; **to be e. for sth** désirer qch vivement; **e. for money** avide d'argent; **to be e. to do** *(want)* tenir (beaucoup) à faire; **e. to help** empressé (à aider) ▪ **eagerly** adv *(work)* avec enthousiasme; *(await)* avec impatience ▪ **eagerness** n impatience f (**to do** de faire); *(zeal)* enthousiasme m (**for sth** pour qch)

eagle ['iːgəl] n aigle m ▪ '**eagle-'eyed** adj au regard d'aigle

ear¹ [ɪə(r)] n oreille f; **to be all ears** être tout ouïe; **up to one's ears in work** débordé de travail; **to play it by e.** improviser; **to give sb a thick e.** donner une gifle à qn ▪ **earache** n mal m d'oreille ▪ **eardrum** n tympan m ▪ **earmuffs** npl protège-oreilles m inv ▪ **earphones** npl écouteurs mpl ▪ **earpiece** n écouteur m ▪ **earplug** n boule f Quiès® ▪ **earring** n boucle f d'oreille ▪ **earshot** n **within e.** à portée de voix ▪ **ear-splitting** adj assourdissant

ear² [ɪə(r)] n *(of corn)* épi m

earl [ɜːl] n comte m

early ['ɜːlɪ] **1** (-ier, -iest) adj *(first)* premier, -ière; *(fruit, season)* précoce; *(death)* prématuré; *(age)* jeune; *(painting, work)* de jeunesse; *(reply)* rapide; *(return, retirement)* anticipé; *(ancient)* ancien, -ienne; **it's e.** *(on clock)* il est tôt; *(referring to meeting, appointment)* c'est tôt; **it's too e. to get up** il est trop tôt pour se lever; **to be e.** *(ahead of time)* être en avance; *(in getting up)* être matinal; **to have an e. meal/night** manger/se coucher de bonne heure; **in e. times** jadis; **in e. summer** au début de l'été; **in the e. nineties** au début des années 90; **to be in one's e. fifties** avoir à peine plus de cinquante ans; **one's e. life** sa jeunesse

2 adv tôt, de bonne heure; *(ahead of time)* en avance; *(die)* prématurément; **as e. as possible** le plus tôt possible; **earlier (on)** plus tôt; **at the earliest** au plus tôt; **as e. as yesterday** déjà hier ▪ **early-'warning system** n Mil système m radar de préalerte

earmark ['ɪəmɑːk] vt *(funds)* assigner (**for** à)

earn [ɜːn] vt gagner; *(interest)* rapporter; **to e. one's living** gagner sa vie ▪ **earnings** npl *(wages)* salaire m; *(profits)* bénéfices mpl

earnest ['ɜːnɪst] **1** adj *(serious)* sérieux, -ieuse; *(sincere)* sincère **2** n **in e.** sérieusement; **it's raining in e.** il pleut pour de bon; **he's in e.** il est sérieux ▪ **earnestness** n sérieux m; *(sincerity)* sincérité f

earth [ɜːθ] n *(ground)* sol m; *(soil)* terre f; Br *(electrical wire)* terre, masse f; **the E.** *(planet)* la Terre; **to fall to e.** tomber à ou par terre; **nothing/nobody on e.** rien/personne au monde; Fam **where/what on e....?** où/que diable...?; Fam **how on e. should I know?** comment veux-tu que je le sache? ▪ **earthquake** n tremblement m de terre ▪ **earthworm** n ver m de terre

earthenware ['ɜːθənweə(r)] n terre f cuite

earthly ['ɜːθlɪ] adj *(existence, possessions)* terrestre; Fam **not an e. chance** pas la moindre chance; Fam **for no e. reason** sans la moindre raison

earthy ['ɜːθɪ] (-ier, -iest) adj *(taste, smell)* terreux, -euse; Fig *(person)* terre-à-terre inv

earwig ['ɪəwɪg] n *(insect)* perce-oreille m

ease [iːz] n *(facility)* facilité f; *(physical)* bien-être m; *(mental)* tranquillité f; **with e.** facilement; **to be at e.** être à l'aise; **to be ill at e.** être mal à l'aise; **my mind is at e.** j'ai l'esprit tranquille; Mil **(stand) at e.!** repos! **2** vt *(pain)* soulager; *(mind)* calmer; *(tension)* réduire; *(restrictions)* assouplir; **to e. sth off/along** enlever/déplacer qch doucement; **to e. oneself through** se glisser par **3** vi **to e. (off** or **up)** *(become less)* *(of pressure)* diminuer; *(of demand)* baisser; *(of pain)* se calmer; *(not work so hard)* se relâcher; **the situation is easing** la situation se détend

easel ['iːzəl] n chevalet m

easily ['iːzɪlɪ] adv facilement; **e. the best** de loin le meilleur/la meilleure; **that could e. be the case** ça pourrait bien être le cas ▪ **easiness** n aisance f

east [iːst] **1** n est m; **(to the) e. of** à l'est de; **the E.** *(Eastern Europe)* l'Est m; *(the Orient)* l'Orient m **2**

adj (coast) est *inv*; *(wind)* d'est; **E.
Africa** l'Afrique *f* orientale; *Formerly* **E.
Germany** l'Allemagne *f* de l'Est **3** *adv* à l'est; *(travel)* vers l'est ▪ **eastbound** *adj (traffic)* en direction de l'est; *Br (carriageway)* est *inv* ▪ **easterly** *adj (point)* est *inv*; *(direction)* de l'est; *(wind)* d'est ▪ **eastern** *adj (coast)* est *inv*; **E. France** l'est *m* de la France; **E. Europe** l'Europe *f* de l'est ▪ **easterner** *n* habitant, -ante *mf* de l'est ▪ **eastward(s)** *adj & adv* vers l'est

Easter ['iːstə(r)] *n* Pâques *fpl*; **Happy E.!** joyeuses Pâques!; **E. egg** œuf *m* de Pâques; **E. week** semaine *f* de Pâques

easy ['iːzɪ] **1** *(-ier, -iest) adj (not difficult)* facile; *(solution)* simple; *(pace)* modéré; *(manners)* naturel, -elle; *(style)* aisé; **an e. life** une vie tranquille; **it's e. to do** c'est facile à faire; **it's e. for them to do it** il leur est facile de faire ça; **to feel e. in one's mind** être tranquille; **to be an e. first** *(in race)* être bon premier; *Br Fam* **I'm e.** ça m'est égal; **e. chair** fauteuil *m* **2** *adv* doucement; **go e. on the salt** vas-y mollo avec le sel; **go e. on him** ne sois pas trop dur avec lui; **take it e.** *(rest)* repose-toi; *(work less)* ne te fatigue pas; *(calm down)* calme-toi; *(go slow)* ne te presse pas ▪ **'easy'going** *adj (carefree)* insouciant; *(easy to get along with)* facile à vivre

eat [iːt] *(pt ate [Br et, eɪt, Am eɪt], pp eaten* ['iːtən]*)* **1** *vt* manger; *(meal)* prendre; **to e. breakfast** prendre le petit déjeuner; *Fig* **to e. one's words** se rétracter; *Fam* **what's eating you?** qu'est-ce que tu tracasse?; **to e. sth up** *(finish)* finir qch; **eaten up with jealousy** dévoré de jalousie **2** *vi* manger; **to e. into sth** *(of acid)* ronger qch; **to e. into one's savings** entamer ses économies; **to e. out** manger dehors; **eating place** restaurant *m* ▪ **eatable** *adj* mangeable ▪ **eater** *n* **big e.** gros mangeur *m*, grosse mangeuse *f*

eau de Cologne [əʊdəkə'ləʊn] *n* eau *f* de Cologne

eaves [iːvz] *npl* avant-toit *m* ▪ **eavesdrop** *(pt & pp* **-pp-***) vti* **to e. (on)** écouter avec indiscrétion

ebb [eb] **1** *n* reflux *m*; **the e. and flow** le flux et le reflux; **e. tide** marée *f* descendante; *Fig* **to be at a low e.** *(of patient, spirits)* être déprimé **2** *vi* refluer; *Fig* **to e. (away)** *(of strength)* décliner

ebony ['ebənɪ] *n* ébène *f*

ebullient [ɪ'bʌlɪənt] *adj* exubérant

EC [iː'siː] *(abbr* **European Community***) n Formerly* CE *f*

eccentric [ɪk'sentrɪk] *adj & n* excentrique *(mf)* ▪ **eccentricity** [eksen'trɪsɪtɪ] *n* excentricité *f*

ecclesiastic [ɪkliːzɪ'æstɪk] *adj & n* ecclésiastique *(m)* ▪ **ecclesiastical** *adj* ecclésiastique

echelon ['eʃəlɒn] *n* échelon *m*

echo ['ekəʊ] **1** *(pl* **-oes***) n* écho *m* **2** *(pt & pp* echoed*) vt (sound)* répercuter; *Fig (repeat)* répéter **3** *vi* résonner *(***with** de*)*; **the explosion echoed** le bruit de l'explosion se répercuta; **the room echoes** il y a de l'écho dans cette pièce

éclair [eɪ'kleə(r)] *n (cake)* éclair *m*

eclectic [ɪ'klektɪk] *adj* éclectique

eclipse [ɪ'klɪps] **1** *n (of sun, moon) & Fig (loss of fame)* éclipse *f* **2** *vt also Fig* éclipser

eco- ['iːkəʊ] *pref* éco- ▪ **ecofriendly** *adj* qui ne nuit pas à l'environnement ▪ **ecotax** *n* écotaxe *f* ▪ **ecotourism** *n* écotourisme *m* ▪ **ecowarrior** *n* écoguerrier, -ière *mf*

ecology [ɪ'kɒlədʒɪ] *n* écologie *f* ▪ **ecological** [iːkə'lɒdʒɪkəl] *adj* écologique ▪ **ecologist** *n* écologiste *mf*

e-commerce [iː'kɒmɜːs] *n Comptr* commerce *m* électronique

economic [iːkə'nɒmɪk] *adj* économique; *(profitable)* rentable ▪ **economical** *adj* économique; *(thrifty)* économe ▪ **economically** *adv* économiquement ▪ **economics** **1** *n* économie *f* **2** *npl (profitability)* aspect *m* financier

economist [ɪ'kɒnəmɪst] *n* économiste *mf*

economize [ɪ'kɒnəmaɪz] *vti* économiser *(***on** sur*)*

economy [ɪ'kɒnəmɪ] *(pl* **-ies***) n (saving, system, thrift)* économie *f*; **new e.** nouvelle économie; *Av* **e. class** classe *f* économique

ecstasy ['ekstəsɪ] *(pl* **-ies***) n (state)* extase *f*; *(drug)* ecstasy *f* ▪ **ecstatic** [ɪk'stætɪk] *adj* fou *(f* folle*)* de joie; **to be e. about** s'extasier sur

Ecuador ['ekwədɔː(r)] *n* l'Équateur *m*

eczema ['eksɪmə] *n Med* eczéma *m*; **to have e.** avoir de l'eczéma

eddy ['edɪ] *(pl* **-ies***) n* tourbillon *m*

edge [edʒ] **1** *n* bord *m*; *(of forest)* lisière *f*; *(of town)* abords *mpl*; *(of page)* marge *f*; *(of knife, blade)* tranchant *m*; **to be on e.** *(of person)* être énervé; **to set sb's teeth on e.** crisper qn; *Fig* **to have the e.** *or* **a slight e.** être légèrement supérieur *(***over** à*)* **2** *vt (clothing)* border *(***with** de*)* **3** *vi* **to e. into** *(move)* se glisser dans; **to e. forward** avancer doucement ▪ **edging** *n (border)* bordure *f*

edgeways ['edʒweɪz] *(Am* **edgewise** ['edʒwaɪz]*) adv* de côté; *Fam* **I can't get a word in e.** je ne peux pas en placer une

edgy ['edʒɪ] *(-ier, -iest) adj* énervé

edible ['edɪbəl] *adj (safe to eat)* comestible; *(fit to eat)* mangeable

edifice ['edɪfɪs] *n (building, organization)* édifice *m*

edify ['edɪfaɪ] *(pt & pp* **-ied***) vt* édifier

Edinburgh ['edɪnbərə] *n* Édimbourg *m ou f*

edit ['edɪt] *vt (newspaper)* diriger; *(article)* corriger; *(prepare for publication)* préparer pour la publication; *(film)* monter; *Comptr* éditer; **to e. (out)** *(cut out)* couper

Note that the French verb **éditer** is a false friend. It means **to publish**.

edition [ɪ'dɪʃən] *n* édition *f*

editor ['edɪtə(r)] *n* (*in charge of newspaper*) rédacteur, -trice *mf* en chef; (*in charge of magazine*) directeur, -trice *mf*; (*of section*) rédacteur, -trice *mf*; (*proofreader*) correcteur, -trice *mf*; (*of film*) monteur, -euse *mf*; Comptr (*software*) éditeur *m*; **sports e.** (*in newspaper*) rédacteur *m* sportif, rédactrice *f* sportive; **the e. in chief** (*of newspaper*) le rédacteur/la rédactrice en chef ▪**editorial** [-'tɔ:rɪəl] **1** *adj* de la rédaction; **e. staff** rédaction *f* **2** *n* éditorial *m*

educate ['edjʊkeɪt] *vt* (*bring up*) éduquer; (*in school*) instruire; (*mind*) former; **to be educated at** faire ses études à ▪**educated** *adj* (*voice*) cultivé; (**well-**)**e.** (*person*) instruit

education [edjʊ'keɪʃən] *n* éducation *f*; (*teaching*) enseignement *m*; (*training*) formation *f*; (*university subject*) pédagogie *f*; **the e. system** le système éducatif ▪**educational** *adj* (*qualification*) d'enseignement; (*method, theory, content*) pédagogique; (*game, film, system*) éducatif, -ive; (*establishment*) scolaire; (*experience*) instructif, -ive; **e. qualifications** diplômes *mpl*

Note that the French noun **éducation** can be a false friend. It refers both to education and to upbringing.

educator ['edjʊkeɪtə(r)] *n* éducateur, -trice *mf*

EEA [i:i:'eɪ] (*abbr* **European Economic Area**) *n* EEE *m*

EEC [i:i:'si:] (*abbr* **European Economic Community**) *n* Formerly CEE *f*

eel [i:l] *n* anguille *f*

eerie ['ɪərɪ] (**-ier, -iest**) *adj* sinistre

efface [ɪ'feɪs] *vt* effacer

effect [ɪ'fekt] **1** *n* (*result, impression*) effet *m* (**on** sur); **to no e.** en vain; **in e.** en fait; **to put sth into e.** mettre qch en application; **to come into e., to take e.** (*of law*) entrer en vigueur; **to take e.** (*of medicine*) agir; **to have an e.** (*of medicine*) faire de l'effet; **to write a letter to the e. that…** écrire une lettre comme quoi…; **or words to that e.** ou quelque chose d'approchant; Formal **personal effects** effets *mpl* personnels **2** *vt* (*change, rescue*) effectuer; (*saving, wish*) réaliser

effective [ɪ'fektɪv] *adj* (*efficient*) efficace; (*actual*) réel (*f* réelle); **to become e.** (*of law*) prendre effet ▪**effectively** *adv* (*efficiently*) efficacement; (*in fact*) effectivement ▪**effectiveness** *n* efficacité *f*

Note that the French word **effectivement** is a false friend and is never used in the sense of **efficiently**. It means **actually**.

effeminate [ɪ'femɪnɪt] *adj* efféminé

effervescent [efə'vesənt] *adj* (*drink*) gazeux, -euse; (*mixture, liquid, youth*) effervescent ▪**effervescence** *n* (*excitement, bubbling*) effervescence *f*; (*of drink*) pétillement *m*

effete [ɪ'fi:t] *adj* (*person*) veule; (*gesture*) efféminé

efficient [ɪ'fɪʃənt] *adj* efficace; (*productive*) performant ▪**efficiency** *n* efficacité *f*; (*of machine*) performances *fpl* ▪**efficiently** *adv* efficacement; **to work e.** (*of machine*) bien fonctionner

effigy ['efɪdʒɪ] (*pl* **-ies**) *n* effigie *f*

effort ['efət] *n* effort *m*; **to make an e.** faire un effort (**to** pour); **it isn't worth the e.** ça n'en vaut pas la peine; Fam **his/her latest e.** sa dernière tentative ▪**effortless** *adj* (*victory, progress*) facile; (*skill, grace*) naturel, -elle; **with e. ease** sans effort ▪**effortlessly** *adv* sans effort

effrontery [ɪ'frʌntərɪ] *n* effronterie *f*

effusive [ɪ'fju:sɪv] *adj* (*person*) expansif, -ive; (*thanks, excuses*) sans fin ▪**effusively** *adv* avec effusion

E-fit® ['i:fɪt] *n* Comptr portrait-robot *m* électronique

eg [i:'dʒi:] (*abbr* **exempli gratia**) p. ex.

egalitarian [ɪgælɪ'teərɪən] *adj* (*society*) égalitaire

egg¹ [eg] *n* œuf *m*; **e. timer** sablier *m* ▪**eggcup** *n* coquetier *m* ▪**egghead** *n* Pej or Hum intello *mf* ▪**eggplant** *n Am* aubergine *f* ▪**eggshell** *n* coquille *f* d'œuf ▪**egg-whisk** *n* fouet *m*

egg² [eg] *vt* **to e. sb on** encourager qn (**to do** à faire)

ego ['i:gəʊ] (*pl* **-os**) *n* **the e.** l'ego *m*; **to have an enormous e.** avoir très haute opinion de soi-même ▪**ego'centric** *adj* égocentrique

egoism ['i:gəʊɪzəm] *n* égoïsme *m* ▪**egoist** *n* égoïste *mf* ▪**ego'istic(al)** *adj* égoïste

egotism ['i:gətɪzəm] *n* égotisme *m* ▪**egotist** *n* égotiste *mf* ▪**egotistic(al)** [i:gə'tɪstɪk(əl)] *adj* égoïste

Egypt ['i:dʒɪpt] *n* l'Égypte *f* ▪**Egyptian** [ɪ'dʒɪpʃən] **1** *adj* égyptien, -ienne **2** *n* Égyptien, -ienne *mf*

eiderdown ['aɪdədaʊn] *n* édredon *m*

eight [eɪt] *adj & n* huit (*m*) ▪**eighth** *adj & n* huitième (*mf*); **an e.** un huitième

eighteen [eɪ'ti:n] *adj & n* dix-huit (*m*) ▪**eighteenth** *adj & n* dix-huitième (*mf*)

eighty ['eɪtɪ] *adj & n* quatre-vingts (*m*); **e.-one** quatre-vingt-un; **in the eighties** dans les années 80 ▪**eightieth** *adj & n* quatre-vingtième (*mf*)

Eire ['eərə] *n* l'Eire *f*

either ['aɪðə(r)] **1** *adj & pron* (*one or other*) l'un(e) ou l'autre; (*with negative*) ni l'un(e) ni l'autre; (*each*) chaque; **on e. side** des deux côtés; **I don't know e. man** *or* **e. of the men** je ne connais ni l'un ni l'autre de ces hommes **2** *adv* **she can't swim e.** elle ne sait pas nager non plus; **I don't e.** (ni) moi non plus; **and it's not so far off e.** et ce n'est pas si loin d'ailleurs **3** *conj* **e.... or** ou... ou, soit... soit; *(with negative)* ni... ni; **it isn't e. green or red** ce n'est ni vert ni rouge

eject [ɪ'dʒekt] **1** *vt (troublemaker)* expulser (**from** de); *(from aircraft, machine)* éjecter **2** *vi (of pilot)* s'éjecter ▪ **ejector** *adj* **e. seat** siège *m* éjectable

eke [i:k]

▸ **eke out** *vt sep (money)* dépenser avec parcimonie; **to e. out a living** gagner péniblement sa vie

elaborate¹ [ɪ'læbərət] *adj (meal)* élaboré; *(scheme)* compliqué; *(description)* détaillé; *(preparation)* minutieux, -ieuse; *(style)* recherché ▪ **elaborately** *adv (plan)* minutieusement; *(decorate)* avec recherche

elaborate² [ɪ'læbəreɪt] **1** *vt (theory)* élaborer **2** *vi* entrer dans les détails (**on** de) ▪ **elaboration** [-'reɪʃən] *n* élaboration *f*

elapse [ɪ'læps] *vi* s'écouler

elastic [ɪ'læstɪk] **1** *adj also Fig* élastique; *Br* **e. band** élastique *m* **2** *n (fabric)* élastique *m* ▪ **elasticity** [i:læs'tɪsɪtɪ] *n* élasticité *f*

elated [ɪ'leɪtɪd] *adj* transporté de joie ▪ **elation** *n* exaltation *f*

elbow ['elbəʊ] **1** *n* coude *m*; *Fam* **e. grease** huile *f* de coude **2** *vt* **to e. one's way** se frayer un chemin en jouant des coudes (**through** à travers) ▪ **elbow-room** *n Fam* **to have enough e.** avoir assez de liberté

elder¹ ['eldə(r)] *adj & n (of two people)* aîné, -ée *(mf)* ▪ **eldest** *adj & n* aîné, -ée *(mf)*; **his/her e. brother** l'aîné de ses frères

elder² ['eldə(r)] *n (tree)* sureau *m*

elderly ['eldəlɪ] **1** *adj* âgé **2** *npl* **the e.** les personnes *fpl* âgées

elect [ɪ'lekt] **1** *vt (by voting)* élire (**to** à); *Formal* **to e. to do sth** choisir de faire qch **2** *adj* **the president e.** le président élu

election [ɪ'lekʃən] **1** *n* élection *f*; **general e.** élections *fpl* législatives **2** *adj (campaign)* électoral; *(day, results)* des élections ▪ **electio'neering** *n* propagande *f* électorale

elective [ɪ'lektɪv] *Univ* **1** *adj (course)* optionnel, -elle **2** *n* cours *m* optionnel

electoral [ɪ'lektərəl] *adj* électoral ▪ **electorate** *n* électorat *m*

electric [ɪ'lektrɪk] *adj* électrique; **e. blanket** couverture *f* chauffante; *Br* **e. fire** radiateur *m* électrique; **e. shock** décharge *f* électrique; **e. shock treatment** électrochoc *m* ▪ **electrical** *adj* électrique; **e. engineer** ingénieur *m* électricien

electrician [ɪlek'trɪʃən] *n* électricien *m*

electricity [ɪlek'trɪsɪtɪ] *n* électricité *f*

electrify [ɪ'lektrɪfaɪ] *(pt & pp* **-ied)** *vt* électrifier; *Fig (excite)* électriser

electrocute [ɪ'lektrəkju:t] *vt* électrocuter

electrode [ɪ'lektrəʊd] *n* électrode *f*

electron [ɪ'lektrɒn] *n* électron *m*

electronic [ɪlek'trɒnɪk] *adj* électronique ▪ **electronics** *n (subject)* électronique *f*

elegant ['elɪgənt] *adj* élégant ▪ **elegance** *n* élégance *f* ▪ **elegantly** *adv* avec élégance

elegy ['elədʒɪ] *(pl* **-ies)** *n* élégie *f*

element ['eləmənt] *n (component, chemical, person)* élément *m*; *(of heater, kettle)* résistance *f*; **an e. of truth** une part de vérité; **the human/ chance e.** le facteur humain/chance; **the elements** *(bad weather)* les éléments *mpl*; **to be in one's e.** être dans son élément

elementary [elɪ'mentərɪ] *adj* élémentaire; *Am (school)* primaire

elephant ['elɪfənt] *n* éléphant *m*

elevate ['elɪveɪt] *vt* élever (**to** à) ▪ **elevation** [-'veɪʃən] *n* élévation *f (of* de); *(height)* altitude *f*

elevator ['elɪveɪtə(r)] *n Am* ascenseur *m*

eleven [ɪ'levən] *adj & n* onze *(m)* ▪ **elevenses** [ɪ'levənzɪz] *n Br Fam* pause-café *f (vers onze heures du matin)* ▪ **eleventh** *adj & n* onzième *(mf)*

elf [elf] *(pl* **elves)** *n* lutin *m*

elicit [ɪ'lɪsɪt] *vt* tirer (**from** de)

eligible ['elɪdʒəbəl] *adj (for post)* admissible (**for** à); *(for political office)* éligible (**for** à); **to be e. for sth** avoir droit à qch; **an e. young man** un beau parti ▪ **eligi'bility** *n* admissibilité *f*; *Pol* éligibilité *f*

eliminate [ɪ'lɪmɪneɪt] *vt* éliminer ▪ **elimination** [-'neɪʃən] *n* élimination *f*

elite [eɪ'li:t] *n* élite *f (of* de)

elk [elk] *n* élan *m*

ellipse [ɪ'lɪps] *n Math* ellipse *f* ▪ **elliptical** *adj* elliptique

elm [elm] *n* orme *m*

elocution [elə'kju:ʃən] *n* élocution *f*

elongate ['i:lɒŋgeɪt] *vt* allonger ▪ **elongated** *adj* allongé

elope [ɪ'ləʊp] *vi (of lovers)* s'enfuir (**with** avec)

eloquent ['eləkwənt] *adj* éloquent ▪ **eloquence** *n* éloquence *f* ▪ **eloquently** *adv* avec éloquence

El Salvador [el'sælvədɔ:(r)] *n* El Salvador *m*

else [els] *adv* d'autre; **somebody/anybody e.** quelqu'un/n'importe qui d'autre; **everybody e.** tous les autres; **nobody/nothing e.** personne/rien d'autre; **something e.** autre chose; **anything e.?** *(in shop)* est-ce qu'il vous faut autre chose?; **anything e. to add?** avez-vous quelque chose d'autre à ajouter?; **somewhere e.,** *Am* **someplace e.** ailleurs, autre part; **anywhere/nowhere e.** n'importe où/nulle part ailleurs; **what e.?** quoi d'autre?;

who e.? qui d'autre?; **how e.?** de quelle autre façon?; **or e.** ou bien, sinon ▪**else'where** adv ailleurs; **e. in the town** dans une autre partie de la ville

elucidate [ɪ'luːsɪdeɪt] vt élucider

elude [ɪ'luːd] vt échapper à ▪**elusive** adj (person) insaisissable; (reply) évasif, -ive

elves [elvz] pl of **elf**

emaciated [ɪ'meɪsɪeɪtɪd] adj émacié

e-mail ['iːmeɪl] **1** n courrier m électronique, e-mail m, mél m; **to send sth by e.** envoyer qch par courrier électronique; **to check one's e.** consulter sa boîte à lettres électronique; **e. address** adresse f électronique **2** vt envoyer un courrier électronique ou un e-mail ou un mél à

emanate ['eməneɪt] vi émaner (**from** de)

emancipate [ɪ'mænsɪpeɪt] vt émanciper ▪**emancipation** [-'peɪʃən] n émancipation f

embalm [ɪm'bɑːm] vt embaumer

embankment [ɪm'bæŋkmənt] n (of path) talus m; (of river) berge f

embargo [ɪm'bɑːgəʊ] (pl **-oes**) n embargo m; **to impose an e. on** mettre l'embargo sur

embark [ɪm'bɑːk] **1** vt (passengers, goods) embarquer **2** vi (s')embarquer; **to e. on sth** s'embarquer dans qch ▪**embarkation** [embɑː'keɪʃən] n embarquement m

embarrass [ɪm'bærəs] vt embarrasser ▪**embarrassing** adj embarrassant ▪**embarrassment** n embarras m

embassy ['embəsɪ] (pl **-ies**) n ambassade f

embattled [ɪm'bætəld] adj assiégé de toutes parts

embedded [ɪm'bedɪd] adj (stick, bullet) enfoncé (**in** dans); (jewel) enchâssé; (in memory) gravé; (in stone) scellé

embellish [ɪm'belɪʃ] vt embellir ▪**embellishment** n embellissement m

embers ['embəz] npl braises fpl

embezzle [ɪm'bezəl] vt (money) détourner ▪**embezzlement** n détournement m de fonds ▪**embezzler** n escroc m

embitter [ɪm'bɪtə(r)] vt (person) aigrir; (relations, situation) envenimer ▪**embittered** adj (person) aigri

emblem ['embləm] n emblème m

embody [ɪm'bɒdɪ] (pt & pp **-ied**) vt (express) exprimer; (represent) incarner ▪**embodiment** n incarnation f (**of** de)

emboss [ɪm'bɒs] vt (paper) gaufrer; (metal) bosseler ▪**embossed** adj (pattern, characters) en relief; **e. paper** papier m gaufré

embrace [ɪm'breɪs] **1** n étreinte f **2** vt (person) étreindre; Fig (belief) embrasser **3** vi s'étreindre

embroider [ɪm'brɔɪdə(r)] vt (cloth) broder; Fig (story, facts) enjoliver ▪**embroidery** n broderie f

embroil [ɪm'brɔɪl] vt **to e. sb in sth** mêler qn à qch

embryo ['embrɪəʊ] (pl **-os**) n embryon m ▪**embryonic** [-ɪ'ɒnɪk] adj Med & Fig à l'état embryonnaire

emend [ɪ'mend] vt corriger

emerald ['emərəld] n émeraude f

emerge [ɪ'mɜːdʒ] vi apparaître (**from** de); (from hole) sortir; (from water) émerger; (of nation) naître; **it emerges that…** il apparaît que… ▪**emergence** n apparition f; (of state, leader) émergence f

emergency [ɪ'mɜːdʒənsɪ] **1** (pl **-ies**) n (situation, case) urgence f; **in an e.** en cas d'urgence; **this is an e.** (speaking on telephone) j'appelle pour une urgence **2** adj (measure, operation) d'urgence; **e. exit/brake** sortie f/ frein m de secours; **e. landing** atterrissage m forcé; **e. powers** (of government) pouvoirs mpl extraordinaires; **e. services** services mpl d'urgence; **e. stop** arrêt m d'urgence; Br **e. ward,** Am **e. room** salle f des urgences

emery ['emərɪ] adj **e. board** lime f à ongles (en carton)

emigrant ['emɪgrənt] n émigrant, -ante mf ▪**emigrate** [-greɪt] vi émigrer ▪**emigration** [-'greɪʃən] n émigration f

eminent ['emɪnənt] adj éminent ▪**eminence** n distinction f; **Your E.** (to cardinal) Votre Éminence ▪**eminently** adv éminemment

emir [e'mɪə(r)] n émir m ▪**emirate** ['emɪrət] n émirat m

emissary ['emɪsərɪ] (pl **-ies**) n émissaire m

emission [ɪ'mɪʃən] n (of gas, light) émission f

emit [ɪ'mɪt] (pt & pp **-tt-**) vt (light, heat) émettre; (smell) dégager

emoticon [ɪ'məʊtɪkɒn] n Comptr émoticon m

emotion [ɪ'məʊʃən] n (strength of feeling) émotion f; (individual feeling) sentiment m

emotional [ɪ'məʊʃənəl] adj (person, reaction) émotif, -ive; (story, speech, plea) émouvant; (moment) d'intense émotion; **an e. state** un état émotionnel ▪**emotionally** adv (to say) avec émotion; **to be e. unstable** avoir des troubles émotifs

emotive [ɪ'məʊtɪv] adj (word) affectif, -ive; (person) émotif, -ive; **an e. issue** une question sensible

empathy ['empəθɪ] n compassion f

emperor ['empərə(r)] n empereur m

emphasis ['emfəsɪs] (pl **-ases** [-əsiːz]) n (in word or phrase) accent m; (insistence) insistance f; **to lay** or **put e. on sth** mettre l'accent sur qch

emphasize ['emfəsaɪz] vt (importance) souligner; (word, fact) insister sur, souligner; (syllable) appuyer sur; **to e. that…** souligner que…

emphatic [em'fætɪk] adj (denial, refusal) (clear) catégorique; (forceful) énergique; **to be e. about sth** insister sur qch; **she was e.** elle a été catégorique ▪**emphatically** adv *(refuse)* catégoriquement; *(forcefully)* énergiquement

empire ['empaɪə(r)] n empire m

empirical [em'pɪrɪkəl] adj empirique ▪**empiricism** n empirisme m

employ [ɪm'plɔɪ] vt *(person, means)* employer ▪**employable** adj susceptible d'être employé; **qualifications make you more e.** il est plus facile de se faire embaucher quand on a des qualifications ▪**employability** [ɪmplɔɪə-'bɪlɪtɪ] n employabilité f ▪**employee** [ɪm'plɔɪiː, emplɔɪ'iː] n employé, -ée mf ▪**employer** n patron, -onne mf ▪**employment** n emploi m; **place of e.** lieu m de travail; **to be in the e. of** être employé par; **e. agency** bureau m de placement

empower [ɪm'paʊə(r)] vt autoriser (**to do** à faire)

empress ['emprɪs] n impératrice f

empty ['emptɪ] **1** (**-ier, -iest**) adj vide; *(threat, promise)* vain; **on an e. stomach** à jeun; **to return e.-handed** revenir les mains vides **2** npl **empties** *(bottles)* bouteilles fpl vides **3** *(pt & pp* **-ied**) vt **to e. (out)** *(box, pocket, liquid)* vider; *(vehicle)* décharger; *(objects from box)* sortir (**from** or **out of** de) **4** vi *(of building, tank)* se vider; **to e. into** *(of river)* se jeter dans ▪**emptiness** n vide m; **I was surprised by the e. of the theatre** j'ai été surpris de trouver le théâtre vide

EMU [iːem'juː] (abbr **Economic and Monetary Union**) n UME f

emulate ['emjʊleɪt] vt imiter ▪**emu'lation** n émulation f

emulsion [ɪ'mʌlʃən] n *(paint)* peinture f acrylique (mate); *Phot* émulsion f

enable [ɪ'neɪbəl] vt **to e. sb to do sth** permettre à qn de faire qch

enact [ɪ'nækt] vt *(law)* promulguer; *(play, part in play)* jouer

enamel [ɪ'næməl] **1** n émail m *(pl* émaux) **2** adj en émail **3** *(Br* **-ll-,** *Am* **-l-)** vt émailler

enamoured *(Am* **enamored)** [ɪ'næməd] adj **e. of** *(thing)* séduit par; *(person)* amoureux, -euse de

encamp [ɪn'kæmp] vi camper ▪**encampment** n campement m

encapsulate [ɪn'kæpsjʊleɪt] vt *(ideas, views)* résumer

encase [ɪn'keɪs] vt *(cover)* envelopper (**in** dans)

enchant [ɪn'tʃɑːnt] vt enchanter ▪**enchanting** adj enchanteur, -eresse ▪**enchantment** n enchantement m

encircle [ɪn'sɜːkəl] vt entourer; *(of army, police)* encercler

encl (abbr **enclosure(s)**) PJ

enclave ['enkleɪv] n enclave f

enclose [ɪn'kləʊz] vt *(send with letter)* joindre (**in** or **with** à); *(fence off)* clôturer; **to e. sth**

with a wall entourer qch d'un mur ▪**enclosed** adj *(receipt, document)* ci-joint; *(market)* couvert; **e. space** espace m clos; **please find e....** veuillez trouver ci-joint...

enclosure [ɪn'kləʊʒə(r)] n *(in letter)* pièce f jointe; *(place, fence)* enceinte f

encompass [ɪn'kʌmpəs] vt *(include)* inclure; *(surround)* entourer

encore ['ɒŋkɔː(r)] **1** exclam & n bis *(m)* **2** vt bisser

encounter [ɪn'kaʊntə(r)] **1** n rencontre f **2** vt *(person, resistance)* rencontrer

encourage [ɪn'kʌrɪdʒ] vt encourager (**to do** à faire) ▪**encouragement** n encouragement m

encroach [ɪn'krəʊtʃ] vi empiéter (**on** or **upon** sur)

encumber [ɪn'kʌmbə(r)] vt encombrer (**with** de) ▪**encumbrance** n embarras m

encyclop(a)edia [ɪnsaɪklə'piːdɪə] n encyclopédie f ▪**encyclop(a)edic** adj encyclopédique

end [end] **1** n *(extremity)* bout m, extrémité f; *(of month, meeting, book)* fin f; *(purpose)* but m; **at an e.** *(discussion, war)* fini; *(period of time)* écoulé; **my patience is at an e.** ma patience est à bout; **in the e.** à la fin; **to come to an e.** prendre fin; **to put an e. to sth, to bring sth to an e.** mettre fin à qch; **there's no e. to it** ça n'en finit plus; *Fam* **no e. of** énormément de; **for days on e.** pendant des jours et des jours; **to stand sth on e.** mettre qch debout **2** adj *(row, house)* dernier, -ière; **e. product** *(industrial)* produit m fini; *Fig* résultat m **3** vt finir, terminer (**with** par); *(rumour, speculation)* mettre fin à **4** vi finir, se terminer; **to e. in failure** se solder par un échec; **to e. in a point** finir en pointe; **to e. up doing sth** finir par faire qch; **to e. up in London** se retrouver à Londres; **he ended up in prison/a doctor** il a fini en prison/médecin

endanger [ɪn'deɪndʒə(r)] vt mettre en danger; **endangered species** espèce f menacée

endear [ɪn'dɪə(r)] vt faire aimer (**to** de); **that's what endears him to me** c'est cela qui me plaît en lui ▪**endearing** adj *(person)* attachant; *(quality)* qui inspire la sympathie ▪**endearment** n mot m tendre; **term of e.** terme m d'affection

endeavour *(Am* **endeavor)** [ɪn'devə(r)] **1** n effort m (**to do** pour faire) **2** vi s'efforcer (**to do** de faire)

ending ['endɪŋ] n fin f; *(of word)* terminaison f; **a happy e.** *(in story)* un heureux dénouement

endive ['endaɪv] n *(curly)* chicorée f; *(smooth)* endive f

endless ['endləs] adj *(speech, series, list)* interminable; *(patience)* infini; *(countless)* innombrable ▪**endlessly** adv interminablement

endorse [ɪnˈdɔːs] *vt (cheque)* endosser; *(action, plan)* approuver; *(claim, application)* appuyer ▪ **endorsement** *n Br (on driving licence)* ≃ point(s) enlevé(s) sur le permis de conduire

endow [ɪnˈdaʊ] *vt (institution)* doter (**with** de); **to be endowed with** *(of person)* être doté de ▪ **endowment** *n* dotation *f*

endurance [ɪnˈdjʊərəns] *n* endurance *f*; **e. test** épreuve *f* d'endurance

endure [ɪnˈdjʊə(r)] **1** *vt (violence)* endurer; *(person, insult)* supporter **2** *vi (last)* survivre ▪ **enduring** *adj* durable

enemy [ˈenəmɪ] **1** *(pl -ies) n* ennemi, -ie *mf* **2** *adj (army, tank)* ennemi

energetic [enəˈdʒetɪk] *adj* énergique; **to feel e.** se sentir plein d'énergie ▪ **energetically** *adv* énergiquement

energy [ˈenədʒɪ] **1** *(pl -ies) n* énergie *f* **2** *adj (resources)* énergétique; **e. crisis** crise *f* de l'énergie

enforce [ɪnˈfɔːs] *vt (law)* faire respecter; *(discipline)* imposer (**on** à) ▪ **enforced** *adj (rest, silence)* forcé

engage [ɪnˈgeɪdʒ] **1** *vt (take on)* engager; **to e. sb in conversation** engager la conversation avec qn; *Br* **to e. the clutch** embrayer **2** *vi* **to e. in** *(launch into)* se lancer dans; *(be involved in)* être mêlé à

engaged [ɪnˈgeɪdʒd] *adj* **(a)** *(occupied) (person, toilet, phone)* occupé; **e. in doing sth** occupé à faire qch; **to be e. in business** être dans les affaires **(b)** **e. (to be married)** fiancé; **to get e.** se fiancer

engagement [ɪnˈgeɪdʒmənt] *n (to marry)* fiançailles *fpl*; *(meeting)* rendez-vous *m inv*; *(undertaking)* engagement *m*; **to have a prior e.** être déjà pris; **e. ring** bague *f* de fiançailles

engaging [ɪnˈgeɪdʒɪŋ] *adj* engageant

engender [ɪnˈdʒendə(r)] *vt* engendrer

engine [ˈendʒɪn] *n (of vehicle, aircraft)* moteur *m*; *(of train)* locomotive *f*; *(of ship)* machine *f*; *Br* **e. driver** *(of train)* mécanicien *m*

> Note that the French word **engin** is a false friend and is rarely a translation for the English word **engine**. Its most common meaning is **machine**.

engineer [endʒɪˈnɪə(r)] **1** *n* ingénieur *m*; *Br (repairer)* dépanneur *m*; *(on ship, train)* mécanicien *m*; **civil e.** ingénieur des travaux publics; **mechanical e.** ingénieur mécanicien **2** *vt (arrange secretly)* manigancer ▪ **engineering** *n* ingénierie *f*; **(civil) e.** génie *m* civil; **(mechanical) e.** mécanique *f*; **e. factory** atelier *m* de construction mécanique

England [ˈɪŋglənd] *n* l'Angleterre *f* ▪ **English** *adj* anglais; **E. teacher** professeur *m* d'anglais; **the E. Channel** la Manche **2** *n (language)* anglais *m*; **the E.** *(people)* les Anglais *mpl*

▪ **Englishman** *(pl -men) n* Anglais *m*
▪ **English-speaking** *adj* anglophone
▪ **Englishwoman** *(pl -women) n* Anglaise *f*

engrave [ɪnˈgreɪv] *vt* graver ▪ **engraver** *n* graveur *m* ▪ **engraving** *n* gravure *f*

engrossed [ɪnˈgrəʊst] *adj* **e. in one's work** absorbé par son travail; **e. in one's book** absorbé dans sa lecture

engulf [ɪnˈgʌlf] *vt* engloutir

enhance [ɪnˈhɑːns] *vt (beauty, prestige)* rehausser; *(value)* augmenter

enigma [ɪˈnɪgmə] *n* énigme *f* ▪ **enigmatic** [enɪgˈmætɪk] *adj* énigmatique

enjoy [ɪnˈdʒɔɪ] *vt (like)* aimer (**doing** faire); *(meal)* savourer; *(benefit from)* jouir de; **to e. the evening** passer une bonne soirée; **to e. oneself** s'amuser; **to e. being in London** se plaire à Londres ▪ **enjoyable** *adj* agréable; *(meal)* excellent ▪ **enjoyably** *adv* agréablement ▪ **enjoyment** *n* plaisir *m*

enlarge [ɪnˈlɑːdʒ] **1** *vt* agrandir **2** *vi* s'agrandir; **to e. (up)on sth** s'étendre sur qch ▪ **enlargement** *n (increase)* & *Phot* agrandissement *m*

enlighten [ɪnˈlaɪtən] *vt* éclairer (**sb on** or **about sth** qn sur qch) ▪ **enlightening** *adj* instructif, -ive ▪ **enlightenment** *n (explanations)* éclaircissements *mpl*; **an age of e.** une époque éclairée

enlist [ɪnˈlɪst] **1** *vt (recruit)* engager; *(supporter)* recruter; *(support)* s'assurer **2** *vi (in the army)* s'engager

enliven [ɪnˈlaɪvən] *vt (meeting)* animer; *(people)* égayer

enmeshed [ɪnˈmeʃt] *adj* empêtré (**in** dans)

enmity [ˈenmɪtɪ] *n* inimitié *f* (**between** entre)

enormous [ɪˈnɔːməs] *adj* énorme; *(explosion, blow)* terrible; *(patience, gratitude)* immense; **an e. success** un immense succès ▪ **enormity** *n (vastness, extent)* énormité *f*; *(atrocity)* atrocité *f* ▪ **enormously** *adv (very much)* énormément; *(very)* extrêmement

enough [ɪˈnʌf] **1** *adj* assez de; **e. time/cups** assez de temps/de tasses **2** *pron* assez; **to have e. to live on** avoir de quoi vivre; **to have e. to drink** avoir assez à boire; **to have had e. of sb/sth** en avoir assez de qn/qch; **it's e. for me to see that...** il me suffit de voir que...; **that's e.** ça suffit **3** *adv (work, sleep)* assez; **big/good e.** assez grand/bon (**to** pour); **strangely e., he left** chose curieuse, il est parti

enquire [ɪnˈkwaɪə(r)] *vti* = **inquire**

enquiry [ɪnˈkwaɪərɪ] *n* = **inquiry**

enrage [ɪnˈreɪdʒ] *vt* mettre en rage

enrapture [ɪnˈræptʃə(r)] *vt* ravir

enrich [ɪnˈrɪtʃ] *vt* enrichir; *(soil)* fertiliser ▪ **enrichment** *n* enrichissement *m*

enrol [ɪnˈrəʊl] *(Am* **enroll)** *(pt & pp -ll-)* **1** *vt* inscrire **2** *vi* s'inscrire (**in/for** à) ▪ **enrolment**

(Am **enrollment**) n inscription f; (people enrolled) effectif m

ensconced [ɪnˈskɒnst] adj bien installé (**in** dans)

ensemble [ɒnˈsɒmbəl] n (musicians, clothes) ensemble m

ensign [ˈensən, ˈensaɪn] n (flag) pavillon m; Am (naval rank) enseigne m de vaisseau (de deuxième classe)

enslave [ɪnˈsleɪv] vt asservir

ensue [ɪnˈsjuː] vi s'ensuivre ▪ **ensuing** adj (in the past) qui a suivi; (in the future) qui suivra

ensure [ɪnˈʃʊə(r)] vt assurer; **to e. that...** s'assurer que...

entail [ɪnˈteɪl] vt (involve) occasionner; (difficulties) comporter; **what does the job e.?** en quoi le travail consiste-t-il?

entangle [ɪnˈtæŋgəl] vt enchevêtrer; **to get entangled in sth** (of person, animal) s'empêtrer dans qch

enter [ˈentə(r)] 1 vt (room, vehicle, army) entrer dans; (road) s'engager dans; (university) entrer à; (race, competition) participer à; (write down) (on list) inscrire (**in** dans; **on** sur); (in accounts book) porter (**in** sur); Comptr (data) entrer; **to e. sb for an exam** inscrire qn à un examen; **to e. a painting in a competition** présenter un tableau à un concours; **it didn't e. my head or mind** ça ne m'est pas venu à l'esprit (**that** que) 2 vi entrer; **to e. for** (exam) se présenter à; (race) se faire inscrire à; **to e. into** (relations) entrer en; (explanation) entamer; (contract) passer (**with** avec); **to e. into a conversation with sb** engager une conversation avec qn; **you don't e. into it** tu n'y es pour rien; **to e. into** or **upon** (career) entrer dans; (negotiations) entamer; (agreement) conclure

enterprise [ˈentəpraɪz] n (undertaking, firm) entreprise f; (spirit, initiative) initiative f ▪ **enterprising** adj (person) entreprenant

entertain [entəˈteɪn] 1 vt amuser, distraire; (guest) recevoir; (idea, possibility) envisager; (doubt, hope) nourrir; **to e. sb to a meal** recevoir qn à dîner 2 vi (receive guests) recevoir ▪ **entertainer** n comique mf ▪ **entertaining** adj amusant ▪ **entertainment** n amusement m; (show) spectacle m

---

Note that the French verb **entretenir** is a false friend and is never a translation for the English verb **to entertain**. Its most common meaning is **to maintain**.

---

enthral(l) [ɪnˈθrɔːl] (pt & pp **-ll-**) vt (delight) captiver

enthuse [ɪnˈθjuːz] vi **to e. over** s'enthousiasmer pour

enthusiasm [ɪnˈθjuːzɪæzəm] n enthousiasme m ▪ **enthusiast** n enthousiaste mf; **jazz e.** passionné, -ée mf de jazz

enthusiastic [ɪnθjuːzɪˈæstɪk] adj enthousiaste; (golfer, photographer) passionné; **to get e.** s'emballer (**about** pour) ▪ **enthusiastically** adv avec enthousiasme

entice [ɪnˈtaɪs] vt attirer (**into** dans); **to e. sb to do sth** inciter qn à faire qch ▪ **enticing** adj séduisant

entire [ɪnˈtaɪə(r)] adj entier, -ière ▪ **entirely** adv entièrement

entirety [ɪnˈtaɪərətɪ] n intégralité f; **in its e.** dans son intégralité

entitle [ɪnˈtaɪtəl] vt **to e. sb to do sth** donner à qn le droit de faire qch; **to e. sb to sth** donner à qn le droit à qch; **that entitles me to believe that...** ça m'autorise à croire que... ▪ **entitled** adj (**a**) **to be e. to do sth** avoir le droit de faire qch; **to be e. to sth** avoir droit à qch (**b**) **a book e....** un livre intitulé... ▪ **entitlement** n one's **e.** son dû

entity [ˈentɪtɪ] (pl **-ies**) n entité f

entourage [ˈɒntʊrɑːʒ] n entourage m

entrails [ˈentreɪlz] npl entrailles fpl

entrance[1] [ˈentrəns] n entrée f (**to** de); (to university, school) admission f (**to** à); **e. examination** examen m d'entrée; **e. fee** droit m d'entrée

entrance[2] [ɪnˈtrɑːns] vt (charm) transporter

entrant [ˈentrənt] n (in race) concurrent, -ente mf; (for exam) candidat, -ate mf

entreat [ɪnˈtriːt] vt implorer (**to do** faire) ▪ **entreaty** (pl **-ies**) n supplication f

entrée [ˈɒntreɪ] n Br Culin entrée f; Am (main dish) plat m principal

entrench [ɪnˈtrentʃ] vt **to e. oneself** (of soldier) & Fig se retrancher

entrepreneur [ɒntrəprəˈnɜː(r)] n entrepreneur m

entrust [ɪnˈtrʌst] vt confier (**to** à); **to e. sb with sth** confier qch à qn

entry [ˈentrɪ] n entrée f; (in race) concurrent, -ente mf; (to be judged in competition) objet m/ œuvre f/projet m soumis au jury; **to gain e. to** pénétrer dans; **e. form** feuille f d'inscription; **'no e.'** (on door) 'entrée interdite'; (on road sign) 'sens interdit'

entwine [ɪnˈtwaɪn] vt entrelacer

enumerate [ɪˈnjuːməreɪt] vt énumérer ▪ **enumeration** [-ˈreɪʃən] n énumération f

enunciate [ɪˈnʌnsɪeɪt] vt (word) articuler; (theory) énoncer ▪ **enunciation** [-ˈeɪʃən] n articulation f; (of theory) énonciation f

envelop [ɪnˈveləp] vt envelopper (**in** dans); **enveloped in mystery** entouré de mystère

envelope [ˈenvələʊp] n enveloppe f

enviable [ˈenvɪəbl] adj enviable

envious [ˈenvɪəs] adj envieux, -ieuse (**of** de); **to be e. of sb** envier qn ▪ **enviously** adv avec envie

environment [ɪnˈvaɪərənmənt] n (social, moral)

milieu *m*; **the e.** *(natural)* l'environnement *m*; **e.-friendly product** produit *m* qui ne nuit pas à l'environnement ▪ **environmental** [-'mentəl] *adj (policy)* de l'environnement; **e. disaster** catastrophe *f* écologique ▪ **environmentalist** [-'mentəlɪst] *n* écologiste *mf* ▪ **environmentally** [-'mentəlɪ] *adv* écologiquement; **e. friendly** qui ne nuit pas à l'environnement

envisage [ɪn'vɪzɪdʒ] *(Am* **envision** [ɪn'vɪʒən]*) vt (imagine)* envisager; *(foresee)* prévoir; **to e. doing sth** envisager de faire qch

envoy ['envɔɪ] *n (messenger)* envoyé, -ée *mf*; *(diplomat)* ministre *m* plénipotentiaire

envy ['envɪ] **1** *n* envie *f* **2** *(pt & pp* **-ied)** *vt* envier; **to e. sb sth** envier qch à qn

ephemeral [ɪ'femərəl] *adj* éphémère

epic ['epɪk] **1** *adj* épique **2** *n (poem, novel)* épopée *f*; *(film)* film *m* à grand spectacle

epidemic [epɪ'demɪk] *n* épidémie *f*

epidural [epɪ'djʊərəl] *n Med* péridurale *f*

epilepsy ['epɪlepsɪ] *n* épilepsie *f* ▪ **epi'leptic** *adj & n* épileptique *(mf)*

epilogue ['epɪlɒg] *n* épilogue *m*

episode ['epɪsəʊd] *n (part of story)* épisode *m*; *(incident)* incident *m* ▪ **episodic** [-'sɒdɪk] *adj* épisodique

epistle [ɪ'pɪsəl] *n* épître *f*

epitaph ['epɪtɑːf] *n* épitaphe *f*

epithet ['epɪθet] *n* épithète *f*

epitome [ɪ'pɪtəmɪ] *n* **to be the e. of sth** être l'exemple même de qch ▪ **epitomize** *vt* incarner

epoch ['iːpɒk] *n* époque *f*

equal ['iːkwəl] **1** *adj* égal **(to** à); **with e. hostility/respect** avec la même hostilité/le même respect; **to be e. to sth** *(in quantity)* égaler qch; *(good enough)* être à la hauteur de qch **2** *n (person)* égal, -ale *mf*; **to treat sb as an e.** traiter qn d'égal à égal; **he doesn't have his e.** il n'a pas son pareil **3** *(Br* **-ll-,** *Am* **-l-)** *vt* égaler **(in** en) ▪ **equals sign** *n* signe *m* d'égalité

equality [ɪ'kwɒlɪtɪ] *n* égalité *f*

equalize ['iːkwəlaɪz] **1** *vt* égaliser; *(chances)* équilibrer **2** *vi (in sport)* égaliser

equalizer ['iːkwəlaɪzə(r)] *n (goal)* but *m* égalisateur

equally ['iːkwəlɪ] *adv (to an equal degree, also)* également; *(divide)* en parts égales; **he's e. stupid** il est tout aussi bête

equanimity [ekwə'nɪmɪtɪ] *n* égalité *f* d'humeur

equate [ɪ'kweɪt] *vt* assimiler **(with** à)

equation [ɪ'kweɪʒən] *n Math* équation *f*

equator [ɪ'kweɪtə(r)] *n* équateur *m*; **at** *or* **on the e.** sous l'équateur ▪ **equatorial** [ekwə'tɔːrɪəl] *adj* équatorial

equestrian [ɪ'kwestrɪən] *adj* équestre

equilibrium [iːkwɪ'lɪbrɪəm] *n* équilibre *m*

equinox ['iːkwɪnɒks, 'ekwɪnɒks] *n* équinoxe *m*

equip [ɪ'kwɪp] *(pt & pp* **-pp-)** *vt (provide with*

equipment) équiper **(with** de); *(prepare)* préparer **(for** pour); **(well-)equipped with** pourvu de; **to be (well-)equipped to do** être compétent pour faire ▪ **equipment** *n* équipement *m*; *(in factory)* matériel *m*

equity ['ekwɪtɪ] *(pl* **-ies)** *n* **(a)** *(fairness)* équité *f* **(b)** *Fin (of shareholders)* fonds *mpl* propres; *(of company)* capital *m* actions; **equities** *(shares)* actions *fpl* ordinaires ▪ **equitable** *adj* équitable

equivalent [ɪ'kwɪvələnt] *adj & n* équivalent *(m)* ▪ **equivalence** *n* équivalence *f*

equivocal [ɪ'kwɪvəkəl] *adj* équivoque

era [*Br* 'ɪərə, *Am* 'erə] *n* époque *f*; *(historical, geological)* ère *f*

eradicate [ɪ'rædɪkeɪt] *vt* éradiquer

erase [*Br* ɪ'reɪz, *Am* ɪ'reɪs] *vt* effacer; *(with eraser)* gommer ▪ **eraser** *n Am* gomme *f*

erect [ɪ'rekt] **1** *adj (upright)* droit **2** *vt (building)* construire; *(statue, monument)* ériger; *(scaffolding)* monter; *(tent)* dresser ▪ **erection** *n* construction *f*; *(of statue)* érection *f*

ERM [iːɑː'rem] *(abbr* **Exchange Rate Mechanism)** *n Formerly =* mécanisme de change

ermine ['ɜːmɪn] *n* hermine *f*

erode [ɪ'rəʊd] *vt (of sea)* éroder; *Fig (confidence)* miner ▪ **erosion** [-ʒən] *n* érosion *f*

erotic [ɪ'rɒtɪk] *adj* érotique ▪ **eroticism** *n* érotisme *m*

err [ɜː(r)] *vi (be wrong)* faire erreur; *(sin)* pécher; **to e. on the side of caution** pécher par excès de prudence

errand ['erənd] *n* commission *f*, course *f*; **to run errands for sb** faire des courses pour qn; **e. boy** garçon *m* de courses

erratic [ɪ'rætɪk] *adj (unpredictable) (behaviour)* imprévisible; *(service, machine)* fantaisiste; *(person)* lunatique; *(irregular) (performance, results)* irrégulier, -ière

erroneous [ɪ'rəʊnɪəs] *adj* erroné

error ['erə(r)] *n (mistake)* erreur *f*; **to do sth in e.** faire qch par erreur; **typing/printing e.** faute *f* de frappe/d'impression

erudite ['erʊdaɪt] *adj* érudit

erupt [ɪ'rʌpt] *vi (of volcano)* entrer en éruption; *(of pimples)* apparaître; *(of war, violence)* éclater ▪ **eruption** *n (of volcano, pimples)* éruption *f* **(of** de); *(of violence, anger)* flambée *f*

escalate ['eskəleɪt] **1** *vt* intensifier **2** *vi (of war, violence)* s'intensifier; *(of prices)* monter en flèche ▪ **esca'lation** *n* escalade *f*; *(of prices)* montée *f* en flèche

escalator ['eskəleɪtə(r)] *n* escalier *m* roulant

escapade ['eskəpeɪd] *n* frasque *f*

escape [ɪ'skeɪp] **1** *n (of gas, liquid)* fuite *f*; *(of person)* évasion *f*; **he had a lucky** *or* **narrow e.** il l'a échappé belle **2** *vt (death, punishment)* échapper à; **her name escapes me** son nom

méchappe; **to e. notice** passer inaperçu **3** *vi*
(of gas, animal) s'échapper (**from** de); *(of
prisoner)* s'évader (**from** de); **to e. unhurt** s'en
tirer indemne; **escaped prisoner** évadé, -ée *mf*
escapism [ɪ'skeɪpɪzəm] *n* évasion *f* (hors de la
réalité) ▪ **escapist** *adj (film, novel)* d'évasion
escort 1 ['eskɔːt] *n (for convoy)* escorte *f; (for
tourist)* guide *m; (of woman)* cavalier *m;* **under
e.** sous escorte; **it's dangerous – she needs
an e.** c'est dangereux – il faut que quelqu'un
l'accompagne **2** [ɪ'skɔːt] *vt* escorter; *(prisoner)*
conduire sous escorte
Eskimo ['eskɪməʊ] **1** *adj* esquimau, -aude **2** *(pl
-os) n* Esquimau, -aude *mf*
esoteric [esəʊ'terɪk] *adj* ésotérique
especially [ɪ'speʃəlɪ] *adv(in particular)* surtout;
(more than normally) particulièrement; *(for
purpose)* (tout) spécialement; **e. as** d'autant
plus que
espionage ['espɪənɑːʒ] *n* espionnage *m*
esplanade ['espləneɪd] *n* esplanade *f*
espouse [ɪ'spaʊz] *vt (cause)* épouser
espresso [e'spresəʊ] *(pl -os) n* express *m*
Esq *(abbr* **Esquire)** *Br* **J. Smith Esq** = Monsieur J.
Smith
essay ['eseɪ] *n (in school)* rédaction *f, (in
university)* dissertation *f* (**on** sur)
essence ['esəns] *n (distinctive quality)* essence *f,
Culin (extract)* extrait *m;* **the e. of sth** *(main
point)* l'essentiel *m* de qch; **in e.** essentiellement
essential [ɪ'senʃəl] **1** *adj (principal)* essentiel,
-ielle; *(necessary)* indispensable, essentiel; **it's
e. that...** il est indispensable que... (*+
subjunctive*) **2** *npl* **the essentials** l'essentiel *m*
(**of** de); *(basic foodstuffs)* les produits *mpl* de
première nécessité; *(of grammar)* les éléments
mpl ▪ **essentially** *adv* essentiellement
establish [ɪ'stæblɪʃ] *vt* établir; *(state, society,
company)* fonder; *(post)* créer ▪ **established**
adj **(well-)e.** solide; *(fact)* reconnu;
(reputation) établi; **she's (well-)e.** *(well-known)*
elle a une réputation établie ▪ **establishment**
n (institution, company) établissement *m;* **the e.
of** *(action)* l'établissement de; *(state)* la
fondation de; *(post)* la création de; **the E.**
(dominant group) les classes *fpl* dirigeantes
estate [ɪ'steɪt] *n (land)* terres *fpl,* propriété *f,
(possessions)* biens *mpl; (property after death)*
succession *f; Br* **e. agency** agence *f*
immobilière; *Br* **e. agent** agent *m* immobilier;
Br **e. car** break *m; Br* **e. duty,** *Am* **e. tax** droits
mpl de succession
esteem [ɪ'stiːm] **1** *n* estime *f;* **to hold sb in high
e.** avoir qn en haute estime **2** *vt* estimer; **highly
esteemed** très estimé
esthetic [es'θetɪk] *adj Am* esthétique
estimate 1 ['estɪmət] *n* évaluation *f, Com* devis
m; **rough e.** chiffre *m* approximatif **2** ['estɪmeɪt]

vt (value) estimer, évaluer; *(consider)* estimer
(**that** que) ▪ **estimation** [-'meɪʃən] *n*
jugement *m; (esteem)* estime *f; (calculation)*
estimation *f;* **in my e.** à mon avis
estranged [ɪ'streɪndʒd] *adj* **her e. husband** son
mari, dont elle vit séparée
Estonia [es'təʊnɪə] *n* Estonie *f* ▪ **Estonian 1** *adj*
estonien, -ienne **2** *n (person)* Estonien, -ienne
mf; (language) estonien *m*
estuary ['estjʊərɪ] *(pl -ies) n* estuaire *m*
etc [et'setərə] *(abbr* **et cetera)** *adv* etc
etch [etʃ] *vti* graver à l'eau forte ▪ **etching** *n
(picture)* eau-forte *f*
eternal [ɪ'tɜːnəl] *adj* éternel, -elle ▪ **eternally**
adv éternellement ▪ **eternity** *n* éternité *f*
ether ['iːθə(r)] *n* éther *m*
ethic ['eθɪk] *n* éthique *f* ▪ **ethical** *adj* moral,
éthique ▪ **ethics** *n* éthique *f,* morale *f; (of
profession)* déontologie *f*
Ethiopia [iːθɪ'əʊpɪə] *n* l'Éthiopie *f* ▪ **Ethiopian
1** *adj* éthiopien, -ienne **2** *n* Éthiopien, -ienne *mf*
ethnic ['eθnɪk] *adj* ethnique; **e. cleansing**
purification *f* ethnique; **e. minority** minorité *f*
ethnique; **e. dancing** danses *fpl* tradi-
tionnelles; **e. music** musique *f* traditionnelle
ethos ['iːθɒs] *n* génie *m*
e-ticket [iː'tɪkɪt] *n Comptr* billet *m* électronique
etiquette ['etɪket] *n* étiquette *f*
etymology [etɪ'mɒlədʒɪ] *n* étymologie *f*
EU [iː'juː] *(abbr* **European Union)** *n* UE *f*
eucalyptus [juːkə'lɪptəs] *n* eucalyptus *m*
eulogy ['juːlədʒɪ] *(pl -ies) n* éloge *m*
euphemism ['juːfəmɪzəm] *n* euphémisme *m*
euphoria [juː'fɔːrɪə] *n* euphorie *f* ▪ **euphoric**
[-'fɒrɪk] *adj* euphorique
euro ['jʊərəʊ] *(pl -os) n (currency)* euro *m;* **e.
area, e. zone** zone *f* euro
Euro- ['jʊərəʊ] *pref* euro- ▪ **Euro-MP** *n* député
m européen ▪ **Euro'sceptic** *(Am* **Euro-
'skeptic)** *n* eurosceptique *mf*
Eurocheque ['jʊərəʊtʃek] *n* eurochèque *m*
Eurocrat ['jʊərəkræt] *n* eurocrate *mf*
Europe ['jʊərəp] *n* l'Europe *f* ▪ **European**
[-'piːən] **1** *adj* européen, -éenne; **E.
Commission** Commission *f* européenne; **E.
Union** Union *f* européenne **2** *n* Européen, -
éenne *mf*
euthanasia [juːθə'neɪzɪə] *n* euthanasie *f*
evacuate [ɪ'vækjʊeɪt] *vt* évacuer ▪ **evacuation** [-'eɪʃən] *n* évacuation *f*
evade [ɪ'veɪd] *vt* éviter, esquiver; *(pursuer)*
échapper à; *(law, question)* éluder; **to e. tax**
frauder le fisc

> Note that the French verb **s'évader** is a false
> friend and is never a translation for the Eng-
> lish verb **to evade.** It means **to escape.**

evaluate [ɪ'væljʊeɪt] *vt* évaluer (**at** à)
▪ **evalu'ation** *n* évaluation *f*

evangelical [iːvænˈdʒelɪkəl] *adj* évangélique ■ **evangelist** [ɪˈvændʒəlɪst] *n* évangéliste *m*

evaporate [ɪˈvæpəreɪt] *vi (of liquid)* s'évaporer; *(of hopes)* s'évanouir; **evaporated milk** lait *m* condensé ■ **evapo'ration** *n* évaporation *f*

evasion [ɪˈveɪʒən] *n (escape)* fuite *f*; *(of pursuer, responsibilities, question)* dérobade *f*; **(tax) e.** évasion *f* fiscale

> Note that the French word **évasion** is a false friend and is rarely a translation for the English word **evasion**. Its most common meaning is **escape**.

evasive [ɪˈveɪsɪv] *adj* évasif, -ive

eve [iːv] *n* **on the e. of** à la veille de

even [ˈiːvən] **1** *adj (equal, flat)* égal; *(smooth)* uni; *(regular)* régulier, -ière; *(temperature)* constant; *(number)* pair; *Fig* **to get e. with sb** prendre sa revanche sur qn; **I'll get e. with him (for that)** je lui revaudrai ça; **we're e.** *(morally)* nous sommes quittes; *(in score)* nous sommes à égalité; **to break e.** *(financially)* s'y retrouver **2** *adv* même; **e. better/more** encore mieux/plus; **e. if** *or* **though…** bien que… (+ *subjunctive*); **e. so** quand même **3** *vt* **to e. sth (out** *or* **up)** égaliser qch ■ **evenly** *adv (equally)* de manière égale; *(uniformly)* uniformément; *(regularly)* régulièrement ■ **evenness** *n (of surface, temper)* égalité *f* ■ **'even-'tempered** *adj* d'humeur égale

evening [ˈiːvnɪŋ] *n* soir *m*; *(referring to duration, event)* soirée *f*; **tomorrow/yesterday e.** demain/hier soir; **in the e.,** *Am* **evenings** le soir; **at seven in the e.** à sept heures du soir; **every Tuesday e.** tous les mardis soir; **all e.** toute la soirée; **good e.!** bonsoir!; **e. meal/paper** repas *m*/journal *m* du soir; **e. class** cours *m* du soir; **e. dress** *(of man)* tenue *f* de soirée; *(of woman)* robe *f* du soir; **e. performance** *(in theatre)* soirée

event [ɪˈvent] *n* événement *m*; *Sport* épreuve *f*; **in the e. of fire** en cas d'incendie; **in any e.** en tout cas; **after the e.** après coup

eventful [ɪˈventfəl] *adj (day, journey, life)* mouvementé; *(occasion)* mémorable

eventual [ɪˈventʃʊəl] *adj (final)* final, définitif, -ive ■ **eventuality** [-tʃʊˈælɪtɪ] *(pl* -**ies)** *n* éventualité *f* ■ **eventually** *adv* finalement; *(some day)* par la suite; **he'll do it e.** il le fera un jour ou l'autre

> Note that the French words **éventuel** and **éventuellement** are false friends and are never translations for the English words **eventual** and **eventually**. They mean **possible** and **possibly**.

ever [ˈevə(r)] *adv* jamais; **have you e. been to Spain?** es-tu déjà allé en Espagne?; **has he e. seen it?** l'a-t-il jamais vu?; **more than e.** plus que jamais; **nothing e.** jamais rien; **hardly e.** presque jamais; **e. ready** toujours prêt; **the first e.** le tout premier; **e. since (1990)** depuis (1990); **e. since then** depuis lors; **for e.** pour toujours; **the best son e.** le meilleur fils du monde; **e. so sorry** vraiment désolé; *Br* **thank you e. so much** merci mille fois; *Br* **it's e. such a pity** c'est vraiment dommage; **she's e. so nice** elle est tellement gentille; **all she e. does is criticize** elle ne fait que critiquer; **why e. not?** mais pourquoi pas?

evergreen [ˈevəgriːn] *n* arbre *m* à feuilles persistantes

everlasting [evəˈlɑːstɪŋ] *adj* éternel, -elle

evermore [evəˈmɔː(r)] *adv Formal* **for e.** à (tout) jamais

every [ˈevrɪ] *adj* chaque; **e. child** chaque enfant; **e. time** chaque fois (**that** que); **e. one** chacun; **e. single one** tous/toutes (sans exception); **e. second** *or* **other day** tous les deux jours; **her e. gesture** ses moindres gestes; **e. bit as big** tout aussi grand (**as** que); **e. so often, e. now and then** de temps en temps; **to have e. confidence in sb** avoir pleine confiance en qn

everybody [ˈevrɪbɒdɪ] *pron* tout le monde; **e. in turn** chacun à son tour ■ **everyday** *adj (happening, life)* de tous les jours; *(ordinary)* banal *(mpl* -als); **in e. use** d'usage courant ■ **everyone** *pron* = **everybody** ■ **everyplace** *adv Am* = **everywhere** ■ **everything** *pron* tout; **e. I have** tout ce que j'ai ■ **everywhere** *adv* partout; **e. she goes** où qu'elle aille

evict [ɪˈvɪkt] *vt* expulser (**from** de) ■ **eviction** *n* expulsion *f*

evidence [ˈevɪdəns] *n (proof)* preuve(s) *f(pl)*; *(testimony)* témoignage *m*; **to give e.** témoigner (**against** contre); **to accept the e.** se rendre à l'évidence; **to show e. of** donner des signes de; **in e.** *(noticeable)* (bien) en vue

> Note that the French word **évidence** is a false friend and is never a translation for the English word **evidence**. It means **obviousness**.

evident [ˈevɪdənt] *adj* évident (**that** que); **it is e. from…** il apparaît de… (**that** que) ■ **evidently** *adv (clearly)* manifestement; *(apparently)* apparemment

> Note that the French word **évidemment** is a false friend and is never a translation for the English word **evidently**. It means **of course**.

evil [ˈiːvəl] **1** *adj (spell, influence, person)* malfaisant; *(deed, advice, system)* mauvais; *(consequence)* funeste **2** *n* mal *m*; **to speak e.** dire du mal (**about** *or* **of** de)

evocative [ɪˈvɒkətɪv] *adj* évocateur, -trice (**of** de)

evoke [ɪ'vəʊk] *vt (conjure up)* évoquer; *(provoke)* susciter

evolution [iːvə'luːʃən] *n* évolution *f*

evolve [ɪ'vɒlv] **1** *vt (system)* mettre au point **2** *vi (of society, idea)* évoluer; *(of plan)* se développer

ewe [juː] *n* brebis *f*

ex [eks] *n Fam (former partner)* ex *mf*

ex- [eks] *pref* ex-; **ex-wife** ex-femme *f*; **ex-minister** ancien ministre *m*

exacerbate [ɪk'sæsəbeɪt] *vt* aggraver; *(pain)* exacerber

exact [ɪg'zækt] **1** *adj* exact; **to be (more) e. about sth** préciser qch **2** *vt (demand)* exiger (**from** de); *(money, promise)* extorquer (**from** à) ▪ **exactly** *adv* exactement

exacting [ɪg'zæktɪŋ] *adj* exigeant

exaggerate [ɪg'zædʒəreɪt] *vti* exagérer ▪ **exaggeration** [-'reɪʃən] *n* exagération *f*

exalt [ɪg'zɔːlt] *vt Formal* exalter ▪ **exaltation** [-'teɪʃən] *n* exaltation *f* ▪ **exalted** *adj (position, rank)* élevé

exam [ɪg'zæm] *(abbr* **examination)** *n* examen *m*

examine [ɪg'zæmɪn] *vt (evidence, patient, question)* examiner; *(accounts, luggage)* vérifier; *(passport)* contrôler; *(student)* interroger ▪ **exami'nation** *n* examen *m*; *(of accounts)* vérification *f*; *(of passport)* contrôle *m*; **to take** *or* **sit an e.** passer un examen; **class e.** devoir *m* sur table ▪ **examiner** *n (for school exam)* examinateur, -trice *mf*

example [ɪg'zɑːmpəl] *n* exemple *m*; **for e.** par exemple; **to set an e.** *or* **a good e.** donner l'exemple (**to** à); **to set a bad e.** donner le mauvais exemple (**to** à); **to make an e. of sb** punir qn pour l'exemple

exasperate [ɪg'zɑːspəreɪt] *vt* exaspérer; **to get exasperated** s'irriter (**at** de) ▪ **exasperation** [-'reɪʃən] *n* exaspération *f*

excavate ['ekskəveɪt] *vt (dig)* creuser; *(uncover)* déterrer; *(site)* faire des fouilles dans ▪ **excavation** [-'veɪʃən] *n (digging)* creusement *m*; *(archaeological)* fouilles *fpl*

exceed [ɪk'siːd] *vt* dépasser; *(one's powers)* excéder

exceedingly [ɪk'siːdɪŋlɪ] *adv* extrêmement

excel [ɪk'sel] *(pt & pp* **-ll-) 1** *vt (be better than)* surpasser **2** *vi* **to e. in** *or* **at sth** exceller en qch; **to e. at** *or* **in doing sth** exceller à faire qch

Excellency ['eksələnsɪ] *(pl* **-ies)** *n* **Your E.** Votre Excellence *f*

excellent ['eksələnt] *adj* excellent ▪ **excellence** *n* excellence *f* ▪ **excellently** *adv* parfaitement, admirablement

except [ɪk'sept] **1** *prep* sauf, excepté; **e. for** à part; **e. that** sauf que...; **e. if...** sauf si...; **to do nothing e... wait** ne rien faire sinon attendre **2** *vt* excepter (**de** from)

exception [ɪk'sepʃən] *n* exception *f*; **with the e.**

of... à l'exception de...; **to take e. to sth** *(object to)* trouver à redire de qch; *(be hurt by)* s'offenser de qch

exceptional [ɪk'sepʃənəl] *adj* exceptionnel, -elle ▪ **exceptionally** *adv* exceptionnellement

excerpt ['eksɜːpt] *n (from film, book)* extrait *m*

excess ['ekses] *n* excès *m*; *(surplus)* excédent *m*; **to eat/drink to e.** manger/boire à l'excès; **a sum in e. of...** une somme qui dépasse...; **e. calories** des calories *fpl* en trop; **e. fare** supplément *m*; **e. baggage** excédent *m* de bagages

excessive [ɪk'sesɪv] *adj* excessif, -ive ▪ **excessively** *adv (too much)* excessivement; *(very)* extrêmement; *(drink, eat)* à l'excès

exchange [ɪks'tʃeɪndʒ] **1** *n* échange *m*; *Fin (of currency)* change *m*; **(telephone) e.** central *m* téléphonique; **in e.** en échange (**for** de); **e. rate** taux *m* de change **2** *vt* échanger (**for** contre)

Exchequer [ɪks'tʃekə(r)] *n Br Pol* **Chancellor of the E.** ≃ Ministre *m* des Finances

excise ['eksaɪz] *n* taxe *f* (**on** sur)

excitable [ɪk'saɪtəbəl] *adj* nerveux, -euse

excite [ɪk'saɪt] *vt (get worked up)* surexciter; *(enthuse)* passionner; *(provoke, stimulate)* exciter ▪ **excited** *adj (happy)* surexcité; *(nervous)* énervé; *(enthusiastic)* enthousiaste; **to get e. (about)** s'exciter (pour); *(angry)* s'énerver (contre) ▪ **excitedly** [-ɪdlɪ] *adv* avec agitation; *(wait)* avec une impatience fébrile ▪ **exciting** *adj (book, adventure)* passionnant

excitement [ɪk'saɪtmənt] *n* agitation *f*; *(enthusiasm)* enthousiasme *m*; **to cause great e.** faire sensation

exclaim [ɪk'skleɪm] *vti* s'écrier (**that** que) ▪ **exclamation** [eksklə'meɪʃən] *n* exclamation *f*; *Br* **e. mark,** *Am* **e. point** point *m* d'exclamation

exclude [ɪk'skluːd] *vt* exclure (**from** de); *(doubt, suspicion)* écarter; **excluding...** à l'exclusion de... ▪ **exclusion** [-ʒən] *n* exclusion *f* (**from** de)

exclusive [ɪk'skluːsɪv] *adj (right, interest, interview, design)* exclusif, -ive; *(club, group)* fermé; **e. of wine** vin non compris ▪ **exclusively** *adv* exclusivement

excommunicate [ekskə'mjuːnɪkeɪt] *vt* excommunier ▪ **excommunication** [-'keɪʃən] *n* excommunication *f*

excrement ['ekskrəmənt] *n* excrément *m*

excruciating [ɪk'skruːʃɪeɪtɪŋ] *adj* atroce

excursion [ɪk'skɜːʃən] *n* excursion *f*

excuse 1 [ɪk'skjuːs] *n* excuse *f*; **to make an e., to make excuses** se trouver une excuse **2** [ɪk'skjuːz] *vt (forgive, justify)* excuser; *(exempt)* dispenser (**from** de); **e. me for asking** permettez-moi de demander; **e. me!** excusez-moi!, pardon!; **you're excused** *(you may go)* tu peux sortir

ex-directory [eksdaɪ'rektərɪ] *adj Br* **to be e.** être sur (la) liste rouge

execute ['eksɪkjuːt] vt (prisoner, order) exécuter; (plan) mettre à exécution ▪ **exe'cution** n exécution f ▪ **exe'cutioner** n bourreau m

executive [ɪɡ'zekjʊtɪv] **1** adj (job) de cadre; (car) de luxe; Br **e. director** directeur m administratif **2** n (person) cadre m; (committee) bureau m. the **e.** (part of government) l'exécutif m; **senior e.** cadre m supérieur; **sales e.** cadre commercial

exemplary [ɪɡ'zemplərɪ] adj exemplaire

exemplify [ɪɡ'zemplɪfaɪ] (pt & pp -ied) vt illustrer

exempt [ɪɡ'zempt] **1** adj (person) dispensé (**from** de) **2** vt dispenser (**from** de; **from doing** de faire) ▪ **exemption** n dispense f (**from** de)

exercise ['eksəsaɪz] **1** n exercice m; **e. bike** vélo m d'appartement; **e. book** cahier m **2** vt exercer; (dog, horse) promener; (caution, restraint) user de **3** vi faire de l'exercice

exert [ɪɡ'zɜːt] vt exercer; (force) employer; **to e. oneself** se donner du mal ▪ **exertion** n effort m; (of force) emploi m

exhale [eks'heɪl] vi expirer

exhaust [ɪɡ'zɔːst] **1** n **e. (fumes)** gaz mpl d'échappement; **e. (pipe)** tuyau m d'échappement **2** vt (person, resources) épuiser ▪ **exhausted** adj (person, resources) épuisé ▪ **exhausting** adj épuisant

exhaustion [ɪɡ'zɔːstʃən] n épuisement m

exhaustive [ɪɡ'zɔːstɪv] adj (list) exhaustif, -ive; (analysis) détaillé; (inquiry) approfondi

exhibit [ɪɡ'zɪbɪt] **1** n objet m exposé; (in court) pièce f à conviction **2** vt (put on display) exposer; (ticket, courage) montrer ▪ **exhibition** [eksɪ'bɪʃən] n exposition f; Fam **to make an e. of oneself** se donner en spectacle ▪ **exhibitionist** [eksɪ'bɪʃənɪst] n exhibitionniste mf

> Note that the French word **exhibition** is a false friend and is never a translation for the English word **exhibition**. It means **flaunting**.

exhibitor [ɪɡ'zɪbɪtə(r)] n exposant, -ante mf

exhilarate [ɪɡ'zɪləreɪt] vt stimuler; (of air) vivifier; (make happy) rendre fou (f folle) de joie ▪ **exhilarating** adj (experience) grisant; (air) vivifiant ▪ **exhila'ration** n joie f

exhort [ɪɡ'zɔːt] vt exhorter (**to do sth** à faire qch)

exhume [eks'hjuːm] vt exhumer

exile ['eɡzaɪl] **1** n (banishment) exil m; (person) exilé, -ée mf **2** vt exiler

exist [ɪɡ'zɪst] vi exister; (live) survivre (**on** avec) ▪ **existing** adj (situation, circumstances) actuel, -uelle; (law) existant

existence [ɪɡ'zɪstəns] n existence f; **to come into e.** être créé; **to be in e.** exister

exit ['eksɪt, 'eɡzɪt] **1** n sortie f **2** vi (leave) & Comptr sortir

exodus ['eksədəs] n inv exode m

exonerate [ɪɡ'zɒnəreɪt] vt (from blame) disculper (**from** de)

exorbitant [ɪɡ'zɔːbɪtənt] adj exorbitant

exorcize ['eksɔːsaɪz] vt exorciser ▪ **exorcism** [-sɪzəm] n exorcisme m

exotic [ɪɡ'zɒtɪk] adj exotique

expand [ɪk'spænd] **1** vt (production, influence) accroître; (knowledge) étendre; (trade, range, idea) développer; (mind) élargir **2** vi (of knowledge) s'étendre; (of trade) se développer; (of production) augmenter; (of gas) se dilater; **to e. on** développer; (**fast** or **rapidly**) **expanding sector** secteur m en (pleine) expansion

expanse [ɪk'spæns] n étendue f

expansion [ɪk'spænʃən] n (economic, colonial) expansion f; (of trade) développement m; (of production) augmentation f; (of gas) dilatation f ▪ **expansionism** n expansionnisme m

expansive [ɪk'spænsɪv] adj (person) expansif, -ive

expatriate [Br eks'pætrɪət, Am eks'peɪtrɪət] adj & n expatrié, -iée (mf)

expect [ɪk'spekt] vt (anticipate) s'attendre à; (think) penser (**that** que); (await) attendre; **to e. sth from sb/sth** attendre qch de qn/qch; **to e. to do sth** compter faire qch; **to e. that...** (anticipate) s'attendre à ce que... (+ subjunctive); **to e. sb to do sth** (anticipate) s'attendre à ce que qn fasse qch; (require) attendre de qn qu'il/elle fasse qch; **to be expecting a baby** attendre un enfant; **as expected** comme prévu

expectancy [ɪk'spektənsɪ] n attente f

expectant [ɪk'spektənt] adj impatient; **e. mother** future mère f

expectation [ekspek'teɪʃən] n espérance f; **in the e. of sth** dans l'attente de qch; **contrary to all expectations** contre toute attente; **to come up to expectations** se montrer à la hauteur

expedient [ɪks'piːdɪənt] **1** adj opportun **2** n expédient m

expedition [ekspɪ'dɪʃən] n expédition f

expel [ɪk'spel] (pt & pp -ll-) vt expulser (**from** de); (from school) renvoyer

expend [ɪk'spend] vt (energy, money) dépenser ▪ **expendable** adj (person) qui n'est pas irremplaçable; (troops) que l'on peut sacrifier

expenditure [ɪk'spendɪtʃə(r)] n (of money, energy) dépense f

expense [ɪk'spens] n frais mpl, dépense f; Com **expenses** frais mpl; **to go to some e.** faire des frais; **at the e. of sb/sth** aux dépens de qn/qch; **to laugh at sb's e.** rire aux dépens de qn; **e. account** note f de frais

expensive [ɪk'spensɪv] adj (goods, hotel, shop)

cher (*f* chère); *(tastes)* de luxe; **to be e.** coûter cher; **an e. mistake** une faute qui coûte cher ■**expensively** *adv* e. **dressed/furnished** habillé/meublé luxueusement; **to do sth e.** faire qch à grands frais

experience [ɪkˈspɪərɪəns] **1** *n* expérience *f*; **from** *or* **by e.** par expérience; **I've had e. of driving** j'ai déjà conduit **2** *vt (emotion)* ressentir; *(hunger, success)* connaître; *(difficulty, remorse)* éprouver ■**experienced** *adj (person)* expérimenté; *(eye, ear)* exercé; **to be e. in sth** s'y connaître en qch

experiment 1 [ɪkˈsperɪmənt] *n* expérience *f* **2** [ɪkˈsperɪment] *vi* expérimenter (**on** sur); **to e. with sth** *(technique, drugs)* essayer qch ■**experimental** [-ˈmentəl] *adj* expérimental

expert [ˈekspɜːt] **1** *n* expert *m* (**on** *or* **in** en) **2** *adj* expert (**in sth** en qch; **in** *or* **at doing** à faire); **e. advice** le conseil d'un expert; **an e. eye** l'œil d'un connaisseur ■**expertise** [-ˈtiːz] *n* compétence *f* (**in** en) ■**expertly** *adv* habilement

expiration [ekspəˈreɪʃən] *n Am* = **expiry**

expire [ɪkˈspaɪə(r)] *vi* expirer ■**expired** *adj (ticket, passport)* périmé

expiry [ɪkˈspaɪərɪ] *(Am* **expiration** [ekspəˈreɪʃən]) *n* expiration *f*; **e. date** *(on ticket)* date *f* d'expiration; *(on product)* date limite d'utilisation

explain [ɪkˈspleɪn] *vt* expliquer (**to** à; **that** que); *(reasons)* exposer; *(mystery)* éclaircir; **e. yourself!** explique-toi!; **to e. sth away** justifier qch ■**explainable** *adj* explicable

explanation [ekspləˈneɪʃən] *n* explication *f*

explanatory [ɪkˈsplænətərɪ] *adj* explicatif, -ive

expletive [ɪkˈspliːtɪv] *n* juron *m*

explicit [ɪkˈsplɪsɪt] *adj* explicite ■**explicitly** *adv* explicitement

explode [ɪkˈspləʊd] **1** *vt (bomb)* faire exploser; *Fig (theory)* discréditer **2** *vi (of bomb)* exploser; *Fig* **to e. with laughter** éclater de rire

exploit 1 [ˈeksplɔɪt] *n* exploit *m* **2** [ɪkˈsplɔɪt] *vt (person, land)* exploiter ■**exploitation** [eksplɔɪˈteɪʃən] *n* exploitation *f*

exploratory [ɪkˈsplɒrətərɪ] *adj (trip)* d'exploration; *(talks, step, surgery)* exploratoire

explore [ɪkˈsplɔː(r)] *vt* explorer; *(causes, possibilities)* examiner ■**exploration** [eksplə-ˈreɪʃən] *n* exploration *f*

explorer [ɪkˈsplɔːrə(r)] *n* explorateur, -trice *mf*

explosion [ɪkˈspləʊʒən] *n* explosion *f*

explosive [ɪkˈspləʊsɪv] **1** *adj (weapon, situation, question)* explosif, -ive **2** *n* explosif *m*

exponent [ɪkˈspəʊnənt] *n (of theory)* avocat, -ate *mf*; *(of music)* interprète *m*

export 1 [ˈekspɔːt] *n (activity)* exportation *f*; **e. goods/permit** marchandises *fpl*/permis *m* d'exportation **2** [ɪkˈspɔːt] *vt* exporter (**to** vers; **from** de) ■**exporter** *n* exportateur, -trice *mf*; *(country)* pays *m* exportateur

expose [ɪkˈspəʊz] *vt (to air, cold, danger)* & *Phot* exposer (**to** à); *(wire)* dénuder; *(plot, scandal)* révéler; *(criminal)* démasquer; **to e. oneself** *(in public place)* s'exhiber ■**exposition** [ekspəˈzɪʃən] *n* exposition *f*

exposure [ɪkˈspəʊʒə(r)] *n* exposition *f* (**to** à); *(of plot)* révélation *f*; *Phot* pose *f*; **to die of e.** mourir de froid; **to get a lot of e.** *(in the media)* faire l'objet d'une importante couverture médiatique

expound [ɪkˈspaʊnd] *vt Formal* exposer

express¹ [ɪkˈspres] *vt* exprimer; **to e. oneself** s'exprimer

express² [ɪkˈspres] **1** *adj (letter, delivery)* exprès *inv*; *(train)* rapide, express *inv*; *(order)* exprès; **with the e. purpose of doing sth 2** *adv (send)* en exprès **3** *n (train)* rapide *m*, express *m inv* ■**expressly** *adv (forbid)* expressément

expression [ɪkˈspreʃən] *n* expression *f*; **an e. of gratitude** un témoignage de gratitude

expressive [ɪkˈspresɪv] *adj* expressif, -ive

expressway [ɪkˈspresweɪ] *n Am* autoroute *f*

expulsion [ɪkˈspʌlʃən] *n* expulsion *f*; *(from school)* renvoi *m*

expurgate [ˈekspəgeɪt] *vt* expurger

exquisite [ɪkˈskwɪzɪt] *adj* exquis ■**exquisite-ly** *adv* d'une façon exquise

ex-serviceman [eks-ˈsɜːvɪsmən] *(pl* **-men***)* *n Br* ancien combattant *m*

extant [ˈekstənt, ekˈstænt] *adj* qui existe encore

extend [ɪkˈstend] **1** *vt (in space)* étendre; *(in time)* prolonger (**by** de); *(hand)* tendre (**to sb** à qn); *(house)* agrandir; *(knowledge)* accroître; *(help, thanks)* offrir (**to** à); **to e. an invitation to** faire une invitation à **2** *vi (in space)* s'étendre (**to** jusqu'à); *(in time)* se prolonger

extension [ɪkˈstenʃən] *n (for table)* rallonge *f*; *(to building)* annexe *f*; *(for telephone)* poste *m*; *(in time)* prolongation *f*; *(for essay)* délai *m* supplémentaire; *(in space)* prolongement *m*; *(of meaning, powers, strike)* extension *f*

extensive [ɪkˈstensɪv] *adj (powers, forests)* vaste; *(repairs, damage)* important; **to make e. use of sth** faire un usage considérable de qch ■**extensively** *adv (very much)* énormément; **to use sth e.** se servir beaucoup de qch

extent [ɪkˈstent] *n (scope)* étendue *f*; *(size)* importance *f*; **to a large** *or* **great e.** dans une large mesure; **to some e.** *or* **a certain e.** dans une certaine mesure; **to such an e. that...** à tel point que...

extenuating [ɪkˈstenjʊeɪtɪŋ] *adj* **e. circum-stances** circonstances *fpl* atténuantes

exterior [ɪkˈstɪərɪə(r)] *adj & n* extérieur *(m)*

exterminate [ɪkˈstɜːmɪneɪt] *vt* exterminer; *(disease)* éradiquer ■**extermi'nation** *n* extermination *f*; *(of disease)* éradication *f*

external [ɪkˈstɜːnəl] *adj (trade, debt, event)*

extérieur; *(wall)* externe; **for e. use** *(on medicine)* à usage externe; *Pol* **e. affairs** affaires *fpl* étrangères

extinct [ɪk'stɪŋkt] *adj (volcano)* éteint; *(species, animal)* disparu ▪ **extinction** *n* extinction *f*

extinguish [ɪk'stɪŋgwɪʃ] *vt* éteindre ▪ **extinguisher** *n* **(fire)** e. extincteur *m*

extol [ɪk'stəʊl] *(pt & pp* **-ll-)** *vt (virtues)* exalter; *(beauty)* chanter

extort [ɪk'stɔːt] *vt (money)* extorquer **(from** à); *(consent)* arracher **(from** à) ▪ **extortion** *n (crime)* extorsion *f* de fonds

extortionate [ɪk'stɔːʃənət] *adj* exorbitant; **that's e.!** c'est du vol!

extra ['ekstrə] **1** *adj (additional)* supplémentaire; **to be e.** *(spare)* être en trop; *(cost more)* être en supplément; **postage is e.** les frais d'envoi sont en sus; **e. care** un soin tout particulier; **e. charge** supplément *m*; *Sport* **e. time** prolongation *f* **2** *adv (more than usual)* extrêmement; **to pay e.** payer un supplément; **wine costs** *or* **is 5 euros e.** il y a un supplément de 5 euros pour le vin; **e. large** *(clothing)* grand patron **3** *n (perk)* à-côté *m*; *(actor in film)* figurant, -ante *mf*; *(on bill)* supplément *m*; **an optional e.** *(for car)* un accessoire en option

extra- ['ekstrə] *pref* extra- ▪ **extra-dry** *adj (champagne)* brut ▪ **extra-fine** *adj* extra-fin ▪ **extra-special** *adj (occasion)* très spécial; *(care)* tout particulier *(f* toute particulière*)* ▪ **extra-strong** *adj* extra-fort

extract 1 ['ekstrækt] *n* extrait *m* **2** [ɪk'strækt] *vt* extraire **(from** de); *(promise)* arracher **(from** à); *(information, money)* soutirer **(from** à) ▪ **extraction** [ɪk'strækʃən] *n* **(a)** *(removal)* extraction *f* **(b)** *(descent)* origine *f*

extra-curricular [ekstrəkə'rɪkjʊlə(r)] *adj Br Sch* extrascolaire

extradite ['ekstrədaɪt] *vt* extrader ▪ **extradition** [-'dɪʃən] *n* extradition *f*

extramarital [ekstrə'mærɪtəl] *adj* extraconjugal

extramural [ekstrə'mjʊərəl] *adj Br Univ* de formation continue

extraneous [ɪk'streɪnɪəs] *adj Formal* accessoire

extranet ['ekstrənet] *n Comptr* extranet *m*

extraordinary [ɪk'strɔːdənərɪ] *adj* extraordinaire ▪ **extraordinarily** *adv* extraordinairement

extravagant [ɪk'strævəgənt] *adj (behaviour,*

idea) extravagant; *(wasteful)* dépensier, -ière; *(tastes)* dispendieux, -ieuse ▪ **extravagance** *n (of behaviour)* extravagance *f*; *(wastefulness)* gaspillage *m*; *(thing bought)* folie *f*

extravaganza [ɪkstrævə'gænzə] *n* spectacle *m* somptueux

extreme [ɪk'striːm] **1** *adj* extrême; **at the e. end** à l'extrémité; **of e. importance** de première importance; **e. sports** sports *mpl* extrêmes **2** *n* extrême *m*; **to carry** *or* **take sth to extremes** pousser qch à l'extrême; **extremes of temperature** températures *fpl* extrêmes ▪ **extremely** *adv* extrêmement

extremist [ɪk'striːmɪst] *adj & n* extrémiste *(mf)* ▪ **extremism** *n* extrémisme *m*

extremity [ɪk'stremɪtɪ] *(pl* **-ies)** *n* extrémité *f*

extricate ['ekstrɪkeɪt] *vt (free)* dégager **(from** de); **to e. oneself from a difficulty** se tirer d'une situation difficile

extrovert ['ekstrəvɜːt] *n* extraverti, -ie *mf*

exuberant [ɪg'zjuːbərənt] *adj* exubérant ▪ **exuberance** *n* exubérance *f*

exude [ɪg'zjuːd] *vt (health, honesty)* respirer

eye [aɪ] **1** *n (pl* **eyes)** œil *m*; **before my very eyes** sous mes yeux; **as far as the e. can see** à perte de vue; **up to one's eyes in debt** endetté jusqu'au cou; **up to one's eyes in work** débordé de travail; **to have one's e. on sth** avoir qch en vue; **to keep an e. on sb/sth** surveiller qn/qch; **to lay** *or* **set eyes on sth** poser les yeux sur qch; **to take one's eyes off sb/sth** quitter qn/qch des yeux; **to catch sb's e.** attirer l'attention de qn; **to make e. contact with sb** regarder qn dans les yeux; **keep your eyes open!, keep an e. out!** ouvre l'œil!; **we don't see e. to e.** nous ne voyons pas les choses du même œil **2** *vt* regarder ▪ **eyeball** *n* globe *m* oculaire ▪ **eyebrow** *n* sourcil *m* ▪ **eye-catching** *adj (title)* accrocheur, -euse ▪ **eye doctor** *n Am* opticien, -ienne *mf* ▪ **eye drops** *npl* gouttes *fpl* (pour les yeux) ▪ **eyelash** *n* cil *m* ▪ **eyelid** *n* paupière *f* ▪ **eyeliner** *n* eye-liner *m* ▪ **eye-opener** *n* **to be an e. for sb** être une révélation pour qn ▪ **eye-piece** *n (of telescope)* oculaire *m* ▪ **eyeshadow** *n* fard *m* à paupières ▪ **eyesight** *n* vue *f* ▪ **eyesore** *n* horreur *f* ▪ **eyestrain** *n* fatigue *f* oculaire ▪ **eye-wash** *n* collyre *m*; *Fam (nonsense)* sottises *fpl* ▪ **eye-witness** *n* témoin *m* oculaire

▸ **eye up** *vt sep* reluquer

ezine, e-zine ['iːziːn] *n Comptr* ezine *m*, e-zine *m*

F, f [ef] n (**a**) (letter) F, f m inv (**b**) Mus fa m

fab [fæb] adj Br Fam super inv, génial

fable ['feɪbəl] n fable f

fabric ['fæbrɪk] n (cloth) tissu m, étoffe f; (of building) structure f; Fig **the f. of society** le tissu social

> Note that the French word **fabrique** is a false friend and is never a translation for the English word **fabric**. Its most common meaning is **factory**.

fabricate ['fæbrɪkeɪt] vt fabriquer ▪**fabri-'cation** n fabrication f

fabulous ['fæbjʊləs] adj (legendary, incredible) fabuleux, -euse

façade [fə'sɑːd] n (of building) & Fig (appearance) façade f

face [feɪs] **1** n (of person) visage m, figure f; (expression) mine f; (of clock) cadran m; (of building) façade f; (of cube, mountain) face f; (of cliff) paroi f; **the f. of the earth** la surface de la terre; **she laughed in my f.** elle m'a ri au nez; **to show one's f.** se montrer; **f. down(wards)** (person) face contre terre; (thing) à l'envers; **to f.** face à face; **in the f. of** devant; (despite) en dépit de; **to save/lose f.** sauver/perdre la face; **to make or pull faces** faire des grimaces; **to tell sb sth to his/her f.** dire qch à qn en face; **f. powder** poudre f; **f. value** (of stamp, coin) valeur f; Fig **to take sth at f. value** prendre qch au pied de la lettre; Br **f. cloth** gant m de toilette

2 vt (danger, enemy, problem) faire face à; **to f., to be facing** (be opposite) être en face de; (of window, door, room) donner sur; **faced with** (prospect, problem) confronté à; (defeat) menacé par; (bill) contraint à payer; **he can't f. leaving** il n'a pas le courage de partir; **let's f. it** soyons réalistes

3 vi **to f. north** (of building) être orienté au nord; **to f. towards** (of person) se tourner vers; **to f. up to** (danger, problem) faire face à; (fact) accepter

faceless ['feɪsləs] adj anonyme

face-lift ['feɪslɪft] n (by surgeon) lifting m; (of building) ravalement m

facet ['fæsɪt] n facette f

facetious [fə'siːʃəs] adj (person) facétieux, -ieuse; **don't be f.!** ne plaisante pas!

facial ['feɪʃəl] **1** adj (expression) du visage **2** n soin m du visage

facile [Br 'fæsaɪl, Am 'fæsəl] adj Pej facile

facilitate [fə'sɪlɪteɪt] vt faciliter

facility [fə'sɪlɪtɪ] (pl -ies) n (ease) facilité f; Comptr option f ▪**facilities** npl (for sports, cooking) équipements mpl; (in harbour, airport) installations fpl; **shopping f.** magasins mpl; **transport f.** moyens mpl de transports; **special f.** conditions fpl spéciales (**for** pour)

fact [fækt] n fait m; **as a matter of f., in f.** en fait; **it's a f.** c'est une réalité; **is that a f.?** c'est vrai?; **to distinguish f. from fiction** distinguer la fiction de la réalité

faction ['fækʃən] n faction f

factor ['fæktə(r)] n facteur m

factory ['fæktərɪ] (pl -ies) n (large) usine f; (small) fabrique f; **arms/porcelain f.** manufacture f d'armes/de porcelaine; **f. farming** élevage m industriel

factual ['fæktʃʊəl] adj basé sur les faits

faculty ['fækəltɪ] (pl -ies) n (of mind, in university) faculté f

fad [fæd] n (fashion) mode f (**for** de); (personal habit) marotte f

fade [feɪd] **1** vt faner **2** vi (of flower, material, colour) se faner; (of light) baisser; **to f. (away)** (of memory, smile) s'effacer; (of sound) s'affaiblir; (of person) dépérir

fag [fæg] n (**a**) Br Fam (cigarette) clope m ou f; **f. end** mégot m (**b**) Am very Fam Pej (homosexual) pédé m

faggot ['fægət] n (**a**) Br (meatball) boulette f de viande (**b**) Am very Fam Pej (homosexual) pédé m

fail [feɪl] **1** n **without f.** sans faute

2 vt (exam) échouer à; (candidate) recaler; **to f. sb** (let down) laisser tomber qn, décevoir qn; **words f. me** les mots me manquent; **to f. to do** (forget) manquer de faire; (not be able) ne pas arriver à faire; **I f. to see the reason** je n'en vois pas la raison

3 vi (of person, plan) échouer; (of business) faire faillite; (of health, sight, light) baisser; (of memory, strength) défaillir; (of brakes) lâcher; (of engine) tomber en panne; (run short) (of supplies) manquer; (of gas, electricity) être coupé; **to f. in an exam** échouer à un examen; **to f. in one's duty** manquer à son devoir ▪**failed** adj (attempt, poet) raté ▪**failing 1** n (fault) défaut m **2** prep à défaut de; **f. this, f. that** à défaut

failure ['feɪljə(r)] n échec m; (of business) faillite f; (of engine, machine) panne f; (of gas) coupure f; (person) raté, -ée mf; **her f. to leave** le fait qu'elle ne soit pas partie; **to end in f.** se solder par un échec

faint [feɪnt] **1** (**-er, -est**) adj (weak) (voice, trace, breeze, hope) faible; (colour) pâle; (idea) vague; **I haven't got the faintest idea** je n'en ai pas la moindre idée; **to feel f.** se sentir mal **2** vi s'évanouir (**with** or **from** de); **she fainted with hunger** elle s'est évanouie tellement elle avait faim ▪**faintly** adv (weakly) faiblement; (slightly) légèrement

faint-hearted [feɪnt'hɑːtɪd] adj timoré

fair[1] [feə(r)] n (trade fair) foire f; Br (funfair) fête f foraine ▪**fairground** n parc m d'attractions

fair[2] [feə(r)] **1** (**-er, -est**) adj (**a**) (just) juste; (game, fight) loyal; **she's f. to him** elle est juste envers lui; **to beat sb f. and square** battre qn à plates coutures; **f. play** fair-play m inv; **that's not f. play!** ce n'est pas du jeu!; **f. enough!** (OK) d'accord!; (rightly so) ça se comprend!; **f. trade** commerce m équitable (**b**) (rather good) assez bon (f bonne); (price) raisonnable; **a f. amount (of)** (a lot) pas mal (de); **f. copy** copie f au propre (**c**) (wind) favorable; (weather) beau (f belle)

2 adv (fight) loyalement; **to play f.** jouer franc jeu ▪**fairly** adv (**a**) (treat) équitablement; (act, fight, get) loyalement (**b**) (rather) assez; **f. sure** presque sûr ▪'**fair-'minded** adj équitable ▪**fairness**[1] n justice f; (of person, decision) impartialité f; **in all f.** en toute justice ▪'**fair-'sized** adj assez grand

fair[3] [feə(r)] adj (hair, person) blond; (complexion, skin) clair ▪'**fair-'haired** adj blond ▪**fairness**[2] n (of hair) blondeur f; (of skin) pâleur f ▪'**fair-'skinned** adj à la peau claire

fairy ['feərɪ] (pl **-ies**) n fée f; Br **f. lights** guirlande f lumineuse (de sapin de Noël) ▪**fairytale** n conte m de fées

faith [feɪθ] n foi f; **to be of the Catholic/etc f.** être de religion catholique/etc; **to have f. in sb** avoir foi en qn; **to put one's f. in** (justice, medicine) avoir foi en; **in good/bad f.** (act) de bonne/mauvaise foi; **f. healer** guérisseur, -euse mf

faithful ['feɪθfəl] adj fidèle ▪**faithfully** adv fidèlement; Br **yours f.,** Am **f. yours** (in letter) veuillez agréer l'expression de mes sentiments distingués ▪**faithfulness** n fidélité f

fake [feɪk] **1** adj faux (f fausse); (elections) truqué **2** n (object) faux m; (person) imposteur m **3** vt (signature) contrefaire **4** vi (pretend) faire semblant

falcon ['fɔːlkən] n faucon m

fall [fɔːl] **1** n (of person, snow, city) chute f; (in price, demand) baisse f; **falls** (waterfall) chutes fpl; Am **the f.** (season) l'automne m

2 (pt **fell,** pp **fallen**) vi tomber; (of price, temperature) baisser; **the dollar is falling** le dollar est en baisse; **her face fell** son visage se rembrunit; **to f. into** (hole, trap) tomber dans; (habit) prendre; **to f. into several categories** se diviser en plusieurs catégories; **to f. off a bicycle** tomber d'une bicyclette; **to f. off** or **down a ladder** tomber d'une échelle; **to f. out of a window** tomber d'une fenêtre; **to f. over sth** tomber en butant contre qch; **to f. on a Monday** tomber un lundi; **the responsibility falls on you** c'est à vous qu'en incombe la responsabilité; **to f. short of sb's expectations** ne pas répondre à l'attente de qn; **to f. short of being** être loin d'être; **to f. victim** devenir victime (**to** de); **to f. asleep** s'endormir; **to f. ill** tomber malade; **to f. due** échoir

▶ **fall apart** vi (of book, machine) tomber en morceaux; (of group) se désagréger; (of person) s'effondrer

▶ **fall away** vi (come off) tomber; (of numbers) diminuer

▶ **fall back on** vt insep (resort to) se rabattre sur

▶ **fall behind** vi (stay behind) rester en arrière; (in work, payments) prendre du retard

▶ **fall down** vi tomber; (of building) s'effondrer

▶ **fall for** vt insep (person) tomber amoureux, -euse de; (trick) se laisser prendre à

▶ **fall in** vi (collapse) s'écrouler

▶ **fall in with** vt insep (tally with) cadrer avec; (agree to) accepter

▶ **fall off** vi (come off) tomber; (of numbers) diminuer

▶ **fall out** vi (quarrel) se brouiller (**with** avec)

▶ **fall over** vi tomber; (of table, vase) se renverser

▶ **fall through** vi (of plan) tomber à l'eau, échouer

fallacious [fə'leɪʃəs] adj faux (f fausse) ▪**fallacy** ['fæləsɪ] (pl **-ies**) n erreur f

fallen ['fɔːlən] **1** pp of **fall 2** adj tombé; (angel) déchu; (woman) perdu; **f. leaf** feuille f morte

fallible ['fæləbəl] adj faillible

fallout ['fɔːlaʊt] n (radioactive) retombées fpl; **f. shelter** abri m antiatomique

fallow ['fæləʊ] adj (land, fields) en jachère

false [fɔːls] adj faux (f fausse); **f. alarm** fausse alerte f; **f. bottom** double fond m; **f. friend** faux ami m; **f. teeth** dentier m ▪**falsehood** n mensonge m ▪**falseness** n fausseté f

falsify ['fɔːlsɪfaɪ] (pt & pp **-ied**) vt (forge) falsifier

falter ['fɔːltə(r)] vi (of step, courage) vaciller; (of voice, speaker) hésiter

fame [feɪm] n renommée f ▪**famed** adj renommé (**for** pour)

familiar [fə'mɪljə(r)] adj (well-known) familier, -ière (**to** à); **to be f. with sb/sth** bien connaître qn/qch; **I'm f. with her voice** sa voix m'est familière; **to make oneself f. with** se familiariser avec; **he looks f. (to me)** je l'ai déjà vu (quelque part)

familiarity [fəmɪlɪˈærətɪ] *n* familiarité *f* (**with** avec); *(of event, sight)* caractère *m* familier

familiarize [fəˈmɪljəraɪz] *vt* familiariser (**with** avec); **to f. oneself with sth** se familiariser avec qch

family [ˈfæmɪlɪ] **1** *(pl* **-ies)** *n* famille *f*; **to start a f.** fonder une famille **2** *adj (name, doctor, jewels)* de famille; *(planning, problems, business)* familial; **f. friend** ami *m*/amie *f* de la famille; **f. man** homme *m* attaché à sa famille; **f. tree** arbre *m* généalogique

famine [ˈfæmɪn] *n* famine *f*

famished [ˈfæmɪʃt] *adj* affamé

famous [ˈfeɪməs] **1** *adj* célèbre (**for** pour) **2** *npl* **the f.** les célébrités *fpl* ▪**famously** *adv Fam (very well)* rudement bien

fan¹ [fæn] **1** *n (held in hand)* éventail *m (pl* -ails); *(mechanical)* ventilateur *m*; **f. belt** *(of vehicle)* courroie *f* de ventilateur; **f. heater** radiateur *m* soufflant **2** *(pt & pp* **-nn-)** *vt (person)* éventer; *(fire, quarrel)* attiser **3** *vi* **to f. out** se déployer (en éventail)

fan² [fæn] *n (of person)* fan *mf*; *(of team)* supporter *m*; **to be a jazz/sports f.** être passionné de jazz/de sport; **f. mail** courrier *m* des admirateurs

fanatic [fəˈnætɪk] *n* fanatique *mf* ▪**fanatical** *adj* fanatique ▪**fanaticism** *n* fanatisme *m*

fanciful [ˈfænsɪfəl] *adj* fantaisiste

fancy [ˈfænsɪ] **1** *(pl* **-ies)** *n (imagination)* imagination *f*; *(whim)* fantaisie *f*; **to take a f. to sb** se prendre d'affection pour qn; **I took a f. to it, it took my f.** j'en ai eu envie; **when the f. takes me** quand ça me chante **2** *adj (jewels, hat, button)* fantaisie *inv*; *(car)* de luxe; *(house, restaurant)* chic *inv*; *(idea)* fantaisiste; *Br* **f. dress** déguisement *m*; *Br* **f. dress party** soirée *f* déguisée **3** *(pt & pp* **-ied)** *vt* **(a)** *Br Fam (want)* avoir envie de; *(like)* aimer; **he fancies her** elle lui plaît; *Fam* **to f. oneself as a writer** se prendre pour un écrivain; *Fam Pej* **she fancies herself!** elle ne se prend pas pour n'importe qui! **(b) to f. that...** *(imagine)* se figurer que...; *(think)* croire que...; *Fam* **f. that!** tiens (donc)!; *Fam* **f. meeting you here!** si je m'attendais à vous rencontrer ici!

fanfare [ˈfænfeə(r)] *n* fanfare *f*

fang [fæŋ] *n (of dog, wolf)* croc *m*; *(of snake)* crochet *m*

fanny [ˈfænɪ] *(pl* **-ies)** *n Am Fam (buttocks)* derrière *m*; **f. pack** banane *f*

fantastic [fænˈtæstɪk] *adj* fantastique; *(price)* astronomique; *(wealth, size)* prodigieux, -ieuse; *(unbelievable)* absurde; *Fam (excellent)* formidable

fantasy [ˈfæntəsɪ] *(pl* **-ies)** *n (dream)* chimère *f*; *(fanciful, sexual)* fantasme *m*; *(imagination)* fantaisie *f* ▪**fantasize** *vi* fantasmer (**about** sur)

Note that the French word **fantaisie** is a false friend and is rarely a translation for the English word **fantasy**.

FAQ [efeɪˈkjuː] *(abbr* **frequently asked questions)** *n Comptr* FAQ *f inv*

far [fɑː(r)] **1** (**farther** *or* **further, farthest** *or* **furthest)** *adj* **the f. side/end** l'autre côté/bout; **it's a f. cry from...** ça n'a rien à voir avec...; **the F. East** l'Extrême-Orient *m*; *Pol* **the f. left/right** l'extrême gauche *f*/droite *f*

2 *adv* **(a)** *(in distance)* loin (**from** de); **how f. is it to Toulouse?** combien y a-t-il d'ici à Toulouse?; **is it f. to...?** sommes-nous/suis-je/ *etc* loin de...?; **how f. are you going?** jusqu'où vas-tu?; **how f. has he got with his work?** où en est-il dans son travail?; **as f. as** jusqu'à; **as f.** *or* **so f. as I know** autant que je sache; **as f.** *or* **so f. as I'm concerned** en ce qui me concerne; **f. from doing sth** loin de faire qch; **f. from it!** loin de là!; **f. away** *or* **off** au loin; **to be f. away** être loin (**from** de); **f. and wide** partout

(b) *(in time)* **as f. back as 1820** dès 1820; **so f.** jusqu'ici; **so f. so good** jusqu'ici, tout va bien; **by f.** de loin; **f. into the night** jusqu'à une heure très avancée de la nuit

(c) *(much)* **f. bigger/more expensive** beaucoup plus grand/plus cher (*f* chère) (**than** que); **f. more/better** beaucoup plus/ mieux (**than** que); **f. advanced** très avancé ▪**far-away** *adj (country)* lointain; *(look)* perdu dans le vague ▪**'far-'fetched** *adj* tiré par les cheveux ▪**'far-'flung, 'far-'off** *adj (country)* lointain ▪**'far-'reaching** *adj* de grande portée ▪**'far-'sighted** *adj* clairvoyant

farce [fɑːs] *n* farce *f* ▪**farcical** *adj* grotesque

fare [feə(r)] **1** *n* **(a)** *(for journey) (in train, bus)* prix *m* du billet; *(in taxi)* prix de la course; *(taxi passenger)* client, -iente *mf* **(b)** *Formal (food)* chère *f* **2** *vi (manage)* se débrouiller

farewell [feəˈwel] **1** *n & exclam* adieu *(m)* **2** *adj (party, speech)* d'adieu

farm [fɑːm] **1** *n* ferme *f*; **to work on a f.** travailler dans une ferme **2** *adj (worker, produce)* agricole; **f. land** terres *fpl* cultivées **3** *vt* cultiver **4** *vi* être agriculteur, -trice ▪**farmer** *n* fermier, -ière *mf*, agriculteur, -trice *mf* ▪**farmhand** *n* ouvrier, -ière *mf* agricole ▪**farmhouse** *n* ferme *f* ▪**farming** *n* agriculture *f*; *(breeding)* élevage *m* ▪**farm worker** *n* ouvrier, -ière *mf* agricole ▪**farmyard** *n* cour *f* de ferme

fart [fɑːt] *Fam* **1** *n* pet *m* **2** *vi* péter

farther [ˈfɑːðə(r)] **1** *comparative of* **far 2** *adj* **at the f. end of** à l'autre bout de **3** *adv* plus loin; **nothing is f. from the truth** rien n'est plus éloigné de la vérité; **f. forward** plus avancé; **to get f. away** s'éloigner ▪ **farthest 1** *superlative of* **far 2** *adj* le plus éloigné **3** *adv* le plus loin

fascinate ['fæsɪneɪt] *vt* fasciner ▪ **fascinating** *adj* fascinant ▪ **fasci'nation** *n* fascination *f*

fascism ['fæʃɪzəm] *n* fascisme *m* ▪ **fascist** *adj & n* fasciste (*mf*)

fashion ['fæʃən] **1** *n* (**a**) (*in clothes*) mode *f*; **in f.** à la mode; **out of f.** démodé; **f. designer** styliste *mf*; (*famous*) couturier *m*; **f. house** maison *f* de couture; **f. show** défilé *m* de mode (**b**) (*manner*) façon *f*; **after a f.** tant bien que mal **2** *vt* (*form*) façonner; (*make*) confectionner ▪ **fashionable** *adj* à la mode ▪ **fashionably** *adv* (*dressed*) à la mode

fast¹ [fɑːst] **1** (**-er, -est**) *adj* rapide; **to be f.** (*of clock*) avancer (**by** de); **f. colour** couleur *f* grand teint *inv*; **f. food** restauration *f* rapide; **f. food restaurant** fast-food *m* **2** *adv* (**a**) (*quickly*) vite; **how f.?** à quelle vitesse? (**b**) **f. asleep** profondément endormi (**c**) **to hold f.** (*of person*) tenir bon

fast² [fɑːst] **1** *n* jeûne *m* **2** *vi* jeûner

fasten ['fɑːsən] **1** *vt* attacher (**to** à); (*door, window*) fermer; **to f. sth down** attacher qch **2** *vi* (*of dress*) s'attacher; (*of door, window*) se fermer ▪ **fastener, fastening** *n* (*clip*) attache *f*; (*hook*) agrafe *f*; (*press stud*) bouton-pression *m*; (*of bag*) fermoir *m*

fastidious [fæ'stɪdɪəs] *adj* difficile

> Note that the French word **fastidieux** is a false friend and is never a translation for the English word **fastidious**. It means **tedious**.

fat [fæt] **1** (**fatter, fattest**) *adj* gras (*f* grasse); (*cheeks, salary, book*) gros (*f* grosse); **to get f.** grossir; *Fam Ironic* **a f. lot of good that will do you!** ça te fera une belle jambe!; *Fam* **f. cat** (*person*) gros salaire *m* **2** *n* graisse *f*; (*on meat*) gras *m*

fatal ['feɪtəl] *adj* mortel, -elle ▪ **fatally** *adv* **f. wounded** mortellement blessé

> Note that the French word **fatalement** is a false friend and is never a translation for the English word **fatally**. It means **inevitably**.

fatality [fə'tælɪtɪ] (*pl* **-ies**) *n* (**a**) (*person*) victime *f* (**b**) (*fate*) fatalité *f*

fate [feɪt] *n* destin *m*, sort *m* ▪ **fated** *adj* **to be f. to do sth** être destiné à faire qch ▪ **fateful** *adj* (*words, day*) fatidique

father ['fɑːðə(r)] **1** *n* père *m*; **F. Christmas** le père Noël; **F. Martin** (*priest*) le Père Martin; **yes, F.** (*to priest*) oui, mon père **2** *vt* (*child*) engendrer ▪ **father-in-law** (*pl* **fathers-in-law**) *n* beau-père *m* ▪ **fatherhood** *n* paternité *f* ▪ **fatherly** *adj* paternel, -elle

fathom ['fæðəm] **1** *n* (*nautical measurement*)

brasse *f* (*= 1,8 m*) **2** *vt* **to f. (out)** (*understand*) comprendre

fatigue [fə'tiːg] **1** *n* (**a**) (*tiredness*) fatigue *f* (**b**) *Mil* **f. (duty)** corvée *f* **2** *vt* fatiguer

fatten ['fætən] *vt* **to f. (up)** engraisser ▪ **fattening** *adj* (*food*) qui fait grossir

fatty ['fætɪ] **1** (**-ier, -iest**) *adj* (*food*) gras (*f* grasse); (*tissue*) adipeux, -euse **2** *n* *Fam* (*person*) gros *m*, grosse *f*

fatuous ['fætʃʊəs] *adj* stupide

faucet ['fɔːsɪt] *n Am* (*tap*) robinet *m*

fault [fɔːlt] **1** *n* (*blame*) faute *f*; (*defect, failing*) défaut *m*; *Geol* faille *f*; **to find f. (with)** trouver à redire (à); **to be at f.** être en faute; **it's your f.** c'est (de) ta faute **2** *vt* **to f. sb/sth** trouver des défauts à qn/à qch

faultless ['fɔːltləs] *adj* irréprochable

faulty ['fɔːltɪ] (**-ier, -iest**) *adj* défectueux, -euse

fauna ['fɔːnə] *n* faune *f*

faux pas [fəʊ'pɑː] *n inv* gaffe *f*

favour ['feɪvə(r)] (*Am* **favor**) **1** *n* (*act of kindness*) service *m*; (*approval*) faveur *f*; **to do sb a f.** rendre service à qn; **in f.** (*fashion*) en vogue; **in f. (with sb)** bien vu (de qn); **it's in her f. to do that** elle a intérêt à faire cela; **in f. of** en faveur de; **to be in f. of sth** être partisan de qch **2** *vt* (*encourage*) favoriser; (*support*) être partisan de; **he favoured me with a visit** il a eu la gentillesse de me rendre visite ▪ **favourable** (*Am* **favorable**) *adj* favorable (**to** à)

favourite ['feɪvərɪt] (*Am* **favorite**) **1** *adj* favori, -ite, préféré **2** *n* favori, -ite *mf* ▪ **favouritism** (*Am* **favoritism**) *n* favoritisme *m*

fawn¹ [fɔːn] **1** *n* (*deer*) faon *m* **2** *adj & n* (*colour*) fauve (*m*)

fawn² [fɔːn] *vi* **to f. (up)on sb** ramper devant qn

fax [fæks] **1** *n* (*message*) télécopie *f*, fax *m*; **f. (machine)** télécopieur *m*, fax *m*; *Comptr* **f. modem** fax modem *m*; **f. number** numéro *m* de fax **2** *vt* (*message*) faxer; **to f. sb** envoyer un fax à qn

fear [fɪə(r)] **1** *n* peur *f*; (*worry*) crainte *f*; **for f. of doing sth** de peur de faire qch; **for f. that...** de peur que... (*+ ne + subjunctive*); **there's no f. of his going** il ne risque pas d'y aller; **there are fears (that) he might leave** on craint qu'il ne parte **2** *vt* craindre; **I f. that he might leave** je crains qu'il ne parte **3** *vi* **to f. for one's life/career** craindre pour sa vie/carrière ▪ **fearful** *adj* (*person*) apeuré; (*noise, pain, consequence*) épouvantable ▪ **fearless** *adj* intrépide ▪ **fearlessness** *n* intrépidité *f* ▪ **fearsome** *adj* effrayant

feasible ['fiːzəbəl] *adj* faisable ▪ **feasi'bility** *n* possibilité *f* (**of doing** de faire); (*of plan*) faisabilité *f*; **f. study** étude *f* de faisabilité

feast [fiːst] **1** *n* festin *m*; (*religious*) fête *f* **2** *vi* **to f. on sth** se régaler de qch

feat [fiːt] *n* exploit *m*; **f. of skill** tour *m* de force

feather ['feðə(r)] **1** *n* plume *f*; **f. duster** plumeau *m* **2** *vt Fig* **to f. one's nest** faire son beurre

feature ['fiːtʃə(r)] **1** *n (of face, person)* trait *m; (of thing, place, machine)* caractéristique *f*; **f. (article)** article *m* de fond; **f. (film)** long métrage *m*; **to be a regular f.** *(in newspaper)* paraître régulièrement **2** *vt (of newspaper, exhibition, film) (present)* présenter; *(portray)* représenter; **a film featuring…** un film ayant pour vedette… **3** *vi (appear)* figurer (**in** dans)

February ['februəri] *n* février *m*

fed [fed] **1** *pt & pp of* **feed 2** *adj Fam* **to be f. up** en avoir marre *ou* ras le bol (**with** de)

federal ['fedərəl] *adj* fédéral ▪ **federate** [-reit] *vt* fédérer ▪ **federation** ['reiʃən] *n* fédération *f*

fee [fiː] *n* **fee(s)** *(of doctor, lawyer)* honoraires *mpl; (of artist)* cachet *m; (for registration, examination)* droits *mpl; (for membership)* cotisation *f*; **to charge a f. (for a job)** se faire payer (pour un travail); **for a small f.** pour une petite somme; **school** *ou* **tuition fees** frais *mpl* d'inscription; **f.-paying school** école *f* privée

feeble ['fiːbəl] **(-er, -est)** *adj* faible; *(excuse, smile)* pauvre; *(attempt)* peu convaincant ▪ **'feeble-'minded** *adj* faible d'esprit

feed [fiːd] **1** *n (animal food)* nourriture *f; (for baby) (from breast)* tétée *f; (from bottle)* biberon *m* **2** *(pt & pp fed) vt* donner à manger à; *(baby) (from breast)* donner la tétée à; *(from bottle)* donner son biberon à; *Fig (machine)* alimenter; **to f. sb sth** faire manger qch à qn; **to f. sth into a machine** introduire qch dans une machine **3** *vi (eat)* manger; **to f. on sth** se nourrir de qch ▪ **feeding** *n* alimentation *f*

feedback ['fiːdbæk] *n (response)* réactions *fpl*

feel [fiːl] **1** *n (touch)* toucher *m; (feeling)* sensation *f*

2 *(pt & pp felt) vt (be aware of)* sentir; *(experience)* éprouver, ressentir; *(touch)* tâter; **to f. that…** penser que…; **to f. one's way** avancer à tâtons

3 *vi* **to f. (about)** *(grope)* tâtonner; *(in pocket)* fouiller (**for sth** pour trouver qch); **it feels hard** c'est dur au toucher; **to f. tired/old** se sentir fatigué/vieux (*f* vieille); **I f. hot/sleepy/hungry** j'ai chaud/sommeil/faim; **she feels better** elle va mieux; **he doesn't f. well** il ne se sent pas bien; **how are you feeling?** comment te sens-tu?; **to f. like sth** avoir envie de qch; **it feels like cotton** on dirait du coton; **to f. as if…** avoir l'impression que…; **what do you f. about…?** que pensez-vous de…?; **I f. bad about it** ça m'ennuie; **what does it f. like?** quelle impression ça (te) fait?; **to f. for sb** plaindre qn; **to f. up to doing sth** *(well enough)* être assez bien pour faire qch; *(competent enough)* se sentir de taille à faire qch

feeler ['fiːlə(r)] *n (of insect)* antenne *f; Fig* **to put out feelers** tâter le terrain

feeling ['fiːlɪŋ] *n (emotion, impression)* sentiment *m; (physical)* sensation *f*, **(sense of) f.** toucher *m*; **to have a f. for** *(person)* avoir de la sympathie pour; *(music, painting)* être sensible à; **to hurt sb's feelings** blesser qn; **no hard feelings!** sans rancune!

feet [fiːt] *pl of* **foot**[1]

feign [feɪn] *vt* feindre

feint [feɪnt] *n (in combat sports)* feinte *f*

feisty ['faɪstɪ] **(-ier, -iest)** *Fam adj* **(a)** *(lively)* plein d'entrain **(b)** *(pugnacious)* contestataire

feline ['fiːlaɪn] *adj & n* félin (*m*)

fell [fel] **1** *pt of* **fall 2** *vt (tree)* abattre; *(opponent)* terrasser

fellow ['feləʊ] *n* **(a)** *(man, boy)* gars *m* **(b)** *(companion)* camarade *mf*; **f. being** semblable *mf*; **f. citizen** concitoyen, -enne *mf*; **f. countryman/f. countrywoman** compatriote *mf*; **f. passenger** compagnon *m* de voyage, compagne *f* de voyage; **f. worker** collègue *mf* **(c)** *(of society)* membre *m; (teacher)* professeur *m; (student)* boursier, -ière *mf*

fellowship ['feləʊʃɪp] *n (friendship)* camaraderie *f; (group)* association *f; (scholarship)* bourse *f* de recherche

felony ['felənɪ] *(pl -ies) n Am Law* crime *m*

felt[1] [felt] *pt & pp of* **feel**

felt[2] [felt] *n* feutre *m* ▪ **'felt-'tip, 'felt-tip 'pen** *n* crayon-feutre *m*

female ['fiːmeɪl] **1** *adj (person, name, voice)* féminin; *(animal)* femelle; **the f. vote** le vote des femmes; **f. student** étudiante *f* **2** *n (woman)* femme *f; (girl)* fille *f; (animal, plant)* femelle *f*

feminine ['femɪnɪn] **1** *adj* féminin **2** *Grammar* féminin *m* ▪ **femi'ninity** *n* féminité *f* ▪ **feminist** *adj & n* féministe (*mf*)

fence [fens] **1** *n* **(a)** *(barrier)* clôture *f; (more solid)* barrière *f; (in race)* obstacle *m* **(b)** *Fam (person)* receleur, -euse *mf* **2** *vt* **to f. (in)** *(land)* clôturer **3** *vi (as sport)* faire de l'escrime ▪ **fencing** *n Sport* escrime *f*

fend [fend] **1** *vi* **to f. for oneself** se débrouiller **2** *vt* **to f. off** *(blow)* parer

fender ['fendə(r)] *n* **(a)** *Am (of car)* aile *f* **(b)** *(for fire)* garde-feu *m inv*

fennel ['fenəl] *n* fenouil *m*

ferment 1 ['fɜːment] *n (substance)* ferment *m; Fig (excitement)* effervescence *f* **2** [fə'ment] *vi* fermenter ▪ **fermentation** [fɜːmen'teɪʃən] *n* fermentation *f*

fern [fɜːn] *n* fougère *f*

ferocious [fə'rəʊʃəs] *adj* féroce ▪ **ferocity** [fə'rɒsɪtɪ] *n* férocité *f*

ferret ['ferɪt] **1** *n (animal)* furet *m* **2** *vt* **to f. out** *(object, information)* dénicher **3** *vi* **to f. about for sth** fouiller pour trouver qch

ferris wheel ['ferɪswiːl] *n* grande roue *f*

ferry ['ferɪ] **1** (*pl* **-ies**) *n* ferry-boat *m*; (*small, for river*) bac *m* **2** (*pt & pp* **-ied**) *vt* transporter

fertile [*Br* 'fɜːtaɪl, *Am* 'fɜːrtəl] *adj* (*land, imagination*) fertile; (*person, animal*) fécond ▪ **fertility** [-'tɪlɪtɪ] *n* fertilité *f*; **f. treatment** traitement *m* de la stérilité

fertilize ['fɜːtɪlaɪz] *vt* (*land*) fertiliser; (*egg, animal*) féconder ▪ **fertilizer** *n* engrais *m*

fervent ['fɜːvənt] *adj* fervent ▪ **fervour** (*Am* **fervor**) *n* ferveur *f*

fester ['festə(r)] *vi* (*of wound*) s'infecter; *Fig* (*of situation*) s'envenimer

festival ['festɪvəl] *n* (*of music, film*) festival *m* (*pl* -als); (*religious*) fête *f*

festive ['festɪv] *adj* de fête; (*mood*) festif, -ive; **the f. season** les fêtes *fpl* de fin d'année ▪ **fe'stivities** *npl* festivités *fpl*

festoon [fe'stuːn] *vt* orner (**with** de)

fetch [fetʃ] *vt* (**a**) (*bring*) aller chercher; **to f. sth in** rentrer qch (**b**) (*be sold for*) rapporter; **it fetched a high price** cela a atteint un prix élevé ▪ **fetching** *adj* (*smile*) charmant

fête [feɪt] **1** *n Br* fête *f* **2** *vt* fêter

fetid ['fetɪd] *adj* fétide

fetish ['fetɪʃ] *n* (*object*) fétiche *m*

fetter ['fetə(r)] *vt* (*hinder*) entraver

fettle ['fetəl] *n* **in fine f.** en pleine forme

fetus ['fiːtəs] *n Am* = **foetus**

feud [fjuːd] *n* querelle *f*

fever ['fiːvə(r)] *n* fièvre *f*; **to have a f.** (*temperature*) avoir de la fièvre; **a high f.** une forte fièvre ▪ **feverish** *adj* (*person, activity*) fiévreux, -euse

few [fjuː] **1** *adj* (**a**) (*not many*) peu de; **f. towns** peu de villes; **f. of them** un petit nombre d'entre eux; **every f. days** tous les trois ou quatre jours; **one of the f. books** l'un des rares livres; **f. and far between** rarissime (**b**) (*some*) **a f.** quelques-un(e)s (**of** de); **a f. towns** quelques villes; **a f. of us** quelques-uns d'entre nous; **a f. more books** encore quelques livres; **quite a f., a good f.** bon nombre de **2** *pron* peu; **f. came** peu sont venus; **the examples are f.** les exemples sont peu nombreux

fewer ['fjuːə(r)] **1** *adj* moins de (**than** que); **f. houses** moins de maisons (**than** que); **no f. than thirty** pas moins de trente; **to be f.** (**than**) être moins nombreux (que) **2** *pron* moins ▪ **fewest** ['fjuːɪst] **1** *adj* le moins de **2** *pron* le moins

fiancé [fɪ'ɒnseɪ] *n* fiancé *m*

fiancée [fɪ'ɒnseɪ] *n* fiancée *f*

fiasco [fɪ'æskəʊ] (*pl* **-os**, *Am* **-oes**) *n* fiasco *m*

fib [fɪb] *Fam* **1** *n* bobard *m* **2** (*pt & pp* **-bb-**) *vi* raconter des bobards ▪ **fibber** *n Fam* menteur, -euse *mf*

fibre ['faɪbə(r)] (*Am* **fiber**) *n* fibre *f*; (*in diet*) fibres *fpl*; **high-f. diet** alimentation *f* riche en

fibres; **f. optics** technologie *f* des fibres optiques ▪ **fibreglass** (*Am* **fiberglass**) *n* fibre *f* de verre

fickle ['fɪkəl] *adj* inconstant

fiction ['fɪkʃən] *n* (*imagination*) fiction *f*; (*works of*) **f.** livres *mpl* de fiction; **that's pure f.** ce sont des histoires ▪ **fictional** *adj* (*character*) fictif, -ive

fictitious [fɪk'tɪʃəs] *adj* fictif, -ive

fiddle ['fɪdəl] **1** *n* (**a**) (*violin*) violon *m* (**b**) *Br Fam* (*dishonest act*) combine *f*; **to be on the f.** traficoter **2** *vt Br Fam* (*accounts*) truquer **3** *vi* (**a**) (*play violin*) jouer du violon (**b**) *Fam* (*waste time*) traînailler; **to f. (about) with sth** tripoter qch ▪ **fiddly** (**-ier, -iest**) *adj Br Fam* minutieux, -ieuse ▪ **fiddler** *n* (**a**) (*violin player*) violoniste *mf* (**b**) *Br Fam* (*swindler*) combinard, -arde *mf*

fidelity [fɪ'delɪtɪ] *n* fidélité *f* (**to** à)

fidget ['fɪdʒɪt] **1** *n* **to be a f.** ne pas tenir en place **2** *vi* **to f. (about)** gigoter; **to f. (about) with sth** tripoter qch ▪ **fidgety** *adj* agité

field [fiːld] *n* champ *m*; (*for sports*) terrain *m*; (*sphere*) domaine *m*; **to have a f. day** (*a good day*) s'en donner à cœur joie; **f. glasses** jumelles *fpl*; *Am* **f. hockey** hockey *m* (*sur* gazon); **f. marshal** ≃ maréchal *m* de France

fiend [fiːnd] *n* démon *m*; *Fam* **a jazz f.** un(e) fana de jazz; *Fam* (*sex*) **f.** obsédé *m* sexuel ▪ **fiendish** *adj* (*cruel*) diabolique; (*difficult, awful*) abominable

fierce [fɪəs] (**-er, -est**) *adj* (*animal, warrior, tone*) féroce; (*attack, wind*) violent ▪ **fierceness** *n* férocité *f*; (*of attack*) violence *f*

fiery ['faɪərɪ] (**-ier, -iest**) *adj* (*person, speech*) fougueux, -ueuse; (*sun, eyes*) ardent; (*taste*) très épicé

fifteen [fɪf'tiːn] *adj & n* quinze (*m*) ▪ **fifteenth** *adj & n* quinzième (*mf*)

fifth [fɪfθ] *adj & n* cinquième (*mf*); **a f.** un cinquième

fifty ['fɪftɪ] *adj & n* cinquante (*m*); **a f.-f. chance** une chance sur deux; **to split the profits f.-f.** partager les bénéfices moitié-moitié ▪ **fiftieth** *adj & n* cinquantième (*mf*)

fig [fɪg] *n* figue *f*; **f. tree** figuier *m*

fight [faɪt] **1** *n* (*between people*) bagarre *f*; (*between boxers, soldiers*) combat *m*; (*struggle*) lutte *f* (**against/for** contre/pour); (*quarrel*) dispute *f*; **to put up a good f.** bien se défendre **2** (*pt & pp* **fought**) *vt* (*person*) se battre contre; (*decision, enemy*) combattre; (*fire, temptation*) lutter contre; **to f. a battle** livrer bataille; *Pol* **to f. an election** se présenter à une élection; **to f. back** (*tears*) retenir; **to f. off** (*attacker, attack*) repousser; (*illness*) lutter contre; **to f. it out** se bagarrer **3** *vi* se battre (**against** contre); (*of soldiers*) combattre; (*struggle*) lutter; (*quarrel*) se disputer; **to f. back** (*retaliate*) se défendre; **to f. over sth** se disputer qch; **to f. against an**

illness/for a cause lutter contre une maladie/ pour une cause

fighter ['faɪtə(r)] *n (determined person)* battant, -ante *mf*; *(in brawl, battle)* combattant, -ante *mf*; *(boxer)* boxeur *m*; *(aircraft)* avion *m* de chasse

fighting ['faɪtɪŋ] *n (brawling)* bagarres *fpl*; *Mil* combat *m*; **f. spirit** combativité *f*; **f. troops** troupes *fpl* de combat

figment ['fɪgmənt] *n* **it's a f. of your imagination** c'est le fruit de ton imagination

figurative ['fɪgjʊrətɪv] *adj (meaning)* figuré; *(art)* figuratif, -ive

figure¹ [Br 'fɪgə(r), Am 'fɪgjə(r)] *n* (**a**) *(numeral)* chiffre *m*; **figures** *(arithmetic)* calcul *m* (**b**) *(shape)* forme *f*; *(outline)* silhouette *f*; **she has a nice f.** elle est bien faite (**c**) *(diagram)* figure *f*; *Br* **f. of eight**, *Am* **f. eight** huit *m*; **f. skating** patinage *m* artistique (**d**) *(expression, word)* **a f. of speech** une figure de rhétorique; *Fig* **it's just a f. of speech** c'est une façon de parler (**e**) *(important person)* personnage *m*

> Note that the French noun **figure** is a false friend when referring to the human body. It means **face**.

figure² [Br 'fɪgə(r), Am 'fɪgjə(r)] **1** *vt* **to f. that...** *(think)* penser que...; *(estimate)* supposer que...; **to f. out** *(person, motive)* arriver à comprendre; *(answer)* trouver; *(amount)* calculer **2** *vi* (**a**) *(appear)* figurer (**on** sur); **to f. on doing sth** compter faire qch (**b**) *Fam* **that figures!** *(makes sense)* ça se tient!

figurehead ['fɪgəhed] *n (of ship)* figure *f* de proue; *Fig & Pej (of organization)* homme *m* de paille

filament ['fɪləmənt] *n* filament *m*

filch [fɪltʃ] *vt Fam* faucher (**from** à)

file¹ [faɪl] **1** *n (tool)* lime *f* **2** *vt* **to f. (down)** limer

file² [faɪl] **1** *n (folder)* chemise *f*; *(documents)* dossier *m* (**on** sur); *(loose-leaf)* classeur *m*; *Comptr* fichier *m*; **to be on f.** figurer au dossier; *Comptr* **f. manager** gestionnaire *m* de fichiers **2** *vt (document)* classer; *(complaint, claim)* déposer **3** *vi* **to f. for divorce** demander le divorce ▪**filing** *adj* **f. cabinet** classeur *m* *(meuble)*; **f. clerk** documentaliste *mf*

file³ [faɪl] **1** *n (line)* file *f*; **in single f.** en file indienne **2** *vi* **to f. in/out** entrer/sortir à la queue leu leu; **to f. past sb/sth** défiler devant qn/qch

Filipino [fɪlɪ'piːnəʊ] **1** *adj* philippin, -ine **2** *n (pl -os)* Philippin, -ine *mf*

fill [fɪl] **1** *n* **to eat one's f.** manger à sa faim; **to have had one's f. of sb/sth** en avoir assez de qn/qch **2** *vt* remplir (**with** de); *(tooth)* plomber; *(time)* occuper; **to f. a need** répondre à un besoin; **to f. a vacancy** pourvoir à un poste vacant; **to be filled with hope** être plein d'espoir; **to f. in** *(form)* remplir; *(hole)*

combler; *(door, window)* condamner; **to f. sb in on sth** mettre qn au courant de qch; **to f. out** *(form)* remplir; **to f. up** *(container, form)* remplir **3** *vi* **to f. (up)** se remplir (**with** de); **to f. in for sb** remplacer qn; **to f. out** *(get fatter)* grossir; **to f. up** *(with petrol)* faire le plein

fillet [Br 'fɪlɪt, Am fɪ'leɪ] **1** *n (of fish, meat)* filet *m* **2** *(Am pt & pp* fɪ'leɪd) *vt (fish)* découper en filets; *(meat)* désosser

filling ['fɪlɪŋ] **1** *adj (meal)* nourrissant **2** *n (in tooth)* plombage *m*; *(in food)* garniture *f*; **f. station** station-service *f*

fillip ['fɪlɪp] *n (stimulus)* coup *m* de fouet

filly ['fɪlɪ] *(pl -ies) n (horse)* pouliche *f*

film [fɪlm] **1** *n* film *m*; *(for camera, layer)* pellicule *f*; *(for food)* film *m* plastique **2** *adj (studio, technician, critic)* de cinéma; **f. club** ciné-club *m*; **f. fan** *or* **buff** cinéphile *mf*; **f. festival** festival *m* du film; **f. library** cinémathèque *f*; **f. maker** cinéaste *mf*; **f. star** vedette *f* de cinéma **3** *vt* filmer **4** *vi (of film maker, actor)* tourner

Filofax® ['faɪləfæks] *n* organiseur *m*

filter ['fɪltə(r)] **1** *n* filtre *m*; *Br (traffic sign)* flèche *f* de dégagement; **f. coffee** café *m* filtre; *BrAut* **f. lane** = voie réservée aux véhicules qui tournent; **f. tip** bout *m* filtre **2** *vt* filtrer **3** *vi* **to f. through** filtrer

filth [fɪlθ] *n* saleté *f*; *Fig (obscenities)* saletés *fpl* ▪**filthy** **1** (**-ier, -iest**) *adj (hands, shoes)* sale; *(language)* obscène; *(habit)* dégoûtant; *Br Fam* **f. weather** un sale temps **2** *adv Fam* **f. rich** pourri de fric

fin [fɪn] *n (of fish, seal)* nageoire *f*; *(of shark)* aileron *m*; *Am (of swimmer)* palme *f*

final ['faɪnəl] **1** *adj (last)* dernier, -ière; *(definite)* définitif, -ive **2** *n Sport* finale *f*; *Univ* **finals** examens *mpl* de dernière année ▪**finalist** *n* finaliste *mf* ▪**finalize** *vt (plan)* mettre au point; *(date)* fixer définitivement; *(deal)* conclure ▪**finally** *adv (lastly)* enfin; *(eventually)* finalement; *(irrevocably)* définitivement

finale [fɪ'nɑːlɪ] *n (musical)* finale *m*

finance ['faɪnæns] **1** *n* finance *f*; **finances** *(of person)* finances *fpl*; *(of company)* situation *f* financière; **f. company** société *f* financière **2** *vt* financer

financial [faɪ'nænʃəl] *adj* financier, -ière; **it was a f. success** ça a rapporté beaucoup d'argent; *Br* **f. year** exercice *m* comptable ▪**financially** *adv* financièrement

financier [faɪ'nænsɪə(r)] *n* financier *m*

find [faɪnd] **1** *n (discovery)* découverte *f* **2** *(pt & pp* found) *vt* trouver; **I f. that...** je trouve que...; **I found him waiting in the hall** je l'ai trouvé qui attendait dans le vestibule; **she was nowhere to be found** elle était introuvable; **he found it impossible to understand her** il avait beaucoup de mal à la comprendre; **£20 all**

found 20 livres logé et nourri; **to f. difficulty doing sth** éprouver de la difficulté à faire qch; **to f. one's feet** *(settle in)* s'adapter; **to f. oneself** *(spiritually)* se trouver

▸ **find out 1** *vt (secret, information)* découvrir; *(person)* prendre en défaut **2** *vi (inquire)* se renseigner (**about** sur); **to f. out about sth** *(discover)* apprendre qch

findings ['faɪndɪŋz] *npl* conclusions *fpl*

fine¹ [faɪn] **1** *n (money)* amende *f*; *(for driving offence)* contravention *f* **2** *vt* **to f. sb £10** infliger une amende de 10 livres à qn

fine² [faɪn] **1** (**-er, -est**) *adj* (**a**) *(thin, not coarse) (hair, needle)* fin; *(gold, metal)* pur; *(feeling)* délicat; *(distinction)* subtil (**b**) *(very good)* excellent; *(beautiful) (weather, statue)* beau *(f* belle); **it's f.** *(weather)* il fait beau; **he's f.** *(healthy)* il va bien; **f. arts** beaux-arts *mpl* **2** *adv* (**a**) *(very well)* très bien; **f.!** très bien! (**b**) *(cut, write)* menu ▪ **finely** *adv (dressed)* magnifiquement; *(embroidered, ground)* finement; *(painted, expressed)* délicatement; **f. chopped** haché menu

finery ['faɪnərɪ] *n (clothes)* parure *f*

finesse [fɪ'nes] *n* finesse *f*

finger ['fɪŋgə(r)] *n* doigt *m*; **to keep one's fingers crossed** croiser les doigts; **little f.** petit doigt *m*, auriculaire *m*; **middle f.** majeur *m*; **f. mark** trace *f* de doigt **2** *vt* tâter ▪ **fingernail** *n* ongle *m* ▪ **fingerprint** *n* empreinte *f* digitale ▪ **fingertip** *n* bout *m* du doigt; **to have sth at one's fingertips** savoir qch sur le bout des doigts

finicky ['fɪnɪkɪ] *adj (precise)* tatillon, -onne; *(difficult)* difficile (**about** sur)

finish ['fɪnɪʃ] **1** *n (end)* fin *f*; *(of race)* arrivée *f*; *(of article, car)* finition *f*; **paint with a matt f.** peinture *f* mate **2** *vt* **to f. sth (off** *or* **up)** finir qch; **to f. doing sth** finir de faire qch; **to f. sb off** *(kill)* achever qn **3** *vi (of meeting, event)* finir, se terminer; *(of person)* finir, terminer; **to f. first** terminer premier; **to have finished with** *(object)* ne plus avoir besoin de; *(situation, person)* en avoir fini avec; **to f. off** *or* **up** *(of person)* finir, terminer; **to f. up** *(end up in)* se retrouver à; **to f. up doing sth** finir par faire qch; **finishing line** *(of race)* ligne *f* d'arrivée; **to put the finishing touches to sth** mettre la dernière main à qch ▪ **finished** *adj (ended, complete, ruined)* fini

finite ['faɪnaɪt] *adj* fini

Finland ['fɪnlənd] *n* la Finlande ▪ **Finn** *n* Finlandais, -aise *mf*, Finnois, -oise *mf* ▪ **Finnish 1** *adj* finlandais, finnois **2** *n (language)* finnois *m*

fir [fɜː(r)] *n* sapin *m*

fire ['faɪə(r)] **1** *n* feu *m*; *(accidental)* incendie *m*; *Br (electric heater)* radiateur *m*; **to light** *or* **make a f.** faire du feu; **to set f. to sb/sth** mettre le feu

à qn/qch; **to catch f.** prendre feu; **on f.** en feu; **f.!** *(alarm)* au feu!; *(to soldiers)* feu!; **to open f.** ouvrir le feu; **f. alarm** sirène *f* d'incendie; *Br* **f. brigade,** *Am* **f. department** pompiers *mpl*; **f. engine** voiture *f* des pompiers; **f. escape** escalier *m* de secours; **f. exit** sortie *f* de secours; **f. station** caserne *f* des pompiers

2 *vt (cannon)* tirer; *(pottery)* cuire; *Fig (imagination)* enflammer; **to f. a gun** tirer un coup de fusil/de pistolet; **to f. questions at sb** bombarder qn de questions; **to f. sb** *(dismiss)* renvoyer qn

3 *vi* tirer (**at** sur); *Fam* **f. away!** *(start speaking)* vas-y!; *Fig Br* **in** *or Am* **on the firing line** en butte aux attaques; **firing squad** peloton *m* d'exécution ▪ **firearm** *n* arme *f* à feu ▪ **firecracker** *n* pétard *m* ▪ **firedoor** *n* porte *f* pare-feu ▪ **fireguard** *n* garde-feu *m inv* ▪ **fireman** (*pl* **-men**) *n* sapeur-pompier *m* ▪ **fireplace** *n* cheminée *f* ▪ **fireproof** *adj (door)* ignifugé ▪ **fireside** *n* **by the f.** au coin du feu; ▪ **firewall** *n Comptr* pare-feu *m inv* ▪ **firewood** *n* bois *m* de chauffage ▪ **firework** *n* fusée *f*; *(firecracker)* pétard *m*; *Br* **f. display** feu *m* d'artifice

firm¹ [fɜːm] *n (company)* entreprise *f*, firme *f*

firm² [fɜːm] **1** (**-er, -est**) *adj (earth, decision)* ferme; *(foundations, faith)* solide; *(character)* résolu; **to be f. with sb** être ferme avec qn **2** *adv* **to stand f.** tenir bon ou ferme ▪ **firmly** *adv (believe)* fermement; *(speak)* d'une voix ferme; *(shut)* bien ▪ **firmness** *n* fermeté *f*

first [fɜːst] **1** *adj (premier, -ière; **I'll do it f. thing in the morning** je le ferai dès le matin; **f. aid** premiers secours *mpl*; **f. cousin** cousin, -ine *mf* germain(e) **2** *adv* d'abord; *(for the first time)* pour la première fois; **f. of all, f. and foremost** tout d'abord; **at f.** d'abord; **to come f.** *(in race)* arriver premier; *(in exam)* être reçu premier **3** *n (person, thing)* premier, -ière *mf*; **from the f.** dès le début; **f. (gear)** *(of vehicle)* première *f*; *Br Univ* **to get a f.** ≃ avoir une licence avec mention très bien ▪ **'first-'class 1** *adj* excellent; *(ticket)* de première classe; *(mail)* ordinaire **2** *adv (travel)* en première ▪ **'first-'hand 1** *adj (news)* de première main; **to have (had) f. experience of sth** avoir fait l'expérience personnelle de qch **2** *adv (hear news)* de première main ▪ **'first-'rate** *adj* excellent

firstly ['fɜːstlɪ] *adv* premièrement

fiscal ['fɪskəl] *adj* fiscal

fish [fɪʃ] **1** *(pl inv or* **-es** [-ɪz]*) n* poisson *m*; **f. bone** arête *f*; **f. bowl** bocal *m*; **f. cake** croquette *f* de poisson; *Br* **f. fingers,** *Am* **f. sticks** bâtonnets *mpl* de poisson; **f. market** marché *m* aux poissons; **f. shop** poissonnerie *f*; **f. tank** aquarium *m*; *Br* **f.-and-chip shop** = magasin où on vend du poisson frit et des frites **2** *vt* **to**

f. sth out *(from water)* repêcher qch; **to f. sb/sth from somewhere** *(remove)* sortir qn/qch de quelque part **3** *vi* pêcher; **to f. for salmon** pêcher le saumon; *Fig* **to f. for compliments** rechercher les compliments ▪**fishing** *n* pêche *f*; **to go f.** aller à la pêche. **f. boat** bateau *m* de pêche; **f. line** ligne *f*; **f. net** *(of fisherman)* filet *m* (de pêche); *(of angler)* épuisette *f*; *Am* **f. pole** canne *f* à pêche; **f. rod** canne à pêche

fisherman ['fɪʃəmən] *(pl* **-men)** *n* pêcheur *m*

fishmonger ['fɪʃmʌŋgə(r)] *n* poissonnier, -ière *mf*

fishy ['fɪʃɪ] *(-ier, -iest) adj (smell, taste)* de poisson; *Fig (suspicious)* louche

fission ['fɪʃən] *n* **nuclear f.** fission *f* nucléaire

fissure ['fɪʃə(r)] *n (in rock)* fissure *f*

fist [fɪst] *n* poing *m* ▪**fistful** *n* poignée *f* (of de)

fit¹ [fɪt] **1** *(fitter, fittest) adj* **(a)** *(healthy)* en forme; **to keep f.** se maintenir en forme **(b)** *(suitable)* propre **(for** à; **to do** à faire); *(worthy)* digne **(for** de; **to do** de faire); *(able)* apte **(for** à; **to do** à faire); **f. to eat** *or* **for eating** mangeable; **to see f. to do sth** juger bon de faire qch; **as you see f.** comme bon vous semblera; *Fam* **I was f. to drop** je ne tenais plus debout **(c)** *Br Fam (attractive)* bien foutu

2 *n* **a good f.** *(clothes)* à la bonne taille; **a close** *or* **tight f.** *(clothes)* ajusté

3 *(pt & pp* **-tt-)** *vt (be the right size for)* aller bien à; *(match)* correspondre à; *(put in)* poser; *(go in)* aller dans; *(go on)* aller sur; **to f. sth on sb** *(garment)* ajuster qch à qn; **to f. sth (on) to sth** *(put)* poser qch sur qch; *(adjust)* adapter qch à qch; *(fix)* fixer qch à qch; **to f. sth (out** *or* **up) with sth** équiper qch de qch; **to f. sth in** *(install)* poser qch; *(insert)* faire entrer qch; **to f. in a customer** *(find time to see)* prendre un client

4 *vi (of clothes, lid, key, plug)* aller; **this shirt fits** cette chemise me/te/*etc* va; **to f. (in)** *(go in)* aller; *(of facts, plans)* cadrer **(with** avec); **he doesn't f. in** il n'est pas à sa place

fit² [fɪt] *n (seizure)* attaque *f*; **to have a f.** avoir une attaque; *Fam (get angry)* piquer une crise; **a f. of coughing** une quinte de toux; **a f. of crying** une crise de larmes; **a f. of enthusiasm** un accès d'enthousiasme; **in fits and starts** par à-coups

fitful ['fɪtfəl] *adj (sleep)* agité

fitness ['fɪtnɪs] *n (health)* santé *f*; *(of remark)* à-propos *m*; *(for job)* aptitude *f* **(for** à)

fitted ['fɪtɪd] *adj Br (cupboard)* encastré; *(garment)* ajusté; **f. carpet** moquette *f*; **f. kitchen** cuisine *f* intégrée; **f. (kitchen) units** éléments *mpl* de cuisine

fitter ['fɪtə(r)] *n Br (of machinery)* monteur, -euse *mf*

fitting ['fɪtɪŋ] **1** *adj (suitable)* approprié **(to** à) **2** *n (of clothes)* essayage *m*; **f. room** cabine *f*

d'essayage ▪**fittings** *npl (in house)* installations *fpl*

five [faɪv] *adj & n* cinq *(m)* ▪**fiver** *n Br Fam* billet *m* de 5 livres

fix [fɪks] **1** *vt (make firm, decide)* fixer **(to** à); *(mend)* réparer; *(deal with)* arranger; *(prepare)* préparer; *Fam (election)* truquer; **to f. one's attention on sb/sth** fixer son attention sur qn/qch; **to f. one's hopes on sb/sth** mettre ses espoirs en qn/qch; **to f. the blame on sb** rejeter la responsabilité sur qn; *Fam* **to f. sb** *(punish)* régler son compte à qn; **to f. sth in my mind** c'est gravé dans mon esprit; **to f. sth (on)** *(lid)* mettre qch en place; **to f. sth up** *(trip)* arranger qch; **to f. sb up with a job** procurer un travail à qn **2** *n Fam (of drug)* dose *f*; *Fam Fig* **her daily chocolate f.** sa dose quotidienne de chocolat; *Fam* **in a f.** dans le pétrin

fixation [fɪk'seɪʃən] *n* fixation *f*

fixed [fɪkst] *adj (price)* fixe; *(resolution)* inébranlable; *(idea)* bien arrêté; *Fam* **how's he f. for cash?** a-t-il de l'argent?; *Fam* **how are you f. for tomorrow?** qu'est-ce que tu fais demain?

fixer ['fɪksə(r)] *n Fam* combinard, -arde *mf*

fixture ['fɪkstʃə(r)] *n* **(a)** *Sport* rencontre *f* **(b)** **fixtures** *(in house)* installations *fpl*

fizz [fɪz] *vi (of drink)* pétiller ▪**fizzy** *(-ier, -iest) adj* gazeux, -euse

fizzle [fɪzəl]

▶ **fizzle out** *vi (of firework)* rater; *Fam (of plan)* tomber à l'eau; *Fam (of enthusiasm)* retomber; *Fam (of custom)* disparaître

flabbergasted ['flæbəgɑːstɪd] *adj Fam* sidéré

flabby ['flæbɪ] *(-ier, -iest) adj (person)* bouffi; *(skin, character)* mou *(f* molle)

flag [flæg] **1** *n (a)* drapeau *m*; *Naut* pavillon *m*; *(for charity)* insigne *m* **2** *(pt & pp* **-gg-)** *vt* marquer; **to f. (down) a taxi** héler un taxi **3** *vi (of person, conversation)* faiblir; *(of plant)* dépérir ▪**flagpole** *n* mât *m*

flagrant ['fleɪgrənt] *adj* flagrant

flagstone ['flægstəʊn] *n* dalle *f*

flair [fleə(r)] *n (intuition)* don *m* **(for** pour); **to have a f. for business** avoir le sens des affaires

flak [flæk] *n Fam* **to get** *or* **take a lot of f.** *(be criticized)* se faire rentrer dedans; **f. jacket** gilet *m* pare-balles

flake [fleɪk] **1** *n (of snow)* flocon *m*; *(of paint)* écaille *f*; *(of soap, metal)* paillette *f* **2** *vi* **to f. (off)** *(of paint)* s'écailler ▪**flaky** *adj Br* **f. pastry** pâte *f* feuilletée

flamboyant [flæm'bɔɪənt] *adj (person)* extraverti

flame [fleɪm] **1** *n* flamme *f*; **to go up in flames** prendre feu; **to burst into flames** s'enflammer; **to be in flames** être en flammes **2** *vi* **to f. (up)** *(of fire, house)* flamber ▪**flaming 1** *adj (a) (sun)* flamboyant **(b)** *Br Fam (damn)* sacré **2** *n Comptr* = échange d'insultes sur Internet

flamingo [flə'mɪŋgəʊ] (*pl* **-os** *or* **-oes**) *n* flamant *m*

flammable ['flæməbəl] *adj* inflammable

flan [flæn] *n* tarte *f*

flank [flæŋk] **1** *n* flanc *m* **2** *vt* flanquer (**with** *or* **by** de)

flannel ['flænəl] *n* (*cloth*) flanelle *f*; *Br* (*face cloth*) gant *m* de toilette; *Br* **flannels** (*trousers*) pantalon *m* de flanelle

flap [flæp] **1** *n* (*noise*) battement *m*; (*of pocket, envelope*) rabat *m*; (*of table*) abattant *m*; (*of door*) battant *m* **2** (*pt & pp* **-pp-**) *vt* **to f. its wings** (*of bird*) battre des ailes **3** *vi* (*of wings, sail, shutter*) battre

flare [fleə(r)] **1** *n* (**a**) (*signal*) signal *m* lumineux; (*rocket*) fusée *f* éclairante (**b**) (**pair of**) **flares** pantalon *m* pattes d'éléphant **2** *vi* (*of fire*) flamboyer; **to f. up** (*of fire*) s'embraser; (*of violence, anger, trouble*) éclater ▪ **flare-up** *n* (*of violence, fire*) flambée *f*; (*of region*) embrasement *m*

flared [fleəd] *adj* (*skirt*) évasé; (*trousers*) (à) pattes d'éléphant

flash [flæʃ] **1** *n* (*of light, genius*) éclair *m*; (*for camera*) flash *m*; **f. of lightning** éclair; **in a f.** en un clin d'œil **2** *vt* (*light*) projeter; (*aim*) diriger (**on/at** sur); (*smile, look*) jeter (**at** à); **to f. sth (around)** montrer qch rapidement; **to f. one's headlights** faire un appel de phares **3** *vi* (*shine*) briller; (*on and off*) clignoter; **to f. past** *or* **by** (*rush*) passer comme un éclair; **flashing lights** clignotants *mpl* ▪ **flashback** *n* retour *m* en arrière ▪ **flashlight** *n* *Am* (*torch*) lampe *f* électrique ▪ **flashy** (**-ier, -iest**) *adj* tape-à-l'œil

flask [flɑːsk] *n* Thermos® *m* ou *f* inv; (*for alcohol*) flasque *f*; (*phial*) fiole *f*

flat¹ [flæt] **1** (**flatter, flattest**) *adj* plat; (*tyre, battery*) à plat; (*drink*) éventé; (*refusal*) net (*f* nette); **f. nose** nez *m* aplati; **f. fee** prix *m* unique; **f. rate** tarif *m* unique: **to put sth (down) f.** mettre qch à plat; **to be f.-footed** avoir les pieds plats

2 *n* (*puncture*) crevaison *f*; (*of hand*) plat *m*; (*in music*) bémol *m*

3 *adv* **to sing f.** chanter trop bas; **to fall f. on one's face** tomber à plat ventre; **to fall f.** (*of joke, play*) tomber à plat; **to fold f.** (*of ironing board*) se (re)plier; **I told him f.** je le lui ai dit carrément; *Fam* **f. broke** complètement fauché; **in two minutes f.** en deux minutes pile; **f. out** (*work*) d'arrache-pied; (*run*) à toute vitesse; **to be lying f. out** être étendu de tout son long ▪ **flatly** *adv* (*deny, refuse*) catégoriquement

flat² [flæt] *n* *Br* (*in building*) appartement *m*

flatmate ['flætmeɪt] *n* *Br* colocataire *mf*

flatten ['flætən] *vt* aplatir; (*crops*) coucher; (*town, buildings*) raser

flatter ['flætə(r)] *vt* flatter; (*of clothes*) avantager

▪ **flattering** *adj* (*remark, words*) flatteur, -euse; (*clothes, colour*) qui avantage ▪ **flattery** *n* flatterie *f*

flatulence ['flætjʊləns] *n* **to have f.** avoir des gaz

flaunt [flɔːnt] *vt* (*show off*) faire étalage de

flautist ['flɔːtɪst] *n* *Br* flûtiste *mf*

flavour ['fleɪvə(r)] (*Am* **flavor**) **1** *n* (*taste*) goût *m*; (*of ice cream*) parfum *m* **2** *vt* (*food*) relever (**with** de); (*ice cream*) parfumer (**with** à); **lemon-flavoured** (parfumé) au citron ▪ **flavouring** (*Am* **flavoring**) *n* (*seasoning*) assaisonnement *m*; (*in cake, ice cream*) parfum *m*

flaw [flɔː] *n* défaut *m* ▪ **flawed** *adj* qui a un défaut/des défauts ▪ **flawless** *adj* parfait

flax [flæks] *n* lin *m* ▪ **flaxen** *adj* (*hair*) blond de lin *inv*

flay [fleɪ] *vt* (*flog*) fouetter; *Fig* (*criticize*) éreinter

flea [fliː] *n* puce *f*; **f. market** marché *m* aux puces

fleck [flek] *n* (*mark*) petite tache *f*

fled [fled] *pt & pp of* **flee**

fledgling ['fledʒlɪŋ] *n* (*bird*) oisillon *m*

flee [fliː] **1** (*pt & pp* **fled**) *vt* (*place*) s'enfuir de; (*danger*) fuir **2** *vi* s'enfuir, fuir

fleece [fliːs] **1** *n* (*of sheep*) toison *f*; (*garment*) (fourrure *f*) polaire *f* **2** *vt* *Fam* (*overcharge*) écorcher; (*cheat*) arnaquer ▪ **fleecy** (**-ier, -iest**) *adj* (*gloves*) molletonné

fleet [fliːt] *n* (*of ships*) flotte *f*; (*of taxis, buses*) parc *m*

fleeting ['fliːtɪŋ] *adj* (*visit, moment*) bref (*f* brève); (*beauty*) éphémère ▪ **fleetingly** *adv* fugitivement, un bref instant

Flemish ['flemɪʃ] **1** *adj* flamand **2** *n* (*language*) flamand *m*; **the F.** (*people*) les Flamands *mpl*

flesh [fleʃ] *n* chair *f*; **in the f.** en chair et en os; **he's your (own) f. and blood** (*child*) c'est la chair de ta chair; (*brother, cousin*) il est de ton sang; **f. wound** blessure *f* superficielle ▪ **fleshy** (**-ier, -iest**) *adj* charnu

flew [fluː] *pt of* **fly²**

flex [fleks] **1** *n* (*wire*) fil *m*; (*for telephone*) cordon *m* **2** *vt* (*limb*) fléchir; (*muscle*) faire jouer

flexible ['fleksɪbəl] *adj* flexible ▪ **flexi'bility** *n* flexibilité *f*

flexitime ['fleksɪtaɪm] *n* horaires *mpl* flexibles *ou* à la carte

flick [flɪk] **1** *n* (*with finger*) chiquenaude *f*; (*with whip*) petit coup *m*; *Br* **f. knife** couteau *m* à cran d'arrêt **2** *vt* (*with whip*) donner un petit coup à; (*with finger*) donner une chiquenaude à; **to f. sth off** (*remove*) enlever qch d'une chiquenaude; **to f. a switch** pousser un bouton; **to f. on/off the light** allumer/éteindre **3** *vi* **to f. over** *or* **through** (*pages*) feuilleter

flicker ['flɪkə(r)] **1** *n* vacillement *m*; **f. of light** lueur *f* vacillante **2** *vi* (*of flame, light*) vaciller

flier ['flaɪə(r)] n (a) (leaflet) prospectus m (b) (person) = personne qui voyage en avion

flies [flaɪz] npl (of trousers) braguette f

flight [flaɪt] n (a) (of bird, aircraft) vol m; **f. to/ from** vol à destination de/en provenance de; **to have a good f.** faire bon voyage; **f. attendant** (man) steward m; (woman) hôtesse f de l'air; **f. deck** cabine f de pilotage; **f. path** trajectoire f de vol (b) (floor) étage m; **f. of stairs** escalier m (c) (escape) fuite f (**from** de); **to take f.** prendre la fuite

flighty ['flaɪtɪ] (-ier, -iest) adj volage

flimsy ['flɪmzɪ] (-ier, -iest) adj (cloth, structure) (light) (trop) léger, -ère; (thin) (trop) mince; (excuse) piètre

flinch [flɪntʃ] vi (with pain) tressaillir; **without flinching** (complaining) sans broncher

fling [flɪŋ] **1** n (affair) aventure f **2** (pt & pp flung) vt jeter; (ball) lancer; **to f. a door open** ouvrir brutalement une porte

flint [flɪnt] n (stone) silex m; (of lighter) pierre f

flip [flɪp] **1** n chiquenaude f; **the f. side** (of record) la face B; **f. chart** tableau m à feuilles **2** (pt & pp -pp-) vt (with finger) donner une chiquenaude à; **to f. a switch** pousser un bouton; **to f. a coin** jouer à pile ou face; **to f. sth over** retourner qch **3** vi **to f. through a book** feuilleter un livre **4** adj Am Fam (impudent) effronté

flip-flops ['flɪpflɒps] npl tongs fpl

flippant ['flɪpənt] adj désinvolte

flipper ['flɪpə(r)] n Br (of swimmer) palme f; (of animal) nageoire f

flipping ['flɪpɪŋ] Br Fam **1** adj (idiot, rain) sacré **2** adv sacrément

flirt [flɜːt] **1** n charmeur, -euse mf **2** vi flirter (**with** avec) ■**flirtation** n flirt m ■**flirtatious** adj (look, smile) charmeur, -euse; **to be f. with sb** flirter avec qn

flit [flɪt] (pt & pp -tt-) vi (fly) voltiger; Fig **to f. in and out** (of person) entrer et sortir rapidement

float [fləʊt] **1** n Fishing bouchon m; (for swimming) flotteur m; (in procession) char m **2** vt (ship) mettre à flot; (wood) faire flotter; (idea, rumour) lancer; (company) introduire en Bourse **3** vi flotter (**on** sur); **to f. down the river** descendre la rivière ■**floating** adj (wood, debt) flottant; (population) fluctuant; **f. voters** électeurs mpl indécis

flock [flɒk] **1** n (of sheep) troupeau m; (of birds) volée f; (of people) foule f; (religious congregation) ouailles fpl **2** vi **to f. round sb** s'attrouper autour de qn; **people are flocking to the exhibition** les gens vont en foule voir l'exposition

flog [flɒg] (pt & pp -gg-) vt (beat) flageller; Br Fam (sell) vendre

flood [flʌd] **1** n inondation f; Fig (of light) flot m; **to be in floods of tears** verser des torrents de

larmes; **the F.** (in the Bible) le Déluge **2** vt (land, bathroom, market) inonder (**with** de); **the river flooded its banks** la rivière est sortie de son lit; **to f. (out)** (house) inonder **3** vi (of river) déborder; **to f. in** (of people, money) affluer; **to f. into** (of tourists) envahir ■**flooding** n inondation(s) f(pl)

floodgate ['flʌdgeɪt] n (in water) vanne f

floodlight ['flʌdlaɪt] **1** n projecteur m **2** (pt & pp -lit) vt illuminer

floor [flɔː(r)] **1** n (of room, forest) sol m; (wooden) plancher m; (storey) étage m; **on the f.** par terre; Br **on the first f.** au premier étage; Am (ground floor) au rez-de-chaussée; **f. polish** cire f; **f. show** spectacle m de cabaret **2** vt (knock down) envoyer au tapis; (puzzle) stupéfier

floorboard ['flɔːbɔːd] n latte f (de plancher)

flop [flɒp] **1** n Fam fiasco m; (play) four m **2** (pt & pp -pp-) vi (fail) (of business, efforts) échouer; (of play, film) faire un four; **to f. down** s'effondrer; **to f. about** s'agiter mollement

floppy ['flɒpɪ] (-ier, -iest) adj (soft) mou (f molle); (clothes) (trop) large; (ears) pendant; Comptr **f. disk** disquette f

flora ['flɔːrə] n (plant life) flore f ■**floral** adj (material, pattern) à fleurs

florid ['flɒrɪd] adj (style) fleuri; (complexion) rubicond

florist ['flɒrɪst] n fleuriste mf

floss [flɒs] n (**dental**) **f.** fil m dentaire

flotilla [fləˈtɪlə] n (of ships) flottille f

flounce [flaʊns] **1** n (on dress, tablecloth) volant m **2** vi **to f. in/out** entrer/sortir brusquement

flounder ['flaʊndə(r)] **1** n (fish) carrelet m **2** vi (in water) patauger; Fig (in speech) perdre pied

flour ['flaʊə(r)] n farine f

flourish ['flʌrɪʃ] **1** n (gesture) grand geste m; (decoration) fioriture f **2** vt (wave) brandir **3** vi (of person, plant) prospérer; (of arts, business) être florissant ■**flourishing** adj (plant) qui prospère; (business) florissant

flout [flaʊt] vt (rules, authority, person) défier

flow [fləʊ] **1** n (of river) courant m; (of tide) flux m; (of current, information, blood) circulation f; (of liquid) écoulement m; **f. of traffic** circulation f; **a f. of visitors/words** un flot de visiteurs/paroles; Fig **to go with the f.** suivre le mouvement; **f. chart** organigramme m **2** vi couler; (of electric current, information) circuler; (of hair, clothes) flotter; (of traffic) s'écouler; **to f. back** (of liquid) refluer; **to f. in** (of people, money) affluer; **to f. into the sea** (of river) se jeter dans la mer ■**flowing** adj (movement, style) fluide; (hair, beard) flottant

flower ['flaʊə(r)] **1** n fleur f; **in f.** en fleur(s); **f. bed** parterre m; **f. pot** pot m de fleurs; **f. shop** fleuriste mf; **f. show** floralies fpl **2** vi fleurir ■**flowered** adj (dress) à fleurs ■**flowering 1** n

floraison f 2 adj (in bloom) en fleurs; (producing flowers) (shrub) à fleurs

flowery ['flaʊərɪ] adj (style) fleuri; (material) à fleurs

flown [fləʊn] pp of **fly²**

flu [fluː] n (influenza) grippe f

fluctuate ['flʌktʃʊeɪt] vi varier ■**fluctuation** [-'eɪʃən] n variation f (**in** de)

flue [fluː] n (of chimney) tuyau m

fluent ['fluːənt] adj (style) fluide; **he's f. in Russian, his Russian is f.** il parle couramment le russe; **to be a f. speaker** s'exprimer avec facilité ■**fluency** n facilité f ■**fluently** adv (write, express oneself) avec facilité; (speak language) couramment

fluff [flʌf] **1** n peluche f **2** vt Fam (bungle) rater ■**fluffy** (**-ier, -iest**) adj (bird) duveteux, -euse; (toy) en peluche

fluid ['fluːɪd] **1** adj fluide; (plans) mal défini; **f. ounce** = 0,03 l **2** n fluide m, liquide m

fluke [fluːk] n Fam coup m de chance; **by a f.** par hasard ■**flukey, fluky** adj Fam (person) chanceux, -euse; **it was a f. guess** c'est par hasard que j'ai/qu'il a /etc deviné juste

flummox ['flʌməks] vt Br Fam scier

flung [flʌŋ] pt & pp of **fling**

flunk [flʌŋk] Am Fam **1** vt (exam) être collé à; (pupil) coller **2** vi (in exam) être collé

flunkey, flunky ['flʌŋkɪ] (pl flunkeys or flunkies) n Fam Pej larbin m

fluorescent [flʊə'resənt] adj fluorescent

fluoride ['flʊəraɪd] n fluorure m; **f. toothpaste** dentifrice m au fluor

flurry ['flʌrɪ] (pl **-ies**) n (of snow) bourrasque f; **a f. of activity** une soudaine activité

flush [flʌʃ] **1** adj (level) de niveau (**with** de); Fam (rich) plein aux as **2** n (**a**) (blush) rougeur f; (of youth, beauty) éclat m; **hot flushes** bouffées fpl de chaleur (**b**) (in cards) flush m (**c**) (in toilet) chasse f d'eau **3** vt **to f. sth** (**out**) (clean) nettoyer qch à grande eau; **to f. the toilet** tirer la chasse d'eau **4** vi (blush) rougir (**with** de) ■**flushed** adj (cheeks) rouge; **f. with success** ivre de succès

fluster ['flʌstə(r)] vt démonter; **to get flustered** se démonter

flute [fluːt] n flûte f ■**flutist** n Am flûtiste mf

flutter ['flʌtə(r)] **1** n Br Fam **to have a f.** (bet) jouer une petite somme (**on** sur) **2** vt **to f. its wings** (of bird) battre des ailes **3** vi (of bird, butterfly) voleter; (of heart) battre; (of flag) flotter

flux [flʌks] n **in a state of f.** en changement constant

fly¹ [flaɪ] (pl **-ies**) n (insect) mouche f

fly² [flaɪ] **1** (pt flew, pp flown) vt (aircraft) piloter; (passengers) transporter; (airline) voyager par; (flag) arborer; (kite) faire voler; **to f. the French flag** battre pavillon français;

to f. the Atlantic traverser l'Atlantique en avion **2** vi (of bird, aircraft) voler; (of passenger) aller en avion; (of time) passer vite; (of flag) flotter; **to f. away** or **off** s'envoler; **to f. out** (of passenger) partir en avion; **to f. out of a room** sortir d'une pièce à toute vitesse; **to f. at sb** (attack) sauter sur qn; **to f. across** or **over** (country, city) survoler; **the door flew open** la porte s'ouvrit brusquement; **I must f.!** il faut que je file! ■**flyby** n (by plane) défilé m aérien ■**fly-by-night** adj (firm) véreux, -euse ■**flyer** n = **flier** ■**flying 1** n (as pilot) pilotage m; (as passenger) voyage m en avion **2** adj (doctor, personnel) volant; **to succeed with f. colours** réussir haut la main; **to get off to a f. start** prendre un très bon départ; **f. saucer** soucoupe f volante; **f. visit** visite f éclair inv; **f. time** heures fpl de vol ■**flyover** n Br (bridge) Toboggan® m ■**flypast** n (by plane) défilé m aérien

fly³ [flaɪ] n Br (on trousers) braguette f

FM [ef'em] (abbr **frequency modulation**) n FM f

foal [fəʊl] n poulain m

foam [fəʊm] **1** n (on sea, mouth) écume f; (on beer) mousse f; **f. bath** bain m moussant; **f. rubber** caoutchouc m Mousse® **2** vi (of sea, mouth) écumer; (of beer, soap) mousser

fob [fɒb] (pt & pp **-bb-**) vt Fam **to f. sb off with an excuse** se débarrasser de qn en lui racontant des salades; **to f. sth off on (to) sb** refiler qch à qn

focal ['fəʊkəl] adj focal

focus ['fəʊkəs] **1** (pl focuses ['fəʊkəsəz] or foci ['fəʊkaɪ]) n (of attention, interest) centre m; (optical, geometrical) foyer m; **the photo is in f./out of f.** la photo est nette/floue; **f. group** groupe-témoin m **2** vt (image, camera) mettre au point; (attention, efforts) concentrer (**on** sur) **3** vi (converge) (of light) converger (**on** sur); **to f. on sb/sth** (with camera) faire la mise au point sur qn/qch **4** vti **to f. (one's eyes) on sb/sth** fixer les yeux sur qn/qch; **to f. (one's attention) on sb/sth** se tourner vers qn/qch

fodder ['fɒdə(r)] n fourrage m

foe [fəʊ] n Literary ennemi, -ie mf

foetus ['fiːtəs] (Am fetus) n fœtus m

fog [fɒg] **1** n brouillard m **2** (pt & pp **-gg-**) vt **to f. the issue** embrouiller la question ■**fogbound** adj bloqué en raison du brouillard ■**foghorn** n corne f de brume ■**foglamp, foglight** n (on vehicle) phare m anti-brouillard inv

fogey ['fəʊgɪ] n = **fogy**

foggy ['fɒgɪ] (**-ier, -iest**) adj brumeux, -euse; **it's f.** il y a du brouillard; **on a f. day** par un jour de brouillard; Fam **I haven't got the foggiest (idea)** je n'en ai pas la moindre idée

fogy ['fəʊgɪ] n old f. vieille baderne f

foible ['fɔɪbəl] n (habit) petite manie f; (weakness) point m faible

foil [fɔɪl] **1** n (**a**) (for cooking) papier m alu; (metal sheet) feuille f de métal (**b**) (person) repoussoir m (**c**) (sword) fleuret m **2** vt (plans) contrecarrer

foist [fɔɪst] vt **to f. sth (off) on sb** refiler qch à qn; **to f. oneself on sb** s'imposer à qn

fold¹ [fəʊld] **1** n (in paper, cloth) pli m **2** vt plier; **to f. away** or **down** or **up** (chair) plier; **to f. back** or **over** (blanket) replier; **to f. one's arms** croiser les bras **3** vi (of chair) se plier; Fam (of business) fermer ses portes; **to f. away** or **down** or **up** (of chair) se plier; **to f. back** or **over** (of blanket) se replier ▪**folding** adj (chair, bed) pliant

fold² [fəʊld] n (for sheep) parc m à moutons; Fig **to return to the f.** rentrer au bercail

-fold [fəʊld] suff **1** adj tenfold par dix **2** adv tenfold dix fois

folder ['fəʊldə(r)] n (file holder) chemise f; (for drawings) carton m à dessins; Comptr répertoire m

foliage ['fəʊlɪɪdʒ] n feuillage m

folk [fəʊk] **1** (Am **folks**) npl gens mpl; Fam **my folks** (parents) mes parents mpl; Fam **hi, folks!** salut tout le monde!; Br **old f.** les vieux mpl **2** adj (dance, costume) folklorique; **f. music** (contemporary) folk m

folklore ['fəʊklɔ:(r)] n folklore m

follow ['fɒləʊ] **1** vt suivre; (career) poursuivre; **followed by** suivi de; **to f. suit** (do the same) faire de même; **to f. sb around** suivre qn partout; **to f. through** (plan, idea) mener à son terme; **to f. up** (idea, story) creuser; (clue, case) suivre; (letter) donner suite à; (remark) faire suivre (**with** de); (advantage) exploiter **2** vi (of person, event) suivre; **it follows that…** il s'ensuit que…; **that doesn't f.** ce n'est pas logique; **to f. on** (come after) suivre ▪**follow-up** n Com (of orders) suivi m (**to** de); (letter) rappel m; **f. visit** (by doctor) visite f de contrôle; **f. treatment** traitement m complémentaire

follower ['fɒləʊə(r)] n (of ideas, politician) partisan m

following ['fɒləʊɪŋ] **1** adj suivant **2** n (of ideas, politician) partisans mpl; **to have a large f.** avoir de nombreux partisans; (of programme) être très suivi **3** prep à la suite de

folly ['fɒlɪ] (pl **-ies**) n folie f

fond [fɒnd] (**-er, -est**) adj (loving) affectueux, -euse; (memory, thought) doux (f douce); **to be (very) f. of sb/sth** aimer beaucoup qn/qch; **with f. regards** (in letter) bien amicalement ▪**fondly** adv tendrement ▪**fondness** n penchant m (**for sth** pour qch); (affection) affection f (**for sb** pour qn)

fondle ['fɒndəl] vt caresser

font [fɒnt] n (**a**) Rel fonts mpl baptismaux (**b**) Typ & Comptr police f de caractères

food [fu:d] **1** n nourriture f; (particular substance) aliment m; (cooking) cuisine f; (for cats, dogs, pigs) pâtée f; (for plants) engrais m; **foods** (foodstuffs) aliments mpl **2** adj (needs, industry) alimentaire; **f. poisoning** intoxication f alimentaire; **f. value** valeur f nutritive

foodstuffs ['fu:dstʌfs] npl denrées fpl alimentaires

fool [fu:l] **1** n imbécile mf; **(you) silly f.!** espèce d'imbécile!; **to make a f. of sb** (ridicule) ridiculiser qn; (trick) rouler qn; **to make a f. of oneself** se couvrir de ridicule; **to be f. enough to do sth** être assez stupide pour faire qch; **to play the f.** faire l'imbécile **2** vt (trick) duper **3** vi **to f. about** or **around** faire l'imbécile; (waste time) perdre son temps; Fam **to f. around** (have affairs) avoir des aventures

foolhardy ['fu:lha:dɪ] adj (rash) téméraire ▪**foolhardiness** n témérité f

foolish ['fu:lɪʃ] adj bête ▪**foolishly** adv bêtement ▪**foolishness** n bêtise f

foolproof ['fu:lpru:f] adj (scheme) infaillible

foot¹ [fʊt] (pl **feet**) n pied m; (of animal) patte f; (unit of measurement) = 30,48 cm, pied m; **at the f. of** (page, stairs) au bas de; (table) au bout de; **on f.** à pied; **to be on one's feet** (standing) être debout; (recovered from illness) être sur pied; **f. brake** (of vehicle) frein m au plancher; **f.-and-mouth disease** fièvre f aphteuse ▪**football** n (soccer) football m; (American game) football américain; (ball) ballon m ▪**footballer** n Br joueur, -euse mf de football ▪**footbridge** n passerelle f ▪**foothills** npl contreforts mpl ▪**foothold** n prise f (de pied); Fig position f; **to gain a f.** (of person) prendre pied (**in** dans) ▪**footlights** npl (in theatre) rampe f ▪**footloose** adj libre de toute attache ▪**footman** (pl **-men**) n valet m de pied ▪**footnote** n note f de bas de page; Fig (extra comment) post-scriptum m inv ▪**footpath** n sentier m ▪**footprint** n empreinte f de pied ▪**footstep** n pas m; **to follow in sb's footsteps** suivre les traces de qn ▪**footstool** n petit tabouret m ▪**footwear** n chaussures fpl

foot² [fʊt] vt (bill) payer

footage ['fʊtɪdʒ] n Cin séquences fpl

footing ['fʊtɪŋ] n (**a**) (balance) **to lose one's f.** perdre l'équilibre (**b**) (level) **to be on an equal f.** être sur un pied d'égalité (**with** avec)

for [fɔ:(r), unstressed fə(r)] **1** prep pour; (for a distance or period of) pendant; (in spite of) malgré; **f. you/me** pour toi/moi; **it's f. tomorrow/f. eating** c'est pour demain/pour manger; **what's it f.?** ça sert à quoi?; **I did it f. love/pleasure** je l'ai fait par amour/par plaisir; **to swim/rush f.** (towards) nager/se précipiter vers; **a train f.** un train à destination de; **the road f. London** la route de Londres; **it's time f. breakfast** c'est l'heure du petit déjeuner; **to come f. dinner** venir dîner; **to sell sth f.** 7

dollars vendre qch 7 dollars; **what's the French f. 'book'?** comment dit-on 'book' en français?; **A f. Alice** A comme Alice; **she walked f. a kilometre** elle a marché pendant un kilomètre; **he was away f. a month** il a été absent pendant un mois; **he won't be back f. a month** il ne sera pas de retour avant un mois; **he's been here f. a month** il est ici depuis un mois; **I haven't seen him f. ten years** voilà dix ans que je ne l'ai vu, je ne l'ai pas vu depuis dix ans; **it's easy f. her to do it** il lui est facile de le faire; **it's f. you to say** c'est à toi de dire; **f. that to be done** pour que ça soit fait **2** *conj (because)* car

forage ['fɒrɪdʒ] *vi* fouiller (**for** pour trouver)

foray ['fɒreɪ] *n* incursion *f* (**into** dans)

forbad [fə'bæd] *pt of* **forbid**

forbade [fə'bæd, fə'beɪd] *pt of* **forbid**

forbearance [fɔː'beərəns] *n Formal* patience *f*

forbid [fə'bɪd] (*pt* **forbad(e)**, *pp* **forbidden** [fə'bɪdən], *pres p* **forbidding**) *vt* interdire, défendre (**sb to do à** qn de faire); **to f. sb sth** interdire qch à qn; **God f.!** Dieu nous en préserve! ■**forbidden** *adj (fruit, region, palace)* défendu; **she is f. to leave** il lui est interdit de partir ■**forbidding** *adj (look, landscape)* sinistre

force [fɔːs] **1** *n* force *f*; **the (armed) forces** les forces armées; **by f.** de force; **by sheer f.** par la force; **in f.** *(rule)* en vigueur; *(in great numbers)* en force **2** *vt* forcer (**to do** à faire); *(impose)* imposer (**on** à); *(door, lock)* forcer; *(confession)* arracher (**from** à); **to f. one's way into** entrer de force dans; **to f. back** *(enemy, demonstrators)* faire reculer; *(tears)* refouler; **to f. down** *(aircraft)* forcer à atterrir; **to f. sth into sth** faire entrer qch de force dans qch; **to f. sth out** faire sortir qch de force ■**forced** *adj* **f. to do** obligé ou forcé de faire; **a f. smile** un sourire forcé ■**force-feed** (*pt & pp* **-fed**) *vt* nourrir de force

forceful ['fɔːsfəl] *adj* énergique

forceps ['fɔːseps] *npl* forceps *m*

forcible ['fɔːsɪbəl] *adj (powerful)* puissant; *Law* **f. entry** entrée *f* par effraction ■**forcibly** *adv (by force)* de force; *(argue, express)* avec force

ford [fɔːd] **1** *n* gué *m* **2** *vt (river)* passer à gué

fore [fɔː(r)] *n* **to come to the f.** *(of issue)* passer au premier plan

forearm ['fɔːrɑːm] *n* avant-bras *m inv*

forebode [fɔː'bəʊd] *vt (warn)* présager ■**foreboding** *n (feeling)* pressentiment *m*

forecast ['fɔːkɑːst] **1** *n (of weather)* prévisions *fpl*; *(in racing)* pronostic *m* **2** (*pt & pp* **forecast(ed)**) *vt* prévoir; *(in racing)* pronostiquer

forecourt ['fɔːkɔːt] *n (of hotel)* avant-cour *f*; *(of petrol station)* devant *m*

forefathers ['fɔːfɑːðəz] *npl* aïeux *mpl*

forefinger ['fɔːfɪŋɡə(r)] *n* index *m*

forefront ['fɔːfrʌnt] *n* **in the f. of** au premier plan de

forego [fɔː'ɡəʊ] (*pp* **-gone**) *vt* renoncer à; **it's a foregone conclusion** c'est couru d'avance

foreground ['fɔːɡraʊnd] *n* premier plan *m*

forehead ['fɒrɪd, 'fɔːhed] *n* front *m*

foreign ['fɒrɪn] *adj (language, person, country)* étranger, -ère; *(trade)* extérieur; *(travel, correspondent)* à l'étranger; *Med* **f. body** corps *m* étranger; **F. Minister,** *Br* **F. Secretary** ministre *m* des Affaires étrangères; *Br* **F. Office** ministère *m* des Affaires étrangères ■**foreigner** *n* étranger, -ère *mf*

foreman ['fɔːmən] (*pl* **-men**) *n (worker)* contremaître *m*; *(of jury)* président *m*

foremost ['fɔːməʊst] *adj* principal

forensic [fə'rensɪk] *adj* **f. medicine** médecine *f* légale

forerunner ['fɔːrʌnə(r)] *n (person)* précurseur *m*

foresee [fɔː'siː] (*pt* **-saw**, *pp* **-seen**) *vt* prévoir ■**foreseeable** *adj* prévisible

foreshadow [fɔː'ʃædəʊ] *vt* annoncer

foresight ['fɔːsaɪt] *n* prévoyance *f*

forest ['fɒrɪst] *n* forêt *f*

forestall [fɔː'stɔːl] *vt* devancer

foretaste ['fɔːteɪst] *n* avant-goût *m* (**of** de)

foretell [fɔː'tel] (*pt & pp* **-told**) *vt* prédire

forethought ['fɔːθɔːt] *n* prévoyance *f*

forever [fə'revə(r)] *adv (for always)* pour toujours; *(continually)* sans cesse

forewarn [fɔː'wɔːn] *vt* avertir

foreword ['fɔːwɜːd] *n* avant-propos *m inv*

forfeit ['fɔːfɪt] **1** *n (in game)* gage *m*; *Law* amende *f* **2** *vt (lose)* perdre

forge [fɔːdʒ] **1** *n* forge *f* **2** *vt (a) (metal, alliance)* forger (**b**) *(signature, money)* contrefaire; **to f. a passport** faire un faux passeport **3** *vi* **to f. ahead** *(progress)* aller de l'avant ■**forged** *adj* faux *(f* fausse); **f. money** fausse monnaie *f* ■**forger** *n (of documents, money)* faussaire *m*

forgery ['fɔːdʒərɪ] (*pl* **-ies**) *n* contrefaçon *f*

forget [fə'ɡet] **1** (*pt* **forgot**, *pp* **forgotten**, *pres p* **forgetting**) *vt* oublier (**to do** de faire); *Fam* **f. it!** *(when thanked)* pas de quoi!; *(it doesn't matter)* laisse tomber!; **to f. oneself** s'oublier **2** *vi* oublier; **to f. about sb/sth** oublier qn/qch ■**forget-me-not** *n* myosotis *m*

forgetful [fə'ɡetfəl] *adj* **to be f.** avoir une mauvaise mémoire ■**forgetfulness** *n* manque *m* de mémoire; *(carelessness)* négligence *f*; **in a moment of f.** dans un moment d'oubli

forgive [fə'ɡɪv] (*pt* **-gave**, *pp* **-given**) *vt* pardonner (**sb sth** qch à qn) ■**forgiveness** *n* pardon *m* ■**forgiving** *adj* indulgent

forgo [fɔː'ɡəʊ] (*pp* **-gone**) *vt* renoncer à

forgot [fə'ɡɒt] *pt of* **forget**

forgotten [fə'ɡɒtən] *pp of* **forget**

fork [fɔːk] **1** *n (for eating)* fourchette *f*; *(for gardening, in road)* fourche *f* **2** *vt Fam* **to f. out** *(money)* allonger **3** *vi (of road)* bifurquer; *Fam* **to f. out** *(pay)* casquer (**on** pour) **▪forked** *adj (branch, tongue)* fourchu **▪forklift truck** *n* chariot *m* élévateur

forlorn [fəˈlɔːn] *adj (forsaken)* abandonné; *(unhappy)* triste

form [fɔːm] **1** *n (shape, type, style)* forme *f*; *(document)* formulaire *m*; *Br Sch* classe *f*; **it's good f.** c'est ce qui se fait; **in the f. of** sous forme de; **a f. of speech** une façon de parler; **on f., in good** *or* **top f.** en (pleine) forme **2** *vt (group, basis, character)* former; *(clay)* façonner; *(habit)* contracter; *(obstacle)* constituer; **to f. part of sth** faire partie de qch; **to f. an opinion** se faire une opinion (**of** de) **3** *vi (appear)* se former

formal [ˈfɔːməl] *adj (person, tone)* cérémonieux, -ieuse; *(announcement, dinner, invitation)* officiel, -ielle; *(agreement)* en bonne et due forme; *(denial, logic)* formel, -elle; *(language)* soutenu; **f. dress** tenue *f* de soirée; **f. education** éducation *f* scolaire **▪formality** [-ˈmælɪtɪ] *(pl* **-ies**) *n (procedure)* formalité *f* **▪formally** *adv (declare)* officiellement; **f. dressed** en tenue de soirée

Note that the French word **formellement** is a false friend. Its most common meaning is **strictly**.

format [ˈfɔːmæt] **1** *n* format *m* **2** *(pt & pp* **-tt-)** *vt Comptr* formater

formation [fɔːˈmeɪʃən] *n* formation *f*

formative [ˈfɔːmətɪv] *adj* formateur, -trice

former [ˈfɔːmə(r)] **1** *adj (previous) (president, teacher, job, house)* ancien, -ienne *(before noun)*; *(situation, life)* antérieur; **her f. husband** son ex-mari; **in f. days** autrefois **2** *pron* **the f.** celui-là, celle-là **▪formerly** *adv* autrefois

formidable [ˈfɔːmɪdəbəl] *adj* effroyable

formula [ˈfɔːmjʊlə] *n* (**a**) *(pl* **-as** *or* **-ae** [-iː]) *(rule, symbols)* formule *f*; *Aut* **f. 1** formule 1 (**b**) *(pl* **-as**) *(baby food)* lait *m* en poudre **▪formulate** [-leɪt] *vt* formuler **▪formulation** [-ˈleɪʃən] *n* formulation *f*

forsake [fəˈseɪk] *(pt* **-sook** [-ˈsʊk], *pp* **-saken** [-ˈseɪkən]) *vt Literary* abandonner

fort [fɔːt] *n Mil* fort *m*; *Fam* **to hold the f.** monter la garde

forte [*Br* ˈfɔːteɪ, *Am* fɔːt] *n* fort *m*

forth [fɔːθ] *adv* en avant; **from this day f.** désormais; **and so f.** et ainsi de suite; **to go back and f.** aller et venir

forthcoming [fɔːθˈkʌmɪŋ] *adj* (**a**) *(event)* à venir; *(book, film)* qui va sortir; **my f. book** mon prochain livre (**b**) *(available)* disponible (**c**) *(informative)* expansif, -ive (**about** sur)

forthright [ˈfɔːθraɪt] *adj* franc (*f* franche)

forthwith [fɔːθˈwɪð] *adv Formal* sur-le-champ

fortieth [ˈfɔːtɪəθ] *adj & n* quarantième *(mf)*

fortify [ˈfɔːtɪfaɪ] *(pt & pp* **-ied**) *vt (strengthen)* fortifier; **to f. sb** *(of food, drink)* réconforter qn, remonter qn **▪fortification** [-fɪˈkeɪʃən] *n* fortification *f*

fortitude [ˈfɔːtɪtjuːd] *n* force *f* morale

fortnight [ˈfɔːtnaɪt] *n Br* quinzaine *f* de jours **▪fortnightly 1** *adj Br* bimensuel, -uelle **2** *adv* tous les quinze jours

fortress [ˈfɔːtrɪs] *n* forteresse *f*

fortuitous [fɔːˈtjuːɪtəs] *adj* fortuit

fortunate [ˈfɔːtʃənət] *adj* heureux, -euse; **to be f.** *(of person)* avoir de la chance; **to be f. enough to…** avoir la chance de…; **it's f. (for her) that…** c'est heureux (pour elle) que… (+ *subjunctive*) **▪fortunately** *adv* heureusement

Note that the French adjective **fortuné** is a false friend. It means **wealthy**.

fortune [ˈfɔːtʃuːn] *n (wealth)* fortune *f*; *(luck)* chance *f*; **to have the good f. to do sth** avoir la chance de faire qch; **to tell sb's f.** dire la bonne aventure à qn; **to make one's f.** faire fortune; **to cost a f.** coûter une (petite) fortune **▪fortune-teller** *n* diseur, -euse *mf* de bonne aventure

forty [ˈfɔːtɪ] *adj & n* quarante *(m)*

forum [ˈfɔːrəm] *n* forum *m*; *Comptr* **discussion f.** forum *m* de discussion; **online f.** forum *m* en ligne

forward [ˈfɔːwəd] **1** *adj (position)* avant *inv*; *(movement)* en avant; *Fig (impudent)* effronté **2** *n Sport* avant *m* **3** *adv* en avant; **to go f.** avancer; **to put the clocks f.** avancer les pendules; **from this day f.** à partir d'aujourd'hui **4** *vt (letter)* faire suivre; *(goods)* expédier **▪forward-looking** *adj* progressiste

forwards [ˈfɔːwədz] *adv* = **forward**

fossil [ˈfɒsəl] *n* fossile *m*; **f. fuel** combustible *m* fossile

foster [ˈfɒstə(r)] **1** *vt* (**a**) *(music, art)* encourager (**b**) *(child)* élever en famille d'accueil **2** *adj* **f. child** = enfant placé dans une famille d'accueil; **f. home** *or* **family** famille *f* d'accueil; **f. parents** parents *mpl* nourriciers

fought [fɔːt] *pt & pp of* **fight**

foul [faʊl] **1** (**-er, -est**) *adj* (**a**) *(smell, taste, weather, person)* infect; *(air)* vicié; *(breath)* fétide; *(language)* grossier, -ière; *(place)* immonde; **to be in a f. mood** être d'une humeur massacrante; **to be f.-mouthed** avoir un langage grossier (**b**) *Sport* **f. play** jeu *m* irrégulier; *Law* acte *m* criminel **2** *n Sport* faute *f* **3** *vt* **to f. (up)** *(get dirty)* salir; *(air)* vicier; *Fam* **to f. up** *(ruin)* gâcher

found¹ [faʊnd] *pt & pp of* **find**

found² [faʊnd] *vt (town, party)* fonder; *(opinion,*

suspicions) fonder, baser (**on** sur) ▪**founder¹** *n* fondateur, -trice *mf*

foundation [faʊn'deɪʃən] *n (of city, organization)* fondation *f; (basis)* fondement *m;* **the foundations** *(of building)* les fondations *fpl;* **without f.** sans fondement; **f. (cream)** fond *m* de teint

founder² ['faʊndə(r)] *vi (of ship)* s'échouer

foundry ['faʊndrɪ] *(pl* -**ies**) *n* fonderie *f*

fountain ['faʊntɪn] *n* fontaine *f;* **f. pen** stylo-plume *m*

four [fɔː(r)] *adj & n* quatre *(m);* **on all fours** à quatre pattes; **f.-letter word** gros mot *m* ▪**fourth** *adj & n* quatrième *(mf)*

fourfold ['fɔːfəʊld] **1** *adj* **a f. increase** une augmentation au quadruple **2** *adv* **to increase f.** quadrupler

foursome ['fɔːsəm] *n* groupe *m* de quatre personnes

fourteen [fɔː'tiːn] *adj & n* quatorze *(m)* ▪**fourteenth** *adj & n* quatorzième *(mf)*

fowl [faʊl] *n inv* volaille *f*

fox [fɒks] **1** *n* renard *m* **2** *vt (puzzle)* laisser perplexe; *(deceive)* duper ▪**foxy** *adj Fam (sly)* rusé; *(sexy)* sexy *inv*

foyer ['fɔɪeɪ] *n (in theatre)* foyer *m; (in hotel)* hall *m*

fraction ['frækʃən] *n* fraction *f* ▪**fractionally** *adv* un tout petit peu

fractious ['frækʃəs] *adj* grincheux, -euse

fracture ['fræktʃə(r)] **1** *n* fracture *f* **2** *vt* fracturer; **to f. one's leg** se fracturer la jambe **3** *vi* se fracturer

fragile [*Br* 'frædʒaɪl, *Am* 'frædʒəl] *adj* fragile ▪**fragility** [frə'dʒɪlətɪ] *n* fragilité *f*

fragment ['frægmənt] *n* fragment *m* ▪**fragmented** [-'mentɪd], ▪**fragmentary** [-'mentərɪ] *adj* fragmentaire

fragrant ['freɪgrənt] *adj* parfumé ▪**fragrance** *n* parfum *m*

frail [freɪl] (-**er**, -**est**) *adj (person)* frêle; *(hope, health)* fragile ▪**frailty** *n* fragilité *f*

frame [freɪm] **1** *n (of building)* charpente *f; (of person)* ossature *f; (of picture, bicycle)* cadre *m; (of door, window)* encadrement *m; (of car)* châssis *m; (of spectacles)* monture *f;* **f. of mind** état *m* d'esprit **2** *vt (picture)* encadrer; *Fig (proposals, ideas)* formuler; *Fam* **to f. sb** monter un coup contre qn ▪**framework** *n* structure *f;* **(with)in the f. of** *(context)* dans le cadre de

franc [fræŋk] *n (currency)* franc *m*

France [frɑːns] *n* la France

franchise ['fræntʃaɪz] *n (right to vote)* droit *m* de vote; *(right to sell product)* franchise *f*

Franco- ['fræŋkəʊ] *pref* franco-

frank¹ [fræŋk] (-**er**, -**est**) *adj (honest)* franc *(f* franche) ▪**frankly** *adv* franchement ▪**frankness** *n* franchise *f*

frank² [fræŋk] *vt (letter)* affranchir

frankfurter ['fræŋkfɜːtə(r)] *n* saucisse *f* de Francfort

frantic ['fræntɪk] *adj (activity, shouts, pace)* frénétique; *(attempt, efforts)* désespéré; **f. with joy** fou *(f* folle) de joie ▪**frantically** *adv* frénétiquement; *(run, search)* comme un fou/une folle; *(work)* avec frénésie

fraternal [frə'tɜːnəl] *adj* fraternel, -elle ▪**fraternity** *(pl* -**ies**) *n (brotherliness)* fraternité *f; Am Univ* = association d'étudiants; **the banking/medical f.** la confrérie des banquiers/médecins ▪**fraternize** ['frætənaɪz] *vi* fraterniser (**with** avec)

fraud [frɔːd] *n* (**a**) *(crime)* fraude *f;* **to obtain sth by f.** obtenir qch frauduleusement (**b**) *(person)* imposteur *m* ▪**fraudulent** ['frɔːdjʊlənt] *adj* frauduleux, -euse

fraught [frɔːt] *adj (situation)* tendu; **f. with** plein de

fray [freɪ] **1** *n (fight)* bagarre *f* **2** *vt (garment)* effilocher; *(rope)* user; **my nerves are frayed** j'ai les nerfs à vif; **tempers were frayed** on s'énervait **3** *vi (of garment)* s'effilocher; *(of rope)* s'user

freak [friːk] **1** *n (person)* monstre *m; Fam* **jazz f.** fana *f* de jazz **2** *adj (result, weather)* anormal; **f. accident** accident imprévisible

▸**freak out** *Fam* **1** *vt sep (shock, scare)* faire flipper **2** *vi (panic)* paniquer; *(get angry)* piquer une crise

freckle ['frekəl] *n* tache *f* de rousseur ▪**freckled** *adj* couvert de taches de rousseur

free [friː] **1** (**freer, freest**) *adj (at liberty, not occupied)* libre; *(without cost)* gratuit; *(lavish)* généreux, -euse (**with** de); **to get f.** se libérer; **to be f. to do sth** être libre de faire qch; **to let sb go f.** relâcher qn; **to be f. of sb** être débarrassé de qn; **f. of charge** gratuit; **to have a f. hand** avoir carte blanche (**to do** pour faire); **f. and easy** décontracté; **f. gift** cadeau *m; Football* **f. kick** coup *m* franc; **f. speech** liberté *f* d'expression; **f. trade** libre-échange *m*

2 *adv* **f. (of charge)** gratuitement

3 *(pt & pp* **freed**) *vt (prisoner, country)* libérer; *(trapped person)* dégager; *(untie)* détacher ▪**Freefone®** *n Br (phone number)* ≃ numéro *m* vert ▪**free-for-'all** *n* bagarre *f* ▪**freehold** *n Law* propriété *f* foncière perpétuelle et libre ▪**freelance 1** *adj* indépendant **2** *n* travailleur, -euse *mf* indépendant(e) **3** *adv* **to work f.** travailler en indépendant ▪**freeloader** *n Fam* parasite *m* ▪**Freemason** *n* franc-maçon *m* ▪**Freepost®** *n Br* ≃ correspondance-réponse *f* ▪**free-range** *adj Br* **f. chicken** poulet *m* fermier; *Br* **f. egg** œuf *m* de ferme ▪**freestyle** *n (in swimming)* nage *f* libre ▪**free'thinker** *n* libre penseur, -euse *mf* ▪**freeway** *n Am* autoroute *f* ▪**free-wheel** *vi (on bicycle)* être en roue libre

freebie ['fri:bi:] *n Fam* petit cadeau *m*

freedom ['fri:dəm] *n* liberté *f*; **f. of information** libre accès *m* à l'information; **f. of speech** liberté *f* d'expression; **f. from worry/responsibility** absence *f* de souci/de responsabilité; **f. fighter** guérillero *m*

freely ['fri:lɪ] *adv (speak, act, circulate)* librement; *(give)* sans compter

freeze [fri:z] **1** *n (in weather)* gel *m*; *(of prices, salaries)* blocage *m* **2** *(pt* **froze,** *pp* **frozen)** *vt (food)* congeler; *(credits, river)* geler; *(prices, wages)* bloquer; **frozen food** surgelés *mpl* **3** *vi* geler; *(of person)* s'arrêter net; **f.!** ne bougez plus!; **to f. to death** mourir de froid; **to f. up** or **over** *(of lake)* geler ▪**freeze-dry** *vt* lyophiliser ▪**freezer** *n (deep-freeze)* congélateur *m*; *(ice-box)* freezer *m* ▪**freezing 1** *adj (weather)* glacial; *(hands, feet)* gelé; **it's f.** il gèle; *Fam* **I'm f.!** je gèle! **2** *n* **it's 5 degrees below f.** il fait 5 degrés au-dessous de zéro **3** *adv* **f. cold** très froid; **it's f. cold in here!** on meurt de froid ici!

freight [freɪt] *Com* **1** *n (transport)* fret *m*; *(goods)* cargaison *f*; **f. train** train *m* de marchandises **2** *vt (goods)* transporter ▪**freighter** *n (ship)* cargo *m*

French [frentʃ] **1** *adj* français; *(teacher)* de français; *(embassy)* de France; **F. fries** frites *fpl*; **F. loaf** baguette *f* **2** *n (language)* français *m*; **the F.** *(people)* les Français *mpl* ▪**Frenchman** *(pl* -**men)** *n* Français *m* ▪**French-speaking** *adj* francophone ▪**Frenchwoman** *(pl* -**women)** *n* Française *f*

frenzy ['frenzɪ] *(pl* -**ies)** *n* frénésie *f* ▪**frenzied** *adj (activity)* frénétique; *(person)* affolé; *(attack)* violent

frequency ['fri:kwənsɪ] *(pl* -**ies)** *n* fréquence *f*

frequent 1 ['fri:kwənt] *adj* fréquent; **f. flyer =** personne qui prend souvent l'avion; **f. visitor** habitué, -uée *mf* **(to** de) **2** [frɪ'kwent] *vt* fréquenter ▪**frequently** *adv* fréquemment

fresco ['freskəʊ] *(pl* -**oes** or -**os)** *n* fresque *f*

fresh [freʃ] **1** (-**er,** -**est)** *adj* frais *(f* fraîche); *(new)* nouveau *(f* nouvelle); *Am Fam (cheeky)* insolent; **to get some f. air** prendre l'air; **f.-water fish** poisson *m* d'eau douce **2** *adv* **to be f. from** *(city, country)* arriver tout juste de; *(school, university)* sortir tout juste de ▪**freshly** *adv (arrived, picked)* fraîchement ▪**freshness** *n* fraîcheur *f*

freshen ['freʃən] **1** *vi (of wind)* fraîchir; **to f. up** *(have a wash)* faire un brin de toilette **2** *vt* **to f. up** *(house)* retaper; **to f. sb up** *(of bath, shower)* rafraîchir qn

fresher ['freʃə(r)] *n Br Univ* étudiant, -iante *mf* de première année

freshman ['freʃmən] *(pl* -**men)** *n Am Univ* étudiant, -iante *mf* de première année

fret [fret] *(pt & pp* -**tt-)** *vi (worry)* se faire du souci ▪**fretful** *adj* inquiet, -iète

friar ['fraɪə(r)] *n* moine *m*

friction ['frɪkʃən] *n* friction *f*

Friday ['fraɪdeɪ] *n* vendredi *m*; **Good F.** le Vendredi saint

fridge [frɪdʒ] *n* frigo *m*

fried [fraɪd] **1** *pt & pp of* **fry¹ 2** *adj* frit; **f. egg** œuf *m* sur le plat

friend [frend] *n* ami, -ie *mf*; **to be friends with sb** être ami avec qn; **to make friends with sb** devenir ami avec qn ▪**friendly 1** (-**ier,** -**iest)** *adj* amical; **f. advice** conseils *mpl* d'ami; **to be f. with sb** être ami avec qn; **to be on f. terms with sb** être en bons termes avec qn **2** *n Sport* match *m* amical ▪**friendship** *n* amitié *f*

frieze [fri:z] *n (on building)* frise *f*

fright [fraɪt] *n* peur *f*; **to take f.** prendre peur; **to give sb a f.** faire peur à qn; *Fam* **you look a f.!** tu es à faire peur!

frighten ['fraɪtən] *vt* effrayer, faire peur à; **to f. sb away** or **off** faire fuir qn ▪**frightened** *adj* effrayé; **to be f.** avoir peur **(of** de) ▪**frightening** *adj* effrayant

frightful ['fraɪtfəl] *adj* affreux, -euse ▪**frightfully** *adv* terriblement

frigid ['frɪdʒɪd] *adj (greeting, manner)* glacial; *(woman)* frigide

frill [frɪl] *n* volant *m*; **no frills** *(machine, holiday)* rudimentaire; *(ceremony)* sans chichis

fringe [frɪndʒ] *n* **(a)** *(of hair, on clothes)* frange *f* **(b)** *(of forest)* lisière *f*; *(of town)* abords *mpl*; **on the fringes of society** en marge de la société; **f. benefits** avantages *mpl* divers; **f. group** groupuscule *m*; *Br* **f. theatre** théâtre *m* expérimental

Frisbee® ['frɪzbi:] *n* Frisbee® *m*

frisk [frɪsk] **1** *vt (search)* fouiller **2** *vi* **to f. (about)** gambader

frisky ['frɪskɪ] (-**ier,** -**iest)** *adj (lively)* vif *(f* vive)

fritter ['frɪtə(r)] **1** *n Culin* beignet *m* **2** *vt* **to f. away** gaspiller

frivolous ['frɪvələs] *adj* frivole ▪**frivolity** [-'vɒlɪtɪ] *(pl* -**ies)** *n* frivolité *f*

frizzy ['frɪzɪ] *adj (hair)* crépu

fro [frəʊ] *adv* **to go to and f.** aller et venir

frock [frɒk] *n (dress)* robe *f*; *(of monk)* froc *m*

Frog [frɒg] *n Br Fam (French person) =* terme injurieux désignant un Français

frog [frɒg] *n* grenouille *f*; **f.'s legs** cuisses *fpl* de grenouille; *Fam* **to have a f. in one's throat** avoir un chat dans la gorge ▪**'frogman** *(pl* -**men)** *n* homme-grenouille *m*

frolic ['frɒlɪk] *(pt & pp* -**ck-)** *vi* **to f. (about)** gambader ▪**frolics** *npl (playing)* gambades *fpl*; *(pranks)* gamineries *fpl*

from [frɒm, *unstressed* frəm] *prep* **(a)** *(expressing origin)* de; **a letter f. sb** une lettre de qn; **to suffer f. sth** souffrir de qch; **where are you f.?** d'où êtes-vous?; **I come f. Portugal** je viens du Portugal; **a train f. Paris** un train en provenance de Paris; **to be 10 m (away)** f. the **house** être à 10 m de la maison; **f. York to London** de York à Londres

(**b**) (*expressing time*) à partir de; **f. today (on), as** f. **today** à partir d'aujourd'hui; **f. then on** depuis ce jour-là; **f. the beginning** dès le début

(**c**) (*expressing range*) **f.... to...** de... à...; **f. six to seven o'clock** de six à sept heures; **f. morning till night** du matin au soir; **they take children** f. **the age of five** ils acceptent les enfants à partir de cinq ans

(**d**) (*expressing source*) de; **to take/borrow sth f. sb** prendre/emprunter qch à qn; **to drink f. a cup** boire dans une tasse

(**e**) (*expressing removal*) de; **to take sth f. sb** prendre qch à qn; **to take sth f. a box** prendre qch dans une boîte; **to take sth f. the table** prendre qch sur la table

(**f**) (*according to*) d'après; **f. what I saw...** d'après ce que j'ai vu...

(**g**) (*on behalf of*) de la part de; **tell her f. me** dis-lui de ma part

front [frʌnt] **1** *n* devant *m*; (*of boat, car*) avant *m*; (*of building*) façade *f*; (*of crowd*) premier rang *m*; *Mil & Pol* front *m*; *Br* **on the sea f.** sur le front de mer; **in f. of sb/sth** devant qn/qch; **in f.** devant; (*further ahead*) en avant; (*in race*) en tête; **I sat in the f.** (*of car*) j'étais assis à l'avant; *Fig* **it's just a f.** (*appearance*) ce n'est qu'une façade; *Met* **cold/warm f.** front froid/chaud **2** *adj* (*tooth, garden*) de devant; (*car seat*) avant *inv*; (*row, page*) premier, -ière; **f. door** porte *f* d'entrée; *Mil* **f. line** front *m*; *Br* **f. room** (*lounge*) salon *m*; **f. view** vue *f* de face; *Aut* **f.-wheel drive** traction *f* avant **3** *vt* (*organization*) être à la tête de; (*government*) diriger; (*TV programme*) présenter **4** *vi* **to f. on to** (*of windows*) donner sur ▪**frontrunner** *n Fig* favori, -ite *mf*

frontage ['frʌntɪdʒ] *n* façade *f*

frontal ['frʌntəl] *adj Anat & (attack)* frontal

frontier ['frʌntɪə(r)] *n* frontière *f*; **f. town** ville *f* frontalière

frost [frɒst] **1** *n* gel *m* **2** *vi* **to f. up** (*of window*) se couvrir de givre

frostbite ['frɒstbaɪt] *n* gelure *f* ▪**frostbitten** *adj* gelé

frosted ['frɒstɪd] *adj* (**a**) (*glass*) dépoli (**b**) *Am* (*cake*) glacé

frosting ['frɒstɪŋ] *n Am* (*icing on cake*) glaçage *m*

frosty ['frɒstɪ] (**-ier, -iest**) *adj* (*air, night*) glacé; (*window*) givré; *Fig* (*welcome*) glacial; **it's f.** il gèle

froth [frɒθ] **1** *n* (*on beer*) mousse *f*; (*on waves*) écume *f* **2** *vi* (*liquid*) mousser ▪**frothy** (**-ier, -iest**) *adj* (*beer*) mousseux, -euse

frown [fraʊn] **1** *n* froncement *m* de sourcils **2** *vi* froncer les sourcils; *Fig* **to f. (up)on** désapprouver

froze [frəʊz] *pt of* **freeze**

frozen ['frəʊzən] *pp of* **freeze**

frugal ['fruːgəl] *adj* frugal ▪**frugally** *adv* frugalement

fruit [fruːt] *n* fruit *m*; **some f.** (*one item*) un fruit; (*more than one*) des fruits; **to like f.** aimer les fruits; **f. basket/bowl** corbeille *f*/coupe *f* à fruits; **f. drink** boisson *f* aux fruits; **f. juice** jus *m* de fruit; **f. salad** salade *f* de fruits; **f. tree** arbre *m* fruitier; *Br* **f. machine** (*for gambling*) machine *f* à sous ▪**fruitcake** *n* cake *m*; *Br Fam* cinglé, -ée *mf*

fruitful ['fruːtfəl] *adj* (*meeting, discussion*) fructueux, -ueuse ▪**fruitless** *adj* (*attempt, search*) infructueux, -ueuse

fruition [fruː'ɪʃən] *n* **to come to f.** (*of plan*) porter ses fruits

fruity ['fruːtɪ] (**-ier, -iest**) *adj* (*taste*) de fruit

frumpish ['frʌmpɪʃ], **frumpy** ['frʌmpɪ] *adj Fam* **to be f.** faire mémère

frustrate [frʌ'streɪt] *vt* (*person*) frustrer; (*plans*) contrarier ▪**frustrated** *adj* (*person*) frustré; ▪**frustrating** *adj* frustrant ▪**frustration** *n* frustration *f*

fry[1] [fraɪ] **1** (*pt & pp* **fried**) *vt* faire frire **2** *vi* frire ▪**frying** *n* friture *f*; **f. pan** poêle *f* (à frire) ▪**fry-up** *n Br Fam* = bacon, œufs, saucisses, tomates etc frits ensemble

fry[2] [fraɪ] *n* **small f.** (*people*) menu fretin *m*

ft *abbr* (*unit of measurement*) = **foot**[1], **feet**

fuddy-duddy ['fʌdɪdʌdɪ] *n Fam* **he's an old f.** c'est un vieux schnock

fudge [fʌdʒ] **1** *n* (*sweet*) caramel *m* mou **2** *vt* **to f. the issue** éluder une question

fuel [fjʊəl] **1** *n* combustible *m*; (*for engine*) carburant *m*; **f. oil** mazout *m*; **f. tank** (*in vehicle*) réservoir *m* **2** (*Br* **-ll-**, *Am* **-l-**) *vt* (*stove*) alimenter; (*vehicle, plane, ship*) ravitailler (en combustible); *Fig* (*anger, hatred*) attiser; **to be fuelled by diesel** (*of engine*) marcher au gazole

fugitive ['fjuːdʒɪtɪv] *n* fugitif, -ive *mf*

fugue [fjuːg] *n Mus* fugue *f*

fulfil [fʊl'fɪl] (*Am* **fulfill**) (*pt & pp* **-ll-**) *vt* (*ambition, dream*) réaliser; (*condition, duty*) remplir; (*desire, need*) satisfaire; **to f. oneself** s'épanouir ▪**fulfilling** *adj* satisfaisant ▪**fulfilment** (*Am* **fulfillment**) *n* (*of ambition*) réalisation *f* (**of** de); (*satisfaction*) épanouissement *m*

full [fʊl] **1** (**-er, -est**) *adj* plein (**of** de); (*bus, theatre, hotel, examination*) complet, -ète; (*amount*) intégral; (*day, programme*) chargé; (*skirt*) bouffant; **to be f.** (*up*) (*of person*) n'avoir plus faim; (*of hotel*) être complet; **to wait a f. hour** attendre une heure entière; **to pay (the) f. fare** *or* **price** payer plein tarif; **to lead a f. life** mener une vie bien remplie; **at f. speed** à toute vitesse; **f. house** (*in theatre*) salle *f* comble; **f. member** membre à part entière; **f. name** nom *m* et prénom *m*; *Br* **f. stop** point *m*

2 *n* in f. *(pay)* intégralement; *(read, publish)* en entier; *(write)* en toutes lettres; **the text in f.** le texte intégral; **to live life to the f.** vivre pleinement **3** *adv* **to know f. well** savoir fort bien; **f. in the face** *(hit)* en pleine figure ■ **full-back** *n Sport* arrière *m* ■ '**full-'blown** *adj (row)* vrai; **to have f. AIDS** avoir le SIDA ■ '**full-'grown** *adj* adulte ■ '**full-'length** *adj (portrait)* en pied; *(dress)* long *(f* longue); **f. film** long métrage *m* ■ '**full-'scale** *adj (model)* grandeur nature *inv; (operation)* de grande envergure ■ '**full-'sized** *adj (model)* grandeur nature *inv* ■ '**full-'time** *adj & adv (work)* à plein temps

fullness ['fʊlnɪs] *n (of details)* abondance *f; (of dress)* ampleur *f;* **in the f. of time** avec le temps

fully ['fʊlɪ] *adv (completely)* entièrement; *(understand)* parfaitement; *(at least)* au moins ■ '**fully-'fledged** *(Am* '**full-'fledged)** *adj (engineer, teacher)* diplômé; *(member)* à part entière ■ '**fully-'grown** *adj* adulte

fulsome ['fʊlsəm] *adj (praise)* excessif, -ive; **a f. apology** de plates excuses

fumble ['fʌmbəl] *vi* **to f. (about)** *(grope)* tâtonner; *(search)* fouiller (**for** pour trouver); **to f. (about) with sth** tripoter qch

fume [fjuːm] *vi* **(a)** *(give off fumes)* fumer **(b) to be fuming** *(of person)* rager ■ **fumes** *npl* émanations *fpl; (from car)* gaz *mpl* d'échappement

Note that the French verb **fumer** is a false friend. Its most common meaning is **to smoke**.

fumigate ['fjuːmɪgeɪt] *vt* désinfecter (par fumigation)

fun [fʌn] *n* plaisir *m;* **for f., for the f. of it** pour le plaisir; **to be (good or great) f.** être (très) amusant; **to have (some) f.** s'amuser; **to make f. of sb/sth** se moquer de qn/qch; **to spoil sb's f.** empêcher qn de s'amuser

function ['fʌŋkʃən] **1** *n (role, duty) & Comptr* fonction *f; (party)* réception *f; (ceremony)* cérémonie *f* **2** *vi* fonctionner; **to f. as** faire fonction de ■ **functional** *adj* fonctionnel, -elle

fund [fʌnd] **1** *n (of money)* fonds *m; Fig (of information)* mine *f;* **funds** fonds *mpl;* **f. manager** gestionnaire *mf* de fonds **2** *vt* financer

fundamental [fʌndə'mentəl] *adj* fondamental **2** *npl* **fundamentals** principes *mpl*

funeral ['fjuːnərəl] *n* enterrement *m; (grandiose)* funérailles *fpl;* **f. service/march** service *m*/marche *f* funèbre; *Br* **f. parlour,** *Am* **f. home** entreprise *f* de pompes funèbres

funfair ['fʌnfeə(r)] *n Br* fête *f* foraine

fungus ['fʌŋgəs] *(pl* **-gi** [-gaɪ]) *n (plant)* champignon *m; (on walls)* moisissure *f*

funicular [fjʊ'nɪkjʊlə(r)] *n* funiculaire *m*

funky ['fʌŋkɪ] *adj Fam* cool *inv*

funnel ['fʌnəl] *n* **(a)** *(of ship)* cheminée *f* **(b)** *(for filling)* entonnoir *m*

funny ['fʌnɪ] **(-ier, -iest)** *adj (amusing)* drôle; *(strange)* bizarre; **a f. idea** une drôle d'idée; **there's some f. business going on** il y a quelque chose de louche; **to feel f.** ne pas se sentir très bien ■ **funnily** *adv (amusingly)* drôlement; *(strangely)* bizarrement; **f. enough, I was just about to…** bizarrement, j'étais sur le point de…

fur [fɜː(r)] **1** *n* **(a)** *(of animal, for wearing)* fourrure *f; (of dog, cat)* poil *m;* **f. coat** manteau *m* de fourrure **(b)** *Br (in kettle, boiler)* tartre *m* **2** *(pt & pp* **-rr-)** *vi Br* **to f. (up)** *(of kettle)* s'entartrer

furious ['fjʊərɪəs] *adj (violent, angry)* furieux, -ieuse *(with or at* contre); *(efforts, struggle)* violent; **at a f. speed** à une allure folle ■ **furiously** *adv* furieusement; *(struggle)* avec acharnement; *(drive, rush)* à une allure folle

furlong ['fɜːlɒŋ] *n (measurement)* = 201 m

furnace ['fɜːnɪs] *n (forge)* fourneau *m; Fig (hot room)* fournaise *f*

furnish ['fɜːnɪʃ] *vt* **(a)** *(room, house)* meubler **(b)** *Formal (supply)* fournir (**sb with sth** qch à qn) ■ **furnishings** *npl* ameublement *m*

furniture ['fɜːnɪtʃə(r)] *n* meubles *mpl;* **a piece of f.** un meuble; **f. shop** magasin *m* d'ameublement

Note that the French noun **fourniture** is a false friend. Its most common meaning is **supplies**.

furrow ['fʌrəʊ] *n (in earth, on brow)* sillon *m*

furry ['fɜːrɪ] *adj (animal)* à poil; *(toy)* en peluche

further ['fɜːðə(r)] **1** *adv & adj* = **farther 2** *adj (additional)* supplémentaire; **a f. case** *(another)* un autre cas; **without f. delay** sans plus attendre; **until f. notice** jusqu'à nouvel ordre; **for f. information…** pour de plus amples renseignements…; *Br* **f. education** = enseignement supérieur dispensé par un établissement autre qu'une université **3** *adv (more)* davantage; *Formal (besides)* en outre; **f. to my letter…** suite à ma lettre…; **he did not question us any f.** il ne nous a pas interrogés davantage **4** *vt (cause, research, career)* promouvoir ■ **further'more** *adv Formal* en outre ■ **furthest** *adj & adv* = **farthest**

furtive ['fɜːtɪv] *adj* sournois

fury ['fjʊərɪ] *n (violence, anger)* fureur *f*

fuse [fjuːz] **1** *n (wire)* fusible *m; (of bomb)* amorce *f* **2** *vt (melt)* fondre; *(join)* fusionner; *Br* **to f. the lights** faire sauter les plombs **3** *vi (of metals)* fondre; *(of organizations)* fusionner; *Br* **the lights have fused** les plombs ont sauté

fused [fjuːzd] *adj Br* **f. plug** fiche *f* avec fusible incorporé

fuselage ['fjuːzəlɑːʒ] *n* fuselage *m*

fusion ['fjuːʒən] *n* fusion *f*

fuss [fʌs] **1** *n* histoires *fpl*; **what a (lot of) f.!** quelle histoire!; **to kick up** *or* **make a f.** faire des histoires; **to make a f. of sb** être aux petits soins pour qn **2** *vi* faire des histoires; **to f. about** s'activer; **to f. over sb** être aux petits soins pour qn ▪**fusspot** (*Am* **fussbudget**) *n Fam* chichiteux, -euse *mf* ▪**fussy** (**-ier, -iest**) *adj* exigeant (**about** sur); **I'm not f.** *(I don't mind)* ça m'est égal

fusty [ˈfʌstɪ] (**-ier, -iest**) *adj (smell)* de renfermé

futile [*Br* ˈfjuːtaɪl, *Am* ˈfjuːtəl] *adj (remark)* futile; *(attempt)* vain ▪**fu'tility** *n* futilité *f*

futon [ˈfuːtɒn] *n* futon *m*

future [ˈfjuːtʃə(r)] **1** *n* avenir *m*; *Grammar* futur *m*; **in (the) f.** à l'avenir **2** *adj* futur; **my f. wife** ma future épouse; **the f. tense** le futur; **at a** *or* **some f. date** à une date ultérieure

fuze [fjuːz] *n & vti Am* = **fuse**

fuzz [fʌz] *n (on face, legs)* duvet *m*; *Am (of fabric)* peluches *fpl*

fuzzy [ˈfʌzɪ] (**-ier, -iest**) *adj* (**a**) *(unclear) (picture, idea)* flou (**b**) *Am (material, coat)* pelucheux, -euse (**c**) *(hair)* crépu

FYI [efwaɪˈaɪ] *(abbr* **for your information***)* à titre indicatif

G, g [dʒiː] *n* (**a**) (*letter*) G, g *m inv* (**b**) *Mus* sol *m* ▪**G-string** *n* string *m*

gab [gæb] *n Fam* **to have the gift of the g.** (*be talkative*) avoir la langue bien pendue; (*speak persuasively*) avoir de la tchatche

gabardine [gæbəˈdiːn] *n* (*material, coat*) gabardine *f*

gabble [ˈgæbəl] **1** *n* **a g. of conversation** un bruit de conversation **2** *vi* (*chatter*) jacasser; (*indistinctly*) bredouiller

gable [ˈgeɪbəl] *n* pignon *m*

gad [gæd] (*pt & pp* **-dd-**) *vi* **to g. about** *or* **around** vadrouiller

gadget [ˈgædʒɪt] *n* gadget *m*

Gaelic [ˈgeɪlɪk, ˈgælɪk] *adj & n* gaélique (*m*)

gaffe [gæf] *n* (*blunder*) gaffe *f*

gag [gæg] **1** *n* (**a**) (*on mouth*) bâillon *m* (**b**) *Fam* (*joke*) blague *f* **2** (*pt & pp* **-gg-**) *vt* (*person*) bâillonner; *Fig* (*press*) museler **3** *vi* (*choke*) s'étouffer (**on** avec); (*retch*) avoir des haut-le-cœur

gaggle [ˈgægəl] *n* troupeau *m*

gaiety [ˈgeɪtɪ] *n* gaieté *f* ▪**gaily** *adv* gaiement

gain [geɪn] **1** *n* (*increase*) augmentation *f* (**in** de); (*profit*) gain *m*; *Fig* avantage *m* **2** *vt* (*obtain, win*) gagner; (*experience, reputation*) acquérir; **to g. speed/weight** prendre de la vitesse/du poids; **to g. support** (*of person, idea*) recueillir de plus en plus d'opinions favorables **3** *vi* (*of clock*) avancer; **to g. in popularity** devenir populaire; **to g. on sb** gagner du terrain sur qn; **to g. by sth** bénéficier de qch

gainful [ˈgeɪnfəl] *adj* **g. employment** emploi *m* rémunéré

gainsay [geɪnˈseɪ] (*pt & pp* **-said** [-sed]) *vt Formal* (*person*) contredire; (*facts*) nier

gait [geɪt] *n* démarche *f*

gala [*Br* ˈgɑːlə, *Am* ˈgeɪlə] *n* gala *m*; *Br* **swimming g.** concours *m* de natation

galaxy [ˈgæləksɪ] (*pl* **-ies**) *n* galaxie *f*

gale [geɪl] *n* grand vent *m*

gall [gɔːl] **1** *n* (*bitterness*) fiel *m*; (*impudence*) culot *m*; **g. bladder** vésicule *f* biliaire **2** *vt* (*annoy*) irriter

gallant [ˈgælənt] *adj* (*brave*) brave; (*polite*) galant ▪**gallantry** *n* (*bravery*) bravoure *f*; (*politeness*) galanterie *f*

galleon [ˈgælɪən] *n Hist* (*ship*) galion *m*

gallery [ˈgælərɪ] (*pl* **-ies**) *n* (*room, shop, in theatre*) galerie *f*; (*museum*) musée *m*; (*for public, press*) tribune *f*

galley [ˈgælɪ] (*pl* **-eys**) *n Hist* (*ship*) galère *f*; (*kitchen*) cuisine *f*

Gallic [ˈgælɪk] *adj* (*French*) français

galling [ˈgɔːlɪŋ] *adj* humiliant

gallivant [ˈgælɪvænt] *vi Fam* **to g. (about)** vadrouiller

gallon [ˈgælən] *n* gallon *m* (*Br = 4,5 l, Am = 3,8 l*)

gallop [ˈgæləp] **1** *n* galop *m* **2** *vi* galoper; **to g. away** (*rush off*) partir en vitesse; **galloping inflation** inflation *f* galopante

gallows [ˈgæləʊz] *n* potence *f*

gallstone [ˈgɔːlstəʊn] *n Med* calcul *m* biliaire

galore [gəˈlɔː(r)] *adv Fam* à gogo

galvanize [ˈgælvənaɪz] *vt* (*metal, person*) galvaniser

Gambia [ˈgæmbɪə] *n* **The G.** la Gambie

gambit [ˈgæmbɪt] *n* **opening g.** (*ploy*) manœuvre *f* d'approche

gamble [ˈgæmbəl] **1** *n* (*risk*) coup *m* risqué; **to take a g.** prendre un risque **2** *vt* (*bet*) parier, jouer; **to g. sth away** (*lose*) perdre qch au jeu **3** *vi* jouer (**on** sur; **with** avec); **to g. on the horses** jouer aux courses; **to g. on sth** (*count on*) miser sur qch ▪**gambler** *n* joueur, -euse *mf* ▪**gambling** *n* jeu *m*

game¹ [geɪm] *n* (**a**) (*activity*) jeu *m*; (*of football, cricket*) match *m*; (*of tennis, chess, cards*) partie *f*; **to have a g. of football/tennis** faire un match de football/une partie de tennis; *Br* **games** (*in school*) le sport; *Br* **games teacher** professeur *m* d'éducation physique; **g. show** jeu *m* télévisé (**b**) (*animals, birds*) gibier *m*; *Fig* **to be fair g. for sb** être une proie idéale pour qn

game² [geɪm] *adj* (*brave*) courageux, -euse; **to be g. (to do sth)** être partant (pour faire qch)

gamekeeper [ˈgeɪmkiːpə(r)] *n* garde-chasse *m*

gammon [ˈgæmən] *n Br* jambon *m*

gammy [ˈgæmɪ] *adj Fam* **a g. leg** une patte folle

gamut [ˈgæmət] *n Mus & Fig* gamme *f*

gang [gæŋ] **1** *n* (*of children, friends*) bande *f*; (*of workers*) équipe *f*; (*of criminals*) gang *m* **2** *vi* **to g. up on** *or* **against** se mettre à plusieurs contre

Ganges [ˈgændʒiːz] *n* **the G.** le Gange *m*

gangling [ˈgæŋglɪŋ] *adj* dégingandé

gangrene [ˈgæŋgriːn] *n* gangrène *f*

gangster [ˈgæŋstə(r)] *n* gangster *m*

gangway ['gæŋweɪ] *n Br* passage *m*; *(in train, plane)* couloir *m*; *(on ship)* passerelle *f*; *(in bus, cinema, theatre)* allée *f*; **g.!** dégagez!

gaol [dʒeɪl] *n & vt Br* = **jail**

gap [gæp] *n (space)* espace *m* (**between** entre); *(in wall, fence)* trou *m*; *(in time)* intervalle *m*; *(in knowledge)* lacune *f*; **the g. between** *(difference)* l'écart *m* entre; *Br* **g. year** = année que s'accorde un étudiant avant son entrée à l'université ou à la fin de ses études

gape [geɪp] *vi (stare)* rester bouche bée; **to g. at sb/sth** regarder qn/qch bouche bée ▪ **gaping** *adj* béant

garage [*Br* 'gæra:(d)ʒ, 'gærɪdʒ, *Am* gə'ra:ʒ] *n* garage *m*

garbage ['ga:bɪdʒ] *n Am* ordures *fpl*; **g. can** poubelle *f*; **g. man** *or* **collector** éboueur *m*

garbled ['ga:bəld] *adj* confus

garden ['ga:dən] **1** *n* jardin *m*; **gardens** *(park)* parc *m*; **g. centre** jardinerie *f*; **g. party** garden-party *f*; **g. produce** produits *mpl* maraîchers **2** *vi* jardiner, faire du jardinage ▪ **gardener** *n* jardinier, -ière *mf* ▪ **gardening** *n* jardinage *m*

gargle ['ga:gəl] *vi* se gargariser

gargoyle ['ga:gɔɪl] *n Archit* gargouille *f*

garish [*Br* 'geərɪʃ, *Am* 'gærɪʃ] *adj (clothes)* voyant; *(colour)* criard; *(light)* cru

garland ['ga:lənd] *n* guirlande *f*

garlic ['ga:lɪk] *n* ail *m*; **g. bread** = pain chaud à l'ail; **g. sausage** saucisson *m* à l'ail

garment ['ga:mənt] *n* vêtement *m*

garnish ['ga:nɪʃ] **1** *n* garniture *f* **2** *vt* garnir (**with** de)

garret ['gærət] *n* mansarde *f*

garrison ['gærɪsən] *n* garnison *f*

garrulous ['gærələs] *adj (talkative)* loquace

garter ['ga:tə(r)] *n (round leg)* jarretière *f*; *Am (attached to belt)* jarretelle *f*; *(for men)* fixe-chaussette *m*

gas [gæs] **1** *n* gaz *m inv*; *Am (gasoline)* essence *f*; *Med (for operation)* anesthésique *m*; *Am Fam* **for a g.** pour rire; **g. chamber** chambre *f* à gaz; *Br* **g. cooker** cuisinière *f* à gaz; *Br* **g. heater, g. fire** radiateur *m* à gaz; **g. heating** chauffage *m* au gaz; **g. mask** masque *m* à gaz; **g. pipe** tuyau *m* de gaz; **g. ring** *(burner)* brûleur *m*; *Am* **g. station** station-service *f*; **g. stove** *(large)* cuisinière *f* à gaz; *(portable)* réchaud *m* à gaz; *Am* **g. tank** réservoir *m* à essence **2** *(pt & pp* **-ss-)** *vt (person)* asphyxier; *(deliberately)* gazer **3** *vi Fam (talk)* bavarder ▪ **gasman** *(pl* **-men)** *n* employé *m* du gaz ▪ **gasworks** *n Br* usine *f* à gaz

gasbag ['gæsbæg] *n Fam (chatterbox)* bavard, -arde *mf*

gash [gæʃ] **1** *n* entaille *f* **2** *vt (skin)* entailler; **to g. one's knee** se faire une blessure profonde au genou

gasket ['gæskɪt] *n (in engine)* joint *m* de culasse

gasoline ['gæsəli:n] *n Am* essence *f*

gasp [ga:sp] **1** *n* halètement *m*; *(of surprise)* sursaut *m* **2** *vt* dire d'une voix pantelante **3** *vi* avoir le souffle coupé (**with** *or* **in** de); **to g. for breath** haleter

gassy ['gæsɪ] *(-ier, -iest)* *adj* gazeux, -euse

gastric ['gæstrɪk] *adj* gastrique; **g. flu** grippe *f* gastro-intestinale

gastronomy [gæ'strɒnəmɪ] *n* gastronomie *f* ▪ **gastronomic** *adj* gastronomique

gate [geɪt] *n (in garden, field)* barrière *f*; *(made of metal)* grille *f*; *(of castle, city, airport)* porte *f*; *(at stadium)* entrée *f*; **gate(s)** *(of park)* grilles *fpl*

gâteau ['gætəʊ] *(pl* **-eaux** [-əʊz]) *n Br (cake)* gros gâteau *m* à la crème

gatecrash ['geɪtkræʃ] *vt* **to g. a party** s'inviter à une réception

gateway ['geɪtweɪ] *n* entrée *f*; **the g. to success** le chemin du succès

gather ['gæðə(r)] **1** *vt* **(a)** *(people, objects)* rassembler; *(pick up)* ramasser; *(flowers, fruit)* cueillir; *(information)* recueillir; **to g. speed** prendre de la vitesse; **to g. in** *(crops, harvest)* rentrer; *(exam papers)* ramasser; **to g. (up) one's strength** rassembler ses forces; **to g. up papers** ramasser des papiers **(b)** *(understand)* **I g. that...** je crois comprendre que... **(c)** *(sew pleats in)* froncer **2** *vi (of people)* se rassembler; *(of clouds)* se former; *(of dust)* s'accumuler; **to g. round** *(come closer)* s'approcher; **to g. round sb** entourer qn

gathering ['gæðərɪŋ] *n (group)* rassemblement *m*

gaudy ['gɔ:dɪ] *(-ier, -iest)* *adj* voyant

gauge [geɪdʒ] **1** *n (instrument)* jauge *f*; *(of railway track)* écartement *m*; *Fig* **to be a g. of sth** permettre de jauger qch **2** *vt* évaluer

gaunt [gɔ:nt] *adj* décharné

gauntlet ['gɔ:ntlɪt] *n* gant *m*; **to run the g. of sth** s'exposer à qch

gauze [gɔ:z] *n* gaze *f*

gave [geɪv] *pt of* **give**

gawk [gɔ:k], **gawp** [gɔ:p] *vi* **to g. at sb/sth** regarder qn/qch bouche bée

gay [geɪ] *(-er, -est)* **1** *adj* **(a)** *(homosexual)* homosexuel, -uelle, gay *inv*; **g. rights** les droits *mpl* des homosexuels **(b)** *Old-fashioned (cheerful)* gai **2** *n* homosexuel, -elle *mf*

gaze [geɪz] **1** *n* regard *m* **2** *vi* **to g. at sb/sth** regarder fixement qn/qch

gazelle [gə'zel] *n* gazelle *f*

gazette [gə'zet] *n* journal *m* officiel

gazetteer [gæzə'tɪə(r)] *n* index *m* géographique

gazump [gə'zʌmp] *vt Br* = revenir sur une promesse de vente pour accepter l'offre plus élevée d'une tierce personne

GB [dʒi:'bi:] *(abbr* **Great Britain**) *n* GB

GCSE [dʒi:si:es'i:] *(abbr* **General Certificate of**

Secondary Education) *n Br* = diplôme de fin de premier cycle de l'enseignement secondaire, sanctionnant une matière déterminée

GDP [dʒi:di:'pi:] (*abbr* **gross domestic product**) *n Econ* PIB *m*

gear [gɪə(r)] **1** *n* (**a**) *Fam (equipment)* attirail *m*; *(belongings)* affaires *fpl*; *(clothes)* fringues *fpl* (**b**) *(on car, bicycle)* vitesse *f*; **in g.** *(vehicle)* en prise; **not in g.** au point mort; *Br* **g. lever**, *Am* **g. shift** levier *m* de (changement de) vitesse **2** *vt* **to g. sth to sth** adapter qch à qch; **to be geared (up) to do sth** être prêt à faire qch; **to g. oneself up for sth** se préparer pour qch ▪ **gearbox** *n* boîte *f* de vitesses

gee [dʒi:] *exclam Am Fam* ça alors!

geek [gi:k] *Fam n* ringard, -arde *mf* ▪ **geeky** *adj Fam* ringard, débile

geese [gi:s] *pl of* **goose**

geezer ['gi:zə(r)] *n Br Fam* type *m*

Geiger counter ['gaɪɡəkaʊntə(r)] *n* compteur *m* Geiger

gel [dʒel] *n* gel *m*

gelatin(e) [*Br* 'dʒeləti:n, *Am* -tən] *n* gélatine *f*

gem [dʒem] *n (stone)* pierre *f* précieuse; *Fig (person)* perle *f*; *Fig (thing)* bijou *m* (*pl* -oux); *Ironic (error)* perle *f*

Gemini ['dʒemɪnaɪ] *n (sign)* les Gémeaux *mpl*; **to be (a) G.** être Gémeaux

gen [dʒen] *Br Fam* **1** *n (information)* tuyaux *mpl* **2** (*pt & pp* -nn-) *vi* **to g. up on sb/sth** se rancarder sur qn/qch

gender ['dʒendə(r)] *n Grammar* genre *m*; *(of person)* sexe *m*; **g. discrimination** discrimination *f* fondée sur le sexe

gene [dʒi:n] *n Biol* gène *m*

genealogy [dʒi:nɪ'ælədʒɪ] *n* généalogie *f*

general ['dʒenərəl] **1** *adj* général; **in g.** en général; **the g. public** le grand public; **for g. use** à l'usage du public; *Am* **g. delivery** poste *f* restante; **g.-purpose tool** outil *m* universel **2** *n Mil* général *m*

generality [dʒenə'rælətɪ] (*pl* -ies) *n* généralité *f*

generalize ['dʒenərəlaɪz] *vti* généraliser; **to become generalized** se généraliser ▪ **generalization** [-'zeɪʃən] *n* généralisation *f*

generally ['dʒenərəlɪ] *adv* généralement; **g. speaking** de manière générale

generate ['dʒenəreɪt] *vt (fear, hope, unemployment)* & *Ling* engendrer; *(heat, electricity)* produire; *(interest, ideas)* faire naître; *(income, jobs)* créer

generation [dʒenə'reɪʃən] *n (of people, products)* génération *f*; *(of electricity)* production *f*; **from g. to g.** de génération en génération; **g. gap** conflit *m* des générations

generator ['dʒenəreɪtə(r)] *n* générateur *m*

generous ['dʒenərəs] *adj* généreux, -euse (**with** de); *(helping, meal)* copieux, -ieuse ▪ **generosity** [-'rɒsɪtɪ] *n* générosité *f*

▪ **generously** *adv* généreusement; *(serve with food)* copieusement

genesis ['dʒenəsɪs] *n* genèse *f*

genetic [dʒɪ'netɪk] *adj* génétique; **g. code** code *m* génétique; **g. engineering** génie *m* génétique; **g. fingerprint** empreinte *f* génétique; **g. fingerprinting** analyse *f* de l'empreinte génétique ▪ **genetically** *adv* **g. modified** génétiquement modifié ▪ **genetics** *n* génétique *f*

Geneva [dʒɪ'ni:və] *n* Genève *m ou f*; **G. Convention** Convention *f* de Genève

genial ['dʒi:nɪəl] *adj* cordial

> Note that the French word **génial** is a false friend and is never a translation for the English word **genial**. It means **brilliant**.

genie ['dʒi:nɪ] *n (goblin)* génie *m*

genital ['dʒenɪtəl] *adj* génital ▪ **genitals** *npl* organes *mpl* génitaux

genius ['dʒi:nɪəs] *n (ability, person)* génie *m*; *Ironic* **to have a g. for sth/for doing sth** avoir le génie de qch/de faire qch

genocide ['dʒenəsaɪd] *n* génocide *m*

gent [dʒent] *n Br Fam* monsieur *m*; **gents' shoes** chaussures *fpl* pour hommes; **the gents** les toilettes *fpl* des hommes

genteel [dʒen'ti:l] *adj* distingué

> Note that the French word **gentil** is a false friend and is never a translation for the English word **genteel**. It means **kind**.

gentle ['dʒentəl] (**-er, -est**) *adj (person, sound, slope)* doux (*f* douce); *(hint)* discret, -ète; *(exercise, speed, progress)* modéré; **g. breeze** légère brise *f*; **to be g. to sb** traiter qn avec douceur; **be g. with your sister!** ne sois pas brutal avec ta sœur!; **to be g. with sth** faire attention à qch; **of g. birth** bien né ▪ **gentleness** *n* douceur *f* ▪ **gently** *adv* doucement; *(remind)* gentiment; *(land)* en douceur

> Note that the French word **gentil** is a false friend and is never a translation for the English word **gentle**. It means **kind**.

gentleman ['dʒentəlmən] (*pl* -men) *n* monsieur *m*; *(well-bred)* gentleman *m*

genuine ['dʒenjuɪn] *adj (leather, diamond)* véritable; *(signature, work of art)* authentique; *(sincere)* sincère ▪ **genuinely** *adv (sincerely)* sincèrement; *(surprised)* véritablement

geography [dʒɪ'ɒɡrəfɪ] *n* géographie *f* ▪ **geographical** [dʒɪə'ɡræfɪkəl] *adj* géographique

geology [dʒɪ'ɒlədʒɪ] *n* géologie *f* ▪ **geological** [dʒɪə'lɒdʒɪkəl] *adj* géologique ▪ **geologist** *n* géologue *mf*

geometry [dʒɪ'ɒmɪtrɪ] n géométrie f
■**geometric(al)** [dʒɪə'metrɪk(əl)] adj géométrique

geranium [dʒɪ'reɪnɪəm] n géranium m

geriatric [dʒerɪ'ætrɪk] adj (hospital) gériatrique; **g. ward** service m de gériatrie

germ [dʒɜːm] n (causing disease) microbe m; (seed of plant, idea) germe m; **g. warfare** guerre f bactériologique

German ['dʒɜːmən] **1** adj allemand; **G. teacher** professeur m d'allemand; **G. measles** rubéole f; **G. shepherd** berger m allemand **2** n (**a**) (person) Allemand, -ande mf (**b**) (language) allemand m ■**Germanic** [-'mænɪk] adj germanique ■**Germany** n l'Allemagne f

germinate ['dʒɜːmɪneɪt] vi (of seed, idea) germer

gerund ['dʒerənd] n Grammar gérondif m

gestation [dʒe'steɪʃən] n gestation f; **g. period** période f de gestation

gesticulate [dʒe'stɪkjʊleɪt] vi gesticuler

gesture ['dʒestʃə(r)] **1** n geste m **2** vi **to g. to sb to do sth** faire signe à qn de faire qch

get [get] (pt & Br pp **got**, Am pp **gotten**, pres p **getting**) **1** vt (obtain) obtenir, avoir; (find) trouver; (buy) acheter; (receive) recevoir; (catch) attraper; (bus, train) prendre; (seize) prendre, saisir; (fetch) aller chercher; (put) mettre; (derive) tirer (**from** de); (prepare) préparer; (lead) mener; (hit with fist, stick) atteindre; (reputation) se faire; Fam (understand) piger; Fam (annoy) énerver; **to g. sb to do sth** faire faire qch à qn; **to g. sth done** faire faire qch; **to g. sth built** faire construire qch; **to g. things started** faire démarrer les choses; **to g. sth clean/dirty** nettoyer/salir qch; **to g. sth to sb** (send) faire parvenir qch à qn; **to g. sb to the station** amener qn à la gare; **can I g. you anything?** je te rapporte quelque chose?; **what's that got to do with it?** qu'est-ce que ça a à voir?

2 vi (go) aller (**to** à); (arrive) arriver (**to** à); (become) devenir; **to g. old** vieillir; **to g. better** s'améliorer; **to g. caught/run over** se faire prendre/écraser; **to g. married** se marier; **to g. dressed/washed** s'habiller/se laver; **to g. paid** être payé; **to g. killed** se faire tuer; **where have you got** or Am **gotten to?** où en es-tu?; **you've got to stay** (must) tu dois rester; **to g. to do sth** (succeed in doing) parvenir à faire qch; **I'm getting to understand** (starting) je commence à comprendre; **to g. going** (leave) se mettre en route; (start) se mettre au travail ■**getaway** n (escape) fuite f ■**get-together** n Fam réunion f ■**get-up** n Fam (clothes) accoutrement m

▸**get about, get around** vi se déplacer; (of news) circuler

▸**get across 1** vt sep (message) faire passer; **to**
g. sb across faire traverser qn **2** vi traverser; (of speaker) se faire comprendre (**to** de); **to g. across to sb that...** faire comprendre à qn que...

▸**get along** vi (manage) se débrouiller; (progress) avancer; (be on good terms) s'entendre (**with** avec); (leave) s'en aller

▸**get at** vt insep (reach) atteindre; Fam (taunt) s'en prendre à; **what's he getting at?** où veut-il en venir?

▸**get away** vi (leave) s'en aller; (escape) se sauver; **to g. away with a fine** s'en tirer avec une amende; **he got away with that crime** il n'a pas été inquiété pour ce crime; **there's no getting away from it** c'est comme ça

▸**get back 1** vt sep (recover) récupérer **2** vi (return) revenir; **to g. back at sb, to g. one's own back on sb** (punish) se venger de qn

▸**get by** vi (manage) se débrouiller

▸**get down 1** vi (go down) descendre (**from** de); **to g. down to** (work) se mettre à **2** vt sep (bring down) descendre (**from** de); Fam **to g. sb down** (depress) déprimer qn **3** vt insep **to g. down the stairs/a ladder** descendre l'escalier/d'une échelle

▸**get in 1** vt sep (stock up with) faire provision de; **to g. sb in** (call for) faire venir qn **2** vi (enter) entrer; (come home) rentrer; (enter vehicle or train) monter; (arrive) arriver; (be elected) être élu

▸**get into** vt insep entrer dans; (vehicle, train) monter dans; (habit) prendre; **to g. into bed/a rage** se mettre au lit/en colère

▸**get off 1** vt sep (remove) enlever; (send) expédier; (in court) faire acquitter; Fam **to g. off doing sth** se dispenser de faire qch **2** vt insep **to g. off a chair** se lever d'une chaise; **to g. off a bus** descendre d'un bus **3** vi (leave) partir; (from vehicle or train) descendre (**from** de); (escape) s'en tirer

▸**get on 1** vt sep (shoes, clothes) mettre **2** vt insep (bus, train) monter dans **3** vi (enter bus or train) monter; (manage) se débrouiller; (succeed) réussir; (be on good terms) s'entendre (**with** avec); **how are you getting on?** comment ça va?; **how did you g. on?** (in exam) comment ça s'est passé?; **to be getting on** (in years) se faire vieux (f vieille); **to g. onto sb** (on phone) contacter qn; **to g. on with** (task) continuer

▸**get out 1** vt sep (remove) enlever; (bring out) sortir **2** vi sortir; (from vehicle or train) descendre (**of** or **from** de); **to g. out of** (obligation) échapper à; (danger) se tirer de; (habit) perdre

▸**get over 1** vt sep (ideas) faire passer; **let's g. it over with** finissons-en **2** vt insep (illness) se remettre de; (shock) revenir de

▸**get round 1** vt insep (obstacle) contourner **2**

vi (visit) passer; **to g. round to doing sth** trouver le temps de faire qch
▸**get through 1** *vt sep (communicate)* **to g. sth through to sb** faire comprendre qch à qn **2** *vt insep (hole)* passer par; *(task)* venir à bout de; *(exam, interview)* survivre à; *(food)* consommer **3** *vi (pass)* passer; *(finish)* finir; *(pass exam)* être reçu; **to g. through to sb** *(communicate with)* se faire comprendre de qn; *(on the phone)* obtenir la communication avec qn
▸**get together** *vi (of people)* se réunir
▸**get up 1** *vt sep* **to g. sb up** *(out of bed)* faire lever qn; **to g. sth up** *(bring up)* monter qch **2** *vt insep (ladder, stairs)* monter **3** *vi (rise, stand up)* se lever *(from* de); **to g. up to something** *or* **to mischief** faire des bêtises; **where have you got up to?** *(in book)* où en es-tu?

geyser ['giːzə(r)] *n* **(a)** *Br (water heater)* chauffe-eau *m inv* **(b)** *(spring)* geyser *m*

Ghana ['gɑːnə] *n* le Ghana

ghastly ['gɑːstlɪ] *(-ier, -iest) adj (horrible)* épouvantable; *(pale)* blême

gherkin ['gɜːkɪn] *n* cornichon *m*

ghetto ['getəʊ] *(pl -oes or -os) n* ghetto *m*; *Fam* **g. blaster** radiocassette *m*

ghost [gəʊst] *n* fantôme *m*; **not the g. of a chance** pas la moindre chance; **g. ship** vaisseau *m* fantôme; **g. story** histoire *f* de fantômes; **g. town** ville *f* fantôme ▪**ghostly** *adj* spectral

giant ['dʒaɪənt] **1** *adj (tree, packet)* géant; *(struggle, efforts)* gigantesque; **with g. steps** à pas de géant **2** *n* géant *m*

gibberish ['dʒɪbərɪʃ] *n* baragouin *m*; **to talk g.** dire n'importe quoi

gibe [dʒaɪb] *n* moquerie *f* **2** *vi* **at sb** se moquer de qn

giblets ['dʒɪblɪts] *npl* abats *mpl*

giddy ['gɪdɪ] *(-ier, -iest) adj* **to be** *or* **feel g.** avoir le vertige; **to make sb g.** donner le vertige à qn ▪**giddiness** *n* vertige *m*

gift [gɪft] *n* cadeau *m*; *(talent, donation)* don *m*; *Br* **g. voucher** *or* **token,** *Am* **g. certificate** chèque-cadeau *m* ▪**gifted** *adj* doué *(with* de; **for** pour); **g. child** surdoué, -ée *mf*

gift-wrapped ['gɪftræpt] *adj* sous paquet-cadeau

gig [gɪg] *n Fam (pop concert)* concert *m*

gigabyte ['dʒɪgəbaɪt] *n Comptr* gigaoctet *m*

gigantic [dʒaɪˈgæntɪk] *adj* gigantesque

giggle ['gɪgəl] **1** *n* petit rire *m* bête; **to have the giggles** avoir le fou rire **2** *vi* rire *(bêtement)*

gild [gɪld] *vt* dorer ▪**gilt 1** *adj* doré **2** *n* dorure *f*

gills [gɪlz] *npl (of fish)* ouïes *fpl*

gimmick ['gɪmɪk] *n (trick, object)* truc *m*

gin [dʒɪn] *n (drink)* gin *m*

ginger ['dʒɪndʒə(r)] **1** *adj (hair)* roux *(f* rousse) **2** *n (plant, spice)* gingembre *m*; **g. beer** limonade *f* au gingembre ▪**gingerbread** *n* pain *m* d'épice

gingerly ['dʒɪndʒəlɪ] *adv* avec précaution

gipsy ['dʒɪpsɪ] *(pl -ies) n* bohémien, -ienne *mf*; *(Eastern European)* Tsigane *mf*; *(Spanish)* gitan, -ane *mf*

giraffe [dʒɪˈræf, *Br* dʒɪˈrɑːf] *n* girafe *f*

girder ['gɜːdə(r)] *n (metal beam)* poutre *f*

girdle ['gɜːdəl] *n (corset)* gaine *f*

girl [gɜːl] *n (child)* (petite) fille *f*, fillette *f*; *(young woman)* jeune fille *f*; **English g.** jeune Anglaise *f*; **g. band** girls band *m*; **G. Guide** éclaireuse *f* ▪**girlfriend** *n (of girl)* amie *f*; *(of boy)* petite amie *f* ▪**girlish** *adj* de (jeune) fille

giro ['dʒaɪrəʊ] *(pl -os) n Br* **bank g.** virement *m* bancaire; **g. account** compte *m* courant postal, CCP *m*

girth [gɜːθ] *n (of tree)* circonférence *f*; *(of person)* corpulence *f*

gist [dʒɪst] *n* **to get the g. of sth** saisir l'essentiel de qch

give [gɪv] **1** *n (of fabric)* élasticité *f* **2** *(pt* **gave,** *pp* **given)** *vt* donner; *(as present)* offrir; *(support)* apporter; *(smile, gesture, pleasure)* faire; *(sigh)* pousser; *(look)* jeter; *(blow)* porter; **to g. sth to sb, to g. sb sth** donner/offrir qch à qn; *Fam* **she doesn't g. a damn** elle s'en fiche pas mal; **to g. way** *(of branch, person)* céder; *(of roof)* s'effondrer; *(in vehicle)* céder la priorité **(to** à) **3** *vi* **(a)** *(donate)* donner **(b)** *(of shoes)* se faire; *(of support)* céder
▸**give away** *vt sep (prize)* distribuer; *(money)* donner; *(betray)* trahir
▸**give back** *vt sep (return)* rendre
▸**give in 1** *vt sep (hand in)* remettre **2** *vi (surrender)* céder **(to** à)
▸**give off** *vt sep (smell, heat)* dégager
▸**give onto** *vt insep* donner sur
▸**give out** *vt sep (hand out)* distribuer; *(make known)* annoncer
▸**give over 1** *vt sep (devote)* consacrer **(to** à); **to g. oneself over to** *(despair, bad habit)* s'abandonner à **2** *vi Br Fam* **g. over!** arrête!
▸**give up 1** *vt sep (possessions)* abandonner; *(activity)* renoncer à; *(seat)* céder **(to** à); **to g. up smoking** cesser de fumer **2** *vi* abandonner

given ['gɪvən] **1** *pp of* **give 2** *adj (fixed)* donné; **at a g. time** à un moment donné; **to be g. to doing sth** avoir tendance à faire qch **3** *conj (considering)* étant donné; **g. that...** étant donné que...

glacier [*Br* ˈglæsɪə(r), *Am* ˈgleɪʃər] *n* glacier *m*

glad [glæd] *adj (person)* content **(of/about** de; **that** que + *subjunctive)*; **I'm so g. to know/hear that...** je suis content de savoir/d'apprendre que...; **I would be g. to help you** je serais ravi de vous aider ▪**gladden** *vt* réjouir ▪**gladly** *adv* volontiers

glade [gleɪd] *n Literary* clairière *f*

gladiolus [glædɪ'əʊləs] (*pl* **-li** [-laɪ]) *n* glaïeul *m*

glamour ['glæmə(r)] (*Am* **glamor**) *n* (*of person*) séduction *f*; (*of career*) prestige *m* ▪ **glamorize** *vt* rendre séduisant ▪ **glamorous** *adj* (*person, dress*) élégant; (*job*) prestigieux, -ieuse

glance [glɑːns] **1** *n* coup *m* d'œil **2** *vi* **to g. at sb/sth** jeter un coup d'œil à qn/qch; **to g. off sth** (*of bullet*) ricocher sur qch

gland [glænd] *n* glande *f* ▪ **glandular 'fever** *n* *Br* mononucléose *f* infectieuse

glare [gleə(r)] **1** *n* (*of sun*) éclat *m* aveuglant; (*look*) regard *m* furieux **2** *vi* (*of sun*) briller d'un éclat aveuglant; **to g. at sb** foudroyer qn (du regard) ▪ **glaring** *adj* (*light*) éblouissant; (*sun*) aveuglant; (*eyes*) furieux, -ieuse; **a g. mistake** une faute grossière

glass [glɑːs] **1** *n* verre *m* **2** *adj* (*bottle*) de verre; **g. door** porte *f* vitrée; **g. wool** laine *f* de verre ▪ **glassful** *n* (plein) verre *m*

glasses ['glɑːsɪz] *npl* (*spectacles*) lunettes *fpl*

glaze [gleɪz] **1** *n* (*on pottery*) vernis *m* **2** *vt* (*window*) vitrer; (*pottery*) vernisser ▪ **glazier** *n* vitrier *m*

gleam [gliːm] **1** *n* lueur *f* **2** *vi* luire

glean [gliːn] *vt* (*information, grain*) glaner

glee [gliː] *n* joie *f* ▪ **gleeful** *adj* joyeux, -euse

glen [glen] *n* *Scot* vallon *m*

glib [glɪb] *adj* (*person, excuse*) désinvolte; (*reply*) spécieux, -ieuse

glide [glaɪd] *vi* glisser; (*of aircraft, bird*) planer ▪ **glider** *n* (*aircraft*) planeur *m* ▪ **gliding** *n* (*sport*) vol *m* à voile

glimmer ['glɪmə(r)] **1** *n* (*light, of hope*) faible lueur *f* **2** *vi* luire (faiblement)

glimpse [glɪmps] **1** *n* aperçu *m*; **to catch** *or* **get a g. of sth** entrevoir qch **2** *vt* entrevoir

glint [glɪnt] **1** *n* éclat *m*; (*in eye*) étincelle *f* **2** *vi* (*of light, eye*) briller

glisten ['glɪsən] *vi* (*of wet surface*) briller; (*of water*) miroiter

glitch [glɪtʃ] *n* *Fam* problème *m* (technique)

glitter ['glɪtə(r)] **1** *n* scintillement *m*; (*for make-up, decoration*) paillettes *fpl* **2** *vi* scintiller ▪ **glittering** *adj* scintillant; (*prize, career*) extraordinaire

gloat [gləʊt] *vi* jubiler (**over** à l'idée de)

global ['gləʊbəl] *adj* (*universal*) mondial; (*comprehensive*) global; **g. economy** économie *f* mondiale; **g. village** village *m* planétaire; **g. warming** réchauffement *m* de la planète ▪ **globalization** *n* mondialisation *f*

globe [gləʊb] *n* globe *m*

gloom [gluːm] *n* (*sadness*) morosité *f*; (*darkness*) obscurité *f* ▪ **gloomy** (**-ier, -iest**) *adj* (*sad*) morose; (*dark, dismal*) sombre

glorify ['glɔːrɪfaɪ] (*pt & pp* **-ied**) *vt* (*praise*) glorifier; *Br* **it's a glorified barn** ce n'est guère plus qu'une grange

glorious ['glɔːrɪəs] *adj* (*splendid*) magnifique; (*full of glory*) glorieux, -ieuse

glory ['glɔːrɪ] **1** *n* gloire *f*; (*great beauty*) splendeur *f* **2** *vi* **to g. in sth** se glorifier de qch

gloss [glɒs] **1** *n* (*shine*) lustre *m*; **g. paint** peinture *f* brillante; **g. finish** brillant *m* **2** *vt* **to g. over sth** glisser sur qch ▪ **glossy** (**-ier, -iest**) *adj* brillant; (*photo*) glacé; (*magazine*) de luxe

glossary ['glɒsərɪ] (*pl* **-ies**) *n* glossaire *m*

glove [glʌv] *n* gant *m*; **g. compartment** (*in car*) boîte *f* à gants

glow [gləʊ] **1** *n* (*light*) lueur *f*; (*on cheeks*) couleurs *fpl* **2** *vi* (*of sky, fire, embers*) rougeoyer; *Fig* (*of eyes, person*) rayonner (**with** de) ▪ **glowing** *adj* (*account, terms, reference*) enthousiaste ▪ **glow-worm** *n* ver *m* luisant

glucose ['gluːkəʊs] *n* glucose *m*

glue [gluː] **1** *n* colle *f* **2** *vt* coller (**to/on** à); *Fam* **to be glued to the television** être cloué devant la télévision ▪ **glue-sniffing** *n* inhalation *f* de colle

glum [glʌm] (**glummer, glummest**) *adj* triste

glut [glʌt] **1** *n* (*of goods*) surplus *m* (**of** de) **2** *vt* **the market is glutted** le marché est saturé (**with** de)

glutton ['glʌtən] *n* goinfre *mf*; **g. for punishment** masochiste *mf* ▪ **gluttony** *n* goinfrerie *f*

glycerin ['glɪsərɪn], **glycerine** ['glɪsəriːn] *n* glycérine *f*

GM [dʒiː'em] *abbr* = **genetically modified**

GMO [dʒiːem'əʊ] (*abbr* **genetically modified organism**) *n* OGM *m*

GMT [dʒiːem'tiː] (*abbr* **Greenwich Mean Time**) *n* GMT *f*

gnarled [nɑːld] *adj* noueux, -euse

gnash [næʃ] *vt* **to g. one's teeth** grincer des dents

gnat [næt] *n* moucheron *m*

gnaw [nɔː] *vti* **to g. (at) sth** ronger qch

gnome [nəʊm] *n* gnome *m*; **garden g.** nain *m* de jardin

GNP [dʒiːen'piː] (*abbr* **gross national product**) *n* *Econ* PNB *m*

go [gəʊ] **1** (*pl* **goes**) *n* (*turn*) tour *m*; **to have a go at (doing) sth** essayer (de faire) qch; **at one go** d'un seul coup; **on the go** en mouvement; **to make a go of sth** réussir qch

2 (*3rd person sing present tense* **goes**; *pt* **went**; *pp* **gone**; *pres p* **going**) *vt* (*make sound*) faire; **cows go moo** les vaches font meuh; **to go it alone** se lancer en solo

3 *vi* aller (**to** à; **from** de); (*depart*) partir, s'en aller; (*disappear*) disparaître; (*be sold*) se vendre; (*function*) marcher; (*progress*) aller; (*become*) devenir; (*of time*) passer; (*of hearing, strength*) baisser; (*of fuse*) sauter; (*of light bulb*) griller; (*of material*) s'user; (*of rope*) céder; **to go well/badly** (*of event*) se passer bien/mal;

she's going to do sth *(is about to, intends to)* elle va faire qch; **it's going to rain** il va pleuvoir; **it's all gone** *(finished)* il n'y en a plus; **to go and get sb/sth** *(fetch)* aller chercher qn/qch; **to go and see** aller voir; **to go riding/on a trip** faire du cheval/un voyage; **to let go of sth** lâcher qch; **to go to a doctor/lawyer** aller voir un médecin/un avocat; **to get things going** faire démarrer les choses; **let's get going** allons-y; **is there any beer going?** y a-t-il de la bière?; **it goes to show that…** ça montre que…; **two hours to go** encore deux heures

▸ **go about, go around** *vi (of person)* se promener; *(of rumour)* circuler

▸ **go about** *vt insep (task)* vaquer à; **to go about doing sth** s'y prendre pour faire qch

▸ **go across 1** *vt insep* traverser **2** *vi (cross)* traverser; *(go)* aller *(to* à); **to go across to sb('s)** faire un saut chez qn

▸ **go after** *vt insep (chase)* poursuivre; *(seek)* rechercher; *(job)* essayer d'obtenir

▸ **go against** *vt insep (contradict)* aller à l'encontre de; *(be unfavourable to)* être défavorable à

▸ **go ahead** *vi (take place)* avoir lieu; *(go in front)* passer devant; **to go ahead of sb** devancer qn; **to go ahead with sth** entreprendre qch; **go ahead!** allez-y!

▸ **go along** *vi (proceed)* se dérouler; **to go along with sb/sth** être d'accord avec qn/qch; **we'll see as we go along** nous verrons au fur et à mesure

▸ **go away** *vi* partir, s'en aller

▸ **go back** *vi (return)* revenir; *(step back, retreat)* reculer; **to go back to sleep** se rendormir; **to go back to doing sth** se remettre à faire qch; **to go back to** *(in time)* remonter à; **to go back on one's promise** *or* **word** revenir sur sa promesse

▸ **go by 1** *vt insep (act according to)* se fonder sur; *(judge from)* juger d'après; **to go by the rules** respecter les règles; **to go by the name of…** être connu sous le nom de… **2** *vi* passer

▸ **go down 1** *vt insep (stairs, street)* descendre **2** *vi* descendre; *(fall down)* tomber; *(of ship)* sombrer; *(of sun)* se coucher; *(of temperature, price)* baisser; *(of tyre, balloon)* se dégonfler; **to go down well/badly** être bien/mal reçu; **he has gone down in history as a tyrant** l'histoire a retenu de lui l'image d'un tyran

▸ **go for** *vt insep (fetch)* aller chercher; *(attack)* attaquer; *Fam (like)* avoir un faible pour; **the same goes for you** ça vaut aussi pour toi; *Fam* **g. for it!** vas-y!

▸ **go forward(s)** *vi* avancer

▸ **go in** *vi* (r)entrer; *(of sun)* se cacher; *Br* **to go in for** *(exam)* s'inscrire à; **she doesn't go in for cooking** elle n'est pas très portée sur la cuisine

▸ **go into** *vt insep (enter)* entrer dans; *(examine)* examiner

▸ **go off 1** *vt insep (lose liking for)* se lasser de **2** *vi (leave)* partir; *(go bad)* se gâter; *(of alarm)* se déclencher; *(of bomb)* exploser; **the gun went off** le coup est parti; **the light went off** la lumière s'est éteinte

▸ **go on** *vi* continuer (**doing** à faire); *(travel)* poursuivre sa route; *(happen)* se passer; *(last)* durer; **as time went on** avec le temps; **to go on to sth** passer à qch; *Fam* **to go on at sb** *(nag)* s'en prendre à qn; *Fam* **to go on about sb/sth** parler sans cesse de qn/qch

▸ **go out** *vi* sortir; *(of light, fire)* s'éteindre; *(of tide)* descendre; *(depart)* partir; *(date)* sortir ensemble; **to go out for a meal** aller au restaurant; **to go out with sb** *(date)* sortir avec qn; **to go out to work** travailler (hors de chez soi)

▸ **go over 1** *vt insep* (**a**) *(cross over)* traverser; **the ball went over the wall** la balle est passée par-dessus le mur (**b**) *(examine)* passer en revue; *(speech)* revoir; **to go over sth in one's mind** repasser qch dans son esprit **2** *vi (go)* aller (**to** à); *(to enemy)* passer (**to** à); **to go over to sb** aller vers qn; *(visit)* faire un saut chez qn

▸ **go round 1** *vt insep* **to go round a corner** tourner au coin; **to go round the shops** faire les magasins; **to go round the world** faire le tour du monde **2** *vi (turn)* tourner; *(make a detour)* faire le tour; *(of rumour)* circuler; **to go round to sb's** faire un saut chez qn; **there is enough to go round** il y en a assez pour tout le monde

▸ **go through 1** *vt insep (suffer, undergo)* subir; *(examine)* passer en revue; *(search)* fouiller; *(spend)* dépenser; *(wear out)* user; *(perform)* accomplir; **we've gone through six bottles of wine** nous avons bu six bouteilles de vin; **to go through with sth** aller jusqu'au bout de qch **2** *vi* passer; *(of deal)* être conclu

▸ **go under** *vi (of ship)* couler; *Fig (of firm)* faire faillite

▸ **go up 1** *vt insep* monter **2** *vi* monter; *(explode)* sauter; **to go up in sb's estimation** monter dans l'estime de qn; **to go up to sth** *(approach)* se diriger vers qch; *(reach)* aller jusqu'à qch

▸ **go with** *vt insep* aller de pair avec; **the company car goes with the job** le poste donne droit à une voiture de fonction

▸ **go without** *vt insep* se passer de

goad [gəʊd] *vt* **to g. sb (on)** aiguillonner qn

go-ahead ['gəʊəhed] **1** *adj* dynamique **2** *n* **to get the g.** avoir le feu vert; **to give sb the g.** donner le feu vert à qn

goal [gəʊl] *n* but *m*; **to score a g.** marquer un but ▪**goalie** *n Br Fam Sport* goal *m* ▪**goalkeeper** *n Sport* gardien *m* de but, goal *m* ▪**goalpost** *n* poteau *m* de but

goat [gəʊt] n chèvre f; Fam **to get sb's g.** énerver qn

goatee [gəʊ'tiː] n barbiche f

gobble ['gɒbəl] vt **to g. (up** or **down)** (food) engloutir

go-between ['gəʊbɪtwiːn] n intermédiaire mf

goblet ['gɒblɪt] n verre m à pied

> Note that the French noun **gobelet** is a false friend. It means **tumbler**.

goblin ['gɒblɪn] n lutin m

god [gɒd] n dieu m; **G.** Dieu; Fam **oh G.!, my G.!** mon Dieu!; Fam **thank G.!** heureusement!; Fam **for G.'s sake!** pour l'amour de Dieu!; Fam **the gods** (in theatre) le poulailler ■ **godchild** (pl **-children**) n filleul, -eule mf ■ **goddaughter** n filleule f ■ **goddess** n déesse f ■ **godfather** n parrain m ■ **god-fearing** adj croyant ■ **godforsaken** adj (place) perdu ■ **godmother** n marraine f ■ **godsend** n **to be a g.** être un don du ciel ■ **godson** n filleul m

goddam(n) ['gɒdæm] adj Am Fam foutu

goes [gəʊz] 3rd person sing present tense & npl of **go**

goggle ['gɒgəl] vi **to g. at sb/sth** regarder qn/qch avec des yeux ronds ■ **goggles** npl lunettes fpl (de protection, de plongée) ■ **'goggle-'eyed** adj Fam **to be g.** avoir les yeux ronds

going ['gəʊɪŋ] **1** n (condition of ground) terrain m; **it's hard** or **heavy g.** c'est difficile; **it's slow g.** (at work) ça n'avance pas vite **2** adj **the g. price** le prix pratiqué (**for** pour); **the g. rate** le tarif en vigueur; **the g. salary** le salaire habituel; **a g. concern** une affaire qui tourne ■ **goings-'on** npl Pej activités fpl

go-kart ['gəʊkɑːt] n (for racing) kart m

gold [gəʊld] **1** n or m **2** adj (watch) en or; (coin, dust) d'or; Sport **g. medal** médaille f d'or ■ **golden** adj (of gold colour) doré; **g. rule** règle f d'or; **it's a g. opportunity** c'est une occasion en or ■ **goldmine** n mine f d'or ■ **'gold-'plated** adj plaqué or ■ **goldsmith** n orfèvre m

goldfinch ['gəʊldfɪntʃ] n chardonneret m

goldfish ['gəʊldfɪʃ] n poisson m rouge

golf [gɒlf] n golf m; **g. club** (stick, association) club m de golf; **g. course** parcours m de golf ■ **golfer** n golfeur, -euse mf ■ **golfing** n **to go g.** faire du golf

gondola ['gɒndələ] n (boat) gondole f ■ **gondolier** [-'lɪə(r)] n gondolier m

gone [gɒn] **1** pp of **go 2** Br Fam **it's g. two** il est plus de deux heures ■ **goner** n Fam **to be a g.** être fichu

gong [gɒŋ] n gong m

goo [guː] n Fam truc m visqueux

good [gʊd] **1** (**better, best**) adj bon (f bonne); (kind) gentil, -ille; (well-behaved) sage; **my g. friend** mon cher ami; **a g. fellow** un brave type; **g.!** bon!, bien!; **very g.!** (all right) très bien!; **that isn't g. enough** (bad) ça ne va pas; (not sufficient) ça ne suffit pas; **would you be g. enough to...?** auriez-vous la gentillesse de...?; **that's g. of you** c'est gentil de ta part; **it's g. for us** ça nous fait du bien; **to taste g.** avoir bon goût; **to feel g.** se sentir bien; **to have g. weather** avoir beau temps; **to be g. at French** être bon en français; **to be g. at swimming/telling jokes** savoir bien nager/raconter des blagues; **to be g. with children** savoir s'y prendre avec les enfants; **it's a g. thing (that)...** heureusement que...; **a g. many, a g. deal (of)** beaucoup (de); **as g. as** (almost) pratiquement; **g. afternoon, g. morning** bonjour; (on leaving someone) au revoir; **g. evening** bonsoir; **g. night** bonsoir; (before going to bed) bonne nuit

2 n (advantage, virtue) bien m; **for her (own) g.** pour son bien; **for the g. of your family/career** pour ta famille/carrière; **it will do you (some) g.** ça te fera du bien; **it's no g. crying/shouting** ça ne sert à rien de pleurer/crier; **that's no g.** (worthless) ça ne vaut rien; (bad) ça ne va pas; **what's the g. of crying?** à quoi bon pleurer?; **for g.** (leave, give up) pour de bon ■ **good-for-'nothing** n propre-à-rien mf ■ **'good-'humoured** (Am **-humored**) adj détendu ■ **'good-'looking** adj (person) d'un caractère agréable ■ **'good-'natured** adj (person) d'un caractère agréable

goodbye [gʊd'baɪ] exclam & n au revoir (m inv)

goodness ['gʊdnɪs] n bonté f; **my g.!** mon Dieu!

goods [gʊdz] npl marchandises fpl; **g. train** train m de marchandises

goodwill [gʊd'wɪl] n (willingness) bonne volonté f; (benevolence) bienveillance f

gooey ['guːɪ] adj Fam gluant

goof [guːf] vi Am Fam **to g. (up)** faire une gaffe

goon [guːn] n Br Fam idiot, -iote mf

goose [guːs] (pl **geese**) n oie f; adj Br **pimples** or Am **bumps** chair f de poule ■ **gooseflesh** n chair f de poule

gooseberry ['gʊzbərɪ] (pl **-ies**) n groseille f à maquereau

gorge [gɔːdʒ] **1** n (ravine) gorge f **2** vt **to g. oneself** se gaver (**on** de)

gorgeous ['gɔːdʒəs] adj magnifique

gorilla [gə'rɪlə] n gorille m

gormless ['gɔːmləs] adj Br Fam balourd

gorse [gɔːs] n inv ajoncs mpl

gory ['gɔːrɪ] (**-ier, -iest**) adj (bloody) sanglant; Fig (details) horrible

gosh [gɒʃ] exclam Fam mince (alors)!

gosling ['gɒzlɪŋ] n oison m

go-slow [gəʊ'sləʊ] n Br (strike) grève f du zèle

gospel ['gɒspəl] n évangile m

gossip ['gɒsɪp] **1** n (talk) bavardages mpl; (malicious) cancans mpl; (person) commère f; **g. column** (in newspaper) rubrique f mondaine; échos *mpl* **2** *vi* bavarder; *(maliciously)* colporter des commérages ▪**gossiping, gossipy** *adj* bavard; *(maliciously)* cancanier, -ière

got [gɒt] *pt & Br pp of* **get**

Gothic ['gɒθɪk] *adj & n* gothique (m)

gotten ['gɒtən] *Am pp of* **get**

gouge [gaʊdʒ] *vt* **to g. sb's eye out** arracher l'œil à qn

goulash ['gu:læʃ] *n* goulache *m*

gourmet ['gʊəmeɪ] *n* gourmet *m*; **g. restaurant** restaurant *m* gastronomique

gout [gaʊt] *n (illness)* goutte *f*

govern ['gʌvən] **1** *vt (rule)* gouverner; *(city, province)* administrer; *(emotion)* maîtriser; *(influence)* déterminer **2** *vi (rule)* gouverner; **governing body** conseil *m* d'administration

governess ['gʌvənɪs] *n* gouvernante *f*

government ['gʌvənmənt] **1** *n* gouvernement *m*; **local g.** administration *f* locale **2** *adj (decision, policy)* gouvernemental; **g. loan** emprunt *m* d'État ▪**governmental** [-'mentəl] *adj* gouvernemental

governor ['gʌvənə(r)] *n* gouverneur *m*; *(of school)* administrateur, -trice *mf*; *(of prison)* directeur, -trice *mf*

gown [gaʊn] *n (of woman)* robe *f*; *Br (of judge, lecturer)* toge *f*

GP [dʒi:'pi:] *(abbr* **general practitioner)** *n Br* généraliste *mf*

grab [græb] *(pt & pp* -**bb-***) vt* **to g. (hold of) sb/ sth** saisir qn/qch; **to g. sth from sb** arracher qch à qn; **I'll g. a sandwich later** j'avalerai un sandwich plus tard

grace [greɪs] **1** *n (charm, goodwill, religious mercy)* grâce *f*; *Rel* **to say g.** dire le bénédicité; **to be in sb's good graces** être dans les bonnes grâces de qn; **g. (period)** *(extension)* délai *m* de grâce; **ten days' g.** dix jours de grâce **2** *vt (adorn)* orner; *(honour)* honorer (**with** de) ▪**graceful** *adj (movement, person)* gracieux, -ieuse ▪**gracefully** *adv* avec grâce

gracious ['greɪʃəs] *adj (kind)* aimable (**to** envers); *(elegant)* élégant; *Fam* **good g.!** bonté divine! ▪**graciously** *adv (accept)* de bonne grâce

gradation [*Br* grə'deɪʃən, *Am* greɪ'deɪʃən] *n* gradation *f*

grade [greɪd] **1** *n (a) (rank)* grade *m*; *(in profession)* échelon *m*; *(quality)* qualité *f*; *(of eggs, fruit)* calibre *m*; *Am* **g. crossing** passage *m* à niveau **(b)** *Am Sch (mark)* note *f*; *(year)* classe *f*; *Am* **g. school** école *f* primaire **2** *vt (classify)* classer; *Am (exam)* noter

gradient ['greɪdɪənt] *n (slope)* dénivellation *f*

gradual ['grædʒʊəl] *adj* progressif, -ive; *(slope)* doux *(f* douce) ▪**gradually** *adv* progressivement

graduate¹ **1** ['grædʒʊət] *n Br (from university)* ≃

licencié, -iée *mf*; *Am (from high school)* ≃ bachelier, -ière *mf*; *Am Univ* **g. studies** études *fpl* de troisième cycle **2** ['grædʒʊeɪt] *vi Br (from university)* ≃ obtenir sa licence; *Am (from high school)* ≃ obtenir son baccalauréat; **to g. from sth to sth** passer de qch à qch ▪**graduation** [-'eɪʃən] *n Univ* remise *f* des diplômes

graduate² ['grædʒʊeɪt] *vt (mark with degrees)* graduer ▪**graduated** *adj (tube, thermometer)* gradué

graffiti [grə'fi:tɪ] *npl* graffiti *mpl*

graft¹ [grɑ:ft] **1** *n (technique)* greffe *f*; *(thing grafted)* greffon *m* **2** *vt* greffer (**on to** à)

graft² [grɑ:ft] *n (a) Am Fam (bribe)* pot-de-vin *m* **(b)** *Br Fam* **hard g.** boulot *m*

grain [greɪn] *n (a) (seed, particle)* grain *m*; *(cereals)* céréales *fpl*; *Fig* **a g. of truth** une once de vérité **(b)** *(in wood, leather, paper)* grain *m*; *(in cloth)* fil *m*

gram [græm] *n* gramme *m*

grammar ['græmə(r)] *n* grammaire *f*; **g. (book)** grammaire *f*; **g. school** *Br* ≃ lycée *m*, *Am* ≃ école *f* primaire ▪**grammatical** [grə'mætɪkəl] *adj* grammatical

gramme [græm] *n* gramme *m*

gramophone ['græməfəʊn] *n* phonographe *m*

gran [græn] *n Br Fam* mamie *f*

granary ['grænərɪ] *(pl* -**ies***) n* grenier *m*; *Br* **g. bread** = pain complet

grand [grænd] **1** (-**er**, -**est**) *adj (splendid)* grandiose; *Fam (excellent)* excellent; **with a g. gesture** d'un geste majestueux; **she went on a g. tour of Italy** elle a visité toute l'Italie; **g. duke** grand-duc *m*; **g. piano** piano *m* à queue; **g. total** somme *f* totale **2** *n inv Br Fam* mille livres *fpl*; *Am Fam* mille dollars *mpl* ▪**grandchild** *(pl* -**children***) n* petit-fils *m*, petite-fille *f*; **grandchildren** petits-enfants *mpl* ▪**grand(d)ad** *n Fam* papi *m* ▪**granddaughter** *n* petite-fille *f* ▪**grandfather** *n* grand-père *m* ▪**grandma** [-mɑ:] *n Fam* mamie *f* ▪**grandmother** *n* grand-mère *f* ▪**grandpa** [-pɑ:] *n Fam* papi *m* ▪**grandparents** *npl* grands-parents *mpl* ▪**grandson** *n* petit-fils *m*

grandeur ['grændʒə(r)] *n* grandeur *f*; *(of person, country)* magnificence *f*

grandstand ['grændstænd] *n* tribune *f*

granite ['grænɪt] *n* granit *m*

granny ['grænɪ] *(pl* -**ies***) n Fam* mamie *f*

grant [grɑ:nt] **1** *n* subvention *f*; *(for student)* bourse *f* **2** *vt* accorder (**to** à); *(request)* accéder à; *(prayer, wish)* exaucer; *(admit)* admettre (**that** que); **to take sth for granted** considérer qch comme allant de soi; **to take sb for granted** considérer qn comme faisant partie du décor; **I take it for granted that...** je présume que...

granule ['grænju:l] *n* granule *m* ▪**granulated sugar** [grænjʊleɪtɪd'ʃʊgə(r)] *n* sucre *m* semoule

grape [greɪp] *n* grain *m* de raisin; **some grapes** du raisin; **to eat (some) grapes** manger du raisin; **g. harvest** vendange *f*; **g. juice** jus *m* de raisin

Note that the French word **grappe** is a false friend. It means **bunch** or **cluster**.

grapefruit ['greɪpfruːt] *n* pamplemousse *m*
grapevine ['greɪpvaɪn] *n Fig* **on** *or* **through the g.** par le téléphone arabe
graph [græf, grɑːf] *n* graphique *m*; **g. paper** papier *m* millimétré
graphic ['græfɪk] *adj (description)* très détaillé; *(language)* cru; **in g. detail** de façon très détaillée; **g. artist** graphiste *mf*; **g. arts** arts *mpl* graphiques; **g. design** conception *f* graphique; **g. designer** (concepteur, -trice *f*) graphiste *(mf)* ■ **graphically** *adv (describe)* de façon très détaillée ■ **graphics** *npl* **(computer) g.** graphiques *mpl*
grapple ['græpəl] *vi (with problem)* se débattre **(with** avec)
grasp [grɑːsp] **1** *n (hold)* prise *f*; *(understanding)* compréhension *f*; **within sb's g.** à la portée de qn **2** *vt (seize, understand)* saisir ■ **grasping** *adj (mean)* avide
grass [grɑːs] **1** *n* herbe *f*; *(lawn)* gazon *m*; *Fig* **the g. roots** *(of organization)* la base **2** *vt Fam* **to g. on sb** balancer qn ■ **grasshopper** *n* sauterelle *f* ■ **grassland** *n* prairie *f* ■ **grassy** *adj* herbeux, -euse
grate [greɪt] **1** *n (for fireplace)* grille *f* **2** *vt (cheese, carrot)* râper **3** *vi (of sound)* grincer; **to g. on the ears** écorcher les oreilles; **to g. on sb's nerves** taper sur les nerfs de qn ■ **grater** *n* râpe *f* ■ **grating 1** *adj (sound)* grinçant; *(voice)* éraillé **2** *n (bars)* grille *f*
grateful ['greɪtfəl] *adj* reconnaissant **(to** à; **for** de); *(words, letter)* de remerciement; **I would be g. if you could let me know** je vous serais reconnaissant de m'en informer ■ **gratefully** *adv* avec reconnaissance
gratify ['grætɪfaɪ] *(pt & pp* **-ied)** *vt (whim)* satisfaire; **to g. sb** faire plaisir à qn ■ **gratifi'cation** *n* satisfaction *f* ■ **gratified** *adj (pleased)* satisfait **(by** *or* **with** de; **to do** de faire) ■ **gratifying** *adj* très satisfaisant
gratis ['grætɪs, 'greɪtɪs] *adv* gratis
gratitude ['grætɪtjuːd] *n* gratitude *f* **(for** de)
gratuitous [grə'tjuːɪtəs] *adj (act)* gratuit
gratuity [grə'tjuːɪtɪ] *(pl* **-ies)** *n Formal (tip)* pourboire *m*

Note that the French word **gratuité** is a false friend and is never a translation for the English word **gratuity**. It indicates something that is free of charge.

grave¹ [greɪv] *n* tombe *f* ■ **gravedigger** *n* fossoyeur *m* ■ **gravestone** *n* pierre *f* tombale ■ **graveyard** *n* cimetière *m*

grave² [greɪv] **(-er, -est)** *adj (serious)* grave; *(manner, voice)* solennel, -elle; **to make a g. mistake** se tromper lourdement ■ **gravely** *adv* gravement; **g. concerned** extrêmement inquiet, -iète
gravel ['grævəl] *n* gravier *m*; **g. path** allée *f* de gravier
gravitate ['grævɪteɪt] *vi* **to g. towards sth** *(be drawn to)* être attiré par qch; *(move towards)* se diriger vers qch ■ **gravitation** [-'teɪʃən] *n* gravitation *f*
gravity ['grævɪtɪ] *n* **(a)** *Phys (force)* pesanteur *f* **(b)** *(seriousness)* gravité *f*
gravy ['greɪvɪ] *n* = sauce à base de jus de viande
gray [greɪ] *adj, n & Am* = **grey**
graze¹ [greɪz] **1** *n (wound)* écorchure *f* **2** *vt (scrape)* écorcher
graze² [greɪz] *vi (of cattle)* paître
grease [griːs] **1** *n* graisse *f* **2** *vt* graisser ■ **greaseproof 'paper** *n Br* papier *m* sulfurisé ■ **greasy** **(-ier, -iest)** *adj* graisseux, -euse; *(hair, skin, food)* gras *(f* graisse)
great [greɪt] **(-er, -est)** *adj* grand; *(effort, heat, parcel)* gros *(f* grosse), grand; *Fam (very good)* génial; **to reach a g. age** parvenir à un âge avancé; **to be g. at tennis** être très doué pour le tennis; **a g. deal** *or* **number (of), a g. many** beaucoup (de); **the greatest team** *(best)* la meilleure équipe; **Great Britain** la Grande-Bretagne; **Greater London/Manchester** le grand Londres/Manchester ■ **great-'grand-father** *n* arrière-grand-père *m* ■ **great-'grandmother** *n* arrière-grand-mère *f*
greatly ['greɪtlɪ] *adv* très; **you'll be g. missed** vous nous manquerez beaucoup
greatness ['greɪtnɪs] *n (in size, importance)* grandeur *f*; *(in degree)* intensité *f*
Greece [griːs] *n* la Grèce ■ **Greek 1** *adj* grec *(f* grecque) **2** *n (person)* Grec *m*, Grecque *f*; *(language)* grec *m*
greed [griːd] *n* avidité *f* **(for** de); *(for food)* gourmandise *f*
greedy ['griːdɪ] **(-ier, -iest)** *adj* avide **(for** de); *(for food)* gourmand ■ **greedily** *adv* avidement; *(eat)* goulûment ■ **greediness** *n* = **greed**
green [griːn] **1** **(-er, -est)** *adj* vert; *(pale)* blême; *Fig (immature)* inexpérimenté; *Fam (environmentally friendly)* vert, écolo; **to turn** *or* **go g.** *(of traffic lights)* passer au vert; *(of person, garden, tree)* verdir; *Fig* **to get the g. light** avoir le feu vert; *Fig* **to have g. fingers** *or Am* **a g. thumb** avoir la main verte; *Fig* **g. with envy** vert de jalousie; *Br* **the g. belt** la zone verte; *Am* **g. card** ≃ permis *m* de travail **2** *n (colour)* vert *m*; *(grassy area)* pelouse *f*; **greens** *(vegetables)* légumes *mpl* verts; *Pol* **the G. Party, the Greens** les Verts *mpl* ■ **greenery** *n*

verdure f ▪**greengage** n reine-claude f
▪**greengrocer** n Br marchand, -ande mf de
fruits et légumes ▪**greenhouse** n serre f; **the
g. effect** l'effet m de serre ▪**greenish** adj
verdâtre

Greenland ['gri:nlənd] n le Groenland

greet [gri:t] vt (say hello to) saluer; (welcome)
accueillir ▪**greeting** n accueil m; (more
formal) salutation f; **greetings** (for birthday,
festival) vœux mpl; **greetings card** carte f de
vœux

gregarious [grɪ'geərɪəs] adj sociable; (instinct,
animal) grégaire

> Note that the French adjective **grégaire** is a
> false friend. It never means **sociable**.

gremlin ['gremlɪn] n Fam diablotin m

grenade [grə'neɪd] n (bomb) grenade f

grew [gru:] pt of **grow**

grey [greɪ] 1 adj (-er, -est) gris; Fig (pale)
morne; **to be going g.** grisonner; **g. matter**
matière f grise 2 n gris m 3 vi (of hair)
grisonner ▪**grey-'haired** adj aux cheveux
gris ▪**greyhound** n lévrier m ▪**greyish** adj
grisâtre

grid [grɪd] n (bars) grille f; (on map) quadrillage
m; Br **the (national) g.** le réseau électrique
national

griddle ['grɪdəl] n (for cooking) tôle f

gridlock ['grɪdlɒk] n (traffic jam) embouteillage
m

grief [gri:f] n chagrin m; **to come to g.** échouer;
Fam **good g.!** mon Dieu!

> Note that the French word **grief** is a false
> friend and is never a translation for the Eng-
> lish word **grief**. It means **grievance**.

grievance ['gri:vəns] n grief m; **grievances**
(complaints) doléances fpl; **to have a g.
against sb** avoir à se plaindre de qn

grieve [gri:v] 1 vt affliger 2 vi **to g. for sb/over
sth** pleurer qn/qch

grievous ['gri:vəs] adj Formal grave; Br Law **g.
bodily harm** coups mpl et blessures fpl

grill [grɪl] 1 n (utensil) gril m; (dish) grillade f 2 vt
griller; Fam (question) cuisiner

grille [grɪl] n (bars) grille f; **(radiator) g.** (of
vehicle) calandre f

grim [grɪm] (**grimmer, grimmest**) adj (stern)
sinistre; Fam (bad) lamentable; **g.
determination** une volonté inflexible; **the g.
truth** la triste vérité ▪**grimly** adv (fight) avec
acharnement

grimace ['grɪməs] 1 n grimace f 2 vi grimacer

grime [graɪm] n crasse f ▪**grimy** (-ier, -iest) adj
crasseux, -euse

grin [grɪn] 1 n large sourire m 2 (pt & pp -nn-) vi
avoir un large sourire

grind [graɪnd] 1 n Fam (work) corvée f; **the daily
g.** le train-train quotidien 2 (pt & pp **ground**) vt
(coffee, pepper) moudre; Am (meat) hacher;
(blade, tool) aiguiser; **to g. one's teeth** grincer
des dents 3 vi **to g. to a halt** s'immobiliser;
grinding poverty la misère noire ▪**grinder** n
coffee g. moulin m à café

grip [grɪp] 1 n (hold) prise f; (handle) poignée f;
Fam (of subject) connaissance f; **to have a firm
g. on the situation** avoir la situation bien en
main; **to get a g. on oneself** se ressaisir; Fig
to lose one's g. ne plus être à la hauteur; Fig
to get to grips with sth s'attaquer à qch; **in
the g. of a disease** en proie à une maladie 2
(pt & pp **-pp-**) vt (seize) saisir; (hold)
empoigner; (of tyre) adhérer à; **the audience
was gripped by the play** la pièce a captivé les
spectateurs 3 vi (of tyre) adhérer ▪**gripping**
adj passionnant

gripe [graɪp] vi Fam (complain) rouspéter

grisly ['grɪzlɪ] adj (gruesome) horrible

gristle ['grɪsəl] n (in meat) nerfs mpl

grit [grɪt] 1 n (a) (sand) sable m; (gravel)
gravillons mpl (b) Fam (courage) cran m 2 (pt
& pp **-tt-**) vt (a) (road) sabler (b) **to g. one's
teeth** serrer les dents

grizzly ['grɪzlɪ] (pl **-ies**) n **g. (bear)** grizzli m

groan [grəʊn] 1 n (of pain) gémissement m; (of
dissatisfaction) grognement m 2 vi (with pain)
gémir; (complain) grogner

grocer ['grəʊsə(r)] n épicier, -ière mf; **g.'s shop**
épicerie f ▪**groceries** npl (food) provisions fpl
▪**grocery** (pl **-ies**) n Am (shop) épicerie f

groggy ['grɒgɪ] (**-ier, -iest**) adj Fam groggy inv

groin [grɔɪn] n aine f

groom [gru:m] 1 n (a) (bridegroom) marié m (b)
(for horses) lad m 2 vt (horse) panser; **to g. sb
for sth** préparer qn pour qch; **well-groomed**
(person) très soigné

groove [gru:v] n (in wood, metal) rainure f; (in
record) sillon m

grope [grəʊp] vi **to g. (about) for sth** chercher
qch à tâtons

gross [grəʊs] 1 adj (a) (total) (weight, income,
profit) brut; Econ **g. domestic product** produit
m intérieur brut (b) (-er, -est) (coarse)
grossier, -ière; (injustice) flagrant; **g. error**
erreur f grossière (c) Fam (disgusting)
dégueulasse 2 n inv grosse f 3 vt gagner brut
▪**grossly** adv (negligent) extrêmement;
(exaggerated) grossièrement; (unfair) vraiment; **g. overweight** obèse

grotesque [grəʊ'tesk] adj grotesque

grotto ['grɒtəʊ] (pl **-oes** or **-os**) n grotte f

grotty ['grɒtɪ] (**-ier, -iest**) adj Br Fam minable

ground¹ [graʊnd] 1 n (earth) terre f, sol m; (land)
terrain m; (estate) terres fpl; **grounds** (gardens)
parc m; Fig (reasons) motifs mpl; **on the g.**
(lying, sitting) par terre; **to gain/lose g.**

gagner/perdre du terrain; *Fig* **to hold one's g.** tenir bon; **g. crew** *(at airport)* personnel *m* au sol; *Br* **g. floor** rez-de-chaussée *m inv*; **g. frost** gelée *f* blanche; **g. rules** règles *fpl* de base **2** *vt (aircraft)* interdire de vol ▪**grounding** *n (basis)* fondement *m*; *(basic knowledge)* bases *fpl* (**in** de) ▪**groundless** *adj* sans fondement ▪**groundnut** *n* arachide *f* ▪**groundsheet** *n* tapis *m* de sol ▪**groundswell** *n* lame *f* de fond ▪**groundwork** *n* travail *m* préparatoire

ground² [graʊnd] **1** *pt & pp of* **grind 2** *adj (coffee)* moulu; *Am* **g. meat** viande *f* hachée **3** *npl* **(coffee) grounds** marc *m* (de café)

group [gruːp] **1** *n* groupe *m*; **g. decision** décision *f* collective **2** *vt* **to g. (together)** grouper **3** *vi* se grouper ▪**grouping** *n (group)* groupe *m*

grouse¹ [graʊs] *n inv (bird)* tétras *m*

grouse² [graʊs] *vi Fam (complain)* rouspéter

grove [graʊv] *n* bosquet *m*

grovel ['grɒvəl] *(Br* -ll-*, Am* -l-*) vi (be humble)* ramper, s'aplatir (**to** devant)

grow [graʊ] **1** *(pt* **grew**, *pp* **grown)** *vt (vegetables)* cultiver; **to g. a beard** se laisser pousser la barbe **2** *vi (of person)* grandir; *(of plant, hair)* pousser; *(of economy, feeling)* croître; *(of firm, town)* se développer; *(of gap, family)* s'agrandir; **to g. fat(ter)** grossir; **to g. old** vieillir; **to g. to like sth** finir par aimer qch; **to g. into a man** devenir un homme; **to g. up** grandir; **when I g. up** quand je serai grand; **he's grown out of his shoes** ses chaussures sont maintenant trop petites pour lui; **it'll g. on you** *(of music, book)* tu finiras par t'y intéresser ▪**grower** *n (person)* cultivateur, -trice *mf* (**of** de) ▪**growing** *adj (child)* en pleine croissance; *(number, discontent)* grandissant ▪**grown** *adj (man, woman)* adulte ▪**grown-up 1** ['grəʊnʌp] *n* grande personne *f* **2** ['grəʊn'ʌp] *adj (ideas, behaviour)* d'adulte

growl [graʊl] **1** *n* grognement *m* **2** *vi* grogner (**at** contre)

grown [grəʊn] *pp of* **grow**

growth [grəʊθ] *n* croissance *f*; *(increase)* augmentation *f* (**in** de); *(lump)* grosseur *f* (**on** à); **a week's g. of beard** une barbe de huit jours

grub [grʌb] *n* (**a**) *Fam (food)* bouffe *f* (**b**) *(insect)* larve *f*

grubby ['grʌbɪ] *(-ier, -iest) adj* sale

grudge [grʌdʒ] **1** *n* rancune *f*; **to have a g. against sb** garder rancune à qn **2** *vt* **to g. sb sth** donner qch à qn à contrecœur; **to g. doing sth** faire qch à contrecœur; **he grudges her her success** il lui en veut parce qu'elle a réussi ▪**grudging** *adj* accordé à contrecœur ▪**grudgingly** *adv* à contrecœur

gruelling ['grʊəlɪŋ] *(Am* **grueling**) *adj (journey, experience)* épuisant

gruesome ['gruːsəm] *adj* horrible

gruff [grʌf] *(-er, -est) adj* bourru

grumble ['grʌmbəl] *vi (complain)* grommeler; **to g. about** sth rouspéter contre qch

grumpy ['grʌmpɪ] *(-ier, -iest) adj* grincheux, -euse

grunt [grʌnt] **1** *n* grognement *m* **2** *vti* grogner

GSM [dʒiːesˈem] *(abbr* **global system for mobile communications**) *n Tel* GSM *m*; **G. network** réseau *m* GSM

guarantee [gærənˈtiː] **1** *n* garantie *f* **2** *vt* garantir (**against** contre); *(vouch for)* se porter garant de; **to g. sb that...** garantir à qn que... ▪**guarantor** [-tɔː(r)] *n* garant, -ante *mf*

guard [gɑːd] **1** *n (supervision)* garde *f*; *(sentry)* garde *m*; *(on train)* chef *m* de train; **under g.** sous surveillance; **on one's g.** sur ses gardes; **on g. (duty)** de garde; **to stand g.** monter la garde; **to catch sb off his g.** prendre qn au dépourvu **2** *vt (protect)* garder; **to g. sb from danger** protéger qn d'un danger **3** *vt insep* **to g. against** *(protect oneself)* se prémunir contre; *(prevent)* empêcher; **to g. against doing sth** se garder de faire qch ▪**guarded** *adj (cautious)* prudent

guardian ['gɑːdɪən] *n Law (of child)* tuteur, -trice *mf*; *(protector)* gardien, -ienne *mf*; **g. angel** ange *m* gardien

Guatemala [gwætɪˈmɑːlə] *n* le Guatemala

Guernsey ['gɜːnzɪ] *n* Guernesey *m ou f*

guerrilla [gəˈrɪlə] *n (person)* guérillero *m*; **g. warfare** guérilla *f*

> Note that the French word **guérilla** is a false friend and is never a translation for the English word **guerrilla**. It means **guerrilla warfare**.

guess [ges] **1** *n (estimate)* estimation *f*; **to make or take a g.** deviner; **at a g.** à vue de nez **2** *vt* deviner (**that** que); *(suppose)* supposer, croire **3** *vi* deviner; **to g. right** deviner juste; **to g. wrong** se tromper; *Am* **I g. (so)** je crois ▪**guesswork** *n* conjecture *f*; **by g.** au juger

guest [gest] *n* invité, -ée *mf*; *(in hotel)* client, -iente *mf*; *(at meal)* convive *mf*; **be my g.!** je t'en prie!; **g. room** chambre *mf* d'amis; **g. speaker** conférencier, -ière *mf* ▪**guesthouse** *n* pension *f* de famille

guffaw [gəˈfɔː] *vi* rire bruyamment

guidance ['gaɪdəns] *n (advice)* conseils *mpl*

guide [gaɪd] **1** *n (person)* guide *m*; *(indication)* indication *f*; **g. (book)** guide *m*; *Br* **G.** éclaireuse *f*; *Br* **g. dog** chien *m* d'aveugle **2** *vt (lead)* guider; **guiding principle** principe *m* directeur ▪**guided** *adj (missile, rocket)* guidé; **g. tour** visite *f* guidée ▪**guidelines** *npl* directives *fpl*

guild [gɪld] *n* association *f*; *Hist* corporation *f*

guile [gaɪl] *n* ruse *f*

guillotine ['gɪlətiːn] *n (for execution)* guillotine *f*; *Br (for paper)* massicot *m*

guilt [gɪlt] *n* culpabilité *f* ∎ **guilty** (**-ier, -iest**) *adj* coupable; **to find sb g./not g.** déclarer qn coupable/non coupable

guinea pig ['gɪnɪpɪg] *n (animal) & Fig* cobaye *m*

guise [gaɪz] *n* **under the g. of** sous l'apparence de

guitar [gɪ'tɑː(r)] *n* guitare *f* ∎ **guitarist** *n* guitariste *mf*

gulf [gʌlf] *n (in sea)* golfe *m; (chasm)* gouffre *m* (**between** entre); **the G.** le golfe Persique; **the G. War** la guerre du Golfe

gull [gʌl] *n* mouette *f*

gullet ['gʌlɪt] *n* gosier *m*

gullible ['gʌlɪbəl] *adj* crédule

gully ['gʌlɪ] *(pl* **-ies)** *n* petit ravin *m*

gulp [gʌlp] **1** *n* (**a**) *(of drink)* gorgée *f;* **in** *or* **at one g.** d'un coup (**b**) *(of surprise)* serrement *m* de gorge **2** *vt* **to g. (down)** engloutir **3** *vi (with surprise)* avoir la gorge serrée

gum¹ [gʌm] *n (in mouth)* gencive *f*

gum² [gʌm] **1** *n* (**a**) *(glue)* colle *f; (from tree)* gomme *f* (**b**) *(for chewing)* chewing-gum *m* **2** *(pt & pp* **-mm-)** *vt* coller

gumption ['gʌmpʃən] *n Fam (courage)* cran *m; (common sense)* jugeote *f*

gun [gʌn] **1** *n* pistolet *m; (rifle)* fusil *m; (firing shells)* canon *m* **2** *(pt & pp* **-nn-)** *vt sep* **to g. down** abattre ∎ **gunfight** *n* fusillade *f* ∎ **gunfire** *n* coups *mpl* de feu; *(in battle)* tir *m* d'artillerie ∎ **gunman** *(pl* **-men)** *n* homme *m* armé ∎ **gunner** *n* artilleur *m* ∎ **gunpoint** *n* **to hold sb at g.** tenir qn sous la menace d'une arme ∎ **gunpowder** *n* poudre *f* à canon ∎ **gunshot** *n* coup *m* de feu; **g. wound** blessure *f* par balle

gung-ho [gʌŋ'həʊ] *adj* **g. about sth** très enthousiaste à l'idée de qch

gurgle ['gɜːgəl] **1** *n* gargouillement *m; (of baby)* gazouillis *m* **2** *vi (of water)* gargouiller; *(of baby)* gazouiller

guru ['guːruː] *n* gourou *m*

gush [gʌʃ] **1** *n* jaillissement *m* **2** *vi* **to g. (out)** jaillir (**of** de)

gust [gʌst] **1** *n (of wind)* rafale *f; (of hot air)* bouffée *f* **2** *vi (of wind)* souffler par rafales

gusto ['gʌstəʊ] *n* **with g.** avec entrain

gut [gʌt] **1** *n (inside body)* intestin *m; Fam* guts *(insides)* entrailles *fpl; (courage)* cran *m; Fam* **he hates your guts** il ne peut pas te sentir **2** *(pt & pp* **-tt-)** *vt (of fire)* ravager

gutter ['gʌtə(r)] *n (on roof)* gouttière *f; (in street)* caniveau *m* ∎ **guttering** *n* gouttières *fpl*

guttural ['gʌtərəl] *adj* guttural

guy [gaɪ] *n Fam (man)* type *m*

guzzle ['gʌzəl] *vt (eat)* engloutir; *(drink)* siffler

gym [dʒɪm] *n* gym *f; (gymnasium)* gymnase *m;* **g. shoes** chaussures *fpl* de gym ∎ **gymnasium** [-'neɪzɪəm] *n* gymnase *m* ∎ **gymnast** *n* gymnaste *mf* ∎ **gym'nastics** *n* gymnastique *f*

gynaecology [gaɪnɪ'kɒlədʒɪ] *(Am* **gynecology)** *n* gynécologie *f* ∎ **gynaecologist** *(Am* **gynecologist)** *n* gynécologue *mf*

gypsy ['dʒɪpsɪ] *n* = **gipsy**

gyrate [dʒaɪ'reɪt] *vi* tournoyer

H, h [eɪtʃ] *n (letter)* H, h *m inv*; **H bomb** bombe *f* H

haberdasher ['hæbədæʃə(r)] *n Br (selling sewing items)* mercier, -ière *mf*; *Am (men's outfitter)* chemisier *m* ▪ **haberdashery** (*pl* **-ies**) *n* mercerie *f*; *Am* chemiserie *f*

habit ['hæbɪt] *n* (**a**) *(custom, practice)* habitude *f*; **to be in/get into the h. of doing sth** avoir/ prendre l'habitude de faire qch; **to make a h. of doing sth** avoir pour habitude de faire qch (**b**) *Fam (addiction)* accoutumance *f*; **a h.-forming drug** une drogue qui crée une accoutumance (**c**) *(of monk, nun)* habit *m*

habitable ['hæbɪtəbəl] *adj* habitable ▪ **habitat** [-tæt] *n (of animal, plant)* habitat *m* ▪ **habi'tation** *n* habitation *f*; **fit for (human) h.** habitable

habitual [hə'bɪtʃʊəl] *adj* habituel, -uelle; *(smoker, drunk)* invétéré ▪ **habitually** *adv* habituellement

hack¹ [hæk] *vt (cut)* hacher ▪ **hacker** *n Comptr* pirate *m* informatique
▸ **hack into** *vt insep Comptr* **to h. into a system** pirater un système

hack² [hæk] *n Pej* **h. (writer)** écrivaillon *m*

hackneyed ['hæknɪd] *adj (saying)* rebattu

had [hæd] *pt & pp of* **have**

haddock ['hædək] *n* aiglefin *m*; **smoked h.** haddock *m*

haemorrhage ['hemərɪdʒ] (*Am* **hemorrhage**) *n* hémorragie *f*

haemorrhoids ['hemərɔɪdz] (*Am* **hemorrhoids**) *npl Med* hémorroïdes *fpl*

hag [hæg] *n Pej (old)* **h.** vieille taupe *f*

haggard ['hægəd] *adj* hâve

haggle ['hægəl] *vi* marchander; **to h. over sth** marchander qch; **to h. over the price of sth** chicaner sur le prix de qch ▪ **haggling** *n* marchandage *m*

Hague [heɪg] *n* **The H.** La Haye

hail¹ [heɪl] **1** *n* grêle *f*; *Fig* **a h. of bullets** une pluie de balles **2** *vi* **it's hailing** il grêle ▪ **hailstone** *n* grêlon *m*

hail² [heɪl] **1** *vt (greet)* saluer (**as** comme); *(taxi)* héler **2** *vt insep* **to h. from** *(of person)* être originaire de; *(of ship, train)* être en provenance de

hair [heə(r)] *n (on head)* cheveux *mpl*; *(on body, of animal)* poils *mpl*; **a h.** *(on head)* un cheveu; *(on body, of animal)* un poil; **by a h.'s breadth** de

justesse; **h. straighteners** défriseur *m* ▪ **hairbrush** *n* brosse *f* à cheveux ▪ **hairclip, hairslide** *n Br* barrette *f* ▪ **haircut** *n* coupe *f* de cheveux; **to have a h.** se faire couper les cheveux ▪ **hairdo** (*pl* **-dos**) *n Fam* coiffure *f* ▪ **hairdresser** *n* coiffeur, -euse *mf* ▪ **hairdryer** *n* sèchecheveux *m inv* ▪ **hairgrip** *n* pince *f* à cheveux ▪ **hairnet** *n* résille *f* ▪ **hairpiece** *n* postiche *m* ▪ **hairpin** *n* épingle *f* à cheveux; **h. bend** *(in road)* virage *m* en épingle à cheveux ▪ **hair-raising** *adj* à faire dresser les cheveux sur la tête ▪ **hair-splitting** *n* ergotage *m* ▪ **hairspray** *n* laque *f* ▪ **hairstyle** *n* coiffure *f*

-haired [heəd] *suff* **long-/red-h.** aux cheveux longs/roux

hairy ['heərɪ] (**-ier, -iest**) *adj (person, animal, body)* poilu; *Fam (frightening)* effrayant

hake [heɪk] *n* colin *m*

half [hɑːf] **1** (*pl* **halves**) *n* moitié *f*; *(part of match)* mi-temps *f*; *Br (half fare)* demi-tarif *m*; *Br (beer)* demi *m*; **h. (of) the apple** la moitié de la pomme; **h. past one** une heure et demie; **ten and a h.** dix et demi; **ten and a h. weeks** dix semaines et demie; **h. a day** une demi-journée; **h. a dozen** une demi-douzaine; **to cut in h.** couper en deux; **to go halves with sb** partager avec qn

2 *adj* demi; **h. board** demi-pension *f*; **a h.-day** une demi-journée; **a h.-dozen** une demi-douzaine; **h. fare** demi-tarif *m*; **at h. price** à moitié prix; **h. man h. beast** mi-homme mi-bête

3 *adv (dressed, full)* à moitié; **h.-asleep** à moitié endormi; *Br Fam* **he isn't h. lazy** il est rudement paresseux; **h. as much as** moitié moins que; **h. as much again** moitié plus ▪ **halfback** *n Sport* demi *m* ▪ **half-'baked** *adj Fam (idea)* à la manque ▪ **half-'dozen** *n* demi-douzaine *f* ▪ **'half-'hearted** *adj (person, manner)* peu enthousiaste; *(effort)* timide ▪ **half-'hour** *n* demi-heure *f* ▪ **half-light** *n* demi-jour *m* ▪ **half-'mast** *n* **at h.** *(flag)* en berne ▪ **'half-'open** *adj* entrouvert ▪ **'half-'price** *adj & adv* à moitié prix ▪ **half-'term** *n Br Sch* congé *m* de milieu de trimestre ▪ **half-'time** *n (in game)* mi-temps *f* ▪ **'half'way** *adv (between)* à mi-chemin (**between** entre); **to fill sth h.** remplir qch à moitié; **to be h. through a book** être à la moitié d'un livre ▪ **halfwit** *n* imbécile *mf* ▪ **halfwitted** *adj* imbécile

halibut ['hælɪbət] *n (fish)* flétan *m*

hall [hɔːl] *n (room)* salle *f*; *(entrance room)* entrée *f*; *(of hotel)* hall *m*; *(mansion)* manoir *m*; *(for meals, in British university)* réfectoire *m*; *Br Univ* **h. of residence** résidence *f* universitaire

hallelujah [hælɪ'luːjə] *n & exclam* alléluia *(m)*

hallmark ['hɔːlmɑːk] *n (on metal)* poinçon *m*; *Fig (typical quality)* signe *m*

hallo [hə'ləʊ] *exclam* = **hello**

Hallowe'en [hæləʊ'iːn] *n* Halloween *m*

hallucination [həluːsɪ'neɪʃən] *n* hallucination *f*

hallway ['hɔːlweɪ] *n* entrée *f*

halo ['heɪləʊ] *(pl* -**oes** *or* -**os**) *n* auréole *f*

halogen ['hælədʒən] *n* **h. lamp** lampe *f* halogène

halt [hɔːlt] **1** *n* halte *f*; **to call a h. to sth** mettre fin à qch; **to come to a h.** s'arrêter **2** *exclam* halte! **3** *vt* arrêter **4** *vi (of soldiers)* faire halte; *(of production)* s'arrêter ■**halting** *adj (voice)* hésitant

halve [hɑːv] *vt (reduce by half)* réduire de moitié; *(divide in two)* diviser en deux

ham [hæm] *n* (**a**) *(meat)* jambon *m*; **h. and eggs** œufs *mpl* au jambon; **h. sandwich** sandwich *m* au jambon (**b**) *Pej (actor)* cabotin, -ine *mf*

hamburger ['hæmbɜːgə(r)] *n* hamburger *m*

ham-fisted [hæm'fɪstɪd] *adj Fam* maladroit

hamlet ['hæmlɪt] *n* hameau *m*

hammer ['hæmə(r)] **1** *n* marteau *m* **2** *vt (nail)* enfoncer (**into** dans); *(metal)* marteler; *Fam (defeat)* écraser; *Fam (criticize)* démolir; **to h. sth out** *(agreement, plan)* mettre au point qch **3** *vi* frapper (au marteau); **to h. on the door** frapper à la porte à coups redoublés ■**hammered** *adj Br Fam (drunk)* bourré ■**hammering** *n Fam (defeat)* raclée *f*

hammock ['hæmək] *n* hamac *m*

hamper ['hæmpə(r)] **1** *n Br (for food)* panier *m*; *Am (laundry basket)* panier *m* à linge **2** *vt (hinder)* gêner

hamster ['hæmstə(r)] *n* hamster *m*

hand¹ [hænd] **1** *n* (**a**) *(part of the body)* main *f*; **to hold sth in one's h.** tenir qch à la main; **to hold hands** se tenir par la main; **by h.** *(make, sew)* à la main; **to deliver sth by h.** remettre qch en mains propres; **at** *or* **to h.** *(within reach)* à portée de la main; **(close) at h.** *(person)* tout près; **the situation is in h.** la situation est bien en main; **the matter is in h.** l'affaire *f* en question; **to have money in h.** avoir de l'argent disponible; **work in h.** travail *m* en cours; **on h.** *(ready for use)* disponible; *Fig* **to have sb on one's hands** avoir qn sur les bras; **on the right h.** du côté droit (**of** de); **on the one h....** d'une part...; **on the other h....** d'autre part...; **hands up!** *(in attack)* haut les mains!; *(to schoolchildren)* levez la main!; **hands off!** bas les pattes!; *Fig* **my hands are full** je suis très occupé; **to lend sb a (helping) h.** donner un coup de main à qn; **to get out of h.** *(of child)* devenir impossible; *(of situation)* devenir incontrôlable; **h. in h.** la main dans la main; *Fig* **it goes h. in h. with...** *(together with)* cela va de pair avec...; **at first h.** de première main; **to win hands down** gagner haut la main (**b**) *(worker)* ouvrier, -ière *mf*; *(of clock)* aiguille *f*; *Cards* jeu *m*; *(style of writing)* écriture *f* **2** *adj (luggage, grenade)* à main; *(cream, lotion)* pour les mains ■**handbag** *n* sac *m* à main ■**handball** *n* handball *m* ■**handbook** *n (manual)* manuel *m*; *(guide)* guide *m* ■**handbrake** *n* frein *m* à main ■**handcuff** *vt* passer les menottes à; **to be handcuffed** avoir les menottes aux poignets ■**handcuffs** *npl* menottes *fpl* ■'**hand'made** *adj* fait à la main ■'**hand'picked** *adj (team member)* trié sur le volet ■**handrail** *n* rampe *f* ■**handshake** *n* poignée *f* de main ■**hands-on** *adj (experience)* pratique ■**handwriting** *n* écriture *f* ■'**hand'written** *adj* écrit à la main

hand² [hænd] *vt (give)* donner (**to** à); **to h. sth down** *(give)* passer qch; **to be handed down from generation to generation** se transmettre de génération en génération; **to h. sth in** remettre qch; **to h. sth out** distribuer qch; **to h. sth over** remettre qch; **to h. sth round** faire circuler qch

handful ['hændfʊl] *n (bunch, group)* poignée *f*; *Fig* **she's (quite) a h.** elle n'est pas facile

handicap ['hændɪkæp] **1** *n (disadvantage) & Sport* handicap *m* **2** *(pt & pp* -**pp**-) *vt* handicaper ■**handicapped** *adj (disabled)* handicapé

handicraft ['hændɪkrɑːft] *n (skill)* artisanat *m*; *(object)* objet *m* artisanal

handiwork ['hændɪwɜːk] *n (skill)* travail *m* manuel; *(result)* ouvrage *m*

handkerchief ['hæŋkətʃɪf] *(pl* -**chiefs**) *n* mouchoir *m*

handle ['hændəl] **1** *n (of door)* poignée *f*; *(of knife)* manche *m*; *(of cup)* anse *f*; *(of saucepan)* queue *f*; *(of pump)* bras *m* **2** *vt (manipulate)* manier; *(touch)* toucher à; *(deal with)* s'occuper de; *(vehicle, ship)* manœuvrer; *(difficult thing)* s'y prendre avec **3** *vi* **to h. well** *(of machine)* être maniable

handlebars ['hændəlbɑːz] *npl* guidon *m*

handout ['hændaʊt] *n (leaflet)* prospectus *m*; *(money)* aumône *f*

handsome ['hænsəm] *adj (person, building)* beau *(f* belle); *(profit, sum)* considérable; *(gift)* généreux, -euse ■**handsomely** *adv (generously)* généreusement

handy ['hændɪ] (-**ier**, -**iest**) *adj (convenient)* commode; *(useful)* pratique; *(within reach)* à portée de la main; *(skilful)* habile (**at doing** à faire); **to come in h.** être utile; **to keep sth h.** avoir qch sous la main; **the flat is h. for the**

shops l'appartement est près des commerces ■ **handyman** (*pl* **-men**) *n* homme *m* à tout faire
hang[1] [hæŋ] **1** *n Fam* **to get the h. of sth** piger qch (*pt & pp* **hung**) *vt* suspendre (**on/from** à); (*on hook*) accrocher (**on** *or* **from** à); (*wallpaper*) poser; **to h. sth with sth** (*decorate with*) orner qch de qch **3** *vi* (*dangle*) pendre; (*of threat*) planer; (*of fog, smoke*) flotter ■ **hanging** *adj* suspendu (**from** à); **h. on the wall** accroché au mur ■ **hang-up** *n Fam* complexe *m*
► **hang about, hang around** *vi* (*loiter*) traîner; *Fam* (*wait*) poireauter
► **hang down** *vi* (*dangle*) pendre; (*of hair*) tomber
► **hang on 1** *vi* (*hold out*) tenir le coup; *Fam* (*wait*) patienter; **to h. on to sth** garder qch **2** *vt insep* (*depend on*) dépendre de
► **hang out 1** *vt sep* (*washing*) étendre **2** *vi* (*from pocket, box*) dépasser; *Fam* (*spend time*) traîner
► **hang together** *vi* (*of facts*) se tenir; (*of plan*) tenir debout
► **hang up 1** *vt sep* (*picture*) accrocher **2** *vi* (*on phone*) raccrocher
hang[2] [hæŋ] (*pt & pp* **hanged**) **1** *vt* (*criminal*) pendre (**for** pour) **2** *vi* (*of criminal*) être pendu ■ **hanging** *n* (*execution*) pendaison *f* ■ **hangman** (*pl* **-men**) *n* bourreau *m*; (*game*) le pendu
hangar ['hæŋə(r)] *n* hangar *m*
hanger ['hæŋə(r)] *n* (**coat**) **h.** cintre *m* ■ **hanger-on** (*pl* **hangers-on**) *n* parasite *m*
hang-glider ['hæŋɡlaɪdə(r)] *n* deltaplane *m* ■ **hang-gliding** *n* vol *m* libre
hangnail ['hæŋneɪl] *n* envie *f*
hangover ['hæŋəʊvə(r)] *n Fam* (*after drinking*) gueule *f* de bois
hanker ['hæŋkə(r)] *vi* **to h. after** *or* **for sth** avoir envie de qch ■ **hankering** *n* forte envie *f*
hankie, hanky ['hæŋkɪ] (*pl* **-ies**) *n Fam* mouchoir *m*
hanky-panky [hæŋkɪ'pæŋkɪ] *n inv Fam* (*sexual behaviour*) galipettes *fpl*; (*underhand behaviour*) entourloupettes *fpl*
haphazard [hæp'hæzəd] *adj* (*choice, decision*) pris au hasard; (*attempt*) mal organisé ■ **haphazardly** *adv* n'importe comment
hapless ['hæplɪs] *adj Literary* infortuné
happen ['hæpən] *vi* arriver, se produire; **to h. to sb** arriver à qn; **I h. to know, it (so) happens that I know** il se trouve que je le sais; **do you h. to have...?** est-ce que par hasard vous avez...?; **what happened?** que s'est-il passé?; **whatever happens** quoi qu'il arrive ■ **happening** *n* événement *m*
happily ['hæpɪlɪ] *adv* joyeusement; (*contentedly*) tranquillement; (*fortunately*) heureusement; **h. married couple** couple *m* heureux
happiness ['hæpɪnəs] *n* bonheur *m*

happy ['hæpɪ] (**-ier, -iest**) *adj* heureux, -euse (**to do** de faire; **about** de); **I'm not h. about it** ça ne me plaît pas; **H. New Year!** bonne année!; **h. birthday/Christmas!** joyeux anniversaire/Noël! ■ **'happy-go-'lucky** *adj* insouciant
harass [*Br* 'hærəs, *Am* hə'ræs] *vt* harceler ■ **harassment** *n* harcèlement *m*; **sexual h.** harcèlement *m* sexuel

> Note that the French verb **harasser** is a false friend and is never a translation for the English verb **to harass**. It means **to exhaust**.

harbour ['hɑːbə(r)] (*Am* **harbor**) **1** *n* port *m* **2** *vt* (*fugitive*) cacher; (*hope, suspicion*) nourrir; **to h. a grudge against sb** garder rancune contre qn
hard [hɑːd] (**-er, -est**) **1** *adj* (*not soft, severe*) dur; (*difficult*) difficile, dur; (*water*) calcaire; **to be h. on sb** être dur avec qn; **to find it h. to sleep** avoir du mal à dormir; **to be h. of hearing** être dur d'oreille; **it was h. work persuading him** ça n'a pas été facile de le convaincre; *Fam* **h. up** (*broke*) fauché; **to be h. up for sth** manquer de qch; **no h. feelings!** sans rancune!; **h. cash** espèces *fpl*; *Comptr* **h. copy** copie *f* sur papier; **h. core** (*of group*) noyau *m* dur; *Comptr* **h. disk** disque *m* dur; **h. drugs** drogues *fpl* dures; **h. evidence** preuves *fpl* tangibles; **h. frost** forte gelée *f*; **h. labour** travaux *mpl* forcés; **h. shoulder** (*on motorway*) bande *f* d'arrêt d'urgence; **h. worker** gros travailleur *m*
2 *adv* (*work*) dur; (*pull, push, hit*) fort; (*study*) assidûment; (*rain*) à verse; **to look h. at sb/sth** regarder fixement qn/qch; **to look h.** (*seek*) chercher bien; **to think h.** réfléchir bien; **to try h.** faire de son mieux; **h. at work** en plein travail; **h. by** tout près de; **to feel h. done by** se sentir brimé ■ **'hard-and-'fast** *adj* (*rule*) strict ■ **'hardback** *n* livre *m* relié ■ **'hardboard** *n* aggloméré *m* ■ **'hard-'boiled** *adj* (*egg*) dur ■ **'hard-core** *adj* (*supporter*) inconditionnel, -elle ■ **'hard-'earned** *adj* (*money*) durement gagné; (*rest*) bien mérité ■ **'hard'headed** *adj* réaliste ■ **'hard'wearing** *adj* résistant ■ **'hard-'working** *adj* travailleur, -euse
harden ['hɑːdən] **1** *vt* endurcir; **to become hardened to sth** s'endurcir à qch **2** *vi* (*of substance, attitude*) durcir ■ **hardened** *adj* (*criminal*) endurci
hardly ['hɑːdlɪ] *adv* à peine; **h. had I arrived when...** j'étais à peine arrivé que...; **h. anyone/anything** presque personne/rien; **h. ever** presque jamais
hardness ['hɑːdnɪs] *n* dureté *f*
hardship ['hɑːdʃɪp] *n* (*ordeal*) épreuve *f*; **to live in h.** vivre dans la misère
hardware ['hɑːdweə(r)] *n inv* quincaillerie *f*;

Comptr & Mil matériel *m*; **h. shop** *or Am* **store** quincaillerie

hardy ['hɑːdɪ] (**-ier, -iest**) *adj* résistant

hare [heə(r)] *n* lièvre *m* ▪ **harebrained** *adj* (*person*) écervelé; (*idea*) insensé

harem [hɑːˈriːm] *n* harem *m*

hark [hɑːk] *vi Literary* écouter; *Fam* **to h. back to sth** évoquer qch

harm [hɑːm] **1** *n* (*hurt*) mal *m*; (*wrong*) tort *m*; **to do sb h.** faire du mal à qn; **he means no h.** il ne veut pas faire de mal; **she'll come to no h.** il ne lui arrivera rien; **out of h.'s way** en lieu sûr **2** *vt* (*physically*) faire du mal à; (*health, interests, cause*) nuire à; (*object*) abîmer ▪ **harmful** *adj* (*influence*) néfaste; (*substance*) nocif, -ive ▪ **harmless** *adj* (*person, treatment*) inoffensif, -ive; (*hobby, joke*) innocent

harmonica [hɑːˈmɒnɪkə] *n* harmonica *m*

harmonium [hɑːˈməʊnɪəm] *n* harmonium *m*

harmonize ['hɑːmənaɪz] **1** *vt* harmoniser **2** *vi* s'harmoniser

harmony ['hɑːmənɪ] (*pl* **-ies**) *n* harmonie *f* ▪ **harmonious** [hɑːˈməʊnɪəs] *adj* harmonieux, -ieuse

harness ['hɑːnɪs] **1** *n* (*for horse, baby*) harnais *m* **2** *vt* (*horse*) harnacher; *Fig* (*resources*) exploiter

harp [hɑːp] **1** *n* harpe *f* **2** *vi Fam* **to h. on about sth** revenir sans arrêt sur qch

harpoon [hɑːˈpuːn] **1** *n* harpon *m* **2** *vt* harponner

harpsichord ['hɑːpsɪkɔːd] *n* clavecin *m*

harrowing ['hærəʊɪŋ] *adj* (*story, memory*) poignant; (*experience*) très éprouvant; (*account, cry, sight*) déchirant

harsh [hɑːʃ] (**-er, -est**) *adj* (*person, treatment*) dur; (*winter, climate*) rude; (*sound, voice*) strident; (*light*) cru; **to be h. with sb** être dur envers qn ▪ **harshly** *adv* durement ▪ **harshness** *n* dureté *f*; (*of winter, climate*) rigueur *f*; (*of sound*) discordance *f*

harvest ['hɑːvɪst] **1** *n* moisson *f*; (*of fruit*) récolte *f* **2** *vt* moissonner; (*fruit*) récolter

has [hæz] *see* **have** ▪ **has-been** *n Fam Pej* has been *mf inv*

hash [hæʃ] **1** *n* (**a**) (*food*) hachis *m*; *Fam* **to make a h. of sth** faire un beau gâchis de qch; **h. browns** = pommes de terre râpées et sautées (**b**) *Fam* (*hashish*) hasch *m* (**c**) *Br Tel* **h. sign** dièse *m* **2** *vt* **to h. (up)** hacher

hashish ['hæʃiːʃ] *n* haschisch *m*

hassle ['hæsəl] *Fam* **1** *n* embêtements *mpl*; **it's too much h.** c'est trop compliqué **2** *vt* embêter

haste [heɪst] *n* hâte *f*; **in h.** à la hâte; **to make h.** se hâter

hasten ['heɪsən] **1** *vt* hâter **2** *vi* se hâter (**to do** de faire)

hasty ['heɪstɪ] (**-ier, -iest**) *adj* (*departure, removal*) précipité; (*visit*) rapide; (*decision, work*) hâtif, -ive ▪ **hastily** *adv* (*write, prepare*) hâtivement; (*say, eat*) précipitamment

hat [hæt] *n* chapeau *m*; (*woollen*) bonnet *m*; *Fam* **that's old h.** c'est vieux; *Sport* **to score** *or* **get a h. trick** (*of goals*) marquer trois buts au cours d'un match; **h. stand** portemanteau *m*

hatch [hætʃ] **1** *n* serving h. passe-plat *m* **2** *vt* faire éclore; *Fig* (*plot*) tramer **3** *vi* (*of chick, egg*) éclore

hatchback ['hætʃbæk] *n* (*car*) (*three-door*) trois-portes *f inv*; (*five-door*) cinq-portes *f inv*; (*door*) hayon *m*

hatchet ['hætʃɪt] *n* hachette *f*

hate [heɪt] **1** *n* haine *f* **2** *vt* haïr, détester; **to h. doing** *or* **to do sth** détester faire qch; **I h. to say it but...** ça m'ennuie de le dire mais... ▪ **hateful** *adj* odieux, -ieuse ▪ **hatred** ['heɪtrɪd] *n* haine *f*

haughty ['hɔːtɪ] (**-ier, -iest**) *adj* hautain ▪ **haughtily** *adv* avec hauteur

haul [hɔːl] **1** *n* (*fish caught*) prise *f*; (*of thief*) butin *m*; **a long h.** (*trip*) un long voyage **2** *vt* (**a**) (*pull*) tirer (**b**) (*goods*) transporter par camion ▪ **haulage** ['hɔːlɪdʒ] *n* transport *m* routier; (*cost*) frais *mpl* de transport ▪ **haulier** (*Am* **hauler**) *n* transporteur *m* routier

haunt [hɔːnt] **1** *n* (*place*) lieu *m* de rendez-vous; (*of criminal*) repaire *m* **2** *vt* hanter ▪ **haunted** *adj* (*house*) hanté ▪ **haunting** *adj* obsédant

have [hæv] **1** *npl* **the haves and (the) have-nots** les riches *mpl* et les pauvres *mpl*

2 (*3rd person sing present tense* **has**; *pt & pp* **had**; *pres p* **having**) *vt* avoir; (*meal, bath, lesson*) prendre; **he has (got) a big house** il a une grande maison; **she doesn't h.** *or* **hasn't got a car** elle n'a pas de voiture; **to h. a drink** prendre un verre; **to h. a walk/dream** faire une promenade/un rêve; **to h. a wash** se laver; **to h. a swim** se baigner; **to h. a pleasant holiday** passer d'agréables vacances; **to h. a party** faire une soirée; **to h. a cold** être enrhumé; **to h. flu** avoir la grippe; **will you h. some tea?** est-ce que tu veux du thé?; **to h. sth to do** avoir qch à faire; **to let sb h. sth** donner qch à qn; **he had me by the hair** il me tenait par les cheveux; **I won't h. this** (*allow*) je ne tolérerai pas ça; **to h. it from sb that...** tenir de qn que...; *Fam* **to h. had it with sb/sth** en avoir assez de qn/qch; *Fam* **you've had it!** tu es fichu!; *Fam* **I've been had** (*cheated*) je me suis fait avoir; **to h. gloves/a dress on** porter des gants/une robe; **to h. a lot on** avoir beaucoup à faire; **to h. sb over** *or* **round** inviter qn chez soi

3 *v aux* avoir; (*with* **entrer, monter, sortir** *etc &* *pronominal verbs*) être; **to h. decided** avoir décidé; **to h. gone** être allé; **to h. cut oneself** s'être coupé; **she has been punished** elle a été punie, on l'a punie; **I've just done it** je viens de le faire; **I haven't seen it yet,** *Formal* **I h. not seen it yet** je ne l'ai pas encore vu; **to h. to do**

sth *(must)* devoir faire qch; **I've got to go, I h. to go** je dois partir, il faut que je parte; **I don't h. to go** je ne suis pas obligé de partir; **to h. sb do sth** faire faire qch à qn; **to h. sth done** faire faire qch; **to h. one's hair cut** se faire couper les cheveux; **he's had his suitcase brought up** il a fait monter sa valise; **I've had my car stolen** on m'a volé mon auto; **I've been doing it for months** je le fais depuis des mois; **you h. told me, haven't you?** tu le lui as dit, n'est-ce pas?; **you've seen this film before – no I haven't!** tu as déjà vu ce film – mais non!; **you haven't done the dishes – yes I h.!** tu n'as pas fait la vaisselle – mais si, je l'ai faite!; **after he had eaten** *or* **after having eaten, he left** après avoir mangé, il partit

▸ **have on** *vt sep* **(a)** *(be wearing)* porter **(b)** *Fam (fool)* **to h. sb on** faire marcher qn **(c)** *(have arranged)* **to h. a lot on** avoir beaucoup à faire; **to h. nothing on** n'avoir rien de prévu

▸ **have out** *vt sep* **(a)** *(have removed)* **to h. a tooth out** se faire arracher une dent **(b)** *(resolve)* **to h. it out with sb** s'expliquer avec qn

haven ['heɪvən] *n* refuge *m*

haven't ['hævənt] = **have not**

haversack ['hævəsæk] *n* sac *m* à dos

havoc ['hævək] *n* ravages *mpl*; **to wreak** *or* **cause h.** faire des ravages; **to play h. with sth** *(plans)* chambouler qch

hawk¹ [hɔːk] *n (bird)* & *Pol* faucon *m*

hawk² [hɔːk] *vt* **to h. one's wares** *(from door to door)* faire du porte-à-porte ▪ **hawker** *n* colporteur, -euse *mf*

hawthorn ['hɔːθɔːn] *n* aubépine *f*

hay [heɪ] *n* foin *m* ▪ **hayfever** *n* rhume *m* des foins ▪ **haystack** *n* meule *f* de foin

haywire ['heɪwaɪə(r)] *adj* **to go h.** *(of machine)* se détraquer; *(of plan)* mal tourner

hazard ['hæzəd] **1** *n* risque *m*; **to be a health h.** présenter un risque pour la santé; **it's a fire h.** ça risque de provoquer un incendie; *Br Aut* **h. (warning) lights** feux *mpl* de détresse **2** *vt (fortune, remark)* risquer ▪ **hazardous** *adj* dangereux, -euse

> Note that the French word **hasard** is a false friend and is never a translation for the English word **hazard**. It means **chance**.

haze [heɪz] **1** *n* brume *f*; *Fig* **in a h.** *(confused)* dans le brouillard **2** *vt Am Univ (student)* bizuter ▪ **hazing** *n Am Univ* bizutage *m*

hazel ['heɪzəl] **1** *n (tree)* noisetier *m* **2** *adj* **to have h. eyes** avoir les yeux noisette ▪ **hazelnut** *n* noisette *f*

hazy ['heɪzɪ] (**-ier, -iest**) *adj (weather)* brumeux, -euse; *(photo, idea)* flou; **h. sunshine** soleil *m* voilé; **to be h. about sth** *(remember vaguely)* n'avoir qu'un vague souvenir de qch

he [hiː] **1** *pron* il; *(stressed)* lui; **he wants** il veut; **he's a happy man** c'est un homme heureux; **if I were he** si j'étais lui; **he and I** lui et moi **2** *n Fam (male)* mâle *m*; **he-bear** ours *m* mâle; *Fam* **it's a he** *(baby)* c'est un garçon

head [hed] **1** *n (of person, hammer)* tête *f*; *(leader)* chef *m*; *Br (headmaster)* directeur *m*; *Br (headmistress)* directrice *f*; *(of bed)* chevet *m*, tête *f*; *(of arrow)* pointe *f*; *(subject heading)* rubrique; **(tape) h.** *(of tape recorder, VCR)* tête magnétique; **h. of hair** chevelure *f*; **h. of state** chef *m* d'État; **h. first** la tête la première; **at the h. of** *(in charge of)* à la tête de; **at the h. of the table** en bout de table; **at the h. of the list** en tête de liste; **at the h. of the page** en haut de la page; **it didn't enter my h.** ça ne m'est pas venu à l'esprit **(that** que); **to take it into one's h. to do sth** se mettre en tête de faire qch; **to have a good h. for business** avoir le sens des affaires; *Fam* **to shout one's h. off** crier à tue-tête; **it's above my h.** ça me dépasse; **to keep one's h.** garder son sang-froid; **to lose one's h.** perdre la tête; **to go off one's h.** devenir fou *(f* folle); **it's coming to a h.** *(of situation)* ça devient critique; **heads or tails?** pile ou face?; **per h., a h.** *(each)* par personne; **h. cold** rhume *m* de cerveau

2 *adj* **h. gardener** jardinier *m* en chef; **h. office** siège *m* social; **h. waiter** maître *m* d'hôtel; **to have a h. start over** avoir beaucoup d'avance sur

3 *vt (group, firm)* être à la tête de; *(list, poll)* être en tête de; *(vehicle)* diriger **(towards** vers); *Football* **to h. the ball** faire une tête; **to h. sb off** détourner qn de son chemin; **to h. sth off** éviter qch; *Am* **to be headed for** se diriger vers **4** *vi* **to h. for, to be heading for** *(place)* se diriger vers ▪ **headache** *n* mal *m* de tête; *Fig (problem)* casse-tête *m inv*; **to have a h.** avoir mal à la tête ▪ **headdress** *n (ornamental)* coiffe *f* ▪ **headlamp, headlight** *n (of vehicle)* phare *m* ▪ **headline** *n (of newspaper, TV news)* titre *m*; **to hit the headlines** faire la une des journaux ▪ **headlong** *adv (fall)* la tête la première; *(rush)* tête baissée ▪ **head'master** *n Br Sch* directeur *m* ▪ **head'mistress** *n Br Sch* directrice *f* ▪ **'head-'on** *adv & adj* de front ▪ **headphones** *npl* écouteurs *mpl* ▪ **headquarters** *npl (of company, political party)* siège *m* (social); *(of army, police)* quartier *m* général, QG *m* ▪ **headrest** *n* appuie-tête *m inv* ▪ **headscarf** *(pl* **-scarves)** *n* foulard *m* ▪ **headstrong** *adj* têtu ▪ **headway** *n* **to make h.** faire des progrès

headed ['hedɪd] *adj Br* **h. (note)paper** papier *m* à en-tête

-headed ['hedɪd] *suff* **two-h.** *(monster)* à deux têtes; **curly-h.** aux cheveux frisés

header ['hedə(r)] *n Football* (coup *m* de) tête *f*

headhunter ['hedhʌntə(r)] n Com chasseur m de têtes

heading ['hedɪŋ] n (of chapter, page) titre m; (of subject) rubrique f; (printed on letter) en-tête m

heady ['hedɪ] (**-ier, -iest**) adj (wine, perfume) capiteux, -euse; (atmosphere) enivrant

heal [hiːl] **1** vt (wound) cicatriser; Fig (person, sorrow) guérir **2** vi **to h. (up)** (of wound) cicatriser **• healer** n guérisseur, -euse mf

health [helθ] n santé f; **in good/bad h.** en bonne/mauvaise santé; **h. care** soins mpl médicaux; Br **h. centre** dispensaire m; **h. food** produit m de culture biologique; **h. food shop** or Am **store** magasin m de produits biologiques; **h. resort** station f climatique; Br **the (National) H. Service** ≃ la Sécurité Sociale

healthy ['helθɪ] (**-ier, -iest**) adj (person) en bonne santé; (food, attitude) sain; (appetite) robuste

heap [hiːp] **1** n tas m; Fam **heaps of** (money, people) des tas de; Fam **to have heaps of time** avoir largement le temps **2** vt entasser; **to h. sth on sb** (praise, gifts) couvrir qn de qch; (insults, work) accabler qn de qch; **a heaped spoonful** une cuillerée bien pleine

hear [hɪə(r)] (pt & pp **heard** [hɜːd]) **1** vt entendre; (listen to) écouter; (learn) apprendre (**that** que); **I heard him come** or **coming** je l'ai entendu venir; **have you heard the news?** connais-tu la nouvelle?; **to h. it said that…** entendre dire que…; **I h. you're not well** j'ai appris que vous n'alliez pas bien; **to h. sb out** écouter qn jusqu'au bout; **h., h.!** bravo!
2 vi entendre; **to h. from sb** avoir des nouvelles de qn; **I've heard of** or **about him** j'ai entendu parler de lui; **she wouldn't h. of it** elle ne voulait pas en entendre parler; **I won't h. of it!** pas question! **• hearing** n (**a**) (sense) ouïe f; **hard of h.** dur d'oreille; **h. aid** audiophone m (**b**) (of committee) séance f; Law (inquiry) audition f; **to give sb a fair h.** laisser qn s'expliquer

hearsay ['hɪəseɪ] n **by h.** par ouï-dire; **it's only h.** ce ne sont que des on-dit

hearse [hɜːs] n corbillard m

heart [hɑːt] n cœur m; Cards **hearts** cœur m; (**off) by h.** (know) par cœur; **at h.** au fond; **the h. of the matter** le fond du problème; **to lose h.** perdre courage; **to one's h.'s content** tout son soûl; **his h. is set on it** il y tient; **his h. is set on doing it** il tient à le faire; **h. attack** crise f cardiaque; **h. disease** maladie f de cœur; **h. failure** arrêt m cardiaque; **h. surgeon** chirurgien, -ienne mf cardiologue **• heartache** n chagrin m **• heartbeat** n battement m de cœur; (rhythm) pouls m **• heartbreaking** adj navrant **• heartbroken** adj inconsolable **• heartburn** n (indigestion) brûlures fpl d'estomac **• heartfelt** adj sincère

• heartlands npl (of country) cœur m, centre m
• heartthrob n Fam idole f

hearten ['hɑːtən] vt encourager **• heartening** adj encourageant

hearth [hɑːθ] n foyer m

hearty ['hɑːtɪ] (**-ier, -iest**) adj (appetite, meal) gros (f grosse) **• heartily** adv (eat) avec appétit; (laugh, detest) de tout son cœur; (approve, agree) absolument

heat [hiːt] **1** n (**a**) chaleur f; (heating) chauffage m; (of oven) température f; **in the h. of the argument** dans le feu de la discussion; **at low h., on a low h.** (cook) à feu doux; **h. wave** vague f de chaleur (**b**) (in competition) éliminatoire f; **it was a dead h.** ils sont arrivés ex aequo **2** vti **to h. (up)** chauffer **• heated** adj (swimming pool) chauffé; (argument) animé; **the house is centrally h.** la maison a le chauffage central **• heatedly** adv avec passion **• heating** n chauffage m; **central h.** chauffage m central

heater ['hiːtə(r)] n radiateur m

heath [hiːθ] n (land) lande f

heathen ['hiːðən] adj & n Rel païen, païenne (mf)

heather ['heðə(r)] n bruyère f

heave [hiːv] **1** n (effort) effort m **2** vt (lift) soulever avec effort; (pull) tirer fort; (push) pousser fortement; Fam (throw) balancer; **to h. a sigh** pousser un soupir **3** vi (of stomach, chest) se soulever; Fam (feel sick) avoir des haut-le-cœur

heaven ['hevən] n paradis m, ciel m; **in h.** au paradis; Fig (overjoyed) aux anges; Fam **h. knows why…** Dieu sait pourquoi…; Fam **good heavens!** mon Dieu!; Fam **it was h.** c'était divin **• heavenly** adj Fam (pleasing) divin; **h. body** corps m céleste

heavily ['hevɪlɪ] adv (walk, tax) lourdement; (breathe) bruyamment; (smoke, drink) beaucoup; **h. in debt** lourdement endetté; **to rain h.** pleuvoir à verse; **to snow h.** neiger beaucoup; **to depend h. on** dépendre beaucoup de; **to be h. defeated** subir une lourde défaite; **to be h. involved in sth** être lourdement impliqué dans qch

heavy ['hevɪ] (**-ier, -iest**) adj lourd; (work, cold) gros (f grosse); (rain, concentration) fort; (traffic) dense; (film, text) difficile; (timetable, schedule) chargé; **how h. are you?** combien pesez-vous?; **h. snow** d'abondantes chutes de neige; **to be a h. drinker/smoker** boire/fumer beaucoup; **to be h. on** Br **petrol** or Am **gas** (of vehicle) consommer beaucoup; **it's h. going** c'est difficile; Br **h. goods vehicle** poids m lourd **• heaviness** n pesanteur f, lourdeur f **• heavyweight** n Boxing poids m lourd; Fig personnage m important

Hebrew ['hiːbruː] **1** adj hébraïque **2** n (language) hébreu m
Hebrides ['hebrɪdiːz] n the H. les Hébrides fpl
heck [hek] n Fam zut!; **what the h.!** et puis zut!; **a h. of a lot** des masses
heckle ['hekəl] vt interpeller ▪**heckler** n chahuteur, -euse mf ▪**heckling** n chahut m
hectic ['hektɪk] adj (busy) agité; (eventful) mouvementé; **h. life** vie f trépidante
he'd [hiːd] = he had, he would
hedge [hedʒ] **1** n (in garden, field) haie f **2** vi (answer evasively) ne pas se mouiller
hedgehog ['hedʒhɒg] n hérisson m
hedgerow ['hedʒrəʊ] n Br haie f
heed [hiːd] **1** n **to pay h. to sth, to take h. of sth** tenir compte de qch **2** vt tenir compte de ▪**heedless** adj **to be h. of sth** ne pas tenir compte de qch
heel [hiːl] n (**a**) (of foot, shoe) talon m; Br **down at h.,** Am **down at the heels** (shabby) miteux, -euse; **h. bar** cordonnerie f express (**b**) Am Fam (person) salaud m
hefty ['heftɪ] (**-ier, -iest**) adj (large, heavy) gros (f grosse); (person) costaud
heifer ['hefə(r)] n génisse f
height [haɪt] n (of person) taille f; (of mountain, aircraft) altitude f; **to be afraid of heights** avoir le vertige; **the h. of** (success, fame, glory) l'apogée m de; (folly, pain) le comble de; **at the h. of** (summer, storm) au cœur de; **it's the h. of fashion** c'est la dernière mode
heighten ['haɪtən] vt (tension, interest) augmenter
heinous ['heɪnəs] adj Formal (crime) atroce

> Note that the French word **haineux** is a false friend and is never a translation for the English word **heinous**. It means **full of hatred**.

heir [eə(r)] n héritier m; **to be h. to sth** l'héritier de qch ▪**heiress** n héritière f ▪**heirloom** n **a family h.** un objet de famille
held [held] pt & pp of **hold**
helicopter ['helɪkɒptə(r)] n hélicoptère m ▪**heliport** n héliport m
hell [hel] n enfer m; Fam **a h. of a lot (of sth)** énormément (de qch); Fam **a h. of a nice guy** un type super; Fam **what the h. are you doing?** qu'est-ce que tu fous?; Fam **to h. with him!** qu'il aille se faire voir!; Fam **h.!** zut! ▪**hellbent** adj Br Fam **to be h. on doing** or **to do sth** vouloir à tout prix faire qch ▪**hellish** adj Fam infernal
he'll [hiːl] = he will, he shall
hello [hə'ləʊ] exclam bonjour!; (answering phone) allô!
helm [helm] n (of ship) barre f
helmet ['helmɪt] n casque m
help [help] **1** n aide f; Br (cleaning woman)

femme f de ménage; (office or shop workers) employés, -ées mfpl; **with the h. of sth** à l'aide de qch; **to be of h. to sb** aider qn; **to cry** or **shout for h.** appeler à l'aide; **h.!** au secours! **2** vt aider; **to h. sb do** or **to do sth** aider qn à faire qch; **to h. oneself (to sth)** se servir (de qch); **to h. sb out** aider qn; **to h. sb up** aider qn à monter; **I can't h. laughing** je ne peux pas m'empêcher de rire; **he can't h. being bald** ce n'est pas sa faute s'il est chauve; **it can't be helped** on n'y peut rien **3** vi aider; **to h. out** donner un coup de main ▪**helper** n assistant, -ante mf ▪**helping** n (serving) portion f
helpful ['helpfəl] adj (person) serviable; (useful) utile
helpless ['helpləs] adj (powerless) impuissant; (disabled) impotent ▪**helplessly** adv (struggle) en vain
helpline ['helplaɪn] n service m d'assistance téléphonique
helter-skelter [heltə'skeltə(r)] **1** n (slide) toboggan m **2** adv **to run h.** courir comme un fou/une folle
hem [hem] **1** n ourlet m **2** (pt & pp -mm-) vt (garment) ourler; **to be hemmed in** (surrounded) être cerné (**by** de)
he-man ['hiːmæn] n Fam mâle m
hemisphere ['hemɪsfɪə(r)] n hémisphère m
hemorrhage ['hemərɪdʒ] n Am = haemorrhage
hemorrhoids ['hemərɔɪdz] npl Am = haemorrhoids
hemp [hemp] n chanvre m
hen [hen] n poule f; **h. bird** oiseau m femelle; Br **to have a h. night** or **party** enterrer sa vie de jeune fille
hence [hens] adv (**a**) (thus) d'où (**b**) (from now) **ten years h.** d'ici dix ans ▪**hence'forth** adv Formal désormais
henchman ['hentʃmən] (pl **-men**) n Pej acolyte m
henpecked ['henpekt] adj (husband) mené par le bout du nez
hepatitis [hepə'taɪtɪs] n Med hépatite f
her [hɜː(r)] **1** pron la, l'; (after prep, 'than', 'it is') elle; (to) h. (indirect) lui; **I see h.** je la vois; **I saw h.** je l'ai vue; **I gave it to h.** je le lui ai donné; **with h.** avec elle **2** possessive adj son, sa, pl ses; **h. husband** son mari; **h. sister** sœur; **h. parents** ses parents
herald ['herəld] vt annoncer
heraldry ['herəldrɪ] n héraldique f
herb [Br hɜːb, Am ɜːb] n herbe f aromatique; Br **h. tea** tisane f ▪**herbal** adj **h. tea** tisane f
herd [hɜːd] **1** n troupeau m **2** vt (cattle, people) rassembler
here [hɪə(r)] **1** adv ici; **h. it/he is** le voici; **h. she comes!** la voilà!; **h. comes the teacher** voici le professeur qui arrive; **h. is a good example**

voici un bon exemple; **h. are my friends** voici mes amis; **I won't be h. tomorrow** je ne serai pas là demain; **summer is h.** c'est l'été; **h. and there** çà et là; **h. you are!** *(take this)* tenez!; **h.'s to you!** *(toast)* à la tienne! **2** *exclam* **h.!** *(giving sb sth)* tenez! ▪ **here'after** *adv Formal (below)* ci-après; *(in the future)* dorénavant ▪ **hereby** *adv Formal (declare)* par le présent acte; *(in writing)* par la présente ▪ **here'with** *adv Formal (with letter)* ci-joint

heredity [hɪ'redɪtɪ] *n* hérédité *f* ▪ **hereditary** *adj* héréditaire

heresy ['herəsɪ] *(pl -ies) n* hérésie *f* ▪ **heretic** *n* hérétique *mf*

heritage ['herɪtɪdʒ] *n* patrimoine *m*

hermetic [hɜ:'metɪk] *adj* hermétique ▪ **hermetically** *adv* hermétiquement

hermit ['hɜ:mɪt] *n* ermite *m*

hernia ['hɜ:nɪə] *n Med* hernie *f*

hero ['hɪərəʊ] *(pl -oes) n* héros *m* ▪ **heroic** [hɪ'rəʊɪk] *adj* héroïque ▪ **heroics** [hɪ'rəʊɪks] *npl (action)* coup *m* d'éclat ▪ **heroine** ['herəʊɪn] *n* héroïne *f* ▪ **heroism** ['herəʊɪzəm] *n* héroïsme *m*

heroin ['herəʊɪn] *n (drug)* héroïne *f*

heron ['herən] *n* héron *m*

herring ['herɪŋ] *n* hareng *m*; *Fig* **a red h.** une diversion

hers [hɜ:z] *possessive pron* le sien, la sienne, *pl* les sien(ne)s; **this hat is h.** ce chapeau est à elle *ou* est le sien; **a friend of h.** un ami à elle

herself [hɜ:'self] *pron* elle-même; *(reflexive)* se, s'; *(after prep)* elle; **she did it h.** elle l'a fait elle-même; **she cut h.** elle s'est coupée; **she thinks of h.** elle pense à elle

hesitant ['hezɪtənt] *adj* hésitant ▪ **hesitantly** *adv* avec hésitation

hesitate ['hezɪteɪt] **1** *vt* **to h. to do sth** hésiter à faire qch **2** *vi* hésiter (**over** *or* **about** sur) ▪ **hesi'tation** *n* hésitation *f*

heterogeneous [hetərəʊ'dʒi:nɪəs] *adj* hétérogène

heterosexual [hetərəʊ'seksjʊəl] *adj & n* hétérosexuel, -uelle *(mf)*

het up [het'ʌp] *adj Fam* énervé

hew [hju:] *(pp hewn [hju:n] or hewed) vt* tailler

hexagon ['heksəgən] *n* hexagone *m* ▪ **hexagonal** [-'sægənəl] *adj* hexagonal

hey [heɪ] *exclam (calling sb)* hé!, ohé!; *(expressing surprise, annoyance)* ho!

heyday ['heɪdeɪ] *n* apogée *m*; **in its h.** à son apogée; **in his h.** au sommet de sa gloire

hi [haɪ] *exclam Fam* salut!

hiatus [haɪ'eɪtəs] *n (interruption)* interruption *f*; *(in conversation)* silence *m*

hibernate ['haɪbəneɪt] *vi* hiberner ▪ **hibernation** [-'neɪʃən] *n* hibernation *f*

hiccup, hiccough ['hɪkʌp] **1** *n* hoquet *m*; *Fig (in plan)* accroc *m*; **to have (the) hiccups** *or* **(the) hiccoughs** avoir le hoquet **2** *vi* hoqueter

hick [hɪk] *n Am Fam Pej (peasant)* plouc *mf*

hide¹ [haɪd] *(pt hid [hɪd], pp hidden [hɪdən])* **1** *vt* cacher (**from** à) **2** *vi* **to h. (away** *or* **out)** se cacher (**from** de) ▪ **hide-and-'seek** *n* cache-cache *m inv*; **to play h.** jouer à cache-cache

hide² [haɪd] *n (skin)* peau *f*

hideaway ['haɪdəweɪ] *n* cachette *f*

hideous ['hɪdɪəs] *adj (ugly)* hideux, -euse; *(horrific)* horrible ▪ **hideously** *adv* horriblement

hide-out ['haɪdaʊt] *n* cachette *f*

hiding¹ ['haɪdɪŋ] *n* **to go into h.** se cacher; **h. place** cachette *f*

hiding² ['haɪdɪŋ] *n Fam* **a good h.** *(thrashing)* une bonne raclée

hierarchy ['haɪərɑ:kɪ] *(pl -ies) n* hiérarchie *f*

hi-fi ['haɪfaɪ] **1** *n (system, equipment)* chaîne *f* hi-fi; *(sound reproduction)* hi-fi *f inv* **2** *adj* hi-fi *inv*

high [haɪ] **1** *(-er, -est) adj* haut; *(speed)* grand; *(price, standards)* élevé; *(number, ideal)* grand, élevé; *(voice, tone)* aigu *(f* aiguë); *(wind)* violent; *(meat, game)* faisandé; *Fam (on drugs)* défoncé; **to be 5 m h.** avoir 5 m de haut; **h. and mighty** arrogant; **to be in h. spirits** être plein d'entrain; **it is h. time that you went** il est grand temps que tu y ailles; *Fam* **to leave sb h. and dry** laisser qn en plan; **h. fever** forte fièvre *f*; *Sport* **h. jump** saut *m* en hauteur; **h. noon** plein midi *m*; **h. priest** grand prêtre *m*; **h. school** ≃ lycée *m*; *Am* **h. school diploma** diplôme *m* de fin d'études secondaires; **h. spot** *(of visit, day)* point *m* culminant; *(of show)* clou *m*; *Br* **h. street** grand-rue *f*; **h. summer** plein été; **h. table** table *f* d'honneur; **h. tea** = dîner pris tôt dans la soirée; **h. tide** marée *f* haute **2** *adv* **h. (up)** *(fly, throw, aim)* haut; **feelings were running h.** la tension montait

3 *n* sommet *m*; **a new h., an all-time h.** *(peak)* un nouveau record; **to be on a h.** *(from drugs)* planer; *(from success)* être sur un petit nuage ▪ **highchair** *n* chaise *f* haute ▪ **high-'class** *adj (service)* de premier ordre; *(building)* de luxe; *(person)* raffiné ▪ **high-'five** *n Fam* = tape amicale donnée dans la paume de quelqu'un, bras levé, en signe de victoire ▪ **high-'flier, high-'flyer** *n* jeune loup *m* ▪ **high-'handed** *adj* tyrannique ▪ **high-'minded** *adj* noble ▪ **high-'pitched** *adj (sound)* aigu *(f* aiguë) ▪ **high-'powered** *adj (engine, car)* très puissant; *(job)* à hautes responsabilités ▪ **high-'profile** *adj (person)* très en vue; *(campaign)* de grande envergure ▪ **high-'rise** *adj Br* **h. building** tour *f* ▪ **high-'speed** *adj* ultrarapide; **h. train** train *m* à grande vitesse ▪ **high-'strung** *adj Am* nerveux, -euse ▪ **high-'tech** *adj (appliance)* perfectionné; *(industry)* de pointe ▪ **high-'up** *adj Fam (important)* haut placé

highbrow ['haɪbraʊ] adj & n intellectuel, -uelle (mf)

higher ['haɪə(r)] 1 adj (number, speed, quality) supérieur (**than** à); **h. education** enseignement m supérieur 2 adv (fly, aim) plus haut (**than** que) 3 n Scot Sch **H.** = diplôme de fin d'études secondaires sanctionnant une matière déterminée

highlands ['haɪləndz] npl régions fpl montagneuses

highlight ['haɪlaɪt] 1 n (of visit, day) point m culminant; (of show) clou m; **highlights** (in hair) mèches fpl 2 vt souligner; (with marker) surligner ▪**highlighter** n (pen) surligneur m

highly ['haɪlɪ] adv (very) très; (recommend) chaudement; **h. paid** très bien payé; **to speak h. of sb** dire beaucoup de bien de qn; Br **h. strung** hypersensible

Highness ['haɪnɪs] n His/Her Royal **H.** Son Altesse f

highroad ['haɪrəʊd] n Br Old-fashioned grand-route f; Fig **the h. to success** la voie du succès

highway ['haɪweɪ] n Am (main road) nationale f; (motorway) autoroute f; Br **public h.** voie f publique; Br **H. Code** code m de la route

hijack ['haɪdʒæk] 1 n détournement m 2 vt (plane) détourner ▪**hijacker** n (of plane) pirate m de l'air ▪**hijacking** n (air piracy) piraterie f aérienne; (hijack) détournement m

hike [haɪk] 1 n (a) (walk) randonnée f (b) Fam (increase) hausse f 2 vt Fam (price) augmenter 3 vi faire de la randonnée ▪**hiker** n randonneur, -euse mf ▪**hiking** n randonnée f; **to go h.** faire de la randonnée

hilarious [hɪ'leərɪəs] adj hilarant

hill [hɪl] n colline f, (slope) pente f ▪**hillbilly** (pl -ies) n Am Fam péquenaud, -aude mf ▪**hillside** n **on the h.** à flanc de coteau ▪**hilly** (-ier, -iest) adj vallonné

hilt [hɪlt] n (of sword) poignée f; Fig **to the h.** au maximum

him [hɪm] pron le, l'; (after prep, 'than', 'it is') lui; **(to) h.** (indirect) lui; **I see h.** je le vois; **I saw h.** je l'ai vu; **I gave it to h.** je le lui ai donné; **with h.** avec lui

himself [hɪm'self] pron lui-même; (reflexive) se, s'; (after prep) lui; **he did it h.** il l'a fait lui-même; **he cut h.** il s'est coupé; **he thinks of h.** il pense à lui

hind [haɪnd] adj **h. legs** pattes fpl de derrière ▪**hindquarters** npl arrière-train m

hinder ['hɪndə(r)] vt (obstruct) gêner; (delay) retarder; **to h. sb from doing sth** empêcher qn de faire qch ▪**hindrance** n obstacle m

hindsight ['haɪndsaɪt] n **with h.** avec le recul

Hindu ['hɪnduː] 1 adj hindou 2 n Hindou, -oue mf

hinge [hɪndʒ] 1 n gond m, charnière f 2 vt insep **to h. on** (depend on) dépendre de ▪**hinged** adj à charnière(s)

hint [hɪnt] 1 n (insinuation) allusion f; (sign) signe m; (clue) indice m; **hints** (advice) conseils mpl; **to drop sb a h.** faire une allusion à l'intention de qn 2 vt laisser entendre (**that** que) 3 vt insep **to h. at sb/sth** faire allusion à qn/qch

hip¹ [hɪp] n hanche f ▪**hipsters** (Am **hip-huggers**) (trousers) pantalon m (à) taille basse

hip² [hɪp] adj (trendy) branché

hip-hop ['hɪphɒp] n (music) hip-hop m inv

hippie ['hɪpɪ] n hippie m f

hippopotamus [hɪpə'pɒtəməs] n hippopotame m ▪**hippo** n Fam hippopotame m

hire ['haɪə(r)] 1 n location f; **for h.** à louer; Br (sign on taxi) 'libre'; **on h.** en location; Br **h. purchase** achat m à crédit; Br **on h. purchase** à crédit 2 vt (vehicle) louer; (worker) engager; **to h. sth out** louer qch

his [hɪz] 1 possessive pron le sien, la sienne, pl les sien(ne)s; **this hat is h.** ce chapeau est à lui ou est le sien; **a friend of h.** un ami à lui 2 possessive adj son, sa, pl ses

Hispanic [hɪ'spænɪk] Am 1 adj hispano-américain 2 n Hispano-Américain, -aine mf

hiss [hɪs] 1 n sifflement m; **hisses** (booing) sifflets mpl 2 vti siffler ▪**hissing** n sifflement m

history ['hɪstərɪ] (pl -ies) n (study, events) histoire f; **to make h., to go down in h.** (of event) faire date; (of person) entrer dans l'histoire; **medical h.** antécédents mpl médicaux ▪**historian** [hɪ'stɔːrɪən] n historien, -ienne mf ▪**historic(al)** [hɪ'stɒrɪk(əl)] adj historique

histrionic [hɪstrɪ'ɒnɪk] adj Pej théâtral ▪**histrionics** npl Pej scène f

hit [hɪt] 1 n (blow) coup m; (in shooting) tir m réussi; (success) succès m; Comptr (visit to website) hit m, contact m; **to score a direct h.** taper dans le mille; **h. man** tueur m à gages; **h. list** liste f noire; **h. (song)** hit m 2 (pt & pp hit, pres p hitting) vt (beat) frapper; (bump into) heurter; (reach) atteindre; (affect) toucher; (problem, difficulty) rencontrer; Fam **h. it off** s'entendre bien (**with sb** avec qn) 3 vi frapper; **to h. back** riposter (**at** à); Fam **to h. out at sb** (physically) frapper qn; (verbally) s'en prendre à qn; **to h. (up)on sth** (solution, idea) trouver qch ▪**'hit-and-run driver** n chauffard m (qui prend la fuite) ▪**'hit-or-'miss** adj (chancy, random) aléatoire

hitch [hɪtʃ] 1 n (difficulty) problème m 2 vt (fasten) accrocher (**to** à) 3 vti to **h. (a ride)**, Br **to h. a lift** faire du stop (**to** jusqu'à) ▪**hitchhike** vi faire du stop (**to** jusqu'à) ▪**hitchhiker** n auto-stoppeur, -euse mf ▪**hitchhiking** n auto-stop m

hitherto [hɪðə'tuː] adv jusqu'ici

HIV [eɪtʃaɪ'viː] (abbr **human immunodeficiency virus**) n (virus) VIH m; **HIV positive/negative** séropositif, -ive/séronégatif, -ive

hive [haɪv] 1 n ruche f 2 vt **to h. off** (separate) séparer

HMS ['eɪtʃemes] (*abbr* **Her/His Majesty's Ship**) *n Br* = abréviation précédant le nom des navires de la marine britannique

hoard [hɔːd] **1** *n* réserve *f*; *(of money)* trésor *m* **2** *vt* amasser

hoarding ['hɔːdɪŋ] *n Br (for advertising)* panneau *m* d'affichage

hoarse [hɔːs] (**-er, -est**) *adj* enroué

hoax [həʊks] **1** *n* canular *m* **2** *vt* faire un canular à

hob [hɒb] *n (on stove)* plaque *f* chauffante

hobble ['hɒbəl] *vi* boitiller

hobby ['hɒbɪ] (*pl* **-ies**) *n* passe-temps *m inv* ▪ **hobbyhorse** *n (favourite subject)* dada *m*

hobnob ['hɒbnɒb] (*pt & pp* **-bb-**) *vi Fam* **to h. with sb** frayer avec qn

hobo ['həʊbəʊ] (*pl* **-oes** *or* **-os**) *n Am* vagabond, -onde *mf*

hock [hɒk] *Fam* **1** *n* **in h.** *(object)* au clou **2** *vt* mettre au clou

hockey ['hɒkɪ] *n* hockey *m*; *Br (field hockey)* hockey sur gazon; *Am (ice hockey)* hockey sur glace; **h. stick** crosse *f* de hockey

hocus-pocus [həʊkəs'pəʊkəs] *n (deception)* tromperie *f*; *(talk)* paroles *fpl* trompeuses

hoe [həʊ] **1** *n* binette *f*, houe *f* **2** (*pt & pp* **hoed**) *vt* biner

hog [hɒg] **1** *n (pig)* porc *m* châtré; *Fam* **to go the whole h.** aller jusqu'au bout **2** (*pt & pp* **-gg-**) *vt Fam* monopoliser

Hogmanay [hɒgmə'neɪ] *n Scot* la Saint Sylvestre

hoist [hɔɪst] **1** *n (device)* appareil *m* de levage **2** *vt* hisser

hold [həʊld] **1** *n (grip)* prise *f*; *(of ship)* cale *f*; *(of plane)* soute *f*; **to get h. of** *(grab)* saisir; *(contact)* joindre; *(find)* trouver; *Fam* **to get a h. of oneself** se maîtriser; **to be on h.** *(of project)* être en suspens; **to put sb on h.** *(on phone)* mettre qn en attente

2 (*pt & pp* **held**) *vt* tenir; *(heat, attention)* retenir; *(post)* occuper; *(record)* détenir; *(title, opinion)* avoir; *(party, exhibition)* organiser; *(ceremony, mass)* célébrer; *(contain)* contenir; *(keep)* garder; **to h. sb prisoner** retenir qn prisonnier; **to h. one's breath** retenir son souffle; **I h. that...** *(believe)* je maintiens que...; **to h. one's own** se défendre; **h. the line!** *(on phone)* ne quittez pas!; **h. it!** *(stay still)* ne bouge pas!; **to be held** *(of event)* avoir lieu

3 *vi (of nail, rope)* tenir; *(of weather)* se maintenir; **the same holds for you** cela vaut aussi pour toi ▪ **hold-up** *n (attack)* hold-up *m inv*; *Br (traffic jam)* ralentissement *m*; *(delay)* retard *m*

▸ **hold back** *vt sep (restrain)* retenir; *(hide)* cacher (**from sb** à qn)

▸ **hold down** *vt sep (price)* bloquer; *(person on ground)* maintenir au sol; **to h. down a job** *(keep)* garder un emploi; *(occupy)* avoir un emploi

▸ **hold forth** *vi Pej (talk)* disserter

▸ **hold in** *vt sep* **to h. one's stomach in** rentrer son ventre

▸ **hold off** **1** *vt sep (enemy)* tenir à distance **2** *vi* **if the rain holds off** s'il ne pleut pas

▸ **hold on** **1** *vt sep (keep in place)* tenir en place **2** *vi (wait)* patienter; *(stand firm)* tenir bon; **h. on!** *(on phone)* ne quittez pas!; **h. on (tight)!** tenez bon!

▸ **hold on to** *vt insep (cling to)* tenir bien; *(keep)* garder

▸ **hold out** **1** *vt sep (offer)* offrir; *(hand)* tendre **2** *vi (resist)* résister; *(last)* durer

▸ **hold over** *vt sep (postpone)* remettre

▸ **hold together** *vt sep (nation, group)* assurer l'union de

▸ **hold up** *vt sep (raise)* lever; *(support)* soutenir; *(delay)* retarder; *(rob)* attaquer

holdall ['həʊldɔːl] *n Br* fourre-tout *m inv*

holder ['həʊldə(r)] *n* (**a**) *(of passport, degree, post)* titulaire *mf*; *(of record, card, ticket)* détenteur, -trice *mf* (**b**) *(container)* support *m*

hole [həʊl] **1** *n* trou *m*; *Fam (town, village)* bled *m*, trou; *Fam (room)* baraque *f* **2** *vt (ship)* faire une brèche dans **3** *vi Fam* **to h. up** *(hide)* se terrer

holiday ['hɒlɪdeɪ] **1** *n Br* **holiday(s)** *(from work, school)* vacances *fpl*; **a h.** *(day off)* un congé; **a (public** *or* **bank) h.,** *Am* **a legal h.** un jour férié; **a religious h.** une fête; **a month's h.** un mois de vacances; **on h.** en vacances; **to be/go on h.** être/partir en vacances; **holidays with pay** congés *mpl* payés **2** *adj (camp, clothes)* de vacances; **h. home** résidence *f* secondaire; **h. season** saison *f* touristique ▪ **holidaymaker** *n Br* vacancier, -ière *mf*

holiness ['həʊlɪnəs] *n* sainteté *f*

Holland ['hɒlənd] *n* la Hollande

hollow ['hɒləʊ] **1** *adj* creux *(f* creuse); *(victory)* faux *(f* fausse); *(promise)* vain **2** *n* creux *m* **3** *adv* **to sound h.** sonner creux **4** *vt* **to h. sth out** évider qch

holly ['hɒlɪ] *n* houx *m*

holocaust ['hɒləkɔːst] *n* holocauste *m*

hologram ['hɒləgræm] *n* hologramme *m*

holster ['həʊlstə(r)] *n* étui *m* de revolver

holy ['həʊlɪ] (**-ier, -iest**) *adj* saint; *(bread, water)* bénit; *(ground)* sacré; **the H. Bible** la Sainte Bible

homage ['hɒmɪdʒ] *n* hommage *m*; **to pay h. to sb** rendre hommage à qn

home[1] [həʊm] **1** *n* maison *f*; *(country)* patrie *f*; *(for old soldiers, sailors)* foyer *m*; **old people's h.** maison *f* de retraite; **at h.** à la maison, chez soi; **to feel at h.** se sentir chez soi; **make yourself at h.** faites comme chez vous; **to play at h.** *(of football team)* jouer à domicile; **at h. and abroad** dans notre pays et à l'étranger; **far from h.** loin de chez soi; **a broken h.** un foyer désuni; **a good h.** une bonne famille; **to**

make one's h. in France s'installer en France; **my h. is here** j'habite ici

2 *adv* à la maison, chez soi; **to go** *or* **come (back) h.** rentrer chez soi; **to be h.** être rentré; **to drive sb h.** ramener qn; **to drive a nail h.** enfoncer complètement un clou; *Fig* **to bring sth h. to sb** faire voir qch à qn

3 *adj (pleasures, atmosphere, cooking)* familial; *(visit, match)* à domicile; *(product, market)* national; **h. address** adresse *f* personnelle; **h. banking** banque *f* à domicile; **h. computer** ordinateur *m* domestique; **h. economics** économie *f* domestique; *Br* **h. help** aide *f* ménagère; **h. life** vie *f* de famille; **h. loan** prêt *m* immobilier; *Br Pol* **H. Office** ≃ ministère *m* de l'Intérieur; **h. owner** propriétaire *mf*; *Comptr* **h. page** page *f* d'accueil; **h. rule** autonomie *f*; *Br Pol* **H. Secretary** ≃ ministre *m* de l'Intérieur; **h. team** équipe *f* qui reçoit; **h. town** ville *f* natale ▪ **homecoming** *n* retour *m* (au foyer) ▪ **'home'grown** *adj (fruit, vegetables)* du jardin; *(not grown abroad)* du pays ▪ **homeland** *n* patrie *f* ▪ **homeloving** *adj* casanier, -ière ▪ **'home'made** *adj* (fait) maison *inv* ▪ **homesick** *adj* **to be h.** avoir le mal du pays ▪ **homesickness** *n* mal *m* du pays

home² [həʊm] *vi* **to h. in on sth** se diriger automatiquement sur qch

homeless ['həʊmlɪs] **1** *adj* sans abri **2** *npl* **the h.** les sans-abri *mpl*

homely ['həʊmlɪ] **(-ier, -iest)** *adj (comfortable)* agréable et sans prétention; *Am (ugly)* sans charme

homeopathic [həʊmɪəʊ'pæθɪk] *adj* homéopathique ▪ **homeopath** *n* homéopathe *mf* ▪ **homeopathy** [-ɪ'ɒpəθɪ] *n* homéopathie *f*

homeward ['həʊmwəd] **1** *adj (trip)* de retour **2** *adv* **h.-bound** sur le chemin de retour

homework ['həʊmwɜːk] *n Sch* devoirs *mpl*

homey ['həʊmɪ] **(-ier, -iest)** *adj Am Fam* accueillant

homicide ['hɒmɪsaɪd] *n* homicide *m*

homogeneous [həʊmə'dʒiːnɪəs] *adj* homogène

homosexual [həʊmə'sekʃʊəl] *adj & n* homosexuel, -uelle *(mf)* ▪ **homosexuality** [-ʊ'ælɪtɪ] *n* homosexualité *f*

Honduras [hɒn'djʊərəs] *n* le Honduras

honest ['ɒnɪst] *adj* honnête (**with** avec); *(profit, money)* honnêtement gagné; **the h. truth** la vérité vraie; **to earn an h. living** gagner honnêtement sa vie; **to be h., I don't know** franchement, je ne sais pas ▪ **honestly** *adv* honnêtement; **h.!** *(showing annoyance)* vraiment! ▪ **honesty** *n* honnêteté *f*

honey ['hʌnɪ] *n* miel *m*; *esp Am Fam (person)* chéri, -ie *mf* ▪ **honeycomb** [-kəʊm] *n* rayon *m* de miel ▪ **honeymoon** *n* voyage *m* de noces ▪ **honeysuckle** *n* chèvrefeuille *m*

Hong Kong [hɒŋ'kɒŋ] *n* Hongkong *m ou f*

honk [hɒŋk] **1** *n* coup *m* de Klaxon® **2** *vi (of driver)* klaxonner

honorary ['ɒnərərɪ] *adj (member)* honoraire; *(title)* honorifique

honour ['ɒnə(r)] *(Am* **honor**) **1** *n* honneur *m*; **in h. of** en l'honneur de; **to have the h. of doing sth** avoir l'honneur de faire qch; *Br Univ* **honours degree** diplôme *m* universitaire **2** *vt* honorer (**with** de)

honourable ['ɒnərəbəl] *(Am* **honorable**) *adj* honorable

hood [hʊd] *n* (**a**) *(of coat)* capuche *f*; *(with eyeholes)* cagoule *f*; *Br (of car, pram)* capote *f*; *Am (car bonnet)* capot *m*; *(above stove)* hotte *f* (**b**) *Am Fam (gangster)* truand *m* ▪ **hooded** *adj (person)* encapuchonné; *(coat)* à capuchon

hoodlum ['huːdləm] *n Fam* voyou *m (pl* -ous)

hoodwink ['hʊdwɪŋk] *vt Fam* embobiner

hoof [huːf] *(pl* **hoofs** [huːfs] *or* **hooves** [huːvz]) *n* sabot *m*

hoo-ha ['huːhɑː] *n Fam* tintouin *m*

hook [hʊk] **1** *n* crochet *m*; *(on clothes)* agrafe *f*; *Fishing* hameçon *m*; **off the h.** *(phone)* décroché; *Fam* **to let** *or* **get sb off the h.** tirer qn d'affaire **2** *vt* **to h. (on** *or* **up)** accrocher (**to** à); **to h. a computer up** connecter un ordinateur ▪ **hooked** *adj (nose, beak)* crochu; *(end, object)* recourbé; *Fam* **to be h. on sth** être accro à qch; *Fam* **to be h. on sb** *(infatuated with)* être entiché de qn; *Fam* **to be h. on drugs** être accro

hooker ['hʊkə(r)] *n Am Fam* prostituée *f*

hook(e)y ['hʊkɪ] *n Am Fam* **to play h.** sécher (les cours)

hooligan ['huːlɪgən] *n* hooligan *m* ▪ **hooliganism** *n* hooliganisme *m*

hoop [huːp] *n* cerceau *m*

hoot [huːt] **1** *n* huée *f*; *Br (of vehicle)* coup *m* de Klaxon® **2** *vti (jeer)* huer **3** *vi Br (of vehicle)* klaxonner; *(of train)* siffler; *(of owl)* hululer ▪ **hooter** *n Br (of vehicle)* Klaxon® *m*; *(of factory)* sirène *f*; *Fam (nose)* pif *m*

hoover® ['huːvə(r)] **1** *n Br* aspirateur *m* **2** *vt Br (room)* passer l'aspirateur dans; *(carpet)* passer l'aspirateur sur; **to h. sth up** *(dust, crumbs)* enlever qch à l'aspirateur

hop [hɒp] **1** *n (leap)* saut *m* **2** *(pt & pp* **-pp-**) *vi (jump)* sautiller; *(on one leg)* sauter à cloche-pied; **h. in!** *(car)* allez! grimpe!; **he hopped onto the first train** il a sauté dans le premier train **3** *vt* espérer; **h. it!** fiche le camp!

hope [həʊp] **1** *n* espoir *m* **2** *vt* **to h. to do sth** espérer faire qch; **to h. that...** espérer que... **3** *vi* espérer; **to h. for sth** espérer qch; **I h. so/not** j'espère que oui/non ▪ **hopeful** ['həʊpfʊl] **1** *adj (person)* optimiste; *(situation)* encourageant; **to be h. that...** avoir bon espoir que... **2** *n* **a young h.** un jeune espoir ▪ **hopefully** *adv* avec un peu de chance; **to do sth h.** faire

qch plein d'espoir ▪**hopeless** ['həʊpləs] *adj*
désespéré; *Fam (useless, bad)* nul (*f* nulle)
▪**hopelessly** *adv (lost, out-of-date)*
complètement; *(in love)* éperdument; *(live, act)* sans espoir

hops [hɒps] *npl (for beer)* houblon *m*

hopscotch ['hɒpskɒtʃ] *n* marelle *f*

horde [hɔːd] *n* horde *f*

horizon [hə'raɪzən] *n* horizon *m*; **on the h.** à
l'horizon ▪**horizontal** [hɒrɪ'zɒntəl] *adj*
horizontal ▪**horizontally** [hɒrɪ'zɒntəlɪ] *adv*
horizontalement

hormone ['hɔːməʊn] *n* hormone *f*; **h.
replacement therapy** hormonothérapie *f* de
substitution

horn [hɔːn] 1 *n (of animal)* corne *f*; *(on vehicle)*
Klaxon® *m*; *(musical instrument)* cor *m* 2 *vi Am
Fam* **to h. in** mêler son grain de sel (**on** à);
(interrupt) interrompre

hornet ['hɔːnɪt] *n* frelon *m*

horny ['hɔːnɪ] *(-ier, -iest) adj very Fam
(aroused)* excité

horoscope ['hɒrəskəʊp] *n* horoscope *m*

horrendous [hə'rendəs] *adj* horrible

horrible ['hɒrəbəl] *adj* horrible ▪**horribly** *adv*
horriblement

horrid ['hɒrɪd] *adj (unpleasant)* affreux, -euse;
(unkind) méchant

horrific [hə'rɪfɪk] *adj* horrible

horrify ['hɒrɪfaɪ] *(pt & pp -ied) vt* horrifier

horror ['hɒrə(r)] *n* horreur *f*; *Fam (little)* **h.**
(child) petit monstre *m*; **h. film** film *m*
d'horreur; **h. story** histoire *f* épouvantable

hors d'œuvre [ɔː'dɜːv] *(pl inv or* **hors
d'œuvres**) *n* hors-d'œuvre *m inv*

horse [hɔːs] *n* (a) *(animal)* cheval *m*; **to go h.
riding** faire du cheval; **h. racing** courses *fpl*; **h.
show** concours *m* hippique (b) **h. chestnut**
(fruit) marron *m* ▪**horseback** *n* **on h.** à
cheval; *Am* **to go h. riding** faire du cheval
▪**horseman** *(pl* -men) *n* cavalier *m*
▪**horseplay** *n* chahut *m* ▪**horsepower** *n*
(unit) cheval-vapeur *m* ▪**horseradish** *n* raifort
m ▪**horseshoe** *n* fer *m* à cheval ▪**horsewoman** *(pl* -women) *n* cavalière *f*

horticulture ['hɔːtɪkʌltʃə(r)] *n* horticulture *f*
▪**horti'cultural** *adj* horticole

hose [həʊz] 1 *n (pipe)* tuyau *m*; **garden h.** tuyau
d'arrosage 2 *vt* arroser (au jet d'eau); **to h. sth
down** *(car)* laver qch au jet ▪**hosepipe** *n Br*
tuyau *m* d'arrosage

hosiery [*Br* 'həʊzɪərɪ, *Am* 'həʊʒərɪ] *n* bonneterie *f*

hospice ['hɒspɪs] *n (hospital)* = établissement
pour malades en phase terminale

hospitable [hɒ'spɪtəbəl] *adj* hospitalier, -ière (**to**
envers) ▪**hospitality** [-'tælɪtɪ] *n* hospitalité *f*

hospital ['hɒspɪtəl] *n* hôpital *m*; **in h.,** *Am* **in the
h.** à l'hôpital; **h. bed** lit *m* d'hôpital; **h. staff/
services** personnel *m*/services *mpl*

hospitalier(s) ▪**hospitalize** *vt* hospitaliser

host¹ [həʊst] 1 *n (of guests)* hôte *m*; *(on TV or
radio show)* présentateur, -trice *mf*; *Comptr (of
Web site)* hébergeur, -euse *mf*; **h. country** pays
m d'accueil 2 *vt (party)* donner; *(programme)*
présenter; *Comptr (Web site)* héberger

host² [həʊst] *n* **a h. of** *(many)* une foule de

hostage ['hɒstɪdʒ] *n* otage *m*; **to take sb h.**
prendre qn en otage; **to be held h.** être retenu
en otage

hostel ['hɒstəl] *n* foyer *m*; **(youth) h.** auberge *f*
de jeunesse

hostess ['həʊstɪs] *n (in house, nightclub)*
hôtesse *f*; **(air) h.** hôtesse *f* (de l'air)

hostile [*Br* 'hɒstaɪl, *Am* 'hɒstəl] *adj* hostile (**to**
or **towards** à) ▪**hos'tility** *n* hostilité *f* (**to**
or **towards** envers); **hostilities** *(in battle)*
hostilités *fpl*

hot¹ [hɒt] *(hotter, hottest) adj* chaud; *(spice)*
fort; *(temperament)* passionné; *Fam (news)*
dernier, -ière; **to be** or **feel h.** avoir chaud; **it's
h.** il fait chaud; *Fam* **to be h.** être calé en qch;
(knowledgeable) être calé en qch; *Fam* **not so
h.** *(bad)* pas fameux, -euse; *Sport* **h. favourite**
grand(e) favori(te) *mf*; **h. pants** mini-short *m*
▪**hotbed** *n Pej* foyer *m* (**of** de) ▪**'hot-
'blooded** *adj* passionné ▪**hotcake** *n Am
(pancake)* crêpe *f* ▪**hotdog** *n* hot dog *m*
▪**hothead** *n* tête *f* brûlée ▪**'hot'headed** *adj*
exalté ▪**hothouse** *n* serre *f* (chaude) ▪**hotly**
adv passionnément ▪**hotplate** *n* chauffe-plat
m; *(on stove)* plaque *f* chauffante ▪**hotshot** 1
adj **a h. pool player** un joueur de billard
super-doué; **a h. lawyer** un as du barreau 2 *n
(expert)* as *m*; *Br (VIP)* gros bonnet *m*; *Am (show-
off)* personne *f* suffisante ▪**'hot-'tempered**
adj emporté ▪**hot-'water bottle** *n* bouillotte *f*
▪**hot²** [hɒt] *(pt & pp -tt-) vi Fam* **to h. up** *(increase)*
s'intensifier; *(become dangerous or excited)*
s'envenimer

hotchpotch ['hɒtʃpɒtʃ] *n Fam* fatras *m*

hotel [həʊ'tel] *n* hôtel *m*; **h. room/bed** chambre
f/lit *m* d'hôtel; **the h. trade** l'industrie *f* hôtelière
▪**hotelier** [həʊ'telɪə] *n* hôtelier, -ière *mf*

houmous ['hʊməs] *n* = **hummus**

hound [haʊnd] 1 *n (dog)* chien *m* de chasse 2 *vt
(pursue)* traquer; *(bother, worry)* harceler

hour ['aʊə(r)] *n* heure *f*; **half an h.** une demi-
heure; **a quarter of an h.** un quart d'heure;
paid 20 euros an h. payé 20 euros (de)
l'heure; **10 miles an h.** 10 miles à l'heure;
open all hours ouvert à toute heure; **h. hand**
(of watch, clock) petite aiguille *f*

hourly ['aʊəlɪ] 1 *adj (rate, pay)* horaire; **an h. bus/
train** un bus/train toutes les heures 2 *adv* toutes
les heures; **h. paid, paid h.** payé à l'heure

house 1 [haʊs] *(pl* -ses [-zɪz]) *n* maison *f*;
(audience in theatre) salle *f*, auditoire *m*; *Br Pol*
the H. of Commons la Chambre des

communes; *Br Pol* **the H. of Lords** la Chambre des lords; *Br Pol* **the Houses of Parliament** le Parlement; *Am Pol* **the H. of Representatives** la Chambre des représentants; **at/to my h.** chez moi; **on the h.** *(free of charge)* aux frais de la maison; *Br* **h. doctor** interne *mf*; **h. guest** invité, -ée *mf*; **h. plant** plante *f* d'intérieur; **h. prices** prix *mpl* de l'immobilier; **h. wine** vin *m* de la maison

2 [haʊz] *vt* loger; *(of building)* abriter ▪ **houseboat** *n* péniche *f* aménagée ▪ **housebound** *adj* confiné chez soi ▪ **housebreaking** *n (crime)* cambriolage *m* ▪ **housebroken** *adj Am (pet)* propre ▪ **housefly** *(pl* **-flies)** *n* mouche *f* (domestique) ▪ **household** *n* ménage *m*; **h. chores** tâches *fpl* ménagères; **a h. name** un nom très connu ▪ **householder** *n (owner)* propriétaire *mf*; ▪ **househusband** *n* homme *m* au foyer ▪ **housekeeper** *n (employee)* gouvernante *f* ▪ **housekeeping** *n* ménage *m* ▪ **houseman** *(pl* **-men)** *n Br Med* interne *m* ▪ **house-proud** *adj* qui s'occupe méticuleusement de sa maison ▪ **housetrained** *adj Br (pet)* propre ▪ **house-warming** *n & adj* **h. (party)** pendre la crémaillère ▪ **housewife** *(pl* **-wives)** *n* ménagère *f* ▪ **housework** *n* ménage *m*

housing [haʊzɪŋ] *n* logement *m*; *(houses)* logements *mpl*; **h. crisis** crise *f* du logement; *Br* **h. estate** lotissement *m*; *(council-owned)* cité *f*

hovel ['hɒvəl] *n* taudis *m*

hover ['hɒvə(r)] *vi (of bird, aircraft, danger)* planer; **to h. (around)** *(of person)* rôder

hovercraft ['hɒvəkra:ft] *n* aéroglisseur *m*

how [haʊ] *adv* comment; **h. kind!** comme c'est gentil!; **h. long/high is...?** quelle est la longueur/hauteur de...?; **h. much?, h. many?** combien?; **h. much time?** combien de temps?; **h. many apples?** combien de pommes?; **h. about a walk?** si on faisait une promenade?; **h. about some coffee?** (si on prenait) du café?; **h. about me?** et moi?; **h. do you do** *(greeting)* bonjour; *Fam* **h.'s that?, h. so?, h. come?** comment ça?

howdy ['haʊdɪ] *exclam Am Fam* salut!

however [haʊ'evə(r)] **1** *adv* **h. big he may be** si grand soit-il; **h. she may do it, h. she does it** de quelque manière qu'elle le fasse; **h. that may be** quoi qu'il en soit; **h. did she find out?** comment bien a-t-elle pu l'apprendre? **2** *conj* cependant

howl [haʊl] **1** *n* hurlement *m*; *(of baby)* braillement *m*; *(of wind)* mugissement *m*; **h. of laughter** éclat *m* de rire **2** *vi* hurler; *(of baby)* brailler; *(of wind)* mugir

howler ['haʊlə(r)] *n Fam (mistake)* gaffe *f*

HP [eɪtʃ'pi:] *Br abbr* = **hire purchase**

hp *(abbr* **horsepower)** CV

HQ [eɪtʃ'kju:] *(abbr* **headquarters)** *n* QG *m*

hub [hʌb] *n (of wheel)* moyeu *m*; *Fig* centre *m* ▪ **hubcap** *n (of wheel)* enjoliveur *m*

hubbub ['hʌbʌb] *n* brouhaha *m*

huckleberry ['hʌkəlbərɪ] *(pl* **-ies)** *n Am* myrtille *f*

huddle ['hʌdəl] *vi* **to h. (together)** se blottir (les uns contre les autres)

hue [hju:] *n* **(a)** *(colour)* teinte *f* **(b)** **h. and cry** tollé *m*

huff [hʌf] *n Fam* **in a h.** *(offended)* fâché

hug [hʌg] **1** *n* **to give sb a h.** serrer qn (dans ses bras) **2** *(pt & pp* **-gg-)** *vt (person)* serrer dans ses bras; **to h. the kerb/coast** serrer le trottoir/la côte

huge [hju:dʒ] *adj* énorme ▪ **hugely** *adv* énormément

hulk [hʌlk] *n (person)* mastodonte *m*

hullabaloo [hʌləbə'lu:] *(pl* **-oos)** *n Fam (noise)* raffut *m*

hullo [hʌ'ləʊ] *exclam Br* bonjour!; *(answering phone)* allô!; *(surprise)* tiens!

hum [hʌm] **1** *n (of insect)* bourdonnement *m* **2** *(pt & pp* **-mm-)** *vt (tune)* fredonner **3** *vi (of insect)* bourdonner; *(of person)* fredonner; *(of engine)* ronronner

human ['hju:mən] **1** *adj* humain; **h. being** être *m* humain; **h. rights** droits *mpl* de l'homme **2** *n* être *m* humain ▪ **humanly** *adv* humainement

humane [hju:'meɪn] *adj (kind)* humain ▪ **humanely** *adv* humainement

humanitarian [hju:mænɪ'teərɪən] *adj & n* humanitaire *(mf)*

humanity [hju:'mænətɪ] *n (human beings, kindness)* humanité *f*

humble ['hʌmbəl] **1** *adj* humble **2** *vt* humilier ▪ **humbly** *adv* humblement

humdrum ['hʌmdrʌm] *adj* monotone

humid ['hju:mɪd] *adj* humide ▪ **hu'midify** *(pt & pp* **-ied)** *vt* humidifier ▪ **hu'midity** *n* humidité *f*

humiliate [hju:'mɪlɪeɪt] *vt* humilier ▪ **humiliation** [-'eɪʃən] *n* humiliation *f*

humility [hju:'mɪlətɪ] *n* humilité *f*

hummus ['hʌməs] *n Culin* houmous *m*

humorist ['hju:mərɪst] *n* humoriste *mf*

humorous ['hju:mərəs] *adj (book, writer)* humoristique; *(person, situation)* drôle ▪ **humorously** *adv* avec humour

humour ['hju:mə(r)] *(Am* **humor)** **1** *n (fun)* humour *m*; *Formal (temper)* humeur *f*; **to have a sense of h.** avoir le sens de l'humour; **in a good h.** de bonne humeur **2** *vt* **to h. sb** faire plaisir à qn

hump [hʌmp] **1** *n (lump, mound in road)* bosse *f*; *Br Fam* **to have the h.** *(be depressed)* avoir le cafard; *(be angry)* être en rogne **2** *vt Fam (carry)* trimbaler ▪ **'humpback(ed) 'bridge** *n Br* pont en dos d'âne

hunch [hʌntʃ] **1** *n Fam (intuition)* intuition *f* **2** *vt* **to h. one's shoulders** rentrer les épaules ▪ **hunchback** *n* bossu, -ue *mf*

hundred ['hʌndrəd] *adj & n* cent *(m)*; **a h. pages**

cent pages; **two h. pages** deux cents pages;
hundreds of des centaines de ▪**hundredfold**
1 adj centuple **2** adv au centuple ▪**hundredth**
adj & n centième (mf)

hung [hʌŋ] pt & pp of **hang**¹

Hungary ['hʌŋgərɪ] n la Hongrie ▪**Hungarian**
[-'geərɪən] **1** adj hongrois **2** n (person)
Hongrois, -oise mf; (language) hongrois m

hunger ['hʌŋgə(r)] n faim f; **h. strike** grève f de
la faim ▪**hungrily** adv avidement ▪**hungry**
(-ier, -iest) adj to be or feel h. avoir faim; **to
go h.** souffrir de la faim; **to make sb h.** donner
faim à qn; **h. for sth** avide de qch

hunk [hʌŋk] n gros morceau m

hunt [hʌnt] **1** n (search) recherche f (**for** de); (for
animals) chasse f **2** vt (animals) chasser;
(pursue) poursuivre; **to h. down** (animal,
fugitive) traquer; **to h. out** (information)
dénicher **3** vi (kill animals) chasser; **to h. for
sth** rechercher qch ▪**hunter** n chasseur m
▪**hunting** n chasse f

hurdle ['hɜ:dəl] n (fence in race) haie f; Fig
(problem) obstacle m

hurl [hɜ:l] vt (throw) jeter, lancer (**at** à); **to h.
oneself at sb** se ruer sur qn; **to h. insults** or
abuse at sb lancer des insultes à qn

hurray [hʊ'reɪ] exclam hourra!

hurricane [Br 'hʌrɪkən, Am 'hʌrɪkeɪn] n ouragan m

hurry ['hʌrɪ] **1** n hâte f; **in a h.** à la hâte; **to be
in a h.** être pressé; **to be in a h. to do sth** avoir
hâte de faire qch; **there's no h.** rien ne presse
2 (pt & pp -ied) vt (person) presser; (work)
hâter; **to h. one's meal** manger à toute vitesse;
to h. sb out faire sortir qn à la hâte; **he was
hurried to hospital** on l'a transporté
d'urgence à l'hôpital
3 vi se dépêcher, se presser (**to do** de faire); **to
h. up** se dépêcher; **to h. back** se dépêcher de
revenir; **to h. out** sortir à la hâte; **to h.
towards sb/sth** se précipiter vers qn/qch
▪**hurried** adj (steps, decision) précipité; (work)
fait à la hâte; (visit) éclair inv; **to be h.** (in a
hurry) être pressé m

hurt [hɜ:t] **1** adj (wounded, offended) blessé **2** n
(emotional) blessure f **3** (pt & pp hurt) vt
(physically) faire du mal à; (causing a wound)
blesser; (emotionally) faire de la peine à;
(reputation, chances) nuire à; **to h. sb's feelings**
blesser qn **4** vi faire mal; **where does it h.?** où
avez-vous mal?; **his arm hurts (him)** son bras
lui fait mal ▪**hurtful** adj (remark) blessant

hurtle ['hɜ:təl] vi **to h. along** aller à toute
vitesse; **to h. down the street** dévaler la rue

husband ['hʌzbənd] n mari m

hush [hʌʃ] **1** n silence m **2** exclam chut! **3** vt
(person) faire taire; (baby) calmer; **to h. up**
(scandal) étouffer ▪**hushed** adj (voice) étouffé;
(silence) profond ▪'**hush-'hush** adj Fam top
secret inv

husk [hʌsk] n (of rice, grain) enveloppe f

husky ['hʌskɪ] (-ier, -iest) adj (voice) rauque

hussy ['hʌsɪ] (pl -ies) n Old-fashioned or Hum
gourgandine f

hustle ['hʌsəl] **1** n **h. and bustle** effervescence f
2 vt (shove, push) **to h. sb away** emmener qn de
force **3** vi Am (work busily) se démener (**to get
sth** pour avoir qch)

hut [hʌt] n cabane f; (dwelling) hutte f

hutch [hʌtʃ] n (for rabbit) clapier m

hyacinth ['haɪəsɪnθ] n jacinthe f

hybrid ['haɪbrɪd] adj & n hybride (m)

hydrangea [haɪ'dreɪndʒə] n hortensia m

hydrant ['haɪdrənt] n (fire) h. bouche f d'incendie

hydraulic [haɪ'drɔ:lɪk] adj hydraulique

hydrocarbon [haɪdrəʊ'kɑ:bən] n hydrocarbure m

hydroelectric [haɪdrəʊɪ'lektrɪk] adj hydroélectrique

hydrogen ['haɪdrədʒən] n Chem hydrogène m

hyena [haɪ'i:nə] n (animal) hyène f

hygiene ['haɪdʒi:n] n hygiène f ▪**hy'gienic** adj
hygiénique ▪**hygienist** n (dental) h.
spécialiste mf de l'hygiène dentaire

hymn [hɪm] n cantique m

hype [haɪp] n Fam (publicity) battage m publicitaire

hyper- ['haɪpə(r)] pref hyper- ▪**hyperlink** n
Comptr hyperlien m ▪**hypermarket** n hypermarché m

hyphen ['haɪfən] n trait m d'union
▪**hyphenate** vt mettre un trait d'union à
▪**hyphenated** adj (word) à trait d'union

hypnosis [hɪp'nəʊsɪs] n hypnose f
▪**hypnotism** ['hɪpnətɪzəm] n hypnotisme m
▪**hypnotist** ['hɪpnətɪst] n hypnotiseur m
▪**hypnotize** ['hɪpnətaɪz] vt hypnotiser

hypoallergenic [haɪpəʊælə'dʒenɪk] adj hypoallergénique

hypochondriac [haɪpə'kɒndrɪæk] n hypocondriaque mf

hypocrisy [hɪ'pɒkrɪsɪ] n hypocrisie f
▪**hypocrite** ['hɪpəkrɪt] n hypocrite mf
▪**hypocritical** [hɪpə'krɪtɪkəl] adj hypocrite

hypodermic [haɪpə'dɜ:mɪk] adj hypodermique

hypothermia [haɪpə'θɜ:mɪə] n Med hypo-
thermie f

hypothesis [haɪ'pɒθɪsɪs] (pl -theses [-θɪsi:z])
n hypothèse f ▪**hypothetical** [haɪpə'θetɪkəl]
adj hypothétique

hysteria [hɪ'stɪərɪə] n hystérie f ▪**hysterical**
[hɪ'sterɪkəl] adj (very upset) qui a une crise de
nerfs; Fam (funny) tordant; **to become h.** avoir
une crise de nerfs ▪**hysterically** [hɪ'sterɪkəlɪ]
adv (cry) sans pouvoir s'arrêter; **to laugh h.** rire
aux larmes ▪**hysterics** [hɪ'sterɪks] npl (tears)
crise f de nerfs; (laughter) fou rire m; **to be in h.**
avoir une crise de nerfs; (with laughter) être
écroulé de rire; **he had us in h.** il nous a fait
tordre de rire

I¹, i [aɪ] *n (letter)* I, i *m inv*

I² [aɪ] *pron* je, j'; *(stressed)* moi; **I want** je veux; **she and I** elle et moi

IAEA [aɪeɪiː'eɪ] *(abbr International Atomic Energy Agency) n* AIEA *f*

ice¹ [aɪs] **1** *n* glace *f; (on road)* verglas *m; Br* **black i.** *(on road)* verglas **2** *vi* **to i.** *(over or up) (of lake)* geler; *(of window)* se givrer **■ iceberg** *n* iceberg *m* **■ icebox** *n Am (fridge)* réfrigérateur *m; Br (in fridge)* freezer *m* **■ 'ice-'cold** *adj* glacial; *(drink)* glacé **■ ice 'cream** *n* glace *f* **■ ice cube** *n* glaçon *m* **■ iced** *adj (tea, coffee)* glacé **■ ice hockey** *n* hockey *m* sur glace **■ ice-skating** *n* patinage *m* (sur glace)

ice² [aɪs] *vt Br (cake)* glacer **■ icing** *n Br (on cake)* glaçage *m*

Iceland ['aɪslənd] *n* l'Islande *f* **■ Icelandic** [-'lændɪk] **1** *adj* islandais **2** *n (language)* islandais *m*

icicle ['aɪsɪkəl] *n* glaçon *m (de gouttière etc)*

icon ['aɪkɒn] *n* icône *f*

icy ['aɪsɪ] *(-ier, -iest) adj (road)* verglacé; *(ground)* gelé; *(water, hands)* glacé

ID [aɪ'diː] *n* pièce *f* d'identité

I'd [aɪd] = **I had, I would**

idea [aɪ'dɪə] *n* idée *f*; **I have an i. that...** j'ai l'impression que...; **that's my i. of rest** c'est ce que j'appelle du repos; *Fam* **that's the i.!** c'est ça!; **not the slightest** *or* **foggiest i.** pas la moindre idée

ideal [aɪ'dɪəl] *adj & n* idéal *(m)*

idealism [aɪ'dɪəlɪzəm] *n* idéalisme *m* **■ idealist** *n* idéaliste *mf* **■ idea'listic** *adj* idéaliste **■ idealize** *vt* idéaliser

ideally [aɪ'dɪəlɪ] *adv* idéalement; **i., we should stay** l'idéal, ce serait que nous restions

identical [aɪ'dentɪkəl] *adj* identique (**to** *or* **with** à)

identify [aɪ'dentɪfaɪ] *(pt & pp -ied) vt* identifier; **to i. (oneself) with** s'identifier avec **■ identification** [-fɪ'keɪʃən] *n* identification *f*; **to have (some) i.** *(document)* avoir une pièce d'identité

identikit [aɪ'dentɪkɪt] *n* portrait-robot *m*

identity [aɪ'dentɪtɪ] *(pl -ies) n* identité *f*; **i. card** carte *f* d'identité; **i. disc** plaque *f* d'identité

ideology [aɪdɪ'ɒlədʒɪ] *(pl -ies) n* idéologie *f* **■ ideological** [aɪdɪə'lɒdʒɪkəl] *adj* idéologique

idiocy ['ɪdɪəsɪ] *n* idiotie *f*

idiom ['ɪdɪəm] *n (phrase)* expression *f* idiomatique; *(language)* idiome *m* **■ idio'matic** *adj* idiomatique

idiosyncrasy [ɪdɪə'sɪŋkrəsɪ] *(pl -ies) n* particularité *f*

idiot ['ɪdɪət] *n* idiot, -iote *mf* **■ idiotic** [-'ɒtɪk] *adj* idiot, bête **■ idiotically** [-'ɒtɪkəlɪ] *adv* idiotement

idle ['aɪdəl] **1** *adj (unoccupied)* désœuvré; *(lazy)* oisif, -ive; *(promise)* vain; *(pleasure, question)* futile, vain; *(rumour)* sans fondement; **to lie i.** *(of machine)* être au repos; **an i. moment** un moment de loisir **2** *vt* **to i. away the** *or* **one's time** passer son temps à ne rien faire **3** *vi (of engine, machine)* tourner au ralenti **■ idleness** *n (inaction)* inactivité *f*; *(laziness)* oisiveté *f* **■ idler** *n* paresseux, -euse *mf* **■ idly** *adv (lazily)* paresseusement; *(suggest, say)* négligemment

idol ['aɪdəl] *n* idole *f* **■ idolize** *vt (adore)* idolâtrer

idyllic [aɪ'dɪlɪk] *adj* idyllique

ie [aɪ'iː] *(abbr id est)* c'est-à-dire

if [ɪf] *conj* si; **if he comes** s'il vient; **even if** même si; **if so** c'est le cas; **if not** sinon; **if only I were rich** si seulement j'étais riche; **if only to look** ne serait-ce que pour regarder; **as if** comme si; **as if nothing had happened** comme si de rien n'était; **as if to say** comme pour dire; **if necessary** s'il le faut

igloo ['ɪgluː] *(pl -oos) n* igloo *m*

ignite [ɪg'naɪt] **1** *vt* mettre le feu à **2** *vi* prendre feu **■ ignition** [-'nɪʃən] *n (in vehicle)* allumage *m*; **to switch on/off the i.** mettre/couper le contact; **i. key** clef *f* de contact

ignominious [ɪgnə'mɪnɪəs] *adj* ignominieux, -ieuse

ignoramus [ɪgnə'reɪməs] *n* ignare *mf*

ignorance ['ɪgnərəns] *n* ignorance *f* (**of** de) **■ ignorant** *adj* ignorant (**of** de) **■ ignorantly** *adv* par ignorance

ignore [ɪg'nɔː(r)] *vt* ignorer; **just i. him!** ne fais pas attention à lui!

iguana [ɪg'wɑːnə] *n* iguane *m*

ilk [ɪlk] *n* **of that i.** de cet acabit

ill [ɪl] **1** *adj (sick)* malade; *(bad)* mauvais; **i. will** malveillance *f* **2** *npl* **ills** maux *mpl* **3** *adv* mal; **to speak i. of sb** dire du mal de qn **■ ill-ad'vised** *adj (person)* malavisé; *(decision)* peu judicieux, -ieuse **■ 'ill-'fated** *adj (day)* fatal; *(enterprise)* malheureux, -euse ▪ **ill-gotten** adj i. gains biens mpl mal acquis ▪ **'ill-in'formed** adj mal renseigné ▪ **ill-'mannered** adj mal élevé ▪ **'ill-'natured** adj (mean, unkind) désagréable ▪ **'ill-'timed** adj inopportun ▪ **ill-'treat** vt maltraiter

I'll [aɪl] = **I will, I shall**

illegal [ɪ'li:gəl] adj illégal ▪ **illegality** [ɪlɪ-'gælɪtɪ] n illégalité f

illegible [ɪ'ledʒəbəl] adj illisible

illegitimate [ɪlɪ'dʒɪtɪmət] adj illégitime ▪ **illegitimacy** n illégitimité f

illicit [ɪ'lɪsɪt] adj illicite

illiterate [ɪ'lɪtərət] adj & n analphabète (mf) ▪ **illiteracy** n analphabétisme m

illness [ɪlnɪs] n maladie f

illogical [ɪ'lɒdʒɪkəl] adj illogique

illuminate [ɪ'lu:mɪneɪt] vt (monument) illuminer; (street, question) éclairer ▪ **illumi'nation** n (lighting) éclairage m; Br **the illuminations** (decorative lights) les illuminations fpl

illusion [ɪ'lu:ʒən] n illusion f (**about** sur); **to have the i. that...** avoir l'illusion que...; **I'm not under any i. about...** je ne me fais aucune illusion sur... ▪ **illusive, illusory** adj illusoire

illustrate ['ɪləstreɪt] vt (with pictures, examples) illustrer (**with** de) ▪ **illu'stration** n illustration f

illustrious [ɪ'lʌstrɪəs] adj illustre

image ['ɪmɪdʒ] n image f; **(public) i.** (of company) image f de marque; **he's the (living** or **spitting** or **very) i. of his brother** c'est tout le portrait de son frère ▪ **imagery** n imagerie f

imaginable [ɪ'mædʒɪnəbəl] adj imaginable; **the worst thing i.** le pire que l'on puisse imaginer

imaginary [ɪ'mædʒɪnərɪ] adj imaginaire

imagination [ɪmædʒɪ'neɪʃən] n imagination f

imaginative [ɪ'mædʒɪnətɪv] adj (plan, novel) original; (person) imaginatif, -ive

imagine [ɪ'mædʒɪn] vt imaginer (**that** que); **to i. sb doing sth** imaginer qn faisant qch; **you're imagining things!** tu te fais des idées!

imbalance [ɪm'bæləns] n déséquilibre m

imbecile [Br 'ɪmbəsi:l, Am 'ɪmbəsəl] adj & n imbécile (mf) ▪ **imbecility** [-'sɪlɪtɪ] n imbécillité f

imbibe [ɪm'baɪb] vt Formal absorber

imbued [ɪm'bju:d] adj Formal **i. with** (ideas) imprégné de; (feelings) empreint de

IMF [aɪem'ef] (abbr **International Monetary Fund**) n FMI m

imitate ['ɪmɪteɪt] vt imiter ▪ **imi'tation** n imitation f; Br **i. jewellery,** Am **i. jewelry** faux bijoux mpl; **i. leather** similicuir m

imitative ['ɪmɪtətɪv] adj (sound) imitatif, -ive; (person) imitateur, -trice

imitator ['ɪmɪteɪtə(r)] n imitateur, -trice mf

immaculate [ɪ'mækjʊlət] adj impeccable

immaterial [ɪmə'tɪərɪəl] adj sans importance (**to** pour)

immature [ɪmə'tʃʊə(r)] adj (person) immature; (fruit) vert

immeasurable [ɪ'meʒərəbəl] adj incommensurable

immediate [ɪ'mi:dɪət] adj immédiat ▪ **immediacy** n immédiateté f ▪ **immediately 1** adv (at once) tout de suite, immédiatement; (concern, affect) directement; **it's i. above/ below** c'est juste au-dessus/en dessous **2** conj Br (as soon as) dès que

immense [ɪ'mens] adj immense ▪ **immensely** adv (rich) immensément; (painful) extrêmement; **to enjoy oneself i.** s'amuser énormément ▪ **immensity** n immensité f

immerse [ɪ'mɜ:s] vt (in liquid) plonger; Fig **to i. oneself in sth** se plonger dans qch ▪ **immersion** n immersion f; Br **i. heater** chauffe-eau m inv électrique

immigrate ['ɪmɪgreɪt] vi immigrer ▪ **immigrant** adj & n immigré, -ée (mf) ▪ **immi'gration** n immigration f; **i. control** contrôle m de l'immigration

imminent ['ɪmɪnənt] adj imminent ▪ **imminence** f imminence f

immobile [Br ɪ'məʊbaɪl, Am ɪ'məʊbəl] adj immobile ▪ **immo'bility** n immobilité f ▪ **immobilize** [-bɪlaɪz] vt immobiliser

immoderate [ɪ'mɒdərət] adj immodéré

immodest [ɪ'mɒdɪst] adj impudique

immoral [ɪ'mɒrəl] adj immoral ▪ **immorality** [ɪmə'rælɪtɪ] n immoralité f

immortal [ɪ'mɔ:təl] adj immortel, -elle ▪ **immortality** [-'tælɪtɪ] n immortalité f ▪ **immortalize** vt immortaliser

immune [ɪ'mju:n] adj Med (to disease) immunisé (**to** contre); **i. system** système m immunitaire; Fig **i. to criticism** imperméable à la critique ▪ **immunity** n immunité f ▪ **immunize** ['ɪmjʊnaɪz] vt immuniser (**against** contre)

immutable [ɪ'mju:təbəl] adj immuable

imp [ɪmp] n lutin m; **(you) little i.!** (to child) petit coquin!

impact 1 ['ɪmpækt] n impact m; **on i.** au moment de l'impact; **to make an i. on sb/sth** avoir un impact sur qn/qch **2** [ɪm'pækt] vt (collide with) heurter; (influence) avoir un impact sur

impair [ɪm'peə(r)] vt (sight, hearing) diminuer, affaiblir; (relations, chances) compromettre

impale [ɪm'peɪl] vt empaler (**on** sur)

impart [ɪm'pɑ:t] vt Formal (heat, light) donner; (knowledge, news) transmettre (**to** à)

impartial [ɪm'pɑ:ʃəl] adj impartial ▪ **impartiality** [-ʃɪ'ælɪtɪ] n impartialité f

impassable [ɪm'pɑ:səbəl] adj (road) impraticable; (river) infranchissable

impasse [Br æm'pɑ:s, Am 'ɪmpæs] n (situation) impasse f

impassioned [ɪm'pæʃənd] *adj (speech, request)* passionné

impassive [ɪm'pæsɪv] *adj* impassible ▪ **impassively** *adv* impassiblement

impatient [ɪm'peɪʃənt] *adj* impatient (**to do** de faire); **to get i. (with sb)** s'impatienter (contre qn) ▪ **impatience** *n* impatience *f* ▪ **impatiently** *adv* avec impatience, impatiemment

impeccable [ɪm'pekəbəl] *adj (manners, person)* impeccable ▪ **impeccably** *adv* impeccablement

impede [ɪm'piːd] *vt* gêner; **to i. sb from doing** *(prevent)* empêcher qn de faire

impediment [ɪm'pedɪmənt] *n* obstacle *m*; **speech i.** défaut *m* d'élocution

impel [ɪm'pel] (**-ll-**) *vt (drive)* pousser; *(force)* obliger (**to do** à faire)

impending [ɪm'pendɪŋ] *adj* imminent

impenetrable [ɪm'penɪtrəbəl] *adj (forest, mystery)* impénétrable

imperative [ɪm'perətɪv] **1** *adj (need, tone)* impérieux, -ieuse; **it is i. that he should come** il faut impérativement qu'il vienne **2** *n* *Grammar* impératif *m*

imperceptible [ɪmpə'septəbəl] *adj* imperceptible (**to** à)

imperfect [ɪm'pɜːfɪkt] **1** *adj* imparfait; *(goods)* défectueux, -ueuse **2** *adj & n* *Grammar* **i. (tense)** imparfait *(m)* ▪ **imperfection** [-pə'fekʃən] *n* imperfection *f*

imperial [ɪm'pɪərɪəl] *adj* impérial; *Br* **i. measure** = système de mesure anglo-saxon utilisant les miles, les pints etc ▪ **imperialism** *n* impérialisme *m*

imperil [ɪm'perɪl] (*Br* **-ll-**, *Am* **-l-**) *vt* mettre en péril

imperious [ɪm'pɪərɪəs] *adj* impérieux, -ieuse

impersonal [ɪm'pɜːsənəl] *adj* impersonnel, -elle

impersonate [ɪm'pɜːsəneɪt] *vt (pretend to be)* se faire passer pour; *(imitate)* imiter ▪ **imperso'nation** *n* imitation *f* ▪ **impersonator** *n (mimic)* imitateur, -trice *mf*

impertinent [ɪm'pɜːtɪnənt] *adj* impertinent (**to** envers) ▪ **impertinence** *n* impertinence *f* ▪ **impertinently** *adv* avec impertinence

impervious [ɪm'pɜːvɪəs] *adj also Fig* imperméable (**to** à)

impetuous [ɪm'petjʊəs] *adj* impétueux, -ueuse

impetus ['ɪmpɪtəs] *n* impulsion *f*

impinge [ɪm'pɪndʒ] *vi* **to i. on sth** *(affect)* affecter qch; *(encroach on)* empiéter sur qch

impish ['ɪmpɪʃ] *adj* espiègle

implacable [ɪm'plækəbəl] *adj* implacable

implant 1 ['ɪmplɑːnt] *n* *Med* implant *m* **2** [ɪm'plɑːnt] *vt Med* implanter (**in** dans); *(ideas)* inculquer (**in** à)

implement¹ ['ɪmplɪmənt] *n (tool)* instrument *m*; *(utensil)* ustensile *m*; **farm implements** matériel *m* agricole

implement² ['ɪmplɪment] *vt (carry out)* mettre en œuvre ▪ **implemen'tation** *n* mise *f* en œuvre

implicate ['ɪmplɪkeɪt] *vt* impliquer (**in** dans) ▪ **impli'cation** *n (consequence)* conséquence *f*; *(involvement)* implication *f*; *(innuendo)* insinuation *f*; *(impact)* portée *f*; **by i.** implicitement

implicit [ɪm'plɪsɪt] *adj (implied)* implicite; *(absolute)* absolu ▪ **implicitly** *adv* implicitement

implore [ɪm'plɔː(r)] *vt* implorer (**sb to do** qn de faire)

imply [ɪm'plaɪ] (*pt & pp* **-ied**) *vt (insinuate)* insinuer (**that** que); *(presuppose)* supposer (**that** que); *(involve)* impliquer (**that** que) ▪ **implied** *adj* implicite

impolite [ɪmpə'laɪt] *adj* impoli ▪ **impoliteness** *n* impolitesse *f*

import 1 ['ɪmpɔːt] *n* (**a**) *(item, activity)* importation *f* (**b**) *Formal (importance)* importance *f* **2** [ɪm'pɔːt] *vt (goods) & Comptr* importer (**from** de) ▪ **importer** *n* importateur, -trice *mf*

importance [ɪm'pɔːtəns] *n* importance *f*; **to be of i.** avoir de l'importance; **of no i.** sans importance

important [ɪm'pɔːtənt] *adj* important (**to/for** pour); **it's i. that...** il est important que... (+ *subjunctive*); **to become more i.** prendre de l'importance ▪ **importantly** *adv (speak)* d'un air important; **but, more i....** mais, plus important...

> Note that the French adjective **important** can be a false friend. It also means **large**, **considerable**.

impose [ɪm'pəʊz] **1** *vt (conditions, silence)* imposer (**on** à); *(fine, punishment)* infliger (**on sb** à qn); *(tax)* prélever (**on** sur) **2** *vi (take advantage)* s'imposer; **to i. on sb** abuser de la gentillesse de qn ▪ **imposition** [-pə'zɪʃən] *n* imposition *f* (**of** de); *(inconvenience)* dérangement *m*

imposing [ɪm'pəʊzɪŋ] *adj* imposant

impossible [ɪm'pɒsəbəl] **1** *adj* impossible (**to do** à faire); **it is i. (for us) to do it** il (nous) est impossible de le faire; **it is i. that...** il est impossible que...(+ *subjunctive*); **to make it i. for sb to do sth** mettre qn dans l'impossibilité de faire qch **2** *n* **to do the i.** faire l'impossible ▪ **impossi'bility** (*pl* **-ies**) *n* impossibilité *f* ▪ **impossibly** *adv (extremely)* incroyablement

impostor [ɪm'pɒstə(r)] *n* imposteur *m*

impotent ['ɪmpətənt] *adj* impuissant ▪ **impotence** *n* impuissance *f*

impound [ɪm'paʊnd] *vt (of police)* saisir; *(vehicle)* mettre à la fourrière

impoverish [ɪm'pɒvərɪʃ] *vt* appauvrir • **impoverished** *adj* appauvri

impracticable [ɪm'præktɪkəbəl] *adj* impraticable, irréalisable

impractical [ɪm'præktɪkəl] *adj* peu réaliste

imprecise [ɪmprɪ'saɪs] *adj* imprécis

impregnable [ɪm'pregnəbəl] *adj (fortress)* imprenable; *Fig (argument)* inattaquable

impregnate ['ɪmpregneɪt] *vt (soak)* imprégner (**with** de); *(fertilize)* féconder

impresario [ɪmprɪ'sɑːrɪəʊ] *(pl -os) n* impresario *m*

impress [ɪm'pres] *vt (person)* impressionner; **to i. sth on sb** faire comprendre qch à qn; **to i. sth on sth** imprimer qch sur qch; **to be impressed with** *or* **by sb/sth** être impressionné par qn/qch

impression [ɪm'preʃən] *n* impression *f*; **to be under** *or* **have the i. that…** avoir l'impression que…; **to make a good/bad i. on sb** faire une bonne/mauvaise impression à qn • **impressionable** *adj (person)* impressionnable; *(age)* où l'on est impressionnable

impressionist [ɪm'preʃənɪst] *n (mimic)* imitateur, -trice *mf*; *(artist)* impressionniste *mf*

impressive [ɪm'presɪv] *adj* impressionnant

imprint 1 ['ɪmprɪnt] *n* empreinte *f* **2** [ɪm'prɪnt] *vt* imprimer; **the words are imprinted on my memory** ces mots restent gravés dans ma mémoire

imprison [ɪm'prɪzən] *vt* emprisonner • **imprisonment** *n* emprisonnement *m*; **life i.** la prison à vie

improbable [ɪm'prɒbəbəl] *adj (unlikely)* improbable; *(unbelievable)* invraisemblable • **improba'bility** *(pl -ies) n* improbabilité *f*; *(of story)* invraisemblance *f*

impromptu [ɪm'prɒmptjuː] **1** *adj (speech, party)* improvisé **2** *adv (unexpectedly)* à l'improviste; *(ad lib)* au pied levé

improper [ɪm'prɒpə(r)] *adj* (**a**) *(indecent)* indécent (**b**) *(use, purpose)* mauvais; *(behaviour)* déplacé; *Law* **i. practices** pratiques *fpl* malhonnêtes • **impropriety** [-prə'praɪətɪ] *n (of behaviour)* inconvenance *f*; *(of language)* impropriété *f*

improve [ɪm'pruːv] **1** *vt* améliorer; *(technique, invention)* perfectionner; **to i. sb's looks** embellir qn; **to i. one's chances** augmenter ses chances; **to i. one's English** se perfectionner en anglais; **to i. one's mind** se cultiver **2** *vi* s'améliorer; *(of business)* reprendre; **to i. on sth** *(do better than)* faire mieux que qch • **improvement** *n* amélioration *f* (**in** de); *(progress)* progrès *mpl*; **there has been some** *or* **an i.** il y a du mieux; **to be an i. on sth** *(be better than)* être meilleur que qch

improvise ['ɪmprəvaɪz] *vti* improviser • **improvi'sation** *n* improvisation *f*

impudent ['ɪmpjʊdənt] *adj* impudent • **impudence** *n* impudence *f*

impulse ['ɪmpʌls] *n* impulsion *f*; **on i.** sur un coup de tête • **im'pulsive** *adj (person)* impulsif, -ive; *(remark)* irréfléchi • **im'pulsively** *adv (act)* de manière impulsive

impunity [ɪm'pjuːnɪtɪ] *n* impunité *f*; **with i.** impunément

impure [ɪm'pjʊə(r)] *adj* impur • **impurity** *(pl -ies) n* impureté *f*

in [ɪn] **1** *prep* (**a**) dans; **in the box/the school** dans la boîte/l'école; **in an hour('s time)** dans une heure; **in the garden** dans le jardin, au jardin; **in luxury** dans le luxe; **in so far as** dans la mesure où

(**b**) à; **in school** à l'école; **in Paris** à Paris; **in the USA** aux USA; **in Portugal** au Portugal; **in fashion** à la mode; **in pencil** au crayon; **in ink** à l'encre; **in my opinion** à mon avis; **in spring** au printemps; **the woman in the red dress** la femme à la robe rouge

(**c**) en; **in summer/secret/French** en été/secret/français; **in Spain** en Espagne; **in May** en mai; **in 2003** en 2003; **in season** *(fruit)* de saison; **in an hour** *(during an hour)* en une heure; **in doing sth** en faisant qch; **dressed in black** habillé en noir; **in all** en tout

(**d**) de; **in a soft voice** d'une voix douce; **the best in the class** le meilleur/la meilleure de la classe; **an increase in salary** une augmentation de salaire; **at six in the evening** à six heures du soir

(**e**) chez; **in children/adults/animals** chez les enfants/les adultes/les animaux; **in Shakespeare** chez Shakespeare

(**f**) **in the rain** sous la pluie; **in the morning** le matin; **he hasn't done it in months/years** ça fait des mois/années qu'il ne l'a pas fait; **in an hour** *(at the end of an hour)* au bout d'une heure; **one in ten** un sur dix; **in tens** dix par dix; **in hundreds/thousands** par centaines/milliers; **in here** ici; **in there** là-dedans

2 *adv* **to be in** *(home)* être là; *(of train)* être arrivé; *(in fashion)* être en vogue; *(in power)* être au pouvoir; **day in, day out** jour après jour; **in on a secret** au courant d'un secret; **we're in for some rain/trouble** on va avoir de la pluie/des ennuis; *Fam* **it's the in thing** c'est à la mode

3 *npl* **the ins and outs of** les moindres détails de

in- [ɪn] *pref* in-

inbox *n Comptr (for e-mail)* boîte *f* de réception

inability [ɪnə'bɪlɪtɪ] *(pl -ies) n* incapacité *f* (**to do** de faire)

inaccessible [ɪnək'sesəbəl] *adj* inaccessible

inaccurate [ɪn'ækjʊrət] *adj* inexact • **inaccuracy** *(pl -ies) n* inexactitude *f*

inaction [ɪn'ækʃən] *n* inaction *f*

inactive [ɪn'æktɪv] *adj* inactif, -ive ▪ **inac'tivity** *n* inactivité *f*

inadequate [ɪn'ædɪkwət] *adj* (*quantity*) insuffisant; (*person*) pas à la hauteur; (*work*) médiocre ▪ **inadequacy** (*pl* **-ies**) *n* insuffisance *f* ▪ **inadequately** *adv* insuffisamment

inadmissible [ɪnəd'mɪsəbəl] *adj* inadmissible

inadvertently [ɪnəd'vɜːtəntlɪ] *adv* par inadvertance

inadvisable [ɪnəd'vaɪzəbəl] *adj* (*action*) à déconseiller; **it is i. to go out alone** il est déconseillé de sortir seul

inane [ɪ'neɪn] *adj* inepte

inanimate [ɪn'ænɪmət] *adj* inanimé

inappropriate [ɪnə'prəʊprɪət] *adj* (*unsuitable*) (*place, clothes*) peu approprié; (*remark, moment*) inopportun

inarticulate [ɪnɑː'tɪkjʊlət] *adj* (*person*) incapable de s'exprimer; (*sound*) inarticulé

inasmuch as [ɪnəz'mʌtʃəz] *conj Formal* (*because*) dans la mesure où; (*to the extent that*) en ce sens que

inattentive [ɪnə'tentɪv] *adj* inattentif, -ive (**to** à)

inaudible [ɪn'ɔːdɪbəl] *adj* inaudible

inaugural [ɪ'nɔːgjʊrəl] *adj* (*speech, meeting*) inaugural

inaugurate [ɪ'nɔːgjʊreɪt] *vt* (*building, policy*) inaugurer; (*official*) installer (dans ses fonctions) ▪ **inaugu'ration** *n* inauguration *f*; (*of official*) investiture *f*

inauspicious [ɪnɔː'spɪʃəs] *adj* peu propice

inborn [ɪn'bɔːn] *adj* inné

inbred [ɪn'bred] *adj* (*quality*) inné; (*person*) de parents consanguins

Inc (*abbr* **Incorporated**) *Am Com* ≃ SARL

incalculable [ɪn'kælkjʊləbəl] *adj* incalculable

incandescent [ɪnkæn'desənt] *adj* incandescent

incapable [ɪn'keɪpəbəl] *adj* incapable (**of doing** de faire); **i. of pity** inaccessible à la pitié

incapacitate [ɪnkə'pæsɪteɪt] *vt* rendre infirme ▪ **incapacity** (*pl* **-ies**) *n* (*inability*) incapacité *f*

incarcerate [ɪn'kɑːsəreɪt] *vt* incarcérer ▪ **incarce'ration** *n* incarcération *f*

incarnate 1 [ɪn'kɑːnət] *adj* incarné 2 [ɪn'kɑːneɪt] *vt* incarner ▪ **incar'nation** *n* incarnation *f*

incendiary [ɪn'sendɪərɪ] *adj* **i. device** *or* **bomb** bombe *f* incendiaire

incense¹ ['ɪnsens] *n* (*substance*) encens *m*

incense² [ɪn'sens] *vt* rendre furieux, -ieuse

> Note that the French verb **encenser** is a false friend and is never a translation for the English word **to incense**. It means **to praise lavishly**.

incentive [ɪn'sentɪv] *n* motivation *f*; (*payment*) prime *f*; **to give sb an i. to work** encourager qn à travailler

incessant [ɪn'sesənt] *adj* incessant ▪ **incessantly** *adv* sans cesse

> Note that the French word **incessamment** is a false friend. It means **very shortly**.

incest ['ɪnsest] *n* inceste *m* ▪ **in'cestuous** *adj* incestueux, -ueuse

inch [ɪntʃ] 1 *n* pouce *m* (=2,54 cm); **a few inches from the edge** à quelques centimètres du bord; **within an i. of death** à deux doigts de la mort; **i. by i.** petit à petit 2 *vti* **to i. (one's way) forward** avancer tout doucement

incidence ['ɪnsɪdəns] *n* (*frequency*) taux *m*; (*of disease*) incidence *f*

incident ['ɪnsɪdənt] *n* incident *m*; (*in book, film*) épisode *m*

incidental [ɪnsɪ'dentəl] *adj* (*additional*) accessoire; **it's i. to the main plot** c'est secondaire par rapport à l'intrigue principale; **i. expenses** faux frais *mpl*; **i. music** (*in film*) musique *f* ▪ **incidentally** *adv* (*by the way*) au fait; (*additionally*) accessoirement

incinerate [ɪn'sɪnəreɪt] *vt* (*refuse, leaves*) incinérer ▪ **incinerator** *n* incinérateur *m*

incision [ɪn'sɪʒən] *n* incision *f*

incisive [ɪn'saɪsɪv] *adj* incisif, -ive

incisor [ɪn'saɪzə(r)] *n* (*tooth*) incisive *f*

incite [ɪn'saɪt] *vt* inciter (**to do** à faire) ▪ **incitement** *n* incitation *f* (**to do** à faire)

inclination [ɪnklɪ'neɪʃən] *n* (*liking*) inclination *f*; (*desire*) envie *f* (**to do** de faire); **to have no i. to do sth** n'avoir aucune envie de faire qch

incline 1 ['ɪnklaɪn] *n* (*slope*) pente *f* 2 [ɪn'klaɪn] *vt* (*bend, tilt*) incliner; **to be inclined to do sth** (*feel a wish to*) avoir bien envie de faire qch; (*tend to*) avoir tendance à faire qch; **to be inclined towards** (*indulgence*) incliner à; (*opinion*) pencher pour; **to i. sb to do sth** inciter qn à faire qch 3 *vi* **to i. to** *or* **towards sth** pencher pour qch

include [ɪn'kluːd] *vt* (*contain*) comprendre, inclure; (*in letter*) joindre; **my invitation includes you** mon invitation s'adresse aussi à vous; **to be included** être compris; (*on list*) être inclus ▪ **including** *prep* y compris; **not i.** sans compter; **i. service** service *m* compris

inclusion [ɪn'kluːʒən] *n* inclusion *f*

inclusive [ɪn'kluːsɪv] *adj* inclus; **from the fourth to the tenth of May i.** du quatre au dix mai inclus; **to be i. of** comprendre; **i. of tax** toutes taxes comprises; **i. charge** *or* **price** prix *m* global

incognito [ɪnkɒg'niːtəʊ] *adv* incognito

incoherent [ɪnkəʊ'hɪərənt] *adj* incohérent ▪ **incoherently** *adv* (*speak, act*) de façon incohérente

income ['ɪŋkʌm] *n* revenu *m* (**from** de); **private i.** rentes *fpl*; **i. support** ≃ RMI *m*; **i. tax** impôt *m* sur le revenu

incoming [ˈɪnkʌmɪŋ] *adj (tenant, president)* nouveau (*f* nouvelle); **i. calls** *(on telephone)* appels *mpl* de l'extérieur; **i. mail** courrier *m* à l'arrivée; **i. tide** marée *f* montante

incommunicado [ɪnkəmjuːnɪˈkɑːdəʊ] *adj* injoignable

incomparable [ɪnˈkɒmpərəbəl] *adj* incomparable

incompatible [ɪnkəmˈpætəbəl] *adj* incompatible (**with** avec); ▪**incompati'bility** *n* incompatibilité *f*

incompetent [ɪnˈkɒmpɪtənt] *adj* incompétent ▪**incompetence** *n* incompétence *f*

incomplete [ɪnkəmˈpliːt] *adj* incomplet, -ète

incomprehensible [ɪnkɒmprɪˈhensəbəl] *adj* incompréhensible

inconceivable [ɪnkənˈsiːvəbəl] *adj* inconcevable

inconclusive [ɪnkənˈkluːsɪv] *adj* peu concluant

incongruous [ɪnˈkɒŋgrʊəs] *adj (building, colours)* qui jure(nt) (**with** avec); *(remark, attitude)* incongru

inconsequential [ɪnkɒnsɪˈkwenʃəl] *adj* sans importance

inconsiderate [ɪnkənˈsɪdərət] *adj (action, remark)* inconsidéré; *(person)* sans égards pour les autres

inconsistent [ɪnkənˈsɪstənt] *adj (person)* incohérent; *(uneven)* irrégulier, -ière; **to be i. with sth** ne pas concorder avec qch ▪**inconsistency** *(pl* **-ies***)* *n (in argument)* incohérence *f*; *(between reports)* contradiction *f*; *(uneven quality)* irrégularité *f*

> Note that the French word **inconsistant** is a false friend. It means **thin** or **runny**.

inconsolable [ɪnkənˈsəʊləbəl] *adj* inconsolable

inconspicuous [ɪnkənˈspɪkjʊəs] *adj* qui passe inaperçu ▪**inconspicuously** *adv* discrètement

incontinent [ɪnˈkɒntɪnənt] *adj* incontinent

inconvenience [ɪnkənˈviːnɪəns] **1** *n (bother)* dérangement *m*; *(disadvantage)* inconvénient *m* **2** *vt* déranger

inconvenient [ɪnkənˈviːnɪənt] *adj (moment)* mauvais; *(arrangement)* peu commode; *(building)* mal situé; **it's i. (for me) to...** ça me dérange de...; **that's very i.** c'est très gênant ▪**inconveniently** *adv (arrive, happen)* à un moment gênant; **i. situated** mal situé

incorporate [ɪnˈkɔːpəreɪt] *vt (contain)* contenir; *(introduce)* incorporer (**into** dans); *Am* **incorporated society** société *f* anonyme, société à responsabilité limitée

incorrect [ɪnkəˈrekt] *adj* incorrect; **you're i.** vous avez tort

incorrigible [ɪnˈkɒrɪdʒəbəl] *adj* incorrigible

incorruptible [ɪnkəˈrʌptəbəl] *adj* incorruptible

increase [ɪnˈkriːs] **1** [ˈɪnkriːs] *n* augmentation *f* (**in** *or* **of** de); **on the i.** en hausse **2** *vt* augmenter; **to i. one's efforts** redoubler d'efforts **3** *vi* augmenter; **to i. in weight** prendre du poids; **to i. in price** augmenter ▪**increasing** *adj* croissant ▪**increasingly** *adv* de plus en plus

incredible [ɪnˈkredəbəl] *adj* incroyable ▪**incredibly** *adv* incroyablement

incredulous [ɪnˈkredjʊləs] *adj* incrédule

increment [ˈɪnkrəmənt] *n* augmentation *f*

incriminate [ɪnˈkrɪmɪneɪt] *vt* incriminer ▪**incriminating** *adj* compromettant

incubate [ˈɪnkjʊbeɪt] **1** *vt (eggs)* couver **2** *vi (of illness)* être en période d'incubation ▪**incu'bation** *n* incubation *f* ▪**incubator** *n (for baby)* couveuse *f*

incumbent [ɪnˈkʌmbənt] **1** *n (of administrative position)* titulaire *mf* **2** *adj* **it is i. upon him/her to...** il lui incombe de...

incur [ɪnˈkɜː(r)] *(pt & pp* **-rr-***)* *vt (expenses)* encourir; *(loss)* subir; *(debt)* contracter; *(criticism, anger)* s'attirer

incurable [ɪnˈkjʊərəbəl] *adj* incurable

incursion [ɪnˈkɜːʃən] *n* incursion *f* (**into** dans)

indebted [ɪnˈdetɪd] *adj (financially)* endetté; **i. to sb for sth/for doing sth** redevable à qn de qch/d'avoir fait qch

indecent [ɪnˈdiːsənt] *adj (obscene)* indécent; *Br* **i. assault** attentat *m* à la pudeur ▪**indecency** *(pl* **-ies***)* *n* indécence *f*; *Br Law* outrage *m* à la pudeur ▪**indecently** *adv* indécemment

indecisive [ɪndɪˈsaɪsɪv] *adj (person, answer)* indécis ▪**inde'cision** *n* ▪**indecisiveness** *n* indécision *f*

indeed [ɪnˈdiːd] *adv* en effet; **very good i.** vraiment très bon; **yes i.!** bien sûr!; **thank you very much i.!** merci infiniment!

indefensible [ɪndɪˈfensəbəl] *adj* indéfendable

indefinable [ɪndɪˈfaɪnəbəl] *adj* indéfinissable

indefinite [ɪnˈdefɪnət] *adj (duration, number)* indéterminé; *(plan)* mal défini ▪**indefinitely** *adv* indéfiniment

indelible [ɪnˈdeləbəl] *adj (ink, memory)* indélébile; **i. pen** stylo *m* à encre indélébile

indelicate [ɪnˈdelɪkət] *adj* indélicat

indemnify [ɪnˈdemnɪfaɪ] *(pt & pp* **-ied***)* *vt* indemniser (**for** de) ▪**indemnity** *(pl* **-ies***)* *n (compensation)* indemnité *f*; **an i. against** *(protection)* une garantie contre

indented [ɪnˈdentɪd] *adj (edge, coastline)* découpé ▪**inden'tation** *n* dentelure *f*, découpure *f*; *Typ* alinéa *m*

independence [ɪndɪˈpendəns] *n* indépendance *f*

independent [ɪndɪˈpendənt] *adj* indépendant (**of** de); *(opinions, reports)* de sources différentes ▪**independently** *adv* de façon indépendante; **i. of** indépendamment de

indescribable [ɪndɪ'skraɪbəbəl] *adj* indescriptible

indestructible [ɪndɪ'strʌktəbəl] *adj* indestructible

indeterminate [ɪndɪ'tɜːmɪnət] *adj* indéterminé

index ['ɪndeks] **1** *n* (*in book*) index *m*; (*in library*) fichier *m*; (*number, sign*) indice *m*; **i. card** fiche *f*; **i. finger** index **2** *vt* (*classify*) classer ▪**'index-'linked** *adj* (*wages*) indexé (**to** sur)

India ['ɪndɪə] *n* l'Inde *f* ▪**Indian 1** *adj* indien, -ienne **2** *n* Indien, -ienne *mf*

indicate ['ɪndɪkeɪt] *vt* indiquer (**that** que); **I was indicating right** (*in vehicle*) j'avais mis mon clignotant droit ▪**indi'cation** *n* (*sign*) signe *m*; (*information*) indication *f*; **there is every i. that…** tout porte à croire que…

indicative [ɪn'dɪkətɪv] **1** *adj* **to be i. of** (*symptomatic*) être symptomatique de **2** *n* *Grammar* indicatif *m*

indicator ['ɪndɪkeɪtə(r)] *n* (*sign*) indication *f* (**of** de); *Br* (*in vehicle*) clignotant *m*

indict [ɪn'daɪt] *vt* *Law* inculper (**for** de) ▪**indictment** *n* inculpation *f*

Indies ['ɪndɪz] *npl* **the West I.** les Antilles *fpl*

indifferent [ɪn'dɪfərənt] *adj* indifférent (**to** à); (*mediocre*) médiocre ▪**indifference** *n* indifférence *f* (**to** à) ▪**indifferently** *adv* indifféremment

indigenous [ɪn'dɪdʒɪnəs] *adj* indigène

indigestion [ɪndɪ'dʒestʃən] *n* troubles *mpl* digestifs; (**an attack of) i.** une indigestion ▪**indigestible** *adj* indigeste

indignant [ɪn'dɪgnənt] *adj* indigné (**at** *or* **about** de); **to become i.** s'indigner ▪**indignantly** *adv* avec indignation ▪**indignation** *n* indignation *f*

indignity [ɪn'dɪgnɪtɪ] *n* indignité *f*

indigo ['ɪndɪgəʊ] *n* & *adj* (*colour*) indigo (*m*) *inv*

indirect [ɪndaɪ'rekt] *adj* indirect ▪**indirectly** *adv* indirectement

indiscreet [ɪndɪ'skriːt] *adj* indiscret, -ète ▪**indiscretion** [-'skreʃən] *n* indiscrétion *f*

indiscriminate [ɪndɪ'skrɪmɪnət] *adj* (*person*) qui manque de discernement; **to be i. in one's praise** distribuer les compliments à tort et à travers ▪**indiscriminately** *adv* (*at random*) au hasard; (*without discrimination*) sans discernement

indispensable [ɪndɪ'spensəbəl] *adj* indispensable (**to** à)

indisposed [ɪndɪ'spəʊzd] *adj* (*unwell*) indisposé

indisputable [ɪndɪ'spjuːtəbəl] *adj* incontestable

indistinct [ɪndɪ'stɪŋkt] *adj* indistinct

indistinguishable [ɪndɪ'stɪŋgwɪʃəbəl] *adj* indifférenciable (**from** de)

individual [ɪndɪ'vɪdʒʊəl] **1** *adj* (*separate, personal*) individuel, -uelle; (*specific*)

particulier, -ière **2** *n* (*person*) individu *m* ▪**individuality** [-ʊ'ælɪtɪ] *n* (*distinctiveness*) individualité *f* ▪**individually** *adv* (*separately*) individuellement; (*unusually*) de façon (très) personnelle

individualist [ɪndɪ'vɪdʒʊəlɪst] *n* individualiste *mf* ▪**individua'listic** *adj* individualiste

indivisible [ɪndɪ'vɪzəbəl] *adj* indivisible

Indo-China [ɪndəʊ'tʃaɪnə] *n* l'Indochine *f*

indoctrinate [ɪn'dɒktrɪneɪt] *vt* endoctriner ▪**indoctri'nation** *n* endoctrinement *m*

indolent ['ɪndələnt] *adj* indolent ▪**indolence** *n* indolence *f*

indomitable [ɪn'dɒmɪtəbəl] *adj* (*will, energy*) domptable

Indonesia [ɪndəʊ'niːzɪə] *n* l'Indonésie *f* ▪**Indonesian 1** *adj* indonésien, -ienne **2** *n* (*person*) Indonésien, -ienne *mf*; (*language*) indonésien *m*

indoor ['ɪndɔː(r)] *adj* (*games, shoes*) d'intérieur; (*swimming pool*) couvert ▪**in'doors** *adv* à l'intérieur; **to go/come i.** rentrer

induce [ɪn'djuːs] *vt* (*persuade*) persuader (**to do** de faire); (*cause*) provoquer; **to i. labour** (*in pregnant woman*) déclencher l'accouchement

indulge [ɪn'dʌldʒ] **1** *vt* (*sb's wishes*) satisfaire; (*child*) gâter; **to i. oneself** se faire plaisir **2** *vi* **to i. in sth** (*ice cream, cigar*) s'offrir qch; (*hobby, vice*) s'adonner à qch ▪**indulgence** *n* indulgence *f* ▪**indulgent** *adj* indulgent (**to** envers)

industrial [ɪn'dʌstrɪəl] *adj* industriel, -ielle; (*legislation*) du travail; *Br* **i. action** grève *f*; *Br* **to take i. action** se mettre en grève; *Br* **i. estate,** *Am* **i. park** zone *f* industrielle; **i. relations** relations *fpl* patronat-salariés; **i. tribunal** ≃ conseil *m* de prud'hommes ▪**industrialist** *n* industriel *m* ▪**industrialized** *adj* industrialisé

> Note that the French adjective **industriel** never refers to the relationship between employers and employees.

industrious [ɪn'dʌstrɪəs] *adj* travailleur, -euse

industry ['ɪndəstrɪ] (*pl* **-ies**) *n* (*economic sector*) industrie *f*; (*hard work*) application *f*

inebriated [ɪn'iːbrɪeɪtɪd] *adj* ivre

inedible [ɪn'edəbəl] *adj* immangeable

ineffective [ɪnɪ'fektɪv] *adj* (*measure*) inefficace; (*person*) incapable ▪**ineffectiveness** *n* inefficacité *f*

ineffectual [ɪnɪ'fektʃʊəl] *adj* (*measure*) inefficace; (*person*) incompétent

inefficient [ɪnɪ'fɪʃənt] *adj* (*person, measure*) inefficace; (*machine*) peu performant ▪**inefficiency** *n* inefficacité *f*

ineligible [ɪn'elɪdʒəbəl] *adj* (*candidate*) inéligible; **to be i. for sth** (*scholarship*) ne pas avoir droit à qch

inept [ɪˈnept] *adj (incompetent)* incompétent; *(foolish)* inepte

inequality [ɪnɪˈkwɒlətɪ] *(pl* **-ies)** *n* inégalité *f*

inert [ɪˈnɜːt] *adj* inerte ▪ **inertia** [-ʃə] *n* inertie *f*

inescapable [ɪnɪˈskeɪpəbəl] *adj (outcome)* inéluctable; *(conclusion)* incontournable

inevitable [ɪnˈevɪtəbəl] *adj* inévitable ▪ **inevitably** *adv* inévitablement

inexcusable [ɪnɪkˈskjuːzəbəl] *adj* inexcusable

inexhaustible [ɪnɪgˈzɔːstəbəl] *adj* inépuisable

inexorable [ɪnˈeksərəbəl] *adj* inexorable

inexpensive [ɪnɪkˈspensɪv] *adj* bon marché *inv*

inexperience [ɪnɪkˈspɪərɪəns] *n* inexpérience *f* ▪ **inexperienced** *adj* inexpérimenté

inexplicable [ɪnɪkˈsplɪkəbəl] *adj* inexplicable

inexpressible [ɪnɪkˈspresəbəl] *adj* inexprimable

inextricable [ɪnɪkˈstrɪkəbəl] *adj* inextricable

infallible [ɪnˈfæləbəl] *adj* infaillible ▪ **infalli'bility** *n* infaillibilité *f*

infamous [ˈɪnfəməs] *adj (well-known)* tristement célèbre; *(crime, rumour)* infâme ▪ **infamy** *n* infamie *f*

infancy [ˈɪnfənsɪ] *n* petite enfance *f*; **to be in its i.** *(of art, technique)* en être à ses premiers balbutiements

infant [ˈɪnfənt] *n* bébé *m*; *Br* **i. school** = école primaire pour enfants de cinq à sept ans

infantile [ˈɪnfəntaɪl] *adj Pej* infantile

infantry [ˈɪnfəntrɪ] *n* infanterie *f*

infatuated [ɪnˈfætʃʊeɪtɪd] *adj* entiché (**with** de) ▪ **infatu'ation** *n (with person)* tocade *f* (**for** *or* **with** pour)

infect [ɪnˈfekt] *vt (wound, person)* infecter; *(water, food)* contaminer; **to get** *or* **become infected** s'infecter; **to i. sb with sth** transmettre qch à qn ▪ **infection** *n* infection *f*

infectious [ɪnˈfekʃəs] *adj (disease)* infectieux, -ieuse; *(person)* contagieux, -ieuse; *(laughter)* communicatif, -ive

infer [ɪnˈfɜː(r)] *(pt & pp* **-rr-)** *vt* déduire (**from** de; **that** que) ▪ **inference** [ˈɪnfərəns] *n* déduction *f*; **by i.** par déduction; **to draw an i. from sth** tirer une conclusion de qch

inferior [ɪnˈfɪərɪə(r)] **1** *adj* inférieur (**to** à); *(goods, work)* de qualité inférieure **2** *n (person)* inférieur, -ieure *mf* ▪ **inferiority** [-rɪˈɒrɪtɪ] *n* infériorité *f*; **i. complex** complexe *m* d'infériorité

infernal [ɪnˈfɜːnəl] *adj* infernal

inferno [ɪnˈfɜːnəʊ] *(pl* **-os)** *n (blaze)* brasier *m*; *(hell)* enfer *m*

infertile [*Br* ɪnˈfɜːtaɪl, *Am* ɪnˈfɜːrtəl] *adj (person, land)* stérile ▪ **infertility** [-ˈtɪlɪtɪ] *n* stérilité *f*

infest [ɪnˈfest] *vt* infester (**with** de); **rat-/shark-infested** infesté de rats/requins

infidelity [ɪnfɪˈdelɪtɪ] *(pl* **-ies)** *n* infidélité *f*

infighting [ˈɪnfaɪtɪŋ] *n* luttes *fpl* intestines

infiltrate [ˈɪnfɪltreɪt] **1** *vt* infiltrer **2** *vi* s'infiltrer

(**into** dans) ▪ **infil'tration** *n* infiltration *f*; *Pol* noyautage *m*

infinite [ˈɪnfɪnɪt] *adj & n* infini *(m)* ▪ **infinitely** *adv* infiniment ▪ **in'finity** *n Math & Phot* infini *m*; *Math* **to i.** à l'infini

infinitive [ɪnˈfɪnɪtɪv] *n Grammar* infinitif *m*

infirm [ɪnˈfɜːm] *adj* infirme

infirmary [ɪnˈfɜːmərɪ] *(pl* **-ies)** *n (hospital)* hôpital *m*; *(sickbay)* infirmerie *f*

infirmity [ɪnˈfɜːmɪtɪ] *(pl* **-ies)** *n (disability)* infirmité *f*

inflame [ɪnˈfleɪm] *vt* enflammer ▪ **inflamed** *adj (throat, wound)* enflammé; **to become i.** s'enflammer

inflammable [ɪnˈflæməbəl] *adj* inflammable ▪ **inflammation** [-fləˈmeɪʃən] *n* inflammation *f* ▪ **inflammatory** *adj (remark, speech)* incendiaire

inflate [ɪnˈfleɪt] *vt (balloon, prices)* gonfler ▪ **inflatable** *adj* gonflable

inflation [ɪnˈfleɪʃən] *n Econ* inflation *f* ▪ **inflationary** *adj Econ* inflationniste

inflection [ɪnˈflekʃən] *n Grammar* flexion *f*; *(of voice)* inflexion *f*

inflexible [ɪnˈfleksəbəl] *adj* inflexible

inflexion [ɪnˈflekʃən] *n Br* = **inflection**

inflict [ɪnˈflɪkt] *vt (punishment, defeat)* infliger (**on** à); *(wound, damage)* occasionner (**on** à); **to i. pain on sb** faire souffrir qn

influence [ˈɪnfluəns] **1** *n* influence *f* (**on** sur); **to have i. over sb** avoir de l'influence sur qn; **under the i. of drink/anger** sous l'empire de la boisson/de la colère **2** *vt* influencer ▪ **influential** [-ˈenʃəl] *adj* influent

influenza [ɪnfluˈenzə] *n* grippe *f*

influx [ˈɪnflʌks] *n* afflux *m* (**of** de)

info [ˈɪnfəʊ] *n Fam* renseignements *mpl* (**on** sur)

inform [ɪnˈfɔːm] **1** *vt* informer (**of** *or* **about** de; **that** que) **2** *vi* **to i. on sb** dénoncer qn ▪ **informed** *adj (person, public)* informé; **to keep sb i. of sth** tenir qn au courant de qch

informal [ɪnˈfɔːməl] *adj (unaffected)* simple; *(casual)* décontracté; *(tone, language)* familier, -ière; *(unofficial)* officieux, -ieuse ▪ **informality** [-ˈmælɪtɪ] *n (unaffectedness)* simplicité *f*; *(casualness)* décontraction *f*; *(of talks)* caractère *m* officieux ▪ **informally** *adv (unaffectedly)* avec simplicité; *(casually)* avec décontraction; *(meet, discuss)* officieusement

informant [ɪnˈfɔːmənt] *n* informateur, -trice *mf*

information [ɪnfəˈmeɪʃən] *n (facts, news)* renseignements *mpl* (**about** *or* **on** sur); *Comptr* information *f*; **a piece of i.** un renseignement, une information; **to get some i.** se renseigner; **the i. superhighway** l'autoroute *f* de l'information; **i. technology** informatique *f*

informative [ɪnˈfɔːmətɪv] *adj* instructif, -ive

informer [ɪnˈfɔːmə(r)] *n (police)* **i.** indicateur, -trice *mf*

infrared [ɪnfrə'red] adj infrarouge

infrequent [ɪn'fri:kwənt] adj peu fréquent ▪**infrequently** adv rarement

infringe [ɪn'frɪndʒ] 1 vt (rule, law) enfreindre à 2 vt insep **to i. upon sth** empiéter sur qch ▪**infringement** n (of rule, law) infraction f (**of** à)

infuriate [ɪn'fjʊərɪeɪt] vt exaspérer ▪**infuriating** adj exaspérant

infuse [ɪn'fju:z] vt (tea) (faire) infuser ▪**infusion** n (drink) infusion f

ingenious [ɪn'dʒi:nɪəs] adj ingénieux, -ieuse ▪**ingenuity** [ɪndʒɪ'nju:ɪtɪ] n ingéniosité f

ingot ['ɪŋgət] n lingot m

ingrained [ɪn'greɪnd] adj (prejudice, attitude) enraciné; **i. dirt** crasse f

ingratiate [ɪn'greɪʃɪeɪt] vt **to i. oneself with sb** s'insinuer dans les bonnes grâces de qn ▪**ingratiating** adj (person, smile) doucereux, -euse

ingratitude [ɪn'grætɪtju:d] n ingratitude f

ingredient [ɪn'gri:dɪənt] n ingrédient m

ingrowing ['ɪngrəʊɪŋ] (Am **ingrown** ['ɪn-grəʊn]) adj (toenail) incarné

inhabit [ɪn'hæbɪt] vt habiter ▪**inhabitable** adj habitable ▪**inhabitant** n habitant, -ante mf

> Note that the French words **inhabitable** and **inhabité** are false friends and are never translations for the English words **inhabitable** and **inhabited**. They mean respectively **uninhabitable** and **uninhabited**.

inhale [ɪn'heɪl] vt (gas, fumes) inhaler; (cigarette smoke) avaler ▪**inhalation** [ɪnhə'leɪʃən] n inhalation f ▪**inhaler** n (for medication) inhalateur m

inherent [ɪn'hɪərənt] adj inhérent (**in** à) ▪**inherently** adv intrinsèquement

inherit [ɪn'herɪt] vt hériter (**from** de); (title) accéder à ▪**inheritance** n héritage m; (legal process) succession f; **cultural i.** patrimoine m

inhibit [ɪn'hɪbɪt] vt (progress, growth) entraver; (of person) inhiber; **to i. sb from doing sth** empêcher qn de faire qch ▪**inhibited** adj (person) inhibé ▪**inhi'bition** n inhibition f

inhospitable [ɪnhɒ'spɪtəbəl] adj inhospitalier, -ière

inhuman [ɪn'hju:mən] adj inhumain ▪**inhumane** [-'meɪn] adj inhumain ▪**inhumanity** [-'mænɪtɪ] n inhumanité f, cruauté f

inimitable [ɪ'nɪmɪtəbəl] adj inimitable

iniquitous [ɪ'nɪkwɪtəs] adj inique ▪**iniquity** (pl -ies) n iniquité f

initial [ɪ'nɪʃəl] 1 adj initial 2 npl **initials** (letters) initiales fpl; (signature) paraphe m 3 (Br -ll-, Am -l-) vt parapher ▪**initially** adv au début, initialement

initiate [ɪ'nɪʃɪeɪt] vt (reform, negotiations) amorcer; (attack, rumour, project) lancer; (policy, period) inaugurer; **to i. sb into a gang** faire subir à qn les épreuves initiatiques d'un gang; Law **to i. proceedings against sb** entamer des poursuites contre qn ▪**initi'ation** n (beginning) amorce f; (induction) initiation f; **i. ceremony** rite m d'initiation ▪**initiator** n initiateur, -trice mf

initiative [ɪ'nɪʃətɪv] n initiative f

inject [ɪn'dʒekt] vt injecter (**into** dans); Fig (enthusiasm) communiquer (**into** à); **to i. sth into sb, to i. sb with sth** faire une piqûre de qch à qn; Fig **to i. new life into sth** donner un nouvel essor à qch ▪**injection** n injection f, piqûre f; **to give sb an i.** faire une piqûre à qn

injunction [ɪn'dʒʌŋkʃən] n Law arrêt m

injure ['ɪndʒə(r)] vt (physically) blesser; (reputation, interest) nuire à; **to i. one's foot** se blesser au pied; **to i. sb's feelings** blesser qn ▪**injured 1** adj blessé **2** npl **the i.** les blessés mpl

> Note that the French verb **injurier** is a false friend and is never a translation for the English verb **to injure**. It means **to insult**.

injurious [ɪn'dʒʊərɪəs] adj préjudiciable (**to** à)

injury ['ɪndʒərɪ] (pl -ies) n (physical) blessure f; Fig (wrong) préjudice m; Sport **i. time** arrêts mpl de jeu

> Note that the French word **injure** is a false friend. It means **insult**.

injustice [ɪn'dʒʌstɪs] n injustice f

ink [ɪŋk] n encre f ▪**inkpot, inkwell** n encrier m ▪**inky** adj couvert d'encre

inkling ['ɪŋklɪŋ] n petite idée f; **to have an i. of sth** avoir une petite idée de qch

inlaid [ɪn'leɪd] adj (with jewels) incrusté (**with** de); (with wood) marqueté

inland 1 ['ɪnlənd, 'ɪnlænd] adj intérieur; Br **the I. Revenue** ≃ le fisc **2** [ɪn'lænd] adv (travel) vers l'intérieur; (live) dans les terres

in-laws ['ɪnlɔ:z] npl belle-famille f

inlet ['ɪnlet] n (of sea) crique f; **i. pipe** tuyau m d'arrivée

in-line skates [ɪnlaɪn'skeɪts] npl rollers mpl (en-ligne) ▪**in-line skating** n roller m (en-ligne)

inmate ['ɪnmeɪt] n (of prison) détenu, -ue mf; (of asylum) interné, -ée mf

inmost ['ɪnməʊst] adj le plus profond (f la plus profonde)

inn [ɪn] n auberge f

innards ['ɪnədz] npl Fam entrailles fpl

innate [ɪ'neɪt] adj inné

inner ['ɪnə(r)] adj intérieur; (feelings) intime; (ear) interne; **i. circle** (of society) initiés mpl; **i. city** quartiers mpl déshérités du centre-ville; **i. tube** chambre f à air ▪**innermost** adj le plus profond (*f* la plus profonde); *(thoughts)* le plus secret (*f* la plus secrète)

inning ['ɪnɪŋ] *n* Baseball tour *m* de batte ▪**innings** *n* inv Cricket tour *m* de batte; *Fig* **a good i.** une longue vie

innkeeper ['ɪnkiːpə(r)] *n* aubergiste *mf*

innocent ['ɪnəsənt] *adj* innocent ▪**innocence** *n* innocence *f* ▪**innocently** *adv* innocemment

innocuous [ɪ'nɒkjʊəs] *adj* inoffensif, -ive

innovate ['ɪnəveɪt] *vi* innover ▪**inno'vation** *n* innovation *f* ▪**innovator** *n* innovateur, -trice *mf*

innuendo [ɪnjʊ'endəʊ] *(pl* -oes *or* -os) *n* insinuation *f*

innumerable [ɪ'njuːmərəbəl] *adj* innombrable

inoculate [ɪ'nɒkjʊleɪt] *vt* vacciner (**against** contre) ▪**inocu'lation** *n* inoculation *f*

inoffensive [ɪnə'fensɪv] *adj* inoffensif, -ive

inoperative [ɪn'ɒpərətɪv] *adj (machine)* arrêté; *(rule)* inopérant

inopportune [ɪn'ɒpətjuːn] *adj* inopportun

inordinate [ɪ'nɔːdɪnət] *adj* excessif, -ive ▪**inordinately** *adv* excessivement

in-patient ['ɪnpeɪʃənt] *n* Br malade *mf* hospitalisé(e)

input ['ɪnpʊt] **1** *n (contribution)* contribution *f*; *Comptr* entrée *f*; *(data)* données *fpl*; *El* puissance *f* d'alimentation **2** *(pt & pp* -put) *vt* Comptr *(data)* entrer

inquest ['ɪnkwest] *n Law* enquête *f*

inquire [ɪn'kwaɪə(r)] **1** *vt* demander; **to i. how to get to...** demander le chemin de... **2** *vi* se renseigner (**about** sur); **to i. after sb** demander des nouvelles de qn; **to i. into sth** faire des recherches sur qch ▪**inquiring** *adj (mind, look)* curieux, -ieuse

inquiry [ɪn'kwaɪərɪ] *(pl* -ies) *n (request for information)* demande *f* de renseignements; *(official investigation)* enquête *f*; **'inquiries'** *(on sign)* 'renseignements'; **to make inquiries** demander des renseignements; *(of police)* enquêter

inquisitive [ɪn'kwɪzɪtɪv] *adj* curieux, -ieuse ▪**inqui'sition** *n (inquiry) & Rel* inquisition *f* ▪**inquisitively** *adv* avec curiosité

inroads ['ɪnrəʊdz] *npl (attacks)* incursions *fpl* (**into** dans); **to make i. into** *(savings, capital)* entamer; *(market)* pénétrer

insane [ɪn'seɪn] *adj* dément, fou (*f* folle); **to go i.** perdre la raison; **to be i. with grief** être fou de chagrin ▪**insanely** *adv* comme un fou (*f* une folle) ▪**insanity** [-'sænɪtɪ] *n* démence *f*

insanitary [ɪn'sænɪtərɪ] *adj* insalubre

insatiable [ɪn'seɪʃəbəl] *adj* insatiable

inscribe [ɪn'skraɪb] *vt* inscrire; *(book)* dédicacer (**to** à) ▪**inscription** [-'skrɪpʃən] *n* inscription *f*; *(in book)* dédicace *f*

inscrutable [ɪn'skruːtəbəl] *adj* impénétrable

insect ['ɪnsekt] *n* insecte *m*; **i. powder/spray**

poudre *f*/bombe *f* insecticide; **i. repellent** anti-moustiques *m inv* ▪**in'secticide** *n* insecticide *m*

insecure [ɪnsɪ'kjʊə(r)] *adj (unsafe)* peu sûr; *(job, future)* précaire; *(person)* angoissé; **to be financially i.** être dans une situation financièrement précaire ▪**insecurity** *n (of job, future)* précarité *f*; *(of person)* angoisse *f*

insemination [ɪnsemɪ'neɪʃən] *n* **artificial i.** insémination artificielle

insensible [ɪn'sensəbəl] *adj (unaware, unconscious)* inconscient (**to** de)

insensitive [ɪn'sensɪtɪv] *adj (person)* insensible (**to** à); *(remark)* indélicat ▪**insensi'tivity** *n* insensibilité *f*

inseparable [ɪn'sepərəbəl] *adj* inséparable (**from** de)

insert [ɪn'sɜːt] *vt* insérer (**in** or **into** dans) ▪**insertion** *n* insertion *f*

inshore **1** ['ɪnʃɔː(r)] *adj* côtier, -ière **2** [ɪn'ʃɔː(r)] *adv (fish)* près des côtes

inside **1** ['ɪnsaɪd] *adj* intérieur; *(information)* obtenu à la source; **the i. lane** Br la voie de gauche, Am la voie de droite **2** ['ɪnsaɪd] *n* intérieur *m*; *Fam* **insides** *(stomach)* entrailles *fpl*; **on the i.** à l'intérieur (**of** de); **i. out** *(clothes)* à l'envers; *(know, study)* à fond; *Fig* **to turn everything i. out** tout chambouler **3** [ɪn'saɪd] *adv* à l'intérieur; *Fam (in prison)* en taule; **come i.!** entrez! **4** [ɪn'saɪd] *prep* à l'intérieur de, dans; *(time)* en moins de

insider [ɪn'saɪdə(r)] *n* initié, -iée *mf*; *Fin* **i. dealing** *or* **trading** délit *m* d'initié

insidious [ɪn'sɪdɪəs] *adj* insidieux, -ieuse

insight ['ɪnsaɪt] *n* perspicacité *f*; *(into question)* aperçu *m*; **to give sb an i. into** *(sb's character)* permettre à qn de comprendre; *(question)* donner à qn un aperçu de

insignia [ɪn'sɪgnɪə] *n* insignes *mpl*

insignificant [ɪnsɪg'nɪfɪkənt] *adj* insignifiant ▪**insignificance** *n* insignifiance *f*

insincere [ɪnsɪn'sɪə(r)] *adj* peu sincère ▪**insincerity** [-'serɪtɪ] *n* manque *m* de sincérité

insinuate [ɪn'sɪnjʊeɪt] *vt (suggest)* insinuer (**that** que); **to i. oneself into sb's good favours** s'insinuer dans les bonnes grâces de qn ▪**insinu'ation** *n* insinuation *f*

insipid [ɪn'sɪpɪd] *adj* insipide

insist [ɪn'sɪst] **1** *vt (maintain)* soutenir (**that** que); **I i. that you come** *or* **on your coming** *(I demand it)* j'insiste pour que tu viennes **2** *vi* insister; **to i. on sth** *(demand)* exiger qch; *(assert)* affirmer qch; **to i. on doing sth** tenir à faire qch

insistence [ɪn'sɪstəns] *n* insistance *f*; **her i. on seeing me** l'insistance qu'elle met à vouloir me voir

insistent [ɪn'sɪstənt] *adj (person, request)* pressant; **to be i. (that)** insister (pour que +

subjunctive); **I was i. about it** j'ai insisté ▪ **insistently** *adv* avec insistance

insolent ['ɪnsələnt] *adj* insolent ▪ **insolence** *n* insolence *f* ▪ **insolently** *adv* insolemment

insoluble [ɪn'sɒljʊbəl] *adj* insoluble

insolvent [ɪn'sɒlvənt] *adj (financially)* insolvable

insomnia [ɪn'sɒmnɪə] *n* insomnie *f* ▪ **insomniac** [-nɪæk] *n* insomniaque *mf*

insomuch as [ɪnsəʊ'mʌtʃəz] *adv* = **inasmuch as**

inspect [ɪn'spekt] *vt* inspecter; *(tickets)* contrôler; *(troops)* passer en revue ▪ **inspection** *n* inspection *f; (of tickets)* contrôle *m; (of troops)* revue *f* ▪ **inspector** *n* inspecteur, -trice *mf; (on train)* contrôleur, -euse *mf*

inspire [ɪn'spaɪə(r)] *vt* inspirer; **to i. sb to do sth** pousser qn à faire qch; **to i. sb with sth** inspirer qch à qn ▪ **inspiration** [-spə'reɪʃən] *n* inspiration *f; (person)* source *f* d'inspiration ▪ **inspired** *adj* inspiré ▪ **inspiring** *adj* exaltant

instability [ɪnstə'bɪlɪtɪ] *n* instabilité *f*

install [ɪn'stɔːl] *(Am* **instal**) *vt* installer ▪ **installation** [-stə'leɪʃən] *n* installation *f*

instalment [ɪn'stɔːlmənt] *(Am* **installment**) *n (part payment)* versement *m; (of serial, story)* épisode *m; (of publication)* fascicule *m;* **to pay by instalments** payer par versements échelonnés; *Am* **to buy on the i. plan** acheter à crédit

instance ['ɪnstəns] *n (example)* exemple *m; (case)* cas *m;* **for i.** par exemple; **in this i.** dans le cas présent; **in the first i.** en premier lieu

> Note that the French noun **instance** is a false friend. It never means **example**.

instant ['ɪnstənt] **1** *adj* immédiat; **i. camera** appareil photo *m* à développement instantané; **i. coffee** café *m* instantané; *Comptr* **i. messaging** messagerie *f* instantanée **2** *n (moment)* instant *m;* **this (very) i.** *(at once)* à l'instant; **the i. that I saw her** dès que je l'ai vue ▪ **instantly** *adv* immédiatement

instantaneous [ɪnstən'teɪnɪəs] *adj* instantané

instead [ɪn'sted] *adv (in place of sth)* à la place; *(in place of sb)* à ma/ta/*etc* place; **i. of sth** au lieu de qch; **i. of doing sth** au lieu de faire qch; **i. of sb** à la place de qn; **i. of him/her** à sa place

instep ['ɪnstep] *n (of foot)* cou-de-pied *m; (of shoe)* cambrure *f*

instigate ['ɪnstɪgeɪt] *vt* provoquer ▪ **insti'gation** *n* instigation *f* ▪ **instigator** *n* instigateur, -trice *mf*

instil [ɪn'stɪl] *(Am* **instill**) *(pt & pp* **-ll-**) *vt (idea)* inculquer (**into** à); *(courage)* insuffler (**into** à); *(doubt)* instiller (**in** à)

instinct ['ɪnstɪŋkt] *n* instinct *m;* **by i.** d'instinct ▪ **in'stinctive** *adj* instinctif, -ive ▪ **in'stinctively** *adv* instinctivement

institute ['ɪnstɪtjuːt] **1** *n* institut *m* **2** *vt (rule, practice)* instituer; *Law (inquiry)* ordonner; *Law* **to i. proceedings against sb** entamer des poursuites contre qn

institution [ɪnstɪ'tjuːʃən] *n (organization, custom)* institution *f; (public, financial, religious, psychiatric)* établissement *m* ▪ **institutional** *adj* institutionnel, -elle

instruct [ɪn'strʌkt] *vt (teach)* enseigner (**sb in sth** qch à qn); **to i. sb about sth** *(inform)* instruire qn de qch; **to i. sb to do** *(order)* charger qn de faire

instruction [ɪn'strʌkʃən] *n (teaching)* instruction *f;* **instructions** *(orders)* instructions *fpl;* **instructions (for use)** mode *m* d'emploi

instructive [ɪn'strʌktɪv] *adj* instructif, -ive

instructor [ɪn'strʌktə(r)] *n (for judo, dance)* professeur *m; (for skiing, swimming)* moniteur, -trice *mf; (military)* instructeur *m; (in American university)* maître-assistant, -ante *mf;* **driving i.** moniteur, -trice *mf* d'auto-école

instrument ['ɪnstrəmənt] *n* instrument *m*

instrumental [ɪnstrə'mentəl] *adj (music)* instrumental; **to be i. in sth/in doing sth** contribuer à qch/à faire qch ▪ **instrumentalist** *n* instrumentiste *mf*

instrumentation [ɪnstrəmən'teɪʃən] *n Mus* orchestration *f*

insubordinate [ɪnsə'bɔːdɪnət] *adj* insubordonné ▪ **insubordi'nation** *n* insubordination *f*

insubstantial [ɪnsəb'stænʃəl] *adj (argument, evidence)* peu solide

insufferable [ɪn'sʌfərəbəl] *adj* intolérable

insufficient [ɪnsə'fɪʃənt] *adj* insuffisant ▪ **insufficiently** *adv* insuffisamment

insular ['ɪnsjʊlə(r)] *adj (climate)* insulaire; *(views)* étroit, borné

insulate ['ɪnsjʊleɪt] *vt (against cold) & El* isoler; *(against sound)* insonoriser; *Fig* **to i. sb from sth** protéger qn de qch; **insulating tape** chatterton *m* ▪ **insu'lation** *n* isolation *f; (against sound)* insonorisation *f; (material)* isolant *m*

insulin ['ɪnsjʊlɪn] *n* insuline *f*

insult 1 ['ɪnsʌlt] *n* insulte *f* (**to** à); **to add i. to injury** pour aggraver les choses **2** [ɪn'sʌlt] *vt* insulter ▪ **in'sulting** *adj (words, offer)* insultant

insuperable [ɪn'suːpərəbəl] *adj* insurmontable

insure [ɪn'ʃʊə(r)] *vt* **(a)** *(house, car, goods)* assurer (**against** contre) **(b)** *Am* = **ensure** ▪ **insurance** *n* assurance *f;* **i. company** compagnie *f* d'assurances; **i. policy** police *f* d'assurance

insurgent [ɪn'sɜːdʒənt] *n* insurgé, -ée *mf*

insurmountable [ɪnsə'maʊntəbəl] *adj* insurmontable

insurrection [ɪnsə'rekʃən] *n* insurrection *f*

intact [ɪnˈtækt] *adj* intact

intake [ˈɪnteɪk] *n (of food)* consommation *f; (of students, schoolchildren)* admissions *fpl; (of recruits)* contingent *m; Tech (of gas, air)* admission *f*

intangible [ɪnˈtændʒəbəl] *adj* intangible

integral [ˈɪntɪgrəl] *adj* intégral; **to be an i. part of sth** faire partie intégrante de qch

integrate [ˈɪntɪgreɪt] **1** *vt* intégrer (**into** dans); **integrated school** école *f* où se pratique la déségrégation raciale **2** *vi* s'intégrer (**into** dans) ▪ **inte'gration** *n* intégration *f*; **(racial) i.** déségrégation *f* raciale

integrity [ɪnˈtegrɪtɪ] *n* intégrité *f*

intellect [ˈɪntɪlekt] *n* intelligence *f*, intellect *m* ▪ **inte'llectual** *adj & n* intellectuel, -uelle *(mf)*

intelligence [ɪnˈtelɪdʒəns] *n* intelligence *f*; *(information)* renseignements *mpl*; **i. service** services *mpl* secrets

intelligent [ɪnˈtelɪdʒənt] *adj* intelligent ▪ **intelligently** *adv* intelligemment

intelligentsia [ɪntelɪˈdʒentsɪə] *n* intelligentsia *f*

intelligible [ɪnˈtelɪdʒəbəl] *adj* intelligible ▪ **intelligi'bility** *n* intelligibilité *f*

intemperance [ɪnˈtempərəns] *n* intempérance *f*

intend [ɪnˈtend] *vt (gift, remark)* destiner (**for** à); **to be intended for sb** être destiné à qn; **to be intended to do sth** être destiné à faire qch; **to i. to do sth** avoir l'intention de faire qch; **I i. you to stay** mon intention est que vous restiez ▪ **intended** *adj (deliberate)* voulu; *(planned)* prévu; *(effect)* escompté; **was that i.?** était-ce intentionnel?

intense [ɪnˈtens] *adj* intense; *(interest)* vif *(f vive)*; *(person)* passionné ▪ **intensely** *adv (look at)* intensément; *Fig (very)* extrêmement

intensify [ɪnˈtensɪfaɪ] *(pt & pp* **-ied)** **1** *vt* intensifier **2** *vi* s'intensifier ▪ **intensification** [-fɪˈkeɪʃən] *n* intensification *f*

intensity [ɪnˈtensɪtɪ] *n* intensité *f*

intensive [ɪnˈtensɪv] *adj* intensif, -ive; **in i. care** en réanimation; **i. care unit** service *m* de réanimation

intent [ɪnˈtent] **1** *adj (look)* intense; **to be i. on doing** être résolu à faire; **i. on one's task** absorbé par son travail **2** *n* intention *f*; **to all intents and purposes** quasiment

intention [ɪnˈtenʃən] *n* intention *f* (**of doing** de faire); **to have every i. of doing sth** avoir la ferme intention de faire qch

intentional [ɪnˈtenʃənəl] *adj* intentionnel, -elle; **it wasn't i.** ce n'était pas fait exprès ▪ **intentionally** *adv* intentionnellement, exprès

inter [ɪnˈtɜː(r)] *(pt & pp* **-rr-)** *vt* enterrer

inter- [ˈɪntə(r)] *pref* inter-

interact [ɪntərˈækt] *vi (of person)* communiquer (**with** avec); *(of several people)* communiquer entre eux/elles; *(of ideas)* être interdépendant(e)s; *(of chemicals)* réagir (**with** avec) ▪ **interaction** *n* interaction *f* ▪ **interactive** *adj Comptr* interactif, -ive

intercede [ɪntəˈsiːd] *vi* intercéder (**with** auprès de)

intercept [ɪntəˈsept] *vt* intercepter ▪ **interception** *n* interception *f*

interchange [ˈɪntətʃeɪndʒ] *n Br (on road)* échangeur *m*

interchangeable [ɪntəˈtʃeɪndʒəbəl] *adj* interchangeable

inter-city [ɪntəˈsɪtɪ] *adj Br* **i. service** grandes lignes *fpl; Br* **i. train** train *m* de grandes lignes

intercom [ˈɪntəkɒm] *n* Interphone® *m*

interconnected [ɪntəkəˈnektɪd] *adj (facts)* lié(e)s ▪ **interconnecting** *adj* **i. rooms** pièces *fpl* communicantes

intercontinental [ɪntəkɒntɪˈnentəl] *adj* intercontinental

intercourse [ˈɪntəkɔːs] *n (sexual)* rapports *mpl* sexuels

interdependent [ɪntədɪˈpendənt] *adj* interdépendant; *(parts of machine)* solidaire

interest [ˈɪntərest, ˈɪntrɪst] **1** *n* intérêt *m*; *(hobby)* centre *m* d'intérêt; *(money)* intérêts *mpl*; **to take an i. in sb/sth** s'intéresser à qn/qch; **to lose i. in sb/sth** se désintéresser de qn/qch; **to have a financial i. in sth** avoir investi financièrement dans qch; **to act in sb's i.** agir dans l'intérêt de qn; **it's in my i. to do it** j'ai tout intérêt à le faire; **to be of i.** être intéressant; **to be of i. to sb** intéresser qn **2** *vt* intéresser ▪ **interested** *adj* intéressé; **to seem i.** sembler intéressé (**in** par); **to be i. in sb/sth** s'intéresser à qn/qch; **I'm i. in doing that** ça m'intéresse de faire ça; **are you i.?** ça vous intéresse? ▪ **interest-free** *adj (loan)* sans intérêts; *(credit)* gratuit ▪ **interesting** *adj* intéressant ▪ **interestingly** *adv* **i. (enough), she…** curieusement, elle…

interface [ˈɪntəfeɪs] *n Comptr* interface *f*

interfere [ɪntəˈfɪə(r)] *vi (meddle)* se mêler (**in** de); **to i. with sth** *(hinder)* gêner qch; *(touch)* toucher à qch; **don't i.!** ne te mêle pas de ce qui ne te regarde pas! ▪ **interfering** *adj (person)* qui se mêle de tout

interference [ɪntəˈfɪərəns] *n* ingérence *f; TV & Radio* parasites *mpl*

interim [ˈɪntərɪm] **1** *n* **in the i.** entre-temps **2** *adj (measure)* provisoire; *(post)* intérimaire

interior [ɪnˈtɪərɪə(r)] **1** *adj* intérieur; **i. decoration** décoration *f* (d'intérieurs) **2** *n* intérieur *m; Am Pol* **Department of the I.** ministère *m* de l'Intérieur

interjection [ɪntəˈdʒekʃən] *n* interjection *f*

interlock [ɪntəˈlɒk] *vi (of machine parts)* s'emboîter

interloper [ˈɪntələʊpə(r)] *n* intrus, -use *mf*

interlude ['ɪntəluːd] *n (on TV)* interlude *m; (in theatre)* intermède *m; (period of time)* intervalle *m*

intermarry [ɪntə'mærɪ] *(pt & pp -ied) vi* se marier *(au sein d'une même famille)* ▪ **intermarriage** *n (within a family)* mariage *m* consanguin; *(with member of another group)* mariage

intermediary [ɪntə'miːdɪərɪ] *(pl -ies) adj & n* intermédiaire *(mf)*

intermediate [ɪntə'miːdɪət] *adj* intermédiaire; *(course, student)* de niveau moyen

interminable [ɪn'tɜːmɪnəbəl] *adj* interminable

intermingle [ɪntə'mɪŋgəl] *vi* se mélanger

intermission [ɪntə'mɪʃən] *n* entracte *m*

intermittent [ɪntə'mɪtənt] *adj* intermittent ▪ **intermittently** *adv* par intermittence

intern 1 ['ɪntɜːn] *n Am Med* interne *mf* **2** [ɪn'tɜːn] *vt (imprison)* interner ▪ **in'ternment** *n Pol* internement *m*

internal [ɪn'tɜːnəl] *adj* interne; *(flight, policy)* intérieur; **i. combustion engine** moteur *m* à combustion interne; *Am* **the I. Revenue Service** ≃ le fisc ▪ **internally** *adv* intérieurement; **'not to be taken i.'** *(medicine)* 'à usage externe'

international [ɪntə'næʃənəl] **1** *adj* international **2** *n (match)* rencontre *f* internationale; *(player)* international *m* ▪ **internationally** *adv* **i. famous** mondialement connu; **i. recognized** reconnu dans le monde entier

Internet ['ɪntənet] *n Comptr* **the I.** l'Internet *m*; **on the I.** sur Internet; **I. access** accès *m* (à l')Internet; **I. service provider** fournisseur *m* d'accès Internet; **I. user** internaute *mf*

interplanetary [ɪntə'plænɪtərɪ] *adj* interplanétaire

interplay ['ɪntəpleɪ] *n* interaction *f (of or between* de)

interpret [ɪn'tɜːprɪt] **1** *vt* interpréter **2** *vi (translate for people)* faire l'interprète ▪ **interpre'tation** *n* interprétation *f* ▪ **interpreter** *n* interprète *mf*

interrelated [ɪntərɪ'leɪtɪd] *adj* lié ▪ **interrelation** *n* corrélation *f*

interrogate [ɪn'terəgeɪt] *vt* interroger ▪ **interro'gation** *n* interrogation *f; (by police)* interrogatoire *m* ▪ **interrogator** *n* interrogateur, -trice *mf*

interrogative [ɪntə'rɒgətɪv] *adj & n Grammar* interrogatif, -ive *(m)*

interrupt [ɪntə'rʌpt] **1** *vt* interrompre **2** *vi* **I'm sorry to i.** je suis désolé de vous interrompre ▪ **interruption** *n* interruption *f*

intersect [ɪntə'sekt] **1** *vt* couper **2** *vi* se couper ▪ **intersection** *n* intersection *f; (of roads)* croisement *m*

interspersed [ɪntə'spɜːst] *adj* **i. with sth** parsemé de qch; **weeks of work i. with visits to the theatre** des semaines de travail entrecoupées de sorties au théâtre

intertwine [ɪntə'twaɪn] **1** *vt* entrelacer **2** *vi* s'entrelacer

interval ['ɪntəvəl] *n* intervalle *m; Br (in theatre, cinema)* entracte *m; (time)* de temps à autre; *(space)* par intervalles; **at five-minute intervals** toutes les cinq minutes; **bright or sunny intervals** éclaircies *fpl*

intervene [ɪntə'viːn] *vi (of person)* intervenir *(in* dans); *(of event)* survenir; **ten years intervened** dix années s'écoulèrent; **if nothing intervenes** s'il n'arrive rien entre-temps ▪ **intervention** [-'venʃən] *n* intervention *f*

interview ['ɪntəvjuː] **1** *n* entretien *m (with* avec); *TV & Journ* interview *m ou f;* **to call sb for or to an i.** convoquer qn à un entretien; *TV & Journ* interviewer ▪ **interviewer** *n TV & Journ* intervieweur, -euse *mf; (for research, in canvassing)* enquêteur, -euse *mf*

intestine [ɪn'testɪn] *n* intestin *m*

intimate¹ ['ɪntɪmət] *adj* intime; *(friendship)* profond; *(knowledge)* approfondi ▪ **intimacy** *n* intimité *f* ▪ **intimately** *adv* intimement

intimate² ['ɪntɪmeɪt] *vt (hint at)* faire comprendre; *(make known)* signifier ▪ **inti'mation** *n (announcement)* annonce *f; (hint)* suggestion *f; (sign)* indication *f*

intimidate [ɪn'tɪmɪdeɪt] *vt* intimider ▪ **intimi'dation** *n* intimidation *f*

into ['ɪntuː, *unstressed* 'ɪntə] *prep* **(a)** dans; **to put sth i. sth** mettre qch dans qch; **to go i. a room** entrer dans une pièce; **to go i. detail** entrer dans les détails **(b)** en; **to translate i. French** traduire en français; **to change sb i. sth** changer qn en qch; **to break sth i. pieces** briser qch en morceaux; **to go i. town** aller en ville **(c)** *Math* **three i. six goes two** six divisé par trois fait deux **(d)** *Fam* **to be i. jazz** être branché jazz

intolerable [ɪn'tɒlərəbəl] *adj* intolérable **(that** que + *subjunctive)*

intolerance [ɪn'tɒlərəns] *n* intolérance *f* ▪ **intolerant** *adj* intolérant; **to be i. of sb** être intolérant à l'égard de qn; **to be i. of sth** ne pas tolérer qch

intonation [ɪntə'neɪʃən] *n* intonation *f*

intoxicate [ɪn'tɒksɪkeɪt] *vt* enivrer ▪ **intoxicated** *adj* ivre; *Fig* **to be i. with fame** être ivre de gloire ▪ **intoxi'cation** *n* ivresse *f*

intractable [ɪn'træktəbəl] *adj (person)* intraitable; *(problem)* épineux, -euse

Intranet ['ɪntrənet] *n Comptr* Intranet *m*

intransigent [ɪn'trænsɪdʒənt] *adj* intransigeant ▪ **intransigence** *n* intransigeance *f*

intransitive [ɪn'trænsɪtɪv] *adj Grammar* intransitif, -ive

intravenous [ɪntrə'viːnəs] *adj Med* intraveineux, -euse

in-tray ['ɪntreɪ] *n (in office)* bac *m* du courrier à traiter

intrepid [ɪn'trepɪd] *adj* intrépide

intricate ['ɪntrɪkət] *adj* compliqué ▪ **intricacy** (*pl* -**ies**) *n* complexité *f*

intrigue 1 [' ɪntriːg] *n* (*plot*) intrigue *f* 2 [ɪn'triːg] *vt* (*interest*) intriguer; **I'm intrigued to know...** je suis curieux de savoir... ▪ **intriguing** *adj* (*news, attitude*) curieux, -ieuse

intrinsic [ɪn'trɪnsɪk] *adj* intrinsèque ▪ **intrinsically** *adv* intrinsèquement

introduce [ɪntrə'djuːs] *vt* (*bring in, insert*) introduire (**into** dans); (*programme, subject*) présenter; **to i. sb (to sb)** présenter qn (à qn); **to i. oneself (to sb)** se présenter (à qn); **to i. sb to Dickens/geography** faire découvrir Dickens/la géographie à qn

introduction [ɪntrə'dʌkʃən] *n* introduction *f*; (*of person to person*) présentation *f*; **i. to computing** initiation *f* à l'informatique; **her i. to life abroad** son premier contact avec la vie à l'étranger

introductory [ɪntrə'dʌktərɪ] *adj* (*words, speech*) d'introduction; (*course*) d'initiation; **i. price** prix *m* de lancement

introspective [ɪntrə'spektɪv] *adj* introspectif, -ive ▪ **introspection** *n* introspection *f*

introvert ['ɪntrəvɜːt] *n* introverti, -ie *mf*

intrude [ɪn'truːd] *vi* (*of person*) déranger (**on sb** qn); **to i. on sb's time** abuser du temps de qn; **to i. on sb's privacy** s'immiscer dans la vie privée de qn ▪ **intruder** *n* intrus, -use *mf* ▪ **intrusion** *n* (*bother*) dérangement *m*; (*interference*) intrusion *f* (**into** dans); **forgive my i.** pardonnez-moi de vous avoir dérangé

intuition [ɪntjuː'ɪʃən] *n* intuition *f* ▪ **in'tuitive** *adj* intuitif, -ive

Inuit ['ɪnjuːɪt] 1 *adj* inuit *inv* 2 *n* Inuit *mf inv*

inundate ['ɪnʌndeɪt] *vt* inonder (**with** de); **inundated with work/letters** submergé de travail/lettres ▪ **inun'dation** *n* inondation *f*

invade [ɪn'veɪd] *vt* envahir; **to i. sb's privacy** s'immiscer dans la vie privée de qn ▪ **invader** *n* envahisseur, -euse *mf*

invalid[1] ['ɪnvəlɪd] *adj & n* malade (*mf*); (*disabled person*) infirme (*mf*)

invalid[2] [ɪn'vælɪd] *adj* (*ticket*) non valable ▪ **invalidate** *vt* (*ticket*) annuler; (*election, law*) invalider; (*theory*) infirmer

invaluable [ɪn'væljʊəbəl] *adj* inestimable

invariable [ɪn'veərɪəbəl] *adj* invariable ▪ **invariably** *adv* invariablement

invasion [ɪn'veɪʒən] *n* invasion *f*; **i. of sb's privacy** atteinte *f* à la vie privée de qn

invective [ɪn'vektɪv] *n* invectives *fpl*

inveigh [ɪn'veɪ] *vi Formal* **to i. against sb/sth** invectiver contre qn/qch

inveigle [ɪn'veɪɡəl] *vt* **to i. sb into doing sth** entortiller qn pour qu'il fasse qch

invent [ɪn'vent] *vt* inventer ▪ **invention** *n* invention *f*; (*creativity*) inventivité *f*

▪ **inventive** *adj* inventif, -ive ▪ **inventiveness** *n* inventivité *f* ▪ **inventor** *n* inventeur, -trice *mf*

inventory ['ɪnvəntərɪ] (*pl* -**ies**) *n* inventaire *m*

inverse [ɪn'vɜːs] *adj* inverse; **in i. proportion to sth** inversement proportionnel, -elle à qch

invert [ɪn'vɜːt] *vt* (*order*) intervertir; (*turn upside down*) renverser; *Br* **inverted commas** guillemets *mpl* ▪ **inversion** *n* interversion *f*; *Grammar & Anat* inversion *f*

invest [ɪn'vest] 1 *vt* (*money*) investir (**in** dans); (*time, effort*) consacrer (**in** à); **to i. sb with** (*right, power*) investir qn de 2 *vi* **to i. in** (*company*) investir dans; *Fig* (*car*) se payer ▪ **investment** *n* investissement *m* ▪ **investor** *n* (*in shares*) investisseur *m*

investigate [ɪn'vestɪɡeɪt] 1 *vt* (*examine*) examiner; (*crime*) enquêter sur 2 *vi Fam* **to go and i.** aller voir ce qui se passe ▪ **investi'gation** *n* examen *m*, étude *f*; (*inquiry by journalist, police*) enquête *f* (**of** or **into** sur) ▪ **investigator** *n* (*detective*) enquêteur, -euse *mf*; (*private*) détective *m*

investiture [ɪn'vestɪtʃə(r)] *n* investiture *f*

inveterate [ɪn'vetərət] *adj* invétéré

invidious [ɪn'vɪdɪəs] *adj* (*unfair*) injuste; (*unpleasant*) ingrat, pénible

invigilate [ɪn'vɪdʒɪleɪt] *vi Br* (*in school*) être de surveillance à un examen ▪ **invigilator** *n Br* surveillant, -ante *mf* (*à un examen*)

invigorate [ɪn'vɪɡəreɪt] *vt* revigorer ▪ **invigorating** *adj* vivifiant

invincible [ɪn'vɪnsəbəl] *adj* invincible

invisible [ɪn'vɪzəbəl] *adj* invisible; **i. ink** encre *f* sympathique

invite 1 [ɪn'vaɪt] *vt* inviter (**to do** à faire); (*ask for*) demander; (*criticism*) aller au devant de; **you're inviting trouble** tu cherches les ennuis; **to i. sb out** inviter qn (à sortir); **to i. sb over** inviter qn (à venir) 2 ['ɪnvaɪt] *n Fam* invit' *f* ▪ **invitation** [-və'teɪʃən] *n* invitation *f* ▪ **in'viting** *adj* (*prospect*) engageant; (*food*) appétissant

invoice ['ɪnvɔɪs] 1 *n* facture *f* 2 *vt* (*goods*) facturer; (*person*) envoyer la facture à

invoke [ɪn'vəʊk] *vt* invoquer

involuntary [ɪn'vɒləntərɪ] *adj* involontaire ▪ **involuntarily** *adv* involontairement

involve [ɪn'vɒlv] *vt* (*entail*) entraîner; **to i. sb in sth** impliquer qn dans qch; (*in project*) associer qn à qch; **the job involves going abroad** le poste nécessite des déplacements à l'étranger; **what does the job i.?** en quoi consiste le travail?

involved [ɪn'vɒlvd] *adj* (a) **to be i. in sth** (*crime, affair*) être impliqué dans qch; **to be i. in an accident** avoir un accident; **to be i. in teaching** être dans l'enseignement; **fifty people were i. in the project** cinquante personnes ont pris part au projet; **the police**

became i. la police est intervenue; **to get i. in a book** s'absorber dans un livre; **to be i. with sb** *(emotionally)* avoir une liaison avec qn; **I don't want to get i.** *(be a part of it)* je ne veux pas m'en mêler; *(emotionally)* je ne veux pas m'engager; **the factors i.** *(at stake)* les facteurs en jeu; **the person i.** *(concerned)* la personne en question; **to be directly i.** être directement concerné (**b**) *(complicated)* compliqué

involvement [ɪn'vɒlvmənt] *n* participation *f* (**in** à); *(commitment)* engagement *m* (**in** dans); **emotional i.** liaison *f*

invulnerable [ɪn'vʌlnərəbəl] *adj* invulnérable

inward ['ɪnwəd] **1** *adj & adv (movement, move)* vers l'intérieur **2** *adj (inner) (happiness)* intérieur; *(thoughts)* intime ▪ **inward-looking** *adj* replié sur soi-même ▪ **inwardly** *adv (laugh, curse)* intérieurement ▪ **inwards** *adv* vers l'intérieur

in-your-face [ɪnjə'feɪs] *adj (documentary, film)* sans fard; *(attitude)* agressif, -ive

iodine [*Br* 'aɪədiːn, *Am* 'aɪədaɪn] *n Chem* iode *m*; *(antiseptic)* teinture *f* d'iode

iota [aɪ'əʊtə] *n (of truth, guilt)* once *f*

IOU [aɪəʊ'juː] *(abbr* **I owe you)** *n* reconnaissance *f* de dette

IQ [aɪ'kjuː] *(abbr* **intelligence quotient)** *n* QI *m inv*

Iran [ɪ'rɑːn, ɪ'ræn] *n* l'Iran *m* ▪ **Iranian** [ɪ'reɪnɪən, *Am* ɪ'rɑːnɪən] **1** *adj* iranien, -ienne **2** *n* Iranien, -ienne *mf*

Iraq [ɪ'rɑːk] *n* l'Irak *m* ▪ **Iraqi 1** *adj* irakien, -ienne **2** *n* Irakien, -ienne *mf*

irascible [ɪ'ræsəbəl] *adj* irascible

irate [aɪ'reɪt] *adj* furieux, -ieuse

Ireland ['aɪələnd] *n* l'Irlande *f* ▪ **Irish** ['aɪərɪʃ] **1** *adj* irlandais **2** *n (language)* irlandais *m*; **the I.** *(people)* les Irlandais *mpl* ▪ **Irishman** *(pl* -men*)* *n* Irlandais *m* ▪ **Irishwoman** *(pl* -women*)* *n* Irlandaise *f*

iris ['aɪərɪs] *n (plant, of eye)* iris *m*

irk [ɜːk] *vt* agacer ▪ **irksome** *adj* agaçant

iron ['aɪən] **1** *n* fer *m*; *(for clothes)* fer à repasser; **i. and steel industry** sidérurgie *f*; **an i. will** volonté de fer; **the I. Curtain** le rideau de fer; *Br* **old i., scrap i.** ferraille *f* **2** *vt (clothes)* repasser; *Fig* **to i. out difficulties** aplanir les difficultés ▪ **ironing** *n* repassage *m*; **i. board** planche *f* à repasser

ironmonger ['aɪənmʌŋgə(r)] *n* quincaillier, -ière *mf*; **i.'s shop** quincaillerie *f* ▪ **ironmongery** *n* quincaillerie *f*

ironwork ['aɪənwɜːk] *n* ferronnerie *f*

irony ['aɪərənɪ] *n* ironie *f* ▪ **ironic(al)** [aɪ'rɒnɪk(əl)] *adj* ironique

irradiate [ɪ'reɪdɪeɪt] *vt (subject to radiation)* irradier; **irradiated food** aliments *mpl* irradiés

irrational [ɪ'ræʃənəl] *adj* irrationnel, -elle

irreconcilable [ɪrekən'saɪləbəl] *adj (people)* irréconciliable; *(views, laws)* inconciliable

irrefutable [ɪrɪ'fjuːtəbəl] *adj (evidence)* irréfutable

irregular [ɪ'regjʊlə(r)] *adj* irrégulier, -ière ▪ **irregularity** [-'lærɪtɪ] *(pl* -ies*)* *n* irrégularité *f*

irrelevant [ɪ'reləvənt] *adj* sans rapport (**to** avec); *(remark)* hors de propos; **that's i.** ça n'a rien à voir (avec la question) ▪ **irrelevance** *n* manque *m* de rapport

irreparable [ɪ'repərəbəl] *adj (harm, loss)* irréparable

irreplaceable [ɪrɪ'pleɪsəbəl] *adj* irremplaçable

irrepressible [ɪrɪ'presəbəl] *adj (laughter, urge)* irrépressible

irreproachable [ɪrɪ'prəʊtʃəbəl] *adj* irréprochable

irresistible [ɪrɪ'zɪstəbəl] *adj (person, charm)* irrésistible

irresolute [ɪ'rezəluːt] *adj* irrésolu, indécis

irrespective [ɪrɪ'spektɪv] *prep* **i. of** indépendamment de

irresponsible [ɪrɪ'spɒnsəbəl] *adj (act)* irréfléchi; *(person)* irresponsable ▪ **irresponsibly** *adv (behave)* de façon irresponsable

irretrievable [ɪrɪ'triːvəbəl] *adj (loss, mistake, situation)* irréparable

irreverent [ɪ'revərənt] *adj* irrévérencieux, -ieuse

irreversible [ɪrɪ'vɜːsəbəl] *adj (process)* irréversible; *(decision)* irrévocable

irrevocable [ɪ'revəkəbəl] *adj* irrévocable

irrigate ['ɪrɪgeɪt] *vt* irriguer ▪ **irri'gation** *n* irrigation *f*

irritable ['ɪrɪtəbəl] *adj (easily annoyed)* irritable

irritant ['ɪrɪtənt] *n (to eyes, skin)* irritant *m*

irritate ['ɪrɪteɪt] *vt (annoy, inflame)* irriter ▪ **irritating** *adj* irritant

irritation [ɪrɪ'teɪʃən] *n (anger, inflammation)* irritation *f*

IRS [aɪɑː'res] *(abbr* **Internal Revenue Service)** *n Am* ≃ le fisc

is [ɪz] *see* **be**

Islam ['ɪzlɑːm] *n* l'Islam *m* ▪ **Islamic** [ɪz'læmɪk] *adj* islamique

island ['aɪlənd] *n* île *f*; **(traffic) i.** refuge *m* (pour piétons) ▪ **islander** *n* insulaire *mf*

isle [aɪl] *n* île *f*; **the British Isles** les îles Britanniques

isn't ['ɪzənt] = **is not**

isolate ['aɪsəleɪt] *vt* isoler (**from** de) ▪ **isolated** *adj (remote, unique)* isolé ▪ **iso'lation** *n* isolement *m*; **in i.** isolément

ISP [aɪes'piː] *(abbr* **Internet Service Provider)** *n* Comptr fournisseur *m* d'accès Internet

Israel ['ɪzreɪl] *n* Israël *m* ▪ **Is'raeli 1** *adj* israélien, -ienne **2** *n* Israélien, -ienne *mf*

issue ['ɪʃuː] **1** *n (of newspaper, magazine)* numéro *m*; *(matter)* question *f*; *(of stamps, banknotes)* émission *f*; **at i.** *(at stake)* en cause;

to make an i. *or* a big i. of sth faire toute une affaire de qch; **to take i. with sb** exprimer son désaccord à qn **2** *vt (book)* publier; *(tickets)* distribuer; *(passport)* délivrer; *(order)* donner; *(warning)* lancer; *(stamps, banknotes)* émettre; *(supply)* fournir (**with** de; **to** à); **to i. a statement** faire une déclaration **3** *vi Formal* **to i. from** *(of smell, water)* se dégager de; *(of noise)* provenir de

> Note that the French word **issue** is a false friend and is never a translation for the English word **issue**. It means **exit**.

IT [aɪˈtiː] *(abbr* **information technology)** *n* informatique *f*

it [ɪt] *pron* (**a**) *(subject)* il, elle; *(object)* le, la, l'; **(to) it** *(indirect object)* lui; **it bites** *(dog)* il mord; **I've done it** je l'ai fait (**b**) *(impersonal)* il; **it's snowing** il neige; **it's hot** il fait chaud (**c**) *(non-specific)* ce, cela, ça; **it's good** c'est bon; **it was pleasant** c'était agréable; **who is it?** qui est-ce?; **that's it!** *(I agree)* c'est ça!; *(it's done)* ça y est!; **to consider it wise to do sth** juger prudent de faire qch; **it was Paul who...** c'est Paul qui...; **she's got it in her to succeed** elle est capable de réussir; **to have it in for sb** en vouloir à qn (**d**) **of it, from it, about it** en; **in it, to it, at it** y; **on it** dessus; **under it** dessous

italic [ɪˈtælɪk] *adj* italique ▪ **italics** *npl* italique *m*; **in i.** en italique

Italy [ˈɪtəlɪ] *n* l'Italie *f* ▪ **Italian 1** [ɪˈtælɪən] *adj* italien, -ienne **2** *n (person)* Italien, -ienne *mf*; *(language)* italien *m*

itch [ɪtʃ] **1** *n* démangeaison *f*; **to have an i. to do sth** brûler d'envie de faire qch **2** *vi (of person)* avoir des démangeaisons; **his arm itches** son bras le *ou* lui démange; *Fig* **to be itching to do sth** brûler d'envie de faire qch ▪ **itching** *n* démangeaisons *fpl* ▪ **itchy** *adj* **I have an i. hand** j'ai la main qui me démange; **I'm (all) i.** j'ai des démangeaisons

item [ˈaɪtəm] *n (in collection, on list, in newspaper)* article *m*; *(matter)* question *f*; *(on entertainment programme)* numéro *m*; **i. of clothing** vêtement *m*; **news i.** information *f* ▪ **itemize** *vt (invoice)* détailler

itinerant [aɪˈtɪnərənt] *adj (musician, actor)* ambulant; *(judge, preacher)* itinérant

itinerary [aɪˈtɪnərərɪ] *(pl* **-ies)** *n* itinéraire *m*

its [ɪts] *possessive adj* son, sa, *pl* ses ▪ **it'self** *pron* lui-même, elle-même; *(reflexive)* se, s'; **goodness i.** la bonté même; **by i.** tout seul

it's [ɪts] = **it is, it has**

IUD [aɪjuːˈdiː] *(abbr* **intrauterine device)** *n Med* stérilet *m*

I've [aɪv] = **I have**

IVF [aɪviːˈef] *(abbr* **in vitro fertilization)** *n* FIV *f*

ivory [ˈaɪvərɪ] *n* ivoire *m*; **i. statuette** statuette *f* en ivoire

ivy [ˈaɪvɪ] *n* lierre *m*

J, j [dʒeɪ] *n (letter)* J, j *m inv*

jab [dʒæb] **1** *n* coup *m; Br Fam (injection)* piqûre *f* **2** *(pt & pp* **-bb-)** *vt (knife, stick)* enfoncer (**into** dans); *(prick)* piquer (**with** du bout de)

jabber ['dʒæbə(r)] *Fam* **1** *vt* **to j. out** *(excuse)* marmonner **2** *vi* marmonner ▪ **jabbering** *n* bavardage *m*

jack [dʒæk] *n* **(a)** *(for vehicle)* cric *m* **(b)** *Cards* valet *m* **(c) j. of all trades** homme *m* à tout faire ▪ **jack-in-the-box** *n* diable *m* (à ressort)
▸ **jack in** *vt sep Br Fam (job)* plaquer
▸ **jack up** *vt sep (vehicle)* soulever *(avec un cric); Fig (price)* augmenter

jackal ['dʒækɔl] *n* chacal *m (pl* -als)

jackass ['dʒækæs] *n (animal, person)* âne *m*

jackdaw ['dʒækdɔː] *n* choucas *m*

jacket ['dʒækɪt] *n (coat)* veste *f; (of book)* jaquette *f; Br* **j. potato** pomme *f* de terre en robe des champs

jackknife ['dʒæknaɪf] **1** *(pl* -knives*) n* couteau *m* de poche **2** *vi Br (of truck)* se mettre en travers de la route

jackpot ['dʒækpɒt] *n* gros lot *m*

Jacuzzi® [dʒə'kuːzɪ] *n* Jacuzzi® *m*

jade [dʒeɪd] *n (stone)* jade *m*

jaded ['dʒeɪdɪd] *adj* blasé

jagged ['dʒægɪd] *adj* déchiqueté

jaguar [*Br* 'dʒægjʊə(r), *Am* 'dʒægwɑːr] *n* jaguar *m*

jail [dʒeɪl] **1** *n* prison *f* **2** *vt* emprisonner (**for** pour); **to j. sb for ten years** condamner qn à dix ans de prison; **to j. sb for life** condamner qn à perpétuité ▪ **jailer** *n* gardien, -ienne *mf* de prison

jalopy [dʒə'lɒpɪ] *(pl* -ies*) n Am Fam (car)* vieux tacot *m*

jam¹ [dʒæm] *n (preserve)* confiture *f;* **strawberry j.** confiture de fraises ▪ **jamjar** *n* pot *m* à confiture

jam² [dʒæm] **1** *n* **(traffic) j.** embouteillage *m; Fam* **in a j.** *(trouble)* dans le pétrin **2** *(pt & pp* **-mm-)** *vt (squeeze, make stuck)* coincer; *(gun)* enrayer; *(street, corridor)* encombrer; *(broadcast, radio station)* brouiller; **to j. sth into sth** entasser qch dans qch; **to j. people into a room** entasser des gens dans une pièce; **to j. a stick into sth** enfoncer un bâton dans qch; **to j. on the brakes** écraser la pédale de frein **3** *vi* **(a)** *(get stuck)* se coincer; *(of gun)* s'enrayer; *(of crowd)* s'entasser (**into** dans) **(b)**

(of musicians) improviser ▪ **jammed** *adj (machine)* coincé; *(street)* encombré ▪ **'jam-'packed** *adj Br Fam (hall, train)* bourré

Jamaica [dʒə'meɪkə] *n* la Jamaïque

jangle ['dʒæŋgəl] **1** *vi* cliquetis *m* **2** *vi* cliqueter

janitor ['dʒænɪtə(r)] *n Am & Scot (caretaker)* concierge *m*

January ['dʒænjʊərɪ] *n* janvier *m*

Japan [dʒə'pæn] *n* le Japon ▪ **Japanese** [dʒæpə'niːz] **1** *adj* japonais **2** *n (person)* Japonais, -aise *mf; (language)* japonais *m*

jar¹ [dʒɑː(r)] *n (container)* pot *m; (large, glass)* bocal *m*

jar² [dʒɑː(r)] **1** *n (jolt)* choc *m* **2** *(pt & pp* **-rr-)** *vt (shake)* ébranler **3** *vi (of noise)* grincer; *(of musical note)* détonner; *(of colours, words)* jurer (**with** avec); **it jars on my nerves** ça me tape sur les nerfs; **it jars on my ears** cela m'écorche les oreilles ▪ **jarring** *adj (noise, voice)* discordant

jargon ['dʒɑːgən] *n* jargon *m*

jasmine ['dʒæzmɪn] *n* jasmin *m*

jaundice ['dʒɔːndɪs] *n (illness)* jaunisse *f* ▪ **jaundiced** *adj (bitter)* aigri; **to take a j. view of sth** voir qch d'un mauvais œil

jaunt [dʒɔːnt] *n (journey)* balade *f*

jaunty ['dʒɔːntɪ] *(*-ier, -iest*) adj (carefree)* insouciant; *(cheerful, lively)* allègre; *(hat)* coquet, -ette ▪ **jauntily** *adv* avec insouciance; *(cheerfully)* allègrement

javelin ['dʒævlɪn] *n* javelot *m*

jaw [dʒɔː] **1** *n Anat* mâchoire *f; Fam* **to have a j.** tailler une bavette **2** *vi Fam (talk)* papoter

jay [dʒeɪ] *n* geai *m*

jaywalker ['dʒeɪwɔːkə(r)] *n* = piéton qui traverse en dehors des passages cloutés

jazz [dʒæz] **1** *n* jazz *m* **2** *vt Fam* **to j. sth up** *(clothes, room, style)* égayer qch; *(music)* jazzifier qch

JCB® [dʒeɪsiː'biː] *n Br* tractopelle *m* ou *f*

jealous ['dʒeləs] *adj* jaloux, -ouse (**of** de) ▪ **jealousy** *n* jalousie *f*

jeans [dʒiːnz] *npl* **(pair of) j.** jean *m*

Jeep® [dʒiːp] *n* Jeep® *f*

jeer [dʒɪə(r)] **1** *n* raillerie *f;* **jeers** *(boos)* huées *fpl* **2** *vt (boo)* huer; *(mock)* se moquer de **3** *vi* **to j. at sb/sth** *(boo)* huer qn/qch; *(mock)* se moquer de qn/qch ▪ **jeering 1** *adj* railleur, -euse **2** *n (mocking)* railleries *fpl; (of crowd)* huées *fpl*

jell [dʒel] *vi Fam (of ideas)* prendre tournure

jello® ['dʒeləʊ] *n Am (dessert)* gelée *f*

jelly ['dʒelɪ] *(pl* **-ies)** *n (preserve, dessert)* gelée *f*; **j. baby** = bonbon à base de gélatine, en forme de bébé ▪ **jellybean** *n* = bonbon recouvert de sucre, en forme de haricot ▪ **jellyfish** *n* méduse *f*

jeopardy ['dʒepədɪ] *n* danger *m*, péril *m* ▪ **jeopardize** *vt* mettre en danger

jerk¹ [dʒɜːk] **1** *n* secousse *f* **2** *vt (pull)* tirer brusquement; *(in order to move)* déplacer par à-coups **3** *vi* **to j. forward** *(of car)* faire un bond en avant

jerk² [dʒɜːk] *n Am Fam (person)* abruti, -ie *mf*

jerky ['dʒɜːkɪ] *(-ier, -iest) adj* **(a)** *(movement, voice)* saccadé **(b)** *Am Fam (stupid)* stupide, bête ▪ **jerkily** *adv* par saccades

Jersey ['dʒɜːzɪ] *n* Jersey *m ou f*

jersey ['dʒɜːzɪ] *(pl* **-eys)** *n (garment)* tricot *m*; *Football* maillot *m*; *(cloth)* jersey *m*

jest [dʒest] **1** *n* plaisanterie *f*; **in j.** pour rire **2** *vi* plaisanter ▪ **jester** *n Hist (court)* **j.** fou *m* (du roi)

Jesus ['dʒiːzəs] *n* Jésus *m*; **J. Christ** Jésus-Christ *m*

jet [dʒet] **1** *n* **(a)** *(plane)* avion *m* à réaction; **j. engine** réacteur *m*, moteur *m* à réaction; **j. lag** fatigue *f* due au décalage horaire; **j. ski** scooter *m* des mers, jet-ski *m* **(b)** *(steam, liquid)* jet *m* **2** *vi Fam* **to j. off** s'envoler **(to** pour)

jet-black ['dʒet'blæk] *adj* (noir) de jais

jetfoil ['dʒetfɔɪl] *n* hydroglisseur *m*

jet-lagged ['dʒetlægd] *adj Fam* qui souffre du décalage horaire

jettison ['dʒetɪsən] *vt (cargo from ship)* jeter à la mer; *(fuel from plane)* larguer; *Fig (plan, tradition)* abandonner

jetty ['dʒetɪ] *(pl* **-ies)** *n* jetée *f*; *(landing place)* embarcadère *m*

Jew [dʒuː] *n (man)* Juif *m*; *(woman)* Juive *f* ▪ **Jewish** *adj* juif *(f* juive)

jewel ['dʒuːəl] *n* bijou *m (pl* -oux); *(in watch)* rubis *m* ▪ **jewelled** *(Am* **jeweled)** *adj* orné de bijoux ▪ **jeweller** *(Am* **jeweler)** *n* bijoutier, -ière *mf* ▪ **jewellery** *(Am* **jewelry)** *n* bijoux *mpl*

jib [dʒɪb] *(pt & pp* **-bb-)** *vi* rechigner **(at** devant); **to j. at doing sth** rechigner à faire qch

jibe [dʒaɪb] *n & vi =* gibe

jiffy ['dʒɪfɪ] *n Fam* instant *m*

Jiffy bag® ['dʒɪfɪbæg] *n* enveloppe *f* matelassée

jig [dʒɪg] *n (dance, music)* gigue *f*

jigsaw ['dʒɪgsɔː] *n* **j. (puzzle)** puzzle *m*

jilt [dʒɪlt] *vt (lover)* laisser tomber

jingle ['dʒɪŋgəl] **1** *n* tintement *m*; *(in advertisement)* jingle *m* **2** *vt* faire tinter **3** *vi (of keys, bell)* tinter

jinx [dʒɪŋks] *n (person, object)* portemalheur *m inv*; *(spell, curse)* mauvais sort *m*

jitters ['dʒɪtəz] *npl Fam* **to have the j.** être à cran ▪ **jittery** *adj Fam* **to be j.** être à cran

job [dʒɒb] *n (employment, post)* travail *m*, emploi *m*; *(task)* tâche *f*; *Fam (crime)* coup *m*; *Fam* **to have a (hard) j. doing** *or* **to do sth** avoir du mal à faire qch; **to have the j. of doing sth** *(unpleasant task)* être obligé de faire qch; *(for a living)* être chargé de faire qch; *Br Fam* **it's a good j. (that)...** heureusement que... (+ *indicative)*; *Fam* **that's just the j.** c'est juste ce qu'il faut; **out of a j.** au chômage; **j. losses** suppressions *fpl* d'emplois; **j. offer** offre *f* d'emploi

jobcentre ['dʒɒbsentə(r)] *n Br* ≃ agence *f* nationale pour l'emploi

jobless ['dʒɒbləs] *adj* au chômage

jock [dʒɒk] *n Am Fam (sportsman)* sportif *m*

jockey ['dʒɒkɪ] **1** *(pl* **-eys)** *n* jockey *m* **2** *vi* **to j. for position** jouer des coudes

jockstrap ['dʒɒkstræp] *n* slip *m* à coquille

jocular ['dʒɒkjʊlə(r)] *adj* jovial

jog [dʒɒg] **1** *n (shake, jolt)* secousse *f*; *(nudge)* coup *m* de coude **2** *(pt & pp* **-gg-)** *vt (shake)* secouer; *(push)* pousser; *Fig (memory)* rafraîchir **3** *vi Sport* faire du jogging; **to go jogging** aller faire un jogging; **to j. along** *(of vehicle)* cahoter; *(of work)* aller tant bien que mal; *(of person)* faire son petit bonhomme de chemin ▪ **jogging** *n Sport* jogging *m*

john [dʒɒn] *n Am Fam* **the j.** *(lavatory)* le petit coin

join [dʒɔɪn] **1** *n* raccord *m* **2** *vt* **(a)** *(put together)* joindre; *(wires, pipes)* raccorder; *(words, towns)* relier; **to j. sth to sth** joindre qch à qch; *(link)* relier qch à qch; **to j. two things together** relier une chose à une autre; **to j. sb** *(catch up with, meet)* rejoindre qn; *(associate oneself with, go with)* se joindre à qn *(in doing* pour faire); **to j. the sea** *(of river)* rejoindre la mer; **to j. hands** se donner la main; **to j. forces** s'unir **(b)** *(become a member of)* s'inscrire à; *(army, police, company)* entrer dans; **to j. the queue** *or Am* **line** prendre la queue **3** *vi* **(a)** *(of roads, rivers)* se rejoindre; **to j. (together** *or* **up)** *(of objects)* se joindre **(with** à); **to j. in sth** prendre part à qch **(b)** *(become a member)* devenir membre; *Mil* **to j. up** s'engager

joiner ['dʒɔɪnə(r)] *n Br* menuisier *m*

joint [dʒɔɪnt] **1** *n* **(a)** *(in body)* articulation *f*; *Br (meat)* rôti *m*; *Tech* joint *m*; *(in carpentry)* assemblage *m*; **out of j.** *(shoulder)* déboîté **(b)** *Fam (nightclub)* boîte *f* **(c)** *Fam (cannabis cigarette)* joint *m* **2** *adj (decision)* commun; **j. account** compte *m* joint; **j. author** coauteur *m*; **j. efforts** efforts *mpl* conjugués ▪ **jointly** *adv* conjointement

joist [dʒɔɪst] *n* solive *f*

joke [dʒəʊk] **1** n plaisanterie f; (trick) tour m; **it's no j.** (it's unpleasant) ce n'est pas drôle (**doing** de faire) **2** vi plaisanter (**about** sur) ▪ **joker** n plaisantin m; Fam (fellow) type m; Cards joker m ▪ **jokingly** adv (say) en plaisantant

jolly[1] ['dʒɒlɪ] (**-ier, -iest**) adj (happy) gai; Fam (drunk) éméché

jolly[2] ['dʒɒlɪ] adv Br Fam (very) rudement; **j. good!** très bien!

> Note that the French word **joli** is a false friend and is never a translation for the English word **jolly**. It means **pretty**.

jolt [dʒɒlt] **1** n secousse f **2** vt (shake) secouer; **to j. sb into action** secouer les puces à qn **3** vi **to j. (along)** (of vehicle) cahoter

Jordan ['dʒɔːdən] n la Jordanie

jostle ['dʒɒsəl] **1** vt (push) bousculer; **don't j.!** ne bousculez pas! **2** vi (push each other) se bousculer (**for sth** pour obtenir qch)

jot [dʒɒt] (pt & pp **-tt-**) vt **to j. sth down** noter qch ▪ **jotter** n (notepad) bloc-notes m

journal ['dʒɜːnəl] n (periodical) revue f

journalism ['dʒɜːnəlɪzəm] n journalisme m ▪ **journalist** n journaliste mf

journey ['dʒɜːnɪ] **1** (pl **-eys**) n (trip) voyage m; (distance) trajet m; **to go on a j.** partir en voyage **2** vi voyager

> Note that the French word **journée** is a false friend and is never a translation for the English word **journey**. It means **day**.

jovial ['dʒəʊvɪəl] adj jovial

joy [dʒɔɪ] n joie f; **the joys of** (countryside, motherhood) les plaisirs mpl de ▪ **joyful, joyous** adj joyeux, -euse

joyride ['dʒɔɪraɪd] n = virée dans une voiture volée ▪ **joyrider** n = chauffard qui conduit une voiture volée

joystick ['dʒɔɪstɪk] n (of aircraft) manche m à balai; (for computer) manette f (de jeu)

JP [dʒeɪ'piː] abbr Br = **Justice of the Peace**

jubilant ['dʒuːbɪlənt] adj **to be j.** jubiler ▪ **jubilation** n jubilation f

jubilee ['dʒuːbɪliː] n **(golden) j.** jubilé m

Judaism ['dʒuːdeɪɪzəm] n judaïsme m

judder ['dʒʌdə(r)] **1** n vibration f **2** vi (shake) vibrer

judge [dʒʌdʒ] **1** n juge m **2** vti juger; **to j. sb by** or **on sth** juger qn sur ou d'après qch; **judging by...** à en juger par... ▪ **judg(e)ment** n jugement m ▪ **judg(e)mental** adj critique

judicial [dʒuː'dɪʃəl] adj judiciaire

judiciary [dʒuː'dɪʃərɪ] n magistrature f

judicious [dʒuː'dɪʃəs] adj judicieux, -ieuse

judo ['dʒuːdəʊ] n judo m

jug [dʒʌg] n cruche f; (for milk) pot m

juggernaut ['dʒʌgənɔːt] n Br (truck) poids m lourd

juggle ['dʒʌgəl] **1** vt jongler avec **2** vi jongler (**with** avec) ▪ **juggler** n jongleur, -euse mf ▪ **juggling** n jonglerie f

juice [dʒuːs] n jus m; (in stomach) suc m; **j. bar** = bar où l'on sert des jus de fruit; **j. extractor** centrifugeuse f ▪ **juicer** n (manual) presse-fruits m inv; (electric) centrifugeuse f ▪ **juicy** (**-ier, -iest**) adj (fruit) juteux, -euse; (meat) succulent; Fig (story) savoureux, -euse

jukebox ['dʒuːkbɒks] n juke-box m

July [dʒuː'laɪ] n juillet m

jumble ['dʒʌmbəl] **1** n (disorder) fouillis m; Br (unwanted articles) bric-à-brac m inv; Br **j. sale** (used clothes) vente f de charité **2** vt **to j. (up)** (objects, facts) mélanger

jumbo ['dʒʌmbəʊ] **1** adj (packet) géant **2** (pl **-os**) adj & n **j. (jet)** jumbo-jet (m)

jump [dʒʌmp] **1** n (leap) saut m; (start) sursaut m; (increase) hausse f soudaine; Br **j. leads** câbles mpl de démarrage; Am **j. rope** corde f à sauter

2 vt (ditch) sauter; **to j. the lights** (in car) griller un feu rouge; **to j. the rails** (of train) dérailler; Br **to j. the queue** passer avant son tour, resquiller; Am **to j. rope** sauter à la corde

3 vi sauter (**at** sur); (start) sursauter; (of price, heart) faire un bond; **to j. about** sautiller; **to j. across sth** traverser qch d'un bond; **to j. to conclusions** tirer des conclusions hâtives; **to j. in** or **on** (train, vehicle, bus) sauter dans; **j. in** or **on!** montez!; **to j. off** or **out** sauter; (from bus) descendre; **to j. off sth, to j. out of sth** sauter de qch; **to j. out of the window** sauter par la fenêtre; **to j. up** se lever d'un bond ▪ **jumpy** ['dʒʌmpɪ] (**-ier, -iest**) adj nerveux, -euse

jumper ['dʒʌmpə(r)] n Br pull(-over) m; Am (dress) robe f chasuble; Am **j. cables** câbles mpl de démarrage

junction ['dʒʌŋkʃən] n (crossroads) carrefour m; (joining) jonction f; **j. 23** Br (on motorway) (exit) la sortie 23; (entrance) l'entrée f 23

juncture ['dʒʌŋktʃə(r)] n Formal **at this j.** à ce moment-là

June [dʒuːn] n juin m

jungle ['dʒʌŋgəl] n jungle f

junior ['dʒuːnɪə(r)] **1** adj (younger) plus jeune; (in rank, status) subalterne; (teacher, doctor) jeune; **to be sb's j., to be j. to sb** être plus jeune que qn; (in rank, status) être au-dessous de qn; **Smith j.** Smith fils; Br **j. school** école f primaire (entre 7 et 11 ans); Am **j. high (school)** ≃ collège m d'enseignement secondaire **2** n cadet, -ette mf; (in school) petit, -ite mf; Sport junior mf, cadet, -ette mf; **he's three years my j.** il a trois ans de moins que moi

junk [dʒʌŋk] **1** n (unwanted objects) bric-à-brac m inv; (inferior goods) camelote f; (bad film, book) navet m; (nonsense) idioties fpl; **j. food** malbouffe f; **j. mail** prospectus mpl; **j. shop**

boutique *f* de brocanteur **2** *vt Fam (get rid of)* balancer ▪**junkyard** *n* dépôt *m* de ferrailleur

junkie ['dʒʌŋkɪ] *n Fam* drogué, -ée *mf*

jurisdiction [dʒʊərɪs'dɪkʃən] *n* juridiction *f*; **to be within the j. of** être sous la juridiction de

jury ['dʒʊərɪ] (*pl* **-ies**) *n (in competition, court)* jury *m* ▪**juror** *n (in court)* juré *m*

just [dʒʌst] **1** *adv (exactly, slightly)* juste; *(only)* juste, seulement; *(simply)* (tout) simplement; **j. before/after** juste avant/après; **it's j. as I thought** c'est bien ce que je pensais; **j. at that time** à cet instant même; **she has/had j. left** elle vient/venait de partir; **I've j. come from…** j'arrive de…; **I'm j. coming!** j'arrive!; **he'll (only) j. catch the bus** il aura son bus de justesse; **he j. missed it** il l'a manqué de peu; **j. as big/light** tout aussi grand/léger (**as** que); **j. listen!** écoute donc!; **j. a moment!** un instant!; **j. over ten** un peu plus de dix; **j. one** un(e) seul(e) (**of** de); **j. about** *(approximately)* à peu près; *(almost)* presque; **to be j. about to do sth** être sur le point de faire qch **2** *adj (fair)* juste (**to** envers) ▪**justly** *adv (fairly)* avec justice; *(deservedly)* à juste titre

justice ['dʒʌstɪs] *n* justice *f*; *(judge)* juge *m*; **to do j. to a meal** faire honneur à un repas; **it doesn't do you j.** *(hat, photo)* cela ne vous avantage pas; *(attitude)* cela ne vous fait pas honneur; **J. of the Peace** juge *m* de paix

justify ['dʒʌstɪfaɪ] (*pt & pp* **-ied**) *vt* justifier; **to be justified in doing sth** *(have right)* être en droit de faire qch; *(have reason)* être fondé à faire qch; *Typ & Comptr* **left/right justified** justifié à gauche/à droite ▪**justifiable** *adj* justifiable ▪**justifiably** *adv* à juste titre ▪**justification** [-fɪ'keɪʃən] *n* justification *f*

jut [dʒʌt] (*pt & pp* **-tt-**) *vi* **to j. out** faire saillie; **to j. out over sth** *(overhang)* surplomber qch

jute [dʒuːt] *n* jute *m*

juvenile ['dʒuːvənaɪl, *Am* -ənəl] **1** *n Law* mineur, -eure *mf* **2** *adj (court, book)* pour enfants; *Pej (behaviour)* puéril; **j. delinquent** jeune délinquant, -ante *mf*

juxtapose [dʒʌkstə'pəʊz] *vt* juxtaposer ▪**juxtaposition** [-pə'zɪʃən] *n* juxtaposition *f*

K, k [keɪ] *n (letter)* K, k *m inv*

kaleidoscope [kə'laɪdəskəʊp] *n* kaléidoscope *m*

kangaroo [kæŋgə'ruː] *n* kangourou *m*

kaput [kə'pʊt] *adj Fam* kaput *inv*

karaoke [kærɪ'əʊkɪ] *n* karaoké *m*

karat [karət] *n Am* = **carat**

karate [kə'rɑːtɪ] *n Sport* karaté *m*

kebab [kə'bæb] *n* brochette *f*; **doner k.** sandwich *m* grec; **shish k.** chiche-kébab *m*

keel [kiːl] **1** *n (of boat)* quille *f* **2** *vi* **to k. over** *(of boat)* chavirer

keen [kiːn] *adj* (**a**) *Br (eager, enthusiastic)* plein d'enthousiasme; **he's a k. sportsman** c'est un passionné de sport; **to be k. on sth** *(music, sport)* être passionné de qch; **he is k. on her/ the idea** elle/l'idée lui plaît beaucoup; **to be k. on doing sth** *(habitually)* adorer faire qch; *(want to do)* avoir très envie de faire qch (**b**) **to be k. to do sth** avoir très envie de faire qch (**b**) *(edge, appetite)* aiguisé; *(interest, feeling)* vif *(f* vive); *(mind)* pénétrant; *(wind)* glacial; **to have k. eyesight** avoir la vue perçante ▪ **keenly** *adv Br (work)* avec enthousiasme; *(feel, interest)* vivement

keep [kiːp] **1** *(pt & pp kept) vt* garder; *(shop, car)* avoir; *(diary, promise)* tenir; *(family)* entretenir; *(rule)* respecter; *(feast day)* célébrer; *(birthday)* fêter; *(delay, detain)* retenir; *(put)* mettre; **to k. doing sth** continuer à faire qch; **to k. sth clean** garder qch propre; **to k. sth from sb** dissimuler qch à qn; **to k. sb from doing sth** empêcher qn de faire qch; **to k. sb waiting/ working** faire attendre/travailler qn; **to k. sth going** *(engine, machine)* laisser qch en marche; **to k. sb in whisky** fournir qn en whisky; **to k. an appointment** se rendre à un rendez-vous

2 *vi (remain)* rester; *(continue)* continuer; *(of food)* se conserver; **how is he keeping?** comment va-t-il?; **to k. still** rester immobile; **to k. quiet** se tenir tranquille; **to k. left** tenir sa gauche; **to k. from doing sth** s'abstenir de faire qch; **to k. going** continuer à faire qch; **to k. at it** *(keep doing it)* persévérer

3 *n (food)* subsistance *f*; **to have one's k.** être logé et nourri; *Fam* **for keeps** pour toujours

▸ **keep away 1** *vt (person)* éloigner (**from** de) **2** *vi* ne pas s'approcher (**from** de)

▸ **keep back 1** *vt sep (crowd)* contenir; *(delay, withhold)* retarder; *(hide)* cacher (**from** à) **2** *vi* ne pas s'approcher (**from** de)

▸ **keep down** *vt sep (restrict)* limiter; *(control)* maîtriser; *(price, costs)* maintenir bas

▸ **keep in** *vt sep* empêcher de sortir; *(as punishment in school)* garder en retenue

▸ **keep off 1** *vt sep (person)* éloigner; **k. your hands off!** n'y touche pas! **2** *vt insep* **'k. off the grass'** 'défense de marcher sur les pelouses' **3** *vi (not go near)* ne pas s'approcher; **if the rain keeps off** s'il ne pleut pas

▸ **keep on 1** *vt sep (hat, employee)* garder; **to k. on doing sth** continuer à faire qch **2** *vi* **to k. on at sb** harceler qn

▸ **keep out 1** *vt sep* empêcher d'entrer **2** *vi* rester en dehors (**of** de)

▸ **keep to 1** *vt insep (subject, path)* ne pas s'écarter de; *(room)* garder **2** *vi* **to k. to the left** tenir la gauche; **to k. to oneself** rester à l'écart

▸ **keep up 1** *vt sep (continue, maintain)* continuer (**doing** à faire); *(keep awake)* empêcher de dormir; **to k. up appearances** sauver les apparences **2** *vi (continue)* continuer; *(follow)* suivre; **to k. up with sb** *(follow)* aller à la même allure que qn; *(in quality of work)* se maintenir à la hauteur de qn

keeper ['kiːpə(r)] *n (in park, zoo)* & *Football* gardien, -ienne *mf*

keeping ['kiːpɪŋ] *n* **in k. with** conformément à; **to have sth in one's k.** avoir qch sous sa garde

keepsake ['kiːpseɪk] *n* souvenir *m*

keg [keg] *n* baril *m*

kennel ['kenəl] *n Br* niche *f*; *(for boarding dogs)* chenil *m*; *Br* **kennels** chenil *m*

Kenya ['kiːnjə, 'kenjə] *n* le Kenya ▪ **Kenyan 1** *adj* kenyan **2** *n* Kenyan, -ane *mf*

kept [kept] **1** *pt & pp of* **keep 2** *adj* **well** *or* **nicely k.** *(house)* bien tenu

kerb [kɜːb] *n Br* bord *m* du trottoir

kernel ['kɜːnəl] *n (of nut)* amande *f*

kerosene ['kerəsiːn] *n Am (paraffin)* pétrole *m* (lampant); *(aviation fuel)* kérosène *m*

ketchup ['ketʃəp] *n* ketchup *m*

kettle ['ketəl] *n* bouilloire *f*; **the k. is boiling** l'eau bout; **to put the k. on** mettre l'eau à chauffer

key [kiː] **1** *n* clef *f*, clé *f*; *(of piano, typewriter, computer)* touche *f* **2** *adj (industry, post)* clef *f* *inv*, clé f *inv*; **k. person** pivot *m*; *Br Sch* **k. stage** étape f clé de la scolarité **3** *vt* **to k. in** *(data)* saisir ▪**keyboard 1** *n (of piano, computer)* clavier *m*; **k. operator** opérateur, -trice *mf* de saisie **2** *vt (data)* faire la saisie de ▪**keyhole** *n* trou *m* de serrure ▪**keynote** *n (of speech)* point *m* essentiel; **k. speech** discours *m* introductif ▪**keyring** *n* porte-clefs *m inv* ▪**keystone** *n (of policy)* & *Archit* clef f de voûte

keyed [kiːd] *adj* **to be k. up** être surexcité

khaki [ˈkɑːkɪ] *adj* & *n* kaki *(m) inv*

kibbutz [kɪˈbʊts] *(pl* **kibbutzim** [kɪbʊtˈsiːm]*) n* kibboutz *m*

kick [kɪk] **1** *n* coup *m* de pied; *(of horse)* ruade f; *Fam* **to get a k. out of doing sth** prendre son pied à faire qch; *Fam* **for kicks** pour le plaisir; **k. boxing** boxe f française **2** *vt* donner un coup de pied/des coups de pied à; *(of horse)* lancer une ruade à **3** *vi* donner des coups de pied; *(of horse)* ruer ▪**kickback** *n Fam (bribe)* pot-de-vin *m* ▪**kickoff** *n Football* coup *m* d'envoi

▸**kick back** *vt sep (ball)* renvoyer (du pied)

▸**kick down, kick in** *vt sep (door)* démolir à coups de pied

▸**kick off** *vi Football* donner le coup d'envoi; *Fam (start)* démarrer

▸**kick out** *vt sep Fam (throw out)* flanquer dehors

▸**kick up** *vt sep Br Fam* **to k. up a fuss/row** faire des histoires/du vacarme

kid [kɪd] **1** *n* **(a)** *Fam (child)* gosse *mf*; *Am Fam* **my k. brother** mon petit frère **(b)** *(goat)* chevreau *m* **2** *(pt & pp* **-dd-***) vti Fam (joke, tease)* faire marcher; **to k. oneself** se faire des illusions; **to be kidding** plaisanter; **no kidding!** sans blague!

kidnap [ˈkɪdnæp] *(pt & pp* **-pp-***) vt* kidnapper ▪**kidnapper** *n* ravisseur, -euse *mf* ▪**kidnapping** *n* enlèvement *m*

kidney [ˈkɪdnɪ] *(pl* **-eys***) n* rein *m*; *(as food)* rognon *m*; **on a k. machine** sous rein artificiel; **k. failure** insuffisance f rénale; **k. bean** haricot *m* rouge

kill [kɪl] **1** *n* mise f à mort; *(prey)* tableau *m* de chasse **2** *vt (person, animal, plant)* tuer; *Fig (rumour)* étouffer; *Fam (engine)* arrêter; **to k. oneself** se tuer; *Fam* **my feet are killing me** j'ai les pieds en compote; *Journ* **to k. a story** retirer une information; **to k. time** tuer le temps; **to k. off** *(bacteria)* & *Fig* détruire **3** *vi* tuer; *Fam* **I'd k. for a beer** je me damnerais pour une bière ▪**killer** *n* tueur *m*, tueuse f; *Fam (difficult question)* colle f; *Fam (joke)* **this one's a k.** celle-là est à mourir de rire; *Fam (tiring experience)* **that walk was a k.!** cette promenade était vraiment crevante ▪**killing 1** *n (of person)* meurtre *m*; *(of group)* massacre

m; *(of animal)* mise f à mort; **to make a k.** *(financially)* faire un bénéfice énorme **2** *adj Fam (tiring)* tuant; *(amusing)* tordant

killjoy [ˈkɪldʒɔɪ] *n* rabat-joie *m inv*

kiln [kɪln] *n* four *m*

kilo [ˈkiːləʊ] *(pl* **-os***) n* kilo *m* ▪**kilogram(me)** [ˈkɪləʊɡræm] *n* kilogramme *m*

kilobyte [ˈkɪləbaɪt] *n Comptr* kilo-octet *m*

kilometre [kɪˈlɒmɪtə(r)] *(Am* **kilometer***) n* kilomètre *m*

kilowatt [ˈkɪləʊwɒt] *n* kilowatt *m*

kilt [kɪlt] *n* kilt *m*

kimono [kɪˈməʊnəʊ] *(pl* **-os***) n* kimono *m*

kin [kɪn] *n Formal (relatives)* parents *mpl*; **one's next of k.** son plus proche parent

kind[1] [kaɪnd] *n (sort, type)* genre *m*, espèce f *(of* de); **to pay in k.** payer en nature; **what k. of drink is it?** qu'est-ce que c'est comme boisson?; **that's the k. of man he is** il est comme ça; **nothing of the k.!** absolument pas!; *Fam* **k. of worried/sad** plutôt inquiet, -iète/triste; **in a k. of way** d'une certaine façon; **it's the only one of its k., it's one of a k.** c'est unique en son genre; **we are two of a k.** nous nous ressemblons

kind[2] [kaɪnd] *(-er, -est) adj (helpful, pleasant)* gentil, -ille *(to* avec); **that's k. of you** c'est gentil de votre part; **would you be so k. as to…?** auriez-vous la bonté de…? ▪**kind-'hearted** *adj* qui a bon cœur

kindergarten [ˈkɪndəɡɑːtən] *n* jardin *m* d'enfants

kindle [ˈkɪndəl] **1** *vt* allumer **2** *vi* s'allumer

kindly [ˈkaɪndlɪ] *adv* gentiment; **k. wait** ayez la bonté d'attendre; **not to take k. to sth** ne pas apprécier qch **2** *adj (person)* bienveillant

kindness [ˈkaɪndnɪs] *n* gentillesse f

kindred [ˈkɪndrɪd] *adj* du même genre, de la même nature; **k. spirits** âmes *fpl* sœurs

king [kɪŋ] *n* roi *m* ▪**king-size(d)** *adj (pack)* géant; *(bed)* grand format; *(cigarette)* long *(f* longue)

kingdom [ˈkɪŋdəm] *n* royaume *m*; **animal/plant k.** règne *m* animal/végétal

kingfisher [ˈkɪŋfɪʃə(r)] *n* martin-pêcheur *m*

kink [kɪŋk] *n (in rope)* boucle f

kinky [ˈkɪŋkɪ] *(-ier, -iest) adj (person)* qui a des goûts bizarres; *(clothes, tastes)* bizarre

kinship [ˈkɪnʃɪp] *n* parenté f

kiosk [ˈkiːɒsk] *n* kiosque *m*; *Br* **(telephone) k.** cabine f téléphonique

kip [kɪp] *(pt & pp* **-pp-***) Br Fam* **1** *n (sleep)* **to have a k.** piquer un roupillon; **to get some k.** roupiller **2** *vi (sleep)* roupiller

kipper [ˈkɪpə(r)] *n* hareng *m* salé et fumé

kiss [kɪs] **1** *n* baiser *m*; **the k. of life** *(in first aid)* le bouche-à-bouche **2** *vt (person)* embrasser; **to k. sb's hand** baiser la main de qn; **to k. sb goodbye** dire au revoir à qn en l'embrassant **3** *vi* s'embrasser

kit [kɪt] **1** n équipement m, matériel m; (set of articles) trousse f; Br (belongings) affaires fpl; Br (sports clothes) tenue f; **first-aid k.** trousse de pharmacie; **tool k.** trousse à outils; **(do-it-yourself) k.** kit m; **model aircraft k.** maquette f d'avion; **in k. form** en kit **2** (pt & pp -tt-) vt Br **to k. sb out** équiper qn (**with** de) ▪ **kitbag** n sac m de marin; Mil sac à paquetage

kitchen [ˈkɪtʃɪn] n cuisine f; **k. cabinet** buffet m de cuisine; **k. garden** jardin m potager; **k. sink** évier m; **k. units** éléments mpl de cuisine ▪ **kitche'nette** n coin-cuisine m ▪ **kitchenware** n ustensiles mpl de cuisine; (dishes) vaisselle f de cuisine

kite [kaɪt] n (toy) cerf-volant m

kith [kɪθ] n **k. and kin** parents mpl et amis mpl

kitten [ˈkɪtən] n chaton m

kitty [ˈkɪtɪ] (pl -ies) n (a) Fam (cat) minou m (b) (fund) cagnotte f

kiwi [ˈkiːwiː] n (bird, fruit) kiwi m

km (abbr **kilometre**) km

knack [næk] n (skill) talent m; **to have the k. of doing sth** avoir le don de faire qch

knackered [ˈnækəd] adj Br Fam (tired) crevé ▪ **knackering** adj Br Fam crevant

knapsack [ˈnæpsæk] n sac m à dos

knead [niːd] vt (dough) pétrir

knee [niː] n genou m; **to go down on one's knees** s'agenouiller; **k. pad** genouillère f ▪ **kneecap** n rotule f ▪ **'knee-'deep** adj (in water, snow) jusqu'aux genoux ▪ **'knee-'high** adj jusqu'aux genoux ▪ **knees-up** n Br Fam (party) soirée f

kneel [niːl] (pt & pp **knelt** or **kneeled**) vi **to k. (down)** s'agenouiller (**before** devant); **to be kneeling (down)** être à genoux

knell [nel] n Literary glas m

knelt [nelt] pt & pp of **kneel**

knew [n(j)uː] pt of **know**

knickers [ˈnɪkəz] npl Br (underwear) culotte f (de femme)

knick-knack [ˈnɪknæk] n Fam babiole f

knife [naɪf] **1** (pl **knives**) n couteau m; (penknife) canif m **2** vt poignarder

knight [naɪt] **1** n chevalier m; Chess cavalier m **2** vt Br **to be knighted** être fait chevalier ▪ **knighthood** n titre m de chevalier

knit [nɪt] (pt & pp -tt-) **1** vt tricoter; **to k. one's brow** froncer les sourcils **2** vi tricoter; **to k. (together)** (of bones) se ressouder ▪ **knitting** n (activity, material) tricot m; **k. needle** aiguille f à tricoter ▪ **knitwear** n lainages mpl

knob [nɒb] n (on door) poignée f; (on cane) pommeau m; (on radio) bouton m; **k. of butter** noix f de beurre

knock [nɒk] **1** n (blow) coup m; **there's a k. at the door** on frappe à la porte; **I heard a k.** j'ai entendu frapper **2** vt (strike) frapper; (collide with) heurter; Fam (criticize) critiquer; **to k.**

one's head on sth se cogner la tête contre qch; **to k. sb senseless** assommer qn; **to k. sb to the ground** faire tomber qn en le frappant **3** vi (strike) frapper; **to k. against** or **into sth** heurter qch ▪ **knockdown** adj Br **k. price** prix m imbattable ▪ **'knock-'kneed** adj cagneux, -euse ▪ **knockout** n Boxing knock-out m inv; Fam **to be a k.** (of person, film) être formidable

▸ **knock about 1** vt sep (ill-treat) malmener **2** vi Fam (travel) bourlinguer; Fam (lie around, stand around) traîner

▸ **knock back** vt sep Br Fam (drink, glass) s'envoyer (derrière la cravate)

▸ **knock down** vt sep (object, pedestrian) renverser; (house, tree, wall) abattre; (price) baisser

▸ **knock in** vt sep (nail) enfoncer

▸ **knock off 1** vt sep (person, object) faire tomber (**from** de); Fam (do quickly) expédier; Br Fam (steal) piquer; **to k. £5 off (the price)** baisser le prix de 5 livres **2** vi Fam (stop work) s'arrêter de travailler

▸ **knock out** vt sep (make unconscious) assommer; Boxing mettre K.-O.; (beat in competition) éliminer; Fam **to k. oneself out** s'esquinter (**doing** à faire)

▸ **knock over** vt sep (pedestrian, object) renverser

▸ **knock up** vt sep Br Fam (meal) préparer en vitesse

knocker [ˈnɒkə(r)] n (for door) marteau m

knot [nɒt] **1** n (a) (in rope, hair) nœud m; **to tie a k.** faire un nœud; Fig **to tie the k.** se marier (b) Naut (unit of speed) nœud m **2** (pt & pp -tt-) vt nouer ▪ **knotty** (-ier, -iest) adj (rope, hair) plein de nœuds; (wood) noueux, -euse; Fig (problem) épineux, -euse

know [nəʊ] **1** n Fam **to be in the k.** être au courant **2** (pt **knew**, pp **known**) vt (facts, language) savoir; (person, place) connaître; (recognize) reconnaître (**by** à); **to k. that...** savoir que...; **to k. how to do sth** savoir faire qch; **for all I k.** que je sache; **I'll let you k.** je vous le ferai savoir; **I'll have you k. that...** sachez que...; **to k. (a lot) about** (person, event) en savoir long sur; **to k. (a lot) about cars/sewing** s'y connaître en voitures/couture; **I've never known him to complain** je ne l'ai jamais vu se plaindre; **to get to k. (about) sth** apprendre qch; **to get to k. sb** apprendre à connaître qn **3** vi savoir; **I k.** je (le) sais; **I wouldn't k., I k. nothing about it** je n'en sais rien; **to k. about sth** être au courant de qch; **to k. of** (have heard of) avoir entendu parler de; **do you k. of a good dentist?** connais-tu un bon dentiste?; **you (should) k. better than to do that** tu es trop intelligent pour faire ça; **you should have known better** tu aurais dû réfléchir ▪ **know-**

all *n Fam Pej* je-sais-tout *mf inv* ▪ **know-how** *n Fam* savoir-faire *m inv* ▪ **knowing** *adj (smile, look)* entendu ▪ **knowingly** *adv (consciously)* sciemment ▪ **know-it-all** *n Fam Pej* je-sais-tout *mf inv* ▪ **known** *adj* connu; **a k. expert** un expert reconnu; **she is k. to be…** on sait qu'elle est…

knowledge ['nɒlɪdʒ] *n (of fact)* connaissance *f*; *(learning)* connaissances *fpl*, savoir *m*; **to (the best of) my k.** à ma connaissance; **without sb's k.** à l'insu de qn; **to have no k. of sth** ignorer qch; **general k.** culture *f* générale ▪ **knowledgeable** *adj* savant; **to be k. about sth** bien s'y connaître en qch

known [nəʊn] *pp of* **know**

knuckle ['nʌkəl] *n* articulation *f* (du doigt)
▶ **knuckle down** *vi Fam* se mettre au boulot; **to k. down to sth** se mettre à qch

Koran [kə'rɑːn] *n* **the K.** le Coran

Korea [kə'rɪə] *n* la Corée ▪ **Korean 1** *adj* coréen, -éenne **2** *n (person)* Coréen, -éenne *mf*; *(language)* coréen *m*

kosher ['kəʊʃə(r)] *adj Rel (food)* kasher *inv*; *Fam (legitimate)* réglo

kowtow [kaʊ'taʊ] *vi* **to k. to sb** faire des courbettes devant qn

kudos ['kjuːdɒs] *n (glory)* gloire *f*; *(prestige)* prestige *m*

Kuwait [kʊ'weɪt] *n* le Koweït ▪ **Kuwaiti 1** *adj* koweïtien, -ienne **2** *n* Koweïtien, -ienne *mf*

L, l [el] *n* (*letter*) L, l *m inv*; *Br* **L-plate** = plaque apposée sur une voiture pour signaler que le conducteur est en conduite accompagnée

lab [læb] *n Fam* labo *m* ▪ **laboratory** [*Br* ləˈbɒrətərɪ, *Am* ˈlæbrətɔːrɪ] *n* laboratoire *m*; **l. assistant** laborantin, -ine *mf*

label [ˈleɪbəl] **1** *n* étiquette *f*; (*of record company*) label *m* **2** (*Br* **-ll-**, *Am* **-l-**) *vt* étiqueter; *Fig (person)* cataloguer; *Fig* **to l. sb as a liar** qualifier qn de menteur

laborious [ləˈbɔːrɪəs] *adj* laborieux, -ieuse

labour [ˈleɪbə(r)] (*Am* **labor**) **1** *n* (*work*) travail *m*; (*workers*) main-d'œuvre *f*; *Br* **L.** (*political party*) le parti travailliste; **in l.** (*woman*) en train d'accoucher **2** *adj* (*market*) du travail; (*relations*) ouvriers-patronat *inv*; **l. dispute** conflit *m* social; **l. force** effectifs *mpl*; *Am* **l. union** syndicat *m*; **l. unrest** agitation *f* ouvrière **3** *vt* **to l. a point** insister sur un point **4** *vi* (*toil*) peiner (**over** sur) ▪ **laboured** (*Am* **labored**) *adj* (*style*) laborieux, -ieuse ▪ **labourer** (*Am* **laborer**) *n* (*on roads*) manœuvre *m*; (*on farm*) ouvrier *m* agricole

labyrinth [ˈlæbərɪnθ] *n* labyrinthe *m*

lace [leɪs] **1** *n* (**a**) (*cloth*) dentelle *f* (**b**) (*of shoe*) lacet *m* **2** *vt* (**a**) **to l.** (**up**) (*tie up*) lacer (**b**) (*drink*) additionner (**with** de)

lacerate [ˈlæsəreɪt] *vt* lacérer ▪ **laceration** *n* lacération *f*

lack [læk] **1** *n* manque *m* (**of** de); **for l. of sth** à défaut de qch **2** *vt* manquer de **3** *vi* **to be lacking** manquer (**in** de); **they l. for nothing** ils ne manquent de rien

lackey [ˈlækɪ] (*pl* **-eys**) *n Pej* laquais *m*

lacklustre [ˈlæklʌstə(r)] (*Am* **lackluster**) *adj* terne

laconic [ləˈkɒnɪk] *adj* laconique ▪ **laconically** *adv* laconiquement

lacquer [ˈlækə(r)] **1** *n* laque *f* **2** *vt* laquer

lad [læd] *n Fam* (*young man*) jeune gars *m*; (*child*) garçon *m*; **when I was a l.** quand j'étais gamin; **come on lads!** allez les mecs!

ladder [ˈlædə(r)] **1** *n* échelle *f*; *Br* (*in tights*) maille *f* filée **2** *vti Br* filer

laden [ˈleɪdən] *adj* chargé (**with** de)

ladle [ˈleɪdəl] *n* louche *f*
▸ **ladle out** *vt sep* (*soup*) servir (avec une louche)

lady [ˈleɪdɪ] (*pl* **-ies**) *n* dame *f*; **a young l.** jeune fille; (*married*) une jeune dame; **the l. of the house** la maîtresse de maison; **Ladies and Gentlemen!** Mesdames, Mesdemoiselles, Messieurs!; **l. friend** amie *f*; **ladies' night** (*in bar*) = soirée où les femmes ont droit à des réductions; **the ladies' room**, *Br* **the ladies** les toilettes *fpl* pour dames ▪ **lady-in-'waiting** (*pl* **ladies-in-waiting**) *n* dame *f* d'honneur

ladybird [ˈleɪdɪbɜːd] (*Am* **ladybug** [ˈleɪdɪbʌg]) *n* coccinelle *f*

ladylike [ˈleɪdɪlaɪk] *adj* (*manner*) distingué; **she's (very) l.** elle fait très grande dame

lag [læg] **1** *n* **time l.** (*between events*) décalage *m*; (*between countries*) décalage horaire **2** (*pt & pp* **-gg-**) *vt* (*pipe*) isoler **3** *vi* **to l. behind** (*in progress, work*) avoir du retard; (*dawdle*) être à la traîne; **to l. behind sb** être à la traîne derrière qn

lager [ˈlɑːgə(r)] *n Br* bière *f* blonde

lagoon [ləˈguːn] *n* lagune *f*; (*of atoll*) lagon *m*

laid [leɪd] *pt & pp of* **lay³** ▪ **'laid-'back** *adj Fam* cool *inv*

lain [leɪn] *pp of* **lie²**

lair [leə(r)] *n* tanière *f*

lake [leɪk] *n* lac *m*

lamb [læm] *n* agneau *m* ▪ **lambswool** *n* lambswool *m*; **l. sweater** pull *m* en lambswool

lame [leɪm] (**-er, -est**) *adj* (*person, argument*) boiteux, -euse; (*excuse*) piètre; *Fam* (*stupid*) cloche, nouille; **to be l.** boiter; *Am Pol* **l. duck** = candidat sortant non réélu ▪ **lameness** *n Med* claudication *f*; *Fig* (*of excuse*) faiblesse *f*

lament [ləˈment] **1** *n* lamentation *f* **2** *vt* **to l. (over)** se lamenter sur ▪ **lamentable** *adj* lamentable ▪ **lamentation** [læmenˈteɪʃən] *n* lamentation *f*

laminated [ˈlæmɪneɪtɪd] *adj* (*glass*) feuilleté; (*wood, plastic*) stratifié

lamp [læmp] *n* lampe *f* ▪ **lamppost** *n* réverbère *m* ▪ **lampshade** *n* abat-jour *m inv*

lance [lɑːns] **1** *n* (*weapon*) lance *f* **2** *vt* (*abscess*) inciser

land [lænd] **1** *n* terre *f*; (*country*) pays *m*; (*plot of*) **l.** terrain *m*; **on dry l.** sur la terre ferme; **to travel by l.** voyager par voie de terre
2 *adj* (*transport, flora*) terrestre; (*reform, law*) agraire; (*tax*) foncier, -ière
3 *vt* (*passengers, cargo*) débarquer; (*aircraft*) poser; (*blow*) flanquer (**on** à); *Fam* (*job, prize*)

décrocher; *Fam* **to l. sb in trouble** mettre qn dans le pétrin; *Fam* **to be landed with** *(person)* avoir sur les bras; *(fine)* écoper de; *Fam* **to l. sb one** *(hit)* en coller une à qn

4 *vi (of aircraft)* atterrir; *(of ship)* mouiller; *(of passengers)* débarquer; *(of bomb, missile)* tomber; **to l. up in a ditch/in jail** se retrouver dans un fossé/en prison ▪ **landing** *n* (a) *(of aircraft)* atterrissage *m*; *(of cargo, troops)* débarquement *m*; **forced l.** atterrissage *m* forcé; **l. stage** débarcadère *m* (b) *(of staircase)* palier *m* ▪ **landlady** *(pl -ies)* *n* propriétaire *f*; *(of pub)* patronne *f* ▪ **landlocked** *adj* sans accès à la mer ▪ **landlord** *n* propriétaire *m*; *(of pub)* patron *m* ▪ **landmark** *n* point *m* de repère ▪ **landowner** *n* propriétaire *m* foncier ▪ **landslide** *n* *(falling rocks)* glissement *m* de terrain; *(election victory)* raz de marée *m inv* électoral

landed ['lændɪd] *adj (owning land)* terrien, -ienne

landscape ['lændskeɪp] *n* paysage *m*

lane [leɪn] *n* *(in country)* chemin *m*; *(in town)* ruelle *f*; *(division of road)* voie *f*; *(line of traffic)* file *f*; *(for aircraft, shipping, swimming)* couloir *m*; **'get in l.'** *(traffic sign)* 'prenez votre file'

language ['læŋgwɪdʒ] **1** *n (of a people)* langue *f*; *(faculty, style)* langage *m* **2** *adj (laboratory)* de langues; *(teacher, studies)* de langue(s)

languid ['læŋgwɪd] *adj* languissant ▪ **languish** *vi* languir **(for** or **after** après)

lank [læŋk] *adj (hair)* plat et terne

lanky ['læŋkɪ] *(-ier, -iest)* *adj* dégingandé

lantern ['læntən] *n* lanterne *f*; **Chinese l.** lampion *m*

lap [læp] **1** *n* (a) *(of person)* genoux *mpl*; **in the l. of luxury** dans le luxe; **l. dancer** = entraîneuse qui danse nue pour un client (b) *(in race)* tour *m* de piste **2** *(pt & pp -pp-)* *vt* **to l. up** *(drink)* laper; *Fam (like very much)* se délecter de; *Fam (believe)* gober **3** *vi (of waves)* clapoter; **to l. over** *(overlap)* se chevaucher

lapdog ['læpdɒg] *n* chien *m* d'appartement; *Fig* toutou *m*

lapel [lə'pel] *n* revers *m*

lapse [læps] **1** *n* (a) *(in concentration, standards)* baisse *f*; **a l. of memory** un trou de mémoire; **a l. in behaviour** un écart de conduite (b) *(interval)* laps *m* de temps; **a l. of time** un intervalle **(between** entre) **2** *vi* (a) *(of concentration, standards)* baisser; *(of person)* retomber dans un travers; **to l. into silence** se taire; **to l. into bad habits** reprendre de mauvaises habitudes (b) *(expire)* *(of ticket, passport, subscription)* expirer

laptop ['læptɒp] *adj & n* **l. (computer)** ordinateur *m* portable

larceny ['lɑːsənɪ] *n Am Law* vol *m*

lard [lɑːd] *n* saindoux *m*

Note that the French word **lard** is a false friend. Its most common meaning is **bacon**.

---

larder ['lɑːdə(r)] *n* garde-manger *m inv*

large [lɑːdʒ] *(-er, -est)* *adj (big)* grand; *(fat, bulky)* gros (*f* grosse); *(quantity)* grand, important; **to become** or **grow** or **get l.** s'agrandir; *(of person)* grossir; **to a l. extent** en grande partie; **at l.** *(of prisoner, animal)* en liberté; *(as a whole)* en général; **by and l.** dans l'ensemble ▪ **'large-'scale** *adj (operation, reform)* de grande envergure

largely ['lɑːdʒlɪ] *adv* en grande partie

Note that the French word **largement** is a false friend. It means **widely** or **generously** depending on the context.

---

largesse [lɑː'ʒes] *n* largesse *f*

lark¹ [lɑːk] *n (bird)* alouette *f*

lark² [lɑːk] *Fam* **1** *n (joke)* rigolade *f* **2** *vi* **to l. about** faire le fou/la folle

larva ['lɑːvə] *(pl -vae* [-viː]) *n* larve *f*

larynx ['lærɪŋks] *n* larynx *m* ▪ **laryngitis** [-rɪn'dʒaɪtɪs] *n Med* laryngite *f*

lasagne [lə'zænjə] *n* lasagnes *fpl*

lascivious [lə'sɪvɪəs] *adj* lascif, -ive

laser ['leɪzə(r)] *n* laser *m*; **l. beam/printer/pointer** rayon *m*/imprimante *f* /pointeur *m* laser; **l. surgery** chirurgie *f* au laser

lash¹ [læʃ] **1** *n (with whip)* coup *m* de fouet **2** *vt (strike)* fouetter; *(tie)* attacher (**to** à); **the dog lashed its tail** le chien donna un coup de queue **3** *vi Fam* **to l. out** *(spend wildly)* claquer son argent; **to l. out at sb** *(hit)* donner des coups à qn; *(insult)* s'en prendre violemment à qn; *(criticize)* fustiger qn

lash² [læʃ] *n (eyelash)* cil *m*

lashings ['læʃɪŋz] *npl Br Fam* **l. of cream/jam** une tonne de crème/confiture

lass [læs] *n Br* jeune fille *f*

lassitude ['læsɪtjuːd] *n* lassitude *f*

lasso [læ'suː] **1** *(pl -oes* or *-os)* *n* lasso *m* **2** *(pt & pp -oed)* *vt* attraper au lasso

last¹ [lɑːst] **1** *adj* dernier, -ière; **the l. ten lines** les dix dernières lignes; **l. night** *(evening)* hier soir; *(night)* la nuit dernière; **l. name** nom *m* de famille **2** *adv (lastly)* en dernier lieu; *(on the last occasion)* (pour) la dernière fois; **to leave l.** sortir le dernier; **when I saw him l.** la dernière fois que je l'ai vu **3** *n (person, object)* dernier, -ière *mf*; **l. but one** avant-dernier *m* (*f* avant-dernière); **that's the l. of the beer** on a fini la bière; **the day before l.** avant-hier; **at (long) l.** enfin ▪ **last-'ditch** *adj (attempt)* ultime ▪ **last-'minute** *adj (decision)* de dernière minute

last² [lɑːst] *vi* durer; **to l. (out)** *(endure, resist)* tenir (le coup); *(of money, supplies)* suffire; **it lasted me ten years** ça m'a fait dix ans ▪ **lasting** *adj (impression, peace)* durable

lastly ['lɑːstlɪ] *adv* en dernier lieu

latch [lætʃ] **1** *n* loquet *m*; **the door is on the l.** la porte n'est pas fermée à clef **2** *vt insep Fam* **to l. onto** *(understand)* piger; *(grab)* s'accrocher à; *(adopt)* adopter

late¹ [leɪt] **1** (**-er, -est**) *adj (not on time)* en retard (**for** à); *(meal, fruit, season, hour)* tardif, -ive; *(stage)* avancé; *(edition)* dernier, -ière; **to be l. (for sth)** être en retard (pour qch); **to be l. (in) coming** arriver en retard; **to make sb l.** mettre qn en retard; **he's an hour l.** il a une heure de retard; **it's l.** il est tard; **in l. June** in juin; **in the l. nineties** à la fin des années 90; **to be in one's l. forties** approcher de la cinquantaine; **a later edition** *(more recent)* une édition plus récente; **the latest edition** *(last)* la dernière édition; **to take a later train** prendre un train plus tard; **in later life** plus tard (dans la vie); **at a later date** à une date ultérieure; **at the latest** au plus tard

2 *adv (in the day, season)* tard; *(not on time)* en retard; **it's getting l.** il se fait tard; **l. into the night** jusqu'à une heure avancée de la nuit; **l. in the year** vers la fin de l'année; **later (on)** plus tard; **of l.** récemment; **not** *or* **no later than** pas plus tard que

late² [leɪt] *adj* **the l. Mr Smith** feu Monsieur Smith; **our l. friend** notre regretté ami

latecomer ['leɪtkʌmə(r)] *n* retardataire *mf*

lately ['leɪtlɪ] *adv* dernièrement

lateness ['leɪtnəs] *n (of person, train)* retard *m*; **the l. of the hour** l'heure *f* tardive

latent ['leɪtənt] *adj (disease, tendency)* latent

lateral ['lætərəl] *adj* latéral

lathe [leɪð] *n (machine)* tour *m*

lather ['lɑːðə(r)] **1** *n* mousse *f* **2** *vt* savonner **3** *vi* mousser

Latin ['lætɪn] **1** *adj* latin; **L. America** l'Amérique *f* latine **2** *n (person)* Latin, -ine *mf*; *(language)* latin *m* ▪**Latin American, -aine** *adj* d'Amérique latine **2** *n* Latino-Américain, -aine *mf*

latitude ['lætɪtjuːd] *n (on map, freedom)* latitude *f*

latrines [lə'triːnz] *npl esp Mil* latrines *fpl*

latte ['lateɪ] *n* café *m* au lait

latter ['lætə(r)] **1** *adj (later, last-named)* dernier, -ière; *(second)* deuxième; **the l. part of June** la deuxième moitié du mois de juin **2** *n* **the l.** le dernier (*f* la dernière); *(of two)* le second (*f* la seconde) ▪**latterly** *adv (recently)* récemment, dernièrement

lattice ['lætɪs] *n* treillis *m* ▪**latticework** *n* treillis *m*

Latvia ['lætvɪə] *n* Lettonie *f* ▪**Latvian 1** *adj* letton, -onne **2** *n (person)* Letton, -onne *mf*; *(language)* letton *m*

laudable ['lɔːdəbəl] *adj* louable

laugh [lɑːf] **1** *n* rire *m*; **to have a good l.** bien rire **2** *vt* **to l. sth off** tourner qch en plaisanterie; *Fam* **to l. one's head off** être mort de rire **3** *vi* rire (**at/about** de); **to l. to oneself** rire en soi-même ▪**laughing** *adj* riant; **it's no l. matter** il n'y a pas de quoi rire; **to be the l. stock of** être la risée de

laughable ['lɑːfəbəl] *adj* ridicule

laughter ['lɑːftə(r)] *n* rire(s) *m(pl)*; **to roar with l.** rire aux éclats

launch [lɔːntʃ] **1** *n* (**a**) *(motorboat)* vedette *f*; *(pleasure boat)* bateau *m* de plaisance (**b**) *(of ship, rocket, product)* lancement *m*; **l. pad** aire *f* de lancement **2** *vt (ship, rocket, product)* lancer **3** *vi* **to l. (out) into** *(begin)* se lancer dans ▪**launching** *n (of ship, rocket, product)* lancement *m*; **l. pad** aire *f* de lancement

launder ['lɔːndə(r)] *vt (clothes, money)* blanchir ▪**laundering** *n* blanchiment *m*

launderette [lɔːndə'ret] (*Am* **Laundromat®** ['lɔːndrəmæt]) *n* laverie *f* automatique

laundry ['lɔːndrɪ] *n (place)* blanchisserie *f*; *(clothes)* linge *m*; **to do the l.** faire la lessive

laurel ['lɒrəl] *n* laurier *m*; *Fig* **to rest on one's laurels** se reposer sur ses lauriers

lava ['lɑːvə] *n* lave *f*

lavatory ['lævətərɪ] (*pl* **-ies**) *n* toilettes *fpl*

lavender ['lævɪndə(r)] *n* lavande *f*

lavish ['lævɪʃ] **1** *adj* prodigue (**with** de); *(meal, décor, gift)* somptueux, -ueuse; *(expenditure)* excessif, -ive **2** *vt* **to l. sth on sb** couvrir qn de qch ▪**lavishly** *adv (furnish)* somptueusement; **to spend l.** dépenser sans compter

law [lɔː] *n (rule, rules)* loi *f*; *(study, profession, system)* droit *m*; **against the l.** illégal; **to break the l.** enfreindre la loi; **to be above the l.** être au-dessus des lois; **court of l., l. court** cour *f* de justice; **l. and order** l'ordre *m* public; **l. firm** cabinet *m* d'avocat; *Am* **l. school** faculté *f* de droit; **l. student** étudiant, -iante *mf* en droit ▪**law-abiding** *adj* respectueux, -ueuse des lois

lawful ['lɔːfəl] *adj (action, age)* légal; *(wife, claim)* légitime ▪**lawfully** *adv* légalement

lawless ['lɔːləs] *adj (country)* anarchique ▪**lawlessness** *n* anarchie *f*

lawn [lɔːn] *n* pelouse *f*, gazon *m*; **l. mower** tondeuse *f* à gazon; **l. tennis** tennis *m*

lawsuit ['lɔːsuːt] *n* procès *m*

lawyer ['lɔːjə(r)] *n (in court)* avocat, -ate *mf*; *(for wills, sales)* notaire *m*; *(legal expert, author)* juriste *m*

lax [læks] *adj (person)* laxiste; *(discipline, behaviour)* relâché; **to be l. in doing sth** négliger de faire qch ▪**laxity, laxness** *n* laxisme *m*; *(of discipline)* relâchement *m*

laxative ['læksətɪv] *adj* laxatif, -ive **2** *n* laxatif *m*

lay¹ [leɪ] *pt of* **lie²**

lay² [leɪ] *adj (non-religious)* laïque; *(non-specialized) (opinion)* d'un profane; **l. person**

profane *mf* ▪**layman** (*pl* **-men**) *n* (*non-specialist*) profane *mf*

lay³ [leɪ] (*pt & pp* **laid**) **1** *vt* (*put down, place*) poser; (*blanket*) étendre (**over** sur); (*trap*) tendre; (*money*) miser (**on** sur); (*accusation*) porter; (*ghost*) exorciser; (*egg*) pondre; **to l. sth flat** poser qch à plat; *Br* **to l. the table** mettre la table; **to l. a bet** parier; **to l. sth bare** mettre qch à nu; **to l. oneself open to criticism** s'exposer aux critiques; **to l. one's hands on sth** mettre la main sur qch; **to l. a hand** *or* **a finger on sb** lever la main sur qn **2** *vi* (*of bird*) pondre ▪**layabout** *n Fam* fainéant, -éante *mf* ▪**lay-by** (*pl* **-bys**) *n Br* (*for vehicles*) aire *f* de stationnement ▪**layout** *n* disposition *f*; (*of text*) mise *f* en page ▪**lay-over** *n Am* halte *f*

▶**lay down** *vt sep* (*put down*) poser; (*arms*) déposer; (*principle, condition*) établir; **to l. down one's life** sacrifier sa vie (**for** pour); **to l. down the law** dicter sa loi (**to** à)

▶**lay into** *vt insep Fam* (*physically*) rosser; (*verbally*) voler dans les plumes à

▶**lay off 1** *vt sep Fam* **l. sb off** (*worker*) licencier qn **2** *vt insep Fam* (*stop*) arrêter; *Fam* **to l. off sb** (*leave alone*) ficher la paix à **3** *vi Fam* (*desist*) arrêter; **l. off!** (*don't touch*) pas touche!

▶**lay on** *vt sep Br* (*install*) installer; (*supply*) fournir; *Fam* **to l. it on (thick)** y aller un peu fort

▶**lay out** *vt sep* (*garden*) dessiner; (*house*) concevoir; (*prepare*) préparer; (*display*) disposer; *Fam* (*money*) mettre (**on** dans)

layer ['leɪə(r)] *n* couche *f*

laze [leɪz] *vi* **to l. (about** *or* **around**) paresser

lazy ['leɪzɪ] (**-ier, -iest**) *adj* (*person*) paresseux, -euse; (*afternoon*) passé à ne rien faire ▪**lazybones** *n Fam* flemmard, -arde *mf*

lb (*abbr* **libra**) livre *f* (*unité de poids*)

lead¹ [led] *n* (*metal*) plomb *m*; (*of pencil*) mine *f*; **l. pencil** crayon *m* à papier ▪**leaded** *adj* (*petrol*) au plomb ▪**leaden** *adj* **l. sky** ciel *m* de plomb ▪**'lead-'free** *adj* (*petrol, paint*) sans plomb

lead² [liːd] **1** *n* (*distance or time ahead*) avance *f* (**over** sur); (*example*) exemple *m*; (*clue*) indice *m*; (*in film*) rôle *m* principal; *Br* (*for dog*) laisse *f*; (*electric wire*) fil *m* électrique; **to take the l.** (*in race*) prendre la tête; **to be in the l.** (*in race*) être en tête; (*in match*) mener (à la marque); **l. singer** (*in pop group*) chanteur, -euse *mf* vedette **2** (*pt & pp* **led**) *vt* (*guide, conduct, take*) mener, conduire (**to** à); (*team, government*) diriger; (*expedition, attack*) commander; (*procession*) être en tête de; **to l. a happy life** mener une vie heureuse; **to l. sb in/out** faire entrer/sortir qn; **to l. sb to do sth** (*cause, induce*) amener qn à faire qch; **to l. the way** montrer le chemin; **to l. the world** tenir le premier rang mondial; **easily led** influençable **3** *vi* (*of street, door*) mener, conduire (**to** à); (*in race*) être en tête; (*in match*) mener (à la

marque); (*go ahead*) aller devant; **to l. to sth** (*result in*) aboutir à qch; (*cause*) mener à qch; **to l. up to** (*of street*) conduire à, mener à; (*precede*) précéder; (*approach gradually*) en venir à

▶**lead away** *vt sep* emmener

▶**lead back** *vt sep* ramener

▶**lead off** *vt sep* emmener

▶**lead on** *vt sep* (*deceive*) tromper, duper

leader ['liːdə(r)] *n* (**a**) chef *m*; (*of country, party*) dirigeant, -ante *mf*; (*of strike, riot*) meneur, -euse *mf*; (*guide*) guide *m*; **to be the l.** (*in race*) être en tête (**b**) *Br* (*newspaper article*) éditorial *m* ▪**leadership** *n* direction *f*; (*qualities*) qualités *fpl* de chef; (*leaders*) (*of country, party*) dirigeants *mpl*

leading ['liːdɪŋ] *adj* (*best, most important*) principal; **the l. car** la voiture de tête; **a l. figure, a l. light** un personnage marquant; **the l. lady** (*in film*) le premier rôle féminin; *Br* **l. article** (*in newspaper*) éditorial *m*

leaf [liːf] **1** (*pl* **leaves**) *n* feuille *f*; (*of book*) feuillet *m*; (*of table*) rallonge *f* **2** *vi* **to l. through** (*book*) feuilleter ▪**leafy** (**-ier, -iest**) *adj* (*tree*) feuillu

leaflet ['liːflɪt] *n* prospectus *m*; (*containing instructions*) notice *f*

league [liːg] *n* (**a**) (*alliance*) ligue *f*; *Sport* championnat *m*; *Pej* **in l. with** de connivence avec (**b**) *Hist* (*measure*) lieue *f*

leak [liːk] **1** *n* (*in pipe, information*) fuite *f*; (*in boat*) voie *f* d'eau **2** *vt Fig* (*information*) divulguer; **the pipe was leaking gas** du gaz fuyait du tuyau **3** *vi* (*of liquid, pipe, tap*) fuir; (*of ship*) faire eau; *Fig* **to l. out** (*of information*) être divulgué ▪**leakage** [-ɪdʒ] *n* fuite *f*; (*amount lost*) perte *f* ▪**leaky** (**-ier, -iest**) *adj* (*kettle, pipe, tap*) qui fuit; (*roof*) qui a une fuite

lean¹ [liːn] (**-er, -est**) *adj* (*meat*) maigre; (*person*) mince; (*year*) difficile

lean² [liːn] (*pt & pp* **leaned** *or* **leant** [lent]) **1** *vt* **to l. sth on/against sth** appuyer qch sur/contre qch **2** *vi* (*of object*) pencher; (*of person*) se pencher; **to l. against/on sth** (*of person*) s'appuyer contre/sur qch; **to l. back against** s'adosser à; *Fam* **to l. on sb** (*influence*) faire pression sur qn (**to do** pour faire); **to l. forward** (*of person*) se pencher (en avant); **to l. over** (*of person*) se pencher; (*of object*) pencher ▪**leaning** *adj* penché; **l. against** (*resting*) appuyé contre ▪**leanings** *npl* tendances *fpl* (**towards** à) ▪**lean-to** (*pl* **-tos**) *n Br* (*building*) appentis *m*

leap [liːp] **1** *n* (*jump*) bond *m*, saut *m*; *Fig* (*change, increase*) bond *m*; **l. year** année *f* bissextile; **in leaps and bounds** à pas de géant **2** (*pt & pp* **leaped** *or* **leapt**) *vi* bondir, sauter; (*of flames*) jaillir; (*of profits*) faire un bond; **to l. for joy** sauter de joie; **to l. to one's feet, to l. up** se lever d'un bond

leapfrog ['li:pfrɒg] *n* saute-mouton *m*; **to play l.** jouer à saute-mouton

leapt [lept] *pt & pp of* **leap**

learn [lɜːn] (*pt & pp* **learned** *or* **learnt** [lɜːnt]) **1** *vt* apprendre (**that** que); **to l. (how) to do sth** apprendre à faire qch **2** *vi* apprendre; **to l. about sth** (*study*) étudier qch; (*hear about*) apprendre qch ▪**learned** [-ɪd] *adj* savant ▪**learner** *n* (*beginner*) débutant, -ante *mf*; (*student*) étudiant, -iante *mf*; **to be a quick/slow l.** apprendre vite/lentement ▪**learning** *n* (*of language*) apprentissage *m* (**of** de); (*knowledge*) savoir *m*; **l. curve** courbe *f* d'assimilation

lease [li:s] **1** *n* bail *m* (*pl* baux); *Fig* **to give sb a new l. of life** *or Am* **on life** redonner à qn goût à la vie **2** *vt* (*house*) louer à bail (**from/to** à)

leash [li:ʃ] *n* (*of dog*) laisse *f*; **on a l.** en laisse

least [li:st] **1** *adj* **the l.** (*smallest amount of*) le moins de; **he has (the) l. talent** il a le moins de talent (**of all** de tous); **the l. effort/noise** le moindre effort/bruit **2** *n* **the l.** le moins; **at l.** du moins; (*with quantity*) au moins; **at l. that's what she says** du moins, c'est ce qu'elle dit; **not in the l.** pas du tout **3** *adv* (*work, eat*) le moins; **the l. difficult** le/la moins difficile; **l. of all** (*especially not*) surtout pas

leather ['leðə(r)] *n* cuir *m*; **l. jacket** veste *m* en cuir; (**wash**) **l.** peau *f* de chamois ▪**leathe'rette®** *n* similicuir *m*

leave [li:v] **1** *n* (*holiday*) congé *m*; (*of soldier, permission*) permission *f*; **to be on l.** être en congé; (*of soldier*) être en permission; **l. of absence** congé exceptionnel; **to take (one's) l. of sb** prendre congé de qn **2** (*pt & pp* **left**) *vt* (*allow to remain, forget*) laisser; (*depart from*) quitter; **to l. the table** sortir de table; **to l. sb in charge of sb/sth** laisser à qn la garde de qn/qch; **to l. sth with sb** (*entrust, give*) laisser qch à qn; **to leave sb** (*over*) rester; **there's no hope/bread left** il ne reste plus d'espoir/de pain; **l. it to me!** laisse-moi faire!; **I'll l. it (up) to you** je m'en remets à toi **3** *vi* (*go away*) partir (**from** de; **for** pour)

▸**leave behind** *vt sep* **to l. sth behind** (*on purpose*) laisser qch; (*accidentally*) oublier qch; **to l. sb behind** (*not take*) partir sans qn; (*surpass*) dépasser qn; (*in race, at school*) distancer qn

▸**leave off 1** *vt sep* (*lid*) ne pas remettre; *Fam* **to l. off doing sth** (*stop*) arrêter de faire qch **2** *vi Fam* (*stop*) s'arrêter

▸**leave on** *vt sep* (*clothes*) garder

▸**leave out** *vt sep* (*forget to put*) oublier de mettre; (*word, line*) sauter; (*exclude*) exclure

Lebanon ['lebənən] *n* le Liban ▪**Leba'nese** *adj* libanais **2** *n* Libanais, -aise *mf*

lecher ['letʃə(r)] *n* débauché *m* ▪**lecherous** *adj* lubrique

lectern ['lektən] *n* (*for giving speeches*) pupitre *m*; (*in church*) lutrin *m*

lecture ['lektʃə(r)] **1** *n* (*public speech*) conférence *f*; (*as part of series at university*) cours *m* magistral; *Fam* (*scolding*) sermon *m*; **l. hall** *or* **theatre** amphithéâtre *m* **2** *vt Fam* (*scold*) faire la morale à **3** *vi* faire une conférence/un cours; **she lectures in chemistry** elle est professeur de chimie ▪**lecturer** *n* conférencier, -ière *mf*; (*at university*) enseignant, -ante *mf*

Note that the French word **lecture** is a false friend and is never a translation for the English word **lecture**. It means *reading*.

---

led [led] *pt & pp of* **lead²**

ledge [ledʒ] *n* (*on wall, window*) rebord *m*; (*on mountain*) saillie *f*

ledger ['ledʒə(r)] *n* grand livre *m*

leech [li:tʃ] *n* (*animal, person*) sangsue *f*

leek [li:k] *n* poireau *m*

leer [lɪə(r)] **1** *n* (*lustful*) regard *m* lubrique; (*cruel*) regard sadique **2** *vi* **to l. at sb** (*lustfully*) regarder qn d'un air lubrique; (*cruelly*) regarder qn d'un air sadique

leeway ['li:weɪ] *n* marge *f* (de manœuvre)

left¹ [left] *pt & pp of* **leave** ▪**left-'luggage office** *n Br* consigne *f*

left² [left] **1** *adj* (*side, hand*) gauche **2** *n* gauche *f*; **on** *or* **to the l.** à gauche (**of** de) **3** *adv* à gauche ▪**'left-'hand** *adj* de gauche; **on the l. side** à gauche (**of** de); **l. drive** conduite *f* à gauche ▪**'left-'handed** *adj* (*person*) gaucher, -ère ▪**'left-'wing** *adj* (*views, government*) de gauche

leftist ['leftɪst] *n & adj Pol* gauchiste (*mf*)

leftovers ['leftəʊvəz] *npl* restes *mpl*

leg [leg] *n* jambe *f*; (*of dog, bird*) patte *f*; (*of table*) pied *m*; (*of journey*) étape *f*; **l. of chicken** cuisse *f* de poulet; **l. of lamb** gigot *m* d'agneau; **to pull sb's l.** (*make fun of*) mettre qn en boîte; *Fam* **on its last legs** (*machine, car*) prêt à claquer; *Fam* **to be on one's last legs** avoir un pied dans la tombe

legacy ['legəsɪ] (*pl* -**ies**) *n Law & Fig* legs *m*

legal ['li:gəl] *adj* (*lawful*) légal; (*affairs, adviser, mind*) juridique; (*error*) judiciaire; *Br* **l. aid** aide *f* judiciaire; **l. expert** juriste *mf*; **l. proceedings** procès *m* ▪**legality** [lɪ'gælɪtɪ] *n* légalité *f* ▪**legalization** *n* légalisation *f* ▪**legalize** *vt* légaliser ▪**legally** *adv* légalement

legation [lɪ'geɪʃən] *n Pol* légation *f*

legend ['ledʒənd] *n* (*story, inscription*) légende *f* ▪**legendary** *adj* légendaire

leggings ['legɪŋz] *npl* (*of woman*) caleçon *m*; (*of cowboy*) jambières *fpl*

leggy ['legɪ] (-**ier**, -**iest**) *adj* (*person*) tout en jambes

legible ['ledʒɪbəl] *adj* lisible ▪**legibility** *n* lisibilité *f* ▪**legibly** *adv* lisiblement

legion ['liːdʒən] n légion f

legislate ['ledʒɪsleɪt] vi légiférer ▪ **legis'lation** n (laws) législation f; (action) élaboration f des lois; (piece of) l. loi f

legislative ['ledʒɪslətɪv] adj législatif, -ive

legitimate [lɪ'dʒɪtɪmət] adj légitime ▪ **legitimacy** n légitimité f

legless ['legləs] adj Br Fam (drunk) complètement bourré

legroom ['legruːm] n place f pour les jambes

leisure [Br 'leʒə(r), Am 'liːʒər] n **1.** (time) loisirs mpl; **l.** activities loisirs; l. centre or complex centre m de loisirs; **moment of l.** moment m de loisir; **at (one's) l.** à tête reposée ▪ **leisurely** adj (walk, occupation) peu fatigant; (meal, life) tranquille; **at a l. pace, in a l. way** sans se presser

lemon ['lemən] n citron m; Br **l. squash** citronnade f; **l. tea** thé m au citron; **l. tree** citronnier m ▪ **lemo'nade** n Br (fizzy) limonade f; Am (still) citronnade f

lend [lend] (pt & pp lent) vt prêter (**to** à); (support) apporter (**to** à); Fig (charm, colour) donner (**to** à); **to l. an ear to sth** prêter l'oreille à qch; **to l. credibility to sth** rendre qch crédible ▪ **lender** n prêteur, -euse mf ▪ **lending** n prêt m; **l. library** bibliothèque f de prêt

length [leŋθ] n (in space) longueur f; (of road, string) tronçon m; (of cloth) métrage m; (duration) durée f; **a great l. of time** longtemps; **at l.** (at last) enfin; **at (great) l.** (in detail) dans le détail; (for a long time) longuement; **to go to great lengths** se donner beaucoup de mal (**to do** pour faire)

lengthen ['leŋθən] **1** vt (garment) allonger; (holiday, visit) prolonger **2** vi (of days) allonger ▪ **lengthwise** adv dans le sens de la longueur ▪ **lengthy** (-ier, -iest) adj long (f longue)

lenient ['liːnɪənt] adj indulgent (**to** envers) ▪ **leniency** n indulgence f ▪ **leniently** adv avec indulgence

lens [lenz] (pl lenses [-zəz]) n lentille f; (in spectacles) verre m; (of camera) objectif m

Lent [lent] n Rel carême m

lent [lent] pt & pp of **lend**

lentil ['lentɪl] n (seed, plant) lentille f

Leo ['liːəʊ] (pl **Leos**) n (sign) le Lion; **to be (a) L.** être Lion

leopard ['lepəd] n léopard m

leotard ['liːətɑːd] n justaucorps m

leper ['lepə(r)] n lépreux, -euse mf ▪ **leprosy** ['leprəsɪ] n lèpre f

lesbian ['lezbɪən] **1** adj lesbien, -ienne **2** n lesbienne f

lesion ['liːʒən] n Med lésion f

less [les] **1** adj & pron moins (de) (**than** que); **l. time** moins de temps; **she has l. (than you)** elle en a moins (que toi); **l. than a kilo/ten miles** d'un kilo/de dix **2** adv moins (**than** que); **l. (often)** moins souvent; **l. and l.** de moins en moins; **one l.** un(e) de moins **3** prep moins; **l. 2 euros** moins 2 euros

-less [ləs] suff sans; **childless** sans enfants

lessen ['lesən] vti diminuer ▪ **lessening** n diminution f

lesser ['lesə(r)] **1** adj moindre **2** n **the l. of** le/la moindre de

lesson ['lesən] n leçon f; **an English l.** une leçon d'anglais; **I have lessons now** j'ai cours maintenant; Fig **he has learnt his l.** ça lui a servi de leçon

lest [lest] conj Literary de peur que… (+ ne + subjunctive)

let¹ [let] **1** (pt & pp let, pres p letting) vt (allow) **to l. sb do sth** laisser qn faire qch; **to l. sb have sth** donner qch à qn **2** v aux **l. us eat/go, l.'s eat/go** mangeons/partons; **l.'s go for a stroll** allons nous promener; **l. him come** qu'il vienne ▪ **letdown** n déception f ▪ **letup** n répit m

▸ **let away** vt sep (allow to leave) laisser partir

▸ **let down** vt sep (lower) baisser; (hair) dénouer; (dress) rallonger; (tyre) dégonfler; **to l. sb down** (disappoint) décevoir qn; **don't l. me down** tu peux compter sur moi; **the car l. me down** la voiture est tombée en panne

▸ **let in** vt sep (person, dog) laisser entrer; (noise, light) laisser entrer; Br **to l. in the clutch** (in vehicle) embrayer; **to l. sb in on sth** mettre qn au courant de qch; **to l. oneself in for a lot of expense** se laisser entraîner à des dépenses; **to l. oneself in for trouble** s'attirer des ennuis; **what are you letting yourself in for?** sais-tu à quoi tu t'exposes?

▸ **let off** vt sep (firework) tirer; (bomb) faire exploser; (gun) faire partir; **to l. sb off** (allow to leave) laisser partir qn; (not punish) ne pas punir qn; (clear of crime) disculper qn; **to be l. off with a fine** s'en tirer avec une amende; **to l. sb off doing sth** dispenser qn de faire qch

▸ **let on** vi Fam **not to l. on** ne rien dire; Fam **to l. on that…** (admit) avouer que…; (reveal) dire que…

▸ **let out** vt sep (allow to leave) laisser sortir; (prisoner) relâcher; (cry, secret) laisser échapper; (skirt) élargir; **my secretary will l. you out** ma secrétaire va vous reconduire; Br **to l. out the clutch** (in vehicle) débrayer

▸ **let up** vi (of rain, person) s'arrêter

let² [let] (pt & pp let, pres p letting) vt **to l. (off or out)** (house, room) louer ▪ **letting** n (renting) location f

lethal ['liːθəl] adj (blow, dose) mortel, -elle; (weapon) meurtrier, -ière

lethargy ['leθədʒɪ] n léthargie f ▪ **lethargic** [lɪ'θɑːdʒɪk] adj léthargique

letter ['letə(r)] n (message, part of word) lettre f;

man of letters homme *m* de lettres; **l. of introduction** lettre de recommandation; **l. bomb** lettre piégée; **l. opener** coupe-papier *m inv* ∎ **letterbox** *n Br* boîte *f* aux lettres ∎ **letterhead** *n* en-tête *m* ∎ **letterheaded** *adj* **l. paper** papier *m* à en-tête ∎ **lettering** *n (letters)* lettres *fpl*; *(on tomb)* inscription *f*

lettuce ['letɪs] *n* laitue *f*

leukaemia [lu:'ki:mɪə] *(Am* **leukemia**) *n* leucémie *f*; **to have l.** avoir une leucémie

level ['levəl] **1** *n* niveau *m*; **at international l.** à l'échelon international; **at eye l.** à hauteur des yeux; *Fam* **on the l.** *(honest)* régulier, -ière; *(honestly)* franchement **2** *adj (surface)* plat; *(equal in score)* à égalité (**with** avec); *(in height)* à la même hauteur (**with** que); **l. spoonful** cuillerée *f* rase; *Br* **l. crossing** *(for train)* passage *m* à niveau **3** *(Br -ll-, Am -l-) vt (surface, differences)* aplanir; *(plane down)* raboter; *(building)* raser; *(gun)* braquer (**at** sur); *(accusation)* lancer (**at** contre) **4** *vi* **to l. off** *or* **out** *(of prices)* se stabiliser; *Fam* **to l. with sb** être franc (*f* franche) avec qn ∎ **'level-'headed** *adj* équilibré

lever [*Br* 'li:və(r), *Am* 'levər] *n* levier *m* ∎ **leverage** *n (power)* influence *f*

levity ['levɪtɪ] *n* légèreté *f*

levy ['levɪ] **1** *(pl -ies) n (tax)* impôt *m* (**on** sur) **2** *(pt & pp -ied) vt (tax, troops)* lever

lewd [lu:d] *(-er, -est) adj* obscène

liability [laɪə'bɪlɪtɪ] *n Law* responsabilité *f* (**for** de); *(disadvantage)* handicap *m*; *Fin* **liabilities** *(debts)* passif *m*

liable ['laɪəbəl] *adj* **l. to** *(dizziness)* sujet, -ette à; *(fine, tax)* passible de; **to be l. to do sth** risquer de faire qch; **l. for sth** *(responsible)* responsable de qch

liaise [li:'eɪz] *vi* travailler en liaison (**with** avec) ∎ **liaison** [li:'eɪzɒn] *n (contact, love affair)* & *Mil* liaison *f*

liar ['laɪə(r)] *n* menteur, -euse *mf*

libel ['laɪbəl] *Law* **1** *n* diffamation *f*; **l. action** procès *m* en diffamation **2** *(Br -ll-, Am -l-) vt* diffamer (par écrit)

liberal ['lɪbərəl] **1** *adj (open-minded)* & *Pol* libéral; *(generous)* généreux, -euse (**with** de) **2** *n Pol* libéral, -ale *mf* ∎ **liberalism** *n* libéralisme *m*

liberate ['lɪbəreɪt] *vt* libérer ∎ **libe'ration** *n* libération *f* ∎ **liberator** *n* libérateur, -trice *mf*

liberty ['lɪbətɪ] *(pl -ies) n* liberté *f*; **to be at l. to do sth** être libre de faire qch; **to take liberties with sb/sth** prendre des libertés avec qn/qch; *Fam* **what a l.!** *(impudence)* quel culot!

Libra ['li:brə] *n (sign)* la Balance; **to be (a) L.** être Balance

library ['laɪbrərɪ] *(pl -ies) n* bibliothèque *f*; **l. card** carte *f* de bibliothèque ∎ **librarian** [-'breərɪən] *n* bibliothécaire *mf*

> Note that the French words **libraire** and **librairie** are false friends and are never translations for the English words **librarian** and **library**. They mean **bookseller** and **bookshop**.

libretto [lɪ'bretəʊ] *(pl -os) n Mus* livret *m*

Libya ['lɪbɪə] *n* la Libye ∎ **Libyan 1** *adj* libyen, -enne **2** *n* Libyen, -enne *mf*

lice [laɪs] *pl of* **louse**

licence ['laɪsəns] *(Am* **license**) *n* **(a)** *(permit)* permis *m*; *(for trading)* licence *f*; *(for flying)* brevet *m*; **(TV) l.** redevance *f*; **l. plate/number** *(of vehicle)* plaque *f*/numéro *m* d'immatriculation **(b)** *(excessive freedom)* licence *f*

> Note that the French noun **licence** can be a false friend. It also means **bachelor's degree**.

license ['laɪsəns] **1** *n Am* = **licence 2** *vt* accorder un permis/une licence/un brevet à; **to be licensed to carry a gun** avoir un permis de port d'armes; *Br* **licensed premises** débit *m* de boissons; **licensing laws** lois *fpl* relatives aux débits de boissons

licit ['lɪsɪt] *adj* licite

lick [lɪk] **1** *n* coup *m* de langue; **a l. of paint** un coup de peinture **2** *vt* lécher; *Fam (defeat)* écraser; **to l. one's lips** s'en lécher les babines ∎ **licking** *n Fam (defeat)* déculottée *f*

licorice ['lɪkərɪʃ, 'lɪkərɪs] *n* réglisse *f*

lid [lɪd] *n* **(a)** *(of box)* couvercle *m* **(b)** *(of eye)* paupière *f*

lie¹ [laɪ] **1** *n* mensonge *m*; **to tell a l.** dire un mensonge; **to give the l. to sth** *(show as untrue)* démentir qch; **l. detector** détecteur *m* de mensonges **2** *(pt & pp* **lied**, *pres p* **lying**) *vi (tell lies)* mentir; **to l. through one's teeth** mentir effrontément

lie² [laɪ] *(pt* **lay**, *pp* **lain**, *pres p* **lying**) *vi* **(a)** *(of person, animal)* (be in a flat position) être allongé; *(get down)* s'allonger; **to be lying on the grass** être allongé sur l'herbe; **to l. in bed** rester au lit; **he lay asleep** il dormait; **I lay awake all night** je n'ai pas dormi de la nuit; **she lay dead at my feet** elle était étendue morte à mes pieds; *Fig* **to l. low** garder un profil bas; **here lies...** *(on tomb)* ci-gît...

(b) *(of object)* être, se trouver; **snow lay on the hills** il y avait de la neige sur les collines; **to l. in ruins** *(of building)* être en ruines; *(of career)* être détruit; **the problem lies in that...** le problème réside dans le fait que...; **a brilliant future lies before her** un brillant avenir s'ouvre devant elle; **it's lying heavy on my stomach** *(of meal)* cela me pèse sur l'estomac ∎ **'lie-'down** *n Br* **to have a l.** faire une sieste ∎ **'lie-'in** *n Br* **to have a l.** faire la grasse matinée

▸ **lie about, lie around** *vi (of objects, person)* traîner

▸ **lie down** *vi* s'allonger; **to be lying down** être allongé

▸ **lie in** *vi Br Fam* faire la grasse matinée

lieu [lu:] *n* **in l.** à la place; **in l. of sth** au lieu de qch

lieutenant [*Br* lefʹtenənt, *Am* lu:ʹtenənt] *n* lieutenant *m*

life [laɪf] *(pl* **lives**) *n* vie *f; (of battery, machine)* durée *f* de vie; **to come to l.** *(of party, street)* s'animer; **at your time of l.** à ton âge; **loss of l.** perte *f* en vies humaines; **true to l.** conforme à la réalité; **to take one's (own) l.** se donner la mort; **bird l.** les oiseaux *mpl;* **l. annuity** rente *f* viagère; **l. expectancy** espérance *f* de vie; **l. force** force *f* vitale; **l. insurance** assurance-vie *f;* **l. jacket** gilet *m* de sauvetage; *Br* **l. peer** pair *m* à vie; *Am* **l. preserver** ceinture *f* de sauvetage; **l. raft** radeau *m* de sauvetage; **l. span** durée *f* de vie ▪ **lifebelt** *n* ceinture *f* de sauvetage ▪ **lifeblood** *n (of person)* souffle *m* vital; *(of economy)* moteur *m* ▪ **lifeboat** *n* canot *m* de sauvetage ▪ **lifebuoy** *n* bouée *f* de sauvetage ▪ **lifeguard** *n* maître nageur *m* ▪ **lifeless** *adj* sans vie ▪ **lifelike** *adj* très ressemblant ▪ **lifeline** *n* **to be sb's l.** être essentiel, -ielle à la survie de qn ▪ **lifelong** *adj* de toute sa vie; *(friend)* de toujours ▪ **lifesaving** *n* sauvetage *m* ▪ **lifesize(d)** *adj* grandeur nature *inv* ▪ **lifestyle** *n* style *m* de vie ▪ **life-supʹport machine** *n* respirateur *m* artificiel ▪ **lifetime** *n* vie *f;* **l. éternité** *f;* **in my l.** de mon vivant; **it's the chance of a l.** une telle chance ne se présente qu'une fois dans une vie; **the holidays of a l.** des vacances exceptionnelles; **a once-in-a-l. experience** une expérience inoubliable

lift [lɪft] **1** *n Br (elevator)* ascenseur *m;* **to give sb a l.** emmener qn en voiture **(to** à) **2** *vt* lever; *(heavy object)* soulever; *Fig (ban, siege)* lever; *Fig (steal)* piquer **(from** à) **3** *vi (of fog)* se lever ▪ **lift-off** *n (of space vehicle)* décollage *m*

▸ **lift down** *vt sep (take down)* descendre **(from** de)

▸ **lift off** *vt sep (take down)* descendre **(from** de) **2** *vi (of spacecraft)* décoller

▸ **lift out** *vt sep (take out)* sortir

▸ **lift up** *vt sep (arm, object, eyes)* lever; *(heavy object)* soulever

ligament [ʹlɪgəmənt] *n* ligament *m*

light¹ [laɪt] **1** *n* lumière *f; (on vehicle)* feu *m; (vehicle headlight)* phare *m;* **by the l. of sth** à la clarté de qch; **in the l. of...** *(considering)* à la lumière de...; *Fig* **in that l.** sous cet éclairage; **against the l.** à contre-jour; **to bring sth to l.** mettre qch en lumière; **to come to l.** être découvert; **to throw l. on sth** *(matter)* éclaircir qch; **do you have a l.?** *(for cigarette)* est-ce que

vous avez du feu?; **to set l. to sth** mettre le feu à qch; **turn right at the lights** tournez à droite après les feux; **l. bulb** ampoule *f;* **l. switch** interrupteur *m* **2** *adj* **it will soon be l.** il fera bientôt jour **3** *(pt & pp* **lit** *or* **lighted)** *vt (fire, candle, gas)* allumer; *(match)* allumer, gratter; **to l. (up)** *(room)* éclairer; *(cigarette)* allumer **4** *vi* **to l. up** *(of window)* s'allumer ▪ **lighting** *n (act, system)* éclairage *m* ▪ **light-year** *n* année-lumière *f*

light² [laɪt] *adj (bright, not dark)* clair; **a l. green jacket** une veste vert clair ▪ **lightness** *n (brightness)* clarté *f*

light³ [laɪt] *adj (in weight, quantity, strength)* léger; *(task, exercise)* facile; *(low-fat)* allégé; *(low-calorie)* pauvre en calories; **l. rain** pluie *f* fine; **to travel l.** voyager avec peu de bagages ▪ **light-ʹfingered** *adj* chapardeur, -euse ▪ **light-ʹheaded** *adj (giddy, foolish)* étourdi ▪ **light-ʹhearted** *adj* enjoué ▪ **lightness** *n (in weight)* légèreté *f*

lighten [ʹlaɪtən] *vt* **(a)** *(make less dark)* éclaircir **(b)** *(make less heavy)* alléger; *Fig* **to l. sb's load** soulager qn **2** *vi (of sky)* s'éclaircir; *Fam* **to l. up** se détendre

lighter [ʹlaɪtə(r)] *n* briquet *m; (for cooker)* allume-gaz *m inv*

lighthouse [ʹlaɪthaʊs] *n* phare *m*

lightly [ʹlaɪtlɪ] *adv* légèrement; **to get off l.** s'en tirer à bon compte

lightning [ʹlaɪtnɪŋ] **1** *n (flashes of light)* éclairs *mpl; (charge)* foudre *f;* **flash of l.** éclair *m;* **struck by l.** frappé par la foudre **2** *adj (speed)* foudroyant; *(visit)* éclair *inv; Br* **l. conductor,** *Am* **l. rod** paratonnerre *m*

lightweight [ʹlaɪtweɪt] **1** *adj (shoes, fabric)* léger, -ère; *Fig & Pej (person)* pas sérieux, -ieuse **2** *n Boxing* poids *m* léger

like¹ [laɪk] **1** *prep* comme; **l. this** comme ça; **what's he l.?** *(physically, as character)* comment est-il?; **to be** *or* **look l. sb/sth** ressembler à qn/qch; **what was the book l.?** comment as-tu trouvé le livre?; **what does it smell l.?** cela sent quoi?; **I have one l. it** j'en ai un pareil **2** *adv* **nothing l. as big** loin d'être aussi grand **3** *conj Fam (as)* comme; **it's l. I say** c'est comme je te le dis; **do l. I do** fais comme moi **4** *n* **...and the l.** ...et ainsi de suite; **the l. of which we shall never see again** comme on n'en reverra plus; **the likes of you** des gens de ton acabit

like² [laɪk] **1** *vt* aimer (bien) **(to do** *or* **doing** faire); **I l. him** je l'aime bien; **she likes it here** elle se plaît ici; **to l. sb/sth best** aimer mieux qn/qch; **I'd l. to come** *(want)* j'aimerais bien venir; **I'd l. a kilo of apples** je voudrais un kilo de pommes; **would you l. an apple?** voulez-vous une pomme?; **if you l.** si vous voulez;

how would you I. to come? ça te dirait de venir? **2** *npl* **one's likes and dislikes** nos préférences *fpl* ▪ **liking** *n* **a I. for** *(person)* de la sympathie pour; *(thing)* du goût pour; **to my I.** à mon goût

likeable ['laɪkəbəl] *adj* sympathique

likely ['laɪklɪ] **1** (**-ier, -iest**) *adj* (*result, event*) probable; *(excuse)* vraisemblable; *(place)* propice; *(candidate)* prometteur, -euse; *Ironic* **a I. excuse!** la belle excuse!; **it's I. (that) she'll come** il est probable qu'elle viendra; **he's I. to come** il viendra probablement; **he's not I. to come** il ne risque pas de venir **2** *adv* **very I.** très probablement; **not I.!** pas question! ▪ **likelihood** *n* probabilité *f*; **there isn't much I. that...** il y a peu de chances que... (*+ subjunctive*)

liken ['laɪkən] *vt* comparer (**to** à)

likeness ['laɪknɪs] *n* (**a**) *(similarity)* ressemblance *f*; **a family I.** un air de famille; **it's a good I.** c'est très ressemblant (**b**) *(portrait)* portrait *m*

likewise ['laɪkwaɪz] *adv* (*similarly*) de même

lilac ['laɪlək] **1** *(flower, colour)* lilas *m* **2** *adj* *(colour)* lilas *inv*

Lilo® ['laɪləʊ] (*pl* **-os**) *n Br* matelas *m* pneumatique

lilt [lɪlt] *n* (*in song, voice*) modulation *f*

lily ['lɪlɪ] (*pl* **-ies**) *n* lis *m*; **I. of the valley** muguet *m*

limb [lɪm] *n* (*of body*) membre *m*; *Fig* **to be out on a I.** (*in dangerous position*) être sur la corde raide

limber ['lɪmbə(r)] *vi* **to I. up** s'échauffer

limbo ['lɪmbəʊ] *adv* **in I.** (*uncertain, waiting*) dans l'incertitude

lime¹ [laɪm] *n* (**a**) *(fruit)* citron *m* vert; **I. juice** jus *m* de citron vert (**b**) *(tree)* tilleul *m*

lime² [laɪm] *n Chem* chaux *f* ▪ **limestone** *n Geol* calcaire *m*

limelight ['laɪmlaɪt] *n* **to be in the I.** occuper le devant de la scène

limerick ['lɪmərɪk] *n* = poème humoristique de cinq vers

limit ['lɪmɪt] **1** *n* limite *f*; (*restriction*) limitation *f* (**on** de); *Fam* **that's the I.!** c'est le comble!; **within limits** jusqu'à un certain point **2** *vt* limiter (**to** à); **to I. oneself to sth/doing sth** se borner à qch/faire qch ▪ **limi'tation** *n* limitation *f* ▪ **limited** *adj* (*restricted*) limité; *(edition)* à tirage limité; *(mind)* borné; *Br* **I. company** société *f* à responsabilité limitée; *Br* **(public) I. company** (*with shareholders*) société *f* anonyme; **to a I. degree** jusqu'à un certain point ▪ **limitless** *adj* illimité

limousine [lɪmə'ziːn] *n* (*car*) limousine *f* ▪ **limo** *n Fam* limousine *f*

limp¹ [lɪmp] **1** *n* **to have a I.** boiter **2** *vi* (*of person*) boiter; *Fig* **to I. along** (*of vehicle, ship*) avancer tant bien que mal

limp² [lɪmp] (**-er, -est**) *adj* (*soft*) mou (*f* molle); (*flabby*) (*skin*) flasque; (*person, hat*) avachi

limpid ['lɪmpɪd] *adj* limpide

linchpin ['lɪntʃpɪn] *n* (*person*) pivot *m*

line¹ [laɪn] *n* ligne *f*; (*stroke*) trait *m*; (*of poem*) vers *m*; (*wrinkle*) ride *f*; (*track*) voie *f*; (*rope*) corde *f*; (*row*) rangée *f*; (*of vehicles*) file *f*; *Am* (*queue of people*) file, queue *f*; (*family*) lignée *f*; (*of goods*) ligne (de produits); **to learn one's lines** (*of actor*) apprendre son texte; **to be on the I.** (*at other end of phone line*) être au bout du fil; (*at risk*) (*of job*) être menacé; **hold the I.!** (*remain on phone*) ne quittez pas!; **the hot I.** le téléphone rouge; *Am* **to stand in I.** faire la queue; *Fig* **to step** *or* **get out of I.** refuser de se conformer; (*misbehave*) faire une incartade; **out of I. with** (*sb's ideas*) en désaccord avec; **in I. with sth** conforme à qch; **to be in I. for promotion** être sur la liste des promotions; **to take a hard I.** adopter une attitude ferme; **along the same lines** (*work, think, act*) de la même façon; **something along those lines** quelque chose dans ce genre-là; *Fam* **to drop a I.** (*send a letter*) envoyer un mot (**to** à); **where do we draw the I.?** où fixer les limites?; **what I. of business are you in?** vous travaillez dans quelle branche?; **I. dancing** = danse de style country effectuée en rangs

2 *vt* **to I. the street** (*of trees*) border la rue; (*of people*) s'aligner le long du trottoir; **to I. up** (*children, objects*) aligner; (*arrange*) organiser; **to have something lined up** (*in mind*) avoir quelque chose en vue; **lined face** visage *m* ridé; **lined paper** papier *m* réglé

3 *vi* **to I. up** s'aligner; *Am* (*queue up*) faire la queue; **to I. up in twos** se mettre en rangs par deux ▪ **line-up** *n* (*row of people*) file *f*; *Pol* (*of countries*) front *m*; *TV* (*of programmes*) programme *m*; *TV* (*of guests*) plateau *m*; *Am* (*identity parade*) séance *f* d'identification

line² [laɪn] *vt* (*clothes*) doubler; *Fig* **to I. one's pockets** se remplir les poches ▪ **lining** *n* (*of clothes*) doublure *f*; **brake I.** garniture *f* de frein

lineage ['lɪnɪɪdʒ] *n* lignée *f*

linear ['lɪnɪə(r)] *adj* linéaire

linen ['lɪnɪn] *n* (*sheets*) linge *m*; (*material*) (*toile f* de) lin *m*; *Br* **I. basket** panier *m* à linge; *Br* **I. cupboard**, *Am* **I. closet** armoire *f* à linge; **I. sheet** drap *m* de lin

liner ['laɪnə(r)] *n* (**a**) (*ocean*) **I.** paquebot *m* (**b**) *Br* **(dust)bin I.**, *Am* **garbage can I.** sac *m* poubelle

linesman ['laɪnzmən] (*pl* **-men**) *n Football* juge *m* de touche

linger ['lɪŋgə(r)] *vi* **to I. (on)** (*of person*) s'attarder; (*of smell, memory*) persister; (*of doubt*) subsister; **a lingering death** une mort lente

lingo ['lɪŋgəʊ] (*pl* **-oes**) *n Fam* jargon *m*

linguist ['lɪŋgwɪst] *n* (*specialist*) linguiste *mf*; **to**

be a good l. être doué pour les langues ▪ **lin'guistic** *adj* linguistique ▪ **lin'guistics** *n* linguistique *f*

liniment ['lɪnɪmənt] *n* pommade *f*

link [lɪŋk] **1** *n (connection) & Comptr* lien *m*; *(of chain)* maillon *m*; *(by road, rail)* liaison *f* **2** *vt (connect)* relier (**to** à); *(relate, associate)* lier (**to** à); **to l. up** relier; *(computer)* connecter **3** *vi* **to l. up** *(of companies, countries)* s'associer; *(of computers)* se connecter; *(of roads)* se rejoindre ▪ **linkup** *n (of spacecraft)* jonction *f*; *(between TV stations)* liaison *f*

lino ['laɪnəʊ] *(pl* **-os)** *n Br* lino *m* ▪ **linoleum** [lɪ'nəʊlɪəm] *n* linoléum *m*

linseed ['lɪnsiːd] *n* **l. oil** huile *f* de lin

lint [lɪnt] *n (bandage)* tissu *m* ouaté; *(fluff)* peluches *fpl*

lion ['laɪən] *n* lion *m*; **l. cub** lionceau *m*; **l. tamer** dompteur, -euse *mf* de lions ▪ **lioness** *n* lionne *f*

lip [lɪp] *n (of person, wound)* lèvre *f*; *(of cup)* bord *m*; *Fam (impudence)* culot *m*; **to pay l. service to sth** faire semblant de s'intéresser à qch; **l. balm, l. salve** baume *m* pour les lèvres; **l. gloss** brillant *m* à lèvres ▪ **lip-read** *(pt & pp* **-read** [-red]) *vi* lire sur les lèvres ▪ **lipstick** *n* rouge *m* à lèvres

liquefy ['lɪkwɪfaɪ] *(pt & pp* **-ied)** *vt* liquéfier **2** *vi* se liquéfier

liqueur [*Br* lɪ'kjʊə(r), *Am* lɪ'kɜːr] *n* liqueur *f*

liquid ['lɪkwɪd] *n & adj* liquide *(m)*

liquidate ['lɪkwɪdeɪt] *vt (debt, firm) & Fam (kill)* liquider ▪ **liqui'dation** *n* liquidation *f*

liquidizer ['lɪkwɪdaɪzə(r)] *n Br (for fruit juices, purées)* mixeur *m* ▪ **liquidize** *vt Br* passer au mixer

liquor ['lɪkə(r)] *n Am* alcool *m*; **l. store** magasin *m* de vins et de spiritueux

liquorice ['lɪkərɪʃ, 'lɪkərɪs] *n Br* réglisse *f*

lira ['lɪərə] *(pl* **lire** ['lɪəreɪ]) *n* lire *f*

lisp [lɪsp] **1** *n* **to have a l.** zézayer **2** *vi* zézayer

list [lɪst] **1** *n* liste *f* **2** *vt (things)* faire la liste de; *(names)* mettre sur la liste; *(name one by one)* énumérer; *Br* **listed building** monument *m* classé

listen ['lɪsən] *vi* écouter; **to l. to sb/sth** écouter qn/qch; **to l. (out) for** *(telephone, person)* guetter; **to l. in (to)** *(on radio)* écouter ▪ **listener** *n (to radio)* auditeur, -trice *mf*; **to be a good l.** *(pay attention)* savoir écouter ▪ **listening** *n* écoute *f* (**to** de)

listless ['lɪstləs] *adj* apathique ▪ **listlessness** *n* apathie *f*

lit [lɪt] *pt & pp of* **light**¹

litany ['lɪtənɪ] *(pl* **-ies)** *n* litanie *f*

liter ['liːtə(r)] *Am =* **litre**

literal ['lɪtərəl] *adj* littéral; *(not exaggerated)* réel *(f* réelle) ▪ **literally** *adv* littéralement; *(really)* réellement; **he took it l.** il l'a pris au pied de la lettre

literary ['lɪtərərɪ] *adj* littéraire

literate ['lɪtərət] *adj* qui sait lire et écrire; **highly l.** *(person)* très instruit ▪ **literacy** *n (of country)* degré *m* d'alphabétisation; *(of person)* capacité *f* de lire et d'écrire

literature ['lɪtərətʃə(r)] *n* littérature *f*; *(pamphlets)* documentation *f*

lithe [laɪð] *adj* agile

Lithuania [lɪθjʊ'eɪnɪə] *n* Lituanie *f* ▪ **Lithuanian 1** *adj* lituanien, -ienne **2** *n (person)* Lituanien, -ienne *mf*; *(language)* lituanien *m*

litigation [lɪtɪ'geɪʃən] *n Law* litige *m* ▪ **litigant 1** *n* plaideur, -euse *mf* **2** *adj (party)* plaidant ▪ **litigious** *adj* litigieux, -euse

litre ['liːtə(r)] *(Am* **liter)** *n* litre *m*

litter ['lɪtə(r)] **1** *n (rubbish)* détritus *mpl*; *(papers)* papiers *mpl*; *(young animals)* portée *f*; *(for cat)* litière *f*, *Fig (jumble, confusion)* fouillis *m*; *Br* **l. basket** *or* **bin** boîte *f* à ordures **2** *vt Br* **to be littered with sth** être jonché de qch ▪ **litterbug** *n Fam =* personne qui jette des détritus n'importe où

little ['lɪtəl] **1** *n* **l.** peu *m*; **I've l. left** il m'en reste peu; **she eats l.** elle mange peu; **to have l. to say** avoir peu de choses à dire; **I have a l.** j'en ai un peu; **the l. that I have** le peu que j'ai **2** *adj* (**a**) *(small)* petit; **the l. ones** les petits; **a l. bit** un *(petit)* peu (**b**) *(not much)* peu de; **l. time/ money** peu de temps/d'argent; **a l. time/ money** un peu de temps/d'argent **3** *adv (somewhat, rather)* peu; **l. by l.** peu à peu; **as l. as possible** le moins possible; **a l. heavy** un peu lourd; **to work a l.** travailler un peu; **it's a l. better** c'est un peu mieux; **it's l. better** *(not much)* ce n'est guère mieux

liturgy ['lɪtədʒɪ] *(pl* **-ies)** *n* liturgie *f*

live¹ [laɪv] **1** *adj* (**a**) *(electric wire)* sous tension; *(switch)* mal isolé; *(plugged in) (appliance)* branché; *(ammunition)* réel *(f* réelle), de combat; *(bomb)* non explosé; *(coal)* ardent (**b**) *(alive) (animal)* vivant; **a real l. king** un roi en chair et en os **2** *adj & adv Radio & TV* en direct; **a l. broadcast** une émission en direct; **l. audience** public *m*; **a l. recording** un enregistrement public

live² [lɪv] **1** *vt (life)* mener, vivre; *(one's faith)* vivre pleinement; *Fam* **to l. it up** mener la grande vie **2** *vi* vivre; **where do you l.?** où habitez-vous?; **to l. in Paris** habiter (à) Paris

▸ **live down** *vt sep* faire oublier

▸ **live off, live on** *vt insep (eat)* vivre de; *(sponge off)* vivre aux crochets de

▸ **live on** *vi (of memory)* survivre

▸ **live through** *vt insep (experience)* vivre; **to l. through the winter** passer l'hiver

▸ **live up to** *vt insep (one's principles)* vivre selon; *(sb's expectations)* se montrer à la hauteur de

livelihood ['laɪvlɪhʊd] n moyens mpl de subsistance; **my l.** mon gagne-pain; **to earn one's** or **a l.** gagner sa vie

lively ['laɪvlɪ] (**-ier, -iest**) adj (person, style) plein de vie; (street, story) vivant; (mind, colour) vif (f vive); (discussion, conversation) animé; (protest, campaign) vigoureux, -euse ■ **liveliness** n vivacité f

liven ['laɪvən] 1 vt **to l. up** (person) égayer; (party) animer 2 vi **to l. up** (of person, party) s'animer

liver ['lɪvə(r)] n foie m

livery ['lɪvərɪ] n (uniform) livrée f; **in l.** en livrée

livestock ['laɪvstɒk] n bétail m

livid ['lɪvɪd] adj (angry) furieux, -ieuse; (pale) livide; **l. with cold** blême de froid

living ['lɪvɪŋ] 1 adj (alive) vivant; **not a l. soul** (nobody) pas âme qui vive; **within l. memory** de mémoire d'homme; **l. or dead** mort ou vif (f morte ou vive); **the l.** les vivants mpl 2 n (livelihood) vie f; **to make** or **earn a** or **one's l.** gagner sa vie; **to work for a l.** travailler pour vivre; **l. conditions** conditions fpl de vie; **a l. wage** un salaire qui permet de vivre ■ **living room** n salle f de séjour

lizard ['lɪzəd] n lézard m

llama ['lɑːmə] n lama m

load [ləʊd] 1 n (object carried, burden) charge f; (freight) chargement m; (strain, weight) poids m; Fam **a l. of, loads of** (people, money) un tas de; **to take a l. off sb's mind** ôter un grand poids à qn 2 vt (truck, gun) charger (**with** de); **to l. sb down with** (presents) charger qn de; **to l. up** (car, ship) charger (**with** de) 3 vi **to l. (up)** prendre un chargement

loaded ['ləʊdɪd] adj (gun, vehicle) chargé; Fam (rich) plein aux as; **a l. question** une question piège; **the dice are l.** les dés sont pipés; **l. (down) with** (debts) accablé de

loaf [ləʊf] 1 n (pl **loaves**) n pain m 2 vi **to l. (about)** fainéanter ■ **loafer** n (a) (person) fainéant, -éante mf (b) (shoes) mocassin m

loam [ləʊm] n terreau m

loan [ləʊn] n (money lent) prêt m; (money borrowed) emprunt m; **on l. from** prêté par; **(out) on l.** (book) sorti; **may I have the l. of...?** puis-je emprunter...? 2 vt (lend) prêter (**to** à)

loath [ləʊθ] adj **to be l. to do sth** répugner à faire qch

loathe [ləʊð] vt détester (**doing** faire) ■ **loathing** n dégoût m ■ **loathsome** adj répugnant

lobby ['lɒbɪ] 1 (pl **-ies**) n (a) (of hotel) hall m; (of theatre) foyer m (b) (in politics) groupe m de pression 2 (pt & pp **-ied**) vt faire pression sur 3 vi **to l. for sth** faire pression pour obtenir qch

lobe [ləʊb] n lobe m

lobster ['lɒbstə(r)] n homard m; (spiny) langouste f

local ['ləʊkəl] 1 adj local; (regional) régional; (of the neighbourhood) du quartier; **are you l.?** êtes-vous du coin?; **the doctor is l.** le médecin est tout près d'ici; **a l. phone call** (within town) une communication urbaine 2 n Br Fam (pub) bistrot m du coin; **she's a l.** elle est du coin; **the locals** (people) les gens mpl du coin

locality [ləʊ'kælətɪ] (pl **-ies**) n (neighbourhood) environs mpl

localize ['ləʊkəlaɪz] vt localiser ■ **localization** n localisation f

locally ['ləʊkəlɪ] adv dans le quartier

locate [ləʊ'keɪt] vt (find) repérer; (pain, noise, leak) localiser; (situate) situer; **to be located in Paris** être situé à Paris ■ **location** n (site) emplacement m; (act) repérage m; (of pain) localisation f; **on l.** (shoot a film) en extérieur

> Note that the French word **location** is a false friend and is never a translation for the English word **location**. It means **renting** or **rented accommodation** depending on the context.

lock¹ [lɒk] n (of hair) mèche f

lock² [lɒk] 1 n (a) (on door, chest) serrure f; (of gun) cran m de sûreté; (anti-theft) **l.** (on vehicle) antivol m; **under l. and key** (object) sous clef (b) (on canal) écluse f 2 vt (door, car) fermer à clef; **to l. the wheels** (of vehicle) bloquer les roues 3 vi fermer à clef
> ► **lock away** vt sep (prisoner) enfermer; (jewels) mettre sous clef
> ► **lock in** vt sep (person) enfermer; **to l. sb in sth** enfermer qn dans qch
> ► **lock out** vt sep (person) enfermer dehors
> ► **lock up** 1 vt sep (house, car) fermer à clef; (prisoner) enfermer; (jewels) mettre sous clef, enfermer 2 vi fermer à clef

locker ['lɒkə(r)] n (in school) casier m; (for luggage) (at station, airport) casier m de consigne automatique; (for clothes) vestiaire m (métallique); Am Sport **l. room** vestiaire

locket ['lɒkɪt] n médaillon m

lock-out ['lɒkaʊt] n (industrial) lock-out m inv

locksmith ['lɒksmɪθ] n serrurier m

lockup ['lɒkʌp] n Br (garage) garage m

loco ['ləʊkəʊ] adj Am Fam (crazy) cinglé

locomotive [ləʊkə'məʊtɪv] n locomotive f ■ **locomotion** [-'məʊʃən] n locomotion f

locum ['ləʊkəm] n Br (doctor) remplaçant, -ante mf

locust ['ləʊkəst] n sauterelle f

lodge [lɒdʒ] 1 n (house) pavillon m; (of porter) loge f 2 vt (person) loger; **to l. a complaint** porter plainte 3 vi (of bullet) se loger (**in** dans); **to be lodging** (accommodated) être logé (**with** chez)

lodger ['lɒdʒə(r)] n (room and meals) pensionnaire mf; (room only) locataire mf

lodging ['lɒdʒɪŋ] n (accommodation) logement m; **lodgings** (flat) logement m; (room) chambre f; **in lodgings** en meublé

loft [lɒft] n grenier m

lofty ['lɒftɪ] (-ier, -iest) adj (high, noble) élevé; (haughty, superior) hautain

log [lɒg] 1 n (tree trunk) tronc m d'arbre; (for fire) bûche f; **l. cabin** hutte f en rondin; **l. fire** feu m de bois 2 (pt & pp -gg-) vt (facts) noter; **to l. (up)** (distance) couvrir 3 vi Comptr **to l. in/out** entrer/sortir ■ **logbook** n (on ship) journal m de bord; (on plane) carnet m de vol; Br (of vehicle) ≃ carte f grise

loggerheads ['lɒgəhedz] n **at l.** en désaccord (with avec)

logic ['lɒdʒɪk] n logique f ■ **logical** adj logique ■ **logically** adv logiquement

logistics [lə'dʒɪstɪks] n logistique f

logo ['ləʊgəʊ] (pl -os) n logo m

loin [lɔɪn] n (meat) filet m; **l. chop** côtes fpl premières

loincloth ['lɔɪnklɒθ] n pagne m

loins [lɔɪnz] npl (of person) reins mpl

loiter ['lɔɪtə(r)] vi traîner

loll [lɒl] vi (in armchair) se prélasser

lollipop ['lɒlɪpɒp] n sucette f; Br **l. man/lady** = contractuel qui aide les écoliers à traverser la rue ■ **lolly** (pl -ies) n (a) Fam sucette f; (ice) **l.** glace f à l'eau (b) Br Fam (money) fric m

London ['lʌndən] 1 n Londres m ou f 2 adj (taxi) londonien, -ienne ■ **Londoner** n Londonien, -ienne mf

lone [ləʊn] adj solitaire; Fig **l. wolf** solitaire mf ■ **loner** n solitaire mf

loneliness ['ləʊnlɪnəs] n solitude f ■ **lonely** (-ier, -iest) adj (road, house, life) solitaire; (person) seul

lonesome ['ləʊnsəm] adj solitaire

long[1] [lɒŋ] 1 (-er, -est) adj long (f longue); **to be 10 m l.** avoir 10 m de long; **to be six weeks l.** durer six semaines; **how l. is...?** quelle est la longueur de...?; (time) quelle est la durée de...?; **a l. time** longtemps; **in the l. run** à la longue; **a l. face** une grimace; **a l. memory** une bonne mémoire; Sport **l. jump** saut m en longueur

2 adv (a long time) longtemps; **l. before/after** longtemps avant/après; **has he been here l.?** il y a longtemps qu'il est ici?; **how l.?** (in time) combien de temps?; **how l. ago?** il y a combien de temps?; **not l.** peu de temps; **before l.** sous peu; **no longer** ne plus; **she no longer swims** elle ne nage plus; **a bit longer** (wait) encore un peu; **I won't be l.** je n'en ai pas pour longtemps; **don't be l.** dépêche-toi; **at the longest** (tout) au plus; **all summer/winter l.** tout l'été/l'hiver; **l. live the queen!** vive la reine!; **as l. as, so l. as** (provided that) pourvu que (+ subjunctive); **as l. as I live** tant

que je vivrai ■ **long-awaited** adj tant attendu ■ **'long-'distance** adj (race) de fond; (phone call) interurbain; (flight) long-courrier ■ **long-drawn-out** adj interminable ■ **'long'haired** adj aux cheveux longs ■ **'long-'life** adj (battery) longue durée inv; (milk) longue conservation ■ **long-playing** adj **l. record** 33 tours m inv ■ **'long-'range** adj (forecast) à long terme ■ **long'sighted** adj (person) presbyte ■ **'long'standing** adj de longue date ■ **'long'suffering** adj très patient ■ **long-term** adj à long terme ■ **'long'winded** adj (speech, speaker) verbeux, -euse

long[2] [lɒŋ] vi **to l. for sth** avoir très envie de qch; **to l. for sb** languir après qn; **to l. to do sth** avoir très envie de faire qch ■ **longing** n désir m

longevity [lɒn'dʒevɪtɪ] n longévité f

longitude ['lɒndʒɪtjuːd] n longitude f

longways ['lɒŋweɪz] adv en longueur

loo [luː] (pl loos) n Br Fam **the l.** le petit coin

look [lʊk] 1 n (glance) regard m; (appearance) air m, allure f; **good looks** beauté f; **to have a l. (at sth)** jeter un coup d'œil (à qch); **to have a l. (for sth)** chercher (qch); **to have a l. (a)round** regarder; (walk) faire un tour; **let me have a l.** fais voir; **I like the l. of him** il me plaît

2 vt **to l. sb in the face** regarder qn dans les yeux; **to l. sb up and down** toiser qn

3 vi regarder; **to l. tired/happy** (seem) avoir l'air fatigué/heureux; **to l. pretty/ugly** (be) être joli/laid; **to l. one's age** faire son âge; **l. here!** dites donc!; **you l. like** or **as if** or **as though you're tired** tu as l'air fatigué; **it looks like** or **as if** or **as though she won't leave** elle n'a pas l'air de vouloir partir; **it looks like it** c'est probable; **to l. like a child** avoir l'air d'un enfant; **to l. like an apple** avoir l'air d'être une pomme; **you l. like my brother** (resemble) tu ressembles à mon frère; **it looks like rain (to me)** on dirait qu'il va pleuvoir; **what does he l. like?** (describe him) comment est-il?; **to l. well** or **good** (of person) avoir bonne mine; **you l. good in that hat** ce chapeau te va très bien; **that looks bad** (action) ça fait mauvais effet

▸ **look after** vt insep (take care of) s'occuper de; (keep safely) garder (**for sb** pour qn); **to l. after oneself** (keep healthy) faire bien attention à soi; (manage, cope) se débrouiller

▸ **look around** 1 vt insep (town, shops) faire un tour dans 2 vi (have a look) regarder; (walk round) faire un tour

▸ **look at** vt insep regarder; (consider) considérer; (check) vérifier

▸ **look away** vi détourner les yeux

▸ **look back** vi regarder derrière soi; (in time) regarder en arrière

▸ **look down** vi baisser les yeux; (from a height) regarder en bas; **to l. down on** (consider scornfully) regarder de haut

▶ **look for** *vt insep (seek)* chercher

▶ **look forward to** *vt insep (event)* attendre avec impatience; **to l. forward to doing sth** avoir hâte de faire qch

▶ **look in** *vi* regarder à l'intérieur; **to l. in on sb** passer voir qn

▶ **look into** *vt insep (examine)* examiner; *(find out about)* se renseigner sur

▶ **look on 1** *vt insep (consider)* considérer (**as** comme) **2** *vi (watch)* regarder

▶ **look out** *vi (be careful)* faire attention; **to l. out for sb/sth** *(seek)* chercher qn/qch; *(watch)* guetter qn/qch; **to l. (out) on to** *(of window, house)* donner sur

▶ **look over** *vt insep (examine fully)* examiner; *(briefly)* parcourir; *(region, town)* parcourir, visiter

▶ **look round 1** *vt insep (visit)* visiter **2** *vi (have a look)* regarder; *(walk round)* faire un tour; *(look back)* se retourner; **to l. round for sb/sth** *(seek)* chercher qn/qch

▶ **look through** *vt insep (inspect)* passer en revue; **to l. straight through sb** *(not see)* regarder qn sans le voir; *(deliberately)* ignorer qn

▶ **look up 1** *vt sep (word)* chercher; **to l. sb up** *(visit)* passer voir qn **2** *vi (of person)* lever les yeux; *(into the air or sky)* regarder en l'air; *(improve)* of situation) s'améliorer; *Fig* **to l. up to sb** respecter qn

-looking ['lʊkɪŋ] *suff* **pleasant-/tired-l.** à l'air agréable/fatigué

looking-glass ['lʊkɪŋglɑːs] *n* miroir *m*

lookout ['lʊkaʊt] *n (soldier)* guetteur *m*; *(sailor)* vigie *f*; **l. (post)** observatoire *m*; *(on ship)* vigie; **to be on the l.** faire le guet; **to be on the l. for sb/sth** guetter qn/qch; *Fam* **that's your l.!** c'est ton problème!

loom [luːm] **1** *n (weaving machine)* métier *m* à tisser **2** *vi* **to l. (up)** *(of mountain)* apparaître indistinctement; *(of event)* paraître imminent

loony ['luːnɪ] *(pl* **-ies)** *n & adj Fam* dingue *(mf)*

loop [luːp] **1** *n* boucle *f* **2** *vt* **to l. the loop** *(in plane)* faire un looping

loophole ['luːphəʊl] *n (in law)* vide *m* juridique

loose [luːs] **1** **(-er, -est)** *adj (screw, belt, knot)* desserré; *(tooth, stone)* qui bouge; *(page)* détaché; *(clothes)* flottant; *(hair)* dénoué; *(flesh)* flasque; *(wording, translation, link)* vague; *(discipline)* relâché; *(articles for sale)* en vrac; *Br (cheese, tea)* au poids; *Pej (woman)* facile; **there's an animal/prisoner l.** *(having escaped)* il y a un animal échappé/un prisonnier évadé; **l. change** petite monnaie *f*; **l. connection** *(in appliance)* mauvais contact *m*; *Br* **l. covers** housses *fpl*; **l. living** vie *f* dissolue; **to come** or **get l.** *(of knot, screw)* se desserrer; *(of page)* se détacher; *(of tooth)* se mettre à bouger; **to get l.** *(of dog)* se détacher;

to set or **turn l.** *(dog)* lâcher; *Br* **he's at a l. end** il ne sait pas trop quoi faire **2** *n* **on the l.** *(prisoner)* en cavale; *(animal)* en liberté

loosely ['luːslɪ] *adv (hang)* lâchement; *(hold, tie)* sans serrer; *(translate)* de façon approximative; *(link)* vaguement

loosen ['luːsən] **1** *vt (knot, belt, screw)* desserrer; *(rope)* détendre; **to l. one's grip** relâcher son étreinte **2** *vi Sport* **to l. up** faire des exercices d'assouplissement

loot [luːt] **1** *n* butin *m*; *Fam (money)* fric *m* **2** *vt* piller ▪ **looter** *n* pillard, -arde *mf* ▪ **looting** *n* pillage *m*

lop [lɒp] *(pt & pp* **-pp-)** *vt* **to l. (off)** couper

lop-sided [lɒp'saɪdɪd] *adj (crooked)* de travers

loquacious [ləʊˈkweɪʃəs] *adj* loquace

lord [lɔːd] **1** *n* seigneur *m*; *(British title)* lord *m*; **the L.** *(God)* le Seigneur; **L. knows if…** Dieu sait si…; *Fam* **oh L.!, good L.!** mon Dieu!; *Br* **my l.** *(to judge)* Monsieur le juge **2** *vt Fam* **to l. it over sb** traiter qn de haut

lordly ['lɔːdlɪ] *adj* digne d'un grand seigneur; *(arrogant)* hautain

lordship ['lɔːdʃɪp] *n Br* **Your L.** *(to judge)* Monsieur le juge

lore [lɔː(r)] *n* traditions *fpl*

lorry ['lɒrɪ] *(pl* **-ies)** *n Br* camion *m*; *(heavy)* poids *m* lourd; **l. driver** camionneur *m*; **(long-distance) l. driver** routier *m*

lose [luːz] *(pt & pp* lost) *vt* perdre; **to l. interest in sth** se désintéresser de qch; **to l. one's life** trouver la mort (**in** dans); **to have nothing to l.** n'avoir rien à perdre; **to be lost at sea** périr en mer; **to l. one's way, to get lost** *(of person)* se perdre; **the ticket got lost** on a perdu le billet; *Fam* **get lost!** fous le camp!; **that lost us the war/our jobs** cela nous a coûté la guerre/notre travail; **I've lost my bearings** je suis désorienté; *Fig* **you've lost me** je ne vous suis plus; **the clock loses six minutes a day** la pendule retarde de six minutes par jour; *Fam* **to l. it** *(go mad)* perdre la boule; *(lose one's temper)* péter les plombs; *Br Fam* **to l. the plot** perdre la boule

2 *vi* perdre; **to l. out** être perdant; **to l. to sb** *(in contest)* être battu par qn ▪ **loser** *n (in contest)* perdant, -ante *mf*; *Fam (failure in life)* minable *mf*; **to be a good l.** être beau joueur ▪ **losing** *adj (number, team, horse)* perdant; **to fight a l. battle** être battu d'avance

loss [lɒs] *n* perte *f*; **at a l.** *(confused)* perplexe; **to sell sth at a l.** vendre qch à perte; **at a l. to do sth** *(unable)* incapable de faire qch; **to be at a l. (to know) what to say** ne savoir que dire; **to make a l.** *(financially)* perdre de l'argent

lost [lɒst] **1** *pt & pp* of **lose 2** *adj* perdu; *Br* **l. property,** *Am* **l. and found** objets *mpl* trouvés

lot[1] [lɒt] *n (destiny)* sort *m*; *(batch)* lot *m*; *(plot of land)* terrain *m*; **to draw lots** tirer au sort

lot² [lɒt] *n* the l. *(everything)* (le) tout; **the l. of you** vous tous; **a l. of, lots of** beaucoup de; **a l.** beaucoup; **quite a l.** pas mal *(of* de); **such a l.** tellement *(of* de); **what a l. of flowers/water!** regarde toutes ces fleurs/toute cette eau!; **what a l. of flowers you have!** que vous avez de fleurs!; *Br Fam* **a bad l.** *(person)* un sale type; *Fam* **listen, you l.!** écoutez, vous tous!

lotion ['ləʊʃən] *n* lotion *f*

lottery ['lɒtəri] *(pl* -ies*) n* loterie *f*; **l. ticket** billet *m* de loterie

lotto ['lɒtəʊ] *n* loto *m*

loud [laʊd] **1** (-er, -est) *adj (voice, music)* fort; *(noise, cry)* grand; *(laugh)* gros *(f* grosse); *(gaudy)* voyant; **the radio is too l.** la radio est trop forte **2** *adv (shout)* fort; **out l.** tout haut ■**loudly** *adv (speak, laugh, shout)* fort ■**loudmouth** *n Fam (person)* grande gueule *f* ■**loudness** *n (of noise, music, voice)* volume *m* ■**loud'speaker** *n* haut-parleur *m*; *(for speaking to crowd)* porte-voix *m inv*; *(of stereo system)* enceinte *f*

lounge [laʊndʒ] **1** *n (in house, hotel)* salon *m*; **airport l.** salle *f* d'aéroport; *Br* **l. suit** complet-veston *m* **2** *vi (loll in armchair)* se prélasser; **to l. about** *(idle)* paresser; *(stroll)* flâner

louse [laʊs] **1** *n* (a) *(pl* lice) *(insect)* pou *m* (b) *(pl* louses) *Fam (person)* salaud *m* **2** *vt Fam* **to l. sth up** *(spoil)* foutre qch en l'air

lousy ['laʊzɪ] (-ier, -iest) *adj Fam (bad)* nul *(f* nulle); *(food, weather)* dégueulasse; **to feel l.** être mal fichu

lout [laʊt] *n* voyou *m* *(pl* -ous) ■**loutish** *adj (attitude)* de voyou

lovable ['lʌvəbəl] *adj* attachant

love [lʌv] **1** *n* (a) *(feeling)* amour *m*; **in l.** amoureux, -euse (**with** de); **they're in l.** ils s'aiment; **art is their l.** l'art est leur passion; **yes, my l.** oui mon amour; *Fam* **yes, l.!** oui monsieur/madame!; **give him/her my l.** *(greeting)* dis-lui bien des choses de ma part; **l. affair** liaison *f*; **l. life** vie *f* sentimentale (b) *Tennis* rien *m*; **15 l.** 15 à rien **2** *vt (person)* aimer; *(thing, activity)* adorer (**to do** ou **doing** faire) ■**loving** *adj* affectueux, -ueuse

lovely ['lʌvlɪ] (-ier, -iest) *adj (idea, smell)* très bon *(f* bonne); *(weather)* beau *(f* belle); *(pretty)* joli; *(charming)* charmant; *(kind)* gentil, -ille; **the weather's l.** il fait beau; **l. to see you!** je suis ravi de te voir!; **l. and warm/dry** bien chaud/sec *(f* sèche)

lover ['lʌvə(r)] *n (man)* amant *m*; *(woman)* maîtresse *f*; **a l. of music/art** un amateur de musique/d'art; **a nature l.** un amoureux de la nature

lovesick ['lʌvsɪk] *adj* amoureux, -euse

low¹ [ləʊ] **1** (-er, -est) *adj* bas *(f* basse); *(speed, income, intelligence)* faible; *(opinion, quality)* mauvais; **she's l. on** *(money)* elle n'a plus

beaucoup de; **to feel l.** *(depressed)* être déprimé; **in a l. voice** à voix basse; **lower** inférieur; **the lower middle class** la petite bourgeoisie

2 (-er, -est) *adv* bas; **to turn (down) l.** mettre plus bas; **to run l.** *(of supplies)* s'épuiser

3 *n Met* dépression *f*; *Fig* **to reach a new l.** *or* **an all-time l.** *(of prices)* atteindre leur niveau le plus bas ■**low 'beams** *npl Am (of vehicle)* codes *mpl* ■**low-'calorie** *adj (diet)* (à) basses calories ■**low-'cost** *adj* bon marché *inv* ■**'low-'cut** *adj* décolleté ■**lowdown** *n Fam (facts)* tuyaux *mpl* ■**low-down** *adj* méprisable ■**low-'fat** *adj (milk)* écrémé; *(cheese)* allégé ■**low-'key** *adj (discreet)* discret, -ète ■**lowland(s)** *n* basses terres *fpl* ■**low-'level** *adj* bas *(f* basse) ■**low-'lying** *adj (region)* bas *(f* basse) ■**low-'paid** *adj* mal payé ■**low-'salt** *adj (food)* à faible teneur en sel

low² [ləʊ] *vi (of cattle)* meugler

lower ['ləʊə(r)] *vt* baisser; **to l. sb/sth** *(by rope)* descendre qn/qch; **to l. oneself** s'abaisser ■**lowering** *n (drop)* baisse *f*

lowly ['ləʊlɪ] (-ier, -iest) *adj* humble

lox [lɒks] *n Am* saumon *m* fumé

loyal ['lɔɪəl] *adj* loyal (**to** envers) ■**loyalty** *n* loyauté *f*; **l. card** *(for shop)* carte *f* de fidélité

lozenge ['lɒzɪndʒ] *n (tablet)* pastille *f*; *(shape)* losange *m*

LP [el'piː] *(abbr* long-playing record*) n* 33 tours *m inv*

Ltd *(abbr* Limited*) Br Com* ≃ SARL

lubricate ['luːbrɪkeɪt] *vt* lubrifier; *(machine, car wheels)* graisser ■**lubricant** *n* lubrifiant *m* ■**lubri'cation** *n (of machine)* graissage *m*

lucid ['luːsɪd] *adj* lucide

luck [lʌk] *n (chance)* chance *f*; *(good fortune)* (bonne) chance, bonheur *m*; **to be in l.** avoir de la chance; **to be out of l.** ne pas avoir de chance; **to wish sb l.** souhaiter bonne chance à qn; **to try one's l.** tenter sa chance; **bad l.**, malchance *f*; **hard l.!, tough l.!** pas de chance!; **just my l.!** c'est bien ma chance!; **worse l.!** *(unfortunately)* malheureusement

luckily ['lʌkɪlɪ] *adv* heureusement

lucky ['lʌkɪ] (-ier, -iest) *adj (person)* chanceux, -euse; **to be l.** *(of person)* avoir de la chance; **to make a l. guess** tomber juste; **to strike it l.** décrocher le gros lot; **it's l. that...** c'est une chance que... *(+ subjunctive)*; **I've had a l. day** j'ai eu de la chance aujourd'hui; **l. charm** porte-bonheur *m inv*; **l. number** chiffre *m* porte-bonheur; *Fam* **l. devil** veinard, -arde *mf*; **how l.!** quelle chance!

lucrative ['luːkrətɪv] *adj* lucratif, -ive

ludicrous ['luːdɪkrəs] *adj* ridicule

lug [lʌg] *(pt & pp* -gg-*) vt Fam* **to l. sth (around)** trimbaler qch

luggage ['lʌgɪdʒ] *n* bagages *mpl*; **a piece of l.**

un bagage; **hand l.** bagages à main; **l. compartment** compartiment *m* à bagages; *Br* **l. van** *(on train)* fourgon *m*

lugubrious [lu:'gu:brɪəs] *adj* lugubre

lukewarm ['lu:kwɔ:m] *adj* tiède

lull [lʌl] **1** *n* arrêt *m*; *(in storm)* accalmie *f* **2** *vt* apaiser; **to l. sb to sleep** endormir qn en le/la berçant; **to l. sb into a false sense of security** endormir la méfiance de qn

lullaby ['lʌləbaɪ] *(pl -ies)* *n* berceuse *f*

lumbago [lʌm'beɪgəʊ] *n* lumbago *m*

lumber[1] ['lʌmbə(r)] *n (timber)* bois *m* de charpente; *Br (junk)* bric-à-brac *m inv* ▪ **lumberjack** *n* bûcheron *m* ▪ **lumber-room** *n Br* débarras *m*

lumber[2] ['lʌmbə(r)] *vt Br Fam* **to l. sb with sb/ sth** coller qn/qch à qn; **he got lumbered with the job** il s'est appuyé la corvée

luminous ['lu:mɪnəs] *adj (colour, paper, ink)* fluorescent; *(dial, clock)* lumineux, -euse

lump [lʌmp] **1** *n* morceau *m*; *(in soup)* grumeau *m*; *(bump)* bosse *f*; *(swelling)* grosseur *f*; **l. sum** somme *f* forfaitaire **2** *vt* **to l. together** réunir; *Fig & Pej* mettre dans le même sac ▪ **lumpy** *(-ier, -iest) adj (soup)* grumeleux, -euse; *(surface)* bosselé

lunacy ['lu:nəsɪ] *n* folie *f*; **it's (sheer) l.** c'est de la folie

lunar ['lu:nə(r)] *adj* lunaire; **l. eclipse** éclipse *f* de lune; **l. module** module *m* lunaire

lunatic ['lu:nətɪk] **1** *adj* fou *(f* folle*)* **2** *n* fou *m*, folle *f*

Note that the French word **lunatique** is a false friend and is never a translation for the English word **lunatic**. It means **moody**.

lunch [lʌntʃ] **1** *n* déjeuner *m*; **to have l.** déjeuner; **l. break, l. hour, l. time** heure *f* du déjeuner **2** *vi* déjeuner (**on** *or* **off** de) ▪ **lunchbox** *n* = boîte *f* dans laquelle on transporte son déjeuner

luncheon ['lʌnʃən] *n* déjeuner *m*; **l. meat** = tranches de viande à base de porc; *Br* **l. voucher** ticket-repas *m*, ticket-restaurant *m*

lung [lʌŋ] *n* poumon *m*; **l. cancer** cancer *m* du poumon

lunge [lʌndʒ] **1** *n* mouvement *m* brusque en avant **2** *vi* **to l. at sb** se ruer sur qn

lurch [lɜ:tʃ] **1** *n Fam* **to leave sb in the l.** laisser qn dans le pétrin **2** *vi (of person)* tituber; *(of ship, car)* faire une embardée

lure [lʊə(r)] **1** *n (attraction)* attrait *m* **2** *vt* attirer (par la ruse) (**into** dans)

lurid ['lʊərɪd] *adj (story, description)* cru; *(gaudy)* voyant

lurk [lɜ:k] *vi (hide)* être tapi (**in** dans); *(prowl)* rôder; *(of suspicion, fear)* subsister

luscious ['lʌʃəs] *adj (food)* appétissant

lush [lʌʃ] **1** *adj (vegetation)* luxuriant; *(wealthy) (surroundings)* luxueux, -ueuse **2** *n Fam (drunkard)* poivrot, -ote *mf*

lust [lʌst] **1** *n (for person)* désir *m*; *(for object)* convoitise *f* (**for** de); *(for power, knowledge)* soif *f* (**for** de) **2** *vi* **to l. after** *(object, person)* convoiter; *(power, knowledge)* avoir soif de

lustre ['lʌstə(r)] *(Am* **luster)** *n (gloss)* lustre *m*

lusty ['lʌstɪ] *(-ier, -iest) adj* vigoureux, -euse

lute [lu:t] *n* luth *m*

Luxembourg ['lʌksəmbɜ:g] *n* le Luxembourg ▪ **Luxembourgish 1** *adj* luxembourgeois **2** *n (language)* luxembourgeois ▪ **Luxembourger** *n* Luxembourgeois, -oise *mf*

luxuriant [lʌg'zʊərɪənt] *adj* luxuriant

luxuriate [lʌg'zʊərɪeɪt] *vi (laze about)* paresser

luxury ['lʌkʃərɪ] **1** *n* luxe *m* **2** *adj (goods, car, home)* de luxe ▪ **luxurious** [lʌg'zʊərɪəs] *adj* luxueux, -ueuse

Note that the French word **luxure** is a false friend and is never a translation for the English word **luxury**. It means **lust**.

lychee ['laɪtʃi:] *n* litchi *m*

lying ['laɪɪŋ] **1** *pres p of* **lie**[1,2] **2** *n* mensonges *mpl* **3** *adj (person)* menteur, -euse

lynch [lɪntʃ] *vt* lyncher ▪ **lynching** *n* lynchage *m*

lynx [lɪŋks] *n* lynx *m*

lyre ['laɪə(r)] *n* lyre *f*

lyric ['lɪrɪk] *adj* lyrique ▪ **lyrical** *adj (person) (effusive)* lyrique ▪ **lyricism** *n* lyrisme *m* ▪ **lyrics** *npl (of song)* paroles *fpl*

M, m [em] *n (letter)* M, m *m inv*

m *n* (**a**) *(abbr* **metre**) mètre *m* (**b**) *(abbr* **mile**) mile *m*

MA *(abbr* **Master of Arts**) *n Univ* to have an MA in French ≃ avoir une maîtrise de français; **John Smith MA** John Smith, titulaire d'une maîtrise *(en lettres, anglais, droit etc)*

ma'am [mæm] *n* madame *f*

mac [mæk] *(abbr* **mackintosh**) *n Br Fam (rain-coat)* imper *m*

macabre [mə'kɑːbrə] *adj* macabre

macaroni [mækə'rəʊnɪ] *n* macaronis *mpl; Br* **m. cheese,** *Am* **m. and cheese** macaronis au gratin

macaroon [mækə'ruːn] *n* macaron *m*

Mace® [meɪs] *n (gas)* gaz *m* lacrymogène

mace [meɪs] *n Culin (spice)* macis *m*

machinations [mækɪ'neɪʃənz] *npl* machinations *fpl*

machine [mə'ʃiːn] *n (apparatus, car, system)* machine *f;* **change/cash m.** distributeur *m* de monnaie/billets; *Comptr* **m. code** code *m* machine; **m. gun** mitrailleuse *f*

machine-gun [mə'ʃiːngʌn] *(pt & pp* **-nn-)** *vt* mitrailler

machinery [mə'ʃiːnərɪ] *n (machines)* machines *fpl; (works)* mécanisme *m; Fig (of organization)* rouages *mpl*

machinist [mə'ʃiːnɪst] *n (in factory)* opérateur, -trice *mf; (on sewing machine)* mécanicien, -ienne *mf*

macho ['mætʃəʊ] *(pl* **-os)** *adj & n* macho *(m) inv*

mackerel ['mækrəl] *n* maquereau *m*

mackintosh ['mækɪntɒʃ] *n Br* imperméable *m*

macro ['mækrəʊ] *(pl* **-os)** *n Comptr* macro-commande *f*

macrobiotic [mækrəʊbaɪ'ɒtɪk] *adj (diet, food)* macrobiotique

mad [mæd] (**madder, maddest**) *adj* fou *(f* folle); **to go m.** devenir fou; **to be m. at sb** *(angry)* être furieux, -ieuse contre qn; *Fam* **to be m. about** *or* **m. keen on sb/sth** être fou de qn/qch; **to drive sb m.** rendre qn fou; *Fam* **to run/work like m.** courir/travailler comme un fou; **m. cow disease** maladie *f* de la vache folle; **m. dog** chien *m* enragé ▪ **madhouse** *n Fam* maison *f* de fous ▪ **madly** *adv (insanely, desperately)* comme un fou/une folle; *Fam (exciting, interested, jealous)* follement ▪ **madman** *(pl* **-men)** *n* fou *m* ▪ **madness** *n* folie *f* ▪ **madwoman** *(pl* **-women)** *n* folle *f*

Madagascar [mædə'gæskə(r)] *n* Madagascar *f*

madam ['mædəm] *n (married)* madame *f; (unmarried)* mademoiselle *f*

maddening ['mædənɪŋ] *adj* exaspérant

made [meɪd] *pt & pp of* **make** ▪ **'made-to-'measure** *adj Br (garment)* (fait) sur mesure

Madeira [mə'dɪərə] *n (island)* Madère *f; (wine)* madère *m*

madonna [mə'dɒnə] *n Rel* madone *f*

maestro ['maɪstrəʊ] *(pl* **-os)** *n* maestro *m*

Mafia ['mæfɪə] *n* the M. la Mafia

magazine [mægə'ziːn] *n* (**a**) *(periodical, TV/radio broadcast)* magazine *m* (**b**) *(of gun, slide projector)* magasin *m*

maggot ['mægət] *n* asticot *m*

magic ['mædʒɪk] **1** *adj* magique; **m. spell** sort *m;* **the m. word** la formule magique **2** *n* magie *f;* **as if by m.** comme par enchantement ▪ **magical** *adj* magique ▪ **magician** [mə'dʒɪ-ʃən] *n* magicien, -ienne *mf*

magistrate ['mædʒɪstreɪt] *n* magistrat *m*

magnanimous [mæg'nænɪməs] *adj* magnanime

magnate ['mægneɪt] *n* magnat *m*

magnesium [mæg'niːzɪəm] *n Chem* magnésium *m*

magnet ['mægnɪt] *n* aimant *m* ▪ **magnetic** [-'netɪk] *adj* magnétique; **m. tape** bande *f* magnétique ▪ **magnetism** *n* magnétisme *m* ▪ **magnetize** *vt* magnétiser

magnificent [mæg'nɪfɪsənt] *adj* magnifique ▪ **magnificence** *n* magnificence *f* ▪ **magnificently** *adv* magnifiquement

magnify ['mægnɪfaɪ] *(pt & pp* **-ied)** *vt (image)* grossir; *(sound)* amplifier; *Fig (exaggerate)* exagérer; **magnifying glass** loupe *f* ▪ **magni-fication** [-fɪ'keɪʃən] *n* grossissement *m; (of sound)* amplification *f*

magnitude ['mægnɪtjuːd] *n* ampleur *f*

magnolia [mæg'nəʊlɪə] *n (tree)* magnolia *m*

magpie ['mægpaɪ] *n* pie *f*

mahogany [mə'hɒgənɪ] *n (wood, colour)* aca-jou *m*

maid [meɪd] *n (servant)* bonne *f; Am* **m. of honor** *(at wedding)* première demoiselle *f* d'honneur

maiden ['meɪdən] **1** *n Old-fashioned* jeune fille *f* **2** *adj (flight, voyage)* inaugural; **m. name** nom *m* de jeune fille; **m. speech** *(of MP)* premier discours *m*

mail [meɪl] **1** *n (system)* poste *f; (letters)* courrier m; *(e-mails)* méls *mpl*, courrier *m* électronique **2** *adj (bag, train)* postal; **m. order** vente *f* par correspondance; *Br* **m. van** *(vehicle)* camion *m* des postes; *(in train)* fourgon *m* postal **3** *vt* poster; **mailing list** liste *f* d'adresses ▪ **mailbox** *n Am & Comptr* boîte *f* aux lettres ▪ **mailman** *(pl* **-men)** *n Am* facteur *m*

maim [meɪm] *vt* mutiler

main¹ [meɪn] *adj* principal; **the m. thing is to…** l'essentiel est de…; **in the m.** *(generally)* en gros; **m. course** plat *m* de résistance; *Rail* **m. line** grande ligne *f*; **m. road** grande route *f*; *Fam* **m. squeeze** petit ami *m*, petite amie *f* ▪ **mainframe** *n* **m. (computer)** ordinateur *m* central ▪ **mainland** *n* continent *m* ▪ **mainly** *adv* principalement; **they were m. Spanish** la plupart étaient espagnols ▪ **mainstream** *n* tendance *f* dominante

main² [meɪn] *n* **water/gas m.** conduite *f* d'eau/de gaz; **the mains** *(electricity)* le secteur

mainstay ['meɪnsteɪ] *n (of family)* soutien *m*; *(of organization, policy)* pilier *m*

maintain [meɪn'teɪn] *vt (continue)* maintenir; *(machine, road)* entretenir; *(family)* subvenir aux besoins de; *(silence)* garder; **to m. law and order** faire respecter l'ordre public; **to m. that…** affirmer que… ▪ **maintenance** ['meɪntənəns] *n (of vehicle, road)* entretien *m*; *(of tradition, prices, position)* maintien *m*; *Law (alimony)* pension *f* alimentaire

maisonette [meɪzə'net] *n Br* duplex *m*

maître d' [metrə'diː] *n Am (in restaurant)* maître *m* d'hôtel

maize [meɪz] *n Br* maïs *m*

majesty ['mædʒəstɪ] *n* majesté *f*; **Your M.** Votre Majesté ▪ **majestic** [mə'dʒestɪk] *adj* majestueux, -ueuse

major ['meɪdʒə(r)] **1** *adj (main, great) & Mus* majeur; *(accident)* très grave; **a m. road** une grande route *f* **2** *n* **(a)** *Mil (officer)* commandant *m* **(b)** *Am Univ (subject of study)* dominante *f* **3** *vi Am Univ* **to m. in** se spécialiser en

Majorca [mə'jɔːkə] *n* Majorque *f*

majorette [meɪdʒə'ret] *n* **(drum) m.** majorette *f*

majority [mə'dʒɒrɪtɪ] **1** *(pl* **-ies)** *n* majorité *f* (**of** de); **to be in the** *or* **a m.** être majoritaire; **the m. of people** la plupart des gens **2** *adj (vote)* majoritaire

make [meɪk] **1** *(pt & pp* **made)** *vt* faire; *(tool, vehicle)* fabriquer; **to m. a decision** prendre une décision; **to m. sb happy/sad** rendre qn heureux/triste; **to m. sb tired** fatiguer qn; **to m. sth ready** préparer qch; **to m. sth yellow** jaunir qch; **to m. sb do sth** faire faire qch à qn; **to m. oneself heard** se faire entendre; **she made him her husband** elle en a fait son mari; **he'll m. a good doctor** il fera un bon médecin; *Fam* **to m. it** *(succeed)* réussir; **sorry I can't m. it to the meeting** désolé, je ne pourrai pas

assister à la réunion; **what time do you m. it?** quelle heure avez-vous?; **I m. it five o'clock** j'ai cinq heures; **what do you m. of it?** qu'en penses-tu?; **I can't m. anything of it** je n'y comprends rien; **m. my day!** fais-moi plaisir!; *Fam* **she made the train** *(did not miss)* elle a eu le train; **he made 10 euros on it** ça lui a rapporté 10 euros; **to m. good** réussir; **to m. good a loss** compenser une perte; **to m. good the damage** réparer les dégâts; **to m. light of sth** prendre qch à la légère; **to be made of wood** être en bois; **made in France** fabriqué en France

2 *vi* **to m. sure** *or* **certain of sth** s'assurer de qch; **to m. do** *(manage)* se débrouiller (**with** avec); **to m. do with sb/sth** *(be satisfied with)* se contenter de qn/qch; **to m. as if to do sth** *(appear to)* faire mine de faire qch; **to m. believe** *(pretend)* faire semblant; **to m. believe that one is…** faire semblant d'être…

3 *n (brand)* marque *f*; **of French m.** de fabrication française ▪ **make-believe** *n* **it's m.** *(story)* c'est pure invention; **to live in a world of m.** se bercer d'illusions ▪ **makeover** *n (of person)* changement *m* de look; *(of building)* transformation *f* ▪ **make-up** *n (for face)* maquillage *m*; *(of team, group)* constitution *f*; *(of person)* caractère *m*; **to put on one's m.** se maquiller; **to wear m.** se maquiller; **m. artist** maquilleur, -euse *mf*; **m. bag** trousse *f* de maquillage

▸ **make for** *vt insep (go towards)* aller vers

▸ **make off** *vi Fam (leave)* filer

▸ **make out 1** *vt sep (see, hear)* distinguer; *(understand)* comprendre; *(decipher)* déchiffrer; *(cheque, list)* faire; *Fam* **to m. out that…** *(claim)* prétendre que…; **you made me out to be stupid** tu m'as fait passer pour un idiot **2** *vi Fam (manage)* se débrouiller

▸ **make over** *vt sep (transfer)* céder (**to** à); *(change, convert)* transformer (**into** en)

▸ **make up 1** *vt sep (story)* inventer; *(put together)* *(list, collection, bed)* faire; *(prepare)* préparer; *(form)* former, composer; *(loss)* compenser; *(quantity)* compléter; *(quarrel)* régler; **to m. oneself up** se maquiller **2** *vi (of friends)* se réconcilier; **to m. up for** *(loss, damage, fault)* compenser; *(lost time, mistake)* rattraper

maker ['meɪkə(r)] *n (of product)* fabricant, -ante *mf*

makeshift ['meɪkʃɪft] *adj (arrangement, building)* de fortune

making ['meɪkɪŋ] *n (manufacture)* fabrication *f*; *(of dress)* confection *f*; **history in the m.** l'histoire en train de se faire; **the film was three years in the m.** le tournage du film a duré trois ans; **she has the makings of a pianist** elle a tout ce qu'il faut pour devenir pianiste

maladjusted [mælə'dʒʌstɪd] *adj* inadapté

malaise [mæ'leɪz] *n* malaise *m*

malaria [mə'leərɪə] *n Med* malaria *f*

Malaysia [mə'leɪzɪə] *n* la Malaisie

male [meɪl] **1** *adj (child, animal, hormone)* mâle; *(clothes, sex)* masculin; **m. nurse** infirmier *m* **2** *n (person)* homme *m*; *(animal)* mâle *m*

malevolent [mə'levələnt] *adj* malveillant ▪ **malevolence** *n* malveillance *f*

malfunction [mæl'fʌŋkʃən] **1** *n* mauvais fonctionnement *m* **2** *vi* fonctionner mal

malice [ˈmælɪs] *n* méchanceté *f*; **to bear sb m.** vouloir du mal à qn ▪ **malicious** [mə'lɪʃəs] *adj* malveillant; *Law* **m. damage** dommage *m* causé avec intention de nuire ▪ **maliciously** [mə'lɪʃəslɪ] *adv* avec malveillance

> Note that the French words **malice** and **malicieux** are false friends and are never translations for the English words **malice** and **malicious**. They mean respectively **mischief** and **mischievous**.

malign [mə'laɪn] *vt* calomnier; **much maligned** très dénigré

malignant [mə'lɪgnənt] *adj (person)* malveillant; **m. tumour** *or* **growth** tumeur *f* maligne

malingerer [mə'lɪŋgərə(r)] *n* simulateur, -trice *mf*

mall [mɔːl] *n Am* **(shopping) m.** centre *m* commercial

malleable [ˈmælɪəbəl] *adj* malléable

mallet [ˈmælɪt] *n* maillet *m*

malnutrition [mælnjuːˈtrɪʃən] *n (poor diet)* malnutrition *f*; *(lack of food)* sous-alimentation *f* ▪ **malnourished** *adj* sous-alimenté

malpractice [mælˈpræktɪs] *n* faute *f* professionnelle

malt [mɔːlt] *n* malt *m*; **m. vinegar** vinaigre *m* de malt

Malta [ˈmɔːltə] *n* Malte *f* ▪ **Mal'tese 1** *adj* maltais **2** *n (person)* Maltais, -aise *mf*; *(language)* maltais *m*

mammal [ˈmæməl] *n* mammifère *m*

mammoth [ˈmæməθ] **1** *n (animal)* mammouth *m* **2** *adj (huge)* gigantesque

man [mæn] **1** *(pl* **men)** *n (adult male)* homme *m*; *(player in sports team)* joueur *m*; *(humanity)* l'homme; *Chess* pièce *f*; **the m. in the street** l'homme de la rue; **a m.'s jacket** une veste d'homme; **a m. of God** un homme d'église; **a m. of the world** un homme d'expérience; **he's a Bristol m.** *(by birth)* il est de Bristol; **to be m. and wife** être mari et femme; **he took it like a m.** il a pris ça courageusement; *Fam* **my old m.** *(father)* mon père; *(husband)* mon homme **2** *(pt & pp* **-nn-)** *vt (be on duty at)* être de service à; *(machine)* assurer le fonctionnement de; *(plane, ship)* être membre de l'équipage de; *(guns)* servir; **manned spacecraft** engin *m*

spatial habité ▪ **manfully** *adv* vaillamment ▪ **manhood** *n (period)* âge *m* d'homme ▪ **manhunt** *n* chasse *f* à l'homme ▪ **manly** (-ier, -iest) *adj* viril ▪ **'man-'made** *adj (lake, beach)* artificiel, -ielle; *(fibre)* synthétique ▪ **'man-to-'man** *adj & adv (discussion, discuss)* d'homme à homme

manacles [ˈmænɪkəlz] *npl* menottes *fpl*

manage [ˈmænɪdʒ] **1** *vt (company, project)* diriger; *(shop, hotel)* être le gérant de; *(economy, money, time, situation)* gérer; **to m. to do sth** *(succeed)* réussir ou arriver à faire qch; *(by being smart)* se débrouiller pour faire qch; **I'll m. it** j'y arriverai; **I can't m. three suitcases** je ne peux pas porter trois valises **2** *vi (succeed)* y arriver; *(make do)* se débrouiller **(with** avec); **to m. without sb/sth** se passer de qn/qch; **managing director** directeur *m* général ▪ **manageable** *adj (parcel, car)* maniable; *(hair)* facile à coiffer; *(task)* faisable ▪ **management** *n (running, managers)* direction *f*; *(of property, economy)* gestion *f*; *(executive staff)* cadres *mpl*; **business m.** gestion *f* des affaires; **m. consultant** conseiller, -ère *mf* en ou de gestion

manager [ˈmænɪdʒə(r)] *n (of shop, company)* directeur, -trice *mf*; *(of shop, café)* gérant *m*; *(of singer, boxer)* manager *m*

managerial [mænə'dʒɪərɪəl] *adj* directorial; **m. position** poste *m* de direction; **the m. staff** les cadres *mpl*

mandarin [ˈmændərɪn] **1** *adj & n* **m. (orange)** mandarine *(f)* **2** *n Br (official)* mandarin *m*; **M. (Chinese)** *(language)* mandarin *m*

mandate [ˈmændeɪt] *n* mandat *m*

mandatory [ˈmændətərɪ] *adj* obligatoire

mane [meɪn] *n* crinière *f*

maneuver [mə'nuːvər] *n & vti Am* = **manoeuvre**

mangle [ˈmæŋgəl] **1** *n (for clothes)* essoreuse *f* **2** *vt (body)* mutiler

mango [ˈmæŋgəʊ] *(pl* **-oes** *or* **-os)** *n* mangue *f*

mangy [ˈmeɪndʒɪ] *adj (animal)* galeux, -euse

manhandle [mæn'hændəl] *vt (person)* malmener

manhole [ˈmænhəʊl] *n* bouche *f* d'égout; **m. cover** plaque *f* d'égout

mania [ˈmeɪnɪə] *n (liking)* passion *f*; *(psychological)* manie *f*

maniac [ˈmeɪnɪæk] *n* fou *m*, folle *f*

manic [ˈmænɪk] *adj Fig (person)* stressé; *(activity)* frénétique

manicure [ˈmænɪkjʊə(r)] **1** *n* manucure *f* **2** *vt* **to m. one's nails** se faire les ongles

manifest [ˈmænɪfest] **1** *adj (plain)* manifeste **2** *vt (show)* manifester

manifesto [mænɪ'festəʊ] *(pl* **-os** *or* **-oes)** *n Pol* manifeste *m*

manifold [ˈmænɪfəʊld] *adj Literary* multiple

manipulate [mə'nɪpjʊleɪt] *vt* manipuler ▪ **manipu'lation** *n* manipulation *f*

mankind [mæn'kaɪnd] *n* l'humanité *f*

manner ['mænə(r)] *n (way)* manière *f*; *(behaviour)* comportement *m*; **manners** *(social habits)* manières *fpl*; **it's bad manners to stare** il est mal élevé de dévisager les gens; **in this m.** *(like this)* de cette manière; **all m. of people/things** toutes sortes de gens/choses; **to have good/bad manners** être bien/mal élevé

mannered ['mænəd] *adj* maniéré

mannerism ['mænərɪzəm] *n Pej* tic *m*

manoeuvre [mə'nuːvə(r)] *(Am* **maneuver**) **1** *n* manœuvre *f* **2** *vti* manœuvrer ■ **manoeuvra'bility** *(Am* **maneuvra'bility**) *n (of vehicle)* maniabilité *f*

manor ['mænə(r)] *n Br* **m. (house)** manoir *m*

manpower ['mænpaʊə(r)] *n (labour)* main-d'œuvre *f*

mansion ['mænʃən] *n (in town)* hôtel *m* particulier; *(in country)* manoir *m*

manslaughter ['mænslɔːtə(r)] *n Law* homicide *m* involontaire

mantelpiece ['mæntəlpiːs] *n* dessus *m* de cheminée; **on the m.** sur la cheminée

manual ['mænjʊəl] **1** *adj (work, worker)* manuel, -uelle **2** *n (book)* manuel *m*

manufacture [mænjʊ'fæktʃə(r)] **1** *n* fabrication *f*; *(of cars)* construction *f* **2** *vt* fabriquer; *(cars)* construire ■ **manufacturer** *n* fabricant, -ante *mf*; *(of cars)* constructeur *m*

manure [mə'njʊə(r)] *n* fumier *m*

manuscript ['mænjʊskrɪpt] *n* manuscrit *m*

many ['menɪ] **1** *adj* beaucoup de; **m. people/things** beaucoup de gens/choses; **very m., a good** *or* **great m.** un très grand nombre de; **(a good** *or* **great) m. of, (very) m. of** un (très) grand nombre de; **m. times** bien des fois; **m. kinds** toutes sortes (**of** de); **how m.?** combien (de)?; **too m.** trop de; **there were so m. people that…** il y avait tant de monde que…; **as m. books as you like** autant de livres que tu veux **2** *pron* beaucoup; **m. came** beaucoup sont venus; **not m.** pas beaucoup; **too m.** trop; *Fam* **he's had one too m.** il a bu un coup de trop; **m. of them** beaucoup d'entre eux; **there are too m. of them** ils sont trop nombreux; **m. a time** bien des fois; **as m. as fifty** *(up to)* jusqu'à cinquante

map [mæp] **1** *n* carte *f*; *(plan of town, underground)* plan *m* **2** *(pt & pp* **-pp-**) *vt (country, town)* dresser une carte de; **to m. out** *(road)* tracer; *Fig (plan, programme)* élaborer

maple ['meɪpəl] *n (tree, wood)* érable *m*; **m. syrup** sirop *m* d'érable

mar [maː(r)] *(pt & pp* **-rr-**) *vt* gâcher

marathon ['mærəθən] *n* marathon *m*

maraud [mə'rɔːd] *vi* piller ■ **marauder** *n* maraudeur, -euse *mf* ■ **marauding** *adj* en maraude

marble ['mɑːbəl] *n (substance)* marbre *m*; *(toy ball)* bille *f*

March [mɑːtʃ] *n* mars *m*

march [mɑːtʃ] **1** *n* marche *f* **2** *vt* **to m. sb off to prison** emmener qn en prison **3** *vi (of soldiers, demonstrators)* défiler; *(walk in step)* marcher au pas; **to m. past (sb/sth)** défiler (devant qn/qch); *Fig* **to m. in/out** entrer/sortir d'un pas décidé ■ **march past** *n Br* défilé *m*

mare [meə(r)] *n* jument *f*

margarine [mɑːdʒə'riːn] *n* margarine *f* ■ **marge** *n Br Fam* margarine *f*

margin ['mɑːdʒɪn] *n (on page)* marge *f*; *Com* marge bénéficiaire; **to win by a narrow m.** gagner de justesse; **m. of error** marge d'erreur ■ **marginal** *adj* marginal; *(unimportant)* négligeable; *Br Pol* **m. seat** siège *m* à majorité précaire ■ **marginally** *adv* très légèrement

marigold ['mærɪgəʊld] *n* souci *m*

marijuana [mærɪ'wɑːnə] *n* marijuana *f*

marina [mə'riːnə] *n* marina *f*

marinade ['mærɪneɪd] *Culin* **1** *n* marinade *f* **2** *vti* (faire) mariner ■ **marinate** *vti* (faire) mariner

marine [mə'riːn] **1** *adj (life, flora)* marin **2** *n (soldier)* fusilier *m* marin; *Am* marine *m*

marionette [mærɪə'net] *n* marionnette *f*

marital ['mærɪtəl] *adj* conjugal; **m. status** situation *f* de famille

maritime ['mærɪtaɪm] *adj* maritime

marjoram ['mɑːdʒərəm] *n* marjolaine *f*

mark¹ [mɑːk] **1** *n (symbol)* marque *f*; *(stain, trace)* tache *f*, marque; *(token, sign)* signe *m*; *(in test, exam)* note *f*; *(target)* but *m*; *(model of machine, aircraft)* série *f*; **as a m. of respect** en signe de respect; *Fig* **to make one's m.** *(succeed)* faire ses preuves; **she isn't up to the m.** elle n'est pas à la hauteur; **on your marks! get set! go!** à vos marques! prêts! partez! **2** *vt* marquer; *(exam)* noter; **to m. time** *(of soldier)* marquer le pas; *Fig (wait)* piétiner; **m. my words** notez bien ce que je vais dire; **to m. a price down** baisser un prix; **to m. sth off** *(separate)* délimiter qch; *(on list)* cocher qch; **to m. sb out** distinguer qn; **to m. sb out for promotion** désigner qn pour obtenir une promotion; **to m. a price up** augmenter un prix ■ **marked** *adj (noticeable)* marqué ■ **markedly** *adv* visiblement

mark² [mɑːk] *n Formerly (currency)* mark *m*

marker ['mɑːkə(r)] *n (pen)* marqueur *m*; *(flag)* balise *f*; *(bookmark)* signet *m*; *(person)* correcteur, -trice *mf*

market ['mɑːkɪt] **1** *n* marché *m*; **to put sth on the m.** mettre qch en vente; **on the open m.** en vente libre; **on the black m.** au marché noir; **(free) m. economy** économie *f* de marché; *Br* **m. garden** jardin *m* maraîcher; *Br* **m. gardener** maraîcher, -ère *mf*; **m. price** prix *m* courant; **m. share** part *f* de marché; **m. survey** étude *f* de marché; **m. value** valeur *f* marchande **2** *vt* commercialiser ▪**marketable** *adj* commercialisable ▪**marketing** *n* marketing *m*, mercatique *f* ▪**marketplace** *n* (*in village, town*) place *f* du marché; *Econ* marché *m*; **in the m.** sur le marché

markings ['mɑːkɪŋz] *npl* (*on animal*) taches *fpl*; (*on road*) signalisation *f* horizontale

marksman ['mɑːksmən] (*pl* **-men**) *n* tireur *m* d'élite

marmalade ['mɑːməleɪd] *n* confiture *f* d'oranges

maroon [mə'ruːn] *adj* (*colour*) bordeaux *inv*

Note that the French word **marron** is a false friend. When referring to a colour, it means **brown**.

marooned [mə'ruːnd] *adj* abandonné; (*in snowstorm*) bloqué (**by** par)

marquee [mɑː'kiː] *n* grande *f* tente; (*at circus*) chapiteau *m*; *Am* (*awning*) marquise *f*

marquis ['mɑːkwɪs] *n* marquis *m*

marriage ['mærɪdʒ] *n* mariage *m*; **to be related by m. to sb** être parent par alliance de qn; **m. bureau** agence *f* matrimoniale; **m. certificate** extrait *m* d'acte de mariage

marrow ['mærəʊ] *n* (**a**) (*of bone*) moelle *f* (**b**) *Br* (*vegetable*) courge *f*

marry ['mærɪ] **1** (*pt & pp* **-ied**) *vt* épouser, se marier avec; **to m. sb (off)** (*of priest*) marier qn **2** *vi* se marier ▪**married** *adj* marié; **to get m.** se marier; **m. life** vie *f* maritale; **m. name** nom *m* de femme mariée

marsh [mɑːʃ] *n* marais *m*, marécage *m* ▪**marshland** *n* marécages *mpl*

marshal ['mɑːʃəl] **1** *n* (*army officer*) maréchal *m*; *Br* (*at public event*) membre *m* du service d'ordre **2** (*Br* **-ll-**, *Am* **-l-**) *vt* (*troops, vehicles*) rassembler; (*crowd*) canaliser

marshmallow [mɑːʃ'mæləʊ] *n* guimauve *f*

martial ['mɑːʃəl] *adj* martial; **m. arts** arts *mpl* martiaux; **m. law** loi *f* martiale

Martian ['mɑːʃən] *n & adj* martien, -ienne (*mf*)

martyr ['mɑːtə(r)] **1** *n* martyr, -yre *mf* **2** *vt* martyriser ▪**martyrdom** *n* martyre *m*

marvel ['mɑːvəl] **1** *n* (*wonder*) merveille *f*; **it's a m. they survived** c'est un miracle qu'ils aient survécu **2** (*Br* **-ll-**, *Am* **-l-**) *vi* s'émerveiller (**at** de)

marvellous ['mɑːvələs] (*Am* **marvelous**) *adj* merveilleux, -euse

Marxism ['mɑːksɪzəm] *n* marxisme *m* ▪**Marxist** *adj & n* marxiste (*mf*)

marzipan ['mɑːzɪpæn] *n* pâte *f* d'amandes

mascara [mæ'skɑːrə] *n* mascara *m*

mascot ['mæskɒt] *n* mascotte *f*

masculine ['mæskjʊlɪn] *adj* masculin ▪**mascu'linity** *n* masculinité *f*

mash [mæʃ] **1** *n* *Br* (*potatoes*) purée *f* (de pommes de terre); (*for poultry, pigs*) pâtée *f* **2** *vt* **to m. (up)** (*vegetables*) écraser (en purée); **mashed potatoes** purée *f* de pommes de terre

mask [mɑːsk] **1** *n* masque *m* **2** *vt* (*cover, hide*) masquer (**from** à)

masochism ['mæsəkɪzəm] *n* masochisme *m* ▪**masochist** *n* masochiste *mf* ▪**maso'chistic** *adj* masochiste

mason ['meɪsən] *n* (*stonemason, Freemason*) maçon *m* ▪**masonry** *n* maçonnerie *f*

masquerade [mɑːskə'reɪd] **1** *n* (*gathering, disguise*) mascarade *f* **2** *vi* **to m. as sb** se faire passer pour qn

mass¹ [mæs] **1** *n* *Phys & (shapeless substance)* masse *f*; **a m. of** (*many*) une multitude de; *Fam* **I've got masses of things to do** j'ai des tas de choses à faire; *Fam* **there's masses of room** il y a plein de place; *Pol* **the masses** le peuple **2** *adj* (*demonstration, culture*) de masse; (*protests, departure*) en masse; (*unemployment, destruction*) massif, -ive; **m. grave** charnier *m*; **m. hysteria** hystérie *f* collective; **m. media** media *mpl*; **m. murderer** tueur *m* fou; **m. production** production *f* en série **3** *vi* (*of troops, people*) se masser ▪**mass-pro'duce** *vt* fabriquer en série

mass² [mæs] *n* (*church service*) messe *f*

massacre ['mæsəkə(r)] **1** *n* massacre *m* **2** *vt* massacrer

massage ['mæsɑːʒ] **1** *n* massage *m*; *Br* **m. parlour**, *Am* **m. parlor** salon *m* de massage **2** *vt* masser; *Fig* **to m. the figures** manipuler les chiffres ▪**masseur** [-'sɜː(r)] *n* masseur *m* ▪**masseuse** [-'sɜːz] *n* masseuse *f*

massive ['mæsɪv] *adj* (*increase, dose, vote*) massif, -ive; (*amount, building*) énorme; (*heart attack*) foudroyant ▪**massively** *adv* (*increase, reduce*) considérablement

mast [mɑːst] *n* (*of ship*) mât *m*; (*for TV, radio*) pylône *m*

master ['mɑːstə(r)] **1** *n* maître *m*; *Br* (*teacher*) professeur *m*; **old m.** (*painting*) tableau *m* de maître; **I'm my own m.** je ne dépends que de moi; *Univ* **m.'s (degree)** maîtrise *f* (**in** de); **M. of Arts/Science** (*qualification*) ≃ maîtrise ès lettres/sciences; (*person*) ≃ maître *m* ès lettres/sciences; **m. of ceremonies** (*presenter*) animateur, -trice *mf*; **m. card** carte *f* maîtresse; **m. copy** original *m*; **m. key** passe-partout *m inv*; **m. plan** plan *m* d'action **2** *vt* maîtriser; (*subject, situation*) dominer ▪**masterly** *adj* magistral ▪**mastery** *n* maîtrise *f* (**of** de)

mastermind ['mɑːstəmaɪnd] **1** *n* (*person*) cerveau *m* **2** *vt* organiser

masterpiece ['mɑːstəpiːs] *n* chef-d'œuvre *m*

masterstroke ['mɑːstəstrəʊk] *n* coup *m* de maître

mastic ['mæstɪk] *n* (*filler, seal*) mastic *m*

masturbate ['mæstəbeɪt] *vi* se masturber ▪ **mastur'bation** *n* masturbation *f*

mat [mæt] *n* tapis *m*; *(of straw)* natte *f*; *(at door)* paillasson *m*; **(table) m.** *(for plates)* set *m* de table; *(for dishes)* dessous-de-plat *m inv*

match¹ [mætʃ] *n* *(for lighting fire, cigarette)* allumette *f* ▪ **matchbox** *n* boîte *f* d'allumettes ▪ **matchstick** *n* allumette *f*

match² [mætʃ] *n (in sport)* match *m*; **m. point** *(in tennis)* balle *f* de match

match³ [mætʃ] **1** *n (equal)* égal, -ale *mf*; *(marriage)* mariage *m*; **to be a good m.** *(of colours, people)* aller bien ensemble; **he's a good m.** *(man to marry)* c'est un bon parti; **to meet one's m.** trouver son maître **2** *vt (of clothes, colour)* être assorti à; *(coordinate)* assortir; *(equal)* égaler; **to m. up** *(colours, clothes, plates)* assortir; **to m. (up to)** *(equal)* égaler; **to m. up to sb's expectations** répondre à l'attente de qn **3** *vi (of colours, clothes)* être assortis, -ies ▪ **matching** *adj* assorti

mate¹ [meɪt] **1** *n (of animal)* mâle *m*/femelle *f*; *Br (friend)* copain *m*, copine *f*; *Br* **builder's/electrician's m.** aide-maçon/-électricien *m* **2** *vi (of animals)* s'accoupler **(with** avec)

mate² [meɪt] *Chess* **1** *n* mat *m* **2** *vt* mettre mat

material [mə'tɪərɪəl] **1** *adj (needs, world)* matériel, -ielle; *(important)* essentiel, -ielle **2** *n (substance)* matière *f*; *(cloth)* tissu *m*; *(for book)* matériaux *mpl*; **material(s)** *(equipment)* matériel *m*; **building materials** matériaux de construction; **reading m.** de quoi lire ▪ **materialism** *n* matérialisme *m* ▪ **materialist** *n* matérialiste *mf* ▪ **materia'listic** *adj* matérialiste ▪ **materially** *adv* matériellement

materialize [mə'tɪərɪəlaɪz] *vi* se matérialiser; *(of hope, threat)* se réaliser; *(of event)* avoir lieu

maternal [mə'tɜːnəl] *adj* maternel, -elle

maternity [mə'tɜːnɪtɪ] *n* maternité *f*; *Br* **m. allowance** *or* **benefit** allocation *f* de maternité; **m. dress** robe *f* de grossesse; **m. hospital, m. unit** maternité; **m. leave** congé *m* de maternité

mathematical [mæθə'mætɪkəl] *adj* mathématique

mathematician [mæθəmə'tɪʃən] *n* mathématicien, -ienne *mf*

mathematics [mæθə'mætɪks] *n (subject)* mathématiques *fpl*; *(calculations)* calculs *mpl* ▪ **maths** *(Am* **math)** *n Fam* maths *fpl*

matinée ['mætɪneɪ] *n (of play, film)* matinée *f*

matriculate [mə'trɪkjʊleɪt] *vi Univ* s'inscrire ▪ **matricu'lation** *n Univ* inscription *f*

matrimony ['mætrɪmənɪ] *n* mariage *m* ▪ **matrimonial** [-'məʊnɪəl] *adj* matrimonial

matrix ['meɪtrɪks] *(pl* **-ices** [-ɪsiːz]) *n Math & Tech* matrice *f*

matron ['meɪtrən] *n Br (nurse)* infirmière *f* en chef; *Br (in boarding school)* infirmière *f*; *(older woman)* matrone *f*

matt [mæt] *adj (paint, paper)* mat

matted ['mætɪd] *adj (hair)* emmêlé

matter¹ ['mætə(r)] **1** *n (substance)* matière *f*; *(issue, affair)* question *f*; **that's a m. of taste** c'est une question de goût; **and to make matters worse...** et pour aggraver les choses...; **as a m. of fact** en fait; **no m.!** peu importe!; **no m. what she does** quoi qu'elle fasse; **no m. where you go** où que tu ailles; **no m. who you are** qui que vous soyez; **no m. when** quel que soit le moment; **what's the m.?** qu'est-ce qu'il y a?; **what's the m. with you?** qu'est-ce que tu as?; **there's something the m.** il y a quelque chose qui ne va pas; **there's something the m. with my leg** j'ai quelque chose à la jambe; **there's nothing the m. with him** il n'a rien **2** *vi (be important)* importer **(to** à**); it doesn't m. if/when/who...** peu importe si/quand/qui...; **it doesn't m.** ça ne fait rien; **it doesn't m. to me** ça m'est égal

matter² ['mætə(r)] *n Med* pus *m*

matter-of-fact [mætərəv'fækt] *adj (person, manner)* terre à terre *inv*; *(voice)* neutre

matting ['mætɪŋ] *n (material)* nattage *m*; **a piece of m., some m.** une natte

mattress ['mætrəs] *n* matelas *m*

mature [mə'tʃʊə(r)] **1** *adj (person, fruit)* mûr; *(cheese)* fort; *Univ* **m. student** = adulte qui reprend des études **2** *vi (person, fruit)* mûrir; *(of cheese)* se faire; *Fin (of interest)* arriver à échéance ▪ **maturity** *n* maturité *f*

maul [mɔːl] *vt (of animal)* mutiler; *Fig (of person)* malmener

Mauritius [mə'rɪʃəs] *n* l'île *f* Maurice

mausoleum [mɔːsə'lɪəm] *n* mausolée *m*

mauve [məʊv] *adj & n (colour)* mauve *(m)*

maverick ['mævərɪk] *n* non-conformiste *mf*

mawkish ['mɔːkɪʃ] *adj Pej* mièvre

maxim ['mæksɪm] *n* maxime *f*

maximize ['mæksɪmaɪz] *vt* maximaliser

maximum ['mæksɪməm] **1** *(pl* **-ima** [-ɪmə] *or* **-imums**) *n* maximum *m* **2** *adj* maximal

May [meɪ] *n* mai *m*; **M. Day** le Premier Mai

may [meɪ] *(pt* **might** [maɪt]) *v aux*

May et might peuvent s'utiliser indifféremment ou presque dans les expressions de la catégorie **(a)**.

(a) *(expressing possibility)* **he m. come** il se peut qu'il vienne; **I m. or might be wrong** je me trompe peut-être; **he m. or might have lost it** il se peut qu'il l'ait perdu; **I m. or might have forgotten it** je l'ai peut-être oublié; **we m. or might as well go** autant y aller; **she's afraid I m. or might get lost** elle a peur que je ne me perde **(b)** *Formal (for asking permission)* **m. I stay?** puis-je rester?; **m. I?** vous permettez?; **you m. go** tu peux partir **(c)** *Formal (expressing* *wish)* m. **you be happy** sois heureux; **m. the best man win!** que le meilleur gagne!

maybe ['meɪbiː] *adv* peut-être

mayday ['meɪdeɪ] *n (distress signal)* mayday *m*, SOS *m*

mayhem ['meɪhem] *n (chaos)* pagaille *f*

mayonnaise [meɪə'neɪz] *n* mayonnaise *f*

mayor [meə(r)] *n* maire *m* ▪ **mayoress** ['meərɪs] *n* mairesse *f*; *(mayor's wife)* femme *f* du maire

maze [meɪz] *n* labyrinthe *m*

MB [em'biː] *(abbr* **megabyte)** *n Comptr* Mo *m*

MC [em'siː] *abbr* = **master of ceremonies**

MD [em'diː] *n* (**a**) *Br (abbr* **managing director)** directeur, -trice *mf* général, -e (**b**) *(abbr* **Doctor of Medicine)** docteur *m* en médecine

me [miː] *pron* me, m'; *(after prep, 'than', 'it is')* moi; **(to) me** *(indirect)* me, m'; **she knows me** elle me connaît; **he helps me** il m'aide; **he gave it to me** il me l'a donné; **with me** avec moi

meadow ['medəʊ] *n* pré *m*, prairie *f*

meagre ['miːgə(r)] *(Am* **meager)** *adj* maigre

meal¹ [miːl] *n (food)* repas *m*; *Am* **m. ticket** ticket-repas *m*, ticket-restaurant *m*

meal² [miːl] *n (flour)* farine *f*

mealy-mouthed [miːlɪ'maʊðd] *adj Pej* mielleux, -euse

mean¹ [miːn] *(pt & pp* **meant)** *vt (of word, event)* signifier; *(of person)* vouloir dire; *(result in)* entraîner; *(represent)* représenter; **to m. to do sth** avoir l'intention de faire qch; **I know what you m.** je comprends; **I m. it, I m. what I say** je parle sérieusement; **it means a lot to me** c'est très important pour moi; **it means something to me** *(name, face)* ça me dit quelque chose; **I didn't m. to!** je ne l'ai pas fait exprès!; **you were meant to come** vous étiez censé venir; **it's meant to be a good film** il paraît que c'est un bon film; **it was meant for you** ça t'était destiné; **it was meant as a joke** c'était une plaisanterie

mean² [miːn] **(-er, -est)** *adj (miserly)* avare; *(petty)* mesquin; *(nasty)* méchant; *(shabby)* misérable; **she's no m. dancer** c'est une excellente danseuse ▪ **meanness** *n (greed)* avarice *f*; *(nastiness)* méchanceté *f*

mean³ [miːn] **1** *adj (average)* moyen, -enne **2** *n (middle position)* milieu *m*; *Math (average, mid-point)* moyenne *f*

meander [mɪ'ændə(r)] *vi (of river)* faire des méandres

meaning ['miːnɪŋ] *n* sens *m*, signification *f* ▪ **meaningful** *adj* significatif, -ive ▪ **meaningless** *adj* vide de sens; *Fig (absurd)* insensé

means [miːnz] **1** *n (method)* moyen *m* (**to do** *or* **of doing** de faire); **by m. of...** au moyen de...; **by m. of hard work** à force de travail; **by all m.!** *(certainly)* je vous en prie!; **by no m.** nullement; **m. of communication/transport** moyen de communication/transport **2** *npl (wealth)*

moyens *mpl*; **to have independent** *or* **private m.** avoir une fortune personnelle; **to live beyond one's m.** vivre au-dessus de ses moyens

meant [ment] *pt & pp of* **mean¹**

meantime ['miːntaɪm] *adv & n* **(in the) m.** *(at the same time)* pendant ce temps; *(between two events)* entre-temps

meanwhile ['miːnwaɪl] *adv* *(at the same time)* pendant ce temps; *(between two events)* entre-temps

measles ['miːzəlz] *n Med* rougeole *f*

measly ['miːzlɪ] *adj Fam* minable

measure ['meʒə(r)] **1** *n* mesure *f*; *(ruler)* règle *f*; *Br* **made to m.** fait sur mesure **2** *vt* mesurer; **to m. sth out** *(ingredient)* mesurer qch; **to m. sth up** *(plank)* mesurer qch **3** *vi* **to m. up to** *(task)* être à la hauteur de ▪ **measured** *adj (careful)* mesuré ▪ **measuring** *adj* **m. jug** verre *m* gradué; **m. tape** mètre *m* ruban

measurement ['meʒəmənt] *n* mesure *f*; **hip/waist measurement(s)** tour *m* de hanches/de taille

meat [miːt] *n* viande *f*; *(of crab, lobster)* chair *f*; *Fig* substance *f*; **m. diet** régime *m* carné; **m. pie** pâté *m* en croûte ▪ **meatball** *n* boulette *f* de viande ▪ **meaty** **(-ier, -iest)** *adj (fleshy)* charnu; *(flavour)* de viande; *Fig (book, film)* substantiel, -ielle

Mecca ['mekə] *n* La Mecque; *Fig* **a M. for antique-lovers** un paradis pour les passionnés d'objets anciens

mechanic [mɪ'kænɪk] *n* mécanicien, -ienne *mf* ▪ **mechanical** *adj* mécanique; *Fig (reply, gesture)* machinal ▪ **mechanics** *n (science)* mécanique *f*; **the m.** *(working parts)* le mécanisme

> Note that the French word **mécanique** is a false friend and is never a translation for the English word **mechanic**. It means **mechanics**.

mechanism ['mekənɪzəm] *n* mécanisme *m*

mechanize ['mekənaɪz] *vt* mécaniser

medal ['medəl] *n* médaille *f*

medallion [mə'dæljən] *n* médaillon *m*

medallist ['medəlɪst] *(Am* **medalist)** *n* médaillé, -ée *mf*; **to be a gold/silver m.** être médaille d'or/d'argent

meddle ['medəl] *vi (interfere)* se mêler (**in** de); *(tamper)* toucher (**with** à) ▪ **meddlesome** *adj* qui se mêle de tout

media ['miːdɪə] **1** *npl* **the (mass) m.** les médias *mpl*; **m. circus** cirque *m* médiatique; **m. event** événement *m* médiatique; **m. studies** = études en communication et journalisme **2** *pl of* **medium**

mediaeval, medieval [medɪ'iːvəl] *adj* médiéval

median ['mi:dɪən] **1** adj médian **2** n Math médiane m; Am **m. (strip)** (on highway) bande f médiane

mediate ['mi:dɪeɪt] vi servir d'intermédiaire (**between** entre) ■ **medi'ation** n médiation f ■ **mediator** n médiateur, -trice mf

Medicaid ['medɪkeɪd] n Am = assistance médicale aux défavorisés

medical ['medɪkəl] **1** adj médical; (school, studies) de médecine; (student) en médecine; **to seek m. advice** demander conseil à un médecin; **m. examination** examen m médical; **m. insurance** assurance f maladie **2** n (in school, army) visite f médicale; (private) examen m médical

Medicare ['medɪkeə(r)] n Am ≃ assistance f médicale aux personnes âgées

medicated ['medɪkeɪtɪd] adj **m. shampoo** shampooing m traitant

medication [medɪ'keɪʃən] n médicaments mpl; **to take one's m.** prendre ses médicaments; **to be on m.** être en traitement

medicine ['medəsən] n (substance) médicament m; (science) médecine f; **m. cabinet, m. chest** (armoire f à) pharmacie f ■ **medicinal** [mə'dɪsənəl] adj médicinal

> Note that the French word **médecine** never means **remedy**.

medieval [medɪ'i:vəl] adj médiéval

mediocre [mi:dɪ'əʊkə(r)] adj médiocre ■ **mediocrity** [-'ɒkrɪtɪ] n médiocrité f

meditate ['medɪteɪt] vi méditer (**on** sur) ■ **medi'tation** n méditation f

Mediterranean [medɪtə'reɪnɪən] **1** adj méditerranéen, -éenne **2** n **the M.** la Méditerranée

medium ['mi:dɪəm] **1** adj (average, middle) moyen, -enne **2** n (**a**) (pl media ['mi:dɪə]) (of thought) véhicule m; Biol milieu m; (for conveying data or publicity) support m; **through the m. of sb/sth** par l'intermédiaire de qn/qch; **to find a happy m.** trouver le juste milieu (**b**) (pl mediums) (person) médium m ■ **'medium-sized** adj de taille moyenne

medley ['medlɪ] (pl -eys) n mélange m; (of songs, tunes) pot-pourri m

meek [mi:k] (-er, -est) adj docile

meet [mi:t] **1** vt (pt & pp met) (person, team) rencontrer; (by arrangement) retrouver; (pass in street, road) croiser; (fetch) aller chercher; (wait for) attendre; (debt, enemy, danger) faire face à; (need) combler; **to arrange to m. sb** donner rendez-vous à qn; **have you met my husband?** connaissez-vous mon mari? **2** vi (of people, teams, looks) se rencontrer; (by arrangement) se retrouver; (of club, society) se réunir; (of rivers) se rejoindre; (of trains, vehicles) se croiser; **we've never met** nous ne nous connaissons pas **3** n Am Sport réunion f

▸ **meet up** vi (of people) se rencontrer; (by arrangement) se retrouver; **to m. up with sb** rencontrer qn; (by arrangement) retrouver qn

▸ **meet with** vt insep (problem, refusal) se heurter à; (loss) essuyer; (danger) affronter; (accident) avoir; Am **to m. with sb** rencontrer qn; (as arranged) retrouver qn

meeting ['mi:tɪŋ] n (for business) réunion f; (large) assemblée f; (by accident) rencontre f; (by arrangement) rendez-vous m inv; **to be in a m.** être en réunion; **m. place** lieu m de rendez-vous

megabyte ['megəbaɪt] n Comptr mégaoctet m

megalomania [megələʊ'meɪnɪə] n mégalomanie f ■ **megalomaniac** n mégalomane mf

megaphone ['megəfəʊn] n porte-voix m inv

melancholy ['melənkɒlɪ] **1** adj mélancolique **2** n mélancolie f

mellow ['meləʊ] **1** (**-er, -est**) adj (fruit) mûr; (wine) moelleux, -euse; (flavour) suave; (colour, voice) chaud; (person) détendu, serein **2** vi (of person) s'adoucir

melodrama ['melədra:mə] n mélodrame m ■ **melodramatic** [-drə'mætɪk] adj mélodramatique

melody ['melədɪ] (pl -ies) n mélodie f ■ **melodic** [mə'lɒdɪk] adj mélodique ■ **melodious** [mə'ləʊdɪəs] adj mélodieux, -ieuse

melon ['melən] n melon m

melt [melt] **1** vt faire fondre; **to m. down** (metal object) fondre; **melting point** point m de fusion; Fig **melting pot** creuset m **2** vi fondre; **to m. away** (of snow) fondre complètement; **the green melts into the blue** le vert se fond dans le bleu ■ **meltdown** n Phys fusion f

member ['membə(r)] n membre m; Br **M. of Parliament**, Am **M. of Congress** ≃ député m; **she's a m. of the family** elle fait partie de la famille; **m. state** État m membre ■ **membership** n (state) adhésion f (**of** à); (members) membres mpl; (number) nombre m de membres; **m. card** carte f de membre; **m. fee** cotisation f

membrane ['membreɪn] n membrane f

memento [mə'mentəʊ] (pl -os or -oes) n souvenir m

memo ['meməʊ] (pl -os) n note f de service; **m. pad** bloc-notes m ■ **memorandum** [memə'rændəm] n (in office) note f de service; Pol & Com mémorandum m

memoir ['memwɑ:(r)] n (essay) mémoire m ■ **memoirs** npl (autobiography) mémoires mpl

memorabilia [memərə'bɪlɪə] npl souvenirs mpl

memorable ['memərəbəl] adj mémorable

memorial [mə'mɔ:rɪəl] **1** adj commémoratif, -ive; **m. service** commémoration f **2** n mémorial m

memorize ['meməraɪz] vt mémoriser

memory ['memərɪ] (pl -ies) n (faculty) & Comptr

mémoire *f*; *(recollection)* souvenir *m*; **from m.** de mémoire; **to the** *or* **in m. of...** à la mémoire de...

men [men] *pl of* **man** *Am* **the men's room** les toilettes *fpl* pour hommes

menace ['menɪs] **1** *n (danger)* danger *m*; *(threat)* menace *f*; *Fam (nuisance)* plaie *f* **2** *vt* menacer ▪ **menacing** *adj* menaçant ▪ **menacingly** *adv (say)* d'un ton menaçant; *(do)* d'une manière menaçante

menagerie [mɪ'nædʒərɪ] *n* ménagerie *f*

mend [mend] **1** *n (in clothes)* raccommodage *m*; **to be on the m.** *(of patient)* aller mieux **2** *vt (repair)* réparer; *(clothes)* raccommoder; **to m. one's ways** s'amender

menial ['miːnɪəl] *adj (work)* subalterne

meningitis [menɪn'dʒaɪtɪs] *n Med* méningite *f*

menopause ['menəpɔːz] *n* ménopause *f*

menstruate ['menstrʊeɪt] *vi* avoir ses règles ▪ **menstru'ation** *n* menstruation *f*

menswear ['menzweə(r)] *n* vêtements *mpl* pour hommes

mental ['mentəl] *adj* mental; *Br Fam (mad)* dingue; *Br Fam* **to go m.** *(lose one's temper)* péter les plombs; **m. arithmetic** calcul *m* mental; **m. block** blocage *m*; **m. breakdown** dépression *f* nerveuse; **m. hospital** hôpital *m* psychiatrique ▪ **mentally** *adv* mentalement; **he's m. handicapped** c'est un handicapé mental; **she's m. ill** c'est une malade mentale

mentality [men'tælətɪ] *(pl* **-ies)** *n* mentalité *f*

mention ['menʃən] **1** *n* mention *f* **2** *vt* mentionner; **not to m...** sans parler de...; **don't m. it!** il n'y a pas de quoi!; **she has no savings worth mentioning** elle n'a pratiquement pas d'économies

mentor ['mentɔː(r)] **1** *n* mentor *m* **2** *vt* **to m. sb** assumer le rôle de mentor auprès de qn

menu ['menjuː] *n (in restaurant) (list)* carte *f*; *(for set meal)* menu *m*; *Comptr* menu; *Comptr* **m. bar** barre *f* de sélection

MEP [emiː'piː] *(abbr* **Member of the European Parliament)** *n* député *m* du Parlement européen

mercantile ['mɜːkəntaɪl] *adj (activity, law)* commercial; *(nation)* commerçant

mercenary ['mɜːsɪnərɪ] **1** *adj* intéressé **2** *(pl* **-ies)** *n* mercenaire *m*

merchandise ['mɜːtʃəndaɪz] *n* marchandises *fpl*

merchant ['mɜːtʃənt] **1** *n (trader)* négociant, -iante *mf*; *(retailer)* commerçant, -ante *mf*; **wine m.** négociant, -iante en vins; *(retail)* marchand *m* de vins **2** *adj (navy)* marchand; *(seaman)* de la marine marchande; *Br* **m. bank** banque *f* d'affaires; **m. vessel** navire *m* marchand

merciful ['mɜːsɪfəl] *adj* miséricordieux, -ieuse **(to** pour**)** ▪ **mercifully** *adv (fortunately)* heureusement

merciless ['mɜːsɪləs] *adj* impitoyable

mercury ['mɜːkjʊrɪ] *n (metal)* mercure *m*

mercy ['mɜːsɪ] *(pl* **-ies)** *n* pitié *f*; *(of God)* miséricorde *f*; **to beg for m.** demander grâce; **at the m. of** à la merci de; **it's a m. that...** *(stroke of luck)* c'est une chance que...; **m. killing** acte *m* d'euthanasie

mere [mɪə(r)] *adj* simple; **she's a m. child** ce n'est qu'une enfant; **by m. chance** par pur hasard; **the m. sight of them...** leur seule vue... ▪ **merely** *adv* simplement

merge [mɜːdʒ] **1** *vt (companies)* & *Comptr* fusionner **2** *vi (blend)* se mêler **(with** à**)**; *(of roads)* se rejoindre; *(of companies, banks)* fusionner ▪ **merger** *n Com* fusion *f*

meridian [mə'rɪdɪən] *n* méridien *m*

meringue [mə'ræŋ] *n* meringue *f*

merit ['merɪt] **1** *n* mérite *m*; **to judge sth on its merits** juger qch objectivement **2** *vt* mériter

mermaid ['mɜːmeɪd] *n* sirène *f*

merrily ['merɪlɪ] *adv* gaiement ▪ **merriment** *n* gaieté *f*

merry ['merɪ] *(*-**ier,** -**iest)** *adj (happy, drunk)* gai; **M. Christmas!** Joyeux Noël! ▪ **merry-go-round** *n* manège *m* ▪ **merrymaking** *n* réjouissances *fpl*

mesh [meʃ] *n (of net, sieve)* mailles *fpl*; *(fabric)* tissu *m* à mailles

mesmerize ['mezməraɪz] *vt* hypnotiser

mess¹ [mes] *n (confusion)* désordre *m*; *(muddle)* gâchis *m*; *(dirt)* saletés *fpl*; **in a m.** en désordre; *(in trouble)* dans le pétrin; *(in a sorry state)* dans un triste état; **my life's a m.** ma vie est un désastre; **to make a m. of sth** *(do sth badly, get sth dirty)* saloper qch ▪ **mess-up** *n Br Fam (disorder)* gâchis *m*

▸ **mess about, mess around** *Fam* **1** *vt sep* **to m. sb about** *or* **around** *(bother, treat badly)* embêter qn **2** *vi (waste time)* traîner; *(play the fool)* faire l'imbécile; **to m. about** *or* **around with sth** *(fiddle with)* tripoter qch

▸ **mess up** *vt sep Fam* **to m. sth up** *(plans)* ficher qch en l'air; *(hair, room, papers)* mettre qch en désordre

mess² [mes] *n Mil (room)* mess *m*

message ['mesɪdʒ] *n* message *m*; *(noticeboard)* & *Comptr* **m. board** tableau *m* d'affichage ▪ **messaging** *n Comptr* messagerie *f* électronique

messenger ['mesɪndʒə(r)] *n* messager, -ère *mf*; *(in office, hotel)* coursier, -ière *mf*

Messiah [mɪ'saɪə] *n Rel* Messie *m*

messy ['mesɪ] *(*-**ier,** -**iest)** *adj (untidy)* en désordre; *(dirty)* sale; *(job)* salissant; *(handwriting)* peu soigné; *Fig (situation, solution)* confus

met [met] *pt* & *pp of* **meet**

metal ['metəl] *n* métal *m*; **m. detector** détecteur *m* de métaux; **m. ladder** échelle *f* métallique

▪ **metallic** [mə'tælɪk] *adj (sound)* métallique; *(paint)* métallisé; **a m. green car** une voiture vert métallisé ▪ **metalwork** *n (study, craft)* travail *m* des métaux; *(objects)* ferronnerie *f*

metamorphosis [metə'mɔːfəsɪs] *(pl* -oses [-əsiːz]) *n* métamorphose *f*

metaphor ['metəfə(r)] *n* métaphore *f* ▪ **metaphorical** [-'fɒrɪkəl] *adj* métaphorique

metaphysical [metə'fɪzɪkəl] *adj* métaphysique ▪ **metaphysics** *n* métaphysique *f*

mete [miːt] *vt* **to m. out** *(punishment)* infliger (**to** à); **to m. out justice** rendre la justice

meteor ['miːtɪə(r)] *n* météore *m* ▪ **meteoric** [-tɪ'ɒrɪk] *adj* **m. rise** *(of politician, film star)* ascension *f* fulgurante ▪ **meteorite** *n* météorite *f*

meteorology [miːtɪə'rɒlədʒɪ] *n* météorologie *f* ▪ **meteorological** [-rə'lɒdʒɪkəl] *adj* météorologique

meter¹ ['miːtə(r)] *n (device)* compteur *m*; **(parking) m.** parcmètre *m*; *Am* **m. maid** *(for traffic)* contractuelle *f*; *Am* **m. man** contractuel *m*

meter² ['miːtə(r)] *n Am* = **metre**

method ['meθəd] *n* méthode *f* ▪ **methodical** [mɪ'θɒdɪkəl] *adj* méthodique

Methodist ['meθədɪst] *adj & n Rel* méthodiste *(mf)*

methylated ['meθɪleɪtɪd] *adj Br* **m. spirit(s)** alcool *m* à brûler ▪ **meths** *n Br Fam* alcool *m* à brûler

meticulous [mɪ'tɪkjʊləs] *adj* méticuleux, -euse

Met Office ['metɒfɪs] *n Br* ≃ Météo France

metre ['miːtə(r)] *(Am* **meter**) *n* mètre *m* ▪ **metric** ['metrɪk] *adj* métrique

metropolis [mə'trɒpəlɪs] *n (chief city)* métropole *f* ▪ **metropolitan** [metrə'pɒlɪtən] *adj* métropolitain; **the M. Police** la police de Londres

mettle ['metəl] *n* courage *m*

mew [mjuː] *vi (of cat)* miauler

mews [mjuːz] *n Br (street)* ruelle *f*; *Br* **m. flat** = appartement chic aménagé dans une ancienne écurie

Mexico ['meksɪkəʊ] *n* le Mexique ▪ **Mexican 1** *adj* mexicain **2** *n* Mexicain, -aine *mf*

mezzanine ['mezəniːn] *n* **m. (floor)** mezzanine *f*

miaow [miː'aʊ] **1** *n* miaulement *m* **2** *exclam* miaou! **3** *vi* miauler

mice [maɪs] *pl of* **mouse**

mickey ['mɪkɪ] *n Br Fam* **to take the m. out of sb** charrier qn

microbe ['maɪkrəʊb] *n* microbe *m*

microchip ['maɪkrəʊtʃɪp] *n Comptr* microprocesseur *m*

microcosm ['maɪkrəʊkɒzəm] *n* microcosme *m*

microfiche ['maɪkrəʊfiːʃ] *n* microfiche *f*

microfilm ['maɪkrəʊfɪlm] *n* microfilm *m*

microlight ['maɪkrəʊlaɪt] *n (plane)* ULM *m*

microphone ['maɪkrəfəʊn] *n* micro *m*

microprocessor [maɪkrəʊ'prəʊsesə(r)] *n* microprocesseur *m*

microscope ['maɪkrəskəʊp] *n* microscope *m* ▪ **microscopic** [-'skɒpɪk] *adj* microscopique

microwave ['maɪkrəʊweɪv] **1** *n* micro-onde *f*; **m. (oven)** *(four m à)* micro-ondes *m inv* **2** *vt* faire cuire au micro-ondes

mid [mɪd] *adj (in)* **m. June** (à) la mi-juin; **in m. air** en plein ciel; **to be in one's m.-twenties** avoir environ vingt-cinq ans

midday [mɪd'deɪ] **1** *n* midi *m*; **at m.** à midi **2** *adj (sun, meal)* de midi

middle ['mɪdəl] **1** *n* milieu *m*; *Fam (waist)* taille *f*; **(right) in the m. of sth** au (beau) milieu de qch; **I was in the m. of saying...** j'étais en train de dire... **2** *adj (central)* du milieu; **the M. Ages** le Moyen Âge; **the Middle E.** le Moyen-Orient; **in m. age** vers la cinquantaine; **the m. class(es)** les classes moyennes; **the m. ear** l'oreille moyenne; **m. name** deuxième prénom *m* ▪ **'middle-aged** *adj* d'âge mûr ▪ **'middle-'class** *adj* bourgeois ▪ **'middleman** *n* intermédiaire *mf* ▪ **'middle-of-the-'road** *adj (politics, views)* modéré; *(music)* grand public *inv*

middling ['mɪdlɪŋ] *adj (fairly good)* moyen, -enne; *(mediocre)* médiocre

midge [mɪdʒ] *n* moucheron *m*

midget ['mɪdʒɪt] **1** *adj (tiny)* minuscule **2** *n (small person)* nain *m*, naine *f*

Midlands ['mɪdləndz] *npl* **the M.** les Midlands *fpl*

midnight ['mɪdnaɪt] *n* minuit *m*

midmorning [mɪd'mɔːnɪŋ] *n* milieu *m* de matinée

midpoint ['mɪdpɔɪnt] *n* milieu *m*

midriff ['mɪdrɪf] *n (belly)* ventre *m*

midst [mɪdst] *n* **in the m. of** *(middle)* au milieu de; **in our/their m.** parmi nous/eux

midsummer [mɪd'sʌmə(r)] *n* milieu *m* de l'été; *(solstice)* solstice *m* d'été; **M.'s Day** la Saint-Jean

midterm ['mɪdtɜːm] *adj Br Sch & Univ* **m. holidays** vacances *fpl* de milieu de trimestre

midway [mɪd'weɪ] *adj & adv* à mi-chemin

midweek [mɪd'wiːk] *adv* en milieu de semaine

Midwest [mɪd'west] *n Am* **the M.** le Midwest

midwife ['mɪdwaɪf] *(pl* -wives) *n* sage-femme *f*

midwinter [mɪd'wɪntə(r)] *n* milieu *m* de l'hiver; *(solstice)* solstice *m* d'hiver

miffed [mɪft] *adj Fam (offended)* vexé (**at** de)

might¹ [maɪt] *v aux see* **may**

> La forme négative **mightn't** s'écrit **might not** dans un style plus soutenu.

might² [maɪt] *n (strength)* force *f* ▪ **mighty (-ier, -iest) 1** *adj* puissant; *(ocean)* vaste; *Fam (very great)* sacré **2** *adv Am Fam (very)* rudement

migraine ['miːgreɪn, 'maɪgreɪn] *n* migraine *f*

migrate [maɪ'greɪt] *vi (of people)* émigrer; *(of birds)* migrer ▪ **migrant** ['maɪgrənt] *adj & n* **m.**

(worker) (travailleur *m*) immigré *m*, (travailleuse *f*) immigrée *f* ▪ **migration** *n* (*of birds*) migration *f*; (*of people*) émigration *f*

mike [maɪk] (*abbr* **microphone**) *n Fam* micro *m*

mild [maɪld] (**-er, -est**) *adj* (*weather, cheese, soap, person*) doux (*f* douce); (*punishment*) léger, -ère; (*curry*) peu épicé ▪ **mildly** *adv* (*say*) doucement; (*moderately*) légèrement; **to put it m.** pour ne pas dire plus ▪ **mildness** *n* (*of weather*) douceur *f*

mildew ['mɪldjuː] *n* moisissure *f*

mile [maɪl] *n* mile *m* (= 1,6 km); **to see for miles** voir à des kilomètres; **to walk for miles** marcher pendant des kilomètres; **he lives miles away** il habite très loin d'ici; *Br Fam* **miles better** vachement mieux ▪ **mileage** *n* (*distance*) ≃ kilométrage *m*; (*rate of fuel consumption*) consommation *f* ▪ **mileometer** [maɪ'lɒmɪtə(r)] *n Br* ≃ compteur *m* kilométrique ▪ **milestone** *n* ≃ borne *f* kilométrique; *Fig* (*in history, career*) étape *f* importante

militant ['mɪlɪtənt] *adj & n* militant, -ante *(mf)*

military ['mɪlɪtərɪ] **1** *adj* militaire; **m. service** service *m* militaire **2** *n* **the m.** les militaires *mpl*

militate ['mɪlɪteɪt] *vi* **to m. against/in favour of** (*of facts, arguments*) militer contre/pour

militia [mə'lɪʃə] *n* milice *f* ▪ **militiaman** (*pl* **-men**) *n* milicien *m*

milk [mɪlk] **1** *n* lait *m*; **m. bottle** bouteille *f* de lait; **m. chocolate** chocolat *m* au lait; **m. diet** régime *m* lacté; *Br* **m. float** camionnette *f* de laitier; *Br* **m. round** tournée *f* du laitier; **m. shake** milk-shake *m* **2** *vt* (*cow*) traire; *Fig* (*exploit*) exploiter; *Fig* **to m. sb of sth** soutirer qch à qn ▪ **milking** *n* traite *f* ▪ **milkman** (*pl* **-men**) *n* laitier *m* ▪ **milky** (**-ier, -iest**) *adj* (*diet*) lacté; (*coffee, tea*) au lait; (*colour*) laiteux, -euse; **the M. Way** la Voie lactée

mill [mɪl] **1** *n* (*for flour*) moulin *m*; (*textile factory*) filature *f* **2** *vt* (*grind*) moudre ▪ **miller** *n* meunier, -ière *mf*
▸ **mill around** *vi* (*of crowd*) grouiller

millennium [mɪ'lenɪəm] (*pl* **-nia** [-nɪə]) *n* millénaire *m*

millet ['mɪlɪt] *n* millet *m*

milligram(me) ['mɪlɪgræm] *n* milligramme *m*

millimetre ['mɪlimiːtə(r)] (*Am* **millimeter**) *n* millimètre *m*

million ['mɪljən] *n* million *m*; **a m. men** un million d'hommes; **two m.** deux millions; *Fam* **she's one in a m.** elle est unique ▪ **millio'naire** *n* millionnaire *mf* ▪ **millionth** *adj & n* millionième *(mf)*

millstone ['mɪlstəʊn] *n* meule *f*; *Fig* **it's a m. around my neck** c'est un boulet que je traîne

milometer [maɪ'lɒmɪtə(r)] *n Br* ≃ compteur *m* kilométrique

mime [maɪm] **1** *n* (*actor*) mime *mf*; (*art*) mime *m* **2** *vti* mimer; (*of singer*) chanter en play-back

mimic ['mɪmɪk] **1** *n* imitateur, -trice *mf* **2** (*pt & pp* **-ck-**) *vt* imiter ▪ **mimicry** [-krɪ] *n* imitation *f*

minaret [mɪnə'ret] *n* minaret *m*

mince [mɪns] **1** *n* (*meat*) viande *f* hachée; **m. pie** *Br* (*containing meat*) tourte *f* à la viande; (*containing fruit*) = tartelette fourrée aux fruits secs et aux épices **2** *vt* hacher; **not to m. matters** *or* **one's words** ne pas mâcher ses mots ▪ **mincemeat** *n Br* (*meat*) viande *f* hachée; (*dried fruit*) = mélange de fruits secs et d'épices utilisé en pâtisserie ▪ **mincer** *n* (*machine*) hachoir *m*

mind¹ [maɪnd] *n* esprit *m*; (*sanity*) raison *f*; *Br* **to my m.** à mon avis; **to change one's m.** changer d'avis; **to speak one's m.** dire ce que l'on pense; *Br* **to be in two minds** (*undecided*) hésiter; **to bear** *or* **keep sth in m.** garder qch à l'esprit; **to have sb/sth in m.** avoir qn/qch en vue; **to make up one's m.** se décider; *Fam* **to be out of one's m.** avoir perdu la tête; **to be bored out of one's m.** s'ennuyer à mourir; **to bring sth to m.** rappeler qch; **I couldn't get it off my m.** je ne pouvais m'empêcher d'y penser; **it's on my m.** cela me préoccupe; **my m. isn't on the job** je n'ai pas la tête à ce que je fais; **her m. is going** elle perd la tête; *Br* **to have a good m. to do sth** avoir bien envie de faire qch

mind² [maɪnd] **1** *vt Br* (*pay attention to*) faire attention à; (*look after*) garder; **to m. one's language** surveiller son langage; *Fam* **to m. one's p's and q's** bien se tenir; *Br* **m. you don't fall** fais attention à ne pas tomber; *Br* **m. you do it** n'oublie pas de le faire; **I don't m. the cold/noise** le froid/bruit ne me gêne pas; **I don't m. trying** je veux bien essayer; **I wouldn't m. a cup of tea** je prendrais bien une tasse de thé; **I m. that...** ça me gêne que...; **if you don't m. my asking...** si je peux me permettre...; **never m. the car** peu importe la voiture; *Br* **m. you...** remarquez...; **m. your own business!** occupe-toi de tes affaires! **2** *vi* **I don't m.** ça m'est égal; **do you m. if I smoke?** ça vous gêne si je fume?; **never m.!** ça ne fait rien!, tant pis!; *Br* **m. (out)!** (*watch out*) attention!

mind-boggling ['maɪndbɒglɪŋ] *adj* stupéfiant ▪ **-minded** ['maɪndɪd] *suff* **fair-m.** impartial; **like-m.** de même opinion

minder ['maɪndə(r)] *n Fam* (*bodyguard*) gorille *m*

mindful ['maɪndfəl] *adj* **m. of sth/doing** attentif, -ive à qch/à faire

mindless ['maɪndləs] *adj* (*job, destruction*) stupide

mine¹ [maɪn] *possessive pron* le mien, la mienne, *pl* les mien(ne)s; **this hat is m.** ce chapeau est à moi *ou* est le mien; **a friend of m.** un ami à moi, un de mes amis

mine² [maɪn] **1** *n* (**a**) (*for coal, gold*) *& Fig* mine *f* (**b**) (*explosive*) mine *f* **2** *vt* (**a**) (*coal, gold*) extraire (**b**) (*beach, bridge*) miner **3** *vi* **to m. for coal** extraire du charbon ▪ **minefield** *n Mil* champ *m* de mines; *Fig* terrain *m* miné ▪ **miner** *n* mineur *m* ▪ **minesweeper** *n* dragueur *m* de mines ▪ **mining 1** *n* exploitation *f* minière **2** *adj* (*industry, region*) minier, -ière

mineral ['mɪnərəl] *adj & n* minéral (*m*); **m. water** eau *f* minérale

minestrone [mɪnɪ'strəʊnɪ] *n* minestrone *m*

minging ['mɪŋɪŋ] *adj Br very Fam* (*unattractive*) moche; (*disgusting*) dégueulasse ▪ **minger** *n Br Fam* mocheté *f*

mingle ['mɪŋgəl] *vi* (*of things*) se mêler (**with** à); (*of people*) parler un peu à tout le monde; **to m. with the crowd** se mêler à la foule

mingy ['mɪndʒɪ] (**-ier, -iest**) *adj Br Fam* radin

miniature ['mɪnɪtʃ(ə)r] **1** *adj* (*tiny*) minuscule; (*train, model*) miniature *inv* **2** *n* miniature *f*; **in m.** en miniature

minibus ['mɪnɪbʌs] *n* minibus *m*

minicab ['mɪnɪkæb] *n Br* radio-taxi *m*

Minidisc® ['mɪnɪdɪsk] *n* Minidisc® *m*; **M. player** lecteur *m* (de) Minidisc®

minigolf ['mɪnɪgɒlf] *n* minigolf *m*

minim ['mɪnɪm] *n Br Mus* blanche *f*

minima ['mɪnɪmə] *pl of* **minimum**

minimal ['mɪnɪməl] *adj* minimal

minimize ['mɪnɪmaɪz] *vt* minimiser

minimum ['mɪnɪməm] **1** (*pl* **-ima** [-ɪmə] *or* **-imums**) *n* minimum *m* **2** *adj* minimal; **m. wage** salaire *m* minimum

mining ['maɪnɪŋ] *n see* **mine²**

miniskirt ['mɪnɪskɜːt] *n* minijupe *f*

minister¹ ['mɪnɪstə(r)] *n Br* (*politician*) ministre *m*; (*of religion*) pasteur *m* ▪ **ministerial** [-'stɪərɪəl] *adj Br Pol* ministériel, -ielle ▪ **ministry** (*pl* **-ies**) *n Br Pol* ministère *m*; *Rel* **to enter** *or* **join the m.** devenir pasteur

minister² ['mɪnɪstə(r)] *vi* **to m. to sb's needs** subvenir aux besoins de qn

mink [mɪŋk] *n* vison *m*

minor ['maɪnə(r)] **1** *adj* (*unimportant*) & *Mus* mineur; (*operation*) bénin, -igne; (*road*) secondaire **2** *n Law* (*child*) mineur, -eure *mf*; **to be a m.** être mineur(e)

Minorca [mɪ'nɔːkə] *n* Minorque *f*

minority [maɪ'nɒrɪtɪ] **1** (*pl* **-ies**) *n* minorité *f*; **to be in the** *or* **a m.** être minoritaire **2** *adj* minoritaire

mint¹ [mɪnt] **1** *n* **the (Royal) M.** ≃ l'hôtel *m* de la Monnaie; *Fam* **to make a m.** (*of money*) faire une petite fortune **2** *adj* **m. stamp** timbre *m* neuf; **in m. condition** à l'état neuf **3** *vt* (*coins*) frapper

mint² [mɪnt] *n* (*herb*) menthe *f*; (*sweet*) bonbon *m* à la menthe; **m. sauce** sauce *f* à la menthe; **m. tea** infusion *f* de menthe

minus ['maɪnəs] **1** *adj & n* **m. (sign)** (signe *m*) moins *m* **2** *prep* (*with numbers*) moins; *Fam*

(*without*) sans; **it's m. 10 (degrees)** il fait moins 10

minute¹ ['mɪnɪt] *n* (*of time*) minute *f*; **this (very) m.** (*now*) tout de suite; **any m. (now)** d'une minute à l'autre; **m. hand** (*of clock*) grande aiguille *f* ▪ **minutes** *npl* (*of meeting*) procèsverbal *m*

minute² [maɪ'njuːt] *adj* (*tiny*) minuscule; (*detailed*) minutieux, -ieuse

miracle ['mɪrəkəl] *n* miracle *m*; **to work miracles** faire des miracles; **by some m.** par miracle ▪ **miraculous** [mɪ'rækjʊləs] *adj* miraculeux, -euse

mirage ['mɪrɑːʒ] *n* mirage *m*

mire [maɪə(r)] *n Literary* fange *f*; *Fig* (*difficult situation*) bourbier *m*

mirror ['mɪrə(r)] **1** *n* miroir *m*, glace *f*; *Fig* (*representation*) miroir; **(rear view) m.** (*of vehicle*) rétroviseur *m* **2** *vt* (*reflect*) refléter

mirth [mɜːθ] *n Literary* gaieté *f*

misadventure [mɪsəd'ventʃə(r)] *n* mésaventure *f*; *Law* **death by m.** mort *f* accidentelle

misanthropist [mɪ'zænθrəpɪst] *n* misanthrope *mf*

misapprehension [mɪsæprɪ'henʃən] *n* malentendu *m*; **to be under a m.** se méprendre

misappropriate [mɪsə'prəʊprɪeɪt] *vt* (*money*) détourner ▪ **misappropriation** *n* (*of money*) détournement

misbehave [mɪsbɪ'heɪv] *vi* se conduire mal

miscalculate [mɪs'kælkjʊleɪt] **1** *vt* mal calculer **2** *vi* faire une erreur de calcul; *Fig* faire un mauvais calcul ▪ **miscalcu'lation** *n* erreur *f* de calcul

miscarriage [mɪs'kærɪdʒ] *n Med* fausse couche *f*; **to have a m.** faire une fausse couche; *Law* **m. of justice** erreur *f* judiciaire ▪ **miscarry** (*pt & pp* **-ied**) *vi* (*of woman*) faire une fausse couche; *Fig* (*of plan*) avorter

miscellaneous [mɪsə'leɪnɪəs] *adj* divers

mischief ['mɪstʃɪf] *n* espièglerie *f*; **to get into m.** faire des bêtises; **to make m. for sb** créer des ennuis à qn; *Br* **to do oneself a m.** (*harm oneself*) se faire mal

mischievous ['mɪstʃɪvəs] *adj* (*naughty*) espiègle; (*malicious*) méchant ▪

misconception [mɪskən'sepʃən] *n* idée *f* fausse

misconduct [mɪs'kɒndʌkt] *n* (*bad behaviour*) inconduite *f*; *Com* (*bad management*) mauvaise gestion *f*; **(professional) m.** faute *f* professionnelle

misconstrue [mɪskən'struː] *vt* mal interpréter

misdemeanour [mɪsdɪ'miːnə(r)] (*Am* **misdemeanor**) *n* écart *m* de conduite; *Am Law* délit *m*

miser ['maɪzə(r)] *n* avare *mf* ▪ **miserly** *adj* avare

miserable ['mɪzərəbəl] *adj* (*wretched*) misérable; (*unhappy*) malheureux, -euse; (*awful*) affreux, -euse; (*derisory*) (*salary*) dérisoire ▪ **miserably** adv (wretchedly) misérablement; (fail) lamentablement

> Note that the French adjective **misérable** never means **unhappy**. Its most common meaning is **destitute** or **wretched**.

misery ['mɪzərɪ] (pl **-ies**) n (suffering) malheur m; (sadness) détresse f; Fam (sad person) grincheux, -euse mf; **his life is a m.** il est malheureux; **to put an animal out of its m.** achever un animal

> Note that the French word **misère** is a false friend and is never a translation for the English word **misery**. It means **extreme poverty**.

misfire [mɪs'faɪə(r)] vi (of gun) faire long feu; (of engine) avoir des ratés; Fig (of plan) rater

misfit ['mɪsfɪt] n Pej inadapté, -ée mf

misfortune [mɪs'fɔːtʃuːn] n malheur m

misgivings [mɪs'gɪvɪŋz] npl (doubts) doutes mpl (about sur); (fears) craintes fpl (about à propos de)

misguided [mɪs'gaɪdɪd] adj (attempt) malencontreux, -euse; (decision) peu judicieux, -ieuse; **to be m.** (of person) se tromper

mishandle [mɪs'hændəl] vt (device) mal utiliser; (situation) mal gérer; (person) malmener

mishap ['mɪshæp] n incident m; **without m.** sans encombre

misinform [mɪsɪn'fɔːm] vt mal renseigner

misinterpret [mɪsɪn'tɜːprɪt] vt mal interpréter

misjudge [mɪs'dʒʌdʒ] vt (person, distance) mal juger

mislay [mɪs'leɪ] (pt & pp **-laid**) vt égarer

mislead [mɪs'liːd] (pt & pp **-led**) tromper ▪ **misleading** adj trompeur, -euse

mismanage [mɪs'mænɪdʒ] vt mal gérer ▪ **mismanagement** n mauvaise gestion f

misnomer [mɪs'nəʊmə(r)] n terme m impropre

miso ['miːsəʊ] n Culin miso m

misogynist [mɪ'sɒdʒɪnɪst] n misogyne mf ▪ **misogynistic** adj misogyne

misplace [mɪs'pleɪs] vt (lose) égarer; (trust) mal placer ▪ **misplaced** adj (remark) déplacé; **m. accent** accent m mal placé

misprint ['mɪsprɪnt] n faute f d'impression, coquille f

mspronounce [mɪsprə'naʊns] vt mal prononcer

misquote [mɪs'kwəʊt] vt citer incorrectement

misrepresent [mɪsreprɪ'zent] vt (theory) dénaturer; (person) présenter sous un faux jour

Miss [mɪs] n Mademoiselle f; **M. World** Miss Monde

miss [mɪs] 1 n coup m raté; **that was** or **we had a near m.** on l'a échappé belle; Fam **I'll give it a m.** (not go) je n'y irai pas; (not take or drink or eat) je n'en prendrai pas 2 vt (train, target, opportunity) manquer, rater; (not see) ne pas voir; (not understand) ne pas comprendre; (feel the lack of) regretter; **he misses Paris** Paris lui manque; **I m. you** tu me manques; **we'll be missed** on nous regrettera; **I'm missing my wallet!** je n'ai plus mon portefeuille!; **the table is missing a leg** il manque un pied à la table; **don't m. seeing this play** il faut absolument que tu voies cette pièce; **to m. sth out** (accidentally) oublier qch; (intentionally) omettre qch 3 vi manquer ou rater son coup; **to m. out** (lose a chance) rater l'occasion; **to m. out on sth** rater qch

misshapen [mɪs'ʃeɪpən] adj difforme

missile [Br 'mɪsaɪl, Am 'mɪsəl] n (rocket) missile m; (object thrown) projectile m

missing ['mɪsɪŋ] adj (absent) absent; (in war, after disaster) disparu; (object) manquant; **there are two cups/students m.** il manque deux tasses/deux étudiants; **nothing is m.** il ne manque rien; **to go m.** disparaître; Mil **m. in action** porté disparu

mission ['mɪʃən] n mission f

missionary ['mɪʃənərɪ] (pl **-ies**) n Rel missionnaire m

misspell [mɪs'spel] (pt & pp **-ed** or **-spelt**) vt mal écrire

mist [mɪst] 1 n (fog) brume f; (on glass) buée f 2 vi **to m. over** or **up** s'embuer

mistake [mɪ'steɪk] 1 n erreur f, faute f; **to make a m.** faire une erreur; **by m.** par erreur 2 (pt **-took**, pp **-taken**) vt (meaning, intention) se tromper sur; **to m. the date/place** se tromper de date/de lieu; **there's no mistaking his face** il est impossible de ne pas reconnaître son visage; **to m. sb for** prendre qn pour ▪ **mistaken** adj (belief, impression) erroné; **to be m.** (of person) se tromper (about sur) ▪ **mistakenly** adv par erreur

Mister ['mɪstə(r)] n Monsieur m

mistletoe ['mɪsltəʊ] n gui m

mistreat [mɪs'triːt] vt maltraiter

mistress ['mɪstrɪs] n maîtresse f; Br (in secondary school) professeur m

mistrust [mɪs'trʌst] 1 n méfiance f 2 vt se méfier de ▪ **mistrustful** adj méfiant

misty ['mɪstɪ] (**-ier**, **-iest**) adj (foggy) brumeux, -euse; (outline) flou

misunderstand [mɪsʌndə'stænd] (pt & pp **-stood**) vti mal comprendre ▪ **misunderstanding** n (disagreement) mésentente f; (misconception) malentendu m ▪ **misunderstood** adj (person) incompris

misuse 1 [mɪs'juːs] n (of equipment, resources) mauvais emploi m; (of funds) détournement m; (of power) abus m 2 [mɪs'juːz] vt (equipment, resources) mal employer; (funds) détourner; (power) abuser de

mite [maɪt] n (a) (bug) acarien m (b) Fam (poor) little m. (child) pauvre petit, -ite mf (c) Fam a m. tired un tantinet fatigué

mitigate ['mɪtɪgeɪt] *vt* atténuer; *Law* **mitigating circumstances** circonstances *fpl* atténuantes

mitt(en) [mɪt, 'mɪtən] *n (glove)* moufle *f*; **baseball mitt** gant *m* de baseball

mix [mɪks] **1** *n (mixture)* mélange *m* **2** *vt* mélanger; *(cement, drink, cake)* préparer; *(salad)* remuer **3** *vi (blend)* se mélanger; *(of colours)* aller ensemble; **to m. with sb** *(socially)* fréquenter qn; **she doesn't m.** elle n'est pas sociable

▸ **mix up** *vt inv (drinks, papers)* mélanger; *(mistake)* confondre (**with** avec); **I'm getting all mixed up** je ne sais plus où j'en suis; **to be mixed up in sth** être mêlé à qch

mixed [mɪkst] *adj (school, marriage)* mixte; *(results)* divers; *(nuts, chocolates)* assortis; **m. grill** assortiment *m* de grillades; **m. feelings** sentiments *mpl* mitigés; **to be (all) m. up** *(of person)* être désorienté; *(of facts, account)* être confus; **in m. company** en présence de personnes des deux sexes

mixer ['mɪksə(r)] *n* (**a**) *(for cooking)* mixeur *m*; *Br* **m. tap** *(robinet m)* mélangeur *m* (**b**) **to be a good m.** *(of person)* être sociable

mixture ['mɪkstʃə(r)] *n* mélange *m*

mix-up ['mɪksʌp] *n* confusion *f*

mm *(abbr millimetre)* mm

moan [məʊn] **1** *n (sound)* gémissement *m*; *(complaint)* plainte *f* **2** *vi (make sound)* gémir; *(complain)* se plaindre (**to** à; **about** de; **that** que)

moat [məʊt] *n* douve *f*

mob [mɒb] **1** *n (crowd)* foule *f*; *Am Fam* **the M.** la Mafia **2** *(pt & pp* **-bb-**) *vt* prendre d'assaut ▪ **mobster** *n Am Fam* gangster *m*

mobile [*Br* 'məʊbaɪl, *Am* 'məʊbəl] **1** *adj* mobile; *Fam* **to be m.** être motorisé; **m. home** mobile home *m*; **m. library** bibliobus *m*; **m. phone** téléphone *m* portable **2** *n* (**a**) *(Am* ['məʊbiːl])* *(ornament)* mobile *m* (**b**) *(phone)* portable *m* ▪ **mobility** *n* mobilité *f*

mobilize ['məʊbɪlaɪz] *vti* mobiliser ▪ **mobili'zation** *n* mobilisation *f*

moccasin ['mɒkəsɪn] *n* mocassin *m*

mocha [*Br* 'mɒkə, *Am* 'məʊkə] *n* moka *m*

mock [mɒk] **1** *adj (false)* simulé; *Br Sch* **m. exam** examen *m* blanc **2** *vt* se moquer de; *(mimic)* singer ▪ **mocking** *n* moquerie *f* ▪ **mockery** *n (act)* moqueries *fpl*; *(farce, parody)* parodie *f*; **to make a m. of sth** tourner qch en ridicule

mock-up ['mɒkʌp] *n* maquette *f*

mod cons [mɒd'kɒnz] *npl Fam* **with all m.** *(house)* tout confort *inv*

mode [məʊd] *n (manner, way)* & *Comptr* mode *m*; **m. of transport** mode de transport

model ['mɒdəl] **1** *n (example, person)* modèle *m*; *(small version)* maquette *f*; (**fashion**) **m.** mannequin *m*; (**scale**) **m.** modèle réduit **2** *adj* *(behaviour, factory, student)* modèle; *(car, plane)* modèle réduit *inv* **3** *(Br* **-ll-,** *Am* **-l-)** *vt (clay)* modeler; *(hats, dresses)* présenter; *Comptr* modéliser; **to m. sth on** modeler qch sur; **to m. oneself on sb** prendre exemple sur qn **4** *vi (for fashion)* être mannequin; *(pose for artist)* poser ▪ **modelling** *(Am* **modeling**) *n (of statues, in clay)* modelage *m*; **to make a career in m.** faire une carrière de mannequin; **m. clay** pâte *f* à modeler

modem ['məʊdəm] *n Comptr* modem *m*

moderate¹ ['mɒdərət] **1** *adj* modéré **2** *n Pol* modéré, -ée *mf* ▪ **moderately** *adv (in moderation)* modérément; *(averagely)* moyennement

moderate² ['mɒdəreɪt] **1** *vt (diminish, tone down)* modérer **2** *vi (of wind)* se calmer ▪ **moder'ation** *n* modération *f*; **in m.** avec modération

modern ['mɒdən] *adj* moderne; **m. languages** langues *fpl* vivantes ▪ **modernism** *n* modernisme *m*

modernize ['mɒdənaɪz] **1** *vt* moderniser **2** *vi* se moderniser ▪ **moderni'zation** *n* modernisation *f*

modest ['mɒdɪst] *adj (unassuming, moderate)* modeste; *(chaste)* pudique ▪ **modesty** *n (of person)* modestie *f*

modicum ['mɒdɪkəm] *n* **a m. of** un minimum de

modify ['mɒdɪfaɪ] *(pt & pp* **-ied**) *vt* modifier ▪ **modification** [-fɪ'keɪʃən] *n* modification *f* (**to** à)

modulate ['mɒdjʊleɪt] *vt* moduler ▪ **modu-'lation** *n* modulation *f*

module ['mɒdjuːl] *n* module *m*

mogul¹ ['məʊgəl] *n (magnate)* magnat *m*

mogul² ['məʊgəl] *n (in skiing)* bosse *f*

mohair ['məʊheə(r)] *n* mohair *m*; **m. sweater** pull *m* en mohair

moist [mɔɪst] *(-er, -est)* *adj* humide; *(skin, hand)* moite ▪ **moisten** ['mɔɪsən] *vt* humecter

moisture ['mɔɪstʃə(r)] *n* humidité *f*; *(on glass)* buée *f*

moisturize ['mɔɪstʃəraɪz] *vt* hydrater ▪ **moisturizer** *n* crème *f* hydratante

molar ['məʊlə(r)] *n* molaire *f*

molasses [mə'læsɪz] *n Am (treacle)* mélasse *f*

mold [məʊld] *n & vt Am* = **mould**

mole [məʊl] *n* (**a**) *(on skin)* grain *m* de beauté (**b**) *(animal, spy)* taupe *f*

molecule ['mɒlɪkjuːl] *n* molécule *f*

molest [mə'lest] *vt (annoy)* importuner; *Law (child, woman)* agresser (sexuellement)

mollusc ['mɒləsk] *n* mollusque *m*

molt [məʊlt] *vi Am* = **moult**

molten ['məʊltən] *adj (metal, rock)* en fusion

mom [mɒm] *n Am Fam* maman *f* ▪ **mommy** *n Am Fam* maman *f*

moment ['məʊmənt] *n* moment *m*, instant *m*; **at**

the m. en ce moment; **for the m.** pour le moment; **in a m.** dans un instant; **the m. she leaves** dès qu'elle partira; **any m. (now)** d'un instant à l'autre

momentary ['məʊməntərɪ] *adj* momentané ▪ **momentarily** [-'terɪlɪ] *adv (temporarily)* momentanément; *Am (soon)* tout de suite

momentous [məʊ'mentəs] *adj* capital

momentum [məʊ'mentəm] *n (speed)* élan *m*; **to gather** *or* **gain m.** *(of ideas)* gagner du terrain; *(of campaign)* prendre de l'ampleur

Monaco ['mɒnəkəʊ] *n* Monaco *m*

monarch ['mɒnək] *n* monarque *m* ▪ **monarchy** *(pl -ies) n* monarchie *f*

monastery ['mɒnəstərɪ] *n (pl -ies) n* monastère *m*

Monday ['mʌndeɪ] *n* lundi *m*

monetary ['mʌnɪtərɪ] *adj* monétaire

money ['mʌnɪ] *n* argent *m*; **to make m.** *(of person)* gagner de l'argent; *(of business)* rapporter de l'argent; **to get one's m.'s worth** en avoir pour son argent; **he gets** *or* **earns good m.** il gagne bien sa vie; *Fam* **to be in the m.** rouler sur l'or; **m. order** mandat *m* ▪ **moneybox** *n* tirelire *f* ▪ **moneychanger** *n Am (machine)* changeur *m ou* distributeur *m* de monnaie ▪ **moneylender** *n* prêteur, -euse *mf* ▪ **moneymaking** *adj* lucratif, -ive ▪ **moneyspinner** *n Fam (project)* mine *f* d'or

> Note that the French word **monnaie** is a false friend and is rarely a translation for the English word **money**. It means **change** or **currency** depending on the context.

Mongolia [mɒŋ'gəʊlɪə] *n n* Mongolie *f* ▪ **Mongolian** 1 *adj* mongol 2 *n (person)* Mongol, -ole *mf*; *(language)* mongol *m*

mongrel ['mʌŋgrəl] *n* bâtard *m*

monitor ['mɒnɪtə(r)] 1 *n Comptr, TV & Tech (screen, device)* moniteur *m* 2 *vt (broadcast, conversation)* écouter; *(check)* surveiller

monk [mʌŋk] *n* moine *m*

monkey ['mʌŋkɪ] *(pl -eys) n* singe *m*; *Fam* **little m.** *(child)* polisson, -onne *mf*; *Fam* **m. business** *(mischief)* singeries *fpl*; *(dishonest behaviour)* magouilles *fpl*; *Br* **m. nut** cacah(o)uète *f*; **m. wrench** clef *f* anglaise

▸ **monkey about, monkey around** *vi Fam* faire l'imbécile

mono ['mɒnəʊ] 1 *adj (record)* mono *inv* 2 *n* **in m.** en monophonie

monochrome ['mɒnəkrəʊm] *adj & n* monochrome *(m)*

monocle ['mɒnəkəl] *n* monocle *m*

monogamous [mə'nɒgəməs] *adj* monogame ▪ **monogamy** *n* monogamie *f*

monogram ['mɒnəgræm] *n* monogramme *m*

monolingual [mɒnəʊ'lɪŋgwəl] *adj* monolingue

monologue ['mɒnəlɒg] *n* monologue *m*

mononucleosis [mɒnəʊnjuːklɪ'əʊsɪs] *n Am Med* mononucléose *f* infectieuse

monopoly [mə'nɒpəlɪ] *n* monopole *m* ▪ **monopolize** *vt* monopoliser

monosyllable ['mɒnəsɪləbəl] *n* monosyllabe *m* ▪ **monosyllabic** [-'læbɪk] *adj* monosyllabique

monotone ['mɒnətəʊn] *n* **in a m.** sur un ton monocorde

monotony [mə'nɒtənɪ] *n* monotonie *f* ▪ **monotonous** *adj* monotone

monsoon [mɒn'suːn] *n* mousson *f*

monster ['mɒnstə(r)] *n* monstre *m*

monstrous ['mɒnstrəs] *adj* monstrueux, -ueuse ▪ **monstrosity** *(pl -ies)* *n* monstruosité *f*

month [mʌnθ] *n* mois *m*

monthly ['mʌnθlɪ] 1 *adj* mensuel, -uelle; **m. payment** mensualité *f* 2 *(pl -ies) n (periodical)* mensuel *m* 3 *adv* tous les mois

Montreal [mɒntrɪ'ɔːl] *n* Montréal *m ou f*

monument ['mɒnjʊmənt] *n* monument *m* ▪ **monumental** *adj* monumental

moo [muː] 1 *(pl* **moos***) n* meuglement *m* 2 *exclam* meuh! 3 *(pt & pp* **mooed***) vi* meugler

mooch [muːtʃ] *Fam* 1 *vi* **to m. around** flâner 2 *vt Am* **to m. sth off sb** *(cadge)* taper qch à qn

mood [muːd] *n (of person)* humeur *f*; *(of country)* état *m* d'esprit; *Grammar* mode *m*; **in a good/ bad m.** de bonne/mauvaise humeur; **to be in the m. to do** *or* **for doing sth** être d'humeur à faire qch

moody ['muːdɪ] *(-ier, -iest) adj (bad-tempered)* maussade; *(changeable)* lunatique

moon [muːn] *n* lune *f*; **full m.** pleine lune; **once in a blue m.** *(rarely)* tous les trente-six du mois; *Br Fam* **over the m.** aux anges *(about* de) ▪ **moonlight** 1 *n* clair *m* de lune; **by m.** au clair de lune 2 *vi Fam* travailler au noir ▪ **moonlit** *adj (landscape)* éclairé par la lune

moor [mʊə(r)] 1 *n (heath)* lande *f* 2 *vt (ship)* amarrer 3 *vi (of ship)* mouiller ▪ **moorings** *npl Naut (ropes)* amarres *fpl*; *(place)* mouillage *m*

moose [muːs] *n inv (animal)* élan *m*; *(Canadian)* orignal *m*

moot [muːt] *adj* **it's a m. point** c'est discutable

mop [mɒp] 1 *n (for floor)* balai *m* à franges; *(with sponge)* balai-éponge *m*; **dish m.** lavette *f*; *Fam* **m. of hair** tignasse *f* 2 *(pt & pp* **-pp-***) vt* **to m. one's brow** s'essuyer le front; **to m. (up) the floor** laver par terre; **to m. sth up** *(liquid)* éponger qch

mope [məʊp] *vi* **to m. about** broyer du noir

moped ['məʊped] *n* Mobylette® *f*

moral ['mɒrəl] 1 *adj* moral 2 *n (of story)* morale *f*; **morals** *(principles)* morale *f* ▪ **morale** [mə'ræl, *Br* mɒ'rɑːl] *n* moral *m* ▪ **morality** [mə'rælɪtɪ] *n* moralité *f* ▪ **moralize** *vi* moraliser ▪ **morally** *adv* moralement; **m. wrong** immoral

morass [mə'ræs] n *(land)* marais m; *Fig (mess, situation)* bourbier m

moratorium [mɒrə'tɔːrɪəm] n moratoire m (**on** sur)

morbid ['mɔːbɪd] adj morbide ▪ **morbidly** adv de façon morbide

more [mɔː(r)] 1 adj plus de; **m. cars** plus de voitures; **m. water** plus d'eau; **he has m. books than you** il a plus de livres que toi; **a few m. months** quelques mois de plus; **(some) m. tea** encore du thé; **(some) m. details** d'autres détails; **m. than a kilo/ten** plus d'un kilo/de dix 2 adv *(to form comparative of adjectives and adverbs)* plus (**than** que); **m. interesting** plus intéressant; **m. easily** plus facilement; **m. and m.** de plus en plus; **m. or less** plus ou moins 3 pron plus; **have some m.** reprenez-en; **she knows m. than you** elle en sait plus que toi; **she doesn't have any m.** elle n'en a plus; **the m. he shouts, the m. hoarse he gets** plus il crie, plus il s'enroue; **what's m.** qui plus est

moreish ['mɔːrɪʃ] adj Br Fam qui a un goût de revenez-y

moreover [mɔː'rəʊvə(r)] adv de plus

mores ['mɔːreɪz] npl Formal mœurs fpl

morgue [mɔːg] n morgue f

morning ['mɔːnɪŋ] 1 n matin m; *(referring to duration)* matinée f; **in the m.** le matin; *(during the course of the morning)* pendant la matinée; *(tomorrow)* demain matin; **tomorrow/yesterday m.** demain/hier matin; **at seven in the m.** à sept heures du matin; **every Tuesday m.** tous les mardis matin; **in the early m.** au petit matin; **good m.!,** Fam **m.!** bonjour! 2 adj *(newspaper)* du matin; **m. sickness** *(of pregnant woman)* nausées fpl matinales ▪ **mornings** adv Am le matin

Morocco [mə'rɒkəʊ] n le Maroc ▪ **Moroccan** 1 adj marocain 2 n Marocain, -aine mf

moron ['mɔːrɒn] n Fam crétin, -ine mf ▪ **moronic** adj Fam idiot

morose [mə'rəʊs] adj morose

morphine ['mɔːfiːn] n morphine f

Morse [mɔːs] n & adj M. **(code)** morse m

morsel ['mɔːsəl] n morceau m

mortal ['mɔːtəl] adj & n mortel, -elle *(mf)* ▪ **mortality** [-'tælɪtɪ] n mortalité f

mortar ['mɔːtə(r)] n mortier m

mortgage ['mɔːgɪdʒ] 1 n *(from lender's viewpoint)* prêt m immobilier; *(from borrower's viewpoint)* emprunt m immobilier; **m. rate** taux m de crédit immobilier 2 vt *(house, one's future)* hypothéquer

mortician [mɔː'tɪʃən] n Am entrepreneur m de pompes funèbres

mortify ['mɔːtɪfaɪ] *(pt & pp -ied)* vt mortifier; **I was mortified!** j'étais vexé!

mortuary ['mɔːtʃʊərɪ] *(pl -ies)* n morgue f

mosaic [məʊ'zeɪɪk] n mosaïque f

Moscow [Br 'mɒskəʊ, Am 'mɒskaʊ] n Moscou m ou f

Moses ['məʊzɪz] adj M. **basket** couffin m

Moslem ['mɒzlɪm] adj & n = **Muslim**

mosque [mɒsk] n mosquée f

mosquito [mɒ'skiːtəʊ] *(pl -oes or -os)* n moustique m; **m. net** moustiquaire f

moss [mɒs] n mousse f ▪ **mossy** adj moussu

most [məʊst] 1 adj **(a)** *(the majority of)* la plupart de; **m. women** la plupart des femmes **(b)** *(greatest amount of)* **the m.** le plus de; **I have the m. books** j'ai le plus de livres 2 adv **(a)** *(to form superlative of adjectives and adverbs)* plus; **the m. beautiful** le plus beau *(f* la plus belle*)* **(in/of** de*)*; **to talk (the) m.** parler le plus; **what I want m.** ce que je veux par-dessus tout; **m. of all** *(especially)* surtout **(b)** *(very)* extrêmement; **it was m. interesting** c'était extrêmement intéressant 3 pron **(a)** *(the majority)* la plupart; **m. of the people** la plupart des gens; **m. of the time** la plupart du temps; **m. of the cake** la plus grande partie du gâteau; **m. of them** la plupart d'entre eux **(b)** *(greatest amount)* le plus; **he earns the m.** c'est lui qui gagne le plus; **to make the m. of sth** *(situation, talent)* tirer le meilleur parti de qch; *(holiday)* profiter au maximum de qch; **at (the very) m.** tout au plus ▪ **mostly** adv *(in the main)* surtout; *(most often)* le plus souvent

MOT [eməʊ'tiː] *(abbr Ministry of Transport)* n Br = contrôle obligatoire des véhicules de plus de trois ans

motel [məʊ'tel] n motel m

moth [mɒθ] n papillon m de nuit; **(clothes) m.** mite f ▪ **mothball** n boule f de naphtaline ▪ **moth-eaten** adj mité

mother ['mʌðə(r)] 1 n mère f; M.'s **Day** la fête des Mères; **m. tongue** langue f maternelle 2 vt materner ▪ **motherhood** n maternité f ▪ **mother-in-law** *(pl mothers-in-law)* n belle-mère f ▪ **motherly** adj maternel, -elle ▪ **mother-of-'pearl** n nacre f ▪ **mother-to-'be** *(pl mothers-to-be)* n future mère f

motion ['məʊʃən] 1 n *(of arm)* mouvement m; *(in meeting)* motion f; **to set sth in m.** mettre qch en mouvement; **m. picture** film m 2 vti **to m. (to) sb to do sth** faire signe à qn de faire qch ▪ **motionless** adj immobile

motivate ['məʊtɪveɪt] vt *(person, decision)* motiver ▪ **motivated** adj motivé ▪ **moti'vation** n motivation f

motive ['məʊtɪv] n motif m (**for** de); Law mobile m (**for** de)

motley ['mɒtlɪ] adj *(collection)* hétéroclite; *(coloured)* bigarré

motor ['məʊtə(r)] 1 n *(engine)* moteur m; Br Fam *(car)* auto f 2 adj *(industry, vehicle, insurance)* automobile; *(accident)* d'auto; *Br* m. **mechanic** mécanicien-auto *m*; m. **racing** courses *fpl* automobiles; m. **show** salon *m* de l'automobile 3 *vi Br (drive)* voyager en auto ■ **motorbike** *n* moto *f* ■ **motorboat** *n* canot *m* à moteur ■ **motorcade** *n* cortège *m* de voitures ■ **motorcar** *n Br* automobile *f* ■ **motorcycle** *n* moto *f*, motocyclette *f* ■ **motorcyclist** *n* motocycliste *mf* ■ **motoring** *n Br* conduite *f* ■ **motorist** *n Br* automobiliste *mf* ■ **motorized** *adj* motorisé ■ **motorway** *n Br* autoroute *f*

mottled ['mɒtəld] *adj* tacheté

motto ['mɒtəʊ] *(pl* -**oes** *or* -**os)** *n* devise *f*

mould¹ [məʊld] *(Am* **mold)** 1 *n (shape)* moule *m* 2 *vt (clay, person's character)* modeler

mould² [məʊld] *(Am* **mold)** *n (fungus)* moisissure *f* ■ **mouldy** *(Am* **moldy)** *(*-**ier**, -**iest**) *adj* moisi; **to go m.** moisir

moult [məʊlt] *(Am* **molt)** *vi* muer

Mount [maʊnt] *n* M. **Everest** l'Everest; M. **Vesuvius** le Vésuve

mount [maʊnt] 1 *n (frame for photo or slide)* cadre *m*; *(horse)* monture *f* 2 *vt (horse, hill, jewel, photo, demonstration)* monter; *(ladder, tree)* monter à 3 *vi* (**a**) **to m. (up)** *(on horse)* se mettre en selle (**b**) *(increase, rise)* monter; **to m. up** *(add up)* chiffrer (**to** à); *(accumulate) (of debts, bills)* s'accumuler

mountain ['maʊntɪn] 1 *n* montagne *f* 2 *adj (plant, shoes)* de montagne; m. **bike** vélo *m* tout terrain; m. **range** chaîne *f* de montagnes; m. **rescue team** équipe *f* de secours en montagne ■ **mountai'neer** *n* alpiniste *mf* ■ **mountaineering** *n* alpinisme *m* ■ **mountainous** *adj* montagneux, -euse

mourn [mɔːn] *vti* **to m. (for) sb, to m. the loss of sb** pleurer qn; **she's mourning** elle est en deuil ■ **mourner** *n* = personne assistant aux obsèques ■ **mournful** *adj* triste ■ **mourning** *n* deuil *m*; **in m.** en deuil

mouse [maʊs] *(pl* **mice** [maɪs]) *n (animal) & Comptr* souris *f*; Comptr m. **button** bouton *m* de souris; Comptr m. **mat** *or* **pad** tapis *m* de souris ■ **mousetrap** *n* souricière *f*

mousse [muːs] *n* mousse *f*; **chocolate m.** mousse au chocolat

moustache [məˈstɑːʃ] *(Am* **mustache** ['mʌstæʃ]) *n* moustache *f*

mousy ['maʊsɪ] *(*-**ier**, -**iest**) *adj Br Pej (hair)* châtain terne; *Fig (shy)* timide

mouth 1 [maʊθ] *(pl* -**s** [maʊðz]) *n (of person, horse)* bouche *f*; *(of other animals)* gueule *f*; *(of river)* embouchure *f*; *(of cave, harbour)* entrée *f* 2 [maʊð] *vt Pej* débiter ■ **mouthful** ['maʊθfəl] *n (of food)* bouchée *f*; *(of liquid)* gorgée *f* ■ **mouthorgan** *n* harmonica *m* ■ **mouthpiece** *n (of musical instrument)* embouchure *f*;

(spokesperson) porte-parole *m inv* ■ **mouth-wash** *n* bain *m* de bouche ■ **mouth-watering** *adj* appétissant

movable ['muːvəbəl] *adj* mobile

move [muːv] 1 *n* mouvement *m*; *(change of house)* déménagement *m*; *(change of job)* changement *m* d'emploi; *(transfer of employee)* mutation *f*; *(in game)* coup *m*; *(step)* pas *m*; **to make a m.** *(leave)* se préparer à partir; *(act)* passer à l'action; **to make a m. towards sb/sth** se diriger vers qn/qch; **to make the first m.** faire le premier pas; **it's your m.** *(turn)* c'est à toi de jouer; *Fam* **to get a m. on** se grouiller; **on the m.** en marche

2 *vt* déplacer; *(arm, leg)* remuer; *(employee)* muter; *(piece in game)* jouer; *(propose in debate)* proposer (**that** que); **to m. sb** *(emotionally)* émouvoir qn; *(transfer in job)* muter qn; **to m. sb to tears** émouvoir qn jusqu'aux larmes; **to m. house** déménager

3 *vi* bouger; *(change position)* se déplacer (**to** à); *(leave)* partir; *(act)* agir; *(play)* jouer; *(change house)* déménager; **to m. to Paris** aller habiter Paris; **to m. into a house** emménager dans une maison; **to get things moving** faire avancer les choses

▸ **move about, move around** *vi* se déplacer; *(fidget)* remuer

▸ **move along** *vi* avancer

▸ **move away** *vi (go away)* s'éloigner; *(move house)* déménager

▸ **move back** 1 *vt sep (chair)* reculer; *(to its original position)* remettre en place 2 *vi (withdraw)* reculer; *(return)* retourner (**to** à)

▸ **move down** 1 *vt sep (take down)* descendre 2 *vi (come down)* descendre

▸ **move forward** *vt sep & vi* avancer

▸ **move in** *vi (into house)* emménager

▸ **move off** *vi (go away)* s'éloigner; *(of vehicle)* démarrer

▸ **move out** *vi (out of house)* déménager

▸ **move over** 1 *vt sep* pousser 2 *vi (make room)* se pousser

▸ **move up** *vi (on seats)* se pousser

moveable ['muːvəbəl] *adj* mobile; *Law* m. **goods, moveables** biens *mpl* meubles

movement ['muːvmənt] *n* mouvement *m*

movie ['muːvɪ] *n* film *m*; **the movies** *(cinema)* le cinéma; m. **camera** caméra *f*; m. **star** vedette *f* de cinéma; *Am* m. **theater** cinéma *m* ■ **moviegoer** *n* cinéphile *mf*

moving ['muːvɪŋ] *adj* en mouvement; *(vehicle)* en marche; *(touching)* émouvant; m. **part** *(of machine)* pièce *f* mobile

mow [məʊ] *(pp* **mown** [məʊn] *or* **mowed)** *vt (field, wheat)* faucher; **to m. the lawn** tondre le gazon; *Fig* **to m. down** *(kill)* faucher ■ **mower** *n* **(lawn) m.** tondeuse *f* (à gazon)

Mozambique [məʊzæmˈbiːk] *n* le Mozambique

MP [em'piː] *(abbr* **Member of Parliament***) n Br* député *m*

mph [empiː'eɪtʃ] *(abbr* **miles per hour***)* ≃ km/h

MP3 [empiː'θriː] *n Comptr* MP3 *m inv;* **M. file** fichier *m* MP3; **M. player** lecteur *m* (de) MP3

Mr ['mɪstə(r)] *n* Mr Brown M. Brown

Mrs ['mɪsɪz] *n* Mrs Brown Mme Brown

Ms [mɪz] *n* Ms Brown ≃ Mme Brown *(ne renseigne pas sur le statut de famille)*

MS [em'es] **(a)** *(abbr* **multiple sclerosis***) Med* sclérose *f* en plaques **(b)** *(abbr* **Master of Science***) Am Univ* = **MSc**

MSc [emes'siː] *(abbr* **Master of Science***) n Univ* **to have an M. in chemistry** avoir une maîtrise de chimie; **John Smith M.** John Smith, titulaire d'une maîtrise *(en sciences, chimie etc)*

MSP [emes'piː] *(abbr* **Member of the Scottish Parliament***) n* député *m* du parlement écossais

much [mʌtʃ] **1** *adj*

Hormis dans la langue soutenue et dans certaines expressions, ne s'utilise que dans des structures négatives ou interrogatives.

beaucoup de; **not m. time/money** pas beaucoup de temps/d'argent; **how m. sugar do you want?** combien de sucre voulez-vous?; **as m. wine as** autant de vin que; **twice as m. traffic** deux fois plus de circulation; **too m. work** trop de travail; **so m. time** tant *ou* tellement de temps; **this m. wine** ça de vin

2 *adv* beaucoup; **very m.** beaucoup; **not (very) m.** pas beaucoup; **m. better** bien meilleur; **m. more difficult** beaucoup plus difficile; **I love him so m.** je l'aime tellement; **she doesn't say very m.** elle ne dit pas grand-chose; **everything had stayed m. the same** rien n'avait vraiment changé

3 *pron* beaucoup; **not m.** pas beaucoup; **there isn't m. left** il n'en reste pas beaucoup; **it's not m. of a garden** ce n'est pas terrible comme jardin; **twice as m.** deux fois plus; **as m. as possible** autant que possible; **as m. as you like** autant que tu veux; **he knows as m. as you do** il en sait autant que toi; **so m. so that...** à tel point que...; **he had drunk so m. that...** il avait tellement bu que...; *Fam* **that's a bit m.!** c'est un peu fort!

muck [mʌk] *n (manure)* fumier *m; Fig (filth)* saleté *f* ▪ **mucky** (**-ier, -iest***) adj Fam* sale

▸ **muck about, muck around** *Br Fam* **1** *vt sep* **to m. sb about** *or* **around** faire perdre son temps à qn **2** *vi (waste time)* traîner; *(play the fool)* faire l'imbécile; *Br Fam* **to m. about** *or* **around with sth** *(fiddle with)* tripoter qch

▸ **muck in** *vi Br Fam (help)* s'y mettre

▸ **muck up** *vt sep Br Fam (task)* bâcler; *(plans)* chambouler

mucus ['mjuːkəs] *n* mucosités *fpl*

mud [mʌd] *n* boue *f* ▪ **muddy** (**-ier, -iest***) adj (water, road)* boueux *(f* boueuse*); (hands)*

couvert de boue ▪ **mudguard** *n* garde-boue *m inv*

muddle ['mʌdəl] **1** *n* confusion *f;* **to be in a m.** *(person)* ne plus s'y retrouver; *(of things)* être en désordre **2** *vt (person, facts)* mélanger; **to get muddled** s'embrouiller

▸ **muddle through** *vi Fam* se débrouiller

▸ **muddle up** *vt sep (person, facts)* mélanger; **to get muddled up** s'embrouiller

muff [mʌf] *n (for hands)* manchon *m*

muffin ['mʌfɪn] *n Br (teacake)* = petite galette servie chaude et beurrée; *Am (cake)* muffin *m*

muffle ['mʌfəl] *vt (noise)* assourdir ▪ **muffled** *adj (noise)* sourd ▪ **muffler** *n Am (on vehicle)* silencieux *m*

mug¹ [mʌg] *n* **(a)** *(for tea, coffee)* grande tasse *f; (beer)* **m.** chope *f* **(b)** *Fam (face)* gueule *f;* **m. shot** photo *f* d'identité judiciaire **(c)** *Br Fam (fool)* poire *f*

mug² [mʌg] *(pt & pp* **-gg-***) vt (attack in street)* agresser ▪ **mugger** *n* agresseur *m* ▪ **mugging** *n* agression *f*

muggy ['mʌgɪ] (**-ier, -iest***) adj (weather)* lourd

mulberry ['mʌlbərɪ] *(pl* **-ies***) n (fruit)* mûre *f*

mule [mjuːl] *n (male)* mulet *m; (female)* mule *f*

▸ **mull over** *vt sep (think over)* ruminer

mulled wine ['mʌld'waɪn] *n* vin *m* chaud épicé

mullet ['mʌlɪt] *n (fish)* mulet *m; Fam (hairstyle)* = coupe *f* de cheveux longue sur la nuque, courte sur les côtés et en brosse longue sur le dessus; **red m.** rouget *m*

multicoloured *(Am* **multicolored***)* ['mʌltɪkʌləd] *adj* multicolore

multicultural [mʌltɪ'kʌltʃər(ə)l] *adj* multiculturel, -elle

multilingual [mʌltɪ'lɪŋgwəl] *adj (person)* polyglotte; *(country)* plurilingue

multimedia [mʌltɪ'miːdɪə] *adj* multimédia

multimillionaire [mʌltɪmɪljə'neə(r)] *n* multimillionnaire *mf*

multinational [mʌltɪ'næʃənəl] *n & adj* **m. (company)** multinationale *(f)*

multiple ['mʌltɪpəl] **1** *adj* multiple; *Med* **m. sclerosis** sclérose *f* en plaques **2** *n Math* multiple *m*

multiple-choice ['mʌltɪpəl'tʃɔɪs] *adj* à choix multiple

multiplex ['mʌltɪpleks] *n (cinema)* multiplexe *m*

multiply ['mʌltɪplaɪ] *(pt & pp* **-ied***)* **1** *vt* multiplier **2** *vi (of animals, insects)* se multiplier ▪ **multiplication** [-plɪ'keɪʃən] *n* multiplication *f*

multiracial [mʌltɪ'reɪʃəl] *adj* multiracial

multistorey [mʌltɪ'stɔːrɪ] *(Am* **multistoried***) adj (car park)* à plusieurs niveaux

multitude ['mʌltɪtjuːd] *n* multitude *f*

mum [mʌm] *Fam* **1** *n Br* maman *f* **2** *adj* **to keep m. (about sth)** ne pas souffler mot (de qch) ▪ **mummy**¹ *(pl* **-ies***) n Br Fam* maman *f*

mumble ['mʌmbəl] *vti* marmotter

mumbo jumbo ['mʌmbəʊ'dʒʌmbəʊ] *n (nonsense)* âneries *fpl*

mummy² ['mʌmɪ] *(pl -ies) n (embalmed body)* momie *f*

mumps [mʌmps] *n Med* oreillons *mpl*

munch [mʌntʃ] *vti (chew)* mâcher

mundane [mʌn'deɪn] *adj* banal *(mpl -als)*

> Note that the French word **mondain** is a false friend and is never a translation for the English word **mundane**. It refers to people and events in high society.

municipal [mju:'nɪsɪpəl] *adj* municipal ▪ **municipality** [-'pælɪtɪ] *(pl -ies) n* municipalité *f*

munitions [mju:'nɪʃənz] *npl* munitions *fpl*

mural ['mjʊərəl] **1** *adj* mural **2** *n* peinture *f* murale

murder ['mɜ:də(r)] **1** *n* meurtre *m; Fam* **it's m.** *(dreadful)* c'est affreux 2 *vt (kill)* assassiner; *Fig (spoil)* massacrer ▪ **murderer** *n* meurtrier, -ière *mf*, assassin *m* ▪ **murderous** *adj* meurtrier, -ière

murky ['mɜ:kɪ] *(-ier, -iest) adj (water, business, past)* trouble; *(weather)* nuageux, -euse

murmur ['mɜ:mə(r)] **1** *n* murmure *m; (of traffic, conversation)* bourdonnement *m;* **(heart) m.** souffle *m* au cœur **2** *vti* murmurer

muscle ['mʌsəl] **1** *n* muscle *m* **2** *vi* **to m. in** intervenir **(on** dans) ▪ **muscular** ['mʌskjʊlə(r)] *adj (person, arm)* musclé; *(tissue, pain)* musculaire

muse [mju:z] *vi* songer **(on** à)

museum [mju:'zɪəm] *n* musée *m*

mush [mʌʃ] *n (pulp)* bouillie *f; Fig (sentimentality)* mièvrerie *f* ▪ **mushy (-ier, -iest) adj (food)** en bouillie; *Fig (sentimental)* mièvre

mushroom ['mʌʃrʊm] **1** *n* champignon *m* **2** *vi (of buildings, towns)* pousser comme des champignons; *(of problems)* se multiplier

music ['mju:zɪk] *n* musique *f;* **m. centre** chaîne *f* stéréo compacte; **m. critic** critique *m* musical; **m. hall** music-hall *m;* **m. lover** mélomane *mf;* **canned** *or* **piped m.** musique *f* (de fond) enregistrée ▪ **musical 1** *adj* musical; **m. instrument** instrument *m* de musique; **to be (very) m.** être (très) musicien **2** *n (film, play)* comédie *f* musicale ▪ **musician** [-'zɪʃən] *n* musicien, -ienne *mf*

musk [mʌsk] *n* musc *m*

Muslim ['mʊzlɪm], **Moslem** ['mɒzlɪm] *adj & n* musulman, -ane *(mf)*

muslin ['mʌzlɪn] *n* mousseline *f*

mussel ['mʌsəl] *n* moule *f*

must [mʌst] **1** *n* **this is a m.** c'est indispensable;

this film is a m. il faut absolument voir ce film **2** *v aux* (**a**) *(expressing necessity)* **you m.** obey tu dois obéir, il faut que tu obéisses (**b**) *(expressing probability)* **she m. be clever** elle doit être intelligente; **I m. have seen it** j'ai dû le voir; **you m. be joking!** tu veux rire!; **m. you be so silly?** qu'est-ce que tu peux être bête!

mustache ['mʌstæʃ] *n Am* = **moustache**

mustard ['mʌstəd] *n* moutarde *f*

muster ['mʌstə(r)] **1** *vt (gather)* rassembler; *(sum)* réunir **2** *vi* se rassembler

mustn't ['mʌsənt] = **must not**

musty ['mʌstɪ] *(-ier, -iest) adj (smell, taste)* de moisi; **it smells m., it's m.** ça sent le moisi

mutant ['mju:tənt] *n & adj Biol* mutant *m* ▪ **mu'tation** *n Biol* mutation *f*

mute [mju:t] **1** *adj (silent) & Ling* muet *(f* muette) **2** *vt (sound)* assourdir ▪ **muted** *adj (criticism)* voilé; *(colour)* sourd

mutilate ['mju:tɪleɪt] *vt* mutiler ▪ **muti'lation** *n* mutilation *f*

mutiny ['mju:tɪnɪ] **1** *(pl -ies) n* mutinerie *f* **2** *(pt & pp -ied) vi* se mutiner ▪ **mutinous** *adj (troops)* rebelle

mutter ['mʌtə(r)] *vti* marmonner

mutton ['mʌtən] *n (meat)* mouton *m;* **leg of m.** gigot *m*

mutual ['mju:tʃʊəl] *adj (help, love)* mutuel, -uelle; *(friend)* commun; *Am Fin* **m. fund** fonds *m* commun de placement ▪ **mutually** *adv* mutuellement

muzzle ['mʌzəl] **1** *n (device for dog)* muselière *f; (snout)* museau *m; (of gun)* gueule *f* **2** *vt (animal, the press)* museler

my [maɪ] *possessive adj* mon, ma, *pl* mes

myself [maɪ'self] *pron* moi-même; *(reflexive)* me, m'; *(after prep)* moi; **I did it m.** je l'ai fait moi-même; **I wash m.** je me lave; **I think of m.** je pense à moi

mystery ['mɪstərɪ] *(pl -ies) n* mystère *m* ▪ **mysterious** [mɪ'stɪərɪəs] *adj* mystérieux, -ieuse

mystic ['mɪstɪk] *adj & n* mystique *(mf)* ▪ **mystical** *adj* mystique ▪ **mysticism** [-tɪsɪzəm] *n* mysticisme *m* ▪ **mystique** [mɪ'sti:k] *n (mystery, power)* mystique *f* (**of** de)

mystify ['mɪstɪfaɪ] *(pt & pp -ied) vt (bewilder)* déconcerter; *(fool)* mystifier

> Note that the French verb **mystifier** is a false friend. It means **to fool, to take in**.

myth [mɪθ] *n* mythe *m* ▪ **mythical** *adj* mythique ▪ **mytho'logical** *adj* mythologique ▪ **my'thology** *(pl -ies) n* mythologie *f*

N, n [en] *n (letter)* N, n *m inv*; **the nth time** la énième fois

nab [næb] *(pt & pp -bb-) vt Fam (catch, arrest)* coffrer

naff [næf] *adj Br Fam (unfashionable)* ringard

nag [næg] *(pt & pp -gg-) vti* **to n. (at)** sb *(of person)* être sur le dos de qn ■ **nagging 1** *adj (doubt, headache)* tenace **2** *n* plaintes *fpl* continuelles

nail [neɪl] **1** *n* (a) *(of finger, toe)* ongle *m*; **n. brush** brosse *f* à ongles; **n. file** lime *f* à ongles; **n. polish**, *Br* **n. varnish** vernis *m* à ongles (b) *(metal)* clou *m* **2** *vt* clouer; *Fam* **to n. sb** épingler qn; **to n. sth down** *(lid)* clouer qch

naïve [naɪˈiːv] *adj* naïf *(f* naïve)

naked [ˈneɪkɪd] *adj (person)* nu; **to see sth with the n. eye** voir qch à l'œil nu; **n. flame** flamme *f* nue ■ **nakedness** *n* nudité *f*

name [neɪm] *n* nom *m*; *(reputation)* réputation *f*; **my n. is…** je m'appelle…; **in the n. of** au nom de; **to put one's n. down for** *(school, course)* s'inscrire à; **to call sb names** insulter qn; **first n., given n.** prénom *m*; *Fig* **to have a good/bad n.** avoir une bonne/mauvaise réputation **2** *vt* nommer; *(ship, street)* baptiser; *(date, price)* fixer; **to n. sb to do sth** nommer qn pour faire qch; **he was named** *Br* **after** *or* **Am for…** on lui a donné le nom de… ■ **nameless** *adj* anonyme ■ **nameplate** *n* plaque *f*

namely [ˈneɪmlɪ] *adv* à savoir

namesake [ˈneɪmseɪk] *n* homonyme *mf*

nanny [ˈnænɪ] *(pl -ies) n* nurse *f*; *Fam (grandmother)* mamie *f*; **n. goat** chèvre *f*

nap [næp] **1** *n (sleep)* petit somme *m*; **to have** *or* **take a n.** faire un petit somme **2** *(pt & pp -pp-) vi* faire un somme; *Fig* **to catch sb napping** prendre qn au dépourvu

nape [neɪp] *n* **n. (of the neck)** nuque *f*

napkin [ˈnæpkɪn] *n (at table)* serviette *f* ■ **nappy** *(pl -ies) n Br (for baby)* couche *f*; **n. rash** érythème *m* fessier ■ **nappy-liner** *n Br* protège-couche *m*

narcotic [nɑːˈkɒtɪk] *adj & n* narcotique *(m),* stupéfiant *(m); Am* **narcotics (branch)** *(of police force)* brigade *f* des stupéfiants

narrate [nəˈreɪt] *vt* raconter ■ **narrative** [ˈnærətɪv] *n* récit *m* ■ **narrator** *n* narrateur, -trice *mf*

narrow [ˈnærəʊ] **1** *(-er, -est) adj* étroit; *(majority)* faible **2** *vt* **to n. (down)** *(choice, meaning)* limiter **3** *vi (of path)* se rétrécir ■ **narrowly** *adv (only just)* de peu; *(strictly)* strictement; **he n. escaped** *or* **missed being killed** il a bien failli être tué ■ **narrowness** *n* étroitesse *f*

narrow-minded [nærəʊˈmaɪndɪd] *adj* borné

nasal [ˈneɪzəl] *adj* nasal; *(voice)* nasillard

nasty [ˈnɑːstɪ] *(-ier, -iest) adj (bad)* mauvais; *(spiteful)* méchant **(to** *or* **towards** avec) ■ **nastily** *adv (behave)* méchamment ■ **nastiness** *n (malice)* méchanceté *f*

nation [ˈneɪʃən] *n* nation *f* ■ **nation'wide** *adj & adv* dans tout le pays

national [ˈnæʃənəl] **1** *adj* national; **n. anthem** hymne *m* national; *Br* **N. Health Service** ≃ Sécurité *f* sociale; *Br* **n. insurance** contributions *fpl* sociales **2** *n (citizen)* ressortissant, -ante *mf* ■ **nationalist** *n* nationaliste *mf* ■ **nationa'listic** *adj Pej* nationaliste ■ **nationally** *adv* dans tout le pays

nationality *(pl -ies)* [næʃəˈnælɪtɪ] *n* nationalité *f*

nationalize [ˈnæʃənəlaɪz] *vt* nationaliser ■ **nationali'zation** *n* nationalisation *f*

native [ˈneɪtɪv] **1** *adj (country)* natal *(mpl -als); (tribe, plant)* indigène; **n. language** langue *f* maternelle; **to be an English n. speaker** avoir l'anglais comme langue maternelle **2** *n (person)* indigène *mf*; **to be a n. of** être originaire de

Nativity [nəˈtɪvɪtɪ] *n Rel* **the N.** la Nativité; **N. play** = pièce jouée par des enfants et représentant l'histoire de la Nativité; **N. scene** crèche *f*

NATO [ˈneɪtəʊ] *(abbr* **North Atlantic Treaty Organization)** *n Mil* OTAN *f*

natter [ˈnætə(r)] *Br Fam* **1** *n* **to have a n.** bavarder **2** *vi* bavarder

natural [ˈnætʃərəl] **1** *adj* naturel, -elle; *(talent)* inné **2** *n Fam* **to be a n. for sth** être fait pour qch; **he's a n.** *(as actor)* c'est un acteur né ■ **naturalist** *n* naturaliste *mf* ■ **naturally** *adv (unaffectedly, of course)* naturellement; *(by nature)* de nature

naturalize [ˈnætʃərəlaɪz] *vt (person)* naturaliser; **to become naturalized** se faire naturaliser ■ **naturali'zation** *n* naturalisation *f*

nature [ˈneɪtʃə(r)] *n (world, character)* nature *f*;

by n. de nature; **problems of this n.** des problèmes de cette nature; **n. reserve** réserve f naturelle; **n. study** sciences fpl naturelles

naturist ['neɪtʃərɪst] n naturiste mf ▪**naturism** n naturisme m

naught [nɔːt] n Br Math zéro m

naughty ['nɔːtɪ] (**-ier, -iest**) adj (child) vilain; (joke, story) coquin ▪**naughtily** adv (behave) mal; (say) avec malice

nausea [Br 'nɔːzɪə, Am 'nɔːʃə] n nausée f ▪**nauseate** [-zɪeɪt] vt écœurer ▪**nauseating** [-zɪeɪtɪŋ] adj écœurant ▪**nauseous** [Br 'nɔːzɪəs, Am 'nɔːʃəs] adj (smell) nauséabond; Am **to feel n.** (sick) avoir envie de vomir

nautical ['nɔːtɪkəl] adj nautique

naval ['neɪvəl] adj naval (mpl -als); (hospital, power) maritime; (officer) de marine

navel ['neɪvəl] n nombril m

navigate ['nævɪgeɪt] 1 vt (boat) piloter; (river) naviguer sur; Comptr naviguer sur; **to n. the Net** naviguer sur l'Internet 2 vi naviguer ▪**navi'gation** n navigation f ▪**navigator** n (on aircraft, boat) navigateur m

navvy ['nævɪ] (pl **-ies**) n Br (labourer) terrassier m

navy ['neɪvɪ] 1 (pl **-ies**) n marine f 2 adj **n. (blue)** bleu marine inv

Nazi ['nɑːtsɪ] adj & n Pol & Hist nazi, -ie (mf) ▪**Nazism** n nazisme m

NB [en'biː] (abbr **nota bene**) NB

near [nɪə(r)] 1 (**-er, -est**) prep **n. (to)** près de; **n. the bed** près du lit; **to be n. (to) victory/death** frôler la victoire/la mort; **n. (to) the end** vers la fin; **to come n. sb** s'approcher de qn 2 (**-er, -est**) adv près; **quite n., n. at hand** tout près; **n. to sth** près de qch; **to come n. to being killed** manquer d'être tué; **n. enough** (more or less) plus ou moins 3 (**-er, -est**) adj proche; **the nearest hospital** l'hôpital le plus proche; **the nearest way** la route la plus directe; **in the n. future** dans un avenir proche; **to the nearest euro** (calculate) à un euro près; Aut **n. side** côté m gauche, Am côté m droit; **the N. East** le Proche-Orient 4 vt (approach) approcher de; **nearing completion** presque terminé

nearby 1 [nɪə'baɪ] adv tout près 2 ['nɪəbaɪ] adj proche

nearly ['nɪəlɪ] adv presque; **she (very) n. fell** elle a failli tomber; **not n. as clever as** loin d'être aussi intelligent que

near-sighted [nɪə'saɪtɪd] adj myope

neat [niːt] (**-er, -est**) adj (clothes, work) soigné; (room) bien rangé; (style) élégant; Am Fam (good) super inv; **to drink one's whisky n.** boire son whisky sec ▪**neatly** adv (carefully) avec soin; (skilfully) habilement

nebulous ['nebjʊləs] adj (vague) flou

necessary ['nesɪsərɪ] 1 adj nécessaire; **it's n.**

to do it il faut le faire; **to make it n. for sb to do sth** mettre qn dans la nécessité de faire qch; **to do what's n.** faire le nécessaire (**for** pour) 2 n Fam **to do the n.** faire le nécessaire ▪**necessarily** [-'serəlɪ] adv **not n.** pas forcément

necessity [nɪ'sesɪtɪ] (pl **-ies**) n (obligation, need) nécessité f; **out of n.** par nécessité; **to be a n.** être indispensable; **the necessities** (things needed) le nécessaire ▪**necessitate** vt nécessiter

neck [nek] n cou m; (of dress) encolure f; (of bottle) goulot m; (of dress) décolleté m; **to finish n. and n.** (in race) finir au coude à coude ▪**necklace** n collier m ▪**neckline** n encolure f ▪**necktie** n Am cravate f

nectarine ['nektəriːn] n (fruit) nectarine f, brugnon m

née [neɪ] adv **n. Dupont** née Dupont

need [niːd] 1 n besoin m; **in n.** dans le besoin; **to be in n. of sth** avoir besoin de qch; **there's no n. (for you) to do that** tu n'as pas besoin de faire cela; **if n. be** si besoin est 2 vt avoir besoin de; **you n. it** tu en as besoin; **it needs an army** or **an army is needed to do that** il faut une armée pour faire cela; **this sport needs patience** ce sport demande de la patience; **her hair needs cutting** il faut qu'elle se fasse couper les cheveux 3 v aux

La forme modale de **need** est la même à toutes les personnes, et s'utilise avec do/does (**he need only worry about himself**; **need she go?**; **it needn't matter**).

n. I say more? ai-je besoin d'en dire plus?; **I needn't have rushed** ce n'était pas la peine de me presser; **you needn't worry** inutile de t'inquiéter ▪**needy** (**-ier, -iest**) adj nécessiteux, -euse

needle ['niːdəl] 1 n aiguille f; (of record player) saphir m 2 vt Fam (irritate) agacer ▪**needlework** n couture f; (object) ouvrage m

needless ['niːdləs] adj inutile ▪**needlessly** adv inutilement

negate [nɪ'geɪt] vt (nullify) annuler; (deny) nier ▪**ne'gation** n (denial) & Grammar négation f

negative ['negətɪv] 1 adj négatif, -ive 2 n (of photo) négatif m; (word, word group) négation f; (grammatical form) forme f négative; **to answer in the n.** répondre par la négative

neglect [nɪ'glekt] 1 n (of person) négligence f; (of duty) manquement m (**of** à); **in a state of n.** (garden, house) mal tenu 2 vt (person, health, work) négliger; (garden, car) ne pas s'occuper de; (duty) manquer à; **to n. to do sth** négliger de faire qch ▪**neglected** adj (appearance, person) négligé; (garden, house) mal tenu; **to feel n.** se sentir abandonné

negligent ['neglɪdʒənt] adj négligent ▪**negligence** n négligence f ▪**negligently** adv négligemment

negligible ['neglɪdʒəbəl] *adj* négligeable

negotiate [nɪ'gəʊʃ ɪeɪt] **1** *vti (discuss)* négocier **2** *vt (fence, obstacle)* franchir; *(bend) (in vehicle)* négocier ▪**negotiable** *adj* négociable ▪**negoti'ation** *n* négociation *f;* **in n. with** en pourparlers avec ▪**negotiator** *n* négociateur, -trice *mf*

neigh [neɪ] *n* hennissement *m* **2** *vi* hennir

neighbour ['neɪbə(r)] *(Am* **neighbor)** *n* voisin, -ine *mf* ▪**neighbourhood** *(Am* **neighborhood)** *n (district)* quartier *m,* voisinage *m; (neighbours)* voisinage; **in the n. of $10/ kilos** dans les 10 dollars/kilos ▪**neighbouring** *(Am* **neighboring)** *adj* voisin ▪**neighbourly** *(Am* **neighborly)** *adj (feeling)* de bon voisinage; **they're n. (people)** ils sont bons voisins

neither ['naɪðə(r), 'niːðə(r)] **1** *conj* **n.... nor... ni... ni...; n. you nor me** ni toi ni moi; **he n. sings nor dances** il ne chante ni ne danse **2** *adv* **n. will I go** je n'y irai pas non plus; **n. do I/ n. can I** (ni) moi non plus **3** *adj* **n. boy came** aucun des deux garçons n'est venu; **on n. side** ni d'un côté ni de l'autre **4** *pron* **n. (of them)** aucun(e) (des deux)

neon ['niːɒn] *n* néon *m;* **n. lighting/sign** éclairage *m*/enseigne *f* au néon

nephew ['nevjuː, 'nefjuː] *n* neveu *m*

nepotism ['nepətɪzəm] *n* népotisme *m*

nerd [nɜːd] *n Fam (stupid person)* crétin, -ine *mf*

nerve [nɜːv] *n* nerf *m; (courage)* courage *m; Fam (impudence)* culot *m; Fam* **he gets on my nerves** il me tape sur les nerfs; **to have an attack of nerves** *(fear, anxiety)* avoir le trac; *Fam* **she's a bundle** *or* **mass** *or* **bag of nerves** c'est un paquet de nerfs; **n. centre** centre *m* nerveux ▪**nerve-racking** *adj* éprouvant ▪**nervy (-ier, -iest)** *adj Fam (anxious)* nerveux, -euse

nervous ['nɜːvəs] *adj (apprehensive)* nerveux, -euse; **to be n. about sth/doing sth** être nerveux à l'idée de qch/de faire qch; **to have a n. breakdown** faire une dépression nerveuse ▪**nervously** *adv* nerveusement ▪**nervousness** *n* nervosité *f*

nest [nest] **1** *n* nid *m; Fig* **n. egg** pécule *m;* **n. of tables** tables *fpl* gigognes **2** *vi (of bird)* nicher

nestle ['nesəl] *vi* se pelotonner **(up to** contre); **a village nestling in** *(forest, valley)* un village niché dans

Net [net] *n Comptr* **the N.** le Net; **N. user** internaute *mf*

net¹ [net] **1** *n* filet *m;* **n. curtain** voilage *m* **2** *(pt & pp* **-tt-)** *vt (fish)* prendre au filet ▪**netting** *n (nets)* filets *mpl; (mesh)* mailles *fpl*

net² [net] **1** *adj (profit, weight, value)* net *(f* nette) **2** *(pt & pp* **-tt-)** *vt (of person, company)* gagner net; **this venture netted them...** cette entreprise leur a rapporté...

Netherlands ['neðələndz] *npl* **the N.** les Pays-Bas *mpl*

netiquette ['netɪket] *n Comptr* netiquette *f*

nettle ['netəl] *n* ortie *f*

network ['netwɜːk] **1** *n* réseau *m* **2** *vi (make contacts)* établir un réseau de contacts

neurotic [njʊ'rɒtɪk] *adj & n* névrosé, -ée *(mf)*

neuter ['njuːtə(r)] **1** *adj & n Grammar* neutre *(m)* **2** *vt (cat)* châtrer

neutral ['njuːtrəl] **1** *adj* neutre; *(policy)* de neutralité **2** *n (electrical wire)* neutre *m;* **in n. (gear)** *(vehicle)* au point mort ▪**neutrality** [-'trælɪtɪ] *n* neutralité *f* ▪**neutralize** *vt* neutraliser

never ['nevə(r)] *adv (not ever)* (ne) jamais; **she n. lies** elle ne ment jamais; **in (all) my life** jamais de ma vie; **n. again** plus jamais; *Fam* **I n. did it** je ne l'ai pas fait; *Fam* **I n. expected this** je ne m'attendais vraiment pas à ça; *Fam* **well I n.!** ça alors! ▪**'never-'ending** *adj* interminable

nevertheless [nevəðə'les] *adv* néanmoins

new [njuː] *adj* **(a) (-er, -est)** nouveau *(f* nouvelle); *(brand-new)* neuf *(f* neuve); **to be n. to** *(job)* être nouveau dans; *(city)* être un nouveau-venu *(f* nouvelle-venue) dans; **a n. boy** *(in school)* un nouveau; **a n. girl** une nouvelle; **n. look** *(of person)* nouveau look *m; (of company)* nouvelle image *f;* **it's as good as n.** c'est comme neuf; *Fam* **what's n.?** quoi de neuf? **(b)** *(different)* **a n. glass/pen** un autre verre/stylo ▪**newborn** *adj* **a n. baby** un nouveau-né, une nouveau-née ▪**newcomer** [-kʌmə(r)] *n* nouveau-venu *m,* nouvelle-venue *f* **(to** dans) ▪**new-found** *adj* nouveau *(f* nouvelle) ▪**newly** *adv* nouvellement ▪**newlyweds** *n* jeunes mariés *mpl*

news [njuːz] *n* nouvelles *fpl; (in the media)* informations *fpl;* **a piece of n.** une nouvelle; **sports n.** *(newspaper column)* rubrique *f* sportive; **n. agency** agence *f* de presse; **n. stand** kiosque *m* à journaux ▪**newsagent** *n Br* marchand, -ande *mf* de journaux ▪**newscaster** *n Am* présentateur, -trice *mf* de journal ▪**newsdealer** *n Am* marchand, -ande *mf* de journaux ▪**newsflash** *n* flash *m* d'informations ▪**newsletter** *n (of club, group)* bulletin *m* ▪**newspaper** *n* journal *m* ▪**newsprint** *n* papier *m* journal ▪**newsreader** *n Br* présentateur, -trice *mf* de journal ▪**newsreel** *n* actualités *fpl* ▪**newsworthy** *adj* d'intérêt médiatique

newt [njuːt] *n* triton *m*

New Zealand [njuː'ziːlənd] **1** *n* la Nouvelle-Zélande **2** *adj* néo-zélandais ▪**New Zealander** *n* Néo-Zélandais, -aise *mf*

next [nekst] **1** *adj* prochain; *(room, house)* d'à côté; *(following)* suivant; **n. month** *(in the future)* le mois prochain; **he returned the n.**

month il revint le mois suivant; **the n. day** le lendemain; **the n. morning** le lendemain matin; **within the n. ten days** d'ici dix jours; **who's n.?** c'est à qui?; **you're n.** c'est ton tour; **n. (please)!** au suivant!; **the n. size up** la taille au-dessus; **to live n. door** habiter à côté (**to** de); **n.-door neighbour/room** voisin m/pièce f d'à côté **2** n (in series) suivant, -ante mf; **from one year to the n.** d'une année sur l'autre **3** adv (afterwards) ensuite, après; (now) maintenant; **when you come n.** la prochaine fois que tu viendras; **the n. best solution is…** à défaut, il y a une autre solution qui est…; **n. to** (beside) à côté de; **n. to nothing** presque rien

NGO [endʒiː'əʊ] (abbr **non-governmental organization**) n ONG f

NHS [eneitʃ'es] (abbr **National Health Service**) n Br ≃ Sécurité f sociale

nib [nɪb] n (of pen) plume f

nibble ['nɪbəl] **1** n **to have a n. of sth** grignoter qch; Fam **nibbles** amuse-gueules mpl **2** vti grignoter

Nicaragua [nɪkə'rægjʊə] n le Nicaragua

nice [naɪs] (**-er, -est**) adj (pleasant) agréable; (tasty) bon (f bonne); (physically attractive) beau (f belle); (kind) gentil, -ille (**to** avec); **n. and warm** bien chaud; **n. and easy** très facile; **have a n. day!** bonne journée! ▪ **nice-looking** adj beau (f belle) ▪ **nicely** adv (kindly) gentiment; (well) bien

niceties ['naɪsətɪz] npl subtilités fpl

niche [Br niːʃ, Am nɪtʃ] n (recess) niche f; **to make a n. for oneself** faire son trou; (market) **n.** créneau m

nick [nɪk] **1** n (**a**) (on skin, wood) entaille f, (in blade, crockery) brèche f; **in the n. of time** juste à temps; Br Fam **in good n.** en bon état (**b**) Br Fam (prison) taule f **2** vt Br Fam (steal) piquer; (arrest) pincer

nickel ['nɪkəl] n (metal) nickel m; Am (coin) pièce f de 5 cents

nickname ['nɪkneɪm] **1** n (informal) surnom m; (short form) diminutif m **2** vt surnommer

nicotine ['nɪkətiːn] n nicotine f; **n. patch** patch m anti-tabac

niece [niːs] n nièce f

nifty ['nɪftɪ] (**-ier, -iest**) adj Fam (idea, device) génial; (agile) vif (f vive)

Nigeria [naɪ'dʒɪərɪə] n le Nigéria ▪ **Nigerian 1** adj nigérian **2** n Nigérian, -iane mf

niggling ['nɪglɪŋ] adj (trifling) insignifiant; (irksome) irritant; (doubt) persistant

night [naɪt] **1** n nuit f; (evening) soir m; **at n.** la nuit; **by n.** de nuit; **last n.** (evening) hier soir; (night) cette nuit; **to have an early/a late n.** se coucher tôt/tard; **to have a good n.'s sleep** bien dormir; **first n.** (of play) première f; **the last n.** (of play) la dernière **2** adj (work, flight)

de nuit; **n. school** cours mpl du soir; **n. shift** (job) poste m de nuit; (workers) équipe f de nuit; **n. watchman** veilleur m de nuit ▪ **nightcap** n (drink) = boisson alcoolisée ou chaude prise avant de se coucher ▪ **nightclub** n boîte f de nuit ▪ **nightdress, nightgown,** Br Fam **nightie** n chemise f de nuit ▪ **nightfall** n **at n.** à la tombée de la nuit ▪ **nightlife** n vie f nocturne ▪ **nightlight** n veilleuse f ▪ **night-time** n nuit f

nightingale ['naɪtɪŋgeɪl] n rossignol m

nightly ['naɪtlɪ] **1** adv chaque nuit/soir **2** adj de chaque nuit/soir

nightmare ['naɪtmeə(r)] n cauchemar m

nil [nɪl] n (nothing) zéro m; **two n.** deux à zéro; **the risk is n.** le risque est nul

Nile [naɪl] n **the N.** le Nil

nimble ['nɪmbəl] (**-er, -est**) adj (person) souple

nine [naɪn] adj & n neuf (m)

nineteen [naɪn'tiːn] adj & n dix-neuf (m) ▪ **nineteenth** adj & n dix-neuvième (mf)

ninety ['naɪntɪ] adj & n quatre-vingt-dix (m) ▪ **ninetieth** adj & n quatre-vingt-dixième (mf)

ninth [naɪnθ] adj & n neuvième (mf); **a n.** un neuvième

nip [nɪp] **1** n pinçon m; **there's a n. in the air** il fait frisquet **2** (pt & pp **-pp-**) vt (pinch) pincer; **to n. sth in the bud** étouffer qch dans l'œuf **3** vi Br Fam **n. round to sb's house** faire un saut chez qn; **to n. out** sortir un instant

nipper ['nɪpə(r)] n Br Fam (child) gosse mf

nipple ['nɪpəl] n mamelon m; Am (on baby's bottle) tétine f

nippy ['nɪpɪ] (**-ier, -iest**) adj Fam (**a**) (chilly) frais (f fraîche); **it's n.** ça pince (**b**) Br **to be n. (about it)** faire vite

nit [nɪt] n (louse) lente f

nitrogen ['naɪtrədʒən] n azote m

nitty-gritty ['nɪtɪ'grɪtɪ] n Fam **to get down to the n.** entrer dans le vif du sujet

nitwit ['nɪtwɪt] n Fam idiot, -iote mf

no [nəʊ] **1** (pl **noes** or **nos**) n non m inv; **she won't take no for an answer** elle n'accepte pas qu'on lui dise non; **the noes** (in voting) les non **2** adj (not any) pas de; **there's no bread** il n'y a pas de pain; **I have no idea** je n'ai aucune idée; **I have no time to play** je n'ai pas le temps de jouer; **of no importance** sans importance; **with no gloves/hat on** sans gants/chapeau; **there's no knowing…** impossible de savoir…; **'no smoking'** 'défense de fumer'; Fam **no way!** pas question! **3** adv (interjection) non; **no more time** plus de temps; **no more/less than ten** plus/moins de dix; **no more/less than you** pas plus/moins que vous; **you can do no better** tu ne peux pas faire mieux

noble ['nəʊbəl] (**-er, -est**) adj noble; (building) majestueux, -ueuse ▪ **nobility** n noblesse f

■**nobleman** (*pl* **-men**) *n* noble *m*
■**noblewoman** (*pl* **-women**) *n* noble *f*

nobody ['nəʊbɒdɪ] **1** *pron* (ne) personne; **n. came** personne n'est venu; **he knows n.** il ne connaît personne; **n.!** personne! **2** *n* **a n.** une nullité

no-brainer [nəʊ'breɪnə(r)] *n Fam (person)* crétin, -ine *mf*; *(question)* jeu *m* d'enfant

nocturnal [nɒk'tɜːnəl] *adj* nocturne

nod [nɒd] **1** *n* signe *m* de tête **2** *(pt & pp* **-dd-**) *vti* **to n. (one's head)** faire un signe de tête **3** *vi Fam* **to n. off** s'assoupir

no-fly zone [nəʊ'flaɪzəʊn] *n* zone *f* d'exclusion aérienne

noise [nɔɪz] *n* bruit *m*; **to make a n.** faire du bruit ■**noiselessly** *adv* sans bruit

noisy ['nɔɪzɪ] (**-ier, -iest**) *adj (person, street)* bruyant ■**noisily** *adv* bruyamment

nomad ['nəʊmæd] *n* nomade *mf* ■**no'madic** *adj* nomade

nominal ['nɒmɪnəl] *adj* nominal; *(rent, salary)* symbolique

nominate ['nɒmɪneɪt] *vt (appoint)* nommer; *(propose)* proposer (**for** comme candidat à) ■**nomi'nation** *n (appointment)* nomination *f*; *(proposal)* candidature *f* ■**nomi'nee** *n (candidate)* candidat *m*

non-aligned [nɒnə'laɪnd] *adj (country)* non-aligné

nonchalant ['nɒnʃələnt] *adj* désinvolte

non-committal [nɒnkə'mɪtəl] *adj (answer)* de Normand; **to be n.** ne pas s'engager

nonconformist [nɒnkən'fɔːmɪst] *adj & n* non-conformiste *(mf)*

nondescript ['nɒndɪskrɪpt] *adj* très ordinaire

none [nʌn] **1** *pron aucun(e) mf*; *(in filling out a form)* néant; **n. of them** aucun d'eux; **she has n. (at all)** elle n'en a pas (du tout); **n. came** pas un(e) seul(e) n'est venu(e); **n. can tell** personne ne peut le dire; **n. of it** *or* **this** rien (de ceci) **2** *adv* **n. too hot** pas très chaud; **he's n. the wiser (for it)** il n'est pas plus avancé ■**none'the'less** *adv* néanmoins

nonentity [nɒ'nentɪtɪ] (*pl* **-ies**) *n (person)* nullité *f*

nonexistent [nɒnɪg'zɪstənt] *adj* inexistant

non-fiction [nɒn'fɪkʃən] *n* ouvrages *mpl* généraux

nonflammable [nɒn'flæməbəl] *adj* ininflammable

non-iron [nɒn'aɪən] *adj* qui ne se repasse pas

no-nonsense [nəʊ'nɒnsəns] *adj* direct

nonplus [nɒn'plʌs] (*pt & pp* **-ss-**) *vt* dérouter

non-profit-making [nɒn'prɒfɪtmeɪkɪŋ] *(Am* **non-profit** [nɒn'prɒfɪt]) *adj (organization)* à but non lucratif

nonsense ['nɒnsəns] *n* bêtises *fpl*; **that's n.** c'est absurde ■**nonsensical** [-'sensɪkəl] *adj* absurde

non-smoker [nɒn'sməʊkə(r)] *n (person)* non-fumeur, -euse *mf* ■**non-smoking** *adj (area)* non-fumeurs

nonstick ['nɒn'stɪk] *adj (pan)* qui n'attache pas

non-stop ['nɒn'stɒp] **1** *adj* sans arrêt; *(train, flight)* sans escale **2** *adv (work)* sans arrêt; *(fly)* sans escale

noodles ['nuːdəlz] *npl* nouilles *fpl*; *(in soup)* vermicelles *mpl*

nook [nʊk] *n* coin *m*; **in every n. and cranny** dans le moindre recoin

noon [nuːn] **1** *n* midi *m*; **at n.** à midi **2** *adj (sun)* de midi

no-one ['nəʊwʌn] *pron* = **nobody**

noose [nuːs] *n* nœud *m* coulant

nor [nɔː(r)] *conj* ni; **neither you n. me** ni toi ni moi; **she neither drinks n. smokes** elle ne fume ni ne boit; **n. do I/n. can I/***etc* (ni) moi non plus; **n. will I (go)** je n'y irai pas non plus

norm [nɔːm] *n* norme *f*

normal ['nɔːməl] **1** *adj* normal **2** *n* **above/below n.** au-dessus/au-dessous de la normale ■**normality** [-'mælɪtɪ] *n* normalité *f* ■**normalize** *vt* normaliser ■**normally** *adv* normalement

Norman ['nɔːmən] *adj* normand ■**Normandy** *n* la Normandie

north [nɔːθ] **1** *n* nord *m*; **(to the) n. of** au nord de **2** *adj (coast)* nord *inv*; *(wind)* du nord; **N. America/Africa** Amérique *f*/Afrique *f* du Nord; **N. American** *adj* nord-américain; *n* Nord-Américain, -aine *mf* **3** *adv* au nord; *(travel)* vers le nord ■**northbound** *adj (traffic)* en direction du nord; *Br (carriageway)* nord *inv* ■**'north-'east** *n & adj* nord-est *(m)* ■**northerly** ['nɔːðəlɪ] *adj (point)* nord *inv*; *(direction, wind)* du nord ■**northern** ['nɔːðən] *adj (coast)* nord *inv*; *(town)* du nord; **n. France** le nord de la France; **n. Europe** l'Europe *f* du Nord; **N. Ireland** l'Irlande *f* du Nord ■**northerner** ['nɔːðənə(r)] *n* habitant, -ante *mf* du Nord ■**northward(s)** *adj & adv* vers le nord ■**north-'west** *n & adj* nord-ouest *(m)*

Norway ['nɔːweɪ] *n* la Norvège ■**Norwegian** [-'wiːdʒən] **1** *adj* norvégien, -ienne **2** *n (person)* Norvégien, -ienne *mf*; *(language)* norvégien *m*

nose [nəʊz] *n* nez *m*; **her n. is bleeding** elle saigne du nez; *Fig* **to turn one's n. up** faire le dégoûté (**at** devant) **2** *vi Fam* **to n. about** fouiner ■**nosebleed** *n* saignement *m* de nez; **to have a n.** saigner du nez ■**nose-dive** *n (of aircraft)* piqué *m*; *(in prices)* chute *f*

nosey ['nəʊzɪ] (**-ier, -iest**) *adj Fam* indiscret, -ète

nosh [nɒʃ] *Br Fam* **1** *n (light meal)* en-cas *m*; *(food)* bouffe *f* **2** *vi (have a light meal)* grignoter; *(eat)* bouffer

no-smoking [nəʊ'sməʊkɪŋ] *adj (carriage, area)* non-fumeurs

nostalgia [nɒˈstældʒɪə] *n* nostalgie *f* **▪nostalgic** *adj* nostalgique

nostril [ˈnɒstrəl] *n* narine *f*

nosy [ˈnəʊzɪ] *adj* = **nosey**

not [nɒt] *adv*

À l'oral, et à l'écrit dans un style familier, on utilise généralement **not** à la forme contractée lorsqu'il suit un modal ou un auxiliaire (**don't go!**; **she wasn't there**; **he couldn't see me**).

(**a**) (ne) pas; **he's n. there, he isn't there** il n'est pas là; **n. yet** pas encore; **why n.?** pourquoi pas?; **n. one reply** pas une seule réponse; **n. at all** pas du tout; *(after 'thank you')* je vous en prie (**b**) non; **I think/hope n.** je pense/j'espère que non; **n. guilty** non coupable; **isn't she?/don't you?***/etc* non?

notable [ˈnəʊtəbəl] *adj & n* notable (*m*) **▪notably** *adv (noticeably)* notablement; *(particularly)* notamment

notary [ˈnəʊtərɪ] *(pl* **-ies**) *n Law* notaire *m*

notation [nəʊˈteɪʃən] *n* notation *f*

notch [nɒtʃ] **1** *n (in wood)* encoche *f*; *(in belt, wheel)* cran *m* **2** *vt* **to n. up** *(points)* marquer; *(victory)* remporter

note [nəʊt] **1** *n (information, reminder) & Mus* note *f*; *Br (banknote)* billet *m*; *(letter)* mot *m*; **to take (a) n. of sth, to make a n. of sth** prendre note de qch; **actor of n.** acteur *m* remarquable **2** *vt (notice)* remarquer, noter; **to n. sth down** *(word, remark)* noter qch **▪notebook** *n* carnet *m*; *(for school)* cahier *m*; *(pad)* bloc-notes *m* **▪notepad** *n* bloc-notes *m* **▪notepaper** *n* papier *m* à lettres

noted [ˈnəʊtɪd] *adj* éminent; **to be n. for one's beauty** être connu pour sa beauté

noteworthy [ˈnəʊtwɜːðɪ] *adj* remarquable

nothing [ˈnʌθɪŋ] **1** *pron* (ne) rien; **he knows n.** il ne sait rien; **n. happened** il ne s'est rien passé; **n. at all** rien du tout; **n. big** rien de grand; **n. much** pas grand-chose; **n. but problems** rien que des problèmes; **to have n. to do** n'avoir rien à faire; **I've got n. to do with it** je n'y suis pour rien; **I can do n. about it** je n'y peux rien; **there's n. like it** il n'y a rien de tel; **for n.** *(in vain, free of charge)* pour rien; **to have n. on** être tout nu **2** *adv* **to look n. like sb** ne ressembler nullement à qn; **n. like as large** loin d'être aussi grand **3** *n* **a (mere) n.** *(person)* une nullité; *(thing)* un rien; **to come to n.** être anéanti

notice [ˈnəʊtɪs] **1** *n (notification)* avis *m*; *(in newspaper)* annonce *f*; *(sign)* pancarte *f*, écriteau *m*; *(poster)* affiche *f*; *(review of film)* critique *f*; **(advance) n.** préavis *m*; **to give sb (advance) n.** *(inform)* avertir qn (**of** de); **n. (to quit), n. (of dismissal)** congé *m*; **to give (in) one's n.** *(resign)* donner sa démission; **to take n.** faire attention (**of** à); **to bring sth to sb's n.** porter qch à la connaissance de qn; **until**

further n. jusqu'à nouvel ordre; **at short n.** au dernier moment **2** *vt* remarquer (**that** que); **to get noticed** se faire remarquer **3** *vi* remarquer **▪noticeboard** *n Br* tableau *m* d'affichage

Note that the French word **notice** is a false friend and is never a translation for the English word **notice**. Its most common meaning is **directions for use**.

noticeable [ˈnəʊtɪsəbəl] *adj* perceptible

notify [ˈnəʊtɪfaɪ] *(pt & pp* **-ied**) *vt (inform)* avertir (**sb of sth** qn de qch); *(announce)* notifier (**to** à) **▪notification** [-fɪˈkeɪʃən] *n* avis *m*

notion [ˈnəʊʃən] *n* notion *f*; **to have some n. of sth** avoir quelques notions de qch; **to have a n. that...** avoir dans l'idée que... **▪notions** *npl Am (sewing articles)* mercerie *f*

notorious [nəʊˈtɔːrɪəs] *adj* tristement célèbre; *(stupidity, criminal)* notoire **▪notoriety** [-təˈraɪətɪ] *n* triste notoriété *f*

notwithstanding [nɒtwɪðˈstændɪŋ] *Formal* **1** *prep* en dépit de **2** *adv* néanmoins

nougat [ˈnuːgɑː] *n* nougat *m*

nought [nɔːt] *n Br Math* zéro *m*; *Br* **noughts and crosses** *(game)* ≃ morpion *m*

noun [naʊn] *n Grammar* nom *m*

nourish [ˈnʌrɪʃ] *vt* nourrir **▪nourishing** *adj* nourrissant **▪nourishment** *n* nourriture *f*

novel [ˈnɒvəl] **1** *n* roman *m* **2** *adj (new)* nouveau *(f* nouvelle), original **▪novelist** *n* romancier, -ière *mf* **▪novelty** *n* nouveauté *f*

Note that the French noun **nouvelle** is a false friend. It means **short story**.

November [nəʊˈvembə(r)] *n* novembre *m*

novice [ˈnɒvɪs] *n (beginner)* débutant, -ante *mf* (**at** en)

now [naʊ] **1** *adv* maintenant; **right n.** en ce moment; **for n.** pour le moment; **even n.** encore maintenant; **from n. on** désormais; **until n., up to n.** jusqu'ici, jusqu'à maintenant; **before n.** avant; **n. and then** de temps à autre; **n. hot, n. cold** tantôt chaud, tantôt froid; **she ought to be here by n.** elle devrait déjà être ici; **n. n.!** allons, allons! **2** *conj* **n. (that)...** maintenant que...

nowadays [ˈnaʊədeɪz] *adv* de nos jours

nowhere [ˈnəʊweə(r)] *adv* nulle part; **n. else** nulle part ailleurs; **it's n. I know** ce n'est pas un endroit que je connais; **n. near the house** loin de la maison; **n. near enough** loin d'être assez

nozzle [ˈnɒzəl] *n* embout *m*; *(of hose)* jet *m*; *(of petrol pump)* pistolet *m*

NSPCC [enespiːsiːˈsiː] *(abbr* **National Society for the Prevention of Cruelty to Children**) *n Br* = association britannique de protection de l'enfance

nuance [ˈnjuːɑːns] *n* nuance *f*

nub [nʌb] *n (of problem)* cœur *m*

nuclear ['nju:klɪə(r)] *adj* nucléaire; **n. bomb** bombe *f* atomique; **n. power** (énergie *f*) nucléaire *f*; *Br* **n. power station,** *Am* **n. power plant** centrale *f* nucléaire; **n. scientist** chercheur, -euse *mf* en physique nucléaire

nucleus ['nju:klɪəs] (*pl* **-clei** [-klɪaɪ]) *n* noyau *m* (*pl* -aux)

nude [nju:d] **1** *adj* nu **2** *n* nu *m*; **in the n.** tout nu (*f* toute nue)

nudge [nʌdʒ] **1** *n* coup *m* de coude **2** *vt* pousser du coude

nudism ['nju:dɪzəm] *n* nudisme *m* ∎**nudist** *n* nudiste *mf*; **n. camp** camp *m* de nudistes

nudity ['nju:dɪtɪ] *n* nudité *f*

nugget ['nʌgɪt] *n (of gold)* pépite *f*

nuisance ['nju:səns] *n* **to be a n.** être embêtant; **to make a n. of oneself** embêter le monde

null [nʌl] *adj* **n. (and void)** nul (et non avenu) (*f* nulle (et non avenue))

numb [nʌm] **1** *adj (stiff) (hand)* engourdi; *Fig (with fear)* paralysé; *(with shock, horror)* hébété; **n. with cold** engourdi par le froid **2** *vt* engourdir; *Fig (of fear)* paralyser; *(of shock)* hébéter ∎**numbness** *n (of hand)* engourdissement *m*

number ['nʌmbə(r)] **1** *n* nombre *m*; *(of page, house, telephone)* numéro *m*; *(song)* chanson *f*; **a/any n. of** un certain/grand nombre de **2** *vt (assign number to)* numéroter; *(count)* compter; **they n. eight** ils sont au nombre de huit ∎**numbering** *n* numérotage *m* ∎**number-plate** *n Br* plaque *f* d'immatriculation

numeral ['nju:mərəl] **1** *n* chiffre *m* **2** *adj* numéral

numerate ['nju:mərət] *adj* **to be n.** savoir compter

numerical [nju:'merɪkəl] *adj* numérique

numerous ['nju:mərəs] *adj* nombreux, -euse

nun [nʌn] *n* religieuse *f*

nurse [nɜ:s] **1** *n* infirmière *f*, *(for children)* nurse *f* **2** *vt (look after)* soigner; *(suckle)* allaiter; *(cradle)* bercer; *Fig (feeling)* nourrir ∎**nursing** **1** *adj* **the n. staff** le personnel soignant **2** *n (care)* soins *mpl*; *(job)* profession *f* d'infirmière; *Br* **n. home** *(for old people)* maison *f* de retraite

nursery ['nɜ:sərɪ] (*pl* **-ies**) *n (children's room)* chambre *f* d'enfants; *(for plants, trees)* pépinière *f*; **(day) n.** *(school)* garderie *f*; *Br* **n. education** enseignement *m* en maternelle; *Br* **n. nurse** puéricultrice *f*; **n. rhyme** comptine *f*; **n. school** école *f* maternelle

nurture ['nɜ:tʃə(r)] *vt (educate)* éduquer

nut[1] [nʌt] *n (fruit)* = noix, noisette ou autre fruit sec de cette nature; **Brazil n.** noix *f* du Brésil ∎**nutcrackers** *npl* casse-noix *m inv* ∎**nutshell** *n* coquille *f* de noix; *Fig* **in a n.** en un mot

nut[2] [nʌt] *n (for bolt)* écrou *m*; *Fam (head)* caboche *f*

nut[3] [nʌt] *n Fam (crazy person)* cinglé, -ée *mf* ∎**nutcase** *n Fam* cinglé, -ée *mf* ∎**nuts** *adj Fam (crazy)* cinglé ∎**nutter** *n Br Fam (crazy person)* cinglé, -eé *mf*

nutmeg ['nʌtmeg] *n* muscade *f*

nutrient ['nju:trɪənt] *n* élément *m* nutritif

nutrition [nju:'trɪʃən] *n* nutrition *f* ∎**nutritional** *adj* nutritionnel, -elle

nutritious [nju:'trɪʃəs] *adj* nutritif, -ive

nylon ['naɪlɒn] *n* Nylon® *m*; **n. shirt** chemise *f* en Nylon®

nymph [nɪmf] *n* nymphe *f* ∎**nymphomaniac** [nɪmfə'meɪnɪæk] *n* nymphomane *f*

O, o [əʊ] *n* (letter) O, o *m inv; Br Sch Formerly* **O-level** = diplôme de fin de premier cycle de l'enseignement secondaire sanctionnant une matière particulière

oaf [əʊf] *n* balourd *m* ▪ **oafish** *adj* lourdaud

oak [əʊk] *n* (tree, wood) chêne *m*; **o. table** table *f* en chêne

OAP [əʊeɪ'piː] *n* (abbr **old age pensioner**) *n Br* retraité, -ée *mf*

oar [ɔː(r)] *n* aviron *m*, rame *f*

oasis [əʊ'eɪsɪs] *(pl* **oases** [əʊ'eɪsiːz]*) n* oasis *f*

oath [əʊθ] *(pl* **-s** [əʊðz]*) n (promise)* serment *m*; *(profanity)* juron *m*; **to take an o. to do sth** faire le serment de faire qch

oatmeal ['əʊtmiːl] *n Br (flour)* farine *f* d'avoine; *Am (porridge)* bouillie *f* d'avoine

oats [əʊts] *npl* avoine *f*; **(porridge) o.** flocons *mpl* d'avoine

obedient [ə'biːdɪənt] *adj* obéissant ▪ **obedience** *n* obéissance *f* (**to** à) ▪ **obediently** *adv* docilement

obelisk ['ɒbəlɪsk] *n* obélisque *m*

obese [əʊ'biːs] *adj* obèse ▪ **obesity** *n* obésité *f*

obey [ə'beɪ] **1** *vt* obéir à; **to be obeyed** être obéi **2** *vi* obéir

obituary [ə'bɪtʃʊərɪ] *(pl* **-ies**) *n* nécrologie *f*

object¹ [ə'bdʒɪkt] *n (thing)* objet *m*; (aim) but *m*, objet; *Grammar* complément *m* d'objet; **money is no o.** le prix importe peu

object² [ə'bdʒekt] **1** *vt* **to o. that…** objecter que… **2** *vi* émettre une objection; **to o. to sth/to doing sth** ne pas être d'accord avec qch/pour faire qch; **I o.!** je proteste!; **she didn't o. when…** elle n'a fait aucune objection quand…

objection [əb'dʒekʃən] *n* objection *f*; **I've got no o.** je n'y vois pas d'objection

objectionable [əb'dʒekʃənəbəl] *adj* déplaisant

objective [əb'dʒektɪv] **1** *adj (impartial)* objectif, -ive **2** *n (aim, target)* objectif *m* ▪ **objectively** *adv* objectivement ▪ **objectivity** [ɒbdʒek'tɪvɪtɪ] *n* objectivité *f*

objector [əb'dʒektə(r)] *n* opposant, -ante *mf* (**to** à)

obligation [ɒblɪ'geɪʃən] *n* obligation *f*; **to be under an o. to do sth** être dans l'obligation de faire qch; **to be under an o. to sb** avoir une dette envers qn ▪ **obligatory** *adj* obligatoire

oblige [ə'blaɪdʒ] *vt* (**a**) *(compel)* obliger; **to o. sb to do sth** obliger qn à faire qch (**b**) *(help)* rendre service à; **to be obliged to sb** être reconnaissant à qn (**for** de); **much obliged!** merci infiniment! ▪ **obliging** *adj* serviable ▪ **obligingly** *adv* obligeamment

oblique [ə'bliːk] *adj (line, angle, look)* oblique; *(reference, route)* indirect

obliterate [ə'blɪtəreɪt] *vt* effacer

oblivion [ə'blɪvɪən] *n* oubli *m* ▪ **oblivious** *adj* inconscient (**to** *or* **of** de)

oblong ['ɒblɒŋ] **1** *adj (elongated)* oblong (*f* oblongue); *(rectangular)* rectangulaire **2** *n* rectangle *m*

obnoxious [əb'nɒkʃəs] *adj (person, behaviour)* odieux, -ieuse; *(smell)* nauséabond

oboe ['əʊbəʊ] *n* hautbois *m*

obscene [əb'siːn] *adj* obscène ▪ **obscenity** [əb'senətɪ] *(pl* **-ies**) *n* obscénité *f*

obscure [əb'skjʊə(r)] **1** *adj* obscur **2** *vt (hide)* cacher; *(confuse)* obscurcir ▪ **obscurely** *adv* obscurément ▪ **obscurity** *n* obscurité *f*

obsequious [əb'siːkwɪəs] *adj* obséquieux, -ieuse

observance [əb'zɜːvəns] *n (of rule, custom)* observation *f*

observation [ɒbzə'veɪʃən] *n (observing, remark)* observation *f*; *(by police)* surveillance *f*; **under o.** *(hospital patient)* en observation ▪ **observant** *adj* observateur, -trice

observatory [əb'zɜːvətərɪ] *(pl* **-ies**) *n* observatoire *m*

observe [əb'zɜːv] *vt* observer; **to o. the speed limit** respecter la limitation de vitesse ▪ **observer** *n* observateur, -trice *mf*

obsess [əb'ses] *vt* obséder ▪ **obsession** *n* obsession *f*; **to have an o. with** *or* **about sth** avoir l'obsession de qch; **to have an o. with sb** être obsédé par qn ▪ **obsessive** *adj (memory, idea)* obsédant; *(person)* obsessionnel, -elle; **to be o. about sth** être obsédé par qch

obsolete ['ɒbsəliːt] *adj* obsolète; *(design, model)* dépassé ▪ **obsolescence** [-'lesəns] *n* obsolescence *f*; **built-in o.** *(of car, computer)* obsolescence *f* programmée

obstacle ['ɒbstəkəl] *n* obstacle *m*; **o. course** parcours *m* d'obstacles; *Fig* parcours du combattant

obstetrician [ɒbstə'trɪʃən] *n Med* obstétricien, -ienne *mf* ▪ **ob'stetrics** [ɒb'stetrɪks] *n Med* obstétrique *f*

obstinate ['ɒbstɪnət] *adj* obstiné; **to be o.
about doing sth** s'obstiner à vouloir faire qch
▪ **obstinacy** *n* obstination *f* ▪ **obstinately** *adv*
obstinément

obstreperous [əb'strepərəs] *adj* tapageur,
-euse

obstruct [əb'strʌkt] *vt (block) (road, pipe)*
obstruer; *(view)* cacher; *(hinder)* gêner
▪ **obstruction** *n (action)* & *Med, Pol* & *Sport*
obstruction *f; (obstacle)* obstacle *m; (in pipe)*
bouchon *m; (traffic jam)* encombrement *m*
▪ **obstructive** *adj* **to be o.** faire de l'obstruction

obtain [əb'teɪn] **1** *vt* obtenir **2** *vi Formal (of
practice)* avoir cours ▪ **obtainable** *adj (available)* disponible; *(on sale)* en vente

obtrusive [əb'truːsɪv] *adj (person)* importun;
(building) trop en voyant

obtuse [əb'tjuːs] *adj (angle, mind)* obtus

obvious ['ɒbvɪəs] *adj* évident **(that** que); **the o.
thing to do is...** la seule chose à faire, c'est
de... ▪ **obviously** *adv (of course)* évidemment;
(conspicuously) manifestement

occasion [ə'keɪʒən] **1** *n* **(a)** *(time, opportunity)*
occasion *f; (event)* événement *m;* **on the o.
of...** à l'occasion de...; **on o.** parfois; **on one
o.** une fois; **on several occasions** à plusieurs
reprises **(b)** *Formal (cause)* raison *f* **2** *vt Formal*
occasionner

occasional [ə'keɪʒənəl] *adj* occasionnel, -elle;
(showers) intermittent; **she drinks the o.
whisky** elle boit un whisky de temps en temps
▪ **occasionally** *adv* de temps en temps; **very o.**
de temps en temps

occult [ə'kʌlt] **1** *adj* occulte **2** *n* **the o.** l'occulte *m*

occupant ['ɒkjʊpənt] *n (of house, car)* occupant,
-ante *mf; (of bus, plane)* passager, -ère *mf*

occupation [ɒkjʊ'peɪʃən] *n* **(a)** *(pastime)*
occupation *f; (profession)* métier *m* **(b)** *(of
house, land)* occupation *f;* **fit for o.** habitable
▪ **occupational** *adj* **o. hazard** risque *m* du
métier; **o. disease** maladie *f* professionnelle;
o. therapy ergothérapie *f*

occupier ['ɒkjʊpaɪə(r)] *n (of house)* occupant,
-ante *mf (of country)* occupant *m*

occupy ['ɒkjʊpaɪ] *(pt & pp* **-ied)** *vt (space, time,
attention)* occuper; **to keep oneself occupied**
s'occuper **(doing** à faire)

occur [ə'kɜː(r)] *(pt & pp* **-rr-)** *vi (happen)* avoir
lieu; *(of opportunity)* se présenter; *(be found)* se
trouver; **it occurs to me that...** il me vient à
l'esprit que...; **the idea occurred to her to...**
l'idée lui est venue de...

occurrence [ə'kʌrəns] *n* **(a)** *(event)* événement
m **(b)** *(of disease)* incidence *f; Ling (of word)*
occurrence *f*

ocean ['əʊʃən] *n* océan *m; Am* **the o.** la mer
▪ **oceanic** [əʊʃɪ'ænɪk] *adj* océanique

o'clock [ə'klɒk] *adv* **(it's) three o.** (il est) trois
heures

octagon ['ɒktəgən] *n* octogone *m* ▪ **oc'tagonal**
adj octogonal

octave ['ɒktɪv, 'ɒkteɪv] *n Mus* octave *f*

October [ɒk'təʊbə(r)] *n* octobre *m*

octogenarian [ɒktəʊdʒɪ'neərɪən] *n* octogénaire *mf*

octopus ['ɒktəpəs] *n* pieuvre *f*

OD [əʊ'diː] *vi Fam* faire une overdose **(on** de)

odd [ɒd] *adj* **(a)** *(strange)* bizarre, curieux,
-ieuse **(b)** *(number)* impair **(c)** *(left over)* **I have
an o. penny** il me reste un penny; **to be the o.
man out** être à part; **an o. glove/sock** un gant/
une chaussette dépareillé(e); **sixty o.** soixante
et quelques **(d)** *(occasional)* **to find the o.
mistake** trouver de temps en temps une
erreur; **I smoke the o. cigarette** je fume une
cigarette de temps en temps; **at o. moments**
de temps en temps; **o. jobs** petits travaux *mpl;
Br* **o. job man** homme *m* à tout faire ▪ **oddly** *adv*
bizarrement; **o. enough, he was elected**
chose curieuse, il a été élu

oddity ['ɒdɪtɪ] *(pl* **-ies)** *n (person)* excentrique
mf; (object) curiosité *f;* **oddities** *(of language,
situation)* bizarreries *fpl*

oddment ['ɒdmənt] *n Br Com* fin *f* de série

odds [ɒdz] *npl* **(a)** *(in betting)* cote *f; (chances)*
chances *fpl;* **we have heavy o. against us**
nous avons très peu de chances de réussir; *Fam*
it makes no o. ça n'a pas d'importance
(b) *(expressions)* **to be at o. (with sb)** être en
désaccord (avec qn); *Fam* **o. and ends** des
bricoles *fpl*

ode [əʊd] *n* ode *f*

odious ['əʊdɪəs] *adj* odieux, -ieuse

odour ['əʊdə(r)] *(Am* **odor)** *n* odeur *f*
▪ **odourless** *(Am* **odorless)** *adj* inodore

of [əv, *stressed* ɒv] *prep* de, d'; **of the table** de la
table; **of the boy** du garçon; **of the boys** des
garçons; **of a book** d'un livre; **of wood/paper**
de *ou* en bois/papier; **she has a lot of it/of
them** elle en a beaucoup; **I have ten of them**
j'en ai dix; **there are ten of us** nous sommes
dix; **a friend of his** un ami à lui, un de ses
amis; **that's nice of you** c'est gentil de ta part;
of no value/interest sans valeur/intérêt; **a
man of fifty** un homme de cinquante ans; *Br*
the fifth of June le cinq juin

off [ɒf] **1** *adj (light, gas, radio)* éteint; *(tap)*
fermé; *(switched off at mains)* coupé; *(gone
away)* parti; *(removed)* enlevé; *(cancelled)*
annulé; *(not fit to eat or drink)* mauvais; *(milk,
meat)* tourné; **the strike's o.** la grève est
annulée; **I'm o. today** j'ai congé aujourd'hui
2 *adv* **to be o.** *(leave)* partir; **where are you o.
to?** où vas-tu?; **with my/his/etc gloves o.** sans
gants; **a day o.** *(holiday)* un jour de congé; **time
o.** du temps libre; **I have today o.** j'ai congé
aujourd'hui; **5 percent o.** une réduction de 5
pour cent; **hands o.!** pas touche!; **on and o.,**

o. and on *(sometimes)* de temps à autre
3 *prep (from)* de; *(distant)* éloigné de; **to fall o. the wall/ladder** tomber du mur/de l'échelle; **to get o. the bus** descendre du bus; **to take sth o. the table** prendre qch sur la table; **to eat o. a plate** manger dans une assiette; **to keep** or **stay o. the grass** ne pas marcher sur la pelouse; **she's o. her food** elle ne mange plus rien; **o. Dover** *(ship)* au large de Douvres; **it's o. limits** c'est interdit ▪ **offbeat** *adj Fam* original ▪ **offchance** *n* **on the o.** à tout hasard ▪ **off-'colour** *(Am* **off-color**) *adj Br (ill)* patraque; *Am (indecent)* d'un goût douteux ▪ **'off-'duty** *adj* qui n'est pas de service ▪ **'off'hand 1** *adj* désinvolte **2** *adv (immediately)* au pied levé ▪ **off-licence** *n Br* ≃ magasin *m* de vins et de spiritueux ▪ **'off-'line** *adj Comptr (computer)* autonome; *(printer)* déconnecté ▪ **off-'load** *vt (vehicle)* décharger; **to o. sth onto sb** *(task)* se décharger de qch sur qn ▪ **'off-'peak** *adj (traffic)* aux heures creuses; *(rate, price)* heures creuses *inv*; **o. hours** heures *fpl* creuses ▪ **'off-'putting** *adj Br Fam* peu engageant ▪ **offshore** *adj (waters)* proche de la côte; *Fin (account, investment)* offshore ▪ **off'side** *adj Football* **to be o.** être hors jeu ▪ **offspring** *n* progéniture *f* ▪ **'off'stage** *adj & adv* dans les coulisses ▪ **'off-the-'cuff 1** *adj* impromptu **2** *adv* au pied levé ▪ **'off-the-'record** *adj* officieux, -ieuse ▪ **'off-the-'wall** *adj Fam* loufoque ▪ **off-'white** *adj* blanc cassé *inv*

offal ['ɒfəl] *n* abats *mpl*

offence [ə'fens] *(Am* **offense**) *n Law* infraction *f*; *(more serious)* délit *m*; **to take o.** s'offenser (**at** de); **to give o. (to sb)** offenser (qn)

offend [ə'fend] *vt* offenser; **to o. the eye/ear** choquer la vue/l'oreille; **to be offended (at sth)** s'offenser (de qch) ▪ **offender** *n Law (criminal)* délinquant, -ante *mf* ▪ **offending** *adj (object, remark)* incriminé

offense [ə'fens] *n Am* = **offence**

offensive [ə'fensɪv] **1** *adj* choquant; *(smell)* repoussant; **to be o. to sb** se montrer blessant envers qn; *Law* **o. weapon** arme *f* offensive **2** *n* offensive *f*; **to be on the o.** être passé à l'offensive

offer ['ɒfə(r)] **1** *n* offre *f*; **to make sb an o.** faire une offre à qn; **on (special) o.** en promotion; **o. of marriage** demande *f* en mariage **2** *vt* offrir; *(explanation)* donner; *(apologies)* présenter; **to o. sb sth, to o. sth to sb** offrir qch à qn; **to o. to do sth** proposer *ou* offrir de faire qch ▪ **offering** *n (gift)* offrande *f*; *(act)* offre *f*

office ['ɒfɪs] *n* **(a)** *(room)* bureau *m*; *Am (of doctor)* cabinet *m*; *(of lawyer)* étude *f*; **o. block** or **building** immeuble *m* de bureaux; **o. hours** heures *fpl* de bureau; **o. manager** chef *m* de bureau; **o. worker** employé, -ée *mf* de bureau

(b) *(position)* fonctions *fpl*; **to be in o.** être au pouvoir

officer ['ɒfɪsə(r)] *n (in the army, navy)* officier *m*; *(police)* **o.** agent *m* de police

official [ə'fɪʃəl] **1** *adj* officiel, -ielle **2** *n* responsable *mf*; *(civil servant)* fonctionnaire *mf* ▪ **officially** *adv* officiellement

officiate [ə'fɪʃɪeɪt] *vi (preside)* présider; *(of priest)* officier; **to o. at a wedding** célébrer un mariage

officious [ə'fɪʃəs] *adj Pej* trop zélé

offing ['ɒfɪŋ] *n* **in the o.** en perspective

offset ['ɒfset, ɒf'set] *(pt & pp* **offset**, *pres p* **offsetting**) *vt (compensate for)* compenser

offshoot ['ɒfʃuːt] *n (of organization)* ramification *f*; *(of family)* branche *f*

often ['ɒf(t)ən] *adv* souvent; **how o.?** combien de fois?; **how o. do they run?** *(trains, buses)* il y en a tous les combien?; **every so o.** de temps en temps

ogle ['əʊgəl] *vt Pej* reluquer

ogre ['əʊgə(r)] *n* ogre *m*

oh [əʊ] *exclam* oh!, ah!; *(in pain)* aïe!; **oh yes!** mais oui!; **oh yes?** ah oui?, ah bon?

OHP [əʊeɪtʃ'piː] *(abbr* **overhead projector**) *n* rétroprojecteur *m*

oil [ɔɪl] **1** *n (for machine, cooking)* huile *f*; *(petroleum)* pétrole *m*; *(fuel)* mazout *m*; **to paint in oils** faire de la peinture à l'huile **2** *adj (industry, product)* pétrolier, -ière; *(painting, paint)* à l'huile; **o. change** *(in vehicle)* vidange *f*; **o. lamp** lampe *f* à pétrole; **o. refinery** raffinerie *f* de pétrole; **o. slick** *(on sea)* nappe *f* de pétrole; *(on beach)* marée *f* noire; **o. tanker** *(ship)* pétrolier *m*; *(lorry)* camion-citerne *m* **3** *vt (machine)* huiler ▪ **oilcan** *n* burette *f* ▪ **oilfield** *n* gisement *m* de pétrole ▪ **oil-fired** *adj (central heating)* au mazout ▪ **oil-producing** *adj* producteur, -trice de pétrole ▪ **oily** *(-ier, -iest) adj (hands, rag)* graisseux, -euse; *(skin, hair)* gras *(f* grasse); *(food)* huileux, -euse

ointment ['ɔɪntmənt] *n* pommade *f*

OK, okay ['əʊ'keɪ] **1** *adj & adv* = **all right 2** *(pt & pp* **OKed, okayed**, *pres p* **OKing, okaying**) *vt* donner le feu vert à

old [əʊld] **1** *(-er, -est) adj* vieux *(f* vieille); *(former)* ancien, -ienne; **how o. is he?** quel âge a-t-il?; **he's ten years o.** il a dix ans; **he's older than me** il est plus âgé que moi; **an older son** un fils aîné; **the oldest son** le fils aîné; **o. enough to do sth** assez grand pour faire qch; **o. enough to marry/vote** en âge de se marier/de voter; **to get** or **grow old(er)** vieillir; **o. age** vieillesse *f*; *Pej* **o. maid** vieille fille *f*; **o. man** vieillard *m*, vieil homme *m*; **o. people** les personnes *fpl* âgées; **o. people's home** maison *f* de retraite; **o. woman** vieille femme *f*; **the O. World** l'Ancien Monde; *Fam* **any o. how** n'importe comment **2** *npl* **the o.** les personnes *fpl* âgées

olden ['əʊldən] adj **in the o. days** jadis

old-fashioned [əʊld'fæʃənd] adj (out-of-date) démodé; (person) vieux jeu inv; (traditional) d'autrefois

old-timer [əʊld'taɪmə(r)] n Fam (old man) ancien m

olive ['ɒlɪv] 1 n (fruit) olive f 2 adj **o. (green)** vert olive inv; **o. oil** huile f d'olive; **o. tree** olivier m

Olympic [ə'lɪmpɪk] adj **the O. Games** les jeux mpl Olympiques

ombudsman ['ɒmbʊdzmən] (pl **-men**) n ≃ médiateur m de la République

omelet(te) ['ɒmlɪt] n omelette f; **cheese o.** omelette au fromage

omen ['əʊmən] n augure m

ominous ['ɒmɪnəs] adj inquiétant; (event) de mauvais augure; (tone, sky) menaçant; (noise) sinistre

omit [əʊ'mɪt] (pt & pp **-tt-**) vt omettre (**to do** faire) ▪ **omission** n omission f

omnipotent [ɒm'nɪpətənt] adj omnipotent

omniscient [ɒm'nɪsɪənt] adj omniscient

on [ɒn] 1 prep (a) (expressing position) sur; **on the chair** sur la chaise; **on page 4** à la page 4; **on the right/left** à droite/gauche; **to put on (to) sth** mettre sur qch; **to look out on to sth** donner sur qch (b) (about) sur; **an article on sth** un article sur qch (c) (expressing manner or means) **on foot** à pied; **on the blackboard** au tableau; **on the radio** à la radio; **on the train/plane** dans le train/l'avion; **to be on** (course) suivre; (project) travailler à; (salary) toucher; (team, committee) faire partie de; **to keep or stay on** (road, path) suivre; Fam **it's on me!** (I'll pay) c'est moi pour moi! (d) (with time) **on Monday** lundi; **on Mondays** le lundi; **on May 3rd** le 3 mai; **on the evening of May 3rd** le 3 mai au soir; **on my arrival** à mon arrivée (e) (+ present participle) en; **on learning that...** en apprenant que...; **on seeing this** en voyant ceci

2 adv (ahead) en avant; (in progress) en cours; (lid, brake) mis; (light, radio) allumé; (gas, tap) ouvert; (machine) en marche; **she has her hat on** elle a mis son chapeau; **he has something/nothing on** il est habillé/tout nu; **I've got something on** (I'm busy) je suis pris; **the strike is on** la grève aura lieu; **what's on?** (on TV) qu'est-ce qu'il y a à la télé?; (in theatre, cinema) qu'est-ce qu'on joue?; **is the meeting still on?** la réunion doit-elle toujours avoir lieu?; **to play on** continuer à jouer; **he went on and on about it** il n'en finissait pas; Fam **that's just not on!** c'est inadmissible!; **I've been on to him** (on phone) je l'ai eu au bout du fil; **to be on to sb** (of police) être sur la piste de qn; **to be on at sb** s'en prendre à qn (**to do** pour qu'il fasse); **I've been on at them for months to get it fixed**

ça fait des mois que je suis sur leur dos pour qu'ils le fassent réparer ▪ **on-coming** adj (vehicle) qui vient en sens inverse ▪ **'on'going** adj (project, discussion) en cours

once [wʌns] 1 adv (on one occasion) une fois; (formerly) autrefois; **o. a month** une fois par mois; **o. again, o. more** encore une fois; **o. and for all** une fois pour toutes; **o. upon a time** il était une fois; **at o.** (immediately) tout de suite; **all at o.** (suddenly) tout à coup; (at the same time) à la fois 2 conj une fois que; **o. he reached home, he collapsed** une fois arrivé chez lui, il s'effondra ▪ **once-over** n Fam **to give sth the o.** jeter un coup d'œil à qch

one [wʌn] 1 adj (a) un, une; **o. man** un homme; **o. woman** une femme; **page o.** la page un; **twenty-o.** vingt et un (b) (only) seul; **my o. (and only) aim** mon seul (et unique) but (c) (same) le même (f la même); **in the o. bus** dans le même bus

2 pron (a) un, une; **do you want o.?** en veux-tu (un)?; **he's o. of us** c'est celui de nous; **o. of them** l'un d'eux, l'une d'elles; **a big/small o.** un grand/petit; **this book is o. that I've read** ce livre est parmi ceux que j'ai lus; **I'm a teacher and she's o.** too je suis professeur et elle aussi; **this o.** celui-ci, celle-ci; **that o.** celui-là, celle-là; **the o. who/which...** celui/celle qui...; Br Fam **it's Paul's o.** c'est celui de Paul; Br Fam **it's my o.** c'est le mien/la mienne; **another o.** un(e) autre; **I for o.** pour ma part (b) (impersonal) on; **o. knows on sait**; **it helps o.** ça vous aide; **o.'s family** sa famille ▪ **'one-'armed** adj (person) manchot ▪ **one-'eyed** adj borgne ▪ **one-legged** ['wʌn'legɪd] adj unijambiste ▪ **one-man** adj (business, office) pour un seul homme; **o. show** one-man-show m inv ▪ **one-night stand** n Fam (sexual encounter) rencontre m sans lendemain ▪ **'one-'off** (Am **'one-of-a-'kind**) adj Fam unique ▪ **one-parent 'family** n famille f monoparentale ▪ **'one-'sided** adj (biased) partial; (contest) inégal; (decision) unilatéral ▪ **one-time** adj (former) ancien, -ienne ▪ **'one-to-'one** (Am **'one-on-'one**) adj (discussion) en tête-à-tête ▪ **one-track 'mind** n **to have a o.** avoir une idée fixe ▪ **one-'upmanship** n Fam = tendance à s'affirmer supérieur aux autres ▪ **one-way** adj (street) à sens unique; (traffic) en sens unique; **o. ticket** billet m simple

onerous ['əʊnərəs] adj (task) difficile; (taxes) lourd

> Note that the French word **onéreux** is a false friend and is never a translation for the English word **onerous**. It means **expensive**.

oneself [wʌn'self] pron soi-même; (reflexive) se, s'; **to cut o.** se couper; **to do sth all by o.** faire qch tout seul

onion ['ʌnjən] n oignon m

online, on-line [ɒn'laɪn] adj Comptr en ligne; **to go o.** se connecter; **o. banking** banque f par Internet; **o. forum** forum m de discussion; **o. shopping** achats mpl sur Internet

onlooker ['ɒnlʊkə(r)] n spectateur, -trice mf

only ['əʊnlɪ] **1** adj seul; **the o. house** la seule maison; **the o.** one le seul, la seule; **an o. son** un fils unique **2** adv seulement, ne… que; **I o. have ten, I have ten o.** je n'en ai que dix, j'en ai dix seulement; **if o.** si seulement; **not o.** non seulement; **I have o. just seen it** je viens tout juste de le voir; **o. he knows** lui seul le sait **3** conj Fam (but) mais

onset ['ɒnset] n (of disease, winter) début m; (of old age) approche f

onslaught ['ɒnslɔːt] n attaque f (**on** contre)

onto ['ɒntuː, unstressed 'ɒntə] prep = **on to**

onus ['əʊnəs] n inv **the o. is on you to…** c'est à vous qu'il incombe de…

onward(s) ['ɒnwəd(z)] adv en avant; **from that day o.** à partir de ce jour-là

onyx ['ɒnɪks] n onyx m

ooze [uːz] **1** vt laisser suinter **2** vi **to o. (out)** suinter

opal ['əʊpəl] n opale f

opaque [əʊ'peɪk] adj opaque; Fig (unclear) obscur

open ['əʊpən] **1** adj ouvert; (site, view, road) dégagé; (meeting) public, -ique; (competition) ouvert à tous; (post, job) vacant; (attempt, envy) manifeste; (airline ticket) open inv; **in the o. air** au grand air; **in (the) o. country** en rase campagne; **o. spaces** (parks) espaces mpl verts; **it's o. to doubt** c'est douteux; **to be o. to** (criticism, attack) exposé à; (ideas, suggestions) ouvert à; **I've got an o. mind on it** je n'ai pas d'opinion arrêtée là-dessus; **to leave sth o.** (date) ne pas préciser qch **2** n (out) **in the o.** (outside) dehors; **to sleep (out) in the o.** dormir à la belle étoile; **to bring sth (out) into the o.** (reveal) divulguer qch **3** vt ouvrir; (conversation) entamer; (arms, legs) écarter; **to o. sth out** (paper, map) ouvrir qch; **to o. sth up** (door, shop) ouvrir qch **4** vi (of flower, door, eyes) s'ouvrir; (of shop, office, person) ouvrir; (of play) débuter; (of film) sortir; **to o. on to sth** (of window) donner sur qch; **to o. out** (of flower) s'ouvrir; (widen) s'élargir; **to o. up** (of flower, person) s'ouvrir; (of shopkeeper, shop) ouvrir ■ **open-'air** adj (pool) en plein air ■ **open-'heart** adj (operation) à cœur ouvert ■ **open-'minded** adj à l'esprit ouvert ■ **open-'necked** adj (shirt) sans cravate ■ **open-'plan** adj (office) paysager, -ère

opening ['əʊpənɪŋ] **1** n ouverture f; (of flower) éclosion f; (job, trade outlet) débouché m; (opportunity) occasion f favorable; **late-night o.** (of shops) nocturne f **2** adj (time, hours,

speech) d'ouverture; **o. night** (of play, musical) première f

openly ['əʊpənlɪ] adv ouvertement ■ **openness** n (frankness) franchise f

opera ['ɒprə] n opéra m; **o. glasses** jumelles fpl de théâtre; **o. house** opéra

operate ['ɒpəreɪt] **1** vt (machine) faire fonctionner; (service) assurer **2** vi (a) **to o. on sb (for sth)** (of surgeon) opérer qn (de qch); **to be operated on** se faire opérer (**b**) (of machine) fonctionner; (of company) opérer ■ **operating** adj **o. costs** frais mpl d'exploitation; Br **o. theatre**, Am **o. room** salle f d'opération; Comptr **o. system** système m d'exploitation

operation [ɒpə'reɪʃən] n Med, Mil & Math opération f; (of machine) fonctionnement m; **in o.** (machine) en service; (plan) en vigueur; **to have an o.** se faire opérer (**on** or **for** de) ■ **operational** adj opérationnel, -elle

operative ['ɒprətɪv] **1** adj (scheme, measure, law) en vigueur; Med opératoire **2** n (worker) ouvrier, -ière mf

operator ['ɒpəreɪtə(r)] n (on phone, machine) opérateur, -trice mf

opinion [ə'pɪnjən] n opinion f; **to form an o.** se faire une opinion; **in my o.** à mon avis ■ **opinionated** adj dogmatique

opium ['əʊpɪəm] n opium m

opponent [ə'pəʊnənt] n adversaire mf

opportune ['ɒpətjuːn] adj opportun

opportunism ['ɒpətjuːnɪzəm, -'tjuːnɪzəm] n opportunisme m

opportunity [ɒpə'tjuːnɪtɪ] (pl **-ies**) n occasion f (**to do** or **of doing** de faire); **to take the o. to do sth** profiter de l'occasion pour faire qch; **opportunities** (prospects) perspectives fpl; **equal opportunities** égalité f des chances; **to take the o. to do sth** profiter de l'occasion pour faire qch

oppose [ə'pəʊz] vt s'opposer à ■ **opposed** adj opposé (**to** à); **as o. to…** par opposition à… ■ **opposing** adj (characters, viewpoints) opposé; (team) adverse

opposite ['ɒpəzɪt] **1** adj (side) opposé; (house, page) d'en face; **in the o. direction** en sens inverse; **o. number** homologue mf **2** adv en face; **the house o.** la maison d'en face **3** prep **o. (to)** en face de **4** n **the o.** le contraire

opposition [ɒpə'zɪʃən] n opposition f (**to** à); **the o.** (rival camp) l'adversaire m; (in business) la concurrence; **he put up no/considerable o.** il n'a opposé aucune résistance/a fait preuve d'une résistance acharnée

oppress [ə'pres] vt (treat cruelly) opprimer; (of heat, anguish) oppresser ■ **oppressed** npl **the o.** les opprimés mpl ■ **oppression** n oppression f ■ **oppressive** adj (heat) accablant, étouffant; (weather) étouffant; (ruler, regime) oppressif, -ive ■ **oppressor** n oppresseur m

opt [ɒpt] *vi* **to o. for sth** opter pour qch; **to o. do sth** choisir de faire qch; **to o. out** se désengager (**of** de)

optical ['ɒptɪkəl] *adj* optique; *(instrument, illusion)* d'optique; *Comptr* **o. character reader** lecteur *m* optique de caractères

optician [ɒp'tɪʃən] *n (dispensing)* opticien, -ienne *mf*

optimism ['ɒptɪmɪzəm] *n* optimisme *m* ▪ **optimist** *n* optimiste *mf* ▪ **opti'mistic** *adj* optimiste (**about** quant à) ▪ **opti'mistically** *adv* avec optimisme

optimum ['ɒptɪməm] *adj & n* optimum *(m)* ▪ **optimal** *adj* optimal ▪ **optimize** *vt* optimiser

option ['ɒpʃən] *n (choice)* choix *m*; *(school subject)* matière *f* à option; **she has no o.** elle n'a pas le choix ▪ **optional** *adj* facultatif, -ive; **o. extra** *(on car)* option *f*

opulent ['ɒpjʊlənt] *adj* opulent ▪ **opulence** *n* opulence *f*

or [ɔː(r)] *conj* ou; **one or two** un ou deux; **he doesn't drink or smoke** il ne boit ni ne fume; **ten or so** environ dix

oracle ['ɒrəkəl] *n* oracle *m*

oral ['ɔːrəl] **1** *adj* oral **2** *n (exam)* oral *m* ▪ **orally** *adv* oralement; *Med* par voie orale

orange ['ɒrɪndʒ] **1** *n (fruit)* orange *f*; **o. drink** boisson *f* à l'orange; **o. juice** jus *m* d'orange; **o. tree** oranger *m* **2** *adj & n (colour)* orange *(m) inv*

orang-outang [ɔːˌræŋuːˈtæŋ], **orang-utan** [ɔːˌræŋuːˈtæn] *n* orang-outan(g) *m*

oration [ɔːˈreɪʃən] *n* **funeral o.** oraison *f* funèbre

orator ['ɒrətə(r)] *n* orateur *m* ▪ **oratory** *(pl* -ies*)* *n* art *m* oratoire

orbit ['ɔːbɪt] **1** *n (of planet, sphere of influence)* orbite *f* **2** *vt* être en orbite autour de

orchard ['ɔːtʃəd] *n* verger *m*

orchestra ['ɔːkɪstrə] *n* orchestre *m*; *Am* **the o.** *(in theatre)* l'orchestre *m* ▪ **orchestral** [ɔːˈkestrəl] *adj (music)* orchestral; *(concert)* symphonique ▪ **orchestrate** *vt (organize)* & *Mus* orchestrer

orchid ['ɔːkɪd] *n* orchidée *f*

ordain [ɔːˈdeɪn] *vt (priest)* ordonner; *Formal* **to o. that…** décréter que…

ordeal [ɔːˈdiːl] *n* épreuve *f*

order ['ɔːdə(r)] **1** *n (instruction, arrangement)* & *Rel* ordre *m*; *(purchase)* commande *f*; **in o.** *(passport)* en règle; *(drawer, room)* en ordre; **in numerical o.** en ordre numérique; **in working o.** en état de marche; **in o. of age** par ordre d'âge; **in o. to do sth** afin de faire qch; **in o. that…** afin que… (*+ subjunctive*); **out of o.** *(machine)* en panne; *(telephone)* en dérangement; *Com* **to make** or **place an o. (with sb)** passer une commande (à qn); **on o.** *(goods)* commandé; **o. form** bon *m* de commande **2** *vt (meal, goods)* commander; *(taxi)* appeler; **to o. sb to do sth** ordonner à qn de faire qch; **to o. sb around** commander qn **3** *vi (in café)* commander; **are you ready to o.?** avez-vous choisi?

orderly ['ɔːdəlɪ] **1** *adj (tidy) (room, life)* ordonné; *(mind)* méthodique; *(crowd)* discipliné; **in an o. fashion** calmement **2** *(pl* -ies*)* *n (soldier)* planton *m*; *(in hospital)* aide-soignant, -ante *mf*

ordinal ['ɔːdɪnəl] *adj* ordinal

ordinary ['ɔːdənrɪ] *adj* ordinaire; **in o. use** d'usage courant; **in the o. course of events** en temps normal; **in the o. way** normalement; **it's out of the o.** ça sort de l'ordinaire; **she was just an o. tourist** c'était une touriste comme une autre

ordination [ɔːdɪˈneɪʃən] *n Rel* ordination *f*

ordnance ['ɔːdnəns] *n Mil (guns)* artillerie *f*; *Br* **O. Survey** ≃ Institut *m* géographique national

ore [ɔː(r)] *n* minerai *m*

oregano [ɒrɪˈɡɑːnəʊ] *n* origan *m*

organ ['ɔːɡən] *n* (**a**) *(part of body, newspaper)* organe *m* (**b**) *(musical instrument)* orgue *m*

organic [ɔːˈɡænɪk] *adj* organique; *(vegetables, farming)* biologique

organism ['ɔːɡənɪzəm] *n* organisme *m*

organization [ɔːɡənaɪˈzeɪʃən] *n* organisation *f*

organize ['ɔːɡənaɪz] *vt* organiser ▪ **organizer** *n (person)* organisateur, -trice *mf*; **(personal) o.** *(diary)* agenda *m*; *(electronic)* agenda électronique

orgasm ['ɔːɡæzəm] *n* orgasme *m*

orgy ['ɔːdʒɪ] *(pl* -ies*)* *n* orgie *f*

Orient ['ɔːrɪənt] *n* **the O.** l'Orient *m* ▪ **oriental** [ɔːrɪˈentəl] **1** *adj* oriental **2** *n* Oriental, -ale *mf*

orientate ['ɔːrɪənteɪt] *(Am* **orient** ['ɔːrɪənt]*)* *vt* orienter

orifice ['ɒrɪfɪs] *n* orifice *m*

origin ['ɒrɪdʒɪn] *n* origine *f*

original [əˈrɪdʒɪnəl] **1** *adj (novel, innovative)* original; *(first)* d'origine **2** *n (document, painting)* original *m* ▪ **originality** [-ˈnælɪtɪ] *n* originalité *f* ▪ **originally** *adv (at first)* à l'origine; *(in an innovative way)* de façon originale; **where do you come from o.?** d'où êtes-vous originaire?

originate [əˈrɪdʒɪneɪt] **1** *vt* être à l'origine de **2** *vi (begin)* prendre naissance (**in** dans); **to o. from** *(of idea)* émaner de; *(of person)* être originaire de

Orkneys ['ɔːknɪz] *npl* **the O.** les Orcades *fpl*

ornament ['ɔːnəmənt] *n* ornement *m* ▪ **ornamental** [-ˈmentəl] *adj* ornemental ▪ **ornamentation** [-menˈteɪʃən] *n* ornementation *f*

ornate [ɔːˈneɪt] *adj* très orné ▪ **ornately** *adv* de façon très orné; **o. decorated** richement décoré

orphan ['ɔːfən] *n* orphelin, -ine *mf*

■ **orphanage** n orphelinat m ■ **orphaned** adj **to be o.** devenir orphelin
orthodox ['ɔːθədɒks] adj orthodoxe ■ **orthodoxy** n orthodoxie f
orthopaedic (Am **orthopedic**) [ɔːθə'piːdɪk] adj orthopédique ■ **orthopaedics** (Am **orthopedics**) n orthopédie f
Oscar ['ɒskə(r)] n Cin oscar m; **the Oscars** (ceremony) les oscars mpl
oscillate ['ɒsɪleɪt] vi osciller
ostensibly [ɒ'stensɪblɪ] adv soi-disant
ostentation [ɒsten'teɪʃən] n ostentation f ■ **ostentatious** adj prétentieux, -ieuse
osteopath ['ɒstɪəpæθ] n ostéopathe mf ■ **osteopathy** [-'ɒpəθɪ] n ostéopathie f
ostracism ['ɒstrəsɪzəm] n ostracisme m ■ **ostracize** vt frapper d'ostracisme
ostrich ['ɒstrɪtʃ] n autruche f
other ['ʌðə(r)] 1 adj autre; **o. doctors** d'autres médecins; **the o. one** l'autre mf; **I have no o. gloves than these** je n'ai pas d'autres gants que ceux-ci 2 pron **the o.** l'autre mf; **(some) others** d'autres; **some do, others don't** les uns le font, les autres ne le font pas; **none o. than, no o. than** nul autre que 3 adv **o. than** autrement que; **the colour's odd, but o. than that, it's fine** la couleur est bizarre, mais à part ça, ça va ■ **otherwise** 1 adv & conj autrement 2 adj (different) autre
OTT [əʊtiː'tiː] (abbr over the top) adj Br Fam trop inv
otter ['ɒtə(r)] n loutre f
ouch [aʊtʃ] exclam aïe!
ought [ɔːt] v aux

La forme négative **ought not** s'écrit **oughtn't** en forme contractée.

(a) (expressing obligation, desirability) **you o. to leave** tu devrais partir; **I o. to have done it** j'aurais dû le faire; **he said he o. to stay** il a dit qu'il devait rester (b) (expressing probability) **it o. to be ready** ça devrait être prêt
ounce [aʊns] n (unit of weight) = 28,35 g, once f; Fig (bit) once f (**of** de)
our [aʊə(r)] possessive adj notre, pl nos
ours [aʊəz] possessive pron le nôtre, la nôtre, pl les nôtres; **this book is o.** ce livre est à nous ou est le nôtre; **a friend of o.** un de nos amis
ourselves [aʊə'selvz] pron nous-mêmes; (reflexive and after prep) nous; **we wash o.** nous nous lavons; **we told you o.** nous vous l'avons dit nous-mêmes
oust [aʊst] vt évincer (**from** de)
out [aʊt] 1 adv (outside) dehors; (not at home) sorti; (light, fire) éteint; (flower) ouvert; (book) publié; (not in fashion) passé de mode; **to go o. a lot** sortir beaucoup; **to have a day o.** sortir pour la journée; **5 km o.** (from the shore) à 5 km du rivage; **the sun's o.** il fait soleil; **the tide's o.** la marée est basse; **the secret is o.**

on a révélé le secret; **you're o.** (wrong) tu t'es trompé; (in game) tu es éliminé (**of** de); **I was £10 o.** (over) j'avais 10 livres de trop; (under) il me manquait 10 livres; **before the week is o.** avant la fin de la semaine; **to be o. to do sth** chercher à faire qch; **the journey o.** l'aller m; **o. here** ici; **o. there** là-bas; Tennis **o.!** faute!
2 prep **o. of** (outside) hors de; **5 km o.** (away from) à 5 km de; **to be o. of the country** être à l'étranger; **she's o. of town** elle n'est pas en ville; **to look/jump o. of the window** regarder/sauter par la fenêtre; **to drink/take/copy o. of sth** boire/prendre/copier dans qch; **to feel o. of place** ne pas se sentir à sa place; Fam **to feel o. of it** se sentir hors du coup; **made o. of wood** fait en bois; **to make sth o. of a box/rag** faire qch avec une boîte/un chiffon; **o. of danger** hors de danger; **o. of pity/love** par pitié/amour; **four o. of five** quatre sur cinq ■ **'out-and-'out** adj (cheat, liar) achevé; (failure) total ■ **out-of-date** adj (expired) périmé; (old-fashioned) démodé ■ **out-of-'doors** adv dehors ■ **'out-of-the-'way** adj (place) isolé
outbid [aʊt'bɪd] (pt & pp **-bid**, pres p **outbidding**) vt **to o. sb** enchérir avec succès sur qn
outboard ['aʊtbɔːd] adj **o. motor** moteur m hors-bord inv
outbreak ['aʊtbreɪk] n (of war, epidemic) début m; (of violence) flambée f; (of hostilities) déclenchement m; (of fever) accès m
outburst ['aʊtbɜːst] n (of anger, joy) explosion f; (of violence) flambée f; (of laughter) éclat m
outcast ['aʊtkɑːst] n **(social) o.** paria m
outcome ['aʊtkʌm] n résultat m, issue f
outcry ['aʊtkraɪ] (pl **-ies**) n tollé m
outdated [aʊt'deɪtɪd] adj démodé
outdo [aʊt'duː] (pt **-did**, pp **-done**) vt surpasser (**in** en)
outdoor ['aʊtdɔː(r)] adj (life) au grand air; (game) de plein air; (pool, market) découvert ■ **out'doors** 1 adv dehors 2 n **the great o.** les grands espaces mpl
outer ['aʊtə(r)] adj extérieur; **O. London** la grande banlieue de Londres; **o. space** l'espace m intersidéral
outfit ['aʊtfɪt] n (clothes) ensemble m; Fam (group, gang) bande f; Fam (company) boîte f; **sports/ski o.** tenue f de sport/de ski
outgoing ['aʊtgəʊɪŋ] adj (a) (minister) sortant; (mail, ship) en partance; **o. calls** (on phone) appels mpl vers l'extérieur (b) (sociable) sociable ■ **outgoings** npl (expenses) dépenses fpl
outgrow [aʊt'grəʊ] (pt **-grew**, pp **-grown**) vt (habit) passer l'âge de; **to o. sb** grandir plus vite que qn; **she's outgrown her jacket** sa veste est devenue trop petite pour elle

outhouse ['aʊthaʊs] n Br (of mansion, farm) dépendance f; Am (lavatory) cabinets mpl extérieurs

outing ['aʊtɪŋ] n (excursion) sortie f

outlandish [aʊt'lændɪʃ] adj (weird) bizarre; (barbaric) barbare

outlast [aʊt'lɑːst] vt (object) durer plus longtemps que; (person) survivre à

outlaw ['aʊtlɔː] 1 n hors-la-loi m inv 2 vt (ban) proscrire; (person) mettre hors la loi

outlay ['aʊtleɪ] n (expense) dépenses fpl

outlet ['aʊtlet] n (shop) point m de vente; (market for goods) débouché m; (for liquid, of tunnel) sortie f; (electrical) prise f de courant; (for feelings, energy) exutoire m; **factory o.** magasin d'usine; **retail o.** point de vente, magasin m;

outline ['aʊtlaɪn] 1 n (shape) contour m; (of play, novel) résumé m; **rough o.** (of article, plan) esquisse f; **the broad or general or main o.** (of plan, policy) les grandes lignes 2 vt (plan, situation) esquisser; (book, speech) résumer; **to be outlined against sth** se profiler sur qch

outlive [aʊt'lɪv] vt survivre à

outlook ['aʊtlʊk] n inv (for future) perspectives fpl; (point of view) façon f de voir les choses; (of weather) prévisions fpl

outlying ['aʊtlaɪɪŋ] adj (remote) isolé

outmoded [aʊt'məʊdɪd] adj démodé

outnumber [aʊt'nʌmbə(r)] vt l'emporter en nombre sur

outpatient ['aʊtpeɪʃənt] n Br malade mf en consultation externe

outpost ['aʊtpəʊst] n Mil avant-poste m

output ['aʊtpʊt] 1 n (of goods) production f; (computer data) données fpl de sortie; (computer process) sortie f 2 (pt & pp -put) vt produire; (data, information) sortir

outrage ['aʊtreɪdʒ] 1 n (scandal) scandale m; (anger) indignation f (**at** face à); (crime) atrocité f 2 vt (make indignant) scandaliser

outrageous [aʊt'reɪdʒəs] adj (shocking) scandaleux, -euse; (atrocious) atroce; (dress, hat) grotesque

outright 1 [aʊt'raɪt] adv (say, tell) franchement; (refuse) catégoriquement; (be killed) sur le coup; **to buy sth o.** acheter qch au comptant 2 ['aʊtraɪt] adj (failure) total; (refusal) catégorique; (folly) pur; (winner) incontesté

outset ['aʊtset] n **at the o.** au début; **from the o.** dès le départ

outside [aʊt'saɪd] 1 adv dehors, à l'extérieur; **to go o.** sortir 2 prep à l'extérieur de, en dehors de; (in front of) devant; (apart from) en dehors de; **o. my room** or **door** à la porte de ma chambre; **o. office hours** en dehors des heures de bureau 3 n extérieur m 4 ['aʊtsaɪd] adj extérieur; (bus or train seat) côté couloir inv; Br **the o. lane** (on road) la voie de droite, Am la voie de gauche; **an o. chance** une petite chance

outsider [aʊt'saɪdə(r)] n (stranger) étranger, -ère mf; (horse in race) outsider m

outskirts ['aʊtskɜːts] npl banlieue f

outsmart [aʊt'smɑːt] vt être plus malin, -igne que

outspoken [aʊt'spəʊkən] adj (frank) franc (f franche)

outstanding [aʊt'stændɪŋ] adj exceptionnel, -elle; (problem, business) en suspens; (debt) impayé

outstay [aʊt'steɪ] vt **to o. one's welcome** abuser de l'hospitalité de son hôte

outstretched [aʊt'stretʃt] adj (arm) tendu; (wings) déployé

outstrip [aʊt'strɪp] (pt & pp -pp-) vt dépasser

out-tray ['aʊttreɪ] n (in office) corbeille f (du courrier) 'départ'

outward ['aʊtwəd] adj (sign, appearance) extérieur; (movement, look) vers l'extérieur; **o. journey** or **trip** aller m ▪ **outward(s)** adv vers l'extérieur

outweigh [aʊt'weɪ] vt (be more important than) l'emporter sur

outwit [aʊt'wɪt] (pt & pp -tt-) vt être plus malin, -igne que

oval ['əʊvəl] adj & n ovale (m); Am Pol **the O. Office** = le bureau du Président des États-Unis

ovary ['əʊvərɪ] (pl -ies) n Anat ovaire m ▪ **ovarian** [əʊ'veərɪən] adj ovarien, -ienne

ovation [əʊ'veɪʃən] n ovation f; **to give sb a standing o.** se lever pour applaudir qn

oven ['ʌvən] n four m; Fig (hot place) fournaise f; Br **o. glove,** Am **o. mitt** gant m isolant ▪ **oven-proof** adj (dish) allant au four ▪ **oven-ready** adj (meal) prêt à mettre au four

over ['əʊvə(r)] 1 prep (on) sur; (above) au-dessus de; (on the other side of) par-dessus; **the bridge o. the river** le pont qui traverse le fleuve; **to jump/look o. sth** sauter/regarder par-dessus qch; **to fall o. the balcony** tomber du balcon; **o. it** (on) dessus; (above) au-dessus; **to jump o. it** sauter par-dessus; **to fight o. sth** se battre pour qch; **o. the phone** au téléphone; Br **o. the holidays** pendant les vacances; **o. ten days** (more than) plus de dix jours; **men o. sixty** les hommes de plus de soixante ans; **o. and above** en plus de; **he's o. his flu** il est remis de sa grippe

2 adv (above) par-dessus; **jump o.!** sautez par-dessus!; **o. here** ici; **o. there** là-bas; **he's o. in Italy** il est en Italie; **she's o. from Paris** elle est venue de Paris; **to ask sb o.** inviter qn; **to be (all) o.** être terminé; **to start all o. (again)** recommencer à zéro; **a kilo o. o.** (more) un kilo ou plus; **I have ten o.** (left) il m'en reste dix; **there's some bread o.** il reste du pain; **o. and o. (again)** (often) à plusieurs reprises; **to**

do sth all o. again refaire qch; **three times o.** trois fois; **famous the world o.** célèbre dans le monde entier; **children of five and o.** les enfants de cinq ans et plus ■ **over-fa'miliar** *adj* trop familier, -ière ■ **overin'dulge** *vt (desires, whims)* céder trop facilement à; *(person)* trop gâter ■ **over-sub'scribed** *adj (course)* ayant trop d'inscrits

overall ['əʊvərɔːl] **1** *adj (measurement, length)* total; *(result, effort)* global **2** [əʊvər'ɔːl] *adv* dans l'ensemble **3** *n (protective coat)* blouse *f*; *Am (boiler suit)* bleu *m* de travail ■ **overalls** *npl Br (boiler suit)* bleu *m* de travail; *Am (dungarees)* salopette *f*

overawe [əʊvər'ɔː] *vt* intimider

overbalance [əʊvə'bæləns] *vi (of person)* perdre l'équilibre; *(of pile, load)* se renverser

overbearing [əʊvə'beərɪŋ] *adj* autoritaire

overboard ['əʊvəbɔːd] *adv* par-dessus bord; **man o.!** un homme à la mer!

overbook [əʊvə'bʊk] *vt* surbooker

overburden [əʊvə'bɜːdən] *vt* surcharger

overcast [əʊvə'kɑːst] *adj (sky)* nuageux, -euse

overcharge [əʊvə'tʃɑːdʒ] *vt* **to o. sb for sth** faire payer qch trop cher à qn

overcoat ['əʊvəkəʊt] *n* pardessus *m*

overcome [əʊvə'kʌm] *(pt* **-came***, pp* **-come***) vt (problem, disgust)* surmonter; *(shyness, fear, enemy)* vaincre; **to be o. by grief** être accablé de chagrin; **he was o. by emotion** l'émotion eut raison de lui

overcook [əʊvə'kʊk] *vt* faire cuire trop

overcrowded [əʊvə'kraʊdɪd] *adj (house, country)* surpeuplé; *(bus, train)* bondé ■ **overcrowding** *n* surpeuplement *m*

overdo [əʊvə'duː] *(pt* **-did***, pp* **-done***) vt* exagérer; *(overcook)* faire cuire trop; **to o. it** se surmener

overdose ['əʊvədəʊs] **1** *n* overdose *f* **2** *vi* faire une overdose **(on** de); *Fam* **to o. on chocolate** exagérer avec le chocolat

overdraft ['əʊvədrɑːft] *n Fin* découvert *m* ■ **over'drawn** *adj (account)* à découvert

overdress [əʊvə'dres] *vi* s'habiller avec trop de recherche

overdue [əʊvə'djuː] *adj (train, bus)* en retard; *(bill)* impayé; *(book)* qui n'a pas été rendu

overeat [əʊvər'iːt] *(pt* **-ate***, pp* **-eaten***) vi* manger trop

overestimate [əʊvər'estɪmeɪt] *vt* surestimer

overexcited [əʊvərɪk'saɪtɪd] *adj* surexcité

overfeed [əʊvə'fiːd] *(pt & pp* **-fed***) vt* suralimenter

overflow 1 ['əʊvəfləʊ] *n (outlet)* trop-plein *m*; *Fig (of people, objects)* excédent *m* **2** [əʊvə'fləʊ] *vi (of river, bath)* déborder; **to be overflowing with sth** *(of town, shop, house)* regorger de qch

overgrown [əʊvə'grəʊn] *adj* envahi par la végétation; **o. with weeds** envahi par les mauvaises herbes; *Fig & Pej* **you're an o. schoolgirl** tu as la mentalité d'une écolière

overhang [əʊvə'hæŋ] *(pt & pp* **-hung***) 1 vt* surplomber **2** *vi* faire saillie

overhaul 1 ['əʊvəhɔːl] *n* révision *f* **2** [əʊvə'hɔːl] *vt (vehicle, schedule, text)* réviser

overhead 1 ['əʊvəhed] **1** [əʊvə'hed] *adv* au-dessus **2** *adj (cable)* aérien, -ienne **3** *n Am* = **overheads** ■ **overheads** *npl Br (expenses)* frais *mpl* généraux

overhear [əʊvə'hɪə(r)] *(pt & pp* **-heard***) vt (conversation)* surprendre; *(person)* entendre

overheat [əʊvə'hiːt] **1** *vt* surchauffer **2** *vi (of engine)* chauffer

overjoyed [əʊvə'dʒɔɪd] *adj* fou (*f* folle) de joie

overland ['əʊvəlænd] *adj & adv* par voie de terre

overlap [əʊvə'læp] **1** ['əʊvəlæp] *n* chevauchement *m* **2** *(pt & pp* **-pp-***) vt* chevaucher **3** *vi* se chevaucher

overleaf [əʊvə'liːf] *adv* au verso

overload [əʊvə'ləʊd] *vt* surcharger

overlook [əʊvə'lʊk] *vt* **(a)** *(not notice)* ne pas remarquer; *(forget)* oublier; *(disregard)* fermer les yeux sur **(b)** *(of window, house)* donner sur; *(of tower, fort)* dominer

overly ['əʊvəlɪ] *adv* excessivement

overnight 1 [əʊvə'naɪt] *adv (during the night)* pendant la nuit; *Fig (suddenly)* du jour au lendemain; **to stay o.** passer la nuit **2** ['əʊvənaɪt] *adj (train, flight)* de nuit; *(stay)* d'une nuit; *(clothes)* pour une nuit; **o. bag** (petit) sac *m* de voyage

overpass ['əʊvəpɑːs] *n Am (bridge)* Toboggan® *m*

overpopulated [əʊvə'pɒpjʊleɪtɪd] *adj* surpeuplé

overpower [əʊvə'paʊə(r)] *vt* maîtriser ■ **overpowering** *adj (heat, smell)* suffocant; *(charm, desire)* irrésistible

overpriced [əʊvə'praɪst] *adj* trop cher (*f* trop chère)

overrated [əʊvə'reɪtɪd] *adj* surfait

overreach [əʊvə'riːtʃ] *vt* **to o. oneself** trop présumer de ses forces

overreact [əʊvərɪ'ækt] *vi* réagir excessivement

override [əʊvə'raɪd] *(pt* **-rode***, pp* **-ridden***) vt (be more important than)* l'emporter sur; *(invalidate)* annuler; *(take no notice of)* passer outre à ■ **over'riding** *adj (importance)* capital; *(factor)* prédominant

overrule [əʊvə'ruːl] *vt (decision)* annuler; *(argument, objection)* rejeter

overrun [əʊvə'rʌn] *(pt* **-ran***, pp* **-run***, pres p* **-running***) vt (invade)* envahir; *(go beyond)* dépasser

overseas 1 ['əʊvəsiːz] *adj* d'outre-mer; *(trade, debt)* extérieur **2** [əʊvə'siːz] *adv* à l'étranger

oversee [əʊvə'siː] (pt -saw, pp -seen) vt (work) superviser ▪ **overseer** ['əʊvəsɪə(r)] n (foreman) contremaître m

overshadow [əʊvə'ʃædəʊ] vt (make less important) éclipser; (make gloomy) assombrir

overshoot [əʊvə'ʃuːt] (pt & pp -shot) vt dépasser

oversight ['əʊvəsaɪt] n oubli m, omission f

oversimplify [əʊvə'sɪmplɪfaɪ] (pt & pp -ied) vti trop simplifier

oversize(d) ['əʊvəsaɪz(d)] adj trop grand

oversleep [əʊvə'sliːp] (pt & pp -slept) vi ne pas se réveiller à temps

overspend [əʊvə'spend] (pt & pp -spent) vi dépenser trop

overstaffing [əʊvə'stɑːfɪŋ] n sureffectifs mpl

overstate [əʊvə'steɪt] vt exagérer

overstay [əʊvə'steɪ] vt **to o. one's welcome** abuser de l'hospitalité de son hôte

overstep [əʊvə'step] (pt & pp -pp-) vt outrepasser; Fig **to o. the mark** dépasser les bornes

overt ['əʊvɜːt] adj manifeste

overtake [əʊvə'teɪk] (pt -took, pp -taken) 1 vt dépasser; **overtaken by nightfall** surpris par la nuit 2 vi (in vehicle) doubler, dépasser

overtax [əʊvə'tæks] vt (a) **to o. one's brain** se fatiguer la cervelle; **to o. one's strength** abuser de ses forces (b) (person) surimposer; (goods) surtaxer

overthrow 1 ['əʊvəθrəʊ] n renversement m 2 [əʊvə'θrəʊ] (pt -threw, pp -thrown) vt renverser

overtime ['əʊvətaɪm] 1 n heures fpl supplémentaires 2 adv **to work o.** faire des heures supplémentaires

overtones ['əʊvətəʊnz] npl nuance f (of de)

overture ['əʊvətjʊə(r)] n Mus ouverture f; Fig **to make overtures to sb** faire des avances à qn

overturn [əʊvə'tɜːn] 1 vt (chair, table, car) renverser; (boat) faire chavirer; Fig (decision) annuler 2 vi (of car) capoter; (of boat) chavirer

overweight [əʊvə'weɪt] adj trop gros (f trop grosse)

overwhelm [əʊvə'welm] vt (of feelings, heat) accabler; (enemy, opponent) écraser; (amaze) bouleverser ▪ **overwhelmed** adj (overjoyed) ravi (by or with de); **o. with** (work, offers) submergé de; **o. with grief** accablé par le chagrin; **o. by** (kindness, gift) vivement touché par ▪ **overwhelming** adj (heat, grief) accablant; (majority, defeat) écrasant; (desire) irrésis-

tible; (impression) dominant; **the o. majority of people** l'écrasante majorité des gens ▪ **overwhelmingly** adv (vote, reject) en masse; (utterly) carrément

overwork [əʊvə'wɜːk] 1 n surmenage m 2 vt (person) surcharger de travail 3 vi se surmener

overwrite [əʊvə'raɪt] (pt -wrote, pp -written) Comptr 1 n **o. mode** mode m de superposition 2 vt (file) écraser

overwrought [əʊvə'rɔːt] adj (tense) à bout

owe [əʊ] vt devoir; **to o. sb sth, to o. sth to sb** devoir qch à qn; **I'll o. it to you** je te le devrai; **to o. it to oneself to do sth** se devoir de faire qch ▪ **owing 1** adj the money o. **to me** l'argent que l'on me doit 2 prep **o. to** à cause de

owl [aʊl] n hibou m (pl -oux)

own [əʊn] 1 adj propre; **my o. house** ma propre maison 2 pron **my o.** le mien, la mienne; **a house of his o.** sa propre maison, sa maison à lui; **it's my (very) o.** c'est à moi (tout seul); **to do sth on one's o.** faire qch tout seul; **to be (all) on one's o.** être tout seul; **to get one's o. back (on sb)** se venger (de qn); **to come into one's o.** montrer ce dont il est capable 3 vt (possess) posséder; **who owns this ball?** à qui appartient cette balle? 4 vi **to o. up** (confess) avouer; **to o. up to sth** avouer qch

own-brand ['əʊnbrænd] adj Com vendu sous la marque du distributeur

owner ['əʊnə(r)] n propriétaire mf ▪ **ownership** n possession f; **to encourage home o.** encourager l'accession à la propriété; Econ **to be in public o.** appartenir au secteur public

ox [ɒks] (pl **oxen** ['ɒksən]) n bœuf m ▪ **oxtail** n Culin queue f de bœuf

Oxfam ['ɒksfæm] n Br = œuvre de bienfaisance travaillant pour le Tiers Monde; **O. shop** = magasin où l'œuvre de bienfaisance Oxfam vend des articles d'occasion et d'artisanat au profit du tiers-monde

oxide ['ɒksaɪd] n Chem oxyde m ▪ **oxidize** ['ɒksɪdaɪz] Chem 1 vt oxyder 2 vi s'oxyder

oxygen ['ɒksɪdʒən] n oxygène m; **o. mask/tent** masque m/tente f à oxygène

oyster ['ɔɪstə(r)] n huître f

Oz [ɒz] n Fam Australie f ▪ **Ozzie** n Fam Australien, -ienne mf

oz (abbr ounce) once f

ozone ['əʊzəʊn] n Chem ozone m; **o. friendly** (product) qui préserve la couche d'ozone; **o. layer** couche f d'ozone

P, p¹ [piː] *n (letter)* P, p *m inv*

p² [piː] *(abbr* **penny, pence)** *Br* penny *m*/pence *mpl*

PA [piːˈeɪ] *n* **(a)** *(abbr* **personal assistant)** secrétaire *mf* de direction **(b)** *(abbr* **public address)** **PA (system)** système *m* de sonorisation

pace [peɪs] **1** *n (speed)* allure *f; (step, measure)* pas *m;* **to set the p.** donner l'allure; **to keep p. with sb** *(follow)* suivre qn; *(in quality of work)* se maintenir à la hauteur de qn **2** *vi* **to p. up and down** faire les cent pas **▪** *vt (room)* arpenter

pacemaker [ˈpeɪsmeɪkə(r)] *n (for heart)* stimulateur *m* cardiaque

Pacific [pəˈsɪfɪk] *adj (coast)* pacifique; **the P. (Ocean)** le Pacifique, l'océan *m* Pacifique

pacifist [ˈpæsɪfɪst] *n & adj* pacifiste *(mf)*

pacify [ˈpæsɪfaɪ] *(pt & pp* **-ied)** *vt (country)* pacifier; *(crowd, person)* calmer **▪ pacifier** *n Am (of baby)* tétine *f*

pack [pæk] **1** *n* **(a)** *(of cigarettes, washing powder)* paquet *m; (of beer, milk)* & *Rugby* pack *m; (of cards)* jeu *m; (of hounds, wolves)* meute *f; (of runners, cyclists)* peloton *m; (of thieves)* bande *f;* **a p. of lies** un tissu de mensonges; **p. animal** animal *m* de bât; **p. ice** banquise *f* **(b)** *(rucksack)* sac *m* à dos; *(of soldier)* paquetage *m* **2** *vt (fill)* remplir **(with** de); *(excessively)* bourrer; *(object into box, suitcase)* mettre; *(make into package)* empaqueter; *(crush, compress)* tasser; **to p. one's bags** faire ses valises **3** *vi (fill one's bags)* faire sa valise/ses valises **▪ packed** *adj (bus, room)* bondé; *Br* **p. lunch** = déjeuner que l'on emporte à l'école ou au bureau; *Br Fam* **p. out** *(crowded)* bourré **▪ packing** *n (material, action)* emballage *m;* **to do one's p.** faire sa valise/ses valises

▶ pack away *vt sep (tidy away)* ranger

▶ pack down *vt sep (crush, compress)* tasser

▶ pack in *vt sep Br Fam (stop)* arrêter; *(give up)* laisser tomber; **p. it in!** laisse tomber!

▶ pack into 1 *vt sep (cram)* entasser dans; *(put)* mettre dans **2** *vt insep (crowd into)* s'entasser dans

▶ pack off *vt sep Fam (person)* expédier

▶ pack up 1 *vt sep (put into box)* emballer; *(put into suitcase)* mettre dans sa valise; *Fam (give up)* laisser tomber **2** *vi* faire sa valise/ses valises; *Fam (stop)* s'arrêter; *(of machine, vehicle)* tomber en panne

package [ˈpækɪdʒ] **1** *n* paquet *m; (contract)* contrat *m* global; *Br* **p. deal** *or* **holiday** forfait *m (comprenant au moins transport et logement);* **p. tourism** tourisme *m* organisé **2** *vt* emballer **▪ packaging** *n (material, action)* emballage *m*

packet [ˈpækɪt] *n* paquet *m; Fam* **to cost a p.** coûter les yeux de la tête; *Fam* **to make a p.** se faire un fric fou

pact [pækt] *n* pacte *m*

pad [pæd] **1** *n (of cotton wool)* tampon *m; (for writing)* bloc *m; Fam (home)* piaule *f;* **ink p.** tampon encreur; **shin p.** jambière *f;* **shoulder p.** *(in jacket)* épaulette *f* **2** *(pt & pp* **-dd-)** *vt (furniture)* capitonner **(with** avec); *(clothes)* matelasser; **to p. out** *(speech, essay)* étoffer **▪ padded** *adj (armchair)* capitonné; *(jacket)* matelassé **▪ padding** *n (material)* rembourrage *m; (in speech, essay)* remplissage *m*

paddle [ˈpædəl] **1** *n (for canoe)* pagaie *f;* **p. boat** bateau *m* à aubes; **to have a p.** patauger **2** *vt* **to p. a canoe** pagayer **3** *vi (in canoe)* pagayer; *(walk in water)* patauger **▪ paddling pool** *n Br (inflatable)* piscine *f* gonflable; *(in park)* pataugeoire *f*

paddock [ˈpædək] *n* enclos *m; (at racecourse)* paddock *m*

paddy [ˈpædɪ] *(pl* **-ies)** *n* **p.** *(field)* rizière *f*

padlock [ˈpædlɒk] **1** *n* cadenas *m* **2** *vt* cadenasser

paediatrician [piːdɪəˈtrɪʃən] *(Am* **pediatrician)** *n* pédiatre *mf* **▪ paediatrics** [-dɪˈætrɪks] *(Am* **pediatrics)** *n* pédiatrie *f*

paedophile [ˈpiːdəfaɪl] *(Am* **pedophile)** *n* pédophile *mf* **▪ paedophilia** [-ˈfɪlɪə] *(Am* **pedophilia)** *n* pédophilie *f*

pagan [ˈpeɪgən] *adj & n* païen, -enne *(mf)* **▪ paganism** *n* paganisme *m*

page¹ [peɪdʒ] *n (of book)* page *f;* **on p. 6** à la page 6

page² [peɪdʒ] *n Hist (at court)* page *m;* **p. (boy)** *(in hotel)* groom *m; (at wedding)* garçon *m* d'honneur

page³ [peɪdʒ] *vt* **to p. sb** faire appeler qn; *(by electronic device)* biper qn **▪ pager** *n* récepteur *m* d'appel

pageant [ˈpædʒənt] *n* grand spectacle *m* **▪ pageantry** *n* pompe *f*

pagoda [pəˈgəʊdə] *n* pagode *f*

paid [peɪd] **1** *pt & pp* de **pay 2** *adj (person, work)* rémunéré; *Br* **to put p. to sb's hopes** anéantir les espoirs de qn; *Br* **to put p. to sb** *(ruin)* couler qn

pail [peɪl] *n* seau *m*

pain [peɪn] **1** *n (physical)* douleur *f; (emotional)* peine *f;* **to have a p. in one's arm** avoir une douleur au bras; **to be in p.** souffrir; **to go to** *or* **take (great) pains to do sth** se donner du mal pour faire qch; **to go to** *or* **take (great) pains not to do sth** prendre bien soin de ne pas faire qch; *Fam* **to be a p. (in the neck)** être casse-pieds **2** *vt* peiner ▪ **painful** *adj (physically)* douloureux, -euse; *(emotionally)* pénible; *Fam (bad)* nul *(f* nulle) ▪ **painfully** *adv (walk)* avec difficulté; *Fig* **p. shy** d'une timidité maladive; *Fig* **p. boring** ennuyeux, -euse à mourir ▪ **painless** *adj (not painful)* indolore; *Fam (easy)* facile ▪ **painlessly** *adv* sans douleur; *(easily)* sans effort

painkiller ['peɪnkɪlə(r)] *n* calmant *m;* **on painkillers** sous calmants

painstaking ['peɪnzteɪkɪŋ] *adj* minutieux, -ieuse ▪ **painstakingly** *adv* avec un soin minutieux

paint [peɪnt] **1** *n* peinture *f;* **'wet p.'** *(on sign)* 'peinture fraîche'; **p. stripper** décapant *m* **2** *vt* peindre; **to p. sth blue** peindre qch en bleu **3** *vi* peindre ▪ **painter** *n* peintre *m; Br* **p. and decorator,** *Am* **(house) p.** peintre-tapissier *m* ▪ **painting** *n (activity)* la peinture; *(picture)* tableau *m,* peinture *f*

paintball ['peɪntbɔːl] *n* paintball *m* ▪ **paint-balling** *n* **to go p.** faire du paintball

paintbrush ['peɪntbrʌʃ] *n* pinceau *m*

paintwork ['peɪntwɜːk] *n (of building, vehicle)* peinture *f*

pair [peə(r)] **1** *n* paire *f;* **a p. of shorts** un short **2** *vt* **to p. sb with sb** mettre qn avec qn **3** *vi* **to p. off** *(of people)* se mettre deux par deux

pajama(s) [pə'dʒɑːmə(z)] *adj & npl Am =* **pyjama(s)**

Pakistan [pɑːkɪ'stɑːn] *n* le Pakistan ▪ **Pakistani 1** *adj* pakistanais **2** *n* Pakistanais, -aise *mf*

pal [pæl] *n Fam* copain *m,* copine *f* ▪ **pally (-ier, -iest)** *adj Fam* **to be p. with sb** être copain *(f* copine) avec qn

palace ['pælɪs] *n* palais *m* ▪ **palatial** [pə'leɪʃəl] *adj* grandiose

Note that the French word **palace** is a false friend and is never a translation for the English word **palace**. It means **luxury hotel**.

palatable ['pælətəbəl] *adj (food)* agréable au palais; *Fig (idea, fact)* acceptable

palate ['pælɪt] *n (in mouth)* palais *m*

palaver [pə'lɑːvə(r)] *n Br Fam (fuss)* histoire *f*

pale [peɪl] **1 (-er, -est)** *adj* pâle; *Br* **p. ale** = bière blonde **2** *vi* pâlir ▪ **paleness** *n* pâleur *f*

Palestine ['pæləstaɪn] *n* la Palestine ▪ **Pal-estinian** [-'stɪnɪən] **1** *adj* palestinien, -ienne **2** *n* Palestinien, -ienne *mf*

palette ['pælɪt] *n (of artist)* palette *f*

palings ['peɪlɪŋz] *n (fence)* palissade *f*

pall¹ [pɔːl] *n (of smoke)* voile *m*

pall² [pɔːl] *vi (become uninteresting)* perdre son attrait

pallbearer ['pɔːlbeərə(r)] *n =* personne qui aide à porter un cercueil

pallid ['pælɪd] *adj* pâle ▪ **pallor** *n* pâleur *f*

palm¹ [pɑːm] **1** *n (of hand)* paume *f* **2** *vt Fam* **to p. sth off on sb** refiler qch à qn

palm² [pɑːm] *n (symbol)* palme *f;* **p. (tree)** palmier *m;* **p. (leaf)** palme; **P. Sunday** le Dimanche des Rameaux

palmist ['pɑːmɪst] *n* chiromancien, -ienne *mf*

palpable ['pælpəbəl] *adj (obvious)* manifeste

palpitate ['pælpɪteɪt] *vi* palpiter ▪ **palpi'tation** *n* palpitation *f;* **to have** *or* **get palpitations** avoir des palpitations

paltry ['pɔːltrɪ] **(-ier, -iest)** *adj (sum)* dérisoire; *(excuse)* piètre

pamper ['pæmpə(r)] *vt* dorloter; **to p. oneself** se dorloter

pamphlet ['pæmflɪt] *n* brochure *f; (political)* pamphlet *m*

Note that the French word **pamphlet** can be a false friend. It always refers to a satirical tract.

pan [pæn] **1** *n (saucepan)* casserole *f; (for frying)* poêle *f; Br (of lavatory)* cuvette *f; Fam* **to go down the p.** *(work, plans)* s'en aller en fumée **2** *(pt & pp* **-nn-)** *vt Fam (criticize)* descendre en flammes **3** *vi Fam* **to p. out** *(turn out)* marcher

panacea [pænə'sɪə] *n* panacée *f*

panache [pə'næʃ] *n* panache *m*

Panama ['pænəmɑː] *n* le Panama; **the P. Canal** le canal de Panama

pancake ['pænkeɪk] *n* crêpe *f; Br* **P. Day** mardi *m* gras

pancreas ['pæŋkrɪəs] *n Anat* pancréas *m*

panda ['pændə] *n* panda *m*

pandemonium [pændɪ'məʊnɪəm] *n (confusion)* chaos *m; (uproar)* vacarme *m*

pander ['pændə(r)] *vi* **to p. to sb/sth** flatter qn/qch

pane [peɪn] *n* vitre *f*

panel ['pænəl] *n* **(a)** *(of door)* panneau *m;* **(instrument) p.** *(in aircraft, vehicle)* tableau *m* de bord **(b)** *(of judges)* jury *m; (of experts)* comité *m; (of TV or radio guests)* invités *mpl;* **p. game** *(on TV)* jeu *m* télévisé; *(on radio)* jeu radiodiffusé

panelled ['pænəld] *(Am* **paneled)** *adj (room)* lambrissé ▪ **panelling** *(Am* **paneling)** *n* lambris *m*

panellist ['pænəlɪst] *(Am* **panelist)** *n (on radio, TV)* invité, -ée *mf*

pangs [pæŋz] *npl* **p. of conscience** remords *mpl*; **p. of hunger** tiraillements *mpl* d'estomac; **p. of jealousy** affres *fpl* de la jalousie

panic ['pænɪk] **1** *n* panique *f*; **to get into a p.** paniquer **2** (*pt & pp* **-ck-**) *vi* paniquer ▪ **panicky** *adj Fam* **to get p.** paniquer ▪ **panic-stricken** *adj* pris de panique

panorama [pænə'rɑ:mə] *n* panorama *m* ▪ **panoramic** [-'ræmɪk] *adj* panoramique

pansy ['pænzɪ] (*pl* **-ies**) *n* (**a**) (*flower*) pensée *f* (**b**) *Pej* (*effeminate man*) tante *f*

pant [pænt] *vi* haleter

panther ['pænθə(r)] *n* panthère *f*

panties ['pæntɪz] *npl* petite culotte *f*

pantomime ['pæntəmaɪm] *n Br* (*show*) = spectacle de Noël

> Note that the French word **pantomime** is a false friend and is never a translation for the English word **pantomime**. It means **mime**.

pantry ['pæntrɪ] (*pl* **-ies**) *n* (*larder*) garde-manger *m inv*; (*storeroom in hotel, ship*) office *m*

pants [pænts] **1** *npl Br* (*underwear*) slip *m*; *Am* (*trousers*) pantalon *m* **2** *adj Br Fam* nul (*f* nulle) **3** *exclam Br Fam* **oh, p.!** mince!

pantyhose ['pæntɪhəʊz] *n Am* (*tights*) collant *m*

papacy ['peɪpəsɪ] *n* papauté *f* ▪ **papal** *adj* papal

paparazzi [pæpə'rætsɪ] *npl* paparazzi *mpl*

papaya [pə'paɪə] *n* (*fruit*) papaye *f*; (*tree*) papayer *m*

paper ['peɪpə(r)] **1** *n* papier *m*; (*newspaper*) journal *m*; (*wallpaper*) papier peint; (*exam*) épreuve *f* écrite; (*student's exercise*) copie *f*; (*scholarly study, report*) article *m*; **a piece of p.** un bout de papier; **to put sth down on p.** mettre qch par écrit; **brown p.** papier d'emballage; **papers** (*documents*) papiers *m* **2** *adj* (*bag*) en papier; (*cup, plate*) en carton; **p. mill** papeterie *f*; **p. money** papier-monnaie *m*; **p. round** tournée *f* de distribution des journaux; *Br* **p. shop** marchand *m* de journaux; **p. towel** essuie-tout *m inv*; *Comptr* **p. tray** chariot *m* d'alimentation en papier **3** *vt* (*room, wall*) tapisser ▪ **paperback** *n* livre *m* de poche ▪ **paperboy** *n* (*delivering papers*) livreur *m* de journaux ▪ **paperclip** *n* trombone *m* ▪ **paperknife** (*pl* **-knives**) *n* coupe-papier *m* ▪ **paperweight** *n* presse-papiers *m inv* ▪ **paperwork** *n* (*in office*) écritures *fpl*; *Pej* (*red tape*) paperasserie *f*

paprika ['pæprɪkə, pə'pri:kə] *n* paprika *m*

par [pɑ:(r)] *n Golf* par *m*; **to be under/over p.** être en dessous/au-dessus du par; *Fam* **that's p. for the course** c'est ce à quoi il faut s'attendre; *Fig* **on a p.** au même niveau (**with** que); *Fam* **to feel under p.** ne pas être dans son assiette

parable ['pærəbəl] *n* (*story*) parabole *f*

paracetamol [pærə'si:təmɒl] *n* paracétamol *m*; **take two p.** prenez deux cachets de paracétamol

parachute ['pærəʃu:t] **1** *n* parachute *m*; **p. jump** saut *m* en parachute **2** *vt* parachuter **3** *vi* sauter en parachute ▪ **parachutist** *n* parachutiste *mf*

parade [pə'reɪd] **1** *n* (**a**) (*procession*) défilé *m*; **to make a p. of sth** faire étalage de qch; *Mil* **p. ground** terrain *m* de manœuvres (**b**) *Br* (*street*) avenue *f*; **a p. of shops** une rangée de magasins **2** *vt* (*troops*) faire défiler; *Fig* (*wealth, knowledge*) faire étalage de **3** *vi* (*of troops*) défiler; **to p. about** (*of person*) se pavaner

paradise ['pærədaɪs] *n* paradis *m*

paradox ['pærədɒks] *n* paradoxe *m* ▪ **paradoxically** *adv* paradoxalement

paraffin ['pærəfɪn] *n Br* pétrole *m* lampant; *Am* (*wax*) paraffine *f*; *Br* **p. lamp** lampe *f* à pétrole

paragliding ['pærəglaɪdɪŋ] *n* parapente *m*; **to go p.** faire du parapente

paragon ['pærəgən] *n* **p. of virtue** modèle *m* de vertu

paragraph ['pærəgrɑ:f] *n* paragraphe *m*; **'new p.'** (*in dictation*) 'à la ligne'

Paraguay ['pærəgwaɪ] *n* le Paraguay

parakeet ['pærəki:t] *n* perruche *f*

parallel ['pærəlel] **1** *adj Math* parallèle (**with** *or* **to** à); *Fig* (*comparable*) semblable (**with** *or* **to** à); **to run p. to** *or* **with sth** être parallèle à qch **2** *n Math* (*line*) parallèle *f*; *Fig* (*comparison*) & *Geog* parallèle *m* **3** *vt* être semblable à

paralyse (*Am* **paralyze**) ['pærəlaɪz] *vt* paralyser ▪ **paralysis** [pə'ræləsɪs] (*pl* **-yses** [-əsi:z]) *n* paralysie *f* ▪ **paralytic** [pærə'lɪtɪk] **1** *adj & n* paralytique (*mf*) **2** *adj Br Fam* (*very drunk*) ivre mort

paramedic [pærə'medɪk] *n* auxiliaire *mf* médical(e)

parameter [pə'ræmɪtə(r)] *n* paramètre *m*

paramilitary [pærə'mɪlɪtrɪ] *adj & n* paramilitaire (*mf*)

paramount ['pærəmaʊnt] *adj* **of p. importance** de la plus haute importance

paranoia [pærə'nɔɪə] *n* paranoïa *f* ▪ **paranoid** *adj & n* paranoïaque (*mf*)

parapet ['pærəpɪt] *n* parapet *m*

paraphernalia [pærəfə'neɪlɪə] *n* attirail *m*

paraphrase ['pærəfreɪz] **1** *n* paraphrase *f* **2** *vt* paraphraser

paraplegic [pærə'pli:dʒɪk] *n* paraplégique *mf*

parascending ['pærəsendɪŋ] *n* parachute *m* ascensionnel

parasite ['pærəsaɪt] *n* (*person, organism*) parasite *m*

parasol ['pærəsɒl] *n* (*over table, on beach*) parasol *m*; (*lady's umbrella*) ombrelle *f*

paratrooper ['pærətru:pə(r)] *n* parachutiste *m*

parboil [pɑ:'bɔɪl] *vt Culin* faire cuire à demi

parcel ['pɑ:səl] 1 *n* colis *m*, paquet *m*; **to be part and p. of sth** faire partie intégrante de qch; **p. bomb** colis piégé 2 (*Br* **-ll-,** *Am* **-l-**) *vt* **to p. sth out** répartir; **to p. sth up** empaqueter

parch [pɑ:tʃ] *vt* dessécher; **to be parched** (*of person*) être assoiffé; **to make sb parched** donner très soif à qn

parchment ['pɑ:tʃmənt] *n* parchemin *m*

pardon ['pɑ:dən] 1 *n* (*forgiveness*) pardon *m*; *Law* grâce *f*; **I beg your p.** (*apologizing*) je vous prie de m'excuser; **p.?** (*not hearing*) pardon? 2 *vt Law* grâcier; **to p. sb (for sth)** pardonner (qch) à qn; **p. (me)!** (*sorry*) pardon!

pare [peə(r)] *vt* (*trim*) rogner; (*peel*) éplucher; *Fig* **to p. sth down** réduire qch

parent ['peərənt] *n* père *m*/mère *f*; **parents** parents *mpl*; **p. company,** *Br* **p. firm** maison *f* mère ▪ **parental** [pə'rentəl] *adj* parental ▪ **parenthood** *n* paternité *f*/maternité *f*, parentalité *f*

parenthesis [pə'renθəsɪs] (*pl* **-eses** [-əsi:z]) *n* parenthèse *f*

Paris ['pærɪs] *n* Paris *m* ou *f* ▪ **Parisian** [*Br* pə'rɪzɪən, *Am* pə'ri:ʒən] 1 *adj* parisien, -ienne 2 *n* Parisien, -ienne *mf*

parish ['pærɪʃ] 1 *n* (*religious*) paroisse *f*, (*civil*) ≃ commune *f* 2 *adj* (*church, register, hall*) paroissial; **p. council** conseil *m* municipal ▪ **parishioner** [pə'rɪʃənə(r)] *n* paroissien, -ienne *mf*

parity ['pærɪtɪ] *n* égalité *f* (**with** avec; **between** entre)

park¹ [pɑ:k] *n* (*garden*) parc *m*; **p. keeper** gardien, -ienne *mf* de parc; **business/science p.** zone *f* commerciale/scientifique; **national p.** parc national

park² [pɑ:k] 1 *vt* (*vehicle*) garer 2 *vi* (*of vehicle*) se garer; (*remain parked*) stationner ▪ **parking** *n* stationnement *m*; **'no p.'** 'défense de stationner'; **p. bay** place *f* de parking; *Br* **p. lights** (*on car*) feux *mpl* de position; *Am* **p. lot** parking *m*; **p. meter** parcmètre *m*; **p. place** *or* **space** place *f* de parking; **p. ticket** contravention *f*

parka ['pɑ:kə] *n* parka *f* ou *m*

parkland ['pɑ:klænd] *n* espace *m* vert

parkway ['pɑ:kweɪ] *n Am* avenue *f*

parliament ['pɑ:ləmənt] *n* parlement *m*; ▪ **parliamentary** [-'mentərɪ] *adj* parlementaire

parlour ['pɑ:lə(r)] (*Am* **parlor**) *n* (*in mansion*) salon *m*; **p. game** jeu *m* de société

parochial [pə'rəʊkɪəl] *adj Rel* paroissial; *Pej* (*mentality, quarrel*) de clocher; *Pej* (*person*) provincial; *Am* **p. school** école *f* catholique

parody ['pærədɪ] 1 (*pl* **-ies**) *n* parodie *f* 2 (*pt & pp* **-ied**) *vt* parodier

parole [pə'rəʊl] *n Law* **to be (out) on p.** être en liberté conditionnelle

parquet ['pɑ:keɪ] *n* **p. (floor)** parquet *m*

parrot ['pærət] *n* perroquet *m*; *Pej* **p. fashion** comme un perroquet

parry ['pærɪ] 1 (*pl* **-ies**) *n* (*in fencing, boxing*) parade *f* 2 (*pt & pp* **-ied**) *vt* (*blow*) parer; (*question*) éluder

parsley ['pɑ:slɪ] *n* persil *m*

parsnip ['pɑ:snɪp] *n* panais *m*

parson ['pɑ:sən] *n* pasteur *m*

part¹ [pɑ:t] 1 *n* partie *f*; (*quantity in mixture*) mesure *f*; (*of machine*) pièce *f*; (*of serial*) épisode *m*; (*role in play, film*) rôle *m*; *Am* (*in hair*) raie *f*; **to take p.** participer (**in** à); **to take sb's p.** (*side*) prendre parti pour qn; **to be a p. of sth** faire partie de qch; **in p.** en partie; **for the most p.** dans l'ensemble; **on the p. of...** de la part de...; **for my p.** pour ma part; **in these parts** dans ces parages; **p. exchange** reprise *f*; **to take sth in p. exchange** reprendre qch; **p. owner** copropriétaire *mf*; **p. payment** paiement *m* partiel 2 *adv* (*partly*) en partie; **p. silk, p. cotton** soie et coton

part² [pɑ:t] 1 *vt* (*separate*) séparer; (*crowd*) écarter; **to p. one's hair** se faire une raie; **to p. company with sb** (*leave sb*) quitter qn 2 *vi* (*of friends*) se quitter; (*of married couple*) se séparer; **to p. with sth** se défaire de qch ▪ **parting** *n* (*separation*) séparation *f*; *Br* (*in hair*) raie *f*

partake [pɑ:'teɪk] (*pt* **-took,** *pp* **-taken**) *vi Formal* **to p. in sth** prendre part à qch; **to p. of a meal** prendre un repas

partial ['pɑ:ʃəl] *adj* (*not total*) partiel, -ielle; (*biased*) partial (**towards** envers); **to be p. to sth** avoir un faible pour qch ▪ **partiality** [-ʃɪ'ælɪtɪ] (*pl* **-ies**) *n* (*bias*) partialité *f*; (*liking*) faible *m*

participate [pɑ:'tɪsɪpeɪt] *vi* participer (**in** à) ▪ **participant** *n* participant, -ante *mf* ▪ **partici'pation** *n* participation *f*

participle [pɑ:'tɪsɪpəl] *n Grammar* participe *m*

particle ['pɑ:tɪkəl] *n* (*of atom, dust, name*) particule *f*; (*of truth*) grain *m*

particular [pə'tɪkjʊlə(r)] 1 *adj* (*specific, special*) particulier, -ière; (*exacting*) méticuleux, -euse; **this p. book** ce livre en particulier; **to be p. about sth** faire très attention à qch 2 *n* **in p.** en particulier ▪ **particularly** *adv* particulièrement ▪ **particulars** *npl* (*details*) détails *mpl*; **to go into p.** entrer dans les détails; **to take down sb's p.** noter les coordonnées de qn

partisan [*Br* pɑ:tɪ'zæn, *Am* 'pɑ:tɪzən] *n* partisan *m*

partition [pɑ:'tɪʃən] 1 *n* (*of room*) cloison *f*; *Pol* (*of country*) partition *f* 2 *vt* (*country*) partager; **to p. sth off** cloisonner qch

partly ['pɑ:tlɪ] *adv* en partie

partner ['pɑ:tnə(r)] n (in game) partenaire mf; (in business) associé, -iée mf; (of racing driver) coéquipier, -ière mf; (in relationship) compagnon m, compagne f; **(dancing) p.** cavalier, -ière mf ▪ **partnership** n association f; **to take sb into p.** prendre qn comme associé(e); **in p. with** en association avec

partridge ['pɑ:trɪdʒ] n perdrix f

part-time ['pɑ:t'taɪm] adj & adv à temps partiel

party ['pɑ:tɪ] (pl -ies) n (a) (gathering) fête f; **to have** or **throw a p.** donner une fête (b) (group) groupe m; (political) parti m; Law (in contract, lawsuit) partie f; **to be (a) p. to sth** être complice de qch; **p. line** (telephone line) ligne f commune (à plusieurs abonnés); Pol ligne du parti

pass¹ [pɑ:s] n (over mountains) col m

pass² [pɑ:s] n (entry permit) laissez-passer m inv; (for travel) carte f d'abonnement; (in sport) passe f; Fam **to make a p. at sb** faire des avances à qn; Br **to get a p.** (in exam) avoir la moyenne; **p. mark** (in exam) moyenne

pass³ [pɑ:s] 1 vt (move, give) passer (**to** à); (go past) passer devant; (vehicle, runner) dépasser; (exam) être reçu à; (bill, law) voter; **to p. sb** (in street) croiser qn; **to p. the time** passer le temps; **to p. judgement on sb** porter un jugement sur qn; Law **to p. sentence** prononcer le verdict 2 vi (go past, go away) passer (**to** à; **through** par); (overtake in vehicle) dépasser; (in exam) avoir la moyenne; (of time) passer; **he can p. for thirty** on lui donnerait trente ans

▸ **pass along** vi passer
▸ **pass away** vi décéder
▸ **pass by** 1 vt insep (building) passer devant; **to p. by sb** (in street) croiser qn 2 vi passer à côté
▸ **pass off** vt sep **to p. oneself off as sb** se faire passer pour qn
▸ **pass on** 1 vt sep (message, illness, title) transmettre (**to** à) 2 vi **to p. on to sth** (move on to) passer à qch
▸ **pass out** 1 vt sep (hand out) distribuer 2 vi (faint) s'évanouir
▸ **pass over** vt insep (ignore) passer sur
▸ **pass round** vt sep (cakes, document) faire passer; (hand out) distribuer
▸ **pass through** vi passer
▸ **pass up** vt sep (opportunity) laisser passer

passable ['pɑ:səbəl] adj (not bad) passable; (road) praticable; (river) franchissable

passage ['pæsɪdʒ] n (a) (act of passing, way through) passage m; (corridor) couloir m; (by boat) traversée f; **with the p. of time** avec le temps (b) (of text) passage m ▪ **passageway** n (corridor) couloir m; (alleyway, way through) passage m

passbook ['pɑ:sbʊk] n livret m de caisse d'épargne

passenger ['pæsɪndʒə(r)] n passager, -ère mf; (on train) voyageur, -euse mf

passer-by [pɑ:sə'baɪ] (pl **passers-by**) n passant, -ante mf

passing ['pɑ:sɪŋ] 1 adj (vehicle) qui passe; (beauty) passager, -ère; **p. place** (on road) aire f de croisement 2 n (of vehicle, visitor) passage m; (of time) écoulement m; (death) disparition f; **in p.** en passant

passion ['pæʃən] n passion f; **to have a p. for sth** adorer qch; **p. fruit** fruit m de la passion ▪ **passionate** adj passionné ▪ **passionately** adv passionnément

passive ['pæsɪv] 1 adj passif, -ive; **p. smoking** tabagisme m passif 2 n Grammar passif m; **in the p.** au passif

Passover ['pɑ:səʊvə(r)] n Rel la Pâque juive

passport ['pɑ:spɔ:t] n passeport m; **p. control** contrôle m des passeports; **p. photo** photo f d'identité

password ['pɑ:swɜ:d] n mot m de passe

past [pɑ:st] 1 n passé m; **in the p.** autrefois; **it's a thing of the p.** ça n'existe plus 2 adj (gone by) passé; (former) ancien, -ienne; **these p. months** ces derniers mois; **that's all p.** c'est du passé; **to be master at sth** être passé maître dans l'art de qch; Grammar **in the p. tense** au passé 3 prep (in front of) devant; (after) après; (beyond) au-delà de; **it's p. four o'clock** il est quatre heures passées; **to be p. fifty** avoir cinquante ans passés; Fam **to be p. it** avoir fait son temps; Fam **I wouldn't put it p. him** il en est bien capable 4 adv devant; **to go p.** passer; **to run p.** passer en courant

pasta ['pæstə] n pâtes fpl

paste [peɪst] 1 n (a) (mixture) pâte f; (of meat, fish) pâté m (b) (glue) colle f 2 vt coller; **to p. sth up** coller qch

pastel [Br 'pæstəl, Am pæ'stel] 1 n pastel m 2 adj (drawing) au pastel; **p. shade** ton m pastel inv

pasteurized ['pæstʃəraɪzd] adj **p. milk** lait m pasteurisé

pastiche [pæ'sti:ʃ] n pastiche m

pastille [Br 'pæstɪl, Am pæ'sti:l] n pastille f

pastime ['pɑ:staɪm] n passe-temps m inv

pastor ['pɑ:stə(r)] n Rel pasteur m ▪ **pastoral** adj pastoral; Sch **p. care** ≃ tutorat m

pastry ['peɪstrɪ] (pl -ies) n (dough) pâte f; (cake) pâtisserie f ▪ **pastrychef, pastrycook** n pâtissier, -ière mf

pasture ['pɑ:stʃə(r)] n pré m, pâture f

pasty¹ ['pæstɪ] (pl -ies) n (pie) feuilleté m

pasty² ['peɪstɪ] (-ier, -iest) adj (complexion) terreux, -euse

pat [pæt] 1 n (tap) petite tape f; (of animal) caresse f 2 adv **to answer p.** avoir la réponse toute prête; **to know sth off p.** savoir qch sur le bout du doigt 3 (pt & pp -tt-) vt (tap) tapoter; (animal) caresser

patch [pætʃ] **1** *n* (for clothes) pièce *f*; (over eye) bandeau *m*; (tyre) Rustine® *f*; (of colour) tache *f*; (of fog) nappe *f*; (of ice) plaque *f*; **a cabbage p.** un carré de choux; **a p. of blue sky** un coin de ciel bleu; *Fig* **to be going through a bad p.** traverser une mauvaise passe; *Fam* **not to be a p. on** (not as good as) (of person) ne pas arriver à la cheville de; (of thing) n'être rien à côté de **2** *vt* **to p. (up)** (clothing) rapiécer; **to p. sth up** (marriage, friendship) raccommoder; **to p. things up** (after argument) se raccommoder

patchwork ['pætʃwɜːk] *n* patchwork *m*; **p. quilt** couverture *f* en patchwork

patchy ['pætʃɪ] (**-ier, -iest**) *adj* inégal

patent 1 ['peɪtənt] *adj* manifeste; **p. leather** cuir *m* verni **2** ['peɪtənt, 'pætənt] *n* brevet *m* d'invention **3** *vt* (faire) breveter ▪ **patently** *adv* manifestement; **it's p. obvious** c'est absolument évident

paternal [pə'tɜːnəl] *adj* paternel, -elle ▪ **paternity** *n* paternité *f*; **p. leave** congé *m* de paternité; **p. test** test *m* de paternité

path [pɑːθ] *n* (*pl* **-s** [pɑːðz]) *n* chemin *m*; (narrow) sentier *m*; (in park) allée *f*; (of river) cours *m*; (of bullet, rocket, planet) trajectoire *f*; **the storm destroyed everything in its p.** la tempête a tout détruit sur son passage

pathetic [pə'θetɪk] *adj* (useless) lamentable

Note that the French word **pathétique** is never used to mean **useless**. It only means **moving**.

pathology [pə'θɒlədʒɪ] *n* pathologie *f* ▪ **pathological** [pæθə'lɒdʒɪkəl] *adj* pathologique

pathos ['peɪθɒs] *n* pathétique *m*

pathway ['pɑːθweɪ] *n* sentier *m*

patience ['peɪʃəns] *n* (**a**) (quality) patience *f*; **to lose p.** perdre patience (**with sb** avec qn); **I have no p. with him** il m'énerve (**b**) *Br* (card game) réussite *f*; **to play p.** faire une réussite

patient ['peɪʃənt] **1** *adj* patient **2** *n* patient, -iente *mf* ▪ **patiently** *adv* patiemment

patio ['pætɪəʊ] (*pl* **-os**) *n* patio *m*; *Br* **p. doors** portes *f* vitrées (donnant sur un patio)

patriot ['pætrɪət, 'peɪtrɪət] *n* patriote *mf* ▪ **patriotic** [-rɪ'ɒtɪk] *adj* (views, speech) patriotique; (person) patriote ▪ **patriotism** *n* patriotisme *m*

patrol [pə'trəʊl] **1** *n* patrouille *f*; **to be on p.** être de patrouille; **p. boat** patrouilleur *m*; **p. car** voiture *f* de police **2** (*pt & pp* **-ll-**) *vt* patrouiller dans **3** *vi* patrouiller ▪ **patrolman** (*pl* **-men**) *n* *Am* (policeman) agent *m* de police

patron ['peɪtrən] *n* (of arts) protecteur, -trice *mf*; (of charity) patron, -onne *mf*; (customer) client, -iente *mf*; (of theatre) spectateur, -trice *mf*; *Rel* **p. saint** patron, -onne *mf* ▪ **patronage** ['pætrənɪdʒ] *n* (of arts, charity) patronage *m*

Note that the French word **patron** is a false friend and is rarely a translation for the English word **patron**. Its most common meaning is **boss**.

patronize [*Br* 'pætrənaɪz, *Am* 'peɪtrənaɪz] *vt* (**a**) (be condescending towards) traiter avec condescendance (**b**) (store, hotel) fréquenter; (arts) protéger ▪ **patronizing** [*Br* 'pætrənaɪzɪŋ, *Am* 'peɪtrənaɪzɪŋ] *adj* condescendant

patter[1] ['pætə(r)] **1** *n* (of footsteps) petit bruit *m*; (of rain, hail) crépitement *m* **2** *vi* (of rain, hail) crépiter

patter[2] ['pætə(r)] *n* *Fam* (of salesman) baratin *m*

pattern ['pætən] *n* (design) dessin *m*, motif *m*; (in sewing) patron *m*; (in knitting) & *Fig* (norm) modèle *m*; (tendency) tendance *f*; *Fig* **to set a p.** créer un modèle; **p. book** catalogue *m* d'échantillons ▪ **patterned** *adj* (fabric) à motifs

paunch [pɔːntʃ] *n* ventre *m*

pauper ['pɔːpə(r)] *n* indigent, -ente *mf*

pause [pɔːz] **1** *n* pause *f*; (in conversation) silence *m* **2** *vi* (stop) faire une pause; (hesitate) hésiter

pave [peɪv] *vt* (road) paver (**with** de); *Fig* **to p. the way for sth** ouvrir la voie à qch ▪ **paved** *adj* pavé ▪ **paving** *n* (with tiles) carrelage *m*; (with slabs) dallage *m*; **p. stone** pavé *m*

pavement ['peɪvmənt] *n* *Br* (beside road) trottoir *m*; *Am* (roadway) chaussée *f*

pavilion [pə'vɪljən] *n* pavillon *m*

paw [pɔː] **1** *n* (of animal) & *Fam* (of person) patte *f*; *Fam* **keep your paws off!** bas les pattes! **2** *vt* (of animal) donner un coup/des coups de patte à; *Fam* (of person) tripoter

pawn[1] [pɔːn] *n* *Chess* pion *m*

pawn[2] [pɔːn] **1** *n* **in p.** en gage **2** *vt* mettre en gage ▪ **pawnbroker** *n* prêteur, -euse *mf* sur gages ▪ **pawnshop** *n* mont-de-piété *m*

pay [peɪ] **1** *n* paie *f*, salaire *m*; (of soldier) solde *f*; *Br* **p. cheque** chèque *m* de paie; **p. packet** enveloppe *f* de paie; **p. rise** augmentation *f* de salaire; *Br* **p. slip**, *Am* **p. stub** fiche *f* de paie **2** (*pt & pp* **paid**) *vt* (person, money, bill) payer; (sum, deposit) verser; (yield) (of investment) rapporter; **I paid £5 for it** je l'ai payé 5 livres; **to p. sb to do sth** *or* **for doing sth** payer qn pour qu'il fasse qch; **to p. money into one's account** verser de l'argent sur son compte; **to p. attention** faire attention (**to** à); **to p. sb a visit** rendre visite à qn; **to p. sb a compliment** faire un compliment à qn; **to p. homage** *or* **tribute to sb** rendre hommage à qn **3** *vi* payer; **to p. a lot** payer cher; **it pays to be cautious** on a intérêt à être prudent ▪ **payable** *adj* (due) payable; **to make a cheque p. to sb** libeller un chèque à l'ordre de qn ▪ **pay-as-you-earn** *n* *Br* prélèvement *m* de l'impôt à la source ▪ **pay-**

as-you-go *n BrTel (for mobile phone)* paiement *m* par carte prépayée; *Comptr (for Internet acces)* facturation *f* à la durée ▪**paycheck** *n Am* chèque *m* de paie ▪**payday** *n* jour *m* de paie ▪**paying** *adj (guest)* payant; *(profitable)* rentable ▪**payment** *n* paiement *m*; *(of deposit)* versement *m*; *(reward)* récompense *f*; **on p. of 20 euros** moyennant 20 euros ▪**payoff** *n Fam (reward)* récompense *f*; *(bribe)* pot-de-vin *m* ▪**pay-per-'view** *TV* **1** *n* système *m* de télévision à péage **2** *adj* à péage ▪**payphone** *n* téléphone *m* public ▪**payroll** *n* **to be on the p.** faire partie du personnel; **to have twenty workers on the p.** employer vingt ouvriers

▸ **pay back** *vt sep (person, loan)* rembourser; *Fig* **I'll p. you back for this!** tu me le paieras!

▸ **pay for** *vt insep* payer

▸ **pay in** *vt sep (cheque, money)* verser sur un compte

▸ **pay off** **1** *vt sep (debt, person)* rembourser; *(in instalments)* rembourser par acomptes; *(staff, worker)* licencier **2** *vi (of work, effort)* porter ses fruits

▸ **pay out** *vt sep (spend)* dépenser

▸ **pay up** *vi* payer

PAYE [pi:eɪwaɪ'i:] *(abbr* **pay-as-you-earn)** *n Br* prélèvement *m* de l'impôt à la source

PC [pi:'si:] **1** *(abbr* **personal computer)** *n* PC *m* **2** *(abbr* **politically correct)** *adj* politiquement correct

PE [pi:'i:] *(abbr* **physical education)** *n Br* EPS *f*

pea [pi:] *n* pois *m*; **peas,** *Br* **garden** *or* **green peas** petits pois *mpl*

peace [pi:s] *n* paix *f*; **p. of mind** tranquillité *f* d'esprit; **in p.** en paix; **at p.** en paix (**with** avec); **to hold one's p.** garder le silence; *Law* **to disturb the p.** troubler l'ordre public; **I'd like to have some p. and quiet** j'aimerais un peu de silence; **p. talks** pourparlers *mpl* de paix; **p. treaty** traité *m* de paix ▪**peace-keeping** *adj (force)* de maintien de la paix; *(measure)* de pacification ▪**peace-loving** *adj* pacifique ▪**peacetime** *n* temps *m* de paix

peaceable ['pi:səbəl] *adj* pacifique

peaceful ['pi:sfəl] *adj (calm)* paisible; *(non-violent)* pacifique ▪**peacefully** *adv* paisiblement ▪**peacefulness** *n* paix *f*

peach [pi:tʃ] **1** *n (fruit)* pêche *f*; **p. (tree)** pêcher *m* **2** *adj (colour)* pêche *inv*

peacock ['pi:kɒk] *n* paon *m*

peak [pi:k] **1** *n (mountain top)* sommet *m*; *(mountain)* pic *m*; *(of cap)* visière *f*; *Fig (of fame, success)* apogée *m*; **the traffic has reached** *or* **is at its p.** la circulation est à son maximum **2** *adj (hours, period)* de pointe; *(demand, production)* maximum **3** *vi* culminer à

peaked [pi:kt] *adj* **p. cap** casquette *f*

peaky ['pi:kɪ] *(-ier, -iest) adj Br Fam (ill)* patraque

peal [pi:l] **1** *n (of bells)* sonnerie *f*; *(of thunder)* coup *m*; **peals of laughter** éclats *mpl* de rire **2** *vi* **to p. (out)** *(of bells)* sonner à toute volée

peanut ['pi:nʌt] *n* cacah(o)uète *f*; *Fam* **to earn peanuts** gagner des clopinettes; **p. butter** beurre *m* de cacah(o)uètes; **p. oil** huile *f* d'arachide

pear [peə(r)] *n* poire *f*; **p. tree** poirier *m*

pearl [pɜːl] *n* perle *f*; **p. necklace** collier *m* de perles ▪**pearly** *(-ier, -iest) adj (colour)* nacré

peasant ['pezənt] *n & adj* paysan, -anne *(mf)*

peashooter ['pi:ʃu:tə(r)] *n* sarbacane *f*

peat [pi:t] *n* tourbe *f*; **p. bog** tourbière *f*

pebble ['pebəl] *n (stone)* caillou *m (pl* -oux); *(on beach)* galet *m* ▪**pebbly** *adj (beach)* de galets

pecan ['pi:kən] *n (nut)* noix *f* de pécan

peck [pek] **1** *n* coup *m* de bec; *(kiss)* bise *f* **2** *vti* **to p. (at)** *(bird)* picorer; *(person)* donner un coup de bec à; *Fig* **the pecking order** la hiérarchie

peckish ['pekɪʃ] *adj Br Fam* **to be p.** avoir un petit creux

peculiar [pɪ'kju:lɪə(r)] *adj (strange)* bizarre; *(special, characteristic)* particulier, -ère (**to** à) ▪**peculiarity** [-lɪ'ærɪtɪ] *(pl* -ies) *n (feature)* particularité *f*; *(oddity)* bizarrerie *f* ▪**peculiarly** *adv* bizarrement; *(specially)* particulièrement

pedal ['pedəl] **1** *n* pédale *f*; **p. bin** poubelle *f* à pédale; **p. boat** Pédalo® *m*; **p. pushers** *(trousers)* corsaire *m* **2** *(Br* -ll-, *Am* -l-) *vt* **to p. a bicycle** être à bicyclette **3** *vi* pédaler

pedant ['pedənt] *n* pédant, -ante *mf* ▪**pedantic** [pɪ'dæntɪk] *adj* pédant

peddle ['pedəl] *vt (goods, ideas, theories)* colporter; *(drugs)* faire du trafic de ▪**peddler** *n (door-to-door)* colporteur, -euse *mf*; *(in street)* camelot *m*; **(drug) p.** trafiquant, -ante *mf* de drogue

pedestal ['pedɪstəl] *n* piédestal *m*; *Fig* **to put sb on a p.** mettre qn sur un piédestal

pedestrian [pə'destrɪən] **1** *n* piéton *m*; *Br* **p. crossing** passage *m* pour piétons; *Br* **p. precinct** zone *f* piétonnière **2** *adj (speech, style)* prosaïque ▪**pedestrianize** *vt (street)* rendre piétonnier; **pedestrianized street** rue *f* piétonne *ou* piétonnière

pediatrician [pi:dɪə'trɪʃən] *n Am* = **paediatrician** ▪**pediatrics** [-dɪ'ætrɪks] *n Am* = **paediatrics**

pedicure ['pedɪkjʊə(r)] *n* soins *mpl* des pieds

pedigree ['pedɪgri:] **1** *n (of animal)* pedigree *m*; *(of person)* ascendance *f* **2** *adj (animal)* de race

pedlar ['pedlə(r)] *n (door-to-door)* colporteur, -euse *mf*; *(in street)* camelot *m*

pedometer [pɪ'dɒmɪtə(r)] *n* podomètre *m*

pedophile ['pi:dəfaɪl] *n Am* = **paedophile** ▪**pedophilia** [-də'fɪlɪə] *n Am* = **paedophile**

pee [pi:] *Fam* **1** *n* **to have a p.** faire pipi **2** *vi* faire pipi

peek [pi:k] **1** *n* to have a **p. (at)** jeter un coup d'œil furtif (à) **2** *vi* jeter un coup d'œil furtif (**at** à)

peel [pi:l] **1** *n (of vegetable, fruit)* peau *f*; *(of orange, lemon)* écorce *f* **2** *vt (vegetable)* éplucher; *(fruit)* peler; **to keep one's eyes peeled** ouvrir l'œil; **to p. sth off** *(label)* décoller qch **3** *vi (of skin, person)* peler; *(of paint)* s'écailler; **to p. easily** *(of fruit)* se peler facilement ■**peeler** *n* **(potato) p.** épluche-légumes *m inv* ■**peelings** *npl* épluchures *fpl*

peep [pi:p] **1** *n* to have a **p. (at)** jeter un coup d'œil furtif à **2** *vi* jeter un coup d'œil furtif (**at** à); **to p. out** se montrer **3** *vi (of bird)* pépier ■**peephole** *n* judas *m* ■**Peeping 'Tom** *n Fam* voyeur *m*

peer [pɪə(r)] **1** *n (equal)* & *Br (nobleman)* pair *m*; **p. pressure** influence *f* du groupe **2** *vi* **to p. at sb/sth** scruter qn/qch du regard; **to p. into the darkness** scruter l'obscurité ■**peerage** [ˈpɪərɪdʒ] *n Br (rank)* pairie *f*

peeved [pi:vd] *adj* en rogne

peevish [ˈpi:vɪʃ] *adj* irritable

peg [peg] **1** *n (for coat, hat)* patère *f*; *(for clothes)* pince *f* à linge; *(for tent)* piquet *m*; *(wooden)* cheville *f*; *(metal)* fiche *f*; *Br* **to buy sth off the p.** acheter qch en prêt-à-porter **2** *(pt & pp -gg-) vt (clothes)* accrocher; *(prices)* stabiliser

▸ **peg out** *vt sep* **to p. out washing on the line** accrocher du linge sur la corde

pejorative [pɪˈdʒɒrətɪv] *adj* péjoratif, -ive

pekinese [pi:kɪˈni:z] *n (dog)* pékinois *m*

Peking [pi:ˈkɪŋ] *n* Pékin *m ou f*; *Culin* **p. duck** canard *m* laqué

pekingese [pi:kɪˈni:z] *n (dog)* pékinois *m*

pelican [ˈpelɪkən] *n* pélican *m*; *Br* **p. crossing** feux *mpl* à commande manuelle

pellet [ˈpelɪt] *n (of paper, bread)* boulette *f*; *(for gun)* plomb *m*

pelmet [ˈpelmɪt] *n (fabric, wood)* cantonnière *f*

pelt [pelt] **1** *n (skin)* peau *f*; *(fur)* fourrure *f* **2** *vt* bombarder (**with** de) **3** *vi Fam* **(a) it's pelting down** il pleut à verse **(b)** *(go fast)* aller à toute allure

pelvis [ˈpelvɪs] *n Anat* pelvis *m*

pen¹ [pen] **1** *n (for writing)* stylo *m*; **to live by one's p.** vivre de sa plume; **p. friend** or **pal** correspondant, -ante *mf*; **p. name** nom *m* de plume; *Pej* **p. pusher** gratte-papier *m inv* **2** *(pt & pp -nn-) vt* écrire

pen² [pen] *n (for sheep, cattle)* parc *m*

penal [ˈpi:nəl] *adj (code, law)* pénal; *(colony)* pénitentiaire ■**penalize** *vt* pénaliser

penalty [ˈpenəltɪ] *(pl -ies) n (prison sentence)* peine *f*; *(fine)* amende *f*; *Football* penalty *m*; *Rugby* pénalité *f*; *Fig* **to pay the p. for sth** subir les conséquences de qch

penance [ˈpenəns] *n* pénitence *f*

pence [pens] *Br pl of* **penny**

pencil [ˈpensəl] **1** *n* crayon *m*; **in p.** au crayon; **p. case** trousse *f*; **p. sharpener** taille-crayon *m* **2** *(Br -ll-, Am -l-) vt (draw)* dessiner au crayon; *(write)* écrire au crayon; *Fig* **to p. sth in** fixer qch provisoirement

pendant [ˈpendənt] *n (around neck)* pendentif *m*

pending [ˈpendɪŋ] **1** *adj (matter, business)* en attente; *(trial)* en instance **2** *prep (until)* en attendant

pendulum [ˈpendjʊləm] *n* pendule *m*

penetrate [ˈpenɪtreɪt] **1** *vt (substance)* pénétrer; *(secret, plan)* découvrir; *(mystery)* percer **2** *vti* **to p. (into)** *(forest)* pénétrer dans; *(group)* s'infiltrer dans ■**penetrating** *adj (mind, cold)* pénétrant ■**pene'tration** *n* pénétration *f*

penguin [ˈpeŋgwɪn] *n* manchot *m*

penicillin [penɪˈsɪlɪn] *n* pénicilline *f*; **to be on p.** prendre de la pénicilline

peninsula [pəˈnɪnsjʊlə] *n* presqu'île *f*; *(larger)* péninsule *f*

penis [ˈpi:nɪs] *n* pénis *m*

penitent [ˈpenɪtənt] *adj* pénitent ■**penitence** *n* pénitence *f*

penitentiary [penɪˈtenʃərɪ] *(pl -ies) n Am* prison *f* centrale

penknife [ˈpennaɪf] *(pl -knives) n* canif *m*

pennant [ˈpenənt] *n* flamme *f*

penniless [ˈpenɪləs] *adj* sans le sou

penny [ˈpenɪ] *n* **(a)** *(pl -ies) Br (coin)* penny *m*; *Am & Can (cent)* cent *m*; *Fig* **I don't have a p.** je n'ai pas un sou; **you won't get a p.** tu n'auras pas un sou; **it was worth every p.** ça valait vraiment le coup **(b)** *(pl pence) Br (value, currency)* penny *m*; **a ten/fifty pence piece** une pièce de dix/cinquante pence

pension [ˈpenʃən] **1** *n* pension *f*; **(retirement) p.** retraite *f*; *Br* **old age p.** pension de vieillesse; **to retire on a p.** toucher une retraite; **p. fund** fonds *m* de retraite; *Br* **p. scheme** régime de retraite **2** *vt* **to p. sb off** mettre qn à la retraite ■**pensionable** *adj (age)* de la retraite; *(job)* qui donne droit à une retraite ■**pensioner** *n* retraité, -ée *mf*; *Br* **old age p.** retraité, -ée *mf*

pensive [ˈpensɪv] *adj* pensif, -ive

Pentagon [ˈpentəgən] *n Am Pol* **the P.** le Pentagone

pentathlon [penˈtæθlən] *n Sport* pentathlon *m*

penthouse [ˈpenthaʊs] *n* = appartement de luxe au dernier étage d'un immeuble

pent-up [ˈpentˈʌp] *adj (energy, feelings)* refoulé

penultimate [pɪˈnʌltɪmət] *adj* avant-dernier, -ière

peony [ˈpi:ənɪ] *(pl -ies) n (plant)* pivoine *f*

people [ˈpi:pəl] **1** *n (nation)* peuple *m* **2** *npl (as group)* gens *mpl*; *(as individuals)* personnes *fpl*; **the p.** *(citizens)* le peuple; **two p.** deux personnes; **English p.** les Anglais *mpl*; **a lot of**

p. beaucoup de gens; **p. think that...** les gens pensent que... **3** *vt* peupler (**with** de)

pep [pep] *Fam* **1** *n* entrain *m*; **p. talk** petit discours *m* d'encouragement **2** (*pt & pp* **-pp-**) *vt* **to p. sb up** ragaillardir qn

pepper ['pepə(r)] **1** *n* poivre *m*; (*vegetable*) poivron *m*; **p. mill** moulin *m* à poivre; **p. pot** poivrière *f* **2** *vt* poivrer ▪ **peppercorn** *n* grain *m* de poivre ▪ **peppermint** *n* (*flavour*) menthe *f*; (*sweet*) bonbon *m* à la menthe ▪ **peppery** *adj* poivré

per [pɜː(r)] *prep* par; **p. annum** par an; **p. head, p. person** par personne; **50 pence p. kilo** 50 pence le kilo; **40 km p. hour** 40 km à l'heure; *Formal* **as p. your instructions** conformément à vos instructions

perceive [pə'siːv] *vt* (*see, hear*) percevoir; (*notice*) remarquer (**that** que)

percentage [pə'sentɪdʒ] *n* pourcentage *m* ▪ **percent** *adv* pour cent

perception [pə'sepʃən] *n* perception *f* (**of** de) ▪ **perceptible** *adj* perceptible ▪ **perceptive** *adj* (*person*) perspicace; (*study, remark*) pertinent

perch¹ [pɜːtʃ] **1** *n* (*for bird*) perchoir *m* **2** *vi* se percher

perch² [pɜːtʃ] *n* (*fish*) perche *f*

percolate ['pɜːkəleɪt] **1** *vt* (*coffee*) passer; **percolated coffee** = café préparé dans une cafetière à pression **2** *vi* (*of liquid*) passer (**through** par) ▪ **percolator** *n* cafetière *f* à pression; (*in café, restaurant*) percolateur *m*

percussion [pə'kʌʃən] *n Mus* percussion *f*

peremptory [pə'remptərɪ] *adj* péremptoire; (*refusal*) absolu

perennial [pə'renɪəl] **1** *adj* (*plant*) vivace; (*worry*) perpétuel, -uelle; (*beauty*) éternel, -elle **2** *n* plante *f* vivace

perfect ['pɜːfɪkt] **1** *adj* parfait **2** *adj & n Grammar* **p. (tense)** parfait *m* **3** [pə'fekt] *vt* parfaire; (*one's French*) parfaire ses connaissances en ▪ **perfectly** *adv* parfaitement

perfection [pə'fekʃən] *n* (*quality*) perfection *f*; (*of technique*) ▪ mise *f* au point (**of** de); **to p.** à la perfection ▪ **perfectionist** *n* perfectionniste *mf*

perforate ['pɜːfəreɪt] *vt* perforer ▪ **perfo-'ration** *n* perforation *f*

perform [pə'fɔːm] **1** *vt* (*task, miracle*) accomplir; (*duty, function*) remplir; (*play, piece of music*) jouer; **to p. an operation on sb** opérer qn **2** *vi* (*act, play*) jouer; (*sing*) chanter; (*dance*) danser; (*of machine, vehicle*) marcher; **to p. well/badly** (*in job*) bien/mal s'en tirer; **how does she p. under pressure?** comment réagit-elle lorsqu'elle est sous pression? ▪ **performing 1** *adj* (*dog, seal*) savant; **p. arts** arts *mpl* du spectacle **2** *n* (*of play, piece of music*) représentation *f*

performance [pə'fɔːməns] *n* (**a**) (*of play*) représentation *f* (**b**) (*of actor, musician*) interprétation *f*; (*of athlete*) performance *f*; (*of machine*) performances *fpl*; (*of company*) résultats *mpl*; *Fam* **to make a p.** faire toute une histoire; **p. art** performance *f*

performer [pə'fɔːmə(r)] *n* (*entertainer*) artiste *mf*; (*in play, of music*) interprète *mf* (**of** de)

perfume 1 ['pɜːfjuːm] *n* parfum *m* **2** [pə'fjuːm] *vt* parfumer

perfunctory [pə'fʌŋktərɪ] *adj* (*examination, glance*) rapide; (*smile*) mécanique; (*letter*) sommaire

perhaps [pə'hæps] *adv* peut-être; **p. not/so** peut-être que non/que oui; **p. she'll come** peut-être qu'elle viendra, elle viendra peut-être

peril ['perɪl] *n* péril *m*, danger *m*; **at your p.** à vos risques et périls ▪ **perilous** *adj* périlleux, -euse

perimeter [pə'rɪmɪtə(r)] *n* périmètre *m*

period ['pɪərɪəd] **1** *n* (**a**) (*stretch of time*) période *f*; (*historical*) époque *f*; (*school lesson*) heure *f* de cours; **in the p. of a month** en l'espace d'un mois; (*menstruation*) règles *fpl*; **to have one's p.** avoir ses règles (**b**) *Am* (*full stop*) point *m*; **I refuse, p.!** je refuse, un point c'est tout! **2** *adj* (*furniture, costume*) d'époque; *TV* **p. drama** drame *m* historique ▪ **periodic** [-rɪ-'ɒdɪk] *adj* périodique ▪ **periodical** [-rɪ-'ɒdɪkəl] *n* (*magazine*) périodique *m* ▪ **periodically** [-rɪ'ɒdɪkəlɪ] *adv* périodiquement

periphery [pə'rɪfərɪ] (*pl* **-ies**) *n* périphérie *f* ▪ **peripheral** *adj* (*area, vision*) & *Comptr* périphérique; (*question*) sans rapport direct (**to** avec); (*issue, importance*) accessoire ▪ **peripherals** *npl Comptr* périphériques *mpl*

periscope ['perɪskəʊp] *n* périscope *m*

perish ['perɪʃ] *vi* (*of person*) périr; (*of rubber, leather*) se détériorer; (*of food*) s'avarier; **p. the thought!** loin de moi cette pensée! ▪ **perishing** *adj Fam* (*cold, weather*) glacial

perishable ['perɪʃəbəl] *adj* (*food*) périssable ▪ **perishables** *npl* denrées *fpl* périssables

perjure ['pɜːdʒə(r)] *vt Law* **to p. oneself** faire un faux témoignage ▪ **perjurer** *n Law* faux témoin *m* ▪ **perjury** *n Law* faux témoignage *m*; **to commit p.** faire un faux témoignage

perk [pɜːk] **1** *n BrFam* (*in job*) avantage *m* **2** *vt* to **p. sb up** (*revive*) ragaillardir qn; (*cheer up*) remonter le moral à qn **3** *vi* **to p. up** reprendre du poil de la bête ▪ **perky** (**-ier, -iest**) *adj Fam* (*lively*) plein d'entrain; (*cheerful*) guilleret, -ette

perm [pɜːm] **1** *n* permanente *f* **2** *vt* **to have one's hair permed** se faire faire une permanente

permanent ['pɜːmənənt] *adj* permanent; (*address*) fixe; (*ink*) indélébile; **she's p. here** (*of worker*) elle est ici à titre permanent ▪ **permanently** *adv* à titre permanent

permeable ['pɜːmɪəbəl] adj perméable

permeate ['pɜːmɪeɪt] vt (of ideas) se répandre dans; **to p. (through)** sth (of liquid) pénétrer qch

permissible [pə'mɪsəbəl] adj permis

permission [pə'mɪʃən] n permission f, autorisation f (**to do** de faire); **to ask for p. (to do sth)** demander la permission (de faire qch); **to give sb p. (to do sth)** donner la permission à qn (de faire qch)

permissive [pə'mɪsɪv] adj permissif, -ive

permit 1 [pə'mɪt] **1** ['pɜːmɪt] n permis m **2** (pt & pp **-tt-**) vt permettre (**sb to do** à qn de faire) **3** vi **weather permitting** si le temps le permet

permutation [pɜːmjʊ'teɪʃən] n permutation f

pernicious [pə'nɪʃəs] adj pernicieux, -ieuse

pernickety [pə'nɪkətɪ] adj Br Fam (person) pointilleux, -euse; (task) délicat

peroxide [pə'rɒksaɪd] **1** n Chem peroxyde m **2** adj (hair) oxygéné; **p. blonde** blonde f décolorée

perpendicular [pɜːpən'dɪkjʊlə(r)] adj & n perpendiculaire (f)

perpetrate ['pɜːpɪtreɪt] vt (crime) perpétrer • **perpetrator** n auteur m

perpetual [pə'petʃʊəl] adj perpétuel, -uelle • **perpetually** adv perpétuellement • **perpetuate** [-veɪt] vt perpétuer • **perpetuity** [pɜːpɪ'tjuːɪtɪ] n perpétuité f

perplex [pə'pleks] vt rendre perplexe • **perplexed** adj perplexe • **perplexing** adj déroutant

persecute ['pɜːsɪkjuːt] vt persécuter • **perse'cution** n persécution f

persevere [pɜːsɪ'vɪə(r)] vi persévérer (**with** dans) • **perseverance** n persévérance f

Persian ['pɜːʃən, 'pɜːʒən] **1** adj (language, cat) persan; **P. carpet** tapis m persan; **the P. Gulf** le golfe Persique **2** n (language) persan m

persist [pə'sɪst] vi persister (**in doing** à faire; **in sth** dans qch); **to p. in one's belief that...** persister à croire que... • **persistence** n (of person) ténacité f; (of fog, belief) persistance f • **persistent** adj (person) tenace; (fever, smell, rumours) persistant; (noise, attempts) continuel, -uelle; Law **p. offender** récidiviste mf • **persistently** adv (stubbornly) obstinément; (continually) continuellement

person ['pɜːsən] n personne f; **in p.** en personne; **a p. to p. call** (on telephone) une communication avec préavis

personable [pɜːsənəbəl] adj charmant

personal ['pɜːsənəl] adj personnel, -elle; (friend) intime; (life) privé; (indiscreet) indiscret, -ète; **to make a p. appearance** venir en personne; **p. ad** petite annonce f, **p. assistant**, **p. secretary** secrétaire m particulier, secrétaire f particulière; **the p. column** les petites annonces fpl; **p. computer** ordinateur m individuel; **p. hygiene** hygiène f; **p. organizer** agenda m; **p. stereo** baladeur m; **p. trainer** entraîneur, -euse mf personnel(elle)

personality [pɜːsə'nælɪtɪ] (pl **-ies**) n (character, famous person) personnalité f; **a television p.** une vedette de la télévision; **p. disorder** trouble m de la personnalité; **p. test** test m de personnalité

personalize ['pɜːsənəlaɪz] vt personnaliser

personally ['pɜːsənəlɪ] adv personnellement; (in person) en personne; **don't take it p.** n'en faites pas une affaire personnelle

personify [pə'sɒnɪfaɪ] (pt & pp **-ied**) vt personnifier • **personification** [-fɪ'keɪʃən] n personnification f

personnel [pɜːsə'nel] n (staff) personnel m; **p. department** service m du personnel; **p. management** direction f du personnel

perspective [pə'spektɪv] n perspective f; Fig **in (its true) p.** sous son vrai jour

Perspex® ['pɜːspeks] n Br Plexiglas® m

perspire [pə'spaɪə(r)] vi transpirer • **perspiration** [pɜːspə'reɪʃən] n transpiration f

persuade [pə'sweɪd] vt persuader (**sb to do** qn de faire) • **persuasion** n persuasion f; (religious beliefs) religion f; (political beliefs) opinions fpl politiques • **persuasive** adj (person, argument) persuasif, -ive • **persuasively** adv de façon persuasive

pert [pɜːt] adj (a) (nose, breasts) pointu; (bottom) petit et ferme (b) (cheeky) espiègle • **pertly** adv avec impertinence

pertain [pə'teɪn] vi Formal **to p. to** (relate) se rapporter à; (belong) appartenir à

pertinent ['pɜːtɪnənt] adj pertinent • **pertinently** adv pertinemment

perturb [pə'tɜːb] vt troubler

Peru [pə'ruː] n le Pérou • **Peruvian 1** adj péruvien, -ienne **2** n Péruvien, -ienne mf

peruse [pə'ruːz] vt Formal (read carefully) lire attentivement; (skim through) parcourir • **perusal** n Formal lecture f

pervade [pə'veɪd] vt imprégner • **pervasive** adj (feeling) général; (smell) envahissant; (influence) omniprésent

perverse [pə'vɜːs] adj (awkward) contrariant; (sexually deviant) pervers • **perversion** [Br -ʃən, Am -ʒən] n (sexual) perversion f; (of justice, truth) travestissement m • **perversity** (pl **-ies**) n esprit m de contradiction; (sexual deviance) perversité f

pervert 1 ['pɜːvɜːt] n (sexual deviant) pervers, -erse mf **2** [pə'vɜːt] vt pervertir; (mind) corrompre; Law **to p. the course of justice** entraver le bon fonctionnement de la justice

pesky ['peskɪ] (**-ier**, **-iest**) adj Am Fam (troublesome) embêtant

pessimism ['pesɪmɪzəm] n pessimisme m • **pessimist** n pessimiste mf • **pessi'mistic** adj pessimiste ▪ **pessi'mistically** adv avec pessimisme

pest [pest] n (animal) animal m nuisible; (insect) insecte m nuisible; Fam (person) plaie f

pester ['pestə(r)] vt tourmenter; **to p. sb to do sth** harceler qn pour qu'il fasse qch; **to p. sb for sth** harceler qn jusqu'à ce qu'il donne qch

pesticide ['pestɪsaɪd] n pesticide m

pet [pet] **1** n animal m domestique; (favourite person) chouchou, -oute mf; (term of address) petit chou m; **to have** or **keep a p.** avoir un animal chez soi **2** adj (dog, cat) domestique; (tiger) apprivoisé; (favourite) favori, -ite; Br **p. hate** bête f noire; **p. name** petit nom m; **p. shop** animalerie f; **p. subject** dada m **3** (pt & pp -tt-) vt (fondle) caresser **4** vi Fam se peloter

petal ['petəl] n pétale m

peter ['piːtə(r)] vi **to p. out** (of conversation, enthusiasm) tarir; (of scheme) n'aboutir à rien; (of path, stream) disparaître

petite [pə'tiːt] adj (woman) menu

petition [pə'tɪʃən] **1** n (signatures) pétition f; (request to court of law) requête f; Law **p. for divorce** demande f en divorce **2** vt adresser une pétition/une requête à (**for sth** pour demander qch) **3** vi **to p. for sth** faire une pétition pour qch; Law **to p. for divorce** faire une demande de divorce

petrify ['petrɪfaɪ] (pt & pp -ied) vt pétrifier

petrol ['petrəl] n Br essence f; **I've run out of p.** je suis tombé en panne d'essence; **p. can** bidon m d'essence; **p. station** station-service f; **p. tank** réservoir m d'essence

Note that the French word **pétrole** is a false friend and is never a translation for the English word **petrol**. It means **oil**.

petroleum [pə'trəʊlɪəm] n pétrole m; **p. jelly** vaseline f

petticoat ['petɪkəʊt] n jupon m

petty ['petɪ] (-ier, -iest) adj (trivial) insignifiant; (mean) mesquin; **p. cash** petite caisse f; **p. criminal** petit délinquant m; **p. officer** (on ship) second maître m ▪ **pettiness** n (triviality) insignifiance f; (meanness) mesquinerie f

petulant ['petjʊlənt] adj irritable ▪ **petulance** n irritabilité f

Note that the French word **pétulant** is a false friend and is never a translation for the English word **petulant**. It means **exuberant**.

petunia [pɪ'tjuːnɪə] n pétunia m

pew [pjuː] n banc m d'église; Fam **take a p.!** assieds-toi!

pewter ['pjuːtə(r)] n étain m

PGCE [piːdʒiːsiː'iː] (abbr **Postgraduate Certificate in Education**) n Br Univ = diplôme d'enseignement

phallic ['fælɪk] adj phallique

phantom ['fæntəm] n fantôme m

pharmacy ['fɑːməsɪ] (pl -ies) n pharmacie f ▪ **pharmaceutical** [-'sjuːtɪkəl] adj pharmaceutique ▪ **pharmaceuticals** [-'sjuːtɪkəl] npl produits mpl pharmaceutiques ▪ **pharmacist** n pharmacien, -ienne mf

pharynx ['færɪŋks] n Anat pharynx m ▪ **pharyngitis** [-rɪn'dʒaɪtəs] n Med pharyngite f

phase [feɪz] n phase f; **it's just a p.** ça lui passera ▪ **phased** adj progressif, -ive
▸ **phase in** vt sep introduire progressivement
▸ **phase out** vt sep supprimer progressivement

PhD [piːeɪtʃ'diː] (abbr **Doctor of Philosophy**) n (degree) doctorat m (**in** de); (person) docteur m

pheasant ['fezənt] n faisan m

phenomenon [fɪ'nɒmɪnən] (pl -ena [-ɪnə]) n phénomène m ▪ **phenomenal** adj phénoménal

phew [fjuː] exclam (in relief) ouf!; (when hot) pfff!

philanthropist [fɪ'lænθrəpɪst] n philanthrope mf ▪ **philanthropic** [fɪlən'θrɒpɪk] adj philanthropique

philately [fɪ'lætəlɪ] n philatélie f ▪ **philatelist** n philatéliste mf

philharmonic [fɪlə'mɒnɪk] adj & n philharmonique (m)

Philippines ['fɪlɪpiːnz] npl **the P.** les Philippines fpl

philistine ['fɪlɪstaɪn] n béotien, -ienne mf, philistin m

philosophy [fɪ'lɒsəfɪ] (pl -ies) n philosophie f ▪ **philosopher** n philosophe mf ▪ **philosophical** [fɪlə'sɒfɪkəl] adj philosophique; Fig (stoical, resigned) philosophe ▪ **philosophically** [fɪlə'sɒfɪklɪ] adv (say) avec philosophie ▪ **philosophize** vi philosopher (**on** sur)

phlegm [flem] n (in throat) glaires fpl; Fig (calmness) flegme m ▪ **phlegmatic** [fleg'mætɪk] adj flegmatique

phobia ['fəʊbɪə] n phobie f

phone [fəʊn] **1** n téléphone m; **to be on the p.** (be talking) être au téléphone; (have a telephone) avoir le téléphone; **p. call** coup m de téléphone; **to make a p. call** téléphoner (**to** à); **p. book** annuaire m; **p. box**, Br **booth** cabine f téléphonique; **p. number** numéro m de téléphone **2** vt téléphoner (**to** à); **to p. sb (up)** téléphoner à qn; **to p. sb back** rappeler qn **3** vi **to p. (up)** téléphoner; **to p. back** rappeler ▪ **phonecard** n Br carte f de téléphone ▪ **phone-in** n = émission au cours de laquelle les auditeurs ou les téléspectateurs peuvent intervenir par téléphone

phonetic [fə'netɪk] adj phonétique; **p. alphabet** alphabet m phonétique ▪ **phonetics** **1** n (science) phonétique f **2** npl (words) transcription f phonétique

phoney ['fəʊnɪ] Fam **1** (-ier, -iest) adj (jewels, writer) faux (f fausse); (company, excuse) bidon inv; *(attitude)* de faux jeton **2** *n (impostor)* imposteur *m*; *(insincere person)* faux jeton *m*; **it's a p.** *(jewel, coin)* c'est du faux

phosphate ['fɒsfeɪt] *n Chem* phosphate *m*

phosphorus ['fɒsfərəs] *n Chem* phosphore *m*

photo ['fəʊtəʊ] *(pl -os) n* photo *f*; **to take sb's p.** prendre qn en photo; **to have one's p. taken** se faire prendre en photo; **p. album** album *m* de photos

photocopy ['fəʊtəʊkɒpɪ] **1** *(pl -ies) n* photocopie *f* **2** *(pt & pp -ied) vt* photocopier **• photocopier** *n* photocopieuse *f*

photogenic [fəʊtəʊ'dʒenɪk] *adj* photogénique

photograph ['fəʊtəɡrɑːf] **1** *n* photographie *f* **2** *vt* photographier **3** *vi* **to p. well** être photogénique **• photographer** [fə'tɒɡrəfə(r)] *n* photographe *mf* **• photographic** [-'ɡræfɪk] *adj* photographique **• photography** [fə'tɒɡrəfɪ] *n (activity)* photographie *f*

> Note that the French noun **photographe** is a false friend and is never a translation for the English word **photograph**. It means **photographer**.

phrase [freɪz] **1** *n (saying)* expression *f*; *(idiom)* & *Grammar* locution *f*; **p. book** manuel *m* de conversation **2** *vt (verbally)* exprimer; *(in writing)* rédiger

> Note that the French noun **phrase** is a false friend. It means **sentence**.

Phys Ed [fɪz'ed] *(abbr physical education) n Am* EPS *f*

physical ['fɪzɪkəl] **1** *adj* physique; **p. education** éducation *f* physique; **p. examination** visite *f* médicale **2** *n (examination)* visite *f* médicale **• physically** *adv* physiquement; **it's p. impossible** c'est matériellement impossible

physician [fɪ'zɪʃən] *n* médecin *m*

> Note that the French word **physicien** is a false friend and is never a translation for the English word **physician**. It means **physicist**.

physics ['fɪzɪks] *n (science)* physique *f* **• physicist** ['fɪzɪsɪst] *n* physicien, -ienne *mf*

physiology [fɪzɪ'ɒlədʒɪ] *n* physiologie *f* **• physiological** [fɪzɪə'lɒdʒɪkəl] *adj* physiologique

physiotherapy [fɪzɪəʊ'θerəpɪ] *n* kinésithérapie *f* **• physiotherapist** *n* kinésithérapeute *mf*

physique [fɪ'ziːk] *n* physique *m*

piano [pɪ'ænəʊ] *(pl -os) n* piano *m* **• pianist** ['pɪənɪst] *n* pianiste *mf*

piazza [pɪ'ætsə] *n (square)* place *f*

pick¹ [pɪk] **1** *n (choice)* choix *m*; **to take one's p.**

choisir; **the p. of the bunch** le meilleur/la meilleure du lot **2** *vt (choose)* choisir; *(flower, fruit)* cueillir; *(hole)* faire (**in** dans); *(pimple)* tripoter; *(lock)* crocheter; **to p. one's nose** se mettre les doigts dans le nez; **to p. one's teeth** se curer les dents; **to p. a fight** chercher la bagarre (**with** avec); *Fig* **to p. holes in sth** relever les failles dans qch **3** *vi* **to p. and choose** se permettre de choisir

▸ **pick at** *vt insep* **to p. at one's food** picorer

▸ **pick off** *vt sep (remove)* enlever

▸ **pick on** *vt insep (nag, blame)* s'en prendre à

▸ **pick out** *vt sep (choose)* choisir; *(identify)* repérer

▸ **pick up 1** *vt sep (lift up)* ramasser; *(to upright position)* relever; *(person into air, weight)* soulever; *(baby)* prendre dans ses bras; *(cold)* attraper; *(habit, accent, speed)* prendre; *(fetch, collect)* passer prendre; *(radio programme)* capter; *(survivor)* recueillir; *(arrest)* arrêter; *(learn)* apprendre; **to p. up the phone** décrocher le téléphone **2** *vi (improve)* s'améliorer; *(of business)* reprendre; *(of patient)* se remettre; **let's p. up where we left off** reprenons (là où nous en étions restés)

pick² [pɪk] *n (tool)* pic *m*; **ice p.** pic à glace

pickaxe ['pɪkæks] *(Am* **pickax)** *n* pioche *f*

picket ['pɪkɪt] **1** *n* **(a)** *(stake)* piquet *m* **(b)** *(in strike)* **p. (line)** piquet *m* de grève **2** *vt (factory)* installer un piquet de grève aux portes de

pickings ['pɪkɪŋz] *npl (leftovers)* restes *mpl*; *(profits)* bénéfices *mpl*; **rich p.** gros bénéfices

pickle ['pɪkəl] **1** *n* = condiment à base de légumes conservés dans du vinaigre; **pickles** *(vegetables) Br* conserves *fpl* (au vinaigre); *Am* concombres *mpl*, cornichons *mpl*; *Fam* **to be in a p.** être dans le pétrin **2** *vt* conserver dans du vinaigre; **pickled onion** oignon *m* au vinaigre

pick-me-up ['pɪkmiːʌp] *n Fam* remontant *m*

pickpocket ['pɪkpɒkɪt] *n* pickpocket *m*

pick-up ['pɪkʌp] *n* **p.** *(truck)* pick-up *m inv (petite camionnette à plateau)*; **p. point** *(for goods, passengers)* point *m* de ramassage

picky ['pɪkɪ] *(-ier, -iest) adj Fam (choosy)* difficile (**about** sur)

picnic ['pɪknɪk] **1** *n* pique-nique *m*; *Br* **p. basket, p. hamper** panier *m* à pique-nique **2** *(pt & pp -ck-) vi* pique-niquer

pictorial [pɪk'tɔːrɪəl] *adj (representation)* en images; *(periodical)* illustré

picture ['pɪktʃə(r)] **1** *n* image *f*; *(painting)* tableau *m*; *(drawing)* dessin *m*; *(photo)* photo *f*; *Fig (situation)* situation *f*; *Br Fam (film)* film *m*; *Br Fam* **the pictures** le cinéma; **to be the p. of health** respirer la santé; *Fig* **to put sb in the p.** mettre qn au courant; **p. frame** cadre *m*; *Tel* **p. message** message *m* image **2** *vt (in painting, photo)* représenter; *Fig (in words)* décrire; **to p. sth** s'imaginer qch; **to p. sb doing sth** s'imaginer qn en train de faire qch

picturesque [pɪktʃəˈresk] *adj* pittoresque

pidgin [ˈpɪdʒɪn] *n* pidgin *m*; **p. English/French**
≃ petit nègre *m*

pie [paɪ] *n (open)* tarte *f; (with pastry on top)*
tourte *f*; **p. chart** camembert *m*

piece [piːs] **1** *n* morceau *m; (smaller)* bout *m; (in
chess, puzzle)* pièce *f*; **in pieces** en morceaux;
to smash sth to pieces briser qch en
morceaux; **to take sth to pieces** démonter
qch; **to come to pieces** se démonter; *Fig* **to go
to pieces** *(of person)* s'effondrer (complètement); **a p. of news/advice/luck** une
nouvelle/un conseil/une chance; **in one p.**
(object) intact; *(person)* indemne **2** *vt* **to p.
together** *(facts)* reconstituer; *(one's life)* refaire

piecemeal [ˈpiːsmiːl] **1** *adv* petit à petit **2** *adj
(unsystematic)* peu méthodique

pier [pɪə(r)] *n (for walking, with entertainments)*
jetée *f; (for landing)* embarcadère *m*

pierce [pɪəs] *vt* percer; *(of cold, bullet, sword)*
transpercer; **to have one's ears/nose pierced**
se faire percer les oreilles/le nez ▪ **piercing 1**
adj (voice, look) perçant; *(wind)* vif *(f* vive*)* **2** *n*
(body) p. piercing *m*

piety [ˈpaɪətɪ] *n* piété *f*

pig [pɪg] *n (animal)* cochon *m*, porc *m; Fam
(greedy person)* goinfre *m; Fam (unpleasant
man)* salaud *m* **2** *(pt & pp* **-gg-)** *vi Am Fam* **to p.
out** *(overeat)* se goinfrer **(on** de**)** ▪ **piggish** *adj
(dirty)* sale; *(greedy)* goinfre ▪ **piggy** *adj Fam
(greedy)* goinfre; **p. eyes** des yeux de cochon
▪ **piggy bank** *n* tirelire *f (en forme de cochon)*
▪ **pig-'headed** *adj* têtu

pigeon [ˈpɪdʒɪn] *n* pigeon *m*

pigeonhole [ˈpɪdʒɪnhəʊl] **1** *n* casier *m* **2** *vt
(classify, label)* classer; *(person)* étiqueter;
(shelve) mettre en suspens

piggyback [ˈpɪgɪbæk] *n* **to give sb a p.** porter
qn sur son dos

pigment [ˈpɪgmənt] *n* pigment *m* ▪ **pig-
men'tation** *n* pigmentation *f*

pigsty [ˈpɪgstaɪ] *(pl* **-ies)** *n* porcherie *f*

pigtail [ˈpɪgteɪl] *n (hair)* natte *f*

pike [paɪk] *n (fish)* brochet *m*

pilchard [ˈpɪltʃəd] *n* pilchard *m*

pile¹ [paɪl] **1** *n (heap)* tas *m; (stack)* pile *f; Fam* **to
have piles** *or* **a p. of things to do** avoir un tas
de choses à faire; *Fam* **to have piles** *or* **a p. of
work to do** avoir des tonnes de travail à faire;
Fam **to make one's p.** faire fortune **2** *vt*
entasser; *(stack)* empiler **3** *vi Fam* **to p. into a
car** s'entasser dans une voiture
▶ **pile up 1** *vt sep* entasser; *(stack)* empiler **2** *vi
(accumulate)* s'accumuler

pile² [paɪl] *n (of carpet)* poils *mpl*

piles [paɪlz] *npl (illness)* hémorroïdes *fpl*

pile-up [ˈpaɪlʌp] *n Fam (on road)* carambolage *m*

pilfer [ˈpɪlfə(r)] *vti* chaparder ▪ **pilfering** *n*
chapardage *m*

pilgrim [ˈpɪlgrɪm] *n* pèlerin *m*; **the P. fathers** les
Pères Pèlerins *mpl* ▪ **pilgrimage** *n* pèlerinage
m

pill [pɪl] *n* pilule *f*; **to be on the p.** *(for
contraception)* prendre la pilule; **to come off
the p.** arrêter la pilule

pillage [ˈpɪlɪdʒ] **1** *n* pillage *m* **2** *vti* piller

pillar [ˈpɪlə(r)] *n* pilier *m; Br* **p. box** boîte *f* aux
lettres

pillion [ˈpɪlɪən] *adv* **to ride p.** *(on motorbike)*
monter derrière

pillow [ˈpɪləʊ] *n* oreiller *m* ▪ **pillowcase, pillowslip** *n* taie *f* d'oreiller

pilot [ˈpaɪlət] **1** *n (of plane, ship)* pilote *m* **2** *adj* **p.
light** veilleuse *f*; **p. scheme** projet-pilote *m* **3** *vt
(plane, ship)* piloter

pimento [pɪˈmentəʊ] *(pl* **-os)** *n* piment *m*

pimp [pɪmp] *n* proxénète *m*

pimple [ˈpɪmpəl] *n* bouton *m* ▪ **pimply (-ier,
-iest)** *adj* boutonneux, -euse

PIN [pɪn] *(abbr* **personal identification
number)** *n Br* **P. (number)** code *m* confidentiel

pin [pɪn] **1** *n* épingle *f; (for surgery)* broche *f; Br
(drawing pin)* punaise *f; (in machine, grenade)*
goupille *f*; **to have pins and needles** avoir des
fourmis **(in** dans**)**; **p. money** argent *m* de poche
2 *(pt & pp* **-nn-)** *vt (attach)* épingler **(to** à**); *(to
wall)* punaiser **(to** *or* **on** à**); **to p. one's hopes
on sb/sth** mettre tous ses espoirs en qn/qch;
to p. the blame on sb rejeter la responsabilité
sur qn; **to p. sb down** *(immobilize)* immobiliser;
(fix) fixer; *(trap)* coincer; *Fig* **to p. sb down**
forcer qn à s'engager; **to p. sth up** *(notice)* fixer
qch au mur ▪ **pincushion** *n* pelote *f* à épingles

pinafore [ˈpɪnəfɔː(r)] *n Br (apron)* tablier *m;
(dress)* robe *f* chasuble

pinball [ˈpɪnbɔːl] *n* flipper *m*; **p. machine** flipper
m

pincers [ˈpɪnsəz] *npl (tool)* tenailles *fpl*

pinch [pɪntʃ] **1** *n (action)* pincement *m; (of salt)*
pincée *f*; **to give sb a p.** pincer qn; *Br* **at a p.,** *Am*
in a p. à la rigueur; *Fig* **to feel the p.** être gêné **2**
vt pincer; *Br Fam (steal)* piquer **(from** à**); *Fam
(arrest)* pincer **3** *vi (of shoes)* serrer

pine [paɪn] **1** *n (tree, wood)* pin *m*; **p. forest**
pinède *f*; **p. nut** pignon *m* **2** *vi* **to p. for sb/sth**
se languir de qn/qch; **to p. away** languir

pineapple [ˈpaɪnæpəl] *n* ananas *m*

ping [pɪŋ] *n* tintement *m*

ping-pong [ˈpɪŋpɒŋ] *n* ping-pong *m*; **p. table**
table *f* de ping-pong

pink [pɪŋk] *adj & n (colour)* rose *(m)*

pinkie [ˈpɪŋkɪ] *n Am & Scot* petit doigt *m*

pinnacle [ˈpɪnəkəl] *n Fig (of fame, career)*
apogée *m*

pinpoint [ˈpɪnpɔɪnt] *vt (locate)* repérer;
(identify) identifier

pinstripe [ˈpɪnstraɪp] *adj (suit)* rayé

pint [paɪnt] *n* pinte *f (Br = 0,57 l, Am = 0,47 l)*; **a p.
(of beer)** ≃ un demi

pin-up ['pɪnʌp] n Fam (girl) pin-up f inv

pioneer [paɪə'nɪə(r)] **1** n pionnier, -ière mf **2** vt **to p. sth** être le premier/la première à mettre au point qch

pious ['paɪəs] adj (person, deed) pieux (f pieuse)

pip [pɪp] n Br (of fruit) pépin m; Br **the pips** (on radio) les bips mpl sonores

pipe [paɪp] **1** n tuyau m; (for smoking) pipe f; (musical instrument) pipeau m; **the pipes** (bagpipes) la cornemuse; **to smoke a p.** fumer la pipe; **p. cleaner** cure-pipes m inv; **p. dream** chimère f **2** vt (water, oil) transporter par canalisation; **piped music** musiquette f **3** vi Fam **to p. down** (shut up) se taire ▪ **piping 1** n (pipes) canalisations fpl; **length of p.** tuyau m **2** adv **p. hot** très chaud

pipeline ['paɪplaɪn] n (for oil) pipeline m; Fig **to be in the p.** être en préparation

pique [piːk] n dépit m

pirate ['paɪərət] **1** n pirate m **2** adj (radio, ship) pirate ▪ **piracy** n (of ships) piraterie f; (of videos, software) piratage m ▪ **pirated** adj (book, video, CD) pirate

Pisces ['paɪsiːz] n (sign) les Poissons mpl; **to be (a) P.** être Poissons

piss [pɪs] very Fam **1** n pisse f; **to have a p.** pisser; **to take the p. out of sb** se foutre (de la gueule) de qn **2** vi pisser; **it's pissing down** or **with rain** il pleut comme vache qui pisse ▪ **pissed** adj Br Fam (drunk) bourré; Am Fam (angry) en rogne
▸ **piss off** very Fam **1** vt sep (annoy) faire chier; **to be pissed off with sb/sth** en avoir ras le bol de qn/qch; **to be pissed off at sb/about sth** être en pétard contre qn/à cause de qch **2** vi (go away) se casser; **p. off!** fous le camp!

pistachio [pɪ'stæʃɪəʊ] (pl -os) n (nut, flavour) pistache f

pistol ['pɪstəl] n pistolet m

piston ['pɪstən] n (of engine) piston m

pit[1] [pɪt] n (hole) fosse f; (mine) mine f; (of stomach) creux m; Br (in theatre) parterre m; **the pits** (in motor racing) les stands mpl de ravitaillement; Fam **it's the pits** c'est complètement nul

pit[2] [pɪt] n Am (stone of fruit) noyau m (pl -aux); (smaller) pépin m

pit[3] [pɪt] (pt & pp -tt-) vt **to p. oneself against sb** se mesurer à qn

pitch[1] [pɪtʃ] **1** n (a) Football terrain m; (in market) place f (b) (degree) degré m; (of voice) hauteur f; (musical) ton m **2** vt (tent) dresser; (camp) établir; (ball) lancer; **a pitched battle** (between armies) une bataille rangée; Fig une belle bagarre **3** vi (of ship) tanguer **4** vi Fam **to p. in** (cooperate) mettre du sien; **to p. into sb** attaquer qn

pitch[2] [pɪtʃ] n (tar) poix f ▪ **pitch-'black, pitch-'dark** adj noir comme dans un four

pitcher[1] ['pɪtʃə(r)] n pichet m

pitcher[2] ['pɪtʃə(r)] n Sport (in baseball) lanceur m

pitchfork ['pɪtʃfɔːk] n fourche f

pitfall ['pɪtfɔːl] n (trap) piège m

pith [pɪθ] n (of orange) peau f blanche; Fig (essence) moelle f ▪ **pithy** (-ier, -iest) adj concis

pitiful ['pɪtɪfəl] adj pitoyable ▪ **pitiless** adj impitoyable

pitta ['pɪtə] adj & n **p. (bread)** pita m

pittance ['pɪtəns] n (income) salaire m de misère; (sum) somme f dérisoire

> Note that the French word **pitance** is a false friend and is never a translation for the English word **pittance**. It means **sustenance**.

pitted ['pɪtɪd] adj (a) (face) grêlé; **p. with rust** piqué de rouille (b) Am (fruit) dénoyauté

pitter-patter ['pɪtəpætə(r)] n = **patter**[1]

pity ['pɪtɪ] **1** n pitié f; **to take** or **have p. on sb** avoir pitié de qn; **what a p.!** quel dommage!; **it's a p. that...** c'est dommage que... (+ subjunctive) **2** (pt & pp -ied) vt plaindre

pivot ['pɪvət] **1** n pivot m **2** vi pivoter (**on** sur)

pixie ['pɪksɪ] n (fairy) lutin m

pizza ['piːtsə] n pizza f; Br **p. parlour,** Am **p. parlor** pizzeria f ▪ **pizzeria** [piːtsə'riːə] n pizzeria f

placard ['plækɑːd] n (on wall) affiche f; (hand-held) pancarte f

> Note that the French word **placard** is a false friend and is never a translation for the English word **placard**. Its most common meaning is **cupboard**.

placate [Br plə'keɪt, Am 'pleɪkeɪt] vt calmer

place [pleɪs] **1** n endroit m, lieu m; (in street name) rue f; (seat, position, rank) place f; Fam **my p.** chez moi; Fam **my parents' p.** chez mes parents; **to lose one's p.** (in queue) perdre sa place; (in book) perdre sa page; **to change** or **swap** or **trade places** changer de place; **to take the p. of sb/sth** remplacer qn/qch; **to take p.** (happen) avoir lieu; Br **to set** or **lay three places** (at the table) mettre trois couverts; Am **some p.** (somewhere) quelque part; Am **no p.** (nowhere) nulle part; **all over the p.** un peu partout; **in the first p.** (firstly) en premier lieu; **in p. of** à la place de; **out of p.** (remark) déplacé; (object) pas à sa place; **p. of work** lieu m de travail; **p. mat** set m de table; **p. setting** couvert m **2** vt (put, situate, invest) & Sport placer; **to be placed third** se classer troisième; **to p. an order with sb** passer une commande à qn; **to p. sb** (remember, identify) remettre qn

placement ['pleɪsmənt] n stage m

placid ['plæsɪd] adj placide

plagiarize ['pleɪdʒəraɪz] vt plagier ▪ **plagiarism** n plagiat m

plague [pleɪg] 1 *n* (*disease*) peste *f*; (*of insects*) invasion *f*; **to avoid sb/sth like the p.** éviter qn/qch comme la peste 2 *vt* (*of person*) harceler (**with** de)

plaice [pleɪs] *n* (*fish*) carrelet *m*

plaid [plæd] *n* (*fabric*) tissu *m* écossais

plain¹ [pleɪn] 1 (**-er, -est**) *adj* (*clear, obvious*) clair; (*simple*) simple; (*without a pattern*) uni; (*not beautiful*) quelconque; **in p. English** clairement; **in p. clothes** en civil; **to make it p. to sb that…** faire comprendre à qn que…; **I'll be quite p. with you** je vais être franc/franche avec vous; *Fam* **that's p. madness** c'est de la pure folie; **p. chocolate** chocolat *m* noir; **p. flour** farine *f* (*sans levure*); **p. speaking** franc-parler *m* 2 *adv Fam* (*utterly*) complètement ▪ **plainly** *adv* (*clearly*) clairement; (*frankly*) franchement

plain² [pleɪn] *n* (*land*) plaine *f*

plaintiff [ˈpleɪntɪf] *n Law* plaignant, -ante *mf*

plaintive [ˈpleɪntɪv] *adj* plaintif, -ive

plait [plæt] 1 *n* tresse *f*, natte *f* 2 *vt* tresser, natter

plan [plæn] 1 *n* (*proposal, intention*) projet *m*; (*of building, town, essay*) plan *m*; **the best p. would be to…** le mieux serait de…; **to go according to p.** se passer comme prévu; **to have no plans** (*be free*) n'avoir rien de prévu; **to change one's plans** (*decide differently*) changer d'idée 2 (*pt & pp* **-nn-**) *vt* (*arrange*) projeter; (*crime*) comploter; (*building, town*) faire le plan de; (*economy*) planifier; **to p. to do** *or* **on doing sth** (*intend*) projeter de faire qch; **as planned** comme prévu 3 *vi* faire des projets; **to p. for the future** faire des projets d'avenir

plane¹ [pleɪn] *n* (*aircraft*) avion *m*

plane² [pleɪn] 1 *n* (*tool*) rabot *m* 2 *vt* raboter

plane³ [pleɪn] *n* **p. (tree)** platane *m*

plane⁴ [pleɪn] *n* (*level, surface*) & *Fig* plan *m*

planet [ˈplænɪt] *n* planète *f* ▪ **planetarium** [-ˈteərɪəm] *n* planétarium *m* ▪ **planetary** [-tərɪ] *adj* planétaire

plank [plæŋk] *n* planche *f*

planner [ˈplænə(r)] *n* planificateur, -trice *mf*; (*town*) **p.** urbaniste *mf*

planning [ˈplænɪŋ] *n* conception *f*; **family p.** planning *m* familial; **p. permission** permis *m* de construire

plant [plɑːnt] 1 *n* (**a**) (*living thing*) plante *f* (**b**) (*factory*) usine *f*; (*machinery*) matériel *m* 2 *vt* (*tree, flower*) planter; (*crops, field*) semer (**with** en); *Fig* (*bomb*) poser; **to p. sth on sb** (*hide*) cacher qch dans les affaires de qn (*pour le compromettre*) ▪ **plan'tation** *n* (*trees, land*) plantation *f*

plaque [plæk] *n* (*sign*) plaque *f*; (*on teeth*) plaque *f* dentaire

plasma [ˈplæzmə] *n* plasma *m*; *Comptr* **p. screen** écran *m* plasma

plaster [ˈplɑːstə(r)] 1 *n* (**a**) (*on wall*) plâtre *m*; **p.**
of Paris plâtre de Paris; **to put sb's leg in p.** mettre la jambe de qn dans le plâtre; **p. cast** (*for broken bone*) plâtre (**b**) *Br* (*sticking*) **p.** pansement *m* adhésif 2 *vt* (*wall*) plâtrer; **to p. sth with** (*cover*) couvrir qch de ▪ **plastered** *adj Br Fam* (*drunk*) bourré ▪ **plasterer** *n* plâtrier *m*

plastic [ˈplæstɪk] 1 *adj* (*object*) en plastique; (*bullet*) de plastique; **p. bag** sac *m* en plastique; **p. explosive** plastic *m*; **p. surgery** (*cosmetic*) chirurgie *f* esthétique; (*to repair damage*) chirurgie plastique 2 *n* plastique *m*; *Fam* **do they take p.?** est-ce qu'ils acceptent les cartes de crédit?

Plasticine® [ˈplæstɪsiːn] *n Br* pâte *f* à modeler

plate [pleɪt] 1 *n* (*dish*) assiette *f*; (*metal sheet*) plaque *f*; (*book illustration*) gravure *f*; *Fam* **to have a lot on one's p.** avoir du pain sur la planche; **p. glass** vitrage *m* très épais 2 *vt* (*with gold*) plaquer en or; (*with silver*) plaquer en argent ▪ **plateful** *n* assiettée *f*

plateau [ˈplætəʊ] (*pl* **-eaus** [-əʊz] *or* **-eaux**) *n* (*flat land*) plateau *m*

platform [ˈplætfɔːm] *n* (*raised surface*) plate-forme *f*; (*in train station*) quai *m*; (*for speaker*) estrade *f*; (*political programme*) programme *m*; **p. shoes** = chaussures à grosses semelles et à talons hauts, typiques des années 70

platinum [ˈplætɪnəm] 1 *n* (*metal*) platine *m* 2 *adj* **p. (blond(e))** hair cheveux *mpl* blond platine

platitude [ˈplætɪtjuːd] *n* platitude *f*

platonic [pləˈtɒnɪk] *adj* platonique

platoon [pləˈtuːn] *n Mil* section *f*

platter [ˈplætə(r)] *n* (*dish*) plat *m*

plaudits [ˈplɔːdɪts] *npl Literary* (*commendation*) applaudissements *mpl*

plausible [ˈplɔːzəbəl] *adj* (*argument, excuse*) plausible; (*person*) convaincant

play [pleɪ] 1 *n* (*drama*) pièce *f* (*de théâtre*); (*amusement, looseness*) jeu *m*; **to come into p.** entrer en jeu; **a p. on words** un jeu de mots 2 *vt* (*part, tune, card*) jouer; (*game*) jouer à; (*instrument*) jouer de; (*match*) disputer (**with** avec); (*team, opponent*) jouer contre; (*record, compact disc*) passer; (*radio, tape recorder*) faire marcher; *Fig* **to p. the fool** faire l'idiot; *Fig* **to p. a part in doing/in sth** contribuer à faire/à qch; *Fig* **to p. ball with** coopérer avec; *Fam* **to p. it cool** garder son sang-froid 3 *vi* jouer (**with** avec; **at** à); (*of record player, tape recorder*) marcher; *Fam* **what are you playing at?** à quoi tu joues? ▪ **play-act** *vi* jouer la comédie ▪ **playboy** *n* play-boy *m* ▪ **playground** *n Br* (*in school*) cour *f* de récréation; (*in park*) terrain *m* de jeux ▪ **playgroup** *n* garderie *f* ▪ **playmate** *n* camarade *mf* de jeu ▪ **playpen** *n* parc *m* (*pour bébé*) ▪ **playroom** *n* (*in house*) salle *f* de jeux ▪ **playschool** *n* garderie *f* ▪ **plaything** *n* (*toy, person*) jouet *m* ▪ **playtime** *n* (*in school*) récréation f ▪ **playwright** n dramaturge mf

▸ **play about, play around** vi jouer, s'amuser

▸ **play back** vt sep (tape) réécouter

▸ **play down** vt sep minimiser

▸ **play on** vt insep (feelings, fears) jouer sur

▸ **play out** vt sep (scene, fantasy) jouer; Fam **to be played out** (of idea, method) être périmé ou vieux jeu inv

▸ **play up** Fam 1 vi (of child, machine) faire des siennes; **to p. up to sb** faire de la lèche à qn 2 vt sep **to p. sb up** (of child) faire enrager qn

player ['pleɪə(r)] n (in game, of instrument) joueur m, joueuse f; (in theatre) acteur m, actrice f; **clarinet p.** joueur/joueuse f de clarinette

playful ['pleɪfəl] adj (mood, tone) enjoué; (child, animal) joueur (f joueuse) ▪ **playfully** adv (say) en badinant ▪ **playfulness** n enjouement m

playing ['pleɪɪŋ] n jeu m; **p. card** carte f à jouer; **p. field** terrain m de jeux

plc [piːel'siː] (abbr public limited company) n Br Com ≃ SARL f

plea [pliː] n (request) appel m; (excuse) excuse f; Law **to enter a p. of guilty** plaider coupable

plead [pliːd] 1 vt (argue) plaider; (as excuse) alléguer; Law **to p. sb's case** plaider la cause de qn 2 vi (in court) plaider; **to p. with sb (to do sth)** implorer qn (de faire qch); Law **to p. guilty** plaider coupable

pleasant ['plezənt] adj agréable (**to** à avec) ▪ **pleasantly** adv (smile, behave) aimablement; (surprised) agréablement

pleasantries ['plezəntrɪz] npl (jokes) plaisanteries fpl; **to exchange p.** (polite remarks) échanger des politesses

please [pliːz] 1 adv s'il te/vous plaît; **p. sit down** asseyez-vous, je vous prie; **p. do!** bien sûr!, je vous en prie!; **'no smoking p.'** (on sign) 'prière de ne pas fumer' 2 vt **to p. sb** faire plaisir à qn; (satisfy) contenter qn; **easy/hard to p.** facile/difficile (à contenter); **p. yourself!** comme tu veux! 3 vi plaire; **to be eager to p.** vouloir plaire; **do as you p.** fais comme tu veux; **as much/as many as you p.** autant qu'il vous plaira ▪ **pleased** adj content (**with** de); **to be p. to do sth** faire qch avec plaisir; **p. to meet you!** enchanté!; **I'd be p. to!** avec plaisir!; **I'm p. to say that…** je suis heureux/heureuse de vous dire que… ▪ **pleasing** adj agréable, plaisant

pleasure ['pleʒə(r)] n plaisir m; **p. boat** bateau m de plaisance ▪ **pleasurable** adj très agréable

pleat [pliːt] 1 n pli m 2 vt plisser ▪ **pleated** adj plissé

plebiscite ['plebɪsaɪt] n plébiscite m

pledge [pledʒ] 1 n (promise) promesse f (**to do** de faire); (object) gage m 2 vt promettre (**to do** de faire); (as security, pawn) engager

plenty ['plentɪ] n abondance f; **p. of** beaucoup de; **that's p.** (of food) merci, j'en ai assez ▪ **plentiful** adj abondant

plethora ['pleθərə] n pléthore f

pliable ['plaɪəbəl] adj souple

pliers ['plaɪəz] npl pince f

plight [plaɪt] n (crisis) situation f critique; **to be in a sorry p.** être dans une situation désespérée

plimsolls ['plɪmsəʊlz] npl Br tennis mpl

plinth [plɪnθ] n socle m

plod [plɒd] (pt & pp -dd-) vi **to p. (along)** (walk) avancer laborieusement; (work) travailler laborieusement; **to p. through a book** se forcer à lire un livre ▪ **plodding** adj (slow) lent; (step) pesant

plonk¹ [plɒŋk] 1 exclam (thud) vlan!; (splash) plouf! 2 vt Fam **to p. sth (down)** (drop) poser qch

plonk² [plɒŋk] n Br Fam (wine) pinard m

plot [plɒt] 1 n (conspiracy) complot m; (of novel, film) intrigue f; **p. (of land)** parcelle f de terrain; **(vegetable) p.** potager m 2 (pt & pp -tt-) vti comploter (**to do** de faire) 3 vt **to p. (out)** (route) déterminer; (diagram, graph) tracer; (one's position) relever

plough [plaʊ] (Am **plow**) 1 n charrue f; **the P.** (constellation) le Grand Chariot 2 vt (field) labourer; Fig (money) réinvestir; **to p. money back into sth** réinvestir de l'argent dans qch 3 vi labourer; Fig **to p. into sth** (crash into) percuter qch; Fig **to p. through sth** (snow, work) avancer péniblement dans qch ▪ **ploughman** (pl **-men**) n laboureur m; Br **p.'s lunch** = assiette de fromage ou jambon avec du pain, de la salade et des condiments

ploy [plɔɪ] n stratagème m

pluck [plʌk] 1 n courage m 2 vt (hair, feathers) arracher; (flower) cueillir; (fowl) plumer; (eyebrows) épiler; (string of guitar) pincer; **to p. up the courage to do sth** trouver le courage de faire qch ▪ **plucky** (**-ier, -iest**) adj courageux, -euse

plug [plʌg] 1 n (**a**) (of cotton wool, wood) tampon m; (for sink, bath) bonde f; **(wall) p.** (for screw) cheville f (**b**) (electrical) (on device) fiche f; (socket) prise f (de courant); Aut **(spark) p.** bougie f (**c**) Fam (publicity) pub f 2 (pt & pp -**gg**-) vt (**a**) **to p. (up)** (gap, hole) boucher; **to p. sth in** (appliance) brancher qch (**b**) Fam (promote) faire de la pub pour; **to p. away** s'acharner (**at** sur) ▪ **plughole** n trou m d'écoulement

plum [plʌm] n prune f; Fam **a p. job** un boulot en or

plumage ['pluːmɪdʒ] n plumage m

plumb [plʌm] 1 vt Fig **to p. the depths** toucher le fond 2 adv Am Fam (crazy) complètement; **p. in the middle** en plein centre

▸ **plumb in** *vt sep (washing machine)* brancher
plumber ['plʌmə(r)] *n* plombier *m* ▪ **plumbing** *n (job, system)* plomberie *f*
plume [plu:m] *n (feather)* plume *f*, *(on hat)* aigrette *f*; **a p. of smoke** une volute de fumée
plummet ['plʌmɪt] *vi (of prices)* s'effondrer; *(of aircraft)* plonger
plump [plʌmp] **1** *(-er, -est) adj (person, arm)* potelé; *(chicken)* dodu; *(cushion, cheek)* rebondi **2** *vi Fam* **to p. for sth** se décider pour qch
plunder ['plʌndə(r)] **1** *n (act)* pillage *m*; *(goods)* butin *m* **2** *vt* piller
plunge [plʌndʒ] **1** *n (dive)* plongeon *m*; *Fig (decrease)* chute *f*; *Fam* **to take the p.** *(take on difficult task)* se jeter à l'eau; *Fam (get married)* se marier **2** *vt (thrust)* plonger (**into** dans) **3** *vi (dive)* plonger (**into** dans); *Fig (decrease)* chuter ▪ **plunger** *n (for clearing sink)* ventouse *f*
plural ['plʊərəl] **1** *adj (form)* pluriel, -ielle; *(noun)* au pluriel **2** *n* pluriel *m*; **in the p.** au pluriel
plus [plʌs] **1** *prep* plus; *(as well as)* en plus de; **two p. two** deux plus deux **2** *adj (factor, quantity) & El* positif, -ive; **twenty p.** plus de vingt **3** *(pl* **plusses** ['plʌsɪz]*) n* **p. (sign)** *(signe m)* plus *m*; **that's a p.** c'est un plus
plush [plʌʃ] *(-er, -est) adj Fam* luxueux, -ueuse
plutonium [plu:'təʊnɪəm] *n Chem* plutonium *m*
ply [plaɪ] *(pt & pp* **plied***) vt (trade)* exercer; **to p. sb with drink** ne pas arrêter de verser à boire à qn; **to p. sb with questions** bombarder qn de questions
plywood ['plaɪwʊd] *n* contreplaqué *m*
PM [pi:'em] *(abbr* **Prime Minister***) n* Premier ministre *m*
p.m. [pi:'em] *adv (afternoon)* de l'après-midi; *(evening)* du soir
PMS [pi:ɛ'mes] *(abbr* **premenstrual syndrome***) n* syndrome *m* prémenstruel
PMT [pi:ɛm'ti:] *(abbr* **premenstrual tension***) n Br* syndrome *m* prémenstruel
pneumatic [nju:'mætɪk] *adj* **p. drill** marteau-piqueur *m*
pneumonia [nju:'məʊnɪə] *n* pneumonie *f*
poach [pəʊtʃ] **1** *vt (egg)* pocher; *(employee)* débaucher **2** *vi (hunt)* braconner ▪ **poacher** *n (person)* braconnier *m* ▪ **poaching** *n* braconnage *m*
PO Box [pi:'əʊbɒks] *(abbr* **Post Office Box***) n* boîte *f* postale, BP *f*
pocket ['pɒkɪt] **1** *n* poche *f*; **to be out of p.** en être de sa poche; **p. calculator** calculette *f*; **p. money** argent *m* de poche **2** *vt (put in pocket)* empocher; *Fam (steal)* rafler ▪ **pocketbook** *n (notebook)* carnet *m*; *Am (handbag)* sac *m* à main ▪ **pocketful** *n* **a p. of** une pleine poche de
pockmarked ['pɒkmɑ:kt] *adj* grêlé
pod [pɒd] *n* gousse *f*
podgy ['pɒdʒɪ] *(-ier, -iest) adj* grassouillet, -ette
podiatrist [pə'daɪətrɪst] *n Am* pédicure *mf*

podium ['pəʊdɪəm] *n* podium *m*
poem ['pəʊɪm] *n* poème *m* ▪ **poet** *n* poète *m* ▪ **poetic** [pəʊ'etɪk] *adj* poétique ▪ **poetry** *n* poésie *f*
po-faced ['pəʊ'feɪst] *adj Pej (expression, person)* pincé
poignant ['pɔɪnjənt] *adj* poignant
point [pɔɪnt] **1** *n* (**a**) *(of knife, needle)* pointe *f*; *Br* **points** *(for train)* aiguillage *m*; *Br* **(power) p.** prise *f* (de courant) (**b**) *(dot, score, degree, argument)* point *m*; *(location)* endroit *m*; *(importance)* intérêt *m*; **the highest p.** le point le plus haut; **to make a p.** faire une remarque; **to make a p. of doing sth** mettre un point d'honneur à faire qch; **I take your p.** je comprends ce que tu veux dire; **you have a p.** tu as raison; **what's the p.?** à quoi bon?; **there's no p. (in) staying** ça ne sert à rien de rester; **that's not the p.** il ne s'agit pas de ça; **that's beside the p.** ça n'a rien à voir; **to the p.** *(relevant)* pertinent; **to get to the p.** en arriver au fait; **at this p. in time** en ce moment; **at this p., the phone rang** à ce moment-là, le téléphone sonna; **to be on the p. of doing sth** être sur le point de faire qch; **his good points** ses qualités *fpl*; **his bad points** ses défauts *mpl*; **p. of sale** point de vente; **p. of view** point de vue (**c**) *Math* **three p. five** trois virgule cinq
2 *vt (aim)* diriger; *(camera, gun)* braquer (**at** sur); **to p. the way** montrer le chemin (**to** à); *Fig* montrer la voie (**to** à); **to p. one's finger at sb** montrer qn du doigt; **to p. sth out** *(show)* montrer qch; *(error, fact)* signaler qch
3 *vi* **to p. at** *or* **to sb/sth** *(with finger)* montrer qn/qch du doigt; **to p. north** *(of arrow, compass)* indiquer le nord; **to be pointing at sb/sth** *(of gun)* être braqué sur qn/qch; **to be pointing towards sth** *(of car, chair)* être face à qch; **everything points to suicide** tout laisse penser à un suicide
point-blank [pɔɪnt'blæŋk] **1** *adj (refusal)* catégorique; **at p. range** à bout portant **2** *adv (fire)* à bout portant; *(refuse)* (tout) net; *(request)* de but en blanc
pointed ['pɔɪntɪd] *adj* pointu; *(beard)* en pointe; *Fig (remark, criticism)* pertinent; *(incisive)* mordant ▪ **pointedly** *adv (meaningfully)* de façon insistante; *(markedly)* de façon marquée *ou* prononcée
pointer ['pɔɪntə(r)] *n (on dial)* aiguille *f*; *(stick)* baguette *f*; *(clue)* indice *m*; *Fam (advice)* tuyau *m*
pointless ['pɔɪntləs] *adj* inutile ▪ **pointlessly** *adv* inutilement
poise [pɔɪz] **1** *n (composure)* assurance *f*; *(grace)* grâce *f*; *(balance)* équilibre *m* **2** *vt (balance)* tenir en équilibre ▪ **poised** *adj (composed)* calme; *(hanging)* suspendu; *(balanced)* en équilibre; **to be p. to do sth** *(ready)* être prêt à faire qch

poison ['pɔɪzən] **1** *n* poison *m*; *(of snake)* venin *m*; **p. gas** gaz *m* toxique **2** *vt* empoisonner; **to p. sb's mind** corrompre qn ▪**poisoning** *n* empoisonnement *m* ▪**poisonous** *adj (fumes, substance)* toxique; *(snake)* venimeux, -euse; *(plant)* vénéneux, -euse

poke [pəʊk] **1** *n* petit coup *m* **2** *vt (person)* donner un coup à; *(object)* tâter; *(fire)* attiser; **to p. sth into sth** enfoncer qch dans qch; **to p. sb in the eye** mettre le doigt dans l'œil à qn; **to p. one's finger at sb** pointer son doigt vers qn; *Fig* **to p. one's nose into sth** mettre son nez dans qch; **to p. a hole in sth** faire un trou dans qch; **to p. one's head out of the window** passer la tête par la fenêtre; **to p. sb's eye out** crever l'œil à qn **3** *vi* **to p. at sth** *(with finger, stick)* tâter qch; **to p. about** *or* **around in sth** fouiner dans qch

poker[1] ['pəʊkə(r)] *n (for fire)* tisonnier *m*

poker[2] ['pəʊkə(r)] *n Cards* poker *m* ▪**poker-faced** *adj Fam* au visage impassible

poky ['pəʊkɪ] (**-ier, -iest**) *adj Br (small) (house, room)* riquiqui *inv*; *Am (slow)* lent

Poland ['pəʊlənd] *n* la Pologne ▪**Pole** *n* Polonais, -aise *mf* ▪**Polish** ['pəʊlɪʃ] **1** *adj* polonais **2** *n (language)* polonais *m*

polarize ['pəʊləraɪz] *vt (opinion, country)* diviser

Polaroid® ['pəʊlərɔɪd] *n (camera, photo)* Polaroid® *m*

pole[1] [pəʊl] *n (rod)* perche *f*; *(fixed)* poteau *m*; *(for flag)* hampe *f*; *Sport* **p. vault(ing)** saut *m* à la perche

pole[2] [pəʊl] *n Geog* pôle *m*; **North/South P.** pôle Nord/Sud; **the P. Star** l'étoile *f* polaire ▪**polar** *adj* polaire; **p. bear** ours *m* blanc

polemic [pə'lemɪk] *n* polémique *f* ▪**polemical** *adj* polémique

police [pə'liːs] **1** *n* police *f*; **a hundred p.** cent policiers *mpl* **2** *adj (inquiry, dog, State)* policier, -ière; *(protection, intervention)* de la police; *Br* **p. cadet** agent *m* de police stagiaire; **p. car** voiture *f* de police; *Am* **p. chief, chief of p.** commissaire *m* de police; *Am* **the p. department** service *m* de police; **p. force** police; **p. officer** agent *m* de police (*f* femme agent de police); **p. station** poste *m* de police; *Br* **p. van** fourgon *m* cellulaire **3** *vt (city, area)* maintenir l'ordre dans; *(frontier)* contrôler ▪**policeman** (*pl* **-men**) *n* agent *m* de police ▪**policewoman** (*pl* **-women**) *n* femme *f* agent de police

policy ['pɒlɪsɪ] (*pl* **-ies**) *n* (**a**) *(of government, organization)* politique *f*; **it's a matter of p.** c'est une question de principe (**b**) *(insurance)* **p.** police *f* (d'assurance); **p. holder** assuré, -ée *mf*

polio ['pəʊlɪəʊ] *n* polio *f*; **p. victim** polio *mf*

polish ['pɒlɪʃ] **1** *n (for shoes)* cirage *m*; *(for floor, furniture)* cire *f*; *(for nails)* vernis *m*; *Fig*

raffinement *m*; **to give sth a p.** faire briller qch **2** *vt (floor, table, shoes)* cirer; *(metal)* astiquer; *(rough surface)* polir; *Fig (manners)* raffiner; *(style)* polir; *Fam* **to p. off** *(food)* avaler; *(drink)* descendre; *(work)* expédier; **to p. up one's French** travailler son français

polite [pə'laɪt] (**-er, -est**) *adj* poli (**to** *or* **with** avec); **in p. society** chez les gens bien ▪**politely** *adv* poliment ▪**politeness** *n* politesse *f*

politic ['pɒlɪtɪk] *adj Formal (wise)* sage; **the body p.** le corps politique

political [pə'lɪtɪkəl] *adj* politique; **p. asylum** asile *m* politique; **p. correctness** le politiquement correct; **p. prisoner** prisonnier politique ▪**politically** *adv* politiquement; **p. correct** politiquement correct ▪**politicize** *vt* politiser

politician [pɒlɪ'tɪʃən] *n* homme *m*/femme *f* politique

politics ['pɒlɪtɪks] *n* politique *f*; **office p.** intrigues *fpl* de bureau

polka [*Br* 'pɒlkə, *Am* 'pəʊlkə] *n* polka *f*; **p. dot** pois *m*

poll [pəʊl] **1** *n (voting)* scrutin *m*; **to go to the polls** aller aux urnes; *(opinion)* **p.** sondage *m* (d'opinion) **2** *vt (votes)* obtenir; *(people)* sonder ▪**polling** *n (election)* élections *fpl*; **p. booth** isoloir *m*; *Br* **p. station**, *Am* **p. place** bureau *m* de vote

pollen ['pɒlən] *n* pollen *m*

pollute [pə'luːt] *vt* polluer ▪**pollutant** *n* polluant *m* ▪**pollution** *n* pollution *f*; **noise p.** pollution sonore

polo ['pəʊləʊ] *n Sport* polo *m*; **p. neck** *(sweater, neckline)* col *m* roulé; **p. shirt** polo *m*

polyester [pɒlɪ'estə(r)] *n* polyester *m*; **p. shirt** chemise *f* en polyester

Polynesia [pɒlɪ'niːʒə] *n* la Polynésie

polystyrene [pɒlɪ'staɪriːn] *n* polystyrène *m*

polytechnic [pɒlɪ'teknɪk] *n Br Formerly* établissement *m* d'enseignement supérieur

> Note that the French word **Polytechnique** is a false friend and is never a translation for the English word **polytechnic**. It is the name of one of the grandes écoles.

polythene ['pɒlɪθiːn] *n Br* polyéthylène *m*; **p. bag** sac *m* en plastique

polyunsaturated [pɒlɪʌn'sætʃʊreɪtɪd] *adj* polyinsaturé

pomegranate ['pɒmɪgrænɪt] *n (fruit)* grenade *f*

pomp [pɒmp] *n* pompe *f*; **p. and circumstance** (grand) apparat *m*

pompom ['pɒmpɒm] *n* pompon *m*

pompous ['pɒmpəs] *adj* pompeux, -euse

poncho ['pɒntʃəʊ] (*pl* **-os**) *n* poncho *m*

pond [pɒnd] *n* étang *m*; *(smaller)* mare *f*; *(artificial)* bassin *m*

ponder ['pɒndə(r)] **1** vt réfléchir à **2** vi **to p. (over sth)** réfléchir (à qch)

ponderous ['pɒndərəs] adj (movement, person) lourd; (progress) laborieux, -ieuse

pong [pɒŋ] Br Fam **1** n (smell) puanteur f **2** vi puer

pontificate [pɒn'tɪfɪkeɪt] vi pontifier (**about** sur)

pony ['pəʊnɪ] (pl **-ies**) n poney m **•ponytail** n queue f de cheval

poo [pu:] n Fam caca m; **to do** or Br **have a p.** faire caca

poodle ['pu:dəl] n caniche m

poof [pʊf] n Br very Fam Pej pédé m, = terme injurieux désignant un homosexuel

pooh [pu:] exclam bah!

pooh-pooh ['pu:'pu:] vt dédaigner

pool¹ [pu:l] n (puddle) flaque f; (of blood) mare f; (pond) étang m; (for swimming) piscine f

pool² [pu:l] **1** n (of money, helpers) réserve f; (of typists) pool m; Br **the (football) pools** = concours de pronostics des matchs de football **2** vt (share) mettre en commun

pool³ [pu:l] n (game) billard m américain

pooped [pu:pt] adj Am Fam vanné

poor [pʊə(r)] **1** (-er, -est) adj (not rich) pauvre; (bad) mauvais; (chances) maigre; (harvest, reward) faible; **to be in p. health** ne pas bien se porter; **p. thing!** le/la pauvre! **2** npl **the p.** les pauvres mpl **•poorly 1** adv mal; (clothed, furnished) pauvrement **2** adj Br Fam malade

pop¹ [pɒp] **1** exclam pan! **2** n (noise) bruit m sec; **to go p.** faire pan **3** (pt & pp **-pp-**) vt (**a**) (balloon) crever; (cork, button) faire sauter (**b**) Fam (put) mettre **4** vi (**a**) (burst) éclater; (of cork) sauter; (of ears) se déboucher (**b**) Br Fam **to p. in** passer; **to p. off** partir; **to p. out** sortir (un instant); **to p. over** or **round to sb's house** faire un saut (chez qn); **to p. up** surgir

pop² [pɒp] **1** n (music) pop f **2** adj (concert, singer, group) pop inv; **p. art** pop art m

pop³ [pɒp] n Am Fam (father) papa m

pop⁴ [pɒp] n (fizzy drink) soda m

popcorn ['pɒpkɔːn] n pop-corn m

pope [pəʊp] n pape m

pop-eyed [pɒp'aɪd] adj aux yeux écarquillés

poplar ['pɒplə(r)] n (tree, wood) peuplier m

popper ['pɒpə(r)] n Br (fastener) pression f

poppy ['pɒpɪ] (pl **-ies**) n (red, wild) coquelicot m; (cultivated) pavot m

Popsicle® ['pɒpsɪkəl] n Am (ice lolly) ≃ Esquimau® m

popular ['pɒpjʊlə(r)] adj populaire; (fashionable) à la mode; (restaurant) qui a beaucoup de succès; **to be p. with** plaire beaucoup à **•popularity** [-'lærɪtɪ] n popularité f (**with** auprès de) **•popularize** vt populariser; (science, knowledge) vulgariser **•popularly** adv communément

populate ['pɒpjʊleɪt] vt peupler; **highly/ sparsely populated** très/peu peuplé; **populated by** or **with** peuplé de

population [pɒpjʊ'leɪʃən] n population f

populous ['pɒpjʊləs] adj populeux, -euse

pop-up ['pɒpʌp] **1** n Comptr (advert) pop-up m **2** adj **p. book** livre m en relief; Comptr **p. menu** menu m local

porcelain ['pɔːsəlɪn] n porcelaine f

porch [pɔːtʃ] n porche m; Am (veranda) véranda f

porcupine ['pɔːkjʊpaɪn] n porc-épic m

pore [pɔː(r)] **1** n (of skin) pore m **2** vi **to p. over sth** (book, question) étudier qch de près **•porous** adj poreux, -euse

pork [pɔːk] n (meat) porc m; **p. pie** ≃ pâté m en croûte

pornography [pɔː'nɒgrəfɪ] n pornographie f **•porn** n & adj Fam porno (m) inv **•pornographic** [-nə'græfɪk] adj pornographique

porpoise ['pɔːpəs] n marsouin m

porridge ['pɒrɪdʒ] n porridge m; **p. oats** flocons mpl d'avoine

port¹ [pɔːt] **1** n (harbour) port m; **p. of call** escale f **2** adj (authorities, installations) portuaire

port² [pɔːt] n Naut (left-hand side) bâbord m

port³ [pɔːt] n (wine) porto m

portable ['pɔːtəbəl] adj portable

portal ['pɔːtəl] n Comptr portail m

porter ['pɔːtə(r)] n (for luggage) porteur m; (door attendant) chasseur m; (in hospital) brancardier m

portfolio [pɔːt'fəʊlɪəʊ] (pl **-os**) n (for documents) porte-documents m inv; (of shares, government minister) portefeuille m

porthole ['pɔːthəʊl] n hublot m

portion ['pɔːʃən] **1** n partie f; (share, helping) portion f **2** vt **to p. sth out** partager qch

portly ['pɔːtlɪ] (-ier, -iest) adj corpulent

portrait ['pɔːtreɪt, 'pɔːtrɪt] n portrait m; **p. painter** portraitiste mf

portray [pɔː'treɪ] vt (describe) dépeindre; (of actor) interpréter **•portrayal** n (description) tableau m; (by actor) interprétation f

Portugal ['pɔːtjʊgəl] n le Portugal **•Portuguese** [-'giːz] **1** adj portugais **2** n (person) Portugais, -aise mf; (language) portugais m; **the P.** (people) les Portugais

pose [pəʊz] **1** n (position) pose f **2** vt (question) poser; (threat) représenter **3** vi poser (**for** pour); **to p. as a lawyer** se faire passer pour un avocat **•poser** n Fam (person) poseur, -euse mf; (question) colle f **•poseur** [-'zɜː(r)] n (show-off) poseur, -euse mf

posh [pɒʃ] adj Fam (smart) chic inv; (snobbish) snob inv

position [pə'zɪʃən] **1** n (place, posture, opinion) position f; (of building, town) emplacement m;

(job, circumstances) situation f; *(window in bank)* guichet m; **in a p. to do sth** en mesure de faire qch; **in a good p. to do sth** bien placé pour faire qch; **in p.** en place **2** vt *(put)* placer; *(troops)* poster

positive ['pɒzɪtɪv] adj *(person, answer, test)* positif, -ive; *(progress, change)* réel (f réelle); *(evidence)* formel, -elle; *(tone)* assuré; *(certain)* sûr, certain (**of** de; **that** que); Fam **a p. genius** un véritable génie ■ **positively** adv *(identify)* formellement; *(think, react)* de façon positive; *(for emphasis)* véritablement; **to reply p.** *(saying yes)* répondre par l'affirmative

possess [pə'zes] vt posséder ■ **possession** n *(ownership)* possession f; *(thing possessed)* bien m; **to be in p. of sth** être en possession de qch; **to take p. of sth** prendre possession de qch ■ **possessor** n possesseur m

possessive [pə'zesɪv] **1** adj possessif, -ive **2** adj & n Grammar possessif (m)

possibility [pɒsɪ'bɪlɪtɪ] *(pl -ies)* n possibilité f; **there is some p. of...** il y a quelques chances de...; **it's a distinct p.** c'est bien possible

possible ['pɒsəbəl] **1** adj possible; **it is p. (for us) to do it** il (nous) est possible de le faire; **it is p. that...** il est possible que... (+ subjunctive); **as soon as p.** dès que possible; **as much/as many as p.** autant que possible; **if p.** si possible **2** n Fam *(person)* candidat m possible; *(thing)* option f

possibly ['pɒsɪblɪ] adv (a) *(perhaps)* peut-être (b) *(for emphasis)* **to do all one p. can** faire tout son possible (**to do** pour faire); **if you p. can** si cela t'est possible; **he cannot p. stay** il ne peut absolument pas rester

post¹ [pəʊst] **1** n Br *(postal system)* poste f; *(letters)* courrier m; **by p.** par la poste; **to catch/miss the p.** avoir/manquer la levée; **p. office** (bureau m de) poste; **the P. Office** *(government department)* ≃ la Poste **2** vt *(letter)* poster; **to keep sb posted** tenir qn au courant ■ **postbag** n Br sac m postal ■ **postbox** n Br boîte f aux lettres ■ **postcard** n carte f postale ■ **postcode** n Br code m postal ■ **postman** *(pl -men)* n Br facteur m ■ **postmark 1** n cachet m de la poste **2** vt oblitérer

post² [pəʊst] **1** n *(job, place)* poste m **2** vt *(sentry, guard)* poster; Br *(employee)* affecter (**to** à)

post³ [pəʊst] **1** n *(pole)* poteau m; *(of door, bed)* montant m; **finishing** or **winning p.** *(in race)* poteau m d'arrivée **2** vt **to p. (up)** *(notice)* afficher

post- [pəʊst] pref *(prefix)*; **post-1800** après 1800

postage ['pəʊstɪdʒ] n affranchissement m (**to** pour); **p. paid** port m payé; **p. stamp** timbre-poste m

postal ['pəʊstəl] adj *(services)* postal; *(inquiries)* par la poste; *(vote)* par correspondance; **p. district** secteur m postal; Br **p. order** mandat m postal; **p. worker** employé, -ée mf des postes

postdate [pəʊst'deɪt] vt postdater

poster ['pəʊstə(r)] n affiche f; *(for decoration)* poster m

posterior [pɒ'stɪərɪə(r)] n Hum *(buttocks)* postérieur m

posterity [pɒ'sterɪtɪ] n postérité f

postgraduate [pəʊst'grædjʊət] **1** adj de troisième cycle **2** n étudiant, -iante mf de troisième cycle

posthumous ['pɒstjʊməs] adj posthume; **to receive a p. award** recevoir un prix à titre posthume ■ **posthumously** adv à titre posthume

postmortem [pəʊst'mɔːtəm] adj & n **p. (examination)** autopsie f (**on** de)

postnatal ['pəʊstneɪtəl] adj postnatal *(mpl -als)*

postpone [pəʊs'pəʊn] vt reporter ■ **postponement** n report m

postscript ['pəʊstskrɪpt] n post-scriptum m inv

postulate ['pɒstjʊleɪt] vt poser comme hypothèse

posture ['pɒstʃə(r)] **1** n *(of body)* posture f; Fig attitude f **2** vi Pej prendre des poses

postwar ['pəʊstwɔː(r)] adj d'après-guerre

posy ['pəʊzɪ] *(pl -ies)* n petit bouquet m

pot¹ [pɒt] **1** n pot m; *(for cooking)* casserole f; **pots and pans** casseroles fpl; **jam p.** pot à confiture; Fam **to go to p.** aller à la ruine; Fam **gone to p.** *(person, plans)* fichu **2** *(pt & pp -tt-)* vt mettre en pot ■ **pothole** n *(in road)* nid-de-poule m; *(cave)* caverne f ■ **potholer** ['pɒthəʊlə(r)] n Br spéléologue mf ■ **potholing** ['pɒthəʊlɪŋ] n Br spéléologie f ■ **pot'luck** n **to take p.** prendre ce que l'on trouve ■ **potpourri** [pəʊ'pʊərɪ, -pə'riː] n pot-pourri m

pot² [pɒt] n Fam *(drug)* hasch m

potassium [pə'tæsɪəm] n potassium m

potato [pə'teɪtəʊ] *(pl -oes)* n pomme f de terre; Br **p. crisps**, Am **p. chips** chips fpl; **p. peeler** éplucheur m

potbelly ['pɒtbelɪ] *(pl -ies)* n bedaine f ■ **'pot'bellied** adj bedonnant

potent ['pəʊtənt] adj puissant; *(drink)* fort ■ **potency** n puissance f; *(of man)* virilité f

potential [pə'tenʃəl] **1** adj potentiel, -ielle **2** n potentiel m; **to have p.** avoir du potentiel ■ **potentially** adv potentiellement

potion ['pəʊʃən] n potion f

potted ['pɒtɪd] adj (a) *(plant)* en pot; *(food)* en terrine (b) Br *(version)* abrégé

potter ['pɒtə(r)] **1** n *(person)* potier, -ière mf **2** vi Br **to p. about** *(do odd jobs)* bricoler ■ **pottery** n *(art)* poterie f; *(objects)* poteries fpl; **a piece of p.** une poterie

potty¹ ['pɒtɪ] n *(for baby)* pot m; **p. training** apprentissage m de la propreté

potty² ['pɒtɪ] *(-ier, -iest)* adj Br Fam *(mad)* dingue

pouch [paʊtʃ] n bourse f; *(for tobacco)* blague f; *(of kangaroo)* poche f

pouf(fe) [pu:f] *n* pouf *m*

poultice ['pəʊltɪs] *n* cataplasme *m*

poultry ['pəʊltrɪ] *n* volaille *f*

pounce [paʊns] *vi (of animal)* bondir (**on** sur); *(of person)* se précipiter (**on** sur)

pound¹ [paʊnd] *n* (**a**) *(weight)* livre *f* (= *453,6 g*) (**b**) **p. (sterling)** livre *f* (sterling) (**c**) *Am Tel* **p. sign** *(on telephone)* dièse *m*

pound² [paʊnd] *n (for cars, dogs)* fourrière *f*

pound³ [paʊnd] 1 *vt (spices, nuts)* piler; *(meat)* attendrir; *(town)* pilonner 2 *vi (of heart)* battre à tout rompre; **to p. on the door** cogner à la porte

pour [pɔ:(r)] 1 *vt* verser; **to p. sb a drink** verser à boire à qn; **to p. money into sth** investir beaucoup d'argent dans qch 2 *vi* **it's pouring (with rain)** il pleut à verse

▸ **pour down** *vi* **it's pouring down** il pleut à verse

▸ **pour in** 1 *vt sep (liquid)* verser 2 *vi (of water, rain, sunshine)* entrer à flots; *Fig (of people, money)* affluer

▸ **pour off** *vt sep (liquid)* vider

▸ **pour out** 1 *vt sep (liquid)* verser; *Fig (anger, grief)* déverser 2 *vi (of liquid)* se déverser; *Fig (of people)* sortir en masse (**from** de); *(of smoke)* s'échapper (**from** de)

pout [paʊt] 1 *n* moue *f* 2 *vi* faire la moue

poverty ['pɒvətɪ] *n* pauvreté *f*; **extreme p.** la misère; **p. line** seuil *m* de pauvreté ▪ **poverty-stricken** *adj (person)* indigent; *(neighbourhood, conditions)* misérable

powder ['paʊdə(r)] 1 *n* poudre *f*; *Fig* **p. keg** *(dangerous place)* poudrière *f*; **p. puff** houppette *f*; **p. room** toilettes *fpl* pour dames 2 *vt (body, skin)* poudrer; **to p. one's face** *or* **nose** se poudrer ▪ **powdered** *adj (milk, eggs)* en poudre ▪ **powdery** *adj (snow)* poudreux, -euse; *(face)* couvert de poudre

power ['paʊə(r)] 1 *n (ability, authority)* pouvoir *m*; *(strength, nation)* puissance *f*; *(energy)* énergie *f*; *(electric current)* courant *m*; **to be in p.** être au pouvoir; **to have sb in one's p.** tenir qn à sa merci; *Math* **three to the p. of ten** trois puissance dix; *Law* **p. of attorney** procuration *f*; **p. of speech** usage *m* de la parole; *Br* **p. failure** *or* **cut** coupure *f* de courant; **p. point** prise *f* de courant; *Br* **p. station**, *Am* **p. plant** centrale *f* électrique; *Aut* **p. steering** direction *f* assistée 2 *vt (provide with power)* actionner; **to be powered by two engines** être propulsé par deux moteurs ▪ **powerful** ['paʊəfəl] *adj* puissant; *(drug)* fort ▪ **powerfully** *adv* puissamment ▪ **powerless** *adj* impuissant (**to do** à faire)

PR [pi:'ɑ:(r)] *(abbr public relations)* n RP *fpl*; **PR agency** agence *f* conseil en communication

practicable ['præktɪkəbəl] *adj* réalisable

practical ['præktɪkəl] *adj (tool, knowledge, solution)* pratique; **to be p.** *(of person)* avoir l'esprit pratique; **p. joke** farce *f* ▪ **practicality** [-'kælɪtɪ] *n (of person)* sens *m* pratique; **practicalities** *(of situation, scheme)* détails *mpl* pratiques

practically ['præktɪkəlɪ] *adv (almost)* pratiquement

practice ['præktɪs] 1 *n (action, exercise, custom)* pratique *f*; *(in sport)* entraînement *m*; *(of profession)* exercice *m* (**of** de); *(surgery)* centre *m* médical; **in p.** *(in reality)* dans la *ou* en pratique; **to put sth into p.** mettre qch en pratique; **to be out of p.** avoir perdu l'habitude; **to make a p. of doing sth** se faire une règle de faire qch; **to be good/bad p.** être conseillé/déconseillé 2 *vti Am* = **practise**

practise ['præktɪs] *(Am* **practice**) 1 *vt (sport, language, art, religion)* pratiquer; *(medicine, law)* exercer; *(musical instrument)* travailler 2 *vi (of musician)* s'exercer; *(of sportsperson)* s'entraîner; *(of doctor, lawyer)* exercer ▪ **practised** *adj (experienced)* expérimenté; *(ear, eye)* exercé ▪ **practising** *adj (doctor, lawyer)* en exercice; *Rel* pratiquant

practitioner [præk'tɪʃənə(r)] *n* praticien, -ienne *mf*; **general p.** (médecin *m*) généraliste *m*

pragmatic [præg'mætɪk] *adj* pragmatique

prairie ['preərɪ] *n* prairie *f*; **the P.** *(in USA)* la Grande Prairie; *(in Canada)* les Prairies *fpl*

praise [preɪz] 1 *n* éloges *mpl* 2 *vt* faire l'éloge de; *(God)* louer; **to p. sb for doing** *or* **having done sth** louer qn d'avoir fait qch ▪ **praiseworthy** *adj* digne d'éloges

pram [præm] *n Br* landau *m* (*pl* -aus)

prance [prɑ:ns] *vi* **to prance (about)** *(of horse)* caracoler; *(of person)* sautiller; **to p. in/out** entrer/sortir en sautillant

prank [præŋk] *n* farce *f*

prat [præt] *n Br Fam* andouille *f*

prattle ['prætəl] *vi* papoter (**about** de)

prawn [prɔ:n] *n* crevette *f* rose; **p. cocktail** cocktail *m* de crevettes; **p. cracker** beignet *m* de crevette

pray [preɪ] 1 *vt* **to p. that…** prier pour que… (+ *subjunctive*) 2 *vi* prier; **to p. to God** prier Dieu; *Fig* **to p. for good weather** prier pour qu'il fasse beau

prayer [preə(r)] *n* prière *f*

pre- [pri:] *pref* **pre-1800** avant 1800

preach [pri:tʃ] *vti* prêcher; **to p. to sb** prêcher qn; *Fig* faire la morale à qn; **to p. a sermon** faire un sermon ▪ **preacher** *n* prédicateur, -trice *mf* ▪ **preaching** *n* prédication *f*

preamble [pri:'æmbəl] *n* préambule *m*

prearrange [pri:ə'reɪndʒ] *vt* arranger à l'avance

precarious [prɪ'keərɪəs] *adj* précaire

precaution [prɪ'kɔ:ʃən] *n* précaution *f*; **as a p.** par précaution

precede [prɪ'siːd] *vti* précéder ▪ **preceding** *adj* précédent

precedence ['presɪdəns] *n (priority)* priorité *f*; *(in rank)* préséance *f*; **to take p. over sb** avoir la préséance sur qn; **to take p. over sth** passer avant qch

precedent ['presɪdənt] *n* précédent *m*; **to create** *or* **set a p.** créer un précédent

precept ['priːsept] *n* précepte *m*

precinct ['priːsɪŋkt] *n (of convent, palace)* enceinte *f*; *(boundary)* limite *f*; *Br (for shopping)* zone *f* commerçante piétonnière; *Am (electoral district)* circonscription *f*; *Am (police district)* secteur *m*; *Am* **p. station** *(police station)* commissariat *m* de quartier

precious ['preʃəs] **1** *adj* précieux, -ieuse; *Ironic* **her p. little bike** son cher petit vélo **2** *adv* **p. little** très peu de

precipice ['presɪpɪs] *n* précipice *m*

precipitate [prɪ'sɪpɪteɪt] *vt (hasten, throw)* & *Chem* précipiter ▪ **precipi'tation** *n (haste)* & *Chem* précipitation *f*; *(rainfall)* précipitations *fpl*

précis ['preɪsiː, *pl* -iːz] *n inv* précis *m*

precise [prɪ'saɪs] *adj (exact)* précis; *(meticulous)* méticuleux, -euse ▪ **precisely** *adv* précisément; **at three o'clock p.** à trois heures précises ▪ **precision** [-'sɪʒən] *n* précision *f*

preclude [prɪ'kluːd] *vt (prevent)* empêcher *(from doing de faire)*; *(possibility)* exclure

precocious [prɪ'kəʊʃəs] *adj* précoce

preconceived [priːkən'siːvd] *adj* préconçu ▪ **preconception** *n* idée *f* préconçue

precondition [priːkən'dɪʃən] *n* condition *f* préalable

precursor [priː'kɜːsə(r)] *n* précurseur *m*

predate [priː'deɪt] *vt (precede)* précéder; *(put earlier date on)* antidater

predator ['predətə(r)] *n* prédateur *m* ▪ **predatory** *adj* prédateur, -trice

predecessor [priːdɪsesə(r)] *n* prédécesseur *m*

predicament [prɪ'dɪkəmənt] *n* situation *f* difficile

predicate ['predɪkət] *n Grammar* prédicat *m*

predict [prɪ'dɪkt] *vt* prédire ▪ **predictable** *adj* prévisible ▪ **prediction** *n* prédiction *f*

predispose [priːdɪs'pəʊz] *vt* prédisposer *(to do* à faire*)* ▪ **predisposition** [-pə'zɪʃən] *n* prédisposition *f*

predominant [prɪ'dɒmɪnənt] *adj* prédominant ▪ **predominance** *n* prédominance *f* ▪ **predominantly** *adv* en majorité

predominate [prɪ'dɒmɪneɪt] *vi* prédominer *(over* sur*)*

pre-eminent [priː'emɪnənt] *adj* prééminent

pre-empt [priː'empt] *vt* devancer

preen [priːn] *vt* **to p. itself** *(of bird)* se lisser les plumes; **to p. oneself** *(of person)* se faire beau *(f* belle*)*

prefab ['priːfæb] *n Br Fam* préfabriqué *m* ▪ **pre'fabricate** *vt* préfabriquer

preface ['prefɪs] **1** *n (of book)* préface *f* **2** *vt* commencer *(with* par*)*

prefect ['priːfekt] *n Br Sch* = élève chargé de la surveillance

prefer [prɪ'fɜː(r)] *(pt & pp* **-rr-***) vt* préférer *(to* à*)*; **to p. to do sth** préférer faire qch; *Law* **to p. charges** porter plainte

preferable ['prefərəbəl] *adj* préférable *(to* à*)* ▪ **preferably** *adv* de préférence

preference ['prefərəns] *n* préférence *f (for* pour*)*; **in p.** to plutôt que ▪ **preferential** [-'renʃəl] *adj (terms, price)* préférentiel, -ielle; **p. treatment** traitement *m* de faveur

prefix ['priːfɪks] *n Grammar* préfixe *m*

pregnant ['pregnənt] *adj (woman)* enceinte; *(animal)* pleine; **five months p.** enceinte de cinq mois ▪ **pregnancy** *(pl* **-ies***) n* grossesse *f*; **p. test** test *m* de grossesse

prehistoric [priːhɪ'stɒrɪk] *adj* préhistorique

prejudge [priː'dʒʌdʒ] *vt (question)* préjuger de; *(person)* juger sans connaître

prejudice ['predʒədɪs] **1** *n (bias)* préjugé *m*; *Law* **without p. to** sans préjudice de **2** *vt (bias)* prévenir *(against/in favour of* contre/en faveur de*)*; *(harm)* nuire à ▪ **prejudiced** *adj (idea)* partial; **to be p.** avoir des préjugés *(against/in favour of* contre/en faveur de*)* ▪ **preju'dicial** *adj Law* préjudiciable *(to* à*)*

preliminary [prɪ'lɪmɪnərɪ] *adj* préliminaire ▪ **preliminaries** *npl* préliminaires *mpl*

prelude ['preljuːd] *n* prélude *m (to* à*)*

premarital [priː'mærɪtəl] *adj* avant le mariage

premature [*Br* 'premətʃʊə(r), *Am* priːmə'tʃʊər] *adj* prématuré ▪ **prematurely** *adv* prématurément

premeditate [priː'medɪteɪt] *vt* préméditer ▪ **premedi'tation** *n* préméditation *f*

premenstrual [priː'menstrʊəl] *adj* prémenstruel, -elle; *Br* **p. tension**, *Am* **p. syndrome** syndrome *m* prémenstruel

premier [*Br* 'premɪə(r), *Am* prɪ'mɪər] **1** *adj* premier, -ière **2** *n* Premier ministre *m*

première [*Br* 'premɪeə(r), *Am* prɪ'mɪər] *n (of play, film)* première *f*

premise ['premɪs] *n Phil* prémisse *f*

premises ['premɪsɪz] *npl* locaux *mpl*; **on the p.** sur place; **off the p.** en dehors de l'établissement

> Note that the French word **prémices** is a false friend. It never refers to a location.

premium ['priːmɪəm] *n Fin (for insurance)* prime *f*; *(additional sum)* supplément *m*; **at a p.** au prix fort; *Br* **p. bonds** ≃ obligations *fpl* à lots ▪ **premium-rate** *adj Tel (number)* surtaxé

premonition [*Br* premə'nɪʃən, *Am* priːmə'nɪʃən] *n* prémonition *f*

prenatal [priː'neɪtəl] *adj Am* prénatal

prenuptial [priː'nʌpʃəl] *adj* prénuptial; **p.**

agreement contrat *m* de mariage ▪**prenup** *n* *Fam* contrat *m* de mariage

preoccupy [priːˈɒkjʊpaɪ] (*pt & pp* **-ied**) *vt* préoccuper au plus haut point; **to be preoccupied** être préoccupé (**with** par) ▪**preoccu'pation** *n* préoccupation *f* (**with** pour); **to have a p. with sth** être préoccupé par qch

prep [prep] **1** *adj* **p. school** *Br* école *f* primaire privée; *Am* école secondaire privée **2** *n* (*homework*) devoirs *mpl*

pre-packed [priːˈpækt] *adj* (*meat, vegetables*) préemballé

prepaid [priːˈpeɪd] *adj* prépayé

preparation [prepəˈreɪʃən] *n* préparation *f*; **preparations** préparatifs *mpl* (**for** de)

preparatory [prəˈpærətərɪ] *adj* préparatoire; **p. school** *Br* école *f* primaire privée; *Am* école secondaire privée

prepare [prɪˈpeə(r)] **1** *vt* préparer (**sth for** qch pour; **sb for** qn à) **2** *vi* se préparer pour; **to p. to do sth** se préparer à faire qch ▪**prepared** *adj* (*made in advance*) préparé à l'avance; (*ready*) prêt (**to do** à faire); **to be p. for sth** s'attendre à qch

preposition [prepəˈzɪʃən] *n* préposition *f*

prepossessing [priːpəˈzesɪŋ] *adj* avenant

preposterous [prɪˈpɒstərəs] *adj* ridicule

prequel [ˈpriːkwəl] *n Cin* = film qui reprend des thèmes et des personnages d'un film réalisé plus tôt, mais dont l'action se déroule antérieurement aux événements exposés dans le premier film

prerecorded [priːrɪˈkɔːdɪd] *adj* préenregistré

prerequisite [priːˈrekwɪzɪt] *n* (condition *f*) préalable *m*

prerogative [prɪˈrɒgətɪv] *n* prérogative *f*

Presbyterian [prezbɪˈtɪərɪən] *adj & n Rel* presbytérien, -ienne (*mf*) ▪**Presbyterianism** *n Rel* presbytérianisme *m*

preschool [ˈpriːskuːl] *adj* préscolaire

prescribe [prɪˈskraɪb] *vt* (*of doctor*) prescrire ▪**prescribed** *adj* (*textbook*) (inscrit) au programme ▪**prescription** *n* (*for medicine*) ordonnance *f*; (*order*) prescription *f*; **on p.** sur ordonnance; **p. charge** = prix payé sur un médicament prescrit sur ordonnance

presence [ˈprezəns] *n* présence *f*; **in the p. of** en présence de; **p. of mind** présence d'esprit

present¹ [ˈprezənt] **1** *adj* (**a**) (*in attendance*) présent (**at** à; **in** dans); **those p.** les personnes présentes (**b**) (*current*) actuel, -uelle; *Grammar* **the p. tense** le présent **2** *n* **the p.** (*time, tense*) le présent; **for the p.** pour l'instant; **at p.** en ce moment ▪**'present-'day** *adj* actuel, -uelle ▪**presently** *adv* (*soon*) bientôt; *Am* (*now*) actuellement

present² **1** [ˈprezənt] *n* (*gift*) cadeau *m* **2** [prɪˈzent] *vt* (*show, introduce*) présenter (**to** à);

(*concert, film*) donner; (*proof*) fournir; **to p. sb with** (*gift*) offrir à qn; (*prize*) remettre à qn ▪**presentable** [prɪˈzentəbəl] *adj* (*person, appearance*) présentable ▪**presenter** [prɪˈzentə(r)] *n* présentateur, -trice *mf*

presentation [prezənˈteɪʃən] *n* présentation *f*; (*of prize*) remise *f*

preservation [prezəˈveɪʃən] *n* (*of building*) conservation *f*; (*of species*) protection *f*

preservative [prɪˈzɜːvətɪv] *n* conservateur *m*

> Note that the French word **préservatif** is a false friend and is never a translation for the English word **preservative**. It means **condom**.

preserve [prɪˈzɜːv] **1** *n* (*jam*) confiture *f*; (*sphere*) domaine *m* **2** *vt* (*keep, maintain*) conserver; (*fruit*) mettre en conserve; **to p. from** (*protect*) préserver de

preside [prɪˈzaɪd] *vi* présider; **to p. over** *or* **at a meeting** présider une réunion

presidency [ˈprezɪdənsɪ] (*pl* **-ies**) *n* présidence *f*

president [ˈprezɪdənt] *n* (*of country*) président, -ente *mf* ▪**presidential** [-ˈdenʃəl] *adj* présidentiel, -ielle

press¹ [pres] *n* (**a**) **the p.** la presse; **p. agency** agence *f* de presse; **p. campaign** campagne *f* de presse; **p. conference** conférence *f* de presse; **p. release** communiqué *m* de presse (**b**) (*machine*) presse *f*; (*for making wine*) pressoir *m*; (*printing*) **p.** presse; **to go to p.** (*of newspaper*) partir à l'impression

press² [pres] **1** *n* pression *f*; **to give sth a p.** repasser qch; **p. stud** bouton-pression *m* **2** *vt* (*button, doorbell*) appuyer sur; (*tube, lemon*) presser; (*hand*) serrer; (*clothes*) repasser; (*pressurize*) faire pression sur; **to p. sb to do sth** presser qn de faire qch; *Law* **to p. charges** engager des poursuites (**against** contre) **3** *vi* (*push*) appuyer (**on** sur); (*of weight*) faire pression (**on** sur) ▪**press-gang** *vt* **to p. sb into doing sth** forcer qn à faire qch ▪**press-up** *n* (*exercise*) pompe *f*

▸ **press down** *vt insep* (*button*) appuyer sur

▸ **press for** *vt sep* (*demand*) exiger

▸ **press on** *vi* (*carry on*) continuer; **to p. on with one's work** continuer de travailler

pressed [prest] *adj* **to be hard p.** (*in difficulties*) être en difficultés; (*busy*) être débordé; **to be p. for time** être pressé par le temps

pressing [ˈpresɪŋ] *adj* (*urgent*) pressant

pressure [ˈpreʃə(r)] **1** *n* pression *f*; **the p. of work** le stress lié au travail; **to be under p.** être stressé; **to put p. on sb (to do sth)** faire pression sur qn (pour qu'il fasse qch); **p. cooker** Cocotte-Minute® *f*; **p. gauge** manomètre *m*; **p. group** groupe *m* de pression **2** *vt* **to p. sb to do sth** *or* **into doing sth** faire pression sur qn pour qu'il fasse qch

pressurize ['preʃəraɪz] *vt (aircraft)* pressuriser; **pressurized cabin** cabine *f* pressurisée; **to p. sb (into doing sth)** faire pression sur qn (pour qu'il fasse qch)

prestige [pre'sti:ʒ] *n* prestige *m* • **prestigious** [*Br* pre'stɪdʒəs, *Am* -'sti:dʒəs] *adj* prestigieux, -ieuse

presume [prɪ'zju:m] *vt (suppose)* présumer (**that** que); **to p. to do sth** se permettre de faire qch • **presumably** *adv* sans doute; **p. she'll come** je suppose qu'elle viendra • **presumption** [-'zʌmpʃən] *n* présomption *f*

presumptuous [prɪ'zʌmptʃʊəs] *adj* présomptueux, -ueuse

presuppose [pri:sə'pəʊz] *vt* présupposer (**that** que)

pretence [prɪ'tens] (*Am* **pretense**) *n (sham)* simulation *f*; *(claim, affectation)* prétention *f*; **to make a p. of sth/of doing sth** feindre qch/de faire qch; **on** or **under false pretences** sous des prétextes fallacieux

pretend [prɪ'tend] **1** *vt (make believe)* faire semblant (**to do** de faire); *(claim, maintain)* prétendre (**to do** faire; **that** que) **2** *vi* faire semblant; **to p. to sth** prétendre à qch

pretense [prɪ'tens] *n Am* = **pretence**

pretentious [prɪ'tenʃəs] *adj* prétentieux, -euse • **pretension** *n* prétention *f*

pretext ['pri:tekst] *n* prétexte *m*; **on the p. of/ that** sous prétexte de/que

pretty ['prɪtɪ] **1** (*-ier, -iest*) *adj* joli **2** *adv Fam (rather, quite)* assez; **p. well, p. much, p. nearly** *(almost)* pratiquement

prevail [prɪ'veɪl] *vi (predominate)* prédominer; *(be successful)* l'emporter (**over** sur); **to p. (up)on sb to do sth** persuader qn de faire qch • **prevailing** *adj* prédominant; *(wind)* dominant

prevalent ['prevələnt] *adj* très répandu • **prevalence** *n (predominance)* prédominance *f*; *(frequency)* fréquence *f*

prevaricate [prɪ'værɪkeɪt] *vi* tergiverser

prevent [prɪ'vent] *vt* empêcher (**from doing** de faire) • **preventable** *adj* évitable • **prevention** *n* prévention *f* • **preventive** *adj* préventif, -ive

preview ['pri:vju:] *n (of film, painting)* avant-première *f*; *Fig (overall view)* aperçu *m*

previous ['pri:vɪəs] **1** *adj* précédent; **to have p. experience** avoir une expérience préalable; **to have a p. engagement** être déjà pris **2** *adv* **p. to** avant • **previously** *adv* auparavant

pre-war ['pri:'wɔ:(r)] *adj* d'avant-guerre

prey [preɪ] **1** *n* proie *f*; *Fig* **to be (a) p.** to être en proie à **2** *vi* **to p. on** *(person)* prendre pour cible; *(fears, doubts)* exploiter; **to p. on sb's mind** tourmenter qn

price [praɪs] **1** *n* prix *m*; **to pay a high p. for sth** payer cher qch; *Fig* payer chèrement qch; **he** **wouldn't do it at any p.** il ne le ferait à aucun prix **2** *adj (control, war, rise)* des prix; **p. list** tarif *m* **3** *vt* mettre un prix à; **it's priced at £5** ça coûte 5 livres

priceless ['praɪsləs] *adj (invaluable)* qui n'a pas de prix; *Fam (funny)* impayable

pricey ['praɪsɪ] (*-ier, -iest*) *adj Fam* cher (*f* chère)

prick [prɪk] **1** *n (of needle)* piqûre *f* **2** *vt (jab)* piquer (**with** avec); *(burst)* crever; **to p. up one's ears** *(of animal)* dresser les oreilles; *(of person)* tendre l'oreille

prickle ['prɪkəl] *n (of animal)* piquant *m*; *(of plant)* épine *f* • **prickly** (*-ier, -iest*) *adj (plant)* à épines; *(animal)* couvert de piquants; *(beard)* piquant; *Fig (subject)* épineux, -euse; *Fig (person)* susceptible

pride [praɪd] **1** *n (satisfaction)* fierté *f*; *(self-esteem)* amour-propre *m*; *Pej (vanity)* orgueil *m*; **to take p. in sth** mettre toute sa fierté dans qch; **to take p. in doing sth** mettre toute sa fierté à faire qch; **to be sb's p. and joy** faire le bonheur de qn; **to have p. of place** trôner **2** *vt* **to p. oneself on sth/on doing sth** s'enorgueillir de qch/de faire qch

priest [pri:st] *n* prêtre *m* • **priesthood** *n* prêtrise *f*; **to enter the p.** entrer dans les ordres • **priestly** *adj* sacerdotal

prig [prɪg] *n* prêcheur, -euse *mf* • **priggish** *adj* prêcheur, -euse

prim [prɪm] (**primmer, primmest**) *adj* **p. (and proper)** *(person, expression)* collet monté *inv*; *(manner)* guindé

primacy ['praɪməsɪ] *n* primauté *f*

primarily [*Br* 'praɪmərəlɪ, *Am* praɪ'merəlɪ] *adv* essentiellement

primary ['praɪmərɪ] **1** *adj (main)* principal; *(initial)* primaire; **of p. importance** de première importance; **p. education** enseignement *m* primaire; *Br* **p. school** école *f* primaire **2** (*pl* **-ies**) *n Am (election)* primaire *f*

primate ['praɪmeɪt] *n (animal)* primate *m*

prime [praɪm] **1** *adj (principal)* principal; *(importance)* capital; *(excellent)* excellent; **P. Minister** Premier ministre *m*; *Math* **p. number** nombre *m* premier; **p. quality** de premier choix **2** *n* **in the p. of life** dans la fleur de l'âge **3** *vt (gun, pump)* amorcer; *(surface)* apprêter • **primer** *n* (**a**) *(book)* manuel *m* élémentaire (**b**) *(paint)* apprêt *m*

primeval [praɪ'mi:vəl] *adj* primitif, -ive

primitive ['prɪmɪtɪv] *adj (original)* primitif, -ive; *(basic)* de base

primrose ['prɪmrəʊz] *n (plant)* primevère *f*

prince [prɪns] *n* prince *m*; **the P. of Wales** le prince de Galles • **princely** *adj* princier, -ière • **prin'cess** *n* princesse *f*

principal ['prɪnsɪpəl] **1** *adj (main)* principal **2** *n* *(of school)* proviseur *m*; *(of university)* ≃

président, -ente *mf* ▪ **principally** *adv* principalement

principality [prɪnsɪ'pælɪtɪ] (*pl* **-ies**) *n* principauté *f*

principle ['prɪnsɪpəl] *n* principe *m*; **in p.** en principe; **on p.** par principe

print [prɪnt] **1** *n* (*of finger, foot*) empreinte *f*; (*letters*) caractères *mpl*; (*engraving*) estampe *f*; (*photo*) épreuve *f*; (*fabric*) imprimé *m*; **in p.** (*book*) disponible en librairie; **out of p.** (*book*) épuisé **2** *vt* (*book, newspaper*) imprimer; (*photo*) tirer; (*write*) écrire en script; **to p. 5,000 copies of a book** tirer un livre à 5000 exemplaires; **to have a book printed** publier un livre; *Comptr* **to p. out** imprimer ▪ **printed** *adj* imprimé; **p. matter** imprimés *mpl* ▪ **printing** *n* (*technique, industry*) imprimerie *f*; (*action*) tirage *m*; **p. error** faute *f* d'impression ▪ **printout** *n Comptr* sortie *f* papier

printer ['prɪntə(r)] *n* (*person*) imprimeur *m*; (*machine*) imprimante *f*

prior ['praɪə(r)] **1** *adj* antérieur; (*experience*) préalable **2** *adv* **p. to sth** avant qch; **p. to doing sth** avant de faire qch

priority [praɪ'ɒrɪtɪ] (*pl* **-ies**) *n* priorité *f* (**over** sur)

priory ['praɪərɪ] (*pl* **-ies**) *n Rel* prieuré *m*

prise [praɪz] *vt Br* **to p. sth off/open** retirer/ouvrir qch en forçant

prism ['prɪzəm] *n* prisme *m*

prison ['prɪzən] **1** *n* prison *f*; **in p.** en prison **2** *adj* (*life, system*) pénitentiaire; (*camp*) de prisonniers; **p. officer** gardien, -ienne *mf* de prison ▪ **prisoner** *n* prisonnier, -ière *mf*; **to take sb p.** faire qn prisonnier; **p. of conscience** prisonnier d'opinion; **p. of war** prisonnier de guerre

prissy ['prɪsɪ] (**-ier, -iest**) *adj Fam* collet monté *inv*

pristine ['prɪstiːn] *adj* (*immaculate*) impeccable; **in p. condition** en parfait état

privacy ['praɪvəsɪ, *Br* 'prɪvəsɪ] *n* intimité *f*; **to give sb some p.** laisser qn seul

private ['praɪvɪt] **1** *adj* privé; (*lesson, car*) particulier, -ière; (*report, letter*) confidentiel, -ielle; (*personal*) personnel, -elle; (*dinner, wedding*) intime; **a p. citizen** un simple particulier; **p. detective, p. eye, p. investigator** détective *m* privé; *Fam* **p. parts** parties *fpl* (génitales); **p. property** propriété *f* privée; **p. secretary** secrétaire *m* particulier, secrétaire *f* particulière; **p. tutor** professeur *m* particulier; **to be a very p. person** aimer la solitude **2** *n* (**a**) **in p.** (*not publicly*) en privé; (*have dinner, get married*) dans l'intimité (**b**) (*soldier*) simple soldat *m*

privately ['praɪvɪtlɪ] *adv* (*in private*) en privé; (*in one's heart of hearts*) en son for intérieur; (*personally*) à titre personnel; **p. owned** (*company*) privé; (*hotel*) familial; **to be p. educated** faire sa scolarité dans le privé; **to be treated p.** ≃ se faire soigner par un médecin non conventionné

privatize ['praɪvətaɪz] *vt* privatiser ▪ **privati'zation** *n* privatisation *f*

privet ['prɪvɪt] *n* troène *m*

privilege ['prɪvɪlɪdʒ] *n* privilège *m* ▪ **privileged** *adj* privilégié; **to be p. to do sth** avoir le privilège de faire qch

privy ['prɪvɪ] *adj Formal* **to be p. to sth** avoir connaissance de qch

prize¹ [praɪz] *n* prix *m*; (*in lottery*) lot *m*; **the first p.** (*in lottery*) le gros lot ▪ **prizegiving** *n* distribution *f* des prix ▪ **prizewinner** *n* (*in contest*) lauréat, -éate *mf*; (*in lottery*) gagnant, -ante *mf* ▪ **prizewinning** *adj* (*essay, animal*) primé; (*ticket*) gagnant

prize² [praɪz] *vt* (*value*) attacher de la valeur à; **my most prized possession** mon bien le plus précieux

prize³ [praɪz] *vt Am* = **prise**

pro [prəʊ] (*pl* **pros**) *n Fam* (*professional*) pro *mf*

proactive [prəʊ'æktɪv] *adj* qui fait preuve d'initiative

probable ['prɒbəbəl] *adj* probable (**that** que) ▪ **proba'bility** (*pl* **-ies**) *n* probabilité *f*; **in all p.** selon toute probabilité ▪ **probably** *adv* probablement

probation [prə'beɪʃən] *n* **on p.** (*criminal*) en liberté surveillée; (*in job*) en période d'essai; **p. officer** agent *m* de probation ▪ **probationary** *adj* (*in job*) d'essai; (*of criminal*) de liberté surveillée

probe [prəʊb] **1** *n* (*device*) sonde *f*; (*inquiry*) enquête *f* (**into** dans) **2** *vt* (*prod*) sonder; (*inquire into*) enquêter sur **3** *vi* **to p. into sth** (*past, private life*) fouiller dans qch ▪ **probing** *adj* (*question*) perspicace

problem ['prɒbləm] *n* problème *m*; **he's got a drug/a drink p.** c'est un drogué/un alcoolique; *Fam* **no p.!** pas de problème!; **p. child** enfant *mf* à problèmes; **p. page** courrier *m* du cœur ▪ **proble'matic** *adj* problématique

procedure [prə'siːdʒə(r)] *n* procédure *f*

proceed [prə'siːd] *vi* (*go on*) se poursuivre; **to p. to sth** passer à qch; **to p. with sth** poursuivre qch; **to p. to do sth** se mettre à faire qch

proceedings [prə'siːdɪŋz] *npl* (*events*) opérations *fpl*; (*minutes of meeting*) actes *mpl*; **to take (legal) p.** intenter un procès (**against** contre)

proceeds ['prəʊsiːdz] *npl* recette *f*

process ['prəʊses] **1** *n* processus *m*; (*method*) procédé *m*; **by a p. of elimination** par élimination; **in p.** (*work*) en cours; **in the p. of doing sth** en train de faire qch **2** *vt* (*food, data*) traiter; (*film*) développer; **processed**

food aliments *mpl* conditionnés ▪ **processing** *n* traitement *m*; *(of photo)* développement *m*

> Note that the French noun **procès** is a false friend. It only means **trial**.

procession [prə'seʃən] *n* défilé *m*

processor ['prəʊsesə(r)] *n Comptr* processeur *m*; **food p.** robot *m* de cuisine

proclaim [prə'kleɪm] *vt* proclamer (**that** que); **to p. sb king** proclamer qn roi ▪ **proclamation** [prɒklə'meɪʃən] *n* proclamation *f*

procrastinate [prə'kræstɪneɪt] *vi* atermoyer ▪ **procrasti'nation** *n* atermoiements *mpl*

procreate ['prəʊkrɪeɪt] *vt* procréer ▪ **pro-cre'ation** *n* procréation *f*

procure [prə'kjʊə(r)] *vt* **to p. sth (for oneself)** se procurer qch; **to p. sth for sb** procurer qch à qn

prod [prɒd] **1** *n* petit coup *m* **2** (*pt & pp* **-dd-**) *vti* *(poke)* donner un petit coup (dans); *Fig* **to p. sb into doing sth** pousser qn à faire qch

prodigal ['prɒdɪgəl] *adj* prodigue

prodigious [prə'dɪdʒəs] *adj* prodigieux, -ieuse

prodigy ['prɒdɪdʒɪ] (*pl* **-ies**) *n* prodige *m*; **child p.** enfant *mf* prodige

produce[1] [prə'dju:s] *vt* *(create)* produire; *(machine)* fabriquer; *(passport, ticket)* présenter; *(documents, alibi)* fournir; *(from bag, pocket)* sortir; *(film, play, programme)* produire; *(reaction)* entraîner ▪ **producer** *n* producteur, -trice *mf*

produce[2] ['prɒdju:s] *n* *(products)* produits *mpl*

product ['prɒdʌkt] *n* *(article, creation)* & *Math* produit *m*

production [prə'dʌkʃən] *n* production *f*; *(of play)* mise *f* en scène; *Radio* réalisation *f*; **to work on the p. line** travailler à la chaîne

productive [prə'dʌktɪv] *adj* productif, -ive ▪ **productivity** [prɒdʌk'tɪvɪtɪ] *n* productivité *f*

profane [prə'feɪn] **1** *adj* *(secular)* profane; *(language)* grossier, -ière **2** *vt* profaner

profess [prə'fes] *vt* *(declare)* professer; **to p. to be** prétendre être ▪ **professed** *adj* *(self-declared)* avoué

profession [prə'feʃən] *n* profession *f*; **the medical p.** le corps médical; **by p.** de profession ▪ **professional 1** *adj* professionnel, -elle; *(man, woman)* qui exerce une profession libérale; *(army)* de métier; *(diplomat)* de carrière; *(piece of work)* de professionnel **2** *n* professionnel, -elle *mf* ▪ **professionalism** *n* professionnalisme *m* ▪ **professionally** *adv* professionnellement; *(perform, play)* en professionnel

professor [prə'fesə(r)] *n Br* ≃ professeur *m* d'université; *Am* = enseignant d'université

proffer ['prɒfə(r)] *vt Formal (advice)* offrir

proficient [prə'fɪʃənt] *adj* compétent (**in** en) ▪ **proficiency** *n* compétence *f* (**in** en)

profile ['prəʊfaɪl] *n* *(of person, object)* profil *m*; *(description)* portrait *m*; **in p.** de profil; *Fig* **to keep a low p.** garder un profil bas ▪ **profiled** *adj* **to be p. against** se profiler sur

profit ['prɒfɪt] **1** *n* profit *m*, bénéfice *m*; **to sell at a p.** vendre à profit; **p. margin** marge *f* bénéficiaire **2** *vi* **to p. by** *or* **from sth** tirer profit de qch ▪ **profit-making** *adj* *(aiming to make profit)* à but lucratif; *(profitable)* rentable; **non** *or* **not p.** à but non lucratif

profitable ['prɒfɪtəbəl] *adj* *(commercially)* rentable; *Fig (worthwhile)* profitable ▪ **profita'bility** *n* rentabilité *f* ▪ **profitably** *adv* à profit

profiteer [prɒfɪ'tɪə(r)] *Pej* **1** *n* profiteur, -euse *mf* **2** *vi* profiter d'une situation pour faire des bénéfices

profound [prə'faʊnd] *adj* profond ▪ **profoundly** *adv* profondément ▪ **profundity** [-'fʌndɪtɪ] (*pl* **-ies**) *n* profondeur *f*

profuse [prə'fju:s] *adj* abondant ▪ **profusely** *adv* *(bleed)* abondamment; *(flow)* à profusion; *(thank)* avec effusion; **to apologize p.** se confondre en excuses ▪ **profusion** *n* profusion *f*; **in p.** à profusion

progeny ['prɒdʒɪnɪ] (*pl* **-ies**) *n Formal* progéniture *f*

programme ['prəʊgræm] (*Am* **program**) **1** *n* *(for play, political party, computer)* programme *m*; *(on TV, radio)* émission *f* **2** (*pt & pp* **-mm-**) *vt* *(machine)* programmer ▪ **programmer** *n* **(computer) p.** programmeur, -euse *mf* ▪ **programming** *n* **(computer) p.** programmation *f*

progress 1 ['prəʊgres] *n* progrès *m*; **to make (good) p.** faire des progrès; **to make p. in sth** progresser dans qch; **in p.** en cours **2** [prə'gres] *vi* *(advance, improve)* progresser; *(of story, meeting)* se dérouler

progression [prə'greʃən] *n* progression *f*

progressive [prə'gresɪv] *adj* *(gradual)* progressif, -ive; *(company, ideas, political party)* progressiste ▪ **progressively** *adv* progressivement

prohibit [prə'hɪbɪt] *vt* interdire (**sb from doing** à qn de faire); **we're prohibited from leaving** il nous est interdit de partir ▪ **prohibition** [prəʊhɪ'bɪʃən] *n* interdiction *f* ▪ **prohibitive** *adj* prohibitif, -ive

project [prə'dʒekt] **1** ['prɒdʒekt] *n* *(plan, undertaking)* projet *m*; *(at school)* dossier *m*; *Am* **(housing) p.** ≃ cité *f* HLM **2** *vt* *(plan)* prévoir; *(propel, show)* projeter **3** *vi* *(protrude)* dépasser ▪ **projected** *adj* *(planned, forecast)* prévu

projection [prə'dʒekʃən] *n* projection *f*; *(protruding part)* saillie *f* ▪ **projectionist** *n* projectionniste *mf* ▪ **projector** *n* projecteur *m*

proletarian [prəʊlə'teərɪən] **1** *adj* *(class)*

prolétarien, -ienne; *(outlook)* de prolétaire **2** *n* prolétaire *mf* ▪ **proletariat** *n* prolétariat *m*

proliferate [prə'lɪfəreɪt] *vi* proliférer ▪ **prolife'ration** *n* prolifération *f*

prolific [prə'lɪfɪk] *adj* prolifique

prologue ['prəʊlɒg] *n* prologue *m* (**to** de)

prolong [prə'lɒŋ] *vt* prolonger

prom [prɒm] *(abbr* **promenade)** *n* (**a**) *Br (at seaside)* promenade *f* (**b**) *Am (dance)* bal *m* d'étudiants ▪ **proms** *npl Br Fam* **the p.** = festival de concerts-promenades

promenade [prɒmə'nɑːd] *n Br (at seaside)* front *m* de mer

prominent ['prɒmɪnənt] *adj (important)* important; *(nose, chin)* proéminent; *(tooth)* en avant; *(peak, landscape)* en saillie; **in a p. position** en évidence ▪ **prominence** *n (importance)* importance *f* ▪ **prominently** *adv* bien en vue

promiscuous [prə'mɪskjʊəs] *adj* qui a de multiples partenaires ▪ **promiscuity** [prɒmɪs-'kjuːətɪ] *n* promiscuité *f* sexuelle

promise ['prɒmɪs] **1** *n* promesse *f*; **to show p., to be full of p.** promettre **2** *vt* promettre (**to do** de faire); **to p. sth to sb, to p. sb sth** promettre qch à qn **3** *vi* **I p.!** je te le promets!; **p.?** promis? ▪ **promising** *adj* prometteur, -euse; **that looks p.** ça s'annonce bien

promote [prə'məʊt] *vt (raise in rank, encourage)* promouvoir; *(advertise)* faire la promotion de ▪ **promoter** *n (of theory)* défenseur, -euse *mf*; *(of boxing match, show)* organisateur, -trice *mf*; *Com* promoteur *m* ▪ **promotion** *n* promotion *f*

prompt¹ [prɒmpt] **1** *adj (speedy)* rapide; *(punctual)* ponctuel, -uelle; **p. to act** prompt à agir **2** *adv* **at eight o'clock p.** à huit heures précises ▪ **promptly** *adv (rapidly)* rapidement; *(punctually)* ponctuellement; *(immediately)* immédiatement ▪ **promptness** *n* rapidité *f*; *(readiness to act)* promptitude *f*; *(punctuality)* ponctualité *f*

prompt² [prɒmpt] **1** *vt* (**a**) *(cause)* provoquer; **to p. sb to do sth** pousser qn à faire qch (**b**) *(actor)* souffler à **2** *n Comptr* invite *f* ▪ **prompter** *n Theatre* souffleur, -euse *mf*

prone [prəʊn] *adj* (**a**) **to be p. to sth** être sujet, -ette à qch; **to be p. to do sth** avoir tendance à faire qch (**b**) *Formal (lying flat)* sur le ventre

prong [prɒŋ] *n (of fork)* dent *f*

pronoun ['prəʊnaʊn] *n Grammar* pronom *m* ▪ **pro'nominal** *adj* pronominal

pronounce [prə'naʊns] **1** *vt (say, articulate)* prononcer; **to p. that...** déclarer que...; **he was pronounced dead** on l'a déclaré mort **2** *vi (articulate)* prononcer; *(give judgement)* se prononcer (**on** sur) ▪ **pronouncement** *n Formal* déclaration *f* ▪ **pronunciation** [-nʌnsɪ'eɪʃən] *n* prononciation *f*

pronto ['prɒntəʊ] *adv Fam* illico

proof [pruːf] **1** *n (evidence)* preuve *f*; *(of book, photo)* épreuve *f*; *(of drink)* teneur *f* en alcool; **to give p. of sth** prouver qch; **p. of identity** pièce *f* d'identité **2** *adj* **to be p. against sth** être résistant à qch ▪ **proofreader** *n* correcteur, -trice *mf* ▪ **proofreading** *n* correction *f* d'épreuves

prop [prɒp] **1** *n (physical support)* support *m*; *Fig (emotional support)* soutien *m*; *Theatre* accessoire *m* **2** *(pt & pp* **-pp-)** *vt* **to p. sth (up) against sth** appuyer qch contre qch; **to p. sth up** *(building, tunnel)* étayer qch; *Fig (economy, regime)* soutenir qch

propaganda [prɒpə'gændə] *n* propagande *f*

propagate ['prɒpəgeɪt] **1** *vt* propager **2** *vi* se propager

propel [prə'pel] *(pt & pp* **-ll-)** *vt* propulser ▪ **propeller** *n* hélice *f*

propensity [prə'pensɪtɪ] *(pl* **-ies)** *n* propension *f* (**for** à)

proper ['prɒpə(r)] *adj* (**a**) *(correct)* vrai; *(word)* correct; **the village p.** le village proprement dit; *Grammar* **p. noun** nom *m* propre (**b**) *(appropriate)* bon *(f* bonne); *(equipment)* adéquat; *(behaviour)* convenable; **in the p. way** comme il faut (**c**) **p. to sb/sth** *(characteristic of)* propre à qn/qch (**d**) *Br (downright)* véritable ▪ **properly** *adv (suitably)* convenablement; *(correctly)* correctement

property ['prɒpətɪ] **1** *(pl* **-ies)** *n* (**a**) *(land, house)* propriété *f*; *(possessions)* biens *mpl* (**b**) *(quality)* propriété *f* **2** *adj (speculator)* immobilier, -ière; *(tax)* foncier, -ière; **p. developer** promoteur *m* immobilier; **p. market** marché *m* immobilier; **p. owner** propriétaire *m* foncier

prophecy ['prɒfɪsɪ] *(pl* **-ies)** *n* prophétie *f* ▪ **prophesy** [-saɪ] *(pt & pp* **-ied)** *vt* prédire

prophet ['prɒfɪt] *n* prophète *m* ▪ **prophetic** [prə'fetɪk] *adj* prophétique

proportion [prə'pɔːʃən] **1** *n (ratio, part)* proportion *f*; **proportions** *(size)* proportions *fpl*; **in p.** proportionné (**to** avec); **out of p.** disproportionné (**to** par rapport à) **2** *vt* proportionner (**to** à); **well** *or* **nicely proportioned** bien proportionné ▪ **proportional, proportionate** *adj* proportionnel, -elle (**to** à); *Pol* **proportional representation** proportionnelle *f*

proposal [prə'pəʊzəl] *n* proposition *f*; *(plan)* projet *m*; *(for marriage)* demande *f* en mariage ▪ **proposition** [prɒpə'zɪʃən] *n* proposition *f*

propose [prə'pəʊz] **1** *vt* proposer; **to p. to do sth, to p. doing sth** *(suggest)* proposer de faire qch; *(intend)* se proposer de faire qch **2** *vi* **to p. to sb** demander qn en mariage

proprietor [prə'praɪətə(r)] *n* propriétaire *mf* ▪ **proprietary** *adj (article, goods)* de marque déposée; **p. name** marque *f* déposée

propriety [prə'praɪətɪ] n (behaviour) bienséance f; (of conduct, remark) justesse f; **to observe the proprieties** observer les convenances

Note that the French word **propriété** is a false friend and is never a translation for the English word **propriety**. It means **property**.

propulsion [prə'pʌlʃən] n propulsion f

pros [prəʊz] npl **the p. and cons** le pour et le contre

prosaic [prəʊ'zeɪɪk] adj prosaïque

proscribe [prəʊ'skraɪb] vt proscrire

prose [prəʊz] n prose f; Br Sch (translation) thème m; **French p. (translation)** thème m français

prosecute ['prɒsɪkjuːt] vt Law poursuivre (en justice) ▪ **prose'cution** n Law poursuites fpl judiciaires; **the p.** (lawyers) ≃ le ministère public ▪ **prosecutor** n Law **(public) p.** procureur m

prospect[1] ['prɒspekt] n (expectation, thought) perspective f; (chance, likelihood) perspectives fpl; (view) vue f; (future) prospects perspectives d'avenir ▪ **prospective** [prə'spektɪv] adj (potential) potentiel, -ielle; (future) futur

prospect[2] [prə'spekt] 1 vt (land) prospecter 2 vi **to p. for gold** chercher de l'or ▪ **prospector** n prospecteur, -trice mf

prospectus [prə'spektəs] n (publicity leaflet) prospectus m; Br Univ guide m de l'étudiant

prosper ['prɒspə(r)] vi prospérer ▪ **prosperity** [-'sperɪtɪ] n prospérité f ▪ **prosperous** adj prospère

prostate ['prɒsteɪt] n Anat **p. (gland)** prostate f

prostitute ['prɒstɪtjuːt] 1 n (woman) prostituée f; **male p.** prostitué m 2 vt **to p. oneself** se prostituer ▪ **prosti'tution** n prostitution f

prostrate 1 ['prɒstreɪt] adj (prone) sur le ventre 2 [prɒ'streɪt] vt **to p. oneself** se prosterner (**before** devant)

protagonist [prəʊ'tægənɪst] n protagoniste mf

protect [prə'tekt] vt protéger (**from** or **against** de) ▪ **protection** n protection f ▪ **protective** adj (clothes, screen) de protection; (person, attitude) protecteur, -trice (**to** or **towards** envers); Écon (barrier) protecteur; **to be too** or **over p. towards** (child) surprotéger ▪ **protector** n protecteur, -trice mf

protein ['prəʊtiːn] n protéine f

protest [prə'test] **1** ['prəʊtest] n protestation f (**against** contre); **in p.** en signe de protestation (**at** contre); **under p.** contre son gré; **p. vote** vote m de protestation **2** vt protester contre; (one's innocence) protester de; **to p. that...** protester en disant que... **3** vi protester (**against** contre) ▪ **protester** [prə'testə(r)] n contestataire mf

Protestant ['prɒtɪstənt] adj & n protestant, -ante (mf) ▪ **Protestantism** n protestantisme m

protocol ['prəʊtəkɒl] n protocole m

proton ['prəʊtɒn] n Phys proton m

prototype ['prəʊtəʊtaɪp] n prototype m

protracted [prə'træktɪd] adj prolongé

protractor [prə'træktə(r)] n rapporteur m

protrude [prə'truːd] vi dépasser (**from** de); (of tooth) avancer; (of balcony, cliff) faire saillie ▪ **protruding** adj (chin, veins, eyes) saillant; (tooth) qui avance

proud [praʊd] (**-er, -est**) **1** adj (person) fier (f fière) (**of** de) **2** adv **to do sb p.** faire honneur à qn ▪ **proudly** adv fièrement

prove [pruːv] **1** vt prouver (**that** que); **to p. sb wrong** prouver que qn a tort; **to p. oneself** faire ses preuves **2** vi **to p. (to be) difficult** s'avérer difficile ▪ **proven** adj (method) éprouvé

proverb ['prɒvɜːb] n proverbe m ▪ **proverbial** [prə'vɜːbɪəl] adj proverbial

provide [prə'vaɪd] **1** vt (a) (supply) fournir; (service) offrir (**to** à); **to p. sb with sth** fournir qch à qn (b) (stipulate) stipuler **2** vi **to p. for sb** (sb's needs) pourvoir aux besoins de qn; (sb's future) assurer l'avenir de qn; **to p. for sth** (make allowance for) prévoir qch ▪ **provided** conj **p. (that)...** pourvu que... (+ subjunctive) ▪ **providing** conj **p. (that)...** pourvu que... (+ subjunctive)

providence ['prɒvɪdəns] n providence f

province ['prɒvɪns] n province f; Fig (field of knowledge) domaine m; **in the provinces** en province ▪ **provincial** [prə'vɪnʃəl] adj & n provincial, -iale (mf)

provision [prə'vɪʒən] n (clause) disposition f; **the p. of sth** (supplying) l'approvisionnement m en qch; **the provisions** (supplies) les provisions fpl; **to make p. for sth** prévoir qch

provisional [prə'vɪʒənəl] adj provisoire ▪ **provisionally** adv provisoirement

proviso [prə'vaɪzəʊ] (pl **-os**) n condition f

provocative [prə'vɒkətɪv] adj provocateur, -trice ▪ **provocation** n provocation f

provoke [prə'vəʊk] vt provoquer; **to p. sb into doing sth** pousser qn à faire qch ▪ **provoking** adj (annoying) agaçant

prow [praʊ] n (of ship) proue f

prowess ['praʊes] n (bravery) vaillance f; (skill) talent m

prowl [praʊl] **1** n **to be on the p.** rôder **2** vi **to p. (around)** rôder ▪ **prowler** n rôdeur, -euse mf

proximity [prɒk'sɪmɪtɪ] n proximité f

proxy ['prɒksɪ] (pl **-ies**) n procuration f; **by p.** par procuration

Prozac® ['prəʊzæk] n Med Prozac® m

prude [pruːd] n prude f ▪ **prudish** adj pudibond

prudent ['pruːdənt] adj prudent ▪ **prudence** n prudence f ▪ **prudently** adv prudemment

prune[1] [pruːn] n (dried plum) pruneau m

Note that the French word **prune** is a false friend and is never a translation for the English word **prune**. It means **plum**.

prune² [pru:n] *vt (tree, bush)* tailler; *Fig (article, speech)* élaguer ▪ **pruning** *n (of tree)* taille *f*; **p. shears** sécateur *m*

pry [praɪ] 1 *(pt & pp pried) vt Am* **to p. open** forcer (avec un levier) 2 *vi* être indiscret, -ète; **to p. into sth** *(meddle)* mettre son nez dans qch; *(sb's reasons)* chercher à découvrir qch ▪ **prying** *adj* indiscret, -ète; **safe from p. eyes** à l'abri des regards indiscrets

PS [piːˈes] *(abbr postscript) n* PS *m*

psalm [sɑːm] *n* psaume *m*

pseudonym [ˈsjuːdənɪm] *n* pseudonyme *m*

psyche [ˈsaɪkɪ] *n* psychisme *m*

psychiatry [saɪˈkaɪətrɪ] *n* psychiatrie *f* ▪ **psychiatric** [-kɪˈætrɪk] *adj* psychiatrique ▪ **psychiatrist** *n* psychiatre *mf*

psychic [ˈsaɪkɪk] 1 *adj (paranormal)* paranormal; *Fam* **I'm not p.** je ne suis pas devin 2 *n* médium *m*

psycho [ˈsaɪkəʊ] *adj & n Fam* psychopathe *(mf)*

psycho- [ˈsaɪkəʊ] *pref* psycho- ▪ **psychoanalysis** [-əˈnælɪsɪs] *n* psychanalyse *f* ▪ **psychoanalyst** [-ˈænəlɪst] *n* psychanalyste *mf* ▪ **psychobabble** *n Fam* jargon *m* de psy

psychology [saɪˈkɒlədʒɪ] *n* psychologie *f* ▪ **psychological** [-kəˈlɒdʒɪkəl] *adj* psychologique ▪ **psychologist** *n* psychologue *mf*

psychopath [ˈsaɪkəʊpæθ] *n* psychopathe *mf*

psychosis [saɪˈkəʊsɪs] *(pl* **-oses** [-əʊsiːz]*) n Med* psychose *f*

psychosomatic [saɪkəʊsəˈmætɪk] *adj* psychosomatique

psychotherapy [saɪkəʊˈθerəpɪ] *n* psychothérapie *f* ▪ **psychotherapist** *n* psychothérapeute *mf*

psychotic [saɪˈkɒtɪk] *n & adj* psychotique *(mf)*

PTO *(abbr* **please turn over)** TSVP

pub [pʌb] *n Br* pub *m*; **p. quiz** = jeu de culture générale dans un pub

puberty [ˈpjuːbətɪ] *n* puberté *f*

pubic [ˈpjuːbɪk] *adj* du pubis

public [ˈpʌblɪk] 1 *adj* public, -ique; *(library, swimming pool)* municipal; **to make sth p.** rendre qch public; **to go p. with sth** prévéler qch *(à la presse)*; **the company is going p.** la compagnie va être cotée en Bourse; **in the p. eye** très en vue; **p. building** édifice *m* public; **p. figure** personnalité *f* en vue; **p. holiday** jour *m* férié; *Br* **p. house** pub *m*; **p. opinion** l'opinion *f* publique; **p. relations** relations *fpl* publiques; *Br* **p. school** école *f* privée; *Am* école publique; *Am* **p. television** la télévision éducative; **p. transport** transports *mpl* en commun 2 *n* public *m*; **in p.** en public; **the sporting p.** les amateurs *mpl* de sport

publican [ˈpʌblɪkən] *n Br* patron, -onne *mf* d'un pub

publication [pʌblɪˈkeɪʃən] *n* publication *f*

publicity [pʌˈblɪsɪtɪ] *n* publicité *f*

publicize [ˈpʌblɪsaɪz] *vt* faire connaître au public

publicly [ˈpʌblɪklɪ] *adv* publiquement; **p. owned** à capitaux publics

public-spirited [pʌblɪkˈspɪrɪtɪd] *adj* **to be p.** avoir le sens civique

publish [ˈpʌblɪʃ] *vt* publier; **'published weekly'** *(of magazine)* 'paraît toutes les semaines' ▪ **publisher** *n* éditeur, -trice *mf* ▪ **publishing** *n* édition *f*; **the p. of** la publication de; **p. house** maison *f* d'édition

pucker [ˈpʌkə(r)] 1 *vt* **to p. (up)** *(brow)* froncer; *(lips)* pincer 2 *vi* **to p. (up)** *(face)* se rider; *(lips)* se plisser

pudding [ˈpʊdɪŋ] *n (dish)* pudding *m*; *Br (dessert)* dessert *m*

puddle [ˈpʌdəl] *n* flaque *f* (d'eau)

pudgy [ˈpʌdʒɪ] *(-ier, -iest) adj* rondelet, -ette

puerile [*Br* ˈpjʊəraɪl, *Am* ˈpjʊərəl] *adj* puéril

Puerto Rico [pwɜːtəʊˈriːkəʊ] *n* Porto Rico *f*

puff [pʌf] 1 *n (of smoke)* bouffée *f*; *(of wind, air)* souffle *m*; *Fam* **to be out of p.** être essoufflé; **p. pastry,** *Am* **p. paste** pâte *f* feuilletée 2 *vt (smoke)* souffler **(into** dans); **to p. sth out** *(cheeks, chest)* gonfler qch 3 *vi (of person)* souffler; *(of steam engine)* lancer des bouffées de vapeur; **to p. at a cigar** tirer sur un cigare ▪ **puffy** *(-ier, -iest) adj* gonflé

puke [pjuːk] *vi Fam* dégueuler

pukka [ˈpʌkə] *adj Br Fam (genuine)* authentique; *(excellent)* génial, super *inv*

pull [pʊl] 1 *n (attraction)* attraction *f*; *(of water current)* force *f*; *Fam (influence)* influence *f*; **to give sth a p.** tirer qch 2 *vt* (a) *(draw, tug)* tirer; *(tooth)* arracher; *(stopper)* enlever; *(trigger)* appuyer sur; *(muscle)* se froisser; *Fig* **to p. sth apart** *or* **to bits** *or* **to pieces** démolir qch; **to p. a face** faire la grimace; *Fig* **to (get sb to) p. strings** se faire pistonner (par qn) (b) *Br Fam (sexual partner)* emballer 3 *vi* (a) *(tug)* tirer **(on** sur); **to p. into the station** *(of train)* entrer en gare; **to p. clear of sth** s'éloigner de qch (b) *Br Fam (find sexual partner)* faire une touche ▪ **pull-up** *n (exercise on bars or rings)* traction *f*
▸ **pull along** *vt sep (drag)* traîner **(to** jusqu'à)
▸ **pull away** 1 *vt sep (move)* éloigner; *(snatch)* arracher **(from** à) 2 *vi (in vehicle)* démarrer; **to p. away from** s'éloigner de
▸ **pull back** 1 *vt sep* retirer; *(curtains)* ouvrir 2 *vi (withdraw)* se retirer
▸ **pull down** *vt sep (lower)* baisser; *(knock down)* faire tomber; *(demolish)* démolir
▸ **pull in** 1 *vt sep (drag into room)* faire entrer (de force); *(rope)* ramener; *(stomach)* rentrer; *(crowd)* attirer 2 *vi (arrive)* arriver; *(stop in vehicle)* s'arrêter

▸ **pull off** *vt sep* *(remove)* enlever; *Fig (plan, deal)* réaliser; **to p. it off** réussir son coup

▸ **pull on** *vt sep (boots, clothes)* mettre

▸ **pull out 1** *vt sep (tooth, hair)* arracher; *(cork, pin)* enlever (**from** de); *(from pocket, bag)* sortir (**from** de); *(troops)* retirer **2** *vi (of car)* déboîter; *(of train)* partir; *(withdraw)* se retirer (**from** de)

▸ **pull over 1** *vt sep (drag)* traîner (**to** jusqu'à); *(knock down)* faire tomber **2** *vi (in vehicle)* s'arrêter

▸ **pull round** *vi (recover)* se remettre

▸ **pull through** *vi (recover)* s'en tirer

▸ **pull together** *vt sep* **to p. oneself together** se ressaisir

▸ **pull up 1** *vt sep (socks, blinds)* remonter; *(haul up)* hisser; *(plant, tree)* arracher; *(stop)* arrêter; *Fig* **to p. one's socks up** se ressaisir **2** *vi (of car)* s'arrêter

pulley ['pʊlɪ] *(pl -eys) n* poulie *f*

pull-out ['pʊlaʊt] *n (in newspaper)* supplément *m* détachable

pullover ['pʊləʊvə(r)] *n* pull-over *m*

pulp [pʌlp] *n (of fruit)* pulpe *f*; **to reduce sth to a p.** écraser qch; **p. fiction** romans *mpl* de gare

pulpit ['pʊlpɪt] *n* chaire *f*

pulsate [pʌl'seɪt] *vi (beat)* palpiter; *(vibrate)* vibrer ▪ **pulsation** *n* pulsation *f*

pulse [pʌls] *n Med* pouls *m*; *(of light, sound)* vibration *f* ▪ **pulses** *npl (seeds)* légumineuses *fpl*

pulverize ['pʌlvəraɪz] *vt* pulvériser

pumice ['pʌmɪs] *n* **p. (stone)** pierre *f* ponce

pump¹ [pʌmp] **1** *n (machine)* pompe *f*; *Br* **petrol p.**, *Am* **gas p.** pompe *f* à essence; *Br* **(petrol) p. attendant** pompiste *mf* **2** *vt* pomper; *Fig (money, resources)* injecter (**into** dans); *Fam* **to p. sb for information** tirer les vers du nez à qn; *Fam* **to p. iron** faire de la gonflette; **to p. sth in** *(liquid)* refouler qch; **to p. sth out** *(liquid)* pomper qch (**of** de); **to p. air into sth, to p. sth up** *(mattress)* gonfler qch **3** *vi* pomper; *(of heart)* battre

pump² [pʌmp] *n (flat shoe)* escarpin *m*; *(for sports)* tennis *m ou f*

pumpkin ['pʌmpkɪn] *n* potiron *m*; *Am* **p. pie** tarte *f* au potiron

pun [pʌn] *n* jeu *m* de mots

Punch [pʌntʃ] *n* **P. and Judy show** ≃ guignol *m*

punch¹ [pʌntʃ] **1** *n (blow)* coup *m* de poing; *Fig (energy)* punch *m*; *Boxing & Fig* **to pack a p.** avoir du punch; **p. line** *(of joke, story)* chute *f* **2** *vt (person)* donner un coup de poing à; *(sb's nose)* donner un coup de poing sur; *(ball)* frapper d'un coup de poing ▪ **punch-up** *n Br Fam* bagarre *f*

punch² [pʌntʃ] **1** *n (for paper)* perforeuse *f*; *(tool)* poinçon *m*; *(for tickets)* poinçonneuse *f*; *Comptr* **p. card** carte *f* perforée **2** *vt (ticket)*

punch³ [pʌntʃ] *n (drink)* punch *m*

punctilious [pʌŋk'tɪlɪəs] *adj* pointilleux, -euse

punctual ['pʌŋktʃʊəl] *adj* ponctuel, -uelle ▪ **punctuality** [-tʃʊ'ælɪtɪ] *n* ponctualité *f* ▪ **punctually** *adv* à l'heure

punctuate ['pʌŋktʃʊeɪt] *vt* ponctuer (**with** de) ▪ **punctu'ation** *n* ponctuation *f*; **p. mark** signe *m* de ponctuation

puncture ['pʌŋktʃə(r)] **1** *n (in tyre)* crevaison *f*; **to have a p.** crever **2** *vt (tyre)* crever; *(metal)* perforer; *(blister)* percer **3** *vi (of tyre)* crever

pundit ['pʌndɪt] *n* expert *m*

pungent ['pʌndʒənt] *adj* âcre ▪ **pungency** *n* âcreté *f*

punish ['pʌnɪʃ] *vt* punir (**for** de); **to p. sb for doing sth** punir qn pour avoir fait qch ▪ **punishable** *adj* punissable (**by** de) ▪ **punishing** *adj (tiring)* éreintant

punishable ['pʌnɪʃəbəl] *adj* punissable (**by** de)

punishment ['pʌnɪʃmənt] *n* punition *f*; *Law* peine *f*; **as (a) p. for** en punition de; *Fig* **to take a lot of p.** être mis à rude épreuve

punitive ['pjuːnɪtɪv] *adj* punitif, -ive

punk [pʌŋk] **1** *n* **(a)** punk *mf*; **p. (rock)** le punk **(b)** *Am Fam (hoodlum)* voyou *m (pl -ous)* **2** *adj* punk *inv*

punnet ['pʌnɪt] *n Br* barquette *f*

punt¹ [pʌnt] **1** *n* barque *f* à fond plat **2** *vi* **to go punting** faire de la barque ▪ **punter** *n Br (gambler)* parieur, -ieuse *mf* ▪ *Fam (customer)* client *m*, cliente *f* ▪ **punting** *n* canotage *m*

punt² [pʌnt] *n Formerly (currency)* livre *f* irlandaise

puny ['pjuːnɪ] *(-ier, -iest) adj* chétif, -ive

pup [pʌp] *n (dog)* chiot *m*

pupil¹ ['pjuːpəl] *n (student)* élève *mf*

pupil² ['pjuːpəl] *n (of eye)* pupille *f*

puppet ['pʌpɪt] **1** *n* marionnette *f*; **p. show** spectacle *m* de marionnettes **2** *adj (government, leader)* fantoche

puppy ['pʌpɪ] *(pl -ies) n (dog)* chiot *m*

purchase ['pɜːtʃɪs] **1** *n (action, thing bought)* achat *m* **2** *vt* acheter (**from** à qn); **purchasing power** pouvoir *m* d'achat ▪ **purchaser** *n* acheteur, -euse *mf*

Note that the French word **pourchasser** is a false friend and is never a translation for the English word **purchase**. It means **to chase**.

---

pure [pjʊə(r)] *(-er, -est) adj* pur

purée ['pjʊəreɪ] *n* purée *f*

purely ['pjʊəlɪ] *adv* purement; **p. and simply** purement et simplement

purgatory ['pɜːgətrɪ] *n Rel* purgatoire *m*

purge [pɜːdʒ] **1** *n* purge *f* **2** *vt* purger (**of** de)

purify ['pjʊərɪfaɪ] (pt & pp **-ied**) vt purifier ▪ **purification** [-fɪˈkeɪʃən] n purification f ▪ **purifier** n (for water) épurateur m; (for air) purificateur m

purist ['pjʊərɪst] n puriste mf

puritan ['pjʊərɪtən] n & adj puritain, -aine (mf) ▪ **puritanical** [-ˈtænɪkəl] adj puritain

purity ['pjʊərɪtɪ] n pureté f

purl [pɜːl] n maille f à l'envers

purple ['pɜːpəl] 1 adj violet, -ette; **to go** or **turn p.** (of person) devenir cramoisi 2 n violet m

purport [pəˈpɔːt] vt Formal **to p. to be sth** prétendre être qch

purpose ['pɜːpəs] n (a) (aim) but m; **on p.** exprès; **to no p.** inutilement; **to serve no p.** ne servir à rien; **for the purposes of** pour les besoins de (b) (determination) résolution f; **to have a sense of p.** savoir ce que l'on veut ▪ **'purpose-'built** adj construit spéciale- ment

purposeful ['pɜːpəsfəl] adj résolu ▪ **pur- posefully** adv (for a reason) dans un but précis; (resolutely) résolument

purposely ['pɜːpəslɪ] adv exprès

purr [pɜː(r)] 1 n ronron m 2 vi ronronner

purse [pɜːs] 1 n (for coins) porte-monnaie m inv; Am (handbag) sac m à main 2 vt **to p. one's lips** pincer les lèvres

pursue [pəˈsjuː] vt poursuivre; (fame, pleasure) rechercher; (profession) exercer ▪ **pursuer** n poursuivant, -ante mf ▪ **pursuit** n (of person) poursuite f; (of pleasure, glory) quête f; (activity) occupation f; **to go in p. of sb/sth** se lancer à la poursuite de qn/qch

purveyor [pəˈveɪə(r)] n Formal fournisseur m

pus [pʌs] n pus m

push [pʊʃ] 1 n (act of pushing, attack) poussée f; **to give sb/sth a p.** pousser qn/qch; Br Fam **to give sb the p.** (of employer) virer qn; **at a p.** à la rigueur

2 vt pousser (**to** or **as far as** jusqu'à); (button) appuyer sur; (lever) abaisser; (product) faire la promotion de; (theory) promouvoir; Fam (drugs) vendre; **to p. sth into/between** enfoncer qch dans/entre; Fig **to p. sb into doing sth** pousser qn à faire qch; **to p. sth off the table** faire tomber qch de la table (en le poussant); **to p. sb off a cliff** pousser qn du haut d'une falaise; **to p. one's way through the crowd** se frayer un chemin à travers la foule; **to p. a door open** ouvrir une porte (en poussant); **to p. one's luck** y aller un peu fort; Fam **to be pushing forty** friser la quarantaine

3 vi pousser; (on button) appuyer (**on** sur) ▪ **push-button** n bouton m; (of phone) touche f; **p. phone** téléphone m à touches; **p. controls** commandes fpl automatiques ▪ **pushchair** n Br poussette f ▪ **pushover** n Fam **to be a p.** (task) être un jeu d'enfant; (person) être un

adversaire facile ▪ **push-up** n Am (exercise) pompe f

▸ **push about, push around** vt sep Fam **to p. sb about** faire de qn ce que l'on veut

▸ **push aside** vt sep écarter

▸ **push away, push back** vt sep repousser

▸ **push down** vt sep (button) appuyer sur; (lever) abaisser

▸ **push for** vt insep faire pression pour obtenir

▸ **push in** vi Br (in queue) resquiller

▸ **push off** vi Fam ficher le camp

▸ **push on** vi (go on) continuer; **to p. on with sth** continuer qch

▸ **push over** vt sep faire tomber

▸ **push through** vt sep (law) faire adopter

▸ **push up** vt sep (lever, collar) relever; (sleeves) remonter; (increase) augmenter

pushed [pʊʃt] adj **to be p. for time** être très pressé

pusher ['pʊʃə(r)] n Fam (of drugs) dealer m

pushy ['pʊʃɪ] (-ier, -iest) adj Fam batailleur, -euse

puss, pussy ['pʊs, 'pʊsɪ] (pl -ies) n Fam (cat) minou m

put [pʊt] (pt & pp **put**, pres p **putting**) 1 vt mettre; (on flat surface) poser; (problem, argument) présenter (**to** à); (question) poser (**to** à); (say) dire; (estimate) évaluer (**at** à); **to p. pressure on sb/sth** faire pression sur qn/qch; **to p. a mark on sth** faire une marque sur qch; **to p. money on a horse** parier sur un cheval; **to p. a lot of work into sth** beaucoup travailler à qch; **to p. sth well** bien tourner qch; **to p. it bluntly** pour parler franc 2 vi **to p. to sea** prendre la mer ▪ **put-up job** n Fam coup m monté

▸ **put across** vt sep (message, idea) faire comprendre (**to** à)

▸ **put aside** vt sep (money, object) mettre de côté

▸ **put away** vt sep (tidy away) ranger; **to p. sb away** (criminal) mettre qn en prison; (insane person) enfermer qn

▸ **put back** vt sep (replace, postpone) remettre; (telephone receiver) raccrocher; (clock, sched- ule) retarder

▸ **put by** vt sep (money) mettre de côté

▸ **put down** vt sep (on floor, table) poser; (deposit) verser; (revolt) réprimer; (write down) inscrire; (attribute) attribuer (**to** à); (kill) faire piquer; **to p. oneself down** se rabaisser

▸ **put forward** vt sep (clock, meeting, argument) avancer; (opinion) exprimer; (candidate) proposer (**for** à)

▸ **put in** 1 vt sep (into box) mettre dedans; (insert) introduire; (add) ajouter; (install) installer; (claim, application) soumettre; (time) passer (**doing** à faire) 2 vi **to p. in for sth** (new job, transfer) faire une demande de qch; **to p. in (at)** (of ship) faire escale (à)

▸ **put off** *vt sep (postpone)* remettre (à plus tard); *(dismay)* déconcerter; *(make wait)* faire attendre; **to p. off doing sth** retarder le moment de faire qch; **to p. sb off sth** dégoûter qn de qch; **to p. sb off doing sth** ôter à qn l'envie de faire qch

▸ **put on** *vt sep (clothes, shoe, record)* mettre; *(accent)* prendre; *(play, show)* monter; *(gas, radio)* allumer; *(clock)* avancer; **to p. on weight** prendre du poids; *Am* **to p. sb on** *(tease)* faire marcher qn; **she p. me on to you** elle m'a donné votre adresse; **p. me on to him!** *(on phone)* passez-le-moi!

▸ **put out** *vt sep (take outside)* sortir; *(arm, leg, hand)* tendre; *(gas, light)* éteindre; *(inconvenience)* déranger; *(upset)* vexer; *(report, statement)* publier; **to p. one's shoulder out** se démettre l'épaule

▸ **put through** *vt sep* **to p. sb through (to sb)** *(on phone)* passer qn (à qn)

▸ **put together** *vt sep (assemble)* assembler; *(meal, team)* composer; *(file, report)* préparer; *(collection)* rassembler; *Fig* **to p. two and two together** tirer ses conclusions

▸ **put up** *vt sep (lift)* lever; *(tent, fence)* monter; *(statue, ladder)* dresser; *(flag)* hisser; *(building)* construire; *(umbrella)* ouvrir; *(picture, poster)* mettre; *(price, sales, numbers)* augmenter; *(resistance, plea, suggestion)* offrir; *(candidate)* présenter (**for** à); *(guest)* loger; **to p. sth up for sale** mettre qch en vente

▸ **put up with** *vt insep* supporter

putrid ['pju:trɪd] *adj* putride ▪ **putrefy** [-trɪfaɪ] *(pt & pp* **-ied)** *vi* se putréfier

putt [pʌt] *n Golf* putt *m* ▪ **putting** *n Golf* putting *m*; **p. green** green *m*

putty ['pʌtɪ] *n* mastic *m*

puzzle ['pʌzəl] **1** *n (jigsaw)* puzzle *m*; *(game)* casse-tête *m inv*; *(mystery)* mystère *m* **2** *vt* laisser perplexe; **to p. out why/when...** essayer de comprendre pourquoi/quand... **3** *vi* **to p. over sth** essayer de comprendre qch ▪ **puzzled** *adj* perplexe ▪ **puzzling** *adj* bizarre

PVC [pi:vi:'si:] *n* PVC *m*; **P. belt** ceinture *f* en PVC

pygmy ['pɪgmɪ] *(pl* **-ies)** *n* pygmée *m*

pyjama [pɪ'dʒɑːmə] *(Am* **pajama** [pə'dʒɑːmə]) *adj (jacket)* de pyjama ▪ **pyjamas** *(Am* **pajamas**) *npl* pyjama *m*; **a pair of p.** un pyjama; **to be in (one's) p.** être en pyjama

pylon ['paɪlən] *n* pylône *m*

pyramid ['pɪrəmɪd] *n* pyramide *f*

Pyrenees [pɪrə'niːz] *npl* **the P.** les Pyrénées *fpl*

Pyrex® ['paɪreks] *n* Pyrex® *m*; **P. dish** plat *m* en Pyrex®

python ['paɪθən] *n* python *m*

Q, q [kju:] *n (letter)* Q, q *m inv*
QC [kju:'si:] *(abbr Queen's Counsel) n Br Law* = membre haut placé du barreau
quack¹ [kwæk] *n (of duck)* coin-coin *m inv*
quack² [kwæk] *n Pej (doctor)* charlatan *m*
quadrangle ['kwɒdræŋgəl] *n Br (of college, school)* cour *f*
quadruple [kwɒ'dru:pəl] *vti* quadrupler
quadruplets [kwɒ'dru:plɪts] *(Fam* **quads** [kwɒdz]*) npl* quadruplés, -ées *mfpl*
quagmire ['kwægmaɪə(r)] *n* bourbier *m*
quail [kweɪl] *n inv (bird)* caille *f*
quaint [kweɪnt] *(-er, -est) adj (picturesque)* pittoresque; *(old-fashioned)* vieillot, -otte; *(odd)* bizarre
quake [kweɪk] **1** *n Fam* tremblement *m* de terre **2** *vi* trembler **(with** de)
Quaker ['kweɪkə(r)] *n Rel* quaker, -eresse *mf*
qualification [kwɒlɪfɪ'keɪʃən] *n (diploma)* diplôme *m; (skill)* compétence *f; (modification)* précision *f; (for competition)* qualification *f;* **on q.** une fois le diplôme obtenu
qualify ['kwɒlɪfaɪ] *(pt & pp -ied)* **1** *vt* **(a)** *(make competent) & Sport* qualifier **(for** pour qch); **to q. sb to do sth** donner à qn les compétences nécessaires pour faire qch **(b)** *(modify)* nuancer; *Grammar* qualifier **2** *vi Sport* se qualifier **(for** pour); **to q. as a doctor** obtenir son diplôme de médecin; **to q. for sth** *(be eligible)* avoir droit à qch **■qualified** *adj (competent)* compétent; *(having diploma)* diplômé; *(opinion)* nuancé; *(support)* mitigé; **to be q. to do sth** *(be competent)* avoir les compétences requises pour faire qch; *(have diploma)* avoir les diplômes requis pour faire qch; **a q. success** un demi-succès **■qualifying** *adj* **q. exam** examen *m* d'entrée; *Sport* **q. round** épreuve *f* éliminatoire
quality ['kwɒlɪtɪ] *(pl -ies) n* qualité *f;* **q. product** produit *m* de qualité **■qualitative** [-tətɪv] *adj* qualitatif, -ive
qualms [kwɑ:mz] *npl* **to have no q. about doing sth** *(scruples)* n'avoir aucun scrupule à faire qch; *(doubts)* ne pas hésiter une seconde avant de faire qch
quandary ['kwɒndərɪ] *(pl -ies) n* dilemme *m;* **to be in a q.** être bien embarrassé
quantify ['kwɒntɪfaɪ] *(pt & pp -ied) vt* évaluer
quantity ['kwɒntɪtɪ] *(pl -ies) n* quantité *f;* **in q.**

(purchase) en grande(s) quantité(s); **q. surveyor** métreur *m* vérificateur **■quantitative** [-tətɪv] *adj* quantitatif, -ive
quarantine ['kwɒrənti:n] **1** *n* quarantaine *f* **2** *vt* mettre en quarantaine
quarrel ['kwɒrəl] **1** *n* dispute *f*, querelle *f;* **to pick a q. with sb** chercher querelle à qn **2** *(Br* **-ll-,** *Am* **-l-)** *vi* se disputer **(with** avec); **to q. with sth** ne pas être d'accord avec qch **■quarrelling** *(Am* **quarreling)** *n* disputes *fpl* **■quarrelsome** *adj* querelleur, -euse
quarry¹ ['kwɒrɪ] *(pl -ies) n (for stone)* carrière *f*
quarry² ['kwɒrɪ] *(pl -ies) n (prey)* proie *f*
quart [kwɔ:t] *n (liquid measurement) Br* = 1,14 l, *Am* = 0,95 l
quarter¹ ['kwɔ:tə(r)] **1** *n* quart *m; (of fruit, moon)* quartier *m; (division of year)* trimestre *m; Am & Can (money)* pièce *f* de 25 cents; **to divide sth into quarters** diviser qch en quatre; **q. (of a) pound** quart de livre; *Br* **q. past nine,** *Am* **a q. after nine** neuf heures et quart; *Br* **a q. to nine,** *Am* **a q. of nine** neuf heures moins le quart **2** *vt* partager en quatre
quarter² ['kwɔ:tə(r)] **1** *n (district)* quartier *m;* **quarters** *(circles)* milieux *mpl;* **(living) quarters** logements *mpl; (of soldier)* quartiers *mpl;* **from all quarters** de toutes parts **2** *vt (troops)* loger
quarterfinal [kwɔ:tə'faɪnəl] *n Sport* quart *m* de finale
quarterly ['kwɔ:təlɪ] **1** *adj (magazine, payment)* trimestriel, -ielle **2** *adv* tous les trimestres **3** *(pl -ies) n* publication *f* trimestrielle
quartet(te) [kwɔ:'tet] *n (music, players)* quatuor *m;* **(jazz) q.** quartette *m*
quartz [kwɔ:ts] **1** *n* quartz *m* **2** *adj (watch)* à quartz
quash [kwɒʃ] *vt (rebellion)* réprimer; *Law (sentence)* annuler
quasi- ['kweɪzaɪ] *pref* quasi-
quaver ['kweɪvə(r)] **1** *n* **(a)** *Br (musical note)* croche *f* **(b)** *(in voice)* tremblement *m* **2** *vi (of voice)* trembler
quay [ki:] *n* quai *m* **■quayside** *n* **on the q.** sur les quais
queasy ['kwi:zɪ] *(-ier, -iest) adj* **to feel** *or* **be q.** avoir mal au cœur **■queasiness** *n* mal *m* au cœur
Quebec [kwɪ'bek] *n* le Québec

queen [kwi:n] *n* reine *f*; **the Q. Mother** la reine mère

queer ['kwɪə(r)] **1** (**-er, -est**) *adj* (**a**) *(strange)* bizarre (**b**) *Fam Pej (homosexual)* pédé **2** *n Fam Pej (homosexual)* pédé *m*, = terme injurieux désignant un homosexuel

quell [kwel] *vt (revolt)* réprimer

quench [kwentʃ] *vt (fire)* éteindre; *(thirst)* étancher

querulous ['kweruləs] *adj (complaining)* grognon, -onne

query ['kwɪərɪ] **1** *(pl* **-ies)** *n* question *f* **2** *(pt & pp* **-ied)** *vt* mettre en question

quest [kwest] *n* quête *f* (**for** de); **in q. of sth** en quête de qch

question ['kwestʃən] **1** *n* question *f*; **there is some q. of it** il en est question; **there's no q. of it, it's out of the q.** c'est hors de question; **without q.** incontestablement; **the matter/ person in q.** l'affaire/la personne en question; **q. mark** point *m* d'interrogation; **q. master** *(on television, radio)* animateur, -trice *mf* **2** *vt* interroger (**about** sur); *(doubt)* mettre en question; **to q. whether...** douter que... (+ *subjunctive*) ▪**questioning 1** *adj (look)* interrogateur, -trice **2** *n* interrogation *f*

questionable ['kwestʃənəbəl] *adj* discutable

questionnaire [kwestʃə'neə(r)] *n* questionnaire *m*

queue [kju:] *Br* **1** *n (of people)* queue *f*; *(of cars)* file *f*; **to form a q., to stand in a q.** faire la queue **2** *vi* **to q. (up)** faire la queue

quibble ['kwɪbəl] *vi* chipoter *(*about à propos de) ▪**quibbling** *n* chipotage *m*

quiche [ki:ʃ] *n* quiche *f*

quick [kwɪk] **1** (**-er, -est**) *adj (rapid)* rapide; *(clever)* vif *(f* vive); **q. to react** prompt à réagir; **be q.!** fais vite!; **to have a q. shower/meal** se doucher/manger en vitesse; **to be a q. worker** travailler vite; **as q. as a flash** rapide comme l'éclair **2** (**-er, -est**) *adv Fam* vite **3** *n Fig* **to cut sb to the q.** piquer qn au vif ▪**'quick-'tempered** *adj* emporté ▪**'quick'witted** *adj* vif *(f* vive)

quicken ['kwɪkən] **1** *vt* accélérer **2** *vi* s'accélérer

quickie ['kwɪkɪ] *n Fam* **to have a q.** *(drink)* prendre un pot en vitesse

quickly ['kwɪklɪ] *adv* vite

quicksand ['kwɪksænd] *n* sables *mpl* mouvants

quid [kwɪd] *n inv Br Fam (pound)* livre *f*

quiet ['kwaɪət] **1** (**-er, -est**) *adj (silent, still, peaceful)* tranquille, calme; *(machine, vehicle)* silencieux, -ieuse; *(person, voice, music)* doux *(f* douce); **to be or keep q.** *(say nothing)* se taire; *(make no noise)* ne pas faire de bruit; **to keep q. about sth, to keep sth q.** ne rien dire au sujet de qch; **q.!** silence!; **a q. wedding** un mariage célébré dans l'intimité **2** *n Fam* **on the q.** *(secretly)* en cachette

quieten ['kwaɪətən] *Br* **1** *vt* **to q. (down)** calmer **2** *vi* **to q. down** se calmer

quietly ['kwaɪətlɪ] *adv* tranquillement; *(gently, not loudly)* doucement; *(silently)* silencieusement; *(secretly)* en cachette; *(discreetly)* discrètement ▪**quietness** *n (of person, place)* tranquillité *f*

quill [kwɪl] *n (pen)* plume *f* d'oie

quilt [kwɪlt] *n (cover)* édredon *m*; *Br (duvet)* couette *f*

quintessential [kwɪnte'senʃəl] *adj* quintessentiel, -ielle

quintet [kwɪn'tet] *n* quintette *m*

quintuplets [*Br* kwɪn'tju:plɪts, *Am* -'tʌplɪts] *npl* quintuplés, -ées *mfpl*

quip [kwɪp] **1** *n* boutade *f* **2** *(pt & pp* **-pp-**) *vti* plaisanter

quirk [kwɜ:k] *n (of character)* particularité *f*; *(of fate)* caprice *m* ▪**quirky** (**-ier, -iest**) *adj* bizarre

quit [kwɪt] *(pt & pp* quit *or* quitted, *pres p* quitting) **1** *vt (leave)* quitter; *Comptr* sortir de; **to q. doing sth** arrêter de faire qch **2** *vi (give up)* abandonner; *(resign)* démissionner; *Comptr* sortir

quite [kwaɪt] *adv (entirely)* tout à fait; *(really)* vraiment; *(fairly)* assez; **I q. understand** je comprends parfaitement; **q. enough** bien assez; **q. another matter** une tout autre affaire; **q. a genius** un véritable génie; **q. good** *(not bad)* pas mal du tout; **q. (so)!** exactement!; **q. a lot** pas mal (**of** de); **q. a long time ago** il y a pas mal de temps

quits [kwɪts] *adj* quitte (**with** envers); **to call it q.** en rester là

quiver ['kwɪvə(r)] *vi (of person)* frémir (**with** de); *(of voice)* trembler; *(of flame)* vaciller

quiz [kwɪz] **1** *(pl* **-zz-**) *n (on radio)* jeu *m* radiophonique; *(on TV)* jeu télévisé; *(in magazine)* questionnaire *m*; **q. show** *(on radio)* jeu radiophonique; *(on TV)* jeu télévisé **2** *(pt & pp* **-zz-**) *vt* interroger ▪**quizmaster** *n TV & Radio* animateur, -trice *mf*

quizzical ['kwɪzɪkəl] *adj (look, air)* interrogateur, -trice

quorum ['kwɔ:rəm] *n* quorum *m*

quota ['kwəʊtə] *n* quota *m*

quotation [kwəʊ'teɪʃən] *n (from author)* citation *f*; *(estimate)* devis *m*; *(on Stock Exchange)* cote *f*; **q. marks** guillemets *mpl*; **in q. marks** entre guillemets

quote [kwəʊt] **1** *n (from author)* citation *f*; *(estimate)* devis *m*; **in quotes** entre guillemets **2** *vt (author, passage)* citer; *(reference number)* rappeler; *(price)* indiquer; *Fin* **quoted company** société *f* cotée en Bourse **3** *vi* **to q. from** *(author, book)* citer

quotient ['kwəʊʃənt] *n Math* quotient *m*

R, r [ɑː(r)] *n (lettre)* R, r *m inv*
rabbi ['ræbaɪ] *n* rabbin *m*; **chief r.** grand rabbin
rabbit ['ræbɪt] *n* lapin *m*
rabble ['ræbəl] *n* foule *f* bruyante
rabies ['reɪbiːz] *n* rage *f* ■ **rabid** ['ræbɪd] *adj (animal)* enragé; *Fig (communist)* fanatique
raccoon [rə'kuːn] *n* raton *m* laveur
race¹ [reɪs] **1** *n (contest)* course *f* **2** *vt (horse)* faire courir; **to r. (against** *or* **with)** **sb** faire une course avec qn **3** *vi (run)* courir; *(of engine)* s'emballer; *(of pulse)* battre la chamade ■ **racecar** *n Am* voiture *f* de course ■ **racecourse** *n* champ *m* de courses ■ **racehorse** *n* cheval *m* de course ■ **racetrack** *n Br* (for cars, bicycles) piste *f*; *Am (for horses)* champ *m* de courses ■ **racing** *n* courses *fpl*; **r. car/bike** voiture *f*/vélo *m* de course; **r. driver** coureur *m* automobile
race² [reɪs] **1** *n (group)* race *f* **2** *adj (prejudice)* racial; **r. relations** relations *fpl* interraciales ■ **racial** ['reɪʃəl] *adj* racial ■ **racialism** ['reɪʃəlɪzəm] *n* racisme *m* ■ **racism** *n* racisme *m* ■ **racist** *adj & n* raciste *(mf)*
rack [ræk] **1** *n* **(a)** *(for bottles, letters, records)* casier *m*; *(for plates)* égouttoir *m*; *(set of shelves)* étagère *f*; **(luggage) r.** porte-bagages *m inv*; **(roof) r.** *(of car)* galerie *f*; **(drying) r.** séchoir *m* à linge **(b)** *(expression)* **to go to r. and ruin** aller de mal en pis **2** *vt* **to r. one's brains** se creuser la cervelle
racket¹ ['rækɪt] *n (for tennis)* raquette *f*
racket² ['rækɪt] *n Fam* **(a)** *(din)* vacarme *m* **(b)** *(criminal activity)* racket *m* ■ **racke'teer** *n* racketteur *m* ■ **racke'teering** *n* racket *m*
racoon [rə'kuːn] *n* raton *m* laveur
racy ['reɪsɪ] *(-ier, -iest) adj (lively)* savoureux, -euse; *(risqué)* osé
radar ['reɪdɑː(r)] *n* radar *m*; **r. control** contrôle *m* radar *inv*; **r. operator** radariste *mf*
radiant ['reɪdɪənt] *adj (person, face)* resplendissant **(with** de); *(sun)* éclatant ■ **radiance** *n* éclat *m* ■ **radiantly** *adv (shine)* avec éclat; **r. happy** rayonnant de joie
radiate ['reɪdɪeɪt] **1** *vt (heat, light)* dégager; *Fig (joy, health)* être rayonnant de **2** *vi* rayonner **(from** de) ■ **radi'ation** *n (of heat)* rayonnement *m* **(of** de); *(radioactivity)* radiation *f*; **r. sickness** mal *m* des rayons
radiator ['reɪdɪeɪtə(r)] *n (heater)* radiateur *m*

radical ['rædɪkəl] *adj & n* radical, -ale *(mf)*
radii ['reɪdɪaɪ] *pl of* **radius**
radio ['reɪdɪəʊ] **1** *(pl* **-os)** *n* radio *f*; **on the r.** à la radio; **r. cassette (player)** radiocassette *m*; **r. operator** radio *m*; **r. wave** onde *f* hertzienne **2** *(pt & pp* **-oed)** *vt (message)* transmettre par radio **(to** à); **to r. sb** contacter qn par radio ■ **'radio-con'trolled** *adj* radioguidé ■ **radiographer** [-'ɒgrəfə(r)] *n* radiologue *mf* ■ **radiography** [-'ɒgrəfɪ] *n* radiographie *f* ■ **radiologist** [-'ɒlədʒɪst] *n* radiologue *mf* ■ **radiology** [-'ɒlədʒɪ] *n* radiologie *f*
radioactive [reɪdɪəʊ'æktɪv] *adj* radioactif, -ive ■ **radioac'tivity** *n* radioactivité *f*
radish ['rædɪʃ] *n* radis *m*
radius ['reɪdɪəs] *(pl* **-dii)** *n* rayon *m*; **within a r. of 10 km** dans un rayon de 10 km
RAF [ɑːreɪ'ef] *(abbr Royal Air Force) n* = armée de l'air britannique
raffia ['ræfɪə] *n* raphia *m*
raffle ['ræfəl] *n* tombola *f*
raft [rɑːft] *n* radeau *m*
rafter ['rɑːftə(r)] *n* chevron *m*
rag [ræg] *n* **(a)** *(piece of old clothing)* chiffon *m*; **in rags** *(clothes)* en loques; *(person)* en haillons **(b)** *Fam Pej (newspaper)* torchon *m* **(c)** *Br Univ* **r. week** = semaine de divertissements organisés par les étudiants au profit d'œuvres de charité
ragamuffin ['rægəmʌfɪn] *n* polisson, -onne *mf*
rage [reɪdʒ] **1** *n (of person)* rage *f*; *(of sea)* furie *f*; **to fly into a r.** entrer dans une rage folle; *Fam* **to be all the r.** *(of fashion)* faire fureur **2** *vi (be angry)* être furieux, -ieuse; *(of storm, battle)* faire rage ■ **raging** *adj (storm, fever, fire)* violent; **in a r. temper** furieux, -ieuse
ragged ['rægɪd] *adj (clothes)* en loques; *(person)* en haillons; *(edge)* irrégulier, -ière
raid [reɪd] **1** *n (military)* raid *m*; *(by police)* descente *f*; *(by thieves)* hold-up *m inv*; **air r.** raid *m* aérien **2** *vt* faire un raid/une descente/un hold-up dans; *Hum* **to r. the fridge** faire la razzia dans le frigo ■ **raider** *n (criminal)* malfaiteur *m*; **raiders** *(soldiers)* commando *m*
rail [reɪl] **1** *n* **(a)** *(for train)* rail *m*; **by r.** par le train; **to go off the rails** *(of train)* dérailler **(b)** *(rod on balcony)* balustrade *f*; *(on stairs, for spotlight)* rampe *f*; *(curtain rod)* tringle *f* **2** *adj (ticket)* de chemin de fer; *(network)* ferroviaire;

(strike) des cheminots ▪**railcard** n carte f d'abonnement de train

railings ['reɪlɪŋz] npl grille f

railroad ['reɪlrəʊd] Am 1 n (system) chemin m de fer; (track) voie f ferrée 2 adj (ticket) de chemin de fer; (timetable, employee) des chemins de fer; (network, company) ferroviaire; **r. car** voiture f; **r. line** ligne f de chemin de fer; **r. station** gare f

railway ['reɪlweɪ] Br 1 n (system) chemin m de fer; (track) voie f ferrée 2 adj (ticket) de chemin de fer; (timetable, employee) des chemins de fer; (network, company) ferroviaire; **r. carriage** voiture f; **r. line** ligne f de chemin de fer; **r. station** gare f

rain [reɪn] 1 n pluie f; **in the r.** sous la pluie 2 vi pleuvoir; **to r. (down)** (of blows, bullets) pleuvoir; **it's raining** il pleut ▪**rainbow** ['-bəʊ] n arc-en-ciel m ▪**raincheck** n Am Fam **I'll take a r.** (for invitation) ce sera pour une autre fois ▪**raincoat** n imperméable m ▪**raindrop** n goutte f de pluie ▪**rainfall** n (amount) précipitations fpl ▪**rainforest** n forêt f tropicale humide ▪**rainproof** adj imperméable ▪**rainstorm** n pluie f torrentielle ▪**rainwater** n eau f de pluie ▪**rainy** (-ier, -iest) adj pluvieux, -ieuse; (day) de pluie; **the r. season** la saison des pluies

raise [reɪz] 1 vt (lift) lever; (child, family, voice, statue) élever; (crops) cultiver; (salary, price) augmenter; (temperature) faire monter; (question, protest) soulever; (taxes, blockade) lever; **to r. a smile/a laugh** (in others) faire sourire/rire; **to r. sb's hopes** donner trop d'espoir à qn; **to r. money** réunir des fonds; **to r. the alarm** donner l'alarme 2 n Am (pay rise) augmentation f (de salaire)

raisin ['reɪzən] n raisin m sec

> Note that the French word **raisin** is a false friend and is never a translation for the English word **raisin**. It means **grapes**.

rake [reɪk] 1 n râteau m 2 vt (garden) ratisser; **to r. (up)** (leaves) ratisser; Fam **to r. money in** ramasser l'argent à la pelle; **to r. through** (drawers, papers) fouiller dans; **to r. up sb's past** fouiller dans le passé de qn

rally ['rælɪ] 1 (pl -ies) n (political) rassemblement m; (car race) rallye m; (in tennis) échange m 2 (pt & pp -ied) vt (unite, win over) rallier (**to** à); **to r. support** rallier des partisans (**for** autour de); Fig **to r. one's strength** reprendre ses forces 3 vi se rallier (**to** à); (recover) reprendre ses forces; (of share prices) se redresser; **to r. round sb** venir en aide à qn; **rallying point** point m de ralliement

RAM [ræm] (abbr **random access memory**) n Comptr mémoire f vive

ram [ræm] 1 n (animal) bélier m 2 (pt & pp **-mm-**)

vt (vehicle) emboutir; (ship) aborder; **to r. sth into sth** enfoncer qch dans qch

ramble ['ræmbəl] 1 n (hike) randonnée f 2 vi faire une randonnée; **to r. on** divaguer ▪**rambler** n randonneur, -euse m f

rambling ['ræmblɪŋ] adj (a) (house) plein de coins et de recoins; (spread out) vaste; (rose) grimpant (b) (speech) décousu ▪**ramblings** npl divagations fpl

ramification [ræmɪfɪ'keɪʃən] n ramification f

ramp [ræmp] n (for wheelchair) rampe f d'accès; (in garage) pont m (de graissage); (to plane) passerelle f; (on road) petit dos m d'âne

rampage ['ræmpeɪdʒ] n **to go on the r.** (lose control) se déchaîner; (loot) tout saccager

rampant ['ræmpənt] adj endémique

rampart ['ræmpɑːt] n rempart m

ramshackle ['ræmʃækəl] adj délabré

ran [ræn] pt of run

ranch [rɑːntʃ] n ranch m

rancid ['rænsɪd] adj rance

rancour ['ræŋkə(r)] (Am **rancor**) n rancœur f

random ['rændəm] 1 n **at r.** au hasard 2 adj (choice) (fait) au hasard; (sample) prélevé au hasard; (pattern) irrégulier, -ière; Comptr **r. access memory** mémoire f vive; **r. check** (by police) contrôle-surprise m

randy ['rændɪ] (-ier, -iest) adj Br Fam excité

rang [ræŋ] pt of ring[2]

range [reɪndʒ] 1 n (a) (of gun, voice) portée f; (of singer's voice) registre m; (of aircraft, ship) rayon m d'action; (of colours, prices, products) gamme f; (of sizes) choix m; (of temperature) variations fpl; Fig (sphere) champ m (b) (of mountains) chaîne f (c) (stove) fourneau m (d) **(shooting) r.** champ m de tir 2 vi (vary) varier (**from** de; **to** à); (extend) s'étendre

ranger ['reɪndʒə(r)] n **(forest) r.** garde m forestier

rank[1] [ræŋk] 1 n (position, class) rang m; (military grade) grade m; (row) rangée f; (for taxis) station f; Mil **the ranks** les hommes mpl du rang 2 vt placer (**among** parmi) 3 vi compter (**among** parmi) ▪**rank-and-file** n **the r.** (in army) les hommes mpl du rang; (in political party) la base

rank[2] [ræŋk] (-er, -est) adj (a) (foul-smelling) fétide; Br Fam (disgusting) dégueulasse (b) (absolute) total; **he's a r. outsider** il n'est vraiment pas dans la course

rankle ['ræŋkəl] vi **it rankles with me** ça m'est resté sur l'estomac

ransack ['rænsæk] vt (house) mettre sens dessus dessous; (shop, town) piller

ransom ['rænsəm] 1 n rançon f; **to hold sb to r.** rançonner qn 2 vt rançonner

rant [rænt] vi Fam **to r. and rave** tempêter (**at** contre)

rap [ræp] 1 n (a) (blow) coup m sec (b) **r. (music)** rap m 2 (pt & pp **-pp-**) vt (window, *door)* frapper à; *Fig* **to r. sb over the knuckles** taper sur les doigts de qn **3** *vi* (**a**) *(hit)* frapper (**on** à) (**b**) *(sing)* faire du rap ▪ **rapper** *n (singer)* rappeur, -euse *f*

rapacious [rə'peɪʃəs] *adj* rapace

rape [reɪp] **1** *n* viol *m* **2** *vt* violer ▪ **rapist** *n* violeur *m*

rapid ['ræpɪd] *adj* rapide ▪ **rapidity** [rə'pɪdɪtɪ] *n* rapidité *f* ▪ **rapidly** *adv* rapidement

rapids ['ræpɪdz] *npl (of river)* rapides *mpl*

rapport [ræ'pɔː(r)] *n* **to have a good r. with sb** avoir de bons rapports avec qn

rapt [ræpt] *adj (attention)* profond

rapture ['ræptʃə(r)] *n* extase *f*; **to go into raptures** s'extasier (**about** sur) ▪ **rapturous** *adj (welcome, applause)* enthousiaste

rare [reə(r)] *adj* (**a**) (**-er, -est**) rare; **it's r. for her to do it** il est rare qu'elle le fasse (**b**) *(meat)* bleu; **(medium)** r. saignant ▪ **rarely** *adv* rarement ▪ **rarity** *(pl* **-ies**) *n (quality, object)* rareté *f*

rarebit ['reəbɪt] *n Br* **Welsh r.** = toast au fromage

rarefied ['reərɪfaɪd] *adj* raréfié

raring ['reərɪŋ] *adj* **r. to do sth** impatient de faire qch

rascal ['rɑːskəl] *n* coquin, -ine *mf*

rash[1] [ræʃ] *n (on skin) (red patches)* rougeurs *fpl*; *(spots)* (éruption *f* de) boutons *mpl*; **to come out in a r.** faire une éruption de boutons

rash[2] [ræʃ] (**-er, -est**) *adj (imprudent)* irréfléchi ▪ **rashly** *adv* sans réfléchir

rasher ['ræʃə(r)] *n Br* tranche *f (de bacon)*

rasp [rɑːsp] *n (tool)* râpe *f*

raspberry ['rɑːzbərɪ] *(pl* **-ies**) *n (fruit)* framboise *f*; **r. (bush)** framboisier *m*

rasping ['rɑːspɪŋ] *adj (voice)* âpre; *(sound)* grinçant

Rastafarian [ræstə'feərɪən] *n & adj* rastafari *(mf) inv*

rat [ræt] **1** *n* rat *m*; **r. poison** mort-aux-rats *f*; *Fig* **r. race** foire *f* d'empoigne **2** *(pt & pp* **-tt-**) *vi Fam* **to r. on sb** *(denounce)* dénoncer qn

rate [reɪt] **1** *n (level, percentage)* taux *m*; *(speed)* rythme *m*; *(price)* tarif *m*; **exchange/interest r.** taux de change/d'intérêt; **at the r. of** au rythme de; *(amount)* à raison de; **at this r.** *(slow speed)* à ce train-là; **at any r.** en tout cas **2** *vt (regard)* considérer (**as** comme); *(deserve)* mériter; **to r. sb/sth highly** tenir qn/qch en haute estime

rather ['rɑːðə(r)] *adv (preferably, quite)* plutôt; **I'd r. stay** j'aimerais mieux rester (**than** que); **I'd r. you came** j'aimerais mieux que vous veniez; **r. than leave** plutôt que de partir; **r. more tired** un peu plus fatigué (**than** que); **I r. liked it** ça m'a bien aimé; **it's r. nice** c'est bien

ratify ['rætɪfaɪ] *(pt & pp* **-ied**) *vt* ratifier ▪ **ratification** [-fɪ'keɪʃən] *n* ratification *f*

rating ['reɪtɪŋ] *n (classification)* classement *m*; **the ratings** *(for TV, radio)* l'indice *m* d'écoute

ratio ['reɪʃɪəʊ] *(pl* **-os**) *n* rapport *m*

ration ['ræʃən] **1** *n* ration *f*; **rations** *(food)* vivres *mpl* **2** *vt* rationner ▪ **rationing** *n* rationnement *m*

rational ['ræʃənəl] *adj (sensible)* raisonnable; *(sane)* rationnel, -elle ▪ **rationalize** *vt (organize)* rationaliser; *(explain)* justifier ▪ **rationally** *adv (behave)* raisonnablement

rattle ['rætəl] **1** *n* (**a**) *(for baby)* hochet *m* (**b**) *(noise)* cliquetis *m*; *(of gunfire)* crépitement *m* **2** *vt (window)* faire vibrer; *(keys, chains)* faire cliqueter; *Fam* **to r. sb** *(make nervous)* démonter qn; *Fam* **to r. sth off** débiter qch **3** *vi (of window)* vibrer; *(of chains, keys)* cliqueter; *(of gunfire)* crépiter

rattlesnake ['rætəlsneɪk] *n* serpent *m* à sonnette

ratty ['rætɪ] (**-ier, -iest**) *adj Fam* (**a**) *(shabby)* *Am* minable (**b**) *Br* **to get r.** *(annoyed)* prendre la mouche

raucous ['rɔːkəs] *adj (noisy, rowdy)* bruyant

raunchy ['rɔːntʃɪ] (**-ier, -iest**) *adj Fam (lewd)* cochon, -onne; *(sexy)* sexy *inv*

ravage ['rævɪdʒ] *vt* ravager ▪ **ravages** *npl (of old age, time)* ravages *mpl*

rave [reɪv] **1** *adj (review)* dithyrambique **2** *n* rave *f* **3** *vi (talk nonsense)* délirer; **to r. about sb/sth** *(enthuse)* ne pas tarir d'éloges sur qn/qch ▪ **raving** *adj* **to be r. mad** être complètement fou (*f* folle)

raven ['reɪvən] *n* corbeau *m*

ravenous ['rævənəs] *adj* **to be r.** avoir une faim de loup

ravine [rə'viːn] *n* ravin *m*

ravioli [rævɪ'əʊlɪ] *n* ravioli(s) *mpl*

ravishing ['rævɪʃɪŋ] *adj (beautiful)* ravissant ▪ **ravishingly** *adv* **r. beautiful** d'une beauté ravissante

raw [rɔː] (**-er, -est**) *adj (vegetable)* cru; *(sugar, data)* brut; *(skin)* écorché; *(wound)* à vif; *(immature)* inexpérimenté; *(weather)* rigoureux, -euse; **r. material** matière *f* première; *Fam* **to get a r. deal** être mal traité

Rawlplug® ['rɔːlplʌg] *n Br* cheville *f*

ray[1] [reɪ] *n (of light, sun)* rayon *m*; *Fig (of hope)* lueur *f*

ray[2] [reɪ] *n (fish)* raie *f*

rayon ['reɪɒn] **1** *n* rayonne *f* **2** *adj* en rayonne

raze [reɪz] *vt* **to r. sth to the ground** raser qch

razor ['reɪzə(r)] *n* rasoir *m*; **r. blade** lame *f* de rasoir

Rd *(abbr* **road**) rue *f*

re [riː] *prep Com* en référence à; **re your letter** suite à votre lettre

reach [riːtʃ] **1** *n* portée *f*; **within r. of** à portée de; *(near)* à proximité de; **within (easy) r.** *(object)* à portée de main; *(shops)* tout proche **2** *vt (place, aim, distant object)* atteindre, arriver à; *(decision)* prendre; *(agreement)* aboutir à;

(contact) joindre; **to r. a conclusion** arriver à une conclusion; **to r. out one's arm** tendre le bras **3** *vi (extend)* s'étendre (**to** jusqu'à); *(of voice)* porter; **to r. for sth** tendre le bras pour prendre qch; **to r. out** tendre le bras (**for** pour prendre)

react [rɪ'ækt] *vi* réagir (**against** contre; **to** à) ▪ **reaction** *n* réaction *f*

reactionary [rɪ'ækʃənərɪ] *(pl -ies) adj & n* réactionnaire *(mf)*

reactor [rɪ'æktə(r)] *n* réacteur *m*

read [ri:d] **1** *(pt & pp read* [red]*) vt* lire; *(meter)* relever; *(of instrument)* indiquer; *Br Univ (study)* étudier; **the sign reads…** sur le panneau, on peut lire… **2** *vi (of person)* lire (**about** sur); **to r. well** *(of text)* se lire bien; **to r. to sb** faire la lecture à qn **3** *n Fam* **to have a r.** lire; **to be a good r.** être agréable à lire ▪ **readable** *adj (handwriting)* lisible; *(book)* facile à lire ▪ **read-only** *adj Comptr (file)* (à) lecture seule; **r. memory** mémoire *f* morte

▸ **read back** *vt sep* relire

▸ **read for** *vt insep Br (university degree)* préparer

▸ **read out** *vt sep* lire (à haute voix)

▸ **read over** *vt sep* relire

▸ **read through** *vt sep (skim)* parcourir

▸ **read up (on)** *vt insep (study)* étudier

readdress [ri:ə'dres] *vt (letter)* faire suivre

reader ['ri:də(r)] *n* lecteur, -trice *mf*; *(book)* livre *m* de lecture ▪ **readership** *n* nombre *m* de lecteurs

readily ['redɪlɪ] *adv (willingly)* volontiers; *(easily)* facilement ▪ **readiness** *n* empressement *m* (**to do** à faire)

reading ['ri:dɪŋ] *n* lecture *f*; *(of meter)* relevé *m*; **it's light/heavy r.** c'est facile/difficile à lire; **r. book/room** livre *m*/salle *f* de lecture; **r. glasses** lunettes *fpl* de lecture; **r. lamp** *(on desk)* lampe *f* de bureau; *(at bedside)* lampe de chevet; **r. matter** de quoi lire

readjust [ri:ə'dʒʌst] **1** *vt (instrument)* régler; *(salary)* réajuster **2** *vi (of person)* se réadapter (**to** à) ▪ **readjustment** *n* réglage *m*; *(of salary)* réajustement *m*; *(of person)* réadaptation *f*

ready ['redɪ] **1** *(-ier, -iest) adj* prêt (**to do** à faire; **for sth** pour qch); **to get sb/sth r.** préparer qn/qch; **to get r.** se préparer (**for sth** pour qch; **to do** à faire); **r.! steady! go!** à vos marques, prêts, partez!; **r. cash, r. money** argent *m* liquide **2** *n* **to be r.** être tout prêt *(f* toute prête) ▪ **'ready-'cooked** *adj* cuisiné ▪ **'ready-'made** *adj (food)* tout prêt *(f* toute prête); *(excuse)* tout fait *(f* toute faite); **r. clothes** le prêt-à-porter ▪ **'ready-to-'wear** *adj* **r. clothes** le prêt-à-porter

real [rɪəl] **1** *adj* vrai; *(leather)* véritable; *(world, fact, danger)* réel *(f* réelle); **in r. life** dans la réalité; **in r. terms** en termes réels; *Fam* **it's the**

r. thing c'est du vrai de vrai; *Am* **r. estate** immobilier *m* **2** *adv Fam* vraiment; **r. stupid** vraiment bête **3** *n Fam* **for r.** pour de vrai

realism ['rɪəlɪzəm] *n* réalisme *m* ▪ **realist** *n* réaliste *mf* ▪ **rea'listic** *adj* réaliste ▪ **rea-'listically** *adv* avec réalisme

reality [rɪ'ælətɪ] *(pl -ies) n* réalité *f*; **in r.** en réalité; **reality television** télé-réalité *f*

realize ['rɪəlaɪz] *vt* (**a**) *(become aware of)* se rendre compte de; **to r. that…** se rendre compte que… (**b**) *(carry out, convert into cash)* réaliser ▪ **reali'zation** *n* (**a**) *(awareness)* prise *f* de conscience *f* (**b**) *(of dream, plan, assets)* réalisation *f*

really ['rɪəlɪ] *adv* vraiment; **is it r. true?** est-ce bien vrai?

realm [relm] *n (kingdom)* royaume *m*; *Fig (field)* domaine *m*

realtor ['rɪəltə(r)] *n Am* agent *m* immobilier

ream [ri:m] *n (of paper)* rame *f*

reap [ri:p] *vt (field, crop)* moissonner; *Fig (profits)* récolter

reappear [ri:ə'pɪə(r)] *vi* réapparaître

reappraise [ri:ə'preɪz] *vt* réévaluer

rear¹ [rɪə(r)] **1** *n (back part)* arrière *m*; *(of military column)* queue *f*; **in** *or* **at the r.** à l'arrière (**of** de); **from the r.** par derrière **2** *adj (entrance, legs)* de derrière; *(lights, window)* arrière *inv* ▪ **rearguard** *n Mil* arrière-garde *f* ▪ **rearview 'mirror** *n* rétroviseur *m*

rear² [rɪə(r)] **1** *vt (child, animals)* élever; *(one's head)* relever **2** *vi* **to r. (up)** *(of horse)* se cabrer

rearrange [ri:ə'reɪndʒ] *vt (hair, room)* réarranger; *(plans)* changer

reason ['ri:zən] **1** *n (cause, sense)* raison *f*; **the r. for/why** la raison de/pour laquelle; **the r. that…** la raison pour laquelle…; **for no r.** sans raison; **it stands to r.** cela va de soi; **within r.** dans des limites raisonnables; **to have every r. to believe that…** avoir tout lieu de croire que… **2** *vt* **to r. that…** estimer que… **3** *vi* raisonner (**about** sur); **to r. with sb** raisonner qn ▪ **reasoning** *n* raisonnement *m*

reasonable ['ri:zənəbəl] *adj (fair)* raisonnable; *(quite good)* passable ▪ **reasonably** *adv (behave, act)* raisonnablement; *(quite)* plutôt; **r. fit** en assez bonne forme

reassess [ri:ə'ses] *vt* reconsidérer

reassure [ri:ə'ʃʊə(r)] *vt* rassurer ▪ **reas-surance** *n* réconfort *m* ▪ **reassuring** *adj* rassurant

reawaken [ri:ə'weɪkən] **1** *vt (interest, feeling)* faire renaître **2** *vi (of person)* se réveiller de nouveau ▪ **reawakening** *n* réveil *m*

rebate ['ri:beɪt] *n (discount)* rabais *m*; *(refund)* remboursement *m*

rebel ['rebəl] **1** *n* rebelle *mf* **2** *adj (camp, chief, attack)* des rebelles **3** [rɪ'bel] *(pt & pp -ll-) vi* se rebeller (**against** contre) ▪ **rebellion** [rɪ'bel-

jən] *n* rébellion *f* ▪ **rebellious** [rɪ'beljəs] *adj*
rebelle

rebirth ['riːbɜːθ] *n* renaissance *f*

reboot [riː'buːt] Comptr 1 *vt* réamorcer 2 *vi* se
réamorcer, redémarrer

rebound 1 ['riːbaʊnd] *n* (of ball) rebond *m*; Fig
to marry sb on the r. épouser qn à la suite
d'une déception sentimentale 2 [rɪ'baʊnd] *vi*
(of ball) rebondir; Fig (of lies, action) se
retourner (**on** contre)

rebuff [rɪ'bʌf] 1 *n* rebuffade *f* 2 *vt* repousser

rebuild [riː'bɪld] (pt & pp -**built**) *vt* reconstruire

rebuke [rɪ'bjuːk] 1 *n* réprimande *f* 2 *vt*
réprimander

rebut [rɪ'bʌt] (pt & pp -**tt**-) *vt* réfuter

recalcitrant [rɪ'kælsɪtrənt] *adj* récalcitrant

recall [rɪ'kɔːl] 1 *n* (calling back) rappel *m*; **my
powers of r.** (memory) ma mémoire 2 *vt*
(remember) se rappeler (**that** que; **doing** avoir
fait); (call back) rappeler; **to r. sth to sb**
rappeler qch à qn

recant [rɪ'kænt] *vi* se rétracter

recap ['riːkæp] 1 *n* récapitulation *f* 2 (pt & pp
-**pp**-) *vi* récapituler ▪ **recapitulate** [-kə'pɪt-
ʃʊleɪt] *vti* récapituler ▪ **recapitulation** [-kəpɪt-
ʃʊ'leɪʃən] *n* récapitulation *f*

recapture [riː'kæptʃə(r)] 1 *n* (of prisoner)
capture *f* 2 *vt* (prisoner) capturer; (town)
reprendre; (recreate) recréer

recede [rɪ'siːd] *vi* (into the distance) s'éloigner;
(of floods) baisser ▪ **receding** *adj* (forehead,
chin) fuyant; **his hairline is r.** son front se
dégarnit

receipt [rɪ'siːt] *n* (for payment, object) reçu *m*
(**for** de); (in shop, bar) ticket *m* de caisse; (for
letter, parcel) récépissé *m*; **receipts** (at box
office) recette *f*; **on r. of sth** dès réception de qch

receive [rɪ'siːv] *vt* recevoir; (stolen goods)
receler ▪ **receiving** *n* (of stolen goods) recel *m*

receiver [rɪ'siːvə(r)] *n* (**a**) (of phone) combiné
m; (radio) récepteur *m*; **to pick up** or **lift the r.**
(of phone) décrocher (**b**) (of stolen goods)
receleur, -euse *mf*; Br Fin (in bankruptcy)
administrateur *m* judiciaire ▪ **receivership** *n*
Fin **to go into r.** être placé sous règlement
judiciaire

recent ['riːsənt] *adj* récent; (development)
dernier, -ière; **in r. months** au cours des
derniers mois ▪ **recently** *adv* récemment; **as
r. as yesterday** pas plus tard qu'hier

receptacle [rɪ'septəkl] *n* récipient *m*

reception [rɪ'sepʃən] *n* (party, of radio)
réception *f*; (welcome) accueil *m*; **r. (desk)**
réception ▪ **receptionist** *n* réceptionniste *m*

receptive [rɪ'septɪv] *adj* réceptif, -ive (**to** à)

recess [Br rɪ'ses, Am 'riːses] *n* (**a**) (holiday)
vacances *fpl*; Am (between classes) récréation *f*
(**b**) (in wall) renfoncement *m*; (smaller) & Fig
recoin *m*

recession [rɪ'seʃən] *n* récession *f*

recharge [riː'tʃɑːdʒ] *vt* (battery) recharger
▪ **rechargeable** *adj* (battery) rechargeable

recipe ['resɪpɪ] *n* (for food) & Fig recette *f* (**for**
sth de qch; **for doing** pour faire)

recipient [rɪ'sɪpɪənt] *n* (of gift, letter)
destinataire *mf*; (of award) lauréat, -éate *mf*

> Note that the French word **récipient** is a
> false friend and is never a translation for
> the English word **recipient**. It means **con-
> tainer**.

reciprocal [rɪ'sɪprəkəl] *adj* réciproque

reciprocate [rɪ'sɪprəkeɪt] 1 *vt* retourner 2 *vi*
rendre la pareille

recital [rɪ'saɪtəl] *n* (of music) récital *m* (pl -als)

recite [rɪ'saɪt] *vt* (poem) réciter; (list) énumérer
▪ **recitation** [resɪ'teɪʃən] *n* récitation *f*

reckless ['rekləs] *adj* (rash) imprudent; **r. driver**
chauffard *m* ▪ **recklessly** *adv* imprudemment

reckon ['rekən] 1 *vt* (calculate) calculer;
(consider) considérer; Fam (think) penser (**that**
que) 2 *vi* calculer; compter; **to r. with** (take
into account) compter avec; (deal with) avoir
affaire à; **to r. on/without sb/sth** compter sur/
sans qn/qch; **to r. on doing sth** compter faire
qch ▪ **reckoning** *n* calcul *m*

reclaim [rɪ'kleɪm] 1 *vt* (lost property, waste
material, luggage) récupérer; (expenses) se
faire rembourser; **to r. land from the sea**
gagner du terrain sur la mer 2 *n* **'baggage r.'**
(in airport) 'retrait des bagages'

> Note that the French word **réclamer** is a
> false friend and is never a translation for
> the English verb **to reclaim**. It means **to
> claim** or **to demand**.

recline [rɪ'klaɪn] 1 *vt* (head) appuyer (**on** sur) 2
vi (of person) être allongé ▪ **reclining 'seat** *n*
siège *m* à dossier inclinable

recluse [rɪ'kluːs] *n* reclus, -use *mf*

recognition [rekəg'nɪʃən] *n* reconnaissance *f*;
to change beyond or **out of all r.** devenir
méconnaissable; **to gain r.** être reconnu

recognize ['rekəgnaɪz] *vt* reconnaître ▪ **recognizable** *adj* reconnaissable

recoil [rɪ'kɔɪl] *vi* (of gun) reculer; (of person)
avoir un mouvement de recul

recollect [rekə'lekt] *vt* se souvenir de
▪ **recollection** *n* souvenir *m*

recommend [rekə'mend] *vt* (praise, support,
advise) recommander (**to** à; **for** pour); **to r. sb
to do sth** recommander à qn de faire qch
▪ **recommen'dation** *n* recommandation *f*

recompense ['rekəmpens] 1 *n* récompense *f* 2
vt (reward) récompenser

reconcile ['rekənsaɪl] *vt* (person) réconcilier
(**with** or **to** avec); (opinions, facts) concilier; **to**

r. oneself to sth se résigner à qch
▪ **reconciliation** [-sɪlɪ'eɪʃən] n réconciliation f
reconditioned [riː'kənˈdɪʃənd] adj (engine, machine) remis à neuf
reconnaissance [rɪ'kɒnɪsəns] n Mil reconnaissance f ▪ **reconnoitre** [rekə'nɔɪtə(r)] (Am **reconnoiter** [riːkə'nɔɪtər]) vt (land, enemy troops) reconnaître
reconsider [riːkən'sɪdə(r)] 1 vt réexaminer 2 vi réfléchir
reconstruct [riːkən'strʌkt] vt reconstruire; (crime) reconstituer
record ['rekɔːd] 1 n (a) (disc) disque m; **r. company** maison f de disques; **r. library** discothèque f; **r. player** électrophone m (b) Sport (best performance) record m (c) (report) rapport m; (background) antécédents mpl; (file) dossier m; **to make** or **keep a r. of sth** garder une trace écrite de qch; **to have a good safety r.** avoir une bonne réputation en matière de sécurité; **on r.** (fact, event) attesté; **the highest figures on r.** les chiffres les plus élevés jamais enregistrés; **(police) r.** casier m judiciaire; **(public) records** archives fpl
2 adj record inv; **in r. time** en un temps record; **to be at a r. high/low** être à son taux le plus haut/bas
3 [rɪ'kɔːd] vt (on tape, in register) enregistrer; (in diary) noter; (relate) rapporter (**that** que)
4 vi (on tape, of tape recorder) enregistrer ▪ **record-holder** n détenteur, -trice mf du record
recorded [rɪ'kɔːdɪd] adj enregistré; (fact) attesté; (TV broadcast) en différé; Br **to send sth (by) r. delivery** ≃ envoyer qch en recommandé avec accusé de réception
recorder [rɪ'kɔːdə(r)] n (musical instrument) flûte f à bec
recording [rɪ'kɔːdɪŋ] n enregistrement m; **r. studio** studio m d'enregistrement
recount [rɪ'kaʊnt] vt (relate) raconter
re-count ['riːkaʊnt] n (of votes) deuxième décompte m
recoup [rɪ'kuːp] vt récupérer
recourse ['rɪkɔːs] n recours m; **to have r. to** avoir recours à
recover [rɪ'kʌvə(r)] 1 vt (get back) récupérer; (one's appetite, balance) retrouver 2 vi (from illness, shock, surprise) se remettre (**from** de); (of economy, country, stock market) se redresser; (of currency) remonter; (of sales) reprendre ▪ **recovery** (pl **-ies**) n (a) (from illness) rétablissement m; (of economy, stock market) redressement m; **to make a r.** se rétablir (b) (of goods) récupération f; Br **r. vehicle** dépanneuse f
re-create [riːkrɪ'eɪt] vt recréer
recreation [rekrɪ'eɪʃən] n Sch (break) récréation f; **r. ground** terrain m de jeux

▪ **recreational** adj (activity) de loisir; **r. drug** drogue f à usage récréatif; Am **r. vehicle** camping-car m
recrimination [rɪkrɪmɪ'neɪʃən] n récrimination f
recruit [rɪ'kruːt] 1 n recrue f 2 vt recruter ▪ **recruitment** n recrutement m; **r. agency** agence f de recrutement
rectangle ['rektæŋɡəl] n rectangle m ▪ **rectangular** [-'tæŋɡʊlə(r)] adj rectangulaire
rectify ['rektɪfaɪ] (pt & pp **-ied**) vt rectifier ▪ **rectification** [-fɪ'keɪʃən] n rectification f
rector ['rektə(r)] n (priest) pasteur m anglican; Scot Sch ≃ proviseur m
rectum ['rektəm] n rectum m
recuperate [rɪ'kuːpəreɪt] vi (from illness) récupérer ▪ **recupe'ration** n (after illness) rétablissement m
recur [rɪ'kɜː(r)] (pt & pp **-rr-**) vi (of event, problem) se reproduire; (of illness) réapparaître; (of theme) revenir ▪ **recurrence** [-'kʌrəns] n récurrence f ▪ **recurrent** [-'kʌrənt] adj récurrent ▪ **recurring** adj (event, problem) récurrent; (illness) qui réapparaît; (theme, dream) qui revient souvent; **six point six r.** six virgule six à l'infini
recycle [riː'saɪkəl] vt recycler; **recycled paper** papier m recyclé; Comptr **r. bin** corbeille f ▪ **recyclable** adj recyclable ▪ **recycling** n recyclage m; **r. facility** installation f de recyclage; **r. plant** usine f de recyclage
red [red] 1 (**redder, reddest**) adj rouge; (hair) roux (f rousse); Football **r. card** carton m rouge; **the R. Cross** la Croix-Rouge; **r. light** (traffic light) feu m rouge; **the r. light district** le quartier chaud; Fig **r. tape** paperasserie f; **the R. Sea** la mer Rouge 2 n (colour) rouge m; **in the r.** (in debt) dans le rouge ▪ **redden** ['redən] vti rougir ▪ **reddish** adj rougeâtre; (hair) légèrement roux (f rousse) ▪ **red-'faced** adj rougeaud; Fig (with confusion) rouge ▪ **red-'handed** adv **to be caught r.** être pris la main dans le sac ▪ **redhead** n roux m, rousse f ▪ **red-'hot** adj brûlant ▪ **redness** n rougeur f; (of hair) rousseur f
redcurrant [red'kʌrənt] n groseille f
redecorate [riː'dekəreɪt] vt (repaint) refaire la peinture de
redeem [rɪ'diːm] vt (restore to favour, buy back, free) racheter; (debt, loan) rembourser; (gift token, coupon) échanger; **his one redeeming feature is...** la seule chose qui le rachète, c'est... ▪ **redemption** [-'dempʃən] n rachat m; (of debt, loan) remboursement m; Rel rédemption f
redeploy [riːdɪ'plɔɪ] vt (staff) réorganiser; (troops) redéployer
redial [riː'daɪəl] (Br **-ll-**, Am **-l-**) Tel 1 ['riːdaɪəl] n

rappel *m* du dernier numéro **2** *vt* recomposer **3** *vi* recomposer le numéro

redirect [riːdaɪˈrekt] *vt* (*mail*) faire suivre; (*plane, traffic*) dévier

redo [riːˈduː] (*pt* -**did**, *pp* -**done**) *vt* refaire

redolent [ˈredələnt] *adj* **to be r. of** (*smell of*) sentir; (*suggest*) avoir un parfum de

redress [rɪˈdres] *n* **to seek r.** demander réparation (**for** de)

reduce [rɪˈdjuːs] *vt* réduire (**to** à; **by** de); (*temperature, price*) baisser; **at a reduced price** à prix réduit; **to r. speed** ralentir; **to r. sb to silence** réduire qn au silence; **to r. sb to tears** faire pleurer qn; **to be reduced to doing sth** en être réduit à faire qch ▪ **reduction** [-ˈdʌkʃən] *n* (*of temperature, price*) baisse *f*; (*discount*) réduction *f* (**in/on** de/sur)

redundant [rɪˈdʌndənt] *adj* (*not needed*) superflu; *Br* **to make sb r.** licencier qn; **to be made r.** être licencié ▪ **redundancy** (*pl* -**ies**) *n Br* (*of worker*) licenciement *m*; **r. pay(ment)** prime *f* de licenciement

reed [riːd] *n* (**a**) (*plant*) roseau *m* (**b**) (*of musical instrument*) anche *f*

re-educate [riːˈedjʊkeɪt] *vt* (*criminal, limb*) rééduquer

reef [riːf] *n* récif *m*

reek [riːk] **1** *n* relent *m* **2** *vi* **to r.** (**of sth**) puer (qch)

reel [riːl] **1** *n* (*of thread, film*) bobine *f*; (*for fishing line*) moulinet *m* **2** *vt sep* **to r. off** (*names, statistics*) débiter **3** *vi* (*stagger*) chanceler; *Fig* **my head is reeling** la tête me tourne

re-elect [riːɪˈlekt] *vt* réélire

re-enact [riːɪˈnækt] *vt* reconstituer

re-entry [riːˈentri] *n* (*of spacecraft*) rentrée *f*

re-establish [riːɪˈstæblɪʃ] *vt* rétablir

re-examine [riːɪgˈzæmɪn] *vt* réexaminer

ref [ref] (*abbr* referee) *n Fam Sport* arbitre *m*

refectory [rɪˈfektərɪ] (*pl* -**ies**) *n* réfectoire *m*

refer [rɪˈfɜː(r)] (*pt & pp* -**rr**-) **1** *vt* **to r. sth to sb** (*submit*) soumettre qch à qn; **to r. sb to a specialist** envoyer qn voir un spécialiste **2** *vt insep* **to r. to** (*allude to*) faire allusion à; (*mention*) parler de; (*apply to*) s'appliquer à; (*consult*) consulter

referee [refəˈriː] **1** *n Sport* arbitre *m*; **to give the names of two referees** (*for job*) fournir deux références **2** *vti* arbitrer

reference [ˈrefərəns] *n* (*source, consultation*) référence *f*; (*allusion*) allusion *f* (**to** à); (*mention*) mention *f* (**to** de); (*for employer*) lettre *f* de référence; **with** or **in r. to** concernant; *Com* **with** or **in r. to your letter** suite à votre lettre; **for future r.** à titre d'information; **r. book** ouvrage *m* de référence; **r. point** point *m* de repère

referendum [refəˈrendəm] *n* référendum *m*

refill 1 [ˈriːfɪl] *n* (*for notebook*) feuillets *mpl* de

rechange; (*for pen*) cartouche *f*; (*for lighter*) recharge *f*; **would you like a r.?** (*of drink*) je te ressers? **2** [riːˈfɪl] *vt* (*glass*) remplir à nouveau; (*lighter, pen*) recharger

refine [rɪˈfaɪn] **1** *vt* (*oil, sugar, manners*) raffiner; (*technique, machine*) perfectionner **2** *vi* **to r. upon sth** parfaire qch ▪ **refined** *adj* (*person, manners, sugar*) raffiné ▪ **refinement** *n* (*of person, manners*) raffinement *m*; (*of sugar, oil*) raffinage *m*; (*of technique*) perfectionnement *m*; **refinements** (*technical improvements*) améliorations *fpl* ▪ **refinery** (*pl* -**ies**) *n* raffinerie *f*

refit 1 [ˈriːfɪt] *n* (*of ship*) remise *f* en état **2** [riːˈfɪt] (*pt & pp* -**tt**-) *vt* (*ship*) remettre en état

reflate [riːˈfleɪt] *vt* (*economy*) relancer

reflect [rɪˈflekt] **1** *vt* (**a**) (*light, image*) refléter, réfléchir; *Fig* (*portray*) refléter; **to be reflected (in)** (*of light*) se refléter (dans) (**b**) **to r. that…** se dire que… **2** *vi* (**a**) **to r. on sb, to be reflected on sb** (*of prestige, honour*) rejaillir sur qn; **to r. badly on sb** faire du tort à qn; **to r. well on sb** faire honneur à qn (**b**) (*think*) réfléchir (**on** à)

reflection [rɪˈflekʃən] *n* (**a**) (*image*) & *Fig* reflet *m*; *Fig* **it is no r. on your own capabilities** cela ne remet pas en cause vos compétences (**b**) (*thought, criticism*) réflexion (**on** sur); **on r.** tout bien réfléchi

reflector [rɪˈflektə(r)] *n* (*on bicycle, vehicle*) catadioptre *m*

reflex [ˈriːfleks] *n & adj* réflexe (*m*); **r. action** réflexe *m*

reflexion [rɪˈflekʃən] *n Br* = **reflection**

reflexive [rɪˈfleksɪv] *adj Grammar* réfléchi

reflexology [riːflekˈsɒlədʒɪ] *n* réflexologie *f* ▪ **reflexologist** *n* réflexologiste *mf*

refloat [riːˈfləʊt] *vt* (*ship, company*) renflouer

reform [rɪˈfɔːm] **1** *n* réforme *f*; *Am* **r. school** centre *m* d'éducation surveillée **2** *vt* réformer; (*person, conduct*) corriger **3** *vi* (*of person*) se réformer ▪ **reformer** *n* réformateur, -trice *mf*

reformatory [rɪˈfɔːmətərɪ] (*pl* -**ies**) *n Am* centre *m* d'éducation surveillée

refrain [rɪˈfreɪn] **1** *n* (*of song*) & *Fig* refrain *m* **2** *vi* s'abstenir (**from sth** de qch; **from doing** de faire)

refresh [rɪˈfreʃ] *vt* (*of drink*) rafraîchir; (*of bath*) revigorer; (*of sleep, rest*) reposer; **to r. oneself** (*drink*) se rafraîchir; **to r. one's memory** se rafraîchir la mémoire ▪ **refreshing** *adj* (*drink*) rafraîchissant; (*bath*) revigorant; (*sleep*) reposant; (*original*) nouveau (*f* nouvelle) ▪ **refreshments** *npl* rafraîchissements *mpl*

refresher course [rɪˈfreʃəkɔːs] *n* cours *m* de recyclage

refrigerate [rɪˈfrɪdʒəreɪt] *vt* réfrigérer ▪ **refrigerator** *n* (*domestic*) réfrigérateur *m*

refuel [riːˈfjʊəl] **1** (*Br* -**ll**-, *Am* -**l**-) *vt* (*aircraft*)

ravitailler en carburant **2** vi *(of aircraft)* se
ravitailler en carburant
refuge ['rɛfjuːdʒ] n refuge m; **to take r.** se
réfugier (**in** dans)
refugee [rɛfjʊ'dʒiː] n réfugié, -iée mf; **r. camp**
camp m de réfugiés
refund 1 ['riːfʌnd] n remboursement m **2**
[rɪ'fʌnd] vt rembourser
refurbish [riː'fɜːbɪʃ] vt rénover
refusal [rɪ'fjuːzəl] n refus m
refuse¹ [rɪ'fjuːz] **1** vt refuser; **to r. to do sth**
refuser de faire qch; **to r. sb sth** refuser qch à
qn **2** vi refuser
refuse² ['rɛfjuːs] n Br *(rubbish)* ordures fpl;
(industrial waste materials) déchets mpl; **r.
collection** ramassage m des ordures; **r. dump**
dépôt m d'ordures
refute [rɪ'fjuːt] vt réfuter
regain [rɪ'geɪn] vt *(lost ground, favour)*
regagner; *(health, sight)* retrouver; *(power)*
reconquérir; **to r. one's strength** reprendre
des forces; **to r. consciousness** reprendre
connaissance;. **to r. possession of sth**
reprendre possession de qch
regal ['riːgəl] adj royal
regalia [rɪ'geɪlɪə] npl insignes mpl
regard [rɪ'gɑːd] **1** n *(admiration)* respect m;
(consideration) égard m; **to hold sb in high r.**
tenir qn en haute estime; **with r. to** en ce qui
concerne; **without r. to** sans tenir compte de;
to give or **send one's regards to sb**
transmettre son meilleur souvenir à qn **2** vt
(admire, respect) estimer; **to r. sb/sth as...**
considérer qn/qch comme...; **as regards...**
en ce qui concerne... ▪**regarding** prep en ce
qui concerne

Note that the French words **regard** and **regarder** are false friends and are never translations for the English words **regard** and **to
regard**. They mean **look** and **to look at**.

regardless [rɪ'gɑːdləs] **1** adj **r. of...** *(without
considering)* sans tenir compte de... **2** adv *(all
the same)* quand même
regatta [rɪ'gætə] n régate f
regency ['riːdʒənsɪ] *(pl* **-ies)** n régence f
▪**regent** n régent, -ente mf
regenerate [rɪ'dʒenəreɪt] **1** vt régénérer **2** vi
se régénérer
reggae ['regeɪ] **1** n *(music)* reggae m **2** adj
(group, musician) reggae inv
régime [reɪ'ʒiːm] n régime m
regiment 1 ['redʒɪmənt] n régiment m **2**
['redʒɪment] vt régimenter ▪**regimental** [-'men-
təl] adj du régiment ▪**regimentation** [-men-
'teɪʃən] n discipline f draconienne
region ['riːdʒən] n région f; Fig **in the r. of**
(about) environ ▪**regional** adj régional
register ['redʒɪstə(r)] **1** n registre m; *(in school)*

cahier m d'appel; **electoral r.** liste f électorale;
to take the r. *(of teacher)* faire l'appel **2** vt *(birth,
death)* déclarer; *(record, note, speed)* enregistrer; *(vehicle)* immatriculer; *(complaint)*
déposer; *(astonishment, displeasure)* manifester;
Fam *(realize)* réaliser **3** vi *(enrol)* s'inscrire
(**for a course** à un cours); *(at hotel)* signer le
registre; *(of voter)* s'inscrire sur les listes
électorales; Fam **I told him but it didn't r.** je
lui ai dit mais il n'a pas enregistré ▪**registered** adj *(member)* inscrit; *(letter, package)*
recommandé; *(charity)* agréé; **to send sth
by r. post** or Am **mail** envoyer qch en recommandé; **r. trademark** marque f déposée; Br **r.
unemployed** inscrit au chômage
registrar [redʒɪ'strɑː(r)] n Br *(record keeper)*
officier m de l'état civil; *(in university)*
responsable m des inscriptions; *(in hospital)*
chef m de clinique
registration [redʒɪ'streɪʃən] n *(enrolment)*
inscription f; *(of complaint)* enregistrement m;
Br **r. (number)** *(of vehicle)* numéro m
d'immatriculation; Br **r. document** *(of vehicle)*
≃ carte f grise
registry ['redʒɪstrɪ] adj & n Br **r. (office)** bureau
m de l'état civil; **to get married in a r. office** se
marier à la mairie
regress [rɪ'gres] vi régresser ▪**regression** n
régression f
regret [rɪ'gret] **1** n regret m **2** *(pt & pp* **-tt-**) vt
regretter (**to do** de faire; **that** que (+
subjunctive)); **I r. to hear that...** j'ai le regret
d'apprendre que...; **to r. doing sth** regretter
d'avoir fait qch ▪**regretfully** adv **r., I...** à mon
grand regret, je...
regrettable [rɪ'gretəbəl] adj regrettable (**that**
que + *subjunctive)* ▪**regrettably** adv malheureusement; *(poor, ill)* fâcheusement
regroup [riː'gruːp] **1** vt regrouper **2** vi se
regrouper
regular ['regjʊlə(r)] **1** adj **(a)** *(steady, even)*
& Grammar régulier, -ière; *(usual)* habituel,
-uelle; *(price)* normal; *(size)* moyen, -enne;
(listener, reader) fidèle; *(staff)* permanent; Fam
(for emphasis) vrai; **on a r. basis**
régulièrement; Am Fam **a r. guy** un type sympa
(b) *(army, soldier)* régulier, -ière **2** n *(in bar)*
habitué, -uée mf ▪**regularity** [-'lærɪtɪ] n
régularité f ▪**regularly** adv régulièrement
regulate ['regjʊleɪt] vt *(adjust)* régler; *(control)*
réglementer ▪**regu'lation 1** n **(a)** *(rules)* regula-
tions *(rules)* règlement m **(b)** *(regulating)*
réglage m **2** adj *(statutory)* réglementaire
rehabilitate [riːhə'bɪlɪteɪt] vt réhabiliter
▪**rehabili'tation** n réadaptation f
rehash 1 ['riːhæʃ] n resucée f **2** [riː'hæʃ] vt *(text,
film)* remanier
rehearse [rɪ'hɜːs] vti répéter ▪**rehearsal** n
répétition f

reign [reɪn] **1** n règne m; **in** or **during the r. of** sous le règne de **2** vi régner (**over** sur)

reimburse [riːɪmˈbɜːs] vt rembourser (**for** de) ▪ **reimbursement** n remboursement m

rein [reɪn] n **to give sb free r. to do sth** donner carte blanche à qn pour qu'il fasse qch

reincarnation [riːɪnkɑːˈneɪʃən] n réincarnation f

reindeer [ˈreɪndɪə(r)] n inv renne m

reinforce [riːɪnˈfɔːs] vt renforcer (**with** de); **reinforced concrete** béton m armé ▪ **reinforcement** n renforcement m (**of** de); **reinforcements** (troops) renforts mpl

reins [reɪnz] npl (for horse) rênes fpl; (for baby) bretelles fpl de sécurité

reinstate [riːɪnˈsteɪt] vt réintégrer ▪ **reinstatement** n réintégration f

reissue [riːˈɪʃuː] vt (book) rééditer

reiterate [riːˈɪtəreɪt] vt réitérer

reject 1 [ˈriːdʒekt] n (object) rebus m; Fam (person) inadapté, -ée mf; **r. article** article m de deuxième choix; Br **r. shop** soldeur f **2** [rɪˈdʒekt] vt rejeter; (candidate, goods, offer) refuser ▪ **rejection** [rɪˈdʒekʃən] n rejet m; (of candidate, goods, offer) refus m

rejoice [rɪˈdʒɔɪs] vi se réjouir (**over** or **at** de) ▪ **rejoicing** n réjouissance f

rejoin[1] [rɪˈdʒɔɪn] vt (a) (join up with) rejoindre (b) (join again) réintégrer

rejoin[2] [rɪˈdʒɔɪn] vi (retort) répliquer

rejuvenate [rɪˈdʒuːvəneɪt] vt rajeunir

rekindle [riːˈkɪndəl] vt raviver

relapse 1 [ˈriːlæps] n rechute f **2** [rɪˈlæps] vi rechuter; Fig **to r. into** retomber dans

relate [rɪˈleɪt] **1** vt (a) (narrate) raconter (**that** que); (report) rapporter (**that** que) (b) (connect) mettre en rapport (**to** avec) **2** vi **to r. to** (apply to) avoir rapport à; (person) avoir des affinités avec ▪ **related** adj (linked) lié (**to** à); (languages, styles) apparenté; **to be r. to sb** (by family) être parent de qn

relation [rɪˈleɪʃən] n (a) (relative) parent, -ente mf; **what r. are you to him?** quel est ton lien de parenté avec lui? (b) (relationship) rapport m; **international relations** relations fpl internationales; **sexual relations** rapports mpl sexuels

relationship [rɪˈleɪʃənʃɪp] n (within family) lien m de parenté; (between people) relation f; (between countries) relations fpl; (connection) rapport m; **to have a good r. with sb** bien s'entendre avec qn

relative [ˈrelətɪv] **1** n parent, -ente mf **2** adj (comparative) relatif, -ive; (respective) respectif, -ive; **r. to** relativement à; **to be r. to** (depend on) être fonction de ▪ **relatively** adv relativement

Note that the French word **relatif** is a false friend. It is never used to refer to members of one's family.

relax [rɪˈlæks] **1** vt (person, mind) détendre; (grip, pressure) relâcher; (law, control) assouplir **2** vi (of person) se détendre; (of muscle) se relâcher; **r.!** (calm down) du calme! ▪ **relaxed** adj détendu ▪ **relaxing** adj délassant

relaxation [riːlækˈseɪʃən] n (a) (of person) détente f; (of discipline) relâchement m; (of law, control) assouplissement m (b) (as therapy) relaxation f

relay 1 [ˈriːleɪ] n (of workers) équipe f de relais; **to work in relays** se relayer; **r. (race)** (course f de) relais m **2** [riːˈleɪ] vt retransmettre; (information) transmettre (**to** à)

release [rɪˈliːs] **1** n (of prisoner) libération f; (of film, book) sortie f (**of** de); (film) nouveau film m; (record) nouveau disque m; (emotional) soulagement m; Br **to be on general r.** (of film) passer dans toutes les grandes salles **2** vt (person) libérer (**from** de); (bomb) lâcher; (brake) desserrer; (smoke, funds) dégager; (film, record) sortir; (news, facts) communiquer; **to r. sb's hand** lâcher la main de qn

relegate [ˈrelɪgeɪt] vt reléguer (**to** à); Br Sport **to be relegated** (of team) descendre en division inférieure

relent [rɪˈlent] vi (of storm, wind) se calmer; (of person) céder

relentless [rɪˈlentləs] adj implacable

relevant [ˈreləvənt] adj (a) (apt) pertinent; **to be r. to sth** avoir rapport à qch; **that's not r.** ça n'a rien à voir (b) (appropriate) (chapter) correspondant; (authorities) compétent; (qualifications) requis (c) (topical) d'actualité ▪ **relevance** n pertinence f (**to** à); (connection) rapport m (**to** avec)

reliable [rɪˈlaɪəbəl] adj (person, machine) fiable; (information) sûr ▪ **relia'bility** n (of person) sérieux m; (of machine) fiabilité f ▪ **reliably** adv **to be r. informed that...** tenir de source sûre que...

reliance [rɪˈlaɪəns] n (dependence) dépendance f (**on** vis-à-vis de); (trust) confiance f (**on** en) ▪ **reliant** adj **to be r. on** (dependent) dépendre de; (trusting) avoir confiance en

relic [ˈrelɪk] n relique f; Fig **relics** vestiges mpl

relief [rɪˈliːf] **1** n (comfort) soulagement m; (help) secours m; (in art) relief m **2** adj (train, bus) supplémentaire; (work, troops) de secours; **r. map** carte f en relief; Br **r. road** route f de délestage

relieve [rɪˈliːv] vt (alleviate) soulager; (boredom) tromper; (replace) remplacer; (free) libérer; **to r. sb of sth** débarrasser qn de qch; **to r. sb of his duties** relever qn de ses fonctions; **to r. congestion in** (street) décongestionner; Hum **to r. oneself** se soulager

religion [rɪˈlɪdʒən] n religion f ▪ **religious** adj religieux, -ieuse; (war) de religion ▪ **religiously** adv religieusement

relinquish [rɪˈlɪŋkwɪʃ] *vt* *(hope, habit, thought)* abandonner; *(share, claim)* renoncer à

relish [ˈrelɪʃ] **1** *n* *(pickle)* condiments *mpl*; *(liking)* goût *m* (**for** pour); *(pleasure)* plaisir *m*; **to do sth with r.** faire qch avec délectation **2** *vt* savourer

reload [riːˈləʊd] *vt* *(gun, camera)* recharger

relocate [Br riːˈləʊkeɪt, *Am* riːˈləʊkeɪt] *vi* *(of company)* être transféré; *(of person)* se déplacer

reluctant [rɪˈlʌktənt] *adj* *(greeting, gift, promise)* accordé à contrecœur; **to be r. (to do sth)** être réticent (à faire qch) ▪ **reluctance** *n* réticence *f* (**to do** à faire) ▪ **reluctantly** *adv* à contrecœur

rely [rɪˈlaɪ] *(pt & pp* -ied) *vi* **to r. (up)on** *(count on)* compter sur; *(be dependent on)* dépendre de

remain [rɪˈmeɪn] *vi* *(stay behind, continue to be)* rester; *(be left)* subsister ▪ **remaining** *adj* restant ▪ **remains** *npl* restes *mpl*; **mortal r.** dépouille *f* mortelle

remainder [rɪˈmeɪndə(r)] **1** *n* reste *m*; *(book)* invendu *m* soldé **2** *vt (book)* solder

remand [rɪˈmɑːnd] *Law* **1** **on r.** en détention préventive; *Br* **r. centre** centre *m* de détention préventive **2** *vt* **to r. sb (in custody)** placer qn en détention préventive

remark [rɪˈmɑːk] **1** *n* remarque *f* **2** *vt* faire remarquer **3** *vi* **to r. on sth** *(comment)* faire un commentaire sur qch; *(criticize)* faire des remarques sur qch ▪ **remarkable** *adj* remarquable ▪ **remarkably** *adv* remarquablement

> Note that the French verb **remarquer** is a false friend and is never a translation for the English verb **to remark**. It means **to notice**.

remarry [riːˈmærɪ] *(pt & pp* -ied) *vi* se remarier

remedial [rɪˈmiːdɪəl] *adj* **to take r. measures** prendre des mesures; **r. class** cours *m* de rattrapage

remedy [ˈremɪdɪ] **1** *(pl* -ies) *n* remède *m* **2** *(pt & pp* -ied) *vt* remédier à

remember [rɪˈmembə(r)] **1** *vt* se souvenir de, se rappeler; *(commemorate)* commémorer; **to r. that/doing** se rappeler que/d'avoir fait; **to r. to do sth** penser à faire qch; **to r. sb to sb** rappeler qn au bon souvenir de qn **2** *vi* se souvenir, se rappeler ▪ **remembrance** *n Formal (memory)* souvenir *m*; **in r. of** en souvenir de; *Br & Can* **R. Day** *or* **Sunday** ≃ le 11 novembre *(commémoration de la fin des deux guerres mondiales)*

remind [rɪˈmaɪnd] *vt* **to r. sb of sth** rappeler qch à qn; **to r. sb to do sth** rappeler à qn de faire qch; **that** *or* **which reminds me…** à propos… ▪ **reminder** *n (of event, letter)* rappel *m*; **it's a r. (for him/her) that…** c'est pour lui rappeler que…

reminisce [remɪˈnɪs] *vi* évoquer des souvenirs;

to r. about sth évoquer qch ▪ **reminiscent** *adj* **r. of** qui rappelle

remiss [rɪˈmɪs] *adj* négligent

remission [rɪˈmɪʃən] *n Law* remise *f* de peine; *Med* **to be in r.** être en rémission

remit [rɪˈmɪt] *(pt & pp* -tt-) *vt (money)* envoyer ▪ **remittance** [rɪˈmɪtəns] *n (sum)* paiement *m*

remix 1 [ˈriːmɪks] *n* remix *m* **2** [riːˈmɪks] *vt* remixer

remnant [ˈremnənt] *n (remaining part)* reste *m*; *(of civilization, building)* vestige *m*; *(of fabric)* coupon *m*; *(oddment)* fin *f* de série

remodel [riːˈmɒdəl] *(Br* -ll-, *Am* -l-) *vt* remodeler (**on** sur)

remold [ˈriːməʊld] *n Am* = **remould**

remonstrate [ˈremənstreɪt] *vi* **to r. with sb** faire des remontrances à qn

remorse [rɪˈmɔːs] *n* remords *m*; **to feel r.** avoir du *ou* des remords ▪ **remorseless** *adj* impitoyable ▪ **remorselessly** *adv* impitoyablement

remote [rɪˈməʊt] (-er, -est) *adj* **(a)** *(far-off)* (in space) éloigné (**from** de); *(in time)* lointain (**from** de); *Fig (aloof)* distant; **r. control** télécommande *f* **(b)** *(slight)* vague; **not the remotest idea** pas la moindre idée ▪ **remotely** *adv (slightly)* vaguement; **r. situated** isolé; **not r. aware** nullement conscient ▪ **remoteness** *n* éloignement *m*; *(isolation)* isolement *m*; *Fig (aloofness)* attitude *f* distante

remould *(Am* **remold**) [ˈriːməʊld] *n* pneu *m* rechapé

removable [rɪˈmuːvəbəl] *adj (lining)* amovible

removal [rɪˈmuːvəl] *n* **(a)** *(of control, threat)* suppression *f*; *(of politician)* renvoi *m* **(b)** *Br (moving house)* déménagement *m*; *Br* **r. man** déménageur *m*; *Br* **r. van** camion *m* de déménagement

remove [rɪˈmuːv] *vt (clothes, stain, object)* enlever (**from sth** à qn; **from sth** de qch); *Br (furniture)* déménager; *(obstacle, threat, word)* supprimer; *(fear, doubt)* dissiper; *(politician)* renvoyer; **(far) removed from** loin de

remover [rɪˈmuːvə(r)] *n (for nail polish)* dissolvant *m*; *(for paint)* décapant *m*; *(for stains)* détachant *m*

remunerate [rɪˈmjuːnəreɪt] *vt* rémunérer ▪ **remune'ration** *n* rémunération *f*

renaissance [rəˈneɪsəns] *n* renouveau *m*

rename [riːˈneɪm] *vt* rebaptiser; *Comptr (file)* renommer

render [ˈrendə(r)] *vt Formal (give, make)* rendre; *(piece of music)* interpréter; **to r. assistance to sb** prêter main-forte à qn ▪ **rendering** *n (musical)* interprétation *f*; *(translation)* traduction *f*

rendezvous [ˈrɒndɪvuː, *pl* -vuːz] *n inv* rendezvous *m inv*

renegade [ˈrenɪɡeɪd] *n* renégat, -ate *mf*

renege [rɪ'niːg, *Br* rɪ'neɪg] *vi* **to r. on sth** revenir sur qch

renew [rɪ'njuː] *vt* renouveler; *(resume)* reprendre; *(library book)* renouveler le prêt de ■**renewed** *adj (efforts)* renouvelé; *(attempt)* nouveau (*f* nouvelle); **with r. vigour** avec un regain de vigueur

renewable [rɪ'njuːəbəl] *adj* renouvelable

renewal [rɪ'njuːəl] *n* renouvellement *m*; *(of activity, negotiations)* reprise *f*; *(of optimism, strength)* regain *m*

renounce [rɪ'naʊns] *vt (give up)* renoncer à; *(disown)* renier

renovate ['renəveɪt] *vt (house)* rénover; *(painting)* restaurer ■**reno'vation** *n* rénovation *f*; *(of painting)* restauration *f*

renown [rɪ'naʊn] *n* renommée *f* ■**renowned** *adj* renommé (**for** pour)

rent [rent] **1** *n (for house, flat)* loyer *m*; **for r.** à louer **2** *vt* louer; **to r. out** louer; **rented car** voiture *f* de location ■**'rent-'free 1** *adv* sans payer de loyer **2** *adj* exempt de loyer

rental ['rentəl] *n (of television, car)* location *f*; *(of telephone)* abonnement *m*

reopen [riː'əʊpən] *vti* rouvrir ■**reopening** *n* réouverture *f*

reorder [riː'ɔːdə(r)] *vt (goods)* passer une nouvelle commande de

reorganize [riː'ɔːgənaɪz] *vt* réorganiser

rep [rep] *(abbr representative) n Fam (for large company)* représentant, -ante *mf*, VRP *m*; **sales r.** représentant de commerce, VRP

repair [rɪ'peə(r)] **1** *n* réparation *f*; **beyond r.** irréparable; **under r.** en travaux; **in good/bad r.** en bon/mauvais état **2** *vt* réparer ■**repairman** *(pl -men) n* réparateur *m*

reparation [repə'reɪʃən] *n Formal* réparation *f* (**for** de); **reparations** *(after war)* réparations *fpl*

repartee [repɑː'tiː] *n* repartie *f*

repatriate [riː'pætrɪeɪt] *vt* rapatrier (**to** vers)

repay [riː'peɪ] *(pt & pp -paid) vt (pay back)* rembourser; *(kindness)* payer de retour; *(reward)* remercier (**for** de) ■**repayment** *n* remboursement *m*

repeal [rɪ'piːl] *Law* **1** *n* abrogation *f* **2** *vt* abroger

repeat [rɪ'piːt] **1** *n (of event)* répétition *f*; *(on TV, radio)* rediffusion *f* **2** *vt* répéter (**that** que); *(promise, threat)* réitérer; *(class)* redoubler; *(TV programme)* rediffuser; **to r. oneself** se répéter **3** *vi* répéter; **r. after me** répétez après moi; **I r., you're wrong** je le répète, vous avez tort; ■**repeated** *adj (attempts)* répété; *(efforts)* renouvelé ■**repeatedly** *adv* à maintes reprises

repel [rɪ'pel] *(pt & pp -ll-) vt* repousser ■**repellent 1** *adj (disgusting)* repoussant **2** *n* **insect r.** insecticide *m*

repent [rɪ'pent] *vi* se repentir (**of** de) ■**repentance** *n* repentir *m* ■**repentant** *adj* repentant

repercussions [riːpə'kʌʃənz] *npl* répercussions *fpl* (**on** sur)

repertoire ['repətwɑː(r)] *n Theatre & Fig* répertoire *m* ■**repertory** [-təri] *(pl -ies) n Theatre & Fig* répertoire *m*; **r. (theatre)** théâtre *m* de répertoire

repetition [repɪ'tɪʃən] *n* répétition *f* ■**repetitive** [rɪ'petɪtɪv] *adj* répétitif, -ive

rephrase [riː'freɪz] *vt* reformuler

replace [rɪ'pleɪs] *vt (take the place of)* remplacer (**by** *or* **with** par); *(put back)* remettre (à sa place); **to r. the receiver** *(on phone)* raccrocher ■**replacement** *n (substitution)* remplacement *m* (**of** de); *(person)* remplaçant, -ante *mf*; *(machine part)* pièce *f* de rechange

replay 1 ['riːpleɪ] *n Sport* nouvelle rencontre *f*; **(instant** *or* **action) r.** *(on TV)* = répétition d'une séquence précédente **2** [riː'pleɪ] *vt (match)* rejouer

replenish [rɪ'plenɪʃ] *vt (refill)* remplir (de nouveau) (**with** de); **to r. one's supplies** se réapprovisionner

replete [rɪ'pliːt] *adj Formal* **r. with** rempli de; **r. (with food)** rassasié

replica ['replɪkə] *n* réplique *f*

reply [rɪ'plaɪ] **1** *(pl -ies) n* réponse *f*; **in r.** en réponse (**to** à) **2** *(pt & pp -ied) vti* répondre (**to** à; **that** que)

report [rɪ'pɔːt] **1** *n* **(a)** *(analysis)* rapport *m*; *(account)* compte rendu *m*; *(in media)* reportage *m*; *Br* **(school) r.,** *Am* **r. card** bulletin *m* scolaire **(b)** *(of gun)* détonation *f* **2** *vt (information)* rapporter; *(accident, theft)* signaler (**to** à); **to r. sb missing** signaler la disparition de qn; **to r. sb to the police** dénoncer qn à la police; **to r. one's findings (to sb)** faire un rapport (à qn) **3** *vi (give account)* faire un rapport (**on** sur); *(of journalist)* faire un reportage (**on** sur); *(go)* se présenter (**to** à); **to r. to sb** *(be accountable)* rendre compte à qn ■**reported** *adj Grammar* **r. speech** discours *m* indirect; **it is r. that...** on dit que...; **to be r. missing** être porté disparu ■**reportedly** *adv* à ce qu'on dit ■**reporter** *n* reporter *m*

> Note that the French words **report** and **reporter** are false friends and are never translations for the English words **report** and **to report**. Their most common meanings are **postponement** and **to postpone**.

repose [rɪ'pəʊz] *n Literary* repos *m*

repository [rɪ'pɒzɪtəri] *(pl -ies) n* dépôt *m*

repossess [riːpə'zes] *vt* saisir

reprehensible [reprɪ'hensəbəl] *adj* répréhensible

represent [reprɪ'zent] *vt* représenter ▪**represen'tation** *n* représentation *f*

representative [reprɪ'zentətɪv] **1** *adj* représentatif, -ive (**of** de) **2** *n* représentant, -ante *mf*; *Am Pol* ≃ député *m*

repress [rɪ'pres] *vt* réprimer; *(memory, feeling)* refouler; **to be repressed** *(of person)* être un(e) refoulé(e) ▪**repression** *n* répression *f* ▪**repressive** *adj (régime)* répressif, -ive; *(measures)* de répression

reprieve [rɪ'priːv] *Law* **1** *n (cancellation)* commutation *f* de la peine capitale; *(temporary) & Fig* sursis *m* **2** *vt* **to r. sb** *(cancel punishment of)* commuer la peine capitale de qn en réclusion à perpétuité; *(postpone punishment of)* accorder un sursis à qn

reprimand ['reprɪmɑːnd] **1** *n* réprimande *f* **2** *vt* réprimander

reprint 1 ['riːprɪnt] *n* réimpression *f* **2** [riːˈprɪnt] *vt* réimprimer

reprisal [rɪ'praɪzəl] *n* représailles *fpl*; **as a r. for, in r. for** en représailles de

reproach [rɪ'prəʊtʃ] **1** *n (blame)* reproche *m*; **beyond r.** irréprochable **2** *vt* faire des reproches à; **to r. sb with sth** reprocher qch à qn ▪**reproachful** *adj* réprobateur, -trice ▪**reproachfully** *adv* d'un ton/air réprobateur

reprocess [riːˈprəʊses] *vt* retraiter ▪**reprocessing** *n* retraitement *m*; **r. plant** usine *f* de retraitement

reproduce [riːprəˈdjuːs] **1** *vt* reproduire **2** *vi* se reproduire ▪**reproduction** [-ˈdʌkʃən] *n* reproduction *f* ▪**reproductive** [-ˈdʌktɪv] *adj* reproducteur, -trice

reproof [rɪ'pruːf] *n Literary* réprobation *f*

reptile ['reptaɪl] *n* reptile *m*

republic [rɪ'pʌblɪk] *n* république *f* ▪**republican** *adj & n* républicain, -aine *(mf)*

repudiate [rɪ'pjuːdɪeɪt] *vt Formal (behaviour, violence)* condamner; *(offer, accusation)* rejeter; *(idea)* renier; *(spouse)* répudier

repugnant [rɪ'pʌgnənt] *adj* répugnant; **he's r. to me** il me répugne ▪**repugnance** *n* répugnance *f* (**for** pour)

repulse [rɪ'pʌls] *vt* repousser ▪**repulsion** *n* répulsion *f* ▪**repulsive** *adj* repoussant

reputable ['repjʊtəbəl] *adj* de bonne réputation ▪**repute** [rɪ'pjuːt] *n* réputation *f*; **of r.** réputé ▪**reputed** [rɪ'pjuːtɪd] *adj* **she's r. to be wealthy** on la dit riche ▪**reputedly** [rɪ'pjuːtɪdlɪ] *adv* à ce qu'on dit

reputation [repjʊ'teɪʃən] *n* réputation *f*; **to have a r. for being frank** *or* **for frankness** avoir la réputation d'être franc

request [rɪ'kwest] **1** *n* demande *f* (**for** de); **on r.** sur demande; **at sb's r.** à la demande de qn; **by popular r.** à la demande générale; *Br* **r. stop** *(for bus)* arrêt *m* facultatif **2** *vt* demander; **to r. sb to do sth** prier qn de faire qch

requiem ['rekwɪəm] *n* requiem *m inv*

require [rɪ'kwaɪə(r)] *vt (of task, problem, situation)* requérir; *(of person)* avoir besoin de; **to be required to do sth** être tenu de faire qch; **if required** si besoin est/était; **the required qualities** les qualités *fpl* requises ▪**requirement** *n (need)* exigence *f*; *(condition)* condition *f* (requise)

requisite ['rekwɪzɪt] **1** *adj* requis **2** *n* élément *m* essentiel

requisition [rekwɪ'zɪʃən] **1** *n* réquisition *f* **2** *vt* réquisitionner

reroute [riːˈruːt] *vt* dérouter

rerun ['riːrʌn] *n (of film)* reprise *f*; *(of TV programme)* rediffusion *f*

resale ['riːseɪl] *n* revente *f*

reschedule [*Br* riːˈʃedjuːl, *Am* riːˈskedʒʊəl] *vt* changer la date/l'heure de

rescind [rɪ'sɪnd] *vt Law* annuler; *(law)* abroger

rescue ['reskjuː] **1** *n (action)* sauvetage *m* (**of** de); *(help, troops)* secours *mpl*; **to go/come to sb's r.** aller/venir au secours de qn; **to the r.** à la rescousse **2** *adj (team, operation, attempt)* de sauvetage **3** *vt (save)* sauver; *(set free)* délivrer (**from** de) ▪**rescuer** *n* sauveteur *m*

research [rɪ'sɜːtʃ] **1** *n* recherches *fpl* (**on** or **into** sur); **some r.** des recherches; **to do r.** faire de la recherche; **to do r. into sth** faire des recherches sur qch **2** *vi* faire des recherches (**on** or **into** sur) ▪**researcher** *n* chercheur, -euse *mf*

resemble [rɪ'zembəl] *vt* ressembler à ▪**resemblance** *n* ressemblance *f* (**to** avec)

resent [rɪ'zent] *vt* ne pas aimer ▪**resentful** *adj* **to be r.** éprouver du ressentiment ▪**resentment** *n* ressentiment *m*

> Note that the French verb **ressentir** is a false friend. It means **to feel, to experience**.

reservation [rezə'veɪʃən] *n* (a) *(booking)* réservation *f*; **to make a r.** réserver; **do you have a r.?** avez-vous réservé? (b) *(doubt)* réserve *f* (c) *(land for Indians, animals)* réserve *f*

reserve [rɪ'zɜːv] **1** *n* (a) *(reticence)* réserve *f* (b) *(land, stock)* réserve *f*; **r. (player)** *(in team)* remplaçant, -ante *mf*; *Mil* **the reserves** les réservistes *mpl*; **in r.** en réserve; **r. tank** *(of vehicle, aircraft)* réservoir *m* de secours **2** *vt (room, decision)* réserver; *(right)* se réserver; **to r. one's strength** ménager ses forces ▪**reserved** *adj (person, room)* réservé

reservoir ['rezəvwɑː(r)] *n (of water)* réservoir *m*; *Fig* réserve *f*

reset [riː'set] *vt (clock, watch)* mettre à l'heure; *(counter)* remettre à zéro

reshape [riː'ʃeɪp] *vt* réorganiser

reshuffle [riː'ʃʌfəl] *n* réorganisation *f*; *Pol* **(cabinet) r.** remaniement *m* (ministériel)

reside [rɪ'zaɪd] *vi* résider

residence ['rezɪdəns] n (home) résidence f; (of students) foyer m; **to take up r.** s'installer; **in r.** (doctor) sur place; Br (students on campus) sur le campus; Br (in halls of residence) rentrés; Br **r. permit** permis m de séjour

resident ['rezɪdənt] **1** n (of country, street) habitant, -ante mf; (of hotel) pensionnaire mf; (foreigner) résident, -ente mf; Am (doctor) interne mf **2** adj résidant, qui habite sur place; (doctor, nurse) à demeure; **to be r. in London** résider à Londres

residential [rezɪ'denʃəl] adj (neighbourhood) résidentiel, -ielle

residue ['rezɪdjuː] n Chem résidu m; (remainder) reste m ▪**residual** [rɪ'zɪdjʊəl] adj résiduel, -uelle; (pain, doubt) qui persiste

resign [rɪ'zaɪn] **1** vt (job) démissionner de; **to r. oneself to sth/to doing sth** se résigner à qch/ à faire qch **2** vi démissionner (**from** de) ▪**resigned** adj résigné

resignation [rezɪg'neɪʃən] n (from job) démission f; (attitude) résignation f

resilient [rɪ'zɪlɪənt] adj élastique; Fig (person) résistant ▪**resilience** n élasticité f; Fig résistance f

resin ['rezɪn] n résine f

resist [rɪ'zɪst] **1** vt résister à; **to r. doing sth** s'empêcher de faire qch; **she can't r. cakes** elle ne peut pas résister devant les gâteaux **2** vi résister ▪**resistance** n résistance f (**to** à); **r. fighter** résistant, -ante mf ▪**resistant** adj résistant (**to** à); **to be r. to sth** résister à qch

resit Br Sch & Univ **1** ['riːsɪt] n to do a r. repasser un examen; **resits** session f de rattrapage **2** [riː'sɪt] vt (pt & pp -sat, pres p -sitting) (exam) repasser

resolute ['rezəluːt] adj résolu ▪**resolutely** adv résolument ▪**reso'lution** n résolution f

resolve [rɪ'zɒlv] **1** n résolution f **2** vt (problem) résoudre; **to r. to do sth** (of person) se résoudre de faire qch; (of committee) décider de faire qch

resonant ['rezənənt] adj qui résonne; **to be r. with** résonner de ▪**resonance** n résonance f

resonate ['rezəneɪt] vi résonner

resort [rɪ'zɔːt] **1** n (**a**) (holiday place) lieu m de villégiature; Br **seaside r.**, Am **beach r.** station f balnéaire; **ski r.** station de ski (**b**) (recourse) recours m (**to** à); **as a last r., in the last r.** en dernier ressort; **without r. to** sans avoir recours à **2** vi **to r. to sth** avoir recours à qch; **to r. to doing sth** finir par faire qch

resound [rɪ'zaʊnd] vi résonner (**with** de); Fig Literary avoir du retentissement ▪**resounding** adj (noise, failure) retentissant; (success) éclatant

resource [rɪ'sɔːs, rɪ'zɔːs] n ressource f ▪**resourceful** adj ingénieux, -ieuse ▪**resourcefulness** n ingéniosité f

respect [rɪ'spekt] **1** n respect m (**for** pour); (aspect) égard m; **in many respects** à bien des égards; **with r. to, in r. of** en ce qui concerne; **with all due r.** sans vouloir vous/te vexer **2** vt respecter

respectable [rɪ'spektəbəl] adj (decent, fairly large) respectable; (fairly good) honorable ▪**respectability** n respectabilité f ▪**respectably** adv (decently) de manière respectable; (dressed) convenablement; (fairly well) honorablement

respectful [rɪ'spektfəl] adj respectueux, -ueuse (**to** envers; **of** de) ▪**respectfully** adv respectueusement

respective [rɪ'spektɪv] adj respectif, -ive ▪**respectively** adv respectivement

respiration [respɪ'reɪʃən] n respiration f

respite ['respɪt, Br 'respaɪt] n répit m

resplendent [rɪ'splendənt] adj Literary resplendissant

respond [rɪ'spɒnd] vi (answer) répondre (**to** à); (react) réagir (**to** à); **to r. to treatment** bien réagir (au traitement) ▪**response** n (answer) réponse f; (reaction) réaction f; **in r. to** en réponse à

responsible [rɪ'spɒnsəbəl] adj responsable (**for** de); (job) à responsabilités ▪**responsi'bility** (pl -ies) n responsabilité f (**for** de) ▪**responsibly** adv de façon responsable

responsive [rɪ'spɒnsɪv] adj (reacting) qui réagit bien; (alert) éveillé; **r. to** (kindness) sensible à; (suggestion) réceptif, -ive à ▪**responsiveness** n (bonne) réaction f

respray ['riːspreɪ] vt (vehicle) repeindre

rest¹ [rest] **1** n (relaxation) repos m; (support) support m; Mus (pause) silence m; **to have** or **take a r.** se reposer; **to set** or **put sb's mind at r.** tranquilliser qn; **to come to r.** (of ball, car) s'immobiliser; **r. home** maison f de repos; Am **r. room** toilettes fpl **2** vt (lean) poser (**on** sur); (base) fonder (**on** sur); (horse) laisser reposer; **to r. one's eyes** se reposer les yeux **3** vi (relax) se reposer; (be buried) reposer; (lean) être posé (**on** sur); **to r. on** (of argument, roof) reposer sur; **I won't r. till...** je n'aurai de cesse que... (+ subjunctive); **resting place** lieu m de repos

rest² [rest] **1** n (remainder) reste m (**of** de); **the r.** (others) les autres mfpl; **the r. of the men** le reste des hommes **2** vi (remain) **r. assured** soyez assuré (**that** que); **to r. with sb** (of decision, responsibility) incomber à qn

restaurant ['restərɒnt] n restaurant m; Br **r. car** (on train) wagon-restaurant m

restful ['restfəl] adj reposant

restitution [restɪ'tjuːʃən] n (compensation for damage) réparation f

restive ['restɪv] adj agité

restless ['restləs] adj agité ▪**restlessly** adv avec agitation ▪**restlessness** n agitation f

restore [rɪ'stɔː(r)] vt (give back) rendre (**to** à);

(order, peace, rights) rétablir; *(building, painting, monarchy)* restaurer; **to r. sb to health** redonner la santé à qn ▪ **restoration** [restə'reɪʃən] *n (of order, peace)* rétablissement *m*; *(of building, painting, monarchy)* restauration *f*

restrain [rɪ'streɪn] *vt (person, dog)* maîtriser; *(crowd, anger)* contenir; *(passions)* refréner; **to r. sb from doing sth** retenir qn pour qu'il ne fasse pas qch; **to r. oneself (from doing sth)** se retenir (de faire qch) ▪ **restrained** *adj (feelings)* contenu; *(tone)* mesuré; *(manner)* réservé ▪ **restraint** *n (moderation)* mesure *f*; *(restriction)* restriction *f*

restrict [rɪ'strɪkt] *vt* restreindre; **to r. oneself to sth/doing sth** se limiter à qch/à faire qch ▪ **restricted** *adj* restreint; **r. area** *Mil* zone *f* interdite; *(for parking)* ≃ zone bleue ▪ **restriction** *n* restriction *f* **(on** à**)** ▪ **restrictive** *adj* restrictif, -ive

result [rɪ'zʌlt] **1** *n (outcome, success)* résultat *m*; **as a r.** en conséquence; **as a r. of** à la suite de **2** *vi* résulter **(from** de**); to r. in sth** aboutir à qch

resume [rɪ'zjuːm] *vti* reprendre; **to r. doing sth** se remettre à faire qch ▪ **resumption** [-'zʌmpʃən] *n* reprise *f*

résumé ['rezjʊmeɪ] *n (summary)* résumé *m*; *Am* curriculum vitae *m inv*

resurface [riː'sɜːfɪs] **1** *vt (road)* refaire le revêtement de **2** *vi* refaire surface

resurgence [rɪ'sɜːdʒəns] *n* réapparition *f*

resurrect [rezə'rekt] *vt Rel* ressusciter; *Fig (fashion)* remettre au goût du jour ▪ **resurrection** *n Rel* résurrection *f*

resuscitate [rɪ'sʌsɪteɪt] *vt Med* ranimer ▪ **resusci'tation** *n* réanimation *f*

> Note that the French word **ressusciter** is a false friend and is never a translation for the English verb **to resuscitate**. It means **to resurrect**.

retail ['riːteɪl] **1** *n (vente f* au**) détail** *m* **2** *adj (price, shop)* de détail **3** *vt* vendre au détail **4** *vi* se vendre (au détail) **(at** à**)** ▪ **retailer** *n* détaillant *m*

retain [rɪ'teɪn] *vt (keep)* conserver; *(hold in place)* retenir; *(remember)* maintenir ▪ **retainer** *n (fee)* acompte *m*, avance *f*

retaliate [rɪ'tælɪeɪt] *vi* riposter ▪ **retali'ation** *n* représailles *fpl*; **in r. for** en représailles à

retarded [rɪ'tɑːdɪd] *adj* **(mentally) r.** arriéré

retch [retʃ] *vi* avoir des haut-le-cœur

rethink [riː'θɪŋk] *(pt & pp* **-thought)** *vt* repenser

reticent ['retɪsənt] *adj* peu communicatif, -ive ▪ **reticence** *n* réticence *f*

> Note that the French word **réticent** is a false friend and is never a translation for the English word **reticent**. It means **hesitant**.

retina ['retɪnə] *n Anat* rétine *f*

retire [rɪ'taɪə(r)] **1** *vt* mettre à la retraite **2** *vi* **(a)** *(from work)* prendre sa retraite **(b)** *(withdraw)* se retirer **(from** de; **to** à**);** *(go to bed)* aller se coucher ▪ **retired** *adj (no longer working)* retraité ▪ **retirement** *n* retraite *f*; **to take early r.** partir en retraite anticipée; **r. age** l'âge *m* de la retraite; **r. home** maison *f* de retraite ▪ **retiring** *adj* **(a)** *(official, president)* sortant; **r. age** l'âge *m* de la retraite **(b)** *(reserved)* réservé

retort [rɪ'tɔːt] **1** *n* réplique *f* **2** *vti* rétorquer

retrace [riː'treɪs] *vt (past event)* se remémorer; **to r. one's steps** revenir sur ses pas

retract [rɪ'trækt] **1** *vt* **(a)** *(statement)* revenir sur **(b)** *(claws, undercarriage)* rentrer **2** *vi (of person)* se rétracter ▪ **retraction** *n (of statement)* rétractation *f*

retrain [riː'treɪn] **1** *vt* recycler **2** *vi* se recycler ▪ **retraining** *n* recyclage *m*

retread ['riːtred] *n* pneu *m* rechapé

retreat [rɪ'triːt] **1** *n (withdrawal)* retraite *f*; *(place)* refuge *m* **2** *vi* se réfugier; *(of troops)* battre en retraite

retrial [riː'traɪəl] *n Law* nouveau procès *m*

retribution [retrɪ'bjuːʃən] *n* châtiment *m*

> Note that the French word **rétribution** is a false friend and is never a translation for the English word **retribution**. It means **reward**.

retrieve [rɪ'triːv] *vt (recover)* récupérer; *Comptr (file)* ouvrir ▪ **retrieval** *n* récupération *f* **(of** de**)** ▪ **retriever** *n (dog)* retriever *m*

retroactive [retrəʊ'æktɪv] *adj (pay increase)* avec effet rétroactif

retrograde ['retrəgreɪd] *adj* rétrograde

retrospect ['retrəspekt] *n* **in r.** rétrospectivement

retrospective [retrə'spektɪv] **1** *adj* rétrospectif, -ive; *(law, effect)* à effet rétroactif **2** *n (exhibition)* rétrospective *f*

retune [riː'tjuːn] **1** *vt (radio, TV)* régler **2** *vi* **to r. to** *(radio station, wavelength)* régler la radio sur

return [rɪ'tɜːn] **1** *n* retour *m*; *(of goods)* renvoi *m*; *Fin (on investment)* rapport *m*; *(profits)* **returns** bénéfices *mpl*; *Br* **r. (ticket)** (billet *m*) aller et retour *m*; **many happy returns!** bon anniversaire!; **on my r.** à mon retour; **in r.** en échange **(for** de**); by r. of post** par retour du courrier

2 *adj (trip, flight)* (de) retour; **r. match** match *m* retour

3 *vt (give back)* rendre; *(put back)* remettre; *(bring back)* rapporter; *(send back)* renvoyer; *(greeting)* répondre à; *Fin (profit)* rapporter; **'r. to sender'** *(on letter)* 'retour à l'envoyeur'; **to r. sb's call** *(on phone)* rappeler qn; *Law* **to r. a verdict of guilty** déclarer l'accusé coupable

4 *vi (come back)* revenir; *(go back)* retourner;

(go back home) rentrer; **to r. to** *(subject)* revenir à ▪ **returnable** *adj (bottle)* consigné

reunion [riːˈjuːnɪən] *n* réunion *f* ▪ **reu'nite** *vt* réconcilier; **to be reunited with sb** retrouver qn; **they reunited him with his family** ils lui ont fait retrouver sa famille

reuse [riːˈjuːz] *vt* réutiliser

Rev [rev] *(abbr* **Reverend) R. Gray** le révérend Gray

rev [rev] *Fam* **1** *n (of car engine)* tour *m*; **r. counter** compte-tours *m inv* **2** *(pt & pp* **-vv-)** *vt* **to r. the engine (up)** faire monter le régime

revamp [riːˈvæmp] *vt Fam (image)* rajeunir; *(company)* restructurer

reveal [rɪˈviːl] *vt (make known)* révéler (**that** que); *(make visible)* laisser voir ▪ **revealing** *adj (sign, comment)* révélateur, -trice; *(clothing)* qui ne cache pas grand-chose

revel [ˈrevəl] *(Br* **-ll-,** *Am* **-l-)** *vi* faire la fête; **to r. in sth** savourer qch ▪ **reveller** *(Am* **reveler)** *n* noceur, -euse *mf* ▪ **revelling** *(Am* **reveling)**, ▪ **revelry** *n* festivités *fpl*

revelation [revəˈleɪʃən] *n* révélation *f*

revenge [rɪˈvendʒ] **1** *n* vengeance *f*; *Sport* revanche *f*; **to have** *or* **get one's r. (on sb)** se venger (de qn); **in r.** pour se venger **2** *vt* venger

revenue [ˈrevənjuː] *n (income)* revenu *m*; *(from sales)* recettes *fpl*

reverberate [rɪˈvɜːbəreɪt] *vi (of sound)* se répercuter; *(of news)* se propager

revere [rɪˈvɪə(r)] *vt* révérer

reverence [ˈrevərəns] *n* révérence *f*

reverend [ˈrevərənd] **1** *adj Rel* **r. father** révérend père *m* **2** *n* **R. Smith** *(Anglican)* le révérend Smith; *(Catholic)* l'abbé *m* Smith; *(Jewish)* le rabbin Smith

reverent [ˈrevərənt] *adj* respectueux, -ueuse

reversal [rɪˈvɜːsəl] *n (of situation, roles)* renversement *m*; *(of policy, opinion)* revirement *m*; **r. (of fortune)** revers *m* (de fortune)

reverse [rɪˈvɜːs] **1** *adj (opposite)* contraire; *(image)* inverse; **in r. order** dans l'ordre inverse; **r. side** *(of coin)* revers *m*; *(of paper)* verso *m* **2** *n* contraire *m*; *(of coin)* revers *m*; *(of fabric)* envers *m*; *(paper)* verso *m*; *Fig (setback)* revers; **in r. (gear)** *(when driving)* en marche arrière **3** *vt (situation)* renverser; *(order, policy)* inverser; *(decision)* revenir sur; **to r. the car** faire marche arrière; *Br* **to r. the charges** *(when phoning)* téléphoner en PCV **4** *vi Br (in car)* faire marche arrière; **to r. in/out** rentrer/sortir en marche arrière; **to r. into a tree** rentrer dans un arbre en faisant marche arrière

reversible [rɪˈvɜːsəbəl] *adj (fabric)* réversible

revert [rɪˈvɜːt] *vi* **to r. to** revenir à

review [rɪˈvjuː] **1** *n* **(a)** *(of book, film)* critique *f*; *(of troops)* revue *f*; *(of salary, opinion)* révision *f*; **to be under r.** faire l'objet d'une révision **(b)** *(magazine)* revue *f* **2** *vt (book, film)* faire la

critique de; *(troops)* passer en revue; *(situation)* faire le point sur; *(salary, opinion)* réviser ▪ **reviewer** *n* critique *m*

revile [rɪˈvaɪl] *vt Formal* vilipender

revise [rɪˈvaɪz] **1** *vt (opinion, notes, text)* réviser **2** *vi (for exam)* réviser (**for** pour) ▪ **revision** [-ˈvɪʒən] *n* révision *f*

revitalize [riːˈvaɪtəlaɪz] *vt (person)* revigorer

revival [rɪˈvaɪvəl] *n (of custom, business, play)* reprise *f*; *(of hopes)* renaissance *f*; *(of faith, fashion, arts)* renouveau *m*

revive [rɪˈvaɪv] **1** *vt (person, memory, conversation)* ranimer; *(custom, industry)* faire renaître; *(fashion)* relancer **2** *vi (of person)* reprendre connaissance; *(of industry)* connaître un renouveau; *(of hope, interest)* renaître

revoke [rɪˈvəʊk] *vt (law)* abroger; *(decision)* revenir sur; *(contract)* résilier

revolt [rɪˈvəʊlt] **1** *n* révolte *f* **2** *vt (disgust)* révolter **3** *vi (rebel)* se révolter (**against** contre) ▪ **revolting** *adj* dégoûtant; *(injustice)* révoltant

revolution [revəˈluːʃən] *n* révolution *f* ▪ **revolutionary** *(pl* **-ies)** *adj & n* révolutionnaire *(mf)* ▪ **revolutionize** *vt* révolutionner

revolve [rɪˈvɒlv] *vi* tourner (**around** autour de) ▪ **revolving** *adj* **r. chair** fauteuil *m* pivotant; **r. door(s)** porte *f* à tambour

revolver [rɪˈvɒlvə(r)] *n* revolver *m*

revue [rɪˈvjuː] *n (theatrical)* revue *f*

revulsion [rɪˈvʌlʃən] *n (disgust)* dégoût *m*

reward [rɪˈwɔːd] **1** *n* récompense *f* (**for** de) **2** *vt* récompenser (**for** de *ou* pour) ▪ **rewarding** *adj* intéressant

rewind [riːˈwaɪnd] *(pt & pp* **-wound)** **1** *vt (tape, film)* rembobiner **2** *vi (of tape)* se rembobiner

rewire [riːˈwaɪə(r)] *vt (house)* refaire l'installation électrique de

rewrite [riːˈraɪt] *(pt* **-wrote,** *pp* **-written)** *vt* réécrire

rhapsody [ˈræpsədɪ] *(pl* **-ies)** *n* rhapsodie *f*

rhesus [ˈriːsəs] *n* rhésus *m*; **r. positive/negative** rhésus positif/négatif

rhetoric [ˈretərɪk] *n* rhétorique *f* ▪ **rhetorical** [rɪˈtɒrɪkəl] *adj* **r. question** question *f* de pure forme

rheumatism [ˈruːmətɪzəm] *n* rhumatisme *m*; **to have r.** avoir des rhumatismes ▪ **rheumatic** [-ˈmætɪk] *adj (pain)* rhumatismal; *(person)* rhumatisant

Rhine [raɪn] *n* **the R.** le Rhin

rhinoceros [raɪˈnɒsərəs] *n* rhinocéros *m* ▪ **rhino** [ˈraɪnəʊ] *n Fam* rhinocéros *m*

rhododendron [rəʊdəˈdendrən] *n* rhododendron *m*

Rhône [rəʊn] *n* **the R.** le Rhône

rhubarb [ˈruːbɑːb] *n* rhubarbe *f*

rhyme [raɪm] **1** *n* rime *f*; *(poem)* vers *mpl* **2** *vi* rimer (**with** avec)

rhythm ['rɪðəm] *n* rythme *m* ■**rhythmic** ['rɪðmɪk] *adj* rythmé

rib [rɪb] *n (bone)* côte *f*; **to have a broken r.** avoir une côte cassée ■**ribbed** *adj (fabric, jumper)* à côtes

ribbon ['rɪbən] *n* ruban *m*; **to tear sth to ribbons** déchiqueter qch

rice [raɪs] *n* riz *m*; **white/brown/wild r.** riz blanc/complet/sauvage; **basmati r.** riz basmati; **r. pudding** riz au lait ■**ricefield** *n* rizière *f*

rich [rɪtʃ] 1 **(-er, -est)** *adj (person, food)* riche; **to be r. in sth** être riche en qch 2 *npl* **the r.** les riches *mpl* ■**riches** *npl* richesses *fpl* ■**richly** *adv (illustrated, dressed)* richement; **r. deserved** bien mérité ■**richness** *n* richesse *f*

rick [rɪk] *vt* **to r. one's back** se donner un tour de rein

rickets ['rɪkɪts] *n Med* rachitisme *m*

rickety ['rɪkɪtɪ] *adj (furniture)* branlant

rickshaw ['rɪkʃɔː] *n* pousse-pousse *m inv*

ricochet ['rɪkəʃeɪ] 1 *n* ricochet *m* 2 *(pt & pp -tt-)* *vi* ricocher **(off** sur)

rid [rɪd] *(pt & pp* **rid**, *pres p* **ridding)** *vt* débarrasser **(of** de); **to get r. of, to r. oneself of** se débarrasser de ■**riddance** ['rɪdəns] *n Fam* **good r.!** bon débarras!

ridden ['rɪdən] *pp of* **ride**

-ridden ['rɪdən] *suff* **debt-r.** criblé de dettes; **disease-r.** en proie à la maladie

riddle ['rɪdəl] 1 *n (puzzle)* devinette *f*; *(mystery)* énigme *f* 2 *vt* cribler **(with** de); **riddled with mistakes** truffé de fautes

ride [raɪd] 1 *n (on horse)* promenade *f*; *(on bicycle, in car)* tour *m*; *(in taxi)* course *f*; *(on merry-go-round)* tour; **to go for a r.** aller faire un tour; **to give sb a r.** *(in car)* emmener qn en voiture; **to have a r. on** *(bicycle)* monter sur; **it's only a short r. away** ce n'est pas très loin; *Fam* **to take sb for a r.** mener qn en bateau 2 *(pt* **rode**, *pp* **ridden)** *vt (horse, bicycle)* monter à; *(a particular horse)* monter; *(bus, train)* prendre; **to know how to r. a bicycle** savoir faire de la bicyclette; **to r. a bicycle to…** aller à bicyclette à…; *Am Fam* **to r. sb** *(annoy)* harceler qn 3 *vi (on horse)* faire du cheval; *(on bicycle)* faire de la bicyclette; **to go riding** *(on horse)* faire du cheval; **to be riding in a car** être en voiture; **to r. up** *(of skirt)* remonter

rider ['raɪdə(r)] *n* **(a)** *(on horse)* cavalier, -ière *mf*; *(cyclist)* cycliste *mf* **(b)** *Law (to document)* annexe *f*; *(to bill)* clause *f* additionnelle

ridge [rɪdʒ] *n (of mountain)* crête *f*

ridicule ['rɪdɪkjuːl] 1 *n* ridicule *m*; **to hold sb/ sth up to r.** tourner qn/qch en ridicule; **object of r.** objet *m* de risée 2 *vt* tourner en ridicule, ridiculiser ■**ridiculous** *adj* ridicule

riding ['raɪdɪŋ] *n* **(horse) r.** équitation *f*; **r. boots** bottes *fpl* de cheval; **r. school** école *f* d'équitation

rife [raɪf] *adj (widespread)* répandu

riffraff ['rɪfræf] *n* racaille *f*

rifle ['raɪfəl] 1 *n* fusil *m* 2 *vt* **to r. (through)** sth fouiller dans qch

rift [rɪft] *n (in political party)* scission *f*; *(disagreement)* désaccord *m*; *(crack in rock)* fissure *f*

rig [rɪg] 1 *n* **(oil) r.** derrick *m*; *(at sea)* plateforme *f* pétrolière 2 *(pt & pp* **-gg-)** *vt Fam (result, election)* truquer; **to r. up** *(equipment)* installer; *Fam (meeting)* arranger; *Br Fam* **to be rigged out in** être attifé de

rigging ['rɪgɪŋ] *n (on ship)* gréement *m*

right¹ [raɪt] 1 *adj* **(a)** *(correct)* bon *(f* bonne), exact; *(word)* juste; **to be r.** *(of person)* avoir raison **(to do** faire); **it's the r. time** c'est l'heure exacte; **that's r.** c'est ça; **r.!** bon! **(b)** *(appropriate)* bon *(f* bonne); **the r. thing to do** la meilleure chose à faire; **he's the r. man** c'est l'homme qu'il faut *(c) (morally good)* bien *inv*; **to do the r. thing** faire ce qu'il faut **(d)** *(mentally, physically well)* **it doesn't look r.** il y a quelque chose qui ne va pas **(e)** *Br Fam (for emphasis)* véritable; **I felt a r. fool** je me suis vraiment senti stupide **(f)** *Math* **r. angle** angle *m* droit

2 *adv (straight)* (tout) droit; *(completely)* tout à fait; *(correctly)* correctement; **to put sth r.** *(rectify)* corriger qch; *(fix)* arranger qch; **to put things r.** arranger les choses; **to put sb r.** détromper qn; **to remember r.** bien se souvenir; **r. round** tout autour **(sth** de qch); **r. behind** juste derrière; **r. here** ici même; **r. away, r. now** tout de suite; **I'll be r. back** je reviens tout de suite; *Br* **the R. Honourable…** *(to Member of Parliament)* le Très Honorable…

3 *n* **to be in the r.** avoir raison; **r. and wrong** le bien et le mal

4 *vt (error, wrong, boat, car)* redresser

right² [raɪt] 1 *adj (not left) (hand, side)* droit 2 *adv* à droite 3 *n* droite *f*; **on** or **to the r.** à droite **(of** de) ■**'right-'hand** *adj* de droite; **on the r. side** à droite **(of** de); **to be sb's r. man** être le bras droit de qn ■**'right-'handed** *adj (person)* droitier, -ière ■**'right-'wing** *adj Pol* de droite

right³ [raɪt] *n (entitlement)* droit *m* **(to do** faire); **to have a r. to sth** avoir droit à qch; **he's famous in his own r.** il est lui-même célèbre; **to have the r. of way** *(on road)* avoir la priorité

righteous ['raɪtʃəs] *adj (person)* vertueux, -ueuse; *(cause, indignation)* juste

rightful ['raɪtfəl] *adj* légitime ■**rightfully** *adv* légitimement

rightly ['raɪtlɪ] *adv (correctly)* bien; *(justifiably)* à juste titre; **r. or wrongly** à tort ou à raison

rigid ['rɪdʒɪd] *adj* rigide

rigmarole ['rɪgmərəʊl] *n (process)* procédure *f* compliquée

rigour ['rɪgə(r)] *(Am* **rigor)** *n* rigueur *f* ■**rigorous** *adj* rigoureux, -euse

rile [raɪl] *vt* (*annoy*) agacer

rim [rɪm] *n* (*of cup*) bord *m*; (*of wheel*) jante *f*; (*of spectacles*) monture *f*

rind [raɪnd] *n* (*of cheese*) croûte *f*; (*of bacon*) couenne *f*; (*of melon, lemon*) écorce *f*

ring[1] [rɪŋ] **1** *n* (*for finger, curtain*) anneau *m*; (*for finger, with stone*) bague *f*; (*for napkin*) rond *m*; (*on stove*) brûleur *m*; (*of people, chairs*) cercle *m*; (*of criminals*) bande *f*; (*at circus*) piste *f*; *Boxing* ring *m*; **to have rings under one's eyes** avoir les yeux cernés; *Gym* **the rings** les anneaux; *Br* **r. road** périphérique *m* **2** *vt* **to r. (round)** (*surround*) entourer (**with** de)

ring[2] [rɪŋ] **1** *n* (*sound*) sonnerie *f*; **there's a r. at the door** on sonne à la porte; *Fam* **to give sb a r.** passer un coup de fil à qn; **it has a r. of truth (about it)** cela a l'air vrai **2** (*pt* **rang**, *pp* **rung**) *vt* (*bell*) sonner; (*alarm*) déclencher; **to r. sb** (*on phone*) téléphoner à qn; **to r. the bell** sonner; **to r. the doorbell** sonner à la porte; *Fam* **that rings a bell** ça me dit quelque chose **3** *vi* (*of bell, phone, person*) sonner; (*of sound, words*) retentir; (*of ears*) bourdonner; (*make a phone call*) téléphoner; **to r. for sb** sonner qn
■ **ringing 1** *adj Br* **r. tone** (*on phone*) sonnerie *f* **2** *n* (*of bell*) sonnerie *f*; **a r. in one's ears** un bourdonnement dans les oreilles
▸ **ring back 1** *vt sep* **to r. sb back** rappeler qn **2** *vi* rappeler
▸ **ring off** *vi* (*on phone*) raccrocher
▸ **ring out** *vi* (*of bell*) sonner; (*of voice, shout*) retentir
▸ **ring up 1** *vt sep* **to r. sb up** téléphoner à qn **2** *vi* téléphoner

ringleader ['rɪŋliːdə(r)] *n Pej* (*of gang*) chef *m* de bande; (*of rebellion, strike*) meneur, -euse *mf*

ringlet ['rɪŋlɪt] *n* anglaise *f*

rink [rɪŋk] *n* (*for ice-skating*) patinoire *f*; (*for roller-skating*) piste *f*

rinse [rɪns] **1** *n* rinçage *m*; **to give sth a r.** rincer qch **2** *vt* rincer; **to r. one's hands** se rincer les mains; **to r. out** rincer

riot ['raɪət] **1** *n* (*uprising*) émeute *f*; *Fig* **a r. of colour** une explosion de couleurs; **to run r.** se déchaîner; **the r. police** ≃ les CRS *mpl* **2** *vi* (*rise up*) faire une émeute; (*of prisoners*) se mutiner
■ **rioter** *n* émeutier, -ière *mf*; (*vandal*) casseur *m* ■ **rioting** *n* émeutes *fpl*

riotous ['raɪətəs] *adj* (*crowd, party*) tapageur, -euse; **r. living** vie *f* dissolue

rip [rɪp] **1** *n* déchirure *f* **2** (*pt & pp* **-pp-**) *vt* déchirer; **to r. sth off** arracher qch (**from** de); *Fam* (*steal*) faucher qch; *Fam* **to r. sb off** (*deceive*) rouler qn; **to r. sth up** déchirer qch **3** *vi* (*of fabric*) se déchirer; **the explosion ripped through the building** l'explosion souffla dans tout le bâtiment ■ **rip-off** *n Fam* arnaque *f*

ripe [raɪp] (**-er, -est**) *adj* (*fruit*) mûr; (*cheese*) fait ■ **ripen** *vti* mûrir

ripple ['rɪpəl] **1** *n* (*on water*) ride *f*; *Fig* (*of laughter*) cascade *f* **2** *vi* (*of water*) se rider

rise [raɪz] **1** *n* (*in price, pressure*) hausse *f* (**in** de); (*in river*) crue *f*; (*slope in ground*) montée *f*; (*hill*) éminence *f*; (*of leader, party*) ascension *f*; (*of technology, industry*) essor *m*; **his r. to power** son accession au pouvoir; *Br* (*pay*) **r.** augmentation *f* (de salaire); **to give r. to sth** donner lieu à qch **2** (*pt* **rose**, *pp* **risen** ['rɪzən]) *vi* (*of temperature, balloon, price*) monter; (*in society*) s'élever; (*of hope*) grandir; (*of sun, theatre curtain, wind*) se lever; (*of dough*) lever; (*get up from chair or bed*) se lever; **to r. to the surface** remonter à la surface; **the river rises in...** le fleuve prend sa source dans...; **to r. (up)** (*rebel*) se soulever (**against** contre); **to r. to power** accéder au pouvoir; **to r. from the dead** ressusciter; **to r. to the occasion** se montrer à la hauteur de la situation

riser ['raɪzə(r)] *n* **early r.** lève-tôt *mf inv*; **late r.** lève-tard *mf inv*

rising ['raɪzɪŋ] **1** *n* (*of curtain in theatre*) lever *m*; (*revolt*) soulèvement *m*; (*of river*) crue *f* **2** *adj* (*sun*) levant; (*tide*) montant; (*number*) croissant; (*prices*) en hausse; (*artist, politician*) qui monte

risk [rɪsk] **1** *n* risque *m*; **at r.** (*person*) en danger; (*job*) menacé; **at your own r.** à tes risques et périls; **to run the r. of doing sth** courir le risque de faire qch **2** *vt* (*life, reputation*) risquer; **I can't r. going** je ne peux pas prendre le risque d'y aller; **we can't r. it** nous ne pouvons pas prendre ce risque ■ **risky** (**-ier, -iest**) *adj* risqué

rissole ['rɪsəʊl] *n Br Culin* croquette *f*

rite [raɪt] *n* rite *m*; *Rel* **the last rites** les derniers sacrements *mpl* ■ **ritual** ['rɪtʃʊəl] **1** *adj* rituel, -uelle **2** *n* rituel *m*

rival ['raɪvəl] **1** *adj* rival **2** *n* rival, -ale *mf* **3** (*Br* **-ll-**, *Am* **-l-**) *vt* (*compete with*) rivaliser avec (**in** de); (*equal*) égaler (**in** en) ■ **rivalry** (*pl* **-ies**) *n* rivalité *f* (**between** entre)

river ['rɪvə(r)] **1** *n* (*small*) rivière *f*; (*flowing into sea*) fleuve *m*; *Fig* (*of lava, tears*) flot *m*; **the R. Thames** la Tamise **2** *adj* (*port, navigation*) fluvial; **r. bank** rive *f*; **r. bed** lit *m* de rivière/de fleuve ■ **riverside 1** *n* bord *m* de l'eau **2** *adj* au bord de l'eau

rivet ['rɪvɪt] **1** *n* rivet *m* **2** *vt* riveter; *Fig* (*eyes*) fixer (**on** sur); **to be riveted to the TV set** être cloué devant la télé ■ **riveting** *adj Fig* fascinant

Riviera [rɪvɪ'eərə] *n* **the (French) R.** la Côte d'Azur

roach [rəʊtʃ] *n Am* (*cockroach*) cafard *m*

road [rəʊd] **1** *n* route *f*; (*small*) chemin *m*; (*in town*) rue *f*; (*roadway*) chaussée *f*; **the Paris r.** la route de Paris; **by r.** par la route; **down/up the r.** un peu plus loin dans la rue; **to live**

across *or* over the r. habiter en face; **to be on the r. to recovery** être en voie de la guérison **2** *adj (map, safety)* routier, -ière; *(accident)* de la route; *Fam* **r. hog** chauffard *m*; **r. sign** panneau *m* de signalisation; *Br* **r. works**, *Am* **r. work** travaux *mpl* de voirie ▪ **roadblock** *n* barrage *m* routier ▪ **roadside 1** *n* bord *m* de la route **2** *adj* **r. bar** bar *m* situé en bord de route ▪ **roadway** *n* chaussée *f* ▪ **roadworthy** *adj (vehicle)* en état de rouler

roam [rəʊm] **1** *vt* parcourir **2** *vi* errer; **to r. (about) the streets** traîner dans les rues

roar [rɔː(r)] **1** *n (of lion)* rugissement *m*; *(of person)* hurlement *m*; *(of thunder)* grondement *m* **2** *vt* **to r. sth (out)** hurler qch **3** *vi (of lion, wind, engine)* rugir; *(of person, crowd)* hurler; *(of thunder)* gronder; **to r. with laughter** hurler de rire; **to r. past** *(of truck)* passer dans un bruit de tonnerre ▪ **roaring** *adj* **a r. fire** une belle flambée; **a r. success** un succès fou; **to do a r. trade** faire des affaires en or

roast [rəʊst] **1** *n (meat)* rôti *m* **2** *adj* rôti; **r. beef** rosbif *m* **3** *vt (meat, potatoes)* faire rôtir; *(coffee)* faire griller **4** *vi (of meat)* rôtir; *Fam* **it's roasting in here** on cuit ici

rob [rɒb] *(pt & pp* **-bb-**) *vt (person)* voler; *(shop, bank)* dévaliser; *(house)* cambrioler; **to r. sb of sth** voler qch à qn; *Fig (deprive)* priver qn de qch ▪ **robber** *n* voleur, -euse *mf* ▪ **robbery** *(pl* **-ies**) *n* vol *m*; **it's daylight r.!** c'est du vol pur et simple!; **armed r.** vol à main armée

robe [rəʊb] *n (dressing gown)* robe *f* de chambre; *(of priest, judge)* robe

robin [ˈrɒbɪn] *n (bird)* rouge-gorge *m*

robot [ˈrəʊbɒt] *n* robot *m* ▪ **roˈbotic** *adj* robotique ▪ **roˈbotics** *n* robotique *f*

robust [rəʊˈbʌst] *adj* robuste

rock¹ [rɒk] **1** *n (music)* rock *m* **2** *vt (boat)* balancer; *(building)* secouer; **to r. a baby to sleep** bercer un bébé pour qu'il s'endorme **3** *vi (sway)* se balancer; *(of building, ground)* trembler ▪ **rocking chair** *n* fauteuil *m* à bascule ▪ **rocking horse** *n* cheval *m* à bascule

rock² [rɒk] **1** *n (substance)* roche *f*; *(boulder, rock face)* rocher *m*; *Am (stone)* pierre *f*; *Br (sweet)* = sucrerie en forme de bâton parfumée à la menthe; **on the rocks** *(whisky)* avec des glaçons; *(marriage)* en pleine débâcle; **r. climbing** varappe *f*; **r. face** paroi *f* rocheuse ▪ **ˈrock-ˈbottom 1** *n* point le plus bas; **he has reached r.** il a touché le fond **2** *adj (prices)* les plus bas *(f* basses)

rockery [ˈrɒkərɪ] *(pl* **-ies**) *n* rocaille *f*

rocket [ˈrɒkɪt] **1** *n* **(a)** *(missile)* fusée *f* **(b)** *Culin* roquette *f* **2** *vi (of prices, unemployment)* monter en flèche

rocky [ˈrɒkɪ] *(-ier, -iest) adj (road)* rocailleux, -euse; *(hill)* rocheux, -euse; *Fig (relationship)* instable

rod [rɒd] *n (wooden)* baguette *f*; *(metal)* tige *f*; *(of curtain)* tringle *f*; *(for fishing)* canne *f* à pêche

rode [rəʊd] *pt of* **ride**

rodent [ˈrəʊdənt] *n* rongeur *m*

rodeo [*Br* ˈrəʊdɪəʊ, *Am* rəʊˈdeɪəʊ] *(pl* **-os**) *n Am* rodéo *m*

roe [rəʊ] *n* **(a)** *(eggs)* œufs *mpl* de poisson **(b) r. (deer)** chevreuil *m*

rogue [rəʊg] *n (dishonest)* crapule *f*; *(mischievous)* coquin, -ine *mf* ▪ **roguish** *adj (smile)* coquin

role [rəʊl] *n* rôle *m*; **r. model** modèle *m*

roll [rəʊl] **1** *n (of paper)* rouleau *m*; *(of fat, flesh)* bourrelet *m*; *(of drum, thunder)* roulement *m*; *(of ship)* roulis *m*; *(bread)* petit pain *m*; *(list)* liste *f*; **r. of film** pellicule *f*; **r. neck** col *m* roulé **2** *vt (cigarette)* rouler; *(ball)* faire rouler **3** *vi (of ball, ship)* rouler; *(of camera)* tourner; *(of thunder)* gronder; **to r. into a ball** *(of animal)* se rouler en boule; *Fam* **to be rolling in money, to be rolling in it** rouler sur l'or ▪ **rolling** *adj (hills)* ondulant; *(sea)* gros *(f* grosse); **r. pin** rouleau *m* à pâtisserie

▸ **roll down** *vt sep (car window)* baisser; *(sleeves)* redescendre

▸ **roll in** *vi Fam (flow in)* affluer; *(of person)* s'amener

▸ **roll on 1** *vt sep (paint)* appliquer au rouleau **2** *vi Fam* **r. on tonight!** vivement ce soir!

▸ **roll out** *vt sep (dough)* étaler

▸ **roll over 1** *vt sep* retourner **2** *vi (many times)* se rouler; *(once)* se retourner

▸ **roll up 1** *vt sep (map, cloth)* rouler; *(sleeve)* retrousser **2** *vi Fam (arrive)* s'amener

roller [ˈrəʊlə(r)] **1** *n (for hair, painting)* rouleau *m*; **r. coaster** montagnes *fpl* russes; **r. skate** patin *m* à roulettes; **roller-skating** patin *m* à roulettes; **to go r.** faire du patin à roulettes; ▪ **rollerblades** *npl* rollers *mpl* ▪ **rollerblading** *n* roller *m*; **to go r.** faire du roller

rollicking [ˈrɒlɪkɪŋ] **1** *adj* joyeux, -euse (et bruyant) **2** *n Br Fam* **to give sb a r.** engueuler qn

ROM [rɒm] *(abbr* **read only memory**) *n Comptr* mémoire *f* morte

Roman [ˈrəʊmən] **1** *adj* romain **2** *n* Romain, -aine *mf* **3** *adj & n* **R. Catholic** catholique *(mf)*

romance [rəʊˈmæns] **1** *n (love)* amour *m*; *(affair)* aventure *f* amoureuse; *(story)* histoire *f* d'amour; *(charm)* poésie *f* **2** *adj* **R. language** langue *f* romane

Romania [rəʊˈmeɪnɪə] *n* la Roumanie ▪ **Romanian 1** *adj* roumain **2** *n (person)* Roumain, -aine *mf*; *(language)* roumain *m*

romantic [rəʊˈmæntɪk] **1** *adj (of love, tenderness)* romantique; *(fanciful, imaginary)* romanesque **2** *n* romantique *mf* ▪ **romantically** *adv* de façon romantique ▪ **romanticism** *n* romantisme *m*

romp [rɒmp] **1** *n* to have a r. chahuter **2** *vi* s'ébattre; **to r. through an exam** avoir un examen les doigts dans le nez

rompers ['rɒmpəz] *npl (for baby)* barboteuse *f*

roof [ruːf] *n (of building, vehicle)* toit *m; (of tunnel, cave)* plafond *m*; **r. of the mouth** voûte *f* du palais; **r. rack** *(of car)* galerie *f* ▪ **roofing** *n* toiture *f* ▪ **rooftop** *n* toit *m*

rook [rʊk] *n (bird)* freux *m; Chess* tour *f*

rookie ['rʊkɪ] *n Am Fam (new recruit)* bleu *m*

room [ruːm, rʊm] *n* **(a)** *(in house)* pièce *f; (bedroom)* chambre *f; (large, public)* salle *f; Am* **men's r., ladies' r.** toilettes *fpl* **(b)** *(space)* place *f*; **to make r.** faire de la place *(for* pour*);* **there's r. for doubt** le doute est permis; **no r. for doubt** aucun doute possible ▪ **roommate** *n Br (sharing a room)* camarade *mf* de chambre; *Am (sharing a flat)* colocataire *mf* ▪ **roomy** (**-ier, -iest**) *adj* spacieux, -ieuse; *(clothes)* ample

roost [ruːst] **1** *n* perchoir *m* **2** *vi* se percher

rooster ['ruːstə(r)] *n* coq *m*

root [ruːt] **1** *n (of plant, tooth, hair) & Math* racine *f; Fig (origin)* origine *f; (cause)* cause *f*; **to pull sth up by the root(s)** déraciner qch; **to take r.** *(of plant, person)* prendre racine; *Fig* **to find one's roots** retrouver ses racines; *Fig* **to put down (new) roots** *(of person)* s'intégrer; *Am* **r. beer** = boisson gazeuse aux extraits végétaux; **r. cause** cause *f* première **2** *vt* **to r. sth out** supprimer qch **3** *vi (of plant cutting)* s'enraciner; **to r. about** *or* **around for sth** fouiller pour trouver qch; *Fam* **to r. for sb** appuyer qn ▪ **rooted** *adj* **deeply r.** bien enraciné **(in** dans*);* **r. to the spot** *(immobile)* cloué sur place ▪ **rootless** *adj* sans racines

rope [rəʊp] **1** *n* corde *f; (on ship)* cordage *m; Fam* **to know the ropes** connaître son affaire **2** *vt (tie)* lier; *Fam* **to r. sb in** recruter qn; **to r. sth off** *(of police)* interdire l'accès de qch

rop(e)y ['rəʊpɪ] (**-ier, -iest**) *adj Br Fam (thing)* minable; *(person)* patraque

rosary ['rəʊzərɪ] *(pl* **-ies**) *n Rel* rosaire *m*

rose¹ [rəʊz] *n* **(a)** *(flower)* rose *f*; **r. bush** rosier *m* **(b)** *(of watering can)* pomme *f* ▪ **rosebud** *n* bouton *m* de rose

rose² [rəʊz] *pt of* **rise**

rosé ['rəʊzeɪ] *n* rosé *m*

rosemary ['rəʊzmərɪ] *n (plant, herb)* romarin *m*

rosette [rəʊ'zet] *n* rosette *f*

roster ['rɒstə(r)] *n (duty)* liste *f* de service

rostrum ['rɒstrəm] *n* tribune *f; (for prizewinner)* podium *m*

rosy ['rəʊzɪ] (**-ier, -iest**) *adj (pink)* rose; *Fig (future)* prometteur, -euse

rot [rɒt] **1** *n* pourriture *f; Br Fam (nonsense)* inepties *fpl* **2** *(pt & pp* **-tt-**) *vti* pourrir ▪ **rotting** *adj (meat, fruit)* qui pourrit

rota ['rəʊtə] *n* roulement *m*

rotary ['rəʊtərɪ] **1** *adj* rotatif, -ive *(pl* **-ies**) *n*

Am (for traffic) rond-point *m* ▪ **ro'tation** *n* rotation *f*; **in r.** à tour de rôle

rotate [rəʊ'teɪt] **1** *vt* faire tourner; *(crops)* alterner **2** *vi* tourner

rote [rəʊt] *n* **by r.** machinalement

rotten ['rɒtən] *adj (fruit, egg, wood)* pourri; *Fam (bad)* nul *(f* nulle*); Fam (weather)* pourri; *Fam* **to feel r.** *(ill)* être mal fichu

rouble ['ruːbəl] *(Am* **ruble**) *n (currency)* rouble *m*

rouge [ruːʒ] *n Old-fashioned* rouge *m* (à joues)

rough¹ [rʌf] **1** (**-er, -est**) *adj (surface)* rugueux, -ueuse; *(ground)* accidenté; *(manners)* fruste; *(climate, life, voice)* rude; *(wine)* âpre; *(neighbourhood)* dur; *(sea)* agité; *(diamond)* brut; *(brutal)* brutal; *Br (justice)* sommaire; *Fig* **to feel r.** *(ill)* être mal fichu **2** *adv Br* **to sleep/ live r.** coucher/vivre à la dure; **to play r.** jouer avec brutalité **3** *vt Fam* **to r. it** vivre à la dure; *Fam* **to r. sb up** tabasser qn; **to r. up sb's hair** ébouriffer les cheveux de qn ▪ **rough-and- 'ready** *adj (solution)* rudimentaire; *(meal, accommodation)* sommaire ▪ **rough-and- 'tumble** *n* bousculade *f* ▪ **roughen** *vt* rendre rugueux, -ueuse ▪ **roughly¹** *adv (brutally)* brutalement; *(crudely)* grossièrement ▪ **roughness** *n (of surface)* rugosité *f; (of behaviour)* rudesse *f*

rough² [rʌf] **1** (**-er, -est**) *adj (approximate)* approximatif, -ive; **I have a r. idea of what he wants** j'ai une petite idée de ce qu'il veut; **r. guess, r. estimate** approximation *f; Br* **r. book** cahier *m* de brouillon; **r. copy, r. draft** brouillon *m*; **r. paper** papier *m* brouillon **2** *vt* **to r. sth out** *(plan)* ébaucher ▪ **roughly²** *adv (approximately)* à peu près; **r. speaking** en gros

roughage ['rʌfɪdʒ] *n* fibres *fpl* (alimentaires)

roulette [ruː'let] *n* roulette *f*; **Russian r.** roulette *f* russe

round [raʊnd] **1** (**-er, -est**) *adj* rond; *Am* **r. trip** aller (et) retour *m*

2 *adv* autour; **all r., right r.** tout autour; **all year r.** toute l'année; **the long way r.** le chemin le plus long; **the wrong way r.** à l'envers; **the other way r.** dans l'autre sens; **to go r. to sb's** passer chez qn; **to ask sb r.** inviter qn chez soi

3 *prep* autour de; **r. here** par ici; **r. about** *(approximately)* environ; **r. (about) midday** vers midi; **to go r. the corner** tourner le coin; **it's just r. the corner** c'est juste au coin; **to go r. the world** parcourir le monde

4 *n Br (slice)* tranche *f; Br (sandwich)* sandwich *m; (in competition)* manche *f; (of golf)* partie *f; Boxing* round *m; (of talks)* série *f; (of drinks, visits)* tournée *f*; **to be on one's round(s), to do one's round(s)** *(of milkman)* faire sa tournée; *(of doctor)* faire ses visites; *(of policeman)* faire sa ronde; **r. of applause** salve *f* d'applaudissements; **r. of ammunition** cartouche *f*

5 *vt* **to r. a corner** *(in car)* prendre un virage; **to r. sth off** *(meal, speech)* terminer qch (**with** par); **to r. up** *(gather)* rassembler; *(price)* arrondir au chiffre supérieur ▪ **rounded** *adj* arrondi ▪ **roundness** *n* rondeur *m* ▪ **round-'shouldered** *adj* voûté

roundabout ['raʊndəbaʊt] **1** *adj (method, route)* indirect **2** *n Br (at funfair)* manège *m*; *(road junction)* rond-point *m*

rounders ['raʊndəz] *npl Br* = jeu similaire au base-ball

roundup ['raʊndʌp] *n (of criminals)* rafle *f*

rouse [raʊz] *vt (awaken)* éveiller; **roused (to anger)** en colère; **to r. sb to action** inciter qn à agir ▪ **rousing** *adj (welcome)* enthousiaste; *(speech)* vibrant; *(music)* allègre

rout [raʊt] **1** *n* déroute *f* **2** *vt* mettre en déroute

route¹ [ru:t] **1** *n* itinéraire *m*; *(of aircraft, ship)* route *f*; **bus r.** ligne *f* d'autobus **2** *vt (train)* fixer l'itinéraire de

route² [raʊt] *n Am (delivery round)* tournée *f*

routine [ru:'ti:n] **1** *n (habit)* routine *f*; *(on stage)* numéro *m*; *Comptr* sous-programme *m*; **the daily r.** le train-train quotidien; **as a matter of r.** de façon systématique **2** *adj (inquiry, work)* de routine; *(injection) Pej* routinier, -ière

rove [raʊv] **1** *vt* parcourir **2** *vi* rôder ▪ **roving** *adj (life)* nomade; *(ambassador)* itinérant; **r. reporter** reporter *m (qui va sur le terrain)*

row¹ [raʊ] *n (line)* rangée *f*; **two days in a r.** deux jours d'affilée

row² [raʊ] **1** *n* **to go for a r.** canoter; *Am* **r. boat** bateau *m* à rames **2** *vt (boat)* faire aller à la rame; *(person)* transporter en canot **3** *vi (in boat)* ramer ▪ **rowing** *n* canotage *m*; *(as sport)* aviron *m*; *Br* **r. boat** bateau *m* à rames

row³ [raʊ] **1** *n (noise)* vacarme *m*; *(quarrel)* dispute *f* **2** *vi* se disputer (**with** avec)

rowdy ['raʊdɪ] **1** (**-ier, -iest**) *adj* chahuteur, -euse **2** (*pl* **-ies**) *n* chahuteur, -euse *mf*

royal ['rɔɪəl] **1** *adj* royal; **the R. Air Force** = l'armée de l'air britannique **2** *npl Fam* **the royals** la famille royale ▪ **royalist** *adj & n* royaliste *(mf)* ▪ **royally** *adv (treat)* royalement ▪ **royalty** *n (rank, position)* royauté *f*; *(person)* membre *m* de la famille royale **2** *npl* **royalties** *(from book)* droits *mpl* d'auteur; *(from invention, on oil)* royalties *fpl*

rpm [a:pi:'em] *(abbr* **revolutions per minute)** *Aut* tours/minute

RSPCA [a:respi:si:'eɪ] *(abbr* **Royal Society for the Prevention of Cruelty to Animals)** *n Br* ≃ SPA *f*

RSVP [a:resvi:'pi:] *(abbr* **répondez s'il vous plaît)** RSVP

Rt Hon *(abbr* **Right Honourable)** *see* **right¹**

rub [rʌb] **1** *n (massage)* friction *f*; **to give sth a r.** frotter qch **2** *(pt & pp* **-bb-)** *vt* frotter; *Fig* **to r. shoulders with** côtoyer; *Fam* **to r. sb up the**

wrong way prendre qn à rebrousse-poil **3** *vi* frotter

▸ **rub away** *vt sep (mark)* effacer; *(tears)* essuyer

▸ **rub down** *vt sep (person)* frictionner; *(wood, with sandpaper)* poncer

▸ **rub in** *vt sep (cream)* faire pénétrer (en massant); *Fam* **to r. it in** retourner le couteau dans la plaie

▸ **rub off 1** *vt sep (mark)* effacer **2** *vi (of mark)* partir; *Fig (of manners)* déteindre (**on** sur)

▸ **rub out** *vt sep (mark)* effacer

rubber ['rʌbə(r)] *n (substance)* caoutchouc *m*; *Br (eraser)* gomme *f*; *Am Fam (condom)* capote *f*; **r. band** élastique *m*; **r. stamp** tampon *m* ▪ **rubber-'stamp** *vt Pej* approuver (sans discuter) ▪ **rubbery** *adj* caoutchouteux, -euse

rubbing alcohol ['rʌbɪŋælkəhəl] *n Am* alcool *m* à 90°

rubbish ['rʌbɪʃ] **1** *n Br (waste)* ordures *fpl*; *(industrial)* déchets *mpl*; *(junk)* cochonneries *fpl*; *Fig (nonsense)* idioties *fpl*; *Fam* **that's r.** *(absurd)* c'est absurde; *(worthless)* ça ne vaut rien; **r. bin** poubelle *f*; **r. dump** décharge *f* publique **2** *vt Fam* **to r. sb/sth** *(criticize)* dénigrer qn/qch ▪ **rubbishy** *adj Br Fam (book, film)* nul *(f* nulle); *(goods)* de mauvaise qualité

rubble ['rʌbəl] *n* décombres *mpl*

rubella [ru:'belə] *n Med* rubéole *f*

ruble ['ru:bəl] *n Am* = **rouble**

ruby ['ru:bɪ] *(pl* **-ies**) *n (gem)* rubis *m*

rucksack ['rʌksæk] *n* sac *m* à dos

rudder ['rʌdə(r)] *n* gouvernail *m*

ruddy ['rʌdɪ] (**-ier, -iest**) *adj (complexion)* rose; *Br Fam (bloody)* fichu

rude [ru:d] (**-er, -est**) *adj (impolite)* impoli (**to** envers); *(coarse, insolent)* grossier, -ière (**to** envers); *(indecent)* obscène; *(shock)* violent ▪ **rudely** *adv (impolitely)* impoliment; *(coarsely)* grossièrement ▪ **rudeness** *n (impoliteness)* impolitesse *f*; *(coarseness)* grossièreté *f*

> Note that the French word **rude** is a false friend and is never a translation for the English word **rude**. It means **harsh** or **rough**.

rudimentary [ru:dɪ'ment(ə)rɪ] *adj* rudimentaire ▪ **rudiments** ['ru:dɪmənts] *npl* rudiments *mpl*

rueful ['ru:fəl] *adj Literary (voice, smile)* de regret

ruffian ['rʌfɪən] *n* voyou *m (pl* -ous)

ruffle ['rʌfəl] **1** *vt (hair)* ébouriffer; *(water)* troubler; **to r. sb, to r. sb's feathers** *(offend)* froisser qn **2** *n (frill)* ruche *f*

rug [rʌg] *n* tapis *m*; *(over knees)* plaid *m*; *(bedside)* **r.** descente *f* de lit

rugby ['rʌgbɪ] *n* rugby *m*; **r. league** rugby à treize; **r. player** rugbyman *m*; **r. union** rugby à quinze

rugged ['rʌgɪd] *adj (surface)* rugueux, -ueuse;

(terrain, coast) accidenté; *(features, manners)* rude; *Fig (determination)* farouche

rugger ['rʌgə(r)] *n Br Fam* rugby *m*

ruin ['ruːɪn] **1** *n (destruction, rubble, building)* ruine *f*; **in ruins** *(building)* en ruine **2** *vt (health, country, person)* ruiner; *(clothes)* abîmer; *(effect, meal, party)* gâcher ▪ **ruined** *adj (person, country)* ruiné; *(building)* en ruine ▪ **ruinous** *adj* ruineux, -euse

rule [ruːl] **1** *n* **(a)** *(principle)* règle *f*; *(regulation)* règlement *m*; *(government)* autorité *f*; *Br* **against the rules** *or Am* **r.** contraire au règlement; **as a r.** en règle générale; **it's the** *or* **a r. that...** il est de règle que... *(+ subjunctive)* **(b)** *(for measuring)* règle *f* **2** *vt (country)* gouverner; *(decide) (of judge, referee)* décider **(that** que); **to r. sth out** *(exclude)* exclure qch **3** *vi (of king)* régner **(over** sur); *(of judge)* statuer **(against** contre; **on** sur) ▪ **ruled** *adj (paper)* réglé ▪ **ruling 1** *adj (passion, fear)* dominant; **the r. class** la classe dirigeante; *Pol* **the r. party** le parti au pouvoir **2** *n (of judge, referee)* décision *f*

ruler ['ruːlə(r)] *n* **(a)** *(for measuring)* règle *f* **(b)** *(king, queen)* souverain, -aine *mf*; *(political leader)* dirigeant, -ante *mf*

rum [rʌm] *n* rhum *m*

Rumania [ruː'meɪnɪə] *n* = **Romania**

rumble ['rʌmbəl] **1** *n* grondement *m*; *(of stomach)* gargouillement *m* **2** *vi (of train, thunder, gun)* gronder; *(of stomach)* gargouiller

ruminate ['ruːmɪneɪt] *vi Formal* **to r. over sth** *(scheme)* ruminer qch

rummage ['rʌmɪdʒ] *vi* **to r. (about)** farfouiller ▪ **rummage sale** *n Am (used clothes)* vente *f* de charité

rumour ['ruːmə(r)] *(Am* **rumor)** *n* rumeur *f* ▪ **rumoured** *(Am* **rumored)** *adj* **it is r. that...** on dit que...

rump [rʌmp] *n (of horse)* croupe *f*; *(of fowl)* croupion *m*; **r. steak** romsteck *m*

rumple ['rʌmpəl] *vt (clothes)* chiffonner

run [rʌn] **1** *n (series)* série *f*; *(period)* période *f*; *(running)* course *f*; *(outing)* tour *m*; *(journey)* trajet *m*; *(rush)* ruée *f* **(on** sur); *(for skiing)* piste *f*; *(in cricket, baseball)* point *m*; *Cards* suite *f*; *(in stocking)* maille *f* filée; **to go for a r.** aller courir; **on the r.** *(prisoner)* en fuite; **to have the r. of** *(house)* avoir à sa disposition; **in the long/short r.** à long/court terme; *Fam* **to have the runs** avoir la courante

2 *(pt* **ran,** *pp* **run,** *pres p* **running)** *vt (distance, race)* courir; *(machine)* faire fonctionner; *(test)* effectuer; *(business, country)* diriger; *(courses, events)* organiser; *Comptr (program)* exécuter; *(newspaper article)* publier **(on** sur); *(bath)* faire couler; **to r. a temperature** avoir de la fièvre; **to r. one's hand over** passer la main sur; **to r. one's eye over sth** jeter un coup d'œil à qch;

to r. its course *(of illness)* suivre son cours; **to r. sb to the airport** conduire qn à l'aéroport; **to r. a car** avoir une voiture

3 *vi* courir; *(flee)* fuir; *(of river, nose, pen, tap)* couler; *(of colour in washing)* déteindre; *(of ink)* baver; *(melt)* fondre; *(function) (of machine)* marcher; *(idle) (of engine)* tourner; *(of stocking, tights)* filer; **to r. down/in/out** descendre/entrer/sortir en courant; **to go running** faire du jogging; *Am* **to r. for president** être candidat à la présidence; **to r. with blood** ruisseler de sang; **to r. between** *(of bus)* faire le service entre; **the road runs to...** la route va à...; **the river runs into the sea** le fleuve se jette dans la mer; **it runs in the family** ça tient de famille

▸ **run about, run around** *vi* courir çà et là

▸ **run across** *vt insep (meet)* tomber sur

▸ **run along** *vi* **r. along!** filez!

▸ **run away** *vi (flee)* s'enfuir **(from** de)

▸ **run back** *vt sep (person in vehicle)* ramener **(to** à)

▸ **run down** *vt sep (pedestrian)* renverser; *(knock over and kill)* écraser; *Fig (belittle)* dénigrer; *(restrict)* limiter peu à peu

▸ **run in** *vt sep Br (engine)* roder

▸ **run into** *vt insep (meet)* tomber sur; *(crash into) (of vehicle, train)* percuter; **to r. into debt** s'endetter

▸ **run off 1** *vt sep (print)* tirer **2** *vi (flee)* s'enfuir **(with** avec)

▸ **run out 1** *vt sep* **to r. sb out of** *(chase)* chasser qn de **2** *vi (of stocks)* s'épuiser; *(of lease)* expirer; *(of time)* manquer; **to r. out of time/money** manquer de temps/d'argent; **we've r. out of coffee** on n'a plus de café; **I ran out of petrol** *orAm* **gas** je suis tombé en panne d'essence

▸ **run over 1** *vt sep (kill)* écraser; *(knock down)* renverser **2** *vt insep (notes, text)* revoir **3** *vi (of liquid)* déborder

▸ **run round** *vt insep (surround)* entourer

▸ **run through** *vt insep (recap)* revoir

▸ **run up** *vt sep (debts, bill)* laisser s'accumuler

runaway ['rʌnəweɪ] **1** *n* fugitif, -ive *mf* **2** *adj (car, horse)* fou *(f* folle); *(inflation)* galopant; *(victory)* remporté haut la main

run-down [rʌn'daʊn] *adj (weak, tired)* fatigué; *(district)* délabré

rung¹ [rʌŋ] *n (of ladder)* barreau *m*

rung² [rʌŋ] *pp of* **ring²**

runner ['rʌnə(r)] *n (athlete)* coureur *m*; *Br* **r. bean** haricot *m* d'Espagne

runner-up [rʌnər'ʌp] *n (in race)* second, -onde *mf*

running ['rʌnɪŋ] **1** *n* course *f*; *(of machine)* fonctionnement *m*; *(of business, country)* gestion *f*; **to be in/out of the r.** être/ne plus être dans la course **2** *adj* **six days r.** six jours de suite; **r. water** eau *f* courante; **a r. battle**

with *(cancer, landlord)* une lutte de tous les instants avec; **to give a r. commentary (on)** *(on TV)* faire un commentaire en direct (de); **r. costs** *(of factory)* frais *mpl* d'exploitation; *(of car)* dépenses *fpl* courantes

runny ['rʌnɪ] **(-ier, -iest)** *adj (cream, sauce)* liquide; *(nose)* qui coule; **r. omelet(te)** omelette *f* baveuse

run-of-the-mill [rʌnəvðə'mɪl] *adj* ordinaire

run-up ['rʌnʌp] *n* **in the r. to** *(elections, Christmas)* dans la période qui précède

runway ['rʌnweɪ] *n (for aircraft)* piste *f* (d'envol); *Am (for fashion show)* podium *m*

rupture ['rʌptʃə(r)] **1** *n (hernia)* hernie *f*; **the r. of** *(breaking)* la rupture de **2** *vt* rompre; **to r. oneself** se faire une hernie

rural ['rʊərəl] *adj* rural

ruse [ruːz] *n* ruse *f*

rush¹ [rʌʃ] **1** *n (demand)* ruée *f* **(for** vers; **on** sur); *(confusion)* bousculade *f*; **to be in a r.** être pressé **(to do** de faire); **to leave in a r.** partir en vitesse; **the gold r.** la ruée vers l'or; **r. hour** heures *fpl* de pointe; **a r. job** un travail urgent **2** *vt Mil (attack)* prendre d'assaut; **to r. sb** *(hurry)* bousculer qn; **to r. sb to hospital** *or Am* **the hospital** transporter qn d'urgence à l'hôpital; **to r. (through) sth** *(job)* faire qch en vitesse; *(decision)* prendre qch à la hâte; **to be**

rushed into a decision être forcé à prendre une décision à la hâte *vi (move fast, throw oneself)* se ruer **(at** sur; **towards** vers); *(of blood)* affluer **(to** à); *(hurry)* se dépêcher **(to do** de faire); *(of vehicle)* foncer; **to r. out** sortir précipitamment

rush² [rʌʃ] *n (plant)* jonc *m*

rusk [rʌsk] *n Br* biscotte *f*

Russia ['rʌʃə] *n* la Russie ▪ **Russian 1** *adj* russe **2** *n (person)* Russe *mf*; *(language)* russe *m*

russet ['rʌsɪt] *adj* brun roux *inv*

rust [rʌst] **1** *n* rouille *f* **2** *vi* rouiller ▪ **rustproof** *adj* inoxydable ▪ **rusty (-ier, -iest)** *adj* rouillé

rustic ['rʌstɪk] *adj* rustique

rustle¹ ['rʌsəl] **1** *n* bruissement *m* **2** *vt Fam* **to r. sth up** *(meal, snack)* improviser qch; **to r. up support** rassembler des partisans **3** *vi (of leaves)* bruire

rustle² ['rʌsəl] *vt Am (steal)* voler ▪ **rustler** *n Am (thief)* voleur *m* de bétail

rut [rʌt] *n* ornière *f*; *Fig* **to be (stuck) in a r.** être encroûté

rutabaga [ruːtə'beɪgə] *n Am (swede)* rutabaga *m*

ruthless ['ruːθləs] *adj* impitoyable ▪ **ruthlessly** *adv* impitoyablement ▪ **ruthlessness** *n* cruauté *f*

rye [raɪ] *n* seigle *m*; **r. bread** pain *m* de seigle

S, s [es] *n (letter)* S, s *m inv*

Sabbath ['sæbəθ] *n (Jewish)* sabbat *m*; *(Christian)* jour *m* du seigneur

sabbatical [sə'bætɪkəl] **1** *adj (university year, term)* sabbatique **2** *n* **to be on s.** être en congé sabbatique

sabotage ['sæbətɑːʒ] **1** *n* sabotage *m* **2** *vt* saboter ▪ **saboteur** [-'tɜː(r)] *n* saboteur, -euse *mf*

sabre ['seɪbə(r)] *(Am* **saber)** *n* sabre *m*

saccharin ['sækərɪn] *n* saccharine *f*

sachet ['sæʃeɪ] *n* sachet *m*

sack [sæk] **1** *n (bag)* sac *m*; *Fam* **to get the s.** se faire virer; *Fam* **to give sb the s.** virer qn; *Fam* **to hit the s.** se pieuter **2** *vt (town)* mettre à sac; *Fam (dismiss)* virer ▪ **sacking** *n (cloth)* toile *f* à sac; *Fam (dismissal)* renvoi *m*

sacrament ['sækrəmənt] *n Rel* sacrement *m*

sacred ['seɪkrɪd] *adj* sacré

sacrifice ['sækrɪfaɪs] **1** *n* sacrifice *m* **2** *vt* sacrifier **(to** à)

sacrilege ['sækrɪlɪdʒ] *n* sacrilège *m* ▪ **sacrilegious** [-'lɪdʒəs] *adj* sacrilège

sacrosanct ['sækrəʊsæŋkt] *adj Ironic* sacro-saint

sad [sæd] **(sadder, saddest)** *adj* triste ▪ **sadden** *vt* attrister ▪ **sadly** *adv (unhappily)* tristement; *(unfortunately)* malheureusement; **to be s. mistaken** se tromper lourdement ▪ **sadness** *n* tristesse *f*

saddle ['sædəl] **1** *n* selle *f*; *Fig* **to be in the s.** *(in control)* être aux commandes **2** *vt (horse)* seller; *Fam* **to s. sb with sb/sth** refiler qn/qch à qn ▪ **saddlebag** *n* sacoche *f*

sadism ['seɪdɪzəm] *n* sadisme *m* ▪ **sadist** *n* sadique *mf* ▪ **sadistic** [sə'dɪstɪk] *adj* sadique

sae [eseɪ'iː] *(abbr Br* **stamped addressed envelope,** *Am* **self-addressed envelope)** *n* enveloppe *f* timbrée (libellée à ses noms et adresse)

safari [sə'fɑːrɪ] *n* safari *m*; **to go on s.** faire un safari; **s. park** réserve *f* d'animaux sauvages

safe [seɪf] **1 (-er, -est)** *adj (person)* en sécurité; *(equipment, animal)* sans danger; *(place, investment, method)* sûr; *(winner)* assuré; **s. (and sound)** sain et sauf (*f* saine et sauve); **in s. hands** entre de bonnes mains; **to be s. from** être à l'abri de; **... to be on the s. side** ... pour plus de sûreté; **to wish sb a s. journey** souhaiter bon voyage à qn; **it's s. to go out** on peut sortir sans danger; **the safest thing to do is...** le plus sûr est de...; **s. sex** rapports *mpl* sexuels protégés **2** *n (for money, valuables)* coffre-fort *m* ▪ **safe-de'posit box** *n (in bank)* coffre *m* ▪ **safeguard 1** *n* garantie *f* **(against** contre) **2** *vt* sauvegarder **3** *vi* **to s. against sth** se protéger contre qch ▪ **safe-'keeping** *n* **to give sb sth for s.** donner qch à la garde de qn

safely ['seɪflɪ] *adv (without risk)* en toute sécurité; *(drive)* prudemment; *(with certainty)* avec certitude; **to arrive s.** bien arriver

safety ['seɪftɪ] **1** *n* sécurité *f* **2** *adj (belt, device, screen, margin)* de sécurité; *(pin, chain, valve)* de sûreté; **s. curtain** *(in theatre)* rideau *m* de fer; **s. net** *(in circus)* filet *m*; *Fig (safeguard)* mesure *f* de sécurité

saffron ['sæfrən] *n* safran *m*

sag [sæg] *(pt & pp* **-gg-)** *vi (of roof, ground, bed)* s'affaisser; *(of breasts)* tomber; *(of flesh)* être flasque; *(of prices)* baisser

saga ['sɑːɡə] *n* saga *f*

sage[1] [seɪdʒ] *n (plant, herb)* sauge *f*

sage[2] [seɪdʒ] *n (wise man)* sage *m*

Sagittarius [sædʒɪ'teərɪəs] *n (sign)* le Sagittaire; **to be (a) S.** être Sagittaire

Sahara [sə'hɑːrə] *n* **the S. (desert)** le Sahara

said [sed] *pt & pp of* **say**

sail [seɪl] **1** *n (on boat)* voile *f*; *(of mill)* aile *f*; **to set s.** prendre la mer **2** *vt (boat)* commander; *(seas)* parcourir **3** *vi (of person, ship)* naviguer; *(leave)* prendre la mer; *(do as sport)* faire de la voile; **to s. into port** entrer au port; **to s. round the world** faire le tour du monde en bateau; *Fam* **to s. through an exam** réussir un examen haut la main; **the clouds sailed by** les nuages passaient dans le ciel ▪ **sailboard** *n* planche *f* à voile ▪ **sailboat** *n Am* voilier *m* ▪ **sailing** *n (sport)* voile *f*; *(departure)* appareillage *m*; **to go s.** faire de la voile; *Br* **s. boat** voilier *m*

sailor ['seɪlə(r)] *n* marin *m*

saint [seɪnt] *n* saint *m*, sainte *f*; **S. John** saint Jean; **All Saints' Day** la Toussaint ▪ **saintly** **(-ier, -iest)** *adj (life)* de saint

sake [seɪk] *n* **for my/your/his s.** pour moi/toi/lui; **for heaven's** *or* **God's s.!** pour l'amour de Dieu!; **for your own s.** pour ton bien; **(just) for the s. of eating** simplement pour manger

salable [ˈseɪləbəl] *adj Am* vendable

salacious [səˈleɪʃəs] *adj* salace

salad [ˈsæləd] *n* salade *f*; **s. bowl** saladier *m*; *Br* **s. cream** = sorte de mayonnaise; **s. dressing** = sauce pour salade

salamander [ˈsæləmændə(r)] *n* salamandre *f*

salami [səˈlɑːmɪ] *n* salami *m*

salary [ˈsælərɪ] (*pl* **-ies**) *n* salaire *m* • **salaried** *adj* salarié

sale [seɪl] *n* (*action, event*) vente *f*; (*at reduced price*) solde *m*; **the sales** les soldes; **on s.** en vente; **in the sales** en solde; (**up**) **for s.** à vendre; **to put sth up for s.** mettre qch en vente; **s. price** prix *m* de vente; *Br* **sales assistant** vendeur, -euse *mf*; **sales department** service *m* commercial; **sales pitch** arguments *mpl* de vente; *Am* **sales check** *or* **slip** reçu *m* • **saleable** (*Am* **salable**) *adj* vendable • **salesclerk** *n Am* vendeur, -euse *mf* • **salesman** (*pl* **-men**) *n* (*in shop*) vendeur *m*; (*for company*) représentant *m* • **saleswoman** (*pl* **-women**) *n* (*in shop*) vendeuse *f*; (*for company*) représentante *f*

salient [ˈseɪlɪənt] *adj* (*feature, fact*) marquant

saliva [səˈlaɪvə] *n* salive *f* • **salivate** [ˈsælɪveɪt] *vi* saliver

sallow [ˈsæləʊ] (**-er, -est**) *adj* jaunâtre

salmon [ˈsæmən] *n inv* saumon *m*; **s. trout** truite *f* saumonée

salmonella [sælməˈnelə] *n* salmonelle *f*

salon [ˈsælɒn] *n* **beauty s.** institut *m* de beauté; **hairdressing s.** salon *m* de coiffure

saloon [səˈluːn] *n* (*room*) salle *f*; *Am* (*bar*) bar *m*; *Br* **s. car** berline *f*

salt [sɔːlt] **1** *n* sel *m*; **s. beef** bœuf *m* salé; **s. mine** mine *f* de sel; **s. water** eau *f* salée **2** *vt* saler • **saltcellar** *n Br* salière *f* • **'salt-'free** *adj* sans sel • **saltshaker** *n Am* salière *f* • **saltwater** *adj* (*lake*) salé; (*fish*) de mer • **salty** (**-ier, -iest**) *adj* salé

salubrious [səˈluːbrɪəs] *adj Formal* salubre

salute [səˈluːt] **1** *n* salut *m* **2** *vt* (*greet*) & *Mil* saluer **3** *vi* faire un salut

salvage [ˈsælvɪdʒ] **1** *n* (*of ship*) sauvetage *m*; (*of waste material*) récupération *f*; **s. operation** opération *f* de sauvetage **2** *vt* (*ship*) sauver; (*waste material*) récupérer

salvation [sælˈveɪʃən] *n* salut *m*; **the S. Army** l'Armée *f* du salut

same [seɪm] **1** *adj* même; **the (very) s. house as...** (exactement) la même maison que... **2** *pron* the s. le même, la même, *pl* les mêmes; **I would have done the s.** j'aurais fait la même chose; **it's all the s. to me** ça m'est égal **3** *adv* **to look the s.** (*of two things*) sembler pareils; **to taste the s.** avoir le même goût; **all the s.** (*nevertheless*) tout de même • **sameness** *n* monotonie *f*

sample [ˈsɑːmpəl] **1** *n* échantillon *m*; (*of blood*) prélèvement *m* **2** *vt* (*wine, cheese*) goûter; (*public opinion*) sonder; (*piece of music*) sampler

sanatorium [sænəˈtɔːrɪəm] (*pl* **-ria** [-rɪə]) *n Br* sanatorium *m*

sanctify [ˈsæŋktɪfaɪ] (*pt & pp* **-ied**) *vt* sanctifier

sanctimonious [sæŋktɪˈməʊnɪəs] *adj* moralisateur, -trice

sanction [ˈsæŋkʃən] **1** *n* (*penalty*) sanction *f*; *Formal* (*consent*) consentement *m* **2** *vt Formal* (*approve*) sanctionner

sanctity [ˈsæŋktɪtɪ] *n* sainteté *f*; (*of marriage*) caractère *m* sacré

sanctuary [*Br* ˈsæŋktʃʊərɪ, *Am* -erɪ] (*pl* **-ies**) *n Rel* sanctuaire *m*; (*for fugitive, refugee*) refuge *m*; (*for wildlife*) réserve *f*

sand [sænd] **1** *n* sable *m*; **s. castle** château *m* de sable; **s. dune** dune *f* **2** *vt* (*road*) sabler; **to s. (down)** (*wood*) poncer • **sandbag** *n* sac *m* de sable • **sandbank** *n* banc *m* de sable • **sandbox** *n Am* bac *m* à sable • **sander** *n* (*machine*) ponceuse *f* • **sandpaper 1** *n* papier *m* de verre **2** *vt* (*wood*) poncer • **sandpit** *n Br* bac *m* à sable • **sandstone** *n* (*rock*) grès *m* • **sandstorm** *n* tempête *f* de sable

sandal [ˈsændəl] *n* sandale *f*

sandwich [ˈsænwɪdʒ] **1** *n* sandwich *m*; **cheese s.** sandwich au fromage; *Br* **s. bar** snack *m* (*qui ne vend que des sandwichs*); *Br* **s. course** formation *f* professionnelle en alternance **2** *vt* **to be sandwiched between** (*of layer*) être intercalé entre; (*of person, building*) être coincé entre

sandy [ˈsændɪ] (**-ier, -iest**) *adj* (**a**) (*beach*) de sable; (*road, ground*) sablonneux, -euse; (*water*) sableux, -euse (**b**) (*hair*) blond roux *inv*

sane [seɪn] (**-er, -est**) *adj* (*person*) sain d'esprit; (*action, remark*) sensé

sang [sæŋ] *pt of* **sing**

sanguine [ˈsæŋgwɪn] *adj* optimiste

sanitarium [sænɪˈteərɪəm] *n Am* = **sanatorium**

sanitary [*Br* ˈsænɪtərɪ, *Am* -erɪ] *adj* (*fittings, conditions*) sanitaire; (*clean*) hygiénique; *Br* **s. towel**, *Am* **s. napkin** serviette *f* hygiénique

sanitation [sænɪˈteɪʃən] *n* hygiène *f* publique; (*plumbing*) installations *fpl* sanitaires; *Am* **s. department** service *m* de collecte des ordures ménagères

sanity [ˈsænɪtɪ] *n* santé *f* mentale

sank [sæŋk] *pt of* **sink**[2]

Santa Claus [ˈsæntəklɔːz] *n* le père Noël

sap [sæp] **1** *n* (*of tree, plant*) sève *f* **2** (*pt & pp* **-pp-**) *vt* (*weaken*) saper

sapphire [ˈsæfaɪə(r)] *n* (*jewel, needle*) saphir *m*

sarcasm [ˈsɑːkæzəm] *n* sarcasme *m* • **sarcastic** *adj* sarcastique

sardine [sɑːˈdiːn] *n* sardine *f*

Sardinia [sɑːˈdɪnɪə] *n* la Sardaigne

sardonic [sɑːˈdɒnɪk] *adj* sardonique

sari [ˈsɑːrɪ] *n* sari *m*

sarong [sə'rɒŋ] n paréo m

SARS [sɑːz] (abbr **severe acute respiratory syndrome**) n Med SRAS m

SASE [eseɪes'iː] (abbr **self-addressed stamped envelope**) n Am enveloppe f timbrée (libellée à ses noms et adresse)

sash [sæʃ] n (on dress) ceinture f; (of mayor) écharpe f; **s. window** fenêtre f à guillotine

sat [sæt] pt & pp of **sit**

Satan ['seɪtən] n Satan m ▪ **satanic** [sə'tænɪk] adj satanique

satchel ['sætʃəl] n cartable m

satellite ['sætəlaɪt] n satellite m; **s. (country)** pays m satellite; **s. dish** antenne f parabolique, parabole f; **s. picture** (for weather) animation f satellite; **s. television** télévision f par satellite

satin ['sætɪn] n satin m; **s. dress** robe f de ou en satin

satire ['sætaɪə(r)] n satire f (**on** contre) ▪ **satirical** [sə'tɪrɪkəl] adj satirique ▪ **satirist** ['sætɪrɪst] n écrivain m satirique ▪ **satirize** ['sætɪraɪz] vt satiriser, faire la satire de

satisfaction [sætɪs'fækʃən] n satisfaction f ▪ **satisfactory** adj satisfaisant

satisfy ['sætɪsfaɪ] (pt & pp -ied) vt satisfaire; (convince) persuader (**that** que); (condition) remplir; **to s. oneself that...** s'assurer que...; **to be satisfied (with)** être satisfait (de) ▪ **satisfying** adj satisfaisant; (meal, food) substantiel, -ielle

satsuma [sæt'suːmə] n Br mandarine f

saturate ['sætʃəreɪt] vt saturer (**with** de) ▪ **satu'ration** n saturation f; **to reach s. point** arriver à saturation

Saturday ['sætədeɪ] n samedi m

sauce [sɔːs] n (a) sauce f; **mint s.** sauce à la menthe; **s. boat** saucière f (b) Fam (impudence) toupet m ▪ **saucy** (-ier, -iest) adj Fam (impudent) insolent; (risqué) coquin

saucepan ['sɔːspən] n casserole f

saucer ['sɔːsə(r)] n soucoupe f

Saudi Arabia [saʊdɪə'reɪbɪə] n l'Arabie f Saoudite

sauerkraut ['saʊəkraʊt] n choucroute f

sauna ['sɔːnə] n sauna m

saunter ['sɔːntə(r)] vi flâner

sausage ['sɒsɪdʒ] n saucisse f; Br **s. roll** feuilleté m à la viande

sauté ['səʊteɪ] 1 adj sauté 2 (pt & pp -éed) vt faire sauter

savage ['sævɪdʒ] 1 adj (animal, person) féroce; (attack, criticism) violent 2 n Old-fashioned sauvage mf 3 vt (physically) attaquer ▪ **savagery** n (cruelty) sauvagerie f

save[1] [seɪv] 1 vt (rescue) sauver (**from** de); (keep) garder; (money) économiser; (time) gagner; Comptr sauvegarder; **to s. energy** faire des économies d'énergie; **to s. sb's life**

sauver la vie de qn; **to s. sb from doing sth** empêcher qn de faire qch; **to s. sb sth** éviter qch à qn; **to s. up** mettre de l'argent de côté (**for** pour); **God s. the Queen!** vive la reine! 2 vi **to s. (up)** faire des économies (**for/on** pour/sur) 3 n Football arrêt m ▪ **saving** n (of time, money) économie f; **savings** (money saved) économies fpl; **savings account** compte m d'épargne; **savings bank** caisse f d'épargne

save[2] [seɪv] prep Formal (except) hormis

saviour ['seɪvjə(r)] (Am **savior**) n sauveur m

savour ['seɪvə(r)] (Am **savor**) 1 n saveur f 2 vt savourer ▪ **savoury** (Am **savory**) adj (not sweet) salé; Fig (conduct) honorable

saw[1] [sɔː] 1 n scie f 2 (pt **sawed**, pp **sawn** or **sawed**) vt scier; **to s. sth off** scier qch; **a** Br **sawn-off** or Am **sawed-off shotgun** un fusil à canon scié ▪ **sawdust** n sciure f ▪ **sawmill** n scierie f

saw[2] [sɔː] pt of **see**[1]

sawn [sɔːn] pp of **saw**[1]

saxophone ['sæksəfəʊn] n saxophone m

say [seɪ] 1 (pt & pp **said**) vt dire (**to** à; **that** que); (of dial, watch) indiquer; **to s. again** répéter; **it is said that...** on dit que...; **what do you s. to a walk?** que dirais-tu d'une promenade?; **let's s. tomorrow** disons demain; **to s. the least** c'est le moins que l'on puisse dire; **to s. nothing of...** sans parler de...; **that is to s.** c'est-à-dire 2 vi dire; Fam **you don't s.!** sans blague!; Br Old-fashioned **I s.!** dites donc!; Am Fam **s.!** dis donc!; **that goes without saying** ça va sans dire 3 n **to have one's s.** avoir son mot à dire; **to have no s.** ne pas avoir voix au chapitre (**in** concernant)

saying ['seɪɪŋ] n maxime f

scab [skæb] n (of wound) croûte f; Fam (strikebreaker) jaune mf

scaffold ['skæfəld] n (gallows) échafaud m; (for construction work) échafaudage m ▪ **scaffolding** n échafaudage m

scald [skɔːld] 1 n brûlure f 2 vt ébouillanter ▪ **scalding** adj brûlant

scale[1] [skeɪl] 1 n (of instrument, map) échelle f; (of salaries) barème m; Fig (of problem) étendue f; **on a small/large s.** sur une petite/grande échelle; **s. model** modèle m réduit 2 vt **to s. sth down** revoir qch à la baisse

scale[2] [skeɪl] 1 n (on fish) écaille f; (in kettle) dépôt m calcaire 2 vt (fish) écailler

scale[3] [skeɪl] vt (climb) escalader

scales [skeɪlz] npl (for weighing) balance f; **(bathroom) s.** pèse-personne m; **(baby) s.** pèse-bébé m

scallion ['skæljən] n Am (onion) oignon m blanc

scallop ['skɒləp] n coquille f Saint-Jacques

scalp [skælp] n cuir m chevelu

scalpel ['skælpəl] n scalpel m

scam [skæm] n Fam arnaque f

scamp [skæmp] n coquin, -ine mf

scamper ['skæmpə(r)] *vi* **to s. off** *or* **away** détaler

scampi ['skæmpɪ] *n* scampi *mpl*

scan [skæn] **1** *n Med* **to have a s.** *(of pregnant woman)* passer une échographie **2** *(pt & pp* **-nn-)** *vt (read quickly)* parcourir; *(scrutinize)* scruter; *Comptr* passer au scanner ▪ **scanner** *n Med & Comptr* scanner *m*

scandal ['skændəl] *n (outrage)* scandale *m*; *(gossip)* ragots *mpl*; **to cause a s.** faire scandale ▪ **scandalize** *vt* scandaliser ▪ **scandalous** *adj* scandaleux, -euse

Scandinavia [skændɪ'neɪvɪə] *n* la Scandinavie ▪ **Scandinavian 1** *adj* scandinave **2** *n* Scandinave *mf*

scant [skænt] *adj* insuffisant ▪ **scantily** *adv* insuffisamment; **s. dressed** légèrement vêtu ▪ **scanty (-ier, -iest)** *adj* insuffisant

scapegoat ['skeɪpɡəʊt] *n* bouc *m* émissaire

scar [skɑː(r)] **1** *n* cicatrice *f*; **s. tissue** tissu *m* cicatriciel **2** *(pt & pp* **-rr-)** *vt* marquer d'une cicatrice; *Fig (of experience)* marquer; *Fig* **to be scarred for life** être marqué à vie

scarce [skeəs] **(-er, -est)** *adj* rare; **to make oneself s.** filer ▪ **scarceness, scarcity** *n* pénurie *f*

scarcely ['skeəslɪ] *adv* à peine; **he could s. breathe** il pouvait à peine respirer; **s. anything** presque rien; **s. ever** presque jamais

scare [skeə(r)] **1** *n* frayeur *f*; **to give sb a s.** faire peur à qn **2** *vt* faire peur à; **to s. sb off** faire fuir qn ▪ **scared** *adj* effrayé; **to be s. of sb/sth** avoir peur de qn/qch; **to be s. stiff** être mort de peur ▪ **scary (-ier, -iest)** *adj Fam* effrayant; **it's s.** ça fait peur

scarecrow ['skeəkrəʊ] *n* épouvantail *m*

scaremonger ['skeəmʌŋɡə(r)] *n* alarmiste *mf*

scarf [skɑːf] *(pl* **scarves)** *n (long)* écharpe *f*; *(square)* foulard *m*

scarlet ['skɑːlət] *adj* écarlate; **s. fever** scarlatine *f*

scathing ['skeɪðɪŋ] *adj (remark)* acerbe; **to be s. about sb/sth** faire des remarques acerbes sur qn/qch

scatter ['skætə(r)] **1** *vt (clouds, demonstrators)* disperser; *(corn, seed)* jeter à la volée; *(papers)* laisser traîner **2** *vi (of crowd)* se disperser

scatterbrain ['skætəbreɪn] *n* écervelé, -ée *mf*

scatty ['skætɪ] **(-ier, -iest)** *adj Br Fam* écervelé

scavenge ['skævɪndʒ] *vi* **to s. for sth** fouiller pour trouver qch ▪ **scavenger** *n (animal)* charognard *m*

scenario [sɪ'nɑːrɪəʊ] *(pl* **-os)** *n (of film)* scénario *m*

scene [siːn] *n (in book, film, play)* scène *f*; *(of event, crime, accident)* lieu *m*; *(fuss)* scandale *m*; *also Fig* **behind the scenes** dans les coulisses; **on the s.** sur les lieux; **a s. of devastation** un spectacle de dévastation; **to make a s.** faire un scandale

scenery ['siːnərɪ] *(pl* **-ies)** *n (landscape)* paysage *m*; *(in play, film)* décors *mpl*; *Fam* **I need a change of s.** j'ai besoin de changer d'air

scenic ['siːnɪk] *adj* pittoresque; **s. route** route *f* touristique

scent [sent] **1** *n (smell)* odeur *f*; *(perfume)* parfum *m*; *(in hunting)* fumet *m*; **she threw her pursuers off the s.** elle sema ses poursuivants **2** *vt (perfume)* parfumer *(with* de); *(smell)* flairer

scepter ['septər] *n Am* = **sceptre**

sceptic ['skeptɪk] *(Am* **skeptic)** *adj & n* sceptique *(mf)* ▪ **sceptical** *(Am* **skeptical)** *adj* sceptique ▪ **scepticism** *(Am* **skepticism)** *n* scepticisme *m*

sceptre ['septə(r)] *(Am* **scepter)** *n* sceptre *m*

schedule [*Br* 'ʃedjuːl, *Am* 'skedʒʊl] **1** *n (plan)* programme *m*; *(for trains, buses)* horaire *m*; *(list)* liste *f*; **to be on s.** *(train, bus)* être à l'heure; *(person)* être dans les temps; **to be ahead of s.** être en avance sur le programme; **to be behind s.** être en retard sur le programme; **according to s.** comme prévu **2** *vt* prévoir; *(event)* fixer la date/l'heure de ▪ **scheduled** *adj (planned)* prévu; *(service, flight, train)* régulier, -ière; **she's s. to leave at eight** son départ est prévu pour huit heures

scheme [skiːm] **1** *n (plan)* plan *m* **(to do** pour faire); *(plot)* complot *m*; *(arrangement)* arrangement *m*; **(housing) s.** lotissement *m* **2** *vi Pej* comploter ▪ **scheming** *Pej* **1** *adj* intrigant **2** *n* machinations *fpl*

schizophrenia [skɪtsəʊ'friːnɪə] *n* schizophrénie *f* ▪ **schizophrenic** [-'frenɪk] *adj & n* schizophrène *(mf)*

scholar ['skɒlə(r)] *n* érudit, -ite *mf* ▪ **scholarly** *adj* érudit ▪ **scholarship** *n (learning)* érudition *f*; *(grant)* bourse *f* d'études

school [skuːl] **1** *n* école *f*; *(within university)* département *m*; *Am Fam (college)* université *f*; **in** *or* **at s.** à l'école; *Br* **secondary s.,** *Am* **high s.** établissement *m* d'enseignement secondaire **2** *adj (year, book, equipment)* scolaire; **s. bag** cartable *m*; **s. bus** car *m* de ramassage scolaire; **s. fees** frais *mpl* de scolarité; **s. hours** les heures *fpl* de cours; **s. leaver** = jeune qui vient de terminer ses études secondaires; *Am* **s. yard** cour *f* de récréation ▪ **schoolboy** *n* écolier *m* ▪ **schoolchildren** *npl* écoliers *mpl* ▪ **schoolfriend** *n* camarade *mf* de classe ▪ **schoolgirl** *n* écolière *f* ▪ **schooling** *n* scolarité *f* ▪ **schoolmate** *n* camarade *mf* de classe ▪ **schoolroom** *n* salle *f* de classe ▪ **schoolteacher** *n (primary)* instituteur, -trice *mf*; *(secondary)* professeur *m*

schooner ['skuːnə(r)] *n (ship)* goélette *f*

sciatica [saɪ'ætɪkə] *n* sciatique *f*

science ['saɪəns] *n* science *f*; **to study s.** étudier les sciences; **s. teacher** professeur *m* de sciences; **s. fiction** science-fiction *f* ▪ **sci-**

en'tific adj scientifique ▪**scientist** n scientifique mf

sci-fi ['saɪfaɪ] n Fam SF f

Scilly Isles ['sɪlɪaɪlz] npl the S. les Sorlingues fpl

scintillating ['sɪntɪleɪtɪŋ] adj brillant

scissors ['sɪzəz] npl ciseaux mpl; **a pair of s.** une paire de ciseaux

sclerosis [sklɪ'rəʊsɪs] n Med sclérose f

scoff [skɒf] **1** vt to s. at sb/sth se moquer de qn/qch **2** vti Br Fam (eat) bouffer

scold [skəʊld] vt gronder (**for doing** pour avoir fait) ▪**scolding** n to get a s. se faire gronder

scone [skəʊn, skɒn] n Br scone m

scoop [sku:p] **1** n (for flour, sugar) pelle f; (for ice cream) cuillère f; Fam (in newspaper) scoop m; **at one s.** d'un seul coup **2** vt to s. sth out évider qch; **to s. sth up** ramasser qch

scoot [sku:t] vi Fam filer

scooter ['sku:tə(r)] n (for child) trottinette f; (motorcycle) scooter m

scope [skəʊp] n (range) étendue f; (of action) possibilité f; **to give s. for...** (interpretation) laisser le champ libre à...

scorch [skɔ:tʃ] **1** n s. (mark) brûlure f **2** vt roussir ▪**scorcher** n Br Fam jour m de canicule ▪**scorching** adj caniculaire; (sun, sand) brûlant

score¹ [skɔ:(r)] **1** n (in sport) score m; (in music) partition f; (of film) musique f **2** vt (point, goal) marquer; (exam mark) avoir; (piece of music) adapter (**for** pour) **3** vi (score a goal) marquer; (count points) marquer les points ▪**scoreboard** n tableau m d'affichage ▪**scorer** n marqueur m

score² [skɔ:(r)] n **a s.** (twenty) vingt; Fam **scores of** des tas de

score³ [skɔ:(r)] vt (cut line in) entailler; **to s. sth off** or **out** (delete) biffer

scorn [skɔ:n] **1** n mépris m **2** vt mépriser ▪**scornful** adj méprisant; **to be s. of sb/sth** considérer qn/qch avec mépris ▪**scornfully** adv avec mépris

Scorpio ['skɔ:pɪəʊ] n (sign) le Scorpion; **to be (a) S.** être Scorpion

scorpion ['skɔ:pɪən] n scorpion m

Scot [skɒt] n Écossais, -aise mf ▪**Scotland** n l'Écosse f ▪**Scotsman** (pl -men) n Écossais m ▪**Scotswoman** (pl -women) n Écossaise f ▪**Scottish** adj écossais

Scotch [skɒtʃ] n (whisky) scotch m

scotch¹ [skɒtʃ] adj Am **S. tape®** Scotch® m

scotch² [skɒtʃ] vt (rumour) étouffer

scot-free ['skɒt'fri:] adv sans être puni

scoundrel ['skaʊndrəl] n crapule f

scour ['skaʊə(r)] vt (pan) récurer; Fig (streets, house) ratisser (**for** à la recherche de) ▪**scourer** n tampon m à récurer

scourge [skɜ:dʒ] n fléau m

scout [skaʊt] **1** n (soldier) éclaireur m; **(boy) s.** scout m, éclaireur; Am **(girl) s.** éclaireuse f **2** vi to s. round for sth chercher qch; **to s. for talent** dénicher les talents

scowl [skaʊl] vi lancer des regards noirs (**at** à)

scrabble ['skræbəl] vi to s. around for sth chercher qch à tâtons

scraggy ['skrægɪ] (-ier, -iest) adj (bony) maigre

scram [skræm] (pt & pp -mm-) vi Fam se tirer

scramble ['skræmbəl] **1** n (rush) ruée f (**for** vers); (struggle) bousculade f (**for** pour) **2** vt (signal) brouiller; **scrambled eggs** œufs mpl brouillés **3** vi to s. for sth se ruer vers qch; **to s. up a hill** gravir une colline en s'aidant des mains

scrap¹ [skræp] **1** n (**a**) (piece) bout m (**of** de); (of information) bribe f; **scraps** (food) restes mpl; **not a s. of** (truth, good sense) pas une once de; **s. paper** papier m brouillon (**b**) **s. (metal)** ferraille f; **to sell sth for s.** vendre qch à la ferraille; **s. heap** tas m de ferraille; **s. dealer, s. merchant** ferrailleur m; **s. yard** casse f **2** (pt & pp -pp-) vt (get rid of) se débarrasser de; (car) envoyer à la casse; Fig (plan, idea) abandonner

scrap² [skræp] n Fam (fight) bagarre f; **to get into a s. with sb** en venir aux mains avec qn

scrapbook ['skræpbʊk] n album m (de découpages)

scrape [skreɪp] **1** n (on skin) éraflure f; (sound) raclement m; Fam **to get into a s.** se mettre dans le pétrin **2** vt gratter; (skin) érafler; **to s. a living** arriver tout juste à vivre **3** vi to s. against sth frotter contre qch ▪**scraper** n racloir m ▪**scraping** n (of butter) mince couche f

▸ **scrape along** vi (financially) se débrouiller

▸ **scrape away, scrape off** vt sep racler

▸ **scrape through** vt insep & vi to s. through (an exam) passer de justesse (à un examen)

▸ **scrape together** vt sep (money, people) parvenir à rassembler

scratch [skrætʃ] **1** n (mark, injury) éraflure f; (on glass, wood) rayure f; Fam **to start from s.** repartir de zéro; **it isn't up to s.** ce n'est pas au niveau; **he isn't up to s.** il n'est pas à la hauteur **2** vt (to relieve itching) gratter; (by accident) érafler; (glass) rayer; (with claw) griffer; (write, draw) griffonner (**on** sur) **3** vi (of person) se gratter; (of pen, clothes) gratter ▪**scratch-card** n (lottery card) carte f à gratter

scrawl [skrɔ:l] **1** n gribouillis m **2** vt gribouiller

scrawny ['skrɔ:nɪ] (-ier, -iest) adj maigrichon, -onne

scream [skri:m] **1** n hurlement m **2** vt hurler **3** vi hurler; **to s. at sb** crier après qn; **to s. with pain** hurler de douleur

screech [skri:tʃ] **1** n cri m strident **2** vti hurler

screen [skri:n] **1** n (of TV set, computer) écran m; (folding) s. paravent m; Comptr **on s.** à l'écran;

Comptr **s. saver** économiseur m d'écran; *Cin* **s. test** bout m d'essai **2** *vt (hide)* cacher (**from** à qn); *(protect)* protéger (**from** de); *(film)* projeter; *(visitors, calls)* filtrer; *(for disease)* faire subir un test de dépistage à; **to s. off** *(hide)* cacher ▪ **screening** *n (of film)* projection f; *(selection)* tri m; *(for disease)* dépistage m ▪ **screenplay** *n (of film)* scénario m

screw [skru:] **1** *n* vis f; *Fam* **to have a s. loose** avoir une case de moins **2** *vt* visser (**to** à); **to s. sth down** *or* **on** visser qch; **to s. sth off** dévisser qch; **to s. sth up** *(paper)* chiffonner qch; *very Fam (spoil)* foutre en l'air; **to s. up one's eyes** plisser les yeux; **to s. one's face up** faire la grimace ▪ **screwball** *n & adj Am Fam* cinglé, -ée *(mf)* ▪ **screwdriver** *n* tournevis m

scribble ['skrɪbəl] **1** *n* griffonnage m **2** *vti* griffonner

scribe [skraɪb] *n* scribe m

script [skrɪpt] *n* **(a)** *(of film)* script m; *(of play)* texte m; *(in exam)* copie f **(b)** *(handwriting)* script m ▪ **scriptwriter** *n (for films)* scénariste mf; *(for TV or radio)* dialoguiste mf

Scripture(s) ['skrɪptʃə(z)] *n(pl) Rel* les saintes Écritures fpl

scroll [skrəʊl] **1** *n* rouleau m; *(book)* manuscrit m **2** *vi Comptr* défiler; **to s. down/up** défiler vers le bas/haut

scrooge [skru:dʒ] *n* avare m

scrounge [skraʊndʒ] **1** *vt (meal)* se faire payer (**off** *or* **from sb** par qn); *(steal)* taper (**off** *or* **from sb** à qn); **to s. money off** *or* **from sb** taper qn **2** *vi* vivre en parasite; *Pej* **to s. around for sth** essayer de mettre la main sur qch ▪ **scrounger** *n Fam* parasite m

scrub [skrʌb] **1** *n* **(a)** **to give sth a s.** bien frotter qch; *Am* **s. brush** brosse f dure **(b)** *(land)* broussailles fpl **2** *(pt & pp* **-bb-)** *vt (surface)* frotter; *(pan)* récurer; *Fig (cancel)* annuler; **to s. sth off** *(remove)* enlever qch (à la brosse ou en frottant); *Fig* **to s. sth out** *(erase)* effacer qch ▪ **scrubbing brush** *n Br* brosse f dure

scruff [skrʌf] *n Fam (person)* individu m peu soigné; **by the s. of the neck** par la peau du cou ▪ **scruffy** **(-ier, -iest)** *adj (person)* peu soigné

scrum [skrʌm] *n Rugby* mêlée f

scrumptious ['skrʌmpʃəs] *adj Fam* fameux, -euse

scruple ['skru:pəl] *n* scrupule m ▪ **scrupulous** [-pjʊləs] *adj* scrupuleux, -euse ▪ **scrupulously** [-pjʊləslɪ] *adv* scrupuleusement

scrutinize ['skru:tɪnaɪz] *vt (document)* éplucher; *(votes)* vérifier ▪ **scrutiny** *n* examen m minutieux; **to come under s.** être examiné

scuba ['sku:bə] *n* **s. diver** plongeur, -euse mf; **s. diving** la plongée sous-marine

scuff [skʌf] *vt* **to s. (up)** *(shoe)* érafler

scuffle ['skʌfəl] *n* bagarre f

scullery ['skʌlərɪ] *n Br* arrière-cuisine f

sculpt [skʌlpt] *vti* sculpter ▪ **sculptor** *n* sculpteur, -trice mf ▪ **sculpture 1** *n (art, object)* sculpture f **2** *vti* sculpter

scum [skʌm] *n* **(a)** *(of dirt)* crasse f; *(froth)* écume f **(b)** *Fam Pej (people)* racaille f; *(person)* ordure f; **the s. of the earth** le rebut de la société

scupper ['skʌpə(r)] *vt Br (ship, project)* couler

scurrilous ['skʌrɪləs] *adj* calomnieux, -ieuse

scurry ['skʌrɪ] *vi (rush)* courir; **to s. off** se sauver

scurvy ['skɜ:vɪ] *n Med* scorbut m

scuttle ['skʌtəl] **1** *vt (ship)* saborder **2** *vi* **to s. off** filer

scuzzy ['skʌzɪ] **(-ier, -iest)** *adj Am Fam (dirty)* cradingue, cracra *inv*

scythe [saɪð] *n* faux f

sea [si:] **1** *n* mer f; **(out) at s.** en mer; **by s.** par mer; **by** *or* **beside the s.** au bord de la mer; *Fig* **to be all at s.** nager complètement **2** *adj (level, breeze)* de la mer; *(water, fish, salt)* de mer; *(air)* marin; *(battle)* naval *(mpl* -als); *(route)* maritime; **s. bed, s. floor** fond m de la mer; **s. change** changement m radical; **s. horse** hippocampe m; **s. lion** otarie f; **s. urchin** oursin m; **s. voyage** voyage m en mer ▪ **seaboard** *n* littoral m ▪ **seafarer** *n* marin m ▪ **seafood** *n* fruits mpl de mer ▪ **seafront** *n Br* front m de mer ▪ **seagull** *n* mouette f ▪ **seaman** *(pl* **-men)** *n* marin m ▪ **seaport** *n* port m maritime ▪ **seashell** *n* coquillage m ▪ **seashore** *n* rivage m ▪ **seasick** *adj* **to be s.** avoir le mal de mer ▪ **seasickness** *n* mal m de mer ▪ **seaside** *n Br* bord m de la mer; **s. resort** station f balnéaire; **s. town** ville f au bord de la mer ▪ **seaway** *n* route f maritime ▪ **seaweed** *n* algues fpl ▪ **seaworthy** *adj* en état de naviguer

seal¹ [si:l] *n (animal)* phoque m

seal² [si:l] **1** *n (stamp)* sceau m; *(device for sealing)* joint m d'étanchéité; *(on medicine bottle, food container)* = fermeture garantissant la fraîcheur d'un produit; **to give one's s. of approval to sth** donner son approbation à qch **2** *vt (document, container)* sceller; *(stick down)* cacheter; *(make airtight)* fermer hermétiquement; **to s. sb's fate** décider du sort de qn; **to s. off an area** boucler un quartier

seam [si:m] *n (in cloth)* couture f; *(of coal, quartz)* veine f

seamy ['si:mɪ] **(-ier, -iest)** *adj* **the s. side** le côté sordide (**of** de)

séance ['seɪɒns] *n* séance f de spiritisme

search [sɜ:tʃ] **1** *n* recherches fpl (**for** de); *(of place)* fouille f; **in s. of** à la recherche de; *Comptr* **to do a s. for sth** rechercher qch; *Comptr* **s. engine** moteur m de recherche; **s. party** équipe f de secours; *Law* **s. warrant**

mandat *m* de perquisition **2** *vt (person, place)* fouiller (**for** pour trouver); **to s. (through) one's papers for sth** chercher qch dans ses papiers; *Comptr* **to s. a file** rechercher dans un fichier; *Comptr* **to s. a file for sth** rechercher qch dans un fichier **3** *vi* chercher; **to s. for sth** chercher qch; *Comptr* **s. and replace** rechercher et remplacer ▪ **searching** *adj (look)* pénétrant; *(examination)* minutieux, -ieuse ▪ **searchlight** *n* projecteur *m*

season¹ ['si:zən] *n* saison *f*; *(of films)* cycle *m*; **in the peak s., in (the) high s.** en haute saison; **in the low** *or* **off s.** en basse saison; **'season's greetings'** *(on Christmas card)* 'meilleurs vœux de fin d'année'; **s. ticket** abonnement *m*

season² ['si:zən] *vt Culin (food)* assaisonner; *(with spice)* épicer ▪ **seasoning** *n Culin* assaisonnement *m*

seasonable ['si:zənəbəl] *adj (weather)* de saison

seasonal ['si:zənəl] *adj (work, change)* saisonnier, -ière

seasoned ['si:zənd] *adj* (**a**) **a highly s. dish** un plat très relevé (**b**) *(person)* expérimenté; *(soldier)* aguerri

seat [si:t] **1** *n* siège *m*; *(of trousers)* fond *m*; **to take** *or* **have a s.** s'asseoir; *Fig* **to be in the hot s.** être sur la sellette; **s. belt** ceinture *f* de sécurité **2** *vt (at table)* placer; *(on one's lap)* asseoir; **the bus seats 50** il y a 50 places assises dans ce bus; **be seated!** asseyez-vous! ▪ **seated** *adj (sitting)* assis ▪ **seating** *n (seats)* places *fpl* assises; *(positioning)* placement *m*; **s. capacity** nombre *m* de places assises; **s. plan** plan *m* de table

-seater ['si:tə(r)] *suff* **two-seater (car)** voiture *f* à deux places

secateurs [sekə'tɜ:z] *npl Br* sécateur *m*

secession [sɪ'seʃən] *n* sécession *f* ▪ **secede** [-'si:d] *vi* faire sécession *f* (**from** de)

secluded [sɪ'klu:dɪd] *adj (remote)* isolé ▪ **seclusion** *n* solitude *f*

second¹ ['sekənd] **1** *adj* deuxième, second; **every s. week** une semaine sur deux; *Aut* **in s. (gear)** en seconde; **s. to none** sans égal; **to be s. in command** commander en second **2** *adv (say)* deuxièmement; **to come s.** *(in competition)* se classer deuxième; **the s. biggest** le deuxième en ordre de grandeur; **my s. best (choice)** mon deuxième choix **3** *n (in series)* deuxième *mf*, second, -onde *mf*; *(in month)* deux *m*; **Louis the S.** Louis Deux; **seconds** *(goods)* articles *mpl* défectueux; **anyone for seconds?** *(at meal)* est-ce que quelqu'un veut du rab? **4** *vt (motion, proposal)* appuyer ▪ **'second-'class** *adj (ticket on train)* de seconde (classe); *(mail)* non urgent; *(product)* de qualité inférieure ▪ **secondly** *adv* deuxièmement ▪ **'second-'rate** *adj* médiocre

second² ['sekənd] *n (part of minute)* seconde *f*; **s. hand** *(of clock, watch)* trotteuse *f*

second³ [sɪ'kɒnd] *vt Br (employee)* détacher (**to** à) ▪ **secondment** *n Br* détachement *m*; **on s.** en détachement (**to** à)

secondary ['sekəndərɪ] *adj* secondaire; *Br* **s. school** établissement *m* secondaire

second-hand ['sekənd'hænd] **1** *adj* & *adv (not new)* d'occasion **2** *adj (report, news)* de seconde main

secrecy ['si:krəsɪ] *n (discretion, silence)* secret *m*; **in s.** en secret; **to swear sb to s.** faire jurer le silence à qn

secret ['si:krɪt] **1** *adj* secret, -ète; **s. agent** agent *m* secret; **s. service** services *mpl* secrets **2** *n* secret *m*; **in s.** en secret; **it's no s.** tout le monde le sait ▪ **secretive** *adj (person)* secret, -ète; **to be s. about sth** faire des cachotteries à propos de qch ▪ **secretly** *adv* secrètement

secretary [*Br* 'sekrətərɪ, *Am* -erɪ] *(pl* **-ies)** *n* secrétaire *mf*; *Br* **Foreign S.,** *Am* **S. of State** ≃ ministre *m* des Affaires étrangères ▪ **secretarial** [-'teərɪəl] *adj (work)* administratif, -ive; *(job, course)* de secrétariat ▪ **secretariat** [-'teərɪət] *n* secrétariat *m*

secrete [sɪ'kri:t] *vt (discharge)* sécréter ▪ **secretion** *n* sécrétion *f*

sect [sekt] *n* secte *f* ▪ **sectarian** [-'teərɪən] *adj* & *n* sectaire *(mf)*

section ['sekʃən] **1** *n* partie *f*; *(of road)* tronçon *m*; *(of machine)* élément *m*; *(of organization)* département *m*; *(of soldiers)* section *f*; **the sports s.** *(of newspaper)* la rubrique sportive **2** *vt* sectionner

sector ['sektə(r)] *n* secteur *m*

secular ['sekjʊlə(r)] *adj (teaching)* laïque; *(music, art)* profane

secure [sɪ'kjʊə(r)] **1** *adj (investment, place)* en sécurité; *(investment, place)* sûr; *(foothold)* solide; *(door, window)* bien fermé; *(nomination)* assuré; **I feel s. knowing that…** je suis tranquille car je sais que… **2** *vt (fasten)* attacher; *(window, door)* bien fermer; *(position, future)* assurer; *(support, promise)* procurer; **to s. sth against sth** protéger qch de qch; **to s. sth (for oneself)** se procurer qch ▪ **securely** *adv (firmly)* solidement; *(safely)* en sûreté

security [sɪ'kjʊərətɪ] *(pl* **-ies)** *n* sécurité *f*; *Fin (for loan, bail)* garantie *f*; **job s.** sécurité de l'emploi; **to tighten s.** renforcer les mesures de sécurité; **to be a s. risk** être un danger pour la sécurité; **S. Council** Conseil *m* de sécurité; **s. guard** garde *m*; **securities** *(stocks, bonds)* titres *mpl*

sedan [sɪ'dæn] *n Am (saloon)* berline *f*

sedate [sɪ'deɪt] **1** *adj* calme **2** *vt* mettre sous calmants ▪ **sedation** *n* **under s.** sous calmants ▪ **sedative** *n* calmant *m*

sedentary ['sedəntərɪ] *adj* sédentaire

sediment ['sedɪmənt] n sédiment m

sedition [sɪ'dɪʃən] n sédition f ■**seditious** adj séditieux, -ieuse

seduce [sɪ'djuːs] vt séduire ■**seducer** n séducteur, -trice mf ■**seduction** [-'dʌkʃən] n séduction f ■**seductive** [-'dʌktɪv] adj (person, offer) séduisant

see[1] [siː] (pt saw, pp seen) vti voir; **we'll s. on verra**; **I s. what you mean** je vois ce que tu veux dire; **I can s. a hill** je vois une colline; **I don't s. the point** je ne vois pas l'intérêt; **I'll go and s.** je vais voir; **I saw him run(ning)** je l'ai vu courir; **to s. reason** entendre raison; **to s. the joke** comprendre la plaisanterie; **s. you (later)!** à tout à l'heure!; **s. you (soon)!** à bientôt!; **to s. that...** (make sure that) faire en sorte que... (+ subjunctive); (check) s'assurer que... (+ indicative); **to s. sb to the door** accompagner qn jusqu'à la porte
▸ **see about** vt insep (deal with) s'occuper de; (consider) songer à
▸ **see in** vt sep **to s. in the New Year** fêter le Nouvel An
▸ **see off** vt sep (say goodbye to) dire au revoir à
▸ **see out** vt sep accompagner jusqu'à la porte
▸ **see through** vt sep (deal with) mener à bien 2 vt insep **to s. through sb** percer qn à jour
▸ **see to** vt insep (deal with) s'occuper de; (mend) réparer; **to s. to it that...** (make sure that) faire en sorte que... (+ subjunctive); (check) s'assurer que... (+ indicative)

see[2] [siː] n Rel évêché m

seed [siːd] n graine f; (of fruit) pépin m; Fig (source) germe m; Tennis tête f de série; **to go to s.** (of plant) monter en graine ■**seeded** adj Tennis **s. players** têtes fpl de série ■**seedling** n plant m

seedy ['siːdɪ] (-ier, -iest) adj miteux, -euse

seeing ['siːɪŋ] conj **s. (that)** vu que

seek [siːk] (pt & pp sought) vt chercher (**to do** à faire); (ask for) demander (**from** à); **to s. (after)** rechercher; **to s. sb out** dénicher qn

seem [siːm] vi sembler (**to do** faire); **it seems that...** (impression) il semble que... (+ subjunctive); **it seems to me that...** il me semble que... (+ indicative); **we s. to know each other** il me semble qu'on se connaît; **I can't s. to do it** je n'arrive pas à le faire

seeming ['siːmɪŋ] adj apparent ■**seemingly** adv apparemment

seemly ['siːmlɪ] adj Formal bienséant

seen [siːn] pp of **see**[1]

seep [siːp] vi suinter; **to s. into sth** s'infiltrer dans qch ■**seepage** [-ɪdʒ] n (oozing) suintement m; (infiltration) infiltration f (**into** dans)

seesaw ['siːsɔː] n balançoire f à bascule

seethe [siːð] vi **to s. with anger** bouillir de colère; **to s. with people** (of street) grouiller de monde

see-through ['siːθruː] adj transparent

segment ['segmənt] n segment m; (of orange) quartier m

segregate ['segrɪgeɪt] vt séparer (**from** de) ■**segregation** n ségrégation f

Seine [seɪn] n the S. la Seine

seize [siːz] **1** vt saisir; (power, land) s'emparer de **2** vi **to s. (up)on** (offer) sauter sur; **to s. up** (of engine) se bloquer

seizure ['siːʒə(r)] n Law (of goods, property) saisie f; Med crise f; **s. of power** prise f de pouvoir

seldom ['seldəm] adv rarement

select [sɪ'lekt] **1** vt sélectionner **2** adj (exclusive) sélect ■**selection** n sélection f; **a wide s.** un grand choix ■**selective** adj sélectif, -ive

self [self] (pl selves [selvz]) n the s. le moi; Fam **he's back to his old s.** il est redevenu comme avant ■**self-addressed 'envelope** n Am enveloppe f timbrée (libellée à ses noms et adresse) ■**self-as'surance** n assurance f ■**self-as'sured** adj sûr de soi ■**self-catering** n Br (holiday) en appartement meublé; (accommodation) meublé ■**self-centred** (Am **-centered**) adj égocentrique ■**self-cleaning** adj (oven) autonettoyant ■**self-con'fessed** (liar) de son propre aveu ■**self-'confidence** n confiance f en soi ■**self-'confident** adj sûr de soi ■**self-'conscious** adj gêné ■**self-con'tained** adj (flat) indépendant ■**self-con'trol** n maîtrise f de soi ■**self-de'feating** adj qui va à l'encontre du but recherché ■**self-de'fence** (Am **-defense**) n Law légitime défense f; **in s.** en état de légitime défense ■**self-de'nial** n abnégation f ■**self-determi'nation** n auto-détermination f ■**self-'discipline** n autodiscipline f ■**self-em'ployed** adj indépendant ■**self-es'teem** n confiance f en soi ■**self-'evident** adj évident ■**self-ex'planatory** adj qui se passe d'explications ■**self-'governing** adj autonome ■**self-im'portant** adj suffisant ■**self-in'dulgent** adj complaisant ■**self-'interest** n intérêt m personnel ■**self-o'pinionated** adj entêté ■**self-'pity** n **to be full of s.** s'apitoyer sur son propre sort ■**self-'portrait** n autoportrait m ■**self-pos'sessed** adj qui a une grande maîtrise de soi ■**self-'raising flour** (Am **self-'rising flour**) n = farine contenant de la levure chimique ■**self-re'liant** adj indépendant ■**self-re'spect** n amour-propre m ■**self-re'specting** adj qui se respecte ■**self-'righteous** adj suffisant ■**self-'sacrifice** n abnégation f ■**self-'satisfied** adj content de soi ■**self-'service** n & adj libre-service (m inv) ■**self-'starter** n (person) personne f très motivée ■**self-'styled** adj soi-disant inv ■**self-suf'ficient**

adj indépendant ▪**'self-sup'porting** *adj*
(business, person) financièrement indépendant
▪**'self-'tan** *n (cream)* autobronzant *m* ▪**'self-
'taught** *adj* autodidacte
selfish ['selfɪʃ] *adj* égoïste; *(motive)* intéressé
▪**selfishness** *n* égoïsme *m* ▪**selfless** *adj*
désintéressé
sell [sel] **1** *(pt & pp sold) vt* vendre; *Fig (idea)*
faire accepter; **to s. sb sth, to s. sth to sb**
vendre qch à qn; **she sold it to me for £20**
elle me l'a vendu 20 livres **2** *vi (of product)* se
vendre; *(of person)* vendre ▪**sell-by date** *n*
date *f* limite de vente ▪**seller** *n* vendeur, -euse
mf ▪**selling price** *n* prix *m* de vente ▪**sellout** *n*
(**a**) **it was a s.** *(of play, film)* tous les billets ont
été vendus (**b**) *(betrayal)* trahison *f*
▸ **sell back** *vt sep* revendre
▸ **sell off** *vt sep* liquider
▸ **sell out** *vt insep* **to have** or **be sold out of sth**
n'avoir plus de qch; **to be sold out** *(of book, item)*
être épuisé; *(of show, concert)* afficher complet
▸ **sell up** *vi (sell home, business)* tout vendre
Sellotape® ['seləteɪp] *n Br* Scotch® *m*
semantic [sɪ'mæntɪk] *adj* sémantique
▪**semantics** *n* sémantique *f*
semaphore ['seməfɔː(r)] *n* signaux *mpl* à bras
semblance ['sembləns] *n* semblant *m*
semen ['siːmən] *n* sperme *m*
semester [sɪ'mestə(r)] *n* semestre *m*
semi ['semɪ] *n Br Fam (house)* maison *f* jumelée
semi- ['semɪ] *pref* semi-, demi- ▪**semi-auto-
'matic** *adj* semi-automatique ▪**'semibreve**
[-briːv] *n Br (musical note)* ronde *f* ▪**'semicircle**
n demi-cercle *m* ▪**'semi'circular** *adj* semi-
circulaire ▪**semi'colon** *n* point-virgule *m* ▪**'semi-
'conscious** *adj* à demi conscient ▪**'semi-
de'tached** *adj Br* **s. house** maison *f* jumelée
▪**'semi'final** *n* demi-finale *f* ▪**'semi-'skilled**
adj **s. worker** ouvrier *m* spécialisé ▪**'semi-
'skimmed** *adj (milk)* demi-écrémé ▪**'semi
(-'trailer)** *n Am (truck)* semi-remorque *f*
seminar ['semɪnɑː(r)] *n* séminaire *m*
semolina [semə'liːnə] *n* semoule *f*
senate ['senɪt] *n Am Pol* **the S.** le Sénat
▪**senator** [-nətə(r)] *n Am Pol* sénateur *m*
send [send] *(pt & pp* **sent)** *vt* envoyer (**to** à); **to s.
sth to sb, to s. sb sth** envoyer qch à qn; **to s. sb
home** renvoyer qn chez soi; *Fam* **to s. sb
packing** envoyer promener qn ▪**sender** *n*
expéditeur, -trice *mf* ▪**send-off** *n Fam* **to give
sb a good s.** faire des adieux en règle à qn
▪**send-up** *n Br Fam* parodie *f*
▸ **send away 1** *vt sep (person)* renvoyer **2** *vi* **to
s. away for sth** se faire envoyer qch
▸ **send back** *vt sep* renvoyer
▸ **send for** *vt insep* envoyer chercher; *(doctor)*
faire venir
▸ **send in** *vt sep (form, invoice, troops)* envoyer;
(person) faire entrer

▸ **send off 1** *vt sep (letter)* envoyer (**to** à);
(player) expulser **2** *vi* **to s. off for sth** se faire
envoyer qch
▸ **send on** *vt sep (letter)* faire suivre
▸ **send out 1** *vt sep* envoyer **2** *vi* **to s. out for
sth** envoyer chercher qch
▸ **send up** *vt sep Br Fam (parody)* se moquer de
senile ['siːnaɪl] *adj* sénile ▪**senility** [sɪ'nɪlɪtɪ]
n sénilité *f*
senior ['siːnɪə(r)] **1** *adj (in age)* aîné; *(in
position, rank)* supérieur; **to be sb's s., to be s.
to sb** être l'aîné de qn; *(in rank, status)* être le
supérieur de qn; **Brown s.** Brown père; **s.
citizen** personne *f* âgée; **s. partner** associé *m*
principal; *Am* **s. year** *(in school, college)*
dernière année *f* **2** *n* aîné, -ée *mf*; *Am (in last
year of school or college)* étudiant, -iante *mf* de
dernière année; *Sport* senior *mf* ▪**seniority**
[-nɪ'ɒrɪtɪ] *n (in service)* ancienneté *f*; *(in rank)*
supériorité *f*
sensation [sen'seɪʃən] *n* sensation *f* ▪**sensational** *adj* sensationnel, -elle
sense [sens] **1** *n (faculty, awareness, meaning)*
sens *m*; **s. of smell** l'odorat *m*; **s. of hearing**
l'ouïe *f*; **a s. of shame** un sentiment de honte;
a s. of warmth/pleasure une sensation de
chaleur/plaisir; **s. of direction** sens de
l'orientation; **a s. of time** la notion de l'heure;
to have a s. of humour avoir le sens de
l'humour; **to have (good) s.** avoir du bon
sens; **to have the s. to do sth** avoir
l'intelligence de faire qch; **to bring sb to his
senses** ramener qn à la raison; **to make s.** être
logique; **to make s. of sth** comprendre qch **2** *vt*
sentir (**that** que); *(have a foreboding of)*
pressentir
senseless ['sensləs] *adj (pointless)* absurde;
(unconscious) sans connaissance
sensibility [sensɪ'bɪlɪtɪ] *n* sensibilité *f*;
sensibilities *(touchiness)* susceptibilité *f*
sensible ['sensəbəl] *adj (wise)* sensé; *(clothes,
shoes)* pratique

> Note that the French word **sensible** is a false
> friend and is almost never a translation for
> the English word **sensible**. It means sensi-
> tive.

sensitive ['sensɪtɪv] *adj (person)* sensible (**to**
à); *(skin, question)* délicat; *(information)*
confidentiel, -ielle ▪**sensi'tivity** *n* sensibilité
f; *(touchiness)* susceptibilité *f*
sensor ['sensə(r)] *n* détecteur *m*
sensory ['sensərɪ] *adj* sensoriel, -ielle
sensual ['senʃʊəl] *adj* sensuel, -uelle
▪**sensuality** [-ʃʊ'ælɪtɪ] *n* sensualité *f*
▪**sensuous** *adj* sensuel, -uelle
sent [sent] *pt & pp of* **send**
sentence ['sentəns] **1** *n* (**a**) *(words)* phrase *f* (**b**)
(in prison) peine *f*; **to pass s.** prononcer la

sentence; **to serve a s.** purger une peine **2** *vt* *(criminal)* condamner; **to s. sb to three years (in prison)/to death** condamner qn à trois ans de prison/à mort

sentiment ['sentɪmənt] *n* sentiment *m*
∎ **sentimental** [-'mentəl] *adj* sentimental
∎ **sentimentality** [-men'tælɪtɪ] *n* sentimentalité *f*

sentry ['sentrɪ] *(pl* **-ies)** *n* sentinelle *f*; **to be on s. duty** être de garde; **s. box** guérite *f*

separate ['sepəreɪt] **1** ['sepərət] *adj (distinct)* séparé; *(organization)* indépendant; *(occasion, entrance)* différent; *(room)* à part; **they went their s. ways** ils sont partis chacun de leur côté **2** *vt* séparer **(from** de) **3** *vi* se séparer **(from** de) ∎ **separately** ['sepərətlɪ] *adv* séparément ∎ **sepa'ration** *n* séparation *f*

separates ['sepərəts] *npl (clothes)* coordonnés *mpl*

separatist ['sepərətɪst] *n* séparatiste *mf*

September [sep'tembə(r)] *n* septembre *m*

septic ['septɪk] *adj* septique; *(wound)* infecté; **to go s.** s'infecter; **s. tank** fosse *f* septique

sequel ['siːkwəl] *n (book, film)* suite *f*

sequence ['siːkwəns] *n (order)* ordre *m*; *(series)* succession *f*; *(in film)* & Comptr, Mus & Cards séquence *f*; **in s.** dans l'ordre

sequin ['siːkwɪn] *n* paillette *f* ∎ **sequined** *adj* pailleté

Serb [sɜːb] **1** *adj* serbe **2** Serbe *mf* ∎ **Serbia** *n* la Serbie ∎ **Serbo-Croat 1** *adj* serbo-croate **2** *n (person)* Serbo-croate *mf*; *(language)* serbo-croate *m*

serenade [serə'neɪd] **1** *n* sérénade *f* **2** *vt* chanter la sérénade à

serene [sə'riːn] *adj* serein ∎ **serenity** [-'renɪtɪ] *n* sérénité *f*

sergeant ['saːdʒənt] *n* Mil sergent *m*; *(in police)* brigadier *m*

serial ['sɪərɪəl] *n (story, film)* feuilleton *m*; **s. killer** tueur *m* en série; **s. number** numéro *m* de série ∎ **serialize** *vt (in newspaper)* publier en feuilleton; *(on television or radio)* adapter en feuilleton

series ['sɪərɪːz] *n inv* série *f*

serious ['sɪərɪəs] *adj (person)* sérieux, -ieuse; *(illness, mistake)* grave; *(damage)* important; **to be s. about doing sth** envisager sérieusement de faire qch; *Fam* **s. money** un bon paquet d'argent ∎ **seriously** *adv* sérieusement; *(ill, damaged)* gravement; **to take sth/sb s.** prendre qn/qch au sérieux ∎ **seriousness** *n* sérieux *m*; *(of illness, situation)* gravité *f*; *(of damage)* importance *f*; **in all s.** sérieusement

sermon ['sɜːmən] *n* sermon *m*

serrated [sə'reɪtɪd] *adj* en dents de scie

serum ['sɪərəm] *n* sérum *m*

servant ['sɜːvənt] *n* domestique *mf*

serve [sɜːv] **1** *n Tennis* service *m* **2** *vt (country, cause, meal, customer)* servir; *(be useful to)* servir à; *(prison sentence)* purger; *(apprenticeship)* faire; **to s. a purpose** avoir une utilité; *Law* **to s. a summons on sb** remettre une assignation à qn; **it has served me well** ça m'a fait de l'usage; *Fam* **(it) serves you right!** ça t'apprendra!; **to s. up** *or* **out a meal** servir un repas **3** *vi* servir **(as** de); **to s. on** *(committee, jury)* être membre de ∎ **server** *n Tennis* serveur, -euse *mf*; Comptr serveur *m*; **network s.** serveur de réseau

service ['sɜːvɪs] **1** *n (with army, firm, in restaurant)* & Rel & Tennis service *m*; *(of machine)* entretien *m*; *(of car)* révision *f*; **to be at sb's s.** être au service de qn; **to be of s. to sb** être utile à qn; **the (armed) services** les forces *fpl* armées; **s. charge** service; *Br* **s. area** *(on motorway)* aire *f* de service; **s. station** station-service *f* **2** *vt (machine)* entretenir; *(car)* réviser

serviceable ['sɜːvɪsəbəl] *adj (usable)* en état de marche; *(durable)* résistant

serviceman ['sɜːvɪsmən] *(pl* **-men)** *n* militaire *m*

serviette [sɜːvɪ'et] *n Br* serviette *f* de table

servile ['sɜːvaɪl] *adj* servile

serving ['sɜːvɪŋ] *n (of food)* portion *f*; **s. dish** plat *m*

session ['seʃən] *n (meeting, period)* séance *f*; *(university term)* trimestre *m*; *(university year)* année *f* universitaire; **to be in s.** siéger; **the parliamentary s.** la session parlementaire

set [set] **1** *n (of keys, needles, tools)* jeu *m*; *(of stamps, numbers)* série *f*; *(of people)* groupe *m*; *(of facts, laws)* & Math ensemble *m*; *(of books)* collection *f*; *(of dishes)* service *m*; *(of tyres)* train *m*; *(kit)* trousse *f*; *(in theatre)* décor *m*; *(for film)* plateau *m*; *Tennis* set *m*; **s. of teeth** dentition *f*; **chess s.** jeu d'échecs; **construction s.** jeu de construction; **film s.** plateau de tournage; **radio s.** poste *m* de radio; **tea s.** service à thé; **television s., TV s.** téléviseur *m*

2 *adj (time, price)* fixe; *(lunch)* à prix fixe; *(school book)* au programme; *(ideas, purpose)* déterminé; **to be s. on doing sth** être résolu à faire qch; **to be s. on sth** avoir fixé son choix sur qch; **to be s. in one's ways** tenir à ses habitudes; **to be dead s. against sth** être formellement opposé à qch; **to be all s.** être prêt **(to do** pour faire); **to be s. back from the road** *(of house)* être en retrait de la route; **s. menu** menu *m*; **s. phrase** expression *f* figée

3 *(pt & pp* **set,** *pres p* **setting)** *vt (put)* mettre, poser; *(date, limit, task)* fixer; *(homework)* donner **(for sb** à qn); *(jewel)* sertir; *(watch)* régler; *(alarm clock)* mettre **(for** pour); *(bone fracture)* réduire; *(trap)* tendre **(for** à); **to s. a record** établir un record; **to s. a precedent**

créer un précédent; **to have one's hair s.** se faire faire une mise en plis; **to s. sb thinking** faire réfléchir qn; **to s. sb free** libérer qn; **to s. sth on fire** mettre le feu à qch

4 *vi (of sun)* se coucher; *(of jelly)* prendre; *(of bone)* se ressouder ▪ **set-top box** *n TV* décodeur *m* numérique

▸ **set about** *vt insep (begin)* se mettre à; **to s. about doing sth** se mettre à faire qch

▸ **set back** *vt sep (in time)* retarder; *Fam (cost)* coûter

▸ **set down** *vt sep (object)* poser

▸ **set in** *vi (of winter)* s'installer; *(of fog)* tomber

▸ **set off 1** *vt sep (bomb)* faire exploser; *(mechanism)* déclencher; *Fig (beauty, complexion)* rehausser; **to s. sb off crying** faire pleurer qn **2** *vi (leave)* partir

▸ **set out 1** *vt sep (display, explain)* exposer; *(arrange)* disposer **2** *vi (leave)* partir; **to s. out to do sth** avoir l'intention de faire qch

▸ **set up 1** *vt sep (tent, statue)* dresser; *(roadblock)* mettre en place; *(company)* créer; *(meeting)* organiser; *(inquiry)* ouvrir; **to s. sb up in business (as)** installer qn (comme) **2** *vi* **to s. up in business (as)** s'installer (comme)

▸ **set upon** *vt insep (attack)* attaquer

setback ['setbæk] *n* revers *m*

set-square ['setskweə(r)] *n Br* équerre *f* (à dessin)

settee [se'ti:] *n* canapé *m*

setter ['setə(r)] *n* setter *m*

setting ['setɪŋ] *n (surroundings)* cadre *m*; *(of sun)* coucher *m*; *(on machine)* réglage *m*; *Comptr* **settings** paramètres *mpl*

settle ['setəl] **1** *vt (put in place)* installer; *(decide, arrange, pay)* régler; *(date, venue)* fixer; *(nerves)* calmer; *(land)* coloniser; **to s. a matter out of court** régler une affaire à l'amiable; **that settles it!** c'est décidé! **2** *vi (of person, family)* s'installer; *(of dust)* se déposer; *(of bird)* se poser; **to s. into an armchair** s'installer confortablement dans un fauteuil; **to s. into one's job** s'habituer à son travail ▪ **settled** *adj (weather, period)* stable; *(life)* rangé

▸ **settle down** *vi (in chair, house)* s'installer; *(become quieter)* s'assagir; *(of situation)* se calmer; **to s. down in one's job** s'habituer à son travail; **to s. down with sb** mener une vie stable avec qn; **to s. down to work** se mettre au travail

▸ **settle for** *vt insep* se contenter de

▸ **settle in** *vi (in new home)* s'installer; *(in new school)* s'adapter

▸ **settle up** *vi (pay)* régler; **to s. up with sb** régler qn

settlement ['setəlmənt] *n (agreement)* accord *m*; *(payment)* règlement *m*; *(colony)* colonie *f*

settler ['setlə(r)] *n* colon *m*

set-to [set'tu:] *(pl* **-os***) n Br Fam (quarrel)* prise *f* de bec

setup ['setʌp] *n Fam (arrangement)* système *m*

seven ['sevən] *adj & n* sept *(m)* ▪ **seventh** *adj & n* septième *(mf)*

seventeen [sevən'ti:n] *adj & n* dix-sept *(m)* ▪ **seventeenth** *adj & n* dix-septième *(mf)*

seventy ['sevəntɪ] *adj & n* soixante-dix *(m)*; **s.-one** soixante et onze ▪ **seventieth** *adj & n* soixante-dixième *(mf)*

sever ['sevə(r)] *vt* couper; *Fig (relations)* rompre ▪ **severance** *n (of relations)* rupture *f*; **s. pay** indemnité *f* de licenciement

several ['sevərəl] *adj & pron* plusieurs **(of** d'entre)

severe [sə'vɪə(r)] *adj (person, punishment, tone)* sévère; *(winter, training)* rigoureux, -euse; *(illness, injury)* grave; *(blow, pain)* violent; *(cold, frost)* intense; *(weather)* très mauvais; **to have a s. cold** avoir un gros rhume ▪ **severely** *adv (criticize, punish)* sévèrement; *(damaged, wounded)* gravement; **to be s. handicapped** *or* **disabled** être gravement handicapé ▪ **severity** [-'verɪtɪ] *n* sévérité *f*; *(of winter)* rigueur *f*; *(of injury)* gravité *f*; *(of blow)* violence *f*

sew [səʊ] *(pt* **sewed***, pp* **sewn** *or* **sewed***) vt* coudre; **to s. a button on a shirt** coudre un bouton à une chemise; **to s. sth up** recoudre qch ▪ **sewing** *n* couture *f*; **s. machine** machine *f* à coudre

sewage ['su:ɪdʒ] *n* eaux *fpl* d'égout ▪ **sewer** ['su:ə(r)] *n* égout *m*

sewn [səʊn] *pp of* **sew**

sex [seks] **1** *n* sexe *m*; **to have s. with sb** coucher avec qn **2** *adj (education, life, act)* sexuel; *(urge)* **s. appeal** sex-appeal *m*; **s. maniac** obsédé *m* sexuel, obsédée *f* sexuelle; **s. symbol** sex-symbol *m* ▪ **sexism** *n* sexisme *m* ▪ **sexist** *adj & n* sexiste *(mf)* ▪ **sexy** *(-ier, -iest) adj Fam* sexy *inv*

sextet [seks'stet] *n* sextuor *m*

sexual ['sekʃʊəl] *adj* sexuel, -uelle; **s. assault** agression *f* sexuelle; **s. harassment** harcèlement *m* sexuel ▪ **sexuality** [-ʃʊ'ælɪtɪ] *n* sexualité *f* ▪ **sexually** *adv* sexuellement; **s. transmitted disease** *or* **infection** maladie *f* sexuellement transmissible

Seychelles [seɪ'ʃelz] *npl* **the S.** les Seychelles *fpl*

sh [ʃ] *exclam* chut!

shabby ['ʃæbɪ] *(-ier, -iest) adj* miteux, -euse; *(behaviour, treatment)* mesquin ▪ **shabbily** *adv (dressed)* pauvrement ▪ **shabbiness** *n* aspect *m* miteux; *Fig (meanness)* mesquinerie *f*

shack [ʃæk] **1** *n* cabane *f* **2** *vi Fam* **to s. up with sb** vivre à la colle avec qn

shackles ['ʃækəlz] *npl* chaînes *fpl*

shade [ʃeɪd] **1** *n* ombre *f*; *(of colour, meaning, opinion)* nuance *f*; **in the s.** à l'ombre; **a s. faster/taller** un rien plus vite/plus grand; *Fam* **shades** *(glasses)* lunettes *fpl* de soleil **2** *vt (of* *tree*) ombrager; (*protect*) abriter (**from** de) ▪ **shady** (**-ier, -iest**) *adj* (*place*) ombragé; *Fig* (*person, business*) louche

shadow ['ʃædəʊ] **1** *n* ombre *f*; **to cast a s.** projeter une ombre; *Fig* **to cast a s. over sth** jeter une ombre sur qch **2** *adj Br Pol* **s. cabinet** cabinet *m* fantôme; **the S. Education Secretary** = le porte-parole de l'opposition sur les questions de l'éducation **3** *vt* **to s. sb** (*follow*) filer qn ▪ **shadowy** (**-ier, -iest**) *adj* (*form*) vague

shaft [ʃɑːft] *n* (**a**) (*of tool*) manche *m*; **s. of light** rayon *m* de lumière (**b**) (*of mine*) puits *m*; (*of lift*) cage *f*

shaggy ['ʃægɪ] (**-ier, -iest**) *adj* (*hairy*) hirsute

shake¹ [ʃeɪk] **1** *n* secousse *f*; **to give sth a s.** secouer qch; **with a s. of his head** en secouant la tête; *Fam* **in two shakes** en un rien de temps **2** (*pt* **shook,** *pp* **shaken**) *vt* (*move up and down*) secouer; (*bottle, fist*) agiter; (*building*) faire trembler; *Fig* (*belief, resolution*) ébranler; **to s. one's head** faire non de la tête; **to s. hands with sb** serrer la main à qn; **we shook hands** nous nous sommes serré la main; **to s. off** (*dust*) secouer; *Fig* (*illness, pursuer*) se débarrasser de; **to s. up** (*reorganize*) réorganiser de fond en comble; **to s. sb up** secouer qn; **to s. sth out of sth** faire tomber qch de qch (en secouant) **3** *vi* (*of person, windows, voice*) trembler (**with** de) ▪ **shake-up** *n Fam* (*reorganization*) chambardement *m*

shake² [ʃeɪk] *n* (*milk shake*) milk-shake *m*

shaken ['ʃeɪkən] *pp of* **shake¹**

shaky [ʃeɪkɪ] (**-ier, -iest**) *adj* (*voice*) tremblant; (*table, chair*) branlant; (*handwriting*) tremblé; (*health*) précaire

shall [ʃæl, *unstressed* ʃəl]

> On trouve généralement **I/you/he**/*etc* shall sous leurs formes contractées **I'll/you'll/he'll**/ *etc.* La forme négative correspondante est **shan't**, que l'on écrira **shall not** dans des contextes formels.

v aux (**a**) (*expressing future tense*) **I s. come, I'll come** je viendrai; **we s. not come, we shan't come** nous ne viendrons pas (**b**) (*making suggestion*) **s. I leave?** veux-tu que je parte?; **let's go in, s. we?** entrons, tu veux bien? (**c**) *Formal* (*expressing order*) **he s. do it if I order it** il le fera si je l'ordonne

shallot [ʃəˈlɒt] *n Br* échalote *f*

shallow ['ʃæləʊ] (**-er, -est**) **1** *adj* (*water, river*) peu profond; *Fig & Pej* (*argument, person*) superficiel, -ielle **2** *npl* **the shallows** (*of river*) le bas-fond

sham [ʃæm] **1** *n* (*pretence*) comédie *f*; (*person*) imposteur *m*; **to be a s.** (*of jewel*) être faux (*f* fausse); **it's a s.!** (*election promises*) c'est du bidon! **2** *adj* (*false*) faux (*f* fausse); (*illness,*

emotion) feint **3** (*pt & pp* **-mm-**) *vt* feindre **4** *vi* faire semblant

shambles ['ʃæmbəlz] *n* pagaille *f*; **this place is a s.!** quelle pagaille!

shame [ʃeɪm] **1** *n* (*guilt, disgrace*) honte *f*; **it's a s.** c'est dommage (**to do** de faire); **it's a s. (that)…** c'est dommage que… (+ *subjunctive*); **s. on you!** tu devrais avoir honte!; **what a s.!** quel dommage!; **to put sb to s.** faire honte à qn **2** *vt* (*make ashamed*) faire honte à ▪ **'shame'faced** *adj* (*embarrassed*) honteux, -euse

shameful ['ʃeɪmfəl] *adj* honteux, -euse ▪ **shamefully** *adv* honteusement

shameless ['ʃeɪmləs] *adj* impudique; **to be s. about doing sth** n'avoir aucun scrupule à faire qch ▪ **shamelessly** *adv* sans la moindre honte

shammy ['ʃæmɪ] *n Fam* **s. (leather)** peau *f* de chamois

shampoo [ʃæmˈpuː] **1** *n* shampooing *m* **2** *vt* (*carpet*) shampouiner; **to s. sb's hair** faire un shampooing à qn

shandy ['ʃændɪ] *n Br* panaché *m*

shan't [ʃɑːnt] = **shall not**

shanty¹ ['ʃæntɪ] *n* (*hut*) baraque *f*; **s. town** bidonville *m*

shanty² ['ʃæntɪ] *n* **sea s.** chanson *f* de marins

shape [ʃeɪp] **1** *n* forme *f*; **what s. is it?** quelle forme cela a-t-il?; **in the s. of a pear/bell** en forme de poire/cloche; *Fig* **in any s. or form** quel qu'il soit (*f* quelle qu'elle soit); **to take s.** (*of plan*) prendre forme; **to be in good/bad s.** (*of person*) être en bonne/mauvaise forme; (*of business*) marcher bien/mal; **to keep in s.** garder la forme **2** *vt* (*clay*) modeler; (*wood*) façonner (**into** en); *Fig* (*events, future*) influencer **3** *vi* **to s. up** (*of person*) progresser; (*of teams, plans*) prendre forme ▪ **-shaped** *suff* **pearshaped** en forme de poire ▪ **shapeless** *adj* informe ▪ **shapely** (**-ier, -iest**) *adj* bien fait

share [ʃeə(r)] **1** *n* part *f* (**of** or **in** de); *Fin* (*in company*) action *f*; **to have one's (fair) s. of sth** avoir sa part de qch; **to do one's (fair) s.** mettre la main à la pâte **2** *vt* partager; (*characteristic*) avoir en commun; **to s. sth out** partager qch **3** *vi* partager; **to s. in sth** avoir sa part de qch ▪ **shareholder** *n Fin* actionnaire *mf*

shark [ʃɑːk] *n* (*fish, crook*) requin *m*

sharp [ʃɑːp] **1** (**-er, -est**) *adj* (*knife*) bien aiguisé; (*pencil*) bien taillé; (*razor*) qui coupe bien; (*point*) aigu (*f* aiguë); (*claws*) acéré; (*rise, fall*) brusque; (*focus*) net (*f* nette); (*contrast*) marqué; (*eyesight, sound*) perçant; (*taste*) acide; (*intelligent*) vif (*f* vive) **2** *adv* **to stop s.** s'arrêter net; **five o'clock s.** cinq heures pile; **to turn s. right/left** tourner tout de suite à droite/à gauche; *Fam* **look s.!** grouille-toi! **3** *Mus* dièse *m* ▪ **'sharp-'eyed** *adj* observateur,

-trice **■sharply** adj (rise, fall, speak) brusquement; (contrast) nettement **■sharpness** n (of blade) tranchant m; (of picture) netteté f

sharpen [ˈʃɑːpən] vt (pencil) tailler; (knife) aiguiser **■sharpener** n (for pencils) taille-crayon m; (for blades) aiguisoir m

sharpshooter [ˈʃɑːpʃuːtə(r)] n tireur m d'élite

shatter [ˈʃætə(r)] 1 vt (glass) faire voler en éclats; (career, health, hopes) briser 2 vi (of glass) voler en éclats **■shattered** adj Br Fam (exhausted) crevé **■shattering** adj (defeat) accablant; (news, experience) bouleversant

shave [ʃeɪv] 1 n to have a s. se raser; Fig that was a close s. c'était moins une 2 vt (person, head) raser; to s. one's legs se raser les jambes; to s. off one's beard se raser la barbe 3 vi se raser **■shaven** adj rasé (de près) **■shaver** n rasoir m électrique **■shaving** n (strip of wood) copeau m; **s. brush** blaireau m; **s. cream, s. foam** mousse f à raser

shawl [ʃɔːl] n châle m

she [ʃiː] 1 pron elle; **s.** wants elle veut; **she's a happy woman** c'est une femme heureuse; **s. and I** elle et moi 2 n Fam (female) femelle f; **s.-bear** ourse f; **it's a s.** (of baby) c'est une fille

sheaf [ʃiːf] (pl **sheaves** [ʃiːvz]) n (of corn) gerbe f; (of paper) liasse f

shear [ʃɪə(r)] 1 vt tondre 2 npl **shears** cisaille f

sheath [ʃiːθ] (pl **-s** [ʃiːðz]) n (for sword) fourreau m; (for electric cable) gaine f; (contraceptive) préservatif m

shed¹ [ʃed] n (in garden) abri m; (in factory) atelier m

shed² [ʃed] (pt & pp shed, pres p shedding) vt (leaves) perdre; (tears, blood) verser; to s. its skin (of snake) muer; Fig to s. light on sth éclairer qch

she'd [ʃiːd] = she had, she would

sheen [ʃiːn] n lustre m

sheep [ʃiːp] n inv mouton m **■sheepdog** n chien m de berger **■sheepskin** n peau f de mouton; **s. jacket** veste f en peau de mouton

sheepish [ˈʃiːpɪʃ] adj penaud **■sheepishly** adv d'un air penaud

sheer [ʃɪə(r)] adj (pure) pur; (stockings) très fin; (cliff) à pic; **by s. chance** tout à fait par hasard

sheet [ʃiːt] n (on bed) drap m; (of paper) feuille f; (of glass, ice) plaque f; **s. metal** tôle f

sheikh [ʃeɪk] n cheik m

shelf [ʃelf] (pl **shelves** [ʃelvz]) n étagère f; (in shop) rayon m; (on cliff) rebord m; **set of shelves** étagères fpl; Com **s. life** durée f de conservation avant vente

shell [ʃel] 1 n (a) (of egg, snail, nut) coquille f; (of tortoise, lobster) carapace f; (on beach) coquillage m; (of peas) cosse f; (of building) carcasse f (b) (explosive) obus m 2 vt (a) (peas) écosser; (nut, shrimp) décortiquer (b) (town) bombarder (c) Fam to s. out a lot of

money sortir pas mal d'argent **■shelling** n bombardement m **■shell suit** n Br survêtement m (en synthétique brillant)

she'll [ʃiːl] = she will, she shall

shellfish [ˈʃelfɪʃ] 1 n inv (crustacean) crustacé m; (mollusc) coquillage m 2 npl Culin (as food) fruits mpl de mer

shelter [ˈʃeltə(r)] 1 n (place, protection) abri m; to take s. se mettre à l'abri (from de); to seek s. chercher un abri 2 vt abriter (from de); (criminal) accueillir 3 vi s'abriter (from de) **■sheltered** adj (place) abrité; she's had a s. life elle a eu une enfance très protégée

shelve [ʃelv] vt (postpone) mettre au placard

shelving [ˈʃelvɪŋ] n rayonnages mpl

shepherd [ˈʃepəd] 1 n berger m; Br **s.'s pie** ≃ hachis m Parmentier 2 vt to s. sb in faire entrer qn; to s. sb around piloter qn **■shepherdess** n bergère f

sherbet [ˈʃɜːbət] n Br (powder) poudre f acidulée; Am (sorbet) sorbet m

sheriff [ˈʃerɪf] n Am shérif m

sherry [ˈʃerɪ] n sherry m, xérès m

Shetlands [ˈʃetləndz] npl the S. les Shetland fpl

shiatsu, shiatzu [ʃɪˈætsuː] n shiatsu m

shield [ʃiːld] 1 n (for protection) bouclier m; (police badge) badge m; **human s.** bouclier humain 2 vt protéger (from de)

shift [ʃɪft] 1 n (change) changement m (of or in de); (period of work) poste m; (workers) équipe f; **s. key** (on computer, typewriter) touche f des majuscules 2 vt (move) déplacer; (stain) enlever; (employee) muter (to à); to s. places changer de place; to s. the blame on to sb rejeter la responsabilité sur qn; Am to s. gear(s) (in vehicle) changer de vitesse 3 vi bouger; (of stain) partir **■shiftwork** n travail m posté

shiftless [ˈʃɪftləs] adj fainéant

shifty [ˈʃɪftɪ] (-ier, -iest) adj (person) louche; (look) fuyant

shilly-shally [ˈʃɪlɪˈʃælɪ] (pt & pt -ied) vi hésiter

shimmer [ˈʃɪmə(r)] 1 n (of silk) chatoiement m; (of water) miroitement m 2 vi (of silk) chatoyer; (of water) miroiter

shin [ʃɪn] n tibia m; **s. pad** (of hockey player) jambière f

shindig [ˈʃɪndɪg] n Fam nouba f

shine [ʃaɪn] 1 n brillant m; (on metal) éclat m 2 (pt & pp shone) vt (polish) faire briller; (light, torch) braquer 3 vi briller; to s. with joy (of face) rayonner de joie; (of eyes) briller de joie **■shining** adj brillant; a s. example of un parfait exemple de **■shiny** (-ier, -iest) adj brillant

shingle [ˈʃɪŋgəl] n (on beach) galets mpl; (on roof) bardeau m

shingles [ˈʃɪŋgəlz] n Med zona m

ship [ʃɪp] 1 n navire m 2 (pt & pp -pp-) vt (send)

expédier; *(transport)* transporter; *(take on board)* embarquer (**on to** sur) **▪shipbuilding** *n* construction *f* navale **▪shipmate** *n* camarade *m* de bord **▪shipment** *n* cargaison *f* **▪shipping** *n (traffic)* navigation *f; (ships)* navires *mpl;* **s. agent** agent *m* maritime; **s. line** compagnie *f* de navigation **▪shipshape** *adj & adv* en ordre **▪shipwreck** *n* naufrage *m* **▪shipwrecked** *adj* naufragé; **to be s.** faire naufrage **▪shipyard** *n* chantier *m* naval

shire ['ʃaɪə(r)] *n Br* comté *m;* **s. horse** shire *m*

shirk [ʃɜːk] **1** *vt (duty)* se dérober à; *(work)* éviter de faire **2** *vi* tirer au flanc **▪shirker** *n* tire-au-flanc *m inv*

shirt [ʃɜːt] *n* chemise *f; (of woman)* chemisier *m; (of sportsman)* maillot *m* **▪shirtsleeves** *npl* **in (one's) s.** en bras de chemise

shiver ['ʃɪvə(r)] **1** *n* frisson *m;* **to send shivers down sb's spine** donner le frisson à qn **2** *vi* frissonner (**with** de) **▪shivery** *adj* **to be s.** frissonner

shoal [ʃəʊl] *n (of fish)* banc *m*

shock [ʃɒk] **1** *n (impact, emotional blow)* choc *m; (of earthquake)* secousse *f;* **(electric) s.** décharge *f* (électrique); **to be in a s.** être en état de choc; **the news came as a s. to me** la nouvelle m'a stupéfié **2** *adj (wave, tactics, troops)* de choc; **s. absorber** amortisseur *m;* **s. therapy** électrochocs *mpl* **3** *vt (offend)* choquer; *(surprise)* stupéfier **▪shocking** *adj (outrageous)* choquant; *(very bad)* atroce **▪shockingly** *adv (extremely, badly)* atrocement **▪shockproof** *adj* antichoc *inv*

shod [ʃɒd] *pt & pp of* **shoe**

shoddy ['ʃɒdɪ] (**-ier, -iest**) *adj (goods)* de mauvaise qualité **▪shoddily** *adv (made, done)* mal

shoe [ʃuː] **1** *n* chaussure *f; (for horse)* fer *m* à cheval; **(brake) s.** *(in vehicle)* sabot *m* (de frein); *Fig* **I wouldn't like to be in your shoes** je n'aimerais pas être à ta place; **s. polish** cirage *m;* **s. repair shop** cordonnerie *f;* **s. shop** magasin *m* de chaussures **2** *(pt & pp* **shod)** *vt (horse)* ferrer **▪shoehorn** *n* chausse-pied *m* **▪shoelace** *n* lacet *m* **▪shoemaker** *n* fabricant *m* de chaussures; *(cobbler)* cordonnier *m* **▪shoestring** *n Fam* **on a s.** avec trois fois rien

shone [*Br* ʃɒn, *Am* ʃəʊn] *pt & pp of* **shine**

shoo [ʃuː] **1** *(pt & pp* **shooed)** *vt* **to s. (away)** chasser **2** *exclam* ouste!

shook [ʃʊk] *pt of* **shake¹**

shoot [ʃuːt] **1** *n (of plant)* pousse *f* **2** *(pt & pp* **shot)** *vt (bullet)* lancer; *(arrow)* lancer; *(film, scene)* tourner; **to s. sb** *(kill)* tuer qn par balle; *(wound)* blesser qn par balle; *(execute)* fusiller qn **3** *vi (with gun)* tirer (**at** sur); *Football* shooter **▪shooting** **1** *n (shots)* coups *mpl* de feu; *(incident)* fusillade *f; (of film, scene)*

tournage *m* **2** *adj* **s. star** étoile *f* filante **▪shoot-out** *n Fam* fusillade *f*

▶shoot away *vi (of vehicle, person)* partir à toute vitesse

▶shoot back *vi (return fire)* riposter

▶shoot down *vt sep (plane)* abattre

▶shoot off *vi (leave quickly)* filer

▶shoot out *vi (spurt out)* jaillir

▶shoot up *vi (of price)* monter en flèche; *(of plant, child)* pousser vite; *(spurt)* jaillir; *(of rocket)* s'élever; *Fam (inject drugs)* se shooter

shop [ʃɒp] **1** *n* magasin *m; (small)* boutique *f; (workshop)* atelier *m;* **at the baker's s.** à la boulangerie, chez le boulanger; *Br* **s. assistant** vendeur, -euse *mf; Br* **s. floor** *(workers)* ouvriers *mpl; Br* **s. front** devanture *f; Br* **s. steward** délégué, -ée *mf* syndical(e); **s. window** vitrine *f* **2** *(pt & pp* **-pp-)** *vt Br Fam* **to s. sb** balancer qn **3** *vi* faire ses courses (**at** chez); **to s. around** comparer les prix **▪shopkeeper** *n* commerçant, -ante *mf* **▪shoplifter** *n* voleur, -euse *mf* à l'étalage **▪shoplifting** *n* vol *m* à l'étalage **▪shopper** *n (customer)* client *m*, cliente *f; Br (bag)* sac *m* à provisions **▪shopping** **1** *n (goods)* achats *mpl;* **to go s.** faire des courses; **to do one's s.** faire ses courses **2** *adj (street, district)* commerçant; **s. bag/basket** sac *m*/panier *m* à provisions; **s. centre** centre *m* commercial; **s. list** liste *f* des commissions

shore [ʃɔː(r)] **1** *n (of sea)* rivage *m; (of lake)* bord *m;* **on s.** à terre **2** *vt* **to s. up** *(wall)* étayer; *Fig (company, economy)* consolider

shorn [ʃɔːn] *adj (head)* tondu; *Literary* **s. of** *(stripped of)* dénué de

short [ʃɔːt] **1** *(**-er, -est**) adj* court; *(person, distance)* petit; *(syllable)* bref *(f* brève); *(impatient, curt)* brusque; **to be s. of sth** être à court de qch; **we're s. of ten men** il nous manque dix hommes; **s. of a miracle, we won't...** à moins d'un miracle, nous ne...; **money/time is s.** l'argent/le temps manque; **in a s. time** *or* **while** dans un petit moment; **a s. time** *or* **while ago** il y a peu de temps; **I'll stay for a s. time** *or* **while** je resterai un petit moment; **Tony is s. for Anthony** Tony est le diminutif d'Anthony; **he's not far s. of forty** il n'est pas loin de la quarantaine; **in s.** bref; *Br* **s. list** liste *f* de candidats retenus; **s. story** nouvelle *f*

2 *adv* **to cut s.** *(hair)* couper court; *(visit)* abréger; *(person)* couper la parole à; **to stop s. of doing sth** se retenir tout juste de faire qch; **to be running s. of sth** n'avoir presque plus de qch; **to fall s. of sth** ne pas atteindre qch

3 *n Fam El* court-circuit *m* **▪shortbread** *n* sablé *m* **▪'short-'change** *vt (buyer)* ne pas rendre assez de monnaie à **▪'short-'circuit 1** *n* court-circuit *m* **2** *vt* court-circuiter **3** *vi* se mettre en court-circuit ■**shortcoming** n défaut m ■**short cut** n raccourci m ■**shortfall** n manque m ■**shorthand** n sténo f; **in s.** en sténo; **s. typist** sténodactylo f ■**short-'handed** adj à court de personnel ■**short-'lived** adj de courte durée ■**short-'sighted** adj myope; Fig (in one's judgements) imprévoyant ■**short-'sightedness** n myopie f; Fig imprévoyance f ■**'short-'sleeved** adj à manches courtes ■**short-'staffed** adj à court de personnel ■**short-'tempered** adj irascible ■**'short-'term** adj à court terme ■**short-time 'working** n Br chômage m partiel

shortage ['ʃɔːtɪdʒ] n pénurie f; **to have no s. of sth** ne pas manquer de qch

shorten ['ʃɔːtən] vt raccourcir

shortening ['ʃɔːtənɪŋ] n Br Culin matière f grasse

shortly ['ʃɔːtlɪ] adv (soon) bientôt; **s. before/after** peu avant/après

shorts [ʃɔːts] npl **(a pair of) s.** un short; **boxer s.** caleçon m

shot [ʃɒt] 1 pt & pp of **shoot** 2 n (from gun) coup m; (with camera) prise f de vues; Football coup de pied; Fam (injection) piqûre f; **to fire a s.** tirer; **to be a good s.** (of person) être bon tireur; **to have a s. at sth/doing sth** essayer qch/de faire qch; **it's a long s.** c'est un coup à tenter; Fig **like a s.** sans hésiter; Fam **to get s. of sb/sth** (get rid of) se débarrasser de qn/qch ■**shotgun** n fusil m de chasse

should [ʃʊd, unstressed ʃəd]

v aux (**a**) (expressing obligation) **you s. do it** vous devriez le faire; **I s. have stayed** j'aurais dû rester (**b**) (expressing possibility) **the weather s. improve** le temps devrait s'améliorer; **she s. have arrived by now** elle devrait être arrivée à l'heure qu'il est (**c**) (expressing preferences) **I s. like to stay** j'aimerais bien rester; **I s. like to** j'aimerais bien; **I s. hope so** j'espère bien (**d**) (in subordinate clauses) **it's strange (that) she s. say no** il est étrange qu'elle dise non; **he insisted that she s. meet her parents** il a insisté pour qu'elle rencontre ses parents (**e**) (in conditional clauses) **if he s. come, s. he come** s'il vient (**f**) (in rhetorical questions) **why s. you suspect me?** pourquoi me soupçonnez-vous?; **who s. I meet but Martin!** et qui a-t-il fallu que je rencontre? Martin!

shoulder ['ʃəʊldə(r)] 1 n épaule f; **to have round shoulders** être voûté; Fig **to be looking over one's s.** être constamment sur ses gardes; **s.-length hair** cheveux mpl mi-longs; **s. bag** sac m besace; **s. blade** omoplate f; **s. pad** épaulette f; **s. strap** (of garment) bretelle f 2 vt (responsibility) endosser

shout [ʃaʊt] 1 n cri m; **to give sb a s.** appeler qn 2 vt **to s. sth (out)** crier qch; **to s. sb down** empêcher qn de parler 3 vi **to s. (out)** crier; **to s. to sb to do sth** crier à qn de faire qch; **to s. at sb** crier après qn ■**shouting** n (shouts) cris mpl

shove [ʃʌv] 1 n poussée f; **to give sb/sth a s.** pousser qn/qch 2 vt pousser; Fam **to s. sth into sth** fourrer qch dans qch; Fam **to s. sb around** chahuter qn 3 vi pousser; Fam **to s. off** (leave) dégager; Fam **to s. over** (move over) se pousser

shovel ['ʃʌvəl] 1 n pelle f 2 (Br -ll-, Am -l-) vt pelleter; **to s. snow up** or **away** enlever la neige à la pelle; **to s. leaves up** ramasser des feuilles à la pelle; Fam **to s. sth into sth** fourrer qch dans qch

show [ʃəʊ] 1 n (concert, play) spectacle m; (on TV) émission f; Cin séance f; (exhibition) exposition f; (of force, friendship) démonstration f; (pretence) semblant m (**of** de); **to be on s.** être exposé; **to put sth on s.** exposer qch; Br **to give a good s.** (of sportsman, musician, actor) jouer bien; Br Old-fashioned **good s.!** bravo!; **it's (just) for s.** c'est pour épater la galerie; **to make a s. of one's wealth** faire étalage de ses richesses; **to make a s. of being angry** faire semblant d'être en colère; **s. business** le monde du spectacle; Br **s. flat** appartement m témoin; **s. girl** girl f; **s. jumping** jumping m 2 (pt **showed**, pp **shown**) vt montrer (**to** à; **that** que); (in exhibition) exposer; (film) passer; (indicate) indiquer; **to s. sb sth, to s. sth to sb** montrer qch à qn; **to s. sb to the door** reconduire qn; **to s. sb how to do sth** montrer à qn comment faire qch; **it (just) goes to s. that…** ça montre bien que…; Fam **I'll s. him!** je vais lui apprendre! 3 vi (be visible) se voir; (of film) passer; **'now showing'** (film) 'à l'affiche' ■**showcase** n vitrine f ■**showdown** n confrontation f ■**showmanship** n sens m du spectacle ■**show-off** n Pej crâneur, -euse mf ■**showpiece** n joyau m ■**showroom** n magasin m ■**showy** (-ier, -iest) adj voyant

▸ **show around** vt sep **to s. sb around the town** faire visiter la ville à qn; **she was shown around the house** on lui a fait visiter la maison

▸ **show in** vt sep (visitor) faire entrer

▸ **show off** 1 vt sep Pej (display) étaler; (highlight) faire valoir 2 vi Pej crâner

▸ **show out** vt sep (visitor) reconduire

▸ **show round** vt sep = **show around**

▸ **show up** 1 vt sep (embarrass) faire honte à; (reveal) faire ressortir 2 vi (stand out) ressortir (**against** contre); (of error) être visible; Fam (of person) se présenter

shower ['ʃaʊə(r)] 1 n (bathing, device) douche f; (of rain) averse f; (of blows) déluge m; Am (party) réception f (avec remise de cadeaux); **to have**

or **take a s.** prendre une douche; **s. curtain** rideau *m* de douche; **s. gel** gel *m* de douche; **s. head** pomme *f* de douche **2** *vt* **to s. sb with** *(gifts, abuse)* couvrir qn de ■ **showery** *adj* pluvieux, -ieuse

showing ['ʃəʊɪŋ] *n* *(film show)* séance *f*; *(of team, player)* performance *f*

shown [ʃəʊn] *pp of* **show**

shrank [ʃræŋk] *pt of* **shrink**

shrapnel ['ʃræpnəl] *n* éclats *mpl* d'obus

shred [ʃred] **1** *n* lambeau *m*; **to tear sth to shreds** mettre qch en lambeaux; *Fig* **not a s. of truth** pas une once de vérité; *Fig* **not a s. of evidence** pas la moindre preuve **2** *(pt & pp -dd-)* *vt* mettre en lambeaux; *(documents)* déchiqueter; *(food)* couper grossièrement ■ **shredder** *n (for paper)* déchiqueteuse *f*

shrew [ʃruː] *n (animal)* musaraigne *f*; *Pej (woman)* mégère *f*

shrewd [ʃruːd] *(-er, -est)* *adj (person, plan)* astucieux, -ieuse ■ **shrewdly** *adv* astucieusement

shriek [ʃriːk] **1** *n* cri *m* strident **2** *vi* pousser un cri strident; **to s. with pain/laughter** hurler de douleur/de rire

shrift [ʃrɪft] *n* **to get short s.** être traité sans ménagement

shrill [ʃrɪl] *(-er, -est)* *adj* aigu *(f* aiguë)

shrimp [ʃrɪmp] *n* crevette *f*; *Pej (small person)* nabot, -ote *mf*

shrine [ʃraɪn] *n (place of worship)* lieu *m* saint; *(tomb)* tombeau *m*

shrink [ʃrɪŋk] **1** *n Am Fam (psychiatrist)* psy *mf* **2** *(pt* **shrank** *or Am* **shrunk**, *pp* **shrunk** *or* **shrunken)** *vt (of clothes)* faire rétrécir **3** *vi* rétrécir; **to s. from doing sth** répugner à faire qch; **to s. from an obligation** se dérober devant une obligation ■ **shrinkage** [-ɪdʒ] *n (of material)* rétrécissement *m*; *(in sales, profits)* diminution *f* ■ **'shrink-'wrapped** *adj* emballé sous film plastique

shrivel ['ʃrɪvəl] *(Br -ll-, Am -l-)* **1** *vt* **to s. (up)** dessécher **2** *vi* **to s. (up)** se dessécher

shroud [ʃraʊd] **1** *n* linceul *m*; *Fig* **a s. of mystery** un voile de mystère **2** *vt* **to be shrouded in sth** être enveloppé de qch

Shrove Tuesday [ʃrəʊv'tjuːzdɪ] *n Br* Mardi *m* gras

shrub [ʃrʌb] *n* arbuste *m* ■ **shrubbery** *(pl -ies)* *n* massif *m* d'arbustes

shrug [ʃrʌg] **1** *n* haussement *m* d'épaules **2** *(pt & pp -gg-)* *vt* **to s. one's shoulders** hausser les épaules; **to s. sth off** dédaigner qch

shrunk(en) ['ʃrʌŋk(ən)] *pp of* **shrink**

shudder ['ʃʌdə(r)] **1** *n* frémissement *m*; *(of machine)* vibration *f* **2** *vi (of person)* frémir **(with** de); *(of machine)* vibrer; **I s. to think of it** j'ai des frissons quand j'y pense

shuffle ['ʃʌfəl] **1** *vt (cards)* battre **2** *vti* **to s. (one's feet)** traîner les pieds

shun [ʃʌn] *(pt & pp -nn-)* *vt* fuir, éviter

shunt [ʃʌnt] *vt (train, conversation)* aiguiller **(on to** sur); *Fam* **we were shunted (to and fro)** on nous a baladés

shush [ʃʊʃ] *exclam* chut!

shut [ʃʌt] **1** *(pt & pp* **shut**, *pp* **shutting)** *vt* fermer; **to s. one's finger in a door** se prendre le doigt dans une porte **2** *vi (of door)* se fermer; *(of shop, museum)* fermer; **the door doesn't s.** la porte ne ferme pas ■ **shutdown** *n (of factory)* fermeture *f*

▶ **shut away** *vt sep (lock away)* enfermer

▶ **shut down** **1** *vt sep* fermer (définitivement) **2** *vi* fermer (définitivement)

▶ **shut in** *vt sep (lock in)* enfermer

▶ **shut off** *vt sep (gas, electricity)* couper; *(engine)* arrêter; *(road)* fermer; *(isolate)* isoler

▶ **shut out** *vt sep (keep outside)* empêcher d'entrer; *(exclude)* exclure **(of** *or* **from** de); *(view)* boucher; **to s. sb out** enfermer qn dehors

▶ **shut up** **1** *vt sep (close)* fermer; *(confine)* enfermer; *Fam (silence)* faire taire **2** *vi Fam (be quiet)* se taire

shutter ['ʃʌtə(r)] *n (on window)* volet *m*; *(of shop)* store *m*; *(of camera)* obturateur *m*

shuttle ['ʃʌtəl] **1** *n (bus, train, plane)* navette *f*; **s. service** navette **2** *vt* transporter **3** *vi* faire la navette

shuttlecock ['ʃʌtəlkɒk] *n* volant *m*

shy [ʃaɪ] **1** *(-er, -est)* *adj* timide; **to be s. of doing sth** éviter de faire qch à tout prix **2** *vi* **to s. away from sb/from doing sth** éviter qch/de faire qch ■ **shyly** *adj* timidement ■ **shyness** *n* timidité *f*

Siamese [saɪə'miːz] *adj* **S. cat** chat *m* siamois; **S. twins** *(boys)* frères *mpl* siamois; *(girls)* sœurs *fpl* siamoises

sibling ['sɪblɪŋ] *n (brother)* frère *m*; *(sister)* sœur *f*

Sicily ['sɪsɪlɪ] *n* la Sicile ■ **Si'cilian 1** *adj* sicilien, -ienne **2** *n* Sicilien, -ienne *mf*

sick [sɪk] **1** *(-er, -est)* *adj (ill)* malade; *(humour)* de mauvais goût; **to be s.** *(be ill)* être malade; *(vomit)* vomir; **to feel s.** avoir mal au cœur; **to be off** *or* **away s.,** **to be on s. leave** être en congé de maladie; **to be s. of sb/sth** en avoir assez de qn/qch; **to be s. and tired of sb/sth** en avoir ras le bol de qn/qch; **to have a s. mind** avoir l'esprit dérangé; *Fig* **he makes me s.** il m'écœure; *Br* **s. note** mot *m* d'absence *(pour cause de maladie)*; **s. pay** indemnité *f* de maladie **2** *n Br Fam (vomit)* vomi *m* **3** *npl* **the s.** *(sick people)* les malades *mpl* ■ **sickbay** *n* infirmerie *f* ■ **sickbed** *n* lit *m* de malade

sicken ['sɪkən] **1** *vt* écœurer **2** *vi Br* **to be sickening for something** couver quelque chose ■ **sickening** *adj* écœurant

sickie ['sɪkɪ] *n Br Fam* **to take** *or* **pull a s.** se faire porter pâle *(lorsqu'on est bien portant)*

sickly ['sɪklɪ] (**-ier, -iest**) adj maladif, -ive; (pale, faint) pâle; (taste) écœurant

sickness ['sɪknɪs] n (illness) maladie f; (vomiting) vomissements mpl; Br **s. benefit** indemnité f journalière

side [saɪd] **1** n côté m; (of hill, animal) flanc m; (of road, river) bord m; (of beef) quartier m; (of question, character) aspect m; (team) équipe f; **the right s.** (of fabric) l'endroit m; **the wrong s.** (of fabric) l'envers m; **at** or **by the s. of** (nearby) à côté de; **at** or **by my s.** à côté de moi, à mes côtés; **s. by s.** l'un à côté de l'autre; **to move to one's s.** s'écarter; **on this s.** de ce côté; **on the other s.** de l'autre côté; Fam **it's a bit on the big s.** c'est un peu grand; **to take sides with sb** se ranger du côté de qn; **she's on our s.** elle est de notre côté; **to change sides** changer de camp; **to do sth on the s.** (as extra job) faire qch pour arrondir ses fins de mois **2** adj (lateral) latéral; (view, glance) de côté; (street) transversal; (effect, issue) secondaire **3** vi **to s. with sb** se ranger du côté de qn ▪ **sideboard** n buffet m ▪ **sideboards** npl Br (hair) pattes fpl ▪ **sideburns** npl (hair) pattes fpl ▪ **sidecar** n side-car m ▪ **-sided** suff **ten-sided** à dix côtés ▪ **sidekick** n Fam acolyte m ▪ **sidelight** n Br (on vehicle) feu m de position ▪ **sideline** n (activity) activité f secondaire; (around playing field) ligne f de touche ▪ **side-saddle** adv **to ride s.** monter en amazone ▪ **sidestep** (pt & pp **-pp-**) vt éviter ▪ **sidetrack** vt distraire; **to get sidetracked** s'écarter du sujet ▪ **sidewalk** n Am trottoir m ▪ **sideways 1** adv (look, walk) de côté **2** adj **a s. look/move** un regard/mouvement de côté

siding ['saɪdɪŋ] n Rail voie f de garage

sidle ['saɪdəl] vi **to s. up to sb** se glisser vers qn

siege [siːdʒ] n (by soldiers, police) siège m; **to lay s. to a town** assiéger une ville; **under s.** assiégé

siesta [sɪ'estə] n sieste f; **to take** or **have a s.** faire la sieste

sieve [sɪv] **1** n tamis m; (for liquids) passoire f; (for gravel, ore) crible m **2** vt tamiser ▪ **sift 1** vt (flour) tamiser; (stones) cribler; Fig **to s. out the truth** dégager la vérité **2** vi **to s. through** (papers) examiner (à la loupe)

sigh [saɪ] **1** n soupir m **2** vi soupirer; **to s. with relief** pousser un soupir de soulagement **3** vt 'yes', she sighed 'oui', soupira-t-elle

sight [saɪt] **1** n (faculty) vue f; (thing seen) spectacle m; (on gun) viseur m; **to lose s. of sb/sth** perdre qn/qch de vue; **to catch s. of sb/sth** apercevoir qn/qch; **to come into s.** apparaître; **at first s.** à première vue; **by s.** de vue; **on** or **at s.** à vue; **in s.** (target, end, date) en vue; **out of s.** (hidden) caché; (no longer visible) disparu; **to disappear out of s.** or **from s.** disparaître; **keep out of s.!** ne te montre pas!; **he hates the s. of me** il ne peut pas me voir; **it's**

a lovely s. c'est beau à voir; **the (tourist) sights** les attractions fpl touristiques; **to set one's sights on** (job) viser **2** vt (land) apercevoir ▪ **sighted** adj voyant ▪ **sighting** n **to make a s. of sb** apercevoir qn

sightseer ['saɪtsiːə(r)] n touriste mf ▪ **sightseeing** n **to go s., to do some s.** faire du tourisme

sign [saɪn] **1** n signe m; (notice) panneau m; (over shop, pub) enseigne f; **no s. of** aucune trace de; **s. language** langage m des sourds-muets **2** vt (put signature to) signer; (in sign language) dire en langage des sourds-muets **3** vi (write signature) signer; (use sign language) communiquer dans le langage des sourds-muets
▸ **sign away** vt sep (rights, property) renoncer à qch
▸ **sign for** vt insep (letter, delivery) signer pour accuser réception de
▸ **sign in** vi (in hotel) signer le registre (à l'entrée); (at work) pointer (en arrivant)
▸ **sign off** vi (say goodbye) dire au revoir
▸ **sign on** vi Br Fam (register for unemployment benefit) s'inscrire au chômage
▸ **sign out** vi (of hotel) signer le registre (à la sortie); (at work) pointer (en sortant)
▸ **sign up** vi (of soldier, worker) s'engager; (for course) s'inscrire

signal ['sɪgnəl] **1** n signal m; Rail Br **s. box,** Am **s. tower** poste m d'aiguillage **2** (Br **-ll-,** Am **-l-**) vt (be a sign of) indiquer; (make gesture to) faire signe à **3** vi (make gesture) faire signe (**to** à); (of driver) mettre son clignotant; **to s. (to) sb to do sth** faire signe à qn de faire qch ▪ **signalman** (pl **-men**) n Rail aiguilleur m

signature ['sɪgnətʃə(r)] n signature f; Comptr **digital s.** signature électronique ou numérique; **s. tune** indicatif m ▪ **signatory** [-tərɪ] (pl **-ies**) n signataire mf

signet ring ['sɪgnɪtrɪŋ] n chevalière f

significant [sɪg'nɪfɪkənt] adj (important, large) important; (meaningful) significatif, -ive ▪ **significance** n (meaning) signification f; (importance) importance f ▪ **significantly** adv (appreciably) sensiblement; **s., he...** fait significatif, il...

signify ['sɪgnɪfaɪ] (pt & pp **-ied**) vt (mean) signifier (**that** que); (make known) signifier (**to** à)

signpost ['saɪnpəʊst] **1** n poteau m indicateur **2** vt signaliser

Sikh [siːk] adj & n sikh (mf)

silence ['saɪləns] **1** n silence m; **in s.** en silence **2** vt faire taire ▪ **silencer** n (on gun, motorbike) silencieux m

silent ['saɪlənt] adj silencieux, -ieuse; (film, anger) muet (f muette); **to keep** or **be s.** garder le silence (**about** sur) ▪ **silently** adv silencieusement

silhouette [sɪluː'et] n silhouette f ▪**silhou-etted** adj to be s. against se profiler contre
silicon ['sɪlɪkən] n silicium m; **s. chip** puce f électronique; **S. Valley** Silicon Valley f (centre de l'industrie électronique américaine, situé en Californie)
silicone ['sɪlɪkəʊn] n silicone f; **s. implant** implant m mammaire en silicone
silk [sɪlk] n soie f; **s. dress** robe f de ou en soie ▪**silky** (-ier, -iest) adj soyeux, -euse
sill [sɪl] n (of window) rebord m
silly ['sɪlɪ] 1 (-ier, -iest) adj bête, idiot; **to do something s.** faire une bêtise; **to look s.** avoir l'air ridicule; **to laugh oneself s.** mourir de rire 2 adv (act, behave) bêtement ▪**silliness** n bêtise f
silo ['saɪləʊ] (pl -os) n silo m
silt [sɪlt] n vase f
silver ['sɪlvə(r)] 1 n argent m; (plates) argenterie f; Br **£5 in s.** 5 livres en pièces d'argent 2 adj (spoon) en argent, d'argent; (hair, colour) argenté; **s. jubilee** vingt-cinquième anniversaire m; Br **s. paper** papier m d'argent; **s. plate** (articles) argenterie f ▪**'silver-'plated** adj plaqué argent ▪**sil-versmith** n orfèvre m ▪**silverware** n argenterie f ▪**silvery** adj (colour) argenté
similar ['sɪmɪlə(r)] adj semblable (**to** à) ▪**similarity** [-'lærɪtɪ] (pl -ies) n ressemblance f (**between** entre; **to** avec) ▪**similarly** adv de la même façon; (likewise) de même
simile ['sɪmɪlɪ] n comparaison f
simmer ['sɪmə(r)] 1 vt (vegetables) mijoter; (water) laisser frémir 2 vi (of vegetables) mijoter; (of water) frémir; Fig (of revolt, hatred) couver; **to s. with rage** bouillir de rage; Fam **to s. down** se calmer
simper ['sɪmpə(r)] vi minauder
simple ['sɪmpəl] (-er, -est) adj (easy) simple; (unintelligent) simplet, -ette ▪**'simple-'min-ded** adj simple d'esprit ▪**'simple-'minded-ness** n simplicité f d'esprit ▪**simpleton** n simple mf d'esprit ▪**sim'plicity** n simplicité f
simplify ['sɪmplɪfaɪ] (pt & pp -ied) vt simplifier ▪**simplification** [-fɪ'keɪʃən] n simplification f
simplistic [sɪm'plɪstɪk] adj simpliste
simply ['sɪmplɪ] adv (plainly, merely) simplement; (absolutely) absolument
simulate ['sɪmjʊleɪt] vt simuler
simultaneous [Br sɪməl'teɪnɪəs, Am saɪməl'teɪnɪəs] adj simultané ▪**simulta-neously** adv simultanément
sin [sɪn] 1 n péché m 2 (pt & pp -nn-) vi pécher ▪**sinful** adj (act) coupable; (waste) scandaleux, -euse; **that's s.** c'est un péché ▪**sinner** n pécheur, -eresse mf
since [sɪns] 1 prep (in time) depuis; **s. 2003/my departure** depuis 2003/mon départ; **s. then** depuis 2 conj (in time) depuis que; (because)

puisque; **s. she's been here** depuis qu'elle est ici; **it's a year s. I saw him** ça fait un an que je ne l'ai pas vu 3 adv (ever) s. depuis
sincere [sɪn'sɪə(r)] adj sincère ▪**sincerely** adv sincèrement; Br **yours s.,** Am s. (in letter) veuillez agréer, Madame/Monsieur, l'expres-sion de mes salutations distinguées ▪**since-rity** [-'serɪtɪ] n sincérité f
sinew ['sɪnjuː] n Anat tendon m ▪**sinewy** adj (arm, leg) musclé
sing [sɪŋ] (pt **sang**, pp **sung**) vti chanter; **to s. up** chanter plus fort ▪**singer** n chanteur, -euse mf ▪**singing** n (of bird, musical technique) chant m; (way of singing) façon f de chanter; **s. lesson/teacher** leçon f/professeur m de chant
Singapore [sɪŋgə'pɔː(r)] n Singapour m ou f
singe [sɪndʒ] vt (cloth) roussir; (hair) brûler
single ['sɪŋgəl] 1 adj (only one) seul; (room, bed) pour une personne; (unmarried) célibataire; **not a s. book** pas un seul livre; **every s. day** tous les jours sans exception; Br **s. ticket** aller m simple; **s. parent** père m/mère f célibataire; **s.-parent family** famille f monoparentale; Pol **s. party** parti m unique; **s. European market** marché m unique européen 2 n Br (ticket) aller m simple; (record) single m; Tennis **singles** simples mpl; **singles bar** bar m pour célibataires 3 vt **to s. sb out** sélectionner qn ▪**'single-'breasted** [-brestɪd] adj (jacket) droit ▪**single-'decker** n = autobus sans impériale ▪**'single-'handedly** adv tout seul (f toute seule) ▪**'single-'minded** adj (person) résolu; (determination) farouche ▪**'single-'mindedly** adv résolument ▪**single-sex 'school** n Br école f non mixte
singlet ['sɪŋglɪt] n Br maillot m de corps
singly ['sɪŋglɪ] adv (one by one) un à un
singsong ['sɪŋsɒŋ] 1 n **to get together for a s.** se réunir pour chanter 2 adj (voice, tone) chantant
singular ['sɪŋgjʊlə(r)] 1 adj Grammar singulier, -ière; (remarkable) remarquable 2 n singulier m; **in the s.** au singulier
sinister ['sɪnɪstə(r)] adj sinistre
sink¹ [sɪŋk] n (in kitchen) évier m; (in bathroom) lavabo m
sink² [sɪŋk] (pt **sank**, pp **sunk**) 1 vt (ship) couler; (well) creuser; **to s. a knife into sth** enfoncer un couteau dans qch; **to s. money into a company** investir de l'argent dans une société; **a sinking feeling** un serrement de cœur 2 vi (of ship, person) couler; (of water level, sun, price) baisser; (collapse) s'affaisser; **my heart sank** j'ai eu un pincement de cœur; **to s. (down) into** (mud) s'enfoncer dans; (armchair) s'affaler dans; **to s. in** (of ink, water) pénétrer; Fam (of fact, idea) être assimilé; Fam **it hasn't sunk in**

yet je n'ai/il n'a/*etc* pas encore digéré la nouvelle

sinuous ['sɪnjʊəs] *adj* sinueux, -ueuse

sinus [saɪnəs] *n Anat* sinus *m* ▪ **sinusitis** [-'saɪtəs] *n Med* sinusite *f*; **to have s.** avoir une sinusite

sip [sɪp] **1** *n* petite gorgée *f* **2** (*pt & pp* **-pp-**) *vt* siroter

siphon ['saɪfən] **1** *n* siphon *m* **2** *vt* **to s. sth off** (*liquid*) siphonner qch; (*money*) détourner qch

sir [sɜː(r)] *n* monsieur *m*; **S.Walter Raleigh** (*title*) sirWalter Raleigh

siren ['saɪərən] *n* sirène *f*

sirloin ['sɜːlɔɪn] *n* (*beef*) aloyau *m*

sissy ['sɪsɪ] *n Fam* (*boy, man*) femmelette *f*

sister ['sɪstə(r)] *n* sœur *f*; (*nurse*) infirmière-chef *f* ▪ **sister-in-law** (*pl* sisters-in-law) *n* belle-sœur *f* ▪ **sisterly** *adj* fraternel, -elle

sit [sɪt] (*pt & pp* sat, *pres p* sitting) **1** *vt* (*child on chair*) asseoir; *Br* (*exam*) se présenter à **2** *vi* (*of person*) s'asseoir; (*for artist*) poser (**for** pour); (*of assembly*) siéger; **to s. at home** rester chez soi; **to be sitting** (*of person, cat*) être assis; **to be sitting on its perch** (*of bird*) être sur son perchoir; **she was sitting reading, she sat reading** elle était assise à lire

▸ **sit around** *vi* rester assis à ne rien faire

▸ **sit back** *vi* (*in chair*) se caler; (*rest*) se détendre; (*do nothing*) ne rien faire

▸ **sit down 1** *vt* **to s. sb down** asseoir qn **2** *vi* s'asseoir; **to be sitting down** être assis

▸ **sit for** *vt insep Br* (*exam*) se présenter à

▸ **sit in on** *vt insep* (*lecture*) assister à

▸ **sit on** *vt insep* (*jury*) être membre de; *Fam* (*fact*) garder pour soi

▸ **sit out** *vt sep* (*event, dance*) ne pas prendre part à; (*film*) rester jusqu'au bout de

▸ **sit through** *vt insep* (*film*) rester jusqu'au bout de

▸ **sit up** *vi* **to s. up** (*straight*) s'asseoir (bien droit); (*straighten one's back*) se redresser; **to s. up waiting for sb** veiller jusqu'au retour de qn

sitcom ['sɪtkɒm] *n* sitcom *m*

sit-down ['sɪtdaʊn] *adj* **s. meal** repas *m* servi à table; **s. strike** grève *f* sur le tas

site [saɪt] **1** *n* (*position*) emplacement *m*; (*archaeological*) site *m*; (*building*) **s.** chantier *m* (de construction); *Comptr* (**web**) **s.** site *m* (Web) **2** *vt* (*building*) placer

sit-in ['sɪtɪn] *n* (*protest*) sit-in *m inv*

sitter ['sɪtə(r)] *n* (*for child*) baby-sitter *mf*

sitting ['sɪtɪŋ] **1** *n* séance *f*; (*in restaurant*) service *m* **2** *adj* (*committee*) en séance; *Fam* **s. duck** cible *f* facile; **s. tenant** locataire *mf* dans les lieux ▪ **sitting room** *n* salon *m*

situate ['sɪtʃʊeɪt] *vt* situer; **to be situated** être situé ▪ **situ'ation** *n* situation *f*

six [sɪks] *adj & n* six (*m*) ▪ **sixth** *adj & n* sixième (*mf*); *Br Sch* (**lower**) **s. form** ≃ classe *f* de

première; *Br Sch* (**upper**) **s. form** ≃ classe *f* terminale; **a s.** (*fraction*) un sixième

sixteen [sɪk'stiːn] *adj & n* seize (*m*) ▪ **sixteenth** *adj & n* seizième (*mf*)

sixty ['sɪkstɪ] *adj & n* soixante (*m*) ▪ **sixtieth** *adj & n* soixantième (*mf*)

size [saɪz] **1** *n* (*of person, animal, clothes*) taille *f*; (*of shoes, gloves*) pointure *f*; (*of shirt*) encolure *f*; (*measurements*) dimensions *fpl*; (*of fruit, packet*) grosseur *f*; (*of book*) grandeur *f*; (*of town, damage, problem*) étendue *f*; (*of sum*) montant *m*; **hip/chest s.** tour *m* de hanches/de poitrine; **it's the s. of...** c'est grand comme... **2** *vt* **to s. up** (*person*) jauger; (*situation*) évaluer

sizeable ['saɪzəbəl] *adj* non négligeable

sizzle ['sɪzəl] *vi* grésiller ▪ **sizzling** *adj* **s. (hot)** brûlant

skate¹ [skeɪt] **1** *n* patin *m*; *Fam* **to get one's skates on** se dépêcher **2** *vi* (*on ice skates*) faire du patin à glace; (*on roller skates*) faire du roller ▪ **skateboard 1** *n* planche *f* à roulettes, skateboard *m* **2** *vi* faire du skate-board ▪ **skateboarder** *n* personne *f* pratiquant le skate-board ▪ **skater** *n* (*on skates*) patineur, -euse *mf*; (*on skateboard*) personne *f* pratiquant le skate-board ▪ **skating** *n* patinage *m*; **to go s.** faire du patinage; **s. rink** (*for ice-skating*) patinoire *f*; (*for roller-skating*) piste *f*

skate² [skeɪt] *n* (*fish*) raie *f*

skeleton ['skelɪtən] *n* squelette *m*; *Fig* **to have a s. in the closet** avoir un secret honteux; **s. key** passe-partout *m inv*; **s. staff** personnel *m* minimum

skeptic ['skeptɪk] *adj & n Am* sceptique (*mf*) ▪ **skeptical** *adj Am* sceptique ▪ **skepticism** *n* *Am* scepticisme *m*

sketch [sketʃ] **1** *n* (*drawing*) croquis *m*; (*comic play*) sketch *m*; **a rough s. of the situation** un résumé rapide de la situation **2** *vt* **to s. (out)** (*idea, view*) exposer brièvement; *Fig* **to s. in** esquisser **3** *vi* faire un/des croquis ▪ **sketchbook** *n* carnet *m* de croquis ▪ **sketchy** (**-ier, -iest**) *adj* vague

skew [skjuː] *n* **on the s.** de travers

skewer ['skjuːə(r)] **1** *n* (*for large piece of meat*) broche *f*; (*for kebab*) brochette *f* **2** *vt* (*large piece of meat*) embrocher; (*small pieces of meat, vegetables*) mettre sur une brochette

ski [skiː] **1** (*pl* **skis**) *n* ski *m*; **s. boot** chaussure *f* de ski; **s. jump** (*slope*) tremplin *m*; (*jump*) saut *m* à skis; **s. lift** remonte-pente *m*; **s. mask** cagoule *f*, passe-montagne *m*; **s. pants** fuseau *m*; **s. pass** forfait *m* de remonte-pente; **s. resort** station *f* de ski; **s. run** or **slope** piste *f* de ski; **s. tow** téléski *m*; **s. wax** fart *m* **2** (*pt* skied [skiːd], *pres p* **skiing**) *vi* skier, faire du ski ▪ **skier** *n* skieur, -ieuse *mf* ▪ **skiing 1** *n* (*sport*) ski *m* **2** *adj* (*school, clothes*) de ski; *Br* **s. holiday**, *Am* **s. vacation** vacances *fpl* de neige

skid [skɪd] **1** n dérapage m **2** adj Am Fam **to be on s. row** être à la rue **3** (pt & pp **-dd-**) vi déraper; **to s. into sth** déraper et heurter qch

skill [skɪl] n (ability) qualités fpl; (technique) compétence f ▪**skilful** (Am **skillful**) adj habile (**at doing** à faire; **at sth** en qch) ▪**skilled** adj habile (**at doing** à faire; **at sth** en qch); (worker) qualifié; (work) de spécialiste

skillet [ˈskɪlɪt] n Am poêle f (à frire)

skim [skɪm] (pt & pp **-mm-**) **1** vt (milk) écrémer; (soup) écumer; **to s. (over) sth** (surface) effleurer qch; **to s. stones** (on water) faire des ricochets **2** vt insep **to s. through** (book) parcourir **3** adj **s. milk** lait m écrémé ▪**skimmed** adj **s. milk** lait m écrémé

skimp [skɪmp] vi (on food, fabric) lésiner (**on** sur) ▪**skimpy** (**-ier, -iest**) adj (clothes) étriqué; (meal) maigre

skin [skɪn] **1** n peau f; Fig **he has thick s.** c'est un dur; **s. cancer** cancer m de la peau; **s. diving** plongée f sous-marine; **s. test** cuti-(réaction) f **2** (pt & pp **-nn-**) vt (fruit) peler; (animal) écorcher ▪**'skin-'deep** adj superficiel, -ielle ▪**'skin-'tight** adj moulant

skinflint [ˈskɪnflɪnt] n avare mf

skinhead [ˈskɪnhed] n Br skinhead mf

skinny [ˈskɪnɪ] (**-ier, -iest**) adj maigre

skint [skɪnt] adj Br Fam (penniless) fauché

skip¹ [skɪp] **1** n petit saut m **2** (pt & pp **-pp-**) vt (miss, omit) sauter; **to s. classes** sécher les cours **3** vi (hop about) sautiller; Br (with rope) sauter à la corde; Fam **to s. off** filer; Br **skipping rope** corde f à sauter

skip² [skɪp] n Br (for rubbish) benne f

skipper [ˈskɪpə(r)] n (of ship, team) capitaine m

skirmish [ˈskɜːmɪʃ] n accrochage m

skirt [skɜːt] **1** n jupe f **2** vt **to s. round sth** (bypass, go round) contourner qch ▪**skirting board** n Br plinthe f

skittish [ˈskɪtɪʃ] adj espiègle

skittle [ˈskɪtəl] n Br quille f; **skittles** (game) jeu m de quilles; **to play skittles** jouer aux quilles

skive [skaɪv] vi Br Fam tirer au flanc; **to s. off** (slip away) se défiler ▪**skiver** n Br Fam tire-au-flanc m inv

skivvy [ˈskɪvɪ] (pl **-ies**) n Br Fam Pej bonne f à tout faire

skulk [skʌlk] vi **to s. (about)** rôder

skull [skʌl] n crâne m ▪**skullcap** n calotte f

skunk [skʌŋk] n (animal) moufette f; Pej (person) mufle m

sky [skaɪ] n ciel m ▪**'sky-'blue** adj bleu ciel inv ▪**skydiving** n parachutisme m en chute libre ▪**'sky-'high** adj (prices) exorbitant ▪**skylark** n alouette f ▪**skylight** n lucarne f ▪**skyline** n (horizon) horizon m ▪**skyrocket** vi Fam (of prices) monter en flèche ▪**skyscraper** n gratte-ciel m inv

slab [slæb] n (of concrete) bloc m; (thin, flat) plaque f; (of chocolate) tablette f; (of meat) tranche f épaisse; (paving stone) dalle f

slack [slæk] **1** (**-er, -est**) adj (not tight) mou (f molle); (careless) négligent; **to be s.** (of rope) avoir du mou; **trade is s.** le commerce va mal; **in s. periods** en périodes creuses **2** vi **to s. off** (in effort) se relâcher ▪**slackness** n (negligence) négligence f; (laziness) fainéantise f; (of rope) mou m; (of trade) stagnation f

slacken [ˈslækən] **1** vt **to s. (off)** (rope) relâcher; (pace, effort) ralentir **2** vi **to s. (off)** (in effort) se relâcher; (of production, demand, speed, enthusiasm) diminuer

slacker [ˈslækə(r)] n Fam (person) flemmard, -arde mf

slacks [slæks] npl Am pantalon m

slag¹ [slæg] n (from mine) déchets mpl miniers; (from steelworks) crasse f; **s. heap** (near mine) terril m; (near steelworks) crassier m

slag² [slæg] Br very Fam **1** n (woman) salope f **2** vt **to s. sb off** (criticize) débiner qn

slain [sleɪn] pp of **slay**

slalom [ˈslɑːləm] n (ski race) slalom m

slam [slæm] **1** n claquement m **2** (pt & pp **-mm-**) vt (door, lid) claquer; (hit) frapper violemment; Fam (criticize) éreinter; **to s. the door in sb's face** claquer la porte au nez de qn; **to s. sth (down)** (put down) poser qch violemment **3** vi (of door) claquer; **to s. on the brakes** écraser la pédale de frein

slander [ˈslɑːndə(r)] **1** n calomnie f **2** vt calomnier ▪**slanderous** adj calomnieux, -ieuse

slang [slæŋ] **1** n argot m **2** adj (word) d'argot, argotique; **s. expression** expression f argotique ▪**slanging match** n Br Fam échange m d'insultes

slant [slɑːnt] **1** n pente f; Fig (point of view) perspective f; Fig (bias) parti m pris; **on a s.** penché; (roof) en pente **2** vt (writing) incliner; Fig (news) présenter de façon partiale **3** vi (of roof, handwriting) être incliné ▪**slanted, slanting** adj penché; (roof) en pente

slap [slæp] **1** n (with hand) claque f; **a s. in the face** une gifle **2** (pt & pp **-pp-**) vt (person) donner une claque à; **to s. sb's face** gifler qn; **to s. sb's bottom** donner une fessée à qn; **to s. some paint on sth** passer un coup de peinture sur qch; Fig **to s. sb down** remettre qn à sa place **3** adv Fam **s. in the middle** en plein milieu

slapdash [ˈslæpdæʃ] **1** adj (person) négligent; (task) fait à la va-vite **2** adv (carelessly) à la va-vite

slapstick [ˈslæpstɪk] adj & n **s. (comedy)** grosse farce f

slap-up [ˈslæpʌp] adj Br Fam **s. meal** gueuleton m

slash [slæʃ] **1** n entaille f **2** vt (cut) taillader; (reduce) réduire considérablement; **prices slashed** prix mpl sacrifiés

slat [slæt] *n* latte *f*

slate [sleɪt] **1** *n* ardoise *f* **2** *vt Br Fam (book)* démolir

slaughter ['slɔːtə(r)] **1** *n (of people)* massacre *m*; *(of animal)* abattage *m* **2** *vt (people)* massacrer; *(animal)* abattre; *Fam (defeat)* massacrer ▪ **slaughterhouse** *n* abattoir *m*

Slav [slɑːv] **1** *adj* slave **2** *n* Slave *mf* ▪ **Slavic** *adj* slave *m* ▪ **Slavonic** [slə'vɒnɪk] *adj (language)* slave

slave [sleɪv] **1** *n* esclave *mf*; *Hist* **the s. trade** la traite des Noirs; *Fig & Pej* **s. driver** négrier *m* **2** *vi* **to s. (away)** trimer; **to s. away doing sth** s'escrimer à faire qch ▪ **slavery** *n* esclavage *m* ▪ **slavish** *adj* servile

slaver ['slævə(r)] *vi (dribble)* baver (**over** sur)

slay [sleɪ] *(pt* **slew**, *pp* **slain**) *vt Literary* tuer

sleazy ['sliːzɪ] *(-ier, -iest) adj Fam* sordide ▪ **sleaze** *n Fam (in media)* ragots *mpl* sordides; *(in politics)* corruption *f*

sledge [sledʒ] *(Am* **sled** [sled]) *n Br* luge *f*; *(horse-drawn)* traîneau *m*

sledgehammer ['sledʒhæmə(r)] *n* masse *f*

sleek [sliːk] *(-er, -est) adj (smooth)* lisse et brillant; *Pej (manner)* mielleux, -euse

sleep [sliːp] **1** *n* sommeil *m*; **to have a s., to get some s.** dormir; **to go to s.** *(of person)* s'endormir; *Fam (of arm, foot, hand)* s'engourdir; **to put sb to s.** endormir qn; **to put an animal to s.** *(kill)* faire piquer un animal; *Fig* **to send sb to s.** *(bore)* endormir qn **2** *(pt & pp* **slept**) *vi* dormir; **to s. rough** dormir à la dure; *Euph* **to s. with sb** coucher avec qn; **s. tight** *or* **well!** dors bien!; *Fig* **I'll s. on it** la nuit portera conseil **3** *vt* **this flat sleeps six** on peut dormir à six dans cet appartement; **I haven't slept a wink all night** je n'ai pas fermé l'œil de la nuit; *Fam* **to s. it off, to s. off a hangover** cuver son vin ▪ **sleeping** *adj (asleep)* endormi; **s. bag** sac *m* de couchage; **s. car** wagon-lit *m*; **s. pill** somnifère *m* ▪ **sleepover (party)** *n* = soirée entre copines, où les invitées restent dormir chez leur hôte

sleeper ['sliːpə(r)] *n* (**a**) **to be a light/sound s.** avoir le sommeil léger/lourd (**b**) *Br Rail (on track)* traverse *f*; *(bed in train)* couchette *f*; *(train)* train-couchettes *m* ▪ **sleepless** *adj (night)* d'insomnie; *(hours)* sans sommeil

sleepwalker ['sliːpwɔːkə(r)] *n* somnambule *mf* ▪ **sleepwalking** *n* somnambulisme *m*

sleepy ['sliːpɪ] *(-ier, -iest) adj (town, voice)* endormi; **to be s.** *(of person)* avoir sommeil ▪ **sleepiness** *n* torpeur *f*

sleet [sliːt] **1** *n* neige *f* fondue; *Am (sheet of ice)* verglas *m* **2** *vi* **it's sleeting** il tombe de la neige fondue

sleeve [sliːv] *n (of shirt, jacket)* manche *f*; *(of record)* pochette *f*; **long-/short-sleeved** à

manches longues/courtes; *Fig* **he still has something up his s.** il n'a pas dit son dernier mot

sleigh [sleɪ] *n* traîneau *m*; **s. bell** grelot *m* (de traîneau)

sleight [slaɪt] *n* **s. of hand** tour *m* de passe-passe

slender ['slendə(r)] *adj (person)* svelte; *(neck, hand, waist)* fin; *Fig (small, feeble)* faible

slept [slept] *pt & pp of* **sleep**

sleuth [sluːθ] *n Hum (detective)* limier *m*

slew [sluː] **1** *n Am Fam* **a s. of** un tas de **2** *pt of* **slay**

slice [slaɪs] **1** *n* tranche *f*; *Fig (portion)* part *f* **2** *vt* **to s. sth (up)** couper qch en tranches; **to s. sth off** couper qch ▪ **sliced 'bread** *n* pain *m* en tranches

slick [slɪk] **1** *(-er, -est) adj (campaign)* bien mené; *(reply, person)* habile; *(in prices, surface, tyre)* lisse **2** *n (on beach)* marée *f* noire

slide [slaɪd] **1** *n (in playground)* toboggan *m*; *(for hair)* barrette *f*; *Phot* diapositive *f*; *(of microscope)* lamelle *f*; *(in prices, popularity)* baisse *f* **2** *(pt & pp* **slid** [slɪd]) *vt* glisser (**into** dans); *(table, chair)* faire glisser; **s. the lid off** faites glisser le couvercle **3** *vi* glisser; **to s. into a room** se glisser dans une pièce ▪ **sliding** *adj (door, panel)* coulissant; **s. roof** toit *m* ouvrant; **s. scale** échelle *f* mobile

slight [slaɪt] **1** *(-er, -est) adj (small, unimportant)* léger, -ère; *(chance)* faible; *(person)* menu; **the slightest thing** la moindre chose; **not in the slightest** pas le moins du monde **2** *n* affront *m* (**on** à) **3** *vt (offend)* offenser; *(ignore)* bouder

slightly ['slaɪtlɪ] *adv* légèrement; **to know sb s.** connaître qn un peu; **s. built** fluet *(f* fluette)

slim [slɪm] **1** *(slimmer, slimmest) adj* mince **2** *(pt & pp* **-mm-**) *vi Br* suivre un régime ▪ **slimmer** *n Br* personne *f* qui suit un régime amaigrissant ▪ **slimming** *adj Br* **s. diet** régime *m* amaigrissant ▪ **slimness** *n* minceur *f*

slime [slaɪm] *n* vase *f*; *(of snail)* bave *f* ▪ **slimy** *(-ier, -iest) adj (muddy)* boueux *(f* boueuse); *Fig (sticky, smarmy)* visqueux, -euse

sling [slɪŋ] **1** *n (weapon)* fronde *f*; *(for injured arm)* écharpe *f*; **in a s.** en écharpe **2** *(pt & pp* **slung**) *vt (throw)* lancer; **to s. sth over one's shoulder** mettre qch sur son épaule; *Fam* **to s. away** *or* **out** *(throw out)* balancer ▪ **slingshot** *n Am* lance-pierres *m inv*

slip [slɪp] **1** *n (mistake)* erreur *f*; *(garment)* combinaison *f*; *(fall)* chute *f*; **a s. of paper** un bout de papier; *(printed)* un bordereau; **a s. of the tongue** un lapsus; **a s. of a girl** un petit bout de femme; **to give sb the s.** fausser compagnie à qn; *Br* **s. road** bretelle *f* **2** *(pt & pp* **-pp-**) *vt (slide)* glisser (**to** à; **into** dans); **it slipped her notice** ça lui a échappé; **it**

slipped my mind ça m'est sorti de l'esprit; **to have a slipped disc** avoir une hernie discale 3 *vi* glisser; *Fam (of popularity, ratings)* baisser; **to let sth s.** *(chance, oath, secret)* laisser échapper qch

Note that the French noun **slip** is a false friend and is never a translation for the English noun **slip**. It means **underpants**.

▸ **slip away** *vi (escape)* s'éclipser
▸ **slip back** *vi* retourner furtivement
▸ **slip in** *vi (enter)* entrer furtivement
▸ **slip into** *vt insep (room)* se glisser dans; *(bathrobe)* passer; *(habit)* prendre
▸ **slip off** *vt sep (coat)* enlever
▸ **slip on** *vt sep (coat)* mettre
▸ **slip out** *vi (leave)* sortir furtivement; *(for a moment)* sortir (un instant); *(of secret)* s'éventer
▸ **slip past** *vt insep (guard)* passer sans être vu de
▸ **slip through** 1 *vt insep* **to s. through the crowd** se faufiler parmi la foule 2 *vi (of error)* échapper à l'attention de
▸ **slip up** *vi Fam* se planter

slipcover ['slɪpkʌvə(r)] *n Am* housse *f*
slipper ['slɪpə(r)] *n* pantoufle *f*
slippery ['slɪpərɪ] *adj* glissant
slipshod ['slɪpʃɒd] *adj (negligent)* négligent; *(slovenly)* négligé
slip-up ['slɪpʌp] *n Fam* gaffe *f*
slit [slɪt] 1 *n* fente *f* 2 *(pt & pp* slit*, pres p* slitting*)* *vt (cut)* couper; *(tear)* déchirer; **to s. open** *(sack)* éventrer
slither ['slɪðə(r)] *vi* glisser; *(of snake)* se couler
sliver ['slɪvə(r)] *n (of wood)* éclat *m*; *(of cheese)* fine tranche *f*
slob [slɒb] *n Fam (lazy person)* gros fainéant *m*; *(dirty person)* porc *m*
slobber ['slɒbə(r)] 1 *n* bave *f* 2 *vi (of dog, baby)* baver
sloe [sləʊ] *n (fruit)* prunelle *f*; **s. gin** gin *m* à la prunelle
slog [slɒg] *Br Fam* 1 **a (hard) s.** *(effort)* un gros effort; **it was a bit of a s.** ça a été dur 2 *(pt & pp* -gg-*) vt (ball, person)* donner un grand coup à 3 *vi* **to s. (away)** trimer
slogan ['sləʊgən] *n* slogan *m*
slop [slɒp] 1 *(pt & pp* -pp-*) vt* renverser 2 *vi* **to s. (over)** se renverser
slope [sləʊp] 1 *n* pente *f*; *(of mountain)* versant *m*; *(for skiing)* piste *f*; *(slant of handwriting, pipe)* inclinaison *f* 2 *vi (of ground, roof)* être en pente; *(of handwriting)* pencher; **to s. down** *(of path)* descendre en pente ▪ **sloping** *adj (roof)* en pente; *(handwriting)* penché
sloppy ['slɒpɪ] *(-ier, -iest) adj (work, appearance)* négligé; *(person)* négligent; *(sentimental)* sentimental
slosh [slɒʃ] *Fam* 1 *vt (pour, spill)* renverser;

répandre 2 *vi (of liquid)* clapoter; *(spill)* se renverser; **to s. about** *(walk in water, mud)* patauger; *(splash in bath)* barboter ▪ **sloshed** *adj Br Fam (drunk)* bourré
slot [slɒt] 1 *n (slit)* fente *f*; *(in schedule, list)* créneau *m*; **s. machine** *(for vending)* distributeur *m* automatique; *(for gambling)* machine *f* à sous 2 *(pt & pp* -tt-*) vt (insert)* insérer (**into** dans) 3 *vi* s'insérer (**into** dans)
sloth [sləʊθ] *n (animal)* paresseux *m*; *Literary (laziness)* paresse *f* ▪ **slothful** *adj* paresseux, -euse
slouch [slaʊtʃ] 1 *n* **to have a s.** avoir le dos voûté 2 *vi* ne pas se tenir droit; *(have a stoop)* avoir le dos voûté; *(in chair)* être avachi; **don't s.!** tenez-vous droit!; **he slouched out of the room** il est sorti de la pièce en traînant les pieds
Slovakia [sləʊ'vækɪə] *n* la Slovaquie ▪ **Slovak** 1 *adj* slovaque 2 *n (person)* Slovaque *mf*; *(language)* slovaque *m*
Slovenia [sləʊ'viːnɪə] *n* la Slovénie ▪ **Slovenian** 1 *adj* slovène 2 *n (person)* Slovène *mf*; *(language)* slovène *m*
slovenly ['slʌvənlɪ] *adj* négligé
slow [sləʊ] 1 *(-er, -est) adj (not fast)*; **at (a) s. speed** à vitesse réduite; **in s. motion** au ralenti; **to be a s. walker** marcher lentement; **to be s.** *(of clock, watch)* retarder; **to be five minutes s.** retarder de cinq minutes; **to be s. to do sth** être lent à faire qch; **business is s.** les affaires tournent au ralenti 2 *adv* lentement 3 *vt* **to s. sth down** *or* **up** ralentir qch; *(delay)* retarder qch 4 *vi* **to s. down** *or* **up** ralentir ▪ **slowcoach** *n Br Fam* lambin, -ine *mf* ▪ **slow-down** *n* ralentissement *m*; *Am* **s. (strike)** grève *f* perlée ▪ **slowly** *adv* lentement; *(bit by bit)* peu à peu ▪ **'slow-'moving** *adj (vehicle)* lent ▪ **slowness** *n* lenteur *f* ▪ **slowpoke** *n Am Fam* lambin, -ine *mf*
sludge [slʌdʒ] *n* gadoue *f*
slue [sluː] *n Am Fam* = **slew**
slug [slʌg] 1 *n* (**a**) *(mollusc)* limace *f* (**b**) *Am Fam (bullet)* pruneau *m* 2 *(pt & pp* -gg-*) vt Am Fam (hit)* frapper
sluggish ['slʌgɪʃ] *adj (person)* amorphe; *(business)* au ralenti
sluice [sluːs] *n* **s. (gate)** vanne *f*
slum [slʌm] 1 *n (house)* taudis *m*; **the slums** les quartiers *mpl* délabrés 2 *(pt & pp* -mm-*) vt Fam* **to s. it** s'encanailler ▪ **slummy** *(-ier, -iest) adj* sordide
slumber ['slʌmbə(r)] *n Literary* sommeil *m*; *Am* **s. party** = soirée entre copines, où les invitées restent dormir chez leur hôte
slump [slʌmp] 1 *n* baisse *f* soudaine (**in** de); *(in prices)* effondrement *m*; *(economic depression)* crise *f* 2 *vi (of person, prices)* s'effondrer
slung [slʌŋ] *pt & pp of* **sling**

slur [slɜː(r)] **1** n (insult) insulte f; **to cast a s. on sb's reputation** entacher la réputation de qn; **to speak with a s.** manger ses mots **2** (pt & pp **-rr-**) vt mal articuler; **to s. one's words** manger ses mots ▪ **slurred** adj (speech) indistinct

slush [slʌʃ] n (snow) neige f fondue; (mud) gadoue f; Fam (sentimentality) sensiblerie f; Fam Pol **s. fund** caisse f noire ▪ **slushy (-ier, -iest)** adj (road) couvert de neige fondue; Fam (novel, film) guimauve

slut [slʌt] n Fam Pej (immoral woman) salope f

sly [slaɪ] **1** (-er, -est) adj (deceitful) sournois; (cunning, crafty) rusé **2** n **on the s.** en douce

smack [smæk] **1** n (blow) claque f; (on bottom) fessée f **2** vt (person) donner une claque à; **to s. sb's face** gifler qn; **to s. sb('s bottom)** donner une fessée à qn **3** vi **to s. of** (be suggestive of) avoir des relents de **4** adv Fam **s. in the middle** en plein milieu

small [smɔːl] **1** (-er, -est) adj petit; **in the s. hours** au petit matin; **s. change** petite monnaie f; **s. talk** banalités fpl **2** adv (cut, chop) menu; (write) petit **3** n **the s. of the back** la chute des reins ▪ **'small-'minded** adj à l'esprit étroit ▪ **'small-'mindedness** n étroitesse f d'esprit ▪ **smallness** n petitesse f ▪ **small-scale** adj (model) réduit; (research) à petite échelle ▪ **small-time** adj Fam (crook, dealer) petit

smallpox [ˈsmɔːlpɒks] n variole f

smarmy [ˈsmɑːmɪ] (-ier, -iest) adj Fam Pej obséquieux, -ieuse

smart¹ [smɑːt] (-er, -est) adj (in appearance) élégant; (clever) intelligent; (astute) astucieux, -ieuse; (quick) rapide; Fam **s. aleck** je-sais-tout mf inv; **s. card** carte f à puce ▪ **smartly** adv (dressed) avec élégance; (cleverly) avec intelligence; (astutely) astucieusement; (quickly) en vitesse

smart² [smɑːt] vi (sting) brûler

smarten [ˈsmɑːtən] **1** vt **to s. sth up** égayer qch **2** vti **to s. (oneself) up** se faire beau (f belle)

smash [smæʃ] **1** n (accident) collision f; (noise) fracas m; (blow) coup m; Tennis smash m; Fam **s. hit** gros succès m **2** vt (break) briser; (shatter) fracasser; (record) pulvériser; (enemy) écraser; **to s. sth to pieces** fracasser qch; Fam **to s. sb's face (in)** casser la gueule à qn **3** vi **to s. into sth** s'écraser contre qch; **to s. into pieces** éclater en mille morceaux ▪ **smash-and-'grab raid** n Br pillage m de vitrines ▪ **smash-up** n collision f

▸ **smash down, smash in** vt sep (door) enfoncer

▸ **smash into** vt insep (of vehicle) entrer dans

▸ **smash up** vt sep (vehicle) esquinter; (room) saccager

smashing [ˈsmæʃɪŋ] adj (blow) violent; Br Fam (wonderful) génial ▪ **smasher** n Br **to be a (real) s.** Fam être génial

smattering [ˈsmætərɪŋ] n **a s. of French** quelques notions fpl de français

smear [smɪə(r)] **1** n (mark) trace f; (stain) tache f; Med **s. (test)** frottis m (vaginal); **a s. on sb's reputation** une atteinte à la réputation de qn; **s. campaign** campagne f de diffamation; **to use s. tactics** avoir recours à la diffamation **2** vt (coat) enduire (with de); (stain) tacher (with de); (smudge) faire une trace sur; **to s. sb** calomnier qn

smell [smel] **1** n odeur f; (sense of) **s.** odorat m **2** (pt & pp **smelled** or **smelt**) vt sentir; (of animal) flairer **3** vi (stink) sentir mauvais; (have a smell) sentir; **to s. of smoke** sentir la fumée; **smelling salts** sels mpl ▪ **smelly (-ier, -iest)** adj **to be s.** sentir mauvais

smelt¹ [smelt] pt & pp of **smell**

smelt² [smelt] vt (ore) fondre; **smelting works** fonderie f

smidgen [ˈsmɪdʒən] n Fam **a s.** (a little) un brin (of de)

smile [smaɪl] **1** n sourire m **2** vi sourire (at sb à qn; at sth de qch) ▪ **smiling** adj souriant ▪ **smiley 1** adj souriant **2** n Comptr souriant m, émoticon m

smirk [smɜːk] n (smug) sourire m suffisant; (scornful) sourire goguenard

smith [smɪθ] n forgeron m

smithereens [smɪðəˈriːnz] npl **to smash sth to s.** briser qch en mille morceaux

smitten [ˈsmɪtən] adj Literary **to be s. with terror** être terrorisé; **to be s. with remorse** être pris de remords; Fam **to be s.** (in love) être très épris (with de)

smock [smɒk] n blouse f

smog [smɒg] n smog m

smoke [sməʊk] **1** n fumée f; **to have a s.** fumer une cigarette; **s. alarm** or **detector** détecteur m de fumée; Fig **s. screen** rideau m de fumée **2** vt (cigarette) fumer; **to s. a room out** enfumer une pièce; **smoked salmon** saumon m fumé **3** vi fumer; **to s. like a chimney** (of person) fumer comme un pompier; **'no smoking'** 'défense de fumer'; **smoking compartment** (on train) compartiment m fumeurs ▪ **smokeless** adj **s. fuel** combustible m non polluant ▪ **smoker** n fumeur, -euse mf; (train compartment) compartiment m fumeurs ▪ **smokestack** n cheminée f d'usine ▪ **smoky (-ier, -iest)** adj (room, air) enfumé; (ceiling, wall) noirci par la fumée; **it's s. here** il y a de la fumée ici

smooth [smuːð] **1** (-er, -est) adj (surface, skin) lisse; (cream, sauce) onctueux, -ueuse; (sea, flight) calme; Pej (person, manners) doucereux, -euse; **the s. running of** (machine, service, business) la bonne marche de; **to be a s. talker** être beau parleur; **to be a s. operator** savoir y faire **2** vt **to s. sth down** (hair, sheet, paper) lisser qch; **to s. sth out** (paper, sheet, dress) lisser qch; *(crease)* faire disparaître qch; *Fig* **to s. difficulties out** *or* **over** aplanir des difficultés • **smoothly** *adv* sans problèmes • **smoothness** *n* aspect *m* lisse; *(of road)* surface *f* égale

smoothie ['smuːðɪ] *n (drink)* = boisson à base de jus de fruit et de yaourt

smother ['smʌðə(r)] *vt (stifle)* étouffer; **to s. sth in sth** recouvrir qch de qch; *Fig* **to s. sb with kisses** couvrir qn de baisers

smoulder ['smɔʊldə(r)] *(Am* **smolder)** *vi Fig (of fire, passion)* couver • **smouldering** *(Am* **smoldering)** *adj Fig (fire, passion)* qui couve

smudge [smʌdʒ] **1** *n* tache *f* **2** *vt (paper)* faire des taches sur; *(ink)* étaler

smug [smʌg] **(smugger, smuggest)** *adj (smile)* béat; *(person)* content de soi

smuggle ['smʌɡəl] *vt* passer en fraude; **smuggled goods** contrebande *f* • **smuggler** *n* contrebandier, -ière *mf*; *(of drugs)* trafiquant *m* • **smuggling** *n* contrebande *f*

smut [smʌt] *n inv (obscenity)* cochonneries *fpl* • **smutty (-ier, -iest)** *adj (joke)* cochon, -onne

snack [snæk] **1** *n (meal)* casse-croûte *m inv*; **to eat a s.** *or* **snacks** grignoter quelque chose; **s. bar** snack-bar *m* **2** *vi* manger entre les repas; **to s. on sth** grignoter qch

snag [snæɡ] *n (hitch)* problème *m*; *(in cloth)* accroc *m*

snail [sneɪl] *n* escargot *m*; **at a s.'s pace** comme un escargot; *Fam* **s. mail** courrier *m* escargot, = courrier postal

snake [sneɪk] **1** *n* serpent *m*; **snakes and ladders** ≃ jeu *m* de l'oie **2** *vi (of river)* serpenter • **snakebite** *n* morsure *f* de serpent

snap [snæp] **1** *n (sound)* craquement *m*; *Fam (photo)* photo *f*; **s. (fastener)** pression *f*; **cold s.** coup *m* de froid **2** *adj (judgement, decision)* hâtif, -ive **3** *(pt & pp* **-pp-)** *vt (break)* casser net; *(fingers, whip)* faire claquer; **to s. up a bargain** sauter sur une occasion **4** *vi* se casser net; *(of whip)* claquer; *Fig (of person)* parler sèchement (**at** à); **to s. at sb** *(of dog)* essayer de mordre qn; **to s. off** se casser net; *Fam* **s. out of it!** secoue-toi!

snappy ['snæpɪ] **(-ier, -iest)** *adj (pace)* vif *(f* vive); *Fam* **make it s.!** dépêche-toi!; *Fam* **to be a s. dresser** s'habiller classe

snapshot ['snæpʃɒt] *n Fam* photo *f*

snare [sneə(r)] **1** *n* piège *m* **2** *vt* prendre au piège

snarl [snɑːl] **1** *n* grognement *m* **2** *vi* grogner (en montrant les dents) • **snarl-up** *n Fam (traffic jam)* bouchon *m*; *(confusion)* pagaille *f*

snatch [snætʃ] *vt (grab)* saisir; *(steal)* arracher; **to s. sth from sb** arracher qch à qn; **to s. some sleep** dormir un peu

snatches ['snætʃɪz] *npl (bits)* fragments *mpl* (**of** de)

snazzy ['snæzɪ] **(-ier, -iest)** *adj Fam (smart)* chic; **she's a s. dresser** elle s'habille chic

sneak [sniːk] **1** *n Br Fam (telltale)* mouchard, -arde *mf*; **to get a s. preview of sth** voir qch en avant-première **2** *(pt & pp* **sneaked** *or Am* **snuck)** *vi Br Fam (tell tales)* rapporter; **to s. in/ out** entrer/sortir furtivement; **to s. off** s'esquiver • **sneaky (-ier, -iest)** *adj Fam* sournois

sneaker ['sniːkə(r)] *n Am (shoe)* chaussure *f* de sport

sneer [snɪə(r)] **1** *n* ricanement *m* **2** *vi* ricaner; **to s. at sb/sth** se moquer de qn/qch

sneeze [sniːz] **1** *n* éternuement *m* **2** *vi* éternuer

snicker ['snɪkə(r)] *n & vi Am* = **snigger**

snide [snaɪd] *adj* méprisant

sniff [snɪf] **1** *n* **to give sth a s.** renifler qch; **to take a s. at sth** renifler qch **2** *vt* renifler; **to s. glue** sniffer de la colle; *Fam* **it's not to be sniffed at** il ne faut pas cracher dessus **3** *vi* renifler

sniffle ['snɪfəl] **1** *n Fam* **to have a s.** *or* **the sniffles** avoir un petit rhume **2** *vi* renifler

snigger ['snɪɡə(r)] **1** *n (petit)* ricanement *m* **2** *vi* ricaner • **sniggering** *n* ricanements *mpl*

snip [snɪp] **1** *n (cut)* petite entaille *f*; *(piece)* bout *m*; *Br Fam (bargain)* bonne affaire *f* **2** *(pt & pp* **-pp-)** *vt* **to s. sth (off)** couper qch

sniper ['snaɪpə(r)] *n Mil* tireur *m* embusqué *ou* isolé

snippet ['snɪpɪt] *n (of conversation)* bribe *f*

snivel ['snɪvəl] *(Br* **-ll-,** *Am* **-l-)** *vi* pleurnicher • **snivelling** *(Am* **sniveling)** *adj* pleurnicheur, -euse

snob [snɒb] *n* snob *mf* • **snobbery** *n* snobisme *m* • **snobbish** *adj* snob *inv*

snog [snɒɡ] *Br Fam* **1** *n* **to have a s.** se bécoter **2** *vt* bécoter **2** *vi* se bécoter

snooker ['snuːkə(r)] *n (game)* = billard qui se joue avec vingt-deux billes

snoop [snuːp] *vi* **to s. (around)** fourrer son nez partout; **to s. on sb** espionner qn

snooty ['snuːtɪ] **(-ier, -iest)** *adj Fam* prétentieux, -ieuse

snooze [snuːz] **1** *n* petit somme *m*; **to have a s.** faire un petit somme **2** *vi* faire un petit somme

snore [snɔː(r)] **1** *n* ronflement *m* **2** *vi* ronfler • **snoring** *n* ronflements *mpl*

snorkel ['snɔːkəl] **1** *n* tuba *m* **2** *(Br* **-ll-,** *Am* **-l-)** *vi* nager sous l'eau avec un tuba • **snorkelling** *n* plongée *f* avec un tuba; **to go s.** faire de la plongée avec un tuba

snort [snɔːt] **1** *n (of person)* grognement *m*; *(of horse)* ébrouement *m* **2** *vi (of person)* grogner; *(of horse)* s'ébrouer

snot [snɒt] *n Fam* morve *f* • **snotty (-ier, -iest)** *adj Fam (nose)* qui coule; *(handkerchief)* plein de morve; *(child)* morveux, -euse; *(arrogant)* arrogant • **snotty-nosed, snot-nosed** *adj Fam* morveux, -euse

snout [snaʊt] *n* museau *m*

snow [snəʊ] 1 *n* neige *f* 2 *vi* neiger; **it's snowing** il neige 3 *vt* **to be snowed in** être bloqué par la neige; *Fig* **to be snowed under with work** être submergé de travail ▪ **snowball** 1 *n* boule *f* de neige 2 *vi (increase)* faire boule de neige ▪ **snowbound** *adj* bloqué par la neige ▪ **snow-capped** *adj* couronné de neige ▪ **snowdrift** *n* congère *f* ▪ **snowdrop** *n (flower)* perce-neige *m ou f inv* ▪ **snowfall** *n* chute *f* de neige ▪ **snowflake** *n* flocon *m* de neige ▪ **snowman** *(pl* **-men)** *n* bonhomme *m* de neige ▪ **snowmobile** ['snəʊməʊbiːl] *n* motoneige *f* ▪ **snowplough** *(Am* **snowplow)** *n* chasse-neige *m inv* ▪ **snowshoe** *n* raquette *f* ▪ **snowstorm** *n* tempête *f* de neige ▪ **'Snow 'White** *n* Blanche-Neige *f* ▪ **snowy** **(-ier, -iest)** *adj (weather, hills)* neigeux, -euse; *(day)* de neige

snub [snʌb] 1 *n* rebuffade *f* 2 *(pt & pp* **-bb-)** *vt (offer)* rejeter; **to s. sb** snober qn ▪ **snub 'nose** *n* nez *m* retroussé

snuck [snʌk] *Am pt & pp of* sneak

snuff [snʌf] 1 *n* tabac *m* à priser 2 *vt* **to s. (out)** *(candle)* moucher

snuffle ['snʌfəl] *n & vi* = sniffle

snug [snʌg] *(snugger, snuggest) adj (house)* douillet, -ette; *(garment)* bien ajusté; **s. in bed** bien au chaud dans son lit

snuggle ['snʌgəl] *vi* **to s. up to sb** se blottir contre qn

so [səʊ] 1 *adv (to such a degree)* si, tellement **(that** que); *(thus)* ainsi, comme ça; **to work/ drink so much that…** travailler/boire tellement que…; **so much courage** tellement de courage **(that** que); **so many books** tant de livres **(that** que); **so very fast** tellement vite; **ten or so** environ dix; **and so on** et ainsi de suite; **I think so** je crois que oui; **do so!** faites-le!; **is that so?** c'est vrai?; **so am I** moi aussi; **you're late – so I am** tu es en retard – ah oui! tu as raison; **I told you so** je vous l'avais bien dit; *Fam* **so long!** au revoir! 2 *conj (therefore)* donc; *(in that case)* alors; **so what?** et alors?; **so that…** pour que… *(+ subjunctive)*; **so as to do sth** pour faire qch ▪ **So-and-so** *n* Mr S. Monsieur Untel ▪ **so-called** *adj* soi-disant *inv* ▪ **so-so** *adj & adv Fam* comme ci comme ça

soak [səʊk] 1 *n* **to give sth a s.** faire tremper qch 2 *vt (drench)* tremper; *(washing, food)* faire tremper; **to be soaked through** *or* **to the skin** être trempé jusqu'aux os; **to s. sth up** absorber qch 3 *vi (of washing)* tremper; **to s. in** *(of liquid)* s'infiltrer ▪ **soaked** *adj* trempé ▪ **soaking** 1 *adj & adv Fam* trempé 2 *n* **to get a s.** se faire tremper; **to give sth a s.** faire tremper qch

soap [səʊp] 1 *n* savon *m*; **s. opera** feuilleton *m* populaire; **s. powder** lessive *f* 2 *vt* **to s. sth (down)** savonner qch ▪ **soapsuds** *npl* mousse *f* de savon ▪ **soapy** **(-ier, -iest)** *adj* savonneux, -euse

soar [sɔː(r)] *vi (of bird)* s'élever; *(of price)* monter en flèche

sob [sɒb] 1 *n* sanglot *m*; *Fam Pej* **s. story** histoire *f* à vous fondre le cœur 2 *(pt & pp* **-bb-)** *vi* sangloter ▪ **sobbing** *n (sobs)* sanglots *mpl*

sober ['səʊbə(r)] 1 *adj (sensible)* sobre; **he's s.** *(not drunk)* il n'est pas ivre 2 *vti* **to s. up** dessoûler ▪ **sobering** *adj* qui dégrise; **it's a s. thought** ça vous fait réfléchir

soccer ['sɒkə(r)] *n esp Am* football *m*

sociable ['səʊʃəbəl] *adj (person)* sociable; *(evening)* amical ▪ **sociably** *adv (act, reply)* aimablement

social ['səʊʃəl] 1 *adj* social; **to have a good s. life** sortir beaucoup; **s. class** classe *f* sociale; **s. evening** soirée *f*; **s. gathering** réunion *f* mondaine; **s. science(s)** sciences *fpl* humaines; **S. Security** ≃ la Sécurité sociale; **s. security** *(aid)* aide *f* sociale; *Am (retirement pension)* pension *f* de retraite; **the s. services** les services *mpl* sociaux; **s. worker** assistant, -ante *mf* social(e) 2 *n (party)* fête *f*

socialism ['səʊʃəlɪzəm] *n* socialisme *m* ▪ **socialist** *adj & n* socialiste *(mf)*

socialite ['səʊʃəlaɪt] *n* mondain, -aine *mf*

socialize ['səʊʃəlaɪz] *vi* fréquenter des gens; **to s. with sb** fréquenter qn

socially ['səʊʃəlɪ] *adv* socialement; *(meet, behave)* en société; **to see sb s.** fréquenter qn

society [sə'saɪətɪ] 1 *(pl* **-ies)** *n (community, club, companionship)* société *f*; *(school/university club)* club *m*; **(high) s.** haute société *f* 2 *adj (wedding, news)* mondain

sociology [səʊsɪ'ɒlədʒɪ] *n* sociologie *f* ▪ **sociological** [-sɪə'lɒdʒɪkəl] *adj* sociologique ▪ **sociologist** *n* sociologue *mf*

sock [sɒk] 1 *n* chaussette *f* 2 *vt Fam (hit)* donner un coup de poing à

socket ['sɒkɪt] *n Br (of electric plug)* prise *f* de courant; *Br (of lamp)* douille *f*; *(of eye)* orbite *f*

soda ['səʊdə] *n Chem* soude *f*; **baking s.** bicarbonate *m* de soude; *Am* **s. (pop)** boisson *f* gazeuse; **s. (water)** eau *f* de Seltz

sodden ['sɒdən] *adj (ground)* détrempé

sodium ['səʊdɪəm] *n Chem* sodium *m*

sofa ['səʊfə] *n* canapé *m*; **s. bed** canapé-lit *m*

soft [sɒft] **(-er, -est)** *adj (gentle, not stiff)* doux *(f* douce); *(butter, ground, paste, snow)* mou *(f* molle); *(wood, heart, colour)* tendre; *(easy)* facile; *(indulgent)* indulgent; *Fam (cowardly)* poltron, -onne; *Fam (stupid)* ramolli; **to have a s. spot for sb** avoir un faible pour qn; **s. cheese** fromage *m* frais; **s. drink** boisson *f* non alcoolisée; **s. drugs** drogues *fpl* douces; **s. toy** peluche *f*; **s. water** eau *f* douce ▪ **'soft-'boiled** *adj (egg)* à la coque ▪ **'soft-'hearted** *adj* qui se

laisse facilement attendrir ■ **'soft-'spoken** adj
qui a une voix douce

soften ['sɒfən] **1** vt (object) ramollir; (colour,
light, voice, skin) adoucir **2** vi ramollir; (of
colour) s'adoucir ■ **softener** n adoucissant m

softie ['sɒftɪ] n Fam (gentle person) bonne pâte f;
(weakling) mauviette f

softly ['sɒftlɪ] adv doucement ■ **softness** n
douceur f; (of butter, ground, paste) mollesse f

software ['sɒftweə(r)] n inv Comptr logiciel m; **s.**
package progiciel m

soggy ['sɒgɪ] (**-ier, -iest**) adj trempé

soil [sɔɪl] **1** n (earth) terre f **2** vt (dirty) salir **3** vi
(of fabric) se salir

solar ['səʊlə(r)] adj solaire; **s. plexus** plexus m
solaire; **s. power** énergie f solaire; **s. system**
système m solaire

sold [səʊld] pt & pp of **sell**

solder ['sɒldə(r)] **1** n soudure f **2** vt souder

soldier ['səʊldʒə(r)] **1** n soldat m **2** vi **to s. on**
persévérer

sole[1] [səʊl] **1** n (of shoe) semelle f; (of foot)
plante f **2** vt (shoe) ressemeler

sole[2] [səʊl] adj (only) unique; (rights,
representative, responsibility) exclusif, -ive
■ **solely** adv uniquement; **you're s.** to blame
tu es seul coupable

sole[3] [səʊl] n (fish) sole f; **lemon s.** limande f

solemn ['sɒləm] adj solennel, -elle ■ **sol-**
emnity [sə'lemnɪtɪ] n solennité f ■ **solemnly**
adv (promise) solennellement; (say) gravement

solicit [sə'lɪsɪt] **1** vt (seek) solliciter **2** vi (of
prostitute) racoler

solicitor [sə'lɪsɪtə(r)] n Br notaire m

solid ['sɒlɪd] **1** adj (not liquid) solide; (not
hollow) plein; (gold, silver) massif, -ive; **s. line**
ligne f continue **2** adv **frozen s.** complètement gelé; **ten days s.** dix jours d'affilée **3** n
solide m; **solids** (food) aliments mpl solides
■ **solidify** [sə'lɪdɪfaɪ] (pt & pp **-ied**) vi se
solidifier ■ **solidity** [sə'lɪdɪtɪ] n solidité f
■ **solidly** adv (built) solidement; (support, vote)
en masse; (work) sans interruption

solidarity [sɒlɪ'dærətɪ] n solidarité f (**with**
avec)

soliloquy [sə'lɪləkwɪ] (pl **-ies**) n monologue m

solitary ['sɒlɪtərɪ] adj (lonely, alone) solitaire;
(only) seul; **s. confinement** isolement m
cellulaire ■ **solitude** n solitude f

solo ['səʊləʊ] **1** (pl **-os**) n Mus solo m **2** adj
(guitar, violin) solo inv **3** adv (play, sing) en
solo; (fly) en solitaire ■ **soloist** n Mus soliste mf

solstice ['sɒlstɪs] n solstice m

soluble ['sɒljʊbəl] adj (substance, problem)
soluble

solution [sə'lu:ʃən] n (a) (to problem) solution f
(**to** de) (b) (liquid) solution f

solve [sɒlv] vt (problem) résoudre

solvent ['sɒlvənt] **1** adj (financially) solvable **2** n
Chem solvant m; **s. abuse** = usage de solvants
comme stupéfiants ■ **solvency** n (of company)
solvabilité f

Somalia [sə'mɑ:lɪə] n la Somalie

somber adj Am = **sombre**

sombre ['sɒmbə(r)] (Am **somber**) adj sombre

some [sʌm] **1** adj (a) (a certain quantity of) du,
de la, des; **s. wine** du vin; **s. glue** de la colle; **s.**
water de l'eau; **s. dogs** des chiens; **s. pretty**
flowers de jolies fleurs (b) (unspecified) un,
une; **s. man (or other)** un homme
(quelconque); **s. other way** un autre moyen;
for s. reason or other pour une raison ou
pour une autre; **I have been waiting s. time** ça
fait un moment que j'attends; Fam **that's s.**
book! ça, c'est un livre! (c) (a few) quelques;
(in contrast to others) certains; **s. days ago** il y
a quelques jours; **s. people think that...**
certains pensent que...

2 pron (a) (a certain quantity) en; **I want s.** j'en
veux; **do you have s.?** en as-tu?; **s. of my wine**
un peu de mon vin; **s. of the time** une partie du
temps (b) (as opposed to others) certain(e)s;
some say... certains disent...; **s. of the**
guests certains invités

3 adv (about) environ; **s. ten years** environ dix
ans ■ **somebody** pron = **someone** ■ **someday**
adv un jour ■ **somehow** adv (in some way)
d'une manière ou d'une autre; (for some
reason) on ne sait pourquoi ■ **someone** pron
quelqu'un; **s. small** quelqu'un de petit
■ **someplace** adv Am = **somewhere**
■ **something** pron quelque chose; **s. awful**
quelque chose d'affreux; **he's s. of a liar** il est
plutôt menteur **2** adv **she plays s. like...** elle
joue un peu comme...; **it was s. awful** c'était
vraiment affreux ■ **sometime** **1** adv un jour;
s. in May au mois de mai **2** adj (former)
ancien, -ienne ■ **sometimes** adv quelquefois,
parfois ■ **somewhat** adv quelque peu, assez
■ **somewhere** adv quelque part; **s. about**
fifteen (approximately) environ quinze

somersault ['sʌməsɔ:lt] **1** n (on ground)
roulade f; (in air) saut m périlleux **2** vi faire
une roulade; (in air) faire un saut périlleux

son [sʌn] n fils m ■ **son-in-law** (pl **sons-in-law**)
n gendre m

sonar ['səʊnɑ:(r)] n sonar m

sonata [sə'nɑ:tə] n sonate f

song [sɒŋ] n chanson f; (of bird) chant m
■ **songbook** n recueil m de chansons

sonic ['sɒnɪk] adj **s. boom** bang m

sonnet ['sɒnɪt] n sonnet m

soon [su:n] (**-er, -est**) adv (in a short time)
bientôt; (quickly) vite; (early) tôt; **he s. forgot**
about it il l'oublia vite; **s. after** peu après; **as s.**
as... aussitôt que...; **no sooner had he**
spoken than... à peine avait-il parlé que...;
I'd sooner leave je préférerais partir; **I'd just**

as s. leave j'aimerais autant partir; **sooner or later** tôt ou tard

soot [sʊt] *n* suie *f* ▪**sooty (-ier, -iest)** *adj* couvert de suie

soothe [suːð] *vt* calmer ▪**soothing** *adj* calmant

sophisticated [səˈfɪstɪkeɪtɪd] *adj (person, taste)* raffiné; *(machine, method, technology)* sophistiqué

sophomore [ˈsɒfəmɔː(r)] *n Am Univ* étudiant, -iante *mf* de deuxième année

soporific [sɒpəˈrɪfɪk] *adj* soporifique

sopping [ˈsɒpɪŋ] *adj & adv* **s. (wet)** trempé

soppy [ˈsɒpɪ] **(-ier, -iest)** *adj Br Fam (sentimental)* sentimental

soprano [səˈprɑːnəʊ] *(pl* **-os)** *n (singer)* soprano *mf; (voice)* soprano *m*

sorbet [ˈsɔːbeɪ] *n* sorbet *m*

sorcerer [ˈsɔːsərə(r)] *n* sorcier *m* ▪**sorcery** *n* sorcellerie *f*

sordid [ˈsɔːdɪd] *adj* sordide

sore [sɔː(r)] **1 (-er, -est)** *adj (painful)* douloureux, -euse; *Am (angry)* fâché (**at** contre); **to have a s. throat** avoir mal à la gorge; **he's still s.** *(in pain)* il a encore mal; *Am (angry)* il est toujours fâché; *Fig* **it's a s. point** c'est un sujet délicat **2** *n (wound)* plaie *f* ▪**sorely** *adv (tempted)* très; *(regretted)* amèrement; **it's s. needed** on en a un grand besoin ▪**soreness** *n (pain)* douleur *f*

sorrow [ˈsɒrəʊ] *n* chagrin *m* ▪**sorrowful** *adj* triste

sorry [ˈsɒrɪ] **(-ier, -iest)** *adj (sight, state)* triste; **to be s. (about sth)** *(regret)* être désolé (de qch); **to feel** *or* **be s. for sb** plaindre qn; **I'm s. she can't come** je regrette qu'elle ne puisse pas venir; **s.!** pardon!; **s. to keep you waiting** désolé de vous faire attendre; **to say s.** demander pardon (**to** à)

sort¹ [sɔːt] *n* sorte *f;* **a s. of** une sorte de; **all sorts of** toutes sortes de; **what s. of drink is it?** qu'est-ce que c'est comme boisson?; *Br Fam* **he's a good s.** c'est un brave type; **s. of sad** *(somewhat)* plutôt triste

sort² [sɔːt] **1** *vt (papers)* trier; **to s. out** *(classify, select)* trier; *(separate)* séparer (**from** de); *(organize)* ranger; *(problem)* régler; *Br Fam* **to s. sb out** régler son compte à qn **2** *vi* **to s. through letters/magazines** trier des lettres/ magazines; *Br* **sorting office** *(for mail)* centre *m* de tri ▪**sorted** *adj Br Fam* **to be s.** *(psychologically)* être bien dans ses baskets; *(have everything one needs)* être paré; **if I get that pay rise, I'll be s.** si j'obtiens cette augmentation j'aurai plus à m'en faire

SOS [esəʊˈes] *n* SOS *m*

soufflé [ˈsuːfleɪ] *n Culin* soufflé *m*

sought [sɔːt] *pt & pp of* **seek**

soul [səʊl] *n* âme *f;* **not a living s.** pas âme qui vive; *Fig* **a good s.** un brave type; **s. mate** âme *f* sœur ▪**soul-destroying** *adj* abrutissant ▪**soul-searching** *n* examen *m* de conscience

sound¹ [saʊnd] **1** *n* son *m; (noise)* bruit *m;* **I don't like the s. of it** ça ne me plaît pas du tout; **s. archives** phonothèque *f;* **s. barrier** mur *m* du son; **s. bite** petite phrase *f;* **s. effects** bruitage *m;* **s. engineer** ingénieur *m* du son; **s. recording** enregistrement *m* sonore; **s. wave** onde *f* sonore **2** *vt (bell, alarm)* sonner; *(bugle, horn)* sonner de; *(letter, syllable)* prononcer; **to s. one's horn** *(in vehicle)* klaxonner **3** *vi (trumpet, bugle)* sonner; *(seem)* sembler; **to s. like** sembler être; *(resemble)* ressembler à; **it sounds like** *or* **as if...** il semble que... (+ *subjunctive or indicative);* **(it) sounds good!** bonne idée!; *Pej* **to s. off (about sth)** *(boast)* se vanter (de qch); *(complain)* se plaindre (de qch)

sound² [saʊnd] **1 (-er, -est)** *adj (healthy)* sain; *(in good condition)* en bon état; *(basis)* solide; *(argument)* valable; *(advice)* bon (*f* bonne); *(investment)* sûr; **a s. beating** une bonne correction **2** *adv* **s. asleep** profondément endormi ▪**soundly** *adv (asleep, sleep)* profondément; *(reasoned)* solidement; *(beaten)* complètement ▪**soundness** *n (of mind)* santé *f; (of argument)* solidité *f*

sound³ [saʊnd] *vt (test, measure)* sonder; **to s. sb out** sonder qn *(about* sur)

soundproof [ˈsaʊndpruːf] **1** *adj* insonorisé **2** *vt* insonoriser

soundtrack [ˈsaʊndtræk] *n (of film)* bande *f* sonore

soup [suːp] *n* soupe *f;* **s. dish** *or* **plate** assiette *f* creuse; **s. kitchen** soupe *f* populaire; *Fam* **to be in the s.** *(in trouble)* être dans le pétrin

sour [ˈsaʊə(r)] **1 (-er, -est)** *adj* aigre; *(milk)* tourné; **to turn s.** *(of wine)* s'aigrir; *(of milk)* tourner; *(of friendship)* se détériorer; *(of conversation)* tourner au vinaigre; **s. cream** crème *f* aigre; *Fig* **s. grapes** dépit *m* **2** *vi (of temper)* s'aigrir

source [sɔːs] *n (origin)* source *f;* **s. of energy** source d'énergie

south [saʊθ] **1** *n* sud *m;* **(to the) s. of** au sud de **2** *adj (coast)* sud *inv; (wind)* du sud; **S. Africa/ America** *f* l'Afrique/l'Amérique *f* du Sud; **S. African** *adj* sudafricain; *n* Sud-Africain, -aine *mf;* **S. American** *adj* sud-américain; *n* Sud-Américain, -aine *mf* **3** *adv* au sud; *(travel)* vers le sud ▪**southbound** *adj (traffic)* en direction du sud; *Br (carriageway)* sud *inv* ▪**'south-'east** *n & adj* sud-est *(m)* ▪**southerly** [ˈsʌðəlɪ] *adj (point)* sud *inv; (direction, wind)* du sud ▪**southern** [ˈsʌðən] *adj (town)* du sud; *(coast)* sud *inv;* **s. Italy** le sud de l'Italie; **S. Africa** l'Afrique *f* australe ▪**southerner** [ˈsʌðənə(r)] *n* habitant, -ante *mf* du sud ▪**southward(s)** *adj &*

adv vers le sud ▪ **'south-'west** *n & adj* sud-ouest (*m*)

souvenir [suːvəˈnɪə(r)] *n* souvenir *m*

sovereign [ˈsɒvrɪn] **1** *n* souverain, -aine *mf* **2** *adj* (*State, authority*) souverain; (*rights*) de souveraineté ▪ **sovereignty** [-rəntɪ] *n* souveraineté *f*

Soviet [ˈsəʊvɪət] *adj* soviétique; *Formerly* **the S. Union** l'Union *f* soviétique

sow[1] [saʊ] *n* (*pig*) truie *f*

sow[2] [səʊ] (*pt* sowed, *pp* sowed *or* sown [səʊn]) *vt* (*seeds, doubt*) semer; (*land*) ensemencer (**with** de)

soya [ˈsɔɪə] *n Br* soja *m*; **s. bean** graine *f* de soja; **s. sauce, soy sauce** sauce *f* de soja ▪ **soybean** *n Am* graine *f* de soja

sozzled [ˈsɒzəld] *adj Br Fam* (*drunk*) bourré

spa [spaː] *n* (*town*) station *f* thermale; (*spring*) source *f* thermale

space [speɪs] **1** *n* (*gap, emptiness, atmosphere*) espace *m*; (*for parking*) place *f*; **in the s. of two hours** en l'espace de deux heures; **to take up s.** prendre de la place; **blank s.** espace, blanc *m*; **s. bar** (*on keyboard*) barre *f* d'espacement; **s. heater** (*electric*) radiateur *m* **2** *adj* (*voyage, capsule*) spatial; **s. shuttle** navette *f* spatiale **3** *vt* espacer; **evenly spaced** régulièrement espacés ▪ **spacecraft** *n inv* vaisseau *m* spatial ▪ **spaceman** (*pl* -**men**) *n* astronaute *m* ▪ **spaceship** *n* vaisseau *m* spatial ▪ **spacesuit** *n* combinaison *f* spatiale ▪ **spacing** *n Typ* interligne *m*; **in double/single s.** à double/simple interligne

▸ **space out** *vt sep* espacer; *Fam* **to be spaced out** (*dazed*) être dans le coaltar; (*after taking drugs*) planer

spacious [ˈspeɪʃəs] *adj* spacieux, -ieuse

spade [speɪd] *n* (**a**) (*for garden*) bêche *f*; (*of child*) pelle *f* (**b**) *Cards* spade(s) pique *m*

spaghetti [spəˈgetɪ] *n* spaghettis *mpl*; **s. bolognaise** spaghettis bolognaise

Spain [speɪn] *n* l'Espagne *f*

spam [spæm] *Comptr* **1** *n* messages *mpl* publicitaires, pourriels *mpl*; **a s. e-mail** un message publicitaire, un pourriel **2** *vt* spammer ▪ **spammer** *n Comptr* = personne qui envoie des messages publicitaires en masse ▪ **spamming** *n Comptr* spamming *m*

span [spæn] **1** *n* (*of arch*) portée *f*; (*of wings*) envergure *f*; *Fig* (*of life*) durée *f* **2** (*pt & pp* -**nn**-) *vt* (*of bridge*) enjamber; *Fig* (*in time*) couvrir

Spaniard [ˈspænjəd] *n* Espagnol, -ole *mf* ▪ **Spanish 1** *adj* espagnol **2** *n* (*language*) espagnol *m* ▪ **Spanish-A'merican 1** *adj* hispano-américain **2** *n* Hispano-Américain, -aine *mf*

spaniel [ˈspænjəl] *n* épagneul *m*

spank [spæŋk] **1** *n* **to give sb a s.** donner une fessée à qn **2** *vt* donner une fessée à ▪ **spanking** *n* fessée *f*

spanner [ˈspænə(r)] *n Br* (*tool*) clef *f*; **adjustable s.** clef *f* à molette

spar [spaː(r)] (*pt & pp* -**rr**-) *vi* (*of boxer*) s'entraîner (**with** avec)

spare[1] [speə(r)] **1** *adj* (*extra, surplus*) de ou en trop; (*reserve*) de rechange; (*wheel*) de secours; (*available*) disponible; **s. room** chambre *f* d'ami; **s. time** loisirs *mpl* **2** *n* (**part**) (*for vehicle, machine*) pièce *f* détachée **3** *vt* (*do without*) se passer de; (*efforts, sb's feelings*) ménager; **to s. sb** (*not kill*) épargner qn; **to s. sb's life** épargner la vie de qn; **to s. sb sth** (*grief, details*) épargner qch à qn; (*time*) accorder qch à qn; **I can't s. the time** je n'ai pas le temps; **to s. no expense** ne pas regarder à la dépense; **five to s.** (*extra*) cinq de trop; **with five minutes to s.** avec cinq minutes d'avance

spare[2] [speə(r)] *adj* (*lean*) maigre

sparing [ˈspeərɪŋ] *adj* **her s. use of** l'usage modéré qu'elle fait de; **to be s. with the butter** utiliser le beurre avec modération ▪ **sparingly** *adv* en petite quantité

spark [spaːk] **1** *n* étincelle *f*; **s. plug** (*for vehicle*) bougie *f* **2** *vt* **to s. off** (*cause*) provoquer

sparkle [ˈspaːkəl] **1** *n* éclat *m* **2** *vi* étinceler; (*of wine, water, eyes*) pétiller ▪ **sparkler** *n* (*firework*) cierge *m* magique ▪ **sparkling** *adj* (*diamond, metal*) étincelant; (*wine, water, eyes*) pétillant

sparrow [ˈspærəʊ] *n* moineau *m*

sparse [spaːs] *adj* clairsemé ▪ **sparsely** *adv* (*populated, wooded*) peu; **s. furnished** à peine meublé

spartan [ˈspaːtən] *adj* spartiate

spasm [ˈspæzəm] *n* (*of muscle*) spasme *m*; *Fig* (*of coughing, jealousy*) accès *m* ▪ **spas'modic** *adj* (*pain*) spasmodique; *Fig* intermittent

spat [spæt] *pt & pp of* spit

spate [speɪt] *n* **a s. of sth** (*of letters, calls*) avalanche de qch; (*of crimes*) une vague de qch

spatter [ˈspætə(r)] **1** *vt* (*clothes, person*) éclabousser (**with** de) **2** *vi* **to s. over sb** (*of mud*) éclabousser qn

spatula [ˈspætjʊlə] *n* spatule *f*

spawn [spɔːn] **1** *n* (*of fish*) frai *m* **2** *vt Fig* (*bring about*) engendrer **3** *vi* frayer

speak [spiːk] (*pt* spoke, *pp* spoken) *vt* (*language*) parler; (*say*) dire; **to s. one's mind** dire ce que l'on pense **2** *vi* parler (**about** *or* **of** de); (*formally, in assembly*) prendre la parole; **so to s.** pour ainsi dire; **that speaks for itself** c'est évident; **to s. well of sb/sth** dire du bien de qn/qch; **Bob speaking!** (*on telephone*) Bob à l'appareil!; **Mr Thomas? – yes, speaking** (*on telephone*) M. Thomas? – lui-même; **that's spoken for** c'est déjà pris; **to s. out** *or* **up** (*boldly*) parler (franchement); **to s. up** (*more loudly*) parler plus fort ▪ **speaking 1** *n* public

s. l'art *m* oratoire **2** *adj (toy, robot)* parlant; **they're not on s. terms** ils ne se parlent plus; **English-/French-s.** anglophone/francophone

speaker ['spiːkə(r)] *n (at meeting)* intervenant, -ante *mf*; *(at conference)* conférencier, -ière *mf*; *(loudspeaker)* enceinte *f*; **to be a Spanish s.** parler espagnol

spear [spɪə(r)] *n* lance *f* ▪ **spearhead** *vt (attack, campaign)* être le fer de lance de

spearmint ['spɪəmɪnt] **1** *n (plant)* menthe *f* verte **2** *adj (sweet)* à la menthe; *(flavour)* de menthe; *(chewing gum)* mentholé

spec [spek] *n Br Fam* **on s.** à tout hasard

special ['speʃəl] **1** *adj* spécial; *(care, attention)* particulier, -ière; *(favourite)* préféré; *Pol (measures)* extraordinaire; *Br* **by s. delivery** en exprès; **s. effects** effets *mpl* spéciaux; **s. offer** offre *f* spéciale **2** *n* **today's s.** *(in restaurant)* le plat du jour

> Note that the French adjective **spécial** can be a false friend. It also means **peculiar, odd.**

specialist ['speʃəlɪst] **1** *n* spécialiste *mf* (**in** de) **2** *adj (dictionary, knowledge)* spécialisé; *(equipment)* de spécialiste ▪ **speciality** [speʃɪ'ælɪtɪ] *(Am* **specialty** ['speʃəltɪ]) *(pl* **-ies***)* *n* spécialité *f*

specialize ['speʃəlaɪz] *vi* se spécialiser (**in** dans) ▪ **specialized** *adj* spécialisé

specially ['speʃəlɪ] *adv (specifically)* spécialement; *(particularly)* particulièrement

specialty ['speʃəltɪ] *(pl* **-ies***) Am* = **speciality**

species ['spiːʃiːz] *n inv* espèce *f*

specific [spə'sɪfɪk] *adj* précis ▪ **specifically** *adv (explicitly)* expressément; *(exactly)* précisément; *(specially)* spécialement

specify ['spesɪfaɪ] *(pt & pp* **-ied***) vt (state exactly)* préciser; *(stipulate)* stipuler ▪ **specification** [-fɪ'keɪʃən] *n* spécification *f*

specimen ['spesɪmɪn] *n (individual example)* spécimen *m*; *(of urine, blood)* échantillon *m*; **s. signature** spécimen de signature; **s. copy** *(of book)* spécimen

specious ['spiːʃəs] *adj* spécieux, -ieuse

speck [spek] *n (stain)* petite tache *f*; *(of dust)* grain *m*; *(dot)* point *m*

speckled ['spekəld] *adj* tacheté

specs [speks] *npl Br Fam* lunettes *fpl*

spectacle ['spektəkəl] *n (sight)* spectacle *m* ▪ **spectacles** *npl (glasses)* lunettes *fpl*

spectacular [spek'tækjʊlə(r)] *adj* spectaculaire ▪ **spectacularly** *adv* de façon spectaculaire

spectator [spek'teɪtə(r)] *n* spectateur, -trice *mf*

spectre ['spektə(r)] *n* spectre *m* (**of** de)

spectrum ['spektrəm] *(pl* **-tra** [-trə]) *n* spectre *m*; *Fig (range)* gamme *f*

speculate ['spekjʊleɪt] **1** *vt* **to s. that...** *(guess)* conjecturer que... **2** *vi Fin & Phil* spéculer; **to s.**

about *(make guesses)* faire des suppositions sur ▪ **specu'lation** *n* suppositions *fpl*; *Fin & Phil* spéculation *f* ▪ **speculative** [-lətɪv] *adj Fin & Phil* spéculatif, -ive ▪ **speculator** *n Fin* spéculateur, -trice *mf*

sped [sped] *pt & pp of* **speed**

speech [spiːtʃ] *n (talk, lecture)* discours *m* (**on** or **about** sur); *(faculty)* parole *f*; *(diction)* élocution *f*; *(spoken language of group)* langue *f*; **to make a s.** faire un discours; **part of s.** partie *f* du discours; *Grammar* **direct/indirect s.** discours *m* direct/indirect ▪ **speechless** *adj* muet *(f* muette) (**with** de)

speed [spiːd] **1** *n* (**a**) *(rapidity, gear)* vitesse *f*; **at top** or **full s.** à toute vitesse; **s. dating** speed dating *m*, = soirées de rencontre dont chaque participant dispose d'un temps limité pour s'entretenir avec tous les autres; *Tel* **s. dial** numérotation *f* abrégée; **s. limit** *(on road)* limitation *f* de vitesse; **s. skating** patinage *m* de vitesse (**b**) *Fam (amphetamines)* speed *m*, amphés *fpl* **2** *(pt & pp* **sped***) vt* **to s. up** accélérer qch **3** *vi* (**a**) **to s. up** *(of person)* aller plus vite; *(of pace)* s'accélérer; **to s. past sth** passer à toute vitesse devant qch (**b**) *(pt & pp* **speeded***) (exceed speed limit)* faire un excès de vitesse ▪ **speedboat** *n* vedette *f* ▪ **speeding** *n (in vehicle)* excès *m* de vitesse ▪ **speedometer** [spɪ'dɒmɪtə(r)] *n Br (in vehicle)* compteur *m* de vitesse ▪ **speedway** *n Sport* speedway *m*

speedy ['spiːdɪ] *(***-ier**, **-iest***) adj* rapide ▪ **speedily** *adv* rapidement

spell[1] [spel] *n (magic words)* formule *f* magique; **to cast a s. on sb** jeter un sort à qn; **to be under a s.** être envoûté ▪ **spellbound** *adj* fasciné

spell[2] [spel] *n (period)* période *f*; **cold s.** vague *f* de froid

spell[3] [spel] *(pt & pp* **spelled** *or* **spelt** [spelt]) *vt (write)* écrire; *(say aloud)* épeler; *(of letters)* former; *Fig (mean)* signifier; **to be able to s.** savoir l'orthographe; **how do you s. it?** comment ça s'écrit?; **to s. sth out** *(word)* épeler qch; *Fig (explain)* expliquer clairement qch ▪ **spell-checker** *n Comptr* correcteur *m* d'orthographe ▪ **spelling** *n* orthographe *f*; **s. mistake** faute *f* d'orthographe

spelunking [spɪ'lʌŋkɪŋ] *n Am* spéléologie *f* ▪ **spelunker** *n Am* spéléologue *mf*

spend [spend] *(pt & pp* **spent***) vt (money)* dépenser (**on** pour/en); *(time)* passer (**on sth** sur qch; **doing** à faire); *(energy)* consacrer (**on sth** à qch; **doing** à faire) ▪ **spender** *n* **to be a big s.** dépenser beaucoup ▪ **spending** *n* dépenses *fpl*; **s. money** argent *m* de poche ▪ **spendthrift** *n* to be a s. être dépensier, -ière

spent [spent] **1** *pt & pp of* **spend 2** *adj (used)* utilisé; **to be a s. force** ne plus avoir d'influence

sperm [spɜːm] *n* sperme *m*; **s. bank** banque *f* de sperme; **s. donor** donneur *m* de sperme

spew [spju:] *vt Fam* vomir

sphere [sfɪə(r)] *n (of influence, action) & Math & Pol* sphère *f*; **it's outside my s.** ça n'est pas dans mes compétences; **s. of influence** sphère d'influence ■ **spherical** ['sferɪkəl] *adj* sphérique

sphinx [sfɪŋks] *n* sphinx *m*

spice [spaɪs] **1** *n* épice *f*; *Fig (interest)* piquant *m* **2** *vt (food)* épicer; **to s. sth (up)** *(add interest to)* ajouter du piquant à qch ■ **spicy** (**-ier, -iest**) *adj* épicé

spick-and-span [spɪkən'spæn] *adj (clean)* impeccable

spider ['spaɪdə(r)] *n* araignée *f*; **s.'s web** toile *f* d'araignée

spiel [ʃpi:l] *n Fam (of salesman, entertainer)* baratin *m*

spike [spaɪk] **1** *n (of metal)* pointe *f* **2** *vt (pierce)* transpercer ■ **spiky** (**-ier, -iest**) *adj (stem, stick)* garni de piquants; *(hair)* en épis

spill [spɪl] (*pt & pp* spilled *or* spilt [spɪlt]) **1** *vt (liquid)* renverser; *Fam* **to s. the beans** vendre la mèche **2** *vi* se répandre

▶ **spill out** *vt sep (empty)* vider

▶ **spill over** *vi (of liquid)* déborder

spin [spɪn] **1** *n (motion)* tournoiement *m*; *(on ball)* effet *m*; *Fam* **to go for a s.** *(in car)* aller faire un tour; *Pol* **s. doctor** = spécialiste de la communication chargé de présenter l'information de façon à mettre en valeur un parti politique **2** (*pt & pp* spun, *pres p* spinning) *vt (wool, cotton)* filer; *(wheel, top)* faire tourner; *(spin-dry)* essorer; **to s. sth out** *(speech)* faire durer qch **3** *vi* tourner; **to s. round** *(of dancer, wheel, top, planet)* tourner; **my head's spinning** j'ai la tête qui tourne ■ **spinning** *n (by hand)* filage *m*; *Tech (process)* filature *f*; **s. top** toupie *f*; **s. wheel** rouet *m*

spinach ['spɪnɪdʒ] *n* épinards *mpl*

spindle ['spɪndəl] *n* fuseau *m*

spindly ['spɪndlɪ] (**-ier, -iest**) *adj (legs, arms)* grêle

spin-dry ['spɪn'draɪ] *vt* essorer ■ **spin-dryer** *n* essoreuse *f*

spine [spaɪn] *n (backbone)* colonne *f* vertébrale; *(of book)* dos *m*; *(of plant)* épine *f* ■ **spinal** *adj* **s. column** colonne *f* vertébrale; **s. cord** moelle *f* épinière; **s. injury** blessure *f* à la colonne vertébrale ■ **spineless** *adj Fig* mou *(f* molle)

spin-off ['spɪnɒf] *n (result)* retombée *f*; *(TV programme)* = feuilleton tiré d'un film ou d'un autre feuilleton

spinster ['spɪnstə(r)] *n* vieille fille *f*

spiral ['spaɪərəl] **1** *n* spirale *f* **2** *adj* en spirale; *(staircase)* en colimaçon **3** (*Br* -**ll**-, *Am* -**l**-) *vi (of prices)* s'envoler

spire ['spaɪə(r)] *n (of church)* flèche *f*

spirit ['spɪrɪt] **1** *n (soul, ghost, mood)* esprit *m*; *Fig (determination)* courage *m*; **spirits** *(drink)* spiritueux *mpl*; **in good spirits** de bonne humeur; **to break sb's s.** entamer le courage de qn; *Fam* **that's the s.!** à la bonne heure! **2** *adj (lamp)* à alcool; **s. level** niveau *m* (à bulle) **3** *vt* **to s. away** *(person)* faire disparaître (mystérieusement); *Hum (steal)* subtiliser ■ **spirited** *adj (campaign, attack)* vigoureux, -euse; *(person, remark)* énergique

spiritual ['spɪrɪtʃʊəl] **1** *adj* spirituel, -uelle **2** *n Mus (Negro)* **s.** negro spiritual *m* ■ **spiritualism** [-ʊlɪzəm] *n* spiritisme *m* ■ **spiritualist** [-ʊlɪst] *n* spirite *mf*

spit¹ [spɪt] **1** *n (on ground)* crachat *m*; *(in mouth)* salive *f* **2** (*pt & pp* spat *or* spit, *pres p* spitting) *vt* cracher; **to s. sth out** cracher qch; **to be the spitting image of sb** être le portrait (tout craché) de qn **3** *vi* cracher; *(splutter) (of fat, fire)* crépiter

spit² [spɪt] *n (for meat)* broche *f*

spite [spaɪt] **1** *n (dislike)* dépit *m*; **in s. of sb/sth** malgré qn/qch; **in s. of the fact that…** bien que… *(+ subjunctive)* **2** *vt* vexer ■ **spiteful** *adj* vexant

spittle ['spɪtəl] *n* crachat *m*; *(in mouth)* salive *f*

splash [splæʃ] **1** *n (of liquid)* éclaboussure *f*; *(sound)* plouf *m*; *Fig (of colour)* tache *f*; *Fam* **to make a s.** faire sensation; *Comptr* **s. page** page *f* de garde **2** *vt (spatter)* éclabousser (**with** de); **to s. one's face with water** se passer le visage à l'eau **3** *vi (of mud, ink)* faire des éclaboussures; *(of waves)* clapoter; **to s. over sb/sth** éclabousser qn/qch; **to s. (about)** *(in river, mud)* patauger; *(in bath)* barboter; *Fam* **to s. out** *(spend money)* claquer des ronds

spleen [spli:n] *n Anat* rate *f*

splendid ['splendɪd] *adj* splendide ■ **splendour** *(Am* **splendor)** *n* splendeur *f*

splint [splɪnt] *n* attelle *f*

splinter ['splɪntə(r)] *n (of wood, glass)* éclat *m*; *(in finger)* écharde *f*; *Pol* **s. group** groupe *m* dissident

split [splɪt] **1** *n* fente *f*; *(tear)* déchirure *f*; *(of couple)* rupture *f*; *(in political party)* scission *f*; **to do the splits** faire le grand écart; *Fam* **one's s.** *(share)* sa part **2** *adj* **in a s. second** en une fraction de seconde; **s. ends** *(in hair)* fourches *fpl*; **s.-level apartment** duplex *m*; **s.-level house** maison *f* à deux niveaux; **s. personality** dédoublement *m* de la personnalité **3** (*pt & pp* split, *pres p* splitting) *vt (break apart)* fendre; *(tear)* déchirer; **to s. (up)** *(group)* diviser; *(money, work)* partager (**between** entre); **to s. one's head open** s'ouvrir la tête; **to s. one's sides (laughing)** se tordre (de rire); **to s. hairs** *(make trivial distinctions)* couper les cheveux en quatre **4** *vi* se fendre; *(tear)* se déchirer; **to s. (up)** *(of group)* se diviser (**into** en); **to s. off**

(become loose) se détacher (**from** de); **to s. up** *(because of disagreement) (of couple, friends)* se séparer; *(of crowd)* se disperser; **to s. up with sb** rompre avec qn

splitting ['splɪtɪŋ] *adj* **to have a s. headache** avoir un mal de tête épouvantable

splodge [splɒdʒ], **splotch** [splɒtʃ] *n (mark)* tache *f*

splurge [splɜːdʒ] *vi Fam (spend money)* claquer de l'argent

splutter ['splʌtə(r)] *vi (spit) (of person)* crachoter; *(of sparks, fat)* crépiter; *(stammer)* bredouiller

spoil [spɔɪl] *(pt & pp* **spoilt** *or* **spoiled)** *vt (ruin)* gâcher; *(indulge)* gâter; **to s. sb's appetite** couper l'appétit à qn; **to be spoilt for choice** avoir l'embarras du choix ▪ **spoilsport** *n* rabat-joie *m inv*

spoils [spɔɪlz] *npl (rewards)* butin *m*

spoilt [spɔɪlt] *pt & pp of* **spoil**

spoke¹ [spəʊk] *n (of wheel)* rayon *m*

spoke² [spəʊk] *pt of* **speak** ▪ **spoken 1** *pp of* **speak 2** *adj (language)* parlé; **to be softly s.** avoir la voix douce ▪ **spokesman** *(pl* **-men)**, **spokesperson** *(pl* **-people)** *n* porte-parole *m inv* **(for** *or* **of** de) ▪ **spokeswoman** *(pl* **-women)** *n* porte-parole *f inv*

sponge [spʌndʒ] **1** *n* éponge *f*; *Br* **s. bag** trousse *f* de toilette; **s. cake** génoise *f* **2** *vt* **to s. sth down/off** laver/enlever qch avec une éponge; *Fam* **to s. sth off sb** taper qn de qch **3** *vi Fam* **to s. off** *or* **on sb** vivre aux crochets de qn ▪ **sponger** *n Fam* parasite *m* ▪ **spongy** **(-ier, -iest)** *adj* spongieux, -ieuse

sponsor ['spɒnsə(r)] **1** *n* sponsor *m*; *(for membership)* parrain *m*/marraine *f* **2** *vt* sponsoriser; *(student)* financer les études de; *(member)* parrainer ▪ **sponsored** *adj* **s. walk** marche *f* sponsorisée *(pour aider une œuvre de charité)* ▪ **sponsorship** *n* sponsoring *m*; *(of member)* parrainage *m*

spontaneous [spɒn'teɪnɪəs] *adj* spontané ▪ **spontaneity** [-tə'neɪɪtɪ] *n* spontanéité *f* ▪ **spontaneously** *adv* spontanément

spoof [spuːf] *n Fam (parody)* parodie *f* (**on** de)

spooky ['spuːkɪ] **(-ier, -iest)** *adj Fam* qui donne le frisson ▪ **spook** *n (ghost)* fantôme *m*; *Fam (spy)* espion, -ionne

spool [spuːl] *n* bobine *f*

spoon [spuːn] *n* cuillère *f* ▪ **spoonfeed** *(pt & pp* **-fed)** *vt* faire manger à la cuillère; *Fig (help)* mâcher le travail à ▪ **spoonful** *n* cuillerée *f*

sporadic [spə'rædɪk] *adj* sporadique ▪ **sporadically** *adv* sporadiquement

sport¹ [spɔːt] *n* sport *m*; *Fam* **a (good) s.** *(man)* un chic type; *(woman)* une chic fille; **to do** *or* **play** *Br* **s.** *or Am* **sports** faire du sport; **sports club** club *m* de sport; **sports car/ground** voiture *f*/terrain *m* de sport; **sports jacket**

veste *f* sport ▪ **sporting** *adj (attitude, conduct, person)* sportif, -ive; *Fig* **that's s. of you** c'est chic de ta part ▪ **sportsman** *(pl* **-men)** *n* sportif *m* ▪ **sportsmanlike** *adj* sportif, -ive ▪ **sportsmanship** *n* sportivité *f* ▪ **sportswear** *n* vêtements *mpl* de sport ▪ **sportswoman** *(pl* **-women)** *n* sportive *f* ▪ **sporty** **(-ier, -iest)** *adj* sportif, -ive

sport² [spɔːt] *vt (wear)* arborer

spot¹ [spɒt] *n (stain, mark)* tache *f*; *(dot)* point *m*; *(polka dot)* pois *m*; *(drop)* goutte *f*; *(pimple)* bouton *m*; *(place)* endroit *m*; *(advertising)* spot *m* publicitaire; *Fam* **a s. of bother** de petits problèmes; **to have a soft s. for sb** avoir un faible pour qn; **on the s.** sur place; *(at once)* sur le coup; **to be in a tight s.** *(difficulty)* être dans le pétrin; *Br* **(accident) black s.** *(on road)* point *m* noir; **blind s.** *(in vehicle)* angle *m* mort; *Fig* **bright s.** point *m* positif; **s. check** contrôle *m* surprise

spot² [spɒt] *(pt & pp* **-tt-)** *vt (notice)* apercevoir; **well spotted!** bien vu!

spotless ['spɒtləs] *adj (clean)* impeccable ▪ **spotlessly** *adv* **s. clean** impeccable

spotlight ['spɒtlaɪt] *n* projecteur *m*; *(for photography)* spot *m*; **to be in the s.** être sous le feu des projecteurs

spot-on ['spɒt'ɒn] *adj Br Fam* tout à fait exact

spotted ['spɒtɪd] *adj (fur)* tacheté; *(dress)* à pois; *(stained)* taché

spotty ['spɒtɪ] **(-ier, -iest)** *adj (face, person)* boutonneux, -euse; *Am (patchy)* inégal

spouse [spaʊs, spaʊz] *n* époux *m*, épouse *f*

spout [spaʊt] **1** *n (of teapot, jug)* bec *m*; *Br Fam* **to be up the s.** être fichu **2** *vt Pej (say)* débiter **3** *vi* **to s. (out)** *(of liquid)* jaillir

sprain [spreɪn] *n* entorse *f*; **to s. one's ankle/ wrist** se fouler la cheville/le poignet

sprang [spræŋ] *pt of* **spring¹**

sprawl [sprɔːl] **1** *n* **the urban s.** les banlieues *fpl* tentaculaires **2** *vi (of town, person)* s'étaler ▪ **sprawling** *adj (city)* tentaculaire; *(person)* affalé

spray [spreɪ] **1** *n* **(a)** *(can, device)* vaporisateur *m*; *(water drops)* gouttelettes *fpl*; *(from sea)* embruns *mpl* **(b)** *(of flowers)* petit bouquet *m* **2** *vt (liquid, surface)* vaporiser; *(plant, crops)* pulvériser; *(car)* peindre à la bombe

spread [spred] **1** *n (of idea, religion, language)* diffusion *f*; *(of disease)* propagation *f*; *Fam (meal)* festin *m*; **cheese/chocolate s.** fromage *m*/chocolat *m* à tartiner; **full-page s.** *(in newspaper)* double page *f* **2** *(pt & pp* **spread)** *vt (stretch, open out)* étendre; *(legs, fingers)* écarter; *(paint, payment, visits, cards)* étaler; *(sand, fear, knowledge)* répandre; *(news, germ, illness)* propager; **to s. out** *(map, payments, visits)* étaler; *(fingers)* écarter; **to be s. out** *(of city)* s'étendre **3** *vi (of town, fog)* s'étendre; *(of* *fire, epidemic, fear)* se propager; *(of news, fear)* se répandre; **to s. out** *(of people)* se disperser ▪ **spread-'eagled** *adj* bras et jambes écartés ▪ **spreadsheet** *n Comptr* tableur *m*

spree [spri:] *n* **to go on a spending s.** faire des folies dans les magasins

sprig [sprɪg] *n (of parsley)* brin *m*; *(of holly)* branche *f*

sprightly ['spraɪtlɪ] **(-ier, -iest)** *adj* alerte

spring¹ [sprɪŋ] **1** *n (device)* ressort *m*; *(leap)* bond *m* **2** *(pt* **sprang**, *pp* **sprung)** *vt (news)* annoncer brusquement (**on** à); *(surprise)* faire (**on** à); **to s. a leak** *(of boat)* commencer à prendre l'eau **3** *vi (leap)* bondir; **to s. to mind** venir à l'esprit; **to s. into action** passer rapidement à l'action; **to s. from** *(stem from)* provenir de; **to s. up** *(appear)* surgir ▪ **springboard** *n* tremplin *m* ▪ **springy (-ier, -iest)** *adj* souple

spring² [sprɪŋ] *n (season)* printemps *m*; **in (the) s.** au printemps; *Br* **s. onion** oignon *m* nouveau ▪ **spring-cleaning** *n* nettoyage *m* de printemps ▪ **springlike** *adj (weather)* printanier, -ière ▪ **springtime** *n* printemps *m*

spring³ [sprɪŋ] *n (of water)* source *f*; **s. water** eau *f* de source

sprinkle ['sprɪŋkəl] *vt (sand)* répandre (**on** or **over** sur); **to s. sth with water, to s. water on sth** arroser qch; **to s. sth with sth** *(sugar, salt, flour)* saupoudrer qch de qch ▪ **sprinkler** *n (in garden)* arroseur *m* ▪ **sprinkling** *n* **a s. of customers** *(a few)* quelques rares clients

sprint [sprɪnt] **1** *n (race)* sprint *m* **2** *vi (run)* sprinter ▪ **sprinter** *n* sprinter *m*, sprinteuse *f*

sprout [spraʊt] **1** *n* **(Brussels) s.** chou *m* de Bruxelles **2** *vt (leaves)* pousser; *Fig (beard, whiskers)* se laisser pousser **3** *vi (of seed, bulb)* pousser; **to s. up** *(grow)* pousser vite; *(appear)* surgir

spruce¹ [spru:s] **1 (-er, -est)** *adj (neat)* impeccable **2** *vt* **to s. oneself up** se faire beau (*f* belle)

spruce² [spru:s] *n (tree)* épicéa *m*

sprung [sprʌŋ] **1** *pp of* **spring¹ 2** *adj (mattress, seat)* à ressorts

spry [spraɪ] **(spryer, spryest)** *adj* alerte

spud [spʌd] *n Fam (potato)* patate *f*

spun [spʌn] *pt & pp of* **spin**

spur [spɜː(r)] *n (of horse rider)* éperon *m*; *Fig (stimulus)* aiguillon *m*; **to do sth on the s. of the moment** faire qch sur un coup de tête **2** *(pt & pp* **-rr-)** *vt* **to s. sb on** *(urge on)* aiguillonner qn

spurious ['spjʊərɪəs] *adj* faux (*f* fausse)

spurn [spɜːn] *vt* rejeter

spurt [spɜːt] **1** *n (of liquid)* giclée *f*; *(of energy)* regain *m*; **to put on a s.** foncer **2** *vi (of liquid)* gicler; *(of person)* foncer; **to s. out** *(of liquid)* gicler

spy [spaɪ] **1** *(pl* **-ies)** *n* espion, -ionne *mf* **2** *adj*

(story, film) d'espionnage; **s. hole** judas *m*; **s. ring** réseau *m* d'espionnage **3** *(pt & pp* **-ied)** *vt (notice)* repérer **4** *vi* espionner; **to s. on sb** espionner qn ▪ **spying** *n* espionnage *m*

sq *(abbr* **square)** carré

squabble ['skwɒbəl] **1** *n* querelle *f* **2** *vi* se quereller (**over** à propos de) ▪ **squabbling** *n* querelles *fpl*

squad [skwɒd] *n (of workmen, footballers)* équipe *f*; *(of soldiers)* section *f*; *(of police)* brigade *f*; *Br* **s. car** voiture *f* de police

squadron ['skwɒdrən] *n Mil* escadron *m*; *Naut & Av* escadrille *f*

squalid ['skwɒlɪd] *adj* sordide ▪ **squalor** *n (poverty)* misère *f*

squall [skwɔːl] *n (of wind)* rafale *f*

squander ['skwɒndə(r)] *vt (money, resources)* gaspiller; *(time)* perdre

square ['skweə(r)] **1** *n* carré *m*; *(on chessboard, map)* case *f*; *(in town)* place *f*; *Br (drawing implement)* équerre *f*; *Fig* **to be back to s. one** être de retour à la case départ; *Fam (unfashionable person)* ringard, -arde *mf* **2** *adj* carré; *Fam (unfashionable)* ringard; **to be s. with sb** être honnête avec qn; *Fam* **we're (all) s.** nous sommes quittes; **s. corner** angle *m* droit; **s. deal** arrangement *m* équitable; **s. meal** bon repas *m*; *Math* **s. root** racine *f* carrée **3** *vt (settle)* régler; *Math (number)* élever au carré; **to s. sth with sb** arranger qch avec qn **4** *vi (tally)* cadrer (**with** avec); **to s. up to sb/ sth** faire face à qn/qch ▪ **squarely** *adv (honestly)* honnêtement; **to hit sb s. in the face** frapper qn en pleine figure

squash [skwɒʃ] **1** *n (game)* squash *m*; *Am (vegetable)* courge *f*; *Br* **lemon/orange s.** ≃ sirop *m* de citron/d'orange **2** *vt* écraser ▪ **squashy (-ier, -iest)** *adj (fruit)* mou (*f* molle)

squat [skwɒt] **1** *n (dwelling)* squat *m* **2** *adj (person, object, building)* trapu **3** *(pt & pp* **-tt-)** *vi* squatter; **to s. (down)** s'accroupir; **to be squatting (down)** être accroupi ▪ **squatter** *n* squatter *m*

squawk [skwɔːk] **1** *n* cri *m* rauque **2** *vi* pousser un cri rauque

squeak [skwiːk] **1** *n (of animal, person)* cri *m* aigu; *(of door)* grincement *m* **2** *vi (of person)* pousser un cri aigu; *(of door)* grincer ▪ **squeaky (-ier, -iest)** *adj (door)* grinçant; *(shoe)* qui craque; **s. clean** impeccable

squeal [skwiːl] **1** *n* cri *m* perçant **2** *vi* pousser un cri perçant; *(of tyres)* crisser; *Fam* **to s. on sb** balancer qn

squeamish ['skwiːmɪʃ] *adj* de nature délicate

squeeze [skwiːz] **1** *n* **to give sth a s.** presser qch; **to give sb's hand/arm a s.** serrer la main/le bras à qn; **to give sb a s.** serrer qn dans ses bras; *Fam* **it's a tight s.** il n'y a pas beaucoup de place **2** *vt (press)* presser; **to s.**

sb's hand serrer la main à qn; **to s. sth into sth** faire rentrer qch dans qch; **to s. the juice (out)** faire sortir le jus (**of** de); **to s. sth out of sb** (*information, secret*) arracher qch à qn **3** *vi* **to s. through/into sth** (*force oneself*) se glisser par/dans qch; **to s. in** trouver de la place; **to s. up** se serrer (**against** contre) **■squeezer** *n* **lemon s.** presse-citron *m inv*

squelch [skweltʃ] *vi* patauger

squid [skwɪd] *n inv* calmar *m*

squiggle ['skwɪgəl] *n* gribouillis *m*

squint [skwɪnt] **1** *n* (*eye defect*) strabisme *m*; **to have a s.** loucher **2** *vi* loucher; (*in the sunlight*) plisser les yeux

squirm [skwɜːm] *vi* (*wriggle*) se tortiller; **to s. in pain** se tordre de douleur

squirrel [*Br* 'skwɪrəl, *Am* 'skwɜːrəl] *n* écureuil *m*

squirt [skwɜːt] **1** *n* giclée *f*; *Fam* **little s.** (*person*) petit(e) *m* morveux, -euse *mf* **2** *vt* (*liquid*) faire gicler **3** *vi* (*of liquid*) gicler

Sri Lanka [sriː'læŋkə] *n* le Sri Lanka

St *n* (**a**) (*abbr* **Street**) rue *f* (**b**) (*abbr* **Saint**) St *m* (*f* Ste)

stab [stæb] **1** *n* **s. (wound)** coup *m* de couteau **2** (*pt & pp* **-bb-**) *vt* (*with knife*) poignarder; **to s. sb to death** tuer qn d'un coup de couteau **■stabbing** *n* **there has been a s.** quelqu'un a été poignardé; **a s. pain** une douleur lancinante

stability [stə'bɪlɪtɪ] *n* stabilité *f*

stabilize ['steɪbəlaɪz] **1** *vt* stabiliser **2** *vi* se stabiliser **■stabilizer** *n* (*on bicycle*) stabilisateur *m*

stable¹ ['steɪbəl] (**-er, -est**) *adj* stable

stable² ['steɪbəl] *n* écurie *f*

> Note that the French word **étable** is a false friend and is never a translation for the English word **stable**. It means **cowshed**.

stack [stæk] **1** *n* (**a**) (*heap*) tas *m*; *Fam* **stacks of** (*lots of*) des tas de (**b**) **chimney s.** (*of factory*) tuyau *m* de cheminée **2** *npl* **the stacks** (*in library*) la réserve **3** *vt* **to s. (up)** entasser

stadium ['steɪdɪəm] *n* stade *m*

staff [stɑːf] **1** *n* personnel *m*; (*of school, university*) professeurs *mpl*; (*of army*) état-major *m*; *Literary* (*stick*) bâton *m*; **to be on the s.** faire partie du personnel; **member of s., s. member** (*in office*) employé, -ée *mf*; (*in school*) professeur *m*; *Br* **s. meeting** (*in school, university*) conseil *m* des professeurs; *Br* **s. room** (*in school*) salle *f* des professeurs **2** *vt* pourvoir en personnel; **the desk is staffed at all times** il y a toujours quelqu'un au bureau

stag [stæg] *n* cerf *m*; *Br* **s. party** or **night** enterrement *m* de la vie de garçon; **to have a s. party** or **night** enterrer sa vie de garçon

stage¹ [steɪdʒ] **1** *n* (*platform*) scène *f*; **the s.** (*profession*) le théâtre; **on s.** sur scène; **s. door**

entrée *f* des artistes; **s. fright** trac *m* **2** *vt* (*play*) monter; *Fig* organiser; **it was staged** (*not real*) c'était un coup monté **■stagehand** *n* machiniste *m* **■stage-manager** *n* régisseur *m*

stage² [steɪdʒ] *n* (*phase*) stade *m*; **to do sth in (easy) stages** faire qch par étapes; **at an early s.** au début (**of** de); **at this s. in the work** à ce stade des travaux; **at this s.** (*at this moment*) à l'heure qu'il est

> Note that the French word **stage** is a false friend and is never a translation for the English word **stage**. It means **training course**.

stagecoach ['steɪdʒkəʊtʃ] *n Hist* diligence *f*

stagger ['stægə(r)] **1** *vt* (*holidays*) échelonner; (*astound*) stupéfier **2** *vi* (*reel*) chanceler **■staggering** *adj* stupéfiant

stagnant ['stægnənt] *adj* stagnant **■stag'nate** *vi* stagner **■stag'nation** *n* stagnation *f*

staid [steɪd] *adj* collet monté *inv*

stain [steɪn] **1** *n* (*mark*) tache *f*; (*dye*) teinture *f*; **s. remover** détachant *m* **2** *vt* (*mark*) tacher (**with** de); (*dye*) teinter; **stained-glass window** vitrail *m* (*pl* vitraux) **■stainless 'steel** *n* Inox® *m*; **s. knife** couteau *m* en Inox®

stair [steə(r)] *n* **a s.** (*step*) une marche; **the stairs** (*staircase*) l'escalier *m* **■staircase, stairway** *n* escalier *m* **■stairwell** *n* cage *f* d'escalier

stake [steɪk] **1** *n* (**a**) (*post*) pieu *m*; (*for plant*) tuteur *m*; *Hist* **to be burned at the s.** périr sur le bûcher (**b**) (*betting*) enjeu *m*; **to have a s. in sth** (*share*) avoir des intérêts dans qch; **at s.** en jeu; **there's a lot at s.** l'enjeu est considérable **2** *vt* (**a**) **to s. (out)** (*land*) délimiter; **to s. a claim to sth** revendiquer qch (**b**) (*bet*) jouer (**on** sur)

stale [steɪl] (**-er, -est**) *adj* (*bread*) rassis; (*beer*) éventé; (*air*) vicié; (*smell*) âcre; (*news*) vieux (*f* vieille); (*joke*) éculé; (*person*) blasé

stalemate ['steɪlmeɪt] *n Chess* pat *m*; *Fig* impasse *f*

stalk [stɔːk] **1** *n* (*of plant*) tige *f*; (*of fruit*) queue *f* **2** *vt* (*animal, criminal*) traquer; (*celebrity*) harceler **3** *vi* **to s. out** (*walk angrily*) sortir d'un air furieux mais digne **■stalker** *n* = admirateur obsessionnel qui harcèle une célébrité ou une de ses connaissances

stall [stɔːl] **1** *n* (*in market*) étal *m*; *Br* (*for newspapers, flowers*) kiosque *m*; (*in stable*) stalle *f*; *Br* **the stalls** (*in cinema, theatre*) l'orchestre *m* **2** *vt* (*engine, car*) caler **3** *vi* (*of car*) caler; **to s. (for time)** chercher à gagner du temps

stallion ['stæljən] *n* étalon *m*

stalwart ['stɔːlwət] **1** *adj* résolu **2** *n* fidèle *mf*

stamina ['stæmɪnə] *n* résistance *f* physique

stammer ['stæmə(r)] **1** *n* bégaiement *m*; **to have a s.** être bègue **2** *vi* bégayer **3** *vt* **to s. out an apology** balbutier des excuses

stamp [stæmp] **1** *n* (*for letter*) timbre *m*; (*mark*) cachet *m*; *(device)* tampon *m*; *Fig* **to bear the s. of sth** porter l'empreinte de qch; **to be given the s. of approval** être approuvé; **s. album** album *m* de timbres; **s. collector** philatéliste *mf* **2** *vt (document)* tamponner; *(letter)* timbrer; *(metal)* estamper; **to s. one's foot** taper du pied; *Fig* **to s. sth out** *(rebellion, evil)* écraser qch; *(disease)* éradiquer qch; *Br* **stamped addressed envelope** enveloppe *f* timbrée *(libellée à ses noms et adresse)* **3** *vi* **to s. on sth** écraser qch; *Fam* **stamping ground** lieu *m* favori

stampede [stæm'piːd] **1** *n* débandade *f* **2** *vi* se ruer

stance [stɑːns] *n* position *f*

stand [stænd] **1** *n (opinion)* position *f*; *(support)* support *m*; *(stall)* étal *m*; *(at exhibition)* stand *m*; *(at sports ground)* tribune *f*; **to take a s.** prendre position **2** *(pt & pp stood)* *vt (pain, journey)* supporter; *(put straight)* mettre debout; **to s. a chance** avoir des chances; **to s. one's ground** tenir bon; **I can't s. him** je ne peux pas le supporter; **I can't s. it** je ne supporte pas ça; *Br* **to s. sb sth** *(pay for)* payer qch à qn **3** *vi (be upright)* se tenir debout; *(get up)* se mettre debout; *(remain)* rester debout; *(of building)* se trouver; *(of object)* être; **to s. still** se tenir immobile; **to leave sth to s.** *(liquid)* laisser qch reposer; **to s. to do sth** risquer de faire qch; **inflation stands at...** l'inflation s'élève à...; **the offer still stands** l'offre tient toujours
▸ **stand about, stand around** *vi (in street)* traîner
▸ **stand aside** *vi* s'écarter
▸ **stand back** *vi* reculer
▸ **stand by 1** *vt insep (opinion)* s'en tenir à; *(person)* soutenir **2** *vi (do nothing)* rester sans rien faire; *(be ready)* être prêt
▸ **stand down** *vi (withdraw)* se retirer
▸ **stand for** *vt insep (mean)* signifier; *(represent)* représenter; *Br (be candidate for)* être candidat à; *(tolerate)* supporter
▸ **stand in for** *vt insep (replace)* remplacer
▸ **stand out** *vi (be visible)* ressortir (**against** sur)
▸ **stand over** *vt insep (watch closely)* surveiller
▸ **stand up 1** *vt sep* mettre debout; *Fam* **to s. sb up** poser un lapin à qn **2** *vi (get up)* se lever
▸ **stand up for** *vt insep (defend)* défendre
▸ **stand up to** *vt insep (resist)* résister à; *(defend oneself against)* tenir tête à

standard [ˈstændəd] **1** *n (norm)* norme *f*; *(level)* niveau *m*; *(of weight, gold)* étalon *m*; **standards** principes *mpl* moraux; **to be** *or* **come up to s.** *(of person)* être à la hauteur; *(of work)* être au niveau; **s. of living, living standards** niveau de vie **2** *adj (average)* ordinaire; *(model, size)* standard *inv*; *(weight)* étalon *inv*; *(dictionary, book)* classique; **it's s. practice** c'est une

pratique courante; *Br* **s. lamp** lampadaire *m*
▪ **standardize** *vt* standardiser

stand-by [ˈstændbaɪ] **1** *(pl -bys)* *n* **on s.** *(troops, emergency services)* prêt à intervenir; **s. mode** *(of appliance)* mode *f* veille; **in s. mode** en veille **2** *adj (battery)* de réserve; *(plane ticket)* en stand-by

stand-in [ˈstændɪn] *n* remplaçant, -ante *mf* (**for** de); *(actor)* doublure *f* (**for** de)

standing [ˈstændɪŋ] **1** *adj (upright)* debout; *(permanent)* permanent; **I have a s. invitation** je peux y aller quand je veux; **s. joke** plaisanterie *f* classique; *Br* **s. order** virement *m* automatique **2** *n (reputation)* réputation *f*; *(social, professional)* rang *m*; **a friendship of six years' s.** une amitié de six ans; **of long s.** de longue date

stand-offish [stænd'ɒfɪʃ] *adj* distant

standpoint [ˈstændpɔɪnt] *n* point *m* de vue

standstill [ˈstændstɪl] *n* **to bring sth to a s.** immobiliser qch; **to come to a s.** s'immobiliser; **at a s.** immobile; *(negotiations, industry)* paralysé

stand-up [ˈstændʌp] **1** *n (comedy)* spectacle *m* comique; **to do s.** faire des spectacles comiques **2** *adj* **s. comic** *or* **comedian** comique *mf* de scène

stank [stæŋk] *pt of* **stink**

stanza [ˈstænzə] *n* strophe *f*

staple[1] [ˈsteɪpəl] *adj (basic)* de base; **s. food** *or* **diet** nourriture *f* de base

staple[2] [ˈsteɪpəl] **1** *n (for paper)* agrafe *f* **2** *vt* agrafer ▪ **stapler** *n (for paper)* agrafeuse *f*

star [stɑː(r)] **1** *n (in sky, famous person)* star *f*; **the Stars and Stripes** *(flag)* la bannière étoilée; **the S.-Spangled Banner** *(flag)* la bannière étoilée; *(song)* l'hymne *m* national des États-Unis; *Br* **four-s.** *(petrol)* du super; **s. player** vedette *f*; **s. sign** signe *m* du zodiaque **2** *(pt & pp -rr-)* *vt (of film)* avoir pour vedette **3** *vi (of actor, actress)* être la vedette (**in** de)

starboard [ˈstɑːbəd] *n Naut* tribord *m*

starch [stɑːtʃ] **1** *n* amidon *m* **2** *vt* amidonner ▪ **starchy** *(-ier, -iest)* *adj Fam (manner, person)* guindé; **s. food(s)** féculents *mpl*

stardom [ˈstɑːdəm] *n* célébrité *f*

stare [steə(r)] **1** *n* regard *m* fixe **2** *vt* **to be staring sb in the face** *(be obvious)* crever les yeux à qn **3** *vi* **to s. at sb/sth** fixer qn/qch (du regard)

starfish [ˈstɑːfɪʃ] *n* étoile *f* de mer

stark [stɑːk] **1** *(-er, -est)* *adj (place)* désolé; *(fact, reality)* brutal; **to be in s. contrast to** contraster nettement avec; **the s. truth** la vérité toute nue **2** *adv* **s. naked** complètement nu ▪ **starkers** *adj Br Fam* à poil

starling [ˈstɑːlɪŋ] *n* étourneau *m*

starlit [ˈstɑːlɪt] *adj* étoilé

starry [ˈstɑːrɪ] *(-ier, -iest)* *adj* étoilé ▪ **starry-'eyed** *adj* naïf *(f* naïve*)*

start¹ [stɑːt] **1** *n* début *m*; *(of race)* départ *m*; **for a s.** pour commencer; **from the s.** dès le début; **to make a s.** commencer; **to give sb a 10 metre s.** donner 10 mètres d'avance à qn **2** *vt* commencer; *(packet, conversation)* entamer; *(fashion, campaign, offensive)* lancer; *(engine, vehicle)* mettre en marche; *(business)* fonder; **to s. a war** provoquer une guerre; **to s. a fire** *(deliberately)* *(in grate)* allumer un feu; *(accidentally)* provoquer un incendie; **to s. doing** *or* **to do sth** commencer à faire qch **3** *vi* commencer (**with sth** par qch; **by doing** par faire); *(of vehicle)* démarrer; *(leave)* partir (**for** pour); *(in job)* débuter; **to s. with** *(firstly)* pour commencer; **starting from now/10 euros** à partir de maintenant/10 euros ▪ **starting** *adj (point, line, salary)* de départ; **s. place** point *m* de départ; **s. post** *(in race)* ligne *f* de départ ▪ **start-up** *n (of computer)* démarrage *m*; *(of business)* ouverture *f*

▸ **start off 1** *vt sep* **to s. sb off** *(in business)* aider qn à démarrer **2** *vi (leave)* partir (**for** pour); *(in job)* débuter

▸ **start out** *vi (begin)* débuter; *(on journey)* se mettre en route

▸ **start up 1** *vt sep (engine, vehicle)* mettre en marche; *(business)* fonder **2** *vi (of engine, vehicle)* démarrer

start² [stɑːt] **1** *n (movement)* sursaut *m*; **to give sb a s.** faire sursauter qn **2** *vi* sursauter

starter ['stɑːtə(r)] *n (in vehicle)* démarreur *m*; *(in meal)* entrée *f*; *(runner)* partant, -ante *mf*; *(official in race)* starter *m*; *Fam* **for starters** *(firstly)* pour commencer

startle ['stɑːtəl] *vt* faire sursauter

starvation [stɑː'veɪʃən] **1** *n* faim *f* **2** *adj (wage, ration)* de misère; **to be on a s. diet** *(to lose weight)* suivre un régime draconien

starve [stɑːv] **1** *vt (make suffer)* faire souffrir de la faim; *Fig (deprive)* priver (**of** de); **to s. to death** laisser qn mourir de faim **2** *vi (suffer)* souffrir de la faim; **to s. to death** mourir de faim; *Fam* **I'm starving!** je meurs de faim!

stash [stæʃ] *vt Fam* **to s. away** *(hide)* cacher; *(save up)* mettre de côté

state¹ [steɪt] **1** *n* **(a)** *(condition)* état *m*; *(situation)* situation *f*; **not in a (fit) s. to..., in no (fit) s. to...** hors d'état de...; **in (quite) a s.** *(bad shape)* dans un drôle d'état; **to lie in s.** *(of body)* être exposé **(b)** **S.** *(nation)* État *m*; *Fam* **the States** les États-Unis *mpl* **2** *adj (secret, document)* d'État; *(security)* de l'État; *Br (school, education)* public, -ique; **s. visit** voyage *m* officiel; *Am* **S. Department** ≃ ministère *m* des Affaires étrangères ▪ **stateless** *adj* apatride; **s. person** apatride *mf* ▪ **'state-'owned** *adj* étatisé

state² [steɪt] *vt* déclarer (**that** que); *(opinion)* formuler; *(problem)* exposer; *(time, date)* fixer

stately ['steɪtlɪ] (**-ier, -iest**) *adj* imposant; *Br* **s. home** ≃ château *m*

statement ['steɪtmənt] *n* déclaration *f*; *(in court)* déposition *f*; **(bank) s., s. of account** relevé *m* de compte

state-of-the-art ['steɪtəvðiː'ɑːt] *adj (technology)* de pointe; *(computer, television)* ultramoderne

statesman ['steɪtsmən] *(pl* **-men**) *n* homme *m* d'État

static ['stætɪk] **1** *adj* statique **2** *n* électricité *f* statique

station ['steɪʃən] **1** *n (for trains)* gare *f*; *(underground)* station *f*; *(position) & Mil* poste *m*; *(social)* rang *m*; **coach s.** gare *f* routière; **police s.** poste *m* de police; **space/radio s.** station *f* spatiale/de radio; *Am* **s. wagon** break *m* **2** *vt (position)* placer; **to be stationed at/in** *(of troops)* être en garnison à/en ▪ **station master** *n Rail* chef *m* de gare

stationary ['steɪʃənərɪ] *adj (vehicle)* à l'arrêt; *(person)* immobile

stationery ['steɪʃənərɪ] *n (articles)* articles *mpl* de bureau; *(paper)* papier *m* à papeter, -ière *mf*; **s.'s (shop)** papeterie *f* ▪ **stationer** *n* papetier, -ière *mf*; **s.'s (shop)** papeterie *f*

statistic [stə'tɪstɪk] *n (fact)* statistique *f*; **statistics** *(science)* la statistique ▪ **statistical** *adj* statistique

statue ['stætjuː] *n* statue *f* ▪ **statuesque** [-tʃʊ-'esk] *adj* sculptural

stature ['stætʃə(r)] *n (height)* stature *f*; *Fig (importance)* envergure *f*

status ['steɪtəs] *n (position)* situation *f*; *(legal, official)* statut *m*; *(prestige)* prestige *m*; **s. symbol** marque *f* de prestige; **s. quo** statu quo *m inv*

statute ['stætjuːt] *n (law)* loi *f*; **statutes** *(of institution, club)* statuts *mpl* ▪ **statutory** [-tʃʊ-tərɪ] *adj (right, duty)* statutaire; *Br* **s. holiday** fête *f* légale

staunch [stɔːntʃ] (**-er, -est**) *adj (resolute)* convaincu; *(supporter)* ardent ▪ **staunchly** *adv* résolument

stave [steɪv] **1** *n Mus* portée *f* **2** *vt* **to s. sth off** *(disaster, danger)* conjurer qch; **to s. off hunger** tromper la faim

stay [steɪ] **1** *n (visit)* séjour *m* **2** *vi (remain)* rester; *(reside)* loger; *(visit)* séjourner; **to s. put** ne pas bouger ▪ **staying power** *n* endurance *f*

▸ **stay away** *vi* ne pas s'approcher (**from** de); **to s. away from school** ne pas aller à l'école

▸ **stay behind** *vi* rester en arrière

▸ **stay in** *vi (at home)* rester à la maison; *(of nail, screw, tooth)* tenir

▸ **stay out** *vi (outside)* rester dehors; *(not come home)* ne pas rentrer; **to s. out of sth** *(not interfere in)* ne pas se mêler de qch; *(avoid)* éviter qch

▸ **stay up** *vi (at night)* ne pas se coucher; *(of fence)* tenir; **to s. up late** se coucher tard

▸ **stay with** *vt insep (plan, idea)* ne pas lâcher

St Bernard [*Br* sənt'bɜːnəd, *Am* seɪntbər'nɑːrd] *n (dog)* saint-bernard *m inv*

STD [estiː'diː] *(abbr* **sexually transmitted disease)** *n* MST *f*

stead [sted] *n* **to stand sb in good s.** être bien utile à qn; **in sb's s.** à la place de qn

steadfast ['stedfɑːst] *adj* dévoué; *(opponent)* constant

steady ['stedɪ] **1** (**-ier, -iest**) *adj (firm, stable)* stable; *(hand, voice)* assuré; *(progress, speed, demand)* constant; *(relationship)* durable; **to have a s. boyfriend** avoir un copain; **a s. flood** *or* **stream of insults** un flot ininterrompu d'insultes; **to be s. on one's feet** être solide sur ses jambes **2** *adv Fam* **to go s. with sb** sortir avec qn **3** *vt* faire tenir; **to s. one's nerves** se calmer; **to s. oneself** retrouver son équilibre ▪ **steadily** *adv (gradually)* progressivement; *(regularly)* régulièrement; *(continuously)* sans arrêt; *(walk)* d'un pas assuré

steak [steɪk] *n (beef)* steak *m*; *Br* **s. and kidney pie** = tourte aux rognons et à la viande de bœuf ▪ **steakhouse** *n (restaurant)* grill *m*

steal¹ [stiːl] *(pt* stole, *pp* stolen) *vti* voler *(from sb* à qn)

steal² [stiːl] *(pt* stole, *pp* stolen) *vi* **to s. in/out** entrer/sortir furtivement ▪ **stealth** [stelθ] *n* **by s.** furtivement ▪ **stealthy** ['stelθɪ] (**-ier, -iest**) *adj* furtif, -ive

steam [stiːm] **1** *n* vapeur *f*; *(on glass)* buée *f*; *Fam* **to let off s.** se défouler; **s. engine/iron** locomotive *f*/fer *m* à vapeur **2** *vt (food)* cuire à la vapeur; **to get steamed up** *(of glass)* se couvrir de buée; *Fam (of person)* s'énerver **3** *vi (give off steam)* fumer; **to s. up** *(of glass)* s'embuer ▪ **steamer** *n* bateau *m* à vapeur; *(for food)* panier *m* pour cuisson à la vapeur

steamroller ['stiːmrəʊlə(r)] *n* rouleau *m* compresseur

steamship ['stiːmʃɪp] *n* bateau *m* à vapeur

steamy ['stiːmɪ] (**-ier, -iest**) *adj* plein de vapeur; *(window)* embué; *Fam (love affair, relationship)* torride

steel [stiːl] **1** *n* acier *m*; **s. industry** sidérurgie *f*; **s. mill** aciérie *f* **2** *vt* **to s. oneself** s'armer de courage; **to s. oneself against failure** s'endurcir contre l'échec ▪ **steelworks** *n* aciérie *f*

steep [stiːp] **1** (**-er, -est**) *adj (stairs, slope)* raide; *(hill, path)* escarpé; *Fig (price)* excessif, -ive **2** *vt (soak)* tremper (**in** dans); *Fig* steeped in *(history, prejudice)* imprégné de ▪ **steeply** *adv (rise)* en pente raide; *Fig (of prices)* excessivement

steeple ['stiːpəl] *n* clocher *m*

steeplechase ['stiːpəltʃeɪs] *n* steeple-chase *m*

steer [stɪə(r)] **1** *vt* diriger **2** *vi (of person)* conduire; *(of ship)* se diriger (**for** vers); **to s. towards** faire route vers; **to s. clear of sb/sth** éviter qn/qch ▪ **steering** *n (in vehicle)* direction *f*; **s. wheel** volant *m*

stem [stem] **1** *n (of plant)* tige *f*; *(of glass)* pied *m*; *Biol* **s. cell** cellule *f* souche **2** *(pt & pp* -mm-) *vt (stop)* arrêter; **to s. the flow** *or* **tide of sth** endiguer le flot de qch **3** *vi* **to s. from sth** provenir de qch

stench [stentʃ] *n* puanteur *f*

stencil ['stensəl] **1** *n (device)* pochoir *m*; *(artwork)* peinture *f* au pochoir **2** *(Br* -ll-, *Am* -l-) *vt* i peindre au pochoir

stenographer [stə'nɒɡrəfə(r)] *n Am* sténodactylo *f*

step [step] **1** *n (movement, sound)* pas *m*; *(of stairs)* marche *f*; *(on train, bus)* marchepied *m*; *(doorstep)* pas de la porte; *Fig (action)* mesure *f*; **(flight of) steps** *(indoors)* escalier *m*; *(outdoors)* perron *m*; *Br* **(pair of) steps** *(ladder)* escabeau *m*; **s. by s.** pas à pas; **to keep in s.** marcher au pas; *Fig* **to be in s. with** *(opinions)* être en accord avec **2** *(pt & pp* -pp-) *vi (walk)* marcher (**on** sur); **s. this way!** (venez) par ici! ▪ **stepbrother** *n* demi-frère *m* ▪ **stepdaughter** *n* belle-fille *f* ▪ **stepfather** *n* beau-père *m* ▪ **stepmother** *n* belle-mère *f* ▪ **stepsister** *n* demi-sœur *f* ▪ **stepson** *n* beau-fils *m*

▸ **step aside** *vi* s'écarter

▸ **step back** *vi* reculer

▸ **step down** *vi* descendre (**from** de); *Fig (withdraw)* se retirer

▸ **step forward** *vi* faire un pas en avant

▸ **step in** *vi (enter)* entrer; *(into car)* monter; *Fig (intervene)* intervenir

▸ **step into** *vt insep (car)* monter dans

▸ **step off** *vt insep (chair)* descendre de

▸ **step out** *vi (of car)* descendre (**of** de)

▸ **step over** *vt insep (obstacle)* enjamber

▸ **step up** *vt sep (increase)* augmenter; *(speed up)* accélérer

stepladder ['steplædə(r)] *n* escabeau *m*

stepping-stone ['stepɪŋstəʊn] *n (in river)* pierre *f*; *Fig (in career)* tremplin *m*

stereo ['sterɪəʊ] **1** *(pl* -os) *n (hi-fi, record player)* chaîne *f* stéréo; *(sound)* stéréo *f*; **in s.** en stéréo **2** *adj (record)* stéréo *inv*; *(broadcast)* en stéréo ▪ **stereophonic** [-rɪə'fɒnɪk] *adj* stéréophonique

stereotype ['sterɪətaɪp] **1** *n* stéréotype *m* **2** *vt* stéréotyper

sterile [*Br* 'steraɪl, *Am* 'sterəl] *adj* stérile ▪ **sterility** [stə'rɪlɪtɪ] *n* stérilité *f*

sterilize ['sterəlaɪz] *vt* stériliser ▪ **steri-li'zation** *n* stérilisation *f*

sterling ['stɜːlɪŋ] **1** *n Br (currency)* livre *f* sterling **2** *adj (silver)* fin; *Fig (quality, person)* sûr

stern¹ [stɜːn] (**-er, -est**) adj sévère

stern² [stɜːn] n (of ship) arrière m

steroid ['stɪərɔɪd] n stéroïde m

stethoscope ['steθəskəʊp] n stéthoscope m

Stetson ['stetsən] n chapeau m à larges bords

stew [stjuː] **1** n ragoût m; Fig **to be in a s.** être dans le pétrin **2** vt (meat) faire cuire en ragoût; (fruit) faire de la compote de; **stewed fruit** compote f **3** vi cuire ▪ **stewing** adj (pears, apples) à cuire; **s. steak** bœuf m à braiser

steward ['stjuːəd] n (on plane, ship) steward m ▪ **stewardess** n (on plane) hôtesse f

STI [estiː'aɪ] (abbr **sexually transmitted infection**) n MST f

stick¹ [stɪk] n (piece of wood, chalk, dynamite) bâton m; (for walking) canne f; Fam Pej **in the sticks** (countryside) à la cambrousse; Br Fam **to give sb s.** (criticize) taper sur les doigts de qn; (laugh at) se payer la tête de qn; Br Fam **to get** or **take a lot of s.** (be criticized) se faire taper sur les doigts; (be mocked) se faire mettre en boîte

stick² [stɪk] **1** (pt & pp **stuck**) vt (glue) coller; Fam (put) fourrer; Fam (tolerate) supporter; **to s. sth into sth** fourrer qch dans qch; Fig **to s. to one's guns** ne pas en démordre **2** vi coller (**to** à); (of food in pan) attacher (**to** dans); (of drawer) se coincer; **to s. to the facts** s'en tenir aux faits; **to s. to one's principles** rester fidèle à ses principes ▪ **sticking plaster** n Br sparadrap m

▸ **stick around** vi Fam (hang around) rester dans les parages

▸ **stick by** vt insep rester fidèle à

▸ **stick down** vt sep (envelope, stamp) coller; Fam (put down) poser

▸ **stick on** vt sep (stamp, label) coller

▸ **stick out 1** vt sep (tongue) tirer; Fam (head or arm from window) sortir; Fam **to s. it out** (resist) tenir bon **2** vi (of shirt) dépasser; (of tooth) avancer

▸ **stick up** vt sep (notice) coller; Fam (hand) lever

▸ **stick up for** vt insep défendre

sticker ['stɪkə(r)] n autocollant m

stickler ['stɪklə(r)] n **to be a s. for sth** être à cheval sur qch

stick-on ['stɪkɒn] adj autocollant

stick-up ['stɪkʌp] n Fam braquage m

sticky ['stɪkɪ] (**-ier, -iest**) adj collant; (label) adhésif, -ive; Fig (problem, matter) délicat

stiff [stɪf] (**-er, -est**) adj raide; (joint) ankylosé; (brush, paste) dur; Fig (person) guindé; (difficult) difficile; (price) élevé; (whisky) bien tassé; **to have a s. neck** avoir un torticolis; **to feel s.** être courbaturé; Fam **to be bored s.** s'ennuyer à mourir; Fam **frozen s.** complètement gelé

stiffen ['stɪfən] **1** vt raidir **2** vi se raidir

stiffly ['stɪflɪ] adv Fig (coldly) froidement ▪ **stiffness** n raideur f; (hardness) dureté f

stifle ['staɪfəl] **1** vt (feeling, person) étouffer **2** vi **it's stifling** on étouffe

stigma ['stɪgmə] n (moral stain) flétrissure f; **there's no s. attached to...** il n'y a aucune honte à... ▪ **stigmatize** vt stigmatiser

stile [staɪl] n échalier m

stiletto [stɪ'letəʊ] Br **1** (pl **-os** or **-oes**) n (shoe) talon m aiguille **2** adj **s. heels** talons mpl aiguille

still¹ [stɪl] adv encore, toujours; (even) encore; (nevertheless) tout de même; **better s., s. better** encore mieux

still² [stɪl] **1** (**-er, -est**) adj (not moving) immobile; (calm) calme; Br (drink) non gazeux, -euse; **to stand s.** rester tranquille; **s. life** nature f morte **2** n (photo of film) photo f (tirée d'un film); **in the s. of the night** dans le silence de la nuit ▪ **stillborn** adj (baby) mort-né (f mort-née) ▪ **stillness** n immobilité f; (calm) calme m

still³ [stɪl] n (distilling equipment) alambic m

stilt [stɪlt] n (for walking) échasse f

stilted ['stɪltɪd] adj (speech, person) guindé

stimulate ['stɪmjʊleɪt] vt stimuler ▪ **stimulant** n stimulant m ▪ **stimu'lation** n stimulation f ▪ **stimulus** (pl **-li** [-laɪ]) n (encouragement) stimulant m; (physiological) stimulus m inv

sting [stɪŋ] **1** n piqûre f; (insect's organ) dard m **2** (pt & pp **stung**) vt (of insect, ointment, wind) piquer; Fig (of remark) blesser **3** vi piquer ▪ **stinging** adj (pain) cuisant; (remark) cinglant

stingy ['stɪndʒɪ] (**-ier, -iest**) adj avare; **to be s. with** (money, praise) être avare de; (food, wine) lésiner sur ▪ **stinginess** n avarice f

stink [stɪŋk] **1** n puanteur f; Fam **to cause** or **make a s.** (trouble) faire tout un foin **2** (pt & pp **stank** or **stunk**, pp **stunk**) vi puer; Fam (of book, film) être infect; **to s. of smoke** empester la fumée **3** vt **to s. out** (room) empester ▪ **stinker** n Fam (person) peau f de vache; (question, task) vacherie f ▪ **stinking** adj Fam puant

stint [stɪnt] **1** n (period) période f de travail; (share) part f de travail **2** vi **to s. on sth** lésiner sur qch

stipend ['staɪpend] n traitement m

stipulate ['stɪpjʊleɪt] vt stipuler (**that** que) ▪ **stipu'lation** n stipulation f

stir [stɜː(r)] **1** n agitation f; **to give sth a s.** remuer qch; Fig **to cause a s.** faire du bruit **2** (pt & pp **-rr-**) vt (coffee, leaves) remuer; Fig (excite) exciter; (incite) inciter (**sb to do sth** qn à faire); **to s. oneself** se secouer; **to s. sth up** (leaves) remuer qch; (rebellion) attiser qch; **to s. up trouble** semer la zizanie; **to s. up trouble for sb** attirer des ennuis à qn; **to s. things up** envenimer les choses **3** vi (move) remuer, bouger ▪ **stirring** adj (speech) émouvant

stirrup ['stɪrəp] n étrier m

stitch [stɪtʃ] **1** n point m; (in knitting) maille f; (in wound) point de suture; (sharp pain) point de côté; Fam **to be in stitches** être plié (de rire) **2** vt **to s. (up)** (sew up) coudre; Med recoudre; Fam **to s. sb up** (incriminate) faire porter le chapeau à qn

stoat [stəʊt] n hermine f

stock [stɒk] **1** n (supply) provisions fpl; Com stock m; Fin valeurs fpl; (soup) bouillon m; (cattle) bétail m; Fin **stocks and shares** valeurs mobilières; Hist **the stocks** le pilori; **in s.** (goods) en stock; **out of s.** (goods) épuisé; **to be of German s.** être de souche allemande; Fig **to take s.** faire le point (**of** de); **s. reply/size** réponse f/taille f classique; **s. phrase** expression f toute faite; **the S. Exchange** or **Market** la Bourse **2** vt (sell) vendre; (keep in store) stocker; **to s. (up)** (shop) approvisionner; (fridge, cupboard) remplir; **well-stocked** (shop) bien approvisionné; (fridge) bien rempli **3** vi **to s. up** s'approvisionner (**with** en) ▪ **stockbroker** ['stɒkbrəʊkə(r)] n agent m de change ▪ **stockcar** n stock-car m ▪ **stockholder** n Fin actionnaire mf ▪ **stockist** n stockiste m ▪ **stockpile** vt faire des réserves de ▪ **stockroom** n réserve f, magasin m ▪ **stocktaking** n Br Com inventaire m

stockade [stɒ'keɪd] n palissade f

stocking ['stɒkɪŋ] n (garment) bas m

stocky ['stɒkɪ] (**-ier, -iest**) adj trapu

stodge [stɒdʒ] n Fam (food) étouffe-chrétien m inv ▪ **stodgy** (**-ier, -iest**) adj Fam (food) bourratif, -ive; Fig (book) indigeste

stoic ['stəʊɪk] adj & n stoïque (mf) ▪ **stoical** adj stoïque ▪ **stoicism** [-ɪsɪzəm] n stoïcisme m

stoke [stəʊk] vt (fire) entretenir; (furnace) alimenter; (engine) chauffer

stole¹ [stəʊl] n (shawl) étole f

stole² [stəʊl] pt of **steal¹,²**

stolen ['stəʊlən] pp of **steal¹,²**

stolid ['stɒlɪd] adj impassible

stomach ['stʌmək] **1** n ventre m; (organ) estomac m **2** vt (put up with) supporter ▪ **stomach-ache** n mal m de ventre; **to have (a) s.** avoir mal au ventre

stone [stəʊn] **1** n pierre f; (pebble) caillou m; (in fruit) noyau m; (in kidney) calcul m; Br (unit of weight) = 6,348 kg; Fig **it's a stone's throw away** c'est à deux pas d'ici **2** vt (person) lapider; (fruit) dénoyauter ▪ **stonemason** n maçon m

stone- [stəʊn] pref complètement ▪ **'stone-'cold** adj glacé ▪ **stone-'dead** adj raide mort ▪ **'stone-'deaf** adj sourd comme un pot

stoned [stəʊnd] adj Fam (on drugs) défoncé

stony ['stəʊnɪ] (**-ier, -iest**) adj (path) caillouteux, -euse; Br Fam **s. broke** fauché

stood [stʊd] pt & pp of **stand**

stooge [stuːdʒ] n (actor) comparse mf; Pej (flunkey) larbin m; Pej (dupe) pigeon m

stool [stuːl] n tabouret m

stoop¹ [stuːp] n Am (in front of house) perron m; **to have a s.** être voûté

stoop² [stuːp] vi se baisser; Fig **to s. to doing/to sth** s'abaisser à faire/à qch

stop [stɒp] **1** n (place, halt) arrêt m; (for plane, ship) escale f; **to put a s. to sth** mettre fin à qch; **to make a s.** (of vehicle) s'arrêter; (of plane) faire escale; **to bring a car to a s.** arrêter une voiture; **to come to a s.** s'arrêter; **without a s.** sans arrêt; Br **s. light** (on vehicle) stop m; **s. sign** (on road) stop **2** (pt & pp **-pp-**) vt arrêter; (end) mettre fin à; (cheque) faire opposition à; **to s. sb/sth from doing sth** empêcher qn/qch de faire qch **3** vi s'arrêter; (of pain, bleeding) cesser; (stay) rester; **to s. eating** s'arrêter de manger; **to s. snowing** cesser de neiger ▪ **stopgap** n bouche-trou m **2** adj (solution) intérimaire ▪ **stopoff** n halte f; (in plane journey) escale f ▪ **stopover** n arrêt m; (in plane journey) escale f; **to make a s.** faire halte; (of plane) faire escale ▪ **stop-press** adj de dernière minute ▪ **stopwatch** n chronomètre m

▶ **stop by** vi (visit) passer (**sb's** chez qn)

▶ **stop off, stop over** vi (on journey) s'arrêter

▶ **stop up** vt sep (sink, pipe, leak) boucher

stoppage ['stɒpɪdʒ] n (of flow, traffic) arrêt m; (strike) débrayage m; Br (in pay) retenue f; (blockage) obstruction f; Sport **s. time** arrêts mpl de jeu

stopper ['stɒpə(r)] n bouchon m

store [stɔː(r)] **1** n (supply) provision f; Fig (of knowledge) fonds m; (warehouse) entrepôt m; Br (shop) grand magasin m; Am magasin m; **to have sth in s. for sb** réserver qch à qn; **to keep sth in s.** garder qch en réserve; **to set great s. by sth** faire grand cas de qch **2** vt (in warehouse) stocker; (furniture) entreposer; (food) ranger; (heat) emmagasiner; Comptr (in memory) mettre en mémoire ▪ **storage** [-rɪdʒ] n emmagasinage m; **s. space** espace m de rangement; Comptr **s. capacity** capacité f de mémoire

▶ **store away** vt sep (put away, file away) ranger; (furniture) entreposer

▶ **store up** vt sep accumuler

storekeeper ['stɔːkiːpə(r)] n Am (shopkeeper) commerçant, -ante mf; Br (warehouseman) magasinier m

storeroom ['stɔːruːm] n (in house) débarras m; (in office, shop) réserve f

storey ['stɔːrɪ] (pl **-eys**) n Br (of building) étage m

stork [stɔːk] n cigogne f

storm [stɔːm] **1** n (bad weather) tempête f; (thunderstorm) orage m; **s. cloud** nuée f d'orage; *Fig* **a s. of protest** une tempête de protestations; *Mil* **to take sth by s.** prendre qch d'assaut; *Fig* **she took London by s.** elle a eu un succès foudroyant à Londres; *Fam* **to go down a s.** faire un tabac **2** *vt (of soldiers, police)* prendre d'assaut **3** *vi* **to s. out** *(angrily)* sortir comme une furie ■ **stormy (-ier, -iest)** *adj (weather, meeting)* orageux, -euse; *(wind)* d'orage

story¹ ['stɔːrɪ] *(pl -ies)* *n* histoire *f*; *(newspaper article)* article *m*; **s. line** *(plot)* intrigue *f* ■ **storybook** *n* livre *m* d'histoires ■ **story-teller** *n* conteur, -euse *mf*

story² ['stɔːrɪ] *(pl -ies)* *n Am* = **storey**

stout [staʊt] **1** (-er, -est) *adj (person)* corpulent; *(resistance)* acharné; *(shoes)* solide **2** *n Br (beer)* bière *f* brune ■ **stoutness** *n* corpulence *f*

stove [staʊv] *n (for cooking)* cuisinière *f*; *(for heating)* poêle *m*

stow [staʊ] **1** *vt (cargo)* arrimer; **to s. sth away** *(put away)* ranger qch **2** *vi* **to s. away** *(on ship)* voyager clandestinement ■ **stowaway** *n (on ship)* passager, -ère *mf* clandestin(e)

straddle ['strædəl] *vt (chair, fence)* se mettre à califourchon sur; *(step over, span)* enjamber

straggle ['strægəl] *vi* (a) *(of hair)* pendouiller (b) *(lag behind)* être à la traîne; **to s. in** entrer par petits groupes ■ **straggler** *n* retardataire *mf*

straight [streɪt] **1** (-er, -est) *adj* droit; *(hair)* raide; *(honest)* honnête; *(answer)* clair; *(consecutive)* consécutif, -ive; *(conventional)* conformiste; *Fam (heterosexual)* hétéro; **let's get this s.** comprenons-nous bien; **to keep a s. face** garder son sérieux; **to be s. with sb** jouer franc jeu avec qn **2** *n* **the s.** *(on racetrack)* la ligne droite **3** *adv (in straight line)* droit; *(directly)* directement; *(immediately)* tout de suite; **s. away** *(at once)* tout de suite; **s. out, s. off** sans hésiter; **s. opposite** juste en face; *Br* **s. ahead** *or* **on** *(walk)* tout droit; **to look s. ahead** regarder droit devant soi; **to drink whisky s.** boire son whisky sec

straightaway [streɪtə'weɪ] *adv* tout de suite

straighten ['streɪtən] *vt* **to s. (out)** *(wire)* redresser; **to s. (up)** *(tie, hair, room)* arranger; **to s. things out** arranger les choses

straight-faced ['streɪt'feɪst] *adj* impassible

straightforward [streɪt'fɔːwəd] *adj (easy, clear)* simple; *(frank)* franc (f franche)

strain¹ [streɪn] **1** *n* tension *f*; *(mental stress)* stress *m*; *(on ankle)* foulure *f* **2** *vt* (a) *(rope, wire)* tendre excessivement; *(muscle)* se froisser; *(ankle, wrist)* se fouler; *(eyes)* fatiguer; *(voice)* forcer; *Fig (patience, friendship)* mettre à l'épreuve; **to s. one's ears** tendre l'oreille; **to s. one's back** se faire mal au dos; **to s. oneself** *(hurt oneself)* se faire mal; *(tire oneself)* se

fatiguer (b) *(soup)* passer; *(vegetables)* égoutter **3** *vi* faire un effort (**to do** pour faire); **to s. at a rope** tirer sur une corde

strain² [streɪn] *n (of plant)* variété *f*; *(of virus)* souche *f*; *(streak)* tendance *f*

strained [streɪnd] *adj (muscle)* froissé; *(ankle, wrist)* foulé; *(relations)* tendu; *(laugh)* forcé

strainer ['streɪnə(r)] *n* passoire *f*

strait [streɪt] *n Geog* **strait(s)** détroit *m*; **in financial straits** dans l'embarras

straitjacket ['streɪtdʒækɪt] *n* camisole *f* de force

straitlaced ['streɪt'leɪst] *adj* collet monté *inv*

strand [strænd] *n (of wool)* brin *m*; *(of hair)* mèche *f*; *Fig (of story)* fil *m*

stranded ['strændɪd] *adj (person, vehicle)* en rade

strange [streɪndʒ] (-er, -est) *adj (odd)* bizarre; *(unknown)* inconnu ■ **strangely** *adv* étrangement; **s. (enough), she...** chose étrange, elle... ■ **strangeness** *n* étrangeté *f*

stranger ['streɪndʒə(r)] *n (unknown)* inconnu, -ue *mf*; *(outsider)* étranger, -ère *mf*; **he's a s. here** il n'est pas d'ici; **she's a s. to me** elle m'est inconnue

strangle ['stræŋgəl] *vt* étrangler ■ **strangler** *n* étrangleur, -euse *mf*

stranglehold ['stræŋgəlhəʊld] *n* **to have a s. on sth** avoir la mainmise sur qch

strap [stræp] **1** *n* sangle *f*; *(on dress)* bretelle *f*; *(on watch)* bracelet *m*; *(on sandal)* lanière *f* **2** *(pt & pp* -pp-) *vt* **to s. (down** *or* **in)** attacher *(avec une sangle)*
▸ **strap in** *vt sep* attacher avec une ceinture de sécurité

strapping ['stræpɪŋ] *adj* robuste

stratagem ['strætədʒəm] *n* stratagème *m*

strategy ['strætədʒɪ] *(pl -ies)* *n* stratégie *f* ■ **strategic** [strə'tiːdʒɪk] *adj* stratégique

stratum ['strɑːtəm] *(pl -ta* [-tə]) *n* couche *f*

straw [strɔː] *n (from wheat, for drinking)* paille *f*; **that's the last s.!** c'est le comble!

strawberry ['strɔːbərɪ] **1** *(pl -ies)* *n* fraise *f* **2** *adj (flavour, ice cream)* à la fraise; *(jam)* de fraises; *(tart)* aux fraises

stray [streɪ] **1** *adj (animal, bullet)* perdu; **a few s. cars** quelques rares voitures; **s. dog** chien *m* errant **2** *n (dog)* chien *m* errant; *(cat)* chat *m* égaré **3** *vi* s'égarer; **to s. from** *(subject, path)* s'écarter de; **don't s. too far** ne t'éloigne pas

streak [striːk] *n (of paint, dirt)* traînée *f*; *(of light)* rai *m*; *(in hair)* mèche *f*; **to have a mad s.** avoir une tendance à la folie; **to be on a winning s.** être dans une période de chance; **s. of lightning** éclair *m* ■ **streaked** *adj (marked)* strié; *(stained)* taché *(with de)* ■ **streaker** *n Fam* = personne qui court nu(e) en public ■ **streaky (-ier, -iest)** *adj* strié; *Br* **s. bacon** bacon *m* entrelardé

stream [stri:m] **1** *n* *(brook)* ruisseau *m*; *(current)* courant *m*; *(of light, blood)* jet *m*; *(of tears)* torrent *m*; *(of people)* flot *m* **2** *vt* **to s. blood** ruisseler de sang; **to s. pupils** répartir des élèves par niveaux **3** *vi* ruisseler **(with** de**)**; **to s. in** *(of sunlight, people)* entrer à flots

streamer ['stri:mə(r)] *n* *(banner)* banderole *f*; *(for parties)* serpentin *m*

streamline ['stri:mlaɪn] *vt* *(work, method)* rationaliser ▪ **streamlined** *adj* *(shape)* aérodynamique; *(industry, production)* rationalisé

street [stri:t] *n* rue *f*; *Br Fam* **that's (right) up my s.** c'est mon rayon; *Br Fam* **to be streets ahead** dépasser tout le monde; *Fam* **s. cred** look *m* branché; **s. door** porte *f* d'entrée; **s. lamp, s. light** lampadaire *m*; **s. map** plan *m* des rues ▪ **streetcar** *n Am* *(tram)* tramway *m* ▪ **streetwise** *adj Fam* dégourdi

strength [streŋθ] *n* force *f*; *(of wood, fabric)* solidité *f*; *Fig* **on the s. of** sur la base de; **in** *or* **at full s.** *(of troops)* au (grand) complet ▪ **strengthen** *vt* *(building, position)* renforcer; *(body, soul, limb)* fortifier

strenuous ['strenjʊəs] *adj* *(effort, exercise)* vigoureux, -euse; *(work)* fatigant; *(denial)* énergique ▪ **strenuously** *adv* énergiquement

strep [strep] *adj Am* **s. throat** forte angine *f*

stress [stres] **1** *n* *(physical)* tension *f*; *(mental)* stress *m*; *(emphasis)* & *Grammar* accent *m*; **under s.** *(person)* stressé, sous pression; *(relationship)* tendu **2** *vt* insister sur; *(word)* accentuer; **to s. that…** souligner que… ▪ **stressed** *adj Fam* **to be s. (out)** être stressé **3** *vi Fam* stresser ▪ **stressful** *adj* stressant ▪ **stress-related** *adj* **to be s.** être dû (*f* due) au stress

stretch [stretʃ] **1** *n* *(area, duration)* étendue *f*; *(period of time)* période *f*; *(of road)* tronçon *m*; **ten hours at a s.** dix heures d'affilée; **for a long s. of time** *(pendant)* longtemps; *Fam* **to do a three-year s.** *(in prison)* faire trois ans de prison **2** *vt* *(rope, neck)* tendre; *(shoe, rubber)* étirer; *Fig (meaning)* forcer; *(income, supplies)* faire durer; **to s. (out)** *(arm, leg)* tendre; *Fig* **to s. one's legs** se dégourdir les jambes; *Fig* **to s. sb** pousser qn à son maximum; **we're fully stretched at the moment** nous sommes au maximum de nos capacités en ce moment **3** *vi* *(of person, elastic)* s'étirer; *(of influence)* s'étendre; **to s. (out)** *(of rope, plain)* s'étendre ▪ **stretch marks** *npl* vergetures *fpl*

stretcher ['stretʃə(r)] *n* brancard *m*

strew [stru:] *(pt* **strewed,** *pp* **strewed** *or* **strewn** [stru:n]*)* *vt* *(scatter)* éparpiller; **strewn with** *(covered)* jonché de

stricken ['strɪkən] *adj* *(town, region)* sinistré; **s. with grief** accablé par le chagrin; **s. with illness** atteint de maladie

strict [strɪkt] *(-er, -est) adj* *(severe, absolute)*

strict ▪ **strictly** *adv* strictement; **s. forbidden** formellement interdit ▪ **strictness** *n* sévérité *f*

stride [straɪd] **1** *n* pas *m*; *Fig* **to make great strides** faire de grands progrès **2** *(pt* **strode***) vi* **to s. across** *or* **over** enjamber; **to s. along/out** avancer/sortir à grands pas; **to s. up/down a room** arpenter une pièce

strident ['straɪdənt] *adj* strident

strife [straɪf] *n inv* conflits *mpl*

strike [straɪk] **1** *n* *(of workers)* grève *f*; *(of ore, oil)* découverte *f*; *Mil* raid *m*; **to go (out) on s.** se mettre en grève **2** *(pt & pp* **struck***) vt* *(hit, impress)* frapper; *(collide with)* heurter; *(gold, oil)* trouver; *(coin)* frapper; *(match)* craquer; **to s. the time** *(of clock)* sonner l'heure; **to s. a blow** donner un coup; **to s. a balance** trouver un équilibre; **to s. oil** trouver du pétrole; *Fam* **to s. it rich** faire fortune; **it strikes me that…** il me semble que… *(+ indicative)*; **how did it s. you?** quelle impression ça t'a fait? **3** *vi* *(of workers)* faire grève; *(attack)* attaquer; *Fig* **to s. home** faire mouche

▸ **strike at** *vt insep* *(attack)* attaquer

▸ **strike back** *vi* *(retaliate)* riposter

▸ **strike down** *vt sep* *(of illness)* terrasser; *(of bullet)* abattre

▸ **strike off** *vt sep* *(from list)* rayer **(from** de**)**; **to be struck off** *(of doctor)* être radié

▸ **strike out** *vi* **to s. out at sb** essayer de frapper qn

▸ **strike up** *vt sep* **to s. up a friendship** se lier amitié **(with sb** avec qn**)**

striker ['straɪkə(r)] *n* *(worker)* gréviste *mf*; *Football* buteur *m*

striking ['straɪkɪŋ] *adj* *(impressive)* frappant ▪ **strikingly** *adv* *(beautiful, intelligent)* extraordinairement

string [strɪŋ] **1** *n* ficelle *f*; *(of apron)* cordon *m*; *(of violin, racket)* corde *f*; *(of onions)* chapelet *m*; *(of questions)* série *f*; **s. of pearls** collier *m* de perles; **s. of beads** collier; *(for praying)* chapelet; *Fig* **to pull strings** faire jouer ses relations; *Fig* **to pull strings for sb** pistonner qn **2** *adj* *(instrument, quartet)* à cordes; **s. bean** haricot *m* vert **3** *(pt & pp* **strung***) vt* *(beads)* enfiler **4** *vi Fam* **to s. along** *(follow)* suivre ▪ **stringed** *adj* *(musical instrument)* à cordes ▪ **stringy** *(-ier, -iest) adj* *(meat, vegetables)* filandreux, -euse

stringent ['strɪndʒənt] *adj* rigoureux, -euse ▪ **stringency** *n* rigueur *f*

strip [strɪp] **1** *n* *(piece)* bande *f*; *(of metal)* lame *f*; *(of sports team)* tenue *f*; **landing s.** piste *f* d'atterrissage; **s. cartoon** bande dessinée; **s. club** boîte *f* de strip-tease; *Br* **s. lighting** éclairage *m* au néon **2** *(pt & pp* **-pp-***) vt* *(undress)* déshabiller; *(bed)* défaire; *(deprive)* dépouiller **(of** de**)**; **stripped to the waist** torse nu; **to s. (down)** *(machine)* démonter; **to s. off**

(remove) enlever **3** *vi* **to s. (off)** *(get undressed)* se déshabiller ▪ **stripper** n *(woman)* strip-teaseuse f; **(male) s.** strip-teaseur m; **(paint) s.** décapant m ▪ **strip-search 1** n fouille f d'une personne dévêtue **2** *vt* **to s. sb** faire déshabiller qn pour le/la fouiller ▪ **striptease** n strip-tease m

stripe [straɪp] n rayure f; *(indicating rank)* galon m ▪ **striped** *adj* rayé (**with** de) ▪ **stripy** *adj (fabric, pattern)* rayé

strive [straɪv] *(pt* strove, *pp* striven ['strɪvən]) *vi* s'efforcer (**to do** de faire); **for** d'obtenir)

strobe [strəʊb] *adj* **s. lighting** éclairage m stroboscopique

strode [strəʊd] *pt of* **stride**

stroke [strəʊk] **1** n *(movement)* coup m; *(of pen)* trait m; *(of brush)* touche f; *(caress)* caresse f; *Med (illness)* attaque f; **(swimming) s.** nage f; **at a s.** d'un coup; **on the s. of nine** à neuf heures sonnantes; **s. of luck** coup de chance; **s. of genius** coup de génie; **you haven't done a s. of work** tu n'as rien fait; **four-s. engine** moteur m à quatre temps **2** *vt (caress)* caresser

stroll [strəʊl] **1** n promenade f **2** *vi* se promener; **to s. in** entrer sans se presser ▪ **strolling** *adj (musician)* ambulant

stroller ['strəʊlə(r)] n Am *(for baby)* poussette f

strong [strɒŋ] **1** (**-er, -est**) *adj* fort; *(shoes, chair, nerves)* solide; *(interest)* vif (f vive); *(measures)* énergique; *(supporter)* ardent; **they were sixty s.** ils étaient au nombre de soixante **2** *adv* **to be going s.** aller toujours bien ▪ **strong-arm** *adj* **s. tactics** la manière forte ▪ **strong-box** n coffre-fort m ▪ **stronghold** n bastion m ▪ **strongly** *adv (protest, defend)* énergiquement; *(advise, remind, desire)* fortement; **s. built** solide; **to feel s. about sth** être convaincu de qch ▪ **strong-'willed** *adj* résolu

strove [strəʊv] *pt of* **strive**

struck [strʌk] *pt & pp of* **strike**

structure ['strʌktʃə(r)] n structure f; *(building)* édifice m ▪ **structural** *adj* structural; *(building defect)* de construction; **s. damage** *(to building)* dégâts mpl de structure; **s. engineer** ingénieur m civil

struggle ['strʌgəl] **1** n *(fight)* lutte f (**to do** pour faire); **to put up a s.** résister; **to have a s. doing** *or* **to do sth** avoir du mal à faire qch **2** *vi (fight)* lutter (**with** avec); **to be struggling** *(financially)* avoir du mal; **to s. to do sth** s'efforcer de faire qch; **to s. out of** sortir péniblement de; **to s. into** entrer péniblement dans; **to s. along** *or* **on** se débrouiller

strum [strʌm] *(pt & pp* **-mm-**) *vt (guitar)* gratter

strung [strʌŋ] *pt & pp of* **string**

strut¹ [strʌt] *(pt & pp* **-tt-**) *vi* **to s. (about** *or* **around)** se pavaner

strut² [strʌt] n *(for frame)* étai m

stub [stʌb] **1** n *(of pencil, cigarette)* bout m; *(of cheque)* talon m **2** *(pt & pp* **-bb-**) *vt* **to s. one's toe** se cogner l'orteil (**on** *or* **against** contre); **to s. out** *(cigarette)* écraser

stubble ['stʌbəl] n *(on face)* barbe f de plusieurs jours

stubborn ['stʌbən] *adj (person)* têtu; *(determination)* farouche; *(stain)* rebelle ▪ **stubbornness** n *(of person)* entêtement m; *(of determination)* inflexibilité f

stubby ['stʌbɪ] (**-ier, -iest**) *adj (finger)* court et boudiné; *(person)* trapu

stucco ['stʌkəʊ] *(pl* **-os** *or* **-oes**) n stuc m

stuck [stʌk] **1** *pt & pp of* **stick²** **2** *adj (caught, jammed)* coincé; **s. in bed/indoors** cloué au lit/chez soi; **to get s.** être coincé; **I'm s. for an answer** je ne sais que répondre; **to be s. with sb/sth** se farcir qn/qch ▪ **stuck-up** [stʌ'kʌp] *adj Fam* snob inv

stud¹ [stʌd] n *(on football boot)* crampon m; *(earring)* clou m d'oreille; **(collar) s.** bouton m de col ▪ **studded** *adj (boots, tyres)* clouté; *Fig* **s. with** *(covered)* constellé de

stud² [stʌd] n *(farm)* haras m; *(stallion)* étalon m; *Fam (virile man)* mâle m

student ['stju:dənt] **1** n *(at university)* étudiant, -iante mf; *(at school)* élève mf; **music s.** étudiant, -iante en musique **2** *adj (life, protest)* étudiant; *(restaurant, residence, grant)* universitaire

studied ['stʌdɪd] *adj (deliberate)* étudié

studio ['stju:dɪəʊ] *(pl* **-os**) n studio m; *(of artist)* atelier m; **s. audience** public m présent lors de l'enregistrement; *Br* **s. flat,** *Am* **s. apartment** studio

studious ['stju:dɪəs] *adj (person)* studieux, -ieuse ▪ **studiously** *adv (carefully)* avec soin

study ['stʌdɪ] **1** *(pl* **-ies**) n étude f; *(office)* bureau m **2** *(pp & pp* **-ied**) *vt (learn, observe)* étudier **3** *vi* étudier; **to s. to be a doctor** faire des études de médecine; **to s. for an exam** préparer un examen

stuff [stʌf] **1** n *(possessions)* affaires fpl; *(cloth)* étoffe f; *Fam* **some s.** *(substance)* un truc; *Fam* **he knows his s.** il connaît son affaire; *Fam* **this s.'s good, it's good s.** c'est bien **2** *vt (pocket)* remplir (**with** de); *(cushion)* rembourrer (**with** avec); *(animal)* empailler; *(chicken, tomatoes)* farcir; **to s. sth into sth** fourrer qch dans qch; **to s. (up)** *(hole)* colmater; **my nose is stuffed (up)** j'ai le nez bouché ▪ **stuffing** n *(padding)* bourre f; *(for chicken, tomatoes)* farce f

stuffy ['stʌfɪ] (**-ier, -iest**) *adj (room)* qui sent le renfermé; *(person)* vieux jeu inv

stumble ['stʌmbəl] *vi* trébucher; **to s. across** *or* **on** *(find)* tomber sur; **stumbling block** pierre f d'achoppement

stump [stʌmp] n *(of tree)* souche f; *(of limb)* moignon m; *(of pencil)* bout m; *(in cricket)* piquet m

stumped ['stʌmpt] *adj* to be s. by sth *(baffled)* ne savoir que penser de qch

stun [stʌn] *(pt & pp -nn-) vt (make unconscious)* assommer; *Fig (amaze)* stupéfier ▪ **stunned** *adj (amazed)* stupéfait (**by** par) ▪ **stunning** *adj (news)* stupéfiant; *Fam (excellent)* excellent; *Fam (beautiful)* superbe

stung [stʌŋ] *pt & pp of* **sting**

stunk [stʌŋk] *pt & pp of* **stink**

stunt¹ [stʌnt] *n (in film)* cascade *f; (for publicity)* coup *m* de pub; s. man cascadeur *m;* s. woman cascadeuse *f*

stunt² [stʌnt] *vt (growth)* retarder ▪ **stunted** *adj (person)* rabougri

stupefy ['stju:pɪfaɪ] *(pt & pp -ied) vt (of drink)* abrutir; *Fig (amaze)* stupéfier

stupendous [stju:'pendəs] *adj* fantastique

stupid ['stju:pɪd] *adj* stupide; to do/say a s. thing faire/dire une stupidité ▪ **stu'pidity** *n* stupidité *f* ▪ **stupidly** *adv* bêtement

stupor ['stju:pə(r)] *n (daze)* stupeur *f*

sturdy ['stɜ:dɪ] *(-ier, -iest) adj (person, shoe)* robuste ▪ **sturdiness** *n* robustesse *f*

sturgeon ['stɜ:dʒən] *n* esturgeon *m*

stutter ['stʌtə(r)] **1** *n* bégaiement *m;* to have a s. être bègue **2** *vi* bégayer

sty¹ [staɪ] *n (for pigs)* porcherie *f*

sty², **stye** [staɪ] *n (on eye)* orgelet *m*

style [staɪl] **1** *n* style *m; (sophistication)* classe *f;* to have s. avoir de la classe; to live in s. mener grand train **2** *vt (design)* créer; to s. sb's hair coiffer qn ▪ **styling** *n (of hair)* coupe *f* ▪ **stylist** *n (for fashion)* styliste *mf;* (hair) s. coiffeur, -euse *mf*

stylish ['staɪlɪʃ] *adj* chic *inv* ▪ **stylishly** *adv* élégamment

stylistic [staɪ'lɪstɪk] *adj* stylistique

stylized ['staɪlaɪzd] *adj* stylisé

stylus ['staɪləs] *n (of record player)* pointe *f* de lecture

suave [swɑ:v] *(-er, -est) adj* courtois; *Pej* doucereux, -euse

> Note that the French word **suave** is a false friend and is almost never a translation for the English word **suave**. It means **sweet**.

sub- [sʌb] *pref* sous-, sub-

subconscious [sʌb'kɒnʃəs] *adj & n* subconscient *(m)* ▪ **subconsciously** *adv* inconsciemment

subcontract [sʌbkən'trækt] *vt* sous-traiter ▪ **subcontractor** *n* sous-traitant *m*

subdivide [sʌbdɪ'vaɪd] *vt* subdiviser (**into** en) ▪ **subdivision** [-'vɪʒən] *n* subdivision *f*

subdue [səb'dju:] *vt (country, people)* soumettre; *(feelings)* maîtriser ▪ **subdued** *adj (light)* tamisé; *(voice, tone)* bas (*f* basse); *(person)* inhabituellement calme

subheading ['sʌbhedɪŋ] *n* sous-titre *m*

subject¹ ['sʌbdʒɪkt] *n* (**a**) *(matter)* & *Grammar* sujet *m; (at school, university)* matière *f;* s. matter *(topic)* sujet; *(content)* contenu *m* (**b**) *(of monarch)* sujet, -ette *mf; (in experiment)* sujet *m*

subject² [**1** səb'dʒekt] *adj* to be s. to depression/jealousy avoir tendance à la dépression/à la jalousie; it's s. to my agreement c'est sous réserve de mon accord; prices are s. to change les prix peuvent être modifiés **2** [səb'dʒekt] *vt* soumettre (**to** à) ▪ **subjection** [səb'dʒekʃən] *n* soumission *f* (**to** à)

subjective [səb'dʒektɪv] *adj* subjectif, -ive ▪ **subjectively** *adv* subjectivement ▪ **subjectivity** [sʌbdʒek'tɪvɪtɪ] *n* subjectivité *f*

subjugate ['sʌbdʒʊgeɪt] *vt* subjuguer

subjunctive [səb'dʒʌŋktɪv] *n* *Grammar* subjonctif *m*

sublet [sʌb'let] *(pt & pp -let, pres p -letting) vt* sous-louer

sublimate ['sʌblɪmeɪt] *vt* sublimer

sublime [sə'blaɪm] **1** *adj* sublime; *(utter)* suprême **2** *n* sublime *m;* to go from the s. to the ridiculous passer du sublime au grotesque

sub-machine gun [sʌbmə'ʃi:ngʌn] *n* mitraillette *f*

submarine ['sʌbməri:n] *n* sous-marin *m*

submerge [səb'mɜ:dʒ] **1** *vt (flood, overwhelm)* submerger; *(immerse)* immerger (**in** dans) **2** *vi (of submarine)* s'immerger

submit [səb'mɪt] **1** *(pt & pp -tt-) vt* soumettre (**to** à) **2** *vi* se soumettre (**to** à) ▪ **submission** *n* soumission *f* (**to** à) ▪ **submissive** *adj (person)* soumis; *(attitude)* de soumission ▪ **submissively** *adv* avec soumission

subnormal [sʌb'nɔ:məl] *adj (temperature)* audessous de la normale; *Pej (person, behaviour)* arriéré

subordinate [sə'bɔ:dɪnət] **1** *adj* subalterne; s. to subordonné à; *Grammar* s. clause proposition *f* subordonnée **2** *n* subordonné, -ée *mf* **3** [sə'bɔ:dɪneɪt] *vt* subordonner (**to** à) ▪ **subordi'nation** *n* subordination *f* (**to** à)

subpoena [səb'pi:nə] *Law* **1** *n (summons)* citation *f* à comparaître **2** *(pt & pp -aed) vt (witness)* citer à comparaître

subscribe [səb'skraɪb] **1** *vt (money)* donner (**to** à) **2** *vi (pay money)* cotiser (**to** à); to s. to a newspaper s'abonner à un journal; to s. to an opinion souscrire à une opinion ▪ **subscriber** *n (to newspaper, telephone)* abonné, -ée *mf* ▪ **subscription** [-'skrɪpʃən] *n (to newspaper)* abonnement *m; (to club)* cotisation *f*

subsequent ['sʌbsɪkwənt] *adj* ultérieur (**to** à); our s. problems les problèmes que nous avons eus par la suite; s. to *(as a result of)* consécutif, -ive à ▪ **subsequently** *adv* par la suite

subservient [səb'sɜ:vɪənt] *adj* servile

subside [səb'saɪd] *vi (of ground, building)* s'affaisser; *(of wind, flood, fever)* baisser; *(of threat, danger)* se dissiper ▪ **subsidence** *n (of ground)* affaissement *m*

subsidiary [Br səb'sɪdɪərɪ, Am -dɪerɪ] **1** *adj* subsidiaire **2** *(pl -ies) n (company)* filiale *f*

subsidize ['sʌbsɪdaɪz] *vt* subventionner ▪ **subsidy** *(pl -ies) n* subvention *f*

subsist [səb'sɪst] *vi (of doubts)* subsister; **to s. on sth** vivre de qch ▪ **subsistence** *n* subsistance *f*

substance ['sʌbstəns] *n* substance *f*; *(solidity, worth)* fondement *m*; **s. abuse** usage *m* de stupéfiants

substandard [sʌb'stændəd] *adj* de qualité inférieure

substantial [səb'stænʃəl] *adj* important; *(meal)* substantiel, -ielle ▪ **substantially** *adv* considérablement; **s. true** *(to a great extent)* en grande partie vrai; **s. different** très différent

substantiate [səb'stænʃɪeɪt] *vt (statement)* corroborer; *(claim)* justifier

substitute ['sʌbstɪtjuːt] **1** *n (thing)* produit *m* de remplacement; *(person)* remplaçant, -ante *mf* **(for** de); **s. teacher** suppléant, -éante *mf*; **there's no s. for...** rien ne peut remplacer... **2** *vt* **to s. sb/sth for** substituer qn/qch à **3** *vi* **to s. for sb** remplacer qn ▪ **substi'tution** *n* substitution *f*

subterranean [sʌbtə'reɪnɪən] *adj* souterrain

subtitle ['sʌbtaɪtəl] **1** *n (of film)* sous-titre *m* **2** *vt (film)* sous-titrer

subtle ['sʌtəl] **(-er, -est)** *adj* subtil ▪ **subtlety** *n* subtilité *f* ▪ **subtly** *adv* subtilement

subtotal [sʌb'təʊtəl] *n* sous-total *m*

subtract [səb'trækt] *vt* soustraire **(from** de) ▪ **subtraction** *n* soustraction *f*

subtropical [sʌb'trɒpɪkəl] *adj* subtropical

suburb ['sʌbɜːb] *n* banlieue *f*; **the suburbs** la banlieue; **in the suburbs** en banlieue ▪ **suburban** [sə'bɜːbən] *adj (train, house)* de banlieue; *(accent)* de la banlieue ▪ **suburbia** [sə'bɜːbɪə] *n* la banlieue; **in s.** en banlieue

subversive [səb'vɜːsɪv] *adj* subversif, -ive ▪ **subversion** [Br -ʃən, Am -ʒən] *n* subversion *f* ▪ **subvert** *vt (system)* bouleverser; *(person)* corrompre

subway ['sʌbweɪ] *n Br (under road)* passage *m* souterrain; *Am (railroad)* métro *m*

succeed [sək'siːd] **1** *vt* **to s. sb** succéder à qn **2** *vi (follow)* (**in doing** à faire; **in sth** dans qch); **to s. to the throne** monter sur le trône ▪ **succeeding** *adj (in past)* suivant; *(in future)* futur; *(consecutive)* consécutif, -ive

success [sək'ses] *n* succès *m*, réussite *f*; **to make a s. of sth** mener qch à bien; **he was a s.** il a eu du succès; **it was a s.** c'était réussi; **her s. in the exam** sa réussite à l'examen; **s. story** réussite

successful [sək'sesfəl] *adj (effort, venture)* couronné de succès; *(outcome)* heureux, -euse; *(company, businessman)* prospère; *(candidate in exam)* admis, reçu; *(candidate in election)* élu; *(writer, film)* à succès; **to be s.** réussir; **to be s. in doing sth** réussir à faire qch ▪ **successfully** *adv* avec succès

succession [sək'seʃən] *n* succession *f*; **in s.** successivement; **ten days in s.** dix jours consécutifs; **in rapid s.** coup sur coup ▪ **successive** *adj* successif, -ive; **ten s. days** dix jours consécutifs ▪ **successor** *n* successeur *m* (**to** de)

succinct [sək'sɪŋkt] *adj* succinct

succulent ['sʌkjʊlənt] *adj* succulent

succumb [sə'kʌm] *vi* succomber (**to** à)

such [sʌtʃ] **1** *adj (of this or that kind)* tel (*f* telle); **s. a car** une telle voiture; **s. happiness/noise** tant de bonheur/bruit; **there's no s. thing** ça n'existe pas; **I said no s. thing** je n'ai rien dit de tel; **s. as** comme, tel que; **s. and s. a/an** tel ou tel **2** *adv (so very)* si; *(in comparisons)* aussi; **s. long trips** de si longs voyages; **s. a large helping** une si grosse portion; **s. a kind woman as you** une femme aussi gentille que vous **3** *pron* **happiness as s.** le bonheur en tant que tel; **s. was my idea** telle était mon idée ▪ **suchlike** *pron & adj* **...and s.** ...et autres

suck [sʌk] **1** *vt* sucer; *(of baby)* téter; **to s. (up)** *(with straw, pump)* aspirer; **to s. up or in** *(absorb)* absorber **2** *vi (of baby)* téter; **to s. at** *(pencil)* sucer; **to s. at its mother's breast** *(of baby)* téter sa mère; *very Fam* **this city sucks** cette ville est merdique
▸ **suck up to** *vt insep* lécher les bottes à

sucker ['sʌkə(r)] *n (rubber pad)* ventouse *f*; *Fam (fool)* pigeon *m*, dupe *f*; **to be a s. for sth** ne pas savoir résister à qch

suckle ['sʌkəl] **1** *vt (of woman)* allaiter **2** *vi (of baby)* téter

suction ['sʌkʃən] *n* succion *f*

Sudan [suː'dɑːn, -'dæn] *n* (the) **S.** le Soudan ▪ **Sudanese** **1** *adj* soudanais, soudanien, -ienne **2** *n* Soudanais, -aise, Soudanien, -ienne

sudden ['sʌdən] *adj* soudain; **all of a s.** tout à coup ▪ **suddenly** *adv* tout à coup, soudain; *(die)* subitement ▪ **suddenness** *n* soudaineté *f*

suds [sʌdz] *npl* mousse *f* de savon

sue [suː] **1** *vt* poursuivre (en justice) **2** *vi* engager des poursuites judiciaires

suede [sweɪd] *n* daim *m*; **s. coat/shoes** manteau *m*/chaussures *fpl* de daim

suet ['suːɪt] *n* graisse *f* de rognon

suffer ['sʌfə(r)] **1** *vt (loss, damage, defeat)* subir; *(pain)* ressentir; *(tolerate)* supporter **2** *vi* souffrir (**from** de); **your work will s.** ton travail s'en ressentira ▪ **sufferer** *n (from misfortune)* victime *f*; **AIDS s.** malade *mf* du SIDA; **asthma s.** asthmatique *mf* ▪ **suffering** *n* souffrance *f*

suffice [sə'faɪs] *vi* suffire

sufficient [sə'fɪʃənt] *adj* suffisant; **s. money** *(enough)* suffisamment d'argent; **to be s.** suffire ▪ **sufficiently** *adv* suffisamment

suffix ['sʌfɪks] *n Grammar* suffixe *m*

suffocate ['sʌfəkeɪt] **1** *vt* étouffer **2** *vi* suffoquer ▪ **suffo'cation** *n* étouffement *m*; **to die of s.** mourir asphyxié

suffrage ['sʌfrɪdʒ] *n* droit *m* de vote; **universal s.** le suffrage universel

suffused [sə'fjuːzd] *adj* **s. with light/tears** baigné de lumière/larmes

sugar ['ʃʊɡə(r)] **1** *n* sucre *m*; **s. beet/cane/tongs** betterave *f*/canne *f*/pince *f* à sucre; **s. bowl** sucrier *m*; **s. lump** morceau *m* de sucre **2** *vt (tea)* sucrer ▪ **sugar-free** *adj* sans sucre ▪ **sugary** *adj (taste, tone)* sucré

suggest [sə'dʒest] *vt (propose)* suggérer; *(imply)* indiquer ▪ **suggestion** *n* suggestion *f* ▪ **suggestive** *adj* suggestif, -ive; **to be s. of** évoquer

suicide ['suːɪsaɪd] *n* suicide *m*; **to commit s.** se suicider; **s. bomber** terroriste *mf* suicidaire ▪ **sui'cidal** *adj* suicidaire

suit¹ [suːt] *n* (**a**) *(man's)* costume *m*; *(woman's)* tailleur *m*; **flying/diving/ski s.** combinaison *f* de vol/plongée/ski (**b**) *Cards* couleur *f*; *Fig* **to follow s.** faire de même (**c**) *(lawsuit)* procès *m*

suit² [suːt] *vt (please, be acceptable to)* convenir à; *(of dress, colour)* aller (bien) à; *(adapt)* adapter (**to** à); **it suits me to stay ça** m'arrange de rester; **s. yourself!** comme tu voudras!; **suited to** *(job, activity)* fait pour; *(appropriate to)* qui convient à; **they are well suited** *(of couple)* ils sont faits l'un pour l'autre

suitability [suːtə'bɪlətɪ] *n (of remark)* àpropos *m*; *(of person)* aptitude *f* (**for** pour)

suitable ['suːtəbəl] *adj* convenable (**for** à); *(candidate, date)* adéquat; *(example)* approprié; **this film is not s. for children** ce film n'est pas pour les enfants ▪ **suitably** *adv (dress, behave)* convenablement

suitcase ['suːtkeɪs] *n* valise *f*

suite [swiːt] *n (rooms)* suite *f*; **bedroom s.** *(furniture)* chambre *f* à coucher

suitor ['suːtə(r)] *n* soupirant *m*

sulfur ['sʌlfə(r)] *n Am* = **sulphur**

sulk [sʌlk] *vi* bouder ▪ **sulky** (**-ier, -iest**) *adj* boudeur, -euse

sullen ['sʌlən] *adj* maussade ▪ **sullenly** *adv* d'un air maussade

sully ['sʌlɪ] *(pt & pp -ied)* *vt Literary* souiller

sulphur ['sʌlfə(r)] *(Am* **sulfur**) *n Chem* soufre *m*

sultan ['sʌltən] *n* sultan *m*

sultana [sʌl'tɑːnə] *n* raisin *m* de Smyrne

sultry ['sʌltrɪ] *(***-ier, -iest***) adj (heat)* étouffant; *Fig* sensuel, -uelle

sum [sʌm] **1** *n (amount of money)* somme *f*; *(mathematical problem)* problème *m*; **to do sums** *(arithmetic)* faire du calcul; **s. total**

somme totale **2** *(pt & pp* **-mm-**) *vt* **to s. up** *(summarize)* résumer; *(assess)* évaluer **3** *vi* **to s. up** résumer ▪ **summing-'up** *(pl* **summings-up**) *n* résumé *m*

summarize ['sʌməraɪz] *vt* résumer ▪ **summary** **1** *(pl* **-ies**) *n* résumé *m* **2** *adj (brief)* sommaire

summer ['sʌmə(r)] **1** *n* été *m*; **in (the) s.** en été; **Indian s.** été indien **2** *adj* d'été; *Am* **s. camp** colonie *f* de vacances; **s. school** cours *mpl* d'été; *Br* **s. holidays,** *Am* **s. vacation** grandes vacances *fpl* ▪ **summerhouse** *n* pavillon *m* ▪ **summertime** *n* été *m*; **in (the) s.** en été ▪ **summery** *adj (weather, temperature)* estival; *(dress, day)* d'été

summit ['sʌmɪt] *n* sommet *m*

summon ['sʌmən] *vt (call)* appeler; *(meeting, person)* convoquer (**to** à); **to s. sb to do sth** sommer qn de faire qch; **to s. up courage/strength** rassembler son courage/ses forces

summons ['sʌmənz] *Law* **1** *n* assignation *f* à comparaître **2** *vt* assigner à comparaître

sump [sʌmp] *n Br (in engine)* carter *m* à huile

sumptuous ['sʌmptʃʊəs] *adj* somptueux, -ueuse ▪ **sumptuousness** *n* somptuosité *f*

sun [sʌn] **1** *n* soleil *m*; **in the s.** au soleil; **the s. is shining** il fait soleil **2** *(pt & pp* **-nn-**) *vt* **to s. oneself** prendre le soleil ▪ **sunbaked** *adj* brûlé par le soleil ▪ **sunbathe** *vi* prendre un bain de soleil ▪ **sunbeam** *n* rayon *m* de soleil ▪ **sunbed** *n* lit *m* à ultraviolets ▪ **sunblock** *n (cream)* écran *m* total ▪ **sunburn** *n* coup *m* de soleil ▪ **sunburnt** *adj* brûlé par le soleil ▪ **suncream** *n* crème *f* solaire ▪ **sundial** *n* cadran *m* solaire ▪ **sundown** *n* coucher *m* du soleil ▪ **sundrenched** *adj (beach)* brûlé par le soleil ▪ **sunflower** *n* tournesol *m* ▪ **sunglasses** *npl* lunettes *fpl* de soleil ▪ **sunhat** *n* chapeau *m* de soleil ▪ **sunlamp** *n* lampe *f* à bronzer ▪ **sunlight** *n* lumière *f* du soleil ▪ **sunlit** *adj* ensoleillé ▪ **sun lounge** *n (in house)* véranda *f* ▪ **sunrise** *n* lever *m* du soleil ▪ **sunroof** *n (in car)* toit *m* ouvrant ▪ **sunscreen** *n* crème *f* solaire ▪ **sunset** *n* coucher *m* du soleil ▪ **sunshade** *n (on table)* parasol *m*; *(portable)* ombrelle *f* ▪ **sunshine** *n* soleil *m* ▪ **sunspot** *n Br (resort)* lieu *m* de vacances au soleil ▪ **sunstroke** *n* insolation *f* ▪ **suntan** *n* bronzage *m*; **s. lotion/oil** crème *f*/huile *f* solaire ▪ **suntanned** *adj* bronzé ▪ **sun-up** *n Am* lever *m* du soleil

sundae ['sʌndeɪ] *n* coupe *f* glacée

Sunday ['sʌndeɪ] *n* dimanche *m*; **S. school** ≃ catéchisme *m*; **in one's S. best** dans ses habits du dimanche

sundry ['sʌndrɪ] **1** *adj* divers **2** *n* **all and s.** tout le monde ▪ **sundries** *npl Com* articles *mpl* divers

sung [sʌŋ] *pp of* **sing**

sunk [sʌŋk] **1** *pp of* **sink²** **2** *adj Fam* **I'm s.** je suis fichu ▪ **sunken** adj (rock, treasure) submergé; (eyes) cave

sunny ['sʌnɪ] (-ier, -iest) adj (day) ensoleillé; **it's s.** il fait soleil; **s. periods** or **intervals** éclaircies fpl

super ['su:pə(r)] adj Fam super inv

super- ['su:pə(r)] pref super-

superb [su:'pɜːb] adj superbe

supercilious [su:pə'sɪlɪəs] adj hautain

superficial [su:pə'fɪʃəl] adj superficiel, -ielle ▪ **superficially** adv superficiellement

superfluous [su:'pɜːflʊəs] adj superflu

superglue ['su:pəglu:] n colle f extra-forte

superhuman [su:pə'hju:mən] adj surhumain

superimpose [su:pərɪm'pəʊz] vt superposer (**on** à)

superintendent [su:pərɪn'tendənt] n (in police force) commissaire m; (manager) directeur, -trice mf

superior [su:'pɪərɪə(r)] 1 adj supérieur (**to** à); (goods) de qualité supérieure 2 n (person) supérieur, -ieure mf ▪ **superiority** [-rɪ'ɒrɪtɪ] n supériorité f

superlative [su:'pɜːlətɪv] 1 adj sans pareil 2 adj & n Grammar superlatif (m)

superman ['su:pəmæn] (pl **-men**) n surhomme m

supermarket ['su:pəmɑ:kɪt] n supermarché m

supermodel ['su:pəmɒdəl] n supermodel m

supernatural [su:pə'nætʃərəl] adj & n surnaturel, -elle (m)

superpower ['su:pəpaʊə(r)] n Pol superpuissance f

supersede [su:pə'si:d] vt supplanter

supersonic [su:pə'sɒnɪk] adj supersonique

superstar ['su:pəstɑ:(r)] n (in films) superstar f

superstition [su:pə'stɪʃən] n superstition f ▪ **superstitious** adj superstitieux, -ieuse

superstore ['su:pəstɔ:r] n hypermarché m

supertanker ['su:pətæŋkə(r)] n pétrolier m géant

supervise ['su:pəvaɪz] vt (person, work) surveiller; (office, research) superviser ▪ **supervision** [-'vɪʒən] n (of person) surveillance f; (of office) supervision f ▪ **supervisor** n surveillant, -ante mf; (in office) chef m de service; (in store) chef de rayon; Br (in university) directeur, -trice mf de thèse ▪ **supervisory** adj (post) de supervision

supine [su:'paɪn] adj Literary étendu sur le dos

supper ['sʌpə(r)] n (meal) dîner m; (snack) = casse-croûte pris avant d'aller se coucher

supple ['sʌpəl] adj souple ▪ **suppleness** n souplesse f

supplement 1 ['sʌplɪmənt] n supplément m (**to** à) 2 ['sʌplɪment] vt compléter; **to s. one's income** arrondir ses fins de mois ▪ **supplementary** [-'mentərɪ] adj supplémentaire

supplier [sə'plaɪə(r)] n Com fournisseur m; 'obtainable from your usual s.' 'disponible chez votre fournisseur habituel'

> Note that the French word **supplier** is a false friend and is never a translation for the English word **supplier**. It means to **beg**.

supply [sə'plaɪ] 1 (pl **-ies**) n (stock) provision f; **the s. of** (act) la fourniture de; **the s. of gas/electricity/water to…** l'alimentation f en gaz/électricité/eau de…; **to be in short s.** manquer; (food) **supplies** vivres mpl; (office) **supplies** fournitures fpl de bureau; **s. and demand** l'offre f et la demande; **s. ship/train** navire m/train m ravitailleur; Br **s. teacher** suppléant, -éante mf 2 (pt & pp **-ied**) vt (provide) fournir; (with gas, electricity, water) alimenter (**with** en); (equip) équiper (**with** de); **to s. a need** subvenir à un besoin; **to s. sb with sth, to s. sth to sb** fournir qch à qn

support [sə'pɔ:t] 1 n (backing, person supporting) soutien m; (thing supporting) support m; **s. of** (person) en faveur de; (evidence, theory) à l'appui de; **s. tights** bas mpl de contention 2 vt (bear weight of) supporter; (help, encourage) soutenir; (theory, idea) appuyer; (family, wife, husband) subvenir aux besoins de ▪ **supporting** adj (film) qui passe en première partie; **s. cast** seconds rôles mpl

supporter [sə'pɔ:tə(r)] n partisan m; Football supporter m

supportive [sə'pɔ:tɪv] adj **to be s. of sb** être d'un grand soutien à qn

suppose [sə'pəʊz] vti supposer (**that** que); **I'm supposed to be working** je suis censé travailler; **he's supposed to be rich** on le dit riche; **I s. (so)** je pense; **I don't s. so, I s. not** je ne pense pas; **you're tired, I s.** vous êtes fatigué, je suppose; **s. or supposing we go** (suggestion) et si nous partions; **s. or supposing you're right** supposons que tu aies raison ▪ **supposed** adj prétendu ▪ **supposedly** [-ɪdlɪ] adv soi-disant; **he went away, s. to get help** il est parti, soi-disant pour chercher de l'aide ▪ **supposition** [sʌpə'zɪʃən] n supposition f

suppository [Br sə'pɒzɪtərɪ, Am -ɔ:rɪ] (pl **-ies**) n Med suppositoire m

suppress [sə'pres] vt (revolt, feelings, smile) réprimer; (fact, evidence) faire disparaître ▪ **suppression** n (of revolt, feelings) répression f; (of fact) dissimulation f

> Note that the French verb **supprimer** is a false friend and is almost never a translation for the English verb **suppress**. Its most common meaning is to **cancel**.

supreme [su:'pri:m] adj suprême ▪ **supremacy** [sə'preməsɪ] n suprématie f (**over** sur)

supremo [suːˈpriːməʊ] (pl **-os**) n Br Fam grand chef m

surcharge [ˈsɜːtʃɑːdʒ] n (extra charge) supplément m; (on stamp) surcharge f; (tax) surtaxe f

sure [ʃʊə(r)] (**-er, -est**) adj sûr (**of** de; **that** que); **she's s. to accept** c'est sûr qu'elle acceptera; **it's s. to snow** il va sûrement neiger; **to make s. of sth** s'assurer de qch; **for s.** à coup sûr; Fam **s.!, s. thing!** bien sûr!; **s. enough** (in effect) en effet; Am **it s. is cold** il fait vraiment froid; **be s. to do it!** ne manquez pas de le faire! ▪ **surely** adv (certainly) sûrement; **s. he didn't refuse?** il n'a quand même pas refusé?

surety [ˈʃʊərətɪ] n Law caution f

surf [sɜːf] 1 n (waves) ressac m 2 vt Comptr **to s. the Net** naviguer sur l'Internet 3 vi Sport faire du surf ▪ **surfboard** n Sport planche f de surf ▪ **surfer** n Sport surfeur, -euse mf; Comptr (Internet) **s.** internaute mf, surfeur, -euse ▪ **surfing** n Sport surf m; **to go s.** faire du surf

surface [ˈsɜːfɪs] 1 n surface f; **s. area** superficie f, **s. mail** courrier m par voie(s) de terre; **on the s.** (of water) à la surface; Fig (to all appearances) en apparence 2 vt (road) revêtir 3 vi (of swimmer) remonter à la surface; Fam (of person, thing) réapparaître

surfeit [ˈsɜːfɪt] n (excess) excès m (**of** de)

surge [sɜːdʒ] 1 n (of enthusiasm) vague f; (of anger, pride) bouffée f; (rise) (of prices) montée f; (in electrical current) surtension f 2 vi (of crowd, hatred) déferler; (of prices) monter (soudainement); **to s. forward** (of person) se lancer en avant

surgeon [ˈsɜːdʒən] n chirurgien m ▪ **surgery** [-dʒərɪ] n Br (doctor's office) cabinet m; (period, sitting) consultation f; (science) chirurgie f; **to have heart s.** se faire opérer du cœur ▪ **surgical** adj chirurgical; **s. appliance** appareil m orthopédique; Br **s. spirit** alcool m à 90°

surly [ˈsɜːlɪ] (**-ier, -iest**) adj revêche

surmise [səˈmaɪz] vt conjecturer (**that** que)

surmount [səˈmaʊnt] vt surmonter

surname [ˈsɜːneɪm] n nom m de famille

Note that the French word **surnom** is a false friend and is never a translation for the English word **surname**. It means **nickname**.

surpass [səˈpɑːs] vt surpasser (**in** en)

surplus [ˈsɜːpləs] 1 n surplus m 2 adj (goods) en surplus; **some s. material** (left over) un surplus de tissu; **s. stock** surplus mpl

surprise [səˈpraɪz] 1 n surprise f; **to give sb a s.** faire une surprise à qn; **to take sb by s.** prendre qn au dépourvu; **s. visit/result** visite f/résultat m inattendu(e) 2 vt étonner, surprendre ▪ **surprised** adj surpris (**that** que + subjunctive, **at sth** de qch; **at seeing** de voir);

I'm s. at his stupidity sa bêtise m'étonne; **I'm s. to see you** je suis surpris de te voir ▪ **surprising** adj surprenant ▪ **surprisingly** adv étonnamment; **s. (enough), he...** chose étonnante, il...

surreal [səˈrɪəl] adj (surrealist) surréaliste; Fam (strange) délirant ▪ **surrealism** n surréalisme m ▪ **surrealist** adj & n surréaliste (mf)

surrender [səˈrendə(r)] 1 n (of soldiers) reddition f 2 vt (town) livrer; (right, claim) renoncer à 3 vi (give oneself up) se rendre (**to** à)

surreptitious [sʌrəpˈtɪʃəs] adj furtif, -ive

surrogate [ˈsʌrəgət] n substitut m; **s. mother** mère f porteuse ▪ **surrogacy** n maternité f de substitution

surround [səˈraʊnd] vt entourer (**with** de); (of army, police) cerner; **surrounded by** entouré de; **s. sound** son m 3D ▪ **surrounding** adj environnant ▪ **surroundings** npl (of town) environs mpl; (setting) cadre m

surveillance [sɜːˈveɪləns] n surveillance f

survey 1 [ˈsɜːveɪ] n (investigation) enquête f; (of opinion) sondage m; (of house) inspection f; **a (general) s. of** une étude générale de 2 [səˈveɪ] vt (look at) regarder; (review) passer en revue; (house) inspecter; (land) faire un relevé de ▪ **surveying** [səˈveɪɪŋ] n (of land) relevé m ▪ **surveyor** [səˈveɪə(r)] n (of land) géomètre m; (of house) expert m

Note that the French verb **surveiller** is a false friend and is never a translation for the English verb **to survey**. Its most common meaning is **to supervise**.

survive [səˈvaɪv] 1 vt survivre à 2 vi survivre ▪ **survival** n (act) survie f; (relic) vestige m ▪ **survivor** n survivant, -ante mf

susceptible [səˈseptəbl] adj (sensitive) sensible (**to** à); **s. to colds** prédisposé aux rhumes ▪ **suscepti'bility** n sensibilité f; (to colds) prédisposition f

suspect 1 [ˈsʌspekt] n & adj suspect, -ecte (mf) 2 [səˈspekt] vt soupçonner (**sb of sth** qn de qch; **sb of doing** qn d'avoir fait); (have intuition of) se douter de; **I suspected as much** je m'en doutais

suspend [səˈspend] vt (a) (hang) suspendre (**from** à) (b) (service, employee, player) suspendre; (pupil) renvoyer temporairement; Law **suspended sentence** condamnation f avec sursis

suspender [səˈspendə(r)] n Br (for stocking) jarretelle f; Am **suspenders** (for trousers) bretelles fpl; Br **s. belt** porte-jarretelles m inv

suspense [səˈspens] n (uncertainty) incertitude f, (in film, book) suspense m; **to keep sb in s.** tenir qn en haleine

suspension [səˈspenʃən] n (**a**) (of car) suspension f; **s. bridge** pont m suspendu (**b**) *(of service, employee, player)* suspension *f*; *(of pupil)* renvoi *m*

suspicion [sə'spɪʃən] *n* soupçon *m*; **to arouse s.** éveiller les soupçons; **to be under s.** être soupçonné

suspicious [sə'spɪʃəs] *adj (person)* soupçonneux, -euse; *(behaviour)* suspect; **s.-looking** suspect; **to be s. of** *or* **about sth** se méfier de qch ■**suspiciously** *adv (behave)* de manière suspecte; *(consider)* avec méfiance

suss [sʌs] *vt Br Fam* **to s. out** piger

sustain [sə'steɪn] *vt (effort, theory)* soutenir; *(weight)* supporter; *(life)* maintenir; *(damage, loss, attack)* subir; **to s. an injury** être blessé; **a proper breakfast will s. you until lunchtime** un bon petit déjeuner vous permettra de tenir jusqu'à midi ■**sustainable** *adj (growth)* durable

sustenance ['sʌstənəns] *n (means)* subsistance *f*; *(nourishment)* valeur *f* nutritive

swab [swɒb] *n (pad)* tampon *m*; *(specimen)* prélèvement *m*

swagger ['swægə(r)] **1** *n* démarche *f* de fanfaron **2** *vi (walk)* se pavaner

swallow[1] ['swɒləʊ] **1** *vt* avaler; **to s. sth down** *or* **up** avaler qch; *Fig* **to s. a country up** engloutir un pays **2** *vi* avaler

swallow[2] ['swɒləʊ] *n (bird)* hirondelle *f*

swam [swæm] *pt of* **swim**

swamp [swɒmp] **1** *n* marais *m* **2** *vt (flood, overwhelm)* submerger *(with* de) ■**swampy (-ier, -iest)** *adj* marécageux, -euse

swan [swɒn] *n* cygne *m*

swank [swæŋk] *vi Fam (show off)* frimer ■**swanky** *adj Fam (person)* prétentieux, -ieuse; *(restaurant, dinner, hotel)* hyperchic

swap [swɒp] **1** *n* échange *m* **2** *(pt & pp* **-pp-)** *vt* échanger *(for* contre); **to s. seats** *or* **places** changer de place **3** *vi* échanger

swarm [swɔːm] **1** *n (of bees, people)* essaim *m* **2** *vi (of streets, insects, people)* fourmiller *(with* de); **to s. in** *(of people)* accourir en masse

swarthy ['swɔːðɪ] **(-ier, -iest)** *adj* basané

swastika ['swɒstɪkə] *n* croix *f* gammée

swat [swɒt] *(pt & pp* **-tt-)** *vt* écraser

sway [sweɪ] **1** *n* balancement *m*; *Fig* influence *f* **2** *vt* balancer; *Fig (person, public opinion)* influencer **3** *vi* se balancer

swear [sweə(r)] **1** *(pt* **swore**, *pp* **sworn**) *vt (promise)* jurer **(to do** de faire; **that** que); **to s. an oath** prêter serment; **to s. sb to secrecy** faire jurer le silence à qn; **sworn enemies** ennemis *mpl* jurés **2** *vi (take an oath)* jurer **(to sth** de qch); **to s. at sb** injurier qn; **she swears by this lotion** elle ne jure que par cette lotion ■**swearword** *n* juron *m*

▸**swear in** *vt sep Law* **to s. sb in** *(jury, witness)* faire prêter serment à qn

sweat [swet] **1** *n* sueur *f*; *Fam* **no s.!** pas de

problème! **2** *vi* suer ■**sweatshirt** *n* sweatshirt *m* ■**sweatshop** *n* = atelier de confection où les ouvriers sont exploités ■**sweaty (-ier, -iest)** *adj (person)* en sueur; *(clothing)* plein de sueur

▸**sweat out** *vt sep* **to s. out a cold** se débarrasser d'un rhume *(en transpirant)*

sweater ['swetə(r)] *n* pull *m*

Swede [swiːd] *n* Suédois, -oise *mf* ■**Sweden** *n* la Suède ■**Swedish 1** *adj* suédois **2** *n (language)* suédois *m*

swede [swiːd] *n Br (vegetable)* rutabaga *m*

sweep [swiːp] **1** *n (with broom)* coup *m* de balai; *(movement)* geste *m* large; *(of road, river)* courbe *f*; *Fig* **at one s.** d'un seul coup; **to make a clean s.** *(win everything)* tout gagner **2** *(pt & pp* **swept)** *vt (with broom)* balayer; *(chimney)* ramoner; *(river)* draguer **3** *vi* balayer

▸**sweep along** *vt sep (carry off)* emporter

▸**sweep aside** *vt sep (opposition, criticism)* écarter

▸**sweep away** *vt sep (leaves)* balayer; *(carry off)* emporter

▸**sweep off** *vt sep* **to s. sb off** *(take away)* emmener qn **(to** à); **to s. sb off their feet** faire perdre la tête à qn

▸**sweep out** *vt sep (room)* balayer

▸**sweep through** *vt insep (of fear)* saisir; *(of disease)* ravager

▸**sweep up** *vt sep & vi* balayer

sweeping ['swiːpɪŋ] *adj (gesture)* large; *(change)* radical; *(statement)* trop général

sweepstake ['swiːpsteɪk] *n* sweepstake *m*

sweet [swiːt] **1** **(-er, -est)** *adj* doux *(f* douce*)*; *(tea, coffee, cake)* sucré; *(smell)* agréable; *(pretty, kind)* adorable; **to have a s. tooth** aimer les sucreries; **s. pea** pois *m* de senteur; **s. potato** patate *f* douce; *Fam* **s. talk** cajoleries *fpl*, douceurs *fpl* **2** *n Br (piece of confectionery)* bonbon *m*; *Br (dessert)* dessert *m*; **my s.!** *(darling)* mon ange!; *Br* **s. shop** confiserie *f* ■**'sweet-and-'sour** *adj* aigre-doux, -douce ■**sweetcorn** *n Br* maïs *m* ■**'sweet-'smelling** *adj* **to be s.** sentir bon

sweetbreads ['swiːtbredz] *npl* ris *m (de veau, d'agneau)*

sweeten ['swiːtən] *vt (food)* sucrer; *Fig (offer, task)* rendre plus alléchant; *(person)* amadouer ■**sweetener** *n (in food)* édulcorant *m*

sweetheart ['swiːthɑːt] *n* petit(e) ami(e) *mf*; *(darling)* chéri, -ie *mf*

sweetie ['swiːtɪ] *n Fam (darling)* chou *m*

sweetly ['swiːtlɪ] *adv (smile, answer)* gentiment; *(sing)* d'une voix douce ■**sweetness** *n* douceur *f*

swell[1] [swel] **1** *(pt* **swelled**, *pp* **swollen** *or* **swelled)** *vt (river, numbers)* grossir **2** *vi (of hand, leg)* enfler; *(of wood)* gonfler; *(of sails)* se gonfler; *(of river, numbers)* grossir; **to s. up** *(of* *body part)* enfler ▪ **swelling** *n (on body)* enflure *f*

swell² [swel] **1** *n (of sea)* houle *f* **2** *adj Am Fam (excellent)* super *inv*

swelter ['sweltə(r)] *vi* étouffer ▪ **sweltering** *adj* étouffant; **it's s.** on étouffe

swept [swept] *pt & pp of* **sweep**

swerve [swɜːv] *vi (of vehicle)* faire une embardée; *(of player)* faire un écart

swift [swift] **1** (**-er, -est**) *adj* rapide; **to be s. to act** être prompt à agir **2** *n (bird)* martinet *m* ▪ **swiftly** *adv* rapidement ▪ **swiftness** *n* rapidité *f*

swig [swig] *n Fam* lampée *f*; **to take a s.** avaler une lampée

swill [swil] *vt Fam (drink)* écluser; **to s. (out** *or* **down)** rincer à grande eau

swim [swim] **1** *n* **to go for a s.** aller nager **2** (*pt* **swam,** *pp* **swum,** *pres p* **swimming**) *vt (river)* traverser à la nage; *(length, crawl)* nager **3** *vi* nager; *(as sport)* faire de la natation; **to go swimming** aller nager; **to s. away** s'éloigner à la nage ▪ **swimmer** *n* nageur, -euse *mf* ▪ **swimming** *n* natation *f*; **s. cap** *or* **hat** bonnet *m* de bain; *Br* **s. costume** maillot *m* de bain; *Br* **s. pool** piscine *f*; **s. trunks** slip *m* de bain ▪ **swimsuit** *n* maillot *m* de bain

swindle ['swindəl] **1** *n* escroquerie *f* **2** *vt* escroquer; **to s. sb out of money** escroquer de l'argent à qn ▪ **swindler** *n* escroc *m*

swine [swain] *n inv Pej (person)* salaud *m*

swing [swiŋ] **1** *n (in playground)* balançoire *f*; *(movement)* balancement *m*; *(of pendulum)* oscillation *f*; *(in opinion)* revirement *m*; *Golf* swing *m*; **to be in full s.** *(of party)* battre son plein; *Fam* **to get into the s. of things** se mettre dans le bain; *Br* **s. door** porte *f* battante **2** (*pt & pp* **swung**) *vt (arms, legs)* balancer; *(axe)* brandir; *Fam (influence)* influencer; **to s. round** *(car)* faire tourner **3** *vi (sway)* se balancer; *(of pendulum)* osciller; *(turn)* virer; **to s. round** *(turn suddenly)* se retourner; **to s. into action** passer à l'action

swingeing ['swindʒiŋ] *adj Br* énorme

swipe [swaip] **1** *n* grand coup *m* **2** *vt (card)* passer dans un lecteur de cartes; *Fam* **to s. sth** *(steal)* faucher qch (**from sb** à qn) **3** *vi* **to s. at sth** essayer de frapper qch

swirl [swɜːl] **1** *n* tourbillon *m* **2** *vi* tourbillonner

swish [swiʃ] **1** *n (of whip)* sifflement *m*; *(of fabric)* froufrou *m* **2** *adj Fam (posh)* chic *inv* **3** *vi (of whip)* siffler; *(of fabric)* froufrouter

Swiss [swis] **1** *adj* suisse; *Br Culin* **S. roll** roulé *m*; **S. army knife** couteau *m* suisse **2** *n inv* Suisse *m*, Suissesse *f*; **the S.** les Suisses *mpl*

switch [switʃ] **1** *n (electrical)* interrupteur *m*; *(change)* changement *m* (**in** de); *(reversal)* revirement *m* (**in** de) **2** *vt (money, employee)* transférer (**to** à); *(support, affection)* reporter

(to sur); *(exchange)* échanger (**for** contre); **to s. buses** changer de bus; **to s. places** *or* **seats** changer de place **3** *vi* **to s. to** *(change to)* passer à ▪ **switchback** *n* route *f* en lacets ▪ **switchblade** *n Am* couteau *m* à cran d'arrêt ▪ **switchboard** *n Tel* standard *m*; **s. operator** standardiste *mf*

▸ **switch off 1** *vt sep (lamp, gas, radio)* éteindre; *(engine)* arrêter; *(electricity)* couper; **to s. itself off** *(of heating)* s'éteindre tout seul **2** *vi (of appliance)* s'éteindre

▸ **switch on 1** *vt sep (lamp, gas, radio)* allumer; *(engine)* mettre en marche **2** *vi (of appliance)* s'allumer

▸ **switch over** *vi (change TV channels)* changer de chaîne; **to s. over to** *(change to)* passer à

Switzerland ['switsələnd] *n* la Suisse

swivel ['swivəl] **1** (*Br* **-ll-,** *Am* **-l-**) *vi* **to s. (round)** *(of chair)* pivoter **2** *adj* **s. chair** chaise *f* pivotante

swollen ['swəʊlən] **1** *pp of* **swell¹ 2** *adj (leg)* enflé; *(stomach)* gonflé

swoon [swuːn] *vi Literary* se pâmer

swoop [swuːp] **1** *n (of police)* descente *f* **2** *vi* faire une descente (**on** dans); **to s. (down) on** *(of bird)* fondre sur

swop [swɒp] *n & vti* = **swap**

sword [sɔːd] *n* épée *f* ▪ **swordfish** *n* espadon *m*

swore [swɔː(r)] *pt of* **swear**

sworn [swɔːn] *pp of* **swear**

swot [swɒt] *Br Fam Pej* **1** *n* bûcheur, -euse *mf* **2** (*pt & pp* **-tt-**) *vti* **to s. (up)** bûcher; **to s. (up) for an exam** bûcher un examen; **to s. up on sth** bûcher qch

swum [swʌm] *pp of* **swim**

swung [swʌŋ] *pt & pp of* **swing**

sycamore ['sikəmɔː(r)] *n (maple)* sycomore *m*; *Am (plane tree)* platane *m*

sycophant ['sikəfænt] *n Literary* flagorneur, -euse *mf* ▪ **sycophantic** *adj* flagorneur, -euse

syllable ['siləbəl] *n* syllabe *f*

syllabus ['siləbəs] *n* programme *m*

symbol ['simbəl] *n* symbole *m* ▪ **symbolic** [-'bɒlik] *adj* symbolique ▪ **symbolism** *n* symbolisme *m* ▪ **symbolize** *vt* symboliser

symmetry ['simətri] *n* symétrie *f* ▪ **symmetrical** [-'metrikəl] *adj* symétrique

sympathetic [simpə'θetik] *adj (showing pity)* compatissant; *(understanding)* compréhensif, -ive; **s. to sb/sth** *(favourable)* bien disposé à l'égard de qn/qch

> Note that the French adjective **sympathique** is a false friend and is never a translation for the English adjective **sympathetic**. It means **friendly**.

sympathize ['simpəθaiz] *vi* **I s. with you** *(pity)* je suis désolé (pour vous); *(understanding)* je vous comprends ▪ **sympathizer** *n Pol* sympathisant, -ante *mf*

Note that the French verb **sympathiser avec** is a false friend and is almost never a translation for the English verb **to sympathize with**. It means **to be friendly with**.

sympathy ['sɪmpəθɪ] n (pity) compassion f; (understanding) compréhension f; **to have s. for sb** éprouver de la compassion pour qn; **to be in s. with sb's opinion** être en accord avec les opinions de qn

Note that the French noun **sympathie** is a false friend and is rarely a translation for the English noun **sympathy**. It is usually used to convey the idea of liking somebody.

symphony ['sɪmfənɪ] 1 (pl -ies) n symphonie f 2 adj (orchestra, concert) symphonique ▪ **symphonic** [-'fɒnɪk] adj symphonique
symposium [sɪm'pəʊzɪəm] (pl -sia [-zɪə]) n symposium m
symptom ['sɪmptəm] n Med & Fig symptôme m ▪ **sympto'matic** adj symptomatique (of de)
synagogue ['sɪnəgɒg] n synagogue f
synchronize ['sɪŋkrənaɪz] vt synchroniser
syndicate ['sɪndɪkət] n syndicat m
syndrome ['sɪndrəʊm] n Med & Fig syndrome m
synonym ['sɪnənɪm] n synonyme m

▪ **synonymous** [-'nɒnɪməs] adj synonyme (with de)
synopsis [sɪ'nɒpsɪs] (pl -opses [-ɒpsi:z]) n résumé m; (of film) synopsis m
syntax ['sɪntæks] n syntaxe f
synthesis ['sɪnθəsɪs] (pl -theses [-θəsi:z]) n synthèse f
synthesizer ['sɪnθəsaɪzə(r)] n synthétiseur m
synthetic [sɪn'θetɪk] adj synthétique
syphilis ['sɪfɪlɪs] n Med syphilis f
syphon ['saɪfən] n & vt = **siphon**
Syria ['sɪrɪə] n la Syrie ▪ **Syrian 1** adj syrien, -ienne **2** n Syrien, -ienne mf
syringe [sə'rɪndʒ] n seringue f
syrup ['sɪrəp] n sirop m; Br **(golden) s.** mélasse f raffinée ▪ **syrupy** adj sirupeux, -euse
system ['sɪstəm] n (structure) & Comptr système m; (human body) organisme m; (method) méthode f; Fam **to get sth out of one's s.** se sortir qch de la tête; **the digestive s.** l'appareil m digestif; Comptr **s. disk** disque m système; Comptr **s. software** logiciel m système ou d'exploitation; **systems analyst** analyste m programmeur
systematic [sɪstə'mætɪk] adj systématique ▪ **systematically** adv systématiquement

T, t [tiː] *n (letter)* T, t *m inv*

ta [tɑː] *exclam Br Fam* merci!

tab [tæb] *n* (**a**) *(label)* étiquette *f*; *(on file, dictionary)* onglet *m*; *Fam* **to keep tabs on sb** avoir qn à l'œil (**b**) *Am Fam (bill)* addition *f*; **to pick up the t.** payer l'addition (**c**) *(on computer, typewriter)* tabulateur *m*; **t. key** touche *f* de tabulation

tabbouleh [ˈtæbʊleɪ] *n Culin* taboulé *m*

tabby [ˈtæbɪ] *adj* **t. cat** chat *m* tigré

table¹ [ˈteɪbəl] *n* (**a**) *(furniture)* table *f*; **card/ operating t.** table de jeu/d'opération; *Br* **to set** *or* **lay/clear the t.** mettre/débarrasser la table; **(sitting) at the t.** à table; **t. tennis** tennis *m* de table; **t. top** dessus *m* de table; **t. wine** vin *m* de table (**b**) *(list)* table *f*; **t. of contents** table des matières ▪ **tablecloth** *n* nappe *f* ▪ **table mat** *n* set *m* de table ▪ **tablespoon** *n* ≃ cuillère *f* à soupe ▪ **tablespoonful** *n* ≃ cuillerée *f* à soupe

table² [ˈteɪbəl] *vt Br (motion)* présenter; *Am (postpone)* ajourner

tablet [ˈtæblɪt] *n* (**a**) *(pill)* comprimé *m* (**b**) *(inscribed stone)* tablette *f*

tabloid [ˈtæblɔɪd] *n (newspaper)* tabloïd *m*; *Pej* **the t. press** = la presse populaire à scandales

taboo [təˈbuː] *(pl* **-oos)** *adj & n* tabou *(m)*

tabulate [ˈtæbjʊleɪt] *vt* présenter sous forme de tableau

tacit [ˈtæsɪt] *adj* tacite ▪ **tacitly** *adv* tacitement

taciturn [ˈtæsɪtɜːn] *adj* taciturne

tack [tæk] **1** *n (nail)* clou *m*; *Am (thumbtack)* punaise *f*; *Naut (course)* bordée *f*; *Fig* **to change t.** changer de jeu/d'opération; *Fig* **to get down to brass tacks** en venir aux faits **2** *vt* **to t. (down)** clouer; *Fig* **to t. sth on** rajouter qch **3** *vi Naut* louvoyer

tackle [ˈtækəl] **1** *n (gear)* matériel *m*; *Rugby* placage *m*; *Football* tacle *m* **2** *vt (task, problem)* s'attaquer à; *(subject)* aborder; *Rugby* plaquer; *Football* tacler

tacky [ˈtækɪ] *(-ier, -iest) adj (sticky)* collant; *Fam (person)* vulgaire; *(remark)* de mauvais goût

taco [ˈtækəʊ] *(pl* **-os)** *n* crêpe *f* de maïs farcie

tact [tækt] *n* tact *m* ▪ **tactful** *adj (remark)* diplomatique; **to be t.** *(of person)* avoir du tact ▪ **tactfully** *adv* avec tact ▪ **tactless** *adj (person, remark)* qui manque de tact ▪ **tactlessly** *adv* sans tact

tactic [ˈtæktɪk] *n* **a t.** une tactique; **tactics** la tactique ▪ **tactical** *adj* tactique

tactile [ˈtæktaɪl] *adj* tactile

tadpole [ˈtædpəʊl] *n* têtard *m*

tag [tæg] **1** *n (label)* étiquette *f*; **electronic t.** *(for offender)* bracelet *m* électronique *ou* de cheville **2** *(pt & pp* **-gg-)** *vt (label)* étiqueter; *(offender)* mettre un bracelet électronique *ou* de cheville à; *Fam* **to t. sth on** *(add)* rajouter qch *(***to** à) **3** *vi* **to t. along with sb** venir avec qn

Tahiti [təˈhiːtɪ] *n* Tahiti *f*

tai chi [taɪˈtʃiː] *n* tai-chi *m*

tail [teɪl] **1** *n (of animal)* queue *f*; *(of shirt)* pan *m*; **tails, t. coat** queue-de-pie *f*; **the t. end** *(of film)* la fin *(of* de); *(of cloth, string)* le bout *(of* de) **2** *vt Fam (follow)* filer **3** *vi* **to t. off** *(lessen)* diminuer; *Br* **the traffic is tailing back (for miles)** ça bouchonne (sur des kilomètres) ▪ **tailback** *n Br (of traffic)* bouchon *m* ▪ **tailgate** **1** *n Br (of car)* hayon *m* **2** *vt Am* **to t. sb** *(in vehicle)* coller au pare-chocs de qn ▪ **taillight** *n Am (of vehicle)* feu *m* arrière *inv*

tailor [ˈteɪlə(r)] **1** *n (person)* tailleur *m* **2** *vt (garment)* faire; *Fig (adjust)* adapter *(***to** à) ▪ **tailored** *adj* ajusté ▪ **'tailor-'made** *adj* fait sur mesure

tainted [ˈteɪntɪd] *adj (air)* pollué; *(food)* gâté; *Fig (reputation, system)* souillé

Taiwan [taɪˈwɑːn] *n* Taïwan *m ou f* ▪ **Taiwanese 1** *adj* taïwanais **2** *n* Taïwanais, -aise *mf*

take [teɪk] **1** *n (recording of film)* prise *f* **2** *(pt* **took,** *pp* **taken)** *vt* prendre; *(bring)* amener *(***to** à); *(by car)* conduire *(***to** à); *(escort)* accompagner *(***to** à); *(lead away)* emmener *(***to** à); *(of road)* mener *(***to** à); *(prize)* remporter; *(exam)* passer; *(credit card)* accepter; *(contain)* avoir une capacité de; *(tolerate)* supporter; *Math (subtract)* soustraire *(***from** de); **to t. sth to sb** apporter qch à qn; **to t. sb (out) to the theatre** emmener qn au théâtre; **to t. sth with one** emporter qch; **to t. sb home** ramener qn; **it takes an army/courage** il faut une armée/du courage *(***to do** pour faire); **I took an hour to do it** *or* **over it** j'ai mis une heure à le faire; **I t. it that...** je présume que... **3** *vi (of vaccination, fire)* prendre ▪ **takeaway** *Br* **1** *adj (meal)* à emporter **2** *n (shop)* restaurant *m* qui fait des plats à emporter; *(meal)* plat *m* à emporter ▪ **takeoff** *n (of plane)*

décollage *m* ▪ **take-out** *adj & n Am* = **takeaway**
▪ **takeover** *n* (*of company*) rachat *m*; (*of
government, country*) prise *f* de pouvoir; **t. bid**
offre *f* publique d'achat, OPA *f*

▸ **take after** *vt insep* **to t. after sb** ressembler à
qn

▸ **take along** *vt sep* (*object*) emporter; (*person*)
emmener

▸ **take apart** *vt sep* (*machine*) démonter

▸ **take away** *vt sep* (*thing*) emporter; (*person*)
emmener; (*remove*) enlever (**from** à); *Math*
(*subtract*) soustraire (**from** de)

▸ **take back** *vt sep* reprendre; (*return*)
rapporter; (*statement*) retirer; (*accompany*)
ramener (**to** à)

▸ **take down** *vt sep* (*object*) descendre; (*notes*)
prendre

▸ **take in** *vt sep* (*chair, car*) rentrer; (*orphan*)
recueillir; (*skirt*) reprendre; (*distance*) couvrir;
(*include*) inclure; (*understand*) saisir; *Fam*
(*deceive*) rouler

▸ **take off 1** *vt sep* (*remove*) enlever; (*train, bus*)
supprimer; (*lead away*) emmener; (*mimic*)
imiter; *Math* (*deduct*) déduire (**from** de) **2** *vi* (*of
aircraft*) décoller

▸ **take on** *vt sep* (*work, staff, passenger, shape*)
prendre

▸ **take out** *vt sep* (*from pocket*) sortir; (*stain*)
enlever; (*tooth*) arracher; (*insurance policy,
patent*) prendre; **to t. sb out to the theatre**
emmener qn au théâtre; *Fam* **to t. it out on sb**
passer sa colère sur qn

▸ **take over 1** *vt sep* (*become responsible for*)
reprendre; (*buy out*) racheter; (*overrun*)
envahir; **to t. over sb's job** remplacer qn **2** *vi*
(*relieve*) prendre la relève (**from** de); (*succeed*)
prendre la succession (**from** de); (*of dictator,
general*) prendre le pouvoir

▸ **take round** *vt sep* (*bring*) apporter (**to** à);
(*distribute*) distribuer; (*visitor*) faire visiter

▸ **take to** *vt insep* **to t. to doing sth** se mettre à
faire qch; **I didn't t. to him/it** il/ça ne m'a pas
plu

▸ **take up 1** *vt sep* (*carry up*) monter; (*continue*)
reprendre; (*space, time*) prendre; (*offer*)
accepter; (*hobby*) se mettre à; (*hem*) raccourcir
2 *vi* **to t. up with sb** se lier avec qn

taken ['teɪkən] *adj* (*seat*) pris; (*impressed*)
impressionné (**with** *or* **by** par); **to be t. ill**
tomber malade

taking ['teɪkɪŋ] *n* (*capture of town*) prise *f*;
takings (*money*) recette *f*; **it's yours for the t.**
tu n'as plus qu'à accepter

talc [tælk], **talcum powder** ['tælkəmpaʊdə(r)] *n*
talc *m*

tale [teɪl] *n* (*story*) histoire *f*; (*legend*) conte *m*;
(*lie*) salades *fpl*; **to tell tales** rapporter (**on sb**
sur qn)

talent ['tælənt] *n* talent *m*; **to have a t. for** avoir

du talent pour ▪ **talented** *adj* talentueux,
-ueuse

talisman ['tælɪzmən] (*pl* **-mans**) *n* talisman *m*

talk [tɔːk] **1** *n* (*conversation*) conversation *f*
(**about** à propos de); (*lecture*) exposé *m* (**on**
sur); **talks** (*negotiations*) pourparlers *mpl*; **to
have a t. with sb** parler avec qn; **to do the
talking** parler; **there's t. of…** on parle de…; **t.
show** talk-show *m* **2** *vt* (*nonsense*) dire; **to t.
politics** parler politique; **to t. sb into doing/
out of doing sth** persuader qn de faire/de ne
pas faire qch; **to t. sth over** discuter (de) qch;
to t. sb round persuader qn **3** *vi* parler (**to/
about** à/de); (*gossip*) jaser; **to t. down to sb**
parler à qn sur un ton de supériorité
▪ **talkative** *adj* bavard ▪ **talking-to** *n* **to give
sb a t.** passer un savon à qn

talker ['tɔːkə(r)] *n* causeur, -euse *mf*; **she's a
good t.** elle parle bien

tall [tɔːl] (**-er, -est**) *adj* (*person*) grand; (*tree,
house*) haut; **how t. are you?** combien
mesures-tu?; *Fig* **a t. story** une histoire
invraisemblable ▪ **tallness** *n* (*of person*)
grande taille *f*; (*of building*) hauteur *f*

tallboy ['tɔːlbɔɪ] *n Br* grande commode *f*

tally ['tælɪ] (*pt & pp* **-ied**) *vi* correspondre (**with**
à)

talon ['tælən] *n* serre *f*

tambourine [tæmbə'riːn] *n* tambourin *m*

tame [teɪm] **1** (**-er, -est**) *adj* (*animal*)
apprivoisé; *Fig* (*person*) docile; (*book, play*)
fade **2** *vt* (*animal*) apprivoiser; *Fig* (*emotions*)
maîtriser

tamper ['tæmpə(r)] *vt insep* **to t. with** (*lock, car*)
essayer de forcer; (*machine*) toucher à;
(*documents*) trafiquer ▪ **tamper-proof** *adj*
(*lock*) inviolable; (*jar*) à fermeture de sécurité;
t. seal fermeture *f* de sécurité

tampon ['tæmpɒn] *n* tampon *m* (hygiénique)

tan [tæn] **1** *n* (*suntan*) bronzage *m* **2** *adj* (*colour*)
marron clair *inv* **3** (*pt & pp* **-nn-**) *vt* (*skin*) hâler;
(*leather*) tanner **4** *vi* (*of person, skin*) bronzer

tandem ['tændəm] *n* (*bicycle*) tandem *m*; **in t.** en
tandem; **in t. with sth** parallèlement à qch

tang [tæŋ] *n* (*taste*) saveur *f* acidulée; (*smell*)
odeur *f* acidulée ▪ **tangy** (**-ier, -iest**) *adj*
acidulé

tangent ['tændʒənt] *n Math* tangente *f*; **to go off
at a t.** changer de sujet

tangerine [tændʒə'riːn] *n* mandarine *f*

tangible ['tændʒəbəl] *adj* tangible

tangle ['tæŋgəl] *n* enchevêtrement *m*; **to get
into a t.** (*of rope*) s'enchevêtrer; (*of hair*)
s'emmêler; *Fig* (*of person*) s'embrouiller
▪ **tangled** *adj* enchevêtré; (*hair*) emmêlé

tango ['tæŋgəʊ] (*pl* **-os**) *n* tango *m*

tank [tæŋk] *n* (*container*) réservoir *m*; (*military
vehicle*) tank *m*

tankard ['tæŋkəd] *n Br* chope *f*

tanker ['tæŋkə(r)] n (lorry) camion-citerne m; **(oil) t.** (ship) pétrolier m

Tannoy® ['tænɔɪ] n Br **over the T.** au haut-parleur

tantalizing ['tæntəlaɪzɪŋ] adj alléchant

tantamount ['tæntəmaʊnt] adj **it's t. to...** cela équivaut à...

tantrum ['tæntrəm] n caprice m; **to have** or **throw a t.** faire un caprice

Tanzania [tænzə'nɪə] n la Tanzanie

tap¹ [tæp] **1** n Br (for water) robinet m; Fig **on t.** disponible; **t. water** eau f du robinet **2** (pt & pp **-pp-**) vt (resources) puiser dans; (phone) placer sur écoute

tap² [tæp] **1** n (blow) petit coup m; **t. dancing** claquettes fpl **2** (pt & pp **-pp-**) vt (hit) tapoter

tape [teɪp] **1** n (a) (ribbon) ruban m; (sticky or adhesive) **t.** ruban adhésif; **t. measure** mètre m (à) ruban (b) (for recording) bande f; (cassette) cassette f; **t. deck** platine f cassette; **t. recorder** magnétophone m **2** vt (a) (stick) scotcher (b) (record) enregistrer

taper ['teɪpə(r)] **1** n (candle) bougie f filée **2** vi s'effiler; Fig **to t. off** diminuer ■ **tapered** adj (trousers) en fuseau

tapestry ['tæpəstrɪ] n tapisserie f

tapeworm ['teɪpwɜːm] n ver m solitaire

tapioca [tæpɪ'əʊkə] n tapioca m

tar [tɑː(r)] **1** n goudron m **2** (pt & pp **-rr-**) vt goudronner

ta-ra [tæ'rɑː] exclam Br Fam **t.!** au revoir!

tarantula [tə'ræntjʊlə] (pl **-as**) n tarentule f

tardy ['tɑːdɪ] (**-ier, -iest**) adj (belated) tardif, -ive; (slow) lent

target ['tɑːgɪt] **1** n cible f; (objective) objectif m; **t. audience** audience f cible **2** vt (campaign, product) destiner (**at** à); (age group) viser

tariff ['tærɪf] n (tax) tarif m douanier; Br (price list) tarif

tarmac ['tɑːmæk] n Br (on road) macadam m; (runway) piste f

tarnish ['tɑːnɪʃ] vt ternir

tarpaulin [tɑː'pɔːlɪn] n bâche f

tarragon ['tærəgən] n estragon m

tart [tɑːt] **1** (**-er, -est**) adj (sour) aigre **2** n (a) (pie) (large) tarte f; (small) tartelette f (b) Br Fam Pej (prostitute) pute f **3** vt Br Fam Pej **to t. up** (decorate) retaper ■ **tarty** (**-ier, -iest**) adj Br Fam Pej (clothes etc) vulgaire; **to look t.** avoir l'air d'une pute

tartan ['tɑːtən] **1** n tartan m **2** adj (skirt, tie) écossais

tartar¹ ['tɑːtə(r)] adj **t. sauce** sauce f tartare

tartar² ['tɑːtə(r)] n (on teeth) tartre m

task [tɑːsk] n tâche f; **to take sb to t. for sth** reprocher qch à qn ■ **taskforce** n Mil corps m expéditionnaire; Pol commission f spéciale

tassel ['tæsəl] n gland m

taste [teɪst] **1** n goût m; **in good/bad t.** de bon/

mauvais goût; **to have a t. of sth** goûter à qch; **to get a t. for sth** prendre goût à qch; **t. bud** papille f gustative **2** vt (detect flavour of) sentir; (sample) goûter; Fig (experience) goûter à **3** vi **to t. of** or **like sth** avoir un goût de qch; **to t. good** être bon (f bonne) ■ **tasty** (**-ier, -iest**) adj savoureux, -euse

tasteful ['teɪstfəl] adj de bon goût ■ **tastefully** adv avec goût ■ **tasteless** adj (food) insipide; Fig (joke) de mauvais goût

tat¹ [tæt] see **tit¹**

tat² [tæt] n Br Fam (junk) camelote f ■ **tatty** (**-ier, -iest**) adj Br Fam miteux, -euse

ta-ta [tæ'tɑː] exclam Br Fam = **ta-ra**

tattered ['tætəd] adj (clothes) en lambeaux; (person) déguenillé ■ **tatters** npl **in t.** (clothes) en lambeaux

tattoo¹ [tæ'tuː] **1** (pl **-oos**) n (design) tatouage m; **to get a t.** se faire tatouer **2** (pt & pp **-ooed**) vt tatouer

tattoo² [tæ'tuː] (pl **-oos**) n Mil spectacle m militaire

taught [tɔːt] pt & pp of **teach**

taunt [tɔːnt] **1** n raillerie f **2** vt railler

Taurus ['tɔːrəs] n (sign) le Taureau; **to be (a) T.** être Taureau

taut [tɔːt] adj tendu

tavern ['tævən] n taverne f

tawdry ['tɔːdrɪ] (**-ier, -iest**) adj Pej tape-à-l'œil inv

tawny ['tɔːnɪ] adj (colour) fauve; **t. owl** (chouette f) hulotte f

tax¹ [tæks] **1** n (on goods) taxe f, impôt m; Br **road t.** ≃ vignette f automobile **2** adj fiscal; **t. collector** percepteur m; **t. relief** dégrèvement m fiscal; **t. return** déclaration f d'impôt; Br **(road) t. disc** ≃ vignette f automobile **3** vt (person) imposer; (goods) taxer ■ **taxable** adj imposable ■ **tax'ation** n (taxes) impôts mpl; (act) imposition f; **the burden of t.** le poids de l'impôt ■ **'tax-'free** adj exempt d'impôts ■ **taxman** (pl **-men**) n Br Fam percepteur m ■ **taxpayer** n contribuable mf

tax² [tæks] vt (put under strain) mettre à l'épreuve ■ **taxing** adj (journey) éprouvant

taxi ['tæksɪ] **1** n taxi m; **t. cab** taxi; Br **t. rank,** Am **t. stand** station f de taxis **2** vi (of aircraft) rouler

TB [tiː'biː] (abbr **tuberculosis**) n tuberculose f

tea [tiː] n (plant, drink) thé m; Br (snack) goûter m; Br (evening meal) repas m du soir; Br **high t.** dîner m (pris tôt dans la soirée); **to have t.** prendre le thé; Br **t. break** ≃ pause-café f; **t. cloth** torchon m; **t. party** thé m; **t. set** service m à thé; **t. strainer** passoire f à thé; Br **t. towel** torchon m ■ **teabag** n sachet m de thé ■ **teacup** n tasse f à thé ■ **tea leaves** npl feuilles fpl de thé ■ **teapot** n théière f ■ **tearoom** n salon m de thé ■ **teashop** n Br salon *m* de thé ▪**teaspoon** *n* petite cuillère *f* ▪**teaspoonful** *n* cuillerée *f* à café ▪**teatime** *n* l'heure *f* du thé

teach [tiːtʃ] **1** (*pt & pp* **taught**) *vt* apprendre (**sb sth** qch à qn; **that** que); (*in school, at university*) enseigner (**sb sth** qch à qn); **to t. sb (how) to do sth** apprendre à qn à faire qch; **to t. oneself sth** apprendre qch tout seul; *Am* **to t. school** enseigner **2** *vi* enseigner ▪**teaching 1** *n* enseignement *m* **2** *adj* (*staff*) enseignant; (*method, material*) pédagogique; *Br* **t. hospital** centre *m* hospitalo-universitaire; **the t. profession** l'enseignement *m*; (*teachers*) le corps enseignant; **t. qualification** diplôme *m* permettant d'enseigner; **the t. staff** le personnel enseignant

teacher ['tiːtʃə(r)] *n* professeur *m*; (*in primary school*) instituteur, -trice *mf*; *Br* **t. training college** ≃ IUFM *m*

teak [tiːk] *n* teck *m*; **a t. sideboard** un buffet en teck

team [tiːm] **1** *n* équipe *f*; (*of horses, oxen*) attelage *m*; **to be a t. player** avoir l'esprit d'équipe; **t. mate** coéquipier, -ière *mf* **2** *vi* **to t. up** faire équipe (**with sb** avec qn) ▪**teamwork** *n* travail *m* d'équipe

tear¹ [teə(r)] **1** *n* déchirure *f* **2** (*pt* **tore**, *pp* **torn**) *vt* (*rip*) déchirer; (*snatch*) arracher (**from** à); *Fig* **torn between** tiraillé entre; **to t. sth away from sth** arracher qn à qch; **to t. down** (*house*) démolir; **to t. off** *or* **out** arracher; **to t. up** déchirer **3** *vi* (*of cloth*) se déchirer; **to t. along/past/away** aller/passer/partir à toute vitesse

tear² [tɪə(r)] *n* larme *f*; **in tears** en larmes; **close to** *or* **near (to) tears** au bord des larmes ▪**tearful** *adj* (*eyes*) larmoyant; (*person*) en larmes; **in a t. voice** avec des larmes dans la voix ▪**tearfully** *adv* en pleurant ▪**tear gas** *n* gaz *m* lacrymogène

tearaway ['teərəweɪ] *n Br Fam* casse-cou *m inv*

tease [tiːz] **1** *n* (*person*) taquin, -ine *mf* **2** *vt* taquiner ▪**teaser** *n* (*person*) taquin, -ine *mf*; *Fam* (*question*) colle *f* ▪**teasing** *adj* (*remark*) taquin

teat [tiːt] *n Br* (*of animal*) trayon *m*; (*of baby's bottle*) tétine *f*

technical ['teknɪkəl] *adj* technique; *Br* **t. college** ≃ institut *m* universitaire; **t. drawing** dessin *m* industriel ▪**technicality** [-'kælɪtɪ] *n* (*detail*) détail *m* technique ▪**technically** *adv* techniquement

technician ['teknɪʃən] *n* technicien, -ienne *mf*

technique [tek'niːk] *n* technique *f*

techno ['teknəʊ] *n* (*music*) techno *f*

technocrat ['teknəkræt] *n* technocrate *m*

technology [tek'nɒlədʒɪ] (*pl* **-ies**) *n* technologie *f* ▪**technological** [-nə'lɒdʒɪkəl] *adj* technologique

teddy ['tedɪ] *n* **t. (bear)** ours *m* en peluche

tedious ['tiːdɪəs] *adj* fastidieux, -ieuse ▪**tediousness, tedium** *n* ennui *m*

teem [tiːm] *vi* (*swarm*) grouiller (**with** de); **to t. (with rain)** pleuvoir à torrents ▪**teeming** *adj* grouillant; **t. rain** pluie *f* torrentielle

teenage ['tiːneɪdʒ] *adj* (*boy, girl, behaviour*) adolescent; (*fashion, magazine*) pour adolescents ▪**teenager** *n* adolescent, -ente *mf* ▪**teens** *npl* **to be in one's t.** être adolescent

teeny(-weeny) ['tiːnɪ('wiːnɪ)] *adj Fam* (*tiny*) minuscule

tee-shirt ['tiːʃɜːt] *n* tee-shirt *m*

teeter ['tiːtə(r)] *vi* (*be unsteady*) chanceler; *Fig* **to t. on the brink of sth** être au bord de qch

teeth [tiːθ] *pl of* **tooth**

teethe [tiːð] *vi* faire ses dents ▪**teething** *n* poussée *f* dentaire; *Fig* **t. troubles** difficultés *fpl* de mise en route

teetotal [tiː'təʊtəl] *adj* **to be t.** ne jamais boire d'alcool ▪**teetotaller** (*Am* **teetotaler**) *n* personne *f* qui ne boit jamais d'alcool

TEFL ['tefəl] (*abbr* **Teaching English as a Foreign Language**) *n* enseignement *m* de l'anglais langue étrangère

tele- [telɪ] *pref* télé-

telecommunications [telɪkəmjuːnɪˈkeɪʃənz] *npl* télécommunications *fpl*

telegram ['telɪgræm] *n* télégramme *m*

telegraph ['telɪgrɑːf] *adj* **t. pole/wire** poteau *m*/fil *m* télégraphique

telepathy [tə'lepəθɪ] *n* télépathie *f* ▪**telepathic** *adj* télépathique

telephone ['telɪfəʊn] **1** *n* téléphone *m*; **to be on the t.** (*speaking*) être au téléphone **2** *adj* (*call, line, message*) téléphonique; *Br* **t. booth, t. box** cabine *f* téléphonique; **t. directory** annuaire *m* du téléphone; **t. number** numéro *m* de téléphone **3** *vt* (*message*) téléphoner (**to** à); **to t. sb** téléphoner à qn **4** *vi* téléphoner

telephoto ['telɪfəʊtəʊ] *adj Phot* **t. lens** téléobjectif *m*

teleprinter ['telɪprɪntə(r)] *n Br* téléimprimeur *m*

telesales ['telɪseɪlz] *n* télévente *f*

telescope ['telɪskəʊp] *n* télescope *m* ▪**telescopic** [-'skɒpɪk] *adj* télescopique

teleshopping ['telɪʃɒpɪŋ] *n* téléachat *m*

teletext ['telɪtekst] *n* télétexte *m*

television [telɪ'vɪʒən] **1** *n* télévision *f*; **on (the) t.** à la télévision; **to watch (the) t.** regarder la télévision **2** *adj* (*programme, screen*) de télévision; (*interview, report*) télévisé; **t. set** téléviseur *m* ▪**televise** *vt* téléviser

teleworking ['telɪwɜːkɪŋ] *n* télétravail *m* ▪**teleworker** *n* télétravailleur, -euse *mf*

telex ['teleks] **1** *n* (*service, message*) télex *m* **2** *vt* (*message*) télexer

tell [tel] **1** (*pt & pp* **told**) *vt* dire (**sb sth** qch à qn; **that** que); (*story*) raconter; (*distinguish*) distinguer (**from** de); **to t. sb to do sth** dire à qn de faire qch; **to know how to t. the time** savoir lire l'heure; **to t. the difference** voir la différence (**between** entre); **I could t. she was lying** je savais qu'elle mentait; *Fam* **to t. sb off** disputer qn **2** *vi* dire; *(have an effect)* se faire sentir; **to t. of** *or* **about sb/sth** parler de qn/qch; **it's hard to t.** c'est difficile à dire; **you can never t.** on ne sait jamais; *Fam* **to t. on sb** dénoncer qn

teller ['telə(r)] *n (in bank)* guichetier, -ière *mf*

telling ['telɪŋ] *adj (revealing)* révélateur, -trice; *(decisive)* qui porte

telltale ['telteɪl] **1** *adj* révélateur, -trice **2** *n* rapporteur, -euse *mf*

telly ['telɪ] *n Br Fam* télé *f*; **on (the) t.** à la télé

temerity [tə'merɪtɪ] *n* témérité *f*

temp [temp] *Br Fam* **1** *n* intérimaire *mf* **2** *vi* faire de l'intérim

temper ['tempə(r)] **1** *n (mood, nature)* humeur *f*; *(bad mood)* mauvaise humeur; **in a bad t.** de mauvaise humeur; **to have a (bad) t.** avoir un caractère de cochon; **to lose one's t.** se mettre en colère **2** *vt (moderate)* tempérer; *(steel)* tremper

temperament ['tempərəmənt] *n* tempérament *m* ▪ **temperamental** [-'mentəl] *adj (person, machine)* capricieux, -ieuse; *(inborn)* inné

temperance ['tempərəns] *n (in drink)* tempérance *f*

temperate ['tempərət] *adj (climate)* tempéré

temperature ['tempərətʃə(r)] *n* température *f*; *Br* **to have a t.** avoir de la température

tempest ['tempɪst] *n Literary* tempête *f* ▪ **tempestuous** [-'pestjʊəs] *adj (meeting, relationship)* orageux, -euse

template ['templət, -pleɪt] *n* gabarit *m*; *Comptr* modèle *m*

temple¹ ['tempəl] *n (religious building)* temple *m*

temple² ['tempəl] *n Anat* tempe *f*

tempo ['tempəʊ] *(pl* **-os)** *n (of life, work)* rythme *m*; *Mus* tempo *m*

temporal ['tempərəl] *adj* temporel, -elle

temporary [*Br* 'tempərərɪ, *Am* -erɪ] *adj* temporaire; *(secretary)* intérimaire ▪ **temporarily** [*Br* 'tempərərɪlɪ, *Am* tempə'reərɪlɪ] *adv* temporairement

tempt [tempt] *vt* tenter; **tempted to do sth** tenté de faire qch; **to t. sb to do sth** inciter qn à faire qch ▪ **temp'tation** *n* tentation *f* ▪ **tempting** *adj* tentant

ten [ten] *adj & n* dix *(m)*

tenable ['tenəbəl] *adj* défendable; **the post is t. for three years** ce poste peut être occupé pendant trois ans

tenacious [tə'neɪʃəs] *adj* tenace ▪ **tenacity** [-'næsɪtɪ] *n* ténacité *f*

tenant ['tenənt] *n* locataire *mf* ▪ **tenancy** *n (lease)* location *f*; *(period)* occupation *f*

tend¹ [tend] *vi* **to t. to do sth** avoir tendance à faire qch; **to t. towards** incliner vers ▪ **tendency** *(pl* **-ies)** *n* tendance *f* (**to do** à faire)

tend² [tend] *vt (look after)* s'occuper de

tendentious [ten'denʃəs] *adj Pej* tendancieux, -ieuse

tender¹ ['tendə(r)] *adj (soft, delicate, loving)* tendre; *(painful)* sensible ▪ **tenderly** *adv* tendrement ▪ **tenderness** *n* tendresse *f*; *(pain)* (petite) douleur *f*; *(of meat)* tendreté *f*

tender² ['tendə(r)] **1** *n Com (bid)* soumission *f* (**for** pour); **to be legal t.** *(of money)* avoir cours **2** *vt (offer)* offrir; **to t. one's resignation** donner sa démission

tendon ['tendən] *n Anat* tendon *m*

tenement ['tenəmənt] *n* immeuble *m* d'habitation

tenet ['tenɪt] *n* principe *m*

tenfold ['tenfəʊld] **1** *adj* décuple **2** *adv* **to increase t.** être multiplié par dix

tenner ['tenə(r)] *n Br Fam* billet *m* de 10 livres

tennis ['tenɪs] *n* tennis *m*; **t. court** court *m* de tennis

tenor ['tenə(r)] *n* (**a**) *Formal (sense, course)* teneur *f* (**b**) *Mus* ténor *m*

tenpin ['tenpɪn] *adj Br* **t. bowling** bowling *m*

tense¹ [tens] **1** (**-er, -est**) *adj (person, muscle, situation)* tendu **2** *vt* tendre; *(muscle)* contracter **3** *vi* **to t. (up)** *(of person, face)* se crisper ▪ **tension** *n* tension *f*

tense² [tens] *n Grammar* temps *m*; **in the future t.** au futur

tent [tent] *n* tente *f*; *Br* **t. peg**, *Am* **t. stake** piquet *m* de tente; **t. pole** mât *m* de tente

tentacle ['tentəkəl] *n* tentacule *m*

tentative ['tentətɪv] *adj (not definite)* provisoire; *(hesitant)* timide ▪ **tentatively** *adv* provisoirement; *(hesitantly)* timidement

tenterhooks ['tentəhʊks] *npl* **to be on t.** être sur des charbons ardents

tenth [tenθ] *adj & n* dixième *(mf)*; **a t.** un dixième

tenuous ['tenjʊəs] *adj (link, suspicion)* ténu

tepid ['tepɪd] *adj (liquid) & Fig* tiède

term [tɜːm] **1** *n (word)* terme *m*; *(period)* période *f*; *Br (of school or university year)* trimestre *m*; *Am (semester)* semestre *m*; *Pol* **t. (of office)** mandat *m*; **terms** *(conditions)* conditions *fpl*; *(of contract)* termes *mpl*; **terms of reference** *(of commission)* attributions *fpl*; **to be on good/ bad terms** être en bons/mauvais termes (**with sb** avec qn); **to buy sth on easy terms** acheter qch avec facilités de paiement; **in terms of** *(speaking of)* sur le plan de; **in real terms** dans la pratique; **to come to terms with sth** se résigner à qch; **in the long/short/ medium t.** à long/court/moyen terme; **at (full) t.** *(baby)* à terme **2** *vt* appeler

terminal ['tɜːmɪnəl] **1** *n (electronic) & Comptr*

terminal *m*; *(of battery)* borne *f*; **(air) t.** aérogare *f*; **(oil) t.** terminal pétrolier **2** *adj (patient, illness)* en phase terminale; **in its t. stage** *(illness)* en phase terminale ▪ **terminally** *adv* **t. ill** *(patient)* en phase terminale

terminate ['tɜːmɪneɪt] **1** *vt* mettre fin à; *(contract)* résilier; *(pregnancy)* interrompre **2** *vi* se terminer ▪ **termi'nation** *n* fin *f*; *(of contract)* résiliation *f*; *(of pregnancy)* interruption *f*

terminology [tɜːmɪ'nɒlədʒɪ] *(pl* **-ies)** *n* terminologie *f*

terminus ['tɜːmɪnəs] *n* terminus *m*

termite ['tɜːmaɪt] *n (insect)* termite *m*

terrace ['terɪs] *n (next to house, on hill)* terrasse *f*; *Br (houses)* = rangée de maisons attenantes; *Br* **the terraces** *(at football ground)* les gradins *mpl* ▪ **terrace house, terraced house** *n Br* = maison située dans une rangée d'habitations attenantes

terracotta [terə'kɒtə] *n (substance)* terre *f* cuite; *(colour)* ocre *m* foncé

terrain [tə'reɪn] *n Mil & Geol* terrain *m*

terrestrial [tə'restrɪəl] *adj* terrestre; **t. television, t. broadcasting** diffusion *f* hertzienne *ou* terrestre

terrible ['terəbəl] *adj* terrible ▪ **terribly** *adv (badly)* affreusement mal; *(injured)* très gravement

terrier ['terɪə(r)] *n (dog)* terrier *m*

terrific [tə'rɪfɪk] *adj Fam (excellent)* super *inv* ▪ **terrifically** *adv Fam (extremely)* terriblement; *(extremely well)* terriblement bien

terrify ['terɪfaɪ] *(pt & pp* **-ied)** *vt* terrifier; **to be terrified of sb/sth** avoir une peur bleue de qn/qch ▪ **terrifying** *adj* terrifiant

territory ['terɪtərɪ] *(pl* **-ies)** *n* territoire *m* ▪ **territorial** [-'tɔːrɪəl] *adj* territorial; *Br* **the T. Army** = armée de réserve, constituée de volontaires

terror ['terə(r)] *n* terreur *f*; *Fam* **that child is a t.** cet enfant est une vraie terreur ▪ **terrorism** *n* terrorisme *m* ▪ **terrorist** *n & adj* terroriste *(mf)* ▪ **terrorize** *vt* terroriser

terse [tɜːs] *adj* laconique

tertiary ['tɜːʃərɪ] *adj* tertiaire; **t. education** enseignement *m* supérieur

test [test] **1** *n (trial)* essai *m*; *(of product)* test *m*; *Sch & Univ* interrogation *f*; *(by doctor)* examen *m*; *(of blood)* analyse *f*; **to put sb to the t.** mettre qn à l'épreuve; **eye t.** examen de la vue; **driving t.** examen du permis de conduire **2** *adj* **t. pilot/flight** pilote *m*/vol *m* d'essai; **t. drive** *or* **run** essai *m* sur route; *Law* **t. case** précédent *m*; *Cricket* **t. match** match *m* international; **t. tube** éprouvette *f*; **t. tube baby** bébé-éprouvette *m* **3** *vt (try)* essayer; *(product, machine)* tester; *(pupil)* interroger; *(of doctor)* examiner; *(blood)* analyser; *Fig (try out)* mettre à l'épreuve; **to t. sb for AIDS** faire subir à

qn un test de dépistage du SIDA **4** *vi* **to t. positive** *(for drugs)* être positif, -ive

testament ['testəmənt] *n (will)* testament *m*; *(tribute)* preuve *f*; *Rel* **the Old/New T.** l'Ancien/le Nouveau Testament

testicle ['testɪkəl] *n Anat* testicule *m*

testify ['testɪfaɪ] *(pt & pp* **-ied)** *Law* **1** *vt* **to t. that…** témoigner que… **2** *vi* témoigner *(against* contre); **to t. to sth** *(be proof of)* témoigner de qch ▪ **testimonial** [-'məʊnɪəl] *n* références *fpl* ▪ **testimony** ['testɪmənɪ] *(pl* **-ies)** *n* témoignage *m*

testy ['testɪ] **(-ier, -iest)** *adj* irritable

tetanus ['tetənəs] *n Med* tétanos *m*

tetchy ['tetʃɪ] **(-ier, -iest)** *adj* irritable

tête-à-tête [teɪtɑː'teɪt] *n* tête-à-tête *m inv*

tether ['teðə(r)] **1** *n* **at the end of one's t.** à bout **2** *vt (animal)* attacher

text [tekst] **1** *n* texte *m*; *Tel* **t. (message)** texto *m*, SMS *m* **2** *vt* **to t. sb** envoyer un texto *ou* un SMS à qn ▪ **textbook** *n* manuel *m*

textile ['tekstaɪl] *adj & n* textile *(m)*

texture ['tekstʃə(r)] *n (of fabric, cake)* texture *f*; *(of paper, wood)* grain *m*

Thai [taɪ] **1** *adj* thaïlandais **2** *n* Thaïlandais, -aise *mf* ▪ **Thailand** *n* la Thaïlande

Thames [temz] *n* **the T.** la Tamise

than [ðən, *stressed* ðæn] *conj* que; **happier t. me** plus heureux que moi; **less happy t. you** moins heureux que toi; **he has more/less t. you** il en a plus/moins que toi; **she has fewer oranges t. plums** elle a moins d'oranges que de prunes; **more t. six** plus de six

thank [θæŋk] *vt* remercier *(for sth* de qch; *for doing* d'avoir fait); **t. you** merci; **no, t. you** (non) merci; **t. God!, t. heavens!, t. goodness!** Dieu merci! ▪ **thanks** *npl* remerciements *mpl*; **(many) t.!** merci (beaucoup)!; **t. to** *(because of)* grâce à

thankful ['θæŋkfəl] *adj* reconnaissant *(for* de); **to be t. that…** être heureux, -euse que… *(+ subjunctive)* ▪ **thankfully** *adv (gratefully)* avec reconnaissance; *(fortunately)* heureusement ▪ **thankless** *adj* ingrat

thanksgiving [θæŋks'gɪvɪŋ] *n* action *f* de grâce; *Am* **T. (Day)** = 4ème jeudi de novembre, commémorant la première action de grâce des colons anglais

that [ðət, *stressed* ðæt] **1** *conj (souvent omise)* que; **she said (t.) she would come** elle a dit qu'elle viendrait

2 *relative pron*

On peut omettre le pronom relatif **that** sauf s'il est en position sujet.

(subject) qui; *(object)* que; *(with preposition)* lequel, laquelle, *pl* lesquel(le)s; **the boy t. left** le garçon qui est parti; **the book (t.) I read** le livre que j'ai lu; **the carpet (t.) I put it on** le tapis sur lequel je l'ai mis; **the house (t.) she**

told me about la maison dont elle m'a parlé;
the day/morning (t.) she arrived le jour/
matin où elle est arrivée

3 (pl those) demonstrative adj ce, cet (before
vowel or mute h), cette; (opposed to 'this') ce…-
là (f cette…-là); **t. woman** cette femme(-là); **t.
day** ce jour-là; **t. one** celui-là m, celle-là f

4 (pl those) demonstrative pron cela, Fam ça;
give me t. donne-moi ça; **before t.** avant cela;
t.'s right c'est exact; **who's t.?** qui est-ce?; **t.'s
the house** voilà la maison; **what do you mean
by t.?** qu'entends-tu par là?; **t. is (to say)…**
c'est-à-dire…

5 adv Fam (so) si; **not t. good** pas si bon que
ça; **t. high** (pointing) haut comme ça; **it cost t.
much** ça a coûté tant que ça

thatch [θætʃ] n chaume m ▪ **thatched** adj (roof)
de chaume; **t. cottage** chaumière f

thaw [θɔ:] **1** n dégel m **2** vt (snow, ice) faire
fondre; **to t. (out)** (food) se décongeler **3** vi
dégeler; (of snow, ice) fondre; (of food)
décongeler; Fig **to t. (out)** (of person) se dérider

the [ðə, before vowel ði, stressed ði:] definite
article le, l', la, pl les; **t. roof** le toit; **t. man**
l'homme; **t. moon** la lune; **t. orange** l'orange;
t. boxes les boîtes; **t. smallest** le plus petit (f
la plus petite); **of t., from t.** du, de l', de la, pl
des; **to t., at t.** au, à l', à la, pl aux; **Elizabeth t.
Second** Élisabeth Deux

theatre ['θɪətə(r)] (Am **theater**) n (place, art)
théâtre m; Br **(operating) t.** (in hospital) salle f
d'opération; Mil **t. of operations** théâtre des
opérations ▪ **theatregoer** n amateur m de
théâtre ▪ **theatrical** [θɪ'ætrɪkəl] adj théâtral;
t. company troupe f de théâtre

theft [θeft] n vol m

their [ðeə(r)] possessive adj leur, pl leurs; **t.
house** leur maison f ▪ **theirs** possessive pron le
leur, la leur, pl les leurs; **this book is t.** ce livre
est à eux ou est le leur; **a friend of t.** un ami à
eux

them [ðəm, stressed ðem] pron les; (after prep,
'than', 'it is') eux mpl, elles fpl; **(to) t.** (indirect)
leur; **I see t.** je les vois; **I gave it to t.** je le leur
ai donné; **with t.** avec eux/elles; **ten of t.** dix
d'entre eux/elles; **all of t. came** tous sont
venus, toutes sont venues; **I like all of t.** je les
aime tous/toutes

theme [θi:m] n thème m; **t. song** or **tune**
chanson f de générique; **t. park** parc m à thème

themselves [ðəm'selvz, stressed ðem'selvz]
pron eux-mêmes mpl, elles-mêmes fpl;
(reflexive) se, s'; (after prep) eux mpl, elles fpl;
they did it t. ils/elles l'ont fait eux-mêmes/
elles-mêmes; **they cut t.** ils/elles se sont
coupé(e)s; **they wash t.** ils/elles se lavent;
they think of t. ils pensent à eux/elles
pensent à elles

then [ðen] **1** adv (at that time) à cette époque-là,

alors; (just a moment ago) à ce moment-là;
(next) ensuite, puis; (therefore) donc, alors;
from t. on dès lors; **before t.** avant cela; **until
t.** jusque-là, jusqu'alors **2** adj **the t. mayor** le
maire d'alors

theology [θɪ'ɒlədʒɪ] n théologie f ▪ **theological** [θɪə'lɒdʒɪkəl] adj théologique

theorem ['θɪərəm] n théorème m

theory ['θɪərɪ] (pl -ies) n théorie f; **in t.** en
théorie ▪ **theo'retical** adj théorique ▪ **theo-
'retically** adv théoriquement ▪ **theorist** n
théoricien, -ienne mf ▪ **theorize** vi théoriser
(about sur)

therapy ['θerəpɪ] (pl -ies) n thérapeutique
f; (psychological) thérapie f; **to be in
t.** faire une psychothérapie; **speech t.**
orthophonie f ▪ **therapeutic** [-'pju:tɪk] adj
thérapeutique ▪ **therapist** n thérapeute mf;
(psychological) psychothérapeute mf; **speech
t.** orthophoniste mf

there [ðeə(r)] adv là; (down or over) **t.** là-bas;
on t. là-dessus; **she'll be t.** elle y sera; **t. is, t.
are** il y a; (pointing) voilà; **t. he is** le voilà; **t.
she is** la voilà; **t. they are** les voilà; **that man t.**
cet homme-là; **t. (you are)!** (take this) tenez!; **t.,
(t.,) don't cry!** allons, allons, ne pleure pas!
▪ **there'abouts** adv dans les environs; (in
amount) à peu près ▪ **there'after** adv Formal
après cela ▪ **thereby** adv Formal ainsi
▪ **therefore** adv donc ▪ **thereu'pon** adv
Formal sur ce

thermal ['θɜ:məl] adj (underwear) en Thermo-
lactyl®; (energy, unit) thermique

thermometer [θə'mɒmɪtə(r)] n thermomètre m

thermonuclear [θɜ:məʊ'nju:klɪə(r)] adj thermonucléaire

Thermos® ['θɜ:məs] (pl -moses [-məsəz]) n **T.
(flask)** Thermos® m ou f

thermostat ['θɜ:məstæt] n thermostat m

thesaurus [θɪ'sɔ:rəs] n dictionnaire m de
synonymes

these [ði:z] (sing **this**) **1** demonstrative adj ces;
(opposed to 'those') ces…-ci; **t. men** ces
hommes(-ci); **t. ones** ceux-ci mpl, celles-ci fpl
2 demonstrative pron ceux-ci mpl, celles-ci fpl;
t. are my friends ce sont mes amis

thesis ['θi:sɪs] (pl **theses** ['θi:si:z]) n thèse f

they [ðeɪ] pron **(a)** (subject) ils mpl, elles fpl;
(stressed) eux mpl, elles fpl; **t. go** ils/elles vont;
t. are doctors ce sont des médecins **(b)**
(people in general) Fam on; **t. say** on dit ▪ **they'd** =
they had, they would ▪ **they'll** = **they will**

thick [θɪk] **1** (-er, -est) adj épais (f épaisse); Br
Fam (stupid) lourd **2** adv (spread) en couche
épaisse; (grow) dru **3** n **in the t. of battle** au
cœur de la bataille ▪ **thickly** adv (spread) en
couche épaisse; (grow) dru; **t. populated/
wooded** très peuplé/boisé

thicken ['θɪkən] **1** vt épaissir **2** vi (of fog)

s'épaissir; *(of cream, sauce)* épaissir ▪**thick-ness** *n* épaisseur *f*

thicket ['θɪkɪt] *n* fourré *m*

thickset [θɪk'set] *adj (person)* trapu ▪'**thick-'skinned** *adj (person)* peu susceptible

thief [θiːf] *(pl* **thieves)** *n* voleur, -euse *mf*; **stop t.!** au voleur! ▪**thieve** *vti* voler ▪**thieving** 1 *adj* voleur, -euse 2 *n* vol *m*

thigh [θaɪ] *n* cuisse *f* ▪**thighbone** *n* fémur *m*

thimble ['θɪmbəl] *n* dé *m* à coudre

thin [θɪn] 1 (**thinner, thinnest**) *adj (person, slice, paper)* mince; *(soup)* peu épais *(f* peu épaisse); *(crowd, hair)* clairsemé; *(powder)* fin; *Fig (excuse, profit)* maigre 2 *adv (spread)* en couche mince; *(cut)* en tranches minces 3 *(pt & pp* **-nn-)** *vt* **to t. (down)** *(paint)* diluer 4 *vi* **to t. out** *(of crowd, mist)* s'éclaircir ▪**thinly** *adv (spread)* en couche mince; *(cut)* en tranches minces; **t. disguised** à peine déguisé; **t. populated/wooded** peu peuplé/boisé ▪**thinness** *n* minceur *f*

thing [θɪŋ] *n* chose *f*; **one's things** *(belongings, clothes)* ses affaires *fpl*; **it's a funny t.** c'est drôle; **poor little t.!** pauvre petit!; **that's just the t.** voilà exactement ce qu'il faut; **how are things?,** *Fam* how's things? comment ça va?; **I'll think things over** j'y réfléchirai; **for one t.... and for another t....** d'abord... et ensuite ...; *Br* **the tea things** *(set)* le service à thé; *(dishes)* la vaisselle ▪**thingamabob** ['θɪŋəmə-bɒb] *(Br* **thingummy** ['θɪŋəmɪ], **thingy** [θɪŋɪ]) *n Fam* truc *m*, machin *m*

think [θɪŋk] 1 *(pt & pp* **thought)** *vt* penser **(that** que); **I t. so** je pense *ou* crois que oui; **what do you t. of him?** que penses-tu de lui?; **I thought it difficult** j'ai trouvé ça difficile; **to t. out** *(plan, method)* élaborer; *(reply)* réfléchir sérieusement à; **to t. sth over** réfléchir à qch; **to t. sth through** réfléchir à qch sous tous les angles; **to t. sth up** *(invent)* inventer qch 2 *vi* penser **(about/of** à); **to t. (carefully)** réfléchir **(about/of** à); **to t. of doing sth** penser à faire qch; **to t. highly of sb** penser beaucoup de bien de qn; **she doesn't t. much of it** ça ne lui dit pas grand-chose; **to t. better of it** se raviser; **I can't t. of it** je n'arrive pas à m'en souvenir 3 *n Fam* **to have a t.** réfléchir **(about** à); **t.-tank** comité *m* d'experts ▪**thinker** *n* penseur, -euse *mf* ▪**thinking** 1 *adj* **t. person** personne *f* intelligente 2 *n (opinion)* opinion *f*; **to my t.** à mon avis

thinner ['θɪnə(r)] *n* diluant *m*

thin-skinned [θɪn'skɪnd] *adj Fig* susceptible

third [θɜːd] 1 *adj* troisième; **t. party** *or* **person** tiers *m*; **t.-party insurance** assurance *f* au tiers; **the T. World** le tiers-monde 2 *n* troisième *mf*; **a t.** *(fraction)* un tiers 3 *adv* **to come t.** *(in race)* se classer troisième ▪**thirdly** *adv* troisièmement **third-class** ['θɜːd'klɑːs] *adj* de troisième

classe; *Br* **t. degree** ≃ licence *f* avec mention passable ▪'**third-'rate** *adj* très inférieur

thirst [θɜːst] *n* soif *f* **(for** de) ▪**thirsty (-ier, -iest)** *adj* **to be** *or* **feel t.** avoir soif; **to make sb t.** donner soif à qn; *Fig* **to be t. for power** être assoiffé de pouvoir

thirteen [θɜː'tiːn] *adj & n* treize *(m)* ▪**thirteenth** *adj & n* treizième *(mf)*

thirty ['θɜːtɪ] *adj & n* trente *(m)* ▪**thirtieth** *adj & n* trentième *(mf)*

this [ðɪs] 1 *(pl* **these)** *demonstrative adj* ce, cet *(before vowel or mute h)*, cette; *(opposed to 'that')* ce...-ci; **t. book** ce livre(-ci); **t. man** cet homme(-ci); **t. photo** cette photo(-ci); **t. one** celui-ci *m*, celle-ci *f* 2 *(pl* **these)** *demonstrative pron (subject)* ce, ceci; *(object)* ceci; **give me t.** donne-moi ceci; **I prefer t.** je préfère celui-ci; **before t.** avant ceci; **who's t.?** qui est-ce?; **t. is Paul** c'est Paul; *(pointing)* voici Paul 3 *adv (so)* **t. high** *(pointing)* haut comme ceci; **t. far** *(until now)* jusqu'ici

thistle ['θɪsəl] *n* chardon *m*

thong ['θɒŋ] *n (strip of leather)* lanière *f*; *(underwear)* string *m*; *Am* **thongs** *(sandals)* tongs *mpl*

thorax ['θɔːræks] *n Anat* thorax *m*

thorn [θɔːn] *n* épine *f* ▪**thorny (-ier, -iest)** *adj (bush, problem)* épineux, -euse

thorough ['θʌrə] *adj (search, cleaning, preparation)* minutieux, -ieuse; *(knowledge, examination)* approfondi; **to give sth a t. wash** laver qch à fond ▪**thoroughly** *adv (completely)* tout à fait; *(carefully)* avec minutie; *(know, clean, wash)* à fond ▪**thoroughness** *n* minutie *f*

thoroughbred ['θʌrəbred] *n (horse)* pur-sang *m inv*

thoroughfare ['θʌrəfeə(r)] *n* voie *f* de communication; *Br* '**no t.**' 'passage interdit'

those [ðəʊz] 1 *(sing* **that)** *demonstrative adj* ces; *(opposed to 'these')* ces...-là; **t. men** ces hommes(-là); **t. ones** ceux-là *mpl*, celles-là *fpl* 2 *(sing* **that)** *demonstrative pron* ceux-là *mpl*, celles-là *fpl*; **t. are my friends** ce sont mes amis

though [ðəʊ] 1 *conj* bien que (+ *subjunctive)*; **(even) t.** même si; **as t.** comme si; **strange t. it may seem** si étrange que cela puisse paraître 2 *adv (however)* pourtant

thought [θɔːt] 1 *pt & pp of* **think** 2 *n* pensée *f*; **(careful) t.** réflexion *f*; **to have second thoughts** changer d'avis; *Br* **on second thoughts,** *Am* **on second t.** à la réflexion; **I didn't give it another t.** je n'y ai plus pensé

thoughtful ['θɔːtfəl] *adj (considerate, kind)* attentionné; *(pensive)* pensif, -ive ▪**thoughtfully** *adv (considerately)* gentiment; *(pensively)* pensivement ▪**thoughtfulness** *n (consideration)* gentillesse *f*; *(pensiveness)* méditation *f*

thoughtless ['θɔːtləs] *adj (ill-considered)* irréfléchi; *(inconsiderate)* **t. of others** qui

manque d'égards pour les autres
■**thoughtlessly** *adv (without thinking)* sans réfléchir; *(inconsiderately)* sans aucun égard ■**thoughtlessness** *n (lack of forethought)* irréflexion *f*; *(lack of consideration)* manque *f* d'égards

thousand ['θaʊzənd] *adj & n* mille *(m) inv*; **a t. pages** mille pages; **two t. pages** deux mille pages; **thousands of** des milliers de; **they came in their thousands** ils sont venus par milliers

thrash [θræʃ] **1** *vt* **to t. sb** donner une correction à qn; *(defeat)* écraser qn; **to t. out** *(plan)* discuter de **2** *vi* **to t. around** *or* **about** *(struggle)* se débattre ■**thrashing** *n (beating)* correction *f*

thread [θred] **1** *n (yarn) & Fig* fil *m*; *(of screw)* filetage *m* **2** *vt (needle, beads)* enfiler; **to t. one's way between...** se faufiler entre... ■**threadbare** *adj* élimé

threat [θret] *n* menace *f* ■**threaten 1** *vt* menacer (**to do de** faire; **with sth de** qch) **2** *vi* menacer ■**threatening** *adj* menaçant ■**threateningly** *adv (say)* d'un ton menaçant

three [θriː] *adj & n* trois *(m)*; *Br* **t.-piece suite** canapé *m* et deux fauteuils assortis ■**three-'D** *adj (film)* en 3-D ■**three-di'mensional** *adj* à trois dimensions ■**threefold 1** *adj* triple **2** *adv* **to increase t.** tripler ■**three-point 'turn** *n Aut* demi-tour *m* en trois manœuvres ■**'three-'quarters 1** *n* **t. (of)** les trois quarts *mpl* (de) **2** *adv* **it's t. full** c'est aux trois quarts plein ■**threesome** *n* groupe *m* de trois personnes ■**three-way** *adj (division)* en trois; *(conversation)* à trois ■**three-'wheeler** *n (tricycle)* tricycle *m*; *(car)* voiture *f* à trois roues

thresh [θreʃ] *vt* battre

threshold ['θreʃhəʊld] *n* seuil *m*; **pain t.** seuil de résistance à la douleur

threw [θruː] *pt of* **throw**

thrift [θrɪft] *n* économie *f*; *Am* **t. store** = magasin vendant des articles d'occasion au profit d'œuvres charitables ■**thrifty** (**-ier, -iest**) *adj* économe

thrill [θrɪl] **1** *n* frisson *m*; **to get a t. out of doing sth** prendre plaisir à faire qch **2** *vt (delight)* réjouir; *(excite)* faire frissonner ■**thrilled** *adj* ravi (**with sth** de qch; **to do** de faire) ■**thriller** *n* thriller *m* ■**thrilling** *adj* passionnant

thrive [θraɪv] *vi (of business, person, plant)* prospérer; **to t. on sth** avoir besoin de qch pour s'épanouir ■**thriving** *adj (business)* prospère

throat [θrəʊt] *n* gorge *f*; **to clear one's t.** se racler la gorge ■**throaty** *adj (voice)* rauque; *(person)* à la voix rauque

throb [θrɒb] **1** *n (of heart)* battement *m*; *(of engine)* vibration *f*, *(of pain)* élancement *m* **2** *(pt & pp* **-bb-)** *vi (of heart)* palpiter; *(of engine)*

vibrer; **my head is throbbing** j'ai une tête lancinante dans la tête

throes [θrəʊz] *npl* **in the t. of** au milieu de; *(illness, crisis)* en proie à; **in the t. of doing sth** en train de faire qch; **death t.** les affres *fpl* de la mort

thrombosis [θrɒm'bəʊsɪs] *n Med* thrombose *f*; **deep vein t.** thrombose veineuse profonde

throne [θrəʊn] *n* trône *m*

throng [θrɒŋ] **1** *n Literary* foule *f* **2** *vt (station, street)* se presser dans; **it was thronged with people** c'était noir de monde **3** *vi (rush)* affluer

throttle ['θrɒtəl] **1** *n (valve)* papillon *m* des gaz; *(accelerator)* manette *f* des gaz **2** *vt (strangle)* étrangler

through [θruː] **1** *prep (place)* à travers; *(by means of)* par; *(because of)* à cause de; **t. the window/door** par la fenêtre/porte; **t. ignorance** par ignorance; **all t. his life** toute sa vie; **halfway t. the book** à la moitié du livre; **to go** *or* **get t.** *(forest)* traverser; *(hole)* passer par; *(wall)* passer à travers; **to speak t. one's nose** parler du nez; *Am* **Tuesday t. Saturday** de mardi à samedi **2** *adv* à travers; **to go t.** *(of bullet, nail)* traverser; **to let sb t.** laisser passer qn; *Am* **to be t. with sb/sth** *(finished)* en avoir fini avec qn/qch; *Am* **I'm t. with the book** je n'ai plus besoin du livre; **to sleep all night t.** dormir toute la nuit; **t. to** *or* **till** jusqu'à; **French t. and t.** français jusqu'au bout des ongles; **I'll put you t. (to him)** *(on telephone)* je vous le passe **3** *adj (train, ticket)* direct; *Br* **'no t. road'** *(no exit)* 'voie sans issue'

throughout [θruː'aʊt] **1** *prep* **t. the neighbourhood** dans tout le quartier; **t. the day** pendant toute la journée **2** *adv (everywhere)* partout; *(all the time)* tout le temps

throw [θrəʊ] **1** *n (of stone)* jet *m*; *Sport* lancer *m*; *(of dice)* coup *m* **2** *(pt* **threw**, *pp* **thrown**) *vt* jeter **(to/at** à); *(javelin, discus)* lancer; *(image, shadow)* projeter; *(of horse)* désarçonner; *(party)* donner; *Fam (baffle)* déconcerter

▶ **throw away** *vt sep (discard)* jeter; *Fig (life, chance)* gâcher

▶ **throw back** *vt sep (ball)* renvoyer **(to** à); *(one's head)* rejeter en arrière

▶ **throw in** *vt sep Fam (include as extra)* donner en prime

▶ **throw off** *vt sep (get rid of)* se débarrasser de

▶ **throw out** *vt sep (unwanted object)* jeter; *(suggestion)* repousser; *(expel)* mettre à la porte

▶ **throw over** *vt sep (abandon)* abandonner

▶ **throw up** *vi Fam (vomit)* vomir

throwaway ['θrəʊəweɪ] *adj (disposable)* jetable

thrown [θrəʊn] *pp of* **throw**

thrush¹ [θrʌʃ] *n (bird)* grive *f*

thrush² [θrʌʃ] *n Med* muguet *m*

thrust [θrʌst] **1** *n (movement)* mouvement *m* en avant; *(of argument)* idée *f* principale; *(of* *engine)* poussée *f* **2** *(pt & pp* thrust) *vt* **to t. sth into sth** enfoncer qch dans qch; **to t. sb/sth aside** écarter qn/qch; *Fig* **to t. sth (up)on sb** imposer qch à qn

thruway ['θruːweɪ] *n Am* autoroute *f*

thud [θʌd] *n* bruit *m* sourd

thug [θʌg] *n* voyou *m* (*pl* -ous)

thumb [θʌm] **1** *n* pouce *m*; **with a t. index** *(book)* à onglets **2** *vt Fam* **to t. a lift** *or* **a ride** faire du stop **3** *vi* **to t. through a book** feuilleter un livre ■**thumbtack** *n Am* punaise *f*

thump [θʌmp] **1** *n (blow)* coup *m*; *(noise)* bruit *m* sourd **2** *vt (hit)* frapper; *(put down heavily)* poser lourdement; **to t. one's head** se cogner la tête *(on contre)* **3** *vi* frapper, cogner *(on* sur); *(of heart)* battre la chamade ■**thumping** *adj Fam (huge, great)* énorme

thunder ['θʌndə(r)] **1** *n* tonnerre *m* **2** *vi* tonner; **to t. past** *(of train, truck)* passer dans un bruit de tonnerre ■**thunderbolt** *n* éclair *m* suivi d'un coup de tonnerre ■**thunderclap** *n* coup *m* de tonnerre ■**thunderstorm** *n* orage *m* ■**thunderstruck** *adj* abasourdi

Thursday ['θɜːzdeɪ] *n* jeudi *m*

thus [ðʌs] *adv* ainsi

thwart [θwɔːt] *vt* contrecarrer

thyme [taɪm] *n* thym *m*

thyroid ['θaɪrɔɪd] *adj & n Anat* thyroïde *(f)*

tiara [tɪ'ɑːrə] *n (jewellery)* diadème *m*

Tibet [tɪ'bet] *n* leTibet

tic [tɪk] *n* tic *m*

tick¹ [tɪk] **1** *n (of clock)* tic-tac *m inv*; *(mark)* ≃ croix *f*; *(moment)* instant *m* **2** *vt* **to t. (off)** *(on list)* cocher qch; *Fam* **to t. sb off** passer un savon à qn **3** *vi* faire tic-tac; *Br* **to t. over** *(of engine, factory)* tourner au ralenti ■**ticking** *n (of clock)* tic-tac *m inv* ■**ticking-off** *n Br Fam* **to give sb a t.** passer un savon à qn

tick² [tɪk] *n (insect)* tique *f*

tick³ [tɪk] *adv Br Fam* **on t.** à crédit

ticket ['tɪkɪt] *n* billet *m*; *(for bus, metro)* ticket *m*; *Fam (for parking, speeding)* contravention *f*; *Am Pol (list of candidates)* liste *f* électorale; **(price) t.** étiquette *f*; **t. collector** contrôleur, -euse *mf*; **t. holder** personne *f* munie d'un billet; **t. office** guichet *m*; *Am* **t. scalper,** *Br* **t. tout** revendeur, -euse *mf* (en fraude)

tickle ['tɪkəl] **1** *n* chatouillement *m* **2** *vt* chatouiller; *Fig (amuse)* amuser ■**ticklish** *adj (person)* chatouilleux, -euse; *Fig (problem)* délicat

tick-tack-toe [tɪktæk'təʊ] *n Am* morpion *m*

tidal ['taɪdəl] *adj (river)* régi par les marées; **t. wave** raz de marée *m inv*

tidbit ['tɪdbɪt] *n Am* = **titbit**

tiddlywinks ['tɪdlɪwɪŋks] *n* jeu *m* de puce

tide [taɪd] **1** *n* marée *f*; *Fig* **against the t.** à contre-courant; **the rising t. of discontent** le mécontentement grandissant **2** *vt* **to t. sb**

over dépanner qn ■**tidemark** *n Br Fig & Hum (on neck, in bath)* ligne *f* de crasse

tidy ['taɪdɪ] **1** *(-ier, -iest) adj (place, toys)* bien rangé; *(clothes, hair)* soigné; *(person) (methodical)* ordonné; *(in appearance)* soigné; *Fam* **a t. sum** *or* **amount** une jolie somme; **to make sth t.** ranger qch **2** *vt* **to t. sth (up** *or* **away)** ranger qch; **to t. sth out** mettre de l'ordre dans qch; **to t. oneself up** s'arranger **3** *vi* **to t. up** ranger ■**tidily** *adv (put away)* soigneusement, avec soin ■**tidiness** *n (of drawer, desk)* ordre *m*; *(of appearance)* soin *m*

tie [taɪ] **1** *n (garment)* cravate *f*; *(link)* lien *m*; *Am (on railroad track)* traverse *f*; *Sport* égalité *f*; *(drawn match)* match *m* nul **2** *vt (fasten)* attacher *(to* à); *(knot)* faire *(in* à); *(shoe)* lacer **3** *vi Sport* être à égalité; *Football* faire match nul; *(in race)* être ex aequo

▸ **tie down** *vt sep* attacher; **to t. sb down to a date** obliger qn à accepter une date

▸ **tie in** *vi (of facts)* concorder

▸ **tie up** *vt sep (animal)* attacher; *(parcel)* ficeler; *(deal)* conclure; *(money)* immobiliser; *Fig* **to be tied up** *(busy)* être occupé

tier [tɪə(r)] *n (of seats)* gradin *m*; *(of cake)* étage *m*

tiff [tɪf] *n Fam* petite querelle *f*

tiger ['taɪgə(r)] *n* tigre *m*

tight [taɪt] **1** *(-er, -est) adj (clothes, knot, race, bend)* serré; *(control)* strict; *Fam (mean)* radin; *Fam (drunk)* bourré; *Fam* **a t. spot** *or* **corner** une mauvaise passe; **it's a t. squeeze** il y a juste la place **2** *adv (hold, shut)* bien; *(squeeze)* fort; **to sit t.** ne pas bouger; **sleep t.!** dors bien! ■'**tight'fisted** *adj Fam* radin ■'**tight-'fitting** *adj (garment)* ajusté ■'**tight'knit** *adj (community)* uni ■**tightly** *adv (hold)* bien; *(squeeze)* fort ■**tightness** *n (of garment)* étroitesse *f*; *(of control)* rigueur *f*; *(of rope)* tension *f* ■**tightrope** *n* corde *f* raide ■**tightwad** *n Am Fam (miser)* grippe-sou *m*

tighten ['taɪtən] **1** *vt* **to t. (up)** *(bolt)* serrer; *(rope)* tendre; *Fig (security)* renforcer **2** *vi* **to t. up on sth** se montrer plus strict à l'égard de qch

tights [taɪts] *npl Br (garment)* collant *m*

tile [taɪl] **1** *n (on roof)* tuile *f*; *(on wall, floor)* carreau *m* **2** *vt (wall, floor)* carreler ■**tiled** *adj (roof)* de tuiles; *(wall, floor)* carrelé ■**tiler** *n* carreleur *m*

till¹ [tɪl] *prep & conj =* **until**

till² [tɪl] *n Br (for money)* caisse *f* enregistreuse

till³ [tɪl] *vt (land)* labourer

tiller ['tɪlə(r)] *n (of boat)* barre *f*

tilt [tɪlt] **1** *n* inclinaison *f*; **(at) full t.** à toute vitesse **2** *vti* pencher

timber ['tɪmbə(r)] **1** *n Br (wood)* bois *m* (de construction) **2** *adj Br (house)* de bois ■**timberyard** *n Br* entrepôt *m* de bois

time [taɪm] **1** *n* temps *m*; *(period, moment)*

moment *m*; *(age)* époque *f*; *(on clock)* heure *f*; *(occasion)* fois *f*, *Mus* mesure *f*; **in t., with t.** avec le temps; **it's t. to do sth** il est temps de faire qch; **I have no t. to play** je n'ai pas le temps de jouer; **I have no t. to waste** je n'ai pas de temps à perdre; **some of the t.** *(not always)* une partie du temps; **most of the t.** la plupart du temps; **all (of) the t.** tout le temps; **in a year's t.** dans un an; **a long t.** longtemps; **a short t.** peu de temps; **to have a good** *or* **a nice t.** s'amuser *(bien)*; **to have a hard t. doing sth** avoir du mal à faire qch; **to have t. off** avoir du temps libre; **in no t. (at all)** en un rien de temps; **(just) in t.** *(arrive)* à temps *(***for** sth pour qch; **to do** pour faire)*; **in my t.** *(formerly)* de mon temps; **from t. to t.** de temps en temps; **what t. is it?** quelle heure est-il?; **the right** *or* **exact t.** l'heure *f* exacte; **on t.** à l'heure; **at the same t.** en même temps *(***as** que); *(simultaneously)* à la fois; **for the t. being** pour le moment; **at the** *or* **that t.** à ce moment-là; **at the present t.** à l'heure actuelle; **at times** parfois; **at one t.** à un moment donné; **this t. tomorrow** demain à cette heure-ci; **(the) next t. you come** la prochaine fois que tu viendras; **(the) last t.** la dernière fois; **one at a t.** un à un; **t. and (t.) again, t. after t.** encore et encore; **ten times ten** dix fois dix; **t. bomb** bombe *f* à retardement; **t. difference** décalage *m* horaire; **t. lag** *(between events)* décalage; **t. limit** délai *m*; **t. switch** minuterie *f*; **t. zone** fuseau *m* horaire

2 *vt (sportsman, worker)* chronométrer; *(activity, programme)* minuter; *(choose the time of)* choisir le moment de; *(plan)* prévoir ■**time-consuming** *adj* qui prend du temps ■**time-honoured** (*Am* **time-honored**) *adj* consacré (par l'usage) ■**time-share** *n* multipropriété *f*

timeless ['taɪmləs] *adj* intemporel, -elle

timely ['taɪmlɪ] *adj* à propos ■**timeliness** *n* à-propos *m*

timer ['taɪmə(r)] *n (device)* minuteur *m*; *(sand-filled)* sablier *m*; *(built into appliance)* programmateur *m*; *(plugged into socket)* prise *f* programmable

timescale ['taɪmskeɪl] *n* période *f*

timetable ['taɪmteɪbəl] *n* horaire *m*; *(in school)* emploi *m* du temps

timid ['tɪmɪd] *adj* timide ■**timidly** *adv* timidement

timing ['taɪmɪŋ] *n (of sportsman)* chronométrage *m*; *(of election)* moment *m* choisi; *(of musician)* sens *m* du rythme; **what (good) t.!** quelle synchronisation!

tin [tɪn] *n (metal)* étain *m*; *Br (can)* boîte *f*; **cake t.** moule *m* à gâteaux; **t. opener** ouvre-boîtes *m inv*; **t. plate** fer-blanc *m*; **t. soldier** soldat *m* de plomb ■**tinfoil** *n* papier *m* aluminium

tinge [tɪndʒ] *n* pointe *f* ■**tinged** *adj* **t. with sth** teinté de qch

tingle ['tɪŋgəl] *vi* picoter; **it's tingling** ça me picote ■**tingly** *adj* **t. feeling** sensation *f* de picotement

tinker ['tɪŋkə(r)] *vi* **to t.** *(***about** *or* **around)** **with sth** bricoler qch

tinkle ['tɪŋkəl] **1** *n* tintement *m*; *Br Fam* **to give sb a t.** *(phone sb)* passer un coup de fil à qn **2** *vi* tinter

tinned [tɪnd] *adj Br* **t. pears/salmon** poires *fpl*/ saumon *m* en boîte; **t. food** conserves *fpl*

tinny ['tɪnɪ] *(***-ier, -iest***) adj (sound)* métallique

tinsel ['tɪnsəl] *n* guirlandes *fpl* de Noël

tint [tɪnt] *n* teinte *f*; *(for hair)* rinçage *m* ■**tinted** *adj (paper, glass)* teinté

tiny ['taɪnɪ] *(***-ier, -iest***) adj* minuscule

tip¹ [tɪp] *n (end)* bout *m*; *(pointed)* pointe *f*; *Fig* **the t. of the iceberg** la partie visible de l'iceberg

tip² [tɪp] **1** *Br (rubbish dump)* décharge *f*; *Fam* **this room is a real t.** cette pièce est un vrai dépotoir **2** *(pt & pp* **-pp-***) vt (pour)* déverser; **to t. sth up** *or* **over** renverser qch; **to t. sth out** *(liquid, load)* déverser qch (**into** dans) **3** *vi* **to t. (up** *or* **over)** *(tilt)* se renverser; *(overturn)* basculer

tip³ [tɪp] **1** *n (money)* pourboire *m*; *(advice)* conseil *m*; *(information)* tuyau *m* **2** *(pt & pp* **-pp-***) vt (waiter)* donner un pourboire à; **to t. a horse** donner un cheval gagnant; **to t. off** *(police)* prévenir

tip-off ['tɪpɒf] *n* **to get a t.** se faire tuyauter

tipple ['tɪpəl] *Fam* **1** *n (drink)* **what's your t.?** qu'est-ce que vous prenez habituellement? **2** *vi (drink)* picoler

tipsy ['tɪpsɪ] *(***-ier, -iest***) adj (drunk)* éméché, gai

tiptoe ['tɪptəʊ] **1** *n* **on t.** sur la pointe des pieds **2** *vi* marcher sur la pointe des pieds; **to t. into/ out of a room** entrer dans une pièce/sortir d'une pièce sur la pointe des pieds

tiptop ['tɪptɒp] *adj Fam* excellent

tirade [taɪ'reɪd] *n* diatribe *f*

tire¹ ['taɪə(r)] **1** *vt* fatiguer; **to t. sb out** épuiser qn **2** *vi* se fatiguer ■**tired** *adj* fatigué; **to be t. of sth/doing** en avoir assez de qch/de faire; **to get t. of doing sth** se lasser de faire qch ■**tiredness** *n* fatigue *f* ■**tireless** *adj* infatigable ■**tiresome** *adj* ennuyeux, -euse ■**tiring** *adj* fatigant

tire² ['taɪə(r)] *n Am =* **tyre**

tissue ['tɪʃuː] *n (handkerchief)* mouchoir *m* en papier; *Biol* tissu *m*; **t. paper** papier *m* de soie

tit¹ [tɪt] *n* **to give t. for tat** rendre coup pour coup

tit² [tɪt] *n (bird)* mésange *f*

tit³ [tɪt] *n Br very Fam (breast)* nichon *m*; *(idiot)* imbécile *mf*

titbit ['tɪtbɪt] *n Br (food)* bon morceau *m*

titillate ['tɪtɪleɪt] *vt* exciter

title ['taɪtəl] **1** *n (name, claim) & Sport* titre *m*; **t. deeds** titres *mpl* de propriété; **t. role** *(in film, play)* rôle-titre *m* **2** *vt* intituler ▪**titled** *adj (person)* titré ▪**titleholder** *n Sport* tenant, -ante *mf* du titre

titter ['tɪtə(r)] *vi* rire bêtement

tittle-tattle ['tɪtəltætəl] *n Fam* cancans *mpl*

T-junction ['tiːdʒʌŋkʃən] *n Br (of roads)* intersection *f* en T

to [tə, *stressed* tuː] **1** *prep* (**a**) *(towards)* à; *(until)* jusqu'à; **give it to him/her** donne-le-lui; **to go to town** aller en ville; **to go to France/ Portugal** aller en France/au Portugal; **to go to the butcher's** aller chez le boucher; **the road to London** la route de Londres; **the train to Paris** le train pour Paris; **kind/cruel to sb** gentil/cruel envers qn; **to my surprise** à ma grande surprise; **from bad to worse** de mal en pis; **it's ten (minutes) to one** il est une heure moins dix; **ten to one** *(proportion)* dix contre un; **one person to a room** une personne par chambre (**b**) *(with infinitive)* **to say/jump** dire/ sauter; **(in order) to do sth** pour faire qch; **she tried to** elle a essayé; **wife-to-be** future femme *f* (**c**) *(with adjective)* **I'd be happy to do it** je serais heureux de le faire; **it's easy to do** c'est facile à faire **2** *adv* **to push the door to** fermer la porte; **to go** *or* **walk to and fro** aller et venir

toad [təʊd] *n* crapaud *m*

toadstool ['təʊdstuːl] *n* champignon *m* vénéneux

toast¹ [təʊst] **1** *n (bread)* pain *m* grillé; **piece** *or* **slice of t.** tranche *f* de pain grillé **2** *vt (bread)* faire griller ▪**toaster** *n* grille-pain *m inv*

toast² [təʊst] **1** *n (drink)* toast *m* **2** *vt (person)* porter un toast à; *(success, event)* arroser

tobacco [tə'bækəʊ] *(pl* -os*)* *n* tabac *m*; *Am* **t. store** (bureau *m* de) tabac ▪**tobacconist** [-kənɪst] *n* buraliste *mf*; *Br* **t.'s (shop)** (bureau *m* de) tabac *m*

toboggan [tə'bɒgən] *n* luge *f*

> Note that the French word **toboggan** is a false friend. Its most common meaning is **slide** (in a playground).

today [tə'deɪ] *adv* aujourd'hui; **t.'s date** la date d'aujourd'hui

toddle ['tɒdəl] *vi Br Fam* **to t. off** ficher le camp

toddler ['tɒdlə(r)] *n* enfant *mf* (en bas âge)

toddy ['tɒdɪ] *n* **(hot) t.** grog *m*

to-do [tə'duː] *n Fam (fuss)* histoire *f*

toe [təʊ] **1** *n* orteil *m*; *Fig* **on one's toes** vigilant **2** *vt* **to t. the line** bien se tenir; **to t. the party line** respecter la ligne du parti ▪**toenail** *n* ongle *m* de pied

toffee ['tɒfɪ] *n Br* caramel *m* (dur); **t. apple** pomme *f* d'amour

together [tə'geðə(r)] *adv* ensemble; *(at the same time)* en même temps; **t. with** ainsi que ▪**togetherness** *n* harmonie *f*

togs [tɒgz] *npl Fam (clothes)* fringues *fpl*

toil [tɔɪl] **1** *n* labeur *m* **2** *vi* travailler dur

toilet ['tɔɪlɪt] *n Br (room)* toilettes *fpl*; *(bowl, seat)* cuvette *f* des toilettes; *Br* **to go to the t.** aller aux toilettes; **t. flush** chasse *f* d'eau; **t. paper** papier *m* hygiénique; **t. roll** rouleau *m* de papier hygiénique; **t. soap** savon *m* de toilette ▪**toiletries** *npl* articles *mpl* de toilette ▪**toilet-trained** *adj (child)* propre

token ['təʊkən] **1** *n (for vending machine)* jeton *m*; *(symbol)* signe *m*; **as a t. of respect** en signe de respect; **by the same t.** de même; *Br* **book t.** chèque-livre *m* **2** *adj* symbolique

told [təʊld] **1** *pt & pp of* **tell 2** *adv* **all t.** *(taken together)* en tout

tolerable ['tɒlərəbəl] *adj (bearable)* tolérable; *(fairly good)* acceptable ▪**tolerably** *adv (fairly, fairly well)* passablement

tolerant ['tɒlərənt] *adj* tolérant *(of* à l'égard de*)* ▪**tolerance** *n* tolérance *f* ▪**tolerantly** *adv* avec tolérance

tolerate ['tɒləreɪt] *vt* tolérer

toll [təʊl] **1** *n* (**a**) *(fee)* péage *m*; **t. road/bridge** route *f*/pont *m* à péage (**b**) **the death t.** le nombre de morts; *Fig* **to take its t.** faire des dégâts **2** *vi (of bell)* sonner ▪**'toll-'free** *Am* **1** *adj* **t. number** ≃ numéro *m* vert **2** *adv (call)* gratuitement

tomato [*Br* tə'mɑːtəʊ, *Am* tə'meɪtəʊ] *(pl* -oes*)* *n* tomate *f*; **t. sauce** sauce *f* tomate

tomb [tuːm] *n* tombeau *m* ▪**tombstone** *n* pierre *f* tombale

tomboy ['tɒmbɔɪ] *n* garçon *m* manqué

tomcat ['tɒmkæt] *n* matou *m*

tome [təʊm] *n Formal* gros volume *m*

tomfoolery [tɒm'fuːlərɪ] *n* bêtises *fpl*

tomorrow [tə'mɒrəʊ] *adv & n* demain (*m*); **t. morning/evening** demain matin/soir; **the day after t.** après-demain; **a week from t.,** *Br* **a week t.** demain en huit

ton [tʌn] *n* tonne *f*; **metric t.** tonne *f*; *Fam* **tons of** *(lots of)* des tonnes de

tone [təʊn] **1** *n* ton *m*; *(of telephone, radio)* tonalité *f*; *(of answering machine)* signal *m* sonore; *Br* **the engaged t.** *(on telephone)* la sonnerie 'occupé'; **to set the t.** donner le ton; **she's t.-deaf** elle n'a pas d'oreille **2** *vt* **to t. sth down** atténuer qch; **to t. up** *(muscles, skin)* tonifier **3** *vi* **to t. in** *(blend in)* s'harmoniser (**with** avec)

tongs [tɒŋz] *npl* pinces *fpl*; **curling t.** fer *m* à friser; **sugar t.** pince *f* à sucre

tongue [tʌŋ] *n (in mouth, language)* langue *f*; **to say sth t. in cheek** dire qch en plaisantant; **t. twister** ≃ mot ou phrase imprononçable ▪**tongue-tied** *adj* muet (*f* muette)

tonic ['tɒnɪk] *n* (*medicine*) fortifiant *m*; **t. (water)** Schweppes® *m*; **gin and t.** gin-tonic *m*

tonight [tə'naɪt] *adv & n* (*this evening*) ce soir (*m*); (*during the night*) cette nuit (*f*)

tonne [tʌn] *n* (*metric*) tonne *f* ▪**tonnage** ['tʌnɪdʒ] *n* tonnage *m*

tonsil ['tɒnsəl] *n* amygdale *f* ▪**tonsillitis** [-'laɪtɪs] *n* to have t. avoir une angine

too [tuː] *adv* (**a**) (*excessively*) trop; **t. tired to play** trop fatigué pour jouer; **t. much, t. many** trop; **t. much salt** trop de sel; **t. many people** trop de gens; **one t. many** un de trop; *Fam* **t. right!** et comment! (**b**) (*also*) aussi; (*moreover*) en plus

took [tʊk] *pt of* **take**

tool [tuːl] *n* outil *m*; **t. bag, t. kit** trousse *f* à outils; **t. shed** remise *f* ▪**toolbar** *n Comptr* barre *f* d'outils

toot [tuːt] *vti Aut* **to t. (the horn)** klaxonner

tooth [tuːθ] *n* (*pl* **teeth**) *n* dent *f*; **front t.** dent de devant; **back t.** molaire *f*; **milk/wisdom t.** dent de lait/de sagesse; **t. decay** carie *f* dentaire; **to have a sweet t.** aimer les sucreries; *Hum* **long in the t.** (*old*) chenu, vieux (*f* vieille) ▪**toothache** *n* mal *m* de dents; **to have t.** avoir mal aux dents ▪**toothbrush** *n* brosse *f* à dents ▪**toothpaste** *n* dentifrice *m* ▪**toothpick** *n* cure-dents *m inv*

top¹ [tɒp] **1** *n* (*of mountain, tower, tree*) sommet *m*; (*of wall, ladder, page*) haut *m*; (*of table, box, surface*) dessus *m*; (*of list*) tête *f*; (*of bottle, tube*) bouchon *m*; (*bottle cap*) capsule *f*; (*of pen*) capuchon *m*; **pyjama t.** veste *f* de pyjama; **(at the) t. of the class** le premier/la première de la classe; **on t.** dessus; (*in bus*) en haut; **on t. of** sur; *Fig* (*in addition to*) en plus de; **from t. to bottom** de fond en comble; *Fam* **over the t.** (*excessive*) exagéré
2 *adj* (*drawer, shelf*) du haut; (*step, layer*) dernier, -ière; (*upper*) supérieur; (*in rank, exam*) premier, -ière; (*chief*) principal; (*best*) meilleur; **on the t. floor** au dernier étage; **in t. gear** (*vehicle*) en quatrième vitesse; **at t. speed** à toute vitesse; **t. hat** haut-de-forme *m* ▪**'top-'heavy** *adj* trop lourd du haut ▪**'top-'level** (*talks*) au sommet ▪**'top-'notch** *adj Fam* excellent ▪**'top-'ranking** *adj* (*official*) haut placé ▪**'top-'secret** *adj* top secret *inv*

top² [tɒp] (*pt & pp* **-pp-**) *vt* (*exceed*) dépasser; *Br* **to t. up** (*glass*) remplir (de nouveau); (*mobile phone*) recharger le compte de; **and to t. it all…** et pour comble…; **topped with cream** nappé de crème; **topped with cherries** décoré de cerises ▪**topping** *n* (*of pizza*) garniture *f*; **with a t. of cream** nappé de crème

top³ [tɒp] *n* (*spinning*) **t.** toupie *f*

top-up ['tɒpʌp] *n Br* (*for mobile phone*) rechargement *m*; **would you like a t.?** (*when serving drinks*) vous en reprendrez bien un

peu?; *Br Tel* **t. card** (*for mobile phone*) carte *f* de recharge; *Br Univ* **t. fees** = frais de scolarité complémentaires déterminés par chaque université, venant s'ajouter aux frais fixes payés par tous les étudiants britanniques

topaz ['təʊpæz] *n* topaze *f*

topic ['tɒpɪk] *n* sujet *m* ▪**topical** *adj* d'actualité ▪**topicality** [-'kælɪtɪ] *n* actualité *f*

topless ['tɒpləs] *adj* (*woman*) aux seins nus

topography [tə'pɒgrəfɪ] *n* topographie *f*

topple ['tɒpəl] **1** *vt* **to t. sth (over)** faire tomber qch **2** *vi* **to t. (over)** tomber

topside ['tɒpsaɪd] *n Br* (*of beef*) gîte *m*

topsy-turvy [tɒpsɪ'tɜːvɪ] *adj & adv* sens dessus dessous

torch [tɔːtʃ] *n Br* (*electric*) lampe *f* de poche; (*flame*) torche *f* ▪**torchlight 1** *n* **by t.** à la lumière d'une lampe de poche **2** *adj* **t. procession** retraite *f* aux flambeaux

tore [tɔː(r)] *pt of* **tear¹**

torment 1 ['tɔːment] *n* supplice *m* **2** [tɔː'ment] *vt* tourmenter

torn [tɔːn] *pp of* **tear¹**

tornado [tɔː'neɪdəʊ] (*pl* **-oes**) *n* tornade *f*

torpedo [tɔː'piːdəʊ] **1** (*pl* **-oes**) *n* torpille *f*; **t. boat** torpilleur *m* **2** *vt* torpiller

torrent ['tɒrənt] *n* torrent *m* ▪**torrential** [tə'renʃəl] *adj* **t. rain** pluie *f* torrentielle

torrid ['tɒrɪd] *adj* (*weather, love affair*) torride

torso ['tɔːsəʊ] (*pl* **-os**) *n* torse *m*

tortoise ['tɔːtəs] *n* tortue *f* ▪**tortoiseshell** *adj* (*comb*) en écaille; (*spectacles*) à monture d'écaille

tortuous ['tɔːtʃʊəs] *adj* tortueux, -ueuse

torture ['tɔːtʃə(r)] **1** *n* torture *f*; *Fig* **it's (sheer) t.!** quel supplice! **2** *vt* torturer ▪**torturer** *n* tortionnaire *mf*

Tory ['tɔːrɪ] *Br Pol* **1** *n* tory *m* **2** *adj* tory *inv*

toss [tɒs] **1** *n* **with a t. of the head** d'un mouvement brusque de la tête; *Br very Fam* **I don't give a t.** je m'en fous **2** *vt* (*throw*) lancer (**to** à); (*pancake*) faire sauter; **to t. sb (about)** (*of boat, vehicle*) ballotter qn; **to t. a coin** jouer à pile ou face; **to t. back one's head** rejeter la tête en arrière **3** *vi* **to t. (about), to t. and turn** (*in bed*) se tourner et se retourner; **let's t. up, let's t. (up) for it** jouons-le à pile ou face ▪**toss-up** *n Fam* **it's a t. whether she leaves or stays** on ne sait vraiment pas si elle va partir

tot [tɒt] **1** *n* (*tiny*) **t.** tout-petit *m*; *Br* **a t. of whisky** une goutte de whisky **2** (*pt & pp* **-tt-**) *vt Fam* **to t. up** (*total*) additionner

total ['təʊtəl] **1** *adj* total; **the t. sales** le total des ventes **2** *n* total *m*; **in t.** au total **3** (*Br* **-ll-**, *Am* **-l-**) *vt* (*of sum*) s'élever à; *Am Fam* (*car*) bousiller; **to t. (up)** (*find the total of*) totaliser; **that totals $9** ça fait 9 dollars en tout ▪**totally** *adv* totalement

totalitarian [təʊtælɪ'teərɪən] *adj Pol* totalitaire

tote [təʊt] **1** *n Br Fam Sport* pari *m* mutuel **2** *vt Fam (carry)* trimballer ■ **tote bag** *n Am* fourre-tout *m inv*

totter ['tɒtə(r)] *vi* chanceler

touch [tʌʃ] **1** *n (contact)* contact *m*; *(sense)* toucher *m*; *(of painter)* & *Football* & *Rugby* touche *f*; **a t. of** *(small amount)* une pointe de; **to have a t. of flu** être un peu grippé; **to be/ get in t. with sb** être/se mettre en contact avec qn; **to stay in/lose t. with sb** rester en/ perdre contact avec qn; **it's t. and go whether he'll live** on n'est pas sûr du tout qu'il survivra **2** *vt* toucher; *(interfere with, eat)* toucher à; **I don't t. the stuff** *(I hate it)* je n'en bois/mange jamais; *Fig* **there's nothing to t. it** c'est sans égal **3** *vi (of lines, hands, ends)* se toucher; **don't t.!** ne touche pas! ■ **touchdown** *n (of aircraft)* atterrissage *m*; *American Football* but *m* ■ **touched** *adj (emotionally)* touché (**by** de); *Fam (crazy)* cinglé ■ **touching** *adj (moving)* touchant ■ **touchline** *n* ligne *f* de touche ■ **touch-type** *vi* taper au toucher ■ **touch-typing** *n* dactylographie *f* au toucher

► **touch down** *vi (of plane)* atterrir

► **touch on** *vt insep* aborder

► **touch up** *vt sep (photo)* retoucher

touchy ['tʌʃɪ] (**-ier, -iest**) *adj (sensitive)* susceptible (**about** à propos de)

tough [tʌf] **1** (**-er, -est**) *adj (strict, hard)* dur; *(sturdy)* solide; **t. guy** dur *m* à cuire; *Fam* **t. luck!** pas de chance! **2** *n* dur *m* ■ **toughen** *vt (body, person)* endurcir; *(conditions)* durcir ■ **toughness** *n (hardness)* dureté *f*; *(sturdiness)* solidité *f*; *(strength)* force *f*

toupee ['tu:peɪ] *n* postiche *m*

tour [tʊə(r)] **1** *n (journey)* voyage *m*; *(visit)* visite *f*; *(by artist)* tournée *f*; *(on bicycle, on foot)* randonnée *f*; **to be on a t.** *(of tourist)* faire un voyage organisé; **to go on t.** *(of artist)* être en tournée; **(package) t.** voyage organisé; **t. guide** guide *mf*; **t. operator** voyagiste *m* **2** *vt* visiter; *(of artist)* être en tournée en/dans

tourism ['tʊərɪzəm] *n* tourisme *m* ■ **tourist 1** *n* touriste *mf* **2** *adj (region)* touristique; *Av* **t. class** classe *f* touriste; **t. office** syndicat *m* d'initiative ■ **touristy** *adj Fam (trop)* touristique

tournament ['tʊənəmənt] *n Sport* & *Hist* tournoi *m*

tousled ['taʊzəld] *adj (hair)* ébouriffé

tout [taʊt] **1** *n* racoleur, -euse *mf* **2** *vi* **to t. for trade** racoler des clients

tow [təʊ] **1** *n Br* **'on t.',** *Am* **'in t.'** 'en remorque'; *Am* **t. truck** dépanneuse *f* **2** *vt* remorquer; **to t. a car away** *(of police)* mettre une voiture à la fourrière ■ **towpath** *n* chemin *m* de halage ■ **towrope** *n* câble *m* de remorque

toward(s) [tə'wɔːd(z)] *prep* vers; *(of feelings)* envers; **cruel t. sb** cruel envers qn; **the money is going t. a new car** l'argent servira à l'achat d'une nouvelle voiture

towel ['taʊəl] *n* serviette *f* (de toilette); *Br* **t. rail,** *Am* **t. rack** porte-serviettes *m inv* ■ **towelling** *(Am* **toweling)** *n* tissu-éponge *m*; *Am* **(kitchen) t.** essuie-tout *m inv*

tower ['taʊə(r)] **1** *n* tour *f*; *Br* **t. block** tour; *Fig* **ivory t.** tour d'ivoire **2** *vi* **to t. over sb/sth** dominer qn/qch ■ **towering** *adj* immense

town [taʊn] *n* ville *f*; **to go into t.** aller en ville; **country t.** bourg *m*; **t. centre** centre-ville *m*; *Br* **t. clerk** secrétaire *mf* de mairie; *Br* **t. council** conseil *m* municipal; *Br* **t. hall** mairie *f*; *Br* **t. planner** urbaniste *mf*; *Br* **t. planning** urbanisme *m* ■ **township** *n (in South Africa)* township *f*

toxic ['tɒksɪk] *adj* toxique ■ **toxin** *n* toxine *f*

toy [tɔɪ] **1** *n* jouet *m* **2** *adj (gun)* d'enfant; *(house, car, train)* miniature **3** *vi* **to t. with an idea** caresser une idée ■ **toy shop** *n* magasin *m* de jouets

trace [treɪs] **1** *n* trace *f*; **without t.** sans laisser de traces; *Chem* **t. element** oligoélément *m* **2** *vt (diagram, picture)* tracer; *(person)* retrouver la trace de; *(history)* retracer; **to t. sth back to...** faire remonter qch à... ■ **tracing** *n (drawing)* calque *m*; **t. paper** papier-calque *m*

track [træk] **1** *n (mark)* trace *f*; *(trail)* piste *f*; *(path)* chemin *m*, piste; *(for trains)* voie *f*; *(of rocket)* trajectoire *f*; *(of record)* morceau *m*; *Am Sch* classe *f* (de niveau); *Am (racetrack)* champ *m* de courses; **to keep t. of sth** surveiller qch; **to lose t. of** *(friend)* perdre de vue; *(argument)* perdre le fil de; **to be on the right t.** être sur la bonne voie; **off the beaten t.** *(remote)* loin des sentiers battus; *Fam* **to make tracks** filer; *Sport* **t. event** épreuve *f* sur piste; *Fig* **t. record** passé *m* **2** *vt* **to t. (down)** *(find)* retrouver ■ **tracker dog** *n* chien *m* policier ■ **tracking shot** *n Cin* **to do a t.** faire un travelling ■ **track shoes** *npl Am* chaussures *fpl* d'athlétisme ■ **tracksuit** *n* survêtement *m*

tract [trækt] *n (stretch of land)* étendue *f*

traction ['trækʃən] *n Tech* traction *f*

tractor ['træktə(r)] *n* tracteur *m*

trade [treɪd] **1** *n* commerce *m*; *(job)* métier *m*; *(exchange)* échange *m* **2** *adj (fair, balance, route)* commercial; *(price)* de (demi-)gros; *(secret)* de fabrication; *(barrier)* douanier, -ière; *Br* **t. union** syndicat *m*; *Br* **t. unionist** syndicaliste *mf* **3** *vt (exchange)* échanger (**for** contre); **to t. sth in** *(old article)* faire reprendre qch **4** *vi* faire du commerce (**with** avec); **to t. in** *(sugar)* faire le commerce de ■ **trade-in** *n Com* reprise *f* ■ **trademark** *n* marque *f* de fabrique ■ **trade-off** *n (compromise)* compromis *m* ■ **trader** *n Br (shopkeeper)* commerçant, -ante *mf*; *(on Stock Exchange)* opérateur, -trice *mf*; *Br* **street t.** vendeur, -euse *mf* de rue ■ **tradesman** *(pl* **-men)** *n Br* commerçant *m*

trading ['treɪdɪŋ] **1** *n* commerce *m* **2** *adj (port, debts, activity)* commercial; *(nation)* commerçant; *Br* **t. estate** zone *f* industrielle

tradition [trə'dɪʃən] n tradition f ■ **traditional** adj traditionnel, -elle ■ **traditionalist** n traditionaliste mf ■ **traditionally** adv traditionnellement

traffic ['træfɪk] 1 n (a) (on road) circulation f; (air, sea, rail) trafic m; Am **t. circle** rond-point m; Br **t. cone** cône m de signalisation; **t. island** refuge m (pour piétons); **t. jam** embouteillage m; **t. lights** feux mpl (de signalisation); **t. warden** contractuel, -uelle mf (b) Pej (trade) trafic m (**in** de); **drug t.** trafic m de la drogue 2 (pt & pp **-ck-**) vi trafiquer (**in** de) ■ **trafficker** n Pej trafiquant, -ante mf

tragedy ['trædʒədɪ] (pl **-ies**) n tragédie f ■ **tragic** adj tragique ■ **tragically** adv tragiquement

trail [treɪl] 1 n (of smoke, blood, powder) traînée f; (path) piste f, sentier m; **in its t.** (wake) dans son sillage 2 vt (drag) traîner; (caravan) tracter; (follow) suivre 3 vi (drag) traîner; (of plant) ramper; (move slowly) se traîner; Sport **to be trailing (behind)** être mené ■ **trailer** n (a) (for car) remorque f; Am (caravan) caravane f; Am (camper) camping-car m (b) (advertisement for film) bande f annonce

train [treɪn] 1 n (a) (engine, transport) train m; (underground) rame f; **t. set** (toy) petit train m (b) (procession) file f; (of events) suite f; (of dress) traîne f; **my t. of thought** le fil de ma pensée 2 vt (person) former (**to do** à faire); Sport entraîner; (animal) dresser (**to do** à faire); (ear) exercer; **to t. oneself to do sth** s'entraîner à faire qch; **to t. sth on sb/sth** braquer qch sur qn/qch 3 vi Sport s'entraîner; **to t. as a nurse** faire une formation d'infirmière ■ **trained** adj (skilled) qualifié; (nurse, engineer) diplômé; (animal) dressé; (ear) exercé ■ **training** n formation f; Sport entraînement m; (of animal) dressage m; Sport **to be in t.** s'entraîner

trainee [treɪ'niː] n & adj stagiaire (mf)

trainer ['treɪnə(r)] n (of athlete, racehorse) entraîneur m; (of animals) dresseur m; Br **trainers** (shoes) chaussures fpl de sport

traipse [treɪps] vi Fam **to t. around** (tiredly) traîner les pieds; (wander) se balader; **to t. in** se pointer, se ramener

trait [treɪt] n trait m (de caractère)

traitor ['treɪtə(r)] n traître m, traîtresse f

trajectory [trə'dʒektərɪ] (pl **-ies**) n trajectoire f

tram [træm] n tram(way) m

tramp [træmp] 1 n Br (vagrant) clochard, -arde mf; Fam Pej (woman) traînée f; (sound) pas mpl lourds 2 vt (country) parcourir 3 vi marcher d'un pas lourd

trample ['træmpəl] vti **to t. sth (underfoot), to t. on sth** piétiner qch

trampoline [træmpə'liːn] n trampoline m

trance [trɑːns] n **to be in a t.** être en transe; **to go into a t.** entrer en transe

tranquil ['træŋkwɪl] adj tranquille ■ **tranquillity** (Am **tran'quility**) n tranquillité f ■ **tranquillizer** (Am **tranquilizer**) n tranquillisant m

transaction [træn'zækʃən] n opération f, transaction f

transatlantic [trænzət'læntɪk] adj transatlantique

transcend [træn'send] vt transcender ■ **transcen'dental** adj transcendantal

transcribe [træn'skraɪb] vt transcrire ■ **'transcript** n transcription f ■ **tran'scription** n transcription f

transept ['trænsept] n transept m

transfer 1 [træns'fɜː(r)] n transfert m (**to** à); (of political power) passation f; Br (picture, design) décalcomanie f; **credit t.** virement m bancaire 2 (pt & pp **-rr-**) vt transférer (**to** à); (political power) faire passer (**to** à); Br **to t. the charges** téléphoner en PCV 3 vi être transféré (**to** à) ■ **trans'ferable** adj 'not t.' (on ticket) 'titre de transport nominal'

transform [træns'fɔːm] vt transformer (**into** en) ■ **transformation** [-fə'meɪʃən] n transformation f ■ **transformer** n El transformateur m

transfusion [træns'fjuːʒən] n (blood) t. transfusion f (sanguine)

transgenic [trænz'dʒenɪk] adj transgénique

transgress [trænz'gres] vt Formal (law) transgresser ■ **transgression** n transgression f

transient ['trænzɪənt] adj éphémère

transistor [træn'zɪstə(r)] n (device) transistor m; **t. (radio)** transistor

transit ['trænzɪt] n transit m; **in t.** en transit; Br **t. lounge** (in airport) salle f de transit

transition [træn'zɪʃən] n transition f ■ **transitional** adj de transition

transitive ['trænsɪtɪv] adj Grammar transitif

transitory ['trænzɪtərɪ] adj transitoire

translate [træns'leɪt] vt traduire (**from** de; **into** en) ■ **translation** n traduction f ■ **translator** n traducteur, -trice mf

transmit [trænz'mɪt] 1 (pt & pp **-tt-**) vt transmettre 2 vti (broadcast) émettre ■ **transmission** n transmission f; (broadcast) émission f ■ **transmitter** n Radio & TV émetteur m

transparent [træn'spærənt] adj transparent ■ **transparency** n transparence f; Br (photographic slide) diapositive f

transpire [træn'spaɪə(r)] vi (of secret) s'ébruiter; Fam (happen) arriver; **it transpired that...** il s'est avéré que...

> Note that the French word **transpirer** is a false friend. Its most common meaning is **to sweat**.

transplant 1 ['trænsplɑːnt] n (surgical) greffe f, transplantation f 2 [træns'plɑːnt] vt transplanter

transport 1 ['trænspɔːt] n transport m (**of** de); **do you have t.?** es-tu motorisé?; Br **t. café** routier m (restaurant) **2** [træn'spɔːt] vt transporter ■ **transpor'tation** n transport m

transpose [træn'spəʊz] vt transposer ■ **transposition** [-pə'zɪʃən] n transposition f

transsexual [træn(z)'seksjʊəl] adj & n transsexuel, -uelle (mf)

transvestite [trænz'vestaɪt] n travesti m

trap [træp] **1** n piège m; Fam (mouth) gueule f **2** (pt & pp **-pp-**) vt prendre au piège; **to t. one's finger** se coincer le doigt (**in** dans); **to t. sb into doing sth** faire faire qch à qn en usant de ruse ■ **trapdoor** n trappe f ■ **trapper** n (hunter) trappeur m

trapeze [trə'piːz] n trapèze m; **t. artist** trapéziste mf

trappings ['træpɪŋz] npl signes mpl extérieurs

trash [træʃ] n (nonsense) bêtises fpl; (junk) bric-à-brac m inv; Am (waste) ordures fpl; Am (riffraff) racaille f ■ **trash can** n Am poubelle f ■ **trashy** (**-ier, -iest**) adj Fam de pacotille; (magazine, novel) de bas étage

trauma ['trɔːmə, 'traʊmə] n traumatisme m ■ **traumatic** [-'mætɪk] adj traumatisant ■ **traumatize** vt traumatiser

travel ['trævəl] **1** n voyage m; **on my travels** au cours de mes voyages; **t. agency/agent** agence f/agent m de voyages; **t. book** récit m de voyages; **t. documents** titre m de transport; **t. insurance** assurance f voyage; **t. sickness** (in car) mal m de la route; (in aircraft) mal de l'air **2** (Br **-ll-**, Am **-l-**) vt (country, distance, road) parcourir **3** vi (of person) voyager; (of vehicle, light, sound) se déplacer ■ **travelled** (Am **traveled**) adj **to be well** or **widely t.** avoir beaucoup voyagé ■ **traveller** (Am **traveler**) n voyageur, -euse mf; Br **t.'s cheque**, Am **t.'s check** chèque m de voyage ■ **travelling** (Am **traveling**) n voyages mpl **2** adj (bag, clothes) de voyage; (expenses) de déplacement; (musician, circus) ambulant

travelogue ['trævəlɒg] (Am **travelog**) n (book) récit m de voyage

travesty ['trævəstɪ] (pl **-ies**) n parodie f; **a t. of justice** un simulacre de justice

trawler ['trɔːlə(r)] n (ship) chalutier m

tray [treɪ] n plateau m; (in office) corbeille f; **baking t.** plaque f de four

treacherous ['tretʃərəs] adj (road, conditions) très dangereux, -euse; (journey) parsemé d'embûches; (person, action) traître ■ **treacherously** adv (act) traîtreusement; (dangerously) dangereusement ■ **treachery** (pl **-ies**) n traîtrise f

treacle ['triːkəl] n Br mélasse f

tread [tred] **1** n (footstep) pas m; (step of stairs) marche f; (of tyre) chape f **2** (pt **trod**, pp **trodden**) vt marcher sur; **to t. sth into a**

carpet étaler qch sur un tapis (avec ses chaussures); **to t. sth underfoot** fouler qch au pied **3** vi (walk) marcher (**on** sur)

treadmill ['tredmɪl] n tapis m roulant de jogging; Pej & Fig routine f

treason ['triːzən] n trahison f

treasure ['treʒə(r)] **1** n trésor m; **t. hunt** chasse f au trésor **2** vt (value) tenir beaucoup à ■ **treasurer** n trésorier, -ière mf ■ **Treasury** n Br Pol **the T.** ≃ le ministère des Finances

treat [triːt] **1** n (pleasure) plaisir m; (gift) cadeau m; **to give sb a t.** faire plaisir à qn; **it's my t.** c'est moi qui régale; Fam **to work a t.** marcher à merveille **2** vt (person, illness, product) traiter; **to t. sb/sth with care** prendre soin de qn/qch; **to t. sb like a child** traiter qn comme un enfant; **to t. sb to sth** offrir qch à qn

treatise ['triːtɪz] n traité m (**on** de)

treatment ['triːtmənt] n traitement m; **his t. of her** la façon dont il la traite/traitait

treaty ['triːtɪ] (pl **-ies**) n (international) traité m

treble ['trebəl] **1** adj triple; Mus **t. clef** clef f de sol; Mus **t. voice** voix f de soprano **2** n le triple; **it's t. the price** c'est le triple du prix **3** vti tripler

tree [triː] n arbre m; **t.-lined** adj bordé d'arbres ■ **treetop** n cime f (d'un arbre) ■ **tree trunk** n tronc m d'arbre

trek [trek] **1** n (long walk) randonnée f; Fig **it's quite a t. to the shops** ça fait loin à pied jusqu'aux magasins **2** (pt & pp **-kk-**) vi faire de la randonnée; Fig **to t. to the shops** se taper le chemin à pied jusqu'aux magasins

trellis ['trelɪs] n treillage m, treillis m

tremble ['trembəl] vi trembler (**with** de) ■ **tremor** n tremblement m

tremendous [trə'mendəs] adj (huge) énorme; (excellent) formidable ■ **tremendously** adv (very) extrêmement

trench [trentʃ] n Mil tranchée f ■ **trench coat** n trench-coat m

trend [trend] n tendance f (**towards** à); (fashion) mode f; **to set a** or **the t.** lancer une mode ■ **trendy** (**-ier, -iest**) adj Fam branché

trepidation [trepɪ'deɪʃən] n Formal inquiétude f

trespass ['trespəs] vi s'introduire illégalement dans une propriété privée; '**no trespassing**' 'entrée interdite'

> Note that the French verb **trépasser** is a false friend and is never a translation for the English verb **to trespass**. It means **to die**.

tresses ['tresɪz] npl Literary chevelure f

trestle ['tresəl] n tréteau m

trial ['traɪəl] **1** n Law procès m; (test) essai m; (ordeal) épreuve f; **to go** or **be on t.**, **to stand t.** passer en jugement; **to put sb on t.** juger qn; **to be on t.** (of product) être à l'essai; **by t.**

and error par tâtonnements **2** *adj (period, flight, offer)* d'essai; **t. run** essai *m*

triangle ['traɪæŋgəl] *n* triangle *m*; *Am (set-square)* équerre *f* ▪ **triangular** [-'æŋgjʊlə(r)] *adj* triangulaire

tribe [traɪb] *n* tribu *f* ▪ **tribal** *adj* tribal

tribulations [trɪbjʊ'leɪʃənz] *npl* **trials and t.** tribulations *fpl*

tribunal [traɪ'bjuːnəl] *n* tribunal *m*

tributary [*Br* 'trɪbjʊtərɪ, *Am* -erɪ] (*pl* **-ies**) *n* affluent *m*

tribute ['trɪbjuːt] *n* hommage *m*; **to pay t. to** rendre hommage à

trick [trɪk] **1** *n (joke, deception, of conjurer)* tour *m*; *(clever method)* astuce *f*; *(in card game)* pli *m*; **card t.** tour de cartes; **the tricks of the trade** les ficelles *fpl* du métier; **to play a t. on sb** jouer un tour à qn; *Fam* **to do the t.** marcher; **t. photo** photo *f* truquée; **t. question** question *f* piège **2** *vt (deceive)* duper; **to t. sb into doing sth** amener qn à faire qch par la ruse ▪ **trickery** *n* ruse *f*

trickle ['trɪkəl] **1** *n (of liquid)* filet *m*; *Fig* **a t. of** *(letters, people)* un petit nombre de **2** *vi (of liquid)* couler goutte à goutte; *Fig* **to t. in** *(of letters, people)* arriver en petit nombre

tricky ['trɪkɪ] (**-ier, -iest**) *adj (problem)* délicat

tricycle ['traɪsɪkəl] *n* tricycle *m*

trier ['traɪə(r)] *n Fam* **to be a t.** être persévérant

trifle ['traɪfəl] **1** *n (insignificant thing)* bagatelle *f*; *Br (dessert)* = dessert où alternent génoise, fruits en gelée et crème anglaise **2** *adv* **a t. wide** un tantinet trop large **3** *vi* **to t. with** plaisanter avec ▪ **trifling** *adj* insignifiant

trigger ['trɪgə(r)] **1** *n (of gun)* détente *f* **2** *vt* **to t. sth (off)** déclencher qch ▪ **trigger-happy** *adj (person)* qui a la gâchette facile

trilby ['trɪlbɪ] *n Br* **t. (hat)** chapeau *m* en feutre

trilingual [traɪ'lɪŋgwəl] *adj* trilingue

trilogy ['trɪlədʒɪ] (*pl* **-ies**) *n* trilogie *f*

trim [trɪm] **1** (**trimmer, trimmest**) *adj (neat)* soigné; *(slim)* svelte **2** *n* **to give sb's hair a t.** faire une coupe d'entretien à qn; **to keep in t.** garder la forme **3** *(pt & pp* **-mm-**) *vt* couper (un peu); **to t. sth with** orner qch de qch ▪ **trimmings** *npl (on clothes)* garniture *f*; *(of meal)* accompagnements *mpl* traditionnels

Trinity ['trɪnɪtɪ] *n Rel* **the T.** la Trinité

trinket ['trɪŋkɪt] *n* babiole *f*

trio ['triːəʊ] (*pl* **-os**) *n* trio *m*

trip [trɪp] **1** *n (journey)* voyage *m*; *(outing)* excursion *f*; *(stumble)* faux pas *m*; **to take a t. to the shops** aller dans les magasins *(pt & pp* **-pp-**) *vt* **to t. sb up** faire trébucher qn **3** *vi (walk gently)* marcher d'un pas léger; **to t. (over** *or* **up)** trébucher; **to t. over sth** trébucher sur qch

tripe [traɪp] *n (food)* tripes *fpl*; *Fam (nonsense)* bêtises *fpl*

triple ['trɪpəl] **1** *adj* triple **2** *vti* tripler ▪ **triplets** *npl (children)* triplés, -ées *mfpl*

triplicate ['trɪplɪkət] *n* **in t.** en trois exemplaires

tripod ['traɪpɒd] *n* trépied *m*

tripper ['trɪpə(r)] *n Br* **day t.** excursionniste *mf*

trite [traɪt] *adj* banal (*mpl* -als) ▪ **triteness** *n* banalité *f*

triumph ['traɪəmf] **1** *n* triomphe *m* (**over** sur) **2** *vi* triompher (**over** de) ▪ **triumphal** [traɪ'ʌmfəl] *adj* triomphal ▪ **triumphant** [traɪ'ʌmfənt] *adj* triomphant; *(success, welcome, return)* triomphal ▪ **triumphantly** [traɪ'ʌmfəntlɪ] *adv* triomphalement

trivia ['trɪvɪə] *npl* vétilles *fpl* ▪ **trivial** *adj (unimportant)* insignifiant; *(trite)* banal (*mpl* -als) ▪ **triviality** [-vɪ'ælɪtɪ] *n* insignifiance *f*; *(triteness)* banalité *f* ▪ **trivialize** *vt* banaliser

> Note that the French word **trivial** is a false friend. It means **vulgar**.

trod [trɒd] *pt of* **tread**

trodden ['trɒdən] *pp of* **tread**

trolley ['trɒlɪ] (*pl* **-eys**) *n Br* chariot *m*; *Br* **(tea) t.** table *f* roulante; *Am* **t. (car)** tramway *m* ▪ **trolleybus** *n Am* trolley *m*

trombone [trɒm'bəʊn] *n* trombone *m*

troop [truːp] **1** *n* bande *f*; *(of soldiers)* troupe *f*; **the troops** *(soldiers)* les troupes *fpl* **2** *vi* **to t. in/out** entrer/sortir en groupe ▪ **trooper** *n Am (state)* **t.** membre *m* de la police montée ▪ **trooping** *n Br* **t. the colour** salut *m* au drapeau

trophy ['trəʊfɪ] (*pl* **-ies**) *n* trophée *m*

tropic ['trɒpɪk] *n* tropique *m*; **in the tropics** sous les tropiques ▪ **tropical** *adj* tropical

trot [trɒt] **1** *n* trot *m*; *Fam* **on the t.** *(consecutively)* de suite **2** *(pt & pp* **-tt-**) *vt Fam* **to t. sth out** débiter qch **3** *vi* trotter; *Br Fam Hum* **to t. off** *or* **along** *(leave)* se sauver

trouble ['trʌbəl] **1** *n (difficulty)* ennui *m*; *(inconvenience)* problème *m*; *(social unrest, illness)* trouble *m*; **to be in t.** avoir des ennuis; **to get into t.** s'attirer des ennuis; **to have t. with sb/sth** avoir des problèmes avec qn/qch; **to have t. doing sth** avoir du mal à faire qch; **to go to the t. of doing sth** se donner la peine de faire qch; **the t. with you is...** l'ennui avec toi, c'est que...; **it's no t.** pas de problème; *Br* **a spot of t.** un petit problème; **t. spot** point *m* chaud **2** *vt (inconvenience)* déranger; *(worry)* inquiéter; **to t. to do sth** se donner la peine de faire qch; **to t. oneself** se déranger ▪ **troubled** *adj (person)* inquiet, -iète; *(period, region)* agité ▪ **'trouble-'free** *adj* sans souci ▪ **trouble-some** *adj* pénible

troublemaker ['trʌbəlmeɪkə(r)] *n (in school)* élément *m* perturbateur; *(political)* fauteur *m* de troubles

troubleshooter ['trʌbəlʃuːtə(r)] *n Tech* dépanneur *m*; *Pol* conciliateur, -trice *mf*; *(for firm)* expert *m*

trough [trɒf] *n (for drinking)* abreuvoir *m*; *(for feeding)* auge *f*; **t. of low pressure** *(in weather front)* dépression *f*

trounce [traʊns] *vt (defeat)* écraser

troupe [truːp] *n (of actors)* troupe *f*

trousers ['traʊzəz] *npl Br* pantalon *m*; **a pair of t.**, **some t.** un pantalon; **short t.** culottes *fpl* courtes ▪ **trouser suit** *n Br* tailleur-pantalon *m*

trousseau ['truːsəʊ] *(pl -eaux or -eaus* [-əʊz]*) m* trousseau *m*

trout [traʊt] *n inv* truite *f*

trowel ['traʊəl] *n (for cement or plaster)* truelle *f*; *(for plants)* déplantoir *m*

truant ['truːənt] *n (pupil)* élève *mf* qui fait l'école buissonnière; **to play t.** faire l'école buissonnière ▪ **truancy** *n* absentéisme *m* scolaire

> Note that the French word **truand** is a false friend. It means **crook**.

truce [truːs] *n Mil* trêve *f*

truck [trʌk] *n (lorry)* camion *m*; *Br Rail* wagon *m*; **t. driver** camionneur *m*; *Am* **t. farmer** maraîcher, -ère *mf*; *Am* **t. stop** *(restaurant)* routier *m* ▪ **trucker** *n Am* camionneur *m*

truculent ['trʌkjʊlənt] *adj* agressif, -ive

> Note that the French word **truculent** is a false friend. It means **colourful** or **vivid**.

trudge [trʌdʒ] *vi* marcher péniblement

true [truː] **(-er, -est)** *adj* vrai; *(genuine)* véritable; *(accurate)* exact; *(faithful)* fidèle **(to** à); **t. to life** conforme à la réalité; **to come t.** se réaliser; **to hold t.** être vrai **(for** de); *Fam* **too t.!** ah, ça oui!; **t. love** grand amour *m* ▪ **truly** *adv* vraiment; **well and t.** bel et bien; **yours t.** *(in letter)* je vous prie, Madame/Monsieur, d'agréer l'expression de mes sentiments distingués; *Fam Hum* mézigue *m*

truffle ['trʌfəl] *n* truffe *f*

truism ['truːɪzəm] *n* truisme *m*

trump [trʌmp] **1** *n Cards & Fig* atout *m*; **spades are trumps** atout pique **2** *vt* **to t. sth up** inventer qch de toutes pièces

trumpet ['trʌmpɪt] *n* trompette *f*; **t. player** trompettiste *m*

truncate [trʌŋ'keɪt] *vt* tronquer

truncheon ['trʌntʃən] *n Br* matraque *f*

trundle ['trʌndəl] *vti* **to t. along** rouler bruyamment

trunk [trʌŋk] *n (of tree, body)* tronc *m*; *(of elephant)* trompe *f*; *(case)* malle *f*; *Am (of vehicle)* coffre *m*; **trunks** *(for swimming)* slip *m* de bain; *Br* **t. road** route *f* nationale

truss [trʌs] **1** *n (belt, bandage)* bandage *m* herniaire **2** *vt* **to t. sb (up)** ligoter qn

trust [trʌst] **1** *n (faith)* confiance *f* **(in** en); *Fin* trust *m*; *Law* fidéicommis *m*; **to take sth on t.**

accepter qch de confiance **2** *vt (believe in)* faire confiance à; **to t. sb with sth, to t. sth to sb** confier qch à qn; **to t. sb to do sth** laisser à qn le soin de faire qch; **I t. that...** j'espère que...; *Fam* **t. him to say that!** c'est bien de lui! **3** *vi* **to t. in sb** faire confiance à qn; **to t. to luck** s'en remettre au hasard ▪ **trusted** *adj (method)* éprouvé; **he is a t. friend** c'est un ami en qui j'ai une confiance totale ▪ **trusting** *adj* qui fait confiance aux gens

trustee [trʌs'tiː] *n (of school, charity)* administrateur, -trice *mf*; *Law* fidéicommissaire *m*

trustworthy ['trʌstwɜːðɪ] *adj* digne de confiance

truth [truːθ] *(pl -s* [truːðz]*) n* vérité *f*; **to tell the t.** dire la vérité; **there's some t. in...** il y a du vrai dans... ▪ **truthful** *adj (story)* véridique; *(person)* sincère ▪ **truthfully** *adv* sincèrement

try [traɪ] **1** *(pl -ies) n (attempt) & Rugby* essai *m*; **to have a t. at sth/doing sth** essayer qch/de faire qch; **at (the) first t.** du premier coup; **it's worth a t.** ça vaut la peine d'essayer **2** *(pt & pp -ied) vt (attempt, sample)* essayer; *(food, drink)* goûter à; *Law (person)* juger **(for** pour); **to t. doing** *or* **to do sth** essayer de faire qch; **to t. one's hand at sth** s'essayer à; **to t. sb's patience** mettre à l'épreuve la patience de qn **3** *vi* essayer; **to t. hard** faire un gros effort; **t. and come!** essaie de venir! ▪ **trying** *adj* difficile

▸ **try on** *vt sep (clothes, shoes)* essayer

▸ **try out** *vt sep (car, method, recipe)* essayer; *(person)* mettre à l'essai

tsar [zɑː(r)] *n* tsar *m*

T-shirt ['tiːʃɜːt] *n* tee-shirt *m*

tub [tʌb] *n (basin)* baquet *m*; *esp Am (bath)* baignoire *f*; *Br (for ice cream)* pot *m*; *Br (for flower, bush)* bac *m*

tuba ['tjuːbə] *n* tuba *m*

tubby ['tʌbɪ] *(-ier, -iest) adj Fam* grassouillet, -ette

tube [tjuːb] *n* tube *m*; *(of tyre)* chambre *f* à air; *Br Fam* **the t.** *(underground railway)* le métro; **to go down the tubes** *(of money)* être foutu en l'air ▪ **tubing** *n* tuyaux *mpl* ▪ **tubular** *adj* tubulaire

tuberculosis [tjuːbɜːkjʊ'ləʊsɪs] *n Med* tuberculose *f*

TUC [tiːjuː'siː] *(abbr* **Trades Union Congress)** *n Br* = confédération des syndicats britanniques

tuck [tʌk] **1** *n (in garment)* pli *m*; *Br* **t. shop** *(in school)* boutique *f* de friandises **2** *vt (put)* mettre; **to t. sth away** *(put)* ranger qch; *(hide)* cacher qch; **to t. in** *(shirt, blanket)* rentrer; *(child)* border; **to t. one's sleeves up** remonter ses manches **3** *vi Br Fam* **to t. in** *(start eating)* attaquer; **to t. into a meal** attaquer un repas

Tuesday ['tjuːzdeɪ] *n* mardi *m*

tuft [tʌft] *n* touffe *f*

tug [tʌg] **1** *n* **to give sth a t.** tirer sur qch **2** *(pt & pp -gg-) vt (pull)* tirer sur **3** *vi* tirer **(at** *or* **on** sur) ▪ **tug(boat)** *n* remorqueur *m*

tuition [tjuːˈɪʃən] n *(lessons)* cours mpl; *(fee)* frais mpl de scolarité

tulip [ˈtjuːlɪp] n tulipe f

tumble [ˈtʌmbəl] 1 n *(fall)* chute f; **to take a t.** faire une chute; *Fig (of prices)* chuter 2 vi *(of person)* faire une chute; *Fig (of prices)* chuter; **to t. down** s'écrouler ▪ **tumble-dry** vt *Br (clothes)* faire sécher au sèche-linge ▪ **tumble-'dryer, tumble-'drier** n *Br* sèche-linge m inv

tumbledown [ˈtʌmbldaʊn] adj délabré

tumbler [ˈtʌmblə(r)] n verre m droit

tummy [ˈtʌmɪ] n *Fam* ventre m; **to have a t. ache** avoir mal au ventre

tumour [ˈtjuːmə(r)] *(Am tumor)* n tumeur f

tumult [ˈtjuːmʌlt] n tumulte m ▪ **tumultuous** [-ˈmʌltjʊəs] adj tumultueux, -ueuse

tuna [ˈtjuːnə] n **t. (fish)** thon m

tune [tjuːn] 1 n *(melody)* air m; **in t.** *(instrument)* accordé; **out of t.** *(instrument)* désaccordé; **to be or sing in t./out of t.** chanter juste/faux; *Fig* **to be in t. with sb/sth** être en harmonie avec qn/qch; **to the t. of £50** d'un montant de 50 livres 2 vt **to t. (up)** *(instrument)* accorder; *(engine)* régler 3 vi **to t. in** brancher son poste (**to** sur) ▪ **tuning** n *(of engine)* réglage m; *Mus* **t. fork** diapason m

tuneful [ˈtjuːnfəl] adj mélodieux, -ieuse

tuner [ˈtjuːnə(r)] n *(on TV, radio)* tuner m

tunic [ˈtjuːnɪk] n tunique f

Tunisia [tjuːˈnɪzɪə] n la Tunisie ▪ **Tunisian** 1 adj tunisien, -ienne 2 n Tunisien, -ienne mf

tunnel [ˈtʌnəl] 1 n tunnel m; *(in mine)* galerie f 2 *(Br -ll-, Am -l-)* vi creuser un tunnel (**into** dans)

turban [ˈtɜːbən] n turban m

turbine [*Br* ˈtɜːbaɪn, *Am* ˈtɜːrbɪn] n turbine f

turbulence [ˈtɜːbjʊləns] n *(of crowd)* agitation f; *(when flying)* turbulence f ▪ **turbulent** adj *(crowd)* agité; *(flight)* turbulent

tureen [*Br* tjʊˈriːn, *Am* təˈriːn] n *(soup)* **t.** soupière f

turf [tɜːf] 1 n *(grass)* gazon m; **the t.** *(horseracing)* le turf; *Br* **t. accountant** bookmaker m 2 vt *Br Fam* **to t. sb out** *(get rid of)* jeter qn dehors

turgid [ˈtɜːdʒɪd] adj *(style)* ampoulé

Turkey [ˈtɜːkɪ] n la Turquie ▪ **Turk** n Turc m, Turque f ▪ **Turkish** 1 adj turc (f turque); **T. bath/coffee** bain m/café m turc; **T. delight** loukoum m 2 n *(language)* turc m

turkey [ˈtɜːkɪ] n *(pl -eys)* *(bird)* dinde f

turmoil [ˈtɜːmɔɪl] n *(of person)* émoi m; *(of country)* agitation f; **to be in t.** *(of person)* être dans tous ses états; *(of country)* être en ébullition

turn [tɜːn] 1 n *(of wheel, in game, queue)* tour m; *(in road)* tournant m; *(of events, mind)* tournure f; *(performance)* numéro m; *Br Fam (fit)* crise f; **to take turns** se relayer; **to take it in turns to do sth** se relayer pour faire qch; **in t.** à tour de rôle; **in one's t.** à son tour; **by turns** tour à tour; **it's**

your t. (to play) c'est à toi (de jouer); **to do sb a good t.** rendre service à qn; **the t. of the century** le tournant du siècle; **t. of phrase** tournure de phrase

2 vt tourner; *(mechanically)* faire tourner; *(mattress, pancake)* retourner; **to t. sb/sth into sb/sth** changer qn/qch en qn/qch; **to t. sth red/black** rougir/noircir qch; **to t. sth on sb** *(aim)* braquer qch sur qn; **she has turned twenty** elle a vingt ans passés; **it has turned seven** il est sept heures passées; **it turns my stomach** cela me soulève le cœur

3 vi *(of wheel, driver)* tourner; *(of person)* se retourner; **to t. red/black** rougir/noircir; **to t. nasty** *(of person)* devenir méchant; *(of situation)* mal tourner; **to t. to sb** se tourner vers qn; **to t. into sb/sth** devenir qn/qch; **to t. against sb** se retourner contre qn ▪ **turn-off** n *(on road)* sortie f; *Fam* **to be a t.** être rébarbatif, -ive; *(sexually)* couper l'envie ▪ **turn-on** n *Fam* **it's a real t.** *(sexually)* c'est excitant ▪ **turnout** n *(people)* assistance f; *(at polls)* participation f ▪ **turnover** n *Com (sales)* chiffre m d'affaires; *(of stock)* rotation f; *(of staff)* renouvellement m; *Br* **apple t.** chausson m aux pommes ▪ **turn-up** n *Br (on trousers)* revers m

▸ **turn around** vi *(of person)* se retourner; *(in vehicle)* faire demi-tour

▸ **turn away** 1 vt sep *(eyes)* détourner (**from** de); *(person)* refuser 2 vi se détourner

▸ **turn back** 1 vt sep *(sheets)* rabattre; *(person)* refouler; *(clock)* retarder 2 vi *(return)* faire demi-tour

▸ **turn down** vt sep *(gas, radio)* baisser; *(fold down)* rabattre; *(refuse)* rejeter

▸ **turn in** 1 vt sep *(lost property)* rapporter à la police; *(person)* livrer à la police 2 vi *Fam (go to bed)* aller au pieu

▸ **turn off** 1 vt sep *(light, radio)* éteindre; *(tap)* fermer; *(machine)* arrêter; *Fam* **to t. sb off** dégoûter qn 2 vi *(leave road)* sortir

▸ **turn on** 1 vt sep *(light, radio)* allumer; *(tap)* ouvrir; *(machine)* mettre en marche; *Fam* **to t. sb on** *(sexually)* exciter qn 2 vi **to t. on sb** *(attack)* attaquer qn

▸ **turn out** 1 vt sep *(light)* éteindre; *(pocket, box)* vider; *(produce)* produire 2 vi *(go out)* se déplacer; **it turns out that...** il s'avère que...; **she turned out to be...** elle s'est révélée être...

▸ **turn over** 1 vt sep *(page)* tourner 2 vi *(of vehicle, person)* se retourner; *(of car)* faire un tonneau

▸ **turn round** 1 vt sep *(head)* tourner; *(object)* retourner; *(situation)* renverser 2 vi *(of person)* se retourner; *(in vehicle)* faire demi-tour

▸ **turn up** 1 vt sep *(radio, heat)* mettre plus fort; *(collar)* remonter 2 vi *(arrive)* arriver; *(be found)* être retrouvé

turncoat [ˈtɜːnkəʊt] n renégat, -ate mf

turning ['tɜːnɪŋ] *n Br (street)* petite rue *f*; *(bend in road)* tournant *m*; *Br Aut* **t. circle** rayon *m* de braquage; *Fig* **t. point** tournant *m*

turnip ['tɜːnɪp] *n* navet *m*

turnpike ['tɜːnpaɪk] *n Am* autoroute *f* à péage

turnstile ['tɜːnstaɪl] *n* tourniquet *m*

turntable ['tɜːnteɪbəl] *n* platine *f*

turpentine ['tɜːpəntaɪn] *n* térébenthine *f* ▪ **turps** *n Br Fam* térébenthine *f*

turquoise ['tɜːkwɔɪz] *adj* turquoise *inv*

turret ['tʌrɪt] *n* tourelle *f*

turtle ['tɜːtəl] *n Br* tortue *f* de mer; *Am* tortue *f* ▪ **turtle dove** *n* tourterelle *f* ▪ **turtleneck 1** *adj (sweater)* à col montant **2** *n* col *m* montant

tusk [tʌsk] *n* défense *f*

tussle ['tʌsəl] *n* bagarre *f*

tutor ['tjuːtə(r)] **1** *n* professeur *m* particulier; *(in British university)* directeur, -trice *mf* d'études; *(in American university)* assistant, -ante *mf* **2** *vt* donner des cours particuliers à ▪ **tutorial** [-'tɔːrɪəl] *n Univ* ≃ travaux *mpl* dirigés

tuxedo [tʌk'siːdəʊ] *(pl -os) n Am* smoking *m*

TV [tiː'viː] *n* télé *f*; **on TV** à la télé

twaddle ['twɒdəl] *n Fam* fadaises *fpl*

twang [twæŋ] **1** *n (sound)* vibration *f*; *(nasal voice)* ton *m* nasillard **2** *vi (of wire)* vibrer

twee [twiː] *adj Br Fam Pej* cucul (la praline) *inv*

tweed [twiːd] *n* tweed *m*; **t. jacket** veste *f* en tweed

tweezers ['twiːzəz] *npl* pince *f* à épiler

twelve [twelv] *adj & n* douze (*m*) ▪ **twelfth** *adj & n* douzième (*mf*)

twenty ['twentɪ] *adj & n* vingt (*m*) ▪ **twentieth** *adj & n* vingtième (*mf*)

twerp [twɜːp] *n Br Fam* crétin, -ine *mf*

twice [twaɪs] *adv* deux fois; **t. as heavy (as…)** deux fois plus lourd (que…); **t. a month, t. monthly** deux fois par mois

twiddle ['twɪdəl] *vti* **to t. (with)** sth tripoter qch; **to t. one's thumbs** se tourner les pouces

twig[1] [twɪg] *n (of branch)* brindille *f*

twig[2] [twɪg] *(pt & pp -gg-) vti Br Fam* piger

twilight ['twaɪlaɪt] *n* crépuscule *m*

twin [twɪn] **1** *n* jumeau, jumelle *f*; **identical t.** vrai jumeau, vraie jumelle; **t. beds** lits *mpl* jumeaux; **t. brother** frère *m* jumeau; **t. sister** sœur *f* jumelle; *Br* **t. town** ville *f* jumelée **2** *(pt & pp -nn-) vt (town)* jumeler

twine [twaɪn] **1** *n (string)* ficelle *f* **2** *vi (twist)* s'enrouler (**round** autour de)

twinge [twɪndʒ] *n* **a t. (of pain)** un élancement; **a t. of remorse** un peu de remords

twinkle ['twɪŋkəl] **1** *n* scintillement *m*; *(in eye)* pétillement *m* **2** *vi (of star)* scintiller; *(of eye)* pétiller

twirl [twɜːl] **1** *vt* faire tournoyer; *(moustache)* tortiller **2** *vi* tournoyer

twist [twɪst] **1** *n (action)* tour *m*; *(bend)*

tortillement *m*; *(in road)* tournant *m*; *Fig (in story)* tour inattendu; **t. of lemon** rondelle *f* de citron; **twists and turns** *(of road)* tours et détours *mpl*; *(of events)* rebondissements *mpl* **2** *vt (wire, arm)* tordre; *(roll)* enrouler (**round** autour de); *(weave together)* entortiller; **to t. one's ankle** se tordre la cheville; *Fig* **to t. sb's arm** forcer la main à qn; **to t. sth off** *(lid)* dévisser qch **3** *vi (wind)* s'entortiller (**round sth** autour de qch); *(of road, river)* serpenter ▪ **twisted** *adj (person, mind, logic)* tordu ▪ **twister** *n Am (tornado)* tornade *f*

twit [twɪt] *n Br Fam* andouille *f*

twitch [twɪtʃ] **1** *n (jerk)* secousse *f*; *(nervous)* tic *m* **2** *vi (of person)* avoir un tic; *(of muscle)* se contracter nerveusement

twitter ['twɪtə(r)] **1** *n (of bird)* pépiement *m* **2** *vi* pépier

two [tuː] *adj & n* deux (*m*) ▪ **two-cycle** *adj Am (engine)* à deux temps ▪ **'two-di'mensional** *adj* à deux dimensions ▪ **'two-'faced** *adj Fig* hypocrite ▪ **'two-'legged** [-legɪd] *adj* bipède ▪ **two-piece** *adj (suit, swimsuit)* deux pièces ▪ **two-'seater** *n (car)* voiture *f* à deux places ▪ **two-way** *adj* **t. mirror** miroir *m* sans tain; **t. radio** émetteur-récepteur *m*; **t. traffic** circulation *f* dans les deux sens

twofold ['tuːfəʊld] **1** *adj* double **2** *adv* **to increase t.** doubler

twosome ['tuːsəm] *n* couple *m*

tycoon [taɪ'kuːn] *n* magnat *m*

type[1] [taɪp] *n* (**a**) *(sort)* genre *m*, type *m*; **blood t.** groupe *m* sanguin (**b**) *(print)* caractères *mpl*; **in large t.** en gros caractères ▪ **typeface** *n* police *f* de caractères ▪ **typeset** *(pt & pp -set, pres p -setting) vt* composer ▪ **typesetter** *n* compositeur, -trice *mf*

type[2] [taɪp] **1** *vti (write)* taper (à la machine) **2** *vt* **to t. sth in** *(on computer)* entrer qch au clavier; **to t. sth out** *(letter)* taper qch ▪ **typewriter** *n* machine *f* à écrire ▪ **typewritten** *adj* dactylographié ▪ **typing** *n* dactylographie *f*; **a page of t.** une page dactylographiée; **t. error** faute *f* de frappe ▪ **typist** *n* dactylo *f*

typhoid ['taɪfɔɪd] *n Med* **t. (fever)** typhoïde *f*

typhoon [taɪ'fuːn] *n* typhon *m*

typical ['tɪpɪkəl] *adj* typique (**of** de); **that's t. (of him)!** c'est bien lui! ▪ **typically** *adv* typiquement ▪ **typify** *(pt & pp -ied) vt* caractériser

typo ['taɪpəʊ] *(pl -os) n Fam (misprint)* coquille *f*

tyranny ['tɪrənɪ] *n* tyrannie *f* ▪ **tyrannical** [-'rænɪkəl] *adj* tyrannique ▪ **tyrant** ['taɪərənt] *n* tyran *m*

tyre ['taɪə(r)] *n Br* pneu *m*; **t. pressure** pression *f* des pneus

U, u [juː] *n (letter)* U, u *m inv*
ubiquitous [juːˈbɪkwɪtəs] *adj* omniprésent
udder [ˈʌdə(r)] *n* pis *m*
UFO [juːefˈəʊ, ˈjuːfəʊ] *(pl* **UFOs**) *(abbr* **unidentified flying object**) *n* OVNI *m*
Uganda [juːˈgændə] *n* l'Ouganda *m* ▪**Ugandan 1** *adj* ougandais **2** *n* Ougandais, -aise
ugh [ʌх] *exclam* berk!
ugly [ˈʌglɪ] (**-ier, -iest**) *adj* laid ▪**ugliness** *n* laideur *f*
UK [juːˈkeɪ] *(abbr* **United Kingdom**) *n* RU *m*, Royaume-Uni *m*
Ukraine [juːˈkreɪn] *n* the U. l'Ukraine *f*
ulcer [ˈʌlsə(r)] *n* ulcère *m* ▪**ulcerated** *adj* ulcéré
ulterior [ʌlˈtɪərɪə(r)] *adj* ultérieur; **u. motive** arrière-pensée *f*
ultimate [ˈʌltɪmət] *adj (last)* final; *(supreme, best)* absolu; **the u. holidays** les vacances *fpl* idéales ▪**ultimately** *adv (finally)* finalement; *(basically)* en fin de compte
ultimatum [ʌltɪˈmeɪtəm] *n* ultimatum *m*; **to give sb an u.** lancer un ultimatum à qn
ultra- [ˈʌltrə] *pref* ultra-
ultramarine [ʌltrəməˈriːn] *adj & n* **u. (blue)** (bleu *(m)* d')outremer *(m)*
ultramodern [ʌltrəˈmɒdən] *adj* ultramoderne
ultrasound [ˈʌltrəsaʊnd] *n* ultrason *m*; *Fam* **to have an u.** passer une échographie
ultraviolet [ʌltrəˈvaɪələt] *adj* ultraviolet, -ette
umbilical [ʌmˈbɪlɪkəl] *adj* **u. cord** cordon *m* ombilical
umbrage [ˈʌmbrɪdʒ] *n Literary* **to take u.** prendre ombrage (**at** de)
umbrella [ʌmˈbrelə] *n* parapluie *m*; **u. stand** porte-parapluies *m inv*

> Note that the French word **ombrelle** is a false friend. It means **sunshade**.

umpire [ˈʌmpaɪə(r)] **1** *n* arbitre *m* **2** *vt* arbitrer
umpteen [ʌmpˈtiːn] *adj Fam* **u. times** je ne sais combien de fois ▪**umpteenth** *adj Fam* énième
UN [juːˈen] *(abbr* **United Nations**) *n* ONU *f*
unabashed [ʌnəˈbæʃt] *adj* imperturbable
unabated [ʌnəˈbeɪtɪd] *adj* **to continue u.** continuer avec la même intensité
unable [ʌnˈeɪbəl] *adj* **to be u. to do sth** être incapable de faire qch; **he's u. to swim** il ne sait pas nager
unabridged [ʌnəˈbrɪdʒd] *adj* intégral

unacceptable [ʌnəkˈseptəbəl] *adj* inacceptable; **it's u. that...** il est inacceptable que... *(+ subjunctive)*
unaccompanied [ʌnəˈkʌmpənɪd] *adj (person)* non accompagné; *(singing)* sans accompagnement
unaccountable [ʌnəˈkaʊntəbəl] *adj* inexplicable ▪**unaccountably** *adv* inexplicablement
unaccounted [ʌnəˈkaʊntɪd] *adj* **to be u. for** rester introuvable
unaccustomed [ʌnəˈkʌstəmd] *adj* inaccoutumé; **to be u. to sth/to doing sth** ne pas être habitué à qch/à faire qch
unadulterated [ʌnəˈdʌltəreɪtɪd] *adj* pur; *(food)* naturel, -elle
unaided [ʌnˈeɪdɪd] *adv* sans aide
unanimity [juːnəˈnɪmɪtɪ] *n* unanimité *f* ▪**unanimous** [-ˈnænɪməs] *adj* unanime ▪**unanimously** *adv* à l'unanimité
unannounced [ʌnəˈnaʊnst] **1** *adj* non annoncé **2** *adv* sans prévenir
unappetizing [ʌnˈæpɪtaɪzɪŋ] *adj* peu appétissant
unapproachable [ʌnəˈprəʊtʃəbəl] *adj* inaccessible
unarmed [ʌnˈɑːmd] *adj* non armé; **u. combat** combat *m* à mains nues
unashamed [ʌnəˈʃeɪmd] *adj (person)* sans honte; *(look, curiosity)* non dissimulé; **she's u. about it** elle n'en a pas honte ▪**unashamedly** [-ɪdlɪ] *adv* sans aucune honte
unassailable [ʌnəˈseɪləbəl] *adj (castle)* imprenable; *(argument, reputation)* inattaquable
unassuming [ʌnəˈsjuːmɪŋ] *adj* sans prétention
unattached [ʌnəˈtætʃt] *adj (not connected)* détaché; *(without partner)* sans attaches
unattainable [ʌnəˈteɪnəbəl] *adj* inaccessible
unattended [ʌnəˈtendɪd] *adv* **to leave sb/sth u.** laisser qn/qch sans surveillance
unattractive [ʌnəˈtræktɪv] *adj* peu attrayant
unauthorized [ʌnˈɔːθəraɪzd] *adj* non autorisé
unavailable [ʌnəˈveɪləbəl] *adj* non disponible; **to be u.** ne pas être disponible
unavoidable [ʌnəˈvɔɪdəbəl] *adj* inévitable ▪**unavoidably** *adv* inévitablement; **to be u. detained** être retardé pour des raisons indépendantes de sa volonté
unaware [ʌnəˈweə(r)] *adj* **to be u. of sth** ignorer qch; **to be u. that...** ignorer que... ▪**unawares** *adv* **to catch sb u.** prendre qn au dépourvu
unbalanced [ʌnˈbælənst] *adj (mind, person)* instable

unbearable [ʌn'beərəbəl] *adj* insupportable
 ▪ **unbearably** *adv* insupportablement
unbeatable [ʌn'biːtəbəl] *adj* imbattable
 ▪ **unbeaten** *adj (player)* invaincu; *(record)* jamais battu
unbeknown [ʌnbɪ'nəʊn] *adj* **u. to sb** à l'insu de qn
unbelievable [ʌnbɪ'liːvəbəl] *adj* incroyable
 ▪ **unbelieving** *adj* incrédule
unbias(s)ed [ʌn'baɪəst] *adj* impartial
unblock [ʌn'blɒk] *vt (sink, pipe)* déboucher
unbolt [ʌn'bəʊlt] *vt (door)* déverrouiller
unborn ['ʌn'bɔːn] *adj* **u. child** enfant *mf* à naître
unbounded [ʌn'baʊndɪd] *adj* sans borne(s)
unbreakable [ʌn'breɪkəbəl] *adj* incassable
 ▪ **unbroken** *adj (intact)* intact; *(continuous)* continu; *(record)* jamais battu
unbridled [ʌn'braɪdəld] *adj* débridé
unburden [ʌn'bɜːdən] *vt* **to u. oneself** se confier **(to** à**)**
unbutton [ʌn'bʌtən] *vt* déboutonner
uncalled-for [ʌn'kɔːldfɔː(r)] *adj* déplacé
uncanny [ʌn'kænɪ] *(-ier, -iest) adj* étrange
unceasing [ʌn'siːsɪŋ] *adj* incessant ▪ **un-ceasingly** *adv* sans cesse
unceremoniously [ʌnserɪ'məʊnɪəslɪ] *adv (to treat sb)* sans ménagement; *(show sb out)* brusquement
uncertain [ʌn'sɜːtən] *adj* incertain; **to be u. about sth** ne pas être certain de qch; **it's u. whether** *or* **that...** il n'est pas certain que... *(+ subjunctive)*; **I'm u. whether to stay (or not)** je ne sais pas très bien si je dois rester (ou pas) ▪ **uncertainty** *(pl* **-ies***) n* incertitude *f*
unchanged [ʌn'tʃeɪndʒd] *adj* inchangé ▪ **unchanging** *adj* immuable
uncharitable [ʌn'tʃærɪtəbəl] *adj* peu charitable
unchecked [ʌn'tʃekt] *adj* sans que rien ne soit fait
uncivil [ʌn'sɪvəl] *adj* impoli
uncivilized [ʌn'sɪvɪlaɪzd] *adj* non civilisé
unclaimed [ʌn'kleɪmd] *adj (luggage)* non réclamé
uncle ['ʌŋkəl] *n* oncle *m*
unclear [ʌn'klɪə(r)] *adj* vague; *(result)* incertain; **it's u. whether...** on ne sait pas très bien si...
uncomfortable [ʌn'kʌmftəbəl] *adj* inconfortable; *(heat, experience)* désagréable; *(silence)* gêné; **to feel u.** *(physically)* ne pas être à l'aise; *(ill at ease)* être mal à l'aise ▪ **uncomfortably** *adv* inconfortablement; *(unpleasantly)* désagréablement
uncommitted [ʌnkə'mɪtɪd] *adj* indécis
uncommon [ʌn'kɒmən] *adj* peu commun ▪ **uncommonly** *adv (very)* extraordinairement; **not u.** *(fairly often)* assez souvent
uncommunicative [ʌnkə'mjuːnɪkətɪv] *adj* peu communicatif, -ive
uncomplicated [ʌn'kɒmplɪkeɪtɪd] *adj* simple
uncompromising [ʌn'kɒmprəmaɪzɪŋ] *adj* intransigeant

unconcerned [ʌnkən'sɜːnd] *adj* indifférent
unconditional [ʌnkən'dɪʃənəl] *adj* sans condition
unconfirmed [ʌnkən'fɜːmd] *adj* non confirmé
unconnected [ʌnkə'nektɪd] *adj* sans lien
unconscious [ʌn'kɒnʃəs] **1** *adj (person)* sans connaissance; *(desire)* inconscient; **to be u. of sth** ne pas avoir conscience de qch **2** *n* **the u.** l'inconscient *m* ▪ **unconsciously** *adv* inconsciemment
uncontrollable [ʌnkən'trəʊləbəl] *adj* incontrôlable ▪ **uncontrollably** *adv (laugh, sob)* sans pouvoir s'arrêter
unconventional [ʌnkən'venʃənəl] *adj* non conformiste
unconvinced [ʌnkən'vɪnst] *adj* **to be** *or* **remain u.** ne pas être convaincu **(of** de**)** ▪ **un-convincing** *adj* peu convaincant
uncooked [ʌn'kʊkt] *adj* cru
uncooperative [ʌnkəʊ'ɒpərətɪv] *adj* peu coopératif, -ive
uncork [ʌn'kɔːk] *vt* déboucher
uncouth [ʌn'kuːθ] *adj* fruste
uncover [ʌn'kʌvə(r)] *vt* découvrir
unctuous ['ʌŋktʃʊəs] *adj (insincere)* onctueux, -ueuse
uncut [ʌn'kʌt] *adj (film, play, version)* intégral; *(diamond)* brut
undamaged [ʌn'dæmɪdʒd] *adj* intact
undated [ʌn'deɪtɪd] *adj* non daté
undaunted [ʌn'dɔːntɪd] *adj* nullement impressionné
undecided [ʌndɪ'saɪdɪd] *adj (person)* indécis **(about** sur**)**; **I'm u. whether to do it or not** je n'ai pas décidé si je le ferai ou non
undefeated [ʌndɪ'fiːtɪd] *adj* invaincu
undeniable [ʌndɪ'naɪəbəl] *adj* indéniable
under ['ʌndə(r)] **1** *prep* sous; *(less than)* moins de; **children u. nine** les enfants de moins de neuf ans; **u. there** là-dessous; **u. it** dessous; **u. (the command of) sb** sous les ordres de qn; **u. the terms of the agreement** selon l'accord; **u. the circumstances** dans ces circonstances; **to be u. age** être mineur; **to be u. discussion/ repair** être en discussion/réparation; **to be u. way** *(in progress)* être en cours; *(on the way)* être en route; **to get u. way** *(of campaign)* démarrer; **to be u. the impression that...** avoir l'impression que... **2** *adv* au-dessous
undercarriage ['ʌndəkærɪdʒ] *n* train *m* d'atterrissage
undercharge [ʌndə'tʃɑːdʒ] *vt* se tromper dans l'addition de *(à l'avantage du client)*; **I undercharged him (for it)** je ne (le) lui ai pas fait payer assez
underclothes ['ʌndəkləʊðz] *npl* sous-vêtements *mpl*
undercoat ['ʌndəkəʊt] *n* sous-couche *f*
undercooked [ʌndə'kʊkt] *adj* pas assez cuit
undercover ['ʌndəkʌvə(r)] *adj* secret, -ète

undercurrent [ˈʌndəkʌrənt] *n (in sea)* courant *m* sous-marin; **an u. of discontent** un mécontentement sous-jacent

undercut [ʌndəˈkʌt] *(pt & pp* **-cut,** *pres p* **-cutting)** *vt* vendre moins cher que

underdeveloped [ʌndədɪˈveləpt] *adj (country, region)* sous-développé

underdog [ˈʌndədɒg] *n (politically, socially)* opprimé, -ée *mf*; *(likely loser)* outsider *m*

underdone [ʌndəˈdʌn] *adj (food)* pas assez cuit; *(steak)* saignant

underestimate [ʌndərˈestɪmeɪt] *vt* sousestimer

underfed [ʌndəˈfed] *adj* sous-alimenté

underfoot [ʌndəˈfʊt] *adv* sous les pieds; **to trample sth u.** piétiner qch

undergo [ʌndəˈgəʊ] *(pt* **-went,** *pp* **-gone)** *vt* subir; **to u. surgery** être opéré

undergraduate [ʌndəˈgrædʒʊət] *n* étudiant, -iante *mf* de licence

underground [ˈʌndəgraʊnd] **1** *adj* souterrain; *Fig (secret)* clandestin **2** *n Br (railway)* métro *m*; *Pol (organization)* résistance *f* **3** [ʌndəˈgraʊnd] *adv* sous terre; *Fig* **to go u.** *(of fugitive)* passer dans la clandestinité

undergrowth [ˈʌndəgrəʊθ] *n* brousailles *fpl*

underhand [ʌndəˈhænd] *adj* sournois

underlie [ʌndəˈlaɪ] *(pt* **-lay,** *pp* **-lain,** *pres p* **-lying)** *vt* sous-tendre ▪ **underlying** *adj* sous-jacent

underline [ʌndəˈlaɪn] *vt* souligner

underling [ˈʌndəlɪŋ] *n Pej* subalterne *mf*

undermine [ʌndəˈmaɪn] *vt (weaken)* saper

underneath [ʌndəˈniːθ] **1** *prep* sous **2** *adv* (en) dessous; **the book u.** le livre d'en dessous **3** *n* **the u. (of)** le dessous (de)

undernourished [ʌndəˈnʌrɪʃt] *adj* sous-alimenté

underpants [ˈʌndəpænts] *npl (male underwear)* slip *m*

underpass [ˈʌndəpaːs] *n (for pedestrians)* passage *m* souterrain; *(for vehicles)* passage inférieur

underpay [ʌndəˈpeɪ] *vt* sous-payer ▪ **underpaid** *adj* sous-payé

underprice [ʌndəˈpraɪs] *vt* vendre au-dessous de sa valeur

underprivileged [ʌndəˈprɪvɪlɪdʒd] *adj* défavorisé

underrate [ʌndəˈreɪt] *vt* sous-estimer

underscore [ʌndəˈskɔː(r)] *vt* souligner

undersecretary [ʌndəˈsekrətərɪ] *n Pol* soussecrétaire *m*

undershirt [ˈʌndəʃɜːt] *n Am* maillot *m* de corps

underside [ˈʌndəsaɪd] *n* **the u. (of)** le dessous (de)

undersigned [ˈʌndəsaɪnd] *adj* **I, the u.** je soussigné(e)

undersized [ʌndəˈsaɪzd] *adj* trop petit

underskirt [ˈʌndəskɜːt] *n* jupon *m*

understaffed [ʌndəˈstɑːft] *adj (office, organization)* **to be u.** manquer de personnel

understand [ʌndəˈstænd] *(pt & pp* **-stood)** *vti* comprendre; **I u. that...** je crois comprendre que...; **I've been given to u. that...** on m'a fait comprendre que...; **to make oneself understood** se faire comprendre ▪ **understanding 1** *n (act, faculty)* compréhension *f*; *(agreement)* accord *m*, entente *f*; *(sympathy)* entente; **on the u. that...** à condition que... *(+ subjunctive)* **2** *adj (person)* compréhensif, -ive ▪ **understood** *adj (agreed)* entendu; *(implied)* sous-entendu

understandable [ʌndəˈstændəbəl] *adj* compréhensible ▪ **understandably** *adv* naturellement

understatement [ˈʌndəsteɪtmənt] *n* euphémisme *m*

understudy [ˈʌndəstʌdɪ] *(pl* **-ies)** *n* doublure *f*

undertake [ʌndəˈteɪk] *(pt* **-took,** *pp* **-taken)** *vt (task)* entreprendre; *(responsibility)* assumer; **to u. to do sth** entreprendre de faire qch ▪ **undertaking** *n (task)* entreprise *f*; *(promise)* promesse *f*

undertaker [ˈʌndəteɪkə(r)] *n* entrepreneur *m* de pompes funèbres

undertone [ˈʌndətəʊn] *n* **in an u.** à mi-voix; *Fig* **an u. of** *(criticism, sadness)* une nuance de

undervalue [ʌndəˈvæljuː] *vt* sous-évaluer; **it's undervalued at £10** ça vaut plus que 10 livres

underwater 1 [ʌndəˈwɔːtə(r)] *adj* de plongée **2** [ʌndəˈwɔːtə(r)] *adv* sous l'eau

underwear [ˈʌndəweə(r)] *n* sous-vêtements *mpl*

underweight [ʌndəˈweɪt] *adj (person)* trop maigre

underworld [ˈʌndəwɜːld] *n* **the u.** *(criminals)* la pègre

undeserved [ʌndɪˈzɜːvd] *adj* immérité

undesirable [ʌndɪˈzaɪərəbəl] *adj & n* indésirable *(mf)*

undetected [ʌndɪˈtektɪd] *adj (crime)* non découvert; **to go u.** *(of crime)* ne pas être découvert; *(of person)* passer inaperçu

undies [ˈʌndɪz] *npl Fam* dessous *mpl*

undignified [ʌnˈdɪgnɪfaɪd] *adj* indigne

undisciplined [ʌnˈdɪsɪplɪnd] *adj* indiscipliné

undiscovered [ʌndɪˈskʌvəd] *adj* **to remain u.** *(of crime, body)* ne pas être découvert

undisputed [ʌndɪˈspjuːtɪd] *adj* incontesté

undistinguished [ʌndɪˈstɪŋgwɪʃt] *adj* médiocre

undisturbed [ʌndɪˈstɜːbd] *adj* **to leave sb u.** ne pas déranger qn

undivided [ʌndɪˈvaɪdɪd] *adj* **my u. attention** toute mon attention

undo [ʌnˈduː] *(pt* **-did,** *pp* **-done)** *vt* défaire; *(bound person)* détacher; *(parcel)* ouvrir; *(mistake, damage)* réparer; *Comptr (command)* annuler ▪ **undoing** *n* ruine *f* ▪ **undone** [ʌnˈdʌn] *adj* **to come u.** *(of knot)* se défaire; **to leave sth u.** *(work)* ne pas faire qch

undoubted [ʌnˈdaʊtɪd] *adj* indubitable ▪ **undoubtedly** *adv* indubitablement

undreamt-of [ʌnˈdremtɒv] *adj* inimaginable

undress [ʌn'dres] **1** *vt* déshabiller; **to get undressed** se déshabiller **2** *vi* se déshabiller

undrinkable [ʌn'drɪnkəbəl] *adj* imbuvable

undue [ʌn'dju:] *adj* excessif, -ive **• unduly** *adv* excessivement

undulating ['ʌndjʊleɪtɪŋ] *adj* (*movement*) onduleux, -euse; (*countryside*) vallonné

undying [ʌn'daɪɪŋ] *adj* (*love*) éternel, -elle

unearned [ʌn'ɜ:nd] *adj* **u. income** rentes *fpl*

unearth [ʌn'ɜ:θ] *vt* (*from ground*) déterrer; *Fig* (*discover*) mettre à jour

unearthly [ʌn'ɜ:θlɪ] *adj* mystérieux, -ieuse; *Fam* **at an u. hour** à une heure impossible

uneasy [ʌn'i:zɪ] *adj* (*person*) mal à l'aise; (*sleep*) agité; (*silence*) gêné

uneatable [ʌn'i:təbəl] *adj* (*bad*) immangeable; (*poisonous*) non comestible

uneconomic(al) [ʌni:kə'nɒmɪk(əl)] *adj* peu économique

uneducated [ʌn'edjʊkeɪtɪd] *adj* (*person*) sans éducation; (*accent*) populaire

unemotional [ʌnɪ'məʊʃənəl] *adj* impassible; (*speech*) sans passion

unemployed [ʌnɪm'plɔɪd] **1** *adj* au chômage **2** *npl* **the u.** les chômeurs *mpl* **• unemployment** *n* chômage *m*; **u. rate** taux *m* de chômage

unending [ʌn'endɪŋ] *adj* interminable

unenthusiastic [ʌnɪnθju:zɪ'æstɪk] *adj* peu enthousiaste

unenviable [ʌn'envɪəbəl] *adj* peu enviable

unequal [ʌn'i:kwəl] *adj* inégal; **to be u. to the task** ne pas être à la hauteur de la tâche **• unequalled** (*Am* **unequaled**) *adj* (*incomparable*) inégalé

unequivocal [ʌnɪ'kwɪvəkəl] *adj* sans équivoque **• unequivocally** *adv* sans équivoque

unerring [ʌn'ɜ:rɪŋ] *adj* infaillible

unethical [ʌn'eθɪkəl] *adj* contraire à l'éthique

uneven [ʌn'i:vən] *adj* inégal **• unevenly** *adv* inégalement

uneventful [ʌnɪ'ventfəl] *adj* sans histoires

unexceptionable [ʌnɪk'sepʃənəbəl] *adj* irréprochable

unexpected [ʌnɪk'spektɪd] *adj* inattendu **• unexpectedly** *adv* (*arrive*) à l'improviste; (*fail, succeed*) contre toute attente

unexplained [ʌnɪk'spleɪnd] *adj* inexpliqué

unfailing [ʌn'feɪlɪŋ] *adj* (*optimism, courage*) à toute épreuve; (*supply*) inépuisable

unfair [ʌn'feə(r)] *adj* injuste (**to sb** envers qn); (*competition*) déloyal **• unfairly** *adv* injustement **• unfairness** *n* injustice *f*

unfaithful [ʌn'feɪθfəl] *adj* infidèle (**to** à)

unfamiliar [ʌnfə'mɪlɪə(r)] *adj* inconnu; **to be u. with sth** ne pas connaître qch

unfashionable [ʌn'fæʃənəbəl] *adj* démodé

unfasten [ʌn'fɑ:sən] *vt* défaire

unfavourable [ʌn'feɪvərəbəl] (*Am* **unfavorable**) *adj* défavorable

unfeeling [ʌn'fi:lɪŋ] *adj* insensible

unfinished [ʌn'fɪnɪʃt] *adj* inachevé; **to have some u. business** avoir une affaire à régler

unfit [ʌn'fɪt] *adj* (*unsuitable*) inapte; (*in bad shape*) pas en forme; **to be u. to do sth** être incapable de faire qch; **u. for human consumption** impropre à la consommation; **u. mother** mère *f* indigne

unflagging [ʌn'flægɪŋ] *adj* (*optimism, zeal*) inépuisable; (*interest, attention*) sans faille

unflappable [ʌn'flæpəbəl] *adj* *Br Fam* imperturbable

unflattering [ʌn'flætərɪŋ] *adj* peu flatteur, -euse

unflinching [ʌn'flɪntʃɪŋ] *adj* (*courage*) inépuisable; (*resolve, loyalty, support*) à toute épreuve

unfold [ʌn'fəʊld] **1** *vt* déplier; (*wings*) déployer; *Fig* (*intentions, plan*) dévoiler **2** *vi* (*of story, view*) se dérouler

unforeseeable [ʌnfɔ:'si:əbəl] *adj* imprévisible **• unforeseen** *adj* imprévu

unforgettable [ʌnfə'getəbəl] *adj* inoubliable

unforgivable [ʌnfə'gɪvəbəl] *adj* impardonnable **• unforgiving** *adj* impitoyable

unfortunate [ʌn'fɔ:tʃənət] *adj* malchanceux, -euse; (*event*) fâcheux, -euse; **you were u.** tu n'as pas eu de chance **• unfortunately** *adv* malheureusement

unfounded [ʌn'faʊndɪd] *adj* (*rumour, argument*) sans fondement

unfriendly [ʌn'frendlɪ] *adj* peu aimable (**to** avec) **• unfriendliness** *n* froideur *f*

unfulfilled [ʌnfʊl'fɪld] *adj* (*desire*) insatisfait; (*plan, dream*) non réalisé; (*condition*) non rempli

unfurl [ʌn'fɜ:l] *vt* déployer

unfurnished [ʌn'fɜ:nɪʃt] *adj* non meublé

ungainly [ʌn'geɪnlɪ] *adj* (*clumsy*) gauche

unglued [ʌn'glu:d] *adj* *Am Fam* **to come u.** (*confused*) perdre les pédales, s'affoler

ungodly [ʌn'gɒdlɪ] *adj* (*sinful*) impie; *Fam* **at an u. hour** à une heure impossible

ungracious [ʌn'greɪʃəs] *adj* peu aimable

ungrammatical [ʌngrə'mætɪkəl] *adj* non grammatical

ungrateful [ʌn'greɪtfəl] *adj* ingrat

unguarded [ʌn'gɑ:dɪd] *adj* (*place*) sans surveillance; **in an u. moment** dans un moment d'inattention

unhappy [ʌn'hæpɪ] (**-ier, -iest**) *adj* (*sad, unfortunate*) malheureux, -euse; (*not pleased*) mécontent; **to be u. about doing sth** ne pas vouloir faire qch **• unhappily** *adv* (*unfortunately*) malheureusement **• unhappiness** *n* tristesse *f*

unharmed [ʌn'hɑ:md] *adj* indemne

unhealthy [ʌn'helθɪ] (**-ier, -iest**) *adj* (*person*) maladif, -ive; (*climate, place, job*) malsain; (*lungs*) malade

unheard-of [ʌn'hɜ:dɒv] *adj* (*unprecedented*) inouï

unheeded [ʌn'hiːdɪd] *adj* **it went u.** on n'en a pas tenu compte

unhelpful [ʌn'helpfəl] *adj (person)* peu serviable; *(advice)* peu utile

unhinged [ʌn'hɪndʒd] *adj (person, mind)* déséquilibré

unholy [ʌn'həʊlɪ] (**-ier, -iest**) *adj* impie; *Fam (noise)* de tous les diables

unhook [ʌn'hʊk] *vt (picture, curtain)* décrocher; *(dress)* dégrafer

unhoped-for [ʌn'həʊptfɔː(r)] *adj* inespéré

unhurried [ʌn'hʌrɪd] *adj (movement)* lent; *(stroll, journey)* fait sans hâte

unhurt [ʌn'hɜːt] *adj* indemne

unhygienic [ʌnhaɪ'dʒiːnɪk] *adj* contraire à l'hygiène

unicorn ['juːnɪkɔːn] *n* licorne *f*

unidentified [ʌnaɪ'dentɪfaɪd] *adj* **u. flying object** objet *m* volant non identifié

uniform ['juːnɪfɔːm] **1** *n* uniforme *m* **2** *adj (regular)* uniforme; *(temperature)* constant ▪ **uniformed** *adj (police officer)* en uniforme ▪ **uni'formity** *n* uniformité *f* ▪ **uniformly** *adv* uniformément

unify ['juːnɪfaɪ] (*pt & pp* **-ied**) *vt* unifier ▪ **unification** [-fɪ'keɪʃən] *n* unification *f*

unilateral [juːnɪ'lætərəl] *adj* unilatéral

unimaginable [ʌnɪ'mædʒɪnəbəl] *adj* inimaginable ▪ **unimaginative** *adj (person, plan)* qui manque d'imagination

unimpaired [ʌnɪm'peəd] *adj* intact

unimportant [ʌnɪm'pɔːtənt] *adj* sans importance

uninformative [ʌnɪn'fɔːmətɪv] *adj* peu instructif, -ive

uninhabitable [ʌnɪn'hæbɪtəbəl] *adj* inhabitable ▪ **uninhabited** *adj* inhabité

uninhibited [ʌnɪn'hɪbɪtɪd] *adj (person)* sans complexes

uninitiated [ʌnɪ'nɪʃɪeɪtɪd] *npl* **the u.** les non-initiés *mpl*

uninjured [ʌn'ɪndʒəd] *adj* indemne

uninspiring [ʌnɪn'spaɪərɪŋ] *adj (subject)* pas très inspirant

unintelligible [ʌnɪn'telɪdʒəbəl] *adj* inintelligible

unintended [ʌnɪn'tendɪd] *adj* involontaire

unintentional [ʌnɪn'tenʃənəl] *adj* involontaire

uninterested [ʌn'ɪntrɪstɪd] *adj* indifférent (**in** à) ▪ **uninteresting** *adj* inintéressant

uninterrupted [ʌnɪntə'rʌptɪd] *adj* ininterrompu

uninvited [ʌnɪn'vaɪtɪd] *adv (arrive)* sans invitation ▪ **uninviting** *adj* peu attrayant

union ['juːnɪən] **1** *n* union *f*; *(trade union)* syndicat *m* **2** *adj* syndical; **u. member** syndicaliste *mf*; **the U. Jack** = le drapeau britannique ▪ **unionist** *n* **Br trade u.**, **Am labor u.** syndicaliste *mf* ▪ **unionize** *vt* syndiquer

unique [juː'niːk] *adj* unique ▪ **uniquely** *adv (remarkably)* exceptionnellement

unisex ['juːnɪseks] *adj (clothing, hairdresser's)* unisexe

unison ['juːnɪsən] *n* **in u.** à l'unisson (**with** de)

unit ['juːnɪt] *n* unité *f*; *(of furniture)* élément *m*; *(system)* bloc *m*; *(group, team)* groupe *m*; **psychiatric/heart u.** *(of hospital)* service *m* de psychiatrie/cardiologie; **research u.** centre *m* de recherche; *Br Fin* **u. trust** fonds *m* commun de placement

unite [juː'naɪt] **1** *vt* unir; *(country, party)* unifier; **the United Kingdom** le Royaume-Uni; **the United Nations** les Nations *fpl* unies; **the United States (of America)** les États-Unis *mpl* (d'Amérique) **2** *vi* s'unir

unity ['juːnətɪ] *n (cohesion)* unité *f*; *Fig (harmony)* harmonie *f*

universal [juːnɪ'vɜːsəl] *adj* universel, -elle ▪ **universally** *adv* universellement

universe ['juːnɪvɜːs] *n* univers *m*

university [juːnɪ'vɜːsɪtɪ] **1** (*pl* **-ies**) *n* université *f*; **to go to u.** aller à l'université; *Br* **at u.** à l'université **2** *adj (teaching, town, restaurant)* universitaire; *(student, teacher)* d'université

unjust [ʌn'dʒʌst] *adj* injuste

unjustified [ʌn'dʒʌstɪfaɪd] *adj* injustifié

unkempt [ʌn'kempt] *adj* négligé

unkind [ʌn'kaɪnd] *adj* pas gentil (*f* pas gentille) (**to sb** avec qn) ▪ **unkindly** *adv* méchamment

unknowingly [ʌn'nəʊɪŋlɪ] *adv* inconsciemment

unknown [ʌn'nəʊn] **1** *adj* inconnu; **u. to me, he had left** il était parti, ce que j'ignorais **2** *n (person)* inconnu, -ue *mf*; *Phil* **the u.** l'inconnu *m*; *Math & Fig* **u. (quantity)** inconnue *f*

unlawful [ʌn'lɔːfəl] *adj* illégal

unleaded [ʌn'ledɪd] *adj* sans plomb

unleash [ʌn'liːʃ] *vt (dog)* détacher; *Fig (emotion)* susciter

unless [ʌn'les] *conj* à moins que (+ *subjunctive*); **u. she comes** à moins qu'elle ne vienne; **u. you work harder, you'll fail** à moins de travailler plus dur, vous échouerez

unlicensed [ʌn'laɪsənst] *adj Br* **u. premises** = établissement qui n'a pas de licence de débit de boissons

unlike [ʌn'laɪk] *prep* **to be u. sb/sth** ne pas être comme qn/qch; **u. her brother, she...** à la différence de son frère, elle...; **it's very u. him to...** ça ne lui ressemble pas du tout de...

unlikely [ʌn'laɪklɪ] *adj* improbable; *(unbelievable)* invraisemblable; **she's to win** il est peu probable qu'elle gagne; **in the u. event of an accident...** dans le cas fort peu probable d'un accident...

unlimited [ʌn'lɪmɪtɪd] *adj* illimité

unlisted [ʌn'lɪstɪd] *adj Am (phone number)* sur (la) liste rouge

unload [ʌn'ləʊd] *vti* décharger

unlock [ʌn'lɒk] *vt* ouvrir

unlucky [ʌn'lʌkɪ] (**-ier, -iest**) *adj (person)* malchanceux, -euse; *(number, colour)* qui porte malheur; **you're u.** tu n'as pas de chance ▪ **unluckily** *adv* malheureusement

unmade [ʌn'meɪd] *adj (bed)* défait

unmanageable [ʌn'mænɪdʒəbəl] *adj (child)* difficile; *(hair)* difficile à coiffer; *(package, large book, size)* peu maniable

unmanned [ʌn'mænd] *adj (spacecraft)* inhabité

unmarked [ʌn'mɑːkt] *adj (grave)* sans inscription; *Br* **u. police car** voiture *f* banalisée

unmarried [ʌn'mærɪd] *adj* non marié

unmask [ʌn'mɑːsk] *vt* démasquer

unmentionable [ʌn'menʃənəbəl] *adj* dont il ne faut pas parler

unmistakable [ʌnmɪ'steɪkəbəl] *adj (obvious)* indubitable; *(face, voice)* caractéristique

unmitigated [ʌn'mɪtɪgeɪtɪd] *adj (disaster)* absolu; *(folly)* pur

unmoved [ʌn'muːvd] *adj* **to be u. by sth** rester insensible à qch

unnamed [ʌn'neɪmd] *adj (person)* anonyme; *(thing)* sans nom

unnatural [ʌn'nætʃərəl] *adj (abnormal)* anormal; *(love)* contre nature; *(affected)* affecté ▪ **unnaturally** *adv* **not u.** naturellement

unnecessary [ʌn'nesəsərɪ] *adj* inutile; *(superfluous)* superflu

unnerve [ʌn'nɜːv] *vt* troubler

> Note that the French verb **énerver** is a false friend. It means **to irritate** or **to make nervous** depending on the context.

unnoticed [ʌn'nəʊtɪst] *adv* **to go u.** passer inaperçu

unobstructed [ʌnəb'strʌktɪd] *adj (road, view)* dégagé

unobtainable [ʌnəb'teɪnəbəl] *adj* impossible à obtenir

unobtrusive [ʌnəb'truːsɪv] *adj* discret, -ète

unoccupied [ʌn'ɒkjʊpaɪd] *adj (house, person)* inoccupé; *(seat)* libre

unofficial [ʌnə'fɪʃəl] *adj* officieux, -ieuse; *(visit)* privé; *(strike)* sauvage ▪ **unofficially** *adv* officieusement

unorthodox [ʌn'ɔːθədɒks] *adj* peu orthodoxe

unpack [ʌn'pæk] **1** *vt (suitcase)* défaire; *(contents)* déballer; *(box)* ouvrir **2** *vi* défaire sa valise

unpaid [ʌn'peɪd] *adj (bill, sum)* impayé; *(work, worker)* bénévole; *(leave)* non payé

unpalatable [ʌn'pælətəbəl] *adj (food)* qui n'est pas bon *(f* bonne) à manger; *Fig (truth)* désagréable à entendre

unparalleled [ʌn'pærəleld] *adj* sans égal

unperturbed [ʌnpə'tɜːbd] *adj* nullement déconcerté

unplanned [ʌn'plænd] *adj* imprévu

unpleasant [ʌn'plezənt] *adj* désagréable (**to sb** avec qn)

unplug [ʌn'plʌg] *(pt & pp* **-gg-**) *vt (appliance)* débrancher; *(unblock)* déboucher

unpopular [ʌn'pɒpjʊlə(r)] *adj* impopulaire; **to be u. with sb** ne pas plaire à qn

unprecedented [ʌn'presɪdentɪd] *adj* sans précédent

unpredictable [ʌnprɪ'dɪktəbəl] *adj* imprévisible; *(weather)* indécis

unprepared [ʌnprɪ'peəd] *adj (meal, room)* non préparé; *(speech)* improvisé; **to be u. for sth** *(not expect)* ne pas s'attendre à qch

unprepossessing [ʌnpriːpə'zesɪŋ] *adj* peu avenant

unpretentious [ʌnprɪ'tenʃəs] *adj* sans prétentions

unprincipled [ʌn'prɪnsɪpəld] *adj* sans scrupules

unprofessional [ʌnprə'feʃənəl] *adj (person, behaviour)* pas très professionnel, -elle

unprovoked [ʌnprə'vəʊkt] *adj* gratuit

unpublished [ʌn'pʌblɪʃt] *adj (text, writer)* inédit

unpunished [ʌn'pʌnɪʃt] *adv* **to go u.** rester impuni

unqualified [ʌn'kwɒlɪfaɪd] *adj (teacher)* non diplômé; *(support)* sans réserve; *(success, liar)* parfait; **to be u. to do sth** ne pas être qualifié pour faire qch

unquestionable [ʌn'kwestʃənəbəl] *adj* incontestable ▪ **unquestionably** *adv* incontestablement

unravel [ʌn'rævəl] *(Br* **-ll-,** *Am* **-l-)** *vt (threads)* démêler; *Fig (mystery)* éclaircir

unreal [ʌn'rɪəl] *adj* irréel, -éelle

unrealistic [ʌn'rɪəlɪstɪk] *adj* irréaliste

unreasonable [ʌn'riːzənəbəl] *adj (person, attitude)* déraisonnable; *(price)* excessif, -ive

unrecognizable [ʌn'rekəgnaɪzəbəl] *adj* méconnaissable

unrelated [ʌnrɪ'leɪtɪd] *adj (facts)* sans rapport (**to** avec); **we're u.** il n'y a aucun lien de parenté entre nous

unrelenting [ʌnrɪ'lentɪŋ] *adj* incessant; *(person)* tenace

unreliable [ʌnrɪ'laɪəbəl] *adj* peu fiable

unremarkable [ʌnrɪ'mɑːkəbəl] *adj* quelconque

unrepentant [ʌnrɪ'pentənt] *adj* impénitent; **the murderer was u.** le meurtrier n'a manifesté aucun remords

unreservedly [ʌnrɪ'zɜːvɪdlɪ] *adv* sans réserve

unrest [ʌn'rest] *n* agitation *f*, troubles *mpl*

unrestricted [ʌnrɪ'strɪktɪd] *adj* illimité; **u. access** libre accès *m* (**to** à)

unrewarding [ʌnrɪ'wɔːdɪŋ] *adj* ingrat; *(financially)* peu rémunérateur, -trice

unripe [ʌn'raɪp] *adj (fruit)* qui n'est pas mûr

unrivalled [ʌn'raɪvəld] *(Am* **unrivaled**) *adj* hors pair *inv*

unroll [ʌn'rəʊl] **1** *vt* dérouler **2** *vi* se dérouler

unruffled [ʌn'rʌfəld] *adj* imperturbable

unruly [ʌn'ruːlɪ] *(-ier, -iest)* *adj* indiscipliné

unsafe [ʌn'seɪf] *adj (place, machine)*

dangereux, -euse; *(person)* en danger; **u. sex** rapports *mpl* sexuels non protégés

unsaid [ʌn'sed] *adj* **to leave sth u.** passer qch sous silence

unsaleable *(Am* **unsalable)** [ʌn'seɪləbəl] *adj* invendable

unsatisfactory [ʌnsætɪs'fæktərɪ] *adj* peu satisfaisant ▪ **un'satisfied** *adj* insatisfait; **u. with sb/sth** peu satisfait de qn/qch

unsavoury [ʌn'seɪvərɪ] *(Am* **unsavory)** *adj (person, place)* peu recommandable

unscathed [ʌn'skeɪðd] *adj* indemne

unscheduled [*Br* ʌn'ʃedju:ld, *Am* ʌn'skedjʊld] *adj* imprévu

unscrew [ʌn'skru:] *vt* dévisser

unscrupulous [ʌn'skru:pjʊləs] *adj (person)* peu scrupuleux, -euse; *(action)* malhonnête

unseemly [ʌn'si:mlɪ] *adj* inconvenant

unseen [ʌn'si:n] **1** *adj* invisible **2** *n Br Sch & Univ* traduction *f* à vue **3** *adv* **to do sth u.** faire qch sans qu'on vous voie

unselfish [ʌn'selfɪʃ] *adj (person, motive)* désintéressé

unsettle [ʌn'setəl] *vt (person)* troubler ▪ **unsettled** *adj (weather, situation)* instable; *(person)* troublé; *(in a job)* mal à l'aise

unshak(e)able [ʌn'ʃeɪkəbəl] *adj* inébranlable

unshaven [ʌn'ʃeɪvən] *adj* pas rasé

unsightly [ʌn'saɪtlɪ] *adj* laid

unskilled [ʌn'skɪld] *adj* non qualifié

unsociable [ʌn'səʊʃəbəl] *adj* peu sociable

unsocial [ʌn'səʊʃəl] *adj* **to work u. hours** travailler en dehors des heures de bureau

unsolved [ʌn'sɒlvd] *adj (mystery)* inexpliqué; *(crime)* dont l'auteur n'est pas connu

unsophisticated [ʌnsə'fɪstɪkeɪtɪd] *adj* simple

unsound [ʌn'saʊnd] *adj (construction)* peu solide; *(method)* peu sûr; *(decision)* peu judicieux, -ieuse; *Law* **to be of u. mind** ne pas jouir de toutes ses facultés mentales

unspeakable [ʌn'spi:kəbəl] *adj* indescriptible

unspecified [ʌn'spesɪfaɪd] *adj* non spécifié

unsporting [ʌn'spɔ:tɪŋ] *adj* qui n'est pas fair-play

unstable [ʌn'steɪbəl] *adj* instable

unsteady [ʌn'stedɪ] *adj (hand, voice, step)* mal assuré; *(table, ladder)* bancal *(mpl* -als) ▪ **unsteadily** *(walk)* d'un pas mal assuré

unstinting [ʌn'stɪntɪŋ] *adj (generosity)* sans bornes; *(praise)* sans réserve

unstoppable [ʌn'stɒpəbəl] *adj* qu'on ne peut arrêter

unstuck [ʌn'stʌk] *adj* **to come u.** *(of stamp)* se décoller; *Br Fam (of person, plan)* se casser la figure

unsuccessful [ʌnsək'sesfʊl] *adj (attempt)* infructueux, -ueuse; *(outcome, candidate)* malheureux, -euse; *(application)* non retenu; **to be u.** ne pas réussir *(in doing* à faire); *(of*

book, film, artist) ne pas avoir de succès ▪ **unsuccessfully** *adv* en vain, sans succès

unsuitable [ʌn'su:təbəl] *adj* qui ne convient pas *(for* à); *(example)* peu approprié; *(manners, clothes)* peu convenable; **to be u. for sth** ne pas convenir à qch ▪ **unsuited** *adj* **to be u. to sth** ne pas être fait pour qch; **they're u. to each other** ils ne sont pas compatibles

unsupervised [ʌn'su:pəvaɪzd] *adv (play)* sans surveillance

unsure [ʌn'ʃʊə(r)] *adj* incertain *(of or about* de)

unsuspecting [ʌnsə'spektɪŋ] *adj* qui ne se doute de rien

unswerving [ʌn'swɜ:vɪŋ] *adj* à toute épreuve

unsympathetic [ʌnsɪmpə'θetɪk] *adj* peu compatissant *(to* à); **u. to a cause/request** insensible à une cause/requête

untangle [ʌn'tæŋgəl] *vt (rope, hair)* démêler

untapped [ʌn'tæpt] *adj (resources)* inexploité

untenable [ʌn'tenəbəl] *adj (position, argument)* indéfendable

unthinkable [ʌn'θɪŋkəbəl] *adj* impensable, inconcevable

untidy [ʌn'taɪdɪ] *(-ier, -iest) adj (clothes, hair)* peu soigné; *(room)* en désordre; *(person)* désordonné ▪ **untidily** *adv* sans soin

untie [ʌn'taɪ] *vt (person, hands)* détacher; *(knot, parcel)* défaire

until [ʌn'tɪl] **1** *prep* jusqu'à; **u. now** jusqu'à présent; **u. then** jusque-là; **not u. tomorrow** pas avant demain; **I didn't see her u. Monday** c'est seulement lundi que je l'ai vue **2** *conj* jusqu'à ce que *(+ subjunctive)*; **u. she comes** jusqu'à ce qu'elle vienne; **do nothing u. I come** ne fais rien avant que je vienne

untimely [ʌn'taɪmlɪ] *adj (remark, question)* inopportun; *(death)* prématuré

untiring [ʌn'taɪərɪŋ] *adj* infatigable

untold [ʌn'təʊld] *adj (wealth, quantity)* incalculable; *(beauty)* immense

untoward [ʌntə'wɔ:d] *adj* fâcheux, -euse

untranslatable [ʌntræns'leɪtəbəl] *adj* intra-duisible

untroubled [ʌn'trʌbəld] *adj (calm)* calme

untrue [ʌn'tru:] *adj* faux *(f* fausse) ▪ **'untruth** *n* mensonge *m* ▪ **un'truthful** *adj (person)* menteur, -euse; *(statement)* mensonger, -ère

unusable [ʌn'ju:zəbəl] *adj* inutilisable

unused¹ [ʌn'ju:zd] *adj (new)* neuf *(f* neuve); *(not in use)* inutilisé

unused² [ʌn'ju:st] *adj* **u. to sth/to doing** peu habitué à qch/à faire

unusual [ʌn'ju:ʒʊəl] *adj (not common)* inhabituel, -uelle; *(strange)* étrange ▪ **unusually** *adv* exceptionnellement

unveil [ʌn'veɪl] *vt* dévoiler ▪ **unveiling** *n (ceremony)* inauguration *f*

unwanted [ʌn'wɒntɪd] *adj* non désiré

unwarranted [ʌnˈwɒrəntɪd] *adj* injustifié
unwavering [ʌnˈweɪvərɪŋ] *adj* inébranlable
unwelcome [ʌnˈwelkəm] *adj (news)* fâcheux, -euse; *(gift, visit)* inopportun; *(person)* importun
unwell [ʌnˈwel] *adj* souffrant
unwieldy [ʌnˈwiːldɪ] *adj (package)* encombrant; *(system)* lourd
unwilling [ʌnˈwɪlɪŋ] *adj* to be u. to do sth être réticent à faire qch ▪ **unwillingly** *adv* à contrecœur
unwind [ʌnˈwaɪnd] *(pt & pp -wound)* 1 *vt (thread)* dérouler 2 *vi* se dérouler; *Fam (relax)* décompresser
unwise [ʌnˈwaɪz] *adj* imprudent ▪ **unwisely** *adv* imprudemment
unwitting [ʌnˈwɪtɪŋ] *adj* involontaire ▪ **unwittingly** *adv* involontairement
unworkable [ʌnˈwɜːkəbəl] *adj (idea)* impraticable
unworthy [ʌnˈwɜːðɪ] *adj* indigne (**of** de)
unwrap [ʌnˈræp] *(pt & pp -pp-)* *vt* déballer
unwritten [ʌnˈrɪtən] *adj (agreement)* verbal
unyielding [ʌnˈjiːldɪŋ] *adj* inflexible
unzip [ʌnˈzɪp] *(pt & pp -pp-)* *vt (clothes)* ouvrir (la fermeture Éclair® de); *Comptr (file)* dézipper, décompresser

up [ʌp] 1 *adv* en haut; **to come/go up** monter; **to walk up and down** marcher de long en large; **up there** là-haut; **up above** au-dessus; **up on the roof** sur le toit; **further** *or* **higher up** plus haut; **up to** *(as far as)* jusqu'à; **to be up to doing sth** *(capable of)* être de taille à faire qch; *(in a position to)* être à même de faire qch; **to be a goal up** avoir un but d'avance; **it's up to you to do it** c'est à toi de le faire; **it's up to you** *(you decide)* c'est à toi de décider; **where are you up to?** *(in book)* où en es-tu?; *Fam* **what are you up to?** que fais-tu?; *Fam* **to be well up in** *(versed in)* s'y connaître en; *Fam* **up (with) the workers!** vive(nt) les travailleurs!

2 *prep* **up a hill** en haut d'une colline; **up a tree** dans un arbre; **up a ladder** sur une échelle; **to go up the stairs** monter les escaliers; **to live up the street** habiter plus loin dans la rue; *Fig* **to be up against sth** avoir affaire à qch

3 *adj (out of bed)* levé; **we were up all night** nous sommes restés debout toute la nuit; **the two weeks were up** les deux semaines étaient terminées; **your time's up** c'est terminé; *Fam* **what's up?** qu'est-ce qu'il y a?; **to be up and running** être opérationnel, -elle

4 *npl* **ups and downs** des hauts et des bas *mpl*

5 *(pt & pp -pp-)* *vt Fam (price, offer)* augmenter ▪ **up-and-'coming** *adj* qui monte ▪ **'up'beat** *adj Fam* optimiste ▪ **upbringing** *n* éducation *f* ▪ **upcoming** *adj Am* imminent ▪ **update 1** [ˈʌpdeɪt] *n* mise *f* à jour 2 [ʌpˈdeɪt] *vt* mettre à jour ▪ **upgrade 1** [ˈʌpɡreɪd] *n (new model)* nouvelle version *f*; *Comptr (hardware)* augmentation *f* de puissance; *(software)* mise *f* à jour 2 [ʌpˈɡreɪd] *vt (improve)* améliorer; *(promote)* promouvoir; *Comptr (hardware)* augmenter la puissance de; *(software)* mettre à jour 3 *vi* **to u. to a new model** *(of car, computer, mobile phone)* passer à un modèle supérieur ▪ **uphill 1** [ʌpˈhɪl] *adv* **to go u.** monter 2 [ˈʌphɪl] *adj Fig (struggle, task)* pénible ▪ **up'hold** *(pt & pp -held)* *vt (decision)* maintenir ▪ **upkeep** *n* entretien *m* ▪ **uplift 1** [ˈʌplɪft] *n* élévation *f* spirituelle 2 [ʌpˈlɪft] *vt* élever ▪ **up'lifting** *adj* édifiant ▪ **up-'market** *adj Br (car, product)* haut de gamme *inv*; *(area, place)* chic *inv* ▪ **upright 1** *adv (straight)* droit 2 *adj (vertical, honest)* droit 3 *n (post)* montant *m* ▪ **uprising** *n* insurrection *f* ▪ **up'root** *vt (plant, person)* déraciner ▪ **upside 'down** *adv* à l'envers; **to turn sth u.** retourner qch; *Fig* **mettre qch sens dessus dessous** ▪ **upstairs 1** [ʌpˈsteəz] *adv* en haut; **to go u.** monter 2 [ˈʌpsteəz] *adj (people, room)* du dessus ▪ **up'stream** *adv* en amont ▪ **upsurge** *n (of interest)* recrudescence *f*; *(of anger)* accès *m* ▪ **uptake** *n Fam* **to be quick on the u.** piger vite ▪ **'up'tight** *adj Fam (tense)* crispé; *(inhibited)* coincé ▪ **'up-to-'date** *adj* moderne; *(information)* à jour; *(well-informed)* au courant (**on** de) ▪ **'up-to-the-'minute** *adj (news, information)* de dernière minute; *(style, fashion)* dernier cri *inv* ▪ **upturn** *n (improvement)* amélioration *f* (**in** de) ▪ **upturned** *adj (nose)* retroussé ▪ **upward** *adj (movement)* ascendant; *(path)* qui monte; *(trend)* à la hausse ▪ **upwards** *adv* vers le haut; **from 5 euros u.** à partir de 5 euros; **u. of fifty** cinquante et plus

upheaval [ʌpˈhiːvəl] *n* bouleversement *m*
upholster [ʌpˈhəʊlstə(r)] *vt (pad)* rembourrer; *(cover)* recouvrir ▪ **upholsterer** *n* tapissier *m* ▪ **upholstery** *n (padding)* rembourrage *m*; *(covering)* revêtement *m*; *(in car)* sièges *mpl*
upon [əˈpɒn] *prep* sur
upper [ˈʌpə(r)] 1 *adj* supérieur; **u. class** aristocratie *f*; **to have/get the u. hand** avoir/prendre le dessus; *Br Theatre* **u. circle** deuxième balcon *m* 2 *n (of shoe)* empeigne *f* ▪ **'upper-'class** *adj* aristocratique ▪ **uppermost** *adj* le plus haut *(f* la plus haute*)*; **it was u. in my mind** c'était la première de mes préoccupations
uppity [ˈʌpətɪ] *adj Fam* crâneur, -euse
uproar [ˈʌprɔː(r)] *n* tumulte *m*
upset 1 [ʌpˈset] *(pt & pp -set, pres p -setting)* *vt (knock over, spill)* renverser; *(person, plans, schedule)* bouleverser 2 *adj (unhappy)* bouleversé (**about** par); **to have an u. stomach** avoir l'estomac dérangé 3 [ˈʌpset] *n (disturbance)* bouleversement *m*; *(surprise)*

défaite *f*; **to have a stomach u.** avoir l'estomac dérangé ▪ **upsetting** *adj* bouleversant

upshot ['ʌpʃɒt] *n* résultat *m*

upstart ['ʌpstɑːt] *n Pej* parvenu, -ue *mf*

upstate [ʌp'steɪt] *Am* **1** *adj* du nord *(d'un État)*; **u. New York** le nord de l'État de New York **2** *adv* **to go u.** aller vers le nord *(d'un État)*

uptight [ʌp'taɪt] *adj (nervous)* nerveux, -euse; *(inhibited)* coincé

uranium [jʊ'reɪnɪəm] *n* uranium *m*

urban ['ɜːbən] *adj* urbain

urbane [ɜː'beɪn] *adj* courtois

urchin ['ɜːtʃɪn] *n* polisson, -onne *mf*

urge [ɜːdʒ] **1** *n* forte envie *f*; **to have an u. to do sth** avoir très envie de faire qch **2** *vt* **to u. sb to do sth** presser qn de faire qch; **to u. sb on to do sth** encourager qn à faire qch

urgency ['ɜːdʒənsɪ] *n* urgence *f*; *(of tone, request)* insistance *f*; **it's a matter of u.** il y a urgence ▪ **urgent** *adj* urgent; **to be in u. need of sth** avoir un besoin urgent de qch ▪ **urgently** *adv* d'urgence

urinal [jʊ'raɪnəl] *n* urinoir *m*

urine ['jʊərɪn] *n* urine *f* ▪ **urinate** *vi* uriner

URL [juːɑːr'el] *(abbr* **uniform resource locator**) *n Comptr* URL *m*

urn [ɜːn] *n* urne *f*; *(for coffee or tea)* fontaine *f*

Uruguay ['jʊərəgwaɪ] *n* l'Uruguay *m*

US [juː'es] *(abbr* **United States**) *n* **the US** les USA *mpl*

us [əs, *stressed* ʌs] *pron* nous; **(to) us** *(indirect)* nous; **she sees us** elle nous voit; **she saw us** elle nous a vus; **he gave it to us** il nous l'a donné; **with us** avec nous; **all of us** nous tous; **let's** *or* **let us eat!** mangeons!

USA [juːes'eɪ] *(abbr* **United States of America**) *n* **the U.** les USA *mpl*

usage ['juːsɪdʒ] *n* usage *m*

use 1 [juːs] *n (utilization)* emploi *m*, usage *m*; *(ability, permission to use)* emploi; **to have the u. of sth** avoir l'usage de qch; **to make (good) u. of sth** faire (bon) usage de qch; **to be of u. to sb** être utile à qn; **in u.** en usage; **not in u., out of u.** hors d'usage; **ready for u.** prêt à l'emploi; **it's no u. crying** ça ne sert à rien de pleurer; **what's the u. of worrying?** à quoi bon s'inquiéter?; **I have no u. for it** je n'en ai pas l'usage; *Fam* **he's no u.** il est nul **2** [juːz] *vt (utilize)* utiliser, se servir de; *(force, diplomacy)* avoir recours à; *(electricity)* consommer; **it's used to do** *or* **for doing sth** ça sert à faire qch; **it's used as...** ça sert de...; **to u. sth up** *(food, fuel)* finir; *(money)* dépenser **3** *v aux* ▪ **used to** [juːstə] **I used to sing** avant, je chantais; **she u. to jog every Sunday** elle faisait du jogging tous les dimanches ▪ **use-by date** ['juːz-] *n* date *f* limite de consommation

used 1 [juːzd] *adj (second-hand)* d'occasion;

(stamp) oblitéré **2** [juːst] *adj* **to be u. to sth/to doing sth** être habitué à qch/à faire qch; **to get u. to sb/sth** s'habituer à qn/qch

useful ['juːsfəl] *adj* utile **(to** à); **to come in u.** être utile; **to make oneself u.** se rendre utile ▪ **usefulness** *n* utilité *f* ▪ **useless** *adj* inutile; *(unusable)* inutilisable; *(person)* nul *(f* nulle) **(at** en)

user ['juːzə(r)] *n (of train, telephone)* usager *m*; *(of road, machine, dictionary)* utilisateur, -trice *mf*; **end u.** utilisateur final ▪ **'user-'friendly** *adj* convivial

> Note that the French verb **user** is a false friend. Its most common meaning is **to wear out**.

usher ['ʌʃə(r)] **1** *n (in church, theatre)* ouvreur *m*; *(in court)* huissier *m* **2** *vt* **to u. sb in** faire entrer qn

USSR [juːeses'ɑː(r)] *(abbr* **Union of Soviet Socialist Republics**) *n Formerly* URSS *f*

usual ['juːʒʊəl] **1** *adj* habituel, -uelle; **as u.** comme d'habitude; **you're not your u. self today** tu n'es pas aussi gai que d'habitude aujourd'hui **2** *n Fam* **the u.** *(food, excuse)* la même chose que d'habitude ▪ **usually** *adv* d'habitude

usurer ['juːʒərə(r)] *n* usurier, -ière *mf*

usurp [juːˈzɜːp] *vt* usurper

utensil [juːˈtensəl] *n* ustensile *m*; **kitchen u.** ustensile de cuisine

uterus ['juːtərəs] *n Anat* utérus *m*

utilitarian [juːtɪlɪ'teərɪən] *adj* utilitaire

utility [juːˈtɪlətɪ] *n (usefulness)* utilité *f*; **(public) utilities** services *mpl* publics; *Am* **utilities** *(service charges)* charges *fpl*; *Comptr* **u. (program)** utilitaire *m*; **u. room** pièce *f* de rangement

utilize ['juːtɪlaɪz] *vt* utiliser ▪ **utili'zation** *n* utilisation *f*

utmost ['ʌtməʊst] **1** *adj* **the u. ease** *(greatest)* la plus grande facilité; **the u. danger/limit** *(extreme)* un danger/une limite extrême; **it is of the u. importance that...** il est de la plus haute importance que... *(+ subjunctive)* **2** *n* **to do one's u.** faire de son mieux **(to do** pour faire)

utopia [juːˈtəʊpɪə] *n* utopie *f* ▪ **utopian** *adj* utopique

utter¹ ['ʌtə(r)] *adj* total; *(folly, lie)* pur; **it's u. nonsense** c'est complètement absurde ▪ **utterly** *adv* complètement

utter² ['ʌtə(r)] *vt (cry, sigh)* pousser; *(word)* prononcer; *(threat)* proférer ▪ **utterance** *n (act)* énonciation *f*; *(words spoken)* déclaration *f*; *Ling* énoncé *m*

U-turn ['juːtɜːn] *n (in vehicle)* demi-tour *m*; *Fig (change of policy)* virage *m* à 180°

V, v [viː] *n (letter)* V, v *m inv*

vacant ['veɪkənt] *adj (room, seat)* libre; *(post)* vacant; *(look)* absent; *Br* **'situations v.'** *(in newspaper)* 'offres d'emploi' ▪ **vacancy** *(pl -ies)* *n (post)* poste *m* vacant; *(room)* chambre *f* libre; **'no vacancies'** *(in hotel)* 'complet' ▪ **vacantly** *adv* d'un air absent

> Note that the French word **vacances** is a false friend. It means **holiday**.

vacate [*Br* və'keɪt, *Am* 'veɪkeɪt] *vt* quitter

vacation [veɪ'keɪʃən] *n Am* vacances *fpl*; **to take a v.** prendre des vacances ▪ **vacationer** *n Am* vacancier, -ière *mf*

vaccinate ['væksɪneɪt] *vt* vacciner ▪ **vacci-nation** *n* vaccination *f* ▪ **vaccine** [-'siːn] *n* vaccin *m*

vacillate ['væsɪleɪt] *vi* hésiter

vacuum ['vækjʊəm] **1** *n* vide *m*; **v. cleaner** aspirateur *m*; *Br* **v. flask** Thermos® *m ou f* **2** *vt (room)* passer l'aspirateur dans; *(carpet)* passer l'aspirateur sur ▪ **vacuum-packed** *adj* emballé sous vide

vagabond ['vægəbɒnd] *n* vagabond, -onde *mf*

vagary ['veɪgərɪ] *(pl -ies)* *n* caprice *m*

vagina [və'dʒaɪnə] *n Anat* vagin *m* ▪ **vaginal** *adj* vaginal

vagrant ['veɪgrənt] *n Law* vagabond, -onde *mf* ▪ **vagrancy** *n Law* vagabondage *m*

vague [veɪg] *(-er, -est) adj* vague; *(outline, photo)* flou; **I haven't got the vaguest idea** je n'en ai pas la moindre idée; **he was v. (about it)** il est resté vague ▪ **vaguely** *adv* vaguement

vain [veɪn] *(-er, -est) adj* (a) *(attempt, hope)* vain; **in v.** en vain; **her efforts were in v.** ses efforts ont été inutiles (b) *(conceited)* vaniteux, -euse

valentine ['væləntaɪn] *n (card)* carte *f* de la Saint-Valentin; **(Saint) V.'s Day** la Saint-Valentin

valet ['vælɪt, 'væleɪ] *n* valet *m* de chambre

valiant ['væljənt] *adj* vaillant ▪ **valour** *(Am* **valor)** *n* bravoure *f*

valid ['vælɪd] *adj* valable ▪ **validate** [və'lɪdɪtɪ] *vt* valider ▪ **validity** [və'lɪdɪtɪ] *n* validité *f*

valley ['vælɪ] *(pl -eys)* *n* vallée *f*

valuable ['væljʊəbəl] **1** *adj (object)* de valeur; *Fig (help, time)* précieux, -ieuse **2** *npl* **valuables** objets *mpl* de valeur

value ['væljuː] **1** *n* valeur *f*; **to be of v.** avoir de la valeur; **to be good v. (for money)** être d'un bon rapport qualité-prix; *Br* **v.-added tax** taxe *f* sur la valeur ajoutée **2** *vt (appreciate)* apprécier; *(assess)* évaluer ▪ **valuation** [-jʊ'eɪʃən] *n (assessment)* évaluation *f*; *(by expert)* expertise *f*

valve [vælv] *n (of machine, car)* soupape *f*; *(of pipe, tube)* valve *f*; *(of heart)* valvule *f*

vampire ['væmpaɪə(r)] *n* vampire *m*

van [væn] *n (vehicle)* camionnette *f*, fourgonnette *f*; *Br Rail* fourgon *m*

vandal ['vændəl] *n* vandale *mf* ▪ **vandalism** *n* vandalisme *m* ▪ **vandalize** *vt* saccager

vanguard ['vængɑːd] *n* **in the v. of** à l'avant-garde de

vanilla [və'nɪlə] **1** *n* vanille *f* **2** *adj (ice cream)* à la vanille; **v. flavour** parfum *m* vanille

vanish ['vænɪʃ] *vi* disparaître; **to v. into thin air** se volatiliser

vanity ['vænɪtɪ] *n* vanité *f*; **v. case** vanity-case *m*

vantage point ['vɑːntɪdʒpɔɪnt] *n* point *m* de vue; *Fig* position *f* objective

vapour ['veɪpə(r)] *(Am* **vapor)** *n* vapeur *f*

variable ['veərɪəbəl] *adj & n* variable *(f)*

variance ['veərɪəns] *n* **at v.** en désaccord (**with** avec)

variant ['veərɪənt] **1** *adj* différent **2** *n* variante *f*

variation [veərɪ'eɪʃən] *n* variation *f*

varicose ['værɪkəʊs] *adj* **v. veins** varices *fpl*

variety [və'raɪətɪ] *n* (a) *(diversity)* variété *f*; **a v. of** toutes sortes de; **a v. of articles/products** toute une gamme d'articles/de produits (b) *(entertainment)* variétés *fpl*; **v. show** spectacle *m* de variétés

various ['veərɪəs] *adj* divers ▪ **variously** *adv* diversement

varnish ['vɑːnɪʃ] **1** *n* vernis *m* **2** *vt* vernir

vary ['veərɪ] *(pt & pp -ied) vti* varier (**in/with** en/selon) ▪ **varied** *adj* varié ▪ **varying** *adj* variable

vase [*Br* vɑːz, *Am* veɪs] *n* vase *m*

vasectomy [və'sektəmɪ] *n* vasectomie *f*

Vaseline® ['væsəliːn] *n* vaseline *f*

vast [vɑːst] *adj* immense ▪ **vastly** *adv* à l'extrême; *(superior)* infiniment ▪ **vastness** *n* immensité *f*

VAT [viːeɪ'tiː, væt] *(abbr* **value added tax**) *n Br* TVA *f*

vat [væt] *n* cuve *f*

Vatican ['vætɪkən] *n* the V. le Vatican

vault¹ [vɔːlt] *n (roof)* voûte *f; (tomb)* caveau *m; (cellar)* cave *f; (in bank)* salle *f* des coffres

vault² [vɔːlt] *vti (jump)* sauter

VCR [viːsiːˈɑː(r)] *n (abbr* **video cassette recorder)** *n* magnétoscope *m*

VD [viːˈdiː] *(abbr* **venereal disease)** *n* maladie *f* vénérienne

VDU [viːdiːˈjuː] *(abbr* **visual display unit)** *n* Comptr moniteur *m*

veal [viːl] *n* veau *m*

veer [vɪə(r)] *vi (of car)* virer; *(of wind)* tourner; *(of road)* décrire un virage; **to v. off the road** quitter la route

veg [vedʒ] *npl Br Fam* légumes *mpl*

vegan ['viːɡən] *adj & n* végétalien, -ienne *(mf)*

vegeburger ['vedʒɪbɜːɡə(r)] *n* hamburger *m* végétarien

vegetable ['vedʒtəbəl] *n* légume *m;* **v. fat** graisse *f* végétale; **v. garden** potager *m;* **v. kingdom** règne *m* végétal; **v. oil** huile *f* végétale ▪ **vegetation** [vedʒɪˈteɪʃən] *n* végétation *f*

vegetate ['vedʒɪteɪt] *vi Pej (of person)* végéter

vegetarian [vedʒɪˈteərɪən] *adj & n* végétarien, -ienne *(mf)* ▪ **veggie** [vedʒɪ] *adj & n Br Fam* végétarien, -ienne *(mf)*

vehement ['viːəmənt] *adj* véhément ▪ **vehemently** *adv* avec véhémence

vehicle ['viːɪkəl] *n* véhicule *m*

veil [veɪl] **1** *n (covering)* & Fig voile *m* **2** *vt* voiler ▪ **veiled** *adj* voilé

vein [veɪn] *n (in body, rock)* veine *f; (in leaf)* nervure *f; Fig* **in a similar v.** de la même veine

Velcro® ['velkrəʊ] *n* Velcro® *m*

velocity [vəˈlɒsɪtɪ] *n* vélocité *f*

velvet ['velvɪt] **1** *n* velours *m* **2** *adj* de velours ▪ **velvety** *adj* velouté

vendetta [venˈdetə] *n* vendetta *f*

vending machine ['vendɪŋməʃiːn] *n* distributeur *m* automatique

vendor ['vendə(r)] *n* vendeur, -euse *mf*

veneer [vəˈnɪə(r)] *n (wood)* placage *m; Fig (appearance)* vernis *m*

venerable ['venərəbəl] *adj* vénérable ▪ **venerate** *vt* vénérer

venereal [vəˈnɪərɪəl] *adj* vénérien, -ienne

venetian [vəˈniːʃən] *adj* **v. blind** store *m* vénitien

Venezuela [venɪˈzweɪlə] *n* le Venezuela

vengeance ['vendʒəns] *n* vengeance *f;* **to take v. on sb** se venger de qn; *Fig* **with a v.** de plus belle

venison ['venɪsən] *n* venaison *f*

venom ['venəm] *n (poison)* & Fig venin *m* ▪ **venomous** *adj (snake, speech)* venimeux, -euse

vent [vent] **1** *n* conduit *m; Fig* **to give v. to sth** donner libre cours à qch **2** *vt* **to v. one's anger on sb** décharger sa colère sur qn

ventilate ['ventɪleɪt] *vt* ventiler, aérer ▪ **venti'lation** *n* ventilation *f*, aération *f* ▪ **ventilator** *n* ventilateur *m; Med* respirateur *m; Med* **to be on a v.** être branché sur un respirateur

ventriloquist [venˈtrɪləkwɪst] *n* ventriloque *mf*

venture ['ventʃə(r)] **1** *n* entreprise *f* (hasardeuse); *Fin* **v. capital** capital-risque *m* **2** *vt* risquer; **to v. to do sth** se risquer à faire qch **3** *vi* s'aventurer (**into** dans)

venue ['venjuː] *n (for meeting, concert)* salle *f; (for football match)* stade *m*

> Note that the French word **venue** is a false friend and is never a translation for the English word **venue**. It means **arrival**.

veranda(h) [vəˈrændə] *n* véranda *f*

verb [vɜːb] *n* verbe *m* ▪ **verbal** *adj* verbal

verbatim [vɜːˈbeɪtɪm] *adj & adv* mot pour mot

verbose [vɜːˈbəʊs] *adj* verbeux, -euse

verdict ['vɜːdɪkt] *n* verdict *m*

verge [vɜːdʒ] **1** *n Br (of road)* bord *m;* **on the v. of ruin/tears** au bord de la ruine/des larmes; **on the v. of a discovery** à la veille d'une découverte; **to be on the v. of doing sth** être sur le point de faire qch **2** *vi* **to v. on** friser; *(of colour)* tirer sur

verify ['verɪfaɪ] *(pt & pp* -ied*) vt* vérifier ▪ **verification** [-fɪˈkeɪʃən] *n* vérification *f*

veritable ['verɪtəbəl] *adj Formal* véritable

vermin ['vɜːmɪn] *n (animals)* animaux *mpl* nuisibles; *(insects, people)* vermine *f*

vermouth ['vɜːməθ] *n* vermouth *m*

vernacular [vəˈnækjʊlə(r)] *n* langue *f* vernaculaire

versatile [*Br* 'vɜːsətaɪl, *Am* 'vɜːrsətəl] *adj* polyvalent ▪ **versatility** [-ˈtɪlɪtɪ] *n* polyvalence *f*

> Note that the French word **versatile** is a false friend and is never a translation for the English word **versatile**. It means **changeable**.

verse [vɜːs] *n (poetry)* vers *mpl; (stanza)* strophe *f; (of Bible)* verset *m*

versed [vɜːst] *adj* **(well) v. in sth** versé dans qch

version [*Br* 'vɜːʃən, *Am* 'vɜːrʒən] *n* version *f*

versus ['vɜːsəs] *prep (in sport, law)* contre; *(compared to)* comparé à

vertebra ['vɜːtɪbrə] *(pl* -ae [-iː]*) n* vertèbre *f*

vertical ['vɜːtɪkəl] **1** *adj* vertical **2** *n* verticale *f* ▪ **vertically** *adv* verticalement

vertigo ['vɜːtɪɡəʊ] *n* vertige *m*

verve [vɜːv] *n* verve *f*

very ['verɪ] **1** *adv* très; **v. little** très peu; **v. much** beaucoup; **I'm v. hot** j'ai très chaud; **the v. first** le tout premier *(f* la toute première); **the v. next day** le lendemain même; **at the v. least/most** tout au moins/plus; **at the v. latest** au plus

tard 2 *adj (emphatic use)* **this v. house** cette maison même; **at the v. end** tout à la fin; **to the v. end** jusqu'au bout; **those were her v. words** c'est ce qu'elle a dit mot pour mot
vespers ['vespəz] *npl (church service)* vêpres *fpl*
vessel ['vesəl] *n (ship)* vaisseau *m; (container)* récipient *m*
vest [vest] *n Br* maillot *m* de corps; *Am (waistcoat)* gilet *m*

> Note that the French word **veste** is a false friend and is never a translation for the English word **vest**. It means **jacket**.

vested ['vestɪd] *adj* **to have a v. interest in sth** avoir un intérêt personnel dans qch
vestige ['vestɪdʒ] *n* vestige *m*; **not a v. of truth** pas une once de vérité
vestry ['vestrɪ] *(pl* **-ies)** *n (in church)* sacristie *f*
vet¹ [vet] *n* vétérinaire *mf* ■ **veterinarian** [vetərɪ'neərɪən] *n Am* vétérinaire *mf* ■ **veterinary** ['vetərɪnərɪ] *adj* vétérinaire; *Br* **v. surgeon** vétérinaire *mf*
vet² [vet] *(pt & pp* **-tt-)** *vt Br* faire une enquête sur
vet³ [vet] *n Am Fam Mil* ancien combattant *m*
veteran ['vetərən] **1** *n Mil* ancien combattant *m*; *Fig* vétéran *m* **2** *adj* de longue date; **v. golfer** golfeur expérimenté
veto ['viːtəʊ] **1** *(pl* **-oes)** *n* veto *m inv*; **right or power of v.** droit *m* de veto **2** *(pt & pp* **-oed)** *vt* mettre son veto à
VHF [viːeɪtʃ'ef] *(abbr* **very high frequency)** *n* **on V.** en VHF *f*
VHS [viːeɪtʃ'es] *(abbr* **video home system)** *n* VHS *m*
via [Br 'vaɪə, Am 'viːə] *prep* via, par
viable ['vaɪəbəl] *adj* viable ■ **via'bility** *n* viabilité *f*
viaduct ['vaɪədʌkt] *n* viaduc *m*
Viagra® [vaɪ'ægrə] *n Med* Viagra® *m*
vibrant ['vaɪbrənt] *adj (person)* plein de vie; *(speech)* vibrant; *(colour)* vif *(f* vive)
vibrate [vaɪ'breɪt] *vi* vibrer ■ **vibration** *n* vibration *f* ■ **vibrator** *n* vibromasseur *m*
vicar ['vɪkə(r)] *n (in Church of England)* pasteur *m* ■ **vicarage** [-rɪdʒ] *n* presbytère *m*
vicarious [vɪ'keərɪəs] *adj* indirect ■ **vicariously** *adv* indirectement
vice¹ *(Am* **vise)** [vaɪs] *n (tool)* étau *m*
vice² [vaɪs] *n (depravity, fault)* vice *m*; **the v. squad** ≃ la brigade des mœurs
vice- [vaɪs] *pref* vice- ■ **vice-'chancellor** *n (of British university)* président *m* ■ **vice-'president** *n* vice-président, -ente *mf*
vice versa [vaɪs(ɪ)'vɜːsə] *adv* vice versa
vicinity [və'sɪnɪtɪ] *n* environs *mpl*; **in the v. of** aux environs de
vicious ['vɪʃəs] *adj (malicious)* méchant; *(violent)* brutal; **v. circle** cercle *m* vicieux ■ **viciously** *adv (spitefully)* méchamment;

(violently) brutalement ■ **viciousness** *n (spite)* méchanceté *f; (violence)* brutalité *f*

> Note that the French word **vicieux** is a false friend. It means **depraved** or **underhand** depending on the context.

vicissitudes [vɪ'sɪsɪtjuːdz] *npl* vicissitudes *fpl*
victim ['vɪktɪm] *n* victime *f*; **to be the v. of** être victime de; **to fall v. to a disease** contracter une maladie
victimize ['vɪktɪmaɪz] *vt* persécuter ■ **victimi'zation** *n* persécution *f*
Victorian [vɪk'tɔːrɪən] **1** *adj* victorien, -ienne **2** *n* Victorien, -ienne *mf*
victory ['vɪktərɪ] *(pl* **-ies)** *n* victoire *f* ■ **victor** ['vɪktər] *n Old-fashioned* vainqueur *m* ■ **victorious** [-'tɔːrɪəs] *adj* victorieux, -ieuse
video ['vɪdɪəʊ] **1** *(pl* **-os)** *n (medium)* vidéo *f; (cassette)* cassette *f* vidéo; *(recorder)* magnétoscope *m*; **on v.** sur cassette vidéo; **to make a v. of** faire une cassette vidéo de **2** *adj (camera)* vidéo *inv*; **v. cassette** cassette *f* vidéo; **v. game** jeu *m* vidéo; **v. recorder** magnétoscope *m*; **v. shop** *(for renting videos)* vidéoclub *m* **3** *(pt & pp* **-oed)** *vt (on camcorder)* filmer en vidéo; *(on video recorder)* enregistrer *(sur magnétoscope)* ■ **videodisc** *n* vidéodisque *m* ■ **videotape 1** *n* bande *f* vidéo **2** *vt* enregistrer sur magnétoscope
vie [vaɪ] *(pres p* **vying)** *vi* **to v. with sb (for sth/ to do sth)** rivaliser avec qn (pour qch/pour faire qch)
Vienna [vɪ'enə] *n* Vienne *m ou f*
Vietnam [Br vjet'næm, Am -'nɑːm] *n* le Viêt Nam ■ **Vietnamese** [-nə'miːz] **1** *adj* vietnamien, -ienne **2** *n* Vietnamien, -ienne *mf*
view [vjuː] **1** *n* vue *f; (opinion)* opinion *f*; **to come into v.** apparaître; **in full v. of everyone** à la vue de tous; **in my v.** *(opinion)* à mon avis; **in v. of** *(considering)* étant donné; **on v.** *(exhibit)* exposé; **with a v. to doing sth** dans l'intention de faire qch **2** *vt (regard)* considérer; *(look at)* voir; *(house)* visiter ■ **viewer** *n* **(a)** *TV* téléspectateur, -trice *mf* **(b)** *(for slides)* visionneuse *f* ■ **viewfinder** *n (in camera)* viseur *m* ■ **viewpoint** *n* point *m* de vue
vigil ['vɪdʒɪl] *n* veillée *f*

> Note that the French word **vigile** is a false friend. Its most common meaning is **security guard**.

vigilant ['vɪdʒɪlənt] *adj* vigilant ■ **vigilance** *n* vigilance *f*
vigilante [vɪdʒɪ'læntɪ] *n Pej* = membre d'une milice privée
vigour ['vɪgə(r)] *(Am* **vigor)** *n* vigueur *f* ■ **vigorous** *adj* vigoureux, -euse
vile [vaɪl] **(-er, -est)** *adj (unpleasant)* abominable; *(food, drink)* infect

vilify ['vɪlɪfaɪ] (pt & pp -ied) vt calomnier

villa ['vɪlə] n villa f

village ['vɪlɪdʒ] n village m **•villager** n villageois, -oise mf

villain ['vɪlən] n (scoundrel) scélérat m; (in story, play) méchant m **•villainous** adj diabolique

vindicate ['vɪndɪkeɪt] vt justifier **•vindication** n justification f

vindictive [vɪn'dɪktɪv] adj vindicatif, -ive

vine [vaɪn] n vigne f; **v. grower** viticulteur, -trice mf **•vineyard** ['vɪnjəd] n vigne f

vinegar ['vɪnɪgə(r)] n vinaigre m

vintage ['vɪntɪdʒ] **1** n (year) année f; (wine) cru m **2** adj (wine) de cru; (car) de collection (datant généralement des années 1920)

vinyl ['vaɪnəl] n vinyle m; **the album is available on v.** l'album existe sur vinyle; **v. seats** sièges mpl en vinyle

viola ['vɪəʊlə] n alto m

violate ['vaɪəleɪt] vt (agreement) violer **•vio'lation** n violation f

violence ['vaɪələns] n violence f **•violent** adj violent; **to take a v. dislike to sb/sth** se prendre d'une aversion violente pour qn/qch **•violently** adv violemment; Br **to be v. sick** être pris de violents vomissements

violet ['vaɪələt] **1** adj (colour) violet, -ette **2** n (colour) violet m; (plant) violette f

violin [vaɪə'lɪn] n violon m; **v. concerto** concerto m pour violon **•violinist** n violoniste mf

VIP [viːaɪ'piː] (abbr very important person) n VIP mf

viper ['vaɪpə(r)] n vipère f

viral ['vaɪrəl] adj viral

virgin ['vɜːdʒɪn] **1** n vierge f; **to be a v.** être vierge **2** adj (territory, forest) vierge; **v. snow** neige f d'une blancheur virginale **•vir'ginity** n virginité f; **to lose one's v.** perdre sa virginité

Virgo ['vɜːgəʊ] n (sign) la Vierge; **to be (a) V.** être Vierge

virile [Br 'vɪraɪl, Am 'vɪrəl] adj viril **•virility** [-'rɪlɪtɪ] n virilité f

virtual ['vɜːtʃʊəl] adj quasi; Comptr virtuel, -uelle; **v. reality** réalité f virtuelle **•virtually** adv (in fact) en fait; (almost) quasiment

virtue ['vɜːtʃuː] n (goodness, chastity) vertu f; (advantage) mérite m; **by v. of** en vertu de **•virtuous** [-tʃʊəs] adj vertueux, -ueuse

virtuoso [vɜːtʃʊ'əʊsəʊ] (pl -si [-siː]) n virtuose mf **•virtuosity** [-tʃʊ'ɒsɪtɪ] n virtuosité f

virulent ['vɪrʊlənt] adj virulent **•virulence** n virulence f

virus ['vaɪərəs] n Med & Comptr virus m

Visa® ['viːzə] n **V. (card)** carte f Visa®

visa ['viːzə] n visa m

vis-à-vis [viːzə'viː] prep vis-à-vis de

viscount ['vaɪkaʊnt] n vicomte m **•viscountess** n vicomtesse f

viscous ['vɪskəs] adj visqueux, -euse

vise [vaɪs] n Am = **vice¹**

visible ['vɪzəbəl] adj visible **•visi'bility** n visibilité f **•visibly** adv visiblement

vision ['vɪʒən] n (eyesight) vue f; (foresight) clairvoyance f; (apparition) vision f; Fig **a man of v.** un homme clairvoyant **•visionary** (pl -ies) adj & n visionnaire (mf)

visit ['vɪzɪt] **1** n visite f; **to pay sb a v.** rendre visite à qn **2** vt (place) visiter; (person) rendre visite à **3** vi **to be visiting** être de passage; **to go visiting** aller en visites; Br **v. hours/card** heures fpl/carte f de visite **•visitor** n visiteur, -euse mf; (guest) invité, -ée mf

visor ['vaɪzə(r)] n visière f

vista ['vɪstə] n vue f; Fig (of future) perspective f

visual ['vɪʒʊəl] adj visuel, -uelle; **v. aid** support m visuel; **v. arts** arts mpl plastiques; Comptr **v. display unit** console f de visualisation **•visualize** vt (imagine) visualiser; (foresee) envisager

vital ['vaɪtəl] adj vital; **it's v. that...** il est vital que... (+ subjunctive); **of v. importance** d'une importance vitale; Hum **v. statistics** (of woman) mensurations fpl **•vitally** adv **v. important** d'une importance vitale

vitality [vaɪ'tælɪtɪ] n vitalité f

vitamin [Br 'vɪtəmɪn, Am 'vaɪtəmɪn] n vitamine f; **with added vitamins** vitaminé; **v. pill** comprimé m de vitamines

vitriol ['vɪtrɪəl] n (acid, bitter speech) vitriol m **•vitriolic** [-ɪ'ɒlɪk] adj au vitriol

viva ['vaɪvə] n Br Univ oral m

vivacious [vɪ'veɪʃəs] adj enjoué

vivid ['vɪvɪd] adj vif (f vive); (description) vivant; (memory) clair **•vividly** adv (describe) de façon vivante; **to remember sth v.** se souvenir clairement de qch

vivisection [vɪvɪ'sekʃən] n vivisection f

vixen ['vɪksən] n renarde f

V-neck [viː'nek] **1** adj à col en V **2** n col m en V

vocabulary [Br və'kæbjʊlərɪ, Am -erɪ] n vocabulaire m

vocal ['vəʊkəl] **1** adj (cords, music) vocal; (outspoken) franc (f franche); (noisy, critical) qui se fait entendre **2** n **on vocals** au chant **•vocalist** n chanteur, -euse mf

vocation [vəʊ'keɪʃən] n vocation f **•vocational** adj professionnel, -elle; **v. course** (short) stage m de formation professionnelle; (longer) enseignement m professionnel; **v. school** établissement m d'enseignement professionnel; **v. training** formation f professionnelle

vociferous [və'sɪfərəs] adj bruyant

vodka ['vɒdkə] n vodka f; **v. and orange** vodka orange

vogue [vəʊg] n vogue f; **in v.** en vogue

voice [vɔɪs] **1** n voix f; **at the top of one's v.** à tue-tête; **I've lost my v.** je n'ai plus de voix **2** vt (opinion, feelings) exprimer ▪ **voiceless** adj Med aphone ▪ **voicemail** n Tel (service) messagerie f vocale; (message) message m vocal

void [vɔɪd] **1** n vide m **2** adj Law (deed, contract) nul (f nulle); Literary **v. of** dépourvu de

volatile [Br 'vɒlətaɪl, Am 'vɒlətəl] adj (person) inconstant; (situation) explosif, -ive

volcano [vɒl'keɪnəʊ] (pl -oes) n volcan m ▪ **volcanic** [-'kænɪk] adj volcanique

volition [və'lɪʃən] n Formal **of one's own v.** de son propre gré

volley ['vɒlɪ] n (of gunfire) salve f; (of blows) volée f; Fig (of insults) bordée f; Tennis volée f ▪ **volleyball** n Sport volley(-ball) m

volt [vəʊlt] n volt m ▪ **voltage** [-tɪdʒ] n voltage m

volume ['vɒljuːm] n (book, capacity, loudness) volume m; **at full v.** (TV, radio) à fond; **v. control** (on TV, radio) bouton m de réglage du volume ▪ **voluminous** [və'luːmɪnəs] adj volumineux, -euse

voluntary [Br 'vɒləntərɪ, Am -erɪ] adj volontaire; (unpaid) bénévole; **v. redundancy** départ m volontaire ▪ **voluntarily** adv volontairement; (on an unpaid basis) bénévolement

volunteer [vɒlən'tɪə(r)] **1** n volontaire mf; (for charity) bénévole mf **2** vt (information) donner spontanément **3** vi se porter volontaire (**for sth** pour qch; **to do** pour faire); (for the army) s'engager (**for** dans)

voluptuous [və'lʌptʃʊəs] adj voluptueux, -ueuse

vomit ['vɒmɪt] **1** n vomi m **2** vti vomir

voracious [və'reɪʃəs] adj vorace

vote [vəʊt] **1** n (choice) vote m; (election) scrutin m; (paper) voix f; **to put sth to the v.** soumettre qch au vote; **to take a v. on sth** voter sur qch; **to have the v.** avoir le droit de vote; **they got 12 percent of the v.** ils ont obtenu 12 pour cent des voix; **v. of no confidence** motion f de censure; **v. of thanks** discours m de remerciement **2** vt (funds, bill) voter; (person) élire; **to v. sb in** élire qn; **to be voted president** être élu président **3** vi voter; **to v. Labour/Democrat** voter travailliste/démocrate ▪ **voter** n (elector) électeur, -trice mf ▪ **voting** n (of funds) vote m (**of** de); (polling) scrutin m

vouch [vaʊtʃ] vi **to v. for sb/sth** répondre de qn/qch

voucher ['vaʊtʃə(r)] n Br coupon m, bon m; **gift v.** chèque-cadeau m

vow [vaʊ] **1** n vœu m **2** vt jurer (**to** à); **to v. to do sth** jurer de faire qch

vowel ['vaʊəl] n voyelle f

voyage ['vɔɪɪdʒ] n voyage m

vulgar ['vʌlgə(r)] adj vulgaire ▪ **vulgarity** [-'gærɪtɪ] n vulgarité f

vulnerable ['vʌlnərəbəl] adj vulnérable ▪ **vulnera'bility** n vulnérabilité f

vulture ['vʌltʃə(r)] n vautour m

W, w [ˈdʌbəljuː] n (letter) W, w m inv

wacky [ˈwækɪ] (**-ier, -iest**) adj Fam farfelu

wad [wɒd] n (of papers, banknotes) liasse f; (of cotton wool) morceau m

waddle [ˈwɒdəl] vi Fig (of duck, person) se dandiner

wade [weɪd] vi **to w. through** (mud, water) patauger dans; Fig (book) venir péniblement à bout de ▪ **wading pool** n Am (inflatable) piscine f gonflable; (purpose-built) pataugeoire f

wafer [ˈweɪfə(r)] n (biscuit) gaufrette f; Rel hostie f; **w.-thin** (slice) mince comme du papier à cigarette

waffle¹ [ˈwɒfəl] n (cake) gaufre f

waffle² [ˈwɒfəl] Br Fam **1** n remplissage m **2** vi faire du remplissage

waft [wɒft] vi (of smell, sound) parvenir

wag¹ [wæg] (pt & pp **-gg-**) **1** vt remuer, agiter; **to w. one's finger at sb** menacer qn du doigt **2** vi remuer; **its tail was wagging** (of dog) il remuait la queue; Fam **tongues are wagging** les langues vont bon train

wag² [wæg] n Fam (joker) farceur, -euse mf

wage [weɪdʒ] **1** n **wage(s)** salaire m, paie f; **a living w.** un salaire qui permet de vivre; **w. claim** revendication f salariale; **w. earner** salarié, -iée mf; **w. freeze** gel m des salaires; **w. increase** augmentation f de salaire; Br **w. packet** (envelope) enveloppe f de paie; (money) paie **2** vt **to w. war** faire la guerre (**on** à); **to w. a campaign against smoking** mener une campagne antitabac

wager [ˈweɪdʒə(r)] **1** n pari m **2** vt parier (**that** que)

waggle [ˈwægəl] vti remuer

wag(g)on [ˈwægən] n Br (of train) wagon m (découvert); (horse-drawn) charrette f; Fam **to be on the w.** (no longer drinking) être au régime sec; Fam **to fall off the w.** (start drinking again) se remettre à boire

waif [weɪf] n (child) enfant mf abandonné(e); (very thin girl) fille f excessivement maigre

wail [weɪl] **1** n (of person) gémissement m; (of siren) hurlement m **2** vi (of person) gémir; (of siren) hurler

waist [weɪst] n taille f ▪ **waistband** n ceinture f ▪ **waistcoat** n Br gilet m ▪ **waistline** n taille f

wait [weɪt] **1** n attente f; **to lie in w. for sb** guetter qn **2** vt attendre; **to w. one's turn** attendre son tour **3** vi (**a**) attendre; **to w. for sb/sth** attendre qn/qch; **to keep sb waiting** faire attendre qn; **w. till** or **until I've gone, w. for me to go** attends que je sois parti; **w. and see!** tu verras bien!; **I can't w. to see her** j'ai vraiment hâte de la voir (**b**) **to w. at table** servir à table; **to w. on sb** servir qn ▪ **waiting 1** n attente f; Br **'no w.'** (on sign) 'arrêt interdit' **2** adj **w. list/room** liste f/salle f d'attente ▪ **waitlist** vt Am mettre sur la liste d'attente

▸ **wait about, wait around** vi attendre; **to w. about** or **around for sb/sth** attendre qn/qch

▸ **wait behind** vi rester

▸ **wait up** vi veiller; **to w. up for sb** attendre le retour de qn pour aller se coucher

waiter [ˈweɪtə(r)] n serveur m ▪ **waitress** n serveuse f

waive [weɪv] vt (renounce) renoncer à; **to w. a requirement for sb** dispenser qn d'une condition requise

wake¹ [weɪk] (pt **woke**, pp **woken**) **1** vt **to w. sb (up)** réveiller qn **2** vi **to w. (up)** se réveiller; **to w. up to sth** prendre conscience de qch ▪ **waking** adj **to spend one's w. hours working** passer ses journées à travailler

wake² [weɪk] n (of ship) sillage m; Fig **in the w. of sth** à la suite de qch

wake³ [weɪk] n (before funeral) veillée f mortuaire

waken [ˈweɪkən] vt réveiller

Wales [weɪlz] n le pays de Galles

walk [wɔːk] **1** n (short) promenade f; (long) marche f; (gait) démarche f; (pace) pas m; (path) avenue f; **to go for a w., to take a w.** aller se promener; **to take sb for a w.** emmener qn se promener; **to take the dog for a w.** promener le chien; **five minutes' w. (away)** à cinq minutes à pied; Fig **from all walks of life** de tous les milieux **2** vt **to w. the dog** promener le chien; **to w. sb home** raccompagner qn; **to w. sb to** (place) accompagner qn à; **to w. the streets** battre le pavé; **I walked 3 miles** j'ai fait presque 5 km à pied **3** vi marcher; (as opposed to cycling, driving) aller à pied; (for exercise, pleasure) se promener; **to w. home** rentrer à pied; **w.!** (don't run) ne cours pas! ▪ **walker** n marcheur, -euse mf; (for pleasure) promeneur, -euse mf

▪ **walking 1** n marche f (à pied) **2** adj Fig **a w. corpse/dictionary** (person) un cadavre/ dictionnaire ambulant; **at a w. pace** au pas; **w. shoes** chaussures fpl de marche; **w. stick** canne f ▪ **walkout** n (strike) grève f surprise; (from meeting) départ m en signe de protestation ▪ **walkover** n Fam **it was a w.** c'était du gâteau ▪ **walkway** n passage m couvert; **moving w.** trottoir m roulant

▸ **walk away** vi s'en aller (from de); Fig **to w. away with a prize** remporter un prix

▸ **walk in** vi entrer; **to w. into a tree** rentrer dans un arbre; **to w. into a trap** tomber dans un piège

▸ **walk off** vi s'en aller; **to w. off with sth** (steal) partir avec qch; (win easily) remporter qch

▸ **walk out** vi (leave) sortir; Br (of workers) se mettre en grève; **to w. out on sb** quitter qn

▸ **walk over 1** vi **to w. over to** (go up to) s'approcher de **2** vt insep Fam **to w. over sb** marcher sur les pieds de qn

walkie-talkie [wɔːkɪˈtɔːkɪ] n talkie-walkie m

Walkman® [ˈwɔːkmən] (pl **-mans**) n baladeur m

wall [wɔːl] **1** n mur m; (of cabin, tunnel, stomach) paroi f; Fig **a. w. of smoke** un rideau de fumée; Fig **to go to the w.** faire faillite; Fam **I might as well talk to the w.** c'est comme si je parlais à un mur **2** adj (map, hanging) mural **3** vt **to w. a door up** murer une porte ▪ **walled** adj **w. city** ville f fortifiée ▪ **wallflower** n (plant) giroflée f; Fig **to be a w.** (of person) faire tapisserie ▪ **wallpaper 1** n papier m peint **2** vt tapisser ▪ **'wall-to-wall 'carpet(ing)** n moquette f

wallet [ˈwɒlɪt] n portefeuille m

wallop [ˈwɒləp] Fam **1** n beigne f **2** vt filer une beigne à

wallow [ˈwɒləʊ] vi se vautrer; Fig **to w. in self-pity** s'apitoyer sur son sort

wally [ˈwɒlɪ] (pl **-ies**) n Br Fam (idiot) andouille f

walnut [ˈwɔːlnʌt] n (nut) noix f; (tree, wood) noyer m

walrus [ˈwɔːlrəs] (pl **-ruses** [-rəsəz]) n morse m

waltz [Br wɔːls, Am wɒlts] **1** n valse f **2** vi valser

wan [wɒn] adj blême

wand [wɒnd] n (magic) **w.** baguette f magique

wander [ˈwɒndə(r)] **1** vt **to w. the streets** errer dans les rues **2** vi (of thoughts) vagabonder; (of person) errer, vagabonder; **to w. from** (path, subject) s'écarter de; **to w. around the town** se promener dans la ville; **to w. in/out** entrer/ sortir tranquillement; **my mind's wandering** je suis distrait ▪ **wanderer** n vagabond, -onde mf ▪ **wandering** adj (life) vagabond; (tribe) nomade

▸ **wander about, wander around** vi (roam) errer, vagabonder; (stroll) flâner

▸ **wander off** vi (go away) s'éloigner; **to w. off the path/the subject** s'écarter du chemin/du sujet

wane [weɪn] **1** n **to be on the w.** (of moon) décroître; (of fame, enthusiasm, power) décliner **2** vi (of moon) décroître; (of fame, strength) décliner

wangle [ˈwæŋgəl] vt Br Fam (obtain) se débrouiller pour avoir; (through devious means) carotter (from à)

want [wɒnt] **1** n (lack) manque m (of de); (poverty) besoin m; **for w. of** par manque de; **for w. of money/time** faute d'argent/de temps; **for w. of anything better** faute de mieux **2** vt vouloir (to do faire); Fam (need) avoir besoin de; **I w. him to go** je veux qu'il parte; **the lawn wants cutting** la pelouse a besoin d'être tondue; Br **you w. to try** (should) tu devrais essayer; **you're wanted on the phone** on vous demande au téléphone; Br **'situations wanted'** (in newspaper) 'demandes d'emploi' **3** vi **to w. for nothing** ne manquer de rien ▪ **wanted** adj (criminal, man) recherché par la police; **to feel w.** sentir qu'on vous aime ▪ **wanting** adj **to be w. in sth** manquer de qch; **to be found w.** (of person) se révéler incapable; (of thing) laisser à désirer

wanton [ˈwɒntən] adj (gratuitous) gratuit; Old-fashioned (immoral) impudique

WAP [wæp] (abbr **wireless applications protocol**) n Tel WAP m

war [wɔː(r)] **1** n guerre f; **at w.** en guerre (with avec); **to go to w.** entrer en guerre (with avec); **to declare w.** déclarer la guerre (on à); **the First/Second World W.** la Première/ Deuxième Guerre mondiale **2** adj (wound, crime, criminal, correspondent) de guerre; **w. memorial** monument m aux morts ▪ **warfare** n guerre f ▪ **warlike** adj guerrier, -ière ▪ **warmonger** [-mʌŋgə(r)] n belliciste mf ▪ **warring** adj (countries) en guerre ▪ **wartime** n **in w.** en temps m de guerre

warble [ˈwɔːbəl] vi gazouiller

ward¹ [wɔːd] n (in hospital) salle f; Br (electoral division) circonscription f électorale; Law **w. of court** pupille mf sous tutelle judiciaire

ward² [wɔːd] vt **to w. off** (blow, anger) éviter; (danger) chasser

warden [ˈwɔːdən] n (of institution, hostel) directeur, -trice mf; Br (of park) gardien, -ienne mf

warder [ˈwɔːdə(r)] n Br gardien m (de prison)

wardrobe [ˈwɔːdrəʊb] n (cupboard) penderie f; (clothes) garde-robe f

warehouse [ˈweəhaʊs] (pl **-ses** [-zɪz]) n entrepôt m

wares [weəz] npl marchandises fpl

warily [ˈweərɪlɪ] adv avec précaution

warm [wɔːm] **1** (**-er, -est**) adj chaud; Fig (welcome, thanks) chaleureux, -euse; **to be** or **feel w.** avoir chaud; **to get w.** (of person, room) se réchauffer; (of food, water) chauffer; **it's w.** (of weather) il fait chaud **2** vt (faire) chauffer;

to w. oneself by the fire se chauffer près du feu; **to w. some water** faire chauffer de l'eau **3** vi Fig **to w. to sb** se prendre de sympathie pour qn ▪ **'warm-'hearted** adj chaleureux, -euse ▪ **warmly** adv (dress) chaudement; Fig (welcome, thank) chaleureusement ▪ **warmth** n chaleur f ▪ **warm-up** n (of athlete) échauffement m

▸ **warm up 1** vt (person, food) réchauffer; (engine) faire chauffer **2** vi (of person, room, engine) se réchauffer; (of athlete) s'échauffer; (of food, water) chauffer; (of weather) faire plus chaud

warn [wɔːn] vt avertir, prévenir (**that** que); **to w. sb against** or **of sth** mettre qn en garde contre qch; **to w. sb against doing sth** déconseiller à qn de faire qch ▪ **warning** n (caution) avertissement m; (advance notice) avis m; **without w.** sans prévenir; **gale/storm w.** avis de coup de vent/de tempête; **a word** or **note of w.** une mise en garde; **w. light** (on appliance) voyant m lumineux; Br (hazard) w. **lights** feux mpl de détresse; **w. triangle** triangle m de présignalisation

warp [wɔːp] **1** vt (wood) gauchir; Fig (judgement, person) pervertir; **a warped mind** un esprit tordu **2** vi (of door) gauchir

warpath ['wɔːpɑːθ] n Fam **to be on the w.** en vouloir à tout le monde

warrant ['wɒrənt] **1** n Law mandat m; **I have a w. for your arrest** j'ai un mandat d'arrêt contre vous; **search w.** mandat de perquisition **2** vt (justify) justifier; **I w. you that...** je vous assure que... ▪ **warranty** (pl **-ies**) n Com garantie f; **under w.** sous garantie

warren ['wɒrən] n (rabbit) w. garenne f

warrior ['wɒrɪə(r)] n guerrier, -ière mf

Warsaw ['wɔːsɔː] n Varsovie m ou f

warship ['wɔːʃɪp] n navire m de guerre

wart [wɔːt] n verrue f

wary ['weərɪ] (**-ier, -iest**) adj prudent; **to be w. of sb/sth** se méfier de qn/qch; **to be w. of doing sth** hésiter beaucoup à faire qch

was [wəz, stressed wɒz] pt of **be**

wash [wɒʃ] **1** n (action) lavage m; (of ship) remous m; **to have a w.** se laver; **to give sth a w.** laver qch; **to be in the w.** être au lavage **2** vt laver; (of sea) baigner; **to w. one's hands** se laver les mains (**of sth** de qch); **to w. sb/sth ashore** rejeter qn/qch sur le rivage **3** vi (have a wash) se laver; Fam **that won't w.!** ça ne marche pas! ▪ **washbasin** n Br lavabo m ▪ **washcloth** n Am gant m de toilette ▪ **washed-'out** adj Fam (tired) lessivé ▪ **washed-'up** adj Fam (all) w. (person, plan) fichu ▪ **washroom** n Am toilettes fpl

▸ **wash away 1** vt sep (stain) faire partir (en lavant); **to w. sb/sth away** (of sea) emporter qn/qch **2** vi (of stain) partir (au lavage)

▸ **wash down** vt sep (car, deck) laver à grande eau; (food) arroser (**with** de)

▸ **wash off 1** vt sep enlever **2** vi partir

▸ **wash out 1** vt sep (bowl, cup) rincer; (stain) faire partir (en lavant) **2** vi (of stain) partir (au lavage)

▸ **wash up 1** vt sep Br (dishes, forks) laver **2** vi Br (do the dishes) faire la vaisselle; Am (have a wash) se débarbouiller

washable ['wɒʃəbəl] adj lavable

washer ['wɒʃə(r)] n (ring) joint m

washing ['wɒʃɪŋ] n (action) lavage m; (clothes) linge m; **to do the w.** faire la lessive; **w. line** corde f à linge; **w. machine** machine f à laver; Br **w. powder** lessive f ▪ **washing-'up** n Br vaisselle f; **to do the w.** faire la vaisselle; **w. liquid** liquide m vaisselle

washout ['wɒʃaʊt] n Fam (event) bide m

wasp [wɒsp] n guêpe f

waste [weɪst] **1** n (action) gaspillage m; (of time) perte f; (rubbish) déchets mpl; **wastes** (land) étendues fpl désertiques; Br **w. disposal unit** broyeur m d'ordures; Br **w. ground** (in town) terrain m vague; **w. land** (uncultivated) terres fpl incultes; (in town) terrain vague; **w. material** or **products** déchets mpl; **w. pipe** tuyau m d'évacuation **2** vt (money, food) gaspiller; (time) perdre; (opportunity) gâcher; **to w. no time doing sth** ne pas perdre de temps pour faire qch; **to w. one's life** gâcher sa vie **3** vi **to w. away** dépérir ▪ **wastage** n gaspillage m; (losses) pertes fpl ▪ **wasted** adj (effort) inutile; (body) émacié; Fam (drunk) bourré; Fam (drugged) défoncé

wastebin ['weɪstbɪn] n (in kitchen) poubelle f

wasteful ['weɪstfəl] adj (person) gaspilleur, -euse; (process) peu économique

wastepaper [weɪst'peɪpə(r)] n vieux papiers mpl; **w. basket** corbeille f à papier

watch [wɒtʃ] **1** n (**a**) (clock) montre f (**b**) (over suspect, baby) garde f; (guard) sentinelle f; (on ship) quart m; **to keep a close w. on sb/sth** surveiller qn/qch de près; **to keep w.** faire le guet; **to be on w.** monter la garde **2** vt regarder; (observe) observer; (suspect, baby, luggage) surveiller; (be careful of) faire attention à; **w. it!** attention! **3** vi regarder; **to w. out for sb/sth** guetter qn/qch; **to w. out** (take care) faire attention (**for** à); **w. out!** attention!; **to w. over** surveiller ▪ **watchdog** n chien m de garde ▪ **watchmaker** n horloger, -ère mf ▪ **watchman** (pl **-men**) n gardien m ▪ **watchstrap** n bracelet m de montre ▪ **watchtower** n tour f de guet

watchful ['wɒtʃfəl] adj vigilant

water ['wɔːtə(r)] **1** n under w. (road, field) inondé; (swim) sous l'eau; Fig **it doesn't hold w.** (of theory) ça ne tient pas debout; Fig **in hot w.** dans le pétrin; **w. cannon** canon m à eau; **w. chestnut** macre f; **w. heater** chauffe-eau m *inv; Br* w. **ice** sorbet *m;* w. **lily** nénuphar *m;* w. **main** conduite *f* d'eau; w. **pistol** pistolet *m* à eau; *Sport* w. **polo** water-polo *m;* w. **power** énergie *f* hydraulique; *Br* w. **rates** taxes *fpl* sur l'eau; w. **skiing** ski *m* nautique; w. **tank** réservoir *m* d'eau; w. **tower** château *m* d'eau; w. **wings** brassards *mpl* de natation

2 *vt (plant)* arroser; **to w. sth down** *(wine)* diluer qch; *(text)* édulcorer qch

3 *vi (of eyes)* larmoyer; **it makes my mouth w.** ça me met l'eau à la bouche ▪**watercolour** *(Am* **-color)** *n* aquarelle *f* ▪**watercress** *n* cresson *m* (de fontaine) ▪**waterfall** *n* cascade *f* ▪**waterfront** *n (by sea)* front *m* de mer; *(by river)* bord *m* de l'eau ▪**watering** *n (of plant)* arrosage *m;* w. **can** arrosoir *m* ▪**waterline** *n (on ship)* ligne *f* de flottaison ▪**waterlogged** *adj (clothes)* trempé; *(land)* détrempé ▪**watermark** *n* filigrane *m* ▪**watermelon** *n* pastèque *f* ▪**waterproof** *adj* imperméable; *(watch)* étanche ▪**water-repellent** *adj* imperméable ▪**watershed** *n Fig (turning point)* tournant *m; BrTV* **the (nine o'clock) w.** = l'heure après laquelle l'émission de programmes destinés aux adultes est autorisée ▪**watertight** *adj (container)* étanche ▪**waterway** *n* voie *f* navigable ▪**waterworks** *n* station *f* hydraulique

watery ['wɔ:təri] *adj (soup)* trop liquide; *(coffee, tea)* insipide; *(colour)* délavé; *(eyes)* larmoyant

watt [wɒt] *n* watt *m*

wave [weɪv] **1** *n (of water, crime)* vague *f; (in hair)* ondulation *f; (sign)* signe *m* (de la main); *Radio & Phys* onde *f; Fig* **to make waves** faire des vagues **2** *vt (arm, flag)* agiter; *(stick)* brandir; **to w. goodbye to sb** faire au revoir de la main à qn; **to w. sb on** faire signe à qn d'avancer; **to w. sth aside** *(objection)* écarter qch **3** *vi (of person)* faire signe (de la main); *(of flag)* flotter; **to w. to sb** *(signal)* faire signe de la main à qn; *(greet)* saluer qn de la main ▪**waveband** *n Radio* bande *f* de fréquences ▪**wavelength** *n Radio* longueur *f* d'onde; *Fig* **on the same w.** sur la même longueur d'onde

waver ['weɪvə(r)] *vi (of person, flame)* vaciller

wavy ['weɪvɪ] **(-ier, -iest)** *adj (line)* qui ondule; *(hair)* ondulé

wax¹ [wæks] **1** *n* cire *f; (for ski)* fart *m* **2** *adj (candle, doll)* de cire; w. **crayon** crayon *m* (gras); *Am* w. **paper** *(for wrapping)* papier *m* paraffiné **3** *vt (street, ski)* farter; *(car)* lustrer; *(legs)* épiler ▪**waxwork** *n (dummy)* moulage *m* de cire; **waxworks** musée *m* de cire

wax² [wæks] *vi (of moon)* croître; *Literary* **to w. lyrical** devenir lyrique

way [weɪ] **1** *n* **(a)** *(path, road)* chemin *m* **(to** de); *(direction)* sens *m,* direction *f; (street)* rue *f;* **the w. in** l'entrée *f;* **the w. out** la sortie; **the w. to the station** le chemin pour aller à la gare; **to ask sb**

the w. demander son chemin à qn; **to show sb the w.** montrer le chemin à qn; **to lose one's w.** se perdre; **I'm on my w.** *(coming)* j'arrive; *(going)* je pars; **to stand in sb's w.** barrer le passage à qn; **to make one's w. towards** se diriger vers; **to make w. for sb** faire de la place à qn; **out of the w.** *(isolated)* isolé; **to get out of the w.** s'écarter; *Fig* **to go out of one's w. to help sb** se mettre en quatre pour aider qn; *Fig* **to find a w. out of a problem** trouver une solution à un problème; **to go part of the w.** faire un bout de chemin; **to go all the w.** aller jusqu'au bout; **we talked all the w.** nous avons parlé pendant tout le chemin; **to give w.** céder; *Br (in vehicle)* céder le passage **(to** à); **it's a long w. away** *or* **off** c'est très loin; **it's the wrong w. up** c'est dans le mauvais sens; **do it the other w. round** fais le contraire; **this w.** par ici; **that w.** par là; **which w.?** par où? **(b)** *(manner)* manière *f;* **in this w.** de cette manière; **in a w.** d'une certaine manière; **by w. of** *(via)* par; *Fig (as)* comme; *Fig* **by the w.** à propos; **to find a w. of doing sth** trouver une manière de faire qch; **to get one's w.** arriver à ses fins; **to be in a good/bad w.** aller bien/mal; *Fam* **no w.!** *(certainly not)* pas question!; *Am Fam* **w. to go!** c'est géant!; **w. of life** mode *m* de vie

2 *adv Fam* **w. behind** très en arrière; **w. ahead** très en avance **(of** sur)

waylay [weɪ'leɪ] *(pt & pp* **-laid)** *vt (attack)* agresser; *Fig (stop)* arrêter au passage

way-out [weɪ'aʊt] *adj Fam* excentrique

wayside ['weɪsaɪd] *n* **by the w.** au bord de la route

wayward ['weɪwəd] *adj* difficile

WC [dʌbəlju:'si:] *n* W.-C. *mpl*

we [wi:] *pron* nous; *(indefinite)* on; **we go** nous allons; **we teachers** nous autres professeurs; **WE are right, not you** *(stressed)* nous, nous avons raison, pas vous; **we all make mistakes** tout le monde peut se tromper

weak [wi:k] **(-er, -est)** *adj* faible; *(tea, coffee)* léger, -ère; **to have a w. heart** avoir le cœur fragile; **to be w. at sth** *(school subject)* être faible en qch ▪**weakly** *adv* faiblement ▪**weakness** *n* faiblesse *f; (of heart)* fragilité *f; (fault)* point *m* faible; **to have a w. for sb/sth** avoir un faible pour qn/qch

weaken ['wi:kən] **1** *vt* affaiblir **2** *vi* s'affaiblir

weakling ['wi:klɪŋ] *n (in body)* mauviette *f; (in character)* faible *mf*

weak-willed ['wi:k'wɪld] *adj* sans volonté

weal [wi:l] *n* trace *f* de coup

wealth [welθ] *n* richesse *f; Fig* **a w. of sth** une abondance de qch ▪**wealthy** **1** **(-ier, -iest)** *adj* riche **2** *npl* **the w.** les riches *mpl*

wean [wi:n] *vt (baby)* sevrer

weapon ['wepən] *n* arme *f;* **weapons of mass destruction** armes *fpl* de destruction massive; **weapons inspector** inspecteur, -trice *mf* du désarmement ▪**weaponry** *n* armes *fpl*

wear [weə(r)] **1** n (**a**) men's w. vêtements mpl pour hommes; **evening** w. tenue f de soirée (**b**) (use) usure f; **to get a lot of w. out of sth** porter qch longtemps; **w. and tear** usure naturelle **2** (pt **wore**, pp **worn**) vt (garment, glasses) porter; Fig (patience) user; **to w. black** porter du noir; **to have nothing to w.** n'avoir rien à se mettre **3** vi (of clothing) s'user; **to w. thin** s'user; Fig **that excuse is wearing thin** cette excuse ne prend plus; **to w. well** (of clothing, film) bien vieillir ▪ **wearing** adj lassant
▸ **wear away 1** vt sep (clothes, patience) user **2** vi (of material) s'user; (of colours, ink) s'effacer
▸ **wear down 1** vt sep user; Fig **to w. sb down** avoir qn à l'usure **2** vi s'user
▸ **wear off** vi (of colour, pain) disparaître
▸ **wear on** vi (of time) s'écouler
▸ **wear out 1** vt sep (clothes, patience) user; **to w. sth out** épuiser qch **2** vi (of clothes) s'user; Fig (of patience) s'épuiser

weary ['wɪərɪ] **1** (-ier, -iest) adj las (f lasse) (**of doing** de faire) **2** vi se lasser (**of** de) ▪ **wearily** adv avec lassitude ▪ **weariness** n lassitude f

weasel ['wiːzəl] n belette f

weather ['weðə(r)] **1** n temps m; **what's the w. like?** quel temps fait-il?; **in hot/cold w.** par temps chaud/froid; **under the w.** (ill) patraque **2** adj **w. chart/conditions/station** carte f/conditions fpl/station f météorologique(s); **w. forecast** prévisions fpl météorologiques; **w. report** (bulletin m) météo f **3** vt (storm, hurricane) essuyer; Fig (crisis) surmonter ▪ **weatherbeaten** adj (face, person) hâlé ▪ **weathergirl** n (on TV, radio) présentatrice f météo ▪ **weatherman** (pl -men) n (on TV, radio) présentateur m météo ▪ **weathervane** n girouette f

weave [wiːv] **1** n (style) tissage m **2** (pt **wove**, pp **woven**) vt (cloth, plot) tisser; (basket, garland) tresser **3** vi tisser; Fig **to w. in and out of** (crowd, cars) se faufiler entre ▪ **weaver** n tisserand, -ande mf ▪ **weaving** n tissage m

web [web] n (of spider) toile f; Fig (of lies) tissu m; Comptr **the W.** le Web, la Toile; **w. designer** concepteur, -trice mf de sites Web; **w. page** page f Web; **w. site** site m Web ▪ **webbed** adj (foot) palmé ▪ **webbing** n (in chair) sangles fpl ▪ **webcam** n Comptr Webcam m, caméra f Internet ▪ **webcast** Comptr **1** n webcast m **2** vt diffuser sur Internet ▪ **weblog** n Comptr Weblog m ▪ **webmaster** n Comptr Webmestre m ▪ **webzine** n Comptr Webzine m

wed [wed] (pt & pp **-dd-**) **1** vt (marry) épouser; Fig (qualities) allier (**to** à) **2** vi se marier ▪ **wedded** adj (bliss, life) conjugal

we'd [wiːd] = **we had, we would**

wedding ['wedɪŋ] **1** n mariage m; **golden/silver w.** noces fpl d'or/d'argent **2** adj (anniversary, present, cake) de mariage; (dress) de mariée; (night) de noces; **his/her w. day** le jour de son mariage; Br **w. ring**, Am **w. band** alliance f

wedge [wedʒ] **1** n (of wheel, table) cale f; (for splitting) coin m; (of cake) part f; **w. heel** (of shoe) semelle f compensée **2** vt (wheel, table) caler; (push) enfoncer (**into** dans); **to w. a door open** maintenir une porte ouverte avec une cale; **wedged (in) between** coincé entre

wedlock ['wedlɒk] n **born out of w.** illégitime

Wednesday ['wenzdeɪ] n mercredi m

wee¹ [wiː] adj Scot Fam (tiny) tout petit (f toute petite)

wee² [wiː] Br Fam **1** n pipi m; **to do** or **have a w.** faire pipi **2** vi faire pipi

weed [wiːd] **1** n (plant) mauvaise herbe f; Fam (weak person) mauviette f **2** vti désherber; Fig **to w. sth out** éliminer qch (**from** de) ▪ **weedkiller** n désherbant m ▪ **weedy** (-ier, -iest) adj Fam (person) malingre

week [wiːk] n semaine f; **the w. before last** pas la semaine dernière, celle d'avant; **the w. after next** pas la semaine prochaine, celle d'après; **tomorrow w.** demain en huit ▪ **weekday** n jour m de semaine

weekend [wiːk'end] n week-end m; **at** or **over** or Am **on the w.** ce week-end; (every weekend) le week-end

weekly ['wiːklɪ] **1** adj hebdomadaire **2** adv toutes les semaines **3** n (magazine) hebdomadaire m

weep [wiːp] (pt & pp **wept**) vti pleurer; **to w. for sb** pleurer qn ▪ **weeping 'willow** n saule m pleureur

wee(-)wee ['wiːwiː] n Br Fam pipi m; **to do a w.** faire pipi

weft [weft] n trame f

weigh [weɪ] **1** vt peser; **to w. sb/sth down** (with load) surcharger qn/qch (**with** de); **to w. down a branch** (of fruit) faire plier une branche; **to be weighed down by** (of branch) plier sous le poids de; Fig **weighed down with worry** accablé de soucis; **to w. up** (goods, chances) peser **2** vi peser; **how much do you w.?** combien pèses-tu?; **it's weighing on my mind** ça me tracasse; **to w. down on sb** (of worries) accabler qn ▪ **weighing-machine** n balance f

weight [weɪt] **1** n poids m; **by w.** au poids; **to put on w.** grossir; **to lose w.** maigrir; Fig **to carry w.** (of argument) avoir du poids; Fig **to pull one's w.** faire sa part du travail **2** vt **to w. sth (down)** (hold down) faire tenir qch avec un poids; **to w. sb/sth down with sth** (overload) surcharger qn/qch de qch ▪ **weightlifter** n haltérophile mf ▪ **weightlifting** n haltérophilie f

weighting ['weɪtɪŋ] n Fin pondération f; **London w.** = indemnité de résidence à Londres

weightless ['weɪtləs] adj (in space) en apesanteur ▪**weightlessness** n apesanteur f

weighty ['weɪtɪ] (**-ier, -iest**) adj (heavy) lourd; Fig (serious, important) grave

weir [wɪə(r)] n barrage m

weird [wɪəd] (**-er, -est**) adj bizarre ▪**weirdo** ['wɪədəʊ] (pl **-os**) n Fam type m bizarre

welcome ['welkəm] **1** adj (person, news, change) bienvenu; **to make sb w.** faire un bon accueil à qn; **to feel w.** se sentir le/la bienvenu(e); **w.! bienvenue!; w. home!** ça fait plaisir de te revoir!; **you're always w.** vous êtes toujours le/la bienvenu(e); **you're w.!** (after 'thank you') il n'y a pas de quoi!; **you're w. to use my bike** mon vélo est à ta disposition **2** n accueil m; **to give sb a warm w.** faire un accueil chaleureux à qn **3** vt (person) souhaiter la bienvenue à; (news, change) accueillir favorablement ▪**welcoming** adj accueillant; (speech, words) de bienvenue

weld [weld] **1** n soudure f **2** vt souder ▪**welder** n soudeur, -euse mf ▪**welding** n soudure f

welfare ['welfeə(r)] n (wellbeing) bien-être m; Am Fam **to be on w.** recevoir l'aide sociale; Br **the W. State** l'État m providence; **w. work** assistance f sociale

well¹ [wel] **1** n (for water, oil) puits m; (of stairs, lift) cage f **2** vi **to w. up** (tears) monter

well² [wel] **1** (**better, best**) adj bien; **to be w.** aller bien; **to get w.** se remettre; **it's just as w....** heureusement que...; **all's w.** tout va bien; **that's all very w. but...** tout ça c'est très bien mais...

2 adv bien; **w. before/after** bien avant/après; **to speak w. of sb** dire du bien de qn; **you'd do w. to refuse** tu ferais bien de refuser; **she might (just) as w. have left** elle aurait mieux fait de partir; **to be w. aware of sth** avoir parfaitement conscience de qch; **it's w. worth the effort** ça vaut vraiment la peine; **w. done!** bravo!; **as w.** (also) aussi; **as w. as** aussi bien que; **as w. as two cats, he has...** en plus de deux chats, il a...

3 exclam eh bien!; **w., w.!** (surprise) tiens, tiens!; huge, enfin, **w. quite big** énorme, enfin, assez grand ▪**well-be'haved** adj sage ▪**well-'being** n bien-être m ▪**well-'built** adj (person, car) solide ▪**well-'dressed** adj bien habillé ▪**well-'fed** adj bien nourri ▪**well-'founded** adj fondé ▪**well-'heeled** adj Fam cossu ▪**well-in'formed** adj bien informé ▪**well-'known** adj (bien) connu ▪**well-'mannered** adj bien élevé ▪**well-'matched** adj assorti ▪**well-'meaning** adj bien intentionné ▪**well-'off** adj riche ▪**well-'paid** adj bien payé ▪**well-'read** adj instruit ▪**well-'spoken** adj qui parle bien ▪**well-'thought-of** adj bien considéré ▪**well-thought-'out** adj bien conçu ▪**well-'timed** adj opportun ▪**well-to-'do** adj aisé ▪**well-'tried** adj (method) éprouvé ▪**well-'trodden** adj (path) battu ▪**wellwisher** n sympathisant, -ante mf ▪**well-'woman clinic** n Br centre m de dépistage gynécologique ▪**well-'worn** adj (clothes, carpet) très usé

we'll [wiːl] = we will, we shall

wellington ['welɪŋtən] n Br **w. (boot)** botte f de caoutchouc ▪**welly** (pl **-ies**) n Br Fam botte f de caoutchouc

Welsh [welʃ] **1** adj gallois; Br **W. rabbit** or **rarebit** = toast au fromage **2** n (language) gallois m; **the W.** (people) les Gallois mpl ▪**Welshman** (pl **-men**) n Gallois m ▪**Welshwoman** (pl **-women**) n Galloise f

welsh [welʃ] vi **to w. on** (debt, promise) ne pas honorer

wench [wentʃ] n Old-fashioned & Hum jeune fille f

wend [wend] vt Literary **to w. one's way** s'acheminer (**to** vers)

went [went] pt of **go**

wept [wept] pt & pp of **weep**

were [wə(r), stressed wɜː(r)] pt of **be**

we're [wɪə(r)] = we are

werewolf ['weəwʊlf] (pl **-wolves**) n loup-garou m

west [west] **1** n ouest m; **(to the) w. of** à l'ouest de; Pol **the W.** l'Occident m **2** adj (coast) ouest inv; (wind) d'ouest; **W. Africa** l'Afrique f occidentale; Formerly **W. Germany** l'Allemagne f de l'Ouest; **W. Indian** adj antillais; n Antillais, -aise mf; **the W. Indies** les Antilles fpl; Br **the W. Country** le sud-ouest de l'Angleterre **3** adv à l'ouest; (travel) vers l'ouest ▪**westbound** adj (traffic) en direction de l'ouest; Br (carriageway) ouest inv ▪**westerly** adj (point) ouest inv; (direction) de l'ouest; (wind) d'ouest ▪**western 1** adj (coast) ouest inv; Pol (culture) occidental; **W. Europe** l'Europe f de l'Ouest **2** n (film) western m ▪**westerner** n habitant, -ante mf de l'Ouest; Pol occidental, -ale mf ▪**westernize** vt occidentaliser ▪**westward** adj & adv vers l'ouest ▪**westwards** adv vers l'ouest

wet [wet] **1** (**wetter, wettest**) adj mouillé; (weather) pluvieux, -ieuse; (day) de pluie; Fam (feeble) minable; **to get w.** se mouiller; **to be w. through** être trempé; **it's w.** (raining) il pleut; **'w. paint'** (on sign) 'peinture fraîche'; **the ink is w.** l'encre est fraîche; Fig **w. blanket** rabat-joie m inv; **w. nurse** nourrice f; **w. suit** combinaison f de plongée **2** n **the w.** (rain) la pluie; (damp) l'humidité f **3** (pt & pp **-tt-**) vt mouiller

we've [wiːv] = we have

whack [wæk] Fam **1** n (blow) grand coup m **2** vt donner un grand coup à ▪**whacked** adj Br Fam **w. (out)** (tired) nase ▪**whacking** adj Br Fam (big) énorme

whale [weɪl] n baleine f ■ **whaling** n pêche f à la baleine

wham [wæm] exclam vlan!

wharf [wɔːf] (pl wharfs or wharves) n (for ships) quai m

what [wɒt] 1 adj quel, quelle, pl quel(le)s; **w. book?** quel livre?; **w. a fool!** quel idiot!; **I know w. book it is** je sais quel livre c'est; **w. little she has** le peu qu'elle a 2 pron (a) (in questions) (subject) qu'est-ce qui; (object) (qu'est-ce) que; (after prep) quoi; **w.'s happening?** qu'est-ce qui se passe?; **w. does he do?** qu'est-ce qu'il fait?, que fait-il?; **w. is it?** qu'est-ce que c'est?; **w.'s that book?** c'est quoi, ce livre?; **w.!** (surprise) quoi!, comment!; **w.'s it called?** comment ça s'appelle?; **w. for?** pourquoi?; **w. about me?** et moi?; **w. about going out for lunch?** si on allait déjeuner? (b) (in relative construction) (subject) ce qui; (object) ce que; **I know w. will happen/w. she'll do** je sais ce qui arrivera/ce qu'elle fera; **w. happens is…** ce qui arrive, c'est que…; **w. I need…** ce dont j'ai besoin…

whatever [wɒt'evə(r)] 1 adj **w. (the) mistake** quelle que soit l'erreur; **of w. size** de n'importe quelle taille; **no chance w.** pas la moindre chance; **nothing w.** rien du tout 2 pron (no matter what) quoi que (+ subjunctive); **w. you do** quoi que tu fasses; **w. happens** quoi qu'il arrive; **do w. is important** fais tout ce qui est important; **do w. you want** fais tout ce que tu veux

whatsit [ˈwɒtsɪt] n Fam machin m

whatsoever [wɒtsəʊ'evə(r)] adj **for no reason w.** sans aucune raison; **none w.** aucun

wheat [wiːt] n blé m ■ **wheatgerm** n germe m de blé

wheedle [ˈwiːdəl] vt **to w. sb** enjôler qn (into doing pour qu'il/elle fasse); **to w. sth out of sb** obtenir qch de qn par la flatterie

wheel [wiːl] 1 n roue f; **to be at the w.** être au volant 2 vt (push) pousser 3 vi (turn) tourner; (of person) se retourner brusquement; Fam **to w. and deal** faire des combines ■ **wheelbarrow** n brouette f ■ **wheelchair** n fauteuil m roulant ■ **wheelclamp** n sabot m de Denver

wheeze [wiːz] 1 n (noise) respiration f sifflante; Br Fam (trick) combine f 2 vi respirer bruyamment ■ **wheezy** (-ier, -iest) adj poussif, -ive

whelk [welk] n bulot m

when [wen] 1 adv quand 2 conj (with time) quand, lorsque; (whereas) alors que; **w. I came into the room** quand ou lorsque je suis entré dans la pièce; **w. I finish, w. I've finished** quand j'aurai fini; **the day/moment w.** le jour/moment où; Fam **say w.!** (when pouring drink) dis-moi stop!

whenever [wen'evə(r)] 1 adv n'importe quand

2 conj (at whatever time) quand; (each time that) chaque fois que

where [weə(r)] 1 adv où; **w. are you from?** d'où êtes-vous? 2 conj où; (whereas) alors que; **I found it w. she'd left it** je l'ai trouvé là où elle l'avait laissé; **the place/house w. I live** l'endroit/la maison où j'habite; **I went to w. he was** je suis allé à l'endroit où il était; **that's w. you'll find it** c'est là que tu le trouveras ■ **whereabouts** 1 [weərə'baʊts] adv où 2 [ˈweərəbaʊts] n his w. l'endroit m où il est ■ **where'as** conj alors que ■ **where'by** adv Formal par quoi ■ **whereu'pon** adv Literary sur quoi ■ **wherewithal** [ˈweəwɪðɔːl] n **to have the w. to do sth** avoir les moyens de faire qch

wherever [weər'evə(r)] 1 adv n'importe où 2 conj **w. you go** (everywhere) partout où tu iras, où que tu ailles; **I'll go w. you like** j'irai (là) où vous voudrez

whet [wet] (pt & pp -tt-) vt (appetite, desire) aiguiser

whether [ˈweðə(r)] conj si; **I don't know w. to leave** je ne sais pas si je dois partir; **w. she does it or not** qu'elle le fasse ou non; **w. now or tomorrow** que ce soit maintenant ou demain; **it's doubtful w….** il est douteux que… (+ subjunctive)

which [wɪtʃ] 1 adj (in questions) quel, quelle, pl quel(le)s; **w. hat?** quel chapeau?; **w. one?** lequel/laquelle?; **in w. case** auquel cas 2 relative pron (subject) qui; (object) que; (after prep) lequel, laquelle, pl lesquel(le)s; (referring to a whole clause) (subject) ce qui; (object) ce que; **the house w. is old…** la maison qui est vieille…; **the book w. I like…** le livre que j'aime…; **the table w. I put it on…** la table sur laquelle je l'ai mis…; **the film of w. she was speaking** le film dont ou duquel elle parlait; **she's ill, w. is sad** elle est malade, ce qui est triste; **he lies, w. I don't like** il ment, ce que je n'aime pas; **after w.** (whereupon) après quoi 3 interrogative pron (in questions) lequel, laquelle, pl lesquel(le)s; **w. of us?** lequel/laquelle d'entre nous?; **w. are the best of these books?** quels sont les meilleurs de ces livres? 4 pron **w. (one)** (the one that) (subject) celui qui, celle qui, pl ceux qui, celles qui; (object) celui que; **I know w. (ones) you want** je sais ceux/celles que vous désirez

whichever [wɪtʃ'evə(r)] 1 adj (no matter which) **take w. books interest you** prenez les livres qui vous intéressent; **take w. one you like** prends celui/celle que tu veux 2 pron (no matter which) quel que soit celui qui (f quelle que soit celle qui); **w. you choose…** quel que soit celui que tu choisiras…; **take w. you want** prends celui/celle que tu veux

whiff [wɪf] n odeur f

while [waɪl] 1 conj (when) pendant que;

(although) bien que (+ *subjunctive*); *(as long as)* tant que; *(whereas)* tandis que; **w. eating** en mangeant **2** *n* **a w.** un moment; **all the w.** tout le temps; **it's not worth my w.** ça n'en vaut pas la peine **3** *vt* **to w. away the time** passer le temps (**doing** à faire) • **whilst** [waɪlst] *conj Br* = **while**

whim [wɪm] *n* caprice *m*; **on a w.** sur un coup de tête

whimper ['wɪmpə(r)] **1** *n* gémissement *m*; **without a w.** sans broncher **2** *vi* gémir

whimsical ['wɪmzɪkəl] *adj (look, idea)* bizarre; *(person)* fantasque

whine [waɪn] **1** *n* gémissement *m* **2** *vi* gémir

whip [wɪp] **1** *n* fouet *m*; *Br Pol* chef *m* de file **2** *(pt & pp* **-pp-***) vt* fouetter; *Fam (defeat)* battre à plates coutures; **whipped cream** crème *f* fouettée • **whipround** *n Br Fam* collecte *f*
► **whip off** *vt sep Fam (clothes)* enlever rapidement
► **whip out** *vt sep Fam* sortir brusquement (**from** de)
► **whip round** *vi Fam (turn quickly)* se retourner brusquement
► **whip up** *vt sep (interest)* susciter; *(eggs)* fouetter; *Fam (meal)* préparer rapidement

whirl [wɜːl] **1** *n* tourbillon *m* **2** *vt* **to w. sb/sth (round)** faire tourbillonner qn/qch **3** *vi* **to w. (round)** tourbillonner • **whirlpool** *n* tourbillon *m* • **whirlwind** *n* tourbillon *m*

whirr [wɜː(r)] **1** *n* ronflement *m* **2** *vi* ronfler

whisk [wɪsk] **1** *n (for eggs)* fouet *m* **2** *vt* battre; **to w. away** *or* **off** *(object)* enlever rapidement; *(person)* emmener rapidement

whiskers ['wɪskəz] *npl (of animal)* moustaches *fpl*; *(of man)* favoris *mpl*

whisky ['wɪskɪ] *(Am* **whiskey***) n* whisky *m*

whisper ['wɪspə(r)] **1** *n* chuchotement *m* **2** *vti* chuchoter; **to w. sth to sb** chuchoter qch à l'oreille de qn; **w. to me!** chuchote à mon oreille!

whist [wɪst] *n Br (card game)* whist *m*

whistle ['wɪsəl] **1** *n* sifflement *m*; *(object)* sifflet *m*; **to blow the** *or* **one's w.** siffler, donner un coup de sifflet; **to give a w.** siffler **2** *vti* siffler; **to w. for** *(dog, taxi)* siffler

Whit [wɪt] *adj Br* **W. Sunday** la Pentecôte

white [waɪt] **1** (-**er, -est***) adj* blanc *(f* blanche); **to go** *or* **turn w.** blanchir; *Br* **w. coffee** café *m* au lait; *Fig* **w. elephant** = chose coûteuse et peu rentable; **w. lie** pieux mensonge *m*; **w. man** Blanc *m*; **w. woman** Blanche *f*; **w. spirit** white-spirit *m* **2** *n (colour, of egg, eye)* blanc *m*; *(person)* Blanc *m*, Blanche *f* • **white-'collar worker** *n* col *m* blanc • **whiten** *vti* blanchir • **whiteness** *n* blancheur *f* • **whitewash 1** *n (paint)* badigeon *m* à la chaux; *Fig (of events, faults)* camouflage *m* **2** *vt (paint)* badigeonner à la chaux; *Fig (person)* blanchir; *Fig (events, faults)* camoufler

whiting ['waɪtɪŋ] *n inv (fish)* merlan *m*

Whitsun ['wɪtsən] *n Br* la Pentecôte

whittle ['wɪtəl] *vt* **to w. down** *(wood)* tailler (au couteau); *Fig (price)* réduire

whizz [wɪz] **1** *vi (rush)* aller à toute vitesse; **to w. past** *or* **by** passer à toute vitesse; **to w. through the air** *(of bullet, spear)* fendre l'air **2** *adj Fam* **w. kid** petit prodige *m*

WHO [dʌb(ə)ljuːeɪtʃ'əʊ] *(abbr* **World Health Organization***) n* OMS *f*

who [huː] *pron* qui; **w. did it?** qui est-ce qui a fait ça?; **the woman w. came** la femme qui est venue; **w. did you see?** qui as-tu vu?; **w. were you talking to?** à qui est-ce que tu parlais?

whodunit [huː'dʌnɪt] *n Fam* polar *m*

whoever [huː'evə(r)] *pron (no matter who) (subject)* qui que ce soit qui; *(object)* qui que ce soit que; **w. has seen this** *(anyone who)* quiconque a vu cela; **w. you are** qui que vous soyez; **this man, w. he is** cet homme, quel qu'il soit; **w. did that?** qui donc a fait ça?

whole [həʊl] **1** *adj* entier, -ière; **the w. time** tout le temps; **the w. apple** toute la pomme, la pomme tout entière; **the w. truth** toute la vérité; **the w. world** le monde entier; **the w. lot** le tout; **to swallow sth w.** avaler qch sans le mâcher **2** *n* totalité *f*; **the w. of the village** le village tout entier, tout le village; **the w. of the night** toute la nuit; **on the w., as a w.** dans l'ensemble • **wholefood** *n* aliment *m* complet • **'whole-'hearted** *adj* sans réserve • **wholemeal** *(Am* **wholewheat***) adj (bread)* complet, -ète • **wholesome** *adj (food, climate)* sain

wholesale ['həʊlseɪl] **1** *n* **to deal in w.** faire la vente en gros **2** *adj (price)* de gros; *Fig (destruction)* en masse; **w. business** *or* **trade** commerce *m* de gros **3** *adv (buy or sell one article)* au prix de gros; *(in bulk)* en gros; *Fig (destroy)* en masse • **wholesaler** *n* grossiste *mf*

wholly ['həʊlɪ] *adv* entièrement

whom [huːm] *pron Formal (object)* que; *(in questions and after prep)* qui; **w. did she see?** qui a-t-elle vu?; **the man w. you know** l'homme que tu connais; **with w.** avec qui; **the man of w. we were speaking** l'homme dont nous parlions

whooping cough ['huːpɪŋkɒf] *n* coqueluche *f*

whoops [wʊps] *exclam* houp-là!

whopping ['wɒpɪŋ] *adj Br Fam (big)* énorme • **whopper** *n Br Fam* chose *f* énorme

whore [hɔː(r)] *n very Fam* putain *f*

whose [huːz] *possessive pron & adj* à qui, de qui; **w. book is this?, w. is this book?** à qui est ce livre?; **w. daughter are you?** de qui es-tu la fille?; **the woman w. book I have** la femme dont j'ai le livre; **the man w. mother I spoke to** l'homme à la mère de qui j'ai parlé

why [waɪ] **1** *adv* pourquoi; **w. not?** pourquoi pas? **2** *conj* **the reason w. they...** la raison pour laquelle ils... **3** *npl* **the whys and wherefores** le pourquoi et le comment **4** *exclam (surprise)* tiens!

wick [wɪk] *n (of candle, lighter, oil lamp)* mèche *f*; *BrFam* **it/she gets on my w.** ça/elle me tape sur les nerfs

wicked ['wɪkɪd] *adj (evil)* méchant; *Fig (dreadful)* affreux, -euse; *Br Fam (excellent)* génial ▪ **wickedness** *n* méchanceté *f*

wicker ['wɪkə(r)] *n* osier *m*; **w. basket** panier *m* d'osier; **w. chair** fauteuil *m* en osier ▪ **wickerwork** *n (objects)* vannerie *f*

wicket ['wɪkɪt] *n (cricket stumps)* guichet *m*

wide [waɪd] **1** (**-er, -est**) *adj* large; *(ocean, desert)* vaste; *(choice, variety, knowledge)* grand; **to be 3 m w.** avoir 3 m de large **2** *adv (fall, shoot)* loin du but; **w. open** *(eyes, mouth, door)* grand ouvert; **w. awake** complètement réveillé ▪ **widely** *adv (travel)* beaucoup; *(broadcast, spread)* largement; **w. different** très différent; **it's w. thought that...** on pense généralement que... ▪ **widen 1** *vt* élargir **2** *vi* s'élargir

widespread ['waɪdspred] *adj* répandu

widow ['wɪdəʊ] *n* veuve *f* ▪ **widowed** *adj* **to be w.** *(of man)* devenir veuf; *(of woman)* devenir veuve; **her w. uncle** son oncle qui est veuf ▪ **widower** *n* veuf *m*

width [wɪdθ] *n* largeur *f*

wield [wi:ld] *vt (brandish)* brandir; *(handle)* manier; *Fig* **to w. power** exercer le pouvoir

wife [waɪf] *(pl* **wives)** *n* femme *f*, épouse *f* ▪ **wife-to-'be** *n* future femme *f*

wig [wɪg] *n* perruque *f*

wiggle ['wɪgəl] **1** *vt* remuer **2** *vi (of worm)* se tortiller; *(of tail)* remuer

wild [waɪld] **1** (**-er, -est**) *adj (animal, flower, region)* sauvage; *(sea)* déchaîné; *(idea)* fou *(f* folle); *(enthusiasm)* délirant; **w. with joy/anger** fou de joie/colère; **to be w.** *(of person)* mener une vie agitée; **to be w. about sb** *(very fond of)* être dingue de qn; *Fam* **I'm not w. about it** ça ne m'emballe pas; *Am* **the W. West** le Far West **2** *adv* **to grow w.** *(of plant)* pousser à l'état sauvage; **to run w.** *(of animals)* courir en liberté; *(of crowd)* se déchaîner **3** *n* **in the w.** à l'état sauvage; **in the wilds** en pleine brousse ▪ **wildcard character** *n Comptr* caractère *m* joker ▪ **wildcat 'strike** *n* grève *f* sauvage ▪ **wild-'goose chase** *n* fausse piste *f* ▪ **wildlife** *n* nature *f*

wilderness ['wɪldənəs] *n (region)* région *f* sauvage; *(overgrown garden)* jungle *f*

wildly ['waɪldlɪ] *adv (cheer)* frénétiquement; *(guess)* au hasard; *(for emphasis)* extrêmement

wilful ['wɪlfəl] *(Am* **willful)** *adj (intentional, obstinate)* volontaire ▪ **wilfully** *adv* volontairement

will¹ [wɪl]

v aux (expressing future tense) **he w. come, he'll come** il viendra; **you w. not come, you won't come** tu ne viendras pas; **w. you have some tea?** veux-tu du thé?; **w. you be quiet!** veux-tu te taire!; **yes I w.!** oui!; **it won't open** ça ne s'ouvre pas

will² [wɪl] **1** *n (resolve, determination)* volonté *f*; *(legal document)* testament *m*; **ill w.** mauvaise volonté; **free w.** libre arbitre *m*; **of one's own free w.** de son plein gré; **against one's w.** à contrecœur; **at w.** à volonté; *(cry)* à la demande **2** *vt Old-fashioned (intend, wish)* vouloir (**that** que + *subjunctive*); **to w. oneself to do sth** faire un effort de volonté pour faire qch

willing ['wɪlɪŋ] *adj (helper, worker)* plein de bonne volonté; *(help, advice)* spontané; **to be w. to do sth** bien vouloir faire qch; **to show w.** faire preuve de bonne volonté ▪ **willingly** *adv (with pleasure)* volontiers; *(voluntarily)* de son plein gré ▪ **willingness** *n* bonne volonté *f*; **her w. to do sth** *(enthusiasm)* son empressement *m* à faire qch

willow ['wɪləʊ] *n (tree, wood)* saule *m*

willowy ['wɪləʊɪ] *adj (person)* svelte

willpower ['wɪlpaʊə(r)] *n* volonté *f*

willy-nilly [wɪlɪ'nɪlɪ] *adv* bon gré mal gré

wilt [wɪlt] *vi (of plant)* dépérir; *Fig (of enthusiasm)* décliner

wily [waɪlɪ] (**-ier, -iest**) *adj* rusé

wimp [wɪmp] *n Fam (weakling)* mauviette *f* ▪ **wimpy** *adj Fam (physically)* malingre; *(mentally)* poule mouillée *inv*; **he's so w.!** quelle mauviette!

win [wɪn] **1** *n (victory)* victoire *f* **2** *(pt & pp* **won,** *pres p* **winning)** *vt (money, race, prize)* gagner; *(victory)* remporter; *(fame)* acquérir; *(friends)* se faire; *Br* **to w. sb over** *or* **round** gagner qn (**to** à) **3** *vi* gagner ▪ **winning 1** *adj (number, horse)* gagnant; *(team)* victorieux, -ieuse; *(goal)* décisif, -ive; *(smile)* engageant **2** *npl* **winnings** gains *mpl*

wince [wɪns] *vi* faire une grimace; **without wincing** sans sourciller

winch [wɪntʃ] **1** *n* treuil *m* **2** *vt* **to w. (up)** hisser

wind¹ [wɪnd] **1** *n* vent *m*; *(breath)* souffle *m*; **to have w.** *(in stomach)* avoir des gaz; **to get w. of sth** avoir vent de qch; *Mus* **w. instrument** instrument *m* à vent **2** *vt* **to w. sb** *(of blow)* couper le souffle à qn ▪ **windbreak** *n* brise-vent *m inv* ▪ **windcheater** *(Am* **windbreaker)** *n* coupe-vent *m inv* ▪ **windfall** *n (piece of fruit)* fruit *m* abattu par le vent; *Fig (unexpected money)* aubaine *f* ▪ **windmill** *n* moulin *m* à vent ▪ **windpipe** *n Anat* trachée *f* ▪ **windscreen** *(Am*

windshield) n (of vehicle) pare-brise m inv; **w. wiper** essuie-glace m ▪**windsurfer** n (person) véliplanchiste mf; (board) planche f à voile ▪**windsurfing** n **to go w.** faire de la planche à voile ▪**windswept** adj (street) balayé par le vent ▪**windy** (-ier, -iest) adj it's w. (of weather) il y a du vent; **w. day** jour m de grand vent; **w. place** endroit m plein de vent

wind² [waɪnd] **1** (pt & pp **wound**) vt (roll) enrouler (**round** autour de); (clock) remonter; **to w. a cassette back** rembobiner une cassette **2** vi (of river, road) serpenter ▪**winding** adj (road) sinueux, -ueuse; (staircase) en colimaçon
▸ **wind down 1** vt sep (car window) baisser **2** vi Fam (relax) se détendre
▸ **wind up 1** vt sep (clock) remonter; (meeting, speech) terminer; Br Fam **to w. sb up** (tease) faire marcher qn; (irritate) foutre en rogne **2** vi (end up) finir (**doing** par faire); **to w. up with sb/sth** se retrouver avec qn/qch

window [ˈwɪndəʊ] n fenêtre f; (pane) vitre f; (of shop) vitrine f; (counter) guichet m; **to go w.-shopping** faire du lèche-vitrines; **w. of opportunity** ouverture f; Br **French w.** porte-fenêtre f; **w. box** jardinière f; Br **w. cleaner**, Am **w. washer** laveur, -euse mf de vitres; **w. dresser** étalagiste mf; Br **w. ledge** rebord m de fenêtre; Am **w. shade** store m ▪**windowpane** n vitre f, carreau m ▪**windowsill** n rebord m de fenêtre

wind-up [ˈwaɪndʌp] n Br Fam **is this a w.?** c'est une plaisanterie?

wine [waɪn] **1** n vin m; **w. bar/bottle** bar m/ bouteille f à vin; **w. cellar** cave f à vin; **w. grower** viticulteur, -trice mf; **w. list** carte f des vins; **w. taster** dégustateur, -trice mf; **w. tasting** dégustation f; **w. waiter** sommelier m **2** vt **to w. and dine sb** inviter qn dans de bons restaurants ▪**wineglass** n verre m à vin ▪**wine-growing** adj viticole

wing [wɪŋ] n aile f; **the wings** (in theatre) les coulisses fpl; Fig **to take sb under one's w.** prendre qn sous son aile ▪**winged** adj ailé ▪**winger** n Football ailier m ▪**wingspan** n envergure f

wink [wɪŋk] **1** n clin m d'œil **2** vi faire un clin d'œil (**at** à); (of light) clignoter

winkle [ˈwɪŋkəl] n bigorneau m

winner [ˈwɪnə(r)] n gagnant, -ante mf; Fam **that book is a w.** ce livre est assuré d'avoir du succès

winter [ˈwɪntə(r)] **1** n hiver m; **in (the) w.** en hiver; **a w.'s day** un jour d'hiver **2** adj d'hiver ▪**wintertime** n hiver m ▪**wintry** adj hivernal; **w. day** jour m d'hiver

wipe [waɪp] **1** n lingette f; **to give sth a w.** essuyer qch **2** vt essuyer; **to w. one's feet/ hands** s'essuyer les pieds/les mains; **to w. sth away** or **off** or **up** (liquid) essuyer qch; **to w.**

sth out (clean) essuyer qch; (destroy) anéantir qch; (erase) effacer qch **3** vi **to w. up** (dry the dishes) essuyer la vaisselle ▪**wiper** n essuie-glace m

wire [ˈwaɪə(r)] **1** n fil m; **w. mesh** or **netting** toile f métallique **2** vt **to w. (up)** (house) faire l'installation électrique de; **to w. sth (up) to sth** (connect electrically) relier qch à qch; **to w. a hall (up) for sound** sonoriser une salle ▪**wiring** n (system) installation f électrique; (wires) fils mpl électriques

wirecutters [ˈwaɪəkʌtəz] npl pince f coupante

wireless [ˈwaɪələs] **1** n Old-fashioned (set) Br TSF f **2** adj Comptr sans fil

wiry [ˈwaɪərɪ] (-ier, -iest) adj (person) petit et musclé

wisdom [ˈwɪzdəm] n sagesse f; **w. tooth** dent f de sagesse

wise [waɪz] (-er, -est) adj (in knowledge) sage; (advisable) prudent; (learned) savant; **to be none the wiser** ne pas être plus avancé; Fam **to be w. to** être au courant de; Fam **w. guy** gros malin m ▪**wisecrack** n Fam (joke) vanne f ▪**wisely** adv sagement

-wise [waɪz] suff (with regard to) **health-w./ money-w.** côté santé/argent

wish [wɪʃ] **1** n (specific) souhait m, vœu m; (general) désir m; **to make a w.** faire un vœu; **to do sth against sb's wishes** faire qch contre le souhait de qn; **best wishes, all good wishes** (on greetings card) meilleurs vœux; (in letter) amitiés fpl; **send him my best wishes** fais-lui mes amitiés **2** vt souhaiter (**to do** faire); **to w. sb well** souhaiter à qn que tout se passe bien; **I w. (that) you could help me** je voudrais que vous m'aidiez; **I w. she could come** j'aurais bien aimé qu'elle vienne; **I w. I hadn't done that** je regrette d'avoir fait ça; **if you w.** si tu veux; **I w. you (a) happy birthday/(good) luck** je vous souhaite bon anniversaire/bonne chance; **I w. I could** si seulement je pouvais **3** vi **to w. for sth** souhaiter qch; **I wished for him to recover quickly** j'ai souhaité qu'il se rétablisse vite; **as you w.** comme vous voudrez ▪**wishbone** n bréchet m ▪**wishful** adj it's w. **thinking** tu prends tes désirs pour des réalités

wishy-washy [ˈwɪʃɪwɒʃɪ] adj (taste, colour) délavé

wisp [wɪsp] n (of smoke) traînée f; (of hair) mèche f; (of straw) brin m; Hum **a (mere) w. of a girl** une fillette toute menue ▪**wispy** adj (hair) fin; (clouds) vaporeux, -euse

wisteria [wɪˈstɪərɪə] n glycine f

wistful [ˈwɪstfəl] adj nostalgique ▪**wistfully** adv avec nostalgie

wit [wɪt] n (humour) esprit m; (person) homme m/femme f d'esprit; **wits** (intelligence) intelligence f; **he didn't have the w. to do it** il n'a pas eu l'intelligence de le faire; **to be at**

one's wits' or **w.'s end** ne plus savoir que faire; **to have/keep one's wits about one** avoir/conserver toute sa présence d'esprit

witch [wɪtʃ] n sorcière f; **w. doctor** sorcier m guérisseur (f sorcière guérisseuse) ▪ **witch-craft** n sorcellerie f ▪ **witch-hunt** n Pol chasse f aux sorcières

with [wɪð] prep (**a**) (expressing accompaniment) avec; **come w. me** viens avec moi; **w. no hat/gloves** sans chapeau/gants; **I'll be right w. you** je suis à vous dans une seconde; Fam **I'm w. you** (I understand) je te suis; Fam **to be w. it** (up-to-date) être dans le vent (**b**) (at the house, flat of) chez; **she's staying w. me** elle loge chez moi; Fig **it's a habit w. me** c'est une habitude chez moi (**c**) (expressing cause) de; **to tremble w. fear** trembler de peur; **to be ill w. measles** être malade de la rougeole (**d**) (expressing instrument, means) **to write w. a pen** écrire avec un stylo; **to walk w. a stick** marcher avec une canne; **to fill w. sth** remplir de qch; **satisfied w. sb/sth** satisfait de qn/qch; **w. my own eyes** de mes propres yeux; **w. two hands** à deux mains (**e**) (in description) à; **a woman w. blue eyes** une femme aux yeux bleus (**f**) (despite) malgré; **w. all his faults** malgré tous ses défauts

withdraw [wɪð'drɔː] 1 (pt -drew, pp -drawn) vt retirer (**from** de) 2 vi se retirer (**from** de) ▪ **withdrawal** n retrait m; **to suffer from w. symptoms** (of drug addict) être en manque ▪ **withdrawn** adj (person) renfermé

wither ['wɪðə(r)] vi (of plant) se flétrir ▪ **withered** adj (plant) flétri; (limb) atrophié; (old man) desséché ▪ **withering** adj (look) foudroyant; (remark) cinglant

withhold [wɪð'həʊld] (pt & pp -held) vt (permission, help) refuser (**from** à); (decision) différer; (money) retenir (**from** de); (information) cacher (**from** à)

within [wɪð'ɪn] 1 prep (inside) à l'intérieur de; **w. 10 km (of)** (less than) à moins de 10 km (de); (inside an area of) dans un rayon de 10 km (de); **w. a month** (return) avant un mois; (finish) en moins d'un mois; **it's w. my means** c'est dans mes moyens; **to live w. one's means** vivre selon ses moyens; **w. sight** en vue 2 adv à l'intérieur

without [wɪð'aʊt] 1 prep sans; **w. a tie** sans cravate; **w. doing sth** sans faire qch; **to do w. sth** se passer de qch 2 adv **to do w.** se priver

withstand [wɪð'stænd] (pt & pp -stood) vt résister à

witness ['wɪtnɪs] 1 n (person) témoin m; **to bear w. to sth** témoigner de qch; Br **w. box**, Am **w. stand** barre f des témoins 2 vt (accident) être témoin de; (document) signer (pour attester l'authenticité de)

witty ['wɪtɪ] (-ier, -iest) adj spirituel, -uelle ▪ **witticism** n mot m d'esprit

wizard ['wɪzəd] n magicien m; Fig (genius) as m ▪ **wizardry** n Fig génie m

wizened ['wɪzənd] adj ratatiné

WMD [dʌbəljuːem'diː] (abbr weapons of mass destruction) npl ADM fpl

wobble ['wɒbəl] vi (of chair) branler; (of jelly, leg) trembler; (of wheel) tourner de façon irrégulière; (of person) chanceler ▪ **wobbly** adj (table, chair) branlant; (person) chancelant

woe [wəʊ] n malheur m ▪ **woeful** adj affligé

wok [wɒk] n wok m

woke [wəʊk] pt of **wake**[1]

woken ['wəʊkən] pp of **wake**[1]

wolf [wʊlf] 1 (pl wolves) n loup m; **w. whistle** = sifflement admiratif au passage de quelqu'un 2 vt **to w. (down)** (food) engloutir

woman ['wʊmən] (pl women) n femme f; **young w.** jeune femme; **she's a London w.** c'est une Londonienne; **w. friend** amie f; **women's** (clothes, attitudes, magazine) féminin; **women's rights** droits mpl des femmes ▪ **womanhood** n (quality) féminité f; **to reach w.** devenir une femme ▪ **womanizer** n Pej coureur m de jupons ▪ **womanly** adj féminin

womb [wuːm] n Anat utérus m

women ['wɪmɪn] pl of **woman**

won [wʌn] pt & pp of **win**

wonder ['wʌndə(r)] 1 n (marvel) merveille f; (feeling) émerveillement m; **to work wonders** (of medicine) faire merveille; **in w.** avec émerveillement; **it's no w.** ce n'est pas étonnant (**that** que + subjunctive); **it's a w. she wasn't killed** c'est un miracle qu'elle n'ait pas été tuée 2 vt (ask oneself) se demander (**if** si; **why** pourquoi); **I w. that...** je m'étonne que... (+ subjunctive) 3 vi (**a**) (ask oneself questions) s'interroger (**about** au sujet de ou sur); **I was just wondering** je réfléchissais (**b**) Literary (be amazed) s'étonner (**at** de)

wonderful ['wʌndəfəl] adj merveilleux, -euse ▪ **wonderfully** adv (+ adj) merveilleusement; (+ verb) à merveille

wonky ['wɒŋkɪ] (-ier, -iest) adj Br Fam (table) déglingué; (hat, picture) de travers

won't [wəʊnt] = **will not**

woo [wuː] (pt & pp wooed) vt (woman) courtiser; (voters) chercher à plaire à

wood [wʊd] n (material, forest) bois m; Fig **we're not out of the woods yet** nous ne sommes pas encore tirés d'affaire ▪ **woodcut** n gravure f sur bois ▪ **wooded** adj boisé ▪ **wooden** adj en bois; Fig (manner, dancer, actor) raide ▪ **woodland** n région f boisée ▪ **woodlouse** (pl -lice) n cloporte m ▪ **woodpecker** n pic m ▪ **woodwind** n **the w.** (musical instruments) les bois mpl ▪ **woodwork** n (school subject) menuiserie f ▪ **woodworm** n (larvae) ver m du

bois; **it has w.** c'est vermoulu ▪**woody (-ier,
-iest)** *adj (hill)* boisé; *(stem)* ligneux, -euse

wool [wʊl] *n* laine *f*; **w. cloth/garment** tissu *m*/
vêtement *m* de laine ▪**woollen** *(Am* **woolen)**
1 *adj (dress)* en laine **2** *npl* **woollens** *(Am*
woolens) *(garments)* lainages *mpl* ▪**woolly
(-ier, -iest) 1** *adj* en laine; *Fig (unclear)*
nébuleux, -euse **2** *n BrFam (garment)* lainage *m*

word [wɜːd] **1** *n* mot *m*; *(promise)* parole *f*;
words *(of song)* paroles *fpl*; **to have a w. with
sb** parler à qn; **to keep one's w.** tenir sa
promesse; **in other words** autrement dit; **w.
for w.** *(report)* mot pour mot; *(translate)* mot à
mot; **by w. of mouth** de bouche à oreille; **to
receive w. from sb** avoir des nouvelles de qn; **to
send w. that...** faire savoir que...; **to leave
w. that...** faire dire que...; **the last w. in** *(latest
development)* le dernier cri en matière de; **w.
processing** traitement *m* de texte; **w.
processor** machine *f* à traitement de texte **2**
vt (express) formuler ▪**wording** *n* termes *mpl*
▪**wordy (-ier, -iest)** *adj* prolixe

wore [wɔː(r)] *pt of* **wear**

work [wɜːk] **1** *n* travail *m*; *(literary, artistic)*
œuvre *f*; **works** *(construction)* travaux *mpl*; **to
be at w.** travailler; **it's hard w. (doing that)** ça
demande beaucoup de travail (de faire ça); **to
be out of w.** être sans travail; **a day off w.** un
jour de congé; **he's off w. today** il n'est pas allé
travailler aujourd'hui; **'w. in progress'** *(on sign)*
'travaux'; **the works** *(of clock)* le mécanisme *m*;
w. permit permis *m* de travail; **w. station** poste *m*
de travail; **w. of art** œuvre *f* d'art
2 *vt (person)* faire travailler; *(machine)* faire
marcher; *(mine)* exploiter; *(metal, wood)* travailler
3 *vi (of person)* travailler; *(of machine)*
marcher, fonctionner; *(of drug)* agir; **to w.
loose** *(of knot, screw)* se desserrer; **to w.
towards** *(result, agreement, aim)* travailler à
▪**workable** *adj* possible ▪**workaholic**
[-ə'hɒlɪk] *n Fam* bourreau *m* de travail
▪**workbench** *n* établi *m* ▪**workday** *n Am* jour
m ouvrable ▪**workforce** *n* main-d'œuvre *f*
▪**workload** *n* charge *f* de travail ▪**workman**
(pl **-men)** *n* ouvrier *m* ▪**workmanship** *n*
travail *m* ▪**workmate** *n Br* camarade *mf* de
travail ▪**workout** *n Sport* séance *f*
d'entraînement ▪**workshop** *n (place, study
course)* atelier *m* ▪**workshy** [-ʃaɪ] *adj Br* peu
enclin au travail ▪**'work-to-'rule** *n Br* grève *f*
du zèle
▸**work at** *vt insep (improve)* travailler
▸**work off** *vt sep (debt)* payer en travaillant;
(excess fat) se débarrasser de (par l'exercice);
(anger) passer
▸**work on 1** *vt insep (book, problem)* travailler
à; *(French)* travailler **2** *vi* continuer à travailler
▸**work out 1** *vt sep (calculate)* calculer;
(problem) résoudre; *(plan)* préparer; *(under-*

stand) comprendre **2** *vi (succeed)* marcher; *(do
exercises)* s'entraîner; **it works out at 50 euros**
ça fait 50 euros
▸**work up 1** *vt sep* **to w. up enthusiasm**
s'enthousiasmer (**for** pour); **I worked up an
appetite** ça m'a ouvert l'appétit; **to w. one's
way up** *(rise socially)* faire du chemin; **to get
worked up** s'énerver **2** *vi* **to w. up to sth** se
préparer à qch

worker ['wɜːkə(r)] *n* travailleur, -euse *mf*;
(manual) ouvrier, -ière *mf*; **(office) w.** employé,
-ée *mf* (de bureau); **blue-collar w.** col *m* bleu

working ['wɜːkɪŋ] **1** *adj (day, clothes)* de travail;
Br **Monday is a w. day** on travaille le lundi; **in w.
order** en état de marche; **a w. wife** une femme
qui travaille; **w. class** classe *f* ouvrière; **w.
conditions** conditions *fpl* de travail; **w.
population** population *f* active **2** *npl* **the
workings** *(of)* le mécanisme *m* de
▪**'working-'class** *adj* ouvrier, -ière

world [wɜːld] **1** *n* monde *m*; **all over the w.** dans
le monde entier; **the richest in the w.** le/la plus
riche du monde; **to think the w. of sb** adorer
énormément qn; **it did me the** *or* **a w. of good**
ça m'a beaucoup fait du bien; **why in the w....?**
pourquoi diable...?; *Fam* **out of this w.**
(wonderful) extra *inv* **2** *adj (war, production)*
mondial; *(champion, record)* du monde;
Football **the W. Cup** la Coupe du Monde; **W.
Health Organization** Organisation *f* mondiale
de la santé; **W. Trade Organization** Organisation mondiale du Commerce ▪**'world-
'famous** *adj* de renommée mondiale ▪**worldly**
adj (pleasures) de ce monde; *(person)* qui a l'expérience du monde ▪**'world'wide 1** *adj*
mondial; **the W. Web** le Worldwide Web **2** *adv*
dans le monde entier

worm [wɜːm] **1** *n & Comptr* ver *m* **2** *vt* **to w. one's
way into** s'insinuer dans; **to w. sth out of sb**
soutirer qch à qn ▪**wormeaten** *adj (wood)*
vermoulu; *(fruit)* véreux, -euse

worn [wɔːn] **1** *pp of* **wear 2** *adj (clothes, tyre)* usé
▪**'worn-'out** *adj (object)* complètement usé;
(person) épuisé

worry ['wʌrɪ] **1** *(pl* **-ies)** *n* souci *m*; **it's a w.** ça
me cause du souci; *Fam* **no worries!** pas de
problème! **2** *(pt & pp* **-ied)** *vt* inquiéter; **to w.
oneself sick** se ronger les sangs **3** *vi*
s'inquiéter (**about sth** de qch; **about sb** pour
qn) ▪**worried** *adj* inquiet, -iète (**about** au
sujet de); **to be w. sick** se ronger les sangs
▪**worrier** *n* anxieux, -ieuse *mf* ▪**worrying** *adj*
inquiétant

worse [wɜːs] **1** *adj* pire (**than** que); **to get w.** se
détériorer; **he's getting w.** *(in health)* il va de
plus en plus mal; *(in behaviour)* il se conduit de
plus en plus mal **2** *adv* plus mal (**than** que); **to
go from bad to w.** aller de mal en pis; **I could do
w.** j'aurais pu tomber plus mal; **she's w. off**

(than before) sa situation est pire (qu'avant); *(financially)* elle est encore plus pauvre (qu'avant) **3** *n* there's w. to come le pire reste à venir; **a change for the w.** une détérioration

worsen ['wɜːsən] **1** *vt* aggraver **2** *vi* empirer

worship ['wɜːʃɪp] **1** *n* culte *m*; *Br* his W. the Mayor Monsieur le Maire **2** *(pt & pp -pp-)* *vt* *(person, god)* adorer; *Pej (money)* avoir le culte de **3** *vi (pray)* faire ses dévotions **(at à)** ▪**worshipper** *n (in church)* fidèle *mf*; *(of person)* adorateur, -trice *mf*

worst [wɜːst] **1** *adj (den;* the w. book I've ever read le plus mauvais livre que j'aie jamais lu **2** *adv* (the) w. le plus mal; to come off w. *(in struggle)* avoir le dessous **3** *n* the w. (one) *(object, person)* le/la pire, le/la plus mauvais(e); the w. (thing) is that… le pire, c'est que…; at (the) w. au pire; to be at its w. *(of crisis)* avoir atteint son paroxysme; the situation is at its w. la situation est on ne peut plus mauvaise; to get the w. of it *(in struggle)* avoir le dessous; the w. is yet to come on n'a pas encore vu le pire

worth [wɜːθ] **1** *adj* to be w. sth valoir qch; how much *or* what is it w.? ça vaut combien?; it's w. a great deal *or* a lot avoir beaucoup de valeur; the film's (well) w. seeing le film vaut la peine d'être vu **2** *n* valeur *f*; to buy 50 pence w. of chocolates acheter pour 50 pence de chocolats; to get one's money's w. en avoir pour son argent ▪**worthless** *adj* qui ne vaut rien

worthwhile ['wɜːθ'waɪl] *adj (book, film)* qui vaut la peine d'être lu/vu; *(activity)* qui vaut la peine; *(plan, contribution)* valable; *(cause)* louable; *(satisfying)* qui donne des satisfactions

worthy ['wɜːðɪ] **1** *(-ier, -iest)* *adj (person)* digne; *(cause, act)* louable; to be w. of sb/sth être digne de qn/qch **2** *n (person)* notable *m*

would [wʊd, *unstressed* wəd]

On trouve généralement I/you/he/etc would sous leurs formes contractées I'd/you'd/he'd/ etc. La forme négative correspondante est wouldn't, que l'on écrira would not dans les contextes formels.

v aux (**a**) *(expressing conditional tense)* I w. stay if I could je resterais si je le pouvais; he w. have done it il l'aurait fait; I said she'd come j'ai dit qu'elle viendrait (**b**) *(willingness, ability)* w. you help me, please? veux-tu bien m'aider?; she wouldn't help me elle n'a pas voulu m'aider; w. you like some tea? prendrez-vous du thé?; the car wouldn't start la voiture ne démarrait pas (**c**) *(expressing past habit)* I w. see her every day je la voyais chaque jour ▪**would-be** *adj (musician, actor)* en puissance

wound¹ [wuːnd] **1** *n* blessure *f* **2** *vt (hurt)* blesser; the wounded les blessés *mpl*

wound² [waʊnd] *pt & pp of* **wind²**

wove [wəʊv] *pt of* **weave**

woven ['wəʊvən] *pp of* **weave**

wow [waʊ] *exclam Fam* oh là là!

wrangle ['ræŋgəl] *n* dispute *f* **2** *vi* se disputer

wrap [ræp] **1** *n (shawl)* châle *m*; *Am* plastic w. film *m* plastique **2** *(pt & pp -pp-)* *vt* to w. (up) envelopper; *(parcel)* emballer; *Fig* wrapped up in *(engrossed)* absorbé par **3** *vti* to w. (oneself) up *(dress warmly)* s'emmitoufler ▪**wrapper** *n (of sweet)* papier *m* ▪**wrapping** *n (action, material)* emballage *m*; w. paper papier *m* d'emballage

wrath [rɒθ] *n Literary* courroux *m*

wreak [riːk] *vt* to w. vengeance on se venger de; to w. havoc faire des ravages

wreath [riːθ] *(pl -s* [riːðz]) *n* couronne *f*

wreck [rek] **1** *n (ship)* épave *f*; *(sinking)* naufrage *m*; *(train)* train *m* accidenté; *(person)* épave *f* (humaine); to be a nervous w. être à bout de nerfs **2** *vt (break, destroy)* détruire; *(ship)* provoquer le naufrage de; *Fig (spoil)* gâcher; *Fig (career, hopes)* briser ▪**wreckage** [-ɪdʒ] *n (of plane, train)* débris *mpl* ▪**wrecker** *n Am (truck)* dépanneuse *f*

wren [ren] *n (bird)* roitelet *m*

wrench [rentʃ] **1** *n* faux mouvement *m*; *Fig (emotional)* déchirement *m*; *Am (tool)* clef *f* (à écrous); *(adjustable)* w. clef à molette **2** *vt (tug at)* tirer sur; to w. sth from sb arracher qch à qn; to w. one's ankle se tordre la cheville

wrest [rest] *vt* to w. sth from sb arracher qch à qn

wrestle ['resəl] *vi* lutter **(with sb** avec qn); *Fig* to w. with a problem se débattre avec un problème ▪**wrestler** *n* lutteur, -euse *mf*; *(in all-in wrestling)* catcheur, -euse *mf* ▪**wrestling** *n* lutte *f*; (all-in) w. *(with relaxed rules)* catch *m*

wretch [retʃ] *n (unfortunate person)* malheureux, -euse *mf*; *(rascal)* misérable *mf* ▪**wretched** [-ɪd] *adj (poor, pitiful)* misérable; *(dreadful)* affreux, -euse; *Fam (annoying)* maudit

wriggle ['rɪgəl] **1** *vt (toes, fingers)* tortiller; to w. one's way out of a situation se sortir d'une situation **2** *vi* to w. (about) se tortiller; *(of fish)* frétiller; to w. out of sth couper à qch

wring [rɪŋ] *(pt & pp* wrung) *vt* to w. (out) *(clothes)* essorer; to w. one's hands se tordre les mains; *Fam* I'll w. your neck je vais te tordre le cou; *Fig* to w. sth out of sb arracher qch à qn; to be wringing wet être trempé

wrinkle ['rɪŋkəl] **1** *n (on skin)* ride *f*; *(in cloth, paper)* pli *m* **2** *vt (skin)* rider; *(cloth, paper)* plisser **3** *vi (of skin)* se rider; *(of cloth)* faire des plis ▪**wrinkled** *adj (skin)* ridé; *(cloth)* froissé

wrist [rɪst] *n* poignet *m* ▪**wristwatch** *n* montre-bracelet *f*

writ [rɪt] *n Law* ordre *m*; to issue a w. against sb assigner qn en justice

write [raɪt] (*pt* **wrote**, *pp* **written**) *vti* écrire; **to w. to sb** écrire à qn ▪**write-off** *n Br* **to be a (complete) w.** (*of vehicle*) être bon pour la casse ▪**'write-pro'tected** *adj Comptr* protégé en écriture ▪**write-up** *n* (*of play*) critique *f*
▸ **write away for** *vt insep* (*details*) écrire pour demander
▸ **write back** *vi* répondre
▸ **write down** *vt sep* noter
▸ **write in 1** *vt sep* (*insert*) inscrire **2** *vi* (*send letter*) écrire
▸ **write off** *vt sep* (*debt*) annuler
▸ **write out** *vt sep* (*list, recipe*) noter; (*cheque*) faire
▸ **write up** *vt sep* (*notes*) rédiger; (*diary*) tenir
writer ['raɪtə(r)] *n* auteur *m* (**of** de); (*literary*) écrivain *m*
writhe [raɪð] *vi* (*in pain*) se tordre (**in** de)
writing ['raɪtɪŋ] *n* (*handwriting, action, profession*) écriture *f*; **writings** (*of author*) écrits *mpl*; **to put sth (down) in w.** mettre qch par écrit; **w. desk** secrétaire *m*; **w. pad** bloc-notes *m*; **w. paper** papier *m* à lettres
written ['rɪtən] *pp of* **write**
wrong [rɒŋ] **1** *adj* (*sum, idea*) faux (*f* fausse); (*direction, time*) mauvais; (*unfair*) injuste; **to be w.** (*of person*) avoir tort (**to do** de faire); **it's w. to swear** (*morally*) c'est mal de jurer; **it's the w. road** ce n'est pas la bonne route; **you're the w. man for the job** tu n'es pas l'homme qu'il faut pour ce travail; **the clock's w.** la pendule n'est pas à l'heure; **something's w.** quelque chose ne va pas; **something's w. with the phone** le

téléphone ne marche pas bien; **something's w. with her leg** elle a quelque chose à la jambe; **nothing's w.** tout va bien; **what's w. with you?** qu'est-ce que tu as?; **the w. way round** *or* **up** à l'envers; *Fig* **to rub sb up the w. way** prendre qn à rebrousse-poil
2 *adv* mal; **to go w.** (*of plan*) mal tourner; (*of vehicle, machine*) tomber en panne; (*of clock, watch, camera*) se détraquer; (*of person*) se tromper; **to get the date w.** se tromper de date; **to get the w. number** (*on phone*) se tromper de numéro
3 *n* (*injustice*) injustice *f*; (*evil*) mal *m*; **to be in the w.** être dans son tort; **right and w.** le bien et le mal
4 *vt* faire du tort à ▪**wrongdoer** *n* (*criminal*) malfaiteur *m* ▪**wrongful** *adj* (*accusation*) injustifié; **w. arrest** arrestation *f* arbitraire ▪**wrongfully** *adv* à tort ▪**wrongly** *adv* (*inform, translate*) mal; (*accuse, condemn, claim*) à tort
wrote [rəʊt] *pt of* **write**
wrought [rɔːt] *adj* **w. iron** fer *m* forgé ▪**'wrought-'iron** *adj* en fer forgé
wrung [rʌŋ] *pt & pp of* **wring**
wry [raɪ] (**wryer, wryest**) *adj* ironique; **to pull a w. face** grimacer ▪**wryly** *adv* d'un air ironique
WTO [dʌb(ə)ljuːtiːˈəʊ] (*abbr* **World Trade Organization**) *n* OMC *f*
WWW [dʌb(ə)ljuːdʌb(ə)ljuːˈdʌb(ə)ljuː] (*abbr* **World Wide Web**) *n Comptr* WWW *m*
WYSIWYG [wiziwig] (*abbr* **what you see is what you get**) *adj & n Comptr* wysiwyg (*m inv*)

X, x [eks] *n (letter)* X, x *m inv*
xenophobia [*Br* zenə'fəʊbɪə, *Am* ziːnəʊ-] *n* xénophobie *f* ▪ **xenophobic** *adj* xénophobe
Xerox® ['zɪərɒks] **1** *n (copy)* photocopie *f* **2** *vt* photocopier

Xmas ['krɪsməs] *n Fam* Noël *m*
X-ray ['eksreɪ] **1** *n (picture)* radio *f; (radiation)* rayon *m* X; **to have an X.** passer une radio **2** *vt* radiographier
xylophone ['zaɪləfəʊn] *n* xylophone *m*

Y, y [waɪ] *n (letter)* Y, y *m inv* ▪ **Y-fronts** slip *m* ouvert
yacht [jɒt] *n (sailing boat)* voilier *m; (large private boat)* yacht *m* ▪ **yachting** *n* voile *f*
Yank [jæŋk], **Yankee** ['jæŋkɪ] *n Fam* Ricain, -aine *mf*
yank [jæŋk] *Fam* **1** *n* coup *m* sec **2** *vt* tirer d'un coup sec; **to y. sth off** *or* **out** arracher qch
yap [jæp] *(pt & pp* **-pp-**) *vi (of dog)* japper; *Fam (of person)* jacasser
yard¹ [jɑːd] *n (of house, farm, school, prison)* cour *f; (for working)* chantier *m; (for storage)* dépôt *m* de marchandises; *Am (garden)* jardin *m; Br (builder's) y.* chantier de construction
yard² [jɑːd] *n (measure)* yard *m (= 91,44 cm)* ▪ **yardstick** *n (criterion)* critère *m*
yarn [jɑːn] *n (thread)* fil *m; Fam (tale)* histoire *f* à dormir debout
yawn [jɔːn] **1** *n* bâillement *m* **2** *vi* bâiller ▪ **yawning** *adj (gap)* béant
yeah [jeə] *adv Fam* ouais
year [jɪə(r)] *n* an *m*, année *f; (of wine)* année; **school/tax y.** année scolaire/fiscale; **this y.** cette année; **in the y. 2001** en (l'an) 2001; **y. in y. out** chaque année; **over the years** au fil des ans; **years ago** il y a des années; **he's ten years old** il a dix ans; **New Y.** Nouvel An; **New Y.'s Day** le jour de l'An; **New Y.'s Eve** la Saint-Sylvestre ▪ **yearbook** *n* almanach *m* ▪ **yearly 1** *adj* annuel, -uelle **2** *adv* annuellement; **twice y.** deux fois par an
yearn [jɜːn] *vi* **to y. for sb** languir après qn; **to y. for sth** désirer ardemment qch; **to y. to do sth** brûler de faire qch ▪ **yearning** *n (desire)* désir *m* ardent; *(nostalgia)* nostalgie *f*
yeast [jiːst] *n* levure *f*

yell [jel] **1** *n* hurlement *m* **2** *vti* **to y. (out)** hurler; **to y. at sb** *(scold)* crier après qn
yellow ['jeləʊ] **1** *adj (in colour)* jaune; *Fam (cowardly)* trouillard; *Football* **y. card** carton *m* jaune; *Med* **y. fever** fièvre *f* jaune; **the Y. Pages**® les pages *fpl* jaunes **2** *n* jaune *m* **3** *vi* jaunir ▪ **yellowish** *adj* jaunâtre
yelp [jelp] **1** *n* jappement *m* **2** *vi* japper
Yemen ['jemən] *n* le Yémen
yen¹ [jen] *n* **to have a y. for sth/to do sth** avoir envie de qch/de faire qch
yen² [jen] *n (currency)* yen *m*
yes [jes] **1** *adv* oui; *(after negative question)* si; **aren't you coming? – y.(, I am)!** tu ne viens pas? – mais si! **2** *n* oui *m inv*
yesterday ['jestədeɪ] **1** *adv* hier **2** *n* hier *m;* **y. morning/evening** hier matin/soir; **the day before y.** avant-hier
yet [jet] **1** *adv* (**a**) *(still)* encore; *(already)* déjà; **she hasn't arrived (as) y.** elle n'est pas encore arrivée; **the best y.** le meilleur jusqu'ici; **y. more complicated** *(even more)* encore plus compliqué; **y. another mistake** encore une erreur; **not (just) y.** pas pour l'instant (**b**) *(in questions)* **has he come y.?** est-il arrivé? **2** *conj (nevertheless)* pourtant
yew [juː] *n (tree, wood)* if *m*
Yiddish ['jɪdɪʃ] *n & adj* yiddish *(m) inv*
yield [jiːld] **1** *n (of field, shares)* rendement *m; (of mine)* production *f* **2** *vt (result)* donner; *(interest)* rapporter; *(territory, right)* céder; **to y. a profit** rapporter **3** *vi (surrender)* se rendre; **to y. to force** céder devant la force; **to y. to temptation** céder à la tentation; *Am* **'y.'** *(road sign)* 'cédez le passage'

yippee [jɪ'piː] *exclam* youpi!

YMCA [waɪemsiː'eɪ] (*abbr* **Young Men's Christian Association**) *n* = association chrétienne proposant hébergement et activités sportives

yob [jɒb], **yobbo** ['jɒbəʊ] (*pl* **yob(bo)s**) *n Br Fam* loubard *m*

yoga ['jəʊgə] *n* yoga *m*

yog(h)urt [*Br* 'jɒgət, *Am* 'jəʊgərt] *n* yaourt *m*

yoke [jəʊk] *n* (*for oxen*) & *Fig* joug *m*

yokel ['jəʊkəl] *n Pej* plouc *m*

yolk [jəʊk] *n* jaune *m* (d'œuf)

yonder ['jɒndə(r)] *adv Literary* là-bas

you [juː] *pron* (**a**) (*subject*) (*pl, polite form sing*) vous; (*familiar form sing*) tu; (*object*) vous; te, t'; *pl* vous; (*after prep, 'than', 'it is'*) vous; toi; *pl* vous; **(to) y.** (*indirect*) vous; te, t'; *pl* vous; **y. are** vous êtes/tu es; **I see y.** je vous/te vois; **I gave it to y.** je vous/te l'ai donné; **with y.** avec vous/toi; **y. teachers** vous autres professeurs; **y. idiot!** espèce d'imbécile! (**b**) (*indefinite*) on; (*object*) vous; te, t'; *pl* vous; **y. never know** on ne sait jamais; **it surprises y.** cela surprend ▪ **you'd** = **you had, you would** ▪ **you'll** = **you will, you shall**

young [jʌŋ] **1** (**-er, -est**) *adj* jeune; **she's two years younger than me** elle a deux ans de moins que moi; **my young(er) brother** mon (frère) cadet; **my young(er) sister** ma (sœur) cadette; **her youngest brother** le cadet de ses frères; **my youngest sister** la cadette de mes sœurs; **the youngest son/daughter** le cadet/ la cadette; **to be y. at heart** être jeune d'esprit; **y. people** les jeunes *mpl* **2** *n* (*of animals*) petits *mpl*; **the y.** (*people*) les jeunes *mpl*; **she's my youngest** (*daughter*) c'est ma petite dernière ▪ **young-looking** *adj* qui a l'air jeune ▪ **youngster** *n* jeune *mf*

your [jɔː(r)] *possessive adj* (*polite form sing, polite and familiar form pl*) votre, *pl* vos; (*familiar form sing*) ton, ta, *pl* tes; (*one's*) son, sa, *pl* ses

yours [jɔːz] *possessive pron* le vôtre, la vôtre, *pl* les vôtres; (*familiar form sing*) le tien, la tienne, *pl* les tien(ne)s; **this book is y.** ce livre est à vous *ou* est le vôtre *ou* ce livre est à toi *ou* est le tien; **a friend of y.** un ami à vous/toi

yourself [jɔː'self] *pron* (*polite form*) vous-même; (*familiar form*) toi-même; (*reflexive*) vous; te, t'; (*after prep*) vous; toi; **you wash y.** tu te laves/vous vous lavez ▪ **yourselves** *pron pl* vous-mêmes; (*reflexive and after prep*) vous; **did you cut y.?** est-ce que vous vous êtes coupés?

youth [juːθ] (*pl* **-s** [juːðz]) *n* (*age*) jeunesse *f*; (*young man*) jeune *m*; **y. club** centre *m* de loisirs pour les jeunes; **y. hostel** auberge *f* de jeunesse ▪ **youthful** *adj* (*person*) jeune; (*quality, smile*) juvénile ▪ **youthfulness** *n* jeunesse *f*

you've [juːv] = **you have**

yo-yo ['jəʊjəʊ] (*pl* **yo-yos**) *n* Yo-Yo® *m inv*

yuck [jʌk] *exclam Fam* berk! ▪ **yucky** (**-ier, -iest**) *adj Fam* dégueulasse

yum-yum [jʌm'jʌm] *exclam Fam* miam-miam! ▪ **yummy** (**-ier, iest**) *adj Fam* super bon (*f* super bonne)

yuppie ['jʌpɪ] *n* yuppie *mf*; **y. area** quartier *m* riche et branché ▪ **yuppify** *vt Fam* (*place*) rendre chic et branché

Z, z [*Br* zed, *Am* ziː] *n* (*letter*) Z, z *m inv*.

zany ['zeɪnɪ] (**-ier, -iest**) *adj* loufoque

zap [zæp] (*pt & pp* **-pp-**) *vt Fam Comptr* effacer ▪ **zapper** *n Fam* (*for TV channels*) télécommande *f*

zeal [ziːl] *n* zèle *m* ▪ **zealous** ['zeləs] *adj* zélé; (*supporter*) ardent

zebra ['ziːbrə, *Br* 'zebrə] *n* zèbre *m*; *Br* **z. crossing** passage *m* pour piétons

Zen [zen] **1** *n* zen *m* **2** *adj* zen

zenith ['zenɪθ] *n* zénith *m*

zero ['zɪərəʊ] (*pl* **-os**) *n* zéro *m*; *Fig* **z. hour** (*for military operation*) l'heure *f* H; *Pol* **z. tolerance** tolérance *f* zéro

zest [zest] *n* (*enthusiasm*) enthousiasme *m*; (*of lemon, orange*) zeste *m*

zigzag ['zɪgzæg] **1** *n* zigzag *m* **2** *adj & adv* en zigzag **3** (*pt & pp* **-gg-**) *vi* zigzaguer

Zimbabwe [zɪm'bɑːbweɪ] *n* le Zimbabwe

zinc [zɪŋk] *n* zinc *m*

zip [zɪp] **1** *n* (**a**) *Br* **z. (fastener)** fermeture *f* Éclair®; **z. pocket** poche *f* à fermeture Éclair®; *Comptr* **z. drive** lecteur *m* Zip®; **z. file** fichier *m* zippé (**b**) *Fam* (*vigour*) punch *m* **2** *adj Am* **z. code** code *m* postal **3** (*pt & pp* **-pp-**) *vt* to z. sth (up) remonter la fermeture Éclair® de qch; *Comptr* **to z. a file** zipper *ou* compresser un fichier **4** *vi* to z. past (*of car*) passer en trombe; (*of bullet*) passer en sifflant; **to z. through a book** lire un livre à toute

vitesse ▪**zipper** *n Am* fermeture *f* Éclair®
▪**zippy** *adj* plein de punch
zit [zɪt] *n Fam (pimple)* bouton *m*
zodiac [ˈzəʊdɪæk] *n* zodiaque *m*
zombie [ˈzɒmbɪ] *n Fam* zombi *m*
zone [zəʊn] *n* zone *f*
zonked [zɒŋkt] *adj Fam* z. (out) *(exhausted)*
cassé; *(drugged)* défoncé
zoo [zuː] *(pl* **zoos)** *n* zoo *m* ▪**zoological**

[zuːəˈlɒdʒɪkəl] *adj* zoologique ▪**zoologist**
[zuːˈɒlədʒɪst] *n* zoologiste *mf* ▪**zoology**
[zuːˈɒlədʒɪ] *n* zoologie *f*
zoom [zuːm] **1** *n* z. lens zoom *m* **2** *vi* to z. in *(of camera)* faire un zoom avant (**on** sur); *Fam* to z. **past** passer comme une flèche
zucchini [zuːˈkiːnɪ] *(pl* **-ni** *or* **-nis)** *n Am* courgette *f*
zwieback [ˈzwiːbæk] *n Am (rusk)* biscotte *f*

FRENCH VERB CONJUGATIONS

Regular Verbs

	-ER verbs	**-IR verbs**	**-RE verbs**
Infinitive	*donn/er*	*fin/ir*	*vend/re*
1 Present	je donne	je finis	je vends
	tu donnes	tu finis	tu vends
	il donne	il finit	il vend
	nous donnons	nous finissons	nous vendons
	vous donnez	vous finissez	vous vendez
	ils donnent	ils finissent	ils vendent
2 Imperfect	je donnais	je finissais	je vendais
	tu donnais	tu finissais	tu vendais
	il donnait	il finissait	il vendait
	nous donnions	nous finissions	nous vendions
	vous donniez	vous finissiez	vous vendiez
	ils donnaient	ils finissaient	ils vendaient
3 Past historic	je donnai	je finis	je vendis
	tu donnas	tu finis	tu vendis
	il donna	il finit	il vendit
	nous donnâmes	nous finîmes	nous vendîmes
	vous donnâtes	vous finîtes	vous vendîtes
	ils donnèrent	ils finirent	ils vendirent
4 Future	je donnerai	je finirai	je vendrai
	tu donneras	tu finiras	tu vendras
	il donnera	il finira	il vendra
	nous donnerons	nous finirons	nous vendrons
	vous donnerez	vous finirez	vous vendrez
	ils donneront	ils finiront	ils vendront
5 Subjunctive	je donne	je finisse	je vende
	tu donnes	tu finisses	tu vendes
	il donne	il finisse	il vende
	nous donnions	nous finissions	nous vendions
	vous donniez	vous finissiez	vous vendiez
	ils donnent	ils finissent	ils vendent
6 Imperative	donne	finis	vends
	donnons	finissons	vendons
	donnez	finissez	vendez
7 Present participle	donnant	finissant	vendant
8 Past participle	donné	fini	vendu

Note The conditional is formed by adding the following endings to the infinitive: **-ais**, **-ais**, **-ait**, **-ions**, **-iez**, **-aient**. The final **e** is dropped in infinitives ending **-re**.

(i)

IRREGULAR FRENCH VERBS

Listed below are those verbs considered to be the most useful. Forms and tenses not given are fully derivable, such as the third person singular of the present tense which is normally formed by substituting 't' for the final 's' of the first person singular, eg 'crois' becomes 'croit', 'dis' becomes 'dit'. Note that the endings of the past historic fall into three categories, the 'a' and 'i' categories shown at *donner*, and at *finir* and *vendre*, and the 'u' category which has the following endings: -us, -ut, -ûmes, -ûtes, -urent. Most of the verbs listed below form their past historic with 'u'.

The imperfect may usually be formed by adding -ais, -ait, -ions, -iez, -aient to the stem of the first person plural of the present tense, eg 'je buvais' etc may be derived from 'nous buvons' (stem 'buv-' and ending '-ons'); similarly, the present participle may generally be formed by substituting -ant for -ons (eg buvant). The future may usually be formed by adding -ai, -as, -a, -ons, -ez, -ont to the infinitive or to an infinitive without final 'e' where the ending is -re (eg conduire). The imperative usually has the same forms as the second persons singular and plural and first person plural of the present tense.

1 = Present   2 = Imperfect   3 = Past historic   4 = Future
5 = Subjunctive   6 = Imperative   7 = Present participle
8 = Past participle   n = nous   v = vous   † verbs conjugated with **être** only

abattre	*like*	**battre**
absoudre	1 j'absous, n absolvons 2 j'absolvais
	3 j'absolus *(rarely used)* 5 j'absolve 7 absolvant
	8 absous, absoute
†s'abstenir	*like*	**tenir**
abstraire	1 j'abstrais, n abstrayons 2 j'abstrayais 3 none 5 j'abstraie
	7 abstrayant 8 abstrait
accourir	*like*	**courir**
accroître	*like*	**croître** *except* 8 accru
accueillir	*like*	**cueillir**
acquérir	1 j'acquiers, n acquérons 2 j'acquérais 3 j'acquis
	4 j'acquerrai 5 j'acquière 7 acquérant 8 acquis
adjoindre	*like*	**joindre**
admettre	*like*	**mettre**
advenir	*like*	**venir** *(third person only)*
†aller	1 je vais, tu vas, il va, n allons, v allez, ils vont 4 j'irai
	5 j'aille, n allions, ils aillent 6 va, allons, allez *(but note* vas-y)
apercevoir	*like*	**recevoir**
apparaître	*like*	**connaître**
appartenir	*like*	**tenir**
apprendre	*like*	**prendre**
asseoir	1 j'assieds, il assied, n asseyons, ils asseyent 2 j'asseyais
	3 j'assis 4 j'assiérai 5 j'asseye 7 asseyant 8 assis
astreindre	*like*	**atteindre**
atteindre	1 j'atteins, n atteignons, ils atteignent 2 j'atteignais
	3 j'atteignis 4 j'atteindrai 5 j'atteigne 7 atteignant 8 atteint
avoir	1 j'ai, tu as, il a, n avons, v avez, ils ont 2 j'avais 3 j'eus
	4 j'aurai 5 j'aie, il ait, n ayons, ils aient 6 aie, ayons, ayez
	7 ayant 8 eu
battre	1 je bats, il bat, n battons 5 je batte
boire	1 je bois, n buvons, ils boivent 2 je buvais 3 je bus
	5 je boive, n buvions 7 buvant 8 bu

bouillir		1 je bous, n bouillons, ils bouillent 2 je bouillais 3 je bouillis 5 je bouille 7 bouillant
braire		(*defective*) 1 il brait, ils braient 4 il braira, ils brairont
circonscrire	*like*	**écrire**
circonvenir	*like*	**tenir**
clore	*like*	**éclore**
combattre	*like*	**battre**
commettre	*like*	**mettre**
comparaître	*like*	**connaître**
complaire	*like*	**plaire**
comprendre	*like*	**prendre**
compromettre	*like*	**mettre**
concevoir	*like*	**recevoir**
conclure		1 je conclus, n concluons, ils concluent 5 je conclue
concourir	*like*	**courir**
conduire		1 je conduis, n conduisons 3 je conduisis 5 je conduise 8 conduit
confire	*like*	**suffire**
connaître		1 je connais, il connaît, n connaissons 3 je connus 5 je connaisse 7 connaissant 8 connu
conquérir	*like*	**acquérir**
consentir	*like*	**mentir**
construire	*like*	**conduire**
contenir	*like*	**tenir**
contraindre	*like*	**craindre**
contredire	*like*	**dire** *except* 1 v contredisez
convaincre	*like*	**vaincre**
convenir	*like*	**tenir**
corrompre	*like*	**rompre**
coudre		1 je couds, ils coud, n cousons, ils cousent 3 je cousis 5 je couse 7 cousant 8 cousu
courir		1 je cours, n courons 3 je courus 4 je courrai 5 je coure 8 couru
couvrir		1 je couvre, n couvrons 2 je couvrais 5 je couvre 8 couvert
craindre		1 je crains, n craignons, ils craignent 2 je craignais 3 je craignis 4 je craindrai 5 je craigne 7 craignant 8 craint
croire		1 je crois, n croyons, ils croient 2 je croyais 3 je crus 5 je croie, n croyions 7 croyant 8 cru
croître		1 je crois, il croît, n croissons 2 je croissais 3 je crûs 5 je croisse 7 croissant 8 crû, crue
cueillir		1 je cueille, n cueillons 2 je cueillais 4 je cueillerai 5 je cueille 7 cueillant
cuire		1 je cuis, n cuisons 2 je cuisais 3 je cuisis 5 je cuise 7 cuisant 8 cuit
débattre	*like*	**battre**
décevoir	*like*	**recevoir**
déchoir		(*defective*) 1 je déchois 2 *none* 3 je déchus 4 je déchoirai 6 *none* 7 *none* 8 déchu
découdre	*like*	**coudre**
découvrir	*like*	**couvrir**
décrire	*like*	**écrire**
décroître	*like*	**croître** *except* 8 décru
†se dédire	*like*	**dire**
déduire	*like*	**conduire**
défaillir		1 je défaille, n défaillons 2 je défaillais 3 je défaillis 5 je défaille 7 défaillant 8 défailli
défaire	*like*	**faire**
démentir	*like*	**mentir**

démettre	*like*	mettre
†se départir	*like*	mentir
dépeindre	*like*	atteindre
déplaire	*like*	plaire
déteindre	*like*	atteindre
détenir	*like*	tenir
détruire	*like*	conduire
†devenir	*like*	tenir
†se dévêtir	*like*	vêtir
devoir	1 je dois, n devons, ils doivent 2 je devais 3 je dus 4 je devrai 5 je doive, n devions 6 *not used* 7 devant 8 dû, due, *pl* dus, dues	
dire	1 je dis, n disons, v dites 2 je disais 3 je dis 5 je dise 7 disant 8 dit	
disconvenir	*like*	tenir
disjoindre	*like*	joindre
disparaître	*like*	connaître
dissoudre	*like*	absoudre
distraire	*like*	abstraire
dormir	*like*	mentir
†échoir	(*defective*) 1 il échoit 2 *none* 3 il échut, ils échurent 4 il échoira 6 *none* 7 échéant 8 échu	
éclore	1 il éclôt, ils éclosent 8 éclos	
éconduire	*like*	conduire
écrire	1 j'écris, n écrivons 2 j'écrivais 3 j'écrivis 5 j'écrive 7 écrivant 8 écrit	
élire	*like*	lire
émettre	*like*	mettre
émouvoir	*like*	mouvoir *except* 8 ému
enclore	*like*	éclore
encourir	*like*	courir
endormir	*like*	mentir
enduire	*like*	conduire
enfreindre	*like*	atteindre
†s'enfuir	*like*	fuir
enjoindre	*like*	joindre
†s'enquérir	*like*	acquérir
†s'ensuivre	*like*	suivre (*third person only*)
entreprendre	*like*	prendre
entretenir	*like*	tenir
entrevoir	*like*	voir
entrouvrir	*like*	couvrir
envoyer	4 j'enverrai	
†s'éprendre	*like*	prendre
équivaloir	*like*	valoir
éteindre	*like*	atteindre
être	1 je suis, tu es, il est, n sommes, v êtes, ils sont 2 j'étais 3 je fus 4 je serai 5 je sois, n soyons, ils soient 6 sois, soyons, soyez 7 étant 8 été	
étreindre	*like*	atteindre
exclure	*like*	conclure
extraire	*like*	abstraire
faillir	(*defective*) 3 je faillis 4 je faillirai 8 failli	
faire	1 je fais, n faisons, v faites, ils font 2 je faisais 3 je fis 4 je ferai 5 je fasse 7 faisant 8 fait	
falloir	(*impersonal*) 1 il faut 2 il fallait 3 il fallut 4 il faudra 5 il faille 6 *none* 7 *none* 8 fallu	
feindre	*like*	atteindre

foutre	1 je fous, n foutons 2 je foutais 3 *none* 5 je foute 7 foutant 8 foutu
frire	(*defective*) 1 je fris, tu fris, il frit 4 je frirai 6 fris 8 frit (*for other persons and tenses use* faire frire)
fuir	1 je fuis, n fuyons, ils fuient 2 je fuyais 3 je fuis 5 je fuie 7 fuyant 8 fui
geindre	*like* **atteindre**
haïr	1 je hais, il hait, n haïssons
inclure	*like* **conclure**
induire	*like* **conduire**
inscrire	*like* **écrire**
instruire	*like* **conduire**
interdire	*like* **dire** *except* 1 v interdisez
interrompre	*like* **rompre**
intervenir	*like* **tenir**
introduire	*like* **conduire**
joindre	1 je joins, n joignons, ils joignent 2 je joignais 3 je joignis 4 je joindrai 5 je joigne 7 joignant 8 joint
lire	1 je lis, n lisons 2 je lisais 3 je lus 5 je lise 7 lisant 8 lu
luire	*like* **nuire**
maintenir	*like* **tenir**
maudire	1 je maudis, n maudissons 2 je maudissais 3 je maudis 4 je maudirai 5 je maudisse 7 maudissant 8 maudit
méconnaître	*like* **connaître**
médire	*like* **dire** *except* 1 v médisez
mentir	1 je mens, n mentons 2 je mentais 5 je mente 7 mentant
mettre	1 je mets, n mettons 2 je mettais 3 je mis 5 je mette 7 mettant 8 mis
moudre	1 je mouds, il moud, n moulons 2 je moulais 3 je moulus 5 je moule 7 moulant 8 moulu
†mourir	1 je meurs, n mourons, ils meurent 2 je mourais 3 je mourus 4 je mourrai 5 je meure, n mourions 7 mourant 8 mort
mouvoir	1 je meus, n mouvons, ils meuvent 2 je mouvais 3 je mus 4 je mouvrai 5 je meuve, n mouvions 8 mû, mue, *pl* mus, mues
†naître	1 je nais, il naît, n naissons 2 je naissais 3 je naquis 4 je naîtrai 5 je naisse 7 naissant 8 né
nuire	1 je nuis, n nuisons 2 je nuisais 3 je nuisis 5 je nuise 7 nuisant 8 nui
obtenir	*like* **tenir**
offrir	*like* **couvrir**
omettre	*like* **mettre**
ouvrir	*like* **couvrir**
paître	(*defective*) 1 il paît 2 ils paissait 3 *none* 4 il paîtra 5 il paisse 7 paissant 8 *none*
paraître	*like* **connaître**
parcourir	*like* **courir**
parfaire	*like* **faire** (*present tense, infinitive and past participle only*)
†partir	*like* **mentir**
†parvenir	*like* **tenir**
peindre	*like* **atteindre**
percevoir	*like* **recevoir**
permettre	*like* **mettre**
plaindre	*like* **craindre**
plaire	1 je plais, il plaît, n plaisons 2 je plaisais 3 je plus 5 je plaise 7 plaisant 8 plu
pleuvoir	(*impersonal*) 1 il pleut 2 il pleuvait 3 il plut 4 il pleuvra 5 il pleuve 6 *none* 7 pleuvant 8 plu
poindre	(*defective*) 1 il point 4 il poindra 8 point

poursuivre	*like*	**suivre**
pourvoir	*like*	**voir** *except* 3 je pourvus *and* 4 je pourvoirai
pouvoir		1 je peux *or* je puis, tu peux, il peut, n pouvons, ils peuvent
		2 je pouvais 3 je pus 4 je pourrai 5 je puisse 6 *not used*
		7 pouvant 8 pu
prédire	*like*	**dire** *except* v prédisez
prendre		1 je prends, il prend, n prenons, ils prennent 2 je prenais 3 je pris
		5 je prenne 7 prenant 8 pris
prescrire	*like*	**écrire**
pressentir	*like*	**mentir**
prévaloir	*like*	**valoir** *except* 5 je prévale
prévenir	*like*	**tenir**
prévoir	*like*	**voir** *except* 4 je prévoirai
produire	*like*	**conduire**
promettre	*like*	**mettre**
promouvoir	*like*	**mouvoir** *except* 8 promu
proscrire	*like*	**écrire**
†provenir	*like*	**tenir**
rabattre	*like*	**battre**
rasseoir	*like*	**asseoir**
réapparaître	*like*	**connaître**
recevoir		1 je reçois, n recevons, ils reçoivent 2 je recevais 3 je reçus
		4 je recevrai 5 je reçoive, n recevions, ils reçoivent 7 recevant
		8 reçu
reconduire	*like*	**conduire**
reconnaître	*like*	**connaître**
reconquérir	*like*	**acquérir**
reconstruire	*like*	**conduire**
recoudre	*like*	**coudre**
recourir	*like*	**courir**
recouvrir	*like*	**couvrir**
récrire	*like*	**écrire**
recueillir	*like*	**cueillir**
†redevenir	*like*	**tenir**
redire	*like*	**dire**
réduire	*like*	**conduire**
réécrire	*like*	**écrire**
réélire	*like*	**lire**
refaire	*like*	**faire**
rejoindre	*like*	**joindre**
relire	*like*	**lire**
reluire	*like*	**nuire**
remettre	*like*	**mettre**
†renaître	*like*	**naître**
rendormir	*like*	**mentir**
renvoyer	*like*	**envoyer**
†se repaître	*like*	**paître**
reparaître	*like*	**connaître**
†repartir	*like*	**mentir**
repeindre	*like*	**atteindre**
repentir	*like*	**mentir**
reprendre	*like*	**prendre**
reproduire	*like*	**conduire**
résoudre		1 je résous, n résolvons 2 je résolvais 3 je résolus
		5 je résolve 7 résolvant 8 résolu
ressentir	*like*	**mentir**
resservir	*like*	**mentir**
ressortir	*like*	**mentir**
restreindre	*like*	**atteindre**

retenir	*like*	**tenir**
retransmettre	*like*	**mettre**
†revenir	*like*	**tenir**
revêtir	*like*	**vêtir**
revivre	*like*	**vivre**
revoir	*like*	**voir**

rire 1 je ris, n rions   2 je riais   3 je ris   5 je rie, n riions   7 riant   8 ri

rompre *regular except* 1 il rompt

rouvrir	*like*	**couvrir**
satisfaire	*like*	**faire**

savoir 1 je sais, n savons, il savent   2 je savais   3 je sus   4 je saurai
5 je sache   6 sache, sachons, sachez   7 sachant   8 su

séduire	*like*	**conduire**
sentir	*like*	**mentir**
servir	*like*	**mentir**
sortir	*like*	**mentir**
souffrir	*like*	**couvrir**
soumettre	*like*	**mettre**
sourire	*like*	**rire**
souscrire	*like*	**écrire**
soustraire	*like*	**abstraire**
soutenir	*like*	**tenir**
†se souvenir	*like*	**tenir**
subvenir	*like*	**tenir**

suffire 1 je suffis, n suffisons   2 je suffisais   3 je suffis   5 je suffise
7 suffisant   8 suffi

suivre 1 je suis, n suivons   2 je suivais   3 je suivis   5 je suive
7 suivant   8 suivi

surprendre	*like*	**prendre**
†survenir	*like*	**tenir**
survivre	*like*	**vivre**

taire 1 je tais, n taisons   2 je taisais   3 je tus   5 je taise   7 taisant
8 tu

teindre *like* **atteindre**

tenir 1 je tiens, ne tenons, ils tiennent   2 je tenais
3 je tins, tu tins, il tint, n tînmes, v tîntes, ils tinrent
4 je tiendrai   5 je tienne   7 tenant   8 tenu

traduire	*like*	**conduire**
traire	*like*	**abstraire**
transcrire	*like*	**écrire**
transmettre	*like*	**mettre**
transparaître	*like*	**connaître**
tressaillir	*like*	**défaillir**

vaincre 1 je vaincs, il vainc, n vainquons   2 je vainquais   3 je vainquis
5 je vainque   7 vainquant   8 vaincu

valoir 1 je vaux, il vaut, n valons   2 je valais   3 je valus   4 je vaudrai
5 je vaille   6 *not used*   7 valant   8 valu

†venir *like* **tenir**

vêtir 1 je vêts, n vêtons   2 je vêtais   5 je vête   7 vêtant   8 vêtu

vivre 1 je vis, n vivons   2 je vivais   3 je vécus   5 je vive   7 vivant
8 vécu

voir 1 je vois, n voyons   2 je voyais   3 je vis   4 je verrai
5 je voie, n voyions   7 voyant   8 vu

vouloir 1 je veux, il veut, n voulons, ils veulent   2 je voulais
3 je voulus   4 je voudrai   5 je veuille
6 veuille, veuillons, veuillez   7 voulant   8 voulu

VERBES ANGLAIS IRRÉGULIERS

Infinitif	Prétérit	Participe passé
arise	arose	arisen
awake	awoke	awoken
awaken	awoke, awakened	awakened, awoken
be	were/was	been
bear	bore	borne
beat	beat	beaten
become	became	become
begin	began	begun
bend	bent	bent
beseech	besought, beseeched	besought, beseeched
bet	bet, betted	bet, betted
bid	bade, bid	bidden, bid
bind	bound	bound
bite	bit	bitten
bleed	bled	bled
blow	blew	blown
break	broke	broken
breed	bred	bred
bring	brought	brought
build	built	built
burn	burnt, burned	burnt, burned
burst	burst	burst
bust	bust, busted	bust, busted
buy	bought	bought
cast	cast	cast
catch	caught	caught
chide	chided, chid	chided, chidden
choose	chose	chosen
cleave	cleaved, cleft, clove	cleaved, cleft, cloven
cling	clung	clung
clothe	clad, clothed	clad, clothed
come	came	come
cost	cost	cost
creep	crept	crept
crow	crowed, crew	crowed
cut	cut	cut
deal	dealt	dealt
dig	dug	dug
dive	dived, *Am* dove	dived
do	did	done
draw	drew	drawn
dream	dreamt, dreamed	dreamt, dreamed
drink	drank	drunk
drive	drove	driven
dwell	dwelt	dwelt
eat	ate	eaten
fall	fell	fallen
feed	fed	fed
feel	felt	felt
fight	fought	fought
find	found	found
flee	fled	fled

Verbes anglais irréguliers

Infinitif	Prétérit	Participe passé
fling	flung	flung
fly	flew	flown
forget	forgot	forgotten
forgive	forgave	forgiven
forsake	forsook	forsaken
freeze	froze	frozen
get	got	got, *Am* gotten
gild	gilded, gilt	gilded, gilt
gird	girded, girt	girded, girt
give	gave	given
go	went	gone
grind	ground	ground
grow	grew	grown
hang	hung/hanged	hung/hanged
have	had	had
hear	heard	heard
hew	hewed	hewn, hewed
hide	hid	hidden
hit	hit	hit
hold	held	held
hurt	hurt	hurt
keep	kept	kept
kneel	knelt	knelt
knit	knitted, knit	knitted, knit
know	knew	known
lay	laid	laid
lead	led	led
lean	leant, leaned	leant, leaned
leap	leapt, leaped	leapt, leaped
learn	learnt, learned	learnt, learned
leave	left	left
lend	lent	lent
let	let	let
lie	lay	lain
light	lit	lit
lose	lost	lost
make	made	made
mean	meant	meant
meet	met	met
mow	mowed	mown
pay	paid	paid
plead	pleaded, *Am* pled	pleaded, *Am* pled
prove	proved	proved, proven
put	put	put
quit	quit	quit
read	read	read
rend	rent	rent
rid	rid	rid
ride	rode	ridden
ring	rang	rung
rise	rose	risen
run	ran	run
saw	sawed	sawn, sawed
say	said	said
see	saw	seen
seek	sought	sought
sell	sold	sold
send	sent	sent

Verbes anglais irréguliers

Infinitif	Prétérit	Participe passé
set	set	set
sew	sewed	sewn
shake	shook	shaken
shear	sheared	shorn, sheared
shed	shed	shed
shine	shone	shone
shit	shitted, shat	shitted, shat
shoe	shod	shod
shoot	shot	shot
show	showed	shown
shrink	shrank	shrunk
shut	shut	shut
sing	sang	sung
sink	sank	sunk
sit	sat	sat
slay	slew	slain
sleep	slept	slept
slide	slid	slid
sling	slung	slung
slink	slunk	slunk
slit	slit	slit
smell	smelled, smelt	smelled, smelt
smite	smote	smitten
sow	sowed	sown, sowed
speak	spoke	spoken
speed	sped, speeded	sped, speeded
spell	spelt, spelled	spelt, spelled
spend	spent	spent
spill	spilt, spilled	spilt, spilled
spin	span	spun
spit	spat, *Am* spit	spat, *Am* spit
split	split	split
spoil	spoilt, spoiled	spoilt, spoiled
spread	spread	spread
spring	sprang	sprung
stand	stood	stood
stave in	staved in, stove in	staved in, stove in
steal	stole	stolen
stick	stuck	stuck
sting	stung	stung
stink	stank, stunk	stunk
strew	strewed	strewed, strewn
stride	strode	stridden
strike	struck	struck
string	strung	strung
strive	strove	striven
swear	swore	sworn
sweep	swept	swept
swell	swelled	swollen, swelled
swim	swam	swum
swing	swung	swung
take	took	taken
teach	taught	taught
tear	tore	torn
tell	told	told
think	thought	thought
thrive	thrived, throve	thrived
throw	threw	thrown

Verbes anglais irréguliers

Infinitif	Prétérit	Participe passé
thrust	thrust	thrust
tread	trod	trodden
wake	woke	woken
wear	wore	worn
weave	wove, weaved	woven, weaved
weep	wept	wept
wet	wet, wetted	wet, wetted
win	won	won
wind	wound	wound
wring	wrung	wrung
write	wrote	written

Français–Anglais
French–English

A, a [ɑ] *nm inv* A, a; **connaître un sujet de A à Z** to know a subject inside out; **A1** *(autoroute) Br* ≃ M1, *Am* ≃ I1

a [a] *voir* **avoir**

à [a] *prép*

> **à + le = au** [o], **à + les = aux** [o]

(**a**) *(indique la direction)* to; **aller à Paris** to go to Paris; **partir au Venezuela** to leave for Venezuela; **au lit!** off to bed!

(**b**) *(indique la position)* at; **être au bureau/à la ferme/à Paris** to be at *or* in the office/on *or* at the farm/in Paris; **à la maison** at home; **à l'horizon** on the horizon

(**c**) *(dans l'expression du temps)* **à 8 heures** at 8 o'clock; **au vingt-et-unième siècle** in the twenty-first century; **à mon arrivée** on (my) arrival; **à lundi!** see you (on) Monday!

(**d**) *(dans les descriptions)* **l'homme à la barbe** the man with the beard; **verre à liqueur** liqueur glass

(**e**) *(introduit le complément d'objet indirect)* **donner qch à qn** to give sth to sb, to give sb sth; **penser à qn/qch** to think about *or* of sb/sth

(**f**) *(devant infinitif)* **apprendre à lire** to learn to read; **avoir du travail à faire** to have work to do; **maison à vendre** house for sale; **'à louer'** *Br* 'to let', *Am* 'to rent'; **prêt à partir** ready to leave

(**g**) *(indique l'appartenance)* **un ami à moi** a friend of mine; **c'est (son livre) à lui** it's his (book); **c'est à vous de…** *(il vous incombe de)* it's up to you to…; *(c'est votre tour)* it's your turn to…; **à toi!** your turn!

(**h**) *(indique le moyen, la manière)* **à bicyclette** by bicycle; **à la main** by hand; **à pied** on foot; **au crayon** in pencil; **au galop** at a gallop; **à la française** in the French style; **deux à deux** two by two

(**i**) *(indique la conséquence)* **laid à faire peur** hideously ugly; **c'était à mourir de rire** it was hilarious

(**j**) *(prix)* **pain à 1 euro** loaf for 1 euro

(**k**) *(poids)* **vendre au kilo** to sell by the kilo

(**l**) *(vitesse)* **100 km à l'heure** 100 km an *or* per hour

(**m**) *(pour appeler)* **au voleur!** (stop) thief!; **au feu!** (there's a) fire!

(**n**) *(avec de)* to; **de Paris à Lyon** from Paris to Lyons; **du lundi au vendredi** from Monday to Friday, *Am* Monday through Friday

abaisser [abese] **1** *vt (levier, pont-levis)* to lower; *(store)* to pull down; **a. qn** to humiliate sb **2 s'abaisser** *vpr* (**a**) *(barrière)* to lower; **s'a. à faire qch** to stoop to doing sth (**b**) *(être en pente)* to slope down

abandon [abɑ̃dɔ̃] *nm (d'un enfant, d'un projet)* abandonment; *(d'un lieu)* neglect; *(de sportif)* withdrawal; *(pouvoir, combat)* abandon; *Ordinat* abort; **à l'a.** in a neglected state; **a. de poste** desertion of one's post

abandonner [abɑ̃dɔne] **1** *vt (personne, animal, lieu)* to desert, to abandon; *(projet)* to abandon; *(cours)* to withdraw from; **a. ses études** to drop out (of school); **a. le navire** to abandon ship; **a. qch à qn** to give sb sth **2** *vi (renoncer)* to give up; *(sportif)* to withdraw **3 s'abandonner** *vpr (se détendre)* to let oneself go; **s'a. au sommeil** to drift off to sleep

abasourdi, -ie [abazurdi] *adj* stunned

abat-jour [abaʒur] *nm inv* lampshade

abats [aba] *nmpl* offal; *(de volaille)* giblets

abattant [abatɑ̃] *nm (de table)* flap; *(des toilettes)* lid

abattis [abati] *nmpl* giblets

abattoir [abatwar] *nm* slaughterhouse

abattre* [abatr] **1** *vt (mur)* to knock down; *(arbre)* to cut down; *(personne, gros gibier)* to kill; *(animal de boucherie)* to slaughter; *(animal blessé ou malade)* to destroy; *(avion)* to shoot down; *Fig (déprimer)* to demoralize; *Fig (épuiser)* to exhaust **2 s'abattre** *vpr (tomber)* to crash down (**sur** on); *(pluie)* to pour down (**sur** on); *(oiseau)* to swoop down (**sur** on) ▪ **abattage** *nm (d'arbre)* felling; *(de vache)* slaughter(ing) ▪ **abattement** *nm (faiblesse)* exhaustion; *(désespoir)* dejection; **a. fiscal** tax allowance

> Il faut noter que le nom anglais **abatement** est un faux ami. Il signifie **apaisement**.

abattu, -ue [abaty] *adj (triste)* dejected; *(faible)* exhausted

abbaye [abei] *nf* abbey

abbé [abe] *nm (d'abbaye)* abbot; *(prêtre)* priest

abcès [apsɛ] *nm* abscess

abdiquer [abdike] *vti* to abdicate ▪ **abdication** *nf* abdication

abdomen [abdɔmɛn] *nm* abdomen ▪ **abdominal, -e, -aux, -ales** *adj* abdominal ▪ **abdominaux** *nmpl* abdominal muscles; **faire des a.** to do abdominal exercises

abeille [abɛj] *nf* bee

aberrant, -ante [aberɑ̃, -ɑ̃t] *adj* absurd ■ **aberration** *nf* (*égarement*) aberration; (*idée*) ludicrous idea; **dire des aberrations** to talk utter nonsense

abhorrer [abɔre] *vt Littéraire* to abhor

abîme [abim] *nm* abyss; *Fig* **être au bord de l'a.** to be on the brink of disaster

abîmer [abime] **1** *vt* to spoil, to damage **2 s'abîmer** *vpr* (*object*) to get spoilt; (*fruit*) to go bad; **s'a. les yeux** to ruin one's eyesight; *Littéraire* **s'a. en mer** to be engulfed by the sea

abject, -e [abʒɛkt] *adj* despicable

abjurer [abʒyre] *vti* to abjure

ablation [ablɑsjɔ̃] *nf* removal

ablutions [ablysjɔ̃] *nfpl Littéraire ou Hum* **faire ses a.** to perform one's ablutions

abnégation [abnegɑsjɔ̃] *nf* self-sacrifice, abnegation

abois [abwa] **aux abois** *adv* (*animal*) at bay

abolir [abɔlir] *vt* to abolish ■ **abolition** *nf* abolition

abominable [abɔminabl] *adj* appalling ■ **abominablement** [-əmɑ̃] *adv* appallingly; (*laid*) hideously

abondant, -ante [abɔ̃dɑ̃, -ɑ̃t] *adj* plentiful, abundant ■ **abondamment** *adv* abundantly; (*parler*) at length ■ **abondance** *nf* abundance (**de** of); **en a.** in abundance; **des années d'a.** years of plenty ■ **abonder** *vi* to be plentiful; **a. en qch** to abound in sth; **a. dans le sens de qn** to agree entirely with sb

abonné, -ée [abɔne] *nmf* (*d'un journal, du téléphone*) subscriber; (*de train, d'un théâtre*) & *Sport* season-ticket holder; (*du gaz*) consumer ■ **abonnement** *nm* (*de journal*) subscription; (*de téléphone*) line rental; (*de train, de théâtre*) season ticket ■ **s'abonner** *vpr* (*à un journal*) to subscribe (**à** to); *Rail & Théâtre* to buy a season ticket

abord [abɔr] *nm* (**a**) (*accès*) **d'un a. facile** easy to approach; **abords** (*d'un bâtiment*) surroundings; (*d'une ville*) outskirts; **aux abords de la ville** on the outskirts of the town (**b**) (*vue*) **au premier a., de prime a.** at first sight; **d'a., tout d'a.** (*pour commencer*) at first, to begin with; (*premièrement*) first (and foremost) ■ **abordable** *adj* (*prix, marchandises*) affordable; (*personne*) approachable

aborder [abɔrde] **1** *vt* (*personne, lieu, virage*) to approach; (*problème*) to tackle; (*navire*) (*attaquer*) to board; (*se mettre le long de*) to come alongside **2** *vi* to land ■ **abordage** *nm* (*d'un bateau*) (*assaut*) boarding; (*pour s'amarrer*) coming alongside

aborigène [abɔriʒɛn] *nm* (*d'un pays*) native; **les Aborigènes d'Australie** the (Australian) Aborigines

abortif, -ive [abɔrtif, -iv] *adj voir* **pilule**

aboutir [abutir] *vi* (**a**) (*réussir*) to be successful; **nos efforts n'ont abouti à rien** our efforts came to nothing (**b**) **a. à qch** (*avoir pour résultat*) to result in sth; **a. à un endroit** to lead to a place ■ **aboutissants** *nmpl voir* **tenants** ■ **aboutissement** *nm* (*résultat*) outcome; (*succès*) success

aboyer [abwaje] *vi* to bark ■ **aboiement** *nm* bark; **aboiements** barking

abrasif, -ive [abrazif, -iv] *adj & nm* abrasive

abréger [abreʒe] *vt* (*récit*) to shorten; (*visite*) to cut short; (*mot*) to abbreviate ■ **abrégé** *nm* (*d'un texte*) summary; (*livre*) abstract; **en a.** (*mot*) in abbreviated form

abreuver [abrœve] **1** *vt* (*cheval*) to water **2 s'abreuver** *vpr* to drink ■ **abreuvoir** *nm* (*lieu*) watering place; (*récipient*) drinking trough

abréviation [abrevjɑsjɔ̃] *nf* abbreviation

abri [abri] *nm* shelter; **mettre qn/qch à l'a.** to shelter sb/sth; **se mettre à l'a.** to take shelter; **être à l'a. de qch** to be sheltered from sth; **être à l'a. du besoin** to have no financial worries; **sans a.** homeless; **a. de jardin** garden shed

Abribus® [abribys] *nm* bus shelter

abricot [abriko] *nm* apricot ■ **abricotier** *nm* apricot tree

abriter [abrite] **1** *vt* (*protéger*) to shelter (**de** from); (*loger*) to house **2 s'abriter** *vpr* to (take) shelter (**de** from); **s'a. du soleil** to shade oneself from the sun

abroger [abrɔʒe] *vtJur* to repeal ■ **abrogation** *nJur* repeal

abrupt, -e [abrypt] *adj* (*pente, rocher*) steep; *Fig* (*personne*) abrupt

abrutir [abrytir] *vt* (*hébéter*) to daze; **a. qn de travail** to work sb to the point of exhaustion ■ **abruti, -ie 1** *adj Fam* (*bête*) idiotic; **a. par l'alcool** stupefied with drink **2** *nmf* idiot ■ **abrutissant, -ante** *adj* mind-numbing

absence [apsɑ̃s] *nf* (*d'une personne*) absence; (*manque*) lack ■ **absent, -ente 1** *adj* (*personne*) absent (**de** from); (*chose*) missing; **avoir un air a.** to be miles away **2** *nmf* absentee ■ **absentéisme** *nm* absenteeism ■ **s'absenter** *vpr* to go away

absolu, -ue [apsɔly] *adj* absolute ■ **absolument** *adv* absolutely; **il faut a. y aller** you simply MUST go!

absolution [apsɔlysjɔ̃] *nf Rel* absolution

absorber [apsɔrbe] *vt* (*liquid*) to absorb; (*nourriture*) to eat; (*boisson*) to drink; (*médicament*) to take; **son travail l'absorbe** she is engrossed in her work ■ **absorbant, -ante** *adj* (*papier*) absorbent; (*travail, lecture*) absorbing ■ **absorption** *nf* (*de liquide*) absorption; (*de nourriture*) eating; (*de boisson*) drinking; (*de médicament*) taking

absoudre* [apsudr] *vt Rel ou Littéraire* **a. qn de qch** to forgive sb sth

abstenir* [apstənir] *s'abstenir* vpr (*ne pas voter*) to abstain; **s'a. de qch/de faire qch** to refrain from sth/from doing sth ▪ **abstention** nf Pol abstention

abstinence [apstinɑ̃s] nf abstinence

abstrait, -aite [apstrɛ, -ɛt] adj abstract ▪ **abstraction** nf abstraction; **faire a. de qch** to disregard sth

absurde [apsyrd] **1** adj absurd **2** nm **l'a. de cette situation** the absurdity of this situation ▪ **absurdité** nf absurdity; **dire des absurdités** to talk nonsense

abus [aby] nm (*excès*) overindulgence (**de** in); (*pratique*) abuse (**de** of); **a. de pouvoir** abuse of power; **a. d'alcool** alcohol abuse; **a. de tabac** excessive smoking; **a. de confiance** breach of trust; Fam **il y a de l'a.** that's going too far! ▪ **abuser 1** vi to go too far; **a. de** (*situation, personne*) to take unfair advantage of; (*autorité*) to abuse; (*nourriture*) to overindulge in; **a. du tabac** to smoke too much **2** s'abuser vpr **si je ne m'abuse** if I am not mistaken

> Il faut noter que le verbe anglais **to abuse** est un faux ami. Il ne s'emploie jamais dans le sens d'**exagérer**.

abusif, -ive [abyzif, -iv] adj excessive; (*mère*) possessive; **emploi a.** (*d'un mot*) improper use

acabit [akabi] nm Péj **de cet a.** of that type

académie [akademi] nf academy; (*administration scolaire*) ≃ local education authority; **a. de musique** school of music; **l'A. française** = learned society responsible for promoting the French language and imposing standards ▪ **académicien, -ienne** nmf = member of the Académie française ▪ **académique** adj Péj (*style*) conventional

acajou [akaʒu] nm mahogany

acariâtre [akarjɑtr] adj cantankerous

acarien [akarjɛ̃] nm dust mite

accablement [akɑbləmɑ̃] nm dejection

accabler [akɑble] vt to overwhelm (**de** with); **a. qn de travail** to overload sb with work; **a. qn de reproches** to heap criticism on sb; **accablé de dettes** (over)burdened with debt; **accablé de chaleur** overcome by heat ▪ **accablant, -ante** adj (*chaleur*) oppressive; (*témoignage*) damning

accalmie [akalmi] nf lull

accaparer [akapare] vt (*personne, conversation*) to monopolize

accéder [aksede] vi **a. à** (*lieu*) to reach; (*responsabilité, rang*) to gain; (*requête*) to comply with; Ordinat (*programme*) to access; **a. au trône** to accede to the throne

accélérer [akselere] **1** vt (*travaux*) to speed up; (*allure, pas*) to quicken; Fig **a. le mouvement** to get a move on **2** vi (*en voiture*) to accelerate **3** s'accélérer vpr to speed up ▪ **accélérateur** nm (*de voiture, d'ordinateur*) accelerator ▪ **accélération** nf acceleration; (*de travaux*) speeding up

accent [aksɑ̃] nm accent; (*sur une syllabe*) stress; Fig **mettre l'a. sur qch** to stress sth; **a. aigu/ circonflexe/grave** acute/circumflex/grave (accent); **a. tonique** stress ▪ **accentuation** nf (*sur lettre*) accentuation; (*de phénomène*) intensification ▪ **accentuer 1** vt (*syllabe*) to stress; (*lettre*) to put an accent on; Fig (*renforcer*) to emphasize **2** s'accentuer vpr to become more pronounced

accepter [aksɛpte] vt to accept; **a. de faire qch** to agree to do sth ▪ **acceptable** adj (*recevable*) acceptable ▪ **acceptation** nf acceptance

acception [aksɛpsjɔ̃] nf (*de mot*) meaning; **sans a. de race** irrespective of race

accès [aksɛ] nm (**a**) (*approche*) & Ordinat access (**à** to); **être facile d'a.** to be easy to reach; **avoir a. à qch** to have access to sth; **'a. interdit'** 'no entry'; **'a. aux quais'** 'to the trains' (**b**) Ordinat (*à une page Web*) hit (**c**) (*de folie, colère*) fit; (*de fièvre*) bout; **a. de toux** coughing fit ▪ **accessible** adj (*lieu, livre*) accessible; (*personne*) approachable ▪ **accession** nf accession (**à** to); **a. à la propriété** home ownership

accessoire [akseswar] adj minor ▪ **accessoires** nmpl (*de théâtre*) props; (*de mode, de voiture*) accessories; **a. de toilette** toiletries ▪ **accessoirement** adv if necessary; (*en plus*) also

accident [aksidɑ̃] nm accident; **a. d'avion** plane crash; **a. de chemin de fer** train crash; **a. de la route** road accident; **a. du travail** industrial accident; **a. de parcours** hitch; **par a.** by accident, by chance ▪ **accidenté, -ée 1** adj (*terrain*) uneven; (*voiture*) damaged **2** nmf accident victim ▪ **accidentel, -elle** adj accidental ▪ **accidentellement** adv (*par hasard*) accidentally

acclamer [aklame] vt to cheer ▪ **acclamations** nfpl cheers

acclimater [aklimate] **1** vt to acclimatize, Am to acclimate (**à** to) **2** s'acclimater vpr to become acclimatized or Am acclimated (**à** to) ▪ **acclimatation** nf acclimatization, Am acclimation (**à** to)

accointances [akwɛ̃tɑ̃s] nfpl contacts

accolade [akɔlad] nf (*embrassade*) embrace; (*signe*) curly bracket

accoler [akɔle] vt (*mettre ensemble*) to put side by side

accommoder [akɔmɔde] **1** vt (*nourriture*) to prepare; (*restes*) to use up **2** vi (*œil*) to focus **3** s'accommoder vpr **s'a. de qch** to put up with sth ▪ **accommodant, -ante** adj accommodating

Il faut noter que le verbe anglais **to accom-modate** est un faux ami. Il ne signifie jamais **accommoder**.

accompagner [akɔ̃paɲe] *vt (personne)* to accompany; **a. qn à la gare** *(en voiture)* to take sb to the station; **a. qn au piano** to accompany sb on the piano ■ **accompagnateur, -trice** *nmf (musical)* accompanist; *(de touristes)* guide ■ **accompagnement** [-ɔ̃mɑ̃] *nm Mus* accompaniment

accomplir [akɔ̃plir] *vt (tache)* to carry out; *(exploit)* to accomplish; *(terminer)* to complete ■ **accompli, -ie** *adj* accomplished

accord [akɔr] *nm (traité, entente)* & *Grammaire* agreement; *(autorisation)* consent; *(musical)* chord; **arriver à un a.** to reach an agreement; **être d'a.** to agree (**avec** with); **d'a.!** all right!

accordéon [akɔrdeɔ̃] *nm* accordion; *Fig* **en a.** *(chaussette)* at half-mast

accorder [akɔrde] **1** *vt (instrument)* to tune; **a. qch à qn** *(faveur)* to grant sb sth; *(augmentation)* to award sb sth; *(prêt)* to authorize sth to sb; *Grammaire* **a. qch avec qch** to make sth agree with sth; **a. la plus grande importance à qch** to attach the utmost importance to sth; *Formel* **il est timide, je vous l'accorde** he is shy, I must admit **2** **s'accorder** *vpr (se mettre d'accord)* to agree (**avec** with, **sur** on); *Grammaire (mots)* to agree (**avec** with); **s'a. qch** to allow oneself sth; **on s'accorde à penser que...** there is a general belief that...

accoster [akɔste] **1** *vt (personne)* to approach **2** *vi Naut* to dock

accotement [akɔtmɑ̃] *nm (de route)* verge; *(de voie ferrée)* shoulder

accoucher [akuʃe] **1** *vt* **a. qn** to deliver sb's baby **2** *vi* to give birth (**de** to); *Fam* **accouche!** spit it out! ■ **accouchement** *nm* delivery ■ **accoucheur** *nm (médecin)* **a.** obstetrician

accouder [akude] **s'accouder** *vpr* **s'a. à** *ou* **sur qch** to lean one's elbows on sth ■ **accoudoir** *nm* armrest

accoupler [akuple] **s'accoupler** *vpr (animaux)* to mate ■ **accouplement** [-ɔ̃mɑ̃] *nm (d'animaux)* mating

accourir* [akurir] *vi* to run up

accoutrement [akutrəmɑ̃] *nm Péj* rig-out

accoutumer [akutyme] **1** *vt* **a. qn à qch** to accustom sb to sth **2** **s'accoutumer** *vpr* to get accustomed (**à** to) ■ **accoutumance** *nf (adaptation)* familiarization (**à** with); *Méd (dépendance)* addiction ■ **accoutumé, -ée** *adj* usual; **comme à l'accoutumée** as usual

accréditer [akredite] *vt (ambassadeur)* to accredit; *(rumeur)* to lend credence to

accro [akro] *adj Fam (drogué)* addicted (**à** to)

accroc [akro] *nm (déchirure)* tear; *(difficulté)* hitch; **sans a.** without a hitch

accrocher [akrɔʃe] **1** *vt (déchirer)* to catch; *(fixer)* to hook (**à** onto); *(suspendre)* to hang up (**à** on); *(pare-chocs)* to clip **2** *vi (achopper)* to hit a stumbling block; *(se remarquer)* to grab one's attention **3** **s'accrocher** *vpr (se fixer)* to fasten; *Fam (persévérer)* to stick at it; *Fam (se disputer)* to clash; **s'a. à qn/qch** *(s'agripper)* to cling to sb/sth; *Fam* **accroche-toi, tu n'as pas tout entendu!** brace yourself, you haven't heard everything yet! ■ **accrochage** *nm (de véhicules)* minor accident; *Fam (dispute)* clash ■ **accrocheur, -euse** *adj (personne)* tenacious; *(titre, slogan)* catchy

accroître* [akrwatr] **1** *vt* to increase **2** **s'accroître** *vpr* to increase ■ **accroissement** *nm* increase (**de** in)

accroupir [akrupir] **s'accroupir** *vpr* to squat (down) ■ **accroupi, -ie** *adj* squatting

accueil [akœj] *nm* reception ■ **accueillant, -ante** *adj* welcoming ■ **accueillir*** *vt (personne, proposition)* to greet; *(sujet: hôtel)* to accommodate

acculer [akyle] *vt* **a. qn à qch** to drive sb to sth; **acculé à la faillite** forced into bankruptcy

accumuler [akymyle] *vt*, **s'accumuler** *vpr* to accumulate ■ **accumulateur** *nm* battery ■ **accumulation** *nf* accumulation

accuser [akyze] **1** *vt (dénoncer)* to accuse; *(tendance, baisse)* to show; *(faire ressortir)* to bring out; **a. qn de qch/de faire qch** to accuse sb of sth/of doing sth; **a. réception** to acknowledge receipt (**de** of); *Fig* **a. le coup** to be obviously shaken **2** **s'accuser** *vpr (se déclarer coupable)* to confess (**de** to) ■ **accusateur, -trice** *adj (regard)* accusing **2** *nmf* accuser ■ **accusation** *nf* accusation; **porter une a. contre qn** to make an accusation against sb ■ **accusé, -ée 1** *adj (trait)* prominent **2** *nmf* **l'a.** the accused; *(au tribunal)* the defendant

acerbe [asɛrb] *adj* acerbic; **d'un ton a.** sharply

acéré, -ée [asere] *adj (lame)* sharp

acétone [aseton] *nf* acetone

achalandé, -ée [aʃalɑ̃de] *adj* **bien a.** *(magasin)* well-stocked

acharner [aʃarne] **s'acharner** *vpr* **s'a. sur** *ou* **contre qn** *(persécuter)* to be always after sb; **s'a. sur qn** *(sujet: meurtrier)* to savage sb; *(sujet: examinateur)* to give sb a hard time; **s'a. à faire qch** to try very hard to do sth ■ **acharné, -ée** *adj (effort, travail)* relentless; *(combat)* fierce ■ **acharnement** [-ɔ̃mɑ̃] *nm* relentlessness; *(dans un combat)* fury; **avec a.** relentlessly

achat [aʃa] *nm* purchase; **faire l'a. de qch** to buy sth; **achats** *(provisions, paquets)* shopping; **aller faire ses achats** to go shopping

acheminer [aʃəmine] **1** vt (marchandises) to ship (**vers** to); (courrier) to handle **2** **s'acheminer** vpr s'a. vers qch to make one's way towards sth

acheter [aʃəte] **1** vti to buy; **a. qch à qn** (faire une transaction) to buy sth from sb; (faire un cadeau) to buy sth for sb **2** **s'acheter** vpr je vais m'acheter une glace I'm going to buy (myself) an ice cream ▪**acheteur, -euse** nmf buyer; (dans un magasin) shopper

achever [aʃəve] vt (**a**) (finir) to end; (travail) to complete; **a. de faire qch** to finish doing sth (**b**) (tuer) (animal blessé ou malade) to put out of its misery; **a. qn** to finish sb off **2** **s'achever** vpr to end ▪**achèvement** [-εvmã] nm completion

Il faut noter que les termes anglais **achievement** et **to achieve** sont des faux amis. Le premier signifie **réussite** et le second ne se traduit jamais par **achever**.

achoppement [aʃɔpmã] nm voir **pierre**

acide [asid] **1** adj acid(ic); (au goût) sour **2** nm acid ▪**acidité** nf acidity; (au goût) sourness

acier [asje] nm steel; **a. inoxydable** stainless steel ▪**aciérie** nf steelworks

acné [akne] nf acne

acolyte [akɔlit] nm Péj accomplice

acompte [akɔ̃t] nm down payment; **verser un a.** to make a down payment

à-côté [akote] (pl **à-côtés**) nm (d'une question) side issue; **à-côtés** (gains) little extras

à-coup [aku] (pl **à-coups**) nm jolt; **sans à-coups** smoothly; **par à-coups** (avancer, travailler) in fits and starts

acoustique [akustik] **1** adj acoustic **2** nf (qualité) acoustics (pluriel)

acquérir* [akerir] vt (acheter) to purchase; (obtenir, prendre) to acquire; **a. de la valeur** to increase in value; **tenir qch pour acquis** to take sth for granted ▪**acquéreur** nm purchaser ▪**acquis** nm experience; **les a. sociaux** social benefits ▪**acquisition** nf (action) acquisition; (bien acheté) purchase

acquiescer [akjese] vi to acquiesce (**à** to)

acquit [aki] nm receipt; **'pour a.'** 'paid'; **par a. de conscience** to ease one's conscience

acquitter [akite] **1** vt (accusé) to acquit; (dette) to pay **2** **s'acquitter** vpr s'a. d'un devoir to fulfil a duty; **s'a. envers qn** to repay sb ▪**acquittement** nm (d'un accusé) acquittal; (d'une dette) payment

âcre [akr] adj (goût) bitter; (odeur) acrid

acrobate [akrɔbat] nmf acrobat ▪**acrobatie** [-basi] nf acrobatics (sing); **acrobaties aériennes** aerobatics (sing) ▪**acrobatique** adj acrobatic

acrylique [akrilik] adj & nm acrylic

acte [akt] nm (action) & Théâtre act; Jur deed; **faire a. de candidature à un emploi** to apply for a job; **prendre a. de qch** to take note of sth; **a. terroriste** terrorist act; **a. unique européen** Single European Act; **actes** (de procès) proceedings; Jur **a. d'accusation** bill of indictment; **a. de mariage** marriage certificate; **a. de naissance** birth certificate; **a. de vente** bill of sale

acteur [aktœr] nm actor

actif, -ive [aktif, -iv] **1** adj active **2** nm Grammaire active; Com (d'une entreprise) assets; **avoir qch à son a.** to have sth to one's name

action [aksjɔ̃] nf action; (en Bourse) share; **bonne a.** good deed; **passer à l'a.** to take action ▪**actionnaire** nmf Fin shareholder

actionner [aksjɔne] vt (mettre en marche) to start up; (faire fonctionner) to operate

activer [aktive] **1** vt (accélérer) to speed up; (feu) to stoke; Ordinat (option) to select **2** **s'activer** vpr (être actif) to be busy; Fam (se dépêcher) to get a move on

activiste [aktivist] nmf activist

activité [aktivite] nf activity; **en a.** (personne) working; (volcan) active

actrice [aktris] nf actress

actuaire [aktɥer] nmf actuary

actualisation [aktɥalizasjɔ̃] nf (de texte) updating

actualité [aktɥalite] nf (d'un problème) topicality; **l'a.** current affairs; **les actualités** (à la radio, à la télévision) the news; **d'a.** topical

actuel, -elle [aktɥel] adj (présent) present; (d'actualité) topical; **l'a. président** the President in office ▪**actuellement** adv at present

Il faut noter que les termes anglais **actual** et **actually** sont des faux amis. Le premier ne signifie jamais **actuel** et le second se traduit par **en fait**.

acuité [akɥite] nf (de douleur) acuteness; **a. visuelle** keenness of vision

acupuncture [akypɔ̃ktyr] nf acupuncture ▪**acupuncteur, -trice** nmf acupuncturist

adage [adaʒ] nm adage

adapter [adapte] **1** vt to adapt (**à** to) **2** **s'adapter** vpr (s'acclimater) to adapt (**à** to); **s'a. à qn/qch** to get used to sb/sth ▪**adaptable** adj adaptable ▪**adaptateur, -trice** nmf adapter ▪**adaptation** nf adaptation; **faculté d'a.** adaptability

additif [aditif] nm (substance) additive

addition [adisjɔ̃] nf addition (**à** to); (au restaurant) Br bill, Am check ▪**additionner** **1** vt to add (up) (**à** to) **2** **s'additionner** vpr to add up

adepte [adept] nmf follower; **faire des adeptes** to attract a following

adéquat, -ate [adekwa, -wat] adj appropriate; (quantité) adequate

adhérer [adere] *vi* **a. à qch** (*coller*) to stick to sth; (*s'inscrire*) to join sth; **a. à la route** (*pneus*) to grip the road ▪ **adhérence** *nf* (*de pneu*) grip ▪ **adhérent, -ente** *nmf* member

adhésif, -ive [adezif, -iv] **1** *adj* adhesive **2** *nm* adhesive ▪ **adhésion** *nf* (*inscription*) joining (à of); (*accord*) support (à for)

adieu, -x [adjø] *exclam & nm* farewell; **faire ses adieux** to say one's goodbyes

adipeux, -euse [adipø, -øz] *adj* (*tissu*) adipose; (*visage*) fat

adjacent, -ente [adʒasɑ̃, -ɑ̃t] *adj* adjacent (à to)

adjectif [adʒɛktif] *nm* adjective

adjoint, -ointe [adʒwɛ̃, -ɛ̃t] *adj & nmf* assistant; **a. au maire** deputy mayor

adjonction [adʒɔ̃ksjɔ̃] *n* **sans a. de sucre** no added sugar

adjudant [adʒydɑ̃] *nm* warrant officer

adjuger [adʒyʒe] **1** *vt* **a. qch à qn** (*prix, contrat*) to award sth to sb; (*aux enchères*) to knock sth down to sb **2** **s'adjuger** *vpr* **s'a. qch** to appropriate sth

adjurer [adʒyre] *vt Formel* to entreat

ADM [adeɛm] (*abrév* **armes de destruction massive**) *nfpl* WMD

admettre* [admɛtr] *vt* (*accueillir, reconnaître*) to admit; (*autoriser*) to allow; **être admis à un examen** to pass an examination

administrer [administre] *vt* (*gérer*) to administer; (*pays*) to govern; (*justice*) to dispense ▪ **administrateur, -trice** *nmf* (*de société*) director ▪ **administratif, -ive** *adj* administrative ▪ **administration** *nf* administration; **l'A.** (*service public*) ≃ the Civil Service; (*fonctionnaires*) civil servants

admirer [admire] *vt* to admire ▪ **admirable** *adj* admirable ▪ **admirateur, -trice** *nmf* admirer ▪ **admiratif, -ive** *adj* admiring ▪ **admiration** *nf* admiration; **être en a. devant qn/qch** to be filled with admiration for sb/sth

admissible [admisibl] *adj* (*tolérable*) acceptable, admissible; *Scol & Univ* **candidats admissibles** = candidates who have qualified for the oral examination ▪ **admission** *nf* admission (à/dans to)

ADN [adeɛn] (*abrév* **acide désoxyribonucléique**) *nm* DNA

adolescent, -ente [adɔlesɑ̃, -ɑ̃t] **1** *adj* teenage **2** *nmf* adolescent, teenager ▪ **adolescence** *nf* adolescence

adonner [adɔne] **s'adonner** *vpr* **s'a. à qch** to devote oneself to sth; **s'a. à la boisson** to be an alcoholic

adopter [adɔpte] *vt* to adopt ▪ **adoptif, -ive** *adj* (*enfant, patrie*) adopted; (*parents*) adoptive ▪ **adoption** *nf* adoption; **pays d'a.** adopted country

adorer [adɔre] **1** *vt* (*dieu*) to worship; (*chose, personne*) to adore; **a. faire qch** to adore doing sth **2** **s'adorer** *vpr* **ils s'adorent** they adore each other ▪ **adorable** *adj* adorable ▪ **adoration** *nf* adoration; **être en a. devant qn** to worship sb

adosser [adose] **1** *vt* **a. qch à qch** to lean sth against sth **2** **s'adosser** *vpr* **s'a. à qch** to lean (back) against sth

adoucir [adusir] **1** *vt* (*voix, traits, peau*) to soften; (*chagrin*) to ease **2** **s'adoucir** *vpr* (*temps*) to turn milder; (*voix*) to soften; (*caractère*) to mellow ▪ **adoucissement** *nm* **a. de la température** rise in temperature

adrénaline [adrenalin] *nf* adrenalin(e)

adresse [adrɛs] *nf* **(a)** (*domicile*) address; **a. électronique** e-mail address **(b)** (*habileté*) skill

adresser [adrese] **1** *vt* (*lettre, remarque*) to address (à to); **a. qch à qn** (*lettre*) to send sth; (*compliment*) to present sb with sth; **a. la parole à qn** to speak to sb; **on m'a adressé à vous** I have been referred to you **2** **s'adresser** *vpr* **s'a. à qn** (*parler*) to speak to sb; (*aller trouver*) to go and see sb; (*être destiné à*) to be aimed at sb

Adriatique [adriatik] *nf* **l'A.** the Adriatic

adroit, -oite [adrwa, -wat] *adj* (*habile*) skilful; (*réponse*) clever

ADSL [adeɛsɛl] (*abrév* **Asynchronous Digital Subscriber Line**) *nf* ADSL

adulation [adylasjɔ̃] *nf* adulation

adulte [adylt] **1** *adj* (*personne, animal, attitude*) adult **2** *nmf* adult, grown-up

adultère [adyltɛr] *nm* adultery

advenir* [advənir] (*aux* **être**) *v impersonnel* to happen; **a. de qn** (*devenir*) to become of sb; **advienne que pourra** come what may

adverbe [advɛrb] *nm* adverb ▪ **adverbial, -e, -aux, -ales** *adj* adverbial

adversaire [advɛrsɛr] *nmf* opponent ▪ **adverse** *adj* opposing

adversité [advɛrsite] *nf* adversity

aérer [aere] **1** *vt* (*pièce, lit, linge*) to air **2** **s'aérer** *vpr* to get some fresh air ▪ **aération** *nf* ventilation ▪ **aéré, -ée** *adj* (*pièce*) airy; (*texte*) nicely spaced

aérien, -ienne [aerjɛ̃, -jɛn] *adj* (*transport, attaque, défense*) air; (*photo*) aerial; (*câble*) overhead; (*léger*) airy

aéro- [aero] *préf* aero- ▪ **aérobic** *nf* aerobics (*sing*) ▪ **aéro-club** (*pl* **aéro-clubs**) *nm* flying club ▪ **aérodrome** *nm* aerodrome ▪ **aérodynamique** *adj* streamlined ▪ **aérogare** *nf* air terminal ▪ **aéroglisseur** *nm* hovercraft ▪ **aéronautique 1** *adj* aeronautic(al) **2** *nf* aeronautics (*sing*) ▪ **Aéronavale** *nf Br* ≃ Fleet Air Arm, *Am* ≃ Naval Air Service ▪ **aéroport** *nm* airport ▪ **aéroporté, -ée** *adj* airborne ▪ **aérosol** *nm* aerosol ▪ **aérospatial,**

-ale, -aux, -ales 1 *adj* aerospace **2** *nf* **aérospatiale** aerospace science

affable [afabl] *adj* affable

affaiblir [afeblir] *vt*, **s'affaiblir** *vpr* to weaken • **affaiblissement** *nm* weakening

affaire [afɛr] *nf (question)* matter, affair; *(marché)* deal; *(firme)* concern, business; *(histoire, scandale)* affair; *(procès)* case; **affaires** *(commerce)* business *(sing)*; *(effets personnels)* belongings; **les Affaires étrangères** *Br* ≃ the Foreign Office, *Am* ≃ the State Department; **avoir a. à qn/qch** to have to deal with sb/sth; **faire une bonne a.** to get a bargain; **tirer qn d'affaire** to get sb out of trouble; **c'est mon a.** that's my business; **ça fera l'a.** that will do nicely; **c'est toute une a.!** it's quite a business!; **a. de cœur** love affair

affairer [afɛre] **s'affairer** *vpr* to busy oneself; **s'a. autour de qn** to fuss around sb • **affairé, -ée** *adj* busy

affaisser [afese] **s'affaisser** *vpr (personne, bâtiment)* to collapse; *(sol)* to subside • **affaissement** [-ɛsmã] *nm (du sol)* subsidence

affaler [afale] **s'affaler** *vpr* to collapse; **affalé dans un fauteuil** slumped in an armchair

affamé, -ée [afame] *adj* starving

affecter [afɛkte] *vt* **(a)** *(employé)* to appoint *(à* to*)*; *(soldat)* to post *(à* to*)*; *(fonds, crédits, locaux)* to assign *(à* to*)* **(b)** *(feindre, émouvoir, frapper)* to affect; **a. de faire qch** to pretend to do sth • **affectation** *nf (d'employé)* appointment *(à* to*)*; *(de soldat)* posting *(à* to*)*; *(de fonds)* assignment *(à* to*)*; *Péj (pose, simulacre)* affectation • **affecté, -ée** *adj Péj (manières, personne)* affected

affectif, -ive [afɛktif, -iv] *adj* emotional

affection [afɛksjɔ̃] *nf (attachement)* affection; *(maladie)* ailment; **avoir de l'a. pour qn** to be fond of sb • **affectionner** *vt* to be fond of

affectueux, -ueuse [afɛktɥø, -ɥøz] *adj* affectionate

affermir [afɛrmir] *vt (autorité)* to strengthen; *(muscles)* to tone up; *(voix)* to steady

affiche [afiʃ] *nf (officielle)* notice; *(publicitaire)* poster; **être à l'a.** *(spectacle)* to be on • **affichage** *nm* bill-posting; *Ordinat* display; **'a. interdit'** 'post no bills' • **afficher** *vt (avis, affiche)* to put up; *(prix, horaire, résultat) & Ordinat (message)* to display; *Péj (sentiment)* to show; **a. complet** *(spectacle)* to be sold out

affilée [afile] **d'affilée** *adv* in a row

affiler [afile] *vt* to sharpen

affilier [afilje] **s'affilier** *vpr* **s'a. à qch** to join sth • **affiliation** *nf* affiliation

affiner [afine] **1** *vt (métal, goût)* to refine **2** **s'affiner** *vpr (goût)* to become more refined; *(visage)* to get thinner

affinité [afinite] *nf* affinity

affirmatif, -ive [afirmatif, -iv] **1** *adj (réponse) & Grammaire* affirmative; **il a été a. à ce sujet** he was quite positive about it **2** *nf* **répondre par l'affirmative** to answer yes

affirmer [afirme] **1** *vt (manifester)* to assert; *(soutenir)* to maintain **2** **s'affirmer** *vpr (personne)* to assert oneself; *(tendance)* to be confirmed • **affirmation** *nf* assertion

affleurer [aflœre] *vi* to appear on the surface

affliger [afliʒe] *vt (peiner)* to distress; *(atteindre)* to afflict *(de* with*)*

affluence [aflyãs] *nf (de personnes)* crowd; *(de marchandises)* abundance

affluent [aflyã] *nm* tributary

affluer [aflye] *vi (sang)* to rush *(à* to*)*; *(gens)* to flock *(vers* to*)*

afflux [afly] *nm (de sang)* rush; *(de visiteurs)* flood; *(de capitaux)* influx

affoler [afɔle] **1** *vt* to throw into a panic **2** **s'affoler** *vpr* to panic • **affolant, -ante** *adj* terrifying • **affolement** *nm* panic

affranchir [afrãʃir] *vt (timbrer)* to put a stamp on; *(émanciper)* to free • **affranchissement** *nm (tarif)* postage

affréter [afrete] *vt* to charter

affreux, -euse [afrø, -øz] *adj (laid)* hideous; *(atroce)* dreadful; *Fam (épouvantable)* awful • **affreusement** *adv* horribly; *(en intensif)* awfully

affriolant, -ante [afriɔlã, -ãt] *adj* alluring

affront [afrɔ̃] *nm* insult; **faire un a. à qn** to insult sb

affronter [afrɔ̃te] **1** *vt* to confront; *(mauvais temps)* to brave; **a. la colère de qn** to brave the wrath of sb **2** **s'affronter** *vpr (ennemis, équipes)* to clash • **affrontement** *nm* confrontation

affubler [afyble] *vt Péj* **a. qn de qch** to set sb up in sth

affût [afy] *nm Fig* **à l'a. de** on the lookout for

affûter [afyte] *vt* to sharpen

Afghanistan [afganistã] *nm* **l'A.** Afghanistan

afin [afɛ̃] **1** *prép* **a. de faire qch** in order to do sth **2** *conj* **a. que...** *(+ subjunctive)* so that...

Afrique [afrik] *nf* **l'A.** Africa • **africain, -aine 1** *adj* African **2** *nmf* **A., Africaine** African

agacer [agase] *vt (personne)* to irritate • **agaçant, -ante** *adj* irritating

âge [ɑʒ] *nm* age; **quel â. as-tu?** how old are you?; **avant l'â.** before one's time; **d'un certain â.** middle-aged; **d'un â. avancé** elderly; **l'â. adulte** adulthood • **âgé, -ée** *adj* old; **être â. de six ans** to be six years old; **un enfant â. de six ans** a six-year-old child

agence [aʒãs] *nf* agency; *(de banque)* branch; **a. de recrutement** recruitment agency; **a. de voyage** travel agent's; **a. immobilière** *Br* estate agent's, *Am* real estate office; **a. matrimoniale** dating agency

agencer [aʒãse] *vt* to arrange; **bien agencé** *(maison, pièce)* well laid-out; *(phrase)* well put-together ■**agencement** *nm (de maison)* layout

agenda [aʒɛ̃da] *nm Br* diary, *Am* datebook; **a. électronique** electronic organizer

> Il faut noter que le nom anglais **agenda** est un faux ami. Il signifie **ordre du jour**.

agenouiller [aʒnuje] **s'agenouiller** *vpr* to kneel (down); **être agenouillé** to be kneeling (down)

agent [aʒɑ̃] *nm (employé, espion)* agent; **a. (de police)** police officer; **a. de change** stockbroker; **a. immobilier** *Br* estate agent, *Am* real estate agent; **a. secret** secret agent

aggloméré [aglɔmere] *nm* chipboard

agglomérer [aglɔmere] **s'agglomérer** *vpr* to bind together ■**agglomération** *nf (ville)* built-up area, town; **l'a. parisienne** Paris and its suburbs

agglutiner [aglytine] **s'agglutiner** *vpr (personnes)* to congregate

aggraver [agrave] **1** *vt (situation, maladie)* to make worse; *(difficultés)* to increase **2** **s'aggraver** *vpr (situation, maladie)* to get worse; *(état de santé)* to deteriorate; *(difficultés)* to increase ■**aggravation** *nf (de maladie)* aggravation; *(de conflit)* worsening

agile [aʒil] *adj* agile, nimble ■**agilité** *nf* agility, nimbleness

agir [aʒir] **1** *vi* to act; *Jur* **a. au nom de qn** to act on behalf of sb **2** **s'agir** *v impersonnel* **de quoi s'agit-il?** what is it about?; **il s'agit d'argent** it's a question of money; **il s'agit de se dépêcher** we have to hurry ■**agissements** *nmpl Péj* dealings

agitation [aʒitasjɔ̃] *nf (inquiétude)* agitation; *(bougeotte)* restlessness; *(troubles)* unrest

agiter [aʒite] **1** *vt (remuer)* to stir; *(secouer)* to shake; *(brandir)* to wave; *(troubler)* to agitate **2** **s'agiter** *vpr (enfant)* to fidget; **s'a. dans son sommeil** to toss and turn in one's sleep ■**agitateur, -trice** *nmf* agitator ■**agité, -ée** *adj (mer)* rough; *(personne)* restless; *(enfant)* fidgety; *(period)* unsettled

agneau, -x [aɲo] *nm* lamb

agonie [agɔni] *nf* death throes; **être à l'a.** to be at death's door ■**agoniser** *vi* to be dying

> Il faut noter que les termes anglais **agony** et **to agonize** sont des faux amis. Le premier signifie **douleur atroce** ou **angoisse** selon le contexte, et le second se traduit par **se faire beaucoup de souci**.

agrafe [agraf] *nf (pour vêtement)* hook; *(pour papiers)* staple ■**agrafer** *vt (vêtement)* to fasten; *(papiers)* to staple ■**agrafeuse** *nf* stapler

agrandir [agrɑ̃dir] **1** *vt (rendre plus grand)* to enlarge; *(grossir)* to magnify; **ça agrandit la pièce** it makes the room look bigger **2**

s'agrandir *vpr (entreprise)* to expand; *(ville)* to grow ■**agrandissement** *nm (d'entreprise)* expansion; *(de ville)* growth; *(de maison)* extension; *(de photo)* enlargement

agréable [agreabl] *adj* pleasant ■**agréablement** [-əmɑ̃] *adv* pleasantly

agréer [agree] *vt (fournisseur)* to approve; **veuillez a. l'expression de mes salutations distinguées** *(dans une lettre)* *Br* yours faithfully, yours sincerely, *Am* faithfully yours, sincerely yours ■**agréé, -ée** *adj (fournisseur, centre)* approved

agrégation [agregasjɔ̃] *nf* = competitive examination for recruitment of lycée and university teachers ■**agreg** *nf Fam* = agrégation ■**agrégé, -ée** *nmf* = teacher who has passed the agrégation

agrément [agremɑ̃] *nm (attrait)* charm; *(accord)* assent; **voyage d'a.** pleasure trip ■**agrémenter** *vt* to adorn (**de** with); **a. un récit d'anecdotes** to pepper a story with anecdotes

> Il faut noter que le nom anglais **agreement** est un faux ami. Il signifie **accord**.

agrès [agrɛ] *nmpl (de voilier)* tackle; *(de gymnastique) Br* apparatus, *Am* equipment

agresser [agrese] *vt* to attack; *(peau)* to damage; **se faire a.** to be attacked; *(pour son argent)* to be mugged ■**agresseur** *nm* attacker; *(dans un conflit)* aggressor ■**agression** *nf* attack; *(pour de l'argent)* mugging; *(d'un État)* aggression; **être victime d'une a.** to be attacked; *(pour son argent)* to be mugged; **a. sexuelle** sexual assault

agressif, -ive [agresif, -iv] *adj* aggressive ■**agressivité** *nf* aggressiveness

agricole [agrikɔl] *adj* agricultural; *(ouvrier, machine)* farm; *(peuple)* farming; **travaux agricoles** farm work

agriculteur [agrikyltœr] *nm* farmer ■**agriculture** *nf* farming, agriculture

agripper [agripe] **1** *vt* to clutch **2** **s'agripper** *vpr* **s'a. à qn/qch** to cling on to sb/sth

agronomie [agrɔnɔmi] *nf* agronomics *(sing)*

agrume [agrym] *nm* citrus fruit

aguerri, -ie [ageri] *adj* seasoned, hardened

aguets [agɛ] **aux aguets** *adv* on the lookout

aguicher [agiʃe] *vt* to seduce ■**aguichant, -ante** *adj* seductive

ahurir [ayrir] *vt (étonner)* to astound; **avoir l'air ahuri** to look astounded ■**ahuri, -ie** *nmf* idiot

ai [ɛ] *voir* **avoir**

aide [ɛd] **1** *nf* help, assistance; **à l'a. de qch** with the aid of sth; **appeler à l'a.** to call for help; **venir en a. à qn** to help sb; **a. humanitaire** aid **2** *nmf (personne)* assistant; **a. familiale** *Br* home help, *Am* mother's helper; **a. de camp** aide-de-camp ■**aide-mémoire** *nm inv* notes ■**aide-soignante** *(mpl* aides-soignants, *fpl* aides-soignantes) *nf Br* nursing auxiliary, *Am* nurse's aid

aider [ede] **1** *vt* to help; **a. qn à faire qch** to help sb to do sth **2 s'aider** *vpr* **s'a. de qch** to use sth

aïe [aj] *exclam* ouch!

AIEA [aiəa] (*abrév* **Agence internationale de l'énergie atomique**) *nf* IAEA

aie(s), aient [ɛ] *voir* **avoir**

aïeul, -e [ajœl] *nmf Littéraire* grandfather, *f* grandmother

aïeux [ajø] *nmpl Littéraire* forefathers

aigle [ɛgl] *nm* eagle

aiglefin [ɛgləfɛ̃] *nm* haddock

aigre [ɛgr] *adj* (*acide*) sour; (*parole*) cutting; **d'un ton a.** sharply ▪ **aigre-doux, -douce** (*mpl* **aigres-doux**, *fpl* **aigres-douces**) *adj* (*sauce*) sweet and sour ▪ **aigreur** *nf* (*de goût*) sourness; (*de ton*) sharpness; **aigreurs d'estomac** heartburn

aigrette [ɛgrɛt] *nf* (*d'oiseau*) crest; (*panache*) plume

aigrir [ɛgrir] **s'aigrir** *vpr* (*vin*) to turn sour; (*caractère*) to sour ▪ **aigri, -ie** *adj* (*personne*) embittered

aigu, -uë [egy] *adj* (*douleur, crise, accent*) acute; (*son*) high-pitched

aiguille [eguij] *nf* (*à coudre*) needle; (*de montre*) hand; (*de balance*) pointer; **a. (rocheuse)** peak; **a. de pin** pine needle

aiguiller [eguije] *vt* (*train*) *Br* to shunt, *Am* to switch; *Fig* (*personne*) to steer (**vers** towards) ▪ **aiguillage** *nm* (*appareil*) *Br* points, *Am* switches ▪ **aiguilleur** *nm* (*de trains*) signalman; **a. du ciel** air-traffic controller

aiguillon [eguijɔ̃] *nm* (*dard*) sting; (*stimulant*) spur ▪ **aiguillonner** *vt* (*stimuler*) to spur on; (*curiosité*) to arouse

aiguiser [egize] *vt* (*outil*) to sharpen; *Fig* (*appétit*) to whet

ail [aj] *nm* garlic

aile [ɛl] *nf* wing; (*de moulin*) sail; (*de voiture*) *Br* wing, *Am* fender; *Fig* **battre de l'a.** to be struggling ▪ **ailé, -ée** [ele] *adj* winged ▪ **aileron** *nm* (*de requin*) fin; (*d'avion*) aileron; (*d'oiseau*) pinion ▪ **ailier** [elje] *nm Football* winger; *Rugby* wing

aille(s), aillent [aj] *voir* **aller¹**

ailleurs [ajœr] *adv* somewhere else, elsewhere; **partout a.** everywhere else; **d'a.** (*du reste*) besides, anyway; **par a.** (*en outre*) moreover; (*par d'autres côtés*) in other respects

ailloli [ajɔli] *nm* garlic mayonnaise

aimable [emabl] *adj* (*gentil*) kind; **vous êtes bien a.** it's very kind of you ▪ **aimablement** [-əmã] *adv* kindly

aimant¹ [emã] *nm* magnet ▪ **aimanter** *vt* to magnetize

aimant², -ante [emã, -ãt] *adj* loving

aimer [eme] **1** *vt* to love; **a. bien qn/qch** to like

sb/sth; **a. faire qch** to like doing sth; **j'aimerais qu'il vienne** I would like him to come; **a. mieux** to prefer; **j'aimerais mieux qu'elle reste** I'd rather she stayed **2 s'aimer** *vpr* **ils s'aiment** they're in love

aine [ɛn] *nf* groin

aîné, -ée 1 [ene] *adj* (*de deux enfants*) elder; (*de plus de deux*) eldest **2** *nmf* (*de deux enfants*) elder; (*de plus de deux*) eldest; **c'est mon a.** he's older than me

ainsi [ɛ̃si] *adv* (*de cette façon*) in this way; (*alors*) so; **a. que...** as well as...; **et a. de suite** and so on; **pour a. dire** so to speak; *Rel* **a. soit-il!** amen!

air [ɛr] *nm* (**a**) (*gaz, ciel*) air; **prendre l'a.** to get some fresh air; **au grand a.** in the fresh air; **en plein a.** outside; **en l'a.** (*jeter*) (up) in the air; (*paroles, menaces*) empty; **regarder en l'a.** to look up; *Fam* **ficher qch en l'a.** to mess sth up; **dans l'a.** (*grippe, idées*) about, around (**b**) (*expression*) look, appearance; **avoir l'a. fatigué/content** to look tired/happy; **avoir l'a. de s'ennuyer** to look bored; **avoir l'a. de dire la vérité** to look as if one is telling the truth; **a. de famille** family likeness (**c**) (*mélodie*) tune; **a. d'opéra** aria

Air Bag® [ɛrbag] *nm Aut* airbag

aire [ɛr] *nf* (*surface*) & *Math* area; (*d'oiseau*) eyrie; **a. d'atterrissage** landing strip; **a. de jeux** (*children's*) play area; **a. de lancement** launch pad; **a. de repos** (*sur autoroute*) rest area; **a. de stationnement** lay-by

airelle [ɛrɛl] *nf* (*rouge*) cranberry

aisance [ɛzɑ̃s] *nf* (*facilité*) ease; (*prospérité*) affluence

aise [ɛz] *nf* **à l'a.** (*dans un vêtement*) comfortable; (*dans une situation*) at ease; (*fortuné*) comfortably off; **aimer ses aises** to like one's comforts; **mal à l'a.** uncomfortable, ill at ease ▪ **aisé, -ée** [eze] *adj* (*fortuné*) comfortably off; (*facile*) easy ▪ **aisément** *adv* easily

aisselle [ɛsɛl] *nf* armpit

ait [ɛ] *voir* **avoir**

ajonc [aʒɔ̃] *nm* gorse

ajouré, -ée [aʒure] *adj* (*dentelle, architecture*) openwork

ajourner [aʒurne] *vt* to postpone; (*après le début de la séance*) to adjourn ▪ **ajournement** [-əmã] *nm* postponement

ajout [aʒu] *nm* addition (**à** to) ▪ **ajouter 1** *vti* to add (**à** to) **2 s'ajouter** *vpr* **s'a. à qch** to add to sth

ajuster [aʒyste] *vt* (*appareil, outil*) to adjust; (*coiffure*) to arrange; (*coup*) to aim; (*adapter*) to fit (**à** to); (*vêtement*) to alter ▪ **ajusté, -ée** *adj* (*vêtememt*) close- *or* tight-fitting ▪ **ajusteur** *nm* (*ouvrier*) fitter

alaise [alɛz] *nf* (*waterproof*) undersheet

alambic [alãbik] *nm Chim, Ind* still

alambiqué, -ée [alãbike] *adj* convoluted

alangui [alãgi] *adj* languid

alarme [alarm] *nf* alarm; **sonner l'a.** to sound the alarm; **a. antivol/d'incendie** burglar/fire alarm ▪**alarmer 1** *vt* to alarm **2 s'alarmer** *upr* **s'a. de qch** to become alarmed at sth

Albanie [albani] *nf* **l'A.** Albania ▪**albanais, -aise 1** *adj* Albanian **2** *nmf* **A., Albanaise** Albanian

albâtre [albatr] *nm* alabaster

albatros [albatros] *nm* albatross

albinos [albinos] *nmf & adj inv* albino

album [albɔm] *nm* album; **a. de photos** photo album

alcalin, -ine [alkalɛ̃, -in] *adj Chim* alkaline

alchimie [alʃimi] *nf* alchemy

alcool [alkɔl] *nm Chim* alcohol; *(spiritueux)* spirits; **a. à 90°** *Br* surgical spirit, *Am* rubbing alcohol; **a. à brûler** *Br* methylated spirits, *Am* wood alcohol; **a. de poire** pear brandy ▪**alcoolique** *adj & nmf* alcoholic ▪**alcoolisée** *adj* **f boisson a.** alcoholic drink; **boisson non a.** soft drink ▪**alcoolisme** *nm* alcoholism ▪**Alcootest®** *nm* breath test; *(appareil)* Breathalyzer®

alcôve [alkov] *nf* alcove

aléas [alea] *nmpl* hazards ▪**aléatoire** *adj (résultat)* uncertain; *(sélection, nombre) & Ordinat* random

alentour [alãtur] *adv* round about, around; **les villages a.** the surrounding villages ▪**alentours** *nmpl* surroundings; **aux a. de la ville** in the vicinity of the town; **aux a. de midi** around midday

alerte [alɛrt] **1** *adj (leste)* sprightly; *(éveillé)* alert **2** *nf* alarm; **en état d'a.** on the alert; **donner l'a.** to give the alarm; **a. à la bombe** bomb scare; **fausse a.** false alarm ▪**alerter** *vt* to alert (**sur** to)

algèbre [alʒɛbr] *nf* algebra

Alger [alʒe] *nm* f Algiers

Algérie [alʒeri] *nf* **l'A.** Algeria ▪**algérien, -ienne 1** *adj* Algerian **2** *nmf* **A., Algérienne** Algerian

algues [alg] *nfpl* seaweed

alias [aljas] *adv* alias

alibi [alibi] *nm* alibi

aliéner [aljene] **1** *vt* to alienate **2 s'aliéner** *upr* **s'a. qn** to alienate sb ▪**aliéné, -ée** *nmf* insane person

aligner [aliɲe] **1** *vt* to line up; *(politique)* to align (**sur** with) **2 s'aligner** *upr (personnes)* to line up; *(pays)* to align oneself (**sur** with) ▪**alignement** [-əmã] *nm* alignment; **être dans l'a. de qch** to be in line with sth

aliment [alimã] *nm* food ▪**alimentaire** *adj (ration, industrie)* food; **produits alimentaires** foodstuffs ▪**alimentation** *nf (action)* feeding; *(en eau, électricité)* supply(ing); *(régime)* diet; *(nourriture)* food; **magasin d'a.** grocer's,

grocery store; **a. papier** *(d'imprimante)* paper feed ▪**alimenter** *vt (nourrir)* to feed; *(fournir)* to supply (**en** with); *(débat, feu)* to fuel

alinéa [alinea] *nm (texte)* paragraph

alité, -ée [alite] *adj* bedridden

allaiter [alete] *vt (femme)* to breast-feed; *(sujet: animal)* to suckle

allant [alã] *nm* energy

allécher [aleʃe] *vt* to tempt

allée [ale] *nf (de parc)* path; *(de ville)* avenue; *(de cinéma, de supermarché)* aisle; *(devant une maison)* driveway; **allées et venues** comings and goings

allégation [alegasjɔ̃] *nf* allegation

alléger [aleʒe] *vt (impôt)* to reduce; *(fardeau)* to lighten ▪**allégé, -ée** *adj (fromage)* low-fat

allégorie [alegori] *nf* allegory

allègre [alegr] *adj* lively, cheerful ▪**allégresse** *nf* joy

alléguer [alege] *vt (excuse)* to put forward

alléluia [aleluja] *nm* hallelujah

Allemagne [almaɲ] *nf* **l'A.** Germany ▪**allemand, -ande 1** *adj* German **2** *nmf* **A., Allemande** German **3** *nm (langue)* German

aller[1*] [ale] **1** *(aux être)* *vi* to go; **a. à Paris** to go to Paris; **a. à la pêche** to go fishing; **a. faire qch** to go and do sth; **va voir!** go and see!; **a. à qn** *(convenir à)* to suit sb; **a. avec** *(vêtement)* to go with; **a. bien/mieux** *(personne)* to be well/better; **comment vas-tu?, (comment) ça va?** how are you?; **ça va!** all right!, fine!; **allez-y** go ahead; **j'y vais** I'm coming; **allons (donc)!** come on!, come off it!; **allez! au lit!** go to bed!; **ça va de soi** that's obvious **2** *v aux (futur proche)* **a. faire qch** to be going to do sth; **il va venir** he'll come; **il va partir** he's about to leave **3 s'en aller** *upr (personne)* to go away; *(tache)* to come out

aller[2] [ale] *nm* outward journey; **a. (simple)** *Br* single (ticket), *Am* one-way (ticket); **a. (et) retour** *Br* return (ticket), *Am* round-trip (ticket)

allergie [alɛrʒi] *nf* allergy ▪**allergique** *adj* allergic (**à** to).

alliage [aljaʒ] *nm* alloy

alliance [aljãs] *nf (anneau)* wedding ring; *(mariage)* marriage; *(de pays)* alliance

allier [alje] **1** *vt (associer)* to combine (**à** with); *(pays)* to ally (**à** with); *(famille)* to unite by marriage; **a. l'intelligence à la beauté** to combine intelligence and beauty **2 s'allier** *upr (couleurs)* to combine; *(pays)* to become allied (**à** with); **s'a. contre qn/qch** to unite against sb/sth ▪**allié, -ée** *nmf* ally

alligator [aligatɔr] *nm* alligator

allô [alo] *exclam* hello!

allocation [alɔkasjɔ̃] *nf (somme)* allowance; **a. (de) chômage** unemployment benefit; **a. (de) logement** housing benefit; **allocations familiales** child benefit

allocution [alɔkysjɔ̃] nf address
allonger [alɔ̃ʒe] **1** vt (bras) to stretch out; (jupe) to lengthen; (sauce) to thin; **a. le pas** to quicken one's pace **2** vi (jours) to get longer **3 s'allonger** vpr (jours) to get longer; (personne) to lie down ■**allongé, -ée** adj (étiré) elongated; **être a.** to be lying down
allouer [alwe] vt **a. qch à qn** (ration) to allocate sb sth; (indemnité) to grant sb sth
allumer [alyme] **1** vt (feu, pipe) to light; (électricité, radio) to switch on; (incendie) to start; Fig (passion) to arouse; **laisser la cuisine allumée** to leave the light on in the kitchen **2 s'allumer** vpr (lumière, lampe) to come on; **où est-ce que ça s'allume?** where does it switch on? ■**allumage** nm (de feu) lighting; (de moteur) ignition ■**allume-gaz** nm inv gas lighter ■**allumeuse** nf Fam (femme) teaser
allumette [alymɛt] nf match
allure [alyr] nf (vitesse) speed; (démarche) gait, walk; (maintien) bearing; **à toute a.** at top speed; **avoir de l'a.** to look stylish; **avoir des allures de malfrat** to look like a crook

> Il faut noter que le nom anglais **allure** est un faux ami. Il signifie **attrait**.

allusion [alyzjɔ̃] nf allusion (**à** to); (voilée) hint; **faire a. à qch** to allude to sth; (en termes voilés) to hint at sth
almanach [almana] nm almanac
aloi [alwa] nm **de bon a.** (succès) deserved; (plaisanterie) in good taste
alors [alɔr] adv (donc) so; (à ce moment-là) then; (dans ce cas) in that case; **a. que...** (lorsque) when...; (tandis que) whereas...; **et a.?** so what?; **a., tu viens?** are you coming then?
alouette [alwɛt] nf (sky)lark
alourdir [alurdir] **1** vt (chose) to make heavier; Fig (phrase) to make cumbersome; (charges) to increase **2 s'alourdir** vpr to get heavy
aloyau [alwajo] nm sirloin
alpage [alpaʒ] nm mountain pasture ■**Alpes** nfpl **les A.** the Alps ■**alpestre, alpin, -ine** adj alpine
alphabet [alfabɛ] nm alphabet; **a. phonétique** phonetic alphabet ■**alphabétique** adj alphabetical ■**alphabétisation** nf teaching of literacy
alphanumérique [alfanymerik] adj alphanumeric
alpinisme [alpinism] nm mountaineering; **faire de l'a.** to go mountaineering ■**alpiniste** nmf mountaineer
altercation [alterkasjɔ̃] nf altercation
altérer [altere] **1** vt (a) (viande, vin) to spoil; (santé) to damage (**b**) (changer) to affect **2 s'altérer** vpr (santé, relations) to deteriorate
alternatif, -ive [alternatif, -iv] adj (successif) alternating; (de remplacement) alternative

■**alternative** nf alternative ■**alternativement** adv alternately
alterner [alterne] **1** vt (crops) to rotate **2** vi (se succéder) to alternate (**avec** with); (personnes) to take turns (**avec** with) ■**alternance** nf alternation; **en a.** alternately
Altesse [altɛs] nf **son A. royale** His/Her Royal Highness
altier, -ière [altje, -jɛr] adj haughty
altitude [altityd] nf altitude; **en a.** at altitude; **prendre de l'a.** to climb
alto [alto] nm (instrument) viola
altruisme [altrɥism] nm altruism ■**altruiste** adj altruistic
aluminium [alyminjɔm] nm Br aluminium, Am aluminum; **papier (d')a.** tinfoil
alunir [alynir] vi to land on the moon
alvéole [alveɔl] nf (de ruche) cell; (dentaire) socket ■**alvéolé, -ée** adj honeycombed
amabilité [amabilite] nf kindness; **auriez-vous l'a. de...?** would you be so kind as to...?
amadouer [amadwe] vt to coax
amaigrir [amegrir] vt to make thin(ner); **régime amaigrissant** slimming or weight loss diet ■**amaigri, -ie** adj thin(ner) ■**amaigrissement** nm (involontaire) weight loss; (volontaire) dieting, Br slimming
amalgame [amalgam] nm (mélange) combination ■**amalgamer** vt (confondre) to lump together
amande [amɑ̃d] nf almond
amant [amɑ̃] nm lover
amarre [amar] nf (mooring) rope; **amarres** moorings ■**amarrer** vt (bateau) to moor
amas [ama] nm heap, pile ■**amasser 1** vt to amass **2 s'amasser** vpr (preuves, foule) to build up; (neige) to pile up
amateur [amatœr] nm **1** (non professionnel) amateur; **a. de tennis** tennis enthusiast; **a. d'art** art lover; **faire de la photo en a.** to be an amateur photographer; Péj **c'est du travail d'a.** it's amateurish work **2** adj **une équipe a.** an amateur team; ■**amateurisme** nm Sport amateurism
amazone [amazon] nf horsewoman; **monter en a.** to ride sidesaddle
ambages [ɑ̃baʒ] **sans ambages** adv without beating about the bush
ambassade [ɑ̃basad] nf embassy ■**ambassadeur, -drice** nmf ambassador; **l'a. de France au Japon** the French ambassador to Japan
ambiance [ɑ̃bjɑ̃s] nf atmosphere; Fam **mettre de l'a.** to liven things up ■**ambiant, -ante** adj surrounding; (gaieté, enthousiasme) pervading; **température a.** room temperature
ambidextre [ɑ̃bidɛkstr] adj ambidextrous
ambigu, -uë [ɑ̃bigy] adj ambiguous ■**ambiguïté** [-gɥite] nf ambiguity
ambitieux, -ieuse [ɑ̃bisjø, -jøz] adj ambitious

■**ambition** *nf* ambition ■**ambitionner** *vt* to aspire to; **il ambitionne de faire/d'être...** his ambition is to do/be...

ambre [ãbr] *nm (résine)* amber

ambulance [ãbylãs] *nf* ambulance ■**ambulancier, -ière** *nmf* ambulance driver

ambulant, -ante [ãbylã, -ãt] *adj Br* travelling, *Am* traveling, itinerant; **marchand a.** (street) hawker

âme [ɑm] *nf* soul; **de toute mon â.** with all my heart; **en mon â. et conscience** to the best of my knowledge and belief; **rendre l'â.** to give up the ghost; **avoir charge d'âmes** to be responsible for human life; **je n'ai rencontré â. qui vive** I didn't meet a (living) soul; **â. sœur** soul mate

améliorer [ameljɔre] *vt,* **s'améliorer** *vpr* to improve ■**amélioration** *nf* improvement

amen [amɛn] *adv* amen

aménager [amenaʒe] *vt (changer)* to adjust, *(maison)* to convert (**en** into) ■**aménagement** *nm (changement)* adjustment; *(de pièce)* conversion (**en** into); **a. du temps de travail** flexibility of working hours; **a. du territoire** regional development

amende [amãd] *nf* fine; **infliger une a. à qn** to impose a fine on sb; **faire a. honorable** to apologize

amender [amãde] **1** *vt (texte de loi)* to amend **2** **s'amender** *vpr* to mend one's ways

amener [amne] **1** *vt (apporter)* to bring; *(causer)* to bring about; *(tirer à soi)* to pull in; **a. qn à faire qch** *(sujet: personne)* to get sb to do sth; **ce qui nous amène à parler de...** which brings us to the issue of... **2** **s'amener** *vpr Fam* to turn up

amenuiser [amənɥize] **s'amenuiser** *vpr* to dwindle; *(écart)* to get smaller

amer, -ère [amɛr] *adj* bitter ■**amèrement** *adv* bitterly

Amerindien, -ienne [amerãdjɛ̃, -jɛn] *nmf* American Indian

Amérique [amerik] *nf* l'A. America; l'A. du Nord/du Sud North/South America; l'A. latine Latin America ■**américain, -aine** **1** *adj* American **2** *nmf* A., **Américaine** American

amerrir [amerir] *vi* to make a sea landing

amertume [amɛrtym] *nf* bitterness

améthyste [ametist] *nf* amethyst

ameublement [amœbləmã] *nm (meubles)* furniture

ameuter [amøte] *vt (personnes)* to bring out; **elle va a. tout le quartier si elle continue à hurler comme ça!** she'll have the whole neighbourhood out if she carries on shouting like that!

ami, -ie [ami] **1** *nmf* friend; **petit a.** boyfriend; **petite amie** girlfriend **2** *adj* friendly; **être a. avec qn** to be friends with sb

amiable [amjabl] **à l'amiable 1** *adj* amicable **2** *adv* amicably

amiante [amjãt] *nm* asbestos

amical, -e, -aux, -ales [amikal, -o] *adj* friendly ■**amicale** *nf* association ■**amicalement** *adv* in a friendly manner

amidon [amidɔ̃] *nm* starch ■**amidonner** *vt* to starch

amincir [amɛ̃sir] **1** *vt* to make thin(ner); **cette robe t'amincit** that dress makes you look thinner **2** **s'amincir** *vpr* to become thinner

amiral, -aux [amiral, -o] *nm* admiral

amitié [amitje] *nf* friendship; **prendre qn en a.** to befriend sb; **faites-moi l'a. de le lui dire** would you be so kind as to tell him?; **mes amitiés à votre mère** best wishes to your mother

ammoniaque [amɔnjak] *nf (liquide)* ammonia

amnésie [amnezi] *nf* amnesia ■**amnésique** *adj* amnesic

amniocentèse [amnjosɛtɛz] *nf Méd* amniocentesis

amnistie [amnisti] *nf* amnesty

amocher [amɔʃe] *vt Fam (personne)* to beat up; **se faire a.** to get beaten up

amoindrir [amwɛ̃drir] *vt,* **s'amoindrir** *vpr* to diminish

amollir [amɔlir] *vt,* **s'amollir** *vpr* to soften

amonceler [amɔ̃sle] *vt,* **s'amonceler** *vpr* to pile up; *(preuves)* to accumulate ■**amoncellement** [-sɛlmã] *nm* heap, pile

amont [amɔ̃] *adv* **en amont** upstream (**de** from)

amoral, -e, -aux, -ales [amɔral, -o] *adj* amoral

amorce [amɔrs] *nf (début)* start; *(de pêcheur)* bait; *(détonateur)* detonator; *(de pistolet d'enfant)* cap ■**amorcer 1** *vt (commencer)* to start; *(hameçon)* to bait; *(bombe)* to arm; *Ordinat* to boot up **2** **s'amorcer** *vpr* to start

amorphe [amɔrf] *adj* listless, apathetic

amortir [amɔrtir] *vt (coup)* to absorb; *(bruit)* to deaden; *(chute)* to break; *(achat)* to recoup the costs of; *Fin (dette)* to pay off; *Football* to trap ■**amortissement** *nm (d'un emprunt)* redemption ■**amortisseur** *nm (de véhicule)* shock absorber

amour [amur] *nm (sentiment, liaison)* love; **avec a.** lovingly; **faire qch par a. pour qn** to do sth out of love for sb; **faire l'a. avec qn** to make love with sb; **pour l'a. du ciel!** for heaven's sake!; **mon a.** my darling, my love; **tu es un a.!** you're an angel!; **à tes amours!** *(quand on éternue)* bless you! ■**s'amouracher** *vpr Péj* to become infatuated (**de** with) ■**amoureux, -euse 1** *adj* **être a. de qn** to be in love with sb; **tomber a. de qn** to fall in love with sb; **vie amoureuse** love life **2** *nm* boyfriend; **un couple d'a.** a pair of lovers ■**amour-propre** *nm* self-respect

amovible [amɔvibl] *adj* removable, detachable

ampère [ɑ̃pɛr] *nm Él* ampere

amphétamine [ɑ̃fetamin] *nf* amphetamine

amphi [ɑ̃fi] *nm Fam Univ* lecture hall

amphibie [ɑ̃fibi] *adj* amphibious

amphithéâtre [ɑ̃fiteatr] *nm (romain)* amphitheatre; *(à l'université)* lecture hall *or Br* theatre

ample [ɑ̃pl] *adj (vêtement)* full; *(geste)* sweeping; **de plus amples renseignements** more detailed information; **jusqu'à plus a. informé** until further information is available ▪ **amplement** [-əmɑ̃] *adv* amply, fully; **c'est a. suffisant** it is more than enough ▪ **ampleur** *nf (de vêtement)* fullness; *(importance)* scale, extent; **prendre de l'a.** to grow in size

amplifier [ɑ̃plifje] **1** *vt (son)* to amplify; *(phénomène)* to intensify **2 s'amplifier** *upr (son)* to increase; *(phénomène)* to intensify ▪ **amplificateur** *nm* amplifier ▪ **amplification** *nf (de son)* amplification; *(de phénomène)* intensification

amplitude [ɑ̃plityd] *nf (de désastre)* magnitude; *(variation)* range

ampoule [ɑ̃pul] *nf (électrique)* (light) bulb; *(sur la peau)* blister; *(de médicament)* phial

ampoulé, -ée [ɑ̃pule] *adj (style)* bombastic

amputer [ɑ̃pyte] *vt (membre)* to amputate; *Fig* to slash; **a. qn de la jambe** to amputate sb's leg ▪ **amputation** *nf (de membre)* amputation

amuse-gueule [amyzgœl] *nm inv* appetizer

amuser [amyze] **1** *vt* to amuse; **cette histoire l'a beaucoup amusé** he found the story very amusing **2 s'amuser** *upr* to amuse oneself; **s'a. avec qn/qch** to play with sb/sth; **s'a. à faire qch** to amuse oneself doing sth; **bien s'a.** to have a good time ▪ **amusant, -ante** *adj* amusing ▪ **amusement** *nm* amusement

amygdales [amidal] *nfpl* tonsils

an [ɑ̃] *nm* year; **il a dix ans** he's ten (years old); **par a.** per year; **en l'an 2000** in the year 2000; **bon a., mal a.** on average over the years

anabolisant [anabɔlizɑ̃] *nm* anabolic steroid

anachronisme [anakrɔnism] *nm* anachronism ▪ **anachronique** *adj* anachronistic

anagramme [anagram] *nf* anagram

analogie [analɔʒi] *nf* analogy ▪ **analogue** *adj* similar (**à** to)

analphabète [analfabɛt] *adj & nmf* illiterate ▪ **analphabétisme** *nm* illiteracy

analyse [analiz] *nf* analysis; **a. grammaticale** parsing; **a. du sang/d'urine** blood/urine test; **être en a.** *(en traitement)* to be in analysis ▪ **analyser** *vt* to analyse; *(phrase)* to parse ▪ **analytique** *adj* analytical

ananas [anana(s)] *nm* pineapple

anarchie [anarʃi] *nf* anarchy ▪ **anarchique** *adj* anarchic ▪ **anarchiste 1** *adj* anarchistic **2** *nmf* anarchist

anathème [anatɛm] *nm (condamnation) & Rel* anathema

anatomie [anatɔmi] *nf* anatomy ▪ **anatomique** *adj* anatomical

ancestral, -e, -aux, -ales [ɑ̃sɛstral, -o] *adj* ancestral

ancêtre [ɑ̃sɛtr] *nm* ancestor

anche [ɑ̃ʃ] *nf Mus* reed

anchois [ɑ̃ʃwa] *nm* anchovy

ancien, -ienne [ɑ̃sjɛ̃, -jɛn] **1** *adj (vieux)* old; *(meuble)* antique; *(qui n'est plus)* former, old; *(dans une fonction)* senior; **dans l'a. temps** in the old days; **a. élève** *Br* former pupil, *Am* alumnus; **a. combattant** *Br* ex-serviceman, *Am* veteran **2** *nmf (par l'âge)* elder; **c'est un a. de la maison** he's been in the firm for a long time ▪ **anciennement** *adv* formerly ▪ **ancienneté** *nf (âge)* age; *(expérience)* seniority

ancre [ɑ̃kr] *nf* anchor; **jeter l'a.** to (cast) anchor; **lever l'a.** to weigh anchor ▪ **ancrer** *vt* (**a**) *(navire)* to anchor; **être ancré** to be at anchor (**b**) *Fig (idée, sentiment)* to become rooted; **ancré dans** rooted in

Andorre [ɑ̃dɔr] *nf* Andorra

andouille [ɑ̃duj] *nf* (**a**) *Culin* chitterlings sausage (**b**) *Fam (idiot)* twit

âne [ɑn] *nm (animal)* donkey; *Péj (personne)* ass

anéantir [aneɑ̃tir] *vt (ville)* to destroy; *(armée)* to crush; *(espoirs)* to shatter ▪ **anéanti, -ie** *adj (épuisé)* exhausted; *(accablé)* overwhelmed; **a. par le chagrin** overcome by grief ▪ **anéantissement** *nm (de ville)* destruction; *(d'espoir)* shattering; **dans un état d'a. total** utterly crushed

anecdote [anɛkdɔt] *nf* anecdote ▪ **anecdotique** *adj* anecdotal

anémie [anemi] *nf* an(a)emia ▪ **anémique** *adj* an(a)emic

anémone [anemɔn] *nf* anemone

ânerie [ɑnri] *nf (parole)* stupid remark; *(action)* stupid act

anesthésie [anɛstezi] *nf* an(a)esthesia; **être sous a.** to be under ana(e)sthetic; **a. générale/locale** general/local an(a)esthetic ▪ **anesthésier** *vt* to an(a)esthetize ▪ **anesthésiste** *nmf Br* an(a)esthetist, *Am* anesthesiologist

aneth [anɛt] *nm* dill

ange [ɑ̃ʒ] *nm* angel; **être aux anges** to be in seventh heaven; **a. gardien** guardian angel ▪ **angélique 1** *adj* angelic **2** *nf Culin* angelica

angine [ɑ̃ʒin] *nf* sore throat; **a. de poitrine** angina (pectoris)

anglais, -aise [ɑ̃glɛ, -ɛz] **1** *adj* English **2** *nmf* **A., Anglaise** Englishman, Englishwoman; **les A.** the English **3** *nm (langue)* English **4** *nf Fam* **filer à l'anglaise** to slip away

angle [ɑ̃gl] *nm (point de vue) & Math* angle; *(coin de rue)* corner; **la maison qui fait l'a.** the house on the corner; *Aut* **a. mort** blind spot

Angleterre [ɑ̃glətɛr] *nf* **l'A.** England

anglican, -ane [ãglikã, -an] *adj & nmf* Anglican

anglicisme [ãglisism] *nm* Anglicism

anglo- [ãglɔ] *préf* Anglo- ▪ **anglo-normand, -ande** *adj* **les îles anglo-normandes** the Channel Islands ▪ **anglophile** *adj & nmf* anglophile ▪ **anglophone 1** *adj* English-speaking **2** *nmf* English speaker ▪ **anglo-saxon, -onne** (*mpl* anglo-saxons, *fpl* anglo-saxonnes) *adj & nmf* Anglo-Saxon

angoisse [ãgwas] *nf* anguish; **une crise d'a.** an anxiety attack; *Fam* **c'est l'a.!** what a drag! ▪ **angoissant, -ante** *adj* (*nouvelle*) distressing; (*attente*) agonizing; (*livre*) frightening ▪ **angoissé, -ée** *adj* (*personne*) anxious; (*cri, regard*) anguished ▪ **angoisser 1** *vt* **a. qn** to make sb anxious **2** *vi Fam* to get worked up **3** **s'angoisser** *vpr* to get anxious

angora [ãgɔra] *nm* (*laine*) angora; **pull en a.** angora sweater

anguille [ãgij] *nf* eel

angulaire [ãgylɛr] *adj* **pierre a.** cornerstone ▪ **anguleux, -euse** *adj* (*visage*) angular

animal, -aux [animal, -o] **1** *nm* animal; **a. domestique** pet **2** *adj* (*règne, graisse*) animal

animateur, -trice [animatœr, -tris] *nmf* (*de télévision, de radio*) presenter; (*de club*) leader

animer [anime] **1** *vt* (*débat, groupe*) to lead; (*jeu télévisé*) to present; (*désir, ambition*) to drive; **la joie qui animait son visage** the joy which made his/her face light up **2** **s'animer** *vpr* (*rue*) to come to life; (*visage*) to light up; (*conversation*) to get more lively ▪ **animation** *nf* (*vie*) life; (*divertissement*) event; *Cin* animation; **parler avec a.** to speak animatedly; **mettre de l'a. dans une soirée** to liven up a party ▪ **animé, -ée** *adj* (*personne, réunion, conversation*) lively; (*rue, quartier*) busy

animosité [animozite] *nf* animosity

anis [ani(s)] *nm* (*boisson, parfum*) aniseed; **boisson à l'a.** aniseed drink ▪ **anisette** *nf* anisette

ankylose [ãkiloz] *nf* stiffness ▪ **ankylosé, -ée** *adj* stiff ▪ **s'ankyloser** *vpr* to stiffen up

annales [anal] *nfpl* annals; *Fig* **rester dans les a.** to go down in history

anneau, -x [ano] *nm* (*bague*) ring; (*de chaîne*) link; *Gym* **les anneaux** the rings

année [ane] *nf* year; **les années 90** the nineties; **bonne a.!** Happy New Year!

annexe [anɛks] **1** *nf* (*bâtiment*) annexe; (*de lettre*) enclosure; (*de livre*) appendix; **document en a.** enclosed document **2** *adj* (*pièces*) enclosed; (*revenus*) supplementary; **bâtiment a.** annex(e) ▪ **annexer** *vt* (*pays*) to annex; (*document*) to append

annihiler [aniile] *vt* (*ville, armée*) to annihilate

anniversaire [anivɛrsɛr] **1** *nm* (*d'événement*) anniversary; (*de naissance*) birthday; **gâteau d'a.** birthday cake **2** *adj* **date a.** anniversary

annonce [anɔ̃s] *nf* (*déclaration*) announcement; (*publicitaire*) advertisement; (*indice*) sign; **passer une a. dans un journal** to put an advert in a newspaper; **petites annonces** classified advertisements, *Br* small ads, *Am* want ads ▪ **annoncer 1** *vt* (*déclarer*) to announce; (*dans la presse*) (*soldes, exposition*) to advertise; (*indiquer*) to herald; **a. qn** (*visiteur*) to show sb in **2** **s'annoncer** *vpr* **ça s'annonce bien/mal** things aren't looking too bad/good ▪ **annonceur** *nm* (*publicitaire*) advertiser ▪ **annonciateur, -trice** *adj* **signes annonciateurs de crise** signs that a crisis is on the way

Annonciation [anɔ̃sjasjɔ̃] *nf* **l'A.** Annunciation

annoter [anɔte] *vt* to annotate ▪ **annotation** *nf* annotation

annuaire [anɥɛr] *nm* (*d'organisme*) yearbook; (*liste d'adresses*) directory; **a. téléphonique** telephone directory; **a. électronique** electronic phone directory

annuel, -elle [anɥɛl] *adj* annual, yearly ▪ **annuellement** *adv* annually ▪ **annuité** *nf* (*d'emprunt*) annual repayment

annulaire [anɥlɛr] *nm* ring finger

annuler [anɥle] **1** *vt* (*commande, rendez-vous*) & *Ordinat* to cancel; (*dette*) to write off; (*mariage*) to annul; (*jugement*) to quash; *Ordinat* (*opération*) to undo **2** **s'annuler** *vpr* to cancel each other out ▪ **annulation** *nf* (*de commande, de rendez-vous*) cancellation; (*de dette*) writing off; (*de mariage*) annulment; (*de jugement*) quashing; *Ordinat* deletion

anoblir [anɔblir] *vt* to ennoble

anodin, -ine [anɔdɛ̃, -in] *adj* (*remarque*) harmless; (*personne*) insignificant; (*blessure*) slight

anomalie [anɔmali] *nf* (*bizarrerie*) anomaly; (*difformité*) abnormality

ânonner [ɑnɔne] *vt* to stumble through

anonymat [anɔnima] *nm* anonymity; **garder l'a.** to remain anonymous ▪ **anonyme** *adj & nmf* anonymous

anorak [anɔrak] *nm* anorak

anorexie [anɔrɛksi] *nf Méd* anorexia ▪ **anorexique** *adj & nmf Méd* anorexic

anormal, -e, -aux, -ales [anɔrmal, -o] *adj* (*non conforme*) abnormal; (*mentalement*) mentally handicapped; (*injuste*) unfair

ANPE [aɛnpeø] (*abrév* **agence nationale pour l'emploi**) *nf* = French State employment agency

anse [ɑ̃s] *nf* (a) (*de tasse, de panier*) handle (b) (*baie*) cove

antagonisme [ãtagɔnism] *nm* antagonism ▪ **antagoniste 1** *adj* antagonistic **2** *nmf* antagonist

antan [ãtã] **d'antan** *adj Littéraire* of yesteryear

antarctique [ãtarktik] **1** *adj* Antarctic **2** *nm* **l'A.** the Antarctic, Antarctica

antécédent [ātesedā] *nm Grammaire* ante-cedent; **antécédents** *(de personne)* past re-cord; **antécédents médicaux** medical history

antenne [āten] *nf (de radio, de satellite)* aerial, antenna; *(d'insecte)* antenna, feeler; *(société)* branch; **être à l'a.** to be on the air; **rendre l'a.** to hand over; **hors a.** off the air; *Mil* **a. chirurgicale** field hospital; **a. parabolique** satellite dish

antérieur, -e [āterjœr] *adj (période)* former; *(année)* previous; *(date)* earlier; *(placé devant)* front; **membre a.** forelimb; **a. à qch** prior to sth ■**antérieurement** *adv* previously ■**antério-rité** *nf* precedence

anthologie [ātɔlɔʒi] *nf* anthology

anthropologie [ātrɔpɔlɔʒi] *nf* anthropology

anthropophage [ātrɔpɔfaʒ] *nm* cannibal ■**anthropophagie** *nf* cannibalism

antiaérien, -ienne [ātiaerjē, -jɛn] *adj* **canon a.** anti-aircraft gun; **abri a.** air-raid shelter

antiatomique [ātiatɔmik] *adj* **abri a.** fallout shelter

antibiotique [ātibjɔtik] *nm* antibiotic; **sous antibiotiques** on antibiotics

antibrouillard [ātibrujar] *adj & nm (phare)* **a.** fog lamp

anticancéreux, -euse [ātikāserø, -øz] *adj* **centre a.** cancer hospital

antichambre [ātiʃābr] *nf* antechamber

antichoc [ātiʃɔk] *adj inv* shock-proof

anticiper [ātisipe] *vti* **a. (sur)** to anticipate ■**anticipation** *nf* anticipation; **par a.** in advance; **d'a.** *(roman, film)* science-fiction ■**anticipé, -ée** *adj (retraite, retour)* early; *(paiement)* advance; **avec mes remerciements anticipés** thanking you in advance

anticlérical, -e, -aux, -ales [ātiklerikal, -o] *adj* anticlerical

anticommuniste [ātikɔmynist] *adj* anticom-munist

anticonformiste [ātikɔ̃fɔrmist] *adj & nmf* nonconformist

anticonstitutionnel, -elle [ātikɔ̃stitysjɔnɛl] *adj* unconstitutional

anticorps [ātikɔr] *nm* antibody

anticyclone [ātisiklɔn] *nm* anticyclone

antidémocratique [ātidemɔkratik] *adj* undemo-cratic

antidépresseur [ātidepresœr] *nm* antidepres-sant

antidérapant, -ante [ātiderapā, -āt] *adj (sur-face, pneu)* non-skid; *(semelle)* non-slip

antidopage [ātidɔpaʒ] *adj* **contrôle a.** drug test

antidote [ātidɔt] *nm* antidote

antigel [ātiʒɛl] *nm* antifreeze

antihistaminique [ātiistaminik] *adj Méd* anti-histamine

anti-inflammatoire [ātiɛ̃flamatwar] *adj Méd* anti-inflammatory

Antilles [ātij] *nfpl* **les A.** the West Indies ■**antillais, -aise 1** *adj* West Indian **2** *nmf* **A.**, Antillaise West Indian

antilope [ātilɔp] *nf* antelope

antimite [ātimit] *nm* **de l'a.** mothballs

antimondialiste [ātimɔ̃djalist] *adj & nmf* antiglobalist ■**antimondialisme** *nm* anti-globalization

antinucléaire [ātinykleer] *adj* anti-nuclear

Antiope [ātjɔp] *n* = French Teletext system providing subtitles for the deaf

antioxydant, -ante [ātiɔksidā, -āt] *adj & nm* antioxydant

antipathie [ātipati] *nf* antipathy ■**antipath-ique** *adj* unpleasant; **elle m'est a.** I find her unpleasant

antipelliculaire [ātipelikylɛr] *adj* shampooing **a.** anti-dandruff shampoo

antipodes [ātipɔd] *nmpl* antipodes; **être aux a. de** to be on the other side of the world from; *Fig* to be the exact opposite of

antipoison [ātipwazɔ̃] *adj inv Méd* **centre a.** poisons unit

antique [ātik] *adj (de l'Antiquité)* ancient ■**antiquaire** *nmf* antique dealer ■**antiquité** *nf (objet ancien)* antique; **l'a. grecque/romaine** ancient Greece/Rome; **antiquités** *(dans un musée)* antiquities

antirabique [ātirabik] *adj Méd* anti-rabies

antireflet [ātireflɛ] *adj inv* non-reflecting

antirides [ātirid] *adj inv* anti-wrinkle

antirouille [ātiruj] *adj inv* antirust

antisèche [ātisɛʃ] *nf Fam* crib sheet

antisémite [ātisemit] *adj* anti-Semitic ■**anti-sémitisme** *nm* anti-Semitism

antiseptique [ātiseptik] *adj & nm* antiseptic

antisocial, -e, -aux, -ales [ātisɔsjal, -o] *adj* antisocial

antitabac [ātitaba] *adj inv* **lutte a.** anti-smoking campaign

antiterroriste [ātiterɔrist] *adj* anti-terrorist

antithèse [ātitez] *nf* antithesis

antivariolique [ātivarjɔlik] *adj Méd* **vaccin a.** smallpox vaccine

antivol [ātivɔl] *nm* anti-theft device

antre [ātr] *nm (de lion)* den

anus [anys] *nm* anus

Anvers [āver(s)] *nm ou f* Antwerp

anxiété [āksjete] *nf* anxiety ■**anxieux, -ieuse 1** *adj* anxious **2** *nmf* worrier

août [u(t)] *nm* August ■**aoûtien, -ienne** [ausjē, -jɛn] *nmf* August *Br* holidaymaker *or Am* vacationer

apaiser [apeze] **1** *vt (personne)* to calm (down); *(douleur)* to soothe; *(craintes)* to allay **2 s'apaiser** *upr (personne, colère)* to calm down; *(tempête, douleur)* to subside ■**apaisant, -ante** *adj* soothing

apanage [apanaʒ] *nm* prerogative

aparté [aparte] *nm Théâtre* aside; *(dans une réunion)* private exchange; **en a.** in private
apartheid [aparted] *nm* apartheid
apathie [apati] *nf* apathy ▪ **apathique** *adj* apathetic
apatride [apatrid] *nmf* stateless person
apercevoir* [apɛrsəvwar] **1** *vt* to see; *(brièvement)* to catch a glimpse of **2 s'apercevoir** *vpr* **s'a. de qch** to realize sth; **s'a. que…** to realize that… ▪ **aperçu** *nm (idea)* general idea; **donner à qn un a. de la situation** to give sb a general idea of the situation
apéritif [aperitif] *nm* aperitif; **prendre un a.** to have a drink before lunch/dinner ▪ **apéro** *nm Fam* aperitif
apesanteur [apəzɑ̃tœr] *nf* weightlessness
à-peu-près [apøprɛ] *nm inv* rough approximation
apeuré, -ée [apœre] *adj* frightened, scared
aphone [afɔn] *adj* voiceless; **je suis a. aujourd'hui** I've lost my voice today
aphorisme [afɔrism] *nm* aphorism
aphrodisiaque [afrɔdizjak] *nm & adj* aphrodisiac
aphte [aft] *nm* mouth ulcer ▪ **aphteuse** *adj f* **fièvre a.** foot-and-mouth disease
apiculture [apikyltyr] *nf* beekeeping ▪ **apiculteur, -trice** *nmf* beekeeper
apitoyer [apitwaje] **1** *vt* **a. qn** to move sb to pity **2 s'apitoyer** *vpr* **s'a. sur qn** to feel sorry for sb; **s'a. sur son sort** to feel sorry for oneself ▪ **apitoiement** *nm* pity
aplanir [aplanir] *vt (terrain, route)* to level; *(difficulté)* to iron out
aplatir [aplatir] **1** *vt* to flatten **2 s'aplatir** *vpr (être plat)* to be flat; *(devenir plat)* to go flat; **s'a. contre qch** to flatten oneself against sth; *Fam* **s'a. devant qn** to grovel to sb ▪ **aplati, -ie** *adj* flat
aplomb [aplɔ̃] *nm (assurance)* self-confidence; *Péj* cheek; **mettre qch d'a.** to stand sth up straight; **je ne me sens pas d'a. aujourd'hui** I'm not feeling myself today
apnée [apne] *nf* **plonger en a.** to dive without breathing apparatus
apocalypse [apɔkalips] *nf* apocalypse; **d'a.** *(vision)* apocalyptic ▪ **apocalyptique** *adj* apocalyptic
apogée [apɔʒe] *nm (d'orbite)* apogee; *Fig* **être à l'a. de sa carrière** to be at the height of one's career
apolitique [apɔlitik] *adj* apolitical
apollon [apɔlɔ̃] *nm (bel homme)* Adonis
apologie [apɔlɔʒi] *nf (défense)* apologia (**de** for); *(éloge)* eulogy; **faire l'a. de qch** to eulogize sth

> Il faut noter que le nom anglais **apology** est un faux ami. Il signifie **excuses**.

apoplexie [apɔplɛksi] *nf* apoplexy
apostolat [apɔstɔla] *nm (mission)* vocation
apostrophe [apɔstrɔf] *nf* (**a**) *(signe)* apostrophe (**b**) *(interpellation)* rude remark ▪ **apostropher** *vt (pour attirer l'attention)* to shout at
apothéose [apɔteoz] *nf (consécration)* crowning glory; **finir en a.** to end spectacularly
apôtre [apotr] *nm* apostle
apparaître* [aparɛtr] *(aux être)* *vi (se montrer, sembler)* to appear; **il m'est apparu en rêve** he appeared to me in a dream; **il m'apparaît comme le seul capable d'y parvenir** he seems to me to be the only person capable of doing it
apparat [apara] *nm* pomp; **tenue d'a.** ceremonial dress
appareil [aparɛj] *nm (instrument, machine)* apparatus; *(téléphone)* telephone; *(avion)* aircraft; **l'a. de la justice** the legal system; *Hum* **dans le plus simple a.** in one's birthday suit; **qui est à l'a.?** *(au téléphone)* who's speaking?; **a. (dentaire)** *(correctif)* brace; *Anat* **a. digestif** digestive system; **a. photo** camera; **a. photo numérique** digital camera; **appareils ménagers** household appliances
apparence [aparɑ̃s] *nf* appearance; **en a.** outwardly; **sous l'a. de** under the guise of; **sauver les apparences** to keep up appearances ▪ **apparemment** [-amɑ̃] *adv* apparently ▪ **apparent, -ente** *adj* apparent
apparenter [aparɑ̃te] **s'apparenter** *vpr (ressembler)* to be akin (**à** to) ▪ **apparenté, -ée** *adj (allié)* related; *(semblable)* similar
apparition [aparisjɔ̃] *nf (manifestation)* appearance; *(fantôme)* apparition; **faire son a.** *(personne)* to make one's appearance
appartement [apartəmɑ̃] *nm Br* flat, *Am* apartment
appartenir* [apartənir] **1** *vi* to belong (**à** to) **2** *v impersonnel* **il vous appartient de prendre la décision** it's up to you to decide ▪ **appartenance** *nf (de groupe)* belonging (**à** to); *(de parti)* membership (**à** of)
appât [apɑ] *nm (amorce)* bait; *Fig (attrait)* lure; **l'a. du gain** the lure of money ▪ **appâter** *vt (hameçon)* to bait; *(animal)* to lure; *Fig (personne)* to entice
appauvrir [apovrir] **1** *vt* to impoverish **2 s'appauvrir** *vpr* to become impoverished ▪ **appauvrissement** *nm* impoverishment
appel [apɛl] *nm (cri, attrait)* call; *(invitation) & Jur* appeal; *Mil (recrutement)* call-up; *(pour sauter)* take-off; **faire l'a.** *(à l'école)* to take the register; *Mil* to have a roll call; **faire a. à qn** to appeal to sb; *(plombier, médecin)* to send for sb; *Jur* **faire a. d'une décision** to appeal against a decision; *Fig* **la décision est sans a.** the decision is final; *Com* **lancer un a. d'offre** to invite bids; **a. au secours** call for help; **a. d'air**

draught; **a. gratuit** *Br* freefone call, *Am* toll-free call; **a. téléphonique** telephone call

appeler [aple] **1** *vt (personne, nom)* to call; *(en criant)* to call out to; *Mil (recruter)* to call up; *(nécessiter)* to call for; **a. qn à l'aide** to call to sb for help; **a. qn au téléphone** to call sb; **a. un taxi** to call for a taxi; **a. qn à faire qch** *(inviter)* to call on sb to do sth; **être appelé à témoigner** to be called upon to give evidence; **il est appelé à de hautes fonctions** he is marked out for high office; **en a. à** to appeal to **2 s'appeler** *vpr* to be called; **comment vous appelez-vous?** what's your name?; **je m'appelle David** my name is David ▪**appellation** [apɛlɑsjɔ̃] *nf (nom)* term; **a. contrôlée** *(de vin)* guaranteed vintage ▪**appelé** *nm Mil* conscript

> Il faut noter que le verbe anglais **to appeal** est un faux ami. Il ne signifie jamais **appeler**.

appendice [apɛ̃dis] *nm (du corps, de livre)* appendix; *(d'animal)* appendage ▪**appendicite** *nf* appendicitis

appesantir [apəzɑ̃tir] **s'appesantir** *vpr* to become heavier; **s'a. sur** *(sujet)* to dwell upon

appétit [apeti] *nm* appetite (**de** for); **mettre qn en a.** to whet sb's appetite; **couper l'a. à qn** to spoil sb's appetite; **manger de bon a.** to tuck in; **bon a.!** enjoy your meal! ▪**appétissant, -ante** *adj* appetizing

applaudir [aplodir] *vti* to applaud; **a. à qch** *(approuver)* to applaud sth ▪**applaudissements** *nmpl* applause

applicable [aplikabl] *adj* applicable (**à** to) ▪**application** *nf (action, soin)* application; *(de loi)* enforcement; **mettre une théorie en a.** to put a theory into practice; **mettre une loi en a.** to enforce a law; **entrer en a.** to come into force

applique [aplik] *nf* wall light

appliquer [aplike] **1** *vt* to apply (**à/sur** to); *(loi, décision)* to enforce **2 s'appliquer** *vpr (se concentrer)* to apply oneself (**à** to); **s'a. à faire qch** to take pains to do sth; **cette décision s'applique à...** *(concerne)* this decision applies to... ▪**appliqué, -ée** *adj (personne)* hardworking; *(écriture)* careful; *(sciences)* applied

appoint [apwɛ̃] *nm* (**a**) **faire l'a.** to give the exact money (**b**) **radiateur d'a.** extra radiator; **salaire d'a.** extra income

appointements [apwɛ̃tmɑ̃] *nmpl* salary

> Il faut noter que le nom anglais **appointment** est un faux ami. Il signifie **rendez-vous** ou nomination selon le contexte.

apport [apɔr] *nm* contribution (**à** to)

apporter [apɔrte] *vt* to bring (**à** to); *(preuve)* to provide; *(modification)* to bring about; **je te l'ai apporté** I brought it to you

apposer [apoze] *vt (sceau, signature)* to affix (**à** to); *(affiche)* to put up ▪**apposition** *nf Grammaire* apposition

apprécier [apresje] *vt (aimer, percevoir)* to appreciate; *(évaluer)* to estimate; *Fam* **je n'ai pas apprécié** I wasn't too pleased ▪**appréciable** *adj* appreciable ▪**appréciation** *nf (opinion de professeur)* comment (**sur** on); *(évaluation)* valuation; *(augmentation de valeur)* appreciation; **laisser qch à l'a. de qn** to leave sth to sb's discretion

appréhender [apreɑ̃de] *vt (craindre)* to dread (**de faire** doing); *(arrêter)* to arrest; *(comprendre)* to grasp ▪**appréhension** *nf (crainte)* apprehension (**de** about)

apprendre* [aprɑ̃dr] *vti (étudier)* to learn; *(nouvelle)* to hear; *(mariage, mort)* to hear of; **a. à faire qch** to learn to do sth; **a. qch à qn** *(enseigner)* to teach sb sth; *(informer)* to tell sb sth; **a. à qn à faire qch** to teach sb to do sth; **a. que...** to learn that...; *(être informé)* to hear that...

apprenti, -ie [aprɑ̃ti] *nmf* apprentice ▪**apprentissage** *nm (professionnel)* training; *(chez un artisan)* apprenticeship; *(d'une langue)* learning (**de** of); *Fig* **faire l'a. de qch** to learn about sth

apprêter [aprete] **s'apprêter** *vpr* to get ready (**à faire** to do)

apprivoiser [aprivwaze] **1** *vt* to tame **2 s'apprivoiser** *vpr* to become tame ▪**apprivoisé, -ée** *adj* tame

approbation [aprɔbasjɔ̃] *nf* approval ▪**approbateur, -trice** *adj* approving

approche [aprɔʃ] *nf* approach; **approches** *(de ville)* outskirts; **à l'a. de la vieillesse** as old age draws/drew nearer

approcher [aprɔʃe] **1** *vt (objet)* to bring up; *(personne)* to approach, to get close to; **a. qch de qn** to bring sth near to sb **2** *vi* to approach, to get closer; **a. de qn/qch** to approach sb/sth; **la nuit approchait** it was beginning to get dark; **approche, je vais te montrer** come here, I'll show you **3 s'approcher** *vpr* to approach, to get closer; **s'a. de qn/qch** to approach sb/sth; **il s'est approché de moi** he came up to me ▪**approchant, -ante** *adj* similar

approfondir [aprɔfɔ̃dir] *vt (trou, puits)* to dig deeper; *(question, idée)* to go thoroughly into ▪**approfondi, -ie** *adj (étude, examen)* thorough

approprié, -ée [aprɔprije] *adj* appropriate (**à** for)

approprier [aprɔprije] **s'approprier** *vpr* **s'a. qch** to appropriate sth

approuver [apruve] *vt (facture, contrat)* to approve; *(décision, choix)* to approve of

approvisionner [aprɔvizjɔne] **1** *vt (ville, armée)* to supply (**en** with); *(magasin)* to stock (**en** with); *(compte bancaire)* to pay money into; **le compte n'est plus approvisionné** the account is no longer in credit **2 s'approvisionner** *vpr* to get supplies (**en** of) ▪ **approvisionnement** *nm* (*d'une ville, d'une armée*) supplying (**en** with); (*d'un magasin*) stocking (**en** with)

approximatif, -ive [aprɔksimatif, -iv] *adj* approximate ▪ **approximation** *nf* approximation ▪ **approximativement** *adv* approximately

appui [apɥi] *nm* support; **prendre a. sur qch** to lean on sth; **à l'a. de qch** in support of sth; **preuves à l'a.** with supporting evidence; **a. de fenêtre** window sill ▪ **appui-tête** (*pl* **appuis-tête**) *nm* headrest

appuyer [apɥije] **1** *vt* (*poser*) to lean, to rest; *Fig* (*candidat*) to support, to back; *Fig* (*proposition*) to second; **a. qch sur qch** (*poser*) to rest sth on sth; (*presser*) to press sth on sth **2** *vi* (*presser*) to press; **a. sur un bouton** to press a button; **a. sur la pédale de frein** to put one's foot on the brake, to apply the brake **3 s'appuyer** *vpr* **s'a. sur qch** to lean on sth, to rest on sth; *Fig* (*compter*) to rely on sth; *Fig* (*être basé sur*) to be based on sth; *Fam* **s'a. qch** (*corvée*) to be lumbered with ▪ **appuyé, -ée** *adj* (*plaisanterie*) *Br* laboured, *Am* labored; **lancer à qn des regards appuyés** to stare intently at sb

âpre [apr] *adj* sour; *Fig* (*concurrence, lutte*) fierce; **être â. au gain** to be money-grabbing ▪ **âpreté** [-əte] *nf* sourness; *Fig* (*concurrence, lutte*) fierceness

après [aprɛ] **1** *prép* (*dans le temps*) after; (*dans l'espace*) beyond; **a. un an** after a year; **a. le pont** beyond the bridge; **a. coup** after the event; **a. tout** after all; **a. quoi** after which; **a. avoir mangé** after eating; **a. qu'il t'a vu** after he saw you; **jour a. jour** day after day; **d'a.** (*selon*) according to **2** *adv* after(wards); **l'année d'a.** the following year; **et a.?** (*et ensuite*) and then what?; (*et alors*) so what? ▪ **après-demain** *adv* the day after tomorrow ▪ **après-guerre** *nm* post-war period; **d'a.** post-war ▪ **après-midi** *nm ou f inv* afternoon; **trois heures de l'a.** three o'clock in the afternoon ▪ **après-rasage** (*pl* **après-rasages**) *nm* aftershave ▪ **après-shampooing** *nm inv* conditioner ▪ **après-ski** (*pl* **après-skis**) *nm* snowboot ▪ **après-vente** *adj inv Com* **service a.** aftersales service

Il faut noter que le nom anglais **après-ski** est un faux ami. Il désigne les activités récréatives auxquelles on se livre après une séance de ski.

a priori [aprijɔri] *adv* in principle

à-propos [aprɔpo] *nm* aptness; **avoir l'esprit d'a.** to have presence of mind

apte [apt] *adj* **a. à qch/à faire qch** fit for sth/for doing sth; *Mil* **a. au service** fit for military service ▪ **aptitude** *nf* aptitude (**à** *ou* **pour** for);

avoir des aptitudes pour qch to have an aptitude for sth

aquagym [akwaʒim] *nf* aquarobics (*sing*)

aquarelle [akwarɛl] *nf Br* watercolour, *Am* watercolor

aquarium [akwarjɔm] *nm* aquarium

aquatique [akwatik] *adj* aquatic

aqueduc [akdyk] *nm* aqueduct

aquilin [akilɛ̃] *adj m* **nez a.** aquiline nose

arabe [arab] **1** *adj* (*peuple, monde, littérature*) Arab; (*langue*) Arabic; **chiffres arabes** Arabic numerals **2** *nmf* **A.** Arab **3** *nm* (*langue*) Arabic ▪ **Arabie** *nf* **l'A.** Arabia; **l'A. Saoudite** Saudi Arabia

arabesque [arabɛsk] *nf* arabesque

arable [arabl] *adj* arable

arachide [araʃid] *nf* peanut, groundnut

araignée [arɛɲe] *nf* spider

arbalète [arbalɛt] *nf* crossbow

arbitraire [arbitrɛr] *adj* arbitrary

arbitre [arbitr] *nm Football* referee; *Tennis* umpire; *Jur* arbitrator; (*maître absolu*) arbiter; *Phil* **libre a.** free will ▪ **arbitrage** *nm Football* refereeing; *Tennis* umpiring; *Jur* arbitration ▪ **arbitrer** *vt* (*match de football*) to referee; (*partie de tennis*) to umpire; (*litige*) to arbitrate

arborer [arbɔre] *vt* (*insigne, vêtement*) to sport

arbre [arbr] *nm* (*végétal*) tree; *Tech* shaft; **a. fruitier** fruit tree; **a. à cames** camshaft; **a. de transmission** transmission shaft ▪ **arbrisseau, -x** *nm* shrub ▪ **arbuste** *nm* shrub

arc [ark] *nm* (*arme*) bow; (*voûte*) arch; (*de cercle*) arc ▪ **arcade** *nf* archway; **arcades** (*de place*) arcade; **l'a. sourcilière** the arch of the eyebrows

arc-boutant [arkbutã] (*pl* **arcs-boutants**) *nm* flying buttress ▪ **s'arc-bouter** *vpr* **s'a. contre qch** to brace oneself against sth

arceau, -x [arso] *nm* (*de voûte*) arch

arc-en-ciel [arkãsjɛl] (*pl* **arcs-en-ciel**) *nm* rainbow

archaïque [arkaik] *adj* archaic

archange [arkãʒ] *nm* archangel

arche [arʃ] *nf* (*voûte*) arch; **l'a. de Noé** Noah's ark

archéologie [arkeɔlɔʒi] *nf* archaeology ▪ **archéologique** *adj* archaeological ▪ **archéologue** *nmf* archaeologist

archer [arʃe] *nm* archer

archet [arʃɛ] *nm* (*de violon*) bow

archétype [arketip] *nm* archetype

archevêque [arʃəvɛk] *nm* archbishop

archicomble [arʃikɔbl] *adj Fam* jam-packed, *Br* chock-a-block

archi-connu [arʃikɔny] *adj Fam* very well-known

archiduc [arʃidyk] *nm* archduke ▪ **archiduchesse** *nf* archduchess

archipel [arʃipɛl] *nm* archipelago

archiplein, -pleine [arʃiplɛ̃, -plɛn] *adj* jam-packed, *Br* chock-a-block

architecte [arʃitɛkt] *nm* architect ▪ **architecture** *nf* architecture

archives [arʃiv] *nfpl* archives, records ▪ **archiviste** *nmf* archivist

arctique [arktik] **1** *adj* arctic **2** *nm* l'A. the Arctic

ardent, -ente [ardɑ̃, -ɑ̃t] *adj (tempérament)* fiery; *(désir)* burning; *(soleil)* scorching ▪ **ardemment** [-amɑ̃] *adv* fervently; **désirer a. qch** to yearn for sth ▪ **ardeur** *nf (énergie) Br* fervour, *Am* fervor; *(du soleil)* intense heat

ardoise [ardwaz] *nf* slate

ardu, -ue [ardy] *adj* arduous

are [ar] *nm (mesure)* ≃ 100 square *Br* metres *or Am* meters

arène [arɛn] *nf (pour taureaux)* bullring; *(romaine)* arena; **arènes** bullring; *(romaines)* amphitheatre; *Fig* **a. politique** political arena

arête [arɛt] *nf (de poisson)* bone; *(de cube, dé)* edge; *(de montagne)* ridge

argent [arʒɑ̃] **1** *nm (métal)* silver; *(monnaie)* money; **a. liquide** cash; **a. de poche** pocket money **2** *adj (couleur)* silver ▪ **argenté, -ée** *adj (plaqué)* silver-plated; *(couleur)* silvery ▪ **argenterie** *nf* silverware

Argentine [arʒɑ̃tin] *nf* l'A. Argentina ▪ **argentin, -ine 1** *adj* Argentinian **2** *nmf* A., Argentine Argentinian

argile [arʒil] *nf* clay ▪ **argileux, -euse** *adj* clayey

argot [argo] *nm* slang ▪ **argotique** *adj (terme)* slang; *(texte)* full of slang

arguer [argɥe] *vi Littéraire* **a. de qch** to put forward sth as an argument ▪ **argumentation** *nf* arguments, argumentation ▪ **argumenter** *vi* to argue

argument [argymɑ̃] *nm* argument

Argus [argys] *nm* l'A. (de l'Automobile) = French car buyers' guide

aride [arid] *adj (terre)* arid, barren; *(sujet)* dry

aristocrate [aristɔkrat] *nmf* aristocrat ▪ **aristocratie** [-asi] *nf* aristocracy ▪ **aristocratique** *adj* aristocratic

arithmétique [aritmetik] **1** *adj* arithmetical **2** *nf* arithmetic

arlequin [arləkɛ̃] *nm* Harlequin

armateur [armatœr] *nm* shipowner

armature [armatyr] *nf (charpente)* framework; *(de lunettes, de tente)* frame

arme [arm] *nf* weapon; **prendre les armes** to take up arms; *Fig* **à armes égales** on equal terms; *Fig* **faire ses premières armes** to earn one's spurs; **a. à feu** firearm; **a. biologique** biological weapon; **a. blanche** knife; **armes de destruction massive** weapons of mass destruction; **a. nucléaire** nuclear weapon ▪ **armes** *nfpl (blason)* (coat of) arms

armée [arme] *nf* army; **être dans l'armée** to be

in the army; **être à l'a.** to be doing one's military service; **a. de l'air** air force; **a. de terre** army; **a. active/de métier** regular/professional army

armer [arme] **1** *vt (personne)* to arm (**de** with); *(fusil)* to cock; *(appareil photo)* to set; *(navire)* to commission **2** **s'armer** *upr* to arm oneself (**de** with); **s'a. de patience** to summon up one's patience ▪ **armements** [-amɑ̃] *nmpl (armes)* armaments

armistice [armistis] *nm* armistice

armoire [armwar] *nf (penderie) Br* wardrobe, *Am* closet; **a. à pharmacie** medicine cabinet

armoiries [armwari] *nfpl (coat of)* arms

armure [armyr] *nf Br* armour, *Am* armor

armurier [armyrje] *nm (vendeur)* gun dealer

arnaque [arnak] *nf Fam* rip-off ▪ **arnaquer** *vt Fam* to rip off; **se faire a.** to get ripped off

aromathérapie [arɔmaterapi] *nf* aromatherapy

arôme [arom] *nm (goût) Br* flavour, *Am* flavor; *(odeur)* aroma ▪ **aromate** *nm (herbe)* herbe; *(épice)* spice ▪ **aromatique** *adj* aromatic

arpenter [arpɑ̃te] *vt (mesurer)* to survey; *(parcourir)* to pace up and down ▪ **arpenteur** *nm (land)* surveyor

arqué, -ée [arke] *adj (sourcil)* arched; *(nez)* hooked; **jambes arquées** bow legs

arraché [araʃe] *nm* **gagner à l'a.** to snatch victory

arrache-pied [araʃpje] **d'arrache-pied** *adv* relentlessly

arracher [araʃe] *vt (plante, arbre)* to uproot; *(pommes de terre)* to lift; *(clou, dent, mauvaise herbe)* to pull out; *(page)* to tear out; *(vêtement, masque)* to tear off; **a. qch à qn** *(objet, enfant)* to snatch sth from sb; *(aveu, argent, promesse)* to force sth out of sb; **a. un bras à qn** *(obus)* to blow sb's arm off; **a. qn de son lit** to drag sb out of bed; **se faire a. une dent** to have a tooth out ▪ **arrachage** *nm (de plantes)* uprooting; *(de pommes de terre)* lifting; *(de clou, de dent)* pulling up

arranger [arɑ̃ʒe] **1** *vt (meuble, fleurs)* to arrange; *(maison)* to put in order; *(col)* to straighten; *(réparer)* to repair; *(organiser)* to arrange, to organize; *(différend)* to settle; *Fam* **a. qn** *(maltraiter)* to give sb a going over; **je vais a. ça** I'll fix that; **ça m'arrange** that suits me (fine) **2** **s'arranger** *upr (se mettre d'accord)* to come to an agreement; *(finir bien)* to turn out fine; *(s'organiser)* to manage; **arrangez-vous pour être là** make sure you're there ▪ **arrangeant, -ante** *adj* accommodating ▪ **arrangement** *nm (disposition) & Mus* arrangement; *(accord)* agreement

arrestation [arɛstɑsjɔ̃] *nf* arrest

arrêt [arɛ] *nm (halte, endroit)* stop; *(action)* stopping; *Jur* judgement; **temps d'a.** pause; **à l'a.** stationary; **sans a.** continuously; **a. du cœur** cardiac arrest; *Sport* **a. de jeu** stoppage;

a. de mort death sentence; **a. de travail** *(grève)* stoppage; *(congé)* sick leave ▪ **arrêt-maladie** *nm* sick leave

arrêté¹ [arete] *nm (décret)* order, decree

arrêté², -ée [arete] *adj (idées, projet)* fixed; *(volonté)* firm

arrêter [arete] **1** *vt (personne, animal, véhicule)* to stop; *(criminel)* to arrest; *(moteur)* to turn off; *(date)* to fix; *(études)* to give up **2** *vi* to stop; **a. de faire qch** to stop doing sth; **il n'arrête pas de critiquer** he's always criticizing **3 s'arrêter** *vpr* to stop; **s'a. de faire qch** to stop doing sth

arrhes [ar] *nfpl (acompte)* deposit

arrière [arjɛr] **1** *nm (de maison)* back, rear; *(de bâteau)* stern; *Football* full back; **à l'a.** in/at the back **2** *adj inv (siège)* back, rear; **feu a.** rear light **3** *adv* **en a.** *(marcher, tomber)* backwards; *(rester)* behind; *(regarder)* back, behind; **en a. de qn/qch** behind sb/sth ▪ **arrière-boutique** *(pl* **arrière-boutiques)** *nm* back room ▪ **arrière-garde** *(pl* **arrière-gardes)** *nf* rearguard ▪ **arrière-goût** *(pl* **arrière-goûts)** *nm* aftertaste ▪ **arrière-grand-mère** *(pl* **arrière-grands-mères)** *nf* great-grandmother ▪ **arrière-grand-père** *(pl* **arrière-grands-pères)** *nm* great-grandfather ▪ **arrière-pays** *nm inv* hinterland ▪ **arrière-pensée** *(pl* **arrière-pensées)** *nf* ulterior motive ▪ **arrière-plan** *nm* background; **à l'a.** in the background ▪ **arrière-saison** *(pl* **arrière-saisons)** *nf Br* late autumn, *Am* late fall ▪ **arrière-train** *(pl* **arrière-trains)** *nm (d'animal)* hindquarters; *Fam (de personne)* rump

arriéré, -ée [arjere] **1** *adj (dans ses idées, dans son développement)* backward; *(impayé) (loyer)* in arrears; *(dette)* outstanding **2** *nm (dette)* arrears ▪ **arriérer** *vt (paiement)* to defer

arrimer [arime] *vt (fixer)* to rope down; *Naut* to stow

arriver [arive] **1** *(aux être) vi (venir)* to arrive; **a. à** *(lieu)* to reach; *(résultat)* to achieve; **l'eau m'arrive aux chevilles** the water comes up to my ankles; **a. à faire qch** to manage to do sth; **en a. à faire qch** to get to the point of doing sth **2** *v impersonnel (survenir)* to happen; **a. à qn** happen to sb; **il m'arrive d'oublier** I sometimes forget; **qu'est-ce qu'il t'arrive?** what's wrong with you? ▪ **arrivage** *nm* consignment ▪ **arrivant, -ante** *nmf* new arrival ▪ **arrivée** *nf* arrival; *(ligne, poteau)* winning post ▪ **arriviste** *nmf Péj* social climber

arrobas [arɔbas], **arrobase** [arɔbaz] *nf Ordinat (dans une adresse électronique)* at (sign)

arrogant, -ante [arɔgɑ̃, -ɑ̃t] *adj* arrogant ▪ **arrogance** *nf* arrogance

arroger [arɔʒe] **s'arroger** *vpr (droit)* to claim

arrondir [arɔ̃dir] *vt (somme, chiffre, angle, jupe)* to round off; **a. qch** to make sth round; **a. à l'euro supérieur/inférieur** to round up/down

to the nearest euro; *Fam* **a. ses fins de mois** to supplement one's income ▪ **arrondi, -ie** *adj* round

arrondissement [arɔ̃dismɑ̃] *nm* = administrative subdivision of Paris, Lyons and Marseilles

arroser [aroze] *vt (terre, plante)* to water; *(pelouse)* to sprinkle; *(repas)* to wash down; *(succès)* to drink to ▪ **arrosage** *nm (de terre, de plante)* watering; *(de pelouse)* sprinkling ▪ **arrosoir** *nm* watering can

arsenal, -aux [arsənal, -o] *nm Mil* arsenal; *Fam (panoplie)* gear

arsenic [arsənik] *nm* arsenic

art [ar] *nm* art; **film/critique d'a.** art film/critic; **arts martiaux** martial arts; **arts ménagers** home economics; **arts plastiques** fine arts; **arts du spectacle** performing arts

Arte [arte] *n* = French-German TV channel showing cultural programmes

artère [artɛr] *nf (veine)* artery; *(rue)* main road

artichaut [artiʃo] *nm* artichoke; **fond d'a.** artichoke heart

article [artikl] *nm (de presse, de contrat, de traité) & Grammaire* article; *Com* item; **à l'a. de la mort** at death's door; **a. de fond** feature (article); **articles de toilette** toiletries; **articles de voyage** travel goods

articuler [artikyle] **1** *vt (mot)* to articulate **2 s'articuler** *vpr (membre)* to articulate; *(idées)* to connect; **s'a. autour de qch** *(théorie)* to centre on ▪ **articulation** *nf (de membre)* joint; *(prononciation)* articulation

artifice [artifis] *nm* trick

artificiel, -ielle [artifisjɛl] *adj* artificial ▪ **artificiellement** *adv* artificially

artillerie [artijri] *nf* artillery ▪ **artilleur** *nm* artilleryman

artisan [artizɑ̃] *nm* craftsman, artisan ▪ **artisanal, -e, -aux, -ales** *adj* métier a. craft; **objet a.** object made by craftsmen; **bombe artisanale** homemade bomb ▪ **artisanat** *nm* craft industry

artiste [artist] *nmf* artist; *(acteur, musicien)* performer ▪ **artistique** *adj* artistic

as [as] *nm (carte, champion)* ace; **a. du volant/de la mécanique** crack driver/mechanic; *Fam* **être plein aux as** to be loaded

ascendant [asɑ̃dɑ̃] **1** *adj* ascending; *(mouvement)* upward **2** *nm (influence)* influence; **ascendants** ancestors ▪ **ascendance** *nf (ancêtres)* ancestry

ascenseur [asɑ̃sœr] *nm Br* lift, *Am* elevator

ascension [asɑ̃sjɔ̃] *nf (escalade)* ascent; *Rel* **l'A.** Ascension Day

ascète [asɛt] *nmf* ascetic ▪ **ascétique** *adj* ascetic

Asie [azi] *nf* **l'A.** Asia ▪ **asiatique 1** *adj* Asian **2** *nmf* **A.** Asian

asile [azil] *nm (abri)* refuge, shelter; *(pour*

vieillards) home; *Péj* **a. (d'aliénés)** (lunatic) asylum; **a. politique** (political) asylum; **a. de paix** haven of peace

aspect [aspɛ] *nm (air)* appearance; *(angle)* point of view; *(perspective)* & *Grammaire* aspect

asperger [aspɛrʒe] **1** *vt (par jeu ou accident)* to splash (**de** with); *(pour humecter)* to spray (**de** with); **se faire a.** to get splashed **2 s'asperger** *upr* **s'a. de parfum** to splash oneself with perfume

asperges [aspɛrʒ] *nfpl* asparagus

aspérité [asperite] *nf (de surface)* rough part

asphalte [asfalt] *nm* asphalt

asphyxie [asfiksi] *nf* asphyxiation ▪ **asphyxier 1** *vt* to asphyxiate **2 s'asphyxier** *upr* to suffocate; *(volontairement)* to suffocate oneself

aspirant [aspirã] *nm (candidat)* candidate

aspirateur [aspiratœr] *nm* vacuum cleaner, *Br* Hoover®; **passer l'a. dans la maison** to vacuum or *Br* hoover the house

aspirer [aspire] **1** *vt (liquide)* to suck up; *(air, parfum)* to breathe in, to inhale **2** *vi* **a. à qch** *(bonheur, gloire)* to aspire to sth ▪ **aspiration** *nf (inhalation)* inhalation; *(ambition)* aspiration (**à** for) ▪ **aspiré, -ée** *adj (son, lettre)* aspirate(d)

aspirine [aspirin] *nf* aspirin

assagir [asaʒir] **s'assagir** *upr* to settle down

assaillir [asajir] *vt* to attack; **a. qn de questions** to bombard sb with questions ▪ **assaillant** *nm* attacker, assailant

assainir [asenir] *vt (purifier)* to clean up; *(marché, économie)* to stabilize

assaisonner [asezɔne] *vt* to season ▪ **assaisonnement** *nm* seasoning

assassin [asasɛ̃] *nm* murderer; *(de politicien)* assassin ▪ **assassinat** *nm* murder; *(de politicien)* assassination ▪ **assassiner** *vt* to murder; *(politicien)* to assassinate

assaut [aso] *nm* attack, assault; *Mil* charge; **donner l'a. à** to storm; **prendre qch d'a.** *Mil* to take sth by storm; *Fig (buffet)* to make a run for sth

assécher [aseʃe] **1** *vt* to drain **2 s'assécher** *upr* to dry up

assemblée [asãble] *nf (personnes réunies)* gathering; *(réunion)* meeting; **a. générale** *(de compagnie)* annual general meeting; **l'A. nationale** *Br* ≃ the House of Commons, *Am* ≃ the House of Representatives

assembler [asãble] **1** *vt* to put together, to assemble **2 s'assembler** *upr* to gather ▪ **assemblage** *nm (montage)* assembly; *(réunion d'objets)* collection

asséner [asene] *vt* **a. un coup à qn** to deliver a blow to sb

assentiment [asãtimã] *nm* assent

asseoir* [aswar] **1** *vt (personne)* to seat (**sur** on); *Fig (autorité, réputation)* to establish **2** *vi* **faire a. qn** to ask sb to sit down **3 s'asseoir** *upr* to sit (down)

assermenté, -ée [asɛrmãte] *adj* sworn; *(témoin)* under oath

assertion [asɛrsjɔ̃] *nf* assertion

asservir [asɛrvir] *vt* to enslave

assez [ase] *adv* (**a**) *(suffisamment)* enough; **a. de pain/de gens** enough bread/people; **j'en ai a.** I've had enough (**de** of); **a. grand/intelligent** big/clever enough (**pour faire** to do) (**b**) *(plutôt)* quite, rather

assidu, -ue [asidy] *adj (toujours présent)* regular; *(appliqué)* diligent; **a. auprès de qn** attentive to sb ▪ **assiduité** *nf (d'élève)* regularity; **poursuivre qn de ses assiduités** to force one's attention on sb ▪ **assidûment** *adv (régulièrement)* regularly; *(avec application)* diligently

assiéger [asjeʒe] *vt (ville, magasin, guichet)* to besiege; *(personne)* to pester

assiette [asjɛt] *nf* (**a**) *(récipient)* plate; *Culin* **a. anglaise** *Br* (assorted) cold meats, *Am* cold cuts (**b**) *(à cheval)* seat; *Fam* **il n'est pas dans son a.** he's feeling out of sorts ▪ **assiettée** *nf* plateful

assigner [asiɲe] *vt (attribuer)* to assign (**à** to); *(en justice)* to summon; **a. qn à résidence** to place sb under house arrest ▪ **assignation** *nf* *Jur* summons

assimiler [asimile] **1** *vt (aliments, connaissances, immigrés)* to assimilate **2 s'assimiler** *upr (immigré)* to assimilate ▪ **assimilation** *nf* assimilation

assis, -ise¹ [asi, -iz] *(pp de asseoir) adj* sitting (down), seated; *(situation)* secure; **rester a.** to remain seated; **place assise** seat

assise² [asiz] *nf (base)* foundation; **assises** *(d'un parti)* congress; *Jur* **les assises** Assize Court, *Br* ≃ crown court, *Am* ≃ circuit court

assistance [asistãs] *nf* (**a**) *(public)* audience (**b**) *(aide)* assistance; **être à l'A. publique** *(enfant)* to be in care

assister [asiste] **1** *vt (aider)* to assist **2** *vi* **a. à** *(réunion, cours)* to attend; *(accident)* to witness ▪ **assistant, -ante** *nmf* assistant; **a. personnel** personal assistant; **a. social** social worker; **a. maternel** *Br* child minder, *Am* baby-sitter ▪ **assisté, -ée** *adj* **a. par ordinateur** computer-assisted, computer-aided

> Il faut noter que le verbe anglais **to assist** est un faux ami. Il n'a jamais le sens de **être présent** (à un événement).

association [asɔsjasjɔ̃] *nf* association; *Com* partnership; **a. de parents d'élèves** parent-teacher association; **a. sportive** sports club

associer [asɔsje] **1** *vt* to associate (**à** with); **a. qn à** *(travaux, affaire)* to involve sb in; *(profits)* to give sb a share in **2 s'associer** *upr* to join forces (**à** *ou* **avec** with); *Com* **s'a. avec qn** to enter into partnership with sb; **s'a. à un projet**

to join in a project; **s'a. à la peine de qn** to share sb's grief ▪ **associé, -ée 1** *nmf* partner, associate **2** *adj* **membre a.** associate member

assoiffé, -ée [aswafe] *adj* thirsty (**de** for)

assombrir [asɔ̃brir] **1** *vt (obscurcir)* to darken; *(attrister)* to cast a shadow over **2 s'assombrir** *vpr (ciel, visage)* to cloud over; *(personne)* to become gloomy

assommer [asɔme] *vt* **a. qn** to knock sb unconscious; *Fig (ennuyer)* to bore sb to death ▪ **assommant, -ante** *adj* deadly boring

Assomption [asɔ̃psjɔ̃] *nf Rel* **l'A.** the Assumption

assortir [asɔrtir] *vt (harmoniser)* to match; *Com (magasin)* to stock ▪ **assorti, -ie** *adj (objet semblable)* matching; *(bonbons)* assorted; **époux bien assortis** well-matched couple; **bien a.** *(magasin)* well-stocked; **a. de** accompanied by ▪ **assortiment** *nm* assortment

assoupir [asupir] **s'assoupir** *vpr* to doze off

assouplir [asuplir] **1** *vt(cuir, chaussure, muscles)* to make supple; *Fig (réglementation)* to relax **2 s'assouplir** *vpr (personne, chaussure, cuir)* to get supple ▪ **assouplissement** *nm* **exercices d'a.** stretching exercises

assourdir [asurdir] *vt (personne)* to deafen; *(son)* to muffle ▪ **assourdissant, -ante** *adj* deafening

assouvir [asuvir] *vt* to satisfy

assujettir [asyʒetir] *vt (soumettre)* to subject (**à** to); *(peuple)* to subjugate; *(objet)* to fix (**à** to); **être assujetti à l'impôt** to be liable for tax

assumer [asyme] **1** *vt(tâche, rôle, responsabilité)* to assume, to take on; *(risque, conséquences)* to take **2** *vi Fam* **tu vas devoir a.** you'll have to live with it **3 s'assumer** *vpr* to come to terms with oneself

---

Il faut noter que le verbe anglais **to assume** est un faux ami. Il signifie le plus souvent **supposer**.

---

assurance [asyrɑ̃s] *nf (confiance)* (self-)assurance; *(promesse)* assurance; *(contrat)* insurance; **prendre une a.** to take out insurance; **a. au tiers/tous risques** third-party/comprehensive insurance; **a. maladie/vie** health/life insurance

assurer [asyre] **1** *vt (garantir) Br* to ensure, *Am* to insure; *(par un contrat)* to insure; *(fixer)* to secure; **a. qn de qch, a. qch à qn** to assure sb of sth; **a. à qn que...** to assure sb that...; **a. les fonctions de directeur** to be manager; **un service régulier est assuré** there is a regular service **2 s'assurer** *vpr (par un contrat)* to insure oneself; *s'a.* **l'aide de qn** to secure sb's help; **s'a. de qch/que...** to make sure of sth/ that... ▪ **assuré, -ée 1** *adj (succès)* guaranteed; *(pas, voix)* firm; *(air, personne)* confident **2** *nmf* policyholder ▪ **assurément** *adv* certainly ▪ **assureur** *nm* insurer

astérisque [asterisk] *nm* asterisk

asthme [asm] *nm* asthma; **crise d'a.** asthma attack ▪ **asthmatique** *adj & nmf* asthmatic

asticot [astiko] *nm Br* maggot, *Am* worm

asticoter [astikɔte] *vt Fam* to bug

astiquer [astike] *vt* to polish

astre [astr] *nm* star

astreindre* [astrɛ̃dr] **1** *vt* **a. qn à faire qch** to compel sb to do sth **2 s'astreindre** *vpr* **s'a. à un régime sévère** to stick to a strict diet; **s'a. à faire qch** to force oneself to do sth ▪ **astreignant, -ante** *adj* exacting ▪ **astreinte** *nf* constraint

astrologie [astrɔlɔʒi] *nf* astrology ▪ **astrologique** *adj* astrological ▪ **astrologue** *nm* astrologer

astronaute [astrɔnot] *nmf* astronaut ▪ **astronautique** *nf* space travel

astronomie [astrɔnɔmi] *nf* astronomy ▪ **astronome** *nm* astronomer ▪ **astronomique** *adj* astronomical

astuce [astys] *nf (truc)* trick; *(plaisanterie)* witticism; *(jeu de mots)* pun; *(finesse)* astuteness; **il y a une a.** there's a trick to it; **je ne saisis pas l'a.** I don't get it ▪ **astucieux, -ieuse** *adj* clever

atelier [atəlje] *nm (d'ouvrier)* workshop; *(de peintre)* studio; *(personnel)* workshop staff; *(groupe de travail)* work-group; **a. de carrosserie** bodyshop; **a. de montage** assembly shop; **a. de réparation** repair shop

atermoyer [atermwaje] *vi* to procrastinate

athée [ate] **1** *adj* atheistic **2** *nmf* atheist ▪ **athéisme** *nm* atheism

athénée [atene] *nm Belg Br* secondary school, *Am* high school

Athènes [atɛn] *nm ou f* Athens

athlète [atlɛt] *nmf* athlete ▪ **athlétique** *adj* athletic ▪ **athlétisme** *nm* athletics *(sing)*

atlantique [atlɑ̃tik] **1** *adj* Atlantic **2** *nm* **l'A.** the Atlantic

atlas [atlɑs] *nm* atlas

atmosphère [atmɔsfɛr] *nf* atmosphere ▪ **atmosphérique** *adj* atmospheric

atome [atom] *nm* atom; *Fig* **avoir des atomes crochus avec qn** to hit it off with sb ▪ **atomique** [atɔmik] *adj* atomic

atomiser [atɔmize] *vt (liquide)* to spray ▪ **atomiseur** *nm* spray

atone [atɔn] *adj (inerte)* lifeless; *(regard)* vacant

atours [atur] *nmpl Littéraire* finery; **paré de ses plus beaux a.** in all her finery

atout [atu] *nm* trump; *Fig (avantage)* asset; **a. cœur** hearts are trumps; *Fig* **avoir tous les atouts dans son jeu** to hold all the winning cards

âtre [ɑtr] *nm (foyer)* hearth

atroce [atrɔs] *adj* atrocious; *(douleur)* excruciating; *(rêve)* dreadful ▪ **atrocité** *nf (cruauté)* atrociousness; **les atrocités de la guerre** wartime atrocities

atrophie [atrɔfi] *nf* atrophy ▪**atrophié, -iée** *adj* atrophied

attabler [atable] **s'attabler** *vpr* to sit down at a/the table ▪**attablé, -ée** *adj* (seated) at the table

attache [ataʃ] *nf (lien)* fastener; **attaches** *(amis)* links; **être sans attaches** to be unattached; **je n'avais plus aucune a. dans cette ville** there was nothing to keep me in this town

attaché-case [ataʃekɛz] *(pl* attachés-cases) *nm* attaché case

attachement [ataʃmɑ̃] *nm (affection)* attachment **(à** to)

attacher [ataʃe] **1** *vt* **a. qch à qch** to fasten sth to sth; *(avec de la ficelle)* to tie sth to sth; *(avec une chaîne)* to chain sth to sth; **a. ses lacets** to do one's shoelaces up; **a. de l'importance/de la valeur à qch** to attach great importance/value to sth **2** *vi (en cuisant)* to stick to the pan **3 s'attacher** *vpr (se fixer)* to be fastened; **s'a. à une tâche** to apply oneself to a task; **s'a. à qn** to get attached to sb; **je ne veux pas m'a.** *(sentimentalement)* I don't want to commit myself ▪**attachant, -ante** *adj* engaging ▪**attaché, -ée 1** *adj (fixé)* fastened; *(chien)* chained up; **être a. à qn** to be attached to sb; **les avantages attachés à une fonction** the benefits attached to a post **2** *nmf* attaché; **a. culturel/militaire** cultural/military attaché; **a. de presse** press officer

attaque [atak] *nf* attack; **passer à l'a.** to go on the offensive; *Fam* **d'a.** on top form; **a. aérienne** air raid; **a. à main armée** armed robbery

attaquer [atake] **1** *vt (physiquement, verbalement)* to attack; *(difficulté, sujet)* to tackle; *(morceau de musique)* to strike up; *Jur* **a. qn en justice** to bring an action against sb **2** *vi* to attack **3 s'attaquer** *vpr* **s'a. à** *(adversaire)* to attack; *(problème)* to tackle ▪**attaquant, -ante** *nmf* attacker

attarder [atarde] **s'attarder** *vpr* to linger; **s'a. à des détails** to dwell over details; **ne nous attardons pas sur ce point** let's not dwell on that point ▪**attardé, -ée** *adj (enfant)* mentally retarded; **il ne restait plus que quelques passants attardés** there were only a few people still about

atteindre* [atɛ̃dr] **1** *vt (parvenir à)* to reach; *(cible)* to hit; *(idéal)* to achieve; **être atteint d'une maladie** to be suffering from a disease; **le poumon est atteint** the lung is affected; *Fig* **rien ne l'atteint** nothing affects him/her; *Fam* **il est très atteint** *(fou)* he's completely bonkers **2** *vi* **a. à la perfection** to be close to perfection

atteinte [atɛ̃t] *nf* attack (à on); **porter a. à** to undermine; **hors d'a.** *(objet, personne)* out of reach

atteler [atle] **1** *vt (bêtes)* to harness; **a. une voiture** to hitch up horses to a carriage **2 s'atteler** *vpr* **s'a. à une tâche** to apply oneself to a task ▪**attelage** *nm (bêtes)* team

attelle [atɛl] *nf* splint

attenant, -ante [atnɑ̃, -ɑ̃t] *adj* **a. (à)** adjoining

attendre [atɑ̃dr] **1** *vt (personne, train)* to wait for, **a. son tour** to wait one's turn; **elle attend un bébé** she's expecting a baby; **le bonheur qui nous attend** the happiness that awaits us; **a. que qn fasse qch** to wait for sb to do sth; **a. qch de qn** to expect sth from sb; **se faire a.** *(personne)* to keep people waiting; *(réponse, personne)* to be a long time coming **2** *vi* to wait; **faire a. qn** to keep sb waiting; *Fam* **attends voir!** let me see!; **en attendant** meanwhile; **en attendant que...** (+ subjunctive) until... **3 s'attendre** *vpr* **s'a. à qch/à faire qch** to expect sth/to do sth; **s'a. à ce que qn fasse qch** to expect sb to do sth; **je m'y attendais** I expected as much; **il fallait s'y a.** it was only to be expected ▪**attendu, -ue 1** *adj (prévu)* expected; *(avec joie)* eagerly-awaited **2** *prép Formel* considering; **a. que...** considering that...

attendrir [atɑ̃drir] **1** *vt (émouvoir)* to move; *(viande)* to tenderize **2 s'attendrir** *vpr* to be moved **(sur** by) ▪**attendri, -ie** *adj* compassionate ▪**attendrissant, -ante** *adj* moving

attentat [atɑ̃ta] *nm* attack; **a. à la bombe** bombing; *Jur* **a. à la pudeur** indecent assault ▪**attenter** *vi* **a. à** to make an attempt on; **a. à ses jours** to attempt suicide

attente [atɑ̃t] *nf (fait d'attendre)* waiting; *(période)* wait; **une a. prolongée** a long wait; **en a.** *(au téléphone)* on hold; **être dans l'a. de** to be waiting for; **dans l'a. de vous rencontrer** *(dans une lettre)* I look forward to meeting you; **contre toute a.** against all expectations; **répondre aux attentes de qn** to live up to sb's expectations

attentif, -ive [atɑ̃tif, -iv] *adj* attentive; **a. à qch** to pay attention to sth; **écouter d'une oreille attentive** to listen attentively ▪**attentivement** *adv* attentively

attention [atɑ̃sjɔ̃] *nf (soin, amabilité)* attention; **faire a. à qch** to pay attention to sth; **faire a. à sa santé** to look after one's health; **faire a. (à ce) que...** (+ subjunctive) to be careful that...; **a.!** watch out!; **a. à la voiture!** watch out for the car!; **à l'a. de qn** *(sur lettre)* for the attention of sb; **être plein d'attentions envers qn** to be very attentive towards sb ▪**attentionné, -ée** *adj* considerate

atténuer [atenɥe] **1** *vt (effet, douleur)* to reduce; *(lumière)* to dim **2 s'atténuer** *vpr (douleur)* to ease; *(lumière)* to fade

atterrer [atere] *vt* to appal

atterrir [aterir] *vi* to land; **a. en catastrophe** to make an emergency landing; *Fam* **a. dans un**

bar to land up in a bar ▪**atterrissage** *nm* landing; **a. forcé** forced landing

attester [ateste] *vt* to testify to; **a. que...** to testify that... ▪**attestation** *nf (document)* certificate

attifer [atife] *vt Fam* to dress (**de** in)

attirail [atiraj] *nm* equipment; *Fam Péj* gear

attirance [atirɑ̃s] *nf* attraction (**pour** for)

attirer [atire] **1** *vt (sujet: aimant, planète, personne)* to attract; *(sujet: matière, pays)* to appeal to; **a. l'attention de qn** to catch sb's attention; **a. l'attention de qn sur qch** to draw sb's attention to sth; **a. les regards** to catch the eye; **a. des ennuis à qn** to cause trouble for sb; **a. qn dans un coin** to take sb into a corner; **a. qn dans un piège** to lure sb into a trap **2 s'attirer** *upr (mutuellement)* to be attracted to each other; **s'a. des ennuis** to get oneself into trouble; **s'a. la colère de qn** to incur sb's anger ▪**attirant, -ante** *adj* attractive

attiser [atize] *vt (feu)* to poke; *Fig (désir, colère)* to stir up

attitré, -ée [atitre] *adj (représentant)* appointed; *(marchand)* regular

attitude [atityd] *nf (conduite, position)* attitude; *(affectation)* pose

attraction [atraksjɔ̃] *nf (force, centre d'intérêt)* attraction

attrait [atrɛ] *nm* attraction

attrape [atrap] *nf (farce)* trick ▪**attrape-nigaud** *(pl* attrape-nigauds*) nm (ruse)* trick

attraper [atrape] **1** *vt (ballon, maladie, voleur, train)* to catch; **a. froid** to catch cold; **se faire a.** to be caught; *Fam (gronder)* to get a good talking to; **se laisser a.** *(duper)* to get taken in **2 s'attraper** *upr (maladie)* to be caught

attrayant, -ante [atrɛjɑ̃, -ɑ̃t] *adj* attractive

attribuer [atribɥe] **1** *vt (allouer)* to assign (**à** to); *(prix, bourse)* to award (**à** to); *(œuvre, crime)* to attribute (**à** to); **a. de l'importance à qch** to attach importance to sth **2 s'attribuer** *upr* to claim ▪**attribuable** *adj* attributable (**à** to) ▪**attribution** *nf (allocation)* assigning (à to); *(de prix)* awarding (**à** to); *(d'une œuvre, d'un crime)* attribution (**à** to); **attributions** *(fonctions)* duties; **entrer dans les attributions de qn** to be part of sb's duties

attribut [atriby] *nm (adjectif)* predicate adjective; *(caractéristique)* attribute

attrister [atriste] *vt* to sadden

attrouper [atrupe] *vt,* **s'attrouper** *upr* to gather ▪**attroupement** *nm (de manifestants etc)* crowd

au [o] *voir* **à**

aubaine [obɛn] *nf (bonne)* **a.** godsend

aube [ob] *nf* dawn; **dès l'a.** at the crack of dawn

aubépine [obepin] *nf* hawthorn

auberge [obɛrʒ] *nf* inn; *Fam* **on n'est pas sorti de l'a.** we're not out of the woods yet; **a. de** jeunesse youth hostel ▪**aubergiste** *nmf* innkeeper

aubergine [obɛrʒin] *nf Br* aubergine, *Am* eggplant

aucun, -une [okœ̃, -yn] **1** *adj* no, not any; **il n'a a. talent** he has no talent; **a. professeur n'est venu** no teacher came **2** *pron* none; **il n'en a a.** he has none (at all); **a. d'entre nous** none of us; **a. des deux** neither of the two; *Littéraire* **d'aucuns** some (people) ▪**aucunement** *adv* not at all

audace [odas] *nf (courage)* daring, boldness; *(impudence)* audacity; **audaces** *(de style)* daring innovations; **avoir toutes les audaces** to do the most daring things ▪**audacieux, -ieuse** *adj (courageux)* daring, bold

au-dedans [odədɑ̃] *adv* inside

au-dehors [odəɔr] *adv* outside

au-delà [odəla] **1** *adv* beyond; **100 euros mais pas a.** 100 euros but no more **2** *prép* **a. de** beyond **3** *nm* **l'a.** the next world

au-dessous [odəsu] **1** *adv (à l'étage inférieur)* downstairs; *(moins, dessous)* below, under **2** *prép* **a. de** *(dans l'espace)* below, under, beneath; *(âge, prix)* under; *(température)* below; *Fig* **être a. de tout** to be beneath contempt

au-dessus [odəsy] **1** *adv* above; *(à l'étage supérieur)* upstairs **2** *prép* **a. de** above; *(âge, température, prix)* over; *(posé sur)* on top of; **vivre a. de ses moyens** to live beyond one's means

au-devant [odəvɑ̃] *prép* **aller a. de** *(personne)* to go to meet; *(danger)* to court; *(désirs de qn)* to anticipate

audible [odibl] *adj* audible

audience [odjɑ̃s] *nf (entretien)* audience; *(de tribunal)* hearing; *Jur* **l'a. est suspendue** the case is adjourned

audio [odjo] *adj inv (cassette)* audio ▪**audiophone** *nm* hearing aid ▪**audiovisuel, -elle 1** *adj (méthodes)* audiovisual; *(de la radio, de la télévision)* radio and television **2** *nm* **l'a.** radio and television

auditeur, -trice [oditœr, -tris] *nmf (de radio)* listener; *Univ* **a. libre** auditor *(student allowed to attend classes but not to sit examinations)*

audition [odisjɔ̃] *nf (ouïe)* hearing; *(d'acteurs)* audition; **passer une a.** to have an audition; *Jur* **a. des témoins** examination of the witnesses ▪**auditionner** *vti* to audition ▪**auditoire** *nm* audience ▪**auditorium** *nm* concert hall; *(studio)* recording studio

auge [oʒ] *nf (feeding)* trough

augmenter [ɔgmɑ̃te] **1** *vt* to increase (**de** by); **a. qn** to give sb a *Br* rise *or Am* raise **2** *vi* to increase (**de** by); *(prix, population)* to rise ▪**augmentation** *nf* increase (**de** in/of); **a. de salaire** *Br* (pay) rise, *Am* raise; **être en a.** to be on the increase

augure [ɔgyr] *nm (présage)* omen; *(devin)* augur; **être de bon/mauvais a.** to be a good/bad omen • **augurer** *vt* **a. bien/mal de qch** to augur well/ill for sth

aujourd'hui [oʒurdɥi] *adv* today; *(de nos jours)* nowadays, today; **a. en quinze** two weeks from today; **jusqu'à a.** to this very day; **les problèmes d'a.** today's problems

aumône [omon] *nf* alms; **faire l'a. à qn** to give alms to sb

aumônier [omonje] *nm* chaplain

auparavant [oparavã] *adv (avant)* before (-hand); *(d'abord)* first

auprès [oprɛ] **auprès de** *prép (assis, situé)* by, next to; *(en comparaison de)* compared to; **se renseigner a. de qn** to ask sb; **ambassadeur a. des Nations unies** ambassador to the United Nations

auquel [okɛl] *voir* **lequel**

aura, aurait [ora, orɛ] *voir* **avoir**

auréole [ɔreɔl] *nf (de saint)* halo; *(tache)* ring

auriculaire [ɔrikylɛr] *nm* little finger

aurore [ɔrɔr] *nf* dawn, daybreak; **à l'a.** at dawn; *Fam* **aux aurores** at the crack of dawn

ausculter [ɔskylte] *vt (malade, cœur)* to listen to

auspices [ɔspis] *nmpl* **sous les a. de** under the auspices of

aussi [osi] **1** *adv* (**a**) *(comparaison)* as; **a. lourd que...** as heavy as... (**b**) *(également)* too, as well; **moi a.** so do/can/am I; **a. bien que...** as well as... (**c**) *(tellement)* so; **un repas a. délicieux** such a delicious meal (**d**) *(quelque)* **a. bizarre que cela paraisse** however odd this may seem **2** *conj (donc)* therefore

aussitôt [osito] *adv* immediately, straight away; **a. que...** as soon as...; **a. habillé, il partit** as soon as he was dressed, he left; **a. dit, a. fait** no sooner said than done

austère [ɔstɛr] *adj (vie, style)* austere; *(vêtement)* severe • **austérité** *nf (de vie, de style)* austerity; *(de vêtement)* severity; **mesure d'a.** austerity measures

austral, -e, -als, -ales [ɔstral] *adj* southern

Australie [ɔstrali] *nf* **l'A.** Australia • **australien, -ienne 1** *adj* Australian **2** *nmf* **A., Australienne** Australian

autant [otã] *adv* (**a**) **a. de... que** *(quantité)* as much... as; *(nombre)* as many... as; **il a a. d'argent/de pommes que vous** he has as much money/as many apples as you (**b**) **a. de** *(tant de)* so much; *(nombre)* so many; **je n'ai jamais vu a. d'argent/de pommes** I've never seen so much money/so many apples; **pourquoi manges-tu a.?** why are you eating so much? (**c**) **a. que** *(quantité)* as much as; *(nombre)* as many as; **il lit a. que vous/que possible** he reads as much as you/as much as possible; **il n'a jamais souffert a.** he's never suffered as *or* so much; **a. que je sache** as far as I know (**d**) *(expressions)* **d'a. (plus) que...** all the more (so) since...; **d'a. moins que...** even less since...; **a. dire que...** which amounts to saying...; **a. avouer** we/you might as well confess; **en faire a.** to do the same; **pour a.** *(malgré cela)* for all that; **j'aimerais a. aller au musée** I'd just as soon go to the museum

autel [otɛl] *nm* altar

auteur [otœr] *nm (de livre)* author, writer; *(de chanson)* composer; *(de tableau)* painter; *(de crime)* perpetrator; *(d'accident)* cause

authenticité [otãtisite] *nf* authenticity • **authentifier** *vt* to authenticate • **authentique** *adj* genuine, authentic

autiste [otist] *adj* autistic

autobiographie [otobjɔgrafi] *nf* autobiography • **autobiographique** *adj* autobiographical

autobronzant, -e [otobrɔzɑ̃, -ɑ̃t] **1** *adj* self-tanning **2** *nm (crème)* self-tan

autobus [otobys] *nm* bus

autocar [otokar] *nm* bus, *Br* coach

autochtone [ɔtɔkton] *adj & nmf* native

autocollant, -ante [otokɔlɑ̃, -ɑ̃t] **1** *adj* self-adhesive; *(enveloppe, timbre)* self-seal **2** *nm* sticker

autocrate [otokrat] *nm* autocrat • **autocratique** *adj* autocratic

autocuiseur [otokɥizœr] *nm* pressure cooker

autodéfense [otodefɑ̃s] *nf* self-defence

autodestruction [otodestryksjɔ̃] *nf* self-destruction • **autodestructeur, -trice** *adj* self-destructive

autodidacte [otodidakt] *nmf* self-taught person

auto-école [otoekɔl] *(pl* **auto-écoles**) *nf* driving school

autofinancer [otofinɑ̃se] **s'autofinancer** *vpr* to be self-financing

autogestion [otoʒestjɔ̃] *nf* self-management

autographe [otograf] *nm* autograph

automate [ɔtɔmat] *nm* automaton • **automation, automatisation** *nf* automation • **automatiser** *vt* to automate

automatique [ɔtɔmatik] *adj* automatic • **automatiquement** *adv* automatically

automatisme [otomatism] *nm (réflexe)* automatism; *(appareil)* automatic device; **agir par a.** to act automatically

automédication [otomedikasjɔ̃] *nf* selfmedication

automitrailleuse [otomitrajøz] *nf Br* armoured *or Am* armored car

automne [otɔn] *nm* autumn, *Am* fall • **automnal, -e, -aux, -ales** *adj* autumnal

automobile [otomɔbil] **1** *adj (véhicule)* self-propelling **2** *nf* car; **l'a.** *(industrie)* the car industry • **automobiliste** *nmf* motorist

autonettoyant, -ante [otonetwajɑ̃, -ɑ̃t] *adj* **four a.** self-cleaning oven

autonome [otonom] *adj (région)* autonomous, self-governing; *Fig (personne)* self-sufficient; *Ordinat* **calculateur a.** stand-alone (computer) ■ **autonomie** *nf (de région)* autonomy; *(de personne)* self-sufficiency; **a. de vol** *(d'avion)* range

autopsie [otopsi] *nf* autopsy, post-mortem

autoradio [otoradjo] *nm* car radio

autorail [otoraj] *nm* railcar

autoriser [otorize] *vt* **a. qn à faire qch** to authorize *or* permit sb to do sth; **ces découvertes nous autorisent à penser que...** these discoveries entitle us to believe that... ■ **autorisation** *nf (permission)* permission, authorization; *(document)* authorization; **demander à qn l'a. de faire qch** to ask sb permission to do sth; **donner à qn l'a. de faire qch** to give sb permission to do sth; *Admin* **a. de sortie du territoire** = parental authorization for a minor to travel abroad; *Av* **a. de vol** flight clearance ■ **autorisé, -ée** *adj (qualifié)* authoritative; *(permis)* permitted, allowed; **les milieux autorisés** official circles

autorité [otorite] *nf (fermeté, domination, personne)* authority; **faire qch d'a.** to do sth on one's own authority; **faire a. en qch** *(personne)* to be an authority on; **ce livre fait a.** this book is the authoritative work; **les autorités** the authorities ■ **autoritaire** *adj* authoritarian

autoroute [otorut] *nf Br* motorway, *Am* highway, freeway; **a. à péage** *Br* toll motorway, *Am* turnpike (road); *Ordinat* **a. de l'information** information superhighway ■ **autoroutier** *adj* **réseau a.** *Br* motorway *or* *Am* freeway system

autosatisfait, -e [otosatisfɛ] *adj* self-satisfied ■ **autosatisfaction** *nf* self-satisfaction

auto-stop [otostop] *nm* hitchhiking; **faire de l'a.** to hitchhike ■ **auto-stoppeur, -euse** *nmf* hitchhiker

autour [otur] **1** *adv* around; **tout a.** all around **2** *prép* **a. de** around, round; *(environ)* around, round about

autre [otr] *adj & pron* other; **un a. livre** another book; **un a.** another (one); **d'autres** others; **d'autres médecins/livres** other doctors/ books; **as-tu d'autres questions?** have you any other *or* further questions?; **quelqu'un d'a.** somebody else; **personne/rien d'a.** no one/nothing else; **a. chose/part** something/ somewhere else; **qui/quoi d'a.?** who/what else?; **l'un l'a., les uns les autres** each other; **l'un et l'a.** both (of them); **l'un ou l'a.** either (of them); **ni l'un ni l'a.** neither (of them); **les uns... les autres** some... others; **nous/vous autres Anglais** we/you English; **d'un moment à l'a.** any moment (now); **c'était un touriste comme un a.** he was just an ordinary tourist

autrefois [otrəfwa] *adv* in the past, once

autrement [otrəmā] *adv (différemment)* differently; *(sinon)* otherwise; *(plus)* far more (**que** than); **pas a. satisfait** not particularly satisfied

Autriche [otriʃ] *nf* **l'A.** Austria ■ **autrichien, -ienne 1** *adj* Austrian **2** *nmf* **A., Autrichienne** Austrian

autruche [otryʃ] *nf* ostrich

autrui [otrɥi] *pron* others, other people

aux [o] *voir* **à**

auxiliaire [oksiljɛr] **1** *adj (verbe, machine, troupes)* auxiliary **2** *nm (verbe)* auxiliary **3** *nmf (aide)* assistant; *(dans les hôpitaux)* auxiliary; *(dans l'administration)* temporary worker

auxquels, -elles [okɛl] *voir* **lequel**

av. *(abrév* **avenue)** Ave

avachir [avaʃir] **s'avachir** *vpr (soulier, canapé)* to lose its shape; *(personne) (physiquement)* to get flabby; **s'a. dans un fauteuil** to flop into an armchair

avait [avɛ] *voir* **avoir**

aval [aval] *nm* downstream section; **en a.** downstream (**de** from); *Fig* **donner l'a. à un projet** to give one's support to a project

avalanche [avalɑ̃ʃ] *nf* avalanche; *Fig (de lettres)* flood

avaler [avale] **1** *vt* to swallow; *Fig (livre)* to devour; **a. la fumée** to inhale; *Fig* **a. ses mots** to mumble; *Fig* **a. les kilomètres** to eat up the miles **2** *vi* to swallow; **j'ai avalé de travers** it went down the wrong way

avance [avɑ̃s] *nf (progression, acompte)* advance; *(avantage)* lead; **faire une a. à qn** *(donner de l'argent)* to give sb an advance; **faire des avances à qn** *(chercher à séduire)* to make advances to sb; **avoir de l'a. sur qn** to be ahead of sb; **prendre de l'a. sur qn** to take the lead over sb; **à l'a., d'a., par a.** in advance; **en a.** *(arriver, partir)* early; *(avant l'horaire prévu)* ahead (of time); **être en a. pour son âge** to be advanced for one's age; **être en a. sur son temps** to be ahead of one's time; **avoir une heure d'a.** to be an hour early; **avoir un point d'a. sur qn** to be a point ahead of sb; *Scol* **avoir un an d'a.** to be a year ahead

avancé, -ée [avɑ̃se] *adj* advanced; **à un âge/ stade a.** at an advanced age/stage; **à une heure avancée de la nuit** late at night; *Fig* **te voilà bien a.!** a lot of good that's done you!

avancée [avɑ̃se] *nf (saillie)* projection; *(progression, découverte)* advance

avancement [avɑ̃smɑ̃] *nm (de personne)* promotion; *(de travail)* progress

avancer [avɑ̃se] **1** *vt (dans le temps)* to bring forward; *(dans l'espace)* to move forward; *(pion, thèse)* to advance; *(montre)* to put forward; **a. de l'argent à qn** to lend sb money;

Formel ou Hum **l'automobile de Monsieur est avancée** Sir's carriage awaits **2** *vi (aller de l'avant)* to move forward; *(armée)* to advance; *(faire des progrès)* to progress; *(faire saillie)* to jut out (**sur** over); **a. d'un pas** to take a step forward; **a. (de cinq minutes)** *(montre)* to be (five minutes) fast; **j'avance de deux minutes** my watch is two minutes fast; **alors, ça avance?** how is it coming along?; **ça n'avance à rien de pleurer** crying won't help; **faire a. les choses** to get things moving **3** *s'avancer vpr* to move forward; **s'a. vers qch** to head towards sth

avant [avɑ̃] **1** *prép* before; **a. de faire qch** before doing sth; **je vous verrai a. de partir** I'll see you before I leave; **je vous verrai a. que (ne) partiez** I'll see you before you leave; **a. huit jours** within a week; **a. tout** above all; **a. toute chose** first and foremost; **la famille passe a. tout** family comes first

2 *adv (auparavant)* before; *(d'abord)* beforehand; **a. j'avais les cheveux longs** I used to have long hair; **il vaut mieux téléphoner a.** it's better to phone first; **en a.** *(mouvement)* forward; *(en tête)* ahead; **faire un pas en a.** to take a step forward; **en a. de** in front of; **la nuit d'a.** the night before

3 *nm (de navire, de voiture)* front; *Football (joueur)* forward; **à l'a.** in (the) front; **monter à l'a.** to go in (the) front; **aller de l'a.** to get on with it

4 *adj inv (pneu, roue)* front ▪ **avant-bras** *nm inv* forearm ▪ **avant-centre** *(pl* avants-centres*) nm Football* centre-forward ▪ **avant-coureur** *(pl* avant-coureurs*) adj m* precursory ▪ **avant-dernier, -ière** *(mpl* avant-derniers, *fpl* avant-dernières*) adj & nmf* last but one ▪ **avant-garde** *(pl* avant-gardes*) nf (d'armée)* advance guard; **d'a.** *(idée, film)* avant-garde ▪ **avant-goût** *(pl* avant-goûts*) nm* foretaste (**de** of) ▪ **avant-guerre** *nm ou f* pre-war period; **d'a.** pre-war ▪ **avant-hier** [avɑ̃tjɛr] *adv* the day before yesterday ▪ **avant-poste** *(pl* avant-postes*) nm Mil* outpost ▪ **avant-première** *(pl* avant-premières*) nf* preview ▪ **avant-propos** *nm inv* foreword ▪ **avant-veille** *(pl* avant-veilles*) nf* **l'a. (de)** two days before

avantage [avɑ̃taʒ] *nm* advantage; **être/ tourner à l'a. de qn** to be/turn to sb's advantage; **tirer a. de qch** to turn sth to one's advantage; **prendre/conserver l'a.** *(dans une course)* to gain/retain the advantage; **tu aurais a. à être poli** you'd do well to be polite; **avantages en nature** benefits in kind; **avantages sociaux** social security benefits ▪ **avantager** *vt* **a. qn** *(favoriser)* to give sb an advantage over; *(faire valoir)* to show sb off to advantage

avantageux, -euse [avɑ̃taʒø, -øz] *adj (offre)* attractive; *(prix)* reasonable; *(ton)* superior

avare [avar] **1** *adj* miserly; *Fig* **il n'est pas a. de compliments** he's generous with his compliments **2** *nmf* miser ▪ **avarice** *nf* miserliness, avarice

avaries [avari] *nf* damage; **subir une a.** to be damaged ▪ **avarié, -iée** *adj (aliment)* rotten

avatar [avatar] *nm (mésaventure)* misadventure

avec [avɛk] **1** *prép* with; **méchant/aimable a. qn** nasty/kind to sb; **a. enthousiasme** with enthusiasm, enthusiastically; **être bien/mal a. qn** *(s'entendre bien/mal)* to get on well/badly with sb; **diminuer a. l'âge** to decrease with age; **cela viendra a. le temps** it will come in time; *Fam* **et a. ça?** *(dans un magasin)* anything else? **2** *adv Fam* **il est venu a.** *(son parapluie, ses gants)* he came with it/them

avenant, -ante [avnɑ̃, -ɑ̃t] **1** *adj (personne, manières)* pleasing **2** *nm* **à l'a.** in keeping (**de** with)

avènement [avɛnmɑ̃] *nm (d'une ère)* advent; *(d'un roi)* accession

avenir [avnir] *nm* future; **à l'a.** *(désormais)* in future; **d'a.** *(métier)* with good prospects; **assurer l'a. de qn** to make provision for sb

aventure [avɑ̃tyr] *nf* adventure; *(en amour)* affair; **partir à l'a.** to set off in search of adventure; *(sans préparation)* to set out without making plans; **dire la bonne a. à qn** to tell sb's fortune ▪ **s'aventurer** *vpr* to venture (**dans** into) ▪ **aventureux, -euse** *adj (personne, vie)* adventurous; *(projet)* risky ▪ **aventurier, -ière** *nmf* adventurer

avenue [avny] *nf* avenue

avérer [avere] **s'avérer** *vpr (se révéler)* to prove to be; **il s'avère que...** it turns out that... ▪ **avéré, -ée** *adj (fait)* established

averse [avɛrs] *nf* shower

aversion [avɛrsjɔ̃] *nf* aversion (**pour** to)

avertir [avɛrtir] *vt* **a. qn de qch** *(informer)* to inform sb of sth; *(danger)* to warn sb of sth ▪ **averti, -ie** *adj (public)* informed; **te voilà a.!** don't say I didn't warn you! ▪ **avertissement** *nm* warning; *(de livre)* foreword ▪

> Il faut noter que les termes anglais **to advertise** et **advertisement** sont des faux amis. Le premier ne signifie jamais **avertir** et le second se traduit par **publicité** ou **annonce**.

aveu, -x [avø] *nm* confession; **passer aux aveux** to make a confession; **de l'a. de tout le monde...** it is commonly acknowledged that...

aveugle [avœgl] **1** *adj* blind; **devenir a.** to go blind; **avoir une confiance a.** to trust sb implicitly **2** *nmf* blind man, *f* blind woman; **les aveugles** the blind ▪ **aveuglément** [-emɑ̃] *adv* blindly

aveugler [avœgle] *vt (éblouir) & Fig* to blind;

aveuglé par la colère blind with rage ▪ **aveuglement** [-əmɑ̃] *nm (moral, mental)* blindness

aveuglette [avœglɛt] **à l'aveuglette** *adv* blindly; **chercher qch à l'a.** to grope for sth

aviateur, -trice [avjatœr, -tris] *nmf* aviator ▪ **aviation** *nf (secteur)* aviation; *(armée de l'air)* air force; **l'a.** *(activité)* flying

avide [avid] *adj (cupide)* greedy; *(passionné)* eager (**de** for); **a. de sang** bloodthirsty; **a. d'apprendre** eager to learn ▪ **avidement** *adv (voracement)* greedily; *(avec passion)* eagerly ▪ **avidité** *nf (voracité, cupidité)* greed; *(passion)* eagerness

avilir [avilir] *vt* to degrade

avion [avjɔ̃] *nm* plane, aircraft *inv, Br* aeroplane, *Am* airplane; **par a.** *(sur lettre)* airmail; **en a., par a.** *(voyager)* by plane, by air; **a. à réaction** jet; **a. de chasse** fighter (plane); **a. de tourisme** private plane ▪ **avion-cargo** *(pl avions-cargos) nm* freight plane, cargo plane ▪ **avion-suicide** *(pl avions-suicides) nm* suicide plane

aviron [avirɔ̃] *nm* oar; **l'a.** *(sport)* rowing; **faire de l'a.** to row

avis [avi] *nm* opinion; *(communiqué)* notice; *(conseil)* advice; **à mon a.** in my opinion, to my mind; **être de l'a. de qn** to be of the same opinion as sb; **être d'a. de faire qch** to be of a mind to do sth; **changer d'a.** to change one's mind; **sauf a. contraire** unless I/you/*etc* hear to the contrary

aviser [avize] **1** *vt* **a. qn de qch/que...** to inform sb of sth/that... **2 s'aviser** *vpr* **s'a. de qch** to become aware of sth; **s'a. que...** to notice that...; **ne t'avise pas de recommencer!** don't you dare start again! ▪ **avisé, -ée** *adj* wise (**de faire** to do); **bien/mal a.** well-/ill-advised

aviver [avive] *vt (couleur)* to brighten up; *(douleur)* to sharpen; *(querelle)* to stir up

avocat¹, -ate [avɔka, -at] *nmf Jur* lawyer; *Fig* advocate

avocat² [avɔka] *nm (fruit)* avocado (pear)

avoine [avwan] *nf* oats

avoir* [avwar] **1** *v aux* to have; **je l'ai vu** I have *or* I've seen him; **je l'avais vu** I had *or* I'd seen him **2** *vt (posséder)* to have; *(obtenir)* to get; *(porter)* to wear; *Fam (tromper)* to take for a ride; **il a une**

fille he has *or* he's got a daughter; **qu'est-ce que tu as?** what's the matter with you?; **j'ai à lui parler** I have to speak to her; **j'ai à faire** I have things to do; **il n'a qu'à essayer** he only has to try; **a. faim/chaud** to be *or* feel hungry/hot; **a. cinq ans** to be five (years old); **a. du diabète** to be diabetic; **j'en ai pour dix minutes** this will take me ten minutes; *(ne bougez pas)* I'll be with you in ten minutes; **en a. pour son argent** to get one's money's worth; **j'en ai eu pour dix euros** it cost me ten euros; **en a. après** *ou* **contre qn** to have a grudge against sb; *Fam* **se faire a.** to be conned **3** *v impersonnel* **il y a** there is, *pl* there are; **il y a six ans** six years ago; **il n'y a pas de quoi!** *(en réponse à 'merci')* don't mention it!; **qu'est-ce qu'il y a?** what's the matter? **4** *nm* assets, property; *(d'un compte)* credit

avoisiner [avwazine] *vt (dans l'espace)* to border on; *(en valeur)* to be close to ▪ **avoisinant, -ante** *adj Br* neighbouring, *Am* neighboring, nearby

avorter [avɔrte] *vi (subir une IVG)* to have an abortion; *(faire une fausse couche)* to miscarry; *Fig (projet)* to fall through; **(se faire) a.** *(femme)* to have an abortion ▪ **avortement** [-əmɑ̃] *nm* abortion; *Fig (de projet)* failure

avouer [avwe] **1** *vt (crime)* to confess to; **il a fini par a.** he finally confessed; **il faut a. que...** it must be admitted that... **2 s'avouer** *vpr* **s'a. vaincu** to acknowledge defeat ▪ **avoué, -ée 1** *adj (auteur, partisan)* confessed; *(but)* declared **2** *nm Br* ≃ solicitor, *Am* ≃ attorney

avril [avril] *nm* April

axe [aks] *nm (géométrique)* axis; *(essieu)* axle; **les grands axes** *(routes)* the main roads; *Fig* **les grands axes d'une politique** the main thrust of a policy ▪ **axer** *vt* to *Br* centre *or Am* center (**sur** on)

axiome [aksjom] *nm* axiom

ayant [ɛjɑ̃], **ayez** [ɛje], **ayons** [ɛjɔ̃] *voir* **avoir**

azalée [azale] *nf* azalea

azimuts [azimyt] *nmpl Fam* **tous a.** *(guerre, publicité)* all-out

azote [azɔt] *nm* nitrogen

azur [azyr] *nm Littéraire (couleur)* azure; **l'a.** *(ciel)* the sky

azyme [azim] *adj* **pain a.** unleavened bread

B, b [be] *nm inv* B, b
baba¹ [baba] *n* **b. au rhum** rum baba
baba² [baba] *adj inv Fam* flabbergasted
baba cool [babakul] (*pl* **babas cool**) *nmf* hippie
babeurre [babœr] *nm* buttermilk
babillard [babijar] *nm Can Ordinat* bulletin board
babiller [babije] *vi (enfant)* to babble
babines [babin] *nfpl (lèvres)* chops
babiole [babjɔl] *nf (objet)* knick-knack; *(futilité)* trifle
bâbord [babɔr] *nm* port (side); **à b.** to port
babouin [babwɛ̃] *nm* baboon
baby-foot [babifut] *nm inv* table football
baby-sitting [babisitiŋ] *nm* baby-sitting; **faire du b.** to baby-sit **baby-sitter** (*pl* **baby-sitters**) *n mf* baby-sitter
bac¹ [bak] *nm (bateau)* ferry(boat); *(cuve)* tank; **b. à glace** ice tray; **b. à légumes** salad drawer; **b. à sable** sandpit
bac² [bak] *(abrév* **baccalauréat**) *nm Fam* **passer le b.** to take *or Br* sit one's baccalauréat
baccalauréat [bakalɔrea] *nm* = secondary school examination qualifying for entry to university, *Br* ≃ A-levels, *Am* ≃ high school diploma
bâche [baʃ] *nf (de toile)* tarpaulin; *(de plastique)* plastic sheet **bâcher** *vt* to cover (*with a tarpaulin or plastic sheet*)
bachelier, -ière [baʃəlje, -jɛr] *nmf* = student who has passed the "baccalauréat"
bachoter [baʃɔte] *vi Fam* to cram, *Br* to swot **bachotage** *n Fam* cramming, *Br* swotting
bacille [basil] *nm* bacillus
bâcler [bakle] *vt Fam* to botch (up)
bactérie [bakteri] *nf* bacterium **bactériologique** *adj* bacteriological; **la guerre b.** germ warfare
badaud, -aude [bado, -od] *nmf (promeneur)* stroller; *(curieux)* onlooker
badge [badʒ] *nm Br* badge, *Am* button
badigeonner [badiʒɔne] *vt (surface)* to daub (**de** with); *(mur)* to whitewash; *Culin* to brush (**de** with); *(plaie)* to paint (**de** with)
badin, -ine¹ [badɛ̃, -in] *adj* playful **badinage** *nm* banter **badiner** *vi* to jest; **il ne badine pas avec la ponctualité** he's very strict about punctuality
badine² [badin] *nf* switch *(small stick)*

baffe [baf] *nf Fam* clout
baffle [bafl] *nm* speaker
bafouer [bafwe] *vt (person)* to jeer at; *(autorité)* to flout
bafouiller [bafuje] *vti* to stammer
bâfrer [bafre] *vi très Fam* to stuff oneself
bagage [bagaʒ] *nm Fig (connaissances)* knowledge (**en** of); **bagages** *(sacs, valises)* luggage, baggage; **faire ses bagages** to pack (one's bags); **plier bagages** to pack one's bags; **b. à main** piece of hand luggage **bagagiste** *nm* baggage handler
bagarre [bagar] *nf Fam* fight, brawl; **chercher la b.** to look for a fight; **des bagarres éclatèrent** fighting broke out **se bagarrer** *vpr Fam* to fight **bagarreur, -euse** *adj Fam (personne, caractère)* aggressive
bagatelle [bagatɛl] *nf* trifle; **pour la b. de 50 euros** for a mere 50 euros
bagnole [baɲɔl] *nf Fam* car
bagou(t) [bagu] *nm Fam* glibness; **avoir du b.** to have the gift of the gab
bague [bag] *nf (anneau)* ring; *(de cigare)* band; **passer à qn la b. au doigt** to marry sb; **b. de fiançailles** engagement ring **baguer** *vt (oiseau, arbre)* to ring
baguette [bagɛt] *nf (canne)* stick; *(de chef d'orchestre)* baton; *(pain)* French stick; **baguettes** *(de tambour)* drumsticks; *(pour manger)* chopsticks; **mener qn à la b.** to rule sb with a rod of iron; **b. magique** magic wand
bahut [bay] *nm (coffre)* chest; *(buffet)* sideboard; *Fam (lycée)* school
baie¹ [bɛ] *nf Géog* bay
baie² [bɛ] *nf (fruit)* berry
baie³ [bɛ] *nf* **b. vitrée** picture window
baignade [beɲad] *nf (activité)* swimming, *Br* bathing; *(endroit)* bathing place; **'b. interdite'** *(sur panneau)* 'no swimming'
baigner [beɲe] **1** *vt (pied, blessure)* to bathe; *(enfant) Br* to bath, *Am* to bathe; *(sujet: mer)* to wash; **être baigné de sueur/lumière** to be bathed in sweat/light; **un visage baigné de larmes** a face streaming with tears **2** *vi (tremper)* to soak (**dans** in); **les légumes baignent dans la sauce** the vegetables are swimming in the sauce; **il baignait dans son sang** he was lying in a pool of blood; *Fam* **tout baigne (dans l'huile)** everything's hunky dory!

3 se baigner *vpr (nager)* to have a swim; *(se laver)* to have or take a bath ▪ **baigneur, -euse 1** *nmf* swimmer, *Br* bather **2** *nm (poupée)* baby doll ▪ **baignoire** *nf* bath (tub)

bail [baj] *(pl* **baux** [bo]) *nm* lease; *Fam* **ça fait un b. que je ne l'ai pas vu** I haven't seen him for ages ▪ **bailleur** *nm* **b. de fonds** financial backer

bâiller [baje] *vi* to yawn; *(col)* to gape; *(porte)* to be ajar; *Fam* **b. à se décrocher la mâchoire** to yawn one's head off ▪ **bâillement** *nm (de personne)* yawn

bâillon [bajɔ̃] *nm* gag; **mettre un b. à qn** to gag sb ▪ **bâillonner** *vt (victime, presse)* to gag

bain [bɛ̃] *nm* bath; *(de mer, de rivière)* swim, *Br* bathe; **prendre un b.** to have or take a bath; **prendre un b. de soleil** to sunbathe; *Fam* **être dans le b.** to be in the swing of things; **petit/ grand b.** *(de piscine)* small/large pool; **b. de bouche** mouthwash; **b. moussant** bubble bath; *Fig* **b. de sang** bloodbath; **b. de vapeur** steam bath ▪ **bain-marie** *(pl* **bains-marie**) *nm* bain-marie *(cooking pan set over a second pan of boiling water)*

baïonnette [bajɔnɛt] *nf* bayonet

baisemain [bɛzmɛ̃] *nm* **faire un b. à qn** to kiss sb's hand

baiser¹ [beze] *nm* kiss

baiser² [beze] **1** *vt* (**a**) *Littéraire* **b. qn au front/ sur la joue** to kiss sb on the forehead/cheek (**b**) *Vulg (duper, coucher avec)* to screw **2** *vi Vulg* to screw

baisse [bes] *nf* fall, drop (**de** in); **en b.** *(température)* falling; *(popularité)* declining

baisser [bese] **1** *vt (rideau, vitre, prix)* to lower; *(radio, chauffage)* to turn down; **b. la tête** to lower one's head; **b. les yeux** to look down; **b. la voix** to lower one's voice; *Fig* **b. les bras** to give in **2** *vi (prix, niveau, température)* to fall; *(marée)* to ebb; *(malade)* to get weaker; *(vue, mémoire)* to fail; *(popularité, qualité)* to decline; **le jour baisse** night is falling **3 se baisser** *vpr* to bend down; *(pour éviter qch)* to duck

baissier [besje] *adj m Fin* **marché b.** bear market

bajoues [baʒu] *nfpl (d'animal)* chops

bal [bal] *(pl* **bals**) *nm (élégant)* ball; *(populaire)* dance; **b. costumé, b. masqué** fancy dress ball; **b. musette** = dance to accordion music; **b. populaire** = dance, usually outdoors, open to the public

balade [balad] *nf Fam (à pied)* walk; *(en voiture)* drive; **faire une b.** *(à pied)* to go for a walk; *(en voiture)* to go for a drive ▪ **balader 1** *vt Fam (personne)* to take for a walk/drive; *(objet)* to drag around **2** *vi* **envoyer qn b.** to send sb packing **3 se balader** *vpr Fam (à pied)* to go for a walk; *(en voiture)* to go for a drive ▪ **baladeur** *nm* personal stereo ▪ **baladeuse** *nf* inspection lamp

balafre [balafr] *nf (cicatrice)* scar; *(coupure)* gash ▪ **balafrer** *vt* to gash; **visage balafré** scarred face

balai [balɛ] *nm* broom; **donner un coup de b.** to give the floor a sweep; *Fam* **avoir quarante balais** to be forty; *Fam* **du b.!** clear off!; **b. mécanique** carpet sweeper ▪ **balai-brosse** *(pl* **balais-brosses**) *nm* = long-handled scrubbing brush

balaise [balɛz] *adj* = **balèze**

balance [balɑ̃s] *nf* (**a**) *(instrument)* (pair of) scales; *Écon* balance; *Fig* **ça pèse dans la b.** it carries some weight; **b. commerciale** balance of trade (**b**) **la B.** *(signe)* Libra; **être B.** to be (a) Libra (**c**) *Fam (mouchard)* squealer

> Il faut noter que le nom anglais **balance** est un faux ami. Il signifie le plus souvent **équilibre** et ne s'emploie jamais pour désigner un instrument de mesure.

balancer [balɑ̃se] **1** *vt (bras, jambe)* to swing; *(hanches)* to sway; *Fin (compte)* to balance; *Fam (lancer)* to chuck; *Fam (se débarrasser de)* to chuck out; *Fam (dénoncer)* to squeal on; *Fam* **elle a tout balancé** *(tout abandonné)* she's chucked it all in or given it all up **2 se balancer** *vpr (arbre, bateau)* to sway; *(sur une balançoire)* to swing; **se b. d'un pied sur l'autre** to rock from one foot to the other; *Fam* **je m'en balance!** I don't give *Br* a toss or *Am* a rat's ass! ▪ **balancé, -ée** *adj Fam* **être bien b.** *(personne)* to have a good figure ▪ **balancement** *nm* swaying

balancier [balɑ̃sje] *nm (d'horloge)* pendulum; *(de funambule)* balancing pole

balançoire [balɑ̃swar] *nf (suspendue)* swing; *(bascule)* seesaw

balayer [baleje] *vt (pièce)* to sweep; *(feuilles, saletés)* to sweep up; *Fig (objections)* to brush aside; *(sujet: projecteurs)* to sweep; **le vent a balayé les nuages** the wind swept the clouds away; *Fig* **b. devant sa porte** to put one's own house in order ▪ **balayage** *nm (nettoyage)* sweeping; *(coiffure)* highlighting ▪ **balayette** *nf* small brush ▪ **balayeur, -euse¹** *nmf (personne)* road-sweeper ▪ **balayeuse²** *nf (véhicule)* road-sweeper

balbutier [balbysje] *vti* to stammer ▪ **balbutiement** *nm* balbutiement(s) stammering; **en être à ses premiers balbutiements** *(science)* to be in its infancy

balcon [balkɔ̃] *nm* balcony; *(de théâtre)* circle, *Am* mezzanine; **premier/deuxième b.** dress/ upper circle

baldaquin [baldakɛ̃] *nm* canopy

Baléares [balear] *nfpl* **les B.** the Balearic Islands

baleine [balɛn] *nf (animal)* whale; *(de corset)* whalebone; *(de parapluie)* rib ▪ **baleinier** *nm (navire)* whaler ▪ **baleinière** *nf* whaleboat

balèze [balɛz] *adj Fam (grand et fort)* hefty; *(intelligent)* brainy; **b. en maths** brilliant at maths

balise [baliz] *nf Naut* beacon; *Av* light; *(de piste de ski)* marker; *Ordinat* tag; *Naut* **b. flottante** buoy ▪ **balisage** *nm (signaux) Naut* beacons; *Av* lights ▪ **baliser** *vt (chenal)* to beacon; *(aéroport)* to equip with lights; *(route)* to mark ¬out with beacons; *(piste de ski)* to mark out

balistique [balistik] *adj* ballistic

balivernes [balivern] *nfpl* twaddle, nonsense

Balkans [balkɑ̃] *nmpl* **les B.** the Balkans

ballade [balad] *nf (chanson, poème long)* ballad; *(musicale, poème court)* ballade

ballant, -ante [balɑ̃, -ɑ̃t] *adj (bras, jambes)* dangling

ballast [balast] *nm (de route, de voie ferrée)* ballast

balle¹ [bal] *nf (pour jouer)* ball; *(d'arme)* bullet; *Anciennement Fam* **balles** *(francs)* francs; **jouer à la b.** to play ball; *Tennis* **faire des balles** to knock the ball about; *Fig* **saisir la b. au bond** to seize the opportunity; *Fig* **se renvoyer la b.** to pass the buck; **b. de tennis** tennis ball; **b. de break/match** break/match point; **b. à blanc** blank; **b. perdue** stray bullet

balle² [bal] *nf (de coton, de laine)* bale

ballet [balɛ] *nm* ballet ▪ **ballerine** *nf (danseuse)* ballerina; *(chaussure)* pump

ballon [balɔ̃] *nm (balle, dirigeable)* balloon; *(verre)* round glass wine; **jouer au b.** to play with a ball; **souffler dans le b.** *(pour l'Alcootest®)* to blow into the bag; *Fig* **être un b. d'oxygène pour qn** to be a lifesaver for sb; **b. d'essai** pilot balloon; **b. de football** *Br* football, *Am* soccer ball

ballonné [balɔne] *adj m (ventre, personne)* bloated

ballot [balo] *nm (paquet)* bundle; *Fam (imbécile)* idiot

ballottage [balɔtaʒ] *nm Pol* **il y a b.** there will be a second ballot

ballotter [balɔte] *vti (bateau)* to toss about; *(passagers)* to shake about; *Fig* **un enfant ballotté entre son père et sa mère** a child passed backwards and forwards between its mother and father

balluchon [balyʃɔ̃] *nm Fam* **faire son b.** to pack one's bags

balnéaire [balneɛr] *adj* **station b.** *Br* seaside resort, *Am* beach resort

balourd, -ourde [balur, -urd] **1** *adj* oafish **2** *nmf* clumsy oaf

balte [balt] *adj* **les États baltes** the Baltic states

Baltique [baltik] *nf* **la (mer) B.** the Baltic (Sea)

baluchon [balyʃɔ̃] *nm* = **balluchon**

balustrade [balystrad] *nf (clôture)* railing

bambin [bɑ̃bɛ̃] *nm Fam* toddler

bambou [bɑ̃bu] *nm* bamboo

ban [bɑ̃] *nm (applaudissements)* round of applause; **bans** *(de mariage)* banns; **être au b. de la société** to be an outcast from society; **un b. pour...** three cheers for...

banal, -e, -als, -ales [banal] *adj (objet, gens)* ordinary; *(accident)* common; *(idée, remarque)* trite, banal; **pas b.** unusual ▪ **banalité** *nf (d'objet, de gens)* ordinariness; *(d'idée, de remarque)* triteness; *(d'accident)* commonness; **banalités** *(propos)* platitudes

banalisation [banalizaʒɔ̃] *nf* **la b. de qch** the way sth is becoming more common ▪ **banaliser** *vt (rendre commun)* to trivialize; **voiture banalisée** unmarked (police) car

banane [banan] *nf (fruit)* banana; *(petit sac) Br* bum bag, *Am* fanny pack; *(coiffure)* quiff ▪ **bananier** *nm (arbre)* banana tree

banc [bɑ̃] *nm (siège)* bench; *(établi)* work(-bench); *(de poissons)* shoal; **b. des accusés** dock; **b. d'église** pew; **b. d'essai** *Ind* test bed; *Ordinat* benchtest; *Fig* testing ground; *Can* **b. de neige** snowbank; **b. de sable** sandbank

bancaire [bɑ̃kɛr] *adj (opération)* banking; *(chèque, compte)* bank

bancal, -e, -als, -ales [bɑ̃kal] *adj (meuble)* wobbly; *Fig (raisonnement)* unsound

bandage [bɑ̃daʒ] *nm (pansement)* bandage

bandana [bɑ̃dana] *nm* bandana

bande [bɑ̃d] *nf* (**a**) *(de tissu, de papier, de terre)* strip; *(pansement)* bandage; *(motif)* stripe; *(pellicule)* film; *Radio* band; *Ordinat* **à large b.** broadband; **b. (magnétique)** tape; *Aut* **b. d'arrêt d'urgence** *Br* hard shoulder, *Am* shoulder; **b. dessinée** comic strip; *Aut* **b. médiane** central line; *Cin* **b. originale** original soundtrack; *Cin* **b. sonore** sound track (**b**) *(de personnes)* band, group; *(de voleurs)* gang; *(de loups)* pack; *(d'oiseaux)* flock; **une b. d'imbéciles** a bunch of idiots; **faire b. à part** *(agir seul)* to do one's own thing ▪ **bande-annonce** *(pl* bandes-annonces) *nf Cin* trailer (**de** for) ▪ **bande-son** *(pl* bandes-son) *nf Cin* soundtrack

bandeau, -x [bɑ̃do] *nm (pour les cheveux)* headband; *(pour les yeux)* blindfold

bander [bɑ̃de] *vt (blessure, main)* to bandage; *(ressort)* to tighten; *(arc)* to bend; **b. les yeux à qn** to blindfold sb

banderole [bɑ̃drɔl] *nf (de manifestants)* banner; *(publicitaire)* streamer

bandit [bɑ̃di] *nm (escroc)* crook; **b. de grand chemin** highwayman ▪ **banditisme** *nm* crime; **le grand b.** organized crime

bandoulière [bɑ̃duljɛr] *nf (de sac)* shoulder strap; **en b.** slung across the shoulder

banjo [bɑ̃dʒo] *nm* banjo

banlieue [bɑ̃ljø] *nf* suburbs; **la b. parisienne** the suburbs of Paris; **la grande/proche b.** the outer/inner suburbs; **en b.** in the suburbs; **de**

b. *(maison, magasin)* suburban; **train de b.** commuter train ▪ **banlieusard, -arde** *nmf (habitant)* suburbanite; *(voyageur)* commuter

bannière [banjɛr] *nf* banner; **la b. étoilée** the Star-spangled Banner

bannir [banir] *vt (personne, idée)* to banish (**de** from) ▪ **bannissement** *nm* banishment

banque [bɑ̃k] *nf (établissement)* bank; **la b.** *(activité)* banking; **employé de b.** bank clerk; **faire sauter la b.** *(au jeu)* to break the bank; *Ordinat* **b. de données** data bank; *Méd* **b. du sang/du sperme** blood/sperm bank

banqueroute [bɑ̃krut] *nf Jur* bankruptcy; **faire b.** to go bankrupt

banquet [bɑ̃kɛ] *nm* banquet

banquette [bɑ̃kɛt] *nf (siège)* (bench) seat; **b. arrière** *(d'une voiture)* back seat

banquier, -ière [bɑ̃kje, -jɛr] *nmf* banker

banquise [bɑ̃kiz] *nf* ice floe

baptême [batɛm] *nm Rel* christening, baptism; *Fig (de navire)* naming; **b. de l'air** first flight; **b. du feu** baptism of fire ▪ **baptiser** *vt Rel* to christen, to baptize; *Fig (appeler)* to name

baquet [bakɛ] *nm (cuve)* tub

bar¹ [bar] *nm (café, comptoir)* bar

bar² [bar] *nm (poisson)* bass

baragouiner [baragwine] *Fam* **1** *vt (langue)* to speak badly; **qu'est-ce qu'il baragouine?** what's he jabbering (on) about? **2** *vi* to jabber

baraque [barak] *nf (cabane)* hut, shack; *(de foire)* stall; *Fam (maison)* place ▪ **baraqué, -ée** *adj Fam* hefty ▪ **baraquement** *nm* shacks; *Mil* camp

> Il faut noter que le nom anglais **barracks** est un faux ami. Il signifie **caserne**.

baratin [baratɛ̃] *nm Fam (verbiage)* waffle; *(de séducteur)* sweet talk; *(de vendeur)* sales talk, spiel ▪ **baratiner** *vt Fam (pour essayer de séduire)* Br to chat up, Am to hit on

barbant, -ante [barbɑ̃, -ɑ̃t] *adj Fam* boring

barbare [barbar] **1** *adj (cruel, sauvage)* barbaric **2** *nmf* barbarian ▪ **barbarie** *nf (cruauté)* barbarity ▪ **barbarisme** *nm* barbarism

barbe [barb] *nf* beard; **b. de trois jours** stubble; **se faire la b.** to shave; *Fig* **à la b. de** right under sb's nose; **rire dans sa b.** to laugh up one's sleeve; *Fam* **quelle b.!** what a drag!; **b. à papa** *Br* candyfloss, *Am* cotton candy

barbecue [barbəkju] *nm* barbecue; **faire un b.** to have a barbecue

barbelé [barbəle] *adj m* **fil de fer b.** barbed wire ▪ **barbelés** *nmpl* barbed wire

barber [barbe] *Fam* **1** *vt Fam* **b. qn** to bore sb stiff **2** **se barber** *vpr* to be bored stiff

barbiche [barbiʃ] *nf* goatee (beard)

barbiturique [barbityrik] *nm* barbiturate

barboter [barbɔte] **1** *vi* to splash about **2** *vt*

Fam (voler) to pinch ▪ **barboteuse** *nf* romper-suit

barbouiller [barbuje] *vt (salir)* to smear (**de** with); *(peindre)* to daub; *Fam* **avoir l'estomac barbouillé** to feel queasy

barbu, -ue [barby] **1** *adj* bearded **2** *nm* bearded man

barda [barda] *nm Fam* gear; *Mil* kit

barder¹ [barde] *vt Culin* to bard; *Fig* **bardé de décorations** covered with decorations

barder² [barde] *v impersonnel Fam* **ça va b.!** there's going to be trouble!

barème [barɛm] *nm (de notes, de salaires, de prix)* scale; *(pour calculer)* ready reckoner

baril [baril] *nm (de pétrole, de vin)* barrel; *(de lessive)* drum; **b. de poudre** powder keg

bariolé, -ée [barjɔle] *adj Br* multicoloured, *Am* multicolored

barjo(t) [barʒo] **1** *adj inv Fam (fou)* crazy **2** *nmf Br* nutter; *Am* nut

barman [barman] *(pl* **-men** [-men] *ou* **-mans**) *nm Br* barman, *Am* bartender

baromètre [barɔmetr] *nm* barometer

baron [barɔ̃] *nm* baron; *Fig* **b. de la finance** financial tycoon ▪ **baronne** *nf* baroness

baroque [barɔk] **1** *adj (édifice, style, musique)* baroque; *(idée)* bizarre **2** *nm Archit & Mus* **le b.** the baroque

baroud [barud] *nm* **b. d'honneur** last stand ▪ **baroudeur** *nm Fam (combattant)* fighter; *(voyageur)* keen traveller

barouf(le) [baruf(l)] *nm Fam* din

barque [bark] *nf* (small) boat ▪ **barquette** *nf (de fruit)* punnet; *(de plat cuisiné)* container

barrage [baraʒ] *nm (sur l'eau)* dam; **tir de b.** barrage fire; **b. de police** police roadblock; **b. routier** roadblock

barre [bar] *nf (de fer, de bois)* bar; *(de danse)* barre; *(trait)* line, stroke; *Naut (volant de bateau)* helm; **b. chocolatée** *ou* **de chocolat** bar of chocolate; *Mus* **b. de mesure** bar (line); *Jur* **b. des témoins** *Br* witness box, *Am* witness stand; *Jur* **être appelé à la b.** to be called to the witness box; **b. d'appui** *(de fenêtre)* rail; **b. d'espacement** *(de clavier)* space bar; *Ordinat* **b. d'outils** tool bar; *Ordinat* **b. de sélection** menu bar; *Sport* **b. fixe** horizontal bar; *Sport* **barres parallèles** parallel bars

barreau, -x [baro] *nm (de fenêtre, de cage)* bar; *(d'échelle)* rung; *Jur* **le b.** the bar; *Jur* **être reçu** *ou* **admis au b.** to be called to the bar; **être derrière les barreaux** *(en prison)* to be behind bars

barrer [bare] **1** *vt (route, passage, chemin)* to block off; *(porte, fenêtre)* to bar; *(chèque)* to cross; *(mot, phrase)* to cross out; *Naut (bateau)* to steer; **b. le passage** *ou* **la route à qn** to bar sb's way; **'route barrée'** *(sur panneau)* 'road closed'; *Fam* **on est mal barrés!** things don't look good! **2** **se barrer** *vpr Fam* to beat it

barrette [baʀɛt] *nf (pour les cheveux) Br* (hair)slide, *Am* barrette

barreur [baʀœʀ] *nm Naut* helmsman; *(à l'aviron)* cox

barricade [baʀikad] *nf* barricade ▪ **barricader 1** *vt (rue, porte)* to barricade **2 se barricader** *vpr* to barricade oneself (**dans** in)

barrière [baʀjɛʀ] *nf (obstacle)* barrier; *(de passage à niveau)* gate; *(clôture)* fence; *Com* **barrières douanières** trade barriers

barrique [baʀik] *nf* (large) barrel

barrir [baʀiʀ] *vi (éléphant)* to trumpet

baryton [baʀitɔ̃] *nm Mus* baritone

bas¹, basse [bɑ, bɑs] **1** *adj (dans l'espace, en quantité, en intensité)* & *Mus* low; *(origine)* lowly; *Péj (acte)* mean, low; *(besogne)* menial; **à b. prix** cheaply; **au b. mot** at the very least; **enfant en b. âge** young child; **avoir la vue basse** to be short-sighted; *Péj* **le b. peuple** the hoi polloi; *Boxe & Fig* **coup b.** blow below the belt **2** *adv (dans l'espace)* low (down); *(dans une hiérarchie)* low; *(dans un bâtiment)* downstairs; *(parler)* quietly; **plus b.** further or lower down; **parle plus b.** lower your voice, speak more quietly; **voir plus b.** *(sur document)* see below; **en b.** at the bottom; **en b. de** at the bottom of; **mettre b.** *(sujet: animal)* to give birth; **à b. les dictateurs!** down with dictators!; *Fam* **b. les pattes!** hands off! **3** *nm (partie inférieure)* bottom; **l'étagère du b.** the bottom shelf; **au b. de** at the bottom of; **de b. en haut** upwards

bas² [bɑ] *nm (chaussette)* stocking; **b. de contention** elastic stockings

basané, -ée [bazane] *adj (bronzé)* tanned

bas-côté [bɑkote] *(pl* **bas-côtés**) *nm (de route)* verge; *(d'église)* (side)aisle

bascule [baskyl] *nf (balançoire)* seesaw; *(balance)* weighing machine; **cheval/fauteuil à b.** rocking horse/chair ▪ **basculer 1** *vt (chargement)* to tip over; *(benne)* to tip up **2** *vi (tomber)* to topple over; **faire b.** *(personne)* to knock over; *(chargement)* to tip over; **le pays a basculé dans l'anarchie** the country tipped over into anarchy

base [bɑz] *nf (partie inférieure)* & *Chim, Math, Mil* base; *(de parti politique)* rank and file; *(principe)* basis; **jeter les bases de qch** to lay the foundations for sth; **avoir de bonnes bases en anglais** to have a good grounding in English; **produit à b. de lait** milk-based product; **de b.** basic; **militant de b.** rank-and-file militant; **salaire de b.** basic pay; **b. de lancement** launch site; **b. de maquillage** foundation; *Ordinat* **b. de données** database ▪ **baser 1** *vt* to base (**sur** on) **2 se baser** *vpr* **se b. sur qch** to base oneself on sth; **sur quoi te bases-tu pour dire cela?** what basis do you have for saying that?

bas-fond [bɑfɔ̃] *(pl* **bas-fonds**) *nm (de mer, de rivière)* shallow; *Péj* **les bas-fonds** *(de ville)* the rough areas

basic [bazik] *nm Ordinat* BASIC

basilic [bazilik] *nm (plante, aromate)* basil

basilique [bazilik] *nf* basilica

basket-ball [basketbol], *Fam* **basket** [baskɛt] *nm* basketball ▪ **basketteur, -euse** *nmf* basketball player

baskets [baskɛt] *nmpl ou nfpl (chaussures)* baseball boots; *Fam* **bien dans ses b.** very together, *Br* sorted

basque¹ [bask] **1** *adj* Basque **2** *nmf* **B.** Basque

basque² [bask] *nfpl (de veste)* tail; *Fig* **être toujours pendu aux basques de qn** to always be at sb's heels

basse¹ [bas] *voir* **bas¹**

basse² [bas] *nf Mus (contrebasse)* (double) bass; *(guitare)* bass (guitar)

basse-cour [baskuʀ] *(pl* **basses-cours**) *nf (court) Br* farmyard, *Am* barnyard

bassement [bɑsmɑ̃] *adv* basely; **être b. intéressé** to have one's own interests at heart

bassesse [bases] *nf (d'une action)* lowness; *(action)* low act

bassin [basɛ̃] *nm* **(a)** *(pièce d'eau)* ornamental lake; *(de fontaine)* basin; *(de port)* dock; *(récipient)* bowl, basin; **petit b.** *(de piscine)* children's pool; **grand b.** *(de piscine)* large pool **(b)** *(du corps)* pelvis **(c)** *(région)* basin; **b. houiller** coal basin; **le b. parisien** the Paris Basin ▪ **bassine** *nf (en plastique)* bowl

bassiner [basine] *vt Fam (ennuyer)* to bore stiff

basson [basɔ̃] *nm (instrument)* bassoon; *(musicien)* bassoonist

basta [basta] *exclam Fam* that's enough!

bastingage [bastɛ̃gaʒ] *nm Naut* rail

bastion [bastjɔ̃] *nm aussi Fig* bastion

baston [bastɔ̃] *nm ou f Fam* punch-up

bastringue [bastʀɛ̃g] *nm Fam (affaires)* gear; **et tout le b.** and the whole caboodle

bas-ventre [bɑvɑ̃tʀ] *nm* lower abdomen

bat [ba] *voir* **battre**

bât [bɑ] *nm* saddle *(for packhorse)*; *Fig* **c'est là que le b. blesse** there's the rub

bataclan [bataklɑ̃] *nm Fam (affaires)* gear; *Fam* **et tout le b.** and the whole caboodle

bataille [batɑj] *nf (lutte)* battle; *(jeu de cartes)* beggar-my-neighbour; **cheveux en b.** dishevelled hair ▪ **batailler** *vi Fam* **b. pour faire qch** to fight to do sth ▪ **batailleur, -euse** *adj* aggressive

bataillon [batajɔ̃] *nm Mil* batallion

bâtard, -arde [bɑtaʀ, -aʀd] **1** *adj (enfant)* illegitimate; *Péj* bastard; *(solution)* hybrid **2** *nmf (enfant)* illegitimate child; *Péj* bastard; *(chien)* mongrel; *(pain)* = small French stick

bateau, -x [bato] **1** *nm (embarcation)* boat; *(grand)* ship; **faire du b.** to go boating; **prendre le b.** to go/come by boat; *Fig* **mener qn en b.**

to wind sb up; **b. à moteur** motorboat; **b. à voiles** *Br* sailing boat, *Am* sailboat; **b. de pêche** fishing boat; **b. de plaisance** pleasure boat **2** *adj inv Fam (question, sujet)* hackneyed; **col b.** boat neck **▪ bateau-mouche** (*pl* **bateaux-mouches**) *nm* river boat *(on the Seine)* **▪ batelier** *nm* boatman

batifoler [batifɔle] *vi Fam* to lark about

bâtiment [bɑtimɑ̃] *nm (édifice)* building; *(navire)* vessel; **le b., l'industrie du b.** the building trade; **b. de guerre** warship

bâtir [bɑtir] *vt (construire)* to build; *Couture* to tack; **terrain à b.** building site **▪ bâti, -ie** *adj* **bien b.** *(personne)* well-built **2** *nm (charpente)* frame; *Couture* tacking **▪ bâtisse** *nf Péj* ugly building **▪ bâtisseur, -euse** *nmf* builder (**de** of)

bâton [bɑtɔ̃] *nm (canne)* stick; *(de maréchal)* baton; *(d'agent de police) Br* truncheon, *Am* nightstick; *(trait)* vertical line; **donner des coups de b. à qn** to beat sb (with a stick); *Fig* **parler à bâtons rompus** to talk about this and that; *Fig* **mettre des bâtons dans les roues à qn** to put a spoke in sb's wheel; **b. de rouge à lèvres** lipstick; **bâtons de ski** ski sticks *or* poles **▪ bâtonnet** *nm* stick

battage [bataʒ] *nm (du blé)* threshing; *Fam (publicité)* hype

battant¹ [batɑ̃] *nm* (**a**) *(de cloche)* tongue; *(de porte, de volet)* leaf; **porte à deux battants** double door (**b**) *(personne)* fighter

battant², -ante [batɑ̃, -ɑ̃t] *adj* **pluie b.** driving rain; **porte b.** *Br* swing door, *Am* swinging door; **le cœur b.** with a pounding heart

battement [batmɑ̃] *nm* (**a**) *(de tambour)* beat(ing); *(de porte)* banging; *(de paupières)* blink(ing); *(d'ailes)* flapping; **j'entendais les battements de son cœur** I could hear his/her heart beating (**b**) *(délai)* gap; **une heure de b.** an hour gap

batterie [batri] *nf (d'orchestre)* drums; *(ensemble) & Mil, Él* battery; *(de tests, de questions)* series; **être à la b.** *(sujet: musicien)* to be on drums; **élevage en b.** battery farming; **b. de cuisine** kitchen utensils

batteur [batœr] *nm (musicien)* drummer; *(de cuisine)* mixer

battle-dress [batœldrɛs] *nm inv* (pair of) *Br* combat trousers *or Am* combat pants

battre* [batr] **1** *vt (frapper, vaincre)* to beat; *(œufs)* to whisk; *(beurre)* to churn; *(blé)* to thresh; *(record)* to break; *(cartes)* to shuffle; **b. pavillon britannique** to fly the British flag; **b. le tambour** to beat the drum; *Mus* **b. la mesure** to beat time; **b. la campagne** to scour the countryside; **b. des œufs en neige** to whisk eggs stiffly **2** *vi (cœur)* to beat; *(porte, volet)* to bang; **b. des mains** to clap one's hands; **b. des cils** to flutter one's eyelashes; **b. des ailes** to

flap its wings; **le vent fait b. la porte** the wind bangs the door; **j'ai le cœur qui bat** *(d'émotion)* my heart is pounding **3** **se battre** *upr* to fight (**avec** with); **se b. au couteau** to fight with a knife

battu [baty] *adj (femme, enfant)* battered

battue [baty] *nf (à la chasse)* beat; *(pour retrouver qn)* search

baudet [bodɛ] *nm* donkey

baudruche [bodryʃ] *nf* **ballon de b.** balloon

baume [bom] *nm aussi Fig* balm; *Fig* **mettre du b. au cœur de qn** to be a consolation for sb; **b. pour les lèvres** lip balm *or* salve

baux [bo] *voir* **bail**

bavard, -arde [bavar, -ard] **1** *adj (qui parle beaucoup)* chatty; *(indiscret)* indiscreet **2** *nmf (qui parle beaucoup)* chatterbox; *(indiscret)* gossip **▪ bavardage** *nm (action)* chatting; *(commérage)* gossiping; **bavardages** *(paroles)* chats **▪ bavarder** *vi (parler)* to chat; *(commérer)* to gossip

bave [bav] *nf (de personne)* dribble; *(de chien)* slaver; *(de chien enragé)* froth; *(de limace)* slime **▪ baver 1** *vt Fam* **qu'est-ce que tu baves?** what are you rambling *or Br* wittering on about?; *Fam* **en b.** to have a rough time (of it) **2** *vi (personne)* to dribble; *(chien)* to slaver; *(chien enragé)* to foam at the mouth; *(stylo)* to leak;

bavette [bavɛt] *nf (de bébé)* bib; *(de bœuf)* skirt (of beef); *Fam* **tailler une b.** to have a chat

baveux, -euse [bavø, -øz] *adj (bouche)* dribbling; *(omelette)* runny

bavoir [bavwar] *nm* bib

bavure [bavyr] *nf (tache)* smudge; *(erreur)* slip-up; **sans b.** faultless; **b. policière** case of police misconduct

bayer [baje] *vi* **b. aux corneilles** to stare into space

bazar [bazar] *nm (marché)* bazaar; *(magasin)* general store; *Fam (désordre)* shambles *(sing)*; *Fam (affaires)* gear; *Fam* **mettre du b. dans qch** to make a mess of sth; *Fam* **quel b.!** what a shambles!

bazarder [bazarde] *vt Fam (se débarrasser de)* to get shot of; *(jeter)* to chuck out

bazooka [bazuka] *nm* bazooka

BCBG [besebeʒe] *(abrév* **bon chic bon genre)** *adj inv Br* ≃ Sloany, *Am* ≃ preppy

BCG [beseʒe] *n Méd* BCG

BD [bede] *(abrév* **bande dessinée)** *nf* comic strip; *(livre)* comic book

bd *abrév* **boulevard**

béant, -ante [beɑ̃, -ɑ̃t] *adj (plaie)* gaping; *(gouffre)* yawning

béat, -e [bea, -at] *adj Hum (heureux)* blissful; *Péj (niais)* inane; **être b. d'admiration** to be open-mouthed in admiration **▪ béatement** *adv (sourire)* inanely **▪ béatitude** *nf Hum* bliss

béatifier [beatifje] *vt Rel* to beatify

beau, belle [bo, bɛl] (pl **beaux, belles**)

> **bel** is used before masculine singular nouns beginning with a vowel or h mute.

1 adj (**a**) (femme, enfant, fleur, histoire) beautiful; (homme) handsome, good-looking; (spectacle, discours) fine; (maison, voyage, temps) lovely; **une belle somme** a tidy sum; **avoir une belle situation** to have a good job; **se faire b.** to smarten oneself up; **ce n'est pas b. de mentir** it isn't nice to tell lies; **c'est trop b. pour être vrai** it's too good to be true; **c'est le plus b. jour de ma vie!** it's the best day of my life!; **j'ai eu une belle peur** I had an awful fright; **il en a fait de belles!** he got up to some real tricks; très Fam **un b. salaud** a real bastard (**b**) (expressions) **au b. milieu de** right in the middle of; **de plus belle** with a vengeance; **bel et bien** (complètement) well and truly; **je me suis bel et bien trompé** I have indeed made a mistake

2 adv **il fait b.** it's fine; **j'ai b. crier...** it's no use (my) shouting...; **j'ai b. le lui expliquer...** no matter how many times I explain it to him...

3 nm **le b.** (la beauté) beauty; **faire le b.** (chien) to sit up and beg; **le plus b. de l'histoire, c'est que...** the best part of the story is that...; Fam Ironic **c'et du b.!** that's great!

4 nf **belle** (aux cartes) decider; Hum (amie) lady friend; Fam **se faire la b.** to run away; (de prison) to escape ▪ **beau-fils** (pl **beaux-fils**) nm (gendre) son-in-law; (après remariage) stepson ▪ **beau-frère** (pl **beaux-frères**) nm brother-in-law ▪ **beau-père** (pl **beaux-pères**) nm (père du conjoint) father-in-law; (après remariage) stepfather ▪ **beaux-arts** nmpl fine arts; **école des b., les B.** art school ▪ **beaux-parents** nmpl parents-in-law

beaucoup [boku] adv (intensément, en grande quantité) a lot; **aimer b. qch** to like sth very much; **s'intéresser b. à qch** to be very interested in sth; **ça te plaît? – pas b.** do you like it? – not much; **il reste encore b. à faire** there's still a lot to do; **b. d'entre nous** many of us; **b. pensent que...** a lot of people think that...; **b. de** (quantité) a lot of; (nombre) many, a lot of; **pas b. d'argent** not much money; **pas b. de gens** not many people; **avec b. de soin** with great care; **j'en ai b.** (quantité) I have a lot; (nombre) I have lots; **b. plus/moins** much more/less, a lot more/less (**que** than); (nombre) many or a lot more/a lot fewer (**que** than); **b. trop** (quantité) much too much; (nombre) much too many; **beaucoup trop petit** much too small; **de b.** by far

beauf [bof] nm Fam (beau-frère) brother-in-law; Péj = stereotypical narrow-minded, average Frenchman

beauté [bote] nf (qualité, femme) beauty; **en b.** (gagner, finir) magnificently; **être en b.** to be

looking magnificent; **de toute b.** magnificent; **se refaire une b.** to put one's face on

bébé [bebe] nm baby; **faire le b.** to behave like a baby; **b. gazelle/lapin** baby gazelle/rabbit ▪ **bébé-éprouvette** (pl **bébés-éprouvette**) nm test-tube baby

bébête [bebɛt] adj Fam silly

bec [bɛk] nm (d'oiseau) beak, bill; (de pot) lip; (de flûte) mouthpiece; Fam (bouche) mouth; **coup de b.** peck; Fam **tomber sur un b.** to come up against a serious snag; Fam **clouer le b. à qn** to shut sb up; Fam **rester le b. dans l'eau** to be left high and dry; **b. de gaz** gas lamp; **b. verseur** spout ▪ **bec-de-lièvre** (pl **becs-de-lièvre**) nm harelip

bécane [bekan] nf Fam (vélo) bike

bécarre [bekar] nm Mus natural

bécasse [bekas] nf (oiseau) woodcock; Fam (idiote) silly thing

bêche [bɛʃ] nf spade ▪ **bêcher** [beʃe] vt to dig

bêcheur, -euse [beʃœr, -øz] nmf Fam stuck-up person

bécot [beko] nm Fam snog ▪ **bécoter** vt, **se bécoter** vpr Fam to snog

becquée [beke] nf beakful; **donner la b. à** (oiseau) to feed ▪ **becqueter** 1 vt (sujet: oiseau) to peck at 2 vi très Fam (sujet: personne) to eat

bedaine [bədɛn] nf Fam pot(-belly), paunch

bedon [bədɔ̃] nm Fam pot(-belly), paunch ▪ **bedonnant, -ante** adj Fam pot-bellied, paunchy

bée [be] adj f **bouche b.** open-mouthed; **j'en suis resté bouche b.** I was speechless

beffroi [befrwa] nm belfry

bégayer [begeje] vi to stutter, to stammer ▪ **bégaiement** nm stuttering, stammering

bégonia [begɔnja] nm begonia

bègue [bɛg] **1** adj **être b.** to stutter, to stammer **2** nmf stutterer, stammerer

bégueule [begœl] adj prudish

béguin [begɛ̃] nm Fam Vieilli **avoir le b. pour qn** to have taken a fancy to sb

beige [bɛʒ] adj & nm beige

beigne [bɛɲ] nf Fam clout

beignet [beɲɛ] nm Culin fritter; (à la confiture) Br doughnut, Am donut; **b. aux pommes** apple fritter

Beijing [beidʒiŋ] nm ou f Beijing

bel [bɛl] voir **beau**

bêler [bele] vi to bleat ▪ **bêlement** nm bleat; **bêlements** bleating

belette [bəlɛt] nf weasel; Fam (jeune femme) chick, Br bird

Belgique [bɛlʒik] nf **la B.** Belgium ▪ **belge 1** adj Belgian **2** nmf **B.** Belgian

bélier [belje] nm (animal, machine) ram; **le B.** (signe) Aries; **être B.** to be (an) Aries

belle [bɛl] voir **beau** ▪ **belle-famille** (pl **belles-familles**) nf in-laws ▪ **belle-fille** (pl **belles-**

filles nf (épouse du fils) daughter-in-law; (après remariage) stepdaughter ▪**belle-mère** (pl **belles-mères**) nf (mère du conjoint) mother-in-law; (après remariage) stepmother ▪**belle-sœur** (pl **belles-sœurs**) nf sister-in-law

belligérant, -ante [beliʒerã, -ãt] 1 adj belligerent 2 nm **les belligérants** the warring nations

belliqueux, -euse [belikø, -øz] adj (peuple, pays) warlike; (personne, ton) aggressive

belote [bɔlɔt] nf = card game

belvédère [belvedɛr] nm (construction) gazebo; (sur site naturel) viewpoint

bémol [bemɔl] nm Mus flat

ben [bɛ̃] adv Fam **b. oui!** well, yes!; **b. voilà, euh...** yeah, well, er...

bénédiction [benediksjɔ̃] nf Rel & Fig blessing

bénéfice [benefis] nm (financier) profit; (avantage) benefit; **accorder le b. du doute à qn** to give sb the benefit of the doubt; **au b. de** (œuvre de charité) in aid of

bénéficiaire [benefisjɛr] 1 nmf (de chèque) payee; Jur beneficiary 2 adj (entreprise) profit-making; (compte) in credit; **marge b.** profit margin

bénéficier [benefisje] vi **b. de qch** (profiter de) to benefit from sth; (avoir) to have sth; **b. de conditions idéales** to enjoy ideal conditions; **faire b. qn de son expérience** to give sb the benefit of one's experience

bénéfique [benefik] adj beneficial (à to)

Bénélux [benelyks] nm **le B.** the Benelux

benêt [bǝnɛ] 1 adj m simple 2 nm simpleton

bénévole [benevɔl] 1 adj (travail, infirmière) voluntary 2 nmf volunteer, voluntary worker ▪**bénévolat** nm voluntary work

bénin, -igne [benɛ̃, -iɲ] adj (accident, opération) minor; (tumeur) benign

bénir [benir] vt to bless; **(que) Dieu te bénisse!** (may) God bless you! ▪**bénit, -ite** adj eau bénite holy water; pain b. consecrated bread

benjamin, -ine [bɛ̃ʒamɛ̃, -in] nmf youngest child; Sport junior

benne [bɛn] nf (de camion) tipping body; (de mine) tub; (de téléphérique) cable car; **b. à ordures** dustbin lorry

béotien, -ienne [beɔsjɛ̃, -jɛn] nmf Péj philistine

BEP [beǝpe] (abrév **brevet d'études professionnelles**) nm Scol = vocational diploma taken at 18

BEPC [beǝpese] (abrév **brevet d'études du premier cycle**) nm Scol = school leaving certificate taken at 15

béquille [bekij] nf (canne) crutch; (de moto) stand; **marcher avec des béquilles** to be on crutches

bercail [bɛrkaj] nm Hum **rentrer au b.** to return to the fold

berceau, -x [bɛrso] nm (de bébé) cradle; Fig (de civilisation) birthplace

bercer [bɛrse] 1 vt (bébé) to rock; Fig **b. qn de promesses** to delude sb with promises 2 **se bercer** vpr **se b. d'illusions** to delude oneself ▪**berceuse** nf lullaby

béret [berɛ] nm beret

berge[1] [bɛrʒ] nf (rive) bank

berge[2] [bɛrʒ] nf Fam **avoir trente berges** to be thirty

berger, -ère [bɛrʒe] nmf shepherd; **b. allemand** German shepherd, Br Alsatian ▪**bergère** nf shepherdess ▪**bergerie** nf sheepfold

berk [bɛrk] exclam yuck!

berline [bɛrlin] nf (voiture) Br (four-door) saloon, Am sedan

berlingot [bɛrlɛ̃go] nm (bonbon) Br boiled sweet, Am hard candy; (de lait) carton

berlue [bɛrly] nf **avoir la b.** to be seeing things

bermuda [bɛrmyda] nm Bermuda shorts

Bermudes [bɛrmyd] nfpl **les B.** Bermuda

berne [bɛrn] **en berne** adv Naut Br at half-mast, Am at half-staff; Mil furled

berner [bɛrne] vt to fool

besace [bǝzas] nf (de mendiant) bag; **sac b.** = large, soft bag

bésef [bezɛf] adv = **bézef**

besogne [bǝzɔɲ] nf job, task; Fig & Péj **aller vite en b.** to jump the gun ▪**besogneux, -euse** adj Péj (travailleur) plodding

besoin [bǝzwɛ̃] nm need; **avoir b. de qn/qch** to need sb/sth; **avoir b. de faire qch** to need to do sth; **éprouver le b. de faire qch** to feel the need to do sth; **au b., si b. est** if necessary, if need be; **en cas de b.** if need be; **être dans le b.** (très pauvre) to be in need; **faire ses besoins** (personne) to relieve oneself; (animal) to do its business

bestial, -e, -iaux, -iales [bestjal, -jo] adj bestial ▪**bestiaux** nmpl livestock

bestiole [bestjɔl] nf (insecte) Br creepycrawly, Am creepy-crawler

bêta, -asse [beta, -as] adj Fam silly

bétail [betaj] nm livestock

bête[1] [bɛt] adj stupid, silly; Fam **être b. comme ses pieds** to be as thick as two short planks; **ce n'est pas b.** (suggestion) it's not a bad idea; **c'est b., on a loupé le film!** what a shame, we've missed the film!; **c'est b. comme chou!** it's as easy as pie ▪**bêtement** adv stupidly; **tout b.** quite simply ▪**bêtise** [betiz] nf (manque d'intelligence) stupidity; (action, parole) stupid thing; (bagatelle) mere trifle; **faire/dire une b.** to do/say something stupid; **dire des bêtises** to talk nonsense

bête[2] [bɛt] nf animal; (insecte) bug; Fig **chercher la petite b.** to nit-pick; **elle m'a regardé comme une b. curieuse** she looked at me as if I was from another planet; Péj **b. à concours** Br swot, Am grind; **b. à bon dieu** Br ladybird, Am ladybug; **b. de somme** beast of burden; **b. féroce** wild animal; **b. noire** *Br* pet hate, *Am* pet peeve

béton [betɔ̃] *nm* (**a**) *(matériau)* concrete; **mur en b.** concrete wall; **alibi en b.** cast-iron alibi; **b. armé** reinforced concrete (**b**) *Fam* **laisse b.!** drop it!, forget it! ▪ **bétonner** *vt* to concrete; *Fam (préparer avec soin)* to work really hard on ▪ **bétonnière, bétonneuse** *nf* cement mixer

bette [bɛt] *nf* Swiss chard

betterave [bɛtʀav] *nf (plante) Br* beetroot, *Am* beet; **b. sucrière** sugar beet

beugler [bøgle] *vi (taureau)* to bellow; *(vache)* to moo; *Fig (radio)* to blare

beur [bœʀ] *nmf Fam* = North African born in France of immigrant parents

beurre [bœʀ] *nm* butter; **au b.** *(pâtisserie)* made with butter; *Fig* **ça mettra du b. dans les épinards** that will make life a bit easier; *Fig* **il veut le b. et l'argent du b.** he wants to have his cake and eat it; *Fam* **ça compte pour du b.** that doesn't count; **b. d'anchois** anchovy paste ▪ **beurré** *adj très Fam (ivre)* plastered ▪ **beurrer** *vt* to butter ▪ **beurrier** *nm* butter dish

beuverie [bøvʀi] *nf* drinking session

bévue [bevy] *nf* slip-up

bézef [bezɛf] *adv Fam* **il n'y en a pas b.** *(pain, confiture)* there isn't much of it; *(légumes, livres)* there aren't many of them

biais [bjɛ] *nm* (**a**) *(de mur)* slant; *(moyen)* way; *(aspect)* angle; **regarder qn de b.** to look sideways at sb; **traverser en b.** to cross at an angle; **par le b. de** through

biaiser [bjeze] *vi (ruser)* to dodge the issue

bibelot [biblo] *nm* curio, *Br* knick-knack

biberon [bibʀɔ̃] *nm* (feeding) bottle; **nourrir un bébé au b.** to bottle-feed a child

bibi [bibi] *pron Fam (moi)* yours truly

bibine [bibin] *nf Fam (boisson)* dishwater

bible [bibl] *nf* bible; **la B.** the Bible ▪ **biblique** *adj* biblical

bibliobus [biblijɔbys] *nm* mobile library

bibliographie [biblijɔgʀafi] *nf* bibliography

bibliothèque [biblijɔtɛk] *nf (bâtiment, salle)* library; *(meuble)* bookcase; **b. municipale** public library ▪ **bibliothécaire** *nmf* librarian

Bic® [bik] *nm* ballpoint (pen), *Br* biro®

bicarbonate [bikaʀbɔnat] *nm Chim* bicarbonate; **b. de soude** bicarbonate of soda

bicentenaire [bisɑ̃tnɛʀ] *nm Br* bicentenary, *Am* bicentennial

biceps [bisɛps] *nm Fam* **avoir des b.** to have muscles

biche [biʃ] *nf (animal)* female deer, doe; **ma b.** *(ma chérie)* darling

bichonner [biʃɔne] **1** *vt (préparer)* to doll up; *(soigner)* to pamper **2 se bichonner** *vpr* to doll oneself up

bicolore [bikɔlɔʀ] *adj Br* two-coloured, *Am* two-colored

bicoque [bikɔk] *nf Fam (maison)* house

bicyclette [bisiklɛt] *nf* bicycle; **la b.** *(sport)* cycling; **faire de la b.** to go cycling; **aller en ville à b.** to cycle to town; **je ne sais pas faire de la b.** I can't ride a bicycle

bidasse [bidas] *nm très Fam Br* squaddie, *Am* G.I.

bide [bid] *nm Fam (ventre)* belly; **avoir/prendre du b.** to have/develop a belly; **faire un b.** *(film, roman)* to bomb, *Br* to flop

bidet [bidɛ] *nm (cuvette)* bidet

bidoche [bidɔʃ] *nf très Fam* meat

bidon [bidɔ̃] **1** *nm (d'essence, d'huile)* can; *(de lait)* churn; *Fam (ventre)* belly; *Fam* **c'est du b.** it's a load of tosh; **b. d'essence** petrol can, jerry can **2** *adj inv Fam (simulé)* phoney, fake

bidonner [bidɔne] **se bidonner** *vpr Fam* to laugh one's head off ▪ **bidonnant, ante** *adj Fam* hilarious

bidonville [bidɔ̃vil] *nf* shantytown

bidule [bidyl] *nm Fam (chose)* whatsit, thingummy; **B.** *(personne)* what's-his-name, *f* what's-her-name

bien [bjɛ̃] **1** *adv* (**a**) *(convenablement)* well; **il joue b.** he plays well; **je vais b.** I'm fine or well; **écoutez-moi b.!** listen carefully; *Ironique* **ça commence b.!** that's a good start! (**b**) *(moralement)* right; **b. se conduire** to behave (well); **vous avez b. fait** you did the right thing; **tu ferais b. de te méfier** you would be wise to behave (**c**) *(très)* very; **vous arrivez b. tard** you're very late (**d**) *(beaucoup)* a lot, a great deal; **b. plus/moins** much more/less; **b. des gens** a lot of people; **b. des fois** many times; **il faut b. du courage pour…** it takes a lot of courage to…; **tu as b. de la chance** you're really lucky!; **merci b.!** thanks very much! (**e**) *(en intensif)* **regarder qn b. en face** to look sb right in the face; **je sais b.** I'm well aware of it; **je vous l'avais b. dit** I told you so!; **j'y suis b. obligé** I just have to; **nos verrons b.!** we'll see!; **c'est b. fait pour lui** it serves him right; **c'est b. ce que je pensais** that's what I thought; **c'est b. cela** that's right; **c'est b. compris?** is that quite understood?; **c'est b. toi?** is it really you? (**f**) *(locutions)* **b. que…** (+ *subjunctive)* although, though; **b. entendu, b. sûr** of course; **b. sûr que non!** of course, not!; **b. sûr que je viendrai!** of course, I'll come!

2 *adj inv (satisfaisant)* good; *(à l'aise)* comfortable; *(en forme)* well; *(moral)* decent; *(beau)* attractive; **être b. avec qn** *(en bons termes)* to be on good terms with sb; **on est b. ici** it's nice here; **ce n'est pas b. de mentir** it's not nice to lie; **elle est b. sur cette photo** she looks good on this photo; *Fam* **nous voilà b.!** we're in a right mess!

3 *exclam* fine!, right!; **eh b.!** well!

4 *nm Phil & Rel* good; *(chose, capital)* possession; *Jur* asset; **le b. et le mal** good and evil; *Jur* **biens** property; **faire le b.** to do good; **ça te fera du b.** it will do you good; **dire du b. de qn** to speak well of sb; **c'est pour ton b.** it's for your own good; **grand b. te fasse!** much good may it do you!; **biens de consommation** consumer goods; **biens immobiliers** real estate *or* property ▪**bien-aimé, -ée** (*mpl* **bien-aimés,** *fpl* **bien-aimées**) *adj & nmf* beloved ▪**bien-être** *nm* well-being ▪**bien-fondé** *nm* validity ▪**bien-pensant, -ante** (*mpl* **bien-pensants,** *fpl* **bien-pensantes**) *adj & nmf* conformist

bienfaisance [bjɛ̃fəzɑ̃s] *nf* œuvre de b. charity

bienfaisant, -ante [bjɛ̃fəzɑ̃, -ɑ̃t] *adj* (*remède*) beneficial; (*personne*) charitable

bienfait [bjɛ̃fɛ] *nm* (*acte*) kindness; (*avantage*) benefit

bienfaiteur, -trice [bjɛ̃fɛtœr, -tris] *nmf* benefactor

bienheureux, -euse [bjɛ̃nœrø, -øz] *adj* blissful; *Rel* blessed

biennal, -e, -aux, -ales [bjenal, -o] *adj* biennial

bienséant, -ante [bjɛ̃seɑ̃, -ɑ̃t] *adj* proper ▪**bienséance** *nf* propriety

bientôt [bjɛ̃to] *adv* soon; **à b.!** see you soon!; **il est b. dix heures** it's nearly ten o'clock; *Fam* **tu n'as pas b. fini?** have you quite finished?

bienveillant, -ante [bjɛ̃vɛjɑ̃, -ɑ̃t] *adj* kind ▪**bienveillance** *nf* kindness; **avec b.** kindly

bienvenu, -ue [bjɛ̃vny] **1** *adj* (*repos, explication*) welcome **2** *nmf* **soyez le b.!** welcome!; **tu seras toujours le b. chez nous** you'll always be welcome here ▪**bienvenue** *nf* welcome; **souhaiter la b. à qn** to welcome sb

bière¹ [bjɛr] *nf* (*boisson*) beer; **b. blonde** lager; **b. brune** *Br* brown ale, *Am* dark beer; **b. pression** *Br* draught beer, *Am* draft beer

bière² [bjɛr] *nf* (*cercueil*) coffin

biffer [bife] *vt* to cross out

bifteck [biftɛk] *nm* steak; *Fam* **gagner son b.** to earn one's bread and butter; **b. haché** *Br* mince, *Am* mincemeat

bifurquer [bifyrke] *vi* (*route, chemin*) to fork; (*automobiliste*) to turn off ▪**bifurcation** *nf* junction

bigame [bigam] *adj* bigamous ▪**bigamie** *nf* bigamy

bigarré, -ée [bigare] *adj* (*étoffe*) *Br* multicoloured, *Am* multicolored; (*foule*) motley

bigareau, -x [bigaro] *nm* = type of cherry

bigler [bigle] *vi Fam* (*loucher*) to have a squint; **b. sur qch** to have a good look at sth ▪**bigleux, -euse** *adj Fam* (*qui louche*) cross-eyed; (*myope*) short-sighted

bigorneau, -x [bigorno] *nm* winkle

bigot, -ote [bigo, -ɔt] *Péj* **1** *adj* sanctimonious **2** *nmf* (*religious*) bigot

Il faut noter que le terme anglais **bigot** est un faux ami. Il se rapporte au sectarisme religieux et non à une attitude excessivement dévote.

bigoudi [bigudi] *nm* (hair) curler *or* roller

bigrement [bigrəmɑ̃] *adv Fam* (*très*) awfully; (*beaucoup*) a heck of a lot

bihebdomadaire [biɛbdɔmadɛr] *adj* twice-weekly

bijou, -x [biʒu] *nm* jewel; *Fig* gem ▪**bijouterie** [-tri] *nf* (*boutique*) *Br* jeweller's shop, *Am* jewelry shop; (*commerce, fabrication*) jeweller's trade ▪**bijoutier, -ière** *nmf Br* jeweller, *Am* jeweler

bikini® [bikini] *nm* bikini

bilan [bilɑ̃] *nm* (*de situation*) assessment; (*résultats*) results; (*d'un accident*) toll; **faire le b. de la situation** to take stock of the situation; *Com* **déposer son b.** to file one's petition for bankruptcy; **b. de santé** complete check-up; *Fin* **b. (comptable)** balance sheet

bilatéral, -e, -aux, -ales [bilateral, -o] *adj* bilateral

bile [bil] *nf* bile; *Fam* **se faire de la b. (pour qch)** to fret (about sth) ▪**se biler** *upr Fam* to fret

bilingue [bilɛ̃g] *adj* bilingual

billard [bijar] *nm* (*jeu*) billiards; (*table*) billiard table; *Fam* **passer sur le b.** to go under the knife; **b. américain** pool; **b. électrique** pinball

bille [bij] *nf* (*de verre*) marble; (*de billard*) billiard ball; **jouer aux billes** to play marbles; *Fam* **reprendre ses billes** to pull out

billet [bijɛ] *nm* ticket; **b. (de banque)** *Br* (bank)note, *Am* bill; **b. d'avion/de train** plane/train ticket; **b. électronique** e-ticket; **b. de première/seconde** first-class/second-class ticket; **b. aller retour** *Br* return ticket, *Am* round trip ticket; **b. simple** single ticket, *Am* one-way ticket; **b. doux** love letter

billetterie [bijetri] *nf* (*lieu*) ticket office; **b. automatique** (*de billet de transport*) ticket machine

billion [biljɔ̃] *nm* trillion

billot [bijo] *nm* block

bimensuel, -elle [bimɑ̃sɥɛl] *adj* bimonthly, *Br* fortnightly

bimoteur [bimɔtœr] *adj* twin-engined

binaire [binɛr] *adj Math* binary

biner [bine] *vt* to hoe ▪**binette** *nf* hoe; *Fam* (*visage*) mug; *Can Ordinat* smiley

binocle [binɔkl] *nm* pince-nez

biochimie [bjɔʃimi] *nf* biochemistry ▪**biochimique** *adj* biochemical

biodégradable [bjɔdegradabl] *adj* biodegradable

biodiversité [bjɔdivɛrsite] *nf* biodiversity

biographie [bjɔgrafi] *nf* biography ▪**biographe** *nmf* biographer ▪**biographique** *adj* biographical

bio-industrie [bjoɛ̃dystri] (*pl* **bio-industries**) *nf* biotechnology industry

biologie [bjɔlɔʒi] *nf* biology • **biologique** *adj* biological; (*sans engrais chimiques*) organic • **biologiste** *nm* biologist

biotechnologie [bjotɛknɔlɔʒi] *nf* biotechnology

bioterrorisme [bjoterɔrism] *nm* bioterrorism • **bioterroriste** *nmf* bioterrorist

bip [bip] *nm* (*son*) beep; (*appareil*) beeper; **faire b.** to beep

bipède [biped] *nm* biped

bique [bik] *nf Fam* (*chèvre*) nanny goat

biréacteur [bireaktœr] *nm* twin-engine jet

Birmanie [birmani] *nf* la B. Burma • **birman, -ane 1** *adj* Burmese **2** *nmf* **B., Birmane** Burmese

bis¹ [bis] *adv* (*au théâtre*) encore; (*en musique*) repeat; **4 bis** (*adresse*) ≃ 4A

bis², bise [bi, biz] *adj Br* greyish-brown, *Am* grayish-brown

bisbille [bisbij] *nf Fam* squabble; **en b. avec qn** at odds with sb

biscornu, -ue [biskɔrny] *adj* (*objet*) oddly shaped; *Fam* (*idée*) cranky

biscotte [biskɔt] *nf* rusk

biscuit [biskɥi] *nm* (*sucré*) *Br* biscuit, *Am* cookie; **biscuits salés** crackers

bise¹ [biz] *nf* (*vent*) north wind

bise² [biz] *nf Fam* (*baiser*) kiss; **faire la b. à qn** to give sb a kiss; **grosses bises** (*sur une lettre*) love and kisses

biseau, -x [bizo] *nm* (*outil, bord*) bevel; **en b.** bevel-edged

bisexuel, -uelle [biseksɥɛl] *adj* bisexual

bison [bizɔ̃] *nm* bison

bisou [bizu] *nm Fam* kiss; **bisous** (*sur une lettre*) love

bissextile [bisɛkstil] *adj f* **année b.** leap year

bistouri [bisturi] *nm* lancet

bistro(t) [bistro] *nm Fam* bar

bitume [bitym] *nm* (*revêtement*) asphalt

bivouac [bivwak] *nm* bivouac • **bivouaquer** *vi* to bivouac

bizarre [bizar] *adj* odd • **bizarrement** *adv* oddly • **bizarroïde** *adj Fam* weird

bizutage [bizytaʒ] *nm Fam Univ* = playing practical jokes on first-year students, *Am* ≃ hazing • **bizuter** *vt Fam Univ* = to play practical jokes on, *Am* ≃ to haze

blabla [blabla] *nm Fam* claptrap

blafard, -arde [blafar, -ard] *adj* pallid

blague [blag] *nf* (*plaisanterie*) joke; **faire une b. à qn** to play a joke on sb; **raconter des blagues** (*mensonges*) to lie; **sans b.?** no kidding? • **blaguer** *vi Fam* to joke • **blagueur, -euse** *nmf* joker

blaireau, -x [blero] *nm* (*animal*) badger; (*brosse*) shaving brush

blairer [blere] *vt Fam* **je ne peux pas le b.** I can't stand *or Br* stick him

blâme [blɑm] *nm* (*reproche*) blame; (*sanction*) reprimand • **blâmer** *vt* (*désapprouver*) to blame; (*sanctionner*) to reprimand

blanc, blanche [blɑ̃, blɑ̃ʃ] **1** *adj* white; (*peau*) pale; (*page*) blank; **d'une voix blanche** in a toneless voice **2** *nm* (*couleur*) white; (*espace, domino*) blank; (*vin*) white wine; **(article de) b.** (*linge*) linen; **en b.** (*chèque*) blank; **à b.** (*cartouche*) blank; **tirer à b.** to fire blanks; **chauffé à b.** white-hot; **regarder qn dans le b. de yeux** to look sb straight in the eye; **b. d'œuf** egg white; **b. de poulet** chicken breast; **b. cassé** off-white **3** *nm* (*note de musique*) *Br* minim, *Am* half-note **4** *nmf* **B.** (*personne*) White man, *f* White woman; **les B.** the Whites • **blanchâtre** *adj* whitish • **blancheur** *nf* whiteness

blanchiment [blɑ̃ʃimɑ̃] *nm* (*d'argent*) laundering

blanchir [blɑ̃ʃir] **1** *vt* to whiten; (*mur*) to whitewash; (*linge*) to launder; *Culin* to blanch; *Fig* (*argent*) to launder; **b. qn** (*disculper*) to clear sb **2** *vi* to turn white • **blanchiment** *nm* (*d'argent*) laundering • **blanchissage** *nm* (*de linge*) laundering • **blanchisserie** *nf* (*lieu*) laundry

blanquette [blɑ̃kɛt] *nf* **b. de veau** = veal stew in white sauce; **b. de Limoux** = sparkling white wine from Limoux

blasé, -ée [blaze] *adj* blasé

blason [blazɔ̃] *nm* coat of arms

blasphème [blasfɛm] *nf* blasphemy • **blasphématoire** *adj* blasphemous • **blasphémer** *vi* to blaspheme

blatte [blat] *nf* cockroach

blazer [blazœr] *nm* blazer

bld *abrév* boulevard

blé [ble] *nm* wheat, *Br* corn; *Fam* (*argent*) dough

bled [blɛd] *nm Fam* (*lieu isolé*) dump; **dans un b. perdu** in the middle of nowhere

blême [blɛm] *adj* sickly pale; **b. de colère** livid with anger • **blêmir** *vi* to turn pale

> Il faut noter que le verbe anglais **to blemish** est un faux ami. Il ne signifie jamais **devenir pâle**.

blesser [blese] **1** *vt* (*dans un accident*) to injure, to hurt; (*par arme*) to wound; (*offenser*) to hurt **2 se blesser** *vpr* (*par accident*) to hurt *or* injure oneself; (*avec une arme*) to wound oneself; **se b. au bras** to hurt one's arm • **blessant, -ante** *adj* hurtful • **blessé, -ée** *nmf* (*victime d'accident*) injured person; (*victime d'aggression*) wounded person; **les blessés** the injured/wounded • **blessure** *nf* (*dans un accident*) injury; (*par arme*) wound

blette [blɛt] *nf* = **bette**

bleu, -e [blø] (*mpl* -s) **1** *adj* blue; (*steak*) very rare **2** *n (couleur)* blue; *(ecchymose)* bruise; *(fromage)* blue cheese; *Fam (novice)* novice; **b. de travail** *Br* overalls, *Am* overall; **se faire un b. au genou** to bruise one's knee; **b. ciel** sky blue; **b. marine** navy blue; **b. roi** royal blue ▪ **bleuâtre** *adj* bluish ▪ **bleuté, -ée** *adj* bluish

bleuet [bløɛ] *nm (plante)* cornflower

blinder [blɛ̃de] *vt (véhicule)* to *Br* armour-plate or *Am* armor-plate ▪ **blindé, -ée 1** *adj Mil Br* armoured, armour-plated, *Am* armored, armor-plated; *(voiture)* bulletproof; **porte blindée** steel security door; *Fam* **je suis b.** I'm hardened to it **2** *nm Mil Br* armoured or *Am* armored vehicle

bloc [blɔk] *nm (de pierre, de bois)* block; *(de papier)* pad; *(de maison)* & *Pol* bloc; *(masse compacte)* unit; **faire b. contre qn** to join forces against sb; **en b.** *(démissionner)* all together; **tout refuser en b.** to reject everything in its entirety; **à b.** *(visser, serrer)* as tightly as possible; *très Fam* **être au b.** *(en prison)* to be in the clink; **b. opératoire** *Br* operating theatre, *Am* operating room ▪ **bloc-notes** *(pl* **blocs-notes***) nm* notepad

blocage [blɔkaʒ] *nm (de mécanisme)* jamming; *(de freins, de roues)* locking; **b. des prix** price freeze; **faire un b. psychologique** to have a mental block

blocus [blɔkys] *nm* blockade; **lever le b.** to raise the blockade

blog [blɔg] *nm Ordinat* blog

blond, -onde [blɔ̃, -ɔ̃d] **1** *adj (cheveux, personne)* blond; *(sable)* golden **2** *nm (homme)* fair-haired man; *(couleur)* blond; **b. cendré** ash blond; **b. vénitien** strawberry blond **3** *nf (femme)* fair-haired woman, blonde ▪ **blondeur** *nf* fairness, blondness

blondinet, -ette [blɔ̃dinɛ, -ɛt] *adj* fairhaired

bloquer [blɔke] **1** *vt (route, ballon, compte)* to block; *(porte, mécanisme)* to jam; *(roue)* to lock; *(salaires, prix, crédits)* to freeze; *(grouper)* to group together; **b. le passage à qn** to block sb's way; **bloqué par la neige** snowbound; *Fam* **je suis bloqué à l'hôpital** I'm stuck in hospital **2** **se bloquer** *vpr (machine)* to get stuck

blottir [blɔtir] **se blottir** *vpr* to snuggle up; **se b. contre qn** to snuggle up to sb; **blottis les uns contre les autres** huddled up together

blouse [bluz] *nf (tablier)* overall; *(corsage)* blouse; **b. blanche** *(de médecin, de biologiste)* white coat ▪ **blouson** *nm* (lumber-)jacket; *(plus léger)* blouson; **b. en cuir** leather jacket; **b. d'aviateur** bomber jacket

bluff [blœf] *nm* bluff ▪ **bluffer** *vti (aux cartes)* & *Fam* to bluff

blush [blœʃ] *nm* blusher

boa [bɔa] *nm (serpent, tour de cou)* boa

bobard [bɔbar] *nm Fam* tall story

bobine [bɔbin] *nf (de ruban, de fil)* reel; *(de machine à coudre)* bobbin; *(de film, de papier)* roll; *(de machine à écrire)* spool; *Él* coil; *Fam (visage)* mug

bobo [bɔbo] *nm Fam (petite blessure)* cut; **ça fait b.** it hurts

bocage [bɔkaʒ] *nm* bocage *(countryside with many hedges, trees and small fields)*

bocal, -aux [bɔkal, -o] *nm* jar; *(aquarium)* bowl

bock [bɔk] *nm* beer glass

bœuf [bœf] *(pl* **-fs** [bø]*)* **1** *nm (animal)* bullock; *(de trait)* ox *(pl* oxen*)*; *(viande)* beef **2** *adj inv Fam* **faire un effet b.** to make a big impression

bof [bɔf] *exclam Fam* **ça te plaît? – b.! pas tellement** do you like it? – not really, no; **il est chouette, mon nouveau pull – b.** my new sweater's great – I suppose so

bogue [bɔg] *nm Ordinat* bug

bohème [bɔɛm] *adj & nmf* bohemian ▪ **bohémien, -ienne** *adj & nmf* gypsy

boire* [bwar] **1** *vt (sujet: personne)* to drink; *(sujet: plante)* to soak up; *Fig* **b. les paroles de qn** to drink in sb's every word **2** *vi (sujet: personne)* to drink; *(sujet: plante)* to soak in; **b. comme un trou** to drink like a fish; *Fam* **b. un coup** to have a drink; **b. à la bouteille** to drink from the bottle; **b. à petits coups** to sip; **b. au succès de qn** to drink to sb's success; **donner à b. à qn** to give sb a drink; **faire b. les chevaux** to water the horses **3** **se boire** *vpr* to be drunk **4** *nm* **le b. et le manger** food and drink

bois [bwa] *nm (matériau, forêt)* wood; *(de raquette)* frame; **en ou de b.** wooden; **les b.** *(d'un cerf)* the antlers; *(d'un orchestre)* woodwind instruments; *Fig* **ils vont voir de quel b. je me chauffe!** I'll show them!; **petit b.** kindling; **b. de chauffage** firewood; **b. de construction** timber; **b. de lit** bed frame; **b. mort** dead wood ▪ **boisé, -ée** *adj* wooded ▪ **boiseries** *nfpl Br* panelling, *Am* paneling

boisson [bwasɔ̃] *nf* drink

boit [bwa] *voir* **boire**

boîte [bwat] *nf* **(a)** *(récipient)* box; **b. d'allumettes** *(pleine)* box of matches; *(vide)* matchbox; **des haricots en b.** canned or *Br* tinned beans; *Fam* **mettre qn en b.** to pull sb's leg; **b. à bijoux** jewel box; **b. à gants** glove compartment; **b. à lettres** *Br* postbox, *Am* mailbox; **b. à musique** music box; **b. à outils** toolbox; **b. de conserve** can, *Br* tin; *Aut* **b. de vitesse** gearbox; *Av* **b. noire** black box; **b. postale** Post Office Box; *Ordinat* **b. de dialogue** dialog box; *Ordinat* **b. de réception** *(de messages électroniques)* inbox, mailbox; *Tél* **b. vocale** voice mail **(b)** *Fam (entreprise)* firm; *Péj* **b. à bac** crammer; **b. de jazz** jazz club; **b. de nuit** nightclub ▪ **boîtier** *nm (de montre)* case

boiter [bwate] *vi* to limp ▪ **boiteux, -euse** *adj (personne)* lame; *Fig (raisonnement)* shaky

boive [bwav] *subjonctif de* **boire**

bol [bɔl] *nm (récipient, contenu)* bowl; **prendre un b. d'air** to get a good breath of fresh air; *Fam* **avoir du b.** to be lucky; *Fam* **coup de b.** stroke of luck

bolide [bɔlid] *nm (voiture)* racing car

Bolivie [bɔlivi] *nf* la B. Bolivia ▪ **bolivien, -ienne 1** *adj* Bolivian **2** *nmf* B., Bolivienne Bolivian

bombarder [bɔ̃barde] *vt (avec des bombes)* to bomb; *(avec des obus)* to shell; **b. de qn de questions** to bombard sb with questions ▪ **bombardement** [-amã] *nm (avec des bombes)* bombing; *(avec des obus)* shelling ▪ **bombardier** *nm (avion)* bomber

bombe [bɔ̃b] *nf* (a) *(explosif)* bomb; *Fig* **faire l'effet d'une b.** to be a bombshell; **b. atomique** atom(ic) bomb; **b. à eau** water bomb; **b. à retardement** time bomb (b) *(atomiseur)* spray (can) (c) *(chapeau)* riding hat

bomber [bɔ̃be] **1** *vt* **b. le torse** to stick out one's chest **2** *vi (mur)* to bulge; *(planche)* to warp ▪ **bombé, -ée** *adj* bulging

bon¹, bonne [bɔ̃, bɔn] **1** *adj* (a) *(satisfaisant)* good; **avoir de bons résultats** to get good results; **c'est b.** *(d'accord)* that's fine (b) *(agréable)* nice, good; **passer une bonne soirée** to spend a pleasant evening; **il fait b. se reposer** it's nice *or* good to rest; **b. anniversaire!** happy birthday!; **bonne année!** Happy New Year! (c) *(charitable)* kind, good (**avec qn** to sb) (d) *(correct)* right; **le b. choix/ moment/livre** the right choice/moment/book (e) *(apte)* fit; **b. à manger** fit to eat; *Mil* **b. pour le service** fit for duty; **elle n'est bonne à rien** she's useless (f) *(prudent)* wise, good; **juger b. de partir** to think it wise to leave (g) *(compétent)* good; **b. en français** good at French (h) *(profitable) (investissement, conseil, idée)* good; **c'est b. à savoir** it's worth knowing (i) *(valable)* valid; **ce billet est encore b.** this ticket is still valid; **le lait est-il encore b.?** is that milk still all right to drink? (j) *(en intensif)* **un b. rhume** a bad cold; **dix bonnes minutes** a good ten minutes; **j'ai mis un b. moment à comprendre** it took me a while to understand (k) *(locutions)* **à quoi b.?** what's the point?; **quand b. vous semble** whenever you like; **pour de b.** *(partir, revenir)* for good; **tenir b.** *(personne)* to hold out; **avoir qn à la bonne** to have a soft spot for sb; **elle est bien b.!** that's a good one!

2 *nm* **avoir du b.** to have some good points; **un b. à rien** a good-for-nothing; **les bons et les méchants** the goodies and the baddies

3 *adv* **sentir b.** to smell good; **il fait b.** it's nice and warm

4 *exclam* **b.! on y va?** right, shall we go?; **ah b.,** je ne le savais pas really? I didn't know; **ah b.?** is that so?

bon² [bɔ̃] *nm (papier)* coupon, *Br* voucher; *Fin (titre)* bond; **b. d'achat** *Br* gift voucher, *Am* gift certificate; **b. de commande** order form; **b. de réduction** money-off coupon; *Fin* **b. du Trésor** treasury bond

bonasse [bɔnas] *adj* soft

bonbon [bɔ̃bɔ̃] *nm Br* sweet, *Am* candy; **b. à la menthe** mint ▪ **bonbonnière** *nf Br* sweet box, *Am* candy box

bonbonne [bɔ̃bɔn] *nf (bouteille)* demijohn; *(de gaz)* cylinder

bond [bɔ̃] *nm* leap, jump; *(de balle)* bounce; **faire un b.** to leap up; *Fig (prix)* to shoot up; **se lever d'un b.** *(du lit)* to jump out of bed; *(d'une chaise)* to leap up; **faire faux b. à qn** to leave sb in the lurch

bonde [bɔ̃d] *nf (bouchon)* plug; *(trou)* plughole

bondé, -ée [bɔ̃de] *adj* packed, crammed

bondir [bɔ̃dir] *vi* to leap, to jump; **b. sur qn/qch** to pounce on sb/sth; *Fig* **ça me fait b.** it makes me hopping mad

bon enfant [bɔnãfã] *adj inv* easy-going

bonheur [bɔnœr] *nm (bien-être)* happiness; *(chance)* good fortune; **faire le b. de qn** to make sb happy; **porter b. à qn** to bring sb luck; **par b.** luckily; **au petit b.** at random

bonhomie [bɔnɔmi] *nf* good-naturedness

bonhomme [bɔnɔm] *(pl* bonshommes [bɔ̃zɔm]*) nm* fellow, guy; **aller son petit b. de chemin** to be jogging along nicely; **b. de neige** snowman

boniche [bɔniʃ] *nf Péj* maid

boniment [bɔnimã] *nm (discours)* patter; *Fam (mensonge)* tall story

bonjour [bɔ̃ʒur] *nm & exclam (le matin)* good morning; *(l'après-midi)* good afternoon; **dire b. à qn** to say hello to sb; *Fam* **b. l'ambiance!** there was one hell of an atmosphere

bonne¹ [bɔn] *voir* **bon¹**

bonne² [bɔn] *nf (domestique)* maid; **b. d'enfants** nanny

bonnement [bɔnmã] *adv* **tout b.** simply

bonnet [bɔnɛ] *nm (coiffure)* hat; *(de soutien-gorge)* cup; *Fig* **c'est b. blanc blanc b.** it's six of one and half a dozen of the other; *Fam* **gros b.** bigshot; **b. d'âne** *Br* dunce's cap, *Am* dunce cap; **b. de bain** bathing cap ▪ **bonneterie** [-ɛtri] *nf (bas)* hosiery

bonniche [bɔniʃ] *nf =* **boniche**

bonsoir [bɔ̃swar] *nm & exclam (en rencontrant qn)* good evening; *(en quittant qn)* goodbye; *(au coucher)* goodnight

bonté [bɔ̃te] *nf* kindness, goodness; **avoir la b. de faire qch** to be so kind as to do sth

bonus [bɔnys] *nm (de salaire)* bonus; *(d'assurance)* no-claims bonus

bon vivant [bɔ̃vivã] *adj m* **être b.** to enjoy life

boom [bum] *nm (économique)* boom

bord [bɔr] *nm (limite)* edge; *(de chapeau)* brim; *(de verre)* rim; **le b. du trottoir** *Br* the kerb, *Am* the curb; **au b. de la route** at the side of the road; **au b. de la rivière** beside the river; **au b. de la mer** at the seaside; **au b. de la ruine** on the brink *or* verge of ruin; **au b. des larmes** on the verge of tears; **à bord d'un bateau/d'un avion** on board a boat/a plane; **monter à b.** to go on board; **être le seul maître à b.** to be the one in charge; **par-dessus b.** overboard

bordeaux [bɔrdo] **1** *nm (vin)* Bordeaux (wine); *(rouge)* claret **2** *adj inv* maroon

bordée [bɔrde] *nf Naut (salve)* broadside; *Fig (d'injures)* torrent

bordel [bɔrdɛl] *nm très Fam (lieu)* brothel; *(désordre)* mess; **mettre le b. dans qch** to make a mess of sth ▪ **bordélique** *adj très Fam (organisation, pièce)* shambolic; **être b.** *(personne)* to be a slob

border [bɔrde] *vt (lit)* to tuck in; *(sujet: arbres)* to line; **b. qch de qch** to edge sth with sth; **b. qn dans son lit** to tuck sb in

bordereau, -x [bɔrdəro] *nm Fin & Com* note

bordure [bɔrdyr] *nf (bord)* edge; *(de vêtement)* border; **en b. de route** by the roadside

borgne [bɔrɲ] *adj (personne)* one-eyed; *(louche)* shady

borne [bɔrn] *nf (limite)* boundary marker; *(pierre)* boundary stone; *Él* terminal; *Fam (kilomètre)* kilometer; *Fig* **sans bornes** boundless; *Fig* **dépasser les bornes** to go too far; **b. kilométrique** ≃ milestone

borner [bɔrne] **1** *vt (terrrain)* to mark out **2** **se borner** *vpr* **se b. à qch/à faire qch** *(personne)* to restrict oneself to sth/to doing sth; **se b. à qch** *(chose)* to be limited to sth ▪ **borné, -ée** *adj (personne)* narrow-minded; *(esprit)* narrow

Bosnie [bɔzni] *nf* **la B.** Bosnia

bosquet [bɔskɛ] *nm* grove

bosse [bɔs] *nf (de bossu, de chameau)* hump; *(enflure)* bump, lump; *(de terrain)* bump; **se faire une b.** to get a bump; *Fam* **avoir la b. du commerce** to have a good head for business; *Fam* **il a roulé sa b.** he's knocked about a bit

bosseler [bɔsle] *vt (déformer)* to dent

bosser [bɔse] *vi Fam* to work ▪ **bosseur, -euse** *Fam* **1** *adj* hard-working **2** *nmf* hard worker

bossu, -ue [bɔsy] **1** *adj (personne)* hunchbacked **2** *nmf* hunchback

bot [bo] *adj m* **pied b.** club foot

botanique [bɔtanik] **1** *adj* botanical **2** *nf* botany

botte [bɔt] *nf (chaussure)* boot; *(de fleurs, de radis)* bunch; *Fig* **b. secrète** secret weapon; *Fam* **en avoir plein les bottes** to be fed up to the back teeth; **bottes en caoutchouc** rubber boots ▪ **botter** *vt* **botté de cuir** wearing leather boots; *Fam* **b. le derrière à qn** to boot sb up the backside; *Fam* **ça me botte** I like it ▪ **bottillon** *nm*, ▪ **bottine** *nf* ankle boot

Bottin® [bɔtɛ̃] *nm* phone book; **B. mondain** ≃ Who's Who

bouc [buk] *nm (animal)* billy goat; *(barbe)* goatee; **b. émissaire** scapegoat

boucan [bukɑ̃] *nm Fam* din, row; **faire du b.** to kick up a row

bouche [buʃ] *nf* mouth; **de b. à oreille** by word of mouth; *Fig* **faire la fine b.** to be fussy; **b. d'égout** manhole; **b. d'incendie** *Br* fire hydrant, *Am* fireplug; **b. de métro** métro entrance ▪ **bouche-à-bouche** *nm* mouth-to-mouth resuscitation ▪ **bouchée** *nf* mouthful; *Fig* **mettre les bouchées doubles** to really get a move on

boucher¹ [buʃe] **1** *vt (fente, trou)* to fill in; *(conduite, fenêtre)* to block up; *(vue, rue, artère)* to block; *(bouteille)* to cork; *Fam* **ça m'en a bouché un coin** it took the wind out of my sails **2** **se boucher** *vpr (conduite)* to get blocked up; **se b. le nez** to hold one's nose ▪ **bouché, -ée** *adj (conduite)* blocked; *(temps)* overcast; *Fam (personne)* dense; **j'ai le nez b.** my nose is stuffed up ▪ **bouche-trou** *(pl* **bouche-trous)** *nm Fam* stopgap

boucher², -ère [buʃe, -ɛr] *nmf* butcher ▪ **boucherie** *nf* butcher's (shop); *Fig (carnage)* butchery

bouchon [buʃɔ̃] *nm* (a) *(à vis)* cap, top; *(de tonneau)* stopper; *(de liège)* cork; *(de canne à pêche)* float (b) *(embouteillage)* traffic jam ▪ **bouchonner** *vt Fam* **ça bouchonne** *(sur la route)* the traffic's bad

boucle [bukl] *nf (de ceinture)* buckle; *(de cheveu)* curl; *(méandre)* loop; **écouter un disque en b.** to listen to a record over and over again; **b. d'oreille** earring

boucler [bukle] **1** *vt (ceinture, valise)* to buckle; *(quartier)* to seal off; *(maison)* to lock up; *Fam (travail)* to finish off; *Fam (prisonnier)* to bang up; **b. ses valises** *(se préparer à partir)* to pack one's bags; **b. la boucle** *Av* to loop the loop; *Fig* to come full circle; *Fam* **boucle-la!** belt up! **2** *vi (cheveux)* to be curly ▪ **bouclé, -ée** *adj (cheveux)* curly

bouclier [buklije] *nm* shield; **b. humain** human shield

bouddhiste [budist] *adj & nmf* Buddhist ▪ **bouddhisme** *nm* Buddhism

bouder [bude] **1** *vi* to sulk **2** *vt (personne)* to refuse to talk to; **b. une élection** to refuse to vote ▪ **boudeur, -euse** *adj* sulky

boudin [budɛ̃] *nm* **b. noir** *Br* black pudding, *Am* blood sausage; **b. blanc** white pudding ▪ **boudiné, -ée** *adj (doigt)* podgy

boue [bu] *nf* mud ▪ **boueux, -euse** **1** *adj* muddy **2** *nm Fam Br* dustman, *Am* garbage collector

bouée [bwe] *nf Naut* buoy; **b. de sauvetage** lifebelt; **b. (gonflable)** *(d'enfant)* (inflatable) rubber ring

bouffe [buf] *nf Fam (nourriture)* grub ▪ **bouffer**[1] *vti Fam (manger)* to eat

bouffée [bufe] *nf (de fumée)* puff; *(de parfum)* whiff; *Fig (de colère)* outburst; **une b. d'air pur** a breath of fresh air; *Méd* **b. de chaleur** *Br* hot flush, *Am* hot flash

bouffer[2] [bufe] *vi (cheveux)* to have body; *(manche, jupe)* to puff out ▪ **bouffant, -ante** *adj (cheveux)* bouffant; *(vêtements)* baggy; **manche bouffante** puff(ed) sleeve ▪ **bouffi, -ie** *adj (yeux, visage)* puffy

bouffon, -onne [bufɔ̃, -ɔn] **1** *adj* farcical **2** *nm* buffoon ▪ **bouffonneries** *nfpl (actes)* clowning around

bouge [buʒ] *nm Péj (bar)* dive; *(taudis)* hovel

bougeoir [buʒwar] *nm* candlestick

bougeotte [buʒɔt] *nf Fam* **avoir la b.** to be fidgety

bouger [buʒe] **1** *vti* to move; **rester sans b.** to keep still **2 se bouger** *vpr Fam (se déplacer)* to move; *(s'activer)* to get a move on

bougie [buʒi] *nf (en cire)* candle; *(de moteur)* spark plug

bougon, -onne [bugɔ̃, -ɔn] *adj Fam* grumpy ▪ **bougonner** *vi Fam* to grumble

bougre [bugr] *nm Fam* **le pauvre b.** the poor devil ▪ **bougrement** [-əmɑ̃] *adv Fam* damned, *Br* bloody; **il fait b. froid** it's damn *or Br* bloody cold

bouillabaisse [bujabɛs] *nf* = provençal fish soup

bouille [buj] *nf Fam (visage)* mug; **il a une bonne b.** he looks a good sort

bouillie [buji] *nf (pour bébé)* baby food; *(à base de céréales)* baby cereal; **réduire qch en b.** to mash sth

bouillir* [bujir] *vi* to boil; **faire b. qch** to boil sth; **b. de colère** to seethe with anger ▪ **bouillant, -ante** *adj (qui bout)* boiling; *(très chaud, fiévreux)* boiling hot ▪ **bouilli, -ie** *adj* boiled

bouilloire [bujwar] *nf* kettle

bouillon [bujɔ̃] *nm (aliment)* stock; *(bulles)* bubbles; **bouillir à gros bouillons** to boil hard; **b. de culture** culture medium ▪ **bouillonner** *vi* to bubble

bouillotte [bujɔt] *nf* hot-water bottle

boulanger, -ère [bulɑ̃ʒe, -ɛr] *nmf* baker ▪ **boulangerie** *nf* baker's (shop)

boule [bul] *nf (sphère)* ball; **boules** *(jeu)* bowls; **se mettre en b.** *(chat)* to curl up into a ball; *Fam* **perdre la b.** to go off one's head; *Fam* **avoir la b. à zéro** to be a skinhead; *Fam* **avoir les boules** *(être énervé)* to be pissed off; *(avoir peur)* to be wetting oneself; **b. de neige** snowball; *Fig* **faire b. de neige** to snowball; **b. puante** stink bomb; **boules Quiès®** earplugs

bouleau, -x [bulo] *nm (silver) birch; (bois)* birch(wood)

bouledogue [buldɔg] *nm* bulldog

bouler [bule] *vi Fam* **envoyer qn b.** to send sb packing

boulet [bulɛ] *nm (de forçat)* ball and chain; **b. de canon** cannonball

boulette [bulɛt] *nf (de papier)* ball; *(de viande)* meatball; *Fam (gaffe) Br* boob, *Am* blooper

boulevard [bulvar] *nm* boulevard

bouleverser [bulvɛrse] *vt (émouvoir)* to move deeply; *(perturber)* to distress; *(projets, habitudes)* to disrupt; *(vie)* to turn upside down ▪ **bouleversant, -ante** *adj (émouvant)* deeply moving, *(perturbant)* distressing ▪ **bouleversement** [-əmɑ̃] *nm (de projets, d'habitudes)* disruption; *(de personne)* emotion; **bouleversements économiques** economic upheavals

boulimie [bulimi] *nf Méd* bulimia ▪ **boulimique** *adj* **être b.** to have bulimia

boulon [bulɔ̃] *nm* bolt

boulot[1] [bulo] *nm Fam (emploi)* job; *(travail)* work

boulot[2], **-otte** [bulo, -ɔt] *adj Fam* tubby

boum [bum] **1** *exclam & nm* bang **2** *nf Fam (fête) (for teenagers)* party

bouquet [bukɛ] *nm (fleurs)* bunch of flowers; *(d'arbres)* clump; *(de vin)* bouquet; *Fig* **c'est le b.!** that takes the *Br* biscuit *or Am* cake!; **b. final** *(de feu d'artifice)* grand finale

bouquin [bukɛ̃] *nm Fam* book ▪ **bouquiner** *vti Fam* to read ▪ **bouquiniste** *nmf* second-hand bookseller

bourbeux, -euse [burbø, -øz] *adj* muddy ▪ **bourbier** *nm (lieu, situation)* quagmire

bourde [burd] *nf Fam (gaffe)* blunder; **faire une b.** to put one's foot in it

bourdon [burdɔ̃] *nm (insecte)* bumblebee ▪ **bourdonnement** *nm (d'insecte)* buzz(ing); **avoir des bourdonnements d'oreilles** to have a buzzing in one's ears ▪ **bourdonner** *vi (insecte, oreilles)* to buzz

bourg [bur] *nm* market town ▪ **bourgade** *nf* village

bourge [burʒ] *adj Fam (bourgeois)* upper-class

bourgeois, -oise [burʒwa, -waz] **1** *adj* middle-class **2** *nmf* middle-class person ▪ **bourgeoisie** *nf* middle class

bourgeon [burʒɔ̃] *nm* bud ▪ **bourgeonner** *vi* to bud

bourgmestre [burgmɛstr] *nm (en Belgique, en Suisse)* burgomaster, town's chief magistrate

Bourgogne [burgɔɲ] **1** *nf (région)* Burgundy **2** *nm (vin de)* **B.** Burgundy (wine)

bourlinguer [burlɛ̃ge] *vi Fam (voyager)* to knock about

bourrade [burad] *nf* shove

bourrage [buraʒ] *nm Fam* **b. de crâne** brainwashing

bourrasque [burask] *nf* squall, gust of wind; **souffler en bourrasques** to gust

bourratif, -ive [buratif, -iv] *adj Fam* stodgy

bourre [bur] nf (pour rembourrer) stuffing; Fam **à la b.** in a rush

bourreau, -x [buro] nm executioner; Hum **b. des cœurs** ladykiller; **b. de travail** workaholic

bourrelet [burlε] nm (contre les courants d'air) weather strip; **b. de graisse** spare Br tyre or Am tire

bourrer [bure] **1** vt (coussin) to stuff (**de** with); (sac) to cram (**de** with); (pipe) to fill; **b. qn de qch** (gaver) to fill sb up with sth; **b. qn de coups** to beat sb up; Fam **b. le crâne à qn** (élève) to stuff sb's head with facts **2 se bourrer** vpr **se b. de qch** (se gaver) to stuff oneself up with; très Fam **se b. la gueule** to get Br pissed or Am wasted ▪ **bourré, -ée** adj (a) (plein) **b. à craquer** full to bursting; Fam **être b. de complexes** to be a mass of complexes (b) très Fam (ivre) Br pissed, Am wasted

bourricot [buriko] nm small donkey

bourrique [burik] nf she-ass; Fam **faire tourner qn en b.** to drive sb crazy

bourru, -ue [bury] adj surly

bourse [burs] nf (sac) purse; **sans b. délier** without spending a penny; Scol & Univ **b. (d'étude)** grant; **la B.** the Stock Exchange ▪ **boursier, -ière** 1 adj **opération boursière** Stock Exchange transaction 2 nmf (élève, étudiant) grant holder

boursouflé, -ée [bursufle] adj (visage, yeux) puffy

bous [bu] voir **bouillir**

bousculer [buskyle] 1 vt (pousser) to jostle; (presser) to rush; Fig (habitudes) to disrupt 2 **se bousculer** (foule) to push and shove; **les idées se bousculaient dans sa tête** his/her head was buzzing with ideas ▪ **bousculade** nf (agitation) pushing and shoving

bouse [buz] nf **de la b. de vache** cow dung

bousiller [buzije] vt Fam to wreck

boussole [busɔl] nf compass

bout¹ [bu] voir **bouillir**

bout² [bu] nm (extrémité) end; (de langue, de doigt) tip; (morceau) bit; **un b. de temps** a little while; **faire un b. de chemin** to go part of the way; **d'un b. à l'autre** from one end to the other; **au b. de la rue** at the end of the street; **au b. d'un moment** after a while; Fam **au b. du fil** (au téléphone) on the other end; **jusqu'au b.** (lire, rester) (right) to the end; **à b. de forces** exhausted; **à b. de souffle** out of breath; **à b. de bras** at arm's length; **pousser qn à b.** to push sb too far; **venir à b. de** (travail) to get through; (adversaire) to get the better of; **à b. portant** point-blank; **à tout b. de champ** at every possible opportunity; Fig **voir le b. du tunnel** to see the light at the end of the tunnel; Fam **je n'en vois pas le b.** I'm nowhere near the end of it; Cin **b. d'essai** screen test

boutade [butad] nf (plaisanterie) quip

boute-en-train [butɑ̃trɛ̃] nm inv (personne) live wire; **être le b. de la soirée** to be the life and soul of the party

bouteille [butεj] nf bottle; (de gaz) cylinder

boutique [butik] nf Br shop, Am store; (de couturier) boutique; **fermer b.** to shut up shop ▪ **boutiquier, -ière** nmf Br shopkeeper, Am storekeeper

boutoir [butwar] nm **coup de b.** staggering blow

bouton [butɔ̃] nm (bourgeon) bud; (au visage) spot; (de vêtement) button; (de porte, de télévision) knob; **b. de manchette** cufflink; Ordinat **b. de souris** mouse button ▪ **bouton-d'or** (pl boutons-d'or) nm buttercup ▪ **bouton-pression** (pl boutons-pression) nm Br press-stud, Am snap fastener ▪ **boutonner** vt, **se boutonner** vpr (vêtement) to button (up) ▪ **boutonneux, -euse** adj spotty ▪ **boutonnière** nf buttonhole

bouture [butyr] nf cutting

bovin, -ine [bɔvɛ̃, -in] adj bovine ▪ **bovins** nmpl cattle

bowling [boliŋ] nm (jeu) Br tenpin bowling, Am tenpins; (lieu) bowling alley

box [bɔks] (pl **boxes**) nm (d'écurie) stall; (de dortoir) cubicle; (garage) lock-up garage; Jur **b. des accusés** dock

boxe [bɔks] nf boxing; **b. française** kick boxing ▪ **boxer** vi to box ▪ **boxeur** nm boxer

boyau, -x [bwajo] nm (intestin) gut; (corde) catgut; (de vélo) tubular Br tyre or Am tire; (de mine) narrow gallery

boycotter [bɔjkɔte] vt to boycott ▪ **boycottage** nm boycott

boys band [bɔjzbɑ̃d] nm inv boyband

BP [bepe] (abrév **boîte postale**) nf PO Box

bracelet [braslε] nm (bijou) bracelet; (rigide) bangle; (de montre) Br strap, Am band; **b. électronique ou de cheville** electronic tag (for offenders) ▪ **bracelet-montre** (pl bracelets-montres) nm wristwatch

braconner [brakɔne] vi to poach ▪ **braconnage** nm poaching ▪ **braconnier** nm poacher

brader [brade] vt to sell off cheaply ▪ **braderie** nf clearance sale

braguette [bragεt] nf (de pantalon) fly, Br flies

braille [braj] nm Braille; **en b.** in Braille

brailler [braje] vti to yell

braire* [brεr] vi (âne) to bray

braise(s) [brεz] nf(pl) embers ▪ **braiser** [breze] vt Culin to braise

brancard [brɑ̃kar] nm (civière) stretcher; (de charrette) shaft ▪ **brancardier** nm stretcher-bearer

branche [brɑ̃ʃ] nf (d'arbre, d'une science) branch; (de compas) leg; (de lunettes) side piece ▪ **branchages** nmpl (des arbres) branches; (coupés) cut branches

branché, -ée [brɑ̃ʃe] *adj Fam (à la mode)* cool, hip

brancher [brɑ̃ʃe] **1** *vt (à une prise)* to plug in; *(à un réseau)* to connect; *Fam (plaire à)* **ça me branche** I'm really into it; *Fam* **on va en boîte ce soir, ça te branche?** fancy going clubbing tonight? **2 se brancher** *upr* **se b. sur** *(station de radio)* to tune in to ▪ **branchement** *nm (assemblage de fils)* connection

brandade [brɑ̃dad] *nf Culin* = salt cod puréed with garlic, oil and cream

brandir [brɑ̃dir] *vt* to brandish

branle [brɑ̃l] *nm* **mettre qch en b.** to set sth in motion ▪ **branlant, -ante** *adj (chaise, escalier)* rickety ▪ **branle-bas** *nm inv* **b. (de combat)** commotion ▪ **branler** *vi (chaise, escalier)* to be rickety

braquer [brake] **1** *vt (diriger)* to point (**sur** at); *(regard)* to fix (**sur** on); *Fam (banque)* to hold up; **b. qn contre qn/qch** to turn sb against sb/ sth **2** *vi Aut* to turn the steering wheel ▪ **braquage** *nm (de roues)* turning; *Fam (vol)* hold-up; **(angle de) b.** steering lock

braquet [brake] *nm* gear ratio

bras [bra] *nm* arm; **donner le b. à qn** to give sb one's arm; **le b. dessus le b. dessous** arm in arm; **les b. croisés** with one's arms folded; **à b. ouverts** with open arms; **à tour de b.** with all one's might; **b. de chemise** in one's shirtsleeves; *Fig* **avoir le b. long** to have a lot of influence; *Fig* **se retrouver avec qch sur les b.** to be left with sth on one's hands; *Fam* **faire un b. d'honneur à qn** ≃ to stick two fingers up at sb; **prendre qn à b.-le-corps** to seize sb round the waist; **b. de lecture** pickup arm; **b. de mer** arm of the sea; *Fig* **b. droit** *(assistant)* right-hand man

brasier [brazje] *nm* blaze, inferno

brassard [brasar] *nm* armband

brasse [bras] *nf (nage)* breaststroke; *(mouvement)* stroke; **b. papillon** butterfly stroke

brassée [brase] *nf* armful

brasser [brase] *vt (mélanger)* to mix; *(bière)* to brew ▪ **brassage** *nm (mélange)* mixing; *(de la bière)* brewing ▪ **brasserie** *nf (usine)* brewery; *(café)* brasserie

brassière [brasjer] *nf (de bébé) Br* vest, *Am* undershirt

bravade [bravad] *nf* **par b.** out of bravado

brave [brav] **1** *adj (courageux)* brave; *(bon)* good **2** *nm (héros)* brave man ▪ **bravement** *adv (courageusement)* bravely

braver [brave] *vt (personne, lois)* to defy; *(danger, mort)* to brave

bravo [bravo] **1** *exclam* bravo! **2** *nm* **bravos** cheers

bravoure [bravur] *nf* bravery

break [brek] *nm (voiture) Br* estate car, *Am* station wagon

brebis [brəbi] *nf* ewe; **lait/fromage de b.** ewe's

milk/ewe's-milk cheese; *Fig* **b. galeuse** black sheep

brèche [brɛʃ] *nf* gap; *(dans la coque d'un bateau)* hole; **battre qch en b.** to demolish sth

bredouille [brəduj] *adj* empty-handed

bredouiller [brəduje] *vti* to mumble

bref, brève [bref, brɛv] **1** *adj* brief, short **2** *adv* in short; **enfin b....** in a word...

breloque [brələk] *nf (de bracelet)* charm

Brésil [brezil] *nm* **le B.** Brazil ▪ **brésilien, -ienne 1** *adj* Brazilian **2** *nmf* **B., Brésilienne** Brazilian

Bretagne [brətaɲ] *nf* **la B.** Brittany ▪ **breton, -onne 1** *adj* Breton **2** *nmf* **B., Bretonne** Breton

bretelle [brətɛl] *nf* strap; **bretelles** *(de pantalon) Br* braces, *Am* suspenders; **b. (d'accès)** *(route)* access road

breuvage [brœvaʒ] *nm* potion

brève [brɛv] *voir* **bref**

brevet [brəvɛ] *nm (certificat)* certificate; *(diplôme)* diploma; *Scol* **b. des collèges** = general exam taken at 15; **b. (d'invention)** patent ▪ **breveter** *vt* to patent

bribes [brib] *nfpl* **b. de conversation** snatches of conversation

bric-à-brac [brikabrak] *nm inv (vieux objets)* bric-à-brac, odds and ends

bric et de broc [brikedəbrɔk] **de bric et de broc** *adv* haphazardly

bricole [brikɔl] *nf (objet, futilité)* trifle; *Fam* **il va lui arriver des bricoles** he's/she's going to get into a pickle

bricoler [brikɔle] **1** *vt (construire)* to put together; *(réparer)* to tinker with **2** *vi* to do do-it-yourself *or Br* DIY ▪ **bricolage** *nm (travail)* do-it-yourself, *Br* DIY; **faire du b.** to do some DIY ▪ **bricoleur, -euse 1** *adj* **être b.** to be good with one's hands **2** *nmf* handyman, *f* handywoman

bride [brid] *nf (de cheval)* bridle; **aller à b. abattue** to ride full tilt ▪ **brider** *vt (cheval)* to bridle; *(personne, désir)* to curb; **avoir les yeux bridés** to have slanting eyes

bridge [bridʒ] *nm (jeu, prothèse)* bridge

brièvement [brievmɑ̃] *adv* briefly ▪ **brièveté** *nf* brevity

brigade [brigad] *nf (de gendarmerie)* squad; *Mil* brigade; **b. anti-gang** organized crime squad; **b. des stupéfiants** *ou Fam* **des stups** drug squad ▪ **brigadier** *nm (de police)* police sergeant; *Mil* corporal

brigand [brigɑ̃] *nm (bandit)* brigand; *(personne malhonnête)* crook

briguer [brige] *vt (honneur, poste)* to sollicit

brillant, -ante [brijɑ̃, -ɑ̃t] **1** *adj (luisant)* shining; *(couleur)* bright; *(cheveux, cuir)* shiny; *Fig (remarquable)* brilliant **2** *nm* shine; *(diamant)* diamond; **b. à lèvres** lip gloss ▪ **brillamment** [-amɑ̃] *adv* brilliantly

briller [brije] *vi* to shine; **faire b.** *(chaussures)* to polish; **b. de colère** to shine with anger; **b. par son absence** to be conspicuous by one's absence; **b. de mille feux** to sparkle brilliantly

brimer [brime] *vt* to bully ▪ **brimade** *nf (d'élèves)* bullying; *Fig (humiliation)* vexation

brin [brɛ̃] *nm (d'herbe)* blade; *(de persil)* sprig; *(de muguet)* spray; *(de corde, de fil)* strand; *Fig* **un b. de qch** a bit of sth; **faire un b. de toilette** to have a quick wash

brindille [brɛ̃dij] *nf* twig

bringue[1] [brɛ̃g] *nf Fam* **faire la b.** to party

bringue[2] [brɛ̃g] *nf Fam* **grande b.** *(fille)* beanpole

bringuebaler [brɛ̃gbale] *vti Fam* to shake about

brio [brijo] *nm* brilliance; **avec b.** brilliantly

brioche [brijoʃ] *nf* brioche; *Fam (ventre)* paunch ▪ **brioché** *adj* **pain b.** = milk bread

brique [brik] *nf* (a) *(de construction)* brick; **mur de briques** brick wall (b) *Anciennement Fam (10 000 francs)* 10,000 francs

briquer [brike] *vt (nettoyer)* to scrub down

briquet [brike] *nm (cigarette)* lighter

bris [bri] *nm (de verre)* breaking; **b. de glaces** broken windows

brise [briz] *nf* breeze

briser [brize] **1** *vt* to break; *(opposition, résistance)* to crush; *(espoir, carrière)* to wreck; *(fatiguer)* to exhaust; **la voix brisée par l'émotion** his/her voice choked by emotion; **c'est à vous b. le cœur** it's heartbreaking **2 se briser** *vpr* to break ▪ **brisants** *nmpl* reefs ▪ **brise-glace** *nm inv (navire)* ice breaker ▪ **brise-lames** *nm inv* breakwater

britannique [britanik] **1** *adj* British **2** *nmf* **B.** Briton; **les Britanniques** the British

broc [bro] *nm* pitcher, jug

brocante [brokɑ̃t] *nf (commerce)* second-hand trade ▪ **brocanteur, -euse** *nmf* secondhand dealer

broche [broʃ] *nf (pour rôtir)* spit; *(bijou)* brooch; *(pour fracture)* pin; **faire cuire qch à la b.** to spit-roast sth ▪ **brochette** *nf (tige)* skewer; *(plat)* kebab

broché, -ée [broʃe] *adj* **livre b.** paperback

brochet [broʃɛ] *nm* pike

brochure [broʃyr] *nf* brochure, pamphlet

brocolis [brokoli] *nmpl* broccoli

broder [brode] *vt* to embroider (**de** with) ▪ **broderie** *nf (activité)* embroidery; **faire de la b.** to embroider; **des broderies** embroidery

broncher [brɔ̃ʃe] *vi* **sans b.** without batting an eyelid; **il n'a pas bronché** he didn't bat an eyelid

bronches [brɔ̃ʃ] *nfpl* bronchial tubes ▪ **bronchite** *nf* bronchitis; **avoir une b.** to have bronchitis

bronze [brɔ̃z] *nm* bronze

bronzer [brɔ̃ze] *vi* to tan ▪ **bronzage** *nm (sun)* tan

brosse [brɔs] *nf* brush; **donner un coup de b. à**

qch to give sth a brush; **cheveux en b.** crew cut; **b. à dents** toothbrush ▪ **brosser 1** *vt (tapis, cheveux)* to brush; **b. un tableau de qch** to give an outline of sth **2 se brosser** *vpr* **se b. les dents/les cheveux** to brush one's teeth/one's hair

brouette [bruɛt] *nf* wheelbarrow

brouhaha [bruaa] *nm* hubbub

brouillard [brujar] *nm* fog; **il y a du b.** it's foggy

brouille [bruj] *nf* disagreement, quarrel

brouiller [bruje] **1** *vt (idées)* to muddle up; *(vue)* to blur; *(émission radio)* to jam; **les yeux brouillés de larmes** eyes blurred with tears; *Fig* **b. les pistes** to cover one's tracks **2 se brouiller** *vpr (idées)* to get muddled up; *(vue)* to get blurred; *(se disputer)* to fall out (**avec** with); **le temps se brouille** it's clouding over ▪ **brouillé, -ée** *adj (teint)* blotchy; **être b. avec qn** to have fallen out with sb

brouillon, -onne [brujɔ̃, -ɔn] **1** *adj (mal organisé)* disorganized; *(mal présenté)* untidy **2** *nm* rough draft; **(papier) b.** *Br* scrap paper, *Am* scratch paper

broussailles [brusaj] *nfpl* scrub

brousse [brus] *nf* **la b.** the bush

brouter [brute] *vti* to graze

broutille [brutij] *nf* trifle

broyer [brwaje] *vt* to grind; *(doigt, bras)* to crush; *Fig* **b. du noir** to be down in the dumps

bru [bry] *nf* daughter-in-law

brugnon [brynɔ̃] *nm* nectarine

bruine [brɥin] *nf* drizzle ▪ **bruiner** *v impersonnel* to drizzle; **il bruine** it's drizzling

bruissement [brɥismɑ̃] *nm (de feuilles)* rustle, rustling

bruit [brɥi] *nm* noise, sound; *(nouvelle) Br* rumour, *Am* rumor; **faire du b.** to make a noise ▪ **bruitage** *nm Cin* sound effects ▪ **bruiteur, -euse** *nmf* sound effects engineer

brûlant, -ante [brylɑ̃, -ɑ̃t] *adj (objet, soupe)* burning hot; *(soleil)* scorching; *Fig (sujet)* burning

brûlé, -ée [bryle] *nm* **odeur de b.** burnt smell; **sentir le b.** to smell burnt

brûle-pourpoint [brylpurpwɛ̃] **à brûle-pourpoint** *adv* point-blank

brûler [bryle] **1** *vt (sujet: flamme, acide)* to burn; *(électricité, combustible)* to use; *(feu rouge)* to go through; **être brûlé vif** *(être supplicié)* to be burnt at the stake **2** *vi* to burn; *Fig* **b. d'envie de faire qch** to be dying to do sth; *Fig* **b. de désir** to be burning with desire; **attention, ça brûle!** careful, it's hot! **3 se brûler** *vpr* to burn oneself; **se b. la langue** to burn one's tongue ▪ **brûlure** *nf* burn; **brûlures d'estomac** heartburn

brume [brym] *nf* mist, haze ▪ **brumeux, -euse** *adj* misty, hazy; *Fig (obscur)* hazy

brun, brune [brœ̃, bryn] **1** *adj (cheveux)* dark,

brown; *(personne)* dark-haired **2** *nm (couleur)* brown **3** *nmf* dark-haired man, *f* dark-haired woman ▪**brunette** *nf* brunette ▪**brunir** *vi (personne, peau)* to tan; *(cheveux)* to darken

brushing® [brœʃiŋ] *nm* blow-dry; **faire un b. à qn** to blow-dry sb's hair

brusque [brysk] *adj* abrupt ▪**brusquement** [-əmã] *adv* abruptly ▪**brusquer** *vt (décision)* to rush ▪**brusquerie** *nf* abruptness

brut, -e [bryt] *adj (pétrole)* crude; *(diamant)* rough; *(soie)* raw; *(poids, salaire)* gross; *(champagne)* extra-dry; **à l'état b.** in its raw state

brutal, -e, -aux, -ales [brytal, -o] *adj (personnes, manières, paroles)* brutal; *(choc)* violent; *(franchise, réponse)* crude, blunt; *(changement)* abrupt; **être b. avec qn** to be rough with sb ▪**brutalement** *adv (violemment)* brutally; *(avec brusquerie)* roughly; *(soudainement)* abruptly ▪**brutaliser** *vt* to ill-treat ▪**brutalité** *nf (violence, acte)* brutality; *(soudaineté)* abruptness ▪**brute** *nf* brute

Bruxelles [brysɛl] *nm ou f* Brussels

bruyant, -ante [brɥijã, -ãt] *adj* noisy ▪**bruyamment** [-amã] *adv* noisily

bruyère [bryjɛr] *nf (plante)* heather; *(terrain)* heath

BTS [beteɛs] *(abrév* **brevet de technicien supérieur)** *nm Scol* = advanced vocational training certificate

bu, -e [by] *pp de* **boire**

buanderie [bɥãdri] *nf (lieu)* laundry

bûche [byʃ] *nf* log; *Fam* **prendre une b.** *Br* to come a cropper, *Am* to take a spill; **b. de Noël** Yule log ▪**bûcher**[1] *nm (à bois)* woodshed; *(de supplice)* stake

bûcher[2] [byʃe] *Fam* **1** *vt (étudier)* to bone up on, *Br* to swot up **2** *vi Br* to swot, *Am* to grind ▪**bûcheur, -euse** *nmf Fam Br* swot, *Am* grind

bûcheron [byʃrɔ̃] *nm* woodcutter, *Am* lumberjack

budget [bydʒɛ] *nm* budget ▪**budgétaire** *adj* budgetary; *(année)* financial; **déficit b.** budget deficit

buée [bɥe] *nf (sur vitre)* condensation; *(sur miroir)* mist

buffet [byfɛ] *nm (meuble bas)* sideboard; *(meuble haut)* dresser; *(repas)* buffet

buffle [byfl] *nm* buffalo

buis [bɥi] *nm (arbre)* box; *(bois)* boxwood

buisson [bɥisɔ̃] *nm* bush

buissonnière [bɥisɔnjɛr] *adj f* **faire l'école b.** to play *Br* truant *or Am* hookey

bulbe [bylb] *nm* bulb

Bulgarie [bylgari] *nf* **la B.** Bulgaria ▪**bulgare 1** *adj* Bulgarian **2** *nmf* **B.** Bulgarian

bulldozer [byldozœr] *nm* bulldozer

bulle [byl] *nf (d'air, de savon)* bubble; *(de bande dessinée)* balloon; *(décret du pape)* bull; **faire des bulles** to blow bubbles

buller [byle] *vi Fam* to laze about

bulletin [byltɛ̃] *nm (communiqué, revue)* bulletin; *(météo)* report; **b. d'informations** news bulletin; **b. de paie** *ou* **de salaire** *Br* pay slip, *Am* pay stub; **b. de santé** medical bulletin; **b. de vote** ballot paper; **b. météo** weather report; **b. scolaire** *Br* school report, *Am* report card

buraliste [byralist] *nmf (à la poste)* clerk; *(au tabac)* tobacconist

bureau, -x [byro] *nm (table)* desk; *(lieu)* office; *(comité)* committee; **b. de change** bureau de change; **b. de poste** post office; **b. de tabac** *Br* tobacconist's (shop), *Am* tobacco store

bureaucrate [byrokrat] *nmf* bureaucrat ▪**bureaucratie** [-asi] *nf* bureaucracy ▪**bureaucratique** *adj* bureaucratic

Bureautique® [byrotik] *nf* office automation

burette [byrɛt] *nf (pour huile)* oilcan; *(de chimiste)* burette

burin [byrɛ̃] *nm (de graveur)* burin; *(pour découper)* (cold) chisel

buriné, -ée [byrine] *adj (visage)* lined

burlesque [byrlɛsk] *adj (idée)* ludicrous; *(genre)* burlesque

bus[1] [bys] *nm* bus

bus[2] [by] *pt de* **boire**

busqué [byske] *adj m (nez)* hooked

buste [byst] *nm (torse)* chest; *(sculpture)* bust ▪**bustier** *nm (corsage)* bustier

but[1] [by(t)] *nm (objectif)* aim, goal; *(intention)* purpose; *Football* goal; *Fig* **aller droit au b.** to go straight to the point; **dire qch de b. en blanc** to say sth straight out; **c'est le b. de l'opération** that's the point of the operation

but[2] [by] *pt de* **boire**

butane [bytan] *nm* butane

buter [byte] **1** *vt* **(a) b. qn** to put sb's back up **(b)** *très Fam (tuer)* to bump off **2** *vi* **b. contre qch** *(cogner)* to bump into sth; *(trébucher)* to stumble over sth; *Fig (difficulté)* to come up against sth **3 se buter** *vpr (s'entêter)* to dig one's heels in ▪**buté, -ée** *adj* obstinate

butin [bytɛ̃] *nm (de voleur)* loot; *(de pillards)* spoils; *(d'armée)* booty

butiner [bytine] *vi (abeille)* to gather pollen and nectar

butoir [bytwar] *nm (pour train)* buffer; *(de porte)* stopper, *Br* stop

butte [byt] *nf* hillock; *Fig* **être en b. à qch** to be exposed to sth

buvable [byvabl] *adj* drinkable ▪**buveur, -euse** *nmf* drinker; **un grand b.** a heavy drinker

buvard [byvar] *adj & nm* **(papier) b.** blotting paper

buvette [byvɛt] *nf* refreshment bar

buviez [byvje] *voir* **boire**

C, c [se] *nm inv* C, c

c' [s] *voir* **ce**¹

ça [sa] (*abrév* **cela**) *pron démonstratif* (*pour désigner*) that; (*plus près*) this; (*sujet indéfini*) it, that; **qu'est-ce que c'est que ça?** what (on earth) is that/this?; **c'est qui/quoi ça?** who's/what's that?; **où/quand/comment ça?** where?/when?/how?; **ça dépend** it depends; **ça m'ennuie** it annoys me; **ça m'amuse** I find it amusing; **ça va?** how are things?; **ça va!** fine!, OK!; **ça alors!** my goodness!; **ça y est, j'ai fini** that's it, I'm finished; **c'est ça** that's right

çà [sa] **çà et là** *adv* here and there

caban [kabɑ̃] *nm Naut* reefer (jacket)

cabane [kaban] *nf* (*baraque*) hut; (*en rondin*) cabin; (*de jardin*) shed; **c. à outils** tool shed; **c. à lapins** rabbit hutch

cabaret [kabarɛ] *nm* cabaret

cabas [kaba] *nm* shopping bag

cabillaud [kabijo] *nm* (fresh) cod

cabine [kabin] *nf* (*de bateau*) cabin; (*de camion*) cab; (*d'ascenseur*) *Br* cage, *Am* car; **c. de bain** (*de plage*) *Br* beach hut, *Am* cabana; (*de piscine*) cubicle; **c. d'essayage** fitting room; **c. de pilotage** cockpit; (*d'un grand avion*) flight deck; **c. téléphonique** phone box

cabinet [kabinɛ] *nm* (*de médecin*) *Br* surgery, *Am* office; (*de ministre*) departmental staff; **c. de toilette** (small) bathroom; **c. de travail** study; *Fam* **les cabinets** *Br* the loo, *Am* the john; **c. dentaire** dental surgery; **c. juridique** law firm

câble [kɑbl] *nm* cable; *TV* **le c.** cable ▪ **câblé** *adj Fam* (*à la page*) hip ▪ **câbler** *vt TV* (*ville, quartier*) to install cable television in

caboche [kabɔʃ] *nf Fam* (*tête*) nut

cabosser [kabɔse] *vt* (*métal, voiture*) to bash up

caboteur [kabɔtœr] *nm* (*bateau*) coaster

cabotin, -ine [kabɔtɛ̃, -in] *nmf* (*acteur*) ham actor; (*actrice*) ham actress; (*vantard*) show-off

cabrer [kabre] **se cabrer** *vpr* (*cheval*) to rear (up); *Fig* (*personne*) to recoil

cabri [kabri] *nm* (*chevreau*) kid

cabriole [kabrijɔl] *nf* (*saut*) caper; **faire des cabrioles** to caper about

cabriolet [kabrijɔlɛ] *nm* (*auto*) convertible

caca [kaka] *nm Fam* (*en langage enfantin*) *Br* poo, *Am* poop; **faire c.** to do a number two *or Br* a poo

cacah(o)uète [kakawɛt] *nf* peanut

cacao [kakao] *nm* (*boisson*) cocoa

cacatoès [kakatoɛs] *nm* cockatoo

cachalot [kaʃalo] *nm* sperm whale

cache [kaʃ] *nf* hiding place; **c. d'armes** arms cache ▪ **cache-cache** *nm inv* **jouer à c.** to play hide and seek ▪ **cache-nez** *nm inv* scarf

cachemire [kaʃmir] *nm* (*laine*) cashmere

cacher [kaʃe] **1** *vt* to hide (**à** from); **c. la lumière à qn** to stand in sb's light; **il ne cache pas que...** he makes no secret of the fact that...; **je ne vous cache pas que j'ai été surpris** I won't pretend I wasn't surprised; **pour ne rien vous c.** to be completely open with you **2** **se cacher** *vpr* to hide; **sans se c.** openly; **je ne m'en cache pas** I make no secret of it

cachet [kaʃɛ] *nm* (*sceau*) seal; (*de fabrication*) stamp; (*comprimé*) tablet; (*d'acteur*) fee; (*originalité*) distinctive character; **c. de la poste** postmark ▪ **cacheter** *vt* to seal

cachette [kaʃɛt] *nf* hiding place; **en c.** in secret; **en c. de qn** without sb knowing

cachot [kaʃo] *nm* dungeon

cachotteries [kaʃɔtri] *nfpl* **faire des cachotteries** to be secretive ▪ **cachottier, -ière** *adj* secretive

cachou [kaʃu] *nm* = liquorice sweet

cacophonie [kakɔfɔni] *nf* cacophony

cactus [kaktys] *nm* cactus

c.-à-d. (*abrév* **c'est-à-dire**) i.e.

cadavre [kadavr] *nm* corpse ▪ **cadavérique** *adj* (*teint*) deathly pale

caddie® [kadi] *nm Br* trolley, *Am* cart (*for shopping*)

cadeau, -x [kado] *nm* present, gift; **faire un c. à qn** to give sb a present; **faire c. de qch à qn** to make sb a present of sth

cadenas [kadna] *nm* padlock ▪ **cadenasser** *vt* to padlock

cadence [kadɑ̃s] *nf* (*taux, vitesse*) rate; (*de chanson*) rhythm ▪ **cadencé, -ée** *adj* rhythmical

cadet, -ette [kade, -et] **1** *adj* (*de deux*) younger; (*de plus de deux*) youngest **2** *nmf* (*de deux*) younger (one); (*de plus de deux*) youngest (one); *Sport* junior; **c'est le c. de mes soucis!** that's the least of my worries

cadran [kadrɑ̃] *nm* (*de téléphone*) dial; (*de montre*) face; **faire le tour du c.** to sleep round the clock; **c. solaire** sundial

cadre [kadr] *nm* **(a)** (*de photo, de vélo*) frame;

(décor) setting; *(d'imprimé)* box; **dans le c. de** within the framework of; **c. de vie** environment (**b**) *(d'entreprise)* executive, manager; **les cadres** the management; *Mil* the officers
cadrer [kɑdre] **1** *vt (photo)* to Br centre *or Am* center **2** *vi (correspondre)* to tally (**avec** with) ▪ **cadreur** *nm* cameraman
caduc, -uque [kadyk] *adj (feuille)* deciduous; *Jur (accord)* lapsed; *(loi)* null and void
cafard, -arde [kafar, -ard] *nm (insecte)* cockroach; *Fam* **avoir le c.** to feel low
café [kafe] *nm (produit, boisson)* coffee; *(bar)* café; **c. au lait, c. crème** Br white coffee, *Am* coffee with milk; **c. noir** black coffee; **c. soluble** *ou* **instantané** instant coffee; **c. tabac** = café-cum-tobacconist's; **c.-théâtre** *Br* ≃ pub theatre ▪ **caféine** *nf* caffeine ▪ **cafétéria** *nf* cafeteria ▪ **cafetier** *nm* café owner ▪ **cafetière** *nf (récipient)* coffeepot; *(électrique)* coffee machine; **c. à piston** cafetiere
cafouiller [kafuje] *vi Fam (personne)* to get into a muddle; *(moteur)* to misfire ▪ **cafouillage** *nm Fam (confusion)* muddle
cage [kaʒ] *nf (d'oiseau, de zoo)* cage; *(d'ascenseur)* shaft; *Football* goal; **c. d'escalier** stairwell; *Anat* **c. thoracique** rib cage
cageot [kaʒo] *nm* crate
cagibi [kaʒibi] *nm Fam* storage room
cagneux, -euse [kaɲø] *adj* **avoir les genoux c.** to have knock-knees
cagnotte [kaɲɔt] *nf (caisse commune)* kitty; *(de jeux)* pool
cagoule [kagul] *nf (de bandit)* hood; *(d'enfant)* Br balaclava, *Am* ski mask
cahier [kaje] *nm* notebook; *(d'écolier)* exercise book; **c. de brouillon** *Br* rough book, *Am* ≃ scratch-pad; *Scol* **c. d'appel** register
cahin-caha [kaɛ̃kaa] *adv Fam* **aller c.** *(se déplacer)* to struggle along
cahot [kao] *nm* jolt ▪ **cahoté, -ée** *adj* **être c.** to be jolted about ▪ **cahoter** *vi* to jolt along ▪ **cahoteux, -euse** *adj* bumpy
caïd [kaid] *nm Fam (chef de bande)* gang leader; **jouer les caïds** to act high and mighty
caille [kɑj] *nf (oiseau)* quail
cailler [kaje] **1** *vi (lait)* to curdle; *Fam* **ça caille** it's freezing **2 se cailler** *vpr Fam* **on se (les) caille** it's freezing ▪ **caillot** [kajo] *nm (de sang)* clot
caillou, -x [kaju] *nm* stone; *(sur la plage)* pebble; *Fam* **il n'a plus un poil sur le c.** he's as bald as a coot ▪ **caillouteux, -euse** *adj (route)* stony
Caire [kɛr] *nm* **le C.** Cairo
caisse [kɛs] *nf (a) (boîte)* case; *(d'outils)* box; *(cageot)* crate; *(de véhicule)* body; *Fam (voiture)* car; *Mus* **la grosse c.** the bass drum; **c. de résonance** sound box (**b**) *(coffre)* cash box; *(de magasin)* cash desk; *(de supermarché)* checkout; *(argent)* cash (in hand); **faire sa c.** to do the till; **c. d'épargne** savings bank; **c. de**

retraite pension fund; **c. enregistreuse** cash register; **c. noire** slush fund
caissier, -ière [kesje, -jɛr] *nmf* cashier; *(de supermarché)* checkout operator
cajoler [kaʒɔle] *vt* to cuddle ▪ **cajolerie** *nf* cuddle
cajou [kaʒu] *nm* **noix de c.** cashew nut
cake [kek] *nm* fruit cake
calamité [kalamite] *nf (fléau)* calamity; *(malheur)* great misfortune
calandre [kalɑ̃dr] *nf Aut* radiator grille
calcaire [kalkɛr] **1** *adj (eau)* hard; *(terrain)* chalky **2** *nm Géol* limestone; *(dépôt)* fur
calciné, -ée [kalsine] *adj* burnt to a cinder
calcium [kalsjɔm] *nm* calcium
calcul [kalkyl] *nm (**a**) (opérations, estimation)* calculation; *Scol* **le c.** arithmetic; **faire un c.** to make a calculation; *Fig* **faire un mauvais c.** to miscalculate; **c. mental** mental arithmetic (**b**) *Méd* stone; **c. rénal** kidney stone
calculateur [kalkylatœr] *nm Ordinat* calculator ▪ **calculatrice** *nf* **c. (de poche)** *(pocket)* calculator
calculer [kalkyle] *vt (prix, superficie)* to calculate; *(chances, conséquences)* to weigh (up) ▪ **calculé, -ée** *adj (risque)* calculated
calculette [kalkylɛt] *nf (pocket)* calculator
cale [kal] *nf (**a**) (de meuble, de porte)* wedge (**b**) *(de navire)* hold; **c. sèche** dry dock
calé, -ée [kale] *adj Fam (problème)* tough; **être c. en qch** to be well up in sth
calèche [kalɛʃ] *nf* barouche
caleçon [kalsɔ̃] *nm* boxer shorts; **c. long** long johns
calembour [kalɑ̃bur] *nm* pun, play on words
calendrier [kalɑ̃drije] *nm (mois et jours)* calendar; *(programme)* timetable
cale-pied [kalpje] *(pl* cale-pieds*) nm* toe clip
calepin [kalpɛ̃] *nm* notebook
caler [kale] **1** *vt (meuble, porte)* to wedge; *(chargement)* to secure; *Fam* **ça cale (l'estomac)** it fills you up; *Fam* **je suis calé** I'm stuffed *or* full up **2** *vi (moteur)* to stall; *Fam (abandonner)* to give up **3 se caler** *vpr (dans un fauteuil)* to settle oneself comfortably
calfeutrer [kalføtre] **1** *vt (brèches)* to block up **2 se calfeutrer** *vpr* **se c. chez soi** to shut oneself away
calibre [kalibr] *nm (diamètre)* calibre; *(d'œuf, de fruit)* grade; *(outil)* gauge ▪ **calibrer** *vt (œufs, fruits)* to grade
calice [kalis] *nm Rel* chalice
Californie [kalifɔrni] *nf* **la C.** California
califourchon [kalifurʃɔ̃] **à califourchon** *adv* astride; **se mettre à c. sur qch** to sit astride sth
câlin, -ine [kɑlɛ̃, -in] **1** *adj* affectionate **2** *nm* cuddle; **faire un c. à qn** to give sb a cuddle ▪ **câliner** *vt* to cuddle
calleux, -euse [kalø, -øz] *adj* callous

calligraphie [kaligrafi] *nf* calligraphy
calmant [kalmã] *nm (pour les nerfs)* sedative; *(la douleur)* painkiller
calmar [kalmar] *nm* squid
calme [kalm] **1** *adj (flegmatique)* calm, cool; *(tranquille)* quiet; *(mer)* calm **2** *nm* calm(ness); **garder/perdre son c.** to keep/lose one's calm; **dans le c.** *(travailler, étudier)* in peace and quiet; **du c.!** *(taisez-vous)* keep quiet!; *(pas de panique)* keep calm!
calmer [kalme] **1** *vt (douleur)* to soothe; *(inquiétude)* to calm; *(fièvre)* to reduce; *(faim)* to appease; **c. qn** to calm sb down **2 se calmer** *vpr (personne)* to calm down; *(vent)* to die down; *(mer)* to become calm; *(douleur, fièvre)* to subside
calmos [kalmos] *exclam Fam* chill (out)!, take it easy!
calomnie [kalɔmni] *nf (en paroles)* slander; *(par écrit)* libel ■ **calomnier** *vt (en paroles)* to slander; *(par écrit)* to libel ■ **calomnieux, -euse** *adj (paroles)* slanderous; *(écrits)* libellous
calorie [kalɔri] *nf* calorie ■ **calorifique, calorique** *adj* calorific
calorifuge [kalɔrifyʒ] *adj* (heat-)insulating
calot [kalo] *nm (de soldat)* forage cap
calotte [kalɔt] *nf (chapeau rond)* skullcap; *Fam (gifle)* clout; *Géol* **c. glaciaire** ice cap
calque [kalk] *nm (copie)* tracing; *Fig (imitation)* exact copy; **(papier-)c.** tracing paper ■ **calquer** *vt (reproduire)* to trace; *Fig (imiter)* to copy; **il calque sa conduite sur celle de son frère** he models his behaviour on his brother's
calumet [kalyme] *nm* **c. de la paix** peace pipe
calvaire [kalvɛr] *nm Rel* calvary; *Fig* ordeal
calvitie [kalvisi] *nf* baldness
camarade [kamarad] *nmf* friend; *Pol* comrade; **c. de classe** classmate; **c. d'école** school friend; **c. de jeu** playmate ■ **camaraderie** *nf* camaraderie
Cambodge [kɑ̃bɔdʒ] *nm* **le C.** Cambodia
cambouis [kɑ̃bwi] *nm* dirty oil, grease
cambrer [kɑ̃bre] **1** *vt* to arch; **c. les reins** to arch one's back **2 se cambrer** *vpr* to arch one's back ■ **cambrure** *nf (du pied, du dos)* arch
cambrioler [kɑ̃brijɔle] *vt Br* to burgle, *Am* to burglarize ■ **cambriolage** *nm* burglary ■ **cambrioleur, -euse** *nmf* burglar
cambrousse [kɑ̃brus] *nf Fam* country; **en pleine c.** in the middle of nowhere
camée [kame] *nm* cameo
caméléon [kamelã] *nm* chameleon
camelot [kamlo] *nm* street peddler *or Br* hawker, *Am* huckster ■ **camelote** *nf (pacotille)* junk; *(marchandise)* stuff
camembert [kamɑ̃bɛr] *nm (fromage)* Camembert (cheese)
camer [kame] **se camer** *vpr très Fam* to do drugs ■ **came** *nf très Fam* dope, drugs ■ **camé, -ée** *très Fam* **1** *adj* high **2** *nmf* junkie

caméra [kamera] *nf* TV *or* film *or* video camera; **c. Internet** webcam ■ **cameraman** *(pl* **-mans** *ou* **-men)** *nm* cameraman
Caméscope® [kameskɔp] *nm* camcorder
camion [kamjã] *nm Br* lorry, *Am* truck; **c. de déménagement** *Br* removal van, *Am* moving van; **c. frigorifique** refrigerated lorry ■ **camion-benne** *(pl* **camions-bennes)** *nm* dumper truck ■ **camion-citerne** *(pl* **camions-citernes)** *nm Br* tanker, *Am* tank truck ■ **camionnage** *nm Br* (road) haulage, *Am* trucking ■ **camionnette** *nf* van ■ **camionneur** *nm (conducteur) Br* lorry driver, *Am* truck driver; *(entrepreneur) Br* haulier, *Am* trucker
camisole [kamizɔl] *nf* **c. de force** straitjacket
camomille [kamɔmij] *nf (plante)* camomile; *(tisane)* camomile tea
camoufler [kamufle] *vt Mil* to camouflage; *Fig (vérité)* to disguise ■ **camouflage** *nm Mil* camouflage; *Fig (de vérité)* disguising
camp [kɑ̃] *nm (campement)* camp; *(de parti, de jeu)* side; **lever le c.** to strike camp; **c. de concentration** concentration camp; **c. de prisonniers** prison camp; **c. de réfugiés** refugee camp
campagne [kɑ̃paɲ] *nf* **(a)** *(par opposition à la ville)* country; *(paysage)* countryside; **à la c.** in the country; **en pleine c.** deep in the countryside; **en rase c.** in the open country; **c. de presse/publicité** press/publicity campaign ■ **campagnard, -arde** *adj* country **(b)** *Mil, Com & Pol* campaign; *Pol* **entrer en c.** to go on the campaign trail; **c. de presse/publicité** press/publicity campaign ■ **campagnard, -arde** *adj* country
camper [kɑ̃pe] **1** *vi* to camp **2** *vt (chapeau)* to plant; **c. un personnage** *(sujet: acteur)* to play a part effectively **3 se camper** *vpr* to plant oneself **(devant** in front of) ■ **campement** *nm* camp; **établir un c.** to pitch camp ■ **campeur, -euse** *nmf* camper
camphre [kɑ̃fr] *nm* camphor
camping [kɑ̃piŋ] *nm (activité)* camping; *(terrain)* camp(ing) site; **faire du c.** to go camping; **c. sauvage** unauthorized camping ■ **camping-car** *(pl* **camping-cars)** *nm* camper
campus [kɑ̃pys] *nm* campus
camus, -use [kamy] *adj (nez)* flat
Canada [kanada] *nm* **le C.** Canada ■ **canadien, -ienne** **1** *adj* Canadian **2** *nmf* **C., Canadienne** Canadian ■ **canadienne** *nf* fur-lined jacket
canaille [kanaj] **1** *nf* scoundrel **2** *adj (manière, accent)* vulgar
canal, -aux [kanal, -o] *nm (cours d'eau)* canal; *(conduite)* conduit; *Anat & Bot* duct; *Tél, Com & Fig* channel; *Fig* **par le c. de la poste** through the post
canaliser [kanalize] *vt (rivière, fleuve)* to canalize; *Fig (foule, énergie)* to channel ■ **canalisation** *nf (conduite)* pipe
canapé [kanape] *nm* **(a)** *(siège)* sofa, couch **(b)**

(pour l'apéritif) canapé ▪**canapé-lit** *(pl* **canapés-lits)** *nm* sofa bed

canard [kanar] *nm* duck; *(mâle)* drake; *(fausse note)* false note; *Fam (journal)* rag; *Culin* **c. à l'orange** duck à l'orange

canarder [kanarde] *vt Fam* to snipe at

canari [kanari] *nm* canary

cancans [kɑ̃kɑ̃] *nmpl* gossip ▪**cancaner** *vi* to gossip ▪**cancanier, -ière** *adj* gossipy

cancer [kɑ̃sɛr] *nm (maladie)* cancer; **avoir un c.** to have cancer; **c. de l'estomac/du poumon** stomach/lung cancer; **le C.** *(signe)* Cancer; **être C.** to be (a) Cancer ▪**cancéreux, -euse** **1** *adj* cancerous **2** *nmf* cancer patient ▪**cancérigène** *adj* carcinogenic ▪**cancérologue** *nmf* cancer specialist

cancre [kɑ̃kr] *nm Fam* dunce

cancrelat [kɑ̃krəla] *nm* cockroach

candélabre [kɑ̃delɑbr] *nm* candelabra

candeur [kɑ̃dœr] *nf* guilelessness ▪**candide** *adj* guileless

> Il faut noter que les termes anglais **candour** et **candid** sont des faux amis. Ils signifient respectivement **franchise** et **franc**.

candidat, -ate [kɑ̃dida, -at] *nmf (d'examen)* candidate (**à** for); *(de poste)* applicant (**à** for); **être c. aux élections** to stand for election ▪**candidature** *nf (à un poste)* application (**à** for); *(aux élections)* candidacy (**à** for); **poser sa c.** to apply (**à** for); **c. spontanée** unsolicited *or* speculative application

cane [kan] *nf* (female) duck ▪**caneton** *nm* duckling

canette [kanɛt] *nf (bouteille)* bottle; *(boîte)* can; *(bobine)* spool

canevas [kanva] *nm (toile)* canvas; *(de film, de roman)* outline

caniche [kaniʃ] *nm* poodle

canicule [kanikyl] *nf* heatwave ▪**caniculaire** *adj (journée, temps)* scorching

canif [kanif] *nm* penknife

canine [kanin] **1** *adj f (espèce, race)* canine; **exposition c.** dog show **2** *nf (dent)* canine (tooth)

caniveau, -x [kanivo] *nm* gutter

cannabis [kanabis] *nm* cannabis

canne [kan] *nf (tige)* cane; *(pour marcher)* (walking) stick; **c. à pêche** fishing rod; **c. à sucre** sugar cane; **c. blanche** white stick

cannelle [kanɛl] *nf* cinnamon

cannelure [kanlyr] *nf* groove; *(de colonne)* fluting

cannette [kanɛt] *nf* = **canette**

cannibale [kanibal] **1** *nmf* cannibal **2** *adj (tribu)* cannibalistic ▪**cannibalisme** *nm* cannibalism

canoë-kayak [kanɔekajak] *nm* canoeing

canon¹ [kɑ̃ɔ̃] *nm* gun; *(ancien, à boulets)* cannon; *(de fusil)* barrel ▪**cannonade** *nf* gunfire ▪**canonnier** *nm* gunner

canon² [kɑ̃ɔ̃] **1** *nm Rel & Fig (règle)* canon; *Fam (personne)* stunner **2** *adj inv Fam (beau)* gorgeous ▪**canoniser** *vt Rel* to canonize

canot [kano] *nm* boat; **c. de sauvetage** lifeboat; **c. pneumatique** rubber dinghy ▪**canotage** *nm* boating ▪**canoter** *vi* to go boating

cantate [kɑ̃tat] *nf Mus* cantata

cantatrice [kɑ̃tatris] *nf* opera singer

cantine [kɑ̃tin] *nf* **(a)** *(réfectoire)* canteen; *(d'école)* dining hall; **manger à la c.** to have *Br* school dinners *or Am* school lunch **(b)** *(coffre)* trunk

cantique [kɑ̃tik] *nm Rel* hymn

canton [kɑ̃tɔ̃] *nm (en France)* canton *(division of a department)*; *(en Suisse)* canton *(semi-autonomous region)*

cantonade [kɑ̃tɔnad] **à la cantonnade** *adv* to everyone present

cantonner [kɑ̃tɔne] **1** *vt (troupes)* to quarter; **c. qn dans/à** to confine sb to **2 se cantonner** *vpr* **se c. dans/à** to confine oneself to

cantonnier [kɑ̃tɔnje] *nm* roadmender

canular [kanylar] *nm Fam* hoax

canyon [kajɔ̃] *nm* canyon

CAO [seao] *(abrév* **conception assistée par ordinateur)** *nf Ordinat* CAD

caoutchouc [kautʃu] *nm* rubber; *(élastique)* rubber band; *(plante)* rubber plant; **c. Mousse®** foam rubber ▪**caoutchouteux, -euse** *adj Péj* rubbery

CAP [seape] *(abrév* **certificat d'aptitude professionnelle)** *nm Scol* = vocational training certificate

cap [kap] *nm Géog* cape, headland; *Naut (direction)* course; **mettre le c. sur...** to set course for...; **changer de c.** to change course; **franchir** *ou* **doubler un c.** to round a cape; **franchir le c. de la trentaine** to turn thirty; **franchir le c. des mille employés** to pass the thousand-employee mark

capable [kapabl] *adj* capable, able; **c. de qch** capable of sth; **c. de faire qch** able to do sth, capable of doing sth; **elle est bien c. de les oublier!** she's quite capable of forgetting them! ▪**capacité** *nf* capacity; *(aptitude)* ability; **c. d'accueil** *(d'hôtel)* accommodation capacity; **c. de concentration** attention span

cape [kap] *nf* cape; *(grande)* cloak; **roman de c. et d'épée** swashbuckling novel

CAPES [kapɛs] *(abrév* **certificat d'aptitude professionnelle à l'enseignement secondaire)** *nm Univ* = postgraduate teaching certificate

capillaire [kapilɛr] *adj* **huile/lotion c.** hair oil/lotion

capitaine [kapitɛn] *nm* captain

capital, -e, -aux, -ales [kapital, -o] **1** *adj (essentiel)* major **2** *adj f* **lettre capitale** capital letter **3** *nm Fin* capital ▪**capitale** *nf (lettre, ville)* capital

capitaliser [kapitalize] **1** *vt (intérêts)* to capitalize **2** *vi* to save

capitalisme [kapitalism] *nm* capitalism ▪ **capitaliste** *adj & nmf* capitalist

capiteux, -euse [kapitø, -øz] *adj (vin, parfum)* heady

capitonné, -ée [kapitɔne] *adj* padded

capituler [kapityle] *vi* to surrender ▪ **capitulation** *nf* surrender

caporal, -aux [kapɔral, -o] *nm Mil* corporal

capot [kapo] *nm Aut Br* bonnet, *Am* hood

capote [kapɔt] *nf Aut (de décapotable) Br* hood, *Am* top; *(manteau de soldat)* greatcoat; *Fam (préservatif)* condom, *Am* rubber

capoter [kapɔte] *vi (véhicule)* to overturn; *Fam (échouer)* to fall through

cappuccino [kaputʃino] *nm* cappuccino

câpre [kɑpr] *nf* caper

caprice [kapris] *nm* whim; **faire un c.** to throw a tantrum ▪ **capricieux, -euse** *adj (personne)* capricious; *(moteur)* temperamental

Capricorne [kaprikɔrn] *nm* **le C.** *(signe)* Capricorn; **être C.** to be (a) Capricorn

capsule [kapsyl] *nf (spatiale, de médicament)* capsule; *(de bouteille)* cap

capter [kapte] *vt (signal, radio)* to pick up; *(attention)* to capture; *(eaux)* to harness; *Fam (comprendre)* to get

captif, -ive [kaptif, -iv] *adj & nmf* captive ▪ **captivité** *nf* captivity; **en c.** in captivity

captiver [kaptive] *vt* to captivate ▪ **captivant, -ante** *adj* captivating

capture [kaptyr] *nf* capture ▪ **capturer** *vt* to capture

capuche [kapyʃ] *nf* hood ▪ **capuchon** *nm (de manteau)* hood; *(de moine)* cowl; *(de stylo, de tube)* cap, top

caquet [kakɛ] *nm (de poules)* cackle; *Fam* **rabattre le c. à qn** to shut sb up ▪ **caqueter** *vi (poule)* to cackle

car¹ [kar] *conj* because, for

car² [kar] *nm* bus, *Br* coach; **c. de police** police van; **c. de ramassage scolaire** school bus

> Il faut noter que le nom anglais **car** est un faux ami. Il signifie **voiture**.

carabine [karabin] *nf* rifle; **c. à air comprimé** *Br* airgun, *Am* BB gun

carabiné, -ée [karabine] *adj Fam (grippe)* violent; *(rhume)* stinking; *(punition, amende)* very stiff

caracoler [karakɔle] *vi (cheval)* to caracole

caractère¹ [karaktɛr] *nm (lettre)* character; **en petits caractères** in small print; **en caractères gras** in bold characters; **caractères d'imprimerie** block letters

caractère² [karaktɛr] *nm (tempérament, nature)* character, nature; *(attribut)* characteristic; **avoir bon c.** to be good-natured; **avoir mauvais c.** to be bad-tempered

caractériel, -ielle [karakterjɛl] **1** *adj (troubles)* emotional; **enfant c.** problem child **2** *nmf* emotionally disturbed person

caractériser [karakterize] **1** *vt* to characterize **2 se caractériser** *vpr* **se c. par** to be characterized by

caractéristique [karakteristik] *adj & nf* characteristic

carafe [karaf] *nf (pour l'eau, le vin)* carafe; *(pour le whisky)* decanter

carambolage [karɑ̃bɔlaʒ] *nm* pile-up

caramel [karamɛl] *nm* caramel; **des caramels** *(mous)* fudge; *(durs) Br* toffee, *Am* taffy ▪ **caraméliser** *vti* to caramelize

carapace [karapas] *nf (de tortue) & Fig* shell

carat [kara] *nm Br* carat, *Am* karat; **or à 18 carats** *Br* 18-carat *or Am* 18-karat gold

caravane [karavan] *nf (pour camper) Br* caravan, *Am* trailer; *(dans le désert)* caravan ▪ **caravaning, caravanage** *nm* caravanning; **faire du c.** to go caravanning

carbone [karbɔn] *nm* carbon; **(papier) c.** carbon (paper) ▪ **carbonique** *adj* **gaz c.** carbon dioxide; **neige c.** dry ice

carbonisé, -ée [karbɔnize] *adj (nourriture)* burnt to a cinder; **mourir carbonisé** to burn to death

carburant [karbyrɑ̃] *nm* fuel ▪ **carburateur** *nm Aut Br* carburettor, *Am* carburetor

carburer [karbyre] *vi* **mal c.** to be badly tuned; *Fam* **il carbure au café** coffee keeps him going

carcan [karkɑ̃] *nm* yoke

carcasse [karkas] *nf (os)* carcass; *(d'immeuble)* shell; *Fam (de personne)* body

carcéral, -e, -aux, -ales [karseral, -o] *adj* prison

cardiaque [kardjak] **1** *adj (arrêt, massage)* cardiac; **être c.** to have a heart condition **2** *nmf* heart patient

cardigan [kardigɑ̃] *nm* cardigan

cardinal, -e, -aux, -ales [kardinal, -o] **1** *adj (nombre, point, vertu)* cardinal **2** *nm Rel* cardinal

cardiologie [kardjɔlɔʒi] *nf* cardiology ▪ **cardiologue** *nmf* cardiologist; **chirurgien c.** heart surgeon

carême [karɛm] *nm Rel* **le C.** Lent

carence [karɑ̃s] *nf (manque)* deficiency; **c. alimentaire** nutritional deficiency

caresse [karɛs] *nf* caress; **faire des caresses à** *(personne)* to caress; *(animal)* to stroke

caresser [karese] *vt (personne)* to caress; *(animal)* to stroke; *Fig (espoir)* to cherish ▪ **caressant, -ante** *adj* affectionate

cargaison [kargɛzɔ̃] *nf* cargo ▪ **cargo** *nm Naut* freighter

> Il faut noter que le nom anglais **cargo** est un faux ami. Il signifie **cargaison**.

caricature [karikatyr] nf caricature ■**caricatural, -e, -aux, -ales** adj caricatured ■**caricaturer** vt to caricature

carie [kari] nf **c. (dentaire)** tooth decay; **avoir une c.** to have a cavity ■**cariée** adj f **dent c.** decayed tooth

carillon [karijɔ̃] nm (sonnerie) chimes; (horloge) chiming clock; (de porte) door chime ■**carillonner** vi (cloches) to chime

caritatif, -ive [karitatif, -iv] adj charitable

carlingue [karlɛ̃g] nf (d'avion) cabin

carnage [karnaʒ] nm carnage

carnassier, -ière [karnasje, -jɛr] 1 adj flesh-eating 2 nm carnivore

carnaval, -als [karnaval] nm carnival

carnet [karnɛ] nm notebook; (de timbres, chèques, adresses) book; (de tickets de métro) = book of ten tickets; **c. d'adresses** address book; **c. de notes** Br school report, Am report card; **c. de route** logbook; **c. de santé** health record

carnivore [karnivɔr] 1 adj carnivorous 2 nm carnivore

carotte [karɔt] 1 nf carrot; Fam **les carottes sont cuites** we've/he's/etc had it 2 adj inv **roux c.** (cheveux) carroty

carotter [karɔte] vt Fam (objet) to pinch, Br to nick

carpe [karp] nf carp

carpette [karpɛt] nf rug; Fam Péj **c'est une vraie c.** he's a doormat

Il faut noter que le nom anglais **carpet** est un faux ami. Il signifie **moquette**.

carquois [karkwa] nm quiver

carré, -ée [kare] 1 adj square; (épaules) square, broad; **être c. en affaires** to be straightforward in one's business dealings; **mètre c.** square metre 2 nm Géom & Math square; **avoir une coupe au c.** to have one's hair in a bob; Culin **c. d'agneau** rack of lamb; **c. de soie** silk scarf; Cartes **c. de valets** four jacks; Naut **c. des officiers** wardroom

carreau, -x [karo] nm (motif) square; (sur tissu) check; (de céramique) tile; (vitre) (window) pane; Cartes (couleur) diamonds; **tissu à carreaux** check(ed) material; Fam **se tenir à c.** to keep a low profile; Fam **rester sur le c.** to be killed; (être blessé) to be badly injured; (être éliminé) to be given the boot

carrefour [karfur] nm crossroads (sing); giratoire Br roundabout, Am traffic circle

carreler [karle] vt to tile ■**carrelage** nm (sol) tiled floor; (carreaux) tiles

carrelet [karlɛ] nm Br plaice, Am flounder

carrément [karemɑ̃] adv Fam (franchement) straight out; (très) really

carrière [karjɛr] nf (a) (lieu) quarry (b) (métier) career; **faire c. dans** to make a career in

carriole [karjɔl] nf light cart

carrosse [karɔs] nm Hist (horse-drawn) carriage ■**carrosserie** nf (de véhicule) bodywork

carrure [karyr] nf (de personne) build; (de vêtement) width across the shoulders

cartable [kartabl] nm school bag, satchel

carte [kart] nf (a) (carton, document officiel, informatisé) & Ordinat (géographique) map; (marine, météo) chart; Fig **avoir c. blanche** to have a free hand; **c. (à jouer)** (playing) card; **jouer aux cartes** to play cards; **c. à gratter** (de loterie) scratchcard; **c. à puce** smart card; **c. de crédit** credit card; **c. de fidélité** loyalty card; **c. d'identité** identity card; Tél **c. de recharge** (pour téléphone portable) Br top-up card, Am refill card; **c. de séjour** residence permit; Tél **c. de téléphone** phonecard; **c. de visite** Br business card, Am calling card; (professionnelle) business card; **c. de vœux** greetings card; Aut **c. grise** ≃ vehicle registration document; **C. Orange** = combined monthly season ticket for the métro, bus and RER; **c. postale** postcard; Tél **c. prépayée** (pour téléphone portable) Br top-up card, Am refill card; **c. routière** road map (b) (de restaurant) menu; **manger à la c.** to eat à la carte; **c. des vins** wine list

cartel [kartɛl] nm Écon cartel

carter [kartɛr] nm (de moteur) crankcase; (de bicyclette) chain guard

cartilage [kartilaʒ] nm cartilage

carton [kartɔ̃] nm (matière) cardboard; (boîte) cardboard box; **faire un c.** (au tir) to have a shot; Fam (à un examen) to pass with flying colours; **c. à dessin** portfolio; Football **c. jaune/rouge** yellow/red card ■**cartonner** 1 vt (livre) to case; **livre cartonné** hardback 2 vi Fam (à l'école) to get excellent marks (**en** in)

cartouche [kartuʃ] nf cartridge; (de cigarettes) carton ■**cartouchière** nf cartridge belt

cas [kɑ] nm case; **en tout c.** in any case; **en aucun c.** on no account; **en c. de besoin** if need be; **en c. d'accident** in the event of an accident; **en c. d'urgence** in an emergency; **au c. où elle tomberait** if she should fall; **pour le c. où il pleuvrait** in case it rains; **faire c. de/peu de c. de qn/qch** to set great/little store by sb/sth

casanier, -ière [kazanje, -jɛr] adj homeloving; Péj stay-at-home

casaque [kazak] nf (de jockey) blouse

cascade [kaskad] nf (a) (d'eau) waterfall; **en c.** in succession (b) (de cinéma) stunt ■**cascadeur, -euse** nmf stunt man, f stunt woman

case [kaz] nf (a) (de tiroir) compartment; (d'échiquier) square; (de formulaire) box; Fam **il a une c. de vide** he's got a screw loose (b) (hutte) hut

caser [kaze] **1** *vt* (*placer*) to fit in; *Fam* **c. qn** (*établir*) to fix sb up with a job; (*marier*) to marry sb off **2 se caser** *vpr* (*se marier*) to get married and settle down

caserne [kazɛrn] *nf* barracks; **c. de pompiers** fire station

casier [kazje] *nm* compartment; (*pour le courrier*) pigeonhole; (*pour les vêtements etc*) locker; **c. à bouteilles** bottle/record rack; *Jur* **c. judiciaire** criminal *or* police record

casino [kazino] *nm* casino

casque [kask] *nm* helmet; (*de coiffeur*) hairdryer; **c. (à écouteurs)** headphones; **les Casques bleus** the Blue Berets

casquer [kaske] *vi Fam* to fork out

casquette [kaskɛt] *nf* cap

cassation [kasasjɔ̃] *nf Jur* annulment

casse¹ [kas] *nf* (**a**) (*objets cassés*) breakages; **aller à la c.** to go for scrap; *Fam* **il va y avoir de la c.** something will get broken (**b**) (*d'imprimerie*) case; **haut/bas de c.** upper/lower case

casse² [kas] *nm très Fam* (*cambriolage*) break-in

casser [kase] **1** *vt* (**a**) (*briser*) to break; (*noix*) to crack; (*voix*) to strain; *Fam* **c. les pieds à qn** (*agacer*) to get on sb's nerves; *Fam* **c. les oreilles à qn** to deafen sb; *Fam* **c. la figure à qn** to smash sb's face in; *Fam* **c. sa pipe** to kick the bucket; *Fam* **ça ne casse pas des briques** it's nothing to write home about; *Fam* **ça vaut 50 euros à tout c.** it's worth 50 euros at the very most (**b**) *Jur* (*verdict*) to quash; (*mariage*) to annul **2** *vi* to break **3 se casser** *vpr* to break; *Fam* (*partir*) to clear off; **se c. la jambe** to break one's leg; *Fam* **se c. la figure** (*tomber*) to fall flat on one's face; *Fam* **se c. la tête** to rack one's brains; *Fam* **il ne s'est pas cassé** he didn't exhaust himself • **cassant, -ante** *adj* (*fragile*) brittle; (*brusque*) curt, abrupt • **casse-cou** *nmf inv* (*personne*) daredevil • **casse-croûte** *nm inv Fam* snack • **casse-gueule** *adj inv très Fam* (*lieu*) dangerous; (*entreprise*) risky • **casse-noisettes, casse-noix** *nm inv* nutcrackers • **casse-pieds** *nmf inv Fam* (*personne*) pain in the neck • **casse-tête** *nm inv* (*problème*) headache; (*jeu*) puzzle • **casseur** *nm* (*manifestant*) rioter

casserole [kasrɔl] *nf* (*sauce*)pan

Il faut noter que le nom anglais **casserole** est un faux ami. Il signifie **ragoût** ou **cocotte** selon le contexte.

cassette [kasɛt] *nf* (*magnétique*) cassette, tape; **enregistrer qch sur c.** to tape sth; **c. vidéo** video (cassette)

cassis [kasis] *nm* (*fruit*) blackcurrant; (*boisson*) blackcurrant liqueur

cassoulet [kasulɛ] *nm Culin* cassoulet, = stew of beans, pork and goose

cassure [kasyr] *nf* break; *Géol* fault

castagnettes [kastaɲɛt] *nfpl* castanets

caste [kast] *nf* caste

castor [kastɔr] *nm* beaver

castrer [kastre] *vt* to castrate; (*chat, chien*) to neuter

cataclysme [kataklism] *nm* cataclysm • **cataclysmique** *adj* cataclysmic

catacombes [katakɔ̃b] *nfpl* catacombs

catalogue [katalɔg] *nm Br* catalogue, *Am* catalog • **cataloguer** *vt Br* to catalogue, *Am* catalog; *Fig & Péj* to label

catalyseur [katalizœr] *nm Chim & Fig* catalyst

catalytique [katalitik] *adj Aut* **pot c.** catalytic converter

cataplasme [kataplasm] *nm* poultice

catapulte [katapylt] *nf* catapult • **catapulter** *vt* to catapult

cataracte [katarakt] *nf* (*maladie, cascade*) cataract

catastrophe [katastrɔf] *nf* disaster, catastrophe; **en c.** (*à toute vitesse*) in a panic • **catastrophé, -ée** *adj Fam* stunned • **catastrophique** *adj* disastrous, catastrophic

catch [katʃ] *nm* wrestling • **catcheur, -euse** *nmf* wrestler

catéchisme [kateʃism] *nm Rel* catechism

catégorie [kategɔri] *nf* category; (*d'hôtel*) grade

catégorique [kategɔrik] *adj* categorical; **c'est lui, je suis c.** I'm positive it's him • **catégoriquement** *adv* categorically

cathédrale [katedral] *nf* cathedral

catholique [katɔlik] *adj & nmf* (Roman) Catholic; *Fam* **pas (très) c.** shady, *Br* dodgy • **catholicisme** *nm* Catholicism

catimini [katimini] **en catimini** *adv* on the sly

cauchemar [koʃmar] *nm aussi Fig* nightmare; **faire un c.** to have a nightmare

cause [koz] *nf* (*origine*) cause; (*procès, parti*) case; **à c. de qn/qch** because of sb/sth; **pour c. de décès** due to bereavement; **et pour c.!** for a very good reason!; **être en c.** (*sujet à caution*) to be in question; **mettre qn en c.** (*impliquer*) to implicate sb; **mettre qn hors de c.** to clear sb; **faire c. commune avec qn** to join forces with sb; **en tout état de c.** in any case

causer¹ [koze] *vt* (*provoquer*) to cause

causer² [koze] *vi* (*bavarder*) to chat (**de** about); (*cancaner*) to talk; *Ironique* **cause toujours (, tu m'intéresses!)** riveting • **causant, -ante** *adj Fam* chatty • **causerie** *nf* talk • **causette** *nf Fam* **faire la c.** to have a little chat

caustique [kostik] *adj* (*substance, esprit*) caustic

cautériser [koterize] *vt Méd* to cauterize

caution [kosjɔ̃] *nf (d'appartement)* deposit; *Jur* bail; *(personne)* guarantor; *Fig (appui)* backing; *Jur* **sous c.** on bail; **sujet à c.** unconfirmed ▪ **cautionner** *vt Fig (approuver)* to back

> Il faut noter que le nom anglais **caution** est un faux ami. Il signifie **prudence**.

cavalcade [kavalkad] *nf Fam* stampede; *(défilé)* cavalcade

cavale [kaval] *nf Fam* **en c.** on the run ▪ **cavaler** *vi Fam (se démener)* to rush around; **c. après qn** to chase after sb

cavalerie [kavalri] *nf Mil* cavalry

cavalier, -ière [kavalje, -jɛr] **1** *nmf (à cheval)* rider; *Échecs* knight; *(de bal)* partner, escort; *Fig* **faire c. seul** to go it alone **2** *adj (manière, personne)* cavalier

cave[1] [kav] *nf* cellar ▪ **caveau, -x** *nm (sépulture)* burial vault

cave[2] [kav] *adj (yeux)* sunken, hollow

> Il faut noter que le nom anglais **cave** est un faux ami. Il signifie **grotte**.

caverne [kavɛrn] *nf* cave, cavern; **homme des cavernes** caveman

caverneux, -euse [kavɛrnø, -øz] *adj (voix)* deep

caviar [kavjar] *nm* caviar

cavité [kavite] *nf* hollow, cavity

CCP [sesepe] *(abrév* **compte chèque postal**) *nm Br* ≃ PO Giro account, *Am* ≃ Post Office checking account

CD [sede] *(abrév* **disque compact**) *nm inv* CD ▪ **CD-Rom** *nm inv Ordinat* CD-ROM

CDI [sedei] *(abrév* **centre de documentation et d'information**) *nm inv* school library *(with special resources on how to find information)*

CE [seə] **1** *(abrév* **cours élémentaire**) *nm Scol* **CE1** = second year of primary school; **CE2** = third year of primary school **2** *(abrév* **Communauté européenne**) *nf Anciennement* EC

ce[1] [sə]

> **ce** becomes **c'** before a vowel.

pron démonstratif (**a**) *(pour désigner, pour qualifier)* it, that; **c'est facile** it's easy; **c'est exact** that's right; **c'est mon père** that's my father; *(au téléphone)* it's my father; **c'est un médecin** he's a doctor; **ce sont eux qui...** they are the people who...; **qui est-ce?** *(en général)* who is it?; *(en désignant)* who is that?; **c'est à elle de jouer** it's her turn to play; **est-ce que tu viens?** are you coming?; **ce faisant** in so doing; **sur ce** thereupon (**b**) *(après une proposition)* **ce que..., ce qui...** what...; **je sais ce qui est bon/ce que tu veux** I know what is good/what you want; **elle est malade, ce qui est triste/ce que je ne savais pas** she's ill, which is sad/which I didn't know; **ce que c'est beau!** it's so beautiful!

ce[2]**, cette, ces** [sə, sɛt, se]

> **cet** is used before a masculine singular adjective beginning with a vowel or mute h.

adj démonstratif this, that, *pl* these, those; **cet homme** this/that man; **cet homme-ci** this man; **cet homme-là** that man

ceci [səsi] *pron démonstratif* this; **c. étant dit** having said this

cécité [sesite] *nf* blindness

céder [sede] **1** *vt (donner)* to give up (**à** to); *(par testament)* to leave (**à** to); **c. sa place à qn** to give up one's seat to sb; **c. du terrain** to give ground; **'cédez le passage'** *(sur panneau) Br* 'give way', *Am* 'yield'; **'à céder'** 'for sale' **2** *vi (personne)* to give in (**à/devant** to); *(branche, chaise)* to give way

cédérom [sederɔm] *nm Ordinat* CD-ROM

cédille [sedij] *nf* cedilla

cèdre [sɛdr] *nm (arbre, bois)* cedar

CEE [seøø] *(abrév* **Communauté économique européenne**) *nf Anciennement* EEC

CEI [seøi] *(abrév* **Communauté d'États Indépendants**) *nf* CIS

ceinture [sɛ̃tyr] *nf (accessoire)* belt; *(taille)* waist; **la petite C.** = circular bus route around the centre of Paris; **c. de sécurité** *(de véhicule)* seatbelt

ceinturer [sɛ̃tyre] *vt* to grab around the waist

cela [s(ə)la] *pron démonstratif (pour désigner)* that; *(sujet indéfini)* it, that; **c. m'attriste que...** it saddens me that...; **quand/comment c.?** when?/how?; **c'est c.** that is so

célèbre [selɛbr] *adj* famous ▪ **célébrité** *nf* fame; *(personne)* celebrity

célébrer [selebre] *vt* to celebrate ▪ **célébration** *nf* celebration (**de** of)

céleri [sɛlri] *nm* celery ▪ **céleri-rave** *(pl* **céleris-raves**) *nm* celeriac

céleste [selɛst] *adj* celestial, heavenly

célibat [seliba] *nm (de prêtre)* celibacy ▪ **célibataire** **1** *adj (non marié)* single, unmarried **2** *nmf* bachelor, *f* single woman

> Il faut noter que l'adjectif anglais **celibate** est un faux ami. Il signifie **chaste**.

celle *voir* **celui**

cellier [selje] *nm* storeroom

Cellophane® [selɔfan] *nf* cellophane®; **sous c.** cellophane-wrapped

cellule [selyl] *nf (de prison) & Biol* cell; **c. souche** stem cell ▪ **cellulaire** *adj Biol* cell; **téléphone c.** cellular phone

cellulite [selylit] *nf* cellulite

cellulose [selyloz] *nf* cellulose

celtique, celte [sɛltik, sɛlt] *adj* Celtic

celui, celle, ceux, celles [səlɥi, sɛl, sø, sɛl]

pron démonstratif the one, *pl* those, the ones; **c. de Jean** Jean's (one); **ceux de Jean** Jean's (ones), those of Jean; **c. qui appartient à Jean** the one that belongs to Jean; **c.-ci** this one; *(le dernier)* the latter; **c.-là** that one; *(le premier)* the former; **elle alla voir son amie, mais celle-ci était absente** she went to see her friend but she was out

cendre [sɑ̃dr] *nf* ash ▪ **cendrée** *nf (de stade)* cinder track

cendrier [sɑ̃drije] *nm* ashtray

Cendrillon [sɑ̃drijɔ̃] *nf* Cinderella

censé, -ée [sɑ̃se] *adj* **être c. faire qch** to be supposed to do sth

censeur [sɑ̃sœr] *nm (de films, de journaux)* censor; *(de lycée) Br* deputy head, *Am* assistant principal ▪ **censure** *nf (activité)* censorship; *(comité)* board of censors ▪ **censurer** *vt (film)* to censor

> Il faut noter que le verbe anglais **to censure** est un faux ami. Il signifie **critiquer**.

cent [sɑ̃] *adj & nm* a hundred; *(pièce)* cent; **c. pages** a *or* one hundred pages; **deux cents pages** two hundred pages; **deux c. trois pages** two hundred and three pages; **cinq pour c.** five per cent ▪ **centaine** *nf* **une c. (de)** about a hundred; **des centaines de** hundreds of; **plusieurs centaines de gens** several hundred people ▪ **centenaire** 1 *adj* hundred-year-old; **être c.** to be a hundred 2 *nmf* centenarian 3 *nm (anniversaire)* centenary ▪ **centième** *adj & nmf* hundredth

centigrade [sɑ̃tigrad] *adj* centigrade

centime [sɑ̃tim] *nm* centime; *(d'euro)* cent

centimètre [sɑ̃timetr] *nm Br* centimetre, *Am* centimeter; *(ruban)* tape measure

central, -e, -aux, -ales [sɑ̃tral, -o] 1 *adj* central 2 *nm* **c. téléphonique** telephone exchange ▪ **centrale** *nf* **c. électrique** *Br* power station, *Am* power plant; **c. nucléaire** nuclear *Br* power station *or Am* power plant; **c. d'achat** purchasing group ▪ **centraliser** *vt* to centralize

centre [sɑ̃tr] *nm Br* centre, *Am* center; *Football (passe)* cross; **c. de loisirs** leisure centre; **c. de vacances** holiday centre; **c. aéré** outdoor activity centre; **c. commercial** shopping centre; **c. hospitalo-universitaire** ≃ teaching hospital ▪ **centre-ville** *(pl* centres-villes)* *nm Br* town centre, *Am* downtown; *(de grande ville) Br* city centre, *Am* downtown ▪ **centrer** *vt* to *Br* centre *or Am* center

centrifuge [sɑ̃trifyʒ] *adj* centrifugal ▪ **centrifugeuse** *nf (pour fruits)* juice extractor, juicer

centuple [sɑ̃typl] *nm* **x est le c. de y** x is a hundred times y; **au c.** a hundredfold

cep [sep] *nm* vine-stock ▪ **cépage** *nm* vine

cependant [səpɑ̃dɑ̃] *conj* however, yet

céramique [seramik] *nf (matière)* ceramic; *(art)* ceramics *(sing);* **de** *ou* **en c.** ceramic

cerceau, -x [serso] *nm* hoop

cercle [serkl] *nm (forme, groupe)* circle; **le c. polaire arctique** the Arctic Circle; **c. vicieux** vicious circle

cercueil [serkœj] *nm* coffin

céréale [sereal] *nf* cereal

cérébral, -e, -aux, -ales [serebral, -o] *adj* cerebral

cérémonie [seremɔni] *nf* ceremony; **tenue de c.** ceremonial dress; **sans c.** *(inviter, manger)* informally; *Fam* **faire des cérémonies** to stand on ceremony ▪ **cérémonial** *(pl* -als)* *nm* ceremonial ▪ **cérémonieux, -ieuse** *adj* ceremonious

cerf [ser] *nm* stag ▪ **cerf-volant** *(pl* cerfs-volants)* *nm (jeu)* kite

cerise [səriz] *nf* cherry ▪ **cerisier** *nm* cherry tree

cerne [sern] *nm* ring ▪ **cerner** *vt* to surround; *(problème)* to define; **avoir les yeux cernés** to have rings under one's eyes

certain, -aine [sertɛ̃, -en] 1 *adj (sûr)* certain; **il est c. que tu réussiras** you're certain to succeed; **je suis c. de réussir** I'm certain I'll be successful *or* of being successful; **être c. de qch** to be certain of sth 2 *adj indéfini (avant nom)* certain; **un c. temps** a while; **il a un c. charme** he has a certain charm 3 *pron indéfini* **certains pensent que...** some people think that...; **certains d'entre nous** some of us ▪ **certainement** *adv* most probably

> Il faut noter que l'adverbe anglais **certainly** est un faux ami. Il signifie **sans aucun doute**.

certes [sert] *adv* of course, certainly; **c., tout espoir n'est pas perdu ...** we/I/*etc* haven't given up hope, of course, but ...;

certificat [sertifika] *nm* certificate

certifier [sertifje] *vt* to certify; **je vous certifie que...** I assure you that... ▪ **certifié, -ée** *adj (professeur)* qualified

certitude [sertityd] *nf* certainty; **avoir la c. que...** to be certain that...

cerveau, -x [servo] *nm (organe)* brain; *(intelligence)* mind, brain(s); *Fam (de projet)* mastermind

cervelle [servel] *nf (substance)* brain; *(plat)* brains; **se faire sauter la c.** to blow one's brains out

CES [seaes] *(abrév* **collège d'enseignement secondaire)** *nm Anciennement* = secondary school for pupils aged 12 to 15

ces *voir* **ce²**

César [sezar] *nm Cin* = French cinema award

césarienne [sezarjen] *nf Br* Caesarean *or Am* Cesarian (section)

cesser [sese] *vti* to stop; **faire c. qch** to put a stop to sth; **c. de faire qch** to stop doing sth; **il ne cesse de parler** he doesn't stop talking; **cela a cessé d'exister** that has ceased to exist ▪**cessation** *nf* cessation; **c. de paiements** suspension of payments ▪**cesse** *nf* **sans c.** constantly, non-stop ▪**cessez-le-feu** *nm inv* cease-fire

cession [sesjɔ̃] *nf Jur* transfer

c'est-à-dire [setadir] *conj* that is (to say)

cet, cette *voir* **ce²**

ceux *voir* **celui**

chacal, -als [ʃakal] *nm* jackal

chacun, -e [ʃakœ̃, -yn] *pron indéfini* each (one), every one; *(tous le monde)* everyone; **(à) c. son tour!** wait your turn!

chagrin [ʃagrɛ̃] **1** *nm* grief, sorrow; **avoir du c.** to be upset; **faire du c. à qn** to distress sb **2** *adj Littéraire* woeful ▪**chagriner** *vt (peiner)* to grieve; *(contrarier)* to bother

chahut [ʃay] *nm Fam* racket ▪**chahuter** *Fam* **1** *vi* to make a racket **2** *vt (professeur)* to bait; **se faire c.** *(professeur)* to get baited

chai [ʃɛ] *nm* wine and spirits storehouse

chaîne [ʃɛn] *nf (attache, décoration, série)* chain; *(de montagnes)* chain, range; *(d'étoffe)* warp; **collision en c.** *(accident)* multiple collision; **réaction en c.** chain reaction; **travail à la c.** assembly line work; **travailler à la c.** to work on the assembly line; **faire la c.** to form a chain; *Aut* **chaînes** (snow) chains; **c. de montage** assembly line; **c. de télévision** television channel; **c. de vélo** bicycle chain; **c. alimentaire** food chain; **c. (hi-fi)** hi-fi (system) ▪**chaînette** *nf* (small) chain ▪**chaînon** *nm* link

chair [ʃɛr] *nf* flesh; **(couleur) c.** *Br* fleshcoloured, *Am* fleshcolored; **en c. et en os** in the flesh; **bien en c.** plump; **avoir la c. de poule** to have *Br* goose pimples *or Am* goose bumps; **c. à saucisses** sausagemeat

chaire [ʃɛr] *nf (d'université)* chair; *(d'église)* pulpit

chaise [ʃɛz] *nf* chair; **c. longue** deckchair; **c. d'enfant, c. haute** high chair; **c. roulante** wheelchair

chaland [ʃalã] *nm* barge

châle [ʃal] *nm* shawl

chalet [ʃale] *nm* chalet

chaleur [ʃalœr] *nf* heat; *(de personne, de couleur, de voix)* warmth; **coup de c.** heatstroke; **les grandes chaleurs** the hot season; **c. humaine** human warmth ▪**chaleureux, -euse** *adj* warm ▪**chaleureusement** *adv* warmly

challenge [ʃalɑ̃ʒ] *nm Sport* tournament; *(défi)* challenge

chaloupe [ʃalup] *nf* launch

chalumeau, -x [ʃalymo] *nm* blowtorch

chalut [ʃaly] *nm* trawl; **pêcher au c.** to trawl ▪**chalutier** *nm* trawler

chamade [ʃamad] *nf* **mon cœur battait la c.** my heart was beating wildly

chamailler [ʃamaje] **se chamailler** *vpr* to squabble ▪**chamailleries** *nfpl* squabbling

chamarré, -ée [ʃamare] *adj* richly *Br* coloured *or Am* colored

chambarder [ʃãbarde] *vt Fam* to turn upside down

chambouler [ʃãbule] *vt Fam* to turn upside down

chambre [ʃãbr] *nf* bedroom; *(de tribunal)* division; **c. (d'hôtel)** (hotel) room; **garder la c.** to keep to one's room; **auriez-vous une c. libre?** do you have any vacancies?; **c. à coucher** *(pièce)* bedroom; *(mobilier)* bedroom suite; **c. d'ami** spare room; **c. d'hôte** ≃ guest house, bed and breakfast; *Jur* **c. d'accusation** Court of Criminal Appeal; **C. de commerce** Chamber of Commerce; *Pol* **C. des députés** = lower chamber of French Parliament; **c. à air** inner tube; **c. à gaz** gas chamber; **c. forte** strongroom; **c. froide** cold store; **c. noire** darkroom ▪**chambrée** *nf Mil* barrackroom ▪**chambrer** *vt (vin)* to bring to room temperature; *Fam* **c. qn** to pull sb's leg

chameau, -x [ʃamo] *nm* camel

chamois [ʃamwa] *nm (animal)* chamois; **peau de c.** chamois (leather)

champ [ʃã] *nm (étendue)* & *Él, Ordinat* field; *Fig (portée)* scope; **c. de blé** field of wheat, wheatfield; *Fig* **laisser le c. libre à qn** to leave the field free for sb; *Phot* **être dans le c.** to be in shot; **tombé au c. d'honneur** killed in action; **c. de bataille** battlefield; **c. de courses** *Br* racecourse, *Am* racetrack; **c. de foire** fairground; **c. de mines** minefield; **c. de tir** rifle range; **c. magnétique** magnetic field; **c. visuel** field of vision

champagne [ʃãpaɲ] *nm* champagne

champêtre [ʃãpetr] *adj* rustic

champignon [ʃãpiɲɔ̃] *nm (végétal)* mushroom; *Méd* fungus; *Fam* **appuyer sur le c.** *Br* to put one's foot down, *Am* to step on the gas; **c. atomique** mushroom cloud; **c. de Paris** button mushroom; **c. vénéneux** toadstool, poisonous mushroom

champion, -onne [ʃãpjɔ̃, -jɔn] **1** *nmf* champion **2** *adj* **l'équipe championne du monde** the world champions ▪**championnat** *nm* championship

chance [ʃãs] *nf (sort favorable)* luck; *(possibilité)* chance; **avoir de la c.** to be lucky; **ne pas avoir de c.** to be unlucky; **souhaiter bonne c. à qn** to wish sb luck; **tenter sa c.** to try one's luck; **avoir peu de chances de faire qch** to have little chance of doing sth; **il y a de fortes chances que...** there's every chance that...; **c'est une c. que je sois arrivé** it's lucky that I came; **avec un peu de c.** with a bit of luck; **quelle c.!**

what a stroke of luck!; **par c.** luckily
▪ **chanceux, -euse** adj lucky

> Il faut noter que le nom anglais **chance** ne
> signifie jamais **bonne fortune**.

chanceler [ʃɑ̃sle] vi to stagger; Fig (courage,
détermination) to falter ▪ **chancelant, -ante**
adj (pas) unsteady; (mémoire) shaky; (santé)
delicate
chancelier [ʃɑ̃səlje] nm Pol chancellor
▪ **chancellerie** nf (d'ambassade) chancellery
chandail [ʃɑ̃daj] nm sweater
Chandeleur [ʃɑ̃dlœr] nf Rel **la C.** Candlemas
chandelier [ʃɑ̃dəlje] nm (à une branche)
candlestick; (à plusieurs branches) candelabra

> Il faut noter que le nom anglais **chandelier**
> est un faux ami. Il signifie **lustre**.

chandelle [ʃɑ̃dɛl] nf candle; Gym shoulder
stand; Fig **voir trente-six chandelles** to see
stars
change [ʃɑ̃ʒ] nm Fin exchange; Fig **gagner au
c.** to gain on the exchange; Fig **donner le c. à
qn** to put sb off the scent
changer [ʃɑ̃ʒe] **1** vt (modifier, remplacer,
convertir) to change; **c. un bébé** to change a
baby; **c. qn/qch en qn/qch** to change sb/sth
into sb/sth; **c. qch de place** to move sth; **ça lui
changera les idées** that will take his mind off
things; **ça va le c.!** it'll be a change for them!
2 vi to change; **c. de voiture/d'adresse** to
change one's car/address; **c. de train/de côté**
to change trains/sides; **c. de place avec qn** to
change places with sb; **c. de vitesse/de
couleur** to change gear/colour; **c. de sujet** to
change the subject; Ironique **pour c.** for a
change
3 se changer vpr to change (one's clothes); **se
c. les idées** to take one's mind off things; **se c.
en qch** to change into sth ▪ **changeant, -ante**
adj (temps) unsettled; **d'humeur changeante**
moody ▪ **changement** nm change; Aut **c. de
vitesse** (levier) Br gear lever, Am gear shift
▪ **changeur** nm **c. de monnaie** change
machine
chanson [ʃɑ̃sɔ̃] nf song ▪ **chant** nm (art)
singing; (chanson) song; **c. de Noël** Christmas
carol
chanter [ʃɑ̃te] **1** vt (chanson) to sing; (exploits)
to sing of; Fam **qu'est-ce que vous me
chantez là?** what are you on about? **2** vi
(personne, oiseau) to sing; (coq) to crow; **faire
c. qn** to blackmail sb; Fam **si ça te chante** if
you feel like it ▪ **chantage** nm blackmail
▪ **chantant, -ante** adj (air, voix) melodious
▪ **chanteur, -euse** nmf singer

> Il faut noter que le verbe anglais **to chant** est
> un faux ami. Il signifie **scander**.

chantier [ʃɑ̃tje] nm (building) site; (sur route)
roadworks; **mettre qch en c.** to get sth under
way; Fam **quel c.!** (désordre) what a mess!; **c.
naval** shipyard
chantilly [ʃɑ̃tiji] nf whipped cream
chantonner [ʃɑ̃tɔne] vti to hum
chanvre [ʃɑ̃vr] nm hemp
chaos [kao] nm chaos ▪ **chaotique** adj chaotic
chaparder [ʃaparde] vt Fam (voler) to pinch
chapeau, -x [ʃapo] nm hat; (de champignon)
cap; Fig **tirer son c. à qn** to raise one's hat;
prendre un virage sur les chapeaux de roue
to take a corner at top speed; **c.!** well done!; **c.
de paille** straw hat; **c. melon** bowler hat; **c. mou**
Br trilby, Am fedora ▪ **chapelier** nm hatter
chapeauter [ʃapote] vt (contrôler) to head
chapelet [ʃaple] nm rosary; Fig **un c. d'injures** a
stream of abuse
chapelle [ʃapɛl] nf chapel; **c. ardente** chapel of
rest
chapelure [ʃaplyr] nf Culin breadcrumbs
chaperon [ʃaprɔ̃] nm chaperon ▪ **chaperonner** vt to chaperon
chapiteau, -x [ʃapito] nm (de cirque) big top;
(pour expositions) tent, Br marquee; Archit (de
colonne) capital
chapitre [ʃapitr] nm (de livre) & Rel chapter; Fig
sur le c. de on the subject of; Fig **avoir voix au
c.** to have a say in the matter
chaque [ʃak] adj each, every; **c. chose en son
temps** all in good time
char [ʃar] nm (romain) chariot; (de carnaval)
float; Can Fam (voiture) car; Fam **arrête ton c.!**
come off it!; Mil **c. (d'assaut)** tank; **c. à voile**
sand yacht
charabia [ʃarabja] nm Fam gibberish
charade [ʃarad] nf riddle (with verbal clues
corresponding to each syllable of a word to be
guessed)
charbon [ʃarbɔ̃] nm coal; (pour dessiner) & Méd
charcoal; **c. de bois** charcoal; Fig **sur des
charbons ardents** on tenterhooks ▪ **charbon-
nages** nmpl (houillères) collieries ▪ **charbon-
nier, -ière 1** adj **industrie charbonnière** coal
industry **2** nm coal merchant
charcuter [ʃarkyte] vt Fam Péj (opérer) to hack
up
charcuterie [ʃarkytri] nf (magasin) pork
butcher's shop; (aliments) cooked (pork)
meats ▪ **charcutier, -ière** nmf pork butcher
chardon [ʃardɔ̃] nm (plante) thistle
charge [ʃarʒ] nf (poids) load; (responsabilité)
responsibility; (d'une arme) & Él, Mil charge;
(fonction) office; **être en c. de qch** to be in
charge of sth; **prendre qn/qch en c.** to take
charge of sb/sth; **se prendre en c.** to be
responsible for oneself; **être à la c. de qn**
(personne) to be dependent on sb; (frais) to be
payable by sb; **avoir un enfant à c.** a

dependent child; *Fig* **revenir à la c.** to return to the attack; **charges (locatives)** maintenance charges; **charges sociales** *Br* national insurance contributions, *Am* Social Security contributions

charger [ʃarʒe] **1** *vt* (*véhicule, marchandises, arme*) & *Ordinat* to load; (*batterie*) & *Mil* to charge; **c. qn de qch** to entrust sb with; **c. qn de faire qch** to give sb the responsibility of doing sth **2** *vi Ordinat* to load up; *Mil* to charge **3 se charger** *vpr* (*s'encombrer*) to weigh oneself down; **se c. de qn/qch** to take care of sb/sth; **se c. de faire qch** to undertake to do sth ▪ **chargé, -ée 1** *adj* (*véhicule*) loaded (**de** with); (*arme*) loaded; (*journée, programme*) busy; **avoir la langue chargée** to have a furred tongue; **être c. de faire qch** to be responsible for doing sth; **être c. de famille** to have family responsibilities **2** *nmf Univ* **c. de cours** = part-time lecturer ▪ **chargement** [-əmã] *nm* (*action*) loading; (*marchandises*) load; (*de bateau*) cargo ▪ **chargeur** *nm* (*d'arme*) magazine; *Él* (*battery*) charger

chariot [ʃarjo] *nm* (*de supermarché*) *Br* trolley, *Am* cart; (*de ferme*) waggon; (*de machine à écrire*) carriage; **c. à bagages** luggage trolley

charisme [karism] *nm* charisma

charitable [ʃaritabl] *adj* charitable (**envers** towards)

charité [ʃarite] *nf* (*vertu*) charity; **faire la c.** to give to charity; **demander la c.** to ask for charity

charivari [ʃarivari] *nm Fam* hubbub, hullabaloo

charlatan [ʃarlatã] *nm Péj* (*escroc*) charlatan; (*médecin*) quack

charme [ʃarm] *nm* (*attrait*) charm; (*magie*) spell; **avoir du c.** to have charm; **faire du c. à qn** to turn on the charm with sb; **être sous le c.** to be under the spell; *Fig* **se porter comme un c.** to be as fit as a fiddle

charmer [ʃarme] *vt* to charm ▪ **charmant, -ante** *adj* charming ▪ **charmeur, -euse 1** *adj* (*sourire, air*) charming **2** *nmf* charmer; **c. de serpents** snake charmer

charnel, -elle [ʃarnɛl] *adj* carnal

charnier [ʃarnje] *nm* mass grave

charnière [ʃarnjɛr] *nf* hinge; *Fig* **à la c. de deux grandes époques** at the junction of two great eras; **époque c.** transitional period

charnu, -ue [ʃarny] *adj* fleshy

charogne [ʃarɔɲ] *nf* carrion

charpente [ʃarpãt] *nf* framework; (*de personne*) build ▪ **charpenté, -ée** *adj* **bien c.** solidly built ▪ **charpenterie** *nf* carpentry ▪ **charpentier, -ière** *nmf* carpenter

charpie [ʃarpi] *nf* **mettre qch en c.** to tear sth to shreds

charrette [ʃarɛt] *nf* cart ▪ **charrier 1** *vt* (*transporter*) to cart; (*rivière*) to carry along; *Fam*

(*taquiner*) to tease **2** *vi Fam* **faut pas c.!** come off it!

charrue [ʃary] *nf Br* plough, *Am* plow

charte [ʃart] *nf* charter

charter [ʃarter] *nm* (*vol*) charter (flight); (*avion*) charter plane

chas [ʃa] *nm* (*d'une aiguille*) eye

chasse¹ [ʃas] *nf* (*activité*) hunting; (*événement*) hunt; (*poursuite*) chase; **aller à la c.** to go hunting; **faire la c. à** to hunt for; **donner la c. à qn/qch** to give chase to sb/sth; **c. à courre** hunting; **c. à l'homme** manhunt; **c. au trésor** treasure hunt; *Pol* **c. aux sorcières** witch hunt; **c. gardée** private hunting ground

> Il faut noter que le nom anglais **chase** est un faux ami. Il signifie **poursuite**.

chasse² [ʃas] *nf* **c. d'eau** flush; **tirer la c.** to flush the toilet

chassé-croisé [ʃasekrwaze] (*pl* **chassés-croisés**) *nm* (*de personnes*) comings and goings

chasser [ʃase] **1** *vt* (*animal*) to hunt; (*faisan, perdrix*) to shoot; (*papillon*) to chase; **c. qn** (*expulser*) to chase sb away; (*employé*) to dismiss sb **2** *vi* to hunt; *Aut* to skid ▪ **chasse-neige** *nm inv Br* snowplough, *Am* snowplow ▪ **chasseur, -euse 1** *nmf* hunter; **c. de têtes** headhunter **2** *nm* (*d'hôtel*) *Br* pageboy, *Am* bellboy; (*avion*) fighter

> Il faut noter que le verbe anglais **to chase** est un faux ami. Il signifie **poursuivre**.

châssis [ʃasi] *nm* frame; (*d'automobile*) chassis

chaste [ʃast] *adj* chaste ▪ **chasteté** [-əte] *nf* chastity

chat¹ [ʃa] *nm* cat; *Fig* **avoir un c. dans la gorge** to have a frog in one's throat; *Fig* **avoir d'autres chats à fouetter** to have other fish to fry; *Fig* **il n'y avait pas un c.** there wasn't a soul (around); **c. de gouttière** alley cat; **c. perché** (*jeu*) tag; **c. sauvage** wildcat

chat² [tʃat] *nm Ordinat* chat

châtaigne [ʃatɛɲ] *nf* chestnut ▪ **châtaignier** *nm* chestnut tree ▪ **châtain** *adj* (*cheveux*) (chestnut) brown; (*personne*) brown-haired

château, -x [ʃato] *nm* (*forteresse*) castle; (*manoir*) mansion; *Fig* **bâtir des châteaux en Espagne** to build castles in the air *or* sky; *Fig* **c. de cartes** house of cards; **c. d'eau** water tower; **c. fort** fortified castle

châtelain, -aine [ʃatlɛ̃, -ɛn] *nmf Hist* lord of the manor, *f* lady of the manor

châtiment [ʃatimã] *nm* punishment; **c. corporel** corporal punishment

chaton [ʃatɔ̃] *nm* (**a**) (*chat*) kitten (**b**) (*d'arbre*) catkin

chatouilles [ʃatuj] *nfpl* **faire des c. à qn** to tickle sb ▪ **chatouiller** *vt* to tickle; *Fig* (*curiosité*) to arouse ▪ **chatouilleux, -euse**

adj ticklish; *Fig (pointilleux)* sensitive (**sur** about)

chatoyer [ʃatwaje] *vi* to shimmer; *(pierre)* to sparkle

châtrer [ʃatre] *vt* to castrate

chatte [ʃat] *nf* (she-)cat

chaud, -e [ʃo, ʃod] **1** *adj* (**a**) *(modérément)* warm; *(intensément)* hot (**b**) *Fig (couleur)* warm; *(voix)* sultry; *(discussion)* heated; *(partisan)* keen; **elle n'est pas chaude pour le projet** she's not keen on the plan **2** *adv* **j'aime manger c.** I like my food hot **3** *nm (modéré)* warmth; *(intense)* heat; **avoir c.** to be hot; *Fam (échapper de justesse)* to have a narrow escape; **garder qch au c.** to keep sth warm; **il fait c.** it's hot; *Fig* **ça ne me fait ni c. ni froid** it's all the same to me ▪**chaudement** *adv (s'habiller, féliciter)* warmly

chaudière [ʃodjɛr] *nf* boiler

chauffage [ʃofaʒ] *nm* heating; *(de voiture)* heater

chauffard [ʃofar] *nm* reckless driver

chauffer [ʃofe] **1** *vt* to heat (up); *(moteur)* to warm up **2** *vi* to heat (up); *(s'échauffer) (moteur)* to overheat; **faire c. qch** to heat sth up; **ce radiateur chauffe bien** this radiator gives out a lot of heat; *Fam* **ça va c. s'il est en retard!** there'll be trouble if he's late! **3 se chauffer** *upr* to warm oneself; **se c. au mazout** to have oil-fired heating ▪**chauffant, -ante** *adj* **couverture chauffante** electric blanket; **plaque chauffante** hot plate ▪**chauffé, -ée** *adj (piscine)* heated; **la chambre n'est pas chauffée** there's no heating in the bedroom ▪**chauffe-eau** *nm inv* water heater; **c. électrique** immersion heater ▪**chauffe-plat** *(pl* **chauffe-plats)** *nm* hotplate ▪**chaufferie** *nf* boiler room

chauffeur [ʃofœr] *nm (de véhicule)* driver; *(employé)* chauffeur; **c. de taxi** taxi driver

chaume [ʃom] *nm (pour toits)* thatch; *(des céréales)* stubble; **toit de c.** thatched roof ▪**chaumière** *nf (à toit de chaume)* thatched cottage; *(maison pauvre)* cottage

chaussée [ʃose] *nf* road(way)

chausser [ʃose] **1** *vt (chaussures, lunettes, skis)* to put on; *(aller à)* to fit; **c. qn** to put shoes on sb; **c. du 40** to take a size 40 shoe; **souliers qui chaussent bien** shoes that fit well **2 se chausser** *upr* to put one's shoes on ▪**chausse-pied** *(pl* **chausse-pieds)** *nm* shoehorn

chaussette [ʃosɛt] *nf* sock; **en chaussettes** in one's socks

chausson [ʃosɔ̃] *nm (pantoufle)* slipper; *(de danse)* ballet shoe; *(de bébé)* bootee; *Culin* **c. aux pommes** apple turnover

chaussure [ʃosyr] *nf* shoe; **(l'industrie de) la c.** the shoe industry; *Fig* **trouver c. à son pied** to

find the right man/woman; **chaussures à lacets** lace-up shoes; **chaussures à semelles compensées** platform shoes; **chaussures à talons** high-heeled shoes; **chaussures de marche** walking boots; **chaussures de ski** ski boots; **chaussures de sport** sports shoes

chauve [ʃov] **1** *adj* bald **2** *nm* bald(-headed) man

chauve-souris [ʃovsuri] *(pl* **chauves-souris)** *nf* bat

chauvin, -ine [ʃovɛ̃, -in] **1** *adj* chauvinistic **2** *nmf* chauvinist ▪**chauvinisme** *nm* chauvinism

> Il faut noter que le nom anglais **chauvinism** est un faux ami. Il signifie le plus souvent **phallocratie**.

chaux [ʃo] *nf* lime; **blanchir qch à la c.** to whitewash sth; **c. vive** quick lime

chavirer [ʃavire] *vti (bateau)* to capsize; **faire c. un bateau** to capsize a boat

chef [ʃef] *nm* (**a**) *(de parti, de bande)* leader; *(de tribu)* chief; *Fam (patron)* boss; **rédacteur en c.** editor in chief; **le c. du gouvernement** the head of government; *Fam* **se débrouiller comme un c.** to do really well; **c. d'atelier** (shop) foreman; **c. de bureau** office manager; **c. d'entreprise** company head; **c. d'équipe** foreman; **c. d'État** head of state; **c. d'état-major** chief of staff; **c. de famille** head of the family; **c. de file** leader; **c. de gare** station-master; **c. d'orchestre** conductor; **c. de service** departmental head (**b**) *(cuisinier)* chef (**c**) *Jur* **c. d'accusation** charge (**d**) **de son propre c.** on one's own authority

chef-d'œuvre [ʃedœvr] *(pl* **chefs-d'œuvre)** *nm* masterpiece

chef-lieu [ʃefljø] *(pl* **chefs-lieux)** *nm =* administrative centre of a département

cheik(h) [ʃek] *nm* sheik(h)

chemin [ʃəmɛ̃] *nm (route étroite)* path, track; *(itinéraire)* way (**de** to); *Fig (de la gloire)* road; **à mi-c.** half-way; **en c., c. faisant** on the way; **se mettre en c.** to set out; **avoir beaucoup de c. à faire** to have a long way to go; *Fig* **faire son c.** *(idée)* to gain ground; *Fig* **suivre le droit c.** to stay on the straight and narrow; *Fig* **ne pas y aller par quatre chemins** to get straight to the point; **c. de grande randonnée** hiking trail; **c. de terre** track; **c. de traverse** path across the fields ▪**chemin de fer** *(pl* **chemins de fer)** *nm Br* railway, *Am* railroad

cheminée [ʃəmine] *nf (âtre)* fireplace; *(encadrement)* mantelpiece; *(sur le toit)* chimney; *(de navire)* funnel

> Il faut noter que le nom anglais **chimney** ne signifie jamais **âtre** ou **encadrement**.

cheminer [ʃəmine] *vi (personne)* to make one's way; *Fig (idée)* to gain ground ▪**chemine-**

ment nm (de personnes) movement; Fig (de pensée) development

cheminot [ʃəmino] nm Br railwayman, Am railroader

chemise [ʃəmiz] nf (vêtement) shirt; (classeur) folder; Fig **changer de qch comme de c.** to change sth at the drop of a hat; **c. de nuit** (de femme) nightdress ▪ **chemisette** nf short-sleeved shirt ▪ **chemisier** nm (corsage) blouse

chenal, -aux [ʃənal, -o] nm channel

chenapan [ʃənapã] nm Hum scoundrel

chêne [ʃɛn] nm (arbre, bois) oak

chenil [ʃəni(l)] nm Br kennels, Am kennel

chenille [ʃənij] nf (insecte) caterpillar; (de char) caterpillar track

chenu, -e [ʃəny] adj Littéraire (personne) hoary; (arbre) leafless

cheptel [ʃɛptɛl] nm livestock

chèque [ʃɛk] nm Br cheque, Am check; **faire un c.** à qn to write sb a cheque; **payer qch par c.** to pay sth by cheque; Fam **c. en bois** rubber cheque; **c. sans provision** bad cheque; **c. de voyage** Br traveller's cheque, Am traveler's cheque ▪ **chèque-cadeau** (pl **chèques-cadeaux**) nm Br gift voucher, Am gift certificate ▪ **chèque-repas** (pl **chèques-repas**), **chèque-restaurant** (pl **chèques-restaurant**) nm Br luncheon voucher, Am meal ticket ▪ **chéquier** nm Br cheque book, Am checkbook

cher, chère¹ [ʃɛr] 1 adj (a) (aimé) dear (à to); **il a retrouvé son c. bureau** he's back in his beloved office; **C. Monsieur** (dans une lettre) Dear Mr X; (officiel) Dear Sir (b) (coûteux) expensive, dear; Fam **pas c.** cheap; **la vie chère** the high cost of living 2 adv **coûter c.** to be expensive; **payer qch c.** to pay a high price for sth; Fig **payer c. une erreur** to pay dearly for a mistake; Fam **je l'ai eu pour pas c.** I got it cheap; Fig **je donnerais c. pour savoir ce qu'il a dit** I'd give anything to know what he said to them 3 nmf **mon c., ma chère** my dear ▪ **chère²** nf Littéraire **aimer la bonne c.** to be a lover of good food ▪ **chèrement** adv (à un prix élevé) dearly; Fig **il a payé c. sa liberté** his freedom cost him dearly ▪ **cherté** nf high price; **la c. de la vie** the high cost of living

chercher [ʃɛrʃe] 1 vt to look for; (secours, paix) to seek; (dans ses souvenirs) to try to think of; (dans un dictionnaire) to look up; **c. qn du regard** to look around for sb; **c. ses mots** to search for words; **aller c. qn/qch** to (go and) fetch sb/sth; **venir c. qn/qch** to (come and) fetch sb/sth; **c. à faire qch** to try to do sth; **tu l'as bien cherché!** you asked for it!; Fam **ça va c. dans les 10 000 euros** you're talking about something like 10,000 euros; Fam **tu me cherches?** are you looking for a fight? 2 **se chercher** vpr (chercher son identité) to try to

find oneself ▪ **chercheur, -euse** nmf (scientifique) researcher; **c. d'or** gold digger

chérir [ʃerir] vt to cherish ▪ **chéri, -ie** 1 adj dear 2 nmf darling

chérot [ʃero] adj inv Fam pricey

chétif, -ive [ʃetif, -iv] adj (personne) puny

cheval, -aux [ʃəval, -o] nm horse; **à c.** on horseback; **faire du c.** Br to go horse riding, Am to go horseback riding; **être à c. sur qch** to straddle sth; Fig **être à c. sur les principes** to be a stickler for principle; Fig **monter sur ses grands chevaux** to get on one's high horse; Sport **c. d'arçons** vaulting horse; **c. à bascule** rocking horse; **c. de bataille** hobby-horse; **chevaux de bois** merry-go-round; **c. de course** racehorse; **c. de trait** carthorse; Aut **c. (-vapeur)** horsepower

chevaleresque [ʃəvalrɛsk] adj chivalrous

chevalet [ʃəvalɛ] nm (de peintre) easel; (de menuisier) trestle

chevalier [ʃəvalje] nm knight

chevalière [ʃəvaljɛr] nf signet ring

chevaline [ʃəvalin] adj f **boucherie c.** horse butcher's (shop)

chevauchée [ʃəvoʃe] nf (horse) ride

chevaucher [ʃəvoʃe] 1 vt to straddle 2 vi se **chevaucher** vpr to overlap

chevelu, -ue [ʃəvly] adj long-haired ▪ **chevelure** nf (head of) hair

chevet [ʃəvɛ] nm head of the bed; **rester au c. de qn** to stay at sb's bedside; **lampe de c.** bedside lamp; **table de c.** Br bedside table, Am nightstand

cheveu, -x [ʃəvø] nm **un c.** a hair; **cheveux** hair; **avoir les cheveux noirs** to have black hair; Fig **couper les cheveux en quatre** to split hairs; Fig **tiré par les cheveux** (argument) far-fetched

cheville [ʃəvij] nf (partie du corps) ankle; (pour accrocher) peg; (pour boucher un trou) plug; Fam **être en c. avec qn** to be in cahoots with sb; Fig **elle ne vous arrive pas à la c.** she can't hold a candle to you; Fig **c. ouvrière** mainspring

chèvre [ʃɛvr] 1 nf goat; Fam **rendre qn c.** to drive sb round the bend 2 nm goat's cheese ▪ **chevreau, -x** nm kid

chèvrefeuille [ʃɛvrəfœj] nm honeysuckle

chevreuil [ʃəvrœj] nm roe deer; (viande) venison

chevron [ʃəvrɔ̃] nm (poutre) rafter; Mil stripe, chevron; **à chevrons** (tissu, veste) herringbone

chevronné, -ée [ʃəvrɔne] adj experienced

chevroter [ʃəvrɔte] vi (voix) to quaver

chewing-gum [ʃwiŋɡɔm] (pl chewing-gums) nm chewing gum; **un c.** a piece of chewing gum

chez [ʃe] prép **c. qn** at sb's place; **il n'est pas c. lui** he isn't at home; **elle est rentrée c. elle** she's gone home; **faites comme c. vous** make yourself at home; **c. les Suisses/les jeunes**

among the Swiss/the young; **c. Camus** in (the work of) Camus; **c. les mammifères** in mammals; **c'est devenu une habitude c.** elle it's become a habit with her; **c. Mme Dupont** *(adresse)* c/o Mme Dupont ▪ **chez-soi** *nm inv* **son petit c.** one's own little home

chialer [ʃjale] *vi très Fam (pleurer)* to blubber

chiant, -ante [ʃjɑ̃, -ɑ̃t] *adj très Fam (énervant)* bloody annoying; *(ennuyeux)* deadly boring

chic [ʃik] **1** *adj inv* smart, stylish; *Fam (gentil)* decent **2** *nm (élégance)* style; **avoir le c. pour faire qch** to have the knack of doing sth

chicaner [ʃikane] *vi* **c. sur qch** to quibble over sth

chiche [ʃiʃ] *adj (repas)* scanty; *Fam* **tu n'es pas c. d'y aller!** I bet you don't go!; *Fam* **c.!** *(pour défier)* I dare you!; *(pour relever le défi)* you're on! ▪ **chichement** *adv* meanly

chichis [ʃiʃi] *nmpl Fam* **faire des c.** *(compliquer les choses)* to make a lot of fuss; **sans c.** informal, unfussy

chicorée [ʃikɔre] *nf (en poudre)* chicory; **c. sauvage** chicory *inv*; **c. frisée** endive

chien, chienne [ʃjɛ̃, ʃjɛn] *nmf* dog, *f* bitch; *Fig* **se regarder en chiens de faïence** to stare at one another; *Fam* **quel temps de c.!** what foul weather!; *Fam* **une vie de c.** a dog's life; **entre c. et loup** at dusk; **c. d'arrêt** pointer; **c. d'aveugle** *Br* guide dog, *Am* seeing-eye dog; **c. de berger** sheepdog; **c. de chasse** retriever; **c. de garde** guard dog; **c. policier** police dog; **c. de traîneau** husky ▪ **chien-loup** *(pl chiens-loups) nm* wolfhound

chiendent [ʃjɛ̃dɑ̃] *nm (plante)* couch grass; **brosse de c.** scrubbing brush

chiffe [ʃif] *nf Fam* **c'est une c. molle** he's a drip

chiffon [ʃifɔ̃] *nm* rag; **passer un coup de c. sur qch** to give sth a dust; **c. (de poussière)** *Br* duster, *Am* dustcloth ▪ **chiffonner** *vt* to crumple; *Fig (ennuyer)* to bother ▪ **chiffonnier** *nm* rag picker

chiffre [ʃifr] *nm (nombre)* figure, number; *(total)* total; **chiffres romains/arabes** Roman/Arabic numerals; **c. d'affaires** turnover ▪ **chiffrer** *vt (montant)* to work out; *(réparations)* to assess; **message chiffré** coded message **2 se chiffrer** *vpr* **se c. à** to amount to

chignon [ʃiɲɔ̃] *nm* bun, chignon; **se faire un c.** to put one's hair in a bun

Chili [ʃili] *nm* **le C.** Chile ▪ **chilien, -ienne 1** *adj* Chilean **2** *nmf* **C., Chilienne** Chilean

chili [ʃili] *nm Culin* chilli *(con carne)*

chimère [ʃimɛr] *nf Fig (rêve)* pipe dream

chimie [ʃimi] *nf* chemistry ▪ **chimique** *adj* chemical ▪ **chimiste** *nmf* (research) chemist

chimiothérapie [ʃimjɔterapi] *nf Méd* chemotherapy

chimpanzé [ʃɛ̃pɑ̃ze] *nm* chimpanzee

Chine [ʃin] *nf* **la C.** China ▪ **chinois, -oise 1** *adj*

Chinese **2** *nmf* **C., Chinoise** Chinese; **les C.** the Chinese **3** *nm (langue)* Chinese ▪ **chinoiserie** *nf (objet)* Chinese curio; *Fam* **chinoiseries** *(complications)* pointless complications

chiner [ʃine] *vi* to hunt for bargains

chiot [ʃjo] *nm* puppy, pup

chiper [ʃipe] *vt Fam* to swipe, *Br* to pinch (**à** from)

chipie [ʃipi] *nf Fam (femme)* bad-tempered woman; *(petite fille)* little minx; **vieille c.** old cow

chipoter [ʃipɔte] *vi (contester)* to quibble (**sur** about); *(picorer)* to pick at one's food

chips [ʃips] *nf Br* (potato) crisp, *Am* (potato) chip

> Il faut noter que le nom anglais britannique **chips** est un faux ami. Il signifie **frites**.

chiqué [ʃike] *nm Fam* **faire du c.** to put on an act

chiquenaude [ʃiknod] *nf* flick (of the finger)

chirurgie [ʃiryrʒi] *nf* surgery; **c. esthétique** plastic surgery; **c. au laser** laser surgery ▪ **chirurgical, -e, -aux, -ales** *adj* surgical ▪ **chirurgien** *nm* surgeon ▪ **chirurgien-dentiste** *(pl chirurgiens-dentistes) nm* dental surgeon

chlem [ʃlɛm] *nm Sport* **le grand c.** the grand slam

chlinguer [ʃlɛ̃ge] *vi très Fam* to stink

chlore [klɔr] *nm* chlorine ▪ **chlorer** *vt* to chlorinate

chloroforme [klɔrɔfɔrm] *nm* chloroform

choc [ʃɔk] **1** *nm (coup)* impact; *(forte émotion) Méd* shock; *Fig (conflit)* clash; **faire un c. à qn** to give sb a shock; **être sous le c.** to be in shock; **troupes de c.** shock troops; *Méd* **c. opératoire** post-operative shock; **c. pétrolier** oil crisis **2** *adj* **image-c.** shocking image; **'prix-chocs'** *(dans un magasin)* 'drastic reductions'

chocolat [ʃɔkɔla] **1** *nm* chocolate; **gâteau au c.** chocolate cake; **c. à croquer** *Br* plain chocolate, *Am* bittersweet chocolate; **c. au lait** milk chocolate; **c. chaud** hot chocolate; **c. glacé** *Br* choc-ice, *Am* ice-cream bar **2** *adj inv Br* chocolate(-coloured), *Am* chocolate(-colored) ▪ **chocolaté, -ée** *adj* chocolate

chœur [kœr] *nm Rel (chanteurs, nef)* choir; *(d'opéra) & Fig* chorus; **en c.** *(chanter, répéter)* in chorus

choir [ʃwar] *(aux être) vi Littéraire (tomber)* to fall; *Fam* **laisser c. qn** to drop sb

choisir [ʃwazir] *vt* to choose, to pick; **c. de faire qch** to choose to do sth ▪ **choisi, -ie** *adj (œuvres)* selected; *(termes, langage)* careful

choix [ʃwa] *nm* choice; *(assortiment)* selection; **avoir le c.** to have a choice; **faire son c.** to take one's pick; **laisser le c. à qn** to let sb choose; **viande ou poisson au c.** *(sur menu)* choice of meat or fish; **de premier/second c.** top-/second-grade

choléra [kɔlera] *nm Méd* cholera

cholestérol [kɔlɛsterɔl] *nm Méd* cholesterol; *Fam* **avoir du c.** to have high cholesterol

chômer [ʃome] *vi* to be unemployed; *Fig* to do nothing; **vous n'avez pas chômé!** you've not been idle!; **jour chômé** (public) holiday **•chômage** *nm* unemployment; **être au c.** to be unemployed; **être en c. technique** to have been laid off; **s'inscrire au c.** to sign on **•chômeur, -euse** *nmf* unemployed person; **les chômeurs** the unemployed

chope [ʃɔp] *nf (verre)* beer mug, *Br* tankard; *(contenu)* pint

choquer [ʃɔke] *vt (scandaliser)* to shock; **c. qn** *(commotionner)* to shake sb badly **•choquant, -ante** *adj* shocking

choral, -e, -aux *ou* **-als, -ales** [kɔral] *adj* choral **•chorale** *nf (club)* choral society; *(chanteurs)* choir **•choriste** *nmf* chorister

chorégraphe [kɔregraf] *nmf* choreographer **•chorégraphie** *nf* choreography **•chorégraphier** *vt* to choreograph

chose [ʃoz] **1** *nf* thing; **je vais te dire une c.** I'll tell you something; **dis bien des choses de ma part à...** remember me to...; **avant toute c.** first of all **2** *nm Fam* **monsieur C.** Mr What's-his-name **3** *adj inv Fam* **se sentir tout c.** to feel a bit funny

chou, -x [ʃu] *nm* cabbage; **choux de Bruxelles** Brussels sprouts; **mon petit c.!** my darling!; **c. à la crème** cream puff **•chou-fleur** *(pl* **choux-fleurs)** *nm* cauliflower

chouchou, -oute [ʃuʃu, -ut] *nmf Fam (favori)* pet **•chouchouter** *vt Fam* to pamper

choucroute [ʃukrut] *nf* sauerkraut

chouette [ʃwɛt] **1** *nf (oiseau)* owl **2** *adj Fam (chic)* great **3** *exclam* great!

choyer [ʃwaje] *vt* to pamper

chrétien, -ienne [kretjɛ̃, -jɛn] *adj & nmf* Christian **•Christ** [krist] *nm* **le C.** Christ **•christianisme** *nm* Christianity

chrome [krom] *nm* chromium; **chromes** *(de voitures)* chrome **•chromé, -ée** *adj* chromium-plated

chromosome [krɔmozom] *nm* chromosome

chronique¹ [krɔnik] *adj (malade, chômage)* chronic

chronique² [krɔnik] *nf (de journal)* column; *(annales)* chronicle **•chroniqueur** *nm (historien)* chronicler; *(journaliste)* columnist

chronologie [krɔnɔlɔʒi] *nf* chronology **•chronologique** *adj* chronological

chronomètre [krɔnɔmɛtr] *nm* chronometer; *(pour le sport)* stopwatch **•chronométrer** *vt Sport* to time

chrysanthème [krizɑ̃tɛm] *nm* chrysanthemum

CHU [seaʃy] *(abrév* **centre hospitalo-universitaire)** *nm inv* teaching hospital

chuchoter [ʃyʃote] *vti* to whisper **•chuchotement** *nm* whisper; **des chuchotements** whispering

chuinter [ʃwɛ̃te] *vi (siffler)* to hiss

chut [ʃyt] *exclam* sh!, shush!

chute [ʃyt] *nf* fall; *(d'histoire drôle)* punchline; *(de tissu)* scrap; **prévenir la c. des cheveux** to prevent hair loss; **c. d'eau** waterfall; **c. de neige** snowfall; **c. libre** free fall **•chuter** *vi (diminuer)* to fall, to drop; *Fam (tomber)* to fall

Chypre [ʃipr] *nm ou f* Cyprus **•chypriote 1** *adj* Cypriot **2** *nmf* **C.** Cypriot

ci [si] *pron dém* **comme ci comme ça** so so

-ci [si] *adv* **(a)** **par-ci, par-là** here and there **(b)** *voir* **ce², celui**

ci-après [siapre] *adv* below; *Jur* hereinafter **•ci-contre** *adv* opposite **•ci-dessous** *adv* below **•ci-dessus** *adv* above **•ci-joint, -jointe** *(mpl* **ci-joints,** *fpl* **ci-jointes) 1** *adj* **le document c.** the enclosed document **2** *adv* **vous trouverez c. copie de...** please find enclosed a copy of...

cible [sibl] *nf* target; **audience/marché c.** target audience/market **•ciblé, -ée** *adj* well targeted **•cibler** *vt* to target

ciboulette [sibulɛt] *nf* chives *(pluriel)*

cicatrice [sikatris] *nf* scar

cicatriser [sikatrize] *vti,* **se cicatriser** *vpr* to heal **•cicatrisation** *nf* healing

cidre [sidr] *nm* cider; **c. doux/brut** sweet/dry cider

Cie *(abrév* **compagnie)** Co

ciel [sjɛl] *nm* **(a)** *(pl* **ciels)** sky; **à c. ouvert** open-air; **c. de lit** canopy **(b)** *(pl* **cieux** [sjø]) *(paradis)* heaven; **sous d'autres cieux** in other climes

cierge [sjɛrʒ] *nm* candle *(in church)*; **c. magique** sparkler

cigale [sigal] *nf* cicada

cigare [sigar] *nm* cigar **•cigarette** *nf* cigarette

cigogne [sigɔɲ] *nf* stork

cil [sil] *nm* eyelash

cime [sim] *nf (d'arbre)* top; *(de montagne)* peak

ciment [simɑ̃] *nm* cement **•cimenter** *vt* to cement

cimetière [simtjɛr] *nm* cemetery; *(d'église)* graveyard; **c. de voitures** scrapyard

ciné [sine] *nm Fam Br* pictures, *Am* movies **•cinéaste** *nm* film maker **•ciné-club** *(pl* **ciné-clubs)** *nm* film club **•cinéphile** *nmf Br* film *or Am* movie enthusiast

cinéma [sinema] *nm (art, industrie) Br* cinema, *Am* movies; *(salle) Br* cinema, *Am* movie theater; **faire du c.** to be a film actor/actress; **aller au c.** to go to the *Br* cinema *or Am* movies; *Fam* **arrête ton c.!** stop making such a fuss!; **c. d'art et d'essai** art films; **c. muet** silent films **•CinémaScope®** *nm* CinemaScope® **•cinéma-**

thèque *nf* film library ▪ **cinématographique** *adj* film; **industrie c.** film industry ▪ **cinéma-vérité** *nm* cinéma vérité

cinglé, -ée [sɛ̃gle] *adj Fam* crazy

cingler [sɛ̃gle] *vt* to lash ▪ **cinglant, -ante** *adj (pluie)* lashing; *(vent, remarque)* cutting

cinoche [sinɔʃ] *nm Fam Br* cinema, *Am* movie theater

cinq [sɛ̃k] **1** *adj inv* five **2** *nm inv* five; **recevoir qn c. sur c.** to receive sb loud and clear ▪ **cinquième** *adj & nmf* fifth; **un c.** a fifth

cinquante [sɛ̃kɑ̃t] *adj & nm inv* fifty ▪ **cinquantaine** *nf* **une c. (de)** about fifty; **avoir la c.** to be about fifty ▪ **cinquantenaire** *nm (anniversaire)* fiftieth anniversary ▪ **cinquantième** *adj & nmf* fiftieth

cintre [sɛ̃tr] *nm* coathanger ▪ **cintré, -ée** *adj (veste)* fitted

cirage [siraʒ] *nm* (shoe) polish; *Fam* **être dans le c.** to be feeling woozy

circoncire [sirkɔ̃sir] *vt* to circumcise ▪ **circoncis** *adj m* circumcised ▪ **circoncision** *nf* circumcision

circonférence [sirkɔ̃ferɑ̃s] *nf* circumference

circonflexe [sirkɔ̃fleks] *adj voir* **accent**

circonscription [sirkɔ̃skripsjɔ̃] *nf* division, district; **c. (électorale)** *Br* constituency, *Am* district

circonscrire* [sirkɔ̃skrir] *vt (encercler)* to encircle; *(incendie)* to contain

circonspect, -ecte [sirkɔ̃spɛ, -ɛkt] *adj* cautious, circumspect ▪ **circonspection** *nf* caution

circonstance [sirkɔ̃stɑ̃s] *nf* circumstance; **pour/en la c.** for/on this occasion; **en pareilles circonstances** under such circumstances; **de c.** *(habit, parole)* appropriate; *Jur* **circonstances atténuantes** extenuating circumstances ▪ **circonstancié, -ée** *adj* detailed ▪ **circonstanciel, -ielle** *adj voir* **complément**

circuit [sirkɥi] *nm (électrique, sportif)* circuit; *(chemin)* way; **c. automobile** racing circuit; **c. de distribution** distribution network; **c. touristique** (organized) tour

circulaire [sirkylɛr] **1** *adj* circular **2** *nf (lettre)* circular

circulation [sirkylasjɔ̃] *nf (du sang, de l'information, de billets)* circulation; *(d'autos, d'avions)* traffic; **retirer un produit de la c.** to take a product off the market; **c. routière/aérienne** road/air traffic ▪ **circuler** *vi (sang, air, rumeur, lettre)* to circulate; *(voyageur)* to travel; *(train, bus)* to run; **on circule très mal dans Paris** it's very difficult to drive about in Paris; **circulez!** keep moving!

cire [sir] *nf* wax; *(pour meubles)* polish ▪ **cirer** *vt* to polish; *très Fam* **il n'en a rien à c.** he doesn't give a damn! ▪ **cireux, -euse** *adj* waxy

cirque [sirk] *nm (spectacle)* circus; *Fig* **c. médiatique** media circus

cirrhose [siroz] *nf* **c. (du foie)** cirrhosis (of the liver)

cisaille(s) [sizaj] *nf(pl)* (garden) shears ▪ **ciseau, -x** *nm (de menuisier)* chisel; **(une paire de) ciseaux** (a pair of) scissors ▪ **ciseler** *vt* to chisel; *(or, argent)* to chase

citadelle [sitadɛl] *nf* citadel ▪ **citadin, -ine 1** *adj* city; **vie citadine** city life **2** *nmf* city dweller

cité [site] *nf (ville)* city; *(immeubles) Br* housing estate, *Am* housing development; **c. universitaire** *Br* (students') halls of residence, *Am* university dormitory complex

citer [site] *vt (auteur, texte)* to quote; *(énumérer)* to name; *Jur* to summons; *(témoin)* to subpoena; *Mil (soldat)* to mention; **c. qn en exemple** to quote sb as an example ▪ **citation** *nf* quotation; *Jur* **c. à comparaître** *(d'accusé)* summons; *(de témoin)* subpoena

citerne [sitɛrn] *nf* tank

citoyen, -enne [sitwajɛ̃, -ɛn] *nmf* citizen ▪ **citoyenneté** *nf* citizenship

citron [sitrɔ̃] *nm* lemon; **c. pressé** = freshly squeezed lemon juice served with water and sugar; **c. vert** lime ▪ **citronnade** *nf Br* lemon squash, *Am* lemonade ▪ **citronnier** *n* lemon tree

citrouille [sitruj] *nf* pumpkin

civet [sivɛ] *nm Culin (de gibier etc)* stew

civière [sivjɛr] *nf* stretcher

civil, -e [sivil] **1** *adj (guerre, mariage, droits)* civil; *(non militaire)* civilian; *(courtois)* civil; **année civile** calendar year **2** *nm* civilian; **dans le c.** in civilian life; **en c.** *(policier)* in plain clothes; *(soldat)* in civilian clothes ▪ **civilement** *adv* **se marier c.** to have a civil wedding ▪ **civilité** *nf* civility

civilisation [sivilizasjɔ̃] *nf* civilization ▪ **civilisé, -ée** *adj* civilized

civique [sivik] *adj* civic; *Scol* **instruction c.** *Br* ≃ citizenship, *Am* ≃ civics ▪ **civisme** *nm* good citizenship

clair, -e [klɛr] **1** *adj (net, limpide, évident)* clear; *(éclairé, pâle)* light; *(soupe)* thin; **bleu/vert c.** light blue/green; **robe bleu/vert c.** light-blue/-green dress; **par temps c.** on a clear day **2** *adv (voir)* clearly; **il fait c.** it's light **3** *nm* **passer le plus c. de son temps à faire qch** to spend the better part of one's time doing sth; **tirer qch au c.** to clarify sth; **en c.** in plain laguage; **émission en c.** non-crypted broadcast; **c. de lune** moonlight ▪ **clairement** *adv* clearly

clairière [klerjɛr] *nf* clearing

clairon [klerɔ̃] *nm (instrument)* bugle; *(soldat)* bugler ▪ **claironner** *vt (nouvelle)* to trumpet forth

clairsemé, -ée [klɛrsəme] *adj (cheveux, auditoire, population)* sparse

clairvoyant, -ante [klɛrvwajɑ̃, -ɑ̃t] *adj* perceptive

clamer [klame] *vt* to proclaim ▪ **clameur** *nf Br* clamour, *Am* clamor

clan [klɑ̃] *nm* (*tribu*) clan; *Péj* (*groupe*) clique

clandestin, -ine [klɑ̃dɛstɛ̃, -in] *adj* (*rencontre*) clandestine; (*journal, mouvement*) underground; (*travailleur*) illegal; **passager c.** stowaway ▪ **clandestinité** *nf* **entrer dans la c.** to go underground

clapet [klapɛ] *nm* (*de pompe*) valve

clapier [klapje] *nm* (rabbit) hutch

clapoter [klapɔte] *vi* (*vagues*) to lap ▪ **clapotement, clapotis** *nm* (*de vagues*) lapping

claque [klak] *nf* slap; **une paire de claques** a slap; *Fam* **j'en ai ma c.** I've had it up to here!

claquer [klake] **1** *vt* (*porte*) to slam; *Fam* (*dépenser*) to blow; **c. la langue** to click one's tongue **2** *vi* (*porte*) to slam; (*drapeau*) to flap; (*talons*) to click; (*coup de feu*) to ring out; *Fam* (*mourir*) to kick the bucket; **c. des doigts** to snap one's fingers; **c. des mains** to clap; **elle claque des dents** her teeth are chattering; **faire c. sa langue** to click one's tongue **3** *se claquer* *vpr* **se c. un muscle** to pull a muscle ▪ **claquage** *nm* (*blessure*) pulled muscle; **se faire un c.** to pull a muscle ▪ **claqué, -ée** *adj Fam* (*fatiguée*) *Br* knackered, *Am* bushed ▪ **claquement** *nm* (*de porte*) slam(ming); (*de drapeau*) flap(ping)

claquettes [klakɛt] *nfpl* tap dancing; **faire des c.** to do tap dancing

clarifier [klarifje] *vt* to clarify ▪ **clarification** *nf* clarification

clarinette [klarinɛt] *nf* clarinet

clarté [klarte] *nf* (*lumière*) light; (*transparence*) clearness; *Fig* (*d'explications*) clarity; **avec c.** clearly

classe [klɑs] **1** *nf* (*catégorie, qualité, leçon, élèves*) class; **en c. de sixième** *Br* in the first year, *Am* in fifth grade; **aller en c.** to go to school; *Mil* **faire ses classes** to undergo basic training; **avoir de la c.** (*personne*) to have class; (**salle de**) **c.** classroom; **c. de neige** = school study trip to the mountains; **c. verte** = school study trip to the countryside; **de première c.** (*billet, compartiment*) first-class; **c. affaire/économique** business/economy class; **c. ouvrière/moyenne** working/middle class; **c. sociale** social class **2** *adj inv Fam* classy

classer [klɑse] **1** *vt* (*photos, spécimens*) to classify; (*papiers*) to file; (*étudiants*) to grade; **c. une affaire** to consider a matter closed **2** *se classer* *vpr* **se c. parmi les meilleurs** to rank among the best; *Sport* **se c. troisième** to be placed third ▪ **classé, -ée** *adj* (*monument*) listed ▪ **classement** *nm* classification; (*de papiers*) filing; (*rang*) place; *Football, Rugby* table ▪ **classeur** *nm* (*meuble*) filing cabinet; (*portefeuille*) ring binder

classifier [klasifje] *vt* to classify ▪ **classification** *nf* classification

classique [klasik] **1** *adj* (*période*) classical; (*typique, conventionnel*) classic **2** *nm* (*œuvre*) classic; (*auteur*) classical author ▪ **classicisme** *nm* classicism

clause [kloz] *nf Jur* clause

claustrophobie [klostrɔfɔbi] *nf* claustrophobia ▪ **claustrophobe** *adj* claustrophobic

clavecin [klavsɛ̃] *nm* harpsichord

clavicule [klavikyl] *nf* collarbone

clavier [klavje] *nm* keyboard

clé, clef [kle] **1** *nf* (*de porte*) key; (*outil*) *Br* spanner, *Am* wrench; **fermer qch à c.** to lock sth; **sous c.** under lock and key; **prix clés en main** (*de voiture*) on-the-road price; (*de maison*) all-inclusive price; **c. de contact** ignition key; *Mus* **c. de sol** treble clef; *Fig* **c. de voûte** cornerstone **2** *adj* key; **poste/industrie c.** key post/industry

clément, -ente [klemɑ̃, -ɑ̃t] *adj* (*juge*) clement; (*temps*) mild ▪ **clémence** *nf* (*de juge*) clemency; (*de temps*) mildness

clémentine [klemɑ̃tin] *nf* clementine

clerc [klɛr] *nm Rel* cleric; **c. de notaire** ≃ solicitor's clerk ▪ **clergé** *nm* clergy ▪ **clérical, -e, -aux, -ales** *adj* clerical

cliché [kliʃe] *nm* (*photo*) photo; (*negative*) negative; (*idée*) cliché

client, -ente [klijɑ̃, -ɑ̃t] *nmf* (*de magasin*) customer; (*d'avocat*) client; (*de médecin*) patient; (*d'hôtel*) guest; (*de taxi*) fare ▪ **clientèle** *nf* (*de magasin*) customers; (*d'avocat, de médecin*) practice; **accorder sa c. à** to give one's custom to

cligner [kliɲe] *vi* **c. des yeux** to blink; **c. de l'œil** to wink

clignoter [kliɲɔte] *vi* (*lumière, voyant*) to flash; (*étoile*) to twinkle ▪ **clignotant** *nm* (*de voiture*) *Br* indicator, *Am* flasher; **mettre son c.** to indicate

climat [klima] *nm* (*de région*) & *Fig* climate ▪ **climatique** *adj* climatic

climatisation [klimatizasjɔ̃] *nf* air conditioning ▪ **climatisé, -ée** *adj* air-conditioned ▪ **climatiser** *vt* to air-condition

clin d'œil [klɛ̃dœj] (*pl* **clins d'œil**) *nm* wink; **faire un c. d'œil à qn** to wink at sb; **en un c. d'œil** in a flash

clinique [klinik] **1** *adj* clinical **2** *nf* (*hôpital*) clinic

clinquant, -ante [klɛ̃kɑ̃, -ɑ̃t] *adj* flashy

clip [klip] *nm* (*vidéo*) (music) video; (*bijou*) clip

clipart [klipart] *nm Ordinat* clip-art

clique [klik] *nf Fam* (gang) clique

cliquer [klike] *vi Ordinat* to click; **c. sur qch** to click on sth; **c. deux fois** to double-click

cliqueter [klikte] *vi* (*monnaie, clefs*) to jingle; (*épées*) to clink; (*chaînes*) to rattle ▪ **cliquetis**

nm (de monnaie, de clefs) jingling; *(d'épées)* clinking; *(de chaînes)* rattling

clivage [klivaʒ] *nm (dans la société)* divide; *(dans un parti)* split

cloaque [klɔak] *nm* cesspool

clochard, -arde [klɔʃar, -ard] *nmf* tramp

cloche [klɔʃ] **1** *nf (d'église)* bell; *Fam (imbécile)* twit; **déménager à la c. de bois** to do a moonlight flit; **c. à fromage** covered cheese dish **2** *adj Fam* stupid ▪ **clocher 1** *nm (d'église)* bell tower, steeple **2** *vi Fam* **il y a quelque chose qui cloche** there's something wrong somewhere ▪ **clochette** *nf (cloche)* small bell

cloche-pied [klɔʃpje] **à cloche-pied** *adv* **sauter à c.** to hop

cloison [klwazɔ̃] *nf (entre pièces)* partition; ▪ **cloisonner** *vt (pièce)* to partition; *Fig (activités)* to compartmentalize

cloître [klwatr] *nm (partie de monastère)* cloister; *(bâtiment pour moines)* monastery; *(pour religieuses)* convent

clonage [klɔnaʒ] *nm Biol* cloning; **c. humain** human cloning ▪ **clone** *nm Biol* clone ▪ **cloner** *vt Biol* to clone

clope [klɔp] *nf Fam Br* fag, *Am* smoke

clopin-clopant [klɔpɛ̃klɔpɑ̃] *adv* **aller à c.** to hobble along

clopinettes [klɔpinɛt] *nfpl Fam* **des c.** *Br* sod all, *Am* zilch; **gagner des c.** to earn peanuts

cloque [klɔk] *nf (au pied)* blister

clore* [klɔr] *vt (réunion, lettre)* to conclude; *(débat)* to close; *Ordinat* **c. une session** to log off ▪ **clos, -e 1** *adj (porte, volets)* closed; **l'incident est c.** the matter is closed; **espace c.** enclosed space **2** *nm* enclosure

clôture [klotyr] *nf (barrière)* fence; *(de réunion)* conclusion; *(de débat)* closing; *(de Bourse)* close ▪ **clôturer** *vt (terrain)* to enclose; *(session, débats)* to close

clou [klu] *nm (pointe)* nail; *(de spectacle)* main attraction; **les clous** *(passage) Br* the pedestrian crossing, *Am* the crosswalk; *Fam* **des clous!** not a sausage!; **c. de girofle** clove ▪ **clouer** *vt (au mur)* to nail up; *(ensemble)* to nail together; *(caisse)* to nail down; **c. qn au sol** to pin sb down; **cloué au lit** confined to (one's) bed; **cloué sur place** rooted to the spot; *Fam* **c. le bec à qn** to shut sb up ▪ **clouté, -ée** *adj (chaussures)* studded

clown [klun] *nm* clown; **faire le c.** to clown around

club [klœb] *nm (association) & Golf* club

CM [seɛm] *(abrév* **cours moyen***) nm Scol* **CM1** = fourth year of primary school; **CM2** = fifth year of primary school

cm *(abrév* **centimètre***)* cm

coaguler [kɔagyle] *vti,* **se coaguler** *upr (sang)* to clot

coaliser [kɔalize] **se coaliser** *upr* to unite;

(partis) to form a coalition ▪ **coalition** *nf* coalition

coasser [kɔase] *vi (grenouille)* to croak

cobaye [kɔbaj] *nm (animal) & Fig* guinea pig

cobra [kɔbra] *nm* cobra

cocaïne [kɔkain] *nf* cocaine

cocarde [kɔkard] *nf* rosette

cocasse [kɔkas] *adj Fam* comical

coccinelle [kɔksinɛl] *nf (insecte) Br* ladybird, *Am* ladybug; *(voiture)* beetle

coche [kɔʃ] *nm Fam* **louper le c.** to miss the boat

cocher¹ [kɔʃe] *vt Br* to tick (off), *Am* to check

cocher² [kɔʃe] *nm* coachman

cochon, -onne [kɔʃɔ̃, -ɔn] **1** *nm (animal)* pig; *(viande)* pork; **c. d'Inde** guinea pig **2** *nmf (personne sale)* pig **3** *adj (histoire, film)* dirty ▪ **cochonnerie** *nf (chose sans valeur)* trash, *Br* rubbish; *(obscénité)* smutty remark; *(mauvaise nourriture)* muck; **faire des cochonneries** to make a mess ▪ **cochonnet** *nm (aux boules)* jack

cocktail [kɔktɛl] *nm (boisson)* cocktail; *(réunion)* cocktail party; **c. de fruits/de crevettes** fruit/prawn cocktail

coco [kɔko] *nm* (**a**) **noix de c.** coconut (**b**) *Fam* **un drôle de c.** a strange character ▪ **cocotier** *nm* coconut palm

cocon [kɔkɔ̃] *nm* cocoon

cocorico [kɔkɔriko] *exclam & nm* cock-a-doodle-doo; *Fam* **faire c.** to crow

cocotte [kɔkɔt] *nf (marmite)* casserole dish; **C. minute®** pressure cooker

cocu, -e [kɔky] **1** *adj* **il est c.** his wife's cheating on him **2** *nm* cuckold

code [kɔd] *nm (symboles, lois) & Ordinat* code; **passer le c.** *(examen du permis de conduire)* to sit the written part of one's driving test; **codes** *Br* dipped headlights, *Am* low beams; **se mettre en c.** *Br* to dip one's headlights, *Am* to switch on one's low beams; **le C. de la route** *Br* the Highway Code, *Am* the Rules of the Road; *Jur* **c. civil/pénal** civil/penal code; *Jur* **c. du travail** employment legislation; **c. confidentiel** security code; *(de carte bancaire)* PIN; *Biol* **c. génétique** genetic code; **c. postal** *Br* postcode, *Am* zip code ▪ **code-barres** *(pl* **codes-barres***) nm* bar code ▪ **coder** *vt* to code ▪ **codifier** *vt* to codify

coefficient [kɔefisjɑ̃] *nm* coefficient

coéquipier, -ière [kɔekipje, -jɛr] *nmf* team-mate

cœur [kœr] *nm* heart; *Cartes (couleur)* hearts; **avoir mal au c.** to feel sick; **ça me soulève le c.** that turns my stomach; **avoir le c. gros** to have a heavy heart; **avoir bon c.** to be kind-hearted; **ça me tient à c.** that's close to my heart; **être opéré à c. ouvert** to have open-heart surgery; **au c. de la ville** in the heart of the town; **au c. de l'hiver** in the depths of winter; **par c.** (off) by heart; **de bon c.** *(volontiers)* willingly; *(rire)* heartily; **si le c.**

vous en dit if you so desire; **c. d'artichaut** artichoke heart

coexister [kɔegziste] *vi* to coexist ▪ **coexistence** *nf* coexistence

coffre [kɔr] *nm (meuble)* chest; *(pour objets de valeur)* safe; *(de voiture)* Br boot, Am trunk; **c. à bagages** *(d'avion)* baggage compartment; **c. à jouets** toy box ▪ **coffre-fort** *(pl coffres-forts) nm* safe ▪ **coffret** *nm (petit coffre)* box; **c. à bijoux** Br jewellery orAm jewelry box

cogiter [kɔʒite] *vi Hum* to cogitate

cognac [kɔɲak] *nm* cognac

cogner [kɔɲe] **1** *vt (heurter)* to knock; *Fam* **c. qn** *(battre)* to knock about **2** *vi (buter)* to bang (**sur/contre** on); **c. à une porte** to bang on a door **3 se cogner** *vpr* to bang oneself; **se c. la tête contre qch** to bang one's head on sth; **se c. à qch** to bang into sth

cohabiter [kɔabite] *vi* to live together; **c. avec qn** to live with sb ▪ **cohabitation** *nf* living together; *Pol* cohabitation

cohérent, -ente [kɔerã, -ãt] *adj (discours)* coherent; *(attitude)* consistent ▪ **cohérence** *nf (de discours)* coherence; *(d'attitude)* consistency ▪ **cohésion** *nf* cohesion

cohorte [kɔɔrt] *nf (de gens)* horde

cohue [kɔy] *nf* crowd; **dans la c.** amidst the general pushing and shoving

coiffe [kwaf] *nf* headdress

coiffer [kwafe] **1** *vt Fig (surmonter)* to cap; *(service)* to head; **c. qn** to do sb's hair; **c. qn de qch** to put sth on sb's head; **elle est bien coiffée** her hair is lovely **2 se coiffer** *vpr* to do one's hair; **se c. de qch** to put sth on ▪ **coiffeur, coiffeuse¹** *nmf* hairdresser ▪ **coiffeuse²** *nf (meuble)* dressing table ▪ **coiffure** *nf (chapeau)* headgear; *(coupe de cheveux)* hairstyle; *(métier)* hairdressing

coin [kwɛ̃] *nm (angle)* corner; *(endroit)* spot; *(parcelle)* patch; *(cale)* wedge; **faire le c.** to be on the corner; *Fig* **rester dans son c.** to keep to oneself; **du c.** *(magasin, gens)* local; **dans le c.** in the (local) area; **au c. du feu** by the fireside; *Fam* **le petit c.** *(toilettes)* the smallest room in the house ▪ **coin-repas** *(pl coins-repas) nm* dining area

coincer [kwɛ̃se] **1** *vt (mécanisme, tiroir)* to jam; *(caler)* to wedge; *Fam* **c. qn** *(arrêter)* to nick sb **2** *vi (mécanisme, tiroir)* to jam **3 se coincer** *vpr (mécanisme)* to jam; **se c. le doigt dans la porte** to catch one's finger in the door ▪ **coincé, -ée** *adj (mécanisme, tiroir)* stuck, jammed; *Fam (inhibé)* hung up; *Fam* **être c.** *(dans un embouteillage)* to be stuck; *(être occupé)* to be tied up

coïncider [kɔɛ̃side] *vi* to coincide (**avec** with) ▪ **coïncidence** *nf* coincidence

coin-coin [kwɛ̃kwɛ̃] **1** *exclam* quack! quack! **2** *nm inv (de canard)* quacking

coing [kwɛ̃] *nm* quince

coke [kɔk] *nm (combustible)* coke

col [kɔl] *nm (de chemise)* collar; *(de bouteille)* neck; *Géog* col; **c. en V** V-neck; **c. roulé** Br polo neck, Am turtleneck; *Anat* **c. de l'utérus** cervix

colère [kɔlɛr] *nf* anger; **être en c. (contre qn)** to be angry (with sb); **mettre qn en c.** to make sb angry; **se mettre en c.** to get angry (**contre** with); **elle est partie en c.** she left angrily; **faire une c.** *(enfant)* to throw a tantrum ▪ **coléreux, -euse, colérique** *adj (personne)* quick-tempered

colimaçon [kɔlimasõ] *nm* **escalier en c.** spiral staircase

colin [kɔlɛ̃] *nm (merlu)* hake; *(lieu noir)* coley

colique [kɔlik] *nf (douleurs)* severe stomach pains; *(de bébé)* colic

colis [kɔli] *nm* parcel

collaborer [kɔlabɔre] *vi* collaborate (**avec** with); **c. à qch** *(projet)* to take part in sth; *(journal)* to contribute to sth ▪ **collaborateur, -trice** *nmf (aide)* assistant; *(de journal)* contributor ▪ **collaboration** *nf (aide)* collaboration; *(à un journal)* contribution

collage [kɔlaʒ] *nm (œuvre, jeu)* collage

collant, -ante [kɔlã, -ãt] **1** *adj (papier)* sticky; *(vêtement)* skin-tight; *Fam* **qu'est-ce qu'il est c.!** you just can't shake him off! **2** *nm Br* tights, Am pantihose

collation [kɔlasjõ] *nf (repas)* snack

colle [kɔl] *nf (transparente)* glue; *(blanche)* paste; *Fam (question)* poser; *Fam (interrogation)* oral test; *Fam (retenue)* detention

collecte [kɔlɛkt] *nf* collection ▪ **collecter** *vt* to collect

collectif, -ive [kɔlɛktif, -iv] *adj* collective; **billet c.** group ticket; **hystérie/démission collective** mass hysteria/resignation ▪ **collectivement** *adv* collectively ▪ **collectivité** *nf (groupe)* community

collection [kɔlɛksjõ] *nf (de timbres, de vêtements)* collection; **faire la c. de qch** to collect sth ▪ **collectionner** *vt* to collect ▪ **collectionneur, -euse** *nmf* collector

collège [kɔlɛʒ] *nm (école)* school; *Anciennement* **c. d'enseignement secondaire** = secondary school for pupils aged 12 to 15 ▪ **collégien, -ienne** *nmf* schoolboy, *f* schoolgirl

collègue [kɔlɛg] *nmf* colleague

coller [kɔle] **1** *vt (timbre)* to stick; *(à la colle transparente)* to glue; *(à la colle blanche)* to paste; *(enveloppe)* to stick (down); *(deux objets)* to stick together; *(affiche)* to stick up; *(papier peint)* to hang; **c. son oreille contre qch** to press one's ear against sth; *Fam* **c. un élève** *(en punition)* to keep a pupil in; *Fam* **être collé** *(à un examen)* to fail **2** *vi Fam (coïncider)* to tally (**avec** with); **ça colle!** that's OK! **3 se coller** *vpr* **se c.**

contre un mur to flatten oneself against a wall
▪ **colleur, -euse** nmf c. **d'affiches** billposter

collet [kɔlɛ] nm (piège) snare; **prendre qn au c.**
to grab sb by the scruff of the neck; **être c.
monté** to be strait-laced

collier [kɔlje] nm (bijou) necklace; (de chien, de
tuyau) collar; **c. (de barbe)** fringe of beard

colline [kɔlin] nf hill

collision [kɔlizjɔ̃] nf (de véhicules) collision;
entrer en c. avec qch to collide with sth

colloque [kɔlɔk] nm (conférence) seminar

collusion [kɔlyzjɔ̃] nf collusion

colmater [kɔlmate] vt to fill in

colocataire [kɔlɔkater] nmf Br flatmate, Am
roommate

colombages [kɔlɔ̃baʃ] nmpl **maison à c.** half-
timbered house

colombe [kɔlɔ̃b] nf dove

Colombie [kɔlɔ̃bi] nf **la C.** Columbia
▪ **colombien, -ienne** 1 adj Columbian 2 nmf
C., Colombienne Columbian

colon [kɔlɔ̃] nm (pionnier) settler, colonist;
(enfant) child at camp

côlon [kolɔ̃] nm Anat colon

colonial, -e, -aux, -ales [kɔlɔnjal, -jo] adj
colonial ▪ **colonialisme** nm colonialism

colonie [kɔlɔni] nf colony; **c. de vacances** Br
(children's) holiday camp, Am summer camp

coloniser [kɔlɔnize] vt to colonize ▪ **colonisation** nf colonization

colonel [kɔlɔnɛl] nm (d'infanterie) colonel

colonne [kɔlɔn] nf column; **en c. par deux** in
columns of two; Anat **c. vertébrale** spine
▪ **colonnade** nf colonnade

colorer [kɔlɔre] vt to Br colour or Am color;
c. qch en vert to colour sth green ▪ **colorant,
-ante** 1 adj Br colouring, Am coloring 2 nm
(pour teindre) colorant; (alimentaire) Br
colouring, Am coloring ▪ **coloration** nf Br
colouring, Am coloring ▪ **coloré, -ée** adj Br
coloured, Am colored; (teint) ruddy; Fig (style)
Br colourful, Am colorful ▪ **coloriage** nm
(action) Br colouring, Am coloring; (dessin)
drawing; **album de coloriages** Br colouring or
Am coloring book ▪ **colorier** vt (dessin) to Br
colour or Am color (in) ▪ **coloris** nm (nuance) shade

colosse [kɔlɔs] nm giant ▪ **colossal, -e, -aux,
-ales** adj colossal

colporter [kɔlpɔrte] vt (marchandises) to hawk;
(rumeur) to spread ▪ **colporteur** nm hawker

coltiner [kɔltine] se coltiner vpr Fam **se c. qn/
qch** to get landed with sb/sth

colza [kɔlza] nm rape; **huile de c.** rapeseed oil

coma [kɔma] nm coma; **être dans le c.** to be in a
coma

combat [kɔ̃ba] nm (bataille) & Fig fight; (activité)
combat; **c. de boxe** boxing match ▪ **combatif,
-ive** adj combative ▪ **combativité** nf combative-
ness

combattre* [kɔ̃batr] 1 vt (personne, incendie) to
fight (against); (maladie, inflation) to fight 2 vi
to fight ▪ **combattant, -ante** 1 adj (unité,
troupe) fighting 2 nmf combattant; **anciens
combattants** veterans

combien [kɔ̃bjɛ̃] 1 adv (a) (en quantité) how
much; (en nombre) how many; **c. de money**
how much money; **c. de temps** how long; **c.
de gens** how many people; **c. y a-t-il d'ici
à…?** how far is it to…? (b) (comme) how; **tu
verras, c. il est bête** you'll see how silly he is;
tu sais c. je t'aime you know how (much) I
love you 2 nm inv Fam **le c. sommes-nous?**
what's the date?; **tous les c.?** how often?

combinaison [kɔ̃binɛzɔ̃] nf (assemblage)
combination; (vêtement de travail) Br boiler
suit, Am coveralls; (vêtement de femme) catsuit;
(sous-vêtement) slip; **c. de plongée/ski** wet/ski
suit

combine [kɔ̃bin] nf Fam trick

combiner [kɔ̃bine] 1 vt (unir) to combine; Fam
(plan) to concoct 2 se **combiner** vpr to
combine ▪ **combiné** nm (de téléphone) receiver

comble [kɔ̃bl] 1 adj (salle, bus) packed; Théâtre
faire salle c. to have a full house 2 nm **le c. du
bonheur** the height of happiness; **au c. de la
joie** overjoyed; **pour c. de malheur** to cap it
all; **c'est un** ou **le c.!** that's the last straw!
▪ **combles** nmpl (mansarde) attic; **sous les c.** in
the attic

combler [kɔ̃ble] vt (trou) to fill in; (perte) to make
good; (découvert) to pay off; (lacune) to fill;
(désir) to satisfy; **c. son retard** to make up for
lost time; **c. qn de cadeaux** to shower sb with
gifts; **c. qn de joie** to fill sb with joy; **je suis
comblé** I have all I could wish for

combustible [kɔ̃bystibl] 1 adj combustible 2
nm fuel; **c. fossile** fossil fuel ▪ **combustion** nf
combustion

comédie [kɔmedi] nf comedy; **jouer la c.** to act;
Fig to put on an act; **pas de c.!** stop your
nonsense!; **c. musicale** musical ▪ **comédien,
-ienne** nmf actor, f actress

Il faut noter que le nom anglais **comedian**
est un faux ami. Il signifie **comique**.

comestible [kɔmɛstibl] adj edible

comète [kɔmɛt] nf comet

comique [kɔmik] 1 adj (amusant) funny,
comical; (acteur, rôle) comedy; **auteur c.**
comedy writer 2 nm (genre) comedy; (acteur)
comic actor; **c. de situation** situation comedy

comité [kɔmite] nm committee; **en petit c.** in a
small group; **c. d'entreprise** works council

commandant [kɔmɑ̃dɑ̃] nm (de navire) captain;
(grade) (dans l'infanterie) major; (dans l'aviation)
squadron leader; Av **c. de bord** captain

commande [kɔmɑ̃d] nf (a) (achat) order; **sur c.**
to order; **passer une c.** to place an order (b)

Tech (action, manette) control; *Ordinat* command; **les commandes** *(d'avion)* the controls; **prendre les commandes** to take over the controls; *Fig (de compagnie)* to take control; **c. à distance** remote control; **à c. vocale** voice-activated

commandement [kɔmɑ̃dmɑ̃] *nm (ordre, autorité)* command; *Rel* Commandment

commander [kɔmɑ̃de] **1** *vt (diriger, exiger)* to command; *(marchandises)* to order (**à** from); *(machine)* to control **2** *vi* **c. à qn de faire qch** to command sb to do sth; **qui est-ce qui commande ici?** who's in charge here?

commanditaire [kɔmɑ̃diter] *nm (de société) Br* sleeping partner, *Am* silent partner

commando [kɔmɑ̃do] *nm* commando

comme [kɔm] **1** *adv* (**a**) *(devant nom, pronom)* like; **c. moi/elle** like me/her; **c. cela** like that; **qu'as-tu c. diplômes?** what do you have in the way of certificates?; **je l'ai c. professeur** he's my teacher; **les femmes c. les hommes** men and women alike; *Fam* **joli c. tout** very pretty, *Br* ever so pretty; **P c. pomme** p as in pomme; **c. par hasard** as if by chance; **c. quoi** *(disant que)* to the effect that; *(ce qui prouve que)* so, which goes to show that (**b**) *(devant proposition)* as; **il écrit c. il parle** he writes as he speaks; **c. si** as if; **c. pour faire qch** as if to do sth **2** *adv (exclamatif)* **regarde c. il pleut!** look at the rain!; **c. c'est petit!** isn't it small! **3** *conj (cause)* as, since; **c. tu es mon ami...** as or since you're my friend...; **c. elle entrait** (just) as she was coming in

commémorer [kɔmemɔre] *vt* to commemorate ▪ **commémoratif, -ive** *adj* commemorative ▪ **commémoration** *nf* commemoration

commencer [kɔmɑ̃se] *vti* to begin, to start (**à faire** to do, doing; **par qch** with sth; **par faire** by doing); **pour c.** to begin with ▪ **commencement** *nm* beginning, start; **au c.** at the beginning or start

comment [kɔmɑ̃] *adv* how; **c. le sais-tu?** how do you know?; **c. t'appelles-tu?** what's your name?; **c. est-il?** what is he like?; **c. va-t-il?** how is he?; **c. faire?** what's to be done?; **c.?** *(pour faire répéter)* I beg your pardon?; **c.!** *(indignation)* what!; **et c.!** you bet!

commentaire [kɔmɑ̃ter] *nm (remarque)* comment; *(de radio, de télévision)* commentary ▪ **commentateur, -trice** *nmf* commentator ▪ **commenter** *vt* to comment (up)on

commérages [kɔmeraʒ] *nmpl* gossip

commerçant, -ante [kɔmersɑ̃, -ɑ̃t] **1** *nmf* trader; *(de magasin)* shopkeeper **2** *adj* **rue/quartier commerçant(e)** shopping street/area

commerce [kɔmers] *nm (activité, secteur)* trade; *(affaires, magasin)* business; **faire du c. avec** to do business with; **ça se trouve dans le c.** you can buy it in the shops; **c. intérieur/extérieur** home/foreign trade; **c. de détail/gros** retail/wholesale trade; **c. de proximité** *Br* local shop, *Am* local store; *Ordinat* **c. électronique** e-commerce; **c. équitable** fair trade ▪ **commercial, -e, -iaux, -iales** *adj* commercial ▪ **commercialisation** *nf* marketing ▪ **commercialiser** *vt (produit)* to market; *(art)* to commercialize

commère [kɔmer] *nf* gossip

commettre* [kɔmetr] *vt (délit)* to commit; *(erreur)* to make

commis [kɔmi] *nm (de magasin)* shop assistant; *(de bureau)* clerk

commissaire [kɔmiser] *nmf (de course)* steward, *f* stewardess; **c. (de police)** *Br* ≃ police superintendent, *Am* ≃ police captain; **c. aux comptes** government auditor ▪ **commissaire-priseur, commissaire-priseuse** *(mpl* commissaires-priseurs, *fpl* commissaires-priseuses) *nmf* auctioneer ▪ **commissariat** *nm* **c. (de police)** (central) police station

commission [kɔmisjɔ̃] *nf (course)* errand; *(message)* message; *(comité)* committee; *Com (pourcentage)* commission (**sur** on); **faire les commissions** to go shopping; **c. d'enquête** board of inquiry ▪ **commissionnaire** *nm* messenger; *(agent commercial)* agent

commode [kɔmɔd] **1** *adj (pratique)* handy; *(heure, lieu)* convenient; **pas c.** *(pas aimable)* awkward; *(difficile)* tricky **2** *nf Br* chest of drawers, *Am* dresser ▪ **commodément** *adv* comfortably ▪ **commodité** *nf* convenience; **pour plus de c.** for greater convenience

commotion [kɔmosjɔ̃] *nf* shock; *Méd* **c. cérébrale** concussion ▪ **commotionner** *vt* to shake up; *Méd* to concuss

commuer [kɔmɥe] *vt Jur (peine)* to commute (**en** to)

commun, -e [kɔmœ̃, -yn] **1** *adj (non exclusif, répandu, vulgaire)* common; *(frais, cuisine)* shared; *(démarche)* joint; **peu c.** uncommon; **ami c.** mutual friend; **en c.** in common; **mettre qch en c.** to share sth; **vivre/travailler en c.** to live/work together; **elle n'a rien de c. avec les autres** she has nothing in common with the others; **ils n'ont rien de c.** they have nothing in common **2** *nm* **le c. des mortels** ordinary mortals; **hors du c.** out of the ordinary ▪ **communs** *nmpl (bâtiments)* outbuildings ▪ **communément** [kɔmynemɑ̃] *adv* commonly

communauté [kɔmynote] *nf (collectivité)* community; **la C. économique européenne** the European Economic Community; **la C. d'États indépendants** the Commonwealth of Independent States ▪ **communautaire** *adj (de la CE)* Community; **vie c.** community life

commune [kɔmyn] *nf (municipalité)* commune ▪ **communal, -e, -aux, -ales** *adj Br* ≃

council, *Am* ≃ district; **école communale** ≃ local *Br* primary or*Am* grade school

communicatif, -ive [kɔmynikatif, -iv] *adj (personne)* communicative; *(rire)* infectious; **peu c.** uncommunicative

communication [kɔmynikasjɔ̃] *nf* communication; **c. téléphonique** telephone call; **je vous passe la c.** I'll put you through; **la c. est mauvaise** the line is bad

communier [kɔmynje] *vi Rel* to receive Communion ▪ **communion** *nf* communion; *Rel* (Holy) Communion

communiquer [kɔmynike] **1** *vt* to communicate (**à** to); *(maladie)* to pass on (**à** to) **2** *vi (personne, pièces)* to communicate (**avec** with) **3 se communiquer** *upr* to spread (**à** to) ▪ **communiqué** *nm (avis)* communiqué; **c. de presse** press release

communisme [kɔmynism] *nm* communism ▪ **communiste** *adj & nmf* communist

commutateur [kɔmytatœr] *nm (bouton)* switch

compact, -e [kɔ̃pakt] **1** *adj (foule, amas)* dense; *(appareil, véhicule)* compact **2** *nm (CD)* compact disc

compagne [kɔ̃paɲ] *nf (camarade)* companion; *(concubine)* partner

compagnie [kɔ̃paɲi] *nf (présence, société, soldats)* company; **tenir c. à qn** to keep sb company; **en c. de qn** in the company of sb

compagnon [kɔ̃paɲɔ̃] *nm* companion; *(concubin)* partner; **c. de jeu** playmate; **c. de route** travelling companion

comparaître* [kɔ̃paretr] *vi (devant tribunal)* to appear (in court) (**devant** before)

comparer [kɔ̃pare] *vt* to compare (**à** to, with) ▪ **comparable** *adj* comparable (**à** to, with) ▪ **comparaison** *nf* comparison (**avec** with); *(métaphore)* simile; **en c. de...** in comparison with... ▪ **comparatif, -ive 1** *adj* comparative **2** *nm Grammaire* comparative ▪ **comparé, -ée** *adj (littérature, grammaire)* comparative

comparse [kɔ̃pars] *nmf Péj* associate

compartiment [kɔ̃partimɑ̃] *nm* compartment; **c. à bagages** *(de bus)* luggage compartment; **c. fumeurs** smoking compartment; **c. non-fumeurs** no-smoking compartment ▪ **compartimenter** *vt (diviser)* to partition

comparution [kɔ̃parysjɔ̃] *nf Jur* appearance

compas [kɔ̃pa] *nm Math Br* (pair of) compasses, *Am* compass; *Naut* compass

compassé, -ée [kɔ̃pase] *adj (affecté)* starchy, stiff

compassion [kɔ̃pasjɔ̃] *nf* compassion

compatible [kɔ̃patibl] *adj* compatible (**avec** with) ▪ **compatibilité** *nf* compatibility

compatir [kɔ̃patir] *vi* to sympathize; **c. à la douleur de qn** to share in sb's grief ▪ **compatissant, -ante** *adj* compassionate, sympathetic

compatriote [kɔ̃patrijɔt] *nmf* compatriot

compenser [kɔ̃pɑ̃se] **1** *vt (perte, défaut)* to make up for, to compensate for **2** *vi* to compensate; **pour c.** to make up for it, to compensate ▪ **compensation** *nf (de perte)* compensation; **en c.** in compensation (**de** for)

compétent, -ente [kɔ̃petɑ̃, -ɑ̃t] *adj* competent ▪ **compétence** *nf* competence; **compétences** *(connaissances)* skills, abilities

compétition [kɔ̃petisjɔ̃] *nf (rivalité)* competition; *(épreuve sportive)* event; **être en c. avec qn** to compete with sb; **sport de c.** competitive sport ▪ **compétitif, -ive** *adj* competitive ▪ **compétitivité** *nf* competitiveness

compiler [kɔ̃pile] *vt* to compile

complaire* [kɔ̃plɛr] **se complaire** *upr* **se c. dans qch/à faire qch** to delight in sth/in doing sth

complaisant, -ante [kɔ̃plɛzɑ̃, -ɑ̃t] *adj (bienveillant)* kind, obliging; *(satisfait)* complacent ▪ **complaisance** *nf (bienveillance)* kindness; *(vanité)* complacency

complément [kɔ̃plemɑ̃] *nm (reste)* rest; *Grammaire* complement; **un c. d'information** additional information; **c. circonstanciel** adverbial phrase; **c. d'agent** agent; **c. d'objet direct/indirect** direct/indirect object ▪ **complémentaire** *adj* complementary; *(détails)* additional

complet, -ète [kɔ̃plɛ, -ɛt] **1** *adj (entier, absolu)* complete; *(train, hôtel, théâtre)* full; *(pain)* wholemeal **2** *nm (costume)* suit; **la famille au grand c.** the whole family ▪ **complètement** *adv* completely

compléter [kɔ̃plete] **1** *vt (collection, formation)* to complete; *(formulaire)* to fill in; *(somme)* to make up **2 se compléter** *upr* to complement each other

complexe [kɔ̃plɛks] **1** *adj* complex **2** *nm (sentiment, construction)* complex; **avoir des complexes** to have a hang-up ▪ **complexé, -ée** *adj Fam* hung up (**par** about) ▪ **complexité** *nf* complexity

complication [kɔ̃plikasjɔ̃] *nf (ennui) & Méd* complication; *(complexité)* complexity

complice [kɔ̃plis] **1** *nm* accomplice **2** *adj (regard)* knowing; *(silence)* conniving; **être c. de qch** to be a party to sth ▪ **complicité** *nf* complicity

compliment [kɔ̃plimɑ̃] *nm* compliment; **faire des compliments à qn** to pay sb compliments; **mes compliments!** congratulations! ▪ **complimenter** *vt* to compliment (**sur** on)

compliquer [kɔ̃plike] **1** *vt* to complicate **2 se compliquer** *upr (situation)* to get complicated; **se c. la vie** to make life complicated for oneself ▪ **compliqué, -ée** *adj* complicated

complot [kɔ̃plo] *nm* conspiracy (**contre** against) ▪ **comploter** *vti* to plot (**de faire** to do)

comporter [kɔ̃pɔrte] **1** *vt (contenir)* to contain; *(inconvénient)* to involve; *(être constitué de)* to consist of **2 se comporter** *vpr (personne)* to behave; *(voiture)* to handle ▪ **comportement** [-əmɑ̃] *nm Br* behaviour, *Am* behavior

composer [kɔ̃poze] **1** *vt (faire partie de)* to make up; *(musique, poème)* to compose; *(numéro de téléphone)* to dial; *Typ* to set; **être composé de qch** to be made up *or* composed of sth **2** *vi (étudiant)* to take a test; **c. avec** *(ennemi)* to compromise with **3 se composer** *vpr* **se c. de qch** to be made up *or* composed of sth ▪ **composant** *nm (chimique, électronique)* component ▪ **composante** *nf (d'une idée, d'un ensemble)* component ▪ **composé, -ée** *adj & nm* compound

compositeur, -trice [kɔ̃pozitœr, -tris] *nmf (musicien)* composer; *(typographe)* typesetter

composition [kɔ̃pozisjɔ̃] *nf (de musique, de poème)* composing; *Typ* typesetting; *(éléments)* composition; *(d'aliment)* ingredients; *(examen)* test; **être de bonne c.** to be good-natured

composter [kɔ̃pɔste] *vt (billet)* to cancel

compote [kɔ̃pɔt] *nf Br* stewed fruit, *Am* sauce; **c. de pommes** *Br* stewed apples, *Am* applesauce

compréhensible [kɔ̃preɑ̃sibl] *adj (justifié)* understandable; *(clair)* comprehensible ▪ **compréhensif, -ive** *adj* understanding ▪ **compréhension** *nf* understanding

> Il faut noter que l'adjectif anglais **comprehensive** est un faux ami. Il signifie le plus souvent **complet**.

comprendre* [kɔ̃prɑ̃dr] **1** *vt (par l'esprit)* to understand; *(être composé de)* to consist of; *(comporter)* to include; **mal c. qch** to misunderstand sth; **je n'y comprends rien** I can't make head or tail of it; **se faire c.** to make oneself understood **2 se comprendre** *vpr* **ça se comprend** that's understandable

compresse [kɔ̃prɛs] *nf* compress

compresser [kɔ̃prese] *vt* to compress; *Ordinat (fichier)* to compress, to zip ▪ **compresseur** *nm* compressor; **rouleau c.** steamroller ▪ **compression** *nf (de gaz)* compression; *(réduction)* reduction; *Ordinat (de fichier)* zipping

comprimé [kɔ̃prime] *nm (médicament)* tablet

comprimer [kɔ̃prime] *vt (gaz, artère)* to compress; *(dépenses)* to reduce; *Ordinat (fichier)* to compress, to zip

compris, -ise [kɔ̃pri, -iz] **1** *pp voir* **comprendre 2** *adj (inclus)* included (**dans** in); **y c.** including; **c. entre** between

compromettre* [kɔ̃prɔmɛtr] *vt (personne)* to compromise; *(sécurité)* to jeopardize ▪ **compromis** *nm* compromise ▪ **compromission** *nf Péj* compromise

comptabiliser [kɔ̃tabilize] *vt (compter)* to count

comptable [kɔ̃tabl] *nmf* accountant ▪ **comptabilité** *nf (comptes)* accounts; *(science)* book-keeping, accounting; *(service)* accounts department

comptant [kɔ̃tɑ̃] **1** *adv* **payer c.** to pay (in) cash **2** *nm* **acheter au c.** to buy for cash

compte [kɔ̃t] *nm* (**a**) *(de banque, de commerçant)* account; *(calcul)* calculation; **avoir un c. en banque** to have a bank account; **faire ses comptes** to do one's accounts; **c. chèque** *Br* current account, *Am* checking account; **c. à rebours** countdown (**b**) *(expressions)* **pour le c. de** on behalf of; **en fin de c.** all things considered; **à bon c.** *(acheter)* cheap(ly); **s'en tirer à bon c.** to get off lightly; **demander des comptes à qn** to ask sb for an explanation; **avoir un c. à régler avec qn** to have a score to settle with sb; **tenir c. de qch** to take sth into account; **c. tenu de qch** considering sth; **entrer en ligne de c.** to be taken into account; **se rendre c. de qch** to realize sth; **rendre c. de qch** *(exposer)* to report on sth; *(justifier)* to account for sth; **travailler à son c.** to be self-employed; **s'installer à son c.** to start one's own business; *Fig* **être loin du c.** to be wide of the mark; *Fam* **avoir son c.** to have had enough ▪ **compte-gouttes** *nm inv* dropper; *Fig* **au c.** in dribs and drabs

compter [kɔ̃te] *vt (calculer)* to count; *(prévoir)* to allow; *(inclure)* to include; **c. faire qch** *(espérer)* to expect to do sth; *(avoir l'intention de)* to intend to do sth; **c. qch à qn** *(facturer)* to charge sb for sth; **il compte deux ans de service** he has two years' service; **ses jours sont comptés** his/her days are numbered; **sans c....** *(sans parler de)* not to mention... **2** *vi (calculer, être important)* to count; **c. sur qn/qch** to count *or* rely on sb/sth; **c. avec qn/qch** to reckon with sb/sth; **c. parmi les meilleurs** to rank among the best; **à c. de demain** as from tomorrow; **j'y compte bien!** I should hope so! **3 se compter** *vpr* **ses membres se comptent par milliers** it has thousands of members ▪ **compteur** *nm* meter; **c. de gaz** gas meter; **c. Geiger** Geiger counter; *Aut* **c. kilométrique** *Br* mileometer, *Am* odometer; *Aut* **c. de vitesse** speedometer

compte rendu [kɔ̃trɑ̃dy] (*pl* **comptes rendus**) *nm* report; *(de livre, de film)* review

comptoir [kɔ̃twar] *nm (de magasin)* counter; *(de café)* bar; *(dans un pays éloigné)* trading post; **c. de réception** reception desk

compulser [kɔ̃pylse] *vt (notes, archives)* to consult

comte [kɔ̃t] *nm (noble)* count; *(en Grande-Bretagne)* earl ▪ **comté** *nm (subdivision administrative)* county ▪ **comtesse** *nf* countess

con, conne [kɔ̃, kɔn] *très Fam* **1** *adj (idiot) Br* bloody stupid, *Am* goddamn stupid!; **c'est pas**

c.! that's pretty smart! **2** *nmf* stupid bastard, *f* stupid cow

concave [kɔ̃kav] *adj* concave

concéder [kɔ̃sede] *vt (victoire, but)* to concede; **c. qch à qn** to grant sb sth

concentrer [kɔ̃sɑ̃tre] **1** *vt* to concentrate; *(attention, énergie)* to focus **2 se concentrer** *vpr (réfléchir)* to concentrate **▪ concentration** *nf* concentration **▪ concentré, -ée 1** *adj (lait)* condensed; *(solution)* concentrated; *(attentif)* concentrating (hard) **2** *nm* **c. de tomates** tomato purée

concentrique [kɔ̃sɑ̃trik] *adj* concentric

concept [kɔ̃sɛpt] *nm* concept **▪ conception** *nf (d'idée)* conception; *(création)* design; **c. assistée par ordinateur** computer-aided design; **c. graphique** graphic design; **c. de sites Web** web design **▪ concepteur, -trice** *nmf* designer; **c. graphiste** graphic designer; *Ordinat* **c. de sites Web** web designer

concerner [kɔ̃sɛrne] *vt* to concern; **en ce qui me concerne** as far as I'm concerned **▪ concernant** *prép* concerning

concert [kɔ̃sɛr] *nm (de musique)* concert; *Fig (de protestations)* chorus; **de c.** *(agir)* together

concerter [kɔ̃sɛrte] **1** *vt (projet)* to devise together **2 se concerter** *vpr* to consult together **▪ concertation** *nf* consultation **▪ concerté, -ée** *adj (action)* concerted

concerto [kɔ̃sɛrto] *nm Mus* concerto

concession [kɔ̃sesjɔ̃] *nf (compromis)* concession (à to); *(terrain)* plot **▪ concessionnaire** *nmf* dealer

concevoir* [kɔ̃səvwar] **1** *vt (enfant, plan, idée)* to conceive; *(produit)* to design; *(comprendre)* to understand **2 se concevoir** *vpr* **ça se conçoit** that's understandable **▪ concevable** *adj* conceivable

concierge [kɔ̃sjɛrʒ] *nmf* caretaker, *Am* janitor

concile [kɔ̃sil] *nm Rel* council

concilier [kɔ̃silje] **1** *vt (choses)* to reconcile **2 se concilier** *vpr* **se c. la faveur de qn** to win sb's goodwill **▪ conciliant, -ante** *adj* conciliatory **▪ conciliation** *nf* conciliation

concis, -ise [kɔ̃si, -is] *adj* concise **▪ concision** *nf* concision

concitoyen, -enne [kɔ̃sitwajɛ̃, -ɛn] *nmf* fellow citizen

conclure* [kɔ̃klyr] **1** *vt (terminer)* to conclude; *(accord)* to finalize; *(marché)* to clinch; **c. que... (déduire)** to conclude that... **2** *vi* **c. à la culpabilité de qn** to conclude that sb is guilty **▪ concluant, -ante** *adj* conclusive **▪ conclusion** *nf* conclusion; **tirer une c. de qch** to draw a conclusion from sth

concombre [kɔ̃kɔ̃br] *nm* cucumber

concordance [kɔ̃kɔrdɑ̃s] *nf (de preuves)* tallying; *Grammaire* **c. des temps** sequence of tenses

concorder [kɔ̃kɔrde] *vi (preuves, dates, témoignages)* to tally (**avec** with)

concourir* [kɔ̃kurir] *vi Sport* to compete (**pour** for); *(converger)* to converge; **c. à qch/faire qch** to contribute to sth/to do sth

concours [kɔ̃kur] *nm (examen)* competitive examination; *(jeu)* competition; *(aide)* assistance; **c. de beauté** beauty contest; **c. circonstances** combination of circumstances; **c. hippique** horse show

concret, -ète [kɔ̃krɛ, -ɛt] *adj* concrete **▪ concrétiser 1** *vt (rêve)* to realize; *(projet)* to carry out **2 se concrétiser** *vpr* to materialize

conçu, -ue [kɔ̃sy] **1** *pp de* **concevoir 2** *adj* **c. pour faire qch** designed to do sth; **bien c.** well designed

concubine [kɔ̃kybin] *nf Jur* cohabitant **▪ concubinage** *nm* cohabitation; **vivre en c.** to cohabit

concurrent, -ente [kɔ̃kyrɑ̃, -ɑ̃t] *nmf* competitor **▪ concurrence** *nf* competition; **faire c. à** to compete with; **jusqu'à c. de 100 euros** up to the amount of 100 euros **▪ concurrencer** *vt* to compete with **▪ concurrentiel, -ielle** *adj* competitive

condamnation [kɔ̃danɑsjɔ̃] *nf Jur (jugement)* conviction (**pour** for); *(peine)* sentence (**à** to); *(critique)* condemnation; **c. à mort** death sentence

condamner [kɔ̃dane] *vt (blâmer)* to condemn; *Jur* to sentence (**à** to); *(porte)* to block up; *(pièce)* to seal up; **c. qn à une amende** to fine sb; **c. qn à qch** *(forcer à)* to force sb into sth **▪ condamné, -ée 1** *adj (malade)* terminally ill **2** *nmf* convicted person

condenser [kɔ̃dɑse] *vt,* **se condenser** *vpr* to condense **▪ condensation** *nf* condensation

condescendre [kɔ̃desɑ̃dr] *vi* to condescend (**à faire** to do) **▪ condescendance** *nf* condescension **▪ condescendant, -ante** *adj* condescending

condiment [kɔ̃dimɑ̃] *nm* condiment

condisciple [kɔ̃disipl] *nm (écolier)* schoolmate; *(étudiant)* fellow student

condition [kɔ̃disjɔ̃] *nf (état, stipulation, sort)* condition; *(classe sociale)* station; **conditions** *(circonstances)* conditions; *(d'accord, de vente)* terms; **être en bonne c. physique** to be in good shape; **à c. de faire qch, à c. que l'on fasse qch** providing *or* provided (that) one does sth; **sans c.** *(capitulation)* unconditional; *(se rendre)* unconditionally **▪ conditionnel, -elle 1** *adj* conditional **2** *nm Grammaire* conditional

conditionner [kɔ̃disjɔne] *vt (être la condition de)* to govern; *(emballer)* to package; *(personne)* to condition **▪ conditionnement** *nm (emballage)* packaging; *(de personne)* conditioning

condoléances [kɔ̃dɔleɑ̃s] *nfpl* condolences;

présenter ses c. à qn to offer one's condolences to sb

conducteur, -trice [kɔ̃dyktœr, -tris] 1 *nmf (de véhicule, de train)* driver 2 *adj & nm Él* **(corps) c.** conductor; **(fil) c.** lead (wire)

> Il faut noter que le nom anglais **conductor** est un faux ami. Il signifie **chef d'orchestre** ou **contrôleur** selon le contexte.

conduire* [kɔ̃dyir] 1 *vt (troupeau)* to lead; *(voiture)* to drive; *(moto)* to ride; *(eau)* to carry; *(électricité)* to conduct; **c. qn** *(accompagner)* to take sb to; **c. qn au suicide** to drive sb to suicide 2 *vi (en voiture)* to drive; **c. à** *(lieu)* to lead to 3 **se conduire** *vpr* to behave

conduit [kɔ̃dyi] *nm (tuyau)* pipe

conduite [kɔ̃dyit] *nf (de véhicule)* driving **(de** of); *(d'entreprise, d'opération)* management; *(tuyau)* pipe; *(comportement)* behaviour, *Am* behavior; **c. à gauche/droite** *(volant)* left-hand/right-hand drive; **sous la c. de qn** under the guidance of sb; **c. de gaz** gas main

cône [kon] *nm* cone

confection [kɔ̃fɛksjɔ̃] *nf (de vêtement, de repas)* making **(de** of); *(industrie)* clothing industry; **vêtements de c.** ready-to-wear clothes **•confectionner** *vt* to make **•confectionneur, -euse** *nmf* clothes manufacturer

> Il faut noter que le mot anglais **confectioner** est un faux ami. Il signifie **confiseur** ou **pâtissier.**

confédération [kɔ̃federasjɔ̃] *nf* confederation **•confédéré, -ée** *adj* confederate

conférence [kɔ̃ferɑ̃s] *nf (réunion)* conference; *(exposé)* lecture; **c. de presse** press conference **•conférencier, -ière** *nmf* lecturer

conférer [kɔ̃fere] *vt (titre)* to confer (**à** on)

confesser [kɔ̃fese] *Rel* 1 *vt* to confess 2 **se confesser** *vpr* to confess (**à** to) **•confession** *nf* confession **•confessionnal, -aux** *nm Rel* confessional **•confessionnel, -elle** *adj (école)* denominational

confettis [kɔ̃feti] *nmpl* confetti

confiance [kɔ̃fjɑ̃s] *nf* confidence; **faire c. à qn, avoir c. en qn** to trust sb; **de c.** *(mission)* of trust; *(personne)* trustworthy; **en toute c.** *(acheter, dire)* quite confidently; **c. en soi** self-confidence; **avoir c. en soi** to be self-confident **•confiant, -ante** *adj (qui fait confiance)* trusting; *(optimiste)* confident; *(qui a confiance en soi)* self-confident

confidence [kɔ̃fidɑ̃s] *nf* confidence; **faire une c. à qn** to confide in sb **•confident, -ente** *nmf* confidant, *f* confidante **•confidentiel, -ielle** *adj* confidential

confier [kɔ̃fje] 1 *vt* **c. qch à qn** *(laisser)* to entrust sb with sth; *(dire)* to confide sth to sb 2 **se confier** *vpr* **se c. à qn** to confide in sb

configuration [kɔ̃figyrasjɔ̃] *nf (disposition)* layout; *Ordinat* configuration

confiner [kɔ̃fine] 1 *vt* to confine 2 *vi* **c. à** to border on 3 **se confiner** *vpr* **se c. chez soi** to shut oneself up indoors **•confiné, -ée** *adj (atmosphère)* enclosed

confins [kɔ̃fɛ̃] *nmpl* confines; **aux c. de** on the edge of

confirmer [kɔ̃firme] 1 *vt* to confirm (**que** that); **c. qn dans son opinion** to confirm sb in his/her opinion 2 **se confirmer** *vpr (nouvelle)* to be confirmed; *(tendance)* to continue **•confirmation** *nf* confirmation

confiserie [kɔ̃fizri] *nf (magasin) Br* sweetshop, *Am* candy store; **confiseries** *(bonbons) Br* sweets, *Am* candy **•confiseur, -euse** *nmf* confectioner

confisquer [kɔ̃fiske] *vt* to confiscate (**à qn** from sb) **•confiscation** *nf* confiscation

confit, -e [kɔ̃fi] 1 *adj (fruits)* candied 2 *nm* **c. d'oie** potted goose

confiture [kɔ̃fityr] *nf* jam; **c. de fraises** strawberry jam

conflit [kɔ̃fli] *nm* conflict; **conflits sociaux** industrial disputes **•conflictuel, -elle** *adj (intérêts)* conflicting; **situation conflictuelle** situation of potential conflict

confluent [kɔ̃flyɑ̃] *nm* confluence

confondre [kɔ̃fɔ̃dr] 1 *vt (choses, personnes)* to mix up, to confuse; *(consterner)* to astound; *(démasquer)* to confound; **c. qn/qch avec qn/ qch** to mistake sb/sth for sb/sth 2 **se confondre** *vpr (couleurs, intérêts)* to merge; **se c. en excuses** to apologize profusely

conforme [kɔ̃fɔrm] *adj* **c. à** in accordance with; *(modèle)* true to; **copie c. à l'original** exact copy **•conformément** *adv* **c. à** in accordance with

conformer [kɔ̃fɔrme] 1 *vt* to model 2 **se conformer** *vpr* to conform (**à** to)

conformisme [kɔ̃fɔrmism] *nm* conformism **•conformiste** *adj & nmf* conformist **•conformité** *nf* conformity (**à** with)

confort [kɔ̃fɔr] *nm* comfort **•confortable** *adj* comfortable

confrère [kɔ̃frɛr] *nm (de profession)* colleague

confronter [kɔ̃frɔ̃te] *vt (personnes)* to confront; *(expériences, résultats)* to compare; **confronté à** *(difficulté)* confronted with **•confrontation** *nf (face-à-face)* confrontation; *(comparaison)* comparison

confus, -use [kɔ̃fy, -yz] *adj (esprit, situation, explication)* confused; *(bruit)* indistinct; *(gêné)* embarrassed **•confusément** *adv* vaguely **•confusion** *nf (désordre, méprise)* confusion; *(gêne)* embarrassment

> Il faut noter que l'adjectif anglais **confus** est un faux ami. Il signifie **désorienté.**

congé [kɔ̃ʒe] *nm (vacances) Br* holiday, *Am* vacation; *(arrêt de travail)* leave; *(avis de renvoi)* notice; **donner son c. à qn** *(employé, locataire)* to give notice to sb; **prendre c. de qn** to take one's leave of sb; **c. de maladie** sick leave; **c. de maternité** maternity leave; **c. de paternité** paternity leave; **congés payés** *Br* paid holidays, *Am* paid vacation

congédier [kɔ̃ʒedje] *vt* to dismiss

congeler [kɔ̃ʒle] *vt* to freeze ▪ **congélateur** *nm* freezer ▪ **congélation** *nf* freezing

congénital, -e, -aux, -ales [kɔ̃ʒenital, -o] *adj* congenital

congère [kɔ̃ʒɛr] *nf* snowdrift

congestion [kɔ̃ʒɛstjɔ̃] *nf* congestion; **c. cérébrale** stroke ▪ **congestionné, -ée** *adj (visage)* flushed

Congo [kɔ̃go] *nm* **le C.** Congo ▪ **congolais, -aise** *adj* Congolese **2** *nmf* **C., Congolaise** Congolese

congratuler [kɔ̃gratyle] *vt* to congratulate (**sur** on)

congrégation [kɔ̃gregasjɔ̃] *nf Rel* congregation

congrès [kɔ̃grɛ] *nm* conference; **le C.** *(aux États-Unis)* Congress ▪ **congressiste** *nmf* delegate

conifère [kɔnifɛr] *nm* conifer

conique [kɔnik] *adj* conical

conjecture [kɔ̃ʒɛktyr] *nf* conjecture ▪ **conjecturer** *vt* to conjecture

conjoint, -ointe [kɔ̃ʒwɛ̃, -wɛ̃t] **1** *adj* joint **2** *nm* spouse; **conjoints** husband and wife ▪ **conjointement** *adv* jointly

conjonction [kɔ̃ʒɔ̃ksjɔ̃] *nf (union)* union; *Grammaire* conjunction

conjonctivite [kɔ̃ʒɔ̃ktivit] *nf Méd* conjunctivitis

conjoncture [kɔ̃ʒɔ̃ktyr] *nf* circumstances; **la c. économique** the economic situation

conjugal, -e, -aux, -ales [kɔ̃ʒygal, -o] *adj (bonheur)* marital; *(vie)* married; *(devoir)* conjugal

conjuguer [kɔ̃ʒyge] **1** *vt (verbe)* to conjugate; *(efforts)* to combine **2 se conjuguer** *vpr (verbe)* to be conjugated ▪ **conjugaison** *nf Grammaire* conjugation

conjurer [kɔ̃ʒyre] *vt (danger)* to avert; *(mauvais sort)* to ward off; **c. qn de faire qch** to beg sb to do sth ▪ **conjuration** *nf (complot)* conspiracy ▪ **conjuré, -ée** *nmf* conspirator

connaissance [kɔnɛsɑ̃s] *nf (savoir)* knowledge; *(personne)* acquaintance; **à ma c.** to my knowledge; **en c. de cause** with full knowledge of the facts; **avoir c. de qch** to be aware of sth; **avoir des connaissances en histoire** to have a good knowledge of history; **faire la c. de qn** to make sb's acquaintance; **faire c. avec qn** to get to know sb; **prendre c. de qch** to acquaint oneself with sth; **perdre/reprendre c.** to lose/regain consciousness; **sans c.** unconscious ▪ **connaisseur** *nm* connoisseur

connaître* [kɔnɛtr] **1** *vt (personne, endroit, faits, amour)* to know; *(rencontrer)* to meet; *(famine, guerre)* to experience; **faire c. qch** to make sth known; **faire c. qn** *(présenter)* to introduce sb; *(rendre célèbre)* to make sb known; **ne pas c. de limites** to know no bounds **2 se connaître** *vpr* **nous nous connaissons déjà** we've met before; **s'y c. en qch** to know all about sth

connecter [kɔnɛkte] **1** *vt (appareil électrique)* to connect; *Ordinat* **connecté** on line **2 se connecter** *vpr (appareils électriques)* to be connected; *Ordinat (internaute)* to go on line; **se c. à un système** to log on to a system ▪ **connexion** *nf* connection

connerie [kɔnri] *nf très Fam (bêtise)* (damn) stupidity; *(action)* (damn) stupid thing; **dire des conneries** to talk (a load of) crap

connivence [kɔnivɑ̃s] *nf* connivance

connotation [kɔnɔtasjɔ̃] *nf* connotation

connu, -ue [kɔny] **1** *pp de* **connaître 2** *adj (célèbre)* well-known

conquérir* [kɔ̃kerir] *vt (pays, sommet)* to conquer; *(marché)* to capture; **conquis par son charme** won over by his/her charm ▪ **conquérant, -ante** *nmf* conqueror ▪ **conquête** *nf* conquest; **faire la c. de** *(pays)* to conquer

consacrer [kɔ̃sakre] **1** *vt (temps, vie)* to devote (**à** to); *(église)* to consecrate; *(entériner)* to establish **2 se consacrer** *vpr* **se c. à** to devote oneself to

consciemment [kɔ̃sjamɑ̃] *adv* consciously

conscience [kɔ̃sjɑ̃s] *nf* **(a)** *(esprit)* consciousness; **avoir/prendre c. de qch** to be/become aware of sth; **perdre c.** to lose consciousness **(b)** *(morale)* conscience; **avoir bonne/mauvaise c.** to have a clear/guilty conscience; **c. professionnelle** professional integrity ▪ **consciencieux, -euse** *adj* conscientious

conscient, -ente [kɔ̃sjɑ̃, -ɑ̃t] *adj (lucide)* conscious; **c. de qch** aware *or* conscious of sth

conscrit [kɔ̃skri] *nm Mil* conscript ▪ **conscription** *nf Mil* conscription, *Am* draft

consécration [kɔ̃sekrasjɔ̃] *nf (d'église)* consecration; *(aboutissement)* crowning moment

consécutif, -ive [kɔ̃sekytif, -iv] *adj* consecutive; **c. à** following upon ▪ **consécutivement** *adv* consecutively

conseil [kɔ̃sɛj] *nm* **(a)** **un c.** *(recommandation)* a piece of advice; **des conseils** advice **(b)** *(assemblée)* council, committee; **c. d'administration** board of directors; *Scol* **c. de classe** = staff meeting with participation of class representatives; *Pol* **c. des ministres** cabinet meeting

conseiller¹ [kɔ̃seje] *vt (guider)* to advise; **c. qch**

à qn to recommend sth to sb; **c. à qn de faire qch** to advise sb to do sth

conseiller², -ère [kɔ̃seje, -jɛr] *nmf (expert)* consultant, adviser; **c. de gestion** management consultant; **c. d'orientation** careers adviser

consentir* [kɔ̃sɑ̃tir] **1** *vi* **c. à qch/à faire qch** to consent to sth/to do sth **2** *vt (prêt)* to grant (**à** to) • **consentement** *nm* consent

conséquence [kɔ̃sekɑ̃s] *nf* consequence; **en c.** accordingly; **agir en c.** to take appropriate action; **sans c.** *(sans importance)* of no importance

conséquent, -ente [kɔ̃sekɑ̃, -ɑ̃t] *adj (cohérent)* consistent; *Fam (somme)* tidy; **par c.** consequently

conservateur, -trice [kɔ̃sɛrvatœr, -tris] **1** *adj & nmf Pol* Conservative **2** *nmf (de musée)* curator; *(de bibliothèque)* librarian **3** *nm (alimentaire)* preservative • **conservatisme** *nm* conservatism

conservation [kɔ̃sɛrvasjɔ̃] *nf (d'aliments)* preserving

conservatoire [kɔ̃sɛrvatwar] *nm* school, academy

conserve [kɔ̃sɛrv] *nf* conserves canned *or Br* tinned food; **en c.** canned, *Br* tinned

conserver [kɔ̃sɛrve] **1** *vt* to keep; *(droits)* to retain; *(fruits, tradition)* to preserve; **c. son calme** to keep one's calm **2 se conserver** *vpr (aliment)* to keep

considérable [kɔ̃siderabl] *adj* considerable • **considérablement** [-amɑ̃] *adv* considerably

considérer [kɔ̃sidere] *vt* to consider (**que** that); **c. qn/qch comme...** to consider sb/sth as...; **tout bien considéré** all things considered • **considération** *nf (respect)* regard, esteem; **considérations** *(remarques)* observations; **prendre qch en c.** to take sth into consideration

consigne [kɔ̃siɲ] *nf (instructions)* orders; *Mil (punition)* confinement to barracks; *(de bouteille)* deposit; **c. (à bagages)** *Br* left-luggage office, *Am* checkroom; **c. automatique** lockers • **consigné, -ée** *adj (bouteille)* returnable • **consigner** *vt (bouteille)* to charge a deposit on; *(bagages) Br* to deposit in the left-luggage office, *Am* to check; *(écrire)* to record; *(punir) (élève)* to keep in; *(soldat)* to confine to barracks

consistant, -ante [kɔ̃sistɑ̃, -ɑ̃t] *adj (sauce, bouillie)* thick; *(repas)* substantial • **consistance** *nf (de corps)* consistency

Il faut noter que l'adjectif anglais **consistent** est un faux ami. Il signifie le plus souvent **cohérent**.

consister [kɔ̃siste] *vi* **c. en qch** to consist of sth; **c. à faire qch** to consist in doing sth

consœur [kɔ̃sœr] *nf* female colleague

console [kɔ̃sɔl] *nf (d'ordinateur, de jeux)* console

consoler [kɔ̃sɔle] **1** *vt* to comfort, to console **2 se consoler** *vpr* **se c. de qch** to get over sth • **consolation** *nf* comfort, consolation

consolider [kɔ̃sɔlide] *vt (mur, position)* to strengthen • **consolidation** *nf* strengthening

consommateur, -trice [kɔ̃sɔmatœr, -tris] *nmf* consumer; *(au café)* customer • **consommation** *nf (de nourriture, d'électricité)* consumption; *(de voiture)* fuel consumption; *(boisson)* drink

consommé, -ée [kɔ̃sɔme] **1** *adj* consummate **2** *nm Culin* consommé

consommer [kɔ̃sɔme] **1** *vt (aliment, carburant)* to consume; *(mariage)* to consummate **2** *vi (au café)* to drink

consonne [kɔ̃sɔn] *nf* consonant • **consonance** *nf* consonance

consortium [kɔ̃sɔrsjɔm] *nm (entreprises)* consortium

conspirer [kɔ̃spire] *vi (comploter)* to conspire (**contre** against); **c. à faire qch** *(concourir)* to conspire to do sth • **conspirateur, -trice** *nmf* conspirator • **conspiration** *nf* conspiracy

conspuer [kɔ̃spɥe] *vt* to boo

constant, -ante [kɔ̃stɑ̃, -ɑ̃t] **1** *adj* constant **2** *nf Math* **constante** constant • **constamment** [-amɑ̃] *adv* constantly • **constance** *nf (en amour)* constancy

constat [kɔ̃sta] *nm* (official) report; **faire un c. d'échec** to acknowledge failure

constater [kɔ̃state] **1** *vt (observer)* to note (**que** that); *Jur (enregistrer)* to record; *(décès)* to certify **2** *vi* **je ne fais que c.** I'm merely stating a fact • **constatation** *nf (remarque)* observation

constellation [kɔ̃stɛlɑsjɔ̃] *nf* constellation • **constellé, -ée** *adj* **c. d'étoiles** studded with stars

consterner [kɔ̃stɛrne] *vt* to dismay • **consternation** *nf* dismay

constiper [kɔ̃stipe] *vt* to constipate • **constipation** *nf* constipation • **constipé, -ée** *adj* constipated; *Fam (gêné)* ill at ease

constituer [kɔ̃stitɥe] **1** *vt (composer)* to make up; *(équivaloir à)* to constitute; *(former)* to form; **constitué de** made up of **2 se constituer** *vpr* **se c. prisonnier** to give oneself up

constitutif, -ive [kɔ̃stitytif, -iv] *adj* constituent

constitution [kɔ̃stitysjɔ̃] *nf (santé, lois)* constitution; *(de gouvernement)* formation • **constitutionnel, -elle** *adj* constitutional

constructeur [kɔ̃stryktœr] *nm (bâtisseur)* builder; *(fabricant)* maker (**de** of); **c. automobile** car manufacturer • **constructif, -ive** *adj* constructive • **construction** *nf (de pont, de route, de maison)* building, construction (**de** of); *(de phrase)* structure; *(édifice)* building; **en c.** under construction

construire* [kɔ̃stryir] *vt (maison, route)* to build; *(phrase)* to construct

consul [kɔ̃syl] *nm* consul ▪ **consulaire** *adj* consular ▪ **consulat** *nm* consulate

consulter [kɔ̃sylte] **1** *vt* to consult **2** *vi (médecin)* to see patients **3 se consulter** *vpr* to consult each other ▪ **consultatif, -ive** *adj* consultative ▪ **consultation** *nf* consultation; **être en c.** *(médecin)* to be with a patient

consumer [kɔ̃syme] *vt (brûler)* to consume

contact [kɔ̃takt] *nm (relation, personne, toucher)* & *Él, Aut* contact; **être en c. avec qn** to be in contact with sb; **entrer en c. avec qn** to come into contact with sb; **prendre c.** to get in touch (**avec** with); *Aut* **mettre/couper le c.** to switch on/off ▪ **contacter** *vt* to contact

contagieux, -euse [kɔ̃taʒjø, -øz] *adj (maladie, personne)* contagious; *(enthousiasme)* infectious ▪ **contagion** *nf Méd* contagion

contaminer [kɔ̃tamine] *vt* to contaminate ▪ **contamination** *nf* contamination

conte [kɔ̃t] *nm* tale; **c. de fées** fairy tale

contempler [kɔ̃tɑ̃ple] *vt* to gaze at, to contemplate ▪ **contemplation** *nf* contemplation; **être en c. devant qch** to gaze at sth

contemporain, -aine [kɔ̃tɑ̃pɔrɛ̃, -ɛn] *adj & nmf* contemporary

contenance [kɔ̃tnɑ̃s] *nf* (**a**) *(de récipient)* capacity (**b**) *(allure)* bearing; **perdre c.** to lose one's composure

contenir* [kɔ̃tnir] **1** *vt (renfermer)* to contain; *(contrôler)* to hold back, to contain; **le théâtre contient mille places** the theatre seats a thousand **2 se contenir** *vpr* to contain oneself ▪ **contenant** *nm* container ▪ **conteneur** *nm* container

content, -ente [kɔ̃tɑ̃, -ɑ̃t] **1** *adj* pleased, happy (**de** with; **de faire** to do); **être c. de soi** to be pleased with oneself; **non c. de mentir...** not content with lying... **2** *nm* **avoir son c.** to have had one's fill (**de** of)

contenter [kɔ̃tɑ̃te] **1** *vt (satisfaire)* to satisfy; *(faire plaisir à)* to please **2 se contenter** *vpr* **se c. de qch** to content oneself with sth ▪ **contentement** *nm* contentment, satisfaction

contentieux [kɔ̃tɑ̃sjø] *nm (querelles)* dispute; *Jur* litigation; *(service)* legal department

contenu [kɔ̃tny] *nm (de paquet, de bouteille)* contents; *(de lettre, de film)* content

conter [kɔ̃te] *vt* to tell (**à** to) ▪ **conteur, -euse** *nmf* storyteller

contestable [kɔ̃tɛstabl] *adj* debatable

contestataire [kɔ̃tɛstater] **1** *adj Pol* anti-establishment; **étudiant c.** student protester **2** *nmf Pol* protester ▪ **contestation** *nf* protest; **faire de la c.** to protest; **sans c. possible** beyond dispute

conteste [kɔ̃tɛst] **sans conteste** *adv* indisputably

contester [kɔ̃tɛste] **1** *vt* to dispute **2** *vi* **faire qch sans c.** to do sth without protest ▪ **contesté, -ée** *adj (théorie, dirigeant)* controversial

contexte [kɔ̃tɛkst] *nm* context ▪ **contextualiser** *vt* to contextualize

contigu, -uë [kɔ̃tigy] *adj (maisons)* adjoining; **c. à qch** adjoining sth ▪ **contiguïté** *nf* close proximity

continent [kɔ̃tinɑ̃] *nm* continent; *(opposé à une île)* mainland ▪ **continental, -e, -aux, -ales** *adj (climat, plateau)* continental

contingent [kɔ̃tɛ̃ʒɑ̃] *nm Mil* contingent; *(quota)* quota ▪ **contingences** *nfpl* contingencies

continu, -ue [kɔ̃tiny] *adj* continuous ▪ **continuel, -elle** *adj (ininterrompu)* continuous; *(qui se répète)* continual ▪ **continuellement** *adv (de façon ininterrompue)* continuously; *(de façon répétitive)* continually

continuer [kɔ̃tinye] **1** *vt (études, efforts, politique)* to continue, to carry on with; **c. à** *ou* **de faire qch** to continue *or* carry on doing sth **2** *vi* to continue, to go on ▪ **continuation** *nf* continuation; *Fam* **bonne c.!** all the best!, good luck with everything! ▪ **continuité** *nf* continuity

contondant [kɔ̃tɔ̃dɑ̃] *adj m* blunt

contorsion [kɔ̃tɔrsjɔ̃] *nf* contortion ▪ **se contorsionner** *vpr* to contort oneself ▪ **contorsionniste** *nmf* contortionist

contour [kɔ̃tur] *nm* outline

contourner [kɔ̃turne] *vt* to go round; *Fig (difficulté, loi)* to get round

contraception [kɔ̃trasɛpsjɔ̃] *nf* contraception ▪ **contraceptif, -ive** *adj & nm* contraceptive

contracter [kɔ̃trakte] **1** *vt (muscle, habitude, dette)* to contract **2 se contracter** *vpr (muscle)* to contract; *(personne)* to tense up ▪ **contraction** *nf* contraction

contractuel, -elle [kɔ̃traktɥɛl] **1** *adj (politique)* contractual **2** *nmf Br* ≃ traffic warden, *Am* ≃ traffic policeman, *f* traffic policewoman

contradiction [kɔ̃tradiksjɔ̃] *nf* contradiction; **être en c. avec qch** to contradict sth; **avoir l'esprit de c.** to be contrary ▪ **contradictoire** *adj* contradictory; **débat c.** debate

contraindre* [kɔ̃trɛ̃dr] **1** *vt* to compel, to force (**à faire** to do) **2 se contraindre** *vpr* to compel *or* force oneself (**à faire** to do) ▪ **contraignant, -ante** *adj* restricting ▪ **contrainte** *nf (obligation, limitation)* constraint; **sous la c.** under duress; **obtenir qch par la c.** to obtain sth by force

contraire [kɔ̃trɛr] **1** *adj (opposé)* conflicting; **c. à qch** contrary to sth; **en sens c.** in the opposite direction; **vent c.** headwind; **le sort nous est c.** fate is against us **2** *nm* opposite; **(bien) au c.** on the contrary ▪ **contrairement** *adv* **c. à** contrary to; **c. à qn** unlike sb

contrarier [kɔ̃trarje] *vt (projet, action)* to thwart; *(personne)* to annoy ▪ **contrariant, -ante** *adj (situation)* annoying; *(personne)* contrary ▪ **contrariété** *nf* annoyance

contraste [kɔ̃trast] *nm* contrast ▪ **contraster** *vi* to contrast (**avec** with)

contrat [kɔ̃tra] *nm* contract; **passer un c.** to enter into an agreement; **c. emploi-solidarité** = short-term contract subsidized by the French government; **c. de mariage** prenuptial agreement

contravention [kɔ̃travɑ̃sjɔ̃] *nf (amende)* fine; *(pour stationnement interdit)* (parking) ticket

contre [kɔ̃tr] **1** *prép* against; *(en échange de)* (in exchange) for; **échanger qch c. qch** to exchange sth for sth; **fâché c. qn** angry with sb; **six voix c. deux** six votes to two; **Nîmes c. Arras** *(match)* Nîmes versus or against Arras; **sirop c. la toux** cough mixture; **par c.** on the other hand **2** *nm* **(a)** **le pour et le c.** the pros and cons **(b)** *(au volley, au basket)* block ▪ **contre-attaque** *(pl* **contre-attaques)** *nf* counter-attack ▪ **contre-attaquer** *vt* to counter-attack

contrebalancer [kɔ̃trəbalɑ̃se] *vt* to counterbalance; *Fig (compenser)* to offset

contrebande [kɔ̃trəbɑ̃d] *nf (activité)* smuggling; *(marchandises)* contraband; **tabac de c.** smuggled tobacco; **faire de la c.** to smuggle goods; **faire entrer qch en c.** to smuggle in sth ▪ **contrebandier, -ière** *nmf* smuggler

contrebas [kɔ̃trəba] **en contrebas** *adv* (down) below; **en c. de** below

contrebasse [kɔ̃trəbas] *nf (instrument)* double-bass

contrecarrer [kɔ̃trəkare] *vt* to thwart

contrecœur [kɔ̃trəkœr] **à contrecœur** *adv* reluctantly

contrecoup [kɔ̃trəku] *nm* repercussions

contre-courant [kɔ̃trəkurɑ̃] *(pl* **contre-courants)** **à contre-courant** *adv (nager)* against the current

contredire* [kɔ̃trədir] **1** *vt* to contradict **2 se contredire** *vpr (soi-même)* to contradict oneself; *(l'un l'autre)* to contradict each other

contrée [kɔ̃tre] *nf Littéraire (région)* region; *(pays)* land

contre-espionnage [kɔ̃trɛspjɔnaʒ] *nm* counter-espionage

contrefaçon [kɔ̃trəfasɔ̃] *nf (pratique)* counterfeiting; *(produit)* fake ▪ **contrefaire*** *vt (voix, écriture)* to disguise; *(pièce)* to counterfeit; *(signature)* to forge

contreforts [kɔ̃trəfɔr] *nmpl (montagnes)* foothills

contre-indication [kɔ̃trɛ̃dikasjɔ̃] *(pl* **contre-indications)** *nf* contraindication

contre-jour [kɔ̃trəʒur] *nm* **à c.** *(tableau, photo)* against the light; **un effet de c.** a backlit effect

contremaître [kɔ̃trəmɛtr] *nm* foreman

contre-offensive [kɔ̃trɔfɑ̃siv] *(pl* **contre-offensives)** *nf* counter-offensive

contrepartie [kɔ̃trəparti] *nf* compensation; **en c. (de)** in return (for)

contre-performance [kɔ̃trəpɛrfɔrmɑ̃s] *(pl* **contre-performances)** *nf* substandard performance

contre-pied [kɔ̃trəpje] *nm* **prendre le c. de qch** *(dire le contraire de)* to take the opposite view to sth; *Sport* **prendre son adversaire à c.** to wrongfoot one's opponent

contreplaqué [kɔ̃trəplake] *nm* plywood

contrepoids [kɔ̃trəpwa] *nm* counterbalance; **faire c. à qch** to counterbalance sth

contrepoison [kɔ̃trəpwazɔ̃] *nm* antidote

contrer [kɔ̃tre] *vt (personne, attaque)* to counter

contre-révolution [kɔ̃trərevɔlysjɔ̃] *(pl* **contre-révolutions)** *nf* counter-revolution

contresens [kɔ̃trəsɑ̃s] *nm* misinterpretation; *(en traduisant)* mistranslation; **à c.** *(en voiture)* the wrong way; **prendre une rue à c.** to go down/up a street the wrong way

contresigner [kɔ̃trəsiɲe] *vt* to countersign

contretemps [kɔ̃trətɑ̃] *nm* hitch, mishap; *Mus* offbeat; **à c.** off the beat; *Fig* at the wrong moment

contrevenir* [kɔ̃trəvnir] *vi* **c. à** to contravene

contrevérité [kɔ̃trəverite] *nf* untruth

contribuer [kɔ̃tribɥe] *vi* to contribute (**à** to); **c. à faire qch** to help (to) do sth ▪ **contribuable** *nmf* taxpayer ▪ **contribution** *nf* contribution (**à** to); *(impôt)* tax; **contributions** *(administration)* tax office; **mettre qn à c.** to use sb's services

contrit, -e [kɔ̃tri, -it] *adj* contrite ▪ **contrition** *nf* contrition

contrôle [kɔ̃trol] *nm (vérification)* checking (**de** of); *(surveillance)* monitoring; *(maîtrise)* control; *Scol* test; **avoir le c. de qch** to have control of sth; **perdre le c. de son véhicule** to lose control of one's vehicle; **le c. des naissances** birth control; **c. d'identité** identity check; **c. des passeports** passport control; **c. de soi** self-control; **c. fiscal** tax inspection

contrôler [kɔ̃trole] **1** *vt (vérifier)* to check; *(surveiller)* to monitor; *(maîtriser)* to control **2 se contrôler** *vpr* to control oneself ▪ **contrôleur, -euse** *nmf (de train, de bus)* ticket inspector; **c. aérien** air-traffic controller

contrordre [kɔ̃trɔrdr] *nm* **il y a c.** the orders have been changed

controverse [kɔ̃trɔvɛrs] *nf* controversy ▪ **controversé, -ée** *adj* controversial

contumace [kɔ̃tymas] *nf Jur* non-appearance in court; **par c.** in absentia

contusion [kɔ̃tyzjɔ̃] *nf* bruise ▪ **contusionné, -ée** *adj* bruised

convaincre* [kɔ̃vɛ̃kr] *vt* to convince (**de** of); **c.**

qn de faire qch to persuade sb to do sth
■**convaincant, -ante** *adj* convincing
■**convaincu, -e** *adj* convinced (**de** of; **que** that); *(partisan)* committed; **être c. de meurtre** to be found guilty of murder

convalescent, -ente [kɔ̃valesɑ̃, -ɑ̃t] *adj & nmf* convalescent ■**convalescence** *nf* convalescence; **être en c.** to be convalescing

convenable [kɔ̃vnabl] *adj (approprié)* suitable; *(acceptable, décent)* decent ■**convenablement** [-əmɑ̃] *adv (s'habiller, être payé)* decently

convenance [kɔ̃vnɑ̃s] *nf* **faire qch à sa c.** to do sth at one's own convenience; **pour c. personnelle** for personal reasons; **les convenances** *(usages)* the proprieties

convenir* [kɔ̃vnir] **1** *vi* **c. à** *(être fait pour)* to be suitable for; *(plaire à, aller à)* to suit; **c. de qch** *(lieu, prix)* to agree upon sth; *(erreur)* to admit sth; **c. de faire qch** to agree to do sth; **c. que...** to admit that... **2** *v impersonnel* **il convient de...** it is advisable to...; *(selon les usages)* it is proper to...; **il fut convenu que...** *(décidé)* it was agreed that... ■**convenu, -ue** *adj (décidé)* agreed; *Péj (peu original)* conventional; **comme c.** as agreed

convention [kɔ̃vɑ̃sjɔ̃] *nf (accord)* agreement; *(règle)* convention; *Pol (assemblée)* assembly; **c. collective** collective agreement; **de c.** *(sourire)* superficial

conventionné, -ée [kɔ̃vɑ̃sjɔne] *adj (médecin, clinique)* attached to the health system, *Br* ≃ NHS; **médecin non c.** private doctor

conventionnel, -elle [kɔ̃vɑ̃sjɔnɛl] *adj* conventional

convergent, -ente [kɔ̃vɛrʒɑ̃, -ɑ̃t] *adj* convergent ■**convergence** *nf* convergence ■**converger** *vi* to converge (**vers** on)

conversation [kɔ̃vɛrsasjɔ̃] *nf* conversation; **engager la c.** to start a conversation ■**converser** *vi Formel* to converse (**avec** with)

conversion [kɔ̃vɛrsjɔ̃] *nf (changement)* conversion (**en** into); *(à une doctrine)* conversion (**à** to) ■**converti, -ie** *nmf Rel* convert ■**convertible 1** *adj* convertible (**en** into) **2** *nm* sofa bed ■**convertir 1** *vt (changer)* to convert (**en** into); *(à une doctrine)* to convert (**à** to) **2 se convertir** *vpr (à une doctrine)* to be converted (**à** to) ■**convertisseur** *nm Ordinat* **c. analogique numérique** digitizer

convexe [kɔ̃vɛks] *adj* convex

conviction [kɔ̃viksjɔ̃] *nf (certitude, croyance)* conviction; **avoir la c. que...** to be convinced that...

convier [kɔ̃vje] *vt Formel* to invite (**à** to; **à faire** to do)

convive [kɔ̃viv] *nmf* guest

convivial, -e, -aux, -ales [kɔ̃vivjal, -jo] *adj* convivial; *Ordinat* user-friendly

convoi [kɔ̃vwa] *nm (véhicules, personnes)*

convoy; *(train)* train; **c. funèbre** funeral procession

convoiter [kɔ̃vwate] *vt (poste, richesses)* to covet

convoler [kɔ̃vɔle] *vi Hum* **c. en justes noces** to marry

convoquer [kɔ̃vɔke] *vt (témoin)* to summon; *(employé, postulant)* to call in; *(assemblée)* to convene; **c. qn à un examen** to notify sb of an examination ■**convocation** *nf (lettre)* notice to attend; *(d'assemblée)* convening; *Jur* summons; **c. à un examen** notification of an examination

convoyer [kɔ̃vwaje] *vt (troupes)* to convoy; *(fonds)* to transport under armed guard ■**convoyeur** *nm* **c. de fonds** security guard

convulser [kɔ̃vylse] *vt* to convulse ■**convulsif, -ive** *adj* convulsive ■**convulsion** *nf* convulsion

coopérer [kɔɔpere] *vi* to co-operate (**à** in, **avec** with) ■**coopératif, -ive** *adj & nf* cooperative ■**coopération** *nf* co-operation (**entre** between); *Pol* overseas development

coopter [kɔɔpte] *vt* to co-opt

coordonner [kɔɔrdɔne] *vt* to co-ordinate (**à** *ou* **avec** with) ■**coordination** *nf* co-ordination ■**coordonnées** *nfpl (adresse, téléphone)* address and phone number; *Math* co-ordinates

copain [kɔpɛ̃] *nm Fam (camarade)* pal; *(petit ami)* boyfriend; **être c. avec qn** to be pals with sb

copeau, -x [kɔpo] *nm (de bois)* shaving

copie [kɔpi] *nf (manuscrit, double)* copy; *Scol (devoir, examen)* paper; **c. double** double sheet of paper ■**copier** *vt (texte, musique, document) & Scol (à un examen)* to copy (**sur** from); *Ordinat* **c. qch sur disquette** to copy sth to disk ■**copier-coller** *nm inv Ordinat* copy and paste; **faire un c. sur qch** to copy and paste sth ■**copieur, -euse 1** *nmf (élève)* copier **2** *nm (machine)* photocopier

copieux, -euse [kɔpjø, -øz] *adj (repas)* copious; *(portion)* generous

copilote [kɔpilɔt] *nm Av* co-pilot

copine [kɔpin] *nf Fam (camarade)* pal; *(petite amie)* girlfriend; **être c. avec qn** to be pals with sb

copropriété [kɔprɔprijete] *nf* joint ownership; **(immeuble en) c.** *Br* block of flats in joint ownership, *Am* condominium

copulation [kɔpylasjɔ̃] *nf* copulation

coq [kɔk] *nm* cock, *Am* rooster; **c. au vin** coq au vin *(chicken cooked in red wine)*; **passer du c. à l'âne** to jump from one subject to another

coque [kɔk] *nf (de noix)* shell; *(de navire)* hull; *(fruit de mer)* cockle

coquelet [kɔklɛ] *nm* cockerel

coquelicot [kɔkliko] *nm* poppy

coqueluche [kɔklyʃ] *nf (maladie)* whooping cough; *Fig* **être la c. de** to be the darling of

coquet, -ette [kɔkɛ, -ɛt] *adj (intérieur)*

charming; *Fam (somme)* tidy; *(person)* conscious of one's appearance ▪ **coquetterie** *nf (vestimentaire)* consciousness of one's appearance

coquetier [kɔktje] *nm* egg-cup

coquille [kɔkij] *nf* shell; *(faute d'imprimerie)* misprint; *Culin* **c. Saint-Jacques** scallop ▪ **coquillage** *nm (mollusque)* shellfish *inv*; *(coquille)* shell

coquin, -e [kɔkɛ̃, -in] **1** *adj (sourire, air)* mischievous; *(sous-vêtements)* naughty **2** *nmf* rascal

cor [kɔr] *nm (instrument)* horn; *(durillon)* corn; **réclamer qch à c. et à cri** to clamour for sth

corail, -aux [kɔraj, -o] *nm* coral

Coran [kɔrɑ̃] *nm* **le C.** the Koran

corbeau, -x [kɔrbo] *nm (oiseau)* crow

corbeille [kɔrbɛj] *nf* **(a)** *(panier)* basket; *Ordinat* wastebasket, recycle bin, *Am* trash; *Ordinat* **c. d'arrivé** *(pour courrier électronique)* in-box; **c. de fruits** fruit basket; **c. à pain** breadbasket; **c. à papier** wastepaper basket **(b)** *(à la Bourse)* trading floor **(c)** *Théâtre* dress circle

corbillard [kɔrbijar] *nm* hearse

cordage [kɔrdaʒ] *nm (corde)* rope; *(de raquette)* stringing

corde [kɔrd] *nf (lien)* rope; *(de raquette, de violon)* string; **usé jusqu'à la c.** threadbare; **monter à la c.** to climb up a rope; **tenir la c.** *(coureur)* to be on the inside; *Fam* **ce n'est pas dans mes cordes** it's not in my line; **c. à linge** washing *or* clothes line; **c. à sauter** *Br* skipping rope, *Am* jump-rope; **c. raide** tightrope; **cordes vocales** vocal cords ▪ **cordée** *nf (d'alpinistes)* roped party ▪ **cordelette** *nf* cord ▪ **corder** *vt (raquette)* to string

cordial, -e, -aux, -ales [kɔrdjal, -jo] **1** *adj (accueil, personne)* cordial **2** *nm (remontant)* tonic ▪ **cordialité** *nf* cordiality

cordon [kɔrdɔ̃] *nm (de tablier, de sac)* string; *(de rideau)* cord; *(de policiers)* cordon; *Anat* **c. ombilical** umbilical cord ▪ **cordon-bleu** *(pl cordons-bleus) nm Fam* first-class cook

cordonnier [kɔrdɔnje] *nm* shoe repairer ▪ **cordonnerie** *nf (métier)* shoe-repairing; *(boutique)* shoe repairer's shop

Corée [kɔre] *nf* **la C.** Korea ▪ **coréen, -enne 1** *adj* Korean **2** *nmf* **C., Coréenne** Korean

coriace [kɔrjas] *adj (viande, personne)* tough

corne [kɔrn] *nf (d'animal, matière, instrument)* horn; *(au pied, à la main)* hard skin; **faire une c. à une page** to turn down the corner of a page; **c. de brume** foghorn

cornée [kɔrne] *nf Anat* cornea

corneille [kɔrnɛj] *nf* crow

cornemuse [kɔrnəmyz] *nf* bagpipes

corner[1] [kɔrne] *vt (page)* to turn down the corner of; *(abîmer)* to make dog-eared

corner[2] [kɔrner] *nm Football* corner; **tirer un c.** to take a corner

cornet [kɔrne] *nm (glace)* cone, *Br* cornet; **c. (de papier)** (paper) cone; *Mus* **c. (à pistons)** cornet

corniaud [kɔrnjo] *nm (chien)* mongrel; *Fam (imbécile)* twit

corniche [kɔrniʃ] *nf (de rocher)* ledge; *(route)* coast road; *(en haut d'un mur)* cornice

cornichon [kɔrniʃɔ̃] *nm* gherkin

cornu, -ue [kɔrny] *adj (diable, animal)* horned

corollaire [kɔrɔler] *nm (suite)* consequence

corporation [kɔrpɔrasjɔ̃] *nf* corporate body

corporel, -elle [kɔrpɔrel] *adj (besoin)* bodily; *(hygiène)* personal

corps [kɔr] *nm (organisme, cadavre) & Chim* body; *(partie principale)* main part; **c. et âme** body and soul; **à son c. défendant** under protest; **lutter c. à c.** to fight hand to hand; **prendre c.** *(projet)* to take shape; **donner c. à** *(rumeur, idée)* to give substance to; *Naut* **perdu c. et biens** lost with all hands; **c. d'armée/diplomatique** army/diplomatic corps; **c. électoral** electorate; **c. enseignant** teaching profession; **c. gras** fat

corpulent, -ente [kɔrpylɑ̃, -ɑ̃t] *adj* stout, corpulent ▪ **corpulence** *nf* stoutness, corpulence

corpus [kɔrpys] *nm Jur & Ling* corpus

correct, -e [kɔrekt] *adj (exact, courtois)* correct; *Fam (acceptable)* reasonable ▪ **correctement** [-əmɑ̃] *adv (sans faire de fautes, décemment)* correctly; *Fam (de façon acceptable)* reasonably; **gagner c. sa vie** to make a reasonable living

correcteur, -trice [kɔrektœr, -tris] **1** *adj* **verres correcteurs** corrective lenses **2** *nmf (d'examen)* examiner; *(en typographie)* proofreader **3** *nm Ordinat* **c. d'orthographe** spellchecker

correction [kɔreksjɔ̃] *nf (rectification)* correction; *(punition)* beating; *(décence, courtoisie)* correctness; *Scol (de devoirs, d'examens)* marking; **c. d'épreuves** proofreading

correctionnel, -elle [kɔreksjɔnel] **1** *adj* **tribunal c.** criminal court **2** *nf* **correctionnelle** criminal court; **passer en c.** to go before a criminal court

corrélation [kɔrelasjɔ̃] *nf* correlation

correspondance [kɔrespɔ̃dɑ̃s] *nf (relation, lettres)* correspondence; *(de train, d'avion) Br* connection, *Am* transfer

correspondre [kɔrespɔ̃dr] *vi* **c. à qch** to correspond to sth; **c. avec qn** *(par lettres)* to correspond with sb ▪ **correspondant, -ante 1** *adj* corresponding **(à** to) **2** *nm (reporter)* correspondent; *(par lettres)* pen friend, pen pal; *(au téléphone)* caller; **c. de guerre** war correspondent

corrida [kɔrida] *nf* bullfight

corridor [kɔridɔr] *nm* corridor

corriger [kɔriʒe] **1** *vt (texte, erreur, myopie, injustice)* to correct; *(exercice, devoir)* to mark; **c. qn** to give sb a beating; **c. qn de qch** to cure sb of sth **2 se corriger** *upr* to mend one's ways; **se c. de qch** to cure oneself of sth ▪ **corrigé** *nm (d'exercice)* correct answers (**de** to)

corroborer [kɔrɔbɔre] *vt* to corroborate

corroder [kɔrɔde] *vt* to corrode ▪ **corrosif, -ive** *adj* corrosive ▪ **corrosion** *nf* corrosion

corrompre* [kɔrɔ̃pr] *vt (personne, goût)* to corrupt; *(soudoyer)* to bribe ▪ **corrompu, -e** *adj* corrupt ▪ **corruption** *nf (par l'argent)* bribery; *(vice)* corruption

corsage [kɔrsaʒ] *nm* blouse

corsaire [kɔrsɛr] *nm* (**a**) *Hist (marin)* corsair (**b**) *(pantalon)* pedal pushers

Corse [kɔrs] *nf* **la C.** Corsica ▪ **corse 1** *adj* Corsican **2** *nmf* **C.** Corsican

corser [kɔrse] **1** *vt (plat)* to spice up; *Fig (récit)* to liven up **2 se corser** *upr* **ça se corse** things getting complicated ▪ **corsé, -ée** *adj (café) Br* full-flavoured, *Am* full-flavored; *(vin)* full-bodied; *Fig (histoire)* spicy

corset [kɔrsɛ] *nm* corset

cortège [kɔrtɛʒ] *nm (défilé)* procession; **c. funèbre** funeral cortège

corvée [kɔrve] *nf* chore; *Mil* fatigue duty

cosmétique [kɔsmetik] *adj & nm* cosmetic

cosmopolite [kɔsmɔpɔlit] *adj* cosmopolitan

cosmos [kɔsmos] *nm (univers)* cosmos; *(espace)* outer space ▪ **cosmique** *adj* cosmic ▪ **cosmonaute** *nmf* cosmonaut

cosse [kɔs] *nf (de pois)* pod

cossu, -e [kɔsy] *adj (personne)* well-to-do; *(maison, intérieur)* opulent

costard [kɔstar] *nm Fam* suit

costaud, -aude [kɔsto, -od] **1** *adj (personne)* sturdy; *(alcool, épice)* strong **2** *nm* sturdy man

costume [kɔstym] *nm (habit)* costume; *(complet)* suit

cotation [kɔtasjɔ̃] *nf* **c. (en Bourse)** quotation (on the Stock Exchange)

cote [kɔt] *nf (marque de classement)* classification mark; *(valeur)* quotation; *(liste)* share index; *(de cheval)* odds; *(altitude)* altitude; *Fam* **avoir la c.** to be popular; **c. d'alerte** danger level; **c. de popularité** popularity rating

côte [kot] *nf* (**a**) *(os)* rib; **à côtes** *(étoffe)* ribbed; **c. à c.** side by side; **se tenir les côtes (de rire)** to split one's sides (laughing); **c. d'agneau/de porc** lamb/pork chop; **c. de bœuf** rib of beef (**b**) *(de montagne)* slope (**c**) *(littoral)* coast; **la C. d'Azur** the French Riviera

côté [kote] *nm* side; **de l'autre c.** on the other side (**de** of); *(direction)* the other way; **de ce c.** *(passer)* this way; **du c. de** *(près de)* near; **à c.** close by, nearby; *(pièce)* in the other room; *(maison)* next door; **la maison d'à c.** the house

next door; **à c. de qn/qch** next to sb/sth; *(en comparaison de)* compared to sb/sth; **passer à c.** *(balle)* to fall wide (**de** of); **à mes côtés** by my side; **mettre qch de c.** to put sth aside; **venir de tous côtés** to come from all directions; **d'un c.... d'un autre c....** on the one hand... on the other hand...; **de mon c.** for my part; **le bon c. de qch** the bright side of sth; *Fam* **c. argent** moneywise

coteau, -x [kɔto] *nm* hill; *(versant)* hillside

côtelé, -ée [kotle] *adj* **velours c.** corduroy

côtelette [kotlɛt] *nf (d'agneau, de porc)* chop

coter [kɔte] *vt (prix, action)* to quote ▪ **coté, -ée** *adj* **bien c.** highly rated; **c. en Bourse** quoted on the Stock Market

côtier, -ière [kotje, -jɛr] *adj* coastal; *(pêche)* inshore

cotiser [kɔtize] **1** *vi (à un cadeau, pour la retraite)* to contribute (**à** to; **pour** towards) **2 se cotiser** *upr Br* to club together, *Am* to club in ▪ **cotisation** *nf (de club)* dues, subscription; *(de retraite, de chômage)* contribution

coton [kɔtɔ̃] *nm* cotton; **c. hydrophile** *Br* cotton wool, *Am* absorbent cotton ▪ **cotonnade** *nf* cotton fabric

côtoyer [kotwaje] *vt (personnes)* to mix with; *Fig (rivière, forêt)* to border on

cotte [kɔt] *nf* **c. de maille** coat of mail

cou [ku] *nm* neck; **sauter au c. de qn** to throw one's arms around sb; *Fam* **endetté jusqu'au c.** up to one's ears in debt

couche [kuʃ] *nf* (**a**) *(épaisseur)* layer; *(de peinture)* coat; **couches sociales** levels of society; **la c. d'ozone** the ozone layer; *Fam* **il en tient une c.!** he's really stupid (**b**) *(linge de bébé) Br* nappy, *Am* diaper ▪ **couche-culotte** *(pl couches-culottes) nf Br* disposable nappy, *Am* disposable diaper

coucher [kuʃe] **1** *nm (moment)* bedtime; **l'heure du c.** bedtime; **au c.** at bedtime; **c. de soleil** sunset **2** *vt (allonger)* to lay down; **c. qn** to put sb to bed; **c. qn sur son testament** to mention sb in one's will **3** *vi* to sleep (**avec** with) **4 se coucher** *upr (personne)* to go to bed; *(s'allonger)* to lie down; *(soleil)* to set, to go down; **aller se c.** to go to bed ▪ **couchant 1** *adj m* **soleil c.** setting sun **2** *nm* **le c.** *(ouest)* the west ▪ **couché, -ée** *adj* **être c.** to be in bed; *(étendu)* to be lying (down)

couchette [kuʃɛt] *nf (de train)* couchette; *(de bateau)* bunk

couci-couça [kusikusa] *adv Fam* so-so

coucou [kuku] **1** *nm (oiseau)* cuckoo; *(pendule)* cuckoo clock; *(fleur)* cowslip **2** *exclam (me voilà)* peek-a-boo!; *(pour dire bonjour)* cooee!

coude [kud] *nm* elbow; *(tournant)* bend; **donner un coup de c. à qn** to nudge sb; **pousser qn du c.** to nudge sb; **être au c. à c.** to be neck and neck; *Fig* **se serrer les coudes** to stick together

cou-de-pied [kudpje] (*pl* **cous-de-pied**) *nm* instep

coudre* [kudr] *vti* to sew

couenne [kwan] *nf (de lard)* rind

couette¹ [kwɛt] *nf (édredon)* duvet

couette² [kwɛt] *nf Fam (coiffure)* bunch; **se faire des couettes** to put one's hair in bunches

couffin [kufɛ̃] *nm (de bébé) Br* Moses basket, *Am* bassinet

couillon, -onne [kujɔ̃, -ɔn] *nmf très Fam* twat

couiner [kwine] *vi (animal)* to squeal; *(enfant)* to whine

coulée [kule] *nf* **c. de lave** lava flow; **c. de boue** mudslide

couler [kule] **1** *vt* (**a**) *(métal, statue)* to cast; *(liquide, ciment)* to lead; (**b**) *(navire)* to sink; *Fig* **c. qn** to bring sb down **2** *vi* (**a**) *(eau, rivière)* to flow; *(nez, sueur)* to run; *(robinet)* to leak; *Fig* **faire c. un bain** to run a bath; **faire c. le sang** to cause bloodshed; *Fig* **c. de source** to be obvious (**b**) *(bateau, nageur)* to sink; **c. à pic** to sink to the bottom **3 se couler** *vpr* **se c. dans** *(passer)* to slip into; *Fam* **se la c. douce** to take things easy ▪ **coulant, -ante** *adj (fromage)* runny; *Fig (style)* flowing; *Fam (personne)* easy-going

couleur [kulœr] *nf (teinte) Br* colour, *Am* color; *(colorant)* paint; *(pour cheveux)* dye; *Cartes* suit; **couleurs** *(de drapeau, de club)* colours; **de quelle c. est...?** what colour is...?; **prendre des couleurs** to get some colour in one's cheeks; *Fam* **il nous en a fait voir de toutes les couleurs** he gave us a hard time; **homme de c.** coloured man; **boîte de couleurs** paintbox; **photo en couleurs** colour photo; **télévision c.** *ou* **en couleurs** colour television set

couleuvre [kulœvr] *nf* grass snake

coulis [kuli] *nm* **c. de tomates** tomato coulis

coulisse [kulis] *nf (de porte)* runner; **porte à c.** sliding door; *Théâtre* **les coulisses** the wings; *Théâtre & Fig* **dans les coulisses** behind the scenes ▪ **coulissant, -ante** *adj (porte, panneau)* sliding

couloir [kulwar] *nm (de maison, de train)* corridor; *(en natation, en athlétisme)* lane; **c. aérien** air corridor; **c. de bus** bus lane

coup [ku] *nm* (**a**) *(choc)* blow; *(essai)* attempt, go; *Échecs* move; **donner un c. à qn** to hit sb; **se donner un c. contre qch** to knock against sth; **donner un c. de bâton à qn** to hit sb with a stick; **donner un c. de couteau à qn** to knife sb; **c. de pied** kick; **donner un c. de pied à qn** to kick sb; **c. de poing** punch; **donner un c. de poing à qn** to punch sb; *Fig* **donner un c. de main à qn** to give sb a hand; **c. de tête** header; **mauvais c.** piece of mischief; *Fam* **sale c.** dirty trick; *Fam* **c. dur** nasty blow

(**b**) *(action soudaine, événement soudain)* **c. de vent** gust of wind; **donner un c. de frein** to brake; **prendre un c. de soleil** to get sunburned; *Fam* **avoir un c. de barre** to have the munchies; *Fig* **ça a été le c. de foudre** it was love at first sight; **c. de chance** stroke of luck; **c. d'État** coup; *Fam* **c. de pub** publicity stunt; **c. de théâtre** coup de théâtre

(**c**) *(bruit)* **c. de feu** shot; **c. de fusil** shot; **c. de sifflet** whistle; **c. de sonnette** ring; **c. de tonnerre** clap of thunder; **sur le c. de midi** on the stroke of twelve; **l'horloge sonna deux coups** the clock struck two

(**d**) *(expressions)* **après c.** after the event; **sur le c.** *(alors)* at the time; **tué sur le c.** killed outright; **à c. sûr** for certain; **c. sur c.** one after the other; **tout à c., tout d'un c.** suddenly; **d'un seul c.** *(avaler)* in one go; *(soudain)* all of a sudden; **du premier c.** at the first attempt; *Fam* **du c.** and so; **sous le c. de la colère** in a fit of anger; **faire les quatre cents coups** to sow one's wild oats; **tenir le c.** to hold out; **tomber sous le c. de la loi** to be an offence; *Fam* **tenter le c.** to have a go; *Fam* **réussir son c.** to be a great success; *Fam* **il est dans le c.** he's in the know; *Football & Rugby* **c. d'envoi** kickoff; **c. de maître** masterstroke; *Tennis* **c. droit** forehand; *Football* **c. franc** free kick; **c. monté** put-up job

coupable [kupabl] **1** *adj* guilty (**de** of); *(négligence)* culpable; **se sentir c.** to feel guilty **2** *nmf* culprit

coupe¹ [kup] *nf (trophée)* cup; *(récipient)* bowl; **la C. du monde** the World Cup; **c. à champagne** champagne glass

coupe² [kup] *nf (de vêtement)* cut; *(plan)* section; *Fig* **être sous la c. de qn** to be under sb's thumb; **c. de cheveux** haircut ▪ **coupe-faim** *nm inv* appetite suppressant ▪ **coupe-gorge** *nm inv* cut-throat alley ▪ **coupe-ongles** *nm inv* nail clippers ▪ **coupe-papier** *nm inv* paper knife, letter opener ▪ **coupe-vent** *nm inv (blouson) Br* windcheater, *Am* Windbreaker®

couper [kupe] **1** *vt (trancher, supprimer)* to cut; *(arbre)* to cut down; **c. le courant** *(pour réparation)* to switch off the current; *(pour non-paiement)* to cut off the power; **c. la parole à qn** to cut sb short; **c. l'appétit à qn** to spoil sb's appetite; **c. les cheveux à qn** to cut sb's hair; *Fig* **c. les cheveux en quatre** to split hairs; **être coupé du monde** to be cut off from the outside world; **nous avons été coupés** *(au téléphone)* we were cut off; *Fam* **j'en donnerais ma main** *ou* **ma tête à c.** I'd stake my life on it **2** *vi (être tranchant)* to be sharp; *(aux cartes)* to cut; *(prendre un raccourci)* to take a short cut; **c. à travers champs** to cut across country; **c. court à qn** to cut sb short; *Fam* **c. à qch** *(se dérober)* to get out of sth; **ne coupez pas!** *(au* *téléphone)* hold the line! **3 se couper** *vpr (routes)* to intersect; **se c. au doigt** to cut one's finger; **se c. les cheveux** to cut one's hair ▪**coupant, -ante** *adj* sharp ▪**coupé** *nm (voiture)* coupé ▪**couper-coller** *nm inv Ordinat* cut and paste; **faire un c. sur qch** to cut and paste sth

couperet [kupʀɛ] *nm (de boucher)* cleaver; *(de guillotine)* blade

couperosé, -ée [kupʀoze] *adj (visage)* blotchy

couple [kupl] *nm* couple

couplet [kuplɛ] *nm* verse

coupole [kupɔl] *nf* dome

coupon [kupɔ̃] *nm (tissu)* remnant; **c. de réduction** money-off coupon; **c.-réponse** reply coupon

coupure [kupyʀ] *nf (blessure)* cut; **5 000 euros en petites coupures** 5,000 euros in small notes; **c. d'électricité** *ou* **de courant** blackout, *Br* power cut; **c. de presse** newspaper cutting

cour [kuʀ] *nf* (**a**) *(de maison, de ferme)* yard; **c. de récréation** *Br* playground, *Am* schoolyard (**b**) *(de roi, tribunal)* court; **c. d'appel** court of appeal; **c. d'assises** Assize Court, *Br* ≃ crown court, *Am* ≃ circuit court; **c. de cassation** ≃ Supreme Court of Appeal (**c**) **faire la c. à qn** to court sb

courage [kuʀaʒ] *nm* courage; **perdre c.** to lose heart; **s'armer de c.** to pluck up courage; **bon c.!** good luck! ▪**courageux, -euse** *adj (brave)* courageous; *(énergique)* spirited ▪**courageusement** *adv (bravely)* courageously

couramment [kuʀamɑ̃] *adv (parler)* fluently; *(généralement)* commonly

courant, -ante [kuʀɑ̃, -ɑ̃t] **1** *adj (commun)* common; *(en cours)* current; *Com* **le dix c.** the tenth of this month, *Br* the tenth inst. **2** *nm (de rivière)* current; **dans le c. du mois** during the course of the month; **être au c. de qch** to know about sth; **mettre qn au c. de qch** to tell sb about sth; **c. d'air** *Br* draught, *Am* draft; **c. électrique** electric current

> Il faut noter que l'adjectif anglais **current** est un faux ami. Il signifie **actuel**.

courbature [kuʀbatyʀ] *nf* ache; **avoir des courbatures** to be aching (all over) ▪**courbaturé, -ée** *adj* aching (all over)

courbe [kuʀb] **1** *adj* curved **2** *nf* curve; **c. de niveau** contour line ▪**courber 1** *vti* to bend **2 se courber** *vpr (personne)* to bend down; **se c. en deux** to bend double

courge [kuʀʒ] *nf Br* marrow, *Am* squash ▪**courgette** *nf Br* courgette, *Am* zucchini

courir* [kuʀiʀ] **1** *vi* to run; *(à une course automobile)* to race; **c. après qn/qch** to run after sb/sth; **c. à sa perte** to be heading for disaster; **descendre une colline en courant** to run down a hill; *Fam* **faire qch en courant** to do

sth in a rush; **faire c. un bruit** to spread a rumour; **le bruit court que...** rumour has it that...; **le voleur court toujours** the thief is still at large **2** *vt* **c. un risque** to run a risk; **c. le 100 mètres** to run the 100 *Br* metres *or Am* meters; **c. le monde** to roam the world; **c. les théâtres** to go to the theatre all the time; **c. les filles** to chase women ▪**coureur, -euse** *nmf (sportif)* runner; *(cycliste)* cyclist; **c. automobile** racing driver; **c. de jupons** womanizer

couronne [kuʀɔn] *nf (de roi, de reine)* crown; *(pour enterrement)* wreath; *(de dent)* crown ▪**couronnement** [-əmɑ̃] *nm (de roi)* coronation; *Fig (réussite)* crowning achievement ▪**couronner** *vt (roi)* to crown; *(auteur, ouvrage)* to award a prize to; **leurs efforts furent couronnés de succès** their efforts were crowned with success; **et pour c. le tout...** and to crown it all...

courriel [kuʀjɛl] *(abrév* **courrier électronique)** *nm Can Ordinat* e-mail

courrier [kuʀje] *nm (lettres)* mail, *Br* post; **j'ai du c. à faire** I have (some) letters to write; **par retour du c.** *Br* by return of post, *Am* by return mail; *Journ* **c. du cœur** problem page; **c. électronique** e-mail; *Fam* **c. escargot** snail mail

courroie [kuʀwa] *nf (attache)* strap

courroux [kuʀu] *nm Littéraire* wrath

cours [kuʀ] *nm* (**a**) *(de rivière, d'astre)* course; *(de monnaie)* currency; *Fin (d'action)* price; **suivre son c.** to run its course; **suivre le c. de ses pensées** to follow one's train of thoughts; **donner libre c. à qch** to give free rein to sth; **avoir c.** *(monnaie)* to be legal tender; *(pratique)* to be current; **en c.** *(travail)* in progress; *(année)* current; *(affaires)* outstanding; **en c. de route** on the way; **au c. de qch** in the course of sth; **c. d'eau** river, stream (**b**) *(leçon)* class; *(série de leçons)* course; *(conférence)* lecture; *(établissement)* school; **faire c.** to teach; **aller en c.** to go to school; **suivre un c.** to take a course; **c. magistral** lecture; **c. particulier** private lesson; **c. du soir** evening class; *Scol* **c. moyen** = fourth and fifth years of primary school; *Scol* **c. préparatoire** = first year of primary school (**c**) *(allée)* avenue

course¹ [kuʀs] *nf (action de courir)* running; *Sport (épreuve)* race; *(discipline)* racing; *(trajet en taxi)* journey; *(de projectile, de planète)* course; **les courses de chevaux** the races; **faire la c. avec qn** to race sb; *Fam* **il n'est plus dans la c.** he's out of touch; **c. automobile** motor race; **c. cycliste** cycle race

course² [kuʀs] *nf (commission)* errand; **courses** *(achats)* shopping; **faire une c.** to get something from the shops; **faire des courses** to go shopping; **faire les courses** to do the shopping

coursier, -ière [kursje, -jɛr] *nmf* messenger, courier

court, -e [kur, kurt] **1** *adj* short; *Fam* **c'est un peu c.** that's not very much **2** *adv* short; **prendre qn de c.** *(en lui laissant peu de temps)* to give sb short notice; **pris de c.** caught unawares; **on l'appelle Charles tout c.** people just call him Charles; **à c. d'argent** short of money **3** *nm* **c. (de tennis)** tennis court ▪ **court-bouillon** *(pl* **courts-bouillons)** *nm* court-bouillon ▪ **court-circuit** *(pl* **courts-circuits)** *nm* short-circuit ▪ **court-circuiter** *vt* to short-circuit; *Fig Fam* **c. la filière normale** to bypass the usual procedures

courtier, -ière [kurtje, -jɛr] *nmf* broker

courtisan [kurtizɑ̃] *nm Hist* courtier ▪ **courtisane** *nf Littéraire* courtesan ▪ **courtiser** *vt (femme)* to court

courtois, -oise [kurtwa, -waz] *adj* courteous ▪ **courtoisie** *nf* courtesy

couru, -e [kury] *adj (spectacle, lieu)* popular; *Fam* **c'est c. d'avance** it's a sure thing

couscous [kuskus] *nm* couscous

cousin, -ine [kuzɛ̃, -in] **1** *nmf* cousin; **c. germain** first cousin **2** *nm (insecte)* mosquito

coussin [kusɛ̃] *nm* cushion; **c. d'air** air cushion

cousu, -e [kuzy] *adj* sewn; **c. main** hand-sewn

coût [ku] *nm* cost; **le c. de la vie** the cost of living ▪ **coûter** *vti* to cost; **ça coûte combien?** how much is it?, how much does it cost?; *Fig* **ça coûte les yeux de la tête** it costs the earth or an arm and a leg; *Fig* **cette erreur va vous c. cher** that error will cost you dearly; **coûte que coûte** at all costs

couteau, -x [kuto] *nm* knife; *Fig* **être à couteaux tirés avec qn** to be at daggers drawn with sb; *Fig* **retourner le c. dans la plaie** to rub it in; **c. à pain** breadknife; **c.-scie** serrated knife; **c. suisse** Swiss army knife

coûteux, -euse [kutø, -øz] *adj* costly, expensive

coutume [kutym] *nf (habitude, tradition)* custom; **avoir c. de faire qch** to be accustomed to doing sth; **comme de c.** as usual ▪ **coutumier, -ière** *adj* customary

couture [kutyr] *nf (activité)* sewing, needlework; *(raccord)* seam; **faire de la c.** to sew ▪ **couturier** *nm* fashion designer ▪ **couturière** *nf* dressmaker

couvent [kuvɑ̃] *nm (de religieuses)* convent; *(de moines)* monastery; *(pensionnat)* convent school

couver [kuve] **1** *vt (œufs)* to sit on; *Fig (personne)* to mollycoddle; *(maladie)* to be coming down with **2** *vi (poule)* to brood; *(feu) Br* to smoulder, *Am* to smolder; *(mal, complot)* to be brewing ▪ **couvée** *nf (petits oiseaux)* brood; *(œufs)* clutch ▪ **couveuse** *nf (pour nouveaux-nés)* incubator

couvercle [kuvɛrkl] *nm* lid; *(vissé)* cap

couvert¹ [kuvɛr] *nm* (**a**) **mettre le c.** to set or *Br* lay the table; **table de cinq couverts** table set or *Br* laid for five; **couverts** *(ustensiles)* cutlery (**b**) **sous le c. de** *(sous l'apparence de)* under cover of; **se mettre à c.** to take cover

couvert², -e [kuvɛr, -ɛrt] **1** *pp de* **couvrir 2** *adj* covered (**de** with or in); *(ciel)* overcast; **être bien c.** *(habillé chaudement)* to be warmly dressed

couverture [kuvɛrtyr] *nf (de lit)* blanket; *(de livre, de magazine)* cover; *(de bâtiment)* roofing; *Journ* coverage; **c. chauffante** electric blanket; **c. sociale** social security cover

couvrir* [kuvrir] **1** *vt* to cover (**de** with); *(bruit)* to drown; **c. qn de cadeaux** to shower sb with gifts **2 se couvrir** *vpr (s'habiller)* to wrap up; *(se coiffer)* to cover one's head; *(ciel)* to cloud over; **se c. de ridicule** to cover oneself with ridicule ▪ **couvre-chef** *(pl* **couvre-chefs)** *nm Hum* headgear ▪ **couvre-feu** *(pl* **couvre-feux)** *nm* curfew ▪ **couvre-lit** *(pl* **couvre-lits)** *nm* bedspread ▪ **couvreur** *nm* roofer

covoiturage [kovwatyraʒ] *nm* car-pooling

cow-boy [kɔbɔj] *(pl* **cow-boys)** *nm* cowboy

CP [sepe] *(abrév* **cours préparatoire)** *nm Scol* = first year of primary school

CPE [sepeə] *(abrév* **conseiller principal d'éducation)** *nm inv Scol* school administrator

crabe [krab] *nm* crab

crac [krak] *exclam (objet qui casse)* snap!

cracher [kraʃe] **1** *vt* to spit out; **c. du sang** to spit blood **2** *vi (personne)* to spit; *(stylo)* to splutter; *(radio)* to crackle; *Fam* **c. dans la soupe** to bite the hand that feeds one ▪ **crachat** *nm* gob of spit; **crachats** spit ▪ **craché** *adj Fam* **c'est son père tout c.** he's the spitting image of his mother

crachin [kraʃɛ̃] *nm (fine)* drizzle

crack [krak] *nm Fam (champion)* ace; *(drogue)* crack

crade [krad], **cradingue** [kradɛ̃g] *adj Fam* filthy, *Br* grotty

craie [krɛ] *nf (matière)* chalk; *(bâton)* stick of chalk; **écrire qch à la c.** to write sth in chalk

craignos [krɛɲos] *adj Fam (louche)* shady, *Br* dodgy

craindre* [krɛ̃dr] **1** *vt (redouter)* to be afraid of, to fear; *(chaleur, froid)* to be sensitive to; **c. de faire qch** to be afraid of doing sth; **je crains qu'elle ne soit partie** I'm afraid she's left; **ne craignez rien** *(n'ayez pas peur)* don't be afraid; *(ne vous inquiétez pas)* don't worry **2** *vi Fam* **ça craint!** *(c'est ennuyeux)* what a pain!; *(c'est louche)* it's dodgy

crainte [krɛ̃t] *nf* fear; **de c. de faire qch** for fear of doing sth; **de c. qu'on ne l'entende** for fear of being overheard ▪ **craintif, -ive** *adj* timid

cramoisi, -ie [kramwazi] *adj* crimson

crampe [krɑ̃p] nf cramp

crampon [krɑ̃pɔ̃] nm (de chaussure) stud; (pour l'alpinisme) crampon

cramponner [krɑ̃pɔne] **se cramponner** vpr to hold on; **se c. à qn/qch** to hold on to sb/sth

cran [krɑ̃] nm (a) (entaille) notch; (de ceinture) hole; Fig **avancer d'un c.** to go up a notch; **c. d'arrêt** ou **de sûreté** safety catch (b) Fam (courage) guts; **avoir du c.** to have guts (c) Fam **être à c.** (excédé) to be wound up

crâne [krɑn] nm skull; Fam **mets-toi ça dans la c.!** get that into your head! ▪ **crânien, -ienne** adj Anat cranial; **boîte crânienne** skull, cranium

crâner [krɑne] vi Fam to show off

crapaud [krapo] nm toad

crapule [krapyl] nf villain, scoundrel ▪ **crapuleux, -euse** adj (malhonnête) villainous; **crime c.** = crime committed for financial gain

> Il faut noter que l'adjectif anglais **crapulous** est un faux ami. Il signifie **intempérant**.

craqueler [krakle] vt, **se craqueler** vpr to crack

craquer [krake] **1** vt (allumette) to strike **2** vi (branche) to crack; (escalier) to creak; (se casser) to snap; (se déchirer) to rip; Fam (personne) to crack up ▪ **craquements** nmpl cracking/creaking

crasse [kras] **1** nf filth **2** adj (ignorance) crass ▪ **crasseux, -euse** adj filthy

cratère [kratɛr] nm crater

cravache [kravaʃ] nf riding crop

cravate [kravat] nf tie

crawl [krol] nm crawl; **nager le c.** to do the crawl ▪ **crawlé** adj m **dos c.** backstroke

crayeux, -euse [krɛjø, -jøz] adj chalky

crayon [krɛjɔ̃] nm (en bois) pencil; **c. de couleur** coloured pencil; (en cire) crayon; **c. à lèvres** lip pencil

créance [kreɑ̃s] nf debt ▪ **créancier, -ière** nmf creditor

créateur, -trice [kreatœr, -tris] **1** adj creative **2** nmf creator, designer ▪ **créatif, -ive** adj creative ▪ **création** nf creation; **1 000 créations d'emplois** 1,000 new jobs ▪ **créativité** nf creativity

créature [kreatyr] nf (être vivant) creature

crécelle [kresɛl] nf rattle; **quelle c.!** (bavard) what a chatterbox!

crèche [krɛʃ] nf (de Noël) manger, Br crib; (garderie) (day) nursery, Br crèche ▪ **crécher** vi Fam (habiter) to live; (passer la nuit) to crash

crédible [kredibl] adj credible ▪ **crédibilité** nf credibility

crédit [kredi] nm (prêt, influence) credit; **crédits** (somme d'argent) funds; **à c.** on credit; **faire c. à qn** to give sb credit ▪ **créditer** vt (compte) to credit (**de** with); Fig **c. qn de qch** to give sb credit for sth ▪ **créditeur, -trice** adj **solde c.** credit balance; **être c.** to be in credit

crédule [kredyl] adj credulous ▪ **crédulité** nf credulity

créer [kree] vt to create

crémaillère [kremajɛr] nf **pendre la c.** to have a housewarming (party)

crématoire [krematwar] adj **four c.** Br crematorium, Am crematory

crématorium [krematɔrjɔm] nm Br crematorium, Am crematory

crème [krɛm] **1** nf (de lait, dessert, cosmétique) cream; **c. anglaise** custard; **c. Chantilly** whipped cream; **c. glacée** ice cream; **c. à raser** shaving cream; **c. solaire** sun cream, suntan cream **2** adj inv Br cream(-coloured), Am cream(-colored) **3** nm Fam coffee with milk, Br white coffee ▪ **crémerie** nf (magasin) dairy ▪ **crémeux, -euse** adj creamy

créneau, -x [kreno] nm Com niche; TV, Radio slot; **créneaux** (de château) Br crenellations, Am crenelations; **faire un c.** (pour se garer) to reverse into a parking space

créole [kreɔl] **1** adj creole **2** nmf Creole **3** nm (langue) Creole

crêpe [krɛp] **1** nf pancake **2** nm (tissu) crepe; (caoutchouc) crepe (rubber) ▪ **crêperie** nf crêperie, pancake restaurant

crépi, -e [krepi] adj & nm roughcast

crépiter [krepite] vi (feu) to crackle ▪ **crépitement** nm (du feu) crackling

crépu, -e [krepy] adj (cheveux) frizzy

crépuscule [krepyskyl] nm twilight

crescendo [kreʃɛndo] adv & nm crescendo

cresson [kresɔ̃] nm cress; **c. de fontaine** watercress

Crète [krɛt] nf la C. Crete

crête [krɛt] nf (de montagne, d'oiseau, de vague) crest; **c. de coq** cockscomb

crétin, -e [kretɛ̃, -in] nmf Fam cretin

creuser [krøze] **1** vt (trou, puits) to dig; (évider) to hollow (out); Fig (idée) to look into; **c. la terre** to dig **2** vi; Fam **ça creuse** it whets the appetite **3** **se creuser** vpr (joues) to become hollow; Fig (abîme) to form; Fam **se c. la tête** ou **la cervelle** to rack one's brains

creuset [krøze] nm (récipient) crucible; Fig (lieu) melting pot

creux, -euse [krø, -øz] **1** adj (tube, joues, arbre, paroles) hollow; (sans activité) slack; **assiette creuse** soup plate; Fam **avoir le ventre c.** to be hungry **2** nm hollow; (moment) slack period; **le c. des reins** the small of the back; Fig **être au c. de la vague** to have hit rock bottom

crevaison [krəvɛzɔ̃] nf (de pneu) flat, Br puncture

crevasse [krəvas] nf (trou) crack; (de glacier) crevasse; **avoir des crevasses aux mains** to have chapped hands

crève [krɛv] nf très Fam **avoir la c.** to have a stinking cold

crever [krəve] **1** *vt (ballon, bulle)* to burst; *Fam (épuiser)* to wear out; **ça crève le cœur** it's heartbreaking; *Fam* **ça crève les yeux** it sticks out a mile **2** *vi (bulle, ballon, pneu)* to burst; *Fam* **c. de jalousie** to be bursting with jealousy; *Fam* **c. d'ennui/de froid** to be bored/to freeze to death; *Fam* **c. de faim** to be starving; *Fam* **je crève de chaud** I'm boiling ▪ **crevant, -ante** *adj Fam (fatigant)* exhausting ▪ **crevé, -ée** *adj (ballon, pneu)* burst; *Fam (fatigué)* worn out, *Br* dead beat ▪ **crève-cœur** *nm inv* heartbreak

crevette [krəvet] *nf (grise)* shrimp; *(rose)* prawn

cri [kri] *nm (de personne)* cry, shout; *(perçant)* scream; *(d'animal)* cry; **c. de guerre** war cry ▪ **criard, -arde** *adj (son)* shrill; *(couleur)* loud

criant, -ante [krijā, -āt] *adj (injustice, preuve)* glaring; **c. de vérité** *(témoignage)* obviously true

crible [kribl] *nm* sieve ▪ **criblé, -ée** *adj* **c. de balles/dettes** riddled with bullets/debts

cric [krik] *nm* jack

cricket [kriket] *nm* cricket

crier [krije] **1** *vt (injure, ordre)* to shout (**à** to); **c. vengeance** to cry out for vengeance; **c. son innocence** to protest one's innocence **2** *vi (personne)* to shout, to cry out; *(fort)* to scream; *(parler très fort)* to shout; **c. au scandale** to protest; **c. au secours** to shout for help; *Fam* **c. après qn** to shout at sb

crime [krim] *nm* crime; *(assassinat)* murder; **crimes de guerre** war crimes ▪ **criminalité** *nf* crime ▪ **criminel, -elle** **1** *adj* criminal **2** *nmf* criminal; *(assassin)* murderer

crin [krɛ̃] *nm* horsehair; *Fig* **à tous crins** out-and-out ▪ **crinière** *nf* mane

crique [krik] *nf* creek

criquet [krike] *nm* locust

crise [kriz] *nf* crisis; *(de maladie)* attack; *Fam* **faire** *ou* **piquer une c.** to throw a fit; **c. de colère** fit of anger; **c. de conscience** *(moral)* dilemma; **c. de nerfs** fit of hysteria

crisper [krispe] **1** *vt (poing)* to clench; *(muscle)* to tense; *Fam* **c. qn** to irritate sb **2 se crisper** *upr (visage)* to tense; *(personne)* to get tense ▪ **crispant, -ante** *adj Fam* irritating ▪ **crispé, -ée** *adj (personne)* tense

crisser [krise] *vi (pneu, roue)* to squeal; *(neige)* to crunch

cristal, -aux [kristal, -o] *nm* crystal; **cristaux** *(objets)* crystal(ware); *(de sels)* crystals; *Tech* **cristaux liquides** liquid crystal ▪ **cristallin, -ine** *adj (eau, son)* crystal-clear ▪ **cristalliser** *vti*, **se cristalliser** *upr* to crystallize

critère [kriter] *nm* criterion

critérium [kriterjɔm] *nm (épreuve sportive)* heat

critique [kritik] **1** *adj (situation, phase)* critical **2** *nf (reproche)* criticism; *(de film, de livre)* review; **faire la c. de** *(film)* to review; **affronter la c.** to confront the critics **3** *nm* critic ▪ **critiquer** *vt* to criticize

croasser [krɔase] *vi* to caw

Croatie [krɔasi] *nf* **la C.** Croatia ▪ **croate** [krɔat] **1** *adj* Croat, Croatian **2** *nmf* **C.** Croat, Croatian **3** *nm (langue)* Croat, Croatian

croc [kro] *nm (crochet)* hook; *(dent)* fang; *Fam* **avoir les crocs** to be starving

croc-en-jambe [krɔkāʒɑ̃b] *(pl* **crocs-en-jambe)** *nm* trip; **faire un c. à qn** to trip sb up

croche [krɔʃ] *nf Mus Br* quaver, *Am* eighth (note)

croche-pied [krɔʃpje] *nm* trip; **faire un c. à qn** to trip sb up

crochet [krɔʃɛ] *nm (pour accrocher)* & *Boxe* hook; *(aiguille)* crochet hook; *(parenthèse)* square bracket; **faire du c.** to crochet; **faire un c.** *(détour)* to make a detour; *(route)* to make a sudden turn; *Fam* **vivre aux crochets de qn** to live off sb ▪ **crocheter** *vt (serrure)* to pick

crochu, -e [krɔʃy] *adj (nez)* hooked; *(doigts)* claw-like

crocodile [krɔkɔdil] *nm* crocodile

crocus [krɔkys] *nm* crocus

croire* [krwar] **1** *vt* to believe; *(penser)* to think (**que** that); **j'ai cru la voir** I thought I saw her; **je crois que oui** I think *or* believe so; **je n'en crois pas mes yeux** I can't believe my eyes; **à l'en c.** according to him/her **2** *vi (personne, talent, Dieu)* to believe (**à** *ou* **en** in) **3 se croire** *upr* **il se croit malin** he thinks he's smart

croisé¹ [krwaze] *nm Hist* crusader ▪ **croisade** *nf Hist* crusade

croiser [krwaze] **1** *vt (passer)* to pass; *(ligne)* to cross; *(espèce)* to crossbreed; **c. les jambes** to cross one's legs; **c. les bras** to fold one's arms; **c. le regard de qn** to meet sb's gaze; *Fig* **c. les doigts** to keep one's fingers crossed **2** *vi (navire)* to cruise **3 se croiser** *upr (voitures)* to pass each other; *(lignes, routes)* to cross, to intersect; *(lettres)* to cross; *(regards)* to meet ▪ **croisé², -ée** *adj (bras)* folded; *(veston)* double-breasted ▪ **croisement** *nm (de routes)* crossroads *(sing)*, intersection; *(d'animaux)* crossing

croisière [krwazjer] *nf* cruise; **faire une c.** to go on a cruise; **navire de c.** cruise ship

croître* [krwatr] *vi (plante)* to grow; *(augmenter)* to increase, to grow (**de** by); *(lune)* to wax ▪ **croissance** *nf* growth ▪ **croissant, -ante 1** *adj (nombre)* growing **2** *nm* crescent; *(pâtisserie)* croissant

croix [krwa] *nf* cross; **la C.-Rouge** the Red Cross

croquer [krɔke] **1** *vt (manger)* to crunch; *(peindre)* to sketch; **joli à c.** pretty as a picture **2** *vi (fruit)* to be crunchy; **c. dans qch** to bite into sth ▪ **croquant, -ante** *adj* crunchy ▪ **croque-monsieur** *nm inv* = toasted cheese and ham sandwich ▪ **croque-mort** *(pl* **croque-morts)** *nm Fam* undertaker ▪ **croquette** *nf Culin* croquette

croquis [krɔki] *nm* sketch; **faire un c. de qch** to make a sketch of sth

crosse [krɔs] *nf (de fusil)* butt; *(de hockey)* stick; *(d'évêque)* crook

crotte [krɔt] *nf (de mouton, de lapin)* droppings; **c. de chien** dog dirt ▪ **crotté, -ée** *adj* dirty, muddy ▪ **crottin** *nm* dung; *(fromage)* small goat's-milk cheese

crouler [krule] *vi (édifice)* to crumble; **c. sous le poids de qch** to give way under the weight of sth; **c. sous le travail** to be snowed under with work ▪ **croulant, -ante 1** *adj (mur)* crumbling **2** *nm Fam* **vieux c.** old wrinkly

croupe [krup] *nf* rump; **monter en c.** to ride behind ▪ **croupion** *nm (de poulet) Br* parson's nose, *Am* pope's nose

croupier [krupje] *nm* croupier

croupir [krupir] *vi (eau)* to stagnate; **c. en prison** to rot in prison

croustiller [krustije] *vi* to be crunchy; *(pain)* to be crusty ▪ **croustillant, -ante** *adj* crunchy; *(pain)* crusty; *Fig (histoire)* spicy

croûte [krut] *nf (de pain)* crust; *(de fromage)* rind; *(de plaie)* scab; *Fam* **casser la c.** to have a snack; *Fam* **gagner sa c.** to earn one's bread and butter ▪ **croûton** *nm (de pain)* end; **croûtons** *(pour la soupe)* croûtons

croyable [krwajabl] *adj* credible, believable; **pas c.** unbelievable, incredible ▪ **croyance** *nf* belief **(en in)** ▪ **croyant, -ante 1** *adj* **être c.** to be a believer **2** *nmf* believer

CRS [seɛrɛs] *(abrév* **compagnie républicaine de sécurité)** *nm* = French riot policeman; **les CRS** = French riot police

cru¹, crue¹ [kry] *pp de* **croire**

cru², crue² [kry] **1** *adj (aliment)* raw; *(lait)* unpasteurized; *(lumière)* garish; *(propos)* crude; **monter à c.** to ride bareback **2** *nm (vignoble)* vineyard; **un grand c.** *(vin)* a vintage wine; **vin du c.** local wine

cruauté [kryote] *nf* cruelty **(envers to)**

cruche [kryʃ] *nf* pitcher, jug

crucial, -e, -aux, -ales [krysjal, -jo] *adj* crucial

crucifier [krysifje] *vt* to crucify ▪ **crucifix** [krysifi] *nm* crucifix ▪ **crucifixion** *nf* crucifixion

crudité [krydite] *nf (grossièreté)* crudeness ▪ **crudités** *nfpl (légumes)* assorted raw vegetables

crue³ [kry] *nf (montée)* swelling; *(inondation)* flood; **en c.** *(rivière, fleuve)* in spate

cruel, -elle [kryɛl] *adj* cruel **(envers** *ou* **avec** **c)** ▪ **cruellement** *adv* cruelly; **faire c. défaut** to be sadly lacking

crûment [krymɑ̃] *adv (sans détour)* bluntly; *(grossièrement)* crudely

crustacés [krystase] *nmpl Culin* shellfish *inv*

crypte [kript] *nf* crypt

crypté, -ée [kripte] *adj (message)* & *TV* coded

Cuba [kyba] *n* Cuba ▪ **cubain, -aine 1** *adj* Cuban **2** *nmf* **C., Cubaine** Cuban

cube [kyb] **1** *nm* cube; *(de jeu)* building block **2** *adj* **mètre c.** cubic metre ▪ **cubique** *adj* cubic

cueillir* [kœjir] *vt* to pick, to gather; *Fam* **c. qn** to arrest sb ▪ **cueillette** *nf* picking, gathering; *(fruits)* harvest

cuiller, cuillère [kɥijɛr] *nf* spoon; *(mesure)* spoonful; **c. à café, petite c.** teaspoon; **c. à soupe** tablespoon ▪ **cuillerée** *nf* spoonful; **c. à café** teaspoonful; **c. à soupe** tablespoonful

cuir [kɥir] *nm* leather; *(d'éléphant)* hide; **pantalon en c.** leather trousers; **c. chevelu** scalp

cuirasse [kɥiras] *nf Hist* breastplate ▪ **cuirassé** *nm Naut* battleship

cuire* [kɥir] **1** *vt (aliment, plat)* to cook; **c. qch à l'eau** to boil sth; **c. qch au four** to bake sth; *(viande)* to roast sth **2** *vi (aliment)* to cook; **faire c. qch** to cook sth; **faire trop c. qch** to overcook sth; *Fam* **on cuit!** it's baking hot

cuisant, -ante [kɥizɑ̃, -ɑ̃t] *adj (douleur)* burning; *(affront, blessure)* stinging

cuisine [kɥizin] *nf (pièce)* kitchen; *(art)* cookery, cooking; *Fam (intrigues)* scheming; **faire la c.** to do the cooking; **faire de la bonne c.** to be a good cook ▪ **cuisiner** *vti* to cook; *Fam* **c. qn** *(interroger)* to grill sb ▪ **cuisinier, -ière** *nmf* cook ▪ **cuisinière²** *nf (appareil)* stove, *Br* cooker

cuisse [kɥis] *nf* thigh; **c. de poulet** chicken leg; **cuisses de grenouilles** frogs' legs

cuisson [kɥisɔ̃] *nm (d'aliments)* cooking; *(de pain)* baking

cuissot [kɥiso] *nm (de venaison)* haunch

cuit, -e [kɥi, kɥit] **1** *pp de* **cuire 2** *adj* cooked; **bien c.** well done; **trop c.** overcooked; **pas assez c.** undercooked; *Fam* **nous sommes cuits** we're finished; *Fam* **c'est cuit!** we've had it!

cuite [kɥit] *nf Fam* **prendre une c.** to get *Br* pissed *or Am* wasted

cuivre [kɥivr] *nm (rouge)* copper; *(jaune)* brass; *Mus* **les cuivres** the brass ▪ **cuivré, -ée** *adj Br* copper-coloured, *Am* copper-colored

cul [ky] *nm Fam (derrière) Br* arse, *Am* ass; *(de bouteille, de verre)* bottom; **rester sur le c.** to be flabbergasted; **c'est à se taper le c. par terre** it's an absolute scream; **avoir du c.** to be jammy ▪ **cul-de-jatte** *(pl* culs-de-jatte*)* *nm* legless person ▪ **cul-de-sac** *(pl* culs-de-sac*)* *nm* dead end, *Br* cul-de-sac

culasse [kylas] *nf (de moteur)* cylinder head; *(de fusil)* breech

culbute [kylbyt] *nf (saut)* somersault; *(chute)* tumble; **faire la c.** to tumble; *(acrobate)* to somersault ▪ **culbuter** *vi (personne)* to take a tumble

culinaire [kylinɛr] *adj* culinary

culminer [kylmine] *vi (tension, crise)* to peak; **la montagne culmine à 3 000 mètres** the mountain is 3,000 metres at its highest point ■**culminant** *adj* point c. *(de montagne)* highest point

culot [kylo] *nm (d'ampoule, de lampe)* base; *Fam (audace)* nerve, *Br* cheek ■**culotté, -ée** *adj Fam Br* cheeky, *Am* sassy

culotte [kylɔt] *nf (de femme)* knickers, *Am* panties; *(d'enfant)* pants; **culottes courtes** *Br* short trousers, *Am* short pants; **c. de cheval** jodhpurs

culpabiliser [kylpabilize] **1** *vt* **c. qn** to make sb feel guilty **2 se culpabiliser** *vpr* to feel guilty ■**culpabilité** *nf* guilt

culte [kylt] **1** *nm (de dieu)* worship; *(religion)* religion; **c. de la personnalité** personality cult **2** *adj* **film c.** cult film

cultiver [kyltive] **1** *vt (terre, amitié)* to cultivate; *(plantes)* to grow **2 se cultiver** *vpr* to improve one's mind ■**cultivateur, -trice** *nmf* farmer ■**cultivé, -ée** *adj (terre)* cultivated; *(esprit, personne)* cultured, cultivated

culture [kyltyr] *nf* **(a)** *(action)* farming, cultivation; *(de plantes)* growing; **cultures** *(terres)* fields under cultivation; *(plantes)* crops **(b)** *(éducation, civilisation)* & *Biol* culture; **c. générale** general knowledge; **c. physique** physical training ■**culturel, -elle** *adj* cultural

culturisme [kyltyrism] *nm* body-building

cumin [kymɛ̃] *nm* cumin

cumul [kymyl] *nm* **c. des mandats** plurality of offices ■**cumulatif, -ive** *adj* cumulative ■**cumuler** *vt* **c. deux fonctions** to hold two offices

cupide [kypid] *adj* avaricious ■**cupidité** *nf* cupidity

curable [kyrabl] *adj* curable

cure [kyr] *nf* **(a)** *(traitement)* (course of) treatment; **faire une c. de repos** to go/be on a rest cure; **c. d'amaigrissement** slimming treatment; **c. thermale** spa cure **(b)** *(fonction)* office of a parish priest ■**curatif, -ive** *adj (traitement)* curative

curé [kyre] *nm* parish priest

curer [kyre] **1** *vt* to clean out **2 se curer** *vpr* **se c. les dents** to pick one's teeth; **se c. les ongles** to clean one's nails ■**cure-dents** *nm inv* toothpick ■**cure-ongles** *nm inv* nail cleaner

curieux, -euse [kyrjø, -jøz] **1** *adj (bizarre)* curious; *(indiscret)* inquisitive, curious (**de** about); **je serais c. de savoir** I'd be curious to know **2** *nmf* inquisitive person; *(badaud)* onlooker ■**curieusement** *adv* curiously ■**curiosité** *nf* curiosity; *(chose)* curio; **les curiosités d'une ville** the interesting sights of a town

curriculum vitae [kyrikylɔmvite] *nm inv Br* curriculum vitae, *Am* résumé

curseur [kyrsœr] *nm Ordinat* cursor

cutané, -ée [kytane] *adj* **maladie cutanée** skin condition ■**cuti** *nf* skin test

cuve [kyv] *nf (réservoir)* & *Photo* tank; *(de fermentation)* vat ■**cuvée** *nf (récolte)* vintage ■**cuver** *vt Fam* **c. son vin** to sleep it off ■**cuvette** *nf (récipient)* & *Géog* basin; *(des toilettes)* bowl

CV [seve] *(abrév* **curriculum vitae)** *nm Br* CV, *Am* résumé

cyanure [sjanyr] *nm* cyanide

cybercafé [siberkafe] *nm* cybercafé

cybernétique [sibernetik] *nf* cybernetics *(sing)*

cybersexe [siberseks] *nm Ordinat* cybersex

cycle [sikl] *nm* **(a)** *(série, movement)* cycle **(b)** **premier/second c.** *Scol* = lower/upper classes in secondary school; *Univ* = first/last two years of a degree course **(c)** *(bicyclette)* cycle ■**cyclable** *adj* **piste c.** cycle path ■**cyclique** *adj* cyclical

cyclisme [siklism] *nm* cycling ■**cycliste 1** *nmf* cyclist **2** *adj* **course c.** cycle race; **champion c.** cycling champion; **coureur c.** racing cyclist

cyclomoteur [siklɔmɔtœr] *nm* moped

cyclone [siklon] *nm* cyclone

cyclotourisme [sikloturism] *nm* bicycle touring

cygne [siɲ] *nm* swan

cylindre [silɛ̃dr] *nm* cylinder; *(rouleau)* roller ■**cylindrée** *nf* (cubic) capacity ■**cylindrique** *adj* cylindrical

cymbale [sɛ̃bal] *nf* cymbal

cynique [sinik] **1** *adj* cynical **2** *nmf* cynic ■**cynisme** *nm* cynicism

cyprès [siprɛ] *nm* cypress

cypriote [siprijɔt] **1** *adj* Cypriot **2** *nmf* **C.** Cypriot

D, d [de] *nm inv* (**a**) D, d (**b**) *(abrév route départementale)* = designation of a secondary road

dactylo [daktilo] *nf (personne)* typist; *(action)* typing ▪**dactylographie** *nf* typing ▪**dactylographier** *vt* to type

dada [dada] *nm Fam (manie)* hobby-horse

dadais [dade] *nm Fam* **grand d.** big oaf

dahlia [dalja] *nm* dahlia

daigner [deɲe] *vt* **d. faire qch** to deign to do sth

daim [dɛ̃] *nm (animal)* fallow deer; *(mâle)* buck; *(cuir)* suede

dalle [dal] *nf (de pierre)* paving stone; *(de marbre)* slab; *Fam* **que d.** *(rien)* zilch, *Br* sod all; *Fam* **crever la d.** to be starving ▪**dallage** *nm (action, surface)* paving ▪**daller** *vt* to pave

daltonien, -ienne [daltɔnjɛ̃, -jɛn] *adj Br* colour-blind, *Am* color-blind ▪**daltonisme** *nm Br* colour blindness, *Am* color blindness

dam [dam] *nm* **au grand d. de qn** to the great displeasure of sb

dame [dam] *nf (femme)* lady; *Échecs & Cartes* queen; *(au jeu de dames)* king; **dames** *(jeu) Br* draughts, *Am* checkers ▪**damer** *vt Fam* **d. le pion à qn** to put one over on sb ▪**damier** *nm Br* draughtboard, *Am* checkerboard

damner [dane] 1 *vt* to damn 2 **se damner** *vpr* to damn oneself ▪**damnation** *nf* damnation

dandiner [dɑ̃dine] **se dandiner** *vpr* to waddle

dandy [dɑ̃di] *nm* dandy

Danemark [danmark] *nm* **le D.** Denmark ▪**danois, -oise** 1 *adj* Danish 2 *nmf* **D., Danoise** Dane 3 *nm (langue)* Danish

danger [dɑ̃ʒe] *nm* danger; **en d.** in danger; **mettre qn en d.** to endanger sb; **en d. de mort** in mortal danger; **'d. de mort'** *(sur panneau)* 'danger'; **hors de d.** out of danger; *Fam* **pas de d.!** no way! ▪**dangereusement** *adv* dangerously ▪**dangereux, -euse** *adj* dangerous (**pour** to)

dans [dɑ̃] *prép* (**a**) in; *(changement de lieu)* into; *(à l'intérieur de)* inside; **d. le jardin/journal** in the garden/newspaper; **d. la boîte** in *or* inside the box; **d. Paris** in Paris (itself); **mettre qch d. qch** to put sth in(to) sth; **entrer d. une pièce** to go into a room; **d. un rayon de...** within (a radius of)...; **marcher d. les rues** to walk through *or* around the streets (**b**) *(provenance)* from, out of; **boire d. un verre** to drink out of a

glass (**c**) *(exprime la temporalité)* in; **d. deux jours** in two days, in two days' time (**d**) *(exprime une approximation)* **d. les dix euros** about ten euros

danse [dɑ̃s] *nf (mouvement, musique)* dance; **la d.** *(art)* dancing; **d. classique** ballet ▪**danser** *vti* to dance ▪**danseur, -euse** *nmf* dancer; **danseuse étoile** prima ballerina; **en danseuse** *(cycliste)* standing on the pedals

Danube [danyb] *nm* **le D.** the Danube

dard [dar] *nm (d'insecte)* sting ▪**darder** *vt* **le soleil darde ses rayons** the sun is beating down

dare-dare [dardar] *adv Fam* at the double

date [dat] *nf* date; **amitié de longue d.** long-standing friendship; **faire d.** to be a landmark; **en d. du...** dated the...; **d. d'expiration** *Br* expiry date, *Am* expiration date; **d. de naissance** date of birth; **d. limite** deadline; **d. limite de vente** sell-by date ▪**datation** *nf* dating ▪**dater 1** *vt (lettre)* to date **2** *vi* **à d. du 15** as from the 15th; **ça commence à d.** it's beginning to date ▪**dateur** *adj m* **tampon d.** date stamp

datte [dat] *nf* date ▪**dattier** *nm* date palm

daube [dob] *nf* **bœuf en d.** braised beef stew

dauphin [dofɛ̃] *nm (animal)* dolphin

daurade [dorad] *nf* sea bream

davantage [davɑ̃taʒ] *adv* more; **d. de temps/d'argent** more time/money; **nous ne resterons pas d.** we won't stay any longer

de¹ [də]

de becomes **d'** before vowel and h mute; de + le = **du**, de + les = **des**.

prép (**a**) *(complément d'un nom)* of; **les rayons du soleil** the rays of the sun, the sun's rays; **le livre de Paul** Paul's book; **la ville de Paris** the town of Paris; **un livre de Flaubert** a book by Flaubert; **un pont de fer** an iron bridge; **le train de Londres** the London train; **une augmentation de salaire** an increase in salary (**b**) *(complément d'un adjectif)* **digne de qn** worthy of sb; **content de qn/qch** pleased with sb/sth; **heureux de partir** happy to leave (**c**) *(complément d'un verbe)* **parler de qn/qch** to speak of sb/sth; **se souvenir de qn/qch** to remember sb/sth; **décider de faire qch** to decide to do sth; **empêcher qn de faire qch** to stop sb from doing sth; **traiter qn de lâche** to call sb a coward (**d**) *(indique la provenance)* from; **venir/dater de...** to come/date from...; **mes amis du village** my friends from the village, my village friends; **le train de Londres** the train from London; **sortir de qch** to come out of sth (**e**) *(introduit agent)* **accompagné de qn** accompanied by sb; **entouré de qch** surrounded by *or* with sth (**f**) *(introduit le moyen)* **armé de qch** armed with sth; **se nourrir de...** to live on... (**g**) *(introduit la manière)* **d'une voix douce** in a gentle voice (**h**) *(introduit la cause)* **puni de son impatience** punished for his/her impatience; **mourir de faim** to die of hunger; **sauter de joie** to jump for joy (**i**) *(introduit le temps)* **travailler de nuit/de jour** to work by night/by day; **six heures du matin** six o'clock in the morning (**j**) *(mesure)* **avoir six mètres de haut, être haut de six mètres** to be six metres high; **retarder qn/qch de deux heures** to delay sb/ sth by two hours; **homme de trente ans** thirty-year-old man; **gagner vingt euros de l'heure** to earn twenty euros an hour

de² [də] *art partitif* some; **elle boit du vin** she drinks (some) wine; **il ne boit pas de vin** he doesn't drink (any) wine; **est-ce que vous buvez du vin?** do you drink (any) wine?; **elle achète des épinards** she buys (some) spinach; *Fam* **il y en a six de tués** there are six dead; **un(e) de trop** one too many

de³ [də] *art indéfini* **de, des** some; **des fleurs** (some) flowers; **de jolies fleurs** (some) pretty flowers; **d'agréables soirées** (some) pleasant evenings; **je n'ai plus de problème** I haven't got a problem any more

dé [de] *nm (à jouer)* dice; *(à coudre)* thimble; **jouer aux dés** to play dice; *Fig* **les dés sont jetés** the die is cast; **couper qch en dés** to dice sth

déambuler [deɑ̃byle] *vi* to stroll

débâcle [debɑkl] *nf (d'une armée)* rout; *(des glaces)* breaking up; *Fig (de monnaie)* collapse

déballer [debale] *vt* to unpack; *Fam (sentiments)* to pour out **▪ déballage** *nm* unpacking; *Fam (aveu)* outpouring

débandade [debɑ̃dad] *nf* rout

débaptiser [debatize] *vt (rue, chien)* to rename

débarbouiller [debarbuje] **1** *vt* **d. qn** to wash sb's face **2 se débarbouiller** *upr* to wash one's face

débarcadère [debarkadɛr] *nm* landing stage; *(pour marchandises)* wharf

débardeur [debardœr] *nm (vêtement)* vest (top)

débarquer [debarke] **1** *vt (passagers)* to land; *(marchandises)* to unload **2** *vi (passagers)* to disembark; *Fam (être naïf)* to be not quite with it; *Fam* **d. chez qn** to turn up suddenly at sb's place **▪ débarquement** [-əmɑ̃] *nm (de passagers, de troupes)* landing; *(de marchandises)* unloading

débarras [debara] *nm Br* lumber room, *Am* storeroom; *Fam* **bon d.!** good riddance! **▪ débarrasser** **1** *vt (chambre, table)* to clear (**de** of); **d. qn de qch** to relieve sb of sth **2 se débarrasser** *upr* **se d. de qn/qch** to get rid of sb/sth

débat [deba] *nm* debate; *Pol* **débats (parlementaires)** (parliamentary) proceedings **▪ débattre*** **1** *vt* to discuss, to debate; **d. de qch** to discuss sth; **prix à d.** price negotiable **2 se débattre** *upr* to struggle

débauche [deboʃ] *nf* debauchery; *Fig* **une d. de** a wealth *or* profusion of **▪ débauché, -ée** **1** *adj* debauched **2** *nmf* libertine, debauched person

débaucher [deboʃe] *vt* **d. qn** *(licencier)* to lay sb off; *(inciter à la débauche)* to corrupt sb

débile [debil] **1** *adj (faible)* weak; *Fam* **stupid 2** *nmf Fam (imbécile)* moron **▪ débilité** *nf (faiblesse)* debility; *Fam (niaiserie)* stupidity **▪ débiliter** *vt* to debilitate

débiner [debine] *Fam* **1** *vt* to run down **2 se débiner** *upr* to clear off

débit [debi] *nm Fin* debit; *(ventes)* turnover; *(de fleuve)* flow; *(d'orateur)* delivery; *Ordinat* rate; *Ordinat* **à haut d.** broadband; **d. de boissons** bar; **d. de tabac** *Br* tobacconist's (shop), *Am* tobacco store

débiter [debite] *vt (découper)* to cut up (**en** into); *(vendre)* to sell; *(fournir)* to produce; *(compte)* to debit; *Péj (dire)* to spout **▪ débiteur, -trice** **1** *nmf* debtor **2** *adj Fin* **solde d.** debit balance; **son compte est d.** his/her account is in debit

déblais [deblɛ] *nmpl (terre)* earth; *(décombres)* rubble **▪ déblayer** [deblɛje] *vt (terrain, décombres)* to clear

débloquer [debloke] **1** *vt (mécanisme)* to unjam; *(compte, prix)* to unfreeze; *Fin* **d. des crédits** to release funds **2** *vi Fam (dire n'importe quoi)* to talk nonsense

déboires [debwar] *nmpl (déceptions)* disappointments

déboiser [debwaze] *vt (terrain)* to clear of trees

déboîter [debwate] **1** *vt (tuyau)* to disconnect **2** *vi (véhicule)* to pull out **3 se déboîter** *upr* **se d. l'épaule** to dislocate one's shoulder **▪ déboîtement** *nm (d'articulation)* dislocation

débonnaire [debonɛr] *adj* good-natured, easygoing

déborder [deborde] **1** *vi (fleuve, liquide)* to overflow; *(en bouillant)* to boil over; *(en coloriant)* to go over the edge; **l'eau déborde du vase** the vase is overflowing; *Fig* **d. de joie** to be overflowing with joy; **d. de vie** to be bursting with vitality **2** *vt (dépasser)* to go beyond; *(faire saillie)* to stick out from; **débordé de travail** snowed under with work **▪ débordement** [-əmɑ̃] *nm* overflowing; *Fig (de joie)* outburst

débouché [debuʃe] *nm (carrière)* opening; *(marché pour produit)* outlet

déboucher [debuʃe] **1** *vt (bouteille)* to uncork; *(bouchon vissé)* to uncap; *(lavabo, tuyau)* to unblock **2** *vi (surgir)* to emerge (**de** from); **d. sur** *(rue)* to lead out onto/into; *Fig (aboutir à)* to lead to

débouler [debule] *vi Fam (arriver)* to turn up

déboulonner [debulone] *vt* to unbolt

débourser [deburse] *vt (argent)* to lay out; **sans rien d.** without spending a penny

debout [dəbu] *adv (personne)* standing; *(objet)* upright; **mettre qch d.** to stand sth up; **se mettre d.** to stand up; **se tenir** *ou* **rester d.** to stand; **cent ans plus tard, la maison est encore d.** the house is still standing a hundred years later; *Fig* **ça ne tient pas d.** *(théorie)* that doesn't make sense; **être d.** *(hors du lit)* to be up; **d.!** get up!

déboutonner [debutone] **1** *vt* to unbutton **2 se déboutonner** *vpr (personne)* to undo one's coat/jacket/*etc*

débraillé, -ée [debraje] *adj* slovenly

débrancher [debrɑ̃ʃe] *vt* to unplug

débrayer [debreje] *vi* (a) *Aut* to release the clutch (b) *(se mettre en grève)* to stop work ▪ **débrayage** (a) *Aut* declutching (b) *(grève)* stoppage

débridé, -ée [debride] *adj (passion)* unbridled

débris [debri] *nmpl (de voiture, d'avion)* debris; *(de verre, de bois)* fragments

débrouiller [debruje] **1** *vt (fil, mystère)* to unravel **2 se débrouiller** *vpr Fam* to manage; *(en langues, en math)* to get by; **se d. pour faire qch** to manage (somehow) to do sth ▪ **débrouillard, -arde** *adj Fam* resourceful ▪ **débrouillardise** *nf Fam* resourcefulness

débroussailler [debrusaje] *vt (chemin)* to clear of undergrowth; *Fig (question)* to clarify

débusquer [debyske] *vt* to flush out

début [deby] *nm* beginning, start; **au d. (de)** at the beginning (of); **au tout d.** at the very beginning; **dès le d.** (right) from the start *or* beginning; *Théâtre* **faire ses débuts** to make one's debut

débuter [debyte] *vi* to start, to begin (**par** with); *(dans une carrière)* to start out; *Théâtre* to make one's debut ▪ **débutant, -ante 1** *nmf* beginner **2** *adj* novice

deçà [dəsa] **1** *adv* **en deçà** (on) this side **2** *prép* **en d. de** (on) this side of; *Fig* **être en d. de la vérité** to be some way from the truth

décacheter [dekaʃte] *vt (lettre)* to unseal

décadent, -ente [dekadɑ̃, -ɑ̃t] *adj* decadent ▪ **décadence** *nf (état)* decadence; *(processus)* decline

décaféiné, -ée [dekafeine] *adj* decaffeinated

décalcomanie [dekalkɔmani] *nf (image) Br* transfer, *Am* decal

décaler [dekale] **1** *vt (dans le temps)* to change the time of; *(dans l'espace)* to shift, to move **2 se décaler** *vpr* to move, to shift ▪ **décalage** *nm (écart)* gap (**entre** between); *(entre des faits, des idées)* discrepancy; **d. horaire** time difference; **souffrir du d. horaire** to have jet lag

décalquer [dekalke] *vt* to trace

décamper [dekɑ̃pe] *vi Fam* to clear off

décanter [dekɑ̃te] **1** *vt (vin)* to decant **2 se décanter** *vpr (vin)* to settle; *Fig (situation)* to become clearer

décaper [dekape] *vt (avec un produit)* to strip; *(au papier de verre)* to sand (down); *(four)* to clean ▪ **décapant** *nm (pour peinture)* paint stripper; *(pour four)* oven cleaner; *Fig (humour)* caustic

décapiter [dekapite] *vt (personne)* to decapitate

décapotable [dekapɔtabl] *adj & nf* convertible

décapsuler [dekapsyle] *vt* to take the top off ▪ **décapsuleur** *nm* bottle opener

décarcasser [dekarkase] **se décarcasser** *vpr Fam* to sweat blood (**pour faire** to do)

décathlon [dekatlɔ̃] *nm Sport* decathlon

décéder [desede] *vi* to die ▪ **décédé, -ée 1** *adj* deceased **2** *nmf* **le d., la décédée** the deceased

déceler [desle] *vt (trouver)* to detect; *(indiquer)* to indicate

décembre [desɑ̃br] *nm* December

décence [desɑ̃s] *nf (de comportement)* propriety; *(d'habillement)* decency; **avoir la d. de faire qch** to have the decency to do sth ▪ **décemment** [-samɑ̃] *adv (se comporter)* properly; *(s'habiller)* decently ▪ **décent, -ente** *adj (comportement)* proper; *(vêtements)* decent

décennie [deseni] *nf* decade

décentraliser [desɑ̃tralize] *vt* to decentralize ▪ **décentralisation** *nf* decentralization

déception [desɛpsjɔ̃] *nf* disappointment

> Il faut noter que le nom anglais **deception** est un faux ami. Il signifie **tromperie**.

décerner [deserne] *vt (prix)* to award (**à** to)

décès [desɛ] *nm* death

décevoir* [desəvwar] *vt* to disappoint ▪ **décevant, -ante** *adj* disappointing

> Il faut noter que le verbe anglais **to deceive** est un faux ami. Il signifie **tromper**.

déchaîner [deʃene] **1** *vt (colère, violence)* to unleash; **d. l'hilarité** to provoke laughter **2 se déchaîner** *vpr (tempête, vent)* to rage; *(personne)* to fly into a rage (**contre** with) ▪ **déchaîné, -ée** *adj (mer, vent)* raging; *(personne)* wild ▪ **déchaînement** [-ɛnmɑ̃] *nm (des éléments)* fury; *(de passions)* outburst

déchanter [deʃɑ̃te] *vi Fam* to become disillusioned

décharge [deʃarʒ] *nf Jur (d'accusé)* acquittal; **d.**

(électrique) (electric) shock; **d. (publique)** *Br* (rubbish) dump, *Am* (garbage) dump; *Fig* **à la d. de qn** in sb's *Br* defence *or Am* defense

décharger [deʃaʀʒe] **1** *vt (camion, navire, cargaison)* to unload; **d. qn de qch** *(tâche, responsabilité)* to relieve sb of; *Jur (d'accusation)* to acquit sb of sth; **d. son arme sur qn** to fire one's weapon at sb **2 se décharger** *vpr (batterie)* to go flat; **se d. sur qn d'une tâche** to offload a task onto sb **• déchargement** [-əmɑ̃] *nm* unloading

décharné, -ée [deʃaʀne] *adj (visage, corps)* emaciated

déchausser [deʃose] **1** *vt* **d. qn** to take sb's shoes off **2 se déchausser** *vpr (personne)* to take one's shoes off; **avoir les dents qui se déchaussent** to have receding gums

dèche [dɛʃ] *nf Fam* **être dans la d.** to be stony broke

déchéance [deʃeɑ̃s] *nf (déclin)* decline

déchet [deʃɛ] *nm* **il y a du d.** there's some wastage; **déchets** scraps; **déchets radioactifs** radioactive waste

déchiffrer [deʃifʀe] *vt (message, écriture)* to decipher; *(signaux)* to interpret; *Mus* to sight-read

déchiqueter [deʃikte] *vt* to tear to shreds **• déchiqueté, -ée** *adj (tissu)* torn to shreds; *(côte)* jagged

déchirer [deʃiʀe] **1** *vt (accidentellement)* to tear; *(volontairement)* to tear up; *(enveloppe)* to tear open; *Fig (pays, groupe)* to tear apart; **un cri déchira le silence** a loud cry pierced the silence; **un bruit qui déchire le tympan** an ear-splitting noise **2 se déchirer** *vpr (tissu, papier)* to tear; *Fig (couple)* to tear each other apart; **se d. un muscle** to tear a muscle **• déchirant, -ante** *adj (spectacle, dieux)* heartrending **• déchirement** *nm (peine)* heartbreak **• déchirure** *nf* tear; **d. musculaire** torn muscle

déchoir* [deʃwaʀ] *vi (personne)* to demean oneself **• déchu, -ue** *adj* **ange d.** fallen angel; **être d. de qch** to be stripped of sth

décibel [desibɛl] *nm* decibel

décidé, -ée [deside] *adj (personne, air)* determined; *(fixé)* settled; **d'un ton d.** in a decisive tone; **être d. à faire qch** to be determined to do sth

décidément [desidemɑ̃] *adv* really

Il faut noter que l'adverbe anglais **decidedly** est un faux ami. Il signifie le plus souvent **vraiment**.

décider [deside] **1** *vt* **d. quand/que...** to decide when/that...; **d. qn à faire qch** to persuade sb to do sth **2** *vi* **d. de qch** to decide on sth; **d. de faire qch** to decide to do sth; **cet événement décida de sa carrière** the event determined

his/her career **3 se décider** *vpr* **se d. (à faire qch)** to make up one's mind (to do sth); **se d. pour qch** to decide on sth **• décideur, -euse** *nmf* decision-maker

décilitre [desilitʀ] *nm* decilitre

décimal, -e, -aux, -ales [desimal, -o] *adj* decimal **• décimale** *nf* decimal

décimer [desime] *vt* to decimate

décimètre [desimɛtʀ] *nm Br* decimetre, *Am* decimeter; **double d.** ruler

décisif, -ive [desizif, -iv] *adj (bataille)* decisive; *(moment)* critical **• décision** *nf* decision (**de faire** to do); *(fermeté)* determination; **prendre une d.** to make a decision; **avec d.** decisively

déclamer [deklame] *vt* to declaim; *Péj* to spout **• déclamatoire** *adj Péj (style)* declamatory

déclaration [deklaʀasjɔ̃] *nf (annonce)* statement; *(de naissance, de décès)* registration; *(à la police)* report; **faire sa d.** to declare one's love to sb; **d. d'amour** declaration of love; **d. d'impôts** *ou* **de revenus** income tax return; **d. de guerre** declaration of war

déclarer [deklaʀe] **1** *vt (annoncer)* to declare (**que** that); *(naissance, décès, vol)* to register; *Jur* **d. qn coupable** to find sb guilty (**de** of); **d. la guerre** to declare war (**à** on); *Sport* **d. forfait** to scratch; **rien à d.** *(en douane)* nothing to declare **2 se déclarer** *vpr (incendie, maladie)* to break out; *(avouer son amour)* to declare one's love; **se d. pour/contre qch** to declare oneself in favour of/against sth; **se d. surpris** to declare oneself surprised

déclasser [deklase] *vt (livres)* to put out of order; *(hôtel)* to downgrade; *Sport* **d. qn** to relegate sb

déclencher [deklɑ̃ʃe] **1** *vt (appareil)* to start; *(mécanisme)* to activate; *(sonnerie)* to set off; *(révolte, grève, conflit)* to trigger off; *Mil (attaque)* to launch **2 se déclencher** *vpr (alarme, sonnerie)* to go off; *(incendie)* to start **• déclenchement** *nm (d'appareil)* starting; *(de mécanisme)* activation; *(de sonnerie)* setting off

déclic [deklik] *nm (bruit)* click; *Fig (prise de conscience)* **il s'est produit un d. et elle a trouvé la solution** something suddenly clicked and she found the answer

déclin [deklɛ̃] *nm* decline; *(du jour)* close; *(de la lune)* wane; **être en d.** to be in decline

déclinaison [deklinɛzɔ̃] *nf Grammaire* declension

décliner [dekline] **1** *vi (forces)* to decline; *(jour)* to draw to a close **2** *vt Formel (refuser)* to decline; *(identité)* to state; **d. toute responsabilité** to accept no liability

décocher [dekɔʃe] *vt (flèche)* to shoot; *Fig (remarque)* to fire off (**à** at); *Fig (sourire)* to flash (**à** at)

décoder [dekɔde] *vt* to decode; *TV (chaîne)* to

decode, to unscramble ▪**décodeur** *nm* TV decoder; **d. numérique** set-top box

décoiffer [dekwafe] **1** *vt* **d. qn** to mess up sb's hair; **tu es tout décoiffé** your hair's (in) a mess **2 se décoiffer** *vpr (se dépeigner)* to mess up one's hair; *(ôter son chapeau)* to remove one's hat

décoincer [dekwɛ̃se] *vt*, **se décoincer** *vpr (tiroir, mécanisme)* to loosen; *Fam (personne)* to loosen up

décoller [dekɔle] **1** *vt (timbre)* to peel off **2** *vi (avion, économie)* to take off; *Fam* **je ne décollerai pas d'ici tant que…** I'm not budging until… **3 se décoller** *vpr* to peel off ▪**décollage** *nm (d'avion)* takeoff

décolleté, -ée [dekɔlte] **1** *adj (robe)* low-cut **2** *nm (de robe)* low neckline; *(haut des seins)* cleavage ▪**décolletage** *nm* neckline

décoloniser [dekɔlɔnize] *vt* to decolonize ▪**décolonisation** *nf* decolonization

décolorer [dekɔlɔre] **1** *vt (tissu)* to fade; *(cheveux)* to bleach **2 se décolorer** *vpr (tissu)* to fade; **se d. les cheveux** to bleach one's hair ▪**décolorant** *nm* bleaching agent, bleach ▪**décoloration** *nf (de tissu)* fading; *(de cheveux)* bleaching

décombres [dekɔ̃br] *nmpl* ruins, debris

décommander [dekɔmɑ̃de] **1** *vt (marchandises, invitation)* to cancel; *(invité)* to put off **2 se décommander** *vpr* to cancel

décomposer [dekɔ̃poze] **1** *vt Chim* to decompose; *(phrase)* to break down **(en** into); **il est arrivé complètement décomposé** *(par l'émotion)* he arrived quite distraught **2 se décomposer** *vpr (pourrir)* to decompose; *Fig (visage)* to become distorted ▪**décomposition** *nf* decomposition

décompresser [dekɔ̃prese] **1** *vt* to decompress; *Ordinat (fichier)* to unzip **2** *vi Fam (se détendre)* to unwind ▪**décompression** *nf* decompression

décompte [dekɔ̃t] *nm (soustraction)* deduction; *(détail)* breakdown ▪**décompter** *vt* to deduct **(de** from)

déconcentrer [dekɔ̃sɑ̃tre] **se déconcentrer** *vpr* to lose concentration

déconcerter [dekɔ̃sɛrte] *vt* to disconcert

déconfit, -ite [dekɔ̃fi, -it] *adj (personne, mine)* crestfallen ▪**déconfiture** *nf Fam (échec)* defeat

décongeler [dekɔ̃ʒle] *vt* to thaw, to defrost

décongestionner [dekɔ̃ʒɛstjɔne] *vt (rue, poumons)* to relieve congestion in

déconnecter [dekɔnɛkte] *vt (appareil, fil)* to disconnect

déconner [dekɔne] *vi très Fam (mal fonctionner)* to play up; *(dire des bêtises)* to talk garbage; **faire qch pour d.** to do sth for a laugh; **sans d.!** *(réponse)* no kidding!

déconseiller [dekɔ̃seje] *vt* **d. qch à qn** to advise

sb against sth; **d. à qn de faire qch** to advise sb against doing sth; **il est déconseillé de…** it is not advisable to…

déconsidérer [dekɔ̃sidere] *vt* to discredit

décontaminer [dekɔ̃tamine] *vt* to decontaminate

décontenancer [dekɔ̃tnɑ̃se] **1** *vt* to disconcert **2 se décontenancer** *vpr* to become disconcerted

décontracter [dekɔ̃trakte] **1** *vt (muscle)* to relax **2 se décontracter** *vpr* to relax ▪**décontracté, -ée** *adj (ambiance, personne)* relaxed; *(vêtement)* casual ▪**décontraction** *nf* relaxation

déconvenue [dekɔ̃vny] *nf Formel* disappointment

décor [dekɔr] *nm (de maison)* decor; *(paysage)* surroundings; **décors** *(de théâtre, de cinéma)* scenery, set; *Fam* **aller dans le d.** *(véhicule, automobiliste)* to go off the road

décorer [dekɔre] *vt (maison, soldat)* to decorate **(de** with) ▪**décorateur, -trice** *nmf (interior)* decorator; *Théâtre* stage designer; *Cin* set designer ▪**décoratif, -ive** *adj* decorative ▪**décoration** *nf (action, ornement, médaille)* decoration

décortiquer [dekɔrtike] *vt (riz, orge)* to hull; *(crevette, noisette)* to shell; *Fam (texte)* to dissect

découcher [dekuʃe] *vi* to stay out all night

découdre* [dekudr] **1** *vt (ourlet, vêtement)* to unstitch; *(bouton)* to take off **2** *vi Fam* **en d. (avec qn)** to fight it out (with sb) **3 se découdre** *vpr (ourlet, vêtement)* to come unstitched; *(bouton)* to come off

découler [dekule] *vi* **d. de** to follow from; **il en découle que…** it follows that…

découper [dekupe] **1** *vt (viande)* to carve; *(gâteau, papier)* to cut up; **d. un article dans un journal** to cut an article out of a newspaper **2 se découper** *vpr* **se d. sur qch** to stand out against sth ▪**découpage** *nm (de gâteau)* cutting up; *(de viande)* carving; *(image)* cutout ▪**découpé, -ée** *adj (irrégulier)* jagged

décourager [dekuraʒe] **1** *vt (dissuader)* to discourage **(de faire** from doing); *(démoraliser)* to dishearten, to discourage **2 se décourager** *vpr* to get discouraged or disheartened ▪**découragement** *nm* discouragement

décousu, -ue [dekuzy] *adj (ourlet, vêtement)* unstitched; *Fig (propos)* disjointed

découvert, -erte [dekuvɛr, -ɛrt] **1** *adj (terrain)* open; *(tête, épaule)* bare **2** *nm (de compte)* overdraft; **être à d.** to be overdrawn; **compte à d.** overdrawn account; **agir à d.** to act openly

découverte [dekuvɛrt] *nf* discovery; **partir** *ou* **aller à la d. de qch** to go off to explore sth; **faire une d.** to make a discovery

découvrir* [dekuvrir] **1** *vt (trouver, apprendre à*

connaître) to discover; *(secret, vérité, statue)* to uncover; *(casserole)* to take the lid off; *(bras, épaule)* to bare; *(voir)* to have a view of; **d. que...** to discover that...; **faire d. qch à qn** to introduce sb to sth **2 se découvrir** *vpr (dans son lit)* to push the bedcovers off; *(enlever son chapeau)* to take one's hat off; *(ciel)* to clear

décrasser [dekrase] *vt (nettoyer)* to clean; *Fam* **d. qn** to take the rough edges off sb

décrépit, -ite [dekrepi, -it] *adj (personne, maison)* decrepit ▪ **décrépitude** *nf* decrepitude; *(décadence)* decay

décret [dekrɛ] *nm* decree ▪ **décréter** *vt Jur* to decree

décrié, ée [dekrije] *adj* disparaged

décrire* [dekrir] *vt (représenter)* to describe

décrisper [dekrispe] **1** *vt (atmosphere)* to lighten; *(personne)* to relax **2 se décrisper** *vpr* to relax

décrocher [dekrɔʃe] **1** *vt (détacher)* to unhook; *(tableau, rideau)* to take down; *Fam (prix, poste)* to land; **d. (le téléphone)** *(pour répondre)* to pick up the phone; *(pour ne pas être dérangé)* to take the phone off the hook **2** *vi Fam (ne plus se concentrer)* to switch off **3 se décrocher** *vpr (tableau, rideau)* to come unhooked

décroître* [dekrwatr] *vi (forces, nombre, mortalité)* to decrease; *(eaux)* to subside; *(jours)* to get shorter; **aller en décroissant** to be decreasing

décrotter [dekrɔte] *vt (chaussures)* to clean the mud off

décrue [dekry] *nf (de rivière)* drop in level

décrypter [dekripte] *vt* to decipher; *TV* to decode, to unscramble

déçu, -ue [desy] **1** *pp de* **décevoir 2** *adj* disappointed

déculotter [dekylɔte] **se déculotter** *vpr (enlever son pantalon)* to take off one's *Br* trousers *or Am* pants ▪ **déculottée** *nf Fam* thrashing

déculpabiliser [dekylpabilize] *vt* **d. qn** to stop sb feeling guilty

décupler [dekyple] *vti* to increase tenfold

dédaigner [dedɛɲe] *vt (offre, richesse)* to scorn; *(conseil, injure)* to disregard ▪ **dédaigneux, -euse** *adj* scornful, disdainful (**de** of)

dédain [dedɛ̃] *nm* scorn, disdain (**pour/de** for)

dédale [dedal] *nm* maze

dedans [dədɑ̃] **1** *adv* inside; **de d.** from (the) inside; **en d.** on the inside; **tomber d.** *(trou)* to fall in (it); *Fam* **tomber en plein d.** *(être dupé)* to fall right into the trap; *Fam* **je me suis fichu d.** I got it wrong; *Fam* **je me suis fait rentrer d.** *(par un automobiliste)* someone drove straight into me **2** *nm* **le d.** the inside

dédicace [dedikas] *nf* dedication ▪ **dédicacer** *vt (signer)* to sign (**à** for); *(chanson)* to dedicate (**à** to)

dédier [dedje] *vt* to dedicate (**à** to)

dédire* [dedir] **se dédire** *vpr* **se d. d'une promesse** to go back on one's word

dédommager [dedɔmaʒe] *vt* to compensate (**de** for) ▪ **dédommagement** *nm* compensation

dédouaner [dedwane] *vt (marchandises)* to clear through customs; *(personne)* to clear

dédoubler [deduble] **1** *vt (partager)* to split into two **2 se dédoubler** *vpr Hum* **je ne peux pas me d.** I can't be in two places at once ▪ **dédoublement** [-əmɑ̃] *nm* **d. de la personnalité** split personality

dédramatiser [dedramatize] *vt* **d. qch** to make sth less dramatic

déduire* [dedɥir] *vt (retirer)* to deduct (**de** from); *(conclure)* to deduce (**de** from) ▪ **déductible** *adj* deductible ▪ **déduction** *nf (raisonnement, décompte)* deduction

déesse [deɛs] *nf* goddess

défaillir* [defajir] *vi (s'évanouir)* to faint; *(forces, mémoire)* to fail ▪ **défaillance** *nf (évanouissement)* fainting fit; *(faiblesse)* weakness; *(panne)* failure; **avoir une d.** *(s'évanouir)* to faint; *(faiblir)* to feel weak; **d. cardiaque** heart failure ▪ **défaillant, -ante** *adj (forces, santé)* failing; *(cœur)* weak

défaire* [defɛr] **1** *vt (nœud)* to undo; *(valises)* to unpack; *(installation)* to take down; *(coiffure)* to mess up **2 se défaire** *vpr (nœud)* to come undone; **se d. de qch** to get rid of sth ▪ **défait, -aite** *adj (lit)* unmade; *(cheveux) Br* dishevelled, *Am* disheveled; *(visage)* haggard; *(armée)* defeated

défaite [defɛt] *nf* defeat ▪ **défaitisme** *nm* defeatism

défalquer [defalke] *vt* to deduct (**de** from)

défaut [defo] *nm (de personne)* fault, shortcoming; *(de machine)* defect; *(de diamant, de verre, de raisonnement)* flaw; *(désavantage)* drawback; **faire d.** to be lacking; *Jur* to default; **l'argent lui fait d.** he/she is short of money; **à d. de qch** for lack of sth; **ou, à d....** or, failing that...; **prendre qn en d.** to catch sb out; *Math* **total approché par d.** total rounded down; *Ordinat* **police/lecteur par d.** default font/drive; **d. de fabrication** manufacturing fault; **d. de prononciation** speech impediment

défaveur [defavœr] *nf* **être en d. auprès de qn** to be in *Br* disfavour *or Am* disfavor with sb ▪ **défavorable** *adj Br* unfavourable, *Am* unfavorable (**à** to) ▪ **défavorisé, -ée** *adj (milieu)* underprivileged, disadvantaged ▪ **défavoriser** *vt* to put at a disadvantage

défection [defɛksjɔ̃] *nf (de soldat, d'espion)* defection; **faire d.** *(ne pas venir)* to fail to turn up

défectueux, -ueuse [defɛktɥø, -ɥøz] *adj* faulty, defective

défendre [defɑ̃dr] **1** *vt (protéger, soutenir)* to defend (**contre** against); **d. à qn de faire qch**

to forbid sb to do sth; **d. qch à qn** to forbid sb sth **2 se défendre** *vpr* to defend oneself; **se d. de faire qch** to refrain from doing sth; *Fam* **je me défends en anglais** I can get by in English ▪ **défendable** *adj* defensible

défense¹ [defɑ̃s] *nf (protection) Br* defence, *Am* defense; **prendre la d. de qn** to come to sb's defence; *Jur* **assurer la d. de qn** to conduct the case for the defence; **en état de légitime d.** acting in self-defence; **sans d.** *Br* defenceless, *Am* defenseless; **'d. de fumer'** 'no smoking'; **'d. (absolue) d'entrer'** '(strictly) no entry'

défense² [defɑ̃s] *nf (d'éléphant)* tusk

défenseur [defɑ̃sœr] *nm* defender; *Jur* counsel for the defence

défensif, -ive [defɑ̃sif, -iv] **1** *adj* defensive **2** *nf* **sur la défensive** on the defensive

déférence [deferɑ̃s] *nf* deference

déférer [defere] *vt Jur* **d. qn à la justice** to hand sb over to the police

déferler [deferle] *vi (vagues)* to break; **les vacanciers déferlent sur les routes** *Br* holiday-makers *or Am* vacationers are taking to the roads in droves

défi [defi] *nm* challenge (**à** to); **lancer un d. à qn** to challenge sb; **mettre qn au d. de faire qch** to defy sb to do sth; **relever un d.** to take up a challenge

défiance [defjɑ̃s] *nf* mistrust

déficient, -ente [defisjɑ̃, -ɑ̃t] *adj* deficient ▪ **déficience** *nf* deficiency

déficit [defisit] *nm* deficit; **être en d.** to be in deficit; **d. commercial** trade deficit ▪ **déficitaire** *adj (budget)* in deficit; *(entreprise)* loss-making; *(compte)* in debit

défier [defje] **1** *vt (provoquer)* to challenge; *(danger, mort)* to defy; **d. qn à la course** to challenge sb to a race; **d. qn de faire qch** to defy sb to do sth; **des prix qui défient toute concurrence** unbeatable prices **2 se défier** *vpr* **se d. de** to mistrust ▪ **défiance** *nf* mistrust ▪ **défiant, -ante** *adj* mistrustful (**à l'égard de** of)

défigurer [defigyre] *vt (personne, paysage)* to disfigure; *Fig (vérité)* to distort ▪ **défiguré, -ée** *adj (personne)* disfigured

défilé [defile] *nm (cortège)* procession; *(de manifestants)* march; *(de visiteurs)* stream; *Mil* parade; *Géog* pass; **d. de mode** fashion show

défiler¹ [defile] *vi (chars de carnaval)* to march in procession; *(manifestants)* to march; *(touristes)* to stream; *(paysage, jours)* to pass by; *(images)* to flash by; *Mil* to parade; *Ordinat* **d. vers le bas/le haut** to scroll down/up; *Ordinat* **faire d. un document** to scroll through a document

défiler² [defile] **se défiler** *vpr Fam (se dérober)* to slope off

définir [definir] *vt* to define ▪ **défini, -ie** *adj*

definite ▪ **définition** *nf* definition; *(de mots croisés)* clue

définitif, -ive [definitif, -iv] **1** *adj (jugement, version)* final; *(séparation, fermeture)* permanent **2** *nf* **en définitive** in the final analysis ▪ **définitivement** *adv (partir, exclure)* for good

déflagration [deflagrasjɔ̃] *nf* explosion

déflation [deflasjɔ̃] *nf Écon* deflation

déflorer [deflɔre] *vt (personne)* to deflower

défoncer [defɔ̃se] **1** *vt (porte, mur)* to smash in; *(trottoir, route)* to break up **2 se défoncer** *vpr Fam (faire un gros effort)* to sweat blood (**pour faire qch** to do sth); *(drogué)* to get high (**à** on) ▪ **défoncé, -ée** *adj (route)* bumpy; *Fam (drogué)* high, stoned

déformation [defɔrmasjɔ̃] *nf (de membre)* deformation; *(de fait)* distortion; **d. professionnelle** habits acquired through the type of work one does

déformer [defɔrme] **1** *vt (membre)* to deform; *(vêtement, chaussures)* to put out of shape; *(faits, image)* to distort; *(propos)* to twist **2 se déformer** *vpr* to lose its shape ▪ **déformé, -ée** *adj (objet)* misshapen; *(corps)* deformed

défouler [defule] **se défouler** *vpr Fam* to let off steam; **se d. sur qn** to take it out on sb

défraîchi, -ie [defreʃi] *adj (fleur, beauté)* faded; *(vêtement)* shabby

défrayer [defreje] *vt* **d. la chronique** to be the talk of the town

défricher [defriʃe] *vt (terrain)* to clear; *Fig (sujet)* to open up; *Fig* **d. le terrain** to prepare the ground

défriser [defrize] *vt (cheveux)* to straighten; *Fam (personne)* to bug ▪ **défriseur** *nm* hair straighteners *(pluriel)*

défroisser [defrwase] *vt* to smooth out

défroqué, -ée [defrɔke] *adj (prêtre)* defrocked

défunt, -unte [defœ̃, -œ̃t] **1** *adj (mort)* departed; **son d. mari** her late husband **2** *nmf* **le d., la défunte** the deceased

dégager [degaʒe] **1** *vt (passage, voie)* to clear (**de** of); *(odeur, chaleur)* to emit; *(credit)* to release; *Fig (impression)* to give off; **d. qn de (décombres)** to free sb from; *(promesse)* to release sb from; *Football* **d. le ballon en touche** to kick the ball into touch; *Fam* **dégage!** clear off! **2 se dégager** *vpr (odeur, gaz)* to be given off; *(rue, ciel)* to clear; **se d. de (personne)** to free oneself from ▪ **dégagé, -ée** *adj (ciel)* clear; *(allure, ton)* casual; *(vue)* open ▪ **dégagement** *nm (action)* clearing; *(d'odeur, de chaleur)* emission; *Football* clearance

dégaine [degen] *nf Fam (apparence)* strange appearance

dégainer [degene] *vti* to draw

dégarnir [degarnir] **1** *vt* to empty **2 se dégarnir** *vpr (personne)* to go bald; *(salle)* to empty ▪ **dégarni, -ie** *adj (personne)* balding; **avoir le front d.** to have a receding hairline

dégâts [dega] *nmpl* damage; *Fig* **limiter les d.** to limit the damage; **d. collatéraux** collateral damage

dégel [deʒɛl] *nm* thaw ▪ **dégeler** 1 *vt* to thaw; *(surgelé)* to defrost; *(crédits)* to unfreeze 2 *vi* to thaw; **faire d. qch, mettre qch à d.** *(surgelé)* to defrost sth 3 *v impersonnel* to thaw; **il dégèle** it's thawing 4 **se dégeler** *upr Fig (atmosphère)* to become less chilly

dégénérer [deʒenere] *vi* to degenerate **(en** into) ▪ **dégénéré, -ée** *adj & nmf (dépravé)* degenerate ▪ **dégénérescence** *nf* degeneration

dégingandé, -ée [deʒɛ̃gɑ̃de] *adj* gangling, lanky

dégivrer [deʒivre] *vt (réfrigérateur)* to defrost; *(voiture, avion)* to de-ice

déglinguer [deglɛ̃ge] **se déglinguer** *upr Fam* to fall to bits; *(appareil)* to go wrong

dégobiller [degɔbije] *vt très Fam* to puke

dégonfler [degɔ̃fle] 1 *vt (pneu)* to let the air out of 2 **se dégonfler** *upr (pneu)* to go flat; *Fam (personne)* to chicken out ▪ **dégonflé, -ée** 1 *adj (pneu)* flat; *Fam (lâche)* chicken 2 *nmf Fam* chicken

dégorger [degɔrʒe] 1 *vt (évacuer)* to discharge; *(tuyau)* to unblock 2 *vi* **faire d. des concombres** = to remove water from cucumbers by sprinkling them with salt

dégot(t)er [degɔte] *vt Fam* to dig up

dégouliner [deguline] *vi* to trickle

dégourdir [degurdir] 1 *vt (doigts)* to take the numbness out of; *Fig* **d. qn** to teach sb a thing or two 2 **se dégourdir** *upr* to learn a thing or two; **se d. les jambes** to stretch one's legs ▪ **dégourdi, -ie** *adj (malin)* smart

dégoût [degu] *nm* disgust; **le d. de la vie** world-weariness; **éprouver du d. pour qch** to be disgusted by sth

dégoûter [degute] *vt (moralement)* to disgust; *(physiquement)* to turn sb's stomach; **d. qn de qch** to put sb off sth ▪ **dégoûtant, -ante** *adj* disgusting ▪ **dégoûté, -ée** 1 *adj* disgusted; **être d. de qch** to be sick of sth; *Ironique* **il n'est pas d.!** he's not too fussy 2 *nm* **faire le d.** to turn up one's nose

dégradation [degradɑsjɔ̃] *nf (de monument)* defacement; *(de matériel)* damage **(de** to); *Fig (de santé, de situation)* deterioration

dégrader [degrade] 1 *vt (monument)* to deface; *(matériel)* to damage; *Mil* to demote; *Fig (avilir)* to degrade 2 **se dégrader** *upr (édifice, santé, situation)* to deteriorate; *(maison)* to fall into disrepair; *Fig (s'avilir)* to degrade onself ▪ **dégradant, -ante** *adj* degrading ▪ **dégradé** *nm (de couleurs)* gradation

dégrafer [degrafe] 1 *vt (vêtement, bracelet)* to undo 2 **se dégrafer** *upr (vêtement, bracelet)* to come undone

dégraisser [degrese] *vt (bœuf)* to take the fat off; *(bouillon)* to skim; *Fam (entreprise)* to downsize

degré [dəgre] *nm (d'angle, de température)* degree; *(d'alcool)* proof; *(niveau)* stage; *(d'escalier)* step; *(d'échelle)* rung; **au plus haut d.** in the extreme

dégressif, -ive [degresif, -iv] *adj* **tarif d.** tapering rate

dégrèvement [degrɛvmɑ̃] *nm* **d. fiscal** tax relief

dégriffé [degrife] *nm* = reduced-price designer item with its label removed

dégringoler [degrɛ̃gɔle] *Fam* 1 *vt (escalier)* to rush down 2 *vi (personne)* to tumble (down); *(prix)* to slump ▪ **dégringolade** *nf Fam (chute)* tumble; *(de prix)* slump **(de** in)

dégriser [degrize] *vt Fig* **d. qn** to sober sb up

dégrossir [degrosir] *vt (travail)* to rough out; *Fig* **d. qn** to knock the rough edges off sb

déguerpir [degerpir] *vi Fam* to clear off

dégueulasse [degœlas] *adj très Fam (crasseux)* filthy; *(mauvais, désagréable)* disgusting ▪ **dégueulasser** *vt très Fam* to mess up

dégueuler [degœle] *vi très Fam* to puke

déguiser [degize] 1 *vt (pour tromper)* to disguise; **d. qn en** *(costumer)* to dress sb up as 2 **se déguiser** *upr (pour s'amuser)* to dress up **(en** as); *(pour tromper)* to disguise oneself **(en** as) ▪ **déguisement** *nm* disguise; *(de bal costumé)* fancy dress

déguster [degyste] 1 *vt (goûter)* to taste; *(savourer)* to *Br* savour *or Am* savor 2 *vi Fam* **tu vas d.!** you're in for it! ▪ **dégustation** *nf* tasting

déhancher [deɑ̃ʃe] **se déhancher** *upr* to swing one's hips

dehors [dəɔr] 1 *adv* outside; *(pas chez soi)* out; *(en plein air)* out of doors; **en d.** *(s'ouvrir)* outwards; **en d. de la maison** outside the house; **en d. de la ville** out of town; *Fig* **en d. de** *(excepté)* apart from; *Fam* **mettre qn d.** to throw sb out; *(employé)* to fire sb 2 *nm (extérieur)* outside; **au d.** on the outside; *(se pencher)* out; **sous des d. timides** beneath an outward appearance of shyness

déjà [deʒa] *adv* already; **est-il d. parti?** has he left yet *or* already?; **elle l'a d. vu** she's seen it before, she's already seen it; *Fam* **c'est d. pas mal** that's not bad at all; *Fam* **quand partez-vous, d.?** when did you say you're leaving?

déjanter [deʒɑ̃te] *vi très Fam (être fou)* to be off one's rocker ▪ **déjanté, -ée** *adj très Fam* completely mad

déjeuner [deʒœne] 1 *nm* lunch; **petit d.** breakfast; **prendre son d.** to have lunch/breakfast 2 *vi (à midi)* to have lunch; *(le matin)* to have breakfast

déjouer [deʒwe] *vt (intrigue, plans)* to foil

déjuger [deʒyʒe] **se déjuger** *upr* to go back on one's decision

délabrer [delabre] **se délabrer** *upr (édifice)* to fall into disrepair; *(santé)* to deteriorate ▪ **délabré, -ée** *adj (bâtiment)* dilapidated ▪ **délabrement** [-əmɑ̃] *nm (de bâtiment)* dilapidated state

délacer [delase] **1** *vt (chaussure)* to untie **2 se délacer** *upr (chaussure)* to come untied

délai [delɛ] *nm (laps de temps)* time allowed; *(sursis)* extension; **respecter les délais** to meet the deadline; **dans un d. de dix jours** within ten days; **sans d.** without delay; **dans les plus brefs délais** as soon as possible; **dernier d.** final date

> Il faut noter que le nom anglais **delay** est un faux ami. Il signifie **retard**.

délaisser [delese] *vt (négliger)* to neglect; *(abandonner)* to abandon

délasser [delase] *vt,* **se délasser** *upr* to relax ▪ **délassement** *nm* relaxation

délateur, -trice [delatœr, -tris] *nmf* informer

délavé, -ée [delave] *adj (tissu, jean)* faded; *(couleur, ciel)* watery

délayer [deleje] *vt (poudre)* to add water to; *(liquide)* to water down; *Fig (discours, texte)* to pad out

délecter [delɛkte] **se délecter** *upr* **se d. de qch/ à faire qch** to take delight in sth/in doing sth ▪ **délectable** *adj* delectable

déléguer [delege] *vt* to delegate (**à** to) ▪ **délégation** *nf* delegation ▪ **délégué, -ée** *nmf* delegate; *Scol* **d. de classe** = class representative at class meetings

délestage [delɛstaʒ] *nm* **itinéraire de d.** alternative route *(to relieve congestion)*

délester [delɛste] *vt (navire, ballon)* to unballast; *Hum* **d. qn de qch** to relieve sb of sth

délibérer [delibere] *vi (discuter)* to deliberate (**de** about); *(réfléchir)* to deliberate (**sur** upon); *Jur (jury)* to consider its verdict ▪ **délibération** *nf* deliberation ▪ **délibéré, -ée** *adj (intentionnel)* deliberate; **de propos d.** deliberately ▪ **délibérément** *adv* deliberately

délicat, -ate [delika, -at] *adj (santé, travail)* delicate; *(question)* tricky, delicate; *(peau)* sensitive; *(geste)* tactful; *(exigeant)* fussy; **des procédés peu délicats** unscrupulous methods ▪ **délicatement** *adv (légèrement)* delicately; *(avec tact)* tactfully ▪ **délicatesse** *nf (de fleur, de couleur)* delicacy; *(tact)* tact

délice [delis] *nm* delight ▪ **délices** *nfpl Littéraire* delights ▪ **délicieux, -euse** *adj (mets, sensation)* delicious; *(endroit, parfum)* delightful

délié, -ée [delje] **1** *adj (taille)* slim; *(doigts)* nimble **2** *nm (de lettre)* thin stroke

délier [delje] **1** *vt* to untie; *Fig (langue)* to loosen; **d. qn de qch** to release sb from sth **2 se délier** *upr* **les langues se délient** people start talking

délimiter [delimite] *vt (terrain)* to mark off; *(sujet)* to define

délinquant, -ante [delɛ̃kɑ̃, -ɑ̃t] *adj & nmf* delinquent ▪ **délinquance** *nf* delinquency

délire [delir] *nm Méd* delirium; *(exaltation)* frenzy; *Fam* **c'est du d.** it's utter madness ▪ **délirant, -ante** *adj (malade)* delirious; *(joie)* frenzied; *(déraisonnable)* utterly absurd ▪ **délirer** *vi (patient)* to be delirious; *(dire n'importe quoi)* to rave

délit [deli] *nm Br* offence, *Am* offense; **d. d'initié** insider trading *or* dealing

délivrer [delivre] *vt (a) (captif)* to rescue; *(ville)* to liberate; *(peuple)* to set free; **d. qn de qch** to rid sb of sth **(b)** *(marchandises)* to deliver; *(passeport, billet)* to issue (**à** to) ▪ **délivrance** *nf (soulagement)* relief; *(de passeport)* issue

déloger [delɔʒe] *vt (envahisseur)* to drive out (**de** from); *(locataire)* to evict

déloyal, -e, -aux, -ales [delwajal, -jo] *adj* disloyal; *(concurrence)* unfair

delta [dɛlta] *nm (de fleuve)* delta

deltaplane [dɛltaplan] *nm* hang-glider; **faire du d.** to go hang-gliding

déluge [delyʒ] *nm* flood; *(de pluie)* downpour; *Fig (d'injures)* flood, deluge; *Fig (de coups)* shower

déluré, -ée [delyre] *adj (vif)* smart, sharp; *Péj (provocant)* forward

démagogie [demagɔʒi] *nf* demagogy ▪ **démagogue** *nmf* demagogue

demain [dəmɛ̃] *adv* tomorrow; **d. soir** tomorrow evening; **à d.!** see you tomorrow!; *Fam* **ce n'est pas d. la veille** that won't happen for a long time yet

demande [dəmɑ̃d] *nf (requête)* request (**de** for); *Écon* demand; **faire une d. de qch** *(prêt, permis)* to apply for sth; **à la d. générale** by popular demand; **sur d.** on request; **d. en mariage** proposal of marriage; **faire sa d. (en mariage)** to propose; **demandes d'emploi** *(dans le journal)* jobs wanted, *Br* situations wanted

> Il faut noter que le nom anglais **demand** est un faux ami. Il signifie le plus souvent **exigence**.

demander [dəmɑ̃de] **1** *vt* to ask for; *(prix, raison)* to ask; *(exiger)* to demand; *(nécessiter)* to require; **d. le chemin/l'heure** to ask the way/the time; **d. qch à qn** to ask sb for sth; **d. à qn de faire qch** to ask sb to do sth; **d. si/ où...** to ask *or* inquire whether/where...; **ça demande du temps** it takes time; **je peux vous d. votre nom?** may I ask your name?; **d. qn en mariage** to propose (marriage) to sb; **elle est très demandée** she's in great demand; **on te demande!** you're wanted! **2 se demander** *upr* to wonder, to ask oneself (**pourquoi** why, **si** if) ▪ **demandeur, -euse** *nmf* **d. d'emploi** job seeker

Il faut noter que le verbe anglais **to demand** est un faux ami. Il signifie **exiger**.

démanger [demãʒe] *vti* to itch; **le bras me démange** my arm's itching; **ça me démange de lui dire...** *(j'ai très envie de)* I'm itching to tell him/her... ▪ **démangeaison** *nf* itch; **avoir des démangeaisons** to be itching; **j'ai une d. au bras** my arm's itching

démanteler [demãtle] *vt* to break up

démantibuler [demãtibyle] *vt Fam (meuble)* to break up

démaquiller [demakije] **se démaquiller** *vpr* to remove one's make-up ▪ **démaquillant** *nm* cleanser

démarcation [demarkɑsjɔ̃] *nf* demarcation

démarche [demarʃ] *nf (allure)* walk, gait; *(requête)* step; **faire les démarches nécessaires pour...** to take the necessary steps to...; **faire une d. auprès de qn** to approach sb; **d. intellectuelle** thought process

démarcheur, -euse [demarʃœr, -øz] *nmf (vendeur)* door-to-door salesperson

démarquer [demarke] **1** *vt (marchandises)* to mark down **2 se démarquer** *vpr Sport* to lose one's marker; *Fig* **se d. de qn** to distinguish from sb

démarrer [demare] **1** *vi (moteur)* to start; *(voiture)* to move off; *Fig (entreprise)* to get off the ground **2** *vt Fam (moteur, travaux)* to start; *Ordinat* to start up, to boot up ▪ **démarrage** *nm (de moteur)* starting; *(d'ordinateur)* start; **au d.** when moving off; *Fig* **d. en côte** hill start

démasquer [demaske] *vt* to unmask

démêler [demele] *vt* to untangle; *Fig* **d. le vrai du faux** to disentangle the truth from the lies ▪ **démêlé** *nm (dispute)* disagreement; **avoir des démêlés avec la justice** to be in trouble with the law

démembrer [demãbre] *vt (empire)* to break up

déménager [demenaʒe] **1** *vi* to move; *Fam (musique)* to be mind-blowing **2** *vt (meubles)* to move ▪ **déménagement** *nm* move ▪ **déménageur** *nm Br* removal man, *Am* (furniture) mover

démener [demne] **se démener** *vpr (s'agiter)* to thrash about; **se d. pour faire qch** to spare no effort to do sth

dément, -ente [demã, -ãt] **1** *adj* insane; *Fam (formidable)* fantastic **2** *nmf* lunatic ▪ **démence** *nf* insanity ▪ **démentiel, -ielle** *adj* insane

démentir [demãtir] *vt (nouvelle, fait)* to deny; *(être en contradiction avec)* to belie ▪ **démenti** *nm* denial; **opposer un d. à qch** to make a formal denial of sth

démerder [demerde] **se démerder** *vpr très Fam* to get by; **se d. pour faire qch** to manage to do sth

démesure [deməzyr] *nf* excess ▪ **démesuré, -ée** *adj* excessive

démettre* [demetr] **1** *vt* **d. qn de ses fonctions** to remove sb from his/her post **2 se démettre** *vpr* **se d. l'épaule** to dislocate one's shoulder; **se d. de ses fonctions** to resign from one's post

demeurant [dəmœrã] **au demeurant** *adv (malgré tout)* for all that; *(d'ailleurs)* after all

demeure [dəmœr] *nf (belle maison)* mansion; **à d.** permanently; **mettre qn en d. de faire qch** to instruct sb to do sth

demeuré, -ée *adj Fam Péj* halfwitted

demeurer [dəmœre] *vi* (a) *(aux être) (rester)* to remain; **en d. là** *(affaire)* to rest there (b) *(aux avoir) Formel (habiter)* to reside

demi, -ie [dəmi] **1** *adj* half; **une heure et demie** an hour and a half; *(à l'horloge)* half past one, one-thirty

2 *adv* (à) **d. plein** half-full; **à d. nu** half-naked; **dormir à d.** to be half asleep; **ouvrir qch à d.** to open sth halfway

3 *nmf (moitié)* half

4 *nm* **un d.** *(bière)* a beer, *Br* ≃ a half-pint; *Football* midfielder; *Rugby* **d. de mêlée** scrum half

5 *nf* **à la demie** *(à l'horloge)* at half-past ▪ **demi-cercle** *(pl* **demi-cercles)** *nm* semicircle ▪ **demi-douzaine** *(pl* **demi-douzaines)** *nf* **une d. (de)** half a dozen ▪ **demi-écrémé** *adj (lait) Br* semi-skimmed, *Am* semi-skim ▪ **demi-finale** *(pl* **demi-finales)** *nf Sport* semifinal ▪ **demi-frère** *(pl* **demi-frères)** *nm* half brother ▪ **demi-heure** *(pl* **demi-heures)** *nf* **une d.** half an hour ▪ **demi-journée** *(pl* **demi-journées)** *nf* half-day ▪ **demi-mesure** *(pl* **demi-mesures)** *nf* half-measure ▪ **demi-mot** *mn* **comprendre à d.** to take the hint ▪ **demi-pension** *nf Br* half-board, *Am* breakfast and one meal ▪ **demi-pensionnaire** *(pl* **demi-pensionnaires)** *nmf Scol Br* day boarder, *Am* day student ▪ **demi-saison** *(pl* **demi-saisons)** *nf* **de d.** *(vêtement)* spring and autumn ▪ **demi-sel** *adj inv (beurre)* slightly salted; **fromage d.** slightly salted cream cheese ▪ **demi-sœur** *(pl* **demi-sœurs)** *nf* half sister ▪ **demi-tarif** *(pl* **demi-tarifs)** *nm* half-price ▪ **demi-tour** *(pl* **demi-tours)** *nm Br* about turn, *Am* about face; *(en voiture)* U-turn; **faire d.** *(à pied)* to turn back; *(en voiture)* to do a U-turn

déminéralisée [demineralize] *adj f* **eau d.** distilled water

démis, -ise [demi, -miz] *adj* **avoir l'épaule démise** to have a dislocated shoulder

démission [demisjɔ̃] *nf* resignation; **donner sa d.** to hand in one's resignation ▪ **démissionner** *vi* to resign

démobiliser [demɔbilize] *vt* to demobilize ▪ **démobilisation** *nf* demobilization

démocrate [demɔkrat] **1** *adj* democratic **2** *nmf* democrat ▪ **démocratie** [-asi] *nf* democracy ▪ **démocratique** *adj* democratic

démodé, -ée [demode] *adj* old-fashioned

démographie [demɔgrafi] *nf* demography ▪ **démographique** *adj* demographic

demoiselle [dəmwazɛl] *nf (jeune fille)* young lady; *(célibataire)* single woman; **d. d'honneur** *(de mariée)* bridesmaid

démolir [demɔlir] *vt (maison)* to pull down, to demolish; *(jouet)* to wreck; *Fig (théorie, adversaire)* to demolish; *Fam* **d. le portrait à qn** to smash sb's face in ▪ **démolition** *nf* demolition; **en d.** being demolished

démon [demɔ̃] *nm* demon; **le d.** the Devil ▪ **démoniaque** *adj* demonic

démonstratif, -ive [demɔ̃stratif, -iv] **1** *adj* demonstrative **2** *nm Grammaire* demonstrative

démonstration [demɔ̃strasjɔ̃] *nf* demonstration; *Math* **faire la d. de qch** to demonstrate sth; **être en d.** *(appareil)* to be a display model; **d. de force** show of force

démonter [demɔ̃te] **1** *vt (mécanisme, tente)* to dismantle; *(pneu)* to remove; *Fam (déconcerter)* to throw; **une mer démontée** a raging sea **2 se démonter** *vpr (mécanisme)* to come apart; *Fam* **elle ne s'est pas démontée pour si peu** she wasn't so easily thrown

démontrer [demɔ̃tre] *vt* to demonstrate

démoraliser [demɔralize] **1** *vt* to demoralize **2 se démoraliser** *vpr* to become demoralized ▪ **démoralisation** *nf* demoralization

démordre [demɔrdr] *vi* **ne pas d. de qch** to stick to sth

démouler [demule] *vt (gâteau)* to turn out

démuni, -e [demyni] *adj* penniless

démunir [demynir] **1** *vt* **d. qn de qch** to deprive sb of sth **2 se démunir** *vpr* **se d. de qch** to part with sth

démystifier [demistifje] *vt* to demystify

dénationaliser [denasjɔnalize] *vt* to denationalize

dénaturer [denatyre] *vt (propos, faits)* to distort; *(goût)* to alter ▪ **dénaturé, -ée** *adj (parents, goût)* unnatural

dénégation [denegasjɔ̃] *nf* denial

déneiger [deneʒe] *vt* to clear the snow from

dénicher [denife] *vt Fam (objet)* to unearth; *(personne)* to track down

dénier [denje] *vt (responsabilité, faute)* to deny; **d. qch à qn** to deny sb sth

dénigrer [denigre] *vt* to denigrate ▪ **dénigrement** [-əmɑ̃] *nm* denigration

dénivellation [denivelasjɔ̃] *nf* difference in level; **dénivellations** *(relief)* bumps

dénombrer [denɔ̃bre] *vt* to count

dénominateur [denɔminatœr] *nm Math* denominator; **plus petit d. commun** lowest common denominator

dénommer [denɔme] *vt* to name ▪ **dénomination** *nf* designation ▪ **dénommé, -ée** *nmf* **un d. Dupont** a man named Dupont

dénoncer [denɔ̃se] **1** *vt (injustice, abus, malfaiteur)* to denounce **(à** to); *(élève)* to tell on **(à** to) **2 se dénoncer** *vpr (malfaiteur)* to give oneself up **(à** to); *(élève)* to own up **(à** to) ▪ **dénonciation** *nf* denunciation

dénoter [denɔte] *vt* to denote

dénouement [denumɑ̃] *nm (de livre)* ending; *(de pièce de théâtre)* dénouement; *(d'affaire)* outcome

dénouer [denwe] **1** *vt (nœud, corde)* to undo, to untie; *(cheveux)* to let down, to undo; *Fig (intrigue)* to unravel **2 se dénouer** *vpr (nœud)* to come undone; *(cheveux)* to come down

dénoyauter [denwajote] *vt Br* to stone, *Am* to pit

denrée [dɑ̃re] *nf* foodstuff; **denrées alimentaires** foodstuffs; **denrées périssables** perishable goods

dense [dɑ̃s] *adj* dense ▪ **densité** *nf* density

dent [dɑ̃] *nf* tooth *(pl* teeth); *(de roue)* cog; *(de fourchette)* prong; *(de timbre-poste)* perforation; **d. de lait/sagesse** milk/wisdom tooth; **faire ses dents** *(enfant)* to be teething; **coup de d.** bite; **n'avoir rien à se mettre sous la d.** to have nothing to eat; **manger du bout des dents** to pick at one's food; **être sur les dents** *(énervé)* to be on edge; *(surmené)* to be exhausted; *Fam* **avoir une d. contre qn** to have a grudge against sb; **en dents de scie** serrated; *Fig (résultats)* uneven ▪ **dentaire** *adj* dental ▪ **dentée** *adj f* **roue d.** cogwheel

dentelé, -ée [dɑ̃tle] *adj (côte, feuille)* jagged

dentelle [dɑ̃tɛl] *nf* lace

dentier [dɑ̃tje] *nm (set of)* false teeth, dentures

dentifrice [dɑ̃tifris] *nm* toothpaste

dentiste [dɑ̃tist] *nmf* dentist ▪ **dentition** *nf (dents)* (set of) teeth ▪ **denture** *nf* set of teeth

> Il faut noter que le nom anglais **dentures** est un faux ami. Il signifie **dentier**.

dénuder [denyde] *vt* to (lay) bare ▪ **dénudé, -ée** *adj* bare

dénué, -ée [denɥe] *adj* **d. de sens/d'intérêt** devoid of sense/interest

dénuement [denymɑ̃] *nm* destitution; **dans le d.** poverty-stricken

déodorant [deodorɑ̃] *nm* deodorant ▪ **déodoriser** *vt* to deodorize

dépanner [depane] *vt (machine)* to repair; *Fam* **d. qn** to help sb out ▪ **dépannage** *nm* (emergency) repairs; **voiture/service de d.** breakdown vehicle/service ▪ **dépanneur** *nm (de télévision)* repairman; *(de voiture)* breakdown mechanic ▪ **dépanneuse** *nf (voiture) Br* breakdown lorry, *Am* wrecker

dépareillé, -ée [depareje] *adj (chaussure)* odd; *(collection)* incomplete

départ [depar] *nm* departure; *(de course)* start; **les grands départs** the great holiday exodus; **point/ligne de d.** starting point/post; **salaire**

de d. starting salary; **au d.** at the outset, at the start; **dès le d.** (right) from the start; **au d. de Paris** *(excursion)* leaving from Paris; **à mon d. de Paris** when I left Paris

départager [departaʒe] *vt* to decide between

département [departəmɑ̃] *nm* department *(division of local government)* ▪**départe-mental, -e, -aux, -ales** *adj* departmental; **route départementale** secondary road, *Br* ≃ B road

départir* [departir] **se départir** *vpr* **il ne s'est jamais départi de son calme** his calm never deserted him

dépasser [depɑse] **1** *vt (véhicule) Br* to overtake, *Am* to pass; *(endroit)* to go past; *(prévisions, vitesse)* to exceed; **d. qn** *(en hauteur)* to be taller than sb; *(surclasser)* to be ahead of sb; *Fig* **ça me dépasse** that's beyond me **2** *vi (jupon, clou)* to stick out ▪**dépassé, -ée** *adj (démodé)* outdated; *(incapable)* unable to cope ▪**dépassement** *nm (en voiture) Br* overtaking, *Am* passing

dépayser [depeize] *vt Br* to disorientate, *Am* to disorient ▪**dépaysement** *nm* disorientation

dépecer [depəse] *vt (animal)* to cut up

dépêche [depɛʃ] *nf* dispatch ▪**dépêcher 1** *vt* to dispatch **2 se dépêcher** *vpr* to hurry (up); **se d. de faire qch** to hurry to do sth

dépeindre* [depɛ̃dr] *vt* to describe

dépenaillé, -ée [depənaje] *adj (rideau)* ragged, tattered; *(personne)* in rags, in tatters

dépendant, -ante [depɑ̃dɑ̃, -ɑ̃t] dependent (**de** on) ▪**dépendance** *nf* dependence; **sous la d. de qn** under sb's domination ▪**dépendances** *nfpl (bâtiments)* outbuildings

dépendre [depɑ̃dr] *vi* to depend (**de** on, upon); **d. de** *(appartenir à)* to belong to; *(être soumis à)* to be dependent on; **ça dépend de toi** that's up to you

dépens [depɑ̃] *nmpl* **aux d. de** at the expense of; **apprendre qch à ses d.** to learn sth to one's cost

dépense [depɑ̃s] *nf (frais)* expense, expenditure; **faire des dépenses** to spend money; **d. physique** physical exertion ▪**dépenser 1** *vt (argent)* to spend; *(électricité)* to use; *(forces)* to exert **2 se dépenser** *vpr* to burn up energy

dépensier, -ière [depɑ̃sje, -jɛr] *adj* extravagant

déperdition [deperdisjɔ̃] *nf (de chaleur)* loss

dépérir [deperir] *vi (personne)* to waste away; *(plante)* to wither

dépêtrer [depetre] **se dépêtrer** *vpr Fam* to extricate oneself (**de** from)

dépeupler [depœple] **1** *vt* to depopulate **2 se dépeupler** *vpr* to become depopulated ▪**dépeuplement** [-əmɑ̃] *nm* depopulation

dépilatoire [depilatwar] **1** *adj* **crème d.** hair-removing cream **2** *nm* hair-remover

dépister [depiste] *vt (criminel)* to track down; *(maladie)* to detect ▪**dépistage** *nm (de maladie)* screening

dépit [depi] *nm* spite; **par d.** out of spite; **en d. de** in spite of; **en d. du bon sens** *(mal)* atrociously

dépité, -ée [depite] *adj* annoyed

déplacement [deplasmɑ̃] *nm (voyage)* trip; *(d'ouragan, de troupes)* movement; **être en d.** *(homme d'affaires)* to be on a business trip; **frais de d.** *Br* travelling *or Am* traveling expenses

déplacer [deplase] **1** *vt (objet)* to move; *(fonctionnaire)* to transfer **2 se déplacer** *vpr (aiguille d'une montre)* to move; *(personne, animal)* to move (about); *(marcher)* to walk (around); *(voyager)* to travel ▪**déplacé, -ée** *adj (mal à propos)* out of place; **personne déplacée** *(réfugié)* displaced person

déplaire* [deplɛr] **1** *vi* **d. à qn** to displease sb; **ça me déplaît** I don't like it; *Ironique* **n'en déplaise à...** with all due respect to... **2 se déplaire** *vpr* **il se déplaît à Paris** he doesn't like it in Paris ▪**déplaisant, -ante** *adj* unpleasant ▪**déplaisir** *nm* displeasure

déplier [deplije] *vt* to open out, to unfold ▪**dépliant** *nm (prospectus)* leaflet

déplorer [deplɔre] *vt (regretter)* to deplore; **d. que...** (+ *subjunctive*) to deplore the fact that...; **d. la mort de qn** to mourn sb's death ▪**déplorable** *adj* deplorable

déployer [deplwaje] **1** *vt (ailes)* to spread; *(journal, carte)* to unfold; *(troupes)* to deploy **2 se déployer** *vpr (drapeau)* to unfurl ▪**déploiement** *nm (démonstration)* display; *(d'une armée)* deployment

déplumer [deplyme] **se déplumer** *vpr (oiseau)* to *Br* moult *or Am* molt; *Fam (personne)* to go bald ▪**déplumé, -ée** *adj (oiseau)* featherless; *Fam (personne)* bald

dépoli, -ie [depɔli] *adj* **verre d.** frosted glass

déporter [depɔrte] *vt* **d. qn** to send sb to a concentration camp ▪**déportation** *nf* internment ▪**déporté, -ée** *nmf* internee

déposer [depoze] **1** *vt (poser)* to put down; *(gerbe)* to lay; *(brevet)* to register; *(projet de loi)* to introduce; *(souverain)* to depose; **d. qn** *(en voiture)* to drop sb off; **d. une lettre à la poste** to mail a letter; **d. de l'argent sur un compte** to deposit money in an account; **d. les armes** to lay down one's arms; **d. une plainte contre qn** to lodge a complaint against sb **2** *vi Jur* to testify; *(liquide)* to leave a deposit **3 se déposer** *vpr (poussière, lie)* to settle

dépositaire [depoziter] *nmf (vendeur)* agent; *(de secret)* custodian

déposition [depozisjɔ̃] *nf Jur* statement; *(de souverain)* deposing

déposséder [deposede] *vt* to deprive, to dispossess (**de** of)

dépôt [depo] *nm (de vin)* deposit, sediment; *(argent)* deposit; *(entrepôt)* depot; *(prison)* jail; **d. calcaire** *(de bouilloire)* fur; **mettre qch en d.** to put sth in storage; **d. de munitions** munitions depot; **d. d'ordures** *Br* rubbish dump, *Am* garbage dump; **d.-vente** = *Br* secondhand clothes shop, *Am* thrift store

dépotoir [depotwar] *nm* dump; *Fam (classe)* dumping ground

dépouille [depuj] *nf (d'animal)* hide, skin; **les dépouilles** *(butin)* the spoils; **d. (mortelle)** *(de défunt)* mortal remains

dépouiller [depuje] **1** *vt (animal)* to skin; *(analyser)* to go through; **d. qn de qch** to deprive sb of sth; **d. un scrutin** to count the votes **2 se dépouiller** *upr* **se d. de qch** to rid oneself of sth ▪**dépouillé, -ée** *adj (arbre)* bare; *(style)* austere ▪**dépouillement** *nm (de documents)* analysis; *(privation)* deprivation; *(sobriété)* austerity; **d. du scrutin** counting of the votes

dépourvu, -ue [depurvy] *adj* **d. de qch** devoid of sth; **prendre qn au d.** to catch sb off guard

dépoussiérer [depusjere] *vt* to dust

dépraver [deprave] *vt* to deprave ▪**dépravation** *nf* depravity ▪**dépravé, -ée** *adj* depraved

déprécier [depresje] **1** *vt* to undervalue **2 se déprécier** *upr (valeurs, marchandises)* to depreciate ▪**dépréciation** *nf* depreciation

dépression [depresjɔ̃] *nf (creux, maladie)* depression; **zone de d. atmosphérique** trough of low pressure; **d. économique** slump; **d. nerveuse** nervous breakdown; **faire de la d.** to be suffering from depression ▪**dépressif, -ive** *adj* depressive

déprime [deprim] *nf Fam* depression; **avoir un petit coup de d.** to feel a bit low ▪**déprimé, -ée** *adj* depressed ▪**déprimer 1** *vt* to depress **2** *vi Fam* to be feeling low

depuis [dəpɥi] **1** *prép* since; **d. lundi/1990** since Monday/1990; **j'habite ici d. un mois** I've been living here for a month; **d. quand êtes-vous là?, d. combien de temps êtes-vous là?** how long have you been here?; **d. peu/ longtemps** for a short/long time; **je le connais d. toujours** I've known him all my life; *Fam* **d. des siècles** for ages; **d. le temps que je le connais!** I've known him for ages!; **d. Paris jusqu'à Londres** from Paris to London **2** *adv* since (then), ever since **3** *conj* **d. que** since; **d. qu'elle est partie** since she left

député [depyte] *nm Pol* deputy, *Br* ≃ MP, *Am* ≃ representative; **d. du Parlement européen** Member of the European Parliament

déraciner [derasine] *vt (arbre, personne)* to uproot

dérailler [deraje] *vi (train)* to leave the rails; *Fam (personne)* to talk drivel; **faire d. un train** to derail a train ▪**déraillement** *nm (de train)*

derailment ▪**dérailleur** *nm (de bicyclette)* derailleur (gears)

déraisonnable [derɛzɔnabl] *adj* unreasonable ▪**déraisonner** *vi* to talk nonsense

déranger [derɑ̃ʒe] **1** *vt (affaires)* to disturb; *(projets)* to upset; *(vêtements)* to mess up; **je viendrai si ça ne te dérange pas** I'll come if that' all right with you; **ça vous dérange si je fume?** do you mind if I smoke?; **avoir l'estomac dérangé** to have an upset stomach; **il a l'esprit dérangé** he's deranged **2 se déranger** *upr* to put oneself to a lot of trouble (**pour faire** to do); *(se déplacer)* to move; **ne te dérange pas!** don't bother! ▪**dérangement** *nm (gêne)* trouble; **excusez-moi pour le d.** I'm sorry to trouble you; **en d.** *(téléphone)* out of order

déraper [derape] *vi (véhicule)* to skid; *Fam (personne)* to slip ▪**dérapage** *nm* skid; *Fig* **le d. des prix** spiralling prices

dératé [derate] *nm Fam* **courir comme un d.** to run like mad

dérégler [deregle] **1** *vt (mécanisme)* to cause to malfunction **2 se dérégler** *upr (mécanisme)* to go wrong ▪**dérèglement** [-ɛgləmɑ̃] *nm (de mécanisme)* malfunctioning

dérider [deride] *vt*, **se dérider** *upr* to cheer up

> Il faut noter que le verbe anglais **to deride** est un faux ami. Il signifie le plus souvent **ridiculiser**.

dérision [derizjɔ̃] *nf* derision; **tourner qch en d.** to deride sth; **par d.** derisively ▪**dérisoire** *adj (somme)* derisory

dérivatif [derivatif] *nm* distraction (**à** from)

dériver [derive] **1** *vt (cours d'eau)* to divert **2** *vi Naut* to drift; **d. de** *(mot)* to be derived from ▪**dérivation** *nf (de cours d'eau)* diversion ▪**dérive** *nf Naut* drift; **à la d.** adrift ▪**dérivé** *nm (mot, substance)* derivative

dermatologie [dermatolɔʒi] *nf* dermatology ▪**dermatologiste** [-tɔlɔʒist], **dermatologue** [-tɔlɔg] *nmf* dermatologist

dernier, -ière [dɛrnje, -jɛr] **1** *adj (ultime)* last; *(marquant la fin)* final; *(nouvelles, mode)* latest; *(étage)* top; *(degré)* highest; **le d. rang** the back or last row; **de d. ordre** third-rate; **ces derniers mois** these past few months; **les dix dernières minutes** the last ten minutes; **de la dernière importance** of (the) utmost importance; **en d.** last **2** *nmf* last; **ce d.** *(de deux)* the latter; *(de plusieurs)* the last-mentioned; **être le d. de la classe** to be (at the) bottom of the class; **le d. des derniers** the lowest of the low; **le d. de mes soucis** the least of my worries; **avoir le d. mot** to have the last word ▪**dernier-né, dernière-née** *(mpl* **derniers-nés,** *fpl* **dernières-nées)** *nmf* youngest (child) ▪**dernièrement** *adv* recently

dérobade [deʀɔbad] *nf (esquive)* evasion

dérober [deʀɔbe] **1** *vt (voler)* to steal (**à** from); *(cacher)* to hide (**à** from) **2 se dérober** *vpr (s'esquiver)* to slip away; *(éviter de répondre)* to dodge the issue; **se d. à la curiosité de qn** to avoid sb's prying eyes; **se d. aux regards** to hide from view; **ses jambes se sont dérobées sous lui** his legs gave way beneath him ▪**dérobé, -ée** *adj (porte)* hidden; **à la dérobée** on the sly

dérogation [deʀɔgasjɔ̃] *nf* exemption (**à** to)

déroger [deʀɔʒe] *vi* **d. à une règle** to depart from a rule

dérouiller [deʀuje] *Fam* **1** *vt* **d. qn** *(battre)* to thrash sb **2 se dérouiller** *vpr* **se d. les jambes** to stretch one's legs ▪**dérouillée** *nf Fam* belting

dérouler [deʀule] **1** *vt (tapis)* to unroll; *(fil)* to unwind **2 se dérouler** *vpr (tapis)* to unroll; *(fil)* to unwind; *Fig (événement)* to take place ▪**déroulement** *nm (d'action)* unfolding

déroute [deʀut] *nf (d'armée)* rout

dérouter [deʀute] *vt (avion, navire)* to divert, to reroute; *(poursuivant)* to throw off the scent; *Fig (étonner)* to throw

derrière [deʀjɛʀ] **1** *prép & adv* behind; **d. moi** behind me; **assis d.** *(dans une voiture)* sitting in the back; **par d.** *(attaquer)* from behind, from the rear **2** *nm (de maison)* back, rear; *(fesses)* behind; **patte de d.** hind leg; **roue de d.** back *or* rear wheel

des [de] *voir* **de, un**

dès [dɛ] *prép* from; **d. le début** (right) from the start; **d. maintenant** from now on; **d. son enfance** since *or* from childhood; **d. le VIᵉ siècle** as early as *or* as far back as the sixth century; **d. l'aube** (at the crack of) dawn; **d. lors** *(dans le temps)* from then on; *(en conséquence)* consequently; **d. leur arrivée** as soon as they arrive/arrived; **d. qu'elle viendra** as soon as she comes

désabusé, -ée [dezabyze] *adj* disillusioned

désaccord [dezakɔʀ] *nm* disagreement; **être en d. avec qn** to disagree with sb ▪**désaccordé, -ée** *adj (instrument)* out of tune

désaccoutumer [dezakutyme] **se désaccoutumer** *vpr* **se d. de qch** to get out of the habit of sth

désaffecté, -ée [dezafɛkte] *adj* disused

désaffection [dezafɛksjɔ̃] *nf* disaffection (**à l'égard de** with)

désagréable [dezagreabl] *adj* unpleasant

désagréger [dezagreʒe] *vt*, **se désagréger** *vpr* to disintegrate ▪**désagrégation** *nf* disintegration

désagrément [dezagremã] *nm (gêne)* trouble; *(souci, aspect négatif)* problem

désaltérer [dezaltere] **1** *vt* **d. qn** to quench sb's thirst **2 se désaltérer** *vpr* to quench one's thirst ▪**désaltérant, -ante** *adj* thirst-quenching

désamorcer [dezamɔʀse] *vt (bombe, conflit)* to defuse

désappointer [dezapwɛ̃te] *vt Littéraire* to disappoint

désapprouver [dezapʀuve] **1** *vt* to disapprove of **2** *vi* to disapprove ▪**désapprobateur, -trice** *adj* disapproving ▪**désapprobation** *nf* disapproval

désarçonner [dezaʀsɔne] *vt (jockey)* to throw, to unseat; *Fig (déconcerter)* to throw

désarmer [dezaʀme] **1** *vt (soldat, nation)* to disarm; *Fig* **d. qn** *(franchise, attitude)* to disarm sb **2** *vi (pays)* to disarm; **il ne désarme pas** he won't give up ▪**désarmant, -ante** *adj* disarming ▪**désarmé, -ée** *adj (sans défense)* unarmed; *Fig (sans défenses)* helpless ▪**désarmement** [-əmã] *nm (de nation)* disarmament

désarroi [dezaʀwa] *nm* confusion; **être en plein d.** to be in a state of utter confusion

désarticulé, -ée [dezaʀtikyle] *adj (pantin, clown)* double-jointed

désastre [dezastʀ] *nm* disaster ▪**désastreux, -euse** *adj* disastrous

désavantage [dezavãtaʒ] *nm* disadvantage ▪**désavantager** *vt* to put at a disadvantage ▪**désavantageux, -euse** *adj* disadvantageous

désaveu, -x [dezavø] *nm (reniement)* disowning

désavouer [dezavwe] *vt (renier)* to disown

désaxé, -ée [dezakse] **1** *adj (psychiquement)* unbalanced **2** *nmf* unbalanced person

desceller [desele] **1** *vt (pierre)* to loosen **2 se desceller** *vpr* to come loose

descendant, -ante [desãdã, -ãt] **1** *adj* descending **2** *nmf* descendant ▪**descendance** *nf (enfants)* descendants; *(origine)* descent

descendre [desãdʀ] **1** *(aux être)* *vi* to come/go down (**de** from); *(d'un train)* to get off (**de** from); *(d'un arbre)* to climb down (**de** from); *(nuit, thermomètre)* to fall; *(marée)* to go out; **d. de cheval** to dismount; **d. à l'hôtel** to put up at a hotel; **d. chez un ami** to stay with a friend; **d. de** *(être issu de)* to be descended from **2** *(aux avoir)* *vt (escalier)* to come/go down; *(objet)* to bring/take down; *Fam* **d. qn** *(tuer)* to bump sb off

descente [desãt] *nf (d'avion)* descent; *(en parachute)* drop; *(pente)* slope; *(de police)* raid (**dans** upon); **il fut accueilli à sa d. d'avion** he was met as he got off the plane; **d. de lit** bedside rug

descriptif, -ive [deskriptif, -iv] *adj* descriptive ▪**description** *nf* description

désemparé, -ée [dezãpaʀe] *adj (personne)* at a loss

désemplir [dezãpliʀ] *vi* **ce magasin ne désemplit pas** this shop is always crowded

désenchanté, -ée [dezɑ̃ʃɑ̃te] *adj* disillusioned
• **désenchantement** *nm* disenchantment

désencombrer [dezɑ̃kɔ̃bre] *vt (passage)* to clear

désenfler [dezɑ̃fle] *vi (genou, cheville)* to go down, to become less swollen

déséquilibre [dezekilibr] *nm* imbalance; **en d.** unsteady • **déséquilibré, -ée** 1 *adj* unbalanced 2 *nmf* unbalanced person • **déséquilibrer** *vt* to throw off balance; *Fig (esprit, personne)* to unbalance

désert, -erte [dezɛr, -ɛrt] 1 *adj (lieu)* deserted; *(région)* uninhabited; **île déserte** desert island 2 *nm* desert • **désertique** *adj* **région d.** desert region

déserter [dezɛrte] *vti* to desert • **déserteur** *nm* deserter • **désertion** *nf* desertion

désespérer [dezɛspere] 1 *vt* to drive to despair 2 *vi* to despair **(de** *of)* 3 **se désespérer** *vpr* to despair • **désespérant, -ante** *adj (situation, personne)* hopeless • **désespéré, -ée** 1 *adj (personne)* in despair; *(cas, situation, efforts)* desperate 2 *nmf* desparate person • **désespérément** *adv* desperately

désespoir [dezɛspwar] *nm* despair; **au d.** in despair; **en d. de cause** in desperation

déshabiller [dezabije] *vt*, **se déshabiller** *vpr* to undress

déshabituer [dezabitɥe] *vt* **d. qn de qch** to get sb out of the habit of sth

désherber [dezɛrbe] *vti* to weed • **désherbant** *nm* weedkiller

déshériter [dezerite] *vt* to disinherit • **déshérité, -ée** *adj (pauvre)* deprived

déshonneur [dezɔnœr] *nm Br* dishonour, *Am* dishonor

déshonorer [dezɔnɔre] *vt* to disgrace • **déshonorant, -ante** *adj Br* dishonourable, *Am* dishonorable

déshydrater [dezidrate] 1 *vt* to dehydrate 2 **se déshydrater** *vpr* to become dehydrated

désigner [deziɲe] *vt (montrer)* to point to; *(choisir)* to choose; *(nommer)* to appoint; *(signifier)* to designate; **il est tout désigné pour ce travail** he's just the person for the job • **désignation** *nf* designation

désillusion [dezilyzjɔ̃] *nf* disillusion • **désillusionner** *vt* to disillusion

désinfecter [dezɛ̃fɛkte] *vt* to disinfect • **désinfectant, -ante** *nm & adj* disinfectant • **désinfection** *nf* disinfection

désinformation [dezɛ̃fɔrmasjɔ̃] *nf* disinformation

désintégrer [dezɛ̃tegre] **se désintégrer** *vpr* to disintegrate • **désintégration** *nf* disintegration

désintéresser [dezɛ̃terese] **se désintéresser** *vpr* **se d. de qch** to lose interest in sth • **désintéressé, -ée** *adj (altruiste)* disinterested • **désintérêt** *nm* lack of interest

désintoxication [dezɛ̃tɔksikasjɔ̃] *nf* detoxification, *Fam* detox; **faire une cure de d.** to undergo treatment for alcoholism/drug addiction • **désintoxiquer** 1 *vt (alcoolique, drogué)* to treat for alcoholism/drug abuse 2 **se désintoxiquer** *(alcoolique, drogué)* to come off alcohol/drugs

désinvolte [dezɛ̃vɔlt] *adj (dégagé)* casual; *(insolent)* offhand • **désinvolture** *nf* casualness; *(insolence)* offhandedness

désir [dezir] *nm* desire; **prendre ses désirs pour des réalités** to indulge in wishful thinking • **désirable** *adj* desirable • **désirer** *vt* to wish; *(convoiter)* to desire; **je désire venir** I wish to come; **je désire que tu viennes** I want you to come; **ça laisse à d.** it leaves a lot to be desired

désireux, -euse [dezirø, -øz] *adj* **d. de faire qch** anxious to do sth

désister [deziste] **se désister** *vpr* to withdraw • **désistement** [-əmɑ̃] *nm* withdrawal

désobéir [dezɔbeir] *vi* to disobey; **d. à qn** to disobey sb • **désobéissance** *nf* disobedience (**à** to) • **désobéissant, -ante** *adj* disobedient

désobligeant, -ante [dezɔbliʒɑ̃, -ɑ̃t] *adj* disagreeable

désodorisant [dezɔdɔrizɑ̃] *nm* air freshener

désœuvré, -ée [dezœvre] *adj* idle • **désœuvrement** [-əmɑ̃] *nm* idleness

désoler [dezɔle] 1 *vt* to upset 2 **se désoler** *vpr* to be upset **(de** at) • **désolant, -ante** *adj* upsetting • **désolation** *nf (peine)* distress • **désolé, -ée** *adj (région)* desolate; *(affligé)* upset; **être d. que...** (+ *subjunctive*) to be sorry that...; **je suis d. de vous déranger** I'm sorry to disturb you

désolidariser [desɔlidarize] **se désolidariser** *vpr* to dissociate oneself (**de** from)

désopilant, -ante [dezɔpilɑ̃, -ɑ̃t] *adj* hilarious

désordonné, -ée [dezɔrdɔne] *adj (personne, chambre)* untidy

désordre [dezɔrdr] *nm (manque d'ordre)* mess; *(manque d'organisation)* disorder; **en d.** untidy, messy; **de graves désordres** *(émeutes)* serious disturbances

désorganiser [dezɔrganize] *vt* to disorganize • **désorganisation** *nf* disorganization • **désorganisé, -ée** *adj* disorganized

désorienter [dezɔrjɑ̃te] *vt* **d. qn** to bewilder sb

désormais [dezɔrmɛ] *adv* from now on, in future

désosser [dezɔse] *vt (viande)* to bone

despote [dɛspɔt] *nm* despot • **despotique** *adj* despotic

desquels, desquelles [dekɛl] *voir* lequel

dessaisir [desezir] **se dessaisir** *vpr* **se d. de qch** to relinquish sth

dessaler [desale] *vt (poisson)* to remove the salt from *(by soaking)*

dessécher [desefe] **1** *vt (peau)* to dry up; *(végétation)* to wither **2 se dessécher** *vpr (peau)* to dry up; *(végétation)* to wither

dessein [desɛ̃] *nm* intention; **dans le d. de faire qch** with the intention of doing sth; **à d.** intentionally

desserrer [desere] **1** *vt (ceinture)* to loosen; *(poing)* to unclench; *(frein)* to release; *Fig* **il n'a pas desserré les dents** he didn't open his mouth **2 se desserrer** *vpr (ceinture)* to come loose

dessert [desɛr] *nm* dessert, *Br* pudding

desserte [desɛrt] *nf* **assurer la d. de** *(village)* to provide a service to

desservir [deservir] *vt (table)* to clear (away); **d. qn** to do sb a disservice; **le car dessert ce village** the bus stops at this village; **ce quartier est bien desservi** this district is well served by public transport

dessin [desɛ̃] *nm* drawing; *(rapide)* sketch; *(motif)* design, pattern; *(contour)* outline; **d. animé** cartoon; **d. humoristique** *(de journal)* cartoon

dessinateur, -trice [desinatœr, -tris] *nmf* drawer; **d. humoristique** cartoonist; **d. de modes** dress designer; **d. industriel** *Br* draughtsman, *Am* draftsman

dessiner [desine] **1** *vt* to draw; *(rapidement)* to sketch; *(meuble, robe)* to design; *(indiquer)* to outline; **d. (bien) la taille** *(vêtement)* to show off *or* draw attention to the waist **2 se dessiner** *vpr (colline)* to stand out; *(projet)* to take shape

dessoûler [desule] *vti Fam* to sober up

dessous [dəsu] **1** *adv* underneath; **en d.** underneath; **en d. de** below; *Fam* **être en d. de tout** to be worse than useless **2** *nm* underside; *(du pied)* bottom; **des d.** *(sous-vêtements)* underwear; **drap de d.** bottom sheet; **les gens du d.** the people downstairs *or* below ▪**dessous-de-plat** *nm inv* table mat ▪**dessous-de-table** *nm inv* bribe, *Br* backhander

dessus [dəsy] **1** *adv (marcher, écrire)* on it/them; *(monter)* on top (of it/them), on it/them; *(passer)* over it/them; **de d. la table** off *or* from the table **2** *nm* top; *(de chaussure)* upper; **drap de d.** top sheet; **les gens du d.** the people upstairs *or* above; **avoir le d.** to have the upper hand; **reprendre le d.** *(se remettre)* to get over it ▪**dessus-de-lit** *nm inv* bedspread

déstabiliser [destabilize] *vt* to destabilize

destin [destɛ̃] *nm* fate, destiny ▪**destinée** *nf* destiny

destinataire [destinatɛr] *nmf* addressee

destination [destinasjɔ̃] *nf (lieu)* destination; **trains à d. de...** trains to...; **arriver à d.** to reach one's destination

destiner [destine] **1** *vt* **d. qch à qn** to intend sth

for sb; **d. qn à** *(carrière, fonction)* to intend *or* destine sb for; **destiné à mourir** *(condamné)* destined *or* fated to die **2 se destiner** *vpr* **se d. à** *(carrière)* to intend to take up

destituer [destitɥe] *vt (fonctionnaire)* to remove from office ▪**destitution** *nf* removal from office

destroy [destrɔj] *adj Fam (musique)* = loud, fast and aggressive; *(personne)* self-destructive; **avoir une allure complètement d.** to look wasted

destructeur, -trice [destryktœr, -tris] *adj* destructive

destruction [destryksjɔ̃] *nf* destruction

désuet, -uète [desɥe, -ɥɛt] *adj* obsolete ▪**désuétude** *nf* **tomber en d.** *(expression)* to become obsolete

désunir [dezynir] *vt (famille, personnes)* to divide

détachant [detaʃɑ̃] *nm* stain remover

détachement [detaʃmɑ̃] *nm* (**a**) *(indifférence)* detachment (**b**) *(de fonctionnaire)* secondment; *(de troupes)* detachment

détacher¹ [detaʃe] **1** *vt (ceinture, vêtement)* to undo; *(mains, personne)* to untie; *(ôter)* to take off; *(mots)* to pronounce clearly; **d. qn** *(libérer)* to untie sb; *(affecter)* to transfer sb (on assignment) (**à** to); **d. les yeux de qn/qch** to take one's eyes off sb/sth; **'détachez en suivant les pointillés'** 'tear off along the dotted line' **2 se détacher** *vpr (chien, prisonnier)* to break loose; *(se dénouer)* to come undone; **se d. (de qch)** *(fragment)* to come off (sth); **se d. de ses amis** to break away from one's friends; **se d. (sur)** *(ressortir)* to stand out (against) ▪**détaché, -ée** *adj (nœud)* loose, undone; *(air, ton)* detached

détacher² [detaʃe] *vt (linge)* to remove the stains from

détail [detaj] *nm* detail; **en d.** in detail; **entrer dans les détails** to go into detail; **le d. de** *(dépenses)* a breakdown of; **magasin/prix de d.** retail store/price; **vendre au d.** to sell retail

détaillant [detajɑ̃] *nm* retailer

détailler [detaje] *vt (énumérer)* to detail ▪**détaillé, -ée** *adj (récit, description)* detailed; *(facture)* itemized

détaler [detale] *vi Fam* to take off

détartrer [detartre] *vt (chaudière, dents)* to scale

détaxer [detakse] *vt* to exempt from tax; **produit détaxé** duty-free article

détecter [detekte] *vt* to detect ▪**détecteur** *nm* *(appareil)* detector; **d. de fumée** smoke detector ▪**détection** *nf* detection

détective [detektiv] *nm* **d. (privé)** (private) detective

déteindre* [detɛ̃dr] *vi (couleur, tissu)* to run; **ton tablier bleu a déteint sur ma chemise** the blue of your apron has come off on(to) my shirt; *Fig*

d. sur qn *(influencer)* to leave one's mark on sb

dételer [detle] *vt (chevaux)* to unharness

détendre [detɑ̃dr] **1** *vt (corde)* to slacken; *(arc)* to unbend; **d. l'atmosphère** to make the atmosphere less tense; **d. qn** to relax sb **2 se détendre** *vpr (corde)* to slacken; *(arc)* to unbend; *(atmosphère)* to become less tense; *(personne)* to relax ▪ **détendu, -ue** *adj (visage, atmosphère)* relaxed; *(ressort, câble)* slack

détenir* [detənir] *vt (record, pouvoir, titre, prisonnier)* to hold; *(secret, objet volé)* to be in possession of ▪ **détenteur, -trice** *nmf (de record)* holder ▪ **détention** *nf (d'armes)* possession; *(captivité)* detention; **d. provisoire** detention pending trial ▪ **détenu, -ue** *nmf* prisoner

détente [detɑ̃t] *nf* (**a**) *(repos)* relaxation; *(entre deux pays)* détente (**b**) *(saut)* spring (**c**) *(gâchette)* trigger

détergent [detɛrʒɑ̃] *nm* detergent

détériorer [deterjɔre] **1** *vt* to damage **2 se détériorer** *vpr* to deteriorate ▪ **détérioration** *nf* damage (**de** to); *(d'une situation)* deterioration (**de** in)

détermination [detɛrminasjɔ̃] *nf (fermeté)* determination; *(de date, de lieu)* fixing

déterminer [detɛrmine] **1** *vt (préciser)* to determine; *(causer)* to bring about; **d. qn à faire qch** to induce sb to do sth **2 se déterminer** *vpr* **se d. à faire qch** to make up one's mind to do sth ▪ **déterminant, -ante 1** *adj* decisive **2** *nm* Grammaire determiner ▪ **déterminé, -ée** *adj (précis)* specific; *(résolu)* determined

déterrer [detere] *vt* to dig up

détester [detɛste] *vt* to hate, to detest; **d. faire qch** to hate doing *or* to do sth ▪ **détestable** *adj* foul

détonateur [detɔnatœr] *nm* detonator ▪ **détonation** *nf* explosion; *(d'arme)* bang

détonner [detɔne] *vi (contraster)* to clash

détour [detur] *nm (crochet)* detour; *(de route)* bend, curve; **sans d.** *(parler)* without beating about the bush; **faire un d.** to make a detour; **faire des détours** *(route)* to wind

détourner [deturne] **1** *vt (dévier)* to divert; *(avion)* to hijack; *(conversation, sens)* to change; *(fonds)* to embezzle; *(coup)* to ward off; **d. la tête** to turn one's head away; **d. les yeux** to look away; **d. qn de** *(son devoir, ses amis)* to take sb away from; *(sa route)* to lead sb away from **2 se détourner** *vpr* to turn away ▪ **détourné, -ée** *adj (chemin, moyen)* roundabout, indirect ▪ **détournement** [-əmɑ̃] *nm (de cours d'eau)* diversion; **d. d'avion** hijack(ing); **d. de fonds** embezzlement

détracteur, -trice [detraktœr, -tris] *nmf* detractor

détraquer [detrake] **1** *vt (mécanisme)* to put out of order **2 se détraquer** *vpr (machine)* to go wrong; **se d. l'estomac** to upset one's stomach; **se d. la santé** to ruin one's health ▪ **détraqué, -ée 1** *adj (appareil)* out of order; *(cerveau)* deranged **2** *nmf (obsédé)* sex maniac

détremper [detrɑ̃pe] *vt* to soak; **des terres détrempées** waterlogged ground

détresse [detrɛs] *nf* distress; **en d.** *(navire, âme)* in distress; **dans la d.** *(misère)* in (great) distress

détriment [detrimɑ̃] *nm* **au d. de** to the detriment of; **je l'ai appris à mon d.** I found it out to my cost

détritus [detritys] *nmpl Br* rubbish, *Am* garbage

détroit [detrwa] *nm* strait

détromper [detrɔ̃pe] **1** *vt* **d. qn** to put sb right **2 se détromper** *vpr* **détrompez-vous!** don't you believe it!

détrôner [detrone] *vt (souverain)* to dethrone; *(supplanter)* to supersede

détrousser [detruse] *vt Hum* **d. qn** to relieve sb of one's valuables

détruire* [detrɥir] *vt (ravager)* to destroy; *(tuer)* to kill; *(santé)* to ruin, to wreck

dette [dɛt] *nf* debt; **avoir des dettes** to be in debt; **faire des dettes** to run into debt

DEUG [dœg] *(abrév* **diplôme d'études universitaires générales)** *nm* = degree gained after two years' study at university

deuil [dœj] *nm (affliction, vêtements)* mourning; *(décès)* bereavement; **être en d., porter le d.** to be in mourning; **faire son d. de qch** to give sth up as lost

deux [dø] *adj inv & nm inv* two; **d. fois** twice; **mes d. sœurs** both my sisters, my two sisters; **tous (les) d.** both; *Fam* **en moins de d.** in no time (at all) ▪ **deux-pièces** *nm inv (maillot de bain)* bikini; *(appartement)* two-room(ed) *Br* flat *or Am* apartment ▪ **deux-points** *nm inv* colon ▪ **deux-roues** *nm inv* two-wheeled vehicle

deuxième [døzjɛm] *adj & nmf* second ▪ **deuxièmement** *adv* secondly

dévaler [devale] **1** *vt (escalier)* to hurtle down **2** *vi (personne, pièces)* to hurtle down; *(eau, lave)* to rush down

dévaliser [devalize] *vt (personne, banque)* to rob; *(maison)* to burgle

dévaloriser [devalɔrize] **1** *vt (monnaie, diplôme)* to devalue; *(personne, politique)* to discredit **2 se dévaloriser** *vpr (monnaie)* to depreciate; *(personne)* to put oneself down ▪ **dévalorisation** *nf (de diplôme)* loss of value

dévaluer [devalɥe] *vt (monnaie)* to devalue ▪ **dévaluation** *nf Fin* devaluation

devancer [dəvɑ̃se] *vt (concurrent)* to be ahead of; *(question)* to anticipate; *(arriver avant)* to arrive before; *Mil* **d. l'appel** to enlist before call-up

devant [dəvã] **1** *prép & adv* in front (of); **d. l'hôtel** in front of the hotel; **passer d. (l'église)** to go past (the church); **marcher d. (qn)** to walk in front (of sb); **assis d.** *(dans une voiture)* sitting in the front; **par d.** from *or* at the front; **loin d.** a long way ahead *or* in front; **d. le danger** *(confronté à)* in the face of danger; **d. mes yeux/la loi** before my eyes/the law; **l'avenir est d. toi** the future is ahead of you **2** *nm* front; **roue/porte de d.** front wheel/door; **patte de d.** foreleg; **prendre les devants** *(action)* to take the initiative

devanture [dəvãtyr] *nf (vitrine)* window; *(façade)* front

dévaster [devaste] *vt* to devastate ▪ **dévastation** *nf* devastation

déveine [devɛn] *nf Fam* bad luck

développer [devlɔpe] *vt,* **se développer** *vpr* to develop ▪ **développement** *nm* development; *(de photo)* developing; **en plein d.** *(entreprise, pays)* growing fast

devenir* [dəvnir] *(aux être) vi* to become; **d. médecin** to become a doctor; **d. un papillon/ un homme** or to grow into a butterfly/a man; **d. vieux** to get *or* grow old; **d. tout rouge** to go all red; **qu'est-il devenu?** what has become of him/it?; *Fam* **qu'est-ce que tu deviens?** how are you getting on?

dévergonder [devergɔde] **se dévergonder** *vpr* to get into bad ways ▪ **dévergondé, -ée** *adj* shameless

déverser [deverse] **1** *vt (liquide)* to pour out; *(bombes, ordures)* to dump **2 se déverser** *vpr (liquide, rivière)* to empty **(dans** into)

dévêtir [devetir] *vt,* **se dévêtir** *vpr* to undress

dévier [devje] **1** *vt (circulation)* to divert; *(coup, rayons)* to deflect **2** *vi (balle)* to deflect; *(véhicule)* to veer; **d. de sa route** to veer off course ▪ **déviation** *nf (itinéraire provisoire) Br* diversion, *Am* detour; *(modification)* deviation

devin [dəvɛ̃] *nm* soothsayer; *Fam* **je ne suis pas d.** I can't predict what will happen

deviner [dəvine] *vt* to guess **(que** that); *(avenir)* to predict; *(pensée)* to read ▪ **devinette** *nf* riddle

devis [dəvi] *nm* estimate; **faire faire un d. pour qch** to get an estimate for sth

dévisager [devizaʒe] *vt* **d. qn** to stare at sb

devise [dəviz] *nf (légende)* motto; *(monnaie)* currency; **devises étrangères** foreign currency

dévisser [devise] **1** *vt* to unscrew **2** *vi (en montagne)* to fall **3 se dévisser** *vpr (bouchon)* to unscrew; *(par accident)* to come unscrewed

dévoiler [devwale] **1** *vt (statue)* to unveil; *Fig (secret)* to disclose **2 se dévoiler** *vpr (mystère)* to come to light

devoir*¹ [dəvwar] *v aux* (**a**) *(indique la nécessité)* **je dois refuser** I must refuse, I have (got) to refuse; **j'ai dû refuser** I had to refuse (**b**) *(indique une forte probabilité)* **il doit être tard** it must be late; **elle a dû oublier** she must have forgotten; **il ne doit pas être bête** he can't be stupid; **cela devait arriver** it had to happen (**c**) *(indique l'obligation)* **tu dois apprendre tes leçons** you must learn your lessons; **vous devriez rester** you should stay, you ought to stay; **il aurait dû venir** he should have come, he ought to have come (**d**) *(indique l'intention)* **elle doit venir** she's supposed to be coming, she's due to come; **le train devait arriver à midi** the train was due (to arrive) at noon; **je devais le voir** I was (due) to see him

devoir*² [dəvwar] **1** *vt* to owe; **d. qch à qn** to owe sb sth, to owe sth to sb; **l'argent qui m'est dû** the money due to *or* owing to me, the money owed (to) me **2** *se devoir vpr* **comme il se doit** as is proper **3** *nm (obligation)* duty; **présenter ses devoirs à qn** to pay one's respects to sb; *Scol* **devoirs** homework; **faire ses devoirs** to do one's homework; **d. sur table** class examination

dévolu, -ue [devɔly] **1** *adj* **d. à qn** *(pouvoirs, tâche)* assigned to sb **2** *nm* **jeter son d. sur qn/qch** to set one's heart on sb/sth

dévorer [devɔre] *vt (manger)* to devour; *Fig (kilomètres)* to eat up; **d. qn/qch du regard** to devour sb/sth with one's eyes; **être dévoré par la jalousie** to be consumed by jealousy ▪ **dévorant, -ante** *adj (faim)* ravenous; *(passion)* devouring

dévot, -ote [devo, -ɔt] **1** *adj* devout **2** *nmf* devout person ▪ **dévotion** *nf (adoration)* devotion

dévouer [devwe] **se dévouer** *vpr (se sacrifier)* to volunteer; *(se consacrer)* to devote oneself (**à** to) ▪ **dévoué, -ée** *adj (ami, femme)* devoted (**à** to) ▪ **dévouement** [-umã] *nm* devotion; *(de héros)* devotion to duty

dévoyé, -ée [devwaje] *adj & nmf* delinquent

dextérité [dɛksterite] *nf* dexterity, skill

dézipper [dezipe] *vt Ordinat (fichier)* to unzip

diabète [djabet] *nm Méd* diabetes; **avoir du d.** to have diabetes ▪ **diabétique** *adj & nmf* diabetic

diable [djɑbl] *nm* devil; **le d.** the Devil; **habiter au d.** to live miles from anywhere; **faire qch à la d.** to do something anyhow; **se débattre comme un beau d.** to struggle with all one's might; **tirer le d. par la queue** to live from hand to mouth; **c'est bien le d. si...** I'll be damned if...; **quel d., cet enfant!** what a little devil that child is!; **où/pourquoi d....?** where/why the devil...? ▪ **diabolique** *adj* diabolical

diadème [djadɛm] *nm* tiara

diagnostic [djagnɔstik] *nm* diagnosis ▪ **diagnostiquer** *vt* to diagnose

diagonal, -e, -aux, -ales [djagɔnal, -o] *adj* diagonal ▪ **diagonale** *nf* diagonal (line); **en d.**

diagonally; *Fam* **lire qch en d.** to skim through sth

diagramme [djagram] *nm* diagram

dialecte [djalɛkt] *nm* dialect

dialogue [djalɔg] *nm Br* dialogue, *Am* dialog; *(conversation)* conversation ▪ **dialoguer** *vi* to communicate; *Ordinat* to interact

dialyse [djaliz] *nf Méd* dialysis

diamant [djamã] *nm* diamond

diamètre [djamɛtr] *nm* diameter ▪ **diamétralement** *adv* **d. opposés** diametrically opposed

diapason [djapazɔ̃] *nm Mus (appareil)* tuning fork; *Fig* **se mettre au d.** to fall in with the others

diaphane [djafan] *adj* diaphanous

diaphragme [djafragm] *nm* diaphragm

diapositive, *Fam* **diapo** [djapozitiv, djapo] *nf* slide

diarrhée [djare] *nf* diarrhoea; **avoir la d.** to have diarrhoea

diatribe [djatrib] *nf* diatribe

dictateur [diktatœr] *nm* dictator ▪ **dictatorial, -e, -aux, -ales** *adj* dictatorial ▪ **dictature** *nf* dictatorship

dicter [dikte] *vt* to dictate (à to) ▪ **dictée** *nf* dictation; **prendre qch sous la d. de qn** to take sth down at sb's dictation ▪ **Dictaphone**® *nm* dictaphone®

diction [diksjɔ̃] *nf* diction

dictionnaire [diksjɔnɛr] *nm* dictionary

dicton [diktɔ̃] *nm* saying

didactique [didaktik] *adj* didactic

dièse [djɛz] *adj & nm Mus* sharp **2** *nm Ordinat & Tél Br* hash (sign), *Am* pound (sign)

diesel [djezɛl] *adj & nm* **(moteur) d.** diesel (engine)

diète [djɛt] *nf (partielle)* diet; *(totale)* fast; **être à la d.** to be on a diet/to be fasting

diététicien, -ienne [djetetisjɛ̃, -jɛn] *nmf* dietician ▪ **diététique 1** *nf* dietetics *(sing)* **2** *adj* **aliment** *ou* **produit d.** health food; **magasin/restaurant d.** health-food shop/restaurant

dieu, -x [djø] *nm* god; **D.** God; **le bon D.** God; **on lui donnerait le bon D. sans confession** butter wouldn't melt in his mouth; **D. seul le sait!** God only knows!; **D. merci!** thank God!, thank goodness!; *Fam* **laisse-moi tranquille, bon D.!** leave me alone, for God's sake!

diffamation [difamasjɔ̃] *nf (en paroles)* slander; *(par écrit)* libel; **procès en d.** slander/libel trial ▪ **diffamatoire** *adj (paroles)* slanderous; *(écrit)* libellous

différé [difere] *nm* **en d.** *(émission)* prerecorded

différence [diferãs] *nf* difference (**de** in); **à la d. de qn/qch** unlike sb/sth; **faire la d. entre** to make a distinction between

différencier [diferãsje] **1** *vt* to differentiate (**de** from) **2 se différencier** *vpr* to differ (**de** from)

différend [diferã] *nm* difference of opinion

différent, -ente [diferã, -ãt] *adj* different; **différents** *(divers)* different, various; **d. de** different from ▪ **différemment** [-amã] *adv* differently (**de** from)

différentiel, -ielle [diferãsjɛl] *adj* differential

différer [difere] **1** *vt (remettre)* to postpone; *(paiement)* to defer **2** *vi* to differ (**de** from)

difficile [difisil] *adj* difficult; *(exigeant)* fussy; **c'est d. à faire** it's hard *or* difficult to do; **il nous est d. d'accepter** it's hard *or* difficult for us to accept ▪ **difficilement** *adv* with difficulty; **d. lisible** not easy to read

difficulté [difikylte] *nf* difficulty (**à faire** in doing); **en d.** in a difficult situation; **avoir de la d. à faire qch** to have difficulty (in) doing sth

difforme [difɔrm] *adj* deformed, misshapen ▪ **difformité** *nf* deformity

diffus, -use [dify, -yz] *adj (lumière)* diffuse; *(impression)* vague

diffuser [difyze] *vt (émission)* to broadcast; *(nouvelle)* to spread; *(lumière, chaleur)* to diffuse; *(livre)* to distribute ▪ **diffusion** *nf (d'émission)* broadcasting; *(de lumière, de chaleur)* diffusion; *(de livre)* distribution; **d. terrestre** terrestrial broadcasting

digérer [diʒere] **1** *vt* to digest; *Fam (endurer)* to stomach **2** *vi* to digest; **avoir du mal à d.** to have trouble digesting ▪ **digeste** *adj* easily digestible

digestif, -ive [diʒestif, -iv] **1** *adj (tube, sucs)* digestive **2** *nmf* after-dinner liqueur

digestion [diʒestjɔ̃] *nf* digestion

Digicode® [diʒikɔd] *nm* entry code *(for building)*

digital[1], -ale, -aux, -ales [diʒital, -o] *adj Ordinat* digital; **affichage d.** digital display; **montre à affichage d.** digital watch

digital[2], -ale, -aux, -ales [diʒital, -o] *voir* **empreinte**

digne [diɲ] *adj (air, attitude)* dignified; **d. de qn/qch** worthy of sb/sth; **d. d'admiration** worthy of *or* deserving of admiration; **d. de foi** reliable; **il n'est pas d. d'exister** he's not fit to live ▪ **dignement** [-amã] *adv* with dignity; **être d. récompensé** to be justly rewarded

dignitaire [diɲitɛr] *nm* dignitary

dignité [diɲite] *nf* dignity

digression [digresjɔ̃] *nf* digression

digue [dig] *nf* dike, dyke; *(en bord de mer)* sea wall

dilapider [dilapide] *vt* to squander

dilater [dilate] *vt*, **se dilater** *vpr (pupille)* to dilate ▪ **dilatation** *nf (de pupille)* dilation

dilatoire [dilatwar] *adj* **manœuvre d.** delaying tactic

dilemme [dilɛm] *nm* dilemma

dilettante [diletãt] *nmf* dilettante; **faire qch en d.** to dabble in sth

diligence [diliʒɑ̃s] *nf (rapidité)* speedy efficiency; *(véhicule)* stagecoach ▪**diligent, -ente** *adj (prompt)* speedy and efficient; *(soin)* diligent

diluer [dilɥe] *vt (liquide, substance)* to dilute (**dans** in) ▪**dilution** *nf* dilution

diluvienne [dilyvjɛn] *adj f* **pluie d.** torrential rain

dimanche [dimɑ̃ʃ] *nm* Sunday

dimension [dimɑ̃sjɔ̃] *nf (mesure, aspect)* dimension; *(taille)* size; **à deux dimensions** two-dimensional; **prendre les dimensions de qch** to take the measurements of sth

diminuer [diminɥe] **1** *vt* to reduce, to decrease; *(affaiblir)* to weaken; **d. qn** *(rabaisser)* to belittle sb; **il est très diminué depuis l'accident** he has been far less able-bodied since the accident **2** *vi (réserves, nombre)* to decrease, to diminish; *(jours)* to get shorter; *(prix, profits)* to decrease, to drop ▪**diminution** *nf* reduction, decrease (**de** in)

diminutif, -ive [diminytif, -iv] *nm (nom)* diminutive

dinde [dɛ̃d] *nf (volaille, viande)* turkey

dîner [dine] **1** *nm (repas du soir)* dinner; *(repas de midi)* lunch; *(soirée)* dinner party **2** *vi* to have dinner; *Belg, Can* to have lunch

dînette [dinɛt] *nf (jouet)* doll's tea-set; **jouer à la d.** to have a doll's tea party

dingue [dɛ̃g] *Fam* **1** *adj* crazy, nuts; **être d. de qn/qch** to be crazy about sb/sth **2** *nmf* nutcase; **être un d. de moto** to be a motorbike nut

dinosaure [dinozɔr] *nm* dinosaur

diocèse [djosɛz] *nm Rel* diocese

diphtérie [difteri] *nf Méd* diphtheria

diphtongue [diftɔ̃g] *nf* diphthong

diplomate [diplɔmat] **1** *adj* diplomatic **2** *nmf* diplomat ▪**diplomatie** [-asi] *nf (tact)* diplomacy; *(carrière)* diplomatic service ▪**diplomatique** *adj* diplomatic

diplôme [diplom] *nm* diploma; *(d'université)* degree ▪**diplômé, -ée 1** *adj* qualified; *Univ* **être d. (de)** to be a graduate (of) **2** *nmf* holder of a diploma; *Univ* graduate

dire* [dir] **1** *nm* **au d. de** according to; **selon ses dires** according to him/her

2 *vt (mot, avis)* to say; *(vérité, secret, heure)* to tell; **d. des bêtises** to talk nonsense; **d. qch à qn** to tell sb sth, to say sth to sb; **d. à qn que...** to tell sb that..., to say to sb that...; **elle dit que tu mens** she says (that) you're lying; **d. à qn de faire qch** to tell sb to do sth; **d. du mal/du bien de qn** to speak ill/well of sb; **on dirait un château** it looks like a castle; **on dirait du Mozart** it sounds like Mozart; **on dirait du cabillaud** it tastes like cod; **que diriez-vous d'un verre de vin?** what would you say to a glass of wine?; **qu'est-ce que tu en dis?** what do you think?; **on dirait que...** it would seem that...; **ça ne me dit rien de manger chinois** I don't really fancy Chinese food; **ce nom ne me dit rien** that name doesn't ring a bell; **ça ne me dit rien qui vaille** I don't like the look of it; **ça vous dit de rester?** do you feel like staying?; **ça va sans d.** that goes without saying; **c'est beaucoup d.** that's going too far; **dites donc!** look here!; **autrement dit** in other words; **ceci dit** having said this; **à vrai d.** to tell the truth; **à l'heure dite** at the agreed time

3 se dire *vpr* **il se dit malade** he says he's ill; **comment ça se dit en anglais?** how do you say that in English?

direct, -e [dirɛkt] **1** *adj* direct **2** *nm Radio & TV* live broadcasting; **en d. (de)** live (from); *Boxe* **d. du gauche** straight left ▪**directement** [-əmɑ̃] *adv (sans intermédiaire)* directly; *(sans détour)* straight

directeur, -trice [dirɛktœr, -tris] **1** *nmf* director; *(de magasin, de service)* manager; *(de journal)* editor; *(d'école) Br* headmaster, *f* headmistress, *Am* principal; **d. commercial** sales director **2** *adj (principe)* guiding; *(idées)* main; *(équipe)* management

direction [dirɛksjɔ̃] *nf* (**a**) *(sens)* direction; **train en d. de...** train to (**b**) *(de société, de club)* running, management; *(de parti)* leadership; *Aut* steering; **prendre la d. de** *(parti)* to take charge of; **sous la d. de** under the supervision of; *(orchestre)* conducted by; **la d.** *(l'équipe dirigeante)* the management; **un poste de d.** a management post; **d. du personnel** personnel department

directive [dirɛktiv] *nf* directive

dirigeable [diriʒabl] *adj & nm* (**ballon**) **d.** airship, dirigible

dirigeant, -ante [diriʒɑ̃, -ɑ̃t] **1** *adj (classe)* ruling **2** *nm (de pays)* leader; *(d'entreprise, de club)* manager

diriger [diriʒe] **1** *vt (entreprise, club)* to run, to manage; *(pays, parti, cheval)* to lead; *(séance, orchestre)* to conduct; *(travaux, études)* to supervise; *(acteur)* to direct; *(orienter)* to turn (**vers** to); *(arme, lumière)* to point (**sur** at); *(véhicule)* to steer **2 se diriger** *vpr* **se d. vers** *(lieu, objet)* to head for; *(personne)* to go up to; *(dans une carrière)* to go into ▪**dirigisme** *nm* state control

dis, disant [di, dizɑ̃] *voir* **dire**

discerner [disɛrne] *vt (voir)* to make out; *(différencier)* to distinguish (**de** from) ▪**discernement** [-əmɑ̃] *nm* discernment; **sans d.** rashly

disciple [disipl] *nm* disciple

discipline [disiplin] *nf (règle, matière)* discipline ▪**disciplinaire** *adj* disciplinary

discipliner [discipline] **1** *vt (enfant)* to control **2 se discipliner** *vpr* to discipline oneself ▪**discipliné, -ée** *adj* well-disciplined

discontinu, -ue [diskɔ̃tiny] *adj (ligne)* broken; *(bruit)* intermittent ▪ **discontinuer** *vi* **sans d.** without stopping

discorde [diskɔrd] *nf* discord ▪ **discordant, -ante** *adj (son)* discordant; *(témoignages)* conflicting; *(couleurs)* clashing

discothèque [diskɔtɛk] *nf (organisme)* record library; *(club)* disco; **aller en d.** to go to a disco ▪ **disco** *nf Fam (club)* disco; *(musique)* **d.** disco (music)

discours [diskur] *nm* speech; *(écrit littéraire)* discourse; **faire un d.** to make a speech; **tenir de longs d. à qn sur qch** to go on and on to sb about sth

discrédit [diskredi] *nm* discredit; **jeter le d. sur qn** to bring discredit on sb

discréditer [diskredite] **1** *vt* to discredit **2 se discréditer** *vpr (personne)* to discredit oneself

discret, -ète [diskre, -ɛt] *adj (personne, manière)* discreet; *(vêtement)* simple ▪ **discrètement** *adv (avec retenue)* discreetly; *(sobrement)* simply

discrétion [diskresjɔ̃] *nf* discretion; **laisser qch à la d. de qn** to leave sth to sb's discretion; **vin/ pain à d.** unlimited bread/wine

discrimination [diskriminasjɔ̃] *nf* discrimination ▪ **discriminatoire** *adj* discriminatory

disculper [diskylpe] *vt* to exonerate (**de** from)

discussion [diskysjɔ̃] *nf* discussion; **avoir une d. (sur)** to have a discussion (about); **pas de d.!** no argument!

discutable [diskytabl] *adj* questionable

discuter [diskyte] **1** *vt* to discuss; *(contester)* to question **2** *vi* to discuss; *(protester)* to argue; **d. de qch avec qn** to discuss sth with sb **3 se discuter** *vpr* **ça se discute** that's debatable

dise, disent [diz] *voir* **dire**

disette [dizet] *nf* food shortage

diseuse [dizøz] *nf* **d. de bonne aventure** fortune-teller

disgrace [disgras] *nf* **tomber en d.** to fall into disfavour ▪ **disgracier** *vt* to disgrace ▪ **disgracieux, -ieuse** *adj* ungainly

> Il faut noter que l'adjectif anglais **disgraceful** est un faux ami. Il signifie **honteux**.

disjoindre* [disʒwɛ̃dr] *vt* to separate ▪ **disjoint, -ointe** *adj* separated

disjoncter [disʒɔ̃kte] *vi (circuit électrique)* to fuse; *Fam (s'effondrer)* to crack up ▪ **disjoncteur** *nm* circuit breaker

dislocation [dislɔkasjɔ̃] *nf (de membre)* dislocation

disloquer [dislɔke] **1** *vt (membre)* to dislocate; *(empire)* to break up **2 se disloquer** *vpr (empire)* to break up; **se d. le bras** to dislocate one's arm

disons [dizɔ̃] *voir* **dire**

disparaître* [disparetr] *vi* to disappear; *(être porté manquant)* to go missing; *(mourir)* to die; *(coutume)* to die out; **d. en mer** to be lost at sea; **faire d. qch** to get rid of sth ▪ **disparition** *nf* disappearance; *(mort)* death ▪ **disparu, -ue 1** *adj (personne)* missing; **être porté d.** to be reported missing **2** *nmf (absent)* missing person; *(mort)* departed

disparate [disparat] *adj* ill-matched, disparate; *(couleurs)* clashing

disparité [disparite] *nf* disparity (**entre, de** between)

dispensaire [dispɑ̃ser] *nm* community health *Br* centre *or Am* center

dispense [dispɑ̃s] **1** *nf (d'obligation)* exemption ▪ **dispenser** *vt (soins, bienfaits)* to dispense; **d. qn de qch** to exempt sb from sth; **d. qn de faire qch** to exempt sb from doing sth; **je vous dispense de vos réflexions** you can keep your comments to yourselves **2** *vpr* **se d. de faire qch** to get out of sth; **se d. de faire qch** to get out of doing sth

disperser [disperse] **1** *vt (papiers, foule)* to scatter; *(brouillard)* to disperse; *(collection)* to break up **2 se disperser** *vpr (foule)* to scatter, to disperse; **elle se disperse trop** she tries to do too many things at once ▪ **dispersion** *nf (d'armée, de manifestants, de brouillard)* dispersal

disponible [disponibl] *adj (article, place, personne)* available; **es-tu d. ce soir?** are you free tonight? ▪ **disponibilité** *nf* availability; **mise en d.** *(d'un fonctionnaire)* (extended) leave; **disponibilités** *(fonds)* available funds

dispos [dispo] *adj m (personne)* fit and well

disposé, -ée [dispoze] *adj* **bien/mal d.** in a good/bad mood; **bien d. envers** *ou* **à l'égard de qn** well disposed towards sb; **d. à faire qch** disposed to do sth

disposer [dispoze] **1** *vt (objets)* to arrange; *(table)* to lay; **d. qn à (faire) qch** to dispose sb to (do) sth **2** *vi* **d. de qch** to have sth at one's disposal **3 se disposer** *vpr* **se d. à faire qch** to prepare to do sth

> Il faut noter que le verbe anglais **to dispose of** est un faux ami. Il signifie **se débarrasser de**.

dispositif [dispozitif] *nm (mécanisme)* device; **d. policier** police presence

disposition [dispozisjɔ̃] *nf* arrangement; *(tendance)* tendency (**à** to); *(de maison, de page)* layout; *Jur (de loi)* clause; **être** *ou* **rester** *ou* **se tenir à la d. de qn** to be or remain at sb's disposal; **dispositions** *(aptitudes)* ability, aptitude (**pour** for); **prendre ses** *ou* **des dispositions** to make arrangements; *(pour l'avenir)* to make provision; **dans de bonnes dispositions à l'égard de qn** well disposed towards sb

disproportion [disprɔpɔrsjɔ̃] nf disproportion ▪ **disproportionné, -ée** adj disproportionate

dispute [dispyt] nf quarrel ▪ **disputer 1** vt (match) to play; (rallye) to compete in; (combat de boxe) to fight; (droit) to contest; **d. qch à qn** (prix, première place) to fight with sb for or over sth; Fam **d. qn** (gronder) to tell sb off **2 se disputer** vpr to quarrel (**avec** with); (match) to take place; **se d. qch** to fight over sth

disqualifier [diskalifje] vt (équipe, athlète) to disqualify ▪ **disqualification** nf disqualification

disque [disk] nm (de musique) record; (cercle) Br disc, Am disk; Ordinat disk; Sport discus; **mettre un d.** to play a record; **d. compact** Br compact disc, Am compact disk; **d. dur** hard disk ▪ **disquaire** nmf record dealer ▪ **disquette** nf Ordinat floppy (disk), diskette

dissection [disɛksjɔ̃] nf dissection

dissemblable [disɑ̃blabl] adj dissimilar (**à** to)

disséminer [disemine] vt (graines, mines) to scatter ▪ **dissémination** nf scattering

dissension [disɑ̃sjɔ̃] nf dissension

disséquer [diseke] vt to dissect

disserter [diserte] vi **d. sur qch** to discourse on sth; (écrire) to write about sth ▪ **dissertation** nf essay

dissident, -ente [disidɑ̃, -ɑ̃t] adj & nmf dissident ▪ **dissidence** nf dissidence

dissimuler [disimyle] **1** vt (cacher) to conceal (**à** from) **2 se dissimuler** vpr to be hidden ▪ **dissimulation** nf concealment; (duplicité) deceit

dissipation [disipɑsjɔ̃] nf (de brouillard, de malentendu) clearing; (indiscipline) Br misbehaviour, Am misbehavior; Littéraire (débauche) dissipation

dissiper [disipe] **1** vt (nuages) to disperse; (brouillard) to clear; (malentendu) to clear up; (craintes) to dispel; **d. qn** to lead sb astray **2 se dissiper** vpr (nuage) to disperse; (brume) to clear; (craintes) to vanish; (élève) to misbehave ▪ **dissipé, -ée** adj (élève) unruly

dissocier [disɔsje] vt to dissociate (**de** from)

dissolu, -ue [disɔly] adj (vie) dissolute

dissolution [disɔlysjɔ̃] nf dissolution

dissolvant, -ante [disɔlvɑ̃, -ɑ̃t] adj & nm (produit) **d.** solvent; (pour vernis à ongles) nail polish remover

dissoudre* [disudr] vt, **se dissoudre** vpr to dissolve

dissuader [disɥade] vt to dissuade (**de qch** from sth; **de faire** from doing) ▪ **dissuasif, -ive** adj deterrent; **avoir un effet d.** to be a deterrent ▪ **dissuasion** nf dissuasion; Mil **force de d.** deterrent

distance [distɑ̃s] nf distance; **à deux mètres de d.** two metres apart; **à d.** at or from a distance; **garder ses distances** to keep one's distance

(vis-à-vis de from); **tenir qn à d.** to keep sb at a distance; **commandé à d.** remote-controlled; **à quelle d. se trouve la poste?** how far is it to the post office?

distancer [distɑ̃se] vt to outstrip; **se laisser d.** to fall behind

distant, -ante [distɑ̃, -ɑ̃t] adj distant; (personne) aloof, distant; **d. de dix kilomètres** (éloigné) ten kilometres away; (à intervalles) ten kilometres apart

distendre [distɑ̃dr] vt, **se distendre** vpr to stretch

distiller [distile] vt to distil ▪ **distillation** nf distillation ▪ **distillerie** nf (lieu) distillery

distinct, -incte [distɛ̃, -ɛ̃kt] adj (différent) distinct, separate (**de** from); (net) clear, distinct ▪ **distinctement** [-ɑ̃mɑ̃] adv distinctly, clearly ▪ **distinctif, -ive** adj distinctive ▪ **distinction** nf (différence, raffinement) distinction

distinguer [distɛ̃ge] **1** vt (différencier) to distinguish; (voir) to make out; (choisir) to single out; **d. le bien du mal** to tell good from evil **2 se distinguer** vpr (s'illustrer) to distinguish oneself; **se d. de qn/qch (par)** to be distinguishable from sb/sth (by); **se d. par sa beauté** to be conspicuous for one's beauty ▪ **distingué, -ée** adj (bien élevé, éminent) distinguished

distorsion [distɔrsjɔ̃] nf distortion

distraction [distraksjɔ̃] nf (étourderie) absent-mindedness; **ça manque de distractions** there's nothing to do ▪ **distraire* 1** vt (divertir) to entertain; **d. qn (de qch)** to distract sb (from sth) **2 se distraire** vpr to amuse oneself ▪ **distrait, -aite** adj absent-minded ▪ **distraitement** adv absent-mindedly ▪ **distrayant, -ante** adj entertaining

Il faut noter que l'adjectif anglais **distracted** est un faux ami. Il signifie **préoccupé**.

distribuer [distribɥe] vt (donner) & Com to distribute; (courrier) to deliver; (cartes) to deal; (tâches) to allocate; (eau) to supply

distributeur [distribɥtœr] nm Com distributor; **d. automatique** vending machine; **d. de billets** (de train) ticket machine; (de billets de banque) cash machine, ATM

distribution [distribysjɔ̃] nf distribution; (du courrier) delivery; (de l'eau) supply; (acteurs de cinéma) cast; **d. des prix** prizegiving

district [distrikt] nm district

dit¹, dite [di, dit] **1** pp de **dire 2** adj (convenu) agreed; (surnommé) called

dit², dites [di, dit] voir **dire**

diva [diva] nf (chanteuse, célébrité) diva

divaguer [divage] vi (dérailler) to rave ▪ **divagations** nfpl ravings

divan [divɑ̃] nm divan, couch

divergent, -ente [divɛrʒɑ̃, -ɑ̃t] adj (lignes)

divergent; *(opinions)* differing ▪ **divergence** *nf (de lignes)* divergence; *(d'opinions)* difference ▪ **diverger** *vi* to diverge (**de** from)

divers, -erse [diver, -ɛrs] *adj (varié)* varied; **divers(es)** *(plusieurs)* various ▪ **diversement** [-əmɑ̃] *adv* in various ways

diversifier [diversifje] *vt,* **se diversifier** *vpr* to diversify

diversion [diversjɔ̃] *nf* diversion; **faire d.** to create a diversion

diversité [diversite] *nf* diversity

divertir [divertir] 1 *vt* to entertain 2 **se divertir** *vpr* to enjoy oneself ▪ **divertissement** *nm* entertainment, amusement

dividende [dividɑ̃d] *nm Math & Fin* dividend

divin, -ine [divɛ̃, -in] *adj* divine ▪ **divinité** *nf* divinity

diviser [divize] *vt,* **se diviser** *vpr* to divide (**en** into) ▪ **divisible** *adj* divisible ▪ **division** *nf* division

divorce [divɔrs] *nm* divorce ▪ **divorcer** *vi* to get divorced; **d. d'avec qn** to divorce sb ▪ **divorcé, -ée** 1 *adj* divorced (**d'avec** from) 2 *nmf* divorcee

divulguer [divylge] *vt* to divulge ▪ **divulgation** *nf* disclosure

dix [dis] ([di] *before consonant,* [diz] *before vowel) adj & nm* ten ▪ **dixième** [dizjɛm] *adj & nmf* tenth; **un d.** a tenth ▪ **dix-huit** *adj & nm* eighteen ▪ **dix-huitième** *adj & nmf* eighteenth ▪ **dix-neuf** [diznœf] *adj & nm* nineteen ▪ **dix-neuvième** *adj & nmf* nineteenth ▪ **dix-sept** [dissɛt] *adj & nm* seventeen ▪ **dix-septième** *adj & nmf* seventeenth

dizaine [dizen] *nf* **une d. (de)** about ten

do [do] *nm inv (note)* C

docile [dɔsil] *adj* docile ▪ **docilité** *nf* docility

dock [dɔk] *nm (bassin)* dock; *(magasin)* warehouse

docteur [dɔktœr] *nm (en médecine, d'université)* doctor (**en** of) ▪ **doctorat** *nm* doctorate, ≃ PhD (**ès/en** in)

doctrine [dɔktrin] *nf* doctrine

document [dɔkymɑ̃] *nm* document ▪ **documentaire** *adj & nm* documentary ▪ **documentaliste** *nmf* archivist; *(à l'école)* (school) librarian

documentation [dɔkymɑ̃tasjɔ̃] *nf (documents)* documentation, *(brochures)* literature ▪ **documenté, -ée** *adj (personne)* well-informed; **un article solidement d.** a well-documented article ▪ **se documenter** *vpr* to gather information *or* material (**sur** on)

dodeliner [dɔdline] *vi* **d. de la tête** to nod (one's head)

dodo [dodo] *nm Fam (en langage enfantin)* **faire d.** to sleep; **aller au d.** to go beddy-byes

dodu, -ue [dɔdy] *adj* chubby, plump

dogme [dɔgm] *nm* dogma ▪ **dogmatique** *adj* dogmatic ▪ **dogmatisme** *nm* dogmatism

dogue [dɔg] *nm (chien)* mastiff

doigt [dwa] *nm* finger; **d. de pied** toe; **petit d.** little finger, *Am & Scot* pinkie; **un d. de vin** a drop of wine; **à deux doigts de** within an ace of; **montrer qn du d.** to point one's finger at sb; **savoir qch sur le bout du d.** to have sth at one's finger tips; **elle ne lèvera pas le petit d. pour vous aider** she won't lift a finger to help you; **c'est mon petit d. qui me l'a dit** a little bird told me

doigté [dwate] *nm Mus* fingering; *(savoir-faire)* tact

dois, doit [dwa] *voir* **devoir**[1,2]

doléances [dɔleɑ̃s] *nfpl (plaintes)* grievances

dollar [dɔlar] *nm* dollar

domaine [dɔmen] *nm (terres)* estate, domain; *(matière)* field, domain; *Ordinat* domain; **être du d. public** to be in the public domain; *Ordinat* **nom de d.** domain name

dôme [dom] *nm* dome

domestique [dɔmɛstik] 1 *adj (vie, marché, produit, querelle)* domestic; **travaux domestiques** housework; **à usage d.** for domestic use 2 *nmf* servant ▪ **domestiquer** *vt* to domesticate

domicile [dɔmisil] *nm* home; *(demeure légale)* abode; **travailler à d.** to work from home; **livrer à d.** to deliver (to the house); **dernier d. connu** last known address; **sans d. fixe** of no fixed abode; *Jur* **d. conjugal** marital home ▪ **domicilié, -ée** *adj* resident (**à/chez** at)

dominateur, -trice [dɔminatœr, -tris] *adj* domineering ▪ **domination** *nf* domination

dominer [dɔmine] 1 *vt* to dominate; *(situation, sentiment)* to master; *(être supérieur à)* to surpass; **d. la situation** to keep the situation under control; **d. le monde** to rule the world 2 *vi (être le plus fort)* to be dominant; *(être le plus important)* to predominate 3 **se dominer** *vpr* to control oneself ▪ **dominant, -ante** *adj* dominant ▪ **dominante** *nf* dominant feature

dominicain, -aine [dɔminikɛ̃, -ɛn] 1 *adj & nmf Rel* Dominican 2 *adj Géog* Dominican; **la République dominicaine** the Dominican Republic 3 *nmf* **D., Dominicaine** Dominican

dominical, -e, -aux, -ales [dɔminikal, -o] *adj* **repos d.** Sunday rest

domino [dɔmino] *nm* domino; **dominos** *(jeu)* dominoes

dommage [dɔmaʒ] *nm (tort)* harm; **dommages** *(dégâts)* damage; **(c'est) d.!** it's a pity, it's a shame! **(que** that); **quel d.!** what a pity, what a shame!; **c'est (bien) d. qu'elle ne soit pas venue** it's a (great) pity *or* shame she didn't come; **dommages collatéraux** collateral damage; **dommages-intérêts** damages

dompter [dɔ̃te] *vt (animal)* to tame; *(passions, rebelles)* to subdue ▪ **dompteur, -euse** *nmf* tamer

DOM-TOM [dɔmtɔm] *(abrév* **départements et**

territoires d'outre-mer *nmpl* = French overseas departments and territories

don [dɔ̃] *nm (cadeau, aptitude)* gift; *(à un musée, à une œuvre)* donation; **faire le d. de qch** to give sth; **avoir le d. de faire qch** to have the knack for doing sth; **d. du sang** blood donation

donateur, -trice [dɔnatœr, -tris] *nmf* donor ▪ **donation** *nf* donation

donc [dɔ̃(k)] *conj* so, then; *(par conséquent)* so, therefore; **asseyez-vous d.!** *(intensif)* do sit down!; **qui/quoi d.?** who?/what?; **allons d.!** come on!; *Fam* **dis d.!** excuse me!

donne [dɔn] *nf Cartes* deal

données [dɔne] *nfpl Ordinat* data; *(de problème)* facts; **avoir toutes les données du problème** to have all the information on the problem

donner [dɔne] **1** *vt* to give; *(récolte, résultat)* to produce; *(sa place)* to give up; *(cartes)* to deal; *(pièce, film)* to put on; **pourriez-vous me d. l'heure?** could you tell me the time?; **d. un coup à qn** to hit sb; **d. le bonjour à qn** to say hello to sb; **d. qch à réparer** to take sth (in) to be repaired; **d. à manger à qn** *(animal, enfant)* to feed sb; **d. raison à qn** to say sb is right; **elle m'a donné de ses nouvelles** she told me how she was doing; **ça donne soif/faim** it makes you thirsty/hungry; **je lui donne trente ans** I'd say he/she was thirty; **ça n'a rien donné** *(efforts)* it hasn't got us anywhere; *Fam* **c'est donné** it's dirt cheap; **étant donné** *(la situation)* considering, in view of; **étant donné que…** seeing (that), considering (that)…; **à un moment donné** at some stage
2 *vi* **d. sur** *(fenêtre)* to overlook, to look out onto; *(porte)* to open onto; **d. dans** *(piège)* to fall into; *Fam* **ne plus savoir où d. de la tête** not to know which way to turn
3 se donner *vpr (se consacrer)* to devote oneself (**à** to); **se d. du mal** to go to a lot of trouble (**pour faire** to do); **s'en d. à cœur joie** to have a whale of a time

donneur, -euse [dɔnœr, -øz] *nmf (de sang, de sperme, d'organe)* donor; *Cartes* dealer

dont [dɔ̃] (= **de qui, duquel, de quoi**) *pron relatif (personne)* of whom; *(chose)* of which; *(appartenance: personne)* whose, of whom; *(appartenance: chose)* of which, whose; **une mère d. le fils est malade** a mother whose son is ill; **la fille d. il est fier** the daughter he is proud of *or* of whom he is proud; **les outils d. j'ai besoin** the tools I need; **la façon d. elle joue** the way (in which) she plays; **cinq enfants d. deux filles** five children two of whom are daughters, five children including two daughters; **voici ce d. il s'agit** here's what it's about

doper [dɔpe] **1** *vt* to dope **2 se doper** *vpr* to take drugs ▪ **dopage** *nm (action)* doping; *(de sportif)* drug-taking

dorénavant [dɔrenavɑ̃] *adv* from now on

dorer [dɔre] **1** *vt (objet)* to gild; *Fig* **d. la pilule à qn** to sugar the pill for sb **2** *vi (à la cuisson)* to brown **3 se dorer** *vpr* **se d. au soleil** to sunbathe ▪ **doré, -ée** *adj (objet)* gilt, gold; *(couleur)* golden

dorloter [dɔrlɔte] *vt* to pamper, to coddle

dormir* [dɔrmir] *vi* to sleep; *(être endormi)* to be asleep; *Fig (argent)* to lie idle; **avoir envie de d.** to feel sleepy; **dormez tranquille!** set your mind at rest!, rest easy!; **histoire à d. debout** tall story, cock-and-bull story; **eau dormante** stagnant water

dortoir [dɔrtwar] *nm* dormitory

dos [do] *nm (de personne, d'animal)* back; *(de livre)* spine; **'voir au d.'** *(verso)* 'see over'; **voir qn de d.** to have a back view of sb; *Fam* **mettre qch sur le d. de qn** *(accuser qn)* to pin sth on sb; *Fam* **avoir qn sur le d.** to have sb on one's back; *Fam* **j'en ai plein le d.** I'm sick of it

dose [doz] *nf* dose; *(dans un mélange)* proportion; *Fig* **forcer la d.** to overdo it ▪ **dosage** *nm (de médicament)* dosage; *(d'ingrédients)* proportioning ▪ **doser** *vt (médicament, ingrédients)* to measure out ▪ **doseur** *nm* **bouchon d.** measuring cap

dossard [dɔsar] *nm (de sportif)* number *(worn by player/competitor)*

dossier [dɔsje] *nm (de siège)* back; *(documents)* file, dossier; *(classeur)* folder, file

dot [dɔt] *nf* dowry

doter [dɔte] *vt (équiper)* to equip (**de** with); **elle est dotée d'une grande intelligence** she's endowed with great intelligence ▪ **dotation** *nf (d'hôpital)* endowment

douane [dwan] *nf* customs; **passer la d.** to go through customs ▪ **douanier, -ière 1** *nm* customs officer **2** *adj* **union douanière** customs union

doublage [dublaʒ] *nm (de film)* dubbing

double [dubl] **1** *adj* double; *(rôle, avantage)* twofold, double; **en d. exemplaire** in duplicate; **enfermer qn à d. tour** to lock sb in; **fermer une porte à d. tour** to double-lock a door; **doubles rideaux** lined curtains, *Am* (thick) drapes **2** *adv* **double 3** *nm (de personne)* double; *(copie)* copy, duplicate; *(de timbre)* swap, duplicate; **le d. (de)** *(quantité)* twice as much (as); **je l'ai en d.** I have two of them ▪ **double-clic** *nm Ordinat* double click; **faire un d. sur qch** to double click on sth ▪ **doublement** [-əmɑ̃] **1** *adv* doubly **2** *nm (de nombres, de lettres)* doubling

doubler [duble] **1** *vt (augmenter)* to double; *(vêtement)* to line; *(film)* to dub; *(acteur)* to dub the voice of; *(classe à l'école)* to repeat; *(cap)* (*en bateau*) to round **2** *vi (augmenter)* to double; **d. de volume** to double in volume **3** *vti (en voiture) Br* to overtake, *Am* to pass **4 se doubler** *vpr* **se d. de** to be coupled with

doublure [dublyr] *nf (étoffe)* lining; *(au théâtre)* understudy; *(au cinéma)* stand-in

douce [dus] *voir* **doux** ▪ **doucement** *adv (délicatement)* gently; *(bas)* softly; *(lentement)* slowly; *(sans bruit)* quietly; *Fam (assez bien)* so-so ▪ **douceur** *nf (de miel)* sweetness; *(de peau)* softness; *(de temps)* mildness; *(de personne)* gentleness; **douceurs** *(sucreries) Br* sweets, *Am* candy; **la voiture a démarré en d.** the car started smoothly

douche [duʃ] *nf* shower; **prendre une d.** to have *or* take a shower; **être sous la d.** to be in the shower ▪ **doucher 1** *vt* **d. qn** to give sb a shower **2 se doucher** *upr* to have *or* take a shower

doué, -ée [dwe] *adj* gifted, talented (**en** at); **d. de raison** gifted with reason; **être d. pour qch** to have a gift for sth

douille [duj] *nf (d'ampoule)* socket; *(de cartouche)* case

douillet, -ette [duje, -ɛt] *adj (lit) Br* cosy, *Am* cozy; **tu es d.** *(délicat)* you're such a baby

douleur [dulœr] *nf (mal)* pain; *(chagrin)* sorrow, grief ▪ **douloureux, -euse** *adj (maladie, membre, décision, perte)* painful

doute [dut] *nm* doubt; **sans d.** no doubt, probably; **sans aucun d.** without (any) doubt; **mettre qch en d.** to cast doubt on sth; **dans le d.** doubtful; **ça ne fait pas de d.** there is no doubt about it

douter [dute] **1** *vi* to doubt; **d. de qn/qch** to doubt sb/sth; *Fam* **ne d. de rien** to have plenty of self-confidence **2** *vt* **je doute qu'il soit assez fort** I doubt (whether) he's strong enough **3 se douter** *upr* **se d. de qch** to suspected sth; **je m'en doutais bien** I suspected as much

douteux, -euse [dutø, -øz] *adj* doubtful; *(louche, médiocre)* dubious

douve [duv] *nf (de château)* moat

Douvres [duvr] *nm ou f* Dover

doux, douce [du, dus] *adj (miel, son)* sweet; *(peau, lumière, drogue)* soft; *(temps, climat)* mild; *(personne, pente)* gentle; *(émotion, souvenir)* pleasant; **d. comme un agneau** as gentle as a lamb; *Fam* **faire qch en douce** to do sth on the quiet

douze [duz] *adj & nm* twelve ▪ **douzaine** *nf (douze)* dozen; *(environ)* about twelve; **une d. d'œufs** a dozen eggs ▪ **douzième** *adj & nmf* twelfth; **un d.** a twelfth

doyen, -enne [dwajɛ̃, -ɛn] *nmf (d'université, ecclésiastique)* dean; **d. (d'âge)** oldest person

draconien, -ienne [drakɔnjɛ̃, -jɛn] *adj (mesures)* drastic

dragée [draʒe] *nf* sugared almond; *Fig* **tenir la d. haute à qn** to stand up to sb

dragon [dragɔ̃] *nm (animal, personne acariâtre)* dragon; *Hist (soldat)* dragoon

draguer [drage] *vt (rivière)* to dredge; *Fam* **d. qn** *Br* to chat sb up, *Am* to hit on sb ▪ **drague** *nf Fam Br* chatting up, *Am* hitting on; **un lieu de d. idéal** an ideal place for *Br* chatting people up *or Am* hitting on people ▪ **dragueur, -euse 1** *nm (bateau)* dredger; **d. de mines** minesweeper **2** *nmf Fam* **c'est un d.** he's always *Br* chatting up *or Am* hitting on women

drainer [drene] *vt* to drain

drame [dram] *nm (genre littéraire)* drama; *(catastrophe)* tragedy ▪ **dramatique 1** *adj* dramatic; **critique d.** drama critic; **auteur d.** playwright, dramatist **2** *nf* drama ▪ **dramatiser** *vt* to dramatize ▪ **dramaturge** *nmf* dramatist

> Il faut noter que le nom anglais **drama** est un faux ami. Il s'utilise uniquement dans un contexte théâtral.

drap [dra] *nm (de lit)* sheet; *(tissu)* cloth; **d.-housse** fitted sheet; **d. de bain** bath towel; *Fam* **être dans de beaux draps** to be in a fine mess

drapeau, -x [drapo] *nm* flag; **être sous les drapeaux** *(soldat)* to be doing one's military service

draper [drape] **1** *vt* to drape (**de** with) **2 se draper** *upr Fig* **se d. dans sa dignité** to stand on one's dignity

dreadlocks [drɛdlɔks] *nfpl* dreadlocks *(pluriel)*

dresser [drese] **1** *vt (échelle, statue)* to put up, to erect; *(liste)* to draw up; *(piège)* to set, to lay; *(animal)* to train; **d. les oreilles** to prick up one's ears **2 se dresser** *upr (personne)* to stand up; *(statue, montagne)* to rise up ▪ **dressage** *nm* training ▪ **dresseur, -euse** *nmf* trainer

dribbler [drible] *vi Football* to dribble

drogue [drɔg] *nf (stupéfiant)* drug; *Péj (médicament)* medicine; **d. dure/douce** hard/soft drug ▪ **drogué, -ée** *nmf* drug addict ▪ **droguer 1** *vt (victime)* to drug; *(malade)* to dose up **2 se droguer** *upr* to take drugs

droguerie [drɔgri] *nf* hardware *Br* shop *or Am* store ▪ **droguiste** *nmf* hardware dealer

droit¹ [drwa] *nm (privilège)* right; *(d'inscription)* fee(s); **le d.** *(science juridique)* law; **à bon d.** rightly; **avoir d. à qch** to be entitled to sth; **avoir le d. de faire qch** to be entitled to do sth, to have the right to do sth; **d. d'entrée** entrance fee; **droits d'auteur** royalties; **droits de douane** (customs) duty; **droits de l'homme** human rights

droit², droite¹ [drwa, drwat] **1** *adj (route, ligne)* straight; *(angle)* right; *(veston)* single-breasted; *Fig (honnête)* upright **2** *adv* straight; **tout d.** straight *or* right ahead; **aller d. au but** to go straight to the point ▪ **droite²** *nf (ligne)* straight line

droit³, droite³ [drwa, drwat] **1** *adj (côté, bras)* right **2** *nm Boxe (coup)* right ▪ **droite⁴** *nf* **la d.**

(côté) the right (side); *Pol* the right (wing); **à d.**
(tourner) (to the) right; *(rouler, se tenir)* on the
right, on the right(-hand) side; **de d.** *(fenêtre)*
right-hand; *(candidat)* right-wing; **voter à d.** to
vote right-wing; **à d. de** on *or* to the right of; **à
d. et à gauche** *(voyager)* here, there and
everywhere

droitier, -ière [drwatje, -jɛr] **1** *adj* right-
handed **2** *nmf* right-handed person

droiture [drwatyr] *nf* rectitude

drôle [drol] *adj* funny; **d. d'air/de type** funny
look/fellow; **faire une d. de tête** to pull a face
■ **drôlement** *adv* funnily; *Fam (extrêmement)*
terribly, dreadfully

dromadaire [drɔmadɛr] *nm* dromedary

dru, drue [dry] **1** *adj (herbe)* thick, dense **2** *adv*
tomber d. *(pluie)* to pour down heavily;
pousser d. to grow thick(ly)

du [dy] *voir* **de**[1,2]

dû, due [dy] **1** *adj* **d. à qch** due to sth; **en bonne
et due forme** in due form **2** *nm* due

dualité [dɥalite] *nf* duality

dubitatif, -ive [dybitatif, -iv] *adj* doubtful

duc [dyk] *nm* duke ■ **duché** *nm* duchy ■ **duchesse** *nf* duchess

duel [dɥɛl] *nm* duel

dûment [dymɑ̃] *adv* duly

dune [dyn] *nf* (sand) dune

duo [dɥo] *nm Mus* duet; **d. comique** comic duo

dupe [dyp] **1** *adj* **être d. de** to be taken in by; **il
n'est pas d.** he's well aware of it **2** *nf* dupe
■ **duper** *vt* to fool, to dupe

duplex [dyplɛks] *nm Br* maisonette, *Am* duplex;
TV **(émission en) d.** link-up

duplicata [dyplikata] *nm inv* duplicate

duplicité [dyplisite] *nf* duplicity

duquel [dykɛl] *voir* **lequel**

dur, dure [dyr] **1** *adj (substance)* hard; *(difficile)*
hard, tough; *(viande)* tough; *(hiver, ton)* harsh;
(personne) hard, harsh; *(œuf)* hard-boiled;
(brosse, carton) stiff; **d. d'oreille** hard of

hearing; *Fam* **d. à cuire** hard-bitten, tough **2**
adv (travailler) hard; **croire à qch d. comme
fer** to have a cast-iron belief in sth **3** *nm Fam
(personne)* tough guy ■ **durement** *adv* harshly
■ **dureté** *nf (de substance)* hardness; *(d'hiver, de
ton)* harshness; *(de viande)* toughness

durable [dyrabl] *adj* lasting

durant [dyrɑ̃] *prép* during; **d. l'hiver** during the
winter; **des heures d.** for hours and hours

durcir [dyrsir] *vti*, **se durcir** *vpr* to harden
■ **durcissement** *nm* hardening

durée [dyre] *nf (de film, d'événement)* length;
(période) duration; *(de pile électrique)* life; **de
longue d.** *(bonheur)* lasting; **chômage de
longue d.** long-term unemployment; **disque
de longue d.** long-playing record; **pile longue
d.** long-life battery; **de courte d.** *(attente)* short;
(bonheur) short-lived

durer [dyre] *vi* to last; **ça dure depuis...** it's
been going on for...

durillon [dyrijɔ̃] *nm (de la main)* callus; *(du pied)*
corn

DUT [deyte] *(abrév* **diplôme universitaire de
technologie)** *nm* = post-baccalauréat technical qualification awarded after two years

duvet [dyvɛ] *nm (d'oiseau, de visage)* down; *(sac)*
sleeping bag ■ **duveteux, -euse** *adj* downy

DVD [devede] *(abrév* **Digital Versatile Disk,
Digital Video Disk)** *nm inv* DVD

DVD-ROM [devederɔm] *(abrév* **Digital Versatile Disk Read-only Memory)** *nm inv* DVD-ROM

dynamique [dinamik] **1** *adj* dynamic **2** *nf
(force)* dynamic force, thrust ■ **dynamisme**
nm dynamism

dynamite [dinamit] *nf* dynamite ■ **dynamiter**
vt to dynamite

dynamo [dinamo] *nf* dynamo

dynastie [dinasti] *nf* dynasty

dysenterie [disɑ̃tri] *nf Méd* dysentery

dyslexique [dislɛksik] *adj* dyslexic

E, e [ə] *nm inv* E, e

EAO [əao] (*abrév* **enseignement assisté par ordinateur**) *nm inv* CAL

eau, -x [o] *nf* water; **grandes eaux** (*d'un parc*) ornamental fountains; **tout en e.** sweating; **prendre l'e.** to let in water; *Fam* **tomber à l'e.** (*projet*) to fall through; **il est tombé beaucoup d'e.** a lot of rain fell; *Fig* **apporter de l'e. au moulin de qn** to strengthen sb's case; **ça lui fait venir l'e. à la bouche** it makes his/her mouth water; **sports d'e.** vive white-water sports; **e. de Cologne** eau de Cologne; **e. de toilette** toilet water; **e. du robinet** tap water; **e. douce** fresh water; **e. plate** still water; **e. salée** salt water ■ **eau-de-vie** (*pl* **eaux-de-vie**) *nf* brandy ■ **eau-forte** (*pl* **eaux-fortes**) *nf* (*gravure*) etching

ébahir [ebair] *vt* to astound

ébattre [ebatr] **s'ébattre** *vpr* to frolic ■ **ébats** *nmpl* frolicking

ébauche [eboʃ] *nf* (*esquisse*) rough sketch; (*de roman*) outline; (*début*) beginnings; **l'é. d'un sourire** the ghost of a smile ■ **ébaucher** *vt* (*tableau, roman*) to rough out; (*lettre*) to draft; **é. un sourire** to give a faint smile

ébène [ebɛn] *nf* ebony ■ **ébéniste** *nmf* cabinet-maker

éberlué, -uée [ebɛrlɥe] *adj Fam* dumbfounded

éblouir [ebluir] *vt* to dazzle ■ **éblouissement** *nm* (*aveuglement*) dazzle; (*malaise*) fit of dizziness

éborgner [ebɔrɲe] *vt* **é. qn** to put sb's eye out

éboueur [ebwœr] *nm Br* dustman, *Am* garbage collector

ébouillanter [ebujɑ̃te] **1** *vt* to scald **2** **s'ébouillanter** *vpr* to scald oneself

ébouler [ebule] **s'ébouler** *vpr* (*falaise*) to collapse; (*tunnel*) to cave in ■ **éboulement** *nm* (*écroulement*) collapse; (*de mine*) cave-in ■ **éboulis** *nm* (mass of) fallen debris

ébouriffé, -ée [eburife] *adj* (*personne, cheveux*) *Br* dishevelled, *Am* disheveled

ébranler [ebrɑ̃le] **1** *vt* (*mur, confiance, personne*) to shake; (*santé*) to weaken **2** **s'ébranler** *vpr* (*train, cortège*) to move off

ébrécher [ebreʃe] *vt* (*assiette*) to chip; (*lame*) to nick

ébriété [ebrijete] *nf* **en état d'é.** under the influence of drink

ébrouer [ebrue] **s'ébrouer** *vpr* (*chien*) to shake itself; (*cheval*) to snort

ébruiter [ebrɥite] *vt* (*nouvelle*) to spread

EBS [øbeɛs] (*abrév* **encéphalopathie bovine spongiforme**) *nf* BSE

ébullition [ebylisjɔ̃] *nf* boiling; **être en é.** (*eau*) to be boiling; *Fig* (*ville*) to be in turmoil; **porter qch à é.** to bring sth to the boil

écaille [ekaj] *nf* (*de poisson*) scale; (*de tortue, d'huître*) shell ■ **écailler 1** *vt* (*poisson*) to scale; (*huître*) to shell **2** **s'écailler** *vpr* (*peinture*) to peel (off)

écarlate [ekarlat] *adj* scarlet

écarquiller [ekarkije] *vt* **é. les yeux** to open one's eyes wide

écart [ekar] *nm* (*intervalle*) gap, distance; (*différence*) difference (**de** in; **entre** between); **faire le grand é.** to do the splits; **à l'é.** out of the way; **tenir qn à l'é.** to keep sb out of things; **à l'é. de** away from; **écarts de conduite** misbehaviour; **écarts de langage** bad language

écartelé, -ée [ekartəle] *adj* **é. entre** (*tiraillé*) torn between

écartement [ekartəmɑ̃] *nm* (*espace*) gap, distance (**de** between)

écarter [ekarte] **1** *vt* (*objets, personnes*) to move apart; (*jambes, doigts*) to spread; (*rideaux*) to draw (back); (*crainte, idée*) to brush aside; (*candidat, proposition*) to turn down; **é. qch de qch** to move sth away from sth **2** **s'écarter** *vpr* (**a**) (*se séparer*) (*personnes*) to move apart (**de** from); (*foule*) to part (**b**) (*piéton*) to move away (**de** from); (*voiture*) to swerve; **s'é. du sujet** to wander from the subject ■ **écarté, -ée** *adj* (*endroit*) remote; **les jambes écartées** with his/her legs (wide) apart

ecchymose [ekimoz] *nf* bruise

ecclésiastique [eklezjastik] **1** *adj* ecclesiastical **2** *nm* clergyman

écervelé, -ée [esɛrvəle] **1** *adj* scatterbrained **2** *nmf* scatterbrain

échafaud [eʃafo] *nm* scaffold

échafaudage [eʃafodaʒ] *nm* scaffolding; **des échafaudages** scaffolding ■ **échafauder** *vt* (*empiler*) to pile up

échalote [eʃalɔt] *nf* shallot

échancré, -ée [eʃɑ̃kre] *adj* low-cut ■ **échancrure** *nf* low neckline

échange [eʃɑ̃ʒ] *nm* exchange; **en é.** in exchange (**de** for) ■ **échanger** *vt* to exchange (**contre** for)

échangeur [eʃɑ̃ʒœr] *nm* interchange

échantillon [eʃɑ̃tijɔ̃] *nm* sample ▪ **échantillonnage** *nm* sampling ▪ **échantillonner** *vt* to sample

échappatoire [eʃapatwar] *nf* way out

échappement [eʃapmɑ̃] *nm (de véhicule)* **tuyau d'é.** exhaust pipe; **pot d'é.** exhaust

échapper [eʃape] **1** *vi* **é. à qn** to escape from sb; **é. à la mort/un danger** to escape death/danger; **son nom m'échappe** his/her name escapes me; **ça m'a échappé** *(je n'ai pas compris)* I didn't catch it; **ça lui a échappé (des mains)** it slipped out of his/her hands; **laisser é.** *(cri)* to let out; *(objet, occasion)* to let slip **2** *vt* **il l'a échappé belle** he had a narrow escape **3** **s'échapper** *vpr (personne, gaz, eau)* to escape (**de** from) ▪ **échappée** *nf (de cyclistes)* breakaway; *(vue)* vista

écharde [eʃard] *nf* splinter

écharpe [eʃarp] *nf* scarf; *(de maire)* sash; **avoir le bras en é.** to have one's arm in a sling

échasse [eʃas] *nf (bâton)* stilt

échaudé, -ée [eʃode] *adj Fig* **être é.** to get one's fingers burnt

échauffer [eʃofe] **1** *vt (moteur)* to overheat; **é. les esprits** to get people worked up **2** **s'échauffer** *vpr (discussion, sportif)* to warm up ▪ **échauffement** *nm (de moteur)* overheating; *(de sportif)* warm(ing)-up

échauffourée [eʃofure] *nf (bagarre)* clash, brawl, skirmish

échéance [eʃeɑ̃s] *nf (de facture, de dette)* date of payment; **à brève/longue é.** *(projet, emprunt)* short-/long-term; **faire face à ses échéances** to meet one's financial obligations

échéant [eʃeɑ̃] **le cas échéant** *adv* if need be

échec [eʃɛk] *nm (insuccès)* failure; **faire é. à qch** to hold sth in check; **les échecs** *(jeu)* chess; **é.!** check!; **é. et mat!** checkmate!

échelle [eʃɛl] *nf* **(a)** *(marches)* ladder; **faire la courte é. à qn** to give sb *Br* a leg up *or Am* a boost **(b)** *(de carte)* scale; **à l'é. nationale** on a national scale

échelon [eʃlɔ̃] *nm (d'échelle)* rung; *(de fonctionnaire)* grade; *(d'organisation)* echelon; **à l'é. régional/national** on a regional/national level

échelonner [eʃlɔne] **1** *vt (paiements)* to spread **2** **s'échelonner** *vpr* to be spread out

écheveau, -x [eʃ(ə)vo] *nm (de laine)* skein; *Fig (d'une intrigue)* muddle, tangle

échevelé, -ée [eʃəv(ə)le] *adj (ébouriffé)* Br dishevelled, *Am* disheveled; *Fig (course, danse)* wild

échine [eʃin] *nf Anat* backbone, spine; **courber l'é. devant qn** to submit to sb ▪ **s'échiner** *vpr Fam* **s'é. à faire qch** to wear oneself out doing sth

échiquier [eʃikje] *nm (plateau)* chessboard

écho [eko] *nm (d'un son)* echo; **échos** *(dans la presse)* gossip column; **avoir des échos de qch** to hear some news about sth; **se faire l'é. de qch** to echo sth

échographie [ekɔgrafi] *nf* (ultrasound) scan; **passer une é.** to have a scan

échoir* [eʃwar] *vi* **é. à qn** to fall to sb

échouer [eʃwe] **1** *vi* to fail; **é. à** *(examen)* to fail; **faire é. un projet** to wreck a plan; **faire é. un complot** to foil a plot **2** *vi,* **s'échouer** *vpr (navire)* to run aground

éclabousser [eklabuse] *vt* to splash, to spatter (**avec** with) ▪ **éclaboussure** *nf* splash

éclair [eklɛr] **1** *nm* **(a)** *(lumière)* flash; *(d'orage)* flash of lightning; **un é. de génie** a flash *or* stroke of genius **(b)** *(gâteau)* éclair **2** *adj inv* **visite/raid é.** lightning visit/raid

éclairage [eklɛraʒ] *nm* lighting

éclaircie [eklɛrsi] *nf* sunny spell

éclaircir [eklɛrsir] **1** *vt (couleur)* to lighten; *(teint)* to clear; *(mystère)* to clear up; *(sauce)* to thin out **2** **s'éclaircir** *vpr (ciel)* to clear; *(mystère)* to be cleared up; *(cheveux)* to thin; **s'é. la voix** to clear one's throat ▪ **éclaircissement** *nm (explication)* explanation; **demander des éclaircissements sur qch** to ask for an explanation of sth

éclairer [eklere] **1** *vt (pièce)* to light (up); **é. qn** *(avec une lampe)* to give sb some light; *(informer)* to enlighten sb *(*sur* about)*; **é. une situation d'un jour nouveau** to shed *or* throw new light on a situation **2** *vi (lampe)* to give light; **é. bien/mal** to give good/poor light **3** **s'éclairer** *vpr (visage)* to light up; **s'é. à la bougie** to use candlelight; **s'é. à l'électricité** to have electric lighting ▪ **éclairé, -ée** *adj (averti)* enlightened; **bien/mal é.** *(illuminé)* well/badly lit

éclaireur, -euse [eklɛrœr, -øz] **1** *nmf* (boy) scout, *f* (girl) guide **2** *nm (soldat)* scout

éclat [ekla] *nm* **(a)** *(de lumière)* brightness; *(de phare)* glare; *(de diamant)* flash; *(splendeur)* brilliance, radiance; *Fig* **l'é. de la jeunesse** the bloom of youth **(b)** *(de verre, de bois)* splinter; **é. d'obus** shrapnel; **é. de rire** burst of laughter; **éclats de voix** noisy outbursts, shouts

éclatant, -ante [eklatɑ̃, -ɑ̃t] *adj (lumière, couleur, succès)* brilliant; *(beauté, santé)* radiant; *(rire)* loud; **être é. de santé** to be glowing with health

éclater [eklate] *vi (pneu, obus)* to burst; *(bombe, pétard)* to go off, to explode; *(verre)* to shatter; *(guerre, incendie)* to break out; *(orage, scandale)* to break; *(parti)* to break up; **é. de rire** to burst out laughing; **é. en sanglots** to burst into tears ▪ **éclatement** *nm (de pneu)* bursting; *(de bombe)* explosion; *(de parti)* break-up

éclectique [eklɛktik] *adj* eclectic

éclipse [eklips] *nf (de soleil, de lune)* eclipse ▪ **éclipser 1** *vt* to eclipse **2 s'éclipser** *upr (soleil)* to be eclipsed; *Fam (partir)* to slip away

éclopé, -ée [eklɔpe] **1** *adj* lame **2** *nmf* lame person

éclore* [eklɔr] *vi (œuf)* to hatch; *(fleur)* to open (out), to blossom ▪ **éclosion** *nf* hatching; *(de fleur)* opening, blossoming

écluse [eklyz] *nf (de canal)* lock

écobilan [ekɔbilɑ̃] *nm* life-cycle analysis

écœurer [ekœre] *vt* **é. qn** *(aliment)* to make sb feel sick; *(au moral)* to sicken sb ▪ **écœurant, -ante** *adj* disgusting, sickening ▪ **écœurement** *nm (nausée)* nausea; *(indignation)* disgust

écoguerrier, -ière [ekogɛrje, -ɛr] *nmf* ecowarrior

école [ekɔl] *nf* school; *(militaire)* academy; **à l'é.** at school; **aller à l'é.** to go to school; **faire é.** to gain a following; **les grandes écoles** = university-level colleges specializing in professional training; **é. de danse/dessin** dancing/art school; **é. normale** *Br* ≃ teacher training college, *Am* ≃ teachers' college; **é. privée** private school; **é. publique** *Br* state school, *Am* public school ▪ **écolier, -ière** *nmf* schoolboy, *f* schoolgirl

écolo [ekɔlo] *adj & nmf Fam* green

écologie [ekɔlɔʒi] *nf* ecology ▪ **écologique** *adj* ecological, environmental ▪ **écologiste** *adj & nmf* environmentalist

éconduire* [ekɔ̃dɥir] *vt Littéraire (repousser)* to reject

économe [ekɔnɔm] **1** *adj* thrifty, economical **2** *nmf (de collège)* bursar

économie [ekɔnɔmi] *nf (activité, vertu)* economy; **économies** *(argent)* savings; **une é. de** *(gain)* a saving of; **faire une é. de temps** to save time; **faire des économies** to save (up); **faire des économies d'énergie** to conserve or save energy; **nouvelle é.** new economy; **é. de marché** market economy; **é. dirigée** planned economy; **é. libérale** open-market economy ▪ **économique** *adj* **(a)** *(relatif à l'économie)* economic; **science é.** economics *(sing)* **(b)** *(avantageux)* economical ▪ **économiquement** *adv* economically ▪ **économiste** *nmf* economist

économiser [ekɔnɔmize] **1** *vt (forces, argent, énergie)* to save **2** *vi* to economize **(sur** on) ▪ **économiseur d'écran** *nm Ordinat* screen-saver

écoper [ekɔpe] **1** *vt (bateau)* to bail out, *Br* to bale out **2** *vi Fam* **é. de qch** *(punition, amende)* to get sth

écorce [ekɔrs] *nf (d'arbre)* bark; *(de fruit)* peel; **l'é. terrestre** the earth's crust

écorcher [ekɔrʃe] **1** *vt (érafler)* to graze; *(animal)* to flay; *Fig (nom)* to mispronounce;

é. les oreilles à qn to grate on sb's ears **2 s'écorcher** *upr* to graze oneself; **s'é. le genou** to graze one's knee ▪ **écorchure** *nf* graze

Écosse [ekɔs] *nf* l'É. Scotland ▪ **écossais, -aise 1** *adj* Scottish; *(tissu)* tartan; *(whisky)* Scotch **2** *nmf* É., Écossaise Scot

écosser [ekɔse] *vt (pois)* to shell

écotaxe [ekotaks] *nf* ecotax

écotourisme [ekoturism] *nm* ecotourism

écouler [ekule] **1** *vt (se débarrasser de)* to dispose of **2 s'écouler** *upr (eau)* to flow out, to run out; *(temps)* to pass ▪ **écoulé, -ée** *adj (années)* past ▪ **écoulement** *nm (de liquide)* flow; *(de temps)* passage; *(de marchandises)* sale

écourter [ekurte] *vt (séjour, discours)* to cut short; *(texte, tige)* to shorten

écoute [ekut] *nf* listening; **être à l'é.** to be listening (**de** to); **rester à l'é.** to keep listening; **être à l'é. de qn** to listen (sympathetically) to sb; **heure de grande é.** *Radio* peak listening time; *TV* peak viewing time; **écoutes téléphoniques** phone tapping

écouter [ekute] **1** *vt* to listen to; **faire é. qch à qn** *(disque)* to play sb sth **2 s'écouter** *upr* **si je m'écoutais** if I did what I wanted; **il s'écoute parler** he likes the sound of his own voice ▪ **écouteur** *nm (de téléphone)* earpiece; ▪ **écouteurs** *(casque)* headphones

écrabouiller [ekrabuje] *vt Fam* to crush

écran [ekrɑ̃] *nm* screen; **à l'é.** on screen; **le petit é.** television; **é. publicitaire** commercial break; **é. total** sun block

écraser [ekraze] **1** *vt (broyer, vaincre)* to crush; *(fruit, insecte)* to squash; *(cigarette)* to put out; *(piéton)* to run over; **se faire é. par une voiture** to get run over by a car; *Fam* **se faire é.** to be clobbered **2 s'écraser** *upr (avion)* to crash **(contre** into) ▪ **écrasant, -ante** *adj (victoire, chaleur)* overwhelming ▪ **écrasé, -ée** *adj m* squashed; **nez é.** snub nose

écrémer [ekreme] *vt (lait)* to skim; *Fig (choisir)* to cream off the best from ▪ **écrémé, -ée** *adj (lait)* *Br* skimmed, *Am* skim

écrevisse [ekravis] *nf* crayfish *inv*

écrier [ekrije] **s'écrier** *upr* to exclaim, to cry out (**que** that)

écrin [ekrɛ̃] *nm* (jewel) case

écrire* [ekrir] **1** *vt* to write; *(noter)* to write down; **é. à la machine** to type **2** *vi* to write **3 s'écrire** *upr (mot)* to be spelt; **comment ça s'écrit?** how do you spell it? ▪ **écrit** *nm* written document; *(examen)* written examination; **par é.** in writing; **écrits** *(œuvres)* writings

écriteau, -x [ekrito] *nm* notice, sign

écriture [ekrityr] *nf (système)* writing; *(personnelle)* (hand)writing; *Com* **écritures** accounts; **les Écritures** *(la Bible)* the Scriptures

écrivain [ekrivɛ̃] *nm* writer

écrou [ekru] *nm (de boulon)* nut

écrouer [ekrue] *vt* to imprison

écrouler [ekrule] **s'écrouler** *vpr (édifice, blessé)* to collapse; **être écroulé de fatigue** to be dropping with exhaustion; *Fam* **être écroulé (de rire)** to be doubled up (with laughter) ▪**écroulement** *nm* collapse

écru, -ue [ekry] *adj (beige)* écru; *(naturel)* unbleached

ecsta [eksta] *nf Fam (drogue)* E, ecstasy

écueil [ekœj] *nm (rocher)* reef; *Fig (obstacle)* pitfall

écuelle [ekɥɛl] *nf* bowl

éculé, -ée [ekyle] *adj (chaussure)* down-at-heel; *Fig (plaisanterie)* hackneyed

écume [ekym] *nf (de mer, bave d'animal)* foam; *(de pot-au-feu)* scum ▪**écumer 1** *vt (pot-au-feu)* to skim; *(piller)* to plunder **2** *vi* to foam (**de rage** with anger)

écureuil [ekyrœj] *nm* squirrel

écurie [ekyri] *nf* stable

écusson [ekysɔ̃] *nm (en étoffe)* badge

écuyer, -ère [ekɥije, -ɛr] *nmf (cavalier)* rider

eczéma [ɛgzema] *nm Méd* eczema

édenté, -ée [edɑ̃te] *adj* toothless

EDF [ədeɛf] *(abrév* **Électricité de France)** *nf* = French electricity company

édifice [edifis] *nm* edifice ▪**édification** *nf (de monument)* construction; *(instruction morale)* edification ▪**édifier** *vt (bâtiment)* to erect; *(théorie)* to construct; **é. qn** *(moralement)* to edify sb

Édimbourg [edɛ̃bur] *nm ou f* Edinburgh

édit [edi] *nm Hist* edict

éditer [edite] *vt (publier)* to publish; *(annoter) & Ordinat* to edit ▪**éditeur, -trice** *nmf (dans l'édition)* publisher; *(commentateur)* editor ▪**édition** *nf (livre, journal)* edition; *(métier, diffusion)* publishing

> Il faut noter que le verbe anglais **to edit** est un faux ami. Il ne s'emploie jamais pour dire **publier**.

> Il faut noter aussi que le nom anglais **edition** est un faux ami. Il ne désigne jamais l'industrie du livre.

éditorial, -iaux [editorjal, -jo] *nm (article)* editorial, *Br* leader ▪**éditorialiste** *nmf* editorial *or Br* leader writer

édredon [edrədɔ̃] *nm* eiderdown

éducateur, -trice [edykatœr, -tris] *nmf* educator

éducatif, -ive [edykatif, -iv] *adj* educational

éducation [edykasjɔ̃] *nf (enseignement)* education; *(par les parents)* upbringing; **avoir de l'é.** to have good manners; **l'É. nationale** ≃ the Department of Education; **é. physique** physical education *or* training; **é. sexuelle** sex education ▪**éduquer** *vt (à l'école)* to educate; *(à la maison)* to bring up

> Il faut noter que le nom anglais **education** ne fait référence qu'à l'instruction scolaire et à l'enseignement et non à la façon dont on est élevé.

EEE [əəə] *(abrév* **Espace économique européen)** *nm* EEA

effacé, -ée [efase] *adj (modeste)* self-effacing ▪**effacement** *nm (modestie)* self-effacement

effacer [efase] **1** *vt (gommer)* to rub out, to erase; *(en lavant)* to wash out; *(avec un chiffon)* to wipe away; *Fig (souvenir)* to blot out, to erase **2 s'effacer** *vpr (souvenir, couleur)* to fade; *(se placer en retrait)* to step aside

effarer [efare] *vt* to astound ▪**effarant, -ante** *adj* astounding ▪**effarement** *nm* astonishment

effaroucher [efaruʃe] **1** *vt* to scare away **2 s'effaroucher** *vpr* to take fright

effectif, -ive [efɛktif, -iv] **1** *adj (réel)* effective **2** *nm (de classe)* size; *(d'une armée)* (total) strength; *(employés)* staff ▪**effectivement** *adv (en effet)* actually

> Il faut noter que l'adverbe anglais **effectively** est un faux ami. Il signifie **efficacement**.

effectuer [efɛktɥe] *vt (expérience, geste difficile)* to carry out, to perform; *(paiement, trajet)* to make

efféminé, -ée [efemine] *adj* effeminate

effervescent, -ente [efɛrvesɑ̃, -ɑ̃t] *adj (médicament)* effervescent ▪**effervescence** *nf (exaltation)* excitement

effet [efɛ] *nm (résultat)* effect; *(impression)* impression (**sur** on); **en e.** indeed, in fact; **à cet e.** to this end, for this purpose; **sous l'e. de la colère** *(agir)* in anger, out of anger; **faire de l'e.** *(remède)* to be effective; *Tennis* **donner de l'e. à une balle** to put spin on a ball; **il me fait l'e. d'être fatigué** he seems to me to be tired; **ce n'est pas l'e. du hasard si…** it is not simply a matter of chance if…; **e. de commerce** bill of exchange; **e. de serre** greenhouse effect; **e. secondaire** side effect; *Cin* **effets spéciaux** special effects

effets [efɛ] *nmpl (vêtements)* clothes, things

efficace [efikas] *adj (mesure)* effective; *(personne)* efficient ▪**efficacité** *nf (de mesure)* effectiveness; *(de personne)* efficiency

effigie [efiʒi] *nf* effigy; **à l'e. de qn** bearing the image of sb

effilé, -ée [efile] *adj (doigt, lame)* tapering

effilocher [efiloʃe] **s'effilocher** *vpr* to fray

efflanqué, -ée [eflɑ̃ke] *adj* emaciated

effleurer [eflœre] *vt (frôler)* to touch lightly; *Fig (question)* to touch on; **e. qn** *(pensée)* to cross sb's mind

effondrer [efɔ̃dre] **s'effondrer** *vpr (édifice,*

Bourse) to collapse; *(plan)* to fall through; *(personne)* to go to pieces; **avoir l'air effondré** to look completely dejected ▪ **effondrement** *nm (d'édifice, de la Bourse)* collapse; *(de personne)* dejection

efforcer [efɔrse] **s'efforcer** *upr* **s'e. de faire qch** to try hard to do sth

effort [efɔr] *nm* effort; **sans e.** *(réussir)* effortlessly; **faire des efforts** to make an effort; **allons! encore un petit e.!** come on, try again!

effraction [efraksjɔ̃] *nf* **entrer par e.** to break in; **vol avec e.** housebreaking

effranger [efrɑ̃ʒe] **s'effranger** *upr* to fray

effrayer [efreje] **1** *ut* to frighten, to scare **2 s'effrayer** *upr* to be frightened *or* scared ▪ **effrayant, -ante** *adj* frightening, scary

effréné, -ée [efrene] *adj* unrestrained; *(course)* frantic

effriter [efrite] **s'effriter** *upr* to crumble

effroi [efrwa] *nm Littéraire* dread ▪ **effroyable** *adj* dreadful ▪ **effroyablement** [-əmɑ̃] *adv* dreadfully

effronté, -ée [efrɔ̃te] *adj (personne)* impudent ▪ **effronterie** *nf* impudence

effusion [efyzjɔ̃] *nf (manifestation)* effusiveness; **avec e.** effusively; **e. de sang** bloodshed

égal, -e, -aux, -ales [egal, -o] **1** *adj* equal (**à** to); *(uniforme, régulier)* even; **ça m'est é.** it's all the same to me; **combattre à armes égales** to fight on equal terms; *Sport* **faire jeu é.** to be evenly matched; **se trouver à égale distance de** to be equidistant from **2** *nmf (personne)* equal; **traiter qn d'é. à é.** *ou* **en é.** to treat sb as an equal; **sans é.** without match ▪ **également** *adv (au même degré)* equally; *(aussi)* also, as well ▪ **égaler** *ut* to equal, to match (**en** in); **3 plus 4 égale(nt) 7** 3 plus 4 equals 7

égaliser [egalize] **1** *ut (salaire)* to equalize; *(terrain)* to level **2** *vi Sport* to equalize ▪ **égalisation** *nf Sport* equalization; *(de terrain)* levelling

égalité [egalite] *nf* equality; *(régularité)* evenness; *Tennis* deuce; *Sport* **à é. (de score)** even, equal (in points) ▪ **égalitaire** *adj* egalitarian

égard [egar] *nm* **à l'é. de** *(envers)* towards; *(concernant)* with respect *or* regard to; **à cet é.** in this respect; **à certains égards** in some respects; **eu é. à** considering, in consideration of; **par é. pour qn** out of consideration for sb

égarement [egarmɑ̃] *nm (folie)* distraction; **égarements** *(actes immoraux)* wild behaviour

égarer [egare] **1** *ut (objet)* to mislay; *(personne)* to mislead; *(soupçons)* to avert **2 s'égarer** *upr (personne, lettre)* to get lost; *(objet)* to go astray; *(sortir du sujet)* to wander from the point

égayer [egeje] **1** *ut (pièce)* to brighten up; **é. qn** *(réconforter, amuser)* to cheer sb up **2 s'égayer** *upr (s'animer)* to cheer up

égide [eʒid] *nf* **sous l'é. de** under the aegis of

églantier [eglɑ̃tje] *nm* wild rose ▪ **églantine** *nf* wild rose

église [egliz] *nf* church

égocentrique [egɔsɑ̃trik] *adj* egocentric

égoïsme [egɔism] *nm* selfishness ▪ **égoïste 1** *adj* selfish **2** *nmf* selfish person

égorger [egɔrʒe] *ut* to cut *or* slit the throat of

égosiller [egɔzije] **s'égosiller** *upr* to scream one's head off, to bawl out

égotisme [egɔtism] *nm* egotism

égout [egu] *nm* sewer; **eaux d'é.** sewage

égoutter [egute] **1** *ut* to drain **2** *vi*, **s'égoutter** *upr* to drain ▪ **égouttoir** *nm (panier)* drainer

égratigner [egratiɲe] **1** *ut* to scratch **2 s'égratigner** *upr* to scratch oneself ▪ **égratignure** *nf* scratch

égrener [egrəne] *ut (raisins)* to pick the grapes off; *(maïs, pois)* to shell; *Rel* **é. son chapelet** to tell one's beads; **l'horloge égrène les heures** the clock slowly marks the hours

Égypte [eʒipt] *nf* **l'É.** Egypt ▪ **égyptien, -ienne** [-sjɛ̃, -sjɛn] **1** *adj* Egyptian **2** *nmf* **É., Égyptienne** Egyptian

eh [e] *exclam* hey!; **eh bien!** well!

éhonté, -ée [eɔ̃te] *adj* shameless; **mensonge é.** barefaced lie

éjecter [eʒɛkte] *ut* to eject; *Fam* **se faire é.** to get thrown out ▪ **éjectable** *adj* **siège é.** *(d'avion)* ejector seat ▪ **éjection** *nf (de pilote)* ejection

élaborer [elabɔre] *ut (plan, idée)* to develop ▪ **élaboration** *nf (de plan, d'idée)* development

élaguer [elage] *ut (arbre, texte)* to prune

élan¹ [elɑ̃] *nm (vitesse)* momentum; *(course)* run-up; *Fig (impulsion)* boost; **un é. de tendresse** a surge of affection; **prendre son é.** to take a run-up; **d'un seul é.** in one go

élan² [elɑ̃] *nm (animal)* elk

élancé, -ée [elɑ̃se] *adj (personne, taille)* slender

élancer [elɑ̃se] **1** *vi (abcès)* to give shooting pains **2 s'élancer** *upr (bondir)* to rush forward; *Sport* to take a run-up ▪ **élancement** *nm* shooting pain

élargir [elarʒir] **1** *ut (chemin)* to widen; *(vêtement)* to let out; *(esprit, débat)* to broaden **2 s'élargir** *upr (sentier)* to widen out; *(vêtement)* to stretch

élastique [elastik] **1** *adj (objet, gaz, métal)* elastic; *(règlement, notion)* flexible, supple **2** *nm (lien)* rubber band, *Br* elastic band; *(pour la couture)* elastic ▪ **élasticité** *nf* elasticity

élection [elɛksjɔ̃] *nf* election; **é. partielle** by-election ▪ **électeur, -trice** *nmf* voter, elector ▪ **électoral, -e, -aux, -ales** *adj* **campagne électorale** election campaign; **liste électorale** electoral roll ▪ **électorat** *nm (électeurs)* electorate, voters

électricien, -ienne [elektrisjẽ, -jen] *nmf* electrician ■ **électricité** *nf* electricity ■ **électrifier** *vt (voie ferrée)* to electrify ■ **électrique** *adj (pendule, décharge)* & *Fig* electric; *(courant, fil)* electric(al) ■ **électriser** *vt Fig (animer)* to electrify

électrochoc [elektroʃɔk] *nm (traitement)* electric shock treatment

électrocuter [elektrokyte] *vt* to electrocute

électrode [elektrɔd] *nf Él* electrode

électrogène [elektrɔʒen] *adj Él* **groupe é.** generator

électroménager [elektromenaʒe] **1** *adj m* **appareil é.** household electrical appliance **2** *nm* household appliances

électron [elektrɔ̃] *nm* electron ■ **électronicien, -ienne** *nmf* electronics engineer ■ **électronique 1** *adj* electronic; **microscope é.** electron microscope **2** *nf* electronics *(sing)*

électrophone [elektrofon] *nm* record player

élégant, -ante [elegã, -ãt] *adj (bien habillé)* smart, elegant; *(solution)* neat ■ **élégamment** [-amã] *adv* elegantly, smartly ■ **élégance** *nf* elegance; **avec é.** elegantly

élégie [eleʒi] *nf* elegy

élément [elemã] *nm (composante, personne)* & *Chim* element; *(de meuble)* unit; *Math* member; *Fig* **être dans son é.** to be in one's element ■ **élémentaire** [elemãter] *adj* basic; *(cours, école)* elementary

éléphant [elefã] *nm* elephant

élevage [elvaʒ] *nm (production)* breeding *(de* of); *(ferme)* cattle farm; **faire l'é. de** to breed

élévateur, -euse [elevatœr, -øz] *nmf* breeder

éligible [eliʒibl] *adj* eligible *(à* for)

élimé, -ée [elime] *adj (tissu)* threadbare, worn thin

éliminer [elimine] *vt* to eliminate ■ **élimination** *nf* elimination ■ **éliminatoire** *adj* **épreuve é.** *Sport* qualifying round, heat; *Scol* qualifying exam; *Scol* **note é.** disqualifying mark ■ **éliminatoires** *nfpl Sport* qualifying rounds

élire* [elir] *vt* to elect *(à* to)

élision [elizjɔ̃] *nf Ling* elision

élite [elit] *nf* elite *(de* of); **les élites** the elite; **troupes d'é.** crack *or* elite troops

elle [el] *pron personnel* (**a**) *(sujet)* she; *(chose, animal)* it; **elles** they; **e. est** she is/it is; **elles sont** they are (**b**) *(complément)* her; *(chose, animal)* it; **elles** them; **pour e.** for her; **pour elles** for them; **plus grande qu'e./qu'elles** taller than her/them ■ **elle-même** *pron* herself; *(chose, animal)* itself; **elles-mêmes** themselves

ellipse [elips] *nf* ellipse ■ **elliptique** *adj* elliptical

élocution [elɔkysjɔ̃] *nf* diction

éloge [elɔʒ] *nm (compliment)* praise; *(panégyrique)* eulogy; **faire l'é. de** to praise; **é. funèbre** funeral oration ■ **élogieux, -ieuse** *adj* laudatory

éloigné, -ée [elwaɲe] *adj (lieu)* far away, remote; *(date, parent)* distant; **é. de** *(village, maison)* far (away) from; *(très différent)* far removed from

éloignement [elwaɲəmã] *nm* remoteness, distance; *(absence)* separation *(de* from); **avec l'é.** *(avec le recul)* with time

éloigner [elwaɲe] **1** *vt (chose, personne)* to move away *(de* from); *(crainte, idée)* to banish; **é. qn de** *(sujet, but)* to take sb away from **2** **s'éloigner** *vpr (partir)* to move away *(de* from); *(dans le passé)* to become (more) remote; **s'é. de** *(sujet, but)* to wander from

élongation [elɔ̃gasjɔ̃] *nf Méd* pulled muscle; **se faire une é.** to pull a muscle

éloquent, -ente [elɔkã, -ãt] *adj* eloquent ■ **éloquence** *nf* eloquence

élu, -ue [ely] **1** *pp de* **élire 2** *nmf Rel* **le peuple é.** the chosen people **3** *nmf Pol* elected member *or* representative; *Rel* **les élus** the chosen ones; **l'heureux é./l'heureuse élue** *(futur mari, future femme)* the lucky man/woman

élucider [elyside] *vt* to elucidate

élucubrations [elykybrasjɔ̃] *nfpl Péj* flights of fancy

éluder [elyde] *vt* to evade

Élysée [elize] *nm* **(le palais de) l'É.** the Élysée palace *(French President's residence)*

émacié, -iée [emasje] *adj* emaciated

émail, -aux [emaj, -o] *nm* enamel; **casserole en é.** enamel saucepan ■ **émaillé, -ée** *adj* **é. de fautes** peppered with errors

e-mail [imel] *nm* e-mail; **envoyer un e. à qn** to send sb an e-mail, to e-mail sb

émanciper [emãsipe] **1** *vt (femmes)* to emancipate **2** **s'émanciper** *vpr* to become emancipated ■ **émancipation** *nf* emancipation; **l'é. de la femme** the emancipation of women

émaner [emane] *vt* **é. de** to emanate from ■ **émanation** *nf* **des émanations** *(odeurs)* smells; *(vapeurs)* fumes; **émanations toxiques** toxic fumes

émarger [emarʒe] **1** *vt (signer)* to sign **2** *vi (recevoir un salaire)* to draw one's salary

emballer [ɑ̃bale] **1** *vt* (**a**) *(dans une caisse)* to pack; *(dans du papier)* to wrap (up) (**b**) *(moteur)* to race; *Fam* **e. qn** *(passionner)* to grab sb **2 s'emballer** *vpr Fam (personne)* to get carried away; *(cheval)* to bolt; *(moteur)* to race ▪ **emballage** *nm (action)* packing; *(dans du papier)* wrapping; *(caisse)* packaging; **papier d'e.** wrapping paper ▪ **emballé, -ée** *adj Fam* enthusiastic

embarcadère [ɑ̃barkadɛr] *nm* landing stage

embarcation [ɑ̃barkasjɔ̃] *nf* (small) boat

embardée [ɑ̃barde] *nf (de véhicule)* swerve; **faire une e.** to swerve

embargo [ɑ̃bargo] *nm* embargo; **imposer/lever un e.** to impose/lift an embargo

embarquer [ɑ̃barke] **1** *vt (passagers)* to take on board; *(marchandises)* to load; *Fam (voler)* to walk off with; *Fam* **e. qn** *(au commissariat)* to cart sb off **2** *vi*, **s'embarquer** *vpr* to (go on) board; *Fam* **s'e. dans** *(aventure)* to embark on ▪ **embarquement** [-əmɑ̃] *nm (de passagers)* boarding

embarras [ɑ̃bara] *nm (gêne, malaise)* embarrassment; *(difficulté)* difficulty, trouble; **dans l'e.** in an awkward situation; *(financièrement)* in financial difficulties; **n'avoir que l'e. du choix** to be spoilt for choice

embarrasser [ɑ̃barase] **1** *vt (encombrer)* to clutter up; **e. qn** *(empêcher le passage de)* to be in sb's way; *(gêner)* to embarrass sb **2 s'embarrasser** *vpr* **s'e. de** to burden oneself with; *(se soucier)* to bother oneself about ▪ **embarrassant, -ante** *adj (paquet)* cumbersome; *(question)* embarrassing

embauche [ɑ̃boʃ] *nf (action)* hiring; *(travail)* work; **bureau d'e.** employment office ▪ **embaucher** *vt (ouvrier)* to hire, to take on

embaumer [ɑ̃bome] **1** *vt (parfumer)* to give a sweet smell to; *(cadavre)* to embalm **2** *vi* to smell sweet

embellie [ɑ̃beli] *nf* bright spell; *Naut* calm spell

embellir [ɑ̃belir] **1** *vt (pièce, personne)* to make more attractive; *(texte, vérité)* to embellish **2** *vi (jeune fille)* to grow more attractive ▪ **embellissement** *nm (de lieu)* improvement; *(de récit)* embellishment

emberlificoter [ɑ̃berlifikɔte] *vt Fam (empêtrer)* to tangle up; *Fig* **se laisser e. dans** *(affaire)* to get tangled up in

embêter [ɑ̃bete] *Fam* **1** *vt (agacer)* to annoy; *(ennuyer)* to bore **2 s'embêter** *vpr* to get bored ▪ **embêtant, -ante** *adj Fam* annoying ▪ **embêtement** [-ɛtmɑ̃] *nm Fam* problem; **des embêtements** bother, trouble

emblée [ɑ̃ble] **d'emblée** *adv* right away

emblème [ɑ̃blɛm] *nm* emblem

embobiner [ɑ̃bɔbine] *vt Fam (tromper)* to take in

emboîter [ɑ̃bwate] **1** *vt* to fit together; **e. le pas à qn** to follow close on sb's heels; *Fig (imiter)* to follow in sb's footsteps **2 s'emboîter** *vpr* to fit together

embonpoint [ɑ̃bɔ̃pwɛ̃] *nm* stoutness; **avoir de l'e.** to be stout

embouché, -ée [ɑ̃buʃe] *adj Fam* **mal e.** foul-tempered

embouchure [ɑ̃buʃyr] *nf (de fleuve)* mouth; *(d'un instrument à vent)* mouthpiece

embourber [ɑ̃burbe] **s'embourber** *vpr (véhicule)* & *Fig* to get bogged down

embourgeoiser [ɑ̃burʒwaze] **s'embourgeoiser** *vpr (personne)* to become middle-class; *(quartier)* to become gentrified

embout [ɑ̃bu] *nm (de canne)* tip; *(de tuyau)* nozzle

embouteillage [ɑ̃butejaʒ] *nm* traffic jam

embouteillé, -ée [ɑ̃buteje] *adj (rue)* congested; **route embouteillée sur 5 km** road with a 5-km-long traffic jam

emboutir [ɑ̃butir] *vt (voiture)* to crash into; *(métal)* to stamp; **il a eu l'arrière embouti** someone crashed into the back of his car

embranchement [ɑ̃brɑ̃ʃmɑ̃] *nm (de voie)* junction

embraser [ɑ̃braze] **1** *vt* to set ablaze **2 s'embraser** *vpr (prendre feu)* to flare up

embrasser [ɑ̃brase] **1** *vt* **e. qn** *(donner un baiser à)* to kiss sb; *(serrer contre soi)* to embrace or hug sb; **e. une croyance** to embrace a belief; **e. qch du regard** to take sth in at one glance **2 s'embrasser** *vpr* to kiss (each other) ▪ **embrassade** *nf* embrace, hug

Il faut noter que le verbe anglais **to embrace** est un faux ami. Il ne signifie jamais **donner un baiser.**

embrasure [ɑ̃brazyr] *nf (de fenêtre, de porte)* aperture; **dans l'e. de la porte** in the doorway

embrayer [ɑ̃breje] *vi Aut* to engage the clutch ▪ **embrayage** [-ɛjaʒ] *nm (mécanisme, pédale)* clutch

embrigader [ɑ̃brigade] *vt Péj* to dragoon (**dans** into)

embrocher [ɑ̃brɔʃe] *vt (volaille)* to put on a spit; *Fam* **e. qn** *(avec une épée)* to skewer sb

embrouiller [ɑ̃bruje] **1** *vt (fils)* to tangle (up); *(papiers)* to mix up, to muddle (up); **e. qn** to confuse sb, to get sb muddled; **tu vas m'e. les idées** you're going to get me confused **2 s'embrouiller** *vpr* to get confused or muddled (**dans** in or with) ▪ **embrouillamini** *nm Fam* muddle ▪ **embrouille** *nf Fam* muddle; **un sac d'embrouilles** a muddle of the first order

embroussaillé, -ée [ɑ̃brusaje] *adj (barbe, chemin)* bushy

embruns [ɑ̃brœ̃] *nmpl* (sea) spray

embryon [ɑ̃brijɔ̃] *nm* embryo ■**embryonnaire** *adj Méd & Fig* embryonic

embûches [ɑ̃byʃ] *nfpl (difficultés)* traps, pitfalls; **tendre des e. à qn** to set traps for sb; **semé d'e.** full of pitfalls

embuer [ɑ̃bɥe] *vt (vitre, yeux)* to mist up; **des yeux embués de larmes** eyes misted over with tears

embusquer [ɑ̃byske] **s'embusquer** *upr* to lie in ambush ■**embuscade** *nf* ambush

éméché, -ée [emeʃe] *adj Fam (ivre)* tipsy

émeraude [emrod] *nf & adj inv* emerald

émerger [emɛrʒe] *vi* to emerge **(de** from)

émérite [emerit] *adj* **professeur é.** emeritus professor

émerveiller [emɛrveje] **1** *vt* to amaze, to fill with wonder **2 s'émerveiller** *upr* to marvel, to be filled with wonder **(de** at) ■**émerveillement** *nm* wonder, amazement

émettre* [emɛtr] *vt (lumière, son)* to give out, to emit; *(message radio)* to broadcast; *(timbre, monnaie)* to issue; *(opinion, vœu)* to express; *(cri)* to utter; *(chèque)* to draw; *(emprunt)* to float ■**émetteur** *adj & nm Radio* **(poste) é.** transmitter

émeute [emøt] *nf* riot ■**émeutier, -ière** *nmf* rioter

émietter [emjete] *vt,* **s'émietter** *upr (pain)* to crumble

émigrer [emigre] *vi (personne)* to emigrate ■**émigrant, -ante** *nmf* emigrant ■**émigration** *nf* emigration ■**émigré, -ée 1** *nmf* exile, émigré **2** *adj* **travailleur é.** migrant worker

éminent, -ente [eminɑ̃, -ɑ̃t] *adj* eminent ■**éminemment** [-amɑ̃] *adv* eminently ■**éminence** *nf (colline)* hill; **son É. (le cardinal)** *(titre honorifique)* his Eminence (the Cardinal); *Fig* **une é. grise** *(conseiller)* an éminence grise

émir [emir] *nm* emir ■**émirat** *nm* emirate

émissaire [emiser] *nm* emissary

émission [emisjɔ̃] *nf (de radio)* programme; *(diffusion)* transmission; *(de timbre, monnaie)* issue; *(de lumière, de son)* emission **(de** of)

emmagasiner [ɑ̃magazine] *vt* to store (up); *Fig* **e. de l'énergie/des souvenirs** to store energy/memories

emmanchure [ɑ̃mɑ̃ʃyr] *nf* armhole

emmêler [ɑ̃mele] **1** *vt (fil, cheveux)* to tangle (up) **2 s'emmêler** *upr* to get tangled

emménager [ɑ̃menaʒe] *vi (dans un logement)* to move in; **e. dans** to move into ■**emménagement** *nm* moving in

emmener [ɑ̃mne] *vt* to take **(à** to); *(prisonnier)* to take away; **e. qn faire une promenade** to take sb for a walk; **e. qn en voiture** to give sb a *Br* lift *or Am* ride

emmerder [ɑ̃mɛrde] *très Fam* **1** *vt* **e. qn** *(agacer)*

to get on sb's nerves; *(ennuyer)* to bore sb stiff **2 s'emmerder** *upr* to get bored stiff ■**emmerdement** [-amɑ̃] *nm très Fam* bloody nuisance ■**emmerdeur, -euse** *nmf très Fam (personne)* pain in the *Br* arse *or Am* ass

emmitoufler [ɑ̃mitufle] **s'emmitoufler** *upr* to wrap (oneself) up **(dans** in)

emmurer [ɑ̃myre] *vt (personne)* to wall in

émoi [emwa] *nm* emotion; **en é.** in a flutter

émoluments [emɔlymɑ̃] *nmpl (de fonctionnaire)* remuneration

émotion [emosjɔ̃] *nf (sentiment)* emotion; *(frayeur)* fright; **donner des émotions à qn** to give sb a real fright; **aimer les émotions fortes** to love thrills ■**émotif, -ive** *adj* emotional ■**émotionné, -ée** *adj Fam* upset

émousser [emuse] *vt (pointe)* to blunt; *Fig (sentiment)* to dull ■**émoussé, -ée** *adj (pointe)* blunt; *Fig (sentiment)* dulled

émouvoir* [emuvwar] **1** *vt (affecter)* to move, to touch **2 s'émouvoir** *upr* to be moved *or* touched ■**émouvant, -ante** *adj* moving, touching

empailler [ɑ̃paje] *vt (animal)* to stuff

empaler [ɑ̃pale] *vt* to impale

empaqueter [ɑ̃pakte] *vt* to pack

emparer [ɑ̃pare] **s'emparer** *upr* **s'e. de** *(lieu, personne, objet)* to seize; *(sujet: émotion)* to take hold of

empâter [ɑ̃pate] **s'empâter** *upr* to become bloated ■**empâté, -ée** *adj* fleshy, fat

empêcher [ɑ̃peʃe] *vt* to prevent, to stop; **e. qn de faire qch** to prevent *or* stop sb from doing sth; **elle ne peut pas s'e. de rire** she can't help laughing; *Fig* **ça ne m'empêche pas de dormir** I don't lose any sleep over it; **e. l'accès d'un lieu** to prevent access to a place; *Fam* **n'empêche qu'elle a raison** all the same, she's right; *Fam* **n'empêche** all the same ■**empêchement** [-eʃmɑ̃] *nm* hitch; **il a/j'ai eu un e.** something came up

empereur [ɑ̃prœr] *nm* emperor

empester [ɑ̃peste] **1** *vt (tabac)* to stink of; *(pièce)* to stink out; **e. qn** to stink sb out **2** *vi* to stink

empêtrer [ɑ̃petre] **s'empêtrer** *upr* to get entangled **(dans** in)

emphase [ɑ̃faz] *nf* pomposity ■**emphatique** *adj* pompous

empiéter [ɑ̃pjete] *vi* **e. sur** to encroach (up)on ■**empiétement** *nm* encroachment

empiffrer [ɑ̃pifre] **s'empiffrer** *upr Fam* to stuff oneself **(de** with)

empiler [ɑ̃pile] **1** *vt* to pile up **(sur** on) **2 s'empiler** *upr* to pile up **(sur** on); **s'e. dans** *(passagers)* to cram into

empire [ɑ̃pir] *nm (territoires)* empire; *(autorité)* hold, influence; **sous l'e. de la peur** in the grip of fear

empirer [ɑ̃pire] *vi* to worsen, to get worse

empirique [ɑ̃pirik] *adj* empirical ■**empirisme** *nm* empiricism

emplacement [ɑ̃plasmɑ̃] *nm* (*de construction*) site, location; (*de stationnement*) place

emplâtre [ɑ̃plɑtr] *nm* (*pansement*) plaster

emplette [ɑ̃plɛt] *nf* purchase; **faire des emplettes** to do some shopping

emplir [ɑ̃plir] *vt*, **s'emplir** *vpr* to fill (**de** with)

emploi [ɑ̃plwa] *nm* (**a**) (*usage*) use; **e. du temps** timetable (**b**) (*travail*) job; **sans e.** unemployed; **la situation de l'e.** the employment situation

employabilité [ɑ̃plwajabilite] *nf* employability

employer [ɑ̃plwaje] **1** *vt* (*utiliser*) to use; **e. qn** (*occuper*) to employ sb **2** *s'employer* *vpr* (*expression*) to be used; **s'e. à faire qch** to devote oneself to doing sth ■**employé, -ée** *nmf* employee; **e. de banque** bank clerk; **e. de bureau** office worker; **e. de maison** domestic employee; **e. des postes** postal worker ■**employeur, -euse** *nmf* employer

empocher [ɑ̃pɔʃe] *vt* to pocket

empoigner [ɑ̃pwaɲe] **1** *vt* (*saisir*) to grab **2** *s'empoigner* *vpr* to come to blows ■**empoignade** *nf* (*querelle*) fight

empoisonner [ɑ̃pwazɔne] **1** *vt* (*personne, aliment, atmosphère*) to poison; (*empester*) to stink out; *Fam* **e. qn** to get on sb's nerves; *Fam* **e. la vie à qn** to make sb's life a misery **2** *s'empoisonner* *vpr* (*par accident*) to be poisoned; (*volontairement*) to poison oneself; *Fam* (*s'ennuyer*) to get bored stiff ■**empoisonnant, -ante** *adj Fam* (*embêtant*) irritating ■**empoisonnement** *nm* poisoning; *Fam* (*ennui*) problem

emporter [ɑ̃pɔrte] **1** *vt* (*prendre*) to take (**avec soi** with one); (*transporter*) to take away; (*prix, trophée*) to carry off; (*décision*) to carry; (*entraîner*) to carry along *or* away; (*par le vent*) to blow off *or* away; (*par les vagues*) to sweep away; (*par la maladie*) to carry off; **pizza à e.** takeaway pizza; **l'e. sur qn** to get the upper hand over sb; **il l'a emporté** he won; *Fig* **se laisser e.** to get carried away (**par** by); **elle ne l'emportera pas au paradis** she'll soon be smiling on the other side of her face **2** *s'emporter* *vpr* to lose one's temper (**contre** with) ■**emporté, -ée** *adj* (*caractère*) hot-tempered ■**emportement** [-əmɑ̃] *nm* anger; **emportements** fits of anger

empoté, -ée [ɑ̃pɔte] *adj Fam* clumsy

empourprer [ɑ̃purpre] *s'empourprer* *vpr* to turn crimson

empreint, -einte [ɑ̃prɛ̃, -ɛ̃t] *adj Littéraire* **e. de bonté** full of kindness; **e. de danger** fraught with danger

empreinte [ɑ̃prɛ̃t] *nf* (*marque*) & *Fig* mark; **e. digitale** fingerprint; **e. de pas** footprint

empresser [ɑ̃prese] *s'empresser* *vpr* **s'e. de**

faire qch to hasten to do sth; **s'e. auprès de qn** to be attentive to sb ■**empressé, -ée** *adj* attentive ■**empressement** [-esmɑ̃] *nm* (*hâte*) eagerness; (*prévenance*) attentiveness

emprise [ɑ̃priz] *nf* hold (**sur** over)

emprisonner [ɑ̃prizɔne] *vt* to imprison ■**emprisonnement** *nm* imprisonment

emprunt [ɑ̃prœ̃] *nm* (*argent*) loan; *Ling* (*mot*) borrowing; **faire un e.** (*auprès d'une banque*) to take out a loan; **d'e.** borrowed; **nom d'e.** assumed name ■**emprunter** *vt* (*argent, objet*) to borrow (**à qn** from sb); (*route*) to take

emprunté, -ée [ɑ̃prœ̃te] *adj* (*gêné*) ill at ease

empuantir [ɑ̃pɥɑ̃tir] *vt* to make stink

ému, -ue [emy] **1** *pp de* **émouvoir 2** *adj* (*attendri*) moved; (*attristé*) upset; (*apeuré*) nervous; **une voix émue** a voice charged with emotion

émulation [emylasjɔ̃] *nf* (*sentiment*) & *Ordinat* emulation

émule [emyl] *nmf* emulator

en¹ [ɑ̃] *prép* (**a**) (*indique le lieu*) in; (*indique la direction*) to; **être en ville/en France** to be in town/in France; **aller en ville/en France** to go (in)to town/to France (**b**) (*indique le temps*) in; **en février** in February; **en été** in summer; **d'heure en heure** from hour to hour (**c**) (*indique le moyen*) by; (*indique l'état*) in; **en avion** by plane; **en groupe** in a group; **en fleur** in flower; **en congé** on leave; **en mer** at sea; **en guerre** at war (**d**) (*indique la matière*) in; **en bois** made of wood, wooden; **chemise en Nylon®** nylon shirt; **c'est en or** it's (made of) gold (**e**) (*domaine*) **étudiant en lettres** humanities *or Br* arts student; **docteur en médecine** doctor of medicine (**f**) (*comme*) **en cadeau** as a present; **en ami** as a friend (**g**) (+ *participe présent*) **en mangeant/chantant** while eating/singing; **en apprenant que...** on hearing that...; **en souriant** smiling, with a smile; **en ne disant rien** by saying nothing; **sortir en courant** to run out (**h**) (*transformation*) into; **traduire en français** to translate into French

en² [ɑ̃] *pron* (**a**) (*indique la provenance*) from there; **j'en viens** I've just come from there (**b**) (*remplace les compléments introduits par 'de'*) **il en est content** he's pleased with it/him/them; **en parler** to talk about it; **en mourir** to die of *or* from it; **elle m'en frappa** she struck me with it; **il s'en souviendra** he'll remember it (**c**) (*partitif*) some; **j'en ai** I have some; **en veux-tu?** do you want some?; **donne-lui-en** give some to him/her; **je t'en supplie** I beg you (to)

ENA [ena] (*abrév* **École nationale d'administration**) *nf* = university-level college preparing students for senior positions in law and economics ■**énarque** *nmf* = graduate from ENA

encablure [ɑ̃kablyr] *nf* **à quelques encablures**

du rivage a short distance (away) from the shore

encadrer [ɑ̃kadre] *vt (tableau)* to frame; *(entourer d'un trait)* to circle; *(étudiants, troupes)* to supervise; *(personnel)* to manage; *(prisonnier, accusé)* to flank; *Fam* **je ne peux pas l'e.** I can't stand him/her ▪**encadrement** *nm (action)* framing; *(d'étudiants)* supervision; *(de personnel)* management; *(de porte, de photo)* frame; **personnel d'e.** training and supervisory staff

encaissé, -ée [ɑ̃kese] *adj (vallée)* deep

encaisser [ɑ̃kese] *vt (argent, loyer)* to collect; *(chèque)* to cash; *Fam (coup)* to take; *Fam* **je ne peux pas l'e.** I can't stand him/her ▪**encaissement** [-ɛsmɑ̃] *nm (de loyer)* collection; *(de chèque)* cashing

encart [ɑ̃kar] *nm (feuille)* insert; **e. publicitaire** publicity insert

en-cas [ɑ̃ka] *nm inv (repas)* snack

encastrer [ɑ̃kastre] *vt* to build in (**dans** to) ▪**encastré, -ée** *adj* built-in

encaustique [ɑ̃kostik] *nf* wax, polish

enceinte¹ [ɑ̃sɛ̃t] *adj f (femme)* pregnant; **e. de six mois** six months pregnant

enceinte² [ɑ̃sɛ̃t] *nf (muraille)* (surrounding) wall; *(espace)* enclosure; **dans l'e. de** within, inside; **e. (acoustique)** speakers

encens [ɑ̃sɑ̃] *nm* incense ▪**encensoir** *nm* censer

encercler [ɑ̃sɛrkle] *vt (lieu, ennemi)* to surround, to encircle; *(mot)* to circle

enchaîner [ɑ̃ʃene] **1** *vt (animal, prisonnier)* to chain up; *(idées)* to link (up) **2** *vi (continuer à parler)* to continue **3** **s'enchaîner** *vpr (idées)* to be linked (up) ▪**enchaînement** [-ɛnmɑ̃] *nm (succession)* chain, series; *(liaison)* link(ing) (**de** between *or* of); *(en gymnastique, en danse)* enchaînement

enchanter [ɑ̃ʃɑ̃te] *vt (ravir)* to delight, to enchant; *(ensorceler)* to bewitch ▪**enchanté, -ée** *adj (ravi)* delighted (**de** with; **que** + *subjunctive* that); *(magique)* enchanted; **e. (de faire votre connaissance)!** pleased to meet you! ▪**enchantement** *nm (ravissement)* delight; *(sortilège)* magic spell; **comme par e.** as if by magic ▪**enchanteur, -eresse 1** *adj* delightful, enchanting **2** *nm (sorcier)* magician

enchâsser [ɑ̃ʃase] *vt (diamant)* to set

enchère [ɑ̃ʃɛr] *nf (offre)* bid; **vente aux enchères** auction; **mettre qch aux enchères** to put sth up for auction, to auction sth ▪**enchérir** *vi* to make a higher bid; **e. sur qn** to outbid sb

enchevêtrer [ɑ̃ʃvetre] **1** *vt* to (en)tangle **2** **s'enchevêtrer** *vpr* to get entangled (**dans** in) ▪**enchevêtrement** [-ɛtrəmɑ̃] *nm* tangle, entanglement

enclave [ɑ̃klav] *nf* enclave

enclencher [ɑ̃klɑ̃ʃe] *vt Tech* to engage

enclin, -ine [ɑ̃klɛ̃, -in] *adj* **e. à** inclined to

enclos [ɑ̃klo] *nm (terrain, clôture)* enclosure ▪**enclore*** *vt (terrain)* to enclose

enclume [ɑ̃klym] *nf* anvil

encoche [ɑ̃kɔʃ] *nf* notch (**à** in)

encoignure [ɑ̃kwaɲyr] *nf* corner

encoller [ɑ̃kɔle] *vt (papier peint)* to paste

encolure [ɑ̃kɔlyr] *nf (de cheval, vêtement)* neck; *(tour du cou)* collar (size); **robe à e. carrée** square-neck(ed) dress

encombre [ɑ̃kɔ̃br] **sans encombre** *adv* without a hitch

encombrer [ɑ̃kɔ̃bre] **1** *vt (pièce, couloir)* to clutter up (**de** with); *(rue, passage)* to block; **e. qn** to hamper sb **2** **s'encombrer** *vpr* **s'e. de** to load oneself down with ▪**encombrant, -ante** *adj (paquet)* bulky, cumbersome; *(présence)* awkward ▪**encombré, -ée** *adj (lignes téléphoniques, route)* jammed ▪**encombrement** [-əmɑ̃] *nm (d'objets)* clutter; *(embouteillage)* traffic jam; *(volume)* bulk(iness)

encontre [ɑ̃kɔ̃trə] **à l'encontre de** *prép* against

encore [ɑ̃kɔr] *adv* (**a**) *(toujours)* still; **tu es e. là?** are you still here? (**b**) *(avec négation)* **pas e.** not yet; **je ne suis pas e. prêt** I'm not ready yet (**c**) *(de nouveau)* again; **essaie e.** try again (**d**) *(de plus, en plus)* **e. un café** another coffee, one more coffee; **e. une fois** (once) again, once more; **e. un** another (one), one more; **e. du pain** (some) more bread; **que veut-il e.?** what else *or* more does he want?; **e. quelque chose** something else; **qui/quoi e.?** who/what else? (**e**) *(avec comparatif)* even, still; **e. mieux** even better, better still (**f**) *(aussi)* **mais e.** but also (**g**) **si e.** *(si seulement)* if only; **et e.** *(à peine)* if that, only just (**h**) **e. que...** (+ *subjunctive*) although…

encourager [ɑ̃kuraʒe] *vt* to encourage (**à faire** to do) ▪**encourageant, -ante** *adj* encouraging ▪**encouragement** *nm* encouragement

encourir* [ɑ̃kurir] *vt* to incur

encrasser [ɑ̃krase] **1** *vt* to clog up (with dirt) **2** **s'encrasser** *vpr* to get clogged up

encre [ɑ̃kr] *nf* ink; **faire couler beaucoup d'e.** to be much written about; **e. de Chine** *Br* Indian ink, *Am* India ink; **e. sympathique** invisible ink ▪**encrier** *nm* inkpot

encroûter [ɑ̃krute] **s'encroûter** *vpr Péj* to get into a rut

encyclopédie [ɑ̃siklɔpedi] *nf* encyclopedia ▪**encyclopédique** *adj* encyclopedic

endémique [ɑ̃demik] *adj* endemic

endetter [ɑ̃dete] **1** *vt* **e. qn** to get sb into debt **2** **s'endetter** *vpr* to get into debt ▪**endettement** *nm* debts

endeuiller [ɑ̃dœje] *vt (famille, nation)* to plunge into mourning

endiablé, -ée [ɑ̃djable] *adj (rythme)* wild

endiguer [ãdige] *vt (fleuve)* to dyke (up); *Fig (réprimer)* to contain

endimanché, -ée [ãdimãʃe] *adj* in one's Sunday best

endive [ãdiv] *nf* chicory *inv*, endive

endoctriner [ãdɔktrine] *vt* to indoctrinate ▪ **endoctrinement** *nm* indoctrination

endolori, -ie [ãdɔlɔri] *adj* painful

endommager [ãdɔmaʒe] *vt* to damage

endormir* [ãdɔrmir] **1** *vt (enfant)* to put to sleep; *(ennuyer)* to send to sleep; *(soupçons)* to lull; *(douleur)* to deaden **2** **s'endormir** *vpr* to fall asleep, to go to sleep ▪ **endormi, -ie** *adj* asleep, sleeping; *Fam (indolent)* sluggish

endosser [ãdose] *vt (vêtement)* to put on; *(responsabilité)* to assume; *(chèque)* to endorse

endroit [ãdrwa] *nm* (**a**) *(lieu)* place, spot; **à cet e. du récit** at this point in the story; **par endroits** in places (**b**) *(de tissu)* right side; **à l'e.** *(vêtement)* the right way round

enduire* [ãdɥir] *vt* to smear, to coat (**de** with) ▪ **enduit** *nm* coating; *(de mur)* plaster

endurant, -ante [ãdyrã, -ãt] *adj* hardy, tough ▪ **endurance** *nf* stamina; **épreuve d'e.** endurance trial

endurcir [ãdyrsir] **1** *vt* **e. qn à** *(douleur)* to harden sb to **2** **s'endurcir** *vpr (moralement)* to become hard; *(physiquement)* to toughen up ▪ **endurci, -ie** *adj (insensible)* hardened; **célibataire e.** confirmed bachelor

endurer [ãdyre] *vt* to endure, to bear

énergie [enɛrʒi] *nf* energy; **avec é.** *(protester)* forcefully ▪ **énergétique** *adj* aliment é. energy food; **ressources énergétiques** energy resources ▪ **énergique** *adj (dynamique)* energetic; *(remède)* powerful; *(mesure, ton)* forceful ▪ **énergiquement** *adv (protester)* energetically

énergumène [enɛrgymɛn] *nmf Péj* eccentric

énerver [enɛrve] **1** *vt* **é. qn** *(irriter)* to get on sb's nerves; *(rendre nerveux)* to make sb nervous **2** **s'énerver** *vpr* to get worked up ▪ **énervé, -ée** *adj (agacé)* irritated; *(excité)* on edge, agitated ▪ **énervement** [-əmã] *nm (agacement)* irritation; *(excitation)* agitation

> Il faut noter que le verbe anglais **to unnerve** est un faux ami. Il signifie **troubler**.

enfance [ãfãs] *nf* childhood; **petite e.** infancy, early childhood; *Fam* **c'est l'e. de l'art** it's child's play ▪ **enfanter** *vt* to give birth or ▪ **enfantillages** *nmpl* childish *Br* behaviour *or Am* behavior ▪ **enfantin, -ine** *adj (voix, joie)* childlike; *(langage)* children's; *(puéril)* childish; *(simple)* easy

enfant [ãfã] *nmf* child *(pl* children); **attendre un e.** to be expecting a baby; **c'est un e. de...** *(originaire)* he's a native of...; **c'est un jeu d'e.** it's child's play; **e. en bas âge** infant; *Rel* **e. de chœur** altar boy; **e. gâté** spoilt child; **e.**

prodige child prodigy; **e. prodigue** prodigal son; **e. trouvé** foundling; **e. unique** only child

enfer [ãfɛr] *nm* hell; **d'e.** *(bruit, vision)* infernal; **à un train d'e.** at breakneck speed; *Fam* **un plan d'e.** a hell of a (good) plan

enfermer [ãfɛrme] **1** *vt (personne, chose)* to shut up; **e. qn/qch à clef** to lock sb/sth up **2** **s'enfermer** *vpr* **s'e. dans** *(chambre)* to shut oneself (up) in; *Fig (attitude)* to maintain stubbornly; **s'e. à clef** to lock oneself in

enfiévré, -ée [ãfjevre] *adj (front, imagination)* fevered

enfilade [ãfilad] *nf (série)* row, string; **des pièces en e.** a suite of rooms

enfiler [ãfile] *vt (aiguille)* to thread; *(perles)* to string; *Fam (vêtement)* to slip on

enfin [ãfɛ̃] *adv (à la fin)* finally, at last; *(en dernier lieu)* lastly; *(en somme)* in a word; *(de résignation)* well; *Fam* **e. bref...** *(en somme)* in a word...; **mais e.** but; **(mais) e.!** for heaven's sake!; **il est grand, e. pas trop petit** he's tall, well, at least he's not too short

enflammer [ãflame] **1** *vt* to set fire to; *(allumette)* to light; *(irriter)* to inflame; *(imagination)* to stir **2** **s'enflammer** *vpr* to catch fire ▪ **enflammé, -ée** *adj (discours)* fiery

enfler [ãfle] **1** *vt (rivière, membre)* to swell **2** *vi (membre)* to swell (up) ▪ **enflure** *nf* swelling

enfoncer [ãfɔ̃se] **1** *vt (clou)* to bang in; *(pieu)* to drive in; *(porte, voiture)* to smash in; *(chapeau)* to push down; **e. dans qch** *(couteau, mains)* to plunge into sth **2** *vi (s'enliser)* to sink (**dans** into); *(couteau)* to go in **3** **s'enfoncer** *vpr (s'enliser)* to sink (**dans** into); *(couteau)* to go in; **s'e. dans** *(pénétrer)* to disappear into ▪ **enfoncé, -ée** *adj (yeux)* sunken

enfouir [ãfwir] *vt* to bury

enfourcher [ãfurʃe] *vt (cheval)* to mount

enfourner [ãfurne] *vt* to put in the oven

enfreindre* [ãfrɛ̃dr] *vt* to infringe

enfuir* [ãfɥir] **s'enfuir** *vpr* to run away (**de** from)

enfumer [ãfyme] *vt (pièce)* to fill with smoke; *(personne)* to smoke out

engager [ãgaʒe] **1** *vt (discussion, combat)* to start; *(bijou)* to pawn; *(parole)* to pledge; *(clef)* to insert (**dans** into); **e. qn** *(embaucher)* to hire sb; *(lier)* to bind sb; **e. qn dans** *(affaire)* to involve sb in; **e. qn à faire qch** to urge sb to do sth; **e. la partie** to start the match **2** **s'engager** *vpr (dans l'armée)* to enlist; *(prendre position)* to commit oneself; *(partie)* to start; **s'e. à faire qch** to undertake to do sth; **s'e. dans** *(voie)* to enter; *(affaire)* to get involved in; **s'e. dans une aventure** to get involved in an adventure ▪ **engagé, -ée** *adj (écrivain)* committed ▪ **engageant, -ante** *adj* engaging ▪ **engagement** *nm (promesse)* commitment; *(de soldats)* enlistment; *(commencement)* start; *Football* kick-off; **sans e. de votre part** without obligation (on your part); **prendre l'e. de faire qch** to undertake to do sth

> Il faut noter que l'adjectif anglais **engaged** est un faux ami. Il ne s'utilise jamais dans un contexte politique.

engelure [ɑ̃ʒlyr] *nf* chilblain

engendrer [ɑ̃ʒɑ̃dre] *vt (causer)* to generate, to engender; *(procréer)* to father

engin [ɑ̃ʒɛ̃] *nm (machine)* machine; *(outil)* device; **e. explosif** explosive device; **e. spatial** spacecraft

> Il faut noter que le nom anglais **engine** est un faux ami. Il signifie **moteur**.

englober [ɑ̃glɔbe] *vt* to include

engloutir [ɑ̃glutir] *vt (nourriture)* to wolf down; *(bateau, village)* to submerge

engorger [ɑ̃gɔrʒe] *vt* to block up, to clog

engouement [ɑ̃gumɑ̃] *nm* craze (**pour** for)

engouffrer [ɑ̃gufre] **1** *vt Fam (avaler)* to wolf down **2 s'engouffrer** *upr* **s'e. dans** to rush into

engourdir [ɑ̃gurdir] **1** *vt (membre)* to numb; *(esprit)* to dull **2 s'engourdir** *upr (membre)* to go numb; *(esprit)* to become dull(ed) **•engourdissement** *nm* numbness

engrais [ɑ̃grɛ] *nm* fertilizer

engraisser [ɑ̃grese] **1** *vt (animal, personne)* to fatten up **2** *vi Fam* to get fat

engrenage [ɑ̃grənaʒ] *nm Tech* gears; *Fig* chain; *Fig* **pris dans l'e.** caught (up) in the system

engueuler [ɑ̃gœle] *Fam* **1** *vt* **e. qn** to yell at sb, to bawl sb out; **se faire e.** to get bawled out **2 s'engueuler** *upr* to have a row **•engueulade** *nf Fam (réprimande)* bawling out; *(dispute)* row, *Br* slanging match

enhardir [ɑ̃ardir] **1** *vt* to make bolder **2 s'enhardir** *upr* **s'e. à faire qch** to pluck up courage to do sth

énième [ɛnjɛm] *adj Fam* umpteenth

énigme [enigm] *nf (devinette)* riddle; *(mystère)* enigma **•énigmatique** *adj* enigmatic

enivrer [ɑ̃nivre] **1** *vt (soûler)* to intoxicate **2 s'enivrer** *upr* to get drunk (**de** on)

enjamber [ɑ̃ʒɑ̃be] *vt* to step over; *(sujet: pont) (rivière)* to span **•enjambée** *nf* stride

enjeu, -x [ɑ̃ʒø] *nm (mise)* stake; *Fig (de guerre)* stakes; **quel est l'e.?** what is at stake?

enjoindre* [ɑ̃ʒwɛ̃dr] *vt Littéraire* **e. à qn de faire qch** to enjoin sb to do sth

enjôler [ɑ̃ʒole] *vt* to coax

enjoliver [ɑ̃ʒolive] *vt* to embellish

enjoliveur [ɑ̃ʒolivœr] *nm* hubcap

enjoué, -ée [ɑ̃ʒwe] *adj* playful **•enjouement** *nm* playfulness

enlacer [ɑ̃lase] *vt (mêler)* to entwine; *(embrasser)* to clasp

enlaidir [ɑ̃ledir] **1** *vt* to make ugly **2** *vi* to grow ugly

enlevé, -ée [ɑ̃lve] *adj (style, danse)* lively

enlever [ɑ̃l(ə)ve] **1** *vt* to remove; *(meubles)* to take away, to remove; *(vêtement, couvercle)* to take off, to remove; *(tapis)* to take up; *(rideau)* to take down; *(enfant)* to kidnap, to abduct; *(ordures)* to collect **2 s'enlever** *upr (tache)* to come out; *(vernis)* to come off **•enlèvement** [-ɛvmɑ̃] *nm (d'enfant)* kidnapping, abduction; *(d'un objet)* removal; *(des ordures)* collection

enliser [ɑ̃lize] **s'enliser** *upr (véhicule)* & *Fig* to get bogged down (**dans** in)

enneigé, -ée [ɑ̃neʒe] *adj* snow-covered **•enneigement** [-ɛʒmɑ̃] *nm* snow coverage; **bulletin d'e.** snow report

ennemi, -ie [ɛnmi] **1** *nmf* enemy **2** *adj (personne)* hostile (**de** to); **pays/soldat e.** enemy country/soldier

ennui [ɑ̃nɥi] *nm (lassitude)* boredom; *(souci)* problem; **avoir des ennuis** *(soucis)* to be worried; *(problèmes)* to have problems; **l'e., c'est que...** the annoying thing is that...

ennuyer [ɑ̃nɥije] **1** *vt (agacer)* to annoy; *(préoccuper)* to bother; *(lasser)* to bore; **si ça ne t'ennuie pas** if you don't mind **2 s'ennuyer** *upr* to get bored **•ennuyé, -ée** *adj (air)* bored; **je suis très e.** *(confus)* I feel bad (about it) **•ennuyeux, -euse** *adj (contrariant)* annoying; *(lassant)* boring

> Il faut noter que le verbe anglais **to annoy** ne signifie jamais **lasser**. Il signifie **importuner** ou **irriter**.

énoncé [enɔ̃se] *nm (de question)* wording; *(de faits)* statement; *(de sentence)* pronouncement **•énoncer** *vt* to state

enorgueillir [ɑ̃nɔrgœjir] **s'enorgueillir** *upr* **s'e. de qch** to pride oneself on sth

énorme [enɔrm] *adj* enormous, huge **•énormément** *adv (travailler, pleurer)* an awful lot; **je le regrette é.** I'm awfully sorry about it; **il n'a pas é. d'argent** he hasn't got a huge amount of money **•énormité** *nf (de demande, de crime, de somme)* enormity; *(faute)* glaring mistake

enquérir* [ɑ̃kerir] **s'enquérir** *upr* **s'e. de qch** to inquire about sth

enquête [ɑ̃kɛt] *nf (de policiers, de journalistes)* investigation; *(judiciaire, administrative)* inquiry; *(sondage)* survey **•enquêter** *vi (policier, journaliste)* to investigate; **e. sur qch** to investigate sth **•enquêteur, -euse** *nmf (policier)* investigator; *(sondeur)* researcher

enquiquiner [ɑ̃kikine] *vt Fam* to annoy

enraciner [ɑ̃rasine] **s'enraciner** *upr* to take root; **enraciné dans** *(personne, souvenir)* rooted in; **bien enraciné** *(préjugé)* deep-rooted

enrager [ɑ̃raʒe] *vi* to be furious (**de faire** about doing); **faire e. qn** to get on sb's nerves **•enragé, -ée** *adj (chien)* rabid; *Fam (joueur)* fanatical (**de** about) ▪**enrageant, -ante** *adj* infuriating

enrayer [ɑ̃reje] **1** *vt* (*maladie*) to check **2 s'enrayer** *vpr* (*fusil*) to jam

enregistrer [ɑ̃r(ə)ʒistre] *vt* (*par écrit, sur bande*) to record; (*sur registre*) to register; (*constater*) to register; (**faire**) **e. ses bagages** (*à l'aéroport*) to check in, to check one's bags in; **ça enregistre** it's recording ▪**enregistrement** [-əmɑ̃] *nm* (*d'un acte*) registration; (*sur bande*) recording; **l'e. des bagages** (*à l'aéroport*) (baggage) check-in; **se présenter à l'e.** to check in ▪**enregistreur, -euse** *adj* **appareil e.** recording apparatus; **caisse enregistreuse** cash register

enrhumer [ɑ̃ryme] **s'enrhumer** *vpr* to catch a cold; **être enrhumé** to have a cold

enrichir [ɑ̃riʃir] **1** *vt* to enrich (**de** with) **2 s'enrichir** *vpr* (*personne*) to get rich

enrober [ɑ̃rɔbe] *vt* to coat (**de** in); **enrobé de chocolat** chocolate-coated

enrôler [ɑ̃role] *vt*, **s'enrôler** *vpr* to enlist ▪**enrôlement** *nm* enlistment

enrouer [ɑ̃rwe] **s'enrouer** *vpr* to get hoarse ▪**enroué, -ée** *adj* hoarse

enrouler [ɑ̃rule] **1** *vt* (*fil*) to wind; (*tapis, cordage*) to roll up **2 s'enrouler** *vpr* **s'e. dans qch** (*couvertures*) to wrap oneself up in sth; **s'e. sur** *ou* **autour de qch** to wind round sth

ensabler [ɑ̃sable] *vt*, **s'ensabler** *vpr* (*port*) to silt up

ensanglanté, -ée [ɑ̃sɑ̃glɑ̃te] *adj* bloodstained

enseigne [ɑ̃sɛɲ] *nf* (*de magasin*) sign; *Fig* **logés à la même e.** in the same boat; **e. lumineuse** neon sign

enseigner [ɑ̃seɲe] **1** *vt* to teach; **e. qch à qn** to teach sb sth **2** *vi* to teach ▪**enseignant, -ante** [-ɛɲɑ̃, -ɑ̃t] **1** *nmf* teacher **2** *adj* **corps e.** teaching profession ▪**enseignement** [-ɛɲmɑ̃] *nm* education; (*action, métier*) teaching; **être dans l'e.** to be a teacher; **e. par correspondance** distance learning; **e. privé** private education; **e. public** *Br* state *or Am* public education

ensemble [ɑ̃sɑ̃bl] **1** *adv* together; **aller (bien) e.** (*couleurs*) to go together; (*personnes*) to be well-matched **2** *nm* (*d'objets*) group, set; *Math* set; (*vêtement*) outfit; *Mus* ensemble; (*harmonie*) unity; **l'e. du personnel** (*totalité*) the whole (of the) staff; **l'e. des enseignants** all (of) the teachers; **dans l'e.** on the whole; **vue d'e.** general view; **grand e.** (*quartier*) housing *Br* complex *or Am* development

ensemencer [ɑ̃səmɑ̃se] *vt* (*terre*) to sow

ensevelir [ɑ̃səvlir] *vt* to bury

ensoleillé, -ée [ɑ̃sɔleje] *adj* (*endroit, journée*) sunny

ensommeillé, -ée [ɑ̃sɔmeje] *adj* sleepy

ensorceler [ɑ̃sɔrsəle] *vt* (*envoûter, séduire*) to bewitch ▪**ensorcellement** [-ɛlmɑ̃] *nm* (*séduction*) spell

ensuite [ɑ̃sɥit] *adv* (*puis*) next, then; (*plus tard*) afterwards

ensuivre* [ɑ̃sɥivr] **s'ensuivre** *v impersonnel* **il s'ensuit que...** it follows that...; **et tout ce qui s'ensuit** and all the rest of it; **jusqu'à ce que mort s'ensuive** until death

entacher [ɑ̃taʃe] *vt* (*honneur*) to sully

entaille [ɑ̃taj] *nf* (*fente*) notch; (*blessure*) gash, slash ▪**entailler** *vt* to notch; (*blesser*) to gash, to slash

entame [ɑ̃tam] *nf* first slice

entamer [ɑ̃tame] *vt* (*pain, peau*) to cut into; (*bouteille, boîte*) to open; (*négociations*) to enter into; (*capital*) to eat or break into; (*métal, plastique*) to damage; (*résolution, réputation*) to shake

entartrer [ɑ̃tartre] *vt*, **s'entartrer** *vpr* (*chaudière*) *Br* to fur up, *Am* to scale

entasser [ɑ̃tase] *vt*, **s'entasser** *vpr* (*objets*) to pile up, to heap up ▪**entassement** *nm* (*tas*) pile, heap; (*de gens*) crowding

entendement [ɑ̃tɑ̃dmɑ̃] *nm* (*faculté*) understanding

entendre [ɑ̃tɑ̃dr] **1** *vt* to hear; (*comprendre*) to understand; (*vouloir*) to intend; **e. parler de qn/qch** to hear of sb/sth; **e. dire que...** to hear (it said) that...; **e. raison** to listen to reason; **laisser e. à qn que...** to give sb to understand that... **2 s'entendre** *vpr* (*être entendu*) to be heard; (*être compris*) to be understood; **s'e. (sur)** (*être d'accord*) to agree (on); (**bien**) **s'e. avec qn** to get along *or Br* on with sb; **on ne s'entend plus!** (*à cause du bruit*) we can't hear ourselves speak!; **il s'y entend** (*est expert*) he knows all about that

entendu, -ue [ɑ̃tɑ̃dy] *adj* (*convenu*) agreed; (*compris*) understood; (*sourire, air*) knowing; **e.!** all right!; **bien e.** of course

entente [ɑ̃tɑ̃t] *nf* (*accord*) agreement, understanding; (**bonne**) **e.** (*amitié*) harmony

entériner [ɑ̃terine] *vt* to ratify

enterrer [ɑ̃tere] *vt* (*défunt*) to bury; *Fig* (*projet*) to scrap ▪**enterrement** [-ɛrmɑ̃] *nm* burial; (*funérailles*) funeral

en-tête [ɑ̃tɛt] (*pl* **en-têtes**) *nm* (*de papier*) heading; **papier à e.** *Br* headed paper, *Am* letterhead

entêter [ɑ̃tete] **s'entêter** *vpr* to persist (**à faire** in doing) ▪**entêté, -ée** *adj* stubborn ▪**entêtement** [ɑ̃tɛtmɑ̃] *nm* stubbornness; **e. à faire qch** persistence in doing sth

enthousiasme [ɑ̃tuzjasm] *nm* enthusiasm ▪**enthousiasmant, -ante** *adj* exciting ▪**enthousiasmer 1** *vt* to fill with enthusiasm **2 s'enthousiasmer** *vpr* **s'e. pour qch** to get enthusiastic about sth ▪**enthousiaste** *adj* enthusiastic

enticher [ɑ̃tiʃe] **s'enticher** *vpr* **s'e. de qn/qch** to become infatuated with sb/sth

entier, -ière [ɑ̃tje, -jɛr] **1** *adj (total)* whole, entire; *(intact)* intact; *(absolu)* absolute, complete; *(caractère, personne)* uncompromising; **payer place entière** to pay full price; **le pays tout e.** the whole *or* entire country **2** *nm (unité)* whole; **en e., dans son e.** in its entirety, completely ▪ **entièrement** *adv* entirely

entité [ɑ̃tite] *nf* entity

entonner [ɑ̃tɔne] *vt (air)* to start singing

entonnoir [ɑ̃tɔnwar] *nm* funnel

entorse [ɑ̃tɔrs] *nf Méd* sprain; **se faire une e. à la cheville** to sprain one's ankle; *Fig* **faire une e. au règlement** to bend the rules

entortiller [ɑ̃tɔrtije] **1** *vt* to wrap **(dans** in); *Fam* **e. qn** to dupe sb **2 s'entortiller** *vpr (lierre)* to coil **(autour de** round)

entourage [ɑ̃turaʒ] *nm (proches)* circle of family and friends

entourer [ɑ̃ture] **1** *vt* to surround **(de** with); *(envelopper)* to wrap **(de** in); **entouré de** surrounded by; **e. qn de ses bras** to put one's arms round sb; **il est très entouré** *(soutenu)* he has lots of supportive people around him **2 s'entourer** *vpr* **s'e. de** to surround oneself with

entourlouper [ɑ̃turlupe] *vt Fam* **e. qn** to play a dirty trick on sb ▪ **entourloupette** *nf Fam* dirty trick; **faire une e. à qn** to play a dirty trick on sb

entracte [ɑ̃trakt] *nm (de théâtre) Br* interval, *Am* intermission

entraide [ɑ̃trɛd] *nf* mutual aid ▪ **s'entraider** [sɑ̃trede] *vpr* to help each other

entrailles [ɑ̃traj] *nfpl* entrails

entrain [ɑ̃trɛ̃] *nm* get-up-and-go; **plein d'e.** lively; **sans e.** lifeless

entraînant, -ante [ɑ̃trɛnɑ̃, -ɑ̃t] *adj (musique)* lively

entraîner [ɑ̃trene] **1** *vt* **(a)** *(charrier)* to carry away; *(causer)* to bring about; *(dépenses, modifications)* to entail; *(roue)* to drive; **e. qn** *(emmener)* to lead sb away; *(de force)* to drag sb away; *(attirer)* to lure sb; **e. qn à faire qch** to lead sb to do sth; **se laisser e.** to allow oneself to be led astray **(b)** *(athlète, cheval)* to train **(à** for) **2 s'entraîner** *vpr* to train oneself **(à faire qch** to do sth); *Sport* to train ▪ **entraînement** [-ɛnmɑ̃] *nm Sport* training; *(élan)* impulse; *Tech* drive ▪ **entraîneur** [-ɛnœr] *nm (d'athlète)* coach; *(de cheval)* trainer

entrave [ɑ̃trav] *nf Fig (obstacle)* hindrance **(à** to) ▪ **entraver** *vt* to hinder, to hamper

entre [ɑ̃tr] *prép* between; *(parmi)* among(st); **l'un d'e. vous** one of you; **(soit dit) e. nous** between you and me; **se dévorer e. eux** *(réciprocité)* to devour each other; **e. deux âges** middle-aged; **e. autres (choses)** among other things

entrebâiller [ɑ̃trəbaje] *vt (porte)* to open slightly ▪ **entrebâillement** *nm* **par l'e. de la porte** through the half-open door

entrechoquer [ɑ̃trəʃɔke] **s'entrechoquer** *vpr (bouteilles)* to knock against each other

entrecôte [ɑ̃trəkot] *nf* rib steak

entrecouper [ɑ̃trəkupe] *vt (entremêler)* to punctuate **(de** with)

entrecroiser [ɑ̃trəkrwaze] *vt*, **s'entrecroiser** *vpr (fils)* to interlace; *(routes)* to intersect

entre-deux-guerres [ɑ̃trədøgɛr] *nm inv* inter-war period

entrée [ɑ̃tre] *nf (action)* entry, entrance; *(porte)* entrance; *(vestibule)* entrance hall, entry; *(accès)* admission, entry **(de** to); *Ordinat* input; *(plat)* starter; **à son e.** as he/she came in; **faire son e.** to make one's entrance; **à l'e. de l'hiver** at the beginning of winter; **'e. interdite'** 'no entry', 'no admittance'; **'e. libre'** 'admission free'; **e. en matière** *(d'un discours)* opening, introduction; **e. en vigueur** *(d'une loi)* date of application; *Scol* **e. en sixième** *Br* ≃ entering the first form, *Am* ≃ entering the sixth grade; **e. de service** service *or Br* tradesmen's entrance; **e. des artistes** stage door

entrefaites [ɑ̃trəfɛt] *nfpl* **sur ces e.** at that moment

entrefilet [ɑ̃trəfile] *nm* short (news) item

entrejambe [ɑ̃trəʒɑ̃b] *nm* crotch

entrelacer [ɑ̃trəlase] *vt*, **s'entrelacer** *vpr* to intertwine

entremêler [ɑ̃trəmele] *vt*, **s'entremêler** *vpr* to intermingle

entremets [ɑ̃trəmɛ] *nm (plat)* dessert, *Br* sweet

entremetteur, -euse [ɑ̃trəmɛtœr, -øz] *nmf* go-between

entremise [ɑ̃trəmiz] *nf* intervention; **par l'e. de qn** through sb

entreposer [ɑ̃trəpoze] *vt* to store ▪ **entrepôt** *nm* warehouse

entreprendre* [ɑ̃trəprɑ̃dr] *vt (travail, voyage)* to undertake; **e. de faire qch** to undertake to do sth ▪ **entreprenant, -ante** [-ɑ̃nɑ̃] *adj* enterprising; *(galant)* forward

entrepreneur [ɑ̃trəprənœr] *nm (en bâtiment)* contractor

entreprise [ɑ̃trəpriz] *nf (firme)* company, firm; *(opération)* undertaking

entrer [ɑ̃tre] **1** *vi (aux être) (aller)* to go in, to enter; *(venir)* to come in, to enter; **e. dans** to go into; *(pièce)* to come/go into, to enter; *(club)* to join; *(carrière)* to enter, to go into; **e. dans un arbre** *(en voiture)* to crash into a tree; **e. à l'université** to start university; **e. en action** to go into action; **e. en ébullition** to start boiling; **e. dans les détails** to go into detail; **faire/ laisser e. qn** to show/let sb in; **entrez!** come in! **2** *vt Ordinat* **e. des données** to enter data **(dans** into)

entresol [ɑ̃trəsɔl] *nm* mezzanine floor

entre-temps [ɑ̃trətɑ̃] *adv* meanwhile

entretenir* [ɑ̃trət(ə)nir] **1** *vt (voiture, maison, famille)* to maintain; *(relations, souvenir)* to keep; *(sentiment)* to entertain; **e. sa forme/sa santé** to keep fit/healthy; **e. qn de qch** to talk to sb about sth **2 s'entretenir** *upr* **s'e. de** to talk about (**avec** with) **▪entretenu, -ue** *adj* **bien/mal e.** *(maison)* well-kept/badly kept; **femme entretenue** kept woman

> Il faut noter que le verbe anglais **to enter-tain** est un faux ami. Il signifie le plus sou-vent **divertir**.

entretien [ɑ̃trətjɛ̃] *nm (de route, de maison)* maintenance, upkeep; *(dialogue)* conver-sation; *(entrevue)* interview; **entretiens** *(négoci-ations)* talks

entre-tuer [ɑ̃trətɥe] **s'entre-tuer** *upr* to kill each other

entrevoir* [ɑ̃trəvwar] *vt (rapidement)* to catch a glimpse of; *(pressentir)* to foresee

entrevue [ɑ̃trəvy] *nf* interview

entrouvrir* [ɑ̃truvrir] *vt,* **s'entrouvrir** *upr* to half-open **▪entrouvert, -erte** *adj (porte, fenêtre)* half-open

énumérer [enymere] *vt* to list **▪énumération** *nf* listing

envahir [ɑ̃vair] *vt (pays)* to invade; *(marché)* to flood; **e. qn** *(doute, peur)* to overcome sb **▪envahissant, -ante** *adj (voisin)* intrusive **▪envahissement** *nm* invasion **▪envahisseur** *nm* invader

enveloppant, -ante [ɑ̃vlɔpɑ̃, -ɑ̃t] *adj (séduisant)* captivating

enveloppe [ɑ̃vlɔp] *nf (pour lettre)* envelope; *(de colis)* wrapping; *(de pneu)* casing; *Fig (apparence)* exterior; **mettre qch sous e.** to put sth in an envelope; **e. timbrée à votre adresse** *Br* stamped addressed envelope, *Am* stamped self-addressed envelope

envelopper [ɑ̃vlɔpe] **1** *vt* to wrap (up) (**dans** in); **e. la ville** *(brouillard)* to blanket *or* envelop the town; **enveloppé de mystère** shrouded in mystery **2 s'envelopper** *upr* to wrap oneself (up) (**dans** in)

envenimer [ɑ̃v(ə)nime] **1** *vt (plaie)* to make septic; *Fig (querelle)* to embitter **2 s'en-venimer** *upr (plaie)* to turn septic; *Fig* to be-come acrimonious

envergure [ɑ̃vɛrgyr] *nf (d'avion, d'oiseau)* wingspan; *(de personne)* calibre; *(ampleur)* scope; **de grande e.** *(réforme)* far-reaching

envers [ɑ̃vɛr] **1** *prép Br* towards, *Am* toward(s), to; **e. et contre tous** in the face of all opposition **2** *nm (de tissu)* wrong side; *(de médaille)* reverse side; **à l'e.** *(chaussette)* inside out; *(pantalon)* back to front; *(la tête en bas)* upside down; *(à contresens)* the wrong way

envie [ɑ̃vi] *nf (jalousie)* envy; *(désir)* desire; *Fam*

(des ongles) hangnail; **avoir e. de qch** to want sth; **j'ai e. de faire qch** I feel like doing sth; **elle meurt d'e. de faire qch** she's dying to do sth; **ça me fait e.** I really like that **▪envier** *vt* to envy (**qch à qn** sb sth) **▪envieux, -ieuse** *adj* en-vious; **faire des e.** to make people envious

environ [ɑ̃virɔ̃] *adv (à peu près)* about **▪environs** *nmpl* outskirts, surroundings; **aux e. de** *(Paris, Noël, 10 euros)* around, in the vicinity of

environner [ɑ̃virɔne] *vt* to surround **▪environnant, -ante** *adj* surrounding **▪environnement** *nm* environment

envisager [ɑ̃vizaʒe] *vt (considérer)* to consider; *(projeter) Br* to envisage, *Am* to envision; **e. de faire qch** to consider doing sth **▪envisa-geable** *adj* conceivable; **pas e.** unthinkable

envoi [ɑ̃vwa] *nm (action)* sending; *(paquet)* package; *(marchandises)* consignment

envol [ɑ̃vɔl] *nm (d'oiseau)* taking flight; *(d'avion)* take-off **▪envolée** *nf Fig (élan)* flight **▪s'en-voler** *upr (oiseau)* to fly away; *(avion)* to take off; *(chapeau)* to blow away; *Fig (espoir)* to vanish

envoûter [ɑ̃vute] *vt* to bewitch **▪envoûtement** *nm* bewitchment

envoyer* [ɑ̃vwaje] **1** *vt* to send; *(lancer)* to throw; *Fam (gifle)* to give; **e. chercher qn** to send for sb; *Fam* **e. promener qn** to send sb packing **2 s'envoyer** *upr Fam (repas)* to put *or* stash away **▪envoyé, -ée** *nmf* envoy; **e. spécial** *(reporter)* special correspondent **▪envoyeur** *nm* sender; **'retour à l'e.'** *(sur une enveloppe)* 'return to sender'

épagneul, -eule [epaɲœl] *nmf* spaniel

épais, -aisse [epɛ, -ɛs] *adj* thick **▪épaisseur** *nf* thickness; **avoir 1 m d'é.** to be 1 m thick **▪épaissir** [epesir] **1** *vt* to thicken **2** *vi,* **s'épaissir** *upr* to thicken; *(grossir)* to fill out; **le mystère s'épaissit** the mystery is deepening

épancher [epɑ̃ʃe] **1** *vt Fig (cœur)* to pour out **2 s'épancher** *upr* to pour out one's heart **▪épanchement** *nm (aveu)* outpouring

épanouir [epanwir] **s'épanouir** *upr (fleur)* to bloom; *Fig (personne)* to blossom; *(visage)* to beam **▪épanoui, -ouie** *adj (fleur, personne)* in full bloom; *(visage)* beaming **▪épanouisse-ment** *nm (de fleur)* full bloom; *(de personne)* blossoming

épargne [eparɲ] *nf (action, vertu)* saving; *(sommes)* savings **▪épargnant, -ante** *nmf* saver **▪épargner** *vt (argent, provisions)* to save; *(ennemi)* to spare; **e. qch à qn** *(ennuis, chagrin)* to spare sb sth

éparpiller [eparpije] *vt,* **s'éparpiller** *upr* to scatter; *(efforts)* to dissipate **▪épars, -arse** *adj* scattered

épaté, -ée [epate] *adj (nez)* flat

épater [epate] *vt Fam* to astound **▪épatant, -ante** *adj Fam* splendid

épaule [epol] *nf* shoulder ▪ **épauler 1** *vt (fusil)* to raise (to one's shoulder); **é. qn** *(aider)* to back sb up **2** *vi* to take aim ▪ **épaulette** *nf (de veste)* shoulder pad

épave [epav] *nf (bateau, personne)* wreck

épée [epe] *nf* sword

épeler [ep(ə)le] *vt* to spell

éperdu, -ue [eperdy] *adj (regard)* distraught; *(amour)* passionate ▪ **éperdument** *adv (aimer)* madly; **elle s'en moque e.** she couldn't care less

éperon [eprɔ̃] *nm (de cavalier, de coq)* spur ▪ **éperonner** *vt* to spur on

éphémère [efemɛr] *adj* short-lived, ephemeral

épi [epi] *nm (de blé)* ear; *(de cheveux)* tuft of hair

épice [epis] *nf* spice ▪ **épicé, -ée 1** *adj (plat, récit)* spicy **2** *adv* **manger é.** to eat spicy food ▪ **épicer** *vt* to spice

épicier, -ière [episje, -jɛr] *nmf* grocer ▪ **épicerie** *nf (magasin) Br* grocer's (shop), *Am* grocery (store); **é. fine** delicatessen

épidémie [epidemi] *nf* epidemic ▪ **épidémique** *adj* epidemic

épiderme [epidɛrm] *nm* skin

épier [epje] *vt (observer)* to watch closely; *(occasion)* to watch out for; **é. qn** to spy on sb

épilepsie [epilɛpsi] *nf Méd* epilepsy ▪ **épileptique** *adj & nmf* epileptic

épiler [epile] **1** *vt (jambes)* to remove unwanted hair from; *(sourcils)* to pluck **2 s' épiler** *vpr* **s'é. les jambes (à la cire)** to wax one's legs; **s'é. les sourcils** to pluck one's eyebrows ▪ **épilation** *nf (des jambes)* removal of unwanted hair; *(des sourcils)* plucking

épilogue [epilɔg] *nm* epilogue

épinard [epinar] *nm (plante)* spinach; **épinards** spinach

épine [epin] *nf (de plante)* thorn; *(d'animal)* spine, prickle; *Anat* **é. dorsale** spine ▪ **épineux, -euse** *adj (tige, question)* thorny; *(poisson)* spiny

épingle [epɛ̃gl] *nf* pin; *Fig* **tiré à quatre épingles** immaculately turned out; **é. à cheveux** hairpin; **virage en é. à cheveux** hairpin bend; **é. de** *ou* **à nourrice, é. de sûreté** safety pin; **é. à linge** *Br* clothes peg, *Am* clothes pin ▪ **épingler** *vt* to pin; *Fam* **é. qn** *(arrêter)* to nab sb

Épiphanie [epifani] *nf* **l'É.** Epiphany

épique [epik] *adj* epic

épiscopal, -e, -aux, -ales [episkɔpal, -o] *adj* episcopal

épisode [epizɔd] *nm* episode; **feuilleton en six épisodes** serial in six episodes, six-part serial ▪ **épisodique** *adj (intermittent)* occasional; *(accessoire)* minor

épitaphe [epitaf] *nf* epitaph

épithète [epitɛt] *nf* epithet; *Grammaire* attribute

épître [epitr] *nf* epistle

éploré, -ée [eplɔre] *adj (veuve, air)* tearful

éplucher [eplyʃe] *vt (carotte, pomme)* to peel; *(salade)* to clean; *Fig (texte)* to dissect ▪ **épluchure** *nf* peeling

éponge [epɔ̃ʒ] *nf* sponge; *Fig* **jeter l'é.** to throw in the towel ▪ **éponger 1** *vt (liquide)* to mop up; *(surface)* to sponge down; *(dette)* to absorb **2 s'éponger** *vpr* **s'é. le front** to mop one's brow

épopée [epɔpe] *nf* epic

époque [epɔk] *nf (date)* time, period; *(historique)* age; **meubles d'é.** period furniture; **à l'é.** at the *or* that time

épouse [epuz] *nf* wife

épouser [epuze] *vt* to marry; *Fig (cause)* to espouse; *Fig* **é. la forme de qch** to take on the exact shape of sth

épousseter [epuste] *vt* to dust

époustoufler [epustufle] *vt Fam* to astound ▪ **époustouflant, -ante** *adj Fam* astounding

épouvantable [epuvɑ̃tabl] *adj* appalling

épouvantail [epuvɑ̃taj] *nm (de jardin)* scarecrow

épouvante [epuvɑ̃t] *nf* terror ▪ **épouvanter** *vt* to terrify

époux [epu] *nm* husband; **les é.** the husband and wife

éprendre* [eprɑ̃dr] **s'éprendre** *vpr* **s'é. de qn** to fall in love with sb ▪ **épris, -ise** *adj* in love (**de** with)

épreuve [eprœv] *nf (essai, examen)* test; *(sportive)* event; *(malheur)* ordeal, trial; *(photo)* print; *(texte imprimé)* proof; **mettre qn/qch à l'é.** to put sb/sth to the test; **à toute é.** *(patience)* unfailing; *(nerfs)* rock-solid; **à l'é. des balles/du feu** bulletproof/fireproof

éprouver [epruve] *vt (méthode, personne, courage)* to test; *(sentiment)* to feel; *(difficultés)* to meet with ▪ **éprouvant, -ante** *adj (pénible)* trying ▪ **éprouvé, -ée** *adj (remède)* well-tried; *(famille)* sorely tried; *(région)* hard-hit

éprouvette [epruvɛt] *nf* test tube

EPS [əpeɛs] *(abrév* **éducation physique et sportive)** *nf Scol* PE

épuiser [epɥize] **1** *vt (personne, provisions, sujet)* to exhaust **2 s'épuiser** *vpr (réserves, patience)* to run out; **s'é. à faire qch** to exhaust oneself doing sth ▪ **épuisant, -ante** *adj* exhausting ▪ **épuisé, -ée** *adj* exhausted; *(marchandise)* sold out; *(édition)* out of print ▪ **épuisement** *nm* exhaustion

épuisette [epɥizɛt] *nf* landing net

épurer [epyre] *vt (eau, gaz)* to purify; *(minerai)* to refine ▪ **épuration** *nf* purification; *(de minerai)* refining; **station d'é.** purification *Br* works *or Am* plant

équateur [ekwatœr] *nm* equator; **sous l'é.** at the equator ▪ **équatorial, -e, -iaux, -iales** *adj* equatorial

équation [ekwasjɔ̃] *nf Math* equation

équerre [eker] *nf* **é. (à dessin)** *Br* set square, *Am* triangle; **d'é.** straight, square

équestre [ekɛstr] *adj (statue, sports)* equestrian

équilibre [ekilibr] *nm* balance; **mettre qch en é.** to balance sth (**sur** on); **se tenir en é.** to (keep one's) balance; **garder/perdre l'é.** to keep/lose one's balance ▪ **équilibriste** *nmf* tightrope walker

équilibrer [ekilibre] **1** *vt (charge, composition, budget)* to balance **2 s'équilibrer** *upr (équipes)* to balance each other out; *(comptes)* to balance

équinoxe [ekinɔks] *nm* equinox

équipage [ekipaʒ] *nm (de navire, d'avion)* crew

équipe [ekip] *nf* team; *(d'ouvriers)* gang; **faire é. avec qn** to team up with sb; **é. de nuit** night shift; **é. de secours** rescue team ▪ **équipier, -ière** *nmf* team member

équipée [ekipe] *nf* escapade

équiper [ekipe] **1** *vt* to equip (**de** with) **2 s'équiper** *upr* to equip oneself (**de** with) ▪ **équipement** *nm* equipment

équitation [ekitasjɔ̃] *nf Br (horse) riding, Am (horseback) riding;* **faire de l'é.** to go riding

équité [ekite] *nf* fairness ▪ **équitable** *adj* fair, equitable ▪ **équitablement** [-əmɑ̃] *adv* fairly

équivalent, -ente [ekivalɑ̃, -ɑ̃t] *adj & nm* equivalent ▪ **équivalence** *nf* equivalence ▪ **équivaloir*** *vi* **é. à qch** to be equivalent to sth

équivoque [ekivɔk] **1** *adj (ambigu)* equivocal; *(douteux)* dubious **2** *nf* ambiguity; **sans é.** *(déclaration)* unequivocal

érable [erabl] *nm (arbre, bois)* maple

érafler [erafle] *vt* to graze, to scratch ▪ **éraflure** *nf* graze, scratch

éraillé [eraje] *adj (tissu)* frayed; *(surface)* scratched; *(voice)* hoarse; **yeux éraillés** bloodshot eyes

ère [ɛr] *nf* era; **avant notre è.** BC; **en l'an 800 de notre è.** in the year 800 AD

érection [erɛksjɔ̃] *nf* erection

éreinter [erɛ̃te] **1** *vt (fatiguer)* to exhaust; *(critiquer)* to tear to pieces **2 s'éreinter** *upr* **s'é. à faire qch** to wear oneself out doing sth

ergot [ergo] *nm (de coq)* spur

ergoter [ergɔte] *vi* to quibble (**sur** about)

ériger [eriʒe] **1** *vt* to erect **2 s'ériger** *upr* **s'é. en qch** to set oneself up as sth

ermite [ermit] *nm* hermit

érosion [erozjɔ̃] *nf* erosion ▪ **éroder** *vt* to erode

érotique [erɔtik] *adj* erotic ▪ **érotisme** *nm* eroticism

errer [ɛre] *vi* to wander ▪ **errant, -ante** *adj* wandering; **chien/chat e.** stray dog/cat

erreur [ɛrœr] *nf (faute)* mistake, error; **par e.** by mistake; **dans l'e.** mistaken; **sauf e. de ma part** unless I'm mistaken; **faire e.** *(au téléphone)* to dial the wrong number; **e. de calcul** miscalculation; **e. judiciaire** miscarriage of justice ▪ **erroné, -ée** *adj* erroneous

ersatz [ɛrzats] *nm* substitute

éructer [erykte] *vi* to belch

érudit, -ite [erydi, -it] **1** *adj* scholarly, erudite **2** *nmf* scholar ▪ **érudition** *nf* scholarship, erudition

éruption [erypsjɔ̃] *nf (de volcan)* eruption; *(de boutons)* rash

es [ɛ] *voir* **être**

ès [ɛs] *prép* of; **licencié/docteur ès lettres** ≃ BA/PhD

ESB [øɛsbe] *(abrév* **encéphalopathie spongiforme bovine)** *nf* BSE

escabeau, -x [ɛskabo] *nm (marchepied)* stepladder, *Br* (pair of) steps; *(tabouret)* stool

escadre [ɛskadr] *nf Naut* squadron ▪ **escadrille** *nf Av (unité)* flight ▪ **escadron** *nm* squadron

escalade [ɛskalad] *nf* climbing; *(de prix, de violence, de guerre)* escalation ▪ **escalader** *vt* to climb, to scale

escale [ɛskal] *nf Av* stopover; *Naut (lieu)* port of call; **faire e. à** *(avion)* to stop (over) at; *(navire)* to put in at; **vol sans e.** non-stop flight; **e. technique** refuelling stop

escalier [ɛskalje] *nm (marches)* stairs; *(cage)* staircase; **l'e., les escaliers** the stairs; **e. mécanique** *ou* **roulant** escalator; **e. de secours** fire escape; **e. de service** service stairs

escalope [ɛskalɔp] *nf* escalope

escamoter [ɛskamɔte] *vt (faire disparaître)* to make vanish; *(esquiver)* to dodge ▪ **escamotable** *adj Tech* retractable

escampette [ɛskɑ̃pɛt] *nf Fam* **prendre la poudre d'e.** to make off

escapade [ɛskapad] *nf* jaunt; **faire une e.** to go on a jaunt

escargot [ɛskargo] *nm* snail

escarmouche [ɛskarmuʃ] *nf* skirmish

escarpé, -ée [ɛskarpe] *adj* steep ▪ **escarpement** [-əmɑ̃] *nm (côte)* steep slope

escarpin [ɛskarpɛ̃] *nm (soulier)* pump, *Br* court shoe

escient [ɛsjɑ̃] **à bon e.** *adv* wisely

esclaffer [ɛsklafe] **s'esclaffer** *upr* to roar with laughter

esclandre [ɛsklɑ̃dr] *nm (noisy)* scene; **causer un e.** to make a scene

esclave [ɛsklav] *nmf* slave; **être l'e. de qn/qch** to be a slave to sb/sth ▪ **esclavage** *nm* slavery

escompte [ɛskɔ̃t] *nm* discount; **taux d'e.** bank discount rate ▪ **escompter** *vt (espérer)* to anticipate (**faire** doing), to expect (**faire** to do)

escorte [ɛskɔrt] *nf* escort; **sous bonne e.** under escort ▪ **escorter** *vt* to escort

escouade [ɛskwad] *nf Mil* squad

escrime [ɛskrim] *nf Sport* fencing; **faire de l'e.** to fence ▪ **escrimeur, -euse** *nmf* fencer

escrimer [ɛskrime] **s'escrimer** *upr* **s'e. à faire qch** to struggle to do sth

escroc [ɛskro] *nm* crook, swindler ▪ **escroquer** *vt* **e. qn** to swindle sb; **e. qch à qn** to swindle sb out of sth ▪ **escroquerie** *nf (action)* swindling; *(résultat)* swindle; *Fam* **c'est de l'e.!** it's a rip-off!

espace [ɛspas] *nm* space; **e. aérien** air space; **e. vert** garden, park ▪ **espacer 1** *vt* to space out; **espacés d'un mètre** one metre apart **2 s'espacer** *vpr (maisons, visites)* to become less frequent

espadon [ɛspadɔ̃] *nm* swordfish

espadrille [ɛspadrij] *nf* espadrille, rope-soled sandal

Espagne [ɛspaɲ] *nf* **l'E.** Spain ▪ **espagnol, -ole 1** *adj* Spanish **2** *nmf* **E., Espagnole** Spaniard **3** *nm (langue)* Spanish

espèce [ɛspɛs] *nf (race)* species; *(genre)* kind, sort; *Fam* **un e. d'idiot/une e. d'idiote** an idiot; *Fam* **e. d'idiot!** you idiot! ▪ **espèces** *nfpl (argent)* cash; **en e.** in cash

espérance [ɛsperɑ̃s] *nf* hope; **au-delà de nos espérances** beyond our expectations; **répondre aux espérances de qn** to live up to sb's expectations; **e. de vie** life expectancy

espérer [ɛspere] **1** *vt* to hope for; **e. que...** to hope that...; **e. faire qch** to hope to do sth **2** *vi* to hope; **en qn/qch** to trust in sb/sth; **j'espère (bien)!** I hope so!

espiègle [ɛspjɛgl] *adj* mischievous ▪ **espièglerie** [-əri] *nf* mischievousness

espion, -ionne [ɛspjɔ̃, -jɔn] *nmf* spy ▪ **espionnage** *nm* spying, espionage ▪ **espionner 1** *vt* to spy on **2** *vi* to spy

esplanade [ɛsplanad] *nf* esplanade

espoir [ɛspwar] *nm* hope; **avoir l'e. de faire qch** to have hopes of doing sth; **il n'y a plus d'e. (il va mourir)** there's no hope for him; **sans e. (cas)** hopeless; **les espoirs de la danse** the young hopefuls of the dancing world

esprit [ɛspri] *nm (attitude, fantôme)* spirit; *(intellect)* mind; *(humour)* wit; **venir à l'e. de qn** to cross sb's mind; **avoir de l'e.** to be witty; **avoir l'e. large/étroit** to be broad-/narrow-minded; **perdre l'e.** to go out of one's mind

esquimau, -aude, -aux, -audes [ɛskimo, -od] **1** *adj* Eskimo, *Am* Inuit **2** *nmf* **E., Esquimaude** Eskimo, *Am* Inuit **3** *nm* **E.®** *(glace) Br* ≃ choc-ice *(on a stick), Am* ≃ ice-cream bar

esquinter [ɛskɛ̃te] *Fam* **1** *vt (voiture)* to damage; *(blesser)* to hurt **2 s'esquinter** *vpr* **s'e. la jambe** to hurt one's leg; **s'e. la santé** to damage one's health; **s'e. à faire qch** to wear oneself out doing sth

esquisse [ɛskis] *nf (croquis, plan)* sketch ▪ **esquisser** *vt* to sketch; **e. un geste** to make a (slight) gesture

esquiver [ɛskive] **1** *vt (coup, problème)* to dodge **2 s'esquiver** *vpr* to slip away

essai [ɛsɛ] *nm (test)* test, trial; *(tentative) & Rugby* try; *(ouvrage)* essay; **à l'e. (objet)** on a trial basis; **coup d'e.** first attempt

essaim [ɛsɛ̃] *nm* swarm

essayer [ɛseje] **1** *vt* to try **(de faire** to do); *(vêtement)* to try on; *(méthode, restaurant)* to try out **2 s'essayer** *vpr* **s'e. à qch/à faire qch** to try one's hand at sth/at doing sth ▪ **essayage** [-ɛjaʒ] *nm (de vêtement)* fitting

essence [ɛsɑ̃s] *nf (carburant) Br* petrol, *Am* gas; *(extrait) & Phil* essence; **par e.** essentially; **e. sans plomb** unleaded; **e. ordinaire** *Br* two-star petrol, *Am* regular gas

essentiel, -ielle [ɛsɑ̃sjɛl] **1** *adj* essential **(à/pour** for) **2** *nm* **l'e. (le plus important)** the main thing; *(le minimum)* the essentials; **l'e. de** the majority of ▪ **essentiellement** *adv* essentially

essieu, -x [ɛsjø] *nm* axle

essor [ɛsɔr] *nm (d'oiseau)* flight; *(de pays, d'entreprise)* rapid growth; **en plein e.** booming; **prendre son e.** to take off

essorer [ɛsɔre] *vt (linge)* to wring; *(dans une essoreuse)* to spin-dry; *(dans une machine à laver)* to spin ▪ **essoreuse** *nf (à main)* wringer; *(électrique)* spin-dryer

essouffler [ɛsufle] **1** *vt* to make out of breath **2 s'essouffler** *vpr* to get out of breath

essuyer [ɛsɥije] **1** *vt (objet, surface)* to wipe; *(liquide)* to wipe up; *(larmes)* to wipe away; *(défaite)* to suffer; *(refus)* to meet with; **e. la vaisselle** to dry the dishes **2 s'essuyer** *vpr* to wipe oneself; **s'e. les yeux** to wipe one's eyes ▪ **essuie-glace** *(pl* **essuie-glaces)** *nm Br* windscreen wiper, *Am* windshield wiper ▪ **essuie-mains** *nm inv* hand towel

est¹ [ɛ] *voir* **être**

est² [ɛst] **1** *nm* east; **à l'e.** in the east; *(direction)* (to the) east **(de** of); **d'e.** *(vent)* east(erly); **de l'e.** eastern **2** *adj inv (côte)* east(ern)

estafilade [ɛstafilad] *nf* gash

estampe [ɛstɑ̃p] *nf* print

estampille [ɛstɑ̃pij] *nf (de produit)* mark; *(de document)* stamp

esthète [ɛstɛt] *nmf Br* aesthete, *Am* estheste

esthéticienne [ɛstetisjɛn] *nf* beautician

esthétique [ɛstetik] *adj Br* aesthetic, *Am* esthetic

estime [ɛstim] *nf* esteem, regard

estimer [ɛstime] **1** *vt (tableau)* to value **(à** at); *(prix, distance, poids)* to estimate; *(dommages, besoins)* to assess; *(juger)* to consider **(que** that); **e. dangereux de faire qch** to consider it dangerous to do sth; **e. qn** to esteem sb **2 s'estimer** *vpr* **s'e. heureux** to consider oneself happy ▪ **estimable** *adj* respectable ▪ **estimation** *nf (de mobilier)* valuation; *(de prix, de distance, de poids)* estimation; *(de dommages, de besoins)* assessment

estival, -e, -aux, -ales [ɛstival, -o] *adj* **travail e.** summer work ▪ **estivant, -ante** *nmf* *(summer) Br* holidaymaker *or Am* vacationer

estomac [ɛstɔma] *nm* stomach

estomaquer [ɛstɔmake] *vt Fam* to flabbergast

estomper [ɛstɔpe] **1** *vt (rendre flou)* to blur **2** **s'estomper** *upr* to become blurred

Estonie [ɛstɔni] *nf* Estonia ▪ **estonien, -ienne 1** *adj* Estonian **2** *nmf* **E., Estonienne** Estonian **3** *nm (langue)* Estonian

estrade [ɛstrad] *nf* platform

estragon [ɛstragɔ̃] *nm (plante, condiment)* tarragon

estropier [ɛstrɔpje] *vt* to cripple, to maim ▪ **estropié, -iée** *nmf* cripple

estuaire [ɛstɥer] *nm* estuary

esturgeon [ɛstyrʒɔ̃] *nm* sturgeon

et [e] *conj* and; **vingt et un** twenty-one; **et moi?** what about me?

étable [etabl] *nf* cowshed

établi [etabli] *nm* workbench

établir [etablir] **1** *vt (paix, relations, principe)* to establish; *(agence)* to set up; *(liste)* to draw up; *(record)* to set; *(démontrer)* to establish, to prove **2** **s'établir** *upr (pour habiter)* to settle; *(pour exercer un métier)* to set up in business ▪ **établissement** *nm (de paix, de relations, de principe)* establishment; *(entreprise)* business, firm; **é. scolaire** school

étage [etaʒ] *nm (d'immeuble)* floor, *Br* storey, *Am* story; *(de fusée)* stage; **à l'é.** upstairs; **au premier é.** on the *Br* first *or Am* second floor; **maison à deux étages** *Br* two-storeyed *or Am* two-storied house ▪ **s'étager** *upr* to rise in tiers

étagère [etaʒer] *nf* shelf; *(meuble)* shelving unit

étai [ete] *nm Tech* prop

étain [etɛ̃] *nm (métal)* tin; *(de gobelet)* pewter

étais, était [ete] *voir* **être**

étal [etal] *(pl* **étals)** *nm (au marché)* stall

étalage [etalaʒ] *nm* display; *(vitrine)* display window; **faire é. de son savoir** to show off one's knowledge ▪ **étalagiste** *nmf* window dresser

étaler [etale] **1** *vt (disposer)* to lay out; *(en vitrine)* to display; *(beurre)* to spread; *(vacances, paiements)* to stagger; *Fig (érudition)* to show off **2** **s'étaler** *upr Fam (s'affaler)* to sprawl; **s'é. sur** *(congés, paiements)* to be spread over; *Fam* **s'é. de tout son long** to fall flat on one's face ▪ **étalement** *nm (de vacances, de paiements)* staggering

étalon [etalɔ̃] *nm (cheval)* stallion; *(modèle)* standard; **é.-or** gold standard

étanche [etɑ̃ʃ] *adj* watertight; *(montre)* waterproof

étancher [etɑ̃ʃe] *vt (sang)* to stop the flow of; *(soif)* to quench

étang [etɑ̃] *nm* pond

étant [etɑ̃] *p prés de* **être**

étape [etap] *nf (de voyage)* stage; *(lieu)* stop(over); **faire é. à** to stop off *or* over at; **par (petites) étapes** in (easy) stages; *Fig* **brûler les étapes** *(dans sa carrière)* to shoot to the top

état [eta] *nm* (**a**) *(condition, manière d'être)* state; *(inventaire)* statement; **à l'é. brut** in a raw state; **à l'é. neuf** as new; **de son é.** *(métier)* by trade; **en bon é.** in good condition; **en é. de marche** in working order; **en é. de faire qch** in a position to do sth; **hors d'é. de faire qch** not in a position to do sth; **faire é. de qch** to mention sth; **(ne pas) être dans son é. normal** (not) to be one's usual self; **être dans un é. second** to be spaced out; *Fam* **être dans tous ses états** to be in a state; **mettre qn en é. d'arrestation** to put sb under arrest; **remettre qch en é.** to repair sth; **é. d'âme** mood; **é. d'esprit** state *or* frame of mind; **é. de choses** state of affairs; **é. de santé** state of health; **é. des lieux** inventory of fixtures; **é. civil** register office (**b**) *(autorité centrale)* **É.** *(nation)* State ▪ **étatisé, -ée** *adj* state-controlled

état-major [etamaʒɔr] *(pl* **états-majors)** *nm Mil* (general) staff; *(de parti)* senior staff

États-Unis [etazyni] *nmpl* **les É. (d'Amérique)** the United States (of America)

étau, -x [eto] *nm (instrument) Br* vice, *Am* vise

étayer [eteje] *vt (mur)* to shore up; *(théorie)* to support

été[1] [ete] *nm* summer

été[2] [ete] *pp de* **être**

éteindre* [etɛ̃dr] **1** *vt (feu, cigarette)* to put out, to extinguish; *(lampe)* to switch off; *(gaz)* to turn off **2** *vi* to switch off **3** **s'éteindre** *upr (feu)* to go out; *(personne)* to pass away; *(race)* to die out; *(amour)* to die ▪ **éteint, -einte** *adj (feu, bougie)* out; *(lampe, lumière)* off; *(volcan, race, famille)* extinct; *(voix)* faint

étendard [etɑ̃dar] *nm (drapeau)* standard

étendre [etɑ̃dr] **1** *vt (linge)* to hang out; *(nappe)* to spread out; *(beurre)* to spread; *(agrandir)* to extend; **é. le bras** to stretch out one's arm **2** **s'étendre** *upr (personne)* to lie down; *(plaine)* to stretch; *(feu)* to spread; *(pouvoir)* to extend; **s'é. sur qch** *(sujet)* to dwell on sth ▪ **étendu, -ue** *adj (forêt, vocabulaire)* extensive; *(personne)* lying ▪ **étendue** *nf (importance)* extent; *(surface)* area; *(d'eau)* expanse

éternel, -elle [eternɛl] *adj* eternal ▪ **éternellement** *adv* eternally, for ever ▪ **s'éterniser** *upr (débat)* to drag on endlessly; *Fam (visiteur)* to stay for ever ▪ **éternité** *nf* eternity

éternuer [eternɥe] *vi* to sneeze ▪ **éternuement** [-ymɑ̃] *nm* sneeze

êtes [ɛt] *voir* **être**

éther [eter] *nm* ether

Éthiopie [etjɔpi] *nf* **l'É.** Ethiopia ▪ **éthiopien, -ienne 1** *adj* Ethiopian **2** *nmf* **É., Éthiopienne** Ethiopian

éthique [etik] **1** *adj* ethical **2** *nf Phil* ethics *(sing)*; **l'é. puritaine** the Puritan ethic

ethnie [etni] *nf* ethnic group ▪ **ethnique** *adj* ethnic

étinceler [etɛ̃s(ə)le] *vi* to sparkle • **étincelle** *nf* spark; *Fam* **ça va faire des étincelles** sparks will fly

étioler [etjɔle] **s'étioler** *vpr* to wilt

étiquette [etiket] *nf* (**a**) *(marque)* label (**b**) *(protocole)* (diplomatic or court) etiquette • **étiqueter** *vt* to label

étirer [etire] **1** *vt* to stretch **2 s'étirer** *vpr* to stretch (oneself)

étoffe [etɔf] *nf* material, fabric; **avoir l'é. d'un héros** to be the stuff heroes are made of

étoffer [etɔfe] **1** *vt (personne, texte)* to flesh out **2 s'étoffer** *vpr (personne)* to fill out

étoile [etwal] *nf* star; **à la belle é.** in the open; **être né sous une bonne é.** to be born under a lucky star; **é. de mer** starfish; **é. filante** shooting star • **étoilé, -ée** *adj (ciel, nuit)* starry; *(vitre)* cracked *(star-shaped)*

étonner [etɔne] **1** *vt* to surprise **2 s'étonner** *vpr* to be surprised (**de qch** at sth; **que +** *subjunctive* that) • **étonnant, -ante** *adj (ahurissant)* surprising; *(remarquable)* amazing • **étonnement** *nm* surprise

étouffer [etufe] **1** *vt (tuer)* to suffocate; *(bruit)* to muffle; *(feu)* to smother; *Fig (révolte, sentiment)* to stifle; *Fig (scandale)* to hush up **2** *vi* to suffocate; **on étouffe!** it's stifling!; **é. de colère** to choke with anger **3 s'étouffer** *vpr (en mangeant)* to choke (**avec** on); *(mourir)* to suffocate • **étouffant, -ante** *adj (air)* stifling • **étouffement** *nm* suffocation

étourdi, -ie [eturdi] **1** *adj* scatterbrained **2** *nmf* scatterbrain • **étourderie** *nf* absent-mindedness; **une é.** a thoughtless blunder

étourdir [eturdir] *vt* to stun, to daze; *(sujet: vin, vitesse)* to make dizzy • **étourdissant, -ante** *adj (bruit)* deafening; *(beauté)* stunning • **étourdissement** *nm (malaise)* dizzy spell

étourneau, -x [eturno] *nm* starling

étrange [etrɑ̃ʒ] *adj* strange, odd • **étrangement** *adv* strangely, oddly • **étrangeté** *nf* strangeness, oddness

étranger, -ère [etrɑ̃ʒe, -ɛr] **1** *adj (d'un autre pays)* foreign; *(non familier)* strange (**à** to); **il m'est é.** he's unknown to me **2** *nmf (d'un autre pays)* foreigner; *(inconnu)* stranger; **à l'é.** abroad; **de l'é.** from abroad

étrangler [etrɑ̃gle] **1** *vt* **é. qn** *(tuer)* to strangle sb; *(col)* to choke sb **2 s'étrangler** *vpr (de colère, en mangeant)* to choke • **étranglé, -ée** *adj (voix)* choking; *(passage)* constricted • **étranglement** [-əmɑ̃] *nm (de personne)* strangulation

être* [ɛtr] **1** *vi* to be; **il est tailleur** he's a tailor; **est-ce qu'elle vient?** is she coming?; **il vient, n'est-ce pas?** he's coming, isn't he?; **est-ce qu'il aime le thé?** does he like tea?; **nous sommes dix** there are ten of us; **nous sommes le dix** today is the tenth; **où en es-tu?** how far

have you *Br* got *or Am* gotten?; **il a été à Paris** *(il y est allé)* he has been to Paris; **elle est de Paris** she's from Paris; **elle est de la famille** she's one of the family; **il est cinq heures** it's five (o'clock); **il était une fois...** once upon a time, there was...; **c'est à lire pour demain** *(obligation)* this has to be read for tomorrow; **c'est à voir absolument** *(exposition)* it's well worth seeing; **c'est à lui** it's his; **il n'est plus** *(il est mort)* he is dead; **si j'étais vous** if I were or was you; **cela étant** that being so

2 *v aux (avec 'venir', 'partir')* to have/to be; **elle est (déjà) arrivée** she has (already) arrived; **elle est née en 1980** she was born in 1980; **nous y sommes toujours bien reçus** *(passif)* we are always well received

3 *nm (personne)* being; **les êtres chers** the loved ones; **ê. humain** human being; **ê. vivant** living being

étreindre* [etrɛ̃dr] *vt* to grip; *(avec amour)* to embrace • **étreinte** *nf* grip; *(amoureuse)* embrace

étrenner [etrene] *vt* to use for the first time; *(vêtement)* to wear for the first time

étrennes [etren] *nfpl* New Year gift; *(gratification)* ≃ Christmas tip *or Br* box

étrier [etrije] *nm* stirrup; **mettre le pied à l'é. à qn** to help sb get off to a good start

étriper [etripe] **s'étriper** *vpr Fam* to tear each other apart

étriqué, -ée [etrike] *adj (vêtement)* tight; *Fig (esprit, vie)* narrow

étroit, -oite [etrwa, -at] *adj* narrow; *(vêtement)* tight; *(lien, collaboration)* close; **être à l'é.** to be cramped • **étroitement** *adv (surveiller)* closely • **étroitesse** *nf* narrowness; *(de lien)* closeness; **é. d'esprit** narrow-mindedness

étude [etyd] *nf (action, ouvrage)* study; *(de notaire)* office; *Scol (pièce)* study room; *(période)* study period; **à l'é.** *(projet)* under consideration; **faire des études de français** to study French; **faire une é. de marché** to do market research; **é. de cas** case study

étudiant, -iante [etydjɑ̃, -jɑ̃t] **1** *nmf* student; **être é. en droit** to be a law student **2** *adj (vie)* student

étudier [etydje] *vti* to study

étui [etɥi] *nm (à lunettes, à cigarettes)* case; *(de revolver)* holster

étymologie [etimɔlɔʒi] *nf* etymology

eu, eue [y] *pp de* **avoir**

eucalyptus [økaliptys] *nm* eucalyptus

eucharistie [økaristi] *nf Rel* **l'e.** the Eucharist

eugénisme [øʒenism] *nm* eugenics *(sing)*

euh [ø] *exclam* er!, well!

euphémisme [øfemism] *nm* euphemism

euphorie [øfɔri] *nf* euphoria

eurent [yr] *voir* **avoir**

euro [øro] *nm (monnaie)* euro

euro- [øro] *préf* Euro-

eurocrate [ørɔkrat] *nmf* Eurocrat

eurodéputé [ørodepyte] *nm* Euro MP

Europe [ørɔp] *nf* l'E. Europe; l'E. (des vingt-cinq) the European Union (*comprising twenty-five member states*) ▪ **européen, -éenne 1** *adj* European **2** *nmf* E., **Européenne** European

eurosceptique [øroseptik] *nmf Br* Eurosceptic, *Am* Euroskeptic

eut [y] *voir* **avoir**

euthanasie [øtanazi] *nf* euthanasia

eux [ø] *pron personnel (sujet)* they; *(complément)* them; *(réfléchi, emphase)* themselves ▪ **eux-mêmes** *pron* themselves

évacuer [evakɥe] *vt* to evacuate; *(liquide)* to drain off ▪ **évacuation** *nf* evacuation

évader [evade] **s'évader** *vpr* to escape *(de from)* ▪ **évadé, -ée** *nmf* escaped prisoner

> Il faut noter que le verbe anglais **to evade** est un faux ami. Il signifie **éviter**.

évaluer [evalɥe] *vt (fortune)* to estimate; *(meuble)* to value ▪ **évaluation** *nf* estimation; *(de meuble)* valuation

évangile [evãʒil] *nm* gospel; l'É. the Gospel; *Fig* **parole d'é.** gospel (truth) ▪ **évangélique** *adj* evangelical ▪ **évangeliste** *nmf* evangelist; *(auteur de l'un des Évangiles)* Evangelist

évanouir [evanwir] **s'évanouir** *vpr (personne)* to faint; *(espoir, crainte)* to vanish ▪ **évanoui, -ouie** *adj* unconscious ▪ **évanouissement** *nm (syncope)* fainting fit

évaporer [evapɔre] **s'évaporer** *vpr* to evaporate; *Fig (disparaître)* to vanish into thin air ▪ **évaporation** *nf* evaporation

évasé, -ée [evaze] *adj (jupe)* flared

évasif, -ive [evazif, -iv] *adj* evasive

évasion [evazjɔ̃] *nf* escape *(de* from); *(hors de la réalité)* escapism; **é. de capitaux** flight of capital; **é. fiscale** tax evasion

> Il faut noter que le nom anglais **evasion** est un faux ami. Il signifie le plus souvent **dérobade**.

éveil [evɛj] *nm* awakening; **être en é.** to be alert; **donner l'é. à qn** to alert sb; *Scol* **activité d'é.** early-learning activity

éveiller [eveje] **1** *vt (susciter)* to arouse; **é. qn** to awaken sb **2 s'éveiller** *vpr* to awaken (**à** to); *(intelligence)* to develop ▪ **éveillé, -ée** *adj* awake; *(vif)* alert

événement [evenmã] *nm* event

éventail [evãtaj] *nm (instrument)* fan; *(choix)* range; **en é.** *(orteils)* spread out

éventer [evãte] **1** *vt (secret)* to discover; **é. qn** to fan sb **2 s'éventer** *vpr (vin, parfum)* to turn stale; *(bière)* to go flat ▪ **éventé, -ée** *adj (vin, parfum)* stale; *(bière)* flat

éventrer [evãtre] *vt (oreiller)* to rip open; *(animal)* to open up

éventuel, -uelle [evãtɥel] *adj* possible ▪ **éventualité** *nf* possibility; **dans l'é. de** in the event of; **parer à toute é.** to be prepared for all eventualities ▪ **éventuellement** *adv* possibly

> Il faut noter que les termes anglais **eventual** et **eventually** sont des faux amis. Ils signifient respectivement **final** et **finalement**.

évêque [evɛk] *nm* bishop

évertuer [evertɥe] **s'évertuer** *vpr* **s'é. à faire qch** to endeavour to do sth

éviction [eviksjɔ̃] *nf (de concurrent, de président)* ousting; *(de locataire)* eviction

évident, -ente [evidã, -ãt] *adj* obvious (**que** that); *Fam (facile)* easy ▪ **évidemment** [-amã] *adv* obviously ▪ **évidence** *nf* obviousness; **une é.** an obvious fact; **nier l'é.** to deny the obvious; **en é.** in a prominent position; **mettre qch en é.** to highlight sth; **se rendre à l'é.** to face the facts; **à l'é.** obviously

> Il faut noter que les termes anglais **evidently** et **evidence** sont des faux amis. Le premier signifie **manifestement**, et le second signifie le plus souvent **preuve**.

évider [evide] *vt* to hollow out

évier [evje] *nm* (kitchen) sink

évincer [evɛ̃se] *vt (concurrent, président)* to oust *(de* from); *(locataire)* to evict *(de* from)

éviter [evite] *vt* to avoid *(de faire* doing); **é. qch à qn** to spare *or* save sb sth; **je voulais é. que vous ne vous déplaciez pour rien** I wanted to save you coming for nothing

évoluer [evɔlɥe] *vi (changer)* to develop; *(société, idée, situation)* to evolve; *(se déplacer)* to move around; **é. dans un milieu artistique** to move in artistic circles ▪ **évolué, -uée** *adj (pays)* advanced; *(personne)* enlightened ▪ **évolution** *nf (changement)* development; *Biol* evolution; **évolutions** *(mouvements)* movements

évoquer [evɔke] *vt* to evoke ▪ **évocateur, -trice** *adj* evocative ▪ **évocation** *nf* evocation

ex [ɛks] *nmf Fam (mari, femme)* ex

ex- [ɛks] *préf* ex-; **ex-mari** ex-husband

exacerber [ɛgzaserbe] *vt (douleur)* to exacerbate

exact, -e [ɛgzakt] *adj (quantité, poids, nombre)* exact, precise; *(rapport, description)* exact, accurate; *(mot)* right, correct; *(ponctuel)* punctual ▪ **exactement** [-amã] *adv* exactly ▪ **exactitude** *nf (précision, fidélité)* exactness; *(justesse)* correctness; *(ponctualité)* punctuality

exactions [ɛgzaksjɔ̃] *nfpl* atrocities

ex æquo [ɛgzeko] **1** *adj inv Sport* **être classés e.** to tie, to be equally placed **2** *adv* **être troisième e.** to tie for third place

exagérer [ɛgzaʒere] **1** *vt* to exaggerate **2** *vi (parler)* to exaggerate; *(agir)* to go too far

• **exagération** *nf* exaggeration • **exagéré, -ée** *adj* excessive • **exagérément** *adv* excessively

exalter [ɛgzalte] *vt (glorifier)* to exalt; *(passionner)* to stir • **exaltant, -ante** *adj* stirring • **exaltation** *nf (délire)* intense excitement • **exalté, -ée** **1** *adj (sentiment)* impassioned **2** *nmf Péj* fanatic

examen [ɛgzamɛ̃] *nm* examination; **e. blanc** mock exam; **e. médical** medical examination; **e. de la vue** eye test • **examinateur, -trice** *nmf* examiner • **examiner** *vt (considérer, regarder)* to examine

exaspérer [ɛgzaspere] *vt (personne)* to exasperate; *Fig (douleur)* to aggravate • **exaspération** *nf* exasperation

exaucer [ɛgzose] *vt (désir)* to grant; **e. qn** to grant sb's wish

excavation [ɛkskavasjɔ̃] *nf (trou, action)* excavation • **excaver** *vt* to excavate

excéder [ɛksede] *vt (dépasser)* to exceed; **é. qn** *(énerver)* to exasperate sb • **excédent** *nm* surplus, excess; **e. de bagages** excess baggage • **excédentaire** *adj* **poids e.** excess weight

excellent, -ente [ɛksɛlɑ̃, -ɑ̃t] *adj* excellent • **excellence** *nf* excellence; **c'est le chercheur par e.** he's the researcher par excellence; **E.** *(titre)* Excellency • **exceller** *vi* to excel **(en** at)

excentrique [ɛksɑ̃trik] *adj & nmf* eccentric • **excentricité** *nf* eccentricity

excepté, -ée [ɛksɛpte] **1** *prép* except **2** *adj* except (for); **les femmes exceptées** except (for) the women • **excepter** *vt* to except

exception [ɛksɛpsjɔ̃] *nf* exception; **à l'e. de** except (for), with the exception of; **faire e.** to be an exception • **exceptionnel, -elle** *adj* exceptional • **exceptionnellement** *adv* exceptionally

excès [ɛksɛ] *nm* excess; **faire des e. (de table)** to overindulge; **e. de vitesse** speeding; **faire un e. de vitesse** to speed • **excessif, -ive** *adj* excessive • **excessivement** *adv* excessively

excitation [ɛksitasjɔ̃] *nf (agitation)* excitement; **e. à (haine)** incitement to

exciter [ɛksite] **1** *vt (faire naître)* to arouse; **e. qn** *(énerver)* to excite sb; **e. qn à la révolte** to incite sb to revolt **2 s'exciter** *vpr (devenir nerveux)* to get excited • **excitable** *adj* excitable • **excitant, -ante** **1** *adj Fam* exciting **2** *nm* stimulant • **excité, -ée** *adj* excited

exclamer [ɛksklame] **s'exclamer** *vpr* to exclaim • **exclamatif, -ive** *adj* exclamatory • **exclamation** *nf* exclamation

exclure* [ɛksklyr] *vt (écarter)* to exclude *(de* from); *(chasser)* to expel *(de* from); **e. qch** *(rendre impossible)* to preclude sth • **exclu, -ue** *adj (solution)* out of the question; *(avec une date)* exclusive

exclusif, -ive [ɛksklyzif, -iv] *adj (droit, modèle, préoccupation)* exclusive • **exclusivement** *adv* exclusively • **exclusivité** *nf Com* exclusive rights; *(dans la presse)* scoop; **en e.** *(film)* having an exclusive showing **(à** at)

exclusion [ɛksklyzjɔ̃] *nf* exclusion; **à l'e. de** with the exception of

excommunier [ɛkskɔmynje] *vt* to excommunicate • **excommunication** *nf* excommunication

excréments [ɛkskremɑ̃] *nmpl* excrement

excroissance [ɛkskrwasɑ̃s] *nf* excrescence

excursion [ɛkskyrsjɔ̃] *nf* trip, excursion; *(de plusieurs jours)* tour; **faire une e.** to go on a trip/tour

excuse [ɛkskyz] *nf (prétexte)* excuse; **excuses** *(regrets)* apology; **faire des excuses** to apologize **(à** to); **toutes mes excuses** (my) sincere apologies • **excuser 1** *vt (justifier, pardonner)* to excuse **(qn d'avoir fait/qn de faire** sb for doing) **2 s'excuser** *vpr* to apologize **(de** for; **auprès de** to); **excusez-moi!, je m'excuse!** excuse me!

exécrer [ɛgzekre] *vt* to loathe • **exécrable** *adj* atrocious

exécuter [ɛgzekyte] **1** *vt (travail, projet, tâche)* to carry out; *(peinture)* to execute; *Mus (jouer)* to perform; *Ordinat* to run; **e. qn** to execute sb **2 s'exécuter** *vpr* to comply • **exécutant, -ante** *nmf (musicien)* performer; *(ouvrier, employé)* subordinate • **exécution** *nf (de travail)* carrying out; *(de musique)* performance; *(de peinture, de condamné & Ordinat)* execution; **mettre qch à e.** to carry sth out

exécutif [ɛgzekytif] **1** *adj m* **pouvoir e.** executive power **2** *nm* **l'e.** the executive

exemplaire [ɛgzɑ̃plɛr] **1** *adj* exemplary **2** *nm (livre)* copy; **photocopier un document en double e.** to make two photocopies of a document

exemple [ɛgzɑ̃pl] *nm* example; **par e.** for example, for instance; **donner l'e.** to set an example **(à** to); **prendre e. sur qn** to follow sb's example; **faire un e.** to make an example (of someone); **c'est un e. de vertu** he's a model of virtue; *Fam* **(ça) par e.!** good heavens!

exempt, -empte [ɛgzɑ̃, -ɑ̃t] *adj* **e. de** *(dispensé de)* exempt from; *(sans)* free from • **exempter** [ɛgzɑ̃te] *vt* to exempt **(de** from) • **exemption** *nf* exemption

exercer [ɛgzɛrse] **1** *vt (voix, droits)* to exercise; *(autorité, influence)* to exert **(sur** on); *(profession)* *Br* to practise, *Am* to practice; **e. qn à qch** to train sb in sth; **e. qn à faire qch** to train sb to do sth **2** *vi (médecin)* *Br* to practise, *Am* to practice **3 s'exercer** *vpr (s'entraîner)* to train; **s'e. à qch** to *Br* practise *or Am* practice sth; **s'e. à faire qch** to *Br* practise *or Am* practice doing sth

exercice [ɛgzɛrsis] *nm (physique) & Scol* exercise; *Mil* drill; *(de métier)* practice; **l'e. de** *(pouvoir)* the exercise of; **en e.** *(fonctionnaire)* in office; *(médecin)* in practice; **dans l'e. de ses fonctions** in the exercise of one's duties; **faire de l'e., prendre de l'e.** to (take) exercise

exhaler [ɛgzale] *vt (odeur)* to give off

exhaustif, -ive [ɛgzostif, -iv] *adj* exhaustive

exhiber [ɛgzibe] *vt (documents, passeport)* to produce; *Péj (savoir, richesses)* to show off, to flaunt ▪ **exhibition** *nf Péj* flaunting ▪ **exhibitionniste** *nmf* exhibitionist

> Il faut noter que le nom anglais **exhibition** est un faux ami. Il signifie le plus souvent **exposition**.

exhorter [ɛgzɔrte] *vt* to exhort (**à faire** to do)

exhumer [ɛgzyme] *vt (corps)* to exhume; *(vestiges)* to dig up

exiger [ɛgzize] *vt (exiger)* to demand (**de** from); *(nécessiter)* to require; **e. que qch soit fait** to demand that sth be done ▪ **exigeant, -ante** *adj* demanding, exacting ▪ **exigence** *nf (caractère)* exacting nature; *(condition)* demand

exigu, -uë [ɛgzigy] *adj* cramped, tiny ▪ **exiguïté** *nf* crampedness

exil [ɛgzil] *nm* exile; **exilé, -ée** *nmf (personne)* exile ▪ **exiler 1** *vt* to exile **2 s'exiler** *upr* to go into exile

existence [ɛgzistɑ̃s] *nf (fait d'exister)* existence; *(vie)* life; **moyen d'e.** means of existence ▪ **existant, -ante** *adj* existing ▪ **existentialisme** *nm* existentialism ▪ **exister 1** *vi* to exist **2** *v impersonnel* **il existe…** there is/there are…

exode [ɛgzɔd] *nm* exodus; **e. rural** rural depopulation

exonérer [ɛgzɔnere] *vt* to exempt (**de** from); **exonéré d'impôts** exempt from tax ▪ **exonération** *nf* exemption

exorbitant, -ante [ɛgzɔrbitɑ̃, -ɑ̃t] *adj* exorbitant

exorbité, -ée [ɛgzɔrbite] *adj* **yeux exorbités** bulging eyes

exorciser [ɛgzɔrsize] *vt* to exorcize ▪ **exorcisme** *nm* exorcism

exotique [ɛgzɔtik] *adj* exotic ▪ **exotisme** *nm* exoticism

expansif, -ive [ɛkspɑ̃sif, -iv] *adj* expansive

expansion [ɛkspɑ̃sjɔ̃] *nf (de commerce, de pays, de gaz)* expansion; **en (pleine) e.** (rapidly) expanding

expatrier [ɛkspatrije] **s'expatrier** *upr* to leave one's country ▪ **expatrié, -iée** *adj & nmf* expatriate

expectative [ɛkspɛktativ] *nf* **être dans l'e.** to be waiting to see what happens

expédient [ɛkspedjɑ̃] *nm (moyen)* expedient

expédier [ɛkspedje] *vt (envoyer)* to send, to dispatch; *(affaires, client)* to deal promptly with ▪ **expéditeur, -trice** *nmf* sender ▪ **expéditif, -ive** *adj* hasty ▪ **expédition** *nf (envoi)* dispatch; *(voyage)* expedition

expérience [ɛksperjɑ̃s] *nf (connaissance)* experience; *(scientifique)* experiment; **faire l'e. de qch** to experience sth; **avoir de l'e.** to have experience; **être sans e.** to have no experience; **un homme d'e.** a man of experience

expérimenter [ɛksperimɑ̃te] *vt (remède, vaccin)* to try out ▪ **expérimental, -e, -aux, -ales** *adj* experimental ▪ **expérimentation** *nf* experimentation ▪ **expérimenté, -ée** *adj* experienced

expert, -erte [ɛkspɛr, -ɛrt] **1** *adj* expert, skilled (**en** in); **être e. en la matière** to be an expert on the subject **2** *nm* expert (**en** on *or* in); *(d'assurances)* valuer ▪ **expert-comptable** *(pl* **experts-comptables)** *nm Br* ≃ chartered accountant, *Am* ≃ certified public accountant ▪ **expertise** *nf (évaluation)* valuation; *(rapport)* expert's report; *(compétence)* expertise

expier [ɛkspje] *vt (péchés, crime)* to expiate, to atone for ▪ **expiation** *nf* expiation (**de** of)

expirer [ɛkspire] **1** *vti* to breathe out **2** *vi (mourir)* to pass away; *(finir, cesser)* to expire ▪ **expiration** *nf (respiration)* breathing out; *(échéance) Br* expiry, *Am* expiration; **arriver à e.** to expire

explication [ɛksplikɑsjɔ̃] *nf* explanation; *(mise au point)* discussion; *Scol* **e. de texte** textual analysis

explicite [ɛksplisit] *adj* explicit ▪ **explicitement** *adv* explicitly

expliquer [ɛksplike] **1** *vt* to explain (**à** to; **que** that) **2 s'expliquer** *upr* to explain oneself; *(discuter)* to talk things over (**avec** with); **s'e. qch** *(comprendre)* to understand sth; **ça s'explique** that is understandable ▪ **explicable** *adj* understandable ▪ **explicatif, -ive** *adj* explanatory

exploit [ɛksplwa] *nm* feat

exploiter [ɛksplwate] *vt (champs)* to farm; *(ferme, entreprise)* to run; *(mine)* to work; *Fig & Péj (personne, situation)* to exploit ▪ **exploitant, -ante** *nmf* operator; *(directeur)* manager; **e. agricole** farmer ▪ **exploitation** *nf (de champs)* farming; *(de ferme)* running; *(de mine)* working; *Péj* exploitation; *Ordinat* **système d'e.** operating system; **e. agricole** farm; **e. minière** mine

explorer [ɛksplɔre] *vt* to explore ▪ **explorateur, -trice** *nmf* explorer ▪ **exploration** *nf* exploration

exploser [ɛksploze] *vi (gaz, bombe, personne)* to explode; **faire e. qch** to explode sth ▪ **explosif, -ive** *adj & nm* explosive ▪ **explosion** *nf* explosion; *(de colère, joie)* outburst

exporter [ɛkspɔrte] *vt* to export (**vers** to; **de**

from) ■ **exportateur, -trice** 1 *nmf* exporter 2 *adj* exporting ■ **exportation** *nf (produit)* export; *(action)* export(ation); *Ordinat (de fichier)* exporting

exposer [ɛkspoze] 1 *vt (tableau)* to exhibit; *(marchandises)* to display; *(raison, théorie)* to set out; *(vie, réputation)* to risk, to endanger; *Phot (film)* to expose; **e. qch à la lumière** to expose sth to the light; **e. qn à la critique** to expose sb to criticism; **je leur ai exposé ma situation** I explained my situation to them 2 **s'exposer** *vpr* **s'e. au danger** to put oneself in danger; **s'e. à la critique** to lay oneself open to criticism; **ne t'expose pas trop longtemps** don't stay in the sun too long ■ **exposant, -ante** *nmf (artiste, commerçant)* exhibitor ■ **exposé, -ée** 1 *adj* **e. au sud** facing south 2 *nm (compte rendu)* account (**de** of); *(présentation)* talk; *Scol* paper

exposition [ɛkspozisjɔ̃] *nf (d'objets d'art)* exhibition; *(de marchandises)* display; *(au danger)* & *Phot* exposure (**à** to); *(de maison)* aspect

exprès¹ [ɛksprɛ] *adv* on purpose, intentionally; *(spécialement)* specially; **comme (par) un fait e.** almost as if it was meant to be

exprès², -esse [ɛksprɛs] *adj (ordre, condition)* express ■ **expressément** *adv* expressly

exprès³ [ɛksprɛs] *adj inv* **lettre/colis e.** special delivery letter/parcel

express [ɛksprɛs] *adj & nm inv (train)* express; *(café)* espresso

expressif, -ive [ɛkspresif, -iv] *adj* expressive ■ **expression** *nf (phrase, mine)* expression; *Fig* **réduire qch à sa plus simple e.** to reduce sth to its simplest form ■ **exprimer** 1 *vt* to express 2 **s'exprimer** *vpr* to express oneself

exproprier [ɛksproprije] *vt* to expropriate

expulser [ɛkspylse] *vt* to expel (**de** from); *(joueur)* to send off; *(locataire)* to evict ■ **expulsion** *nf* expulsion; *(de joueur)* sending off; *(de locataire)* eviction

expurger [ɛkspyrʒe] *vt* to expurgate

exquis, -ise [ɛkski, -iz] *adj (nourriture)* exquisite

exsangue [ɛksɑ̃g] *adj (visage)* bloodless

extase [ɛkstaz] *nf* ecstasy; **tomber en e. devant qch** to be in raptures over sth ■ **s'extasier** *vpr* to be in raptures (**sur** over or about)

extensible [ɛkstɑ̃sibl] *adj (métal)* tensile; *(tissu)* stretch ■ **extension** *nf (de muscle)* stretching; *(de durée, de contrat)* extension; *(essor)* expansion; **par e.** by extension

exténuer [ɛkstenɥe] *vt (fatiguer)* to exhaust ■ **exténué, -uée** *adj* exhausted

> Il faut noter que le verbe anglais **to extenuate** est un faux ami. Il signifie **atténuer**.

extérieur, -ieure [ɛksterjœr] 1 *adj (monde)* outside; *(surface)* outer, external; *(signe)*

outward, external; *(politique)* foreign; **e. à qch** external to sth; **signe e. de richesse** outward sign of wealth 2 *nm* outside, exterior; **à l'e. (de)** outside; **à l'e. (match)** away; **tourner un film en e.** to shoot a film on location ■ **extérieurement** *adv* externally; *(en apparence)* outwardly ■ **extérioriser** *vt* to express

exterminer [ɛkstermine] *vt* to exterminate ■ **extermination** *nf* extermination

externat [ɛksterna] *nm (école)* day school

externe [ɛkstern] 1 *adj* external 2 *nmf (élève)* day pupil; *Méd* = non-resident hospital medical student, *Am* extern

extincteur [ɛkstɛ̃ktœr] *nm* fire extinguisher ■ **extinction** *nf (de feu)* extinguishing; *(de race)* extinction; **e. de voix** loss of voice

extirper [ɛkstirpe] 1 *vt* to eradicate 2 **s'extirper** *vpr* **s'e. de** *(endroit)* to extricate oneself from

extorquer [ɛkstɔrke] *vt* to extort (**à** from) ■ **extorsion** *nf* extortion; **e. de fonds** extortion

extra [ɛkstra] 1 *adj inv Fam (très bon)* top-quality 2 *nm inv Culin (gâterie)* (extra-special) treat; *(serviteur)* extra hand

extra- [ɛkstra] *préf* extra- ■ **extrafin, -ine** *adj* extra-fine ■ **extrafort, -orte** *adj* extra-strong

extradition [ɛkstradisjɔ̃] *nf* extradition ■ **extrader** *vt* to extradite

extraire* [ɛkstrɛr] *vt* to extract (**de** from); *(charbon)* to mine ■ **extraction** *nf* extraction ■ **extrait** *nm* extract; **e. de compte** statement of account, bank statement; **e. de naissance** birth certificate

extralucide [ɛkstralysid] *adj & nmf* clairvoyant

extranet [ɛkstranet] *nm Ordinat* extranet

extraordinaire [ɛkstraɔrdinɛr] *adj* extraordinary; **si par e.** if by some remote chance ■ **extraordinairement** *adv* exceptionally; *(très, bizarrement)* extraordinarily

extraterrestre [ɛkstraterɛstr] *adj & nmf* extraterrestrial

extravagant, -ante [ɛkstravagɑ̃, -ɑ̃t] *adj (idée, comportement)* extravagant ■ **extravagance** *nf (d'idée, de comportement)* extravagance

extraverti, -ie [ɛkstraverti] *adj & nmf* extrovert

extrême [ɛkstrɛm] 1 *adj* extreme; *Pol* **l'e. droite/gauche** the far *or* extreme right/left 2 *nm* extreme; **pousser qch à l'e.** to take *or* carry sth to extremes ■ **extrêmement** *adv* extremely ■ **Extrême-Orient** *nm* **l'E.** the Far East ■ **extrémiste** *adj & nmf* extremist ■ **extrémité** *nf (bout)* extremity, end; **extrémités** *(pieds et mains)* extremities; **être à la dernière e.** to be on the point of death

exubérant, -ante [ɛgzyberɑ̃, -ɑ̃t] *adj* exuberant ■ **exubérance** *nf* exuberance

exulter [ɛgzylte] *vi* to exult, to rejoice ■ **exultation** *nf* exultation

exutoire [ɛgzytwar] *nm* outlet (**à** for)

ezine, e-zine [izin] *nm Ordinat* ezine, e-zine

F¹, f [ɛf] *nm inv* F, f

F² *abrév* **franc(s)**

fa [fa] *nm (note de musique)* F

fable [fɑbl] *nf* fable

fabricant, -ante [fabrikɑ̃, -ɑ̃t] *nmf* manufacturer ▪ **fabrication** *nf* manufacture; **f. artisanale** production by craftsmen; **de f. artisanale** hand-made; **de f. française** made in France

fabrique [fabrik] *nf* factory

> Il faut noter que le nom anglais **fabric** est un faux ami. Il signifie le plus souvent **tissu**.

fabriquer [fabrike] *vt (objet)* to make; *(en usine)* to manufacture; *Péj (récit)* to fabricate, to make up; *Fam* **qu'est-ce qu'il fabrique?** what's he up to?

fabuler [fabyle] *vi* to make up stories

fabuleux, -euse [fabylø, -øz] *adj (légendaire, incroyable)* fabulous

fac [fak] *nf Fam* university; **à la f.** *Br* at university, *Am* at school, in college

façade [fasad] *nf* façade

face [fas] *nf (visage)* face; *(de cube, de montagne)* side; *(de pièce de monnaie)* head; **en f.** opposite; **en f. de** opposite, facing; *(en présence de)* in front of; **f. à** *(vis-à-vis)* facing; **f. à f.** face to face; **f. à un problème** faced with a problem; **faire f. à** *(situation)* to face up to; **regarder qn en f.** to look sb in the face; **sauver/perdre la f.** to save/lose face; *Fig* **se voiler la f.** to hide from reality; **photo de f.** full-face (photo) ▪ **face-à-face** *nm inv* télévisé face-to-face TV encounter

facétie [fasesi] *nf* joke ▪ **facétieux, -ieuse** [-esjø, -øz] *adj (personne)* facetious

facette [fasɛt] *nf (de diamant, de problème)* facet

fâcher [faʃe] **1** *vt* to anger **2 se fâcher** *vpr* to get angry **(contre** with); **se f. avec qn** to fall out with sb ▪ **fâché, -ée** *adj (air)* angry; *(amis)* on bad terms; **f. avec** *ou* **contre qn** angry with sb; *Fam* **être f. avec l'orthographe** to be a hopeless speller; **f. de qch** sorry about sth ▪ **fâcheux, -euse** *adj (nouvelle)* unfortunate

facho [faʃo] *adj & nmf Fam* fascist

facile [fasil] *adj* easy; *(caractère, humeur)* easy-going; *Péj (banal)* facile; **c'est f. à faire** it's easy to do; **il nous est f. de faire ça** it's easy for us to do that; **f. à vivre** easy to get along with ▪ **facilement** *adv* easily ▪ **facilité** *nf (simplicité)* easiness; *(aisance)* ease; *Com* **facilités de paiement** payment facilities; **avoir des**

facilités pour qch to have an aptitude for sth ▪ **faciliter** *vt* to make easier, to facilitate

façon [fasɔ̃] *nf (a) (manière)* way; **la f. dont elle parle** the way (in which) she talks; **de quelle f.?** how?; **façons** *(comportements)* manners; **une f. de parler** a manner of speaking; **à la f. de** in the fashion of; **de toute f.** anyway, anyhow; **d'une certaine f.** in some way; **de f. à** so as to; **de f. à ce qu'on vous comprenne** so as to be understood, so that you may be understood; **de f. générale** generally speaking; **d'une f. ou d'une autre** one way or another; **à ma f.** my way, (in) my own way; **faire des façons** to make a fuss; **accepter qch sans f.** to accept sth without fuss; **table f. chêne** imitation oak table; **f. cuir** imitation leather **(b)** *(coupe de vêtement)* cut, style

façonner [fasɔne] *vt (travailler, former)* to shape; *(fabriquer)* to make

facteur [faktœr] *nm* **(a)** *(employé) Br* postman, *Am* mailman **(b)** *(élément)* factor ▪ **factrice** *nf Br* postwoman, *Am* mailwoman

factice [faktis] *adj* false; **diamant f.** imitation diamond

faction [faksjɔ̃] *nf (groupe)* faction; **de f.** *(soldat)* on guard duty

facture [faktyr] *nf Com* bill, invoice ▪ **facturer** *vt* to bill, to invoice

facultatif, -ive [fakyltatif, -iv] *adj (travail)* optional; *Scol* **matière/épreuve facultative** *Br* optional *or Am* elective subject/test paper

faculté [fakylte] *nf* **(a)** *(aptitude)* faculty; **une grande f. de travail** a great capacity for work; **facultés mentales** faculties **(b)** *(d'université)* faculty; **à la f.** *Br* at university, *Am* at school, in college

fada [fada] *Fam* **1** *adj* nuts **2** *nm* nutcase

fadaises [fadez] *nfpl* nonsense

fade [fad] *adj* insipid ▪ **fadasse** *adj Fam* wishy-washy

fagot [fago] *nm* bundle of firewood ▪ **fagoter** *vt Péj* to dress

faible [fɛbl] **1** *adj* weak, feeble; *(bruit, voix)* faint; *(vent, chances)* slight; *(quantité, revenus)* small; **f. en anglais** poor at English **2** *nm* weakling; **les faibles** the weak; **f. d'esprit** feeble-minded person; **avoir un f. pour qn** to have a soft spot for sb; **avoir un f. pour qch** to have a weakness for sth ▪ **faiblement** [-əmɑ̃]

adv (protester) weakly; *(éclairer)* faintly
■ **faiblesse** *nf (physique, morale)* weakness; *(de vent)* lightness; *(de revenus)* smallness

faiblir [fɛblir] *vi (forces)* to weaken; *(courage, vue)* to fail; *(vent)* to drop

faïence [fajɑ̃s] *nf (matière)* earthenware;
faïences *(objets)* earthenware

faille¹ [faj] *nf Géol* fault; *Fig* flaw

faille² [faj] *voir* **falloir**

faillible [fajibl] *adj* fallible

faillir* [fajir] *vi* **il a failli tomber** he almost *or* nearly fell; **f. à un devoir** to fail in a duty

faillite [fajit] *nf Com* bankruptcy; *Fig* failure; **faire f.** to go bankrupt

faim [fɛ̃] *nf* hunger; **avoir f.** to be hungry; **donner f. à qn** to make sb hungry; **manger à sa f.** to eat one's fill; **rester sur sa f.** to remain hungry; **mourir de f.** to die of starvation; *Fig (avoir très faim)* to be starving

fainéant, -éante [feneɑ̃, -eɑ̃t] **1** *adj* idle **2** *nmf* idler ■ **fainéanter** *vi* to idle ■ **fainéantise** *nf* idleness

faire* [fɛr] **1** *vt (bruit, faute, gâteau, voyage, repas)* to make; *(devoir, ménage, dégâts)* to do; *(rêve, chute)* to have; *(sourire)* to give; *(promenade, sieste)* to have, to take; *(guerre)* to wage, to make; **ça fait 10 m de large** it's 10 m wide; **ça fait 10 euros** it's *or* that's 10 euros; **2 et 2 font 4** 2 and 2 are 4; **qu'a-t-il fait de…?** what's he done with…?; **que f.?** what's to be done?; **f. du tennis/du piano** to play tennis/the piano; **f. du droit/de la médecine** to study law/ medicine; **f. du bien à qn** to do sb good; **f. du mal à qn** to hurt *or* harm sb; **f. l'idiot** to act *or* play the fool; **il fera un bon médecin** he'll be *or* make a good doctor; **ça ne fait rien** that doesn't matter; **comment as-tu fait pour…?** how did you manage to…?; **il ne fait que travailler** he does nothing but work; **je ne fais que d'arriver** I've just arrived; **'oui', fit-elle** 'yes', she said

2 *vi (agir)* to do; *(paraître)* to look; **f. comme chez soi** to make oneself at home; **faites donc!** please do!; **elle ferait bien de partir** she'd do well to leave; **il fait vieux** he looks old; **il fait (bien) son âge** he looks his age

3 *v impersonnel* **il fait beau/froid** it's fine/cold; **il fait du vent/soleil** it's windy/sunny; **quel temps fait-il?** what's the weather like?; **ça fait deux ans que je ne l'ai pas vu** I haven't seen him for two years, it's (been) two years since I saw him; **ça fait un an que je suis là** I've been here for a year

4 *v aux (+ infinitive)* **f. construire une maison** to have a house built (**à qn** for sb; **par qn** by sb); **f. crier/souffrir qn** to make sb shout/suffer

5 se faire *vpr (fabrication)* to be made; *(activité)* to be done; **se f. couper les cheveux** to have one's hair cut; **se f. tuer/renverser** to get

killed/knocked down; **se f. des illusions** to have illusions; **se f. des amis** to make friends; **se f. vieux** to get old; **il se fait tard** it's getting late; **comment se fait-il que…?** how is it that…?; **ça se fait beaucoup** people do that a lot; **se f. à** to get used to; **ne t'en fais pas!** don't worry! ■ **faire-part** *nm inv* announcement

fais, fait [fɛ] *voir* **faire**

faisable [fəzabl] *adj* feasible

faisan [fəzɑ̃] *nm* pheasant ■ **faisandé, -ée** *adj (gibier)* high

faisceau, -x [fɛso] *nm (rayons)* beam; *Fig* **un f. de preuves** a body of proof; **f. lumineux** beam of light

fait, -e [fɛ, fɛt] **1** *pp de* **faire 2** *adj (fromage)* ripe; *(yeux)* made up; *(ongles)* polished; *(homme)* grown; **tout f.** ready made; **bien f.** *(jambes, corps)* shapely; **c'est bien f. (pour toi)!** it serves you right! **3** *nm (événement)* event; *(donnée, réalité)* fact; **du f. de** on account of; **au f. *(à propos)*** by the way; **en f.** in fact; **en f. de** *(en guise de)* by way of; *(au lieu de)* instead of; **prendre qn sur le f.** to catch sb red-handed *or* in the act; **aller au f., en venir au f.** to get to the point; **faits et gestes** actions; **prendre f. et cause pour qn** to stand up for sb; **mettre qn devant un f. accompli** to present sb with a fait accompli; *Journ* **faits divers** ≃ news in brief

faîte [fɛt] *nm (haut)* top; *Fig (apogée)* height

faites [fɛt] *voir* **faire**

fait-tout [fɛtu] *nm inv* stewpot

falaise [falɛz] *nf* cliff

falloir* [falwar] **1** *v impersonnel* **il faut qn/qch l/ you/we/*etc* need sb/sth; **il lui faut un stylo** he/ she needs a pen; **il faut partir** I/you/we/*etc* have to go; **il faut que je parte** I have to go; **il faudrait qu'elle reste** she ought to stay; **il faut un jour** it takes a day (**pour faire** to do); **comme il faut** proper(ly); **s'il le faut** if need be **2 s'en falloir** *vpr* **il s'en est fallu de peu qu'il ne pleure, peu s'en est fallu qu'il ne pleure** he almost cried; **tant s'en faut** far from it

falsifier [falsifje] *vt (texte)* to falsify ■ **falsification** *nf* falsification

famé, -ée [fame] *adj* **mal f.** of ill repute

famélique [famelik] *adj* half-starved

fameux, -euse [famø, -øz] *adj (célèbre)* famous; *Fam (excellent)* first-class; *Fam* **pas f.** not much good

familial, -e, -iaux, -iales [familjal, -jo] *adj (atmosphère, ennuis)* family; *(entreprise)* family-run

familier, -ière [familje, -jɛr] **1** *adj (connu)* familiar (**à qn** to sb); *(désinvolte)* informal (**avec** with); *(locution)* colloquial **2** *nm (de club)* regular visitor (**de** to) ■ **familiariser 1** *vt* to familiarize (**avec** with) **2 se familiariser** *vpr* to familiarize oneself (**avec** with) ■ **familiarité**

nf (désinvolture) informality; *Péj* **familiarités** liberties

famille [famij] *nf* family; **en f.** with one's family

famine [famin] *nf* famine

fan [fan], **fana** [fana] *nmf Fam* fan; **être f. de** to be crazy about

fanal, -aux [fanal, -o] *nm* lantern

fanatique [fanatik] **1** *adj* fanatical **2** *nmf* fanatic **■ fanatisme** *nm* fanaticism

faner [fane] **se faner** *upr (fleur, beauté)* to fade **■ fané, -ée** *adj* faded

fanfare [fɑ̃far] *nf (orchestre)* brass band; *Fam* **réveil en f.** brutal awakening

fanfaron, -onne [fɑ̃farɔ̃, -ɔn] **1** *adj* boastful **2** *nmf* boaster

fanfreluches [fɑ̃frəlyʃ] *nfpl Péj* frills

fanion [fanjɔ̃] *nm (de club)* pennant

fantaisie [fɑ̃tezi] *nf (caprice)* whim; *(imagination)* imagination; **bijoux f.** costume *Br* jewellery *or Am* jewelry **■ fantaisiste** *adj (pas sérieux)* fanciful; *(excentrique)* unorthodox

> Il faut noter que le nom anglais **fantasy** est un faux ami. Il signifie **rêve**.

fantasme [fɑ̃tasm] *nm* fantasy **■ fantasmer** *vi* to fantasize (**sur** about)

fantasque [fɑ̃task] *adj* whimsical

fantassin [fɑ̃tasɛ̃] *nm* infantryman

fantastique [fɑ̃tastik] *adj (imaginaire, excellent)* fantastic

fantoche [fɑ̃tɔʃ] *nm & adj* puppet

fantôme [fɑ̃tom] **1** *nm* ghost, phantom **2** *adj* **ville/train f.** ghost town/train; **firme f.** bogus company *or* firm

faon [fɑ̃] *nm* fawn

FAQ [efaky] *(abrév* **foire aux questions, frequently asked questions**) *nf Ordinat* FAQ

faramineux, -euse [faraminø, -øz] *adj Fam* fantastic

farce¹ [fars] *nf (tour)* practical joke, prank; *(pièce de théâtre)* farce; **faire une f. à qn** to play a practical joke *or* a prank on sb; **magasin de farces et attrapes** joke shop **■ farceur, -euse** *nmf (blagueur)* practical joker

farce² [fars] *nf Culin* stuffing **■ farcir** *vt (poulet)* to stuff; *Fam* **se f. qn** to put up with sb; **se f. qch** to get landed with sth

fard [far] *nm* make-up **■ farder 1** *vt (maquiller)* to make up **2 se farder** *upr (se maquiller)* to put on one's make-up; **se f. les yeux** to put eyeshadow on

fardeau, -x [fardo] *nm* burden, load

farfelu, -ue [farfəly] *Fam* **1** *adj* weird **2** *nmf* weirdo

farfouiller [farfuje] *vi Fam* to rummage (**dans** through)

fariboles [faribɔl] *nfpl Fam* nonsense

farine [farin] *nf (de blé)* flour; **f. d'avoine** oatmeal **■ farineux, -euse** *adj* floury

farouche [faruʃ] *adj (personne)* shy; *(animal)* timid; *(haine, regard)* fierce **■ farouchement** *adv* fiercely

fascicule [fasikyl] *nm (de publication)* instalment; *(brochure)* brochure

fasciner [fasine] *vt* to fascinate **■ fascination** *nf* fascination

fascisme [faʃism] *nm* fascism **■ fasciste** *adj & nmf* fascist

fasse(s), fassent [fas] *voir* **faire**

faste [fast] **1** *nm Br* splendour, *Am* splendor **2** *adj* **jour/période f.** lucky day/period

fastidieux, -ieuse [fastidjø, -jøz] *adj* tedious

> Il faut noter que l'adjectif anglais **fastidious** est un faux ami. Il signifie **pointilleux**.

fatal, -e, -als, -ales [fatal] *adj (mortel)* fatal; *(inévitable)* inevitable; *(moment, ton)* fateful; **c'était f.!** it was bound to happen! **■ fatalement** *adv* inevitably **■ fataliste 1** *adj* fatalistic **2** *nmf* fatalist **■ fatalité** *nf (destin)* fate **■ fatidique** *adj (jour, date)* fateful

> Il faut noter que les termes anglais **fatally** et **fatality** sont des faux amis. Ils signifient respectivement **mortellement** ou **irrémédiablement**, et **victime**.

fatigant, -ante [fatigɑ̃, -ɑ̃t] *adj (épuisant)* tiring; *(ennuyeux)* tiresome

fatigue [fatig] *nf* tiredness; **tomber de f.** to be dead tired

fatiguer [fatige] **1** *vt (épuiser)* to tire; *(yeux)* to strain; *(ennuyer)* to bore **2** *vi (personne)* to get tired; *(moteur)* to *Br* labour *or Am* labor **3** **se fatiguer** *upr (s'épuiser, se lasser)* to get tired (**de** of); **se f. à faire qch** to tire oneself out doing sth; **se f. les yeux** to strain one's eyes **■ fatigué, -ée** *adj* tired (**de** of)

fatras [fatra] *nm* jumble, muddle

faubourg [fobur] *nm* suburb

fauché, -ée [foʃe] *adj Fam (sans argent)* broke

faucher [foʃe] *vt (herbe)* to mow; *(blé)* to reap; *Fam (voler)* to snatch, *Br* to pinch; *Fig* **f. qn** *(faire tomber brutalement)* to mow sb down **■ faucheuse** *nf (machine)* reaper

faucille [fosij] *nf* sickle

faucon [fokɔ̃] *nm* hawk, falcon

faudra, faudrait [fodra, fodrɛ] *voir* **falloir**

faufiler [fofile] **se faufiler** *upr* to work one's way (**dans** through *or* into; **entre** between)

faune [fon] *nf* wildlife, fauna; *Péj (gens)* set

faussaire [fosɛr] *nm* forger

fausse [fos] *voir* **faux¹** **■ faussement** *adv* falsely

fausser [fose] *vt (réalité)* to distort; *(clé)* to buckle; **f. compagnie à qn** to give sb the slip

fausseté [foste] *nf (de raisonnement)* falseness; *(hypocrisie)* duplicity

faut [fo] *voir* **falloir**

faute [fot] nf (erreur) mistake; (responsabilité) & Tennis fault; Football foul; Fam **c'est de ta f., c'est ta f.** it's your fault; **f. de temps** for lack of time; **f. de mieux** for want of anything better; **en f.** at fault; **sans f.** without fail; **faire une f.** to make a mistake; **f. d'impression** printing error

fauteuil [fotœj] nm armchair; (de président) chair; Fam **arriver dans un f.** to win hands down; Théâtre **f. d'orchestre** seat in the Br stalls or Am orchestra; **f. pivotant** swivel chair; **f. roulant** wheelchair

fauteur [fotœr] nm **f. de troubles** troublemaker

fautif, -ive [fotif, -iv] adj (personne) at fault; (erroné) faulty

fauve [fov] **1** nm big cat; **chasse aux grands fauves** big game hunting **2** adj & nm (couleur) fawn

faux¹, fausse [fo, fos] **1** adj (pas vrai) false, untrue; (inexact) wrong; (inauthentique) false; (monnaie) forged; (tableau) fake; **faire fausse route** to take the wrong road; Fig to be on the wrong track; **faire un f. mouvement** to make a sudden (awkward) movement; **faire une fausse note** (musicien) to play a wrong note; **faire une fausse couche** to have a miscarriage; Fam **avoir tout f.** to get it all wrong; Ling **f. ami** false friend; **f. col** detachable collar; **f. départ** false start; **f. diamant** fake diamond; **f. nez** false nose **2** adv (chanter) out of tune **3** nm (tableau) fake; (document) forgery ▪ **faux-filet** (pl **faux-filets**) nm sirloin ▪ **faux-fuyant** (pl **faux-fuyants**) nm subterfuge ▪ **faux-monnayeur** (pl **faux-monnayeurs**) nm counterfeiter

faux² [fo] nf (instrument) scythe

faveur [favœr] nf Br favour, Am favor; **en f. de** (au profit de) in aid of; **être en f. de qch** to be in favour of sth; **de f.** (billet) complimentary; (traitement, régime) preferential ▪ **favorable** adj Br favourable, Am favorable (à to) ▪ **favori, -ite** adj & nmf Br favourite, Am favorite ▪ **favoriser** vt Br to favour, Am to favor ▪ **favoritisme** nm Br favouritism, Am favoritism

favoris [favori] nmpl sideburns

fax [faks] nm (appareil, message) fax; Ordinat **f. modem** fax modem ▪ **faxer** vt (message) to fax

fébrile [febril] adj feverish ▪ **fébrilité** nf feverishness

fécond, -onde [fekɔ̃, -ɔ̃d] adj (femme, idée) fertile ▪ **fécondation** nf fertilization; **f. in vitro** in vitro fertilization ▪ **féconder** vt to fertilize ▪ **fécondité** nf fertility

fécule [fekyl] nf starch ▪ **féculents** nmpl (aliments) starchy food

fédéral, -e, -aux, -ales [federal, -o] adj federal ▪ **fédération** nf federation ▪ **fédérer** vt to federate

fée [fe] nf fairy ▪ **féerique** adj (personnage, monde) fairy; (vision) enchanting

feindre* [fɛ̃dr] vt to feign; **f. de faire qch** to pretend to do sth ▪ **feint, -e** adj feigned ▪ **feinte** nf (ruse) ruse; Football & Rugby dummy run

fêler [fele] vt, **se fêler** vpr to crack ▪ **fêlure** nf crack

féliciter [felisite] **1** vt to congratulate (**de** ou **sur** on) **2 se féliciter** vpr **se f. de qch** to congratulate oneself on sth ▪ **félicitations** nfpl congratulations (**pour** on)

félin, -ine [felɛ̃, -in] adj & nm feline

femelle [fəmɛl] adj & nf female

féminin, -ine [feminɛ̃, -in] adj (prénom, hormone) female; (trait, intuition, pronom) feminine; (mode, revue, équipe) women's ▪ **féministe** adj & nmf feminist ▪ **féminité** nf femininity

femme [fam] nf woman (pl women); (épouse) wife; **f. d'affaires** businesswoman; **f. de chambre** (chamber)maid; **f. de ménage** cleaning lady; **f. au foyer** housewife; Fam **bonne f.** woman

fémur [femyr] nm thighbone, femur

fendiller [fɑ̃dije] **se fendiller** vpr to crack

fendre [fɑ̃dr] **1** vt (bois) to split; (foule) to force one's way through; (air) to cleave; Fig (cœur) to break; **jupe fendue** slit skirt **2 se fendre** vpr (se fissurer) to crack; Fam **se f. de 50 euros** to fork out 50 euros; Fam **se f. la gueule** to laugh one's head off

fenêtre [fənɛtr] nf window

fenouil [fənuj] nm fennel

fente [fɑ̃t] nf (de tirelire, palissade, jupe) slit; (de rocher) split, crack

féodal, -e, -aux, -ales [feɔdal, -o] adj feudal

fer [fɛr] nm iron; (partie métallique de qch) metal (part); **barre de ou en f.** iron bar; **boîte en f.** can, Br tin; Fig **santé de f.** cast-iron constitution; Fig **main/volonté de f.** iron hand/will; **f. à cheval** horseshoe; **f. forgé** wrought iron; Fig **f. de lance** spearhead; **f. à friser** curling tongs; Fig **f. de lance** spearhead; **f. à repasser** iron ▪ **fer-blanc** (pl **fers-blancs**) nm tin(-plate)

fera, ferait etc [fəra, fərɛ] voir **faire**

férié [ferje] adj m **jour f.** (public) holiday

ferme¹ [fɛrm] nf farm; (maison) farm(house)

ferme² [fɛrm] **1** adj (beurre, décision) firm; (pas, voix) steady; (pâte) stiff; (autoritaire) firm (**avec** with) **2** adv (discuter) keenly; (travailler, boire) hard; **s'ennuyer f.** to be bored stiff ▪ **fermement** [-əmɑ̃] adv firmly

ferment [fɛrmɑ̃] nm ferment ▪ **fermentation** nf fermentation ▪ **fermenter** vi to ferment

fermer [fɛrme] **1** vt to close, to shut; (gaz, radio) to turn or switch off; (vêtement) to do up; (passage) to block; **f. qch à clef** to lock sth; **f. un magasin** (définitivement) to close or shut (down) a shop; **f. la marche** to bring up the rear; Fam **ferme-la!, la ferme!** shut up! **2** vi, **se**

fermer *vpr* to close, to shut ▪**fermé, -ée** *adj (porte, magasin)* closed, shut; *(route, circuit)* closed; *(gaz)* off

fermeté [fɛrməte] *nf* firmness; *(de geste, de voix)* steadiness

fermeture [fɛrmətyr] *nf* closing, closure; *(heure)* closing time; *(mécanisme)* catch; **f. annuelle** annual closure; **f. Éclair®** *Br* zip (fastener), *Am* zipper

fermier, -ière [fɛrmje, -jɛr] 1 *nmf* farmer 2 *adj* **poulet f.** free-range chicken

fermoir [fɛrmwar] *nm* clasp

féroce [feɾɔs] *adj* ferocious ▪**férocité** *nf* ferocity

feront [fəɾɔ̃] *voir* **faire**

ferraille [fɛɾaj] *nf* scrap iron; **mettre qch à la f.** to scrap sth ▪**ferrailleur** *nm* scrap metal dealer *or Br* merchant

ferré, -ée [fere] *adj (canne)* metal-tipped

ferrer [fere] *vt (cheval)* to shoe

ferronnerie [fɛɾɔnri] *nf* ironwork

ferroviaire [feɾɔvjɛr] *adj* **compagnie f.** *Br* railway company, *Am* railroad company; **catastrophe f.** rail disaster

ferry [feri] *(pl ferrys ou ferries)* *nm* ferry

fertile [fɛrtil] *adj (terre, imagination)* fertile; **f. en incidents** eventful ▪**fertiliser** *vt* to fertilize ▪**fertilité** *nf* fertility

fervent, -ente [fɛrvɑ̃, -ɑ̃t] 1 *adj* fervent 2 *nmf* devotee *(de* of*)* ▪**ferveur** *nf* fervour

fesse [fɛs] *nf* buttock; **fesses** *Br* bottom, *Am* butt ▪**fessée** *nf* spanking

festin [fɛstɛ̃] *nm* feast

festival, -als [fɛstival] *nm* festival; *Fig* **nous avons assisté à un vrai f.** we witnessed a dazzling performance

festivités [fɛstivite] *nfpl* festivities

festoyer [fɛstwaje] *vi* to feast

fête [fɛt] *nf (civile)* holiday; *(religieuse)* festival, feast; *(entre amis)* party; **jour de f.** (public) holiday; **air de f.** festive air; **les fêtes (de Noël et du nouvel an)** the Christmas holidays; **faire la f.** to have a good time; **c'est sa f.** it's his/her saint's day; *Fam* **ça va être ta f.!** you're in for it!; **f. de famille** family celebration; **la f. des Mères** Mother's Day; **la f. du Travail** Labour Day; **la f. du village** village fair *or* fête; **f. nationale** national holiday ▪**fêter** *vt (événement)* to celebrate

fétiche [fetiʃ] *nm (objet de culte)* fetish; *Fig (mascotte)* mascot

fétide [fetid] *adj* fetid

feu¹, -x [fø] *nm* fire; *(de réchaud)* burner; *Aut, Naut & Av (lumière)* light; **tous feux éteints** *(rouler)* without lights; **en f.** on fire, ablaze; **mettre le f. à qch** to set fire to sth; **faire du f.** to light *or* make a fire; **prendre f.** to catch fire; **donner du f. à qn** to give sb a light; **avez-vous du f.?** have you got a light?; **faire cuire qch à f. doux** to cook sth on a low heat; *Fig* **dans le f. de la dispute** in the heat of the argument; *Fig*

mettre le f. aux poudres to spark things off; *Fig* **donner le f. vert** to give the go-ahead (**à** to); *Fig* **ne pas faire long f.** not to last very long; **au f.!** (there's a) fire!; *Mil* **f.!** fire!; **feux de croisement** *Br* dipped headlights, *Am* low beams; **feux de détresse** (hazard) warning lights; **feux de position** parking lights; *Aut* **f. rouge** *(lumière)* red light; *(objet)* traffic light; **feux tricolores** traffic lights

feu², -e [fø] *adj* late; **f. ma tante** my late aunt

feuille [fœj] *nf* leaf; *(de papier)* sheet; *(de température)* chart; *(de journal)* newssheet; **f. d'impôt** tax form *or* return; **f. de maladie** = form given by doctor to patient for claiming reimbursement from Social Security; **f. de paie** *Br* pay slip, *Am* pay stub; *Scol* **f. de présence** attendance sheet ▪**feuillage** *nm* leaves, foliage ▪**feuillu, -ue** *adj* leafy

feuillet [fœjɛ] *nm (de livre)* leaf ▪**feuilleté f. au fromage** cheese pastry ▪**feuilleter** *vt (livre)* to flip through

feuilleton [fœjtɔ̃] *nm (roman, film)* serial; **f. télévisé** television serial

feutre [føtr] *nm* felt; *(chapeau)* felt hat; **(crayon) f.** felt-tip(ped) pen ▪**feutré, -ée** *adj (lainage)* matted; *(bruit)* muffled; **à pas feutrés** silently

fève [fɛv] *nf (broad)* bean; *(de la galette des Rois)* charm

février [fevrije] *nm* February

fiable [fjabl] *adj* reliable ▪**fiabilité** *nf* reliability

fiacre [fjakr] *nm Hist* hackney carriage

fiancer [fjɑ̃se] **se fiancer** *vpr* to become engaged (**avec** to) ▪**fiançailles** *nfpl* engagement ▪**fiancé** *nm* fiancé; **fiancés** engaged couple ▪**fiancée** *nf* fiancée

fiasco [fjasko] *nm* fiasco

fibre [fibr] *nf* fibre; **f. de verre** fibreglass; **fibres optiques** optical fibres; **câble en fibres optiques** fibre-optic cable

ficelle [fisɛl] *nf (de corde)* string; *(pain)* = long thin loaf; **les ficelles du métier** the tricks of the trade ▪**ficeler** *vt* to tie up

fiche [fiʃ] *nf* (**a**) *(carte)* index card; *(papier)* form; **f. d'état civil** = administrative record of birth details and marital status; **f. de paie** *Br* pay slip, *Am* pay stub; **f. technique** data record (**b**) *Él (broche)* pin; *(prise)* plug

fiche(r) [fiʃ(e)] *(pp fichu) Fam* 1 *vt (faire)* to do; *(donner)* to give; *(jeter)* to throw; *(mettre)* to put; **f. le camp** to shove off; **fiche-moi la paix!** leave me alone! 2 **se ficher** *vpr* **se f. de qn** to make fun of sb; **je m'en fiche!** I don't give a damn!; **je me suis fichu dedans** I goofed

ficher [fiʃe] *vt (enfoncer)* to drive in; *(mettre sur fiche)* to put on file

fichier [fiʃje] *nm* card index, file; *Ordinat* file; *Ordinat* **f. MP3** MP3 file; *Ordinat* **f. de sauvegarde** backup file

fichu¹, -ue [fiʃy] *adj Fam (mauvais)* lousy,

rotten; *(capable)* able (**de faire** to do); **mal f.** *(malade)* not well; **c'est f.** *(abîmé)* it's had it; **il est f.** *(condamné)* he's had it, *Br* he's done for
fichu² [fiʃy] *nm (étoffe)* (head)scarf
fictif, -ive [fiktif, -iv] *adj* fictitious ▪ **fiction** *nf* fiction
fidèle [fidɛl] **1** *adj* faithful (**à** to) **2** *nmf* faithful supporter; *(client)* regular (customer); **les fidèles** *(croyants)* the faithful; *(à l'église)* the congregation ▪ **fidèlement** *adv* faithfully ▪ **fidélité** *nf* fidelity, faithfulness
fief [fjɛf] *nm* domain
fieffé, -ée [fjefe] *adj* **un f. menteur** an out-and-out liar
fiel [fjɛl] *nm* gall
fier¹ [fje] **se fier** *vpr* **se f. à qn/qch** to trust sb/sth
fier², fière [fjɛr] *adj* proud (**de** of); **avoir fière allure** to cut a fine figure ▪ **fièrement** *adv* proudly ▪ **fierté** *nf* pride
fièvre [fjɛvr] *nf (maladie)* fever; *(agitation)* frenzy; **avoir de la f.** to have a temperature *or* a fever ▪ **fiévreux, -euse** *adj* feverish
figer [fiʒe] **1** *vt (liquide)* to congeal; *Fig* **f. qn** to paralyse sb **2** **se figer** *vpr (liquide)* to congeal; *Fig (sourire, personne)* to freeze ▪ **figé, -ée** *adj (locution)* set, fixed; *(regard)* frozen; *(société)* fossilized
fignoler [fiɲɔle] *vt Fam* to put the finishing touches to
figue [fig] *nf* fig ▪ **figuier** *nm* fig tree
figurant, -ante [figyrɑ̃, -ɑ̃t] *nmf (de film)* extra
figure [figyr] *nf (visage)* face; *(personnage, illustration)* & *Math* figure; **faire f. de favori** to be considered the favourite; **f. de style** stylistic device; **figures imposées** compulsory figures; **figures libres** freestyle ▪ **figurine** *nf* statuette

Il faut remarquer que le nom anglais **figure** est un faux ami lorsqu'il s'applique à une personne. Il signifie **silhouette**.

figurer [figyre] **1** *vt* to represent **2** *vi* to appear **3** **se figurer** *vpr* to imagine; **figurez-vous que…?** would you believe that…? ▪ **figuré, -ée 1** *adj (sens)* figurative **2** *nm* **au f.** figuratively
fil [fil] *nm* **(a)** *(de coton, de pensée)* thread; *(lin)* linen; **de f. en aiguille** bit by bit; *Fig* **cousu de f. blanc** plain for all to see, as plain as day; *Fig* **donner du f. à retordre à qn** to give sb trouble; **f. dentaire** dental floss **(b)** *(métallique)* wire; *Ordinat* **sans f.** wireless; **f. de fer** wire; **f. à plomb** plumbline **(c)** *(de couteau)* edge **(d)** *(expressions)* **au f. de l'eau/des jours** with the current/the passing of time; **au bout du f.** *(au téléphone)* on the line
filaire [filɛr] *nm* corded phone
filament [filamɑ̃] *nm Biol & Él* filament
filandreux, -euse [filɑ̃drø, -øz] *adj (viande, légumes)* stringy

filature [filatyr] *nf (usine)* textile mill; *(surveillance)* shadowing; **prendre qn en f.** to shadow sb
file [fil] *nf* line; *Aut (couloir)* lane; **f. d'attente** *Br* queue, *Am* line; **en f. indienne** in single file; **être en double f.** to be double-parked
filer [file] **1** *vt (coton)* to spin; **f. qn** to shadow sb; *Fam* **f. qch à qn** to give sb sth **2** *vi (partir)* to rush off; *(aller vite)* to speed along; *(temps)* to fly; *(bas, collant)* to run, *Br* to ladder; **f. entre les doigts à qn** to slip through sb's fingers; *Fam* **f. à l'anglaise** *(sans se faire remarquer)* to slip away; *(pour éviter qn ou qch)* to sneak off, *Br* to do a runner; **f. doux** to be obedient; **filez!** beat it!
filet [filɛ] *nm* **(a)** *(en maille)* net; **coup de f.** *(opération de police)* police haul; **f. à bagages** luggage rack; **f. à provisions** string bag **(b)** *(d'eau)* trickle **(c)** *(de poisson, de viande)* fillet
filial, -e, -iaux, -iales [filjal, -jo] *adj* filial ▪ **filiale** *nf* subsidiary (company)
filiation [filjasjɔ̃] *nf (relation)* relationship
filière [filjɛr] *nf (voie obligée)* channels; *(domaine d'études)* field of study; *(organisation clandestine)* network; **suivre la f. normale** to go through the official channels; *(employé)* to work one's way up; *Scol* **suivre la f. scientifique** to study scientific subjects; **remonter la f.** *(police)* to go back through the network (to reach the person at the top)
filigrane [filigran] *nm (sur papier)* watermark
filin [filɛ̃] *nm Naut* rope
fille [fij] *nf (enfant)* girl; *(descendante)* daughter; **petite f.** (little *or* young) girl; **jeune f.** girl, young lady; *Péj* **vieille f.** old maid ▪ **fillette** *nf* little girl
filleul [fijœl] *nm* godson ▪ **filleule** *nf* goddaughter
film [film] *nm (œuvre)* film, movie; *(pour photo)* film; *Fig* **le f. des événements** the sequence of events; *Fam* **se faire un f.** to be living in a dream world; **f. d'aventures** adventure film; **f. muet/parlant** silent/talking film; **f. policier** thriller; **f. plastique** *Br* clingfilm, *Am* plastic wrap ▪ **filmer** *vt (personne, scène)* to film
filon [filɔ̃] *nm Géol* seam; *Fam* **trouver le f.** to strike it lucky
filou [filu] *nm (escroc)* rogue
fils [fis] *nm* son; **f. à papa** daddy's boy
filtre [filtr] *nm* filter; **(à bout) f.** *(cigarette)* filter-tipped; **(bout) f.** filter (tip) ▪ **filtrer 1** *vt* to filter; *(personne, nouvelles)* to screen **2** *vi (liquide)* to filter (through); *(nouvelle)* to leak out
fin¹ [fɛ̃] *nf* **(a)** *(conclusion)* end; **mettre f. à qch** to put an end to sth; **prendre f.** to come to an end; **tirer à sa f.** to draw to a close; **sans f.** endless; **à la f.** in the end; **arrêtez, à la f.!** stop, for heaven's sake!; **f. mai** at the end of May; **f. de semaine** weekend **(b)** *(but)* end, aim; **arriver à ses fins** to achieve one's ends; **à cette f.** to this end

fin², **fine** [fɛ̃, fin] **1** *adj (pointe, tissu)* fine; *(peu épais)* thin; *(plat)* delicate; *(esprit, oreille)* sharp; *(observation)* sharp, fine; *(intelligent)* clever; **au f. fond de** in the depths of; **jouer au plus f. avec qn** to try and be smarter than sb **2** *adv (couper, moudre)* finely; *(écrire)* small

final, -e, -aux *ou* **-als, -ales** [final, -o] *adj* final ▪**finale 1** *nf Sport* final **2** *nm Mus* finale ▪**finalement** *adv* finally ▪**finaliste** *nmf Sport* finalist

finance [finɑ̃s] *nf* finance ▪**financement** *nm* financing ▪**financer** *vt* to finance

financier, -ière [finɑ̃sje, -jɛr] **1** *adj* financial **2** *nm* financier ▪**financièrement** *adv* financially

fine [fin] *nf* liqueur brandy

finement [finmɑ̃] *adv (couper, broder)* finely; *(agir)* cleverly; **f. joué** nicely played

finesse [finɛs] *nf (de pointe)* fineness; *(de taille)* thinness; *(de plat)* delicacy; *(d'esprit, de goût)* finesse; **finesses** *(de langue)* niceties

finir [finir] **1** *vt* to finish; *(discours, vie)* to end, to finish **2** *vi* to finish, to end; **f. bien/mal** to have a happy/an unhappy ending; **f. de faire qch** to finish doing sth; **f. par faire qch** to end up doing sth; **f. par qch** to finish (up) *or* end (up) with sth; **en f. avec qn/qch** to have done with sb/sth; **elle n'en finit pas de pleurer** there's nothing that can make her stop crying; **il finira tout seul** *(il mourra tout seul)* he'll come to a lonely end ▪**fini, -ie 1** *adj (produit)* finished; *(univers)* & *Math* finite; **c'est f.** it's over *or* finished; **il est f.** *(trop vieux)* he's finished **2** *nm (d'objet manufacturé)* finish ▪**finish** *nm inv Sport* finish; **avoir qn au f.** *(à l'usure)* to get sb in the end ▪**finition** *nf Tech (action)* finishing; *(résultat)* finish

Finlande [fɛ̃lɑ̃d] *nf* la F. Finland ▪**finlandais, -aise** *adj* Finnish **2** *nmf* F., **Finlandaise** Finn ▪**finnois, -oise 1** *adj* Finnish **2** *nmf* F., **Finnoise** Finn **3** *nm (langue)* Finnish

fiole [fjɔl] *nf* phial

firme [firm] *nf* firm

fisc [fisk] *nm Br* ≃ Inland Revenue, *Am* ≃ Internal Revenue ▪**fiscal, -e, -aux, -ales** *adj* droit f. tax law; **charges fiscales** taxes; **fraude fiscale** tax fraud *or* evasion ▪**fiscalité** *nf* tax system

fissure [fisyr] *nf* crack ▪**se fissurer** *vpr* to crack

fiston [fistɔ̃] *nm Fam* son, lad

FIV [ɛfive] *(abrév* **fécondation in vitro)** *nf* IVF

fixateur [fiksatœr] *nm Phot* fixer

fixation [fiksasjɔ̃] *nf (action)* fixing; *(dispositif)* fastening, fixing; *(idée fixe)* fixation; **faire une f. sur qn/qch** to be fixated on sb/sth

fixe [fiks] **1** *adj* fixed; *(prix, heure)* set, fixed; **être au beau f.** *(temps)* to be set fair **2** *nm (paie)* fixed salary ▪**fixement** [-əmɑ̃] *adv* **regarder qn/qch f.** to stare at sb/sth

fixer [fikse] **1** *vt (attacher)* to fix (**à** to); *(choix)* to settle; *(date, règle)* to decide, to fix; **f. qn/qch (du regard)** to stare at sb/sth; **être fixé** *(décidé)* to be decided; **comme ça, on est fixé!** *(renseigné)* we've got the picture! **2** **se fixer** *vpr (regard)* to become fixed; *(s'établir)* to settle

flacon [flakɔ̃] *nm* small bottle

flageoler [flaʒɔle] *vi* to shake, to tremble

flageolet [flaʒɔlɛ] *nm (haricot)* flageolet bean

flagrant, -ante [flagrɑ̃, -ɑ̃t] *adj (injustice)* flagrant, blatant; **pris en f. délit** caught in the act *or* red-handed

flair [flɛr] *nm (d'un chien)* (sense of) smell, scent; *(clairvoyance)* intuition, flair ▪**flairer** *vt* to smell, to sniff at; *Fig (discerner)* to smell

flamand, -ande [flamɑ̃, -ɑ̃d] **1** *adj* Flemish **2** *nmf* F., **Flamande** Fleming **3** *nm (langue)* Flemish

flamant [flamɑ̃] *nm* **f. (rose)** flamingo

flambant [flɑ̃bɑ̃] *adv* **f. neuf** brand new

flambeau, -x [flɑ̃bo] *nm* torch

flambée [flɑ̃be] *nf* blaze; *Fig (de colère, des prix)* surge; *(de violence)* flare-up

flamber [flɑ̃be] **1** *vt Méd (aiguille)* to sterilize; *Culin* to flambé; *(poulet)* to singe; **crêpes flambées** flambéed pancakes **2** *vi* to blaze; *Fam (jouer)* to gamble for big money ▪**flambeur** *nm Fam* big-time gambler

flamboyer [flɑ̃bwaje] *vi* to blaze

flamme [flam] *nf* flame; *Fig (ardeur)* fire; **en flammes** on fire

flan [flɑ̃] *nm* baked custard

flanc [flɑ̃] *nm* side; *(d'armée, d'animal)* flank; *Fam* **tirer au f.** to shirk

flancher [flɑ̃ʃe] *vi Fam* to give in

Flandre [flɑ̃dr] *nf* **la F., les Flandres** Flanders

flanelle [flanɛl] *nf* flannel

flâner [flɑne] *vi* to stroll

flanquer [flɑ̃ke] **1** *vt* to flank (**de** with); *Fam (jeter)* to chuck; *Fam (donner)* to give; *Fam* **f. qn à la porte** to kick sb out **2** **se flanquer** *vpr* **se f. par terre** to fall flat on one's face

flaque [flak] *nf (d'eau)* puddle; *(de sang)* pool

flash [flaʃ] *(pl* **flashes**) *nm Phot* flashlight; *Radio & TV* **f. d'informations** (news)flash ▪**flasher** *vi Fam* **f. sur qn/qch** to fall for sb/sth in a big way

flasque [flask] *adj* flabby

flatter [flate] **1** *vt* to flatter **2** **se flatter** *vpr* **se f. de faire qch** to flatter oneself on doing sth ▪**flatté, -ée** *adj* flattered (**de qch** by sth; **de faire** to do; **que** that) ▪**flatterie** *nf* flattery ▪**flatteur, -euse 1** *adj* flattering **2** *nmf* flatterer

fléau, -x [fleo] *nm (catastrophe)* scourge; *Fig (personne)* pain; *Agr* flail

flèche [flɛʃ] *nf* arrow; *(d'église)* spire; **monter en f.** *(prix)* to shoot up ▪**flécher** *vt* to signpost (with arrows) ▪**fléchette** *nf* dart; **fléchettes** *(jeu)* darts

fléchir [fleʃir] **1** *vt (membre)* to bend; *Fig* **f. qn** to sway sb **2** *vi (membre)* to bend; *(poutre)* to sag; *(faiblir)* to give way; *(baisser)* to fall

flegme [flɛgm] *nm* composure ▪**flegmatique** *adj* phlegmatic

flemme [flɛm] *nf Fam* laziness; **il a la f.** he can't be bothered ▪ **flemmard, -arde** *Fam* **1** *adj* lazy **2** *nmf* lazybones

flétrir [fletrir] *vt,* **se flétrir** *vpr* to wither

fleur [flœr] *nf* flower; *(d'arbre, d'arbuste)* blossom; **en fleur(s)** in flower, in bloom; *(arbre)* in blossom; **à fleurs** *(tissu)* floral; **à ou dans la f. de l'âge** in the prime of life; **à f. d'eau** just above the water; **émotions à f. de peau** skin-deep emotions; **avoir les nerfs à f. de peau** to be all on edge; **la fine f. de la marine française** the cream of the French navy; *Fam* **arriver comme une f.** to arrive innocent and unsuspecting; *Fam* **faire une f. à qn** to do sb a favour; **il a un côté f. bleue** he has a romantic side

fleurir [flœrir] **1** *vt (table)* to decorate with flowers; *(tombe)* to lay flowers on **2** *vi (plante)* to flower, to bloom; *(arbre)* to blossom; *Fig (art, commerce)* to flourish ▪ **fleuri, -ie** *adj (fleur, jardin)* in bloom; *(tissu)* floral; *(style)* flowery, florid

fleuriste [flœrist] *nmf* florist

fleuve [flœv] *nm* river

flexible [flɛksibl] *adj* flexible ▪ **flexibilité** *nf* flexibility

flexion [flɛksjɔ̃] *nf (fléchissement)* bending

flic [flik] *nm Fam* cop

flingue [flɛ̃g] *nm Fam* gun ▪ **flinguer** *vt Fam* **f. qn** to gun sb down

flipper [flipœr] *nm (jeu)* pinball; *(appareil)* pinball machine

flocon [flɔkɔ̃] *nm* flake; **il neige à gros flocons** big flakes of snow are falling; **f. de neige** snowflake; **flocons d'avoine** porridge oats ▪ **floconneux, -euse** *adj* fluffy

floraison [flɔrɛzɔ̃] *nf* flowering; **en pleine f.** in full bloom ▪ **floral, -e, -aux, -ales** *adj* floral ▪ **florales** *nfpl* flower show

flore [flɔr] *nf* flora

florissant, -ante [flɔrisɑ̃, -ɑ̃t] *adj* flourishing

flot [flo] *nm (de souvenirs, de larmes)* flood, stream; **les flots** *(la mer)* the waves; **à f.** *(bateau, personne)* afloat; *Fig* **remettre qn à f.** to restore sb's fortunes; *Fig* **couler à flots** *(argent, vin)* to flow freely; **le soleil entrait à flots** the sun was streaming in

flotte [flɔt] *nf (de bateaux, d'avions)* fleet; *Fam (pluie)* rain; *Fam (eau)* water

flottement [flɔtmɑ̃] *nm (hésitation)* indecision

flotter [flɔte] *vi (bateau)* to float; *(drapeau)* to fly; *(cheveux)* to flow; *Fam (pleuvoir)* to rain ▪ **flotteur** *nm* float

flou, -e [flu] **1** *adj (photo)* fuzzy, blurred; *(idée)* vague **2** *nm* fuzziness; *Fig* vagueness; *Phot* **f. artistique** soft focus (effect)

fluctuant, -uante [flyktɥɑ̃, -ɥɑ̃t] *adj (prix, opinions)* fluctuating ▪ **fluctuations** *nfpl* fluctuation(s) (**de** in)

fluet, -uette [flɥɛ, -ɥɛt] *adj* thin, slender

fluide [flɥid] **1** *adj (liquide)* & *Fig* fluid **2** *nm (liquide)* fluid ▪ **fluidité** *nf* fluidity

fluorescent, -ente [flyɔresɑ̃, -ɑ̃t] *adj* fluorescent ▪ **fluo** *adj inv Fam* fluorescent

flûte [flyt] **1** *nf (instrument)* flute; *(verre)* champagne glass **2** *exclam Fam* damn! ▪ **flûtiste** *nmf Br* flautist, *Am* flutist

fluvial, -e, -iaux, -iales [flyvjal, -jo] *adj* river; **navigation/pêche fluviale** river navigation/fishing

flux [fly] *nm (abondance)* flow; **f. et reflux** ebb and flow

focal, -e, -aux, -ales [fɔkal, -o] *adj* focal ▪ **focaliser** *vt* to focus (**sur** on)

fœtus [fetys] *nm Br* foetus, *Am* fetus

foi [fwa] *nf* faith; **sur la f. de** on the strength of; **être de bonne/mauvaise f.** to be sincere/insincere; **avoir la f.** to have faith; **ma f., oui!** yes, indeed!

foie [fwa] *nm* liver; **f. gras** foie gras; **crise de f.** bout of indigestion

foin [fwɛ̃] *nm* hay; *Fam* **faire du f.** *(scandale)* to kick up a fuss

foire [fwar] *nf* fair; *Fam* **faire la f.** to muck about

fois [fwa] *nf* time; **une f.** once; **deux f.** twice; **trois f.** three times; **deux f. trois** two times three; **payer qch en plusieurs f.** to pay for sth in several instalments; **chaque f. que…** whenever…, each time (that)…; **une f. qu'il sera arrivé** *(dès que)* once he has arrived; **une f. pour toutes** once and for all; **à la f.** at the same time, at once; **à la f. riche et heureux** both rich and happy; *Fam* **des f.** sometimes; *Fam* **non mais des f.!** really now!

foison [fwazɔ̃] *nf* **à f.** in abundance ▪ **foisonnement** *nm* abundance ▪ **foisonner** *vi* to abound (**de** ou **en** in)

fol [fɔl] *voir* **fou**

folâtre [fɔlɑtr] *adj* playful ▪ **folâtrer** *vi* to romp, to frolic

folichon, -onne [fɔliʃɔ̃, -ɔn] *adj Fam* **pas f.** not much fun

folie [fɔli] *nf* madness; **faire une f.** to do a foolish thing; *(dépense)* to be very extravagant; **faire des folies pour qn** to do anything for sb; **aimer qn à la f.** to be madly in love with sb; **la f. des grandeurs** delusions of grandeur

folklore [fɔlklɔr] *nm* folklore ▪ **folklorique** *adj (costume)* traditional; *(danse)* folk; *Fam (endroit, soirée)* bizarre

folle [fɔl] *voir* **fou** ▪ **follement** *adv* madly

foncé, -ée [fɔ̃se] *adj* dark

foncer [fɔ̃se] **1** *vi (aller vite)* to tear or charge along; *Fam (s'y mettre)* to get one's head down; **f. sur qn/qch** to swoop on sb/sth **2** *vti (couleur)* to darken ▪ **fonceur, -euse** *nmf Fam* go-getter

foncier, -ière [fɔ̃sje, -jɛr] *adj (fondamental)* fundamental, basic; *(impôt)* land; **crédit f.** land loan ▪ **foncièrement** *adv* fundamentally

fonction [fɔ̃ksjɔ̃] nf (rôle) & Math function; (emploi) office; **en f. de** according to; **faire f. de** (personne) to act as; (objet) to serve or act as; **prendre ses fonctions** to take up one's duties; **la f. publique** the civil service; Ordinat **f. recherche et remplacement** search and replace function; Ordinat **f. de sauvegarde** save function ▪**fonctionnaire** nmf civil servant; **haut f.** high-ranking civil servant ▪**fonctionnel, -elle** adj functional

fonctionner [fɔ̃ksjɔne] vi (machine) to work, to function; (personne) **faire f. qch** to operate sth ▪**fonctionnement** nm (de machine) working; **en état de f.** in working order; Ordinat **f. en réseau** networking

fond [fɔ̃] nm (de boîte, de jardin, de vallée) bottom; (de salle, d'armoire) back; (arrière-plan) background; **au f. de** (boîte, jardin) at the bottom of; (salle) at the back of; Fig **au f., dans le f.** basically; **à f.** (connaître) thoroughly; Fam **à f. la caisse** (très vite) hell for leather; **de f. en comble** from top to bottom; **course/coureur de f.** long-distance race/runner; **ski de f.** cross-country skiing; **bruits de f.** background noise; **toucher le f. (du désespoir)** to have hit rock-bottom; **user ses fonds de culotte sur les bancs d'une école** to spend a great deal of time at a school; **f. de bouteille** (contenu) dregs; **f. de teint** foundation (cream); **f. sonore** background music

fondamental, -e, -aux, -ales [fɔ̃damɑ̃tal, -o] adj fundamental, basic

fonder [fɔ̃de] 1 vt (ville) to found; (commerce) to set up; (famille) to start; **f. qch sur qch** to base sth on sth; **être fondé à croire** to be justified in thinking; **bien fondé** well-founded 2 **se fonder** vpr **se f. sur qch** (sujet: théorie, remarque) to be based on sth; **sur quoi se fonde-t-il pour...?** what are his grounds for...? ▪**fondateur, -trice** nmf founder 2 adj **membre f.** founding member ▪**fondation** nf (création, œuvre) foundation (**de** of); **fondations** (de bâtiment) foundations ▪**fondement** nm foundation

fonderie [fɔ̃dri] nf foundry

fondre [fɔ̃dr] 1 vt (métal) to melt down; (neige) to melt; (cloche) to cast; Fig (couleurs) to blend (**avec** with); **faire f. qch** (sucre) to dissolve sth 2 vi (se liquéfier) to melt; (sucre) to dissolve; **f. en larmes** to burst into tears; **f. sur qch** to swoop on sth 3 **se fondre** vpr **se f. en eau** (glaçon) to melt away; **se f. dans qch** (brume) to merge into sth ▪**fondant, -ante** 1 adj which melts in the mouth 2 nm (bonbon) **un fondant au chocolat** a chocolate fondant ▪**fondu** nm Cin **f. enchaîné** dissolve

fonds [fɔ̃] 1 nm (organisme) fund; (de bibliothèque) collection; **f. de commerce** business; **F. monétaire international** International Monetary Fund 2 nmpl (argent) funds; **être en f.** to be in funds

fondue [fɔ̃dy] nf Culin fondue; **f. bourguignonne** beef fondue; **f. savoyarde** cheese fondue

font [fɔ̃] voir **faire**

fontaine [fɔ̃tɛn] nf (construction) fountain; (source) spring

fonte [fɔ̃t] nf (**a**) (de neige) melting; (d'acier) smelting (**b**) (alliage) cast iron; **en f.** (poêle) cast-iron (**c**) Typ font

fonts [fɔ̃] nmpl Rel **f. baptismaux** font

football [futbol] nm Br football, Am soccer; **f. américain** Br American football, Am football ▪**footballeur, -euse** nmf Br footballer, Am soccer player

footing [futiŋ] nm Sport jogging; **faire du f.** to go jogging

for [fɔr] nm Littéraire **en son f. intérieur** in one's heart of hearts

forage [fɔraʒ] nm drilling, boring

forain [fɔrɛ̃] nm fairground stallholder

forçat [fɔrsa] nm (prisonnier) convict

force [fɔrs] nf (violence) & Phys force; (vigueur) strength; **de toutes ses forces** with all one's strength; **de f.** by force, forcibly; **en f.** (attaquer, venir) in force; **à f. de volonté** through sheer willpower; **à f. de faire qch** through doing sth; Fam **à f., il va se mettre en colère** he'll end up losing his temper; **dans la f. de l'âge** in the prime of life; **par la f. des choses** through force of circumstance; **les forces armées** the armed forces; **les forces de l'ordre** the police; **f. de frappe** strike force

forcé, -ée [fɔrse] adj forced (**de faire** to do); Fam **c'est f.** it's inevitable ▪**forcément** adv inevitably; **pas f.** not necessarily

forcené, -ée [fɔrsəne] 1 adj fanatical 2 nmf maniac

forceps [fɔrsɛps] nm forceps (pluriel)

forcer [fɔrse] 1 vt (obliger) to force; (porte) to force open; (voix) to strain; **f. qn à faire qch** to force sb to do sth; **f. la main à qn** to force sb's hand; Fam **f. la dose** to overdo it 2 vi (appuyer, tirer) to force it; (se surmener) to overdo it 3 **se forcer** vpr to force oneself (**à faire** to do)

forcir [fɔrsir] vi to get bigger

forer [fɔre] vt to drill, to bore

forêt [fɔrɛ] nf forest; **f.-noire** (gâteau) Black Forest gateau; **f. vierge** virgin forest ▪**forestier, -ière** 1 adj **chemin f.** forest road 2 nm forester

forfait [fɔrfɛ] nm (**a**) (prix) all-in price; (de ski) pass; **f. week-end** weekend package (**b**) (crime) heinous crime ▪**forfaitaire** adj (indemnités) basic; **prix f.** all-in price

forge [fɔrʒ] nf forge ▪**forger** vt (métal, liens) to forge; Fig (caractère) to form; Fig (histoire) to make up ▪**forgeron** [-ərɔ̃] nm (black)smith

formaliser [fɔrmalize] **se formaliser** *vpr* to take offence (**de** at)

formalité [fɔrmalite] *nf* formality

format [fɔrma] *nm* format; **f. de poche** pocket format

formater [fɔrmate] *vt Ordinat* to format ▪ **formatage** *nm Ordinat* formatting

formation [fɔrmasjɔ̃] *nf (de roche, de mot)* formation; *(éducation)* education; **f. permanente** continuing education; **f. professionnelle** vocational training ▪ **formateur, -trice 1** *adj* formative **2** *nmf* trainer

forme [fɔrm] *nf (contour)* shape, form; *(manière, bonne santé)* form; **formes** *(de femme)* curves; **en f. de qch** in the shape of sth; **en f. de poire** pear-shaped; **sous f. de qch** in the form of sth; **dans les formes** in the accepted way; **en bonne et due f.** in due form; **en (pleine) f.** *(en bonne santé)* on (top) form; **sans autre f. de procès** without further ado; **prendre f.** to take shape; **y mettre les formes** to do things tactfully

formel, -elle [fɔrmɛl] *adj (structure, logique)* formal; *(démenti)* flat; *(personne, preuve)* positive; *(interdiction)* strict ▪ **formellement** *adv (interdire)* strictly

former [fɔrme] **1** *vt (groupe, caractère)* to form; *(apprenti)* to train **2 se former** *vpr (apparaître)* to form; *(association, liens)* to be formed; *(apprendre son métier)* to train oneself

formidable [fɔrmidabl] *adj (fantastique)* great; *(gigantesque)* tremendous

Il faut noter que l'adjectif anglais **formidable** est un faux ami. Il signifie **redoutable**.

formulaire [fɔrmylɛr] *nm* form

formule [fɔrmyl] *nf Math* formula; *(phrase)* expression; *(solution)* method; **nouvelle f.** *(abonnement, menu)* new-style; **f. magique** magic formula; **f. de politesse** *(au début d'une lettre)* standard opening; *(à la fin d'une lettre)* standard closure ▪ **formulation** *nf* formulation ▪ **formuler** *vt* to formulate

fort¹, -e [fɔr, fɔrt] **1** *adj (vigoureux)* strong; *(gros, important)* large; *(pluie, mer, chute de neige)* heavy; *(voix)* loud; *(fièvre)* high; *(pente)* steep; **être f. en qch** *(doué)* to be good at sth; **il y a de fortes chances que ça réussisse** there's a good chance it will work; **c'est plus f. qu'elle** she can't help it; *Fam* **c'est un peu f.!** that's a bit much! **2** *adv* (**a**) *(frapper)* hard; *(pleuvoir)* hard, heavily; *(parler)* loud(ly); *(serrer)* tight; **sentir f.** to have a strong smell; **respirer f.** to breathe heavily; *Fam* **y aller f.** to overdo it; *Fam* **faire très f.** *(très bien)* to do really brilliantly (**b**) *Littéraire (très)* very; *(beaucoup)* very much **3** *nm (spécialité)* strong point; **au plus f. de qch** *(hiver)* in the depths of sth; *(épidémie)* at the height of sth ▪ **fortement** [-əmã] *adv (désirer, influencer)* strongly; *(tirer, pousser)* hard;

(impressionner) greatly; **f. épicé** highly spiced

fort² [fɔr] *nm Hist & Mil* fort ▪ **forteresse** *nf* fortress

fortifié, -iée [fɔrtifje] *adj (ville, camp)* fortified ▪ **fortification** *nf* fortification

fortifier [fɔrtifje] *vt (mur, ville)* to fortify; *(corps)* to strengthen ▪ **fortifiant** *nm* tonic

fortuit, -uite [fɔrtɥi, -ɥit] *adj* **rencontre fortuite** chance meeting

fortune [fɔrtyn] *nf (richesse, hasard)* fortune; **moyens de f.** makeshift means; **faire f.** to make one's fortune; **dîner à la f. du pot** to take pot luck; **faire contre mauvaise f. bon cœur** to make the best of it ▪ **fortuné, -ée** *adj (riche)* wealthy

Il faut noter que l'adjectif anglais **fortunate** signifie uniquement **qui a de la chance**.

forum [fɔrɔm] *nm* forum; *Ordinat* **f. de discussion** discussion forum; **f. en-ligne** online forum

fosse [fos] *nf (trou)* pit; *(tombe)* grave; **f. d'aisances** cesspool; **f. d'orchestre** orchestra pit; **f. commune** mass grave

fossé [fose] *nm* ditch; *(de château)* moat; *Fig (désaccord)* gulf

fossette [fosɛt] *nf* dimple

fossile [fosil] *nm & adj* fossil; *Fam* **un vieux f.** an old fossil ▪ **fossilisé, -ée** *adj* fossilized ▪ **fossiliser** *vt*, **se fossiliser** *vpr* to fossilize

fossoyeur [foswajœr] *nm* gravedigger

fou, folle [fu, fɔl]

fol is used before masculine singular nouns beginning with a vowel or h mute.

1 *adj (personne, projet)* mad, insane; *(succès, temps)* tremendous; *(envie)* wild, mad; *(espoir)* foolish; *(cheval, camion)* runaway; **f. à lier** raving mad; **f. de qch** *(musique, personne)* mad about sth; **f. de joie** beside oneself with joy; **f. rire** uncontrollable giggling; **avoir le f. rire** to have the giggles **2** *nmf* madman, *f* madwoman **3** *nm (bouffon)* jester; *Échecs* bishop; **faire le f.** to play the fool

foudre [fudr] *nf* **la f.** lightning ▪ **foudroyant, -ante** *adj (succès, vitesse)* staggering; *(regard)* withering ▪ **foudroyer** *vt* to strike; **f. qn du regard** to give sb a withering look

fouet [fwɛ] *nm* whip; *Culin* (egg-)whisk; **coup de f.** lash (with a whip); **de plein f.** head-on ▪ **fouetter** *vt* to whip; *(œufs)* to whisk; *(sujet: pluie)* to lash (against); **crème fouettée** whipped cream

fougère [fuʒɛr] *nf* fern

fougue [fug] *nf* fire, spirit ▪ **fougueux, -euse** *adj* fiery, ardent

fouille [fuj] **1** *nf (de personne, de bagages)* search **2** *nfpl* **fouilles archéologiques** excavations, dig ▪ **fouillé, -ée** *adj* detailed ▪ **fouiller 1** *vt (personne, maison)* to search **2** *vi* **f. dans qch** *(tiroir)* to search through sth **3** *vti (creuser)* to dig

fouillis [fuji] *nm* jumble

fouine [fwin] *nf* stone marten

fouiner [fwine] *vi Fam* to nose about (**dans** in) ▪**fouineur, -euse** *Fam* **1** *adj* nosey **2** *nmf* nosey parker

foulard [fular] *nm* (head)scarf

foule [ful] *nf* crowd; **en f.** in mass; **une f. de** (*objets*) a mass of; **bain de f.** walkabout

foulée [fule] *nf* (*de coureur, de cheval*) stride; *Fam* **dans la f., j'ai vérifié les comptes** while I was at it, I checked the accounts

fouler [fule] **1** *vt* (*raisin*) to press; (*sol*) to tread; **f. qch aux pieds** to trample sth underfoot **2 se fouler** *vpr* **se f. la cheville** to sprain one's ankle; *Fam* **il ne se foule pas** he doesn't exactly exert himself ▪**foulure** *nf* sprain

four [fur] *nm* (*de cuisine*) oven; (*de potier*) kiln; *Fam* (*fiasco*) flop; **faire un f.** to flop; **petit f.** (*gâteau*) petit four, small fancy cake

fourbe [furb] **1** *adj* deceitful **2** *nmf* cheat ▪**fourberie** *nf* deceit

fourbi [furbi] *nm Fam* (*désordre*) mess; (*choses*) stuff

fourbu, -ue [furby] *adj* (*fatigué*) exhausted

fourche [furʃ] *nf* (*outil, embranchement*) fork; **faire une f.** to fork ▪**fourcher** *vi* (*arbre*) to fork; **ma langue a fourché** I made a slip of the tongue ▪**fourchette** *nf* (*pour manger*) fork; (*de salaires*) bracket ▪**fourchu, -ue** *adj* forked; **avoir les cheveux fourchus** to have split ends

fourgon [furgɔ̃] *nm* (*camion*) van; **f. cellulaire** *Br* prison van, *Am* patrol wagon; **f. funéraire** hearse; **f. postal** *Br* postal van, *Am* mail car ▪**fourgonnette** *nf* (small) van

fourguer [furge] *vt Fam* **f. qch à qn** to unload sth onto sb

fourmi [furmi] *nf* (*insecte*) ant; **avoir des fourmis dans les jambes** to have pins and needles in one's legs ▪**fourmilière** *nf* anthill ▪**fourmiller** *vi* to teem, to swarm (**de** with)

fournaise [furnɛz] *nf* furnace

fourneau, -x [furno] *nm* (*de cuisine*) stove; (*de verrier*) furnace

fournée [furne] *nf* (*de pain, de gens*) batch

fournil [furni] *nm* bakehouse

fournir [furnir] **1** *vt* (*approvisionner*) to supply (**en** with); (*alibi, preuve, document*) to provide; (*effort*) to make; **f. qch à qn** to provide sb with sth; **pièces à f.** required documents **2 se fournir** *vpr* **se f. en qch** to get in supplies of sth; **se f. chez qn** to get one's supplies from sb ▪**fourni, -ie** *adj* (*barbe*) bushy; **bien f.** (*boutique*) well-stocked ▪**fournisseur** *nm* (*commerçant*) supplier; *Ordinat* **f. d'accès** access provider ▪**fourniture** *nf* (*action*) supply(ing) (**de** of); **fournitures de bureau** office supplies; **fournitures scolaires** educational stationery

> Il faut noter que le mot anglais **furniture** est un faux ami. Il signifie **meubles**.

fourrage [furaʒ] *nm* fodder

fourrager [furaʒe] *vi Fam* to rummage (**dans** in)

fourré, -ée [fure] **1** *adj* (*gant*) fur-lined; (*gâteau*) jam-/cream-filled; *Fam* **coup f.** (*traîtrise*) stab in the back **2** *nm Bot* thicket

fourreau, -x [furo] *nm* (*gaine*) sheath

fourrer [fure] **1** *vt* (*gâteau, chou*) to fill; (*vêtement*) to fur-line; *Fam* (*mettre*) to stick; **f. son nez dans qch** to poke one's nose into sth **2 se fourrer** *vpr Fam* to put oneself (**dans** in); **se f. dans une sale affaire** to get involved in a nasty business; **se f. le doigt dans l'œil** to kid oneself; **où est-il allé se f.?** where's he got to? ▪**fourre-tout** *nm inv* (*pièce*) junk room; (*sac*) *Br* holdall, *Am* carryall

fourrière [furjɛr] *nf* (*lieu*) pound; **mettre à la f.** (*voiture*) to impound; (*chien*) to put in the pound

fourrure [furyr] *nf* fur; **manteau de f.** fur coat ▪**fourreur** *nm* furrier

fourvoyer [furvwaje] **se fourvoyer** *vpr Littéraire & Fig* to go astray

foutaises [futɛz] *nfpl Fam* crap

foutoir [futwar] *nm Fam* dump

foutre* [futr] *très Fam* **1** *vt* (*mettre*) to stick; (*faire*) to do; (*donner*) to give; **f. qch par terre** to chuck sth on the ground; **f. qn à la porte** to kick sb out; **f. qch en l'air** (*faire échouer*) to screw sth up; **f. le camp** to piss off; **ne rien f.** to do damn all *or Br* bugger all; **je n'en ai rien à f.** I don't give a damn!, *Br* I don't give a toss! **2 se foutre** *vpr* **se f. un coup** to bang oneself; **se f. du monde** to take the piss; **se f. de la gueule de qn** to take the piss out of sb; **je m'en fous** I don't give a damn ▪**foutu, -ue** *adj Fam* (*maudit*) damn; **être f.** (*en mauvais état*) to have had it; **être bien f.** (*beau*) to have a nice body; (*bien conçu*) to be well designed; **être mal f.** (*malade*) to be under the weather; **être f. de faire qch** to be quite likely to do sth

foyer [fwaje] *nm* (*maison*) home; (*d'étudiants*) residence; (*de travailleurs*) hostel; (*de théâtre*) foyer; (*de lunettes*) focus; (*de chaleur, d'infection*) source; (*d'incendie*) seat; (*âtre*) hearth; (*famille*) family; **fonder un f.** to start a family

fracas [fraka] *nm* crash ▪**fracassant, -ante** *adj* (*nouvelle, révélation*) shattering ▪**fracasser** *vt,* **se fracasser** *vpr* to smash

fraction [fraksjɔ̃] *nf* fraction; (*partie*) part ▪**fractionner** *vt,* **se fractionner** *vpr* to split (up)

fracture [fraktyr] *nf* fracture; *Fig* **f. sociale** social fracture ▪**fracturer** **1** *vt* (*porte*) to break open; (*os*) to fracture **2 se fracturer** *vpr* **se f. la jambe** to fracture one's leg

fragile [fraʒil] *adj* (*objet, matériau*) fragile; (*santé, équilibre*) delicate; (*personne*) (*physiquement*) frail; (*mentalement*) sensitive ▪**fragilité** *nf* (*d'objet, de matériau*) fragility; (*de personne*) (*physique*) frailty; (*mentale*) sensitivity

fragment [fragmɑ̃] *nm* fragment

•fragmentaire adj fragmentary **•fragmenter** vt to fragment

frais¹, fraîche [frɛ, frɛʃ] **1** adj (aliment, fleurs, teint) fresh; (vent, air) cool, fresh; (nouvelles) recent; (peinture) wet; **connaître qn de fraîche date** to have known sb for a short time **2** adv **servir f.** (vin) to serve chilled; **f. émoulu de** fresh out of **3** nm **prendre le f.** to get some fresh air; **mettre qch au f.** to put sth in a cool place; (au réfrigérateur) to refrigerate sth; **il fait f.** it's cool **•fraîchement** adv (récemment) newly; (accueillir) coolly **•fraîcheur** nf (d'aliments, du teint) freshness; (de température, d'accueil) coolness **•fraîchir** vi (temps) to freshen

frais² [frɛ] nmpl expenses; **à mes f.** at my (own) expense; **à grands f.** at great expense; **faire des f., se mettre en f.** to go to great expense; **faire les f.** to bear the cost (**de** of); **j'en ai été pour mes f.** I wasted my time and effort; **faux f.** incidental expenses; **f. d'inscription** (d'université) registration fees; (de club) enrolment fee(s); **f. de scolarité** school fees; **f. généraux** Br overheads, Am overhead

fraise [frɛz] nf (fruit) strawberry; (de dentiste) drill **•fraisier** nm (plante) strawberry plant; (gâteau) strawberry cream cake

framboise [frɑ̃bwaz] nf raspberry **•framboisier** nm raspberry bush

franc¹, franche [frɑ̃, frɑ̃ʃ] adj (**a**) (sincère) frank; (visage) open (**b**) (net) (couleur) pure; (cassure) clean (**c**) (zone, ville, port) free **•franchement** adv (sincèrement) frankly; (vraiment) really; (sans ambiguïté) clearly

franc² [frɑ̃] nm (monnaie) franc

France [frɑ̃s] nf la F. France **•français, -aise 1** adj French **2** nmf F. Frenchman; **Française** Frenchwoman; **les F.** the French **3** nm (langue) French

franchir [frɑ̃ʃir] vt (obstacle, difficulté) to get over; (fossé) to jump over; (frontière, ligne d'arrivée) to cross; (porte) to go through; (distance) to cover; Fig (seuil, limite) to exceed

franchise [frɑ̃ʃiz] nf (sincérité) frankness; (exonération) exemption; Com franchise; **en toute f.** quite frankly; **f. postale** ≃ postage paid

franc-maçon [frɑ̃masɔ̃] (pl **francs-maçons**) nm freemason **•franc-maçonnerie** nf freemasonry

franco [frɑ̃ko] adv **f. de port** postage paid

franco- [frɑ̃ko] préf Franco-

francophile [frɑ̃kɔfil] adj & nmf Francophile

francophone [frɑ̃kɔfɔn] **1** adj French-speaking **2** nmf French speaker **•francophonie** nf la f. the French-speaking world

franc-parler [frɑ̃parle] nm **avoir son f.** to speak one's mind

franc-tireur [frɑ̃tirœr] (pl **francs-tireurs**) nm irregular (soldier)

frange [frɑ̃ʒ] nf (de cheveux) Br fringe, Am bangs; (de vêtement) fringe

frangin [frɑ̃ʒɛ̃] nm Fam brother **•frangine** nf Fam sister

franquette [frɑ̃kɛt] nf **à la bonne franquette** without ceremony; **un repas à la bonne f.** a simple meal

frappe [frap] nf (sur machine à écrire) typing; (sur ordinateur) keying; (de monnaie) minting; Football kick; **faute de f.** typing error; Mil **force de f.** strike force

frapper [frape] **1** vt (battre) to strike, to hit; (monnaie) to mint; **f. qn** (impressionner) to strike sb; (impôt, mesure) to hit sb **2** vi (donner un coup) to strike, to hit; **f. du pied** to stamp (one's foot); **f. du poing sur la table** to bang (on) the table; **f. dans ses mains** to clap one's hands; **f. à une porte** to knock on a door; Fig **f. à toutes les portes** to try everywhere; **'entrez sans f.'** (sur une porte) 'go straight in' **3** se **frapper** vpr Fam (s'inquiéter) to get oneself worked up **•frappant, -ante** adj striking **•frappé, -ée** adj (vin) chilled; Fam (fou) crazy; **f. de stupeur** astounded, flabbergasted

frasque [frask] nf escapade, prank; **faire des frasques** to get up to mischief

fraternel, -elle [fratɛrnɛl] adj fraternal, brotherly **•fraterniser** vi to fraternize (**avec** with) **•fraternité** nf fraternity, brotherhood

fraude [frod] nf fraud; **passer qch en f.** to smuggle sth in; **f. électorale** electoral fraud; **f. fiscale** tax evasion **•frauder** vt to defraud; **f. le fisc** to evade tax **2** vi to cheat (**sur** on) **•fraudeur, -euse** nmf defrauder **•frauduleux, -euse** adj fraudulent

frayer [freje] **1** vi (poisson) to spawn **2** se **frayer** vpr se **f. un chemin** to clear a way (**à travers/dans** through)

frayeur [frejœr] nf fright

fredaine [frədɛn] nf escapade, prank; **faire des fredaines** to get up to mischief

fredonner [frədɔne] vti to hum

freezer [frizœr] nm freezer compartment

frein [frɛ̃] nm brake; **donner un coup de f.** to put on the brakes; Fig **mettre un f. à qch** to curb sth; **f. à main** handbrake **•freinage** nm Aut braking **•freiner 1** vt (véhicule) to slow down; (chute) to break; Fig (inflation, production) to curb **2** vi to brake

frelaté, -ée [frəlate] adj (vin) & Fig adulterated

frêle [frɛl] adj frail

frelon [frəlɔ̃] nm hornet

frémir [fremir] vi (personne) to tremble (**de** with); (feuilles) to rustle; (eau chaude) to simmer **•frémissement** nm (de peur) shudder; (de plaisir) thrill; (de colère) quiver; (de feuilles) rustle; (d'eau chaude) simmering

frêne [frɛn] nm (arbre, bois) ash

frénésie [frenezi] nf frenzy **•frénétique** adj frenzied

fréquent, -ente [frekɑ̃, -ɑ̃t] adj frequent

▪**fréquemment** [-amã] *adv* frequently
▪**fréquence** *nf* frequency
fréquenter [frekãte] **1** *vt (lieu)* to frequent; **f. qn** to see sb regularly **2 se fréquenter** *upr (se voir régulièrement)* to see each other socially ▪**fréquentable** *adj* **peu f.** *(personne, endroit)* not very commendable ▪**fréquentation** *nf (de lieu)* frequenting; **fréquentations** *(relations)* company; **avoir de mauvaises fréquentations** to keep bad company ▪**fréquenté, -ée** *adj* **très f.** busy; **mal f.** of ill repute; **bien f.** reputable, of good repute
frère [frɛr] *nm* brother
fresque [frɛsk] *nf* fresco
fret [frɛ] *nm* freight
frétiller [fretije] *vi (poisson, personne)* to wriggle; **f. d'impatience** to quiver with impatience; **f. de joie** to tingle with excitement
fretin [frɔtɛ̃] *nm* **menu f.** *(poissons, personnes)* small fry
friable [frijabl] *adj* crumbly
friand, -e [frijã, -ãd] **1** *adj* **f. de qch** fond of sth **2** *nm (salé)* = small savoury pastry ▪**friandise** *nf Br* titbit, *Am* tidbit
fric [frik] *nm Fam (argent)* dough
friche [friʃ] *nf* fallow land; **laisser une terre en f.** to let a piece of land lie fallow
friction [friksjɔ̃] *nf (massage)* rubdown; *(de cuir chevelu)* scalp massage; *(désaccord)* friction ▪**frictionner** *vt (partie du corps)* to rub; *(personne)* to rub down
Frigidaire® [friʒidɛr] *nm* fridge ▪**frigo** *nm Fam* fridge ▪**frigorifié, -iée** *adj Fam (personne)* frozen stiff ▪**frigorifique** *adj voir* **camion**
frigide [friʒid] *adj* frigid ▪**frigidité** *nf* frigidity
frileux, -euse [frilø, -øz] *adj* **être f.** to feel the cold
frime [frim] *nf Fam* show ▪**frimer** *vi Fam* to show off
frimousse [frimus] *nf Fam* sweet little face; *Ordinat* smiley
fringale [frɛ̃gal] *nf Fam* hunger; **avoir la f.** to be starving
fringant, -ante [frɛ̃gã, -ãt] *adj (personne, allure)* dashing
fringues [frɛ̃g] *nfpl Fam (vêtements)* clothes, gear ▪**se fringuer** *upr Fam* to get dressed
friper [fripe] **1** *vt* to crumple **2 se friper** *upr* to get crumpled ▪**fripé, -ée** *adj* crumpled
fripier, -ière [fripje, -jɛr] *nmf* second-hand clothes dealer
fripon, -onne [fripɔ̃, -ɔn] *Fam* **1** *adj* mischievous **2** *nmf* rascal
fripouille [fripuj] *nf Fam* rogue
friqué, -ée [frike] *adj Fam (riche)* loaded
frire* [frir] **1** *vt* to fry **2** *vi* to fry; **faire f. qch** to fry sth
frise [friz] *nf* frieze
friser [frize] **1** *vt (cheveux)* to curl; *(effleurer)* to skim; **f. les cheveux à qn** to curl sb's hair; **f. la**

trentaine to be close to thirty; **f. la catastrophe** to come within an inch of disaster **2** *vi (cheveux)* to curl; *(personne)* to have curly hair ▪**frisé, -ée** *adj (cheveux)* curly; *(personne)* curly-haired
frisquet, -ette [friskɛ, -ɛt] *adj Fam* chilly; **il fait f.** it's chilly
frisson [frisɔ̃] *nm (de froid, de peur)* shiver; *(de plaisir)* thrill; **avoir des frissons** to shiver; **donner le f. à qn** to give sb the shivers ▪**frissonner** *vi (de froid, de peur)* to shiver
frit, -e [fri, -it] **1** *pp de* **frire 2** *adj* fried ▪**frite** *nf Fam* **avoir la f.** to be on form ▪**frites** *nfpl Br* chips, *Am* French fries ▪**friteuse** *nf* (deep) frier, *Br* chip pan; **f. électrique** electric frier ▪**friture** *nf (mode de cuisson)* frying; *(corps gras)* frying fat; *(aliment)* fried food; *Radio & Tél (bruit)* crackling
frivole [frivɔl] *adj* frivolous ▪**frivolité** *nf* frivolity
froc [frɔk] *nm Fam (pantalon) Br* trousers, *Am* pants
froid, -e [frwa, frwad] **1** *adj* cold **2** *nm* cold; **avoir/prendre f.** to be/catch cold; **avoir f. aux mains** to have cold hands; **démarrer à f.** *(véhicule)* to start (from) cold; **être en f.** to be on bad terms (**avec qn** with sb); *Fig* **n'avoir pas f. aux yeux** to have plenty of nerve; *Fam* **jeter un f.** to cast a chill (**dans** over); **il fait f.** it's cold ▪**froidement** *adv (accueillir)* coldly; *(abattre)* cold-bloodedly; *(répondre)* coolly ▪**froideur** *nf* coldness
froisser [frwase] **1** *vt (tissu)* to crumple, to crease; *Fig* **f. qn** to offend sb **2 se froisser** *upr (tissu)* to crease, to crumple; *Fig* to take offence (**de** at); **se f. un muscle** to strain a muscle
frôler [frole] *vt (effleurer)* to brush against, to touch lightly; *Fig (la mort, la catastrophe)* to come close to
fromage [frɔmaʒ] *nm* cheese; **f. de chèvre** goat's cheese; **f. de tête** *Br* brawn, *Am* headcheese; **f. blanc** fromage frais; **f. frais** soft cheese ▪**fromager, -ère 1** *adj* cheese; **industrie fromagère** cheese industry **2** *nmf (fabricant)* cheesemaker; *(commerçant)* cheese seller ▪**fromagerie** *nf (magasin)* cheese shop
froment [frɔmã] *nm* wheat
fronce [frɔ̃s] *nf* gather ▪**froncement** *nm* **f. de sourcils** frown ▪**froncer** *vt (tissu)* to gather; **f. les sourcils** to frown
fronde [frɔ̃d] *nf (arme)* sling; *(sédition)* revolt
front [frɔ̃] *nm (du visage)* forehead; *(avant), Mil & Pol* front; **de f.** *(heurter)* head-on; *(côte à côte)* abreast; *(à la fois)* (all) at once; **faire f. à qn/qch** to face up to sb/sth; **f. de mer** sea front ▪**frontal, -e, -aux, -ales** *adj (collision)* head-on
frontière [frɔ̃tjer] **1** *nf (entre pays)* border, frontier **2** *adj inv* **ville f.** border town ▪**frontalier, -ière 1** *adj* **ville frontalière** border *or* frontier town **2** *nmf (habitant)*

inhabitant of the border *or* frontier zone; *(travailleur)* cross-border commuter

fronton [frɔ̃tɔ̃] *nm (de monument)* pediment

frotter [frɔte] **1** *vt* to rub; *(plancher)* to scrub; *(allumette)* to strike **2** *vi* to rub (**contre** against) **3 se frotter** *vpr* to rub oneself; **se f. le dos** to scrub one's back; *Fig* **se f. à qn** *(l'attaquer)* to meddle with sb ▪ **frottement** *nm* rubbing; *Tech* friction

froufrou [frufru] *nm (bruit)* rustling; **froufrous** *(de vêtements)* frills

frousse [frus] *nf Fam* fear; **avoir la f.** to be scared ▪ **froussard, -arde** *nmf Fam* chicken

fructifier [fryktifje] *vi (arbre, capital)* to bear fruit; **faire f. son capital** to make one's capital grow ▪ **fructueux, -ueuse** *adj* fruitful

frugal, -e, -aux, -ales [frygal, -o] *adj* frugal ▪ **frugalité** *nf* frugality

fruit [frɥi] *nm* fruit; **des fruits**; **un f.** a piece of fruit; **porter ses fruits** *(placement)* to bear fruit; **fruits de mer** seafood; **fruits rouges** red berries and currants; **fruits secs** dried fruit ▪ **fruité, -ée** *adj* fruity ▪ **fruitier, -ière 1** *adj* **arbre f.** fruit tree **2** *nmf* fruit seller, *Br* fruiterer

frusques [frysk] *nfpl Fam (vêtements)* gear

fruste [fryst] *adj (personne)* rough

frustrer [frystre] *vt* **f. qn** to frustrate sb; **f. qn de qch** to deprive sb of sth ▪ **frustration** *nf* frustration ▪ **frustré, -ée** *adj* frustrated

fuel [fjul] *nm* fuel oil

fugace [fygas] *adj* fleeting

fugitif, -ive [fyʒitif, -iv] **1** *adj (passager)* fleeting **2** *nmf* runaway, fugitive

fugue [fyg] *nf (œuvre musicale)* fugue; **faire une f.** *(enfant)* to run away ▪ **fuguer** *vi Fam* to run away

fuir* [fɥir] **1** *vt (pays)* to flee; *(personne)* to run away from; *(guerre)* to escape; *(responsabilités)* to shirk **2** *vi (s'échapper)* to run away (**devant** from); *(gaz, robinet, stylo)* to leak; *Littéraire (temps)* to fly ▪ **fuite** *nf (évasion)* flight (**devant** from); *(de gaz)* leak; **en f.** on the run; **prendre la f.** to take flight; **f. des cerveaux** brain drain

fulgurant, -ante [fylgyrɑ̃, -ɑ̃t] *adj (progrès)* spectacular; *(vitesse)* lightning; *(douleur)* searing

fumée [fyme] *nf* smoke; *(vapeur)* steam

fumer [fyme] **1** *vt (cigarette, poisson)* to smoke; **f. la pipe** to smoke a pipe **2** *vi (fumeur, feu, moteur)* to smoke; *(liquide brûlant)* to steam ▪ **fumé, -ée** *adj (poisson, verre)* smoked ▪ **fume-cigarette** *nm inv* cigarette holder ▪ **fumeur, -euse** *nmf* smoker

Il faut noter que le verbe anglais **to fume** est un faux ami. Il signifie **fulminer**.

fumet [fymɛ] *nm* aroma

fumeux, -euse [fymø, -øz] *adj Fig (idée)* hazy

fumier [fymje] *nm (engrais)* manure, dung

fumigation [fymigasjɔ̃] *nf* fumigation

fumiste [fymist] *nmf Fam (sur qui on ne peut compter)* clown ▪ **fumisterie** *nf Fam (farce)* con

funambule [fynãbyl] *nmf* tightrope walker

funèbre [fynɛbr] *adj (lugubre)* gloomy; **service/ marche f.** funeral service/march ▪ **funérailles** *nfpl* funeral ▪ **funéraire** *adj (frais)* funeral

funeste [fynɛst] *adj (désastreux)* disastrous

funiculaire [fynikylɛr] *nm* funicular

fur [fyr] **au fur et à mesure** *adv* as one goes along; **au f. et à mesure de vos besoins** as your needs dictate; **au f. et à mesure que…** as…

furent [fyr] *voir* **être**

furet [fyrɛ] *nm* ferret

fureter [fyr(ə)te] *vi Péj* to ferret about

fureur [fyrœr] *nf (colère)* fury, rage; *(passion)* passion (**de** for); **en f.** furious; *Fam* **faire f.** to be all the rage ▪ **furibond, -onde** *adj* furious ▪ **furie** *nf (colère)* fury; *Fig (femme)* shrew; **comme une f.** like a wild thing ▪ **furieux, -ieuse** *adj (en colère)* furious (**contre** with); *(vent)* raging; *Fig (envie)* tremendous

furoncle [fyrɔ̃kl] *nm* boil

furtif, -ive [fyrtif, -iv] *adj* furtive, stealthy

fusain [fyzɛ̃] *nm (crayon, dessin)* charcoal; **dessin au f.** charcoal drawing

fuseau, -x [fyzo] *nm (pantalon)* ski pants; *Tex* spindle; **f. horaire** time zone ▪ **fuselé, -ée** *adj* slender; *(voiture)* streamlined

fusée [fyze] *nf (projectile)* rocket; **f. de détresse** flare, distress signal; **f. éclairante** flare

fuselage [fyzlaʒ] *nm (d'avion)* fuselage

fuser [fyze] *vi (rires)* to burst forth

fusible [fyzibl] *nm Br* fuse; *Am* fuze

fusil [fyzi] *nm* rifle, gun; *(de chasse)* shotgun; **un bon f.** *(personne)* a good shot ▪ **fusillade** *nf (tirs)* gunfire ▪ **fusiller** *vt (exécuter)* to shoot; *Fam (abîmer)* to wreck; *Fam* **f. qn du regard** to look daggers at sb

fusion [fyzjɔ̃] *nf* (**a**) *(de métal)* melting; *Phys* fusion; **point de f.** melting point; **métal en f.** molten metal (**b**) *(de sociétés)* merger ▪ **fusionner** *vti (sociétés)* to merge

fustiger [fystiʒe] *vt (critiquer)* to castigate

fut [fy] *voir* **être**

fût [fy] *nm (tonneau)* barrel, cask; *(d'arbre)* bole

futal, -als [fytal], **fute** [fyt] *nm Fam Br* trousers, *Am* pants

futé, -ée [fyte] *adj* crafty

futile [fytil] *adj (personne)* frivolous; *(occupation, prétexte)* trivial ▪ **futilité** *nf* triviality

futur, -ure [fytyr] **1** *adj* future; **un f. artiste** a budding artist; **f. client** prospective client; **future mère** mother-to-be **2** *nmf* **mon f./ma future** my intended **3** *nm (avenir)* future; *Grammaire* future (tense)

fuyant [fɥijã] *p prés de* **fuir** ▪ **fuyant, -ante** *adj (front, ligne)* receding; *(personne)* evasive; *(yeux)* shifty ▪ **fuyard** *nm* runaway

G, g [ʒe] *nm inv* G, g

gabardine [gabardin] *nf (tissu, imperméable)* gabardine

gabarit [gabari] *nm (dimension)* size

gâcher [gɑʃe] *vt (gâter)* to spoil; *(gaspiller)* to waste; *(plâtre)* to mix; **g. sa vie** to waste one's life ▪ **gâchis** *nm* waste

gâchette [gɑʃɛt] *nf* trigger; **appuyer sur la g.** to pull the trigger

gadget [gadʒɛt] *nm* gadget

gadoue [gadu] *nf* mud

gaffe [gaf] *nf Fam (bévue)* blunder; **faire une g.** to put one's foot in it; **faire g.** to pay attention; **fait g.!** look out! ▪ **gaffer** *vi Fam* to put one's foot in it ▪ **gaffeur, -euse** *nmf Fam* blunderer

gag [gag] *nm* gag

gaga [gaga] *adj Fam* gaga

gage [gaʒ] *nm (garantie)* guarantee; *(au jeu)* forfeit; *(de prêteur sur gages)* pledge; *(preuve)* token; **mettre qch en g.** to pawn sth; **donner qch en g. de fidélité** to give sth as a token of one's fidelity ▪ **gages** *nmpl Vieilli (salaire)* pay; **tueur à g.** hired assassin

gager [gaʒe] *vt Littéraire* **g. que...** to wager that... ▪ **gageure** [gaʒyr] *nf Littéraire* wager

gagnant, -ante [gaɲɑ̃, -ɑ̃t] **1** *adj (billet, cheval)* winning **2** *nmf* winner

gagner [gaɲe] **1** *vt (par le travail)* to earn; *(par le jeu)* to win; *(obtenir)* to gain; *(atteindre)* to reach; *(sujet: feu, épidémie)* to spread to; **g. sa vie** to earn one's living; *Fam* **g. des mille et des cents** to earn a bundle *or Br* a packet; **g. une heure** to save an hour; **g. du temps** *(aller plus vite)* to save time; *(temporiser)* to gain time; **g. du terrain/du poids** to gain ground/weight; **g. de la place** to save space; **g. qn** *(sommeil, faim, panique)* to overcome sb; *Fam* **c'est toujours ça de gagné** that's something, anyway **2** *vi (être vainqueur)* to win; *(croître)* to increase; **g. à être connu** to improve with acquaintance; **g. sur tous les tableaux** to win on all counts ▪ **gagne-pain** *nm inv* livelihood

gai, -e [gɛ] *adj* cheerful; *Fam* **être un peu g.** to be tipsy ▪ **gaiement** *adv* cheerfully ▪ **gaieté** *nf* cheerfulness; **je ne le fais pas de g. de cœur** I don't enjoy doing it

gaillard, -arde [gajar, -ard] **1** *adj (fort)* vigorous; *(grivois)* bawdy **2** *nm (homme)* hearty type; **un grand g.** a strapping man

gain [gɛ̃] *nm (profit)* gain, profit; *(succès)* winning; **gains** *(à la Bourse)* profits; *(au jeu)* winnings; **un g. de temps** a saving of time; **obtenir g. de cause** to win one's case

gaine [gɛn] *nf (sous-vêtement)* girdle; *(étui)* sheath

gala [gala] *nm* gala

galant, -ante [galɑ̃, -ɑ̃t] *adj (homme)* gallant; *(rendez-vous)* romantic ▪ **galanterie** *nf* gallantry

galaxie [galaksi] *nf* galaxy

galbe [galb] *nm* curve ▪ **galbé, -ée** *adj (jambes)* shapely

gale [gal] *nf Méd* **la g.** scabies; *(de chien)* mange ▪ **galeux, -euse** *adj (chien)* mangy

galère [galɛr] *nf Hist (navire)* galley; *Fam (difficultés)* hassle; **c'est la g. pour se garer le samedi** it's a real hassle finding a parking space on Saturdays; **c'est une vraie g.** it's a real pain; *(situation pénible)* **être dans une g.** to be in a mess *or Br* a pickle ▪ **galérer** *vi Fam* to have a hard time

galerie [galri] *nf (passage, salle)* gallery; *(de taupe)* tunnel; *Théâtre* balcony; *Aut (porte-bagages)* roof rack; *Fam* **épater la g.** to show off; **g. d'art** art gallery; **g. marchande** *Br* shopping centre, *Am* (shopping) mall

galet [galɛ] *nm* pebble; **plage de galets** shingle beach

galette [galɛt] *nf (gâteau)* butter biscuit; *(crêpe)* buckwheat pancake; **g. des Rois** Twelfth Night cake

galipette [galipɛt] *nf Fam* somersault

Galles [gal] *nfpl* **pays de G.** Wales ▪ **gallois, -oise** **1** *adj* Welsh **2** *nmf* **G.** Welshman; **Galloise** Welshwoman **3** *nm (langue)* Welsh

gallicisme [galisism] *nm* Gallicism

galon [galɔ̃] *nm (ruban)* braid; *(de soldat)* stripe; *Fam* **prendre du g.** to get promoted

galop [galo] *nm* gallop; **aller au g.** to gallop; *Fig* **g. d'essai** trial run ▪ **galopade** *nf (ruée)* stampede ▪ **galoper** *vi (cheval)* to gallop; *(personne)* to rush; **inflation galopante** galloping inflation

galopin [galɔpɛ̃] *nm Fam* urchin

galvaniser [galvanize] *vt* to galvanize

galvauder [galvode] *vt (talent, avantage)* to misuse

gambade [gɑ̃bad] *nf* leap ▪ **gambader** *vi* to leap *or* frisk about

gambas [gãbas] *nfpl* large prawns

Gambie [gãbi] *nf* **la G.** The Gambia

gamelle [gamɛl] *nf (de chien)* bowl; *(d'ouvrier)* billy(can); *(de soldat)* mess tin; *Fam* **se prendre une g.** *Br* to come a cropper, *Am* to take a spill

gamin, -ine [gamɛ̃, -in] **1** *nmf Fam (enfant)* kid **2** *adj (puéril)* childish ▪**gaminerie** *nf (comportement)* childishness; *(acte)* childish prank

gamme [gam] *nf Mus* scale; *(éventail)* range; **téléviseur haut/bas de g.** top-of-the-range/ bottom-of-the-range television

gammée [game] *adj f* **croix g.** swastika

gang [gãg] *nm* gang ▪**gangster** *nm* gangster

Gange [gãʒ] *nm* **le G.** the Ganges

gangrène [gãgrɛn] *nf Méd* gangrene ▪**se gangrener** [sǝgãgrǝne] *upr* to become gangrenous

gant [gã] *nm* glove; *Fig* **aller comme un g. à qn** *(vêtement)* to fit sb like a glove; *Fig* **jeter/relever le g.** to throw down/take up the gauntlet; **g. de boxe** boxing glove; **g. de toilette** *Br* ≃ facecloth, *Am* ≃ washcloth ▪**ganté, -ée** *adj (main)* gloved; *(personne)* wearing gloves

garage [garaʒ] *nm (pour véhicules)* garage ▪**garagiste** *nmf (mécanicien)* garage mechanic; *(propriétaire)* garage owner

garant, -ante [garã, -ãt] *nmf Jur (personne)* guarantor; **se porter g. de qn** to stand guarantor for sb; **se porter g. de qch** to vouch for sth

garantie [garãti] *nf* guarantee; *Fig (précaution)* safeguard; **être sous g.** to be under guarantee ▪**garantir** *ut* to guarantee; *(emprunt)* to secure; **g. à qn que...** to give sb the guarantee that...; **g. qch de qch** *(protéger)* to protect sth from sth; **je te le garantis** I can vouch for it

garce [gars] *nf Fam Péj* bitch

garçon [garsɔ̃] *nm* boy; *(jeune homme)* young man; *(serveur)* waiter; **de g.** *(comportement)* boyish; **vieux g.** (old) bachelor; **g. de café** waiter; **g. d'honneur** best man; **g. manqué** tomboy ▪**garçonnet** *nm* little boy ▪**garçonnière** *nf* bachelor *Br* flat *or Am* apartment

garde [gard] **1** *nm (gardien)* guard; *(soldat)* guardsman; **g. champêtre** rural policeman; **g. du corps** bodyguard; **g. des Sceaux** Justice Minister

2 *nf* (**a**) *(d'enfants, de bagages)* care, custody *(de* of); **avoir la g. de** to be in charge of; **faire bonne g.** to keep a close watch; **prendre g.** to pay attention (**à qch** to sth); **prendre g. de ne pas faire qch** to be careful not to do sth; **mettre qn en g.** to warn sb (**contre** against); **mise en g.** warning; **être de g.** to be on duty; *(soldat)* to be on guard duty; **médecin de g.** duty doctor; **monter la g.** to mount guard; **être sur ses gardes** to be on one's guard; **g. à vue** police custody (**b**) *(escorte, soldats)* guard

3 *nmf* **g. d'enfants** childminder; **g. de nuit** *(de malade)* night nurse ▪**garde-à-vous** *nm inv Mil* (position of) attention; **se mettre au g.** to stand to attention ▪**garde-boue** *nm inv Br* mudguard, *Am* fender ▪**garde-chasse** *(pl gardes-chasses)* *nm* gamekeeper ▪**garde-côte** *(pl garde-côtes)* *nm (bateau)* coastguard vessel ▪**garde-fou** *(pl garde-fous)* *nm (rambarde)* railings; *(mur)* parapet ▪**garde-malade** *(pl gardes-malades)* *nmf* nurse ▪**garde-manger** *nm inv (armoire)* food safe; *(pièce)* pantry, *Br* larder ▪**garde-robe** *(pl garde-robes)* *nf (habits, armoire)* wardrobe, *Am* closet

garder [garde] **1** *ut (conserver)* to keep; *(vêtement)* to keep on; *(habitude)* to keep up; *(surveiller)* to look after; *(défendre)* to protect; **g. qn à dîner** to get sb to stay for dinner; **g. la chambre** to keep to one's room; **g. le lit** to stay in bed; **g. la tête** to keep a cool head **2 se garder** *upr (aliment)* to keep; **se g. de qch** to beware of sth; **se g. de faire qch** to take care not to do sth

garderie [gardǝri] *nf Br* (day) nursery, *Am* daycare center

gardien, -ienne [gardjɛ̃, -jɛn] *nmf (d'immeuble, d'hôtel)* caretaker, *Am* janitor; *(de prison)* (prison) guard, *Br* warder; *(de zoo, parc)* keeper; *(de musée)* *Br* attendant, *Am* guard; *Fig* **g. de** *(libertés)* guardian of; *Football* **g. de but** goalkeeper; **g.** childminder, baby-sitter; **g. de nuit** night watchman; **g. de la paix** policeman

gardon [gardɔ̃] *nm* roach; *Fig* **frais comme un g.** fresh as a daisy

gare¹ [gar] *nf (pour trains)* station; **g. routière** bus *or Br* coach station

gare² [gar] *exclam* **g. à toi si on l'apprend** woe betide you if anyone finds out; **g. aux orties!** mind the nettles!; **sans crier g.** without warning

garer [gare] **1** *ut (voiture)* to park **2 se garer** *upr (automobiliste)* to park; **se g. de qch** *(se protéger)* to steer clear of sth

gargariser [gargarize] **se gargariser** *upr* to gargle ▪**gargarisme** *nm* gargle

gargote [gargɔt] *nf Péj* cheap restaurant

gargouiller [garguje] *vi (fontaine, eau)* to gurgle; *(ventre)* to rumble ▪**gargouillis, gargouillement** *nm* gurgling; *(de ventre)* rumbling

garnement [garnǝmã] *nm* rascal

garnir [garnir] *ut (équiper)* to fit out (**de** with); *(couvrir)* to cover; *(remplir)* to fill; *(magasin)* to stock (**de** with); *(tiroir)* to line; *(robe, chapeau)* to trim (**de** with); *Culin* to garnish; **garni, -ie** *adj (plat)* served with vegetables; *Fig* **bien g.** *(portefeuille)* well-lined ▪**garniture** *nf Culin* garnish; *Aut* **g. de frein** brake lining; **g. de lit** bedding

garnison [garnizɔ̃] *nf* garrison

garrot [garo] *nm Méd (lien)* tourniquet
gars [gɑ] *nm Fam* fellow, guy
gas-oil [gazwal] *nm* diesel (oil)
gaspiller [gaspije] *vt* to waste ▪ **gaspillage** *nm* waste
gastrique [gastrik] *adj* gastric
gastronome [gastrɔnɔm] *nmf* gourmet ▪ **gastronomie** *nf* gastronomy
gâteau, -x [gɑto] *nm* cake; *Fam* **c'était du g.** *(facile)* it was a piece of cake; **g. de riz** rice pudding; **g. sec** *Br* biscuit, *Am* cookie
gâter [gɑte] **1** *vt* to spoil **2 se gâter** *vpr (aliment, dent)* to go bad; *(temps, situation)* to take a turn for the worse; *(relations)* to turn sour ▪ **gâté, -ée** *adj (dent, fruit)* bad ▪ **gâterie** *nf (cadeau, friandise)* treat
gâteux, -euse [gɑtø, -øz] *adj* senile
gauche¹ [goʃ] **1** *adj (côté, main)* left **2** *nf* **la g.** *(côté)* the left (side); *Pol* the left (wing); **à g.** *(tourner)* (to the) left; *(marcher, se tenir)* to the left, on the left(-hand) side; **de g.** *(fenêtre)* left-hand; *(parti, politique)* left-wing; **à g. de** on or to the left of ▪ **gaucher, -ère 1** *adj* left-handed **2** *nmf* left-hander ▪ **gauchisant, -ante** *adj Pol* left-leaning; **être g.** to have left-wing sympathies ▪ **gauchiste** *adj & nmf Pol* (extreme) leftist
gauche² [goʃ] *adj (maladroit)* awkward ▪ **gauchement** *adv* awkwardly ▪ **gaucherie** *nf* awkwardness
gauchir [goʃir] *vti* to warp
gaufre [gofr] *nf* waffle ▪ **gaufrette** *nf* wafer (biscuit)
Gaule [gol] *nf Hist* **la G.** *(pays)* Gaul ▪ **gaulois, -oise 1** *adj* Gallic; *Fig (propos)* bawdy **2** *nmpl* *Hist* **les G.** the Gauls ▪ **gauloiserie** *nf (plaisanterie)* bawdy joke
gaule [gol] *nf* long pole; *Pêche* fishing rod
gausser [gose] **se gausser** *vpr Littéraire* to mock
gaver [gave] **1** *vt (animal)* to force-feed; *(personne)* to stuff (**de** with) **2 se gaver** *vpr* to stuff oneself (**de** with)
gay [gɛ, ge] *adj & nmf Fam (homosexuel)* gay
gaz [gaz] *nm inv* gas; **réchaud/masque à g.** gas stove/mask; **avoir des g.** to have wind; *Fam* **il y a de l'eau dans le g.** things aren't going too well; **g. carbonique** carbon dioxide; **g. d'échappement** exhaust fumes; **g. lacrymogène** tear gas ▪ **gazeux, -euse** *adj (état)* gaseous; *(boisson, eau)* *Br* fizzy, carbonated ▪ **gazomètre** *nm Br* gasometer, gas storage tank
Gaza [gaza] *nf* Gaza; **la bande de G.** the Gaza Strip
gaze [gaz] *nf* gauze
gazelle [gazɛl] *nf* gazelle
gazer [gaze] **1** *vt (asphyxier)* to gas **2** *vi Fam* **ça gaze?** how's it going?; **ça gaze!** everything's just fine!

gazette [gazɛt] *nf (journal)* newspaper
gazinière [gazinjɛr] *nf Br* gas cooker, *Am* gas stove
gazoduc [gazɔdyk] *nm* gas pipeline
gazole [gazɔl] *nm* diesel oil
gazon [gazɔ̃] *nm (herbe)* grass; *(surface)* lawn
gazouiller [gazuje] *vi (oiseau)* to chirp; *(bébé, ruisseau)* to babble ▪ **gazouillis, gazouille-ment** *nm (d'oiseau)* chirping; *(de bébé)* babbling
GDF [ʒedeɛf] *(abrév* Gaz de France*)* *nm* = French gas company
geai [ʒɛ] *nm* jay
géant, -e [ʒeɑ̃, -ɑ̃t] *adj & nmf* giant
geindre* [ʒɛ̃dr] *vi (gémir)* to moan; *Fam (se plaindre)* to whine
gel [ʒɛl] *nm* (a) *(temps, glace)* frost; *Écon* **g. des salaires** wage freeze (b) *(pour cheveux)* gel ▪ **gelé, -ée** *adj* frozen; *Méd (doigts, mains, pieds)* frostbitten ▪ **gelée** *nf* (a) frost; **g. blanche** ground frost (b) *(de viande)* jelly; *(de fruits)* *Br* jelly, *Am* jello ▪ **geler 1** *vt* to freeze **2** *vi* to freeze; **on gèle ici** it's freezing here **3** *v impersonnel* **il gèle** it's freezing
gélatine [ʒelatin] *nf* gelatine
gélule [ʒelyl] *nf* capsule
Gémeaux [ʒemo] *nmpl* **les G.** *(signe)* Gemini; **être G.** to be (a) Gemini
gémir [ʒemir] *vi* to groan, to moan ▪ **gémissement** *nm* groan, moan
gencive [ʒɑ̃siv] *nf* gum
gendarme [ʒɑ̃darm] *nm* gendarme, policeman; **g. couché** sleeping policeman ▪ **gendarmerie** *nf (corps)* police force; *(local)* police headquarters
gendre [ʒɑ̃dr] *nm* son-in-law
gène [ʒɛn] *nm* gene
gêne [ʒɛn] *nf (trouble physique)* discomfort; *(confusion)* embarrassment; *(dérangement)* inconvenience; **dans la g.** *(à court d'argent)* in financial difficulties
généalogie [ʒenealɔʒi] *nf* genealogy ▪ **généalogique** *adj* genealogical; **arbre g.** family tree
gêner [ʒene] **1** *vt (déranger, irriter)* to bother; *(troubler)* to embarrass; *(mouvement, action)* to hamper; *(circulation)* to hold up; **g. qn** *(vêtement)* to be uncomfortable on sb; *(par sa présence)* to be in sb's way; **ça ne me gêne pas** I don't mind (**si** if) **2 se gêner** *vpr (se déranger)* to put oneself out; **ne te gêne pas pour moi!** don't mind me! ▪ **gênant, -ante** *adj (objet)* cumbersome; *(présence, situation)* awkward; *(bruit, personne)* annoying ▪ **gêné, -ée** *adj (intimidé)* embarrassed; *(silence, sourire)* awkward; *(sans argent)* short of money
général, -e, -aux, -ales [ʒeneral, -o] **1** *adj* general; **en g.** in general **2** *nm Mil* general; **oui, mon g.!** yes, general! ▪ **générale** *nf Théâtre* dress rehearsal ▪ **généralement** *adv*

generally; **g. parlant** broadly *or* generally speaking ▪ **généralité** *nf* generality

généralisation [ʒeneralizasjɔ̃] *nf* generalization ▪ **généraliser 1** *vti* to generalize **2 se généraliser** *upr* to become widespread ▪ **généraliste** *nmf (médecin)* general practitioner, GP

générateur [ʒeneratœr] *nm* *Él* generator

génération [ʒenerasjɔ̃] *nf* generation

génératrice [ʒeneratris] *nf* *Él* generator

générer [ʒenere] *vt* to generate

généreux, -euse [ʒenerø, -øz] *adj* generous (**de** with) ▪ **généreusement** *adv* generously ▪ **générosité** *nf* generosity

générique [ʒenerik] **1** *nm (de film)* credits **2** *adj* **produit g.** generic product

genèse [ʒənɛz] *nf* genesis

genêt [ʒəne] *nm* broom

génétique [ʒenetik] **1** *nf* genetics *(sing)* **2** *adj* genetic; **manipulation g.** genetic engineering ▪ **génétiquement** *adv* genetically; **g. modifié** genetically modified

Genève [ʒənɛv] *nm ou f* Geneva

génial, -e, -iaux, -iales [ʒenjal, -jo] *adj (personne, invention)* brilliant; *Fam (formidable)* great, fantastic

> Il faut noter que l'adjectif anglais **genial** est un faux ami. Il signifie **cordial**.

génie [ʒeni] *nm* (**a**) *(aptitude, personne)* genius; **inventeur de g.** inventor of genius; **avoir le g. pour faire/de qch** to have a genius for doing/ for sth (**b**) **g. civil** civil engineering; **g. génétique/informatique** genetic/computer engineering; **g. militaire** engineering corps (**c**) *(esprit)* genie, spirit; **bon/mauvais g.** good/ evil genie

génital, -e, -aux, -ales [ʒenital, -o] *adj* genital; **organes génitaux** genitals

génocide [ʒenɔsid] *nm* genocide

genou, -x [ʒ(ə)nu] *nm* knee; **être à genoux** to be kneeling (down); **se mettre à genoux** to kneel (down); **prendre qn sur ses genoux** to take sb on one's lap *or* knee; **écrire sur ses genoux** to write on one's lap ▪ **genouillère** *nf* kneepad

genre [ʒɑ̃r] *nm (espèce)* kind, sort; *(attitude)* manner; *Littérature & Cin* genre; *Grammaire* gender; **en tous genres** of all kinds; **ce n'est pas son g.** that's not like him; **le g. humain** mankind

gens [ʒɑ̃] *nmpl* people; **jeunes g.** young people; *(hommes)* young men; **de petites g.** people of humble means; **g. de maison** domestic servants

gentil, -ille [ʒɑ̃ti, -ij] *adj (aimable)* nice (**avec** to); *(sage)* good; **une gentille somme** a nice little sum ▪ **gentillesse** *nf* kindness; **avoir la g. de faire qch** to be kind enough to do sth ▪ **gentiment** *adv (aimablement)* kindly; *(sagement)* nicely

> Il faut noter que les termes anglais **genteel** et **gentle** sont des faux amis. Le premier signifie **respectable** ou **affecté**, le second signifie **doux**.

gentilhomme [ʒɑ̃tijɔm] *(pl* **gentilshommes** [ʒɑ̃tizɔm]*) nm Hist (noble)* gentleman

géographie [ʒeɔgrafi] *nf* geography ▪ **géographique** *adj* geographical

geôlier, -ière [ʒolje, -jɛr] *nmf* jailer

géologie [ʒeɔlɔʒi] *nf* geology ▪ **géologique** *adj* geological ▪ **géologue** *nmf* geologist

géomètre [ʒeɔmɛtr] *nm* surveyor

géométrie [ʒeɔmetri] *nf* geometry; *Fig* **à g. variable** ever-changing ▪ **géométrique** *adj* geometric(al)

géranium [ʒeranjɔm] *nm* geranium

gérant, -ante [ʒerɑ̃, -ɑ̃t] *nmf* manager ▪ **gérance** *nf (gestion)* management

gerbe [ʒɛrb] *nf (de blé)* sheaf; *(de fleurs)* bunch; *(d'eau)* spray; *(d'étincelles)* shower

gercer [ʒɛrse] *vi, se gercer* *upr (peau, lèvres)* to chap; **avoir les lèvres gercées** to have chapped lips ▪ **gerçure** *nf* chap, crack; **avoir des gerçures aux mains** to have chapped hands

gérer [ʒere] *vt* to manage

germain, -aine [ʒɛrmɛ̃, -ɛn] *adj voir* **cousin**

germanique [ʒɛrmanik] *adj* Germanic

germe [ʒɛrm] *nm (microbe)* germ; *(de plante)* shoot; *Fig (d'une idée)* seed, germ ▪ **germer** *vi (graine)* to start to grow; *(pomme de terre)* to sprout; *Fig (idée)* to germinate

gérondif [ʒerɔ̃dif] *nm Grammaire* gerund

gésir [ʒezir] *vi Littéraire (être étendu)* to be lying; **il gît/gisait** he is/was lying; **ci-gît...** *(sur tombe)* here lies...

gestation [ʒɛstasjɔ̃] *nf* gestation

geste [ʒɛst] *nm* gesture; **ne pas faire un g.** *(ne pas bouger)* not to make a move; **faire un g. de la main** to wave one's hand; **faire un g.** *(bouger, agir)* to make a gesture ▪ **gesticuler** *vi* to gesticulate

gestion [ʒɛstjɔ̃] *nf (action)* management; **g. du personnel/de patrimoine/des affaires** personnel/property/business management ▪ **gestionnaire** *nmf* administrator

geyser [ʒezɛr] *nm* geyser

Ghana [gana] *nm* **le G.** Ghana

ghetto [gɛto] *nm* ghetto

gibecière [ʒibɛsjɛr] *nf (de chasseur)* game bag

gibier [ʒibje] *nm* game; **le gros g.** big game; *Fig* **g. de potence** gallows bird

giboulée [ʒibule] *nf* sudden shower; **giboulées de mars** ≃ April showers

gicler [ʒikle] *vi (liquide)* to spurt out; *(boue)* to splash up ▪ **giclée** *nf* spurt ▪ **gicleur** *nm Aut* jet

gifle [ʒifl] *nf* slap in the face ▪ **gifler** *vt* **g. qn** to slap sb in the face

gigantesque [ʒiɡɑ̃tɛsk] adj gigantic

gigogne [ʒiɡɔɲ] adj **tables gigognes** nest of tables; **poupées gigognes** nest of (Russian) dolls

gigot [ʒiɡo] nm leg of mutton/lamb

gigoter [ʒiɡɔte] vi Fam to wriggle, to fidget

gilet [ʒile] nm (cardigan) cardigan; (de costume) Br waistcoat, Am vest; **g. pare-balles** bulletproof vest; **g. de sauvetage** life jacket, life vest

gin [dʒin] nm gin

gingembre [ʒɛ̃ʒɑ̃br] nm ginger

girafe [ʒiraf] nf giraffe

giratoire [ʒiratwar] nm Br roundabout, Am traffic circle

girofle [ʒirɔfl] nm **clou de g.** clove

giroflée [ʒirɔfle] nf wallflower

girouette [ʒirwɛt] nf Br weathercock, Am weathervane

gisait [ʒize] voir **gésir**

gisement [ʒizmɑ̃] nm (de minerai) deposit; **g. de pétrole** oilfield

gît [ʒi] voir **gésir**

gitan, -ane [ʒitɑ̃, -an] nmf gipsy

gîte [ʒit] nm (abri) resting place; **donner le g. et le couvert à qn** to give sb room and board; **g. rural** gîte, = self-catering holiday cottage or apartment

givre [ʒivr] nm frost ▪ **givré, -ée** adj frostcovered; Fam (fou) nuts, crazy ▪ **se givrer** vpr (pare-brise) to ice up, to frost up

glabre [ɡlabr] adj (visage) smooth

glace [ɡlas] nf (a) (eau gelée) ice; (crème glacée) ice cream (b) (vitre) window; (miroir) mirror; Fig **briser la g.** to break the ice; **il est resté de g.** he showed no emotion

glacer [ɡlase] 1 vt (durcir) to freeze; (gâteau) to ice; Fig (sang) to chill; **à vous g. le sang** spinechilling 2 **se glacer** vpr **mon sang s'est glacé dans mes veines** my blood ran cold ▪ **glaçage** nm (de gâteau) icing ▪ **glacé, -ée** adj (eau, pièce) ice-cold, icy; (vent) freezing, icy; (thé, café) iced; (fruit) candied; (papier) glazed; Fig (accueil) icy, chilly; **avoir les pieds glacés** to have icy or frozen feet

glacial, -e, -iaux, -iales [ɡlasjal, -jo] adj icy

glacier [ɡlasje] nm (a) Géol glacier (b) (vendeur) ice-cream seller

glacière [ɡlasjɛr] nf (boîte) icebox

glaçon [ɡlasɔ̃] nm Culin ice cube; Géol block of ice; (sur toit) icicle

glaïeul [ɡlajœl] nm gladiolus

glaire [ɡlɛr] nf Méd phlegm

glaise [ɡlɛz] nf clay

gland [ɡlɑ̃] nm Bot acorn; (pompon) tassel

glande [ɡlɑ̃d] nf gland

glander [ɡlɑ̃de] vi très Fam to laze around ▪ **glandeur, -euse** nmf très Fam layabout

glandouiller [ɡlɑ̃duje] vi très Fam to laze around

glaner [ɡlane] vt (blé, renseignement) to glean

glapir [ɡlapir] vi (chien) to yap

glas [ɡlɑ] nm (de cloche) knell; **on sonne le g.** the bell is tolling

glauque [ɡlok] adj sea-green; Fam (sinistre) creepy

glisse [ɡlis] nf **(sports de) g.** = sports involving sliding motion, eg skiing, surfing etc

glisser [ɡlise] 1 vt (introduire) to slip (**dans** into); (murmurer) to whisper 2 vi (involontairement) to slip; (volontairement) (sur glace) to slide; (sur l'eau) to glide; Fig **g. sur** (sujet) to gloss over; Ordinat **faire g.** (pointeur) to drag; **se laisser g. le long de la gouttière** to slide down the drainpipe; **ça glisse** it's slippery; **ça m'a glissé des mains** it slipped out of my hands 3 **se glisser** vpr **se g. dans/sous qch** to slip into/under sth ▪ **glissade** nf (involontaire) slip; (volontaire) slide ▪ **glissant, -ante** adj slippery ▪ **glissement** nm **g. de terrain** landslide

glissière [ɡlisjɛr] nf Tech runner, slide; **porte à g.** sliding door; Aut **g. de sécurité** crash barrier

global, -e, -aux, -ales [ɡlɔbal, -o] adj total, global; **somme globale** lump sum; Scol **méthode globale** word recognition method ▪ **globalement** adv overall

globe [ɡlɔb] nm globe; **g. oculaire** eyeball; **g. terrestre** (mappemonde) globe

globule [ɡlɔbyl] nm (d'air, d'eau) globule; (de sang) blood cell; **globules blancs/rouges** white/red blood cells

globuleux, -euse [ɡlɔbylø, -øz] adj **yeux g.** bulging eyes

gloire [ɡlwar] nf (renom) glory; (personne célèbre) celebrity; **tirer g. de qch** to glory in sth; **à la g. de qn** in praise of sb ▪ **glorieux, -ieuse** adj glorious ▪ **glorifier** 1 vt to glorify 2 **se glorifier** vpr **se g. de qch** to glory in sth

glossaire [ɡlɔsɛr] nm glossary

glouglou [ɡluɡlu] nm Fam (de liquide) gurgle ▪ **glouglouter** vi Fam to gurgle

glousser [ɡluse] vi (poule) to cluck; (personne) to chuckle ▪ **gloussement** nm clucking; (de personne) chuckling

glouton, -onne [ɡlutɔ̃, -ɔn] 1 adj greedy, gluttonous 2 nmf glutton ▪ **gloutonnerie** nf gluttony

gluant, -e [ɡlyɑ̃, -ɑ̃t] adj sticky

glucose [ɡlykoz] nm glucose

glycérine [ɡliserin] nf glycerine

glycine [ɡlisin] nf (plante) wisteria

gnome [ɡnom] nm gnome

gnon [ɲɔ̃] nm Fam thump; **se prendre un g.** to get thumped

go [ɡo] **tout de go** adv straight away; **répondre tout de go** to answer straight off

goal [ɡol] nm Football goalkeeper

gobelet [ɡɔblɛ] nm tumbler; (de plastique, de papier) cup

gober [gɔbe] *vt (œuf, mouche)* to gulp down; *Fam (croire)* to swallow

godasse [gɔdas] *nf Fam* shoe

godet [gɔdɛ] *nm (récipient)* pot; *Fam (verre)* drink

godillot [gɔdijo] *nm Fam* clodhopper

goéland [gɔelɑ̃] *nm* (sea)gull

goélette [gɔelɛt] *nf* schooner

gogo[1] [gogo] *nm Fam (homme naïf)* sucker

gogo[2] [gogo] **à gogo** *adv Fam* **whisky à g.** whisky galore

goguenard, -arde [gɔgnar, -ard] *adj* mocking

goinfre [gwɛ̃fr] *nmf Fam (glouton)* pig ▪ **se goinfrer** *vpr Fam* to stuff oneself (**de** with); to pig out (**de** on)

golf [gɔlf] *nm Sport* golf; *(terrain)* golf course ▪ **golfeur, -euse** *nmf* golfer

golfe [gɔlf] *nm* gulf, bay

gomme [gɔm] *nf (substance)* gum; *(à effacer)* eraser, *Br* rubber; *Fam* **mettre la g.** *(accélérer)* to get a move on; *(en voiture)* to step on it; *Fam* **à la g.** useless ▪ **gommé, -ée** *adj (papier)* gummed ▪ **gommer** *vt (effacer)* to rub out, to erase

gond [gɔ̃] *nm (de porte)* hinge; *Fig* **sortir de ses gonds** to fly off the handle

gondole [gɔ̃dɔl] *nf (barque, présentoir)* gondola ▪ **gondolier** *nm* gondolier

gondoler [gɔ̃dɔle] **1** *vi (planche)* to warp; *(papier)* to crinkle **2 se gondoler** *vpr (planche)* to warp; *(papier)* to crinkle; *Fam (rire)* to fall about laughing

gonflable [gɔ̃flabl] *adj* inflatable

gonfler [gɔ̃fle] **1** *vt* to swell; *(pneu)* to inflate; *très Fam (énerver)* to get up sb's nose **2** *vi* to swell **3 se gonfler** *vpr* to swell ▪ **gonflé, -ée** *adj* swollen; *Fam* **être g.** *(courageux)* to have plenty of pluck; *(insolent)* to have a lot of nerve ▪ **gonflement** [-əmɑ̃] *nm* swelling

gong [gɔ̃g] *nm* gong

gorge [gɔrʒ] *nf* throat; *Littéraire (poitrine)* bosom; *Géog* gorge; **avoir la g. serrée** to have a lump in one's throat; **rire à g. déployée** to roar with laughter; *Fig* **faire des gorges chaudes de qch** to have a field day pouring scorn on sth

gorgé, -ée [gɔrʒe] *adj* **g. de** *(saturé)* gorged with

gorgée [gɔrʒe] *nf* mouthful; **petite g.** sip; **d'une seule g.** in one gulp

gorger [gɔrʒe] **1** *vt (remplir)* to stuff (**de** with) **2 se gorger** *vpr* **se g. de** to gorge oneself with

gorille [gɔrij] *nm (animal)* gorilla; *Fam (garde du corps)* bodyguard

gosier [gozje] *nm* throat

gosse [gɔs] *nmf Fam (enfant)* kid

gothique [gɔtik] *adj & nm* Gothic

gouache [gwaʃ] *nf (peinture)* gouache

goudron [gudrɔ̃] *nm* tar ▪ **goudronner** *vt* to tar

gouffre [gufr] *nm* abyss

goujat [guʒa] *nm* boor

goulot [gulo] *nm (de bouteille)* neck; **boire au g.** to drink from the bottle

goulu, -ue [guly] *adj* greedy ▪ **goulûment** *adv* greedily

goupille [gupij] *nf (de grenade)* pin

goupiller [gupije] *Fam* **1** *vt (arranger)* to fix up **2 se goupiller** *vpr* **ça s'est bien goupillé** it worked out (well); **ça s'est mal goupillé** it didn't work out

gourde [gurd] *nf (à eau)* water bottle, flask; *Fam Péj (femme niaise)* dope

gourdin [gurdɛ̃] *nm* club, cudgel

gourer [gure] **se gourer** *vpr Fam* to make a mistake

gourmand, -ande [gurmɑ̃, -ɑ̃d] **1** *adj* fond of food; *Fig (intéressé)* greedy; **g. de qch** fond of sth **2** *nmf* hearty eater ▪ **gourmandise** *nf* fondness for food; **gourmandises** *(mets)* delicacies

gourmet [gurmɛ] *nm* gourmet; **fin g.** gourmet

gourmette [gurmɛt] *nf (bracelet)* chain

gousse [gus] *nf* **g. d'ail** clove of garlic

goût [gu] *nm* taste; **de bon g.** in good taste; **sans g.** tasteless; **par g.** by choice; **avoir du g.** *(personne)* to have good taste; **avoir un g. de noisette** to taste of hazelnut; **prendre g. à qch** to take a liking to sth; *Fam* **quelque chose dans ce g.-là!** something of that order!

goûter [gute] **1** *vt (aliment)* to taste; *(apprécier)* to enjoy; **g. à qch** to taste (a little of) sth **2** *vi* to have an afternoon snack, *Br* to have tea **3** *nm* afternoon snack, *Br* tea

goutte [gut] *nf* **(a)** *(de liquide)* drop; **couler g. à g.** to drip **(b)** *Méd* gout ▪ **goutte-à-goutte** *nm inv Méd* drip ▪ **gouttelette** *nf* droplet ▪ **goutter** *vi* to drip

gouttière [gutjɛr] *nf (le long du toit)* gutter; *(le long du mur)* drainpipe

gouvernail [guvɛrnaj] *nm (pale)* rudder; *(barre)* helm

gouvernante [guvɛrnɑ̃t] *nf* governess

gouvernement [guvɛrnəmɑ̃] *nm* government ▪ **gouvernemental, -e, -aux, -ales** *adj* **politique gouvernementale** government policy; **l'équipe gouvernementale** the government

gouverner [guvɛrne] *vti Pol & Fig* to govern, to rule ▪ **gouvernants** *nmpl* rulers ▪ **gouverneur** *nm* governor

grabuge [graby3] *nm Fam* **il y a du g.** there's trouble, *Br* there are ructions

grâce [gras] **1** *nf (charme) & Rel* grace; *Littéraire (faveur) Br* favour, *Am* favor; *(acquittement)* pardon; **de bonne/mauvaise g.** with good/bad grace; **crier g.** to beg for mercy; **donner le coup de g. à** to finish off; **faire g. de qch à qn** to spare sb sth; **être dans les bonnes grâces de**

qn to be in favour with sb; **rendre g. à qn** to give thanks to sb; **délai de g.** period of grace; **g. présidentielle** presidential pardon **2** *prép* **g. à** thanks to

gracier [grasje] *vt (condamné)* to pardon

gracieux, -ieuse [grasjø, -jøz] *adj (élégant)* graceful; *(aimable)* gracious; *(gratuit)* gratuitous; **à titre g.** free (of charge) ▪ **gracieusement** *adv* gracefully; *(aimablement)* graciously; *(gratuitement)* free (of charge)

gracile [grasil] *adj Littéraire* slender

gradation [gradɑsjɔ̃] *nf* gradation

grade [grad] *nm (militaire)* rank; **monter en g.** to be promoted ▪ **gradé** *nm Mil* non-commissioned officer

gradins [gradɛ̃] *nmpl (d'amphithéâtre)* rows of seats; *(de stade) Br* terraces, *Am* bleachers

graduel, -uelle [graduɛl] *adj* gradual

graduer [gradue] *vt (règle)* to graduate; *(augmenter)* to increase gradually

graffiti [grafiti] *nmpl* graffiti

grain [grɛ̃] *nm* (**a**) *(de blé) & Fig* grain; *(de café)* bean; *(de poussière)* speck; *(de chapelet)* bead; **le g.** *(de cuir, de papier)* the grain; *Fam* **avoir un g.** to be not quite right in the head; *Fam* **mettre son g. de sel** to stick one's oar in; **g. de beauté** mole; *(sur le visage)* beauty spot; **g. de raisin** grape (**b**) *(averse)* shower

graine [grɛn] *nf* seed; **mauvaise g.** *(enfant)* rotten lot; *Br* bad lot; **en prendre de la g.** to learn from someone's example

graisse [grɛs] *nf* fat; *(lubrifiant)* grease ▪ **graissage** *nm (de véhicule)* lubrication ▪ **graisser** *vt* to grease ▪ **graisseux, -euse** *adj (vêtement)* greasy, oily; *(bourrelets, tissu)* fatty

grammaire [gramɛr] *nf* grammar; **livre de g.** grammar (book) ▪ **grammatical, -e, -aux, -ales** *adj* grammatical

gramme [gram] *nm* gram(me)

grand, -e [grɑ̃, grɑ̃d] **1** *adj* big, large; *(en hauteur)* tall; *(chaleur, découverte, âge, mérite, ami)* great; *(bruit)* loud; *(différence)* big, great; *(adulte, mûr, plus âgé)* grown-up, big; *(âme)* noble; *(illustre)* great; **le g. frère** *(plus âgé)* big brother; **le g. air** the open air; **il est g. temps que je parte** it's high time that I left; **il n'y avait pas g. monde** there were not many people **2** *adv* **g. ouvert** *(yeux, fenêtre)* wide open; **ouvrir g.** to open wide; **en g.** on a grand or large scale **3** *nmf (à l'école)* senior; *(adulte)* grown-up ▪ **grandement** *adv (beaucoup)* greatly; *(généreusement)* grandly; **avoir g. de quoi vivre** to have plenty to live on ▪ **grand-mère** *(pl* **grands-mères)** *nf* grandmother ▪ **grand-père** *(pl* **grands-pères)** *nm* grandfather ▪ **grand-route** *(pl* **grand-routes)** *nf* main road ▪ **grands-parents** *nmpl* grandparents

grand-chose [grɑ̃ʃoz] *pron* **pas g.** not much

Grande-Bretagne [grɑ̃dbrətaɲ] *nf* **la G.** Great Britain

grandeur [grɑ̃dœr] *nf (importance, gloire)* greatness; *(dimension)* size; *(majesté, splendeur)* grandeur; **avoir la folie des grandeurs** to have delusions of grandeur; **g. d'âme** magnanimity; **g. nature** life-size

grandiose [grɑ̃djoz] *adj* imposing

grandir [grɑ̃dir] **1** *vi (en taille)* to grow; *(en âge)* to grow up; *(bruit)* to grow louder; **g. de 2 cm** to grow 2 cm **2** *vt* **g. qn** *(faire paraître plus grand)* to make sb look taller

grange [grɑ̃ʒ] *nf* barn

granit(e) [granit] *nm* granite

granule [granyl] *nm* granule

graphique [grafik] **1** *adj (signe, art)* graphic **2** *nm* graph; *Ordinat* graphic

grappe [grap] *nf (de fruits)* cluster; **g. de raisin** bunch of grapes

> Il faut noter que le nom anglais **grape** est un faux ami. Il signifie **grain de raisin**.

grappin [grapɛ̃] *nm Fam* **mettre le g. sur qn/qch** to get one's hands on sb/sth

gras, grasse [grɑ, grɑs] **1** *adj (personne, ventre)* fat; *(aliment)* fatty; *(graisseux)* greasy, oily; *(plante, contour)* thick; *(rire)* throaty; *(toux)* loose; **faire la grasse matinée** to have a lie-in **2** *nm (de viande)* fat ▪ **grassement** *adv* **g. payé** handsomely paid ▪ **grassouillet, -ette** *adj* plump

gratifier [gratifje] *vt* **g. qn de qch** to present sb with sth ▪ **gratification** *nf (prime)* bonus

gratin [gratɛ̃] *nm Culin (plat)* = baked dish with a cheese topping; *Fam (élite)* upper crust; **chou-fleur au g.** cauliflower cheese; **g. dauphinois** = sliced potatoes baked with milk; **g. de macaronis** *Br* macaroni cheese, *Am* macaroni and cheese ▪ **gratiner** *vt* to brown

gratis [gratis] *adv* free (of charge)

gratitude [gratityd] *nf* gratitude

gratte-ciel [gratsjɛl] *nm inv* skyscraper

gratte-papier [gratpapje] *nm inv Péj (employé)* pen-pusher

gratter [grate] **1** *vt (avec un outil)* to scrape; *(avec les ongles, les griffes)* to scratch; *(boue)* to scrape off; *(effacer)* to scratch out; *Fam* **ça me gratte** it itches **2** *vi (à la porte)* to scratch; *(tissu)* to be scratchy **3** **se gratter** *upr* to scratch oneself ▪ **grattoir** *nm* scraper

gratuit, -uite [gratɥi, -ɥit] *adj (billet, entrée)* free; *(hypothèse, acte)* gratuitous ▪ **gratuité** *nf* **la g. de l'enseignement** free education ▪ **gratuitement** *adv (sans payer)* free (of charge); *(sans motif)* gratuitously

> Il faut noter que le nom anglais **gratuity** est un faux ami. Il signifie **pourboire**.

gravats [grava] *nmpl* rubble, debris

grave [grav] *adj (maladie, faute)* serious; *(juge, visage)* grave; *(voix)* deep, low; **ce n'est pas g.!** it's not important! ▪ **gravement** *adv (malade, menacé)* seriously; *(dignement)* gravely

graver [grave] *vt (sur métal)* to engrave; *(sur bois)* to carve; *(disque)* to cut; *(dans sa mémoire)* to engrave ▪ **graveur** *nm* engraver; **g. de CD** CD burner or writer

gravier [gravje] *nm* gravel ▪ **gravillon** *nm* piece of gravel; **gravillons** gravel, *Br* (loose) chippings

gravir [gravir] *vt* to climb; *Fig* **g. les échelons** to climb the ladder

gravité [gravite] *nf (de situation)* seriousness; *(solennité)* & *Phys* gravity; **accident sans g.** minor accident; *Phys* **centre de g.** centre of gravity

graviter [gravite] *vi* to revolve *(autour* around) ▪ **gravitation** *nf* gravitation

gravure [gravyr] *nf (image)* print; *(action, art)* engraving; **g. sur bois** *(action)* woodcarving; *(objet)* woodcut

gré [gre] *nm* **à son g.** *(goût)* to his/her taste; *(désir)* as he/she pleases; **de son plein g.** of one's own free will; **de bon g.** willingly; **contre le g. de qn** against sb's will; **bon g. mal g.** whether we/you/*etc* like it or not; **de g. ou de force** one way or another; **au g. de** *(vent)* at the mercy of; *Formel* **savoir g. de qch à qn** to be thankful to sb for sth

Grèce [gres] *nf* **la G.** Greece ▪ **grec, grecque 1** *adj* Greek **2** *nmf* **G., Grecque** Greek **3** *nm (langue)* Greek

greffe [gref] **1** *nf (de peau, d'arbre)* graft; *(d'organe)* transplant **2** *nm Jur* record office ▪ **greffer** *vt (peau)* & *Bot* to graft *(à* on to); *(organe)* to transplant ▪ **greffier** *nm Jur* clerk (of the court) ▪ **greffon** *nm (de peau)* & *Bot* graft

grégaire [greger] *adj* gregarious

> Il faut noter que lorsque l'adjectif anglais **gregarious** s'emploie à propos de personnes, il signifie **sociable**.

grêle¹ [grel] *nf* hail; *Fig* **g. de balles** hail of bullets ▪ **grêlé, -ée** *adj (visage)* pockmarked ▪ **grêler** *v impersonnel* to hail; **il grêle** it's hailing ▪ **grêlon** *nm* hailstone

grêle² [grel] *adj (jambes)* skinny; *(tige)* slender; *(voix)* shrill

grelot [grəlo] *nm* (small) bell

grelotter [grəlote] *vi* to shiver *(de* with)

grenade [grənad] *nf (fruit)* pomegranate; *(projectile)* grenade ▪ **grenadine** *nf* grenadine

grenat [grəna] *adj inv (couleur)* dark red

grenier [grənje] *nm (de maison)* attic; *(pour le fourrage)* granary

grenouille [grənuj] *nf* frog

grès [gre] *nm (roche)* sandstone; *(poterie)* stoneware

grésiller [grezije] *vi (huile)* to sizzle; *(feu, radio)* to crackle

grève¹ [grev] *nf (arrêt du travail)* strike; **se mettre en g.** to go out on strike; **faire g.** to be on strike; **g. de la faim** hunger strike; **g. perlée** *Br* go-slow, *Am* slow-down (strike); **g. sauvage/ sur le tas** wildcat/sit-down strike; **g. tournante** staggered strike; **g. du zèle** *Br* work-to-rule, *Am* rule-book slow-down ▪ **gréviste** *nmf* striker

grève² [grev] *nf (de mer)* shore; *(de rivière)* bank

gribouiller [gribuje] *vti* to scribble ▪ **gribouillis** *nm* scribble

grief [grijef] *nm (plainte)* grievance; **faire g. de qch à qn** to hold sth against sb

> Il faut noter que le nom anglais **grief** est un faux ami. Il signifie **chagrin**.

grièvement [grijevmɑ̃] *adv* seriously, badly

griffe [grif] *nf (ongle)* claw; *(de couturier)* (designer) label; *Fig (style)* stamp; *Fig* **arracher qn des griffes de qn** to snatch sb out of sb's clutches ▪ **griffé, -ée** *adj* **vêtements griffés** designer clothes ▪ **griffer** *vt* to scratch

griffonner [grifone] *vt* to scribble, to scrawl ▪ **griffonnage** *nm* scribble, scrawl

grignoter [grinote] *vti* to nibble

gril [gril] *nm (ustensile de cuisine)* *Br* grill, *Am* broiler ▪ **grillade** [grijad] *nf (viande)* *Br* grilled meat, *Am* broiled meat ▪ **grille-pain** *nm inv* toaster ▪ **griller 1** *vt (viande)* *Br* to grill, *Am* to broil; *(pain)* to toast; *(café)* to roast; *(ampoule électrique)* to blow; *(brûler)* to scorch; *Fam (cigarette)* to smoke; *Fam* **g. un feu rouge** to jump the lights; *Fam* **il est grillé** his game's up **2** *vi (viande)* to grill; *(pain)* to toast; **mettre qch à g.** to put sth on the grill, *Am* to broil sth; **g. d'impatience** to be burning with impatience

grille [grij] *nf (clôture)* railings; *(porte)* gate; *(de fourneau, de foyer)* grate; *Aut (de radiateur)* grille; *Fig (des salaires)* scale; **g. des horaires** schedule; **g. de mots croisés** crossword puzzle grid ▪ **grillage** *nm* wire mesh or netting

grillon [grijɔ̃] *nm* cricket

grimace [grimas] *nf (pour faire rire)* (funny) face; *(de douleur)* grimace; **faire la g.** to pull a face ▪ **grimacer** *vi* to make a face; *(de douleur)* to wince *(de* with)

grimer [grime] **1** *vt (acteur, visage)* to make up **2** **se grimer** *vpr* to put one's make-up on

grimper [grɛ̃pe] **1** *vi* to climb *(à qch* up sth); *Fam (prix)* to rocket **2** *vt (escalier)* to climb ▪ **grimpant, -ante** *adj* **plante grimpante** climbing plant

grincer [grɛ̃se] *vi* to creak; **g. des dents** to grind one's teeth ▪ **grincement** *nm* creaking; **grincements de dents** grinding of teeth

grincheux, -euse [grɛ̃ʃø, -øz] *adj* grumpy

gringalet [grɛ̃galε] *nm Péj* weakling

grippe [grip] *nf (maladie)* flu, influenza; **g.**

intestinale gastric flu; **prendre qn/qch en g.** to take a strong dislike to sb/sth ▪ **grippé, -ée** adj **être g.** to have (the) flu

gripper [gripe] **se gripper** vpr (moteur) to seize up

grippe-sou [gripsu] nm inv skinflint, miser

gris, -e [gri, griz] 1 adj Br grey, Am gray; (temps) dull, grey; (ivre) tipsy 2 nm Br grey, Am gray ▪ **grisaille** nf (caractère morne) dreariness ▪ **grisâtre** adj Br greyish, Am grayish

griser [grize] vt (vin) to make tipsy; (air vif, succès) to exhilarate

grisonner [grizone] vi (cheveux, personne) to go Br grey or Am gray ▪ **grisonnant, -ante** adj Br greying, Am graying; **avoir les tempes grisonnantes** to be going grey at the temples

grisou [grizu] nm firedamp; **coup de g.** firedamp explosion

grive [griv] nf thrush

grivois, -oise [grivwa, -waz] adj bawdy ▪ **grivoiserie** nf (propos) bawdy talk

grizzli [grizli] nm grizzly bear

Groenland [grɔenlɑ̃d] nm **le G.** Greenland

grog [grɔg] nm hot toddy

grogner [grɔɲe] vi (personne) to grumble (**contre** at); (cochon) to grunt ▪ **grogne** nf Fam discontent ▪ **grognement** [-əmɑ̃] nm (de personne) growl; (de cochon) grunt ▪ **grognon, -onne** adj grumpy

groin [grwɛ̃] nm snout

grol(l)e [grɔl] nf très Fam shoe

grommeler [grɔm(ə)le] vti to mutter

gronder [grɔ̃de] 1 vt (réprimander) to scold, to tell off 2 vi (chien) to growl; (tonnerre, camion) to rumble ▪ **grondement** nm (de chien) growl; (de tonnerre) rumble

groom [grum] nm Br page, Am bellboy

gros, grosse [gro, gros] 1 adj (corpulent, important) big; (gras) fat; (épais) thick; (effort, progrès) great; (somme, fortune) large; (averse, rhume, mer) heavy; (faute) serious, gross; (bruit) loud; (traits, laine, fil) coarse; **g. mot** swearword 2 adv **gagner g.** to earn big money; **risquer g.** to take a big risk; **écrire g.** to write big; **en g.** (globalement) roughly; (écrire) in big letters; (vendre) in bulk, wholesale; Fig **en avoir g. sur le cœur** to be bitter 3 nmf (personne) fat man, f fat woman 4 nm **le g. de** the bulk of; **commerce/prix de g.** wholesale trade/prices

groseille [grozɛj] nf redcurrant; **g. à maquereau** gooseberry

grossesse [grosɛs] nf pregnancy

grosseur [grosœr] nf (volume) size; (tumeur) lump

grossier, -ière [grosje, -jɛr] adj (tissu, traits) rough, coarse; (personne, manières) rude, coarse; (erreur) gross; (idée, solution) rough, crude; (ruse, instrument) crude; **être g. envers**

qn to be rude to sb ▪ **grossièrement** adv (calculer) roughly; (répondre) coarsely, rudely; (se tromper) grossly ▪ **grossièreté** nf (incorrection, vulgarité) coarseness; (mot) rude word

grossir [grosir] 1 vt (sujet: verre, loupe) to magnify; Fig (exagérer) to exaggerate 2 vi (personne) to put on weight; (fleuve) to swell; (bosse, foule, nombre) to get bigger; (bruit) to get louder ▪ **grossissant, -ante** adj **verre g.** magnifying glass ▪ **grossissement** nm (augmentation de taille) increase in size; (de microscope) magnification

grossiste [grosist] nmf Com wholesaler

grosso modo [grosomɔdo] adv (en gros) roughly

grotesque [grɔtɛsk] adj ludicrous

grotte [grɔt] nf cave

grouiller [gruje] 1 vi (se presser) to swarm around; **g. de** to swarm with 2 se grouiller vpr Fam (se hâter) to get a move on ▪ **grouillant, -ante** adj swarming (**de** with)

groupe [grup] nm group; **g. sanguin** blood group; **g. scolaire** (bâtiments) school block; **g. témoin** focus group ▪ **groupement** nm (action) grouping; (groupe) group ▪ **grouper** 1 vt to group (together) 2 se grouper vpr (en association) to form a group; **restez groupés** keep together

groupie [grupi] nf Fam groupie

grue [gry] nf (machine, oiseau) crane

gruger [gryʒe] vt to swindle; **se faire g.** to get swindled

grumeau, -x [grymo] nm (dans une sauce) lump ▪ **grumeleux, -euse** adj lumpy

gruyère [gryjɛr] nm Gruyère (cheese)

GSM [ʒeɛsɛm] (abrév **global system for mobile communications**) nm Tél GSM; Belg (téléphone portable) Br mobile (phone), Am cell (phone); **réseau G.** GSM network

Guadeloupe [gwadlup] nf **la G.** Guadeloupe

Guatemala [gwatemala] nm **le G.** Guatemala

gué [ge] nm ford; **passer à g.** to ford

guenilles [gənij] nfpl rags (and tatters)

guépard [gepar] nm cheetah

guêpe [gɛp] nf wasp ▪ **guêpier** nm (nid) wasp's nest; Fig (piège) trap

guère [gɛr] adv **(ne...) g.** (pas beaucoup) not much; (pas longtemps) hardly, scarcely; **il n'a g. d'amis** he hasn't got many friends; **il ne sort g.** he hardly or scarcely goes out; **il n'y a g. plus de six ans** just over six years ago

guéridon [geridɔ̃] nm pedestal table

guérilla [gerija] nf guerrilla warfare ▪ **guérillero** nm guerrilla

> Il faut noter que le nom anglais **guerrilla** est un faux ami. Il signifie **guérillero**.

guérir [gerir] 1 vt (personne, maladie) to cure (**de** of); (blessure) to heal 2 vi (personne) to get better, to recover; *(blessure)* to heal; *(rhume)* to get better **3 se guérir** *vpr* to get better ■ **guéri, -ie** *adj* cured; *Fig* **être g. de qn/qch** to have got rid of sb/sth ■ **guérison** *nf (rétablissement)* recovery ■ **guérisseur, -euse** *nmf* faith healer

guérite [gerit] *nf Mil* sentry box

Guernesey [gɛrn(ə)zɛ] *nf* Guernsey

guerre [gɛr] *nf* war; *(technique)* warfare; **en g.** at war *(avec* with); **faire la g.** to wage *or* make war (**à** *or* against); *(soldat)* to fight; **crime/cri de g.** war crime/cry; *Fig* **c'est de bonne g.** that's fair enough; **g. d'usure** war of attrition ■ **guerrier, -ière 1** *adj* **danse guerrière** war dance; **chant g.** battle song; **nation guerrière** warlike nation **2** *nmf* warrior ■ **guerroyer** *vi Littéraire* to wage war (**contre** on)

guet [gɛ] *nm* **faire le g.** to be on the lookout ■ **guetter** [gete] *vt (occasion)* to watch out for; *(gibier)* to lie in wait for

guet-apens [gɛtapɑ̃] *(pl* **guets-apens**) *nm* ambush

guêtre [gɛtr] *nf* gaiter

gueule [gœl] *nf (d'animal, de canon)* mouth; *Fam (de personne)* mouth; *Fam (visage)* face; *Fam* **avoir la g. de bois** to have a hangover; *Fam* **faire la g.** to sulk; *Fam* **faire une g. d'enterrement** to look really *Br* pissed off *or Am* pissed ■ **gueuler** *vti très Fam* to bawl ■ **gueuleton** *nm Fam (repas)* feast, *Br* blowout

gui [gi] *nm* mistletoe

guichet [giʃɛ] *nm (de gare, de banque)* window; *(de théâtre)* box office; *Théâtre* **on joue à guichets fermés** the performance is sold out; **g. automatique** *(de banque)* cash dispenser ■ **guichetier, -ière** *nmf (de banque) Br* counter clerk, *Am* teller; *(à la gare)* ticket clerk

guide [gid] **1** *nm (personne, livre)* guide; **g.**

touristique tourist guide **2** *nf (éclaireuse)* (Girl) Guide ■ **guider** *vt* to guide ■ **guides** *nfpl (rênes)* reins

guidon [gidɔ̃] *nm* handlebars

guigne [giɲ] *nf Fam (malchance)* bad luck

guignol [giɲɔl] *nm (spectacle)* ≃ Punch and Judy show; *Fam* **faire le g.** to clown around

guillemets [gijmɛ] *nmpl Typ* inverted commas, quotation marks; **entre g.** in inverted commas, in quotation marks

guilleret, -ette [gijrɛ, -ɛt] *adj* lively, perky

guillotine [gijɔtin] *nf* guillotine ■ **guillotiner** *vt* to guillotine

guimauve [gimov] *nf (confiserie)* marshmallow

guimbarde [gɛ̃bard] *nf Fam (voiture) Br* old banger, *Am* (old) wreck

guindé, -ée [gɛ̃de] *adj (peu naturel)* stiff; *(style)* stilted

Guinée [gine] *nf* **la G.** Guinea

guingois [gɛ̃gwa] *adv Fam* **de g.** askew; *Fig* **tout va de g.** everything's going wrong

guirlande [girlɑ̃d] *nf* garland; **g. de Noël** piece of tinsel; **g. lumineuse** string of (fairy) lights

guise [giz] *nf* **agir à sa g.** to do as one pleases; **n'en faire qu'à sa g.** to do just as one pleases; **en g. de** by way of

guitare [gitar] *nf* guitar ■ **guitariste** *nmf* guitarist

guttural, -e, -aux, -ales [gytyral, -o] *adj* guttural

Guyane [gɥijan] *nf* **la G.** Guiana

gymnase [ʒimnaz] *nm* gymnasium ■ **gymnaste** *nmf* gymnast ■ **gymnastique** *nf* gymnastics *(sing)*

gynécologie [ʒinekɔlɔʒi] *nf Br* gynaecology, *Am* gynecology ■ **gynécologue** *nmf Br* gynaecologist, *Am* gynecologist

gyrophare [ʒirofar] *nm* flashing light

H, h [aʃ] *nm inv* H, h; **l'heure H** zero hour; **bombe H** H-bomb

ha [ˈa] *exclam* ah!, oh!; **ha, ha!** *(rire)* ha-ha!

habile [abil] *adj* skilful, *Am* skillful (**à qch** at sth; **à faire** at doing); **h. de ses mains** good with one's hands ▪ **habilement** *adv* skilfully, *Am* skillfully ▪ **habileté** *nf* skill

habilité, -ée [abilite] *adj* (legally) authorized (**à faire** to do)

habiller [abije] **1** *vt* (*vêtir*) to dress (**de** in); (*fournir en vêtements*) to clothe; (*garnir*) to cover (**de** with); **h. qn en soldat** to dress sb up as a soldier; **un rien l'habille** he/she looks good in anything **2 s'habiller** *vpr* to dress, to get dressed; (*avec élégance*) to dress up; **s'h. chez Dior** to buy one's clothes from Dior ▪ **habillé, -ée** *adj* dressed (**de** in; **en** as); (*costume, robe*) smart; **soirée habillée** formal occasion ▪ **habillement** *nm* (*vêtements*) clothes

habit [abi] *nm* (*tenue de soirée*) evening dress, tails; **habits** (*vêtements*) clothes

habitable [abitabl] *adj* (in)habitable; (*maison*) fit to live in

habitat [abita] *nm* (*d'animal, de plante*) habitat; (*conditions*) housing conditions

habitation [abitasjɔ̃] *nf* (*lieu*) dwelling; (*fait de résider*) living

habiter [abite] **1** *vt* (*maison, région*) to live in; (*planète*) to inhabit **2** *vi* to live (**à/en** in) ▪ **habitant, -ante** *nmf* (*de pays*) inhabitant; (*de maison*) occupant ▪ **habité, -ée** *adj* (*région*) inhabited; (*maison*) occupied

habitude [abityd] *nf* habit; **avoir l'h. de qch** to be used to sth; **avoir l'h. de faire qch** to be used to doing sth; **prendre l'h. de faire qch** to get into the habit of doing sth; **prendre de bonnes habitudes** to take on some good habits; **prendre de mauvaises habitudes** to pick up (some) bad habits; **d'h.** usually; **comme d'h.** as usual

habituel, -uelle [abityɛl] *adj* usual, customary ▪ **habituellement** *adv* usually

habituer [abitɥe] **1** *vt* **h. qn à qch** to accustom sb to sth; **être habitué à qch/à faire qch** to be used to sth/to doing sth **2 s'habituer** *vpr* **s'h. à qn/qch** to get used to sb/sth ▪ **habitué, -uée** *nmf* regular; (*de maison*) regular visitor

hache [ˈaʃ] *nf* axe, *Am* ax ▪ **hachette** *nf* hatchet

hacher [ˈaʃe] *vt* (*au couteau*) to chop up; (*avec un appareil*) *Br* to mince, *Am* to grind ▪ **haché, -ée** *adj* (*viande*) *Br* minced, *Am* ground; (*légumes*) chopped; (*style*) jerky ▪ **hachis** *nm* (*viande*) *Br* mince, *Am* ground meat; **h. Parmentier** ≃ cottage pie ▪ **hachoir** *nm* (*couteau*) chopper; (*appareil*) *Br* mincer, *Am* grinder

hachures [ˈaʃyr] *nfpl* hatching ▪ **hachurer** *vt* to hatch

hagard, -arde [ˈagar, -ard] *adj* (*visage*) haggard; (*yeux*) wild

haie [ˈɛ] *nf* (*clôture*) hedge; (*rangée*) row; (*en athlétisme*) hurdle; (*en équitation*) fence; **400 mètres haies** (*en athlétisme*) 400-metre hurdles; **course de haies** (*en équitation*) steeplechase; **h. d'honneur** guard of honour

haillons [ˈajɔ̃] *nmpl* rags; **en h.** in rags

haine [ˈɛn] *nf* hatred, hate; *Fam* **avoir la h.** (*être révolté*) to be full of rage ▪ **haineux, -euse** *adj* full of hatred

---

Il faut noter que l'adjectif anglais **heinous** est un faux ami. Il signifie **atroce**.

---

haïr* [ˈair] *vt* to hate ▪ **haïssable** *adj* hateful

hâle [ˈɑl] *nm* suntan ▪ **hâlé, -ée** *adj* suntanned

haleine [alɛn] *nf* breath; **hors d'h.** out of breath; **perdre h.** to get out of breath; **reprendre h.** to get one's breath back; **tenir qn en h.** to keep sb in suspense; **travail de longue h.** long job

haler [ˈale] *vt* to tow ▪ **halage** *nm* towing; **chemin de h.** towpath

haleter [ˈal(ə)te] *vi* to pant, to gasp ▪ **haletant, -ante** *adj* panting, gasping

hall [ˈol] *nm* (*de maison*) entrance hall; (*d'hôtel*) lobby; (*d'aéroport*) lounge; **h. de gare** station concourse

halle [ˈal] *nf* (covered) market; **les halles** the central food market

hallucination [alysinasjɔ̃] *nf* hallucination ▪ **hallucinant, -ante** *adj* incredible ▪ **halluciner** *vi* to hallucinate; *Fam* **j'hallucine!** I don't believe it!

halo [ˈalo] *nm* halo

halogène [aloʒɛn] *nm* (*lampe*) halogen lamp

halte [ˈalt] **1** *nf* (*arrêt*) stop, *Mil* halt; (*lieu*) stopping place, *Mil* halting place; **faire h.** to stop; **h. routière** (roadside) rest area **2** *exclam* stop!, *Mil* halt!

haltère [altɛr] *nm* dumbbell ▪ **haltérophile** *nmf* weightlifter ▪ **haltérophilie** *nf* weightlifting

hamac ['amak] *nm* hammock

hamburger ['ãbœrgœr] *nm* burger

hameau, -x ['amo] *nm* hamlet

hameçon [ams5] *nm* (fish-)hook; *Fig* **mordre à l'h.** to swallow the bait

hamster ['amster] *nm* hamster

hanche ['ãʃ] *nf* hip

handball ['ãdbal] *nm Sport* handball ▪ **handballeur, -euse** *nmf* handball player

handicap ['ãdikap] *nm (physique, mental)* disability; *Fig* handicap ▪ **handicapé, -ée 1** *adj* disabled **2** *nmf* disabled person; **h. moteur** person with motor impairment; **h. physique/ mental** physically/mentally handicapped person ▪ **handicaper** *vt (physiquement, men- talement)* to disable; *Fig* to handicap

hangar ['ãgar] *nm (entrepôt)* shed; *(pour avions)* hangar; *(de bus)* depot

hanneton ['an(ə)t5] *nm* cockchafer, *Am* June bug; *Fam* **pas piqué des hannetons** *(difficile)* tough; *(bon)* incredible

hanter ['ãte] *vt (sujet: fantôme, souvenir)* to haunt; *Fig (bars)* to hang around ▪ **hanté, -ée** *adj (maison)* haunted ▪ **hantise** *nf* **avoir la h. de qch** to really dread sth

happer ['ape] *vt (saisir)* to snatch; *(par la gueule)* to snap up

haras ['ara] *nm* stud farm

harasser ['arase] *vt* to exhaust ▪ **harassé, -ée** *adj* exhausted

> Il faut noter que le verbe anglais **to harass** est un faux ami. Il signifie **harceler**.

harceler ['arsəle] *vt (importuner)* to harass; *(insister auprès de)* to pester; **h. qn de questions** to pester sb with questions ▪ **harcèlement** *nm* harassment; **h. sexuel** sexual harassment ▪ **harceleur, -euse** *nmf* tormentor; **h. téléphonique** phone pest

hardi, -ie ['ardi] *adj* bold ▪ **hardiesse** *nf* boldness ▪ **hardiment** *adv* boldly

harem ['arɛm] *nm* harem

hareng ['arã] *nm* herring; **h. saur** smoked herring

hargne ['arɲ] *nf* bad temper ▪ **hargneux, -euse** *adj* bad-tempered

haricot ['ariko] *nm* bean; *Fam* **c'est la fin des haricots** it's all over; **h. blanc** haricot bean; **h. rouge** kidney bean; **h. vert** green bean, *Br* French bean

harmonica [armɔnika] *nm* harmonica, mouth organ

harmonie [armɔni] *nf* harmony ▪ **harmonieux, -ieuse** *adj* harmonious ▪ **harmonique** *adj Mus* harmonic ▪ **harmoniser** *vt,* **s'harmoniser** *upr* to harmonize ▪ **harmonium** *nm* harmonium

harnacher ['arnaʃe] *vt (cheval)* to harness ▪ **harnais** *nm (de cheval, de bébé)* harness

harpe ['arp] *nf* harp

harpon ['arp5] *nm* harpoon ▪ **harponner** *vt*

(baleine) to harpoon; *Fam* **h. qn** *(sujet: importun)* to corner sb

hasard ['azar] *nm* **le h.** chance; **un h. a** coincidence; **un heureux h.** a stroke of luck; **un malheureux h.** a rotten piece of luck; **par h.** by chance; **par le plus grand des hasards** by a (sheer) fluke; **au h.** *(choisir, répondre)* at random; *(marcher)* aimlessly; **à tout h.** *(par précaution)* just in case; *(pour voir)* on the off chance; **si par h.** if by any chance; **les hasards de la vie** the fortunes of life ▪ **hasarder 1** *vt (remarque, démarche)* to venture **2 se hasarder** *upr* **se h. dans** to venture into; **se h. à faire qch** to risk doing sth ▪ **hasardeux, -euse** *adj* risky, hazardous

> Il faut noter que le nom anglais **hazard** est un faux ami. Il signifie uniquement **danger**.

haschisch ['aʃiʃ] *nm* hashish

hâte ['ɑt] *nf* haste; **à la h.** hastily; **en (toute) h.** hurriedly; **avoir h. de faire qch** to be eager to do sth ▪ **hâter 1** *vt (pas, départ)* to hasten **2 se hâter** *upr* to hurry *(de faire* to do) ▪ **hâtif, -ive** *adj (trop rapide)* hasty

hausse ['os] *nf* rise *(de* in); **en h.** rising ▪ **hausser 1** *vt (prix, voix)* to raise; *(épaules)* to shrug **2 se hausser** *upr* **se h. sur la pointe des pieds** to stand on tiptoe

haussier ['osje] *adj m voir* **marché**

haut, -e ['o, 'ot] **1** *adj* high; *(en taille)* tall; *(dans le temps)* early; **h. de 5 m** 5 m high *or* tall; **à haute voix, à voix haute** aloud; **en haute mer** out at sea; **la mer est haute** it's high tide; **la haute couture** high fashion; **la haute coiffure** haute coiffure; **la haute société** high society; **la haute bourgeoisie** the upper middle class; **un instrument de haute précision** a precision instrument; **un renseignement de la plus haute importance** news of the utmost importance; **avoir une haute opinion de qn** to have a high opinion of sb; **obtenir qch de haute lutte** to get sth after a hard struggle; **haute trahison** high treason

2 *adv (dans l'espace) & Mus* high; *(dans une hiérarchie)* highly; *(parler)* loud, loudly; **tout h.** *(lire, penser)* out loud; **h. placé** *(personne)* in a high position; **plus h.** *(dans un texte)* above; **gagner h. la main** to win hands down

3 *nm (partie haute)* top; **en h. de** at the top of; **en h.** *(loger)* upstairs; *(regarder)* up; *(mettre)* on (the) top; **d'en h.** *(de la partie haute, du ciel)* from high up, from up above; **avoir 5 mètres de h.** to be 5 metres high *or* tall; *Fig* **des hauts et des bas** ups and downs ▪ **haut-de-forme** *(pl hauts-de-forme)* top hat ▪ **haut- fourneau** *(pl hauts-fourneaux)* *nm* blast- furnace ▪ **haut-le-cœur** *nm inv* **avoir un h.** to retch ▪ **haut-parleur** *(pl haut-parleurs)* *nm Br* loudspeaker, *Am* bullhorn

hautain, -aine ['otɛ̃, -ɛn] *adj* haughty
hautbois ['obwa] *nm* oboe
hautement ['otmɑ̃] *adv (très)* highly ▪ **hauteur** *nf* height; *(colline)* hill; *Péj (orgueil)* haughtiness; **à h. de 10 000 euros** for a sum of 10,000 euros; **à la h. de** *(objet)* level with; *(rue)* opposite; **arriver à la h. de qch** *(mesurer)* to reach (the level of) sth; **à la h. de la situation** up to *or* equal to the situation; **il n'est pas à la h.** he isn't up to it
hâve ['ɑv] *adj* gaunt
havre ['ɑvr] *nm Littéraire* haven; **h. de paix** haven of peace
Haye ['ɛ] *nf* **La H.** The Hague
hayon ['ajɔ̃] *nm (de voiture)* hatchback
hé ['e] *exclam (appel)* hey!; **hé! hé!** *(appréciation, moquerie)* well, well!
hebdomadaire [ɛbdɔmadɛr] *adj & nm* weekly
héberger [ebɛrʒe] *vt (invités)* to put up; *Ordinat (site Web)* to host ▪ **hébergement** [-əmɑ̃] *nm* putting up; **centre d'h.** shelter ▪ **hébergeur, -euse** *nmf Ordinat (de site Web)* host
hébété, -ée [ebete] *adj* dazed
hébreu, -x [ebrø] **1** *adj m* Hebrew **2** *nm (langue)* Hebrew ▪ **hébraïque** *adj* Hebrew
Hébrides [ebrid] *nfpl* **les H.** the Hebrides
hécatombe [ekatɔ̃b] *nf* slaughter
hectare [ektar] *nm* hectare *(= 2.47 acres)*
hégémonie [eʒemɔni] *nf* hegemony
hein ['ɛ̃] *exclam Fam (surprise, interrogation)* eh?; **ne fais plus jamais ça, h.?** don't ever do that again, OK?
hélas ['elɑs] *exclam* unfortunately
héler ['ele] *vt (taxi)* to hail
hélice [elis] *nf (d'avion, de navire)* propeller
hélicoptère [elikɔptɛr] *nm* helicopter ▪ **héliport** *nm* heliport
helvétique [ɛlvetik] *adj* Swiss ▪ **helvétisme** *nm* Swiss French expression
hémicycle [emisikl] *nm Pol* **l'h.** *(de l'Assemblée nationale)* the chamber
hémisphère [emisfɛr] *nm* hemisphere
hémophile [emɔfil] **1** *adj* haemophilic **2** *nm* haemophiliac ▪ **hémophilie** *nf Méd* haemophilia
hémorragie [emɔraʒi] *nf Méd* haemorrhage; *Fig (de capitaux)* drain; **faire une h.** to haemorrhage; **h. cérébrale** stroke
hémorroïdes [emɔrɔid] *nfpl* piles, haemorrhoids
hennir ['enir] *vi (cheval)* to neigh ▪ **hennissement** *nm* neigh; **hennissements** neighing
hépatite [epatit] *nf Méd* hepatitis
herbe [ɛrb] *nf* grass; *(pour soigner)* herb; **mauvaise h.** weed; *Culin* **fines herbes** herbs; **blé en h.** green wheat; *Fig* **poète en h.** budding poet; **couper l'h. sous le pied de qn** to cut the ground from under sb's feet; *Fam*

fumer de l'h. to smoke grass *or* weed ▪ **herbage** *nm* pasture ▪ **herbeux, -euse** *adj* grassy ▪ **herbicide** *nm* weedkiller ▪ **herbivore** *adj* herbivorous
herculéen, -éenne [ɛrkyleɛ̃, -ɛn] *adj* Herculean
hérédité [eredite] *nf Biol* heredity ▪ **héréditaire** *adj* hereditary
hérésie [erezi] *nf* heresy ▪ **hérétique 1** *adj* heretical **2** *nmf* heretic
hérisser ['erise] **1** *vt (poils)* to bristle up; *Fig* **h. qn** *(irriter)* to get sb's back up **2 se hérisser** *vpr (animal, personne)* to bristle; *(poils, cheveux)* to stand on end ▪ **hérissé, -ée** *adj (cheveux)* bristly; *(cactus)* prickly; **h. de** bristling with
hérisson ['erisɔ̃] *nm* hedgehog
hériter [erite] **1** *vt* to inherit (**qch de qn** sth from sb) **2** *vi* **h. de qch** to inherit sth ▪ **héritage** *nm (biens)* inheritance; *Fig (culturel, politique)* heritage; **faire un h.** to come into an inheritance ▪ **héritier** *nm* heir (**de** to) ▪ **héritière** *nf* heiress (**de** to)
hermétique [ermetik] *adj* hermetically sealed; *Fig (obscur)* impenetrable ▪ **hermétiquement** *adv* hermetically
hermine [ermin] *nf (animal, fourrure)* ermine
hernie ['ɛrni] *nf Méd* hernia; **h. discale** slipped disc
héron ['erɔ̃] *nm* heron
héros ['ero] *nm* hero ▪ **héroïne** [erɔin] *nf (femme)* heroine; *(drogue)* heroin ▪ **héroïque** [erɔik] *adj* heroic ▪ **héroïsme** [erɔism] *nm* heroism
hésiter [ezite] *vi* to hesitate (**sur** over *or* about; **entre** between; **à faire** to do) ▪ **hésitant, -ante** *adj* hesitant ▪ **hésitation** *nf* hesitation; **avec h.** hesitatingly
hétéroclite [eterɔklit] *adj* motley
hétérogène [eterɔʒɛn] *adj* mixed
hêtre ['ɛtr] *nm (arbre, bois)* beech
heu ['ø] *exclam (hésitation)* er
heure [œr] *nf (mesure)* hour; *(moment)* time; **quelle h. est-il?** what time is it?; **il est six heures** it's six (o'clock); **six heures moins cinq** five to six; **six heures cinq** *Br* five past six, *Am* five after six; **à l'h.** *(arriver)* on time; *(être payé)* by the hour; **10 km à l'h.** 10 km an hour; **ils devraient être arrivés à l'h. qu'il est** they ought to have arrived by now; **de bonne h.** early; **nouvelle de dernière h.** latest *or* last-minute news; **tout à l'h.** *(futur)* in a few moments, later; *(passé)* a moment ago; **à tout à l'h.!** *(au revoir)* see you soon!; **à toute h.** *(continuellement)* at all hours; **24 heures sur 24** 24 hours a day; **d'h. en h.** hourly, hour by hour; **faire des heures supplémentaires** to work *or* to do overtime; **heures d'affluence, heures de pointe** *(circulation)* rush hour; *(dans les magasins)* peak period; **heures creuses** off-

peak *or* slack periods; **h. d'été** *Br* summer time, *Am* daylight-saving time

heureux, -euse [œrø, -øz] **1** *adj* happy (**de** with); *(chanceux)* lucky, fortunate; *(issue, changement)* successful; *(expression, choix)* apt; **h. de faire qch** happy to do sth; **je suis h. que vous puissiez venir** I'm happy you can come **2** *adv (vivre, mourir)* happily • **heureusement** *adv (par chance)* fortunately, luckily (**pour** for); *(avec succès)* successfully

heurt ['œr] *nm* collision; *Fig (d'opinions)* clash; **sans heurts** smoothly

heurter ['œrte] **1** *vt (cogner)* to hit (**contre** against); *(entrer en collision avec)* to collide with; **h. qn** *(choquer)* to offend sb **2 se heurter** *vpr* to collide (**à** *ou* **contre** against); *Fig* **se h. à qch** to meet with sth • **heurtoir** *nm* (door) knocker

hexagone [ɛgzagɔn] *nm* hexagon; *Fig* **l'H.** France • **hexagonal, -e, -aux, -ales** *adj* hexagonal; *Fam (français)* French

hiatus [jatys] *nm* *Fig* hiatus, gap

hiberner [ibɛrne] *vi* to hibernate • **hibernation** *nf* hibernation

hibou, -x ['ibu] *nm* owl

hic ['ik] *nm Fam* **voilà le h.!** there's the snag!

hideux, -euse ['idø, -øz] *adj* hideous

hier [ijɛr] *adv* yesterday; **h. soir** yesterday evening; **ça ne date pas d'h.** that's nothing new; *Fig* **elle n'est pas née d'h.** she wasn't born yesterday

hiérarchie ['jerarʃi] *nf* hierarchy • **hiérarchique** *adj* hierarchical; **par la voie h.** through the official channels

hi-fi ['ifi] *adj inv & nf inv* hi-fi

hilare [ilar] *adj* grinning • **hilarant, -ante** *adj* hilarious • **hilarité** *nf* hilarity, mirth

hindou, -oue [ɛ̃du] *adj & nmf* Hindu

hip-hop ['ipɔp] *nm inv (musique)* hip-hop

hippie ['ipi] *nmf* hippie

hippique [ipik] *adj* **concours h.** horse show • **hippodrome** *nm Br* racecourse, *Am* race-track

hippopotame [ipɔpɔtam] *nm* hippopotamus, *Fam* hippo

hirondelle [irɔ̃dɛl] *nf (oiseau)* swallow

hirsute [irsyt] *adj (personne, barbe)* shaggy

hispanique [ispanik] *adj* Hispanic

hisser ['ise] **1** *vt* to hoist up **2 se hisser** *vpr* to heave oneself up

histoire [istwar] *nf (science, événements)* history; *(récit)* story; *Fam (affaire)* business, matter; *Fam* **des histoires** *(mensonges)* fibs, stories; *(chichis)* fuss; *Fam* **raconter des histoires** to tell fibs; *Fam* **faire des histoires à qn** to make trouble for sb; *Fam* **c'est toute une h. pour lui faire prendre son bain** it's quite a business getting him/her to have a bath; *Fam* **h. de rire** for a laugh; **sans histoires** *(voyage)* uneventful

historien, -ienne [istɔrjɛ̃, -jɛn] *nmf* historian

historique [istɔrik] **1** *adj (concernant l'histoire)* historical; *(important)* historic **2** *nm* historical account

hiver [ivɛr] *nm* winter • **hivernal, -e, -aux, -ales** *adj* winter; *(temps)* wintry

HLM ['aʃɛlɛm] *(abrév* **habitation à loyer modéré)** *nm ou f Br* ≃ (block of) council flats, *Am* ≃ public housing unit

hocher ['ɔʃe] *vt* **h. la tête** *(pour dire oui)* to nod; *(pour dire non)* to shake one's head • **hochement** *nm* **h. de tête** *(affirmatif)* nod; *(négatif)* shake of the head

hochet ['ɔʃɛ] *nm* rattle

hockey ['ɔkɛ] *nm* hockey; **h. sur glace** ice hockey; **h. sur gazon** *Br* hockey, *Am* field hockey

holà ['ɔla] **1** *exclam* stop! **2** *nm inv* **mettre le h. à qch** to put a stop to sth

hold-up ['ɔldœp] *nm inv* hold-up

Hollande ['ɔlɑ̃d] *nf* **la H.** Holland • **hollandais, -aise 1** *adj* Dutch **2** *nmf* **H.** Dutchman; **Hollandaise** Dutchwoman; **les H.** the Dutch **3** *nm (langue)* Dutch

holocauste [ɔlɔkost] *nm* holocaust

homard ['ɔmar] *nm* lobster

homélie [ɔmeli] *nf* homily

homéopathe [ɔmeɔpat] **1** *adj* homoeopathic **2** *nmf* homeopath • **homéopathie** *nf* homeopathy • **homéopathique** *adj* homeopathic

homicide [ɔmisid] *nm* homicide; **h. involontaire** *ou* **par imprudence** manslaughter; **h. volontaire** murder

hommage [ɔmaʒ] *nm* homage (**à** to); **rendre h. à qn** to pay homage to sb; **faire qch en h. à qn** to do sth as a tribute to sb *or* in homage to sb; **présenter ses hommages à une femme** to pay one's respects to a lady

homme [ɔm] *nm* man *(pl* men); **l'h.** *(genre humain)* man(kind); **des vêtements d'h.** men's clothes; **d'h. à h.** man to man; *Fig* **l'h. de la rue** the man in the street; **il n'est pas h. à vous laisser tomber** he's not the sort of man to let you down; **h. d'affaires** businessman; **h. politique** politician • **homme-grenouille** *(pl* **hommes-grenouilles)** *nm* frogman

homogène [ɔmɔʒɛn] *adj* homogeneous • **homogénéité** *nf* homogeneity

homologue [ɔmɔlɔg] *nmf* counterpart, opposite number

homologuer [ɔmɔlɔge] *vt (décision, accord, record)* to ratify

homonyme [ɔmɔnim] **1** *nm (mot)* homonym **2** *nmf (personne)* namesake

homosexuel, -uelle [ɔmɔsɛksɥɛl] *adj & nmf* homosexual • **homosexualité** *nf* homosexuality

Hongrie ['ɔ̃gri] *nf* **la H.** Hungary • **hongrois, -oise 1** *adj* Hungarian **2** *nmf* **H., Hongroise** Hungarian **3** *nm (langue)* Hungarian

honnête [ɔnɛt] *adj (intègre)* honest; *(vie, gens)* decent; *(prix)* fair ▪ **honnêtement** *adv (avec intégrité)* honestly; *(raisonnablement)* decently; **h., qu'est-ce que tu en penses?** be honest, what do you think? ▪ **honnêteté** *nf (intégrité)* honesty

honneur [ɔnœr] *nm Br* honour, *Am* honor; **en l'h. de qn** in honour of sb; **faire h. à** *(sa famille)* to be a credit to; *(par sa présence)* to do honour to; *(promesse)* to honour; *Fam (repas)* to do justice to; **être à l'h.** to have the place of honour; **donner sa parole d'h.** to give one's word of honour; **mettre un point d'h. à faire qch** to make it a point of honour to do sth; **invité d'h.** guest of honour; **membre d'h.** honorary member

honorable [ɔnɔrabl] *adj Br* honourable, *Am* honorable; *Fig (résultat, salaire)* respectable

honoraire [ɔnɔrɛr] *adj (membre)* honorary ▪ **honoraires** *nmpl* fees

honorer [ɔnɔre] **1** *vt* to *Br* honour *or Am* honor (**de** with); **h. qn** *(conduite)* to be a credit to sb; **h. qn de sa confiance** to put one's trust in sb **2** **s'honorer** *vpr* **s'h. d'avoir fait qch** to pride oneself on having done sth ▪ **honorifique** *adj* honorary

honte [ʼɔt] *nf* shame; **avoir h.** to be *or* feel ashamed (**de qch/de faire** of sth/to do *or* of doing); **faire h. à qn** to put sb to shame; **sans h.** shamelessly ▪ **honteusement** *adv* shamefully ▪ **honteux, -euse** *adj (personne)* ashamed (**de** of); *(conduite, acte)* shameful

hop [ʼɔp] *exclam* **allez h., saute!** go on, jump!; **allez h., tout le monde dehors!** come on, everybody out!

hôpital, -aux [ɔpital, -o] *nm* hospital; **à l'h.** *Br* in hospital, *Am* in the hospital

hoquet [ʼɔkɛ] *nm* hiccup; **avoir le h.** to have the hiccups ▪ **hoqueter** [-əte] *vi* to hiccup

horaire [ɔrɛr] **1** *adj (salaire)* hourly; *(vitesse)* per hour **2** *nm* timetable, schedule; **horaires de travail** working hours

horde [ʼɔrd] *nf* horde

horizon [ɔrizɔ̃] *nm* horizon; *(vue, paysage)* view; **à l'h.** on the horizon ▪ **horizontal, -e, -aux, -ales** *adj* horizontal ▪ **horizontalement** *adv* horizontally

horloge [ɔrlɔʒ] *nf* clock ▪ **horloger, -ère** *nmf* watchmaker ▪ **horlogerie** *nf (magasin)* watchmaker's (shop); *(industrie)* watchmaking

hormis [ʼɔrmi] *prép Littéraire* save, except (for)

hormone [ɔrmɔn] *nf* hormone ▪ **hormonal, -e, -aux, -ales** *adj* **traitement h.** hormone treatment

horoscope [ɔrɔskɔp] *nm* horoscope

horreur [ɔrœr] *nf* horror; **des horreurs** *(propos)* horrible things; **faire h. à qn** to disgust sb; **avoir h. de qch** to hate *or* loathe sth; **quelle h.!** how awful!

horrible [ɔribl] *adj (effrayant)* horrible; *(laid)* hideous ▪ **horriblement** [-əmɑ̃] *adv (défiguré)* horribly; *(cher, froid)* terribly

horrifiant, -iante [ɔrifjɑ̃, -jɑ̃t] *adj* horrifying ▪ **horrifié, -iée** *adj* horrified

horripiler [ɔripile] *vt* to exasperate

hors [ʼɔr] *prép* **h. de** *(maison, boîte)* outside; *Fig (danger, haleine)* out of; **h. de doute** beyond doubt; **h. de soi** *(furieux)* beside oneself; *Fig* **être h. concours** to be in a class of one's own; *Football* **être h. jeu** to be offside ▪ **hors-bord** *nm inv* speedboat; **moteur h.** outboard motor ▪ **hors-d'œuvre** *nm inv (plat)* hors-d'œuvre, starter ▪ **hors-jeu** *nm inv Football* offside ▪ **hors-la-loi** *nm inv* outlaw ▪ **hors-piste** *nm inv Ski* off-piste skiing; **faire du h.** to ski off piste ▪ **hors service** *adj inv (appareil)* out of order ▪ **hors taxe** *adj inv (magasin, objet)* duty-free

hortensia [ɔrtɑ̃sja] *nm* hydrangea

horticulteur, -trice [ɔrtikyltœr, -tris] *nmf* horticulturist ▪ **horticole** *adj* horticultural ▪ **horticulture** *nf* horticulture

hospice [ɔspis] *nm (foyer)* home; *(hôpital)* hospice

hospitalier, -ière [ɔspitalje, -jɛr] *adj (accueillant)* hospitable; **centre h.** hospital (complex); **personnel h.** hospital staff ▪ **hospitaliser** *vt* to hospitalize ▪ **hospitalité** *nf* hospitality

hostile [ɔstil] *adj* hostile (**à** to *or* towards) ▪ **hostilité** *nf* hostility (**envers** to *or* towards); *Mil* **hostilités** hostilities

hôte [ot] **1** *nm (qui reçoit)* host **2** *nmf (invité)* guest ▪ **hôtesse** *nf* hostess; **h. de l'air** air hostess

hôtel [otɛl] *nm* hotel; **h. particulier** mansion, town house; **h. de ville** *Br* town hall, *Am* city hall; **h. des impôts** tax office; **h. des ventes** auction rooms ▪ **hôtelier, -ière 1** *nmf* hotelkeeper, hotelier **2** *adj* **industrie hôtelière** hotel industry ▪ **hôtellerie** *nf (auberge)* inn; *(métier)* hotel trade

hotte [ʼɔt] *nf (panier)* basket *(carried on back)*; *(de cheminée)* hood; **la h. du père Noël** Santa's sack, *Br* Father Christmas's sack; **h. aspirante** extractor hood

houblon [ʼublɔ̃] *nm* **le h.** hops

houille [ʼuj] *nf* coal; **h. blanche** hydroelectric power ▪ **houiller, -ère 1** *adj* **bassin h.** coalfield **2** *nf* colliery, *Br* colliery

houle [ʼul] *nf* swell ▪ **houleux, -euse** *adj (mer)* rough; *Fig (réunion)* stormy

houlette [ʼulɛt] *nf Fig* **sous la h. de qn** under the leadership of sb

houmous [ʼumus] *nm Culin* hummus, houmous

houppette [ʼupɛt] *nf (de poudrier)* powder puff

hourra [ʼura] **1** *exclam* hurray! **2** *nm* hurray

houspiller [ʼuspije] *vt* to tell off

housse ['us] *nf* (protective) cover
houx ['u] *nm* holly
hublot ['yblo] *nm* (de navire, d'avion) porthole
huche ['yʃ] *nf* **h. à pain** bread bin
hue ['y] *exclam* gee up!
huer ['ɥe] *vt* to boo ▪**huées** *nfpl* boos
huile [ɥil] *nf* oil; *Fam* (personne) big shot; *Fig* **mer d'h.** glassy sea; *Fig* **jeter de l'h. sur le feu** to add fuel to the fire; *Fam* **h. de coude** elbow grease; **h. d'arachide/d'olive** groundnut/olive oil; **h. essentielle** essential oil; **h. solaire** suntan oil ▪**huiler** *vt* to oil ▪**huileux, -euse** *adj* oily
huis [ɥi] *nm* **à h. clos** behind closed doors; *Jur* in camera
huissier [ɥisje] *nm* (portier) usher; *Jur* bailiff
huit ['ɥit, 'ɥi *before consonant*] *adj & nm inv* eight; **h. jours** a week; **dimanche en h.** *Br* a week on Sunday, *Am* a week from Sunday ▪**huitaine** *nf* (about) eight; (semaine) week; **une h. (de)** about eight ▪**huitième** *adj, nm & nmf* eighth; *Sport* **h. de finale** last sixteen
huître [ɥitr] *nf* oyster
hululer ['ylyle] *vi* to hoot
humain, -aine [ymɛ̃, -ɛn] **1** *adj (relatif à l'homme)* human; (compatissant) humane **2** *nmpl* **les humains** humans ▪**humainement** *adv* (relatif à l'homme) humanly; (avec bonté) humanely; **h. possible** humanly possible ▪**humanitaire** *adj* humanitarian ▪**humanité** *nf* (genre humain, sentiment) humanity
humble [œbl] *adj* humble ▪**humblement** [-əmɑ̃] *adv* humbly
humecter [ymɛkte] *vt* to moisten
humer ['yme] *vt* (respirer) to breathe in; (sentir) to smell
humeur [ymœr] *nf* (disposition) mood; (caractère) temper; (mauvaise humeur) bad mood; **être de bonne/mauvaise h.** to be in a good/bad mood; **mettre qn de bonne/ mauvaise h.** to put sb in a good/bad mood; **être d'une h. massacrante** to be in a foul mood; **d'h. égale** even-tempered
humide [ymid] *adj* (linge) damp, wet; (climat, temps) humid; **les yeux humides de larmes** eyes moist with tears ▪**humidifier** *vt* to humidify ▪**humidité** *nf* (de maison) dampness; (de climat) humidity
humilier [ymilje] *vt* to humiliate ▪**humiliant, -iante** *adj* humiliating ▪**humiliation** *nf* humiliation ▪**humilité** *nf* humility
humour [ymur] *nm Br* humour, *Am* humor; **avoir de l'h.** *ou* **le sens de l'h.** to have a sense of humour; **h. noir** black humour ▪**humoriste**

nmf humorist ▪**humoristique** *adj (ton)* humorous
huppé, -ée ['ype] *adj Fam (riche)* high-class, *Br* posh
hurler ['yrle] **1** *vt (slogans, injures)* to yell **2** *vi (loup, vent)* to howl; (personne) to scream; *Fig* **h. avec les loups** to follow the crowd ▪**hurlement** [-əmɑ̃] *nm (de loup, de vent)* howl; (de personne) scream
hurluberlu [yrlybɛrly] *nm* oddball
hutte ['yt] *nf* hut
hybride [ibrid] *adj & nm* hybrid
hydrater [idrate] *vt (peau)* to moisturize; **crème hydratante** moisturizing cream
hydraulique [idrolik] *adj* hydraulic
hydravion [idravjɔ̃] *nm* seaplane
hydrocarbure [idrokarbyr] *nm* hydrocarbon
hydroélectrique [idroelɛktrik] *adj* hydroelectric
hydrogène [idrɔʒɛn] *nm* hydrogen
hydrophile [idrɔfil] *adj* **coton h.** *Br* cotton wool, *Am* (absorbent) cotton
hyène [jɛn] *nf* hyena
hygiène [iʒjɛn] *nf* hygiene ▪**hygiénique** *adj* hygienic; (serviette, conditions) sanitary
hymne [imn] *nm* hymn; **h. national** national anthem
hyper- [iper] *préf* hyper- ▪**hyperlien** *nm Ordinat* hyperlink ▪**hypermarché** *nm* hypermarket ▪**hypermétrope** *adj* longsighted ▪**hypertension** *nf* **h. artérielle** high blood pressure; **faire de l'h.** to have high blood pressure
hypnose [ipnoz] *nf* hypnosis ▪**hypnotique** *adj* hypnotic ▪**hypnotiser** *vt* to hypnotize ▪**hypnotiseur** *nm* hypnotist ▪**hypnotisme** *nm* hypnotism
hypoallergénique [ipoalɛrʒenik] *adj* hypoallergenic
hypocalorique [ipokalɔrik] *adj (régime, aliment)* low-calorie
hypocondriaque [ipokɔ̃drijak] *adj & nmf* hypochondriac
hypocrisie [ipokrizi] *nf* hypocrisy ▪**hypocrite** **1** *adj* hypocritical **2** *nmf* hypocrite
hypodermique [ipodɛrmik] *adj* hypodermic
hypokhâgne [ipokaɲ] *nf Scol* = first-year arts class preparing students for the entrance examination for the École normale supérieure
hypothèque [ipotɛk] *nf* mortgage ▪**hypothéquer** *vt (maison)* to mortgage
hypothèse [ipotɛz] *nf* hypothesis; **dans l'h. où…** supposing (that)… ▪**hypothétique** *adj* hypothetical
hystérie [isteri] *nf* hysteria ▪**hystérique** *adj* hysterical

I, i [i] *nm inv* I, i

iceberg [isbɛrg, ajsbɛrg] *nm* iceberg

ici [isi] *adv* here; **par i.** *(passer)* this way; *(habiter)* around here; **jusqu'i.** *(temps)* up to now; *(lieu)* as far as this *or* here; **d'i. à mardi** by Tuesday; **d'i. à une semaine** within a week; **d'i. peu** before long; **i. Dupont!** *(au téléphone)* Dupont here!, this is Dupont!; **je ne suis pas d'i.** I'm a stranger around here; **les gens d'i.** the people from around here, the locals ▪ **ici-bas** *adv* on earth

icône [ikon] *nf Rel & Ordinat* icon

idéal, -e, -aux *ou* **-als, -ales** [ideal, -o] **1** *adj* ideal **2** *n* ideal; **l'i. serait de/que...** the ideal *or* best solution would be to/if... ▪ **idéalement** *adv* ideally ▪ **idéaliser** *vt* to idealize ▪ **idéalisme** *nm* idealism ▪ **idéaliste 1** *adj* idealistic **2** *nmf* idealist

idée [ide] *nf* idea **(de** of; **que** that); **changer d'i.** to change one's mind; **il m'est venu à l'i. que...** it occurred to me that...; **se faire une i. de qch** to get an idea of sth; *Fam* **se faire des idées** to imagine things; **avoir dans l'i. de faire qch** to have it in mind to do sth; **avoir son i. sur qch** to have one's own opinions about sth; **avoir une i. derrière la tête** to have an idea at the back of one's mind; *Fam* **avoir des idées** to be full of good ideas; **i. fixe** obsession; **idées noires** black thoughts

idem [idɛm] *adv* ditto

identifier [idɑ̃tifje] *vt*, **s'identifier** *vpr* to identify **(à** *ou* **avec** with) ▪ **identification** *nf* identification

identique [idɑ̃tik] *adj* identical **(à** to)

identité [idɑ̃tite] *nf* identity

idéologie [ideɔlɔʒi] *nf* ideology ▪ **idéologique** *adj* ideological

idiome [idjom] *nm* idiom ▪ **idiomatique** *adj* idiomatic

idiot, -iote [idjo, -jɔt] **1** *adj* silly, idiotic **2** *nmf* idiot ▪ **idiotie** [-ɔsi] *nf (état)* idiocy; **une i.** *(parole, action)* a silly thing

idole [idɔl] *nf* idol; **i. des jeunes** teen idol

idylle [idil] *nf (amourette)* romance

idyllique [idilik] *adj* idyllic

if [if] *nm* yew (tree)

IFOP [ifɔp] *(abrév* **Institut français d'opinion publique)** *nm* = French market and opinion research institute

igloo [iglu] *nm* igloo

ignare [iɲar] **1** *adj* ignorant **2** *nmf* ignoramus

ignifugé, -ée [iɲifyʒe] *adj* fireproof(ed)

ignoble [iɲɔbl] *adj* vile

ignorant, -ante [iɲɔrɑ̃, -ɑ̃t] *adj* ignorant **(de** of) ▪ **ignorance** *nf* ignorance

ignorer [iɲɔre] *vt* not to know; **j'ignore si...** I don't know if...; **je n'ignore pas les difficultés** I am not unaware of the difficulties; **i. qn** *(mépriser)* to ignore sb ▪ **ignoré, -ée** *adj (inconnu)* unknown

il [il] *pron personnel (personne)* he; *(chose, animal, impersonnel)* it; **il est** he/it is; **il pleut** it's raining; **il est vrai que...** it's true that...; **il y a...** there is/are...; **il y a six ans** six years ago; **il y a une heure qu'il travaille** he has been working for an hour; **qu'est-ce qu'il y a?** what's the matter?, what's wrong?; **il n'y a pas de quoi!** don't mention it!

île [il] *nf* island; **les îles Anglo-Normandes** the Channel Islands; **les îles Britanniques** the British Isles; **l'î. Maurice** Mauritius; *Culin* **î. flottante** floating island *(beaten egg whites served on custard)*

illégal, -e, -aux, -ales [il(l)egal, -o] *adj* illegal ▪ **illégalité** *nf* illegality

illégitime [il(l)eʒitim] *adj (enfant, revendication)* illegitimate; *(demande)* unwarranted

illettré, -ée [il(l)etre] *adj & nmf* illiterate

illicite [il(l)isit] *adj* unlawful, illicit

illico [il(l)iko] *adv Fam* **i. (presto)** pronto

illimité, -ée [il(l)imite] *adj* unlimited

illisible [il(l)izibl] *adj (écriture)* illegible; *(livre)* & *Ordinat* unreadable

illogique [il(l)ɔʒik] *adj* illogical

illuminer [il(l)ymine] **1** *vt* to light up, to illuminate **2 s'illuminer** *vpr (visage, ciel)* to light up ▪ **illumination** *nf (action, lumière)* illumination ▪ **illuminé, -ée** *adj (monument)* floodlit

illusion [il(l)yzjɔ̃] *nf* illusion **(sur** about); **se faire des illusions** to delude oneself **(sur** about); **i. d'optique** optical illusion ▪ **s'illusionner** *vpr* to delude oneself **(sur** about) ▪ **illusionniste** *nmf* conjurer ▪ **illusoire** *adj* illusory

illustre [il(l)ystr] *adj* illustrious

illustrer [il(l)ystre] **1** *vt (livre, récit)* to illustrate **(de** with) **2 s'illustrer** *vpr* to distinguish

oneself (**par** by) ▪ **illustration** *nf* illustration
▪ **illustré, -ée** *adj (livre, magazine)* illustrated

îlot [ilo] *nm (île)* small island; *(maisons)* block

ils [il] *pron personnel mpl* they; **i. sont ici** they are
here

image [imaʒ] *nf* picture; *(ressemblance, symbole)*
image; *(dans une glace)* reflection; **i. de marque**
(de produit) brand image; *(firme)* (public)
image; *Ordinat* **i. de synthèse** computer-
generated image ▪ **imagé, -ée** *adj (style)* full
of imagery

imaginable [imaʒinabl] *adj* imaginable
▪ **imaginaire** *adj* imaginary ▪ **imaginatif,
-ive** *adj* imaginative

imagination [imaʒinasjɔ̃] *nf* imagination; **avoir
de l'i.** to be imaginative

imaginer [imaʒine] **1** *vt (se figurer)* to imagine;
(inventer) to devise **2 s'imaginer** *upr (se figurer)*
to imagine (**que** that); *(se voir)* to picture oneself

imbattable [ɛ̃batabl] *adj* unbeatable

imbécile [ɛ̃besil] **1** *adj* idiotic **2** *nmf* idiot,
imbecile ▪ **imbécillité** *nf (état)* imbecility; **une
i.** *(action, parole)* an idiotic thing

imberbe [ɛ̃bɛrb] *adj* beardless

imbiber [ɛ̃bibe] **1** *vt* to soak (**de** with or in) **2
s'imbiber** *upr* to become soaked (**de** with)

imbriquer [ɛ̃brike] **s'imbriquer** *upr (s'emboîter)*
to overlap

imbroglio [ɛ̃brɔglijo] *nm* imbroglio

imbu, -ue [ɛ̃by] *adj* **i. de soi-même** full of
oneself

imbuvable [ɛ̃byvabl] *adj* undrinkable; *Fam
(personne)* insufferable

imiter [imite] *vt* to imitate; *(signature)* to forge;
i. qn *(pour rire)* to mimic sb; *(faire comme)* to
do the same as sb; *(imitateur professionnel)*
to impersonate sb ▪ **imitateur, -trice** *nmf*
imitator; *(professionnel)* impersonator ▪ **imitation** *nf* imitation

immaculé, -ée [imakyle] *adj (sans tache, sans
péché)* immaculate

immangeable [ɛ̃mɑ̃ʒabl] *adj* inedible

immanquable [ɛ̃mɑ̃kabl] *adj* inevitable

immatriculer [imatrikyle] *vt* to register; **se faire
i.** to register ▪ **immatriculation** *nf* registration

immédiat, -iate [imedja, -jat] **1** *adj* immediate
2 *nm* **dans l'i.** for the time being
▪ **immédiatement** *adv* immediately

immense [imɑ̃s] *adj* immense ▪ **immensément** *adv* immensely ▪ **immensité** *nf* immensity

immerger [imɛrʒe] *vt* to immerse ▪ **immersion**
nf immersion (**dans** in)

immettable [ɛ̃metabl] *adj* unwearable

immeuble [imœbl] *nm* building; *(appartements)*
Br block of flats, *Am* apartment block

immigrer [imigre] *vi* to immigrate ▪ **immigrant, -ante** *nmf* immigrant ▪ **immigration**
nf immigration ▪ **immigré, -ée** *adj & nmf*
immigrant; **travailleur i.** immigrant worker

imminent, -ente [iminɑ̃, -ɑ̃t] *adj* imminent
▪ **imminence** *nf* imminence

immiscer [imise] **s'immiscer** *upr* to interfere
(**dans** in)

immobile [imɔbil] *adj* still, motionless
▪ **immobiliser 1** *vt (blessé)* to immobilize;
(train) to bring to a stop; *(voiture) (avec un
sabot)* to clamp **2 s'immobiliser** *upr* to come
to a stop ▪ **immobilité** *nf* stillness; *(de visage)*
immobility

immobilier, -ière [imɔbilje, -jɛr] **1** *adj* **marché
i.** property market; **vente immobilière** sale of
property **2** *nm* **l'i.** *Br* property, *Am* real estate

immodéré, -ée [i(m)mɔdere] *adj* immoderate

immoler [i(m)mɔle] *Littéraire* **1** *vt (sacrifier)* to
sacrifice **2 s'immoler** *upr* **s'i. par le feu** to die
by setting fire to oneself

immonde [i(m)mɔ̃d] *adj (sale)* foul; *(ignoble,
laid)* vile ▪ **immondices** *nfpl* refuse

immoral, -e, -aux, -ales [i(m)mɔral, -o] *adj*
immoral ▪ **immoralité** *nf* immorality

immortel, -elle [i(m)mɔrtɛl] *adj* immortal; **les
Immortels** the members of the Académie
française ▪ **immortaliser** *vt* to immortalize
▪ **immortalité** *nf* immortality

immuable [i(m)mɥabl] *adj* immutable,
unchanging

immuniser [i(m)mynize] *vt Méd* to immunize
(**contre** against) ▪ **immunitaire** *adj Méd
(déficience, système)* immune ▪ **immunité** *nf
Méd & Pol* immunity; **i. parlementaire**
parliamentary immunity

impact [ɛ̃pakt] *nm* impact (**sur** on)

impair, -aire [ɛ̃pɛr] **1** *adj (nombre)* odd, uneven
2 *nm (maladresse)* blunder

imparable [ɛ̃parabl] *adj (coup)* unavoidable

impardonnable [ɛ̃pardɔnabl] *adj* unforgivable

imparfait, -aite [ɛ̃parfɛ, -ɛt] **1** *adj
(connaissance)* imperfect **2** *nm Grammaire
(temps)* imperfect

impartial, -e, -iaux, -iales [ɛ̃parsjal, -jo]
adj impartial, unbiased ▪ **impartialité** *nf*
impartiality

impartir [ɛ̃partir] *vt* to grant (**à** to); **dans le
temps qui nous est imparti** within the
allotted time

impasse [ɛ̃pas] *nf (rue)* dead end; *Fig (situation)*
impasse; **être dans une i.** to be deadlocked;
faire une i. *(en révisant)* = to miss out part of a
subject when revising

impassible [ɛ̃pasibl] *adj* impassive
▪ **impassibilité** *nf* impassiveness

impatient, -iente [ɛ̃pasjɑ̃, -jɑ̃t] *adj* impatient;
i. de faire qch impatient to do sth
▪ **impatiemment** [-amɑ̃] *adv* impatiently
▪ **impatience** *nf* impatience ▪ **impatienter 1**
vt to annoy **2 s'impatienter** *upr* to get
impatient

impavide [ɛ̃pavid] *adj Littéraire* impassive

impayable [ɛ̃pɛjabl] *adj Fam (comique)* priceless

impayé, -ée [ɛ̃peje] *adj* unpaid

impeccable [ɛ̃pekabl] *adj* impeccable ▪ **impeccablement** [-əmɑ̃] *adv* impeccably

impénétrable [ɛ̃penetrabl] *adj (forêt, mystère)* impenetrable

impénitent, -ente [ɛ̃penitɑ̃, -ɑ̃t] *adj* unrepentant

impensable [ɛ̃pɑ̃sabl] *adj* unthinkable

imper [ɛ̃pɛr] *nm Fam* raincoat, *Br* mac

impératif, -ive [ɛ̃peratif, -iv] *1 adj (consigne, besoin)* imperative; *(ton)* imperious *2 nm Grammaire* imperative

impératrice [ɛ̃peratris] *nf* empress

imperceptible [ɛ̃pɛrsɛptibl] *adj* imperceptible (**à** to)

imperfection [ɛ̃pɛrfɛksjɔ̃] *nf* imperfection

impérial, -e, -iaux, -iales [ɛ̃perjal, -jo] *adj* imperial ▪ **impérialisme** *nm* imperialism

impériale [ɛ̃perjal] *nf (d'autobus)* top deck; **autobus à i.** double-decker (bus)

impérieux, -ieuse [ɛ̃perjø, -jøz] *adj (autoritaire)* imperious; *(besoin)* pressing

impérissable [ɛ̃perisabl] *adj (souvenir)* enduring

imperméable [ɛ̃pɛrmeabl] *1 adj* impervious (**à** to); *(tissu, manteau)* waterproof *2 nm* raincoat, *Br* mackintosh ▪ **imperméabilisé, -ée** *adj* waterproof

impersonnel, -elle [ɛ̃pɛrsɔnɛl] *adj* impersonal

impertinent, -ente [ɛ̃pɛrtinɑ̃, -ɑ̃t] *adj* impertinent (**envers** to) ▪ **impertinence** *nf* impertinence

imperturbable [ɛ̃pɛrtyrbabl] *adj (personne)* imperturbable

impétueux, -ueuse [ɛ̃petɥø, -ɥøz] *adj* impetuous ▪ **impétuosité** *nf* impetuosity

impie [ɛ̃pi] *adj Littéraire* impious

impitoyable [ɛ̃pitwajabl] *adj* merciless

implacable [ɛ̃plakabl] *adj (personne, vengeance)* implacable; *(avancée)* relentless

implant [ɛ̃plɑ̃] *nm Méd* implant; **implants capillaires** hair grafts

implanter [ɛ̃plɑ̃te] *1 vt (installer)* to establish; *(chirurgicalement)* to implant *2* **s'implanter** *vpr* to become established ▪ **implantation** *nf* establishment

implicite [ɛ̃plisit] *adj* implicit ▪ **implicitement** *adv* implicitly

impliquer [ɛ̃plike] *vt (entraîner)* to imply; **i. que...** to imply that...; **i. qn** to implicate sb (**dans** in) ▪ **implication** *nf (conséquence)* implication; *(participation)* involvement

implorer [ɛ̃plɔre] *vt* to implore (**qn de faire** sb to do)

impoli, -ie [ɛ̃pɔli] *adj* rude, impolite ▪ **impolitesse** *nf* impoliteness, rudeness; **une i.** *(acte)* impolite act

impondérable [ɛ̃pɔ̃derabl] *nm* imponderable

impopulaire [ɛ̃pɔpylɛr] *adj* unpopular

import [ɛ̃pɔr] *nm* import

important, -ante [ɛ̃pɔrtɑ̃, -ɑ̃t] *1 adj (personnage, événement)* important; *(quantité, somme, ville)* large; *(dégâts, retard)* considerable *2 nm* **l'i., c'est de...** the important thing is to... ▪ **importance** *nf* importance; *(taille)* size; *(de dégâts)* extent; **attacher de l'i. à qch** to attach importance to sth; **ça n'a pas d'i.** it doesn't matter

> Il faut noter que l'adjectif anglais **important** ne signifie jamais **considérable** et ne se rapporte donc jamais à des proportions ou à une quantité.

importer¹ [ɛ̃pɔrte] *1 vi* to matter (**à** to) *2 v impersonnel* **il importe de faire qch** it's important to do sth; **il importe que vous y soyez** it is important that you're there; **peu importe, n'importe** it doesn't matter; **n'importe qui/quoi/où/quand/comment** anyone/anything/anywhere/any time/anyhow; *Péj* **dire n'importe quoi** to talk nonsense

importer² [ɛ̃pɔrte] *vt (marchandises)* to import (**de** from) ▪ **importateur, -trice** *1 adj* importing *2 nmf* importer ▪ **importation** *nf (objet)* import; *(action)* importing, importation; **d'i.** *(article)* imported

importun, -une [ɛ̃pɔrtœ̃, -yn] *1 adj (personne, question)* importunate; *(arrivée)* ill-timed *2 nmf* nuisance ▪ **importuner** *vt Formel* to bother

imposer [ɛ̃poze] *1 vt (condition)* to impose; *(taxer)* to tax; **i. qch à qn** to impose sth on sb; **i. le respect** to command respect *2 vi* **en i. à qn** to impress sb *3* **s'imposer** *vpr (faire reconnaître sa valeur)* to assert oneself; *(gagner)* to win; *(être nécessaire)* to be essential; *Péj (chez qn)* to impose; **s'i. de faire qch** to make it a rule to do sth ▪ **imposable** *adj Fin* taxable ▪ **imposant, -ante** *adj* imposing ▪ **imposition** *nf Fin* taxation

impossible [ɛ̃pɔsibl] *1 adj* impossible (**à faire** to do); **il (nous) est i. de faire qch** it is impossible (for us) to do sth; **il est i. que...** (+ *subjunctive*) it is impossible that...; **ça m'est i.** I cannot possibly; **i. n'est pas français** there's no such word as 'can't' *2 nm* **tenter l'i.** to attempt the impossible; **faire l'i. pour faire qch** to do everything possible to do sth ▪ **impossibilité** *nf* impossibility

imposteur [ɛ̃pɔstœr] *nm* impostor ▪ **imposture** *nf* deception

impôt [ɛ̃po] *nm* tax; **(service des) impôts** tax authorities; **payer 500 euros d'impôts** to pay 500 euros in tax; **impôts locaux** local taxes; **i. sur le revenu** income tax

impotent, -ente [ɛ̃pɔtɑ̃, -ɑ̃t] *adj* disabled; *(de vieillesse)* infirm

Il faut noter que l'adjectif anglais **impotent** est un faux ami. Il signifie **impuissant**.

impraticable [ɛ̃pratikabl] *adj (chemin)* impassable; *(projet)* impracticable

imprécis, -ise [ɛ̃presi, -iz] *adj* imprecise ▪ **imprécision** *nf* imprecision

imprégner [ɛ̃preɲe] **1** *vt* to impregnate (**de** with); *Fig* **être imprégné de qch** to be full of sth **2 s'imprégner** *vpr* to become impregnated (**de** with)

imprenable [ɛ̃prənabl] *adj (forteresse)* impregnable; *(vue)* unobstructed

imprésario [ɛ̃presarjo] *nm* manager

impression [ɛ̃presjɔ̃] *nf* (**a**) *(sensation)* impression; **avoir l'i. que...** to have the impression that...; **il donne l'i. d'être fatigué** he gives the impression of being tired; **faire bonne i. à qn** to make a good impression on sb (**b**) *(de livre)* printing

impressionner [ɛ̃presjone] *vt (bouleverser)* to upset; *(frapper)* to impress ▪ **impressionnable** *adj* easily upset ▪ **impressionnant, -ante** *adj* impressive

Il faut noter que l'adjectif anglais **impressionable** est un faux ami. Il signifie **influençable**.

impressionnisme [ɛ̃presjɔnism] *nm* impressionism ▪ **impressionniste** *adj & nmf* impressionist

imprévisible [ɛ̃previzibl] *adj (temps, réaction, personne)* unpredictable; *(événement)* unforeseeable ▪ **imprévoyance** *nf* lack of foresight ▪ **imprévoyant, -ante** *adj* lacking in foresight ▪ **imprévu, -ue 1** *adj* unexpected, unforeseen **2** *nm* **en cas d'i.** in case of anything unexpected

imprimer [ɛ̃prime] *vt (livre, tissu)* to print; *(cachet)* to stamp; *Ordinat* to print (out); *Tech* **i. un mouvement à** to impart motion to ▪ **imprimante** *nf* printer; **i. à bulles (d'encre)** bubble-jet printer; **i. laser** laser printer ▪ **imprimé** *nm (formulaire)* printed form; **imprimés** *(journaux, prospectus)* printed matter ▪ **imprimerie** *nf (technique)* printing; *(lieu) Br* printing works, *Am* print shop ▪ **imprimeur** *nm* printer

improbable [ɛ̃prɔbabl] *adj* improbable, unlikely

impromptu, -ue [ɛ̃prɔ̃pty] *adj & adv* impromptu

impropre [ɛ̃prɔpr] *adj* inappropriate; **i. à qch** unfit for sth; **i. à la consommation** unfit for human consumption

improviser [ɛ̃prɔvize] *vti* to improvise ▪ **improvisation** *nf* improvisation

improviste [ɛ̃prɔvist] **à l'improviste** *adv* unexpectedly

imprudent, -ente [ɛ̃prydɑ̃, -ɑ̃t] *adj (personne, action)* rash; **il est i. de...** it is unwise to... ▪ **imprudemment** [-amɑ̃] *adv* rashly ▪ **imprudence** *nf* rashness; **commettre une i.** to do something foolish

impudent, -ente [ɛ̃pydɑ̃, -ɑ̃t] *adj* impudent ▪ **impudence** *nf* impudence

impudique [ɛ̃pydik] *adj* shameless

impuissant, -ante [ɛ̃pɥisɑ̃, -ɑ̃t] *adj* powerless; *Méd* impotent ▪ **impuissance** *nf* powerlessness; *Méd* impotence

impulsif, -ive [ɛ̃pylsif, -iv] *adj* impulsive ▪ **impulsion** *nf* impulse; *Fig* **donner une i. à qch** to give an impetus to sth

impunément [ɛ̃pynemɑ̃] *adv* with impunity ▪ **impuni, -ie** *adj* unpunished

impur, -ure [ɛ̃pyr] *adj* impure ▪ **impureté** *nf* impurity

imputer [ɛ̃pyte] *vt* to attribute (**à** to); *(frais)* to charge (**à** to) ▪ **imputable** *adj* attributable (**à** to)

inabordable [inabɔrdabl] *adj (prix)* prohibitive; *(lieu)* inaccessible; *(personne)* unapproachable

inacceptable [inakseptabl] *adj* unacceptable

inaccessible [inaksesibl] *adj (lieu)* inaccessible; *(personne)* unapproachable

inachevé, -ée [inaʃve] *adj* unfinished

inactif, -ive [inaktif, -iv] *adj (personne)* inactive; *(remède)* ineffective ▪ **inaction** *nf* inaction ▪ **inactivité** *nf* inactivity

inadapté, -ée [inadapte] **1** *adj (socialement)* maladjusted; *(physiquement, mentalement)* handicapped; *(matériel)* unsuitable (**à** for) **2** *nmf (socialement)* maladjusted person

inadmissible [inadmisibl] *adj* inadmissible

inadvertance [inadvɛrtɑ̃s] *nf* **par i.** inadvertently

inaltérable [inalterabl] *adj (matière)* stable; *Fig (sentiment)* unchanging

inamical, -e, -aux, -ales [inamikal, -o] *adj* unfriendly

inanimé, -ée [inanime] *adj (mort)* lifeless; *(évanoui)* unconscious; *(matière)* inanimate

inanité [inanite] *nf (d'effort)* futility; *(de conversation)* inanity

inanition [inanisjɔ̃] *nf* **mourir d'i.** to die of starvation

inaperçu, -ue [inapersy] *adj* **passer i.** to go unnoticed

inapplicable [inaplikabl] *adj (loi)* unenforceable; *(théorie)* inapplicable (**à** to)

inappréciable [inapresjabl] *adj* invaluable

inapte [inapt] *adj (intellectuellement)* unsuited; *(médicalement)* unfit; **être i. à qch** to be unsuited/unfit for sth ▪ **inaptitude** *nf (intellectuelle)* inaptitude; *(médicale)* unfitness (**à** for)

inarticulé, -ée [inartikyle] *adj (son, cri)* inarticulate

inattaquable [inatakabl] *adj* unassailable
inattendu, -ue [inatɑ̃dy] *adj* unexpected
inattentif, -ive [inatɑ̃tif, -iv] *adj* inattentive; **i. à qch** *(indifférent)* heedless of sth • **inattention** *nf* lack of attention; **moment d'i.** lapse of concentration
inaudible [inodibl] *adj* inaudible
inaugurer [inogyre] *vt (édifice)* to inaugurate; *(statue)* to unveil; *(politique)* to implement • **inaugural, -e, -aux, -ales** *adj* inaugural • **inauguration** *nf (d'édifice)* inauguration; *(de statue)* unveiling
inavouable [inavwabl] *adj* shameful
incalculable [ɛ̃kalkylabl] *adj* incalculable
incandescent, -ente [ɛ̃kɑ̃desɑ̃, -ɑ̃t] *adj* incandescent
incapable [ɛ̃kapabl] **1** *adj* incapable; **i. de faire qch** incapable of doing sth **2** *nmf (personne)* incompetent • **incapacité** *nf (impossibilité)* inability (**de faire** to do); *(invalidité)* disability; **être dans l'i. de faire qch** to be unable to do sth
incarcérer [ɛ̃karsere] *vt* to incarcerate • **incarcération** *nf* incarceration
incarné, -ée [ɛ̃karne] *adj (ongle)* ingrown; **être la gentillesse incarnée** to be the very embodiment of kindness
incarner [ɛ̃karne] *vt* to embody; *Cin* **i. le rôle de qn** to play the part of sb • **incarnation** *nf* incarnation
incartade [ɛ̃kartad] *nf* indiscretion
incassable [ɛ̃kasabl] *adj* unbreakable
incendie [ɛ̃sɑ̃di] *nm* fire; **i. criminel** arson; **i. de forêt** forest fire • **incendiaire 1** *adj (bombe)* incendiary; *Fig (paroles)* inflammatory **2** *nmf* arsonist • **incendier** *vt* to set on fire
incertain, -aine [ɛ̃sɛrtɛ̃, -ɛn] *adj (résultat)* uncertain; *(temps)* unsettled; *(entreprise)* chancy; *(contour)* indistinct; *(personne)* indecisive • **incertitude** *nf* uncertainty; **être dans l'i. quant à qch** to be uncertain about sth
incessamment [ɛ̃sesamɑ̃] *adv* very soon
incessant, -ante [ɛ̃sesɑ̃, -ɑ̃t] *adj* incessant
inceste [ɛ̃sɛst] *nm* incest • **incestueux, -ueuse** *adj* incestuous
inchangé, -ée [ɛ̃ʃɑ̃ʒe] *adj* unchanged
incidence [ɛ̃sidɑ̃s] *nf (influence)* impact (**sur** on); *Méd* incidence
incident [ɛ̃sidɑ̃] *nm* incident; *(accroc)* hitch; **i. diplomatique** diplomatic incident; **i. de parcours** minor setback; **i. technique** technical hitch
incinérer [ɛ̃sinere] *vt (cadavre)* to cremate • **incinération** *nf (de cadavre)* cremation
inciser [ɛ̃size] *vt (peau)* to make an incision in; *(abcès)* to lance • **incision** *nf (entaille)* incision
incisif, -ive [ɛ̃sizif, -iv] **1** *adj* incisive **2** *nf (dent)* incisive incisor (tooth)
inciter [ɛ̃site] *vt* to encourage (**à faire** to do); **i. qn à la prudence** *(sujet: événement)* to incline

sb to be cautious • **incitation** *nf* incitement (**à** to)
incliner [ɛ̃kline] **1** *vt (pencher)* to tilt; **i. la tête** *(approuver)* to nod; *(saluer)* to bow one's head; *Fig* **i. qn à faire qch** to incline sb to do sth; *Fig* **i. qn à la prudence** to incline sb to be cautious **2 s'incliner** *vpr (se pencher)* to lean forward; *(pour saluer)* to bow; *(bateau)* to heel over; *(avion)* to bank; *Fig (se soumettre)* to give in (**devant** to) • **inclinaison** *nf* incline, slope • **inclination** *nf (tendance)* inclination; **i. de la tête** *(pour saluer)* nod
inclure* [ɛ̃klyr] *vt* to include; *(dans un courrier)* to enclose (**dans** with) • **inclus, -use** *adj* **du 4 au 10 i.** from the 4th to the 10th inclusive; **jusqu'à lundi i.** *Br* up to and including Monday, *Am* through Monday • **inclusion** *nf* inclusion
incognito [ɛ̃kɔɲito] *adv* incognito; **passer/ rester i.** to go/remain incognito
incohérent, -ente [ɛ̃koerɑ̃, -ɑ̃t] *adj (propos)* incoherent; *(histoire)* inconsistent • **incohérence** *nf (de propos)* incoherence; *(d'histoire)* inconsistency
incollable [ɛ̃kɔlabl] *adj (riz)* non-stick; *Fam (personne)* unbeatable
incolore [ɛ̃kɔlɔr] *adj Br* colourless, *Am* colorless; *(vernis, verre)* clear
incomber [ɛ̃kɔbe] *vi* **i. à qn** *(devoir)* to fall to sb; **il lui incombe de faire qch** it falls to him/her to do sth
incommensurable [ɛ̃kɔmɑ̃syrabl] *adj* immeasurable
incommode [ɛ̃kɔmɔd] *adj (situation)* awkward
incommoder [ɛ̃kɔmɔde] *vt* to bother • **incommodant, -ante** *adj* annoying
incomparable [ɛ̃kɔparabl] *adj* matchless
incompatible [ɛ̃kɔpatibl] *adj* incompatible (**avec** with) • **incompatibilité** *nf* incompatibility; **i. d'humeur** mutual incompatibility
incompétent, -ente [ɛ̃kɔpetɑ̃, -ɑ̃t] *adj* incompetent • **incompétence** *nf* incompetence
incomplet, -ète [ɛ̃kɔplɛ, -ɛt] *adj* incomplete
incompréhensible [ɛ̃kɔpreɑ̃sibl] *adj* incomprehensible • **incompréhension** *nf* incomprehension
incompris, -ise [ɛ̃kɔpri, -iz] **1** *adj* misunderstood **2** *nmf* **être un i.** to be misunderstood
inconcevable [ɛ̃kɔsəvabl] *adj* inconceivable
inconciliable [ɛ̃kɔsiljabl] *adj (théorie)* irreconcilable; *(activité)* incompatible
inconditionnel, -elle [ɛ̃kɔdisjɔnɛl] *adj* unconditional; *(supporter)* staunch
inconfort [ɛ̃kɔfɔr] *nm (matériel)* discomfort • **inconfortable** *adj* uncomfortable
incongru, -ue [ɛ̃kɔgry] *adj* inappropriate
inconnu, -ue [ɛ̃kɔny] **1** *adj* unknown (**de** to) **2**

nmf (étranger) stranger; *(auteur)* unknown **3** *nm*
l'i. the unknown **4** *nf Math* **inconnue** unknown
(quantity)

inconscient, -iente [ɛ̃kɔ̃sjɑ̃, -jɑ̃t] **1** *adj*
(sans connaissance) unconscious; *(imprudent)*
reckless; **i. de qch** unaware of sth **2** *nm* **l'i.**
the unconscious ■ **inconsciemment** [-amɑ̃]
adv (dans l'inconscient) subconsciously ■ **incon-
science** *nf (perte de connaissance)* unconscious-
ness; *(irréflexion)* recklessness

inconséquence [ɛ̃kɔ̃sekɑ̃s] *nf (manque de
prudence)* recklessness; *(manque de cohérence)*
inconsistency

inconsidéré, -ée [ɛ̃kɔ̃sidere] *adj* thoughtless

inconsistant, -ante [ɛ̃kɔ̃sistɑ̃, -ɑ̃t] *adj
(personne)* weak; *(film, roman)* flimsy; *(sauce,
crème)* thin

> Il faut noter que l'adjectif anglais **inconsis-
> tent** est un faux ami. Il signifie **incohérent**.

inconsolable [ɛ̃kɔ̃sɔlabl] *adj* inconsolable
inconstant, -ante [ɛ̃kɔ̃stɑ̃, -ɑ̃t] *adj* fickle
■ **inconstance** *nf* fickleness
incontestable [ɛ̃kɔ̃testabl] *adj* indisputable
■ **incontesté, -ée** *adj* undisputed
incontinent, -ente [ɛ̃kɔ̃tinɑ̃, -ɑ̃t] *adj Méd*
incontinent
incontournable [ɛ̃kɔ̃turnabl] *adj Fig (film)*
unmissable; *(auteur)* who cannot be ignored
incontrôlé, -ée [ɛ̃kɔ̃trole] *adj* unchecked
■ **incontrôlable** *adj (invérifiable)* unverifiable;
(indomptable) uncontrollable
inconvenant, -ante [ɛ̃kɔ̃vnɑ̃, -ɑ̃t] *adj*
improper ■ **inconvenance** *nf* impropriety
inconvénient [ɛ̃kɔ̃venjɑ̃] *nm (désavantage)*
drawback; **je n'y vois pas d'i.** I have no
objection; **l'i. c'est que…** the annoying thing
is that…
incorporer [ɛ̃kɔrpɔre] *vt (insérer)* to insert (**à**
in); *(troupes)* to draft; **i. qch à qch** to blend sth
into sth ■ **incorporation** *nf (mélange)* blending
(de qch dans qch of sth into sth); *Mil*
conscription
incorrect, -ecte [ɛ̃kɔrekt] *adj (inexact)*
incorrect; *(grossier)* impolite; *(inconvenant)*
improper ■ **incorrection** *nf (impolitesse)* impoliteness; *(propos)* impolite remark; *(faute de
grammaire)* mistake
incorrigible [ɛ̃kɔriʒibl] *adj* incorrigible
incorruptible [ɛ̃kɔryptibl] *adj* incorruptible
incrédule [ɛ̃kredyl] *adj* incredulous
■ **incrédulité** *nf* incredulity
increvable [ɛ̃krəvabl] *adj (pneu)* puncture-
proof; *Fam (personne)* tireless
incriminer [ɛ̃krimine] *vt (personne)* to accuse
incroyable [ɛ̃krwajabl] *adj* incredible
■ **incroyablement** [-əmɑ̃] *adv* incredibly
■ **incroyant, -ante 1** *adj* unbelieving **2** *nmf*
unbeliever

incrusté, -ée [ɛ̃kryste] *adj* **i. de** *(orné)* inlaid
with ■ **incrustation** *nf (ornement)* inlay; *(dépôt)* fur ■ **s'incruster** *vpr Fam (chez qn)* to be difficult to get rid of
incubation [ɛ̃kybasjɔ̃] *nf* incubation
inculper [ɛ̃kylpe] *vt Jur (accuser)* to charge (**de**
with) ■ **inculpation** *nf Jur* charge, indictment
■ **inculpé, -ée** *nmf Jur* **l'i.** the accused
inculquer [ɛ̃kylke] *vt* to instil (**à qn** in sb)
inculte [ɛ̃kylt] *adj (terre, personne)* uncultivated
incurable [ɛ̃kyrabl] *adj* incurable
incursion [ɛ̃kyrsjɔ̃] *nf (invasion)* incursion; *Fig
(entrée soudaine)* intrusion
incurvé, -ée [ɛ̃kyrve] *adj* curved
Inde [ɛ̃d] *nf* **l'I.** India
indécent, -ente [ɛ̃desɑ̃, -ɑ̃t] *adj* indecent
■ **indécence** *nf* indecency
indéchiffrable [ɛ̃deʃifrabl] *adj (illisible)*
undecipherable
indécis, -ise [ɛ̃desi, -iz] *adj (personne) (de
caractère)* indecisive; *(ponctuellement)* undecided; *(bataille)* inconclusive; *(contour)* vague
■ **indécision** *nf (de caractère)* indecisiveness;
(ponctuelle) indecision
indéfendable [ɛ̃defɑ̃dabl] *adj* indefensible
indéfini, -ie [ɛ̃defini] *adj (illimité) & Grammaire*
indefinite; *(imprécis)* undefined ■ **indéfiniment** *adv* indefinitely ■ **indéfinissable** *adj*
indefinable
indéformable [ɛ̃defɔrmabl] *adj (vêtement)*
which keeps its shape
indélébile [ɛ̃delebil] *adj* indelible
indélicat, -ate [ɛ̃delika, -at] *adj (grossier)*
insensitive; *(malhonnête)* unscrupulous
■ **indélicatesse** *nf (manque de tact)*
tactlessness
indemne [ɛ̃dɛmn] *adj* unhurt, unscathed
indemniser [ɛ̃dɛmnize] *vt* to compensate (**de**
for) ■ **indemnisation** *nf* compensation
■ **indemnité** *nf (dédommagement)* compensation; *(allocation)* allowance; **i. de licenciement** severance pay, *Br* redundancy payment
indémodable [ɛ̃demɔdabl] *adj* classic,
perennially fashionable
indéniable [ɛ̃denjabl] *adj* undeniable
indépendant, -ante [ɛ̃depɑ̃dɑ̃, -ɑ̃t] *adj*
independent (**de** of); *(chambre)* selfcontained;
(travailleur) self-employed; **i. de ma volonté**
beyond my control ■ **indépendamment**
[-amɑ̃] *adv* independently; **i. de** apart from
■ **indépendance** *nf* independence ■ **indépen-
dantiste** *nmf Pol (activiste)* freedom fighter
indescriptible [ɛ̃deskriptibl] *adj* indescribable
indésirable [ɛ̃dezirabl] *adj & nmf* undesirable
indestructible [ɛ̃dɛstryktibl] *adj* indestructible
indéterminé, -ée [ɛ̃determine] *adj (date, heure)*
unspecified; *(raison)* unknown
index [ɛ̃dɛks] *nm (doigt)* index finger; *(liste) &
Ordinat* index

indexer [ɛ̃dɛkse] *vt Écon* to index-link (**sur** to); *(ajouter un index à)* to index

indicateur, -trice [ɛ̃dikatœr, -tris] 1 *nm Rail* timetable; *Tech* indicator, gauge; *Écon* indicator; *(espion)* informer 2 *adj* **poteau i.** signpost; **panneau i.** road sign

indicatif, -ive [ɛ̃dikatif, -iv] 1 *adj* indicative (**de** of); **à titre i.** for information 2 *nm Radio* theme tune; *Grammaire* indicative; **i. téléphonique** *Br* dialling code, *Am* area code

indication [ɛ̃dikɑsjɔ̃] *nf* indication (**de** of); *(renseignement)* (piece of) information; *(directive)* instruction; **indications:...** *(de médicament)* suitable for...

indice [ɛ̃dis] *nm (signe)* sign; *(d'enquête)* clue; *Radio & TV* **i. d'écoute** audience rating; **i. des prix** price index

indien, -ienne [ɛ̃djɛ̃, -jɛn] 1 *adj* Indian 2 *nmf* **I., Indienne** Indian; **I. d'Amérique** Native American

indifférent, -ente [ɛ̃diferɑ̃, -ɑ̃t] *adj* indifferent (**à** to); **ça m'est i.** it's all the same to me ▪ **indifféremment** [-amɑ̃] *adv* indifferently ▪ **indifférence** *nf* indifference (**à** to)

indigène [ɛ̃diʒɛn] *adj & nmf* native

indigent, -ente [ɛ̃diʒɑ̃, -ɑ̃t] *adj* destitute ▪ **indigence** *nf* destitution

indigeste [ɛ̃diʒɛst] *adj* indigestible ▪ **indigestion** *nf* **avoir une i.** to have a stomach upset

indigne [ɛ̃diɲ] *adj (personne)* unworthy; *(conduite)* shameful; **i. de qn/qch** unworthy of sb/sth ▪ **indignité** *nf (de personne)* unworthiness; *(de conduite)* shamefulness; *(action)* shameful act

indigner [ɛ̃diɲe] 1 *vt* **i. qn** to make sb indignant 2 **s'indigner** *vpr* to be indignant (**de** at) ▪ **indignation** *nf* indignation ▪ **indigné, -ée** *adj* indignant

indigo [ɛ̃digo] *nm & adj inv* indigo

indiquer [ɛ̃dike] *vt (sujet: personne)* to point out; *(sujet: panneau, étiquette)* to show, to indicate; *(sujet: compteur)* to read; *(donner) (date, adresse)* to give; *(recommander)* to recommend; **i. qch du doigt** to point to or at sth; **i. le chemin à qn** to tell sb the way ▪ **indiqué, -ée** *adj (conseillé)* advisable; **à l'heure indiquée** at the appointed time; **il est tout i. pour ce poste** he's the right person for the job

indirect, -ecte [ɛ̃dirɛkt] *adj* indirect ▪ **indirectement** [-əmɑ̃] *adv* indirectly

indiscipline [ɛ̃disiplin] *nf* indiscipline ▪ **indiscipliné, -ée** *adj* unruly

indiscret, -ète [ɛ̃diskrɛ, -ɛt] *adj Péj (curieux)* inquisitive; *(qui parle trop)* indiscreet; **à l'abri des regards indiscrets** safe from prying eyes ▪ **indiscrétion** *nf* indiscretion

indiscutable [ɛ̃diskytabl] *adj* indisputable

indispensable [ɛ̃dispɑ̃sabl] *adj* essential, indispensable (**à qch** for sth); **i. à qn** indispensable to sb

indisponible [ɛ̃dispɔnibl] *adj* unavailable

indisposer [ɛ̃dispoze] *vt (contrarier)* to annoy; **i. qn** *(odeur, climat)* to make sb feel ill ▪ **indisposé, -ée** *adj (malade)* indisposed, unwell ▪ **indisposition** *nf* indisposition

indissoluble [ɛ̃disɔlybl] *adj (liens)* indissoluble

indistinct, -incte [ɛ̃distɛ̃(kt), -ɛ̃kt] *adj* indistinct ▪ **indistinctement** [-ɛ̃ktəmɑ̃] *adv* *(voir, parler)* indistinctly; *(également)* equally

individu [ɛ̃dividy] *nm* individual; *Péj* individual, character

individualiser [ɛ̃dividɥalize] *vt (adapter)* to adapt to individual circumstances

individualiste [ɛ̃dividɥalist] 1 *adj* individualistic 2 *nmf* individualist

individualité [ɛ̃dividɥalite] *nf* individuality

individuel, -uelle [ɛ̃dividɥɛl] *adj* individual; *(maison)* detached ▪ **individuellement** *adv* individually

indivisible [ɛ̃divizibl] *adj* indivisible

Indochine [ɛ̃dɔʃin] *nf* **l'I.** Indo-China

indolent, -ente [ɛ̃dɔlɑ̃, -ɑ̃t] *adj* lazy ▪ **indolence** *nf* laziness

indolore [ɛ̃dɔlɔr] *adj* painless

indomptable [ɛ̃dɔ̃(p)tabl] *adj (animal)* untamable; *Fig (orgueil, volonté)* indomitable ▪ **indompté, -ée** *adj (animal)* untamed

Indonésie [ɛ̃dɔnezi] *nf* **l'I.** Indonesia ▪ **indonésien, -ienne** 1 *adj* Indonesian 2 *nmf (person)* **I., Indonésienne** Indonesian 3 *nm (langue)* Indonesian

indu, -ue [ɛ̃dy] *adj* unwarranted; **à une heure indue** at an ungodly hour; **rentrer à des heures indues** to come home at all hours of the night

indubitable [ɛ̃dybitabl] *adj* indisputable; **c'est i.** there's no doubt about it ▪ **indubitablement** [-əmɑ̃] *adv* undoubtedly

induire* [ɛ̃dɥir] *vt* **i. qn en erreur** to lead sb astray

indulgent, -ente [ɛ̃dylʒɑ̃, -ɑ̃t] *adj* indulgent ▪ **indulgence** *nf* indulgence

industrie [ɛ̃dystri] *nf* industry ▪ **industrialisé, -ée** *adj* industrialized ▪ **industriel, -ielle** 1 *adj* industrial 2 *nm* industrialist

> Il faut noter que l'adjectif anglais **industrial** ne signifie pas toujours **industriel**. Il s'emploie également à propos des relations entre employeurs et employés dans des expressions du type **industrial relations** ou **industrial unrest**.

inébranlable [inebrɑ̃labl] *adj Fig (certitude, personne)* unshakeable

inédit, -ite [inedi, -it] *adj (texte)* unpublished; *Fig (nouveau)* original

ineffable [inefabl] *adj* ineffable

inefficace [inefikas] *adj (mesure)* ineffective; *(personne)* inefficient ▪ **inefficacité** *nf (de mesure)* ineffectiveness; *(de personne)* inefficiency

inégal, -e, -aux, -ales [inegal, -o] *adj (parts, lutte)* unequal; *(sol, humeur)* uneven; *Fig (travail)* inconsistent ▪ **inégalable** *adj* incomparable ▪ **inégalé, -ée** *adj* unequalled ▪ **inégalité** *nf (injustice)* inequality; *(physique)* disparity (**de** in); *(de sol)* unevenness

inélégant, -ante [inelegã, -ãt] *adj (mal habillé)* inelegant; *(discourtois)* discourteous

inéligible [ineliʒibl] *adj* ineligible

inéluctable [inelyktabl] *adj* inescapable

inénarrable [inenarabl] *adj (comique)* indescribably funny

inepte [inɛpt] *adj (remarque, histoire)* inane; *(personne)* inept ▪ **ineptie** [inɛpsi] *nf (de comportement, de film)* inanity; *(remarque)* stupid remark

inépuisable [inepɥizabl] *adj* inexhaustible

inerte [inɛrt] *adj (matière)* inert; *(corps)* lifeless ▪ **inertie** [inɛrsi] *nf Phys* inertia; *(manque d'énergie)* apathy

inespéré, -ée [inɛspere] *adj* unhoped-for

inestimable [inɛstimabl] *adj (objet d'art)* priceless; **d'une valeur i.** priceless

inévitable [inevitabl] *adj* inevitable, unavoidable

inexact, -acte [inɛgzakt] *adj (erroné)* inaccurate; *(calcul)* wrong ▪ **inexactitude** *nf (caractère erroné, erreur)* inaccuracy; *(manque de ponctualité)* unpunctuality

inexcusable [inɛkskyzabl] *adj* inexcusable

inexistant, -ante [inɛgzistã, -ãt] *adj* non-existent

inexorable [inɛgzɔrabl] *adj* inexorable; *(volonté)* inflexible

inexpérience [inɛksperjãs] *nf* inexperience ▪ **inexpérimenté, -ée** *adj* inexperienced

inexplicable [inɛksplikabl] *adj* inexplicable ▪ **inexpliqué, -ée** *adj* unexplained

inexploré, -ée [inɛksplore] *adj* unexplored

inexpressif, -ive [inɛkspresif, -iv] *adj* expressionless

inexprimable [inɛksprimabl] *adj* inexpressible

in extremis [inɛkstremis] *adv* at the very last minute

inextricable [inɛkstrikabl] *adj* inextricable

infaillible [ɛ̃fajibl] *adj* infallible ▪ **infaillibilité** *nf* infallibility

infaisable [ɛ̃fəzabl] *adj (travail)* impossible

infamant, -ante [ɛ̃famã, -ãt] *adj (accusation)* defamatory

infâme [ɛ̃fam] *adj (personne)* despicable; *(acte)* unspeakable; *(taudis)* squalid; *(aliment)* revolting ▪ **infamie** *nf (caractère infâme)* infamy; *(remarque)* slanderous remark

infanterie [ɛ̃fãtri] *nf* infantry

infantile [ɛ̃fãtil] *adj (maladie)* childhood; *Péj (comportement, personne)* infantile

infarctus [ɛ̃farktys] *nm Méd* heart attack

infatigable [ɛ̃fatigabl] *adj* tireless

infect, -ecte [ɛ̃fɛkt] *adj* foul

infecter [ɛ̃fɛkte] **1** *vt (atmosphère)* to contaminate; *Méd* to infect **2 s'infecter** *vpr* to become infected ▪ **infectieux, -ieuse** *adj* infectious ▪ **infection** *nf Méd* infection; *(odeur)* stench

inférieur, -ieure [ɛ̃ferjœr] **1** *adj (étagère, niveau)* bottom; *(étage, lèvre, membre)* lower; *(qualité, marchandises)* inferior; **i. à** *(qualité)* inferior to; *(quantité)* less than; **i. à la moyenne** below average; **à l'étage i.** on the floor below **2** *nmf* inferior ▪ **infériorité** *nf* inferiority

infernal, -e, -aux, -ales [ɛ̃fɛrnal, -o] *adj (de l'enfer)* & *Fig (chaleur, bruit)* infernal; **cet enfant est i.** this child's a little devil

infester [ɛ̃fɛste] *vt* to infest (**de** with) ▪ **infesté, -ée** *adj* **i. de requins/de fourmis** shark-/ant-infested

infidèle [ɛ̃fidɛl] *adj* unfaithful (**à** to) ▪ **infidélité** *nf* unfaithfulness; **une i.** *(acte)* an infidelity

infiltrer [ɛ̃filtre] **1** *vt (party)* to infiltrate **2 s'infiltrer** *vpr (liquide)* to seep (**dans** into); *(lumière)* to filter in; *Fig* **s'i. dans** *(groupe, esprit)* to infiltrate ▪ **infiltration** *nf (de liquide, d'espions)* infiltration

infime [ɛ̃fim] *adj* tiny

infini, -ie [ɛ̃fini] **1** *adj* infinite **2** *nm Math & Phot* infinity; *Phil* infinite; **à l'i.** *(discuter)* ad infinitum; *Math* to infinity ▪ **infiniment** *adv* infinitely; **je regrette i.** I'm very sorry ▪ **infinité** *nf* **une i. de** an infinite number of

infinitif [ɛ̃finitif] *nm Grammaire* infinitive

infirme [ɛ̃firm] **1** *adj* disabled **2** *nmf* disabled person ▪ **infirmité** *nf* disability

infirmer [ɛ̃firme] *vt* to invalidate

infirmerie [ɛ̃firməri] *nf (d'école, de bateau)* sick room; *(de caserne, de prison)* infirmary ▪ **infirmier** *nm* male nurse ▪ **infirmière** *nf* nurse

inflammable [ɛ̃flamabl] *adj* (in)flammable

inflammation [ɛ̃flamasjɔ̃] *nf Méd* inflammation

inflation [ɛ̃flasjɔ̃] *nf Écon* inflation ▪ **inflationniste** *adj Écon* inflationary

infléchir [ɛ̃fleʃir] *vt (courber)* to bend; *(politique)* to change the direction of ▪ **inflexion** *nf (de courbe, de voix)* inflection; **i. de la tête** tilt of the head; *(pour saluer)* nod

inflexible [ɛ̃flɛksibl] *adj* inflexible

infliger [ɛ̃fliʒe] *vt* to inflict (**à** on); *(amende)* to impose (**à** on)

influence [ɛ̃flyãs] *nf* influence; **sous l'i. de la drogue** under the influence of drugs; **sous l'i. de la colère** in the grip of anger ▪ **influençable** *adj* easily influenced, impressionable ▪**influencer** *vt* to influence ▪**influent, -uente** *adj* influential ▪**influer** *vi* **i. sur qch** to influence sth

info [ɛfo] *nf Fam* news item; **les infos** the news (*sing*)

informateur, -trice [ɛ̃fɔrmatœr, -tris] *nmf* informant

informaticien, -ienne [ɛ̃fɔrmatisjɛ̃, -jɛn] *nmf* computer scientist

information [ɛ̃fɔrmasjɔ̃] *nf* information; (*nouvelle*) piece of news; *Jur* (*enquête*) inquiry; *Ordinat* data, information; *Radio & TV* **les informations** the news (*sing*)

informatique [ɛ̃fɔrmatik] **1** *nf* (*science*) computer science, IT; (*technique*) data processing **2** *adj* **programme/matériel i.** computer program/hardware ▪**informatisation** *nf* computerization ▪**informatiser** *vt* to computerize

informe [ɛ̃fɔrm] *adj* shapeless

informer [ɛ̃fɔrme] **1** *vt* to inform (**de** of or about; **que** that) **2 s'informer** *vpr* (*se renseigner*) to inquire (**de** about; **si** if or whether)

inforoute [ɛ̃fɔrut] *nf* information superhighway

infortune [ɛ̃fɔrtyn] *nf* misfortune ▪**infortuné, -ée** *adj* unfortunate

infospectacle [ɛ̃fospɛktakl] *nf* infotainment

infraction [ɛ̃fraksjɔ̃] *nf* (*à un règlement*) infringement; (*délit*) *Br* offence, *Am* offense; **être en i.** to be committing an offence

infranchissable [ɛ̃frɑ̃ʃisabl] *adj* (*mur, fleuve*) impassable; *Fig* (*difficulté*) insurmountable

infrarouge [ɛ̃fraruʒ] *adj* infrared

infrastructure [ɛ̃frastryktyr] *nf* (*de bâtiment*) substructure; (*équipements*) infrastructure

infroissable [ɛ̃frwasabl] *adj* crease-resistant

infructueux, -ueuse [ɛ̃fryktɥø, -ɥøz] *adj* fruitless

infuser [ɛ̃fyze] *vi* (*thé*) to brew; (*tisane*) to infuse; **laisser i. le thé** to leave the tea to brew ▪**infusion** *nf* (*tisane*) herb(al) tea

ingénier [ɛ̃ʒenje] **s'ingénier** *vpr* to strive (**à faire** to do)

ingénieur [ɛ̃ʒenjœr] *nm* engineer; **i. civil/mécanique/électronique** structural/mechanical/electronics engineer; **i. des ponts et chaussées** civil engineer ▪**ingénierie** [-iri] *nf* engineering; **i. mécanique** mechanical engineering

ingénieux, -ieuse [ɛ̃ʒenjø, -jøz] *adj* ingenious ▪**ingéniosité** *nf* ingenuity

ingénu, -ue [ɛ̃ʒeny] *adj* ingenuous

ingérer [ɛ̃ʒere] **s'ingérer** *vpr* to interfere (**dans** in) ▪**ingérence** *nf* interference (**dans** in)

ingrat, -ate [ɛ̃gra, -at] *adj* (*personne*) ungrateful (**envers** to); (*tâche*) thankless; (*sol*) barren; (*visage*) unattractive; **l'âge i.** the awkward age ▪**ingratitude** *nf* ingratitude

ingrédient [ɛ̃gredjɑ̃] *nm* ingredient

inguérissable [ɛ̃gerisabl] *adj* incurable

ingurgiter [ɛ̃gyrʒite] *vt* to gulp down

inhabitable [inabitabl] *adj* uninhabitable ▪**inhabité, -ée** *adj* uninhabited

> Il faut noter que les adjectifs anglais **inhabitable** et **inhabited** sont des faux amis. Ils signifient respectivement **habitable** et **habité**.

inhabituel, -uelle [inabitɥɛl] *adj* unusual

inhalateur [inalatœr] *nm Méd* inhaler ▪**inhalation** *nf* inhalation; **faire des inhalations** to inhale

inhérent, -ente [inerɑ̃, -ɑ̃t] *adj* inherent (**à** in)

inhibé, -ée [inibe] *adj* inhibited ▪**inhibition** *nf* inhibition

inhospitalier, -ière [inɔspitalje, -jɛr] *adj* inhospitable

inhumain, -aine [inymɛ̃, -ɛn] *adj* (*cruel, terrible*) inhuman

inhumer [inyme] *vt* to bury ▪**inhumation** *nf* burial

inimaginable [inimaʒinabl] *adj* unimaginable

inimitable [inimitabl] *adj* inimitable

inimitié [inimitje] *nf* enmity

ininflammable [inɛ̃flamabl] *adj* nonflammable

inintelligent, -ente [inɛ̃teliʒɑ̃, -ɑ̃t] *adj* unintelligent

inintelligible [inɛ̃teliʒibl] *adj* unintelligible

inintéressant, -ante [inɛ̃teresɑ̃, -ɑ̃t] *adj* uninteresting

ininterrompu, -ue [inɛ̃terɔ̃py] *adj* continuous

inique [inik] *adj* iniquitous ▪**iniquité** *nf* iniquity

initial, -e, -iaux, -iales [inisjal, -jo] *adj* initial ▪**initiale** *nf* initial ▪**initialement** *adv* initially

initialiser [inisjalize] *vt Ordinat* (*disque*) to initialize; (*ordinateur*) to boot (up)

initiative [inisjativ] *nf* initiative; **de ma propre i.** on my own initiative

initier [inisje] **1** *vt* (*former*) to introduce (**à** to); (*rituellement*) to initiate (**à** into) **2 s'initier** *vpr* **s'i. à qch** to start learning sth ▪**initiation** *nf* initiation ▪**initié, -iée** *nmf* initiate; **les initiés** the initiated

injecter [ɛ̃ʒɛkte] *vt* to inject (**dans** into); **injecté de sang** bloodshot ▪**injection** *nf* injection

injoignable [ɛ̃ʒwaɲabl] *adj* **il est i.** he cannot be reached

injonction [ɛ̃ʒɔ̃ksjɔ̃] *nf* injunction

injure [ɛ̃ʒyr] *nf* insult; **injures** abuse, insults ▪**injurier** *vt* to insult, to abuse ▪**injurieux, -ieuse** *adj* abusive, insulting (**pour** to)

> Il faut noter que les termes anglais **injury** et **to injure** sont des faux amis. Ils signifient le plus souvent **blessure** et **blesser**.

injuste [ɛ̃ʒyst] *adj (contraire à la justice)* unjust; *(non équitable)* unfair ▪ **injustice** *nf* injustice

injustifiable [ɛ̃ʒystifjabl] *adj* unjustifiable ▪ **injustifié, -iée** *adj* unjustified

inlassable [ɛ̃lasabl] *adj* untiring

inné, -ée [ine] *adj* innate, inborn

innocent, -ente [inɔsɑ̃, -ɑ̃t] **1** *adj* innocent (**de** of) **2** *nmf (non coupable)* innocent person ▪ **innocemment** [-amɑ̃] *adv* innocently ▪ **innocence** *nf* innocence; **en toute i.** in all innocence ▪ **innocenter** *vt* **i. qn** to clear sb (**de** of)

innombrable [inɔ̃brabl] *adj* countless, innumerable; *(foule)* huge

innommable [inɔmabl] *adj (conduite, actes)* unspeakable; *(nourriture, odeur)* vile

innover [inɔve] *vi* to innovate ▪ **innovateur, -trice** **1** *adj* innovative **2** *nmf* innovator ▪ **innovation** *nf* innovation

inoccupé, -ée [inɔkype] *adj* unoccupied

inoculer [inɔkyle] *vt Méd* **i. qch à qn** to inoculate sb with sth; **i. qn contre qch** to inoculate sb against sth ▪ **inoculation** *nf Méd* inoculation

inodore [inɔdɔr] *adj Br* odourless, *Am* odorless

inoffensif, -ive [inɔfɑ̃sif, -iv] *adj* harmless

inonder [inɔ̃de] *vt (lieu)* to flood, to inundate (**de** with); *Fig (marché)* to flood, to inundate (**de** with); **inondé de réclamations** inundated with complaints; **inondé de larmes** *(visage)* streaming with tears; **inondé de soleil** bathed in sunlight ▪ **inondation** *nf* flood; *(action)* flooding

inopérable [inɔperabl] *adj* inoperable

inopérant, -ante [inɔperɑ̃, -ɑ̃t] *adj* ineffective

inopiné, -ée [inɔpine] *adj* unexpected

inopportun, -une [inɔpɔrtœ̃, -yn] *adj* inopportune

inoubliable [inublijabl] *adj* unforgettable

inouï, inouïe [inwi] *adj* incredible

Inox® [inɔks] *nm* stainless steel; **couteau en I.** stainless-steel knife ▪ **inoxydable** *adj (couteau)* stainless-steel

inqualifiable [ɛ̃kalifjabl] *adj* unspeakable

inquiet, -iète [ɛ̃kjɛ, -jɛt] *adj* worried, anxious (**de** about)

inquiéter [ɛ̃kjete] **1** *vt (préoccuper)* to worry **2** **s'inquiéter** *vpr* to worry (**de** about); **s'i. pour qn** to worry about sb ▪ **inquiétant, -ante** *adj* worrying

inquiétude [ɛ̃kjetyd] *nf* anxiety, worry; **avoir quelques inquiétudes** to feel a bit worried

inquisiteur, -trice [ɛ̃kizitœr, -tris] *adj (regard)* inquisitive

insaisissable [ɛ̃sezizabl] *adj* elusive

insalubre [ɛ̃salybr] *adj (climat, habitation)* insalubrious

insanités [ɛ̃sanite] *nfpl (idioties)* complete nonsense

insatiable [ɛ̃sasjabl] *adj* insatiable

insatisfait, -aite [ɛ̃satisfɛ, -ɛt] *adj (personne)* dissatisfied

inscription [ɛ̃skripsjɔ̃] *nf (action)* entering; *(immatriculation)* registration; *(sur écriteau, mur, tombe)* inscription

inscrire* [ɛ̃skrir] **1** *vt (renseignements, date)* to write down; *(dans un journal, sur un registre)* to enter; *(graver)* to inscribe; **i. qn à un club** to *Br* enrol *or Am* enroll sb in a club **2** **s'inscrire** *vpr* to put one's name down; *(à une activité) Br* to enrol, *Am* to enroll (**à** at); *(à l'université)* to register (**à** at); **s'i. à un club** to join a club; **s'i. à un examen** to register for an exam; **s'i. dans le cadre de** to come within the framework of; **s'i. en faux contre qch** to deny sth absolutely

insecte [ɛ̃sɛkt] *nm* insect ▪ **insecticide** *nm & adj* insecticide

insécurité [ɛ̃sekyrite] *nf* insecurity

INSEE [inse] *(abrév* **Institut national de la statistique et des études économiques***) nm* = French national institute of statistics and economic studies

insémination [ɛ̃seminasjɔ̃] *nf Méd* **i. artificielle** artificial insemination

insensé, -ée [ɛ̃sɑ̃se] *adj (projet, idée)* crazy; *(espoir)* wild

insensible [ɛ̃sɑ̃sibl] *adj (indifférent)* insensitive (**à** to); *(imperceptible)* imperceptible ▪ **insensibilité** *nf* insensitivity ▪ **insensiblement** [-amɑ̃] *adv* imperceptibly

inséparable [ɛ̃separabl] *adj* inseparable (**de** from)

insérer [ɛ̃sere] *vt* to insert (**dans** in) ▪ **insertion** [ɛ̃sɛrsjɔ̃] *nf* insertion; **i. professionnelle** integration into the job market

insidieux, -ieuse [ɛ̃sidjø, -jøz] *adj* insidious

insigne [ɛ̃siɲ] *nm* badge; **les insignes de la royauté** the insignia of royalty

insignifiant, -iante [ɛ̃siɲifjɑ̃, -jɑ̃t] *adj* insignificant ▪ **insignifiance** *nf* insignificance

insinuer [ɛ̃sinɥe] **1** *vt Péj* to insinuate (**que** that) **2** **s'insinuer** *vpr (froid)* to creep (**dans** into); *(personne)* to worm one's way (**dans** into); **le doute qui s'insinue dans mon esprit** the doubt that is creeping into my mind ▪ **insinuation** *nf* insinuation

insipide [ɛ̃sipid] *adj* insipid

insister [ɛ̃siste] *vi* to insist (**pour faire** on doing); *Fam (persévérer)* to persevere; **i. sur qch** to stress sth; **i. pour que...** (+ *subjunctive*) to insist that...; **il a beaucoup insisté** he was very insistent ▪ **insistance** *nf* insistence ▪ **insistant, -ante** *adj* insistent

insolation [ɛ̃sɔlasjɔ̃] *nf Méd* sunstroke

insolent, -ente [ɛ̃sɔlɑ̃, -ɑ̃t] *adj (impoli)* insolent; *(luxe)* unashamed ▪ **insolence** *nf* insolence

insolite [ɛ̃sɔlit] *adj* unusual, strange

insoluble [ɛ̃sɔlybl] *adj* insoluble

insolvable [ɛ̃sɔlvabl] *adj Fin* insolvent

insomnie [ɛ̃sɔmni] *nf* insomnia; **avoir des insomnies** to have insomnia; **nuit d'i.** sleepless night ▪ **insomniaque** *nmf* insomniac

insondable [ɛ̃sɔ̃dabl] *adj* unfathomable

insonoriser [ɛ̃sɔnɔrize] *vt* to soundproof ▪ **insonorisation** *nf* soundproofing

insouciant, -iante [ɛ̃susjɑ̃, -jɑ̃t] *adj* carefree; **i. de** unconcerned about ▪ **insouciance** *nf* carefree attitude

insoumis, -ise [ɛ̃sumi, -iz] *adj (personne)* rebellious; *(coutume)* institution; *(école)* private *Mil* absentee

insoupçonnable [ɛ̃supsɔnabl] *adj* beyond suspicion ▪ **insoupçonné, -ée** *adj* unsuspected

insoutenable [ɛ̃sutnabl] *adj (spectacle, odeur)* unbearable; *(théorie)* untenable

inspecter [ɛ̃spɛkte] *vt* to inspect ▪ **inspecteur, -trice** *nmf* inspector ▪ **inspection** *nf* inspection

inspirer [ɛ̃spire] **1** *vt* to inspire; **i. qch à qn** to inspire sb with sth; **i. confiance à qn** to inspire confidence in sb **2** *vi* to breathe in **3 s'inspirer** *vpr* **s'i. de qn/qch** to take one's inspiration from sb/sth ▪ **inspiration** *nf (pour créer, idée)* inspiration; *(d'air)* breathing in ▪ **inspiré, -ée** *adj* inspired; **être bien i. de faire qch** to have the good idea to do sth

instable [ɛ̃stabl] *adj* unstable; *(temps)* changeable ▪ **instabilité** *nf* instability; *(de temps)* changeability

installer [ɛ̃stale] **1** *vt (appareil, meuble)* to install, to put in; *(étagère)* to put up; *(cuisine)* to fit out; **i. qn** *(dans une fonction, dans un logement)* to install sb (**dans** in); **i. qn dans un fauteuil** to settle sb down in an armchair **2 s'installer** *vpr (s'asseoir)* to settle down; *(dans un bureau)* to install oneself; *(médecin)* to set oneself up; **s'i. à la campagne** to settle in the country ▪ **installateur** *nm* fitter ▪ **installation** *nf (de machine)* installation; *(de cuisine)* fitting out; *(de rideaux)* putting in; *(emménagement)* move; **installations** *(appareils)* fittings; *(bâtiments)* facilities

instamment [ɛ̃stamɑ̃] *adv* earnestly

instance [ɛ̃stɑ̃s] *nf (insistance)* plea; *(autorité)* authority; *Jur* proceedings; **en i. de divorce** waiting for a divorce; **courrier en i.** mail waiting to go out

> Il faut noter que le nom anglais **instance** est un faux ami. Il signifie **exemple**.

instant [ɛ̃stɑ̃] *nm* moment, instant; **à l'i.** a moment ago; **à l'i. (même) où...** just as...; **pour l'i.** for the moment; **dès l'i. que...** from the moment that...; *(puisque)* seeing that... ▪ **instantané, -ée 1** *adj* instantaneous; **café i.** instant coffee **2** *nm (photo)* snapshot

instar [ɛ̃star] *nm* **à l'i. de qn** after the fashion of sb

instaurer [ɛ̃stɔre] *vt* to establish

instigateur, -trice [ɛ̃stigatœr, -tris] *nmf* instigator ▪ **instigation** *nf* instigation

instinct [ɛ̃stɛ̃] *nm* instinct; **d'i.** by instinct ▪ **instinctif, -ive** *adj* instinctive

instituer [ɛ̃stitɥe] *vt* to establish

institut [ɛ̃stity] *nm* institute; **i. de beauté** beauty salon, *Am* beauty parlor

instituteur, -trice [ɛ̃stitytœr, -tris] *nmf Br* primary or *Am* elementary school teacher

institution [ɛ̃stitysjɔ̃] *nf (création)* establishment; *(coutume)* institution; *(école)* private school; *Pol* **institutions** institutions ▪ **institutionnel, -elle** *adj* institutional

instructif, -ive [ɛ̃stryktif, -iv] *adj* instructive

instruction [ɛ̃stryksjɔ̃] *nf (éducation)* education; *Mil* training; *Jur* preliminary investigation; **instructions** instructions ▪ **instructeur** *nm* instructor

instruire* [ɛ̃strɥir] **1** *vt* to teach, to educate; *Mil* to train; *Jur* to investigate; **i. qn de qch** to inform sb of sth **2 s'instruire** *vpr* to educate oneself; **s'i. de** to find out about ▪ **instruit, -uite** *adj* educated

instrument [ɛ̃strymɑ̃] *nm* instrument; **i. à vent** wind instrument; **instruments de bord** *(d'avion)* instruments ▪ **instrumental, -e, -aux, -ales** *adj Mus* instrumental ▪ **instrumentiste** *nmf Mus* instrumentalist

insu [ɛ̃sy] *nm* **à l'insu de** without the knowledge of; **à mon/son i.** *(sans m'en/s'en apercevoir)* without being aware of it

insuccès [ɛ̃syksɛ] *nm* failure

insuffisant, -ante [ɛ̃syfizɑ̃, -ɑ̃t] *adj (en quantité)* insufficient; *(en qualité)* inadequate ▪ **insuffisance** *nf (manque)* insufficiency; *(de moyens)* inadequacy; **insuffisances** *(faiblesses)* shortcomings

insulaire [ɛ̃sylɛr] **1** *adj* insular **2** *nmf* islander

insuline [ɛ̃sylin] *nf Méd* insulin

insulte [ɛ̃sylt] *nf* insult (**à** to) ▪ **insulter** *vt* to insult

insupportable [ɛ̃sypɔrtabl] *adj* unbearable

insurger [ɛ̃syrʒe] **s'insurger** *vpr* to rise up (**contre** against) ▪ **insurgé, -ée** *nmf & adj* insurgent ▪ **insurrection** *nf* insurrection, uprising

insurmontable [ɛ̃syrmɔ̃tabl] *adj* insurmountable

intact, -acte [ɛ̃takt] *adj* intact

intangible [ɛ̃tɑ̃ʒibl] *adj (loi, institution)* sacred

intarissable [ɛ̃tarisabl] *adj* inexhaustible

intégral, -e, -aux, -ales [ɛ̃tegral, -o] *adj (paiement)* full; *(édition)* unabridged; **casque i.** full-face crash helmet; **version intégrale** *(de film)* uncut version ▪ **intégralement** *adv* in full, fully ▪ **intégralité** *nf* whole (**de** of); **dans son i.** in full

intègre [ɛ̃tegr] *adj* upright, honest ▪ **intégrité** *nf* integrity

intégrer [ɛtegre] **1** *vt* to integrate (**dans** in); *(école)* to get into **2 s'intégrer** *vpr* to become integrated **■ intégrante** *adj f* **faire partie i. de qch** to be an integral part of sth **■ intégration** *nf (au sein d'un groupe)* integration

intégrisme [ɛtegrism] *nm* fundamentalism

intellectuel, -uelle [ɛtelɛktɥɛl] *adj & nmf* intellectual

intelligent, -ente [ɛteliʒɑ̃, -ɑ̃t] *adj* intelligent, clever **■ intelligemment** [-amɑ̃] *adv* intelligently **■ intelligence** *nf (faculté)* intelligence; **avoir l'i. de faire qch** to have the intelligence to do sth; **vivre en bonne i. avec qn** to be on good terms with sb; *Ordinat* **i. artificielle** artificial intelligence

intelligentsia [inteligɛntsja] *nf* intelligentsia

intelligible [ɛteliʒibl] *adj* intelligible **■ intelligibilité** *nf* intelligibility

intempéries [ɛtɑ̃peri] *nfpl* bad weather

intempestif, -ive [ɛtɑ̃pɛstif, -iv] *adj* untimely

intenable [ɛtnabl] *adj (position)* untenable; *Fam (enfant)* uncontrollable

intendant, -ante [ɛtɑ̃dɑ̃, -ɑ̃t] *nmf Scol* bursar **■ intendance** *nf Scol* bursary

intense [ɛtɑ̃s] *adj* intense; *(circulation)* heavy **■ intensément** *adv* intensely **■ intensif, -ive** *adj* intensive **■ intensité** *nf* intensity

intensifier [ɛtɑ̃sifje] *vt*, **s'intensifier** *vpr* to intensify

intenter [ɛtɑ̃te] *vt Jur* **i. un procès à qn** to institute proceedings against sb

intention [ɛtɑ̃sjɔ̃] *nf* intention; *Jur* intent; **avoir l'i. de faire qch** to intend to do sth; **à l'i. de qn** for sb **■ intentionné, -ée** *adj* **bien i.** well-intentioned; **mal i.** ill-intentioned **■ intentionnel, -elle** *adj* intentional **■ intentionnellement** *adv* intentionally

interactif, -ive [ɛteraktif, -iv] *adj Ordinat* interactive

interaction [ɛteraksjɔ̃] *nf* interaction

intercalaire [ɛterkaler] *adj & nm* **(feuillet) i.** *(de classeur)* divider

intercaler [ɛterkale] *vt* to insert

intercéder [ɛtersede] *vt* to intercede (**auprès de** with; **en faveur de** on behalf of)

intercepter [ɛtersɛpte] *vt* to intercept **■ interception** *nf* interception

interchangeable [ɛterʃɑ̃ʒabl] *adj* interchangeable

interclasse [ɛterklɑs] *nm Scol* = short break between classes

intercontinental, -e, -aux, -ales [ɛterkɔ̃tinɑ̃tal, -o] *adj* intercontinental

interdépendant, -ante [ɛterdepɑ̃dɑ̃, -ɑ̃t] *adj* interdependent

interdire* [ɛterdir] *vt* to forbid (**qch à qn** sb sth); *(film, meeting)* to ban; **i. à qn de faire qch** *(médecin, père)* to forbid sb to do sth; *(santé)* to prevent sb from doing sth **■ interdiction** *nf*

ban (**de** on); **'i. de fumer'** 'no smoking' **■ interdit, -ite** *adj* **(a)** forbidden; **il est i. de...** it is forbidden to...; **'stationnement i.'** *(sur panneau)* 'no parking' **(b)** *(étonné)* disconcerted

intéresser [ɛterese] **1** *vt (captiver)* to interest; *(concerner)* to concern **2 s'intéresser** *vpr* **s'i. à qn/qch** to be interested in sb/sth **■ intéressant, -ante 1** *adj (captivant)* interesting; *(prix)* attractive **2** *nmf Péj* **faire l'i.** to show off **■ intéressé, -ée 1** *adj (avide)* self-interested; *(motif)* selfish; *(concerné)* concerned **2** *nmf* **l'i.** the person concerned

intérêt [ɛtere] *nm* interest; *Fin* **intérêts** interest; **tu as i. à le faire** you'd do well to do it; **sans i.** *(personne, film)* uninteresting

interface [ɛterfas] *nf Ordinat* interface

intérieur, -ieure [ɛterjœr] **1** *adj (escalier, paroi)* interior; *(cour, vie)* inner; *(poche)* inside; *(partie)* internal; *(vol)* internal, domestic; *(mer)* inland **2** *nm (de boîte, de maison)* inside (**de** of); *(de pays)* interior; *(maison)* home; **à l'i. (de)** inside; **à l'i. de nos frontières** within the country; **d'i.** *(vêtement, jeux)* indoor; **femme d'i.** home-loving woman **■ intérieurement** *adv* inwardly

intérim [ɛterim] *nm (travail temporaire)* temporary work; **assurer l'i.** to stand in (**de** for); **président par i.** acting president **■ intérimaire 1** *adj (fonction, employé)* temporary **2** *nmf (travailleur)* temporary worker; *(secrétaire)* temp

intérioriser [ɛterjɔrize] *vt* to internalize

interligne [ɛterliɲ] *nm* line spacing

interlocuteur, -trice [ɛterlɔkytœr, -tris] *nmf (de conversation)* speaker; *(de négociation)* discussion partner; **mon i.** the person I am/was speaking to

interloqué, -ée [ɛterlɔke] *adj* dumbfounded

interlude [ɛterlyd] *nm* interlude

intermède [ɛtermɛd] *nm* interlude

intermédiaire [ɛtermedjer] **1** *adj* intermediate **2** *nm* intermediary; *Com* middleman; **par l'i. de** through; **sans i.** directly

interminable [ɛterminabl] *adj* interminable

intermittent, -ente [ɛtermitɑ̃, -ɑ̃t] *adj* intermittent **■ intermittence** *nf* **par i.** intermittently

internat [ɛterna] *nm (école)* boarding school; *(concours de médecine)* = entrance examination for *Br* a housemanship *or Am* an internship **■ interne 1** *adj (douleur)* internal; *(oreille)* inner **2** *nmf (élève)* boarder; **i. des hôpitaux** *Br* house doctor, *Am* intern

international, -e, -aux, -ales [ɛternasjɔnal, -o] **1** *adj* international **2** *nm (joueur de football)* international

interner [ɛterne] *vt (prisonnier)* to intern; *(aliéné)* to commit **■ internement** [-amɑ̃] *nm (emprisonnement)* internment; *(d'aliéné)* confinement

Internet [ɛtɛrnɛt] *nm* Internet; **sur I.** on the Internet ▪ **internaute** *nmf* Internet surfer

interopérabilité [ɛtɛrɔperabilite] *nf* Ordinat interoperability

interpeller [ɛtɛrpəle] *vt (appeler)* to call out to; *(dans une réunion)* to question; **i. qn** *(police)* to take sb in for questioning; **ce roman m'a interpellé** I can really relate to that novel ▪ **interpellation** *nf* sharp address; *(dans une réunion)* question; **la police a procédé à plusieurs interpellations** the police took several people in for questioning

Interphone® [ɛtɛrfɔn] *nm (de bureau)* intercom; *(d'immeuble)* entryphone

interplanétaire [ɛtɛrplanetɛr] *adj* interplanetary

interposer [ɛtɛrpoze] **s'interposer** *upr (intervenir)* to intervene (**dans** in); **par personne interposée** through an intermediary

interprète [ɛtɛrprɛt] *nmf (traducteur)* interpreter; *(chanteur)* singer; *(musicien, acteur)* performer; *(porte-parole)* spokesman, spokesperson, *f* spokeswoman ▪ **interprétariat** *nm* interpreting ▪ **interprétation** *nf (de texte, de rôle, de rêve)* interpretation; *(traduction)* interpreting ▪ **interpréter** *vt (texte, rôle, musique, rêve)* to interpret; *(chanter)* to sing; **mal i. les paroles de qn** to misinterpret sb's words

interroger [ɛterɔʒe] *vt* to question; *(élève)* to test; Ordinat *(banque de données)* to query ▪ **interrogateur, -trice** *adj (air)* questioning ▪ **interrogatif, -ive** *adj & nm* Grammaire interrogative ▪ **interrogation** *nf (question)* question; *(de prisonnier)* questioning; Scol **i. écrite/orale** written/oral test ▪ **interrogatoire** *nm* interrogation

interrompre* [ɛtɛrɔ̃pr] **1** *vt* to interrupt **2 s'interrompre** *upr* to break off ▪ **interrupteur** *nm* switch ▪ **interruption** *nf* interruption; *(de négociations)* breaking off; **sans i.** continuously; **i. volontaire de grossesse** (voluntary) termination of pregnancy, abortion

intersection [ɛtɛrsɛksjɔ̃] *nf* intersection; *(de routes)* junction

interstice [ɛtɛrstis] *nm* crack, chink

intervalle [ɛtɛrval] *nm (dans l'espace)* gap, space; *(dans le temps)* interval; **dans l'i.** *(entretemps)* in the meantime; **par intervalles** (every) now and then, at intervals

intervenir* [ɛtɛrvənir] *vi (agir, prendre la parole)* to intervene; *(survenir)* to occur; **i. auprès de qn** to intercede with sb; **être intervenu** *(accord)* to be reached ▪ **intervention** *nf* intervention; *(discours)* speech; **i. chirurgicale** operation

intervertir [ɛtɛrvɛrtir] *vt (l'ordre de qch)* to invert; *(objets)* to switch round ▪ **interversion** *nf* inversion

interview [ɛtɛrvju] *nm ou f* interview ▪ **interviewer** [-vjuve] *vt* to interview

intestin [ɛtɛstɛ̃] *nm* intestine ▪ **intestinal, -e, -aux, -ales** *adj* intestinal

intime [ɛtim] **1** *adj* intimate; *(ami)* close; *(toilette)* personal; *(cérémonie)* quiet **2** *nmf* close friend ▪ **intimement** [-əmɑ̃] *adv* intimately; **i. liés** *(problèmes)* closely linked ▪ **intimité** *nf (familiarité)* intimacy; *(vie privée)* privacy; **dans l'i.** in private

> Il faut noter qu'en anglais **to be intimate with someone** signifie le plus souvent **avoir des rapports sexuels avec quelqu'un.**

intimider [ɛtimide] *vt* to intimidate ▪ **intimidation** *nf* intimidation

intituler [ɛtityle] **1** *vt* to give a title to **2 s'intituler** *upr* to be entitled

intolérable [ɛtɔlerabl] *adj* intolerable ▪ **intolérance** *nf* intolerance ▪ **intolérant, -ante** *adj* intolerant

intonation [ɛtɔnasjɔ̃] *nf* Ling intonation

intoxiquer [ɛtɔksike] **1** *vt (empoisonner)* to poison **2 s'intoxiquer** *upr* to poison oneself ▪ **intoxication** *nf (empoisonnement)* poisoning; **i. alimentaire** food poisoning

intraduisible [ɛtradɥizibl] *adj* untranslatable

intraitable [ɛtrɛtabl] *adj* uncompromising

Intranet [ɛtranɛt] *nm* Ordinat Intranet

intransigeant, -ante [ɛtrɑ̃ziʒɑ̃, -ɑ̃t] *adj* intransigent ▪ **intransigeance** *nf* intransigence

intransitif, -ive [ɛtrɑ̃zitif, -iv] *adj & nm* Grammaire intransitive

intraveineux, -euse [ɛtravenø, -øz] Méd **1** *adj* intravenous **2** *nf* **intraveineuse** intravenous injection

intrépide [ɛtrepid] *adj* fearless, intrepid ▪ **intrépidité** *nf* fearlessness

intrigue [ɛtrig] *nf* intrigue; *(de film, roman)* plot ▪ **intrigant, -ante** *nmf* schemer ▪ **intriguer 1** *vt* **i. qn** to intrigue sb **2** *vi* to scheme

intrinsèque [ɛtrɛ̃sɛk] *adj* intrinsic

introduire* [ɛtrodɥir] **1** *vt (insérer)* to insert (**dans** into); *(marchandises)* to bring in; *(réforme, mode)* to introduce; *(visiteur)* to show in; Com **i. sur le marché** to launch onto the market **2 s'introduire** *upr* **s'i. dans une maison** to get into a house ▪ **introduction** *nf (texte, action)* introduction

introspectif, -ive [ɛtrɔspɛktif, -iv] *adj* introspective ▪ **introspection** *nf* introspection

introuvable [ɛtruvabl] *adj (produit)* unobtainable; *(personne)* nowhere to be found

introverti, -ie [ɛtrɔvɛrti] *adj & nmf* introvert

intrus, -use [ɛtry, -yz] *nmf* intruder ▪ **intrusion** *nf* intrusion (**dans** into)

intuition [ɛtɥisjɔ̃] *nf* intuition ▪ **intuitif, -ive** *adj* intuitive

inuit [inɥit] **1** *adj inv* Inuit **2** *nmf inv* **I.** Inuit
inusable [inyzabl] *adj* hard-wearing
inusité, -ée [inyzite] *adj (mot, forme)* uncommon
inutile [inytil] *adj (qui ne sert à rien)* useless; *(précaution, bagage)* unnecessary; **c'est i. de crier** there's no point shouting; **i. de dire que...** needless to say that... ■ **inutilement** *adv* needlessly ■ **inutilité** *nf* uselessness
inutilisable [inytilizabl] *adj* unusable ■ **inutilisé, -ée** *adj* unused
invaincu, -ue [ɛ̃vɛ̃ky] *adj Sport* unbeaten
invalide [ɛ̃valid] **1** *adj* disabled **2** *nmf* disabled person; **i. de guerre** disabled ex-serviceman
invalider [ɛ̃valide] *vt* to invalidate
invariable [ɛ̃varjabl] *adj* invariable ■ **invariablement** [-əmɑ̃] *adv* invariably
invasion [ɛ̃vazjɔ̃] *nf* invasion
invective [ɛ̃vɛktiv] *nf* invective ■ **invectiver** *vt* to hurl abuse at
invendable [ɛ̃vɑ̃dabl] *adj* unsellable ■ **invendu, -ue 1** *adj* unsold **2** *nmpl* **invendus** unsold articles; *(journaux)* unsold copies
inventaire [ɛ̃vɑ̃tɛr] *nm Com (liste)* inventory; *Fig (étude)* survey; *Com* **faire l'i.** to do the stocktaking
inventer [ɛ̃vɑ̃te] *vt (créer)* to invent; *(concept)* to think up; *(histoire, excuse)* to make up ■ **inventeur, -trice** *nmf* inventor ■ **inventif, -ive** *adj* inventive ■ **invention** *nf* invention
inverse [ɛ̃vɛrs] **1** *adj (sens)* opposite; *(ordre)* reverse; *Math* inverse **2** *nm* **l'i.** the reverse, the opposite ■ **inversement** [-əmɑ̃] *adv* conversely ■ **inverser** *vt (ordre)* to reverse ■ **inversion** *nf* inversion
investigation [ɛ̃vɛstigasjɔ̃] *nf* investigation ■ **investigateur, -trice** *nmf* investigator
investir [ɛ̃vɛstir] **1** *vt (capitaux)* to invest (**dans** in); *(édifice, ville)* to besiege; **i. qn d'une mission** to entrust sb with a mission **2** *vi* to invest (**dans** in) ■ **investissement** *nm Fin* investment ■ **investiture** *nf Pol* nomination
invétéré, -ée [ɛ̃vetere] *adj* inveterate
invincible [ɛ̃vɛ̃sibl] *adj* invincible
invisible [ɛ̃vizibl] *adj* invisible
inviter [ɛ̃vite] *vt* to invite; **i. qn à faire qch** *(prier)* to request sb to do sth; *(inciter)* to urge sb to do sth; **i. qn à dîner** to invite sb to dinner ■ **invitation** *nf* invitation ■ **invité, -ée** *nmf* guest
invivable [ɛ̃vivabl] *adj* unbearable; *Fam (personne)* insufferable
involontaire [ɛ̃vɔlɔ̃tɛr] *adj (geste)* involuntary; *(témoin)* unwilling ■ **involontairement** *adv* involuntarily
invoquer [ɛ̃vɔke] *vt (argument)* to put forward; *(loi, texte)* to refer to; *(divinité)* to invoke ■ **invocation** *nf* invocation (**à** to)
invraisemblable [ɛ̃vrɛsɑ̃blabl] *adj (extra-*

ordinaire) incredible; *(alibi)* implausible ■ **invraisemblance** *nf (improbabilité)* unlikelihood; *(d'alibi)* implausibility; **invraisemblances** implausibilities
invulnérable [ɛ̃vylnerabl] *adj* invulnerable
iode [jɔd] *nm* **teinture d'i.** *(antiseptique)* iodine
ira, irait *etc* [ira, irɛ] *voir* **aller¹**
Irak [irak] *nm* **l'I.** Iraq ■ **irakien, -ienne 1** *adj* Iraqi **2** *nmf* **I., Irakienne** Iraqi
Iran [irɑ̃] *nm* **l'I.** Iran ■ **iranien, -ienne 1** *adj* Iranian **2** *nmf* **I., Iranienne** Iranian
irascible [irasibl] *adj* irascible
iris [iris] *nm (plante)* & *Anat* iris
Irlande [irlɑ̃d] *nf* **l'I.** Ireland; **l'I. du Nord** Northern Ireland ■ **irlandais, -aise 1** *adj* Irish **2** *nmf* **I.** Irishman; **Irlandaise** Irishwoman; **les I.** the Irish **3** *nm (langue)* Irish
ironie [irɔni] *nf* irony ■ **ironique** *adj* ironic(al)
iront [irɔ̃] *voir* **aller¹**
irradier [iradje] *vt* to irradiate
irraisonné, -ée [irezɔne] *adj* irrational
irrationnel, -elle [irasjɔnɛl] *adj* irrational
irrattrapable [iratrapabl] *adj (retard)* that cannot be made up
irréalisable [irealizabl] *adj (projet)* impracticable
irréaliste [irealist] *adj* unrealistic
irrecevable [irəsəvabl] *adj Jur (preuve)* inadmissible
irrécupérable [irekyperabl] *adj (objet)* beyond repair; *(personne)* irredeemable
irrécusable [irekyzabl] *adj (preuve)* indisputable; *Jur (témoignage)* unimpeachable
irréductible [iredyktibl] **1** *adj (ennemi)* implacable **2** *nm* die-hard
irréel, -éelle [ireɛl] *adj* unreal
irréfléchi, -ie [irefleʃi] *adj* rash
irréfutable [irefytabl] *adj* irrefutable
irrégulier, -ière [iregylje, -jɛr] *adj (rythme, respiration, verbe, procédure)* irregular; *(sol)* uneven; *(résultats)* inconsistent; **être en situation irrégulière** *(voyageur)* not to hold a valid ticket; *(étranger)* not to have one's residence papers in order ■ **irrégularité** *nf* irregularity; *(de sol)* unevenness
irrémédiable [iremedjabl] *adj* irreparable
irremplaçable [irɑ̃plasabl] *adj* irreplaceable
irréparable [ireparabl] *adj (véhicule)* beyond repair; *(tort, perte)* irreparable
irrépressible [irepresibl] *adj* irrepressible
irréprochable [ireprɔʃabl] *adj* irreproachable
irrésistible [irezistibl] *adj (personne, charme)* irresistible
irrésolu, -ue [irezɔly] *adj (personne)* indecisive; *(problème)* unresolved
irrespect [irɛspɛ] *nm* disrespect ■ **irrespectueux, -ueuse** *adj* disrespectful
irrespirable [irespirabl] *adj (air)* unbreathable; *Fig (atmosphère)* unbearable

irresponsable [iʀɛspɔ̃sabl] *adj (personne)* irresponsible

irrévérencieux, -ieuse [iʀeveʀɑ̃sjø, -jøz] *adj* irreverent

irréversible [iʀevɛʀsibl] *adj* irreversible

irrévocable [iʀevɔkabl] *adj* irrevocable

irriguer [iʀige] *vt* to irrigate ▪ **irrigation** *nf* irrigation

irriter [iʀite] **1** *vt* to irritate **2** **s'irriter** *vpr (s'énerver)* to get irritated (**de/contre** with/at); *(s'enflammer)* to become irritated ▪ **irritable** *adj* irritable ▪ **irritant, -ante** *adj (personne, comportement)* irritating; *(produit)* irritant ▪ **irritation** *nf (colère) & Méd* irritation

irruption [iʀypsjɔ̃] *nf* **faire i. dans** to burst into

Islam [islam] *nm* **l'I.** Islam ▪ **islamique** *adj* Islamic

Islande [islɑ̃d] *nf* **l'I.** Iceland ▪ **islandais, -aise** **1** *adj* Icelandic **2** *nmf* **I., Islandaise** Icelander

isocèle [izɔsɛl] *adj* **triangle i.** isosceles triangle

isoler [izɔle] **1** *vt* to isolate (**de** from); *(du froid) & Él* to insulate **2** **s'isoler** *vpr* to isolate oneself ▪ **isolant, -ante** **1** *adj* insulating **2** *nm* insulating material ▪ **isolation** *nf* insulation; **i. thermique** thermal insulation ▪ **isolé, -ée** *adj (personne, endroit, maison)* isolated; *(du froid)* insulated; **i. de** cut off *or* isolated from ▪ **isolement** *nm (de personne)* isolation ▪ **isolément** *adv (agir)* in isolation; *(interroger des gens)* individually

isoloir [izɔlwaʀ] *nm Br* polling booth, *Am* voting booth

Israël [israɛl] *nm* Israel ▪ **israélien, -ienne** **1** *adj* Israeli **2** *nmf* **I., Israélienne** Israeli ▪ **israélite** **1** *adj* Jewish **2** *nmf* Jew

issu, -ue [isy] *adj* **être i. de** to come from

issue [isy] *nf (sortie)* exit; *Fig (solution)* way out; *(résultat)* outcome; *Fig* **situation sans i.** dead end; **à l'i. de** at the end of; **i. de secours** emergency exit

> Il faut noter que le nom anglais **issue** est un faux ami. Il signifie le plus souvent **problème** ou **question**.

isthme [ism] *nm* isthmus

Italie [itali] *nf* **l'I.** Italy ▪ **italien, -ienne** **1** *adj* Italian **2** *nmf* **I., Italienne** Italian **3** *nm (langue)* Italian

italique [italik] **1** *adj (lettre)* italic **2** *nm* italics; **en i.** in italics

itinéraire [itineʀɛʀ] *nm* route, itinerary; **i. bis** = alternative route recommended when roads are highly congested

itinérant, -ante [itineʀɑ̃, -ɑ̃t] *adj Br* travelling, *Am* traveling

IUFM [iyɛfɛm] *(abrév* **Institut universitaire de formation des maîtres)** *nm Br* ≃ teacher training college, *Am* ≃ teachers' college

IUT [iyte] *(abrév* **institut universitaire de technologie)** *nm* = vocational higher education college

IVG [iveʒe] *(abrév* **interruption volontaire de grossesse)** *nf* (voluntary) abortion *or* termination

ivoire [ivwaʀ] *nm* ivory; **statuette en i.** *ou* **d'i.** ivory statuette

ivre [ivʀ] *adj* drunk (**de** with); *Fig* **i. de joie** wild with joy; **i. de bonheur** wildly happy; **i. mort** blind drunk ▪ **ivresse** *nf* drunkenness; **en état d'i.** under the influence of drink ▪ **ivrogne** *nmf* drunk(ard)

J, j [ʒi] *nm inv* J, j; **le jour J.** D-day

j' [ʒ] *voir* je

jacasser [ʒakase] *vi (personne, pie)* to chatter

jachère [ʒaʃɛr] **en jachère** *adv (champ)* fallow; **être en j.** to lie fallow

jacinthe [ʒasɛ̃t] *nf* hyacinth

Jacuzzi® [ʒakuzi] *nm* Jacuzzi®

jade [ʒad] *nm (pierre)* jade

jadis [ʒadis] *adv Littéraire* in days gone by

jaguar [ʒagwar] *nm* jaguar

jaillir [ʒajir] *vi (liquide)* to gush out; *(étincelles)* to shoot out; *(lumière)* to flash; *(cri)* to burst out

jais [ʒɛ] *nm* **(noir) de j.** jet-black

jalon [ʒalɔ̃] *nm* ranging pole; *Fig* **poser les jalons** to prepare the way (**de** for) ▪**jalonner** *vt (marquer)* to mark out; *(border)* to line

jaloux, -ouse [ʒalu, -uz] *adj* jealous (**de** of) ▪**jalouser** *vt* to envy ▪**jalousie** *nf (sentiment)* jealousy; *(store)* Venetian blind

Jamaïque [ʒamaik] *nf* **la J.** Jamaica

jamais [ʒamɛ] *adv* (**a**) *(négatif)* never; **elle ne sort j.** she never goes out; **sans j. sortir** without ever going out; **j. de la vie!** (absolutely) never! (**b**) *(positif)* ever; **à (tout) j.** for ever; **si j.** if ever; **le film le plus drôle que j'aie j. vu** the funniest film I have ever seen

jambe [ʒɑ̃b] *nf* leg; **à toutes jambes** as fast as one can; *Fig* **prendre ses jambes à son cou** to take to one's heels; **être dans les jambes de qn** to be under sb's feet; *Fam* **faire qch par-dessus la j.** to do sth any old how; *Fam* **ça me fait une belle j.!** a fat lot of good that does me!

jambon [ʒɑ̃bɔ̃] *nm* ham ▪**jambonneau, -x** *nm* knuckle of ham

jante [ʒɑ̃t] *nf* rim

janvier [ʒɑ̃vje] *nm* January

Japon [ʒapɔ̃] *nm* **le J.** Japan ▪**japonais, -aise** **1** *adj* Japanese **2** *nmf* **J., Japonaise** Japanese *inv*; **les J.** the Japanese **3** *nm (langue)* Japanese

japper [ʒape] *vi (chien)* to yap, to yelp

jaquette [ʒakɛt] *nf (d'homme)* morning coat; *(de livre)* jacket

jardin [ʒardɛ̃] *nm* garden; **j. d'enfants** kindergarten; **j. public** gardens ▪**jardinage** *nm* gardening ▪**jardiner** *vi* to do some gardening ▪**jardinerie** *nf* garden centre ▪**jardinier** *nm* gardener ▪**jardinière** *nf (caisse à fleurs)* window box; **j. de légumes** mixed vegetables

jargon [ʒargɔ̃] *nm* jargon

jarret [ʒarɛ] *nm* back of the knee

jarretelle [ʒartɛl] *nf Br* suspender, *Am* garter ▪**jarretière** *nf* garter

jaser [ʒaze] *vi (médire)* to gossip

jasmin [ʒasmɛ̃] *nm* jasmine; **thé au j.** jasmine tea

jatte [ʒat] *nf* bowl

jauge [ʒoʒ] *nf (instrument)* gauge; *Naut* tonnage ▪**jauger** *vt Fig (personne, situation)* to size up

jaune [ʒon] **1** *adj* yellow **2** *nm (couleur)* yellow; *Péj (ouvrier)* yellowbelly; **j. d'œuf** (egg) yolk **3** *adv* **rire j.** to give a forced laugh ▪**jaunâtre** *adj* yellowish ▪**jaunir** *vti* to turn yellow ▪**jaunisse** *nf Méd* jaundice

Javel [ʒavɛl] *nf* **(eau de) J.** bleach

javelot [ʒavlo] *nm* javelin

jazz [dʒaz] *nm* jazz

J.-C. [ʃise] *(abrév* **Jésus-Christ**) *nm* J.C.; **av./ap. J.-C.** BC/AD

je [ʒə]

j' is used before a word beginning with a vowel or h mute.

pron personnel I; **je suis ici** I'm here

jean [dʒin] *nm* (pair of) jeans; **veste/jupe en j.** denim jacket/skirt

Jeep® [dʒip] *nf* Jeep®

je-m'en-foutisme [ʒmɑ̃futism] *nm inv très Fam* couldn't-care-less attitude

jérémiades [ʒeremjad] *nfpl* whining

jerrican [(d)ʒerikan] *nm* jerry can

Jersey [ʒɛrzɛ] *nf* Jersey

jésuite [ʒezɥit] *nm* Jesuit

Jésus-Christ [ʒezykrist] *nm* Jesus Christ; **avant/après J.** BC/AD

jet [ʒɛ] *nm (de pierre)* throwing; *(de vapeur, de liquide)* jet; *(de lumière)* flash; **premier j.** *(ébauche)* first draft; **d'un seul j.** in one go; **j. d'eau** fountain

jetable [ʒətabl] *adj* disposable

jetée [ʒəte] *nf* pier, jetty

jeter [ʒəte] **1** *vt* to throw (**à** to; **dans** into); *(à la poubelle)* to throw away; *(ancre, sort, regard)* to cast; *(bases)* to lay; *(cri)* to utter; *(éclat, lueur)* to give out; *(noter)* to jot down; **j. qch à qn** to throw sth to sb, to throw sb sth; **j. un coup d'œil à qn/ qch** to have a quick look at sb/sth; *Fig* **j. l'argent par les fenêtres** to throw money down the drain; *Fam* **se faire j. de** to get chucked out of; **ça a jeté un froid** it cast a chill; *Fam* **ça en jette!** that's really something!

2 se jeter *vpr (personne)* to throw oneself; **se j. sur qn** to throw oneself at sb; *Fig* to pounce on sb; **se j. sur** *(nourriture)* to pounce on; *(occasion)* to jump at; **se j. contre** *(véhicule)* to crash into; **se j. dans** *(fleuve)* to flow into; **se j. à l'eau** *(plonger)* to jump into the water; *Fig (se décider)* to take the plunge

jeton [ʒətɔ̃] *nm (pièce)* token; *(au jeu)* chip; *Fam* **avoir les jetons** to have the jitters

jeu, -x [ʒø] *nm* (**a**) *(amusement)* play; *(activité) & Tennis* game; *(d'acteur)* acting; *(de musicien)* playing; **le j.** *(au casino)* gambling; **maison de jeux** gambling club; **en j.** *(en cause)* at stake; *(forces)* at work; **entrer en j.** to come into play; **d'entrée de j.** from the outset; *Fig* **tirer son épingle du j.** to play one's game profitably; **elle a beau j. de critiquer** it's easy for her to criticize; **c'est un j. d'enfant!** it's child's play!; **j.-concours** competition; **j. électronique** computer game; **jeux de hasard** games of chance; **j. de mots** play on words, pun; **jeux de société** *(devinettes)* parlour games; *(jeu de l'oie, petits chevaux)* board games; **j. télévisé** television game show; *(avec questions)* television quiz show; **j. vidéo** video game (**b**) *(série complète)* set; *(de cartes)* deck, *Br* pack; *(cartes en main)* hand; **j. d'échecs** *(boîte, pièces)* chess set (**c**) *Tech (de ressort, verrou)* play

jeudi [ʒødi] *nm* Thursday

jeun [ʒœ̃] **à jeun 1** *adv* on an empty stomach **2** *adj* **être à j.** to have eaten no food

jeune [ʒœn] **1** *adj* young; *(apparence)* youthful; **jeunes gens** young people **2** *nmf* young person; **les jeunes** young people ▪**jeunesse** *nf* youth; *(apparence)* youthfulness; **la j.** *(les jeunes)* the young

jeûne [ʒøn] *nm (période)* fast; *(pratique)* fasting ▪**jeûner** *vi* to fast

joaillier, -ière [ʒɔaje, -jɛr] *nmf Br* jeweller, *Am* jeweler ▪**joaillerie** *nf (bijoux) Br* jewellery, *Am* jewelry; *(magasin) Br* jewellery shop, *Am* jewelry store

jockey [ʒɔkɛ] *nm* jockey

jogging [dʒɔgiŋ] *nm Sport* jogging; *(survêtement)* jogging suit; **faire du j.** to jog, to go jogging

joie [ʒwa] *nf* joy, delight; **avec j.** with pleasure, gladly; **faire la j. de qn** to make sb happy

joindre* [ʒwɛ̃dr] **1** *vt (réunir)* to join; *(ajouter)* to add (**à** to); *(dans une enveloppe)* to enclose (**à** with); **j. qn** *(contacter)* to get in touch with sb; **j. les mains** to put one's hands together; *Fig* **j. les deux bouts** to make ends meet **2 se joindre** *vpr* **se j. à qn** to join sb; **se j. à qch** to join in sth ▪**joint, -e 1** *adj* **à pieds joints** with feet together; **les mains jointes** with hands together; **pièces jointes** *(de lettre)* enclosures **2** *nm Tech (articulation)* joint; *(d'étanchéité)* seal; *(de robinet)* washer; *Fam (à fumer)* joint; **j.**

de culasse gasket ▪**jointure** *nf (articulation)* joint

joker [ʒɔkɛr] *nm Cartes* joker

joli, -ie [ʒɔli] *adj* pretty; *(somme)* nice ▪**joliment** *adv* nicely; *Fam (très, beaucoup)* awfully

> Il faut noter que l'adjectif anglais **jolly** est un faux ami. Il signifie **joyeux**.

jonc [ʒɔ̃] *nm (plante)* rush

joncher [ʒɔ̃ʃe] *vt* to strew (**de** with); **jonché de** strewn with

jonction [ʒɔ̃ksjɔ̃] *nf* junction

jongler [ʒɔ̃gle] *vi* to juggle (**avec** with) ▪**jonglerie** *nf* juggling ▪**jongleur, -euse** *nmf* juggler

jonquille [ʒɔ̃kij] *nf* daffodil

Jordanie [ʒɔrdani] *nf* **la J.** Jordan

joue [ʒu] *nf (du visage)* cheek; **mettre qn en j.** to take aim at sb; **en j.!** (take) aim!

jouer [ʒwe] **1** *vt (musique, tour, carte, rôle)* to play; *(pièce de théâtre)* to perform; *(film)* to show; *(parier)* to stake (**sur** on); *(cheval)* to bet on; **j. la finale** to play in the final; **j. les héros** to play the hero; *Fig* **j. son avenir** to risk one's future **2** *vi* to play; *(acteur)* to act; *(au tiercé)* to gamble; *(être important)* to count; **j. au tennis/aux cartes** to play tennis/cards; **j. du piano/du violon** to play the piano/violin; **j. aux courses** to bet on the horses; *Fig* **j. en faveur de qn** to work in sb's favour; **j. des coudes** to elbow one's way through; **faire j. un ressort** to release a spring; **à toi de j.!** it's your turn (to play)! **3 se jouer** *vpr (film, pièce)* to be on; **se j. de qn** to trifle with sb; **se j. des difficultés** to make light of difficulties

jouet [ʒwɛ] *nm* toy; *Fig* **être le j. de qn** to be sb's plaything

joueur, -euse [ʒwœr, -øz] *nmf* player; *(au tiercé)* gambler; **beau j., bon j.** good loser

joufflu, -ue [ʒufly] *adj (visage)* chubby; *(enfant)* chubby-cheeked

joug [ʒu] *nm Agr & Fig* yoke

jouir [ʒwir] *vi (sexuellement)* to have an orgasm; **j. de qch** to enjoy sth; **j. d'une bonne santé** to enjoy good health ▪**jouissance** *nf (plaisir)* enjoyment; *(sexuel)* orgasm; *Jur (usage)* use

joujou, -x [ʒuʒu] *nm Fam (en langage enfantin)* toy

jour [ʒur] *nm (journée, date)* day; *(clarté)* daylight; *(éclairage)* light; *(ouverture)* gap; **il fait j.** it's (day)light; **de j. en j.** day by day; **du j. au lendemain** overnight; **au j. le j.** from day to day; **en plein j., au grand j.** in broad daylight; **de nos jours** nowadays, these days; *Fig* **sous un j. nouveau** in a different light; **les beaux jours** *(l'été)* summer; **mettre qch à j.** to bring sth up to date; **se faire j.** to come to light; **donner le j. à qn** to give birth to sb; **mettre fin**

à ses jours to commit suicide; **quel j. sommes-nous?** what day is it?; **il y a dix ans j. pour j.** ten years ago to the day; *Fam* **elle et lui, c'est le j. et la nuit** she and he are as different as night and day *or Br* as chalk and cheese; **le j. de l'an** New Year's Day

journal, -aux [ʒurnal, -o] *nm* (news)paper; *(spécialisé)* journal; *(intime)* diary; *Radio* **j. parlé** (radio) news *(sing)*; **j. télévisé** (TV) news *(sing)*; *Naut* **j. de bord** logbook ▪ **journalisme** *nm* journalism ▪ **journaliste** *nmf* journalist ▪ **journalistique** *adj (style)* journalistic

journalier, -ière [ʒurnalje, -jɛr] *adj* daily

journée [ʒurne] *nf* day; **pendant la j.** during the day(time); **toute la j.** all day (long) ▪ **journellement** *adv* daily

---

Il faut noter que le nom anglais **journey** est un faux ami. Il signifie **voyage** ou **trajet**.

---

jouxter [ʒukste] *vt* to adjoin

jovial, -e, -iaux, -iales [ʒɔvjal, -jo] *adj* jovial, jolly ▪ **jovialité** *nf* joviality

joyau, -x [ʒwajo] *nm* jewel

joyeux, -euse [ʒwajø, -øz] *adj* joyful; **j. anniversaire!** happy birthday!; **j. Noël!** merry *or Br* happy Christmas! ▪ **joyeusement** *adv* joyfully

jubilé [ʒybile] *nm* jubilee

jubiler [ʒybile] *vi* to be jubilant ▪ **jubilation** *nf* jubilation

jucher [ʒyʃe] *vt*, **se jucher** *vpr* to perch (**sur** on)

judaïsme [ʒydaism] *nm* Judaism

judas [ʒyda] *nm (de porte)* peephole, spyhole

judiciaire [ʒydisjɛr] *adj* judicial; *(autorité)* legal

judicieux, -ieuse [ʒydisjø, -jøz] *adj* judicious

judo [ʒydo] *nm* judo

juge [ʒyʒ] *nmf* judge; **j. d'instruction** examining magistrate; *Football* **j. de touche** linesman, assistant referee

jugé [ʒyʒe] **au jugé** *adv (calculer)* roughly

jugement [ʒyʒmɑ̃] *nm (opinion, discernement)* judgement; *Jur (verdict)* sentence; **porter un j. sur qch** to pass judgement on sth; *Jur* **passer en j.** to stand trial

jugeote [ʒyʒɔt] *nf Fam* common sense

juger [ʒyʒe] **1** *vt (personne, question)* to judge; *(au tribunal)* to try; *(estimer)* to consider (**que** that); **j. utile de faire qch** to consider it useful to do sth **2** *vi* **j. de** to judge; **jugez de ma surprise!** imagine my surprise!

juguler [ʒygyle] *vt (inflation, épidémie)* to check

juif, juive [ʒyif, ʒyiv] **1** *adj* Jewish **2** *nmf* **J.** Jew

juillet [ʒyije] *nm* July

juin [ʒyɛ̃] *nm* June

jumeau, -elle, -x, -elles [ʒymo, -ɛl] **1** *adj* **frère j.** twin brother; **sœur jumelle** twin sister; **lits jumeaux** twin beds; **maisons jumelles** semi-detached houses **2** *nmf* twin ▪ **jumelé,**

-ée *adj* **maison jumelée** semi-detached house; **villes jumelées** *Br* twin(ned) towns *or* cities, *Am* sister cities ▪ **jumeler** *vt (villes) Br* to twin, *Am* to make sister cities ▪ **jumelles** *nfpl (pour regarder)* binoculars; **j. de théâtre** opera glasses

jument [ʒymɑ̃] *nf* mare

jungle [ʒœ̃gl] *nf* jungle

junior [ʒynjɔr] *nm & adj inv Sport* junior

junte [ʒœ̃t] *nf* junta

jupe [ʒyp] *nf* skirt ▪ **jupon** *nm* petticoat

jurer [ʒyre] **1** *vt (promettre)* to swear (**que** that; **de faire** to do) **2** *vi (dire un gros mot) Br* to swear, *Am* to curse (**contre** at); *(contraster)* to clash (**avec** with); **j. de qch** to swear to sth ▪ **juré, -ée 1** *adj* **ennemi j.** sworn enemy **2** *nmJur* juror

juridiction [ʒyridiksjɔ̃] *nf (compétence)* jurisdiction; *(tribunaux)* courts (of law)

juridique [ʒyridik] *adj* legal ▪ **juriste** *nmf* legal expert

juron [ʒyrɔ̃] *nm* swearword

jury [ʒyri] *nm Jur* jury; *(d'examen)* board of examiners

jus [ʒy] *nm (de fruits)* juice; *(de viande)* gravy; *Fam (café)* coffee; *Fam* **prendre du j.** *(électricité)* to get a shock; **j. d'orange** orange juice

jusque [ʒysk] **1** *prép* **jusqu'à** *(espace)* as far as, (right) up to; *(temps)* until, (up) till, to; *(même)* even; **jusqu'à 10 euros** up to 10 euros; **jusqu'en mai** until May; **jusqu'où?** how far?; **jusqu'ici** as far as this; *(temps)* up till now; **jusqu'à présent** up till now; **jusqu'à un certain point** up to a point; **jusqu'à la limite de ses forces** to the point of exhaustion; **j. dans/sous** right into/under; **j. chez moi** as far as my place; *Fam* **en avoir j.-là** to be fed up **2** *conj* **jusqu'à ce qu'il vienne** till he comes

juste [ʒyst] **1** *adj (équitable)* fair, just; *(exact)* right, correct; *(étroit)* tight; *(raisonnement)* sound; **un peu j.** *(quantité, qualité)* barely enough; **très j.!** quite so *or* right! **2** *adv (deviner, compter)* correctly, right; *(chanter)* in tune; *(précisément, à peine)* just; **au j.** exactly; **à trois heures j.** on the stroke of three; **un peu j.** *(mesurer, compter)* a bit on the short side; **calculer trop j. (pour)** not to allow enough (for); **ils ont tout j. fini de manger** they've only just finished eating; **j. comme je** as one would expect **3** *nm (homme)* just man ▪ **justement** [-əmɑ̃] *adv (précisément)* exactly; *(avec justesse, avec justice)* justly; **j. j'allais t'appeler** I was just going to ring you

justesse [ʒystɛs] *nf (exactitude)* accuracy; **de j.** *(éviter, gagner)* just

justice [ʒystis] *nf (équité)* justice; **la j.** *(autorité)* the law; **rendre j. à qn** to do justice to sb; **se faire j.** *(se venger)* to take the law into one's own hands ▪ **justicier, -ière** *nmf* righter of wrongs

justifier [ʒystifje] **1** *vt & Typ & Ordinat* to justify; **justifié à gauche/droite** left/right justified **2 se justifier** *vpr* to justify oneself (**de** of) ▪ **justifiable** *adj* justifiable ▪ **justificatif, -ive** *adj* **pièces justificatives** supporting documents ▪ **justification** *nf* (*explication*) justification; (*preuve*) proof

jute [ʒyt] *nm* (*fibre*) jute

juteux, -euse [ʒytø, -øz] *adj* juicy

juvénile [ʒyvenil] *adj* youthful

juxtaposer [ʒykstapoze] *vt* to juxtapose ▪ **juxtaposition** *nf* juxtaposition

K, k [ka] *nm inv* K, k
kaki [kaki] *adj inv & nm* khaki
kaléidoscope [kaleidɔskɔp] *nm* kaleidoscope
kangourou [kãguru] *nm* kangaroo
karaté [karate] *nm Sport* karate
kart [kart] *nm Sport* (go-)kart ▪ **karting** [-iŋ] *nm Sport* karting
kasher [kaʃɛr] *adj inv Rel* kosher
kayak [kajak] *nm (bateau de sport)* canoe, kayak; **faire du k.** to go canoeing
Kenya [kenja] *nm* **le K.** Kenya
képi [kepi] *nm* kepi
kermesse [kermɛs] *nf* charity fair *or Br* fête; *(en Belgique)* village fair
kérosène [kerozɛn] *nm* kerosine
kibboutz [kibuts] *nm inv* kibbutz
kidnapper [kidnape] *vt* to kidnap ▪ **kidnappeur, -euse** *nmf* kidnapper
kilo [kilo] *nm* kilo ▪ **kilogramme** *nm* kilogram(me)
kilomètre [kilɔmɛtr] *nm* kilometre ▪ **kilométrage** *nm Aut* ≃ mileage ▪ **kilométrique** *adj* **borne k.** ≃ milestone
kilo-octet [kiloɔktɛ] *(pl* **kilo-octets)** *nm Ordinat* kilobyte
kilowatt [kilɔwat] *nm* kilowatt
kimono [kimɔno] *nm* kimono
kinésithérapie [kineziterapi] *nf* physiotherapy ▪ **kinésithérapeute** *nmf* physiotherapist
kiosque [kjɔsk] *nm (à fleurs)* kiosk, *Br* stall; **k. à journaux** newsstand; **k. à musique** bandstand
kit [kit] *nm* (self-assembly) kit; **en k.** in kit form
kiwi [kiwi] *nm (oiseau, fruit)* kiwi
Klaxon® [klaksɔn] *nm* horn ▪ **klaxonner** *vi* to sound one's horn
km *(abrév* **kilomètre)** km ▪ **km/h** *(abrév* **kilomètre-heure)** kph, ≃ mph
k.-o. [kao] *adj inv* **mettre qn k.** to knock sb out
Koweït [kɔwɛjt] *nm* **le K.** Kuwait ▪ **koweïtien, -ienne 1** *adj* Kuwaiti **2** *nmf* **K., Koweïtienne** Kuwaiti
kyrielle [kirjɛl] *nf* **une k. de** *(reproches, fautes)* a long string of; *(vedettes)* a whole series of
kyste [kist] *nm Méd* cyst

L, l [εl] *nm inv* L, l

l', la[1] [l, la] *voir* **le**

la[2] [la] *nm inv (note)* A; *Mus* **donner le la** to give an A

là [la] **1** *adv (là-bas)* there; *(ici)* here; **je reste là** I'll stay here; **c'est là que...** *(lieu)* that's where...; **c'est là ton erreur** that's *or* there's your mistake; **c'est là que j'ai compris** that's when I understood; **là où il est** where he is; **à 5 m de là** 5 m away; **de là son échec** *(cause)* hence his/her failure; **jusque-là** *(lieu)* as far as that; *(temps)* up till then **2** *exclam* **oh là là!** oh dear!; **alors là!** well! **3** *voir* **ce**[2], **celui**

là-bas [labɑ] *adv* over there

label [labɛl] *nm Com* quality label

labeur [labœr] *nm Littéraire* toil

laboratoire [laboratwar] *nm* laboratory; **l. de langues** language laboratory ▪ **labo** *nm Fam* lab

laborieux, -ieuse [labɔrjø, -jøz] *adj (pénible)* laborious; **les masses laborieuses** the toiling masses

labour [labur] *nm Br* ploughing, *Am* plowing ▪ **labourer** *vt (terre) Br* to plough, *Am* to plow; *Fig (griffer)* to furrow ▪ **laboureur** *nm Br* ploughman, *Am* plowman

labyrinthe [labirɛ̃t] *nm* maze, labyrinth

lac [lak] *nm* lake

lacer [lase] *vt* to lace (up) ▪ **lacet** *nm (de chaussure)* lace; *(de route)* sharp bend; **faire ses lacets** to tie one's laces; **route en l.** winding road

lacérer [lasere] *vt (déchirer)* to tear to shreds; *(lacérer)* to lacerate

lâche [lɑʃ] **1** *adj (ressort, nœud)* loose, slack; *Péj (personne, acte)* cowardly **2** *nmf* coward ▪ **lâchement** *adv* in a cowardly manner ▪ **lâcheté** *nf* cowardice; **une l.** *(action)* a cowardly act

lâcher [lɑʃe] **1** *vt (ne plus tenir)* to let go of; *(bombe)* to drop; *(colombe)* to release; *(poursuivant)* to shake off; *(dans une course)* to leave behind; *Fam (ami)* to let down; *(juron, cri)* to let out; **l. prise** to let go; *Fam* **lâche-moi les baskets!** get off my back! **2** *vi (corde)* to break **3** *nm* release ▪ **lâcheur, -euse** *nmf Fam* unreliable person

laconique [lakɔnik] *adj* laconic ▪ **laconiquement** *adv* laconically

lacrymogène [lakrimɔʒɛn] *adj* **gaz l.** tear gas

lacté, -ée [lakte] *adj (produit)* containing milk; **régime l.** milk diet

lacune [lakyn] *nf* gap, deficiency

là-dedans [ladədɑ̃] *adv (lieu)* in there, inside

là-dessous [ladəsu] *adv* underneath

là-dessus [ladəsy] *adv* on there; *(monter)* on top; *(alors)* thereupon

lagon [lagɔ̃] *nm* lagoon ▪ **lagune** *nf* lagoon

là-haut [lao] *adv* up there; *(à l'étage)* upstairs

laid, -e [lɛ, lɛd] *adj (personne, visage, endroit)* ugly; *(ignoble)* not nice ▪ **laideur** *nf* ugliness

laine [lɛn] *nf* wool; **de l., en l.** *Br* woollen, *Am* woolen; **l. de verre** glass wool ▪ **lainage** *nm (vêtement)* jumper; *(étoffe)* woollen material; *Com* **lainages** woollens ▪ **laineux, -euse** *adj* woolly

laïque [laik] **1** *adj (école)* non-denominational; *(vie)* secular; *(tribunal)* lay **2** *nmf (non-prêtre)* layman, *f* laywoman

laisse [lɛs] *nf* lead, leash; **tenir un chien en l.** to keep a dog on a lead

laisser [lese] **1** *vt* to leave; **l. qn partir/entrer** *(permettre)* to let sb go/come in; **l. qch à qn** *(confier, donner)* to leave sth with sb; **laissez-moi le temps de le faire** give me *or* leave me time to do it; **l. qn seul** to leave sb alone; **je vous laisse** *(je pars)* I'm leaving now; **je vous le laisse pour 100 euros** I'll let you have it for 100 euros **2** *se laisser vpr* **se l. aller** to let oneself go; **se l. faire** to be pushed around; **se l. surprendre par l'orage** to get caught out by the storm ▪ **laissé-pour-compte** *(pl* **laissés-pour-compte)** *nm (personne)* misfit, reject ▪ **laisser-aller** *nm inv* carelessness ▪ **laissez-passer** *nm inv (sauf-conduit)* pass

lait [lɛ] *nm* milk; **l. entier/demi-écrémé/écrémé** whole/semi-skimmed/skimmed milk; **frère/sœur de l.** foster-brother/-sister ▪ **laitage** *nm* dairy product ▪ **laiterie** *nf* dairy ▪ **laiteux, -euse** *adj* milky ▪ **laitier, -ière 1** *adj* **produit l.** dairy product **2** *nm (livreur)* milkman; *(vendeur)* dairyman **3** *nf* **laitière** *(femme)* dairywoman

laiton [lɛtɔ̃] *nm* brass

laitue [lety] *nf* lettuce

laïus [lajys] *nm Fam* speech

lama [lama] *nm (animal)* llama

lambeau, -x [lɑ̃bo] *nm* scrap; **mettre qch en**

lambeaux to tear sth to shreds; **tomber en lambeaux** to fall to bits

lambris [lɑ̃bri] *nm Br* panelling, *Am* paneling ▪ **lambrisser** *vt* to panel

lame [lam] *nf (de couteau, de rasoir)* blade; *(de métal)* strip, plate; *(vague)* wave; **l. de fond** groundswell; **l. de parquet** floorboard

lamelle [lamɛl] *nf* thin strip; **l. de verre** *(de microscope)* cover glass

lamenter [lamɑ̃te] **se lamenter** *vpr* to moan; **se l. sur qch** to bemoan sth ▪ **lamentable** *adj (mauvais)* terrible, deplorable; *(voix, cri)* mournful; *(personne)* pathetic ▪ **lamentations** *nfpl (cris, pleurs)* wailing

laminé, -ée [lamine] *adj (métal)* laminated

lampadaire [lɑ̃padɛr] *nm Br* standard lamp, *Am* floor lamp; *(de rue)* street lamp

lampe [lɑ̃p] *nf* lamp; **l. de bureau** desk lamp; **l. de poche** *Br* torch, *Am* flashlight; **l. à pétrole** oil lamp

lampée [lɑ̃pe] *nf Fam* gulp

lampion [lɑ̃pjɔ̃] *nm* paper lantern

lance [lɑ̃s] *nf* spear; **l. d'incendie** fire hose ▪ **lance-flammes** *nm inv* flamethrower ▪ **lance-pierres** *nm inv* catapult; *Am* slingshot

lancer [lɑ̃se] **1** *vt (jeter)* to throw (**à** to); *(fusée, produit, mode, navire)* to launch; *(appel, ultimatum)* to issue; *(cri)* to utter; *(bombe)* to drop; *(regard)* to cast (**à** at); **'au revoir!' nous lança-t-il gaiement** 'goodbye!' he called out to us cheerfully **2 se lancer** *vpr (se précipiter)* to rush; *(se faire connaître)* to make a name for oneself; **se l. dans** *(aventure, discussion)* to launch into; **se l. à la poursuite de qn** to rush off in pursuit of sb **3** *nm Sport* **l. du javelot** throwing the javelin; *Basket* **l. franc** free throw ▪ **lancée** *nf* **continuer sur sa l.** to keep going ▪ **lancement** *nm (de fusée, de produit)* launch(ing)

lancinant, -ante [lɑ̃sinɑ̃, -ɑ̃t] *adj (douleur)* shooting; *(obsédant)* haunting

landau, -s [lɑ̃do] *nm Br* pram, *Am* baby carriage

lande [lɑ̃d] *nf* moor, heath

langage [lɑ̃gaʒ] *nm* language; **l. chiffré** code; *Ordinat* **l. machine/naturel** computer/natural language

lange [lɑ̃ʒ] *nm (couche) Br* nappy, *Am* diaper ▪ **langer** *vt (bébé)* to change

langouste [lɑ̃gust] *nf* crayfish ▪ **langoustine** *nf* Dublin Bay prawn

langue [lɑ̃g] *nf Anat* tongue; *Ling* language; **de l. anglaise/française** English-/French-speaking; *Fam* **mauvaise l.** *(personne)* gossip; *Fig* **tenir sa l.** to keep a secret; *Fig* **donner sa l. au chat** to give up; *Fig* **avoir un cheveu sur la l.** to lisp; *Fig* **avoir la l. bien pendue** to have the gift of the gab; *Fig* **avoir un mot sur le bout de la l.** to have a word on the tip of one's tongue; **l. maternelle** mother tongue; **langues mortes** ancient languages; **langues vivantes** modern languages ▪ **languette** *nf (patte)* tongue

langueur [lɑ̃gœr] *nf (mélancolie)* languor ▪ **languir** *vi* to languish (**après** for *or* after); *(conversation)* to flag; **ne nous fais pas l.** don't keep us in suspense

lanière [lanjɛr] *nf* strap; *(d'étoffe)* strip

lanterne [lɑ̃tɛrn] *nf (lampe)* lantern; *Aut* **lanternes** parking lights, *Br* sidelights; *Fig* **éclairer la l. de qn** to enlighten sb

lanterner [lɑ̃tɛrne] *vi Fam* to dawdle

lapalissade [lapalisad] *nf* statement of the obvious

laper [lape] *vt* to lap up

lapider [lapide] *vt* to stone

lapin [lapɛ̃] *nm* rabbit; **mon (petit) l.** darling, *Am* honey; *Fam* **poser un l. à qn** to stand sb up

laps [laps] *nm* **un l. de temps** a period of time

lapsus [lapsys] *nm* slip of the tongue; **faire un l.** to make a slip

laquais [lakɛ] *nm Hist* footman; *Fig & Péj* lackey

laque [lak] *nf (vernis)* lacquer; *(pour cheveux)* hairspray; *(peinture)* gloss (paint) ▪ **laquer** *vt (objet, cheveux)* to lacquer

laquelle [lakɛl] *voir* **lequel**

larbin [larbɛ̃] *nm Fam Péj* flunkey

larcin [larsɛ̃] *nm* petty theft

lard [lar] *nm (gras)* (pork) fat; *(viande)* bacon ▪ **lardon** *nm Culin* strip of bacon

> Il faut noter que le nom anglais **lard** est un faux ami. Il signifie **saindoux**.

large [larʒ] **1** *adj (route, porte, chaussure)* wide; *(vêtement)* loose-fitting; *(nez, geste)* broad; *(considérable)* large; *(généreux)* generous; **l. de 6 m** 6 m wide; **l. d'esprit** broad-minded; **avoir les idées larges** to be broad-minded; **dans une l. mesure** to a large extent **2** *adv* **compter l.** to allow for more **3** *nm* **avoir 6 m de l.** to be 6 m wide; **le l.** *(mer)* the open sea; **au l. de Cherbourg** off Cherbourg; **être au l. dans** *(vêtement)* to have lots of room in ▪ **largement** [-əmɑ̃] *adv (répandu, critiqué)* widely; *(ouvrir)* wide; *(récompenser, payer, servir)* generously; *(dépasser)* by a long way; **avoir l. le temps** to have plenty of time ▪ **largesse** *nf (générosité)* generosity; **largesses** *(dons)* generous gifts ▪ **largeur** *nf (dimension)* width, breadth; **en l., dans la l.** widthwise; **l. d'esprit** broadmindedness; *Ordinat* **l. de bande** bandwidth

> Il faut noter que l'adverbe anglais **largely** est un faux ami. Il signifie **en grande partie**.

larguer [large] *vt (bombe, parachutiste)* to drop; *Naut* **l. les amarres** to cast off; *Fam* **l. qn** *(abandonner)* to chuck *or* dump sb; *Fam* **je suis largué** *(perdu)* I'm all at sea

larme [larm] *nf* tear; *Fam (goutte)* drop; **avoir les larmes aux yeux** to have tears in one's eyes; **en**

larmes in tears; **rire aux larmes** to laugh till one cries ∎**larmoyer** *vi (yeux)* to water

larve [larv] *nf (d'insecte)* grub

larvé, -ée [larve] *adj (guerre)* latent

larynx [larɛ̃ks] *nm* larynx ∎**laryngite** *nf Méd* laryngitis

las, lasse [lɑ, lɑs] *adj* weary (**de** of) ∎**lassant, -ante** *adj* tiresome ∎**lasser** 1 *vt* to tire 2 se **lasser** *vpr* se **l. de qch/de faire qch** to get tired of sth/of doing sth ∎**lassitude** *nf* weariness

lasagnes [lazaɲ] *nfpl* lasagne

lascar [laskar] *nm Fam* rascal

lascif, -ive [lasif, -iv] *adj* lascivious

laser [lazer] *nm* laser; **rayon/imprimante l.** laser beam/printer

lasso [laso] *nm* lasso; **prendre au l.** to lasso

latent, -ente [latɑ̃, -ɑ̃t] *adj* latent

latéral, -e, -aux, -ales [lateral, -o] *adj* side; **rue latérale** side street

latin, -ine [latɛ̃, -in] 1 *adj* Latin 2 *nmf* L., Latine Latin 3 *nm (langue)* Latin; *Fam* **j'y perds mon l.** I can't make head nor tail of it

latitude [latityd] *nf Géog & Fig* latitude

latrines [latrin] *nfpl* latrines

latte [lat] *nf* lath; *(de plancher)* board

lauréat, -éate [lɔrea, -eat] *nmf* (prize)winner

laurier [lɔrje] *nm (arbre)* laurel; *Culin* bay leaves; *Fig* **s'endormir sur ses lauriers** to rest on one's laurels

lavabo [lavabo] *nm* washbasin; **lavabos** *(toilettes) Br* toilet(s), *Am* washroom

lavande [lavɑ̃d] *nf* lavender

lave [lav] *nf* lava

laver [lave] 1 *vt* to wash; **l. qch à l'eau froide** to wash sth in cold water; *Fig* **l. qn d'une accusation** to clear sb of an accusation 2 se **laver** *vpr* to wash (oneself), *Am* to wash up; se **l. les mains** to wash one's hands; se **l. les dents** to clean one's teeth ∎**lavable** *adj* washable ∎**lavage** *nm* washing; **l. de cerveau** brainwashing ∎**lave-auto** *(pl* lave-autos) *nm Can* carwash ∎**lave-glace** *(pl* lave-glaces) *nm Br* windscreen *or Am* windshield washer ∎**lave-linge** *nm inv* washing machine ∎**laverie** *nf (automatique) Br* launderette, *Am* Laundromat® ∎**lavette** *nf* dishcloth; *Péj (homme)* drip ∎**laveur** *nm* **l. de carreaux** window *Br* cleaner *or Am* washer ∎**lave-vaisselle** *nm inv* dishwasher ∎**lavoir** *nm (bâtiment)* washhouse

laxatif, -ive [laksatif, -iv] *nm & adj* laxative

laxisme [laksism] *nm* laxness ∎**laxiste** *adj* lax

layette [lɛjɛt] *nf* baby clothes

le, la, les [lə, la, le]

l' is used instead of **le** or **la** before a word beginning with a vowel or h mute.

1 *article défini* (**a**) *(pour définir le nom)* the; **le garçon** the boy; **la fille** the girl; **les petits/rouges** the little ones/red ones; **mon ami le**

plus proche my closest friend; **venez, les enfants!** come, children! (**b**) *(avec les généralités, les notions)* **la beauté/vie** beauty/life; **la France** France; **les Français** the French; **les hommes** men; **aimer le café** to like coffee (**c**) *(avec les parties du corps)* **il ouvrit la bouche** he opened his mouth; **se blesser au pied** to hurt one's foot; **avoir les cheveux blonds** to have blond hair (**d**) *(distributif)* **3 euros le kilo** 3 euros a kilo (**e**) *(dans les compléments de temps)* **elle vient le lundi/le matin** she comes on Mondays/in the morning(s); **elle passe le soir** she comes over in the evening(s); **l'an prochain** next year; **une fois l'an** once a year

2 *pron (homme)* him; *(femme)* her; *(chose, animal)* it; **les** them; **je la vois** I see her/it; **je le vois** I see him/it; **je les vois** I see them; **es-tu fatigué? – je le suis** are you tired? – I am; **je le crois** I think so

leader [lidœr] *nm* leader

lécher [leʃe] *vt* to lick 2 se **lécher** *vpr* se **l. les doigts** to lick one's fingers ∎**lèche-vitrines** *nm Fam* **faire du l.** to go window-shopping

leçon [ləsɔ̃] *nf* lesson; **faire la l. à qn** to lecture sb; **servir de l. à qn** to teach sb a lesson

lecteur, -trice [lektœr, -tris] *nmf* reader; *Univ* foreign language assistant; **l. (de) cassettes/CD/DVD** cassette/CD/DVD player; *Ordinat* **l. (de) disques** *ou* **(de) disquettes** disk drive; **l. (de) MP3** MP3 player; *Ordinat* **l. Zip®** zip drive ∎**lecture** *nf* reading; **faire la l. à qn** to read to sb; **de la l.** some reading matter; **donner l. des résultats** to read out the results; **lectures** *(livres)* books; *Ordinat* **l. optique** optical reading

> Il faut noter que le nom anglais **lecture** est un faux ami. Il signifie **conférence**.

légal, -e, -aux, -ales [legal, -o] *adj* legal ∎**légalement** *adv* legally ∎**légaliser** *vt* to legalize ∎**légalité** *nf* legality (**de** of); **agir en toute l.** to act within the law

légataire [legater] *nmf* legatee; **l. universel** sole legatee

légende [leʒɑ̃d] *nf (histoire)* legend; *(de carte)* key; *(de photo)* caption; **entrer dans la l.** to become a legend ∎**légendaire** *adj* legendary

léger, -ère [leʒe, -ɛr] 1 *adj* light; *(bruit, blessure, fièvre, nuance)* slight; *(café, thé, argument)* weak; *(bière, tabac)* mild; *(frivole)* frivolous; *(irréfléchi)* thoughtless 2 *adv* **manger l.** to have a light meal 3 *nf* **agir à la légère** to act thoughtlessly; **prendre qch à la légère** to make light of sth ∎**légèrement** *adv* lightly; *(un peu)* slightly; *(avec désinvolture)* rashly ∎**légèreté** *nf (d'objet, de danseur)* lightness; *(de blessure)* slightness; *(désinvolture)* thoughtlessness

légiférer [leʒifere] *vi* to legislate (**sur** on)

légion [leʒjɔ̃] *nf Mil* legion; *Fig* huge number; **L. d'honneur** Legion of Honour ▪**légionnaire** *nm (de la Légion étrangère)* legionnaire
législatif, -ive [leʒislatif, -iv] *adj* legislative; *(élections)* parliamentary ▪**législation** *nf* legislation ▪**législature** *nf (période)* term of office
légitime [leʒitim] *adj (action, enfant)* legitimate; *(héritier)* rightful; *(colère)* justified; **être en état de l. défense** to be acting in *Br* self-defence *or Am* self-defense ▪**légitimité** *nf* legitimacy
legs [lɛg] *nm Jur* legacy, bequest; *Fig (héritage)* legacy ▪**léguer** *vt* to bequeath (**à** to)
légume [legym] *nm* vegetable
lendemain [lɑ̃dmɛ̃] *nm* **le l.** the next day; **le l. de** the day after; **le l. matin** the next morning; **sans l.** *(succès)* short-lived; **au l. de la guerre** soon after the war
lent, -e [lɑ̃, lɑ̃t] *adj* slow ▪**lentement** *adv* slowly ▪**lenteur** *nf* slowness
lentille [lɑ̃tij] *nf (plante, graine)* lentil; *(verre)* lens; **lentilles de contact** contact lenses
léopard [leɔpar] *nm* leopard
LEP [ɛləp, lɛp] *(abrév* **lycée d'enseignement professionnel)** *nm Anciennement Scol* ≃ technical college
lèpre [lɛpr] *nf* leprosy ▪**lépreux, -euse 1** *adj* leprous **2** *nmf* leper
lequel, laquelle [ləkɛl, lakɛl] *(mpl* **lesquels,** *fpl* **lesquelles** [lekɛl])

lequel and lesquel(le)s contract with **à** to form **auquel** and **auxquel(le)s**, and with **de** to form **duquel** and **desquel(le)s**.

1 *pron relatif (chose, animal)* which; *(personne)* who; *(indirect)* whom; **dans l.** in which; **parmi lesquels** *(choses, animaux)* among which; *(personnes)* among whom **2** *pron interrogatif* which (one); **l. préférez-vous?** which (one) do you prefer?
les [le] *voir* **le**
lesbien, -ienne [lɛsbjɛ̃, -jɛn] **1** *adj* lesbian **2** *nf* **lesbienne** lesbian
léser [leze] *vt (personne)* to wrong
lésiner [lezine] *vi* to skimp (**sur** on)
lésion [lezjɔ̃] *nf* lesion
lessive [lesiv] *nf (produit)* washing powder; *(liquide)* liquid detergent; *(linge)* washing; **faire la l.** to do the washing ▪**lessivé, -ée** *adj Fam* washed out ▪**lessiver** *vt* to wash
lest [lɛst] *nm* ballast; **lâcher du l.** to discharge ballast ▪**lester** *vt* to ballast; *Fam (remplir)* to stuff
leste [lɛst] *adj (agile)* nimble; *(grivois)* risqué
léthargie [letarʒi] *nf* lethargy ▪**léthargique** *adj* lethargic
Lettonie [lɛtɔni] *nf* Latvia ▪**letton, -onne 1** *adj* Latvian **2** *nmf* **L., Lettonne** Latvian **3** *nm (langue)* Latvian
lettre [lɛtr] *nf (missive, caractère)* letter; **en toutes lettres** in full; **obéir à qch à la l.** to

obey sth to the letter; **les lettres** *(discipline)* arts, humanities; **homme de lettres** man of letters; *Fam* **c'est passé comme une l. à la poste** it went off without a hitch; **l. ouverte** open letter ▪**lettré, -ée** *adj* well-read
leucémie [løsemi] *nf Méd Br* leukaemia, *Am* leukemia
leur [lœr] **1** *adj possessif* their; **l. chat** their cat; **leurs voitures** their cars **2** *pron possessif* **le l., la l., les leurs** theirs **3** *pron personnel (indirect)* to them; **donne-l. ta carte** give them your card; **il l. est facile de…** it's easy for them to…
leurre [lœr] *nm (illusion)* illusion ▪**leurrer 1** *vt* to delude **2 se leurrer** *upr* to delude oneself
lever [ləve] **1** *vt (objet)* to lift, to raise; *(blocus, interdiction, immunité parlementaire)* to lift; *(séance)* to close; *(impôts, armée)* to levy; **l. les yeux** to look up **2** *vi (pâte)* to rise; *(blé)* to shoot **3 se lever** *upr* to get up; *(soleil, rideau)* to rise; *(jour)* to break; *(brume)* to clear, to lift **4** *nm* **le l. du jour** daybreak; **le l. du soleil** sunrise; *Théâtre* **l. de rideau** curtain up ▪**levant, -ante 1** *adj (soleil)* rising **2** *nm* **le l.** the east ▪**levé, -ée** *adj* **être l.** *(debout)* to be up ▪**levée** *nf (d'interdiction)* lifting; *(du courrier)* collection; *(d'impôts)* levying; *Fig* **l. de boucliers** public outcry
levier [ləvje] *nm* lever; *Aut* **l. de vitesse** *Br* gear lever, *Am* gearshift
lèvre [lɛvr] *nf* lip; **accepter du bout des lèvres** to accept grudgingly
lévrier [levrije] *nm* greyhound
levure [ləvyr] *nf* yeast
lexique [lɛksik] *nm (glossaire)* glossary
lézard [lezar] *nm* lizard
lézarde [lezard] *nf* crack ▪**lézarder 1** *vt* to crack **2** *vi Fam* to bask in the sun **3 se lézarder** *upr* to crack
liaison [ljɛzɔ̃] *nf (rapport)* connection; *(entre mots) & Mil* liaison; **en l. avec qn** in contact with sb; **assurer la l. entre deux services** to liaise between two departments; **l. aérienne/ferroviaire** air/rail link; **l. amoureuse** love affair; **l. radio/téléphonique** radio/telephone link
liane [ljan] *nf* creeper
liant, -e [ljɑ̃, -ɑ̃t] *adj* sociable
liasse [ljas] *nf* bundle
Liban [libɑ̃] *nm* **le L.** (the) Lebanon ▪**libanais, -aise 1** *adj* Lebanese **2** *nmf* **L., Libanaise** Lebanese
libeller [libele] *vt (contrat)* to word; *(chèque)* to make out ▪**libellé** *nm* wording
libellule [libelyl] *nf* dragonfly
libéral, -e, -aux, -ales [liberal, -o] *adj & nmf* liberal ▪**libéraliser** *vt* to liberalize ▪**libéralisme** *nm Pol* liberalism; *Écon* free-market economics ▪**libéralité** *nf Littéraire (générosité)* generosity; *Jur (don)* gift

libérer [libere] **1** *vt (prisonnier)* to free, to release; *(élève)* to let go; *(pays)* to liberate (**de** from); *(chambre)* to vacate; **l. qn d'un souci** to take the weight off sb's mind **2 se libérer** *vpr* to free oneself (**de** from); **je n'ai pas pu me l. plus tôt** I couldn't get away any earlier ■ **libérateur, -trice 1** *adj* liberating **2** *nmf* liberator ■ **libération** *nf (de prisonnier)* release; *(de pays)* liberation; *Jur* **l. conditionnelle** parole; *Hist* **la L.** the Liberation *(of France from the Germans in 1944-45)*

liberté [liberte] *nf* freedom, liberty; *Jur* **en l. provisoire** on bail; **rendre sa l. à qn** to let sb go; **mettre qn en l.** to set sb free; **mise en l.** release

libraire [librɛr] *nmf* bookseller ■ **librairie** *nf (magasin)* bookshop

> Il faut noter que les termes anglais **librarian** et **library** sont des faux amis. Ils signifient respectivement **bibliothécaire** et **bibliothèque**.

libre [libr] *adj (personne, siège)* free (**de qch** from sth; **de faire** to do); *(voie)* clear; **être l. comme l'air** to be as free as a bird; **avoir les mains libres** to have one's hands free; *Fig* **la voie est l.** the coast is clear; **école l.** independent Catholic school; **radio l.** independent radio; **l. arbitre** free will ■ **libre-échange** *nm Écon* free trade ■ **librement** [-əmɑ̃] *adv* freely ■ **libre-penseur** *(pl* libres-penseurs) *nm* freethinker ■ **libre-service** *(pl* libres-services) *nm (système, magasin)* self-service

Libye [libi] *nf* **la L.** Libya ■ **libyen, -enne 1** *adj* Libyan **2** *nmf* **L., Libyenne** Libyan

licence [lisɑ̃s] *nf Sport* permit; *Com Br* licence, *Am* license; *Univ* (bachelor's) degree; **l. en lettres/sciences** arts/science degree; **l. poétique** poetic licence ■ **licencié, -iée** *adj & nmf* graduate; **l. en lettres/sciences** arts/ science graduate

> Il faut noter que le nom anglais **licence** ne signifie jamais **diplôme**.

licencier [lisɑ̃sje] *vt (employé)* to lay off, *Br* to make redundant ■ **licenciement** *nm* lay-off, *Br* redundancy; **l. économique** lay-off, *Br* redundancy

licorne [likɔrn] *nf* unicorn

lie [li] *nf* dregs

liège [ljɛʒ] *nm (matérielle)* cork; **un bouchon de l.** a cork

lien [ljɛ̃] *nm (rapport)* link, connection; *(attache)* bond; **les liens sacrés du mariage** the sacred bonds of marriage; **l. de parenté** family relationship; *Ordinat* **l. hypertexte** hypertext link

lier [lje] **1** *vt (attacher)* to tie up; *(contrat)* to be binding on; *(personnes)* to bind together; *(événements, paragraphes)* to connect, to link; *Culin (sauce)* to thicken; **l. qn** *(unir, engager)* to bind sb; **avoir les mains liées** to have one's hands tied; **être très lié avec qn** to be great friends with sb **2 se lier** *vpr* **se l. (d'amitié)** to become friends

lierre [ljɛr] *nm* ivy

lieu, -x [ljø] *nm* place; **les lieux** *(locaux)* the premises; **sur les lieux du crime/de l'accident** at the scene of the crime/accident; **être sur les lieux** to be on the spot; **avoir l.** to take place; **donner l. à qch** to give rise to sth; **avoir l. de faire qch** to have good reason to do sth; **il n'y a pas l. de s'inquiéter** there's no need to worry; **tenir l. de qch** to serve as sth; **se plaindre en haut l.** to complain to people in high places; **au l. de** instead of; **au l. de te plaindre** instead of complaining; **en premier l.** in the first place, firstly; **en dernier l.** lastly; **s'il y a l.** if necessary; **l. commun** commonplace; **l. de naissance** place of birth; **l. public** public place; **l. de vacances** *Br* holiday *or Am* vacation destination ■ **lieu-dit** *(pl* lieux-dits) *nm* locality

lieue [ljø] *nf Hist & Naut (mesure)* league

lieutenant [ljøtnɑ̃] *nm* lieutenant

lièvre [ljɛvr] *nm* hare

lifter [lifte] *vt (personne)* to perform a facelift on; *(bâtiment)* to give a facelift to ■ **lifting** *nm* facelift

ligament [ligamɑ̃] *nm* ligament

ligne [liɲ] *nf (trait, contour, de transport)* line; *(belle silhouette)* figure; *(rangée)* row, line; **les grandes lignes** *(de train)* the main lines; *Fig (les idées principales)* the broad outline; **aller à la l.** to begin a new paragraph; *Fig* **sur toute la l.** completely; **(se) mettre en l.** to line up; **être en l.** *(au téléphone)* to be through; **entrer en l. de compte** to be taken into account; *Fam* **garder la l.** to stay slim; **l. d'autobus** bus service; *(parcours)* bus route; **l. de chemin de fer** *Br* railway *or Am* railroad line; **l. de conduite** line of conduct; *Sport* **l. de touche** touchline

lignée [liɲe] *nf* descendants; *Fig* **dans la l. de** in the tradition of

ligoter [ligɔte] *vt* to tie up (**à** to)

ligue [lig] *nf* league ■ **se liguer** *vpr (États)* to form a league (**contre** against); *(personnes)* to gang up (**contre** against)

lilas [lila] *nm & adj inv* lilac

limace [limas] *nf* slug

limaille [limɑj] *nf* filings

limande [limɑ̃d] *nf* dab

lime [lim] *nf (outil)* file; **l. à ongles** nail file ■ **limer** *vt* to file

limier [limje] *nm (chien)* bloodhound; *Fam* **fin l.** *(policier)* sleuth

limitatif, -ive [limitatif, -iv] *adj* restrictive ▪ **limitation** *nf* limitation; **l. de vitesse** speed limit

limite [limit] **1** *nf* limit (à to); *(de propriété)* boundary; **sans l.** unlimited, limitless; **jusqu'à la l. de ses forces** to the point of exhaustion; **à la l.** if absolutely necessary; **dans la l. des stocks disponibles** while stocks last; **ma patience a des limites!** there are limits to my patience! **2** *adj (vitesse, âge)* maximum; **cas l.** borderline case; *Fam* **je suis un peu l.** financièrement I'm a bit short of cash

limiter [limite] **1** *vt (restreindre)* to limit, to restrict (à to); *(territoire)* to bound **2 se limiter** *vpr* **se l. à qch/à faire qch** to limit *or* restrict oneself to sth/to doing sth

limoger [limɔʒe] *vt* to dismiss

limonade [limɔnad] *nf* lemonade *(fizzy)*

limpide [lɛ̃pid] *adj (eau, explication)* clear, crystal-clear ▪ **limpidité** *nf* clearness

lin [lɛ̃] *nm (plante)* flax; *(tissu)* linen; **huile de l.** linseed oil

linceul [lɛ̃sœl] *nm* shroud

linéaire [lineɛr] *adj* linear

linge [lɛ̃ʒ] *nm (vêtements)* linen; *(à laver)* washing; *(morceau de tissu)* cloth; **l. de corps** underwear; **l. de maison** household linen ▪ **lingerie** *nf (de femmes)* underwear; *(pièce)* linen room

lingot [lɛ̃go] *nm* ingot; **l. d'or** gold bar

linguiste [lɛ̃gɥist] *nmf* linguist ▪ **linguistique 1** *adj* linguistic **2** *nf* linguistics *(sing)*

lino [lino] *nm* lino ▪ **linoléum** *nm* linoleum

linotte [linɔt] *nf Fig* **tête de l.** scatterbrain

lion [ljɔ̃] *nm* lion; **le L.** *(signe)* Leo; **être L.** to be (a) Leo ▪ **lionceau, -x** *nm* lion cub ▪ **lionne** *nf* lioness

liquéfier [likefje] *vt*, **se liquéfier** *vpr* to liquefy

liqueur [likœr] *nf* liqueur

> Il faut noter que le nom **liquor** utilisé en américain est un faux ami. Il signifie **alcool**.

liquide [likid] **1** *adj* liquid **2** *nm* liquid; *(argent)* cash; **payer en l.** to pay cash

liquider [likide] *vt (dette, stock)* to clear; *Jur (société)* to liquidate; *Fam (travail, restes)* to polish off; *Fam* **l. qn (tuer)** to liquidate sb ▪ **liquidation** *nf (de dette, de stock)* clearing; *Jur (de société)* liquidation; *Com* **l. totale** stock clearance

lire¹* [lir] **1** *vt* to read; **l. qch à qn** to read sth to sb **2** *vi* to read

lire² [lir] *nf (monnaie)* lira

lis¹ [lis] *nm (plante, fleur)* lily

lis², lisant, lise(nt) *etc* [li, lizɑ̃, liz] *voir* **lire¹**

lisible [lizibl] *adj (écriture)* legible; *(livre)* readable ▪ **lisiblement** [-əmɑ̃] *adv* legibly

lisière [lizjɛr] *nf* edge

lisse [lis] *adj* smooth ▪ **lisser** *vt* to smooth; *(plumes)* to preen

liste [list] *nf* list; **sur (la) l. rouge** *(du téléphone)* Br ex-directory, Am unlisted; **faire une l. de qch** to make (out) a list of sth; **l. d'attente** waiting list; **l. électorale** electoral roll; **l. de mariage** wedding list

lit¹ [li] *nm* bed; **se mettre au l.** to go to bed; **garder le l.** to stay in bed; **faire son l.** to make one's bed; **sortir de son l.** *(rivière)* to burst its banks; **l. de camp** Br camp bed, Am cot; **l. d'enfant** Br cot, Am crib; **lits superposés** bunk beds ▪ **literie** *nf* bedding

lit² [li] *voir* **lire¹**

litanie [litani] *nf* litany

litière [litjɛr] *nf (de chat, de cheval)* litter

litige [litiʒ] *nm (conflit)* dispute; *Jur* lawsuit ▪ **litigieux, -ieuse** *adj* contentious

litre [litr] *nm Br* litre, *Am* liter

littéraire [literɛr] *adj* literary ▪ **littérature** *nf* literature

littéral, -e, -aux, -ales [literal, -o] *adj* literal ▪ **littéralement** *adv* literally

littoral, -e, -aux, -ales [litɔral, -o] **1** *adj* coastal **2** *nm* coast(line)

Lituanie [lityani] *nf* Lithuania ▪ **lituanien, -ienne 1** *adj* Lithuanian **2** *nmf* **L., Lituanienne** Lithuanian **3** *nm (langue)* Lithuanian

liturgie [lityrʒi] *nf* liturgy ▪ **liturgique** *adj* liturgical

livide [livid] *adj (pâle)* pallid

livraison [livrɛzɔ̃] *nf* delivery

livre¹ [livr] **1** *nm* book; **le l., l'industrie du l.** the book industry; *Naut* **l. de bord** logbook; **l. de cuisine** cookery book; **l. de poche** paperback (book) **2** *nf (monnaie, poids)* pound ▪ **livresque** [-ɛsk] *adj (savoir)* acquired from books; *Péj (personne)* bookish

livrée [livre] *nf (de domestique)* livery

livrer [livre] **1** *vt (marchandises)* to deliver (à to); *(secret)* to reveal; **l. qn à la police** to hand sb over to the police; **l. bataille** to join battle **2 se livrer** *vpr (se rendre)* to give oneself up (à to); *(se confier)* to confide (à in); **se l. à** *(habitude, excès)* to indulge in; *(activité)* to devote oneself to; *(désespoir, destin)* to abandon oneself ▪ **livraison** *nf* delivery ▪ **livreur, -euse** *nmf* delivery man, *f* delivery woman

livret [livre] *nm (petit livre)* booklet; *Mus* libretto; **l. de caisse d'épargne** bankbook, *Br* passbook; **l. de famille** family record book *(registering births and deaths)*; **l. scolaire** school report book

lobe [lɔb] *nm Anat* lobe

local, -e, -aux, -ales [lɔkal, -o] **1** *adj* local **2** *nm (pièce)* room; **locaux** *(bâtiment)* premises ▪ **localement** *adv* locally ▪ **localiser** *vt (déterminer)* to locate; *(appel téléphonique)* to trace

localité [lɔkalite] *nf* locality

locataire [lɔkatɛr] *nmf* tenant; *(chez le propriétaire)* Br lodger, Am roomer

location [lɔkasjɔ̃] nf (de maison) (par le locataire) renting; (par le propriétaire) renting out, Br letting; (de voiture) renting, Br hiring; (appartement, maison) rented accommodation; (loyer) rent; (de place de spectacle) booking; **bureau de l.** booking office; **en l.** on hire; **voiture de l.** rented or Br hire(d) car; **l.-vente** (crédit-bail) leasing with option to buy

> Il faut noter que le nom anglais **location** est un faux ami. Il signifie **endroit**.

locomotion [lɔkɔmosjɔ̃] nf moyen de l. means of transport

locomotive [lɔkɔmɔtiv] nf (de train) engine

locuteur, -trice [lɔkytœr, -tris] nmf Ling speaker **■locution** nf phrase

loge [lɔʒ] nf (de concierge) lodge; (d'acteur) dressing-room; Théâtre (de spectateur) box; Fig **être aux premières loges** to have a ringside seat

loger [lɔʒe] 1 vt (recevoir, mettre) to accommodate; (héberger) to put up; **être logé et nourri** to have board and lodging 2 vi (temporairement) to stay; (en permanence) to live 3 **se loger** vpr (trouver à) **se l.** to find somewhere to live; (temporairement) to find somewhere to stay; **la balle se logea dans le mur** the bullet lodged (itself) in the wall **■logement** nm (habitation) accommodation, lodging; (appartement) Br flat, Am apartment; (maison) house; (action) housing; **le l.** housing **■logeur, -euse** nmf landlord, f landlady

loggia [lɔdʒja] nf (balcon) loggia

logiciel [lɔʒisjɛl] nm Ordinat software inv; **un l.** a software package; (programme) a computer program

logique [lɔʒik] 1 adj logical 2 nf logic **■logiquement** adv logically

logistique [lɔʒistik] nf logistics (sing)

logo [lɔgo] nm logo

loi [lwa] nf law; **faire la l.** to lay down the law (à to)

loin [lwɛ̃] adv far (away or off) (de from); **Boston est l. de Paris** Boston is a long way away from Paris; **plus l.** further, farther; (ci-après) further on; **aller l.** (réussir) to go far; **aller trop l.** (exagérer) to go too far; **au l.** in the distance, far away; **de l.** from a distance; (de beaucoup) by far; **c'est l., tout ça** (passé) that was a long time ago; Fig **l. de là** far from it **■lointain, -aine** adj distant, far-off; (ressemblance, rapport) remote

loir [lwar] nm dormouse

loisir [lwazir] nm **avoir le l. de faire qch** to have the time to do sth; **(tout) à l.** (en prenant tout son temps) at leisure; (autant qu'on le désire) as much as one would like; **loisirs** (temps libre) spare time, leisure (time); (distractions) leisure or spare-time activities

Londres [lɔ̃dr] nm ou f London **■londonien, -ienne 1** adj London, of London **2** nmf L., Londonienne Londoner

long, longue [lɔ̃, lɔ̃g] **1** adj long; **être l. (à faire qch)** to be a long time (in doing sth); **l. de 2 m** 2 m long **2** nm **avoir 2 m de l.** to be 2 m long; **(tout) le l. de** (espace) (all) along; **tout le l. de** (temps) throughout; **de l. en large** (marcher) up and down; **en l. et en large** thoroughly; **en l.** lengthwise; **tomber de tout son l.** to fall flat (on one's face) **3** adv **en savoir/en dire l. sur** to know/say a lot about; **leur attitude en disait l.** their attitude spoke volumes **■long-courrier** (pl long-courriers) nm (avion) long-haul aircraft

longer [lɔ̃ʒe] vt (sujet: personne, voiture) to go along; (mur, côte) to hug; (sujet: sentier, canal) to run alongside

longévité [lɔ̃ʒevite] nf longevity

longiligne [lɔ̃ʒiliɲ] adj willowy

longitude [lɔ̃ʒityd] nf longitude

longtemps [lɔ̃tã] adv (for) a long time; **trop/avant l.** too/before long; **aussi l. que** as long as

longue [lɔ̃g] voir **long ■longuement** adv (expliquer) at length; (attendre, réfléchir) for a long time **■longuet, -ette** adj Fam longish **■longueur** nf length; Péj **longueurs** (de texte, de film) drawn-out passages; **à l. de journée** all day long; Radio **l. d'onde** wavelength; Fig **être sur la même l. d'onde** to be on the same wavelength **■longue-vue** (pl longues-vues) nf telescope

look [luk] nm Fam look; **avoir un l. d'enfer** to look great or Br wicked **■looké, -ée** adj Fam **être l. punk/grunge** to have a punky/grungy look

lopin [lɔpɛ̃] nm **l. de terre** plot or patch of land

loquace [lɔkas] adj talkative

loque [lɔk] nf (vêtement) rag; Fig (personne) wreck; **être en loques** to be in rags

loquet [lɔkɛ] nm latch

lorgner [lɔrɲe] vt (avec indiscrétion) to eye; (avec concupiscence) to eye up; (convoiter) to have one's eye on

lors [lɔr] adv **l. de** at the time of; **depuis l., dès l.** from then on; **dès l. que** (puisque) since

lorsque [lɔrsk(ə)] conj when

losange [lɔzɑ̃ʒ] nm (forme) diamond

lot [lo] nm (de marchandises) batch; (de loterie) prize; **gros l.** jackpot **■loterie** nf lottery

loti, -ie [lɔti] adj Fig **bien/mal l.** well-off/badly off

lotion [losjɔ̃] nf lotion

lotissement [lɔtismã] nm (terrain) building plot; (habitations) housing Br estate or Am development

loto [lɔto] nm (jeu) lotto; (jeu national) national lottery

louable [lwabl] adj praiseworthy, laudable

louange [lwɑ̃ʒ] nf praise

louche[1] [luʃ] nf (cuillère) ladle

louche[2] [luʃ] adj (suspect) shady, Br dodgy

loucher [luʃe] vi to squint; Fam **l. sur qch** to eye sth

louer[1] [lwe] vt (prendre en location) (maison, appartement) to rent; (voiture) to rent, Br to hire; (donner en location) (maison, appartement) to rent out, Br to let; (voiture) to rent out, Br to hire out; (réserver) to book; **maison/chambre à l.** house/room to rent or Br to let

louer[2] [lwe] 1 vt (exalter) to praise (**de** for) 2 se **louer** vpr **se l. de qch** to be highly satisfied with sth

loufoque [lufɔk] adj Fam (fou) crazy

loukoum [lukum] nm piece of Turkish delight; **des loukoums** Turkish delight

loup [lu] nm wolf; **avoir une faim de l.** to be ravenous ▪ **loup-garou** (pl **loups-garous**) nm werewolf

loupe [lup] nf magnifying glass

louper [lupe] vt Fam (train) to miss; (examen) to fail, Am to flunk; (travail) to mess up

lourd, -e [lur, lurd] 1 adj heavy (**de** with); (temps, chaleur) close; (faute) gross; (tâche) arduous; (esprit) dull 2 adv **peser l.** (malle) to be heavy ▪ **lourdaud, -aude** 1 adj oafish 2 nmf oaf ▪ **lourdement** [-əmɑ̃] adv heavily; **se tromper l.** to be greatly mistaken ▪ **lourdeur** nf heaviness; (d'esprit) dullness; **avoir des lourdeurs d'estomac** to feel bloated

lourdingue [lurdɛ̃g] adj Fam (personne, plaisanterie) unsubtle

loutre [lutr] nf otter

louve [luv] nf she-wolf ▪ **louveteau, -x** nm (animal) wolf cub; (scout) Cub (Scout)

loyal, -e, -aux, -ales [lwajal, -o] adj (honnête) fair (**envers** to); (dévoué) loyal (**envers** to) ▪ **loyalement** adv (honnête) fairly; (avec dévouement) loyally ▪ **loyauté** nf (honnêteté) fairness; (dévouement) loyalty (**envers** to)

loyer [lwaje] nm rent

lu [ly] pp de **lire**[1]

lubie [lybi] nf whim

lubrifier [lybrifje] vt to lubricate ▪ **lubrifiant** nm lubricant

lubrique [lybrik] adj lustful

lucarne [lykarn] nf (fenêtre) dormer window; (de toit) skylight

lucide [lysid] adj lucid ▪ **lucidité** nf lucidity

lucratif, -ive [lykratif, -iv] adj lucrative

lueur [lqœr] nf (lumière) & Fig glimmer

luge [lyʒ] nf Br sledge, Am sled

lugubre [lygybr] adj gloomy

lui [lqi] pron personnel (a) (objet indirect) (to) him; (femme) (to) her; (chose, animal) (to) it; **je le l. ai montré** I showed it to him/her; **il l. est facile de...** it's easy for him/her to... (b) (complément direct) him; **elle n'aime que l.** she

only loves him; **elle n'écoute ni l. ni personne** she doesn't listen to him or to anybody (c) (après une préposition) him; **pour/avec l.** for/with him; **elle pense à l.** she thinks of him; **il ne pense qu'à lui** he only thinks of himself; **ce livre est à l.** this book is his (d) (dans les comparaisons) **elle est plus grande que l.** she's taller than he is or than him (e) (sujet) **l., il ne viendra pas** (emphatique) HE won't come; **c'est l. qui me l'a dit** he is the one who told me ▪ **lui-même** pron himself; (chose, animal) itself

luire* [lqir] vi to shine ▪ **luisant, -ante** adj (métal) shiny

lumbago [lɔ̃bago] nm lumbago

lumière [lymjɛr] nf light; **à la l. de** by the light of; Fig (grâce à) in the light of; Fig **faire toute la l. sur** to clear up; Fig **mettre en l.** to bring to light; Fam **ce n'est pas une l.** he's/she's not very bright ▪ **luminaire** nm (appareil) lighting appliance

lumineux, -euse [lyminø, -øz] adj (idée, ciel) bright, brilliant; (cadran, corps) luminous; **source lumineuse** light source ▪ **luminosité** nf luminosity

lunaire [lynɛr] adj lunar; **clarté l.** light or brightness of the moon

lunatique [lynatik] adj quirky

> Il faut noter que l'adjectif anglais **lunatic** est un faux ami. Il signifie **fou**.

lundi [lœ̃di] nm Monday

lune [lyn] nf moon; **être dans la l.** to have one's head in the clouds; **l. de miel** honeymoon ▪ **luné, -ée** adj Fam **être bien/mal l.** to be in a good/bad mood

lunette [lynɛt] nf (astronomique) telescope; **lunettes** (de vue) glasses, spectacles; (de protection, de plongée) goggles; **l. arrière** (de voiture) rear window; **lunettes de soleil** sunglasses

lurette [lyrɛt] nf Fam **il y a belle l.** ages ago

luron [lyrɔ̃] nm **c'est un gai l.** he's a bit of a lad

lustre [lystr] nm (lampe) chandelier; (éclat) lustre ▪ **lustré, -ée** adj (par l'usure) shiny ▪ **lustres** nmpl Fam **depuis des l.** for ages and ages

luth [lyt] nm lute

lutin [lytɛ̃] nm elf, pixie

lutte [lyt] nf fight, struggle; Sport wrestling; **l. des classes** class struggle ▪ **lutter** vi to fight, to struggle; Sport to wrestle ▪ **lutteur, -euse** nmf Sport wrestler

luxation [lyksasjɔ̃] nf Méd dislocation; **se faire une l. à l'épaule** to dislocate one's shoulder

luxe [lyks] nm luxury; **un l. de** a wealth of; **article de l.** luxury article; **modèle de l.** de luxe model ▪ **luxueux, -ueuse** adj luxurious

Luxembourg [lyksɑ̃bur] nm **le L.** Luxembourg ▪ **luxembourgeois 1** adj Luxembourgish **2**

nmf **L., Luxembourgeoise** Luxembourger **3** *nm* *(langue)* Luxembourgish

luxure [lyksyr] *nf Littéraire* lust

> Il faut noter que le nom anglais **luxury** est un faux ami. Il signifie **luxe**.

luxuriant, -iante [lyksyrjɑ̃, -jɑ̃t] *adj* luxuriant

luzerne [lyzɛrn] *nf (plante) Br* lucerne, *Am* alfalfa

lycée [lise] *nm Br* ≃ secondary school, *Am* ≃ high school; **l. technique** *ou* **professionnel** technical *or* vocational school ▪ **lycéen, -éenne** *nmf Br* secondary school pupil, *Am* high school student

lymphatique [lɛ̃fatik] *adj Biol* lymphatic; *(apathique)* lethargic

lyncher [lɛ̃ʃe] *vt* to lynch ▪ **lynchage** *nm* lynching

lynx [lɛ̃ks] *nm* lynx; *Fig* **avoir des yeux de l.** to have eyes like a hawk

lyophiliser [ljɔfilize] *vt (café)* to freeze-dry

lyre [lir] *nf* lyre

lyrique [lirik] *adj (poème)* lyric; *Fig (passionné)* lyrical; **artiste l.** opera singer ▪ **lyrisme** *nm* lyricism

lys [lis] *nm (plante, fleur)* lily

M¹, m¹ [ɛm] *nm inv* M, m
M² (*abrév* **Monsieur**) Mr
m² (*abrév* **mètre(s)**) m
m' [m] *voir* **me**
ma [ma] *voir* **mon**
macabre [makɑbr] *adj* macabre, gruesome
macadam [makadam] *nm* (*goudron*) macadam
macaron [makarɔ̃] *nm* (*gâteau*) macaroon; (*insigne*) badge; (*autocollant*) sticker
macaronis [makarɔni] *nmpl* macaroni
macédoine [masedwan] *nf* **m. de légumes** mixed vegetables; **m. de fruits** fruit salad
macérer [masere] *vti* to steep **• macération** *nf* steeping
mâche [maʃ] *nf* lamb's lettuce
mâcher [maʃe] *vt* to chew; **m. le travail à qn** to make sb's task easy; **ne pas m. ses mots** not to mince one's words
machiavélique [makjavelik] *adj* Machiavellian
machin, -ine [maʃɛ̃, -ʃin] *Fam* **1** *nmf* (*personne*) M. what's-his-name; **Machine** what's-her-name **2** *nm* (*chose*) thingy
machinal, -e, -aux, -ales [maʃinal, -o] *adj* (*geste, travail*) mechanical; (*réaction*) automatic **• machinalement** *adv* (*agir*) mechanically; (*réagir*) automatically
machination [maʃinasjɔ̃] *nf* conspiracy
machine [maʃin] *nf* (*appareil*) machine; (*locomotive, moteur*) engine; *Naut* **salle des machines** engine room; **m. à calculer** calculator; **m. à coudre** sewing machine; **m. à écrire** typewriter; **m. à laver** washing machine; **m. à laver la vaisselle** dishwasher; **m. à** *ou* **de traitement de texte** word processor **• machiniste** *nm* (*conducteur*) driver; (*de théâtre*) stagehand
machisme [maʃism] *nm* machismo **• macho** [matʃo] *adj & nm Fam* macho
mâchoire [maʃwar] *nf* jaw
mâchonner [maʃɔne] *vt* to chew
macis [masi] *nm Culin* (*épice*) mace
maçon [masɔ̃] *nm* (*de briques*) bricklayer; (*de pierres*) mason **• maçonnerie** *nf* (*travaux*) building work; (*ouvrage de briques*) brickwork; (*de pierres*) masonry, stonework
macrobiotique [makrobjɔtik] *adj* macrobiotic
macro-commande [makrokɔmɑ̃d] (*pl* **macro-commandes**) *nf Ordinat* macro
maculer [makyle] *vt* to stain (**de** with)

Madagascar [madagaskar] *nf* Madagascar
madame [madam] (*pl* **mesdames**) *nf* (*en apostrophe*) madam; **bonjour mesdames** good morning(, ladies); **M. Legras** Mrs Legras; **M.** (*dans une lettre*) Dear Madam
madeleine [madlɛn] *nf* (*gâteau*) madeleine
mademoiselle [madmwazɛl] (*pl* **mesdemoiselles**) *nf* (*suivi d'un nom*) Miss; **M. Legras** Miss Legras; **merci m.** thank you; **bonjour mesdemoiselles** good morning(, ladies); **M.** (*dans une lettre*) Dear Madam
Madère [madɛr] *nf* (*île*) Madeira
madère [madɛr] *nm* (*vin*) Madeira
madone [madɔn] *nf Rel* Madonna
madrier [madrije] *nm* beam
Maf(f)ia [mafja] *nf* **la M.** the Mafia
magasin [magazɛ̃] *nm Br* shop, *Am* store; (*entrepôt*) warehouse; (*d'arme*) & *Phot* magazine; **grand m.** department store; **en m.** in stock **• magasinier** *nm* warehouseman
magazine [magazin] *nm* (*revue*) magazine
magie [maʒi] *nf* magic **• magicien, -ienne** *nmf* magician **• magique** *adj* (*surnaturel*) magic; (*enchanteur*) magical
magistral, -e, -aux, -ales [maʒistral, -o] *adj* (*démonstration*) masterly; (*erreur*) colossal **• magistralement** *adv* magnificently
magistrat [maʒistra] *nm* magistrate **• magistrature** *nf* magistrature
magma [magma] *nm* (*roche*) magma; *Fig* (*mélange*) jumble
magnanime [maɲanim] *adj* magnanimous
magnat [maɲa] *nm* tycoon, magnate; **m. de la presse** press baron
magner [maɲe] **se magner** *vpr Fam* to get a move on
magnésium [maɲezjɔm] *nm* magnesium
magnétique [maɲetik] *adj* magnetic **• magnétiser** *vt* to magnetize **• magnétisme** *nm* magnetism
magnétophone [maɲetɔfɔn] (*Fam* **magnéto**) *nm* tape recorder; **m. à cassettes** cassette recorder
magnétoscope [maɲetɔskɔp] *nm* video (recorder), *Am* VCR
magnifique [maɲifik] *adj* magnificent **• magnificence** *nf* magnificence **• magnifiquement** *adv* magnificently
magnolia [maɲɔlja] *nm* (*arbre*) magnolia

magot [mago] *nm Fam* hoard

magouille [maguj] *nf Fam* scheming ■ **magouilleur, -euse** *nmf Fam* schemer

magret [magrɛ] *nm* **m. de canard** *Br* fillet *or Am* filet of duck

mai [mɛ] *nm* May

maigre [mɛgr] **1** *adj* (*personne, partie du corps*) thin; (*viande*) lean; (*fromage, yaourt*) low-fat; (*repas, salaire, espoir*) meagre **2** *adv* **faire m.** to abstain from meat ■ **maigreur** *nf* (*de personne*) thinness ■ **maigrichon, -onne** [meg-] *adj Fam* skinny ■ **maigrir** *vi* to get thinner, to lose weight

maille [maj] *nf* (*de tricot*) stitch; (*de filet*) mesh; **m. filée** (*de bas*) run, *Br* ladder; *Fig* **avoir m. à partir avec qn** to have a set-to with sb ■ **maillon** *nm* link

maillet [majɛ] *nm* mallet

maillot [majo] *nm* (*de sportif*) jersey, shirt; **m. de bain** (*de femme*) swimsuit, *Br* swimming costume; (*d'homme*) (swimming) trunks; **m. de corps** *Br* vest, *Am* undershirt; **m. jaune** (*du Tour de France*) yellow jersey

main [mɛ̃] **1** *nf* hand; **à la m.** (*faire, écrire*) by hand; **tenir qch à la m.** to hold sth in one's hand; **sous la m.** handy; **la m. dans la m.** hand in hand; **en mains propres** in person; **donner la m. à qn** to hold sb's hand; *Fig* **avoir la m. heureuse** to be lucky; **avoir le coup de m.** to have the knack; **demander la m. d'une femme** to ask for a woman's hand (in marriage); **faire m. basse sur qch** to get one's hands on sth; **mettre la m. à la pâte** to do one's bit; **ne pas y aller de m. morte** not to pull punches; **en venir aux mains** to come to blows; *Fig* **j'y mettrais ma m. au feu** I'd stake my life on it; **haut les mains!** hands up!; **m. courante** handrail **2** *adj* **fait m.** hand-made ■ **main-d'œuvre** (*pl* **mains-d'œuvre**) *nf* labour ■ **mainmise** *nf Jur* seizure (**de** of)

maint, mainte [mɛ̃, mɛ̃t] *adj Littéraire* **maintes fois, à maintes reprises** many a time

maintenant [mɛ̃tənɑ̃] *adv* now; (*de nos jours*) nowadays; **m. que...** now that...; **dès m.** from now on

maintenir* [mɛ̃tənir] **1** *vt* (*conserver*) to keep, to maintain; (*retenir*) to hold in position; (*foule*) to hold back; (*affirmer*) to maintain (**que** that) **2** **se maintenir** *vpr* (*durer*) to remain; (*malade, vieillard*) to hold up ■ **maintien** *nm* (*action*) maintenance (**de** of); (*allure*) bearing

maire [mɛr] *nmf* mayor ■ **mairie** *nf Br* town hall, *Am* city hall; (*administration*) *Br* town council, *Am* city hall

mais [mɛ] *conj* but; **m. oui, m. si** of course; **m. non** definitely not

maïs [mais] *nm Br* maize, *Am* corn

maison [mɛzɔ̃] **1** *nf* (*bâtiment, famille*) house; (*foyer*) home; (*entreprise*) company; **à la m.** at home; **aller à la m.** to go home; **rentrer à la m.** to go/come (back) home; **m. de la culture** arts centre; **m. d'édition** publishing house; **m. des jeunes et de la culture** = youth club and arts centre; **m. de repos** rest home; **m. de retraite** retirement home, *Br* old people's home; **m. de santé** nursing home; **la M.-Blanche** the White House **2** *adj inv* (*artisanal*) home-made ■ **maisonnée** *nf* household ■ **maisonnette** *nf* small house

maître [mɛtr] *nm* master; **être m. de la situation** to be in control of the situation; **être m. de ses émotions** to have one's emotions under control; **se rendre m. de qch** (*incendie*) to bring sth under control; (*pays*) to conquer sth; **m. d'école** teacher; **m. d'hôtel** (*de restaurant*) head waiter; **m. de maison** host; **m. chanteur** blackmailer; **m. nageur (sauveteur)** swimming instructor (and lifeguard)

maîtresse [mɛtrɛs] **1** *nf* mistress; **être m. de la situation** to be in control of the situation; **m. d'école** teacher; **m. de maison** hostess **2** *adj f* (*idée, poutre*) main; (*carte*) master

maîtrise [mɛtriz] *nf* (*contrôle, connaissance*) mastery (**de** of); (*diplôme*) ≃ master's degree (**de** in); **m. de soi** self-control ■ **maîtriser 1** *vt* (*incendie, passion*) to control; (*peur*) to overcome; (*sujet*) to master; (*véhicule*) to have under control; **m. qn** to overpower sb **2** **se maîtriser** *vpr* to control oneself

majesté [maʒɛste] *nf* majesty; **Votre M.** (*titre*) Your Majesty ■ **majestueux, -ueuse** *adj* majestic

majeur, -eure [maʒœr] **1** *adj* (*important*) & *Mus* major; *Jur* **être m.** to be of age; **la majeure partie de** most of; **en majeure partie** for the most part **2** *nm* (*doigt*) middle finger

majorer [maʒɔre] *vt* to increase ■ **majoration** *nf* (*hausse*) increase (**de** in)

majorette [maʒɔrɛt] *nf* (*drum*) majorette

majorité [maʒɔrite] *nf* majority (**de** of); (*gouvernement*) government, party in office; **en m.** (*pour la plupart*) in the main; **m. civile** majority, coming of age ■ **majoritaire** *adj* majority; **être m.** to be in the majority; **être m. aux élections** to win the elections

Majorque [maʒɔrk] *nf* Majorca

majuscule [maʒyskyl] **1** *adj* capital **2** *nf* capital letter

mal, maux [mal, mo] **1** *nm* (*douleur*) pain; (*préjudice*) harm; (*maladie*) illness; (*malheur*) misfortune; *Phil* **le m.** evil; **avoir m. à la tête/à la gorge** to have a headache/sore throat; **ça me fait m., j'ai m.** it hurts (me); **avoir le m. de mer** to be seasick; **avoir le m. de l'air** to be airsick; **avoir le m. des transports** to be travelsick; **faire du m. à qn** to harm sb; **dire du m. de qn** to speak ill of sb; **avoir du m. à faire qch** to have trouble doing sth; **se donner**

du m. pour faire qch to take pains to do sth; **m. de dents** toothache; **m. de gorge** sore throat; **m. de tête** headache; **m. de ventre** stomach ache; **m. du pays** homesickness; **avoir le m. du pays** to be homesick **2** *adv (avec médiocrité)* badly; *(incorrectement)* wrongly; **aller m.** *(projet)* to be going badly; *(personne)* to be ill; **être m. en point** to be in a bad way; **prendre m.** to catch cold; **m. comprendre** to misunderstand; **se trouver m.** to faint; *Fam* **pas m.** *(beaucoup)* quite a lot (**de** of); **c'est m. de mentir** it's wrong to lie; **de m. en pis** from bad to worse

malade [malad] **1** *adj* ill, sick; *(arbre, dent)* diseased; *(estomac, jambe)* bad **2** *nmf* sick person; *(de médecin)* patient; **les malades** the sick ▪ **maladie** *nf* illness, disease; **m. émergente** new disease; **m. sexuellement transmissible** sexually transmitted disease *or* infection ▪ **maladif, -ive** *adj (personne)* sickly; *(curiosité)* morbid

maladroit, -oite [maladrwa, -wat] *adj (malhabile)* clumsy, awkward; *(indélicat)* tactless ▪ **maladresse** *nf (manque d'habileté)* clumsiness, awkwardness; *(indélicatesse)* tactlessness; *(bévue)* blunder

malaise [malɛz] *nm (angoisse)* uneasiness, malaise; *(indisposition)* feeling of sickness; *(étourdissement)* dizzy spell; **avoir un m.** to feel faint

malaisé, -ée [maleze] *adj* difficult

Malaisie [malɛzi] *nf* **la M.** Malaysia

malaria [malarja] *nf* malaria

malavisé, -ée [malavize] *adj* ill-advised (**de faire** to do)

malaxer [malakse] *vt* to knead

malbouffe [malbuf] *nf Fam* junk food

malchance [malʃɑ̃s] *nf* bad luck; **jouer de m.** to have no luck at all ▪ **malchanceux, -euse** *adj* unlucky

malcommode [malkɔmɔd] *adj* awkward

mâle [mal] **1** *adj (du sexe masculin)* male; *(viril)* manly **2** *nm* male

malédiction [malediksjɔ̃] *nf* curse

maléfice [malefis] *nm* evil spell ▪ **maléfique** *adj* evil

malencontreux, -euse [malɑ̃kɔ̃trø, -øz] *adj* unfortunate

malentendant, -ante [malɑ̃tɑ̃dɑ̃, -ɑ̃t] *nmf* person who is hard of hearing

malentendu [malɑ̃tɑ̃dy] *nm* misunderstanding

malfaçon [malfasɔ̃] *nf* defect

malfaisant, -ante [malfəzɑ̃, -ɑ̃t] *adj* harmful

malfaiteur [malfɛtœr] *nm* criminal

malfamé, -ée [malfame] *adj* disreputable

malformation [malfɔrmasjɔ̃] *nf* malformation

malgré [malgre] *prép* in spite of; **m. tout** for all that, after all; **m. soi** *(à contrecœur)* reluctantly

malhabile [malabil] *adj* clumsy

malheur [malœr] *nm (drame)* misfortune; *(malchance)* bad luck; **par m.** unfortunately; **porter m. à qn** to bring sb bad luck; **faire un m.** to be a big hit ▪ **malheureusement** *adv* unfortunately ▪ **malheureux, -euse 1** *adj (triste)* unhappy, miserable; *(malchanceux)* unlucky; *(candidat)* unsuccessful **2** *nmf (infortuné)* poor wretch; *(indigent)* needy person

malhonnête [malɔnɛt] *adj* dishonest ▪ **malhonnêteté** *nf* dishonesty

malice [malis] *nf* mischievousness ▪ **malicieux, -ieuse** *adj* mischievous

> Il faut noter que les termes anglais **malice** et **malicious** sont des faux amis. Ils signifient respectivement **méchanceté** ou **préméditation** selon le contexte, et **méchant**.

malin, -igne [malɛ̃, -iɲ] *adj (astucieux)* clever, smart; *Méd (tumeur)* malignant; **prendre un m. plaisir à faire qch** to take a malicious pleasure in doing sth; *Ironique* **c'est m.!** that's clever!

malingre [malɛ̃gr] *adj* puny

malintentionné, -ée [malɛ̃tɑ̃sjɔne] *adj* ill-intentioned (**à l'égard de** towards)

malle [mal] *nf (coffre)* trunk; *(de véhicule) Br* boot, *Am* trunk; *Fam* **se faire la m.** to clear off ▪ **mallette** *nf* briefcase

malléable [maleabl] *adj* malleable

mal-logés [malloʒe] *nmpl* **les m.** = people living in inadequate housing conditions

malmener [malmǝne] *vt* to manhandle, to treat badly

malnutrition [malnytrisjɔ̃] *nf* malnutrition

malodorant, -ante [malɔdɔrɑ̃, -ɑ̃t] *adj* smelly

malotru, -ue [malɔtry] *nmf* boor, lout

malpoli, -ie [malpɔli] *adj Fam* rude

malpropre [malprɔpr] *adj (sale)* dirty

malsain, -aine [malsɛ̃, -ɛn] *adj* unhealthy

malséant, -éante [malseɑ̃, -eɑ̃t] *adj Littéraire* unseemly

malt [malt] *nm* malt

Malte [malt] *nf* Malta ▪ **maltais, -aise 1** *adj* Maltese **2** *nmf* **M., Maltaise** Maltese **3** *nm (langue)* Maltese

maltraiter [maltrete] *vt* to ill-treat ▪ **maltraitance** *nf* ill-treatment

malveillant, -ante [malvɛjɑ̃, -ɑ̃t] *adj* malevolent ▪ **malveillance** *nf* malevolence

malvenu, -ue [malvǝny] *adj (déplacé)* uncalled-for

malversation [malvɛrsasjɔ̃] *nf* embezzlement

maman [mamɑ̃] *nf Br* mum, *Am* mom

mamelle [mamɛl] *nf (d'animal)* teat; *(de vache)* udder ▪ **mamelon** *nm (de femme)* nipple; *(colline)* hillock

mamie [mami] *nf* grandma, granny

mammifère [mamifɛr] *nm* mammal

Manche [mɑ̃ʃ] *nf* **la M.** the Channel

manche¹ [mɑ̃ʃ] *nf (de vêtement)* sleeve; *Sport & Cartes* round; *Fam* **faire la m.** to beg; *Fam* **c'est une autre paire de manches!** it's a different ball game ▪ **manchette** *nf (de chemise)* cuff; *(de journal)* headline ▪ **manchon** *nm (en fourrure)* muff

manche² [mɑ̃ʃ] *nm (d'outil)* handle; **m. à balai** broomstick; *(d'avion, d'ordinateur)* joystick

manchot¹, -ote [mɑ̃ʃo, -ɔt] **1** *adj* one-armed **2** *nmf* one-armed person

manchot² [mɑ̃ʃo] *nm (oiseau)* penguin

mandale [mɑ̃dal] *nf très Fam* clout

mandarin [mɑ̃darɛ̃] *nm (langue)* Mandarin; *Péj (personnage influent)* mandarin

mandarine [mɑ̃darin] *nf (fruit)* mandarin (orange)

mandat [mɑ̃da] *nm (de député)* mandate; *(de président)* term of office; *(procuration)* power of attorney; **m. d'amener** = summons; **m. d'arrêt** warrant (**contre qn** for sb's arrest); **m. de perquisition** search warrant; **m. postal** *Br* postal order, *Am* money order ▪ **mandataire** *nmf (délégué)* representative ▪ **mandater** *vt* to delegate; *(député)* to give a mandate to

manège [manɛʒ] *nm* (**a**) *(de foire)* merry-go-round, *Br* roundabout; *Équitation* riding school (**b**) *(intrigue)* game

manette [manɛt] *nf* lever; *Ordinat* **m. (de jeu)** joystick

mangeoire [mɑ̃ʒwar] *nf (feeding)* trough

manger [mɑ̃ʒe] **1** *vt* to eat; *(corroder)* to eat into; *Fig (consommer, dépenser)* to get through **2** *vi* to eat; **donner à m. à qn** to give sb sth to eat; **m. à sa faim** to have enough to eat; **on mange bien ici** the food is good here **3** *nm (nourriture)* food ▪ **mangeable** *adj (médiocre)* eatable ▪ **mangeur, -euse** *nmf* **être un gros m.** to be a big eater

mangue [mɑ̃g] *nf* mango

manie [mani] *nf (habitude)* odd habit; *(idée fixe)* mania (**de** for) ▪ **maniaque 1** *adj* fussy **2** *nmf Br* fusspot, *Am* fussbudget; **un m. de la propreté** a maniac for cleanliness

manier [manje] *vt* to handle ▪ **maniabilité** *nf (de véhicule) Br* manoeuvrability, *Am* maneuverability ▪ **maniable** *adj (outil)* handy; *(véhicule)* easy to handle ▪ **maniement** *nm* handling

manière [manjɛr] *nf* way, manner; **la m. dont elle parle** the way (in which) she talks; **manières** *(politesse)* manners; **faire des manières** *(se faire prier)* to make a fuss; *(être affecté)* to put on airs; **de toute m.** anyway, anyhow; **de cette m.** this way; **de m. à faire qch** so as to do sth; **à ma m.** my way; **à la m. de** in the style of; **d'une m. générale** generally speaking ▪ **maniéré, -ée** *adj* affected

manif [manif] *(abrév* **manifestation**) *nf Fam* demo

manifeste [manifɛst] **1** *adj* manifest, obvious **2** *nm Pol* manifesto ▪ **manifestement** [-əma] *adv* obviously, manifestly

manifester [manifɛste] **1** *vt (exprimer)* to show **2** *vi (protester)* to demonstrate **3** **se manifester** *vpr (maladie, sentiment)* to show or manifest itself; *(personne)* to make oneself known ▪ **manifestant, -ante** *nmf* demonstrator ▪ **manifestation** *nf (défilé)* demonstration; *(réunion, fête)* event; *(de sentiments)* display

manigances [manigɑ̃s] *nfpl* scheming ▪ **manigancer** *vt* to scheme

manipuler [manipyle] *vt (appareils, produits)* to handle; *Péj (personnes)* to manipulate ▪ **manipulation** *nf (d'appareils, de produits)* handling; *Péj (de personnes)* manipulation (**de** of); **manipulations génétiques** genetic engineering

manivelle [manivɛl] *nf* crank

mannequin [mankɛ̃] *nm (personne)* model; *(statue)* dummy

manœuvre [manœvr] **1** *nm (ouvrier)* unskilled worker **2** *nf (opération)* & *Mil Br* manoeuvre, *Am* maneuver; *(intrigue)* scheme ▪ **manœuvrer 1** *vt (véhicule, personne) Br* to manoeuvre, *Am* to maneuver; *(machine)* to operate **2** *vi Br* to manoeuvre, *Am* to maneuver

manoir [manwar] *nm* manor house

manomètre [manɔmɛtr] *nm* pressure gauge

manque [mɑ̃k] *nm (insuffisance)* lack (**de** of); *(lacune)* gap; **par m. de qch** through lack of sth; **être en m.** *(drogué)* to have withdrawal symptoms; **m. à gagner** loss of earnings

manquer [mɑ̃ke] **1** *vt (cible, train, chance)* to miss; *(échouer)* to fail **2** *vi (faire défaut)* to be lacking; *(être absent)* to be missing; *(échouer)* to fail; **m. de** *(pain, argent)* to be short of; *(attention, cohérence)* to lack; **m. à son devoir** to fail in one's duty; **m. à sa parole** to break one's word; *Mil* **m. à l'appel** to miss (the) roll call; **ça manque de sel** there isn't enough salt; **tu me manques** I miss you; **le temps lui manque** he's short of time; **le cœur m'a manqué** my courage failed me; **ça n'a pas manqué, il est arrivé en retard** sure enough, he was late; **je ne manquerai pas de venir** I won't fail to come; **je n'y manquerai pas** I certainly will; **elle a manqué de tomber** she nearly fell; **ne m. de rien** to have all one needs **3** *v impersonnel* **il manque/il nous manque dix tasses** there are/we are ten cups short; **il manque quelques pages** there are a few pages missing; **il ne manquait plus que ça!** that's all I/we/*etc* needed! ▪ **manquant, -ante** *adj* missing ▪ **manqué, -ée** *adj (occasion)* missed; *(tentative)* unsuccessful ▪ **manquement** *nm* breach (**à** of)

mansarde [mãsard] *nf* attic

mansuétude [mãsɥetyd] *nf Littéraire* indulgence

manteau, -x [mãto] *nm* coat; *Fig* **sous le m.** secretly

manucure [manykyr] **1** *nmf (personne)* manicurist **2** *nf (soin)* manicure

manuel, -uelle [manɥɛl] **1** *adj (travail)* manual **2** *nm (livre)* handbook, manual; **m. scolaire** textbook

manufacture [manyfaktyr] *nf* factory ▪ **manufacturé, -ée** *adj (produit)* manufactured

manuscrit [manyskri] *nm* manuscript; *(tapé à la machine)* typescript

manutention [manytãsjõ] *nf* handling ▪ **manutentionnaire** *nmf* packer

mappemonde [mapmõd] *nf (carte)* map of the world; *(sphère)* globe

maquereau, -x [makro] *nm (poisson)* mackerel

maquette [makɛt] *nf (de bâtiment)* (scale) model; *(jouet)* model

maquiller [makije] **1** *vt (personne, visage)* to make up; *(voiture)* to tamper with; *(documents)* to forge **2 se maquiller** *vpr (action)* to put one's make-up on; *(habitude)* to wear make-up ▪ **maquillage** *nm (fard)* make-up; *(action)* making up

maquis [maki] *nm (végétation) & Hist* maquis; **prendre le m.** to take to the hills

maraîcher, -ère [mareʃe, -ɛʃer] **1** *nmf Br* market gardener, *Am* truck farmer **2** *adj* **culture maraîchère** *Br* market gardening, *Am* truck farming

marais [marɛ] *nm* marsh; **m. salant** saltern, saltworks

marasme [marasm] *nm* **m. économique/politique** economic/political stagnation

marathon [maratõ] *nm* marathon

maraudeur, -euse [marodœr, -øz] *nmf* petty thief

marbre [marbr] *nm* marble; **en m.** marble; **rester de m.** to remain impassive ▪ **marbré, -ée** *adj (surface)* marbled; **gâteau m.** marble cake

marc [mar] *nm (eau-de-vie)* marc (brandy); **m. de café** coffee grounds

marchand, -ande [marʃã, -ãd] **1** *nmf Br* shopkeeper, *Am* storekeeper; *(de vins, de charbon)* merchant; *(de voitures, de meubles)* dealer; **m. de journaux** *(dans la rue)* newsvendor; *(dans un magasin) Br* newsagent, *Am* newsdealer; **m. de légumes** *Br* greengrocer, *Am* produce dealer **2** *adj* **prix m.** trade price; **valeur marchande** market value

marchander [marʃãde] **1** *vt (objet, prix)* to haggle over **2** *vi* to haggle ▪ **marchandage** *nm* haggling

marchandises [marʃãdiz] *nfpl* goods, merchandise

marche [marʃ] *nf* (**a**) *(d'escalier)* step, stair (**b**) *(action)* walking; *(promenade)* walk; *Mus* march; *(de train, de véhicule)* movement; *(d'événement)* course; **un train/véhicule en m.** a moving train/vehicle; **la bonne m. de** *(opération, machine)* the smooth running of; **dans le sens de la m.** *(dans un train)* facing forward; **mettre qch en m.** to start sth (up); **faire m. arrière** *(en voiture) Br* to reverse, *Am* to back up; *Fig* to backtrack; **fermer la m.** to bring up the rear; **m. à suivre** procedure

marché [marʃe] *nm* **1** *(lieu) & Écon* market; *(contrat)* deal; *Fig* **par-dessus le m.** into the bargain; **faire son** *ou* **le m.** to go shopping; **vendre qch au m. noir** to sell sth on the black market; **le m. du travail** the labour market; **le M. commun** the Common Market; **le M. unique européen** the Single European Market; **m. des changes** foreign exchange market; **m. immobilier** property market; **m. baissier/haussier** bear/bull market **2** *adj inv* **être bon m.** to be cheap; **c'est meilleur m.** it's cheaper

marchepied [marʃəpje] *nm (de train, de bus)* step

marcher [marʃe] *vi (à pied)* to walk; *(poser le pied)* to step (**dans** in); *(machine)* to run; *(plans)* to work; *(soldats)* to march; **faire m. qch** to operate sth; *Fam* **faire m. qn** to pull sb's leg; *Fam* **ça marche?** how's it going?; *Fam* **elle va m.** *(accepter)* she'll go along (with it) ▪ **marcheur, -euse** *nmf* walker

mardi [mardi] *nm* Tuesday; **M. gras** Shrove Tuesday

mare [mar] *nf (étang)* pond; *(grande quantité)* pool

marécage [marekaʒ] *nm* marsh ▪ **marécageux, -euse** *adj* marshy

maréchal, -aux [mareʃal, -o] *nm* **m. (de France)** field marshal ▪ **maréchal-ferrant** *(pl* **maréchaux-ferrants)** *nm* blacksmith

marée [mare] *nf* tide; *(poissons)* fresh seafood; **m. haute/basse** high/low tide; **m. noire** oil slick

marelle [marɛl] *nf (jeu)* hopscotch; **jouer à la m.** to play hopscotch

marémotrice [maremɔtris] *adj f* tidal; **usine m.** tidal power station

marge [marʒ] *nf (de page)* margin; **en m. de** *(en dehors de)* on the fringes of; **avoir de la m.** to have some leeway; **m. de manœuvre** room for manoeuvre; **m. de sécurité** safety margin ▪ **marginal, -e, -aux, -ales 1** *adj (secondaire)* marginal; *(personne)* on the fringes of society **2** *nmf* dropout

marguerite [margərit] *nf (fleur)* daisy

mari [mari] *nm* husband

mariage [marjaʒ] *nm (union)* marriage;

(cérémonie) wedding; *Fig (de couleurs)* blend; **m. blanc** marriage in name only; **m. de raison** marriage of convenience

marier [marje] **1** *vt (couleurs)* to blend; **m. q n** *(sujet: prêtre, maire)* to marry sb; *(sujet: père)* to marry sb off **2 se marier** *vpr* to get married; **se m. avec qn** to get married to sb, to marry sb ▪ **marié, -iée 1** *adj* married **2** *nm* (bride)groom; **les mariés** the bride and groom; **les jeunes mariés** the newly-weds ▪ **mariée** *nf* bride

marijuana [mariɥana] *nf* marijuana

marin, -ine [marɛ̃, -in] **1** *adj (flore)* marine; *(mille)* nautical; **air/sel m.** sea air/salt; **costume m.** sailor suit **2** *nm* sailor, seaman; **m. pêcheur** (deep-sea) fisherman ▪ **marine 1** *nf* **m. de guerre** navy; **m. marchande** merchant navy **2** *adj & nm inv (bleu)* **m.** *(couleur)* navy (blue)

marina [marina] *nf* marina

marinade [marinad] *nf Culin* marinade ▪ **mariner** *vti Culin* to marinade, to marinate

marionnette [marjɔnɛt] *nf* puppet; *(à fils)* marionette

maritalement [maritalmɑ̃] *adv* **vivre m.** to cohabit

maritime [maritim] *adj (droit, climat)* maritime; **gare m.** harbour station; **port m.** seaport; *Can* **les Provinces maritimes** the Maritime Provinces

marjolaine [marʒɔlɛn] *nf* marjoram

mark [mark] *nm (monnaie)* mark

marmaille [marmɑj] *nf Fam Péj (enfants)* kids

marmelade [marmǝlad] *nf Br* stewed fruit, *Am* fruit compote; *Fig* **en m.** reduced to a pulp

marmite [marmit] *nf (cooking)* pot

marmonner [marmɔne] *vti* to mutter

marmot [marmo] *nm Fam (enfant)* kid

marmotte [marmɔt] *nf* marmot; *Fig* **dormir comme une m.** to sleep like a log

marmotter [marmɔte] *vti* to mumble

Maroc [marɔk] *nm* **le M.** Morocco ▪ **marocain, -aine 1** *adj* Moroccan **2** *nmf* **M., Marocaine** Moroccan

maroquinerie [marɔkinri] *nf (magasin)* leather goods shop ▪ **maroquinier** *nm* leather goods dealer

marotte [marɔt] *nf Fam (passion)* craze

marque [mark] *nf (trace, signe)* mark; *(de confiance)* sign; *(de produit)* brand; *(de voiture)* make; *Sport (points)* score; **de m.** *(hôte, visiteur)* distinguished; *(produit)* of quality; **à vos marques! prêts? partez!** on your marks! get set! go!; **m. de fabrique** trademark; **m. déposée** (registered) trademark

marquer [marke] **1** *vt (par une marque)* to mark; *(écrire)* to note down; *(indiquer)* to show; *Sport (point, but)* to score; **m. les points** to keep (the) score; *Fam* **m. le coup** to mark the event

2 *vi (laisser une trace)* to leave a mark; *(date, événement)* to stand out; *Sport* to score ▪ **marquant, -ante** *adj (remarquable)* outstanding; *(épisode)* significant ▪ **marqué, -ée** *adj (différence, accent)* marked; *(visage)* lined ▪ **marqueur** *nm (stylo)* marker

marquis [marki] *nm* marquis ▪ **marquise** *nf* (**a**) *(personne)* marchioness (**b**) *(auvent)* canopy

marraine [marɛn] *nf* godmother

marre [mar] *adv Fam* **en avoir m.** to be fed up (de with)

marrer [mare] **se marrer** *vpr Fam* to have a good laugh ▪ **marrant, -ante 1** *adj Fam* funny, hilarious **2** *nmf Fam* **c'est un m.** he's a good laugh

marron¹ [marɔ̃] **1** *nm (fruit)* chestnut; *(couleur)* (chestnut) brown; *Fam (coup)* thump; **m. d'Inde** horse chestnut **2** *adj inv (couleur)* (chestnut) brown ▪ **marronnier** *nm* (horse) chestnut tree

---

Il faut noter que le mot anglais **maroon** est un faux ami. Lorsqu'il désigne une couleur, il signifie **bordeaux**.

---

marron², -onne [marɔ̃, -ɔn] *adj (médecin)* quack

mars [mars] *nm* March

marsouin [marswɛ̃] *nm* porpoise

marteau, -x [marto] *nm* hammer; *(de porte)* (door)knocker; **m. piqueur** pneumatic drill ▪ **martèlement** *nm* hammering ▪ **marteler** *vt* to hammer

martial, -e, -iaux, -iales [marsjal, -jo] *adj* martial; **cour martiale** court martial; **loi martiale** martial law

martien, -ienne [marsjɛ̃, -jɛn] *nmf & adj* Martian

martinet [martinɛ] *nm (fouet)* strap

Martinique [martinik] *nf* **la M.** Martinique ▪ **martiniquais, -aise 1** *adj* Martinican **2** *nmf* **M., Martiniquaise** Martinican

martin-pêcheur [martɛ̃pɛʃœr] *nm (pl* **martins-pêcheurs**) *nm* kingfisher

martyr, -yre¹ [martir] **1** *nmf (personne)* martyr **2** *adj* **enfant m.** battered child ▪ **martyre²** *nm (souffrance)* martyrdom; **souffrir le m.** to be in agony ▪ **martyriser** *vt* to torture; *(enfant)* to batter

marxisme [marksism] *nm* Marxism ▪ **marxiste** *adj & nmf* Marxist

mascara [maskara] *nm* mascara

mascarade [maskarad] *nf* masquerade

mascotte [maskɔt] *nf* mascot

masculin, -ine [maskylɛ̃, -in] **1** *adj (sexe, mode, métier)* male; *(trait de caractère, femme)* & *Grammaire* masculine; *(équipe)* men's **2** *nm Grammaire* masculine ▪ **masculinité** *nf* masculinity

masochisme [mazɔfism] *nm* masochism ▪ **masochiste** *(Fam* **maso**) **1** *adj* masochistic **2** *nmf* masochist

masque [mask] *nm* mask; **m. à gaz/oxygène** gas/oxygen mask ▪ **masquer** *vt (dissimuler)* to mask (**à** from); *(cacher à la vue)* to block off

massacre [masakr] *nm (tuerie)* massacre; **jeu de m.** *Br* = Aunt Sally; *Fig* **faire un m.** *(avoir du succès)* to be a runaway success ▪ **massacrer** *vt* to massacre; *Fam (abîmer)* to ruin

massage [masaʒ] *nm* massage

masse [mas] *nf* (**a**) *(volume)* mass; *(gros morceau, majorité)* bulk (**de** of); **de m.** *(culture, communication)* mass; **en m.** en masse; **une m. de** masses of; **les masses** *(peuple)* the masses; *Fam* **des masses de** masses of; *Fam* **pas des masses** *(quantité)* not that much; *(nombre)* not many; *Fam* **être à la m.** to be off one's head (**b**) *(outil)* sledgehammer (**c**) *Él Br* earth, *Am* ground

masser [mase] **1** *vt (rassembler)* to assemble; *(pétrir)* to massage **2 se masser** *vpr (foule)* to form ▪ **masseur** *nm* masseur ▪ **masseuse** *nf* masseuse

massif, -ive [masif, -iv] **1** *adj* massive; *(or, chêne)* solid **2** *nm (d'arbres, de fleurs)* clump; *Géog* massif ▪ **massivement** *adv (voter, répondre)* en masse

massue [masy] *nf* club

mastic [mastik] **1** *nm (pour vitres)* putty; *(pour bois)* filler **2** *adj inv (beige)* putty-coloured

mastiquer¹ [mastike] *vt (vitre)* to putty; *(bois)* to fill

mastiquer² [mastike] *vt (mâcher)* to chew

mastoc [mastɔk] *adj inv Fam Péj* massive

mastodonte [mastɔdɔ̃t] *nm Péj (personne)* colossus; *(objet)* hulking great thing

masturber [mastyrbe] **se masturber** *vpr* to masturbate ▪ **masturbation** *nf* masturbation

masure [mazyr] *nf* hovel

mat¹, mate [mat] *adj (papier, couleur)* matt; *(son)* dull

mat² [mat] *adj m inv & nm* Échecs (check-)mate; **faire m.** to (check)mate; **mettre qn m.** to (check)mate sb

mât [mɑ] *nm (de navire)* mast; *(poteau)* pole

match [matʃ] *nm Sport Br* match, *Am* game; **m. aller** first leg; **m. retour** return leg; **m. nul** draw; **faire m. nul** to draw

matelas [matla] *nm* mattress; **m. pneumatique** air bed ▪ **matelassé, -ée** *adj (tissu)* quilted; *(enveloppe)* padded

matelot [matlo] *nm* sailor

mater¹ [mate] *vt (se rendre maître de)* to bring to heel

mater² [mate] *vt Fam (regarder)* to ogle

matérialiser [materjalize] *vt,* **se matérialiser** *vpr* to materialize ▪ **matérialisation** *nf* materialization

matérialisme [materjalism] *nm* materialism ▪ **matérialiste 1** *adj* materialistic **2** *nmf* materialist

matériau, -x [materjo] *nm* material; **matériaux** *(de construction)* building material(s); *Fig (de roman, d'enquête)* material

matériel, -ielle [materjɛl] **1** *adj (confort, dégâts, besoins)* material; *(organisation, problème)* practical **2** *nm (de camping)* equipment; *Ordinat* **m. informatique** computer hardware ▪ **matériellement** *adv* materially; **m. impossible** physically impossible

maternel, -elle [maternɛl] **1** *adj (amour, femme)* maternal; *(langue)* native **2** *nf* (**école**) **maternelle** *Br* nursery school, *Am* kindergarten ▪ **materner** *vt* to mother ▪ **maternité** *nf (état)* motherhood; *(hôpital)* maternity hospital

mathématique [matematik] *adj* mathematical ▪ **mathématicien, -ienne** *nmf* mathematician ▪ **mathématiques** *nfpl* mathematics *(sing)* ▪ **maths** [mat] *nfpl Fam Br* maths, *Am* math; *Fam* **M. Sup/Spé** = first-/second-year class preparing for the science-orientated "grandes écoles"

matière [matjɛr] *nf (à l'école)* subject; *(de livre)* subject matter; *(substance)* material; *Phys* **la m.** matter; **en m. de qch** as regards sth; **s'y connaître en m. de qch** to be experienced in sth; **en la m.** *(sur ce sujet)* on the subject; **m. plastique** plastic; **m. première** raw material; **matières grasses** fat

Matignon [matiɲɔ̃] *nm* **(l'hôtel) M.** = the French Prime Minister's offices

matin [matɛ̃] *nm* morning; **le m.** *(chaque matin)* in the morning(s); **tous les mardis matin(s)** every Tuesday morning; **le 8 au m.** on the morning of the 8th; **à sept heures du m.** at seven in the morning; **de bon m., au petit m., de grand m.** very early (in the morning); **du m. au soir** from morning till night; **médicament à prendre m., midi et soir** medicine to be taken three times a day ▪ **matinal, -e, -aux, -ales** *adj (heure)* early; **soleil m.** morning sun; **être m.** to be an early riser

matinée [matine] *nf* morning; *Théâtre & Cin* matinée; **dans la m.** in the course of the morning

matos [matos] *nm Fam* gear

matou [matu] *nm* tomcat

matraque [matrak] *nf* bludgeon; *(de policier) Br* truncheon, *Am* nightstick ▪ **matraquage** *nm* **m. publicitaire** hype ▪ **matraquer** *vt (frapper)* to club; *Fig (harceler)* to bombard

matrice [matris] *nf (moule)* & *Math* matrix ▪ **matricielle** *adj f Ordinat* **imprimante m.** dot matrix printer

matricule [matrikyl] **1** *nm* number **2** *adj* **numéro m.** registration number

matrimonial, -e, -iaux, -iales [matrimɔnjal, -jo] *adj* matrimonial

mâture [mɑtyr] *nf (de navire)* masts

maturité [matyrite] *nf* maturity; **arriver à m.** *(fromage, vin)* to mature; *(fruit)* to ripen

maudire* [modir] *vt* to curse ▪ **maudit, -ite** *adj (damné)* cursed; *(insupportable)* damned

maugréer [mogree] *vi* to growl, to grumble (**contre** at)

Maurice [mɔris] *nf* **l'île M.** Mauritius

mausolée [mozole] *nm* mausoleum

maussade [mosad] *adj (personne)* sullen; *(temps)* gloomy

mauvais, -aise [move, -ɛz] **1** *adj* bad; *(santé, vue)* poor; *(méchant)* nasty; *(mal choisi)* wrong; *(mer)* rough; **plus m. que...** worse than...; **le plus m.** the worst; **être m. en anglais** to be bad at English; **être en mauvaise santé** to be in bad *or* ill *or* poor health **2** *adv* **il fait m.** the weather's bad; **ça sent m.** it smells bad **3** *nm* **le bon et le m.** the good and the bad

mauve [mov] *adj & nm (couleur)* mauve

mauviette [movjɛt] *nf Fam (personne)* wimp

maux [mo] *pl de* **mal**

max [maks] *nm inv Fam* **un m.** loads; **un m. de fric** loads of money; **on s'est éclaté un m.** we had *Br* a fantastic time *or Am* a blast

maxime [maksim] *nf* maxim

maximum [maksimɔm] *(pl* **maxima** [-ma] *ou* **maximums) 1** *nm* maximum; **faire le m.** to do one's very best; **au m.** at the most; *Fam* **un m. de gens** *(le plus possible)* as many people as possible; *(énormément)* loads of people **2** *adj* maximum ▪ **maximal, -e, -aux, -ales** *adj* maximum

mayonnaise [majɔnɛz] *nf* mayonnaise

mazout [mazut] *nm (fuel)* oil

me [mə]

m' is used before a vowel or mute h.

pron personnel **(a)** *(complément direct)* me; **il me voit** he sees me **(b)** *(complément indirect)* (to) me; **elle me parle** she speaks to me; **tu me l'as dit** you told me **(c)** *(réfléchi)* myself; **je me lave** I wash myself **(d)** *(avec les pronominaux)* **je me suis trompé** I made a mistake

méandres [meɑ̃dr] *nmpl (de rivière)* meanders

mec [mɛk] *nm Fam (individu)* guy, *Br* bloke

mécanicien [mekanisjɛ̃] *nm* mechanic; *(de train) Br* train driver, *Am* engineer

mécanique [mekanik] **1** *adj* mechanical; **jouet m.** wind-up toy **2** *nf (science)* mechanics *(sing)*; *(mécanisme)* mechanism ▪ **mécanisme** *nm* mechanism

Il faut noter que le nom anglais **mechanic** est un faux ami. Il signifie **mécanicien**.

mécanisation [mekanizasjɔ̃] *nf* mechanization

mécène [mesɛn] *nm* patron (of the arts)

méchant, -ante [meʃɑ̃, -ɑ̃t] *adj (personne, remarque, blessure)* nasty; *(enfant)* naughty; *(chien)* vicious; **être de méchante humeur** to

be in a foul mood; **'attention! chien m.'** 'beware of the dog' ▪ **méchamment** [-amɑ̃] *adv (cruellement)* nastily; *Fam (très)* terribly ▪ **méchanceté** *nf* nastiness; **une m.** *(parole)* a nasty remark; *(acte)* a nasty action

mèche [mɛʃ] *nf* **(a)** *(de cheveux)* lock; **se faire des mèches** to have highlights done *(in one's hair)* **(b)** *(de bougie)* wick; *(de pétard)* fuse; *(de perceuse)* bit; *Fig* **vendre la m.** to spill the beans **(c)** *Fam* **être de m. avec qn** to be in cahoots with sb

méconnaître* [mekɔnɛtr] *vt (fait)* to fail to take into account; *(talent, artiste)* to fail to recognize ▪ **méconnaissable** *adj* unrecognizable ▪ **méconnu, -ue** *adj* unrecognized

mécontent, -ente [mekɔ̃tɑ̃, -ɑ̃t] *adj (insatisfait)* displeased (**de** with); *(contrarié)* annoyed ▪ **mécontentement** *nm (insatisfaction)* displeasure; *(contrariété)* annoyance ▪ **mécontenter** *vt (ne pas satisfaire)* to displease; *(contrarier)* to annoy

Mecque [mɛk] *nf* **La M.** Mecca

médaille [medaj] *nf (décoration, bijou) & Sport* medal; *(portant le nom)* pendant *(with name engraved on it)*; *(de chien)* name tag; *Sport* **être m. d'or/d'argent** to be a gold/silver medallist ▪ **médaillé, -ée** *nmf* medal holder ▪ **médaillon** *nm (bijou)* locket; *(de viande)* medallion

médecin [medsɛ̃] *nm* doctor, physician; **m. de famille** family doctor; **m. généraliste** general practitioner, GP; **m. traitant** consulting physician ▪ **médecine** *nf* medicine; **médecines alternatives** *ou* **douces** alternative medicine; **m. traditionnelle** traditional medicine; **étudiant en m.** medical student ▪ **médical, -e, -aux, -ales** *adj* medical ▪ **médicament** *nm* medicine ▪ **médicinal, -e, -aux, -ales** *adj* medicinal ▪ **médico-légal, -e** *(mpl* **médico-légaux**, *fpl* **médico-légales)** *adj* forensic

Il faut noter que le nom anglais **medicine** signifie également **médicament, remède**.

média [medja] *nm* medium; **les médias** the media ▪ **médiatique** *adj* **campagne/événement m.** media campaign/event ▪ **médiatiser** *vt* to give media coverage to

médiateur, -trice [medjatœr, -tris] *nmf* mediator ▪ **médiation** *nf* mediation

médiéval, -e, -aux, -ales [medjeval, -o] *adj* medieval

médiocre [medjɔkr] *adj* mediocre ▪ **médiocrité** *nf* mediocrity

médire* [medir] *vi* **m. de qn** to speak ill of sb ▪ **médisance** *nf (action)* gossiping; **médisances** *(propos)* gossip

méditer [medite] **1** *vt (réfléchir profondément à)* to contemplate; **m. de faire qch** to be contemplating doing sth **2** *vi* to meditate (**sur**

on) ▪ **méditatif, -ive** *adj* meditative ▪ **méditation** *nf* meditation

Méditerranée [mediterane] *nf* **la M.** the Mediterranean ▪ **méditerranéen, -éenne** *adj* Mediterranean

médium [medjɔm] *nmf (voyant)* medium

méduse [medyz] *nf* jellyfish ▪ **méduser** *vt* to dumbfound

meeting [mitiŋ] *nm* meeting

méfait [mefɛ] *nm* misdemeanour; **les méfaits du temps** the ravages of time

méfier [mefje] **se méfier** *vpr* to be careful; **se m. de qn** not to trust sb; **se m. de qch** to watch out for sth; **méfie-toi!** watch out!, beware! ▪ **méfiance** *nf* distrust, mistrust ▪ **méfiant, -iante** *adj* suspicious, distrustful

mégalomane [megalɔman] *(Fam mégalo) nmf* megalomaniac ▪ **mégalomanie** *nf* megalomania

mégaoctet [megaɔktɛ] *nm Ordinat* megabyte

mégaphone [megafɔn] *nm Br* megaphone, *Am* bullhorn

mégarde [megard] **par mégarde** *adv* inadvertently

mégère [meʒɛr] *nf (femme)* shrew

mégot [mego] *nm* cigarette butt *or* end

mégoter [megɔte] *vi* to skimp (**sur, pour** on); **arrête de m!** don't be stingy!

meilleur, -eure [mejœr] **1** *adj* better (**que** than); **le m. résultat/moment** the best result/ moment **2** *nmf* **le m., la meilleure** the best (one); **pour le m. et pour le pire** for better or for worse **3** *adv* **il fait m.** it's warmer

mél [mel] *nm (courrier)* e-mail

mélancolie [melɑ̃kɔli] *nf* melancholy ▪ **mélancolique** *adj* melancholy

mélange [melɑ̃ʒ] *nm (résultat)* mixture; *(opération)* mixing ▪ **mélanger 1** *vt (mêler)* to mix; *(brouiller)* to mix up **2 se mélanger** *vpr (s'incorporer)* to mix; *(idées)* to get mixed up ▪ **mélangeur** *nm (robinet) Br* mixer tap, *Am* mixing faucet

mélasse [melas] *nf Br* treacle, *Am* molasses; *Fam* **être dans la m.** to be in a mess

mêler [mele] **1** *vt* to mix (**à** with); *(odeurs, thèmes)* to combine; **m. qn à qch** *(affaire, conversation)* to involve sb in sth **2 se mêler** *vpr* to combine (**à** with); **se m. à qch** *(foule)* to mingle with sth; *(conversation)* to join in sth; **se m. de qch** to get involved in sth; **mêle-toi de tes affaires!** mind your own business! ▪ **mêlé, -ée** *adj* mixed (**de** with) ▪ **mêlée** *nf (bataille)* fray; *Rugby* scrum

méli-mélo [melimelo] *(pl* **mélis-mélos)** *nm Fam* jumble, muddle

mélo [melo] *Fam* **1** *adj* melodramatic **2** *nm* melodrama

mélodie [melɔdi] *nf* melody ▪ **mélodieux, -ieuse** *adj* melodious ▪ **mélodique** *adj* melodic ▪ **mélomane** *nmf* music lover

mélodrame [melɔdram] *nm* melodrama ▪ **mélodramatique** *adj* melodramatic

melon [məlɔ̃] *nm (fruit)* melon; **(chapeau) m.** *Br* bowler hat, *Am* derby

membrane [mɑ̃bran] *nf* membrane

membre [mɑ̃br] *nm (bras, jambe)* limb; *(de groupe)* member

même [mɛm] **1** *adj (identique)* same; **en m. temps** at the same time (**que** as); **le m. jour** the same day; **le jour m.** *(exact)* the very day; **il est la bonté m.** he is kindness itself; **lui-m./ vous-m.** himself/yourself **2** *pron* **le/la m.** the same (one); **j'ai les mêmes** I have the same (ones); **cela revient au m.** it amounts to the same thing **3** *adv (y compris, aussi)* even; **m. si...** even if...; **ici m.** in this very place; **tout de m.,** *Fam* **quand m.** all the same; **de m.** likewise; **de m. que...** just as...; **être à m. de faire qch** to be in a position to do sth; **dormir à m. le sol** to sleep on the ground; **boire à m. la bouteille** to drink (straight) from the bottle

mémento [memɛ̃to] *nm (aide-mémoire)* handbook; *(carnet)* diary

mémère [memɛr] *nf Fam Péj* **une grosse m.** a fat old bag

mémoire [memwar] **1** *nf* memory; **de m.** *(citer)* from memory; **de m. d'homme** in living memory; **à la m. de** in memory of; *Ordinat* **m. morte/vive** read-only/random access memory **2** *nm (rapport)* report; *Univ* dissertation; **Mémoires** *(chronique)* memoirs ▪ **mémorable** *adj* memorable

mémorandum [memɔrɑ̃dɔm] *nm (note)* memorandum

mémorial, -iaux [memɔrjal, -jo] *nm (monument)* memorial

menace [mənas] *nf* threat ▪ **menaçant, -ante** *adj* threatening ▪ **menacer** *vt* to threaten (**de faire** to do)

ménage [menaʒ] *nm (entretien)* housekeeping; *(couple)* couple, household; **faire le m.** to do the housework; **faire bon m. avec qn** to get on well with sb ▪ **ménager¹, -ère 1** *adj (équipement)* household **2** *nf* **ménagère** *(femme)* housewife

ménager² [menaʒe] **1** *vt (argent)* to use sparingly; *(forces)* to save; *(entrevue)* to arrange; *(sortie)* to provide; **m. qn** to treat sb carefully; **ne pas m. sa peine** to put in a lot of effort **2 se ménager** *vpr (prendre soin de soi)* to look after oneself; *(se réserver)* to set aside ▪ **ménagement** *nm (soin)* care; **sans m.** *(brutalement)* brutally

ménagerie [menaʒri] *nf* menagerie

mendier [mɑ̃dje] **1** *vt* to beg for **2** *vi* to beg ▪ **mendiant, -iante** *nmf* beggar ▪ **mendicité** *nf* begging

menées [məne] *nfpl* intrigues

mener [məne] **1** *vt (personne)* to take (**à** to);

(course, vie) to lead; *(enquête, tâche)* to carry out; **m. une campagne** to wage a campaign; *Fig* **m. la vie dure à qn** to give sb a hard time; *Fig* **m. qch à bien** to carry sth through; **ça ne mène à rien** it won't get you/us anywhere **2** *vi Sport* to lead; **m. à un lieu** to lead to a place; *Fam* **elle n'en menait pas large** her heart was in her mouth ▪ **meneur, -euse** *nmf (de révolte)* ringleader

méninges [menɛʒ] *nfpl Fam* brains

méningite [menɛʒit] *nf* meningitis

ménopause [menɔpoz] *nf* menopause

menottes [mənɔt] *nfpl* handcuffs; **passer les m. à qn** to handcuff sb

mensonge [mɑ̃sɔ̃ʒ] *nm (propos)* lie; *(action)* lying ▪ **mensonger, -ère** *adj (propos)* untrue; *(publicité)* misleading

menstruation [mɑ̃stryasjɔ̃] *nf* menstruation ▪ **menstruel, -elle** *adj* menstrual

mensuel, -uelle [mɑ̃sɥɛl] **1** *adj* monthly **2** *nm (revue)* monthly ▪ **mensualité** *nf* monthly payment ▪ **mensuellement** *adv* monthly

mensurations [mɑ̃syrasjɔ̃] *nfpl* measurements

mental, -e, -aux, -ales [mɑ̃tal, -o] *adj* mental; **calcul m.** mental arithmetic ▪ **mentalité** *nf* mentality

menthe [mɑ̃t] *nf* mint

mention [mɑ̃sjɔ̃] *nf (fait de citer)* mention; *(à un examen)* ≃ distinction; *Scol* **passable/assez bien/bien/très bien** ≃ C/B/A; **faire m. de qch** to mention sth; **'rayez les mentions inutiles'** 'delete as appropriate' ▪ **mentionner** *vt* to mention

mentir* [mɑ̃tir] *vi* to lie **(à** to) ▪ **menteur, -euse 1** *adj* lying **2** *nmf* liar

menton [mɑ̃tɔ̃] *nm* chin

menu¹ [məny] *nm (de restaurant)* set menu; *Ordinat* menu; **par le m.** in detail; *Ordinat* **m. déroulant** pull-down menu; *Ordinat* **m. local** pop-up menu; *Ordinat* **m. principal** main menu

menu², -ue [məny] **1** *adj (petit)* tiny; *(mince)* slim; *(détail, monnaie)* small **2** *adv (hacher)* small, finely

menuisier [mənɥizje] *nm* carpenter, joiner ▪ **menuiserie** *nf (atelier)* joiner's workshop; *(ouvrage)* woodwork

méprendre [meprɑ̃dr] **se méprendre** *vpr Littéraire* **se m. sur** to be mistaken about ▪ **méprise** *nf* mistake

mépris [mepri] *nm* contempt **(pour** for), scorn **(pour** for); **au m. de qch** without regard to sth; **avoir du m. pour qn** to despise sb ▪ **méprisable** *adj* despicable ▪ **méprisant, -ante** *adj* contemptuous, scornful ▪ **mépriser** *vt* to despise

mer [mɛr] *nf* sea; *Am* ocean; *(marée)* tide; **en (haute) m.** at sea; **par m.** by sea; **aller à la m.** to go to the seaside; **prendre la m.** to set sail;

Fam **ce n'est pas la m. à boire** it's no big deal; **un homme à la m.!** man overboard!

mercantile [mɛrkɑ̃til] *adj Péj* mercenary

mercatique [mɛrkatik] *nf* marketing

mercenaire [mɛrsənɛr] *adj & nm* mercenary

mercerie [mɛrsəri] *nf (magasin) Br* haberdasher's, *Am* notions store; *(marchandise) Br* haberdashery, *Am* notions ▪ **mercier, -ière** *nmf Br* haberdasher, *Am* notions dealer *or* merchant

merci [mɛrsi] **1** *exclam* thank you, thanks **(de** *ou* **pour** for); **non m.** no thank you; **m. bien** thanks very much **2** *nf* **à la m. de qn/qch** at the mercy of sb/sth; **tenir qn à sa m.** to have sb at one's mercy; **sans m.** merciless

mercredi [mɛrkrədi] *nm* Wednesday

mercure [mɛrkyr] *nm* mercury

merde [mɛrd] *Vulg* **1** *nm* shit; **de m.** *(voiture, télé)* shitty, crappy; **être dans la m.** to be in the shit **2** *exclam* shit! ▪ **merder** *vi très Fam (ne pas marcher)* to go down the pan; **j'ai merdé à l'examen** I really screwed up in the exam ▪ **merdique** *adj très Fam* shitty, crappy

mère [mɛr] *nf* mother; *Fam* **la m. Dubois** old Mrs Dubois; *Com* **maison m.** parent company; **m. célibataire** single mother; **m. de famille** wife and mother; **m. porteuse** surrogate mother; **m. poule** mother hen

méridien [meridjɛ̃] *nm* meridian

méridional, -e, -aux, -ales [meridjɔnal, -o] **1** *adj* southern **2** *nmf* southerner

meringue [mərɛ̃g] *nf* meringue

merisier [mərizje] *nm (bois)* cherry

mérite [merit] *nm* merit; *(honneur)* credit; **avoir du m. à faire qch** to deserve credit for doing sth; **homme de m.** *(valeur)* man of worth ▪ **méritant, -ante** *adj* deserving ▪ **mériter** *vt (être digne de)* to deserve; *(demander)* to be worth; **m. de réussir** to deserve to succeed; **m. réflexion** to be worth thinking about; **ce livre mérite d'être lu** this book is worth reading ▪ **méritoire** *adj* commendable

merlan [mɛrlɑ̃] *nm (poisson)* whiting

merle [mɛrl] *nm* blackbird

merlu [mɛrly] *nm* hake

merveille [mɛrvɛj] *nf* wonder, marvel; **à m.** wonderfully (well); *Fig* **faire des merveilles** to work wonders; **les Sept Merveilles du monde** the Seven Wonders of the World

merveilleux, -euse [mɛrvɛjø, -øz] **1** *adj* wonderful, *Br* marvellous, *Am* marvelous **2** *nm* **le m.** the supernatural ▪ **merveilleusement** *adv* wonderfully

mes [me] *voir* **mon**

mésange [mezɑ̃ʒ] *nf (oiseau)* tit

mésaventure [mezavɑ̃tyr] *nf* misadventure

mesdames [medam] *pl de* **madame**

mesdemoiselles [medmwazɛl] *pl de* **mademoiselle**

mésentente [mezɑ̃tɑ̃t] *nf* disagreement

mésestimer [mezɛstime] *vt* to underestimate

mesquin, -ine [mɛskɛ̃, -in] *adj* mean, petty ▪ **mesquinerie** *nf* meanness, pettiness; **une m.** an act of meanness

mess [mɛs] *nm inv Mil (salle)* mess

message [mesaʒ] *nm* message; **m. publicitaire** advertisement; **m. vocal** voicemail (message) ▪ **messager, -ère** *nmf* messenger ▪ **messagerie** *nf* courier company; *Ordinat* **m. électronique** e-mail; *Ordinat* **m. instantanée** instant messaging; **m. vocale** voicemail (service)

messe [mɛs] *nf (office, musique)* mass; **aller à la m.** to go to mass; *Fig* **faire des messes basses** to whisper

messeigneurs [mesɛɲœr] *pl de* **monseigneur**

Messie [mesi] *nm* **le M.** the Messiah

messieurs [mesjø] *pl de* **monsieur**

mesure [məzyr] *nf (dimension)* measurement; *(action)* measuring; *(moyen)* measure; *(retenue)* moderation; *Mus (temps)* time; *Mus (division)* bar; **sur m.** *(vêtement)* made to measure; **être en m. de faire qch** to be in a position to do sth; **être sans commune m. avec qch** to be out of proportion to sth; **prendre la m. de qch** *(problème)* to size sth up; **prendre les mesures de qn** to measure sb; **prendre des mesures** to take measures; **à m. que...** as...; **dans la m. où...** in so far as...; **dans une certaine m.** to a certain extent; **dans la m. du possible** as far as possible

mesurer [məzyre] **1** *vt (dimension, taille)* to measure; *(déterminer)* to assess; *(argent, temps)* to ration **2** *vi* **m.1 m 83** *(personne)* ≃ to be 6 ft tall; *(objet)* to measure 6 ft **3 se mesurer** *upr Fig* **se m. à** *ou* **avec qn** to pit oneself against sb ▪ **mesuré, -ée** *adj (pas, ton)* measured; *(personne)* moderate

met [mɛ] *voir* **mettre**

métal, -aux [metal, -o] *nm* metal ▪ **métallique** *adj (éclat, reflet)* metallic; **pont m.** metal bridge ▪ **métallisé, -ée** *adj* **bleu m.** metallic blue

métallurgie [metalyrʒi] *nf (industrie)* steel industry; *(science)* metallurgy ▪ **métallurgique** *adj* **usine m.** steelworks ▪ **métallurgiste** *nm* metalworker

métamorphose [metamɔrfoz] *nf* metamorphosis ▪ **métamorphoser** *vt*, **se métamorphoser** *upr* to transform (**en** into)

métaphore [metafɔr] *nf* metaphor ▪ **métaphorique** *adj* metaphorical

métaphysique [metafizik] **1** *adj* metaphysical **2** *nf* metaphysics *(sing)*

météo [meteo] *Fam* **1** *nf (bulletin)* weather forecast **2** *nm* **Monsieur M.** the weather man

météore [meteɔr] *nm* meteor ▪ **météorite** *nf* meteorite

météorologie [meteɔrɔlɔʒi] *nf (science)* meteorology; *(service)* weather bureau

▪ **météorologique** *adj* meteorological; **bulletin/station m.** weather report/station

méthode [metɔd] *nf (manière, soin)* method; *(livre)* course ▪ **méthodique** *adj* methodical

méticuleux, -euse [metikylø, -øz] *adj* meticulous

métier [metje] *nm (manuel, commercial)* trade; *(intellectuel)* profession; *(savoir-faire)* experience; **homme de m.** specialist; **tailleur de son m.** tailor by trade; **être du m.** to be in the business; **m. à tisser** loom

métis, -isse [metis] **1** *adj* mixed-race **2** *nmf* person of mixed race

métrage [metraʒ] *nm (action)* measuring; *(tissu)* length; *(de film)* footage; **long m.** feature film; **court m.** short film

mètre [mɛtr] *nm (mesure) Br* metre, *Am* meter; *(règle)* (metre) rule; **m. carré/cube** square/cubic metre; **m. à ruban** tape measure ▪ **métreur** *nm* quantity surveyor ▪ **métrique** *adj (système)* metric

métro [metro] *nm Br* underground, *Am* subway

métropole [metrɔpɔl] *nf (ville)* metropolis; *(pays)* mother country ▪ **métropolitain, -aine** *adj* metropolitan

mets [mɛ] *nm (aliment)* dish

mettable [metabl] *adj* wearable

metteur [metœr] *nm* **m. en scène** director

mettre* [mɛtr] **1** *vt* to put; *(vêtement, lunettes)* to put on; *(chauffage, radio)* to switch on; *(réveil)* to set (**à** for); **m. dix heures à venir** to take ten hours to come; **j'ai mis une heure** it took me an hour; **m. 100 euros** to spend 100 euros (**pour une robe** on a dress); **m. qn en colère** to make sb angry; **m. qn à l'aise** to put sb at ease; **m. qn en liberté** to free sb; **m. qch en bouteilles** to bottle sth; **m. qch plus fort** to turn sth up; **m. de la musique** to put some music on; **m. du soin à faire qch** to take care to do sth; **mettons que...** (+ *subjunctive*) let's suppose that...

2 se mettre *upr (se placer)* to put oneself; *(debout)* to stand; *(assis)* to sit; *(objet)* to go; **se m. en pyjama** to get into one's pyjamas; **se m. à table** to sit (down) at the table; **se m. à l'aise** to make oneself comfortable; **se m. à la cuisine/au salon** to go into the kitchen/dining room; **se m. au travail** to start work; **se m. à faire qch** to start doing sth; **le temps s'est mis au beau/à la pluie** the weather has turned fine/rainy; **se m. en rapport avec qn** to get in touch with sb; *Fam* **se m. le doigt dans l'œil** to be badly mistaken

meuble [mœbl] **1** *adj (terre)* soft **2** *nm* piece of furniture; **meubles** furniture ▪ **meublé** *nm* furnished *Br* flat *or Am* apartment ▪ **meubler** *vt* to furnish; *Fig (remplir)* to fill

meuf [mœf] *nf très Fam* chick, *Br* bird

meugler [møgle] *vi (vache)* to moo ▪ **meugle-**

ment [-əmã] *nm* moo; **meuglements** mooing
meule [møl] *nf (d'herbe)* stack; *(de moulin)* millstone; **m. de foin** haystack
meunier, -ière [mønje, -jɛr] *nmf* miller
meurt [mœr] *voir* **mourir**
meurtre [mœrtr] *nm* murder ▪ **meurtrier, -ière 1** *nmf* murderer **2** *adj* murderous; *(épidémie)* deadly
meurtrir [mœrtrir] *vt* to bruise ▪ **meurtrissure** *nf* bruise
meute [møt] *nf (de chiens)* pack; *Fig (foule)* mob
Mexique [mɛksik] *nm* **le M.** Mexico ▪ **mexicain, -aine 1** *adj* Mexican **2** *nmf* **M., Mexicaine** Mexican
mezzanine [mɛdzanin] *nf (de pièce)* mezzanine floor; *(au théâtre)* Br dress circle, Am mezzanine
mi [mi] *nm inv (note)* E
mi- [mi] *préf* **la mi-mars** mid March; **à mi-distance** midway; **cheveux mi-longs** shoulder-length hair
miaou [mjau] *exclam* miaow ▪ **miaulement** *nm* miaowing ▪ **miauler** [mjole] *vi (chat)* to miaow
mi-bas [miba] *nm inv* knee-high sock
miche [miʃ] *nf (pain)* round loaf
mi-chemin [miʃmɛ̃] **à mi-chemin** *adv* halfway
mi-clos, -close [miklo, -kloz] *(mpl* **mi-clos,** *fpl* **mi-closes)** *adj* half-closed
micmac [mikmak] *nm Fam (manigance)* muddle
mi-corps [mikɔr] **à mi-corps** *adv* (up) to the waist
mi-côte [mikot] **à mi-côte** *adv* halfway up the hill
micro [mikro] *nm (microphone)* mike; *Ordinat* micro(computer) ▪ **microphone** *nm* microphone
microbe [mikrɔb] *nm* germ, microbe
microcosme [mikrɔkɔsm] *nm* microcosm
microfiche [mikrofiʃ] *nf* microfiche
microfilm [mikrɔfilm] *nm* microfilm
micro-informatique [mikroɛ̃fɔrmatik] *nf* microcomputing
micro-ondes [mikrɔɔ̃d] *nm inv* microwave; **four à m.** microwave oven
micro-ordinateur [mikroordinatœr] *(pl* **micro-ordinateurs)** *nm* microcomputer
microprocesseur [mikroprɔsɛsœr] *nm Ordinat* microprocessor
microscope [mikrɔskɔp] *nm* microscope ▪ **microscopique** *adj* microscopic
midi [midi] *nm* **(a)** *(heure)* twelve o'clock, midday; *(heure du déjeuner)* lunchtime; **entre m. et deux heures** at lunchtime; *Fig* **chercher m. à quatorze heures** to make unnecessary complications for oneself **(b)** *(sud)* south; **le M.** the South of France
mie [mi] *nf (de pain)* soft part, crumb
miel [mjɛl] *nm* honey ▪ **mielleux, -euse** *adj Fig (parole, personne)* smooth
mien, mienne [mjɛ̃, mjɛn] **1** *pron possessif* **le**

m., la mienne mine, *Br* my one; **les miens, les miennes** mine, *Br* my ones; **les deux miens** my two **2** *nmpl* **les miens** *(ma famille)* my family
miette [mjɛt] *nf (de pain)* crumb; **réduire qch en miettes** to smash sth to pieces; *Fam* **ne pas perdre une m. de qch** *(conversation)* not to miss a word of sth
mieux [mjø] **1** *adv* better **(que** than); **aller m.** to be (feeling) better; **de m. en m.** better and better; **faire qch à qui m. m.** to try to outdo each other doing sth; **le/la/les m.** *(être)* the best; *(de deux)* the better; **le m. serait de...** the best thing would be to...; **le plus tôt sera le m.** the sooner the better **2** *adj inv* better; *(plus beau)* better-looking; **si tu n'as rien de m. à faire** if you've got nothing better to do **3** *nm (amélioration)* improvement; **faire de son m.** to do one's best; **faites au m.** do the best you can
mièvre [mjɛvr] *adj* insipid
mignon, -onne [miɲɔ̃, -ɔn] *adj (charmant)* cute; *(gentil)* nice
migraine [migrɛn] *nf* headache; *Méd* migraine
migration [migrasjɔ̃] *nf* migration ▪ **migrant, -ante** *adj & nmf* migrant ▪ **migrateur, -trice** *adj* migratory
mijoter [miʒɔte] **1** *vt (avec soin)* to cook (lovingly); *(lentement)* to simmer; *Fam (tramer)* to cook up **2** *vi* to simmer
mil [mil] *adj inv* **l'an deux m.** the year two thousand
milice [milis] *nf* militia ▪ **milicien** *nm* militiaman
milieu, -x [miljø] *nm (centre)* middle; *(cadre, groupe social)* environment; *(entre extrêmes)* middle course; *Phys* medium; **milieux littéraires/militaires** literary/military circles; **au m. de** in the middle of; **au m. du danger** in the midst of danger; **le juste m.** the happy medium; **le m.** *(la pègre)* the underworld
militaire [militɛr] **1** *adj* military **2** *nm* serviceman; *(dans l'armée de terre)* soldier
militer [milite] *vi (personne)* to campaign (**pour** for; **contre** against) ▪ **militant, -ante** *adj & nmf* militant
mille [mil] **1** *adj inv & nm inv* thousand; **m. hommes** a *or* one thousand men; **deux m.** two thousand; **mettre dans le m.** to hit the bull's-eye; **je vous le donne en m.!** you'll never guess! **2** *nm* **m. (marin)** nautical mile ▪ **mille-feuille** *(pl* **mille-feuilles)** *nm Br* ≃ vanilla slice, *Am* ≃ napoleon ▪ **mille-pattes** *nm inv* centipede ▪ **millième** *adj, nm & nmf* thousandth; **un m.** a thousandth ▪ **millier** *nm* thousand; **un m. (de)** a thousand or so; **par milliers** in their thousands
millénaire [milenɛr] *nm* millennium
millésime [milezim] *nm (de vin)* year; *(de pièce de monnaie)* date

millet [mijɛ] *nm* millet

milliard [miljar] *nm* billion ▪ **milliardaire** *adj & nmf* billionaire

millimètre [milimɛtr] *nm* millimetre

million [miljɔ̃] *nm* million; **un m. d'euros** a million euros; **deux millions** two million; **par millions** in millions ▪ **millionième** *adj, nm & nmf* millionth ▪ **millionnaire** *nmf* millionaire

mime [mim] **1** *nm (art)* mime **2** *nmf (artiste)* mime ▪ **mimer** *vti (exprimer)* to mime ▪ **mimique** *nf (mine)* (funny) face

mimétisme [mimetism] *nm* mimicry; **agir par m.** to mimic *or* copy sb's attitudes

mimosa [mimoza] *nm (arbre, fleur)* mimosa

minable [minabl] *adj (lieu, personne)* shabby; *(médiocre)* pathetic

minaret [minarɛ] *nm* minaret

minauder [minode] *vi* to simper

mince [mɛ̃s] **1** *adj* thin; *(élancé)* slim; *(insuffisant)* slight **2** *exclam Fam* **m. (alors)!** *(de déception)* damn!; *(de surprise)* well, blow me! ▪ **minceur** *nf* thinness; *(sveltesse)* slimness ▪ **mincir** *vi* to get slimmer

mine [min] *nf* **(a)** *(physionomie)* look; **avoir bonne/mauvaise m.** to look well/ill; **faire m. de faire qch** *(chagrin, maladie)* to make as if to do sth; **faire grise m.** to look anything but pleased; *Fam* **m. de rien** *(discrètement)* quite casually **(b)** *(gisement)* & *Fig* mine; **m. de charbon** coalmine **(c)** *(de crayon)* lead **(d)** *(engin explosif)* mine; *Mil* **champ de mines** minefield

miner [mine] *vt (terrain)* to mine; *Fig (saper)* to undermine; **m. qn** *(chagrin, maladie)* to wear sb down

minerai [minrɛ] *nm* ore

minéral, -e, -aux, -ales [mineral, -o] *adj & nm* mineral

minéralogique [mineraloʒik] *adj* **plaque m.** *(de véhicule)* Br number *or* Am license plate

minerve [minɛrv] *nf* surgical collar

minet, -ette [minɛ, -ɛt] *nmf Fam (chat)* puss, kitty; *(personne)* trendy

mineur, -eure [minœr] **1** *nm (ouvrier)* miner; **m. de fond** underground worker **2** *adj (secondaire)* & *Mus* minor; *(de moins de 18 ans)* under-age **3** *nmf Jur* minor ▪ **minier, -ière** *adj* **industrie minière** mining industry

miniature [minjatyr] **1** *nf* miniature **2** *adj* **train m.** miniature train

minibus [minibys] *nm* minibus

minichaîne [miniʃɛn] *nf* mini (hi-fi) system

Minidisc® [minidisk] *nm* MiniDisc®; **lecteur M.** Minidisc® player

minigolf [minigɔlf] *nm* minigolf, crazy golf

minijupe [miniʒyp] *nf* miniskirt

minimal, -ale, -aux, -ales [minimal, -o] *adj* minimum

minime [minim] *adj* minimal ▪ **minimiser** *vt* to minimize

minimum [minimɔm] *(pl* **minima** [-ma] *ou* **minimums**) **1** *nm* minimum; **le m. de (force)** the minimum (amount of); **faire le m.** to do the bare minimum; **en un m. de temps** in as short a time as possible; **au (grand) m.** at the very least; **le m. vital** a minimum to live on; **les minima sociaux** = basic income support **2** *adj* minimum

ministère [minister] *nm (département)* ministry; *(gouvernement)* government, cabinet; **m. des Affaires étrangères** *Br* ≃ Foreign Office, *Am* ≃ State Department; **m. de l'Intérieur** *Br* ≃ Home Office, *Am* ≃ Department of the Interior; *Jur* **le m. public** *Br* ≃ the Crown Prosecution Service, *Am* ≃ the District Attorney's Office ▪ **ministériel, -ielle** *adj* ministerial; **remaniement m.** cabinet *or* government reshuffle

ministre [ministr] *nm Pol & Rel* secretary, *Br* minister; **m. des Affaires étrangères** *Br* ≃ Foreign Secretary, *Am* ≃ Secretary of State; **m. de l'Intérieur** *Br* ≃ Home Secretary, *Am* ≃ Secretary of the Interior; **m. de la Justice** *Br* ≃ Lord Chancellor, *Am* ≃ Attorney General; **m. de la Culture** ≃ Arts Minister; **m. d'État** ≃ secretary of state; **m.** ≃ cabinet minister

Minitel® [minitɛl] *nm* = consumer information network accessible via home computer terminal

minois [minwa] *nm (d'enfant, de jeune femme)* (pretty) face

minorer [minɔre] *vt (faire baisser)* to reduce

minorité [minɔrite] *nf* minority; **en m.** in the minority ▪ **minoritaire** *adj* **parti m.** minority party; **être m.** to be in the minority

Minorque [minɔrk] *nf* Minorca

minou [minu] *nm Fam (chat)* puss, kitty

minuit [minɥi] *nm* midnight, twelve o'clock

minus [minys] *nm Fam (incapable)* no-hoper

minuscule [minyskyl] **1** *adj (petit)* tiny, minute **2** *adj & nf* **(lettre)** *n.* small letter

minute [minyt] **1** *nf* minute; **à la m.** *(tout de suite)* this (very) minute; **d'une m. à l'autre** any minute (now) **2** *adj inv* **plats m.** convenience food ▪ **minuter** *vt* to time ▪ **minuterie** *nf (d'éclairage)* time switch ▪ **minuteur** *nm* timer

minutie [minysi] *nf* meticulousness ▪ **minutieux, -ieuse** *adj* meticulous

mioche [mjɔʃ] *nmf Fam (enfant)* kid

mirabelle [mirabɛl] *nf* mirabelle plum

miracle [mirakl] *nm* miracle; **par m.** miraculously ▪ **miraculeux, -euse** *adj* miraculous

mirador [miradɔr] *nm* watchtower

mirage [miraʒ] *nm* mirage

mire [mir] *nf* **point de m.** *(cible)* & *Fig* target

mirettes [mirɛt] *nfpl Fam* eyes

mirifique [mirifik] *adj Hum* fabulous

mirobolant, -ante [mirɔbɔlɑ̃, -ɑ̃t] *adj Fam* fantastic

miroir [mirwar] *nm* mirror ■ **miroiter** *vi* to shimmer

mis, mise¹ [mi, miz] **1** *pp de* mettre **2** *adj* bien **m.** (*vêtu*) well-dressed

misanthrope [mizɑ̃trɔp] *nmf* misanthropist

mise² [miz] *nf* (a) (*placement*) putting; **m. à feu** (*de fusée*) blast-off; **m. au point** (*de rapport*) finalization; *Phot* focusing; (*de moteur*) tuning; (*de technique*) perfecting; *Fig* (*clarification*) clarification; **m. en garde** warning; **m. en marche** starting up; **m. en page(s)** page make-up; *Ordinat* **m. en réseau** networking; **m. en service** putting into service; **m. en scène** *Théâtre* production; *Cin* direction (b) (*argent*) stake (c) (*tenue*) attire (d) **être de m.** to be acceptable

miser [mize] *vt* (*argent*) to stake (**sur** on); **m. sur qn/qch** (*parier*) to bet on sb/sth; (*compter sur*) to count on sb/sth; **m. sur tous les tableaux** to hedge one's bets

misère [mizɛr] *nf* extreme poverty; **être dans la m.** to be poverty-stricken; **gagner une m.** to earn a pittance; **payer qch une m.** to pay next to nothing for sth; **faire des misères à qn** to give sb a hard time ■ **misérable 1** (*pitoyable*) miserable; (*pauvre*) destitute; (*condition, existence*) wretched; (*logement, quartier*) seedy, slummy **2** *nmf* (*indigent*) poor wretch; (*scélérat*) scoundrel ■ **miséreux, -euse 1** *adj* destitute **2** *nmf* pauper

> Il faut noter que le nom anglais **misery** et l'adjectif **miserable** sont des faux amis. Le premier signifie **malheur, tristesse** et le deuxième signifie le plus souvent **malheureux, triste**.

miséricorde [mizerikɔrd] *nf* mercy ■ **miséricordieux, -ieuse** *adj* merciful

miso [miso] *nm* Culin miso

misogyne [mizɔʒin] *nmf* misogynist

missile [misil] *nm* missile

mission [misjɔ̃] *nf* (*tâche, vocation, organisation*) mission; (*d'employé*) task; **partir en m.** (*cadre*) to go away on business; (*diplomate*) to go off on a mission; **m. accomplie** mission accomplished; **m. scientifique** scientific expedition ■ **missionnaire** *nmf & adj* missionary

missive [misiv] *nf Littéraire* (*lettre*) missive

mistral, -als [mistral] *nm* **le m.** the mistral

mite [mit] *nf* moth ■ **mité, -ée** *adj* moth-eaten ■ **miteux, -euse** *adj* shabby

mi-temps [mitɑ̃] **1** *nf inv Sport* (*pause*) half-time; (*période*) half **2** *nm inv* part-time job; **travailler à m.** to work part-time; **prendre un m.** to take on a part-time job

mitigé, -ée [mitiʒe] *adj* (*accueil*) lukewarm; (*sentiments*) mixed

mitonner [mitɔne] *vt* (*cuire à petit feu*) to simmer gently

mitoyen, -enne [mitwajɛ̃, -jɛn] *adj* common, shared; **mur m.** party wall

mitrailler [mitraje] *vt* to machine-gun; *Fam* (*photographier*) to click or snap away at; **m. qn de questions** to bombard sb with questions ■ **mitraillette** *nf* submachine gun ■ **mitrailleur** *adj* **fusil m.** machine gun ■ **mitrailleuse** *nf* machine gun

mi-voix [mivwa] **à mi-voix** *adv* in a low voice

mixer [mikse] *vt* (*ingrédients, film*) to mix; (*rendre liquide*) to blend

mixe(u)r [miksœr] *nm* (*pour mélanger*) (food) mixer; (*pour rendre liquide*) liquidizer

mixte [mikst] *adj* mixed; (*école*) co-educational, *Br* mixed; (*commission*) joint; (*cuisinière*) gas-and-electric

mixture [mikstyr] *nf* mixture

MJC [emʒise] (*abrév* **maison des jeunes et de la culture**) *nf* ≃ youth club and arts centre

MLF [ɛmɛlɛf] (*abrév* **Mouvement de libération des femmes**) *nm* ≃ Women's Liberation Movement

Mlle (*abrév* **Mademoiselle**) Miss, Ms

MM (*abrév* **Messieurs**) Messrs

mm (*abrév* **millimètre(s)**) mm

Mme (*abrév* **Madame**) Mrs, Ms

mobile [mɔbil] **1** *adj* (*pièce, cible*) moving; (*panneau, fête*) movable; (*personne*) mobile; (*feuillets*) loose; **échelle m.** sliding scale **2** *nm* (*décoration*) mobile; (*motif*) motive (**de** for) ■ **mobilité** *nf* mobility

mobilier [mɔbilje] *nm* furniture

mobiliser [mɔbilize] *vt, se* **mobiliser** *vpr* to mobilize ■ **mobilisation** *nf* mobilization

Mobylette® [mɔbilɛt] *nf* moped

mocassin [mɔkasɛ̃] *nm* moccasin

moche [mɔʃ] *adj Fam* (*laid*) ugly; (*mal*) rotten

modalité [mɔdalite] *nf* (*manière*) mode (**de** of); (*de contrat*) clause; **modalités de paiement** conditions of payment

mode¹ [mɔd] *nf* (*tendance*) fashion; (*industrie*) fashion trade; **à la m.** fashionable; **à la m. de** in the manner of; **passé de m.** out of fashion

mode² [mɔd] *nm* (a) (*manière*) & *Ordinat & Mus* mode; **m. d'emploi** instructions; **m. de paiement** means of payment; **m. de transport** mode of transport; **m. de vie** way of life (b) *Grammaire* mood

modèle [mɔdɛl] **1** *nm* (*schéma, exemple, personne*) model; *Tricot* pattern; **grand/petit m.** (*de vêtement*) large/small size; **m. déposé** registered design; **m. réduit** small-scale model **2** *adj* **élève/petite fille m.** model pupil/girl ■ **modeler 1** *vt* to model (**sur** on) **2** **se modeler** *vpr* **se m. sur qn** to model oneself on sb ■ **modéliste** *nmf* stylist, designer

modem [mɔdɛm] *nm Ordinat* modem

modéré, -ée [mɔdere] *adj* moderate ■ **modérément** *adv* moderately

modérer [mɔdere] **1** *vt (passions, désirs)* to moderate, to restrain; *(vitesse, température)* to reduce **2 se modérer** *vpr* to calm down ▪ **modérateur, -trice 1** *adj* moderating **2** *nmf (personne)* moderator ▪ **modération** *nf (retenue)* moderation; *(réduction)* reduction; **avec m.** in moderation; **à consommer avec m.** drink in moderation *(health warning on all products advertising alcoholic drinks)*

moderne [mɔdern] **1** *adj* modern **2** *nm* **le m.** *(mobilier)* modern furniture ▪ **modernisation** *nf* modernization ▪ **moderniser** *vt,* **se moderniser** *vpr* to modernize ▪ **modernisme** *nm* modernism ▪ **modernité** *nf* modernity

modeste [mɔdɛst] *adj* modest ▪ **modestement** [-əmã] *adv* modestly ▪ **modestie** *nf* modesty

modifier [mɔdifje] **1** *vt* to alter, to modify **2 se modifier** *vpr* to alter ▪ **modification** *nf* alteration, modification; **apporter une m. à qch** to make an alteration to sth

modique [mɔdik] *adj (prix, somme)* modest ▪ **modicité** *nf* modesty

modiste [mɔdist] *nmf* milliner

module [mɔdyl] *nm (élément)* unit; *(de vaisseau spatial)* & *Scol* module

moduler [mɔdyle] *vt (son, amplitude)* to modulate; *(ajuster)* to adjust (**en fonction de** in relation to) ▪ **modulation** *nf (de son, d'amplitude)* modulation; *Radio* **m. de fréquence** frequency modulation

moelle [mwal] *nf (d'os)* marrow; *Fig* **jusqu'à la m.** to the core; **m. épinière** spinal cord; **m. osseuse** bone marrow

moelleux, -euse [mwalø, -øz] *adj (lit, tissu)* soft; *(voix, vin)* mellow

mœurs [mœr(s)] *nfpl (morale)* morals; *(habitudes)* customs; **entrer dans les m.** to become part of everyday life

mohair [mɔɛr] *nm* mohair

moi [mwa] **1** *pron personnel* (**a**) *(après une préposition)* me; **pour/avec m.** for/with me; *Fam* **un ami à m.** a friend of mine (**b**) *(complément direct)* me; **laissez-m.** leave me (**c**) *(complément indirect)* (to) me; **montrez-le-m.** show it to me, show me it (**d**) *(sujet)* I; **c'est m. qui vous le dis!** I'm telling you!; **il est plus grand que m.** he's taller than I am *or* than me; **m., je veux bien** that's OK by me **2** *nm inv* self, ego ▪ **moi-même** *pron* myself

moignon [mwaɲɔ̃] *nm* stump

moindre [mwɛ̃dr] *adj (comparatif)* lesser; *(prix)* lower; *(quantité)* smaller; *(vitesse)* slower; **le/la m.** *(superlatif)* the least; **la m. erreur** the slightest mistake; **le m. doute** the slightest *or* least doubt; **pas la m. idée** not the slightest idea; **dans les moindres détails** in the smallest detail; **c'est un m. mal** it's not as bad as it might have been; **c'est la m. des choses** it's the least I/we/*etc* can do

moine [mwan] *nm* monk

moineau, -x [mwano] *nm* sparrow

moins [mwɛ̃] **1** ([mwɛ̃z] *before vowel*) *adv (comparatif)* less (**que** than); **m. de** *(temps, travail)* less (**que** than); *(gens, livres)* fewer (**que** than); *(100 euros)* less than; **le/la/les m.** *(superlatif)* the least; **le m. grand, la m. grande, les m. grand(e)s** the smallest; **pas le m. du monde** not in the least; **de m. en m.** [dəmãzãmwɛ̃] less and less; **au m., du m.** at least; **qch de m., qch en m.** *(qui manque)* sth missing; **dix ans de m.** ten years less; **en m.** *(personne, objet)* less; *(personnes, objets)* fewer; **les m. de vingt ans** those under twenty, the under-twenties; **à m. que...** (+ *subjunctive*) unless… **2** *prép Math* minus; **cinq m. deux** five to two; **il fait m. 10 (degrés)** it's minus 10 (degrees); *Fam* **c'était m. une** it was a close shave

mois [mwa] *nm* month; **au m. de juin** in (the month of) June

moisir [mwazir] *vi* to go *Br* mouldy *or Am* moldy; *Fam (stagner)* to *Br* moulder *or Am* molder away; *(attendre)* to hang about ▪ **moisi, -ie 1** *adj Br* mouldy, *Am* moldy **2** *nm Br* mould, *Am* mold; *(sur un mur)* mildew; **sentir le m.** to smell musty ▪ **moisissure** *nf Br* mould, *Am* mold

moisson [mwasɔ̃] *nf* harvest; **faire la m.** to harvest ▪ **moissonner** *vt (céréales)* to harvest; *(champ)* to reap ▪ **moissonneuse-batteuse** *(pl moissonneuses-batteuses)* *nf* combine harvester

moite [mwat] *adj* sticky ▪ **moiteur** *nf* stickiness

moitié [mwatje] *nf* half; **la m. de la pomme** half (of) the apple; **à m.** *(remplir)* halfway; **à m. plein/vide** half-full/-empty; **à m. prix** (at) half-price; **réduire qch de m.** to reduce sth by half; *Fam* **m.-m.** fifty-fifty; *Fam* **faire m.-m.** to go halves; *Fam (époux, épouse)* **ma m.** my better half

moka [mɔka] *nm (café)* mocha; *(gâteau)* coffee cake

mol [mɔl] *voir* **mou**

molaire [mɔlɛr] *nf* molar

molécule [mɔlekyl] *nf* molecule

molester [mɔlɛste] *vt* to manhandle

> Il faut noter que le verbe anglais **to molest** est un faux ami. Il signifie **faire subir des sévices sexuels à**.

molette [mɔlɛt] *nf* **clé à m.** adjustable wrench *or Br* spanner

mollasse [mɔlas] *adj Fam (flasque)* flabby ▪ **mollasson, -onne** *Fam* **1** *adj* lethargic **2** *nmf* slob

molle [mɔl] *voir* **mou** ▪ **mollement** *adv (sans énergie)* feebly; *(avec lenteur)* gently ▪ **mollesse** *nf (de matelas)* softness; *(de personne)* lethargy ▪ **mollir** *vi (matière)* to soften; *(courage)* to flag

mollet[1] [mɔlɛ] *nm (de jambe)* calf

mollet[2] [mɔlɛ] *adj* œuf m. soft-boiled egg

molleton [mɔltɔ̃] *nm (tissu en coton)* flannelette; *(sous-nappe)* table felt ▪ **molletonné, -ée** *adj* fleece-lined

mollo [mɔlo] *adv Fam* **y aller m.** to take it easy

mollusque [mɔlysk] *nm* mollusc

molosse [mɔlɔs] *nm* big dog

môme [mom] *nmf Fam (enfant)* kid

moment [mɔmɑ̃] *nm (instant, durée)* moment; **un petit m.** a little while; **en ce m.** at the moment; **pour le m.** for the moment, for the time being; **sur le m.** at the time; **à ce m.-là** *(à ce moment précis)* at that (very) moment, at that time; *(dans ce cas)* then; **à un m. donné** at one point; **le m. venu** *(dans le future)* when the time comes; **d'un m. à l'autre** any moment; **dans ces moments-là** at times like that; **par moments** at times; **au m. de partir** when just about to leave; **au m. où...** just as...; **jusqu'au m. où...** until...; **du m. que...** *(puisque)* seeing that...; **arriver au bon m.** to arrive just at the right time; **c'est le m. ou jamais** it's now or never ▪ **momentané, -ée** *adj (temporaire)* momentary; *(bref)* brief ▪ **momentanément** *adv (temporairement)* temporarily; *(brièvement)* briefly

momie [mɔmi] *nf* mummy

mon, ma, mes [mɔ̃, ma, me]

ma becomes mon [mɔ̃] before a vowel or mute h.

adj possessif my; **m. père** my father; **ma mère** my mother; **m. ami(e)** my friend; **mes parents** my parents

Monaco [mɔnako] *nm* Monaco

monarque [mɔnark] *nm* monarch ▪ **monarchie** *nf* monarchy ▪ **monarchique** *adj* monarchic

monastère [mɔnastɛr] *nm* monastery

monceau, -x [mɔ̃so] *nm* heap, pile

mondain, -aine [mɔ̃dɛ̃, -ɛn] *adj (lieu)* fashionable; **réunion mondaine** society gathering; **rubrique mondaine** *(dans le journal)* gossip column; *Péj* **être très m.** *(personne)* to be a great socialite ▪ **mondanités** *nfpl (événements)* social life; *(conversations superficielles)* social chitchat

Il faut noter que l'adjectif anglais **mundane** est un faux ami. Il signifie **terre-à-terre**.

monde [mɔ̃d] *nm* world; *(gens)* people; **dans le m. entier** worldwide, all over the world; **le (grand) m.** (high) society; **tout le m.** everybody; **il y a du m.** there are a lot of people; **un m. fou** a tremendous crowd; **mettre qn au m.** to give birth to sb; **venir au m.** to come into the world; *Fam* **se faire un m. de qch** to get worked up about sth; **pas le moins du m.!** not in the least *or* slightest!; **c'est le m. à l'envers!** the world's gone mad!

▪ **mondial, -e, -iaux, -iales** *adj (crise, renommée)* worldwide; **guerre mondiale** world war ▪ **mondialement** *adv* throughout the world ▪ **mondialisation** *nf* globalization

monégasque [mɔnegask] **1** *adj* Monegasque **2** *nmf* **M.** Monegasque

monétaire [mɔnetɛr] *adj* monetary

mongolien, -ienne [mɔ̃gɔljɛ̃, -jɛn] *Méd* **1** *adj* **être m.** to have Down's syndrome **2** *nmf* person with Down's syndrome ▪ **mongolisme** *nm* Down's syndrome

moniteur, -trice [mɔnitœr, -tris] **1** *nmf* instructor; *(de colonie de vacances)* Br group leader, Am camp counselor **2** *nm Ordinat (écran)* monitor

monnaie [mɔnɛ] *nf (argent)* money; *(d'un pays)* currency; *(pièces)* change; **petite m.** small change; **faire de la m.** to get change; **avoir la m. de 20 euros** to have change for 20 euros; *Fig* **c'est m. courante** it's very frequent; *Ordinat* **m. électronique** electronic money; **m. légale** legal tender; **m. unique** single currency ▪ **monnayer** *vt (talent, information)* to cash in on; *(bien, titre)* to convert into cash

mono [mɔno] *adj inv (disque)* mono

monochrome [mɔnɔkrom] *adj & nm* monochrome

monocle [mɔnɔkl] *nm* monocle

monocorde [mɔnɔkɔrd] *adj* monotonous

monogamie [mɔnɔgami] *nf* monogamy ▪ **monogame** *adj* monogamous

monokini [mɔnokini] *nm* **faire du m.** to go topless

monolingue [mɔnolɛ̃g] *adj* monolingual

monologue [mɔnɔlɔg] *nm Br* monologue, *Am* monolog

mononucléose [mɔnonykleoz] *nf* glandular fever

monoparentale [mɔnoparɑ̃tal] *adj f* **famille m.** one-parent *or* single-parent family ▪ **monoparentalité** *nf* single parenthood

monoplace [mɔnoplas] *adj & nmf* single-seater

monopole [mɔnɔpɔl] *nm* monopoly; **avoir le m. de qch** to have a monopoly on sth ▪ **monopoliser** *vt* to monopolize

monoski [mɔnoski] *nm* mono-ski; **faire du m.** to mono-ski

monosyllabe [mɔnɔsilab] *nm* monosyllable ▪ **monosyllabique** *adj* monosyllabic

monothéisme [mɔnɔteism] *nm* monotheism

monotone [mɔnotɔn] *adj* monotonous ▪ **monotonie** *nf* monotony

monseigneur [mɔ̃sɛɲœr] *(pl messeigneurs) nm (évêque)* My Lord/His Lordship; *(prince)* His/Your Highness

monsieur [məsjø] *(pl messieurs) nm (homme quelconque)* gentleman; **M. Legras** Mr Legras; **oui m.** yes; *(avec déférence)* yes, sir; **oui messieurs** yes(, gentlemen); **bonsoir, mes-**

sieurs-dames! good evening!; **M.** *(dans une lettre)* Dear Sir; **m. tout-le-monde** the man in the street

monstre [mɔ̃str] **1** *nm* monster; **m. sacré** giant **2** *adj Fam (énorme)* colossal ▪ **monstrueux, -ueuse** *adj (mal formé, scandaleux)* monstrous; *(énorme)* huge ▪ **monstruosité** *nf* monstrosity

mont [mɔ̃] *nm* mount; **être toujours par monts et par vaux** to be forever on the move

montage [mɔ̃taʒ] *nm Tech* assembling; *Cin* editing; *(image truquée)* montage; **m. vidéo** video editing

montagne [mɔ̃taɲ] *nf* mountain; **la m.** *(zone)* the mountains; **à la m.** in the mountains; **en haute m.** high in the mountains; *Fig* **une m. de qch** *(grande quantité)* a mountain of sth; *Fig* **se faire une m. de qch** to make a great song and dance about sth; **montagnes russes** *(attraction foraine)* rollercoaster ▪ **montagnard, -arde 1** *nmf* mountain dweller **2** *adj* **peuple m.** mountain people ▪ **montagneux, -euse** *adj* mountainous

montant, -ante 1 *adj (marée)* rising; *(col)* stand-up; **chaussure montante** boot **2** *nm (somme)* amount; *(de barrière)* post; *(d'échelle)* upright; **montants compensatoires** subsidies

mont-de-piété [mɔ̃dpjete] *(pl* **monts-de-piété***) nm* pawnshop; **mettre qch au m.** to pawn sth

monte-charge [mɔ̃tʃarʒ] *(pl* **monte-charges***) nm* service *Br* lift *or Am* elevator

montée [mɔ̃te] *nf (ascension)* climb, ascent; *(chemin)* slope; *(des prix, du fascisme)* rise; **la m. des eaux** the rise in the water level

monte-plats [mɔ̃tpla] *nm inv* dumb waiter

monter [mɔ̃te] **1** *(aux avoir) vt (côte)* to climb (up); *(objet)* to bring/take up; *(cheval)* to ride; *(son)* to turn up; *(tente)* to put up; *(machine)* to assemble; *(bijou, complot)* to mount; *(affaire)* to hatch; *(pièce de théâtre)* to stage; *(film)* to edit; **m. l'escalier** to go/come upstairs *or* up the stairs; **m. qn contre qn** to set sb against sb

2 *(aux être) vi (personne)* to go/come up; *(ballon)* to go up; *(prix)* to rise; *(marée)* to come in; *(avion)* to climb; **faire m. qn** to show sb up; **m. dans un véhicule** to get in(to) a vehicle; **m. dans un train** to get on(to) a train; **m. sur qch** to climb onto sth; **m. sur *ou* à une échelle** to climb up a ladder; **m. sur le trône** to become king/queen; **m. en courant** to run up; *Sport* **m. à cheval** to ride (a horse); **le vin me monte à la tête** wine goes to my head

3 se monter *vpr* **se m. à** *(s'élever à)* to amount to; *Fam* **se m. la tête** to get carried away with oneself ▪ **monté, -ée** *adj (police)* mounted

monteur, -euse [mɔ̃tœr, -øz] *nmf Cin* editor

montre [mɔ̃tr] *nf (instrument)* (wrist-)watch; *Sport & Fig* **course contre la m.** race against

the clock ▪ **montre-bracelet** *(pl* **montres-bracelets***) nf* wristwatch

Montréal [mɔ̃real] *nm ou f* Montreal

montrer [mɔ̃tre] **1** *vt* to show (**à** to); **m. qn/qch du doigt** to point at sb/sth; **m. le chemin à qn** to show sb the way **2 se montrer** *vpr* to show oneself; **se m. courageux** to be courageous

monture [mɔ̃tyr] *nf (de lunettes)* frame; *(de bijou)* setting; *(cheval)* mount

monument [mɔnymɑ̃] *nm* monument; **m. historique** ancient monument; **m. aux morts** war memorial ▪ **monumental, -e, -aux, -ales** *adj (imposant, énorme)* monumental

moquer [mɔke] **se moquer** *vpr* **se m. de qn** to make fun of sb; **se m. de qch** *(rire de)* to make fun of sth; *(ne pas se soucier)* not to care about sth; *Fam* **il se moque du monde** who does he think he is? ▪ **moquerie** *nf* mockery ▪ **moqueur, -euse** *adj* mocking

moquette [mɔkɛt] *nf Br* fitted carpet, *Am* wall-to-wall carpeting

moral, -e, -aux, -ales [mɔral, -o] **1** *adj* moral **2** *nm* **avoir le m.** to be in good spirits; **avoir le m. à zéro** to feel really down; **remonter le m. à qn** to cheer sb up ▪ **morale** *nf (d'histoire)* moral; *(principes)* morals; *(règles)* morality; **faire la m. à qn** to lecture sb ▪ **moralement** *adv* morally ▪ **moraliste** *nmf* moralist ▪ **moralité** *nf (mœurs)* morality; *(de récit)* moral

moratoire [mɔratwar] *nm Jur* moratorium

morbide [mɔrbid] *adj* morbid

morceau, -x [mɔrso] *nm* piece, bit; *(de sucre)* lump; *(de viande)* cut; *(d'une œuvre littéraire)* extract; **tomber en morceaux** to fall to pieces ▪ **morceler** *vt (terrain)* to divide up

mordicus [mɔrdikys] *adv Fam* stubbornly

mordiller [mɔrdije] *vt* to nibble

mordre [mɔrdr] **1** *vti* to bite; **m. qn au bras** to bite sb's arm; **ça mord?** *(poissons)* are the fish biting? **2 se mordre** *vpr Fig* **se m. les doigts d'avoir fait qch** to kick oneself for doing sth ▪ **mordant, -ante 1** *adj (esprit, remarque, froid)* biting; *(personne, ironie)* caustic **2** *nm (causticité)* bite

mordu, -ue [mɔrdy] **1** *pp de* **mordre 2** *nmf Fam* **un m. de jazz** a jazz fanatic

morfondre [mɔrfɔ̃dr] **se morfondre** *vpr* to mope (about)

morgue [mɔrg] *nf (d'hôpital)* mortuary, morgue

moribond, -onde [mɔribɔ̃, -ɔ̃d] **1** *adj* dying **2** *nmf* dying person

morne [mɔrn] *adj (temps)* dismal; *(silence)* gloomy; *(personne)* glum

morose [mɔroz] *adj* morose

morphine [mɔrfin] *nf* morphine

morphologie [mɔrfɔlɔʒi] *nf* morphology

mors [mɔr] *nm (de harnais)* bit; *Fig* **prendre le m. aux dents** to take the bit between one's teeth

morse [mɔrs] nm (code) Morse (code); (animal) walrus

morsure [mɔrsyr] nf bite

mort¹ [mɔr] nf death; **mettre qn à la m.** to put sb to death; **se donner la m.** to take one's own life; **en vouloir à m. à qn** to be dead set against sb; **un silence de m.** a deathly silence; **la m. dans l'âme** (accepter qch) with a heavy heart; **m. subite du nourrisson** Br cot death, Am crib death ■ **mortalité** nf death rate, mortality ■ **mortel, -elle 1** adj (hommes, ennemi, danger) mortal; (accident) fatal; (pâleur) deathly; Fam (ennuyeux) deadly (dull); Fam (excellent) Br wicked, Am awesome **2** nmf mortal **3** adv Fam **on s'est éclatés mortel!** we had a blast!, Br we had a wicked time! ■ **mortellement** adv (blessé) fatally; (ennuyeux) deadly

mort², morte [mɔr, mɔrt] **1** adj (personne, plante, ville) dead; **m. ou vif** dead or alive; **m. de fatigue** dead tired; **m. de froid** numb with cold; **m. de peur** frightened to death; **m. de rire** killing oneself (laughing) **2** nmf dead man, f dead woman; **les morts** the dead; **de nombreux morts** (victimes) many deaths; **le jour** ou **la fête des Morts** All Souls' Day ■ **morte-saison** (pl mortes-saisons) nf off-season ■ **mort-né, -née** (mpl mort-nés, fpl mort-nées) adj (enfant) & Fig stillborn

mortier [mɔrtje] nm mortar

mortifier [mɔrtifje] vt to mortify

mortuaire [mɔrtɥer] adj **couronne m.** funeral wreath

morue [mɔry] nf cod

morve [mɔrv] nf snot ■ **morveux, -euse** adj Fam Péj (enfant) snotty(-nosed)

mosaïque [mɔzaik] nf mosaic

Moscou [mɔsku] nm ou f Moscow

mosquée [mɔske] nf mosque

mot [mo] nm word; **envoyer un m. à qn** to drop sb a line; **m. à** ou **pour m.** word for word; **un bon m.** a witticism; **avoir le dernier m.** to have the last word; **avoir son m. à dire** to have one's say; **m. d'ordre** watchword; **m. de passe** password; **mots croisés** crossword (puzzle)

motard [mɔtar] nm Fam motorcyclist

motel [mɔtel] nm motel

moteur¹ [mɔtœr] nm (de véhicule) engine; (électrique) motor; Ordinat **m. de recherche** search engine

moteur², -trice [mɔtœr, -tris] **1** adj (nerf, muscle) motor; **force motrice** driving force; **voiture à quatre roues motrices** four-wheel drive (car) **2** nf **motrice** (de train) engine

motif [mɔtif] nm (raison) reason (**de** for); (dessin) pattern

motion [mosjɔ̃] nf Pol motion; **m. de censure** motion of censure

motiver [mɔtive] vt (inciter, causer) to motivate; (justifier) to justify ■ **motivation** nf motivation ■ **motivé, -ée** adj motivated

moto [mɔto] nf motorbike ■ **motocycliste** nmf motorcyclist

motorisé, -ée [mɔtɔrize] adj motorized

motte [mɔt] nf (de terre) lump, clod; (de beurre) block

mou, molle [mu, mɔl]

> **mol** is used before masculine singular nouns beginning with a vowel or h mute.

1 adj soft; (sans énergie) feeble **2** nm **avoir du m.** (cordage) to be slack

mouchard, -arde [muʃar, -ard] nmf Fam Br grass, Am fink ■ **moucharder** vt Fam **m. qn** to squeal on sb

mouche [muʃ] nf (insecte) fly; **faire m.** to hit the bull's-eye; **prendre la m.** to fly off the handle; Fam **quelle m. l'a piqué?** what has Br got or Am gotten into him? ■ **moucheron** nm midge

moucher [muʃe] **1** vt **m. qn** to wipe sb's nose **2 se moucher** upr to blow one's nose

moucheté, -ée [muʃte] adj speckled

mouchoir [muʃwar] nm handkerchief; **m. en papier** tissue

moudre* [mudr] vt to grind

moue [mu] nf pout; **faire la m.** to pout

mouette [mwet] nf (sea)gull

moufle [mufl] nf mitten, mitt

mouiller [muje] **1** vt to wet; **se faire m.** to get wet **2** vi Naut to anchor **3 se mouiller** upr to get wet; Fam (prendre position) to stick one's neck out ■ **mouillage** nm Naut (action) anchoring; (lieu) anchorage ■ **mouillé, -ée** adj wet (**de** with)

moule¹ [mul] nm Br mould, Am mold; **m. à gâteaux** Br cake tin, Am cake pan ■ **moulage** nm (action) casting; (objet) cast ■ **moulant, -ante** adj (vêtement) tight-fitting ■ **mouler** vt Br to mould, Am to mold; (statue) to cast; **m. qn** (vêtement) to fit sb tightly ■ **moulure** nf Archit Br moulding, Am molding

moule² [mul] nf (mollusque) mussel

moulin [mulɛ̃] nm mill; **m. à café** coffee grinder; Fam **m. à paroles** chatterbox; **m. à vent** windmill

moulinet [mulinɛ] nm (de canne à pêche) reel; **faire des moulinets** (avec un bâton) to twirl a stick

moulu, -ue [muly] **1** pp de **moudre 2** nmf (café) ground; Fig (éreinté) dead tired

mourir* [murir] **1** (aux être) vi to die (**de** of or from); **m. de froid** to die of exposure; Fig **m. de fatigue/d'ennui** to be dead tired/bored; Fig **m. de peur** to be frightened to death; Fig **m. de rire** to laugh oneself silly; Fig **s'ennuyer à m.** to be bored to death; Fig **je meurs de faim!** I'm starving! **2 se mourir** upr Littéraire to be dying ■ **mourant, -ante 1** adj dying; (voix) faint **2** nmf dying person

mousquetaire [muskətεr] *nm* musketeer

mousse [mus] **1** *nf (plante)* moss; *(écume)* foam; *(de bière)* head; *(de lait)* froth; *(de savon)* lather; **m. à raser** shaving foam; *Culin* **m. au chocolat** chocolate mousse **2** *nm (marin)* ship's boy ▪ **mousser** *vi (bière)* to froth; *(savon)* to lather ▪ **mousseux, -euse 1** *adj (bière)* frothy; *(vin)* sparkling **2** *nm* sparkling wine ▪ **moussu, -ue** *adj* mossy

mousseline [muslin] *nf (tissu)* muslin

mousson [musɔ̃] *nf* monsoon

moustache [mustaʃ] *nf (d'homme) Br* moustache, *Am* mustache; *(de chat)* whiskers ▪ **moustachu, -ue** *adj* with a *Br* moustache or *Am* mustache

moustique [mustik] *nm* mosquito ▪ **moustiquaire** *nf* mosquito net; *(en métal)* screen

moutard [mutar] *nm Fam (enfant)* kid

moutarde [mutard] *nf* mustard

mouton [mutɔ̃] *nm* sheep *inv*; *(viande)* mutton; **moutons** *(écume) Br* white horses, *Am* whitecaps; *(poussière)* fluff; **peau de m.** sheepskin

mouvement [muvmɑ̃] *nm (geste, groupe, déplacement) & Mus* movement; *(élan)* impulse; *(de gymnastique)* exercise; **en m.** in motion; **m. de colère** fit of anger; **mouvements sociaux** workers' protest movements ▪ **mouvementé, -ée** *adj (vie, voyage)* eventful

mouvoir* [muvwar] *vi,* **se mouvoir** *vpr* to move; **mû par** *(mécanisme)* driven by ▪ **mouvant, -ante** *adj (changeant)* changing

moyen¹, -enne [mwajɛ̃, -ɛn] **1** *adj* average; *(format, entreprise)* medium(-sized) **2** *nf* **moyenne** average; **en moyenne** on average; **la moyenne d'âge** the average age; **avoir la moyenne** *(à un examen) Br* to get a pass mark, *Am* to get a pass; *(à un devoir) Br* to get 50 percent, *Am* to get half marks; **le M. Âge** the Middle Ages ▪ **moyennement** *adv* fairly, moderately

moyen² [mwajɛ̃] *nm (procédé, façon)* means, way (**de faire** of doing *or* to do); **moyens** *(capacités mentales)* ability; *(argent, ressources)* means; **il n'y a pas m. de le faire** it's not possible to do it; **je n'ai pas les moyens** *(argent)* I can't afford it; **au m. de qch** by means of sth; **par mes propres moyens** under my own steam; **utiliser les grands moyens** to take extreme measures; **faire avec les moyens du bord** to make do with what one has

moyennant [mwajɛnɑ̃] *prép (pour)* (in return) for; **m. finance** for a fee

moyeu, -x [mwajø] *nm* hub

Mozambique [mɔzɑ̃bik] *nm* **le M.** Mozambique

MP3 [ɛmpetrwa] *nm Ordinat* MP3 *m inv*

MST [ɛmɛste] *(abrév* **maladie sexuellement transmissible)** *nf* STD, STI

mue [my] *nf (d'animal) Br* moulting, *Am* molting; *(de voix)* breaking of the voice ▪ **muer** [mɥe] **1** *vi (animal) Br* to moult, *Am* to molt; *(voix)* to break **2** **se muer** *vpr* **se m. en qch** to change into sth

muet, muette [mɥe, mɥɛt] **1** *adj (infirme)* dumb; *(de surprise)* speechless; *(film)* silent; *(voyelle)* silent, mute **2** *nmf* mute

mufle [myfl] *nm (d'animal)* muzzle; *Fam (personne)* lout

mugir [myʒir] *vi (bœuf)* to bellow; *(vache)* to moo; *Fig (vent)* to howl ▪ **mugissement** *nm* bellow; *(de vache)* moo; **mugissements** *(de bœuf)* bellowing; *(de vache)* mooing; *(de vent)* howling

muguet [mygε] *nm* lily of the valley

mule [myl] *nf (pantoufle, animal)* mule ▪ **mulet** *nm (équidé)* mule; *(poisson)* mullet

multicolore [myltikɔlɔr] *adj* multicoloured

multiculturel, -elle [myltikyltyrɛl] *adj* multicultural

multimédia [myltimedja] *adj & nm* multimedia

multinational, -e, -aux, -ales [myltinasjɔnal, -o] **1** *adj* multinational **2** *nf* **multinationale** multinational (company)

multiple [myltipl] **1** *adj (nombreux)* numerous; *(varié)* multiple; **à de multiples reprises** repeatedly **2** *nm Math* multiple ▪ **multiplication** *nf (calcul)* multiplication; *(augmentation)* increase ▪ **multiplier 1** *vt* to multiply **2** **se multiplier** *vpr* to increase; *(se reproduire)* to multiply

multiplexe [myltipleks] *nm (cinéma)* multiplex

multithérapie [myltiterapi] *nf Méd* combination therapy

multitude [myltityd] *nf* multitude

municipal, -e, -aux, -ales [mynisipal, -o] *adj* municipal ▪ **municipalité** *nf (maires et conseillers)* local council; *(commune)* municipality

munir [mynir] **1** *vt* **m. de qch** *(personne)* to provide with sth **2** **se munir** *vpr* **se m. de qch** to take sth

munitions [mynisjɔ̃] *nfpl* ammunition

muqueuse [mykøz] *nf* mucous membrane

mur [myr] *nm* wall; *Fig* **au pied du m.** with one's back to the wall; **m. du son** sound barrier ▪ **muraille** *nf* (high) wall ▪ **mural, -e, -aux, -ales** *adj* **carte murale** wall map; **peinture murale** mural *(painting)* ▪ **murer 1** *vt (porte)* to wall up; *(jardin)* to wall in **2** **se murer** *vpr Fig* **se m. dans le silence** to retreat into silence

mûr, mûre¹ [myr] *adj (fruit)* ripe; *(personne)* mature; **d'âge m.** middle-aged ▪ **mûrement** *adv* **m. réfléchi** *(décision)* carefully thought-out ▪ **mûrir** *vti (fruit)* to ripen; *(personne)* to mature

mûre² [myr] *nf (baie)* blackberry

muret [myrε] *nm* low wall

murmure [myrmyr] *nm* murmur ▪ **murmurer** *vti* to murmur

musc [mysk] *nm* musk

muscade [myskad] *nf* nutmeg

muscat [myska] *nm (raisin)* muscat (grape); *(vin)* muscatel (wine)

muscle [myskl] *nm* muscle ▪ **musclé, -ée** *adj (bras)* muscular ▪ **musculaire** *adj (force, douleur)* muscular ▪ **musculature** *nf* muscles

museau, -x [myzo] *nm (de chien, de chat)* muzzle; *(de porc)* snout ▪ **museler** *vt (animal, presse)* to muzzle ▪ **muselière** *nf* muzzle

musée [myze] *nm* museum; **m. de peinture** art gallery ▪ **muséum** *nm* natural history museum

musette [myzɛt] *nf (sac)* bag

music-hall [myzikol] *(pl* **music-halls)** *nm (genre, salle)* music hall

musique [myzik] *nf* music ▪ **musical, -e, -aux, -ales** *adj* musical ▪ **musicien, -ienne 1** *nmf* musician **2** *adj* musical

musulman, -ane [myzylmɑ̃, -an] *adj & nmf* Muslim, Moslem

muter [myte] *vt* to transfer ▪ **mutant, -ante** *adj & nmf* mutant ▪ **mutation** *nf (d'employé)* transfer; *Biol* mutation; *Fig* **en pleine m.** undergoing profound change

mutiler [mytile] *vt* to mutilate, to maim; **être mutilé** to be disabled ▪ **mutilation** *nf* mutilation ▪ **mutilé, -ée** *nmf* **m. de guerre** disabled *Br* ex-serviceman *or Am* veteran

mutin¹, -ine [mytɛ̃, -in] *adj (espiègle)* mischievous

mutin² [mytɛ̃] *nm (rebelle)* mutineer ▪ **se mutiner** *vpr* to mutiny ▪ **mutinerie** *nf* mutiny

mutisme [mytism] *nm* silence; *Méd* muteness

mutualité [mytɥalite] *nf* mutual insurance

mutuel, -uelle [mytɥel] **1** *adj (réciproque)* mutual **2** *nf* **mutuelle** mutual insurance company ▪ **mutuellement** *adv* each other

myope [mjɔp] *adj* shortsighted ▪ **myopie** *nf* shortsightedness

myosotis [mjozɔtis] *nm* forget-me-not

myrtille [mirtij] *nf (baie)* bilberry

mystère [mistɛr] *nm* mystery; **faire des mystères** to be mysterious; **faire m. de qch** to make a secret of sth ▪ **mystérieux, -ieuse** *adj* mysterious

mystifier [mistifje] *vt* to take in ▪ **mystification** *nf* hoax

> Il faut noter que le verbe anglais **to mystify** est un faux ami. Il signifie **déconcerter, laisser perplexe.**

mystique [mistik] **1** *adj* mystical **2** *nmf (personne)* mystic ▪ **mysticisme** *nm* mysticism

mythe [mit] *nm* myth ▪ **mythique** *adj* mythical ▪ **mythologie** *nf* mythology ▪ **mythologique** *adj* mythological

mythomane [mitɔman] *nmf* compulsive liar

myxomatose [miksɔmatoz] *nf* myxomatosis

N, n [ɛn] *nm inv* (a) N, n (b) *(abrév* **route nationale)** = designation of major road

n' [n] *voir* **ne**

nacelle [nasɛl] *nf (de ballon)* basket; *(de landau)* carriage, *Br* carrycot

nacre [nakr] *nf* mother-of-pearl ■ **nacré, -ée** *adj* pearly

nage [naʒ] *nf* (swimming) stroke; **traverser une rivière à la n.** to swim across a river; *Fig* **en n.** sweating; **n. libre** freestyle

nageoire [naʒwar] *nf (de poisson)* fin; *(de dauphin)* flipper

nager [naʒe] **1** *vi* to swim; *Fig* **n. dans le bonheur** to be blissfully happy; *Fam* **je nage complètement** I'm all at sea **2** *vt (crawl)* to swim ■ **nageur, -euse** *nmf* swimmer

naguère [nagɛr] *adv Littéraire* not long ago

naïf, naïve [naif, naiv] **1** *adj* naïve **2** *nmf* fool ■ **naïveté** *nf* naïvety

nain, naine [nɛ̃, nɛn] *adj & nmf* dwarf; **n. de jardin** garden gnome

naissance [nesɑ̃s] *nf (de personne, d'animal)* birth; *(de cou)* base; **donner n. à** *(enfant)* to give birth to; *Fig (rumeur)* to give rise to; **de n.** from birth

naître* [nɛtr] *vi* to be born; *(sentiment, difficulté)* to arise *(de* from); *(idée)* to originate; **faire n.** *(soupçon, industrie)* to give rise to; *Littéraire* **n. à qch** to awaken to sth; *Fam* **il n'est pas né de la dernière pluie** he wasn't born yesterday ■ **naissant, -ante** *adj (jour)* dawning

nana [nana] *nf Fam* chick, *Br* bird

nantir [nɑ̃tir] *vt* **n. qn de qch** to provide sb with sth ■ **nanti, -ie 1** *adj* well-to-do **2** *nmpl Péj* **les nantis** the well-to-do

naphtaline [naftalin] *nf* **(boules de) n.** mothballs

nappe [nap] *nf (de table)* tablecloth; **n. de brouillard** fog patch; **n. d'eau** expanse of water; **n. de pétrole** layer of oil; *(de marée noire)* oil slick ■ **napperon** *nm* mat

napper [nape] *vt* to coat *(de* with)

narcotique [narkɔtik] *adj & nm* narcotic

narguer [narge] *vt* to taunt

narine [narin] *nf* nostril

narquois, -oise [narkwa, -waz] *adj* sneering

narration [narasjɔ̃] *nf (genre)* narration; *(récit)* narrative ■ **narrateur, -trice** *nmf* narrator

nasal, -e, -aux, -ales [nazal, -o] *adj* nasal

nase [naz] *Fam* **1** *adj (personne) (fatigué) Br* knackered, *Am* beat; *(idiot) Br* thick, *Am* dumb; *(nul)* crappy, lousy; *(machine)* kaput **2** *nmf* **c'est un n., ce mec** this guy's *Br* bloody useless *orAm* no goddamn use

naseau, -x [nazo] *nm* nostril

nasillard, -arde [nazijar, -ard] *adj (voix)* nasal

natal, -e, -als, -ales [natal] *adj* native

natalité [natalite] *nf* birth rate

natation [natasjɔ̃] *nf* swimming

natif, -ive [natif, -iv] *adj & nmf* native; **être n. de** to be a native of

nation [nasjɔ̃] *nf* nation; **les Nations unies** the United Nations ■ **national, -e, -aux, -ales** *adj* national ■ **nationale** *nf (route) Br* ≃ A road, *Am* ≃ highway ■ **nationaliser** *vt* to nationalize ■ **nationaliste 1** *adj* nationalistic **2** *nmf* nationalist ■ **nationalité** *nf* nationality

natte [nat] *nf (de cheveux) Br* plait, *Am* braid; *(de paille)* mat ■ **natter** *vt Br* to plait, *Am* to braid

naturaliser [natyralize] *vt* to naturalize ■ **naturalisation** *nf* naturalization

nature [natyr] **1** *nf (univers, caractère)* nature; *(campagne)* country; **plus grand que n.** larger than life; **contre n.** unnatural; **en pleine n.** in the middle of the country; **être de n. à faire qch** to be likely to do sth; **payer en n.** to pay in kind; **seconde n.** second nature; **n. morte** still life **2** *adj inv (omelette, yaourt)* plain; *(thé)* without milk ■ **naturaliste** *nmf* naturalist ■ **naturiste** *nmf* naturist

naturel, -elle [natyrɛl] **1** *adj* natural; **mort naturelle** death from natural causes **2** *nm (caractère)* nature; *(simplicité)* naturalness ■ **naturellement** *adv* naturally

naufrage [nofraʒ] *nm* (ship)wreck; **faire n.** *(bateau)* to be wrecked; *(marin)* to be shipwrecked ■ **naufragé, -ée** *nmf* shipwrecked person

nausée [noze] *nf* nausea, sickness; **avoir la n.** to feel sick ■ **nauséabond, -onde** *adj* nauseating, sickening

nautique [notik] *adj* nautical

naval, -e, -als, -ales [naval] *adj* naval; **constructions navales** shipbuilding

navet [navɛ] *nm (légume)* turnip; *Fam* **c'est un n.** it's a load of rubbish; *(film)* it's a turkey

navette [navɛt] *nf (véhicule)* shuttle; **faire la n.** *(véhicule, personne)* to shuttle back and forth (entre between); **n. spatiale** space shuttle

navigable [navigabl] *adj (fleuve)* navigable ▪**navigabilité** *nf (de bateau)* seaworthiness; *(d'avion)* airworthiness

navigant, -ante [navigã, -ãt] *adj Av* **personnel n.** flight crew

navigateur [navigatœr] *nm (marin)* navigator; *Ordinat* browser; **n. solitaire** lone yachtsman ▪**navigation** *nf* navigation; *Ordinat* **n. sur Internet** Internet surfing

naviguer [navige] *vi (bateau)* to sail; **n. sur Internet** to surf the Net

navire [navir] *nm* ship

navrer [navre] *vt* to appal ▪**navrant, -ante** *adj* appalling ▪**navré, -ée** *adj (air)* distressed; **je suis n.** I'm terribly sorry

nazi, -ie [nazi] *adj & nmf Hist* Nazi

ne [nə]

n' before vowel or mute h; used to form negative verb with **pas, jamais, personne, rien** etc.

adv **ne… pas** not; **il ne boit pas** he does not *or* doesn't drink; **elle n'ose (pas)** she doesn't dare; **ne… que** only; **il n'a qu'une sœur** he only has one sister; **je crains qu'il ne parte** I'm afraid he'll leave

né, née [ne] **1** *pp de* **naître** born; **il est né en 1945** he was born in 1945; **née Dupont** née Dupont **2** *adj* born; **c'est un poète-né** he's a born poet

néanmoins [neãmwɛ̃] *adv* nevertheless

néant [neã] *nm* nothingness; *(sur formulaire)* ≃ none

nébuleux, -euse [nebylø, -øz] *adj* hazy

nécessaire [neseser] **1** *adj* necessary **2** *nm* **le n.** the necessities; **faire le n.** to do what's necessary; **n. de couture** sewing kit; **n. de toilette** toilet bag ▪**nécessairement** *adv* necessarily

nécessité [nesesite] *nf* necessity ▪**nécessiter** *vt* to require, to necessitate ▪**nécessiteux, -euse** *adj* needy

nécrologie [nekrɔlɔʒi] *nf* obituary

nectarine [nektarin] *nf* nectarine

néerlandais, -aise [neɛrlãdɛ, -ɛz] **1** *adj* Dutch **2** *nmf* **N.** Dutchman; **Néerlandaise** Dutchwoman **3** *nm (langue)* Dutch

néfaste [nefast] *adj* harmful (**à** to)

négatif, -ive [negatif, -iv] **1** *adj* negative **2** *nm (de photo)* negative ▪**négation** *nf* negation (**de** of); *Grammaire* negative

négligeable [negliʒabl] *adj* negligible; **non n.** *(quantité)* significant

négligent, -ente [negliʒã, -ãt] *adj* careless, negligent ▪**négligence** *nf (défaut)* carelessness, negligence; *(oubli)* oversight

négliger [negliʒe] **1** *vt (personne, travail, conseil)* to neglect; **n. de faire qch** to neglect to do sth **2** **se négliger** *vpr* to neglect oneself, to let oneself go ▪**négligé, -ée 1** *adj (tenue)*

untidy; *(travail)* careless **2** *nm (vêtement)* négligée

négocier [negɔsje] *vti* to negotiate ▪**négociable** *adj* negotiable ▪**négociant, -iante** *nmf* merchant, dealer ▪**négociateur, -trice** *nmf* negotiator ▪**négociation** *nf* negotiation

nègre [nɛgr] **1** *adj (art, sculpture)* Negro **2** *nm (écrivain)* ghost writer

neige [nɛʒ] *nf* snow; **aller à la n.** to go skiing; **n. carbonique** dry ice; **n. fondue** sleet ▪**neiger** *v impersonnel* to snow; **il neige** it's snowing ▪**neigeux, -euse** *adj* snowy

nénuphar [nenyfar] *nm* water lily

néon [neɔ̃] *nm (gaz)* neon; *(enseigne)* neon sign; **éclairage au n.** neon lighting

néophyte [neɔfit] *nmf* novice

néo-zélandais, -aise [neɔzelãdɛ, -ɛz] *(mpl* néo-zélandais, *fpl* néo-zélandaises*)* **1** *adj* New Zealand **2** *nmf* **Néo-Zélandais, Néo-Zélandaise** New Zealander

nerf [nɛr] *nm* nerve; *Fig* **être sur les nerfs** to live on one's nerves; *Fig* **être à bout de nerfs** to be at the end of one's tether; *Fam* **ça me tape sur les nerfs** it gets on my nerves; *Fam* **du n.!, un peu de n.!** buck up! ▪**nerveux, -euse** *adj* nervous ▪**nervosité** *nf* nervousness

nervure [nervyr] *nf (de feuille)* vein

n'est-ce pas [nɛspɑ] *adv* isn't he?/don't you?/won't they?/*etc*; **tu viendras, n.?** you'll come, won't you?; **il fait beau, n.?** the weather's fine, isn't it?

Net [nɛt] *nm* **le N.** the Net ▪**netiquette** *nf Ordinat* netiquette

net, nette [nɛt] **1** *adj (propre)* clean; *(image, refus)* clear; *(écriture)* neat; *(prix, salaire)* net; **n. d'impôt** net of tax; *Fig* **je veux en avoir le cœur n.** I want to get to the bottom of it once and for all **2** *adv (casser, couper)* clean; *(tuer)* outright; *(refuser)* flatly; **s'arrêter n.** to stop dead ▪**nettement** *adv (avec précision)* clearly; *(incontestablement)* definitely; **il va n. mieux** he's much better ▪**netteté** *nf (propreté, précision)* cleanness; *(de travail)* neatness

nettoyer [netwaje] **1** *vt* to clean; *Fam (sujet: cambrioleur)* to clean out **2** **se nettoyer** *vpr* **se n. les oreilles** to clean one's ears ▪**nettoiement** *nm* **service du n.** refuse *or Am* garbage collection service ▪**nettoyage** *nm* cleaning; **n. à sec** dry-cleaning

neuf¹, neuve [nœf, nœv] **1** *adj* new; **quoi de n.?** what's new? **2** *nm* **remettre qch à n.** to make sth as good as new; **il y a du n.** there's been a new development

neuf² [nœf, nœv *before* **heures & ans**] *adj & nm* nine ▪**neuvième** *adj & nmf* ninth

neurone [nøron] *nm* neuron

neutre [nøtr] **1** *adj (pays, personne)* neutral **2** *nm Él* neutral **3** *adj & nm Grammaire* neuter

• **neutraliser** *vt* to neutralize • **neutralité** *nf* neutrality

neutron [nøtrɔ̃] *nm* neutron

neveu, -x [nəvø] *nm* nephew

névralgie [nevralʒi] *nf Méd* neuralgia • **névralgique** *adj Fig* **centre n.** nerve centre

névrose [nevroz] *nf* neurosis • **névrosé, -ée** *adj & nmf* neurotic

nez [ne] *nm* nose; **n. à n.** face to face (**avec** with); **rire au n. de qn** to laugh in sb's face; **parler du n.** to speak through one's nose; *Fig* **mener qn par le bout du n.** to lead sb by the nose; *Fam* **avoir qch sous le n.** to have sth under one's very nose; *Fam* **avoir un verre dans le n.** to have had one too many; *Fam* **mettre le n. dehors** to set foot outside; *Fam* **ça se voit comme le n. au milieu de la figure** it's as plain as the nose on your face

ni [ni] *conj* **ni... ni...** neither... nor...; **ni Pierre ni Paul ne sont venus** neither Peter nor Paul came; **il n'a ni faim ni soif** he's neither hungry nor thirsty; **sans manger ni boire** without eating or drinking; **ni l'un(e) ni l'autre** neither (of them)

niais, niaise [njɛ, njɛz] **1** *adj* silly **2** *nmf* fool • **niaiserie** *nf* silliness; **niaiseries** *(paroles)* nonsense

Nicaragua [nikaragwa] *nm* **le N.** Nicaragua

niche [niʃ] *nf (de chien)* Br kennel, Am doghouse; *(cavité)* niche, recess; **n. écologique** ecological niche

nicher [niʃe] **1** *vi (oiseau)* to nest **2 se nicher** *vpr (oiseau)* to nest; *(se cacher)* to hide oneself • **nichée** *nf (chiens)* litter; *(oiseaux)* brood

nickel [nikɛl] **1** *nm (métal)* nickel **2** *adj inv Fam (propre)* spotless **3** *adv Fam* **faire qch n.** to do sth really well

nicotine [nikɔtin] *nf* nicotine

nid [ni] *nm* nest; **n.-de-poule** pothole

nièce [njɛs] *nf* niece

nier [nje] *vt* **1** to deny (**que** that) **2** *vi (accusé)* to deny the charge

nigaud, -aude [nigo, -od] *nmf* silly fool

Niger [niʒɛr] *nm* **le N.** *(pays)* Niger

Nigéria [niʒerja] *nm* **le N.** Nigeria

Nil [nil] *nm* **le N.** the Nile

n'importe [nɛ̃pɔrt] *voir* **importer¹**

nippon, -one *ou* **-onne** [nipɔ̃, -ɔn] *adj* Japanese

niveau, -x [nivo] *nm (hauteur, étage, degré)* level; *Scol* standard; **au n. de la mer** at sea level; **être au n.** *(élève)* to be up to standard; *Fig* **se mettre au n. de qn** to put oneself on sb's level; **n. à bulle d'air** spirit level; **n. de vie** standard of living • **niveler** *vt (surface)* to level; *(fortunes)* to even out

noble [nɔbl] **1** *adj* noble **2** *nmf* nobleman, *f* noblewoman • **noblement** [-əmã] *adv* nobly • **noblesse** *nf (caractère, classe)* nobility

noce [nɔs] *nf* wedding; *Fam* **faire la n.** to live it up; *Fam* **être à la n.** to have a whale of a time; **noces d'argent/d'or** silver/golden wedding • **noceur, -euse** *nmf Fam* raver

nocif, -ive [nɔsif, -iv] *adj* harmful • **nocivité** *nf* harmfulness

noctambule [nɔktãbyl] *nmf* night owl

nocturne [nɔktyrn] **1** *adj (animal)* nocturnal **2** *nf (de magasin)* late-night opening; *Sport* **(match en) n.** evening match

Noël [nɔɛl] *nm* Christmas; **sapin de N.** Christmas tree; **le père N.** Santa Claus, *Br* Father Christmas

nœud [nø] *nm* **(a)** *(entrecroisement)* knot; *(ruban)* bow; *Fig* **le n. du problème** the crux of the problem; **n. coulant** slipknot; **n. papillon** bow tie **(b)** *Naut (vitesse)* knot

noir, noire [nwar] **1** *adj* black; *(sombre)* dark; *(idées)* gloomy; *(misère)* dire; *Fig* **rue noire de monde** street swarming with people; **il fait n.** it's dark; **roman n.** thriller; **film n.** film noir **2** *nm (couleur)* black; *(obscurité)* dark; **N. (homme)** Black (man); *Fam* **travailler au n.** to moonlight **3** *nf* **noire** *(note)* Br crotchet, Am quarter note; **Noire** *(femme)* Black (woman) • **noirceur** *nf* blackness • **noircir 1** *vt* to blacken **2** *vi,* **se noircir** *vpr* to turn black

noisette [nwazɛt] *nf* hazelnut • **noisetier** *nm* hazel (tree)

noix [nwa] *nf (du noyer)* walnut; *Fam* **à la n.** lousy; **n. de beurre** knob of butter; **n. de coco** coconut

nom [nɔ̃] *nm* name; *Grammaire* noun; **au n. de qn** on sb's behalf; **au n. de la loi** in the name of the law; **sans n.** *(anonyme)* nameless; *(vil)* vile; *Fam* **n. d'un chien!** hell!; **n. de famille** surname; **n. de jeune fille** maiden name

nomade [nɔmad] **1** *adj* nomadic **2** *nmf* nomad

nombre [nɔ̃br] *nm* number; **être au** *ou* **du n. de** to be among; **ils sont au n. de dix** there are ten of them; **le plus grand n. de** the majority of; **bon n. de** a good many; *Math* **n. premier** prime number

nombreux, -euse [nɔ̃brø, -øz] *adj (amis, livres)* numerous, many; *(famille, collection)* large; **peu n.** few; **venir n.** to come in large numbers

nombril [nɔ̃bri] *nm* navel

nominal, -e, -aux, -ales [nɔminal, -o] *adj* nominal

nomination [nɔminasjɔ̃] *nf (à un poste)* appointment; *(pour récompense)* nomination

nommer [nɔme] **1** *vt (appeler)* to name; **n. qn** *(désigner)* to appoint sb (**à un poste** to a post); **n. qn président** to appoint sb chairman **2 se nommer** *vpr (s'appeler)* to be called • **nommément** *adv* by name

non [nɔ̃] *adv* no; **tu viens ou n.?** are you coming or not?; **n. seulement** not only; **n. (pas) que...** *(+ subjunctive)* not that...; **n. sans regret** not without regret; **n. loin** not far; **je crois que n.** I don't think so; **(ni) moi n. plus** neither do/am/can/*etc* I; *Fam* **c'est bien, n.?** it's all right, isn't it?; *Fam* **(ah) ça n.!** definitely not (that)!

nonante [nɔnɑ̃t] *adj & nm inv Belg & Suisse* ninety

nonchalant, -ante [nɔ̃ʃalɑ̃, -ɑ̃t] *adj* nonchalant ▪ **nonchalance** *nf* nonchalance

non-conformiste [nɔ̃kɔ̃fɔrmist] *adj & nmf* nonconformist

non-fumeur, -euse [nɔ̃fymœr, -øz] **1** *adj* non-smoking **2** *nmf* non-smoker

non-lieu [nɔ̃ljø] *nm Jur* **bénéficier d'un n.** to be discharged through lack of evidence

non-polluant, -uante [nɔ̃pɔlyɑ̃, -yɑ̃t] (*mpl* **non-polluants,** *fpl* **non-polluantes**) *adj* environmentally friendly

non-retour [nɔ̃rətur] *nm* **point de n.** point of no return

non-sens [nɔ̃sɑ̃s] *nm inv* absurdity

non-violence [nɔ̃vjɔlɑ̃s] *nf* non-violence

non-voyants [nɔ̃vwajɑ̃] *nmpl* **les n.** the unsighted

nord [nɔr] **1** *nm* north; **au n.** in the north; (*direction*) (to the) north (**de** of); **du n.** (*vent, direction*) northerly; (*ville*) northern; (*gens*) from/in the north; **l'Afrique du N.** North Africa; **l'Europe du N.** Northern Europe; **le grand N.** the Frozen North **2** *adj inv* (*côte*) north; (*régions*) northern ▪ **nord-africain, -aine** (*mpl* **nord-africains,** *fpl* **nord-africaines**) **1** *adj* North African **2** *nmf* **Nord-Africain, Nord-Africaine** North African ▪ **nord-américain, -aine** (*mpl* **nord-américains,** *fpl* **nord-américaines**) **1** *adj* North American **2** *nmf* **Nord-Américain, Nord-Américaine** North American ▪ **nord-est** *nm & adj inv* northeast ▪ **nord-ouest** *nm & adj inv* northwest

nordique [nɔrdik] **1** *adj* Scandinavian **2** *nmf* **N.** Scandinavian; *Can* Northern Canadian

noria [nɔrja] *nf* noria

normal, -e, -aux, -ales [nɔrmal, -o] *adj* normal ▪ **normale** *nf* norm; **au-dessus/au-dessous de la n.** above/below average; *Fam* **N. Sup** = university-level college preparing students for senior posts in teaching ▪ **normalement** *adv* normally ▪ **normaliser** *vt* (*uniformiser*) to standardize; (*relations*) to normalize

normand, -ande [nɔrmɑ̃, -ɑ̃d] **1** *adj* Norman **2** *nmf* **N., Normande** Norman ▪ **Normandie** *nf* **la N.** Normandy

norme [nɔrm] *nf* norm; **normes de sécurité** safety standards

Norvège [nɔrvɛʒ] *nf* **la N.** Norway ▪ **norvégien, -ienne 1** *adj* Norwegian **2** *nmf* **N., Norvégienne** Norwegian **3** *nm* (*langue*) Norwegian

nos [no] *voir* **notre**

nostalgie [nɔstalʒi] *nf* nostalgia ▪ **nostalgique** *adj* nostalgic

notable [nɔtabl] *adj & nm* notable ▪ **notablement** [-əmɑ̃] *adv* notably

notaire [nɔtɛr] *nm* lawyer, *Br* ≃ solicitor, notary

notamment [nɔtamɑ̃] *adv* notably

note [nɔt] *nf* (*annotation, communication*) & *Mus* note; *Scol Br* mark, *Am* grade; (*facture*) *Br* bill, *Am* check; **prendre n. de qch, prendre qch en n.** to make a note of sth; **prendre des notes** to take notes; **n. de frais** expenses

noter [nɔte] *vt* (*remarquer*) to note; (*écrire*) to note down; (*devoir*) *Br* to mark, *Am* to grade

notice [nɔtis] *nf* (*mode d'emploi*) instructions; (*de médicament*) directions

> Il faut noter que le nom anglais **notice** est un faux ami. Il signifie le plus souvent **avertissement** ou **écriteau** selon le contexte.

notifier [nɔtifje] *vt* **n. qch à qn** to notify sb of sth

notion [nɔsjɔ̃] *nf* notion; **notions** (*éléments*) rudiments; **avoir des notions de qch** to know the basics of sth

notoire [nɔtwar] *adj* (*criminel, bêtise*) notorious; (*fait*) well-known ▪ **notoriété** *nf* (*renom*) fame; **il est de n. publique que...** it's common knowledge that...

notre, nos [nɔtr, no] *adj possessif* our ▪ **nôtre 1** *pron possessif* **le/la n., les nôtres** ours **2** *nmpl* **les nôtres** (*parents*) our family; **serez-vous des nôtres ce soir?** will you be joining us this evening?

nouer [nwe] **1** *vt* (*lacets*) to tie; (*cravate*) to knot; *Fig* (*relation*) to establish; **avoir la gorge nouée** to have a lump in one's throat **2 se nouer** *upr* (*intrigue*) to take shape ▪ **noueux, noueuse** *adj* (*bois*) knotty; (*doigts*) gnarled

nougat [nuga] *nm* nougat

nouille [nuj] *nf Fam* (*idiot*) dimwit

nouilles [nuj] *nfpl Culin* noodles

nounours [nunurs] *nm Fam* teddy bear

nourrice [nuris] *nf* (*assistante maternelle*) (children's) nurse, *Br* child minder; (*qui allaite*) wet nurse; **mettre un enfant en n.** to put a child out to nurse

nourrir [nurir] **1** *vt* (*alimenter*) to feed; *Fig* (*espoir*) to cherish; **n. un bébé au sein** to breastfeed a baby **2 se nourrir** *upr* to eat; **se n. de qch** to feed on sth ▪ **nourrissant, -ante** *adj* nourishing

nourrisson [nurisɔ̃] *nm* infant

nourriture [nurityr] *nf* food

nous [nu] *pron personnel* (**a**) (*sujet*) we; **n. sommes ici** we are here (**b**) (*complément direct*) us; **il n. connaît** he knows us (**c**) (*complément indirect*) (to) us; **il n. l'a donné** he gave it to us, he gave us it (**d**) (*réfléchi*) ourselves; **n. n. lavons** we wash ourselves; **n. n. habillons** we get dressed (**e**) (*réciproque*) each other; **n. n. détestons** we hate each other **= nous-mêmes** *pron* ourselves

nouveau, -elle¹, -x, -elles [nuvo, nuvɛl]

nouvel is used before masculine singular nouns beginning with a vowel or mute h.

1 *adj* new; *(mode)* latest; **on craint de nouvelles inondations** *(d'autres)* further flooding is feared **2** *nmf (à l'école)* new boy, *f* new girl **3** *nm* **du n.** something new **4** *adv* **de n., à n.** again **= nouveau-né, -née** *(mpl* **nouveau-nés,** *fpl* **nouveau-nées) 1** *adj* newborn **2** *nmf* newborn baby

nouveauté [nuvote] *nf* novelty; **nouveautés** *(livres)* new books; *(disques)* new releases

nouvelle² [nuvɛl] *nf* **(a) une n.** *(annonce)* a piece of news; **la n. de sa mort** the news of his/her death; **les nouvelles** the news *(sing)*; **les nouvelles sont bonnes/mauvaises** the news is good/bad; **avoir des nouvelles de qn** *(directement)* to have heard from sb; **demander des nouvelles de qn** to inquire about sb **(b)** *(récit)* short story

Il faut noter que le nom anglais **novel** est un faux ami. Il signifie **roman**.

Nouvelle-Calédonie [nuvɛlkaledɔni] *nf* **la N.** New Caledonia

Nouvelle-Zélande [nuvɛlzelãd] *nf* **la N.** New Zealand

novateur, -trice [nɔvatœr, -tris] **1** *adj* innovative **2** *nmf* innovator

novembre [nɔvãbr] *nm* November

novice [nɔvis] *nmf* novice

noyade [nwajad] *nf* drowning

noyau, -x [nwajo] *nm (de fruit)* stone, *Am* pit; *(d'atome, de cellule)* nucleus; *(groupe)* group; **n. dur** *(de groupe)* hard core

noyauter [nwajote] *vt* to infiltrate

noyer¹ [nwaje] **1** *vt (personne)* to drown; *(terres)* to flood; **n. son chagrin (dans l'alcool)** to drown one's sorrows; *Fig* **n. le poisson** to confuse the issue deliberately; *Fig* **être noyé** *(perdu)* to be out of one's depth; *Fig* **noyé dans la masse** lumped in with the rest **2 se noyer** *vpr* to drown; *(se suicider)* to drown oneself; **se n. dans les détails** to get bogged down in details **= noyé, -ée** *nmf* drowned person

noyer² [nwaje] *nm (arbre)* walnut tree

nu, nue [ny] **1** *adj (personne, vérité)* naked; *(mains, chambre)* bare; **tout nu** (stark) naked, (in the) nude; **tête nue, nu-tête** bare-headed; **aller pieds nus** to go barefoot; **se mettre nu** to strip off **2** *nm Art* nude; **mettre qch à nu** to expose sth

nuage [nyaʒ] *nm* cloud; *Fig* **un n. de lait** a drop of milk; *Fig* **être dans les nuages** to have one's head in the clouds **= nuageux, -euse** *adj (ciel)* cloudy

nuance [nyãs] *nf (de couleur)* shade; *(de sens)*

nuance; *(de regret)* tinge **= nuancé, -ée** *adj (jugement)* qualified **= nuancer** *vt (pensée)* to qualify

nucléaire [nykleer] **1** *adj* nuclear **2** *nm* nuclear energy *or* power

nudisme [nydism] *nm* nudism **= nudiste** *nmf* nudist **= nudité** *nf (de personne)* nudity, nakedness; *(de mur)* bareness

nuée [nye] *nf* **une n. de** *(foule)* a horde of; *(groupe compact)* a cloud of

nues [ny] *nfpl* **tomber des n.** to be astounded; **porter qn aux n.** to praise sb to the skies

nuire* [nɥir] *vi* **n. à qn/qch** to harm sb/sth **= nuisible** *adj* harmful **(à** to)

nuit [nɥi] *nf* night; *(obscurité)* dark(ness); **la n.** *(se promener)* at night; **cette n.** *(hier)* last night; *(aujourd'hui)* tonight; **avant la n.** before nightfall; **il fait n.** it's dark; **il fait n. noire** it's pitch-black; **bonne n.!** good night!; **n. d'hôtel** overnight stay in a hotel **= nuitée** *nf* overnight stay

nul, nulle [nyl] **1** *adj (médiocre)* hopeless, useless; *(risque)* non-existent, nil; *Jur (non valable)* null (and void); **être n. en qch** to be hopeless at sth **2** *adj indéfini Littéraire (aucun)* no; **sans n. doute** without any doubt **3** *pron indéfini m Littéraire (aucun)* no one **= nullard, -arde** *nmf très Fam* useless idiot **= nullement** *adv* not at all **= nulle part** *adv* nowhere; **n. ailleurs** nowhere else **= nullité** *nf (d'un élève)* uselessness; *(personne)* useless person

numéraire [nymerɛr] *nm* cash

numéral, -e, -aux, -ales [nymeral, -o] *adj & nm* numeral

numérique [nymerik] *adj* numerical; *(ordinateur, appareil photo, données)* digital; **montre à affichage n.** digital watch

numéro [nymero] *nm (chiffre)* number; *(de journal)* issue, number; *(au cirque)* act; *Tél* **n. vert** *Br* ≃ Freefone® number, *Am* ≃ toll-free number; *Fam* **quel n.!** *(personne)* what a character!; **n. gagnant** *(au jeu)* winning number; **n. de téléphone** telephone number **= numérotage** *nm* numbering **= numérotation** *nf* numbering; *Tél Br* dialling, *Am* dialing; **n. abrégée** speed dial **= numéroter 1** *vt (pages, sièges)* to number **2** *vi Tél* to dial

nu-pieds [nypje] *nmpl* sandals

nuptial, -iale, -iaux, -iales [nypsjal, -jo] *adj (chambre)* bridal; **cérémonie nuptiale** wedding ceremony

nuque [nyk] *nf* back of the neck

nurse [nœrs] *nf Vieilli* nanny

nutritif, -ive [nytritif, -iv] *adj* nutritious **= nutrition** *nf* nutrition

Nylon® [nilɔ̃] *nm (fibre)* nylon; **chemise en N.** nylon shirt

nymphe [nɛ̃f] *nf* nymph **= nymphomane** *nf* nymphomaniac

O, o [o] *nm inv* O, o

oasis [ɔazis] *nf* oasis

obédience [ɔbedjɑ̃s] *nf (politique)* allegiance

obéir [ɔbeir] *vi* to obey; **o. à qn/qch** to obey sb/ sth; **être obéi** to be obeyed; **o. à qn au doigt et à l'œil** to be at sb's beck and call ▪ **obéissance** *nf* obedience (**à** to) ▪ **obéissant, -ante** *adj* obedient

obélisque [ɔbelisk] *nm* obelisk

obèse [ɔbɛz] *adj* obese ▪ **obésité** [ɔbe-] *nf* obesity

objecter [ɔbʒɛkte] *vt* **que…** to object that…; **n'avoir rien à o. à qch** to have no objection to sth; **on m'objecta mon jeune âge** my youth was held against me ▪ **objecteur** *nm* **o. de conscience** conscientious objector ▪ **objection** *nf* objection; **si vous n'y voyez pas d'o.** if you have no objection(s)

objectif, -ive [ɔbʒɛktif, -iv] **1** *adj* objective **2** *nm (but)* objective; *(d'appareil photo)* lens; *Com* **o. de vente** sales target ▪ **objectivement** *adv* objectively ▪ **objectivité** *nf* objectivity

objet [ɔbʒɛ] *nm (chose, sujet, but)* object; **faire l'o. de** *(étude, critiques)* to be the subject of; *(soins, surveillance)* to be given; **sans o.** *(inquiétude)* groundless; **o. d'art** objet d'art; **o. volant non identifié** unidentified flying object; **objets trouvés** *(bureau) Br* lost property, *Am* lost and found

obligation [ɔbligasjɔ̃] *nf (contrainte)* obligation; *Fin* bond; **se trouver dans l'o. de faire qch** to be obliged to do sth; **sans o. d'achat** no purchase necessary ▪ **obligatoire** *adj* compulsory, obligatory; *Fam (inévitable)* inevitable ▪ **obligatoirement** *adv (fatalement)* inevitably; **tu dois o. le faire** you have to do it; **pas o.** not necessarily

obligeant, -ante [ɔbliʒɑ̃, -ɑ̃t] *adj* obliging, kind ▪ **obligeamment** [-amɑ̃] *adv* obligingly ▪ **obligeance** *nf Formel* **avoir l'o. de faire qch** to be so kind as to do sth

obliger [ɔbliʒe] **1** *vt* (**a**) *(contraindre)* to force (**à faire** to do); **être obligé de faire qch** to be obliged to do sth (**b**) *(rendre service à)* to oblige **2** **s'obliger** *upr* **s'o. à faire qch** to force oneself to do sth ▪ **obligé, -ée** *adj (obligatoire)* necessary; *Fam (fatal)* inevitable

oblique [ɔblik] *adj* oblique; *(regard)* sidelong; **en o.** at an (oblique) angle ▪ **obliquer** *vi (véhicule)* to turn off

oblitérer [ɔblitere] *vt (timbre)* to cancel; **timbre oblitéré** used stamp

oblong, -ongue [ɔblɔ̃, -ɔ̃g] *adj* oblong

obnubilé, -ée [ɔbnybile] *adj (obsédé)* obsessed (**par** with)

obole [ɔbɔl] *nf* small contribution

obscène [ɔpsɛn] *adj* obscene ▪ **obscénité** *nf* obscenity

obscur, -ure [ɔpskyr] *adj (sombre)* dark; *(difficile à comprendre, inconnu)* obscure ▪ **obscurcir 1** *vt (pièce)* to darken; *(rendre confus)* to obscure **2** **s'obscurcir** *upr (ciel)* to darken; *(vue)* to grow dim ▪ **obscurément** *adv* obscurely ▪ **obscurité** *nf (noirceur)* darkness; *(anonymat)* obscurity; **dans l'o.** in the dark

obséder [ɔpsede] *vt* to obsess ▪ **obsédant, -ante** *adj* haunting; *(pensée)* obsessive ▪ **obsédé, -ée** *nmf* maniac (**de** for); **o. sexuel** sex maniac

obsèques [ɔpsɛk] *nfpl* funeral; **faire des o. nationales à qn** to give sb a state funeral

obséquieux, -ieuse [ɔpsekjø, -jøz] *adj* obsequious

observateur, -trice [ɔpsɛrvatœr, -tris] **1** *adj* observant **2** *nmf* observer

observation [ɔpsɛrvasjɔ̃] *nf (étude, remarque)* observation; *(reproche)* remark; *(respect)* observance; **en o.** *(malade)* under observation

observatoire [ɔpsɛrvatwar] *nm* observatory; *Mil* observation post

observer [ɔpsɛrve] *vt (regarder, respecter)* to observe; *(remarquer)* to notice; **faire o. qch à qn** to point sth out to sb

obsession [ɔpsesjɔ̃] *nf* obsession ▪ **obsessionnel, -elle** *adj* obsessional

obsolète [ɔpsɔlɛt] *adj* obsolete

obstacle [ɔpstakl] *nm* obstacle; **faire o. à qch** to stand in the way of sth

obstétricien, -ienne [ɔpstetrisjɛ̃, -jɛn] *nmf* obstetrician

obstiner [ɔpstine] **s'obstiner** *upr* to persist (**à faire** in doing) ▪ **obstination** *nf* stubbornness, obstinacy ▪ **obstiné, -ée** *adj* stubborn, obstinate

obstruction [ɔpstryksjɔ̃] *nf* obstruction; *Pol* **faire de l'o.** to be obstructive ▪ **obstruer** *vt* to obstruct

obtempérer [ɔptɑ̃pere] *vi* **o. à qch** to comply with sth

obtenir* [ɔptənir] *vt* to get, to obtain ▪ **obtention** *nf* obtaining

obturateur [ɔptyratœr] *nm (d'appareil photo)* shutter

obtus, -use [ɔpty, -yz] *adj (angle, esprit)* obtuse

obus [ɔby] *nm (projectile)* shell

occasion [ɔkazjɔ̃] *nf* (**a**) *(chance)* chance, opportunity (**de faire** to do); *(moment)* occasion; **à l'o.** when the occasion arises; **à l'o. de qch** on the occasion of sth; **pour les grandes occasions** for special occasions (**b**) *(affaire)* bargain; *(objet non neuf)* second-hand item; **d'o.** second-hand

occasionner [ɔkazjɔne] *vt* to cause; **o. qch à qn** to cause sb sth

occident [ɔksidɑ̃] *nm Pol* **l'O.** the West ▪ **occidental, -e, -aux, -ales 1** *adj Géog & Pol* western **2** *nmpl Pol* **les Occidentaux** Westerners ▪ **occidentalisé, -ée** *adj Pol* westernized

occulte [ɔkylt] *adj* occult

occupant, -ante [ɔkypɑ̃, -ɑ̃t] **1** *adj (armée)* occupying **2** *nmf (habitant)* occupant **3** *nm Mil* **l'o.** the occupying forces

occupation [ɔkypasjɔ̃] *nf (activité, travail) & Mil* occupation; *Hist* **l'O.** the Occupation

occupé, -ée [ɔkype] *adj* busy (**à faire** doing); *(place, maison)* occupied; *(ligne téléphonique)* Br engaged, Am busy

occuper [ɔkype] **1** *vt (bâtiment, pays, temps)* to occupy; *(place)* to take up, to occupy; *(poste)* to hold; **o. qn** *(jeu, travail)* to keep sb busy *or* occupied; *(ouvrier)* to employ sb **2 s'occuper** *vpr* to keep oneself busy (**à faire** doing); **s'o. de** *(affaire, problème)* to deal with; *(politique)* to be engaged in; **s'o. de qn** *(malade)* to take care of sb; *(client)* to see to sb; **est-ce qu'on s'occupe de vous?** *(dans un magasin)* are you being served?; *Fam* **occupe-toi de tes affaires!** mind your own business!

occurrence [ɔkyrɑ̃s] *nf Ling* occurrence; **en l'o.** in this case

océan [ɔseɑ̃] *nm* ocean; *Fig* **un o. de fleurs** a sea of flowers; *Fig* **un o. de larmes** floods of tears; **l'o. Atlantique/Pacifique** the Atlantic/Pacific Ocean ▪ **océanique** *adj* oceanic

ocre [ɔkr] *nm & adj inv* ochre

octane [ɔktan] *nm* octane

octante [ɔktɑ̃t] *adj & num inv Belg & Suisse* eighty

octave [ɔktav] *nf Mus* octave

octet [ɔktɛ] *nm Ordinat* byte; **milliard d'octets** gigabyte

octobre [ɔktɔbr] *nm* October

octogénaire [ɔktɔʒenɛr] *adj & nmf* octogenarian

octogone [ɔktɔgɔn] *nm* octagon ▪ **octogonal, -e, -aux, -ales** *adj* octagonal

octroyer [ɔktrwaje] *vt Littéraire* to grant (**à** to)

oculaire [ɔkylɛr] *adj* **témoin o.** eyewitness ▪ **oculiste** *nmf* eye specialist

ode [ɔd] *nf* ode

odeur [ɔdœr] *nf* smell; *(de fleur)* scent; **une o. de brûlé** a smell of burning ▪ **odorant, -ante** *adj* sweet-smelling ▪ **odorat** *nm* sense of smell

odieux, -ieuse [ɔdjø, -jøz] *adj* odious

œil [œj] *(pl* **yeux** [jø]) *nm* eye; **l'o. du cyclone** the eye of the storm *or* cyclone; **avoir les yeux verts** to have green eyes; **avoir de grands yeux** to have big eyes; **lever/baisser les yeux** to look up/down; *Fig* **fermer les yeux sur qch** to turn a blind eye to sth; **je n'ai pas fermé l'o. de la nuit** I didn't sleep a wink all night; **coup d'o.** *(regard)* look, glance; **jeter un coup d'o. sur qch** to have a look at sth; **à vue d'o.** visibly; **à mes yeux** in my eyes; *Fam* **à l'o.** *(gratuitement)* free; **avoir qch sous les yeux** to have sth before one's very eyes; **regarder qn dans les yeux** to look sb in the eye; **être les yeux dans les yeux** to be gazing into each other's eyes; **faire les gros yeux à qn** to scowl at sb; *Fam* **faire de l'o. à qn** to give sb the eye; **avoir qn à l'o.** *(surveiller)* to keep an eye on sb; **ne pas avoir les yeux dans sa poche** to be very observant; *Fig* **o. poché, o. au beurre noir** black eye; **ouvre l'o.!** keep your eyes open!; *Fam* **mon o.!** *(incrédulité)* my foot!; *Fam* **entre quat'z'yeux** [katzjø] *(en privé)* in private ▪ **œil-de-bœuf** *(pl* **œils-de-bœuf**) *nm* bull's-eye window

œillade [œjad] *nf* wink

œillères [œjɛr] *nfpl (de cheval) Br* blinkers, *Am* blinders

œillet [œjɛ] *nm (fleur)* carnation; *(trou de ceinture)* eyelet

œnologie [enɔlɔʒi, œ-] *nf* oenology

œuf [œf] *(pl* **œufs** [ø]) *nm* egg; **œufs** *(de poissons)* (hard) roe; *Fig* **étouffer qch dans l'o.** to nip sth in the bud; **o. à la coque** boiled egg; **o. de Pâques** Easter egg; **o. dur** hard-boiled egg; **o. sur le plat** fried egg; **œufs brouillés** scrambled eggs

œuvre [œvr] *nf (travail, livre)* work; **être à l'o.** to be at work; **mettre qch en o.** *(loi, système)* to implement sth; **mettre tout en o.** to do everything possible (**pour faire** to do); **se mettre à l'o.** to set to work; **o. d'art** work of art; **o. de charité** *(organisation)* charity ▪ **œuvrer** *vi* to work

offense [ɔfɑ̃s] *nf* insult; *Rel* transgression ▪ **offensant, -ante** *adj* offensive ▪ **offenser 1** *vt* to offend **2 s'offenser** *vpr* **s'o. de qch** to take *Br* offence *or Am* offense at sth

offensif, -ive [ɔfɑ̃sif, -iv] **1** *adj* offensive **2** *nf* **offensive** offensive; **passer à l'o.** to go on the offensive; **offensive du froid** cold snap

offert, -erte [ɔfɛr, -ɛrt] *pp de* **offrir**

office [ɔfis] *nm* (**a**) *Rel* service (**b**) *(établissement)* office, bureau; **o. du tourisme** tourist information centre (**c**) *(charge)* office;

d'o. without having any say; **faire o. de qch** to serve as sth

officiel, -ielle [ɔfisjɛl] *adj & nm* official ▪ **officiellement** *adv* officially

officier [ɔfisje] 1 *nm (dans l'armée)* officer 2 *vi Rel* to officiate

officieux, -ieuse [ɔfisjø, -jøz] *adj* unofficial

offre [ɔfr] *nf* offer; *(aux enchères)* bid; *Fin* tender; *Écon* **l'o. et la demande** supply and demand; *Fin* **appel d'offres** invitation to tender; *Fin* **o. publique d'achat** takeover bid; **offres d'emploi** *(de journal)* job vacancies, *Br* situations vacant ▪ **offrande** *nf* offering

offrir* [ɔfrir] 1 *vt (donner en cadeau)* to give; *(proposer)* to offer; **o. qch à qn** *(donner)* to give sb sth, to give sth to sb; *(proposer)* to offer sb sth, to offer sth to sb; **o. de faire qch** to offer to do sth; **o. sa démission** to tender one's resignation 2 **s'offrir** *vpr (cadeau)* to treat oneself to; *(se proposer)* to offer oneself (**comme** as); **s'o. aux regards** *(spectacle)* to greet one's eyes ▪ **offrant** *nm* **au plus o.** to the highest bidder

offusquer [ɔfyske] 1 *vt* to offend 2 **s'offusquer** *vpr* **s'o. de qch** to take *Br* offence *or Am* offense at sth

ogive [ɔʒiv] *nf (de fusée)* head; *(de roquette)* nose cone; *Archit* rib; **o. nucléaire** nuclear warhead

OGM [ɔʒeɛm] *(abrév* **organisme génétiquement modifié)** *nm* GMO

ogre [ɔgr] *nm* ogre

oh [o] *exclam* oh!

ohé [ɔe] *exclam* hey (there)!

oie [wa] *nf* goose *(pl* geese)

oignon [ɔɲɔ̃] *nm (légume)* onion; *(de fleur)* bulb; *Fam* **en rang d'oignons** in a neat row; *Fam* **occupe-toi de tes oignons!** mind your own business!

oiseau, -x [wazo] *nm* bird; *Hum* **l'o. rare** the ideal person; *Péj* **drôle d'o.** oddball; **'attention! le petit o. va sortir!'** *(photo)* 'watch the birdie!'; **o. de proie** bird of prey

oiseux, -euse [wazø, -øz] *adj (conversation)* idle; *(explication)* unsatisfactory

oisif, -ive [wazif, -iv] *adj* idle ▪ **oisiveté** *nf* idleness

oisillon [wazijɔ̃] *nm* fledgling

oléoduc [ɔleɔdyk] *nm* pipeline

olfactif, -ive [ɔlfaktif, -iv] *adj* olfactory

oligoélément [ɔligoelemɑ̃] *nm* trace element

olive [ɔliv] 1 *nf* olive 2 *adj inv* **(vert) o.** olive (green) ▪ **olivier** *nm (arbre)* olive tree

olympique [ɔlɛ̃pik] *adj* Olympic; **les jeux Olympiques** the Olympic games

ombilical, -e, -aux, -ales [ɔ̃bilikal, -o] *adj* umbilical

ombrage [ɔ̃braʒ] *nm (ombre)* shade; *Littéraire* **prendre o. de qch** to take umbrage at sth

▪ **ombragé, -ée** *adj* shady ▪ **ombrager** *vt* to give shade to ▪ **ombrageux, -euse** *adj (caractère, personne)* touchy

ombre [ɔ̃br] *nf (forme)* shadow; *(zone sombre)* shade; **30° à l'o.** 30° in the shade; *Fig* **dans l'o.** *(comploter)* in secret; *Fig* **rester dans l'o.** to remain in the background; **sans l'o. d'un doute** without the shadow of a doubt; **pas l'o. d'un reproche/remords** not a trace of blame/remorse; *Fig* **il y a une o. au tableau** there's a fly in the ointment; **o. à paupières** eyeshadow

ombrelle [ɔ̃brɛl] *nf* sunshade, parasol

> Il faut noter que le nom anglais **umbrella** est un faux ami. Il signifie **parapluie**.

OMC [ɔemse] *(abrév* **Organisation mondiale du commerce)** *nf* WTO

omelette [ɔmlɛt] *nf* omelet(te); **o. au fromage** cheese omelet(te); **o. norvégienne** baked Alaska

omettre* [ɔmɛtr] *vt* to omit (**de faire** to do) ▪ **omission** *nf* omission

omnibus [ɔmnibys] *adj & nm (train)* **o.** slow train *(stopping at all stations)*

omnipotent, -ente [ɔmnipɔtɑ̃, -ɑ̃t] *adj* omnipotent

omniprésent, -ente [ɔmniprezɑ̃, -ɑ̃t] *adj* omnipresent

omniscient, -iente [ɔmnisjɑ̃, -ɑ̃t] *adj* omniscient

omnisports [ɔmnispɔr] *adj inv* **centre o.** sports centre

omnivore [ɔmnivɔr] 1 *adj* omnivorous 2 *nmf* omnivore

omoplate [ɔmɔplat] *nf* shoulder blade

OMS [ɔemes] *(abrév* **Organisation mondiale de la santé)** *nf* WHO

on [ɔ̃] *(sometimes* **l'on** [lɔ̃]*) pron indéfini (les gens)* they, people; *(nous)* we, one; *(vous)* you, one; **on frappe** someone's knocking; **on dit** they say, people say; **on m'a dit que...** I was told that...; **on me l'a donné** somebody gave it to me

once [ɔ̃s] *nf (mesure) & Fig* ounce

oncle [ɔ̃kl] *nm* uncle

onctueux, -ueuse [ɔ̃ktɥø, -ɥøz] *adj* smooth, creamy

onde [ɔ̃d] *nf (à la radio) & Phys* wave; **grandes ondes** long wave; **ondes courtes/moyennes** short/medium wave; **o. de choc** shock wave; **sur les ondes** *(à l'antenne)* on the radio

ondée [ɔ̃de] *nf* sudden downpour

on-dit [ɔ̃di] *nm inv* rumour, hearsay

ondoyer [ɔ̃dwaje] *vi* to undulate

ondulation [ɔ̃dylasjɔ̃] *nf* undulation; *(de cheveux)* wave ▪ **ondulé, -ée** *adj* wavy ▪ **onduler** *vi* to undulate; *(cheveux)* to be wavy

onéreux, -euse [ɔnerø, -øz] *adj* costly

Il faut noter que le nom anglais **onerous** est un faux ami. Il signifie **lourd, pénible**.

ONG [ɔɛnʒe] (*abrév* **organisation non gouvernementale**) *nf* NGO

ongle [ɔ̃gl] *nm* (finger)nail; **se faire les ongles** to do one's nails

onglet [ɔ̃glɛ] *nm* (*d'un répertoire*) & *Ordinat* tab; **à onglets** (*dictionnaire*) thumb-indexed

ont [ɔ̃] *voir* **avoir**

ONU [ɔny] (*abrév* **Organisation des Nations unies**) *nf* UN

onyx [ɔniks] *nm* onyx

onze [ɔ̃z] *adj & nm* eleven ▪ **onzième** *adj & nmf* eleventh

OPA [ɔpea] *abrév* = **offre publique d'achat**

opale [ɔpal] *nf* opal

opaque [ɔpak] *adj* opaque ▪ **opacité** *nf* opacity

opéra [ɔpera] *nm* (*musique*) opera; (*édifice*) opera house; **o. rock** rock opera ▪ **opéra-comique** (*pl* **opéras-comiques**) *nm* comic opera ▪ **opérette** *nf* operetta

opérateur, -trice [ɔperatœr, -tris] *nmf* (*personne*) operator; *Cin* cameraman; **o. de saisie** keyboarder

opération [ɔperasjɔ̃] *nf* (*action*) & *Méd, Mil* & *Math* operation; *Fin* deal; **faire une o. portes ouvertes** to open one's doors to the public; **o. à cœur ouvert** open-heart surgery ▪ **opérationnel, -elle** *adj* operational ▪ **opératoire** *adj* (*méthode*) operating

opérer [ɔpere] **1** *vt* (*exécuter*) to carry out; (*choix*) to make; (*patient*) to operate on (**de** for); **se faire o.** to have an operation **2** *vi* (*agir*) to work; (*procéder*) to proceed; (*chirurgien*) to operate **3 s'opérer** *vpr* (*se produire*) to take place

ophtalmologue [ɔftalmɔlɔg] *nmf* ophthalmologist

opiner [ɔpine] *vi* **o. (de la tête)** to nod (in agreement)

opiniâtre [ɔpinjatr] *adj* stubborn ▪ **opiniâtreté** [-trate] *nf* stubbornness

opinion [ɔpinjɔ̃] *nf* opinion (**sur** about *or* on); **sans o.** (*de sondage*) don't know; **mon o. est faite** my mind is made up; **o. publique** public opinion

opium [ɔpjɔm] *nm* opium

opportun, -une [ɔpɔrtœ̃, -yn] *adj* opportune, timely ▪ **opportunément** *adv* opportunely ▪ **opportunisme** *nm* opportunism ▪ **opportunité** *nf* timeliness

opposant, -ante [ɔpozɑ̃, -ɑ̃t] *nmf* opponent (**à** of)

opposé, -ée [ɔpoze] **1** *adj* (*direction*) opposite; (*intérêts*) conflicting; (*armées, équipe*) opposing; **être o. à qch** to be opposed to sth **2** *nm* **l'o.** the opposite (**de** of); **à l'o.** (*côté*) on the opposite side (**de** to); **à l'o. de** (*contrairement à*) contrary to

opposer [ɔpoze] **1** *vt* (*résistance, argument*) to put up (**à** against); (*équipes*) to pit against each other; (*armées*) to bring into conflict; (*styles, conceptions*) to contrast; **o. qn à qn** to set sb against sb; **match qui oppose...** match between... **2 s'opposer** *vpr* (*équipes*) to confront each other; (*styles, conceptions*) to contrast; **s'o. à qch** to be opposed to sth; **je m'y oppose** I'm opposed to it

opposition [ɔpozisjɔ̃] *nf* opposition (**à** to); **faire o. à** to oppose; (*chèque*) to stop; **par o. à** as opposed to

oppresser [ɔprese] *vt* (*gêner*) to oppress ▪ **oppressant, -ante** *adj* oppressive ▪ **oppresseur** *nm* oppressor ▪ **oppressif, -ive** *adj* (*loi*) oppressive ▪ **oppression** *nf* oppression ▪ **opprimer** *vt* (*peuple, nation*) to oppress ▪ **opprimés** *nmpl* **les o.** the oppressed

opter [ɔpte] *vi* **o. pour qch** to opt for sth

opticien, -ienne [ɔptisjɛ̃, -jɛn] *nmf* optician

optimiser [ɔptimize] *vt* to optimize

optimisme [ɔptimism] *nm* optimism ▪ **optimiste** *adj* optimistic **2** *nmf* optimist

optimum [ɔptimɔm] *nm & adj* optimum ▪ **optimal, -e, -aux, -ales** *adj* optimal

option [ɔpsjɔ̃] *nf* (*choix*) option; (*chose*) optional extra; *Scol & Univ Br* optional subject, *Am* elective (subject)

optique [ɔptik] **1** *adj* (*nerf*) optic; (*verre, fibres*) optical **2** *nf* optics (*sing*); *Fig* (*aspect*) perspective; **d'o.** (*instrument, appareil*) optical; **dans cette o.** from this perspective

opulent, -ente [ɔpylɑ̃, -ɑ̃t] *adj* opulent ▪ **opulence** *nf* opulence

or[1] [ɔr] *nm* gold; **montre/chaîne en or** gold watch/chain; **règle/âge/cheveux d'or** golden rule/age/hair; **cœur d'or** heart of gold; **mine d'or** gold mine; **affaire en or** bargain; **or noir** (*pétrole*) black gold

or[2] [ɔr] *conj* (*cependant*) now, well

oracle [ɔrakl] *nm* oracle

orage [ɔraʒ] *nm* (thunder)storm ▪ **orageux, -euse** *adj* stormy

oraison [ɔrɛzɔ̃] *nf* prayer; **o. funèbre** funeral oration

oral, -e, -aux, -ales [ɔral, -o] **1** *adj* oral **2** *nm* *Scol & Univ* oral

orange [ɔrɑ̃ʒ] **1** *nf* orange; **o. pressée** (fresh) orange juice **2** *adj & nm inv* (*couleur*) orange ▪ **orangé, -ée** *adj & nm* (*couleur*) orange ▪ **orangeade** *nf* orangeade ▪ **oranger** *nm* orange tree

orang-outan(g) [ɔrãutã] (*pl* **orangs-outan(g)s**) *nm* orang-utan

orateur [ɔratœr] *nm* speaker, orator

orbite [ɔrbit] *nf* (*d'astre*) & *Fig* orbit; (*d'œil*) socket; **mettre qch sur o.** (*fusée*) to put sth into orbit ▪ **orbital, -e, -aux, -ales** *adj* **station orbitale** space station

orchestre [ɔrkɛstr] *nm (classique)* orchestra; *(de jazz)* band; *Théâtre (places) Br* stalls, *Am* orchestra ▪ **orchestration** *nf* orchestration ▪ **orchestrer** *vt (organiser)* & *Mus* to orchestrate

orchidée [ɔrkide] *nf* orchid

ordinaire [ɔrdinɛr] *adj (habituel, normal)* ordinary, *Am* regular; *(médiocre)* ordinary, average; **d'o., à l'o.** usually; **comme d'o., comme à l'o.** as usual ▪ **ordinairement** *adv* usually

ordinal, -e, -aux, -ales [ɔrdinal, -o] *adj* ordinal

ordinateur [ɔrdinatœr] *nm* computer; **o. individuel** personal computer; **o. portable** laptop

ordination [ɔrdinasjɔ̃] *nf Rel* ordination

ordonnance [ɔrdɔnɑ̃s] *nf (de médecin)* prescription; *(de juge)* order, ruling; *(disposition)* arrangement; *(soldat)* orderly

ordonner [ɔrdɔne] *vt* (**a**) *(commander)* to order (**que** + *subjunctive* that); **o. à qn de faire qch** to order sb to do sth (**b**) *(ranger)* to organize (**c**) *(prêtre)* to ordain; **il a été ordonné prêtre** he has been ordained (as) a priest ▪ **ordonné, -ée** *adj (personne, maison)* tidy

ordre [ɔrdr] *nm (organisation, discipline, catégorie, commandement)* & *Fin* order; *(absence de désordre)* tidiness; **en o.** *(chambre)* tidy; **mettre de l'o. dans qch** to tidy sth up; **rentrer dans l'o.** to return to normal; **jusqu'à nouvel o.** until further notice; **de l'o. de** *(environ)* of the order of; **du même o.** of the same order; **donnez-moi un o. de grandeur** give me a rough estimate; **de premier o.** first-rate; **par o. d'âge** in order of age; **assurer le maintien de l'o.** to maintain order; *Rel* **entrer dans les ordres** to take holy orders; *Mil* **à vos ordres!** yes sir!; **o. du jour** agenda; **l'o. public** law and order

ordures [ɔrdyr] *nfpl (déchets) Br* rubbish, *Am* garbage; **mettre qch aux o.** to throw sth out (in the *Br* rubbish *or Am* garbage) ▪ **ordurier, -ière** *adj* filthy

oreille [ɔrɛj] *nf* ear; **faire la sourde o.** to turn a deaf ear; **être tout oreilles** to be all ears; **écouter d'une o. distraite** to listen with half an ear; **dire qch à l'o. de qn** to whisper sth in sb's ear; **être dur d'o.** to be hard of hearing

oreiller [ɔreje] *nm* pillow

oreillons [ɔrɛjɔ̃] *nmpl (maladie)* mumps

ores et déjà [ɔrzedeʒa] **d'ores et déjà** *adv* already

orfèvre [ɔrfɛvr] *nm (d'or)* goldsmith; *(d'argent)* silversmith ▪ **orfèvrerie** [-vrəri] *nf (magasin)* goldsmith's/silversmith's shop; *(objets)* gold/ silver plate

organe [ɔrgan] *nm Anat* & *Fig* organ; *(porte-parole)* mouthpiece ▪ **organique** *adj* organic ▪ **organisme** *nm (corps)* body; *Biol* organism; *(bureaux)* organization

organisateur, -trice [ɔrganizatœr, -tris] *nmf* organizer

organisation [ɔrganizasjɔ̃] *nf (arrangement, association)* organization; **O. mondiale du commerce** World Trade Organization; **O. mondiale de la santé** World Health Organization; **O. des Nations unies** United Nations Organization

organiser [ɔrganize] **1** *vt* to organize **2** **s'organiser** *vpr* to get organized ▪ **organisé, -ée** *adj* organized ▪ **organiseur** *nm* **o. électronique** electronic organizer; **o. personnel** personal organizer

orgasme [ɔrgasm] *nm* orgasm

orge [ɔrʒ] *nf* barley

orgie [ɔrʒi] *nf* orgy

orgue [ɔrg] **1** *nm* organ; **o. de Barbarie** barrel organ **2** *nfpl* **orgues** organ; **grandes orgues** great organ

orgueil [ɔrgœj] *nm* pride ▪ **orgueilleux, -euse** *adj* proud

orient [ɔrjɑ̃] *nm* **l'O.** the Orient, the East; **en O.** in the East ▪ **oriental, -e, -aux, -ales** [ɔrjɑ̃tal, -o] **1** *adj (côte, région)* eastern; *(langue)* oriental **2** *nmf* **O., Orientale** Oriental

orientable [ɔrjɑ̃tabl] *adj (lampe)* adjustable; *(bras de machine)* movable

orientation [ɔrjɑ̃tasjɔ̃] *nf (détermination de position)* orientation; *(de grue, d'antenne)* positioning; *(de maison)* aspect; *(de politique, de recherche)* direction; **avoir le sens de l'o.** to have a good sense of direction; **o. professionnelle** careers guidance

orienter [ɔrjɑ̃te] **1** *vt (bâtiment)* to orientate; *(canon, télescope)* to point (**vers** at); **o. ses recherches sur** to direct one's research on; **être mal orienté** *(élève)* to have been given bad careers advice **2** **s'orienter** *vpr* to get one's bearings; **s'o. vers** *(carrière)* to specialize in ▪ **orienté, -ée** *adj (peu objectif)* slanted; **o. à l'ouest** *(appartement)* facing west

orifice [ɔrifis] *nm* opening

originaire [ɔriʒinɛr] *adj* **être o. de** *(natif)* to be a native of

original, -e, -aux, -ales [ɔriʒinal, -o] **1** *adj (idée, artiste, version)* original **2** *nm (texte, tableau)* original **3** *nmf (personne)* eccentric ▪ **originalité** *nf* originality

origine [ɔriʒin] *nf* origin; **à l'o.** originally; **être à l'o. de qch** to be at the origin of sth; **d'o.** *(pneu)* original; **pays d'o.** country of origin; **être d'o. française** to be of French origin ▪ **originel, -elle** *adj* original

orme [ɔrm] *nm (arbre, bois)* elm

ornement [ɔrnəmɑ̃] *nm* ornament ▪ **ornemental, -e, -aux, -ales** *adj* ornamental

orner [ɔrne] *vt* to decorate (**de** with)

ornière [ɔrnjer] *nf* rut; *Fig* **sortir de l'o.** to get out of trouble

orphelin, -ine [ɔrfəlɛ̃, -in] *nmf* orphan ▪ **orphelinat** *nm* orphanage

ORSEC [ɔrsɛk] (*abrév* **organisation des secours**) **plan O.** = disaster contingency plan

orteil [ɔrtɛj] *nm* toe; **gros o.** big toe

orthodoxe [ɔrtɔdɔks] *adj* orthodox ▪ **orthodoxie** *nf* orthodoxy

orthographe [ɔrtɔgraf] *nf* spelling ▪ **orthographier** *vt* to spell; **mal o. qch** to misspell sth ▪ **orthographique** *adj* orthographic

orthopédie [ɔrtɔpedi] *nf* orthopaedics (*sing*)

orthophonie [ɔrtɔfɔni] *nf* speech therapy ▪ **orthophoniste** *nmf* speech therapist

ortie [ɔrti] *nf* nettle

os [ɔs, *pl o ou* os] *nm* bone; **trempé jusqu'aux os** soaked to the skin; **on lui voit les os** he's all skin and bone; **il ne fera pas de vieux os** he won't make old bones; *Fam* **tomber sur un os** to hit a snag

oscar [ɔskar] *nm* (*récompense*) Oscar; **les oscars** (*cérémonie*) the Oscars

osciller [ɔsile] *vi Tech* to oscillate; (*pendule*) to swing; (*aiguille, flamme*) to flicker; (*bateau*) to rock; *Fig* (*varier*) to fluctuate (**entre** between) ▪ **oscillation** *nf Tech* oscillation; *Fig* (*de l'opinion*) fluctuation

oseille [ozɛj] *nf* (*plante*) sorrel; *Fam* (*argent*) dosh

oser [oze] *vt* to dare; **o. faire qch** to dare (to) do sth ▪ **osé, -ée** *adj* daring

osier [ozje] *nm* wicker; **panier d'o.** wicker basket

ossature [ɔsatyr] *nf* (*du corps*) frame; (*de bâtiment*) & *Fig* framework ▪ **osselets** *nmpl* (*jeu*) jacks, *Br* knucklebones ▪ **ossements** *nmpl* bones

osseux, -euse [ɔsø, -øz] *adj* (*maigre*) bony; **tissu o.** bone tissue

ostensible [ɔstɑ̃sibl] *adj* open ▪ **ostensiblement** [-əmɑ̃] *adv* openly

> Il faut noter que les termes anglais **ostensible** et **ostensibly** sont des faux amis. Ils signifient respectivement **apparent** et **en apparence**.

ostentation [ɔstɑ̃tasjɔ̃] *nf* ostentation ▪ **ostentatoire** *adj* ostentatious

ostéopathe [ɔsteopat] *nmf* osteopath ▪ **ostéopathie** *nf* osteopathy

ostréiculteur, -trice [ɔstreikytœr, -tris] *nmf* oyster farmer

otage [ɔtaʒ] *nm* hostage; **prendre qn en o.** to take sb hostage

OTAN [ɔtɑ̃] (*abrév* **Organisation du traité de l'Atlantique Nord**) *nf* NATO

otarie [ɔtari] *nf* sea lion

ôter [ote] **1** *vt* to take away, to remove (**à qn** from sb); (*vêtement*) to take off; (*déduire*) to take (away) **2 s'ôter** *vpr Fam* **ôte-toi de là!** move yourself!

otite [ɔtit] *nf* ear infection

oto-rhino [ɔtɔrino] (*pl* **oto-rhinos**) *nmf Fam* (*médecin*) ENT specialist

ou [u] *conj* or; **ou bien** or else; **ou elle ou moi** either her or me; **pour ou contre nous** for or against us

où [u] *adv & pron relatif* where; **le jour où...** the day when...; **la table où...** the table on which...; **l'état où...** the condition in which...; **par où?** which way?; **d'où?** where from?; **d'où ma surprise** hence my surprise; **le pays d'où je viens** the country from which I come; **où qu'il soit** wherever he may be

ouate [wat] *nf* (*pour pansement*) *Br* cotton wool, *Am* absorbent cotton

oubli [ubli] *nm* (*trou de mémoire*) oversight; (*lacune*) omission; **tomber dans l'o.** to fall *or* sink into oblivion

oublier [ublije] **1** *vt* to forget (**de faire** to do); (*omettre*) to leave out **2 s'oublier** *vpr* (*traditions*) to be forgotten; *Fig* (*personne*) to forget oneself

oubliettes [ublijɛt] *nfpl* (*de château*) dungeons; **être tombé aux o.** (*personne, projet*) to be long forgotten

oublieux, -ieuse [ublijø, -jøz] *adj* forgetful (**de** of)

ouest [wɛst] **1** *nm* west; **à l'o.** in the west; (*direction*) (to the) west (**de** of); **d'o.** (*vent*) west(erly); **de l'o.** western **2** *adj inv* (*côte*) west; (*région*) western

ouf [uf] *exclam* (*soulagement*) phew!

Ouganda [ugɑ̃da] *nm* **l'O.** Uganda

oui [wi] **1** *adv* yes; **ah, ça o.!** oh yes (indeed!); **tu viens, o. ou non?** are you coming or aren't you?; **je crois que o.** I think so; **si o.** if so **2** *nm inv* **pour un o. pour un non** for the slightest thing

ouï-dire [widir] *nm* hearsay; **par o.** by hearsay

ouïe [wi] *nf* hearing; *Hum* **être tout o.** to be all ears

ouïes [wi] *nfpl* (*de poisson*) gills

ouille [uj] *exclam* ouch!

ouragan [uragɑ̃] *nm* hurricane

ourler [urle] *vt* to hem ▪ **ourlet** [-ɛ] *nm* hem

ours [urs] *nm* bear; **o. blanc** polar bear; *Fig* **o. mal léché** boor; **o. en peluche** teddy bear ▪ **ourse** *nf* she-bear; **la Grande O.** the Great Bear

oursin [ursɛ̃] *nm* sea urchin

ouste [ust] *exclam Fam* scram!

outil [uti] *nm* tool ▪ **outillage** *nm* tools; (*d'une usine*) equipment ▪ **outiller** *vt* to equip

outrage [utraʒ] *nm* insult (**à** to) *Jur* **o. à magistrat** contempt of court ▪ **outrageant, -ante** *adj* insulting

outrance [utrɑ̃s] *nf (excès)* excess; **à o.** to excess ▪ **outrancier, -ière** *adj* excessive

outre [utr] **1** *prép* besides; **o. mesure** unduly **2** *adv* **en o.** besides; **passer o.** to take no notice (**à** of) ▪ **outre-Manche** *adv* across the Channel ▪ **outre-mer** *adv* overseas; **d'o.** *(marché)* overseas; **territoires d'o.** overseas territories

outré, -ée [utre] *adj (révolté)* outraged; *(excessif)* exaggerated

outrepasser [utrəpase] *vt* to go beyond, to exceed

ouvert, -erte [uvɛr, -ɛrt] **1** *pp de* **ouvrir 2** *adj* open; *(robinet, gaz)* on ▪ **ouvertement** [-əmɑ̃] *adv* openly ▪ **ouverture** *nf* opening; *(trou)* hole; *Mus* overture; *Phot (d'objectif)* aperture; **o. d'esprit** open-mindedness

ouvrable [uvrabl] *adj* **jour o.** *Br* working *or Am* work day

ouvrage [uvraʒ] *nm (travail, livre, objet)* work; *(couture)* (needle)work; **un o.** *(travail)* a piece of work ▪ **ouvragé, -ée** *adj (bijou)* finely worked

ouvreuse [uvrøz] *nf* usherette

ouvrier, -ière [uvrije, -jɛr] **1** *nmf* worker; **o. qualifié/spécialisé** skilled/semi-skilled worker; **o. agricole** farm worker **2** *adj*

(législation) industrial; *(quartier, origine)* working-class

ouvrir* [uvrir] **1** *vt* to open; *(gaz, radio)* to turn on; *(hostilités)* to begin; *(appétit)* to whet; *(procession)* to head **2** *vi* to open **3** **s'ouvrir** *vpr (porte, boîte, fleur)* to open; **s'o. la jambe** to cut one's leg open; *Fig* **s'o. à qn** *(perspectives)* to open up for sb ▪ **ouvre-boîtes** *nm inv Br* tin opener, *Am* can opener ▪ **ouvre-bouteilles** *nm inv* bottle opener

ovaire [ɔvɛr] *nm Anat* ovary

ovale [ɔval] *adj & nm* oval

ovation [ɔvasjɔ̃] *nf* (standing) ovation

overdose [ɔvœrdoz] *nf* overdose; **faire un o.** to overdose (**de** on)

ovni [ɔvni] *(abrév* **objet volant non identifié)** *nm* UFO

oxyde [ɔksid] *nm Chim* oxide; **o. de carbone** carbon monoxide ▪ **oxyder** *vt*, **s'oxyder** *vpr* to oxidize

oxygène [ɔksiʒɛn] *nm* oxygen; **masque/tente à o.** oxygen mask/tent ▪ **oxygéné, -ée** *adj* **eau oxygénée** (hydrogen) peroxide; **cheveux blonds oxygénés** peroxide blonde hair, bleached hair ▪ **s'oxygéner** *vpr Fam* to get some fresh air

ozone [ozon] *nm Chim* ozone

P, p [pe] *nm inv* P, p

PAC [pak] (*abrév* **politique agricole commune**) *nf* CAP

pacifier [pasifje] *vt* to pacify ▪ **pacification** *nf* pacification

pacifique [pasifik] **1** *adj* (*manifestation*) peaceful; (*personne, peuple*) peace-loving; (*côte*) Pacific **2** *nm* **le P.** the Pacific

pacifiste [pasifist] *adj & nmf* pacifist

pack [pak] *nm* (*lot*) pack; **des cannettes de bière en p. de six** a six-pack (of beer)

pacotille [pakɔtij] *nf* junk; **de p.** (*marchandise*) shoddy; (*bijou*) paste

Pacs [paks] (*abrév* **Pacte civil de solidarité**) *nm* civil solidarity pact (*bill introduced in 1998 extending the legal rights of married couples to unmarried heterosexual couples and to homosexual couples, particularly with regard to inheritance and taxation*); **faire un P.** to enter into a Pacs agreement ▪ **pacsé, -ée** *nmf* = person who has entered into a civil solidarity pact ▪ **pacser** *vi*, **se pacser** *vpr* = to enter into a civil solidarity pact

pacte [pakt] *nm* pact ▪ **pactiser** *vi* **p. avec qn** to make a pact with sb

pactole [paktɔl] *nm Fam* jackpot

paf [paf] **1** *exclam* bang! **2** *adj inv Fam* (*ivre*) plastered

pagaie [page] *nf* paddle ▪ **pagayer** *vi* to paddle

pagaïe, pagaille [pagaj] *nf* (*désordre*) mess; **en p.** in a mess; **des livres en p.** loads of books; **semer la p.** to cause chaos

page¹ [paʒ] *nf* (*de livre*) page; *Fig* **à la p.** up-to-date; **perdre la p.** to lose one's place; *Fig* **tourner la p.** to make a fresh start; **les pages jaunes** (*de l'annuaire*) the Yellow Pages®; *Ordinat* **p. d'accueil** home page; **p. de garde** *Typ* flyleaf; *Ordinat* splash page; *Ordinat* **p. personnel,** *Fam* **p. perso** personal home page; *Ordinat* **p. précédente/suivante** page up/down; *Radio & TV* **p. de publicité** commercial break; *Ordinat* **p. Web** web page ▪ **page-écran** (*pl* **pages-écrans**) *nf Ordinat* screenful

page² [paʒ] *nm* (*à la cour*) page(boy)

paginer [paʒine] *vt* to paginate ▪ **pagination** *nf* pagination

pagne [paɲ] *nm* loincloth

pagode [pagɔd] *nf* pagoda

paie [pɛ] *nf* pay, wages; *Fam* **ça fait une p. que je ne l'ai pas vu** I haven't seen him for ages

paiement [pemã] *nm* payment

païen, païenne [pajɛ̃, pajɛn] *adj & nmf* pagan, heathen

paillasse [pajas] *nf* (*matelas*) straw mattress; (*d'évier*) *Br* draining board, *Am* drainboard

paillasson [pajasɔ̃] *nm* (door)mat

paille [paj] *nf* straw; (*pour boire*) (drinking) straw; *Fig* **homme de p.** figurehead; *Fig* **feu de p.** flash in the pan; **tirer à la courte p.** to draw lots; *Fig* **sur la p.** penniless

paillette [pajɛt] *nf* (*d'habit*) sequin; **paillettes** (*de savon, lessive*) flakes; (*d'or*) gold dust; (*maquillage*) glitter ▪ **pailleté, -ée** *adj* (*robe*) sequined; (*maquillage*) glittery

pain [pɛ̃] *nm* bread; **un p.** a loaf (of bread); *Fig* **avoir du p. sur la planche** to have a lot on one's plate; **petit p.** roll; **p. au chocolat** pain au chocolat, = chocolate-filled pastry; **p. complet** wholemeal bread; **p. d'épices** ≃ gingerbread; **p. grillé** toast; **p. de mie** sandwich loaf; **p. de savon** bar of soap; **p. de seigle** rye bread; **p. de sucre** sugar loaf

paintball [pɛntbol] *nm* paintball; **faire du p.** to go paintballing

pair, paire¹ [pɛr] **1** *adj* (*numéro*) even **2** *nm* (*personne*) peer; **hors p.** unrivalled; **aller de p.** to go hand in hand (**avec** with); **au p.** (*étudiante*) au pair; **travailler au p.** to work as an au pair

paire² [pɛr] *nf* pair (**de** of)

paisible [pezibl] *adj* (*vie, endroit*) peaceful; (*caractère, personne*) quiet ▪ **paisiblement** [-əmã] *adv* peacefully

paître* [pɛtr] *vi* to graze; *Fam* **envoyer qn p.** to send sb packing

paix [pɛ] *nf* peace; **en p.** (*vivre, laisser*) in peace (**avec** with); **être en p. avec qn** to be at peace with sb; **signer la p. avec qn** to sign a peace treaty with sb; **avoir la p.** to have (some) peace and quiet

Pakistan [pakistã] *nm* **le P.** Pakistan ▪ **pakistanais, -aise 1** *adj* Pakistani **2** *nmf* **P., Pakistanaise** Pakistani

palabrer [palabre] *vi* to talk endlessly ▪ **palabres** *nfpl* endless discussions

palace [palas] *nm* luxury hotel

Il faut noter que le nom anglais **palace** est un faux ami. Il signifie **palais**.

palais [palɛ] *nm (château)* palace; *Anat* palate; **P. de justice** law courts; **p. des sports** sports centre

pâle [pɑl] *adj* pale; **être p. comme un linge** to be as white as a sheet; *Fam* **se faire porter p.** to call in sick

Palestine [palɛstin] *nf* **la P.** Palestine ▪ **palestinien, -ienne** 1 *adj* Palestinian 2 *nmf* **P., Palestinienne** Palestinian

palet [palɛ] *nm (de hockey)* puck

paletot [palto] *nm (manteau)* (short) overcoat

palette [palɛt] *nf (de peintre)* palette; *(pour marchandises)* pallet

pâleur [pɑlœr] *nf (de lumière)* paleness; *(de personne)* pallor ▪ **pâlir** *vi* to turn pale *(de with)*

palier [palje] *nm (niveau)* level; *(d'escalier)* landing; *(phase de stabilité)* plateau; **par paliers** in stages; **être voisins de p.** to live on the same floor

palissade [palisad] *nf* fence

pallier [palje] 1 *vt (difficultés)* to alleviate 2 *vi* **p. à qch** to compensate for sth ▪ **palliatif** *nm* palliative

palmarès [palmarɛs] *nm* prize list; *(de chansons)* charts

palme [palm] *nf (de palmier)* palm (branch); *(de nageur)* flipper; *Fig (symbole)* palm ▪ **palmier** *nm* palm (tree)

palmé, -ée [palme] *adj (patte, pied)* webbed

palombe [palɔ̃b] *nf* wood pigeon

pâlot, -otte [palo, -ɔt] *adj Fam* pale

palourde [palurd] *nf* clam

palper [palpe] *vt* to feel ▪ **palpable** *adj* palpable

palpiter [palpite] *vi (cœur)* to flutter; *(plus fort)* to throb ▪ **palpitant, -ante** *adj (film)* thrilling ▪ **palpitations** *nfpl* palpitations

pâmer [pɑme] **se pâmer** *vpr Fig & Hum* **se p. devant qn/qch** to swoon over sb/sth; **se p. d'aise** to be blissfully happy

pamphlet [pɑ̃flɛ] *nm* lampoon

> Il faut noter que le terme anglais **pamphlet** est un faux ami. Il désigne le plus souvent une **brochure**.

pamplemousse [pɑ̃pləmus] *nm* grapefruit

pan¹ [pɑ̃] *nm (de chemise)* tail; *(de ciel)* patch; **p. de mur** section of wall

pan² [pɑ̃] *exclam* bang!

panacée [panase] *nf* panacea

panachage [panaʃaʒ] *nm* **p. électoral** = voting for candidates from more than one list

panache [panaʃ] *nm (plume)* plume; *(brio)* panache

panaché, -ée [panaʃe] 1 *adj* multicoloured; **p. de blanc** streaked with white 2 *nm* shandy

Panama [panama] *nm* **le P.** Panama

pan-bagnat [pɑ̃baɲa] *(pl* pans-bagnats) *nm* = large round sandwich filled with "salade niçoise"

pancarte [pɑ̃kart] *nf* sign, notice; *(de manifestant)* placard

pancréas [pɑ̃kreas] *nm Anat* pancreas

panda [pɑ̃da] *nm* panda

pané, -ée [pane] *adj Culin* breaded

panier [panje] *nm (ustensile, contenu)* basket; **jeter qch au p.** to throw sth into the wastepaper basket; *Sport* **marquer un p.** to score a basket; **p. à linge** *Br* linen basket, *Am* (clothes) hamper; **p. à salade** *(ustensile)* salad basket; *Fam (voiture de police) Br* black Maria, *Am* paddy wagon ▪ **panier-repas** *(pl* **paniers-repas)** *nm Br* packed lunch, *Am* (brown-bag) lunch

panique [panik] 1 *nf* panic; **pris de p.** panic-stricken 2 *adj* **peur p.** panic ▪ **paniqué, -ée** *adj Fam* in a panic ▪ **paniquer** *vi Fam* to panic

panne [pan] *nf* breakdown; **tomber en p.** to break down; **être en p.** to have broken down; **'en panne'** *(machine, ascenseur)* 'out of order'; **tomber en p. sèche** to run out of *Br* petrol *or Am* gas; **trouver la p.** to locate the cause of the problem; **p. d'électricité** blackout, *Br* power cut

panneau, -x [pano] *nm (écriteau)* sign, notice, board; *(de porte)* panel; *Fam* **tomber dans le p.** to fall into the trap; **p. d'affichage** *Br* notice board, *Am* bulletin board; **p. de signalisation** road sign

panoplie [panɔpli] *nf (déguisement)* outfit; *(gamme)* set

panorama [panɔrama] *nm* panorama ▪ **panoramique** *adj* panoramic; *Cin* **écran p.** wide screen

panse [pɑ̃s] *nf Fam* belly ▪ **pansu, -ue** *adj* potbellied

panser [pɑ̃se] *vt (main)* to bandage; *(plaie)* to dress; *(cheval)* to groom; **p. qn** to dress sb's wounds ▪ **pansement** *nm* dressing; **faire un p. à qn** to put a dressing on sb; **refaire le p.** to change the dressing; **p. adhésif** *Br* (sticking) plaster, Elastoplast®, *Am* Band-aid®

pantalon [pɑ̃talɔ̃] *nm Br* trousers, *Am* pants; **deux pantalons** two pairs of *Br* trousers *or Am* pants

pantelant, -ante [pɑ̃tlɑ̃, -ɑ̃t] *adj* panting

panthère [pɑ̃tɛr] *nf* panther

pantin [pɑ̃tɛ̃] *nm (jouet)* jumping-jack; *Péj (personne)* puppet

pantois, -oise [pɑ̃twa, -waz] *adj* flabbergasted; **elle en est restée pantoise** she was flabbergasted

pantoufle [pɑ̃tufl] *nf* slipper ▪ **pantouflard, -arde** *nmf Fam Br* stay-at-home, *Am* homebody

PAO [peao] *(abrév* **publication assistée par ordinateur)** *nf Ordinat* DTP

paon [pɑ̃] *nm* peacock

papa [papa] *nm* dad(dy); *Fam Péj* **de p.** outdated

paparazzi [paparadzi] *nmpl Journ & Phot Péj* paparazzi *(pluriel)*

papaye [papaj] *nf* papaya ▪ **papayer** *nm (arbre)* papaya

pape [pap] *nm* pope

paperasse [papras] *nf Péj* papers ▪ **paperasserie** *nf Péj* (official) papers; *(procédure)* red tape

papeterie [papetri] *nf (magasin)* stationer's shop; *(articles)* stationery; *(fabrique)* paper mill ▪ **papetier, -ière** *nmf* stationer

papi [papi] *nm* grand(d)ad

papier [papje] *nm (matière)* paper; **un p.** *(feuille)* a piece of paper; *(formulaire)* a form; *(de journal)* an article; *Fam* **être dans les petits papiers de qn** to be in sb's good books; **p. hygiénique** toilet paper; **papiers d'identité** identity papers; **p. journal** newspaper; **p. à lettres** writing paper; **p. peint** wallpaper; **p. recyclé** recycled paper; **p. de verre** sandpaper

papillon [papijɔ̃] *nm (insecte)* butterfly; *Fam (contravention)* (parking) ticket; **p. de nuit** moth

papoter [papɔte] *vi Fam* to chat

paprika [paprika] *nm* paprika

papy [papi] *nm* grand(d)ad

Pâque [pak] *nf Rel* **la P. juive, P.** Passover

paquebot [pakbo] *nm* liner

pâquerette [pakrɛt] *nf* daisy

Pâques [pak] *nm sing & nfpl* Easter; **le lundi de P.** Easter Monday

paquet [pakɛ] *nm (sac)* packet; *(de sucre)* bag; *(de cigarettes) Br* packet, *Am* pack; *(postal)* parcel, package; *Fam* **y mettre le p.** to pull out all the stops

par [par] *prép* **1** *(indique l'agent, la manière, le moyen)* by; **choisi/frappé p. qn** chosen/hit by sb; **p. mer** by sea; **p. le train** by train; **p. le travail/la force** by *or* through work/force; **apprendre p. un ami** to learn from *or* through a friend; **commencer p. qch** *(récit)* to begin with sth; **p. erreur** by mistake; **p. chance** by a stroke of luck; **p. malchance** as ill luck would have it (**b**) *(à travers)* through; **p. la porte/le tunnel** through the door/tunnel; **jeter/regarder p. la fenêtre** to throw/look out (of) the window; **p. ici/là** *(aller)* this/that way; *(habiter)* around here/there; **p. les rues** through the streets (**c**) *(à cause de)* out of, from; **p. pitié/respect** out of pity/respect (**d**) *(pendant)* **p. un jour d'hiver** on a winter's day; **p. ce froid** in this cold; **p. le passé** in the past (**e**) *(distributif)* **dix fois p. an/mois** ten times a or per year/month; **50 euros p. personne** 50 euros per person; **deux p. deux** two by two; **p. deux fois** twice (**f**) *(avec 'trop')* **p. trop aimable** far too kind

para [para] *nm Fam* para(trooper)

parabole [parabɔl] *nf (récit)* parable; *Math* parabola; *TV & Tél Br* satellite dish, *Am* dish antenna

parachever [paraʃve] *vt* to complete

parachute [paraʃyt] *nm* parachute; **saut en p.** parachute jump; **p. ascensionnel** parascending ▪ **parachuter** *vt* to parachute in; *Fam (nommer)* to draft in ▪ **parachutisme** *nm* parachute jumping ▪ **parachutiste** *nmf* parachutist; *(soldat)* paratrooper

parade [parad] *nf (défilé)* parade; *(étalage)* show; *Boxe & Escrime* parry; *Fig (riposte)* reply ▪ **parader** *vi* to show off

paradis [paradi] *nm* heaven; *Fig* paradise ▪ **paradisiaque** *adj Fig (endroit)* heavenly

paradoxe [paradɔks] *nm* paradox ▪ **paradoxal, -e, -aux, -ales** *adj* paradoxical ▪ **paradoxalement** *adv* paradoxically

parafer [parafe] *vt* to initial

paraffine [parafin] *nf* paraffin (wax)

parages [paraʒ] *nmpl Naut* waters; **dans les p. de** in the vicinity of; *Fam* **est-ce qu'elle est dans les p.?** is she around?

paragraphe [paragraf] *nm* paragraph

Paraguay [paragwe] *nm* **le P.** Paraguay

paraître* [parɛtr] **1** *vi (sembler)* to seem, to appear; *(apparaître)* to appear; *(livre)* to come out, to be published **2** *v impersonnel* **il paraît qu'il va partir** it appears *or* seems (that) he's leaving; **à ce qu'il paraît** apparently

parallèle [paralɛl] **1** *adj* parallel (**à** with *or* to); *(police, marché)* unofficial; **mener une vie p.** to lead a secret life **2** *nf* parallel (line) **3** *nm (comparaison) & Géog* parallel; **mettre qch en p. avec qch** to draw a parallel between sth and sth ▪ **parallèlement** *adv* **p. à** parallel to; *(simultanément)* at the same time as

paralyser [paralize] *vt Br* to paralyse, *Am* to paralyze ▪ **paralysie** *nf* paralysis ▪ **paralytique** *adj & nmf* paralytic

paramédical, -e, -aux, -ales [paramedikal, -o] *adj* paramedical

paramètre [paramɛtr] *nm* parameter; *Ordinat* setting ▪ **paramétrage** *nf Ordinat* configuration ▪ **paramétrer** *vt Ordinat* to configure

paramilitaire [paramilitɛr] *adj & nmf* paramilitary

parano [parano] *adj Fam* paranoid

paranoïa [paranɔja] *nf* paranoia ▪ **paranoïaque** *adj & nmf* paranoiac

parapente [parapɑ̃t] *nm (activité)* paragliding; **faire du p.** to go paragliding

parapet [parapɛ] *nm* parapet

parapher [parafe] *vt* to initial

paraphrase [parafraz] *nf* paraphrase ▪ **paraphraser** *vt* to paraphrase

parapluie [paraplyi] *nm* umbrella

parapsychologie [parapsikɔlɔʒi] *nf* parapsychology

parasite [parazit] **1** *nm (organisme, personne)* parasite; **parasites** *(à la radio)* interference **2** *adj* parasitic

parasol [parasɔl] *nm* sunshade, parasol; *(de plage)* beach umbrella

paratonnerre [paratɔner] *nm* lightning *Br* conductor *or Am* rod

paravent [paravã] *nm* screen

parc [park] *nm (jardin)* park; *(de château)* grounds; *(de bébé)* playpen; **p. d'attractions** amusement park; **p. automobile** *(de pays)* number of vehicles on the road; **p. à huîtres** oyster bed; **p. naturel** natural park; **p. de stationnement** *Br* car park, *Am* parking lot

parcelle [parsɛl] *nf* small piece; *(terrain)* plot; *Fig (de vérité)* grain

parce que [parskə] *conj* because

parchemin [parʃəmɛ̃] *nm* parchment

parcimonie [parsimɔni] *nf* **avec p.** parsimoniously ▪ **parcimonieux, -ieuse** *adj* parsimonious

par-ci, par-là [parsiparla] *adv* here, there and everywhere

parcmètre [parkmɛtr] *nm* (parking) meter

parcourir* [parkurir] *vt (lieu)* to walk round; *(pays)* to travel through; *(mer)* to sail; *(distance)* to cover; *(texte)* to glance through; **p. qch des yeux** *ou* **du regard** to glance at sth; **il reste 2 km à p.** there are 2 km to go ▪ **parcours** *nm (itinéraire)* route; **p. de golf** *(terrain)* golf course

par-delà [pardəla] *prép & adv* beyond

par-derrière [parderjer] **1** *prép* behind **2** *adv (attaquer)* from behind; *(se boutonner)* at the back; **passer p.** to go in the back door

par-dessous [pardəsu] *prép & adv* underneath

pardessus [pardəsy] *nm* overcoat

par-dessus [pardəsy] **1** *prép* over; **p. tout** above all; *Fam* **en avoir p. la tête** to be completely fed up **2** *adv* over

par-devant [pardəvã] *adv (attaquer)* from the front; *(se boutonner)* at the front

pardon [pardɔ̃] *nm* forgiveness; **p.!** *(excusez-moi)* sorry!; **p.?** *(pour demander)* excuse me?, *Am* pardon me?; **demander p.** to apologize (**à** to) ▪ **pardonnable** *adj* forgivable ▪ **pardonner** *vt* to forgive; **p. qch à qn** to forgive sb for sth; **elle m'a pardonné d'avoir oublié** she forgave me for forgetting

pare-balles [parbal] *adj inv* **gilet p.** bulletproof *Br* jacket *or Am* vest

pare-brise [parbriz] *nm inv Br* windscreen, *Am* windshield

pare-chocs [parʃɔk] *nm inv* bumper

pare-feu [parfø] *nm inv (de cheminée)* fireguard; *Ordinat* firewall; **porte p.** firedoor

pareil, -eille [parɛj] **1** *adj* (**a**) *(identique)* the same; **p. à** the same as (**b**) *(tel)* such; **en p. cas** in such cases **2** *adv Fam* the same; **on a tous fait p.** we all did the same (thing) **3** *nmf (personne)* equal; **sans p.** unparalleled, unique; **il n'a pas son p.** he's second to none **4** *nf* **rendre la pareille à qn** *(se venger)* to get one's own back on sb ▪ **pareillement** *adv (de la même manière)* in the same way; *(aussi)* likewise; **p.!** *(en réponse à des vœux)* you too!, same to you!

parement [parmã] *nm (de vêtement)* facing

parent, -ente [parã, -ãt] **1** *nmf (oncle, tante, cousin)* relative, relation **2** *nmpl* **parents** *(père et mère)* parents **3** *adj* related (**de** to) ▪ **parental, -e, -aux, -ales** *adj* parental ▪ **parentalité** *nf* parenthood ▪ **parenté** *nf* relationship; **avoir un lien de p.** to be related

parenthèse [parãtɛz] *nf (signe)* bracket, parenthesis; *Fig (digression)* digression; **entre parenthèses** in brackets

paréo [pareo] *nm (de plage)* sarong

parer¹ [pare] **1** *vt (coup)* to parry **2** *vi* **p. à toute éventualité** to be prepared for any eventuality; **p. au plus pressé** to attend to the most urgent things first

parer² [pare] *vt (orner)* to adorn (**de** with)

paresse [pares] *nf* laziness ▪ **paresser** *vi* to laze about ▪ **paresseux, -euse 1** *adj* lazy **2** *nmf* lazy person **3** *nm (animal)* sloth

parfaire* [parfer] *vt* to finish off ▪ **parfait, -aite** *adj* perfect ▪ **parfaitement** *adv (sans fautes, complètement)* perfectly; *(certainement)* certainly

parfois [parfwa] *adv* sometimes

parfum [parfœ̃] *nm (essence)* perfume; *(senteur)* fragrance; *(de glace)* flavour; *Fam* **être au p.** to be in the know ▪ **parfumé, -ée** *adj (savon, fleur, mouchoir)* scented; **p. au café** coffee-flavoured ▪ **parfumer 1** *vt (embaumer)* to scent; *(glace)* to flavour (**à** with) **2 se parfumer** *vpr* to put perfume on ▪ **parfumerie** *nf (magasin)* perfumery

pari [pari] *nm* bet; **faire un p.** to make a bet; **p. mutuel** *Br* ≃ tote, *Am* ≃ pari-mutuel ▪ **parier** *vti* to bet (**sur** on; **que** that); **il y a fort à p. que...** the odds are that... ▪ **parieur, -ieuse** *nmf* better

Paris [pari] *nm ou f* Paris ▪ **parisien, -ienne 1** *adj* Parisian **2** *nmf* **P., Parisienne** Parisian

parité [parite] *nf* parity

parjure [parʒyr] **1** *nm* perjury **2** *nmf* perjurer ▪ **se parjurer** *vpr* to perjure oneself

parka [parka] *nm ou f* parka

parking [parkiŋ] *nm Br* car park, *Am* parking lot; **'p. payant'** *Br* ≃ 'pay-and-display car park'

parlement [parləmã] *nm* **le P.** Parliament ▪ **parlementaire 1** *adj* parliamentary **2** *nmf* member of parliament

parlementer [parləmãte] *vi* to negotiate (**avec** with)

parler [parle] **1** *vi* to talk, to speak (**de** about *or* of; **à** to); **sans p. de...** not to mention...; **p. par gestes** to use sign language; **n'en parlons plus!** let's forget it!; *Fam* **tu parles!** you bet! **2** *vt (langue)* to speak; **p. affaires** to talk business

3 se parler *vpr* (*langue*) to be spoken; (*l'un l'autre*) to talk to each other **4** *nm* speech; (*régional*) dialect ▪ **parlant, -ante** *adj* (*film*) talking; (*regard*) eloquent ▪ **parlé, -ée** *adj* (*langue*) spoken

parloir [parlwar] *nm* visiting room

parmi [parmi] *prép* among(st)

parodie [parɔdi] *nf* parody ▪ **parodier** *vt* to parody

paroi [parwa] *nf* wall; (*de rocher*) (rock) face

paroisse [parwas] *nf* parish ▪ **paroissien, -ienne** *nmf* parishioner

parole [parɔl] *nf* (*mot, promesse*) word; (*faculté, langage*) speech; **paroles** (*de chanson*) words, lyrics; **adresser la p. à qn** to speak to sb; **prendre la p.** to speak; **demander la p.** to ask to speak; **tenir p.** to keep one's word; **je te crois sur p.** I take your word for it; *Jur* **libéré sur p.** free(d) on parole; **ma p.!** my word!

paroxysme [parɔksism] *nm* **atteindre son p.** to reach its peak

parpaing [parpɛ̃] *nm* breeze block

parquer [parke] *vt* (*bœufs*) to pen in; *Péj* (*gens*) to confine

parquet [parkɛ] *nm* (*sol*) wooden floor; *Jur* public prosecutor's office

parrain [parɛ̃] *nm* *Rel* godfather; (*de sportif, de club*) sponsor ▪ **parrainer** *vt* (*sportif, membre*) to sponsor

pars [par] *voir* **partir**

parsemer [parsəme] *vt* to scatter (**de** with)

part¹ [par] *voir* **partir**

part² [par] *nf* (*portion*) share, part; (*de gâteau*) slice; **prendre p. à** (*activité*) to take part in; (*la joie de qn*) to share; **faire p. de qch à qn** to inform sb of sth; **de toutes parts** on all sides; **de p. et d'autre** on both sides; **d'une p.…. d'autre p.** on (the) one hand…; on the other hand…; **d'autre p.** (*d'ailleurs*) moreover; **de p. en p.** right through; **de la p. de qn** from sb; **c'est de la p. de qui?** (*au téléphone*) who's calling?; **pour ma p.** as for me; **à p.** (*mettre*) aside; (*excepté*) apart from; (*personne*) different; **une place à p.** a special place; **prendre qn à p.** to take sb aside; **membre à p. entière** full member

partage [partaʒ] *nm* (*action*) dividing up; (*de gâteau, de responsabilités*) sharing out; **faire le p. de qch** to divide sth up; **recevoir qch en p.** to be left sth (*in a will*)

partager [partaʒe] **1** *vt* (*avoir en commun*) to share (**avec** with); (*répartir*) to divide (up); **p. qch en deux** to divide sth in two; **p. l'avis de qn** to share sb's opinion **2 se partager** *vpr* (*bénéfices*) to share (between themselves); **se p. entre** to divide one's time between ▪ **partagé, -ée** *adj* (*amour*) mutual; **être p.** to be torn; **les avis sont partagés** opinions are divided

partance [partɑ̃s] **en partance** *adv* (*train*) about to depart; **en p. pour…** for…

partant, -ante [partɑ̃, -ɑ̃t] **1** *nmf* (*coureur, cheval*) starter **2** *adj Fam* **je suis p.!** count me in!

partenaire [partənɛr] *nmf* partner; **partenaires sociaux** workers and managers ▪ **partenariat** *nm* partnership

parterre [partɛr] *nm* (*de fleurs*) flower bed; *Théâtre Br* stalls, *Am* orchestra; *Fam* (*sol*) floor

parti [parti] *nm* (*camp*) side; **prendre le p. de qn** to take sb's side; **tirer p. de qch** to make good use of sth; **p. (politique)** (political) party; **p. pris** bias; **un beau p.** (*personne*) a good match

partial, -e, -iaux, -iales [parsjal, -jo] *adj* biased ▪ **partialité** *nf* bias

participe [partisip] *nm Grammaire* participle

participer [partisipe] *vi* **p. à** (*jeu*) to take part in, to participate in; (*bénéfices, joie*) to share (in); (*financièrement*) to contribute to ▪ **participant, -ante** *nmf* participant ▪ **participation** *nf* participation; (*d'élection*) turnout; *Fin* interest; **p. aux frais** contribution towards costs; **p. aux bénéfices** profit-sharing

particularité [partikylarite] *nf* peculiarity

particule [partikyl] *nf* particle; **avoir un nom à p.** to have a double-barrelled name

particulier, -ière [partikylje, -jɛr] **1** *adj* (*propre*) characteristic (**à** of); (*remarquable*) unusual; (*soin, intérêt*) particular; (*maison, voiture, leçon*) private; *Péj* (*bizarre*) peculiar; **en p.** (*surtout*) in particular; (*à part*) in private; **cas p.** special case **2** *nm* private individual; **vente de p. à p.** private sale ▪ **particulièrement** *adv* particularly; **tout p.** especially

partie [parti] *nf* (*morceau*) part; (*jeu*) game; (*domaine*) field; *Jur* party; **une p. de cartes** a game of cards; **en p.** partly, in part; **en grande p.** mainly; **faire p. de** to be a part of; (*club*) to belong to; (*comité*) to be on; **ça n'a pas été une p. de plaisir** it was no picnic; **ce n'est que p. remise** we'll do it another time ▪ **partiel, -ielle** **1** *adj* partial **2** *nm Univ* end-of-term exam ▪ **partiellement** *adv* partially

partir* [partir] (*aux* **être**) *vi* (*s'en aller*) to go, to leave; (*se mettre en route*) to set off; (*s'éloigner*) to go away; (*douleur*) to go, to disappear; (*coup de feu*) to go off; (*flèche*) to shoot off; (*tache*) to come out; (*bouton, peinture*) to come off; (*moteur*) to start; **p. en voiture** to go by car, to drive; **p. en courant** to run off; **p. de** (*lieu*) to leave from; (*commencer par*) to start (off) with; **p. de rien** to start with nothing; **à p. de** (*date, prix*) from; **à p. de maintenant** from now on; **je pars du principe que…** I'm working on the assumption that…; **ça partait d'un bon sentiment** it was with the best of intentions; **je pars!** I'm going!; **c'est parti!** off we go! ▪ **parti, -ie** *adj* **bien p.** off to a good start

partisan [partizɑ̃] **1** *nm* supporter; (*combattant*)

partisan 2 *adj (esprit)* partisan; **être p. de qch/ de faire qch** to be in favour of sth/of doing sth
partition [paʁtisjɔ̃] *nf Mus* score
partout [paʁtu] *adv* everywhere; **p. où je vais** everywhere *or* wherever I go; **un peu p.** all over the place; *Football* **3 buts p.** 3 all; *Tennis* **15 p.** 15 all
paru, -ue [paʁy] *pp de* **paraître** ▪ **parution** *nf* publication
parure [paʁyʁ] *nf (ensemble)* set
parvenir* [paʁvəniʁ] *(aux être) vi* **p. à** *(lieu)* to reach; *(objectif)* to achieve; **p. à faire qch** to manage to do sth ▪ **parvenu, -ue** *nmf Péj* upstart
parvis [paʁvi] *nm* square *(in front of church)*
pas[1] [pɑ] *adv (de négation)* **(ne...) p.** not; **je ne sais p.** I do not *or* don't know; **je n'ai p. compris** I didn't understand; **je voudrais ne p. sortir** I would like not to go out; **p. de pain/de café** no bread/coffee; **p. du tout** not at all; **elle chantera – p. moi!** she'll sing – not me!
pas[2] [pɑ] *nm* (**a**) *(enjambée)* step; *(allure)* pace; *(bruit)* footstep; *(trace)* footprint; **p. à p.** step by step; **à p. de loup** stealthily; **à deux p. (de)** close by; **aller au p.** to go at a walking pace; **rouler au p.** *(véhicule)* to crawl along; **marcher au p. (cadencé)** to march in step; **faire un faux p.** *(en marchant)* to trip; *Fig (faute)* to make a faux pas; *Fig* **faire le premier p.** to make the first move; **faire ses premiers p.** to take one's first steps; **faire les cent p.** to pace up and down; **revenir sur ses p.** to retrace one's steps; **marcher à grands p.** to stride along; **le p. de la porte** the doorstep (**b**) *(de vis)* pitch (**c**) **le p. de Calais** the Straits of Dover
pascal, -e, -als *ou* **-aux, -ales** [paskal, -o] *adj* **semaine pascale** Easter week
passable [pasabl] *adj* passable, fair ▪ **passablement** [-əmɑ̃] *adv* fairly
passage [pasaʒ] *nm (chemin, extrait)* passage; *(ruelle)* alley(way); *(traversée)* crossing; **être de p. dans une ville** to be passing through a town; **p. clouté** *ou* **pour piétons** *Br* (pedestrian) crossing, *Am* crosswalk; **p. souterrain** underpass, *Br* subway; **p. à niveau** *Br* level crossing, *Am* grade crossing; **'p. interdit'** 'no through traffic'; **'cédez le p.'** *(au carrefour)* *Br* 'give way', *Am* 'yield'; **p. pluvieux** rainy spell
passager, -ère [pasaʒe, -ɛʁ] **1** *adj* momentary **2** *nmf* passenger; **p. clandestin** stowaway
passant, -ante [pasɑ̃, -ɑ̃t] **1** *adj (rue)* busy **2** *nmf* passer-by **3** *nm (de ceinture)* loop
passe [pas] *nf Football* pass; *Fig* **une mauvaise p.** a bad patch; *Fig* **être en p. de faire qch** to be on the way to doing sth
passé, -ée [pase] **1** *adj (temps)* past; *(couleur)* faded; **la semaine passée** last week; **il est dix heures passées** it's after *or Br* gone ten o'clock;

être p. *(personne)* to have been (and gone); *(orage)* to be over; **avoir vingt ans passés** to be over twenty; **p. de mode** out of fashion **2** *nm (temps, vie passée)* past; *Grammaire* past (tense); **par le p.** in the past **3** *prép* after; **p. huit heures** after eight o'clock
passe-montagne [pasmɔ̃taɲ] *(pl passe-montagnes) nm Br* balaclava, *Am* ski mask
passe-partout [paspaʁtu] **1** *nm inv* master key **2** *adj inv* all-purpose
passe-passe [paspas] *nm inv* **tour de p.** conjuring trick
passeport [paspɔʁ] *nm* passport
passer [pase] **1** *(aux avoir) vt (pont, frontière)* to go over; *(porte, douane)* to go through; *(ballon)* to pass; *(vêtement)* to slip on; *(film)* to show; *(disque)* to play; *(vacances)* to spend; *(examen)* to take; *(thé)* to strain; *(café)* to filter; *(commande)* to place; *(accord)* to conclude; *(visite médicale)* to have; *(omettre)* to leave out; **p. qch à qn** *(prêter)* to pass sth to sb; *(caprice)* to grant sb sth; **p. un coup d'éponge sur qch** to give sth a sponge; **p. son tour** to miss a turn; *Aut* **p. la seconde** to change into second; **p. sa colère sur qn** to vent one's anger on sb; **p. son temps à faire qch** to spend one's time doing sth; **j'ai passé l'âge de faire ça** I'm too old to do that; **je vous le passe** *(au téléphone)* I'm putting you through to him
2 *(aux être) vi (se déplacer)* to go past; *(disparaître)* to go; *(facteur, laitier)* to come; *(temps)* to pass (by), to go by; *(film, programme)* to be on; *(douleur, mode)* to pass; *(couleur)* to fade; *(courant)* to flow; *(loi)* to be passed; **laisser p. qn** to let sb through; **p. prendre qn** to pick sb up; **p. voir qn** to drop in on sb; **p. de qch à qch** to go from sth to sth; **p. devant qn/ qch** to go past sb/sth; **p. par Paris** to pass through Paris; **p. chez le boulanger** to go round to the baker's; **p. à la radio** to be on the radio; **p. à l'ennemi** to go over to the enemy; **p. pour** *(riche)* to be taken for; **faire p. qn pour** to pass sb off as; **faire p. qch sous/dans qch** to slide/push sth under/into sth; **faire p. un réfugié** to smuggle a refugee **(en Suisse** to Switzerland); **p. sur** *(détail)* to pass over; *Scol* **p. dans la classe supérieure** to move up a class; *Aut* **p. en seconde** to change into second; **p. capitaine** to be promoted to captain; **dire qch en passant** to mention sth in passing
3 se passer *vpr (se produire)* to happen; **se p. de qn/qch** to do without sb/sth; **cela se passe de commentaires** it needs no comment; **ça s'est bien passé** it went off well
passerelle [pasʁɛl] *nf (pont)* footbridge; **p. d'embarquement** *(de navire)* gangway; *(d'avion)* steps
passe-temps [pastɑ̃] *nm inv* pastime

passeur, -euse [pɑsœr, -øz] *nmf (batelier)* ferryman, *f* ferrywoman; *(contrebandier)* smuggler

passible [pasibl] *adj Jur* **p. de** liable to

passif, -ive [pasif, -iv] **1** *adj* passive **2** *nm* (**a**) *Grammaire* passive (**b**) *Fin* liabilities • **passivité** *nf* passiveness, passivity

passion [pɑsjɔ̃] *nf* passion; **avoir la p. des voitures** to have a passion for cars • **passionnel, -elle** *adj* **crime p.** crime of passion

passionner [pɑsjɔne] **1** *vt* to fascinate **2 se passionner** *vpr* **se p. pour qch** to have a passion for sth • **passionnant, -ante** *adj* fascinating • **passionné, -ée 1** *adj* passionate; **p. de qch** passionately fond of sth **2** *nmf* fan (**de** of) • **passionnément** *adv* passionately

passoire [paswar] *nf (pour liquides)* sieve; *(à thé)* strainer; *(à légumes)* colander

pastel [pastɛl] *adj inv & nm* pastel

pastèque [pastɛk] *nf* watermelon

pasteur [pastœr] *nm Rel* pastor

pasteurisé, -ée [pastœrize] *adj* pasteurized

pastiche [pastiʃ] *nm* pastiche

pastille [pastij] *nf* pastille; *(médicament)* lozenge

pastis [pastis] *nm* pastis

pastoral, -e, -aux, -ales [pastɔral, -o] *adj* pastoral

patate [patat] *nf Fam (pomme de terre)* potato, *Br* spud; *Fig (idiot)* clot; **p. douce** sweet potato

patatras [patatra] *exclam* crash!

pataud, -aude [pato, -od] *adj Fam* clumsy

patauger [patoʒe] *vi (s'embourber)* to squelch; *(barboter)* to splash about; *Fam (s'embrouiller)* to flounder • **pataugeoire** *nf* paddling pool

patch [patʃ] *nm Méd* patch; **p. anti-tabac** nicotine patch

pâte [pat] *nf (pour tarte)* pastry; *(pour pain)* dough; *(pour gâteau)* mixture; **fromage à p. molle** soft cheese; **p. d'amandes** marzipan; **p. de fruits** fruit jelly; **p. à frire** batter; **p. à modeler** *Br* modelling *or Am* modeling clay; **p. brisée** shortcrust pastry; **p. feuilletée** puff pastry; **pâtes (alimentaires)** pasta

pâté [pate] *nm (charcuterie)* pâté; *(tache d'encre)* blot; **p. en croûte** meat pie; **p. de sable** sand castle; **p. de maisons** block of houses

pâtée [pate] *nf (pour chien)* dog food; *(pour chat)* cat food; *Fam* **prendre la p.** to get thrashed

patelin [patlɛ̃] *nm Fam* village

patent, -ente [patɑ̃, -ɑ̃t] **1** *adj* patent, obvious **2** *nf Com* **patente** *Br* licence, *Am* license *(to exercise a trade or profession)* • **patenté, -ée** *adj Com* licensed • **patenter** *vt Com* to license

patère [patɛr] *nf (coat)* peg

paternel, -elle [patɛrnɛl] *adj* paternal • **paternalisme** *nm* paternalism • **paternité**

nf (état) paternity, fatherhood; *(de livre)* authorship; **test de p.** paternity test

pâteux, -euse [patø, -øz] *adj* doughy; **avoir la langue pâteuse** to have a furred tongue

pathétique [patetik] *adj* moving

> Il faut noter que l'adjectif anglais **pathetic** est un faux ami. Il signifie le plus souvent **lamentable**.

pathologie [patɔlɔʒi] *nf* pathology • **pathologique** *adj* pathological

patibulaire [patibylɛr] *adj* **avoir une mine p.** to look sinister

patience [pasjɑ̃s] *nf* patience; **avoir de la p.** to be patient; **perdre p.** to lose patience; **faire une p.** *(jeu de cartes)* to play (a game of) patience

patient, -iente [pasjɑ̃, -jɑ̃t] **1** *adj* patient **2** *nmf (malade)* patient • **patiemment** [-amɑ̃] *adv* patiently • **patienter** *vi* to wait

patin [patɛ̃] *nm (de patineur)* skate; *(pour parquet)* cloth pad; **p. à glace** ice skate; **p. à roulettes** roller skate; **p. de frein** brake shoe

patine [patin] *nf* patina

patiner [patine] *vi Sport* to skate; *(véhicule)* to skid; *(roue)* to spin around; *(embrayage)* to slip • **patinage** *nm Sport* skating; **p. artistique** figure skating; **p. de vitesse** speed skating • **patineur, -euse** *nmf* skater • **patinoire** *nf* skating rink, ice rink

pâtir [patir] *vi* **p. de** to suffer because of

pâtisserie [patisri] *nf (gâteau)* pastry, cake; *(magasin)* cake shop; *(art)* pastry-making • **pâtissier, -ière 1** *nmf* pastry chef; *(commerçant)* confectioner **2** *adj* **crème pâtissière** confectioner's custard

patois [patwa] *nm* patois

patraque [patrak] *adj Fam* out of sorts

patriarche [patrijarʃ] *nm* patriarch

patrie [patri] *nf* homeland

patrimoine [patrimwan] *nm* heritage; *(biens)* property; *Biol* **p. génétique** genotype

patriote [patrijɔt] **1** *adj* patriotic **2** *nmf* patriot • **patriotique** *adj* patriotic • **patriotisme** *nm* patriotism

patron, -onne [patrɔ̃, -ɔn] **1** *nmf (chef)* boss; *(propriétaire)* owner (**de** of); *(gérant)* manager, *f* manageress; *(de bar)* landlord, *f* landlady; *Rel* patron saint **2** *nm Couture* pattern

> Il faut noter que le nom anglais **patron** est un faux ami. Il signifie le plus souvent **client**.

patronage [patrɔnaʒ] *nm (protection)* patronage; *(centre)* youth club

patronat [patrɔna] *nm* employers • **patronal, -e, -aux, -ales** *adj* employers'

patronyme [patrɔnim] *nm* family name

patrouille [patruj] *nf* patrol • **patrouiller** *vi* to patrol

patte [pat] *nf* (**a**) *(membre)* leg; *(de chat, de chien)* paw; **marcher à quatre pattes** to walk on all fours (**b**) *(languette)* tab; *(de poche)* flap ▪ **pattes** *nfpl (favoris)* sideburns

pâturage [patyraʒ] *nm* pasture

pâture [patyr] *nf Fig* **donner qn en p. à qn** to serve sb up to sb

paume [pom] *nf* palm

paumer [pome] *vt Fam* to lose ▪ **paumé, -ée** *Fam* **1** *adj* lost **2** *nmf* loser

paupière [popjɛr] *nf* eyelid

paupiette [popjɛt] *nf* **p. de veau** veal olive

pause [poz] *nf (arrêt)* break; *(en parlant)* pause

pauvre [povr] **1** *adj (personne, sol, excuse)* poor; *(meubles)* shabby; **p. en** *(calories)* low in; *(ressources)* low on **2** *nmf* poor man, *f* poor woman; **les pauvres** the poor ▪ **pauvrement** [-əmã] *adv* poorly ▪ **pauvreté** [-əte] *nf* poverty

pavaner [pavane] **se pavaner** *vpr* to strut about

paver [pave] *vt* to pave ▪ **pavage** *nm (travail, revêtement)* paving ▪ **pavé** *nm* **un p.** a paving stone; *Fig* **sur le p.** on the streets

pavillon [pavijɔ̃] *nm* (**a**) *(maison)* detached house; *(d'hôpital)* wing; *(d'exposition)* pavilion; **p. de chasse** hunting lodge (**b**) *(drapeau)* flag; **p. de complaisance** flag of convenience

pavoiser [pavwaze] *vi Fam* to gloat

pavot [pavo] *nm* poppy; **graines de p.** poppy seeds

payable [pejabl] *adj* payable

paye [pɛj] *nf* pay, wages ▪ **payement** *nm* payment

payer [peje] **1** *vt (personne, somme)* to pay; *(service, objet)* to pay for; *(récompenser)* to repay; **se faire p.** to get paid; *Fam* **p. qch à qn** *(offrir en cadeau)* to treat sb to sth; *Fam* **tu me le paieras!** you'll pay for this! **2** *vi* to pay **3 se payer** *vpr* **se p. qch** to treat oneself to sth; *Fam* **se p. la tête de qn** to take the mickey out of sb ▪ **payant, -ante** *adj (hôte, spectateur)* paying; **l'entrée est payante** there's a charge for admission

pays [pei] *nm* country; *(région)* region; **du p.** *(vin, gens)* local

paysage [peizaʒ] *nm* landscape, scenery ▪ **paysagiste** *nmf (jardinier)* landscape gardener

paysan, -anne [peizã, -an] **1** *nmf* farmer; *Péj* peasant **2** *adj* **coutume paysanne** rural or country custom; **le monde p.** the farming community

Pays-Bas [peibɑ] *nmpl* **les P.** the Netherlands

PCV [peseve] *(abrév* **paiement contre vérification**) *nm* **(appel en) P.** *Br* reverse-charge call, *Am* collect call; **téléphoner en P.** *Br* to reverse the charges, *Am* to call collect

P-DG [pedeʒe] *(abrév* **président-directeur général**) *nm Br* MD, *Am* CEO

péage [peaʒ] *nm (droit)* toll; *(lieu)* tollbooth; **pont à p.** toll bridge; *TV* **chaîne à p.** pay channel

peau, -x [po] *nf* skin; *(de fruit)* peel, skin; *(cuir)* hide; *(fourrure)* pelt; *Fig* **faire p. neuve** to turn over a new leaf; *Fig* **se mettre dans la p. de qn** to put oneself in sb's shoes; *Fam* **avoir qn dans la p.** to be crazy about sb; *Fam* **être bien dans sa p.** to feel good about oneself; *Fam* **laisser sa p. dans** *(aventure)* to lose one's life in; *Fam* **j'aurai sa p.!** I'll get him!

péché [peʃe] *nm* sin; **p. mignon** weakness ▪ **pécher** *vi* to sin; **p. par orgueil** to be too proud ▪ **pécheur, -eresse** *nmf* sinner

pêche¹ [pɛʃ] *nf (activité)* fishing; *(poissons)* catch; **p. à la ligne** angling; **aller à la p.** to go fishing ▪ **pêcher¹** **1** *vt (attraper)* to catch; *(chercher à prendre)* to fish for; *Fam (dénicher)* to dig up **2** *vi* to fish ▪ **pêcheur** *nm* fisherman; *(à la ligne)* angler

pêche² [pɛʃ] *nf (fruit)* peach; **avoir une peau de p.** to have soft, velvety skin; *Fam* **avoir la p.** to be on top form ▪ **pêcher²** *nm (arbre)* peach tree

pectoraux [pɛktoro] *nmpl* chest muscles, pectorals

pécule [pekyl] *nm* savings

pécuniaire [pekynjɛr] *adj* financial

pédagogie [pedagoʒi] *nf (discipline)* pedagogy ▪ **pédagogique** *adj* educational ▪ **pédagogue** *nmf* teacher

pédale [pedal] *nf* (**a**) *(de voiture, de piano)* pedal; *Fam* **mettre la p. douce** to go easy; *Fam* **perdre les pédales** to lose one's marbles; **p. de frein** brake pedal (**b**) *Fam Péj (homosexuel)* queer, = offensive term used to refer to a male homosexual ▪ **pédaler** *vi* to pedal; *Fam* **p. dans la semoule** to be all at sea

Pédalo® [pedalo] *nm* pedal boat, pedalo

pédant, -ante [pedã, -ãt] **1** *adj* pedantic **2** *nmf* pedant

pédé [pede] *nm très Fam Péj (homosexuel)* queer, = offensive term used to refer to a male homosexual

pédestre [pedɛstr] *adj* **randonnée p.** hike

pédiatre [pedjatr] *nmf Br* paediatrician, *Am* pediatrician ▪ **pédiatrie** *f Br* paediatrics, *Am* pediatrics *(sing)*

pédicure [pedikyr] *nmf Br* chiropodist, *Am* podiatrist

pedigree [pedigre] *nm* pedigree

pédophile [pedofil] *nmf Br* paedophile, *Am* pedophile ▪ **pédophilie** *nf Br* paedophilia, *Am* pedophilia

pègre [pɛgr] *nf* **la p.** the underworld

peigne [pɛɲ] *nm* comb; **se donner un coup de p.** to give one's hair a comb; *Fig* **passer qch au p. fin** to go through sth with a fine-tooth comb ▪ **peigner** **1** *vt (cheveux)* to comb; **p. qn** to comb sb's hair **2 se peigner** *vpr* to comb one's hair

peignoir [pɛɲwar] *nm Br* dressing gown, *Am* bathrobe; **p. de bain** bathrobe

peinard, -arde [penar, -ard] *adj Fam* quiet (and easy)

peindre* [pɛ̃dr] **1** *vt* to paint; *Fig (décrire)* to depict; **p. qch en bleu** to paint sth blue **2** *vi* to paint

peine [pɛn] *nf* (**a**) *(châtiment)* punishment; **p. de mort** death penalty; **p. de prison** prison sentence; **'défense d'entrer sous p. d'amende'** 'trespassers will be prosecuted' (**b**) *(chagrin)* sorrow; **avoir de la p.** to be upset; **faire de la p. à qn** to upset sb (**c**) *(effort)* trouble; *(difficulté)* difficulty; **se donner de la p.** *ou* **beaucoup de p.** to go to a lot of trouble (**pour faire** to do); **avec p.** with difficulty; **ça vaut la p. d'attendre** it's worth waiting; **ce n'est pas** *ou* **ça ne vaut pas la p.** it's not worth it (**d**) **à p.** hardly, scarcely; **à p. arrivée, elle...** no sooner had she arrived than she... ▪ **peiner 1** *vt* to upset **2** *vi* to labour

peintre [pɛ̃tr] *nm (artiste)* painter; **p. en bâtiment** painter and decorator ▪ **peinture** *nf (tableau, activité)* painting; *(matière)* paint; **p. à l'huile** oil painting; **'p. fraîche'** 'wet paint' ▪ **peinturlurer** *vt Fam* to daub with paint

péjoratif, -ive [peʒɔratif, -iv] *adj* pejorative

Pékin [pekɛ̃] *nm ou f* Peking, Beijing

pékinois [pekinwa] *nm (chien)* Pekin(g)ese

pelage [pəlaʒ] *nm* coat, fur

pelé, -ée [pəle] *adj* bare

pêle-mêle [pɛlmɛl] *adv* higgledy-piggledy

peler [pəle] **1** *vt* to peel **2** *vi (personne, peau)* to peel; *Fam* **ça pèle** it's freezing (cold)

pèlerin [pɛlrɛ̃] *nm* pilgrim ▪ **pèlerinage** *nm* pilgrimage

pélican [pelikɑ̃] *nm* pelican

pelisse [pəlis] *nf* fur-lined coat

pelle [pɛl] *nf* shovel; *(d'enfant)* spade; **p. à tarte** cake slice; *Fam* **à la p.** by the bucketload; *Fam* **ramasser** *ou* **prendre une p.** to fall flat on one's face ▪ **pelletée** *nf* shovelful ▪ **pelleteuse** *nf* mechanical shovel

pellicule [pelikyl] *nf (pour photos)* film; *(couche)* thin layer; **pellicules** *(de cheveux)* dandruff

pelote [pəlɔt] *nf (de laine)* ball; *(à épingles)* pincushion; *Sport* **p. basque** pelota

peloter [pəlɔte] *vt Fam* to grope

peloton [p(ə)lɔtɔ̃] *nm (de ficelle)* ball; *(de cyclistes)* pack; *Mil* platoon; **le p. de tête** the leaders; **p. d'exécution** firing squad

pelotonner [pəlɔtɔne] **se pelotonner** *upr* to curl up (into a ball)

pelouse [pəluz] *nf* lawn

peluche [pəlyʃ] *nf (tissu)* plush; **(jouet en) p.** soft toy; **chien en p.** furry dog; **peluches** *(de pull)* fluff, lint ▪ **pelucher** *vi* to pill

pelure [pəlyr] *nf (de légumes)* peelings; *(de fruits)* peel

pénal, -e, -aux, -ales [penal, -o] *adj* penal ▪ **pénaliser** *vt* to penalize ▪ **pénalité** *nf* penalty

penalty [penalti] *nm Football* penalty

penaud, -aude [pəno, -od] *adj* sheepish

penchant [pɑ̃ʃɑ̃] *nm (préférence)* penchant (**pour** for); *(tendance)* propensity (**pour** for)

pencher [pɑ̃ʃe] **1** *vt (objet)* to tilt; *(tête)* to lean **2** *vi (arbre)* to lean over; *Fig* **p. pour qch** to incline towards sth **3** **se pencher** *vpr* to lean over; **se p. par la fenêtre** to lean out of the window; **se p. sur qch** *(problème)* to examine sth ▪ **penché, -ée** *adj* leaning

pendable [pɑ̃dabl] *adj* **faire un tour p.** to play a wicked trick (**à qn** on sb)

pendaison [pɑ̃dɛzɔ̃] *nf* hanging

pendant¹ [pɑ̃dɑ̃] *prép (au cours de)* during; **p. la nuit** during the night; **p. deux mois** for two months; **p. tout le trajet** for the whole journey; **p. que...** while...

pendentif [pɑ̃dɑ̃tif] *nm (collier)* pendant

penderie [pɑ̃dri] *nf Br* wardrobe, *Am* closet

pendre [pɑ̃dr] **1** *vti* to hang (**à** from); **p. qn** to hang sb **2** **se pendre** *vpr (se suicider)* to hang oneself; *(se suspendre)* to hang (**à** from) ▪ **pendant², -ante 1** *adj* hanging; *(langue)* hanging out; *Fig (en attente)* pending **2** *nm* **p. (d'oreille)** drop earring; **le p. de** the companion piece to ▪ **pendu, -ue** *adj (objet)* hanging (**à** from); *Fam* **être p. au téléphone** to be never off the phone

pendule [pɑ̃dyl] **1** *nf* clock **2** *nm (balancier)* pendulum

pénétrer [penetre] **1** *vi* **p. dans** to enter; *(profondément)* to penetrate (into) **2** *vt (sujet: pluie)* to penetrate **3** **se pénétrer** *vpr* **se p. d'une idée** to become convinced of an idea ▪ **pénétrant, -ante** *adj (vent, froid)* piercing; *(esprit)* penetrating ▪ **pénétration** *nf* penetration

pénible [penibl] *adj (difficile)* difficult; *(douloureux)* painful, distressing; *(ennuyeux)* tiresome ▪ **péniblement** [-əmɑ̃] *adv* with difficulty

péniche [peniʃ] *nf* barge

pénicilline [penisilin] *nf* penicillin

péninsule [penɛ̃syl] *nf* peninsula

pénis [penis] *nm Anat* penis

pénitence [penitɑ̃s] *nf (punition)* punishment; *Rel (peine)* penance; *(regret)* penitence; **faire p.** to repent ▪ **pénitent, -ente** *nmf Rel* penitent

pénitencier [penitɑ̃sje] *nm* prison, *Am* penitentiary ▪ **pénitentiaire** *adj* **régime p.** prison system

pénombre [penɔ̃br] *nf* half-light

pense-bête [pɑ̃sbɛt] *(pl pense-bêtes) nm Fam* reminder

pensée [pɑ̃se] *nf* (**a**) *(idée)* thought; **à la p. de**

faire qch at the thought of doing sth (**b**) *(fleur)* pansy

penser [pãse] **1** *vi (réfléchir)* to think (**à** *or* about); **p. à qn/qch** to think of *or* about sb/sth; **p. à faire qch** *(ne pas oublier)* to remember to do sth; **p. à tout** to think of everything; **penses-tu!** what an idea! **2** *vt (estimer)* to think (**que** that); *(concevoir)* to think out; **je pensais rester** I was thinking of staying; **je pense réussir** I hope to succeed; **que pensez-vous de...?** what do you think of *or* about...?; **p. du bien de qn/qch** to think highly of sb/sth ▪ **pensant, -ante** *adj* thinking; **bien p.** orthodox ▪ **penseur** *nm* thinker ▪ **pensif, -ive** *adj* thoughtful, pensive

pension [pãsjõ] *nf* (**a**) *(école)* boarding school; **mettre un enfant en p.** to send a child to boarding school (**b**) *(hôtel)* **p. de famille** boarding house; **p. complète** *Br* full board, *Am* American plan (**c**) *(allocation)* pension; **p. alimentaire** maintenance, alimony ▪ **pensionnaire** *nmf (élève, résident)* boarder ▪ **pensionnat** *nm* boarding school ▪ **pensionné, -ée** *nmf* pensioner

> Il faut noter que le nom anglais **pensioner** est un faux ami. Il signifie le plus souvent **retraité**.

pentagone [pɛ̃tagɔn] *nm Am Mil* **le P.** the Pentagon

pente [pãt] *nf* slope; **être en p.** to be sloping; *Fig* **être sur une mauvaise p.** to be going downhill ▪ **pentu, -ue** *adj* sloping

Pentecôte [pãtkot] *nf Rel Br* Whitsun, *Am* Pentecost

pénurie [penyri] *nf* shortage (**de** of)

pépé [pepe] *nm* grandpa

pépère [pepɛr] *Fam* **1** *nm* grand(d)ad **2** *adj (lieu)* quiet; *(emploi)* cushy

pépier [pepje] *vi* to cheep, to chirp

pépin [pepɛ̃] *nm (de fruit) Br* pip, *Am* seed, pit; *Fam (ennui)* hitch; *Fam (parapluie)* umbrella, *Br* brolly

pépinière [pepinjɛr] *nf (pour plantes)* nursery; *Fig (école)* training ground (**de** for)

pépite [pepit] *nf (d'or)* nugget; **p. de chocolat** chocolate chip

péquenaud, -aude [pekno, -od] *nmf Fam* peasant

perçant, -ante [pɛrsã, -ãt] *adj (cri, froid)* piercing; *(vue)* sharp

percée [pɛrse] *nf (ouverture)* opening; *Mil, Sport & Tech* breakthrough

perce-neige [pɛrsənɛʒ] *nm ou f inv* snowdrop

perce-oreille [pɛrsɔrɛj] *(pl perce-oreilles) nm* earwig

percepteur [pɛrseptœr] *nm* tax collector ▪ **perceptible** *adj* perceptible (**à** to) ▪ **perception** *nf* (**a**) *(bureau)* tax office;

(d'impôt) collection (**b**) *(sensation)* perception

percer [pɛrse] **1** *vt (trouer)* to pierce; *(avec une perceuse)* to drill; *(trou, ouverture)* to make; *(abcès)* to lance; *(secret)* to uncover; *(mystère)* to solve; **p. une dent** *(bébé)* to cut a tooth; **p. qch à jour** to see through sth **2** *vi (soleil)* to break through; *(abcès)* to burst; *(acteur)* to make a name for oneself ▪ **perceuse** *nf* drill

percevoir* [pɛrsəvwar] *vt* (**a**) *(sensation)* to perceive; *(son)* to hear (**b**) *(impôt)* to collect

perche [pɛrʃ] *nf* (**a**) *(bâton)* pole; *Sport* **saut à la p.** pole vaulting; *Fig* **tendre la p. à qn** to throw sb a line; *Fam* **une grande p.** *(personne)* a beanpole (**b**) *(poisson)* perch ▪ **perchiste** *nmf Sport* pole vaulter

percher [pɛrʃe] **1** *vi (oiseau)* to perch; *(volailles)* to roost **2** *vt Fam (placer)* to perch **3** **se percher** *vpr (oiseau, personne)* to perch ▪ **perchoir** *nm* perch; *(de volailles)* roost; *Fam Pol* = seat of the president of the "Assemblée nationale"

percolateur [pɛrkɔlatœr] *nm* percolator

percussion [pɛrkysjõ] *nf Mus* percussion

percutant, -ante [pɛrkytã, -ãt] *adj Fig* forceful

percuter [pɛrkyte] **1** *vt (véhicule)* to crash into **2** *vi* **p. contre** to crash into **3** **se percuter** *vpr* to crash into each other

perdant, -ante [pɛrdã, -ãt] **1** *adj* losing **2** *nmf* loser

perdition [pɛrdisjõ] **en perdition** *adv (navire)* in distress

perdre [pɛrdr] **1** *vt* to lose; *(habitude)* to get out of; **p. qn/qch de vue** to lose sight of sb/sth; **il a perdu son père** he lost his father; **sa passion du jeu l'a perdu** his passion for gambling was his undoing **2** *vi* to lose; **j'y perds** I lose out **3** **se perdre** *vpr (s'égarer)* to get lost; *(disparaître)* to die out; **se p. dans les détails** to get lost in details; *Fig* **je m'y perds** I'm lost; *Fig* **nous nous sommes perdus de vue** we lost touch ▪ **perdu, -ue** *adj (égaré)* lost; *(gaspillé)* wasted; *(malade)* finished; *(lieu)* out-of-the-way; **à ses moments perdus** in one's spare time; **c'est du temps p.** it's a waste of time

perdrix [pɛrdri] *nf* partridge

père [pɛr] *nm* father; **de p. en fils** from father to son; **Dupont p.** Dupont senior; *Fam* **le p. Jean** old John; *Rel* **le p. Martin** Father Martin; *Rel* **mon p.** father; **p. de famille** father

péremption [perãpsjõ] *nf* **date de p.** use-by date

péremptoire [perãptwar] *adj* peremptory

perfection [pɛrfɛksjõ] *nf* perfection; **à la p.** to perfection

perfectionner [pɛrfɛksjɔne] **1** *vt* to improve, to perfect **2** **se perfectionner** *vpr* **se p. en anglais** to improve *or* perfect one's English ▪ **perfectionné, -ée** *adj* advanced ▪ **perfectionnement** *nm* improvement (**de** in; **par rapport à** on); **cours de p.** proficiency course

perfectionniste [pɛrfɛksjɔnist] *nmf* perfectionist

perfide [pɛrfid] *adj* perfidious ▪ **perfidie** *nf Littéraire (déloyauté)* perfidiousness

perforer [pɛrfɔre] *vt (pneu, intestin)* to perforate; *(billet)* to punch; **carte perforée** punch card ▪ **perforation** *nf* perforation; *(trou)* punched hole ▪ **perforatrice** *nf (pour papier)* (hole) punch ▪ **perforeuse** *nf* (hole) punch

performance [pɛrfɔrmɑ̃s] *nf* performance; *Fig (exploit)* achievement ▪ **performant, -ante** *adj* highly efficient

perfusion [pɛrfyzjɔ̃] *nf* drip; **être sous p.** to be on a drip

péricliter [periklite] *vi* to collapse

péridurale [peridyral] *adj f & nf (anesthésie)* p. epidural; **accoucher sous p.** to give birth under an epidural

péril [peril] *nm* danger, peril; **à tes risques et périls** at your own risk; **mettre qch en p.** to endanger sth ▪ **périlleux, -euse** *adj* dangerous, perilous

périmer [perime] *vi,* **se périmer** *vpr* **laisser qch (se) p.** to allow sth to expire ▪ **périmé, -ée** *adj (billet)* expired; *(nourriture)* past its sell-by date

périmètre [perimɛtr] *nm* perimeter

période [perjɔd] *nf* period; **p. d'essai** trial period ▪ **périodique 1** *adj* periodic **2** *nm (revue)* periodical

péripétie [peripesi] *nf Littéraire* event

périphérie [periferi] *nf (limite)* periphery; *(banlieue)* outskirts

périphérique [periferik] **1** *adj* peripheral; **radio p.** = radio station broadcasting from outside France **2** *nm & adj (boulevard)* p. *Br* ring road, *Am* beltway ▪ **périphériques** *nmpl Ordinat* peripherals

périphrase [perifrɑz] *nf* circumlocution

périple [peripl] *nm* trip, tour

périr [perir] *vi* to perish ▪ **périssable** *adj (denrée)* perishable

périscope [periskɔp] *nm* periscope

perle [pɛrl] *nf (bijou)* pearl; *(de bois, de verre)* bead; *Fig (personne)* gem; *Ironique (erreur)* howler ▪ **perler** *vi (sueur)* to form in beads

permanent, -ente [pɛrmanɑ̃, -ɑ̃t] **1** *adj* permanent; *Cin (spectacle)* continuous; *(comité)* standing **2** *nf (coiffure)* **permanente** perm ▪ **permanence** *nf* permanence; *(salle d'étude)* study room; *(service, bureau)* duty office; **être de p.** to be on duty; **en p.** permanently

perméable [pɛrmeabl] *adj* permeable (**à** to)

permettre* [pɛrmɛtr] **1** *vt* to allow, to permit; **p. à qn de faire qch** to allow sb to do sth; **permettez!** excuse me!; **vous permettez?** may I? **2 se permettre** *vpr* **se p. qch** to allow oneself sth; **se p. de faire qch** to take the

liberty of doing sth; **je ne peux pas me p.** I can't afford it

permis, -ise [pɛrmi, -iz] **1** *adj* allowed, permitted **2** *nm Br* licence, *Am* license, permit; **p. de conduire** *Br* driving licence, *Am* driver's license; **passer son p. de conduire** to take one's driving test; **p. de construire** planning permission; **p. de séjour** residence permit; **p. de travail** work permit

permission [pɛrmisjɔ̃] *nf* permission; *Mil* leave; **en p.** on leave; **demander la p.** to ask permission (**de faire** to do)

permuter [pɛrmyte] **1** *vt (lettres, chiffres)* to transpose **2** *vi* to exchange posts ▪ **permutation** *nf (de lettres, de chiffres)* transposition

pernicieux, -ieuse [pɛrnisjø, -jøz] *adj* pernicious

pérorer [perɔre] *vi Péj* to hold forth

Pérou [peru] *nm* **le P.** Peru

perpendiculaire [pɛrpɑ̃dikylɛr] *adj & nf* perpendicular (**à** to)

perpétrer [pɛrpetre] *vt* to perpetrate

perpétuel, -uelle [pɛrpetɥɛl] *adj* perpetual; *(membre)* permanent ▪ **perpétuellement** *adv* perpetually ▪ **perpétuer** *vt* to perpetuate ▪ **perpétuité** *adv* **à p.** in perpetuity; **condamnation à p.** life sentence

perplexe [pɛrplɛks] *adj* perplexed, puzzled ▪ **perplexité** *nf* perplexity

perquisition [pɛrkizisjɔ̃] *nf* search ▪ **perquisitionner** *vi* to make a search

perron [pɛrɔ̃] *nm* steps *(leading to a building)*

perroquet [pɛrɔke] *nm* parrot

perruche [pɛryʃ] *nf Br* budgerigar, *Am* parakeet

perruque [peryk] *nf* wig

pers [pɛr] *adj m Littéraire* blue-green

persan, -ane [pɛrsɑ̃, -an] **1** *adj* Persian **2** *nm (langue)* Persian

persécuter [pɛrsekyte] *vt* to persecute ▪ **persécution** *nf* persecution

persévérer [pɛrsevere] *vi* to persevere (**dans** in) ▪ **persévérance** *nf* perseverance ▪ **persévérant, -ante** *adj* persevering

persienne [pɛrsjɛn] *nf* shutter

persil [pɛrsi] *nm* parsley ▪ **persillé, -ée** *adj (plat)* sprinkled with parsley

Persique [pɛrsik] *adj* **le golfe P.** the Persian Gulf

persister [pɛrsiste] *vi* to persist (**à faire** in doing; **dans qch** in sth) ▪ **persistance** *nf* persistence ▪ **persistant, -ante** *adj* persistent; **à feuilles persistantes** evergreen

personnage [pɛrsɔnaʒ] *nm (de fiction, individu)* character; *(personnalité)* important person; **p. célèbre** celebrity; **p. officiel** VIP

personnaliser [pɛrsɔnalize] *vt* to personalize; *(voiture, ordinateur)* to customize

personnalité [pɛrsɔnalite] *nf (caractère, personnage)* personality; **avoir de la p.** to have lots of personality

personne [pɛrsɔn] **1** *nf* person; **deux personnes** two people; **grande p.** grown-up, adult; **p. âgée** elderly person; **les personnes âgées** the elderly; **en p.** in person; **être bien de sa p.** to be good-looking; **être content de sa petite p.** to be pleased with oneself **2** *pron indéfini (de négation)* **(ne...) p.** nobody, no one; **je ne vois p.** I don't see anybody *or* anyone; **je ne saura** nobody *or* no one will know; **mieux que p.** better than anybody *or* anyone

personnel, -elle [pɛrsɔnɛl] **1** *adj* personal; *(joueur, jeu)* individualistic **2** *nm (de firme, d'école)* staff; *(d'usine)* workforce; **service du p.** personnel (department); **manquer de p.** to be understaffed; **p. au sol** ground personnel ▪ **personnellement** *adv* personally

personnifier [pɛrsɔnifje] *vt* to personify ▪ **personnification** *nf* personification

perspective [pɛrspɛktiv] *nf (de dessin)* perspective; *(idée)* prospect (**de** of); *Fig (point de vue)* viewpoint; *Fig* **en p.** in prospect; *Fig* **à la p. de faire qch** at the prospect of doing sth; **perspectives d'avenir** future prospects

perspicace [pɛrspikas] *adj* shrewd ▪ **perspicacité** *nf* shrewdness

persuader [pɛrsɥade] *vt* **p. qn (de qch)** to persuade sb (of sth); **p. qn de faire qch** to persuade sb to do sth; **être persuadé de qch/que...** to be convinced of sth/that... ▪ **persuasif, -ive** *adj* persuasive ▪ **persuasion** *nf* persuasion

perte [pɛrt] *nf* loss; *(destruction)* ruin; **une p. de temps** a waste of time; **à p. de vue** as far as the eye can see; **en pure p.** to no purpose; **vendre qch à p.** to sell sth at a loss; *Fig* **courir à sa p.** to be heading for disaster; **vouloir la p. de qn** to seek sb's destruction; **p. sèche** dead loss

pertinent, -ente [pɛrtinɑ̃, -ɑ̃t] *adj* relevant, pertinent ▪ **pertinemment** [-amɑ̃] *adv* **savoir qch** to know sth for a fact ▪ **pertinence** *nf* relevance, pertinence

perturber [pɛrtyrbe] *vt (trafic, cérémonie)* to disrupt; *(personne)* to disturb ▪ **perturbateur, -trice 1** *adj* disruptive **2** *nmf* troublemaker ▪ **perturbation** *nf* disruption; **p. atmosphérique** atmospheric disturbance

péruvien, -ienne [peryvjɛ̃, -jɛn] **1** *adj* Peruvian **2** *nmf* **P., Péruvienne** Peruvian

pervenche [pɛrvɑ̃ʃ] *nf (plante)* periwinkle; *Fam (contractuelle) Br* (woman) traffic warden, *Am* meter maid

pervers, -erse [pɛrvɛr, -ɛrs] **1** *adj* perverse **2** *nmf* pervert ▪ **perversion** *nf* perversion ▪ **perversité** *nf* perversity ▪ **pervertir** *vt* to pervert

pesage [pəzaʒ] *nm Sport (vérification)* weigh-in; *(lieu)* weighing room

pesant, -ante [pəzɑ̃, -ɑ̃t] **1** *adj* heavy, weighty **2** *nm* **valoir son p. d'or** to be worth one's weight in gold ▪ **pesamment** [-amɑ̃] *adv* heavily ▪ **pesanteur** *nf* heaviness; *Phys* gravity

pesée [pəze] *nf* weighing; *Boxe* weigh-in; *(pression)* force

peser [pəze] **1** *vt* to weigh; **p. le pour et le contre** to weigh up the pros and the cons; **p. ses mots** to weigh one's words; *Fig* **tout bien pesé** all things considered **2** *vi* to weigh; **p. 2 kilos** to weigh 2 kilos; **p. lourd** to be heavy; *Fig (argument)* to carry weight; **p. sur** *(appuyer)* to press on; *(influer)* to bear upon; **p. sur qn** *(menace)* to hang over sb; **p. sur l'estomac** to lie heavy on the stomach; *Fam* **elle pèse 20 millions** she's worth 20 million ▪ **pèse-bébé** *(pl* **pèse-bébés)** *nm* baby scales ▪ **pèse-personne** *(pl* **pèse-personnes)** *nm* (bathroom) scales

pessimisme [pesimism] *nm* pessimism ▪ **pessimiste 1** *adj* pessimistic **2** *nmf* pessimist

peste [pɛst] *nf (maladie)* plague; *Fig (personne)* pest

> Il faut noter que le nom anglais **pest** est un faux ami. Il ne désigne jamais une maladie.

pester [pɛste] *vi* **p. contre qn/qch** to curse sb/sth

pestilentiel, -ielle [pɛstilɑ̃sjɛl] *adj* stinking

pétale [petal] *nm* petal

pétanque [petɑ̃k] *nf (jeu)* ≃ bowls

pétarades [petarad] *nfpl (de véhicule)* backfiring ▪ **pétarader** *vi (véhicule)* to backfire

pétard [petar] *nm (feu d'artifice)* firecracker, *Br* banger; *Fam (pistolet)* shooter

péter [pete] *Fam* **1** *vt (casser)* to bust; **p. la forme** to be full of beans; **p. les plombs** to blow one's top **2** *vi (exploser)* to blow up; *(casser)* to bust; *(personne)* to fart ▪ **pétante** *adj* f *Fam* **à une heure p.** at one o'clock on the dot

pétiller [petije] *vi (yeux, vin)* to sparkle ▪ **pétillant, -ante** *adj (eau, vin, yeux)* sparkling

petit, -ite [pəti, -it] **1** *adj* small, little; *(de taille, distance, séjour)* short; *(bruit, coup, rhume)* slight; *(somme)* small; *(accident)* minor; *(mesquin)* petty; **tout p.** tiny; **un p. Français** a French boy; **une bonne petite employée** a good little worker; **mon p. frère** my little brother; **Fam se faire tout p.** to make oneself inconspicuous; **c'est une petite nature** he's/she's a weak sort of person; *Scol* **les petites classes** the lower classes **2** *nmf (little)* boy, f *(little)* girl; *(personne)* small person; *Scol* junior; **petits** *(d'animal)* young; *(de chien)* pups; *(de chat)* kittens **3** *adv* **écrire p.** to write small; **p. à p.** little by little ▪ **petit-beurre** *(pl* **petits-beurre)** *nm Br* butter biscuit, *Am* butter cookie ▪ **petit-bourgeois, petite-bourgeoise** *(mpl* **petits-bourgeois**, *fpl* **petites-bourgeoises)** *adj Péj* lower middle-class ▪ **petite-fille** *(pl* **petites-filles)** *nf* granddaughter ▪ **petitesse** *nf (de taille)* smallness; *(mesquinerie)* pettiness ▪ **petit-fils** *(pl petits-fils)* nm grandson ▪ **petits-enfants** nmpl grandchildren ▪ **petit-suisse** *(pl petits-suisses)* nm = small dessert of thick fromage frais

pétition [petisjɔ̃] *nf* petition

pétrifier [petrifje] *vt* to petrify

pétrin [petrɛ̃] nm *Fam* **être dans le p.** to be in a mess, *Br* to be in a pickle

pétrir [petrir] *vt* to knead

pétrole [petrɔl] nm oil, petroleum; **p. lampant** *Br* paraffin, *Am* kerosine ▪ **pétrolier, -ière** 1 *adj* **industrie pétrolière** oil industry 2 nm oil tanker ▪ **pétrolifère** *adj* **gisement p.** oilfield

> Il faut noter que le nom anglais **petrol** est un faux ami. Il signifie **essence**.

pétulant, -ante [petylɑ̃, -ɑ̃t] *adj* exuberant

> Il faut noter que l'adjectif anglais **petulant** est un faux ami. Il signifie le plus souvent **irascible**.

pétunia [petynja] nm petunia

peu [pø] 1 *adv (avec un verbe)* not much; *(avec un adjectif, un adverbe)* not very; *(un petit nombre)* few; **elle mange p.** she doesn't eat much; **p. intéressant/souvent** not very interesting/often; **p. ont compris** few understood; **p. de sel/de temps** not much salt/time, little salt/time; **p. de gens/de livres** few people/books; **p. à p.** little by little, gradually; **à p. près** more or less; **p. après/avant** shortly after/before; **sous p.** shortly; **pour p. que...** *(+ subjunctive)* if by chance... 2 nm **un p.** a little, a bit; **un p. grand** a bit big; **un p. de fromage** a little cheese, a bit of cheese; **un p. de sucre** a bit of sugar, a little sugar; **un (tout) petit p.** a (tiny) little bit; **le p. de fromage que j'ai** the little cheese I have; **reste encore un p.** stay a little longer; **pour un p. je l'aurais jeté dehors** I very nearly threw him out

peuplade [pœplad] *nf* tribe

peuple [pœpl] nm *(nation, citoyens)* people; **les gens du p.** ordinary people

peupler [pœple] *vt (habiter)* to inhabit ▪ **peuplé, -ée** *adj (région)* inhabited (**de** by); **très/peu p.** highly/sparsely populated; *Fig* **p. de qch** full of sth ▪ **peuplement** [-əmɑ̃] nm *(action)* populating; **zone de p.** area of population

peuplier [pøplije] nm *(arbre, bois)* poplar

peur [pœr] *nf* fear; **avoir p.** to be afraid or frightened (**de qn/qch** of sb/sth; **de faire qch** to do sth or of doing sth); **faire p. à qn** to frighten or scare sb; **de p. qu'il ne parte** for fear that he would leave; **de p. de faire qch** for fear of doing sth ▪ **peureux, -euse** *adj* easily frightened

peut [pø] *voir* **pouvoir** 1

peut-être [pøtɛtr] *adv* perhaps, maybe; **p. qu'il viendra, p. viendra-t-il** perhaps or maybe he'll come; **p. que oui** perhaps; **p. que non** perhaps not

peuvent, peux [pœv, pø] *voir* **pouvoir** 1

phallique [falik] *adj* phallic ▪ **phallocrate** nm *Péj* male chauvinist (pig)

pharaon [faraɔ̃] nm *Hist* Pharaoh

phare [far] 1 nm *(pour bateaux)* lighthouse; *(de véhicule)* headlight; **faire un appel de phares** to flash one's lights 2 *adj* **épreuve-p.** star event

pharmacie [farmasi] *nf (magasin)* Br chemist's shop, *Am* drugstore; *(science)* pharmacy; *(armoire)* medicine cabinet ▪ **pharmaceutique** *adj* pharmaceutical ▪ **pharmacien, -ienne** nmf *Br* chemist, pharmacist, *Am* druggist

pharynx [farɛ̃ks] nm pharynx ▪ **pharyngite** *nf Méd* pharyngitis

phase [faz] *nf* phase; *Méd* **cancer en p. terminale** terminal cancer; *Fig* **être en p.** to see eye to eye

phénomène [fenɔmɛn] nm phenomenon; *Fam (personne)* character ▪ **phénoménal, -e, -aux, -ales** *adj Fam* phenomenal

philanthrope [filɑ̃trɔp] nmf philanthropist ▪ **philanthropique** *adj* philanthropic

philatélie [filateli] *nf* stamp collecting, philately ▪ **philatéliste** nmf stamp collector, philatelist

philharmonique [filarmɔnik] *adj* philharmonic

Philippines [filipin] *nfpl* **les P.** the Philippines

philosophe [filɔzɔf] 1 nmf philosopher 2 *adj* philosophical ▪ **philosopher** *vi* to philosophize (**sur** about) ▪ **philosophie** *nf* philosophy ▪ **philosophique** *adj* philosophical

philtre [filtr] nm love potion

phobie [fɔbi] *nf* phobia; **avoir la p. de qch** to have a phobia of sth

phonétique [fɔnetik] 1 *adj* phonetic 2 *nf* phonetics *(sing)*

phonographe [fɔnɔɡraf] nm *Br* gramophone, *Am* phonograph

phoque [fɔk] nm *(animal)* seal

phosphate [fɔsfat] nm *Chim* phosphate

phosphore [fɔsfɔr] nm *Chim* phosphorus ▪ **phosphorescent, -ente** *adj* phosphorescent

photo [fɔto] 1 *nf (cliché)* photo; *(art)* photography; **prendre une p. de qn/qch, prendre qn/qch en p.** to take a photo of sb/sth; *Fam* **il veut ma p.?** who does he think he's staring at?; **p. d'identité** ID photo; **p. de mode** fashion photo 2 *adj inv* **appareil p.** camera ▪ **photogénique** *adj* photogenic ▪ **photographe** nmf photographer ▪ **photographie** *nf (art)* photography; *(cliché)* photograph ▪ **photo-**

graphier *vt* to photograph; **se faire p.** to have one's photo taken ▪ **photographique** *adj* photographic

> Il faut noter que le nom anglais **photograph** est un faux ami. Il signifie **photographie**, **cliché**.

photocopie [fɔtɔkɔpi] *nf* photocopy ▪ **photocopier** *vt* to photocopy ▪ **photocopieur** *nm*, **photocopieuse** *nf* photocopier
Photomaton® [fɔtɔmatɔ̃] *nm* photo booth
phrase [fraz] *nf* sentence

> Il faut noter que le nom anglais **phrase** est un faux ami. Il signifie **expression**.

physicien, -ienne [fizisjɛ̃, -jɛn] *nmf* physicist

> Il faut noter que le nom anglais **physician** est un faux ami. Il signifie **médecin**.

physiologie [fizjɔlɔʒi] *nf* physiology ▪ **physiologique** *adj* physiological
physionomie [fizjɔnɔmi] *nf* face
physique [fizik] **1** *adj* physical **2** *nm (de personne)* physique **3** *nf (science)* physics *(sing)* ▪ **physiquement** *adv* physically
phytothérapie [fitɔterapi] *nf* herbal medicine
piaffer [pjafe] *vi (cheval)* to paw the ground; *Fig* **p. d'impatience** to fidget impatiently
piailler [pjaje] *vi (oiseau)* to cheep; *Fam (enfant)* to squeal
piano [pjano] *nm* piano; **jouer du p.** to play the piano; **p. droit/à queue** upright/grand piano ▪ **pianiste** *nmf* pianist ▪ **pianoter** *vi* **sur qch** *(table)* to drum one's fingers on sth
piaule [pjol] *nf Fam (chambre)* pad
PIB [peibe] *nm (abrév* **produit intérieur brut)** *nm Écon* GDP
pic [pik] *nm (cime)* peak; *(outil)* pick(axe); *(oiseau)* woodpecker; **couler à p.** to sink like a stone; **tomber à p.** *(falaise)* to go straight down; *Fam* to come at the right moment; **p. à glace** ice pick
pichenette [piʃnɛt] *nf* flick
pichet [piʃɛ] *nm Br* jug, *Am* pitcher
pickpocket [pikpɔkɛt] *nm* pickpocket
picoler [pikɔle] *vi Fam* to booze ▪ **picoleur, -euse** *nmf Fam* boozer
picorer [pikɔre] *vt* to peck
picoter [pikɔte] *vt* **j'ai la gorge qui (me) picote** I've got a tickle in my throat; **la fumée lui picotait les yeux** the smoke was stinging his eyes ▪ **picotement** *nm (de gorge)* tickling; *(dans les yeux)* stinging
pie [pi] **1** *nf (oiseau)* magpie; *Fam (personne)* chatterbox **2** *adj inv (cheval)* piebald
pièce [pjɛs] *nf (de maison)* room; *(morceau, objet)* piece; *(de pantalon)* patch; *(écrit de dossier)* document; **p. (de monnaie)** coin; **p. (de**

théâtre) play; **5 euros (la) p.** 5 euros each; **travailler à la p.** to do piecework; **mettre qch en pièces** to tear sth to pieces; **p. à conviction** exhibit *(in criminal case)*; **p. d'eau** ornamental lake; *(petite)* ornamental pond; **p. d'identité** proof of identity; **p. montée** = large tiered wedding cake; **pièces détachées** *ou* **de rechange** spare parts; **pièces justificatives** supporting documents
pied [pje] *nm (de personne)* foot *(pl* feet); *(de lit, d'arbre, de colline)* foot; *(de meuble)* leg; *(de verre, de lampe)* base; *(d'appareil photo)* stand; *(de salade)* head; **à p.** on foot; **aller à p.** to walk, to go on foot; **au p. de** at the foot *or* bottom of; *Fig* **au p. de la lettre** literally; **sur p.** *(personne)* up and about; **sur un p. d'égalité** on an equal footing; **sur le p. de guerre** on a war footing; *Fam* **comme un p.** dreadfully; **avoir p.** to be within one's depth; **avoir le p. marin** to be a good sailor; **avoir bon p. bon œil** to be hale and hearty; **faire un p. de nez à qn** to thumb one's nose at sb; **mettre qch sur p.** to set sth up; **attendre qn de p. ferme** to be ready and waiting for sb; **être à p. d'œuvre** to be ready to get on with the job; **faire qch au p. levé** to do sth at a moment's notice; *Fam* **ça lui fera les pieds!** that will serve him/her right!; *Fam* **c'est le p.!** it's fantastic! ▪ **pied-noir** *(pl* **pieds-noirs)** *nmf Fam* = French settler in North Africa
piédestal, -aux [pjedɛstal, -o] *nm* pedestal
piège [pjɛʒ] *nm (pour animal)* & *Fig* trap ▪ **piéger** *vt (animal)* to trap; *(voiture)* to booby-trap; **voiture/lettre piégée** car/letter bomb
piercing [pirsiŋ] *nm (body)* piercing
pierre [pjɛr] *nf* stone; *(de bijou)* gem, stone; **maison en p.** stone house; **geler à p. fendre** to freeze hard; *Fig* **faire d'une p. deux coups** to kill two birds with one stone; **p. à briquet** flint *(for lighter)*; **p. d'achoppement** stumbling block; **p. précieuse** precious stone, gem ▪ **pierreries** *nfpl* gems, precious stones ▪ **pierreux, -euse** *adj* stony
piété [pjete] *nf* piety
piétiner [pjetine] **1** *vt* **p. qch** *(en trépignant)* to stamp on sth; *(en marchant)* to trample on sth **2** *vi (ne pas avancer)* to stand around; **p. d'impatience** to stamp one's feet impatiently
piéton, -onne [pjetɔ̃, -ɔn] **1** *nmf* pedestrian **2** *adj* **rue p.** pedestrian(ized) street; **zone p.** pedestrian precinct ▪ **piétonnier, -ière** *adj* **rue p.** pedestrian(ized) street; **zone p.** pedestrian precinct
piètre [pjɛtr] *adj Littéraire (compagnon)* wretched; *(excuse)* paltry
pieu, -x [pjø] *nm (piquet)* post, stake; *Fam (lit)* bed; **aller au p.** to hit the sack
pieuvre [pjœvr] *nf* octopus
pieux, pieuse [pjø, pjøz] *adj* pious

pif [pif] *nm Fam (nez)* conk; **faire qch au p.** to do sth by guesswork ▪ **pifomètre** *nm Fam* **faire qch au p.** to do sth by guesswork

pif(f)er [pife] *vt Fam* **je ne peux pas le p.** I can't stomach him

pigeon [piʒɔ̃] *nm* pigeon; *Fam (personne)* sucker; **p. voyageur** carrier pigeon

piger [piʒe] *Fam* **1** *vt (comprendre)* to get **2** *vi (comprendre)* to get it

pigment [pigmɑ̃] *nm* pigment ▪ **pigmentation** *nf* pigmentation

pignon¹ [piɲɔ̃] *nm (de mur)* gable; *Fig* **avoir p. sur rue** to be of some standing

pignon² [piɲɔ̃] *nm (graine)* pine nut

pile [pil] **1** *nf* (**a**) **p. (électrique)** battery; **radio à piles** battery radio (**b**) *(tas)* pile; **en p.** in a pile (**c**) *(de pièce)* **p. (ou face)?** heads (or tails)?; **jouer à p. ou face** to toss up **2** *adv Fam* **s'arrêter p.** to stop dead; *Fam* **à deux heures p.** at two on the dot

piler [pile] **1** *vt (broyer)* to crush; *(amandes)* to grind **2** *vi Fam (en voiture)* to slam on the brakes ▪ **pilonner** *vt (bombarder)* to bombard

pilier [pilje] *nm* pillar

piller [pije] *vt* to loot, to pillage ▪ **pillage** *nm* looting, pillaging ▪ **pillard, -arde** *nmf* looter

pilon [pilɔ̃] *nm (de poulet)* drumstick

pilote [pilɔt] **1** *nmf (d'avion, de bateau)* pilot; *(de voiture)* driver; **p. automatique** automatic pilot; **p. de chasse** fighter pilot; **p. d'essai** test pilot; **p. de ligne** airline pilot **2** *adj* **usine(-) p.** pilot factory ▪ **pilotage** *nm* piloting; **p. automatique** automatic piloting ▪ **piloter** *vt (avion)* to fly, to pilot; *(bateau)* to pilot; *(voiture)* to drive; *Fig* **p. qn** to show sb around

pilotis [pilɔti] *nmpl* **construit sur p.** built on piles

pilule [pilyl] *nf* pill; **prendre la p.** to be on the pill; **arrêter la p.** to come off the pill; **p. abortive** abortion pill; **p. du lendemain** morning-after pill

piment [pimɑ̃] *nm* chilli; *Fig* spice ▪ **pimenté, -ée** *adj (plat) & Fig* spicy

pimpant, -ante [pɛ̃pɑ̃, -ɑ̃t] *adj* smart

pin [pɛ̃] *nm (arbre, bois)* pine; **pomme de p.** pine cone; *(de sapin)* fir cone

pinacle [pinakl] *nm* **être au p.** to be at the top

pinailler [pinaje] *vi Fam* to nitpick (**sur** over)

pinard [pinar] *nm Fam (vin)* wine

pince [pɛ̃s] *nf (outil)* pliers; *(sur vêtement)* dart; *(de crustacé)* pincer; *Fam* **serrer la p. à qn** to shake sb's hand; *Fam* **à pinces** on foot; **p. à cheveux** hair clip; **p. à épiler** tweezers; **p. à linge** (clothes) *Br* peg *or Am* pin; **p. à sucre** sugar tongs; **p. à vélo** bicycle clip

pinceau, -x [pɛ̃so] *nm* (paint)brush; *Fam* **s'emmêler les pinceaux** to get all muddled up

pincer [pɛ̃se] **1** *vt* to pinch; *(cordes d'un instrument)* to pluck; *Fam* **p. qn** *(arrêter)* to catch sb; *Fam* **se faire p.** to get caught **2 se pincer** *vpr* **se p. le doigt** to get one's finger caught (**dans** in); **se p. le nez** to hold one's nose ▪ **pincé, -ée** *adj (air)* stiff; *(sourire)* tight-lipped ▪ **pincée** *nf* pinch (**de** of) ▪ **pince-sans-rire** *nmf inv* person with a dry sense of humour ▪ **pincettes** *nfpl (à feu)* (fire) tongs; *(d'horloger)* tweezers; *Fig* **il n'est pas à prendre avec des p.** he's like a bear with a sore head

pinède [pinɛd] *nf* pine forest

pingouin [pɛ̃gwɛ̃] *nm* auk; *(manchot)* penguin

ping-pong [piŋpɔ̃g] *nm* ping-pong, table tennis

pingre [pɛ̃gr] *adj* stingy

pin's [pinz] *nm inv* badge

pinson [pɛ̃sɔ̃] *nm* chaffinch

pintade [pɛ̃tad] *nf* guinea fowl

pinter [pɛ̃te] **se pinter** *vpr très Fam* to get trashed *or* wasted

pin-up [pinœp] *nf inv* pin-up

pioche [pjɔʃ] *nf (outil)* pick(axe); *Cartes* stock, pile ▪ **piocher** *vt (creuser)* to dig (with a pick); **p. une carte** to draw a card (from the pack)

pion [pjɔ̃] *nm (au jeu de dames)* piece; *Échecs & Fig* pawn; *Fam (surveillant)* supervisor *(paid to supervise pupils outside class hours)*

pionnier [pjɔnje] *nm* pioneer

pipe [pip] *nf (de fumeur)* pipe; **fumer la p.** to smoke a pipe

pipeau, -x [pipo] *nm (flûte)* pipe

pipelette [piplɛt] *nf Fam* gossip

piper [pipe] *vt* **ne pas p. mot** to keep mum

pipi [pipi] *nm Fam* **faire p.** to pee

pique [pik] **1** *nm Cartes (couleur)* spades **2** *nf (allusion)* cutting remark; *(arme)* pike

pique-assiette [pikasjet] *(pl* **pique-assiettes**) *nmf Fam* scrounger

pique-nique [piknik] *(pl* **pique-niques**) *nm* picnic ▪ **pique-niquer** *vi* to picnic

piquer [pike] **1** *vt (percer)* to prick; *(langue, yeux)* to sting; *(sujet: moustique)* to bite; *(coudre)* to stitch; *Fam (voler)* to pinch; **p. qch dans** *(enfoncer)* to stick sth into; **la fumée me pique les yeux** the smoke is making my eyes sting; *Fam* **p. qn** *(faire une piqûre à)* to give sb an injection; **faire p. un chien** to have a dog put to sleep; *Fig* **p. qn au vif** to cut sb to the quick; **p. la curiosité de qn** to arouse sb's curiosity; *Fam* **p. une colère** to fly into a rage; *Fam* **p. une crise (de nerfs)** to throw a fit; *Fam* **p. une tête** to dive; *Fam* **p. un cent mètres** to sprint off **2** *vi (avion)* to dive; *(moutarde)* to be hot; *Fig* **p. du nez** *(s'assoupir)* to nod off **3 se piquer** *vpr* to prick oneself; *Fam (se droguer)* to shoot up; **se p. au doigt** to prick one's finger; **se p. au jeu** to get into it; *Littéraire* **se p. de faire qch** to pride oneself on doing sth ▪ **piquant, -ante 1** *adj (au goût)* spicy, hot; *(plante, barbe)* prickly; *(détail)* spicy **2** *nm (de plante)* prickle, thorn; *(d'animal)* spine ▪**piqué, -ée 1** *adj (meuble)* worm-eaten; *Fam (fou)* crazy **2** *nm Av* **descente en p.** nosedive

piquet [pikɛ] *nm (pieu)* stake, post; *(de tente)* peg; **envoyer qn au p.** to send sb to stand in the corner; **p. de grève** picket

piquette [pikɛt] *nf Péj (vin)* cheap wine; *Fam* **prendre la p.** to get a hammering

piqûre [pikyr] *nf (d'abeille)* sting; *(de moustique)* bite; *(d'épingle)* prick; *(de tissu)* stitching; *(de rouille)* spot; *Méd* injection; **faire une p. à qn** to give sb an injection

pirate [pirat] **1** *nm (des mers)* pirate; **p. de l'air** hijacker; *Ordinat* **p. informatique** hacker **2** *adj* **radio p.** pirate radio; **édition/CD p.** pirated edition/CD ▪**piratage** *nm* pirating; *Ordinat* **p. informatique** hacking ▪**pirater** *vt (enregistrement)* to pirate; *Ordinat* to hack; **p. un système** to hack into a system ▪**piraterie** *nf (sur les mers)* piracy; **p. aérienne** hijacking; *Ordinat* **p. informatique** hacking

pire [pir] **1** *adj* worse (**que** than); **c'est de p. en p.** it's getting worse and worse **2** *nmf* **le/la p.** the worst (one); **le p. de tout** the worst thing of all; **au p.** at the (very) worst; **s'attendre au p.** to expect the (very) worst

pirogue [pirɔg] *nf* canoe, dugout

pis[1] [pi] *nm (de vache)* udder

pis[2] [pi] **1** *adj Littéraire* worse **2** *adv* **aller de mal en p.** to go from bad to worse **3** *nm Littéraire* **le p.** the worst ▪**pis-aller** *nm inv* stopgap (solution)

piscine [pisin] *nf* swimming pool

pissenlit [pisɑ̃li] *nm* dandelion

pisser [pise] *vi Fam* to have a pee

pistache [pistaʃ] *nf (graine, parfum)* pistachio

piste [pist] *nf (traces)* track, trail; *(indices)* lead; *(de magnétophone) & Sport* track; *(de cirque)* ring; *(de ski)* run, piste; *(pour chevaux) Br* racecourse, *Am* racetrack; **être sur la p. de qn** to be on sb's track; *Sport* **tour de p.** lap; **jeu de p.** treasure hunt; **p. d'atterrissage** runway; **p. cyclable** *Br* cycle path, *Am* bicycle path; **p. de danse** dance floor

pistolet [pistɔlɛ] *nm* gun, pistol; *(de peintre)* spray gun; **p. à eau** water pistol

piston [pistɔ̃] *nm (de véhicule)* piston; *Fam* stringpulling; **avoir du p.** to have connections ▪**pistonner** *vt Fam (appuyer)* to pull strings for

pitié [pitje] *nf* pity; **avoir de la p. pour qn** to pity sb; **il me fait p.** I feel sorry for him; **être sans p.** to be ruthless ▪**piteux, -euse** *adj* pitiful; **en p. état** in a sorry state ▪**pitoyable** *adj* pitiful

piton [pitɔ̃] *nm (d'alpiniste)* piton; **p. (rocheux)** (rocky) peak

pitre [pitr] *nm* clown ▪**pitreries** [-əri] *nfpl* clowning

pittoresque [pitɔrɛsk] *adj* picturesque

pivoine [pivwan] *nf* peony

pivot [pivo] *nm (axe, d'argumentation)* pivot ▪**pivoter** *vi* to pivot, to swivel; **faire p. qch** to swivel sth round

pixel [piksɛl] *nm Ordinat* pixel

pizza [pidza] *nf* pizza ▪**pizzeria** *nf* pizzeria

PJ [peʒi] **1** *(abrév* **police judiciaire)** *nf Br* ≃ CID, *Am* ≃ FBI **2** *(abrév* **pièces jointes)** enc, encl

placage [plakaʒ] *nm (en bois)* veneer; *Rugby* tackle

placard [plakar] *nm (armoire) Br* cupboard, *Am* closet; **p. publicitaire** large display advertisement ▪**placarder** *vt (affiche)* to stick up

> Il faut noter que le nom anglais **placard** est un faux ami. Il signifie **pancarte**.

place [plas] *nf (endroit, rang) & Sport* place; *(lieu public)* square; *(espace)* room; *(siège)* seat; *(emploi)* job, post; **à la p.** instead (**de** of); **à votre p.** in your place; **se mettre à la p. de qn** to put oneself in sb's position; **sur p.** on the spot; *Fin* **sur la p. de Paris** on the Paris market; **en p.** *(objet)* in place; **mettre qch en p.** to put sth in place; **il ne tient pas en p.** he can't keep still; *Fig* **remettre qn à sa p.** to put sb in his/her place; **changer de p.** to change places; **changer qch de p.** to move sth; **faire de la p. (à qn)** to make room (for sb); **faire p. à qn/qch** to give way to sb/sth; **faire p. nette** to have a clearout; **prendre p.** to take a seat; **p. de parking** parking space; **p. de train/bus** train/bus fare; **p. assise** seat; **p. financière** financial market; **p. forte** fortress

placer [plase] **1** *vt (mettre)* to put, to place; *(faire asseoir)* to seat; *(trouver un emploi à)* to place; *(argent)* to invest (**dans** in); *(vendre)* to sell; **je n'ai pas pu p. un mot** I couldn't get a word in *Br* edgeways or *Am* edgewise **2 se placer** *vpr (debout)* to stand; *(s'asseoir)* to sit; *(objet)* to be put or placed; *(cheval, coureur)* to be placed; *Sport* **se p. troisième** to come third ▪**placé, -ée** *adj (objet) & Sport* placed; **bien/mal p. pour faire qch** well/badly placed to do sth; **les gens haut placés** people in high places ▪**placement** *nm (d'argent)* investment; **bureau de p.** *(d'école)* placement office

placide [plasid] *adj* placid

plafond [plafɔ̃] *nm* ceiling ▪**plafonner** *vi (prix)* to peak; *(salaires)* to have reached a ceiling (**à** of) ▪**plafonnier** *nm* ceiling light

plage [plaʒ] *nf (grève)* beach; *(surface)* area; *(de disque)* track; **p. de sable** sand beach; **p. arrière** *(de voiture)* back shelf; **p. horaire** time slot

plagiat [plaʒja] *nm* plagiarism ▪**plagier** *vt* to plagiarize

plaid [plɛd] *nm* travelling rug

plaider [plede] *vti Jur (défendre)* to plead; **p. coupable** to plead guilty ▪**plaideur, -euse**

nmfJur litigant ▪ **plaidoirie** *nfJur* speech for the Br defence *or Am* defense ▪ **plaidoyer** *nm Jur* speech for the Br defence *or Am* defense; *Fig* plea

plaie [plɛ] *nf* wound; *Fig (fléau)* affliction; *(personne)* nuisance

plaignant, -ante [plɛɲã, -ãt] *nmfJur* plaintiff

plaindre* [plɛ̃dr] **1** *vt* to feel sorry for, to pity **2 se plaindre** *vpr (protester)* to complain (**de** about; **que** that); **se p. de** *(douleur)* to complain of ▪ **plainte** *nf* complaint; *(gémissement)* moan; Jur **porter p. contre qn** to lodge a complaint against sb; Jur **p. contre X** complaint against person or persons unknown

plaine [plɛn] *nf* plain

plain-pied [plɛ̃pje] **de plain-pied** *adv* on the same level (**avec** as); *(maison)* single-storey

plaintif, -ive [plɛ̃tif, -iv] *adj* plaintive

plaire* [plɛr] **1** *vi* **elle me plaît** I like her; **ça me plaît** I like it; **je fais ce qui me plaît** I do whatever I want **2** *v impersonnel* **il me plaît de le faire** I like doing it; **s'il vous/te plaît** please; **comme il vous plaira** as you like it **3 se plaire** *vpr (l'un l'autre)* to like each other; **se p. à Paris** to like it in Paris

plaisance [plɛzãs] *nf* **navigation de p.** yachting ▪ **plaisancier** *nm* yachtsman

plaisant, -ante [plɛzã, -ãt] **1** *adj (drôle)* amusing; *(agréable)* pleasing **2** *nm* **mauvais p.** joker ▪ **plaisanter** *vi* to joke (**sur** about); **on ne plaisante pas avec la drogue** drugs are no joking matter; **tu plaisantes!** you're joking! ▪ **plaisanterie** *nf* joke; **par p.** for a joke; **elle ne comprend pas la p.** she can't take a joke ▪ **plaisantin** *nm* joker

plaisir [plɛzir] *nm* pleasure; **faire p. à qn** to please sb; **pour le p.** for the fun of it; **au p. (de vous revoir)** see you again sometime; **faites-moi le p. de...** would you be good enough to...

plan¹ [plã] *nm (projet, dessin, organisation)* plan; *(de ville)* map; *Math* plane; **au premier p.** in the foreground; *Phot* **au second p.** in the background; *Fig* **passer au second p.** to be forced into the background; **sur le p. politique, au p. politique** from the political viewpoint; **sur le même p.** on the same level; **de premier p.** of importance, major; *Fam* **laisser qn en p.** to leave sb in the lurch; *Fam* **un bon p.** *(combine)* a good trick; *Phot & Cin* **gros p.** close-up; **p. d'eau** stretch of water; *Fin* **p. d'épargne** savings plan; **p. social =** corporate restructuring plan, usually involving job losses

plan², plane [plã, plan] *adj (plat)* even, flat

planche [plãʃ] *nf (en bois)* plank; *(plus large)* board; *(illustration)* plate; **faire la p.** to float on one's back; **monter sur les planches** *(au théâtre)* to go on the stage; **p. à repasser/à dessin** ironing/drawing board; **p. à roulettes**

skateboard; **faire de la p. à roulettes** to skateboard; **p. à voile** sailboard; **faire de la p. à voile** to go windsurfing; **p. de surf** surfboard

plancher¹ [plãʃe] *nm* floor; **prix p.** minimum price

plancher² [plãʃe] *vi Fam Scol* to have an exam

planer [plane] *vi (oiseau, planeur)* to glide; *Fam (se sentir bien)* to be floating on air; *(après s'être drogué)* to be high; *Fig* **p. sur qn/qch** *(mystère, danger)* to hang over sb/sth ▪ **planeur** *nm (avion)* glider

planète [planɛt] *nf* planet ▪ **planétaire** *adj* planetary ▪ **planétarium** *nm* planetarium

planifier [planifje] *vt Écon* to plan ▪ **planification** *nf Écon* planning ▪ **planning** *nm (emploi du temps)* schedule; **p. familial** family planning

planisphère [planisfɛr] *nm* planisphere

planque [plãk] *nf Fam (travail)* cushy job; *(lieu)* hideout ▪ **planquer** *vt,* **se planquer** *vpr Fam* to hide

plant [plã] *nm (de plante)* seedling

plantation [plãtasjõ] *nf (action)* planting; *(exploitation agricole)* plantation

plante [plãt] *nf Bot* plant; **jardin des plantes** botanical gardens; **p. du pied** sole (of the foot); **p. verte, p. d'appartement** house plant

planter [plãte] **1** *vt (fleur, arbre)* to plant; *(clou, couteau)* to drive in; *(tente, drapeau)* to put up; *(mettre)* to put (**sur** on; **contre** against); *Fam* **p. là qn** to dump sb **2** *vi Fam Ordinat (ordinateur)* to crash **3 se planter** *vpr Fam (tomber)* to come a cropper; *Fam (se tromper)* to get it wrong; **se p. devant qn/qch** to stand in front of sb/sth ▪ **planté, -ée** *adj (debout)* standing; *Fam* **ne la laissez pas plantée là** don't leave her standing there; **bien p.** *(robuste)* sturdy; *Fam Ordinat* **être p.** *(réseau, ordinateur)* to be down

planteur [plãtœr] *nm* plantation owner

planton [plãtõ] *nm Mil* orderly

plantureux, -euse [plãtyrø, -øz] *adj (femme)* buxom

plaque [plak] *nf* plate; *(de verre, de métal)* sheet, plate; *(de verglas)* sheet; *(de marbre)* slab; *(de chocolat)* bar; *(commémorative)* plaque; *(sur la peau)* blotch; *Fam* **à côté de la p.** wide of the mark; **p. chauffante** hotplate; **p. dentaire** (dental) plaque; *Aut* **p. minéralogique, p. d'immatriculation** Br number *or Am* license plate; *Fig* **p. tournante** centre

plaquer [plake] **1** *vt (métal, bijou)* to plate; *(bois)* to veneer; *(cheveux)* to plaster down; *Rugby* to tackle; *(aplatir)* to flatten (**contre** against); *Fam* **p. qn** to ditch sb; *Fam* **tout p.** to chuck it all in **2 se plaquer** *vpr* **se p. contre** to flatten oneself against ▪ **plaquage** *nm Rugby* tackle ▪ **plaqué, -ée 1** *adj (bijou)* plated; **p. or** gold-plated **2** *nm* **p. or** gold plate

plasma [plasma] *nm Biol* plasma

plastic [plastik] *nm* plastic explosive
▪ **plastiquer** *vt* to bomb

plastifier [plastifje] *vt* to laminate

plastique [plastik] *adj & nm* plastic; **en p.** plastic

plastron [plastrɔ̃] *nm* shirt front

plat, plate [pla, plat] **1** *adj* flat; *(mer)* calm, smooth; *(ennuyeux)* flat, dull; **à fond p.** flat-bottomed; **à p. ventre** flat on one's face; **à p.** *(pneu, batterie)* flat; *Fam (épuisé)* run down; **poser qch à p.** to lay sth (down) flat; *Fig* **tomber à p.** *(être un échec)* to fall flat; **faire à qn de plates excuses** to make a humble apology to sb; **assiette plate** dinner plate; **calme p.** dead calm **2** *nm* (**a**) *(de la main)* flat; (**b**) *(récipient, nourriture)* dish; *(partie du repas)* course; *Fig* **mettre les petits plats dans les grands** to put on a marvellous spread; *Fam* **en faire tout un p.** to make a song and dance about it; **p. cuisiné** ready meal; **p. du jour** today's special; **p. principal** *ou* **de résistance** main course ▪ **plate-bande** *(pl* **plates-bandes**) *nf* flower bed; *Fam* **marcher sur les plates-bandes de qn** to tread on sb's toes ▪ **plate-forme** *(pl* **plates-formes**) *nf* platform; **p. pétrolière** oil rig

platane [platan] *nm* plane tree

plateau, -x [plato] *nm* tray; *(de balance)* pan; *(de tourne-disque)* turntable; *TV & Cin* set; *Géog* plateau; **p. à fromages** cheeseboard ▪ **plateau-repas** *(pl* **plateaux-repas**) *nm* meal on a tray

platine¹ [platin] **1** *nm (métal)* platinum **2** *adj inv* platinum; **blond p.** platinum blond ▪ **platiné, -ée** *adj (cheveux)* platinum-blond(e)

platine² [platin] *nf (d'électrophone, de magnétophone)* deck; **p. laser** CD player

platitude [platityd] *nf (propos)* platitude

plâtre [plɑtr] *nm (matière)* plaster; **un p.** *(de jambe cassée)* a plaster cast; **dans le p.** *(jambe, bras)* in plaster; **les plâtres** *(de maison)* the plasterwork; *Fam* **essuyer les plâtres** to put up with the teething problems ▪ **plâtrer** *vt (mur)* to plaster; *(membre)* to put in plaster ▪ **plâtrier** *nm* plasterer

plausible [plozibl] *adj* plausible

play-back [plɛbak] *nm inv* **chanter en p.** to mime

plébiscite [plebisit] *nm* plebiscite

plein, pleine [plɛ̃, plɛn] **1** *adj (rempli, complet)* full; *(solide)* solid; **p. de** full of; **p. à craquer** full to bursting; **en pleine mer** out at sea, on the open sea; **en pleine figure** right in the face; **en pleine nuit** in the middle of the night; **en p. jour** in broad daylight; **en p. hiver** in the depths of winter; **en p. soleil** in the full heat of the sun; **en pleine campagne** in the heart of the country; **être en p. travail** to be hard at work; **à la pleine lune** at full moon; **travailler à p.**

temps to work full-time; *Fam* **être p. aux as** to be loaded; **p. sud** due south; **p. tarif** full price; *(de transport)* full fare **2** *adv* **des billes p. les poches** pockets full of marbles; **du chocolat p. la figure** chocolate all over one's face; *Fam* **p. de lettres/d'argent** *(beaucoup de)* lots *or* loads of letters/money **3** *nm Aut* **faire le p.** **(d'essence)** to fill up (the tank); **battre son p.** *(fête)* to be in full swing ▪ **pleinement** *adv* fully

pléonasme [pleɔnasm] *nm* pleonasm

pléthore [pletɔr] *nf* plethora

pleurer [plœre] **1** *vi* to cry, to weep (**sur** over); **p. de rire** to laugh till one cries **2** *vt (personne)* to mourn (for); **p. toutes les larmes de son corps** to cry one's eyes out ▪ **pleurnicher** *vi Fam* to whine ▪ **pleurs** *mpl* **en p.** in tears

pleuvoir* [pløvwar] **1** *v impersonnel* to rain; **il pleut** it's raining; *Fig* **il pleut des cordes** it's raining cats and dogs **2** *vi (coups)* to rain down (**sur** on)

Plexiglas® [plɛksiglas] *nm Br* Perspex®, *Am* Plexiglas®

pli [pli] *nm* (**a**) *(de papier, de rideau, de la peau)* fold; *(de jupe, de robe)* pleat; *(de pantalon, de bouche)* crease; **(faux) p.** crease; **mise en plis** set *(hairstyle)*; *Fam* **ça n'a pas fait un p.** there was no doubt about it (**b**) *(enveloppe)* envelope; *(lettre)* letter; **sous p. séparé** under separate cover (**c**) *Cartes* trick; **faire un p.** to take a trick (**d**) *(habitude)* habit; **prendre le p. de faire qch** to get into the habit of doing sth

plier [plije] **1** *vt (draps, vêtements)* to fold; *(parapluie)* to fold up; *(courber)* to bend; **p. qn à** to submit sb to; **p. bagages** to pack one's bags (and leave); **être plié en deux** *(de douleur)* to be doubled up **2** *vi (branche)* to bend **3** **se plier** *(lit, chaise)* to fold up; **se p. à** to submit to ▪ **pliable** *adj* foldable ▪ **pliage** *nm (manière)* fold; *(action)* folding ▪ **pliant, pliante 1** *adj (chaise)* folding **2** *nm* folding stool

plinthe [plɛ̃t] *nf (de mur) Br* skirting board, *Am* baseboard

plisser [plise] *vt (tissu, jupe)* to pleat; *(lèvres)* to pucker; *(front)* to wrinkle; *(yeux)* to screw up ▪ **plissé, -ée** *adj (tissu, jupe)* pleated

plomb [plɔ̃] *nm (métal)* lead; *(fusible)* fuse; *(pour rideau)* lead weight; **plombs** *(de chasse)* lead shot; **tuyau de p.** *ou* **en p.** lead pipe; *Fig* **de p.** *(sommeil)* heavy; *(soleil)* blazing; *(ciel)* leaden; *Fig* **avoir du p. dans l'aile** to be in a bad way; *Fig* **ça lui mettra du p. dans la cervelle** that will knock some sense into him

plombe [plɔ̃b] *nf Fam* hour

plomber [plɔ̃be] *vt (dent)* to fill; *(mettre des plombs à)* to weigh with lead ▪ **plombage** *nm (de dent)* filling

plombier [plɔ̃bje] *nm* plumber ▪ **plomberie** *nf (métier, installations)* plumbing

plonger [plɔ̃ʒe] **1** *vi (personne)* to dive (**dans**

into); *(oiseau, avion)* to dive (**sur** onto); *Fig (route)* to plunge **2** *vt (enfoncer)* to plunge (**dans** into); **plongé dans ses pensées** deep in thought; **plongé dans l'obscurité** plunged into darkness **3 se plonger** *vpr* **se p. dans** *(lecture)* to immerse oneself in ▪ **plonge** *nf Fam* **faire la p.** to wash the dishes, *Br* to wash up ▪ **plongeant, -ante** *adj (décolleté)* plunging; **vue plongeante** bird's-eye view ▪ **plongée** *nf* diving; *(de sous-marin)* dive; **p. sous-marine** skin *or* scuba diving ▪ **plongeoir** *nm* diving board ▪ **plongeon** *nm* dive; **faire un p.** to dive ▪ **plongeur, -euse** *nmf (nageur)* diver; *Fam (de restaurant)* dishwasher, *Br* washer-up

plouc [pluk] *Fam* **1** *adj Br* naff, *Am* lame **2** *nm* yokel, *Am* hick

plouf [pluf] *exclam* splash!

ployer [plwaje] *vi Littéraire* to bend

plu [ply] *pp de* **plaire, pleuvoir**

pluie [plɥi] *nf* rain; **sous la p.** in the rain; *Fig* **une p. de pierres/coups** a shower of stones/blows; *Fam* **parler de la p. et du beau temps** to talk of this and that; **p. fine** drizzle; **pluies acides** acid rain

plume [plym] *nf (d'oiseau)* feather; *Hist (pour écrire)* quill (pen); *(pointe de stylo)* nib; *Fam* **vivre de sa p.** to live by one's pen ▪ **plumage** *nm* plumage ▪ **plumeau, -x** *nm* feather duster ▪ **plumer** *vt (volaille)* to pluck; *Fig* **p. qn** *(voler)* to fleece sb ▪ **plumier** *nm* pencil box

plupart [plypar] **la plupart** *nf* most; **la p. des cas** most cases; **la p. du temps** most of the time; **la p. d'entre eux** most of them; **pour la p.** mostly

pluriel, -ielle [plyrjɛl] *Grammaire* **1** *adj* plural **2** *nm* plural; **au p.** in the plural

plurilingue [plyrilɛ̃g] *adj* multilingual

plus¹ [ply] ([plyz] *before vowel*, [plys] *in end position*) *adv* (**a**) *(comparatif)* more (**que** than); **p. d'un kilo/de dix** more than a kilo/ten; **p. de thé** more tea; **p. beau/rapidement** more beautiful/rapidly (**que** than); **p. tard** later; **p. petit** smaller; **de p. en p.** more and more; **de p. en p. vite** quicker and quicker; **p. ou moins** more or less; **en p.** in addition (**de** to); **au p.** at most; **de p.** more (**que** than); *(en outre)* moreover; **les enfants de p. de dix ans** children over ten; **j'ai dix ans de p. qu'elle** I'm ten years older than she is; **il est p. de cinq heures** it's after five (o'clock); **p. il crie, p. il s'enroue** the more he shouts, the more hoarse he gets (**b**) *(superlatif)* **le p.** (the) most; **le p. beau** the most beautiful (**de** in); *(de deux)* the more beautiful; **le p. grand** the biggest (**de** in); *(de deux)* the bigger; **j'ai le p. de livres** I have (the) most books; **j'en ai le p.** I have the most

plus² [ply] *adv (négation)* (**ne...**) **p.** no more; **il**

n'a p. de pain he has no more bread, he doesn't have any more bread; **il n'y a p. rien** there's nothing left; **tu n'es p. jeune** you're not young any more *or* any longer, you're no longer young; **elle ne le fait p.** she no longer does it, she doesn't do it any more *or* any longer; **je ne la reverrai p.** I won't see her again; **je ne voyagerai p. jamais** I'll never travel again

plus³ [plys] **1** *conj* plus; **deux p. deux font quatre** two plus two are four; **il fait p. 2 (degrés)** it's 2 degrees above freezing **2** *nm* **le signe p.** the plus sign

plusieurs [plyzjœr] *adj & pron* several

plus-que-parfait [plyskəparfɛ] *nm Grammaire* pluperfect

plus-value [plyvaly] *(pl* **plus-values***) nf (bénéfice)* profit

plutonium [plytɔnjɔm] *nm* plutonium

plutôt [plyto] *adv* rather (**que** than)

pluvieux, -ieuse [plyvjø, -jøz] *adj* rainy, wet

PME [peɛmø] *(abrév* **petite et moyenne entreprise***) nf* small company

PMU [peɛmy] *(abrév* **Pari mutuel urbain***) nm =* state-run betting system

PNB [peɛnbe] *(abrév* **produit national brut***) nm Écon* GNP

pneu [pnø] *(pl* **pneus***) nm (de roue) Br* tyre, *Am* tire; **p. neige** snow tyre; **p. pluie** wet-weather tyre ▪ **pneumatique** *adj (qui fonctionne à l'air)* pneumatic; *(gonflable)* inflatable

pneumonie [pnømɔni] *nf* pneumonia

poche [pɔʃ] *nf (de vêtement)* pocket; *(de kangourou)* pouch; *(sac)* bag; **poches** *(sous les yeux)* bags; **faire des poches** *(pantalon)* to be baggy; *Fam* **faire les poches à qn** to go through sb's pockets; **j'ai cinq euros en p.** I have five euros on me; **elle connaît Paris comme sa poche** she knows Paris like the back of her hand; *Fam* **c'est dans la p.** it's in the bag ▪ **pochette** *nf (sac)* bag; *(d'allumettes)* book; *(de disque)* sleeve; *(sac à main)* (clutch) bag; *(mouchoir)* pocket handkerchief

pocher [pɔʃe] *vt (œufs)* to poach; *Fam* **p. l'œil à qn** to give sb a black eye

podium [pɔdjɔm] *nm* podium

podomètre [pɔdɔmɛtr] *nm* pedometer

poêle [pwal] **1** *nm (chauffage)* stove **2** *nf* **p. (à frire)** frying pan

poème [pɔɛm] *nm* poem ▪ **poésie** *nf (art)* poetry; *(poème)* poem ▪ **poète 1** *nm* poet **2** *adj* **femme p.** (woman) poet ▪ **poétique** *adj* poetic

pognon [pɔɲɔ̃] *nm Fam* dough, cash

poids [pwa] *nm* weight; *Sport* shot; **au p.** by weight; *Fig* **de p.** *(argument)* influential; **prendre/perdre du p.** to gain/lose weight; *Sport* **lancer le p.** to put the shot; *Fig* **faire deux poids deux mesures** to apply double standards; **p. lourd** *(camion) Br* lorry, *Am* truck;

Boxe (personne) heavyweight; *Boxe* **p. plume** featherweight

poignant, -ante [pwaɲɑ̃, -ɑ̃t] *adj* poignant

poignard [pwaɲar] *nm* dagger; **coup de p.** stab ▪ **poignarder** *vt* to stab

poigne [pwaɲ] *nf* grip; *Fig* **avoir de la p.** to be firm

poignée [pwaɲe] *nf (quantité)* handful (**de** of); *(de porte, de casserole)* handle; *(d'épée)* hilt; **p. de main** handshake

poignet [pwaɲɛ] *nm* wrist; *(de chemise)* cuff

poil [pwal] *nm* hair; *(pelage)* coat; **poils** *(de brosse)* bristles; *(de tapis)* pile; *Fam* **à p.** stark naked; *Fam* **à un p. près** very nearly; *Fam* **au p.** great; *Fam* **de bon/mauvais p.** in a good/bad mood; *Fam* **de tout p.** of all kinds; **p. à gratter** itching powder ▪ **poilu, -ue** *adj* hairy

poinçon [pwɛ̃sɔ̃] *nm (outil)* awl; *(marque)* hallmark ▪ **poinçonner** *vt (billet)* to punch; *(bijou)* to hallmark ▪ **poinçonneuse** *nf (machine)* punching machine

poindre* [pwɛ̃dr] *vi Littéraire (jour)* to dawn

poing [pwɛ̃] *nm* fist; **dormir à poings fermés** to sleep like a log

point¹ [pwɛ̃] *nm (lieu, score, question)* point; *(sur i, à l'horizon)* dot; *(tache)* spot; *(de notation)* mark; *Couture* stitch; **être sur le p. de faire qch** to be about to do sth; **à p. nommé** *(arriver)* at the right moment; **à p.** *(steak)* medium rare; **déprimé au p. que...** depressed to such an extent that...; **mettre au p.** *(appareil photo)* to focus; *(moteur)* to tune; *(technique)* to perfect; *Fig (éclaircir)* to clarify; **être au p.** to be up to scratch; **au p. où j'en suis...** at the stage I've reached...; **au plus haut p.** extremely; **au p. mort** *Aut* in neutral; *Fig* at a standstill; *Fig* **faire le p.** to take stock; *Fig* **mettre les points sur les i** to make oneself perfectly clear; **un p., c'est tout!** that's final!; *Am* period!; **p. de côté** stitch; **p. de départ** starting point; **p. de vente** point of sale; **p. de vue** *(opinion)* point of view, viewpoint; *(endroit)* viewing point; **p. du jour** daybreak; **p. d'exclamation** exclamation *Br* mark *ou Am* point; **p. d'interrogation** question mark; **points de suspension** suspension points; **p. chaud** hot spot; **p. faible/fort** weak/strong point; **p. final** *Br* full stop, *Am* period; **p. noir** *(comédon)* blackhead; *(embouteillage)* blackspot ▪ **point-virgule** *(pl* **points-virgules)** *nm* semicolon

point² [pwɛ̃] *adv Littéraire* = **pas¹**

pointe [pwɛ̃t] *nf (extrémité)* tip, point; *(clou)* nail; *Géog* headland; *Fig (maximum)* peak; **une p. d'humour** a touch of humour; **sur la p. des pieds** on tiptoe; **en p.** pointed; **de p.** *(technologie, industrie)* state-of-the-art; **vitesse de p.** top speed; *Fig* **à la p. de** *(progrès)* in or at the forefront of; **faire des pointes** *(danseuse)* to dance on points; **p. d'asperge** asparagus tip; **p. de vitesse** burst of speed

pointer [pwɛ̃te] **1** *vt (cocher) Br* to tick off, *Am* to check (off); *(braquer)* to point (**sur/vers** at); **p. les oreilles** to prick up its ears **2** *vi (employé) (à l'arrivée)* to clock in; *(à la sortie)* to clock out; *(jour)* to dawn; **p. vers** to rise towards **3 se pointer** *vpr Fam (arriver)* to show up ▪ **pointage** *nm (sur une liste)* ticking off; *(au travail* (à l'arrivée)* clocking in; *(à la sortie)* clocking out

pointillé [pwɛ̃tije] *nm* dotted line; **ligne en p.** dotted line

pointilleux, -euse [pwɛ̃tijø, -øz] *adj* fussy, particular

pointu, -ue [pwɛ̃ty] *adj (en pointe)* pointed; *(voix)* shrill; *Fig (spécialisé)* specialized

pointure [pwɛ̃tyr] *nf* size

poire [pwar] *nf (fruit)* pear; *Fam (figure)* mug; *Fam (personne)* sucker; *Fig* **couper la p. en deux** to meet each other halfway ▪ **poirier** *nm* pear tree

poireau, -x [pwaro] *nm* leek

poireauter [pwarote] *vi Fam* to hang around

pois [pwa] *nm (légume)* pea; *(dessin)* (polka) dot; **à p.** *(vêtement)* polka-dot; **petits p.** *Br* (garden) peas, *Am* peas; **p. de senteur** sweet pea; **p. chiche** chickpea

poison [pwazɔ̃] *nm* poison

poisse [pwas] *nf Fam* bad luck

poisseux, -euse [pwasø, -øz] *adj* sticky

poisson [pwasɔ̃] *nm* fish; **les Poissons** *(signe)* Pisces; **être Poissons** to be (a) Pisces; **p. d'avril** April fool; **p. rouge** goldfish ▪ **poissonnerie** *nf* fish shop ▪ **poissonnier, -ière** *nmf* fishmonger

poitrine [pwatrin] *nf* chest; *(seins)* bust; *Culin (de veau)* breast

poivre [pwavr] *nm* pepper ▪ **poivré, -ée** *adj* peppery ▪ **poivrer** *vt* to pepper ▪ **poivrier** *nm (plante)* pepper plant; *(ustensile)* pepper pot ▪ **poivrière** *nf* pepper pot

poivron [pwavrɔ̃] *nm* pepper, capsicum

poivrot, -ote [pwavro, -ɔt] *nmf Fam* drunk

poker [pɔkɛr] *nm Cartes* poker

polar [pɔlar] *nm Fam (roman, film)* whodunnit

polariser [pɔlarize] *vt* to polarize

pôle [pol] *nm Géog* pole; **p. Nord/Sud** North/South Pole; *Fig* **p. d'attraction** centre of attraction ▪ **polaire** *1 adj* polar; **laine p.** fleece, fleecy material *2 nf (veste)* fleece

polémique [pɔlemik] **1** *adj* polemical **2** *nf* controversy, polemic

poli, -ie [pɔli] *adj (courtois)* polite (**avec** to or with); *(lisse)* polished ▪ **poliment** *adv* politely

police [pɔlis] *nf police*; **faire la p.** to keep order (**dans** in); **p. d'assurance** insurance policy; *Typ & Ordinat* **p. de caractères** font; **p. judiciaire** police investigation department; **p. mondaine** vice squad; **p. secours** emergency services ▪ **policier, -ière 1** *adj* **enquête policière**

police inquiry; **roman p.** detective novel **2** *nm* policeman, detective

polichinelle [pɔliʃinɛl] *nm (marionnette)* Punch; *Péj (personne)* buffoon; **secret de P.** open secret

polio [pɔljo] *(abrév* **poliomyélite)** *nf Méd* polio ▪ **poliomyélite** *nf Méd* poliomyelitis

polir [pɔlir] *vt* to polish

polisson, -onne [pɔlisɔ̃, -ɔn] **1** *adj* naughty **2** *nmf* rascal

politesse [pɔlitɛs] *nf* politeness; **par p.** out of politeness

politique [pɔlitik] **1** *adj* political; **homme/ femme p.** politician **2** *nf (activité, science)* politics *(sing); (mesure)* policy; **faire de la p.** to be in politics **3** *nmf* politician ▪ **politicien, -ienne** *nmf Péj* politician ▪ **politiser** *vt* to politicize

pollen [pɔlɛn] *nm* pollen

polluer [pɔlɥe] *vt* to pollute ▪ **polluant** *nm* pollutant ▪ **pollueur, -ueuse 1** *adj* polluting **2** *nmf* polluter ▪ **pollution** *nf* pollution

polo [pɔlo] *nm (chemise)* polo shirt; *Sport* polo

polochon [pɔlɔʃɔ̃] *nm Fam* bolster

Pologne [pɔlɔɲ] *nf* **la P.** Poland ▪ **polonais, -aise 1** *adj* Polish **2** *nmf* **P., Polonaise** Pole **3** *nm (langue)* Polish

poltron, -onne [pɔltrɔ̃, -ɔn] **1** *adj* cowardly **2** *nmf* coward

polycopier [pɔlikɔpje] *vt* to duplicate ▪ **polycopié** *nm Univ* duplicated course material

polyester [pɔliɛstɛr] *nm* polyester; **chemise en p.** polyester shirt

polygame [pɔligam] *adj* polygamous ▪ **polygamie** *nf* polygamy

polyglotte [pɔliglɔt] *adj & nmf (personne)* multilingual

Polynésie [pɔlinezi] *nf* **la P.** Polynesia

polytechnique [pɔliteknik] *adj & nf* **École p., P.** = "grande école" specializing in technology ▪ **polytechnicien, -ienne** *nmf* = student or graduate of the "École polytechnique"

> Il faut noter que le nom anglais **polytechnic** est un faux ami. Il désigne un établissement comparable à un IUT.

polyvalent, -ente [pɔlivalɑ̃, -ɑ̃t] **1** *adj (salle)* multi-purpose; *(personne)* versatile **2** *adj & nf Can* **(école) polyvalente** *Br* ≃ secondary school, *Am* ≃ high school

pommade [pɔmad] *nf* ointment

pomme [pɔm] *nf* **(a)** *(fruit)* apple; *Anat* **p. d'Adam** Adam's apple; **p. de terre** potato; **pommes chips** potato *Br* crisps *or Am* chips; **pommes frites** *Br* chips, *Am* French fries; **pommes vapeur** steamed potatoes **(b)** *(d'arrosoir)* rose **(c)** *(locutions) Fam* **tomber dans les pommes** to faint; *Fam* **être haut comme trois pommes** to be knee-high to a grasshopper; *Fam* **ma p.** *(moi)* yours truly ▪ **pommier** *nm* apple tree

pommeau, -x [pɔmo] *nm (de canne)* knob

pommette [pɔmɛt] *nf* cheekbone; **pommettes saillantes** high cheekbones

pompe¹ [pɔ̃p] **1** *nf (machine)* pump; *Fam (chaussure)* shoe; *Sport Br* press-up, *Am* push-up; *Fam* **coup de p.** (sudden) feeling of exhaustion; *Fam* **il est à côté de ses pompes** he's not with it; **p. à essence** *Br* petrol *or Am* gas station; **p. à incendie** fire engine; **p. à vélo** bicycle pump **2** *nfpl* **pompes funèbres** undertaker's; **entrepreneur des pompes funèbres** *Br* undertaker, *Am* mortician

pompe² [pɔ̃p] *nf (splendeur)* pomp; **en grande p.** with great ceremony

pomper [pɔ̃pe] **1** *vt (eau, air)* to pump; *(faire monter)* to pump up; *(évacuer)* to pump out; *Fam (copier)* to crib *(sur* from); *Fam* **p. qn** *(épuiser)* to do sb in; *Fam* **tu me pompes (l'air)** you're getting on my nerves **2** *vi* to pump; *Fam (copier)* to crib *(sur* from)

pompeux, -euse [pɔ̃pø, -øz] *adj* pompous

pompier [pɔ̃pje] *nm* fireman; **voiture des pompiers** fire engine

pompiste [pɔ̃pist] *nmf Br* petrol *or Am* gas station attendant

pompon [pɔ̃pɔ̃] *nm* pompom

pomponner [pɔ̃pɔne] **se pomponner** *vpr Fam* to doll oneself up

ponce [pɔ̃s] *nf* **pierre p.** pumice stone ▪ **poncer** *vt (au papier de verre)* to sand (down) ▪ **ponceuse** *nf (machine)* sander

ponctuation [pɔ̃ktɥasjɔ̃] *nf* punctuation ▪ **ponctuer** *vt* to punctuate **(de** with)

ponctuel, -uelle [pɔ̃ktɥɛl] *adj (à l'heure)* punctual; *(unique) Br* one-off, *Am* one-of-a-kind ▪ **ponctualité** *nf* punctuality

pondéré, -ée [pɔ̃dere] *adj (personne)* level-headed ▪ **pondération** *nf (modération)* level-headedness

pondre [pɔ̃dr] *vt (œuf)* to lay; *Fam Péj (livre, discours)* to turn out

poney [pɔne] *nm* pony

pont [pɔ̃] *nm* bridge; *(de bateau)* deck; *Fig* **faire le p.** to make a long weekend of it *(taking the working day(s) between a bank holiday and a weekend)*; **p. aérien** airlift ▪ **pont-levis** *(pl* **ponts-levis)** *nm* drawbridge

ponte [pɔ̃t] **1** *nf (d'œufs)* laying **2** *nm Fam (personne)* big shot

pontife [pɔ̃tif] *nm Rel* **(souverain) p.** the Supreme Pontiff ▪ **pontifical, -e, -aux, -ales** *adj* papal

ponton [pɔ̃tɔ̃] *nm* pontoon

pop [pɔp] *nf & adj inv (musique)* pop

pop-up [pɔpœp] *nm Ordinat* pop-up

popote [pɔpɔt] *nf Fam (cuisine)* cooking

populace [pɔpylas] *nf Péj* rabble
populaire [pɔpylɛr] *adj (personne, gouvernement)* popular; *(quartier, milieu)* working-class; *(expression)* vernacular ▪ **populariser** *vt* to popularize ▪ **popularité** *nf* popularity (**auprès de** with)
population [pɔpylasjɔ̃] *nf* population ▪ **populeux, -euse** *adj* crowded
porc [pɔr] *nm (animal)* pig; *(viande)* pork; *Péj (personne)* swine
porcelaine [pɔrsəlɛn] *nf* china, porcelain
porc-épic [pɔrkepik] *(pl* **porcs-épics***) nm* porcupine
porche [pɔrʃ] *nm* porch
porcherie [pɔrʃəri] *nf Br* pigsty, *Am* pigpen
pore [pɔr] *nm* pore ▪ **poreux, -euse** *adj* porous
pornographie [pɔrnɔɡrafi] *nf* pornography ▪ **pornographique** *adj* pornographic
port [pɔr] *nm* (a) *(pour bateaux)* port, harbour; *Ordinat* port; *Fig* **arriver à bon p.** to arrive safely (b) *(d'armes)* carrying; *(de barbe)* wearing; *(prix)* carriage, postage; *(attitude)* bearing
portable [pɔrtabl] **1** *adj (ordinateur)* portable; *(téléphone)* mobile **2** *nm (ordinateur)* laptop; *(téléphone)* *Br* mobile, *Am* cell
portail [pɔrtaj] *nm (de jardin)* gate; *(de cathédrale)* & *Ordinat* portal
portant, -ante [pɔrtɑ̃, -ɑ̃t] *adj* **bien p.** in good health
portatif, -ive [pɔrtatif, -iv] *adj* portable
porte [pɔrt] *nf* door, *(de jardin, de ville, de slalom)* gate; **Alger, p. de...** Algiers, gateway to...; **trouver p. close** to find nobody in; **faire du p.-à-p.** to go from door to door selling/canvassing/*etc*; **mettre qn à la p.** *(jeter dehors)* to throw sb out; *(renvoyer)* to fire sb; **p. à tambour** revolving door; **p. d'embarquement** *(d'aéroport)* (departure) gate; **p. d'entrée** front door; **p. cochère** carriage entrance
porte-à-faux [pɔrtafo] *nm inv* **en p.** unstable
portée [pɔrte] *nf* (a) *(de fusil)* range; *Fig* scope; **à la p. de qn** within reach of sb; *Fig (richesse, plaisir)* within sb's grasp; **à p. de la main** within reach; **à p. de voix** within earshot; **hors de p.** out of reach (b) *(animaux)* litter (c) *(impact)* significance (d) *Mus* stave
portefeuille [pɔrtəfœj] *nm Br* wallet, *Am* billfold; *(de ministre, d'actions)* portfolio
portemanteau, -x [pɔrtmɑ̃to] *nm (sur pied)* coat stand; *(crochet)* coat rack
porter [pɔrte] **1** *vt* to carry; *(vêtement, lunettes)* to wear; *(moustache, barbe)* to have; *(trace, responsabilité, fruits)* to bear; *(regard)* to cast; *(coup)* to strike; *(sentiment)* to have (**à** for); *(inscrire)* to enter; **p. qch à qn** to take/bring sth to sb; **p. bonheur/malheur** to bring good/bad luck; **p. une attaque contre qn** to attack sb; **p. son attention sur qch** to turn one's attention to

sth; **tout (me) porte à croire que...** everything leads me to believe that...; **se faire p. malade** to report sick
2 *vi (voix)* to carry; *(coup)* to strike home; **p. sur** *(concerner)* to be about; *(accent)* to fall on
3 se porter *upr (vêtement)* to be worn; **se p. bien** to be well; **comment te portes-tu?** how are you?; **se p. candidat** *Br* to stand *or Am* to run as a candidate ▪ **portant, -ante** *adj* **bien p.** in good health ▪ **porté, -ée** *adj* **p. à croire** inclined to believe; **p. sur qch** fond of sth ▪ **porte-avions** *nm inv* aircraft carrier ▪ **porte-bagages** *nm inv* luggage rack ▪ **porte-bébé** *(pl* **porte-bébés***) nm* baby carrier ▪ **porte-bonheur** *nm inv* (lucky) charm ▪ **porte-cartes** *nm inv* card-holder ▪ **porte-clefs** *nm inv* key ring ▪ **porte-documents** *nm inv* briefcase ▪ **porte-drapeau** *(pl* **porte-drapeaux***) nm* standard bearer ▪ **porte-fenêtre** *(pl* **portes-fenêtres***) nf Br* French window, *Am* French door ▪ **porte-jarretelles** *nm inv Br* suspender *or Am* garter belt ▪ **porte-monnaie** *nm inv Br* purse, *Am* change purse ▪ **porte-parapluies** *nm inv* umbrella stand ▪ **porte-parole** *nmf inv* spokesperson (**de** for) ▪ **porte-plume** *nm inv* penholder ▪ **porte-revues** *nm inv* newspaper rack ▪ **porte-savon** *(pl* **porte-savons***) nm* soapdish ▪ **porte-serviettes** *nm inv Br* towel rail, *Am* towel rack ▪ **porte-voix** *nm inv* megaphone, *Am* bullhorn
porteur, -euse [pɔrtœr, -øz] **1** *nm (de bagages)* porter **2** *nmf (malade)* carrier; *(de nouvelles, de chèque)* bearer; *Méd* **p. sain** = carrier who doesn't have the symptoms of the disease **3** *adj* **marché p.** growth market
portier [pɔrtje] *nm* doorkeeper, porter ▪ **portière** *nf (de véhicule, de train)* door ▪ **portillon** *nm* gate
portion [pɔrsjɔ̃] *nf* portion
portique [pɔrtik] *nm Archit* portico; *(pour agrès)* crossbeam
porto [pɔrto] *nm (vin)* port
Porto Rico [pɔrtoriko] *nm ou f* Puerto Rico
portrait [pɔrtrɛ] *nm (peinture, dessin, photo)* portrait; *(description)* description; **faire le p. de qn** to do sb's portrait; *Fig* **c'est tout le p. de son père** he's the spitting image of his father ▪ **portrait-robot** *(pl* **portraits-robots***) nm* Photofit®, Identikit® picture; *Ordinat* **p. électronique** E-fit®
portuaire [pɔrtɥɛr] *adj* **installations portuaires** port *or* harbour facilities
Portugal [pɔrtyɡal] *nm* **le P.** Portugal ▪ **portugais, -aise 1** *adj* Portuguese **2** *nmf* **P., Portugaise** Portuguese *inv*; **les P.** the Portuguese **3** *nm (langue)* Portuguese
pose [poz] *nf* (a) *(de rideau, de papier peint)* putting up; *(de moquette)* laying (b) *(pour*

photo, portrait) pose; *Phot* exposure; **prendre la p.** to pose

posé, -ée [poze] *adj (calme)* composed, staid **=posément** *adv* calmly

poser [poze] 1 *vt* to put down; *(papier peint, rideaux)* to put up; *(mine, moquette, fondations)* to lay; *(bombe)* to plant; *(conditions, principe)* to lay down; **p. qch sur qch** to put sth on sth; **p. une question à qn** to ask sb a question; **p. un problème à qn** to pose a problem for sb; **p. sa candidature** *(à une élection)* to put oneself forward as a candidate; *(à un emploi)* to apply (**à** for) 2 *vi (modèle)* to pose (**pour** for) 3 **se poser** *vpr (oiseau, avion)* to land; *(problème, question)* to arise; **se p. sur** *(sujet: regard)* to rest on; **se p. des questions** to ask oneself questions

positif, -ive [pozitif, -iv] *adj* positive **=positivement** *adv* positively **=positiver** *vi Fam* to look on the bright side

position [pozisjɔ̃] *nf* position; *Fig* **prendre p.** to take a stand (**contre** against); *Fig* **rester sur ses positions** to stand one's ground

posologie [pozɔlɔʒi] *nf Méd* dosage

posséder [posede] *vt (biens, talent)* to possess; *(sujet)* to have a thorough knowledge of; *(langue)* to have mastered; *Fam (duper)* to take in **=possesseur** *nm* possessor; owner **=possessif, -ive** *adj & nm Grammaire* possessive **=possession** *nf* possession; **en p. de qch** in possession of sth; **être en pleine p. de ses moyens** to be at the peak of one's powers; **prendre p. de qch** to take possession of sth

possibilité [posibilite] *nf* possibility; **avoir la p. de faire qch** to have the chance *or* opportunity of doing sth; **avoir de grandes possibilités** to have great potential

possible [posibl] 1 *adj* possible (**à faire** to do); **il (nous) est p. de le faire** it is possible (for us) to do it; **il est p. que...** (+ *subjunctive*) it is possible that...; **si p.** if possible; **le plus tôt p.** as soon as possible; **autant que p.** as far as possible; **le plus p.** as much/as many as possible; **le moins de détails p.** as few details as possible 2 *nm* **faire (tout) son p.** to do one's utmost (**pour faire** to do)

postal, -e, -aux, -ales [postal, -o] *adj* postal; *(train)* mail

postdater [postdate] *vt* to postdate

poste¹ [post] *nf (service)* mail, *Br* post; *(bureau)* post office; **la P.** the postal services; **par la p.** by mail, *Br* by post; **mettre qch à la p.** to mail *or Br* post sth; **p. aérienne** airmail; **p. restante** poste restante, *Am* general delivery

poste² [post] *nm* (**a**) *(lieu, emploi)* post; **être à son p.** to be at one's post; **p. d'aiguillage** *Br* signal box, *Am* signal tower; **p. d'essence** *Br* petrol *or Am* gas station; **p. d'incendie** fire point; **p. de pilotage** cockpit; **p. de police**

police station; **p. de secours** first-aid post; *Ordinat* **p. de travail** workstation (**b**) **p. (de radio/télévision)** radio/television set (**c**) *(de standard)* extension

poster¹ [poste] *vt (lettre) Br* to post, *Am* to mail

poster² [poste] 1 *vt (sentinelle, troupes)* to post, to station 2 **se poster** *vpr* to take up a position

poster³ [pɔstɛʀ] *nm* poster

postérieur, -ieure [posterjœr] 1 *adj (dans le temps)* later; *(de derrière)* back; **p. à** after 2 *nm Fam (derrière)* posterior

postérité [posterite] *nf* posterity

posthume [postym] *adj* posthumous; **à titre p.** posthumously

postiche [postiʃ] 1 *adj* false 2 *nm* hairpiece

postier, -ière [postje, -jɛʀ] *nmf* postal worker

postillonner [postijɔne] *vi* to splutter **=postillons** *nmpl* **envoyer des p.** to splutter

post-scriptum [postskriptɔm] *nm inv* post-script

postuler [postyle] 1 *vt Math* to postulate 2 *vi* **p. à un emploi** to apply for a job **=postulant, -ante** *nmf* applicant (**à** for)

posture [postyr] *nf* posture; **être en fâcheuse p.** to be in an awkward situation

pot [po] *nm* pot; *(en verre)* jar; *(en carton)* carton; *(de bébé)* potty; *Fam* **prendre un p.** to have a drink; *Fam* **avoir du p.** to be lucky; **p. à eau** water jug; **p. de chambre** chamber pot; **p. d'échappement** *Br* exhaust pipe, *Am* tail pipe; **p. de fleurs** *(récipient)* flowerpot

potable [pɔtabl] *adj* drinkable; *Fam (passable)* tolerable; **eau p.** drinking water

potage [pɔtaʒ] *nm* soup

potager, -ère [pɔtaʒe, -ɛʀ] 1 *adj* **jardin p.** vegetable garden; **plante potagère** vegetable 2 *nm* vegetable garden

potasser [pɔtase] *vt Fam (examen)* to bone up for

potassium [pɔtasjɔm] *nm* potassium

pot-au-feu [pɔtofø] *nm inv* = beef stew with vegetables

pot-de-vin [podvɛ̃] (*pl* **pots-de-vin**) *nm* bribe

pote [pɔt] *nm Fam (ami)* pal

poteau, -x [pɔto] *nm* post; **p. électrique** electricity pylon; **p. indicateur** signpost; **p. télégraphique** telegraph pole

potelé, -ée [pɔtle] *adj* plump, chubby

potence [pɔtɑ̃s] *nf (gibet)* gallows *(sing)*

potentiel, -ielle [pɔtɑ̃sjɛl] *adj & nm* potential

poterie [pɔtri] *nf (art, objets)* pottery; *(objet)* piece of pottery; **faire de la p.** to make pottery **=potier, -ière** *nmf* potter

potin [pɔtɛ̃] *nm Fam (bruit)* row; **faire du p.** to kick up a row **=potins** *nmpl (ragots)* gossip

potion [posjɔ̃] *nf* potion

potiron [pɔtirɔ̃] *nm* pumpkin

pot-pourri [popuri] (*pl* **pots-pourris**) *nm (fleurs séchées)* potpourri; *(chansons)* medley

pou, -x [pu] *nm* louse; **poux** lice

poubelle [pubɛl] *nf Br* dustbin, *Am* garbage can; **mettre qch à la p.** to throw sth out

pouce [pus] *nm (doigt)* thumb; *Fam* **coup de p.** helping hand; *Fam* **se tourner les pouces** to twiddle one's thumbs

poudre [pudr] *nf (poussière, explosif)* powder; **en p.** *(lait)* powdered; *(chocolat)* drinking; **p. à récurer** scouring powder ▪**poudrer 1** *vt* to powder **2 se poudrer** *vpr* to powder one's face ▪**poudreux, -euse 1** *adj* powdery **2** *nf* **poudreuse** *(neige)* powder snow ▪**poudrier** *nm (powder)* compact ▪**poudrière** *nf (entrepôt)* powder magazine; *Fig (région)* powder keg

pouf [puf] **1** *exclam* thump! **2** *nm (siège)* pouf

pouffer [pufe] *vi* **p. (de rire)** to burst out laughing

pouilleux, -euse [pujø, -øz] *adj (personne)* filthy; *(quartier)* squalid

poulailler [pulaje] *nm* hen house; *Fam Théâtre* **le p.** the gods

poulain [pulɛ̃] *nm* foal; *Fig* protégé

poule[1] [pul] *nf (animal)* hen; *Culin* fowl; *Péj (femme)* tart, *Am* broad; *Fam* **ma p.** darling; *Péj* **p. mouillée** wimp

poule[2] [pul] *nf (groupe)* group

poulet [pulɛ] *nm (animal)* chicken; *Fam (policier)* cop

pouliche [puliʃ] *nf* filly

poulie [puli] *nf* pulley

poulpe [pulp] *nm* octopus

pouls [pu] *nm Méd* pulse; **prendre le p. de qn** to take sb's pulse

poumon [pumɔ̃] *nm* lung; **à pleins poumons** *(respirer)* deeply; **p. d'acier** iron lung

poupe [pup] *nf Naut* stern, poop; *Fig* **avoir le vent en p.** to have the wind in one's sails

poupée [pupe] *nf* doll; **jouer à la p.** to play with dolls

poupin [pupɛ̃] *adj* **visage p.** baby face

poupon [pupɔ̃] *nm (bébé)* baby; *(poupée)* baby doll

pour [pur] **1** *prép* for; **p. toi/moi** for you/me; **faites-le p. lui** do it for him, do it for his sake; **partir p. Paris/l'Italie** to leave for Paris/Italy; **elle part p. cinq ans** she's leaving for five years; **elle est p.** she's all for it, she's in favour of it; **p. faire qch** (in order) to do sth; **p. que tu le voies** so (that) you may see it; **p. quoi faire?** what for?; **trop poli p. faire qch** too polite to do sth; **assez grand p. faire qch** big enough to do sth; **p. femme/base** as a wife/basis; **p. affaires** on business; **p. cela** for that reason; **p. ma part** as for me; **jour p. jour/heure p. heure** to the day/hour; **dix p. cent** ten percent; **acheter p. 2 euros de bonbons** to buy 2 euros' worth of *Br* sweets *or Am* candies; **p. intelligent qu'il soit** however clever he may be; **je n'y suis p.**

rien! it's got nothing to do with me!; *Fam* **c'est fait p.** that's what it's there for **2** *nm* **le p. et le contre** the pros and cons

pourboire [purbwar] *nm* tip

pourcentage [pursɑ̃taʒ] *nm* percentage

pourchasser [purʃase] *vt* to pursue

> Il faut noter que le verbe anglais **to purchase** est un faux ami. Il signifie **acheter**.

pourparlers [purparle] *nmpl* negotiations, talks; **p. de paix** peace talks

pourpre [purpr] *adj & nm* crimson

pourquoi [purkwa] **1** *adv & conj* why; **p. pas?** why not? **2** *nm inv* reason (**de** for); **le p. et le comment** the whys and wherefores

pourra, pourrait [pura, purɛ] *voir* **pouvoir 1**

pourrir [purir] **1** *vt* to rot; *Fig* **p. qn** to spoil sb **2** *vi* to rot ▪**pourri, -ie** *adj (fruit, temps, personne)* rotten; *Fam* **être p. de fric** to be stinking rich ▪**pourriture** *nf* rot

pourriel [purjɛl] *nm Fam Ordinat* spam e-mail; **pourriels** spam

poursuite [pursɥit] **1** *nf (chasse)* pursuit; *(continuation)* continuation; **se lancer à la p. de qn** to set off in pursuit of sb **2** *nfpl Jur* **poursuites (judiciaires)** legal proceedings (**contre** against); **engager des poursuites contre qn** to start proceedings against sb

poursuivre* [pursɥivr] **1** *vt (chercher à atteindre)* to pursue; *(sujet: idée, crainte)* to haunt; *(sujet: malchance)* to dog; *(harceler)* to pester; *(continuer)* to continue, to go on with; *Jur* **p. qn (en justice)** to bring proceedings against sb; *(au criminel)* to prosecute sb **2 se poursuivre** *vpr* to continue, to go on ▪**poursuivant, -ante** *nmf* pursuer

pourtant [purtɑ̃] *adv* yet, nevertheless; **et p.** and yet

pourtour [purtur] *nm* perimeter

pourvoir* [purvwar] **1** *vt* to provide (**de** with); **être pourvu de** to be provided with **2 p. à** *(besoins)* to provide for **3 se pourvoir** *vpr Jur* **se p. en cassation** to take one's case to the Court of Appeal ▪**pourvoyeur, -euse** *nmf* supplier

pourvu [purvy] **pourvu que** *conj* (**a**) *(condition)* provided (that) (**b**) *(souhait)* **p. qu'elle soit là!** I just hope (that) she's there!

pousse [pus] *nf (croissance)* growth; *(bourgeon)* shoot, sprout; **pousses de bambou** bamboo shoots

poussée [puse] *nf (pression)* pressure; *(coup)* push; *(d'ennemi)* thrust, push; *(de fièvre)* outbreak; *(de l'inflation)* upsurge

pousser [puse] **1** *vt (presser)* to push; *(moteur)* to drive hard; **p. qn du coude** to nudge sb with one's elbow; **p. qn à qch** to drive sb to sth; **p. qn à faire qch** *(sujet: faim)* to drive sb to do sth; *(sujet: personne)* to urge sb to do sth; **poussé**

par la curiosité prompted by curiosity; **p. un cri** to shout; **p. un soupir** to sigh 2 *vi (presser)* to push; *(croître)* to grow; **faire p. qch** *(plante)* to grow sth; **se laisser p. les cheveux** to let one's hair grow; **p. jusqu'à Paris** to push on as far as Paris 3 **se pousser** *vpr (pour faire de la place)* to move over **• poussé, -ée** *adj (travail, études)* thorough

poussette [puset] *nf Br* pushchair, *Am* stroller

poussière [pusjɛr] *nf* dust; **une p.** a speck of dust; *Fam* **faire la p.** *ou* **les poussières** to do the dusting; *Fam* **10 euros et des poussières** just over 10 euros **• poussiéreux, -euse** *adj* dusty

poussif, -ive [pusif, -iv] *adj* wheezy

poussin [pusɛ̃] *nm (animal)* chick

poutre [putr] *nf (en bois)* beam; *(en acier)* girder **• poutrelle** *nf* girder

pouvoir* [puvwar] 1 *v aux (être capable de)* can, to be able to; *(avoir la permission)* can, may, to be allowed; **je peux deviner** I can guess, I'm able to guess; **tu peux entrer** you may *or* can come in; **il peut être sorti** he may *or* might be out; **elle pourrait/pouvait venir** she might/ could come; **j'ai pu l'obtenir** I managed to get it; **j'aurais pu l'obtenir** I could have *Br* got *or Am* gotten it; **je n'en peux plus** *(de fatigue)* I'm utterly exhausted 2 *v impersonnel* **il peut neiger** it may snow; **il se peut qu'elle parte** she might leave 3 *nm (puissance, attributions)* power; **au p.** *(parti)* in power; **il n'est pas en mon p. de vous aider** it's not in my power to help you; **p. d'achat** purchasing power; **les pouvoirs publics** the authorities

poux [pu] *pl de* **pou**

pragmatique [pragmatik] *adj* pragmatic

praire [prɛr] *nf* clam

prairie [preri] *nf* meadow

praline [pralin] *nf* praline **• praliné, -ée** *adj (glace)* praline-flavoured

praticable [pratikabl] *adj (route)* passable; *(terrain)* playable

praticien, -ienne [pratisjɛ̃, -jɛn] *nmf* practitioner

pratique [pratik] 1 *adj (méthode, personne)* practical; *(outil)* handy; **avoir l'esprit p.** to be practically minded 2 *nf (application, procédé, coutume)* practice; *(expérience)* practical experience; **la p. de la natation/du golf** swimming/golfing; **mettre qch en p.** to put sth into practice; **dans la p.** *(en réalité)* in practice **• pratiquement** *adv (presque)* practically; *(en réalité)* in practice

pratiquer [pratike] 1 *vt (religion)* to *Br* practise *or Am* practice; *(activité)* to take part in; *(langue)* to use; *(sport)* to play; *(ouverture)* to make; *(opération)* to carry out; **p. la natation** to go swimming 2 *vi (médecin, avocat)* to *Br* practise

or Am practice **• pratiquant, -ante** 1 *adj* practising 2 *nmf* practising Christian/Jew/ Muslim/*etc*

pré [pre] *nm* meadow

préalable [prealabl] 1 *adj* prior, previous; **p. à** prior to 2 *nm* precondition, prerequisite; **au p.** beforehand **• préalablement** [-əmɑ̃] *adv* beforehand

préambule [preɑ̃byl] *nm* preamble; *Fig* **sans p., elle annonça que…** without any warning, she announced that…

PréAO [preao] *(abrév* **présentation assistée par ordinateur)** *nf Ordinat* computer-assisted presentation

préau, -x [preo] *nm (de cour d'école)* covered area; *(salle)* hall

préavis [preavi] *nm* (advance) notice (**de** of); **p. de grève** strike notice; **p. de licenciement** notice of dismissal

précaire [prekɛr] *adj* precarious; *(santé)* delicate **• précarité** *nf* precariousness; **p. de l'emploi** lack of job security

précaution [prekosjɔ̃] *nf (mesure)* precaution; *(prudence)* caution; **par p.** as a precaution; **pour plus de p.** to be on the safe side; **prendre des précautions** to take precautions **• précautionneux, -euse** *adj* careful

précédent, -ente [presedɑ̃, -ɑ̃t] 1 *adj* previous 2 *nmf* previous one 3 *nm* precedent; **sans p.** unprecedented **• précédemment** [-amɑ̃] *adv* previously **• précéder** *vti* to precede

précepte [presept] *nm* precept

précepteur, -trice [preseptœr, -tris] *nmf* (private) tutor

prêcher [preʃe] *vti* to preach

précieux, -ieuse [presjø, -jøz] *adj* precious

précipice [presipis] *nm* chasm, abyss; *(de ravin)* precipice

précipiter [presipite] 1 *vt (hâter)* to hasten; *(jeter)* to hurl down; *Fig* to plunge (**dans** into) 2 **se précipiter** *vpr (se jeter)* to rush (**vers/sur** towards/at); *(se hâter)* to rush; **les événements se sont précipités** things started happening quickly **• précipitamment** [-amɑ̃] *adv* hastily **• précipitation** *nf* haste; **précipitations** *(pluie)* precipitation **• précipité, -ée** *adj* hasty

précis, -ise [presi, -iz] 1 *adj* precise, exact; *(mécanisme)* accurate, precise; **à deux heures précises** at two o'clock sharp *or* precisely 2 *nm (résumé)* summary; *(manuel)* handbook **• précisément** *adv* precisely **• précision** *nf* precision; *(de mécanisme, d'information)* accuracy; *(détail)* detail; **donner des précisions sur qch** to give precise details about sth; **demander des précisions sur qch** to ask for further information about sth

préciser [presize] 1 *vt* to specify (**que** that) 2 **se préciser** *vpr* to become clear(er)

précoce [prekɔs] *adj (enfant)* precocious; *(fruit,*

été) early ▪ **précocité** *nf* precociousness; *(de fruit)* earliness

préconçu, -ue [prekɔ̃sy] *adj* preconceived

préconiser [prekɔnize] *vt* to advocate (**que** that)

précurseur [prekyrsœr] **1** *nm* forerunner, precursor **2** *adj* **signe p.** forewarning

prédécesseur [predesesœr] *nm* predecessor

prédestiné, -ée [predestine] *adj* predestined (**à faire** to do)

prédicateur [predikatœr] *nm* preacher

prédilection [predileksjɔ̃] *nf* predilection; **de p.** favourite

prédire* [predir] *vt* to predict (**que** that) ▪ **prédiction** *nf* prediction

prédisposer [predispoze] *vt* to predispose (**à qch** to sth; **à faire** to do) ▪ **prédisposition** *nf* predisposition (**à** to)

prédominer [predɔmine] *vi* to predominate ▪ **prédominance** *nf* predominance ▪ **prédominant, -ante** *adj* predominant

préfabriqué, -ée [prefabrike] *adj* prefabricated

préface [prefas] *nf* preface (**de** to) ▪ **préfacer** *vt* to preface

préfecture [prefɛktyr] *nf* prefecture; **la P. de police** police headquarters ▪ **préfectoral, -e, -aux, -ales** *adj* = relating to a 'préfecture' or 'préfet'

préférable [preferabl] *adj* preferable (**à** to)

préférence [preferɑ̃s] *nf* preference (**pour** for); **de p.** preferably; **de p. à** in preference to ▪ **préférentiel, -ielle** *adj* preferential

préférer [prefere] *vt* to prefer (**à** to); **p. faire qch** to prefer to do sth; **je préférerais rester** I would rather stay, I would prefer to stay ▪ **préféré, -ée** *adj & nmf* favourite

préfet [prefe] *nm* prefect *(chief administrator in a "département")*; **p. de police** = chief commissioner of police

préfigurer [prefigyre] *vt* to herald, to foreshadow

préfixe [prefiks] *nm* prefix

préhistoire [preistwar] *nf* prehistory ▪ **préhistorique** *adj* prehistoric

préjudice [preʒydis] *nm (à une cause)* prejudice; *(à une personne)* harm; **porter p. à qn** to do sb harm ▪ **préjudiciable** *adj* prejudicial (**à** to)

> Il faut noter que le nom anglais **prejudice** est un faux ami. Il signifie le plus souvent **préjugé.**

préjugé [preʒyʒe] *nm* prejudice; **avoir des préjugés** to be prejudiced (**contre** against)

prélasser [prelɑse] **se prélasser** *vpr* to lounge

prélever [prel(ə)ve] *vt (échantillon)* to take (**sur** from); *(somme)* to deduct (**sur** from) ▪ **prélèvement** *nm (d'échantillon)* taking; *(de somme)* deduction; **p. automatique** *Br* direct

debit, *Am* automatic deduction; **prélèvements obligatoires** = tax and social security contributions

préliminaire [prelimin ɛr] **1** *adj* preliminary **2** *nmpl* **préliminaires** preliminaries

prélude [prelyd] *nm* prelude (**à** to)

prématuré, -ée [prematyre] **1** *adj* premature **2** *nmf* premature baby ▪ **prématurément** *adv* prematurely

préméditer [premedite] *vt* to premeditate ▪ **préméditation** *nf* premeditation; **meurtre avec p.** premeditated murder

prémices [premis] *nfpl Littéraire* **les p. de** the (very) beginnings of

premier, -ière [prəmje, -jɛr] **1** *adj* first; *(enfance)* early; *(page de journal)* front; *(qualité)* prime; *(état)* original; *(notion, cause)* basic; *(danseuse, rôle)* leading; *(marche)* bottom; **le p. rang** the front row; **les trois premiers mois** the first three months; **à la première occasion** at the earliest opportunity; **en p.** firstly; **P. ministre** Prime Minister **2** *nm (étage) Br* first *or Am* second floor; **le p. juin** June the first; **le p. de l'an** New Year's Day **3** *nmf* first (one); **arriver le p.** *ou* **en p.** to arrive first; **être le p. de la classe** to be (at the) top of the class **4** *nf* **première** *(wagon, billet)* first class; *(vitesse)* first (gear); *(événement historique)* first; *(de chaussure)* insole; *Théâtre* opening night; *Cin* première; *Scol Br* ≃ lower sixth, *Am* ≃ eleventh grade ▪ **premièrement** *adv* firstly

prémisse [premis] *nf* premise

> Il faut noter que le nom anglais **premises** est un faux ami. Il signifie **locaux.**

prémonition [premɔnisjɔ̃] *nf* premonition ▪ **prémonitoire** *adj* premonitory

prémunir [premynir] **se prémunir** *vpr Littéraire* **se p. contre qch** to guard against sth

prenant, -ante [prənɑ̃, -ɑ̃t] *adj (film)* engrossing; *(travail)* time-consuming

prénatal, -e, -als, -ales [prenatal] *adj Br* antenatal, *Am* prenatal

prendre* [prɑ̃dr] **1** *vt* to take (**à qn** from sb); *(attraper)* to catch; *(repas, boisson, douche)* to have; *(nouvelles)* to get; *(air)* to put on; *(accent)* to pick up; *(pensionnaire)* to take in; *(bonne, assistant)* to take on; **p. qch dans un tiroir** to take sth out of a drawer; **p. qn pour** to take sb for; **p. feu** to catch fire; **p. du temps/une heure** to take time/an hour; **p. de la place** to take up room; **p. du poids/de la vitesse** to put on weight/gather speed; **p. l'air** *(se promener)* to get some fresh air; **p. l'eau** *(bateau, chaussure)* to be leaking; **passer p. qn** to come and get sb; *Fam* **p. un coup de poing dans la figure** to get a punch in the face; **qu'est-ce qui te prend?** what's *Br* got *or Am* gotten into you?; **à tout p.** on the whole **2** *vi (feu)* to catch; *(ciment, gelée)* to set; *(greffe, vaccin, plante)* to take; *(mode)* to catch on; **p. sur soi** to restrain oneself **3 se prendre** *vpr (médicament)* to be taken; *(s'accrocher)* to get caught; **se p. les pieds dans qch** to get one's feet caught in sth; **s'y p. bien avec qn** to know how to handle sb; **s'en p. à qn** to take it out on sb; *Fig* **je me suis pris au jeu** I got really caught up in it

preneur, -euse [prənœr, -øz] *nmf (acheteur)* taker, buyer; **p. d'otages** hostage taker

prénom [prenɔ̃] *nm* first name ▪ **prénommer** *vt* to name; **il se prénomme Daniel** his first name is Daniel

préoccuper [preɔkype] **1** *vt (inquiéter)* to worry **2 se préoccuper** *vpr* **se p. de qn/qch** to concern oneself with sb/sth ▪ **préoccupant, -ante** *adj* worrying ▪ **préoccupation** *nf* preoccupation, concern ▪ **préoccupé, -ée** *adj* worried (**par** about)

prépa [prepa] *nf Fam Scol* = preparatory class *(for the entrance exam to the "grandes écoles")*

préparatifs [preparatif] *nmpl* preparations (**de** for) ▪ **préparation** *nf* preparation ▪ **préparatoire** *adj* preparatory

préparer [prepare] **1** *vt* to prepare (**qch pour** sth for); *(examen)* to study for; **p. qch à qn** to prepare sth for sb; **p. qn à** *(examen)* to prepare or coach sb for; **plats tout préparés** ready-cooked meals **2 se préparer** *vpr (être imminent)* to be in the offing; *(s'apprêter)* to prepare oneself (**à** *ou* **pour qch** for sth); **se p. à faire qch** to prepare to do sth; **se p. qch** *(boisson)* to make oneself sth

prépondérant, -ante [prepɔ̃derɑ̃, -ɑ̃t] *adj* predominant ▪ **prépondérance** *nf* predominance

préposer [prepoze] *vt* **p. qn à qch** to appoint sb to sth ▪ **préposé, -ée** *nmf* employee; *(facteur)* postman, *f* postwoman

préposition [prepozisjɔ̃] *nf Grammaire* preposition

préretraite [prerətret] *nf* early retirement

prérogative [prerɔgativ] *nf* prerogative

près [prɛ] *adv* **p. de qn/qch** near sb/sth, close to sb/sth; **p. de deux ans** nearly two years; **p. de partir** about to leave; **tout p.** nearby (**de qn/qch** sb /sth), close by (**de qn/qch** sb /sth); **de p.** *(suivre, examiner)* closely; **à peu de chose p.** more or less; **à cela p.** except for that; **voici le chiffre à un euro p.** here is the figure, give or take a euro; **calculer à l'euro p.** to calculate to the nearest euro

présage [prezaʒ] *nm* omen, sign ▪ **présager** *vt (annoncer)* to presage; **ça ne présage rien de bon** it doesn't bode well

presbyte [presbit] *adj* long-sighted ▪ **presbytie** [-bisi] *nf* long-sightedness

presbytérianisme [presbiterjanism] *nm* Presbyterianism ▪ **presbytérien, -ienne** [-jɛ̃, -jɛn] *adj & nmf* Presbyterian

préscolaire [preskɔlɛr] *adj* preschool

prescrire* [preskrir] *vt (médicament)* to prescribe ▪ **prescription** *nf (ordonnance)* prescription

préséance [preseɑ̃s] *nf* precedence (**sur** over)

présence [prezɑ̃s] *nf* presence; *(à l'école)* attendance (**à** at); **en p. de** in the presence of; **faire acte de p.** to put in an appearance; **p. d'esprit** presence of mind

présent¹, -ente [prezɑ̃, -ɑ̃t] **1** *adj (non absent, actuel)* present **2** *nm (temps)* present; *Grammaire* present (tense); **à p.** at present, now; **dès à p.** as from now

présent² [prezɑ̃] *nm Littéraire (cadeau)* present; **faire p. de qch à qn** to present sth to sb

présenter [prezɑ̃te] **1** *vt (montrer)* to show, to present; *(facture)* to submit; *(arguments)* to present; **p. qn à qn** to introduce sb to sb **2** *vi Fam* **elle présente bien** she looks good **3 se présenter** *vpr (dire son nom)* to introduce oneself (**à** to); *(chez qn)* to show up; *(occasion)* to arise; **se p. à** *(examen)* to take, *Br* to sit for; *(élections)* to run in; *(emploi)* to apply for; *(autorités)* to report to; **ça se présente bien** it looks promising ▪ **présentable** *adj* presentable ▪ **présentateur, -trice** *nmf* presenter ▪ **présentation** *nf* presentation; *(de personnes)* introduction; **faire les présentations** to make the introductions; **p. de mode** fashion show

présentoir [prezɑ̃twar] *nm* display unit

préservatif [prezervatif] *nm* condom

Il faut noter que le nom anglais **preservative** est un faux ami. Il signifie **agent de conservation**.

préserver [prezerve] *vt* to protect, to preserve (**de** from) ▪ **préservation** *nf* protection, preservation

présidence [prezidɑ̃s] *nf (de nation)* presidency; *(de firme)* chairmanship ▪ **président, -ente** *nmf (de nation)* president; *(de firme)* chairman, *f* chairwoman; **p.-directeur général** *Br* (chairman and) managing director, *Am* chief executive officer; **p. du jury** *(d'examen)* chief examiner; *(tribunal)* foreman of the jury ▪ **présidentiel, -ielle** *adj* presidential

présider [prezide] *vt (réunion)* to chair; *(conseil)* to preside over

présomption [prezɔ̃psjɔ̃] *nf* presumption

présomptueux, -ueuse [prezɔ̃ptɥø, -ɥøz] *adj* presumptuous

presque [presk] *adv* almost, nearly; **p. jamais/ rien** hardly ever/anything

presqu'île [preskil] *nf* peninsula

presse [pres] *nf Tech* press; *Typ* (printing) press; **la p.** *(journaux)* the press; **la p. à sensation** the tabloids; **conférence de p.** press conference

pressentir* [presɑ̃tir] *vt (deviner)* to sense (**que**

that) ▪ **pressentiment** nm presentiment; (de malheur) foreboding

presser [prese] 1 vt (serrer) to squeeze; (raisin) to press; (sonnette, bouton) to press, to push; **p. qn to hurry sb; p. qn de questions** to bombard sb with questions; **p. qn de faire qch** to urge sb to do sth; **p. le pas** to speed up 2 vi **le temps presse** there's not much time left; **rien ne presse** there's no hurry 3 **se presser** vpr (se hâter) to hurry (**de faire** to do); (se serrer) to squeeze (together); (se grouper) to crowd (**autour de** around) ▪ **pressant, -ante** adj urgent, pressing ▪ **pressé, -ée** adj (personne) in a hurry; (air) hurried ▪ **presse-citron** nm inv lemon squeezer ▪ **presse-fruits** nm inv juicer ▪ **presse-papiers** nm inv paperweight; Ordinat clipboard ▪ **presse-purée** nm inv potato masher

pressing [presiŋ] nm dry cleaner's

pression [presjɔ̃] nf Tech pressure; (bouton) snap (fastener); Fam (bière) Br draught beer, Am draft beer; **faire p. sur qn** to put pressure on sb, to pressurize sb; **subir des pressions** to be under pressure

pressoir [preswar] nm (instrument) press

pressuriser [presyrize] vt (avion) to pressurize ▪ **pressurisation** nf pressurization

prestance [prestɑ̃s] nf presence

prestataire [prestater] nmf **p. de service** service provider; Ordinat **p. d'accès** access provider

prestation [prestasjɔ̃] nf (a) (allocation) benefit; **prestations** (services) services; **prestations sociales** Br social security benefits, Am welfare payments (b) (de comédien) performance

prestidigitateur, -trice [prestidiʒitatœr, -tris] nmf conjurer ▪ **prestidigitation** nf tour de p. conjuring trick

prestige [prestiʒ] nm prestige ▪ **prestigieux, -ieuse** adj prestigious

présumer [prezyme] vt to presume (**que** that); **p. de qch** to overestimate sth

présupposer [presypoze] vt to presuppose (**que** that)

prêt¹, prête [prɛ, prɛt] adj (préparé) ready (**à faire** to do; **à qch** for sth); **être fin p.** to be all set; **être p. à tout** to be prepared to do anything ▪ **prêt-à-porter** [pretaporte] nm ready-to-wear clothes

prêt² [prɛ] nm (somme) loan

prétendre [pretɑ̃dr] 1 vt (déclarer) to claim (**que** that); (vouloir) to intend (**faire** to do); **à ce qu'il prétend** according to him; **on le prétend fou** they say he's mad 2 vi **p. à** (titre) to lay claim to 3 **se prétendre** vpr to claim to be ▪ **prétendant** nm (amoureux) suitor ▪ **prétendu, -ue** adj (progrès) so-called; (coupable) alleged ▪ **prétendument** adv supposedly

Il faut noter que le verbe anglais **to pretend** est un faux ami. Il signifie le plus souvent **faire semblant**.

prétentieux, -ieuse [pretɑ̃sjø, -jøz] adj pretentious ▪ **prétention** nf (vanité) pretension; (revendication, ambition) claim; **sans p.** (film, robe) unpretentious

prêter [prete] 1 vt (argent, objet) to lend (**à** to); (aide) to give (**à** to); (propos, intention) to attribute (**à** to); **p. attention** to pay attention (**à** to); **p. serment** to take an oath; **p. main-forte à qn** to lend sb a hand 2 vi **p. à confusion** to give rise to confusion 3 **se prêter** vpr **se p. à** (consentir) to agree to; (convenir) to lend itself to ▪ **prêteur, -euse** [pretœr, -øz] nmf lender; **p. sur gages** pawnbroker

prétérit [preterit] nm Grammaire preterite (tense)

prétexte [pretekst] nm excuse, pretext; **sous p. de/que** on the pretext of/that; **sous aucun p.** under no circumstances ▪ **prétexter** vt to plead (**que** that)

prêtre [pretr] nm priest

preuve [prœv] nf piece of evidence; **preuves** evidence; **faire p. de qch** to prove sth; **faire p. de courage** to show courage; **faire ses preuves** (personne) to prove oneself; (méthode) to be tried and tested; **p. d'amour** token of love

prévaloir* [prevalwar] vi to prevail (**sur** over)

prévenant, -ante [prevnɑ̃, -ɑ̃t] adj considerate

prévenir* [prevnir] vt (a) (mettre en garde) to warn; (aviser) to inform (**de** of or about) (b) (maladie) to prevent; (accident) to avert ▪ **préventif, -ive** adj preventive; **détention préventive** custody ▪ **prévention** nf prevention; **p. routière** road safety ▪ **prévenu, -ue** nmf Jur defendant, accused

prévisible [previzibl] adj foreseeable

prévision [previzjɔ̃] nf forecast; **en p. de** in expectation of; **prévisions météorologiques** weather forecast

prévoir* [prevwar] vt (météo) to forecast; (difficultés, retard, réaction) to expect; (organiser) to plan; **un repas est prévu** a meal is provided; **la réunion est prévue pour demain** the meeting is scheduled for tomorrow; **comme prévu** as planned; **plus tôt que prévu** earlier than expected; **prévu pour** (véhicule, appareil) designed for

prévoyant, -ante [prevwajɑ̃, -ɑ̃t] adj far-sighted ▪ **prévoyance** nf foresight

prier [prije] 1 vi Rel to pray 2 vt (Dieu) to pray to; (supplier) to beg; **p. qn de faire qch** to ask sb to do sth; **je vous en prie** please; (en réponse à 'merci') don't mention it; **sans se faire p.** without hesitation; **il ne s'est pas fait p.** he didn't need much persuading

prière [prijɛr] *nf Rel* prayer; *(demande)* request; **p. de répondre** please answer

primaire [primɛr] **1** *adj* primary; **école p.** *Br* primary school, *Am* elementary school **2** *nm Scol Br* primary *or Am* elementary education; **être en p.** to be at *Br* primary *or Am* elementary school

primauté [primote] *nf* primacy

prime [prim] **1** *nf (sur salaire)* bonus; *(d'État)* subsidy; **en p.** *(cadeau)* as a free gift; **p. (d'assurance)** (insurance) premium; **p. de fin d'année** ≃ Christmas bonus; **p. de licenciement** severance allowance; **p. de transport** transport allowance **2** *adj* **de p. abord** at the very first glance

primé, -ée [prime] *adj (film, animal)* prizewinning

primer [prime] *vi* to come first; **p. sur qch** to take precedence over sth

primeurs [primœr] *nfpl* early fruit and vegetables

primevère [primvɛr] *nf* primrose

primitif, -ive [primitif, -iv] *adj (société, art)* primitive; *(état, sens)* original

primo [primo] *adv* first(ly)

primordial, -e, -iaux, -iales [primɔrdjal, -jo] *adj* vital (**de faire** to do)

prince [prɛ̃s] *nm* prince ▪ **princesse** *nf* princess ▪ **princier, -ière** *adj* princely ▪ **principauté** *nf* principality

principal, -e, -aux, -ales [prɛ̃sipal, -o] **1** *adj* main, principal; *(rôle)* leading **2** *nm (de collège)* principal, *Br* headmaster, *f* headmistress; **le p.** *(l'essentiel)* the main thing ▪ **principalement** *adv* mainly

principe [prɛ̃sip] *nm* principle; **en p.** theoretically, in principle; **par p.** on principle

printemps [prɛ̃tɑ̃] *nm* spring; **au p.** in the spring ▪ **printanier, -ière** *adj* **température printanière** spring-like temperature

priorité [prijɔrite] *nf* priority (**sur** over); *Aut* right of way; *Aut* **avoir la p.** to have (the) right of way; *Aut* **p. à droite** right of way to traffic coming from the right; **'cédez la p.'** *Br* 'give way', *Am* 'yield'; **en p.** as a matter of priority ▪ **prioritaire** *adj* **secteur p.** priority sector; **être p.** to have priority; *Aut* to have (the) right of way

pris, prise¹ [pri, priz] **1** *pp de* **prendre 2** *adj (place)* taken; **avoir le nez p.** to have a blocked nose; **être p.** *(occupé)* to be busy; *(candidat)* to be accepted; **p. de** *(peur)* seized with; **p. de panique** panic-stricken

prise² [priz] *nf (action)* taking; *(objet saisi)* catch; *(manière d'empoigner)* grip; *(de judo)* hold; *(de tabac)* pinch; **lâcher p.** to lose one's grip; *Fig* **être aux prises avec qn/qch** to be struggling with sb/sth; **p. de sang** blood test; **faire une p. de sang à qn** to take a blood

sample from sb; *Él* **p. (de courant)** *(mâle)* plug; *(femelle)* socket; *Él* **p. multiple** adaptor; **p. de conscience** awareness; **p. de contact** first meeting; *Fig* **p. de position** stand; **p. d'otages** hostage-taking; *Cin & TV* **p. de son** sound recording; *Cin & Phot* **p. de vue** *(action)* shooting; *(de tournage)* take; *(cliché)* shot

priser¹ [prize] **1** *vt* **p. du tabac** to take snuff **2** *vi* to take snuff

priser² [prize] *vt Littéraire (estimer)* to prize

prisme [prism] *nm* prism

prison [prizɔ̃] *nf* prison, jail; *(peine)* imprisonment; **être en p.** to be in prison *or* in jail; **mettre qn en p.** to put sb in prison, to jail sb ▪ **prisonnier, -ière** *nmf* prisoner; **faire qn p.** to take sb prisoner; **p. de guerre** prisoner of war; **p. d'opinion** prisoner of conscience; **p. politique** political prisoner

privation [privasjɔ̃] *nf* deprivation (**de** of); **privations** *(manque)* hardship

privatiser [privatize] *vt* to privatize ▪ **privatisation** *nf* privatization

privé, -ée [prive] **1** *adj* private **2** *nm* **le p.** the private sector; *Scol* the private education system; **en p.** in private; **dans le p.** privately; *(travailler)* in the private sector

priver [prive] **1** *vt* to deprive (**de** of) **2 se priver** *vpr* **se p. de** to do without, to deprive oneself of

privilège [privilɛʒ] *nm* privilege ▪ **privilégié, -iée** *adj* privileged

prix [pri] *nm (coût)* price; *(récompense)* prize; **à tout p.** at all costs; **à aucun p.** on no account; **hors de p.** exorbitant; **attacher du p. à qch** to attach importance to sth; **faire un p. à qn** to give sb a special price; **p. de revient** cost price; **p. de vente** selling price

proactif, -ive [prɔaktif, -iv] *adj* proactive

probable [prɔbabl] *adj* likely, probable; **peu p.** unlikely ▪ **probabilité** *nf* probability, likelihood; **selon toute p.** in all probability ▪ **probablement** [-əmɑ̃] *adv* probably

probant, -ante [prɔbɑ̃, -ɑ̃t] *adj* conclusive

probité [prɔbite] *nf* integrity

problème [prɔblɛm] *nm* problem ▪ **problématique** *adj* problematic

procédé [prɔsede] *nm (technique)* process; *(méthode)* method; **p. de fabrication** manufacturing process

procéder [prɔsede] *vi (agir)* to proceed; **p. à** *(enquête, arrestation)* to carry out; **p. par élimination** to follow a process of elimination ▪ **procédure** *nf (méthode)* procedure; *(règles juridiques)* procedure; *(procès)* proceedings

procès [prɔsɛ] *nm Jur (criminel)* trial; *(civil)* lawsuit; **faire un p. à qn** to take sb to court

Il faut noter que le nom anglais **process** est un faux ami. Il signifie le plus souvent **processus**, **procédé**.

processeur [prɔsesœr] *nm Ordinat* processor
procession [prɔsesjɔ̃] *nf* procession
processus [prɔsesys] *nm* process
procès-verbal [prɔsɛverbal] (*pl* **procès-verbaux** [-o]) *nm (amende)* fine; *(constat)* report; *(de réunion)* minutes
prochain, -aine [prɔʃɛ̃, -ɛn] **1** *adj* next; *(mort, arrivée)* impending; *(mariage)* forthcoming; **un jour p.** one day soon **2** *nf Fam* **je descends à la prochaine** I'll get off at the next station; **à la prochaine!** see you soon! **3** *nm (semblable)* fellow (man) ▪ **prochainement** *adv* shortly, soon
proche [prɔʃ] *adj (dans l'espace)* near, close; *(dans le temps)* near, imminent; *(parent, ami)* close; **p. de** near (to), close to; **de p. en p.** step by step; **le P.-Orient** the Middle East ▪ **proches** *nmpl* close relations
proclamer [prɔklame] *vt* to proclaim (**que** that); **p. qn roi** to proclaim sb king ▪ **proclamation** *nf* proclamation
procréer [prɔkree] *vi* to procreate ▪ **procréation** *nf* procreation; **p. médicalement assistée** assisted conception
procuration [prɔkyrasjɔ̃] *nf* power of attorney; **par p.** by proxy
procurer [prɔkyre] **1** *vt* **p. qch à qn** *(sujet: personne)* to get sth for sb; *(sujet: chose)* to bring sb sth **2 se procurer** *vpr* **se p. qch** to obtain sth
procureur [prɔkyrœr] *nm* **p. de la République** *Br* ≃ public prosecutor, *Am* ≃ district attorney
prodige [prɔdiʒ] *nm (miracle)* wonder; *(personne)* prodigy; **tenir du p.** to be extraordinary ▪ **prodigieux, -ieuse** *adj* prodigious
prodigue [prɔdig] *adj (dépensier)* wasteful; *(généreux)* lavish (**de** with)
prodiguer [prɔdige] *vt* **p. qch à qn** to lavish sth on sb; **p. des conseils à qn** to pour out advice to sb
production [prɔdyksjɔ̃] *nf* production; *(produit)* product; *(d'usine)* output ▪ **producteur, -trice** **1** *nmf* producer **2** *adj* producing; **pays p. de pétrole** oil-producing country ▪ **productif, -ive** *adj* productive ▪ **productivité** *nf* productivity
produire* [prɔdɥir] **1** *vt (marchandise, émission, gaz)* to produce; *(effet, résultat)* to produce, to bring about **2 se produire** *vpr (événement)* to happen, to occur; *(acteur)* to perform ▪ **produit** *nm (article)* product; *(de vente, de collecte)* proceeds; **p. chimique** chemical; **p. de consommation courante** basic consumer product; *Écon* **p. intérieur brut** gross domestic product; *Écon* **p. national brut** gross national product; **produits agricoles** farm produce; **produits de beauté** cosmetics; **produits ménagers** cleaning products

proéminent, -ente [prɔeminɑ̃, -ɑ̃t] *adj* prominent
prof [prɔf] *nm Fam* teacher
profane [prɔfan] **1** *adj* secular **2** *nmf* lay person
profaner [prɔfane] *vt* to desecrate ▪ **profanation** *nf* desecration
proférer [prɔfere] *vt* to utter
professer [prɔfese] *vt* to profess (**que** that)
professeur [prɔfesœr] *nm* teacher; *(à l'université)* professor; **p. principal** *Br* class or form teacher, *Am* homeroom teacher
profession [prɔfesjɔ̃] *nf* occupation, profession; *(manuelle)* trade; **sans p.** not gainfully employed; **de p.** *(chanteur)* professional; **p. libérale** profession; **p. de foi** *Rel* profession of faith; *Fig* declaration of principles ▪ **professionnel, -elle** **1** *adj* professional; *(enseignement)* vocational **2** *nmf* professional
profil [prɔfil] *nm* profile; **de p.** (viewed) from the side; **p. de poste** job description ▪ **se profiler** *vpr* to be outlined (**sur** against)
profit [prɔfi] *nm* profit; **tirer p. de qch** to benefit from sth; **mettre qch à p.** to put sth to good use; **au p. des pauvres** in aid of the poor ▪ **profitable** *adj* profitable (**à** to) ▪ **profiter** *vi* **p. de** to take advantage of; **p. de la vie** to make the most of life; **p. à qn** to benefit sb ▪ **profiteur, -euse** *nmf Péj* profiteer
profond, -onde [prɔfɔ̃, -ɔ̃d] **1** *adj* deep; *(joie, erreur)* profound; *(cause)* underlying; **p. de 2 m** 2 m deep **2** *adv* deep **3** *nm* **au plus p. de la terre** in the depths of the earth ▪ **profondément** *adv* deeply; *(dormir)* soundly; *(triste, ému)* profoundly; *(creuser)* deep ▪ **profondeur** *nf* depth; **faire 6 m de p.** to be 6 m deep; **à 6 m de p.** at a depth of 6 m; **en p.** *(étude)* in-depth
profusion [prɔfyzjɔ̃] *nf* profusion; **à p.** in profusion
progéniture [prɔʒenityr] *nf* offspring
progiciel [prɔʒisjɛl] *nm Ordinat* (software) package
programmable [prɔgramabl] *adj* programmable ▪ **programmation** *nf Radio & TV* programme planning; *Ordinat* programming
programmateur [prɔgramatœr] *nm Tech* automatic control (device)
programme [prɔgram] *nm Br* programme, *Am* program; *(de parti politique)* manifesto; *Scol* curriculum; *(d'un cours)* syllabus; *Ordinat* program ▪ **programmer** *vt Ordinat* to program; *Radio, TV & Cin* to schedule ▪ **programmeur, -euse** *nmf* (computer) programmer
progrès [prɔgrɛ] *nm & nmpl* progress; **faire des p.** to make (good) progress ▪ **progresser** *vi* to progress ▪ **progressif, -ive** *adj* progressive ▪ **progression** *nf* progression ▪ **progressiste**

adj & nmf progressive ▪ **progressivement** *adv* progressively

prohiber [prɔibe] *vt* to prohibit, to forbid ▪ **prohibitif, -ive** *adj* prohibitive ▪ **prohibition** *nf* prohibition

proie [prwa] *nf* prey; *Fig* **être la p. de qn** to fall prey to sb; **être la p. des flammes** to be consumed by fire; *Fig* **en p. au doute** racked with doubt

projecteur [prɔʒɛktœr] *nm (de monument, stade)* floodlight; *(de prison, d'armée)* searchlight; *Théâtre* spotlight; *Cin* projector

projectile [prɔʒɛktil] *nm* missile

projection [prɔʒɛksjɔ̃] *nf (d'objet, de film)* projection; *(séance)* screening

projet [prɔʒɛ] *nm (intention)* plan; *(étude)* project; **faire des projets d'avenir** to make plans for the future; **p. de loi** bill

projeter [prɔʒte] *vt (lancer)* to project; *(liquide, boue)* to splash; *(lumière)* to flash; *(film)* to show; *(ombre)* to cast; *(prévoir)* to plan; **p. de faire qch** to plan to do sth

prolétaire [prɔletɛr] *nmf* proletarian ▪ **prolétariat** *nm* proletariat ▪ **prolétarien, -ienne** *adj* proletarian

proliférer [prɔlifere] *vi* to proliferate ▪ **prolifération** *nf* proliferation

prolifique [prɔlifik] *adj* prolific

prolixe [prɔliks] *adj* verbose, wordy

prologue [prɔlɔg] *nm* prologue (**de** to)

prolonger [prɔlɔ̃ʒe] **1** *vt (vie, débat, séjour)* to prolong; *(mur, route)* to extend **2 se prolonger** *vpr (séjour)* to be prolonged; *(réunion)* to go on; *(rue)* to continue ▪ **prolongation** *nf (de séjour)* extension; *Football* **prolongations** extra time ▪ **prolongement** *nm (de rue)* continuation; *(de mur)* extension; **prolongements** *(d'affaires)* repercussions

promenade [prɔmnad] *nf (à pied)* walk; *(courte)* stroll; *(avenue)* promenade; **faire une p.** to go for a walk; **faire une p. à cheval** to go for a ride

promener [prɔmne] **1** *vt (personne, chien)* to take for a walk; *(visiteur)* to show around; **p. qch sur qch** *(main, regard)* to run sth over sth **2 se promener** *vpr (à pied)* to go for a walk ▪ **promeneur, -euse** *nmf* stroller, walker

promesse [prɔmɛs] *nf* promise; **tenir sa p.** to keep one's promise

promettre* [prɔmɛtr] **1** *vt* to promise (**qch à qn sb** sth; **que** that); **p. de faire qch** to promise to do sth; **c'est promis** it's a promise **2** *vi Fig* to be promising **3 se promettre** *vpr* **se p. qch** *(à soi-même)* to promise oneself sth; *(l'un l'autre)* to promise each other sth; **se p. de faire qch** *(à soi-même)* to resolve to do sth ▪ **prometteur, -euse** *adj* promising

promontoire [prɔmɔ̃twar] *nm* headland

promoteur [prɔmɔtœr] *nm* **p. (immobilier)** property developer

promotion [prɔmosjɔ̃] *nf* (**a**) *(avancement)* & *Com* promotion; **en p.** *(produit)* on (special) offer; **p. sociale** upward mobility (**b**) *(d'une école) Br* year, *Am* class ▪ **promouvoir*** *vt (personne, produit)* to promote; **être promu** *(employé)* to be promoted (**à** to)

prompt, prompte [prɔ̃, prɔ̃t] *adj* prompt; **p. à faire qch** quick to do sth ▪ **promptitude** *nf* promptness

promulguer [prɔmylge] *vt* to promulgate

prôner [prone] *vt* to advocate

pronom [prɔnɔ̃] *nm Grammaire* pronoun ▪ **pronominal, -e, -aux, -ales** *adj Grammaire* pronominal

prononcer [prɔnɔ̃se] **1** *vt (articuler)* to pronounce; *(dire)* to utter; *(discours)* to deliver; *(jugement)* to pronounce **2 se prononcer** *vpr (mot)* to be pronounced; *(personne)* to give one's opinion (**sur** about *or* on); **se p. pour/ contre qch** to come out in favour of/against sth ▪ **prononcé, -ée** *adj* pronounced, marked ▪ **prononciation** *nf* pronunciation

pronostic [prɔnɔstik] *nm* forecast; *Méd* prognosis ▪ **pronostiquer** *vt* to forecast

propagande [prɔpagɑ̃d] *nf* propaganda

propager [prɔpaʒe] *vt*, **se propager** *vpr* to spread ▪ **propagation** *nf* spreading

propension [prɔpɑ̃sjɔ̃] *nf* propensity (**à qch** for sth; **à faire** to do)

prophète [prɔfɛt] *nm* prophet ▪ **prophétie** [-fesi] *nf* prophecy ▪ **prophétique** *adj* prophetic

propice [prɔpis] *adj* favourable (**à** to); **le moment p.** the right moment

proportion [prɔpɔrsjɔ̃] *nf* proportion; **respecter les proportions** to get the proportions right; **en p. de** in proportion to; **hors de p.** out of proportion (**avec** with); **l'affaire a pris des proportions considérables** the affair has blown up into a scandal ▪ **proportionné, -ée** *adj* proportionate (**à** to); **bien p.** wellproportioned ▪ **proportionnel, -elle 1** *adj* proportional **2** *nf* **proportionnelle** *(scrutin)* proportional representation

propos [prɔpo] *nm (sujet)* subject; *(intention)* purpose; **des p.** *(paroles)* talk, words; **à p. de qn/qch** about sb/sth; **à tout p.** constantly; **à p.** *(arriver)* at the right time; **à p.!** by the way!; **c'est à quel p.?** what is it about?; **juger à p. de faire qch** to consider it fit to do sth

proposer [prɔpoze] **1** *vt (suggérer)* to suggest, to propose (**qch à qn** sth to sb; **que** + *subjunctive* that); *(offrir)* to offer (**qch à qn** sb sth; **de faire** to do); **je te propose de rester** I suggest (that) you stay **2 se proposer** *vpr* to offer one's services; **se p. pour faire qch** to offer to do sth; **se p. de faire qch** to propose to do sth ▪ **proposition** *nf* suggestion, proposal; *(offre)* offer; *Grammaire* clause; **faire une p. à qn** to make a suggestion to sb

propre¹ [prɔpr] **1** *adj* clean; *(soigné)* neat; *(enfant)* toilet-trained; *(animal)* Br house-trained, *Am* house-broken; **p. comme un sou neuf** spick and span **2** *nm* **mettre qch au p.** to make a fair copy of sth; *Fam* **c'est du p.!** what a shocking way to behave! ▪ **proprement¹** [-əmã] *adv (avec propreté)* cleanly; *(avec soin)* neatly ▪ **propreté** [-əte] *nf* cleanliness; *(soin)* neatness

propre² [prɔpr] **1** *adj (à soi)* own; **mon p. argent** my own money; **ses propres mots** his/her very words; **être p. à qn/qch** *(particulier)* to be characteristic of sb/sth; **être p. à qch** *(adapté)* to be suitable for sth; **au sens p.** literally **2** *nm* **le p. de** *(qualité)* the distinctive quality of; **au p.** *(au sens propre)* literally ▪ **proprement²** [-əmã] *adv (strictement)* strictly; **à p. parler** strictly speaking; **le village p. dit** the village proper

> Il faut noter que l'adjectif anglais **proper** est un faux ami. Il ne se rapporte jamais à la propreté.

propriétaire [prɔprijetɛr] *nmf* owner; *(de location)* landlord, *f* landlady; **p. foncier** landowner

propriété [prɔprijete] *nf (fait de posséder)* ownership; *(chose possédée)* property; *(caractéristique)* property; **p. littéraire** copyright; **p. privée** private property

> Il faut noter que le nom anglais **propriety** est un faux ami. Il signifie **bienséance**.

propulser [prɔpylse] *vt* to propel ▪ **propulsion** *nf* propulsion; **sous-marin à p. nucléaire** nuclear-powered submarine

prosaïque [prɔzaik] *adj* prosaic

proscrire* [prɔskrir] *vt* to proscribe, to ban ▪ **proscrit, -ite** *nmf Littéraire (banni)* exile

prose [proz] *nf* prose

prospecter [prɔspɛkte] *vt (sol)* to prospect; *(clients)* to canvass ▪ **prospecteur, -trice** *nmf* prospector ▪ **prospection** *nf (de sol)* prospecting; *Com* canvassing

prospectus [prɔspɛktys] *nm* leaflet

prospère [prɔspɛr] *adj* prosperous; *(santé)* glowing ▪ **prospérer** *vi* to prosper ▪ **prospérité** *nf* prosperity

prostate [prɔstat] *nf Anat* prostate (gland)

prosterner [prɔstɛrne] **se prosterner** *upr* to prostrate oneself *(devant* before)

prostituer [prɔstitɥe] **1** *vt* to prostitute **2 se prostituer** *upr* to prostitute oneself ▪ **prostitué** *nm* male prostitute ▪ **prostituée** *nf* prostitute ▪ **prostitution** *nf* prostitution

prostré, -ée [prɔstre] *adj* prostrate

protagoniste [prɔtagɔnist] *nmf* protagonist

protecteur, -trice [prɔtɛktœr, -tris] **1** *nmf* protector; *(mécène)* patron **2** *adj (geste, crème)* protective; *Péj (ton, air)* patronizing

▪ **protection** *nf* protection; **de p.** *(écran)* protective; **assurer la p. de qn** to ensure sb's safety; **p. de l'environnement** protection of the environment; **p. sociale** social welfare system ▪ **protectionnisme** *nm Écon* protectionism

protéger [prɔteʒe] **1** *vt* to protect *(de* from; **contre** against) **2 se protéger** *upr* to protect oneself ▪ **protégé** *nm* protégé ▪ **protège-cahier** *(pl* protège-cahiers*)* *nm* exercise book cover ▪ **protégée** *nf* protégée

protéine [prɔtein] *nf* protein

protestant, -ante [prɔtɛstã, -ãt] *adj & nmf* Protestant ▪ **protestantisme** *nm* Protestantism

protester [prɔtɛste] *vi* to protest *(contre* against); **p. de son innocence** to protest one's innocence ▪ **protestataire** *nmf* protester ▪ **protestation** *nf* protest *(contre* against); **en signe de p.** as a protest; **protestations d'amitiés** protestations of friendship

prothèse [prɔtɛz] *nf* prosthesis; **p. auditive** hearing aid; **p. dentaire** false teeth

protocole [prɔtɔkɔl] *nm* protocol

prototype [prɔtɔtip] *nm* prototype

protubérance [prɔtyberãs] *nf* protuberance

proue [pru] *nf* bows, prow

prouesse [prues] *nf* feat

prouver [pruve] *vt* to prove *(que* that)

Provence [prɔvãs] *nf* **la P.** Provence ▪ **provençal, -e, -aux, -ales 1** *adj* Provençal **2** *nmf* **P., Provençale** Provençal

provenir* [prɔvənir] *vi* **p. de** to come from ▪ **provenance** *nf* origin; **en p. de** from

proverbe [prɔvɛrb] *nm* proverb ▪ **proverbial, -e, -iaux, -iales** *adj* proverbial

providence [prɔvidãs] *nf* providence ▪ **providentiel, -ielle** *adj* providential

province [prɔvɛs] *nf* province; **la p.** the provinces; **en p.** in the provinces; **de p.** *(ville)* provincial ▪ **provincial, -e, -iaux, -iales** *adj & nmf* provincial

proviseur [prɔvizœr] *nm Br* headmaster, *f* headmistress, *Am* principal

provision [prɔvizjɔ̃] *nf* **(a)** *(réserve)* supply, stock; **provisions** *(nourriture)* shopping; **panier/sac à provisions** shopping basket/bag; **faire des provisions de qch** to stock up on sth **(b)** *(somme)* credit; *(acompte)* deposit

provisoire [prɔvizwar] *adj* temporary; **à titre p.** temporarily ▪ **provisoirement** *adv* temporarily, provisionally

provoquer [prɔvɔke] *vt (incendie, mort)* to cause; *(réaction)* to provoke; *(colère, désir)* to arouse; **p. un accouchement** to induce labour ▪ **provocant, -ante** *adj* provocative ▪ **provocateur** *nm* troublemaker ▪ **provocation** *nf* provocation

proxénète [prɔksenɛt] *nm* pimp

proximité [prɔksimite] *nf* closeness, proximity; **à p.** close by; **à p. de** close to; **de p.** local

Prozac® [prɔzak] *nm* Prozac®

prude [pryd] **1** *adj* prudish **2** *nf* prude

prudent, -ente [prydã, -ãt] *adj (personne)* cautious, careful; *(décision)* sensible ▪**prudemment** [-amã] *adv* cautiously, carefully ▪**prudence** *nf* caution, care; **par p.** as a precaution

prune [pryn] *nf (fruit)* plum; *Fam* **pour des prunes** for nothing ▪**pruneau, -x** *nm* prune ▪**prunier** *nm* plum tree

---

Il faut noter que le nom anglais **prune** est un faux ami. Il signifie **pruneau**.

---

prunelle [prynɛl] *nf (de l'œil)* pupil; **il y tient comme à la p. de ses yeux** it's the apple of his eye

P.-S. [pɛɛs] *(abrév* **post-scriptum)** PS

psaume [psom] *nm* psalm

pseudonyme [psødɔnim] *nm* pseudonym

psychanalyse [psikanaliz] *nf* psychoanalysis ▪**psychanalyste** *nmf* psychoanalyst

psychédélique [psikedelik] *adj* psychedelic

psychiatre [psikjatr] *nmf* psychiatrist ▪**psychiatrie** *nf* psychiatry ▪**psychiatrique** *adj* psychiatric

psychique [psiʃik] *adj* psychic

psychologie [psikɔlɔʒi] *nf* psychology ▪**psychologique** *adj* psychological ▪**psychologue** *nmf* psychologist; **p. scolaire** educational psychologist

psychopathe [psikopat] *nmf* psychopath

psychose [psikoz] *nf* psychosis

psychothérapie [psikoterapi] *nf* psychotherapy; **faire une p.** to be in therapy ▪**psychothérapeute** *nmf* psychotherapist

PTT [petete] *(abrév* **Postes, Télécommunications et Télédiffusion)** *nfpl Anciennement* ≃ Post Office and Telecommunications Service

pu [py] *pp de* **pouvoir 1**

puant, puante [pɥã, pɥãt] *adj* stinking ▪**puanteur** *nf* stink, stench

pub [pyb] *nf Fam (secteur)* advertising; *(annonce)* ad

puberté [pybɛrte] *nf* puberty

public, -ique [pyblik] **1** *adj* public; **dette publique** national debt **2** *nm (de spectacle)* audience; **le grand p.** the general public; **film grand p.** film suitable for the general public; **en p.** in public; *(émission)* before a live audience; *Écon* **le p.** the public sector ▪**publiquement** *adv* publicly

publication [pyblikasjɔ̃] *nf (action, livre)* publication; **p. assistée par ordinateur** desktop publishing ▪**publier** *vt* to publish

publicité [pyblisite] *nf (secteur)* advertising; *(annonce)* advertisement, advert; *Radio & TV* commercial; **agence de p.** advertising

agency; **faire de la p. pour qch** to advertise sth ▪**publicitaire 1** *adj* **agence p.** advertising agency; **film p.** promotional film **2** *nmf* advertising executive

puce [pys] *nf (insecte)* flea; *Ordinat (micro-)*chip; **le marché aux puces, les puces** the flea market; *Fig* **mettre la p. à l'oreille de qn** to make sb suspicious

pudeur [pydœr] *nf* modesty; **par p.** out of a sense of decency ▪**pudibond, -onde** *adj* prudish ▪**pudique** *adj* modest

puériculture [pɥerikyltyr] *nf* child care ▪**puériculteur, -trice** *nmf* nursery nurse

puéril, -ile [pɥeril] *adj* puerile ▪**puérilité** *nf* puerility

puis [pɥi] *adv* then; **et p.** *(ensuite)* and then; *(en plus)* and besides

puiser [pɥize] **1** *vt* to draw (**à/dans** from) **2** *vi* **p. dans qch** to dip into sth

puisque [pɥisk(ə)] *conj* since, as

puissant, -ante [pɥisã, -ãt] *adj* powerful ▪**puissamment** [-amã] *adv* powerfully ▪**puissance** *nf (force, nation) & Math* power; **les grandes puissances** the great powers; **en p.** *(meurtrier)* potential; *Math* **dix p. quatre** ten to the power of four

puisse(s), puissent [pɥis] *voir* **pouvoir 1**

puits [pɥi] *nm* well; *(de mine)* shaft; *Fig* **un p. de science** a fount of knowledge; **p. de pétrole** oil well

pull-over [pylɔver] *(pl* **pull-overs)**, **pull** [pyl] *nm* sweater, *Br* jumper

pulluler [pylyle] *vi (abonder)* to swarm

pulmonaire [pylmɔner] *adj* pulmonary

pulpe [pylp] *nf (de fruits)* pulp

pulsation [pylsasjɔ̃] *nf (heart)*beat

pulsion [pylsjɔ̃] *nf* impulse; **p. de mort** death wish

pulvériser [pylverize] *vt (vaporiser)* to spray; *(broyer) & Fig* to pulverize; *Fam Sport* **p. un record** to smash a record ▪**pulvérisateur** *nm* spray ▪**pulvérisation** *nf (de liquide)* spraying

puma [pyma] *nm* puma

punaise [pynɛz] *nf (insecte)* bug; *(clou) Br* drawing pin, *Am* thumbtack ▪**punaiser** *vt Fam* to pin up

punch *nm* (**a**) [pɔ̃ʃ] *(boisson)* punch (**b**) [pœnʃ] *Fam (énergie)* punch

punir [pynir] *vt* to punish; **p. qn de qch** *(bêtise, crime)* to punish sb for sth; **p. qn de mort** to punish sb with death ▪**punition** *nf* punishment

punk [pœnk] *adj inv & nmf* punk

pupille [pypij] **1** *nf (de l'œil)* pupil **2** *nmf (enfant)* ward

pupitre [pypitr] *nm (d'écolier)* desk; *(d'orateur)* lectern; *Ordinat* console; *Ordinat* **p. de visualisation** visual display unit

pur, pure [pyr] *adj* pure; *(alcool)* neat, straight ▪ **purement** *adv* purely; **p. et simplement** purely and simply ▪ **pureté** *nf* purity

purée [pyre] *nf* purée; **p. (de pommes de terre)** mashed potatoes, *Br* mash

purgatoire [pyrgatwar] *nm* purgatory

purge [pyrʒ] *nf (à des fins médicales, politiques)* purge

purger [pyrʒe] *vt (patient)* to purge; *(radiateur)* to bleed; *(peine de prison)* to serve

purifier [pyrifje] *vt* to purify ▪ **purification** *nf* purification; **p. ethnique** ethnic cleansing

purin [pyrɛ̃] *nm* liquid manure

puriste [pyrist] *nmf* purist

puritain, -aine [pyritɛ̃, -ɛn] *adj & nmf* puritan

pur-sang [pyrsɑ̃] *nm inv* thoroughbred

pus[1] [py] *nm (liquide)* pus, matter

pus[2]**, put** [py] *voir* **pouvoir 1**

putain [pytɛ̃] *Vulg* **1** *nf* whore **2** *exclam* **p.!** shit!

putois [pytwa] *nm* polecat

putréfier [pytrefje] *vt,* **se putréfier** *vpr* to putrefy ▪ **putréfaction** *nf* putrefaction

puzzle [pœzl] *nm* (jigsaw) puzzle

P.-V. [peve] *(abrév* **procès-verbal**) *nm Fam* (parking) ticket

PVC [pevese] *nm (matière plastique)* PVC

pygmée [pigme] *nmf* pygmy

pyjama [piʒama] *nm Br* pyjamas, *Am* pajamas; **un p.** a pair of *Br* pyjamas *or Am* pajamas; **être en p.** to be in *Br* pyjamas *or Am* pajamas

pylône [pilon] *nm* pylon

pyramide [piramid] *nf* pyramid

Pyrénées [pirene] *nfpl* **les P.** the Pyrenees

Pyrex® [pireks] *nm* Pyrex®; **plat en P.** Pyrex® dish

pyromane [pirɔman] *nmf* arsonist

python [pitɔ̃] *nm* python

Q, q [ky] *nm inv* Q, q

QCM [kyseɛm] (*abrév* **questionnaire à choix multiple**) *nm* multiple-choice questionnaire

QI [kyi] (*abrév* **quotient intellectuel**) *nm inv* IQ

qu' [k] *voir* **que**

quadragénaire [kwadraʒener] (*Fam* **quadra** [kwadra]) **1** *adj* **être q.** to be in one's forties **2** *nmf* person in his/her forties

quadrillage [kadrijaʒ] *nm (de carte)* grid

quadriller [kadrije] *vt (quartier, ville)* to put under tight surveillance; *(papier)* to mark into squares ▪ **quadrillé, -ée** *adj (papier)* squared

quadrupède [k(w)adryped] *adj & nm* quadruped

quadruple [k(w)adrypl] **1** *adj* quadruple, fourfold **2** *nm* **le q. (de)** *(quantité)* four times as much (as); *(nombre)* four times as many (as) ▪ **quadrupler** *vti* to quadruple ▪ **quadruplés, -ées** *nmfpl* quadruplets

quai [kɛ] *nm (de port)* quay; *(de fleuve)* embankment; *(de gare, de métro)* platform

qualification [kalifikɑsjɔ̃] *nf (action, d'équipe, de sportif)* qualification; *(désignation)* description ▪ **qualificatif** *1 adj Grammaire* qualifying **2** *nm (mot)* term

qualifier [kalifje] **1** *vt (équipe)* to qualify (**pour** qch for sth; **pour faire** to do); *(décrire)* to describe (**de** as) **2 se qualifier** *vpr (équipe)* to qualify (**pour** for) ▪ **qualifié, -iée** *adj (équipe)* that has qualified; **q. pour faire qch** qualified to do sth

qualité [kalite] *nf (de personne, de produit)* quality; *(occupation)* occupation; **produit de q.** quality product; **de bonne q.** of good quality; **en q. de** in his/her/*etc* capacity as; **q. de vie** quality of life ▪ **qualitatif, -ive** *adj* qualitative

quand [kɑ̃] *conj & adv* when; **q. je viendrai** when I come; **à q. le mariage?** when's the wedding?; **q. bien même vous le feriez** even if you did it; *Fam* **q. même** all the same

quant [kɑ̃] **quant à** *prép* as for

quantifier [kɑ̃tifje] *vt* to quantify ▪ **quantitatif, -ive** *adj* quantitative

quantité [kɑ̃tite] *nf* quantity; **une q., des quantités** *(beaucoup)* a lot (**de** of); **en q.** in abundance

quarante [karɑ̃t] *adj & nm inv* forty; **un q.-cinq tours** *(disque)* a single ▪ **quarantaine** *nf* (a)

une **q. (de)** *(nombre)* (about) forty; **avoir la q.** *(âge)* to be about forty (**b**) *Méd* quarantine; **mettre qn en q.** to quarantine sb ▪ **quarantième** *adj & nmf* fortieth

quart [kar] *nm* (**a**) *(fraction)* quarter; **q. de litre** quarter litre, quarter of a litre; **q. d'heure** quarter of an hour; **une heure et q.** an hour and a quarter; **il est une heure et q.** it's a quarter *Br* past *or Am* after one; **une heure moins le q.** (a) quarter to one; *Fam* **passer un mauvais q. d'heure** to have a bad time of it; *Sport* **quarts de finale** quarter finals (**b**) *Naut* watch; **être de q.** to be on watch ▪ **quart-monde** *nm* **le q.** the least developed countries

quarté [karte] *nm* = system of betting on four horses in the same race

quartette [kwartet] *nm* jazz quartet

quartier [kartje] *nm* (**a**) *(de ville)* district; **de q.** local; **les beaux quartiers** the fashionable district; **q. général** headquarters (**b**) *(de lune)* quarter; *(de pomme)* piece; *(d'orange)* segment (**c**) *(expressions)* **ne pas faire de q.** to give no quarter; **avoir q. libre** to be free

quartz [kwarts] *nm* quartz; **montre à q.** quartz watch

quasi [kazi] *adv* almost ▪ **quasi-** *préf* **quasi-obscurité** near darkness; **la quasi-totalité des membres** almost all the members ▪ **quasiment** *adv* almost

quatorze [katɔrz] *adj & nm inv* fourteen ▪ **quatorzième** *adj & nmf* fourteenth

quatre [katr] *adj & nm inv* four; *Fig* **se mettre en q.** to bend over backwards (**pour faire** to do); *Fam* **manger comme q.** to eat like a horse; *Fam* **un de ces q.** some day soon; *Fam* **q. heures** *(goûter)* afternoon snack ▪ **quatrième** *adj & nm* fourth

quatre-vingt [katrəvɛ̃] *adj & nm* eighty; **quatre-vingts ans** eighty years; **q.-un** eighty-one; **page q.** page eighty ▪ **quatre-vingt-dix** *adj & nm inv* ninety

quatuor [kwatɥɔr] *nm* quartet; **q. à cordes** string quartet

quat'zyeux [katzjø] **entre quat'zyeux** *adv* in private

que [kə]

que becomes **qu'** before a vowel or mute h.

1 *conj* (**a**) *(complétif)* that; **je pense qu'elle restera** I think (that) she'll stay; **qu'elle vienne**

ou non whether she comes or not; **qu'il s'en aille!** let him leave!; **ça fait un an q. je suis là** I've been here for a year; **ça fait un an q. je suis parti** I left a year ago (**b**) (*de comparaison*) than; (*avec 'aussi', 'même', 'tel', 'autant'*) as; **plus/moins âgé q. lui** older/younger than him; **aussi sage/fatigué q. toi** as wise/tired as you; **le même q. Pauline** the same as Pauline (**c**) (**ne...**) **que** only; **tu n'as qu'un euro** you only have one euro **2** *adv* (**ce**) **qu'il est bête!** (*comme*) he's really stupid!; **q. de gens!** what a lot of people! **3** *pron relatif* (*chose*) that, which; (*personne*) that, whom; (*temps*) when; **le livre q. j'ai** the book (that *or* which) I have; **l'ami q. j'ai** the friend (that *or* whom) I have; **un jour qu'il faisait beau** one day when the weather was fine **4** *pron interrogatif* what; **q. fait-il?, qu'est-ce qu'il fait?** what is he doing?; **qu'est-ce qui est dans ta poche?** what's in your pocket?; **q. préférez-vous?** which do you prefer?

Québec [kebɛk] *nm* **le Q.** Quebec ▪ **québecois, -oise** *1 adj* (of *or* from) Quebec **2** *nmf* **Q., Québécoise** Quebec(k)er **3** *nm* (*langue*) Quebec French

quel, quelle [kɛl] **1** *adj interrogatif* (*chose*) what, which; (*personne*) which; **q. livre préférez-vous?** which *or* what book do you prefer?; **q. est cet homme?** who is that man?; **je sais q. est ton but** I know what your aim is; **je ne sais à q. employé m'adresser** I don't know which clerk to ask **2** *pron interrogatif* which (one); **q. est le meilleur?** which (one) is the best? **3** *adj exclamatif* **q. idiot!** what a fool!; **q. joli bébé!** what a pretty baby! **4** *adj relatif* **q. qu'il soit** (*chose*) whatever it may be; (*personne*) whoever it *or* he may be

quelconque [kɛlkɔ̃k] **1** *adj indéfini* any; **donne-moi un livre q.** give me any book; **sous un prétexte q.** on some pretext or other **2** *adj* (*insignifiant*) ordinary

quelque [kɛlk] **1** *adj indéfini* some; **quelques** some, a few; **les quelques amies qu'elle a** the few friends she has; **sous q. prétexte que ce soit** on whatever pretext; **q. numéro qu'elle choisisse** whichever number she chooses **2** *adv* (*environ*) about, some; **q. peu** somewhat; **q. grand qu'il soit** however tall he may be; *Fam* **100 euros et q.** 100 euros and a bit, 100-odd euros

quelque chose [kɛlkəʃoz] *pron indéfini* something; **q. d'autre** something else; **q. de grand** something big; **q. de plus pratique/de moins lourd** something more practical/less heavy; **ça m'a fait q.** it touched *or* moved me

quelquefois [kɛlkəfwa] *adv* sometimes

quelque part [kɛlkəpar] *adv* somewhere; (*dans les questions*) anywhere

quelques-uns, -unes [kɛlkəzœ̃, -yn] *pron* some, a few

quelqu'un [kɛlkœ̃] *pron indéfini* someone, somebody; (*dans les questions*) anyone, anybody; **q. d'intelligent** someone clever

quémander [kemɑ̃de] *vt* to beg for

qu'en-dira-t-on [kɑ̃diratɔ̃] *nm* **le q.** gossip

querelle [kərɛl] *nf* quarrel; **chercher q. à qn** to try to pick a fight with sb ▪ **se quereller** *vpr* to quarrel ▪ **querelleur, -euse** *adj* quarrelsome

question [kɛstjɔ̃] *nf* (*interrogation*) question; (*affaire*) matter, question; **il est q. qu'ils déménagent** there's some talk about them moving; **il a été q. de vous** we/they talked about you; **il n'en est pas q.** it's out of the question; **en q.** in question; **hors de q.** out of the question; **remettre qch en q.** to call sth into question; **q. de confiance** vote of confidence ▪ **questionnaire** *nm* questionnaire ▪ **questionner** *vt* to question (**sur** about)

quête [kɛt] *nf* (**a**) (*collecte*) collection; **faire la q.** to collect money (**b**) (*recherche*) quest (**de** for); **en q.** de in quest *or* search of ▪ **quêter** [kete] **1** *vt* to seek **2** *vi* to collect money

queue [kø] *nf* (**a**) (*d'animal*) tail; (*de fleur, de fruit*) stalk; (*de poêle*) handle; (*de train, de cortège*) rear; **être en q. de classement** to be bottom of the table; **faire une q. de poisson à qn** to cut in front of sb; **à la q. leu leu** in single file; **ça n'a ni q. ni tête** it just doesn't make sense; **q. de cheval** (*coiffure*) ponytail (**b**) (*file*) *Br* queue, *Am* line; **faire la q.** *Br* to queue up, *Am* to stand in line (**c**) (*de billard*) cue ▪ **queue-de-pie** (*pl* **queues-de-pie**) *nf* (*veste*) tail coat, *Fam* tails

qui [ki] **1** *pron interrogatif* (*personne*) who; (*en complément*) whom; **q. (est-ce qui) est là?** who's there?; **q. désirez-vous voir?, q. est-ce que vous désirez voir?** who(m) do you want to see?; **à q. est ce livre?** whose book is this?; **q. encore?, q. d'autre?** who else?; **je demande q. a téléphoné** I'm asking who phoned **2** *pron relatif* (**a**) (*sujet*) (*personne*) who, that; (*chose*) which, that; **l'homme q. est là** the man who's here *or* that's here; **la maison q. se trouve en face** the house which is *or* that's opposite (**b**) (*sans antécédent*) **q. que vous soyez** whoever you are; **amène q. tu veux** bring along anyone you like *or* whoever you like; **q. que ce soit** anyone (**c**) (*après une préposition*) **la femme de q. je parle** the woman I'm talking about; **l'ami sur l'aide de q. je compte** the friend on whose help I rely

quiche [kiʃ] *nf* quiche; **q. lorraine** quiche lorraine

quiconque [kikɔ̃k] *pron* (*sujet*) whoever; (*complément*) anyone

quiétude [kjetyd] *nf Littéraire* quiet; **en toute q.** (*sans souci*) with an easy mind

quignon [kiɲɔ̃] *nm* chunk

quille [kij] *nf* (*de navire*) keel; (*de jeu*) (bowling) pin, *Br* skittle; *Fam (jambe)* pin; **jouer aux quilles** to bowl, *Br* to play skittles

quincaillier, -ière [kɛ̃kaje, -jɛr] *nmf* hardware dealer, *Br* ironmonger ▪ **quincaillerie** *nf (magasin)* hardware shop; *(objets)* hardware

quinine [kinin] *nf* quinine

quinquennal, -e, -aux, -ales [kɛ̃kenal, -o] *adj* **plan q.** five-year plan ▪ **quinquennat** *nm Pol* five-year term (of office)

quinte [kɛ̃t] *nf* **q. (de toux)** coughing fit

quintessence [kɛ̃tesɑ̃s] *nf* quintessence

quintette [kɛ̃tet] *nm* quintet

quintuple [kɛ̃typl] **1** *adj* **q. de** fivefold **2** *nm* **le q. (de)** *(quantité)* five times as much (as); *(nombre)* five times as many (as) ▪ **quintupler** *vti* to increase fivefold ▪ **quintuplés, -ées** *nmfpl* quintuplets

quinze [kɛ̃z] *adj & nm inv* fifteen; **q. jours** two weeks, *Br* a fortnight; *Rugby* **le q. de France** the French fifteen ▪ **quinzaine** *nf* **une q. (de)** (about) fifteen; **une q. (de jours)** two weeks, *Br* a fortnight ▪ **quinzième** *adj & nmf* fifteenth

quiproquo [kiprɔko] *nm* mix-up

quittance [kitɑ̃s] *nf (reçu)* receipt; **q. de loyer** rent receipt

quitte [kit] *adj* quits (**envers** with); **q. à faire qch** even if it means doing sth; **en être q. pour qch** to get off *or* escape with sth

quitter [kite] **1** *vt (personne, lieu, poste)* to leave; *(vêtement)* to take off; **q. la route** to go off the road; **ne pas q. qn des yeux** to keep one's eyes on sb **2** *vi* **ne quittez pas!** *(au téléphone)* hold the line! **3 se quitter** *vpr* to part; **ils ne se quittent plus** they are inseparable

qui-vive [kiviv] **sur le qui-vive** *adv* on the alert

quoi [kwa] *pron* what; *(après une préposition)* which; **à q. penses-tu?** what are you thinking about?; **après q.** after which; **ce à q. je m'attendais** what I was expecting; **de q. manger** something to eat; *(assez)* enough to eat; **de q. écrire** something to write with; **q. que je dise** whatever I say; **q. qu'il advienne** whatever happens; **q. qu'il en soit** be that as it may; **il n'y a pas de q.!** *(en réponse à 'merci')* don't mention it!; **q.?** what?; *Fam* **c'est un idiot, q.!** he's a fool!; **et puis q. encore!** really, what next!

quoique [kwak] *conj* (al)though; **quoiqu'il soit pauvre** (al)though he's poor

quolibet [kɔlibe] *nm Littéraire* gibe

quorum [kwɔrɔm] *nm* quorum

quota [kwɔta] *nm* quota

quote-part [kɔtpar] *(pl* **quotes-parts)** *nf* share

quotidien, -ienne [kɔtidjɛ̃, -jɛn] **1** *adj* daily **2** *nm* daily (paper) ▪ **quotidiennement** *adv* daily

quotient [kɔsjɑ̃] *nm* quotient

R, r [er] *nm inv* R, r
rab [rab] *nm Fam (nourriture)* extra; **faire du r.**
(au travail) to put in a bit of overtime
rabâcher [rabɑʃe] **1** *vt* to repeat endlessly **2** *vi*
to say the same thing over and over again
rabais [rabɛ] *nm* reduction, discount; **faire un r.
à qn** to give sb a discount
rabaisser [rabese] **1** *vt (dénigrer)* to belittle **2 se
rabaisser** *vpr* to belittle oneself
rabat-joie [rabaʒwa] *nm inv* killjoy
rabattre* [rabatr] **1** *vt (col)* to turn down;
(couvercle) to close; *(strapontin) (pour s'asseoir)*
to fold down; *(en se levant)* to fold up; *(gibier)* to
drive **2 se rabattre** *vpr (se refermer)* to close;
(strapontin) to fold down; *(véhicule)* to pull
back in; *Fig* **se r. sur qch** to fall back on sth
rabbin [rabɛ̃] *nm Rel* rabbi
rabibocher [rabibɔʃe] *Fam* **1** *vt* to patch things
up between **2 se rabibocher** *vpr* to patch
things up (**avec** with)
rabiot [rabjo] *nm* = **rab**
râblé, -ée [rɑble] *adj* stocky
rabot [rabo] *nm (outil)* plane ▪ **raboter** *vt* to
plane
raboteux, -euse [rabɔtø, -øz] *adj* uneven
rabougri, -ie [rabugri] *adj (personne, plante)*
stunted
rabrouer [rabrue] *vt* to snub
racaille [rakɑj] *nf* scum, riff-raff
raccommoder [rakɔmɔde] **1** *vt (linge)* to mend;
(chaussette) to darn; *Fam (personnes)* to patch
things up between **2 se raccommoder** *vpr*
Fam to patch things up (**avec** with)
▪ **raccommodage** *nm (de linge)* mending; *(de
chaussette)* darning
raccompagner [rakɔ̃paɲe] *vt* to take back, to
accompany
raccord [rakɔr] *nm (dispositif)* connection; *(de
papier peint)* join; *(de peinture)* touch-up
▪ **raccordement** [-əmɑ̃] *nm (action, lien)*
connection ▪ **raccorder** *vt, se raccorder* *vpr*
to link up (**à** to)
raccourcir [rakursir] **1** *vt* to shorten **2** *vi* to get
shorter ▪ **raccourci** *nm* short cut; **en r.** in brief
raccrocher [rakrɔʃe] **1** *vt (objet tombé)* to hang
back up; *(téléphone)* to put down **2** *vi (au
téléphone)* to hang up; *Fam (sportif)* to retire **3
se raccrocher** *vpr* **se r. à qch** to catch hold of
sth; *Fig* to cling to sth

race [ras] *nf (ethnie)* race; *(animale)* breed;
chien de r. pedigree dog ▪ **racé, -ée** *adj
(cheval)* thoroughbred; *(personne)* distinguished
▪ **racial, -e, -iaux, -iales** *adj* racial
▪ **racisme** *nm* racism ▪ **raciste** *adj & nmf*
racist
rachat [raʃa] *nm (de voiture, d'appartement)*
repurchase; *(de firme)* buy-out; *Rel* atonement
▪ **racheter** **1** *vt (acheter davantage)* to buy
some more; *(remplacer)* to buy another; *(firme)*
to buy out; *(péché)* to atone for; *(faute)* to make
up for **2 se racheter** *vpr* to make amends, to
redeem oneself
racine [rasin] *nf (de plante, de personne)* & *Math*
root; **prendre r.** to take root
racket [raket] *nm Fam* racket
raclée [rakle] *nf Fam* thrashing; **prendre une r.**
to get a thrashing
racler [rakle] **1** *vt* to scrape; *(peinture, boue)* to
scrape off **2 se racler** *vpr* **se r. la gorge** to clear
one's throat ▪ **raclette** *nf (outil)* scraper; *(plat)*
raclette *(Swiss dish consisting of potatoes and
melted cheese)* ▪ **racloir** *nm* scraper
racoler [rakɔle] *vt (sujet: prostituée)* to solicit
▪ **racolage** *nm (de prostituée)* soliciting
▪ **racoleur, -euse** *adj (publicité)* eye-catching
raconter [rakɔ̃te] *vt (histoire, mensonge)* to tell;
(événement) to tell about; **r. qch à qn** *(histoire)*
to tell sb sth; *(événement)* to tell sb about sth; **r.
à qn que...** to tell sb that...; *Fam* **qu'est-ce que
tu racontes?** what are you talking about?
▪ **racontars** *nmpl* gossip
racornir [rakɔrnir] *vt, se racornir* *vpr (durcir)* to
harden; *(dessécher)* to shrivel
radar [radar] *nm* radar; **contrôle r.** radar speed
check; *Fam* **être au r.** to be on automatic pilot
rade [rad] *nf* harbour; *Fam* **laisser qn en r.** to
leave sb in the lurch; *Fam* **tomber en r.** to
break down
radeau, -x [rado] *nm* raft
radiateur [radjatœr] *nm* radiator; **r. électrique**
electric heater
radiation [radjɑsjɔ̃] *nf Phys* radiation;
(suppression) removal (**de** from) ▪ **radier** *vt* to
strike off (**de** from)
radical, -e, -aux, -ales [radikal, -o] **1** *adj*
radical **2** *nm (de mot)* stem
radieux, -ieuse [radjø, -jøz] *adj (personne,
visage, soleil)* radiant; *(temps)* glorious

radin, -ine [radɛ̃, -in] *Fam* **1** *adj* stingy, *Br* tight **2** *nmf* skinflint

radio [radjo] **1** *nf* (**a**) *(poste)* radio; *(station)* radio station; **à la r.** on the radio; **r. libre** = independent radio station (**b**) *Méd* X-ray; **passer une r.** to have an X-ray; **faire passer une r. à qn** to give sb an X-ray **2** *nm (opérateur)* radio operator ■ **radio-réveil** *(pl* **radios-réveils)** *nm* radio alarm clock ■ **radio-taxi** *(pl* **radio-taxis)** *nm Br* minicab

radioactif, -ive [radjoaktif, -iv] *adj* radioactive ■ **radioactivité** *nf* radioactivity

radiodiffuser [radjodifyse] *vt* to broadcast ■ **radiodiffusion** *nf* broadcasting

radiographie [radjografi] *nf (photo)* X-ray; *(technique)* radiography ■ **radiographier** *vt* to X-ray ■ **radiologie** *nf Méd* radiology ■ **radiologue** *nmf (technicien)* radiographer; *(médecin)* radiologist

radioguidé, -ée [radjogide] *adj* radio-controlled

radiophonique [radjofɔnik] *adj* **émission r.** radio broadcast ■ **radiotélévisé, -ée** *adj* broadcast on radio and television

radis [radi] *nm* radish; **r. noir** black radish; *Fam* **je n'ai plus un r.** I'm broke *or Br* skint

radoter [radɔte] **1** *vt Fam* to rabbit on about **2** *vi (rabâcher)* to rabbit on; *(divaguer)* to ramble on ■ **radotage** *nm (divagations)* rambling

radoucir [radusir] **se radoucir** *upr (personne)* to calm down; *(temps)* to become milder ■ **radoucissement** *nm (du temps)* milder spell

rafale [rafal] *nf (vent)* gust; *(de mitrailleuse)* burst; **par rafales** in gusts

raffermir [rafermir] **1** *vt (autorité)* to strengthen; *(muscles)* to tone up **2** **se raffermir** *upr (muscle)* to become stronger

raffiné, -ée [rafine] *adj* refined ■ **raffinement** *nm* refinement

raffiner [rafine] *vt* to refine ■ **raffinage** *nm* refining ■ **raffinerie** *nf* refinery

raffoler [rafɔle] *vi Fam* **r. de qch** to be mad about sth

raffut [rafy] *nm Fam* din; **faire du r.** to make a din

rafiot [rafjo] *nm Fam Péj (bateau)* old tub

rafistoler [rafistɔle] *vt Fam* to patch up

rafle [rafl] *nf* raid ■ **rafler** *vt Fam* to swipe

rafraîchir [rafrɛʃir] **1** *vt (rendre frais)* to chill; *(pièce)* to air; *(raviver)* to freshen up; **r. la mémoire à qn** to refresh sb's memory **2** *vi* to cool down **3** **se rafraîchir** *upr (temps)* to get cooler; *(se laver)* to freshen up; *Fam (boire)* to have a cold drink ■ **rafraîchissant, -ante** *adj* refreshing ■ **rafraîchissement** *nm (de température)* cooling; *(boisson)* cold drink

ragaillardir [ragajardir] *vt Fam* to buck up

rage [raʒ] *nf (colère)* rage; *(maladie)* rabies; **faire r.** *(incendie, tempête)* to rage; **r. de dents** violent toothache ■ **rageant, -ante** *adj Fam* infuriating ■ **rager** *vi Fam (personne)* to fume ■ **rageur, -euse** *adj (ton)* furious

ragots [rago] *nmpl Fam* gossip

ragoût [ragu] *nm Culin* stew

ragoûtant, -ante [ragutɑ̃, -ɑ̃t] *adj* **peu r.** *(plat)* unappetizing; *(personne)* unsavoury

rai [rɛ] *nm (de lumière)* ray

raid [rɛd] *nm* raid; **r. aérien** air raid

raide [rɛd] **1** *adj (rigide, guindé)* stiff; *(côte, escalier)* steep; *(cheveux)* straight; *(corde)* taut **2** *adv (grimper)* steeply; **tomber r.** to fall to the ground; **tomber r. mort** to drop (down) dead ■ **raideur** *nf (rigidité)* stiffness; *(de côte)* steepness ■ **raidillon** *nm (chemin)* steep path; *(partie de route)* steep rise ■ **raidir** **1** *vt (bras, jambe)* to brace; *(corde)* to tauten **2** **se raidir** *upr (membres)* to stiffen; *(corde)* to tauten; *(personne)* to tense up

raie¹ [rɛ] *nf (motif)* stripe; *(de cheveux) Br* parting, *Am* part

raie² [rɛ] *nf (poisson)* skate

rail [raj] *nm* rail; **le r.** *(chemins de fer)* rail; **r. de sécurité** crash barrier

railler [raje] *vt* to mock ■ **raillerie** *nf* gibe ■ **railleur, -euse** *adj* mocking

rainure [renyr] *nf* groove

raisin [rɛzɛ̃] *nm* raisin(s) grapes; **r. sec** raisin

Il faut noter que le nom anglais **raisin** est un faux ami. Il signifie **raisin sec.**

---

raison [rɛzɔ̃] *nf* (**a**) *(faculté, motif)* reason; **la r. de mon absence** the reason for my absence; **la r. pour laquelle je…** the reason (why) I…; **pour raisons de famille/de santé** for family/health reasons; **en r. de** *(cause)* on account of; **à r. de** *(proportion)* at the rate of; **à plus forte r.** all the more so; **plus que de r.** *(boire)* much too much; **r. de plus** all the more reason *(***pour faire** to do *or* for doing); **avoir r. de qn/qch** to get the better of sb/sth; **se faire une r.** to resign oneself (**b**) **avoir r.** to be right *(***de faire** to do *or* in doing); **donner r. à qn** to agree with sb; *(événement)* to prove sb right; **avec r.** rightly

raisonnable [rɛzɔnabl] *adj* reasonable ■ **raisonnablement** [-amã] *adv* reasonably

raisonner [rɛzɔne] **1** *vt* **r. qn** to reason with sb **2** *vi (penser)* to reason; *(discuter)* to argue ■ **raisonné, -ée** *adj (choix)* reasoned ■ **raisonnement** *nm (faculté, activité)* reasoning; *(argumentation)* argument

rajeunir [raʒœnir] **1** *vt (moderniser)* to modernize; **r. qn** *(faire paraître plus jeune)* to make sb look younger; *(donner moins que son âge à)* to underestimate how old sb is **2** *vi* to look younger ■ **rajeunissement** *nm (après traitement)* rejuvenation; *(de population)* decrease in age

rajout [raʒu] *nm* addition ■ **rajouter** *vt* to add (**à** to); *Fig* **en r.** to exaggerate

rajuster [raʒyste] **1** *vt (vêtements, lunettes)* to straighten, to adjust **2 se rajuster** *vpr* to tidy oneself up

râle [ral] *nm (de mourant)* death rattle ▪ **râler** *vi (mourant)* to give a death rattle; *Fam (protester)* to moan ▪ **râleur, -euse** *nmf Fam* moaner

ralentir [ralɑ̃tir] *vti* to slow down ▪ **ralenti** *nm Cin & TV* slow motion; **au r.** in slow motion; *(travailler)* at a slower pace; **tourner au r.** *(moteur, usine) Br* to tick over, *Am* to turn over ▪ **ralentissement** *nm* slowing down; *(embouteillage)* hold-up

rallier [ralje] **1** *vt (réunir)* to rally; *(regagner)* to return to; **r. qn à qch** *(convertir)* to win sb over to sth **2 se rallier** *vpr* **se r. à** *(avis)* to come round to; *(cause)* to rally to

rallonge [ralɔ̃ʒ] *nf (de table)* extension; *(fil électrique)* extension (lead) ▪ **rallonger** *vti* to lengthen

rallumer [ralyme] **1** *vt (feu, pipe)* to light again; *(lampe)* to switch on again; *(conflit, haine)* to rekindle **2 se rallumer** *vpr (lumière)* to come back on; *(guerre, incendie)* to flare up again

rallye [rali] *nm (course automobile)* rally

ramage [ramaʒ] *nm (d'oiseau)* song ▪ **ramages** *nmpl (dessin)* foliage

ramassé, -ée [ramase] *adj (trapu)* stocky; *(concis)* compact

ramasser [ramase] **1** *vt (prendre par terre, réunir)* to pick up; *(ordures, copies)* to collect; *(fruits, coquillages)* to gather; *(gifle, rhume, amende)* to get **2 se ramasser** *vpr (se pelotonner)* to curl up; *(se relever)* to pick oneself up; *Fam (tomber)* to fall flat on one's face; *Fam (échouer)* to fail ▪ **ramassage** *nm (d'ordures)* collection; *(de fruits)* gathering; **r. scolaire** school bus service

ramassis [ramasi] *nm Péj* **r. de** *(voyous, vieux livres)* bunch of

rambarde [rɑ̃bard] *nf* guardrail

rame [ram] *nf (aviron)* oar; *(de métro)* train; *(de papier)* ream ▪ **ramer** *vi* to row; *Fam (peiner)* to sweat blood ▪ **rameur, -euse** *nmf* rower

rameau, -x [ramo] *nm* branch; *Rel* **le dimanche des Rameaux, les Rameaux** Palm Sunday

ramener [ramne] **1** *vt (amener)* to bring back; *(raccompagner)* to take back; *(remettre en place)* to put back; *(paix, ordre, calme)* to restore; **r. qch à qch** to reduce sth to sth; **r. qn à la vie** to bring sb back to life; *Fam* **r. sa fraise** to show off **2 se ramener** *vpr Fam (arriver)* to roll up; **se r. à qch** *(se réduire)* to boil down to sth

ramification [ramifikasjɔ̃] *nf* ramification

ramollir [ramɔlir] *vt,* **se ramollir** *vpr* to soften ▪ **ramolli, -ie** *adj* soft; *(personne)* soft-headed

ramoner [ramɔne] *vt (cheminée)* to sweep ▪ **ramonage** *nm (chimney)* sweeping ▪ **ramoneur** *nm (chimney)* sweep

rampe [rɑ̃p] *nf (d'escalier)* banister; *(pente)* slope; **être sous les feux de la r.** to be in the limelight; **r. d'accès** *(de pont)* access ramp; **r. de lancement** launching ramp

ramper [rɑ̃pe] *vi* to crawl; *Péj* **r. devant qn** to grovel to sb

rancard [rɑ̃kar] *nm Fam (rendez-vous)* meeting

rancart [rɑ̃kar] *nm Fam* **mettre qch au r.** to chuck sth out

rance [rɑ̃s] *adj* rancid ▪ **rancir** *vi* to go rancid

ranch [rɑ̃tʃ] *nm* ranch

rancœur [rɑ̃kœr] *nf* rancour, resentment

rançon [rɑ̃sɔ̃] *nf* ransom; *Fig* **la r. de la gloire** the price of fame ▪ **rançonner** *vt* to hold to ransom

rancune [rɑ̃kyn] *nf* spite; **garder r. à qn** to bear sb a grudge; **sans r.!** no hard feelings! ▪ **rancunier, -ière** *adj* spiteful

randonnée [rɑ̃dɔne] *nf (à pied)* hike; *(en vélo)* ride

rang [rɑ̃] *nm (rangée)* row; *(classement, grade)* rank; *Hum* **en r. d'oignons** in a row; **par r. de taille** in order of size; **de haut r.** high-ranking; **se mettre en r.** to line up (**par trois** in threes) ▪ **rangée**[1] *nf* row

ranger [rɑ̃ʒe] **1** *vt (papiers, vaisselle)* to put away; *(chambre)* to tidy (up); *(classer)* to rank (**parmi** among); **r. par ordre alphabétique** to arrange in alphabetical order **2 se ranger** *vpr (se disposer)* to line up; *(s'écarter)* to stand aside; *(voiture)* to pull over; *(s'assagir)* to settle down; **se r. à l'avis de qn** to come round to sb's opinion ▪ **rangé, -ée**[2] *adj (chambre)* tidy; *(personne)* steady ▪ **rangement** *nm* putting away; *(de chambre)* tidying (up); **rangements** *(placards)* storage space; **faire du r.** to do some tidying up

ranimer [ranime] *vt (personne) (après évanouissement)* to bring round; *(après arrêt cardiaque)* to resuscitate; *(feu)* to rekindle; *(souvenir)* to reawaken; *(débat)* to revive

rap [rap] *nm (musique)* rap ▪ **rappeur, -euse** *nmf (chanteur)* rapper

rapace [rapas] **1** *nm (oiseau)* bird of prey **2** *adj (personne)* grasping

rapatrier [rapatrije] *vt* to repatriate ▪ **rapatriement** *nm* repatriation

râpe [rap] *nf Culin* grater; *(lime)* rasp ▪ **râpé, -ée 1** *adj (fromage, carottes)* grated; *(vêtement)* threadbare; *Fam* **c'est r.** we've had it **2** *nm* grated cheese ▪ **râper** *vt (fromage)* to grate; *(bois)* to rasp

rapetisser [raptise] **1** *vt (rendre plus petit)* to make smaller; *(faire paraître plus petit)* to make look smaller **2** *vi (vêtement, personne)* to shrink

râpeux, -euse [rapø, -øz] *adj* rough

raphia [rafja] *nm* raffia

rapide [rapid] **1** *adj* fast; *(progrès)* rapid; *(esprit, lecture)* quick; *(pente)* steep **2** *nm (train)* express (train); *(de fleuve)* rapid ∎**rapidement** *adv* quickly, rapidly ∎**rapidité** *nf* speed

rapiécer [rapjese] *vt* to patch

rappel [rapɛl] *nm* *(de diplomate)* recall; *(d'événement, de promesse)* reminder; *(de salaire)* back pay; *(au théâtre)* curtain call; *(vaccin)* booster; *Sport* **descendre en r.** to abseil down; **r. à l'ordre** call to order

rappeler [rap(ə)le] **1** *vt* *(pour faire revenir, au téléphone)* to call back; *(souvenir, diplomate)* to recall; **r. qch à qn** to remind sb of sth **2** *vi (au téléphone)* to call back **3 se rappeler** *upr* **se r. qn/qch**; **se r. que…** to remember that…

rappliquer [raplike] *vi Fam (arriver)* to roll up

rapport [rapɔr] *nm* **(a)** *(lien)* connection, link; **par r. à** compared with; **sous ce r.** in this respect; **se mettre en r. avec qn** to get in touch with sb; **ça n'a aucun r.!** it has nothing to do with it!; **rapports** *(entre personnes)* relations; **rapports (sexuels)** (sexual) intercourse **(b)** *(profit)* return, yield **(c)** *(compte rendu)* report

rapporter [rapɔrte] **1** *vt (rendre)* to bring back; *(remporter)* to take back; *(raconter)* to report; *(profit)* to yield; **r. de l'argent** to be profitable; **r. qch à qn** *(financièrement)* to bring sb in sth; *(moralement)* to bring sb sth; **on rapporte que…** it is reported that… **2** *vi (chien)* to retrieve; *Péj (moucharder)* to tell tales **3 se rapporter** *upr* **se r. à qch** to relate to sth; **s'en r. à qn/qch** to rely on sb/sth ∎**rapporteur, -euse 1** *nmf Péj (mouchard)* telltale **2** *nm (de commission)* reporter; *(instrument)* protractor

rapprocher [raprɔʃe] **1** *vt (objet)* to move closer (**de** to); *(réconcilier)* to bring together; *(réunir)* to join; *(comparer)* to compare (**de** to or with) **2** ∎**se rapprocher** *upr* to get closer (**de** to); *(se réconcilier)* to be reconciled; *(ressembler)* to be similar (**de** to) ∎**rapproché, -ée** *adj* close; *(yeux)* close-set ∎**rapprochement** *nm (réconciliation)* reconciliation; *(rapport)* connection

rapt [rapt] *nm* abduction

raquette [rakɛt] *nf (de tennis)* racket; *(de pingpong)* bat; *(de neige)* snowshoe

rare [rar] *adj* rare; *(argent, main-d'œuvre)* scarce; *(barbe, végétation)* sparse; **c'est r. qu'il pleuve ici** it rarely rains here ∎**se raréfier** *upr (denrées)* to get scarce ∎**rarement** *adv* rarely, seldom ∎**rareté** *nf (objet rare)* rarity; *(de main-d'œuvre)* scarcity; *(de phénomène)* rareness

RAS [erɑɛs] *(abrév* **rien à signaler)** *Fam* nothing to report

ras, rase [rɑ, rɑz] **1** *adj (cheveux)* closecropped; *(herbe, barbe)* short; *(mesure)* full; **à r. bord** to the brim; **pull (au) r. du cou** crew-neck sweater **2** *nm* **au r. de, à r. de** level with; **voler au r. du sol** to fly close to the ground **3** *adv*

(coupé) short; *Fam* **en avoir r. le bol** to be fed up (**de** with)

raser [rɑze] **1** *vt (menton, personne)* to shave; *(barbe, moustache)* to shave off; *(démolir)* to raze to the ground; *(frôler)* to skim; *Fam (ennuyer)* to bore **2 se raser** *upr* to shave ∎**rasage** *nm* shaving ∎**rasé, -ée** *adj* **être bien r.** to be clean-shaven ∎**raseur, -euse** *nmf Fam* bore

rasoir [rɑzwar] **1** *nm* razor; *(électrique)* shaver **2** *adj inv Fam* boring

rassasier [rasazje] *vt (faim, curiosité)* to satisfy

rassembler [rasɑ̃ble] **1** *vt (gens, objets)* to gather (together); *(courage)* to muster; **r. ses esprits** to collect oneself **2 se rassembler** *upr* to gather, to assemble ∎**rassemblement** [-əmɑ̃] *nm (action, groupe)* gathering

rasseoir* [raswar] **se rasseoir** *upr* to sit down again

rassis, -ise [rasi, -iz] *adj (pain)* stale ∎**rassir** *vi* to go stale

rassurer [rasyre] **1** *vt* to reassure **2 se rassurer** *upr* **rassure-toi** don't worry ∎**rassurant, -ante** *adj* reassuring

rat [ra] *nm* rat; *Fig* **r. de bibliothèque** bookworm; **petit r. de l'Opéra** ballet student *(at the Opéra de Paris)*

ratatiner [ratatine] **se ratatiner** *upr* to shrivel up; *(vieillard)* to become wizened

ratatouille [ratatuj] *nf Culin* **r. (niçoise)** ratatouille

rate [rat] *nf Anat* spleen

râteau, -x [rɑto] *nm* rake

râtelier [rɑtəlje] *nm (pour outils, pour armes)* rack; *Fam (dentier)* set of false teeth

rater [rate] **1** *vt (bus, cible, occasion)* to miss; *(travail, gâteau)* to ruin; *(examen)* to fail; *(vie)* to waste; *Fam* **il n'en rate pas une** he's always putting his foot in it **2** *vi Fam* to fail; **ça n'a pas raté!** sure enough, it happened! ∎**raté, -ée 1** *nmf* loser **2** *nmpl* **avoir des ratés** *(moteur)* to backfire

ratifier [ratifje] *vt* to ratify ∎**ratification** *nf* ratification

ration [rasjɔ̃] *nf* ration ∎**rationnement** *nm* rationing ∎**rationner** *vt* to ration

rationaliser [rasjɔnalize] *vt* to rationalize ∎**rationalisation** *nf* rationalization

rationnel, -elle [rasjɔnɛl] *adj* rational

ratisser [ratise] *vt (allée)* to rake; *(feuilles)* to rake up; *Fam (fouiller)* to comb; *Fam* **se faire r.** *(au jeu)* to be cleaned out

raton [ratɔ̃] *nm* **r. laveur** raccoon

RATP [eratepe] *(abrév* **Régie autonome des transports parisiens)** *nf* = Parisian transport authority

rattacher [rataʃe] **1** *vt (lacets)* to tie up again; *(région)* to unite (**à** with); *(idée)* to link (**à** to) **2 se rattacher** *upr* **se r. à** to be linked to

▪ **rattachement** nm (de région) uniting (**à** with)

rattraper [ratrape] **1** vt to catch; (prisonnier) to recapture; (erreur) to correct; **r. qn** (rejoindre) to catch up with sb; **r. le temps perdu** to make up for lost time **2 se rattraper** vpr (se retenir) to catch oneself in time; (après une faute) to make up for it; **se r. à qch** to catch hold of sth ▪ **rattrapage** nm Scol **cours de r.** remedial class

rature [ratyr] nf crossing-out, deletion ▪ **raturer** vt to cross out, to delete

rauque [rok] adj (voix) hoarse

ravages [ravaʒ] nmpl devastation; (du temps, de maladie) ravages; **faire des r.** to wreak havoc; (femme) to break hearts ▪ **ravager** vt to devastate

ravaler [ravale] vt (façade) to clean; (sanglots, salive) to swallow; Fig (colère) to stifle; Littéraire (avilir) to lower (**à** to) ▪ **ravalement** nm cleaning

ravi, -ie [ravi] adj delighted (**de** with; **de faire** to do; **que** that)

ravier [ravje] nm hors d'œuvre dish

ravigoter [ravigɔte] vt Fam **r. qn** to put new life into sb

ravin [ravɛ̃] nm ravine

ravioli(s) [ravjɔli] nmpl ravioli

ravir [ravir] vt (emporter) to snatch (**à** from); (plaire à) to delight; **chanter à r.** to sing delightfully ▪ **ravissant, -ante** adj delightful ▪ **ravissement** nm (extase) ecstasy ▪ **ravisseur, -euse** nmf kidnapper

raviser [ravize] **se raviser** vpr to change one's mind

ravitailler [ravitaje] **1** vt (personnes) to supply; (avion) to refuel **2 se ravitailler** vpr to get in supplies ▪ **ravitaillement** nm (action) supplying; (d'avion) refuelling; (denrées) supplies

raviver [ravive] vt (feu, sentiment) to rekindle; (douleur) to revive; (couleur) to brighten up

rayer [reje] vt (érafler) to scratch; (mot) to cross out; **r. qn d'une liste** to cross sb off a list ▪ **rayé, -ée** adj (verre, disque) scratched; (tissu, pantalon) striped ▪ **rayure** nf (éraflure) scratch; (motif) stripe; **à rayures** striped

rayon [rejɔ̃] nm (**a**) (de lumière) ray; (de cercle) radius; (de roue) spoke; **dans un r. de** within a radius of; **r. X** X-ray; **r. d'action** range; **r. de soleil** sunbeam (**b**) (d'étagère) shelf; (de magasin) department; (de ruche) honeycomb (**c**) (expressions) Fam **elle en connaît un r.** she's well clued up about it ▪ **rayonnage** nm shelving, shelves

rayonner [rejɔne] vi (avenue, douleur) to radiate; (dans une région) to travel around (from a central base); (soleil) to beam; Fig **r. de joie** to beam with joy ▪ **rayonnant, -ante** adj (soleil) radiant; Fig (visage) beaming (**de** with)

▪ **rayonnement** nm (du soleil) radiance; (influence) influence

raz de marée [rɑdmare] nm inv tidal wave; Fig (bouleversement) upheaval; **r. électoral** landslide

razzia [ra(d)zja] nf Fam **faire une r. sur qch** to raid sth

ré [re] nm inv Mus (note) D

réacteur [reaktœr] nm (d'avion) jet engine; (nucléaire) reactor

réaction [reaksjɔ̃] nf reaction; **moteur à r.** jet engine; **r. en chaîne** chain reaction ▪ **réactionnaire** adj & nmf reactionary

réadapter [readapte] vt, **se réadapter** vpr to readjust (**à** to) ▪ **réadaptation** nf readjustment

réaffirmer [reafirme] vt to reaffirm

réagir [reaʒir] vi to react (**contre** against; **à** to); Fig (se secouer) to shake oneself out of it

réaliser [realize] **1** vt (projet) to realize; (rêve, ambition) to fulfil; (bénéfices, économies) to make; (film) to direct; (se rendre compte) to realize (**que** that) **2 se réaliser** vpr (vœu) to come true; (personne) to fulfil oneself ▪ **réalisable** adj (plan) workable; (rêve) attainable ▪ **réalisateur, -trice** nmf (de film) director ▪ **réalisation** nf (de projet) realization; (de rêve) fulfilment; (de film) direction; (œuvre) achievement

réalisme [realism] nm realism ▪ **réaliste 1** adj realistic **2** nmf realist

réalité [realite] nf reality; **en r.** in reality

réanimation [reanimasjɔ̃] nf resuscitation; (service de) **r.** intensive care unit ▪ **réanimer** vt to resuscitate

réapparaître* [reaparetr] vi to reappear ▪ **réapparition** nf reappearance

réarmer [rearme] **1** vt (fusil) to reload **2** vi (pays) to rearm ▪ **réarmement** [-əmɑ̃] nm rearmament

rébarbatif, -ive [rebarbatif, -iv] adj forbidding, Br off-putting

rebâtir [rəbɑtir] vt to rebuild

rebattu, -ue [rəbaty] adj (sujet) hackneyed

rebelle [rəbɛl] **1** adj (enfant, esprit) rebellious; (mèche) unruly; (fièvre) stubborn; **être r. à** (sujet: enfant) to resist; (sujet: organisme) to be resistant to **2** nmf rebel ▪ **se rebeller** vpr to rebel (**contre** against) ▪ **rébellion** nf rebellion

rebelote [rəbəlɔt] exclam Fam here we go again!

rebiffer [rəbife] **se rebiffer** vpr Fam to hit back (**contre** at)

rebiquer [rəbike] vi Fam (mèche, col) to stick up

reboiser [rəbwaze] vt to reforest

rebond [rəbɔ̃] nm bounce; (par ricochet) rebound ▪ **rebondir** vi to bounce; (par ricochet) to rebound; Fam (se remettre) to recover; **faire r. qch** (affaire, discussion) to get sth going again ▪ **rebondissement** nm new development (**de** in)

rebondi, -ie [rəbɔ̃di] *adj* chubby

rebord [rəbɔr] *nm* edge; *(de plat)* rim; *(de vêtement)* hem; **r. de fenêtre** windowsill

reboucher [rəbuʃe] *vt (flacon)* to put the top back on; *(trou)* to fill in again

rebours [rəbur] **à rebours** *adv* the wrong way; **comprendre à r.** to get the wrong end of the stick; **compte à r.** countdown

rebrousse-poil [rəbruspwal] **à rebrousse-poil** *adv Fig* **prendre qn à r.** to rub sb up the wrong way

rebrousser [rəbruse] *vt* **r. chemin** to turn back

rebuffade [rəbyfad] *nf* rebuff

rébus [rebys] *nm* rebus

rebut [rəby] *nm* **mettre qch au r.** to throw sth out; *Péj* **le r. de la société** the dregs of society

rebuter [rəbyte] *vt (décourager)* to put off; *(déplaire)* to disgust ▪**rebutant, -ante** *adj* off-putting

récalcitrant, -ante [rekalsitrã, -ãt] *adj* recalcitrant

recaler [rəkale] *vt Fam Scol* **r. qn** to fail sb; *Fam Scol* **être recalé, ou faire r.** to fail

récapituler [rekapityle] *vti* to recap, to sum up ▪**récapitulation** *nf* recap, summing up

recel [rəsɛl] *nm* receiving stolen goods ▪**receler, recéler** *vt (mystère, secret)* to conceal; *(objet volé)* to receive; *(criminel)* to harbour ▪**receleur, -euse, recéleur, -euse** *nmf* receiver *(of stolen goods)*

recenser [rəsãse] *vt (population)* to take a census of; *(objets)* to make an inventory of; *(votes)* to count ▪**recensement** *nm (de population)* census; *(d'objets)* inventory; *(de votes)* counting

récent, -ente [resã, -ãt] *adj* recent ▪**récemment** [-amã] *adv* recently

récépissé [resepise] *nm (reçu)* receipt

récepteur [reseptœr] *nm (téléphone)* receiver ▪**réceptif, -ive** *adj* receptive (**à** to) ▪**réception** *nf (accueil, soirée) & Radio* reception; *(de lettre)* receipt; *(d'hôtel)* reception (desk); **dès r.** de on receipt of; **avec accusé de r.** with acknowledgement of receipt ▪**réceptionniste** *nmf* receptionist

récession [resesjɔ̃] *nf Écon* recession

recette [rəsɛt] *nf Culin & Fig* recipe (**de** for); *(argent, bénéfice)* takings; *(bureau)* tax office; **recettes** *(gains)* takings; *Fig* **faire r.** to be a success

recevoir* [rəsəvwar] **1** *vt (amis, lettre, proposition, coup de téléphone)* to receive; *(gifle, coup)* to get; *(client)* to see; *(candidat)* to admit; *(station de radio)* to pick up; **r. la visite de qn** to have a visit from sb; **être reçu à un examen** to pass an exam; **être reçu premier** to come first **2** *vi (faire une fête)* to have guests; *(médecin)* to see patients ▪**recevable** *adj (excuse)* admissible ▪**receveur, -euse** *nmf*

(de bus) (bus) conductor; **r. des Postes** postmaster, *f* postmistress

rechange [rəʃãʒ] **de rechange** *adj (outil, pièce)* spare; *(solution)* alternative; **des vêtements de r.** a change of clothes

rechapé, -ée [rəʃape] *adj* **pneu r.** retread

réchapper [reʃape] *vi* **r. de qch** to survive sth

recharge [rəʃarʒ] *nf (de stylo)* refill ▪**rechargeable** *adj (briquet)* refillable; *(pile)* rechargeable ▪**recharger** *vt (fusil, appareil photo, camion)* to reload; *(briquet, stylo)* to refill; *(batterie, pile)* to recharge; *(crédit du téléphone portable) Br* to top up, *Am* to refill

réchaud [reʃo] *nm* (portable) stove

réchauffer [reʃofe] **1** *vt (personne, aliment)* to warm up **2 se réchauffer** *vpr (personne)* to get warm; *(temps)* to get warmer ▪**réchauffement** *nm (de température)* rise (**de** in); **le r. de la planète** global warming

rêche [rɛʃ] *adj* rough

recherche [rəʃɛrʃ] *nf* (**a**) *(quête)* search (**de** for); *(du pouvoir)* quest (**de** for); **à la r. de** in search of; **se mettre à la r. de qn/qch** to go in search of sb/sth (**b**) *(scientifique)* research (**sur** into); **faire de la r.** to do research (**c**) **recherches** *(de police)* search, hunt; **faire des recherches** to make inquiries (**d**) *(raffinement)* elegance

rechercher [rəʃɛrʃe] *vt (personne, objet)* to search for; *(emploi)* to look for; *(honneurs, faveurs)* to seek; *Ordinat* to do a search for ▪**recherché, -ée** *adj* (**a**) *(très demandé)* in demand; *(rare)* sought-after; **r. pour meurtre** wanted for murder (**b**) *(élégant)* elegant

rechigner [rəʃiɲe] *vi Fam* **r. à qch** to balk at sth; **faire qch en rechignant** to do sth with a bad grace

rechute [rəʃyt] *nf* relapse; **faire une r.** to have a relapse ▪**rechuter** *vi* to have a relapse

récidive [residiv] *nf (de malfaiteur)* repeat *Br* offence *or Am* offense; *(de maladie)* recurrence (**de** of) ▪**récidiver** *vi (malfaiteur)* to reoffend; *(maladie)* to recur ▪**récidiviste** *nmf (malfaiteur)* repeat offender

récif [resif] *nm* reef

récipient [resipjã] *nm* container

> Il faut noter que le nom anglais **recipient** est un faux ami. Il signifie **destinataire**.

réciproque [resiprɔk] *adj (sentiments)* mutual; *(concessions)* reciprocal ▪**réciproquement** *adv* mutually; **et r.** and vice versa

récit [resi] *nm (histoire)* story; *(compte rendu)* account; **faire le r. de qch** to give an account of sth

récital, -als [resital] *nm* recital

réciter [resite] *vt* to recite ▪**récitation** *nf* recitation

réclame [reklam] *nf (publicité)* advertising;

(annonce) advertisement; **en r.** on special offer
réclamer [reklame] **1** *vt (demander)* to ask for; *(exiger)* to demand; *(droit, allocation)* to claim; *(nécessiter)* to require **2** *vi* to complain **3 se réclamer** *upr (se recommander)* to mention sb's name **■réclamation** *nf* complaint; **faire une r.** to make a complaint; **(bureau des) réclamations** complaints department

> Il faut noter que le verbe anglais **to reclaim** est un faux ami. Il signifie le plus souvent **récupérer**.

reclasser [rǝklɑse] *vt (fiches)* to reclassify; *(chômeur)* to find a new job for
reclus, -use [rǝkly, -yz] **1** *adj* cloistered; **vivre r.** to lead a cloistered life **2** *nmf* recluse
réclusion [reklyzjɔ̃] *nf* **r. (criminelle)** imprisonment; **r. (criminelle) à perpétuité** life imprisonment
recoiffer [rǝkwafe] **se recoiffer** *upr (se repeigner)* to redo one's hair
recoin [rǝkwɛ̃] *nm (de lieu)* nook; *(de mémoire)* recess
recoller [rǝkɔle] *vt (objet cassé)* to stick back together; *(enveloppe)* to stick back down
récolte [rekɔlt] *nf (action)* harvesting; *(produits)* harvest, *Fig (de documents)* crop; **faire la r.** to harvest the crops **■récolter** *vt* to harvest; *Fig (recueillir)* to collect
recommandable [rǝkɔmɑ̃dabl] *adj* **peu r.** *(personne)* undesirable; *(endroit)* disreputable
recommandation [rǝkɔmɑ̃dasjɔ̃] *nf (appui, conseil)* recommendation
recommander [rǝkɔmɑ̃de] **1** *vt (appuyer)* to recommend (**à** to; **pour** for); **r. à qn de faire qch** to advise sb to do sth; **r. son âme à Dieu** to commend one's soul to God **2 se recommander** *upr* **se r. de qn** to give sb's name as a reference **■recommandé, -ée 1** *adj (lettre)* registered **2** *nm* **en r.** registered
recommencer [rǝkɔmɑ̃se] *vti* to start *or* begin again **■recommencement** *nm* renewal **(de** of)
récompense [rekɔ̃pɑ̃s] *nf* reward **(pour** *ou* **de** for); *(prix)* award; **en r. de qch** as a reward for sth **■récompenser** *vt* to reward **(de** *ou* **pour** for)
réconcilier [rekɔ̃silje] **1** *vt* to reconcile **(avec** with) **2 se réconcilier** *upr* to become reconciled, *Br* to make it up **(avec** with). **■réconciliation** *nf* reconciliation
reconduire* [rǝkɔ̃dɥir] *vt (contrat)* to renew; *(politique)* to continue; **r. qn (à la porte)** to show sb out; **r. qn à la frontière** to escort sb back to the border **■reconduction** *nf (de contrat)* renewal
réconfort [rekɔ̃fɔr] *nm* comfort **■réconfortant, -ante** *adj* comforting **■réconforter** *vt* to comfort

reconnaissable [rǝkɔnɛsabl] *adj* recognizable **(à qch** by sth)
reconnaissant, -ante [rǝkɔnɛsɑ̃, -ɑ̃t] *adj* grateful **(à qn de qch** to sb for sth) **■reconnaissance** *nf (gratitude)* gratitude **(pour** for); *(de droit, de gouvernement)* recognition; *Mil* reconnaissance; *Mil* **partir en r.** to go off on reconnaissance; **r. de dette** IOU; *Ordinat* **r. vocale** speech recognition
reconnaître* [rǝkɔnɛtr] **1** *vt (identifier, admettre)* to recognize **(à qch** by sth); *(enfant, erreur)* to acknowledge; *(terrain)* to reconnoitre; **être reconnu coupable** to be found guilty **2 se reconnaître** *upr (soi-même)* to recognize oneself; *(l'un l'autre)* to recognize each other; **se r. coupable** to acknowledge one's guilt **■reconnu, -ue** *adj* recognized
reconquérir* [rǝkɔ̃kerir] *vt (territoire)* to reconquer; *(liberté)* to win back
reconsidérer [rǝkɔ̃sidere] *vt* to reconsider
reconstituant, -uante [rǝkɔ̃stitɥɑ̃, -ɥɑ̃t] *adj & nm* tonic
reconstituer [rǝkɔ̃stitɥe] *vt (armée, parti)* to reconstitute; *(crime, quartier)* to reconstruct; *(faits)* to piece together; *(fortune)* to build up again **■reconstitution** *nf (de crime)* reconstruction; **r. historique** historical reconstruction
reconstruire* [rǝkɔ̃strɥir] *vt* to rebuild **■reconstruction** *nf* rebuilding
reconvertir [rǝkɔ̃vertir] **1** *vt (entreprise)* to convert; *(personne)* to retrain **2 se reconvertir** *upr (personne)* to retrain; **se r. dans qch** to retrain for a new career in sth **■reconversion** *nf (d'usine)* conversion; *(de personne)* retraining
recopier [rǝkɔpje] *vt (mettre au propre)* to copy out; *(faire un double de)* to recopy
record [rǝkɔr] *nm & adj inv* record
recoucher [rǝkuʃe] **se recoucher** *upr* to go back to bed
recoudre* [rǝkudr] *vt (bouton)* to sew back on; *(vêtement, plaie)* to stitch up
recouper [rǝkupe] **1** *vt (couper de nouveau)* to recut; *(confirmer)* to confirm **2 se recouper** *upr (témoignages)* to tally **■recoupement** *nm* crosscheck; **par r.** by crosschecking
recourber [rǝkurbe] *vt,* **se recourber** *upr* to bend **■recourbé, -ée** *adj (bec)* curved; *(nez)* hooked
recours [rǝkur] *nm* recourse; **avoir r. à** *(chose)* to resort to; *(personne)* to turn to; **en dernier r.** as a last resort; *Jur* **r. en cassation** appeal **■recourir*** *vi* **r. à** *(moyen, violence)* to resort to; *(personne)* to turn to
recouvrer [rǝkuvre] *vt (santé, bien)* to recover; *(vue)* to regain
recouvrir* [rǝkuvrir] *vt (revêtir, inclure)* to cover **(de** with); *(couvrir de nouveau)* to re-cover; *(enfant)* to cover up again

récréation [rekreasjɔ̃] *nf (détente)* recreation; *Scol Br* break, *Am* recess; *(pour les plus jeunes)* playtime

récrier [rekrije] **se récrier** *upr Littéraire* to protest (**contre** about)

récriminer [rekrimine] *vi* to complain bitterly (**contre** about) ▪ **récriminations** *nfpl* recriminations

récrire* [rekrir] *vt (lettre)* to rewrite

recroqueviller [rəkrɔkvije] **se recroqueviller** *upr (personne)* to curl up

recrudescence [rəkrydesɑ̃s] *nf* renewed outbreak (**de** of)

recrue [rəkry] *nf* recruit ▪ **recrutement** *nm* recruitment ▪ **recruter** *vt* to recruit

rectangle [rektɑ̃gl] *nm* rectangle ▪ **rectangulaire** *adj* rectangular

rectifier [rektifje] *vt (calcul, erreur)* to correct; *(compte)* to adjust; *Fig* **le tir** to take a slightly different tack ▪ **rectificatif** *nm* correction ▪ **rectification** *nf (de calcul, d'erreur)* correction; **faire une r.** to make a correction

recto [rekto] *nm* front; **r. verso** on both sides

rectorat [rektɔra] *nm Br* ≃ local education authority, *Am* ≃ board of education

reçu, -ue [rəsy] **1** *pp de* **recevoir 2** *adj (idée)* received; *(candidat)* successful **3** *nm (récépissé)* receipt

recueil [rəkœj] *nm (de poèmes, de chansons)* collection (**de** of)

recueillir* [rəkœjir] **1** *vt (argent, renseignements)* to collect; *(suffrages)* to win; *(personne, animal)* to take in **2 se recueillir** *upr* to meditate; *(devant un monument)* to stand in silence ▪ **recueillement** *nm* meditation ▪ **recueilli, -ie** *adj* meditative

recul [rəkyl] *nm (d'armée, de négociateur, de maladie)* retreat; *(de canon)* recoil; *(déclin)* decline; **avoir un mouvement de r.** to recoil; *Fig* **manquer de r.** to be too closely involved; *Fig* **prendre du r.** to stand back from things ▪ **reculade** *nf Fig & Péj* climb-down

reculer [rəkyle] **1** *vi (personne)* to move back; *(automobiliste)* to reverse, *Am* to back up; *(armée)* to retreat; *(épidémie)* to lose ground; *(glacier)* to recede; *(renoncer)* to back down, to retreat; *(diminuer)* to decline; **faire r. la foule** to move the crowd back; *Fig* **il ne recule devant rien** nothing daunts him **2** *vt (meuble)* to move back; *(paiement, décision)* to postpone ▪ **reculé, -ée** *adj (endroit, temps)* remote

reculons [rəkylɔ̃] **à reculons** *adv* backwards

récupérer [rekypere] **1** *vt (objet prêté)* to get back, to recover; *(bagages)* & *Ordinat* to retrieve; *(forces)* to recover; *(recycler)* to salvage; *Péj (détourner à son profit)* to exploit; **r. des heures supplémentaires** to take time off in lieu **2** *vi (reprendre des forces)* to recover ▪ **récupération** *nf (d'objet)* recovery; *(de déchets)* salvage; *Péj (d'idée)* exploitation

récurer [rekyre] *vt* to scour

récuser [rekyze] **1** *vt* to challenge **2 se récuser** *upr* to decline to comment

recycler [rəsikle] **1** *vt (matériaux)* to recycle; *(personne)* to retrain **2 se recycler** *upr (personne)* to retrain ▪ **recyclable** *adj* recyclable ▪ **recyclage** *nm (de matériaux)* recycling; *(de personne)* retraining

rédacteur, -trice [redaktœr, -tris] *nmf (d'un acte)* writer; *(de journal)* editor; **r. en chef** *(de journal)* editor (in chief) ▪ **rédaction** *nf (action)* writing; *(de contrat)* drawing up; *Scol (devoir de français)* essay, composition; *(journalistes)* editorial staff; *(bureaux)* editorial offices

reddition [redisjɔ̃] *nf* surrender

redécouvrir [rədekuvrir] *vt (auteur, ouvrage)* to rediscover

redemander [rədəmɑ̃de] *vt (en reposant une question)* to ask again; *(pour en avoir plus)* to ask for more; **r. qch à qn** *(pour le récupérer)* to ask sb for sth back

redémarrer [rədemare] *vi (voiture)* to start again; *Ordinat* to reboot; **faire r. une voiture** to start a car again

rédemption [redɑ̃psjɔ̃] *nf Rel* redemption

redescendre [rədesɑ̃dr] **1** *(aux avoir)* *vt (objet)* to bring/take back down **2** *(aux être)* *vi* to come/go back down

redevable [rədəvabl] *adj* **être r. de qch à qn** to be indebted to sb for sth

redevance [rədəvɑ̃s] *nf (de télévision)* licence fee

redevenir* [rədəvənir] *(aux être)* *vi* to become again

rediffusion [rədifyzjɔ̃] *nf (de film)* repeat

rédiger [rediʒe] *vt* to write; *(contrat)* to draw up

redire* [rədir] **1** *vt* to repeat **2** *vi* **avoir** *ou* **trouver à r. à qch** to find fault with sth ▪ **redite** *nf* pointless repetition; **un texte plein de redites** a very repetitive text

redondant, -ante [rədɔ̃dɑ̃, -ɑ̃t] *adj* redundant

redonner [rədɔne] *vt (rendre)* to give back; *(donner plus)* to give more

redoubler [rəduble] **1** *vt* to increase; *Scol* **r. une classe** to repeat a year *or Am* a grade; **à coups redoublés** *(frapper)* harder and harder **2** *vi Scol* to repeat a year *or Am* a grade; *(colère)* to intensify; **r. de patience** to be much more patient ▪ **redoublant, -ante** *nmf* pupil repeating a year *or Am* a grade ▪ **redoublement** *nm* [-əmɑ̃] increase (**de** in)

redouter [rədute] *vt* to dread (**de faire** doing) ▪ **redoutable** *adj (adversaire, arme)* formidable; *(maladie)* dreadful

redresser [rədrese] **1** *vt (objet tordu)* to straighten (out); *(économie, situation, tort)* to put right; **r. la tête** to hold up one's head **2 se redresser** *vpr (personne)* to straighten up; *(pays, économie)* to recover ▪ **redressement** [-ɛsmã] *nm (pays)* recovery; **plan de r.** recovery plan; **r. fiscal** tax adjustment

réduction [redyksjɔ̃] *nf* reduction (**de** in); *(rabais)* discount; **r. du temps de travail** = reduction of the working week in France from 39 to 35 hours

réduire* [reduir] **1** *vt* to reduce (**à** to; **de** by); **r. qch en cendres** to reduce sth to ashes; **r. qn à qch** *(misère, désespoir)* to reduce sb to sth **2** *vi (sauce)* to reduce **3 se réduire** *vpr* **se r. à** *(se ramener à)* to come down to; **se r. en cendres** to be reduced to ashes ▪ **réduit, -uite 1** *adj (prix, vitesse)* reduced; *(moyens)* limited **2** *nm (pièce)* small room

réécrire* [reekrir] *vt* to rewrite

rééduquer [reedyke] *vt (personne)* to rehabilitate; *(partie du corps)* to re-educate ▪ **rééducation** *nf (de personne)* rehabilitation; *(de membre)* re-education; **faire de la r.** to have physiotherapy

réel, réelle [reel] **1** *adj* real **2** *nm* **le r.** reality ▪ **réellement** *adv* really

réélire* [reelir] *vt* to re-elect

réévaluer [reevalɥe] *vt (monnaie)* to revalue; *(salaires)* to reassess ▪ **réévaluation** *nf (de monnaie)* revaluation; *(de salaires)* reassessment

réexpédier [reekspedje] *vt (faire suivre)* to forward; *(à l'envoyeur)* to return

refaire* [rəfɛr] **1** *vt (exercice, travail)* to do again, to redo; *(chambre)* to do up; *(erreur, voyage)* to make again; *Fam (duper)* to take in; **r. sa vie** to make a new life for oneself; **r. du riz** to cook some more rice; **r. le monde** to put the world to rights; *Méd* **se faire r. le nez** to have one's nose reshaped, *Fam* to have a nose job **2 se refaire** *vpr* **se r. une santé** to recover

réfection [refɛksjɔ̃] *nf* repair

réfectoire [refɛktwar] *nm* dining hall, refectory

référence [referãs] *nf* reference; **faire r. à qch** to refer to sth

référendum [referãdɔm] *nm* referendum

référer [refere] **1** *vi* **en r. à** to refer the matter to **2 se référer** *vpr* **se r. à** to refer to

refermer [rəfɛrme] *vt*, **se refermer** *vpr* to close *or* shut again

refiler [rəfile] *vt Fam* **r. qch à qn** *(donner)* to palm sth off on sb; *(maladie)* to give sb sth

réfléchir [refleʃir] **1** *vt (image, lumière)* to reflect; **r. que...** to realize that... **2** *vi* to think (**à** *ou* **sur** about) **3 se réfléchir** *vpr* to be reflected ▪ **réfléchi, -ie** *adj (personne)* thoughtful; *(action, décision)* carefully thought-out; *Grammaire (verbe, pronom)* reflexive; **c'est tout r.** my mind is made up; **tout bien r.** all things considered

reflet [rəflɛ] *nm (image) & Fig* reflection; *(lumière)* glint; **reflets** *(de cheveux)* highlights ▪ **refléter 1** *vt* to reflect **2 se refléter** *vpr* to be reflected

refleurir [rəflœrir] *vi* to flower again

réflexe [reflɛks] *nm & adj* reflex

réflexion [reflɛksjɔ̃] *nf (d'image, de lumière)* reflection; *(pensée)* thought, reflection; *(remarque)* remark; **faire une r. à qn** to make a remark to sb; **r. faite, à la r.** on second *Br* thoughts *or Am* thought

réflexologie [reflɛksɔlɔʒi] *nf* reflexology ▪ **réflexologiste** *nmf* reflexologist

refluer [rəflɥe] *vi (eaux)* to flow back; *(marée)* to ebb; *(foule)* to surge back ▪ **reflux** *nm (de marée)* ebb; *(de foule)* backward surge

réforme [refɔrm] *nf* reform ▪ **réformateur, -trice** *nmf* reformer ▪ **réformer** *vt (loi)* to reform; *(soldat)* to discharge as unfit

refouler [rəfule] *vt (personnes)* to force *or* drive back; *(étrangers)* to turn away; *(sentiment)* to repress; *(larmes)* to hold back ▪ **refoulé, -ée** *adj* repressed

réfractaire [refraktɛr] *adj (rebelle)* insubordinate

refrain [rəfrɛ̃] *nm (de chanson)* chorus, refrain; *Fam* **c'est toujours le même r.** it's always the same old story

refréner [refrene] *vt* to curb

réfrigérer [refriʒere] *vt* to refrigerate ▪ **réfrigérant, -ante** *adj Fam (accueil)* icy ▪ **réfrigérateur** *nm* refrigerator ▪ **réfrigération** *nf* refrigeration

refroidir [rəfrwadir] **1** *vt* to cool (down); *Fig (ardeur)* to cool; *très Fam (tuer)* to kill; *Fam* **ça m'a refroidi** *(déçu)* it dampened my enthusiasm **2** *vi (devenir froid)* to get cold; *(devenir moins chaud)* to cool down **3 se refroidir** *vpr (temps)* to get colder; *Fig (ardeur)* to cool ▪ **refroidissement** *nm (de la température)* drop in temperature; *(de l'eau)* cooling; *(rhume)* chill

refuge [rəfyʒ] *nm* refuge; *(de montagne)* (mountain) hut; *(pour piétons)* traffic island ▪ **réfugié, -iée** *nmf* refugee ▪ **se réfugier** *vpr* to take refuge

refus [rəfy] *nm* refusal; *Fam* **ce n'est pas de r.** I won't say no ▪ **refuser 1** *vt* to refuse (**qch à qn** sb sth; **de faire** to do); *(offre, invitation)* to turn down; *(proposition)* to reject; *(candidat)* to fail; *(client)* to turn away **2 se refuser** *vpr (plaisir)* to deny oneself; **ne rien se r.** not to stint oneself; **se r. à l'évidence** to shut one's eyes to the facts; **se r. à faire qch** to refuse to do sth

> Il faut noter que le nom anglais **refuse** est un faux ami. Il signifie **ordures**.

réfuter [refyte] *vt* to refute

regagner [rəgaɲe] *vt (récupérer)* to regain, to

get back; *(revenir à)* to get back to; **r. le temps perdu** to make up for lost time ▪**regain** *nm (renouveau)* renewal; **un r. d'énergie** renewed energy

régal, -als [regal] *nm* treat ▪**régaler 1** *vt* to treat to a delicious meal **2 se régaler** *vpr* **je me régale** *(en mangeant)* I'm really enjoying it; *(je m'amuse)* I'm having a great time

regard [rəgar] *nm (coup d'œil, expression)* look; **jeter** *ou* **lancer un r. sur** to glance at; **au r. de la loi** in the eyes of the law; **en r.** *(en face)* opposite

> Il faut noter que le nom anglais **regard** est un faux ami. Il ne correspond jamais au français **regard**.

regarder [rəgarde] **1** *vt* to look at; *(émission, film)* to watch; *(considérer)* to consider, to regard (**comme** as); *(concerner)* to concern; **r. qn fixement** to stare at sb; **r. qn faire qch** to watch sb do sth; **ça ne te regarde pas!** it's none of your business! **2** *vi (observer)* to look; **r. autour de soi** to look round; **r. par la fenêtre** *(du dedans)* to look out of the window; **r. à la dépense** to be careful with one's money; **y r. à deux fois avant de faire qch** to think twice before doing sth **3 se regarder** *vpr (soi-même)* to look at oneself; *(l'un l'autre)* to look at each other; **se r. dans les yeux** to look into each other's eyes ▪**regardant, -ante** *adj Fam (avare)* careful with money

> Il faut noter que le verbe anglais **to regard** est un faux ami. Il ne signifie jamais **regarder**.

régate [regat] *nf* regatta
régence [reʒɑ̃s] *nf* regency
régénérer [reʒenere] *vt* to regenerate
régenter [reʒɑ̃te] *vt* **vouloir tout r.** to want to run the whole show
régie [reʒi] *nf (entreprise)* state-owned company; *Théâtre* stage management; *TV (organisation)* production management; *(lieu)* control room
regimber [rəʒɛ̃be] *vi* to balk (**contre** at)
régime [reʒim] *nm (politique)* (form of) government; *(de moteur)* speed; *(de bananes)* bunch; **r. (alimentaire)** diet; **se mettre au r.** to go on a diet; **suivre un r.** to be on a diet; *Fig* **à ce r.** at this rate
régiment [reʒimɑ̃] *nm (de soldats)* regiment; *Fam* **un r. de** *(quantité)* a host of
région [reʒjɔ̃] *nf* region, area; **la r. parisienne** the Paris region ▪**régional, -e, -aux, -ales** *adj* regional
régir [reʒir] *vt (déterminer)* to govern
régisseur [reʒisœr] *nm (de propriété)* manager; *Théâtre* stage manager; *Cin & TV* assistant production manager
registre [rəʒistr] *nm* register

réglable [reglabl] *adj* adjustable ▪**réglage** *nm (de siège, de machine)* adjustment; *(de moteur, de télévision)* tuning
règle [regl] *nf* (**a**) *(principe)* rule; **en r.** *(papiers d'identité)* in order; **en r. générale** as a (general) rule; **dans les règles de l'art** according to the book (**b**) *(instrument)* ruler ▪**règles** *nfpl (de femme)* (monthly) period
règlement [regləmɑ̃] *nm* (**a**) *(règles)* regulations; **contraire au r.** against the *Br* rules *or Am* rule (**b**) *(de conflit)* settling; *(paiement)* payment; *Fig* **r. de comptes** settling of scores ▪**réglementaire** *adj* in accordance with the regulations; *Mil* **tenue r.** regulation uniform ▪**réglementation** *nf (action)* regulation; *(règles)* regulations ▪**réglementer** *vt* to regulate
régler [regle] **1** *vt (problème, conflit)* to settle; *(mécanisme)* to adjust; *(moteur, télévision)* to tune; *(payer)* to pay; **r. qn** to settle up with sb; *Fig* **r. son compte à qn** to settle old scores with sb **2** *vi* to pay **3 se régler** *vpr* **se r. sur qn** to model oneself on sb ▪**réglé, -ée** *adj (vie)* ordered; *(papier)* ruled
réglisse [reglis] *nf Br* liquorice, *Am* licorice
réglo [reglo] **1** *adj inv Fam (personne)* on the level; *(opération)* kosher, legit **2** *adv* fair and square
règne [rɛɲ] *nm (de souverain)* reign; *(animal, minéral, végétal)* kingdom ▪**régner** *vi (roi, silence)* to reign (**sur** over); *(prédominer)* to prevail; **faire r. l'ordre** to maintain law and order
regorger [rəgɔrʒe] *vi* **r. de** to be overflowing with
régresser [regrese] *vi* to regress ▪**régression** *nf* regression; **en r.** on the decline
regret [rəgrɛ] *nm* regret; **à r.** with regret; **avoir le r.** *ou* **être au r. de faire qch** to be sorry to do sth ▪**regrettable** *adj* regrettable ▪**regretter** [rəgrete] *vt* to regret; **r. qn** to miss sb; **je regrette, je le regrette** I'm sorry; **r. que...** *(+ subjunctive)* to be sorry that...
regrouper [rəgrupe] *vt,* **se regrouper** *vpr* to gather together
régulariser [regylarize] *vt (situation)* to regularize
régulation [regylasjɔ̃] *nf* control
régulier, -ière [regylje, -jɛr] *adj (intervalles, traits du visage, clergé) & Grammaire* regular; *(constant)* steady; *(écriture)* even; *(légal)* legal; *Fam (honnête)* on the level ▪**régularité** *nf (exactitude)* regularity; *(constance)* steadiness; *(de décision)* legality ▪**régulièrement** *adv (à intervalles fixes)* regularly; *(avec constance)* steadily; *(selon la loi)* legitimately
réhabiliter [reabilite] *vt (délinquant)* to rehabilitate; *(accusé)* to clear
réhabituer [reabitɥe] **se réhabituer** *vpr* **se r. à**

qch/à faire qch to get used to sth/to doing sth again

rehausser [rəose] *vt (mur)* to make higher; *(teint)* to set off

réimpression [reɛ̃presjɔ̃] *nf (action)* reprinting; *(résultat)* reprint

rein [rɛ̃] *nm* kidney; **les reins** *(dos)* the lower back; **avoir mal aux reins** to have lower back pain; *Méd* **r. artificiel** kidney machine

reine [rɛn] *nf* queen; **la r. Élisabeth** Queen Elizabeth; **la r. mère** the queen mother ▪ **reine-claude** *(pl reines-claudes) nf* greengage

réinsertion [reɛ̃sɛrsjɔ̃] *nf* reintegration; **r. sociale** rehabilitation

réintégrer [reɛ̃tegre] *vt (fonctionnaire)* to reinstate; *(lieu)* to return to

réitérer [reitere] *vt* to repeat

rejaillir [rəʒajir] *vi* to spurt out; *Fig* **r. sur qn** to reflect on sb

rejet [rəʒɛ] *nm (refus)* & *Méd* rejection ▪ **rejeter** *vt (relancer)* to throw back; *(offre, candidature, greffe, personne)* to reject; *(épave)* to cast up; *(blâme)* to shift (**sur** on to); *(vomir)* to bring up ▪ **rejeton** *nm Fam (enfant)* kid

rejoindre* [rəʒwɛ̃dr] **1** *vt (personne)* to meet; *(fugitif)* to catch up with; *(rue, rivière)* to join; *(lieu)* to reach; *(régiment)* to return to; *(concorder avec)* to coincide with **2 se rejoindre** *vpr (personnes)* to meet up; *(rues, rivières)* to join up

rejouer [rəʒwe] *vt (match)* to replay

réjouir [reʒwir] **1** *vt* to delight **2 se réjouir** *vpr* to be delighted (**de** at; **de faire** to do) ▪ **réjoui, -ie** *adj* joyful ▪ **réjouissance** *nf* rejoicing; **réjouissances** festivities ▪ **réjouissant, -ante** *adj* delightful

relâche [rəlaʃ] *nf Théâtre* & *Cin* (temporary) closure; **faire r.** *Théâtre* & *Cin* to be closed; *Naut* to put in (**dans un port** at a port); **sans r.** without a break

relâcher [rəlaʃe] **1** *vt (corde, étreinte)* to loosen; *(discipline)* to relax; *(efforts)* to let up; *(prisonnier)* to release **2** *vi Naut* to put into port **3 se relâcher** *vpr (corde)* to slacken; *(discipline)* to become lax; *(employé)* to slack off ▪ **relâché, -ée** *adj* lax ▪ **relâchement** *nm (de corde)* slackening; *(de discipline)* relaxation

relais [rəlɛ] *nm (dispositif émetteur)* relay; *Sport* (**course de**) **r.** relay (race); **passer le r. à qn** to hand over to sb; **prendre le r.** to take over (**de** from); **r. routier** *Br* transport café, *Am* truck stop

relance [rəlɑ̃s] *nf (reprise)* revival ▪ **relancer** *vt (lancer à nouveau)* to throw again; *(rendre)* to throw back; *(production)* to boost; *(moteur, logiciel)* to restart; *(client)* to follow up

relater [rəlate] *vt Littéraire* to relate (**que** that)

relatif, -ive [rəlatif, -iv] *adj* relative (**à** to)

▪ **relativement** *adv (assez)* relatively; **r. à** compared to

relation [rəlasjɔ̃] *nf (rapport)* relationship; *(ami)* acquaintance; **être en r. avec qn** to be in touch with sb; **avoir des relations** *(amis influents)* to have contacts; **r. de travail** colleague; **r. (amoureuse)** (love) affair; **relations extérieures** foreign affairs; **relations internationales** international relations; **relations publiques** public relations; **relations sexuelles** (sexual) intercourse

relaxe [rəlaks] *adj Fam* laid-back **se relaxer** *vpr* to relax ▪ **relaxation** *nf* relaxation

relayer [rəleje] **1** *vt (personne)* to take over from; *(émission)* to relay **2 se relayer** *vpr* to take turns (**pour faire** doing); *Sport* to take over from one another

reléguer [rəlege] *vt (objet)* to relegate (**à** to); *Fig* **r. qch au second plan** to push sth into the background

relent [rəlɑ̃] *nm* stench

relevé [rəlve] *nm* list; *(de compteur)* reading; **r. de compte** bank statement; *Scol* **r. de notes** list of *Br* marks or *Am* grades

relève [rəlɛv] *nf* relief; **prendre la r.** to take over (**de** from)

relèvement [rəlɛvmɑ̃] *nm (d'économie, de pays)* recovery; *(de salaires)* raising

relever [rəlve] **1** *vt (ramasser)* to pick up; *(personne)* to help back up; *(pays)* to revive; *(col)* to turn up; *(manches)* to roll up; *(copies)* to collect; *(faute)* to pick out; *(empreinte)* to find; *(défi)* to accept; *(sauce)* to spice up; *(copier)* to note down; *(compteur)* to read; *(relayer)* to relieve; *(rehausser)* to enhance; *(augmenter)* to raise; **r. la tête** to look up; **r. qn de ses fonctions** to relieve sb of his/her duties **2** *vi* **r. de** *(dépendre de)* to come under; *(maladie)* to be recovering from **3 se relever** *vpr (après une chute)* to get up; **se r. de qch** to get over sth

relief [rəljɛf] *nm (de paysage)* relief; **en r.** in relief; *Fig* **mettre qch en r.** to highlight sth ▪ **reliefs** *nmpl (de repas)* remains

relier [rəlje] *vt* to connect, to link (**à** to); *(idées, faits)* to link together; *(livre)* to bind

religion [rəliʒjɔ̃] *nf* religion ▪ **religieux, -ieuse 1** *adj* religious; **mariage r.** church wedding **2** *nm (moine)* monk ▪ **religieuse** *nf (femme)* nun; *(gâteau)* ≃ cream puff

relique [rəlik] *nf* relic

relire* [rəlir] *vt* to reread

reliure [rəljyr] *nf (couverture)* binding; *(art)* bookbinding

relooker [rəluke] *vt Fam* to revamp

reluire* [rəlɥir] *vi* to shine, to gleam; **faire r. qch** to polish sth up ▪ **reluisant, -ante** *adj* shiny; *Fig* **peu r.** far from brilliant

reluquer [rəlyke] *vt Fam* to eye up

remâcher [rəmɑʃe] *vt Fig (souvenirs)* to brood over

remanier [rəmanje] *vt (texte)* to revise; *(ministère)* to reshuffle ▪ **remaniement** *nm (de texte)* revision; *r.* **ministériel** cabinet reshuffle

remarier [rəmarje] **se remarier** *upr* to remarry ▪ **remariage** *nm* remarriage

remarquable [rəmarkabl] *adj* remarkable (**par** for) ▪ **remarquablement** [-əmɑ̃] *adv* remarkably

remarque [rəmark] *nf* remark; **faire une r.** to make a remark

remarquer [rəmarke] *vt (apercevoir)* to notice (**que** that); *(dire)* to remark (**que** that); **faire r. qch** to point sth out (**à** to); **se faire r.** to attract attention; *Fam* **remarque, il n'est pas le seul!** mind you, he's not the only one!

> Il faut noter que le verbe anglais **to remark** est un faux ami. Il signifie uniquement **faire remarquer**.

remballer [rɑ̃bale] *vt* to repack; *Fam* **il s'est fait r.** he was sent packing

rembarrer [rɑ̃bare] *vt Fam* to snub

remblai [rɑ̃blɛ] *nm* embankment ▪ **remblayer** *vt (route)* to bank up

rembobiner [rɑ̃bɔbine] *vt,* **se rembobiner** *upr* to rewind

rembourrer [rɑ̃bure] *vt (fauteuil, matelas)* to stuff ▪ **rembourrage** *nm (action, matière)* stuffing

rembourser [rɑ̃burse] *vt (personne)* to pay back; *(billet, frais)* to refund ▪ **remboursement** [-əmɑ̃] *nm* repayment; *(de billet)* refund; **envoi contre r.** cash on delivery

remède [rəmɛd] *nm* cure, remedy (**contre** for) ▪ **remédier** *vi* **r. à qch** to remedy sth

remémorer [rəmemɔre] **se remémorer** *upr* to remember

remercier [rəmɛrsje] *vt* (**a**) *(dire merci à)* to thank (**de** *ou* **pour qch** for sth); **je vous remercie d'être venu** thank you for coming; **non, je vous remercie** no thank you (**b**) *Euph (congédier)* to ask to leave ▪ **remerciements** *nmpl* thanks

remettre* [rəmɛtr] **1** *vt (replacer)* to put back; *(vêtement)* to put back on; *(télévision)* to turn on again; *(disque)* to put on again; *(différer)* to postpone (**à** until); *(ajouter)* to add (**dans** to); **r. qch à qn** *(lettre, télégramme)* to deliver sth to sb; *(rapport)* to submit sth to sb; *(démission)* to hand sth in to sb; **r. qn en liberté** to set sb free; **r. qch en question** *ou* **en cause** to call sth into question; **r. qch en état** to repair sth; **r. qch à jour** to bring sth up to date; **r. une montre à l'heure** to set a watch to the correct time; *Fig* **r. les pendules à l'heure** to clear things up; **je ne vous remets pas** I can't place you; *Fam* **r. ça** to start again **2** **se remettre** *upr* **se r. en question**

to question oneself; **se r. à qch** to start sth again; **se r. à faire qch** to start to do sth again; **se r. de qch** to recover from sth; **s'en r. à qn** to rely on sb

réminiscences [reminisɑ̃s] *nfpl* (vague) recollections

remise [rəmiz] *nf* (**a**) *(de lettre)* delivery; **r. à neuf** *(de machine)* reconditioning; **r. en cause** *ou* **question** questioning; **r. en état** *(de maison)* restoration; *Football* **r. en jeu** throw-in (**b**) *(rabais)* discount (**c**) *Jur* **r. de peine** reduction of sentence (**d**) *(local)* shed

remiser [rəmize] *vt* to put away

rémission [remisjɔ̃] *nf (de péché, de maladie)* & *Jur* remission; **sans r.** *(travailler)* relentlessly

remix [rəmiks] *nm (d'un disque)* remix ▪ **remixer** *vt (disque)* to remix

remmener [rɑ̃mne] *vt* to take back

remontée [rəmɔ̃te] *nf (de pente)* ascent; *(d'eau, de prix)* rising; **r. mécanique** ski lift

remonter [rəmɔ̃te] **1** *(aux être)* *vi* to come/go back up; *(niveau, prix)* to rise again, to go back up; *(dans le temps)* to go back (**à** to); **r. dans** *(voiture)* to get back in(to); *(bus, train)* to get back on(to); **r. sur** *(cheval, vélo)* to get back on(to); **r. à dix ans** to go back ten years **2** *(aux avoir)* *vt (escalier, pente)* to come/go back up; *(porter)* to bring/take back up; *(montre)* to wind up; *(relever)* to raise; *(col)* to turn up; *(objet démonté)* to put back together, to reassemble; *(garde-robe)* to restock; **r. qn** *(ragaillardir)* to buck sb up; **r. le moral à qn** to cheer sb up; *Fig* **r. la pente** to get back on to one's feet *(after a hard struggle)*; *Fam* **être (très) remonté contre qn** to be (really) furious with *or* mad at sb; *Fam* **se faire r. les bretelles** to get rapped over the knuckles ▪ **remontant** *nm* tonic, pick-me-up ▪ **remonte-pente** *(pl* **remonte-pentes)** *nm* ski lift

remontoir [rəmɔ̃twar] *nm* winder

remontrance [rəmɔ̃trɑ̃s] *nf* remonstrance; **faire des remontrances à qn** to remonstrate with sb

remontrer [rəmɔ̃tre] *vt* to show again; **en r. à qn** to prove one's superiority over sb

remords [rəmɔr] *nm* remorse; **avoir du** *ou* **des r.** to feel remorse

remorque [rəmɔrk] *nf (de voiture)* trailer; **prendre qch en r.** to take sth in tow; *Fig* **être à la r.** to lag behind ▪ **remorquer** *vt (voiture, bateau)* to tow ▪ **remorqueur** *nm* tug(boat)

remous [rəmu] *nm (de rivière)* eddy; *Fig* **faire des r.** to cause a stir

rempailler [rɑ̃paje] *vt (chaise)* to reseat

rempart [rɑ̃par] *nm* rampart; **remparts** (city) walls

remplacer [rɑ̃plase] *vt* to replace (**par** with); *(professionnellement)* to stand in for ▪ **remplaçant, -ante** *nmf (personne)* replacement;

(enseignant) substitute teacher, *Br* supply teacher; *(joueur)* substitute ■ **remplacement** *nm* replacement; **en r. de** in place of

remplir [rɑ̃plir] **1** *vt* to fill (up) (**de** with); *(formulaire)* to fill out *or Br* in; *(promesse)* to fulfil **2 se remplir** *vpr* to fill (up) (**de** with) ■ **remplissage** *nm* filling (up); *Péj* **faire du r.** to pad

remporter [rɑ̃pɔrte] *vt (objet)* to take back; *(prix, victoire)* to win; *(succès)* to achieve

remuer [rəmɥe] **1** *vt (bouger)* to move; *(café)* to stir; *(salade)* to toss; *(terre)* to turn over; **r. qn** *(émouvoir)* to move sb **2** *vi* to move; *(gigoter)* to fidget **3 se remuer** *vpr* to move; *Fam (se démener)* to have plenty of get-up-and-go ■ **remuant, -uante** *adj (enfant)* hyperactive ■ **remue-ménage** *nm inv* commotion ■ **remue-méninges** *nm inv* brainstorming; **un r.** a brainstorming session

rémunérer [remynere] *vt (personne)* to pay; *(travail)* to pay for ■ **rémunérateur, -trice** *adj* remunerative ■ **rémunération** *nf* payment (**de** for)

renâcler [rənakle] *vi Fam* **r. à faire qch** to balk at doing sth

renaître* [rənɛtr] *vi (personne)* to be born again; *(espoir, industrie)* to revive; *Fig* **r. de ses cendres** to rise from its ashes ■ **renaissance** *nf* rebirth; *(des arts)* renaissance

renard [rənar] *nm* fox

renchérir [rɑ̃ʃerir] *vi (dire plus)* to go one better (**sur** than)

rencontre [rɑ̃kɔ̃tr] *nf (de personnes)* meeting; *(match) Br* match, *Am* game; **amours de r.** casual love affairs, flings; **aller à la r. de qn** to go to meet sb ■ **rencontrer 1** *vt (personne)* to meet; *(difficulté, obstacle)* to come up against, to encounter; *(trouver)* to come across **2 se rencontrer** *vpr* to meet

rendement [rɑ̃dmɑ̃] *nm (de champ)* yield; *(d'investissement)* return, yield; *(de personne, de machine)* output

rendez-vous [rɑ̃devu] *nm inv (rencontre)* appointment; *(amoureux)* date; *(lieu)* meeting place; **donner r. à qn** to arrange to meet sb; **prendre r. avec qn** to make an appointment with sb; **recevoir sur r.** *(médecin)* to see patients by appointment

rendormir* [rɑ̃dɔrmir] **se rendormir** *vpr* to go back to sleep

rendre [rɑ̃dr] **1** *vt (restituer)* to give back, to return (**à** to); *(son)* to give; *(jugement)* to deliver; *(armes)* to surrender; *(invitation)* to return; *(santé)* to restore; *(rembourser)* to pay back; *(exprimer)* to render; *(vomir)* to bring up; **r. célèbre/plus grand** to make famous/bigger; **r. la monnaie à qn** to give sb his/her change; **r. sa liberté à qn** to set sb free; **r. la justice** to dispense justice; **r. l'âme** to pass away; **r. les armes** to surrender **2** *vi (vomir)* to vomit;

(arbre, terre) to yield **3 se rendre** *vpr (criminel)* to give oneself up (**à** to); *(soldats)* to surrender (**à** to); *(aller)* to go (**à** to); **se r. à l'évidence** *(être lucide)* to face facts; **se r. malade/utile** to make oneself ill/useful ■ **rendu, -ue** *adj* **être r.** *(arrivé)* to have arrived

renégat, -ate [renega, -at] *nmf* renegade

rênes [rɛn] *nfpl* reins

renfermer [rɑ̃fɛrme] **1** *vt* to contain **2 se renfermer** *vpr* to withdraw into oneself ■ **renfermé, -ée 1** *adj (personne)* withdrawn **2** *nm* **sentir le r.** to smell musty

renflé, -ée [rɑ̃fle] *adj* bulging ■ **renflement** [-əmɑ̃] *nm* bulge

renflouer [rɑ̃flue] *vt (navire)* to refloat; **r. les caisses de l'État** to replenish the State coffers

renfoncement [rɑ̃fɔ̃s(ə)mɑ̃] *nm* recess; **dans le r. d'une porte** in a doorway

renforcer [rɑ̃fɔrse] *vt* to strengthen, to reinforce ■ **renforcement** [-əmɑ̃] *nm* reinforcement, strengthening

renfort [rɑ̃fɔr] *nm* **des renforts** *(troupes)* reinforcements; *Fig (aide)* backup, additional help; *Fig* **à grand r. de** with (the help of) a great deal of

renfrogner [rɑ̃frɔɲe] **se renfrogner** *vpr* to scowl ■ **renfrogné, -ée** *adj* scowling

rengaine [rɑ̃gɛn] *nf Fam Péj* **la même r.** the same old story

rengorger [rɑ̃gɔrʒe] **se rengorger** *vpr* to strut

renier [rənje] *vt (ami, pays)* to disown; *(foi)* to deny ■ **reniement** *nm (d'ami, de pays)* disowning; *(de foi)* denial

renifler [rənifle] *vti* to sniff ■ **reniflement** [-əmɑ̃] *nm (bruit)* sniff

renne [rɛn] *nm* reindeer

renom [rənɔ̃] *nm* renown; **de r.** *(ouvrage, artiste)* famous, renowned ■ **renommé, -ée** *adj* famous, renowned (**pour** for) ■ **renommée** *nf* fame, renown

renoncer [rənɔ̃se] *vi* **r. à qch** to give sth up, to abandon sth; **r. à faire qch** to give up doing sth ■ **renoncement** *nm*, **renonciation** *nf* renunciation (**à** of)

renouer [rənwe] **1** *vt (lacet)* to tie again; *(conversation)* to resume **2** *vi* **r. avec qch** *(tradition)* to revive sth; **r. avec qn** to take up with sb again

renouveau, -x [rənuvo] *nm* revival

renouveler [rənuvle] **1** *vt* to renew; *(erreur, expérience)* to repeat **2 se renouveler** *vpr (incident)* to happen again, to recur; *(cellules, sang)* to be renewed ■ **renouvelable** [-vlabl] *adj* renewable ■ **renouvellement** [-ɛlmɑ̃] *nm* renewal

rénover [renɔve] *vt (édifice, meuble)* to renovate; *(institution)* to reform ■ **rénovation** *nf (d'édifice, de meuble)* renovation; *(d'institution)* reform

renseigner [rɑ̃seɲe] **1** *vt* to give some information to (**sur** about) **2 se renseigner** *upr* to make inquiries (**sur** about) **• renseignement** [-ɛɲəmɑ̃] *nm* piece of information; **renseignements** information; **les renseignements (téléphoniques)** *Br* directory inquiries, *Am* information; **prendre** *ou* **demander des renseignements** to make inquiries

rentable [rɑ̃tabl] *adj* profitable **• rentabilité** *nf* profitability

rente [rɑ̃t] *nf* (private) income; *(pension)* pension; **avoir des rentes** to have private means **• rentier, -ière** *nmf* person of private means

rentrée [rɑ̃tre] *nf (retour)* return; **r. des classes** start of the new school year; **rentrées d'argent** (cash) receipts; **r. parlementaire** reopening of Parliament

rentrer [rɑ̃tre] **1** *(aux* **être)** *vi (entrer)* to go/come in; *(entrer de nouveau)* to go/come back in; *(chez soi)* to go/come (back) home; *(argent)* to come in; **r. en France** to return to France; **r. de vacances** to come back from holiday; **en rentrant de l'école** on my/his/her/*etc* way home from school; **r. dans qch** *(pénétrer)* to get into sth; *(sujet: voiture)* to crash into sth; **r. dans une catégorie** to fall into a category; **r. en classe** to go back to school; **r. dans ses frais** to recover one's expenses; *Fam* **je lui suis rentré dedans** I laid into him/her **2** *(aux* **avoir)** *vt (linge, troupeau)* to bring/take in; *(chemise)* to tuck in; *(larmes)* to stifle; *(griffes)* to retract **• rentré, -ée** *adj (colère)* suppressed

renverse [rɑ̃vɛrs] **à la renverse** *adv (tomber)* backwards

renverser [rɑ̃vɛrse] **1** *vt (faire tomber)* to knock over; *(liquide)* to spill; *(piéton)* to run over; *(tendance, situation)* to reverse; *(gouvernement)* to overthrow; *(tête)* to tilt back **2 se renverser** *upr (récipient)* to fall over; *(véhicule)* to overturn **• renversant, -ante** *adj Fam* astounding **• renversement** [-əmɑ̃] *nm (de situation, de tendance)* reversal; *(de gouvernement)* overthrow

renvoi [rɑ̃vwa] *nm (de marchandise, de lettre)* return; *(d'employé)* dismissal; *(d'élève)* expulsion; *(ajournement)* postponement; *(de texte)* cross-reference; *(rot)* belch, burp **• renvoyer*** *vt (lettre, cadeau)* to send back, to return; *(employé)* to dismiss; *(élève)* to expel; *(balle)* to throw back; *(lumière, image)* to reflect; *(ajourner)* to postpone (**à** until)

réorganiser [reɔrganize] *vt* to reorganize **• réorganisation** *nf* reorganization

réouverture [reuvɛrtyr] *nf* reopening

repaire [rəpɛr] *nm* den

repaître* [rəpɛtr] **se repaître** *upr Fig* **se r. de qch** to revel in sth

répandre [repɑ̃dr] **1** *vt (liquide)* to spill; *(nouvelle, joie)* to spread; *(odeur)* to give off; *(lumière, larmes, sang, chargement)* to shed; *(gravillons)* to scatter; *(dons, bienfaits)* to lavish **2 se répandre** *upr (nouvelle, peur)* to spread; *(liquide)* to spill; **se r. dans** *(fumée, odeur)* to spread through **• répandu, -ue** *adj (opinion, usage)* widespread

reparaître* [rəparɛtr] *vi* to reappear

réparer [repare] *vt (objet, machine)* to repair, to mend; *(faute)* to make amends for; *(dommage)* to make good; **faire r. qch** to get sth repaired **• réparable** *adj (machine)* repairable **• réparateur, -trice 1** *nmf* repairer **2** *adj (sommeil)* refreshing **• réparation** *nf (action)* repairing; *(résultat)* repair; *(dédommagement)* reparation; **en r.** under repair; **faire des réparations** to do some repairs

reparler [rəparle] *vi* **r. de qch** to talk about sth again

repartie [rəparti] *nf* retort

repartir* [rəpartir] *(aux* **être)** *vi (continuer)* to set off again; *(s'en retourner)* to go back; *(machine)* to start again; **r. à** *ou* **de zéro** to go back to square one

répartir [repartir] *vt (poids, charge)* to distribute; *(tâches, vivres)* to share (out); *(classer)* to divide (up); *(étaler dans le temps)* to spread (out) (**sur** over) **• répartition** *nf (de poids)* distribution; *(de tâches)* sharing; *(classement)* division

repas [rəpa] *nm* meal; **prendre un r.** to have a meal

repasser [rəpase] **1** *vi* to come/go back; **r. chez qn** to drop in on sb again **2** *vt (montagne, frontière)* to go across again; *(examen)* to take again, *Br* to resit; *(leçon)* to go over; *(film)* to show again; *(disque, cassette)* to play again; *(linge)* to iron **• repassage** *nm* ironing

repêcher [rəpeʃe] *vt (objet)* to fish out; *Fam (candidat)* to let through

repeindre* [rəpɛ̃dr] *vt* to repaint

repenser [rəpɑ̃se] *vt* to rethink

repentir [rəpɑ̃tir] *nm* repentance **• se repentir*** *upr Rel* to repent (**de** of); **se r. de qch/ d'avoir fait qch** *(regretter)* to regret sth/doing sth **• repentant, -ie** *adj* repentant

répercuter [reperkyte] **1** *vt (son)* to reflect; *(augmentation)* to pass **2 se répercuter** *upr (son, lumière)* to be reflected; *Fig* **se r. sur** to have repercussions on **• répercussion** *nf (conséquence)* repercussion

repère [rəpɛr] *nm* mark; **point de r.** *(espace, temps)* reference point **• repérer 1** *vt (endroit)* to locate; *Fam (remarquer)* to spot **2 se repérer** *upr* to get one's bearings

répertoire [repɛrtwar] *nm (liste)* index; *(carnet)* (indexed) notebook; *Théâtre* repertoire; *Ordinat (de fichiers)* directory **• répertorier** *vt* to list

répéter [repete] **1** *vt* to repeat; *(pièce de théâtre,* *rôle, symphonie)* to rehearse; **r. à qn que...** to tell sb again that...; **je te l'ai répété cent fois** I've told you a hundred times **2** *vi (redire)* to repeat; *(acteur)* to rehearse **3 se répéter** *upr (radoter)* to repeat oneself; *(événement)* to happen again **▪ répétitif, -ive** *adj* repetitive **▪ répétition** *nf (redite)* repetition; *Théâtre* rehearsal; **r. générale** dress rehearsal

repiquer [rəpike] *vt (plante)* to plant out; *(disque)* to record

répit [repi] *nm* rest, respite; **sans r.** ceaselessly

replacer [rəplase] *vt* to replace, to put back

replanter [rəplɑ̃te] *vt* to replant

replet, -ète [rəplɛ, -ɛt] *adj (personne)* podgy

repli [rəpli] *nm (de vêtement, de terrain)* fold; *(d'armée)* withdrawal; *(de monnaie)* fall

replier [rəplije] **1** *vt (objet)* to fold up; *(couteau)* to fold away; *(ailes)* to fold; *(jambes)* to tuck up **2 se replier** *vpr (objet)* to fold up; *(armée)* to withdraw; *Fig* **se r. sur soi-même** to withdraw into oneself

réplique [replik] *nf (réponse)* retort; *(d'acteur)* lines; *(copie)* replica; **sans r.** *(argument)* unanswerable **▪ répliquer 1** *vt* **r. que...** to reply that... **2** *vi* to reply; *(avec impertinence)* to answer back

répondre [repɔ̃dr] **1** *vi* to answer, to reply; *(avec impertinence)* to answer back; *(réagir)* to respond (**à** to); **r. à qn** to answer sb, to reply to sb; *(avec impertinence)* to answer sb back; **r. à** *(lettre, question, objection)* to answer, to reply to; *(besoin)* to meet; *(salut)* to return; *(correspondre à)* to correspond to; **r. au téléphone** to answer the phone; **r. de qn/qch** to answer for sb/sth **2** *vt (remarque)* to answer *or* reply with; **r. que...** to answer *or* reply that... **▪ répondant** *nm Fam* **avoir du r.** to have money behind one **▪ répondeur** *nm* **r. (téléphonique)** answering machine

> Il faut noter que le verbe anglais **to respond** est un faux ami. Il signifie le plus souvent **réagir**.

réponse [repɔ̃s] *nf* answer, reply; *(réaction)* response (**à** to); **en r. à** in answer *or* reply to

report [rəpɔr] *nm (transcription)* transfer; *(de somme)* carrying forward; *(de rendez-vous)* postponement

> Il faut noter que le nom anglais **report** est un faux ami. Il signifie **rapport**.

reportage [rəpɔrtaʒ] *nm (article, émission)* report; *(métier)* reporting

reporter¹ [rəpɔrte] **1** *vt (objet)* to take back; *(réunion)* to put off, to postpone (**à** until); *(transcrire)* to transfer (**sur** to); *(somme)* to carry forward (**sur** to) **2 se reporter** *upr* **se r. à** *(texte)* to refer to; **se r. sur** *(sujet: colère)* to be transferred to

> Il faut noter que le verbe anglais **to report** est un faux ami. Il ne signifie jamais **reporter**.

reporter² [rəpɔrter] *nm* reporter

repos [rəpo] *nm (détente)* rest; *(tranquillité)* peace; *Mil* **r.!** at ease!; **jour de r.** day off; **de tout r.** *(situation)* safe

reposer [rəpoze] **1** *vt (objet)* to put back down; *(problème, question)* to raise again; *(délasser)* to rest, to relax; **r. sa tête sur** *(appuyer)* to lean one's head on **2** *vi (être enterré)* to lie; **r. sur** *(bâtiment)* to be built on; *(théorie)* to be based on; **laisser r.** *(liquide)* to allow to settle **3 se reposer** *upr* to rest; **se r. sur qn** to rely on sb **▪ reposant, -ante** *adj* restful, relaxing **▪ reposé, -ée** *adj* rested

repousser [rəpuse] **1** *vt (en arrière)* to push back; *(sur le côté)* to push away; *(attaque, ennemi)* to beat off; *(réunion)* to put off; *(offre)* to reject; *(dégoûter)* to repel **2** *vi (cheveux, feuilles)* to grow again **▪ repoussant, -ante** *adj* repulsive

répréhensible [repreɑ̃sibl] *adj* reprehensible

reprendre* [rəprɑ̃dr] **1** *vt (objet)* to take back; *(évadé, ville)* to recapture; *(passer prendre)* to pick up again; *(activité)* to take up again; *(refrain)* to take up; *(vêtement)* to alter; *(corriger)* to correct; *(blâmer)* to admonish; *(pièce de théâtre)* to put on again; **r. de la viande/un œuf** to take some more meat/ another egg; **r. sa place** *(retourner s'asseoir)* to return to one's seat; **r. ses esprits** to come round; **r. des forces** to get one's strength back; *Fam* **on ne m'y reprendra plus** I won't be caught out doing that again **2** *vi (plante)* to take root again; *(recommencer)* to start again; *(affaires)* to pick up; *(en parlant)* to go on, to continue **3 se reprendre** *upr (se ressaisir)* to get a grip on oneself; *(se corriger)* to correct oneself; **s'y r. à deux/plusieurs fois** to have another go/several goes (at it)

représailles [rəprezaj] *nfpl* reprisals, retaliation

représenter [rəprezɑ̃te] **1** *vt* to represent; *(pièce de théâtre)* to perform **2 se représenter** *upr (s'imaginer)* to imagine **▪ représentant, -ante** *nmf* representative; **r. de commerce** sales representative **▪ représentatif, -ive** *adj* representative (**de** of) **▪ représentation** *nf* representation; *Théâtre* performance

répression [represjɔ̃] *nf (d'émeute)* suppression; *(mesures de contrôle)* repression **▪ répressif, -ive** *adj* repressive

réprimer [reprime] *vt (sentiment, révolte)* to suppress

réprimande [reprimɑ̃d] *nf* reprimand **▪ réprimander** *vt* to reprimand

repris [rəpri] *nm* **r. de justice** hardened criminal

reprise [rəpriz] *nf (recommencement)* resumption; *Théâtre* revival; *(de film, d'émission)* repeat; *Boxe* round; *(de l'économie)* recovery; *(de locataire)* = money for fixtures and fittings *(paid by outgoing tenant)*; *(de marchandise)* taking back; *(pour nouvel achat)* part exchange, trade-in; **faire une r. à qch** to mend sth; **à plusieurs reprises** on several occasions ▪ **repriser** *vt (chaussette)* to mend

réprobation [reprɔbasjɔ̃] *nf* disapproval ▪ **réprobateur, -trice** *adj* disapproving

reproche [rəprɔʃ] *nm* reproach; **faire des reproches à qn sur qch** to reproach sb for sth; **sans r.** beyond reproach ▪ **reprocher 1** *vt* **r. qch à qn** to blame *or* reproach sb for sth; **qu'as-tu à r. à ce livre?** what do you have against this book? **2 se reprocher** *vpr* **n'avoir rien à se r.** to have nothing to reproach *or* blame oneself for

reproduire* [rəprɔdɥir] **1** *vt (modèle, son)* to reproduce **2 se reproduire** *vpr (animaux)* to reproduce; *(incident)* to happen again ▪ **reproducteur, -trice** *adj* reproductive ▪ **reproduction** *nf (d'animaux, de son)* reproduction; *(copie)* copy

réprouver [repruve] *vt* to condemn

reptile [rɛptil] *nm* reptile

repu, -ue [rəpy] *adj (rassasié)* satiated

république [repyblik] *nf* republic ▪ **républicain, -aine** *adj & nmf* republican

répudier [repydje] *vt* to repudiate

répugnant, -ante [repyɲɑ̃, -ɑ̃t] *adj* repulsive ▪ **répugnance** *nf* repugnance, loathing (**pour** for); *(manque d'enthousiasme)* reluctance ▪ **répugner** *vi* **r. à qn** to be repugnant to sb; **r. à faire qch** to be loath to do sth

répulsion [repylsjɔ̃] *nf* repulsion

réputation [repytasjɔ̃] *nf* reputation; **avoir la r. d'être franc** to have a reputation for being frank *or* for frankness; **connaître qn de r.** to know sb by reputation ▪ **réputé, -ée** *adj (célèbre)* renowned (**pour** for); **r. pour être très intelligent** reputed to be very intelligent

requérir [rəkerir] *vt (nécessiter)* to require; *(solliciter)* to request; *(peine de prison)* to call for ▪ **requis, -ise** *adj* required, requisite

requête [rəkɛt] *nf* request; *Jur (auprès d'un juge)* petition

requiem [rekɥijɛm] *nm inv* requiem

requin [rəkɛ̃] *nm (poisson) & Fig* shark

requinquer [rəkɛ̃ke] *vt Fam* to perk up

réquisition [rekizisjɔ̃] *nf* requisition ▪ **réquisitionner** *vt* to requisition, to commandeer

réquisitoire [rekizitwar] *nm Jur* prosecution address; *(critique)* indictment (**contre** of)

RER [ɛrøɛr] *(abrév* **Réseau express régional)** *nm* = express rail network serving Paris and its suburbs

rescapé, -ée [rɛskape] **1** *adj* surviving **2** *nmf* survivor

rescousse [rɛskus] **à la rescousse** *adv* to the rescue

réseau, -x [rezo] *nm* network; *Ordinat* **en r.** networked; **r. d'espionnage** spy ring *or* network

réservation [rezɛrvasjɔ̃] *nf* reservation, booking; **faire une r.** to make a booking

réserve [rezɛrv] *nf (provision, discrétion)* reserve; *(entrepôt)* storeroom; *(de bibliothèque)* stacks; *(de chasse, de pêche)* preserve; *(restriction)* reservation; *Mil* **la r.** the reserve; **en r.** in reserve; **sans r.** *(admiration)* unqualified; **sous r. de** subject to; **sous toutes réserves** without guarantee; **r. indienne** (native American) reservation; **r. naturelle** nature reserve

réserver [rezɛrve] **1** *vt* to reserve; *(garder)* to save, to keep (**à** for); *(marchandises)* to put aside (**à** for); *(sort, surprise)* to hold in store (**à** for) **2 se réserver** *vpr* **se r. pour qch** to save oneself for sth; **se r. de faire qch** to reserve the right to do sth ▪ **réservé, -ée** *adj (personne, place, chambre)* reserved

réservoir [rezɛrvwar] *nm (lac)* reservoir; *(cuve)* tank; **r. d'essence** *Br* petrol *or Am* gas tank

résidence [rezidɑ̃s] *nf* residence; **r. secondaire** second home; **r. universitaire** *Br* hall of residence, *Am* dormitory ▪ **résident, -ente** *nmf* resident; **un r. français en Irlande** a French national resident in Ireland ▪ **résidentiel, -ielle** *adj (quartier)* residential ▪ **résider** *vi* to reside; **r. dans** *(consister en)* to lie in

résidu [rezidy] *nm* residue

résigner [reziɲe] **se résigner** *vpr* to resign oneself (**à qch** to sth; **à faire** to doing) ▪ **résignation** *nf* resignation

résilier [rezilje] *vt (contrat)* to terminate ▪ **résiliation** *nf* termination

résille [rezij] *nf* hairnet

résine [rezin] *nf* resin

résistance [rezistɑ̃s] *nf* resistance (**à** to); *Hist* **la R.** the Resistance

résister [reziste] *vi* **r. à** *(attaque, agresseur, tentation)* to resist; *(chaleur, fatigue, souffrance)* to withstand; *(mauvais traitement)* to stand up to; **r. à l'analyse** to stand up to analysis ▪ **résistant, -ante 1** *adj* tough; **r. à la chaleur** heat-resistant; **r. au choc** shockproof **2** *nmf Hist* Resistance fighter

résolu, -ue [rezɔly] **1** *pp de* **résoudre 2** *adj* determined, resolute; **r. à faire qch** determined to do sth ▪ **résolument** *adv* resolutely ▪ **résolution** *nf (décision)* resolution; *(fermeté)* determination

résonance [rezonɑ̃s] *nf* resonance

résonner [rezone] *vi (cri)* to resound; *(salle, voix)* to echo (**de** with)

résorber [rezɔrbe] **1** *vt (excédent)* to absorb; *(chômage)* to reduce **2 se résorber** *upr (excédent)* to be absorbed; *(chômage)* to be reduced ▪ **résorption** *nf (de surplus, de déficit)* absorption

résoudre* [rezudr] **1** *vt (problème)* to solve; *(difficulté)* to resolve; **r. de faire qch** to resolve to do sth **2 se résoudre** *upr* **se r. à faire qch** to resolve to do sth

respect [rɛspɛ] *nm* respect (**pour/de** for); **mes respects à...** my regards *or* respects to...; **tenir qn en r.** to hold sb in check ▪ **respectabilité** *nf* respectability ▪ **respectable** *adj (honorable, important)* respectable ▪ **respecter** *vt* to respect; **qui se respecte** self-respecting; **r. la loi** to abide by the law; **faire r. la loi** to enforce the law ▪ **respectueusement** *adv* respectfully ▪ **respectueux, -ueuse** *adj* respectful (**envers** to; **de** of)

respectif, -ive [rɛspɛktif, -iv] *adj* respective ▪ **respectivement** *adv* respectively

respirer [rɛspire] **1** *vi* to breathe; *Fig (être soulagé)* to breathe again **2** *vt* to breathe (in); *Fig (exprimer)* to radiate ▪ **respiration** *nf* breathing; *(haleine)* breath; *Méd* **r. artificielle** artificial respiration ▪ **respiratoire** *adj* **troubles respiratoires** breathing difficulties

resplendir [rɛsplɑ̃dir] *vi* to shine; *(visage)* to glow (**de** with) ▪ **resplendissant, -ante** *adj (personne, visage)* radiant (**de** with)

responsable [rɛspɔ̃sabl] **1** *adj* responsible (**de qch** for sth; **devant qn** to sb) **2** *nmf (chef)* person in charge; *(dans une organisation)* official; *(coupable)* person responsible (**de** for) ▪ **responsabilité** *nf* responsibility; *(légale)* liability

resquiller [rɛskije] *vi (au cinéma)* to sneak in without paying; *(dans le métro)* to dodge paying one's fare

ressaisir [rəsezir] **se ressaisir** *upr* to pull oneself together

ressasser [rəsase] *vt (ruminer)* to brood over; *(répéter)* to keep trotting out

ressemblance [rəsɑ̃blɑ̃s] *nf* likeness, resemblance (**avec** to) ▪ **ressemblant, -ante** *adj* lifelike ▪ **ressembler** **1** *vi* **r. à** to look like, to resemble; **cela ne lui ressemble pas** *(ce n'est pas son genre)* that's not like him/her **2 se ressembler** *upr* to look alike

ressentiment [rəsɑ̃timɑ̃] *nm* resentment

ressentir* [rəsɑ̃tir] **1** *vt* to feel **2 se ressentir** *upr* **se r. de qch** *(personne)* to feel the effects of sth; *(travail)* to show the effects of sth

> Il faut noter que le verbe anglais **to resent** est un faux ami. Il signifie **ne pas aimer du tout**.

resserre [rəsɛr] *nf* storeroom; *(remise)* shed
resserrer [rəsere] **1** *vt (nœud, boulon)* to

tighten; *Fig (liens)* to strengthen **2 se resserrer** *upr (nœud)* to tighten; *(amitié)* to become closer; *(route)* to narrow

resservir* [rəsɛrvir] **1** *vt (plat)* to serve (up) again; **r. qn** to give sb another helping **2** *vi (outil)* to come in useful (again) **3 se resservir** *upr* **se r. de** *(plat)* to have another helping of

ressort [rəsɔr] *nm (objet)* spring; *(énergie)* spirit; **du r.** to be within the competence of; **en dernier r.** *(décider)* as a last resort

ressortir* [rəsɔrtir] **1** *(aux être)* *vi (personne)* to go/come back out; *(film)* to be shown again; *(voir)* to stand out; **faire r. qch** to bring sth out; **il ressort de...** *(résulte)* it emerges from... **2** *(aux avoir)* *vi (vêtement)* to get out again

ressortissant, -ante [rəsɔrtisɑ̃, -ɑ̃t] *nmf* national

ressource [rəsurs] **1** *nfpl* **ressources** *(moyens, argent)* resources; **être sans ressources** to be without means; **ressources humaines** human resources **2** *nf (possibilité)* possibility (**de faire** of doing); **avoir de la r.** to be resourceful; **en dernière r.** as a last resort

ressusciter [resysite] **1** *vi* to rise from the dead **2** *vt (mort)* to raise

> Il faut noter que le verbe anglais **to resuscitate** est un faux ami. Il ne signifie jamais **ressusciter**.

restant, -ante [rɛstɑ̃, -ɑ̃t] **1** *adj* remaining **2** *nm* **le r.** the rest, the remainder; **un r. de viande** some leftover meat

restaurant [rɛstɔrɑ̃] *nm* restaurant

restaurer [rɛstɔre] **1** *vt (réparer, rétablir)* to restore **2 se restaurer** *upr* to have something to eat ▪ **restaurateur, -trice** *nmf (hôtelier, hôtelière)* restaurant owner; *(de tableaux)* restorer ▪ **restauration** *nf (hôtellerie)* catering; *(de tableau)* restoration

reste [rɛst] *nm* rest, remainder (**de** of); **restes** remains (**de** of); *(de repas)* leftovers; **un r. de fromage** some leftover cheese; **au r., du r.** moreover, besides; **avoir qch de r.** to have sth to spare; **il est parti sans demander son r.** he left without further ado

rester [rɛste] *(aux être)* *vi* to stay, to remain; *(calme, jeune)* to keep, to stay, to remain; *(subsister)* to be left, to remain; **il reste du pain** there's some bread left (over); **il me reste une minute** I have one minute left; **l'argent qui lui reste** the money he/she has left; **reste à savoir** it remains to be seen; **il me reste deux choses à faire** I still have two things to do; **il me reste à vous remercier** it remains for me to thank you; **il n'en reste pas moins que...** the fact remains that...; **en r. à** to stop at; **restons-en là** let's leave it at that; **r. sur sa faim** to remain hungry; **celá m'est resté sur l'estomac** *(plat)* it's lying heavy on my stomach; *Fam* **elle a failli y r.** that was very nearly the end of her

restituer [rɛstitɥe] *vt (rendre)* to return (**à** to); *(argent)* to repay; *(son)* to reproduce; *(passé)* to re-create ▪ **restitution** *nf (d'objet)* return; *(de son)* reproduction; *(du passé)* re-creation

restreindre* [rɛstrɛ̃dr] **1** *vt* to restrict (**à** to) **2 se restreindre** *vpr (domaine)* to become more restricted; *(faire des économies)* to cut down ▪ **restreint, -einte** *adj* restricted (**à** to); *(espace)* limited ▪ **restrictif, -ive** *adj* restrictive ▪ **restriction** *nf* restriction; **sans r.** *(approuver)* unreservedly

résultat [rezylta] *nm* result; **avoir qch pour r.** to result in sth ▪ **résulter 1** *vi* **r. de** to result from **2** *v impersonnel* **il en résulte que...** the result of this is that...

résumer [rezyme] **1** *vt (abréger)* to summarize; *(récapituler)* to sum up **2 se résumer** *vpr (orateur)* to sum up; **se r. à qch** *(se réduire à)* to boil down to sth ▪ **résumé** *nm* summary; **en r.** in short

> Il faut noter que le verbe anglais **to resume** est un faux ami. Il signifie **recommencer**.

résurgence [rezyrʒɑ̃s] *nf* resurgence (**de** in)
résurrection [rezyrɛksjɔ̃] *nf* resurrection

rétablir [retablir] **1** *vt (communications, ordre)* to restore; *(vérité)* to re-establish; *(employé)* to reinstate **2 se rétablir** *vpr (ordre)* to be restored; *(malade)* to recover ▪ **rétablissement** *nm (d'ordre, de dynastie)* restoration; *(de vérité)* re-establishment; *(de malade)* recovery

retaper [rətape] *vt Fam (maison, voiture)* to do up; *(lit)* to straighten; *(malade)* to buck up

retard [rətar] *nm (de personne)* lateness; *(sur un programme)* delay; *(de région)* backwardness; **en r.** late; **en r. dans qch** behind in sth; **en r. sur qn/qch** behind sb/sth; **rattraper** *ou* **combler son r.** to catch up; **avoir du r.** to be late; *(sur un programme)* to be behind (schedule); *(montre)* to be slow; **avoir une heure de r.** to be an hour late; **prendre du r.** *(montre)* to lose (time); *(personne)* to fall behind; **sans r.** without delay; *Fam* **il a toujours un métro de r.** he's slow on the uptake

retardataire *nmf* latecomer
retarder [rətarde] **1** *vt (faire arriver en retard)* to delay; *(date, montre, départ)* to put back; **r. qn** *(dans une activité)* to put sb behind **2** *vi (montre)* to be slow; **r. de cinq minutes** to be five minutes slow; *Fig* **r. (sur son temps)** *(personne)* to be behind the times ▪ **retardé, -ée** *adj (enfant)* backward

retenir* [rətənir] **1** *vt (personne)* to keep; *(eau, chaleur)* to retain; *(cotisation)* to deduct (**sur** from); *(suggestion)* to adopt; *(larmes, foule)* to hold back; *Math (chiffre)* to carry; *(se souvenir*

de) to remember; *(réserver)* to reserve; **r. qn par le bras** to hold sb back by the arm; **r. qn prisonnier** to keep sb prisoner; **r. l'attention de qn** to catch sb's attention; **r. qn de faire qch** to stop sb (from) doing sth; **votre candidature n'a pas été retenue** your application was unsuccessful **2 se retenir** *vpr (se contenir)* to restrain oneself; **se r. de faire qch** to stop oneself (from) doing sth; **se r. à qn/qch** to cling to sb/sth

retentir [rətɑ̃tir] *vi* to ring out (**de** with); *Fig* **r. sur qch** to have an impact on sth ▪ **retentissant, -ante** *adj (succès, échec)* resounding; *(scandale)* major ▪ **retentissement** *nm (effet)* impact; **avoir un grand r.** *(film)* to create a stir

retenue [rətəny] *nf (modération)* restraint; *(de salaire)* deduction; *Math (chiffre)* figure carried over; *Scol (punition)* detention; **en r.** in detention

réticent, -ente [retisɑ̃, -ɑ̃t] *adj* hesitant, unwilling ▪ **réticence** *nf* hesitation, unwillingness

> Il faut noter que l'adjectif anglais **reticent** est un faux ami. Il signifie **discret**.

rétine [retin] *nf* retina

retirer [rətire] **1** *vt* to withdraw; *(faire sortir)* to take out; *(ôter)* to take off; *(éloigner)* to take away; *(aller chercher)* to pick up; **r. qch à qn** *(permis)* to take sth away from sb; **r. qch de qch** *(gagner)* to derive sth from sth **2 se retirer** *vpr* to withdraw (**de** from); *(mer)* to ebb ▪ **retiré, -ée** *adj (lieu, vie)* secluded

retomber [rətɔ̃be] *vi* to fall again; *(après un saut)* to land; *(intérêt)* to slacken; **r. dans** *(l'oubli, le chaos)* to sink back into; *(le péché)* to lapse into; **r. malade** to fall ill again; **r. sur qn** *(responsabilité, frais)* to fall on sb; *Fam (rencontrer)* to bump into sb again; *Fig* **r. sur ses pieds** to land on one's feet ▪ **retombées** *nfpl (radioactives)* fallout; *Fig (conséquences)* repercussions

rétorquer [retɔrke] *vt* **r. que...** to retort that...
retors, -orse [rətɔr, -ɔrs] *adj* wily, crafty
rétorsion [retɔrsjɔ̃] *nf* retaliation; **mesure de r.** reprisal

retouche [rətuʃ] *nf (de vêtement)* alteration; *(de photo)* touching up ▪ **retoucher** *vt (vêtement, texte)* to alter; *(photo, tableau)* to touch up

retour [rətur] *nm* return; *(trajet)* return journey; *(de fortune)* reversal; **être de r.** to be back (**de** from); **en r.** *(en échange)* in return; **par r. du courrier** *Br* by return (of post), *Am* by return mail; **à mon r.** when I get/got back (**de** from); **r. à l'envoyeur** return to sender; *Fig* **r. de flamme** backlash; **match r.** return *Br* match *or Am* game

retourner [rəturne] **1** *(aux avoir)* *vt (matelas,*

steak) to turn over; *(terre)* to turn; *(vêtement, sac)* to turn inside out; *(tableau)* to turn round; *(compliment, lettre)* to return; *Fam (maison)* to turn upside down; **r. qch contre qn** *(argument)* to turn sth against sb; *(arme)* to turn sth on sb; *Fam* **r. qn** *(bouleverser)* to upset sb; *Fam* **savoir de quoi il retourne** to know what it's all about **2** *(aux être) vi* to go back, to return **3 se retourner** *vpr (pour regarder)* to turn round; *(sur le dos)* to turn over; *(dans son lit)* to toss and turn; *(voiture)* to overturn; **s'en r.** to go back; *Fig* **se r. contre** to turn against ▪ **retournement** [-əmã] *nm (de situation)* turnaround

retracer [rətrase] *vt (événement)* to recount

rétracter [retrakte] *vt,* **se rétracter** *vpr* to retract ▪ **rétractation** *nf* retraction

retrait [rətrɛ] *nm* withdrawal; *(de bagages, de billets)* collection; *(des eaux)* receding; **en r.** *(maison)* set back; **ligne en r.** indented line; **commencer un paragraphe en r.** to indent a paragraph; **rester en r.** to stay in the background

retraite [rətrɛt] *nf (d'employé)* retirement; *(pension)* (retirement) pension; *(refuge)* retreat, refuge; *(d'une armée)* retreat; **mettre qn à la r.** to pension sb off; **prendre sa r.** to retire; **être à la r.** to be retired; *Mil & Fig* **battre en r.** to beat a retreat; **r. aux flambeaux** torchlight procession; **r. anticipée** early retirement ▪ **retraité, -ée 1** *adj* retired **2** *nmf* senior citizen, *Br* (old age) pensioner

retraitement [rətrɛtmã] *nm* reprocessing; **usine de r. (des déchets nucléaires)** (nuclear) reprocessing plant

retrancher [rətrã ʃe] **1** *vt (passage, nom)* to remove (**de** from); *(argent, quantité)* to deduct (**de** from) **2 se retrancher** *vpr (soldats)* to dig in; *Fig* **se r. dans/derrière qch** to hide in/behind sth ▪ **retranchement** *nm Fig* **pousser qn dans ses derniers retranchements** to drive sb to the wall

retransmettre* [rətrãsmɛtr] *vt* to broadcast ▪ **retransmission** *nf* broadcast

rétrécir [retresir] **1** *vt (vêtement)* to take in **2** *vi (au lavage)* to shrink **3 se rétrécir** *vpr (rue)* to narrow ▪ **rétréci, -ie** *adj (route)* narrow

rétribuer [retribɥe] *vt (personne)* to pay; *(travail)* to pay for ▪ **rétribution** *nf* payment, remuneration

> Il faut noter que le nom anglais **retribution** est un faux ami. Il signifie **châtiment**.

rétro [retro] *adj inv (personne, idée)* retro

rétroactif, -ive [retroaktif, -iv] *adj* retroactive; **augmentation avec effet r.** retroactive (pay) increase

rétrograde [retrograd] *adj* retrograde ▪ **rétrograder 1** *vt (fonctionnaire, officier)* to

demote **2** *vi (automobiliste)* to change down

rétroprojecteur [retroprozɛktœr] *nm* overhead projector

rétrospectif, -ive [retrɔspɛktif, -iv] **1** *adj* retrospective **2** *nf* ▪ **rétrospective** retrospective ▪ **rétrospectivement** *adv* in retrospect

retrousser [rətruse] *vt (manches)* to roll up; *(jupe)* to tuck up ▪ **retroussé, -ée** *adj (nez)* turned-up, snub

retrouver [rətruve] **1** *vt (objet)* to find again; *(personne)* to meet again; *(forces, santé)* to regain; *(se rappeler)* to recall; *(découvrir)* to rediscover **2 se retrouver** *vpr (être)* to find oneself; *(trouver son chemin)* to find one's way (**dans** round); *(se rencontrer)* to meet; **se r. à la rue** to find oneself homeless; **je me suis retrouvé rue d'Assas** I ended up in rue d'Assas; **je ne m'y retrouve plus!** I'm completely lost! ▪ **retrouvailles** *nfpl* reunion

rétroviseur [retrovizœr] *nm* rear-view mirror

Réunion [reynjɔ̃] *nf* **la R.** Réunion

réunion [reynjɔ̃] *nf (séance)* meeting; *(d'objets)* collection, gathering; *(jonction)* joining; **être en r.** to be in a meeting; **r. de famille** family gathering; *Scol* **r. de parents d'élèves** parents meeting

réunir [reynir] **1** *vt (objets)* to put together; *(documents)* to gather together; *(fonds)* to raise; *(amis, famille)* to get together; *(après une rupture)* to reunite; *(avantages, qualités)* to combine; **r. qch à qch** to join sth to sth **2 se réunir** *vpr (personnes, routes)* to meet; **se r. autour de qn/qch** to gather round sb/sth

réussir [reysir] **1** *vt (bien faire)* to make a success of; *(examen)* to pass **2** *vi* to succeed, to be successful (**à faire** in doing); *(à un examen)* to pass; **r. à qn** to work out well for sb; *(aliment, climat)* to agree with sb; **r. à un examen** to pass an exam ▪ **réussi, -ie** *adj* successful ▪ **réussite** *nf* success; *Cartes* **faire des réussites** to play patience

revaloir [rəvalwar] *vt* **je vous le revaudrai** *(en bien ou en mal)* I'll pay you back

revaloriser [rəvalɔrize] *vt (monnaie)* to revalue; *(salaires, profession)* to upgrade ▪ **revalorisation** *nf (de monnaie)* revaluation; *(de salaires, de profession)* upgrading

revanche [rəvã ʃ] *nf* revenge; *(de match)* return game; **prendre sa r. (sur qn)** to get one's revenge (on sb); **en r.** on the other hand

rêve [rɛv] *nm* dream; **faire un r.** to have a dream; **fais de beaux rêves!** sweet dreams!; **maison/voiture de r.** dream house/car ▪ **rêvasser** *vi* to daydream

revêche [rəvɛ ʃ] *adj* bad-tempered

réveil [revɛj] *nm (de personnes)* waking; *Fig* awakening; *(pendule)* alarm (clock); **à son r.** on waking

réveiller [revɛje] **1** *vt (personne)* to wake (up);

Fig (douleur) to revive; *Fig (sentiment, souvenir)* to revive **2 se réveiller** *upr (personne)* to wake (up); *(nature)* to reawaken; *Fig (douleur)* to come back ■**réveillé, -ée** *adj* awake

réveillon [revɛjɔ̃] *nm (repas)* midnight supper; *(soirée)* midnight party *(on Christmas Eve or New Year's Eve)* ■**réveillonner** *vi* to see in Christmas/the NewYear

révéler [revele] **1** *vt* to reveal (**que** that) **2 se révéler** *upr (personne)* to reveal oneself; *(talent)* to be revealed; **se r. facile** to turn out to be easy ■**révélateur, -trice** *adj* revealing; **r. de qch** indicative of sth ■**révélation** *nf (action, découverte)* revelation; *(personne)* discovery; **faire des révélations** to disclose important information

revenant [rəvənɑ̃] *nm* ghost; *Fam* **tiens! un r.!** hello, stranger!

revendiquer [rəvɑ̃dike] *vt* to claim; *(attentat)* to claim responsibility for ■**revendicatif, -ive** *adj* **mouvement r.** protest movement ■**revendication** *nf* claim

revendre [rəvɑ̃dr] *vt* to resell; *Fig* **avoir (de) qch à r.** to have sth to spare ■**revendeur, -euse** *nmf* retailer; *(d'occasion)* second-hand dealer; **r. (de drogue)** drug pusher ■**revente** *nf* resale

revenir* [rəvənir] *(aux être)* *vi (personne)* to come back, to return; *(mot)* to crop up; *(date)* to come round again; **r. à 50 euros** to come to 50 euros; **le dîner nous est revenu à 50 euros** the dinner cost us 50 euros; **r. cher** to work out expensive; **r. à** *(activité, sujet)* to go back to, to return to; *(se résumer à)* to boil down to; **r. à qn** *(forces, mémoire)* to come back to sb; *(honneur)* to fall to sb; **r. à soi** to come round or to; **r. de** *(surprise)* to get over; **r. sur** *(décision, promesse)* to go back on; *(passé, question)* to go back over; **r. sur ses pas** to retrace one's steps; **faire r. qch** *(aliment)* to brown sth; *Fam* **sa tête ne me revient pas** I don't like the look of him; *Fam* **je n'en reviens pas!** I can't get over it!; *Fig* **elle revient de loin** she's been at death's door

revenu [rəvəny] *nm* income (**de** from); *(d'un État)* revenue (**de** from)

rêver [reve] **1** *vt* to dream (**que** that) **2** *vi* to dream (**de** of; **de faire** of doing) ■**rêvé, -ée** *adj* ideal

réverbération [reverberasjɔ̃] *nf (de lumière)* reflection; *(de son)* reverberation

réverbère [reverber] *nm* street lamp

révérence [reverɑ̃s] *nf (respect)* reverence; *(salut de femme)* curtsey; **faire une r.** to curtsey ■**révérer** *vt* to revere

révérend, -ende [reverɑ̃, -ɑ̃d] *adj & nm Rel* reverend

rêverie [revri] *nf* daydream

revers [rəver] *nm (de veste)* lapel; *(de pantalon)* *Br* turn-up, *Am* cuff; *(d'étoffe)* wrong side; *(de pièce)* reverse; *(coup du sort)* setback; *Sport (au* tennis)* backhand; **d'un r. de la main** with the back of one's hand; *Fig* **le r. de la médaille** the other side of the coin

reverser [rəverse] *vt (café, vin)* to pour more; *Fig (argent)* to transfer (**sur un compte** into an account)

réversible [reversibl] *adj* reversible

revêtir* [rəvetir] *vt* to cover (**de** with); *(habit)* to don; *(route)* to surface; *(caractère, forme)* to assume; **r. qn** *(habiller)* to dress sb (**de** in); **r. un document de** *(signature)* to provide a document with ■**revêtement** *nm (surface)* covering; *(de route)* surface

rêveur, -euse [revœr, -øz] **1** *adj* dreamy **2** *nmf* dreamer

revient [rəvjɛ̃] *nm* **prix de r.** *Br* cost price, *Am* wholesale price

revigorer [rəvigore] *vt (personne)* to revive

revirement [rəvirmɑ̃] *nm (changement) Br* about-turn, *Am* about-face; *(de situation, d'opinion, de politique)* reversal

réviser [revize] *vt (leçon) Br* to revise, *Am* to review; *(machine, voiture)* to service; *(jugement, règlement)* to review ■**révision** *nf (de leçon) Br* revision, *Am* review; *(de machine)* service; *(de jugement)* review

revisser [rəvise] *vt (bouchon)* to screw back again

revivre* [rəvivr] **1** *vt (incident)* to relive **2** *vi* to live again; **faire r. qch** to revive sth

révocation [revokasjɔ̃] *nf (de fonctionnaire)* dismissal; *(de contrat)* revocation

revoici [rəvwasi] *prép* **me r.** here I am again

revoilà [rəvwala] *prép* **la r.** there she is again

revoir* [rəvwar] *vt* to see (again); *(texte, leçon)* to revise; **au r.** goodbye

révolte [revolt] *nf (révolte)* ■**révoltant, -ante** *adj (honteux)* revolting ■**révolté, -ée** *nmf* rebel ■**révolter 1** *vt* to appal **2 se révolter** *upr* to rebel, to revolt (**contre** against)

révolu, -ue [revoly] *adj (époque)* past; **avoir trente ans révolus** to be over thirty

révolution [revolysjɔ̃] *nf (changement, rotation)* revolution ■**révolutionnaire** *adj & nmf* revolutionary ■**révolutionner** *vt (transformer)* to revolutionize

revolver [revolver] *nm* revolver

révoquer [revoke] *vt (fonctionnaire)* to dismiss; *(contrat)* to revoke

revue [rəvy] *nf (magazine)* magazine; *(spécialisée)* journal; *(spectacle)* revue; *Mil* review; **passer qch en r.** to review sth

révulser [revylse] *vt* to repulse, to disgust ■**révulsé, -ée** *adj (visage)* contorted; *(yeux)* rolled back

rez-de-chaussée [redəʃose] *nm inv Br* ground floor, *Am* first floor

rhabiller [rabije] **se rhabiller** *upr* to get dressed again

rhapsodie [rapsɔdi] *nf* rhapsody

Rhésus [rezys] *nm* **R. positif/négatif** Rhesus positive/negative

rhétorique [retɔrik] *nf* rhetoric

Rhin [rɛ̃] *nm* **le R.** the Rhine

rhinocéros [rinɔserɔs] *nm* rhinoceros

rhododendron [rɔdɔdɛ̃drɔ̃] *nm* rhododendron

Rhône [ron] *nm* **le R.** the Rhône

rhubarbe [rybarb] *nf* rhubarb

rhum [rɔm] *nm* rum

rhumatisme [rymatism] *nm* rheumatism; **avoir des rhumatismes** to have rheumatism ▪ **rhumatisant, -ante** *adj & nmf* rheumatic ▪ **rhumatismal, -e, -aux, -ales** *adj* rheumatic

rhume [rym] *nm* cold; **r. de cerveau** head cold; **r. des foins** hay fever

ri [ri] *pp de* **rire**

riant, riante [rjɑ̃, rjɑ̃t] **1** *p prés de* **rire 2** *adj* cheerful, smiling

ribambelle [ribɑ̃bɛl] *nf* (*de mots*) long string; (*d'enfants, de visiteurs*) string, crowd

ricaner [rikane] *vi* (*sarcastiquement*) *Br* to snigger, *Am* to snicker; (*bêtement*) to giggle

riche [riʃ] **1** *adj* (*personne, pays, aliment*) rich; **r. en** (*vitamines, minérai*) rich in **2** *nmf* rich person; **les riches** the rich ▪ **richement** *adv* (*vêtu, illustré*) richly ▪ **richesse** *nf* (*de personne, de pays*) wealth; (*d'étoffe, de sol, de vocabulaire*) richness; **richesses** (*trésor*) riches; (*ressources*) wealth

ricin [risɛ̃] *nm* **huile de r.** castor oil

ricocher [rikɔʃe] *vi* to rebound, to ricochet ▪ **ricochet** *nm* rebound, ricochet; **faire des ricochets (sur l'eau)** to skim stones; *Fig* **par r.** indirectly

rictus [riktys] *nm* grimace

ride [rid] *nf* (*de visage*) wrinkle; (*sur l'eau*) ripple ▪ **ridé, -ée** *adj* (*visage, peau*) wrinkled ▪ **rider 1** *vt* (*visage, peau*) to wrinkle; (*eau*) to ripple **2 se rider** *upr* (*visage, peau*) to wrinkle

rideau, -x [rido] *nm* curtain; (*métallique*) shutter; *Fig* (*écran*) screen (**de** of)

ridicule [ridikyl] **1** *adj* ridiculous, ludicrous **2** *nm* (*moquerie*) ridicule; (*absurdité*) ridiculousness; **tourner qn/qch en r.** to ridicule sb/sth ▪ **ridiculiser 1** *vt* to ridicule **2 se ridiculiser** *upr* to make a fool of oneself

rien [rjɛ̃] **1** *pron* nothing; **il ne sait r.** he knows nothing, he doesn't know anything; **r. du tout** nothing at all; **r. d'autre/de bon** nothing else/good; **r. de tel** nothing like it; **il n'y avait r. que des filles** there were only girls there; **de r.!** (*je vous en prie*) don't mention it!; **ça ne fait r.** it doesn't matter; **trois fois r.** next to nothing; **avoir qch pour r.** (*à bas prix*) to get sth for next to nothing; **pour r. au monde** never in a thousand years; **comme si de r. n'était** as if nothing had happened; **il n'en est r.** (*ce n'est pas vrai*) nothing of the kind; *Fam* **je n'en ai r. à**

faire I couldn't care less **2** *nm* (mere) nothing, trifle; **un r. de** a little; **en un r. de temps** in no time; **un r. trop petit** just a bit too small; **pleurer pour un r.** to cry at the slightest thing

rieur, rieuse [rijœr, rijøz] *adj* cheerful

rigide [riʒid] *adj* rigid; (*carton*) stiff; *Fig* (*personne*) inflexible; (*éducation*) strict ▪ **rigidité** *nf* rigidity; (*de carton*) stiffness; (*de personne*) inflexibility; (*d'éducation*) strictness

rigole [rigɔl] *nf* (*conduit*) channel; (*filet d'eau*) rivulet

rigoler [rigɔle] *vi Fam* to laugh; (*s'amuser*) to have a laugh; (*plaisanter*) to joke (**avec** about); **tu rigoles?** are you kidding? ▪ **rigolade** *nf Fam* fun; **prendre qch à la r.** to make a joke out of sth ▪ **rigolo, -ote** *nf* **1** *adj* funny **2** *nmf* joker

rigueur [rigœr] *nf* (*d'analyse*) rigour; (*de climat*) harshness; (*de personne*) strictness; **être de r.** to be the rule; **à la r.** if necessary; *Fig* **tenir r. à qn de qch** to hold sth against sb ▪ **rigoureux, -euse** *adj* (*analyse*) rigorous; (*climat, punition*) harsh; (*personne, morale, neutralité*) strict

rillettes [rijɛt] *nfpl Culin* potted meat

rime [rim] *nf* rhyme ▪ **rimer** *vi* to rhyme (**avec** with); **ça ne rime à rien** it makes no sense

Rimmel® [rimɛl] *nm* mascara

rincer [rɛ̃se] *vt* to rinse; (*verre*) to rinse (out) ▪ **rinçage** *nm* rinsing; (*pour les cheveux*) rinse ▪ **rince-doigts** *nm inv* finger bowl

ring [riŋ] *nm* (boxing) ring

ringard, -arde [rɛ̃gar, -ard] *Fam* **1** *adj* (*démodé*) uncool, *Br* sad **2** *nmf* geek, nerd

ripaille [ripaj] *nf Fam* **faire r.** to have a blow-out

riposte [ripɔst] *nf* (*réponse*) retort; (*attaque*) counterattack ▪ **riposter 1** *vt* **r. que...** to retort that... **2** *vi* to counterattack; **r. à** (*attaque*) to counter; (*insulte*) to reply to

riquiqui [rikiki] *adj inv Fam* tiny

rire* [rir] **1** *nm* laugh; **rires** laughter; **le fou r.** the giggles **2** *vi* to laugh (**de** at); (*s'amuser*) to have a good time; (*plaisanter*) to joke; **r. aux éclats** to roar with laughter; **faire qch pour r.** to do sth for a joke *or* laugh **3 se rire** *upr Littéraire* **se r. de qch** (*se jouer de*) to make light of sth

ris [ri] *nm Culin* **r. de veau** calf's sweetbread

risée [rize] *nf* mockery; **être la r. de** to be the laughing stock of

risible [rizibl] *adj* laughable

risque [risk] *nm* risk; **au r. de faire qch** at the risk of doing sth; **les risques du métier** occupational hazards; **à vos risques et périls** at your own risk; **assurance tous risques** comprehensive insurance

risquer [riske] **1** *vt* to risk; (*question*) to venture; **r. le tout pour le tout** to go for broke; **r. de faire qch** to stand a good chance of doing sth; **ça risque de durer longtemps** that may well last for a long time; **qu'est-ce que tu risques?**

what have you got to lose? **2 se risquer** *vpr* se **r. à faire qch** to dare to do sth; **se r. dans qch** to venture into sth ▪ **risqué, -ée** *adj (dangereux)* risky; *(osé)* risqué

ristourne [risturn] *nf* discount

rite [rit] *nm* rite; *Fig (habitude)* ritual ▪ **rituel, -uelle** *adj & nm* ritual

rivage [rivaʒ] *nm* shore

rival, -e, -aux, -ales [rival, -o] *adj & nmf* rival ▪ **rivaliser** *vi* to compete (**avec** with; **de** in) ▪ **rivalité** *nf* rivalry

rive [riv] *nf (de fleuve)* bank; *(de lac)* shore

river [rive] *vt(attacher)* to rivet; *Fig* **il a les yeux rivés sur elle** his eyes are glued to her ▪ **rivet** *nm* rivet

riverain, -aine [rivərɛ̃, -ɛn] **1** *adj (de rivière)* riverside; *(de lac)* lakeside **2** *nmf (près d'une rivière)* riverside resident; *(près d'un lac)* lakeside resident; *(de rue)* resident

rivière [rivjɛr] *nf* river; **r. de diamants** diamond necklace

rixe [riks] *nf* brawl

riz [ri] *nm* rice; **r. blanc/complet/sauvage** white/brown/wild rice; **r. basmati** basmati rice; **r. au lait** rice pudding ▪ **rizière** *nf* paddy (field), rice-field

RMI [ɛrɛmi] *(abrév* **revenu minimum d'insertion)** *nm Br* ≃ income support, *Am* ≃ welfare ▪ **RMiste** *nmf Br* ≃ person on income support, *Am* ≃ person on welfare

RN *abrév* **route nationale**

robe [rɔb] *nf (de femme)* dress; *(d'ecclésiastique, de juge)* robe; *(de professeur)* gown; *(pelage)* coat; **r. de soirée** *ou* **du soir** evening dress; **r. de grossesse/de mariée** maternity/wedding dress; **r. de chambre** *Br* dressing gown, *Am* bathrobe; **pomme de terre en r. des champs** jacket potato, baked potato

robinet [rɔbinɛ] *nm Br* tap, *Am* faucet

robot [rɔbo] *nm* robot; **r. ménager** food processor ▪ **robotique** *nf* robotics *(sing)*

robuste [rɔbyst] *adj* robust ▪ **robustesse** *nf* robustness

roc [rɔk] *nm* rock

rocade [rɔkad] *nf (route)* bypass

rocaille [rɔkaj] *nf (terrain)* rocky ground; *(de jardin)* rockery ▪ **rocailleux, -euse** *adj* rocky, stony; *(voix)* harsh

rocambolesque [rɔkɑ̃bɔlɛsk] *adj* fantastic

roche [rɔʃ] *nf* rock

rocher [rɔʃe] *nm (bloc, substance)* rock ▪ **rocheux, -euse** *adj* rocky

rock [rɔk] **1** *nm (musique)* rock **2** *adj inv* **chanteur/opéra r.** rock singer/opera ▪ **rockeur, -euse** *nmf (musicien)* rock musician

rodéo [rɔdeo] *nm (de chevaux)* rodeo

roder [rɔde] *vt(moteur, voiture) Br* to run in, *Am* to break in; *Fig* **être rodé** *(personne)* to have *Br*

got *or Am* gotten the hang of things ▪ **rodage** *nm Br* running in, *Am* breaking in

rôder [rode] *vi* to be on the prowl ▪ **rôdeur, -euse** *nmf* prowler

rogne [rɔɲ] *nf Fam* bad temper; **être en r.** to be cross; **se mettre en r.** to get mad

rogner [rɔɲe] **1** *vt (ongles)* to trim, to clip; *Fig (économies)* to eat away at; *Fig* **r. les ailes à qn** to clip sb's wings **2** *vi* **r. sur qch** *(réduire)* to cut down on sth ▪ **rognures** *nfpl (de cuir, de métal)* trimmings

rognon [rɔɲɔ̃] *nm* kidney

roi [rwa] *nm* king; **fête des Rois** Twelfth Night

roitelet [rwatlɛ] *nm (oiseau)* wren

rôle [rol] *nm* role, part; *(de père)* job; **à tour de r.** in turn

roller [rolœr] *nm* rollerblading, in-line skating; **faire du r.** to go rollerblading *or* in-line skating ▪ **rollers (en ligne)** *nmpl* rollerblades, in-line skates

romain, -aine¹ [rɔmɛ̃, -ɛn] **1** *adj* Roman **2** *nmf* **R., Romaine** Roman

romaine² [rɔmɛn] *nf (laitue) Br* cos (lettuce), *Am* romaine

roman¹ [rɔmɑ̃] *nm* novel; *Fig (histoire)* story; **r. d'aventures/d'amour** adventure/love story; **r.-fleuve** saga; **r. noir** thriller; **r.-photo** photostory ▪ **romancé, -ée** *adj (histoire)* fictional ▪ **romancier, -ière** *nmf* novelist

roman², -ane [rɔmɑ̃, -an] *adj (langue)* Romance; *Archit* Romanesque

---

Il faut noter que l'adjectif anglais **Roman** est un faux ami. Il signifie **romain**.

---

romanesque [rɔmanɛsk] *adj* romantic; *(incroyable)* fantastic

romanichel, -elle [rɔmaniʃɛl] *nmf* gipsy

romantique [rɔmɑ̃tik] *adj & nmf* romantic ▪ **romantisme** *nm* romanticism

romarin [rɔmarɛ̃] *nm* rosemary

rompre* [rɔ̃pr] **1** *vt* to break; *(pourparlers, relations)* to break off; *(digue)* to burst **2** *vi (casser)* to break; *(digue)* to burst; *(fiancés)* to break it off; **r. avec la tradition** to break with tradition **3 se rompre** *vpr (corde)* to break; *(digue)* to burst ▪ **rompu, -ue** *adj (fatigué)* exhausted; **r. à qch** *(expérimenté)* used to sth

romsteck [rɔmstɛk] *nm* rump steak

ronces [rɔ̃s] *nfpl (branches)* brambles

ronchonner [rɔ̃ʃɔne] *vi Fam* to grumble

rond, ronde¹ [rɔ̃, rɔ̃d] **1** *adj* round; *(gras)* plump; *Fam (ivre)* plastered; **chiffre r.** whole number; **ouvrir des yeux ronds** to be wide-eyed with astonishment, to look astonished; *Fam* **r. comme une queue de pelle** *Br* rat-arsed, *Am* stewed to the gills **2** *adv* **10 euros tout r.** 10 euros exactly **3** *nm (cercle)* circle; *Fam* **ronds** *(argent)* money; **r. de serviette** napkin ring; **en r.** *(s'asseoir)* in a circle; *Fig*

tourner en r. to go round and round ▪ **rond-de-cuir** (*pl* **ronds-de-cuir**) *nm Péj* pen-pusher ▪ **rondelet, -ette** *adj* chubby; *Fig* (*somme*) tidy ▪ **rondement** *adv* (*efficacement*) briskly; (*franchement*) bluntly; **mener qch r.** to make short work of sth ▪ **rond-point** (*pl* **ronds-points**) *nm Br* roundabout, *Am* traffic circle

ronde² [rɔ̃d] *nf* (*de soldat*) round; (*de policier*) beat; (*danse*) round (dance); *Mus Br* semibreve, *Am* whole note; **à la r.** around; **faire sa r.** (*gardien*) to do one's rounds

rondelle [rɔ̃dɛl] *nf* (*tranche*) slice; *Tech* washer

rondeur [rɔ̃dœr] *nf* roundness; (*du corps*) plumpness, **rondeurs** (*de femme*) curves; (*embonpoint*) plumpness

rondin [rɔ̃dɛ̃] *nm* log

ronflant, -ante [rɔ̃flɑ̃, -ɑ̃t] *adj Péj* (*langage*) high-flown

ronfler [rɔ̃fle] *vi* (*personne*) to snore; (*moteur*) to hum ▪ **ronflement** [-əmɑ̃] *nm* (*de personne*) snore; (*de moteur*) hum; **ronflements** snoring; (*de moteur*) humming

ronger [rɔ̃ʒe] **1** *vt* to gnaw (at); (*ver, mer, rouille*) to eat into; **r. qn** (*maladie, chagrin*) to consume sb; *Fig* **r. son frein** to champ at the bit **2 se ronger** *upr* **se r. les ongles** to bite one's nails; *Fam* **se r. les sangs** to worry oneself sick ▪ **rongeur** *nm* rodent

ronronnement [rɔ̃rɔnmɑ̃] (*Fam* **ronron**) *nm* purr ▪ **ronronner** *vi* to purr

roquefort [rɔkfɔr] *nm* Roquefort

roquette [rɔkɛt] *nf Mil & Culin* rocket

rosaire [rozɛr] *nm Rel* rosary

Rosbif [rɔzbif] *nmf Fam* (*Britannique*) Brit, = pejorative or humorous term used to refer to a British person

rosbif [rɔzbif] *nm* **du r.** (*rôti*) roast beef; (*à rôtir*) roasting beef; **un r.** a joint of roast/roasting beef

rose [roz] **1** *adj* (*couleur*) pink; (*situation, teint*) rosy **2** *nm* (*couleur*) pink; **vieux r.** soft pink; **r. bonbon** bright pink **3** *nf* (*fleur*) rose; *Fam* **envoyer qn sur les roses** to send sb packing; *Fam* **découvrir le pot aux roses** to find out what's been going on ▪ **rosé, -ée 1** *adj* pinkish **2** *adj & nm* (*vin*) rosé ▪ **roseraie** *nf* rose garden ▪ **rosier** *nm* rosebush

roseau, -x [rozo] *nm* reed

rosée [roze] *nf* dew

rosette [rozɛt] *nf* (*d'un officier*) rosette; (*nœud*) bow

rosser [rɔse] *vt* **r. qn** to beat sb up

rossignol [rɔsiɲɔl] *nm* (*oiseau*) nightingale; (*crochet*) picklock

rot [ro] *nm Fam* burp, belch ▪ **roter** *vi Fam* to burp, to belch

rotation [rɔtasjɔ̃] *nf* rotation; (*de stock*) turnover ▪ **rotatif, -ive 1** *adj* rotary **2** *nf* **rotative** rotary press

rotin [rɔtɛ̃] *nm* rattan; **chaise en r.** rattan chair

rôtir [rotir] **1** *vti* to roast; **faire r. qch** to roast sth **2 se rôtir** *upr Fam* **se r. au soleil** to roast in the sun ▪ **rôti** *nm* **du r.** roasting meat; (*cuit*) roast meat; **un r.** a joint; **r. de porc/de bœuf** (*joint of*) roast pork/beef ▪ **rôtissoire** *nf* (*roasting*) spit

rotule [rɔtyl] *nf* kneecap; *Fam* **être sur les rotules** to be *Br* knackered *or Am* beat

roturier, -ière [rɔtyrje, -jɛr] *nmf* commoner

rouage [rwaʒ] *nm* (*de montre*) (working) part; *Fig* (*d'organisation*) workings

roublard, -arde [rublar, -ard] *adj Fam* wily

rouble [rubl] *nm* (*monnaie*) rouble

roucouler [rukule] *vi* to coo

roue [ru] *nf* wheel; **r. dentée** cogwheel; **faire la r.** (*paon*) to spread its tail; **être en r. libre** to freewheel; **les deux roues** two-wheeled vehicles

rouer [rwe] *vt* **r. qn de coups** to beat sb black and blue

rouet [rwɛ] *nm* spinning wheel

rouge [ruʒ] **1** *adj* red; (*fer*) red-hot **2** *nm* (*couleur*) red; *Fam* (*vin*) red wine; **le feu est au r.** the (traffic) lights are at red; **r. à lèvres** lipstick; **r. à joues** rouge, *Br* blusher ▪ **rougeâtre** *adj* reddish ▪ **rougeaud, -aude** *adj* red-faced ▪ **rouge-gorge** (*pl* **rouges-gorges**) *nm* robin

rougeole [ruʒɔl] *nf* measles (*sing*)

rougeoyer [ruʒwaje] *vi* to turn red

rouget [ruʒɛ] *nm* red mullet

rougeur [ruʒœr] *nf* redness; (*due à la honte*) blush; (*due à l'émotion*) flush; **rougeurs** (*irritation*) rash, red blotches

rougir [ruʒir] **1** *vt* (*visage*) to redden; (*ciel, feuilles*) to turn red **2** *vi* (*de honte*) to blush (**de** with); (*d'émotion*) to flush (**de** with)

rouille [ruj] **1** *nf* rust **2** *adj inv* (*couleur*) rust (-coloured) ▪ **rouillé, -ée** *adj* rusty ▪ **rouiller 1** *vi* to rust **2 se rouiller** *upr* to rust; *Fig* (*esprit, sportif*) to get rusty

roulade [rulad] *nf Culin* roulade; **r. de poisson** rolled fish; *Sport* **r. avant/arrière** forward/backward roll; **faire une r.** to do a roll

rouleau, -x [rulo] *nm* (*outil, vague*) roller; (*de papier, de pellicule*) roll; **r. à pâtisserie** rolling pin; **r. compresseur** steamroller

roulement [rulmɑ̃] *nm* (*bruit*) rumbling, rumble; (*de tambour, de tonnerre, d'yeux*) roll; (*ordre*) rotation; **par r.** in rotation; *Tech* **r. à billes** ball bearing

rouler [rule] **1** *vt* to roll; (*crêpe, ficelle, manches*) to roll up; *Fam* **r. qn** (*duper*) to cheat sb **2** *vi* (*balle*) to roll; (*train, voiture*) to go, to travel; (*conducteur*) to drive; **r. sur** (*conversation*) to turn on; *Fig* **r. sur l'or** to be rolling in it; *Fam* **ça roule!** everything's fine! **3 se rouler** *upr* to roll; **se r. dans** (*couverture*) to roll oneself (up) in

▪ **roulant, -ante** adj (escalier, trottoir) moving; (meuble) on wheels; Fig **un feu r. de questions** a barrage of questions ▪ **roulé** nm (gâteau) Swiss roll

roulette [rulɛt] nf (de meuble) castor; (de dentiste) drill; (jeu) roulette

roulis [ruli] nm (de navire) roll

roulotte [rulɔt] nf (de gitan) caravan

Roumanie [rumani] nf **la R.** Romania ▪ **roumain, -aine 1** adj Romanian **2** nmf **R., Roumaine** Romanian **3** nm (langue) Romanian

round [rawnd, rund] nm Boxe round

roupiller [rupije] vi Fam to snooze, Br to kip ▪ **roupillon** nm Fam snooze, Br kip; **faire ou piquer un r.** to have a snooze or Br a kip

rouquin, -ine [rukɛ̃, -in] Fam **1** adj red-haired **2** nmf redhead

rouspéter [ruspete] vi Fam to grumble ▪ **rouspéteur, -euse** nmf Fam grumbler

rousse [rus] voir **roux**

rousseur [rusœr] nf (de chevelure) redness; **tache de r.** freckle ▪ **roussi** nm **ça sent le r.** there's a smell of burning ▪ **roussir 1** vt (brûler) to scorch, to singe **2** vi (feuilles) to turn brown

rouste [rust] nf Fam good hiding

routard, -arde [rutar, -ard] nmf Fam backpacker

route [rut] nf road (de to); (itinéraire) way, route; Fig (chemin) path; **grand-r., grande r.** main road; **code de la r.** Br Highway Code, Am traffic regulations; **en r.** on the way, en route; **en r.!** let's go!; **par la r.** by road; Fig **sur la bonne r.** on the right track; Fig **faire fausse r.** to be on the wrong track; **mettre qch en r.** (voiture) to start sth (up); **se mettre en r.** to set out (**pour** for); **une heure de r.** (en voiture) an hour's drive; **faire r. vers Paris** to head for Paris; **faire de la r.** to do a lot of driving; **bonne r.!** have a good trip!; Fig **leurs routes se sont croisées** their paths crossed; **r. des vins** wine trail; **r. départementale** secondary road, Br B road; **r. nationale** Br main road, A-road, Am (state) highway

routier, -ière [rutje, -jɛr] **1** adj **carte/sécurité routière** road map/safety; **réseau r.** road network **2** nm (camionneur) (long-distance) Br lorry or Am truck driver; (restaurant) Br transport café, Am truck stop

routine [rutin] nf routine; **contrôle de r.** routine check ▪ **routinier, -ière** adj **travail r.** routine work; **être r.** (personne) to be set in one's ways

rouvrir* [ruvrir] vti, **se rouvrir** vpr to reopen

roux, rousse [ru, rus] **1** adj (cheveux) red, ginger; (personne) red-haired **2** nmf redhead

royal, -e, -aux, -ales [rwajal, -jo] adj (famille, palais) royal; (cadeau, festin) fit for a king; (salaire) princely ▪ **royalement** adv (traiter) royally; Fam **je m'en fiche r.** I don't give a

damn (about it) ▪ **royaliste** adj & nmf royalist

royaume [rwajom] nm kingdom ▪ **Royaume-Uni** nm **le R.** the United Kingdom

royauté [rwajote] nf (monarchie) monarchy

RSVP [ɛrɛsvepe] (abrév **répondez s'il vous plaît**) RSVP

ruban [rybã] nm ribbon; (de chapeau) band; **r. adhésif** sticky or adhesive tape

rubéole [rybeɔl] nf rubella, Fam German measles (sing)

rubis [rybi] nm (pierre) ruby; (de montre) jewel

rubrique [rybrik] nf (article de journal) column; (catégorie, titre) heading; (partie) section

ruche [ryʃ] nf beehive

rude [ryd] adj (pénible) tough; (hiver, voix) harsh; (rêche) rough ▪ **rudement** adv (parler, traiter) harshly; (frapper, tomber) hard; Fam (très) awfully ▪ **rudesse** nf harshness

> Il faut noter que l'adjectif anglais **rude** est un faux ami. Il signifie **grossier**.

rudiments [rydimã] nmpl rudiments ▪ **rudimentaire** adj rudimentary

rudoyer [rydwaje] vt to treat harshly

rue [ry] nf street; **être à la r.** (sans domicile) to be on the streets ▪ **ruelle** nf alley(way)

ruer [rɥe] **1** vi (cheval) to kick (out) **2 se ruer** vpr (foncer) to rush (**sur** at) ▪ **ruée** nf rush; **la r. vers l'or** the gold rush

rugby [rygbi] nm rugby; **r. à quinze** rugby union; **r. à treize** rugby league ▪ **rugbyman** [rygbiman] (pl **-men** [-mɛn]) nm rugby player

rugir [ryʒir] vi to roar ▪ **rugissement** nm roar

rugueux, -euse [rygø, -øz] adj rough ▪ **rugosité** nf roughness; **rugosités** (aspérités) rough spots

ruine [rɥin] nf (décombres, destruction, faillite) ruin; **en r.** (bâtiment) in ruins; **tomber en r.** (bâtiment) to become a ruin; (mur) to crumble ▪ **ruiner 1** vt (personne, santé, pays) to ruin **2 se ruiner** vpr (perdre tout son argent) to ruin oneself; (dépenser beaucoup d'argent) to spend a fortune ▪ **ruineux, -euse** adj (goûts, projet) ruinously expensive; (dépense) ruinous; **ce n'est pas r.** it won't ruin me/you/etc

ruisseau, -x [rɥiso] nm stream; (caniveau) gutter ▪ **ruisseler** vi to stream (**de** with)

rumeur [rymœr] nf (murmure) murmur; (nouvelle) rumour

ruminer [rymine] **1** vt (herbe) to chew; Fig (méditer) to mull over **2** vi (vache) to chew the cud; Fig to brood

rumsteck [rɔmstɛk] nm rump steak

rupture [ryptyr] nf breaking; (de fiançailles, de relations) breaking off; (de pourparlers) breakdown (**de** in); (brouille) break-up; Méd rupture; **être en r. de stock** to be out of stock; **r. de contrat** breach of contract

rural, -e, -aux, -ales [ryral, -o] adj

(population) rural; **vie/école rurale** country life/school ▪**ruraux** *nmpl* country people

ruse [ryz] *nf (subterfuge)* trick; **la r.** *(habileté)* cunning; *(fourberie)* trickery ▪**rusé, -ée 1** *adj* cunning, crafty **2** *nmf* **c'est un r.** he's a cunning *or* crafty one ▪**ruser** *vi* to resort to trickery

Russie [rysi] *nf* **la R.** Russia ▪**russe 1** *adj* Russian **2** *nmf* **R.** Russian **3** *nm (langue)* Russian

rustique [rystik] *adj (meuble)* rustic

rustre [rystr] *nm* lout, churl

rut [ryt] **en rut** *nm (animal) Br* on heat, *Am* in heat

rutabaga [rytabaga] *nm Br* swede, *Am* rutabaga

rutilant, -ante [rytilã, -ãt] *adj* gleaming

RV *abrév* **rendez-vous**

rythme [ritm] *nm* rhythm; *(de travail)* rate; *(allure)* pace; **au r. de trois par jour** at the rate of three a day ▪**rythmé, -ée, rythmique** *adj* rhythmic(al)

S, s [ɛs] *nm inv* S, s

s' [s] *voir* **se, si**

SA (*abrév* **société anonyme**) *nf Com Br* ≃ plc, *Am* ≃ Inc

sa [sa] *voir* **son²**

sabbat [saba] *nm* Sabbath

sabbatique [sabatik] *adj* (*repos, année*) sabbatical; **prendre un congé s.** to take a sabbatical

sable [sabl] *nm* sand; **sables mouvants** quicksands ▪ **sabler** *vt* (*route*) to sand; *Fam* **s. le champagne** to celebrate with champagne ▪ **sableux, -euse** *adj* sandy

sablier [sablije] *nm* hourglass; *Culin* egg timer ▪ **sablière** *nf* (*carrière*) sand quarry

sablonneux, -euse [sablɔnø, -øz] *adj* sandy

sablé [sable] *nm* shortbread *Br* biscuit *or Am* cookie ▪ **sablée** *adj f* **pâte sablée** shortcrust pastry

saborder [sabɔrde] *vt* (*navire*) to scuttle; *Fig* (*entreprise*) to scupper

sabot [sabo] *nm* (*de cheval*) hoof; (*chaussure*) clog; **s. de Denver** wheel clamp

saboter [sabɔte] *vt* (*machine, projet*) to sabotage ▪ **sabotage** *nm* sabotage; **un acte de s.** an act of sabotage ▪ **saboteur, -euse** *nmf* saboteur

sabre [sabr] *nm* sabre

sabrer [sabre] *vt Fam* (*critiquer*) to slate; **se faire s. à un examen** to mess up *or Am* flunk an exam

sac [sak] *nm* bag; (*grand, en toile*) sack; **s. à main** handbag; **s. à dos** rucksack; **s. de couchage** sleeping bag; **s. de voyage** travel bag; *Fig* **prendre qn la main dans le s.** to catch sb red-handed; *Fam* **je les mets dans le même s.** in my opinion they're as bad as each other; *Fam* **l'affaire est dans le s.!** it's in the bag!; **mettre une ville à s.** to sack a town

saccade [sakad] *nf* jerk, jolt; **par saccades** in fits and starts ▪ **saccadé, -ée** *adj* jerky

saccager [sakaʒe] *vt* (*détruire*) to wreck havoc in; (*piller*) to sack

saccharine [sakarin] *nf* saccharin

sacerdoce [sasɛrdɔs] *nm Rel* priesthood; *Fig* vocation

sachant, sache(s), sachent [saʃɑ̃, saʃ] *voir* **savoir**

sachet [saʃɛ] *nm* (small) bag; (*de lavande*) sachet; **s. de thé** teabag

sacoche [sakɔʃ] *nf* bag; (*de vélo, de moto*) saddlebag; (*d'écolier*) satchel

sacquer [sake] *vt Fam* (*renvoyer*) to sack; (*élève*) to give a bad *Br* mark *or Am* grade to; *Fam* **je ne peux pas le s.** I can't stand him

sacre [sakr] *nm* (*de roi*) coronation; (*d'évêque*) consecration ▪ **sacrer** *vt* (*roi*) to crown; (*évêque*) to consecrate

sacré, -ée [sakre] *adj* (*saint*) sacred; *Fam* **un s. menteur** a damned *or Br* bloody liar; *Fam* **elle a eu une sacrée vie** she's had quite a life ▪ **sacrément** *adv Fam* (*très*) damn(ed), *Br* bloody; (*beaucoup*) a hell of a lot

sacrement [sakrəmɑ̃] *nm Rel* sacrament

sacrifice [sakrifis] *nm* sacrifice ▪ **sacrifier 1** *vt* to sacrifice (**à** to) **2** *vi* **s. à la mode** to be a slave to fashion **3 se sacrifier** *upr* to sacrifice oneself (**pour** for)

sacrilège [sakrilɛʒ] **1** *adj* sacrilegious **2** *nm* sacrilege

sacristie [sakristi] *nf* vestry

sacro-saint, -sainte [sakrɔsɛ̃, -sɛ̃t] (*mpl* **sacro-saints**, *fpl* **sacro-saintes**) *adj Ironique* sacrosanct

sadisme [sadism] *nm* sadism ▪ **sadique 1** *adj* sadistic **2** *nmf* sadist

safari [safari] *nm* safari; **faire un s.** to go on safari

safran [safrɑ̃] *nm* saffron

sagace [sagas] *adj* shrewd ▪ **sagacité** *nf* shrewdness

sage [saʒ] **1** *adj* (*avisé*) wise; (*calme*) good; (*robe*) sober **2** *nm* wise man ▪ **sage-femme** (*pl* **sages-femmes**) *nf* midwife ▪ **sagement** *adv* (*raisonnablement*) wisely; (*avec calme*) quietly ▪ **sagesse** *nf* (*philosophie*) wisdom; (*calme*) good behaviour

Sagittaire [saʒiter] *nm* **le S.** (*signe*) Sagittarius; **être S.** to be (a) Sagittarius

Sahara [saara] *nm* **le S.** the Sahara (desert)

saigner [seɲe] **1** *vi* to bleed; **s. du nez** to have a nosebleed **2 se saigner** *upr Fig* **se s. aux quatre veines** to bleed oneself dry ▪ **saignant, -ante** [seɲɑ̃, -ɑ̃t] *adj* (*viande*) rare ▪ **saignée** *nf Méd* blood-letting ▪ **saignement** [seɲəmɑ̃] *nm* bleeding; **s. de nez** nosebleed

saillant, -ante [sajɑ̃, -ɑ̃t] *adj* projecting; *Fig* (*trait*) salient ▪ **saillie** *nf* (*partie avant*) projection

sain, saine [sɛ̃, sɛn] *adj* healthy; *(jugement)* sound; *(nourriture)* wholesome, healthy; **s. et sauf** safe and sound ■**sainement** *adv (vivre)* healthily; *(raisonner)* sanely

saint, sainte [sɛ̃, sɛ̃t] **1** *adj (lieu)* holy; *(personne)* saintly; **s. Jean** Saint John; **la Sainte Vierge** the Blessed Virgin **2** *nmf* saint ■**saint-bernard** *nm inv (chien)* St Bernard ■**Saint-Esprit** *nm* le S. the Holy Spirit ■**saint-frusquin** *nm Fam* **tout le s.** the whole caboodle ■**saint-glinglin à la saint-glinglin** *adv Fam* never in a month of Sundays ■**saint-honoré** *nm inv Culin* Saint-Honoré *(choux pastry ring filled with confectioner's custard)* ■**Saint-Sylvestre** *nf* la S. New Year's Eve

sainteté [sɛ̃tǝte] *nf (de lieu)* holiness; *(de personne)* saintliness; **Sa S.** *(le pape)* His Holiness

sais [sɛ] *voir* **savoir**

saisie [sezi] *nf (de biens)* seizure; *Ordinat* **s. de données** data capture, keyboarding

saisir [sezir] **1** *vt* to take hold of; *(brusquement)* to grab; *(occasion)* to seize, to grasp; *(comprendre)* to grasp; *Jur* to seize; *(viande)* to seal; *Fig (frapper)* to strike **2 se saisir** *vpr* **se s. de qn/qch** to take hold of sb/sth; *(brusquement)* to grab sb/sth ■**saisissant, -ante** *adj (film)* gripping; *(contraste, ressemblance)* striking ■**saisissement** *nm (émotion)* shock

saison [sezɔ̃] *nf* season; **en/hors s.** in/out of season; **en haute/basse s.** in the high/low season; **la s. des pluies** the rainy season ■**saisonnier, -ière** *adj* seasonal

sait [sɛ] *voir* **savoir**

salade [salad] *nf (laitue)* lettuce; *Fam (désordre)* mess; **s. composée** mixed salad; **s. de fruits** fruit salad; **s. niçoise** salade niçoise *(lettuce, tomatoes, tuna, olives, anchovies, eggs)*; **s. verte** green salad; ■**salades** *nfpl Fam (mensonges)* whoppers ■**saladier** *nm* salad bowl

salaire [saler] *nm (mensuel)* salary

salaison [salezɔ̃] *nf Culin* salting; **salaisons** *(denrées)* salted meats

salamandre [salamɑ̃dr] *nf* salamander

salami [salami] *nm* salami

salarial, -e, -iaux, -iales [salarjal, -jo] *adj* **accord s.** wage agreement ■**salarié, -ée 1** *adj (payé mensuellement)* salaried **2** *nmf (payé mensuellement)* salaried employee; **salariés** *(de société)* employees

salaud [salo] *nm Vulg* bastard

sale [sal] *adj* dirty; *(dégoûtant)* filthy; *(mauvais)* nasty; *Fam* **s. coup** dirty trick; *Fam* **s. temps** filthy weather; *Fam* **avoir une s. gueule** to look rotten ■**salement** *adv (se conduire, manger)* disgustingly ■**saleté** *nf (manque de soin)* dirtiness; *(crasse)* dirt; *Fam (camelote)* junk; **saletés** *(détritus)* Br rubbish, Am garbage; *(obscénités)* filth; **faire des saletés** to make a mess

saler [sale] *vt* to salt ■**salé, -ée** *adj (goût, plat)* salty; *(aliment)* salted; *Fig (grivois)* spicy; *Fam (excessif)* steep ■**salière** *nf Br* saltcellar, *Am* saltshaker

salir [salir] **1** *vt* to (make) dirty; *Fig (réputation, mémoire)* to sully **2 se salir** *vpr* to get dirty ■**salissant, -ante** *adj (travail)* dirty, messy; *(étoffe)* that shows the dirt ■**salissure** *nf* dirty mark

salive [saliv] *nf* saliva ■**saliver** *vi* to salivate

salle [sal] *nf* room; *(très grande, publique)* hall; *(de cinéma) Br* cinema, *Am* movie theater; *(d'hôpital)* ward; *(public de théâtre)* audience, house; **s. à manger** dining room; **s. de bain(s)** bathroom; **s. de classe** classroom; **s. de concert** concert hall; **s. de jeux** *(pour enfants)* playroom; *(de casino)* gaming room; **s. de spectacle** auditorium; **s. d'embarquement** *(d'aéroport)* departure lounge; *Com* **s. d'exposition** showroom; **s. des fêtes** community hall; **s. d'opération** *(d'hôpital)* operating *Br* theatre *or Am* room; **s. des professeurs** staff room; **s. des ventes** auction room

salon [salɔ̃] *nm* living room, *Br* lounge; *(exposition)* show; **s. de coiffure/de beauté** hairdressing/beauty salon; **s. de thé** tea room

salope [salɔp] *nf Vulg (femme)* bitch ■**saloper** *vt Fam (salir)* to mess up ■**saloperie** [-pri] *nf Fam (action)* dirty trick; *(camelote)* junk; **dire des saloperies sur qn** to bitch about sb

salopette [salɔpɛt] *nf Br* dungarees, *Am* overalls

salsifis [salsifi] *nf* salsify

saltimbanque [saltɛ̃bɑ̃k] *nmf* circus performer

salubre [salybr] *adj* healthy ■**salubrité** *nf* healthiness; **s. publique** public health

saluer [salɥe] *vt* to greet; *(en partant)* to take one's leave of; *(de la main)* to wave to; *(de la tête)* to nod to; *Mil* to salute

salut [saly] **1** *nm* greeting; *(de la main)* wave; *(de la tête)* nod; *Mil* salute; *(sauvegarde)* rescue; *Rel* salvation **2** *exclam Fam (bonjour)* hi!; *(au revoir)* bye! ■**salutation** *nf* greeting

salutaire [salyter] *adj* salutary

salve [salv] *nf* salvo

samedi [samdi] *nm* Saturday

SAMU [samy] *(abrév* **service d'aide médicale d'urgence)** *nm* emergency medical service

sanatorium [sanatɔrjɔm] *nm Br* sanatorium, *Am* sanitarium

sanctifier [sɑ̃ktifje] *vt* to sanctify

sanction [sɑ̃ksjɔ̃] *nf (approbation, peine)* sanction ■**sanctionner** *vt (approuver)* to sanction; *(punir)* to punish

sanctuaire [sɑ̃ktɥer] *nm* sanctuary

sandale [sɑ̃dal] *nf* sandal

sandwich [sɑ̃dwitʃ] *nm* sandwich; **s. au fromage** cheese sandwich

sang [sɑ̃] *nm* blood; **être en s.** to be covered in blood; *Fig* **avoir du s. bleu** to have blue blood; *Fig* **avoir le s. chaud** to be hot-tempered; *Fam* **se faire du mauvais s.** to worry; *Fig* **mon s. n'a fait qu'un tour** my heart missed a beat ▪ **sang-froid** *nm inv* self-control; **garder son s.** to keep calm; **avec s.** calmly; **tuer qn de s.** to kill sb in cold blood ▪ **sanglant, -ante** *adj* bloody

sangle [sɑ̃gl] *nf* strap

sanglier [sɑ̃glije] *nm* wild boar

sanglot [sɑ̃glo] *nm* sob ▪ **sangloter** *vi* to sob

sangsue [sɑ̃sy] *nf* leech

sanguin, -ine [sɑ̃gɛ̃, -in] **1** *adj* (*tempérament*) full-blooded; **vaisseau s.** blood vessel **2** *nf* **sanguine** (*fruit*) blood orange

sanguinaire [sɑ̃giner] *adj* blood-thirsty

sanitaire [saniter] *adj* (*conditions*) sanitary; (*personnel*) medical; **installation s.** bathroom fittings; **règlement s.** health regulations

sans [sɑ̃] ([sɑ̃z] *before vowel and mute* h) *prép* without; **s. faire qch** without doing sth; **s. qu'il le sache** without him *or* his knowing; **s. cela, s. quoi** otherwise; **s. plus** (but) no more than that; **s. faute/exception** without fail/exception; **s. importance/travail** unimportant/unemployed; **s. argent/manches** penniless/sleeveless; **ça va s. dire** that goes without saying ▪ **sans-abri** *nmf inv* homeless person; **les s.** the homeless ▪ **sans-cœur** *nmf inv Fam* heartless person ▪ **sans-faute** *nm inv Équitation* clear round; *Fig* **faire un s.** not to put a foot wrong ▪ **sans-gêne 1** *adj inv* inconsiderate **2** *nm inv* inconsiderate person ▪ **sans-papiers** *nmf inv* illegal immigrant

santé [sɑ̃te] *nf* health; **en bonne/mauvaise s.** in good/bad health; **(à votre) s.!** (*en trinquant*) cheers!; **boire à la s. de qn** to drink to sb's (good) health; **la s. publique** public health

santiag [sɑ̃tjag] *nf Fam* cowboy boot

saoul [su] *adj & nm* = **soûl**

saper [sape] *vt* to undermine; **s. le moral à qn** to sap sb's morale

sapeur-pompier [sapœrpɔ̃pje] (*pl* **sapeurs-pompiers**) *nm* fireman

saphir [safir] *nm* sapphire

sapin [sapɛ̃] *nm* (*arbre, bois*) fir; **s. de Noël** Christmas tree

sarbacane [sarbakan] *nf* (*jouet*) peashooter

sarcasme [sarkasm] *nm* sarcasm; (*remarque*) sarcastic remark ▪ **sarcastique** *adj* sarcastic

sarcler [sarkle] *vt* (*jardin*) to weed

Sardaigne [sardɛɲ] *nf* **la S.** Sardinia ▪ **sarde 1** *adj* Sardinian **2** *nmf* **S.** Sardinian

sardine [sardin] *nf* sardine; **sardines à l'huile** sardines in oil; *Fam* **serrés comme des sardines** packed together like sardines

sardonique [sardɔnik] *adj* sardonic

SARL [ɛsaɛrɛl] (*abrév* **société à responsabilité limitée**) *nf* limited liability company, *Br* ≃ Ltd, *Am* ≃ Inc

sarment [sarmɑ̃] *nm* vine shoot

sarrasin [sarazɛ̃] *nm* (*plante*) buckwheat

sas [sas] *nm* (*de bateau, d'avion*) airlock; **s. de sécurité** security screen

Satan [satɑ̃] *nm* Satan ▪ **satané, -ée** *adj Fam* (*maudit*) damned ▪ **satanique** *adj* satanic

satellite [satelit] *nm* satellite; **télévision par s.** satellite television

satiété [sasjete] *nf* **à s.** (*boire, manger*) one's fill

satin [satɛ̃] *nm* satin ▪ **satiné, -ée** *adj* satiny

satire [satir] *nf* satire (**contre** on) ▪ **satirique** *adj* satirical ▪ **satiriser** *vt* to satirize

satisfaction [satisfaksjɔ̃] *nf* satisfaction; **donner s. à qn** to give sb (complete) satisfaction ▪ **satisfaire*** *vt* to satisfy **2** *vi* **s. à qch** (*conditions*) to satisfy sth; (*obligation*) to *Br* fulfil *or Am* fulfill sth ▪ **satisfaisant, -ante** *adj* (*acceptable*) satisfactory ▪ **satisfait, -faite** *adj* satisfied (**de** with)

saturer [satyre] *vt* to saturate (**de** with) ▪ **saturation** *nf* saturation; **arriver à s.** to reach saturation point

satyre [satir] *nm Fam* sex maniac

sauce [sos] *nf* sauce; **s. tomate** tomato sauce ▪ **saucière** *nf* sauce boat, *Br* gravy boat

saucisse [sosis] *nf* sausage; **s. de Francfort** frankfurter; **s. de Strasbourg** = type of beef sausage ▪ **saucisson** *nm* (cold) sausage

sauf¹ [sof] *prép* except; **s. avis contraire** unless you hear otherwise; **s. erreur** if I'm not mistaken

sauf², sauve [sof, sov] *adj* **avoir la vie sauve** to be unharmed

sauge [soʒ] *nf* sage

saugrenu, -ue [sogrəny] *adj* preposterous

saule [sol] *nm* willow; **s. pleureur** weeping willow

saumâtre [somɑtr] *adj* (*eau*) brackish

saumon [somɔ̃] **1** *nm* salmon **2** *adj inv* (*couleur*) salmon (pink)

saumure [somyr] *nf* brine

sauna [sona] *nm* sauna

saupoudrer [sopudre] *vt* to sprinkle (**de** with)

saur [sɔr] *adj m* **hareng s.** smoked herring

saura, saurait [sora, sore] *voir* **savoir**

saut [so] *nm* jump, leap; **faire un s.** to jump, to leap; *Fam* **faire un s. chez qn** to drop in on sb; **au s. du lit** first thing in the morning; **s. à la corde** *Br* skipping, *Am* jumping rope; **s. à l'élastique** bungee jumping; **s. en hauteur** high jump; **s. en longueur** *Br* long jump, *Am* broad jump; **s. en parachute** parachute jump; (*activité*) parachute jumping

sauté, -ée [sote] *adj & nm Culin* sauté

sauter [sote] **1** *vt* (*franchir*) to jump (over); (*mot, repas, classe, ligne*) to skip **2** *vi* (*personne, animal*) to jump, to leap; (*bombe*) to go off, to explode; *(fusible)* to blow; *(bouton)* to come off; **faire s. qch** *(pont, mine)* to blow sth up; *(serrure)* to force sth; *Fig (gouvernement)* to bring sth down; *Culin* to sauté sth; **s. à la corde** *Br* to skip, *Am* to jump rope; **s. en parachute** to do a parachute jump; *Fig* **s. sur l'occasion** to jump at the opportunity; **ça saute aux yeux** it's obvious; *Fam* **elle m'a sauté dessus** she pounced on me ▪ **saute-mouton** *nm inv* leapfrog

sauterelle [sotrɛl] *nf* grasshopper

sautes [sot] *nfpl (d'humeur, de température)* sudden changes *(de* in)

sautiller [sotije] *vi* to hop about

sautoir [sotwar] *nm (de stade)* jumping area

sauvage [sovaʒ] *adj (animal, plante)* wild; *(tribu, homme)* primitive; *(cruel)* savage; *(farouche)* unsociable; *(illégal)* unauthorized ▪ **sauvagerie** *nf (insociabilité)* unsociability; *(cruauté)* savagery

sauve [sov] *adj voir* **sauf²**

sauvegarde [sovgard] *nf* safeguard (**contre** against); *Ordinat* backup ▪ **sauvegarder** *vt* to safeguard; *Ordinat* to save

sauver [sove] **1** *vt (personne)* to save, to rescue (**de** from); *(matériel)* to salvage; **la vie à qn** to save sb's life **2 se sauver** *upr (s'enfuir)* to run away; *(s'échapper)* to escape; *Fam (partir)* to go ▪ **sauvetage** *nm (de personne)* rescue ▪ **sauveteur** *nm* rescuer ▪ **sauveur** *nm* saviour

sauvette [sovɛt] **à la sauvette** *adv (pour ne pas être vu)* on the sly; **vendre qch à la s.** to peddle sth illegally on the streets

savane [savan] *nf* savanna

savant, -ante [savɑ̃, -ɑ̃t] **1** *adj (érudit)* learned; *(habile)* clever **2** *nm (scientifique)* scientist ▪ **savamment** [-amɑ̃] *adv (avec érudition)* learnedly; *(avec habileté)* cleverly

savate [savat] *nf Fam (pantoufle)* slipper

saveur [savœr] *nf (goût)* flavour; *Fig (piment)* savour

Savoie [savwa] *nf* **la S.** Savoy

savoir* [savwar] **1** *vt* to know; *(nouvelle)* to have heard; **s. lire/nager** to know how to read/ swim; **faire s. à qn que…** to inform sb that…; **à s.** *(c'est-à-dire)* that is, namely; **pas que je sache** not that I know of, not as far as I know; **je n'en sais rien** I have no idea, I don't know; **en s. long sur qn/qch** to know a lot about sb/ sth **2** *nm (culture)* learning, knowledge ▪ **savoir-faire** *nm inv* know-how ▪ **savoir-vivre** *nm inv* good manners

savon [savɔ̃] *nm* soap; *Fam* **passer un s. à qn** to give sb a telling-off ▪ **savonner** *vt* to wash with soap ▪ **savonnette** *nf* bar of soap ▪ **savonneux, -euse** *adj* soapy

savourer [savure] *vt* to savour ▪ **savoureux, -euse** *adj* tasty; *Fig (histoire)* juicy

savoyard, -arde [savwajar, -ard] **1** *adj* Savoyard **2** *nmf* **S., Savoyarde** Savoyard

saxophone [saksɔfɔn] *nm* saxophone

sbire [sbir] *nm Péj* henchman

scabreux, -euse [skabrø, -øz] *adj* obscene

scalp [skalp] *nm (chevelure)* scalp ▪ **scalper** *vt* to scalp

scalpel [skalpɛl] *nm* scalpel

scandale [skɑ̃dal] *nm* scandal; **faire s.** *(sujet: livre, événement)* to cause a scandal; **faire un s.** *(sujet: personne)* to make a scene ▪ **scandaleux, -euse** *adj* scandalous ▪ **scandaliser 1** *vt* to scandalize, to shock **2 se scandaliser** *upr* to be shocked or scandalized (**de** by)

scander [skɑ̃de] *vt (vers)* to scan; *(slogan)* to chant

Scandinavie [skɑ̃dinavi] *nf* **la S.** Scandinavia ▪ **scandinave 1** *adj* Scandinavian **2** *nmf* **S.** Scandinavian

scanner 1 [skanɛr] *nm Ordinat & Méd* scanner; *Ordinat* **passer qch au s.** to scan sth; *Méd* **faire un s.** *(d'un médecin)* to do a scan; *(d'un patient)* to have a scan **2** [skane] *vt Ordinat* to scan

scaphandre [skafɑ̃dr] *nm (de plongeur)* diving suit; *(de cosmonaute)* spacesuit; **s. autonome** aqualung ▪ **scaphandrier** *nm* diver

scarabée [skarabe] *nm* beetle

scarlatine [skarlatin] *nf* scarlet fever

scarole [skarɔl] *nf* endive

sceau, -x [so] *nm* seal ▪ **sceller** *vt (document)* to seal ▪ **scellés** *nmpl (cachets de cire)* seals; **mettre les s.** to seal

scélérat, -ate [selera, -at] *nmf Littéraire* scoundrel

scénario [senarjo] *nm* script, screenplay ▪ **scénariste** *nmf* scriptwriter

scène [sɛn] *nf* **(a)** *(de théâtre)* scene; *(plateau)* stage; *(action)* action; **mettre qch en s.** *(pièce)* to stage sth; *(film)* to direct sth; **entrer en s.** *(acteur)* to come on; *Fig* **sur la s. internationale** on the international scene **(b)** *(dispute)* scene; **faire une s.** to make a scene; **elle m'a fait une s.** she made a scene; **s. de ménage** domestic (quarrel)

scepticisme [sɛptisism] *nm Br* scepticism, *Am* skepticism ▪ **sceptique 1** *adj Br* sceptical, *Am* skeptical **2** *nmf Br* sceptic, *Am* skeptic

schéma [ʃema] *nm* diagram; *Fig* outline ▪ **schématique** *adj* schematic; *Péj* oversimplified ▪ **schématiser** *vt* to schematize; *Péj* to oversimplify

schizophrène [skizɔfrɛn] *adj & nmf* schizophrenic

sciatique [sjatik] *nf* sciatica

scie [si] *nf (outil)* saw; **s. électrique** power saw; **s. musicale** musical saw ▪ **scier** *vt* to saw ▪ **scierie** *nf* sawmill

sciemment [sjamɑ̃] *adv* knowingly

science [sjɑ̃s] *nf* science; *(savoir)* knowledge; **étudier les sciences** to study science;

sciences humaines social sciences; **sciences naturelles** biology ▪**science-fiction** *nf* science fiction ▪**scientifique 1** *adj* scientific **2** *nmf* scientist

scinder [sɛ̃de] *vt, se scinder vpr* to split up (**en** into)

scintiller [sɛ̃tije] *vi* to sparkle; *(étoile)* to twinkle ▪**scintillement** *nm* sparkling; *(d'étoile)* twinkling

scission [sisjɔ̃] *nf (de parti)* split (**de** in); **s. de l'atome** splitting of the atom

sciure [sjyr] *nf* sawdust

sclérose [skleroz] *nf Méd* sclerosis; *Fig* ossification; **s. en plaques** multiple sclerosis ▪**sclérosé, -ée** *adj Fig (société)* ossified

scolaire [skɔlɛr] *adj* **année s.** school year; **enfant d'âge s.** child of school age; **progrès scolaires** academic progress ▪**scolariser** *vt (enfant)* to send to school ▪**scolarité** *nf* schooling; **certificat de s.** certificate of attendance *(at school or university)*; **pendant ma s.** when I was at school

scoliose [skɔljoz] *nf Méd* curvature of the spine

scooter [skuter] *nm* (motor) scooter; **s. des mers** jet ski

scorbut [skɔrbyt] *nm Méd* scurvy

score [skɔr] *nm* score

scories [skɔri] *nfpl (résidu)* slag

scorpion [skɔrpjɔ̃] *nm* scorpion; **le S.** *(signe)* Scorpio; **être S.** to be (a) Scorpio

Scotch [skɔtʃ] *(ruban adhésif) Br* Sellotape®, *Am* Scotch tape® ▪**scotcher** *vt Br* to sellotape, *Am* to tape; *Fam* **être scotché devant la télé** to be glued to the TV; *Fam (stupéfaire)* **ça m'a vraiment scotché!** I was staggered *or Br* gobsmacked!

scotch [skɔtʃ] *nm (boisson)* Scotch

scout, -e [skut] *adj & nm* scout ▪**scoutisme** *nm (activité)* scouting

script [skript] *nm (écriture)* printing; *Cin* script

scripte [skript] *nmf Cin* continuity man, *f* girl

scrupule [skrypyl] *nm* scruple; **sans scrupules** unscrupulous; *(agir)* unscrupulously ▪**scrupuleusement** *adv* scrupulously ▪**scrupuleux, -euse** *adj* scrupulous

scruter [skryte] *vt* to scrutinize

scrutin [skrytɛ̃] *nm (vote)* ballot; *(élection)* poll; *(système)* voting system; **premier tour de s.** first ballot *or* round; **s. majoritaire** first-past-the-post voting system

sculpter [skylte] *vt (statue, pierre)* to sculpt; *(bois)* to carve; **s. qch dans qch** to sculpt/ carve sth out of sth ▪**sculpteur** *nm* sculptor ▪**sculptural, -e, -aux, -ales** *adj (beauté, femme)* statuesque ▪**sculpture** *nf (art, œuvre)* sculpture; **s. sur bois** woodcarving

SDF [ɛsdeɛf] *(abrév* **sans domicile fixe)** *nmf inv* person of no fixed abode

se [sə]

---

pron personnel (**a**) *(complément direct)* himself; *(féminin)* herself; *(non humain)* itself; *(indéfini)* oneself, *pl* themselves; **il se lave** he washes himself; **ils** *ou* **elles se lavent** they wash themselves (**b**) *(indirect)* to himself/herself/ itself/oneself; **se dire qch** to say sth to oneself; **il se lave les mains** he washes his hands; **elle se lave les mains** she washes her hands (**c**) *(réciproque)* each other; *(indirect)* to each other; **ils s'aiment** they love each other; **ils** *ou* **elles se parlent** they speak to each other (**d**) *(passif)* **ça se fait** that is done; **ça se vend bien** it sells well

séance [seɑ̃s] *nf (de cinéma)* showing, performance; *(d'assemblée, de travail)* session; **s. de pose** sitting; **s. tenante** at once

seau, -x [so] *nm* bucket; **s. à glace** ice bucket

sec, sèche [sɛk, sɛʃ] **1** *adj* dry; *(fruits, légumes)* dried; *(ton)* curt; *(maigre)* lean; *Fig (cœur)* hard; **frapper un coup s.** to knock sharply; **bruit s.** snap **2** *adv (boire) Br* neat, *Am* straight; *(frapper, pleuvoir)* hard **3** *nm* **à s.** dry; *Fam (sans argent)* broke; **au s.** in a dry place

sécateur [sekatœr] *nm* pruning shears, *Br* secateurs

sécession [sesesjɔ̃] *nf* secession; **faire s.** to secede

sèche [sɛʃ] *voir* **sec**

sécher [seʃe] **1** *vt* to dry; *Fam (cours)* to skip, to cut **2** *vi* to dry; *Fam (ne pas savoir)* to be stumped; *Fam (être absent) Br* to bunk off, *Am* to play hookey **3** *se sécher vpr* to dry oneself ▪**séchage** *nm* drying ▪**sèche-cheveux** *nm inv* hair dryer ▪**sèche-linge** *nm inv Br* tumble dryer, *Am* (clothes) dryer

sécheresse [seʃrɛs] *nf (d'air, de sol, de peau)* dryness; *(de ton)* curtness; *(manque de pluie)* drought

séchoir [seʃwar] *nm (appareil)* dryer; **s. à linge** clothes horse

second, -onde¹ [səgɔ̃, -ɔ̃d] **1** *adj & nmf* second **2** *nm (adjoint)* second in command; *(étage) Br* second floor, *Am* third floor **3** *nf* **seconde** *Rail* second class; *Scol Br* ≃ fifth form, *Am* ≃ tenth grade; *Aut (vitesse)* second (gear) ▪**secondaire** *adj* secondary; **école s.** *Br* secondary school, *Am* high school

seconde² [səgɔ̃d] *nf (instant)* second

seconder [səgɔ̃de] *vt* to assist

secouer [səkwe] **1** *vt (statue)* to shake; *(poussière)* to shake off; **s. qn** *(maladie, nouvelle)* to shake sb up; **s. qch de qch** *(enlever)* to shake sth out of sth; **s. la tête** *(réponse affirmative)* to nod *(yes)*; *(réponse négative)* to shake one's head **2** **se secouer** *vpr Fam (faire un effort)* to snap out of it

secourir [səkurir] *vt* to assist, to help ▪**secourable** *adj* helpful ▪**secourisme** *nm* first aid ▪ **secouriste** *nmf* first-aid worker

secours [səkur] *nm* help; *(financier, matériel)* aid; *Mil* **les s.** *(renforts)* relief; **premiers s.** first aid; **au s.!** help!; **porter s. à qn** to give sb help; **roue de s.** spare wheel

secousse [səkus] *nf* jolt, jerk; *(de tremblement de terre)* tremor

secret, -ète [səkrɛ, -ɛt] **1** *adj* secret; *(cachottier)* secretive **2** *nm* secret; *(discrétion)* secrecy; **s. d'État** state secret; **en s.** in secret, secretly; **dans le s.** *(au courant)* in on the secret; **au s.** *(en prison)* in solitary confinement

secrétaire [səkreter] **1** *nmf* secretary; **s. d'État** Secretary of State; **s. de mairie** town clerk; **s. médicale** medical secretary; *Journ* **s. de rédaction** *Br* sub-editor, *Am* copyreader **2** *nm* *(meuble)* writing desk ▪ **secrétariat** *nm* *(bureau)* secretary's office; *(d'organisation internationale)* secretariat; *(métier)* secretarial work; **école/travail de s.** secretarial school/work

sécréter [sekrete] *vt Biol* to secrete ▪ **sécrétion** *nf* secretion

secte [sɛkt] *nf* sect ▪ **sectaire** *adj & nmf Péj* sectarian

secteur [sɛktœr] *nm (zone)* area; *Écon* sector; *Él* mains; **branché sur s.** plugged into the mains; *Écon* **s. primaire/secondaire/tertiaire** primary/secondary/tertiary sector

section [sɛksjɔ̃] *nf* section; *(de ligne d'autobus)* stage; *Mil* platoon ▪ **sectionner** *vt (diviser)* to divide (into sections); *(couper)* to sever

séculaire [sekylɛr] *adj (tradition)* age-old

séculier, -ière [sekylje, -jɛr] *adj* secular

secundo [səgɔ̃do] *adv* secondly

sécurité [sekyrite] *nf (absence de danger)* safety; *(tranquillité)* security; **s. routière** road safety; **S. sociale** *Br* Social Security, *Am* Welfare; **s. de l'emploi** job security; **en s.** *(hors de danger)* safe; *(tranquille)* secure ▪ **sécuriser** *vt* to re-assure

sédatif [sedatif] *nm* sedative

sédentaire [sedɑ̃ter] *adj* sedentary

sédiment [sedimɑ̃] *nm* sediment

séditieux, -ieuse [sedisjø, -jøz] *adj* seditious ▪ **sédition** *nf* sedition

séduire* [sedɥir] *vt* to charm; *(plaire à)* to appeal to; *(abuser de)* to seduce ▪ **séduisant, -ante** *adj* attractive ▪ **séducteur, -trice 1** *adj* seductive **2** *nmf* seducer, *f* seductress ▪ **séduction** *nf* attraction; **pouvoir de s.** power of attraction

> Il faut noter que le verbe anglais **to seduce** est un faux ami. Il ne signifie jamais **charmer**.

segment [sɛgmɑ̃] *nm* segment ▪ **segmenter** *vt* to segment

ségrégation [segregasjɔ̃] *nf* segregation

seiche [sɛʃ] *nf* cuttlefish

seigle [sɛgl] *nm* rye; **pain de s.** rye bread

seigneur [sɛɲœr] *nm Hist (noble, maître)* lord; *Rel* **le S.** the Lord

sein [sɛ̃] *nm* breast; *Littéraire* bosom; **bout de s.** nipple; **donner le s. à** *(enfant)* to breastfeed; **au s. de** within

Seine [sɛn] *nf* **la S.** the Seine

séisme [seism] *nm* earthquake

seize [sɛz] *adj & nm inv* sixteen ▪ **seizième** *adj & nmf* sixteenth; *Sport* **les seizièmes de finale** the first round *(of a four-round knockout competition)*

séjour [seʒur] *nm* stay; **s. linguistique** language-learning trip; **(salle de) s.** living room ▪ **séjourner** *vi* to stay

sel [sɛl] *nm* salt; *Fig (piquant)* spice; **sels (à respirer)** (smelling) salts; **s. de mer** sea salt; **sels de bain** bath salts

sélect, -e [selɛkt] *adj Fam* select

sélectif, -ive [selɛktif, -iv] *adj* selective ▪ **sélection** *nf* selection ▪ **sélectionner** *vt* to select ▪ **sélectionneur** *nm* selector

self(-service) [sɛlf(sɛrvis)] *nm* self-service restaurant

selle [sɛl] *nf (de cheval, de vélo)* saddle ▪ **seller** [sele] *vt* to saddle

selles [sɛl] *nfpl Méd* **les s.** stools, *Br* motions

sellette [selɛt] *nf Fam* **sur la s.** in the hot seat

selon [səlɔ̃] *prép* according to; **s. que...** depending on whether...; *Fam* **c'est s.** it (all) depends

semailles [səmɑj] *nfpl (travail)* sowing; *(période)* seedtime

semaine [səmɛn] *nf* week; **en s.** in the week; **à la s.** by the week, weekly; *Fam* **vivre la petite s.** to live from day to day

sémantique [semɑ̃tik] **1** *adj* semantic **2** *nf* semantics

sémaphore [semafɔr] *nm (pour trains)* semaphore signal; *Naut* signal station

semblable [sɑ̃blabl] **1** *adj* similar (**à** to); **de semblables propos** such remarks **2** *nm* fellow creature; **toi et tes semblables** you and your kind

semblant [sɑ̃blɑ̃] *nm* **faire s.** to pretend (**de faire** to do); **un s. de** a semblance of

sembler [sɑ̃ble] **1** *vi* to seem (**à** to); **il (me) semble vieux** he seems *or* looks old (to me); **s. faire qch** to seem to do sth **2** *v impersonnel* **il semble que...** it seems that...; **il me semble que...** it seems to me that...; **quand bon lui semble** when he/she sees fit

semelle [səmɛl] *nf (de chaussure)* sole; *(intérieure)* insole; *Fig* **ne pas quitter qn d'une s.** to be always at sb's heels

semer [səme] *vt (graines)* to sow; *Fig (répandre)* to spread; *(poursuivant)* to shake off; *Fig* **semé de** strewn with ▪ **semence** *nf* seed

semestre [səmɛstr] *nm* half-year; *Univ* semester **▪ semestriel, -ielle** *adj* half-yearly

séminaire [seminɛr] *nm Univ* seminar; *Rel* seminary

semi-remorque [səmirəmɔrk] (*pl* **semi-remorques**) *nm* (*camion*) *Br* articulated lorry, *Am* semi(-trailer), trailer truck

semis [səmi] *nm* sowing; (*terrain*) seedbed; (*plant*) seedling

sémite [semit] **1** *adj* Semitic **2** *nmf* **S.** Semite **▪ sémitique** *adj* (*langue*) Semitic

semonce [səmɔ̃s] *nf* reprimand; **coup de s.** warning shot

semoule [səmul] *nf* semolina

sempiternel, -elle [sɑ̃pitɛrnɛl] *adj* endless, ceaseless

sénat [sena] *nm* senate **▪ sénateur** *nm* senator

sénile [senil] *adj* senile **▪ sénilité** *nf* senility

senior [senjɔr] *nm & adj inv Sport* senior

sens [sɑ̃s] *nm* (**a**) (*faculté, raison, instinct*) sense; **avoir le s. de l'humour** to have a sense of humour; **avoir du bon s.** to be sensible; **cela tombe sous le s.** that's obvious; **à mon s.** to my mind; **s. commun, bon sens** common sense (**b**) (*signification*) meaning, sense; **ça n'a pas de s.** that doesn't make sense; **dans un certain s.** in a way (**c**) (*direction*) direction; *Aut* **s. giratoire** *Br* roundabout, *Am* traffic circle; **s. interdit** *ou* **unique** (*rue*) one-way street; **'s. interdit'** 'no entry'; **à s. unique** (*rue*) one-way; **s. dessus dessous** [sɑ̃d(ə)syd(ə)su] upside down; **dans le s. des aiguilles d'une montre** clockwise; **dans le s. inverse des aiguilles d'une montre** *Br* anticlockwise, *Am* counterclockwise

sensation [sɑ̃sasjɔ̃] *nf* feeling, sensation; **faire s.** to create a sensation; *Péj* **à s.** (*film, roman*) sensational **▪ sensationnel, -elle** *adj* sensational; *Fam* (*excellent*) fantastic

sensé, -ée [sɑ̃se] *adj* sensible

sensible [sɑ̃sibl] *adj* sensitive (**à** to); (*douloureux*) tender, sore; (*perceptible*) perceptible; (*progrès, différence*) noticeable **▪ sensiblement** [-əmɑ̃] *adv* (*notablement*) noticeably; (*à peu près*) more or less **▪ sensibiliser** *vt* **s. qn à qch** (*problème*) to make sb aware of sth **▪ sensibilité** *nf* sensitivity

---

Il faut noter que l'adjectif anglais **sensible** est un faux ami. Il signifie **sensé**.

---

sensoriel, -ielle [sɑ̃sɔrjɛl] *adj* sensory

sensuel, -elle [sɑ̃sɥɛl] *adj* sensual **▪ sensualité** *nf* sensuality

sentence [sɑ̃tɑ̃s] *nf Jur* (*jugement*) sentence; (*maxime*) maxim

senteur [sɑ̃tœr] *nf* (*odeur*) scent

sentier [sɑ̃tje] *nm* path

sentiment [sɑ̃timɑ̃] *nm* feeling; **avoir le s.**

que... to have a feeling that...; **faire du s.** to be sentimental; **meilleurs sentiments** (*sur une carte de visite*) best wishes **▪ sentimental, -e, -aux, -ales** *adj* sentimental; **vie sentimentale** love life **▪ sentimentalité** *nf* sentimentality

sentinelle [sɑ̃tinɛl] *nf* sentry

sentir* [sɑ̃tir] **1** *vt* (*douleur*) to feel; (*odeur*) to smell; (*danger*) to sense; **s. le moisi/le parfum** to smell musty/of perfume; **s. le poisson** to smell of fish; **se faire s.** (*effet*) to make itself felt; *Fam* **je ne peux pas le s.** I can't stand him **2** *vi* to smell; **s. bon/mauvais** to smell good/bad **3 se sentir** *vpr* **se s. fatigué/humilié** to feel tired/humiliated **▪ senti, -ie** *adj* **bien s.** (*remarque*) hard-hitting

séparation [separasjɔ̃] *nf* separation; (*départ*) parting

séparer [separe] **1** *vt* to separate (**de** from); (*cheveux*) to part; **plus rien ne nous sépare de la victoire** nothing stands between us and victory **2 se séparer** *vpr* (*couple*) to separate; (*assemblée, cortège*) to disperse, to break up; (*se détacher*) to split off; **se s. de** (*objet aimé, chien*) to part with **▪ séparé, -ée** *adj* (*distinct*) separate; (*époux*) separated (**de** from) **▪ séparément** *adv* separately

sept [sɛt] *adj & nm inv* seven **▪ septième** *adj & nmf* seventh; **un s.** a seventh

septante [sɛptɑ̃t] *adj Belg & Suisse* seventy

septembre [sɛptɑ̃br] *nm* September

septennat [sɛptena] *nm Pol* seven-year term (of office)

septentrional, -e, -aux, -ales [sɛptɑ̃trijɔnal, -o] *adj* northern

sépulcre [sepylkr] *nm* (*tombeau*) sepulchre

sépulture [sepyltyr] *nf* burial; (*lieu*) burial place

séquelles [sekɛl] *nfpl* (*de maladie*) after-effects; (*de guerre*) aftermath

séquence [sekɑ̃s] *nf* sequence; *Cartes* run; **s. de film** film sequence

séquestrer [sekɛstre] *vt* **s. qn** to keep sb locked up

sera, serait [səra, sərɛ] *voir* **être**

Serbie [sɛrbi] *nf* **la S.** Serbia **▪ serbe 1** *adj* Serbian **2** *nmf* **S.** Serb **▪ serbo-croate** (*pl* **serbo-croates**) **1** *adj* Serbo-Croat **2** *nmf* **S.** Serbo-Croat **3** *nm* (*langue*) Serbo-Croat

serein, -eine [sərɛ̃, -ɛn] *adj* serene **▪ sérénité** *nf* serenity

sérénade [serenad] *nf* serenade

sergent [sɛrʒɑ̃] *nm Mil* sergeant

série [seri] *nf* series; (*ensemble*) set; *Fig* **s. noire** series of disasters; **de s.** (*article, voiture*) standard; **fin de s.** discontinued line; **fabrication en s.** mass production; **numéro hors s.** special issue

sérieux, -ieuse [serjø, -jøz] **1** *adj* (*personne, doute*) serious; (*de bonne foi*) genuine, serious; (*fiable*) reliable; (*bénéfices*) substantial; **de**

sérieuses chances de... a good chance of... **2** *nm (application)* seriousness; *(fiabilité)* reliability; **prendre qn/qch au s.** to take sb/sth seriously; **garder son s.** to keep a straight face; **se prendre (trop) au s.** to take oneself (too) seriously ▪ **sérieusement** *adv* seriously

serin [sərɛ̃] *nm* canary

seriner [sərine] *vt Fig* **s. qch à qn** to repeat sth to sb over and over again

seringue [sərɛ̃g] *nf* syringe

serment [sɛrmɑ̃] *nm (affirmation solennelle)* oath; *(promesse)* pledge; **prêter s.** to take an oath; **faire le s. de faire qch** to swear to do sth; *Jur* **sous s.** on or under oath

sermon [sɛrmɔ̃] *nm (de prêtre)* sermon; *Péj (discours)* lecture ▪ **sermonner** *vt (faire la morale à)* to lecture

séropositif, -ive [seropozitif, -iv] *adj Méd* HIV positive ▪ **séronégatif, -ive** *adj Méd* HIV negative

serpent [sɛrpɑ̃] *nm* snake; **s. à sonnette** rattlesnake

serpenter [sɛrpɑ̃te] *vi (sentier)* to meander

serpentin [sɛrpɑ̃tɛ̃] *nm (ruban)* streamer

serpillière [sɛrpijɛr] *nf* floor cloth

serre [sɛr] *nf* greenhouse ▪ **serres** *nfpl (d'oiseau)* claws, talons

serrement [sɛrmɑ̃] *nm* **s. de cœur** heavy-hearted feeling

serrer [sɛre] *vt (tenir)* to grip; *(nœud, vis)* to tighten; *(poing)* to clench; *(taille)* to hug; *(frein)* to apply; *(rapprocher)* to close up; **s. la main à qn** to shake hands with sb; **s. les rangs** to close ranks; *Fig* **s. les dents** to grit one's teeth; **s. qn** *(embrasser)* to hug sb; *(sujet: vêtement)* to be too tight for sb; **s. qn de près** *(talonner)* to be close behind sb **2** *vi* **s. à droite** to keep (to the) right **3 se serrer** *vpr (se rapprocher)* to squeeze up; **se s. contre** to squeeze up against ▪ **serré, -ée** *adj (nœud, budget, vêtement)* tight; *(gens)* packed (together); *(lutte)* close; *(rangs)* serried; *(écriture)* cramped; *Fig* **avoir le cœur s.** to have a heavy heart ▪ **serre-livres** *nm inv* book-end ▪ **serre-tête** *nm inv* headband

serrure [sɛryr] *nf* lock ▪ **serrurier** *nm* locksmith

sertir [sɛrtir] *vt (diamant)* to set

sérum [serɔm] *nm* serum

servante [sɛrvɑ̃t] *nf* (maid)servant

serveur, -euse [sɛrvœr, -øz] *nmf (de restaurant, de café)* waiter, waitress; *(de bar) Br* barman, *f* barmaid, *Am* bartender; *Ordinat* server; **s. de réseau** network server

serviable [sɛrvjabl] *adj* helpful, obliging ▪ **serviabilité** *nf* helpfulness

service [sɛrvis] *nm* service; *(travail)* duty; *(pourboire)* service (charge); *(d'entreprise)* department; *Tennis* serve, service; **un s.** *(aide)*

a favour; **rendre s.** to be of service (**à qn** to sb); **rendre un mauvais s. à qn** to do sb a disservice; **être de s.** to be on duty; *Tennis* **être au s.** to be serving; **faire son s. (militaire)** to do one's military service; **à votre s.!** at your service!; **s. à café/à thé** coffee/tea set; **s. (non) compris** service (not) included; **s. après-vente** aftersales service; **s. d'ordre** *(policiers)* police; **s. public** civil service

serviette [sɛrvjɛt] *nf (pour s'essuyer)* towel; *(sac)* briefcase; **s. de bain/de toilette** bath/hand towel; **s. de table** napkin, *Br* serviette; **s. hygiénique** sanitary *Br* towel or *Am* napkin ▪ **serviette-éponge** *(pl* **serviettes-éponges)** *nf* terry towel

servile [sɛrvil] *adj* servile; *(imitation)* slavish ▪ **servilité** *nf* servility; slavishness

servir* [sɛrvir] **1** *vt* to serve *(qch à qn* sb with sth, sth to sb); *(convive)* to wait on **2** *vi* to serve; **s. à qch/à faire qch** to be used for sth/to do or for doing sth; **ça ne sert à rien** it's useless, it's no good or use *(de faire* doing); **à quoi ça sert de protester** what's the use or good of protesting; **s. de qch** to be used for sth, to serve as sth; **ça me sert à faire qch/de qch** I use it to do or for doing sth/as sth; **s. à qn de guide** to act as a guide to sb **3 se servir** *vpr (à table)* to help oneself *(de* to); **se s. de qch** *(utiliser)* to use sth

serviteur [sɛrvitœr] *nm* servant ▪ **servitude** *nf (esclavage)* servitude; *Fig (contrainte)* constraint

ses [se] *voir* **son²**

session [sesjɔ̃] *nf* session

set [sɛt] *nm Tennis* set; **s. de table** place mat

seuil [sœj] *nm (entrée)* doorway; *Fig (limite)* threshold; *Fig* **au s. de** on the threshold of

seul, seule [sœl] **1** *adj (sans compagnie)* alone; *(unique)* only; **tout s.** by oneself, on one's own, all alone; **se sentir s.** to feel lonely or alone; **la seule femme** the only woman; **un s. chat** only one cat; **une seule fois** only once; **pas un s. livre** not a single book; **seuls les garçons, les garçons seuls...** only the boys... **2** *adv (tout)* **s.** *(rentrer, vivre)* by oneself, alone, on one's own; *(parler)* to oneself; **s. à s.** *(parler)* in private **3** *nmf* **le s., la seule** the only one; **un s., une seule** only one, one only; **pas un s.** not (a single) one

seulement [sœlmɑ̃] *adv* only; **non s.... mais encore...** not only... but (also)...; **pas s.** *(même)* not even

sève [sɛv] *nf (de plante)* & *Fig* sap

sévère [sever] *adj; (parents, professeur, juge)* strict ▪ **sévèrement** *adv* severely; *(éduquer)* strictly ▪ **sévérité** *nf* severity; *(de parents)* strictness

sévices [sevis] *nmpl* ill-treatment; **s. à enfant** child abuse

sévir [sevir] *vi Fig (fléau)* to rage; **s. contre qch** to deal severely with sth

sevrer [səvre] *vt (enfant)* to wean

sexe [sɛks] *nm (catégorie, sexualité)* sex; *(organes)* genitals ▪ **sexisme** *nm* sexism ▪ **sexiste** *adj & nmf* sexist ▪ **sexualité** *nf* sexuality ▪ **sexuel, -elle** *adj* sexual; **éducation/vie sexuelle** sex education/life ▪ **sexy** *adj inv Fam* sexy

sextuor [sɛkstɥɔr] *nm* sextet

seyant, -ante [sejɑ̃, -ɑ̃t] *adj (vêtement)* becoming

shampooing [ʃɑ̃pwɛ̃] *nm* shampoo; **s. colorant** rinse; **faire un s. à qn** to shampoo sb's hair

shérif [ʃerif] *nm (aux États-Unis)* sheriff

shiatsu [ʃiatsu] *nm* shiatsu, shiatsu

shooter [ʃute] **1** *vti Football* to shoot **2 se shooter** *vpr Fam (drogué)* to shoot up

short [ʃɔrt] *nm (pair of)* shorts

si¹ [si]

si becomes **s'** [s] before **il, ils**.

1 *conj* **if**; **si je pouvais** if I could; **s'il vient** if he comes; **si j'étais roi** if I were *or* was king; **je me demande si…** I wonder whether *or* if…; **si on restait?** *(suggestion)* what if we stayed?; **si je dis ça, c'est que…** I say this because…; **si ce n'est que…** *(sauf que)* apart from the fact that…; **si oui** if so; **si non** if not; **si seulement** if only; **même si** even if **2** *adv* **(a)** *(tellement)* so; **pas si riche que toi/que tu crois** not as rich as you/as you think; **un si bon dîner** such a good dinner; **si grand qu'il soit** however big he may be; **si bien que…** so much so that… **(b)** *(après négative)* yes; **tu ne viens pas? – si!** you're not coming? – yes (I am)!

si² [si] *nm inv (note)* B

siamois, -oise [sjamwa, -waz] *adj* Siamese; **frères s., sœurs siamoises** Siamese twins

Sicile [sisil] *nf* **la S.** Sicily

SIDA [sida] *(abrév* **syndrome immuno-déficitaire acquis)** *nm* AIDS; **malade/virus du S.** AIDS sufferer/virus ▪ **sidéen, -enne** *nmf* AIDS sufferer

sidérer [sidere] *vt Fam* to stagger

sidérurgie [sideryrʒi] *nf* iron and steel industry ▪ **sidérurgique** *adj* **industrie s.** iron and steel industry

siècle [sjɛkl] *nm* century; *(époque)* age; *Fam* **depuis des siècles** for ages (and ages)

siège [sjɛʒ] *nm* **(a)** *(meuble, centre) & Pol* seat; *(d'autorité, de parti)* headquarters; **s. social** head office **(b)** *Mil* siege; **faire le s. de** to lay siege to ▪ **siéger** *vi (assemblée)* to sit

sien, sienne [sjɛ̃, sjɛn] **1** *pron possessif* **le s., la sienne, les sien(ne)s** *(d'homme)* his; *(de femme)* hers; *(de chose)* its; **les deux siens** his/her two **2** *nmpl* **les siens** *(sa famille)* one's family **3** *nfpl* **faire des siennes** *(personne, machine)* to act up

sieste [sjɛst] *nf* siesta; **faire la s.** to have a nap

siffler [sifle] **1** *vi* to whistle; *(avec un sifflet)* to blow one's whistle; *(gaz, serpent)* to hiss **2** *vt (chanson)* to whistle; *(chien)* to whistle at; *Sport (faute, fin de match)* to blow one's whistle for; *(acteur, pièce)* to boo; *Fam (boisson)* to knock back; **se faire s.** *(acteur)* to be booed ▪ **sifflement** [-əmɑ̃] *nm* whistling; *(de serpent, de gaz)* hissing

sifflet [siflɛ] *nm (instrument)* whistle; **sifflets** *(de spectateurs)* booing ▪ **siffloter** *vti* to whistle

sigle [sigl] *nm (initiales)* abbreviation; *(acronyme)* acronym

signal, -aux [siɲal, -o] *nm* signal; **s. d'alarme** alarm signal; **s. lumineux** warning light; **s. sonore** *(au téléphone)* beep; *(pour avertir)* warning sound

signalement [siɲalmɑ̃] *nm* description, particulars

signaler [siɲale] **1** *vt (faire remarquer)* to point out **(à qn** to sb; **que** that); *(avec un panneau)* to signpost; *(rapporter à la police)* to report **(à** to) **2 se signaler** *vpr* **se s. par qch** to distinguish oneself by sth

signalétique [siɲaletik] *adj* **fiche s.** personal details card

signalisation [siɲalizasjɔ̃] *nf (sur les routes)* signposting; *(pour les trains)* signals; *(pour les avions)* lights and marking; **s. routière** *(signaux)* road signs

signature [siɲatyr] *nf* signature; *(action)* signing; *Ordinat* **s. électronique** *ou* **numérique** digital signature ▪ **signataire** *nmf* signatory

signe [siɲ] *nm (indice)* sign, indication; **en s. de protestation** as a sign of protest; **faire s. à qn** *(geste)* to motion (to) sb **(de faire** to do); *(contacter)* to get in touch with sb; **faire s. que oui** to nod (one's head); **faire s. que non** to shake one's head; **faire le s. de croix** to make the sign of the cross; **ne pas donner s. de vie** to give no sign of life; **s. particulier/de ponctuation** distinguishing/punctuation mark; **s. astrologique** astrological sign

signet [siɲɛ] *nm (de livre, de page Web)* bookmark; *Ordinat* **créer un s. sur une page** to bookmark a page

signification [siɲifikasjɔ̃] *nf* meaning ▪ **significatif, -ive** *adj* significant, meaningful; **s. de qch** indicative of sth

signifier [siɲifje] *vt* to mean **(que** that); **s. qch à qn** *(notifier)* to notify sb of sth

silence [silɑ̃s] *nm* silence; *Mus* rest; **en s.** in silence; **garder le s.** to keep quiet *or* silent **(sur** about) ▪ **silencieux, -ieuse 1** *adj* silent **2** *nm (de voiture) Br* silencer, *Am* muffler; *(d'arme)* silencer ▪ **silencieusement** *adv* silently

silex [silɛks] *nm* flint

silhouette [silwɛt] *nf* outline; *(en noir)* silhouette; *(du corps)* figure

silicium [silisjɔm] *nm* silicon; **pastille de s.** silicon chip ▪ **silicone** *nf* silicone

sillage [sijaʒ] *nm (de bateau)* wake; *Fig* **dans le s. de** in the wake of

sillon [sijɔ̃] *nm (de champ)* furrow; *(de disque)* groove

sillonner [sijone] *vt (parcourir)* to criss-cross

silo [silo] *nm* silo

simagrées [simagre] *nfpl* airs and graces; *(minauderies)* fuss

similaire [similɛr] *adj* similar ▪ **similitude** *nf* similarity

similicuir [similikɥir] *nm* imitation leather, leatherette

simple [sɛ̃pl] **1** *adj (facile, crédule, sans prétention)* simple; *(composé d'un élément)* single; *(employé, particulier)* ordinary; *Fam* **c'est s. comme bonjour** it's as easy as pie **2** *nmf* **s. d'esprit** simpleton **3** *nm Tennis* singles; **passer du s. au double** to double ▪ **simplement** [-əmɑ̃] *adv* simply ▪ **simplicité** *nf* simplicity

simplifier [sɛ̃plifje] *vt* to simplify ▪ **simplification** *nf* simplification

simpliste [sɛ̃plist] *adj* simplistic

simulacre [simylakr] *nm* **ce fut un s. de procès** the trial was a farce

simuler [simyle] *vt (reproduire)* to simulate; *(feindre)* to feign ▪ **simulateur, -trice** *nmf (hypocrite)* faker; *(malade)* malingerer **2** *nm (appareil)* simulator ▪ **simulation** *nf (de phénomène)* simulation; *(action)* feigning

simultané, -ée [simyltane] *adj* simultaneous ▪ **simultanément** *adv* simultaneously

sincère [sɛ̃sɛr] *adj* sincere ▪ **sincèrement** *adv* sincerely ▪ **sincérité** *nf* sincerity; **en toute s.** quite sincerely

sinécure [sinekyr] *nf Fam* **ce n'est pas une s.** it's no rest cure

Singapour [sɛ̃gapur] *nm* Singapore

singe [sɛ̃ʒ] *nm* monkey; **grand s.** ape ▪ **singer** *vt (imiter)* to ape, to mimic ▪ **singeries** *nfpl* antics; **faire des s.** to monkey around

singulariser [sɛ̃gylarize] **se singulariser** *vpr* to draw attention to oneself

singulier, -ière [sɛ̃gylje, -jer] **1** *adj (peu ordinaire)* peculiar, odd; **combat s.** single combat **2** *adj & nm Grammaire* singular; **au s.** in the singular ▪ **singularité** *nf* peculiarity ▪ **singulièrement** *adv (notamment)* particularly; *(beaucoup)* extremely

sinistre [sinistr] **1** *adj (effrayant)* sinister; *(triste)* grim **2** *nm* disaster; *(incendie)* fire; *Jur (dommage)* damage ▪ **sinistré, -ée 1** *adj (population, région)* disaster-stricken **2** *nmf* disaster victim

sinon [sinɔ̃] *conj (autrement)* otherwise, or else; *(sauf)* except *(que* that); *(si ce n'est)* if not

sinueux, -ueuse [sinɥø, -ɥøz] *adj* winding ▪ **sinuosités** *nfpl* twists (and turns)

sinus [sinys] *nm inv Anat* sinus ▪ **sinusite** *nf* sinusitis; **avoir une s.** to have sinusitis

siphon [sifɔ̃] *nm* siphon; *(d'évier)* trap, *Br* U-bend

siphonné, -ée [sifone] *adj Fam* round the bend, crazy

sirène [sirɛn] *nf (d'usine)* siren; *(femme)* mermaid

sirop [siro] *nm* syrup; *(à diluer)* (fruit) cordial; **s. contre la toux** cough mixture ▪ **syrupeux, -euse** *adj* syrupy

siroter [sirote] *vt Fam* to sip

sismique [sismik] *adj* seismic; **secousse s.** earth tremor

site [sit] *nm (endroit)* site; *(pittoresque)* beauty spot; **s. classé** conservation area; *Ordinat* **s. de bavardage** chatroom; **s. touristique** place of interest; *Ordinat* **s. (Web)** (web)site

sitôt [sito] *adv* **s. que...** as soon as...; **s. levée, elle partit** as soon as she was up, she left; **s. après** immediately after; **pas de s.** not for some time

situation [sitɥasjɔ̃] *nf* situation, position; *(emploi)* position; **s. de famille** marital status ▪ **situé, -ée** *adj (maison)* situated *(à* in) ▪ **situer 1** *vt (placer)* to situate; *(trouver)* to locate; *(dans le temps)* to set **2 se situer** *vpr (se trouver)* to be situated

six [sis] ([si] *before consonant,* [siz] *before vowel) adj & nm inv* six ▪ **sixième** [sizjɛm] **1** *adj & nmf* sixth; **un s.** a sixth **2** *nf Scol Br* ≃ first form, *Am* ≃ sixth grade

Skaï® [skaj] *nm* imitation leather, leatherette

skateboard [skɛtbɔrd] *nm* skateboard; **faire du s.** to go skateboarding

sketch [skɛtʃ] *(pl* **sketches**) *nm (de théâtre)* sketch

ski [ski] *nm (objet)* ski; *(sport)* skiing; **faire du s.** to ski; **s. alpin** downhill skiing; **s. de fond** cross-country skiing; **s. nautique** water-skiing ▪ **skiable** *adj. (piste)* skiable, fit for skiing ▪ **skier** *vi* to ski ▪ **skieur, -ieuse** *nmf* skier

slalom [slalɔm] *nm Sport* slalom; **faire du s.** to slalom

slave [slav] **1** *adj* Slav, Slavic; *(langue)* Slavonic **2** *nmf* **S.** Slav **3** *nm (langue)* Slavonic

slip [slip] *nm (d'homme)* (under)pants, briefs; *(de femme) Br* pants, *Am* panties; **s. de bain** (swimming) trunks; *(de bikini®)* briefs

> Il faut noter que le nom anglais **slip** est un faux ami. Il ne signifie jamais **culotte**.

slogan [slɔgɑ̃] *nm* slogan

Slovaquie [slɔvaki] *nf* **la S.** Slovakia ▪ **slovaque 1** *adj* Slovak **2** *nmf* **S.** Slovak **3** *nm (langue)* Slovak

Slovénie [slɔveni] *nf* **la S.** Slovenia ▪ **slovène 1**

adj Slovenian **2** *nmf* S. Slovenian **3** *nm (langue)* Slovenian

slow [slo] *nm* slow (dance)

SMIC [smik] *(abrév* **salaire minimum interprofessionnel de croissance)** *nm* guaranteed minimum wage ▪ **smicard, -arde** *nmf Fam* minimum wage earner

smoking [smɔkiŋ] *nm (veston, costume)* dinner jacket, *Am* tuxedo

SMS [εsεmεs] *(abrév* **short message service)** *nm Tél* text (message); **envoyer un SMS à qn** to text sb, to send sb a text

snack(-bar) [snak(bar)] *nm* snack bar

SNCF [εsεnseεf] *(abrév* **Société nationale des chemins de fer français)** *nf* = French national railway company

sniffer [snife] *vt Fam (colle)* to sniff

snob [snɔb] **1** *adj* snobbish **2** *nmf* snob ▪ **snober** *vt* s. qn to snub sb ▪ **snobinard, -arde 1** *adj* stuck-up, snobbish **2** *nmf* stuck-up person, snob ▪ **snobisme** *nm* snobbery

sobre [sɔbr] *adj* sober ▪ **sobriété** *nf* sobriety

sobriquet [sɔbrikε] *nm* nickname

sociable [sɔsjabl] *adj* sociable ▪ **sociabilité** *nf* sociability

social, -e, -iaux, -iales [sɔsjal, -jo] *adj* social ▪ **socialisme** *nm* socialism ▪ **socialiste** *adj & nmf* socialist

société [sɔsjete] *nf (communauté)* society; *(compagnie)* company; **s. anonyme** *Br* (public) limited company, *Am* corporation ▪ **sociétaire** *nmf (membre)* member

sociologie [sɔsjɔlɔʒi] *nf* sociology ▪ **sociologique** *adj* sociological ▪ **sociologue** *nmf* sociologist

socle [sɔkl] *nm (de statue, de colonne)* plinth, pedestal; *(de lampe)* base

socquette [sɔkεt] *nf* ankle sock, *Am* bobby sock

soda [sɔda] *nm Br* fizzy drink, *Am* soda (pop)

sœur [sœr] *nf* sister; *(religieuse)* sister, nun; *Fam* **bonne s.** nun; *Fam* **et ta s.!** get lost!

sofa [sɔfa] *nm* sofa, settee

soi [swa] *pron personnel* oneself; **chacun pour s.** every man for himself; **en s.** *(concept)* in itself; **chez s.** at home; **prendre sur s.** to get a grip on oneself; **cela va de soi** it's self-evident **(que** that) ▪ **soi-même** *pron* oneself

soi-disant [swadizɑ̃] **1** *adj inv* so-called **2** *adv* supposedly

soie [swa] *nf (tissu)* silk; *(de porc)* bristle ▪ **soierie** *nf (tissu)* silk; *(activité)* silk trade

soient [swa] *voir* **être**

SOFRES [sɔfrεs] *(abrév* **Société française d'enquêtes par sondages)** *nf* = French opinion poll company

soif [swaf] *nf* thirst **(de** for); **avoir s.** to be thirsty; *Fig* **avoir s. de liberté** to thirst for freedom; **donner s. à qn** to make sb thirsty

soigner [swaɲe] **1** *vt* to look after, to take care of; *(sujet: médecin) (malade, maladie)* to treat; *(présentation, travail)* to take care over; **se faire s.** to have (medical) treatment **2** *se soigner* *vpr* to take care of oneself, to look after oneself ▪ **soigné, -ée** *adj (personne, vêtement)* neat, tidy; *(travail)* careful

soigneux, -euse [swaɲø, -øz] *adj (attentif)* careful **(de** with); *(propre)* neat, tidy ▪ **soigneusement** *adv* carefully

soin [swε̃] *nm (attention)* care; *Méd* **soins** treatment, care; **soins de beauté** beauty care *or* treatment; **les premiers soins** first aid; **avoir** *ou* **prendre s. de qch/de faire qch** to take care of sth/to do sth; **être aux petits soins avec qn** to wait hand and foot on sb; **aux bons soins de** *(sur lettre)* care of, c/o; **avec s.** carefully, with care

soir [swar] *nm* evening; **le s.** *(chaque soir)* in the evening(s); **à neuf heures du s.** at nine in the evening; **repas du s.** evening meal ▪ **soirée** *nf* evening; *(réunion)* party; **s. dansante** dance

sois, soit¹ [swa] *voir* **être**

soit² [swa] **1** *conj (à savoir)* that is (to say); **s.... s....** either... or...; *Math* **s. une droite...** given a straight line... **2** *adv (oui)* very well

soixante [swasɑ̃t] *adj & nm inv* sixty ▪ **soixantaine** *nf* **une s. (de)** *(nombre)* (about) sixty; **avoir la s.** *(âge)* to be about sixty ▪ **soixantième** *adj & nmf* sixtieth

soixante-dix [swasɑ̃tdis] *adj & nm inv* seventy ▪ **soixante-dixième** *adj & nmf* seventieth

soja [sɔʒa] *nm (plante)* soya; **graines de s.** soya bean; **germes** *ou* **pousses de s.** beansprouts; **sauce de s.** soy sauce

sol¹ [sɔl] *nm* ground; *(plancher)* floor; *(territoire, terrain)* soil

sol² [sɔl] *nm inv (note)* G

solaire [sɔlεr] *adj* solar; **crème/huile s.** sun (-tan) lotion/oil; **maison s.** solar-heated house; *Anat* **plexus s.** solar plexus; **système s.** solar system

solarium [sɔlarjɔm] *nm (établissement)* solarium; *(terrasse)* sun terrace

soldat [sɔlda] *nm* soldier; **simple s.** private

solde [sɔld] **1** *nm (de compte, à payer)* balance; **en s.** *(acheter)* in the sales, *Am* on sale; **soldes** *(marchandises)* sale goods; *(vente)* (clearance) sale(s); **faire les soldes** to go round the sales **2** *nf (de soldat)* pay; *Fig Péj* **à la s. de qn** in sb's pay

solder [sɔlde] **1** *vt (articles)* to clear, to sell off; *(compte)* to pay the balance of **2** *se solder* *vpr* **se s. par un échec** to end in failure ▪ **soldé, -ée** *adj (article)* reduced

sole [sɔl] *nf (poisson)* sole

soleil [sɔlεj] *nm* sun; *(chaleur, lumière)* sunshine; *(fleur)* sunflower; **au s.** in the sun; **il fait s.** it's sunny

solennel, -elle [sɔlanɛl] *adj* solemn **•solen-nellement** *adv* solemnly **•solennité** [-anite] *nf* solemnity

Solex® [sɔlɛks] *nm* moped

solfège [sɔlfɛʒ] *nm* music theory

solidaire [sɔlidɛr] *adj* **être s.** *(ouvriers)* to show solidarity (**de** with); *(pièce de machine)* to be interdependent (**de** with) **•solidairement** *adv* jointly **•se solidariser** *vpr* to show solidarity (**avec** with) **•solidarité** *nf (entre personnes)* solidarity

solide [sɔlid] **1** *adj (mur, voiture, état)* solid; *(amitié)* strong; *(argument, nerfs)* sound; *(personne)* sturdy **2** *nm (corps)* solid **•solidement** *adv* solidly **•se solidifier** *vpr* to solidify **•solidité** *nf (d'objet)* solidity; *(d'argument)* soundness

soliste [sɔlist] *nmf Mus* soloist

solitaire [sɔlitɛr] **1** *adj (par choix)* solitary; *(involontairement)* lonely **2** *nmf* loner; **en s.** on one's own **•solitude** *nf* solitude; **aimer la s.** to like being alone

solive [sɔliv] *nf* joist, beam

solliciter [sɔlisite] *vt (audience)* to request; *(emploi)* to apply for; **s. qn** *(faire appel à)* to appeal to sb *(de faire* to do); **être (très) sollicité** *(personne)* to be in (great) demand **•sollicitation** *nf* request

sollicitude [sɔlisityd] *nf* solicitude, concern

solo [sɔlo] *adj inv & nm Mus* solo

solstice [sɔlstis] *nm* solstice

soluble [sɔlybl] *adj (substance, problème)* soluble

solution [sɔlysjɔ̃] *nf (de problème)* solution (**de** to); *(mélange chimique)* solution

solvable [sɔlvabl] *adj Fin* solvent **•solvabilité** *nf Fin* solvency

> Il faut noter que l'adjectif anglais **solvable** est un faux ami. Il signifie **soluble**.

solvant [sɔlvɑ̃] *nm* solvent

Somalie [sɔmali] *nf* **la S.** Somalia

sombre [sɔ̃br] *adj* dark; *(triste)* sombre, gloomy; **il fait s.** it's dark

sombrer [sɔ̃bre] *vi (bateau)* to sink; *Fig* **s. dans** *(folie, sommeil)* to sink into

sommaire [sɔmɛr] **1** *adj* summary; *(repas)* basic **2** *nm (table des matières)* contents

sommation [sɔmasjɔ̃] *nf Jur* summons; *(de policier)* warning

somme [sɔm] **1** *nf* sum; **faire la s. de** to add up; **en s., s. toute** in short **2** *nm (sommeil)* nap; **faire un s.** to have a nap

sommeil [sɔmɛj] *nm* sleep; **avoir s.** to feel sleepy; **être en plein s.** to be fast asleep; *Fig* **laisser qch en s.** to put sth on hold **•sommeiller** *vi* to doze; *Fig (faculté, qualité)* to lie dormant

sommelier [sɔməlje] *nm* wine waiter

sommer [sɔme] *vt* **s. qn de faire qch** to summon sb to do sth

sommes [sɔm] *voir* **être**

sommet [sɔmɛ] *nm top; (de montagne)* summit, top; *Fig (de la gloire)* height, summit; **conférence au s.** summit (conference)

sommier [sɔmje] *nm (de lit)* base; **s. à ressorts** sprung base

somnambule [sɔmnɑ̃byl] *nmf* sleepwalker; **être s.** to sleepwalk **•somnambulisme** *nm* sleepwalking

somnifère [sɔmnifɛr] *nm* sleeping pill

somnolence [sɔmnɔlɑ̃s] *nf* drowsiness, sleepiness **•somnolent, -ente** *adj* drowsy, sleepy **•somnoler** *vi* to doze

somptuaire [sɔ̃ptɥɛr] *adj* extravagant

somptueux, -ueuse [sɔ̃ptɥø, -ɥøz] *adj* sumptuous **•somptuosité** *nf* sumptuousness

son¹ [sɔ̃] *nm (bruit)* sound; **s. 3D** surround sound

son² [sɔ̃] *nm (de grains)* bran

son³, sa, ses [sɔ̃, sa, se]

> **sa** becomes **son** [sɔ̃n] before a vowel or mute h.

adj possessif (d'homme) his; *(de femme)* her; *(de chose)* its; *(indéfini)* one's; **s. père/sa mère** his/her/one's father/mother; **s. ami(e)** his/her/one's friend

sonate [sɔnat] *nf Mus* sonata

sondage [sɔ̃daʒ] *nm (de terrain)* drilling; **s. (d'opinion)** (opinion) poll

sonde [sɔ̃d] *nf Géol* drill; *Naut* sounding line; *Méd* probe; *(pour l'alimentation)* (feeding) tube; **s. spatiale** space probe

sonder [sɔ̃de] *vt (rivière)* to sound; *(terrain)* to drill; *Méd* to probe; *Fig (personne, l'opinion)* to sound out

songe [sɔ̃ʒ] *nm* dream

songer [sɔ̃ʒe] **1** *vi* **s. à qch/à faire qch** to think of sth/of doing sth **2** *vt* **s. que...** to think that... **•songeur, -euse** *adj* thoughtful, pensive

sonner [sɔne] **1** *vi* to ring; *(cor, cloches)* to sound; **on a sonné (à la porte)** someone has rung the (door)bell; **midi a sonné** it has struck twelve **2** *vt (cloche)* to ring; *(domestique)* to ring for; *(cor)* to sound; *(l'heure)* to strike; *Fam (assommer)* to knock out **•sonnant, -ante** *adj* **en espèces sonnantes et trébuchantes** in hard cash, in coin of the realm; **à cinq heures sonnantes** on the stroke of five **•sonné, -ée** *adj Fam (fou)* crazy; *(assommé)* dazed, groggy

sonnerie [sɔnri] *nf (de téléphones, de cloche)* ring(ing); *(de téléphone portable)* ringtone; *(de cor)* sound; *(appareil)* bell

sonnette [sɔnɛt] *nf* bell; **coup de s.** ring; **s. d'alarme** alarm (bell)

sonnet [sɔnɛ] *nm (poème)* sonnet

sonore [sɔnɔr] *adj (rire)* loud; *(salle, voix)* resonant; **effet s.** sound effect **•sonorité** *nf (de salle)* acoustics; *(de violon)* tone

sonorisation [sɔnɔrizasjɔ̃] nf (matériel) sound equipment; **système de s.** PA (system) ▪ **sonoriser** vt (salle) to wire for sound; (film) to add the soundtrack to

sont [sɔ̃] voir **être**

sophistiqué, -ée [sɔfistike] adj sophisticated

soporifique [sɔpɔrifik] adj (médicament, discours) soporific

soprano [sɔprano] Mus 1 nmf (personne) soprano 2 nm (voix) soprano

sorbet [sɔrbɛ] nm sorbet

sorcellerie [sɔrsɛlri] nf witchcraft, sorcery ▪ **sorcier** 1 nm sorcerer 2 adj m Fam **ce n'est pas s.!** it's dead easy! ▪ **sorcière** nf witch

sordide [sɔrdid] adj (acte, affaire) sordid; (maison) squalid

sornettes [sɔrnɛt] nfpl Péj (propos) twaddle, nonsense

sort [sɔr] nm (destin) fate; (condition) lot; (maléfice) spell

sortable [sɔrtabl] adj Fam **tu n'es pas s.!** I really can't take you anywhere!

sortant, -ante [sɔrtɑ̃, -ɑ̃t] adj (numéro) winning; (député) outgoing

sorte [sɔrt] nf sort, kind (**de** of); **toutes sortes de** all sorts or kinds of; **en quelque s.** in a way, as it were; **de (telle) s. que tu apprennes** so that or in such a way that you may learn; **de la s.** (de cette façon) in that way; **faire en s. que…** (+ subjunctive) to see to it that…

sortie [sɔrti] nf (porte) exit, way out; (action de sortir) leaving, exit, departure; (de scène) exit; (promenade à pied) walk; (en voiture) drive; (excursion) outing, trip; Ordinat output; (de film, de disque) release; (de livre, de modèle) appearance; (de devises) export; **sorties** (argent) outgoings; **à la s. de l'école** when the children come out of school; **l'heure de la s. de qn** the time at which sb leaves; **être de s.** to be out; **s. de bain** bathrobe; **s. de secours** emergency exit

sortilège [sɔrtilɛʒ] nm (magic) spell

sortir* [sɔrtir] 1 (aux **être**) vi to go out, to leave; (pour s'amuser) to go out; (film, modèle) to come out; (numéro gagnant) to come up; **s. de** (endroit) to leave; (université) to be a graduate of; (famille, milieu) to come from; (légalité, limites) to go beyond; (compétence) to be outside; (sujet) to stray from; (gonds, rails) to come off; **s. de table** to leave the table; **s. de terre** (plante, fondations) to come up; **s. de l'ordinaire** ou **du commun** to be out of the ordinary; **s. indemne** to escape unhurt (**de** from) 2 (aux **avoir**) vt to take out (**de** of); (film, modèle, livre) to bring out; Fam (dire) to come out with; Fam (expulser) to throw out 3 se **sortir** vpr **s'en s.** (malade) to pull through 4 nm **au s. de l'hiver** at the end of winter; **au s. du lit** on getting out of bed

SOS [ɛsoɛs] nm SOS; **lancer un SOS** to send (out) an SOS

sosie [sozi] nm (personne) double; **c'est le s. de son père** he's the double or the spitting image of his father

sot, sotte [so, sɔt] 1 adj silly, foolish 2 nmf fool ▪ **sottement** adv foolishly ▪ **sottise** nf silliness, foolishness; (action, parole) silly or foolish thing; **faire des sottises** to do silly things

> Il faut noter que le nom anglais **sot** est un faux ami. Il signifie **ivrogne**.

sou [su] nm Hist (pièce) sou; Fam **sous** (argent) money; **elle n'a pas un** ou **le s.** she doesn't have a penny; Fig **n'avoir pas un s. de bon sens** not to have an ounce of common sense; **dépenser jusqu'à son dernier s.** to spend one's last penny; **machine à sous** slot machine

soubresaut [subrəso] nm (sudden) start, jolt

souche [suʃ] nf (d'arbre) stump; (de carnet) stub, counterfoil; (de famille) founder; (de virus) strain

souci [susi] nm (inquiétude) worry, concern; (préoccupation) concern (**de** for); **se faire du s.** to worry, to be worried; **ça lui donne du s.** it worries him/her; **se soucier** vpr **se s. de** to be worried or concerned about; Fam **se s. de qch comme de l'an quarante** not to give a hoot about sth ▪ **soucieux, -euse** adj worried, concerned (**de qch** about sth); **s. de plaire** anxious to please

soucoupe [sukup] nf saucer; **s. volante** flying saucer

soudain, -aine [sudɛ̃, -ɛn] 1 adj sudden 2 adv suddenly ▪ **soudainement** adv suddenly ▪ **soudaineté** nf suddenness

Soudan [sudɑ̃] nm **le S.** Sudan

soude [sud] nf soda; **s. caustique** caustic soda

souder [sude] 1 vt (par alliage) to solder; (par soudure autogène) to weld; Fig (groupes) to unite (closely); **lampe à s.** blowlamp 2 se **souder** vpr (os) to knit (together) ▪ **soudure** nf (par alliage) soldering; (autogène) welding

soudoyer [sudwaje] vt to bribe

souffle [sufl] nm (d'air, de vent) breath, puff; (respiration) breathing; (de bombe) blast; Fig (inspiration) inspiration; **reprendre son s.** to get one's breath back ▪ **souffler** 1 vi to blow; (haleter) to puff; **laisser s. qn** (se reposer) to give sb time to catch his/her breath 2 vt (bougie) to blow out; (fumée, poussière, verre) to blow; (par une explosion) to blast; (chuchoter) to whisper; Fam (étonner) to stagger; **s. une réplique à qn** (acteur) to give sb a prompt; **ne pas s. mot** not to breathe a word ▪ **soufflet** nm (de forge) bellows; (de train, d'autobus) concertina vestibule ▪ **souffleur, -euse** nmf (de théâtre) prompter

soufflé [sufle] *nm Culin* soufflé

souffrance [sufrɑ̃s] *nf* suffering; **en s.** *(colis)* unclaimed; *(travail)* pending

souffreteux, -euse [sufrətø, -øz] *adj* sickly

souffrir* [sufrir] **1** *vi* to suffer; **s. de** to suffer from; **faire s. qn** *(physiquement)* to hurt sb; *(moralement)* to make sb suffer; **ta réputation en souffrira** your reputation will suffer **2** *vt* *(endurer)* to suffer; *(exception)* to admit of; *Fam* **je ne peux pas le s.** I can't bear him ▪ **souffrant, -ante** *adj* unwell

soufre [sufr] *nm Br* sulphur, *Am* sulfur

souhait [swe] *nm* wish; **à vos souhaits!** *(après un éternuement)* bless you!; **à s.** perfectly ▪ **souhaitable** *adj* desirable ▪ **souhaiter** [swete] *vt (bonheur)* to wish for; **s. qch à qn** to wish sb sth; **s. faire qch** to hope to do sth; **s. que...** (+ *subjunctive)* to hope that...

souiller [suje] *vt* to soil, to dirty; *Fig (déshonorer)* to tarnish ▪ **souillon** *nf Littéraire* slut

soûl, soûle [su, sul] **1** *adj* drunk **2** *nm* **tout son s.** *(boire)* to one's heart's content ▪ **soûler** *vt* **s. qn** to get sb drunk **3 se soûler** *upr* to get drunk

soulager [sulaʒe] *vt* to relieve **(de** of) ▪ **soulagement** *nm* relief

soulever [suləve] **1** *vt* to lift (up); *(poussière, question)* to raise; *(peuple)* to stir up; *(sentiment)* to arouse; **cela me soulève le cœur** it makes me feel sick **2 se soulever** *upr (personne)* to lift oneself (up); *(se révolter)* to rise up ▪ **soulèvement** [-ɛvmɑ̃] *nm (révolte)* uprising

soulier [sulje] *nm* shoe; *Fam* **être dans ses petits souliers** to feel awkward

souligner [suliɲe] *vt (d'un trait)* to underline; *(faire remarquer)* to emphasize

soumettre* [sumɛtr] **1** *vt (pays, rebelles)* to subdue; *(rapport, demande)* to submit **(à** to); **s. qn à** *(assujettir)* to subject sb to **2 se soumettre** *upr* to submit **(à** to) ▪ **soumis, -ise** *adj (docile)* submissive; **s. à** subject to ▪ **soumission** *nf (à une autorité)* submission; *(docilité)* submissiveness

soupape [supap] *nf* valve; **s. de sécurité** safety valve

soupçon [supsɔ̃] *nm* suspicion; *Fig* **un s. de** *(quantité)* a hint or touch of; **au-dessus de tout s.** above suspicion ▪ **soupçonner** *vt* to suspect **(de** of; **d'avoir fait** of doing) ▪ **soupçonneux, -euse** *adj* suspicious

soupe [sup] *nf* soup; *Fam* **être s. au lait** to be hot-tempered; **s. populaire** soup kitchen ▪ **soupière** *nf* (soup) tureen

soupente [supɑ̃t] *nf (sous un toit)* loft

souper [supe] **1** *nm* supper **2** *vi* to have supper

soupeser [supəze] *vt (objet dans la main)* to feel the weight of; *Fig (arguments)* to weigh up

soupir [supir] *nm* sigh ▪ **soupirant** *nm Hum* suitor ▪ **soupirer** *vi* to sigh

soupirail, -aux [supiraj, -o] *nm* basement window

souple [supl] *adj (corps, personne)* supple; *(branche)* flexible ▪ **souplesse** *nf (de corps)* suppleness; *(de branche)* flexibility

source [surs] *nf* **(a)** *(point d'eau)* spring; **prendre sa s.** *(rivière)* to rise **(à** at) **(b)** *(origine)* source; **s. d'énergie** source of energy; **tenir qch de s. sûre** to have sth on good authority

sourcil [sursi] *nm* eyebrow ▪ **sourciller** *vi Fig* **ne pas s.** not to bat an eyelid

sourd, sourde [sur, surd] **1** *adj (personne)* deaf **(à** to); *(douleur)* dull; **bruit s.** thump; **lutte sourde** secret struggle; *Fam* **s. comme un pot** deaf as a post **2** *nmf* deaf person ▪ **sourd-muet, sourde-muette** *(mpl* **sourds-muets**, *fpl* **sourdes-muettes**) **1** *adj* deaf-and-dumb **2** *nmf* deaf mute

sourdine [surdin] *nf Mus (dispositif)* mute; *Fig* **en s.** quietly, secretly

souricière [surisjer] *nf* mousetrap; *Fig* trap

sourire* [surir] **1** *nm* smile; **faire un s. à qn** to give sb a smile **2** *vi* to smile **(à** at); **s. à qn** *(fortune)* to smile on sb ▪ **souriant, -ante 1** *adj (visage)* smiling, smiley; *(personne)* cheerful **2** *nm Ordinat* smiley, emoticon

souris [suri] *nf (animal)* & *Ordinat* mouse *(pl* mice)

sournois, -oise [surnwa, -waz] *adj* sly, underhand ▪ **sournoisement** *adv* slyly ▪ **sournoiserie** *nf* slyness

sous [su] *prép (position)* under, underneath, beneath; *(rang)* under; **s. la pluie** in the rain; **nager s. l'eau** to swim underwater; **s. calmants** under sedation; **s. cet angle** from that point of view; **s. le nom de** under the name of; **s. Charles X** under Charles X; **s. peu** *(bientôt)* shortly

sous-alimenté, -ée [suzalimɑ̃te] *(mpl* **sous-alimentés**, *fpl* **sous-alimentées)** *adj* underfed, malnourished ▪ **sous-alimentation** *nf* undernourishment, malnutrition

sous-bois [subwa] *nm* undergrowth

sous-chef [suʃɛf] *(pl* **sous-chefs)** *nmf* second-in-command

souscrire* [suskrir] *vi* **s. à** *(payer, approuver)* to subscribe to ▪ **souscription** *nf* subscription

sous-développé, -ée [sudevlɔpe] *(mpl* **sous-développés**, *fpl* **sous-développées)** *adj (pays)* underdeveloped

sous-directeur, -trice [sudirɛktœr, -tris] *(pl* **sous-directeurs)** *nmf* assistant manager

sous-emploi [suzɑ̃plwa] *nm* underemployment

sous-entendre [suzɑ̃tɑ̃dr] *vt* to imply ▪ **sous-entendu** *(pl* **sous-entendus)** *nm* insinuation

sous-estimer [suzɛstime] *vt* to underestimate

sous-jacent, -ente [suʒasɑ̃, -ɑ̃t] (*mpl* **sous-jacents**, *fpl* **sous-jacentes**) *adj* underlying

sous-louer [sulwe] *vt* (*sujet: locataire*) to sublet

sous-main [sumɛ̃] *nm inv* desk blotter; **en s.** secretly

sous-marin, -ine [sumarɛ̃, -in] (*mpl* **sous-marins**, *fpl* **sous-marines**) 1 *adj* underwater 2 *nm* submarine

sous-officier [suzɔfisje] (*pl* **sous-officiers**) *nm* non-commissioned officer

sous-payer [supeje] *vt* to underpay

sous-préfet [suprefe] (*pl* **sous-préfets**) *nm* subprefect ▪ **sous-préfecture** *nf* subprefecture

sous-produit [suprɔdɥi] (*pl* **sous-produits**) *nm* by-product

soussigné, -ée [susiɲe] *adj & nmf* undersigned; **je s.** I the undersigned

sous-sol [susɔl] (*pl* **sous-sols**) *nm* (*d'immeuble*) basement

sous-titre [sutitr] (*pl* **sous-titres**) *nm* subtitle ▪ **sous-titrer** *vt* (*film*) to subtitle

soustraire* [sustrɛr] 1 *vt* to remove; *Math* to take away, to subtract (**de** from); **s. qn à** (*danger*) to shield *or* protect sb from 2 **se soustraire** *upr* **s. à** to escape from; (*devoir, obligation*) to avoid ▪ **soustraction** *nf Math* subtraction

sous-traiter [sutrete] *vt* to subcontract ▪ **sous-traitance** *nf* travailler en s. avec qn to work as a subcontractor with sb ▪ **sous-traitant** *nm* subcontractor

sous-verre [suver] *nm inv* (*encadrement*) (frameless) glass mount

sous-vêtement [suvɛtmɑ̃] *nm* undergarment; **sous-vêtements** underwear

soutane [sutan] *nf* (*de prêtre*) cassock

soute [sut] *nf* (*de bateau*) hold

soutenir* [sutənir] *vt* to support, to hold up; (*opinion*) to uphold, to maintain; (*candidat*) to back; (*effort*) to sustain; (*thèse*) to defend; (*regard*) to hold; **s. que...** to maintain that... ▪ **soutenu, -ue** *adj* (*attention, effort*) sustained; (*langue*) formal

souterrain, -aine [suterɛ̃, -ɛn] 1 *adj* underground 2 *nm* underground passage

soutien [sutjɛ̃] *nm* support; (*personne*) supporter; **s. de famille** breadwinner ▪ **soutien-gorge** (*pl* **soutiens-gorge**) *nm* bra

soutirer [sutire] *vt* **s. qch à qn** to extract sth from sb

souvenir [suvnir] *nm* memory, recollection; (*objet*) memento; (*cadeau*) keepsake; (*pour touristes*) souvenir; **en s. de** in memory of ▪ **se souvenir*** *upr* **se s. de qn/qch** to remember sb/sth; **se s. que...** to remember that...

souvent [suvɑ̃] *adv* often; **peu s.** seldom; **le plus s.** usually, more often than not

souverain, -aine [suvərɛ̃, -ɛn] 1 *adj*

(*puissance, état, remède*) sovereign; (*bonheur, mépris*) supreme 2 *nmf* sovereign ▪ **souveraineté** *nf* sovereignty

soviétique [sɔvjetik] *Anciennement* 1 *adj* Soviet; **l'Union s.** the Soviet Union 2 *nmf* Soviet citizen

soyeux, -euse [swajø, -jøz] *adj* silky

soyons, soyez [swajɔ̃, swaje] *voir* **être**

SPA [ɛspea] (*abrév* **Société protectrice des animaux**) *nf Br* ≃ RSPCA, *Am* ≃ ASPCA

spacieux, -ieuse [spasjø, -jøz] *adj* spacious, roomy

spaghettis [spageti] *nmpl* spaghetti

spammer [spame] *vt Ordinat* to spam, to send spam to ▪ **spamming** *nm Ordinat* spamming

sparadrap [sparadra] *nm* (*pour pansement*) *Br* sticking plaster, Elastoplast®, *Am* Band-Aid®

spasme [spasm] *nm* spasm ▪ **spasmodique** *adj* spasmodic

spatial, -e, -iaux, -iales [spasjal, -jo] *adj* **station spatiale** space station; **engin s.** spaceship, spacecraft; **combinaison spatiale** spacesuit

spatule [spatyl] *nf* spatula

speaker [spikœr], **speakerine** [spikrin] *nmf* (*de télévision, de radio*) announcer

spécial, -e, -iaux, -iales [spesjal, -jo] *adj* special; (*bizarre*) peculiar ▪ **spécialement** *adv* (*exprès*) specially; (*en particulier*) especially, particularly; *Fam* **pas s.** not particularly, not especially

> Il faut noter qu'en anglais l'adjectif **special** ne s'emploie jamais à propos de quelque chose d'inhabituel ou d'étrange.

spécialiser [spesjalize] **se spécialiser** *upr* to specialize (**dans** in) ▪ **spécialisation** *nf* specialization ▪ **spécialiste** *nmf* specialist ▪ **spécialité** *nf Br* speciality, *Am* specialty

spécifier [spesifje] *vt* to specify (**que** that)

spécifique [spesifik] *adj* specific

spécimen [spesimen] *nm* specimen; (*livre*) specimen copy

spectacle [spɛktakl] *nm* (a) (*vue*) sight, spectacle; *Péj* **se donner en s.** to make an exhibition of oneself (b) (*représentation*) show; **le s.** (*industrie*) show business ▪ **spectateur, -trice** *nmf* spectator; (*au théâtre, au cinéma*) member of the audience; (*témoin*) witness; **spectateurs** (*au théâtre, au cinéma*) audience

spectaculaire [spɛktakyler] *adj* spectacular

spectre [spɛktr] *nm* (*fantôme*) *Br* spectre, *Am* specter; *Phys* spectrum

spéculer [spekyle] *vi* to speculate; *Fig* **s. sur** (*compter sur*) to bank *or* rely on ▪ **spéculateur, -trice** *nmf* speculator ▪ **spéculatif, -ive** *adj* speculative ▪ **spéculation** *nf* speculation

speed [spid] *Fam* 1 *adj* (*nerveux*) hyper 2 *nm* (*amphétamines*) speed ▪ **speeder** *vi Fam* (*être* *drogué)* to be on speed; *(se dépêcher)* to get a move on

spéléologie [speleɔlɔʒi] *nf (activité) Br* potholing, caving, *Am* spelunking **▪ spéléologue** *nmf Br* potholer, *Am* spelunker

sperme [spɛrm] *nm* sperm, semen

sphère [sfɛr] *nf (boule, domaine)* sphere **▪ sphérique** *adj* spherical

sphinx [sfɛ̃ks] *nm* sphinx

spirale [spiral] *nf* spiral

spirite [spirit] *nmf* spiritualist **▪ spiritisme** *nm* spiritualism

spirituel, -uelle [spirityɛl] *adj (amusant)* witty; *(pouvoir, vie)* spiritual

spiritueux [spirityø] *nmpl (boissons)* spirits

splendide [splɑ̃did] *adj* splendid **▪ splendeur** *nf* splendour

spongieux, -ieuse [spɔ̃ʒjø, -jøz] *adj* spongy

spontané, -ée [spɔ̃tane] *adj* spontaneous **▪ spontanéité** *nf* spontaneity **▪ spontanément** *adv* spontaneously

sporadique [spɔradik] *adj* sporadic

sport [spɔr] *nm* sport; **faire du s.** to do or play *Br* sport *or Am* sports; **(de) s.** *(chaussures, vêtements)* casual, sports; **voiture/terrain de s.** sports car/ground; **sports de combat** combat sports; **sports d'équipe** team sports; **sports extrêmes** extreme sports; **sports d'hiver** winter sports; **aller aux sports d'hiver** to go skiing; **sports mécaniques** motor sports *(on land, in the air, on water)*; **sports nautiques** water sports; **sports de plein air** outdoor sports **▪ sportif, -ive 1** *adj (personne)* fond of *Br* sport *or Am* sports; *(attitude, esprit)* sporting; *(association, journal, résultats)* sports, sporting; *(allure)* athletic **2** *nmf* sportsman, *f* sportswoman **▪ sportivité** *nf* sportsmanship

spot [spɔt] *nm (lampe)* spotlight; *Fam (endroit)* spot; **s. publicitaire** commercial

sprint [sprint] *nm Sport* sprint **▪ sprinter** *Sport* **1** *vt* to sprint **2** [-œr] *nm* sprinter **▪ sprinteuse** *nf Sport* sprinter

square [skwar] *nm* public garden

squash [skwaʃ] *nm (jeu)* squash

squat [skwat] *nm* squat **▪ squatteur, -euse** *nmf* squatter **▪ squatter 1** *vi* to squat **2** [-œr] *nm* squatter

squelette [skəlɛt] *nm* skeleton **▪ squelettique** *adj (personne, maigreur)* skeletal; *(exposé)* sketchy

SRAS [sras] *(abrév* **syndrome respiratoire aigu sévère)** *nm Méd* SARS

stable [stabl] *adj* stable **▪ stabilisateur** *nm* stabilizer **▪ stabiliser** *vt,* **se stabiliser** *vpr* to stabilize **▪ stabilité** *nf* stability

stade [stad] *nm Sport* stadium; *(phase)* stage

stage [staʒ] *nm (période)* training period; *(cours)* (training) course; **faire un s.** to undergo training; **être en s.** to be on a training course;

s. de formation training period; **s. professionnel** *ou* **en entreprise** *Br* work placement, *Am* internship **▪ stagiaire** *adj & nmf* trainee

> Il faut noter que le nom anglais **stage** est un faux ami.

stagner [stagne] *vi* to stagnate **▪ stagnant, -ante** *adj* stagnant **▪ stagnation** *nf* stagnation

stalle [stal] *nf (d'écurie, d'église)* stall

stand [stɑ̃d] *nm (d'exposition)* stand, stall; *Sport* **s. de ravitaillement** pit; **s. de tir** *(de foire)* shooting range; *(militaire)* firing range

standard [stɑ̃dar] **1** *nm (téléphonique)* switchboard **2** *adj inv (modèle)* standard **▪ standardiser** *vt* to standardize **▪ standardiste** *nmf* (switchboard) operator

standing [stɑ̃diŋ] *nm* standing, status; **immeuble de (grand) s.** luxury *Br* block of flats *or Am* apartment building

starter [startɛr] *nm (de véhicule)* choke; *Sport* starter

station [stasjɔ̃] *nf (de métro, d'observation, de radio)* station; *(de bus)* stop; **s. de taxis** *Br* taxi rank, *Am* taxi stand; **s. debout** standing (position) **▪ station-service** *(pl* **stations-service)** *nf* service station, *Br* petrol *or Am* gas station

stationnaire [stasjɔnɛr] *adj* stationary

stationner [stasjɔne] *vi (être garé)* to be parked; *(se garer)* to park **▪ stationnement** *nm* parking; **'s. interdit'** *(sur panneau)* 'no parking'

statique [statik] *adj* static

statistique [statistik] **1** *adj* statistical **2** *nf (donnée)* statistic; **la s.** *(science)* statistics *(sing)*

statue [staty] *nf* statue **▪ statuette** *nf* statuette

statuer [statɥe] *vi* **s. sur** *(juge)* to rule on

statu quo [statykwo] *nm inv* status quo

stature [statyr] *nf* stature

statut [staty] *nm (position)* status; **statuts** *(règles)* statutes **▪ statutaire** *adj* statutory

steak [stɛk] *nm* steak

stencil [stɛnsil] *nm* stencil

sténo [steno] *nf (personne)* stenographer; *(sténographie)* shorthand, stenography; **prendre qch en s.** to take sth down in shorthand **▪ sténodactylo** *nf Br* shorthand typist, *Am* stenographer **▪ sténographie** *nf* shorthand, stenography

stéréo [stereo] **1** *nf* stereo; **en s.** in stereo **2** *adj inv (disque)* stereo **▪ stéréophonique** *adj* stereophonic

stéréotype [stereɔtip] *nm* stereotype **▪ stéréotypé, -ée** *adj* stereotyped **▪ stéréotyper** *vt* to stereotype

stérile [steril] *adj* sterile; *(terre)* barren **▪ stérilisation** *nf* sterilization **▪ stériliser** *vt* to sterilize **▪ stérilité** *nf* sterility; *(de terre)* barrenness

stérilet [sterilɛ] *nm* IUD, coil

stéroïde [steʀɔid] *nm* steroid

stéthoscope [stetɔskɔp] *nm* stethoscope

steward [stiwaʀt] *nm* (*d'avion, de bateau*) steward

stigmate [stigmat] *nm Fig* mark, stigma (**de** of) ▪ **stigmatiser** *vt* (*dénoncer*) to stigmatize

stimuler [stimyle] *vt* to stimulate ▪ **stimulant** *nm Fig* stimulus; (*médicament*) stimulant ▪ **stimulateur** *nm* **s. cardiaque** pacemaker ▪ **stimulation** *nf* stimulation

stimulus [stimylys] (*pl* stimuli [-li]) *nm* (*physiologique*) stimulus (*pl* stimuli)

stipuler [stipyle] *vt* to stipulate (**que** that) ▪ **stipulation** *nf* stipulation

stock [stɔk] *nm* stock (**de** of); **en s.** in stock ▪ **stockage** *nm* stocking ▪ **stocker** *vt* (*provisions*) to stock

stoïque [stɔik] *adj* stoical ▪ **stoïcisme** *nm* stoicism

stop [stɔp] **1** *exclam* stop! **2** *nm Aut* (*panneau*) stop sign; (*feu arrière de véhicule*) *Br* brake light, *Am* stoplight; *Fam* **faire du s.** to hitchhike; *Fam* **prendre qn en s.** to give sb a *Br* lift or *Am* ride ▪ **stopper** *vti* to stop

store [stɔʀ] *nm Br* blind, *Am* (window) shade; (*de magasin*) awning

strabisme [stʀabism] *nm* squint

strapontin [stʀapɔ̃tɛ̃] *nm* tip-up or folding seat

stratagème [stʀataʒɛm] *nm* stratagem, ploy

stratège [stʀatɛʒ] *nm* strategist ▪ **stratégie** *nf* strategy ▪ **stratégique** *adj* strategic

stress [stʀɛs] *nm inv* stress ▪ **stressant, -ante** *adj* stressful ▪ **stressé, -ée** *adj* under stress, *Fam* stressed (out) ▪ **stresser 1** *vt* to put under stress, *Fam* to stress (out) **2** *vi Fam* to stress

strict, -e [stʀikt] *adj* (*principes, professeur*) strict; (*tenue, vérité*) plain; **le s. minimum** the bare minimum; **mon droit le plus s.** my basic right; **dans la plus stricte intimité** in the strictest privacy ▪ **strictement** [-əmɑ̃] *adv* strictly; (*vêtu*) plainly

strident, -ente [stʀidɑ̃, -ɑ̃t] *adj* shrill, strident

strie [stʀi] *nf* (*sillon*) groove; (*de couleur*) streak ▪ **strier** *vt* to streak

string [stʀiŋ] *nm* (*slip*) G-string, thong

strip-tease [stʀiptiz] *nm* striptease ▪ **strip-teaseur** *nm* (*male*) stripper ▪ **strip-teaseuse** *nf* stripper

strophe [stʀɔf] *nf* verse, stanza

structure [stʀyktyʀ] *nf* structure ▪ **structural, -e, -aux, -ales** *adj* structural ▪ **structurer** *vt* to structure

STS [ɛstɛɛs] (*abrév* **section de technicien supérieur**) *nf* = two-year advanced vocational course, taken after the baccalauréat

stuc [styk] *nm* stucco

studieux, -ieuse [stydjø, -jøz] *adj* studious; (*vacances*) devoted to study

studio [stydjo] *nm* (*de cinéma, de télévision, de*

peintre) studio; (*logement*) *Br* studio flat, *Am* studio apartment

stupéfait, -aite [stypefɛ, -ɛt] *adj* amazed, astounded (**de** at, by) ▪ **stupéfaction** *nf* amazement

stupéfier [stypefje] *vt* to amaze, to astound ▪ **stupéfiant, -ante 1** *adj* amazing, astounding **2** *nm* drug, narcotic

stupeur [stypœʀ] *nf* (*étonnement*) amazement; (*inertie*) stupor

stupide [stypid] *adj* stupid ▪ **stupidement** *adv* stupidly ▪ **stupidité** *nf* stupidity; (*action, parole*) stupid thing

style [stil] *nm* style; **meubles de s.** period furniture ▪ **stylisé, -ée** *adj* stylized ▪ **styliste** *nmf* stylist ▪ **stylistique** *adj* stylistic

stylé, -ée [stile] *adj* (*personnel*) well-trained

stylo [stilo] *nm* pen; **s. à bille** ballpoint (pen), *Br* biro®; **s. à encre, s.-plume** fountain pen

su, sue [sy] *pp de* **savoir**

suave [sɥav] *adj* (*odeur, voix*) sweet

subalterne [sybaltɛʀn] *adj & nmf* subordinate

subconscient, -ente [sypkɔ̃sjɑ̃, -ɑ̃t] *adj & nm* subconscious

subdiviser [sybdivize] *vt* to subdivide (**en** into) ▪ **subdivision** *nf* subdivision

subir [sybiʀ] *vt* to undergo; (*conséquences, défaite, perte, tortures*) to suffer; (*influence*) to be under; **faire s. qch à qn** to subject sb to sth; *Fam* **s. qn** (*supporter*) to put up with sb

subit, -ite [sybi, -it] *adj* sudden ▪ **subitement** *adv* suddenly

subjectif, -ive [sybʒɛktif, -iv] *adj* subjective ▪ **subjectivement** *adv* subjectively ▪ **subjectivité** *nf* subjectivity

subjonctif [sybʒɔ̃ktif] *nm Grammaire* subjunctive

subjuguer [sybʒyge] *vt* to subjugate, to subdue; (*envoûter*) to captivate

sublime [syblim] *adj & nm* sublime ▪ **sublimer** *vt* (*passion*) to sublimate

submerger [sybmɛʀʒe] *vt* to submerge; *Fig* (*envahir*) to overwhelm; *Fig* **submergé de travail** snowed under with work; **submergé par** (*ennemi, foule*) swamped by ▪ **submersible** *nm* submarine

subodorer [sybɔdɔʀe] *vt Fam* to scent

subordonner [sybɔʀdɔne] *vt* to subordinate (**à** to) ▪ **subordination** *nf* subordination ▪ **subordonné, -ée 1** *adj* subordinate (**à** to); **être s. à** (*dépendre de*) to depend on **2** *nmf* subordinate **3** *nf Grammaire* **subordonnée** subordinate clause

subreptice [sybʀɛptis] *adj* surreptitious ▪ **subrepticement** *adv* surreptitiously

subside [sypsid] *nm* grant, subsidy

subsidiaire [sybsidjɛʀ] *adj* subsidiary; **question s.** (*de concours*) deciding question

subsister [sybziste] **1** *vi* (*chose*) to remain;

(personne) to subsist **2** *v impersonnel* to remain; **il subsiste un doute/une erreur** there remains some doubt/an error ▪ **subsistance** *nf* subsistence

substance [sypstãs] *nf* substance; *Fig* **en s.** in essence ▪ **substantiel, -ielle** *adj* substantial

substantif [sypstãtif] *nm Grammaire* noun

substituer [sypstitɥe] **1** *vt* to substitute (**à** for) **2 se substituer** *vpr* **se s. à qn** to take the place of sb, to substitute for sb ▪ **substitution** *nf* substitution; **produit de s.** substitute (product); **maternité de s.** surrogacy

substitut [sypstity] *nm (produit)* substitute (**de** for); *(magistrat)* deputy public prosecutor

subterfuge [sypterfyʒ] *nm* subterfuge

subtil, -e [syptil] *adj* subtle ▪ **subtilité** *nf* subtlety

subtiliser [syptilize] *vt Fam (dérober)* to make off with

subvenir* [sybvənir] *vi* **s. à** *(besoins, frais)* to meet

subvention [sybvãsjɔ̃] *nf* subsidy ▪ **subventionner** *vt* to subsidize

subversif, -ive [sybvɛrsif, -iv] *adj* subversive ▪ **subversion** *nf* subversion

suc [syk] *nm (gastrique, de fruit)* juice; *(de plante)* sap

succédané [syksedane] *nm* substitute (**de** for)

succéder [syksede] **1** *vi* **s. à qn** to succeed sb; **s. à qch** to follow sth, to come after sth **2 se succéder** *vpr (choses, personnes)* to follow one another

succès [syksɛ] *nm* success; **s. de librairie** *(livre)* best-seller; **avoir du s.** to be successful; **à s.** *(auteur, film)* successful; **avec s.** successfully

successeur [syksesœr] *nm* successor ▪ **successif, -ive** *adj* successive ▪ **successivement** *adv* successively ▪ **succession** *nf* succession (**de** of, **à** to); *(série)* sequence (**de** of); *(patrimoine)* inheritance, estate; **prendre la s. de qn** to succeed sb

succinct, -incte [syksɛ̃, -ɛ̃t] *adj* succinct, brief

succion [sy(k)sjɔ̃] *nf* suction

succomber [sykɔ̃be] *vi (mourir)* to die; **s. à** *(céder à)* to succumb to; **s. à ses blessures** to die of one's wounds

succulent, -ente [sykylã, -ãt] *adj* succulent

succursale [sykyrsal] *nf (de magasin, de banque)* branch; **magasin à succursales multiples** chain store

sucer [syse] *vt* to suck ▪ **sucette** *nf* lollipop; *(pour bébé)* Br dummy, Am pacifier

sucre [sykr] *nm* sugar; *(morceau)* sugar lump; **s. cristallisé** granulated sugar; **s. en morceaux** lump sugar; **s. en poudre, s. semoule** Br caster sugar, Am finely ground sugar; **s. d'orge** barley sugar

sucrer [sykre] *vt* to sugar, to sweeten ▪ **sucré, -ée** *adj* sweet, sugary; *(artificiellement)* sweetened; *Fig (doucereux)* sugary, syrupy

sucrerie [sykrəri] *nf (usine)* sugar refinery; **sucreries** *(bonbons)* Br sweets, Am candy

sucrier, -ière [sykrije, -jɛr] **1** *adj* **industrie sucrière** sugar industry **2** *nm (récipient)* sugar bowl

sud [syd] **1** *nm* south; **au s.** in the south; *(direction)* (to the) south (**de** of); **du s.** *(vent, direction)* southerly; *(ville)* southern; *(gens)* from *or* in the south; **l'Afrique du S.** South Africa **2** *adj inv (côte)* south(ern) ▪ **sudafricain, -aine** *(mpl* sud-africains, *fpl* sudafricaines) **1** *adj* South African **2** *nmf* **S.-Africain, S.-Africaine** South African ▪ **sudaméricain, -aine** *(mpl* sud-américains, *fpl* sud-américaines) **1** *adj* South American **2** *nmf* **S.-Américain, S.-Américaine** South American ▪ **sud-est** *nm & adj inv* south-east ▪ **sud-ouest** *nm & adj inv* south-west

Suède [sɥɛd] *nf* **la S.** Sweden ▪ **suédois, -oise** **1** *adj* Swedish **2** *nmf* **S., Suédoise** Swede **3** *nm (langue)* Swedish

suer [sɥe] **1** *vi* to sweat; *Fam* **faire s. qn** to get on sb's nerves; *Fam* **se faire s.** to be bored stiff **2** *vt Fig* **s. sang et eau** to sweat blood ▪ **sueur** *nf* sweat; **(tout) en s.** sweating; *Fam* **avoir des sueurs froides** to break out in a cold sweat

suffire* [syfir] **1** *vi* to be enough (**à** for); **ça suffit!** that's enough! **2** *v impersonnel* **il suffit de faire qch** one only has to do sth; **il suffit d'une goutte/d'une heure pour faire qch** a drop/an hour is enough to do sth; **il ne me suffit pas de faire qch** I'm not satisfied with doing sth **3 se suffire** *vpr* **se s. à soi-même** to be self-sufficient

suffisance [syfizãs] *nf (vanité)* conceit

suffisant, -ante [syfizã, -ãt] *adj (satisfaisant)* sufficient, adequate; *(vaniteux)* conceited ▪ **suffisamment** [-amã] *adv* sufficiently; **s. de** enough, sufficient

suffixe [syfiks] *nm Grammaire* suffix

suffoquer [syfɔke] *vti* to choke, to suffocate; *Fig* **s. qn** *(étonner)* to astound sb, to stagger sb ▪ **suffocant, -ante** *adj* stifling, suffocating ▪ **suffocation** *nf* suffocation; *(sensation)* feeling of suffocation

suffrage [syfraʒ] *nm Pol (voix)* vote; **s. universel** universal suffrage; **suffrages exprimés** *(valid)* votes cast; *Fig* **remporter tous les suffrages** to win universal approval

suggérer [sygʒere] *vt (proposer)* to suggest (**à** to; **de faire** doing; **que** + *subjunctive* that); *(évoquer)* to suggest ▪ **suggestif, -ive** *adj* suggestive ▪ **suggestion** *nf* suggestion

suicide [sɥisid] *nm* suicide ▪ **suicidaire** *adj* suicidal ▪ **suicidé, -ée** *nmf* suicide (victim) ▪ **se suicider** *vpr* to commit suicide

suie [sɥi] *nf* soot

suif [sɥif] *nm* tallow

suinter [sɥɛ̃te] *vi* to ooze ▪**suintement** *nm* oozing

suis [sɥi] *voir* **être, suivre**

Suisse [sɥis] *nf* **la S.** Switzerland; **S. allemande/romande** German-speaking/French-speaking Switzerland ▪**suisse 1** *adj* Swiss **2** *nmf* **S.** Swiss; **les Suisses** the Swiss ▪**Suissesse** *nf* Swiss (woman)

suite [sɥit] *nf* (*reste*) rest; (*continuation*) continuation; (*de film, de roman*) sequel; (*série*) series, sequence; (*appartement, escorte*) & *Mus* suite; (*cohérence*) order; **suites** (*séquelles*) effects; (*résultats*) consequences; **faire s. (à)** to follow; **donner s. à** (*demande*) to follow up; **prendre la s. de qn** to take over from sb; **attendre la s.** to wait and see what happens next; **avoir de la s. dans les idées** to be single-minded (of purpose); **par la s.** afterwards; **par s. de** as a result of; **à la s.** one after another; **à la s. de** (*derrière*) behind; (*événement, maladie*) as a result of; **de s.** (*deux jours*) in a row

suivant¹, -ante [sɥivɑ̃, -ɑ̃t] **1** *adj* next, following; (*ci-après*) following **2** *nmf* next (one); **au s.!** next!, next person! ▪**suivant²** *prép* (*selon*) according to

suivi, -ie [sɥivi] *adj* (*régulier*) regular, steady; (*cohérent*) coherent; **peu/très s.** (*cours*) poorly/well attended

suivre* [sɥivr] **1** *vt* to follow; (*accompagner*) to go with, to accompany; (*cours*) to attend, to go to; (*malade*) to treat; **s. qn/qch des yeux** *ou* **du regard** to watch sb/sth; **s. l'exemple de qn** to follow sb's example; **s. le mouvement** to follow the crowd; **s. l'actualité** to follow events *or* the news **2** *vi* to follow; **faire s.** (*courrier, lettre*) to forward; **'à s.'** 'to be continued'; **comme suit** as follows **3 se suivre** *vpr* to follow each other

sujet¹, -ette [syʒɛ, -ɛt] **1** *adj* **s. à** (*maladie*) subject to; **s. à caution** (*information, nouvelle*) unconfirmed **2** *nmf* (*personne*) subject

sujet² [syʒɛ] *nm* (**a**) (*question*) & *Grammaire* subject; (*d'examen*) question; **au s. de** about; **à quel s.?** about what? (**b**) (*raison*) cause; **sujet(s) de dispute** grounds for dispute (**c**) (*individu*) subject; **un brillant s.** a brilliant student

sulfurique [sylfyrik] *adj* (*acide*) *Br* sulphuric, *Am* sulfuric

sultan [syltɑ̃] *nm* sultan

summum [sɔmɔm] *nm Fig* (*comble*) height

super [sypɛr] **1** *adj inv Fam* (*bon*) great, super **2** *nm* (*supercarburant*) *Br* four-star (petrol), *Am* premium *ou* hi(gh)-test gas ▪**supercarburant** *nm* high-octane *Br* petrol *or Am* gasoline ▪**supergrand** *nm Fam Pol* superpower

superbe [sypɛrb] *adj* superb

supercherie [sypɛrʃəri] *nf* deception

supérette [sypɛrɛt] *nf* convenience store, mini-market

superficie [sypɛrfisi] *nf* surface; (*dimensions*) area ▪**superficiel, -ielle** *adj* superficial ▪**superficiellement** *adv* superficially

superflu, -ue [sypɛrfly] *adj* superfluous

supérieur, -e [sypɛrjœr] **1** *adj* (*étages, partie*) upper; (*qualité, air, ton*) superior; **à l'étage s.** on the floor above; **s. à** (*meilleur que*) superior to, better than; (*plus grand que*) above, greater than; **s. à la moyenne** above average; **études supérieures** higher *or* university studies **2** *nmf* superior ▪**supériorité** *nf* superiority

superlatif, -ive [sypɛrlatif, -iv] *adj* & *nm Grammaire* superlative

supermarché [sypɛrmarʃe] *nm* supermarket

superposer [sypɛrpoze] *vt* (*objets*) to put on top of each other; (*images*) to superimpose ▪**superposition** *nf Ordinat* **mode de s.** overwrite mode

superproduction [sypɛrprɔdyksjɔ̃] *nf* (*film*) blockbuster

superpuissance [sypɛrpɥisɑ̃s] *nf Pol* superpower

supersonique [sypɛrsɔnik] *adj* supersonic

superstar [sypɛrstar] *nf* superstar

superstitieux, -ieuse [sypɛrstisjø, -jøz] *adj* superstitious ▪**superstition** *nf* superstition

superviser [sypɛrvize] *vt* to supervise

supplanter [syplɑ̃te] *vt* to take the place of

suppléer [syplee] *vi* **s. à** (*compenser*) to make up for ▪**suppléant, -ante** *adj* & *nmf* (*personne*) substitute, replacement; (*professeur*) **s.** substitute *or Br* supply teacher

supplément [syplemɑ̃] *nm* (*argent*) extra charge, supplement; (*de revue, de livre*) supplement; **en s.** extra; **un s. de** (*information, de travail*) extra, additional; **payer un s.** to pay extra, to pay a supplement ▪**supplémentaire** *adj* extra, additional

supplication [syplikasjɔ̃] *nf* plea, entreaty

supplice [syplis] *nm* torture; *Fig* **au s.** in agony ▪**supplicier** *vt* to torture

supplier [syplije] *vt* **s. qn de faire qch** to beg sb to do sth; **je vous en supplie!** I beg you! ▪**suppliant, -ante** *adj* (*regard*) imploring

support [sypɔr] *nm* support; (*d'instrument*) stand; *Fig* (*moyen*) medium; **s. audio-visuel** audio-visual aid

supporter¹ [sypɔrte] *vt* (*malheur, conséquences*) to bear, to stand, to endure; (*chaleur*) to withstand; (*plafond*) to support; (*frais*) to bear; (*affront*) to suffer; **je ne peux pas la s.** I can't bear *or* stand her ▪**supportable** *adj* bearable; (*excusable, passable*) tolerable

supporter² [sypɔrtɛr] *nm* (*de football*) supporter

supposer [sypoze] *vt* to suppose, to assume (**que** that); (*impliquer*) to imply (**que** that); **à**

s. *ou* **en supposant que...** *(+ subjunctive)* supposing (that)... ■**supposition** *nf* assumption, supposition

suppositoire [sypozitwar] *nm* suppository

suppression [sypresjɔ̃] *nf* removal; *(de mot)* deletion; *(de train)* cancellation; *(d'emplois)* axing

supprimer [syprime] **1** *vt* to get rid of, to remove; *(mot, passage)* to cut out, to delete; *(train)* to cancel; *(tuer)* to do away with; **s. des emplois** to axe jobs; **s. qch à qn** to take sth away from sb **2 se supprimer** *vpr (se suicider)* to do away with oneself

> Il faut noter que le verbe anglais **to suppress** est un faux ami. Il signifie **réprimer** ou **interdire**.

supputer [sypyte] *vt* to calculate

suprématie [sypremasi] *nf* supremacy

suprême [syprɛm] *adj* supreme

sur [syr] *prép* on, upon; *(par-dessus)* over; *(au sujet de)* on, about; **six s. dix** six out of ten; **un jour s. deux** every other day; **six mètres s. dix** six metres by ten; **coup s. coup** blow after *or* upon blow; **s. ce** after which, and then; *(maintenant)* and now; **s. votre gauche** to *or* on your left; **mettre/monter s. qch** to put/climb on (to) sth; **aller s. ses vingt ans** to be approaching twenty; **être s. le départ** to be about to leave

sûr, sûre [syr] *adj* sure, certain *(de* of; *que* that); *(digne de confiance)* reliable; *(lieu)* safe; *(avenir)* secure; *(goût)* discerning; *(jugement)* sound; *(main)* steady; **c'est s. que...** *(+ indicative)* it's certain that...; **s. de soi** self-assured; *Fam* **être s. de son coup** to be quite sure of oneself; **bien s.!** of course!

surabondant, -ante [syrabɔ̃dɑ̃, -ɑ̃t] *adj* overabundant

suranné, -ée [syrane] *adj* outmoded

surcharge [syrʃarʒ] *nf* **(a)** *(poids)* excess weight; **s. de travail** extra work; **en s.** *(passagers)* extra **(b)** *(correction)* alteration *(à payer)* surcharge ■**surcharger** *vt (voiture, personne)* to overload *(de* with)

surchauffer [syrʃofe] *vt* to overheat

surchoix [syrʃwa] *adj inv* top-quality

surclasser [syrklase] *vt* to outclass

surcroît [syrkrwa] *nm* increase *(de* in); **de s., par s.** in addition

surdité [syrdite] *nf* deafness

surdose [syrdoz] *nf (de drogue)* overdose

surdoué, -ée [syrdwe] **1** *adj* exceptionally gifted **2** *nmf* gifted child

surélever [syrelve] *vt* to raise

sûrement [syrmɑ̃] *adv* certainly; *(sans danger)* safely

surenchère [syrɑ̃ʃɛr] *nf (offre d'achat)* higher bid ■**surenchérir** *vi* to bid higher *(sur* than)

surestimer [syrɛstime] *vt* to overestimate; *(tableau)* to overvalue

sûreté [syrte] *nf* safety; *(de l'État)* security; *(garantie)* surety; *(de geste)* sureness; *(de jugement)* soundness; **être en s.** to be safe; **mettre qn/qch en s.** to put sb/sth in a safe place; **pour plus de s.** to be on the safe side

surexcité, -ée [syrɛksite] *adj* overexcited

surf [sœrf] *nm Sport* surfing; **faire du s.** to surf, to go surfing ■**surfer** *vi Sport* to surf; *Ordinat* **s. sur le Net** to surf the Net ■**surfeur, -euse** *nmf Sport & Ordinat* surfer

surface [syrfas] *nf* surface; *(étendue)* (surface) area; **faire s.** *(sous-marin)* to surface; **(magasin à) grande s.** hypermarket; **de s.** *(politesse)* superficial

surfait, -aite [syrfɛ, -ɛt] *adj* overrated

surgelé, -ée [syrʒəle] *adj* frozen ■**surgelés** *nmpl* frozen foods

surgir [syrʒir] *vi* to appear suddenly *(de* from); *(problème)* to crop up

surhomme [syrɔm] *nm* superman ■**surhumain, -aine** *adj* superhuman

sur-le-champ [syrləʃɑ̃] *adv* immediately

surlendemain [syrlɑ̃dəmɛ̃] *nm* **le s.** two days later; **le s. de** two days after

surligner [syrliɲe] *vt* to highlight ■**surligneur** *nm* highlighter (pen)

surmener [syrməne] *vt*, **se surmener** *vpr* to overwork ■**surmenage** *nm* overwork

surmonter [syrmɔ̃te] *vt (être placé sur)* to surmount; *Fig (obstacle, peur)* to overcome

surnager [syrnaʒe] *vi* to float

surnaturel, -elle [syrnatyrɛl] *adj & nm* supernatural

surnom [syrnɔ̃] *nm* nickname ■**surnommer** *vt* to nickname

> Il faut noter que le nom anglais **surname** est un faux ami. Il signifie **nom de famille**.

surnombre [syrnɔ̃br] *nm* **en s.** too many; **je suis en s.** I am one too many

surpasser [syrpase] **1** *vt* to surpass *(en* in) **2 se surpasser** *vpr* to surpass oneself

surpeuplé, -ée [syrpœple] *adj* overpopulated

surplace [syrplas] *nm* **faire du s.** *(dans un embouteillage) & Fig* to be hardly moving

surplomb [syrplɔ̃] *nm* **en s.** overhanging ■**surplomber** *vti* to overhang

surplus [syrply] *nm* surplus

surprendre [syrprɑ̃dr] **1** *vt (étonner)* to surprise; *(prendre sur le fait)* to catch; *(secret)* to discover; *(conversation)* to overhear **2 se surprendre** *vpr* **se s. à faire qch** to find oneself doing sth ■**surprenant, -ante** *adj* surprising ■**surpris, -ise** *adj* surprised *(de* at; *que* + *subjunctive* that); **je suis s. de te voir** I'm surprised to see you ■**surprise** *nf* surprise; **prendre qn par s.** to catch sb unawares

surproduction [syrprɔdyksjɔ̃] *nf* overproduction

surréaliste [syrrealist] *adj & nmf (poète, peintre)* surrealist; *Fam (bizarre)* surrealistic **•surréalisme** *nm* surrealism

sursaut [syrso] *nm* (sudden) start *ou* jump; **s. d'énergie** burst of energy; **se réveiller en s.** to wake (up) with a start **•sursauter** *vi* to jump, start

sursis [syrsi] *nm (à l'armée)* deferment; *Fig (répit)* reprieve; **un an (de prison) avec s.** a one-year suspended sentence

surtaxe [syrtaks] *nf* surcharge **•surtaxé, -ée** *adj Tél (numéro)* premium-rate

surtout [syrtu] *adv* especially; *(avant tout)* above all; **s. pas** certainly not; *Fam* **s. que** especially since *ou* as…

surveiller [syrveje] **1** *vt (garder)* to watch, to keep an eye on; *(contrôler)* to supervise; *(épier)* to watch; *Fig* **s. son langage/sa santé** to watch one's language/health **2 se surveiller** *vpr* to watch oneself **•surveillance** *nf* watch (**sur** over); *(de travaux, d'ouvriers)* supervision; *(de police)* surveillance **•surveillant, -ante** *nmf (de lycée)* supervisor (in charge of discipline); *(de prison)* (prison) guard, *Br* warder; *(de chantier)* supervisor; **s. de plage** lifeguard

> Il faut noter que les termes anglais **surveyor** et **to survey** sont des faux amis. Le premier signifie **géomètre** et le second ne se traduit jamais par **surveiller**.

survenir* [syrvənir] *vi (arriver)* to occur; *(personne)* to turn up

survêtement [syrvetmɑ̃] *nm* tracksuit

survie [syrvi] *nf* survival **•survivre*** *vi* to survive (**à qch** sth); **s. à qn** to outlive sb **•survivance** *nf (chose)* survival, relic **•survivant, -ante** *nmf* survivor

survol [syrvɔl] *nm* **le s. de** *(en avion)* flying over; *Fig (question)* the overview of **•survoler** *vt* to fly over; *Fig (question)* to skim over

survolté, -ée [syrvɔlte] *adj (surexcité)* overexcited

sus [sys] **en sus** *adv Littéraire* in addition

susceptible [syseptibl] *adj (ombrageux)* touchy, sensitive; **s. de** *(interprétations)* open to; **s. de faire qch** likely *ou* liable to do sth; *(capable)* able to do sth **•susceptibilité** *nf* touchiness, sensitivity

susciter [sysite] *vt (sentiment)* to arouse; *(ennuis, obstacles)* to create

suspect, -ecte [syspɛ, -ɛkt] **1** *adj* suspicious, suspect; **s. de qch** suspected of sth **2** *nm* suspect **•suspecter** *vt (personne)* to suspect (**de qch** of sth; **de faire** of doing); *(sincérité)* to question, to suspect

suspendre [syspɑ̃dr] **1** *vt (accrocher)* to hang (up) (**à** on); *(destituer, interrompre, différer)* to

suspend **2 se suspendre** *vpr* **se s. à** to hang from **•suspendu, -ue** *adj* **s. à** hanging from; **pont s.** suspension bridge; *Fig* **être s. aux paroles de qn** to hang upon sb's every word **•suspension** *nf (d'hostilités, d'employé, de véhicule)* suspension

suspens [syspɑ̃] **en suspens** *adv (affaire, travail)* in abeyance; *(en l'air)* suspended

suspense [syspɛns] *nm* suspense

suspicion [syspisjɔ̃] *nf* suspicion

susurrer [sysyre] *vti* to murmur

suture [sytyr] *nf* suture; *Méd* **point de s.** stitch **•suturer** *vt* to stitch up

svelte [svɛlt] *adj* slender **•sveltesse** *nf* slenderness

SVP [ɛsvepe] *(abrév* **s'il vous plaît)** please

syllabe [silab] *nf* syllable

symbole [sɛ̃bɔl] *nm* symbol **•symbolique** *adj* symbolic; *(salaire, cotisation, loyer)* nominal; **geste s.** symbolic *ou* token gesture **•symboliser** *vt* to symbolize **•symbolisme** *nm* symbolism

symétrie [simetri] *nf* symmetry **•symétrique** *adj* symmetrical

sympa [sɛ̃pa] *adj inv Fam* nice

sympathie [sɛ̃pati] *nf (affinité)* liking; *(condoléances)* sympathy; **avoir de la s. pour qn** to be fond of sb **•sympathique** *adj* nice; *(accueil)* friendly **•sympathisant, -ante** *nmf (de parti politique)* sympathizer **•sympathiser** *vi* to get along well, *Br* to get on well (**avec** with)

> Il faut noter que les termes anglais **sympathy, sympathetic** et **to sympathize** sont des faux amis. Ils signifient respectivement **compassion, compréhensif** et **compatir**.

symphonie [sɛ̃fɔni] *nf* symphony **•symphonique** *adj* symphonic; **orchestre s.** symphony orchestra

symposium [sɛ̃pozjɔm] *nm* symposium

symptôme [sɛ̃ptom] *nm Méd & Fig* symptom **•symptomatique** *adj* symptomatic (**de** of)

synagogue [sinagɔg] *nf* synagogue

synchroniser [sɛ̃krɔnize] *vt* to synchronize

syncope [sɛ̃kɔp] *nf (évanouissement)* blackout; **tomber en s.** to black out

syndicat [sɛ̃dika] *nm (d'ouvriers)* (*Br* trade *or Am* labor) union; *(de patrons)* association; **s. d'initiative** tourist (information) office **•syndical, -e, -aux, -ales** *adj* **réunion syndicale** (*Br* trade *or Am* labor) union meeting **•syndicalisme** *nm Br* trade *or Am* labor unionism **•syndicaliste 1** *nmf Br* trade *or Am* labor unionist **2** *adj* **esprit/idéal s.** union spirit/ideal

syndiquer [sɛ̃dike] **1** *vt* to unionize **2 se syndiquer** *vpr (adhérer)* to join a (*Br* trade *or Am* labor) union **•syndiqué, -ée** *nmf (Br* trade *or Am* labor) union member

syndrome [sɛ̃drom] *nm Méd & Fig* syndrome; **s. immunodéficitaire acquis** acquired immune deficiency syndrome; **syndrome prémenstruel** premenstrual syndrome, *Br* premenstrual tension

synonyme [sinɔnim] **1** *adj* synonymous (**de** with) **2** *nm* synonym

syntaxe [sɛ̃taks] *nf (grammaire)* syntax

synthèse [sɛ̃tez] *nf* synthesis ▪ **synthétique** *adj* synthetic

synthétiseur [sɛ̃tetizœr] *nm* synthesizer

syphilis [sifilis] *nf Méd* syphilis

Syrie [siri] *nf* la S. Syria ▪ **syrien, -ienne 1** *adj* Syrian **2** *nmf* S., **Syrienne** Syrian

système [sistɛm] *nm (structure, réseau) & Anat* system; **le s. immunitaire** the immune system; **le s. nerveux** the nervous system; *Fam* **le s. D** resourcefulness; *Ordinat* **s. d'exploitation** operating system ▪ **systématique** *adj* systematic ▪ **systématiquement** *adv* systematically

T, t [te] *nm inv* T, t

t' [t] *voir* **te**

ta [ta] *voir* **ton¹**

tabac [taba] *nm* tobacco; *(magasin) Br* tobacconist's (shop), *Am* tobacco store; *Fam* **faire un t.** to be a big hit; *Fam* **passer qn à t.** to beat sb up; *Fam* **passage à t.** beating up; **t. à priser** snuff ▪ **tabasser** *vt Fam* to beat up; **se faire t.** to get beaten up

table [tabl] *nf* (a) *(meuble)* table; *(d'école)* desk; **mettre/débarrasser la t.** to set *or Br* lay/clear the table; **être à t.** to be sitting at the table; **à t.!** food's ready!; *Fig* **faire t. rase** to make a clean sweep (**de** of); **mettre qn sur t. d'écoute** to tap sb's phone; **t. à repasser** ironing board; **t. de nuit/d'opération/de jeu** bedside/operating/ card table; **t. basse** coffee table; **t. ronde** *(réunion)* (round-table) conference; **t. roulante** *Br* (tea) trolley, *Am* (serving) cart (b) *(liste)* table; **t. des matières** table of contents

tableau, -x [tablo] *nm* (a) *(peinture)* picture, painting; *(image, description)* picture; *(scène de théâtre)* scene; **t. de maître** *(peinture)* old master (b) *(panneau)* board; *(liste)* list; *(graphique)* chart; **t. (noir)** (black)board; **t. d'affichage** *Br* noticeboard, *Am* bulletin board; **t. de bord** *(de véhicule)* dashboard; *(d'avion)* instrument panel; **t. des départs/arrivées** *(de gare, d'aéroport)* departures/arrivals board; *Scol* **avoir le t. d'honneur** *Br* to get one's name on the merit list, *Am* to make the honor roll

tabler [table] *vi* **t. sur qch** to count *or* rely on sth

tablette [tablet] *nf* *(de chocolat)* bar, slab; *(de lavabo)* shelf; *(de cheminée)* mantelpiece

tableur [tablœr] *nm Ordinat* spreadsheet

tablier [tablije] *nm* (a) *(vêtement)* apron; *(d'écolier)* smock; *Fig* **rendre son t.** to hand in one's notice (b) *(de pont)* roadway

tabou [tabu] *adj & nm* taboo

taboulé [tabule] *nm Culin* tabbouleh

tabouret [taburɛ] *nm* stool

tabulateur [tabylatœr] *nm* *(d'ordinateur, de machine à écrire)* tabulator

tac [tak] *nm* **répondre du t. au t.** to give tit for tat

tache [taʃ] *nf* mark; *(salissure)* stain; *Péj* **faire t.** *(détonner)* to jar, to stand out; *Fig* **faire t. d'huile** to spread ▪ **tacher** *vt, se tacher* *vpr (tissu)* to stain

tâche [taʃ] *nf* task, job; **être à la t.** to be on piecework; *Fig* **se tuer à la t.** to work oneself to death; **tâches ménagères** housework

tâcher [taʃe] *vi* **t. de faire qch** to try to do sth

tâcheron [taʃrɔ̃] *nm Péj* drudge

tacheté, -ée [taʃte] *adj* speckled (**de** with)

tacite [tasit] *adj* tacit ▪ **tacitement** *adv* tacitly

taciturne [tasityrn] *adj* taciturn

tacot [tako] *nm Fam (voiture)* (old) wreck, *Br* banger

tact [takt] *nm* tact; **avoir du t.** to be tactful

tactile [taktil] *adj* tactile

tactique [taktik] **1** *adj* tactical **2** *nf* tactics *(sing)*; **une t.** a tactic

tag [tag] *nm* tag *(spray-painted graffiti)* ▪ **taguer** *vti* to tag, to spray-paint ▪ **tagueur, -euse** *nmf* graffiti artist, tagger

Tahiti [taiti] *nm* Tahiti ▪ **tahitien, -ienne** [taisjɛ̃, -jɛn] **1** *adj* Tahitian **2** *nmf* **T., Tahitienne** Tahitian

tai-chi [tajʃi] *nm* tai chi

taie [te] *nf* **t. d'oreiller** pillowcase, pillowslip

taillade [tajad] *nf* gash, slash ▪ **taillader** *vt* to gash, to slash

taille¹ [taj] *nf* (a) *(hauteur)* height; *(dimension, mesure)* size; **de haute t.** *(personne)* tall; **de petite t.** short; **de t. moyenne** medium-sized; *Fig* **être de t. à faire qch** to be capable of doing sth; *Fam* **de t.** *(erreur, objet)* enormous (b) *(ceinture)* waist; **tour de t.** waist measurement

taille² [taj] *nf* cutting; *(de haie)* trimming; *(d'arbre)* pruning ▪ **taillé, -ée** *adj* **t. en athlète** built like an athlete; *Fig* **t. pour faire qch** cut out for doing sth ▪ **tailler** **1** *vt* to cut; *(haie, barbe)* to trim; *(arbre)* to prune; *(crayon)* to sharpen; *(vêtement)* to cut out **2** **se tailler** *upr* (a) **se t. la part du lion** to take the lion's share (b) *Fam (partir)* to beat it

taille-crayon [tajkrɛjɔ̃] *nm inv* pencil-sharpener

tailleur [tajœr] *nm (personne)* tailor; *(costume)* suit

taillis [taji] *nm* copse, coppice

tain [tɛ̃] *nm (de glace)* silvering; **glace sans t.** two-way mirror

taire* [tɛr] **1** *vt* to say nothing about **2** *vi* **faire t. qn** to silence sb **3** **se taire** *upr (ne rien dire)* to keep quiet (**sur qch** about sth); *(cesser de parler)* to stop talking, to fall silent; **tais-toi!** be quiet!

Taïwan [tajwan] *nm ou f* Taiwan ▪ **taïwanais, -aise1** *adj* Taiwanese **2** *nmf* T., Taïwanaise Taiwanese

talc [talk] *nm* talcum powder, talc

talé, -ée [tale] *adj (fruit)* bruised

talent [talɑ̃] *nm* talent; **avoir du t.** to be talented ▪ **talentueux, -ueuse** *adj* talented

talion [taljɔ̃] *nm* **la loi du t.** an eye for an eye

talisman [talismɑ̃] *nm* talisman

talkie-walkie [talkiwalki] *(pl* **talkies-walkies)** *nm* walkie-talkie

taloche [talɔʃ] *nf Fam (gifle)* clout

talon [talɔ̃] *nm* **(a)** *(de chaussure)* heel; **tourner les talons** to walk away; **c'est son t. d'Achille** it's his Achilles' heel; **(chaussures à) talons hauts** high heels, high-heeled shoes; **talons aiguilles** stiletto heels **(b)** *(de chèque)* stub, counterfoil; *(bout de pain)* crust; *(de jambon)* heel ▪ **talonnette** *nf (pour chaussure)* heel pad

talonner [talɔne] **1** *vt (fugitif)* to follow on the heels of **2** *vi Rugby* to heel

talus [taly] *nm* slope

tambour [tɑ̃bur] *nm (de machine, instrument de musique)* drum; *(personne)* drummer; **sans t. ni trompette** quietly, without fuss ▪ **tambourin** *nm* tambourine ▪ **tambouriner** *vi (avec les doigts)* to drum **(sur** on)

tamis [tami] *nm* sieve ▪ **tamiser** *vt (farine)* to sift; *(lumière)* to filter

Tamise [tamiz] *nf* **la T.** the Thames

tampon [tɑ̃pɔ̃] *nm* **(a)** *(marque, instrument)* stamp; **t. dateur** date stamp; **t. encreur** ink pad; **lettre à renvoyer avant minuit le t. de la poste faisant foi** letter to be postmarked no later than midnight **(b)** *(bouchon)* plug, stopper; *(de coton)* wad, pad; *(pour pansement)* swab; **t. (hygiénique** *ou* **périodique)** tampon; **t. à récurer** scouring pad **(c)** *(de train)* & *Fig* buffer; **état t.** buffer state

tamponner [tɑ̃pɔne] **1** *vt (lettre, document)* to stamp; *(visage)* to dab; *(plaie)* to swab; *(train, voiture)* to crash into **2** **se tamponner** *vpr* to crash into each other ▪ **tamponneuses** *adj fpl* **autos t.** Dodgems®, bumper cars

tam-tam [tamtam] *(pl* **tam-tams)** *nm (tambour)* tom-tom

tandem [tɑ̃dɛm] *nm (bicyclette)* tandem; *Fig (duo)* duo; **travailler en t.** to work in tandem

tandis [tɑ̃di] **tandis que** *conj (simultanéité)* while; *(contraste)* whereas, while

tangent, -ente [tɑ̃ʒɑ̃, -ɑ̃t] *adj* tangential **(à** to); *Fam (juste)* touch and go ▪ **tangente** *nf* tangent

tangible [tɑ̃ʒibl] *adj* tangible

tango [tɑ̃go] *nm* tango

tanguer [tɑ̃ge] *vi (bateau, avion)* to pitch ▪ **tangage** *nm (de bateau, d'avion)* pitching

tanière [tanjɛr] *nf* den, lair

tank [tɑ̃k] *nm* tank

tanker [tɑ̃kɛr] *nm (navire)* tanker

tanner [tane] *vt (cuir)* to tan ▪ **tanné, -ée** *adj (visage)* weather-beaten

tant [tɑ̃] *adv (travailler)* so much **(que** that); **t. de** *(pain, temps)* so much **(que** that); *(gens, choses)* so many **(que** that); **t. de fois** so often, so many times; **t. que** *(autant que)* as much as; *(aussi fort que)* as hard as; *(aussi longtemps que)* as long as; **t. que** *(considéré comme)* as; **t. bien que mal** more or less, somehow or other; **t. mieux!** so much the better!; **t. pis!** too bad!; **t. mieux pour toi!** good for you!; **t. pis pour toi!** too bad (for you)!; **t. soit peu** (even) remotely *or* slightly; **un t. soit peu** somewhat; **t. s'en faut** far from it

tante [tɑ̃t] *nf* aunt

tantinet [tɑ̃tinɛ] *nm & adv* **un t.** a tiny bit **(de** of)

tantôt [tɑ̃to] *adv* **(a)** **t....t...** sometimes... sometimes... **(b)** *(cet après-midi)* this afternoon

tapage [tapaʒ] *nm* din, disturbance ▪ **tapageur, -euse** *adj (bruyant)* rowdy; *(criard)* flashy

tape [tap] *nf* slap

tape-à-l'œil [tapalœj] *adj inv Fam* flashy, showy

taper [tape] **1** *vt (enfant, cuisse)* to slap; *(table)* to bang; **t. qch à la machine** to type sth; **t. au toucher** to touch-type; *Fam* **t. qn** *(emprunter de l'argent à)* to cadge money off sb **2** *vi (soleil)* to beat down; **t. du pied** to stamp one's foot; **t. à la porte** to knock on the door; **t. à la machine** to type; **t. sur qch** to bang on sth; *Fam* **t. sur qn** *(critiquer)* to knock sb; *Fam* **t. sur les nerfs de qn** to get on sb's nerves; *Fam* **t. dans** *(provisions)* to dig into; *Fam* **t. dans l'œil à qn** to take sb's fancy **3 se taper** *vpr Fam (travail)* to get landed with; *Fam (nourriture)* to scoff; *(boisson)* to sink; **je me taperais bien une bière** I could murder a beer; **très** *Fam (s'en moquer)* **elle s'en tape** she doesn't give *Br* a toss *or Am* a rat's ass ▪ **tapant, -ante** *adj* **à huit heures tapantes** at eight sharp

tapeur, -euse [tapœr, -øz] *nmf Fam* scrounger

tapioca [tapjɔka] *nm* tapioca

tapir [tapir] **se tapir** *vpr* to crouch ▪ **tapi, -ie** *adj* crouching, crouched

tapis [tapi] *nm* carpet; **envoyer qn au t.** *(abattre)* to floor sb; **mettre qch sur le t.** *(sujet)* to bring sth up for discussion; **dérouler le t. rouge** to put out the red carpet; **t. de bain** bath mat; **t. de sol** earth mat; *Ordinat* **t. de souris** mouse mat; **t. roulant** *(pour marchandises)* conveyor belt; *(pour personnes)* moving walkway ▪ **tapis-brosse** *(pl* **tapis-brosses)** *nm* doormat

tapisser [tapise] *vt (mur)* to (wall)paper; *(de tentures)* to hang with tapestry; *Fig (recouvrir)* to cover ▪ **tapisserie** *nf (papier peint)* wallpaper; *(broderie)* tapestry; *Fig* **faire t.** *(jeune* *fille)* to be a wallflower ■**tapissier, -ière** *nmf (qui pose des tissus)* upholsterer

tapoter [tapɔte] **1** *vt* to tap; *(joue)* to pat **2** *vi* **t. sur** to tap (on)

taquin, -ine [takɛ̃, -in] *adj* teasing ■**taquiner** *vt* to tease ■**taquineries** *nfpl* teasing

tarabiscoté, -ée [tarabiskɔte] *adj* overelaborate

tarabuster [tarabyste] *vt (idée)* to trouble

tarauder [tarode] *vt* to gnaw at

tard [tar] *adv* late; **plus t.** later (on); **au plus t.** at the latest; **sur le t.** late in life

tarder [tarde] **1** *vi (lettre, saison)* to be a long time coming; **sans t.** without delay; **t. à faire qch** to take one's time doing sth; **elle ne va pas t.** she won't be long **2** *v impersonnel* **il me tarde de le faire** I can't wait to do it, I'm dying to do it

tardif, -ive [tardif, -iv] *adj* late; *(regrets)* belated ■**tardivement** *adv* late

tare [tar] *nf (poids)* tare; *Fig (défaut)* defect ■**taré, -ée** *adj Fam (fou)* mad

tarentule [tarɑ̃tyl] *nf* tarantula

targuer [targe] **se targuer** *upr* **se t. de qch/de faire qch** to pride oneself on sth/on doing sth

tarif [tarif] *nm (prix)* rate; *(de train)* fare; *(tableau)* price list, *Br* tariff; **plein t.** full price; *(de train, bus)* full fare ■**tarification** *nf* pricing

tarir [tarir] *vti,* **se tarir** *upr (fleuve)* & *Fig* to dry up; *Fig* **ne pas t. d'éloges sur qn** to rave about sb

tarot [taro] *nm* tarot

tartare [tartar] *adj* **sauce t.** tartar(e) sauce

tarte [tart] **1** *nf (open)* pie, tart; *Fam* **ce n'est pas de la t.!** it isn't easy! **2** *adj inv Fam (sot)* silly ■**tartelette** [-ɔlɛt] *nf (small)* tart

tartine [tartin] *nf* slice of bread; **t. de beurre/de confiture** slice of bread and butter/jam ■**tartiner** *vt (beurre)* to spread; **fromage à t.** cheese spread

tartre [tartr] *nm (de bouilloire)* scale, *Br* fur; *(de dents)* tartar

tas [tɑ] *nm* pile, heap; **mettre qch en t.** to pile or heap sth up; *Fam* **un ou des t. de *(beaucoup)*** loads of; *Fam* **apprendre sur le t.** to learn on the job

tasse [tɑs] *nf* cup; **t. à café** coffee cup; **t. à thé** teacup; *Fam* **boire la t.** to swallow a mouthful *(when swimming)*

tasser [tɑse] **1** *vt* to pack (**dans** into); *(terre)* to pack down; *Fam* **un café bien tassé *(fort)*** a strong coffee **2** **se tasser** *upr (se serrer)* to squeeze up; *(sol)* to sink, to collapse; *(se voûter)* to become bowed; *Fam* **ça va se t.** *(s'arrangera)* things will settle down

tâter [tɑte] **1** *vt* to feel; *Fig* **t. le terrain** to see how the land lies **2** *vi* **t. de *(prison, métier)*** to have a taste of **3** **se tâter** *upr (hésiter)* to be in two minds

tatillon, -onne [tatijɔ̃, -ɔn] *adj Fam* finicky

tâtonner [tɑtɔne] *vi* to grope about ■**tâtonnement** *nm* **par t.** *(procéder)* by trial and error ■**tâtons** *adv* **avancer à t.** to feel one's way (along); **chercher qch à t.** to grope for sth

tatouer [tatwe] *vt (corps, dessin)* to tattoo; **se faire t.** to get a tattoo; **se faire t. un bateau sur le bras** to get a boat tattooed on one's arm ■**tatouage** *nm (dessin)* tattoo; *(action)* tattooing

taudis [todi] *nm* slum

taule [tol] *nf Fam (prison) Br* nick, *Am* can

taupe [top] *nf (animal, espion)* mole ■**taupinière** *nf* molehill

taureau, -x [tɔro] *nm* bull; **le T.** *(signe)* Taurus; **être T.** to be (a) Taurus ■**tauromachie** *nf* bullfighting

taux [to] *nm* rate; **t. d'alcool/de cholestérol** alcohol/cholesterol level; **t. d'intérêt/de change** interest/exchange rate; **t. de natalité/de mortalité** birth/death rate

taverne [tavɛrn] *nf* tavern

taxe [taks] *nf (impôt)* tax; **t. à la valeur ajoutée** value-added tax ■**taxation** *nf* taxation

taxer [takse] *vt (produit, personne, firme)* to tax; **t. qn de qch** to accuse sb of sth; *Fam* **t. qch à qn** *(voler)* to cadge sth off sb ■**taxé, -ée** *adj (produit)* taxed

taxi [taksi] *nm* taxi

tchador [tʃadɔr] *nm (voile)* chador

tchatcher [tʃatʃe] *vi Fam* to chat ■**tchatche** *nf Fam* **avoir de la t.** to have the gift of the gab ■**tchatcheur, -euse** *nmf Fam* smooth talker

Tchécoslovaquie [tʃekɔslɔvaki] *nf Anciennement* **la T.** Czechoslovakia ■**tchèque 1** *adj* Czech; **la République t.** the Czech Republic **2** *nmf* **T.** Czech **3** *nm (langue)* Czech

TD [tede] *(abrév* **travaux dirigés)** *nm Scol & Univ* ≃ tutorial

te [tə]

t' is used before a word beginning with a vowel or h mute.

pron personnel (**a**) *(complément direct)* you; **je te vois** I see you (**b**) *(indirect)* (to) you; **il te parle** he speaks to you; **elle te l'a dit** she told you (**c**) *(réfléchi)* yourself; **tu te laves** you wash yourself

technicien, -ienne [tɛknisjɛ̃, -jɛn] *nmf* technician ■**technique 1** *adj* technical **2** *nf* technique ■**techniquement** *adv* technically ■**technocrate** *nm* technocrat ■**technologie** *nf* technology; **haute t.** high tech(nology) ■**technologique** *adj* technological

teck [tɛk] *nm (bois)* teak

teckel [tekɛl] *nm* dachshund

tee-shirt [tiʃœrt] *nm* tee-shirt, T-shirt

teindre* [tɛ̃dr] **1** *vt* to dye; **t. qch en rouge** to dye sth red **2** **se teindre** *upr* **se t. (les cheveux)** to dye one's hair

teint [tɛ̃] *nm (de visage)* complexion; **bon** *ou* **grand t.** *(tissu) Br* colourfast, *Am* colorfast; *Fig Hum* **bon t.** *(catholique)* staunch

teinte [tɛ̃t] *nf* shade, tint ∎**teinter 1** *vt* to tint; *(bois)* to stain **2 se teinter** *vpr Fig* **se t. de** *(remarque, ciel)* to be tinged with

teinture [tɛ̃tyr] *nf* dyeing; *(produit)* dye ∎**teinturerie** [-rri] *nf (boutique)* (dry) cleaner's ∎**teinturier, -ière** *nmf* dry cleaner

tel, telle [tɛl] *adj* such; **un t. livre/homme** such a book/man; **un t. intérêt** such interest; **de tels mots** such words; **t. que** such as, like; **t. que je l'ai laissé** just as I left it; **laissez-le t. quel** leave it just as it is; **en tant que t., comme t.** as such; **t. ou t.** such and such; **rien de t. que…** (there's) nothing like…; **rien de t.** nothing like it; **t. père t. fils** like father like son

télé [tele] *nf FamTV, Br* telly; **à la t.** onTV, *Br* on (the) telly; **regarder la t.** to watchTV *or Br* on (the) telly ∎**téléfilm** *nm Br* TV film, *Am* TV movie ∎**télé-réalité** *nf* realityTV

téléachat [teleaʃa] *nm (d'articles présentés à la télévision)* teleshopping; *(sur Internet)* on-line shopping

télébenne [teleben] *nf,* **télécabine** [telekabin] *nf (cabine, système)* cable car

Télécarte® [telekart] *nf* phone card

télécharger [teleʃarʒe] *vt Ordinat* to download ∎**téléchargement** *nm* downloading, download

télécommande [telekɔmɑ̃d] *nf* remote control ∎**télécommander** *vt* to operate by remote control

télécommunications [telekɔmynikɑsjɔ̃] *nfpl* telecommunications

téléconférence [telekɔ̃ferɑ̃s] *nf Tél* conference call

télécopie [telekɔpi] *nf* fax ∎**télécopieur** *nm* fax (machine)

télégramme [telegram] *nm* telegram

télégraphe [telegraf] *nm* telegraph ∎**télégraphie** *nf* telegraphy ∎**télégraphier** *vt (message)* to wire, to cable (**que** that) ∎**télégraphique** *adj* **poteau/fil t.** telegraph pole/wire; *Fig* **style t.** telegraphic style

téléguider [telegide] *vt* to operate by remote control ∎**téléguidage** *nm* remote control

télématique [telematik] *nf* telematics *(sing)*

téléobjectif [teleɔbʒɛktif] *nm Phot* telephoto lens

télépathie [telepati] *nf* telepathy ∎**télépathique** *adj* telepathic

téléphérique [teleferik] *nm* cable car

téléphone [telefɔn] *nm* (tele)phone; **coup de t.** (phone) call; **passer un coup de t. à qn** to give sb a ring *or* a call; **au t.** on the (tele)phone; **avoir le t.** to be on the (tele)phone; **t. portable** mobile phone; **t. sans fil** cordless phone; *Fig* **apprendre qch par le t. arabe** to hear about sth on *or* through the grapevine ∎**téléphoner 1** *vt (nouvelle)* to (tele)phone (**à** to) **2** *vi* to (tele)phone; **t. à qn** to (tele)phone sb, to call sb (up) ∎**téléphonique** *adj* **appel t.** (tele)phone call

téléprompteur [teleprɔ̃ptœr] *nm* teleprompter, *Br* autocue

télescope [teleskɔp] *nm* telescope ∎**télescopique** *adj* telescopic

télescoper [teleskɔpe] **1** *vt (voiture, train)* to smash into **2 se télescoper** *vpr (voiture, train)* to concertina

téléscripteur [teleskriptœr] *nm Br* teleprinter, *Am* teletypewriter

télésiège [telesjɛʒ] *nm* chair lift

téléski [teleski] *nm* ski lift *or* tow

téléspectateur, -trice [telespɛktatœr, -tris] *nmf* (television) viewer

télétravail [teletravaj] *nm* teleworking ∎**télétravailleur, -euse** *nmf* teleworker

télévente [televɑ̃t] *nf* telesales

téléviser [televize] *vt* to televise ∎**téléviseur** *nm* television (set) ∎**télévision** *nf* television; **à la t.** on (the) television; **regarder la t.** to watch (the) television; **programme de t.** television programme; **t. à circuit fermé** closed-circuit television

télex [telɛks] *nm (service, message)* telex

telle [tɛl] *voir* **tel** ∎**tellement** *adv (si)* so; *(tant)* so much; **t. grand que…** so big that…; **crier t. que…** to shout so much that…; **t. de travail** so much work; **t. de soucis** so many worries; **tu aimes ça? – pas t.** *(pas beaucoup)* do you like it? – not much *or* a lot; **personne ne peut le supporter, t. il est bavard** nobody can stand him, he talks so much

tellurique [telyrik] *adj* **secousse t.** earth tremor

téméraire [temerɛr] *adj* reckless ∎**témérité** *nf* recklessness

témoigner [temwaɲe] **1** *vt (gratitude)* to show (**à qn** (to) sb); **t. que…** *(attester)* to testify that… **2** *vi Jur* to give evidence, to testify (**contre** against); **t. de qch** *(personne, attitude)* to testify to sth ∎**témoignage** *nm Jur* evidence, testimony; *(récit)* account; **faux t.** *(délit)* perjury; *Fig (d'affection)* token, sign (**de** of); **en t. de qch** as a token of sth

témoin [temwɛ̃] **1** *nm* (**a**) *Jur* witness; **t. à charge** witness for the prosecution; **être t. de qch** to witness sth (**b**) *(de relais)* baton **2** *adj* **appartement t.** *Br* show flat, *Am* model apartment

tempe [tɑ̃p] *nf Anat* temple

tempérament [tɑ̃peramɑ̃] *nm (caractère)* temperament; **acheter qch à t.** to buy sth on *Br* hire purchase *or Am* on the installment plan

tempérance [tɑ̃perɑ̃s] *nf* temperance

température [tãperatyr] *nf* temperature; **avoir de la t.** to have a temperature

tempérer [tãpere] *vt (ardeurs)* to moderate ▪ **tempéré, -ée** *adj (climat, zone)* temperate

tempête [tãpɛt] *nf* storm; **t. de neige** snowstorm, blizzard

tempêter [tãpete] *vi (crier)* to storm, to rage (**contre** against)

temple [tãpl] *nm (romain, grec)* temple; *(protestant)* church

tempo [tempo] *nm* tempo

temporaire [tãpɔrɛr] *adj* temporary ▪ **temporairement** *adv* temporarily

temporel, -elle [tãpɔrɛl] *adj* temporal; *(terrestre)* worldly

temporiser [tãpɔrize] *vi* to play for time

temps¹ [tã] *nm (durée, période, moment)* time; *Grammaire* tense; *(étape)* stage; **en t. de guerre** in wartime, in time of war; **avoir/trouver le t.** to have/find (the) time (**de faire** to do); **il est t.** it is time (**de faire** to do); **il était t.!** it was about time (too)!; **il est (grand) t. que vous partiez** it's (high) time you left; **ces derniers t.** lately; **de t. en t.** [dətãzãtã], **de t. à autre** [dətãzaotr] from time to time, now and again; **en t. utile** [ãtãzytil] in due course; **en t. voulu** in due course; **en même t.** at the same time (**que** as); **à t.** *(arriver)* in time; **à plein t.** *(travailler)* full-time; **à t. partiel** *(travailler)* part-time; **dans le t.** *(autrefois)* in the old days; **avec le t.** *(à la longue)* in time; **tout le t.** all the time; **de mon t.** in my time; **pendant un t.** for a while *or* time; *Fam* **par les t. qui courent** at the present time; **t. d'arrêt** pause, break; **t. libre** free time; *Fig* **t. mort** lull

temps² [tã] *nm (climat)* weather; **il fait beau/mauvais t.** the weather's fine/bad; **quel t. fait-il?** what's the weather like?

tenable [tənabl] *adj* bearable

tenace [tənas] *adj* stubborn, tenacious ▪ **ténacité** *nf* stubbornness, tenacity

tenailler [tənaje] *vt (faim, remords)* to torture

tenailles [tənaj] *nfpl (outil)* pincers

tenancier, -ière [tənãsje, -jɛr] *nmf (d'hôtel)* manager, *f* manageress

tenant, -ante [tənã, -ãt] **1** *nmf* **le t. du titre** *(champion)* the title holder **2** *nm (partisan)* supporter (**de** of) ▪ **tenants** *nmpl* **les t. et les aboutissants d'une question** the ins and outs of a question

tendance [tãdãs] *nf (penchant)* tendency; *(évolution)* trend (**à** towards); **avoir t. à faire qch** to tend to do sth, to have a tendency to do sth

tendancieux, -ieuse [tãdãsjø, -jøz] *adj Péj* tendentious

tendeur [tãdœr] *nm (à bagages)* elastic strap, *Am* bungee

tendon [tãdɔ̃] *nm Anat* tendon

tendre¹ [tãdr] **1** *vt* to stretch; *(main)* to hold out (**à qn** to sb); *(bras, jambe)* to stretch out; *(cou)* to strain, to crane; *(muscle)* to tense; *(arc)* to bend; *(piège)* to set, to lay; *(filet)* to spread; **t. qch à qn** to hold sth out to sb; *Fig* **t. l'oreille** to prick up one's ears **2** *vi* **t. à qch/à faire qch** to tend towards sth/to do sth **3 se tendre** *vpr (rapports)* to become strained ▪ **tendu, -ue** *adj (corde)* tight, taut; *(personne, situation, muscle)* tense; *(rapports)* strained

tendre² [tãdr] *adj (personne)* affectionate (**avec** to); *(parole, regard)* tender, loving; *(viande)* tender; *(bois, couleur)* soft; **depuis ma plus t. enfance** from my earliest childhood ▪ **tendrement** [-əmã] *adv* tenderly, lovingly ▪ **tendresse** *nf (affection)* affection, tenderness ▪ **tendreté** [-əte] *nf (de viande)* tenderness

ténèbres [tenɛbr] *nfpl* **les t.** the darkness ▪ **ténébreux, -euse** *adj* dark, gloomy; *(mystérieux)* mysterious

teneur [tənœr] *nf (de lettre)* content; **t. en alcool** alcohol content (**de** of)

tenir* [tənir] **1** *vt (à la main)* to hold; *(promesse, comptes, hôtel)* to keep; *(rôle)* to play; *(propos)* to utter; **t. sa droite** *(conducteur)* to keep to the right; **t. la route** *(véhicule)* to hold the road; *Fig* **t. sa langue** to hold one's tongue; **t. qch propre/chaud** to keep sth clean/hot; **je le tiens!** *(je l'ai attrapé)* I've got him!; **je le tiens de Louis** *(fait)* I got it from Louis; *(caractère héréditaire)* I get it from Louis **2** *vi (nœud)* to hold; *(neige, coiffure)* to last, to hold; *(résister)* to hold out; *(offre)* to stand; **t. à qn/qch** to be attached to sb/sth; **t. à la vie** to value life; **t. à faire qch** to be anxious to do sth; **t. dans qch** *(être contenu)* to fit into sth; **t. de qn** to take after sb; **tenez!** *(prenez)* here (you are)!; **tiens!** *(surprise)* well!, hey!; **ça tient à sa maladie** it's due to his/her illness **3** *v impersonnel* **il ne tient qu'à vous de le faire** it's up to you to do it **4 se tenir** *vpr (avoir lieu)* to be held; *(rester)* to remain; **se t. debout** to stand (up); **se t. droit** to stand up/sit up straight; **se t. par la main** to hold hands; **se t. bien** to behave oneself; **se t. à qch** to hold on to sth; **s'en t. à qch** *(se limiter à)* to stick to sth; **savoir à quoi s'en t.** to know what's what; *Fig* **tout se tient** it all hangs together

tennis [tenis] **1** *nm* tennis; *(terrain)* (tennis) court; **t. de table** table tennis **2** *nmpl (chaussures) Br* tennis shoes

ténor [tenɔr] *nm Mus* tenor

tension [tãsjɔ̃] *nf* tension; **t. artérielle** blood pressure; **avoir de la t.** to have high blood pressure

tentacule [tãtakyl] *nm* tentacle

tente [tãt] *nf* tent

tenter¹ [tãte] *vt (essayer)* to try; **t. de faire qch** to try *or* attempt to do sth ▪ **tentative** *nf* attempt;

t. d'assassinat attempted murder; **t. de suicide** suicide attempt

tenter² [tɑ̃te] *vt (faire envie à)* to tempt; **tenté de faire qch** tempted to do sth ▪ **tentant, -ante** *adj* tempting ▪ **tentation** *nf* temptation

tenture [tɑ̃tyr] *nf (wall)* hanging; *(de porte)* drape, curtain

tenu, -ue¹ [təny] **1** *pp de* **tenir 2** *adj* **t. de faire qch** obliged to do sth; **bien/mal t.** *(maison)* well/badly kept

ténu, -ue² [teny] *adj (fil)* fine; *(soupçon, différence)* tenuous; *(voix)* thin

tenue [təny] *nf* (a) *(vêtements)* clothes, outfit; **être en petite t.** to be scantily dressed; **t. de combat** *(uniforme)* battledress; **t. de soirée** evening dress (b) *(conduite)* (good) behaviour; *(maintien)* posture (c) *(de maison, d'hôtel)* running; *(de comptes)* keeping (d) **t. de route** *(de véhicule)* road-holding

ter [tɛr] *adj* **4 t.** *(adresse)* ≃ 4B

térébenthine [terebɑ̃tin] *nf* turpentine

Tergal® [tergal] *nm Br*Terylene®, *Am* Dacron®

tergiverser [tɛrʒivɛrse] *vi* to equivocate

terme [tɛrm] *nm* (a) *(mot)* term (b) *(date limite)* time (limit); *(fin)* end; **mettre un t. à qch** to put an end to sth; **à court/long t.** *(conséquences, projet)* short-/long-term; **être né avant/à t.** to be born prematurely/at (full) term (c) **moyen t.** *(solution)* middle course (d) **en bons/mauvais termes** on good/bad terms **(avec qn** with sb) (e) *(loyer)* rent; *(jour)* rent day; *(période)* rental period

terminal, -e, -aux, -ales [tɛrminal, -o] **1** *adj* final; *(phase de maladie)* terminal **2** *adj & nf Scol* **(classe) terminale** *Br* ≃ sixth form, *Am* ≃ twelfth grade **3** *nm (d'ordinateur, pétrolier)* terminal

terminer [tɛrmine] **1** *vt* to end; *(achever)* to finish, to complete **2 se terminer** *vpr* to end **(par** with; **en** in) ▪ **terminaison** *nf (de mot)* ending

terminologie [tɛrminɔlɔʒi] *nf* terminology

terminus [tɛrminys] *nm* terminus

termite [tɛrmit] *nm* termite

terne [tɛrn] *adj (couleur, journée)* dull, drab; *(personne)* dull ▪ **ternir 1** *vt (métal, réputation)* to tarnish; *(meuble, miroir)* to dull **2 se ternir** *vpr (métal)* to tarnish

terrain [terɛ̃] *nm (sol) & Fig* ground; *(étendue)* land; *(à bâtir)* plot, site; *(pour opérations militaires) & Géol* terrain; **un t.** a piece of land; **céder/gagner/perdre du t.** *(armée) & Fig* to give/gain/lose ground; *Fig* **trouver un t. d'entente** to find a common ground; *Fig* **être sur son t.** to be on familiar ground; **t. d'aviation** airfield; **t. de camping** campsite; **t. de football/rugby** football/rugby pitch; **t. de golf** golf course; **t. de jeu(x)** *(pour enfants)* playground; *(stade) Br* playing field, *Am*

athletic field; **t. de sport** *Br* sports ground, *Am* athletic field; **t. vague** waste ground, *Am* vacant lot

terrasse [teras] *nf (balcon, plate-forme)* terrace; *(toit)* terrace (roof); *(de café) Br* pavement or *Am* sidewalk area; **à la t.** outside (the café)

terrassement [terasmɑ̃] *nm (travail)* excavation

terrasser [terase] *vt (adversaire)* to floor; *Fig (accabler)* to overcome

terrassier [terasje] *nm* labourer

terre [tɛr] *nf (matière, monde)* earth; *(sol)* ground; *(opposé à mer, étendue)* land; **terres** *(domaine)* land, estate; *Él Br* earth, *Am* ground; **la t.** *(le monde)* the earth; **la T.** *(planète)* Earth; **à ou par t.** *(tomber)* to the ground; *(poser)* on the ground; **par t.** *(assis, couché)* on the ground; **aller à t.** *(marin)* to go ashore; **sous t.** underground; **t. cuite** (baked) clay, earthenware; **poterie en t. cuite** earthenware pottery; **t. battue** *(de court de tennis)* clay ▪ **terre-à-terre** *adj inv* down-to-earth ▪ **terre-plein** (pl **terres-pleins**) *nm* (earth) platform; *(de route) Br* central reservation, *Am* median strip

terreau [tero] *nm* compost

terrer [tere] **se terrer** *vpr (fugitif, animal)* to go to earth

terrestre [terɛstr] *adj (vie, joies)* earthly; **animal/transport t.** land animal/transportation

terreur [terœr] *nf* terror ▪ **terrible** *adj* awful, terrible; *Fam (formidable)* terrific; *Fam* **pas t.** nothing special ▪ **terriblement** [-əmɑ̃] *adv (extrêmement)* terribly

terreux, -euse [terø, -øz] *adj (goût)* earthy; *(couleur, teint)* muddy

terrien, -ienne [terjɛ̃, -jɛn] **1** *adj* land-owning; **propriétaire t.** landowner **2** *nmf (habitant de la terre)* earthling

terrier [terje] *nm (de lapin)* burrow; *(chien)* terrier

terrifier [terifje] *vt* to terrify ▪ **terrifiant, -ante** *adj* terrifying

terrine [terin] *nf (récipient)* terrine; *(pâté)* pâté

territoire [teritwar] *nm* territory ▪ **territorial, -e, -iaux, iales** *adj* territorial; **eaux territoriales** territorial waters

terroir [terwar] *nm (sol)* soil; *(région)* region; **accent du t.** rural accent

terroriser [terɔrize] *vt* to terrorize ▪ **terrorisme** *nm* terrorism ▪ **terroriste** *adj & nmf* terrorist

tertiaire [tɛrsjɛr] *adj* tertiary

tertre [tɛrtr] *nm* hillock, mound

tes [te] *voir* **ton¹**

tesson [tesɔ̃] *nm* **t. de bouteille** piece of broken bottle

test [tɛst] *nm* test ▪ **tester** *vt (élève, produit)* to test

testament [tɛstamɑ̃] nm (document) will; Fig (œuvre) testament; Rel **Ancien/Nouveau T.** Old/NewTestament

testicule [tɛstikyl] nm Anat testicle

tétanos [tetanos] nm tetanus

têtard [tetar] nm tadpole

tête [tɛt] nf head; (visage) face; (cerveau) brain; (de lit, de clou, de cortège) head; (de page, de liste) top, head; Football header; **à t. reposée** at one's leisure; **à la t. de** (entreprise, parti) at the head of; (classe) at the top of; **de la t. aux pieds** from head or top to toe; **t. nue** bareheaded; **en t.** (d'une course) in the lead; **tenir à qn** (s'opposer à) to stand up to sb; **faire la t.** (bouder) to sulk; Football **faire une t.** to head the ball; **avoir/faire une drôle de t.** to have/ give a funny look; **tomber la t. la première** to fall headlong or head first; **calculer qch de t.** to work sth out in one's head; **se mettre dans la t. de faire qch** to get it into one's head to do sth; Fig **perdre la t.** to lose one's head; Fam **se payer la t. de qn** to make fun of sb; Fam **j'en ai par-dessus la t.** I've had enough of it; Fam **ça me prend la t.** it gets under my skin; Fam **tu n'as pas de t.!** you're a scatterbrain!; **t. nucléaire** nuclear warhead ▪**tête-à-queue** nm inv faire un t. (en voiture) to spin right round ▪**tête-à-tête** nm inv tête-à-tête; **en t.** in private ▪**tête-bêche** adv head to tail

téter [tete] vt (lait, biberon) to suck; **t. sa mère** to feed or suck at one's mother's breast; **donner à t. à un bébé** to feed or suckle a baby ▪**tétée** nf (de bébé) feed ▪**tétine** nf (de biberon) Br teat, Am nipple; (sucette) Br dummy, Am pacifier ▪**téton** nm Fam (de femme) tit

têtu, -ue [tety] adj stubborn, obstinate

texte [tɛkst] nm text; (de théâtre) lines; (de chanson) words ▪**textuel, -elle** adj (traduction) literal ▪**textuellement** adv word for word

textile [tɛkstil] adj & nm textile

texto [tɛksto] nm Tél text (message); **envoyer un t. à qn** to send sb a text, to text sb

texture [tɛkstyr] nf texture

TGV [teʒeve] abrév = **train à grande vitesse**

Thaïlande [tailɑ̃d] nf **la T.** Thailand ▪**thaïlandais, -aise** 1 adj Thai 2 nmf T., ThaïlandaiseThai

thé [te] nm (boisson, réunion) tea ▪**théière** nf teapot

théâtre [teatr] nm (art, lieu) Br theatre, Am theater; (œuvres) drama; Fig (d'un crime) scene; **faire du t.** to act ▪**théâtral, -e, -aux, -ales** adj theatrical

thème [tem] nm theme; Scol (traduction) translation (into a foreign language), Br prose (composition)

théologie [teɔlɔʒi] nf theology ▪**théologique** adj theological

théorème [teɔrɛm] nm theorem

théorie [teɔri] nf theory; **en t.** in theory ▪**théoricien, -ienne** nmf theorist, theoretician ▪**théorique** adj theoretical ▪**théoriquement** adv theoretically

thérapeutique [terapøtik] 1 adj therapeutic 2 nf (traitement) therapy ▪**thérapie** nf therapy

thermal, -e, -aux, -ales [tɛrmal, -o] adj **station thermale** spa; **eaux thermales** hot or thermal springs

thermique [tɛrmik] adj (énergie, unité) thermal

thermomètre [tɛrmɔmɛtr] nm thermometer

thermonucléaire [tɛrmɔnykleɛr] adj thermonuclear

Thermos® [tɛrmɔs] nm ou f Thermos® (Br flask or Am bottle)

thermostat [tɛrmɔsta] nm thermostat

thèse [tɛz] nf (proposition, ouvrage) thesis

thon [tɔ̃] nm tuna (fish)

thorax [tɔraks] nm Anat thorax

thrombose [trɔ̃boz] nf Méd thrombosis; **t. véineuse profonde** deep vein thrombosis

thym [tɛ̃] nm (plante, aromate) thyme

thyroïde [tirɔid] adj & nf Anat thyroid

Tibet [tibɛ] nm le **T.** Tibet

tibia [tibja] nm shinbone, tibia

tic [tik] nm (contraction) twitch, tic; Fig (manie) mannerism

ticket [tikɛ] nm ticket; **t. de caisse** receipt; **t. de quai** (de gare) platform ticket; **t. modérateur** = portion of the cost of medical treatment paid by the patient ▪**ticket-repas** (pl tickets-repas), **ticket-restaurant** (pl tickets-restaurant) nm Br luncheon voucher, Am meal ticket

tic-tac [tiktak] exclam & nm inv tick-tock

tiède [tjɛd] adj lukewarm, tepid; (vent, climat) mild; (accueil, partisan) half-hearted ▪**tiédeur** nf tepidness; (de vent) mildness; (d'accueil) half-heartedness ▪**tiédir** vti (refroidir) to cool down; (réchauffer) to warm up

tien, tienne [tjɛ̃, tjɛn] 1 pron possessif **le t., la tienne, les tien(ne)s** yours; **les deux tiens** your two 2 nmpl **les tiens** (ta famille) your family

tiens, tient [tjɛ̃] voir **tenir**

tiercé [tjɛrse] nm **jouer/gagner au t.** = to bet/ win on the horses; **pari t.** = forecast of the first three horses

tiers, tierce [tjɛr, tjɛrs] 1 adj third 2 nm (fraction) third; (personne) third party; **t. provisionnel** interim tax payment (one third of previous year's tax) ▪**Tiers-Monde** nm le **T.** the Third World

tifs [tif] nmpl Fam hair

tige [tiʒ] nf (de plante) stem, stalk; (barre) rod

tignasse [tiɲas] nf Fam mop (of hair)

tigre [tigr] nm tiger ▪**tigresse** nf tigress

tigré, -ée [tigre] adj (rayé) striped

tilleul [tijœl] nm (arbre) lime tree; (infusion) lime-blossom tea

timbale [tɛ̃bal] *nf* (**a**) *(gobelet)* (metal) tumbler; *Fam* **décrocher la t.** to hit the jackpot (**b**) *(instrument)* kettledrum

timbre [tɛ̃br] *nm* (**a**) *(vignette)* stamp; *(pour traitement médicale)* patch (**b**) *(sonnette)* bell (**c**) *(d'instrument, de voix)* tone (quality) ▪ **timbré, -ée** *adj (lettre)* stamped; *Fam (fou)* crazy ▪ **timbre-poste** *(pl* **timbres-poste)** *nm* (postage) stamp ▪ **timbrer** *vt (lettre)* to put a stamp on; *(document)* to stamp

timide [timid] *adj (gêné)* shy; *(protestations)* timid ▪ **timidement** *adv* shyly; *(protester)* timidly ▪ **timidité** *nf* shyness

timoré, -ée [timɔre] *adj* timorous, fearful

tintamarre [tɛ̃tamar] *nm Fam* din, racket

tinter [tɛ̃te] *vi (cloche)* to tinkle; *(clefs, monnaie)* to jingle; *(verres)* to chink ▪ **tintement** *nm (de cloche)* tinkling; *(de clefs)* jingling; *(de verres)* chinking

tique [tik] *nf (insecte)* tick

tiquer [tike] *vi Fam (personne)* to wince

tir [tir] *nm (sport)* shooting; *(action)* firing, shooting; *Football* shot; **t. (forain)** shooting *or* rifle range; **t. à l'arc** archery

tirade [tirad] *nf (au théâtre) & Fig Br* monologue, *Am* monolog

tirage [tiraʒ] *nm* (**a**) *(de journal)* circulation; *(de livre)* print run; *Typ Phot (impression)* printing (**b**) *(de loterie)* draw; **t. au sort** drawing lots (**c**) *(de cheminée) Br* draught, *Am* draft

tirailler [tiraje] **1** *vt* to pull at; *Fig* **tiraillé entre** *(possibilités)* torn between **2** *vi* **j'ai la peau qui tiraille** my skin feels tight ▪ **tiraillement** *nm (crampe)* cramp

tirant [tirɑ̃] *nm* **t. d'eau** *(de bateau) Br* draught, *Am* draft

tire [tir] *nf* (**a**) **vol à la t.** pickpocketing (**b**) *Fam (voiture)* car

tirelire [tirlir] *nf Br* moneybox, *Am* coin bank

tirer [tire] **1** *vt* to pull; *(langue)* to stick out; *(trait, rideaux, conclusion)* to draw; *(balle)* to fire; *(gibier)* to shoot; *(journal, épreuves de livre, photo)* to print; **t. qch de qch** to pull sth out of sth; *(nom, origine)* to derive sth from sth; *(produit)* to extract sth from sth; **t. qn de qch** *(danger, lit)* to get sb out of sth; *Fig* **je vous tire mon chapeau** I take my hat off to you **2** *vi* to pull (**sur** on, at); *(faire feu)* to shoot, to fire (**sur** at); *Football* to shoot; *(cheminée)* to draw; **t. au sort** to draw lots; **t. à sa fin** to draw to a close; **t. sur le vert** to verge on green; *Fig* **t. à boulets rouges sur qn** to go for sb hammer and tongs **3** *se tirer vpr Fam (partir)* to make tracks; **se t. de qch** *(travail, problème)* to cope with sth; *(danger, situation)* to get out of sth; **se t. d'affaire** to get out of trouble; *Fam* **s'en t.** *(de malade)* to pull through; *(financièrement)* to make it ▪ **tiré, -ée** *adj (traits, visage)* drawn; *Fig* **t. par les cheveux** far-fetched ▪ **tire-au-**

flanc *nm inv Fam (paresseux)* shirker ▪ **tire-bouchon** *(pl* **tire-bouchons)** *nm* corkscrew ▪ **tire-d'aile** *adv* **à t.** swiftly ▪ **tire-fesses** *nm inv Fam* T-bar *(ski lift)*

tiret [tire] *nm (trait)* dash

tireur [tirœr] *nm* gunman; **un bon t.** a good shot; **t. d'élite** marksman; **t. isolé** sniper ▪ **tireuse** *nf* **t. de cartes** fortune-teller

tiroir [tirwar] *nm (de commode)* drawer ▪ **tiroir-caisse** *(pl* **tiroirs-caisses)** *nm* till, cash register

tisane [tizan] *nf* herbal tea

tison [tizɔ̃] *nm (fire)* brand ▪ **tisonner** *vt* to poke ▪ **tisonnier** *nm* poker

tisser [tise] *vt* to weave ▪ **tissage** *nm (action)* weaving ▪ **tisserand, -ande** *nmf* weaver

tissu [tisy] *nm* material, cloth; *Biol* tissue; **du t.-éponge** *Br* (terry) towelling, *Am* toweling; *Fig* **un t. de mensonges** a web of lies; **le t. social** the social fabric

titre [titr] *nm (nom, qualité)* title; *Fin* security; *(diplôme)* qualification; **(gros) t.** *(de journal)* headline; **à quel t.?** *(pour quelle raison)* on what grounds?; **à ce t.** *(en cette qualité)* as such; *(pour cette raison)* therefore; **à aucun t.** on no account; **au même t.** in the same way **(que** as); **à t. d'exemple** as an example; **à t. exceptionnel** exceptionally; **à t. privé** in a private capacity; **à t. provisoire** temporarily; **à t. indicatif** for general information; **à juste t.** rightly; **t. de noblesse** title (of nobility); **t. de propriété** title deed; **t. de transport** ticket

titrer [titre] *vt (film)* to title; *(journal)* to run as a headline ▪ **titré, -ée** *adj (personne)* titled

tituber [titybe] *vi* to stagger

titulaire [titylɛr] **1** *adj (enseignant)* tenured; **être t. de** *(permis)* to be the holder of; *(poste)* to hold **2** *nmf (de permis, de poste)* holder (**de** of) ▪ **titularisation** *nf* granting of tenure ▪ **titulariser** *vt (fonctionnaire)* to give tenure to

toast [tost] *nm (pain grillé)* piece *or* slice of toast; *(allocution)* toast; **porter un t. à** to drink (a toast) to

toboggan [tɔbɔgɑ̃] *nm (d'enfant)* slide; *Can (traîneau)* toboggan; *(voie de circulation) Br* flyover, *Am* overpass

toc [tɔk] **1** *exclam* **t. t.!** knock knock! **2** *nm* **du t.** *(camelote)* junk, trash; **bijou en t.** imitation jewel

tocard [tɔkar] *nm Fam* dead loss

tocsin [tɔksɛ̃] *nm* alarm bell

tohu-bohu [tɔybɔy] *nm (bruit)* hubbub; *(confusion)* confusion

toi [twa] *pron personnel* (**a**) *(après une préposition)* you; **avec t.** with you (**b**) *(sujet)* you; **t., tu peux** you may; **c'est t. qui...** it's you who... (**c**) *(réfléchi)* **assieds-t.** sit (yourself) down; **dépêche-t.** hurry up ▪ **toi-même** *pron* yourself

toile [twal] *nf* (**a**) *(étoffe)* cloth; *(à voile, sac)* canvas; *(à draps)* linen; **une t.** a piece of cloth or canvas; *Théâtre & Fig* **t. de fond** backdrop; **t. de jute** hessian; **t. cirée** oilcloth (**b**) *(tableau)* painting, canvas (**c**) **t. d'araignée** (spider's) web, cobweb (**d**) *Ordinat* **la T.** the Web (**e**) *Fam* **se faire une t.** to go to the *Br* cinema or *Am* movies

toilette [twalet] *nf* *(action)* wash(ing); *(vêtements)* clothes, outfit; **faire sa t.** to wash (and dress); **les toilettes** *(W.C.) Br* the toilet(s), *Am* the bathroom, the men's/ladies' room

toiser [twaze] *vt* to eye scornfully

toison [twazɔ̃] *nf* *(de mouton)* fleece

toit [twa] *nm* roof; **t. ouvrant** sunroof • **toiture** *nf* roof(ing)

tôle [tol] *nf* sheet metal; **une t.** a metal sheet; **t. ondulée** corrugated iron

tolérer [tɔlere] *vt* *(permettre)* to tolerate; *(à la douane)* to allow • **tolérable** *adj* tolerable • **tolérance** *nf* tolerance; *(à la douane)* allowance; *Pol* **t. zéro** zero tolerance • **tolérant, -ante** *adj* tolerant (**à l'égard de** of)

tollé [tɔle] *nm* outcry

tomate [tɔmat] *nf* tomato

tombe [tɔ̃b] *nf* grave; *(avec monument)* tomb • **tombale** *adj f* **pierre t.** gravestone, tombstone • **tombeau, -x** *nm* tomb

tomber [tɔ̃be] *(aux être) vi* to fall; *(température)* to drop, to fall; *(vent)* to drop (off); *(robe)* to hang down; **t. malade** to fall ill; **t. par terre** to fall (down); **faire t.** *(personne)* to knock over; *(gouvernement, prix)* to bring down; **laisser t.** *(objet)* to drop; *Fig* **laisser t. qn** to let sb down; **se laisser t. dans un fauteuil** to drop into an armchair; *Fig* **tu tombes bien/mal** you've come at the right/wrong time; **t. de sommeil** *ou* **de fatigue** to be ready to drop; **t. un lundi** to fall on a Monday; **t. sur qch** *(trouver)* to come across sth; *Fam* **t. de haut** to be bitterly disappointed • **tombée** *nf* **la t. de la nuit** nightfall

tombola [tɔ̃bɔla] *nf* raffle, tombola

tome [tɔm] *nm* *(livre)* volume

tomme [tɔm] *nf* = cheese made in Savoie

ton¹, ta, tes [tɔ̃, ta, te]

ta becomes **ton** [tɔ̃] before a vowel or mute h.

adj possessif your; **t. père** your father; **ta mère** your mother; **t. ami(e)** your friend

ton² [tɔ̃] *nm* *(de voix)* tone; *(de couleur)* shade, tone; *Mus (gamme)* key; *(hauteur de son) & Ling* pitch; **de bon t.** *(goût)* in good taste; *Fig* **donner le t.** to set the tone • **tonalité** *nf* *(timbre, impression)* tone; *(de téléphone) Br* dialling tone, *Am* dial tone

tondre [tɔ̃dr] *vt* *(mouton)* to shear; *(gazon)* to mow; *Fam* **t. qn** *(escroquer)* to fleece sb • **tondeuse** *nf* shears; *(à cheveux)* clippers; **t. (à gazon)** (lawn)mower

tongs [tɔ̃g] *nfpl* *(sandales)* flip-flops, *Am* thongs

tonifier [tɔnifje] *vt* *(muscles, peau)* to tone up; *(personne)* to invigorate • **tonifiant, -ante** *adj* *(crème, exercice)* toning; *(activité, climat)* invigorating

tonique [tɔnik] **1** *adj* *(froid, effet)* tonic, invigorating; *Ling (accent)* tonic **2** *nm* *(médicament)* tonic; *(cosmétique)* tonic lotion

tonitruant, -ante [tɔnitryɑ̃, -ɑ̃t] *adj Fam (voix)* booming

tonnage [tɔnaʒ] *nm (de navire)* tonnage

tonne [tɔn] *nf (poids)* metric ton, tonne; *Fam* **des tonnes de** *(beaucoup)* tons of

tonneau, -x [tɔno] *nm* (**a**) *(récipient)* barrel, cask (**b**) *(acrobatie)* roll; **faire un t.** to roll over (**c**) *Fam* **du même t.** of the same kind

tonnelle [tɔnel] *nf* arbour, bower

tonner [tɔne] **1** *vi (canons)* to thunder; *Fig (crier)* to thunder, to rage (**contre** against) **2** *v impersonnel* **il tonne** it's thundering • **tonnerre** *nm* thunder; *Fam* **du t.** *(excellent)* fantastic

tonte [tɔ̃t] *nf (de moutons)* shearing; *(de gazon)* mowing

tonton [tɔ̃tɔ̃] *nm Fam* uncle

tonus [tɔnys] *nm (énergie)* energy, vitality; **t. musculaire** muscle tone

top [tɔp] *nm (signal sonore)* beep; **les tops** the pips; *Fam* **c'est le t. (du t.)!** it's the best!, *Br* it's the business!

topaze [tɔpaz] *nf* topaz

topinambour [tɔpinɑ̃bur] *nm* Jerusalem artichoke

topo [tɔpo] *nm Fam (exposé)* rundown

topographie [tɔpɔɡrafi] *nf* topography

toquade [tɔkad] *nf Fam (pour un objet)* craze (**pour** for); *(pour une personne)* crush (**pour** on)

toque [tɔk] *nf (de fourrure)* fur hat; *(de jockey)* cap; *(de cuisinier)* hat

toquer [tɔke] **se toquer** *vpr Fam* **se t. de qn** to go crazy over sb • **toqué, -ée** *adj Fam (fou)* crazy

torche [tɔrʃ] *nf (flamme)* torch; **t. électrique** *Br* torch, *Am* flashlight

torcher [tɔrʃe] *vt Fam (enfant)* to wipe; *(travail)* to botch

torchon [tɔrʃɔ̃] *nm (à vaisselle) Br* tea towel, *Am* dish towel

tordre [tɔrdr] **1** *vt* to twist; *(linge, cou)* to wring; *(barre)* to bend **2 se tordre** *vpr* to twist; *(barre)* to bend; **se t. de douleur** to be doubled up with pain; **se t. (de rire)** to split one's sides (laughing); **se t. la cheville** to twist or sprain one's ankle • **tordant, -ante** *adj Fam (drôle)* hilarious • **tordu, -ue** *adj* twisted; *(esprit)* warped

tornade [tɔrnad] *nf* tornado

torpeur [tɔrpœr] *nf* torpor

torpille [tɔrpij] *nf* torpedo • **torpiller** *vt (navire,* *projet)* to torpedo ▪ **torpilleur** *nm* torpedo boat

torréfier [tɔrefje] *vt (café)* to roast ▪ **torréfaction** *nf* roasting

torrent [tɔrɑ̃] *nm* torrent; *Fig* **un t. de larmes** floods of tears; **il pleut à torrents** it's pouring (down) ▪ **torrentiel, -ielle** *adj (pluie)* torrential

torride [tɔrid] *adj (chaleur)* torrid

torsade [tɔrsad] *nf (de cheveux)* twist, coil ▪ **torsader** *vt* to twist

torse [tɔrs] *nm Anat* chest; *(statue)* torso; **t. nu** stripped to the waist

torsion [tɔrsjɔ̃] *nf* twisting

tort [tɔr] *nm (dommage)* wrong; *(défaut)* fault; **avoir t.** to be wrong (**de faire** to do, in doing); **tu as t. de fumer!** you shouldn't smoke!; **être dans son t.** *ou* **en t.** to be in the wrong; **donner t. à qn** *(accuser)* to blame sb; *(faits)* to prove sb wrong; **faire du t. à qn** to harm sb; **à t.** wrongly; **à t. ou à raison** rightly or wrongly; **parler à t. et à travers** to talk nonsense

torticolis [tɔrtikɔli] *nm* **avoir le t.** to have a stiff neck

tortillard [tɔrtijar] *nm Fam* local train

tortiller [tɔrtije] **1** *vt* to twist; *(moustache)* to twirl **2** *vi Fam* **il n'y a pas à t.** there's no two ways about it **3 se tortiller** *vpr (ver, personne)* to wriggle

tortionnaire [tɔrsjɔnɛr] *nm* torturer

tortue [tɔrty] *nf Br* tortoise, *Am* turtle; *(de mer)* turtle; *Fam (personne) Br* slowcoach, *Am* slowpoke

tortueux, -ueuse [tɔrtɥø, -ɥøz] *adj* tortuous

torture [tɔrtyr] *nf* torture ▪ **torturer** *vt* to torture; *Fam* **se t. les méninges** to rack one's brains

tôt [to] *adv* early; **au plus t.** at the earliest; **le plus t. possible** as soon as possible; **t. ou tard** sooner or later; **je n'étais pas plus t. sorti que…** no sooner had I gone out than…

total, -e, -aux, -ales [tɔtal, -o] *adj & nm* total; **au t.** all in all, in total; *(somme toute)* all in all ▪ **totalement** *adv* totally, completely ▪ **totaliser** *vt* to total ▪ **totalité** *nf* entirety; **la t. de** all of; **en t.** *(détruit)* entirely; *(payé)* fully

totalitaire [tɔtalitɛr] *adj (État, régime)* totalitarian

toubib [tubib] *nm Fam (médecin)* doctor

touche [tuʃ] *nf (de clavier)* key; *(de téléphone)* (push-)button; *(de peintre)* touch; *Football & Rugby* throw-in; *Pêche* bite; **téléphone à touches** push-button phone; **une t. de** *(un peu de)* a touch or hint of

toucher [tuʃe] **1** *nm (sens)* touch; **au t.** to the touch **2** *vt* to touch; *(paie)* to draw; *(chèque)* to cash; *(cible)* to hit; *(émouvoir)* to touch, to move; *(concerner)* to affect; **t. le fond (du désespoir)** to hit rock bottom **3** *vi* **t. à** to touch; *(sujet)* to touch on; *(but, fin)* to approach **4 se toucher**

vpr (lignes, mains) to touch ▪ **touchant, -ante** *adj (émouvant)* moving, touching ▪ **touche-à-tout** *nmf inv (qui a plusieurs occupations)* dabbler

touffe [tuf] *nf (de cheveux, d'herbe)* tuft ▪ **touffu, -ue** *adj (barbe, haie)* thick, bushy; *Fig (livre)* dense

touiller [tuje] *vt Fam (salade)* to toss

toujours [tuʒur] *adv (exprime la continuité, la répétition)* always; *(encore)* still; **pour t.** for ever; **essaie t.!** *(quand même)* try anyway!; **t. est-il que…** [tuʒurzetilkə] the fact remains that…

toupet [tupɛ] *nm Fam (audace)* nerve, *Br* cheek

toupie [tupi] *nf (spinning)* top; *Fam* **vieille t.** *(femme)* old bag

tour¹ [tur] *nf (bâtiment) & Ordinat* tower; *(immeuble)* tower block, high-rise; *Échecs* castle, rook

tour² [tur] *nm* **(a)** *(mouvement, ordre, tournure)* turn; *(de magie)* trick; *(excursion)* trip, outing; *(à pied)* stroll, walk; *(en voiture)* drive; **t. (de piste)** *(de course)* lap; **faire un t. d'honneur** *(sportif)* to do a lap of honour; **de dix mètres de t.** ten metres round; **faire le t. de** to go round; *(question, situation)* to review; **faire le t. du monde** to go round the world; **faire un t.** *(à pied)* to go for a stroll or walk; *(en voiture)* to go for a drive; **jouer** *ou* **faire un t. à qn** to play a trick on sb; *Fam* **avoir plus d'un t. dans son sac** to have more than one trick up one's sleeve; **c'est mon t.** it's my turn; **à qui le tour?** whose turn (is it)?; **à son t.** in (one's) turn; **à t. de rôle** in turn; **à t.** in turn, by turns; **t. de cartes** card trick; **t. d'horizon** survey; **t. de poitrine** chest size **(b)** *Tech* lathe; *(de potier)* wheel

tourbe [turb] *nf* peat ▪ **tourbière** *nf* peat bog

tourbillon [turbijɔ̃] *nm (de vent)* whirlwind; *(d'eau)* whirlpool; *(de sable)* swirl; *Fig (tournoiement)* whirl ▪ **tourbillonner** *vi* to whirl

tourelle [turɛl] *nf* turret

tourisme [turism] *nm* tourism; **faire du t.** to go touring; **agence de t.** tourist agency; **t. écologique** ecotourism; **t. organisé** package tourism ▪ **touriste** *nmf* tourist ▪ **touristique** *adj* **guide/menu t.** tourist guide/menu; **circuit** *ou* **route t.** scenic route

tourment [turmɑ̃] *nm* torment ▪ **tourmenté, -ée** *adj (mer, vie)* turbulent; *(expression, visage)* anguished; *(paysage)* wild ▪ **tourmenter 1** *vt* to torment **2 se tourmenter** *vpr* to worry

tourmente [turmɑ̃t] *nf (troubles)* turmoil

tournage [turnaʒ] *nm (de film)* shooting, filming

tourne-disque [turnədisk] *(pl* **tourne-disques)** *nm* record player

tournedos [turnədo] *nm* tournedos

tournée [turne] *nf (de facteur, de boissons)* round; *(spectacle)* tour; **faire sa t.** to do one's rounds; **faire la t. de** (*magasins, musées*) to go to, *Br* to go round

tournemain [turnəmɛ̃] **en un tournemain** *adv Littéraire* in an instant

tourner [turne] **1** *vt* to turn; (*film*) to shoot, to make; (*difficulté*) to get round; **t. qn/qch en ridicule** to ridicule sb/sth; **t. le dos à qn** to turn one's back on sb **2** *vi* to turn; (*tête, toupie*) to spin; (*Terre*) to revolve, to turn; (*moteur, usine*) to run; (*lait*) to go off; **t. autour de** (*objet*) to go round; (*maison, personne*) to hang around; (*question*) to centre on; **t. bien/mal** (*évoluer*) to turn out well/badly; **t. au froid** (*temps*) to turn cold; **t. à l'aigre** (*ton, conversation*) to turn nasty; *Fig* **t. autour du pot** to beat around the bush; *Fam* **t. de l'œil** to faint; *Fam* **faire t. qn en bourrique** to drive sb crazy; **ça me fait t. la tête** (*vin*) it goes to my head; (*manège*) it makes my head spin; **silence! on tourne** quiet, we're filming *or* shooting! **3 se tourner** *vpr* to turn (**vers** to, towards) ▪**tournant, -ante** **1** *adj* **pont t.** swing bridge **2** *nm* (*de route*) bend; *Fig* (*moment*) turning point (**de** in)

tournesol [turnəsɔl] *nm* sunflower

tourneur [turnœr] *nm* (*ouvrier*) turner

tournevis [turnəvis] *nm* screwdriver

tourniquet [turnikɛ] *nm* (*barrière*) turnstile; (*pour arroser*) sprinkler; *Méd* tourniquet

tournis [turni] *nm Fam* **avoir le t.** to feel giddy; **donner t. à qn** to make sb giddy

tournoi [turnwa] *nm* (*de tennis*) & *Hist* tournament

tournoyer [turnwaje] *vi* to swirl (round)

tournure [turnyr] *nf* (*expression*) turn of phrase; **t. d'esprit** way of thinking; **t. des événements** turn of events; **prendre t.** to take shape

tourte [turt] *nf* pie

tourterelle [turtərɛl] *nf* turtledove

Toussaint [tusɛ̃] *nf* **la T.** All Saints' Day

tousser [tuse] *vi* to cough

tout, toute, tous, toutes [tu, tut, tu, tut] **1** *adj* all; **tous les livres** all the books; **t. l'argent/le temps/le village** all the money/time/village; **toute la nuit** all night, the whole (of the) night; **tous (les) deux** both; **tous (les) trois** all three; **t. un problème** quite a problem

2 *adj indéfini* (*chaque*) every, each; (*n'importe quel*) any; **tous les ans/jours** every *or* each year/day; **tous les deux mois** every two months, every second month; **tous les cinq mètres** every five metres; **à toute heure** at any time; **t. homme** [tutɔm] every *or* any man

3 *pron pl* **tous** [tus] all; **ils sont tous là, tous sont là** they're all there

4 *pron m sing* **tout** everything; **dépenser t.** to spend everything, to spend it all; **t. ce qui est là** everything that's here; **t. ce que je sais** everything that *or* all that I know; **en t.** (*au total*) in all

5 *adv* (*tout à fait*) quite; (*très*) very; **t. simplement** quite simply; **t. petit** very small; **t. neuf** brand new; **t. seul** all alone; **t. droit** straight ahead; **t. autour** all around, right round; **t. au début** right at the beginning; **le t. premier** the very first; **t. au plus/moins** at the very most/least; **t. en chantant** while singing; **t. rusé qu'il est** *ou* **soit** however sly he may be; **t. à coup** suddenly, all of a sudden; **t. à fait** completely, quite; **t. de même** all the same; **t. de même!** (*indignation*) really!; **t. de suite** at once

6 *nm* **le t.** everything, the lot; **un t.** a whole; **le t. est que...** (*l'important*) the main thing is that...; **pas du t.** not at all; **rien du t.** nothing at all; **du t. au t.** (*changer*) entirely, completely ▪**tout-à-l'égout** *nm inv* mains drainage ▪**tout-puissant, toute-puissante** (*mpl* **tout-puissants**, *fpl* **toutes-puissantes**) *adj* all-powerful ▪**tout-terrain 1** (*pl* **tout-terrains**) *adj* **véhicule t.** off-road *or* all-terrain vehicle; **vélo t.** mountain bike **2** *nm* **faire du t.** to do off-road racing

toutefois [tutfwa] *adv* nevertheless, however

toutou [tutu] *nm Fam* (*chien*) doggie

toux [tu] *nf* cough

toxicomane [tɔksikɔman] *nmf* drug addict ▪**toxicomanie** *nf* drug addiction

toxine [tɔksin] *nf* toxin ▪**toxique** *adj* toxic

TP [tepe] (*abrév* **travaux pratiques**) *nmpl Scol & Univ* practical work

trac [trak] *nm* **le t.** (*peur*) the jitters; (*de candidat*) exam nerves; (*d'acteur*) stage fright; **avoir le t.** to be nervous

tracas [traka] *nm* worry ▪**tracasser** *vt*, **se tracasser** *vpr* to worry ▪**tracasseries** *nfpl* annoyances

trace [tras] *nf* (*quantité, tache, vestige*) trace; (*marque*) mark; (*de fugitif*) trail; **traces** (*de bête, de pneus*) tracks; **traces de pas** footprints; **disparaître sans laisser de traces** to disappear without trace; *Fig* **suivre** *ou* **marcher sur les traces de qn** to follow in sb's footsteps

tracer [trase] *vt* (*dessiner*) to draw; (*écrire*) to trace; **t. une route** to mark out a route; (*frayer*) to open up a route ▪**tracé** *nm* (*plan*) layout; (*ligne*) line

trachée [traʃe] *nf Anat* windpipe

tract [trakt] *nm* leaflet

tractations [traktasjɔ̃] *nfpl* dealings

tracter [trakte] *vt* to tow ▪**tracteur** *nm* tractor

traction [traksjɔ̃] *nf Tech* traction; *Gymnastique* pull-up; **t. arrière/avant** (*voiture*) rear-/front-wheel drive

tradition [tradisjɔ̃] *nf* tradition ▪**traditionnel, -elle** *adj* traditional

traduire* [tradɥir] *vt* to translate (**de** from, **en** into); *Fig* (*exprimer*) to express; **t. qn en justice**

to bring sb before the courts ■**traducteur, -trice** *nmf* translator ■**traduction** *nf* translation ■**traduisible** *adj* translatable

trafic [trafik] *nm (automobile, ferroviaire)* traffic; *(de marchandises)* traffic, trade; **faire le t. de** to traffic in, trade in ■**trafiquant, -ante** *nmf* trafficker, dealer; **t. d'armes/de drogue** arms/ drug trafficker *or* dealer ■**trafiquer** *vt Fam (produit)* to tamper with

tragédie [traʒedi] *nf (pièce de théâtre, événement)* tragedy ■**tragique** *adj* tragic; **prendre qch au t.** *(remarque)* to take sth too much to heart ■**tragiquement** *adv* tragically

trahir [trair] **1** *vt* to betray; *(secret)* to give away, to betray; *(sujet: forces)* to fail **2 se trahir** *vpr* to give oneself away ■**trahison** *nf* betrayal; *(crime)* treason; **haute t.** high treason

train [trɛ̃] *nm* **(a)** *(de voyageurs, de marchandises)* train; **t. à grande vitesse** high-speed train; **t. autocouchettes** car-sleeper; **t. corail** express train; **t. couchettes** sleeper; **Fig prendre le t. en marche** to jump on the bandwagon **(b) en t.** *(en forme)* on form; **se mettre en t.** to get (oneself) into shape; **être en t. de faire qch** to be (busy) doing sth; **mettre qch en t.** to get sth going, to start sth off **(c)** *(allure)* pace; **t. de vie** lifestyle **(d)** *(de pneus)* set; *(de péniches, de véhicules)* string **(e) t. d'atterrissage** *(d'avion)* undercarriage ■**train-train** *nm inv Fam* **le t. quotidien** the daily grind

traînailler [trenɑje], **traînasser** [trenɑse] *vi Fam* to dawdle; *(errer)* to hang around ■**traînard, -arde** *nmf Br* slowcoach, *Am* slowpoke

traîne [trɛn] *nf (de robe)* train; *Fam* **à la t.** *(en arrière)* lagging behind

traîneau, -x [treno] *nm* sleigh, *Br* sledge, *Am* sled

traînée [trene] *nf (de peinture, dans le ciel)* streak; *Fam (prostituée)* tart; *Fig* **se répandre comme une t. de poudre** to spread like wildfire

traîner [trene] **1** *vt* to drag; *(wagon)* to pull; **faire t. qch en longueur** to drag sth out **2** *vi (jouets, papiers)* to lie around; *(s'attarder)* to lag behind, to dawdle; *(errer)* to hang around; *(subsister)* to linger on; **t. par terre** *(robe)* to trail (on the ground); **t. en longueur** to drag on **3 se traîner** *vpr (avancer)* to drag oneself (along); *(par terre)* to crawl; *(durer)* to drag on ■**traînant, -ante** *adj (voix)* drawling

traire* [trer] *vt (vache)* to milk

trait [trɛ] *nm* line; *(en dessinant)* stroke; *(caractéristique)* feature, trait; **traits** *(du visage)* features; **d'un t.** *(boire)* in one gulp, in one go; **avoir t. à qch** to relate to sth; **t. de génie/ d'esprit** flash of genius/wit; **t. d'union** hyphen

traite [tret] *nf (de vache)* milking; *(lettre de change)* bill, draft; **d'une (seule) t.** *(sans interruption)* in one go; **t. des Noirs** slave trade; **t. des Blanches** white slave trade

traité [trete] *nm (accord)* treaty; *(ouvrage)* treatise *(sur* on); **t. de paix** peace treaty

traiter [trete] **1** *vt (se comporter envers, soigner)* to treat; *(problème, sujet)* to deal with; *(marché)* to negotiate; *(matériau, produit)* to treat, to process; **t. qn de lâche** to call sb a coward; **t. qn de tous les noms** to call sb all the names under the sun **2** *vi* to negotiate, to deal *(avec* with); **t. de** *(sujet)* to deal with ■**traitement** [tretmɑ̃] *nm (de personne, de maladie)* treatment; *(de matériau)* processing; *(gains)* salary; **t. de données/de texte** data/word processing; **machine à t. de texte** word processor

traiteur [tretœr] *nm (fournisseur)* caterer; **chez le t.** at the delicatessen

traître [tretr] **1** *nm* traitor; **en t.** treacherously **2** *adj (dangereux)* treacherous; **être t. à une cause** to be a traitor to a cause ■**traîtrise** *nf* treachery

trajectoire [traʒɛktwar] *nf* path, trajectory

trajet [traʒɛ] *nm* journey; *(distance)* distance; *(itinéraire)* route

trame [tram] *nf (de récit)* framework; *(de tissu)* weft; **usé jusqu'à la t.** threadbare

tramer [trame] **1** *vt (évasion)* to plot; *(complot)* to hatch **2 se tramer** *vpr* **il se trame quelque chose** something's afoot

trampoline [trɑ̃pɔlin] *nm* trampoline

tramway [tramwɛ] *nm Br* tram, *Am* streetcar

tranche [trɑ̃ʃ] *nf (morceau)* slice; *(bord)* edge; *(partie)* portion; *(de salaire, d'impôts)* bracket; **t. d'âge** age bracket

tranchée¹ [trɑ̃ʃe] *nf* trench

trancher [trɑ̃ʃe] **1** *vt* to cut; *(difficulté, question)* to settle **2** *vi (décider)* to decide; *(contraster)* to contrast *(sur* with) ■**tranchant, -ante 1** *adj (couteau)* sharp; *(ton)* curt **2** *nm (cutting)* edge; *Fig* **à double t.** double-edged ■**tranché, -ée²** *adj (couleurs)* distinct; *(opinion)* clearcut

tranquille [trɑ̃kil] *adj* quiet; *(mer)* calm, still; *(esprit)* easy; *Fam (certain)* confident; **avoir la conscience t.** to have a clear conscience; **je suis t.** *(rassuré)* my mind is at rest; **soyez t.** don't worry; **laisser qch/qn t.** to leave sth/sb alone ■**tranquillement** *adv* calmly

tranquilliser [trɑ̃kilize] *vt* to reassure; **tranquillisez-vous** set your mind at rest ■**tranquillisant** *nm Méd* tranquillizer

tranquillité [trɑ̃kilite] *nf* (peace and) quiet; *(d'esprit)* peace of mind

transaction [trɑ̃zaksjɔ̃] *nf (opération)* transaction; *Jur* compromise

transatlantique [trɑ̃zatlɑ̃tik] **1** *adj* transatlantic **2** *nm (paquebot)* transatlantic liner; *(chaise)* deckchair ■**transat** [trɑ̃zat] *nm (chaise)* deckchair

transcender [trɑ̃sɑ̃de] vt to transcend ▪ **transcendant, -ante** adj transcendent

transcrire* [trɑ̃skrir] vt to transcribe ▪ **transcription** nf transcription; (document) transcript

transe [trɑ̃s] nf **en t.** (mystique) in a trance; (excité) very exited; **entrer en t.** to go into a trance

transférer [trɑ̃sfere] vt to transfer (**à** to) ▪ **transfert** nm transfer

transfigurer [trɑ̃sfigyre] vt to transfigure

transformer [trɑ̃sfɔrme] **1** vt to transform; (maison) & Rugby to convert; (matière première) to process; (robe) to alter; **t. qch en qch** to turn sth into sth **2 se transformer** vpr to change, to be transformed (**en** into) ▪ **transformateur** nm Él transformer ▪ **transformation** nf change, transformation; (de maison) alteration

transfuge [trɑ̃sfyʒ] nmf defector

transfusion [trɑ̃sfyzjɔ̃] nf **t. (sanguine)** (blood) transfusion

transgénique [trɑ̃sʒenik] adj transgenic

transgresser [trɑ̃sgrese] vt (ordres) to disobey; (loi) to infringe ▪ **transgression** nf (de loi) infringement; (d'ordres) disobeying

transi, -ie [trɑ̃zi] adj (personne) numb with cold; **t. de peur** Br paralysed or Am paralyzed with fear

transiger [trɑ̃ziʒe] vi to compromise

transistor [trɑ̃zistɔr] nm transistor

transit [trɑ̃zit] nm transit; **en t.** in transit ▪ **transiter 1** vt (marchandises) to transit **2** vi to pass in transit

transitif, -ive [trɑ̃zitif, -iv] adj & nm Grammaire transitive

transition [trɑ̃zisjɔ̃] nf transition ▪ **transitoire** adj (qui passe) transient; (provisoire) transitional

translucide [trɑ̃slysid] adj translucent

transmettre* [trɑ̃smetr] **1** vt (message, héritage) to pass on (**à** to); Radio & TV (informations) to transmit; (émission) to broadcast **2 se transmettre** vpr (maladie, tradition) to be passed on ▪ **transmetteur** nm (appareil) transmitter ▪ **transmission** nf transmission

transparaître* [trɑ̃sparetr] vi to show (through)

transparent, -ente [trɑ̃sparɑ̃, -ɑ̃t] adj clear, transparent ▪ **transparence** nf transparency; **voir qch par t.** to see sth showing through

transpercer [trɑ̃sperse] vt to pierce

transpirer [trɑ̃spire] vi (suer) to sweat, to perspire; Fig (information) to leak out ▪ **transpiration** nf perspiration

transplanter [trɑ̃splɑ̃te] vt (organe, plante) to transplant ▪ **transplantation** nf transplantation; (greffe d'organe) transplant

transport [trɑ̃spɔr] nm (action) transport, transportation (**de** of); **transports** (moyens)

transport; **transports en commun** public transport; **frais de t.** transport costs; **moyen de t.** means of transport

transporter [trɑ̃spɔrte] vt (passagers, troupes, marchandises) to transport, to carry; **t. qn d'urgence à l'hôpital** to rush sb Br to hospital or Am to the hospital ▪ **transporteur** nm **t. (routier)** Br haulier, Am trucker

transposer [trɑ̃spoze] vt to transpose ▪ **transposition** nf transposition

transsexuel, -elle adj & nmf transsexual

transvaser [trɑ̃svaze] vt to decant

transversal, -e, -aux, -ales [trɑ̃sversal, -o] adj transverse, transversal; **rue transversale** cross street

trapèze [trapez] nm (de cirque) trapeze ▪ **trapéziste** nmf trapeze artist

trappe [trap] nf (de plancher) trap door

trappeur [trapœr] nm trapper

trapu, -ue [trapy] adj (personne) stocky, thickset; Fam (problème) tough

traquenard [traknar] nm trap

traquer [trake] vt to hunt (down)

traumatiser [tromatize] vt to traumatize ▪ **traumatisant, -ante** adj traumatic ▪ **traumatisme** nm (choc) trauma; **t. crânien** severe head injury

travail, -aux [travaj, -o] nm (activité, lieu) work; (à effectuer) job, task; (emploi) job; (façonnage) working (**de** of); (ouvrage, étude) work, publication; Écon & Méd labour; **travaux** work; (dans la rue) Br roadworks, Am roadwork; (aménagement) alterations; Scol & Univ **travaux dirigés** ≃ tutorial; **travaux forcés** hard labour; Scol **travaux manuels** arts and crafts; **travaux ménagers** housework; Scol & Univ **travaux pratiques** practical work; **travaux publics** public works

travailler [travaje] **1** vi (personne) to work (**à qch** on sth); (bois) to warp **2** vt (discipline, rôle, style) to work on; (façonner) to work; Fam (inquiéter) to worry; **t. la terre** to work the land ▪ **travaillé, -ée** adj (style) elaborate ▪ **travailleur, -euse 1** adj hard-working **2** nmf worker

travailliste [travajist] Pol **1** adj Labour **2** nmf member of the Labour party

travelling [travliŋ] nm Cin (mouvement de la caméra) tracking; (plan) tracking shot

travers [traver] **1** prép & adv **à t.** through; **en t. (de)** across **2** adv **de t.** (chapeau, nez) crooked; Fig **aller de t.** to go wrong; **comprendre de t.** to misunderstand; **regarder qn de t.** (avec suspicion) to look askance at sb; **j'ai avalé de t.** it went down the wrong way **3** nm (défaut) failing

traverse [travers] nf (de voie ferrée) Br sleeper, Am tie

traverser [traverse] vt to cross; (foule, période,

mur) to go through ■**traversée** *nf (voyage)* crossing

traversin [travɛrsɛ̃] *nm* bolster

travesti [travɛsti] *nm (acteur)* female impersonator; *(homosexuel)* transvestite

travestir [travɛstir] *vt* to disguise; *(pensée, vérité)* to misrepresent ■**travestissement** *nm* disguise

trébucher [trebyʃe] *vi* to stumble (**sur** over); **faire t. qn** to trip sb (up)

trèfle [trɛfl] *nm (plante)* clover; *Cartes (couleur)* clubs

treille [trɛj] *nf* climbing vine

treillis [trɛji] *nm* (**a**) *(treillage)* lattice(work); *(en métal)* wire mesh (**b**) *(tenue militaire)* combat uniform

treize [trɛz] *adj & nm inv* thirteen ■**treizième** *adj & nmf* thirteenth

tréma [trema] *nm* diaeresis

trembler [trɑ̃ble] *vi* to shake, to tremble; *(de froid, peur)* to tremble (**de** with); *(flamme, lumière)* to flicker; *(voix)* to tremble, to quaver; *(avoir peur)* to be afraid (**que** + *subjunctive* that); **t. pour qn** to fear for sb; **t. de tout son corps** to shake all over, to tremble violently ■**tremblement** [-əmɑ̃] *nm (action, frisson)* shaking, trembling; **t. de terre** earthquake ■**trembloter** *vi* to quiver

trémolos [tremɔlo] *nmpl* **avec des t. dans la voix** with a tremor in one's voice

trémousser [tremuse] **se trémousser** *vpr* to wriggle (about)

trempe [trɑ̃p] *nf* **un homme de sa t.** a man of his calibre; *Fam* **mettre une t. à qn** to give sb a thrashing

tremper [trɑ̃pe] **1** *vt* to soak, to drench; *(plonger)* to dip (**dans** in); *(acier)* to temper **2** *vi* to soak; **faire t. qch** to soak sth; *Péj* **t. dans** *(participer)* to be mixed up in **3 se tremper** *vpr Fam (se baigner)* to take a dip ■**trempette** *nf Fam* **faire t.** to take a dip

tremplin [trɑ̃plɛ̃] *nm Sport & Fig* springboard

trente [trɑ̃t] *adj & nm inv* thirty; **un t.-trois tours** *(disque)* an LP; **se mettre sur son t. et un** to get all dressed up; *Fam* **il n'y en a pas t.-six** there aren't that many of them; *Fam* **tous les t.-six du mois** once in a blue moon; *Fam* **être au t.-sixième dessous** to be (feeling) really down ■**trentaine** *nf* **une t. (de)** *(nombre)* (about) thirty; **avoir la t.** *(âge)* to be about thirty ■**trentième** *adj & nmf* thirtieth

trépas [trepa] *nm Littéraire* death; **passer de vie à t.** to pass away

trépidant, -ante [trepidɑ̃, -ɑ̃t] *adj (vie)* hectic

trépied [trepje] *nm* tripod

trépigner [trepiɲe] *vi* to stamp (one's feet)

très [trɛ] ([trɛz] *before vowel or mute h*) *adv* very; **t. aimé/critiqué** *(with past participle)* much or greatly liked/criticized

trésor [trezɔr] *nm* treasure; **le T. (public)** *(service)* public revenue (department); *(finances)* public funds; **des trésors de patience** boundless patience ■**trésorerie** [-rri] *nf (bureaux d'un club)* accounts department; *(gestion)* accounting; *(capitaux)* funds ■**trésorier, -ière** *nmf* treasurer

tressaillir* [tresajir] *vi (frémir)* to shake, to quiver; *(de joie, de peur)* to tremble (**de** with); *(sursauter)* to jump, to start ■**tressaillement** *nm (frémissement)* quiver; *(de joie)* trembling; *(de surprise)* start

tressauter [tresote] *vi (sursauter)* to start, to jump

tresse [trɛs] *nf (cordon)* braid; *(cheveux) Br* plait, *Am* braid ■**tresser** [trese] *vt* to braid; *(cheveux) Br* to plait, *Am* to braid

tréteau, -x [treto] *nm* trestle

treuil [trœj] *nm* winch

trêve [trɛv] *nf (de combat)* truce; *Fig (répit)* respite; **la T. des confiseurs** the Christmas and New Year political truce; **t. de plaisanteries!** joking apart!

tri [tri] *nm* sorting (out); **faire le t. de** to sort (out); **(centre de) t.** *(des postes)* sorting office ■**triage** *nm* sorting (out)

triangle [trijɑ̃gl] *nm* triangle ■**triangulaire** *adj* triangular

tribord [tribɔr] *nm (de bateau, d'avion)* starboard

tribu [triby] *nf* tribe ■**tribal, -e, -aux, -ales** *adj* tribal

tribulations [tribylasjɔ̃] *nfpl* tribulations

tribunal, -aux [tribynal, -o] *nm Jur* court; *(militaire)* tribunal

tribune [tribyn] *nf (de salle publique)* gallery; *(de stade)* (grand)stand; *(d'orateur)* rostrum; **t. libre** *(de journal)* open forum

tribut [triby] *nm* tribute (**à** to)

tributaire [tribytɛr] *adj Fig* **t. de** dependent on

tricher [triʃe] *vi* to cheat ■**tricherie** *nf* cheating, trickery; **une t.** a piece of trickery ■**tricheur, -euse** *nmf Br* cheat, *Am* cheater

tricolore [trikɔlɔr] *adj (cocarde)* red, white and blue; **le drapeau/l'équipe t.** the French flag/ team

tricot [triko] *nm (activité, ouvrage)* knitting; *(chandail)* sweater, *Br* jumper; *(ouvrage)* piece of knitting; **en t.** knitted; **t. de corps** *Br* vest, *Am* undershirt ■**tricoter** *vti* to knit

tricycle [trisikl] *nm* tricycle

trier [trije] *vt (lettres)* to sort; *(vêtements)* to sort through

trifouiller [trifuje] *vi Fam* to rummage around

trilingue [trilɛ̃g] *adj* trilingual

trilogie [trilɔʒi] *nf* trilogy

trimbal(l)er [trɛ̃bale] *Fam* **1** *vt* to cart around **2 se trimbal(l)er** *vpr* to trail around

trimer [trime] *vi Fam* to slave (away)

trimestre [trimɛstr] nm quarter; Scol term; Scol **premier/second/troisième t.** Br autumn orAm fall/winter/summer term ■ **trimestriel, -ielle** adj (revue) quarterly; **bulletin t.** end-of-term Br report orAm report card

tringle [trɛ̃gl] nf rod; **t. à rideaux** curtain rod

Trinité [trinite] nf **la T.** (fête) Trinity; (dogme) the Trinity

trinquer [trɛ̃ke] vi to chink glasses; **t. à la santé de qn** to drink to sb's health

trio [trijo] nm (groupe) & Mus trio

triomphe [trijɔ̃f] nm triumph (sur over); **porter qn en t.** to carry sb shoulder-high ■ **triomphal, -e, -aux, -ales** adj triumphal ■ **triomphant, -ante** adj triumphant ■ **triompher** vi to triumph (**de** over); (jubiler) to be jubilant

tripes [trip] nfpl Culin tripe; Fam guts ■ **tripier, -ière** nmf tripe butcher

triple [tripl] **1** adj treble, triple; Sport **t. saut** triple jump **2** nm **le t.** three times as much (**de** as) ■ **tripler** vti to treble, to triple ■ **triplés, -ées** nmfpl triplets

tripot [tripo] nm gambling den

tripoter [tripote] vt Fam to mess around with, Br to fiddle with

trique [trik] nf cudgel

triste [trist] adj sad; (morne) dreary; (lamentable) unfortunate ■ **tristement** [-əmɑ̃] adv sadly ■ **tristesse** nf sadness; (du temps) dreariness

triturer [trityre] vt (broyer) to grind; Fam (manipuler) to fiddle with

trivial, -e, -iaux, -iales [trivjal, -jo] adj coarse, vulgar ■ **trivialité** nf coarseness, vulgarity

> Il faut noter que l'adjectif anglais **trivial** est un faux ami. Il signifie **insignifiant**.

troc [trɔk] nm exchange; (système économique) barter

troène [trɔɛn] nm privet

trognon [trɔɲɔ̃] nm (de fruit) core; (de chou) stump

trois [trwa] adj & nm inv three; **les t. quarts (de)** three-quarters (of) ■ **troisième 1** adj & nmf third; **le t. âge** (vieillesse) the retirement years; **personne du t. âge** senior citizen **2** nf Scol Br **la t.** ≃ fourth year, Am ≃ eighth grade; Aut (vitesse) third gear ■ **troisièmement** adv thirdly ■ **trois-pièces** nm inv (appartement) three room(ed) Br flat orAm apartment

trombe [trɔ̃b] nf **trombe(s) d'eau** (pluie) rainstorm, downpour; Fig **entrer en t.** to burst in like a whirlwind

trombone [trɔ̃bon] nm (instrument) trombone; (agrafe) paper clip

trompe [trɔ̃p] nf (d'éléphant) trunk; (d'insecte) proboscis; (instrument de musique) horn

tromper [trɔ̃pe] **1** vt (abuser) to fool (**sur** about); (être infidèle à) to be unfaithful to; (échapper à) to elude **2 se tromper** vpr to be mistaken; **se t. de route/de train** to take the wrong road/train; **se t. de date/de jour** to get the date/day wrong; **c'est à s'y t.** you can't tell the difference ■ **trompe-l'œil** nm inv trompe-l'œil; **en t.** trompe-l'œil ■ **tromperie** [-pri] nf deceit, deception ■ **trompeur, -euse** adj (apparences) deceptive, misleading; (personne) deceitful

trompette [trɔ̃pɛt] nf trumpet ■ **trompettiste** nmf trumpet player

tronc [trɔ̃] nm (d'arbre) & Anat trunk; (boîte) collection box

tronche [trɔ̃ʃ] nf Fam face, mug; **il a une drôle de t.** he's really odd-looking; **faire la t.** to sulk; **ce mec-là, c'est une t.!** that guy's really brainy!

tronçon [trɔ̃sɔ̃] nm section ■ **tronçonner** vt to cut into sections ■ **tronçonneuse** nf chainsaw

trône [tron] nm throne ■ **trôner** vi Fig (vase, personne) to occupy the place of honour

tronquer [trɔ̃ke] vt (mot, texte) to shorten

trop [tro] adv (avec adjectif, adverbe) too; (avec verbe) too much; **t. dur/loin** too hard/far; **t. fatigué pour jouer** too tired to play; **boire/lire t.** to drink/read too much; **t. de sel** too much salt; **t. de gens** too many people; **du fromage en t.** too much cheese; **des œufs en t.** too many eggs; **un euro/verre en t.** one euro/glass too many; **t. souvent** too often; **t. peu** not enough; Fig **se sentir de t.** to feel in the way; Fam **en faire t.** to overdo it ■ **trop-plein** (pl **trop-pleins**) nm (excédent) overflow; (dispositif) overflow pipe

trophée [trɔfe] nm trophy

tropique [trɔpik] nm tropic; **les tropiques** the tropics; **sous les tropiques** in the tropics ■ **tropical, -e, -aux, -ales** adj tropical

troquer [trɔke] vt to exchange (**contre** for)

trot [tro] nm trot; **aller au t.** to trot; Fam **au t.** (sans traîner) at the double ■ **trotter** [trɔte] vi (cheval) to trot; Fig (personne) to trot about

trotteuse [trɔtøz] nf (de montre) second hand ■ **trotteur, -euse** nmf (cheval) trotter

trottiner [trɔtine] vi (personne) to trot along

trottinette [trɔtinɛt] nf (jouet) scooter; Fam (voiture) little car

trottoir [trɔtwar] nm Br pavement, Am sidewalk; **t. roulant** moving walkway

trou [tru] nm hole; (d'aiguille) eye; Fam Péj (village) dump, hole; Fig (manque) gap (**dans** in); **t. d'homme** (ouverture) manhole; **t. de (la) serrure** keyhole; Fig **t. de mémoire** memory lapse

trouble [trubl] **1** adj (liquide) cloudy; (image) blurred; (affaire) shady **2** adv **voir t.** to see things blurred **3** nm Littéraire (émoi, émotion) agitation; (désarroi) distress; (désordre) confusion; **troubles** (de santé) trouble; (révolte) disturbances, troubles

troubler [truble] **1** *vt* to disturb; *(vue)* to blur; *(liquide)* to make cloudy; *(esprit)* to unsettle; *(projet)* to upset; *(inquiéter)* to trouble **2 se troubler** *vpr (liquide)* to become cloudy; *(candidat)* to become flustered ▪ **troublant, -ante** *adj (détail)* disturbing, disquieting ▪ **trouble-fête** *nmf inv* killjoy, spoilsport

trouer [true] *vt* to make a hole/holes in; *(silence, ténèbres)* to cut through ▪ **trouée** *nf* gap; *(de ciel)* patch

trouille [truj] *nf Fam* **avoir la t.** to be scared stiff ▪ **trouillard, -arde** *adj Fam (poltron)* chicken

troupe [trup] *nf (de soldats)* troop; *(groupe)* group; *(de théâtre)* company, troupe; **la t., les troupes** *(armée)* the troops

troupeau, -x [trupo] *nm (de vaches)* & *Fig Péj* herd; *(de moutons)* flock

trousse [trus] *nf (étui)* case, kit; *(d'écolier)* pencil case; **t. à outils** toolkit; **t. à pharmacie** first-aid kit; **t. de toilette** toilet bag

trousseau, -x [truso] *nm (de mariée)* trousseau; **t. de clefs** bunch of keys

trousses [trus] *nfpl Fig* **aux t. de qn** on sb's heels

trouvaille [truvaj] *nf* (lucky) find

trouver [truve] **1** *vt* to find; **aller/venir t. qn** to go/come and see sb; **je trouve que…** I think that…; **comment la trouvez-vous?** what do you think of her? **2 se trouver** *vpr* to be; *(être situé)* to be situated; **se t. dans une situation difficile** to find oneself in a difficult situation; **se t. mal** *(s'évanouir)* to faint; **se t. petit** to consider oneself small **3** *v impersonnel* **il se trouve que…** it happens that…

truand [tryɑ̃] *nm* crook

> Il faut noter que le nom anglais **truant** est un faux ami. Il désigne un élève qui fait l'école buissonnière.

truander [tryɑ̃de] *vi Fam (tricher)* to cheat

truc [tryk] *nm Fam (chose)* thing; *(astuce)* trick; *(moyen)* way; **avoir/trouver le t.** to have/get the knack (**pour faire** of doing) ▪ **trucage** *nm* = **truquage**

truchement [tryʃmɑ̃] *nm* **par le t. de qn** through (the intermediary of) sb

truculent, -ente [trykylɑ̃, -ɑ̃t] *adj (langage, personnage)* colourful

> Il faut noter que l'adjectif anglais **truculent** est un faux ami. Il signifie **agressif**.

truelle [tryɛl] *nf* trowel

truffe [tryf] *nf (champignon)* truffle; *(de chien)* nose

truffer [tryfe] *vt (remplir)* to stuff (**de** with) ▪ **truffé, -ée** *adj (pâté)* (garnished) with truffles; *Fig* **t. de** *(balles, fautes)* riddled with; *(citations)* peppered with

truie [trɥi] *nf* sow

truite [trɥit] *nf* trout

truquer [tryke] *vt (photo)* to fake; *(élections, match)* to rig ▪ **truquage** *nm (de cinéma)* (special) effect; *(action)* faking; *(d'élections)* rigging ▪ **truqué, -ée** *adj (élections, match)* rigged; **photo truquée** fake photo; *Cin* **scène truquée** scene with special effects

trust [trœst] *nm Com (cartel)* trust

tsar [dzar] *nm* tsar, czar

TSF [teɛsɛf] *(abrév* **télégraphie sans fil)** *nf Vieilli (poste de radio)* wireless

tsigane [tsigan] **1** *adj* gipsy **2** *nmf* **T.** gipsy

TSVP [teɛsvepe] *(abrév* **tournez s'il vous plaît)** PTO

TTC [tetese] *(abrév* **toutes taxes comprises)** inclusive of tax

tu¹ [ty] *pron personnel* you *(familiar form of address)*

tu² [ty] *pp de* **taire**

tuba [tyba] *nm (instrument de musique)* tuba; *(de plongée)* snorkel

tube [tyb] *nm* tube; *Fam (chanson, disque)* hit; **t. à essai** test tube; *Fam* **marcher à pleins tubes** *(stéréo)* to be going full blast ▪ **tubulaire** *adj* tubular

tuberculose [tybɛrkyloz] *nf* TB, tuberculosis ▪ **tuberculeux, -euse** *adj* tubercular; **être t.** to have TB *or* tuberculosis

TUC [tyk] *(abrév* **travail d'utilité collective)** *nm* = community work project for unemployed young people

tuer [tɥe] **1** *vt* to kill; *Fam (épuiser)* to wear out **2 se tuer** *vpr* to kill oneself; *(dans un accident)* to be killed; *Fig* **se t. à faire qch** to wear oneself out doing sth ▪ **tuant, -ante** *adj Fam (fatigant)* exhausting ▪ **tuerie** *nf* slaughter ▪ **tueur, -euse** *nmf* killer; **t. en série** serial killer

tue-tête [tytɛt] **à tue-tête** *adv* at the top of one's voice

tuile [tɥil] *nf* tile; *Fam (malchance)* (stroke of) bad luck

tulipe [tylip] *nf* tulip

tuméfié, -ée [tymefje] *adj* swollen

tumeur [tymœr] *nf* tumour

tumulte [tymylt] *nm (de la foule)* commotion; *(des passions)* turmoil ▪ **tumultueux, -ueuse** *adj* turbulent

tunique [tynik] *nf* tunic

Tunisie [tynizi] *nf* **la T.** Tunisia ▪ **tunisien, -ienne 1** *adj* Tunisian **2** *nmf* **T., Tunisienne** Tunisian

tunnel [tynɛl] *nm* tunnel; **le t. sous la Manche** the Channel Tunnel

turban [tyrbɑ̃] *nm* turban

turbine [tyrbin] *nf* turbine

turbulences [tyrbylɑ̃s] *nfpl (tourbillons)* turbulence

turbulent, -ente [tyrbylɑ̃, -ɑ̃t] *adj (enfant)* boisterous

turfiste [tyrfist] *nmf* racegoer, *Br* punter

turlupiner [tyrlypine] *vt Fam* **t. qn** to bother sb

Turquie [tyrki] *nf* **la T.** Turkey ▪ **turc, turque 1** *adj* Turkish **2** *nmf* **T., Turque** Turk **3** *nm (langue)* Turkish

turquoise [tyrkwaz] *adj inv* turquoise

tuteur, -trice [tytœr, -tris] **1** *nmf (de mineur)* guardian **2** *nm (bâton)* stake, prop ▪ **tutelle** *nf Jur* guardianship; *Fig* protection

tutoyer [tytwaje] *vt* **t. qn** to address sb using the familiar "tu" form ▪ **tutoiement** *nm* = use of the familiar "tu" *(instead of the more formal "vous")*

tutu [tyty] *nm* tutu

tuyau, -x [tyijo] *nm* pipe; *Fam (conseil)* tip; **t. d'arrosage** hose(pipe); **t. de cheminée** flue; **t. d'échappement** *(de véhicule)* exhaust (pipe) ▪ **tuyauter** *vt Fam* **t. qn** *(conseiller)* to give sb a tip ▪ **tuyauterie** [-tri] *nf (tuyaux)* piping

TVA [tevea] *(abrév* **taxe à la valeur ajoutée)** *nf* VAT

tympan [tɛ̃pɑ̃] *nm* eardrum

type [tip] **1** *nm (genre)* type; *Fam (individu)* fellow, guy, *Br* bloke; *Fig* **le t. même de** the very model of **2** *adj inv* typical; **lettre t.** standard letter ▪ **typique** *adj* typical (**de** of) ▪ **typiquement** *adv* typically

typé, -ée [tipe] *adj* **il est très t.** *(il est italien)* he looks typically Italian

typhoïde [tifɔid] *nf* typhoid (fever)

typhon [tifɔ̃] *nm* typhoon

typographie [typɔgrafi] *nf* typography, printing ▪ **typographe** *nmf* typographer ▪ **typographique** *adj* typographical

tyran [tirɑ̃] *nm* tyrant ▪ **tyrannie** *nf* tyranny ▪ **tyrannique** *adj* tyrannical ▪ **tyranniser** *vt* to tyrannize

tzigane [tzigan] **1** *adj* gipsy **2** *nmf* **T.** gipsy

U, u [y] *nm inv* U, u
UE [yø] (*abrév* **Union européenne**) *nf* EU
Ukraine [ykrɛn] *nf* l'U. the Ukraine
ulcère [ylsɛr] *nm* ulcer ▪ **ulcérer** *vt Fig* u. qn
(*irriter*) to make sb seethe
ULM [yɛlɛm] (*abrév* **ultraléger motorisé**) *nm inv*
Av microlight
ultérieur, -e [ylterjœr] *adj* later, subsequent (**à**
to) ▪ **ultérieurement** *adv* later (on), subsequently
ultimatum [yltimatɔm] *nm* ultimatum; **lancer
un u. à qn** to give sb an ultimatum
ultime [yltim] *adj* last; (*préparatifs*) final
ultramoderne [yltramɔdɛrn] *adj* high-tech
ultrasensible [yltrasɑ̃sibl] *adj* ultra-sensitive
ultrason [yltrasɔ̃] *nm* ultrasound
ultraviolet, -ette [yltravjɔlɛ, -ɛt] *adj & nm*
ultraviolet
un, une [œ̃, yn] **1** *art indéfini* a; (*devant voyelle*)
an; **une page** a page; **un ange** [œ̃nɑ̃ʒ] an angel
2 *adj* one; **la page un** page one; **un kilo** one
kilo; **un jour** one day; **un type (quelconque)**
some *or* a fellow **3** *pron & nmf* one; **l'un** one;
les uns some; **le numéro un** number one; **j'en
ai un** I have one; **l'un d'eux, l'une d'elles** one
of them; *Journ* **la une** front page; *Fam* **j'ai eu
une de ces peurs!** I was really scared!
unanime [ynanim] *adj* unanimous ▪ **unanimité** *nf* unanimity; **à l'u.** unanimously
Unetelle [yntɛl] *nf voir* **Untel**
uni, -ie [yni] *adj* (*famille, couple*) close; (*surface*)
smooth; (*couleur, étoffe*) plain
unième [ynjɛm] *adj* (*after a number*) (-)first;
trente et u. thirty-first; **cent u.** hundred and
first
unifier [ynifje] *vt* to unify ▪ **unification** *nf*
unification
uniforme [ynifɔrm] **1** *adj* (*expression*) uniform;
(*sol*) even; (*mouvement*) regular **2** *nm* uniform
▪ **uniformément** *adv* uniformly ▪ **uniformiser** *vt* to standardize ▪ **uniformité** *nf* (*de
couleurs*) uniformity; (*monotonie*) monotony
unijambiste [yniʒɑ̃bist] **1** *adj* one-legged **2**
nmf one-legged man/woman
unilatéral, -e, -aux, -ales [ynilateral, -o] *adj*
(*décision*) unilateral; (*contrat*) one-sided;
(*stationnement*) on one side of the road/street
only
union [ynjɔ̃] *nf* (*de partis, de consommateurs*)

union, association; (*entente*) unity; (*mariage*)
marriage; **l'U. européenne** the European
Union; **u. libre** cohabitation; **u. monétaire**
monetary union
unique [ynik] *adj* (**a**) (*fille, fils*) only; (*espoir,
souci*) only, sole; (*prix, parti, salaire, marché*)
single; **son seul et u. souci** his/her one and
only worry (**b**) (*exceptionnel*) unique; *Fam*
(*drôle*) priceless; **u. en son genre** completely
unique ▪ **uniquement** *adv* only, just
unir [ynir] **1** *vt* (*personnes, territoires*) to unite;
(*marier*) to join in marriage; (*efforts, qualités*) to
combine (**à** with); **l'amitié qui nous unit** the
friendship that unites us **2 s'unir** *vpr*
(*s'associer*) to unite; (*se marier*) to be joined in
marriage; **s'u. à qn** to join forces with sb
unisexe [ynisɛks] *adj* unisex
unisson [ynisɔ̃] **à l'unisson** *adv* in unison (**de**
with)
unité [ynite] *nf* (*de mesure, élément, régiment*)
unit; (*cohésion*) unity; **u. de longueur** unit of
measurement; **u. de production** production
unit; *Univ* **u. de valeur** credit; *Ordinat* **u.
centrale** central processing unit ▪ **unitaire**
adj (*prix*) per unit
univers [ynivɛr] *nm* universe; *Fig* world
▪ **universalité** *nf* universality ▪ **universel,
-elle** *adj* universal ▪ **universellement** *adv*
universally
université [ynivɛrsite] *nf* university; **à l'u.** *Br* at
university, *Am* in college ▪ **universitaire 1** *adj*
ville/restaurant u. university town/refectory
2 *nmf* academic
Untel, Unetelle [œ̃tɛl, yntɛl] *nmf* what's-his-
name, *f* what's-her-name
uranium [yranjɔm] *nm* uranium
urbain, -aine [yrbɛ̃, -ɛn] *adj* urban
▪ **urbaniser** *vt* to urbanize ▪ **urbanisme** *nm Br*
town planning, *Am* city planning ▪ **urbaniste**
nmf Br town planner, *Am* city planner
urgent, -ente [yrʒɑ̃, -ɑ̃t] *adj* urgent ▪ **urgence**
nf (*de décision, de tâche*) urgency; (*cas d'hôpital*)
emergency; **d'u.** urgently; **mesures d'u.**
emergency measures; *Pol* **état d'u.** state of
emergency; *Méd* **(service des) urgences**
(*d'hôpital*) *Br* casualty (department), *Am*
emergency room, ER; **il y a u.** it's a matter of
urgency ▪ **urgentiste** *nmf Méd* emergency
doctor

urine [yrin] *nf* urine ▪ **uriner** *vi* to urinate ▪ **urinoir** *nm* (public) urinal

urne [yrn] *nf (vase)* urn; *(pour voter)* ballot box; **aller aux urnes** to go to the polls

URSS [yereses, yrs] *(abrév* **Union des républiques socialistes soviétiques)** *nf Anciennement* l'U. the USSR

urticaire [yrtiker] *nf* nettle rash

Uruguay [yrygwe] *nm* l'U. Uruguay

us [ys] *nmpl* **les us et coutumes** the ways and customs

usage [yzaʒ] *nm (utilisation)* use; *(coutume)* custom; *(de mot)* usage; **faire u. de qch** to make use of sth; **faire bon u. de qch** to put sth to good use; **faire de l'u.** *(vêtement)* to wear well; **d'u.** *(habituel)* customary; **à l'u. de** for (the use of); **hors d'u.** out of order; **je n'en ai pas l'u.** I have no use for it ▪ **usagé, -ée** *adj (vêtement)* worn; *(billet)* used ▪ **usager** *nm* user

user [yze] **1** *vt (vêtement)* to wear out; *(personne)* to wear down; *(consommer)* to use (up) **2** *vi* **u. de qch** to use sth **3 s'user** *vpr (tissu, machine)* to wear out; *(talons, personne)* to wear down ▪ **usé, -ée** *adj (tissu)* worn out; *(sujet)* stale; *(personne)* worn out; **eaux usées** dirty *or* waste water

usine [yzin] *nf* factory; **u. à gaz** gasworks; **u. métallurgique** ironworks

usiner [yzine] *vt Tech* to machine

usité, -ée [yzite] *adj* in common use; **peu u.** little used

ustensile [ystãsil] *nm* implement, tool; **u. de cuisine** kitchen utensil

usuel, -elle [yzɥel] *adj* everyday ▪ **usuels** *nmpl (de bibliothèque)* reference books

usure [yzyr] *nf (de pneu)* wear; *(de sol)* wearing away; *Fig* **avoir qn à l'u.** to wear sb down

usurier, -ière [yzyrje, -jɛr] *nmf* usurer

usurper [yzyrpe] *vt* to usurp ▪ **usurpateur, -trice** *nmf* usurper

utérus [yterys] *nm Anat* womb, uterus

utile [ytil] *adj* useful (à to); **puis-je vous être u.?** what can I do for you? ▪ **utilement** *adv* usefully

utiliser [ytilize] *vt* to use ▪ **utilisable** *adj* usable ▪ **utilisateur, -trice** *nmf* user; **u. final** end-user ▪ **utilisation** *nf* use ▪ **utilité** *nf* usefulness; **d'une grande u.** very useful; **déclaré d'u. publique** state-approved

utilitaire [ytiliter] **1** *adj* utilitarian; **véhicule u.** utility vehicle **2** *nf Ordinat* utility

utopie [ytɔpi] *nf (idéal)* utopia; *(projet, idée)* utopian plan/idea ▪ **utopique** *adj* utopian

UV [yve] *(abrév* **ultraviolet)** *nm inv* UV; **faire des UV** *(pour bronzer)* to go on a sunbed

V, v [ve] *nm inv* V, v

va [va] *voir* **aller¹**

vacances [vakɑ̃s] *nfpl Br* holiday(s), *Am* vacation; **en v.** *Br* on holiday, *Am* on vacation; **partir en v.** to go on *Br* holiday *or Am* vacation; **prendre des v.** to take a holiday; **les grandes v.** the summer *Br* holidays *or Am* vacation ▪ **vacancier, -ière** *nmf Br* holidaymaker, *Am* vacationer

vacant, -ante [vakɑ̃, -ɑ̃t] *adj* vacant

vacarme [vakarm] *nm* din, uproar

vaccin [vaksɛ̃] *nm* vaccine; **faire un v. à qn** to vaccinate sb ▪ **vaccination** *nf* vaccination ▪ **vacciner** *vt* to vaccinate; **se faire v.** to get vaccinated (**contre** against); *Fam* **je suis vacciné** I've learnt my lesson

vache [vaʃ] **1** *nf* cow; *Fam Péj (femme méchante)* bitch, cow; *Fam Péj (homme méchant)* pig; **v. laitière** dairy cow; **maladie de la v. folle** mad cow disease; *Fam* **la v.!** *(d'admiration)* wow!; *(de surprise) Br* blimey!, *Am* gee (whiz)! **2** *adj Fam (méchant)* nasty, bitchy ▪ **vachement** *adv Fam (très)* dead, bloody, *Am (beaucoup)* a hell of a lot ▪ **vacherie** *nf Fam (action)* nasty trick; *(parole)* nasty remark

vaciller [vasije] *vi* to sway; *(flamme, lumière)* to flicker; *(mémoire)* to fail ▪ **vacillant, -ante** *adj (lumière)* flickering; *(démarche)* staggering; *(mémoire)* failing

vadrouille [vadruj] *nf Fam* **en v.** roaming about ▪ **vadrouiller** *vi Fam* to roam about

va-et-vient [vaevjɛ̃] *nm inv (mouvement)* movement to and fro; *(de personnes)* comings and goings

vagabond, -onde [vagabɔ̃, -ɔ̃d] **1** *nmf (clochard)* vagrant, tramp **2** *adj* wandering ▪ **vagabondage** *nm* vagrancy ▪ **vagabonder** *vi* to roam, to wander; *Fig (pensée)* to wander

vagin [vaʒɛ̃] *nm Anat* vagina ▪ **vaginal, -ale** *adj Anat* vaginal

vagir [vaʒir] *vi (bébé)* to cry

vague¹ [vag] **1** *adj* vague; *(regard)* vacant; *(souvenir)* dim, vague **2** *nm* vagueness; **regarder dans le v.** to gaze into space, to gaze vacantly; **rester dans le v.** to be vague; **avoir du v. à l'âme** to be melancholy ▪ **vaguement** *adv* vaguely

vague² [vag] *nf (de mer)* & *Fig* wave; **v. de chaleur** heat wave; *Fig* **v. de fond** ground swell; **v. de froid** cold spell *or* snap

vaillant, -ante [vajɑ̃, -ɑ̃t] *adj (courageux)* brave, valiant; *(vigoureux)* healthy ▪ **vaillamment** [-amɑ̃] *adv* valiantly ▪ **vaillance** *nf* bravery

vaille, vailles *voir* **valoir** ▪ **vaille que vaille** *adv* somehow or other

vain, vaine [vɛ̃, vɛn] *adj (sans résultat)* futile; *(mots, promesse)* empty; *(vaniteux)* vain; **en v.** in vain ▪ **vainement** *adv* in vain

vaincre* [vɛ̃kr] *vt (adversaire)* to defeat; *(en sport)* to beat; *Fig (maladie, difficulté)* to overcome ▪ **vaincu, -ue** *nmf* defeated man/woman; *(de match)* loser ▪ **vainqueur 1** *nm* victor; *(de match)* winner **2** *adj m* victorious

vais [ve] *voir* **aller¹**

vaisseau, -x [veso] *nm Anat* vessel; *(bateau)* ship, vessel; **v. spatial** spaceship

vaisselier [vesəlje] *nm (meuble) Br* dresser, *Am* hutch

vaisselle [vesel] *nf* crockery; **faire la v.** to do the washing up, to do the dishes

val [val] *(pl* **vals** *ou* **vaux** [vo]*) nm* valley

valable [valabl] *adj (billet, motif)* valid; *Fam (remarquable, rentable)* worthwhile

valet [valɛ] *nm Cartes* jack; **v. de chambre** valet

valeur [valœr] *nf (prix, qualité)* value; *(mérite)* worth; *(poids)* weight; *Fin* **valeurs** securities; **la v. de** *(équivalent)* the equivalent of; **avoir de la v.** to be valuable; **prendre de la v.** to increase in value; **mettre qch en v.** *(faire ressortir)* to highlight sth; **personne de v.** person of merit; **objets de v.** valuables; **v. refuge** safe investment

valide [valid] *adj (personne)* fit, able-bodied; *(billet)* valid ▪ **valider** *vt* to validate; *(titre de transport)* to stamp; *Ordinat (option)* to confirm ▪ **validité** *nf* validity

valise [valiz] *nf* suitcase; **v. diplomatique** diplomatic *Br* bag *or Am* pouch; **faire ses valises** to pack (one's bags)

vallée [vale] *nf* valley ▪ **vallon** *nm* small valley ▪ **vallonné, -ée** *adj (région)* undulating

valoir* [valwar] **1** *vi (avoir pour valeur)* to be worth; *(s'appliquer)* to apply (**pour** to); **v. mille euros/cher** to be worth a thousand euros/a lot; **un vélo vaut bien une auto** a bicycle is just as good as a car; **il vaut mieux rester** it's better to stay; **il vaut mieux que j'attende** I'd better wait; *Fam* **ça ne vaut rien** it's no good; *Fam* **ça vaut la peine** *ou* **le coup** it's worth while (**de faire** doing); **faire v. qch** *(faire ressortir)* to highlight sth; *(argument)* to put sth forward; *(droit)* to assert sth; **se faire v.** to get oneself noticed **2** *vt* **v. qch à qn** *(ennuis)* to bring sb sth **3** **se valoir** *upr (objets, personnes)* to be as good as each other; *Fam* **ça se vaut** it's all the same

valse [vals] *nf* waltz • **valser** *vi* to waltz • **valseur, -euse** *nmf* waltzer

valve [valv] *nf* valve

vampire [vãpir] *nm* vampire

vandale [vãdal] *nmf* vandal • **vandalisme** *nm* vandalism

vanille [vanij] *nf* vanilla; **glace à la v.** vanilla ice cream • **vanillé, -ée** *adj* vanilla-flavoured; **sucre v.** vanilla sugar

vanité [vanite] *nf (orgueil)* vanity; *Littéraire (futilité)* futility • **vaniteux, -euse** *adj* vain, conceited

vanne [van] *nf (d'écluse)* sluice gate, floodgate; *Fam (remarque)* dig, jibe; *Fam* **envoyer une v. à qn** to have a dig at sb

vanné, -ée [vane] *adj Fam (fatigué) Br* knackered, shattered, *Am* beat

vannerie [vanri] *nf (fabrication)* basket-weaving; *(objets)* basketwork

vanter [vãte] **1** *vt* to praise **2** **se vanter** *upr* to boast, to brag (**de** about, of); *Fam* **il n'y a pas de quoi se v.** there's nothing to brag *or* boast about • **vantard, -arde 1** *adj* boastful **2** *nmf* boaster, braggart • **vantardise** *nf (caractère)* boastfulness; *(propos)* boast

va-nu-pieds [vanypje] *nmf inv* beggar, down-and-out, *Br* tramp

vapeur [vapœr] *nf (brume, émanation)* vapour; **v. (d'eau)** steam; **cuire qch à la v.** to steam sth; **bateau à v.** steamboat • **vaporeux, -euse** *adj (atmosphère)* steamy; *(tissu)* flimsy

vaporiser [vaporize] *vt* to spray • **vaporisateur** *nm (appareil)* spray

vaquer [vake] *vi* **v. à qch** to attend to sth; **v. à ses occupations** to go about one's business

varappe [varap] *nf* rock climbing • **varapper** *vi* to rock climb • **varappeur, -euse** *nmf* rock climber

vareuse [varøz] *nf (d'uniforme)* tunic

variable [varjabl] **1** *adj* variable; *(humeur, temps)* changeable **2** *nf* variable • **variante** *nf* variant • **variation** *nf* variation

varicelle [varisɛl] *nf* chickenpox

varices [varis] *nfpl* varicose veins

varier [varje] *vti* to vary (**de** from) • **varié, -ée** *adj (diversifié)* varied; *(vocabulaire)* wide

variété [varjete] *nf* variety; **spectacle de variétés** *(chansons)* variety show

variole [varjɔl] *nf* smallpox

vas [va] *voir* **aller**[1]

vasculaire [vaskylɛr] *adj* vascular

vase[1] [vaz] *nm (récipient)* vase

vase[2] [vaz] *nf (boue)* mud, silt • **vaseux, -euse** *adj (boueux)* muddy, silty; *Fam (faible)* under the weather, *Br* off colour; *Fam (idées)* woolly

vaseline [vazlin] *nf* Vaseline®

vasistas [vazistas] *nm* fanlight

vasouillard, -arde [vazujar, -ard] *adj Fam* confused, muddled

vaste [vast] *adj* vast, huge

Vatican [vatikã] *nm* **le V.** the Vatican

va-tout [vatu] *nm inv* **jouer son v.** to stake one's all

vaudeville [vodvil] *nm Théâtre* light comedy

vau-l'eau [volo] **à vau-l'eau** *adv* **aller à v.** to go to rack and ruin

vaurien, -ienne [vorjɛ̃, -jɛn] *nmf* good-for-nothing

vaut [vo] *voir* **valoir**

vautour [votur] *nm* vulture

vautrer [votre] **se vautrer** *upr (personne)* to sprawl; **se v. dans la boue/le vice** to wallow in the mud/in vice

va-vite [vavit] **à la va-vite** *adv Fam* in a rush

veau, -x [vo] *nm (animal)* calf; *(viande)* veal; *(cuir)* calfskin; *Fam (voiture)* really slow car

vécu, -ue [veky] **1** *pp de* **vivre 2** *adj (histoire)* real-life **3** *nm* real-life experience

vedette [vədɛt] *nf* (**a**) *(célébrité)* star; **avoir la v., être en v.** *(dans un spectacle)* to top the bill (**b**) *(bateau)* launch

végétal, -e, -aux, -ales [veʒetal, -o] **1** *adj* **huile végétale** vegetable oil; **règne v.** vegetable kingdom **2** *nm* plant • **végétalien, -ienne** *adj & nmf* vegan • **végétarien, -ienne** *adj & nmf* vegetarian • **végétation** *nf* vegetation • **végétations** *nfpl Méd* adenoids

végéter [veʒete] *vi Péj (personne)* to vegetate

véhément, -ente [veemã, -ãt] *adj* vehement • **véhémence** *nf* vehemence

véhicule [veikyl] *nm* vehicle; **v. tout-terrain** off-road *or* all-terrain vehicle • **véhiculer** *vt* to convey

veille [vɛj] *nf* (**a**) *(jour précédent)* **la v. (de qch)** the day before (sth); **la v. de Noël** Christmas Eve; **à la v. de qch** *(événement)* on the eve of sth; *Fam* **ce n'est pas demain la v.** that's not going to happen for quite a while (**b**) *(état)* wakefulness; *Ordinat* standby mode; **en (mode) v.** in standby mode

veillée [veje] *nf (soirée)* evening; *(de mort)* vigil; **v. d'armes** knightly vigil

veiller [veje] **1** *vi* to stay up *or* awake; *(sentinelle)* to keep watch; **v. à qch** to see to sth; **v. à ce que...** *(+ subjunctive)* to make sure that...; **v. sur qn** to watch over sb; *Fig* **v. au grain** to keep an eye open for trouble **2** *vt (malade)* to sit up with • **veilleur** *nm* **v. de nuit**

night watchman ▪**veilleuse** nf (de voiture) Br sidelight, Am parking light; (de cuisinière) pilot light; (lampe allumée la nuit) nightlight; Fam **mets-la en v.!** put a sock in it!

veinard, -arde [vɛnar, -ard] nmf Fam lucky devil

veine [vɛn] nf Anat, Bot & Géol vein; Fam (chance) luck; Fam **avoir de la v.** to be lucky or Br jammy

vêler [vele] vi to calve

véliplanchiste [veliplɑ̃ʃist] nmf windsurfer

velléité [veleite] nf vague desire

vélo [velo] nm bike, bicycle; (activité) cycling; **faire du v.** to cycle, to go cycling; **v. tout-terrain** mountain bike ▪**vélodrome** nm velodrome ▪**vélomoteur** nm moped

velours [vəlur] nm velvet; **v. côtelé** corduroy ▪**velouté, -ée 1** adj velvety; (au goût) mellow, smooth **2** nm (texture) smoothness; **v. d'asperges** cream of asparagus soup

velu, -ue [vəly] adj hairy

venaison [vənɛzɔ̃] nf venison

vénal, -e, -aux, -ales [venal, -o] adj mercenary

vendange [vɑ̃dɑ̃ʒ] nf (récolte) grape harvest; (raisin récolté) grapes (harvested); **une bonne v.** a good vintage; **vendanges** (période) grape-harvesting time; **faire les vendanges** to pick the grapes ▪**vendanger** vi to pick the grapes ▪**vendangeur, -euse** nmf grape picker

vendetta [vɑ̃deta] nf vendetta

vendre [vɑ̃dr] **1** vt to sell; **v. qch à qn** to sell sb sth, to sell sth to sb; **v. qch 10 euros** to sell sth for 10 euros; **'à v.'** 'for sale' **2 se vendre** vpr to be sold; **ça se vend bien** it sells well ▪**vendeur, -euse** nmf (de magasin) Br sales or shop assistant, Am sales clerk; (non professionnel) seller

vendredi [vɑ̃drədi] nm Friday; **V. saint** Good Friday

vénéneux, -euse [venenø, -øz] adj poisonous

vénérable [venerabl] adj venerable ▪**vénérer** vt to venerate

vénérien, -ienne [venerjɛ̃, -jɛn] adj venereal

venger [vɑ̃ʒe] **1** vt to avenge **2 se venger** vpr to get one's revenge (**de qn** on sb; **de qch** for sth) ▪**vengeance** nf revenge, vengeance ▪**vengeur, -eresse 1** adj vengeful **2** nmf avenger

venin [vənɛ̃] nm poison, venom; Fig venom ▪**venimeux, -euse** adj poisonous, venomous; Fig (haineux) venomous

venir* [vənir] **1** (aux **être**) vi to come (**de** from); **v. faire qch** to come to do sth; **viens me voir** come and see me; **je viens/venais d'arriver** I've/I'd just arrived; **en v. à** (conclusion) to come to; **où veux-tu en v.?** what are you getting or driving at?; **les jours qui viennent** the coming days; **faire v. qn** to send for sb; **une idée m'est venue** an idea occurred to me; **d'où vient que...?** how is it that...? **2** v

impersonnel **s'il venait à pleuvoir** if it happened to rain

vent [vɑ̃] nm wind; **il y a** ou **il fait du v.** it's windy; **avoir v. de qch** to get wind of sth; Fam **dans le v.** (à la mode) hip, with it

vente [vɑ̃t] nf sale; **en v.** (en magasin) on sale; **mettre qch en v.** to put sth up for sale; **v. aux enchères** auction (sale); **v. de charité** charity sale; **v. par correspondance** mail order

ventilateur [vɑ̃tilatœr] nm (électrique) fan; (de voiture) blower ▪**ventilation** nf ventilation ▪**ventiler** vt to ventilate

ventouse [vɑ̃tuz] nf (de sangsue) sucker; (de plastique) suction pad

ventre [vɑ̃tr] nm stomach, belly; (utérus) womb; (de cruche) bulge; **à plat v.** flat on one's face; **avoir/prendre du v.** to have/get a paunch; **avoir mal au v.** to have a sore stomach; Fam **il n'a rien dans le v.** he has no guts ▪**ventru, -ue** adj (personne) pot-bellied; (objet) bulging

ventriloque [vɑ̃trilɔk] nmf ventriloquist

venu, -ue [vəny] **1** pp de venir **2** adj **bien v.** (à propos) timely; **mal v.** untimely **3** nmf **nouveau v., nouvelle venue** newcomer; **le premier v.** (just) anyone **4** nf **venue** (de personne, de printemps) coming; **dès sa venue au monde** since he/she came into the world

> Il faut noter que le nom anglais **venue** est un faux ami. Il désigne un lieu de réunion.

vêpres [vɛpr] nfpl Rel vespers

ver [vɛr] nm (animal) & Ordinat worm; (larve) grub; (de fruits, de fromage) maggot; Fig **tirer les vers du nez à qn** to drag it out of sb; **v. à soie** silkworm; **v. de terre** (earth)worm; **v. luisant** glow-worm; **v. solitaire** tapeworm

véracité [verasite] nf truthfulness

véranda [verɑ̃da] nf veranda(h); (en verre) conservatory

verbaliser [verbalize] vi (policier) to record the details of an offence

verbe [vɛrb] nm verb ▪**verbal, -e, -aux, -ales** adj (promesse, expression) verbal

verbeux, -euse [vɛrbø, -øz] adj Péj verbose ▪**verbiage** nm Péj verbiage

verdâtre [vɛrdɑtr] adj greenish

verdeur [vɛrdœr] nf (de fruit, de vin) tartness; (de vieillard) sprightliness; (de langage) crudeness

verdict [vɛrdikt] nm verdict

verdir [vɛrdir] vti to turn green ▪**verdoyant, -ante** adj green ▪**verdure** nf (végétation) greenery; **théâtre de v.** open-air theatre

véreux, -euse [verø, -øz] adj (fruit) wormy, maggoty; Fig (malhonnête) dubious, shady

verger [vɛrʒe] nm orchard

vergetures [vɛrʒətyr] nfpl stretch marks

verglas [vɛrgla] nm Br (black) ice, Am glaze ▪**verglacé, -ée** adj (route) icy

vergogne [vɛrgɔɲ] **sans vergogne 1** *adj* shameless **2** *adv* shamelessly

véridique [veridik] *adj* truthful

vérifier [verifje] **1** *vt* to check, to verify; *(comptes)* to audit **2 se vérifier** *vpr* to prove correct ▪**vérifiable** *adj* verifiable ▪**vérification** *nf* checking, verification; *(de comptes)* audit(ing)

vérité [verite] *nf (de déclaration)* truth; *(de personnage, de tableau)* trueness to life; *(sincérité)* sincerity; **en v.** in fact; **dire la v.** to tell the truth

véritable [veritabl] *adj (histoire, ami)* true, real; *(cuir, or, nom)* real, genuine; *(en intensif)* real ▪**véritablement** [-əmā] *adv* really

verlan [vɛrlā] *nm* back slang *(in which the syllables of words are inverted)*

vermeil, -eille [vɛrmej] *adj* bright red; **carte vermeil** = senior citizen's rail pass

vermicelle [vɛrmisɛl] *nm Culin (nouille)* vermicelli; **vermicelles chinois** Chinese noodles

vermine [vɛrmin] *nf (insectes, racaille)* vermin

vermoulu, -ue [vɛrmuly] *adj* worm-eaten

vermouth [vɛrmut] *nm* vermouth

verni, -ie [vɛrni] *adj (meuble, parquet)* varnished; *Fam (chanceux)* lucky

vernir [vɛrnir] *vt (bois)* to varnish; *(céramique)* to glaze ▪**vernis** *nm* varnish; *(pour céramique)* glaze; *Fig (apparence)* veneer; **v. à ongles** nail polish *or Br* varnish ▪**vernissage** *nm (d'exposition)* opening

verra, verrait [vera, verɛ] *voir* **voir**

verre [vɛr] *nm (substance, récipient)* glass; **boire** *ou* **prendre un v.** to have a drink; **porter des verres** to wear glasses; **gravure sous v.** glass-mounted engraving; **v. de bière** glass of beer; **v. à bière/à vin** beer/wine glass; **v. à dents** toothbrush glass *or* mug; **v. de contact** contact lens ▪**verrerie** *nf (objets)* glassware

verrou [veru] *nm* bolt; **fermer qch au v.** to bolt sth; **sous les verrous** behind bars ▪**verrouiller** *vt (porte)* to bolt; *(quartier)* to seal off

verrue [very] *nf* wart; **v. plantaire** verruca

vers¹ [vɛr] *prép (direction)* toward(s); *(approximation)* around, about

vers² [vɛr] *nm (de poème)* line; **des vers** *(poésie)* verse

versant [vɛrsā] *nm* slope, side

versatile [vɛrsatil] *adj* fickle

> Il faut noter que l'adjectif anglais **versatile** est un faux ami. Il signifie **polyvalent**.

verse [vɛrs] **à verse** *adv* pleuvoir à v. to pour (down); **la pluie tombait à v.** the rain was coming down in torrents

versé, -ée [vɛrse] *adj Littéraire* **v. dans** well-versed in

Verseau [vɛrso] *nm (signe)* Aquarius; **être V.** to be (an) Aquarius

verser [vɛrse] **1** *vt* to pour (out); *(larmes, sang)* to shed; *(argent)* to pay (**sur un compte** into an account) **2** *vi (véhicule)* to overturn ▪**versement** [-əmā] *nm* payment ▪**verseur** *adj* **bec v.** spout

verset [vɛrse] *nm* verse

version [vɛrsjɔ̃] *nf (de film, d'incident)* version; *Scol (traduction)* translation *(into one's mother tongue)*, *Br* unseen; *Cin* **en v. originale** in the original language; **en v. française** dubbed *(into French)*

verso [vɛrso] *nm* back (of the page); **'voir au v.'** 'see overleaf'

vert, verte [vɛr, vɛrt] **1** *adj* green; *(pas mûr)* unripe; *(vin)* too young; *Fig (vieillard)* sprightly; *Fam (écologiste)* green, eco-friendly; **aller en classe verte** to go on a school trip to the countryside; *Fig* **en dire des vertes et des pas mûres** to say some pretty shocking things **2** *nm* green; **se mettre au v.** to go go to the country (to recuperate); *Pol* **les Verts** the Greens

vertèbre [vɛrtɛbr] *nf* vertebra

vertement [vɛrtəmā] *adv* sharply

vertical, -e, -aux, -ales [vɛrtikal, -o] *adj & nf* vertical; **à la verticale** vertically ▪**verticalement** *adv* vertically

vertige [vɛrtiʒ] *nm (étourdissement)* (feeling of) dizziness *or* giddiness; *(peur du vide)* vertigo; **vertiges** dizzy spells; **avoir le v.** to be *or* feel dizzy *or* giddy; **donner le v. à qn** to make sb (feel) dizzy *or* giddy ▪**vertigineux, -euse** *adj (hauteur)* giddy, dizzy; *Fig (très grand)* staggering

vertu [vɛrty] *nf* virtue; **en v. de** in accordance with ▪**vertueux, -euse** *adj* virtuous

verve [vɛrv] *nf (d'orateur)* verve

verveine [vɛrvɛn] *nf (plante)* verbena, *(tisane)* verbena tea

vésicule [vezikyl] *nf* **v. biliaire** gall bladder

vessie [vesi] *nf* bladder

veste [vɛst] *nf* jacket, coat

vestiaire [vɛstjɛr] *nm (de théâtre)* cloakroom; *(de piscine, de stade)* changing room, *Am* locker room

vestibule [vɛstibyl] *nm* (entrance) hall

vestiges [vɛstiʒ] *nmpl (ruines)* remains; *(traces)* relics

vestimentaire [vɛstimāter] *adj* **dépense v.** clothing expenditure; **élégance v.** sartorial elegance

veston [vɛstɔ̃] *nm (suit)* jacket

vêtement [vɛtmā] *nm* garment, article of clothing; **vêtements** clothes; **vêtements de sport** sportswear; **industrie du v.** clothing industry

vétéran [veterā] *nm* veteran

vétérinaire [veteriner] **1** *adj* veterinary **2** *nmf* vet, *Br* veterinary surgeon, *Am* veterinarian

vétille [vetij] *nf* trifle, triviality

vêtir* [vetir] *vt*, **se vêtir** *vpr* to dress ▪ **vêtu, -ue** *adj* dressed (**de** in)

veto [veto] *nm inv* veto; **opposer son v. à qch** to veto sth

vétuste [vetyst] *adj* dilapidated

veuf, veuve [vœf, vœv] **1** *adj* widowed **2** *nm* widower **3** *nf* widow

veuille(s), veuillent [vœœj] *voir* **vouloir**

veule [vøl] *adj Littéraire* effete

veut, veux [vø] *voir* **vouloir**

vexer [vɛkse] **1** *vt* to upset, to hurt **2 se vexer** *vpr* to get upset (**de** at) ▪ **vexant, -ante** *adj* upsetting, hurtful; *(contrariant)* annoying ▪ **vexation** *nf* humiliation

> Il faut noter que le verbe anglais **to vex** est un faux ami. Il signifie **fâcher, chagriner**.

VF [veɛf] *(abrév* **version française)** *nf* **film en VF** film dubbed into French

viable [vjabl] *adj (entreprise, enfant)* viable ▪ **viabilité** *nf* viability

viaduc [vjadyk] *nm* viaduct

viager, -ère [vjaʒe, -ɛr] **1** *adj* **rente viagère** life annuity **2** *nm* life annuity

Viagra® [vjagra] *nm Méd* Viagra®

viande [vjɑ̃d] *nf* meat

vibrer [vibre] *vi* to vibrate; *(être ému)* to be stirred (**de** with); **faire v. qn** to stir sb; **sa voix vibrait de colère** his/her voice was shaking with anger ▪ **vibrant, -ante** *adj (hommage)* stirring ▪ **vibration** *nf* vibration ▪ **vibromasseur** *nm* vibrator

vicaire [vikɛr] *nm (anglican)* curate

vice [vis] *nm (perversité)* vice; *(défectuosité)* defect; *Jur* **v. de forme** flaw, legal technicality

vice versa [vis(e)vɛrsa] *adv* vice versa

vicié, -ée [visje] *adj (personne)* corrupt; *(air, atmosphère)* polluted ▪ **vicier** *vt (personne)* to corrupt, *(air, atmosphère)* to pollute

vicieux, -ieuse [visjø, -jøz] *adj (pervers)* depraved; *(perfide)* underhand

> Il faut noter que l'adjectif anglais **vicious** est un faux ami. Il signifie **méchant**.

vicinal, -e, -aux, -ales [visinal, -o] *adj* **chemin v.** minor road, *Br* byroad

vicissitudes [visisityd] *nfpl* vicissitudes

vicomte [vikɔ̃t] *nm* viscount ▪ **vicomtesse** *nf* viscountess

victime [viktim] *nf* victim; *(d'accident)* casualty; **être v. de** *(accident, attentat)* to be the victim of

victoire [viktwar] *nf* victory; *(en sport)* win ▪ **victorieux, -ieuse** *adj* victorious; *(équipe)* winning

victuailles [viktɥaj] *nfpl* provisions

vidange [vidɑ̃ʒ] *nf* emptying, draining; *(de véhicule)* oil change ▪ **vidanger** *vt* to empty, to drain

vide [vid] **1** *adj* empty **2** *nm (espace)* empty

space; *(d'emploi du temps)* gap; *Phys* vacuum; **regarder dans le v.** to stare into space; **emballé sous v.** vacuum-packed; **à v.** empty

vidéo [video] *adj inv & nf* video ▪ **vidéocassette** *nf* video (cassette) ▪ **vidéoclip** *nm (music)* video

vidéodisque [videodisk] *nm Br* videodisc, *Am* videodisk

vider [vide] **1** *vt* to empty; *(lieu)* to vacate; *(poisson, volaille)* to gut; *Fam* **v. qn** *(chasser)* to throw sb out; *(épuiser)* to tire sb out; *Fam* **j'ai vidé mon sac** I got it off my chest **2 se vider** *vpr* to empty ▪ **vidé, -ée** *adj Fam (fatigué)* exhausted ▪ **vide-ordures** *nm inv Br* rubbish or *Am* garbage chute ▪ **vide-poches** *nm inv (de véhicule)* glove compartment ▪ **videur** *nm Fam (de boîte de nuit)* bouncer

vie [vi] *nf* life; *(durée)* lifetime; **en v.** living; **à v., pour la v.** for life; **donner la v. à qn** to give birth to sb; *Fig* **avoir la v. dure** *(préjugés)* to die hard

vieil, vieille [vjɛj] *voir* **vieux**

vieillard [vjɛjar] *nm* old man; **les vieillards** old people ▪ **vieillerie** *nf (objet)* old thing; *(idée)* old idea ▪ **vieillesse** *nf* old age

vieillir [vjejir] **1** *vi* to grow old; *(changer)* to age; *(théorie, mot)* to become old-fashioned **2** *vt* **v. qn** *(vêtement)* to make sb look old(er) ▪ **vieilli, -ie** *adj (démodé)* old-fashioned ▪ **vieillissant, -ante** *adj* ageing ▪ **vieillissement** *nm* ageing

vieillot, -otte [vjɛjo, -ɔt] *adj* old-fashioned

Vienne [vjɛn] *nm ou f* Vienna

viens, vient [vjɛ̃] *voir* **venir**

vierge [vjɛrʒ] **1** *adj (femme, neige)* virgin; *(feuille de papier, film)* blank; **être v.** *(femme, homme)* to be a virgin **2** *nf* virgin; **la V.** *(signe)* Virgo; **être V.** to be (a) Virgo

Vietnam, Viêt Nam [vjɛtnam] *nm* **le V.** Vietnam ▪ **vietnamien, -ienne 1** *adj* Vietnamese **2** *nmf* **V., Vietnamienne** Vietnamese

vieux, vieille, vieux, vieilles [vjø, vjɛj]

> **vieil** is used before masculine singular nouns beginning with a vowel or mute h.

1 *adj* old; **être v. jeu** *(adj inv)* to be old-fashioned; *Péj* **v. garçon** bachelor; *Péj* **vieille fille** old maid; **se faire v.** to get old **2** *nm* old man; **les vieux** old people; *Fam* **mon v.!** *(mon ami) Br* mate!, pal! **3** *nf* **vieille** old woman; *Fam* **ma vieille!** *(mon amie)* dear!

vif, vive [vif, viv] **1** *adj (personne)* lively; *(imagination)* vivid; *(intelligence, vent, douleur)* sharp; *(intérêt, satisfaction)* great; *(couleur, lumière)* bright; *(froid)* biting; *(pas, mouvement)* quick; **brûler qn v.** to burn sb alive **2** *nm* **entrer dans le v. du sujet** to get to the heart of the matter; **à v.** *(plaie)* open; **piqué au v.** *(vexé)* cut to the quick

vigie [viʒi] *nf (matelot)* lookout; *(poste)* lookout post

vigilant, -ante [viʒilɑ̃, -ɑ̃t] *adj* vigilant ▪ **vigilance** *nf* vigilance

vigile [viʒil] *nm* watchman

> Il faut noter que le nom anglais **vigil** est un faux ami. Il ne signifie jamais **gardien**.

vigne [viɲ] *nf (plante)* vine; *(plantation)* vineyard; **pied de v.** vine (stock) ▪ **vigneron, -onne** [-ərɔ̃, -ɔn] *nmf* wine grower ▪ **vignoble** *nm* vineyard; *(région)* vineyards

vignette [viɲɛt] *nf (de véhicule)* road tax sticker, *Br* ≃ road tax disc; *(de médicament)* label *(for reimbursement by Social Security)*

vigueur [vigœr] *nf* vigour; **entrer/être en v.** *(loi)* to come into/be in force ▪ **vigoureux, -euse** *adj (personne, style)* vigorous; *(bras)* sturdy

vilain, -aine [vilɛ̃, -ɛn] *adj (laid)* ugly; *(peu sage)* naughty; *(impoli)* rude

villa [vila] *nf* villa

village [vilaʒ] *nm* village ▪ **villageois, -oise** *nmf* villager

ville [vil] *nf* town; *(grande)* city; **aller/être en v.** to go (in)to/be in town; **v. d'eaux** spa (town)

villégiature [vileʒjatyr] *nf* **lieu de v.** *Br* holiday resort, *Am* vacation resort

vin [vɛ̃] *nm* wine; **v. ordinaire** *ou* **de table** table wine; **v. d'honneur** reception *(in honour of sb)* ▪ **vinicole** *adj (région)* wine-growing

vinaigre [vinɛgr] *nm* vinegar ▪ **vinaigrette** *nf (sauce)* vinaigrette, *Br* French dressing, *Am* Italian dressing

vindicatif, -ive [vɛ̃dikatif, -iv] *adj* vindictive

vingt [vɛ̃] ([vɛ̃t] before vowel or mute h and in numbers 22-29) *adj & nm inv* twenty; **v. et un** twenty-one ▪ **vingtaine** *nf* **une v. (de)** *(nombre)* about twenty ▪ **vingtième** *adj & nmf* twentieth

vinyle [vinil] *nm* vinyl

viol [vjɔl] *nm (de personne)* rape; *(de lieu)* violation ▪ **violation** *nf* violation ▪ **violenter** *vt* to rape ▪ **violer** *vt (femme)* to rape; *(tombe)* to desecrate; *(secret)* to divulge ▪ **violeur** *nm* rapist

violent, -ente [vjɔlɑ̃, -ɑ̃t] *adj* violent; *(effort)* strenuous ▪ **violemment** [-amɑ̃] *adv* violently ▪ **violence** *nf* violence; **acte de v.** act of violence

violet, -ette [vjɔlɛ, -ɛt] 1 *adj & nm (couleur)* purple 2 *nf* **violette** *(fleur)* violet ▪ **violacé, -ée** *adj* purplish-blue; **v. par le froid** blue with cold

violon [vjɔlɔ̃] *nm* violin; *Fig* **accordons nos violons** let's make sure we get our stories straight ▪ **violoncelle** *nm* cello ▪ **violoncelliste** *nmf* cellist ▪ **violoniste** *nmf* violinist

vipère [vipɛr] *nf* adder, viper

virage [viraʒ] *nm (de route)* bend; *(de véhicule)* turn; *Fig (revirement)* change of course

virée [vire] *nf Fam (en voiture)* drive

virer [vire] 1 *vi* to turn; **v. au bleu** to turn blue 2 *vt Fin (somme)* to transfer *(à* to); *Fam* **v. qn** to chuck *or* kick sb out; *(d'un travail)* to fire sb; **v. qch** to get rid of sth, to chuck sth out ▪ **virement** *nm Fin* transfer

virevolter [virvɔlte] *vi* to spin round

virginité [virʒinite] *nf* virginity

virgule [virgyl] *nf (ponctuation)* comma; *Math* (decimal) point; **2 v. 5** 2 point 5

viril, -e [viril] *adj* virile; *(force, attribut)* male ▪ **virilité** *nf* virility

virtuel, -elle [virtɥɛl] *adj* potential; *(image)* virtual; **réalité virtuelle** virtual reality ▪ **virtuellement** *adv (potentiellement)* potentially; *(très probablement)* virtually

> Il faut noter que l'adverbe anglais **virtually** ne s'emploie jamais dans le sens de **potentiellement**.

virtuose [virtɥoz] *nmf* virtuoso ▪ **virtuosité** *nf* virtuosity

virulent, -ente [virylɑ̃, -ɑ̃t] *adj* virulent ▪ **virulence** *nf* virulence

virus [virys] *nm Méd & Ordinat* virus

vis¹ [vi] *voir* **vivre, voir**

vis² [vis] *nf* screw

visa [viza] *nm (de passeport)* visa; **v. de censure** *(de film)* certificate

visage [vizaʒ] *nm* face

vis-à-vis [vizavi] 1 *prép* **v. de** *(en face de)* opposite; *(envers)* towards; *(comparé à)* compared to 2 *nm inv (personne)* person opposite

viscères [visɛr] *nmpl* intestines ▪ **viscéral, -e, -aux, -ales** *adj Fig (haine)* deep-seated

viscosité [viskozite] *nf* viscosity

viser [vize] 1 *vt (cible)* to aim at; *(concerner)* to be aimed at; *(document)* to stamp 2 *vi* to aim *(à* at); **v. à faire qch** to aim to do sth ▪ **visées** *nfpl Fig (desseins)* aims; **avoir des visées sur qn/qch** to have designs on sb/sth ▪ **viseur** *nm Phot* viewfinder; *(d'arme)* sight

visible [vizibl] *adj* visible; **v. à l'œil nu** visible to the naked eye ▪ **visibilité** *nf* visibility ▪ **visiblement** [-amɑ̃] *adv* visibly

visière [vizjɛr] *nf (de casquette)* peak; *(en plastique)* eyeshade; *(de casque)* visor

vision [vizjɔ̃] *nf (conception, image)* vision; *(sens)* sight; *Fam* **avoir des visions** to be seeing things ▪ **visionnaire** *adj & nmf* visionary ▪ **visionner** *vt (film)* to view ▪ **visionneuse** *nf (pour diapositives)* viewer

visite [vizit] *nf* visit; *(personne)* visitor; *(examen)* inspection; **rendre v. à qn, faire une v. à qn** to visit sb; **avoir de la v.** to have a visitor/visitors; **heures de v.** visiting hours; **v. (à domicile)** *(de médecin)* (house) call; **v. médicale** medical examination; **v. guidée** guided tour ▪ **visiter**

vt (lieu touristique, patient) to visit; *(examiner)* to inspect ▪**visiteur, -euse** *nmf* visitor

vison [vizɔ̃] *nm* mink

visqueux, -euse [viskø, -øz] *adj* viscous; *(surface)* sticky

visser [vise] *vt* to screw on

visu [vizy] **de visu** *adv Littéraire* with one's own eyes

visuel, -elle [vizɥɛl] *adj* visual ▪**visualiser** *vt* to visualize; *Ordinat (afficher)* to display

vit [vi] *voir* **vivre, voir**

vital, -e, -aux, -ales [vital, -o] *adj* vital ▪**vitalité** *nf* vitality

vitamine [vitamin] *nf* vitamin ▪**vitaminé, -ée** *adj* vitamin-enriched

vite [vit] *adv (rapidement)* quickly, fast; *(sous peu)* soon; **v.!** quick(ly)! ▪**vitesse** *nf* speed; *(de moteur)* gear; **à toute v.** at top *or* full speed; *Fam* **en v.** quickly

viticole [vitikɔl] *adj (région)* wine-growing ▪**viticulteur, -trice** *nmf* wine grower ▪**viticulture** *nf* wine growing

vitre [vitr] *nf (window)pane; (de véhicule, de train)* window ▪**vitrage** *nm (vitres)* windows ▪**vitrail, -aux** *nm* stained-glass window ▪**vitré, -ée** *adj* **porte vitrée** glass door ▪**vitreux, -euse** *adj Fig (regard, yeux)* glassy ▪**vitrier** *nm* glazier

vitrine [vitrin] *nf (de magasin)* (shop) window; *(meuble)* display cabinet

vitriol [vitrijɔl] *nm* vitriol

vivable [vivabl] *adj Fam (personne)* easy to live with; *(endroit)* fit to live in

vivace [vivas] *adj (plante)* perennial; *Fig (souvenir)* vivid ▪**vivacité** *nf* liveliness; *(d'imagination)* vividness; *(d'intelligence)* sharpness; *(de couleur)* brightness; *(emportement)* petulance; **v. d'esprit** quick-wittedness

vivant, -ante [vivɑ̃, -ɑ̃t] **1** *adj (en vie)* alive, living; *(récit, rue, enfant)* lively; *(être, matière, preuve)* living **2** *nm* **de son v.** in one's lifetime; **les vivants** the living

vivats [viva] *nmpl* cheers

vive¹ [viv] *voir* **vif**

vive² [viv] *exclam* **v. le roi!** long live the king!

vivement [vivmɑ̃] *adv* quickly; *(répliquer)* sharply; *(regretter)* deeply; **v. demain!** I can hardly wait for tomorrow!, *Br* roll on tomorrow!; **v. qu'il parte** I'll be glad when he's gone

vivier [vivje] *nm* fish pond

vivifier [vivifje] *vt* to invigorate

vivisection [viviseksjɔ̃] *nf* vivisection

vivoter [vivɔte] *vi Fam* to struggle to get by

vivre* [vivr] **1** *vi* to live; **elle vit encore** she's still alive *or* living; **faire v. qn** *(famille)* to support sb; **v. vieux** to live to be old; **facile/difficile à v.** easy/hard to get along with; **v. de** *(fruits)* to live on; *(travail)* to live by; **avoir de quoi v.** to have enough to live on **2** *vt (vie)* to live; *(aventure, époque)* to live through; *(éprouver)* to experience ▪**vivres** *nmpl* food, supplies

vlan [vlɑ̃] *exclam* bang!, wham!

VO [veo] *(abrév* **version originale)** *nf* **film en VO** film in the original language

vocabulaire [vɔkabylɛr] *nm* vocabulary

vocal, -e, -aux, -ales [vɔkal, -o] *adj* vocal ▪**vocalises** *nfpl* **faire des v.** to do voice exercises

vocation [vɔkɑsjɔ̃] *nf* vocation, calling

vociférer [vɔsifere] *vti* to shout angrily ▪**vociférations** *nfpl* shouting

vodka [vɔdka] *nf* vodka; **v. orange** *(verre)* vodka and orange

vœu, -x [vø] *nm (souhait)* wish; *(promesse)* vow; **faire un v.** to make a wish; **faire le v. de faire qch** to vow to do sth; **tous mes vœux!** best wishes!

vogue [vɔg] *nf* fashion, vogue; **en v.** in vogue ▪**voguer** *vi Littéraire* to sail

voici [vwasi] *prép* here is/are; **me v.** here I am; **me v. triste** I'm sad now; **v. dix ans** ten years ago; **v. dix ans que…** it's ten years since…

voie [vwa] *nf (route)* road; *(rails)* track, line; *(partie de route)* lane; *(chemin)* way; *(de gare)* platform; *(de communication)* line; *(moyen)* means, way; *(diplomatique)* channels; *Fig* **préparer la v.** to pave the way; *Fig* **sur la bonne v.** on the right track; **en v. de** in the process of; **pays en v. de développement** developing country; **v. sans issue** dead end; **v. navigable** waterway; **v. publique** public highway

voilà [vwala] *prép* there is/are; **les v.** there they are; **v., j'arrive!** all right, I'm coming!; **le v. parti** he has left now; **v. dix ans** ten years ago; **v. dix ans que…** it's ten years since…; **et v.!** there you go!

voile¹ [vwal] *nm (étoffe, coiffure)* & *Fig* veil ▪**voilage** *nm* net curtain ▪**voilé, -ée** *adj (femme, allusion)* veiled; *(photo, lumière)* hazy ▪**voiler¹ 1** *vt (visage, vérité)* to veil **2 se voiler** *vpr (personne)* to wear a veil; *(ciel, regard)* to cloud over

voile² [vwal] *nf (de bateau)* sail; *(sport)* sailing; **faire de la v.** to sail ▪**voilier** *nm* sailing boat; *(de plaisance)* yacht ▪**voilure** *nf* sails

voiler² [vwale] *vt,* **se voiler** *vpr (roue)* to buckle

voir* [vwar] **1** *vt* to see; **faire** *ou* **laisser v. qch** to show sth; **v. qn faire qch** to see sb do/doing sth; *Fam* **je ne peux pas la v.** I can't stand the sight of her; *Fam* **elle lui en a fait v. de toutes les couleurs** she made his/her life a misery **2** *vi* **fais v.** let me see, show me; **voyons!** *(sois raisonnable)* come on!; **on verra bien** *(attendons)* we'll see; **ça n'a rien à v. avec ça** it's got nothing to do with that; **y v. clair** *(comprendre)* to see clearly **3 se voir** *vpr (soi-*

même) to see oneself; *(se fréquenter)* to see each other; *(objet, attitude)* to be seen; *(reprise, tache)* to show; **ça se voit** that's obvious

voire [vwar] *adv* indeed

voirie [vwari] *nf (service des ordures)* refuse collection; *(routes)* public highways

voisin, -ine [vwazɛ̃, -in] **1** *adj (pays, village)* Br neighbouring, *Am* neighboring; *(maison, pièce)* next *(de* to); *(idée, état)* similar *(de* to) **2** *nmf* Br neighbour, *Am* neighbor **•voisinage** *nm (quartier, voisins)* Br neighbourhood, *Am* neighborhood; *(proximité)* closeness, proximity **•voisiner** *vi* **v. avec** to be side by side with

voiture [vwatyr] *nf* car; *(de train)* carriage, Br coach, *Am* car; *(charrette)* cart; **en v.!** *(dans le train)* all aboard!; **v. de course/de tourisme** racing/private car; **v. d'enfant** Br pram, *Am* baby carriage

voix [vwa] *nf* voice; *(d'électeur)* vote; **à v. basse** in a whisper; **à haute v.** aloud; **à portée de v.** within earshot; *Fig* **avoir v. au chapitre** to have a say (in the matter); *Fig* **rester sans v.** to remain speechless

vol [vɔl] *nm* **(a)** *(d'avion, d'oiseau)* flight; *(groupe d'oiseaux)* flock, flight; **à v. d'oiseau** as the crow flies; **attraper qch au v.** to catch sth in the air; **v. aller-retour** Br return flight, *Am* round-trip flight; **v. habité** manned flight; **v. libre** hang-gliding; **à voile** gliding **(b)** *(délit)* theft; **v. à main armée** armed robbery; **v. à l'étalage** shoplifting; **c'est du v.!** *(trop cher)* it's daylight robbery! **•vol-au-vent** *nm inv Culin* vol-au-vent

volage [vɔlaʒ] *adj* flighty, fickle

volaille [vɔlaj] *nf* **la v.** poultry; **une v.** a fowl

volatile [vɔlatil] *nm* winged creature

volatiliser [vɔlatilize] **se volatiliser** *vpr* to vanish into thin air

volcan [vɔlkɑ̃] *nm* volcano **•volcanique** *adj* volcanic

voler¹ [vɔle] *vi (oiseau, avion)* to fly; *Fig (courir)* to rush **•volant, -ante 1** *adj (tapis)* flying; **feuille volante** loose sheet **2** *nm (de véhicule)* (steering) wheel; *(de badminton)* shuttlecock; *(de jupe)* flounce **•volée** *nf (de flèches)* flight; *(groupe d'oiseaux)* flock, flight; *(de coups)* thrashing; *Tennis & Football* volley; **sonner à toute v.** to ring out

voler² [vɔle] **1** *vt (prendre)* to steal *(à* from); **v. qn** to rob sb; *Fam* **tu ne l'as pas volé!** it serves you right! **2** *vi (prendre)* to steal

volet [vɔlɛ] *nm (de fenêtre)* shutter; *(de programme)* section, part

voleter [vɔlte] *vi* to flutter

voleur, -euse [vɔlœr, -øz] **1** *nmf* thief; **au v.!** stop, thief! **2** *adj* thieving

volière [vɔljɛr] *nf* aviary

volley-ball [vɔlebol] *nm* volleyball **•volleyeur, -euse** *nmf* volleyball player

volontaire [vɔlɔ̃ter] **1** *adj (geste, omission)* deliberate; *(travail)* voluntary; *(opiniâtre)* Br wilful, *Am* willful **2** *nmf* volunteer **•volontairement** *adv (spontanément)* voluntarily; *(exprès)* deliberately

volontariat [vɔlɔ̃tarja] *nm* voluntary work

volonté [vɔlɔ̃te] *nf (faculté, intention)* will; *(détermination)* willpower; *(souhait)* wish; **bonne v.** willingness; **mauvaise v.** unwillingness; **à v.** *(quantité)* as much as desired

volontiers [vɔlɔ̃tje] *adv* gladly, willingly; **v.!** *(oui)* I'd love to!

volt [vɔlt] *nm* volt **•voltage** *nm* voltage

volte-face [vɔltafas] *nf inv* Br about turn, *Am* about face; *Fig (changement d'opinion)* U-turn; **faire v.** to turn round; *Fig* to do a U-turn

voltige [vɔltiʒ] *nf* acrobatics

voltiger [vɔltiʒe] *vi (feuilles)* to flutter

volubile [vɔlybil] *adj* voluble

volume [vɔlym] *nm (de boîte, de son, livre)* volume **•volumineux, -euse** *adj* bulky, voluminous

volupté [vɔlypte] *nf* sensual pleasure **•voluptueux, -ueuse** *adj* voluptuous

vomir [vɔmir] **1** *vt* to bring up, to vomit; *Fig (exécrer)* to loathe **2** *vi* to vomit, Br to be sick **•vomi** *nm Fam* vomit **•vomissements** *nmpl* **avoir des v.** to vomit **•vomitif, -ive** *adj* emetic

vont [vɔ̃] *voir* **aller¹**

vorace [vɔras] *adj* voracious

vos [vo] *voir* **votre**

vote [vɔt] *nm (action)* vote, voting; *(suffrage)* vote; *(de loi)* passing; Br **bureau de v.** polling station, *Am* polling place **•votant, -ante** *nmf* voter **•voter 1** *vt (loi)* to pass; *(crédits)* to vote **2** *vi* to vote

votre, vos [vɔtr, vo] *adj possessif* your **•vôtre 1** *pron possessif* **le** *ou* **la v., les vôtres** yours; **à la v.!** cheers! **2** *nmpl* **les vôtres** *(votre famille)* your family

voudra, voudrait [vudra, vudrɛ] *voir* **vouloir**

vouer [vwe] **1** *vt (promettre)* to vow *(à* to); *(consacrer)* to dedicate *(à* to); *(condamner)* to doom *(à* to) **2** **se vouer** *vpr* **se v. à** to dedicate oneself to

vouloir* [vulwar] *vt* to want *(***faire** to do); **je veux qu'il parte** I want him to go; **v. dire** to mean *(***que** that); **je voudrais un pain** I'd like a loaf of bread; **je voudrais rester** I'd like to stay; **je veux bien attendre** I don't mind waiting; **veuillez attendre** kindly wait; **ça ne veut pas bouger** it won't move; **voulez-vous me suivre** will you follow me; **si tu veux** if you like *or* wish; **en v. à qn d'avoir fait qch** to be angry with sb for doing sth; **l'usage veut que...** *(+ subjunctive)* custom dictates that...; **v. du bien à qn** to wish sb well; **que voulez-vous!** *(résignation)* what can you expect!; **sans le v.** unintentionally; **ne pas v. de qn/qch** not to want sb/sth ▪ **voulu, -ue** *adj (requis)* required; *(délibéré)* deliberate, intentional

vous [vu] *pron personnel* (**a**) *(sujet, complément direct)* you; **v. êtes ici** you are here; **il v. connaît** he knows you (**b**) *(complément indirect)* (to) you; **il v. l'a donné** he gave it to you, he gave you it (**c**) *(réfléchi)* yourself, *pl* yourselves; **v. v. lavez** you wash yourself/ yourselves (**d**) *(réciproque)* each other; **v. v. aimez** you love each other ▪ **vous-même** *pron* yourself ▪ **vous-mêmes** *pron pl* yourselves

voûte [vut] *nf (arch)* vault; **v. d'ogive** vault ▪ **voûté, -ée** *adj (personne)* bent, stooped

vouvoyer [vuvwaje] *vt* **v. qn** to address sb as "vous" ▪ **vouvoiement** *nm* = use of the formal "vous" *(instead of the more familiar "tu")*

voyage [vwajaʒ] *nm* trip, journey; *(par mer)* voyage; **aimer les voyages** to like *Br* travelling *or Am* traveling; **faire un v., partir en v.** to go on a trip; **être en v.** to be (away) travelling; **bon v.!** have a pleasant trip!; **v. de noces** honeymoon; **v. organisé** (package) tour ▪ **voyager** *vi* to travel ▪ **voyageur, -euse** *nmf Br* traveller, *Am* traveler; *(passager)* passenger; **v. de commerce** travelling salesman, *Br* commercial traveller ▪ **voyagiste** *nm* tour operator

voyant, -ante¹ [vwajɑ̃, -ɑ̃t] **1** *adj (couleur)* gaudy, loud **2** *nm (signal)* (warning) light; *(d'appareil électrique)* pilot light

voyant, -ante² [vwajɑ̃, -ɑ̃t] *nmf* clairvoyant

voyelle [vwajɛl] *nf* vowel

voyeur, -euse [vwajœr, -øz] *nmf* voyeur, *f* voyeuse

voyou [vwaju] *nm* hooligan

vrac [vrak] **en vrac** *adv (en désordre)* in a muddle; *(au poids)* loose

vrai [vrɛ] **1** *adj* true; *(réel)* real; *(authentique)* genuine **2** *adv* **dire v.** to be right (in what one says) **3** *nm (vérité)* truth ▪ **vraiment** *adv* really

vraisemblable [vrɛsɑ̃blabl] *adj (probable)* likely, probable; *(crédible)* credible ▪ **vraisemblablement** [-ɑ̃mɑ̃] *adv* probably ▪ **vraisemblance** *nf* likelihood; *(crédibilité)* credibility

vrille [vrij] *nf (outil)* gimlet; *(acrobatie)* (tail)spin; **descendre en v.** *(avion)* to spin down; *Fam* **partir en v.** *(projet)* to go down the pan

vrombir [vrɔ̃bir] *vi* to hum ▪ **vrombissement** *nm* hum(ming)

VRP [veɛrpe] *(abrév* **voyageur représentant placier)** *nm* sales rep

VTT [vetete] *(abrév* **vélo tout terrain)** *nm inv* mountain bike

vu, -ue [vy] **1** *pp de* **voir 2** *adj* **bien vu** well thought of; **mal vu** frowned upon **3** *prép* in view of; **vu que...** seeing that...

vue [vy] *nf (sens)* (eye)sight; *(panorama, photo, idée)* view; **en v.** *(proche)* in sight; *(en évidence)* on view; *Fig (personne)* in the public eye; **avoir qn/qch en v.** to have sb/sth in mind; **à v.** *(tirer)* on sight; *(payable)* at sight; **à première v.** at first sight; **à v. d'œil** *(grandir)* visibly; *Fam* **à v. de nez** at a rough guess; **de v.** *(connaître)* by sight; **en v. de faire qch** with a view to doing sth; **v. d'ensemble** overall view

vulgaire [vylgɛr] *adj (grossier)* vulgar; *(ordinaire)* common ▪ **vulgairement** *adv (grossièrement)* vulgarly; *(appeler)* commonly ▪ **vulgariser** *vt* to popularize ▪ **vulgarité** *nf* vulgarity

vulnérable [vylnerabl] *adj* vulnerable ▪ **vulnérabilité** *nf* vulnerability

W, w [dubləve] *nm inv* W, w

wagon [vagɔ̃] *nm (de voyageurs)* carriage, *Br* coach, *Am* car; *(de marchandises) Br* wagon, *Am* freight car ▪**wagon-lit** (*pl* **wagons-lits**) *nm* sleeping car, sleeper ▪**wagon-restaurant** (*pl* **wagons-restaurants**) *nm* dining *or* restaurant car

Walkman® [wɔkman] *nm* Walkman®, personal stereo

wallon, -onne [walɔ̃, -ɔn] **1** *adj* Walloon **2** *nmf* **W., Wallonne** Walloon

WAP [wap] (*abrév* **wireless applications protocol**) *nm Tél* WAP

water-polo [watɛrpɔlo] *nm* water polo

watt [wat] *nm Él* watt

W.-C. [(dublə)vese] *nmpl Br* toilet, *Am* men's/ladies' room

Web [wɛb] *nm Ordinat* **le W.** the Web ▪**Webcam** *nm Ordinat* webcam ▪**Weblog** *nm Ordinat* weblog ▪**Webmestre** *nm Ordinat* webmaster ▪**Webzine** *nm Ordinat* webzine

week-end [wikɛnd] (*pl* **week-ends**) *nm* weekend; **partir en w.** to go away for the weekend

western [wɛstɛrn] *nm* western

whisky [wiski] (*pl* **-ies** *ou* **-ys**) *nm Br* whisky, *Am* whiskey

WWW [dubləvedubləvedubləve] (*abrév* **World Wide Web**) *nm Ordinat* WWW

wysiwyg [wiziwig] (*abrév* **what you see is what you get**) *adj & nm Ordinat* WYSIWYG

X, x [iks] *nm inv (lettre, personne ou nombre inconnus)* X, x; *Fam (ecstasy)* E; **x fois** umpteen times; **film classé X** adults-only film, *Br* '18' film, *Am* X-rated film; **accoucher sous X** to give birth anonymously; **naître sous X** to be born to an unidentified mother

xénophobe [gsenɔfɔb] **1** *adj* xenophobic **2** *nmf* xenophobe ▪**xénophobie** *nf* xenophobia

xérès [gzeres] *nm* sherry

xylophone [gsilɔfɔn] *nm* xylophone

Y, y¹ [igrek] *nm inv* Y, y

y² [i] **1** *adv* there; *(dedans)* in it/them; *(dessus)* on it/them; **elle y vivra** she'll live there; **j'y entrai** I entered (it); **allons-y** let's go; **j'y suis!** *(je comprends)* now I get it! **2** *pron* **j'y pense** I'm thinking about it; **je m'y attendais** I was expecting it; **ça y est!** that's it!; **je n'y suis pour rien** I have nothing to do with it

yacht [jɔt] *nm* yacht ▪**yachting** *nm* yachting

yaourt [jaurt] *nm* yoghurt

Yémen [jemen] *nm* **le Y.** Yemen

yen [jɛn] *nm* yen

yeux [jø] *voir* **œil**

yiddish [jidiʃ] *nm & adj* Yiddish

yoga [jɔga] *nm* yoga; **faire du y.** to do yoga

yog(h)ourt [jɔgurt] *nm* = **yaourt**

Yo-Yo [jojo] *nm inv* yoyo

Z, z [zɛd] *nm inv* Z, z

Zaïre [zair] *nm* **le Z.** Zaïre

zapper [zape] *vi Fam* to channel-hop *or* channel-surf ▪ **zapping** *nm Fam* **faire du z.** to channel-hop *or* channel-surf

zèbre [zebr] *nm* zebra ▪ **zébré, -ée** [ze-] *adj* striped, streaked (**de** with) ▪ **zébrures** [ze-] *nfpl* stripes

zèle [zɛl] *nm* zeal; **faire du z.** to overdo it ▪ **zélé, -ée** *adj* zealous

zen [zɛn] **1** *nm* Zen **2** *adj* Zen; *Fam* **rester z.** *(serein)* to stay cool

zénith [zenit] *nm* zenith

zéro [zero] *nm (chiffre)* zero, *Br* nought; *(de numéro de téléphone)* 0 [əʊ]; *(température)* zero; *(rien)* nothing; *Fig (personne)* nonentity; *Football* **deux buts à z.** *Br* two nil, *Am* two zero

zeste [zɛst] *nm* **un z. de citron** a piece of lemon zest *or* peel

zézayer [zezeje] *vi* to lisp

zibeline [ziblin] *nf (fourrure)* sable

zieuter, zyeuter [zjøte] *vt Fam* to eye up, to check out

zigzag [zigzag] *nm* zigzag; **en z.** *(route)* zigzag(ging) ▪ **zigzaguer** *vi* to zigzag

Zimbabwe [zimbabwe] *nm* **le Z.** Zimbabwe

zinc [zɛ̃g] *nm (métal)* zinc; *Fam (comptoir)* bar; *Fam (avion)* plane

zinzin [zɛ̃zɛ̃] *Fam* **1** *adj inv (fou)* nuts **2** *nm (chose)* whatsit

zipper [zipe] *vt Ordinat* to zip ▪ **zippé, -ée** *adj Ordinat* **fichier z.** zip file

zizanie [zizani] *nf* discord; **semer la z.** to sow discord

zodiaque [zɔdjak] *nm* zodiac; **signe du z.** sign of the zodiac

zona [zona] *nm Méd* shingles *(sing)*

zone [zon] *nf* zone; **de seconde z.** second-rate; *Fam* **la z.** *(bidonvilles)* the slums; **z. euro** euro zone *or* area; **z. fumeurs/non-fumeurs** smoking/no-smoking area; **z. industrielle** industrial *Br* estate *or Am* park; **z. scientifique** science park ▪ **zonard** *nm Fam (marginal)* dropout ▪ **zoner** *vi Fam* to hang about

zoo [zo(o)] *nm* zoo ▪ **zoologie** [zɔɔ-] *nf* zoology ▪ **zoologique** *adj* zoological; **parc z.** zoo ▪ **zoologiste** *nmf* zoologist

zoom [zum] *nm (objectif)* zoom lens

zozo [zozo] *nm Fam* fool

zozoter [zozɔte] *vi Fam* to lisp

zut [zyt] *exclam Fam* blast!